Features

You may visit us on the Web at
http://www.census.gov/compendia/smadb

ACKNOWLEDGMENTS

Glenn W. King, Chief of the Statistical Compendia Branch, was responsible for the technical supervision and coordination of this volume, with the assistance of **Aonghas M. St. Hilaire**. **Myra D. Smith** was responsible for text preparation and processing of state tables. **Kathleen P. Denton** was responsible for text preparation and processing of metro tables. **Kathleen A. Siemer** was responsible for computer operations and data processing. Assisting with data compilation and review was **Kristen M. Iversen**. Data entry and other support activities were provided by **Connie J. Nadzadi** and **Daphanie M. Smallwood**. **Connie J. Nadzadi** was responsible for the coding and preparation of all tables for printing. Subject development and analytical review were provided by **Lars B. Johanson**, **Rosemary E. Clark**, **Richard P. Kersey**, **Stacey M. Lowe**, and **Jean F. Mullin**.

Maps were designed and produced by **Connie Beard** and **Jessica Dobrowolski** of the Cartographic Operations Branch within the Geography Division.

Michael T. Browne, **Wanda K. Cevis**, and **Linda Chen** of the Administrative and Customer Services Division, **Walter C. Odom**, Chief, provided publications and printing management, graphics design and composition, and editorial review for print and electronic media. General direction and production management were provided by **James R. Clark**, Assistant Division Chief.

The cooperation of many contributors to this volume is gratefully acknowledged. The source notes below each table and in Appendix A credit the various government and private agencies that have furnished information for the *State and Metropolitan Area Data Book*. In a few instances, contributors have requested that their data be designated as subject to copyright restrictions as indicated in the source notes. Permission to use copyright material should be obtained directly from the copyright owner.

State and Metropolitan Area Data Book: 2006

6th Edition

Issued July 2006

U.S. Department of Commerce
Carlos M. Gutierrez,
Secretary

David A. Sampson,
Deputy Secretary

Economics and Statistics
Administration
Vacant,
Under Secretary for Economic Affairs

U.S. CENSUS BUREAU
Charles Louis Kincannon,
Director

SUGGESTED CITATION

U.S. Census Bureau,
*State and Metropolitan
Area Data Book: 2006*
(6th edition).
Washington, DC, 2006.

ECONOMICS
AND STATISTICS
ADMINISTRATION

**Economics
and Statistics
Administration**
Vacant,
Under Secretary
for Economic Affairs

U.S. CENSUS BUREAU
Charles Louis Kincannon,
Director
Hermann Habermann,
Deputy Director and
Chief Operating Officer

Ted A. Johnson,
Associate Director for Administration
and Chief Financial Officer

Walter C. Odom,
Chief, Administrative
and Customer Services Division

U.S. GOVERNMENT PRINTING OFFICE OFFICIAL EDITION NOTICE

This is the official U.S. Government edition of this publication and is herein identified to certify
its authenticity. The Superintendent of Documents of the U.S. Government Printing Office
requests that any reprinted edition clearly be labeled as a copy of the authentic work. Use of the
0-16 ISBN prefix is for U.S. Government Printing Office official editions only.

ISBN: 0-16-076304-5

NATIONAL BIBLIOGRAPHY OF U.S. GOVERNMENT PUBLICATIONS

State and Metropolitan Area Data Book: 2006—6 ed.
   Includes index.
   ISBN 0-16-076304-5
   ISBN 978-0-16-076304-5
   ISSN 0276-6566
1. United States—Statistics. I. United States. Census Bureau.

HA 202.S84 2006
317.3

Library of Congress Card No. 80-600018

http://purl.access.gpo.gov/GPO/

For sale by Superintendent of Documents, U.S. Government Printing Office
Internet: <bookstore.gpo.gov>;   Phone: toll-free 1-866-512-1800; DC area 202-512-1800;
Fax: 202-512-2250;
Mail: Stop SSOP, Washington, DC 20402-0001

Preface

The *State and Metropolitan Area Data Book* (SMADB), published periodically since 1979, is a local area supplement to the *Statistical Abstract of the United States*. This 2006 edition is the sixth in the series. Earlier editions were published in 1979, 1982, 1986, 1991, and 1997–98.

The SMADB is a convenient summary of statistics on the social and economic structure of the states, metropolitan areas, and micropolitan areas in the United States. It is designed to serve as a statistical reference and guide to other data publications and sources. The latter function is served by the source citations appearing below each table and in Appendix A, Source Notes and Explanations.

This volume includes a selection of data from many statistical publications and electronic sources, including most of the federal statistical agencies, nonprofit organizations, and private businesses in some cases. Publications and Internet sites listed as sources usually contain additional detail and more comprehensive discussions of definitions and concepts than can be presented here. Data not available in printed publications issued by the contributing agency but obtained from Web sites are identified in the source notes using the "Suggested Citation Styles for our Internet Information" found on the Census Bureau's Web site at <http://www.census.gov/main/www/citation.html>. More information on the subjects covered in the tables so noted may generally be obtained from the source, including more methodological information about how the numbers are collected or produced.

Changes in this edition. The major change in this edition is in the metropolitan area concept itself. Over time, the concept and nomenclature for metropolitan areas has changed from the original 1910 "metropolitan districts" to what was called standard metropolitan area in 1949 to standard metropolitan statistical areas, or SMSAs, in 1959. SMSAs lasted until 1983, when a new set of acronyms and concepts such as MSA, CMSA, PMSA, and NECMAs came into existence. These lasted until the recent Office of Management and Budget announcement effective June 6, 2003, created the current metropolitan and micropolitan statistical areas. For information about this announcement, see our Appendix C on Geographic Concepts and Codes. Tables B and C cover the metropolitan areas, while Table D presents micropolitan areas.

Information for states has been expanded substantially in comparison with the prior edition. There is extensive information from the Census Bureau's new American Community Survey on topics such as households, marital status, mobility, language spoken at home, foreign born, educational attainment, income, poverty, and housing characteristics that updates many statistics previously only available from the decennial census. There is an interesting, brand-new table with cost-of-living indicators that consolidates many variables in this area. Health data has been expanded to cover many of the key indicators such as obesity, drug use, and alcohol use. Election results from 2004 are also included.

We made a special effort to include material from the 2002 Economic Census for retail and accommodation and food services and also the latest population estimates. To help highlight all this information, you will find a Rankings section in this publication and on our Web site at <http://www.census.gov/compendia/smadb/>.

In order to help users understand more about the data, we have a new appendix B, entitled Limitations of the Data and Methodology. You will find descriptions about the survey universe and frequency, along with some basic information about the data collection operation and sampling and nonsampling errors, if applicable. Sources of additional information and Web links to that information are also included.

States. Data are presented for the United States, the 50 states, and the District of Columbia. 1,539 data items are presented for these areas in tables A-1 through A-87. The states and the District of Columbia are presented in alphabetic order under the U.S. total.

Metropolitan areas and metropolitan divisions. Data are presented for the 390 metropolitan areas and metropolitan divisions defined as of January 1, 1992, as well as the United States, the 50 states, and the District of Columbia. 139 data items are presented for these areas in tables B-1 through B-11.

Metropolitan areas and metropolitan divisions with their county components. Data are presented for 46 data items in tables C-1 through C-4. The counties and county equivalents are presented under their respective metropolitan area or metropolitan division.

Micropolitan areas. Data are presented in table D-1 covering 13 variables and 575 areas.

Appendixes. Appendix A presents a discussion of source notes and explanations for the data items in tables A through D. Appendix B covers data collection and methodological information for the first time in this publication. Appendix C presents a discussion of the geographic concepts and codes relevant to this volume, as well as the current definitions for metropolitan areas.

For additional information on data presented, please consult the source publications available in local libraries, write to the agency indicated in the source notes, or visit the Internet site listed. Contact the Census Bureau only if it is cited as the source.

Statistics for the nation. Extensive data at the national level can be found in the *Statistical Abstract of the United States: 2006*, an annual national data book, released each fall. *U.S.A. Statistics in Brief*, a pocket-size pamphlet highlighting many statistical series in the *Abstract*, is available separately; single copies of this pamphlet can be obtained

free from the U.S. Census Bureau, Customer Services Center, Washington, DC 20233 (telephone 301-763-4100). The *Statistical Abstract* and *U.S.A. Statistics in Brief* may be on our Web site at <http://www.census.gov/compendia /statab/>.

Statistics for counties and cities. Data for counties and cities may be found in the *County and City Data Book 2000* or the U.S.A. Counties database on our Web site at <http://www.census.gov/statab/www/ccdb.html> and <http://censtats.census.gov/usa/usa.shtml>.

State and Metropolitan Area Data Book User Survey—inserted in this edition is the first user survey in order to ask you for suggestions on various aspects of the SMADB. Your input will help us to maintain the usefulness of the Compendia program. If the questionnaire is missing and you would like to participate in the survey, you may obtain one on the SMADB Web site at <http://www.census.gov/compendia/smadb/>.

Contents

States—Con.

Metropolitan Areas

Metropolitan Areas With Component Counties

Micropolitan Areas

Appendixes

Guide to Tabular Presentation

EXAMPLE OF TABLE STRUCTURE FROM:

Table A-78. States — **Federal Government**

Geographic area	Nonfarm employment (BLS)[1] (1,000)			Federal earnings (BEA)[2] (mil. dol.)						Federal funds and grants					
				Civilian			Military			Total (mil. dol.)		Defense, 2003		Selected object categories, 2003 (mil. dol.)		
	2004	2003	2000	2004	2003	2001	2004	2003	2001	2003	2000	Percent	Per capita (dol.)	Direct payments for individuals	Grants to state and local government	Salaries and wages
United States . . .	[3]2,728.0	[3]2,761.0	[3]2,865.0	223,754	219,213	201,864	117,323	109,607	84,859	2,009,585	1,604,670	14.9	1,030	1,073,228	435,050	207,293
Alabama	51.1	50.3	53.4	4,031	4,009	3,681	1,933	1,831	1,338	36,871	29,250	21.4	1,757	19,930	6,649	3,224
Alaska	17.1	17.1	17.1	1,395	1,338	1,239	1,575	1,405	1,108	7,944	5,963	29.0	3,556	1,625	3,022	1,617
Arizona	50.9	50.5	48.7	3,981	3,681	3,292	2,021	1,891	1,399	37,801	29,282	26.2	1,771	18,675	7,235	3,335
Arkansas	20.8	21.0	22.4	1,522	1,474	1,368	890	823	525	18,340	14,847	7.9	530	11,596	4,541	1,339
California	250.2	255.4	272.9	20,080	19,849	18,596	13,004	12,322	9,995	219,706	175,967	17.9	1,106	110,716	51,329	20,611

[1]Bureau of Labor Statistics.
[2]Bureau of Economic Analysis.
[3]United States totals differ from the sum of the state figures because of differing benchmarks among states and differing industrial and geographic stratification.

Survey, Census, or Data Collection Method: Employment—Based on the Current Employment Statistics (CES) survey; for information, see Appendix B, Limitations of the Data and Methodology, and Internet site <http://www.bls.gov/opub/hom/homch2_a.htm>; Earnings—Based on the Regional Economic Information System; for information, see Internet site <http://www.bea.gov/bea/regional/articles/spi2003/>; Federal funds and grants—Based on information systems in various federal government agencies; for information, see Internet site <http://www.census.gov/govs/www/cffr.html>.

Sources: Employment—U.S. Bureau of Labor Statistics, Current Employment Statistics Program, see Internet site <http://www.bls.gov/sae/home.htm>; Earnings—U.S. Bureau of Economic Analysis, *Survey of Current Business*, April 2005, and see Internet site <http://www.bea.gov/bea/regional/spi/>; Federal funds and grants—U.S. Census Bureau, *Consolidated Federal Funds Report*, annual, see Internet site <http://www.census.gov/govs/www/cffr.html>.

Unit indicators show the specified quantities in which data items are presented. They are used for two primary reasons. Sometimes data are not available in absolute form. Other times, we round the numbers in order to save space to show more data, as in the case above.

If no unit indicator is shown, data presented are in absolute form (see Table B-1 for an example). When needed,

unit indicators are found in the column or spanner headings for the data items as shown above.

Footnotes below the bottom rule of table pages give information relating to specific data items or figures within the table.

Examples of Unit Indicator Interpretation From Table

Geographic area	Year	Item	Unit indicator	Number shown	Multiplier
United States	2004	Nonfarm employment	(1,000)	2,728.0	1,000
United States	2003	Federal funds and grants	(mil. dol.)	2,009,585	$1,000,000

To Determine the Figure, It Is Necessary to Multiply the Number Shown by the Unit Indicator

Nonfarm employment, 2004 = 2,728.0 * 1,000 or 2,728,000 (over 2 million).

Federal funds and grants, 2003 = 2,009,585 * 1,000,000 or 2,009,585,000,000 (over 2 trillion dollars).

In many tables, details will not add to the totals shown because of rounding.

EXPLANATION OF SYMBOLS AND TERMS

The following symbols, used in the tables throughout this book, are explained in condensed form in footnotes on the tables where they appear.

–	Represents zero or rounds to less than half the unit of measurement shown.
B	Base figure too small to meet statistical standards for reliability of a derived figure.
D	Figure withheld to avoid disclosure pertaining to a specific organization or individual.
NA	Data not enumerated, tabulated, or otherwise available separately.
S	Figure does not meet publication standards for reasons other than that covered by symbol B, above.
X	Figure not applicable because column heading and stub line make entry impossible, absurd, or meaningless.
Z	Entry would amount to less than half the unit of measurement shown.

The following terms are also used throughout this publication:

Averages. An average is a single number or value that is often used to represent the "typical value" of a group of numbers. It is regarded as a measure of "location" or "central tendency" of a group of numbers.

The *arithmetic* mean is the type of average used most frequently. It is derived by summing the individual item values of a particular group and dividing the total by the number of items. The arithmetic mean is often referred to simply as the "mean" or "average."

The *median* of a group of numbers is the middle number or value when each item in the group is arranged according to size (lowest to highest or vice versa); it generally has the same number of items above it as well as below it. If there is an even number of items in the group, the median is taken to be the average of the two middle numbers.

Rates. A rate is a quantity or amount of an item measured in relation to a specified number of units of another item. For example, unemployment rate is the number of unemployed persons per 100 persons in the civilian labor force. Examples of other rates found in this publication include birth rate, which is the number of births per 1,000 population; infant death rate, the number of infant deaths per 1,000 live births; and crime rate, which is the number of serious offenses per 100,000 population.

A *per capita* figure represents a specific type of rate computed for every person in a specified group (or population). It is derived by taking the total for a data item (such as income, taxes, or retail sales) and dividing it by the number of persons in the specified population.

Ranks. Various data items in Table A, States and Table B, Metropolitan Areas of this publication are ranked from highest to lowest with a rank of 1 representing the highest rank. In both tables, when areas share the same rank, the next lower rank is omitted.

In Table A, only the 50 states are ranked; the District of Columbia is not included in the state rankings. In Table B, only 361 metropolitan statistical areas (MSAs) are ranked. Not ranked are the 29 metropolitan divisions, which make up 11 metropolitan statistical areas. Areas not ranked are indicated by an "X" in the data cell.

Index numbers. An index number is a measure of difference or change, usually expressed as a percent, relating one quantity (the variable) of a specified kind to another quantity of the same kind. Index numbers are widely used to express changes in prices over periods of time but may also be used to express differences between related subjects for a single point in time.

To compute a price index, a base year or period is selected. The base year price (of the commodity or service) is then designated as the base or reference price to which the prices for other years or periods are related. Many price indexes use the year 2000 as the base year; in tables, this is shown as "2000=100." A method of expressing the price relationship is: The price of a set of one or more items for a related year (e.g., 1990) divided by the price of the same set of items for the base year (e.g., 2000). The result multiplied by 100 provides the index number. When 100 is subtracted from the index number, the result equals the percent change in price from the base year.

Current and constant dollars. Statistics in some tables are expressed in both current and constant dollars (see, for example, Table A-42). Current dollar figures reflect actual prices or costs prevailing during the specified year(s). Constant dollar figures are estimates representing an effort to remove the effects of price changes from statistical series reported in dollar terms. In general, constant dollar series are derived by dividing current dollar estimates by the appropriate price index for the appropriate period (for example, the Consumer Price Index). The result is a series as it would presumably exist if prices were the same throughout, as in the base year; in other words, as if the dollar had constant purchasing power. Any changes in this constant dollar series would reflect only changes in real volume of output, income, expenditures, or other measure.

Major Federal Data Contacts

To help *State and Metropolitan Area Data Book* users find more data and information about statistical publications, we are issuing this list of contacts for federal agencies with major statistical programs. The intent is to give a single, first-contact point of entry for users of statistics. These agencies will provide general information on their statistical programs and publications, as well as specific information on how to order their publications. We are also including the Internet (World Wide Web) addresses for many of these agencies. These URLs were current in September 2005.

Executive Office of the President

Office of Management and Budget
Administrator
Office of Information and Regulatory Affairs
Office of Management and Budget
725 17th Street, NW
Washington, DC 20503
Information: 202-395-3080
Internet address: http://www.whitehouse.gov/omb

Department of Agriculture

Economic Research Service
U.S. Department of Agriculture
1800 M St., NW
Room North 3050
Washington, DC 20036-5831
Information and Publications: 202-694-5050
Internet address: http://www.ers.usda.gov/

National Agricultural Statistics Service
U.S. Department of Agriculture
1400 Independence Ave., SW
Room 5829
Washington, DC 20250
Information hotline: 1-800-727-9540
Internet address: http://www.nass.usda.gov/

Department of Commerce

U.S. Census Bureau
Customer Services Branch
Washington, DC 20233
Information and Publications: 301-763-4636
Internet address: http://www.census.gov/

Bureau of Economic Analysis
U.S. Department of Commerce
Washington, DC 20230
Information and Publications: 202-606-9900
Internet address: http://www.bea.gov/

Department of Commerce—Con.

International Trade Administration
Trade Statistics Division
Office of Trade and Economic Analysis
Room 2814 B
Washington, DC 20230
Information and Publications: 202-482-2185
Internet address: http://www.ita.doc.gov/

Department of Defense

Department of Defense
Office of the Assistant Secretary of Defense
(Public Affairs)
Room 3A750
Attention: Directorate for Public Communications
1400 Defense Pentagon
Washington, DC 20301-1400
Information: 703-697-5737
Internet address:
   http://siadapp.dior.whs.mil/index.html

Department of Education

National Center for Education Statistics
U.S. Department of Education
400 Maryland Avenue, SW
Washington, DC 20202-5621
Education Information and Statistics: 1-800-424-1616
Education Publications: 1-877-433-7827
Internet address: http://www.ed.gov/

Department of Energy

Energy Information Administration
National Energy Information Center
U.S. Department of Energy
1000 Independence Ave., SW
1E238-EI-30
Washington, DC 20585
Information and Publications: 202-586-8800
Internet address: http://www.eia.doe.gov/

Department of Health and Human Services

Health Resources and Services Administration
HRSA Office of Communications
5600 Fishers Lane
Room 14-45
Rockville, MD 20857
Information Center: 301-443-3376
Internet address: http://www.hrsa.gov/

Substance Abuse Mental Health Services Administration
U.S. Department of Health and Human Services
5600 Fishers Lane
Room 12-105
Rockville, MD 20857
Information: 301-443-4795
Publications: 1-800-729-6686
Internet address: http://www.samhsa.gov/

Centers for Disease Control and Prevention
Office of Public Affairs
1600 Clifton Road, NE
Atlanta, GA 30333
Public Inquiries: 1-800-311-3435
Internet address: http://www.cdc.gov/

Centers for Medicare and Medicaid Services (CMS)
Office of Public Affairs
U.S. Department of Health and Human Services
Humphrey Building
200 Independence Ave., SW
Room 303D
Washington, DC 20201
Media Relations: 202-690-6145
Internet address: http://www.cms.gov/

National Center for Health Statistics
U.S. Department of Health and Human Services
Centers for Disease Control and Prevention
National Center for Health Statistics
Data Dissemination Branch
6525 Belcrest Rd.
Room 1064
Hyattsville, MD 20782
Information: 301-458-INFO
Internet address: http://www.cdc.gov/nchs

Administration for Children and Families
370 L'Enfant Promenade, SW
Washington, DC 20201
Information and Publications: 202-401-2337
Internet address: http://www.acf.hhs.gov/

Department of Homeland Security

Bureau of Citizenship and Immigration Services
U.S. Department of Homeland Security
425 I St., NW
Room 4034
Washington, DC 20536
Information and Publications: 202-305-1613
Internet address: http://www.uscis.gov/graphics/

Department of the Interior

Geological Survey
Earth Science Information Center
Geological Survey
U.S. Department of the Interior
507 National Center
Reston, VA 20192
Information and Publications: 1-888-275-8747
Internet address for minerals:
  http://minerals.usgs.gov/
Internet address for other materials:
  http://ask.usgs.gov/

National Park Service
WASO-TNT
P.O. Box 25287
Denver, CO 80225-0287
Information and Publications: 303-751-3727
Internet address: http://www2.nature.nps.gov/

Department of Justice

Bureau of Justice Statistics
Statistics Division
810 7th St., NW
2nd Floor
Washington, DC 20531
Information and Publications: 202-307-0765
Internet address: http://www.ojp.usdoj.gov/bjs/

National Criminal Justice Reference Service
Box 6000
Rockville, MD 20849-6000
Information and Publications: 301-519-5500
Publications: 1-800-732-3277
Internet address: http://www.ncjrs.org/

Federal Bureau of Investigation
U.S. Department of Justice
J. Edgar Hoover FBI Building
935 Pennsylvania Ave., NW
Washington, DC 20535-0001
National Press Office: 202-324-3000
Information and Publications: 202-324-3691
Research and Communications Unit: 202-324-5611
Internet address: http://www.fbi.gov/

U.S. Census Bureau

Department of Labor

Bureau of Labor Statistics
Office of Publications and Special Studies Services
Division of Information
Bureau of Labor Statistics
2 Massachusetts Ave., NE
Room 2850
Washington, DC 20212
Information and Publications: 202-691-5200
Internet address: http://www.bls.gov/

Department of Transportation

Bureau of Transportation Statistics
400 7th St., SW, Room 3430
Washington, DC 20590
Products: 202-366-3282
Statistical Information: 1-800-853-1351
Internet address: http://www.bts.gov/

Federal Highway Administration
Office of Public Affairs
Federal Highway Administration
U.S. Department of Transportation
400 7th St., SW
Washington, DC 20590
Information: 202-366-0660
Internet address: http://www.fhwa.dot.gov/

National Highway Traffic Safety Administration
Office of Public and Consumer Affairs
U.S. Department of Transportation
400 7th St., SW
Washington, DC 20590
Information: 202-366-4000
Publications: 202-366-8892
Internet address: http://www.nhtsa.dot.gov/

Department of the Treasury

Internal Revenue Service
Statistics of Income Division
Internal Revenue Service
P.O. Box 2608
Washington, DC 20013-2608
Information and Publications: 202-874-0410
Internet address:
  http://www.irs.gov/taxstats/index.html

Department of Veterans Affairs

Department of Veterans Affairs
Office of Public Affairs
Department of Veterans Affairs
810 Vermont Ave., NW
Washington, DC 20420
Information: 202-273-5400
Internet address: http://www.va.gov/

Independent Agencies

Environmental Protection Agency
Information Resource Center, Room M2904
Environmental Protection Agency
1200 Pennsylvania Ave., NW
Mail Code 3201
Washington, DC 20460
Information: 202-260-9152
Internet address: http://www.epa.gov/

National Science Foundation
Office of Legislation and Public Affairs
National Science Foundation
4201 Wilson Boulevard
Arlington, Virginia 22230
Information: 703-292-5111
Publications: 703-292-8129
Internet address: http://www.nsf.gov/

Social Security Administration
6400 Security Blvd
Baltimore, MD 21235
Information and Publications: 1-800-772-1213
Internet address: http://www.ssa.gov/

Federal Communications Commission
445 12th Street, SW
Washington, DC 20554
Information and Publications: 1-888-225-5322
Internet address: http://www.fcc.gov/

National Credit Union Administration
1775 Duke Street
Alexandria, VA 22314-3428
Information and Publications: 703-518-6300
Internet address: http://www.ncua.gov/

Federal Deposit Insurance Corporation
550 17th Street, NW
Washington, DC 20429-9990
Information and Publications: 202-736-0000
Internet address: http://www.fdic.gov/

Other Related Internet Sites

http://www.fedstats.gov/

http://firstgov.gov/

States

Table A

Page

Note:

Table A presents data for the United States, states, and the District of Columbia. Data are presented for 1,539 items with the states listed in alphabetic order. For a more detailed listing of subjects covered in these tables, see Table of Contents.

You may visit us on the Web at
http://www.census.gov/compendia/smadb

States

Table A

Table A-1. States — **Area and Population**

Geographic area	Area, 2000 (sq. mi.)		Population				Rank			Per square mile of land area[3]			Number, 2000–2005 (1,000)			Percent change	
	Total	Rank	2005 (1,000)	2004 (1,000)	2000[1] (1,000)	1990[2] (1,000)	2005	2000	1990	2005	2000	1990	Net change, total[4]	Net international migration	Net internal migration	2000–2005	1990–2000
United States ...	3,794,083	(X)	296,410	293,657	281,425	248,791	(X)	(X)	(X)	83.8	79.6	70.3	14,985.8	6,333.9	(X)	5.3	13.1
Alabama	52,419	30	4,558	4,525	4,447	4,040	23	23	22	89.8	87.6	79.6	110.5	25.9	10.5	2.5	10.1
Alaska	663,267	1	664	658	627	550	47	48	49	1.2	1.1	1.0	36.7	5.8	–4.6	5.9	14.0
Arizona	113,998	6	5,939	5,740	5,131	3,665	17	20	24	52.3	45.2	32.3	808.7	168.1	408.2	15.8	40.0
Arkansas	53,179	29	2,779	2,750	2,673	2,351	32	33	33	53.4	51.3	45.1	105.8	21.9	35.7	4.0	13.7
California	163,696	3	36,132	35,842	33,872	29,811	1	1	1	231.7	217.2	191.1	2,260.5	1,415.9	–664.5	6.7	13.6
Colorado	104,094	8	4,665	4,602	4,302	3,294	22	24	26	45.0	41.5	31.8	363.2	112.2	47.7	8.4	30.6
Connecticut	5,543	48	3,510	3,499	3,406	3,287	29	29	27	724.5	702.9	678.5	104.7	76.0	–34.3	3.1	3.6
Delaware	2,489	49	844	830	784	666	45	45	46	431.8	401.1	341.0	59.9	11.2	27.9	7.6	17.6
District of Columbia	68	(X)	551	554	572	607	(X)	(X)	(X)	8,966.1	9,316.4	9,884.4	–21.5	20.6	–53.6	–3.8	–5.7
Florida	65,755	22	17,790	17,385	15,983	12,938	4	4	4	329.9	296.4	239.9	1,807.0	528.1	1,057.6	11.3	23.5
Georgia	59,425	24	9,073	8,918	8,187	6,478	9	10	11	156.7	141.4	111.9	885.8	192.8	232.7	10.8	26.4
Hawaii	10,931	43	1,275	1,262	1,212	1,108	42	42	41	198.5	188.6	172.6	63.7	30.1	–13.1	5.3	9.3
Idaho	83,570	14	1,429	1,395	1,294	1,007	39	39	42	17.3	15.6	12.2	135.1	14.5	61.3	10.4	28.5
Illinois	57,914	25	12,763	12,712	12,420	11,431	5	5	6	229.6	223.4	205.6	343.7	328.0	–391.0	2.8	8.7
Indiana	36,418	38	6,272	6,227	6,081	5,544	15	14	14	174.9	169.5	154.6	191.5	55.7	–17.0	3.1	9.7
Iowa	56,272	26	2,966	2,953	2,926	2,777	30	30	30	53.1	52.4	49.7	40.0	29.4	–41.1	1.4	5.4
Kansas	82,277	15	2,745	2,734	2,689	2,478	33	32	32	33.5	32.9	30.3	55.9	38.2	–57.8	2.1	8.5
Kentucky	40,409	37	4,173	4,142	4,042	3,687	26	25	23	105.0	101.7	92.8	131.1	27.4	32.2	3.2	9.6
Louisiana	51,840	31	4,524	4,507	4,469	4,222	24	22	21	103.8	102.6	96.9	54.7	20.2	–89.5	1.2	5.9
Maine	35,385	39	1,322	1,315	1,275	1,228	40	40	38	42.8	41.3	39.8	46.6	5.0	36.8	3.7	3.8
Maryland	12,407	42	5,600	5,561	5,297	4,781	19	19	19	573.0	541.9	489.1	303.9	109.0	9.8	5.7	10.8
Massachusetts	10,555	44	6,399	6,407	6,349	6,016	13	13	13	816.2	809.8	767.4	49.6	162.7	–236.4	0.8	5.5
Michigan	96,716	11	10,121	10,104	9,938	9,295	8	8	8	178.2	175.0	163.6	182.4	122.9	–165.1	1.8	6.9
Minnesota	86,939	12	5,133	5,097	4,919	4,376	21	21	20	64.5	61.8	55.0	213.3	70.8	–16.8	4.3	12.4
Mississippi	48,430	32	2,921	2,901	2,845	2,575	31	31	31	62.3	60.6	54.9	76.4	10.7	–10.6	2.7	10.5
Missouri	69,704	21	5,800	5,760	5,597	5,117	18	17	15	84.2	81.2	74.3	203.6	42.7	27.0	3.6	9.4
Montana	147,042	4	936	927	902	799	44	44	44	6.4	6.2	5.5	33.5	2.1	18.9	3.7	12.9
Nebraska	77,354	16	1,759	1,748	1,711	1,578	38	38	36	22.9	22.3	20.5	47.5	22.2	–26.2	2.8	8.4
Nevada	110,561	7	2,415	2,333	1,998	1,202	35	35	39	22.0	18.2	10.9	416.6	66.1	270.9	20.8	66.3
New Hampshire	9,350	46	1,310	1,299	1,236	1,109	41	41	40	146.1	137.8	123.7	74.2	11.1	40.9	6.0	11.4
New Jersey	8,721	47	8,718	8,685	8,414	7,748	10	9	9	1,175.3	1,134.4	1,044.5	303.6	290.2	–194.9	3.6	8.6
New Mexico	121,590	5	1,928	1,903	1,819	1,515	36	36	37	15.9	15.0	12.5	109.3	28.0	9.5	6.0	20.1
New York	54,556	27	19,255	19,281	18,977	17,991	3	3	2	407.8	401.9	381.0	277.8	667.0	–1,001.1	1.5	5.5
North Carolina	53,819	28	8,683	8,540	8,046	6,632	11	11	10	178.3	165.2	136.2	636.8	158.2	232.4	7.9	21.3
North Dakota	70,700	19	637	636	642	639	48	47	47	9.2	9.3	9.3	–5.5	3.7	–18.6	–0.9	0.5
Ohio	44,825	34	11,464	11,450	11,353	10,847	7	7	7	280.0	277.3	264.9	110.9	75.1	–177.2	1.0	4.7
Oklahoma	69,898	20	3,548	3,524	3,451	3,146	28	27	28	51.7	50.3	45.8	97.2	36.5	–15.4	2.8	9.7
Oregon	98,381	9	3,641	3,591	3,421	2,842	27	28	29	37.9	35.6	29.6	219.6	72.3	77.8	6.4	20.4
Pennsylvania	46,055	33	12,430	12,394	12,281	11,883	6	6	5	277.3	274.0	265.1	148.6	102.5	–28.0	1.2	3.4
Rhode Island	1,545	50	1,076	1,080	1,048	1,003	43	43	43	1,029.9	1,003.2	960.3	27.9	19.0	–5.0	2.7	4.5
South Carolina	32,020	40	4,255	4,198	4,012	3,486	25	26	25	141.3	133.2	115.8	243.3	36.4	115.1	6.1	15.1
South Dakota	77,117	17	776	771	755	696	46	46	45	10.2	9.9	9.2	21.1	4.0	–0.7	2.8	8.5
Tennessee	42,143	36	5,963	5,893	5,689	4,877	16	16	17	144.7	138.0	118.3	273.7	50.0	109.7	4.8	16.7
Texas	268,581	2	22,860	22,472	20,852	16,986	2	2	3	87.3	79.6	64.9	2,008.2	663.2	218.7	9.6	22.8
Utah	84,899	13	2,470	2,421	2,233	1,723	34	34	35	30.1	27.2	21.0	236.4	50.0	–33.8	10.6	29.6
Vermont	9,614	45	623	621	609	563	49	49	48	67.4	65.8	60.8	14.2	4.4	3.5	2.3	8.2
Virginia	42,774	35	7,567	7,481	7,079	6,189	12	12	12	191.1	178.8	156.3	488.4	140.0	103.5	6.9	14.4
Washington	71,300	18	6,288	6,207	5,894	4,867	14	15	18	94.5	88.6	73.1	393.6	134.2	81.0	6.7	21.1
West Virginia	24,230	41	1,817	1,813	1,808	1,793	37	37	34	75.5	75.1	74.5	8.5	3.7	10.5	0.5	0.8
Wisconsin	65,498	23	5,536	5,504	5,364	4,892	20	18	16	101.9	98.8	90.1	172.5	46.1	14.6	3.2	9.6
Wyoming	97,814	10	509	506	494	454	50	50	50	5.2	5.1	4.7	15.5	2.3	1.8	3.1	8.9

X Not applicable.

[1]The April 1, 2000, Population Estimates base reflects modifications to the Census 2000 population as documented in the Count Question Resolution program and geographic program revisions.
[2]The April 1, 1990, census counts include corrections processed through August 1997 and results of special censuses and test censuses, and do not include adjustments for census coverage errors.
[3]Persons per square mile were calculated on the basis of land area data from the 2000 census.
[4]The estimated components of population change will not sum to the numerical population change due to the process of controlling to national totals.

Survey, Census, or Data Collection Method: Based on the Census of Population and Housing; for information, see Appendix B, Limitations of the Data and Methodology, and Internet sites <http://www.census.gov/main/www/cen2000.html> and <http://www.census.gov/popest/topics/methodology/>.

Sources: Area—U.S. Census Bureau, 2000 Census of Population and Housing, *Summary Population and Housing Characteristics*, Series PHC-1; and unpublished data on American FactFinder; Population—U.S. Census Bureau, 1990 Census of Population and Housing, Population and Housing Unit Counts (CPH-2); "Time Series of Intercensal State Population Estimates: April 1, 1990 to April 1, 2000" (CO-EST2001-12-00), published 11 April 2002; Internet site <http://www.census.gov/popest/archives/2000s/vintage_2001/CO-EST2001-12/CO-EST2001-12-00.html>; and "Annual Estimates of the Population for the United States and States, and for Puerto Rico: April 1, 2000 to July 1, 2005" (NST-EST2005-01), published 22 December 2005; Internet site <http://www.census.gov/popest/states/NST-ann-est.html>; Rank—"Table 2: Cumulative Estimates of Population Change for the United States and States, and for Puerto Rico and State Rankings: April 1, 2000 to July 1, 2005" (NST-EST2005-02), published 22 December 2005; Internet site <http://www.census.gov/popest/states/NST-pop-chg.html>; Population change—U.S. Census Bureau, "Table 4: Cumulative Estimates of the Components of Population Change for the United States and States: April 1, 2000 to July 1, 2005" (NST-EST2005-04), published 22 December 2005; Internet site <http://www.census.gov/popest/states/NST-comp-chg.html>.

Table A-2. States — **Population by Residence**

Geographic area	Metropolitan and micropolitan area population					Nonmetropolitan area population[1]				Urban			
										Number (1,000)		Percent of total population	
	2004 (1,000)	2000[2] (1,000)	1990[3] (1,000)	Percent of total, 2004	Percent change, 2000–2004	2004 (1,000)	2000[2] (1,000)	1990[3] (1,000)	Percent change, 2000–2004	2000	1990	2000	1990
United States . . .	**274,114**	**262,060**	**230,747**	**93.3**	**4.6**	**19,542**	**19,364**	**17,971**	**0.9**	**222,361**	**194,097**	**79.0**	**78.0**
Alabama	4,036	3,945	3,559	89.1	2.3	494	503	482	−1.7	2,466	2,293	55.4	56.8
Alaska	489	461	398	74.5	5.9	167	166	152	0.7	411	335	65.6	61.0
Arizona	5,549	4,944	3,512	96.6	12.2	195	187	153	4.6	4,524	3,170	88.2	86.5
Arkansas	2,166	2,082	1,802	78.7	4.0	587	591	549	−0.7	1,404	1,223	52.5	52.0
California	35,637	33,628	29,540	99.3	6.0	257	243	218	5.5	31,990	27,888	94.4	93.7
Colorado	4,209	[4]3,922	2,989	91.5	8.4	392	380	306	3.0	3,633	2,760	84.5	83.8
Connecticut	3,504	3,406	3,287	100.0	2.9	–	–	–	–	2,988	2,859	87.7	87.0
Delaware	830	784	666	100.0	6.0	–	–	–	–	628	528	80.1	79.2
District of Columbia	554	572	607	100.0	−3.2	–	–	–	–	572	607	100.0	100.0
Florida	17,013	15,620	12,645	97.8	8.9	384	363	293	5.9	14,270	11,387	89.3	88.0
Georgia	8,017	7,411	5,822	90.8	8.2	812	776	656	4.7	5,864	4,454	71.6	68.7
Hawaii	1,263	1,211	1,108	100.0	4.2	(Z)	(Z)	(Z)	−14.3	1,108	1,003	91.5	90.5
Idaho	1,198	1,103	846	86.0	8.6	195	191	161	2.3	859	626	66.4	62.2
Illinois	12,096	11,796	10,809	95.1	2.5	617	624	622	−1.0	10,910	9,877	87.8	86.4
Indiana	5,870	5,715	5,198	94.1	2.7	368	366	346	0.5	4,304	3,834	70.8	69.1
Iowa	2,133	2,090	1,939	72.2	2.0	822	836	838	−1.7	1,787	1,650	61.1	59.4
Kansas	2,312	2,248	2,029	84.5	2.8	424	440	448	−3.8	1,921	1,722	71.4	69.5
Kentucky	3,130	3,036	2,734	75.5	3.1	1,016	1,006	953	1.0	2,254	2,059	55.8	55.9
Louisiana	4,207	4,156	3,917	93.2	1.2	309	312	303	−1.1	3,246	3,078	72.6	72.9
Maine	928	893	845	70.4	3.9	390	382	383	2.0	513	523	40.2	42.6
Maryland	5,477	5,218	4,708	98.5	5.0	81	79	73	2.5	4,559	4,063	86.1	85.0
Massachusetts	6,391	6,325	5,999	99.6	1.0	26	25	18	5.2	5,801	5,443	91.4	90.5
Michigan	9,314	9,153	8,601	92.1	1.8	799	785	694	1.7	7,419	6,986	74.7	75.2
Minnesota	4,442	4,266	3,750	87.1	4.1	659	654	626	0.7	3,490	3,019	70.9	69.0
Mississippi	2,255	2,196	1,969	77.7	2.7	648	648	606	−0.1	1,387	1,262	48.8	49.1
Missouri	4,958	4,810	4,392	86.2	3.1	796	787	725	1.2	3,883	3,561	69.4	69.6
Montana	598	574	495	64.6	4.2	328	328	304	0.2	488	450	54.1	56.4
Nebraska	1,387	1,339	1,198	79.4	3.6	360	373	381	−3.4	1,194	1,061	69.8	67.2
Nevada	2,245	1,916	1,137	96.1	17.2	90	82	64	9.4	1,829	1,050	91.5	87.4
New Hampshire	1,253	1,192	1,074	96.4	5.1	47	44	35	7.1	732	635	59.3	57.2
New Jersey	8,699	8,414	7,730	100.0	3.4	–	–	–	–	7,939	7,227	94.4	93.5
New Mexico	1,803	1,717	1,430	94.7	5.0	100	102	85	−1.5	1,364	1,137	75.0	75.0
New York	18,794	18,547	17,574	97.7	1.3	433	430	417	0.7	16,603	15,719	87.5	87.4
North Carolina	7,827	7,352	6,030	91.6	6.5	715	695	602	2.9	4,849	3,833	60.2	57.8
North Dakota	437	435	410	68.8	0.5	198	208	228	−4.7	359	341	55.9	53.4
Ohio	10,947	10,849	10,377	95.5	0.9	512	504	470	1.6	8,782	8,411	77.4	77.5
Oklahoma	2,965	2,891	2,610	84.1	2.6	559	560	536	−0.2	2,255	2,050	65.3	65.2
Oregon	3,454	3,281	2,719	96.1	5.3	140	140	123	0.2	2,694	2,129	78.7	74.9
Pennsylvania	12,022	11,899	11,518	96.9	1.0	384	382	365	0.4	9,464	9,126	77.1	76.8
Rhode Island	1,081	1,048	1,003	100.0	3.1	–	–	–	–	953	903	90.9	89.9
South Carolina	3,923	3,735	3,230	93.4	5.0	276	277	256	−0.5	2,427	2,145	60.5	61.5
South Dakota	548	527	469	71.1	4.0	223	228	227	−2.1	391	350	51.9	50.3
Tennessee	5,280	5,080	4,350	89.5	3.9	621	610	527	1.9	3,620	3,056	63.6	62.7
Texas	21,079	19,465	15,723	93.7	8.3	1,411	1,386	1,264	1.8	17,204	13,791	82.5	83.3
Utah	2,262	2,107	1,618	94.7	7.3	127	126	105	1.3	1,970	1,496	88.2	86.8
Vermont	458	449	417	73.7	1.9	163	159	146	2.5	232	226	38.2	40.2
Virginia	6,639	6,269	5,434	89.0	5.9	821	810	755	1.3	5,170	4,426	73.0	71.5
Washington	5,981	5,678	4,689	96.4	5.3	222	216	178	3.0	4,831	3,891	82.0	79.9
West Virginia	1,360	1,348	1,315	74.9	0.9	456	461	478	−1.1	833	840	46.1	46.9
Wisconsin	4,734	4,604	4,205	85.9	2.8	775	759	687	2.1	3,664	3,291	68.3	67.3
Wyoming	362	352	320	71.6	3.0	144	142	133	1.5	321	304	65.1	67.1

– Represents zero. Z Less than 500.

[1]Represents the area outside of metropolitan and micropolitan areas.
[2]The April 1, 2000, Population Estimates base reflects modifications to the Census 2000 population as documented in the Count Question Resolution program and geographic program revisions.
[3]The April 1, 1990, census counts include corrections processed through August 1997 and results of special censuses and test censuses, and do not include adjustments for census coverage errors.
[4]Colorado state total includes Broomfield city.

Survey, Census, or Data Collection Method: Based on the Census of Population and Housing; for information, see Appendix B, Limitations of the Data and Methodology, and Internet sites <http://www.census.gov/main/www/cen2000.html> and <http://www.census.gov/popest/topics/methodology/>.

Sources: Metropolitan, micropolitan, and nonmetropolitan area population—U.S. Census Bureau, "Annual Estimates of the Population for Counties: April 1, 2000 to July 1, 2004" (CO-EST2004-01), published 14 April 2005; Internet site <http://www.census.gov/popest/counties/CO-EST2004-01.html>; and 2000 Census of Population and Housing, Population and Housing Unit Counts PHC-1; Urban population—U.S. Census Bureau, 2000 Census of Population and Housing, Population and Housing Unit Counts PHC-3, see Internet site <http://www.census.gov/prod/cen2000/index.html>.

Table A-3. States — **Population Projections**

Geographic area	Number (1,000) 2005	2006	2007	2008	2009	2010	2015	2020	2025	2030	Rank 2010	2020	Percent change 2000–2010	2010–2020	2020–2030
United States . . .	**295,507**	**298,217**	**300,913**	**303,598**	**306,272**	**308,936**	**322,366**	**335,805**	**349,439**	**363,584**	(X)	(X)	**9.8**	**8.7**	**8.3**
Alabama	4,527	4,541	4,555	4,569	4,583	4,596	4,663	4,729	4,800	4,874	24	24	3.4	2.9	3.1
Alaska	661	667	674	680	687	694	733	774	821	868	47	47	10.7	11.6	12.0
Arizona	5,868	6,016	6,167	6,321	6,478	6,637	7,495	8,456	9,532	10,712	14	13	29.4	27.4	26.7
Arkansas	2,777	2,797	2,817	2,837	2,856	2,875	2,969	3,060	3,151	3,240	32	31	7.5	6.4	5.9
California	36,039	36,449	36,857	37,262	37,666	38,067	40,123	42,207	44,305	46,445	1	1	12.4	10.9	10.0
Colorado	4,618	4,661	4,704	4,747	4,789	4,832	5,049	5,279	5,523	5,792	22	22	12.3	9.3	9.7
Connecticut	3,503	3,520	3,536	3,550	3,564	3,577	3,635	3,676	3,691	3,689	29	29	5.0	2.7	0.4
Delaware	837	846	856	866	875	884	927	963	991	1,013	45	45	12.9	8.9	5.1
District of Columbia	551	547	543	538	534	530	506	481	455	433	(X)	(X)	-7.4	-9.3	-9.8
Florida	17,510	17,845	18,186	18,534	18,889	19,252	21,204	23,407	25,912	28,686	4	3	20.5	21.6	22.6
Georgia	8,926	9,060	9,193	9,326	9,458	9,589	10,231	10,844	11,439	12,018	9	8	17.1	13.1	10.8
Hawaii	1,277	1,291	1,305	1,318	1,329	1,341	1,386	1,412	1,439	1,466	42	41	10.7	5.3	3.8
Idaho	1,407	1,429	1,451	1,473	1,495	1,517	1,630	1,741	1,853	1,970	39	39	17.3	14.8	13.1
Illinois	12,699	12,747	12,792	12,836	12,877	12,917	13,097	13,237	13,341	13,433	5	5	4.0	2.5	1.5
Indiana	6,250	6,280	6,309	6,337	6,365	6,392	6,518	6,627	6,721	6,810	16	17	5.1	3.7	2.8
Iowa	2,974	2,982	2,990	2,998	3,004	3,010	3,026	3,020	2,993	2,955	30	33	2.9	0.4	-2.2
Kansas	2,752	2,763	2,774	2,785	2,795	2,805	2,853	2,891	2,919	2,940	33	35	4.4	3.0	1.7
Kentucky	4,163	4,185	4,206	4,227	4,246	4,265	4,351	4,424	4,490	4,555	26	26	5.5	3.7	3.0
Louisiana	4,534	4,552	4,568	4,584	4,599	4,613	4,674	4,719	4,762	4,803	23	25	3.2	2.3	1.8
Maine	1,319	1,327	1,335	1,342	1,350	1,357	1,389	1,409	1,414	1,411	41	42	6.4	3.8	0.2
Maryland	5,601	5,662	5,723	5,783	5,844	5,905	6,208	6,498	6,763	7,022	19	18	11.5	10.0	8.1
Massachusetts	6,519	6,548	6,575	6,601	6,626	6,649	6,759	6,856	6,939	7,012	13	15	4.7	3.1	2.3
Michigan	10,207	10,255	10,301	10,345	10,388	10,429	10,599	10,696	10,714	10,694	8	10	4.9	2.6	0.0
Minnesota	5,175	5,223	5,272	5,322	5,371	5,421	5,668	5,901	6,109	6,306	21	21	10.2	8.9	6.9
Mississippi	2,916	2,928	2,940	2,951	2,961	2,971	3,014	3,045	3,069	3,092	31	32	4.5	2.5	1.6
Missouri	5,765	5,797	5,829	5,860	5,891	5,922	6,070	6,200	6,315	6,430	18	19	5.8	4.7	3.7
Montana	933	940	947	955	962	969	999	1,023	1,037	1,045	44	44	7.4	5.6	2.2
Nebraska	1,744	1,750	1,755	1,760	1,765	1,769	1,789	1,803	1,813	1,820	38	37	3.4	1.9	1.0
Nevada	2,352	2,418	2,484	2,552	2,621	2,691	3,058	3,452	3,863	4,282	34	30	34.6	28.3	24.0
New Hampshire	1,315	1,329	1,343	1,357	1,371	1,386	1,457	1,525	1,586	1,646	40	40	12.1	10.0	8.0
New Jersey	8,745	8,804	8,861	8,915	8,968	9,018	9,256	9,462	9,637	9,802	11	11	7.2	4.9	3.6
New Mexico	1,902	1,919	1,936	1,951	1,966	1,980	2,042	2,084	2,107	2,100	36	36	8.9	5.3	0.7
New York	19,258	19,305	19,346	19,383	19,415	19,444	19,547	19,577	19,540	19,477	3	4	2.5	0.7	-0.5
North Carolina	8,702	8,830	8,958	9,087	9,216	9,346	10,011	10,709	11,449	12,228	10	9	16.1	14.6	14.2
North Dakota	635	636	636	636	637	637	635	630	621	607	49	49	-0.9	-1.0	-3.7
Ohio	11,478	11,500	11,522	11,541	11,560	11,576	11,635	11,644	11,606	11,551	7	7	2.0	0.6	-0.8
Oklahoma	3,521	3,536	3,550	3,564	3,578	3,592	3,662	3,736	3,821	3,913	28	28	4.1	4.0	4.8
Oregon	3,596	3,633	3,671	3,710	3,750	3,791	4,013	4,260	4,536	4,834	27	27	10.8	12.4	13.5
Pennsylvania	12,427	12,461	12,494	12,525	12,555	12,584	12,711	12,787	12,802	12,768	6	6	2.5	1.6	-0.1
Rhode Island	1,087	1,093	1,099	1,106	1,111	1,117	1,140	1,154	1,158	1,153	43	43	6.5	3.4	-0.1
South Carolina	4,239	4,282	4,324	4,365	4,406	4,447	4,642	4,823	4,990	5,149	25	23	10.8	8.5	6.8
South Dakota	772	775	778	781	784	786	797	802	802	800	46	46	4.2	2.0	-0.2
Tennessee	5,965	6,018	6,071	6,124	6,178	6,231	6,502	6,781	7,073	7,381	17	16	9.5	8.8	8.8
Texas	22,775	23,149	23,524	23,899	24,274	24,649	26,586	28,635	30,865	33,318	2	2	18.2	16.2	16.4
Utah	2,418	2,453	2,488	2,523	2,559	2,595	2,783	2,990	3,226	3,485	35	34	16.2	15.2	16.6
Vermont	631	635	640	644	648	653	673	691	703	712	48	48	7.2	5.9	3.1
Virginia	7,553	7,645	7,736	7,828	7,919	8,010	8,467	8,917	9,364	9,825	12	12	13.2	11.3	10.2
Washington	6,205	6,267	6,332	6,399	6,469	6,542	6,951	7,432	7,996	8,625	15	14	11.0	13.6	16.0
West Virginia	1,819	1,822	1,825	1,827	1,829	1,829	1,823	1,801	1,766	1,720	37	38	1.2	-1.5	-4.5
Wisconsin	5,554	5,590	5,625	5,660	5,694	5,727	5,883	6,005	6,088	6,151	20	20	6.8	4.8	2.4
Wyoming	507	510	513	515	518	520	528	531	529	523	50	50	5.3	2.1	-1.5

See footnotes at end of table.

Table A-3. States — **Population Projections**—Con.

Geographic area	Males per 100 females, 2010	Population by age (1,000)										Percent of population in 2010	
		Under 18 years		18 to 44 years		45 to 64 years		65 to 74 years		75 years and over		Under 18 years	65 years and over
		2005	2010	2005	2010	2005	2010	2005	2010	2005	2010		
United States . . .	**96.6**	**73,639**	**74,432**	**112,360**	**113,248**	**72,812**	**81,012**	**18,624**	**21,270**	**18,072**	**18,974**	**24.1**	**13.0**
Alabama	93.5	1,112	1,092	1,657	1,605	1,155	1,251	321	354	281	295	23.8	14.1
Alaska	104.2	183	184	264	270	170	184	27	35	17	21	26.5	8.1
Arizona	100.4	1,533	1,688	2,185	2,349	1,384	1,678	406	516	359	406	25.4	13.9
Arkansas	95.9	691	703	1,007	996	697	765	201	227	181	185	24.4	14.3
California	98.2	9,462	9,497	14,357	14,787	8,319	9,391	1,990	2,333	1,910	2,060	24.9	11.5
Colorado	102.1	1,153	1,189	1,861	1,863	1,148	1,263	240	282	216	235	24.6	10.7
Connecticut	93.7	838	814	1,277	1,257	909	990	223	253	256	262	22.8	14.4
Delaware	93.2	199	202	311	309	216	249	59	68	52	57	22.9	14.1
District of Columbia	90.5	117	114	246	237	124	118	32	32	32	29	21.5	11.5
Florida	95.4	3,863	4,086	6,089	6,315	4,541	5,431	1,484	1,773	1,533	1,646	21.2	17.8
Georgia	98.7	2,361	2,502	3,623	3,724	2,086	2,382	473	564	383	417	26.1	10.2
Hawaii	99.9	307	316	471	477	329	357	85	101	85	90	23.6	14.3
Idaho.	100.5	380	400	531	554	338	381	82	99	76	82	26.4	12.0
Illinois	96.9	3,230	3,197	4,916	4,842	3,033	3,277	756	826	765	774	24.7	12.4
Indiana	97.1	1,596	1,596	2,354	2,328	1,533	1,656	386	425	380	386	25.0	12.7
Iowa	97.1	721	711	1,076	1,049	741	800	203	217	233	233	23.6	14.9
Kansas	99.3	702	699	1,024	1,004	667	727	171	185	188	190	24.9	13.4
Kentucky	96.9	1,005	1,002	1,573	1,540	1,066	1,165	278	309	242	249	23.5	13.1
Louisiana	94.8	1,185	1,172	1,706	1,665	1,104	1,194	282	313	257	270	25.4	12.6
Maine	94.8	282	269	470	462	374	413	97	110	96	102	19.8	15.6
Maryland	92.6	1,384	1,406	2,153	2,212	1,421	1,568	331	386	311	332	23.8	12.2
Massachusetts	92.6	1,525	1,484	2,486	2,440	1,649	1,817	406	454	452	454	22.3	13.7
Michigan	97.3	2,555	2,487	3,833	3,822	2,573	2,785	624	699	622	635	23.8	12.8
Minnesota	99.4	1,277	1,290	2,003	2,027	1,278	1,433	301	343	316	327	23.8	12.4
Mississippi	94.6	771	759	1,084	1,052	706	781	189	209	165	170	25.6	12.8
Missouri.	95.4	1,418	1,411	2,134	2,111	1,443	1,578	391	432	379	390	23.8	13.9
Montana	99.1	215	212	326	324	263	287	66	77	64	68	21.9	15.0
Nebraska	97.9	445	446	642	619	425	460	111	119	122	125	25.2	13.8
Nevada	100.7	593	665	894	961	598	735	157	199	110	131	24.7	12.3
New Hampshire.	97.3	307	304	489	494	360	408	82	97	76	82	22.0	12.9
New Jersey	94.8	2,103	2,088	3,285	3,252	2,212	2,446	564	632	582	600	23.2	13.7
New Mexico	94.6	488	479	684	669	491	553	129	153	111	126	24.2	14.1
New York	93.4	4,607	4,421	7,380	7,227	4,762	5,144	1,243	1,346	1,266	1,306	22.7	13.6
North Carolina.	97.2	2,152	2,269	3,363	3,471	2,150	2,445	554	641	483	520	24.3	12.4
North Dakota	101.1	149	142	231	223	161	174	43	46	50	51	22.3	15.3
Ohio	95.4	2,819	2,744	4,220	4,123	2,917	3,121	758	816	763	771	23.7	13.7
Oklahoma	97.5	890	895	1,293	1,264	873	938	243	266	222	229	24.9	13.8
Oregon	98.8	844	863	1,360	1,412	944	1,022	220	263	228	231	22.8	13.0
Pennsylvania	93.6	2,844	2,748	4,444	4,385	3,242	3,496	893	960	1,004	997	21.8	15.5
Rhode Island	92.7	256	249	408	410	271	300	68	76	83	82	22.3	14.1
South Carolina	94.9	1,038	1,036	1,577	1,579	1,095	1,226	289	343	240	263	23.3	13.6
South Dakota	100.3	195	194	278	269	189	209	51	55	58	60	24.7	14.6
Tennessee	94.9	1,449	1,479	2,248	2,249	1,522	1,673	403	461	345	368	23.7	13.3
Texas	98.4	6,317	6,785	9,068	9,417	5,122	5,859	1,216	1,426	1,052	1,162	27.5	10.5
Utah	100.4	771	819	979	1,021	460	520	108	127	99	108	31.6	9.0
Vermont.	97.4	140	132	230	232	179	195	42	50	41	43	20.3	14.3
Virginia	96.0	1,827	1,880	2,940	2,997	1,918	2,139	463	554	404	441	23.5	12.4
Washington	98.8	1,491	1,488	2,410	2,481	1,602	1,777	353	429	350	367	22.8	12.2
West Virginia	96.0	392	382	640	618	508	536	145	156	135	136	20.9	16.0
Wisconsin.	98.1	1,334	1,319	2,095	2,076	1,404	1,561	351	392	369	380	23.0	13.5
Wyoming	100.6	119	116	183	177	142	154	34	40	30	33	22.4	14.0

X Not applicable.

Survey, Census, or Data Collection Method: Based on calculations using National Center for Health Statistics (NCHS) fertility and mortality rates, state migration patterns derived from the Internal Revenue Service (IRS) and Census 2000, and international migration derived from the Population Estimates Program and data on the foreign-born population in Census 2000; for information, see Internet site <http://www.census.gov/population/www/methodep.html>.

Source: U.S. Census Bureau, "State Interim Population Projections by Age and Sex: 2004–2030," published 21 April 2005. See Internet site <http://www.census.gov/population/www/projections/projectionsagesex.html>.

Geographic area	Population by age, 2004 (1,000)										
	Total	Under 5 years	5 to 17 years	18 to 24 years	25 to 34 years	35 to 44 years	45 to 54 years	55 to 64 years	65 to 74 years	75 to 84 years	85 years and over
United States . . .	**293,655**	**20,071**	**53,207**	**29,245**	**40,032**	**44,109**	**41,619**	**29,079**	**18,463**	**12,971**	**4,860**
Alabama	4,530	296	798	456	603	651	648	480	325	207	66
Alaska	655	50	138	74	81	102	107	61	26	13	4
Arizona	5,744	450	1,097	571	830	800	719	545	396	250	86
Arkansas	2,753	186	491	280	360	385	376	294	205	128	48
California	35,894	2,634	6,962	3,596	5,253	5,541	4,860	3,225	1,950	1,359	514
Colorado	4,601	339	840	457	717	709	668	421	241	154	56
Connecticut	3,504	213	626	311	409	565	532	374	217	175	82
Delaware	830	54	140	84	110	128	119	87	58	38	13
District of Columbia	554	35	75	58	108	82	72	56	34	24	9
Florida	17,397	1,091	2,912	1,549	2,142	2,530	2,380	1,865	1,475	1,073	380
Georgia	8,829	679	1,654	902	1,364	1,392	1,189	803	477	275	95
Hawaii	1,263	89	210	126	161	180	186	138	79	68	25
Idaho	1,393	103	269	157	185	192	194	135	83	53	22
Illinois	12,714	891	2,348	1,260	1,798	1,905	1,782	1,210	761	540	219
Indiana	6,238	431	1,170	632	826	907	886	614	388	279	105
Iowa	2,954	181	500	316	369	418	436	301	203	158	72
Kansas	2,736	189	495	299	359	388	392	260	170	129	55
Kentucky	4,146	267	714	413	568	621	605	439	281	179	59
Louisiana	4,516	324	841	503	598	642	639	441	280	188	60
Maine	1,317	68	215	124	146	205	216	155	95	69	25
Maryland	5,558	375	1,020	521	711	895	829	573	326	226	83
Massachusetts	6,417	396	1,069	598	880	1,030	937	652	396	322	136
Michigan	10,113	650	1,884	997	1,306	1,514	1,496	1,020	612	460	175
Minnesota	5,101	332	908	531	678	793	755	488	300	217	98
Mississippi	2,903	208	541	323	391	405	397	284	193	121	40
Missouri	5,755	371	1,013	589	751	845	826	592	392	274	100
Montana	927	53	156	99	107	128	152	107	66	42	18
Nebraska	1,747	122	313	191	229	244	249	167	111	85	36
Nevada	2,335	169	435	210	355	355	310	239	154	84	24
New Hampshire.	1,300	73	232	122	149	216	209	141	79	56	22
New Jersey	8,699	581	1,575	744	1,095	1,416	1,275	886	543	420	163
New Mexico	1,903	133	359	206	236	266	275	199	126	77	27
New York	19,227	1,246	3,326	1,825	2,633	2,993	2,741	1,970	1,226	913	354
North Carolina.	8,541	600	1,518	828	1,242	1,289	1,175	856	555	356	121
North Dakota	634	36	103	77	81	85	97	63	43	34	16
Ohio	11,459	730	2,049	1,128	1,464	1,684	1,702	1,177	747	570	208
Oklahoma	3,524	242	618	385	470	488	493	363	249	161	54
Oregon	3,595	226	626	350	506	511	537	379	227	163	70
Pennsylvania	12,406	719	2,118	1,185	1,471	1,823	1,869	1,325	864	742	291
Rhode Island	1,081	62	182	112	139	166	159	110	65	60	26
South Carolina	4,198	280	744	429	568	611	594	451	286	175	59
South Dakota	771	52	139	87	93	106	111	74	52	39	18
Tennessee	5,901	385	1,007	576	828	887	852	629	407	248	84
Texas	22,490	1,843	4,424	2,400	3,336	3,338	2,981	1,952	1,214	756	246
Utah	2,389	233	507	313	399	291	268	170	111	71	26
Vermont	621	31	104	62	70	95	105	74	41	28	11
Virginia	7,460	498	1,307	748	1,015	1,173	1,093	778	453	291	103
Washington	6,204	387	1,099	635	859	956	933	631	357	243	103
West Virginia	1,815	101	284	173	227	252	284	217	144	102	33
Wisconsin.	5,509	338	970	575	696	840	826	550	349	256	111
Wyoming	507	31	86	57	61	69	84	57	33	21	7

See footnotes at end of table.

Geographic area	Population under 18 years (1,000)			Population 65 years and over (1,000)			Percent of population by age						Males per 100 females, 2004
							Under 18 years			65 years and over			
	2004	2000	1990[1]	2004	2000	1990[1]	2004	2000	1990[1]	2004	2000	1990[1]	
United States . . .	**73,278**	**72,295**	**63,941**	**36,294**	**34,992**	**31,082**	**25.0**	**25.7**	**25.7**	**12.4**	**12.4**	**12.5**	**96.9**
Alabama	1,095	1,124	1,064	598	580	520	24.2	25.3	26.3	13.2	13.0	12.9	94.1
Alaska	188	191	173	42	36	22	28.7	30.4	31.4	6.4	5.7	4.0	107.1
Arizona	1,547	1,367	986	732	668	476	26.9	26.6	26.9	12.7	13.0	13.0	100.1
Arkansas	677	680	624	381	374	349	24.6	25.4	26.5	13.8	14.0	14.8	96.1
California	9,596	9,250	7,822	3,823	3,596	3,113	26.7	27.3	26.3	10.7	10.6	10.5	99.6
Colorado	1,179	1,101	864	451	416	328	25.6	25.6	26.2	9.8	9.7	10.0	101.8
Connecticut	839	842	754	474	470	444	23.9	24.7	22.9	13.5	13.8	13.5	94.3
Delaware	194	195	164	109	102	80	23.3	24.8	24.6	13.1	13.0	12.1	95.1
District of Columbia	110	115	119	67	70	77	19.8	20.1	19.5	12.1	12.2	12.7	89.7
Florida	4,003	3,646	2,884	2,928	2,808	2,356	23.0	22.8	22.3	16.8	17.6	18.2	96.1
Georgia	2,333	2,169	1,736	847	785	651	26.4	26.5	26.8	9.6	9.6	10.0	97.8
Hawaii	299	296	282	172	161	124	23.7	24.4	25.4	13.6	13.3	11.2	99.6
Idaho	372	369	309	159	146	121	26.7	28.5	30.7	11.4	11.3	12.0	100.6
Illinois	3,238	3,246	2,961	1,521	1,500	1,429	25.5	26.1	25.9	12.0	12.1	12.5	96.5
Indiana	1,600	1,574	1,461	772	753	694	25.7	25.9	26.3	12.4	12.4	12.5	96.9
Iowa	680	734	721	433	436	426	23.0	25.1	25.9	14.7	14.9	15.3	96.9
Kansas	683	713	663	355	356	342	25.0	26.5	26.8	13.0	13.2	13.8	98.6
Kentucky	980	995	957	519	505	465	23.6	24.6	26.0	12.5	12.5	12.6	96.3
Louisiana	1,165	1,220	1,233	528	517	467	25.8	27.3	29.2	11.7	11.6	11.1	94.5
Maine	282	301	310	190	183	163	21.4	23.6	25.3	14.4	14.4	13.3	95.4
Maryland	1,395	1,356	1,168	635	599	514	25.1	25.6	24.4	11.4	11.3	10.8	93.9
Massachusetts	1,464	1,500	1,361	854	860	815	22.8	23.6	22.6	13.3	13.5	13.5	93.8
Michigan	2,533	2,596	2,468	1,247	1,219	1,104	25.1	26.1	26.5	12.3	12.3	11.9	96.6
Minnesota	1,240	1,287	1,170	615	594	546	24.3	26.2	26.7	12.1	12.1	12.5	98.6
Mississippi	750	775	750	353	344	319	25.8	27.3	29.1	12.2	12.1	12.4	94.3
Missouri	1,385	1,428	1,319	766	755	715	24.1	25.5	25.8	13.3	13.5	14.0	95.5
Montana	208	230	223	127	121	106	22.5	25.5	27.9	13.7	13.4	13.3	99.5
Nebraska	435	450	430	232	232	223	24.9	26.3	27.2	13.3	13.6	14.1	97.7
Nevada	604	512	299	262	219	127	25.9	25.6	24.8	11.2	11.0	10.5	103.7
New Hampshire	305	310	280	157	148	125	23.5	25.0	25.2	12.1	12.0	11.2	97.3
New Jersey	2,156	2,088	1,817	1,126	1,113	1,026	24.8	24.8	23.5	12.9	13.2	13.2	94.9
New Mexico	492	509	449	229	212	162	25.9	28.0	29.6	12.1	11.7	10.7	96.8
New York	4,572	4,690	4,292	2,493	2,449	2,340	23.8	24.7	23.9	13.0	12.9	13.0	93.8
North Carolina	2,118	1,964	1,616	1,032	969	800	24.8	24.4	24.4	12.1	12.0	12.1	96.7
North Dakota	139	161	176	93	94	91	21.9	25.0	27.5	14.7	14.7	14.2	99.7
Ohio	2,779	2,888	2,808	1,525	1,508	1,403	24.3	25.4	25.9	13.3	13.3	12.9	94.9
Oklahoma	860	892	840	464	456	423	24.4	25.9	26.7	13.2	13.2	13.4	97.6
Oregon	852	847	727	460	438	390	23.7	24.7	25.6	12.8	12.8	13.7	98.8
Pennsylvania	2,837	2,922	2,807	1,897	1,919	1,821	22.9	23.8	23.6	15.3	15.6	15.3	94.1
Rhode Island	244	248	227	151	152	150	22.6	23.6	22.6	13.9	14.5	14.9	93.2
South Carolina	1,025	1,010	925	520	485	394	24.4	25.2	26.5	12.4	12.1	11.3	95.0
South Dakota	191	203	199	109	108	102	24.8	26.8	28.6	14.2	14.3	14.7	98.9
Tennessee	1,391	1,399	1,222	738	703	616	23.6	24.6	25.1	12.5	12.4	12.6	95.7
Texas	6,267	5,887	4,858	2,217	2,073	1,708	27.9	28.2	28.6	9.9	9.9	10.1	99.2
Utah	740	719	629	208	190	149	31.0	32.2	36.5	8.7	8.5	8.7	100.8
Vermont	135	148	144	81	78	66	21.7	24.2	25.5	13.0	12.7	11.7	96.9
Virginia	1,805	1,738	1,511	847	792	661	24.2	24.6	24.4	11.4	11.2	10.7	96.9
Washington	1,486	1,514	1,267	703	662	573	24.0	25.7	26.0	11.3	11.2	11.8	99.5
West Virginia	385	402	445	278	277	268	21.2	22.3	24.8	15.3	15.3	14.9	95.6
Wisconsin	1,308	1,369	1,292	716	703	650	23.7	25.5	26.4	13.0	13.1	13.3	98.0
Wyoming	117	129	136	61	58	47	23.1	26.1	30.0	12.1	11.7	10.4	101.4

[1]The April 1, 1990, data shown here do not reflect the corrections referred to in footnote 2 of Table A-1.

Survey, Census, or Data Collection Method: Based on the Census of Population and Housing; for information, see Appendix B, Limitations of the Data and Methodology, and sites <http://www.census.gov/main/www/cen2000.html> and <http://www.census.gov/popest/topics/methodology/>.

Source: U.S. Census Bureau, "State Single Year of Age and Sex Population Estimates: April 1, 2000 to July 1, 2004—RESIDENT"; see Internet site <http://www.census.gov/popest/states/files/SC-EST2004-AGESEX_RES.csv>; and "Age and Sex for States and for Puerto Rico: April 1, 2000 to July 1, 2004"; see Internet site <http://www.census.gov/popest/states/asrh/SC-est2004-02.html>; and "Table ST-99-9 Population Estimates for the U.S., Regions, and States by Selected Age Groups and Sex: Annual Time Series, July 1, 1990 to July 1, 1999," published 9 March 2000; see Internet site <http://www.census.gov/popest/archives/1990s/ST-99-09.txt>.

Geographic area	All races (1,000)		White alone (1,000)		Black or African American alone (1,000)		American Indian, Alaska Native alone (1,000)		Asian alone (1,000)		Native Hawaiian and Other Pacific Islander alone (1,000)		Two or more races (1,000)		Hispanic or Latino origin (1,000)		Non-Hispanic White alone (1,000)	
	2004	2000¹	2004	2000¹	2004	2000¹	2004	2000¹	2004	2000¹	2004	2000¹	2004	2000¹	2004	2000¹	2004	2000¹
United States ...	**293,655**	**281,425**	**236,058**	**228,107**	**37,502**	**35,705**	**2,825**	**2,664**	**12,326**	**10,589**	**506**	**463**	**4,439**	**3,898**	**41,322**	**35,306**	**197,841**	**195,577**
Alabama	4,530	4,447	3,235	3,196	1,194	1,159	23	23	37	32	2	2	39	36	98	76	3,148	3,131
Alaska	655	627	464	446	24	23	104	99	30	26	4	3	31	30	32	26	438	426
Arizona	5,744	5,131	5,033	4,519	203	169	289	267	123	98	10	9	86	70	1,609	1,296	3,510	3,292
Arkansas	2,753	2,673	2,238	2,183	434	421	20	18	26	21	2	2	32	29	121	87	2,126	2,103
California	35,894	33,872	27,710	26,365	2,437	2,381	417	403	4,326	3,817	149	138	855	768	12,443	10,967	15,982	16,058
Colorado	4,601	4,302	4,154	3,904	189	173	52	50	116	99	6	6	82	71	879	736	3,334	3,218
Connecticut	3,504	3,406	2,983	2,933	352	334	12	11	108	86	3	2	46	39	372	320	2,658	2,656
Delaware	830	784	625	601	169	154	3	3	21	17	(Z)	(Z)	11	9	48	37	583	570
District of Columbia	554	572	207	197	319	349	2	2	17	16	(Z)	(Z)	8	7	47	45	168	161
Florida	17,397	15,983	14,022	13,037	2,726	2,429	74	59	352	279	14	11	209	167	3,305	2,683	10,920	10,510
Georgia	8,829	8,187	5,863	5,535	2,613	2,371	27	24	230	178	7	5	90	73	598	435	5,319	5,145
Hawaii	1,263	1,212	335	314	28	23	4	4	528	511	114	116	254	244	100	88	295	282
Idaho...........	1,393	1,294	1,331	1,239	8	6	20	18	14	12	2	1	19	17	124	102	1,215	1,143
Illinois	12,714	12,420	10,101	9,922	1,926	1,902	39	37	505	435	8	7	135	117	1,775	1,530	8,414	8,471
Indiana	6,238	6,081	5,530	5,428	548	516	18	17	73	61	3	2	66	56	269	215	5,280	5,230
Iowa	2,954	2,926	2,807	2,792	68	63	10	10	42	38	1	1	26	23	104	82	2,710	2,715
Kansas	2,736	2,689	2,445	2,415	161	157	26	26	57	48	2	2	44	41	220	188	2,239	2,239
Kentucky	4,146	4,042	3,747	3,668	311	299	9	9	37	30	2	2	40	34	77	60	3,678	3,615
Louisiana	4,516	4,469	2,896	2,894	1,492	1,458	27	26	62	56	2	1	37	33	124	108	2,789	2,803
Maine	1,317	1,275	1,277	1,240	10	7	7	7	11	9	(Z)	(Z)	12	11	12	9	1,266	1,232
Maryland	5,558	5,297	3,583	3,494	1,615	1,500	18	17	258	216	3	3	81	68	298	228	3,325	3,301
Massachusetts	6,417	6,349	5,581	5,604	435	406	18	18	295	246	5	5	83	70	494	429	5,181	5,257
Michigan	10,113	9,938	8,232	8,138	1,451	1,426	60	60	220	181	4	3	146	130	375	324	7,896	7,849
Minnesota	5,101	4,919	4,583	4,474	212	180	59	56	172	146	3	2	72	61	179	143	4,421	4,345
Mississippi	2,903	2,845	1,780	1,762	1,069	1,036	13	12	21	19	1	1	18	16	49	40	1,739	1,730
Missouri.........	5,755	5,597	4,916	4,805	661	635	26	26	75	63	4	3	73	65	148	119	4,781	4,698
Montana	927	902	844	824	3	3	60	56	5	5	1	(Z)	14	13	22	18	826	809
Nebraska	1,747	1,711	1,609	1,586	75	70	17	16	27	23	1	1	19	16	120	94	1,497	1,497
Nevada	2,335	1,998	1,927	1,683	176	140	33	28	128	94	12	9	58	45	532	394	1,429	1,312
New Hampshire.......	1,300	1,236	1,250	1,196	12	10	3	3	22	16	1	(Z)	12	10	28	20	1,225	1,178
New Jersey	8,699	8,414	6,690	6,588	1,260	1,212	27	24	607	494	7	6	108	90	1,294	1,117	5,549	5,605
New Mexico	1,903	1,819	1,612	1,553	45	38	192	179	24	21	2	2	28	25	823	765	827	821
New York	19,227	18,977	14,216	14,161	3,361	3,346	103	101	1,249	1,105	18	17	279	246	3,077	2,868	11,746	11,881
North Carolina......	8,541	8,046	6,332	5,999	1,861	1,753	110	102	148	118	6	5	83	70	518	379	5,861	5,659
North Dakota......	634	642	586	597	5	4	33	31	4	4	(Z)	(Z)	6	6	10	8	578	590
Ohio	11,459	11,353	9,768	9,749	1,362	1,318	26	26	159	136	4	3	140	122	252	217	9,547	9,562
Oklahoma	3,524	3,451	2,770	2,722	272	264	284	276	54	48	3	3	140	139	223	179	2,570	2,563
Oregon	3,595	3,421	3,267	3,127	64	58	49	48	122	104	10	9	83	75	343	275	2,948	2,872
Pennsylvania	12,406	12,281	10,693	10,675	1,304	1,259	22	20	267	225	5	4	115	97	476	394	10,288	10,346
Rhode Island	1,081	1,048	962	942	66	60	6	6	29	25	1	1	16	14	112	91	870	869
South Carolina	4,198	4,012	2,868	2,739	1,233	1,190	16	14	44	37	2	2	35	30	130	95	2,753	2,658
South Dakota	771	755	684	674	6	5	67	62	5	4	(Z)	(Z)	9	9	15	11	671	665
Tennessee	5,901	5,689	4,763	4,626	991	938	17	16	71	58	3	3	56	48	167	124	4,611	4,515
Texas	22,490	20,852	18,726	17,453	2,633	2,454	153	139	718	587	24	20	235	199	7,781	6,670	11,190	10,987
Utah	2,389	2,233	2,241	2,100	23	19	32	31	45	39	17	16	31	28	253	202	2,003	1,911
Vermont.........	621	609	602	591	4	3	2	2	6	5	(Z)	(Z)	7	6	6	6	597	587
Virginia	7,460	7,079	5,502	5,277	1,483	1,411	24	23	330	268	5	5	115	96	426	330	5,122	4,988
Washington	6,204	5,894	5,290	5,082	216	199	101	97	388	331	28	25	180	160	527	442	4,809	4,680
West Virginia	1,815	1,808	1,728	1,723	58	58	4	4	10	10	(Z)	(Z)	15	14	15	12	1,714	1,712
Wisconsin.........	5,509	5,364	4,967	4,865	328	309	51	48	106	91	2	2	56	49	237	193	4,749	4,689
Wyoming	507	494	480	469	4	4	12	11	3	3	(Z)	(Z)	6	6	34	32	449	440

See footnotes at end of table.

Geographic area	Percent of total, 2004								Percent change, 2000–2004							
	White alone	Black or African American alone	American Indian, Alaska Native alone	Asian alone	Native Hawaiian, Other Pacific Islander alone	Two or more races	Hispanic or Latino origin	Non-Hispanic White alone	White alone	Black or African American alone	American Indian, Alaska Native alone	Asian alone	Native Hawaiian, Other Pacific Islander alone	Two or more races	Hispanic or Latino origin	Non-Hispanic White alone
United States . . .	**80.4**	**12.8**	**1.0**	**4.2**	**0.2**	**1.5**	**14.1**	**67.4**	**3.5**	**5.0**	**6.0**	**16.4**	**9.3**	**13.9**	**17.0**	**1.2**
Alabama	71.4	26.4	0.5	0.8	(Z)	0.9	2.2	69.5	1.2	3.1	0.5	14.5	11.6	9.4	29.7	0.5
Alaska	70.7	3.6	15.8	4.5	0.6	4.7	4.9	66.9	3.8	4.1	4.9	15.9	10.0	3.6	25.3	2.8
Arizona	87.6	3.5	5.0	2.1	0.2	1.5	28.0	61.1	11.4	20.3	8.4	25.9	21.4	21.7	24.2	6.6
Arkansas	81.3	15.8	0.7	0.9	0.1	1.2	4.4	77.2	2.5	3.3	7.4	24.3	18.4	11.5	39.1	1.1
California	77.2	6.8	1.2	12.1	0.4	2.4	34.7	44.5	5.1	2.3	3.3	13.4	8.1	11.4	13.5	-0.5
Colorado	90.3	4.1	1.1	2.5	0.1	1.8	19.1	72.5	6.4	9.1	5.6	17.9	17.5	16.4	19.4	3.6
Connecticut	85.1	10.1	0.3	3.1	0.1	1.3	10.6	75.9	1.7	5.4	9.8	25.5	19.9	17.1	16.1	0.1
Delaware	75.3	20.4	0.4	2.6	0.1	1.3	5.8	70.2	4.0	10.2	9.1	28.9	26.2	20.7	29.2	2.4
District of Columbia	37.4	57.7	0.3	3.0	0.1	1.5	8.5	30.3	5.1	-8.6	-4.5	6.5	-9.2	9.3	5.1	3.9
Florida	80.6	15.7	0.4	2.0	0.1	1.2	19.0	62.8	7.6	12.2	23.9	26.2	27.4	24.8	23.2	3.9
Georgia	66.4	29.6	0.3	2.6	0.1	1.1	6.8	60.2	5.9	10.2	14.3	28.8	27.7	22.8	37.5	3.4
Hawaii	26.5	2.2	0.3	41.8	9.1	20.1	7.9	23.3	6.7	20.4	12.1	3.3	-1.4	4.1	13.8	4.3
Idaho	95.5	0.6	1.4	1.0	0.1	1.3	8.9	87.2	7.4	32.6	7.9	14.5	11.8	12.4	21.8	6.2
Illinois	79.5	15.1	0.3	4.0	0.1	1.1	14.0	66.2	1.8	1.3	6.7	15.9	10.2	15.6	16.0	-0.7
Indiana	88.7	8.8	0.3	1.2	(Z)	1.1	4.3	84.6	1.9	6.2	5.3	20.1	19.0	18.4	25.5	1.0
Iowa	95.0	2.3	0.3	1.4	(Z)	0.9	3.5	91.7	0.5	6.7	8.8	12.8	11.3	13.6	26.2	-0.2
Kansas	89.4	5.9	1.0	2.1	0.1	1.6	8.1	81.9	1.2	2.5	0.8	17.9	15.2	9.1	17.0	(Z)
Kentucky	90.4	7.5	0.2	0.9	(Z)	1.0	1.9	88.7	2.2	4.0	3.1	21.4	19.0	16.0	28.5	1.8
Louisiana	64.1	33.0	0.6	1.4	(Z)	0.8	2.8	61.8	0.1	2.4	4.8	10.4	9.8	10.5	15.3	-0.5
Maine	96.9	0.7	0.6	0.8	(Z)	0.9	0.9	96.1	3.0	32.6	3.8	16.4	15.0	12.5	33.3	2.8
Maryland	64.5	29.1	0.3	4.6	0.1	1.5	5.4	59.8	2.6	7.7	6.4	19.4	20.2	19.0	30.6	0.7
Massachusetts	87.0	6.8	0.3	4.6	0.1	1.3	7.7	80.8	-0.4	7.0	5.1	19.7	11.9	17.7	15.3	-1.4
Michigan	81.4	14.3	0.6	2.2	(Z)	1.4	3.7	78.1	1.2	1.7	0.3	21.6	21.3	11.8	15.8	0.6
Minnesota	89.9	4.1	1.2	3.4	0.1	1.4	3.5	86.7	2.4	17.6	5.9	18.4	19.3	16.8	25.1	1.7
Mississippi	61.3	36.8	0.5	0.7	(Z)	0.6	1.7	59.9	1.1	3.2	13.0	12.4	11.6	13.5	24.0	0.5
Missouri	85.4	11.5	0.5	1.3	0.1	1.3	2.6	83.1	2.3	4.2	2.7	18.3	13.4	12.1	24.9	1.8
Montana	91.1	0.4	6.4	0.5	0.1	1.5	2.4	89.1	2.5	23.4	5.6	5.0	4.7	2.9	20.8	2.0
Nebraska	92.1	4.3	0.9	1.5	0.1	1.1	6.9	85.7	1.5	6.8	5.9	18.7	18.4	14.7	27.1	(Z)
Nevada	82.5	7.5	1.4	5.5	0.5	2.5	22.8	61.2	14.5	25.7	16.8	37.2	31.3	30.1	35.0	8.9
New Hampshire	96.2	0.9	0.2	1.7	(Z)	0.9	2.1	94.3	4.5	23.3	4.8	33.9	27.8	19.7	34.2	4.0
New Jersey	76.9	14.5	0.3	7.0	0.1	1.2	14.9	63.8	1.6	3.9	10.9	22.8	18.4	19.8	15.9	-1.0
New Mexico	84.7	2.4	10.1	1.3	0.1	1.5	43.3	43.5	3.8	16.5	7.4	13.4	14.6	8.7	7.6	0.7
New York	73.9	17.5	0.5	6.5	0.1	1.5	16.0	61.1	0.4	0.5	1.9	13.1	7.4	13.3	7.3	-1.1
North Carolina	74.1	21.8	1.3	1.7	0.1	1.0	6.1	68.6	5.6	6.2	7.7	25.7	20.9	19.4	36.6	3.6
North Dakota	92.4	0.7	5.2	0.7	(Z)	0.9	1.5	91.1	-1.7	10.2	5.1	12.8	5.2	0.8	25.3	-2.1
Ohio	85.2	11.9	0.2	1.4	(Z)	1.2	2.2	83.3	0.2	3.4	1.8	17.3	13.1	14.7	16.2	-0.1
Oklahoma	78.6	7.7	8.1	1.5	0.1	4.0	6.3	72.9	1.8	3.0	3.0	12.1	10.5	1.3	24.4	0.3
Oregon	90.9	1.8	1.4	3.4	0.3	2.3	9.5	82.0	4.5	9.6	3.2	17.2	11.9	10.4	24.7	2.6
Pennsylvania	86.2	10.5	0.2	2.2	(Z)	0.9	3.8	82.9	0.2	3.6	10.7	18.3	18.2	17.7	20.7	-0.6
Rhode Island	89.1	6.1	0.6	2.7	0.1	1.5	10.3	80.5	2.1	10.1	7.7	13.5	11.9	15.8	23.1	0.1
South Carolina	68.3	29.4	0.4	1.1	0.1	0.8	3.1	65.6	4.7	3.6	8.9	19.4	23.3	17.6	37.2	3.6
South Dakota	88.7	0.8	8.6	0.7	(Z)	1.2	2.0	87.1	1.4	20.9	6.5	16.7	4.9	5.2	38.4	0.9
Tennessee	80.7	16.8	0.3	1.2	(Z)	0.9	2.8	78.1	2.9	5.7	6.8	22.1	16.8	16.2	34.9	2.1
Texas	83.3	11.7	0.7	3.2	0.1	1.0	34.6	49.8	7.3	7.3	10.7	22.4	19.6	18.3	16.7	1.9
Utah	93.8	0.9	1.3	1.9	0.7	1.3	10.6	83.8	6.7	16.3	3.3	15.5	8.7	12.4	25.6	4.8
Vermont	96.9	0.6	0.4	1.0	(Z)	1.1	1.0	96.0	1.8	14.6	-6.3	17.7	11.4	6.5	16.5	1.7
Virginia	73.8	19.9	0.3	4.4	0.1	1.5	5.7	68.7	4.3	5.1	6.9	23.1	19.3	20.1	29.3	2.7
Washington	85.3	3.5	1.6	6.3	0.5	2.9	8.5	77.5	4.1	8.7	4.6	17.3	11.4	12.1	19.3	2.7
West Virginia	95.2	3.2	0.2	0.6	(Z)	0.8	0.8	94.4	0.3	0.5	1.7	6.3	(Z)	10.4	19.1	0.1
Wisconsin	90.2	5.9	0.9	1.9	(Z)	1.0	4.3	86.2	2.1	6.0	6.5	16.2	17.5	13.9	23.0	1.3
Wyoming	94.8	0.9	2.4	0.6	0.1	1.2	6.7	88.6	2.3	12.8	7.1	12.1	8.8	7.0	6.8	1.9

Z Less than 500 or .05%.

[1]April 1, 2000, Population Estimates base reflects changes to the Census 2000 population from the Count Question Resolution program and geographic program revisions.

Survey, Census, or Data Collection Method: Based on the Census of Population and Housing; for information, see Appendix B, Limitations of the Data and Methodology, and Internet sites <http://www.census.gov/main/www/cen2000.html> and <http://www.census.gov/popest/topics/methodology/>.

Source: U.S. Census Bureau, "State Population Estimates with Sex, 6 Race Groups (5 Race Alone Groups and One Group with Two or More Race Groups) and Hispanic Origin: April 1, 2000 to July 1, 2004" (SC-EST2004-6RACE), published 11 August 2005; <http://www.census.gov/popest/datasets.html>; "Table 4: Annual Estimates of the Population by Race Alone and Hispanic or Latino Origin for the United States and States: July 1, 2004" (SC-EST2004-04), published 11 August 2005; <http://www.census.gov/popest/states/asrh/SC-EST2004-04.html>.

Table A-6. States — **Households**

Geographic area	Total households (1,000) 2003	Total households (1,000) 2000	2003, percent — Family households — Total[1] — Family households, total	With own children under 18 years	Married-couple families Total	With own children under 18 years	Female householder, no husband present Total	With own children under 18 years	Nonfamily households Total	Householder living alone Total	65 years and over	Households with one or more persons— Under 18 years	65 years and over	Persons per household 2003	Persons per household 2000
United States . . .	**108,420**	**104,819**	**67.4**	**32.2**	**50.4**	**22.4**	**12.6**	**7.7**	**32.6**	**26.8**	**9.1**	**35.4**	**23.0**	**2.61**	**2.61**
Alabama	1,743	1,727	68.5	30.6	50.5	20.6	14.1	8.3	31.5	28.1	9.9	34.3	23.9	2.52	2.51
Alaska	229	223	68.2	38.3	50.4	26.4	11.8	7.8	31.8	25.1	4.7	42.3	13.3	2.75	2.73
Arizona	2,049	1,914	67.9	32.4	50.0	21.1	12.7	8.3	32.1	24.7	8.3	36.2	24.1	2.67	2.62
Arkansas	1,076	1,043	68.6	30.1	52.1	20.2	12.5	7.8	31.5	26.7	10.2	33.4	25.1	2.46	2.49
California	11,857	11,389	68.4	35.3	50.0	25.0	12.9	7.7	31.6	24.3	7.7	39.2	21.8	2.92	2.90
Colorado	1,821	1,703	66.5	33.4	52.0	24.4	9.7	6.6	33.6	26.9	7.2	36.4	17.9	2.44	2.47
Connecticut	1,323	1,291	68.3	33.2	51.1	23.2	13.8	8.5	31.7	25.7	9.5	35.6	24.1	2.55	2.55
Delaware	304	295	65.9	30.1	49.8	21.0	11.9	7.3	34.1	27.3	9.4	33.5	24.2	2.61	2.57
District of Columbia	247	244	45.6	20.6	22.5	8.1	19.4	11.1	54.4	45.5	10.5	24.8	20.3	2.14	2.20
Florida	6,638	6,290	65.4	27.9	48.2	18.2	12.7	7.6	34.6	28.1	11.1	31.3	29.7	2.50	2.48
Georgia	3,153	2,947	68.7	33.9	49.9	22.9	14.6	9.1	31.3	26.6	7.0	37.7	18.7	2.68	2.70
Hawaii	419	387	68.9	28.2	51.6	20.5	12.0	5.8	31.1	24.6	8.3	33.8	27.8	2.91	3.04
Idaho	503	469	71.6	35.2	59.3	27.4	8.6	6.0	28.4	21.8	7.8	37.9	21.4	2.65	2.69
Illinois	4,625	4,540	67.0	32.5	50.5	23.6	12.6	7.2	33.0	27.8	9.4	35.7	22.6	2.67	2.66
Indiana	2,351	2,301	67.5	31.8	52.8	22.6	11.0	7.2	32.5	26.9	9.4	34.7	22.1	2.56	2.56
Iowa	1,158	1,141	65.5	29.9	53.9	22.3	8.4	5.8	34.5	28.2	10.7	32.0	24.4	2.45	2.47
Kansas	1,059	1,036	67.0	32.0	53.1	23.4	9.9	6.4	33.0	28.0	9.6	34.6	22.3	2.50	2.52
Kentucky	1,607	1,578	69.9	31.9	53.6	22.4	12.3	7.4	30.1	25.8	9.5	34.8	22.8	2.49	2.49
Louisiana	1,673	1,656	68.9	32.8	47.2	19.7	17.4	11.0	31.2	26.4	9.0	37.3	21.9	2.61	2.62
Maine	535	523	65.0	28.6	50.8	19.6	10.2	6.7	35.0	28.6	10.7	30.6	24.9	2.37	2.37
Maryland	2,048	1,977	68.4	33.1	49.3	22.5	14.6	8.3	31.6	25.4	7.9	37.0	21.4	2.62	2.61
Massachusetts	2,436	2,410	65.1	31.7	48.7	22.6	12.6	7.3	35.0	28.5	10.5	34.2	24.3	2.55	2.54
Michigan	3,884	3,809	66.9	32.0	50.8	22.4	12.1	7.6	33.1	28.0	9.3	34.7	22.6	2.53	2.54
Minnesota	2,012	1,937	66.3	32.6	53.3	24.4	9.2	5.9	33.7	27.9	9.1	34.4	21.2	2.45	2.47
Mississippi	1,056	1,029	70.0	33.0	47.8	20.2	17.8	10.7	30.0	25.8	9.8	38.3	23.6	2.64	2.67
Missouri	2,285	2,236	67.4	30.8	51.5	21.3	11.4	7.1	32.6	26.6	9.5	33.9	23.2	2.42	2.43
Montana	366	360	65.1	29.1	52.5	20.8	9.0	5.9	34.9	28.1	10.3	31.4	23.4	2.44	2.44
Nebraska	675	664	65.2	30.7	53.7	23.8	8.4	5.3	34.8	28.7	10.8	32.8	22.7	2.50	2.50
Nevada	834	746	64.5	31.4	47.8	21.5	11.2	7.2	35.5	26.5	7.9	34.6	21.5	2.65	2.63
New Hampshire	493	470	68.6	32.8	54.7	23.8	9.6	6.5	31.4	24.2	8.4	35.3	21.0	2.54	2.55
New Jersey	3,123	3,033	70.7	33.8	53.5	25.1	12.9	6.9	29.4	24.8	9.5	37.0	25.2	2.70	2.71
New Mexico	698	662	67.7	33.7	48.7	22.0	13.5	8.6	32.3	26.7	8.5	37.4	23.0	2.63	2.69
New York	7,119	7,009	65.3	31.2	45.5	20.5	15.0	8.6	34.7	28.8	10.0	34.5	24.7	2.61	2.62
North Carolina	3,271	3,084	68.3	31.7	50.6	21.2	13.4	8.2	31.7	26.2	8.7	35.5	22.2	2.49	2.53
North Dakota	254	250	63.2	28.3	52.1	21.2	8.0	5.5	36.8	31.3	11.3	29.9	24.1	2.39	2.48
Ohio	4,480	4,392	66.6	31.2	50.4	21.3	12.4	7.9	33.5	28.9	9.6	33.7	23.4	2.49	2.52
Oklahoma	1,341	1,316	67.8	31.4	52.1	22.2	11.8	7.2	32.2	27.5	10.1	35.2	23.2	2.53	2.54
Oregon	1,409	1,374	64.6	29.9	50.3	21.1	10.3	6.7	35.4	27.5	9.1	32.3	22.3	2.47	2.43
Pennsylvania	4,801	4,718	66.0	29.4	49.4	20.4	12.1	6.8	34.1	29.0	11.7	32.2	27.3	2.48	2.51
Rhode Island	412	407	64.5	30.5	46.9	20.9	13.3	7.7	35.5	29.6	11.5	33.3	25.4	2.52	2.48
South Carolina	1,568	1,503	68.8	31.3	49.9	20.1	14.9	9.2	31.2	26.6	8.1	35.4	22.7	2.56	2.58
South Dakota	299	286	66.4	31.3	54.4	23.5	8.6	6.0	33.6	28.0	10.8	33.1	24.0	2.46	2.54
Tennessee	2,296	2,219	67.5	30.7	50.6	20.9	12.7	7.7	32.5	27.9	9.0	34.1	22.5	2.48	2.50
Texas	7,635	7,332	70.9	36.7	53.0	26.2	13.5	8.5	29.1	24.4	7.4	40.9	19.9	2.82	2.77
Utah	752	710	75.7	42.0	62.4	33.9	8.9	5.7	24.3	18.9	6.4	44.9	18.6	3.07	3.09
Vermont	242	240	64.3	29.4	50.4	20.5	9.7	6.4	35.7	27.5	9.4	31.6	22.9	2.47	2.45
Virginia	2,790	2,676	67.8	31.8	51.8	23.1	12.1	6.9	32.2	26.1	7.9	34.9	21.3	2.56	2.56
Washington	2,382	2,278	64.2	30.8	49.2	21.2	10.3	7.0	35.8	28.3	8.4	33.1	20.1	2.51	2.53
West Virginia	732	720	67.0	27.2	51.7	18.6	11.8	6.8	33.0	28.6	11.1	30.5	26.4	2.41	2.45
Wisconsin	2,159	2,086	64.8	29.8	51.5	21.5	9.4	6.3	35.2	28.3	9.5	32.0	22.7	2.46	2.50
Wyoming	199	192	67.0	30.1	54.3	22.5	8.2	5.2	33.0	27.2	8.5	32.6	21.0	2.45	2.50

[1]Includes male householder, no spouse present, not shown separately.

Survey, Census, or Data Collection Method: Based on the American Community Survey; for information, see Appendix B, Limitations of the Data and Methodology, and Internet site <http://www.census.gov/acs/www/AdvMeth/index.htm>.

Source: U.S. Census Bureau, American Community Survey, Multi-Year Profiles 2003—General Demographics, accessed 24 June 2005. See Internet site <http://www.census.gov/acs/www/Products/Profiles/Chg/2003/ACS/index.htm>.

Geographic area	Males 15 years and over						Females 15 years and over					
		Percent						Percent				
	Total	Never married	Now married, except separated	Separated	Widowed	Divorced	Total	Never married	Now married, except separated	Separated	Widowed	Divorced
United States ...	107,433	30.4	56.6	1.7	2.5	8.9	114,911	24.8	51.6	2.6	9.7	11.3
Alabama	1,643	27.5	57.9	1.5	2.6	10.4	1,830	21.9	51.3	2.7	12.1	12.0
Alaska	242	32.4	53.5	1.6	1.9	10.7	234	23.8	54.2	2.6	5.2	14.3
Arizona	2,065	30.2	55.4	2.0	2.2	10.2	2,124	23.7	52.3	2.3	9.1	12.7
Arkansas	1,008	24.9	59.4	1.8	2.8	11.1	1,081	19.7	54.7	2.3	12.0	11.3
California	13,149	34.3	53.9	1.6	2.1	8.0	13,648	27.4	50.3	2.9	8.2	11.2
Colorado	1,739	29.0	57.5	1.7	1.7	10.1	1,751	22.8	55.3	1.8	7.0	13.2
Connecticut	1,279	30.4	58.3	0.9	2.4	8.0	1,401	26.4	51.1	1.7	9.1	11.8
Delaware	299	31.2	56.2	1.6	2.7	8.3	328	25.9	50.9	2.5	9.3	11.5
District of Columbia	201	50.1	35.1	3.4	2.9	8.6	235	46.0	28.2	4.8	10.1	10.9
Florida	6,412	27.8	56.7	1.7	3.0	10.7	6,955	22.1	50.2	2.8	11.5	13.4
Georgia	3,154	30.5	56.4	1.6	2.2	9.3	3,359	25.7	51.4	2.3	8.5	12.1
Hawaii	480	33.5	54.1	1.5	2.6	8.3	495	26.2	52.4	1.4	9.7	10.3
Idaho	507	25.3	62.0	1.2	2.3	9.3	520	20.0	59.7	1.4	8.5	10.4
Illinois	4,651	32.4	55.9	1.3	2.5	7.9	4,980	26.7	50.9	2.0	9.9	10.5
Indiana	2,264	27.6	58.2	1.3	2.3	10.7	2,424	22.3	53.5	1.6	10.0	12.6
Iowa	1,108	27.7	59.3	1.2	2.1	9.8	1,162	20.8	57.2	1.3	10.1	10.6
Kansas	1,010	28.0	59.9	1.1	2.2	8.9	1,061	21.3	56.3	1.7	9.6	11.1
Kentucky	1,530	25.4	60.5	1.3	2.6	10.2	1,649	19.4	55.7	2.4	10.6	12.0
Louisiana	1,604	31.8	54.4	2.0	3.0	8.7	1,788	26.1	47.7	2.5	11.1	12.7
Maine	502	26.4	58.8	1.2	2.8	10.8	539	21.9	53.6	1.4	10.7	12.5
Maryland	2,000	31.9	55.9	2.5	2.4	7.3	2,227	27.2	49.4	3.2	9.6	10.7
Massachusetts	2,372	32.7	55.7	1.7	3.0	7.0	2,612	28.2	49.0	2.7	10.0	10.1
Michigan	3,725	30.2	57.1	0.9	2.2	9.5	4,012	26.0	51.6	1.6	9.6	11.3
Minnesota	1,917	30.2	58.2	0.9	2.0	8.7	1,980	24.7	55.4	1.3	8.4	10.2
Mississippi	1,017	29.5	55.5	2.5	2.8	9.8	1,138	25.0	47.6	4.1	11.3	12.1
Missouri	2,102	27.9	58.2	1.4	2.2	10.2	2,273	22.6	53.4	2.2	10.2	11.6
Montana	353	27.9	58.3	1.3	2.5	10.0	366	21.5	55.5	1.3	9.9	11.8
Nebraska	648	28.1	59.2	1.0	2.5	9.2	678	21.6	56.6	1.3	9.7	10.8
Nevada	867	30.9	52.8	2.0	2.5	11.8	852	22.0	52.1	2.1	9.0	14.8
New Hampshire	491	27.1	58.8	0.9	1.9	11.3	514	22.4	55.9	1.1	8.3	12.3
New Jersey	3,179	30.9	58.2	1.9	2.6	6.3	3,480	26.2	52.3	2.6	10.2	8.7
New Mexico	692	30.9	54.1	1.8	2.8	10.5	733	24.3	50.1	3.3	9.2	13.1
New York	7,035	35.2	53.2	2.4	2.6	6.5	7,822	29.9	46.1	4.4	10.3	9.4
North Carolina	3,082	28.3	58.2	2.6	2.5	8.4	3,320	22.8	52.6	3.5	10.7	10.4
North Dakota	243	31.7	57.5	0.6	2.2	8.1	248	22.7	56.9	0.8	10.8	8.9
Ohio	4,222	29.3	56.6	1.4	2.7	10.0	4,590	24.3	51.9	2.0	10.1	11.8
Oklahoma	1,282	26.2	58.9	1.5	2.6	10.8	1,386	19.8	54.7	2.2	10.4	12.9
Oregon	1,361	28.5	55.8	2.1	2.5	11.2	1,423	22.3	52.7	2.4	9.8	12.9
Pennsylvania	4,576	30.0	56.1	2.2	3.3	8.4	5,033	24.7	50.6	2.6	12.1	10.0
Rhode Island	397	32.0	54.0	1.2	3.3	9.5	439	26.7	47.7	2.5	11.7	11.4
South Carolina	1,499	28.1	57.8	2.4	2.7	9.1	1,665	25.1	50.8	4.0	10.0	10.0
South Dakota	283	29.4	59.6	0.8	2.0	8.2	294	20.8	58.5	1.1	10.7	8.9
Tennessee	2,172	26.7	58.8	1.6	2.7	10.2	2,357	21.6	52.7	2.4	10.3	13.0
Texas	7,965	28.8	59.0	1.9	2.1	8.2	8,349	23.5	53.5	3.3	8.6	11.2
Utah	838	29.3	60.9	1.2	1.6	7.1	847	23.9	59.8	1.3	6.2	8.8
Vermont	239	29.8	55.9	1.0	2.4	10.9	251	24.9	52.0	1.0	9.4	12.7
Virginia	2,728	29.8	58.0	2.2	2.3	7.6	2,932	23.9	52.5	3.5	9.2	10.9
Washington	2,339	30.3	55.5	1.3	2.3	10.6	2,422	23.6	52.3	1.9	8.1	14.1
West Virginia	696	27.1	57.9	1.3	2.7	11.0	751	19.6	53.6	2.2	12.3	12.4
Wisconsin	2,072	31.0	56.1	1.0	2.5	9.3	2,157	24.8	54.2	1.3	9.1	10.6
Wyoming	194	26.7	58.9	1.4	2.4	10.7	197	20.3	57.3	1.3	8.2	12.9

Survey, Census, or Data Collection Method: Based on the American Community Survey; for information, see Appendix B, Limitations of the Data and Methodology, and Internet site <http://www.census.gov/acs/www/AdvMeth/index.htm>.

Source: U.S. Census Bureau, American Community Survey, Multi-Year Profiles 2003—Social Characteristics, accessed 24 June 2005. See Internet site <http://www.census.gov/acs/www/Products/Profiles/Chg/2003/ACS/index.htm>.

Table A-8. States — Residence 1 Year Ago, Immigrants, and Language Spoken at Home

Geographic area	Residence one year ago		Immigrants												Language spoken at home, 2003		
	Population 1 year and over, 2003 (1,000)	Percent who lived in same house	Total				Leading countries of origin, 2003								Population 5 years and over (1,000)	Language other than English, percent	
			2003	2002	2001	2000	Mexico	India	China	Philippines	Vietnam	El Salvador	Cuba	Bosnia and Herzegovina		Total	Spanish
United States ...	279,118	84.9	[1]703,542	[1]1,063,732	[1]1,064,318	[1]849,807	[1]115,585	[1]50,228	[1]40,568	[1]45,250	[1]22,087	[1]28,231	[1]9,262	[1]6,155	263,230	18.4	11.3
Alabama	4,331	85.2	1,689	2,570	2,257	1,904	250	114	113	77	65	13	11	9	4,088	3.4	2.0
Alaska...........	620	80.8	1,188	1,564	1,401	1,374	69	14	43	405	22	11	4	–	582	12.6	2.9
Arizona	5,376	80.4	10,955	17,719	16,362	11,980	5,722	322	299	433	278	146	99	156	5,032	26.4	20.7
Arkansas	2,614	81.9	1,903	2,535	2,572	1,596	688	84	63	72	74	351	(D)	–	2,461	4.6	3.2
California	34,161	84.7	175,579	291,216	282,957	217,753	51,269	9,508	11,573	18,134	9,230	13,683	300	199	32,116	40.8	27.0
Colorado	4,385	81.6	10,661	12,060	12,494	8,216	3,275	468	632	240	418	156	17	84	4,124	15.0	10.7
Connecticut	3,322	87.7	8,274	11,243	12,148	11,346	84	722	403	299	129	46	32	179	3,158	17.7	8.3
Delaware	781	86.8	1,487	1,862	1,850	1,570	101	244	99	61	21	26	3	(D)	738	10.2	5.2
District of Columbia	523	84.3	2,491	2,723	3,043	2,542	29	85	132	215	28	416	4	5	495	17.8	9.7
Florida...........	16,419	82.4	52,770	90,819	104,715	98,391	1,567	1,219	694	1,668	571	411	6,303	519	15,572	24.2	17.7
Georgia	8,324	84.2	10,794	20,555	19,431	14,778	1,482	1,023	387	340	447	133	32	244	7,780	10.6	6.1
Hawaii	1,205	85.0	4,899	5,503	6,313	6,056	51	13	397	3,050	175	3	–	(D)	1,137	23.6	1.4
Idaho............	1,310	81.4	1,686	2,236	2,296	1,922	586	38	107	56	25	12	–	145	1,230	10.4	7.2
Illinois	12,166	85.9	32,413	47,235	48,296	36,180	6,044	4,536	1,609	2,116	391	251	42	336	11,442	20.2	11.9
Indiana	5,933	83.6	5,241	6,853	6,010	4,128	901	437	346	230	105	100	8	129	5,596	7.8	3.6
Iowa	2,807	85.1	3,419	5,591	5,029	3,052	693	215	307	77	190	86	(D)	429	2,661	5.6	3.0
Kansas	2,605	81.6	3,804	4,508	4,030	4,582	883	415	212	134	240	77	11	12	2,450	8.2	4.5
Kentucky	3,948	85.3	3,038	4,681	4,548	2,989	232	248	194	150	81	11	331	191	3,733	4.0	1.9
Louisiana	4,300	85.8	2,214	3,199	3,778	3,016	133	171	118	101	225	16	65	18	4,039	7.9	2.2
Maine	1,260	87.1	992	1,269	1,186	1,133	17	28	95	84	37	17	(D)	4	1,204	7.4	0.7
Maryland	5,306	86.6	17,770	23,751	22,060	17,705	324	1,339	1,071	1,284	329	1,440	28	22	5,007	13.0	4.7
Massachusetts	6,141	87.8	20,127	31,615	28,965	23,483	124	1,463	1,718	350	683	829	28	65	5,822	19.3	6.6
Michigan	9,697	86.5	13,515	21,787	21,528	16,773	625	1,864	762	451	237	37	143	317	9,178	8.6	2.7
Minnesota	4,855	85.6	8,406	13,522	11,166	8,671	398	651	386	419	364	57	8	162	4,591	9.2	3.0
Mississippi	2,747	84.8	729	1,155	1,340	1,083	77	74	44	49	57	8	9	(D)	2,578	3.0	1.6
Missouri..........	5,459	83.7	6,160	8,610	7,616	6,053	439	449	379	261	265	25	35	661	5,160	5.3	1.9
Montana	883	85.7	453	422	488	493	23	4	28	30	3	–	(D)	–	840	4.1	1.3
Nebraska	1,664	82.4	2,827	3,657	3,850	2,230	882	119	108	70	212	93	9	51	1,569	7.9	4.9
Nevada	2,175	81.7	6,336	9,499	9,618	7,827	1,730	83	232	1,159	87	420	263	26	2,045	24.0	17.4
New Hampshire......	1,237	86.8	1,868	3,009	2,595	2,001	22	206	174	101	23	9	(D)	131	1,179	8.1	1.6
New Jersey	8,335	88.2	40,699	57,721	59,920	40,013	569	7,442	1,688	2,639	431	631	413	40	7,887	26.3	13.0
New Mexico	1,810	83.1	2,336	3,399	5,207	3,973	1,256	77	56	65	84	12	61	(D)	1,708	36.0	28.2
New York	18,378	89.5	89,538	114,827	114,116	106,061	1,198	4,138	8,356	1,830	463	4,065	257	470	17,395	27.5	14.1
North Carolina.....	8,037	84.3	9,451	12,910	13,918	9,251	1,175	868	749	419	323	181	35	95	7,557	8.2	5.2
North Dakota	602	87.3	331	776	558	420	9	14	11	14	12	–	–	40	573	5.8	1.4
Ohio	10,988	85.6	9,787	13,875	14,725	9,263	274	1,743	767	417	182	29	9	222	10,396	5.6	1.8
Oklahoma	3,354	83.6	2,385	4,229	3,492	4,586	543	175	91	107	191	10	5	5	3,163	6.9	4.0
Oregon	3,435	80.8	6,946	12,125	9,638	8,543	1,487	336	503	301	430	71	96	50	3,257	12.5	7.2
Pennsylvania	11,783	88.5	14,606	19,473	21,441	18,148	514	1,964	1,314	473	567	71	56	219	11,218	8.1	3.0
Rhode Island	1,027	88.5	2,492	3,067	2,820	2,526	30	71	94	48	28	56	3	11	976	19.4	8.6
South Carolina	3,962	84.3	1,942	2,966	2,882	2,267	186	198	105	209	44	6	3	5	3,736	4.9	2.7
South Dakota	726	85.4	487	902	671	465	33	27	26	24	15	(D)	–	43	683	4.9	1.5
Tennessee	5,613	84.4	3,367	5,694	6,257	4,882	281	308	203	221	110	66	18	127	5,310	4.7	2.5
Texas	21,203	83.1	53,412	88,365	86,315	63,840	25,342	2,770	1,221	1,995	2,201	2,369	282	177	19,751	32.5	28.2
Utah	2,264	82.3	3,159	4,889	5,247	3,710	755	65	166	74	129	78	9	105	2,083	11.9	7.8
Vermont..........	593	86.9	550	1,007	954	810	5	30	38	16	19	3	(D)	45	567	5.1	0.6
Virginia	7,054	84.4	19,726	25,411	26,876	20,087	474	2,036	1,000	1,154	691	1,581	48	160	6,667	12.0	4.8
Washington	5,915	81.1	17,935	25,704	23,085	18,486	1,965	1,231	960	1,626	1,076	86	18	165	5,600	13.7	5.4
West Virginia	1,746	89.0	483	636	737	573	13	87	32	32	10	3	(D)	–	1,664	2.1	0.8
Wisconsin.........	5,256	84.9	4,357	6,498	8,477	5,057	603	453	345	228	56	15	14	77	4,978	7.8	3.9
Wyoming	481	82.2	253	281	308	248	75	4	21	17	5	–	–	–	456	5.0	3.5

– Represents zero.   D Figures withheld to avoid disclosure.

[1]U.S. totals include data for U.S. Armed Services Posts, U.S. Possessions, and Unknown.

Survey, Census, or Data Collection Method: Residence and language spoken—Based on the American Community Survey; for information, see Appendix B, Limitations of the Data and Methodology, and Internet site <http://www.census.gov/acs/www/AdvMeth/index.htm>;   Immigrants—Based on U.S. application Citizenship and Immigration Services (USCIS)-based case management systems that compile information supplied by aliens on the forms they are required to submit when applying for a legal status; for information, see Internet site <http://uscis.gov/graphics/shared/statistics/yearbook/index.htm>.

Sources: Residence and language spoken—U.S. Census Bureau, American Community Survey, Multi-Year Profiles 2003—Social Characteristics, accessed 24 June 2005. See Internet site <http://www.census.gov/acs/www/Products/Profiles/Chg/2003/ACS/index.htm>;   Immigrants—U.S. Department of Homeland Security, Office of Immigration Statistics, *2003 Yearbook of Immigration Statistics*, see Internet site <http://uscis.gov/graphics/shared/aboutus/statistics/ybpage.htm>.

Geographic area	Total population (1,000)	Percent			Foreign born											
									Percent							
									Born in —							
									Asia						Latin America	
		Born in state of residence	Born in different state	Foreign born	Total (1,000)	Not a citizen	Entered 1990 or later	Europe	Total	China	India	Korea	Philippines	Vietnam	Total	Mexico
United States . . .	282,910	59.6	27.3	11.9	33,534	58.6	49.4	14.2	27.3	5.1	3.9	2.8	4.3	3.2	52.3	29.9
Alabama	4,385	73.9	22.9	2.4	105	67.6	64.1	18.3	24.7	11.1	3.8	4.7	0.2	0.8	43.5	31.9
Alaska	630	38.2	53.7	6.1	38	46.0	46.3	20.0	50.8	2.9	1.2	9.8	28.0	0.6	18.5	7.6
Arizona	5,471	35.4	49.6	13.8	757	70.1	56.4	9.5	12.4	1.8	1.4	1.2	2.1	2.3	72.6	67.1
Arkansas	2,650	61.8	34.6	3.2	83	72.6	60.1	11.0	22.5	1.9	2.1	1.1	1.3	6.3	60.2	51.7
California	34,651	51.2	21.2	26.5	9,187	58.4	43.0	7.5	34.3	7.0	2.8	3.2	7.2	4.7	54.8	43.2
Colorado	4,448	42.1	47.0	9.7	433	67.1	60.0	16.1	19.8	4.0	0.8	5.6	1.5	3.7	57.4	50.0
Connecticut	3,371	56.2	29.6	11.4	385	56.1	46.5	34.1	21.0	3.8	6.2	1.0	1.8	1.7	36.1	4.8
Delaware	792	49.7	42.8	6.1	49	57.5	55.5	21.7	34.4	4.5	14.5	2.5	4.8	0.6	35.3	19.0
District of Columbia	529	41.5	42.6	14.9	79	69.7	61.3	15.8	17.5	2.9	1.6	1.1	3.1	1.9	50.8	2.8
Florida	16,618	33.8	45.9	17.6	2,928	54.2	46.8	11.3	9.2	1.2	1.6	0.6	1.6	1.5	74.0	7.4
Georgia	8,438	58.3	32.8	7.9	667	69.3	67.2	11.3	25.3	3.6	4.5	3.5	1.6	5.0	54.1	34.9
Hawaii	1,222	58.7	21.7	17.0	208	42.9	43.3	6.0	77.6	10.6	0.2	6.5	44.8	2.0	4.2	3.1
Idaho	1,333	48.8	44.7	5.9	79	68.0	66.0	17.2	18.0	3.4	3.2	5.8	1.7	0.9	57.6	51.0
Illinois	12,329	66.3	19.5	13.3	1,634	57.1	50.6	25.0	23.6	3.7	5.4	2.3	4.4	1.8	48.7	40.7
Indiana	6,017	71.8	24.0	3.7	221	68.0	66.3	19.5	27.2	3.3	5.4	3.5	3.9	0.9	46.7	37.2
Iowa	2,840	74.4	21.9	3.3	94	68.8	68.8	17.7	36.6	6.0	5.2	4.2	2.6	8.2	39.3	31.6
Kansas	2,642	59.4	34.4	5.5	144	63.0	63.6	9.6	40.6	7.1	9.7	3.0	2.2	6.2	40.9	32.4
Kentucky	4,003	72.8	24.2	2.3	92	70.7	70.1	26.2	37.1	2.3	7.7	10.3	2.4	1.0	28.6	17.1
Louisiana	4,361	79.9	16.5	3.0	130	53.2	43.6	12.3	44.8	6.2	5.8	3.1	2.5	15.4	36.8	6.3
Maine	1,271	64.0	32.1	3.0	38	42.3	33.2	29.8	18.8	2.9	1.3	1.0	3.5	5.7	4.5	0.8
Maryland	5,372	48.8	39.5	10.6	571	55.3	53.1	14.9	35.4	7.7	6.2	4.4	3.8	2.7	33.7	4.4
Massachusetts	6,219	65.0	19.1	13.7	850	52.9	48.0	30.7	26.5	6.3	5.0	1.1	1.5	4.2	32.1	0.6
Michigan	9,826	75.2	18.3	5.9	582	58.2	56.2	25.0	44.7	4.0	10.0	4.3	3.4	1.5	18.2	11.2
Minnesota	4,920	69.1	24.2	6.1	299	58.5	57.5	16.9	41.3	3.2	5.3	4.5	2.5	5.4	21.1	13.9
Mississippi	2,785	73.0	24.9	1.6	44	67.4	58.7	15.3	33.4	5.5	7.7	1.3	3.5	9.0	47.4	27.6
Missouri	5,535	66.6	29.4	3.4	188	58.7	60.7	25.8	38.1	6.2	5.8	2.4	3.4	5.9	23.0	13.1
Montana	892	55.2	42.2	1.8	16	44.0	36.6	40.0	21.2	4.2	0.3	3.7	4.0	2.1	9.6	4.6
Nebraska	1,688	68.4	26.2	4.8	80	66.2	66.9	11.7	32.6	5.1	2.1	3.1	2.2	8.5	47.5	34.7
Nevada	2,208	23.2	58.5	17.2	380	66.0	54.8	8.2	25.2	1.9	0.8	2.1	11.7	1.2	62.2	48.4
New Hampshire	1,252	42.2	51.8	5.1	63	56.4	46.2	32.0	27.8	4.6	8.1	2.6	2.0	0.9	16.6	3.9
New Jersey	8,444	53.2	25.5	19.2	1,621	53.6	50.2	21.2	28.6	5.0	9.0	3.4	4.4	0.7	43.6	4.4
New Mexico	1,838	50.7	38.3	10.0	184	73.2	50.6	7.5	8.8	1.8	1.2	1.3	1.6	0.3	77.9	74.5
New York	18,601	65.5	11.2	20.8	3,874	49.1	44.4	20.1	24.7	8.0	3.4	2.7	2.0	0.5	50.1	4.0
North Carolina	8,147	63.8	29.2	6.2	503	76.5	70.8	11.5	21.9	3.9	5.2	2.1	1.2	2.9	57.2	41.0
North Dakota	609	71.3	25.3	2.7	16	50.5	51.9	26.5	28.2	7.3	8.1	3.6	4.2	1.0	15.6	6.7
Ohio	11,135	74.2	21.9	3.4	377	51.7	50.7	34.2	36.4	6.5	9.9	3.1	1.8	2.1	16.0	7.9
Oklahoma	3,397	61.0	33.6	4.5	153	65.5	61.2	10.7	31.9	2.7	4.0	4.3	1.6	9.9	51.7	45.4
Oregon	3,482	45.3	45.1	8.7	301	63.3	54.2	19.3	27.4	4.7	3.8	4.8	2.3	5.3	45.0	39.5
Pennsylvania	11,922	77.7	16.6	4.6	553	49.3	49.9	29.8	38.1	4.8	8.6	5.9	2.6	5.7	22.2	7.2
Rhode Island	1,037	60.3	26.1	11.6	120	52.6	40.7	29.6	17.5	2.8	1.6	1.0	1.1	0.7	36.3	2.3
South Carolina	4,009	61.2	34.5	3.4	135	63.6	54.7	19.2	25.2	3.0	3.3	3.8	4.1	4.2	43.1	27.5
South Dakota	735	67.4	30.4	1.7	13	55.5	55.2	31.3	29.2	4.7	1.5	2.9	7.1	5.9	18.9	8.5
Tennessee	5,689	64.0	32.3	3.1	178	68.3	66.6	14.4	35.5	5.1	7.3	3.8	1.2	3.1	42.5	31.5
Texas	21,548	61.0	22.2	15.6	3,358	68.9	52.7	4.5	16.4	2.5	2.7	1.2	1.6	3.2	75.4	66.8
Utah	2,310	63.3	28.5	7.3	167	68.6	60.2	14.4	16.0	1.9	2.8	1.7	0.4	4.8	56.7	43.7
Vermont	598	55.7	39.9	3.5	21	45.6	49.2	38.1	22.5	6.0	2.4	1.8	0.5	7.4	6.9	0.6
Virginia	7,152	51.2	38.2	9.2	657	59.6	56.6	15.6	40.7	3.6	5.4	5.9	5.6	5.5	32.8	4.9
Washington	5,990	47.6	40.7	10.3	614	55.4	51.5	19.8	42.9	5.8	4.9	5.7	10.5	6.2	26.2	20.4
West Virginia	1,766	72.5	25.7	1.5	26	49.8	42.9	17.7	42.3	1.7	12.5	10.6	5.3	2.6	27.3	7.3
Wisconsin	5,316	71.1	24.1	4.2	225	62.1	56.0	22.2	32.2	3.5	6.1	3.5	3.3	1.2	40.6	30.8
Wyoming	487	43.3	53.8	2.2	11	63.6	51.9	28.2	18.2	6.8	3.2	3.1	1.6	–	44.0	37.1

– Represents zero.

Survey, Census, or Data Collection Method: Based on the American Community Survey; for information, see Appendix B, Limitations of the Data and Methodology, and Internet site <http://www.census.gov/acs/www/AdvMeth/index.htm>.

Source: U.S. Census Bureau, American Community Survey, Multi-Year Profiles 2003—Social Characteristics, accessed 24 June 2005, see Internet site <http://www.census.gov/acs/www/Products/Profiles/Chg/2003/ACS/index.htm>; and "PCT027. Place of Birth for the Foreign-Born Population," see Internet site <http://factfinder.census.gov/servlet/DatasetMainPageServlet?_program=ACS&_lang=en&_ts=>.

Geographic area	Total			Rate[1]			Percent with low birth weight[2]			Percent to teenage mothers[3]			Percent to unmarried women		
	2003 prel.	2000	1990	2003 prel.	2000	1990	2003 prel.	2000	1990	2003 prel.	2000	1990	2003 prel.	2000	1990
United States . . .	4,091,063	4,058,814	4,158,212	14.1	14.4	16.7	7.9	7.6	7.0	10.3	11.8	12.8	34.6	33.2	26.6
Alabama	59,621	63,299	63,487	13.2	14.2	15.7	10.0	9.7	8.4	13.9	15.7	18.2	35.0	34.3	30.1
Alaska	10,122	9,974	11,902	15.6	15.9	21.6	6.0	5.6	4.8	10.6	11.8	9.7	34.6	33.0	26.2
Arizona	91,005	85,273	68,995	16.3	16.6	18.8	7.1	7.0	6.4	12.9	14.3	14.2	41.5	39.3	32.7
Arkansas	38,159	37,783	36,457	14.0	14.1	15.5	8.9	8.6	8.2	15.1	17.3	19.7	38.0	35.7	29.4
California	540,995	531,959	612,628	15.2	15.7	20.6	6.6	6.2	5.8	9.3	10.6	11.6	33.5	32.7	31.6
Colorado	69,363	65,438	53,525	15.2	15.2	16.2	9.0	8.4	8.0	9.8	11.7	11.3	26.7	25.0	21.2
Connecticut	42,848	43,026	50,123	12.3	12.6	15.2	7.5	7.4	6.6	6.7	7.8	8.2	30.1	29.3	26.6
Delaware	11,264	11,051	11,113	13.8	14.1	16.7	9.4	8.6	7.6	10.8	12.3	11.9	42.0	37.9	29.0
District of Columbia	7,606	7,666	11,850	13.5	13.4	19.5	10.9	11.9	15.1	11.4	14.2	17.8	53.5	60.3	64.9
Florida	212,286	204,125	199,339	12.5	12.8	15.4	8.5	8.0	7.4	10.9	12.6	13.9	39.9	38.2	31.7
Georgia	136,012	132,644	112,666	15.7	16.2	17.4	9.0	8.6	8.7	11.9	13.9	16.7	38.1	37.0	32.8
Hawaii	18,114	17,551	20,489	14.4	14.5	18.5	8.6	7.5	7.1	8.4	10.3	10.5	33.4	32.2	24.8
Idaho	21,802	20,366	16,433	16.0	15.7	16.3	6.5	6.7	5.7	9.6	11.6	12.3	22.3	21.6	16.7
Illinois	182,590	185,036	195,790	14.4	14.9	17.1	8.3	7.9	7.6	9.7	11.4	13.1	35.3	34.5	31.7
Indiana	86,600	87,699	86,214	14.0	14.4	15.6	7.8	7.4	6.6	11.0	12.5	14.5	37.1	34.7	26.2
Iowa	38,182	38,266	39,409	13.0	13.1	14.2	6.6	6.1	5.4	8.7	10.0	10.2	29.9	28.0	21.0
Kansas	39,493	39,666	39,020	14.5	14.8	15.7	7.4	6.9	6.2	10.4	12.0	12.3	31.5	29.0	21.5
Kentucky	55,281	56,029	54,362	13.4	13.9	14.8	8.7	8.2	7.1	12.5	14.1	17.5	33.8	31.0	23.6
Louisiana	65,298	67,898	72,192	14.5	15.2	17.1	10.7	10.3	9.2	14.9	17.0	17.6	47.6	45.6	36.8
Maine	13,861	13,603	17,359	10.6	10.7	14.1	6.5	6.0	5.1	8.2	9.4	10.8	33.6	31.0	22.6
Maryland	74,856	74,316	80,245	13.6	14.0	16.8	9.1	8.6	7.8	8.6	9.9	10.5	34.8	34.6	29.6
Massachusetts	80,250	81,614	92,654	12.5	12.9	15.4	7.6	7.1	5.9	5.9	6.6	8.0	27.8	26.5	24.7
Michigan	130,937	136,171	153,700	13.0	13.7	16.5	8.2	7.9	7.6	9.5	10.5	13.5	34.7	33.3	26.2
Minnesota	70,157	67,604	68,013	13.9	13.7	15.5	6.3	6.1	5.1	7.1	8.3	8.0	27.7	25.8	20.9
Mississippi	42,362	44,075	43,563	14.7	15.5	16.9	11.4	10.7	9.6	16.2	18.8	21.3	46.5	46.0	40.5
Missouri	77,079	76,463	79,260	13.5	13.7	15.5	8.0	7.6	7.1	11.4	13.1	14.4	35.6	34.6	28.6
Montana	11,416	10,957	11,613	12.4	12.1	14.5	6.8	6.2	6.2	10.6	11.6	11.5	32.2	30.8	23.7
Nebraska	25,924	24,646	24,380	14.9	14.4	15.4	6.9	6.8	5.3	9.0	10.2	9.8	29.7	27.2	20.7
Nevada	33,644	30,829	21,599	15.0	15.4	18.0	8.1	7.2	7.2	11.3	12.7	12.6	39.0	36.4	25.4
New Hampshire.	14,393	14,609	17,569	11.2	11.8	15.8	6.2	6.3	4.9	5.7	6.8	7.2	24.8	24.7	16.9
New Jersey	116,269	115,632	122,289	13.5	13.7	15.8	8.1	7.7	7.0	6.2	7.1	8.4	29.5	28.9	24.3
New Mexico	27,845	27,223	27,402	14.9	15.0	18.1	8.5	8.0	7.4	16.5	17.4	16.3	48.4	45.6	35.4
New York	254,187	258,737	297,576	13.2	13.6	16.5	7.9	7.7	7.6	7.0	8.2	9.1	36.5	36.6	33.0
North Carolina.	118,308	120,311	104,525	14.1	14.9	15.8	9.0	8.8	8.0	11.4	13.0	16.2	35.3	33.3	29.4
North Dakota	7,975	7,676	9,250	12.6	12.0	14.5	6.5	6.4	5.5	7.9	9.2	8.6	28.6	28.3	18.4
Ohio	151,983	155,472	166,913	13.3	13.7	15.4	8.3	7.9	7.1	10.5	12.1	13.8	36.1	34.6	28.9
Oklahoma	50,484	49,782	47,649	14.4	14.4	15.1	7.7	7.5	6.6	13.9	15.9	16.2	36.9	34.3	25.2
Oregon	45,975	45,804	42,891	12.9	13.4	15.1	6.1	5.6	5.0	9.1	11.3	12.0	31.7	30.1	25.7
Pennsylvania	140,660	146,281	171,961	11.4	11.9	14.5	7.9	7.7	7.1	9.0	9.9	10.3	33.9	32.7	28.6
Rhode Island	13,192	12,505	15,195	12.3	11.9	15.1	8.7	7.2	6.2	8.2	10.2	10.5	35.6	35.5	26.3
South Carolina	55,658	56,114	58,610	13.4	14.0	16.8	10.0	9.7	8.7	13.3	15.3	17.1	41.3	39.8	32.7
South Dakota	11,035	10,345	10,999	14.4	13.7	15.8	6.6	6.2	5.1	9.4	11.6	10.8	34.2	33.5	22.9
Tennessee	78,901	79,611	74,962	13.5	14.0	15.4	9.4	9.2	8.2	13.2	14.7	17.6	37.2	34.5	30.2
Texas	381,239	363,414	316,423	17.2	17.4	18.6	7.9	7.4	6.9	13.8	15.3	15.6	34.2	30.5	17.5
Utah	49,870	47,353	36,277	21.2	21.2	21.1	6.5	6.6	5.7	6.7	8.9	10.3	17.2	17.3	13.5
Vermont	6,591	6,500	8,273	10.6	10.7	14.7	7.1	6.1	5.3	6.4	8.0	8.5	29.9	28.1	20.1
Virginia	101,226	98,938	99,352	13.7	14.0	16.1	8.2	7.9	7.2	8.9	9.9	11.7	30.4	29.9	26.0
Washington	80,474	81,036	79,251	13.1	13.7	16.3	6.1	5.6	5.3	8.5	10.2	10.4	28.8	28.2	23.7
West Virginia	20,908	20,865	22,585	11.5	11.5	12.6	8.6	8.3	7.1	12.3	15.9	17.8	34.6	31.7	25.4
Wisconsin.	70,053	69,326	72,895	12.8	12.9	14.9	6.8	6.5	5.9	9.0	10.2	10.2	30.4	29.3	24.2
Wyoming	6,708	6,253	6,985	13.4	12.7	15.4	8.9	8.3	7.4	12.1	13.5	13.6	32.6	28.8	19.8

[1]Per 1,000 estimated population.
[2]Less than 2,500 grams (5 pounds 8 ounces).
[3]Defined as mothers who are 19 years of age or younger.

Survey, Census, or Data Collection Method: Based on the National Vital Statistics System; for information, see Appendix B, Limitations of the Data and Methodology, and Internet site <http://www.cdc.gov/nchs/nvss.htm>.

Source: U.S. National Center for Health Statistics, *Vital Statistics of the United States,* annual; *National Vital Statistics Report* (NVSR), formerly *Monthly Vital Statistics Report*; see also <http://www.cdc.gov/nchs/nvss.htm>.

Table A-11. States — Births and Birth Rates by Race and Hispanic Origin and Fertility Rate: 2002

Geographic area	Births								Birth rates[1]						
	All races[2]	White Total	White Non-Hispanic	Black Total	Black Non-Hispanic	American Indian	Asian or Pacific Islander	His-panic[3]	All races[2]	White, non-Hispanic	Black, non-Hispanic	American Indian	Asian or Pacific Islander	His-panic[3]	Fertility rate[4]
United States ...	4,021,726	3,174,760	2,298,156	593,691	578,335	42,368	210,907	876,642	13.9	11.7	16.1	13.8	16.5	22.6	64.8
Alabama	58,967	39,978	37,402	18,292	18,276	164	533	2,569	13.1	11.9	15.4	6.4	13.1	29.8	61.2
Alaska	9,938	6,377	4,427	432	267	2,438	691	799	15.4	13.0	14.9	22.3	20.6	28.3	73.5
Arizona	87,837	77,043	39,033	2,779	2,545	5,701	2,314	37,938	16.1	11.6	15.1	19.1	17.8	25.7	77.8
Arkansas	37,437	29,209	26,001	7,427	7,415	257	544	3,050	13.8	12.3	17.0	12.5	19.9	31.4	66.6
California	529,357	428,549	164,649	32,653	31,450	3,033	65,122	263,061	15.1	10.3	13.4	6.3	14.8	22.0	68.3
Colorado	68,418	62,425	41,858	2,934	2,761	662	2,397	21,029	15.2	12.5	14.7	11.2	18.6	25.7	69.3
Connecticut	42,001	34,654	27,685	5,195	4,932	224	1,928	6,982	12.1	10.4	15.1	16.8	18.5	20.2	58.8
Delaware	11,090	7,925	6,629	2,708	2,684	29	428	1,316	13.7	11.3	17.2	8.4	20.4	31.9	62.2
District of Columbia . . .	7,498	2,677	1,733	4,620	4,563	7	194	954	13.1	10.9	13.6	(S)	10.3	18.2	52.9
Florida.	205,579	152,855	102,294	46,238	45,257	1,075	5,411	51,619	12.3	9.5	17.7	14.5	15.2	17.1	62.5
Georgia	133,300	85,809	68,269	42,777	42,001	326	4,388	16,819	15.6	13.0	17.3	11.1	20.2	32.6	68.4
Hawaii	17,477	3,953	3,200	475	442	171	12,878	2,422	14.0	9.7	13.5	37.5	15.5	26.6	68.6
Idaho.	20,970	20,151	17,074	103	100	377	339	2,788	15.6	14.7	12.8	17.7	19.4	24.5	73.8
Illinois	180,622	140,163	99,346	31,833	31,604	264	8,362	41,022	14.3	11.7	16.5	5.7	16.4	24.4	66.1
Indiana	85,081	74,309	67,894	9,332	9,271	157	1,283	6,169	13.8	12.9	17.3	7.6	16.5	26.1	64.8
Iowa	37,559	35,112	32,709	1,263	1,243	234	950	2,390	12.8	12.1	17.5	21.3	19.8	26.7	61.7
Kansas	39,412	34,904	29,563	2,890	2,846	448	1,170	5,023	14.5	13.3	17.2	14.6	19.4	24.3	68.7
Kentucky	54,233	48,399	46,811	4,943	4,923	103	788	1,630	13.3	12.8	15.8	9.9	20.1	23.7	60.5
Louisiana	64,872	36,757	35,428	26,659	26,611	412	1,044	1,383	14.5	12.6	18.1	14.5	15.6	12.1	65.4
Maine	13,559	13,049	12,852	174	167	116	220	167	10.5	10.3	18.7	14.0	18.9	16.2	49.8
Maryland	73,323	45,198	39,093	24,214	24,007	239	3,672	6,062	13.4	11.6	15.7	11.8	14.4	23.6	60.6
Massachusetts	80,645	66,689	58,313	8,344	6,635	191	5,421	9,592	12.5	11.1	17.4	8.9	18.8	20.5	56.7
Michigan	129,967	102,590	93,831	22,440	22,217	683	4,254	7,265	12.9	12.0	15.3	9.3	19.1	20.8	60.7
Minnesota	68,025	58,023	52,744	4,862	4,750	1,358	3,782	4,646	13.6	12.1	23.8	21.3	22.2	29.3	62.0
Mississippi	41,518	22,618	21,749	18,202	18,191	268	430	823	14.5	12.6	17.2	20.4	18.0	19.2	65.7
Missouri.	75,251	62,374	59,079	11,028	10,983	353	1,496	3,267	13.3	12.4	16.6	11.1	18.2	25.7	62.1
Montana	11,049	9,512	8,967	37	32	1,395	105	382	12.1	11.2	7.9	22.7	16.1	20.0	60.3
Nebraska	25,383	22,980	19,121	1,442	1,416	403	558	3,313	14.7	13.1	18.9	23.0	19.0	32.0	69.5
Nevada	32,571	26,979	15,638	2,611	2,534	540	2,441	11,386	15.0	11.2	16.9	15.4	20.0	24.6	72.5
New Hampshire.	14,442	13,691	12,690	225	182	48	478	503	11.3	10.9	16.3	12.1	23.4	22.4	52.4
New Jersey	114,751	84,493	61,741	19,952	18,010	172	10,134	24,664	13.4	11.0	15.4	5.6	17.9	20.2	63.5
New Mexico	27,753	23,281	8,759	511	475	3,548	413	14,623	15.0	10.6	13.1	18.6	14.9	18.4	70.7
New York	251,415	181,212	130,189	49,590	45,206	693	19,920	54,700	13.1	11.1	15.1	5.6	15.8	17.8	59.8
North Carolina	117,335	85,210	70,234	27,571	27,434	1,657	2,897	15,064	14.1	12.1	15.1	14.9	19.6	33.9	65.4
North Dakota	7,757	6,762	6,499	90	87	815	90	149	12.2	11.3	16.0	25.2	17.7	18.2	58.7
Ohio	148,720	122,887	117,990	22,547	22,354	288	2,998	4,817	13.0	12.3	16.5	8.8	17.4	21.0	61.7
Oklahoma	50,387	39,508	34,370	4,704	4,676	5,160	1,015	5,259	14.4	13.0	16.5	16.4	16.2	27.3	68.8
Oregon	45,192	41,047	32,949	941	897	804	2400	8,040	12.8	11.2	13.2	14.0	17.5	25.7	61.9
Pennsylvania	142,850	117,817	108,620	20,265	19,727	353	4,415	8,696	11.6	10.5	15.9	14.1	16.6	20.9	56.4
Rhode Island	12,894	11,036	7,356	1,145	1,027	157	556	2,328	12.1	10.0	19.9	22.7	18.1	23.5	54.6
South Carolina	54,570	35,373	32,203	18,183	18,143	168	846	3,175	13.3	11.9	14.8	10.3	17.6	29.1	60.7
South Dakota	10,698	8,657	8,376	103	103	1,805	133	318	14.1	12.5	14.3	27.3	21.5	27.7	68.3
Tennessee	77,482	59,627	55,316	16,304	16,267	157	1,394	4,348	13.4	12.0	16.8	8.5	18.9	31.1	62.2
Texas	372,450	317,150	137,618	41,642	41,007	834	12,824	178,968	17.1	12.3	16.7	5.2	18.3	24.5	77.1
Utah	49,182	46,572	39,533	339	312	685	1586	6,952	21.2	20.1	13.7	19.4	24.0	31.0	90.6
Vermont.	6,387	6,239	6,131	44	43	10	94	32	10.4	10.4	10.2	(S)	14.6	5.5	48.9
Virginia	99,672	71,415	61,694	22,084	21,920	125	6,048	9,790	13.7	12.1	15.0	4.6	18.8	25.9	61.9
Washington	79,028	66,519	53,387	3,393	3,263	1,920	7,196	12,349	13.0	11.3	14.4	16.8	17.3	25.2	60.2
West Virginia	20,712	19,877	19,749	679	677	11	145	84	11.5	11.6	11.0	(S)	11.9	6.7	57.0
Wisconsin.	68,560	58,979	53,820	6,418	6,349	1,051	2,112	5,295	12.6	11.3	19.5	19.2	19.4	25.3	59.0
Wyoming	6,550	6,147	5,540	54	53	279	70	622	13.1	12.4	11.2	22.5	17.9	18.6	63.6

S Figure does not meet standards of reliability or precision; based on fewer than 20 births or fewer than 1,000 women in specified group.

[1] Per 1,000 estimated population.
[2] Includes other races not shown separately.
[3] Persons of Hispanic origin may be any race. Births by Hispanic origin of mother.
[4] Number of births per 1,000 women age 15–44 years estimated.

Survey, Census, or Data Collection Method: Based on the National Vital Statistics System; for information, see Appendix B, Limitations of the Data and Methodology, and Internet site <http://www.cdc.gov/nchs/nvss.htm>.

Source: U.S. National Center for Health Statistics, *Vital Statistics of the United States*, annual; and *National Vital Statistics Report* (NVSR), formerly *Monthly Vital Statistics Report*, and unpublished data. See also Internet site <http://www.cdc.gov/nchs/nvss.htm>.

Geographic area	All races								Number of deaths by race, 2002			
	Number (1,000)				Rate[1]						Asian or Pacific Islander	American Indian, Eskimo, or Aleut
	2002	2001	2000	1990	2002	2001	2000	1990	White	Black		
United States . . .	2,443	2,416	2,403	2,148	8.5	8.5	8.5	8.6	2,102,589	290,051	38,332	12,415
Alabama	46	45	45	39	10.3	10.1	10.1	9.7	34,727	11,225	71	46
Alaska	3	3	3	2	4.7	4.7	4.6	4.0	2,155	88	90	697
Arizona	43	41	41	29	7.8	7.7	7.9	7.9	39,977	970	272	1,597
Arkansas	29	28	28	25	10.5	10.3	10.6	10.5	24,392	3,976	94	51
California	235	234	230	214	6.7	6.8	6.8	7.2	198,718	18,726	16,061	1,060
Colorado	29	28	27	22	6.5	6.4	6.3	6.6	27,757	1,022	285	146
Connecticut	30	30	30	28	8.7	8.7	8.8	8.4	27,920	1,999	145	58
Delaware	7	7	7	6	8.5	8.9	8.8	8.7	5,698	1,110	40	13
District of Columbia	6	6	6	7	10.2	10.4	10.5	12.0	1,136	4,655	58	2
Florida	168	167	164	134	10.0	10.2	10.3	10.4	149,141	17,842	657	174
Georgia	65	64	64	52	7.6	7.7	7.8	8.0	47,256	17,730	362	101
Hawaii	9	8	8	7	7.1	6.8	6.8	6.1	2,400	68	6,300	33
Idaho	10	10	10	7	7.4	7.4	7.4	7.4	9,733	25	52	113
Illinois	107	105	107	103	8.5	8.4	8.6	9.0	88,997	16,437	1,163	70
Indiana	55	55	55	50	9.0	9.0	9.1	8.9	50,838	4,441	86	31
Iowa	28	28	28	27	9.5	9.5	9.6	9.7	27,503	372	75	28
Kansas	25	25	25	22	9.2	9.1	9.2	9.0	23,470	1,313	94	144
Kentucky	41	40	40	35	9.9	9.8	9.8	9.5	37,916	2,701	70	10
Louisiana	42	42	41	38	9.4	9.3	9.2	8.9	28,808	12,935	170	71
Maine	13	12	12	11	9.8	9.7	9.7	9.0	12,593	23	25	53
Maryland	44	44	44	38	8.1	8.1	8.3	8.0	31,633	11,740	518	79
Massachusetts	57	57	57	53	8.9	8.9	8.9	8.8	54,031	2,329	530	38
Michigan	88	86	87	79	8.7	8.6	8.7	8.5	74,310	12,733	351	401
Minnesota	39	38	38	35	7.7	7.6	7.7	7.9	37,061	769	315	365
Mississippi	29	28	29	25	10.0	9.9	10.1	9.8	19,232	9,477	65	79
Missouri	56	55	55	50	9.9	9.8	9.8	9.8	50,002	5,680	186	72
Montana	9	8	8	7	9.4	9.1	9.0	8.6	8,035	17	17	437
Nebraska	16	15	15	15	9.1	8.8	8.8	9.4	15,111	476	43	108
Nevada	17	16	15	9	7.8	7.8	7.6	7.8	15,194	1,112	464	157
New Hampshire	10	10	10	8	7.7	7.8	7.8	7.7	9,785	30	25	13
New Jersey	74	75	75	70	8.6	8.8	8.9	9.1	63,387	9,508	1,055	59
New Mexico	14	14	13	11	7.7	7.7	7.4	7.0	13,079	241	50	974
New York	158	159	158	169	8.3	8.3	8.3	9.4	132,850	22,129	2,942	197
North Carolina	72	71	72	57	8.7	8.6	8.9	8.6	55,897	15,271	230	629
North Dakota	6	6	6	6	9.3	9.5	9.1	8.9	5,646	12	4	230
Ohio	110	108	108	99	9.6	9.5	9.5	9.1	97,547	11,854	316	49
Oklahoma	36	35	35	30	10.2	10.0	10.2	9.7	31,381	2,199	128	1,794
Oregon	31	30	30	25	8.8	8.7	8.6	8.8	30,107	382	335	295
Pennsylvania	130	130	131	122	10.6	10.5	10.7	10.3	117,679	11,985	506	53
Rhode Island	10	10	10	10	9.6	9.5	9.6	9.5	9,854	304	62	26
South Carolina	38	37	37	30	9.2	9.0	9.2	8.5	26,792	10,802	103	39
South Dakota	7	7	7	6	9.1	9.1	9.3	9.1	6,386	12	6	494
Tennessee	57	55	55	46	9.8	9.6	9.7	9.5	47,895	8,515	164	32
Texas	156	153	150	125	7.1	7.1	7.2	7.4	134,753	19,286	1,342	143
Utah	13	13	12	9	5.7	5.6	5.5	5.3	12,709	95	172	140
Vermont	5	5	5	5	8.2	8.5	8.4	8.2	5,049	16	5	5
Virginia	57	56	56	48	7.8	7.8	8.0	7.8	44,715	11,757	685	39
Washington	45	45	44	37	7.5	7.5	7.4	7.6	42,295	1,138	1,332	573
West Virginia	21	21	21	19	11.7	11.6	11.7	10.8	20,351	649	12	4
Wisconsin	47	47	46	43	8.6	8.6	8.7	8.7	44,632	1,865	191	293
Wyoming	4	4	4	3	8.4	8.2	7.9	7.1	4,056	10	8	100

See footnotes at end of table.

Geographic area	Number				Infant deaths — Rate[2]										
					All races[3]				White			Black		
	2002	2001	2000	1990	2002	2001	2000	1990	2002	2001	2000	2002	2001	2000
United States . . .	**28,034**	**27,568**	**28,035**	**38,351**	**7.0**	**6.8**	**6.9**	**9.2**	**5.8**	**5.7**	**5.7**	**14.4**	**14.0**	**14.1**
Alabama	539	567	596	688	9.1	9.4	9.4	10.8	7.1	6.8	6.6	13.9	15.1	15.4
Alaska	55	81	68	125	5.5	8.1	6.8	10.5	4.2	5.8	5.8	(B)	(B)	(B)
Arizona	559	592	573	610	6.4	6.9	6.7	8.8	6.2	6.1	6.2	13.0	22.8	17.6
Arkansas	312	309	316	336	8.3	8.3	8.4	9.2	6.9	6.8	7.0	13.9	14.5	13.7
California	2,889	2,830	2,894	4,844	5.5	5.4	5.4	7.9	5.2	5.0	5.1	12.9	12.9	12.9
Colorado	415	388	404	472	6.1	5.8	6.2	8.8	5.5	5.5	5.6	21.1	12.8	19.5
Connecticut	274	260	282	398	6.5	6.1	6.6	7.9	5.5	4.7	5.6	14.2	16.9	14.4
Delaware	96	115	102	112	8.7	10.7	9.2	10.1	7.3	8.0	7.9	12.9	19.9	14.8
District of Columbia	85	81	92	245	11.3	10.6	12.0	20.7	(B)	(B)	(B)	14.5	15.0	16.1
Florida	1,548	1,495	1,425	1,918	7.5	7.3	7.0	9.6	5.8	5.5	5.4	13.6	13.5	12.6
Georgia	1,192	1,146	1,126	1,392	8.9	8.6	8.5	12.4	6.6	6.2	5.9	13.7	13.3	13.9
Hawaii	127	106	142	138	7.3	6.2	8.1	6.7	(B)	6.0	6.5	(B)	(B)	(B)
Idaho.	128	129	153	143	6.1	6.2	7.5	8.7	6.1	6.3	7.5	(B)	(B)	(B)
Illinois	1,339	1,413	1,568	2,104	7.4	7.7	8.5	10.7	5.6	6.0	6.6	16.3	15.5	17.1
Indiana	657	650	685	831	7.7	7.5	7.8	9.6	6.8	6.8	6.9	15.3	13.7	15.8
Iowa	199	212	247	319	5.3	5.6	6.5	8.1	5.1	5.5	6.0	(B)	(B)	21.1
Kansas	281	287	268	329	7.1	7.4	6.8	8.4	6.5	6.5	6.4	15.2	20.5	12.2
Kentucky	392	325	401	461	7.2	5.9	7.2	8.5	6.6	5.6	6.7	14.2	9.7	12.7
Louisiana	665	643	608	799	10.3	9.8	9.0	11.1	6.9	6.5	5.9	15.0	14.4	13.3
Maine	59	84	66	108	4.4	6.1	4.9	6.2	4.3	5.7	4.8	(B)	(B)	(B)
Maryland	551	594	562	766	7.5	8.1	7.6	9.5	5.3	5.5	4.8	12.3	13.7	13.2
Massachusetts	395	405	376	650	4.9	5.0	4.6	7.0	4.5	4.6	4.0	9.1	9.6	9.9
Michigan	1,057	1,069	1,119	1,641	8.1	8.0	8.2	10.7	6.0	6.1	6.0	18.5	17.0	18.2
Minnesota	364	361	378	496	5.4	5.3	5.6	7.3	5.0	4.8	4.8	10.3	9.6	14.6
Mississippi	428	445	470	529	10.3	10.5	10.7	12.1	6.9	7.0	6.8	14.8	14.9	15.3
Missouri.	637	558	547	748	8.5	7.4	7.2	9.4	7.1	5.9	5.9	17.1	16.5	14.7
Montana	83	74	67	105	7.5	6.7	6.1	9.0	7.1	6.7	5.5	(B)	(B)	(B)
Nebraska	178	168	180	202	7.0	6.8	7.3	8.3	6.1	6.4	6.4	20.8	(B)	20.3
Nevada	197	180	201	181	6.0	5.7	6.5	8.4	5.1	5.1	6.0	18.4	17.1	12.7
New Hampshire.	72	56	84	125	5.0	3.8	5.7	7.1	5.3	3.8	5.5	(B)	(B)	(B)
New Jersey	655	747	733	1,102	5.7	6.5	6.3	9.0	4.5	5.1	5.0	12.8	14.2	13.6
New Mexico	174	174	180	246	6.3	6.4	6.6	9.0	5.7	6.3	6.3	(B)	(B)	(B)
New York	1,519	1,482	1,656	2,851	6.0	5.8	6.4	9.6	5.4	5.1	5.4	9.9	9.7	10.9
North Carolina.	959	1,009	1,038	1,109	8.2	8.5	8.6	10.6	5.9	6.1	6.3	15.6	15.8	15.7
North Dakota	49	67	62	74	6.3	8.8	8.1	8.0	5.6	8.0	7.5	(B)	(B)	(B)
Ohio.	1,180	1,161	1,187	1,640	7.9	7.7	7.6	9.8	6.2	6.2	6.3	17.7	16.4	15.4
Oklahoma	410	366	425	438	8.1	7.3	8.5	9.2	7.1	6.5	7.9	17.2	15.0	16.9
Oregon	260	246	255	354	5.8	5.4	5.6	8.3	5.6	5.5	5.5	(B)	(B)	(B)
Pennsylvania	1,091	1,033	1,039	1,643	7.6	7.2	7.1	9.6	6.6	6.1	5.8	15.1	14.4	15.7
Rhode Island	90	86	79	123	7.0	6.8	6.3	8.1	6.4	6.1	5.9	(B)	(B)	(B)
South Carolina	507	496	488	683	9.3	8.9	8.7	11.7	6.0	5.9	5.4	15.8	15.0	14.8
South Dakota	70	78	57	111	6.5	7.4	5.5	10.1	4.9	6.1	4.3	(B)	(B)	(B)
Tennessee	727	681	724	771	9.4	8.7	9.1	10.3	7.0	6.7	6.8	18.3	16.2	18.0
Texas	2,368	2,171	2,065	2,552	6.4	5.9	5.7	8.1	5.6	5.2	5.1	13.5	12.0	11.4
Utah	273	232	248	271	5.6	4.8	5.2	7.5	5.5	4.9	5.1	(B)	(B)	(B)
Vermont.	28	35	39	53	4.4	5.5	6.4	6.4	4.5	5.6	6.1	(B)	(B)	(B)
Virginia	741	747	682	1,013	7.4	7.6	6.9	10.2	5.5	5.4	5.4	14.6	15.8	12.4
Washington	456	459	421	621	5.8	5.8	5.2	7.8	5.5	5.7	4.9	12.7	12.9	9.4
West Virginia	188	148	158	223	9.1	7.2	7.6	9.9	8.5	7.2	7.4	(B)	(B)	(B)
Wisconsin.	472	491	457	598	6.9	7.1	6.6	8.2	5.6	5.9	5.5	18.9	17.8	17.2
Wyoming	44	36	42	60	6.7	5.9	6.7	8.6	6.8	5.9	6.5	(B)	(B)	(B)

B Base figure too small to meet statistical standards.

[1]Rates based on enumerated resident population as of April 1 for 1990 and 2000; estimated resident population as of July 1 for all other years.
[2]Deaths per 1,000 live births.
[3]Includes other races not shown separately.

Survey, Census, or Data Collection Method: Based on the National Vital Statistics System; for information, see Appendix B, Limitations of the Data and Methodology, and Internet site <http://www.cdc.gov/nchs/nvss.htm>.

Source: U.S. National Center for Health Statistics, *Vital Statistics of the United States*, annual; *National Vital Statistics Report* (NVSR), formerly *Monthly Vital Statistics Report*; see also <http://www.cdc.gov/nchs/nvss.htm>.

Table A-13. States — Death Rates by Cause: 2002

Geographic area	HIV[2]	Malignant neoplasms	Diabetes mellitus	Alzheimer's disease	Diseases of the heart	Cerebro-vascular diseases	Pneumonia and influenza	Chronic lower respiratory diseases	Chronic liver diseases and cirrhosis	Accidents and adverse effects — Total	Accidents and adverse effects — Motor vehicle	Intentional self-harm (suicide)	Assault (homicide)	Injury by firearms
United States . . .	**4.9**	**193.2**	**25.4**	**20.4**	**241.7**	**56.4**	**22.8**	**43.3**	**9.5**	**37.0**	**15.7**	**11.0**	**6.1**	**10.5**
Alabama	4.2	216.2	33.1	26.5	294.1	71.3	27.1	51.9	9.5	49.7	24.9	11.5	9.3	16.1
Alaska	(B)	111.1	13.4	9.5	88.1	24.5	7.9	22.1	8.5	53.7	17.4	20.5	6.2	19.7
Arizona	3.0	171.5	22.6	26.3	198.9	46.5	24.2	47.2	12.3	47.2	20.3	16.2	9.2	17.7
Arkansas	3.0	231.8	29.3	20.3	307.4	82.4	28.6	53.2	8.2	48.4	25.6	13.9	7.2	16.3
California	4.1	154.2	19.4	15.4	195.9	50.2	23.1	36.1	10.7	28.8	12.1	9.2	7.1	9.7
Colorado	2.3	141.7	14.6	21.2	142.6	42.5	16.7	41.0	9.2	40.2	17.3	16.1	4.1	11.5
Connecticut	5.4	207.0	19.5	16.5	254.7	53.8	25.7	42.0	9.2	34.2	10.1	7.5	2.8	4.2
Delaware	8.7	200.8	26.6	15.9	237.6	50.2	20.8	43.3	10.9	36.2	15.0	9.2	4.7	9.2
District of Columbia	40.8	227.4	33.5	18.7	291.8	48.9	14.2	23.3	15.4	35.0	10.2	5.4	40.1	34.2
Florida	10.3	234.2	27.4	24.2	294.6	61.4	19.7	54.2	12.9	44.3	19.1	14.0	6.0	11.3
Georgia	8.3	163.3	18.4	17.8	204.8	49.8	20.9	36.9	8.1	38.9	17.8	10.6	7.9	13.2
Hawaii	2.1	156.2	16.4	11.3	201.8	65.2	19.8	21.3	6.3	31.6	9.7	9.6	3.1	2.9
Idaho	(B)	159.4	24.0	23.7	188.8	54.9	19.8	44.4	7.8	45.6	22.1	15.1	2.4	12.2
Illinois	3.9	196.3	23.9	19.0	244.6	57.0	23.3	38.3	8.5	33.5	12.5	9.1	8.1	9.8
Indiana	1.9	208.9	27.4	23.9	248.8	60.4	22.1	50.9	8.3	34.9	15.6	12.1	6.3	11.7
Iowa	1.0	220.4	25.0	30.6	278.6	75.8	32.1	53.8	7.5	37.2	14.5	10.7	1.9	6.8
Kansas	1.4	197.4	28.2	27.8	246.0	67.9	25.7	50.3	6.9	41.9	20.7	12.7	4.7	9.9
Kentucky	2.4	230.6	30.9	24.8	285.8	62.4	30.2	58.7	9.2	51.1	22.6	13.2	4.8	13.3
Louisiana	8.1	210.6	39.6	24.8	249.5	57.9	21.3	37.8	8.1	47.2	21.4	11.1	13.5	19.5
Maine	(B)	247.7	31.2	39.6	244.9	63.6	24.5	61.1	9.0	39.5	16.6	12.8	(B)	6.8
Maryland	11.2	190.4	27.8	15.9	220.0	51.5	20.5	35.6	8.1	24.4	13.2	8.7	9.9	11.3
Massachusetts	3.6	216.5	22.1	24.4	229.3	55.4	32.5	42.7	9.4	22.0	8.8	6.8	2.9	3.2
Michigan	2.4	198.8	27.7	19.5	265.3	57.8	20.2	44.1	9.9	32.7	13.8	11.0	6.9	10.9
Minnesota	1.1	183.5	26.2	23.7	171.4	53.9	17.9	39.3	6.4	38.4	14.8	9.9	2.5	6.1
Mississippi	6.4	211.3	23.4	20.0	315.5	67.1	27.9	48.0	8.0	57.2	30.6	11.9	10.6	17.1
Missouri	2.2	217.2	28.6	20.9	294.5	68.5	28.5	50.5	7.6	46.6	21.4	12.2	6.5	12.3
Montana	(B)	210.1	23.1	31.3	213.8	70.3	28.0	63.3	14.0	57.6	28.0	20.2	2.5	14.7
Nebraska	1.2	198.5	22.7	26.6	245.3	63.8	24.2	54.0	7.3	44.1	19.5	11.6	2.9	8.1
Nevada	3.5	181.1	15.8	11.6	203.4	44.9	16.9	54.0	12.3	39.6	17.8	19.5	8.1	17.0
New Hampshire	(B)	198.3	24.4	24.4	217.7	49.2	18.6	45.3	8.2	28.0	9.8	10.4	(B)	6.0
New Jersey	8.9	207.5	29.5	17.7	262.0	46.8	23.0	33.6	8.5	30.3	9.1	6.4	3.9	4.8
New Mexico	1.9	165.3	31.4	17.5	181.1	38.5	20.1	46.2	17.1	59.6	22.8	18.8	8.7	16.4
New York	10.3	191.4	20.5	9.4	295.8	39.8	28.0	36.4	7.0	24.3	8.8	6.4	4.8	5.2
North Carolina	5.8	194.8	26.5	23.6	222.6	63.2	22.8	44.2	8.8	44.5	20.3	11.9	7.7	13.7
North Dakota	(B)	203.9	33.7	46.4	255.9	74.0	25.5	50.8	9.9	38.8	17.5	14.4	(B)	9.1
Ohio	2.1	220.4	33.7	22.8	274.8	63.5	21.8	53.1	9.2	36.3	14.0	11.3	4.8	9.4
Oklahoma	2.6	213.9	30.5	21.6	321.4	69.5	26.2	56.9	12.3	45.2	21.9	14.3	5.6	12.9
Oregon	2.6	205.8	29.6	31.9	206.2	75.1	18.9	52.4	10.4	39.7	13.1	14.7	3.0	10.6
Pennsylvania	4.0	242.0	30.1	22.9	315.0	69.5	24.0	48.8	9.4	38.3	14.1	10.9	5.2	9.9
Rhode Island	2.2	224.7	24.6	24.7	290.6	56.6	29.8	48.7	12.0	25.9	8.9	8.0	4.0	5.1
South Carolina	7.3	202.9	27.1	23.5	235.2	68.7	22.2	46.0	9.4	48.0	24.9	10.7	7.9	13.8
South Dakota	(B)	205.2	25.6	21.9	254.5	68.1	31.5	50.3	9.9	45.7	24.4	12.4	2.9	8.0
Tennessee	6.0	215.9	30.2	22.4	279.9	68.7	29.5	51.9	10.5	47.3	21.6	13.4	8.1	15.6
Texas	4.9	156.9	26.0	17.4	199.5	48.4	16.9	35.4	10.5	37.8	18.5	10.6	6.5	10.6
Utah	(B)	102.6	22.2	13.1	128.5	39.0	18.3	26.0	5.7	30.8	14.2	14.7	2.3	8.9
Vermont	(B)	198.5	28.2	26.4	222.2	54.3	18.0	44.8	10.7	38.9	12.7	14.9	(B)	10.1
Virginia	3.6	186.5	21.4	18.8	205.0	54.3	20.3	37.7	8.2	34.0	13.2	11.0	5.4	11.1
Washington	2.0	178.9	24.6	36.2	183.6	61.8	14.9	44.8	8.7	36.3	12.5	13.4	3.5	9.4
West Virginia	1.1	258.2	47.0	22.5	343.5	69.9	23.7	68.2	11.6	53.1	23.0	15.3	5.3	15.0
Wisconsin	1.4	199.0	24.9	24.7	237.5	63.9	23.7	42.9	8.0	41.8	16.0	11.5	3.5	8.2
Wyoming	(B)	172.2	29.1	24.5	201.5	48.7	27.1	65.0	14.0	58.0	31.5	21.1	4.6	19.0

B Figure does not meet standards of reliability or precision.

[1] Deaths per 100,000 resident population enumerated as of July 1.
[2] Human immunodeficiency virus.

Survey, Census, or Data Collection Method: National Vital Statistics System; for information, see Appendix B, Limitations of the Data and Methodology, and Internet site <http://www.cdc.gov/nchs/nvss.htm>.

Source: U.S. National Center for Health Statistics, *National Vital Statistics Report* (NVSR), formerly *Monthly Vital Statistics Report*; see also <http://www.cdc.gov/nchs/nvss.htm>.

Table A-14. States — **Marriages and Divorces—Number and Rate**

Geographic area	Marriages[1]						Divorces[2]					
	Number (1,000)			Rate per 1,000 population[3]			Number (1,000)			Rate per 1,000 population[3]		
	2004	2000	1990	2004	2000	1990	2004	2000	1990	2004	2000	1990
United States[4]...	**2,178.4**	**2,329.0**	**2,443.0**	**7.4**	**8.3**	**9.8**	**(NA)**	**(NA)**	**1,182.0**	**3.7**	**4.2**	**4.7**
Alabama	40.6	45.0	43.3	9.0	10.3	10.6	21.5	23.5	25.3	4.7	5.4	6.1
Alaska	5.4	5.6	5.7	8.3	8.9	10.2	3.1	2.7	2.9	4.8	4.4	5.5
Arizona	37.9	38.7	37.0	6.6	7.9	10.0	24.4	21.6	25.1	4.2	4.4	6.9
Arkansas	35.7	41.1	35.7	13.0	16.0	15.3	17.4	17.9	16.8	6.3	6.9	6.9
California[5]	172.3	196.9	236.7	4.8	5.9	7.9	(NA)	(NA)	128.0	(NA)	(NA)	4.3
Colorado	34.5	35.6	31.5	7.5	8.6	9.8	20.2	(NA)	18.4	4.4	(NA)	5.5
Connecticut	16.5	19.4	27.8	4.7	5.9	7.9	10.3	6.5	10.3	2.9	2.0	3.2
Delaware	5.1	5.1	5.6	6.1	6.7	8.4	3.1	3.2	3.0	3.7	4.2	4.4
District of Columbia	2.9	2.8	4.7	5.3	5.4	8.2	0.9	1.5	2.7	1.7	3.0	4.5
Florida	156.4	141.9	142.3	9.0	9.3	10.9	82.7	81.9	81.7	4.8	5.3	6.3
Georgia	64.5	56.0	64.4	7.3	7.1	10.3	(NA)	30.7	35.7	(NA)	3.9	5.5
Hawaii	28.4	25.0	18.1	22.5	21.2	16.4	(NA)	4.6	5.2	(NA)	3.9	4.6
Idaho	15.2	14.0	15.0	10.9	11.0	13.9	7.1	6.9	6.6	5.1	5.4	6.5
Illinois	77.8	85.5	97.1	6.1	7.0	8.8	33.1	39.1	44.3	2.6	3.2	3.8
Indiana	48.4	34.5	54.3	7.8	5.8	9.6	(NA)	(NA)	(NA)	(NA)	(NA)	(NA)
Iowa	20.5	20.3	24.8	6.9	7.0	9.0	8.3	9.4	11.1	2.8	3.3	3.9
Kansas	19.1	22.2	23.4	7.0	8.3	9.2	9.1	10.6	12.6	3.3	4.0	5.0
Kentucky	36.8	39.7	51.3	8.9	10.0	13.5	20.5	21.6	21.8	4.9	5.4	5.8
Louisiana	30.2	40.5	41.2	6.7	9.3	9.6	(NA)	(NA)	(NA)	(NA)	(NA)	(NA)
Maine	10.9	10.5	11.8	8.3	8.3	9.7	4.7	5.8	5.3	3.6	4.6	4.3
Maryland	37.7	40.0	46.1	6.8	7.7	9.7	17.1	17.0	16.1	3.1	3.3	3.4
Massachusetts	41.2	37.0	47.8	6.4	6.0	7.9	14.1	18.6	16.8	2.2	3.0	2.8
Michigan	62.6	66.4	76.1	6.2	6.7	8.2	35.0	39.4	40.2	3.5	4.0	4.3
Minnesota	30.1	33.4	33.7	5.9	6.9	7.7	14.2	14.8	15.4	2.8	3.1	3.5
Mississippi	17.8	19.7	24.3	6.1	7.1	9.4	13.1	14.4	14.4	4.5	5.2	5.5
Missouri	36.5	43.7	49.3	6.3	7.9	9.6	21.9	26.5	26.4	3.8	4.8	5.1
Montana	6.8	6.6	7.0	7.4	7.4	8.6	3.5	2.1	4.1	3.8	2.4	5.1
Nebraska	12.9	13.0	12.5	7.4	7.8	8.0	6.4	6.4	6.5	3.6	3.8	4.0
Nevada	145.8	144.3	123.4	62.4	76.7	99.0	14.8	18.1	13.3	6.4	9.6	11.4
New Hampshire	9.8	11.6	10.6	7.6	9.5	9.5	5.0	7.1	5.3	3.9	5.8	4.7
New Jersey	50.1	50.4	58.0	5.8	6.1	7.6	26.0	25.6	23.6	3.0	3.1	3.0
New Mexico	14.1	14.5	13.2	7.4	8.3	8.8	8.8	9.2	7.7	4.6	5.3	4.9
New York	124.4	162.0	169.3	6.5	8.9	8.6	57.8	62.8	57.9	3.0	3.4	3.2
North Carolina	65.9	65.6	52.1	7.7	8.5	7.8	37.7	36.9	34.0	4.4	4.8	5.1
North Dakota	4.1	4.6	4.8	6.5	7.3	7.5	1.8	2.0	2.3	2.8	3.2	3.6
Ohio	75.9	88.5	95.8	6.6	7.9	9.0	42.4	49.3	51.0	3.7	4.4	4.7
Oklahoma	22.8	15.6	33.2	6.5	4.6	10.6	(NA)	12.4	24.9	(NA)	3.7	7.7
Oregon	29.0	26.0	25.2	8.1	7.8	8.9	14.8	16.7	15.9	4.1	5.0	5.5
Pennsylvania	65.1	73.2	86.8	5.3	6.1	7.1	30.7	37.9	40.1	2.5	3.2	3.3
Rhode Island	8.2	8.0	8.1	7.6	8.0	8.1	3.3	3.1	3.8	3.0	3.1	3.7
South Carolina	34.5	42.7	55.8	8.2	10.9	15.9	13.4	14.4	16.1	3.2	3.7	4.5
South Dakota	6.5	7.1	7.7	8.4	9.6	11.1	2.5	2.7	2.6	3.2	3.6	3.7
Tennessee	67.5	88.2	66.6	11.4	15.9	13.9	29.8	33.8	32.3	5.0	6.1	6.5
Texas	176.3	196.4	182.8	7.8	9.6	10.5	81.9	85.2	94.0	3.6	4.2	5.5
Utah	13.2	24.1	19.0	5.5	11.1	11.2	9.3	9.7	8.8	3.9	4.5	5.1
Vermont	6.0	6.1	6.1	9.6	10.2	10.9	2.4	5.1	2.6	3.9	8.6	4.5
Virginia	62.5	62.4	71.3	8.4	9.0	11.4	30.1	30.2	27.3	4.0	4.3	4.4
Washington	40.1	40.9	48.6	6.5	7.0	9.5	25.2	27.2	28.8	4.1	4.7	5.9
West Virginia	13.2	15.7	13.2	7.3	8.7	7.2	8.6	9.3	9.7	4.7	5.2	5.3
Wisconsin	34.1	36.1	41.2	6.2	6.8	7.9	17.0	17.6	17.8	3.1	3.3	3.6
Wyoming	4.8	4.9	4.8	9.4	10.3	10.7	2.7	2.8	3.1	5.3	5.9	6.6

NA Not available.

[1]Data include marriage licenses for some states.
[2]Includes annulments and divorce petitions filed or legal separations for some states.
[3]Based on total resident population enumerated as of April 1 for 1990 and 2000; estimated as of July 1 for 2004.
[4]U.S. totals for the number of divorces are estimates that include states not reporting (CA, CO, IN, and LA).
[5]Marriage data include nonlicensed marriages registered.

Survey, Census, or Data Collection Method: Based on the National Vital Statistics System; for information, see Appendix B, Limitations of the Data and Methodology, and Internet site <http://www.cdc.gov/nchs/nvss.htm>.

Source: U.S. National Center for Health Statistics, *Vital Statistics of the United States*, annual; *National Vital Statistics Report* (NVSR), formerly *Monthly Vital Statistics Report*; see also <http://www.cdc.gov/nchs/nvss.htm>.

Geographic area	Number of hospitals			Beds (1,000)			Patients admitted (1,000)			Outpatient visits (mil.)			Personnel (1,000)		
	2003	2000	1990	2003	2000	1990	2003	2000	1990	2003	2000	1990	2002	2000	1990
United States . . .	**4,895**	**4,915**	**5,384**	**813.3**	**823.6**	**928.1**	**34,783**	**33,089**	**31,181**	**563.1**	**521.4**	**301.3**	**3,489**	**3,332**	**3,420**
Alabama	107	108	120	15.6	16.4	18.6	709	680	597	8.9	8.0	4.6	63	60	59
Alaska	19	18	16	1.5	1.4	1.2	46	47	37	1.4	1.3	0.4	7	6	4
Arizona	61	61	61	10.8	10.9	9.9	603	539	396	6.7	5.3	2.7	46	44	36
Arkansas	88	83	86	9.9	9.8	10.9	388	368	347	4.6	4.4	2.2	37	36	33
California	370	389	445	74.3	72.7	80.5	3,474	3,315	3,063	48.0	44.9	29.7	320	288	311
Colorado	68	69	69	9.5	9.4	10.4	444	397	335	7.0	6.7	3.5	45	40	39
Connecticut	34	35	35	7.2	7.7	9.6	372	349	355	6.8	6.7	4.2	36	34	44
Delaware	6	5	8	2.0	1.8	2.0	97	83	84	2.0	1.5	1.0	12	9	10
District of Columbia	10	11	11	3.4	3.3	4.5	135	129	158	1.6	1.3	1.3	19	19	20
Florida	203	202	224	50.7	51.2	50.7	2,296	2,119	1,639	22.0	21.8	11.6	203	194	172
Georgia	146	151	163	24.6	23.9	25.7	926	863	888	12.8	11.2	6.8	98	92	89
Hawaii	24	21	18	3.1	3.1	2.9	112	100	96	1.9	2.5	1.8	13	12	12
Idaho	39	42	43	3.4	3.5	3.2	136	123	97	2.8	2.2	1.1	14	11	10
Illinois	192	196	210	35.0	37.3	45.8	1,594	1,531	1,499	27.0	25.1	16.4	157	161	174
Indiana	112	109	113	18.9	19.2	21.8	712	700	727	15.0	14.1	8.7	79	76	84
Iowa	116	115	124	11.0	11.8	14.3	363	360	385	9.7	9.2	4.1	41	41	44
Kansas	134	129	138	10.6	10.8	11.8	331	310	305	6.0	5.3	2.9	34	32	35
Kentucky	103	105	107	14.9	14.8	15.9	600	582	532	8.5	8.7	4.4	56	56	50
Louisiana	127	123	140	17.8	17.5	19.1	690	654	607	10.8	10.0	5.4	70	70	63
Maine	37	37	39	3.7	3.7	4.5	149	147	146	3.9	3.2	1.9	17	16	18
Maryland	51	49	52	11.6	11.2	13.6	645	587	562	6.5	6.0	4.6	56	52	59
Massachusetts	79	80	101	16.0	16.6	21.7	785	740	811	19.6	16.7	9.9	99	93	101
Michigan	144	146	176	25.8	26.1	33.9	1,168	1,106	1,069	27.0	24.9	15.3	122	123	135
Minnesota	131	135	152	16.4	16.7	19.4	615	571	530	9.1	7.3	4.4	46	41	56
Mississippi	92	95	103	13.0	13.6	12.9	416	425	396	4.0	3.7	2.2	40	40	34
Missouri	119	119	135	19.3	20.1	24.3	831	773	737	15.7	14.8	6.5	86	83	89
Montana	53	52	55	4.3	4.3	4.6	107	99	105	2.7	2.6	0.8	12	11	11
Nebraska	85	85	90	7.5	8.2	8.5	212	209	188	3.7	3.4	1.6	25	24	24
Nevada	25	22	21	4.3	3.8	3.4	213	199	116	2.3	2.2	1.1	16	16	11
New Hampshire.	28	28	27	2.8	2.9	3.5	118	111	125	3.1	2.8	1.6	15	13	14
New Jersey	78	80	95	22.8	25.3	28.9	1,108	1,074	1,132	14.7	16.3	9.7	98	101	108
New Mexico	37	35	37	3.7	3.5	4.2	166	174	153	4.5	3.1	1.8	20	16	14
New York	207	215	235	64.7	66.4	74.7	2,499	2,416	2,322	48.0	46.4	29.3	307	301	310
North Carolina	113	113	120	23.3	23.1	22.0	987	971	784	14.5	12.4	6.1	107	105	88
North Dakota	40	42	50	3.6	3.9	4.4	88	89	96	1.8	1.7	0.5	12	11	11
Ohio	163	163	190	33.0	33.8	43.1	1,458	1,404	1,512	30.0	26.9	17.1	161	151	172
Oklahoma	108	108	111	11.0	11.1	12.4	450	429	382	5.5	4.7	2.3	41	42	42
Oregon	58	59	70	6.8	6.6	8.1	342	330	302	8.2	7.3	3.4	33	31	33
Pennsylvania	201	207	238	40.9	42.3	52.6	1,824	1,796	1,796	33.0	31.8	21.2	186	179	211
Rhode Island	11	11	12	2.4	2.4	3.2	122	119	127	2.0	2.1	1.2	11	11	15
South Carolina	61	63	69	11.1	11.5	11.3	506	495	413	7.4	7.8	3.4	49	45	41
South Dakota	50	48	69	4.4	4.3	4.2	103	99	94	1.5	1.7	0.7	13	11	11
Tennessee	125	121	134	20.3	20.6	23.6	813	737	798	10.0	10.3	5.2	78	79	80
Texas	414	403	428	57.3	55.9	59.2	2,550	2,367	1,986	32.3	29.4	13.6	244	227	203
Utah	42	42	42	4.4	4.3	4.4	215	194	175	4.5	4.5	2.4	21	19	18
Vermont	14	14	15	1.5	1.7	1.7	52	52	58	2.2	1.2	0.7	8	6	6
Virginia	84	88	97	17.2	16.9	20.0	758	727	706	11.2	9.5	5.8	72	71	71
Washington	85	84	91	11.2	11.1	12.0	516	505	492	10.3	9.6	4.9	53	50	49
West Virginia	57	57	59	7.8	8.0	8.4	296	288	277	5.8	5.2	2.8	30	29	28
Wisconsin.	121	118	129	14.8	15.3	18.6	588	558	597	11.8	10.9	5.9	54	49	62
Wyoming	23	24	27	1.8	1.9	2.2	53	48	48	0.9	0.9	0.5	6	6	5

Survey, Census, or Data Collection Method: Based on the American Hospital Association Annual Survey of Hospitals; for information, see Internet site <http://www.healthforum.com/>.

Source: Health Forum, An American Hospital Association Company, Chicago, IL, *Hospital Statistics*, 2005 edition, and prior years (copyright).

Table A-16. States — Health Care Services, Physicians, and Nurses

Geographic area	Health care services, 2002[1] Establishments				Employees (1,000)				Annual payroll (mil. dol.)	Physicians[2] Number		Rate per 100,000 population[3]		Nurses Number		Rate per 100,000 population[3]	
	Total	Ambulatory health care services	Hospitals	Nursing and residential care facilities	Total	Ambulatory health care services	Hospitals	Nursing and residential care facilities		2003	2000	2003	2000	2001	1992	2001	1992
United States ...	563,216	487,747	7,569	67,900	12,809	4,917	5,122	2,771	462,184	858,510	802,156	295	285	2,262,020	1,907,100	793	743
Alabama	7,281	6,423	136	722	186	71	80	35	6,387	10,434	9,887	232	222	36,400	28,900	815	696
Alaska	1,354	1,150	30	174	27	9	15	3	1,271	1,545	1,362	238	217	4,930	3,600	780	611
Arizona	10,192	8,997	103	1,092	183	80	69	34	6,944	13,641	12,250	244	239	34,880	28,300	659	723
Arkansas	4,967	4,327	106	534	122	39	58	25	3,952	6,121	5,711	224	214	19,860	15,600	738	646
California	72,583	63,969	622	7,992	1,222	532	466	224	48,507	104,261	97,213	294	287	185,550	175,800	537	568
Colorado	9,353	8,457	99	797	168	74	61	32	6,498	13,051	11,692	287	272	33,510	27,800	757	795
Connecticut	7,567	6,552	57	958	192	73	60	59	7,555	13,834	13,279	397	390	32,740	31,800	954	963
Delaware	1,556	1,412	16	128	39	16	16	7	1,558	2,284	2,099	279	268	7,280	6,300	915	907
District of Columbia	1,507	1,276	23	208	50	11	32	7	2,225	4,607	4,488	826	785	8,600	9,000	1,510	1,506
Florida	37,751	34,489	362	2,900	694	299	251	143	25,191	50,000	46,013	294	288	129,610	96,900	793	710
Georgia	14,383	12,982	213	1,188	321	130	138	53	11,621	21,075	19,324	243	236	58,600	44,700	698	656
Hawaii	2,644	2,507	31	106	44	20	18	6	1,796	4,358	3,887	349	321	8,680	8,300	710	716
Idaho	2,756	2,435	55	266	52	19	21	11	1,625	2,642	2,370	193	183	8,400	6,300	636	588
Illinois	22,665	20,140	278	2,247	557	194	242	121	20,440	37,608	35,943	297	289	104,830	94,000	837	804
Indiana	10,604	8,907	188	1,509	290	95	128	68	9,749	14,716	13,461	237	221	49,590	40,900	809	721
Iowa	5,470	4,247	129	1,094	158	42	63	52	4,852	6,318	5,927	215	203	30,190	26,400	1,030	937
Kansas	5,321	4,209	147	965	139	47	53	39	4,386	6,743	6,486	247	241	24,680	19,900	914	786
Kentucky	7,583	6,553	164	866	189	67	82	40	6,281	10,215	9,468	248	234	34,920	26,200	858	696
Louisiana	8,481	7,316	228	937	215	70	102	42	6,698	12,878	12,207	287	273	36,690	24,700	821	575
Maine	3,124	2,313	48	763	(D)	24	(4)	21	(D)	3,995	3,598	305	282	13,390	10,800	1,041	872
Maryland	11,375	9,953	103	1,319	233	89	88	56	8,798	24,806	23,449	450	443	43,340	39,100	806	794
Massachusetts	13,346	10,835	155	2,356	393	129	163	101	14,908	30,603	28,886	477	455	75,580	66,200	1,182	1,098
Michigan	19,842	16,395	216	3,231	449	168	190	92	16,381	26,459	25,209	262	254	83,950	68,200	839	719
Minnesota	9,244	6,557	170	2,517	289	109	100	81	10,313	15,591	14,257	308	290	46,990	41,600	943	925
Mississippi	4,144	3,614	134	396	114	34	62	19	3,760	5,820	5,399	202	190	22,290	14,000	780	534
Missouri	10,641	8,912	173	1,556	292	96	130	67	9,650	14,779	14,061	258	251	52,970	40,800	939	782
Montana	2,123	1,748	65	310	41	13	19	10	1,300	2,425	2,188	264	243	7,620	6,000	841	727
Nebraska	3,207	2,627	105	475	91	25	41	25	2,871	4,643	4,300	267	251	15,970	13,400	929	831
Nevada	3,950	3,605	47	298	65	32	25	8	2,637	4,691	4,025	209	201	10,840	7,700	517	570
New Hampshire	2,295	1,981	40	274	61	24	26	12	2,236	3,846	3,438	298	278	11,190	10,600	889	948
New Jersey	19,851	18,213	158	1,480	392	164	153	75	15,575	29,053	27,462	336	326	71,500	67,700	841	859
New Mexico	3,153	2,692	67	394	68	28	27	13	2,311	5,031	4,565	268	251	11,630	10,600	635	664
New York	40,692	36,069	357	4,266	1,002	394	389	219	39,010	81,199	78,524	423	414	165,580	161,600	868	886
North Carolina	13,672	11,181	186	2,305	372	140	143	89	12,889	23,530	21,118	279	262	72,050	50,200	879	728
North Dakota	1,148	868	55	225	(D)	9	(5)	14	(D)	1,691	1,603	267	250	6,460	6,000	1,015	940
Ohio	21,562	18,461	245	2,856	591	208	231	153	20,205	32,150	30,229	281	266	103,870	90,200	912	834
Oklahoma	6,965	5,783	176	1,006	155	55	61	39	4,730	6,792	6,565	194	190	22,890	17,100	660	531
Oregon	7,964	6,277	70	1,617	144	57	49	37	5,277	10,741	9,312	301	272	26,040	23,700	750	792
Pennsylvania	26,209	22,260	364	3,585	667	228	267	172	23,028	40,542	39,603	328	322	132,120	116,300	1,074	965
Rhode Island	2,395	1,941	29	425	61	19	25	18	2,124	4,091	3,814	380	364	11,160	9,500	1,054	938
South Carolina	6,595	5,676	96	823	158	56	70	32	5,666	10,510	9,689	253	242	28,130	20,800	693	575
South Dakota	1,477	1,133	69	275	47	12	23	12	1,529	1,831	1,708	239	226	8,440	7,000	1,113	982
Tennessee	10,359	9,055	187	1,117	261	99	111	51	9,449	16,547	15,360	283	270	48,880	37,000	850	733
Texas	38,777	34,950	626	3,201	864	399	329	135	29,801	50,840	46,904	230	225	129,710	95,200	608	536
Utah	4,453	4,010	65	378	87	35	36	15	2,701	5,514	5,041	234	226	13,830	10,200	606	555
Vermont	1,384	1,181	18	185	(D)	14	(5)	7	(D)	2,578	2,318	416	381	5,820	5,200	949	908
Virginia	12,228	10,931	164	1,133	277	110	113	54	10,121	22,373	20,362	304	288	55,440	45,400	772	708
Washington	12,308	10,519	122	1,667	250	111	88	52	9,366	18,580	16,693	303	283	45,170	40,000	754	775
West Virginia	3,697	3,104	80	513	93	31	44	18	2,847	4,587	4,442	253	246	15,850	12,800	880	709
Wisconsin	9,900	7,580	163	2,157	278	109	99	70	9,886	15,246	13,954	279	260	49,610	41,800	918	832
Wyoming	1,118	975	29	114	(D)	7	(6)	4	(D)	1,095	1,013	218	205	3,780	3,200	765	686

D Withheld to avoid disclosure.

[1]Includes Ambulatory health care services (NAICS 621), Hospitals (NAICS 622), and Nursing and residential care facilities (NAICS 623).
[2]Includes inactive physicians and physicians not classified. Excludes physicians with addresses unknown.
[3]Based on U.S. Census Bureau estimates as of July 1.
[4]25,000–49,999 employees.
[5]10,000–24,999 employees.
[6]5,000–9,999 employees.

Survey, Census, or Data Collection Method: Health care services—Based on the Regional Economic Information System; for information, see Internet site <http://www.census.gov/epcd/cbp/view/cbpview.html>; Physicians—For information, see Internet site <http://www.ama-assn.org/>; Nurses—For information, see Internet site <http://www.bhpr.hrsa.gov/>.

Sources: Health care services—U.S. Census Bureau, *County Business Patterns*, annual, see Internet site <http://www.census.gov/epcd/cbp/view/cbpview.html>; Physicians—American Medical Association, Chicago, IL, *Physician Characteristics and Distribution in the U.S.*, annual (copyright); Nurses—U.S. Department of Health and Human Services, Health Resources and Services Administration, unpublished data.

Table A-17. States — Persons With and Without Health Insurance Coverage

	Persons									Children					
Geographic area	Total persons covered (1,000)			Number not covered (1,000)			Percent of persons not covered			Number not covered (1,000)			Percent of children not covered		
	2003	2000[1]	1990	2003	2000[1]	1990	2003	2000[1]	1990	2003	2000[1]	1990	2003	2000[1]	1990
United States . . .	**243,320**	**239,714**	**214,167**	**44,961**	**39,804**	**34,719**	**15.6**	**14.2**	**13.9**	**8,373**	**8,617**	**8,504**	**11.4**	**11.9**	**13.0**
Alabama	3,798	3,797	3,364	629	582	710	14.2	13.3	17.4	95	107	197	8.7	9.4	17.8
Alaska	523	508	422	122	117	77	18.9	18.7	15.4	24	29	19	12.3	15.4	12.5
Arizona	4,626	4,330	2,974	951	869	547	17.0	16.7	15.5	223	197	145	14.6	13.8	16.3
Arkansas	2,206	2,272	1,999	465	379	421	17.4	14.3	17.4	71	80	132	10.5	11.6	19.6
California	28,895	27,705	24,116	6,499	6,299	5,683	18.4	18.5	19.1	1,196	1,445	1,424	12.5	15.1	17.5
Colorado	3,708	3,721	2,872	772	620	495	17.2	14.3	14.7	159	164	152	13.7	14.5	15.9
Connecticut	3,065	3,041	3,040	357	330	226	10.4	9.8	6.9	71	57	31	8.3	6.8	3.8
Delaware	729	706	594	91	72	96	11.1	9.3	13.9	17	13	19	8.5	6.7	11.8
District of Columbia	475	476	461	79	78	109	14.3	14.0	19.2	12	11	27	11.4	9.8	18.9
Florida	13,849	13,188	10,807	3,071	2,829	2,376	18.2	17.7	18.0	616	662	562	15.5	17.6	18.1
Georgia	7,162	6,958	5,381	1,409	1,166	971	16.4	14.3	15.3	314	226	202	13.7	10.1	11.9
Hawaii	1,126	1,089	1,021	127	113	81	10.1	9.4	7.3	23	21	20	7.4	7.1	7.1
Idaho	1,107	1,091	891	253	199	159	18.6	15.4	15.2	51	56	51	13.7	14.8	15.2
Illinois	10,810	10,597	10,432	1,818	1,704	1,272	14.4	13.9	10.9	320	338	296	10.0	10.8	9.8
Indiana	5,296	5,342	4,893	853	674	587	13.9	11.2	10.7	143	175	166	9.0	11.6	12.1
Iowa	2,593	2,609	2,560	329	253	225	11.3	8.8	8.1	60	53	39	8.6	7.2	5.5
Kansas	2,389	2,364	2,240	294	289	272	11.0	10.9	10.8	45	74	86	6.4	11.0	11.9
Kentucky	3,537	3,457	3,148	574	545	480	14.0	13.6	13.2	107	90	139	10.5	8.9	15.5
Louisiana	3,517	3,577	3,247	912	789	797	20.6	18.1	19.7	182	184	191	15.2	14.9	18.4
Maine	1,150	1,131	1,097	133	138	139	10.4	10.9	11.2	17	25	40	6.0	8.7	12.3
Maryland	4,731	4,714	4,134	762	547	601	13.9	10.4	12.7	114	143	165	8.1	10.3	14.0
Massachusetts	5,685	5,744	5,306	682	549	530	10.7	8.7	9.1	118	92	71	7.9	6.4	5.4
Michigan	8,838	8,935	8,329	1,080	901	865	10.9	9.2	9.4	147	138	161	5.8	5.6	6.6
Minnesota	4,633	4,496	3,987	444	399	389	8.7	8.1	8.9	77	68	72	6.2	5.5	6.2
Mississippi	2,343	2,420	2,138	511	380	531	17.9	13.6	19.9	92	68	156	12.1	8.7	18.6
Missouri	5,004	5,000	4,575	620	524	665	11.0	9.5	12.7	103	101	191	7.3	7.1	13.1
Montana	739	742	705	177	150	115	19.4	16.8	14.0	38	35	32	17.7	15.3	13.0
Nebraska	1,532	1,533	1,479	195	154	138	11.3	9.1	8.5	31	30	34	7.0	6.9	7.4
Nevada	1,824	1,704	1,017	426	344	201	18.9	16.8	16.5	103	89	50	17.4	16.1	14.9
New Hampshire	1,133	1,130	978	131	103	107	10.3	8.4	9.9	17	22	17	5.5	7.3	6.8
New Jersey	7,378	7,372	6,974	1,201	1,021	773	14.0	12.2	10.0	237	171	160	11.0	8.6	8.5
New Mexico	1,457	1,364	1,185	414	435	339	22.1	24.2	22.2	65	93	98	13.2	18.5	22.0
New York	16,104	15,732	15,873	2,866	3,056	2,176	15.1	16.3	12.1	432	499	394	9.4	10.8	8.5
North Carolina	6,829	6,912	5,506	1,424	1,084	883	17.3	13.6	13.8	249	203	190	11.9	10.1	12.8
North Dakota	563	553	595	69	71	40	10.9	11.3	6.3	11	15	8	7.5	10.1	4.3
Ohio	9,885	9,930	9,798	1,362	1,248	1,123	12.1	11.2	10.3	236	288	262	8.3	10.4	9.0
Oklahoma	2,737	2,743	2,520	701	641	574	20.4	18.9	18.6	154	147	159	17.9	16.8	19.6
Oregon	2,957	2,987	2,531	613	433	360	17.2	12.7	12.4	113	97	118	13.5	11.2	16.1
Pennsylvania	10,771	11,017	10,887	1,384	1,047	1,218	11.4	8.7	10.1	239	189	269	8.4	6.7	9.0
Rhode Island	946	959	841	108	77	105	10.2	7.4	11.1	13	9	16	5.2	3.8	8.1
South Carolina	3,481	3,493	2,848	584	480	550	14.4	12.1	16.2	92	88	152	8.9	8.7	17.9
South Dakota	659	656	616	91	81	81	12.2	11.0	11.6	16	18	20	8.4	9.6	10.4
Tennessee	5,131	5,030	4,254	778	615	673	13.2	10.9	13.7	150	92	162	10.8	6.6	12.6
Texas	16,484	15,973	13,316	5,374	4,748	3,569	24.6	22.9	21.1	1,264	1,398	1,003	20.0	23.0	20.8
Utah	2,055	1,961	1,585	298	281	156	12.7	12.5	9.0	69	63	46	9.0	8.6	7.0
Vermont	553	549	511	58	52	54	9.5	8.6	9.5	5	6	9	3.9	4.0	6.4
Virginia	6,424	6,178	5,329	962	814	996	13.0	11.6	15.7	162	194	291	8.9	10.9	16.3
Washington	5,147	5,080	4,328	944	792	557	15.5	13.5	11.4	125	142	115	8.4	9.2	9.2
West Virginia	1,491	1,524	1,561	296	250	249	16.6	14.1	13.8	34	43	61	8.4	10.8	13.8
Wisconsin	4,836	4,914	4,497	593	406	321	10.9	7.6	6.7	104	58	70	7.7	4.3	5.7
Wyoming	411	410	405	78	76	58	15.9	15.7	12.5	15	16	14	12.5	13.1	10.3

[1]Implementation of Census 2000-based population controls. Sample expanded by 28,000 households.

Survey, Census, or Data Collection Method: Based on the Annual Social and Economic Supplement to the Current Population Survey; for information, see Internet site <http://www.census.gov/hhes/income/p60_226sa.pdf>.

Source: U.S. Census Bureau, Current Population Reports, annual, and unpublished data.

Health Conditions and Chronic Disease-Related Characteristics and Diabetes

Geographic area	High blood pressure (percent)		High blood cholesterol (percent)		Cigarette smoking[1] (percent)		Heavy drinking[2] (percent)		Above healthy weight[3] (percent)		Obesity[4] (percent)		Diagnosed diabetes (percent)		No leisure time physical activity in the past month (percent)	
	2001	1991	2001	1991	2003	1991	2001	1991	2001	1991	2001	1991	2001	1991	2001	1991
United States[5]...	25.6	21.0	30.2	26.2	22.1	24.2	5.1	3.4	58.9	46.2	21.4	12.9	6.5	4.8	25.4	28.0
Alabama	31.6	26.7	32.9	25.8	25.3	22.9	4.2	3.2	61.6	46.8	24.9	14.4	9.6	5.1	31.2	34.2
Alaska	21.8	19.2	28.7	31.2	26.3	26.9	5.8	4.1	63.3	48.7	22.9	13.6	4.0	4.3	21.1	22.1
Arizona	23.6	19.1	30.3	27.2	21.0	24.2	6.1	3.6	56.0	41.3	19.3	11.8	6.1	3.8	21.9	24.3
Arkansas	29.7	22.9	29.9	26.4	24.8	26.9	4.6	2.5	59.5	47.5	23.0	13.5	7.8	4.8	31.5	36.0
California	23.3	20.2	31.7	25.7	16.8	20.1	6.2	4.1	59.4	44.6	22.6	10.8	6.5	4.8	26.6	23.3
Colorado	21.6	19.0	29.4	24.1	18.5	24.3	5.5	4.1	51.7	35.8	15.5	8.9	4.6	2.9	19.2	18.6
Connecticut	24.0	22.1	29.8	27.6	18.7	23.0	5.2	4.0	55.1	43.1	18.2	11.4	6.3	4.6	24.0	25.8
Delaware	27.2	21.9	30.5	30.5	21.9	26.5	7.1	4.0	59.1	50.1	21.4	15.7	7.1	4.9	25.7	31.5
District of Columbia	29.0	20.3	29.0	20.3	22.3	22.3	6.1	3.1	52.1	46.6	20.2	16.2	8.3	6.7	24.2	39.4
Florida	26.9	20.3	31.0	24.9	23.9	25.0	5.5	3.8	55.8	45.1	19.2	10.6	8.2	5.1	27.7	28.5
Georgia	26.9	20.9	31.9	22.3	22.8	21.9	3.9	2.0	59.4	47.1	23.1	9.8	6.9	5.6	27.3	39.9
Hawaii	24.1	21.2	25.1	30.0	17.3	20.7	5.1	5.2	51.4	40.4	18.3	10.5	6.2	6.5	18.9	23.4
Idaho	24.6	19.3	30.3	25.7	19.0	21.7	4.2	2.2	59.3	45.7	21.0	12.3	5.4	3.7	21.0	22.1
Illinois	24.8	22.2	29.4	27.2	24.3	24.5	5.5	2.0	58.6	46.7	21.7	13.6	6.6	5.1	26.5	36.1
Indiana	25.8	24.5	30.1	27.4	26.1	25.2	4.4	3.4	60.0	49.3	25.1	15.7	6.5	5.4	26.2	26.9
Iowa	25.5	20.5	30.4	24.5	21.7	21.6	4.7	3.5	59.8	46.2	23.4	15.0	5.7	3.8	25.9	30.1
Kansas	23.9	(NA)	29.2	(NA)	20.4	(NA)	4.8	(NA)	57.0	(NA)	22.2	(NA)	5.8	(NA)	26.7	(NA)
Kentucky	30.1	22.5	31.1	30.2	30.8	30.9	2.7	3.3	62.1	48.6	24.8	13.7	6.7	4.8	33.4	42.0
Louisiana	27.6	20.9	27.6	24.6	26.6	25.0	4.1	4.6	60.3	49.4	25.0	16.5	7.6	6.3	35.6	32.6
Maine	25.2	21.6	30.3	26.2	23.6	26.9	5.5	3.4	58.7	47.0	20.0	12.8	6.7	4.2	23.2	34.9
Maryland	26.3	19.9	31.1	24.7	20.2	22.6	5.2	3.2	57.0	43.6	20.4	11.9	6.9	5.2	24.2	27.8
Massachusetts	23.6	21.7	29.7	26.5	19.2	22.9	7.0	5.2	54.4	43.1	17.1	9.3	5.6	4.4	22.8	25.2
Michigan	27.3	23.9	33.6	31.5	26.2	27.8	5.9	4.9	60.2	50.7	25.8	16.3	7.2	5.4	23.4	28.6
Minnesota	22.3	19.9	30.2	24.9	21.1	24.2	5.8	3.6	60.5	45.2	20.4	11.3	4.4	3.7	17.1	23.7
Mississippi	31.3	29.9	31.0	25.7	25.6	24.8	4.5	2.8	63.8	48.9	27.1	16.2	9.3	7.0	33.4	42.6
Missouri	26.5	23.8	31.3	25.2	27.3	25.5	4.8	4.5	59.4	45.7	23.8	12.6	6.6	4.1	27.5	36.3
Montana	26.8	18.5	29.0	27.8	19.9	22.7	4.4	3.9	56.8	43.0	19.2	10.1	5.6	4.9	21.9	16.6
Nebraska	22.6	23.4	27.8	24.2	21.3	22.3	4.3	3.0	59.1	47.7	21.2	13.8	5.2	4.8	31.4	25.2
Nevada	25.6	(NA)	36.5	(NA)	25.2	(NA)	7.8	(NA)	56.5	(NA)	19.9	(NA)	5.7	(NA)	22.6	(NA)
New Hampshire	22.8	19.7	31.0	29.3	21.2	24.1	6.3	5.5	56.0	42.5	19.9	10.9	5.4	4.7	19.5	21.3
New Jersey	26.1	21.1	30.2	25.3	19.5	22.6	4.0	3.9	57.7	43.0	20.0	10.4	7.1	4.3	26.6	31.4
New Mexico	20.0	14.8	24.8	23.3	22.0	16.7	5.0	2.6	57.1	40.2	20.3	8.5	6.2	3.4	25.8	33.7
New York	26.0	21.5	30.1	25.0	21.6	24.2	5.0	2.5	56.0	45.8	20.8	13.8	6.6	5.2	28.7	34.3
North Carolina	27.2	18.3	28.9	24.8	24.8	24.5	4.1	3.0	58.8	46.1	23.1	13.9	6.7	6.3	26.4	33.4
North Dakota	24.1	18.6	29.6	26.1	20.5	20.2	4.8	2.5	61.5	47.5	20.6	13.7	5.1	4.4	23.2	28.0
Ohio	26.6	19.0	32.8	23.8	25.4	23.1	5.4	3.4	60.1	49.3	22.8	16.2	7.2	4.5	26.2	39.7
Oklahoma	28.5	24.3	29.6	26.8	25.2	25.6	3.5	2.3	61.6	47.8	23.2	12.5	7.7	4.0	32.8	36.7
Oregon	24.9	19.5	32.1	26.5	21.0	21.3	5.9	3.7	58.2	45.2	21.6	12.0	5.7	4.8	20.8	19.6
Pennsylvania	28.1	23.6	32.5	26.6	25.5	25.8	5.2	5.2	60.4	50.3	22.6	15.1	6.7	6.5	24.7	26.4
Rhode Island	25.4	22.0	33.1	28.2	22.4	25.4	7.5	4.9	56.0	42.4	18.1	10.2	6.4	5.6	24.9	28.0
South Carolina	28.8	23.9	27.8	26.8	25.5	23.9	5.5	1.3	59.8	49.0	23.0	14.5	8.1	6.5	26.4	36.1
South Dakota	24.1	18.7	29.5	24.9	22.7	23.1	3.9	2.7	59.4	48.6	21.6	13.1	6.1	3.4	25.4	27.1
Tennessee	29.3	23.0	33.2	24.3	25.7	28.5	2.5	1.3	58.9	47.1	24.2	13.2	7.7	7.2	35.1	38.8
Texas	25.6	20.6	31.8	26.1	22.1	22.1	5.4	5.1	61.3	45.9	25.2	13.0	7.1	4.7	27.1	27.0
Utah	22.3	19.6	29.0	24.6	12.0	14.4	3.1	3.3	54.8	41.4	19.9	10.5	4.3	3.9	16.5	20.8
Vermont	21.4	22.1	29.5	28.1	19.6	22.6	6.8	3.6	52.1	44.6	18.1	10.7	5.1	4.5	20.3	26.6
Virginia	25.8	15.6	30.7	29.9	22.1	22.2	5.1	2.9	57.6	40.0	21.4	10.7	6.0	4.2	23.2	25.2
Washington	24.4	19.0	29.2	26.5	19.5	24.2	5.0	3.4	56.0	41.9	19.9	11.0	5.7	5.0	17.1	20.6
West Virginia	32.5	24.4	37.7	30.4	27.4	25.5	3.0	1.9	63.0	49.4	25.3	15.6	8.8	6.0	31.7	42.3
Wisconsin	24.1	22.0	29.7	26.9	22.1	26.9	8.7	5.0	59.1	48.9	22.7	13.1	5.6	4.9	20.7	25.0
Wyoming	22.4	(NA)	30.5	(NA)	24.6	(NA)	5.2	(NA)	55.6	(NA)	19.9	(NA)	4.5	(NA)	21.2	(NA)

NA Not available.

[1]Has smoked 100 cigarettes or more and currently smokes.
[2]Having consumed an average of more than 2 drinks for males and more than 1 drink for females per day in the past month.
[3]Overweight is defined as having a body mass index greater than or equal to 25.0 and less than or equal to 99.8 kg/m^2.
[4]In adults age 20 years and over. Obesity is defined as having a body mass index greater than or equal to 30.0 and less than or equal to 99.8 kg/m^2.
[5]Represents median value among the states and DC.

Survey, Census, or Data Collection Method: Based on the Behavioral Risk Factor Surveillance System (BRFSS); for information, see Internet site <http://www.cdc.gov/brfss/>.

Source: U.S. Centers for Disease Control and Prevention, Atlanta, GA, *Morbidity and Mortality Weekly Report*, Vol. 53, No. 44, November 12, 2004; Vol. 52, No. 53, January 9, 2004; and *Supplemental Summaries* Vol. 52, No. SS-8, August 22, 2003; see Internet site <http://www.cdc.gov/mmwr/>.

Table A-19. States — State Public Health, Children Immunized, and STDs and AIDS

Geographic area	State direct public health expenditures						Percent of children age 19–35 months who were immunized			Percent of adults age 65 years and over who received influenza vaccine[1]		
	Total (mil. dol.)		Per capita[4] (dol.)		Percent of total state health							
	2003	2000	2003	2000	2003	2000	2003–2004	2001–2002	2000–2001	2003	2002	2001
United States . . .	10,664.9	7,656.0	36.7	27.2	3.0	2.9	80.5	73.1	74.2	[7]70.2	[7]68.7	[7]67.3
Alabama	309.2	209.5	68.7	47.1	6.2	5.4	82.6	77.0	77.7	70.2	64.8	65.9
Alaska	8.6	37.5	13.3	59.8	0.7	3.0	78.2	71.7	75.1	66.5	69.5	62.8
Arizona	124.7	267.8	22.4	52.2	2.3	6.6	78.2	70.1	67.8	68.9	69.7	61.8
Arkansas	88.5	140.1	32.4	52.4	2.9	4.5	79.5	69.6	67.9	71.0	69.0	63.2
California	1,676.8	467.3	47.3	13.8	4.3	1.7	79.3	71.7	74.0	72.5	71.5	68.9
Colorado	18.7	99.9	4.1	23.2	0.6	3.2	70.9	69.2	72.7	74.2	73.3	77.4
Connecticut	214.5	161.2	61.5	47.3	4.1	4.1	92.4	77.4	77.6	74.3	71.4	69.1
Delaware	40.1	37.4	49.0	47.7	3.0	4.0	82.9	73.4	78.6	70.0	71.5	67.6
District of Columbia	(X)	(X)	(X)	(X)	(X)	(X)	78.2	67.8	68.1	63.0	58.7	55.5
Florida	353.6	(NA)	20.8	(NA)	2.3	(NA)	84.0	70.5	72.5	65.9	57.0	54.9
Georgia	323.6	44.4	37.3	5.4	3.0	0.6	78.9	79.3	81.4	67.0	59.3	62.2
Hawaii	83.7	32.0	67.0	26.4	4.0	2.1	82.9	78.1	72.8	71.6	73.9	79.0
Idaho	25.2	14.4	18.4	11.1	2.2	1.6	80.8	65.0	70.4	70.3	65.1	65.1
Illinois	167.9	114.2	13.3	9.2	1.3	1.1	83.3	76.4	71.2	63.3	61.1	62.2
Indiana	110.7	121.3	17.9	19.9	2.0	2.7	79.3	71.6	76.6	66.1	66.3	65.7
Iowa	53.9	15.2	18.3	5.2	2.0	0.8	82.2	77.5	80.5	77.5	73.5	72.8
Kansas	47.7	55.7	17.5	20.7	1.7	2.7	79.1	71.6	72.9	70.8	68.6	68.5
Kentucky	95.6	97.1	23.2	24.0	1.9	2.4	84.2	77.3	74.8	69.1	65.7	60.9
Louisiana	136.4	133.1	30.4	29.8	2.1	2.8	72.6	66.2	68.9	68.3	57.3	56.1
Maine	67.3	41.6	51.4	32.6	3.2	2.7	82.0	73.9	78.4	74.8	73.8	71.5
Maryland	129.4	112.2	23.5	21.2	1.9	2.2	83.7	78.6	70.6	68.4	65.9	67.3
Massachusetts	138.5	322.1	21.6	50.7	1.8	4.4	88.1	80.9	78.6	74.9	72.6	70.6
Michigan	239.4	188.7	23.7	19.0	2.1	1.9	80.9	73.3	73.8	67.5	67.7	60.4
Minnesota	180.2	93.0	35.6	18.9	2.6	2.1	85.9	74.0	77.9	80.3	76.6	70.1
Mississippi	117.7	116.5	40.8	41.0	2.8	4.0	87.3	79.6	77.7	69.0	63.0	61.8
Missouri	198.6	96.0	34.7	17.2	2.6	1.8	83.3	72.7	75.4	69.9	68.7	67.5
Montana	52.7	14.0	57.4	15.5	5.6	1.9	78.4	71.9	76.1	72.8	67.6	73.1
Nebraska	51.7	36.6	29.8	21.4	2.4	2.2	82.4	78.5	78.3	73.6	68.2	70.1
Nevada	51.2	43.0	22.8	21.5	3.1	4.3	71.5	74.4	66.0	60.0	60.3	63.3
New Hampshire	39.2	37.5	30.4	30.3	2.8	3.3	83.9	79.6	79.5	73.9	72.3	69.4
New Jersey	813.1	508.2	94.1	60.4	6.4	5.6	78.8	69.0	73.7	67.2	69.1	64.5
New Mexico	23.6	64.2	12.6	35.3	1.0	3.7	77.9	61.2	65.5	72.4	66.6	70.0
New York	1,369.0	961.5	71.3	50.7	3.1	2.9	83.3	75.3	74.8	68.0	64.7	62.5
North Carolina	298.6	442.6	35.5	55.0	2.8	5.1	86.2	80.7	80.6	68.8	68.1	66.1
North Dakota	16.3	13.8	25.7	21.5	2.1	2.2	78.4	77.4	81.9	73.0	73.9	70.0
Ohio	271.2	242.3	23.7	21.3	2.0	2.6	81.7	71.7	71.9	68.0	66.6	63.4
Oklahoma	79.1	74.1	22.6	21.5	2.3	2.9	77.0	68.6	67.3	75.8	72.7	72.7
Oregon	124.5	32.3	34.9	9.4	3.2	1.2	80.6	72.7	71.4	70.5	68.0	71.7
Pennsylvania	610.3	459.1	49.3	37.4	3.2	3.1	84.1	75.8	81.5	69.2	70.5	63.8
Rhode Island	46.7	16.9	43.4	16.1	2.5	1.1	88.0	81.3	81.0	76.2	73.7	72.6
South Carolina	171.3	182.4	41.3	45.5	3.1	4.3	80.5	76.7	79.5	69.3	69.4	66.2
South Dakota	5.3	2.7	6.9	3.6	0.7	0.5	81.7	78.0	76.0	77.9	74.2	74.1
Tennessee	198.4	174.4	33.9	30.7	2.5	3.1	79.0	78.0	80.1	69.1	71.6	65.6
Texas	926.0	787.7	41.9	37.8	3.7	4.0	73.7	66.7	67.7	67.7	61.0	61.8
Utah	70.2	57.2	29.8	25.6	4.6	4.8	71.5	74.3	68.3	74.8	71.1	68.7
Vermont	14.6	12.4	23.6	20.4	1.7	1.8	83.2	81.1	78.7	74.1	73.6	71.5
Virginia	200.2	267.6	27.2	37.8	3.7	6.3	81.7	67.0	79.1	69.6	65.3	65.3
Washington	158.2	143.4	25.8	24.3	2.0	2.3	76.8	70.7	73.2	73.4	65.1	72.5
West Virginia	31.4	18.6	17.3	10.3	1.4	0.9	83.3	74.6	75.0	69.1	65.8	61.7
Wisconsin	53.3	45.3	9.7	8.4	1.0	1.0	80.5	77.4	78.4	72.1	74.0	70.4
Wyoming	38.4	–	76.5		5.4	–	80.1	74.6	78.8	72.6	70.6	69.6

See footnotes at end of table.

Geographic area	AIDS[2] cases reported						STD[3] cases, 2003			
	Number			Rate[5]						
	2003	2002	2000	2003	2002	2000	Total[6]	Chlamydia	Gonorrhea	Syphilis
United States ...	43,704	42,336	40,307	15.0	14.7	14.3	1,246,906	877,478	335,104	34,270
Alabama	472	433	482	10.5	9.7	10.8	24,078	14,209	9,303	566
Alaska	23	35	23	3.5	5.5	3.7	4,481	3,900	573	8
Arizona	614	633	443	11.0	11.6	8.6	17,507	12,819	3,580	1,106
Arkansas	188	239	194	6.9	8.8	7.2	12,403	7,856	4,251	296
California	5,903	4,228	4,696	16.6	12.1	13.8	147,593	117,428	25,963	4,202
Colorado	366	326	339	8.0	7.2	7.8	16,037	13,039	2,854	144
Connecticut	736	611	614	21.1	17.7	18.0	12,714	9,393	3,114	207
Delaware	213	193	220	26.1	23.9	28.0	4,210	3,035	1,128	47
District of Columbia	961	926	873	170.6	162.7	152.9	6,006	3,168	2,508	330
Florida	4,666	4,979	4,905	27.4	29.8	30.6	64,640	42,382	18,974	3,282
Georgia	1,907	1,471	1,231	22.0	17.2	15.0	55,524	35,686	17,686	2,152
Hawaii	110	131	115	8.7	10.6	9.5	6,802	5,480	1,263	59
Idaho	26	31	22	1.9	2.3	1.7	2,479	2,366	68	45
Illinois	1,730	2,111	1,758	13.7	16.8	14.1	71,487	48,294	21,817	1,376
Indiana	507	491	382	8.2	8.0	6.3	24,131	17,075	6,681	375
Iowa	77	90	92	2.6	3.1	3.1	8,091	6,491	1,554	46
Kansas	116	71	127	4.3	2.6	4.7	9,973	7,249	2,647	77
Kentucky	219	304	210	5.3	7.4	5.2	11,720	7,981	3,578	160
Louisiana	1,041	1,163	661	23.2	26.0	14.8	34,396	20,970	11,850	1,576
Maine	52	28	40	4.0	2.2	3.1	2,284	2,030	233	21
Maryland	1,570	1,848	1,455	28.5	33.9	27.4	25,838	16,831	8,032	974
Massachusetts	757	808	1,185	11.8	12.6	18.6	14,849	11,301	2,901	644
Michigan	680	795	761	6.7	7.9	7.6	47,397	32,572	13,965	860
Minnesota	177	162	184	3.5	3.2	3.7	14,111	10,714	3,202	195
Mississippi	508	436	428	17.6	15.2	15.0	18,956	12,193	6,328	435
Missouri	403	388	452	7.1	6.8	8.1	27,569	18,570	8,792	207
Montana	7	17	16	0.8	1.9	1.8	2,669	2,547	122	–
Nebraska	59	71	77	3.4	4.1	4.5	6,389	4,739	1,623	27
Nevada	277	313	283	12.4	14.4	14.0	8,200	5,830	2,221	149
New Hampshire	37	39	30	2.9	3.1	2.4	1,778	1,616	125	37
New Jersey	1,516	1,456	1,875	17.5	17.0	22.2	25,202	16,169	7,944	1,089
New Mexico	109	86	144	5.8	4.6	7.9	8,854	7,480	1,169	205
New York	6,684	6,741	6,301	34.8	35.2	33.2	83,758	57,222	22,166	4,360
North Carolina	1,083	1,045	674	12.9	12.6	8.3	42,153	26,187	15,116	848
North Dakota	3	3	3	0.5	0.5	0.5	1,760	1,655	103	2
Ohio	775	773	588	6.8	6.8	5.2	65,540	42,522	22,537	481
Oklahoma	213	205	353	6.1	5.9	10.2	15,918	11,013	4,552	353
Oregon	242	300	208	6.8	8.5	6.1	8,808	7,688	1,000	118
Pennsylvania	1,895	1,789	1,658	15.3	14.5	13.5	49,864	37,291	11,866	706
Rhode Island	102	107	99	9.5	10.0	9.4	4,063	3,000	973	90
South Carolina	774	822	789	18.7	20.0	19.6	23,713	14,623	8,518	548
South Dakota	13	11	8	1.7	1.4	1.1	2,839	2,608	226	5
Tennessee	837	772	839	14.3	13.3	14.7	29,775	20,380	8,519	876
Texas	3,379	3,076	2,631	15.3	14.2	12.6	97,794	69,200	24,595	3,996
Utah	73	68	148	3.1	2.9	6.6	4,379	3,893	412	72
Vermont	16	12	38	2.6	1.9	6.2	1,158	1,060	97	1
Virginia	777	948	872	10.5	13.0	12.3	29,057	19,439	9,066	552
Washington	525	471	496	8.6	7.8	8.4	19,789	16,797	2,753	239
West Virginia	94	82	61	5.2	4.5	3.4	3,443	2,585	847	11
Wisconsin	184	187	213	3.4	3.4	4.0	23,716	17,942	5,663	111
Wyoming	8	11	11	1.6	2.2	2.2	1,011	960	46	4

– Represents zero. NA Not available. X Not applicable.

[1]Refers to the number of persons age 65 years and over who reported receiving influenza vaccine during the preceding year.
[2]Acquired Immunodeficiency Syndrome.
[3]Sexually transmitted disease.
[4]Based on enumerated resident population as of April 1 for 2000; estimated resident population as of July 1 for 2003.
[5]Per 100,000 population.
[6]Includes cases of chancroid not shown here.
[7]Represents median value among the states and DC.

Survey, Census, or Data Collection Method: State public health expenditures—Based on surveys completed by governors' state budget officers in the 50 states; for information, see Internet site <http://www.nasbo.org/>; Influenza vaccine—Based on the Behavioral Risk Factor Surveillance System (BRFSS) survey; for information, see Internet site <http://www.cdc.gov/brfss/>; AIDS—Based on confidential name-based registeries of state and local health departments; for information, see Internet site <http://www.cdc.gov/hiv/stats/2003SurveillanceReport/TechnicalNotes.htm>; STDs— Based on STD control programs and health departments in the 50 states, the District of Columbia, selected cities, 3,140 U.S. counties, U.S. dependencies and possessions, and independent nations in free association with the United States; for information, see Internet site <http://www.cdc.gov/nchstp/od/nchstp.html>.

Sources: State public health expenditures—Milbank Memorial Fund, the National Association of State Budget Officers, and the Reforming States Group, *2002–2003 State Health Care Expenditure Report* (copyright) and *2000–2001 State Health Care Expenditure Report* (copyright); Children immunized—U.S. Centers for Disease Control and Prevention, Atlanta, GA, *National Immunization Survey*, accessed 4 March 2005, see <http://www.cdc.gov/nip/coverage/>; Adults who received vaccine—U.S. Centers for Disease Control and Prevention, Atlanta, GA, *Morbidity and Mortality Weekly Report*, Vol. 53, No. 43, November 5, 2004; Vol. 52, No. 41, October 17, 2003; Vol. 51, No. 45, November 15, 2002, see <http://www.cdc.gov/mmwr/>; AIDS—U.S. Centers for Disease Control and Prevention, Atlanta, GA, *HIV/AIDS Surveillance Report*, annual, see <http://www.cdc.gov/hiv/stats/hasrlink.htm>; STDs—U.S. Centers for Disease Control and Prevention, *Sexually Transmitted Disease Surveillance*, annual, see <http://www.cdc.gov/nchstp/od/nchstp.html>.

Geographic area	Total (1,000)				Prekindergarten through grade 8 (1,000)				Grades 9 through 12 (1,000)				Enrollment rate[1]			
	2002	2000	1995	1990	2002	2000	1995	1990	2002	2000	1995	1990	2002	2000	1995	1990
United States . . .	**48,202**	**47,204**	**44,840**	**41,217**	**34,135**	**33,688**	**32,341**	**29,878**	**14,067**	**13,515**	**12,500**	**11,338**	**90.4**	**88.8**	**91.5**	**91.2**
Alabama	740	740	746	722	534	539	539	527	206	201	207	195	90.8	89.6	95.3	93.2
Alaska	134	133	128	114	94	94	93	85	40	39	34	29	94.9	93.4	94.9	97.4
Arizona	938	878	744	640	660	641	549	479	277	237	195	161	88.6	88.4	90.1	93.3
Arkansas	451	450	453	436	319	318	322	314	132	132	131	123	90.6	90.2	94.6	95.8
California	6,356	6,141	5,536	4,950	4,529	4,408	4,041	3,615	1,828	1,733	1,495	1,336	92.6	90.5	92.7	92.6
Colorado	752	725	656	574	534	517	479	420	217	208	177	154	91.0	89.7	92.6	94.6
Connecticut	570	562	518	469	406	406	384	347	164	156	134	122	91.3	90.7	91.7	90.2
Delaware	116	115	108	100	82	81	77	73	34	34	31	27	81.6	80.3	86.6	87.2
District of Columbia	76	69	80	81	59	54	62	61	17	15	18	19	99.2	84.0	105.8	100.6
Florida	2,540	2,435	2,176	1,862	1,809	1,760	1,614	1,370	731	675	563	492	89.7	89.7	91.0	92.6
Georgia	1,496	1,445	1,311	1,152	1,089	1,060	966	849	407	385	345	303	92.1	91.4	95.7	93.7
Hawaii	184	184	187	172	131	132	136	123	53	52	52	49	86.3	84.8	88.5	87.4
Idaho	249	245	243	221	173	170	170	160	75	75	74	61	91.5	90.3	95.2	96.9
Illinois	2,084	2,049	1,944	1,821	1,488	1,474	1,390	1,310	597	575	553	512	88.5	86.4	88.0	86.9
Indiana	1,004	989	977	955	714	703	684	676	290	286	293	279	85.9	85.8	90.6	90.4
Iowa	482	495	502	484	326	334	344	345	156	161	158	139	92.6	91.3	93.2	92.1
Kansas	471	471	463	437	322	323	329	320	149	147	134	117	92.2	90.0	91.6	92.5
Kentucky	661	666	660	636	477	471	468	459	184	194	192	177	91.4	91.4	92.9	90.5
Louisiana	730	743	797	785	537	547	580	586	194	197	217	199	84.2	82.6	88.8	88.1
Maine	204	207	214	215	142	146	156	155	63	61	58	60	91.6	90.3	93.6	96.5
Maryland	867	853	806	715	610	609	590	527	256	244	215	188	85.6	84.9	89.1	89.1
Massachusetts	983	975	915	834	701	703	675	604	282	273	240	230	90.2	88.5	89.9	88.8
Michigan	1,785	1,721	1,641	1,584	1,254	1,222	1,192	1,145	531	498	450	440	93.7	89.5	88.8	90.3
Minnesota	847	854	835	756	568	578	586	546	279	277	249	211	90.6	89.5	90.8	91.3
Mississippi	493	498	506	502	360	364	366	372	132	134	140	131	88.9	87.5	91.8	91.3
Missouri	924	913	890	817	653	645	636	588	272	268	254	228	88.9	86.5	87.9	86.5
Montana	150	155	166	153	101	105	116	111	49	50	49	42	90.6	89.1	93.6	94.1
Nebraska	285	286	290	274	195	195	203	198	90	91	87	76	88.1	86.2	88.6	88.7
Nevada	369	341	265	201	271	251	196	150	99	90	69	51	90.8	91.8	95.7	98.6
New Hampshire	208	208	194	173	144	147	142	126	64	61	52	46	88.7	89.1	89.7	89.1
New Jersey	1,367	1,313	1,197	1,090	979	968	880	784	389	346	317	306	87.9	85.9	86.2	85.9
New Mexico	320	320	330	302	224	225	229	208	96	95	100	94	86.5	85.0	91.8	94.4
New York	2,888	2,882	2,813	2,598	2,017	2,029	1,980	1,828	871	853	833	770	85.8	84.8	88.6	86.6
North Carolina	1,336	1,294	1,183	1,087	964	945	871	783	372	348	312	304	90.3	90.4	92.2	94.8
North Dakota	104	109	119	118	69	72	82	85	35	37	37	33	92.9	90.9	93.2	92.6
Ohio	1,838	1,835	1,836	1,771	1,284	1,294	1,297	1,258	554	541	539	514	87.8	86.1	88.3	88.0
Oklahoma	625	623	616	579	449	445	446	425	176	178	171	154	97.8	95.4	95.5	95.1
Oregon	554	546	528	472	382	379	376	340	172	167	152	132	88.2	87.5	90.1	90.6
Pennsylvania	1,817	1,814	1,788	1,668	1,242	1,258	1,257	1,172	575	556	531	496	84.6	82.8	84.6	83.5
Rhode Island	159	157	150	139	113	114	110	102	47	44	40	37	87.2	85.6	88.2	87.5
South Carolina	695	677	646	622	501	493	463	452	194	184	182	170	93.2	90.9	94.5	93.9
South Dakota	128	129	145	129	87	88	101	95	41	41	43	34	87.7	85.3	94.5	89.9
Tennessee	928	909	894	825	674	668	651	598	254	241	243	226	91.4	88.8	94.7	93.5
Texas	4,260	4,060	3,748	3,383	3,080	2,943	2,757	2,511	1,180	1,117	991	872	97.0	94.9	98.9	98.4
Utah	489	481	477	447	343	333	328	325	147	148	149	122	95.5	94.5	97.3	97.8
Vermont	100	102	106	96	68	70	75	71	32	32	30	25	92.5	90.5	96.0	94.3
Virginia	1,177	1,145	1,080	999	832	816	788	728	346	329	292	270	90.6	89.5	93.6	94.2
Washington	1,015	1,005	957	840	697	694	680	613	318	310	277	227	91.1	89.8	92.9	94.1
West Virginia	282	286	307	322	200	201	211	224	82	85	96	98	96.5	95.6	96.2	95.7
Wisconsin	881	879	870	798	592	595	603	566	290	285	267	232	87.9	86.0	86.8	86.1
Wyoming	88	90	100	98	60	60	69	71	28	30	31	27	95.4	92.7	97.0	97.7

[1]Percent of persons ages 5–17 years. Based on enumerated resident population as of April 1, 1990 and 2000, and estimated resident population as of July 1 for 2001 and 2002.

Survey, Census, or Data Collection Method: Based on the NCES Common Core of Data (CCD); for information, see Internet site <http://www.nces.ed.gov/ccd/>.

Source: U.S. National Center for Education Statistics, *Digest of Education Statistics*, annual, see Internet site <http://www.nces.ed.gov/>.

Public Elementary and Secondary Schools—Finances and Teachers

Geographic area	Receipts, 2003–2004 (mil. dol.)						Expenditures, 2003–2004						Teachers,[1] 2003–2004			
		Revenue receipts							Current expenditures				Number (1,000)		Average salary ($1,000)	
			Source							Average per pupil in average daily attendance						
	Total	Total	Federal	State	Local	Non-revenue receipts[2]	Total[3] (mil. dol.)	Per capita[4] (dol.)	Elementary and secondary day schools (mil. dol.)	Amount (dol.)	Rank	Capital outlay (mil. dol.)	Elementary[5]	Secondary[5]	Elementary[5]	Secondary[5]
United States . . .	488,447	452,795	38,856	217,140	196,798	35,653	471,965	1,623	397,015	8,807	(X)	47,707	[6]1,781.9	[6]1,264.7	[6]46.4	[6]47.1
Alabama	5,613	5,328	639	2,977	1,711	285	5,499	1,221	4,887	6,953	43	417	[6]28.0	[6]20.5	[6]37.9	[6]38.7
Alaska	1,443	1,285	161	817	308	157	1,418	2,187	1,314	11,432	6	38	5.1	2.7	51.5	52.2
Arizona	7,145	7,049	552	3,589	2,907	96	6,346	1,137	5,154	5,595	49	774	30.8	14.7	41.8	41.8
Arkansas	3,596	3,535	391	1,851	1,293	61	3,160	1,158	2,715	6,663	45	353	15.6	16.4	37.4	41.1
California	70,408	60,595	6,501	35,401	18,692	9,813	58,752	1,657	47,771	7,860	32	7,888	220.7	85.2	56.4	56.4
Colorado	7,557	6,489	426	2,797	3,267	1,067	7,272	1,599	6,079	8,651	25	856	22.4	22.5	43.3	43.2
Connecticut	7,469	7,457	436	2,967	4,055	12	7,469	2,142	6,784	12,394	2	476	30.3	12.7	56.9	58.1
Delaware	1,429	1,254	82	804	369	175	1,380	1,687	1,161	10,347	11	155	3.8	3.9	49.0	49.7
District of Columbia	827	827	115	–	712	–	1,042	1,869	867	14,621	(X)	169	4.1	1.6	57.0	57.0
Florida.	22,752	21,161	2,220	9,195	9,746	1,591	21,869	1,286	17,380	7,181	40	3,349	74.6	73.6	40.6	40.6
Georgia	14,299	13,883	1,227	6,335	6,320	416	14,299	1,648	12,347	8,671	24	1,718	62.5	41.1	45.4	46.9
Hawaii	2,138	2,106	173	1,901	32	32	1,683	1,347	1,510	9,019	22	65	6.0	5.3	45.5	45.5
Idaho.	1,700	1,650	150	1,000	500	50	1,700	1,244	1,585	6,779	44	80	7.2	6.9	41.1	41.1
Illinois	20,325	18,240	1,408	5,546	11,286	2,085	29,528	2,334	20,299	10,866	9	2,316	89.9	40.1	50.9	61.8
Indiana	10,471	9,763	642	4,908	4,212	709	10,191	1,644	8,502	9,138	21	793	32.1	27.7	45.8	45.8
Iowa	4,535	4,251	312	1,965	1,974	285	4,139	1,407	3,503	7,696	35	529	16.5	18.3	38.6	40.2
Kansas	4,760	4,274	345	2,138	1,791	486	3,863	1,418	3,435	8,189	29	258	16.0	16.6	38.6	38.6
Kentucky	5,205	5,196	620	3,031	1,545	10	5,203	1,263	4,736	8,298	28	291	27.7	11.6	40.0	40.8
Louisiana	6,442	5,779	782	2,811	2,185	664	6,144	1,367	5,282	7,840	33	721	35.3	15.1	37.9	37.9
Maine	2,247	2,132	201	891	1,039	115	2,247	1,716	2,051	10,961	8	142	10.7	5.0	39.8	40.0
Maryland	9,278	9,074	663	3,458	4,953	205	8,971	1,627	7,983	9,824	16	700	32.7	22.5	50.2	48.5
Massachusetts	12,228	12,227	838	4,722	6,667	1	11,602	1,807	10,562	11,445	5	482	28.0	37.2	53.2	53.2
Michigan	17,055	16,713	944	11,204	4,566	342	18,954	1,880	14,857	9,416	19	3,010	49.2	45.9	54.4	54.4
Minnesota	9,716	8,612	543	6,138	1,931	1,105	9,417	1,860	7,469	9,513	17	1,253	26.6	25.7	45.8	44.3
Mississippi	3,586	3,436	513	1,869	1,053	150	3,394	1,178	2,994	6,556	46	312	18.3	12.4	35.7	35.7
Missouri	8,609	7,972	697	2,577	4,698	637	7,366	1,288	6,203	7,548	37	765	33.2	31.8	38.1	37.9
Montana	1,279	1,251	148	590	512	28	1,205	1,312	1,141	8,631	26	47	6.9	3.4	37.2	37.2
Nebraska	2,230	2,209	157	892	1,159	21	2,385	1,373	2,089	7,947	30	233	13.5	7.1	38.4	38.4
Nevada	3,617	3,025	216	965	1,844	592	3,399	1,516	2,552	6,177	48	659	11.8	8.2	41.9	42.7
New Hampshire.	2,309	2,075	121	961	993	234	2,103	1,632	1,878	9,902	15	174	10.5	4.6	42.7	42.7
New Jersey	18,297	18,143	520	6,892	10,731	154	16,449	1,903	15,728	11,847	4	310	39.7	67.8	54.4	56.3
New Mexico	2,998	2,901	512	2,002	387	97	3,022	1,608	2,547	8,772	23	433	15.3	6.2	37.7	38.9
New York	39,242	38,500	2,400	17,500	18,600	742	39,309	2,046	34,832	12,408	1	2,400	111.0	113.0	54.7	55.8
North Carolina.	10,268	9,422	1,015	6,035	2,371	846	10,382	1,233	9,344	7,511	38	923	61.7	26.3	43.2	43.2
North Dakota	938	847	111	307	429	91	833	1,316	676	7,112	41	81	5.2	2.5	35.8	34.8
Ohio	21,487	18,546	1,167	8,472	8,908	2,941	19,065	1,667	16,673	10,102	13	1,767	80.6	37.2	47.5	47.4
Oklahoma	4,600	4,343	553	2,358	1,432	257	4,078	1,163	3,740	6,405	47	268	20.4	18.8	34.8	35.3
Oregon	4,776	4,402	468	2,354	1,580	374	4,934	1,384	4,217	8,575	27	504	17.8	9.9	49.2	49.2
Pennsylvania	19,552	19,374	1,529	7,007	10,839	178	20,008	1,617	16,866	9,949	14	1,934	61.9	56.5	51.9	51.8
Rhode Island	1,496	1,496	55	553	888	–	1,715	1,594	1,640	10,976	7	37	8.3	5.3	52.3	52.3
South Carolina	6,809	6,004	640	2,769	2,595	804	5,899	1,422	4,767	7,395	39	829	31.8	13.3	39.3	40.0
South Dakota	1,092	1,006	159	339	507	86	1,017	1,329	887	7,611	36	106	6.3	2.7	33.3	33.1
Tennessee	6,523	6,191	709	2,804	2,679	332	6,309	1,079	5,980	6,983	42	113	42.4	16.2	40.0	41.1
Texas	39,680	35,387	3,882	13,644	17,862	4,292	37,498	1,696	30,905	7,698	34	4,787	148.9	140.6	40.0	40.9
Utah	3,023	3,022	279	1,756	987	1	3,103	1,319	2,479	5,556	50	470	11.7	9.9	39.0	39.0
Vermont	1,232	1,182	95	801	286	50	1,206	1,948	1,055	12,157	3	77	4.7	4.3	41.7	42.3
Virginia	12,110	11,310	770	4,588	5,951	800	12,012	1,631	10,381	9,401	20	830	56.9	41.7	42.8	44.9
Washington	9,553	8,758	829	5,457	2,473	795	9,574	1,561	7,511	7,904	31	1,664	29.3	23.6	45.5	45.4
West Virginia	2,837	2,728	321	1,641	765	110	2,785	1,538	2,530	9,509	18	70	13.7	6.1	38.2	39.0
Wisconsin.	10,675	9,413	522	5,052	3,838	1,262	9,813	1,792	8,345	10,293	12	954	41.3	18.8	42.7	43.3
Wyoming	991	970	94	506	370	20	952	1,896	820	10,413	10	126	3.2	3.4	39.6	39.5

– Represents zero.   X Not applicable.

[1] Full-time equivalent.
[2] Amount received by local education agencies from the sales of bonds and real property and equipment, loans, and proceeds from insurance adjustments.
[3] Includes interest on school debt and other current expenditures not shown separately.
[4] Based on U.S. Census Bureau estimated resident population as of July 1, 2003.
[5] Schools classified by type of organization rather than by grade-group; elementary includes kindergarten.
[6] There is some duplication in elementary and secondary levels.

Survey, Census, or Data Collection Method: For information, see Internet site <http://www.nea.org/index.html>.

Source: National Education Association, Washington, DC, Estimates of School Statistics Database (copyright).

Table A-22. States — **Public High School Graduates and Educational Attainment**

Geographic area	Public high school graduates[1] (1,000)				Educational attainment, 2003						
					Population 25 years and over (1,000)	Percent of persons 25 years and over, by highest level completed					
	2004 estimate	2000	1995	1990		Not a high school graduate	High school graduate	Some college, but no degree	Associate's degree	Bachelor's degree	Advanced degree[2]
United States . . .	2,757.5	2,553.8	2,273.5	2,320.3	184,395	16.4	29.8	20.3	7.0	16.9	9.7
Alabama	37.6	37.8	36.3	40.5	2,867	21.2	30.8	20.4	6.5	13.8	7.3
Alaska	7.1	6.6	5.8	5.4	379	8.8	30.2	27.0	7.4	17.3	9.4
Arizona	57.0	38.3	31.0	32.1	3,435	16.5	26.1	25.6	7.5	15.6	8.7
Arkansas	26.9	27.3	24.6	26.5	1,719	20.3	35.5	20.4	4.8	12.3	6.8
California	342.6	309.9	255.2	236.3	21,986	19.8	21.9	21.7	7.4	18.7	10.4
Colorado	42.9	38.9	32.4	33.0	2,888	11.9	23.8	22.5	7.1	22.3	12.4
Connecticut	34.4	31.6	26.4	27.9	2,286	12.4	29.8	16.8	6.4	20.3	14.3
Delaware	6.8	6.1	5.2	5.6	525	14.0	33.3	18.4	6.7	17.2	10.4
District of Columbia	3.2	2.7	3.0	3.6	378	18.3	19.3	15.5	2.7	21.2	22.9
Florida	129.0	106.7	89.8	88.9	11,327	16.0	30.1	21.0	7.9	16.1	9.0
Georgia	69.7	62.6	56.7	56.6	5,361	19.1	30.2	19.6	5.4	16.7	9.0
Hawaii	10.3	10.4	9.4	10.3	817	12.2	30.2	20.8	8.6	19.0	9.2
Idaho	15.5	16.2	14.2	12.0	824	12.1	29.7	26.1	8.1	16.0	8.0
Illinois	121.3	111.8	105.2	108.1	7,993	14.8	29.0	21.1	7.0	17.3	10.8
Indiana	57.6	57.0	56.1	60.0	3,860	16.3	36.8	19.4	6.6	13.0	8.0
Iowa	33.8	33.9	31.3	31.8	1,876	11.1	36.9	20.8	8.7	15.7	6.8
Kansas	30.0	29.1	26.1	25.4	1,687	11.2	30.2	23.3	6.6	18.9	9.8
Kentucky	36.2	36.8	37.6	38.0	2,647	21.3	35.1	19.4	5.7	11.1	7.6
Louisiana	36.2	38.4	36.5	36.1	2,739	21.1	32.2	21.2	4.2	14.6	6.7
Maine	13.4	12.2	11.5	13.8	883	11.7	36.5	17.8	8.2	17.4	8.5
Maryland	53.0	47.8	41.4	41.6	3,549	13.2	27.5	18.4	6.4	19.3	15.2
Massachusetts	57.9	53.0	47.7	55.9	4,252	12.3	27.9	16.5	7.5	20.8	15.1
Michigan	106.3	97.7	84.6	93.8	6,396	12.9	32.2	22.8	7.8	15.1	9.2
Minnesota	59.8	57.4	49.4	49.1	3,214	9.2	29.4	22.3	8.6	21.1	9.5
Mississippi	23.6	24.2	23.8	25.2	1,747	22.6	31.3	20.8	6.7	12.6	6.1
Missouri	57.0	52.8	48.9	49.0	3,614	14.6	33.5	21.5	6.4	15.4	8.7
Montana	10.5	10.9	10.1	9.4	591	9.5	32.7	25.0	7.1	18.2	7.5
Nebraska	20.0	20.1	18.0	17.7	1,086	10.3	31.9	24.4	8.1	17.4	7.9
Nevada	16.2	14.6	10.0	9.5	1,437	17.9	31.7	25.2	5.7	12.8	6.7
New Hampshire	13.3	11.8	10.1	10.8	847	10.6	29.9	19.1	10.1	19.6	10.7
New Jersey	88.3	74.4	67.4	69.8	5,659	14.7	31.2	16.4	5.6	20.3	11.8
New Mexico	18.1	18.0	14.9	14.9	1,156	19.7	27.4	22.6	6.6	13.4	10.4
New York	150.9	141.7	132.4	143.3	12,503	16.8	29.5	16.1	7.9	17.2	12.6
North Carolina	71.4	62.1	59.5	64.8	5,356	19.9	29.2	18.9	7.7	16.5	7.8
North Dakota	7.8	8.6	7.8	7.7	401	11.6	30.2	23.6	9.5	18.7	6.4
Ohio	116.3	111.7	109.4	114.5	7,324	14.0	37.3	19.0	6.7	14.8	8.1
Oklahoma	36.7	37.6	33.3	35.6	2,185	16.7	32.4	22.6	6.4	14.7	7.2
Oregon	32.5	30.2	26.7	25.5	2,319	12.3	27.3	26.6	7.5	17.2	9.2
Pennsylvania	121.6	114.0	104.1	110.5	8,110	14.4	39.4	15.4	6.7	15.4	8.8
Rhode Island	9.3	8.5	7.8	7.8	701	18.4	28.6	16.6	7.3	18.4	10.7
South Carolina	32.1	31.6	30.7	32.5	2,634	18.5	31.5	19.6	7.2	15.7	7.5
South Dakota	9.1	9.3	8.4	7.7	470	11.4	33.9	22.8	8.9	17.2	5.9
Tennessee	43.6	41.6	43.6	46.1	3,789	18.9	34.3	19.9	5.4	14.0	7.5
Texas	236.7	212.9	170.3	172.5	13,189	22.2	26.3	21.0	5.9	16.4	8.1
Utah	29.9	32.5	27.7	21.2	1,276	10.0	26.1	28.5	9.2	17.7	8.5
Vermont	7.0	6.7	5.9	6.1	411	11.4	33.3	15.6	7.8	19.9	12.1
Virginia	71.7	65.6	58.3	60.6	4,732	15.5	27.1	19.0	6.1	19.8	12.4
Washington	60.4	57.6	49.3	45.9	3,945	10.3	25.7	25.4	8.4	20.2	10.0
West Virginia	17.1	19.4	20.1	21.9	1,217	21.7	40.3	16.2	4.9	10.5	6.5
Wisconsin	62.3	58.5	51.7	52.0	3,489	12.9	34.6	20.4	8.3	15.8	8.0
Wyoming	5.7	6.5	5.9	5.8	318	9.7	32.6	25.6	8.5	16.1	7.6

[1]For school year ending in year shown.
[2]Graduate or professional degree.

Survey, Census, or Data Collection Method: Public high school graduates—Based on the NCES Common Core of Data (CCD); for information, see Internet site <http://www.nces.ed.gov/ccd/>; Attainment—Based on the American Community Survey; for information, see Appendix B, Limitations of the Data and Methodology, and Internet site <http://www.census.gov/acs/www/AdvMeth/index.htm>.

Sources: Public high school graduates—U.S. National Center for Education Statistics, *Digest of Education Statistics*, annual;   Attainment—U.S. Census Bureau, American Community Survey, Multi-Year Profiles 2003—Social Characteristics, accessed 24 June 2005. See Internet site <http://www.census.gov/acs/www/Products/Profiles/Chg/2003/ACS/index.htm>.

Table A-23. States — **Institutions of Higher Education**

Geographic area	Fall enrollment[1] (1,000)									State appropriations for higher education, 2003–2004				
	Total			Public			Private			Full-time equivalent enrollment[2] (1,000)	Educational appropriations[3] (mil. dol.)	Educational appropriations per full-time equivalent enrollment (dol.)	Net tuition[4] (mil. dol.)	Net tuition as a percent of total educational revenue (educational appropriations plus net tuition)
	2002	2000	1990	2002	2000	1990	2002	2000	1990					
United States[5]...	16,612	15,312	13,819	12,752	11,753	10,845	3,860	3,560	2,974	9,916.6	56,597.1	5,716	30,646.0	35.1
Alabama	246	234	219	218	207	196	29	27	23	183.3	860.4	4,693	781.7	47.6
Alaska	30	28	30	28	27	28	1	1	2	37.6	198.1	5,269	61.5	23.7
Arizona	402	342	264	307	285	248	94	58	16	211.2	1,203.3	5,699	572.9	32.3
Arkansas	127	115	90	114	102	79	14	13	12	97.7	511.0	5,233	277.9	35.2
California	2,474	2,257	1,809	2,121	1,928	1,595	353	329	214	1,623.5	9,908.6	6,103	2,447.8	19.8
Colorado	282	264	227	234	218	201	49	46	26	161.2	516.1	3,202	749.9	59.2
Connecticut	171	161	169	109	101	110	62	60	59	70.0	624.4	8,916	393.2	38.6
Delaware	49	44	42	37	34	34	12	10	8	31.0	182.6	10,907	248.7	57.7
District of Columbia	91	73	80	6	5	13	85	67	68	(X)	(X)	(X)	(X)	(X)
Florida	792	708	588	618	557	489	174	151	99	526.7	2,261.0	4,293	995.4	30.6
Georgia	398	346	252	317	272	196	80	74	55	210.0	1,728.5	8,231	300.3	14.8
Hawaii	65	60	56	48	45	46	17	16	11	35.4	339.0	9,566	83.5	19.8
Idaho	72	66	52	58	54	41	14	12	11	49.8	301.2	6,050	85.2	22.0
Illinois	777	744	729	554	534	551	223	210	178	378.1	2,562.5	6,777	487.2	16.0
Indiana	342	314	285	259	240	224	83	74	61	218.4	1,114.5	5,103	1,089.8	49.4
Iowa	203	189	171	146	135	118	57	54	53	117.7	618.6	5,255	554.7	47.3
Kansas	188	180	164	168	160	149	20	20	15	110.2	654.8	5,940	366.4	35.9
Kentucky	225	188	178	189	152	147	37	36	31	144.7	920.3	6,360	401.7	30.4
Louisiana	232	224	187	198	189	158	35	35	29	183.3	923.2	5,037	357.4	27.9
Maine	63	58	57	45	41	42	18	18	16	34.5	203.7	5,900	169.3	45.4
Maryland	300	274	260	247	224	221	53	50	39	165.5	890.0	5,378	954.6	51.7
Massachusetts	431	421	418	188	183	186	243	238	232	137.5	965.4	7,021	552.8	36.4
Michigan	606	568	570	496	468	487	110	100	82	357.6	2,127.6	5,950	2,159.0	50.4
Minnesota	324	293	254	236	219	199	88	75	55	189.8	1,056.3	5,564	756.1	41.7
Mississippi	147	137	123	134	125	109	13	12	14	145.9	580.6	3,980	322.7	35.7
Missouri	348	321	290	214	202	200	134	120	90	138.1	970.7	7,031	586.8	37.7
Montana	45	42	36	41	37	32	4	5	4	35.8	140.1	3,915	138.6	49.7
Nebraska	117	112	113	92	89	95	25	24	18	71.3	390.5	5,475	239.8	38.1
Nevada	96	88	62	90	83	61	6	5	(Z)	57.2	448.2	7,834	126.7	22.0
New Hampshire	69	62	60	41	36	32	28	26	27	30.5	101.1	3,316	128.7	56.0
New Jersey	362	336	324	289	267	262	72	69	63	195.5	1,627.5	8,326	899.9	35.6
New Mexico	121	111	86	112	101	83	9	9	2	79.6	444.8	5,586	88.4	16.6
New York	1,107	1,043	1,048	611	583	617	497	460	431	487.3	3,247.2	6,663	1,758.0	35.1
North Carolina	447	405	352	368	329	285	79	75	67	315.2	2,111.3	6,699	695.7	24.8
North Dakota	46	40	38	41	36	35	5	4	3	36.2	157.3	4,345	106.6	40.4
Ohio	588	550	558	442	411	428	146	138	130	378.7	1,772.1	4,680	1,733.3	49.4
Oklahoma	198	178	173	171	154	151	27	24	22	133.4	649.9	4,872	289.6	30.8
Oregon	205	183	166	174	155	144	31	28	21	124.4	593.7	4,772	628.8	51.4
Pennsylvania	655	610	604	370	339	343	284	270	261	322.7	1,727.9	5,355	1,973.6	53.3
Rhode Island	77	75	78	39	38	42	39	37	36	27.8	171.9	6,180	178.0	50.9
South Carolina	202	186	159	168	156	131	34	30	28	137.1	692.8	5,053	344.5	33.2
South Dakota	48	43	34	38	35	27	10	8	8	28.1	124.0	4,408	128.2	50.8
Tennessee	262	264	226	194	203	175	68	61	51	169.4	856.1	5,053	684.6	44.4
Texas	1,152	1,034	901	1,007	897	802	146	137	99	812.9	4,293.6	5,282	1,844.2	30.0
Utah	179	164	121	136	123	86	43	41	35	108.6	548.4	5,048	277.7	33.6
Vermont	37	35	36	21	20	21	15	15	15	17.8	45.8	2,575	168.9	78.7
Virginia	405	382	353	337	314	291	68	68	62	257.7	1,178.0	4,571	1,011.1	46.2
Washington	339	321	263	293	274	228	46	47	36	220.0	1,212.2	5,509	388.9	24.3
West Virginia	94	88	85	80	76	74	14	12	11	69.5	287.3	4,135	229.3	44.4
Wisconsin	329	307	300	268	250	254	61	57	46	218.9	1,300.5	5,941	780.3	37.5
Wyoming	33	30	31	31	29	31	2	1	1	22.2	252.4	11,358	46.3	15.5

X Not applicable. Z Less than 500.

[1]Data for 2000–2002 are for 4-year and 2-year degree-granting institutions that participated in Title IV federal financial programs.
[2]Includes degree enrollment and enrollment in public postsecondary programs resulting in a certificate or other formal recognition. Includes summer sessions. Excludes medical enrollments.
[3]State and local appropriations for public postsecondary education. Includes state-funded financial aid to students attending in-state public institutions. Excludes sums for research, agriculture experiment stations and cooperative extensions, and teaching hospitals and medical schools.
[4]Excludes discounts, waivers, and state-appropriated aid to students attending in-state public institutions. Excludes medical student tuition.
[5]U.S. totals for fall enrollment include U.S. military service schools not distributed by state.

Survey, Census, or Data Collection Method: Fall enrollment—Based on Integrated Postsecondary Education Data System (IPEDS), "Fall Enrollment" surveys; for information, see Appendix B, Limitations of the Data and Methodology, and Internet site <http://nces.ed.gov/ipeds/>; Appropriations—For information, see Internet site <http://www.sheeo.org>.

Sources: Fall enrollment—U.S. National Center for Education Statistics, *Digest of Education Statistics*, annual; Appropriations—State Higher Education Executive Officers, Denver, CO (copyright).

State and Metropolitan Area Data Book: 2006

U.S. Census Bureau

Table A-24. States — Degree-Granting Institutions and Educational Services

Geographic area	Degrees conferred, 2001–2002 Total	Public	Private	Bachelor's	Full-time faculty on 9/10-month contracts, 2002–2003 Total	Average salary (dol.) Total	Professors	Establishments 2002	2001	2000	Number of employees 2002	2001	2000	Annual payroll (mil. dol.) 2002	2001	2000
United States ...	2,494,009	1,590,282	903,727	1,291,900	425,370	61,330	83,466	73,701	70,878	68,014	2,701,675	2,612,430	2,532,324	71,962	67,098	61,923
Alabama	38,118	31,656	6,462	20,314	6,668	51,449	71,756	779	758	737	19,735	21,126	20,055	410	395	363
Alaska	2,734	2,508	226	1,377	868	53,957	69,244	191	217	211	2,568	2,663	2,641	61	59	52
Arizona	47,792	30,737	17,055	22,014	5,984	63,106	84,159	1,465	1,351	1,231	30,549	27,103	24,486	804	672	564
Arkansas	17,416	14,467	2,949	10,078	3,897	46,690	64,275	472	481	470	11,519	11,419	11,060	192	182	170
California	276,647	190,638	86,009	131,152	43,069	73,010	95,997	9,577	9,367	8,976	289,079	278,019	262,446	8,336	7,717	7,110
Colorado	41,423	29,761	11,662	23,216	6,363	58,952	80,197	1,657	1,571	1,528	28,991	29,933	28,168	715	690	635
Connecticut	28,317	13,239	15,078	14,809	5,892	73,968	97,218	1,107	1,048	992	54,033	51,644	54,598	1,799	1,686	1,594
Delaware	8,097	5,647	2,450	4,936	1,532	69,519	100,724	238	227	194	6,356	6,249	5,773	163	152	138
District of Columbia	19,789	466	19,323	8,591	3,590	73,300	98,763	461	445	437	43,813	40,175	40,127	1,535	1,259	1,261
Florida	131,097	89,450	41,647	56,351	14,068	57,364	74,114	4,340	4,152	3,898	106,611	101,100	95,333	2,671	2,507	2,267
Georgia	54,600	36,314	18,286	29,999	10,235	58,028	79,660	1,936	1,802	1,691	71,580	65,033	63,775	1,983	1,686	1,532
Hawaii	10,014	6,062	3,952	4,901	1,929	60,383	77,416	479	444	432	15,776	13,870	13,182	400	355	323
Idaho	10,960	7,319	3,641	4,913	1,983	49,423	62,625	305	262	255	7,398	6,928	6,649	132	117	108
Illinois	118,919	65,172	53,747	57,430	19,396	62,824	86,537	2,980	2,935	2,832	123,813	123,072	121,108	3,577	3,353	3,220
Indiana	57,560	38,014	19,546	33,947	10,232	58,843	80,420	1,253	1,186	1,139	50,176	47,125	46,778	1,041	968	895
Iowa	35,364	22,140	13,224	19,388	5,773	55,593	76,004	647	616	604	32,193	32,458	31,700	575	546	497
Kansas	28,168	22,483	5,685	14,787	5,043	51,397	69,867	666	625	604	18,182	16,561	16,417	354	321	300
Kentucky	30,006	21,980	8,026	16,401	6,094	51,849	67,836	815	793	773	26,756	25,850	25,261	480	462	423
Louisiana	33,584	25,487	8,097	20,312	6,749	52,155	74,178	975	966	944	33,346	33,067	32,419	803	778	710
Maine	9,310	5,690	3,620	5,793	2,187	54,815	73,255	443	419	389	13,378	13,070	12,683	315	289	258
Maryland	44,758	32,021	12,737	23,316	7,296	63,162	83,105	1,733	1,674	1,550	61,224	57,922	54,213	1,921	1,815	1,547
Massachusetts	89,431	28,696	60,735	43,097	15,573	75,337	96,053	2,305	2,239	2,204	170,326	168,115	165,177	5,320	5,011	4,543
Michigan	92,703	67,873	24,830	47,929	13,792	64,458	83,235	1,977	1,942	1,905	61,891	58,138	55,905	1,337	1,232	1,175
Minnesota	47,319	29,068	18,251	24,706	9,039	58,628	79,795	1,468	1,394	1,322	52,784	51,210	48,247	1,115	1,031	956
Mississippi	23,762	20,040	3,722	11,899	4,638	46,453	62,582	583	566	509	16,007	15,057	14,703	256	244	229
Missouri	60,317	29,001	31,316	32,082	8,416	54,978	75,475	1,335	1,292	1,271	62,412	59,231	58,398	1,612	1,569	1,518
Montana	7,989	7,080	909	5,277	1,701	49,168	63,686	265	263	250	5,219	4,927	4,937	90	82	76
Nebraska	19,184	12,798	6,386	10,639	3,093	54,206	75,545	489	463	448	17,826	14,566	15,638	417	328	301
Nevada	8,641	7,387	1,254	4,489	1,776	64,394	76,914	429	400	361	4,590	4,269	4,026	112	103	144
New Hampshire	12,839	5,987	6,852	7,249	2,216	61,496	74,718	531	499	480	24,303	23,227	22,294	635	543	488
New Jersey	53,869	38,210	15,659	28,376	9,167	70,373	96,319	2,767	2,667	2,558	84,346	80,113	77,012	2,420	2,285	2,074
New Mexico	13,371	11,140	2,231	6,432	2,512	49,858	66,537	511	485	464	9,922	9,135	9,581	207	196	184
New York	213,498	94,602	118,896	99,488	33,661	68,793	91,832	5,636	5,355	5,282	310,310	303,908	294,954	9,333	8,855	8,342
North Carolina	63,132	45,503	17,629	36,071	15,580	53,542	84,810	1,844	1,712	1,610	71,105	67,646	63,762	1,948	1,790	1,747
North Dakota	7,842	6,558	1,284	4,810	1,621	44,594	58,953	146	149	144	4,953	4,720	4,631	79	70	64
Ohio	95,915	61,782	34,133	52,748	17,404	59,451	79,093	2,662	2,578	2,478	98,623	95,773	93,525	2,184	2,095	1,871
Oklahoma	30,171	23,922	6,249	16,232	5,051	49,733	66,149	684	661	658	18,088	17,954	17,013	351	334	312
Oregon	27,311	19,700	7,611	14,450	5,155	53,686	70,786	1,109	1,036	992	37,493	33,742	32,136	829	753	686
Pennsylvania	122,771	55,843	66,928	68,999	22,270	66,268	89,443	2,932	2,851	2,700	201,321	203,762	196,127	5,595	5,420	4,977
Rhode Island	14,972	5,141	9,831	8,845	2,633	68,779	86,216	344	326	298	19,932	19,007	18,564	596	551	498
South Carolina	29,399	22,639	6,760	16,886	6,457	51,365	72,655	884	821	771	23,645	22,801	21,416	446	415	379
South Dakota	7,400	5,573	1,827	4,365	1,489	46,180	62,889	169	162	155	7,628	7,407	7,047	146	136	119
Tennessee	41,752	26,569	15,183	23,480	8,369	53,408	72,249	1,030	984	945	44,363	44,624	43,296	1,241	1,136	904
Texas	144,512	110,332	34,180	79,595	26,687	56,545	79,381	4,457	4,293	4,159	121,094	111,361	113,150	3,234	2,950	2,777
Utah	31,757	20,998	10,759	18,188	3,923	58,199	76,802	644	589	561	25,989	25,195	24,345	537	500	437
Vermont	7,886	3,548	4,338	4,673	1,552	53,220	69,456	334	318	307	13,030	12,676	12,292	273	266	249
Virginia	59,272	44,452	14,820	32,948	10,621	59,380	78,208	2,029	1,986	1,869	52,916	54,063	51,549	1,341	1,267	1,148
Washington	53,898	42,073	11,825	24,462	8,252	55,831	76,769	1,916	1,856	1,824	39,964	40,717	39,140	841	820	753
West Virginia	14,746	11,747	2,999	9,022	2,662	49,414	62,502	262	255	250	7,912	8,885	9,389	127	117	111
Wisconsin	48,977	36,932	12,045	28,783	10,206	60,843	77,250	1,310	1,273	1,237	45,069	44,326	43,883	1,045	960	873
Wyoming	4,700	3,837	863	1,655	1,006	52,694	74,146	130	124	115	1,538	1,488	1,315	31	29	25

Survey, Census, or Data Collection Method: Degrees conferred—Based on the Fall 2003 Integrated Postsecondary Education Data System (IPEDS); for information, see Appendix B, Limitations of the Data and Methodology; Faculty—Based on the Winter 2002–2003 Integrated Postsecondary Education Data System (IPEDS); Educational services—Based on tabulations of data extracted from the U.S. Census Bureau's Business Register, see Internet site <http://www.census.gov/epcd/cbp/view/cbpview.html>.

Sources: Degrees conferred—U.S. National Center for Education Statistics, *Digest of Education Statistics 2003*, NCES 2005-025, December 2004; Faculty—U.S. National Center for Education Statistics, *Staff in Postsecondary Institutions, Fall 2002, and Salaries of Full-Time Instructional Faculty, 2002–03*, 2005-167, November 2004; Educational services—U.S. Census Bureau, *County Business Patterns*, annual; see Internet site <http://www.census.gov/epcd/cbp/view/cbpview.html>.

Geographic area	Violent				Property			
	2003	2002	2000	1990	2003	2002	2000	1990
United States . . .	1,381,259	1,423,677	1,425,486	1,820,127	10,435,523	10,455,277	10,182,584	12,655,486
Alabama	19,331	19,931	21,620	28,630	182,241	180,400	180,539	169,974
Alaska	3,850	3,627	3,554	2,885	24,280	24,118	23,087	25,457
Arizona	28,638	30,171	27,281	23,911	314,335	318,296	271,811	265,229
Arkansas	12,431	11,501	11,904	12,511	98,710	101,171	98,115	101,897
California	205,551	208,388	210,531	311,051	1,215,086	1,176,484	1,056,183	1,654,186
Colorado	15,706	15,882	14,367	17,328	179,340	180,054	156,937	182,106
Connecticut	10,736	10,807	11,058	18,201	90,801	93,426	99,033	158,867
Delaware[5]	5,379	4,836	5,363	4,365	27,667	26,967	29,727	31,344
District of Columbia[4]	9,060	9,322	8,626	14,919	32,678	36,477	33,000	50,470
Florida	124,280	128,721	129,777	160,990	757,696	777,236	780,377	978,944
Georgia	39,422	39,271	41,319	48,996	369,501	346,559	347,630	389,165
Hawaii	3,400	3,262	2,954	3,113	65,867	71,976	60,033	64,563
Idaho	3,316	3,419	3,267	2,776	39,742	39,128	38,069	38,069
Illinois[5]	70,456	75,759	81,196	110,575	415,593	430,479	445,278	567,841
Indiana	21,856	22,001	21,230	26,275	208,034	208,965	206,905	233,376
Iowa	8,020	8,388	7,796	8,321	87,178	92,877	86,834	105,550
Kansas[5]	10,771	10,229	10,470	11,093	108,777	100,768	108,057	117,571
Kentucky[5]	10,777	11,101	11,903	14,386	110,418	108,590	107,723	107,208
Louisiana	29,062	29,690	30,440	37,914	195,569	198,838	211,904	235,822
Maine	1,422	1,396	1,397	1,759	32,078	32,985	32,003	43,647
Maryland	38,778	42,015	41,663	43,940	209,418	217,105	213,422	234,842
Massachusetts	30,196	31,137	30,230	44,300	164,018	167,753	161,901	274,442
Michigan	51,524	54,306	55,159	73,468	330,356	335,060	353,297	483,764
Minnesota	13,288	13,428	13,813	13,392	157,691	164,026	157,798	185,185
Mississippi	9,380	9,858	10,267	8,758	107,195	109,584	103,644	90,803
Missouri[5]	26,968	30,557	27,419	36,602	229,004	230,520	225,919	225,422
Montana[5]	3,351	3,197	2,807	1,273	28,428	28,751	32,198	34,702
Nebraska	5,026	5,428	5,606	5,209	64,552	68,178	64,479	61,290
Nevada	13,765	13,856	10,474	7,222	96,109	83,896	74,823	65,652
New Hampshire	1,916	2,056	2,167	1,459	26,448	26,250	27,901	38,976
New Jersey	31,599	32,252	32,298	50,057	219,799	227,715	233,637	371,023
New Mexico	12,470	13,719	13,786	11,821	77,301	80,477	86,605	89,448
New York	89,265	95,030	105,111	212,458	431,448	442,091	483,078	932,416
North Carolina	38,246	39,118	40,051	41,332	359,660	353,708	355,921	322,306
North Dakota	493	496	523	472	13,286	14,762	14,171	18,196
Ohio	38,103	40,128	37,935	54,904	416,317	428,976	420,939	470,469
Oklahoma	17,758	17,587	17,177	17,222	151,208	148,128	140,125	158,889
Oregon	10,520	10,298	12,000	14,405	170,230	161,145	153,780	146,073
Pennsylvania	49,216	49,578	51,584	51,213	300,641	300,868	316,274	361,805
Rhode Island	3,074	3,051	3,121	4,334	32,231	35,342	33,323	49,378
South Carolina	32,908	33,761	33,225	34,050	185,671	183,808	181,290	176,729
South Dakota	1,325	1,350	1,259	1,133	15,299	15,992	16,252	19,116
Tennessee	40,177	41,562	40,233	32,698	255,833	249,399	237,985	213,648
Texas	122,201	126,018	113,653	129,343	1,016,422	1,004,274	919,658	1,200,151
Utah	5,845	5,488	5,711	4,892	99,362	97,641	94,247	92,620
Vermont	682	658	691	716	13,621	14,942	17,494	23,713
Virginia	20,375	21,256	19,943	21,694	199,731	207,783	194,405	253,063
Washington	21,276	20,964	21,788	24,410	291,544	288,967	279,144	278,440
West Virginia	4,661	4,221	5,723	3,036	42,714	41,099	41,344	41,855
Wisconsin	12,095	12,238	12,700	12,948	157,747	164,749	159,424	202,052
Wyoming	1,314	1,364	1,316	1,367	16,648	16,494	14,969	17,732

See footnotes at end of table.

Geographic area	Offenses by type per 100,000 population,[1] 2003								
	Violent crimes					Property crimes			
	Total	Murder[2]	Forcible rape	Robbery	Aggravated assault	Total	Burglary	Larceny/theft	Motor vehicle theft
United States . . .	**475.0**	**5.7**	**32.1**	**142.2**	**295.0**	**3,588.4**	**740.5**	**2,414.5**	**433.4**
Alabama	429.5	6.6	36.8	134.2	251.9	4,049.1	960.8	2,756.0	332.3
Alaska	593.4	6.0	92.5	68.4	426.5	3,742.2	594.2	2,770.7	377.3
Arizona	513.2	7.9	33.3	136.5	335.5	5,632.4	1,050.3	3,560.9	1,021.3
Arkansas	456.1	6.4	33.1	81.7	334.8	3,621.4	913.6	2,487.3	220.5
California	579.3	6.8	28.2	179.7	364.6	3,424.3	682.8	2,061.4	680.1
Colorado	345.1	3.9	41.6	82.1	217.6	3,940.9	711.3	2,730.8	498.8
Connecticut	308.2	3.0	18.7	119.0	167.5	2,606.7	448.1	1,842.1	316.5
Delaware[3]	658.0	2.9	43.2	169.9	442.0	3,384.4	729.8	2,302.3	352.3
District of Columbia[4]	1,608.1	44.2	48.6	699.5	815.8	5,800.3	829.1	3,213.4	1,757.8
Florida	730.2	5.4	39.5	185.2	500.1	4,452.0	1,002.7	2,970.1	479.2
Georgia	453.9	7.6	25.7	161.8	258.8	4,254.6	909.2	2,846.0	499.4
Hawaii	270.4	1.7	29.2	92.9	146.5	5,237.5	907.2	3,562.9	767.4
Idaho	242.7	1.8	37.2	17.9	185.8	2,908.7	570.2	2,147.5	190.9
Illinois[5]	556.8	7.1	32.9	188.2	328.6	3,284.4	618.7	2,335.6	330.1
Indiana	352.8	5.5	27.8	103.3	216.2	3,357.7	671.1	2,351.4	335.2
Iowa	272.4	1.6	25.9	38.1	206.8	2,961.1	596.0	2,174.9	190.2
Kansas[5]	395.5	4.5	38.3	82.5	270.2	3,994.0	803.6	2,904.8	285.6
Kentucky[5]	261.7	4.6	25.6	77.6	153.9	2,681.5	671.6	1,782.4	227.5
Louisiana	646.3	13.0	41.1	157.2	435.0	4,349.5	998.1	2,909.3	442.2
Maine	108.9	1.2	27.1	22.1	58.4	2,456.7	503.9	1,841.3	111.5
Maryland	703.9	9.5	24.7	241.5	428.3	3,801.4	701.4	2,439.2	660.8
Massachusetts	469.4	2.2	27.9	124.1	315.1	2,549.5	539.7	1,613.3	396.5
Michigan	511.2	6.1	54.1	111.7	339.3	3,277.3	677.2	2,067.1	533.1
Minnesota	262.6	2.5	41.2	77.2	141.8	3,116.8	547.4	2,297.4	272.0
Mississippi	325.5	9.3	37.4	104.8	174.1	3,720.4	1,035.6	2,374.2	310.6
Missouri	472.8	5.0	24.4	108.7	334.5	4,014.5	717.1	2,794.9	502.4
Montana[5]	365.2	3.3	26.8	32.5	302.6	3,098.0	405.6	2,484.7	207.7
Nebraska	289.0	3.2	28.5	66.8	190.5	3,711.4	579.1	2,780.2	352.1
Nevada	614.2	8.8	39.0	230.3	336.1	4,288.4	980.6	2,378.0	929.8
New Hampshire	148.8	1.4	33.2	37.1	77.1	2,053.9	353.5	1,551.5	148.9
New Jersey	365.8	4.7	15.3	154.7	191.0	2,544.4	503.0	1,641.3	400.2
New Mexico	665.2	6.0	50.0	104.0	505.2	4,123.6	1,025.2	2,711.3	387.1
New York	465.2	4.9	19.7	186.3	254.3	2,248.3	393.4	1,619.3	235.6
North Carolina	454.9	6.1	25.4	145.5	278.0	4,278.0	1,197.6	2,760.5	319.9
North Dakota	77.8	1.9	23.8	8.0	44.0	2,096.1	306.2	1,619.8	170.1
Ohio	333.2	4.6	40.1	147.7	140.8	3,640.5	830.1	2,451.9	358.5
Oklahoma	505.7	5.9	42.7	91.8	365.3	4,306.0	992.3	2,944.7	369.0
Oregon	295.5	1.9	34.2	80.1	179.3	4,782.3	804.2	3,444.6	533.5
Pennsylvania	398.0	5.3	28.8	145.4	218.6	2,431.3	436.0	1,724.8	270.4
Rhode Island	285.6	2.3	46.9	77.1	159.3	2,995.0	513.3	2,074.0	407.7
South Carolina	793.5	7.2	44.4	136.7	605.1	4,477.1	1,050.9	3,046.1	380.1
South Dakota	173.4	1.3	46.3	13.6	112.1	2,001.7	375.9	1,511.4	114.4
Tennessee	687.8	6.8	35.7	160.4	484.9	4,379.4	1,082.0	2,845.3	452.1
Texas	552.5	6.4	36.2	167.4	342.5	4,595.3	993.7	3,157.7	444.0
Utah	248.6	2.5	37.9	53.4	154.8	4,225.5	713.1	3,182.2	330.2
Vermont	110.2	2.3	19.5	9.7	78.7	2,200.1	477.8	1,618.0	104.3
Virginia	275.8	5.6	24.0	90.3	155.9	2,704.1	391.5	2,070.0	242.5
Washington	347.0	3.0	46.7	93.3	204.0	4,754.9	950.3	3,142.1	662.5
West Virginia	257.5	3.5	16.4	40.3	197.3	2,359.4	562.2	1,602.6	194.7
Wisconsin	221.0	3.3	21.9	80.1	115.7	2,882.6	485.4	2,172.1	225.1
Wyoming	262.1	2.8	27.1	16.8	215.5	3,321.3	520.9	2,641.2	159.2

[1]Based on resident population estimated as of July 1 for 2003.
[2]Includes nonnegligent manslaughter.
[3]Forcible rape figures furnished by the state-level uniform crime reporting (UCR) program administered by the Delaware State Bureau of Investigation were not in accordance with the national UCR guidelines; therefore, it was necessary that the forcible rape count be estimated for 2000.
[4]Includes offenses reported by the police at the National Zoo for 2000 through 2003 and by Metro Transit Police for 2002 and 2003.
[5]Complete data were not available; therefore, it was necessary for the crime counts to be estimated for Illinois and Kentucky for 2000 through 2003 and for Kansas and Montana for 2000.

Survey, Census, or Data Collection Method: Based on the Uniform Crime Reporting Program; for information, see Appendix B, Limitations of the Data and Methodology.

Source: U.S. Federal Bureau of Investigation, *Crime in the United States*, annual. See also <http://www.fbi.gov/ucr/02cius.htm> (released 27 October 2003).

Table A-26. States — Juvenile Arrests, Child Abuse Cases, and Prisoners

Geographic area	Juvenile arrest rate,[1] 2003				Child abuse and neglect cases reported and investigated, 2003			Prisoners under jurisdiction of federal and state authorities (Dec. 31)			Prisoners executed		Prisoners under death sentence			
						Number of children subject of investi-gation[3]	Number of victims[4]	2003				1977 to 2004				
	Violent crime	Prop-erty crime	Drug abuse	Weap-ons	Number of reports[2]			Number	Rate[5]	2000	2004		2003	2002	2001	2000
United States . . .	**291**	**1,442**	**594**	**116**	**[6]1,576,390**	**[6]2,856,284**	**[6]787,156**	**[7]1,470,045**	**506**	**[7]1,391,261**	**59**	**944**	**[8]3,374**	**[8]3,562**	**[8]3,577**	**[8]3,601**
Alabama	126	764	236	31	18,015	29,679	9,290	29,253	650	26,332	2	30	192	191	186	185
Alaska	243	2,202	487	85	10,575	10,575	7,996	[9]4,527	698	[9]4,173	([10])	([10])	([10])	([10])	([10])	([10])
Arizona	223	1,774	820	72	33,649	76,269	4,838	[11]31,170	559	[11]26,510	–	22	123	117	124	119
Arkansas	130	1,282	328	64	19,747	44,666	7,232	13,084	480	11,915	1	26	40	42	40	40
California	364	1,180	523	181	(NA)	(NA)	(NA)	164,487	464	163,001	–	10	629	613	605	587
Colorado	231	2,051	777	168	29,362	43,217	8,137	19,671	433	16,833	–	1	3	5	6	6
Connecticut	290	1,347	479	90	32,802	50,115	12,256	[9]19,846	569	[9]18,355	–	–	7	7	7	7
Delaware	595	1,583	769	147	5,469	12,497	1,236	[9]6,794	830	[9]6,921	([10])	13	16	14	14	15
District of Columbia	(NA)	(NA)	(NA)	(NA)	4,673	11,000	2,518	[12]	(NA)	[12]7,456	([10])	([10])	([10])	([10])	([10])	([10])
Florida	524	2,128	765	109	157,474	351,499	138,499	[11]79,594	468	[11]71,319	2	59	364	366	373	371
Georgia	266	1,411	536	153	71,501	121,269	43,923	[11]47,208	544	[11]44,232	2	36	111	115	116	122
Hawaii	197	1,387	424	36	3,894	8,230	4,046	[9]5,828	467	[9]5,053	([10])	([10])	([10])	([10])	([10])	([10])
Idaho	160	2,158	482	122	6,264	9,458	1,527	5,887	431	5,535	–	1	19	20	20	21
Illinois	944	2,074	2,457	383	59,280	134,919	28,344	43,418	343	45,281	–	12	2	159	159	164
Indiana	317	1,219	438	28	34,388	52,195	21,205	23,069	372	20,125	–	11	35	37	34	41
Iowa	251	2,099	408	45	24,172	36,544	13,303	[11]8,546	290	[11]7,955	([10])	([10])	([10])	([10])	([10])	([10])
Kansas	131	1,055	455	25	15,840	24,250	5,682	9,132	335	8,344	–	–	6	5	4	4
Kentucky	229	1,435	588	56	45,348	69,201	18,178	16,622	404	14,919	–	2	35	36	36	39
Louisiana	355	1,842	570	61	25,480	41,726	11,432	36,047	802	35,207	–	27	87	90	85	89
Maine	78	1,866	562	26	5,152	9,425	4,719	2,013	154	1,679	([10])	([10])	([10])	([10])	([10])	([10])
Maryland	505	1,950	1,235	224	(NA)	(NA)	16,688	23,791	432	23,538	1	4	11	15	15	16
Massachusetts	269	512	337	28	39,692	83,270	36,558	10,232	159	10,722	([10])	([10])	([10])	([10])	([10])	([10])
Michigan	166	947	325	53	74,675	195,583	28,690	49,358	490	47,718	([10])	([10])	([10])	([10])	([10])	([10])
Minnesota	176	1,860	579	102	17,587	25,878	9,230	7,865	155	6,238	([10])	([10])	([10])	([10])	([10])	([10])
Mississippi	136	1,497	526	70	15,998	24,503	5,940	23,182	804	20,241	–	6	66	65	64	61
Missouri.	295	1,728	680	87	55,580	84,383	10,183	30,303	530	27,543	–	61	52	66	72	78
Montana	202	2,175	295	32	9,023	14,966	1,951	3,620	394	3,105	–	2	5	6	6	6
Nebraska	96	1,820	581	83	7,160	14,767	3,875	4,040	233	3,895	–	3	7	7	7	11
Nevada	(NA)	(NA)	(NA)	(NA)	13,641	28,148	4,578	10,543	470	10,063	2	11	84	82	86	88
New Hampshire.	71	674	452	9	6,878	9,697	1,043	2,434	189	2,257	–	–	–	–	–	–
New Jersey	386	934	688	214	42,762	77,915	8,123	27,246	315	29,784	–	–	14	14	16	16
New Mexico	220	1,367	749	174	15,278	25,259	6,238	6,223	331	5,342	–	1	2	2	3	5
New York	264	1,218	569	70	149,841	253,866	75,784	65,198	339	70,199	–	–	5	5	6	6
North Carolina.	310	1,582	522	179	60,466	120,194	32,847	33,560	399	31,266	4	34	195	206	215	215
North Dakota	45	1,866	322	33	3,899	5,900	1,494	1,239	196	1,076	([10])	([10])	([10])	([10])	([10])	([10])
Ohio	150	1,222	443	70	68,399	108,816	47,444	44,778	391	45,833	7	15	209	207	204	201
Oklahoma	217	1,591	469	81	36,641	63,935	12,529	22,821	651	23,181	6	75	102	112	114	132
Oregon	149	1,721	520	53	20,552	32,694	10,368	12,715	357	10,580	–	2	28	27	26	25
Pennsylvania	402	1,222	559	123	23,601	23,601	4,571	40,890	331	36,847	–	3	230	240	241	240
Rhode Island	288	1,372	579	160	7,012	10,362	3,290	[9]3,527	328	[9]3,286	([10])	([10])	([10])	([10])	([10])	([10])
South Carolina	47	214	183	73	18,449	39,396	11,143	23,719	572	21,778	4	32	71	72	73	66
South Dakota	108	1,743	773	82	5,534	9,925	4,346	3,026	396	2,616	–	–	4	5	5	3
Tennessee	223	1,064	472	100	(NA)	46,522	9,421	25,403	435	22,166	–	1	96	96	95	98
Texas	185	1,282	590	64	133,827	215,602	50,522	166,911	755	166,719	23	336	453	449	453	450
Utah	216	2,511	568	183	20,113	31,679	12,366	5,763	245	5,637	–	6	10	11	11	11
Vermont.	81	559	322	11	2,936	3,632	1,233	[9]1,944	314	[9]1,697	([10])	([10])	([10])	([10])	([10])	([10])
Virginia	106	844	377	88	15,975	31,915	6,485	35,067	476	30,168	5	94	27	23	26	30
Washington	246	2,088	530	113	30,222	47,713	6,020	16,148	263	14,915	–	4	10	10	9	11
West Virginia	40	382	157	7	19,604	43,523	8,875	4,758	263	3,856	([10])	([10])	([10])	([10])	([10])	([10])
Wisconsin.	184	2,813	842	176	55,573	41,377	10,174	22,614	413	20,754	([10])	([10])	([10])	([10])	([10])	([10])
Wyoming	88	1,885	769	80	2,381	4,529	786	1,872	373	1,680	–	1	1	2	2	2

– Represents zero. NA Not available.

[1]Arrest rate is defined as the number of arrests of persons under age 18 for every 100,000 persons ages 10–17.
[2]The number of investigations includes assessments. The number of investigations is based on the total number of investigations that received a disposition in 2001.
[3]The number of children subject of an investigation of assessment is based on the total number of children for whom an alleged maltreatment was substantiated, indicated, or assessed to have occurred or the child was at risk of occurrence.
[4]Victims are defined as children subject of a substantiated, indicated, or alternative response-victim maltreatment.
[5]Per 100,000 resident population estimated as of July 1.
[6]Includes estimates for states that did not report.
[7]State-level data excludes federal inmates.
[8]Includes federal cases not distributed by state. Excludes persons held under Armed Forces jurisdiction with a military death sentence for murder.
[9]Includes both jail and prison inmates. (State has combined jail and prison system.)
[10]State did not have death penalty as of December 31 of year shown.
[11]Numbers are for custody rather than jurisdiction counts.
[12]The transfer of responsibility for sentenced felons from the District of Columbia to the federal systems was completed by year end 2001.

Survey, Census, or Data Collection Method: Juvenile arrests—Based on analysis of arrest data from FBI reports and population data from the U.S. Census Bureau; for information, see the following report at <http://www.ncjrs.org/pdffiles1/ojjdp/209735.pdf>;   Child abuse and neglect—Based on the National Child Abuse and Neglect Data System (NCANDS); for information, see Internet site <http://www.acf.dhhs.gov/programs/cb/pubs/cm03/chapterone.htm>;   Prisoners under jurisdiction and capital punishment—Based on the National Prisoner Statistics (NPS) system; for information, see Internet site <http://www.ojp.usdoj.gov/bjs/correct.htm#nps>.

Sources: Juvenile arrests—Office of Justice Programs, *Juvenile Arrests 2003*, see Internet site <http://www.ncjrs.org/pdffiles1/ojjdp/209735.pdf>;   Child abuse and neglect—U.S. Department of Health and Human Services, Administration on Children, Youth and Families. *Child Maltreatment 2003* (Washington, DC: U.S. Government Printing Office, 2003);   Prisoners under jurisdiction—U.S. Bureau of Justice Statistics, *Prisoners in 2003*, and earlier issues, see Internet site <http://www.ojp.usdoj.gov/bjs/abstract/p03.htm>;   Capital punishment—U.S. Bureau of Justice Statistics, *Capital Punishment*, annual, see Internet site <http://www.ojp.usdoj.gov/bjs/correct.htm>.

Geographic area	Full-time equivalent employment (March)							Expenditures[1]		
	2002		2000	Per 10,000 population, 2002				2002		2000 ($1,000)
	Number	Percent of total state and local		Total justice system	Police protection	Judicial and legal	Corrections	Total ($1,000)	Percent of state and local	
United States . . .	**1,994,120**	**12.7**	**1,940,571**	**69.5**	**31.0**	**14.1**	**24.4**	**150,414,874**	**7.4**	**132,635,690**
Alabama	25,712	9.6	25,298	57.4	29.2	11.4	16.9	1,487,133	5.2	1,321,833
Alaska	4,815	9.5	4,693	75.1	25.9	20.5	28.6	570,594	6.1	481,705
Arizona	41,002	15.8	39,345	75.4	31.6	17.1	26.7	3,035,958	9.7	2,662,075
Arkansas	16,697	11.1	15,172	61.7	28.3	11.0	22.5	967,933	6.6	835,961
California	232,735	13.1	226,448	66.5	28.6	15.7	22.1	26,208,117	9.0	22,128,975
Colorado	28,833	12.0	26,869	64.1	28.3	13.3	22.5	2,313,314	7.3	1,979,115
Connecticut	22,685	12.5	23,986	65.6	29.9	12.6	23.1	1,902,173	6.9	1,665,917
Delaware	7,100	15.2	6,353	88.1	30.9	19.7	37.5	542,389	9.1	485,081
District of Columbia	6,348	14.4	7,235	222.4	151.2	15.9	55.2	617,112	7.9	680,407
Florida	131,541	16.7	127,600	78.8	35.5	18.4	24.9	9,403,902	9.5	8,407,384
Georgia	62,641	13.2	60,195	73.3	28.4	12.8	32.1	4,002,823	7.7	3,179,612
Hawaii	8,922	12.7	8,701	71.9	29.4	22.6	19.9	625,776	6.7	556,441
Idaho	8,423	10.9	7,365	62.7	28.1	12.5	22.2	593,029	7.8	500,098
Illinois	89,990	13.8	86,731	71.5	35.7	14.4	21.4	6,212,482	7.1	5,777,158
Indiana	35,364	10.8	33,189	57.4	25.9	10.1	21.4	2,120,127	5.8	1,894,617
Iowa	14,718	8.3	14,919	50.1	24.5	10.7	15.0	1,076,379	5.6	977,082
Kansas	18,145	10.2	18,906	66.9	31.7	13.1	22.2	1,074,566	6.4	985,103
Kentucky	22,543	9.8	22,371	55.1	23.5	14.8	16.9	1,458,516	5.9	1,388,829
Louisiana	37,385	13.4	36,601	83.5	35.9	17.2	30.5	2,107,569	7.6	1,967,772
Maine	6,083	8.3	5,724	47.0	24.9	7.3	14.9	406,412	4.7	355,751
Maryland	39,436	13.8	37,870	72.4	31.7	13.5	27.2	3,112,413	8.7	2,713,505
Massachusetts	43,394	13.1	44,731	67.6	37.2	14.5	15.8	3,308,516	6.5	2,901,028
Michigan	63,749	12.3	61,472	63.5	26.4	12.4	24.6	5,183,326	7.5	4,550,728
Minnesota	25,982	9.2	24,272	51.7	22.4	12.1	17.2	2,189,440	5.4	1,907,219
Mississippi	17,044	9.3	17,786	59.5	30.6	8.9	20.0	941,720	5.4	850,076
Missouri	39,930	12.8	38,350	70.4	31.9	13.0	25.5	2,207,140	6.7	1,916,548
Montana	4,925	9.4	4,841	54.1	25.0	12.0	17.1	368,512	6.6	326,155
Nebraska	9,993	8.8	9,309	57.8	27.1	10.6	20.2	636,613	5.1	562,621
Nevada	15,597	16.8	14,702	72.0	31.0	14.6	26.3	1,474,713	10.6	1,258,843
New Hampshire	6,671	10.1	7,146	52.4	27.4	9.2	15.8	423,984	6.0	394,551
New Jersey	74,083	15.3	69,960	86.4	41.2	25.2	20.0	5,108,651	8.0	4,659,648
New Mexico	14,703	12.4	14,096	79.4	31.1	18.0	30.3	972,289	7.7	864,578
New York	182,248	15.0	177,474	95.3	46.4	16.6	32.3	14,115,834	7.1	12,371,653
North Carolina	54,456	11.5	52,656	65.6	28.2	8.0	29.4	3,229,175	6.2	3,010,205
North Dakota	3,038	7.7	3,019	47.9	22.4	12.3	13.3	187,061	4.5	164,036
Ohio	79,699	12.9	80,094	69.9	29.5	17.8	22.5	5,590,723	7.0	5,220,319
Oklahoma	21,819	10.6	22,213	62.5	30.5	11.7	20.4	1,356,546	6.5	1,222,839
Oregon	22,530	12.3	21,554	64.0	25.2	13.6	25.2	1,999,667	7.2	1,799,118
Pennsylvania	77,954	13.8	74,925	63.2	25.7	14.3	23.2	6,042,329	7.0	5,510,353
Rhode Island	6,420	12.2	6,426	60.1	31.8	11.8	16.6	499,682	6.3	455,578
South Carolina	28,065	11.7	28,447	68.4	32.6	9.6	26.2	1,504,863	5.4	1,391,012
South Dakota	3,804	8.9	3,813	50.0	22.9	10.2	16.9	242,075	5.7	208,732
Tennessee	36,453	11.9	34,375	63.0	30.3	10.6	22.1	2,087,237	5.7	1,943,166
Texas	155,437	12.4	150,718	71.5	27.9	11.1	32.6	9,750,308	7.5	8,314,329
Utah	13,095	10.6	12,318	56.5	23.8	11.6	21.1	1,057,381	6.8	934,625
Vermont	2,784	7.3	2,934	45.2	19.1	10.2	15.8	214,139	5.1	183,612
Virginia	49,031	11.9	48,070	67.3	26.6	10.1	30.5	3,354,056	7.7	2,934,733
Washington	35,146	11.0	34,250	57.9	23.3	12.8	21.8	2,807,823	5.6	2,530,340
West Virginia	6,500	7.0	7,519	36.0	20.0	11.8	4.2	513,269	4.3	462,998
Wisconsin	34,490	11.9	34,031	63.4	29.7	10.7	23.0	2,920,922	7.4	2,594,282
Wyoming	3,962	9.6	3,499	79.4	36.5	14.9	28.0	288,163	6.6	247,344

See footnotes at end of table.

| Geographic area | Expenditures[1] | | | | State prison expenditures, fiscal year 2001[2] (dol.) | | | | |
| | Per capita, 2002 (dol.) | | | | Expenditures (1,000) | | | Annual operating costs | |
	Total justice system	Police protection	Judicial and legal	Corrections	Total	Operating	Capital	Per inmate	Per resident
United States . . .	**524**	**225**	**109**	**191**	**29,491,268**	**28,374,273**	**1,116,995**	**22,650**	**100**
Alabama	332	159	71	103	228,871	221,774	7,097	8,128	50
Alaska	889	412	204	273	[3]154,650	[3]154,156	[3]494	[3]36,730	[3]243
Arizona	558	231	120	206	618,571	609,910	8,661	22,476	115
Arkansas	358	149	72	137	199,003	192,611	6,392	15,619	72
California	749	290	201	257	4,166,573	4,107,844	58,729	25,053	119
Colorado	514	238	86	190	466,551	435,037	31,514	25,408	98
Connecticut	550	226	140	184	[3]523,960	[3]506,905	[3]17,055	[3]26,856	[3]148
Delaware	673	237	132	304	[3]166,327	[3]162,397	[3]3,930	22,802	[3]204
District of Columbia	2,162	1,348	205	609	143,700	143,700	([4])	26,670	251
Florida	563	263	99	202	1,484,799	1,453,799	31,000	20,190	89
Georgia	468	182	80	207	923,505	900,918	22,586	19,860	107
Hawaii	504	205	172	127	[3]117,101	[3]117,101	([5])	[3]21,637	[3]96
Idaho	442	179	92	171	95,494	92,821	2,673	16,319	70
Illinois	494	256	88	149	1,011,311	996,738	14,573	21,844	80
Indiana	344	145	62	137	477,628	449,406	28,222	21,841	73
Iowa	367	156	98	112	188,391	186,298	2,093	22,997	64
Kansas	396	176	87	133	199,843	182,655	17,189	21,381	68
Kentucky	357	133	77	147	288,438	274,404	14,034	17,818	67
Louisiana	471	199	99	173	479,260	459,686	19,573	12,951	103
Maine	314	140	62	112	76,479	75,133	1,346	44,379	58
Maryland	571	245	95	231	645,620	632,749	12,872	26,398	118
Massachusetts	515	224	116	175	413,071	404,862	8,209	37,718	63
Michigan	516	197	109	210	1,582,611	1,573,273	9,338	32,525	157
Minnesota	436	203	104	129	253,385	239,953	13,432	36,836	48
Mississippi	329	161	55	113	266,196	264,503	1,693	12,795	93
Missouri	389	180	66	144	436,081	362,429	73,652	12,867	64
Montana	405	187	84	134	71,994	71,169	825	21,898	79
Nebraska	369	155	65	149	126,857	99,865	26,992	25,321	58
Nevada	680	300	148	232	182,092	180,834	1,258	17,572	86
New Hampshire	333	166	76	90	62,754	60,279	2,475	25,949	48
New Jersey	596	282	126	187	799,560	768,661	30,899	27,347	91
New Mexico	525	221	103	201	149,077	148,249	828	28,035	81
New York	738	351	143	244	2,807,259	2,547,452	259,807	36,835	134
North Carolina	389	181	67	141	863,892	840,347	23,545	26,984	103
North Dakota	295	122	79	94	26,796	24,219	2,577	22,425	38
Ohio	490	212	119	159	1,277,622	1,201,269	76,354	26,295	106
Oklahoma	389	163	65	161	384,060	377,378	6,682	16,309	109
Oregon	568	219	114	235	404,255	399,436	4,819	36,060	115
Pennsylvania	490	199	93	199	1,203,219	1,183,668	19,551	31,900	96
Rhode Island	468	224	97	147	[3]124,333	[3]121,167	[3]3,165	[3]38,503	[3]114
South Carolina	367	176	52	139	405,238	373,249	31,989	16,762	92
South Dakota	318	139	57	123	37,529	37,030	499	13,853	49
Tennessee	361	169	73	119	421,807	421,807	([6])	18,206	73
Texas	449	171	75	202	2,315,899	2,270,959	44,940	13,808	106
Utah	456	190	104	162	133,963	133,683	281	24,574	59
Vermont	347	149	69	129	[3]46,128	[3]44,867	[3]1,261	[3]25,178	[3]73
Virginia	460	180	90	191	723,767	699,104	24,663	22,942	97
Washington	463	180	94	189	488,314	459,814	28,500	30,168	77
West Virginia	284	104	69	112	61,944	61,194	750	14,817	34
Wisconsin	537	234	87	216	709,292	599,080	110,212	28,622	111
Wyoming	578	243	114	220	56,199	48,431	7,768	28,845	98

[1]For the fiscal year ending on September 30 of the year shown.

[2]Forty-six states and the District of Columbia began their fiscal years in July and ended them in June. Exceptions included Alabama and Michigan, October to September; New York, April to March; and Texas, September to August. May not add to total due to rounding.

[3]States have integrated jail-prison systems.

[4]Reported no capital outlays during FY 2001, a transition period during which its sentenced felons were being transferred to the Federal Bureau of Prisons.

[5]State budget officials excluded nonrecurring expenditures from the category.

[6]The state spent capital amounts from sources outside its Department of Corrections.

Survey, Census, or Data Collection Method: Based on the U.S. Census Bureau's Annual Government Finance Survey and Annual Survey of Public Employment; for information, see Internet site <http://www.ojp.usdoj.gov/bjs/eande.htm>.

Source: U.S. Bureau of Justice Statistics, *Justice Expenditure and Employment Extracts, 2002*, and prior years; and *State Prison Expenditures, 2001*; see also <http://www.ojp.usdoj.gov/bjs/>.

Geographic area	Civilian noninstitutionalized population 16 years and over (1,000)						Civilian labor force (1,000)		
	2004			2003	2000	1990	Total, 2004		
	Total	Male	Female				Number	Male	Female
United States[1] **. . .**	**223,357**	**107,710**	**115,647**	**221,168**	**212,577**	**189,164**	**147,401**	**78,980**	**68,421**
Alabama	3,484	1,651	1,833	3,442	3,381	3,072	2,179	1,156	1,023
Alaska	465	233	232	459	437	372	331	179	152
Arizona	4,266	2,101	2,166	4,131	3,845	2,777	2,778	1,536	1,242
Arkansas	2,102	1,008	1,094	2,071	2,027	1,781	1,308	707	601
California	26,768	13,117	13,650	26,490	25,132	22,598	17,551	9,691	7,860
Colorado	3,468	1,718	1,750	3,440	3,259	2,489	2,525	1,383	1,142
Connecticut	2,700	1,287	1,413	2,680	2,597	2,574	1,790	942	848
Delaware	643	306	337	625	598	512	426	220	206
District of Columbia	443	203	240	454	457	485	299	150	149
Florida	13,521	6,480	7,041	13,211	12,484	10,261	8,411	4,507	3,904
Georgia	6,534	3,142	3,392	6,431	6,090	4,873	4,399	2,389	2,010
Hawaii	946	455	491	944	902	809	612	317	295
Idaho	1,039	512	527	1,013	951	729	706	383	323
Illinois	9,641	4,650	4,991	9,583	9,352	8,691	6,386	3,407	2,979
Indiana	4,725	2,290	2,435	4,679	4,599	4,182	3,160	1,674	1,486
Iowa	2,307	1,124	1,183	2,286	2,237	2,088	1,620	846	774
Kansas	2,069	1,008	1,061	2,049	2,003	1,823	1,480	795	685
Kentucky	3,194	1,534	1,660	3,153	3,086	2,799	1,977	1,057	920
Louisiana	3,377	1,589	1,788	3,348	3,292	3,073	2,058	1,076	982
Maine	1,055	507	547	1,039	997	939	696	362	334
Maryland	4,223	1,986	2,237	4,181	3,997	3,691	2,883	1,489	1,394
Massachusetts	5,036	2,402	2,634	5,028	4,934	4,713	3,399	1,770	1,629
Michigan	7,748	3,738	4,010	7,706	7,522	7,015	5,114	2,720	2,394
Minnesota	3,943	1,937	2,006	3,896	3,736	3,271	2,941	1,557	1,384
Mississippi	2,169	1,021	1,147	2,138	2,100	1,894	1,335	698	637
Missouri	4,424	2,120	2,303	4,352	4,239	3,861	3,017	1,572	1,445
Montana	730	359	370	714	688	596	486	256	230
Nebraska	1,331	649	682	1,318	1,285	1,162	990	523	467
Nevada	1,759	886	874	1,686	1,520	939	1,175	657	518
New Hampshire	1,018	497	521	1,005	951	848	724	387	337
New Jersey	6,666	3,183	3,483	6,619	6,442	6,046	4,388	2,356	2,032
New Mexico	1,436	692	744	1,401	1,344	1,118	911	484	427
New York	14,906	7,065	7,841	14,891	14,551	14,079	9,370	4,964	4,406
North Carolina	6,439	3,082	3,357	6,328	6,108	5,096	4,243	2,270	1,973
North Dakota	497	245	252	490	487	463	359	189	170
Ohio	8,828	4,225	4,603	8,771	8,628	8,231	5,884	3,106	2,778
Oklahoma	2,671	1,284	1,387	2,646	2,582	2,347	1,714	916	798
Oregon	2,800	1,375	1,425	2,770	2,643	2,194	1,850	1,010	840
Pennsylvania	9,702	4,621	5,082	9,663	9,494	9,206	6,260	3,310	2,950
Rhode Island	848	402	445	844	814	776	562	287	275
South Carolina	3,193	1,510	1,683	3,142	3,028	2,612	2,077	1,075	1,002
South Dakota	586	287	299	576	562	501	431	224	207
Tennessee	4,564	2,187	2,378	4,501	4,359	3,765	2,894	1,529	1,365
Texas	16,388	7,971	8,417	16,047	15,200	12,604	10,989	6,088	4,901
Utah	1,697	839	858	1,660	1,581	1,159	1,206	668	538
Vermont	499	243	256	494	475	429	353	184	169
Virginia	5,605	2,660	2,945	5,532	5,304	4,656	3,766	1,975	1,791
Washington	4,777	2,338	2,440	4,697	4,466	3,676	3,240	1,746	1,494
West Virginia	1,452	700	752	1,442	1,431	1,398	795	426	369
Wisconsin	4,280	2,093	2,187	4,224	4,092	3,677	3,071	1,615	1,456
Wyoming	395	196	199	387	374	330	282	152	130

See footnotes at end of table.

Geographic area	Civilian labor force (1,000)								
	Total			Employed					
				2004					
	2003	2000	1990	Number	Male	Female	2003	2000	1990
United States[1]...	**146,510**	**142,583**	**125,840**	**139,252**	**74,524**	**64,728**	**137,736**	**136,891**	**118,793**
Alabama	2,133	2,161	1,903	2,053	1,096	957	2,009	2,073	1,783
Alaska	331	319	270	306	165	141	305	299	251
Arizona	2,707	2,507	1,788	2,637	1,458	1,179	2,553	2,406	1,694
Arkansas	1,279	1,256	1,126	1,231	669	562	1,205	1,203	1,050
California	17,414	16,870	15,169	16,466	9,076	7,390	16,223	16,034	14,294
Colorado	2,480	2,359	1,769	2,389	1,305	1,084	2,325	2,297	1,678
Connecticut	1,805	1,739	1,815	1,702	895	807	1,706	1,698	1,725
Delaware	420	417	362	409	211	198	404	403	347
District of Columbia	298	309	332	275	137	138	277	292	312
Florida	8,195	7,859	6,466	8,021	4,302	3,719	7,764	7,559	6,061
Georgia	4,341	4,233	3,300	4,194	2,280	1,914	4,135	4,084	3,129
Hawaii	612	608	551	591	304	287	589	583	538
Idaho	691	662	494	669	362	307	654	631	467
Illinois	6,361	6,472	5,932	5,997	3,203	2,794	5,934	6,181	5,561
Indiana	3,169	3,143	2,831	2,993	1,587	1,406	3,001	3,051	2,689
Iowa	1,620	1,605	1,459	1,545	809	736	1,548	1,561	1,393
Kansas	1,447	1,409	1,270	1,398	754	644	1,366	1,356	1,215
Kentucky	1,979	1,953	1,748	1,874	998	876	1,856	1,871	1,641
Louisiana	2,042	2,028	1,877	1,934	1,008	926	1,915	1,927	1,767
Maine	694	674	631	664	344	320	660	651	598
Maryland	2,880	2,802	2,583	2,762	1,431	1,331	2,751	2,703	2,465
Massachusetts	3,414	3,367	3,226	3,226	1,664	1,562	3,216	3,277	3,022
Michigan	5,054	5,157	4,620	4,758	2,517	2,241	4,695	4,967	4,262
Minnesota	2,929	2,823	2,390	2,800	1,470	1,330	2,786	2,733	2,276
Mississippi	1,322	1,318	1,176	1,252	659	593	1,237	1,244	1,085
Missouri	3,014	2,950	2,608	2,844	1,479	1,365	2,846	2,854	2,457
Montana	473	468	408	462	242	220	452	446	384
Nebraska	976	952	817	953	504	449	937	926	798
Nevada	1,149	1,064	656	1,125	629	496	1,090	1,016	623
New Hampshire	717	695	620	698	372	326	685	677	585
New Jersey	4,371	4,287	4,072	4,178	2,245	1,933	4,115	4,129	3,865
New Mexico	893	851	712	860	457	403	841	809	664
New York	9,300	9,180	8,809	8,823	4,672	4,151	8,705	8,764	8,340
North Carolina	4,230	4,114	3,498	4,016	2,154	1,862	3,957	3,959	3,352
North Dakota	351	347	319	347	181	166	339	337	306
Ohio	5,869	5,805	5,389	5,514	2,901	2,613	5,506	5,571	5,079
Oklahoma	1,710	1,659	1,521	1,630	874	756	1,614	1,608	1,435
Oregon	1,852	1,815	1,506	1,710	930	780	1,702	1,721	1,425
Pennsylvania	6,186	6,086	5,827	5,911	3,103	2,808	5,835	5,832	5,510
Rhode Island	569	543	526	532	271	261	538	521	494
South Carolina	2,013	1,965	1,722	1,935	1,004	931	1,878	1,896	1,639
South Dakota	424	409	351	416	216	200	409	398	338
Tennessee	2,903	2,864	2,401	2,747	1,452	1,295	2,742	2,750	2,269
Texas	10,927	10,365	8,594	10,332	5,718	4,614	10,196	9,913	8,042
Utah	1,188	1,134	820	1,142	633	509	1,121	1,096	784
Vermont	352	335	309	340	177	163	336	327	294
Virginia	3,767	3,573	3,220	3,619	1,901	1,718	3,612	3,491	3,077
Washington	3,160	3,051	2,537	3,037	1,637	1,400	2,927	2,899	2,406
West Virginia	796	809	756	753	401	352	748	765	691
Wisconsin	3,069	2,992	2,599	2,917	1,526	1,391	2,897	2,891	2,486
Wyoming	277	267	236	271	146	125	265	257	224

[1]United States totals differ from the sum of the state figures because of different benchmarks among states.

Survey, Census, or Data Collection Method: Based on the Current Population Survey (CPS); for information, see Appendix B, Limitations of the Data and Methodology, and the following document at <http://www.census.gov/prod/2002pubs/tp63rv.pdf>.

Source: U.S. Bureau of Labor Statistics, *Geographic Profile of Employment and Unemployment, 2004 Annual Averages*; see Internet site <http://www.bls.gov/gps/> (accessed 2 August 2005); data for prior years, Local Unemployment Statistics Program, see Internet site <http://www.bls.gov/lau/> (accessed 7 September 2005).

Table A-29. States — **Civilian Labor Force and Unemployment**

Geographic area	Employment/ population ratio, 2004[1]		Unemployment												Participation rate, 2004[3]	
			Total (1,000)						Rate[2]							
			2004			2003	2000	1990	2004			2003	2000	1990		
	Male	Female	Total	Male	Female				Total	Male	Female				Male	Female
United States[4]. . .	**69.2**	**56.0**	**8,149**	**4,455**	**3,694**	**8,774**	**5,692**	**7,047**	**5.5**	**5.6**	**5.4**	**6.0**	**4.0**	**5.6**	**73.3**	**59.2**
Alabama	66.3	52.2	126	60	66	124	89	121	5.8	5.3	6.4	5.8	4.1	6.3	70.0	55.8
Alaska	70.6	60.9	25	14	11	26	20	19	7.5	7.9	7.2	7.7	6.2	7.0	76.6	65.6
Arizona	69.4	54.4	141	78	63	154	101	94	5.1	5.0	5.1	5.7	4.0	5.3	73.1	57.4
Arkansas	66.3	51.4	77	39	38	75	53	76	5.9	5.5	6.4	5.9	4.2	6.8	70.1	54.9
California	69.2	54.1	1,084	614	470	1,190	836	874	6.2	6.3	6.0	6.8	5.0	5.8	73.9	57.6
Colorado	76.0	61.9	137	79	58	155	63	91	5.4	5.7	5.1	6.2	2.6	5.1	80.5	65.3
Connecticut	69.5	57.1	88	48	40	99	41	90	4.9	5.1	4.7	5.5	2.4	4.9	73.3	60.0
Delaware	69.3	58.6	17	9	8	17	14	15	3.9	3.9	4.0	4.0	3.3	4.2	72.0	61.1
District of Columbia	67.2	57.7	25	14	11	21	18	20	8.2	9.0	7.4	7.2	5.7	6.0	73.9	62.3
Florida	66.4	52.8	390	205	185	431	300	405	4.6	4.5	4.7	5.3	3.8	6.3	69.6	55.4
Georgia	72.6	56.4	205	109	96	206	149	171	4.7	4.6	4.8	4.7	3.5	5.2	76.0	59.2
Hawaii	66.8	58.4	21	13	8	24	25	13	3.4	4.1	2.7	3.9	4.0	2.4	69.7	60.1
Idaho	70.5	58.4	37	22	15	37	31	27	5.3	5.8	4.7	5.3	4.6	5.5	74.8	61.3
Illinois	68.9	56.0	389	204	185	427	290	371	6.1	6.0	6.2	6.7	4.5	6.3	73.3	59.7
Indiana	69.3	57.7	167	87	80	168	91	142	5.3	5.2	5.4	5.3	2.9	5.0	73.1	61.0
Iowa	72.0	62.2	75	37	38	72	44	66	4.6	4.4	4.9	4.4	2.7	4.5	75.3	65.4
Kansas	74.7	60.7	82	42	40	81	52	55	5.5	5.2	5.9	5.6	3.7	4.3	78.9	64.5
Kentucky	65.1	52.8	103	59	44	123	82	107	5.2	5.6	4.8	6.2	4.2	6.1	68.9	55.4
Louisiana	63.4	51.8	124	68	56	128	101	110	6.0	6.3	5.7	6.3	5.0	5.9	67.7	54.9
Maine	67.8	58.5	32	18	14	35	23	33	4.7	5.1	4.2	5.0	3.4	5.3	71.4	61.0
Maryland	72.1	59.5	121	57	64	128	100	118	4.2	3.9	4.6	4.5	3.6	4.6	75.0	62.3
Massachusetts	69.3	59.3	172	104	68	198	90	204	5.1	5.9	4.2	5.8	2.7	6.3	73.7	61.9
Michigan	67.3	55.9	356	203	153	358	190	358	7.0	7.5	6.4	7.1	3.7	7.7	72.8	59.7
Minnesota	75.9	66.3	140	86	54	143	90	114	4.8	5.5	3.9	4.9	3.2	4.8	80.3	69.0
Mississippi	64.5	51.7	83	40	43	85	74	90	6.2	5.6	6.8	6.4	5.6	7.7	68.4	55.5
Missouri	69.8	59.3	173	93	80	168	96	151	5.7	5.9	5.6	5.6	3.3	5.8	74.1	62.7
Montana	67.2	59.4	24	14	10	21	22	25	4.9	5.6	4.3	4.4	4.8	6.0	71.2	62.0
Nebraska	77.7	65.8	37	19	18	39	26	19	3.8	3.7	3.8	4.0	2.7	2.3	80.7	68.5
Nevada	71.0	56.8	50	28	22	59	48	33	4.2	4.2	4.2	5.1	4.5	5.1	74.2	59.3
New Hampshire.	74.7	62.6	27	16	11	32	18	35	3.7	4.0	3.3	4.5	2.6	5.6	77.9	64.7
New Jersey	70.5	55.5	210	111	99	256	158	208	4.8	4.7	4.9	5.9	3.7	5.1	74.0	58.4
New Mexico	66.1	54.1	51	26	25	53	42	48	5.6	5.4	5.8	5.9	5.0	6.8	69.9	57.5
New York	66.1	52.9	548	294	254	595	417	469	5.8	5.9	5.8	6.4	4.5	5.3	70.3	56.2
North Carolina.	69.9	55.5	227	116	111	273	154	145	5.4	5.1	5.6	6.5	3.8	4.2	73.6	58.8
North Dakota	73.8	65.9	12	8	4	13	10	13	3.4	4.2	2.5	3.6	2.9	4.0	77.1	67.6
Ohio	68.6	56.8	370	205	165	363	234	310	6.3	6.6	5.9	6.2	4.0	5.7	73.5	60.4
Oklahoma	68.1	54.5	84	42	42	95	52	86	4.9	4.5	5.3	5.6	3.1	5.7	71.3	57.6
Oregon	67.6	54.8	140	80	60	151	94	81	7.6	8.0	7.1	8.1	5.2	5.4	73.5	59.0
Pennsylvania	67.2	55.3	350	207	143	351	254	317	5.6	6.3	4.8	5.7	4.2	5.4	71.6	58.1
Rhode Island	67.5	58.5	30	16	14	31	22	32	5.4	5.5	5.2	5.4	4.1	6.1	71.5	61.7
South Carolina	66.5	55.3	142	71	71	135	69	84	6.9	6.7	7.1	6.7	3.5	4.9	71.2	59.5
South Dakota	75.4	66.8	16	8	8	15	11	13	3.7	3.5	3.8	3.5	2.7	3.7	78.1	69.4
Tennessee	66.4	54.5	147	77	70	161	114	132	5.1	5.1	5.1	5.5	4.0	5.5	69.9	57.4
Texas	71.7	54.8	657	370	287	731	452	552	6.0	6.1	5.9	6.7	4.4	6.4	76.4	58.2
Utah	75.4	59.4	64	35	29	67	38	36	5.3	5.2	5.4	5.7	3.4	4.4	79.5	62.7
Vermont	72.9	63.6	13	7	6	16	9	15	3.7	4.0	3.4	4.5	2.6	4.9	75.9	65.8
Virginia	71.5	58.3	147	75	72	155	81	143	3.9	3.8	4.0	4.1	2.3	4.4	74.3	60.8
Washington	70.0	57.4	202	108	94	233	152	131	6.2	6.2	6.3	7.4	5.0	5.1	74.7	61.2
West Virginia	57.2	46.8	42	24	18	48	44	65	5.3	5.8	4.7	6.0	5.5	8.6	60.8	49.1
Wisconsin	72.9	63.6	155	90	65	172	101	113	5.0	5.6	4.4	5.6	3.4	4.3	77.2	66.6
Wyoming	74.7	62.6	11	6	5	12	10	13	3.8	3.4	4.2	4.4	3.8	5.3	77.3	65.3

[1]Civilian employment as a percent of civilian noninstitutionalized population.
[2]Percent unemployed of the civilian labor force.
[3]Percent of civilian noninstitutionalized population of each specified group in the civilian labor force.
[4]United States totals differ from the sum of the state figures because of different benchmarks among states.

Survey, Census, or Data Collection Method: Based on the Current Population Survey (CPS); for information, see Appendix B, Limitations of the Data and Methodology, and the following document at <http://www.census.gov/prod/2002pubs/tp63rv.pdf>.

Source: U.S. Bureau of Labor Statistics, *Geographic Profile of Employment and Unemployment, 2004 Annual Averages*; see Internet site <http://www.bls.gov/gps/> (accessed 2 August 2005); data for prior years, Local Unemployment Statistics Program, see Internet site <http://www.bls.gov/lau/> (accessed 7 September 2005).

Geographic area	Total, (1,000)	Management, professional, and related occupations (1,000)		Service occupations (1,000)	Sales and office occupations (1,000)		Natural resources, construction, and maintenance occupations (1,000)			Production, transportation, and material moving occupations (1,000)	
		Management, business, and financial operations occupations	Professional and related occupations		Sales and related occupations	Office and administrative support occupations	Farming, fishing, and forestry occupations	Construction and extraction occupations	Installation, maintenance, and repair occupations	Production occupations	Transportation and material moving occupations
United States[1]...	**137,736**	**19,934**	**27,995**	**22,086**	**15,960**	**19,536**	**1,050**	**8,114**	**5,041**	**9,700**	**8,320**
Alabama	2,023	267	389	292	212	288	(B)	123	82	217	135
Alaska	305	40	64	51	27	45	6	23	14	12	23
Arizona	2,539	393	500	416	361	350	(B)	164	93	134	117
Arkansas	1,186	160	198	170	135	161	(B)	61	53	128	101
California	16,283	2,407	3,424	2,579	1,968	2,375	231	879	536	1,013	873
Colorado	2,328	392	478	363	283	308	(B)	161	79	116	134
Connecticut	1,704	275	397	255	196	257	(B)	95	48	107	72
Delaware	399	61	81	62	41	66	(B)	25	14	24	23
District of Columbia	281	58	96	44	17	40	(B)	8	4	(B)	10
Florida	7,744	1,103	1,461	1,375	1,038	1,155	45	535	300	323	410
Georgia	4,207	605	813	595	526	540	(B)	306	181	343	282
Hawaii	592	86	105	126	64	93	(B)	35	23	20	34
Idaho	655	79	120	118	76	91	19	44	29	39	41
Illinois	5,908	849	1,180	904	653	869	(B)	349	220	457	406
Indiana	3,024	393	527	435	339	432	(B)	174	142	337	232
Iowa	1,540	225	296	231	164	228	(B)	66	53	157	98
Kansas	1,357	214	273	212	142	189	(B)	79	55	102	79
Kentucky	1,836	245	353	301	196	255	(B)	88	74	172	134
Louisiana	1,904	214	379	348	217	261	(B)	141	88	127	116
Maine	658	81	129	115	74	88	11	41	29	51	39
Maryland	2,773	500	691	419	287	389	(B)	158	79	105	137
Massachusetts	3,217	527	796	498	351	440	(B)	196	86	184	128
Michigan	4,674	578	929	815	491	651	(B)	236	154	515	285
Minnesota	2,778	483	607	398	309	373	(B)	168	87	188	149
Mississippi	1,229	140	215	197	127	166	(B)	83	54	131	97
Missouri	2,850	395	583	435	352	416	(B)	194	107	174	183
Montana	452	81	80	77	48	59	10	36	16	19	26
Nebraska	937	163	167	139	106	135	(B)	55	39	61	57
Nevada	1,082	134	160	271	140	140	(B)	91	42	45	57
New Hampshire	688	106	158	94	86	87	(B)	41	27	54	32
New Jersey	4,118	702	913	583	503	640	(B)	190	117	187	271
New Mexico	840	110	178	149	94	110	13	62	32	39	53
New York	8,726	1,217	1,986	1,616	954	1,239	32	450	263	493	476
North Carolina	3,957	532	788	583	438	503	44	274	145	387	261
North Dakota	333	54	61	59	38	45	7	18	13	16	22
Ohio	5,552	758	1,052	970	650	791	(B)	271	198	468	381
Oklahoma	1,600	241	305	245	170	229	(B)	106	77	111	98
Oregon	1,707	237	318	287	214	245	35	83	56	120	113
Pennsylvania	5,826	824	1,267	863	630	876	(B)	283	215	460	380
Rhode Island	543	69	112	103	61	75	(B)	26	16	48	29
South Carolina	1,866	244	318	313	235	248	(B)	106	95	174	123
South Dakota	410	68	70	69	47	56	(B)	23	14	33	21
Tennessee	2,740	397	492	404	325	392	(B)	161	102	239	211
Texas	10,173	1,368	1,925	1,660	1,219	1,462	101	685	412	702	639
Utah	1,118	161	214	159	140	177	(B)	65	43	77	74
Vermont	335	53	78	53	33	41	(B)	23	14	23	14
Virginia	3,620	609	856	520	410	475	(B)	214	140	199	182
Washington	2,903	448	631	453	323	400	40	169	109	165	164
West Virginia	739	78	140	128	86	106	(B)	54	38	46	60
Wisconsin	2,905	422	525	451	306	394	(B)	159	111	313	195
Wyoming	266	39	44	40	29	35	(B)	26	15	12	23

B Base figure too small to meet statistical standards for reliability.

[1]The sum of the states does not equal the U.S. total due to independent population controls.

Survey, Census, or Data Collection Method: Based on the Current Population Survey; for information, see Appendix B, Limitations of the Data and Methodology, and the following document at <http://www.census.gov/prod/2002pubs/tp63rv.pdf>.

Source: U.S. Bureau of Labor Statistics, Local Area Unemployment Statistics, *Geographic Profile of Employment and Unemployment, 2003* (published August 2005). See Internet site <http://www.bls.gov/gps/>.

Table A-31. States — **Private Industry Employment and Pay**

Geographic area	Employment Total (1,000)				Employment Percent change		Average annual pay Total (dol.)				Rank		Average annual pay Percent change	
	2003	2002	2001	2000	2002–2003	2000–2003	2003	2002	2001	2000	2003	2000	2002–2003	2000–2003
United States ...	107,066	107,577	109,305	110,015	−0.48	−2.68	37,508	36,539	36,157	35,337	(X)	(X)	2.65	6.14
Alabama	1,483	1,492	1,519	1,542	−0.63	−3.80	31,567	30,523	29,532	28,491	34	35	3.42	10.80
Alaska	216	212	210	207	1.76	4.26	36,504	35,950	35,034	33,500	17	18	1.54	8.97
Arizona	1,903	1,877	1,892	1,904	1.40	−0.05	34,602	33,640	33,165	32,432	21	20	2.86	6.69
Arkansas	931	936	946	952	−0.61	−2.26	28,494	27,710	26,935	26,032	44	46	2.83	9.46
California	12,447	12,462	12,668	12,632	−0.12	−1.47	41,864	40,777	40,937	41,175	5	5	2.67	1.67
Colorado	1,777	1,814	1,873	1,868	−2.07	−4.86	38,891	37,988	38,214	37,553	10	7	2.38	3.56
Connecticut	1,390	1,409	1,430	1,461	−1.32	−4.81	48,935	47,389	47,733	46,068	1	2	3.26	6.22
Delaware	348	348	353	353	−0.05	−1.62	40,884	39,494	38,680	36,607	6	10	3.52	11.68
District of Columbia	421	420	417	419	0.22	0.53	56,075	54,034	52,903	49,828	(X)	(X)	3.78	12.54
Florida	6,213	6,150	6,154	6,084	1.03	2.12	32,915	31,816	31,038	30,031	29	29	3.45	9.60
Georgia	3,157	3,189	3,268	3,292	−1.01	−4.10	36,863	36,007	35,574	34,686	16	16	2.38	6.28
Hawaii............	454	445	446	443	2.15	2.40	31,974	30,947	29,816	29,179	30	31	3.32	9.58
Idaho............	468	466	467	463	0.58	1.21	28,272	27,758	27,478	27,623	46	38	1.85	2.35
Illinois	4,887	4,952	5,077	5,139	−1.31	−4.91	40,574	39,739	39,235	38,246	7	6	2.10	6.09
Indiana	2,427	2,444	2,486	2,553	−0.68	−4.92	33,395	32,575	31,759	31,022	26	25	2.52	7.65
Iowa	1,178	1,186	1,202	1,219	−0.69	−3.43	30,220	29,158	28,371	27,501	39	39	3.64	9.89
Kansas	1,049	1,064	1,083	1,083	−1.44	−3.16	31,794	31,061	30,468	29,646	31	30	2.36	7.25
Kentucky	1,423	1,426	1,448	1,479	−0.19	−3.76	31,658	30,727	29,934	28,773	32	33	3.03	10.03
Louisiana	1,493	1,489	1,514	1,515	0.30	−1.45	30,615	30,024	29,206	28,013	35	36	1.97	9.29
Maine	492	493	496	496	−0.08	−0.74	30,229	29,239	28,397	27,280	38	41	3.39	10.81
Maryland	1,984	1,977	1,980	1,972	0.33	0.58	39,155	37,873	37,047	35,407	9	13	3.38	10.59
Massachusetts	2,739	2,790	2,862	2,866	−1.83	−4.44	46,569	45,305	45,561	45,049	3	3	2.79	3.37
Michigan	3,680	3,746	3,833	3,959	−1.76	−7.04	39,484	38,162	37,556	37,227	8	9	3.46	6.06
Minnesota	2,206	2,214	2,241	2,260	−0.34	−2.38	38,693	37,519	36,778	35,513	11	12	3.13	8.95
Mississippi	864	874	884	916	−1.19	−5.65	27,138	26,313	25,597	24,833	48	47	3.14	9.28
Missouri..........	2,201	2,215	2,242	2,270	−0.64	−3.07	33,944	33,264	32,630	31,598	23	22	2.04	7.42
Montana	314	310	307	306	1.24	2.53	25,659	24,813	24,122	23,184	50	50	3.41	10.68
Nebraska..........	724	724	735	737	0.08	−1.70	29,924	29,054	28,034	27,471	40	40	2.99	8.93
Nevada	949	918	921	902	3.47	5.27	34,320	33,035	32,197	31,387	22	23	3.89	9.34
New Hampshire.......	520	521	531	530	−0.19	−1.74	37,685	36,594	35,955	35,250	14	14	2.98	6.91
New Jersey	3,262	3,276	3,306	3,320	−0.41	−1.76	45,981	44,872	44,151	43,646	4	4	2.47	5.35
New Mexico	571	566	562	564	0.91	1.19	28,941	28,187	27,683	26,518	43	43	2.67	9.14
New York	6,804	6,849	7,020	7,073	−0.66	−3.81	47,902	47,031	47,659	46,224	2	1	1.85	3.63
North Carolina.......	3,093	3,133	3,193	3,260	−1.25	−5.10	33,313	32,490	31,910	30,998	27	26	2.53	7.47
North Dakota	252	250	251	254	0.74	−0.95	27,197	26,120	25,324	24,319	47	48	4.12	11.83
Ohio	4,524	4,576	4,686	4,775	−1.14	−5.26	34,607	33,701	32,885	32,191	20	21	2.69	7.51
Oklahoma	1,121	1,145	1,171	1,173	−2.13	−4.49	29,264	28,160	27,615	26,617	41	42	3.92	9.94
Oregon	1,315	1,320	1,343	1,363	−0.40	−3.55	33,819	33,066	32,751	32,488	24	19	2.28	4.10
Pennsylvania	4,754	4,791	4,849	4,860	−0.78	−2.19	36,483	35,277	34,544	33,629	18	17	3.42	8.49
Rhode Island	408	404	405	405	0.93	0.74	34,865	33,240	32,179	31,206	19	24	4.89	11.73
South Carolina	1,454	1,455	1,477	1,507	−0.02	−3.50	30,241	29,485	28,796	27,776	37	37	2.56	8.87
South Dakota	296	295	297	305	0.24	−3.18	26,751	25,915	25,139	24,291	49	49	3.23	10.13
Tennessee	2,205	2,209	2,242	2,288	−0.20	−3.65	33,495	32,471	31,457	30,527	25	27	3.15	9.72
Texas	7,588	7,662	7,789	7,748	−0.97	−2.07	37,442	36,766	36,794	35,681	15	11	1.84	4.94
Utah	857	858	872	870	−0.10	−1.50	30,522	30,011	29,702	28,925	36	32	1.70	5.52
Vermont..........	245	247	250	249	−0.78	−1.81	31,572	30,613	29,918	28,691	33	34	3.13	10.04
Virginia	2,788	2,786	2,826	2,823	0.08	−1.23	38,142	36,750	36,525	34,967	13	15	3.79	9.08
Washington	2,158	2,153	2,209	2,248	0.21	−3.99	38,673	37,988	37,397	37,249	12	8	1.80	3.82
West Virginia	542	548	552	551	−0.94	−1.64	28,359	27,819	27,322	26,292	45	45	1.94	7.86
Wisconsin..........	2,307	2,310	2,341	2,379	−0.13	−3.00	32,998	32,118	31,180	30,304	28	28	2.74	8.89
Wyoming	183	182	181	176	0.76	4.21	29,148	28,293	27,630	26,502	42	44	3.02	9.98

X Not applicable.

Survey, Census, or Data Collection Method: Based on the Quarterly Census of Employment and Wages (QCEW) program (ES-202). For information, see Internet site <http://www.bls.gov/cew/cewbultn03.htm>.

Source: U.S. Bureau of Labor Statistics, *Employment and Wages, Annual Averages*, annual, 2003 edition. See Internet sites <http://www.bls.gov/cew/cewbultn03.htm> and <http://www.bls.gov/cew/home.htm> for prior years.

Geographic area	Private industry employment, 2003 (1,000)															Government employment, 2003 (1,000)
	Total[1]	Construction	Manufacturing	Wholesale trade	Retail trade	Transportation and warehousing	Information	Finance and insurance	Real estate and rental and leasing	Professional and technical services	Management of companies and enterprises	Educational services	Health care and social assistance	Arts, entertainment, and recreation	Accommodation and food services	
United States . . .	107,066	6,672	14,460	5,589	14,931	3,946	3,181	5,782	2,045	6,639	1,660	2,016	13,722	1,817	10,345	20,730
Alabama	1,483	100	294	77	229	48	32	71	24	86	10	16	169	15	140	341
Alaska	216	17	12	6	34	19	7	8	5	11	1	2	31	4	26	76
Arizona	1,903	176	176	93	277	63	50	115	43	104	21	28	212	29	204	369
Arkansas	931	51	206	45	129	55	20	36	13	31	24	8	126	9	79	185
California	12,447	785	1,532	646	1,589	406	472	611	273	910	256	228	1,270	235	1,161	2,361
Colorado	1,777	150	156	92	240	61	85	104	46	139	20	22	188	40	205	341
Connecticut	1,390	62	199	65	192	38	40	123	20	88	28	44	215	24	101	235
Delaware	348	24	36	14	52	9	7	39	6	26	11	3	43	9	30	55
District of Columbia . . .	421	13	3	4	17	3	25	17	10	91	2	32	51	6	44	230
Florida	6,213	445	387	313	922	196	172	330	154	386	65	86	770	157	651	1,035
Georgia	3,157	196	450	205	445	147	123	154	58	194	52	51	327	37	312	626
Hawaii	454	28	15	17	65	24	11	16	12	22	7	12	52	11	88	115
Idaho	468	37	62	24	73	15	9	18	7	29	7	4	55	8	47	107
Illinois	4,887	273	716	301	626	211	135	312	84	331	76	105	604	81	417	811
Indiana	2,427	145	572	118	335	99	41	104	35	86	27	37	299	45	226	395
Iowa	1,178	65	220	65	181	45	34	80	15	37	9	22	156	20	105	227
Kansas	1,049	63	172	59	151	40	47	55	15	52	10	10	144	13	96	236
Kentucky	1,423	83	266	73	211	76	30	64	20	57	14	14	195	18	138	291
Louisiana	1,493	119	156	76	224	68	29	64	34	70	22	21	206	37	162	362
Maine	492	31	64	21	86	14	11	27	7	22	6	9	89	8	50	99
Maryland	1,984	167	148	91	297	61	50	109	47	202	9	50	276	34	185	450
Massachusetts	2,739	137	326	135	355	71	91	176	44	219	65	116	425	45	242	402
Michigan	3,680	189	717	172	517	100	70	158	56	249	68	52	474	62	335	641
Minnesota	2,206	125	345	129	301	75	60	137	37	118	60	34	317	36	195	370
Mississippi	864	50	179	35	139	36	15	33	12	29	10	8	101	13	110	233
Missouri	2,201	138	311	118	313	88	68	117	40	113	67	40	292	43	220	415
Montana	314	23	19	15	54	10	8	15	5	16	1	4	49	9	43	79
Nebraska	724	46	102	41	108	34	21	50	10	34	14	9	96	11	67	151
Nevada	949	100	44	34	120	36	16	36	22	43	8	4	71	28	276	131
New Hampshire	520	29	80	27	96	13	12	27	8	25	6	16	71	11	50	84
New Jersey	3,262	159	347	231	465	154	102	203	57	257	62	61	430	47	271	588
New Mexico	571	47	36	22	91	17	16	23	10	41	5	6	81	8	74	175
New York	6,804	317	611	351	852	215	275	514	179	506	120	257	1,134	125	517	1,421
North Carolina	3,093	211	601	163	432	109	75	138	47	146	61	46	364	46	292	626
North Dakota	252	16	23	18	41	8	8	15	3	9	3	1	44	3	27	63
Ohio	4,524	230	845	235	628	152	97	232	70	226	88	79	638	68	419	757
Oklahoma	1,121	63	143	55	170	41	32	55	23	57	12	13	157	13	113	291
Oregon	1,315	77	194	75	184	48	34	59	27	61	25	20	162	20	131	249
Pennsylvania	4,754	246	716	227	664	186	123	270	68	277	64	160	764	76	392	717
Rhode Island	408	21	58	16	53	9	11	25	6	19	8	16	70	7	42	65
South Carolina	1,454	112	276	63	224	47	27	64	25	62	10	17	140	25	169	313
South Dakota	296	19	38	17	48	9	7	24	3	8	3	3	49	6	34	69
Tennessee	2,205	115	411	127	313	131	50	102	35	98	24	35	264	28	219	394
Texas	7,588	552	902	458	1,082	319	239	406	169	451	41	87	934	96	763	1,621
Utah	857	68	111	40	130	38	29	50	15	50	19	15	90	16	84	185
Vermont	245	15	37	10	40	7	6	10	3	12	(Z)	9	40	4	29	50
Virginia	2,788	218	305	113	404	101	101	129	56	290	68	45	297	43	266	623
Washington	2,158	144	262	112	299	77	91	102	47	129	32	27	265	42	203	495
West Virginia	542	33	65	23	88	16	13	22	7	23	3	5	98	9	57	136
Wisconsin	2,307	124	505	113	319	91	50	126	27	89	39	26	312	34	212	381
Wyoming	183	20	9	7	30	7	4	7	3	7	1	1	19	3	28	58

See footnotes at end of table.

Geographic area	Private industry average annual pay, 2003 (dol.)															Government average annual pay, 2003 (dol.)
	Total[1]	Construction	Manufacturing	Wholesale trade	Retail trade	Transportation and warehousing	Information	Finance and insurance	Real estate and rental and leasing	Professional and technical services	Management of companies and enterprises	Educational services	Health care and social assistance	Arts, entertainment, and recreation	Accommodation and food services	
United States . . .	**37,508**	**39,509**	**45,916**	**50,835**	**23,804**	**37,436**	**58,002**	**64,956**	**35,054**	**59,877**	**72,270**	**34,418**	**35,167**	**27,016**	**14,228**	**39,094**
Alabama	31,567	32,185	37,700	42,690	21,111	32,632	42,921	46,125	27,546	51,238	56,525	25,622	33,409	15,416	11,238	35,148
Alaska	36,504	52,526	34,574	41,679	25,444	44,987	44,923	45,317	27,567	46,282	60,228	27,256	34,964	15,135	16,769	41,483
Arizona	34,602	34,941	50,578	50,072	25,594	37,269	43,672	50,386	33,391	50,011	59,269	31,152	37,562	28,859	14,342	37,393
Arkansas	28,494	29,684	31,886	40,502	18,991	32,386	36,517	39,716	22,910	40,511	61,459	24,153	30,131	13,400	10,424	30,896
California	41,864	42,518	53,712	52,049	28,258	39,421	73,737	73,848	39,997	67,589	65,006	34,202	39,619	41,695	15,775	46,434
Colorado	38,891	39,315	50,855	53,806	24,562	37,822	66,529	58,284	35,604	61,505	74,427	30,015	36,601	28,474	14,283	39,211
Connecticut	48,935	48,046	58,051	66,464	27,873	36,906	57,480	104,235	42,956	70,820	105,496	43,772	38,981	23,583	16,031	44,741
Delaware	40,884	38,909	50,147	58,380	23,055	32,307	51,284	67,140	33,694	66,791	68,251	31,190	39,265	20,695	14,408	41,398
District of Columbia	56,075	46,578	65,153	72,135	26,720	40,502	78,914	99,036	51,245	86,453	130,233	45,060	44,573	42,936	23,542	68,368
Florida	32,915	35,266	40,926	47,951	23,967	35,560	47,447	53,572	33,595	50,377	65,959	29,733	36,167	28,020	15,275	37,318
Georgia	36,863	36,904	39,546	53,672	23,597	43,568	59,681	58,097	37,176	57,166	65,057	35,374	36,097	28,707	13,592	35,430
Hawaii	31,974	49,555	31,441	40,473	23,994	36,279	45,433	51,035	34,404	49,554	60,718	29,154	36,703	20,434	21,518	40,695
Idaho	28,272	30,658	39,511	35,465	21,355	27,972	34,433	39,417	21,816	43,547	61,043	29,137	28,851	14,702	10,544	30,447
Illinois	40,574	49,150	46,257	54,786	23,772	39,218	54,491	69,304	41,246	65,811	88,417	36,143	35,650	25,715	13,857	40,336
Indiana	33,395	38,494	45,452	44,122	20,921	34,118	40,479	45,527	27,744	43,940	61,543	27,205	33,429	24,933	11,264	33,283
Iowa	30,220	35,521	39,864	39,352	19,937	32,517	36,681	45,647	27,744	40,305	53,662	25,109	29,885	16,022	10,079	33,242
Kansas	31,794	34,219	41,279	43,505	20,347	32,903	50,675	45,631	26,840	42,814	53,534	26,415	30,411	13,981	11,062	30,129
Kentucky	31,658	34,130	41,391	42,457	20,325	40,738	35,729	43,953	25,792	43,458	70,826	24,745	32,600	18,280	11,953	32,820
Louisiana	30,615	33,115	45,564	39,881	20,136	37,532	36,617	38,018	30,421	43,180	47,734	28,313	29,223	24,450	12,300	31,472
Maine	30,229	33,594	40,237	42,612	21,343	30,451	38,408	45,438	26,973	43,019	52,413	31,230	31,270	16,866	13,123	33,336
Maryland	39,155	42,272	50,326	54,870	25,434	36,596	57,915	63,918	39,677	61,983	65,159	37,943	37,294	22,529	16,047	47,429
Massachusetts	46,569	51,501	58,363	64,353	26,086	36,250	68,222	87,960	44,808	74,863	67,844	44,607	39,690	28,973	16,688	44,642
Michigan	39,484	43,128	55,473	53,535	22,980	42,897	49,168	51,486	29,360	62,909	82,592	28,014	35,935	23,737	11,944	39,139
Minnesota	38,693	45,334	46,591	54,560	22,135	42,045	49,511	64,154	34,787	58,546	79,149	30,130	35,497	23,603	12,284	38,111
Mississippi	27,138	29,551	31,988	37,869	19,152	31,853	35,038	37,842	21,517	40,020	51,721	23,675	31,175	18,951	13,902	29,273
Missouri	33,944	39,371	41,388	45,904	21,406	35,767	46,654	47,611	28,447	53,342	64,442	27,295	32,814	28,149	12,188	32,963
Montana	25,659	31,728	34,606	34,186	20,057	28,522	33,362	37,909	20,064	36,817	37,144	19,948	29,250	13,889	10,662	31,853
Nebraska	29,924	33,498	34,696	38,716	19,539	33,317	43,590	42,941	25,058	44,905	56,334	22,252	31,973	13,124	10,402	32,581
Nevada	34,320	41,722	41,456	47,875	26,045	29,870	46,018	50,670	31,718	56,749	123,478	29,765	40,691	24,334	25,448	42,627
New Hampshire	37,685	42,061	48,237	60,426	25,053	31,243	56,188	60,463	36,518	57,697	71,839	36,189	36,288	17,211	14,754	35,063
New Jersey	45,981	50,350	56,131	64,298	28,136	39,910	68,855	78,260	43,086	69,479	95,015	40,244	39,674	27,433	18,393	48,401
New Mexico	28,941	30,541	39,507	38,231	21,674	31,846	38,600	39,174	25,859	52,979	42,440	24,971	35,089	16,741	11,737	34,313
New York	47,902	48,702	48,342	57,796	25,687	37,313	70,317	124,633	42,907	70,153	107,642	36,820	35,983	37,834	17,788	44,108
North Carolina	33,313	32,646	39,105	46,646	21,946	35,439	48,545	58,019	29,650	49,821	68,260	33,115	32,803	23,875	12,193	34,614
North Dakota	27,197	32,547	34,085	36,126	19,268	30,064	37,228	36,582	19,951	35,969	46,909	20,809	29,457	11,579	9,633	29,360
Ohio	34,607	38,369	45,908	47,284	22,503	35,828	46,811	49,505	29,343	49,402	69,216	27,904	33,446	22,647	11,492	38,417
Oklahoma	29,264	30,570	37,680	38,823	20,207	36,619	38,600	37,162	28,117	41,318	52,409	26,035	29,144	14,960	10,725	31,374
Oregon	33,819	38,402	45,056	50,090	23,321	33,551	50,372	51,289	26,642	48,204	61,660	25,257	34,683	20,443	13,260	37,786
Pennsylvania	36,483	41,869	44,346	50,018	22,522	34,465	51,152	56,243	35,519	58,664	67,745	38,131	34,503	23,111	12,756	40,393
Rhode Island	34,865	43,480	39,152	49,771	23,845	30,815	52,781	53,872	33,275	52,718	83,882	37,097	33,878	20,563	14,108	46,165
South Carolina	30,241	32,454	39,035	42,825	21,695	32,560	39,742	42,092	28,021	45,901	54,050	25,594	33,008	15,563	12,411	33,118
South Dakota	26,751	30,188	32,080	35,698	19,402	28,918	33,094	35,712	20,198	35,707	59,693	23,939	31,466	13,095	10,143	29,191
Tennessee	33,495	35,239	40,159	44,859	23,107	39,116	41,394	53,071	31,519	47,763	51,655	36,599	35,505	30,034	13,498	34,062
Texas	37,442	37,301	48,771	53,164	24,453	41,704	52,996	54,473	35,473	60,697	64,151	33,153	33,155	24,465	13,865	34,751
Utah	30,522	30,526	38,015	42,805	21,373	36,144	40,869	43,219	26,353	47,455	47,745	33,348	30,365	18,175	11,533	33,810
Vermont	31,572	33,416	44,256	44,233	22,395	31,639	37,230	49,853	27,530	47,283	59,466	31,056	30,314	16,449	15,062	34,608
Virginia	38,142	36,268	40,655	52,721	22,624	35,844	67,400	61,366	34,958	66,598	72,245	31,019	34,947	19,624	13,585	40,568
Washington	38,673	39,477	50,537	49,073	26,042	40,379	104,387	57,963	29,571	56,908	69,785	27,822	33,409	22,592	14,330	40,537
West Virginia	28,359	30,911	40,919	38,892	18,913	34,030	36,864	32,958	23,010	36,266	44,937	23,894	29,656	16,871	11,335	32,984
Wisconsin	32,998	40,248	42,048	44,662	20,260	32,369	39,661	46,484	26,810	47,631	68,231	33,244	34,252	20,156	10,210	36,016
Wyoming	29,148	32,986	37,501	38,721	19,892	32,155	28,988	37,394	24,913	36,325	73,646	21,614	29,738	14,715	11,910	32,363

Z Fewer than 500.

[1]Includes data for industries not shown and unclassified establishments.

Survey, Census, or Data Collection Method: Based on the Quarterly Census of Employment and Wages (QCEW) program (ES-202); for information, see Internet site <http://www.bls.gov/cew/cewbultn03.htm>.

Source: U.S. Bureau of Labor Statistics, *Employment and Wages, Annual Averages, 2003,* annual. See Internet site <http://www.bls.gov/cew/cewbultn03.htm>.

Table A-33. States — **Union Membership**

Geographic area	Union members (1,000)			Workers covered by union (1,000)			Percent of workers								
							Union members			Covered by union			Private sector union members		
	2004	2000	1990	2004	2000	1990	2004	2000	1990	2004	2000	1990	2004	2000	1990
United States . . .	**15,471.6**	**16,258.2**	**16,739.8**	**17,087.3**	**17,944.1**	**19,057.8**	**12.5**	**13.5**	**16.1**	**13.8**	**14.9**	**18.3**	**7.9**	**9.0**	**11.9**
Alabama[1]	181.3	180.8	194.6	213.1	197.6	230.0	9.7	9.6	12.3	11.5	10.5	14.5	5.7	5.8	10.4
Alaska	53.9	56.8	46.9	60.0	64.3	52.6	20.1	21.9	23.1	22.4	24.8	25.9	10.9	12.8	14.0
Arizona[1]	145.3	129.7	111.6	183.2	147.8	135.5	6.3	6.4	7.8	7.9	7.3	9.5	3.9	4.2	4.9
Arkansas[1]	50.9	61.5	91.4	65.3	70.9	107.6	4.8	5.8	10.3	6.2	6.7	12.2	3.2	4.0	8.7
California	2,384.7	2,295.1	2,219.4	2,587.6	2,546.0	2,569.1	16.5	16.0	18.4	18.0	17.7	21.3	9.4	9.7	13.0
Colorado	172.0	173.2	153.6	191.3	193.0	176.6	8.4	9.0	10.5	9.3	10.0	12.0	5.2	6.0	7.3
Connecticut	234.7	245.8	272.0	255.8	262.5	303.3	15.3	16.3	17.7	16.6	17.4	19.8	7.3	9.4	11.7
Delaware	46.1	46.9	46.8	49.2	51.7	52.7	12.4	13.3	14.9	13.2	14.6	16.8	7.7	8.9	11.3
District of Columbia	32.7	35.9	41.4	37.5	40.2	50.7	12.7	14.7	16.1	14.5	16.5	19.7	8.8	9.5	11.6
Florida[1]	414.2	433.6	416.9	532.9	553.6	545.7	6.0	6.8	8.1	7.7	8.7	10.5	2.8	3.3	4.3
Georgia[1]	242.2	228.1	186.9	282.3	267.0	230.7	6.4	6.3	6.9	7.5	7.4	8.5	4.3	4.6	5.7
Hawaii	126.4	123.5	130.8	132.2	129.1	141.4	23.7	24.8	29.1	24.8	26.0	31.5	16.2	14.4	21.4
Idaho[1]	32.8	40.7	37.0	44.4	48.0	43.0	5.8	7.6	9.4	7.9	9.0	11.0	3.7	5.5	7.3
Illinois	908.3	1,046.3	1,059.1	970.6	1,100.6	1,155.6	16.8	18.6	20.8	17.9	19.5	22.7	12.1	14.1	16.5
Indiana	310.7	418.4	480.0	337.5	460.6	516.2	11.4	15.6	19.9	12.4	17.1	21.4	9.0	13.1	18.6
Iowa[1]	141.0	181.8	183.6	170.7	215.1	238.6	10.5	13.6	15.5	12.7	16.1	20.1	7.2	10.5	11.6
Kansas[1]	103.0	108.5	119.0	131.7	134.5	154.6	8.4	9.0	11.3	10.8	11.2	14.7	6.1	8.0	9.4
Kentucky	163.7	208.0	206.4	197.2	234.5	223.6	9.6	12.0	14.3	11.6	13.6	15.5	7.5	10.1	12.5
Louisiana[1]	129.3	121.9	116.1	157.2	154.8	141.4	7.6	7.1	7.7	9.3	9.0	9.4	4.8	5.5	5.8
Maine	63.7	78.1	88.5	74.4	92.2	107.5	11.3	14.0	17.5	13.2	16.6	21.2	5.9	8.0	9.7
Maryland	272.0	353.3	319.9	312.9	405.5	374.2	10.9	14.6	14.5	12.5	16.7	17.0	6.0	7.8	10.5
Massachusetts	393.3	406.3	471.7	429.9	444.9	505.1	13.5	14.3	17.6	14.7	15.7	18.8	7.7	7.9	10.7
Michigan	929.8	938.3	974.0	965.6	985.3	1,038.8	21.6	20.8	25.4	22.4	21.8	27.1	15.9	15.7	20.2
Minnesota	424.2	419.0	395.7	443.4	434.3	429.7	17.5	18.2	20.3	18.3	18.8	22.0	11.1	12.3	14.0
Mississippi[1]	52.9	67.7	75.7	70.1	104.3	92.0	4.8	6.0	7.9	6.3	9.3	9.6	4.0	5.4	7.5
Missouri	314.8	337.9	299.2	356.5	365.3	342.8	12.4	13.2	13.7	14.0	14.2	15.7	10.9	12.1	13.1
Montana	42.7	51.2	54.5	46.1	57.8	61.7	11.7	13.9	18.1	12.6	15.7	20.5	5.5	8.2	12.4
Nebraska[1]	69.2	64.9	74.7	83.3	89.4	104.1	8.3	8.4	11.0	10.0	11.5	15.3	5.0	4.6	5.2
Nevada[1]	126.0	150.9	85.9	143.9	165.3	96.9	12.5	17.1	16.3	14.3	18.8	18.4	10.0	13.8	13.2
New Hampshire	60.9	59.8	59.6	68.3	66.7	67.4	9.9	10.4	11.5	11.0	11.6	13.0	4.8	6.3	6.6
New Jersey	744.8	762.0	827.2	813.5	800.7	902.8	19.8	20.8	24.1	21.6	21.8	26.3	11.6	13.1	17.3
New Mexico	49.0	56.2	38.4	65.3	69.7	52.2	6.7	8.1	7.0	8.9	10.1	9.5	3.4	5.5	6.7
New York	1,995.8	1,958.0	2,083.7	2,084.6	2,036.4	2,270.2	25.3	25.5	28.2	26.4	26.5	30.7	15.1	15.3	18.2
North Carolina[1]	97.0	124.1	150.6	126.5	148.4	187.2	2.7	3.6	5.2	3.6	4.4	6.5	1.6	2.4	3.8
North Dakota[1]	22.4	17.6	29.6	26.2	21.1	37.8	7.7	6.5	12.0	9.0	7.8	15.3	4.1	3.7	7.4
Ohio	758.6	879.0	968.5	820.3	955.1	1,076.7	15.2	17.3	21.0	16.4	18.8	23.3	10.5	12.3	17.6
Oklahoma[2]	86.2	93.8	130.3	100.2	108.0	158.7	6.1	6.8	10.6	7.1	7.8	12.9	3.5	4.4	7.1
Oregon	223.5	234.4	237.3	243.2	251.0	273.4	15.2	16.1	20.4	16.5	17.2	23.4	8.1	9.8	13.5
Pennsylvania	792.7	869.6	1,023.0	841.7	925.7	1,136.9	15.0	16.9	20.4	15.9	18.0	22.7	9.7	11.2	15.6
Rhode Island	79.4	79.6	78.6	82.6	82.5	84.6	16.3	18.2	18.2	17.0	18.8	19.6	8.8	9.9	10.8
South Carolina[1]	53.5	70.3	67.3	74.3	88.8	89.5	3.0	4.0	4.6	4.2	5.1	6.1	2.6	2.8	3.7
South Dakota[1]	20.8	18.2	22.3	26.8	22.2	30.2	6.0	5.5	8.4	7.7	6.7	11.3	2.9	2.5	4.6
Tennessee[1]	164.2	211.5	235.5	191.0	238.8	283.2	6.7	8.9	11.7	7.7	10.0	14.1	4.9	6.7	9.8
Texas[1]	457.3	505.4	446.9	572.8	645.1	589.8	5.0	5.8	6.4	6.3	7.4	8.4	2.7	3.8	4.7
Utah[1]	57.5	69.3	61.5	66.6	84.9	85.3	5.8	7.3	9.4	6.7	9.0	13.0	2.9	4.5	5.3
Vermont	28.7	28.2	29.9	33.3	33.9	35.9	9.8	10.3	12.6	11.4	12.4	15.2	4.2	5.1	6.5
Virginia[1]	176.1	179.1	230.4	217.8	227.0	298.6	5.3	5.6	8.4	6.6	7.1	10.9	3.4	3.9	6.3
Washington	509.8	470.8	466.4	535.7	516.1	531.0	19.3	18.2	22.8	20.3	19.9	26.0	13.2	11.8	16.9
West Virginia	99.4	102.9	121.8	109.6	111.4	138.0	14.2	14.3	19.3	15.7	15.5	21.9	10.5	12.4	18.7
Wisconsin	414.3	446.0	451.2	439.1	473.1	474.0	16.0	17.6	20.6	16.9	18.7	21.6	10.4	11.7	15.1
Wyoming[1]	17.8	17.9	26.5	21.9	21.6	33.1	8.0	8.3	13.5	9.8	10.0	16.8	5.3	5.5	8.8

[1]Right-to-work state.
[2]Passed right-to-work law in 2001.

Survey, Census, or Data Collection Method: Based on the Current Population Survey; for information, see Appendix B, Limitations of the Data and Methodology, and Internet sites
<http://www.bna.com/bnaplus/labor/laborrpts.html> and <http://www.unionstats.com>.

Source: The Bureau of National Affairs, Inc., Washington, DC, Union Membership and Earnings Data Book: Compilations from the Current Population Survey, 2004 and prior annual editions (copyright by BNA PLUS); authored by Barry Hirsch of Trinity University, San Antonio, TX, and David Macpherson of Florida State University. See Internet sites
<http://www.bna.com/bnaplus/labor/laborrpts.html> and <http://www.unionstats.com>.

Table A-34. States — Median Income of Households in Constant (2003) Dollars and Distribution by Income Level

Geographic area	Median household income in (2003) dollars				Total number of house-holds, 2003 (1,000)	Percent of households by income level, 2003									
	2003	2002	2001	2000		Under $10,000	$10,000– $14,999	$15,000– $24,999	$25,000– $34,999	$35,000– $49,999	$50,000– $74,999	$75,000– $99,999	$100,000– $149,999	$150,000– $199,999	$200,000 and over
United States ...	43,564	44,049	43,937	44,270	108,420	9.01	6.40	12.69	12.17	15.76	19.10	10.87	8.95	2.68	2.37
Alabama	35,158	35,937	34,919	35,576	1,743	13.98	8.22	14.39	13.19	16.76	16.11	8.76	5.96	1.35	1.28
Alaska	52,499	57,567	58,292	56,586	229	4.29	6.03	9.78	11.93	15.22	21.21	14.07	12.24	3.21	2.02
Arizona	40,762	41,907	42,190	41,171	2,049	8.84	6.66	13.64	13.73	16.84	18.40	9.90	7.58	2.40	2.02
Arkansas	34,246	35,218	34,094	35,312	1,076	11.49	8.36	15.27	15.95	16.76	17.05	7.60	5.37	1.17	0.99
California	50,220	50,574	50,009	49,699	11,857	7.47	5.26	11.56	10.95	14.52	18.92	11.80	11.80	4.09	3.63
Colorado	50,538	49,017	49,237	49,445	1,821	7.18	5.15	10.98	11.46	14.56	21.73	12.18	10.69	3.08	2.99
Connecticut	56,803	57,539	58,427	57,693	1,323	6.13	5.21	9.24	9.72	13.45	19.63	14.11	12.52	4.69	5.31
Delaware	50,583	50,883	50,979	50,983	304	5.45	5.36	11.43	10.86	16.22	20.56	13.28	11.80	3.13	1.91
District of Columbia	42,118	44,668	42,264	43,534	247	14.94	5.95	10.79	10.72	13.59	16.45	8.83	9.61	4.37	4.75
Florida	39,871	40,050	39,561	40,626	6,638	9.10	7.29	14.40	13.06	16.95	17.92	9.88	7.19	2.19	2.01
Georgia	42,742	42,725	43,932	44,048	3,153	9.71	6.15	12.49	12.79	15.97	19.25	10.59	8.49	2.37	2.21
Hawaii	50,787	51,400	51,897	54,904	419	8.23	4.51	9.65	11.16	15.46	20.29	13.01	11.56	3.56	2.58
Idaho..........	39,492	38,034	38,462	40,093	503	7.89	6.44	15.76	14.95	16.41	19.60	10.33	6.08	1.26	1.28
Illinois	47,977	47,458	47,853	48,737	4,625	8.08	5.76	11.29	11.16	15.46	20.10	11.97	10.02	3.30	2.87
Indiana	42,067	42,573	43,349	43,496	2,351	8.15	6.38	13.41	13.53	16.70	21.08	10.82	6.67	1.76	1.51
Iowa	40,526	40,020	40,989	40,767	1,158	8.12	7.22	13.44	13.89	17.60	20.51	9.79	6.61	1.55	1.28
Kansas	41,075	40,789	40,333	42,970	1,059	8.75	6.63	14.14	13.33	16.45	20.00	9.71	7.38	2.07	1.56
Kentucky	34,368	35,650	34,831	35,029	1,607	13.07	8.99	14.55	14.15	15.82	17.63	8.13	5.41	1.11	1.15
Louisiana	34,141	34,092	34,763	32,981	1,673	14.77	9.21	15.50	11.27	14.86	16.56	9.04	6.01	1.50	1.28
Maine	39,838	40,676	39,011	38,980	535	8.97	6.50	14.16	14.10	18.66	19.87	9.35	6.18	0.98	1.24
Maryland	57,218	56,858	55,761	55,796	2,048	6.30	4.30	8.98	9.70	14.17	19.47	13.99	14.51	4.78	3.78
Massachusetts	53,610	56,367	54,718	53,204	2,436	8.48	5.95	9.60	9.60	12.77	18.63	13.76	13.05	4.40	3.78
Michigan	44,407	44,723	46,036	46,305	3,884	8.32	6.00	12.31	12.42	16.27	19.79	11.47	9.21	2.40	1.81
Minnesota	50,100	50,320	51,560	50,986	2,012	6.54	5.24	10.62	11.08	16.41	22.30	12.65	9.99	2.94	2.23
Mississippi	32,466	32,566	33,456	34,947	1,056	14.50	9.34	15.53	13.68	16.53	15.89	7.38	4.85	0.98	1.31
Missouri..........	40,725	40,967	40,593	39,661	2,285	9.17	6.64	13.48	13.32	17.45	20.13	9.86	7.05	1.51	1.40
Montana	35,399	35,980	34,052	35,438	366	9.26	9.49	16.10	14.60	18.26	17.70	7.94	4.53	1.06	1.05
Nebraska	41,406	40,725	41,178	39,899	675	9.13	6.98	13.02	12.87	18.40	20.04	10.56	6.30	1.33	1.38
Nevada	45,395	44,846	45,418	45,481	834	7.04	5.83	12.15	13.31	16.60	19.69	11.89	9.44	2.20	1.86
New Hampshire.......	53,910	55,456	54,693	54,199	493	7.05	5.12	9.48	9.27	14.95	22.08	14.41	12.27	3.19	2.18
New Jersey	58,588	60,031	58,429	57,727	3,123	5.88	4.73	9.43	8.70	13.63	19.10	13.42	14.64	5.58	4.88
New Mexico	34,805	36,721	35,561	35,602	698	12.60	8.91	14.28	14.46	16.70	16.25	7.80	6.31	1.52	1.17
New York..........	46,195	45,703	45,567	46,691	7,119	10.00	6.43	11.75	10.89	13.97	18.41	11.30	10.14	3.51	3.60
North Carolina	38,234	38,972	40,296	40,302	3,271	11.05	6.86	13.74	14.13	16.97	17.90	9.47	6.64	1.64	1.62
North Dakota	37,554	36,895	36,483	36,768	254	10.29	7.97	14.86	13.70	17.52	20.03	8.15	4.89	1.11	1.48
Ohio	41,350	41,353	42,212	42,453	4,480	8.93	7.10	13.55	12.92	16.34	19.99	10.34	7.64	1.82	1.38
Oklahoma	35,129	36,228	35,154	36,309	1,341	11.97	7.67	16.26	13.94	17.38	17.11	7.95	5.41	1.25	1.07
Oregon	40,319	41,207	42,012	41,769	1,409	9.34	6.81	14.81	12.43	16.53	19.83	9.25	7.20	2.05	1.75
Pennsylvania	41,478	41,899	42,333	42,319	4,801	8.68	6.97	13.42	13.25	16.35	19.15	10.31	7.97	2.06	1.82
Rhode Island	48,854	46,653	44,373	46,750	412	8.91	6.91	10.94	10.42	13.69	20.89	12.93	10.13	3.26	1.92
South Carolina	38,467	38,739	40,143	38,894	1,568	11.07	6.97	14.66	12.86	16.47	17.96	10.11	6.77	1.86	1.26
South Dakota	38,415	38,068	38,140	37,174	299	9.26	7.23	13.62	14.95	20.04	19.84	7.81	4.88	1.35	1.01
Tennessee	38,247	37,913	37,541	39,035	2,296	11.23	7.15	13.48	14.07	16.51	18.26	9.44	6.64	1.75	1.47
Texas	40,674	42,184	41,915	42,069	7,635	10.00	6.68	13.97	12.69	15.56	18.20	10.01	8.21	2.47	2.21
Utah	46,873	47,505	47,873	48,461	752	5.90	5.29	11.20	12.80	17.98	21.40	12.82	8.96	2.04	1.60
Vermont..........	43,697	44,745	43,636	43,207	242	7.53	6.46	13.23	12.86	17.10	20.82	11.54	7.36	1.64	1.48
Virginia	50,805	49,879	50,396	50,276	2,790	7.28	4.65	11.37	10.31	15.51	20.14	12.39	11.65	3.68	3.00
Washington	46,868	46,983	47,579	48,120	2,382	7.61	5.40	11.86	11.50	16.80	20.71	11.88	9.66	2.39	2.21
West Virginia	31,008	31,626	30,548	31,102	732	14.88	10.29	16.64	13.36	15.56	15.08	8.41	4.24	0.94	0.59
Wisconsin..........	44,084	44,667	44,649	45,140	2,159	7.49	6.10	12.85	12.71	17.00	22.53	11.16	7.09	1.68	1.38
Wyoming	43,332	41,925	40,479	41,191	199	7.05	6.59	13.80	12.08	17.97	21.55	11.42	6.70	1.66	1.18

Survey, Census, or Data Collection Method: Based on the American Community Survey; for information, see Appendix B, Limitations of the Data and Methodology, and Internet site <http://www.census.gov/acs/www/AdvMeth/index.htm>.

Source: U.S. Census Bureau, American Community Survey, Multi-Year Profiles 2003—Economic Characteristics, accessed 24 June 2005. See Internet site <http://www.census.gov/acs/www/Products/Profiles/Chg/2003/ACS/index.htm>.

Median Income of Families in Constant (2003) Dollars and Distribution by Income Level

Geographic area	Median family income in (2003) dollars				Total number of families, 2003 (1,000)	Percent of families by income level, 2003									
	2003	2002	2001	2000		Under $10,000	$10,000–$14,999	$15,000–$24,999	$25,000–$34,999	$35,000–$49,999	$50,000–$74,999	$75,000–$99,999	$100,000–$149,999	$150,000–$199,999	$200,000 and over
United States ...	**52,273**	**52,764**	**52,754**	**52,904**	**73,058**	**5.45**	**4.18**	**10.40**	**11.37**	**16.00**	**21.51**	**13.32**	**11.33**	**3.41**	**3.03**
Alabama	43,307	43,249	43,075	43,507	1,194	8.31	5.55	12.48	13.08	17.52	19.94	11.59	8.07	1.70	1.77
Alaska	61,117	67,256	64,509	63,190	156	3.09	3.36	8.48	9.61	14.62	23.76	15.78	14.88	3.81	2.60
Arizona	47,219	48,524	48,792	48,876	1,390	6.63	4.74	11.61	13.48	16.25	20.31	12.00	9.72	2.66	2.60
Arkansas	41,072	42,843	41,534	42,168	738	7.23	5.44	13.06	15.76	18.82	20.26	10.00	6.76	1.51	1.16
California	56,530	57,486	56,350	56,681	8,106	5.02	3.96	10.40	10.57	14.37	19.42	13.37	13.86	4.74	4.27
Colorado	59,252	58,481	58,263	59,373	1,210	4.17	3.04	8.79	10.57	13.93	23.35	14.57	13.67	4.06	3.85
Connecticut	69,917	70,421	70,807	69,729	904	3.61	3.00	6.16	8.27	12.63	20.54	16.80	15.87	6.12	7.01
Delaware	61,270	58,936	59,278	58,919	200	2.83	2.76	7.51	9.50	16.10	22.42	16.36	15.79	4.21	2.52
District of Columbia	50,243	50,073	49,030	48,890	113	12.23	5.83	10.74	9.47	11.52	15.17	9.84	10.94	7.20	7.06
Florida	47,442	47,617	46,899	48,340	4,339	5.14	4.68	12.44	12.60	17.65	20.80	12.20	9.06	2.84	2.60
Georgia	50,647	50,503	50,983	49,968	2,165	6.12	4.71	10.70	11.65	16.13	21.49	12.84	10.67	2.94	2.76
Hawaii	60,647	59,977	60,691	63,139	289	4.42	2.51	7.59	9.12	15.80	22.65	15.82	14.99	4.09	3.00
Idaho	46,783	45,683	44,029	46,983	360	4.50	4.94	12.11	13.88	18.17	23.31	12.71	7.58	1.58	1.22
Illinois	57,385	57,916	58,326	58,993	3,097	4.85	3.48	8.83	10.26	15.24	22.01	14.30	12.91	4.26	3.87
Indiana	51,338	51,872	52,547	52,411	1,587	4.23	3.55	9.96	12.30	17.98	24.80	13.99	8.89	2.29	2.02
Iowa	51,336	50,634	50,662	50,463	758	3.89	3.42	9.76	12.18	18.78	25.45	13.36	9.21	2.11	1.83
Kansas	51,157	51,353	49,588	52,737	709	3.97	3.42	10.74	12.94	17.43	23.91	12.72	9.97	2.79	2.12
Kentucky	41,898	43,838	42,556	43,018	1,123	8.28	6.85	12.44	13.53	17.91	20.92	10.33	6.82	1.45	1.47
Louisiana	41,831	41,696	42,296	41,095	1,152	10.02	7.16	13.42	10.94	16.16	19.62	11.21	7.81	1.99	1.67
Maine	48,541	48,086	45,610	48,911	348	4.42	4.38	10.72	12.92	19.33	24.66	12.37	8.22	1.33	1.64
Maryland	69,087	66,985	67,027	66,966	1,401	3.76	2.53	6.52	8.53	13.08	19.84	16.64	17.81	6.31	4.99
Massachusetts	67,527	68,411	67,933	65,908	1,585	4.43	3.43	7.08	8.20	12.07	20.01	16.92	16.99	5.64	5.23
Michigan	55,018	55,118	55,977	56,264	2,600	4.99	3.84	8.67	11.46	16.05	22.50	14.67	12.15	3.22	2.44
Minnesota	61,417	61,534	61,679	61,308	1,334	3.60	2.48	7.00	9.05	15.29	26.13	16.09	13.55	3.88	2.92
Mississippi	39,182	39,372	40,983	42,857	739	9.14	7.67	13.88	13.38	17.75	19.27	9.63	6.25	1.31	1.73
Missouri	49,441	50,779	50,059	47,951	1,539	4.58	3.68	11.48	12.41	18.49	23.64	12.35	9.45	2.16	1.77
Montana	44,503	44,939	41,898	43,997	238	4.74	5.70	12.50	14.36	20.86	22.43	10.58	5.89	1.53	1.41
Nebraska	50,756	50,606	50,866	49,791	440	4.81	3.51	9.15	11.77	19.69	25.15	13.84	8.25	1.85	1.98
Nevada	52,502	51,183	52,407	52,454	538	5.24	2.71	9.69	12.76	16.79	21.49	14.31	11.84	2.75	2.43
New Hampshire.	63,439	65,816	64,767	64,493	338	3.32	2.76	7.03	8.49	14.54	24.31	17.23	15.45	4.12	2.74
New Jersey	70,263	72,082	69,856	69,904	2,206	3.74	2.58	6.86	7.34	12.98	19.86	15.23	18.13	7.00	6.28
New Mexico	41,661	43,586	41,645	42,816	473	7.90	7.33	12.85	14.07	17.75	18.41	10.21	8.04	2.01	1.41
New York	55,309	55,615	54,650	55,887	4,650	6.06	4.47	10.08	10.32	13.92	20.38	13.40	12.48	4.35	4.54
North Carolina.	45,540	46,926	48,003	47,555	2,235	6.70	4.66	12.05	13.58	17.86	20.63	11.71	8.48	2.22	2.11
North Dakota	48,386	48,072	47,976	45,833	161	4.87	4.49	10.79	12.34	19.11	26.19	11.59	6.96	1.63	2.04
Ohio	51,522	50,356	52,507	52,297	2,982	5.53	4.08	10.17	11.63	16.63	23.84	13.51	10.36	2.49	1.77
Oklahoma	43,259	44,234	43,266	43,523	909	7.18	5.03	13.68	13.72	18.37	21.21	10.77	7.05	1.68	1.31
Oregon	49,800	51,534	50,345	49,324	911	5.35	4.38	12.21	11.36	16.90	23.63	11.87	9.27	2.63	2.40
Pennsylvania	51,339	52,152	52,461	51,689	3,166	5.04	3.41	10.08	12.43	17.36	22.78	13.26	10.46	2.82	2.38
Rhode Island	60,165	56,977	56,598	57,732	265	4.90	3.17	9.18	8.99	13.43	22.79	16.51	14.05	4.39	2.59
South Carolina	47,081	47,411	48,935	46,857	1,079	6.91	5.13	12.44	11.81	16.53	21.01	12.98	9.00	2.52	1.68
South Dakota	46,824	47,245	47,529	47,582	199	4.09	3.75	10.22	13.99	21.86	25.53	10.83	6.53	1.88	1.31
Tennessee	46,654	46,735	45,155	47,448	1,549	6.23	4.81	11.43	13.19	17.82	21.95	11.68	8.68	2.28	1.93
Texas	47,479	48,967	48,772	48,595	5,414	6.67	5.21	12.53	12.38	15.51	19.89	11.92	10.15	3.02	2.72
Utah	52,481	52,405	54,017	54,916	570	3.74	2.71	9.30	11.05	19.09	23.80	15.26	10.87	2.31	1.86
Vermont.	52,895	54,203	51,771	51,328	156	2.86	4.01	11.49	11.59	16.95	24.62	14.51	10.01	2.30	1.67
Virginia	60,174	58,980	59,585	58,824	1,891	4.11	2.72	9.08	9.26	15.29	21.57	14.88	14.42	4.80	3.86
Washington	56,461	57,508	58,218	58,146	1,529	4.45	3.53	8.87	10.20	16.39	23.37	14.59	12.42	3.31	2.86
West Virginia	38,568	39,545	38,876	37,375	490	9.22	7.63	13.91	14.02	17.21	19.05	11.35	5.44	1.34	0.84
Wisconsin.	54,500	54,140	54,044	55,892	1,400	3.93	3.48	9.13	11.35	16.79	26.36	15.14	9.76	2.15	1.89
Wyoming	51,627	51,716	50,105	49,977	133	4.02	3.85	9.95	11.39	18.61	25.90	13.97	8.58	2.19	1.53

Survey, Census, or Data Collection Method: Based on the American Community Survey; for information, see Appendix B, Limitations of the Data and Methodology, and Internet site <http://www.census.gov/acs/www/AdvMeth/index.htm>.

Source: U.S. Census Bureau, American Community Survey, Multi-Year Profiles 2003—Economic Characteristics, accessed 24 June 2005. See Internet site <http://www.census.gov/acs/www/Products/Profiles/Chg/2003/ACS/index.htm>.

State and Metropolitan Area Data Book: 2006

U.S. Census Bureau

Table A-36. States — Poverty Status of Families and Individuals in the Past 12 Months

Geographic area	Number below poverty in the past 12 months (1,000)								Percent below poverty in the past 12 months							
	Families				Individuals				Families				Individuals			
	2003	2002	2001	2000	2003	2002	2001	2000	2003	2002	2001	2000	2003	2002	2001	2000
United States . . .	**7,143**	**6,952**	**6,631**	**6,615**	**35,846**	**34,763**	**33,420**	**33,311**	**9.8**	**9.6**	**9.2**	**9.3**	**12.7**	**12.4**	**12.1**	**12.2**
Alabama	164	163	157	146	748	722	716	672	13.7	13.3	13.0	12.4	17.1	16.6	16.5	15.6
Alaska	13	10	8	11	61	48	44	55	8.0	6.1	5.4	6.8	9.7	7.7	7.2	9.1
Arizona	166	145	140	150	839	752	710	780	11.9	10.5	10.7	11.6	15.4	14.2	13.7	15.6
Arkansas	89	85	85	96	421	401	402	439	12.1	11.5	11.8	13.0	16.0	15.3	15.4	17.0
California	849	793	763	832	4,610	4,452	4,298	4,520	10.5	10.0	9.7	10.7	13.4	13.0	12.8	13.7
Colorado	88	79	77	64	433	425	411	363	7.3	6.7	6.8	5.7	9.8	9.7	9.6	8.7
Connecticut	58	49	47	51	273	249	242	254	6.4	5.5	5.3	5.8	8.1	7.5	7.3	7.7
Delaware	12	12	14	14	69	64	75	70	5.8	5.8	7.1	6.7	8.7	8.2	9.8	9.3
District of Columbia	21	18	17	17	105	93	97	94	18.5	15.7	16.2	15.4	19.9	17.5	18.1	17.5
Florida	422	414	391	387	2,174	2,083	1,995	1,987	9.7	9.6	9.3	9.3	13.1	12.8	12.5	12.8
Georgia	234	222	195	206	1,125	1,053	947	999	10.8	10.5	9.2	10.0	13.4	12.7	11.7	12.6
Hawaii	21	23	23	19	132	122	124	103	7.4	7.9	7.9	6.8	10.9	10.1	10.4	8.8
Idaho	35	33	33	26	183	180	154	144	9.8	9.6	9.4	7.7	13.8	13.8	12.0	11.4
Illinois	265	270	244	262	1,389	1,414	1,351	1,335	8.5	8.7	8.0	8.6	11.3	11.6	11.2	11.1
Indiana	119	123	116	113	633	649	579	592	7.5	7.7	7.3	7.1	10.6	10.9	9.8	10.1
Iowa	53	59	54	53	286	316	274	281	6.9	7.7	7.0	7.0	10.1	11.2	9.7	10.0
Kansas	51	58	55	43	284	317	295	247	7.1	8.3	7.9	6.2	10.8	12.1	11.3	9.5
Kentucky	159	143	135	148	696	619	607	640	14.2	12.8	12.3	13.5	17.4	15.6	15.4	16.4
Louisiana	191	184	173	182	882	815	820	862	16.6	16.1	15.2	16.0	20.3	18.8	19.1	20.0
Maine	26	33	28	22	133	139	132	124	7.6	9.1	7.9	6.6	10.5	11.1	10.6	10.1
Maryland	86	85	81	89	439	428	424	477	6.1	6.1	6.0	6.6	8.2	8.1	8.1	9.3
Massachusetts	118	105	102	110	582	554	536	586	7.5	6.6	6.5	7.1	9.4	8.9	8.7	9.6
Michigan	224	216	206	196	1,118	1,078	1,024	975	8.6	8.4	7.9	7.7	11.4	11.0	10.6	10.1
Minnesota	75	73	76	66	383	415	376	328	5.6	5.5	5.7	5.1	7.8	8.5	7.8	6.9
Mississippi	121	122	109	104	553	549	513	498	16.4	16.1	14.9	14.2	19.9	19.9	18.6	18.2
Missouri	133	133	128	118	646	654	637	606	8.6	8.8	8.5	7.7	11.7	11.9	11.7	11.2
Montana	24	25	28	23	126	129	128	117	9.9	10.4	11.6	9.5	14.2	14.6	14.6	13.4
Nebraska	36	36	31	28	182	183	170	158	8.2	7.9	7.1	6.5	10.8	11.0	10.3	9.6
Nevada	47	50	37	34	252	251	200	194	8.7	9.5	7.2	6.9	10.4	11.8	9.7	9.9
New Hampshire	17	15	13	11	96	79	73	63	5.1	4.6	4.1	3.5	7.7	6.4	6.0	5.3
New Jersey	145	127	138	126	704	628	653	651	6.6	5.8	6.4	6.0	8.4	7.5	7.9	7.9
New Mexico	70	72	66	64	340	342	315	320	14.8	15.6	14.3	14.2	18.6	18.9	17.7	18.0
New York	499	487	487	491	2,501	2,418	2,452	2,391	10.7	10.6	10.5	10.7	13.5	13.1	13.4	13.1
North Carolina	239	241	231	203	1,136	1,143	1,110	1,018	10.7	11.0	10.5	9.6	14.0	14.2	14.1	13.1
North Dakota	13	13	13	14	71	76	74	71	8.4	8.1	8.1	8.1	11.7	12.5	12.1	11.6
Ohio	280	273	251	246	1,343	1,314	1,211	1,216	9.4	9.2	8.5	8.4	12.1	11.9	11.0	11.1
Oklahoma	112	105	109	100	546	504	518	459	12.4	11.4	12.2	11.0	16.1	15.0	15.5	13.8
Oregon	88	89	88	84	481	454	452	439	9.7	9.9	9.7	9.5	13.9	13.2	13.4	13.2
Pennsylvania	260	258	254	247	1,296	1,246	1,270	1,240	8.2	8.1	8.0	7.8	10.9	10.5	10.7	10.5
Rhode Island	22	22	23	23	117	110	122	108	8.2	8.1	9.0	8.5	11.3	10.7	12.0	10.7
South Carolina	121	122	104	123	563	563	524	557	11.3	11.3	9.9	11.7	14.1	14.2	13.4	14.4
South Dakota	14	17	16	16	81	83	84	83	7.2	8.7	8.3	8.4	11.1	11.4	11.6	11.5
Tennessee	164	178	174	158	780	817	797	745	10.6	11.6	11.2	10.5	13.8	14.5	14.3	13.5
Texas	712	682	636	639	3,508	3,305	3,093	3,056	13.1	12.8	12.1	12.3	16.3	15.6	15.0	15.1
Utah	43	46	34	40	244	238	190	192	7.6	7.9	6.2	7.2	10.6	10.5	8.6	8.8
Vermont	10	9	12	12	57	51	61	63	6.4	5.4	7.5	7.5	9.7	8.5	10.4	10.7
Virginia	126	141	134	124	642	699	647	630	6.6	7.5	7.2	6.8	9.0	9.9	9.3	9.2
Washington	121	128	120	127	654	672	627	667	7.9	8.4	8.0	8.6	11.0	11.4	10.8	11.6
West Virginia	76	63	70	72	326	302	300	327	15.5	13.2	14.3	14.7	18.5	17.2	17.2	18.6
Wisconsin	101	95	93	75	554	511	510	461	7.2	6.7	6.8	5.6	10.5	9.7	9.8	8.9
Wyoming	10	10	11	10	47	53	54	55	7.3	7.6	8.3	7.9	9.7	11.0	11.4	11.4

Survey, Census, or Data Collection Method: Based on the American Community Survey; for information, see Appendix B, Limitations of the Data and Methodology, and Internet site <http://www.census.gov/acs/www/AdvMeth/index.htm>.

Source: U.S. Census Bureau, American Community Survey, Multi-Year Profiles 2003—Economic Characteristics, accessed 24 June 2005. See Internet site <http://www.census.gov/acs/www/Products/Profiles/Chg/2003/ACS/index.htm>.

Table A-37. States — Housing—Units and Characteristics

Geographic area	Total housing units (1,000) 2004	2000[1]	1990[2]	Units in structure, percent 1-unit detached	1-unit attached	Mobile home	Year built, percent 1990 or later	1970 to 1989	Prior to 1950	Occupied units Total units (1,000)	Vehicles available, percent None	1	2	3 or more	House heating fuel, percent Utility gas	Electricity
United States ...	122,672	115,905	102,262	60.9	5.6	7.2	20.8	32.3	22.1	108,420	9.0	33.3	38.4	19.2	50.8	31.3
Alabama	2,059	1,964	1,670	67.4	1.7	14.3	24.9	36.6	13.2	1,743	6.8	32.9	38.3	22.1	37.6	47.9
Alaska	272	261	233	59.1	7.6	7.6	23.2	56.9	4.7	229	9.9	32.3	38.3	19.4	48.2	10.6
Arizona	2,458	2,189	1,659	59.2	5.4	13.1	36.1	43.6	3.9	2,049	7.2	38.6	37.8	16.4	35.9	58.0
Arkansas	1,233	1,173	1,001	71.3	2.1	12.6	26.6	35.5	13.4	1,076	8.1	33.1	39.3	19.5	49.2	35.8
California	12,805	12,215	11,183	57.1	7.1	4.4	16.5	35.3	17.4	11,857	7.8	32.5	38.3	21.4	69.2	21.2
Colorado	2,011	1,808	1,477	63.8	6.3	5.4	27.5	38.0	13.1	1,821	5.2	29.9	40.9	24.0	75.4	16.4
Connecticut	1,414	1,386	1,321	57.7	6.1	1.0	10.4	28.3	32.9	1,323	8.7	32.8	38.8	19.8	29.4	16.1
Delaware	367	343	290	56.2	13.0	11.2	25.1	31.1	17.0	304	6.5	32.8	41.2	19.5	37.5	27.9
District of Columbia	277	275	278	12.5	26.7	0.1	4.2	11.9	55.2	247	37.5	42.2	16.4	4.0	65.3	27.4
Florida	8,009	7,303	6,100	52.9	5.8	10.8	28.0	45.9	5.7	6,638	7.0	40.5	38.7	13.9	5.3	89.5
Georgia	3,673	3,282	2,638	65.7	2.4	11.7	35.2	35.0	10.3	3,153	7.4	32.3	39.3	21.1	48.2	37.9
Hawaii	483	461	390	52.4	5.6	0.2	19.1	42.8	9.3	419	9.4	36.5	36.3	17.8	2.5	32.7
Idaho	579	528	413	71.4	2.3	11.6	28.9	35.1	16.0	503	3.2	24.7	42.3	29.9	47.0	30.4
Illinois	5,094	4,886	4,506	58.5	5.3	2.9	15.7	24.9	32.1	4,625	10.2	35.0	38.0	16.8	81.7	11.7
Indiana	2,691	2,532	2,246	71.2	3.3	6.6	22.0	26.0	28.2	2,351	6.9	31.4	39.3	22.5	61.1	24.1
Iowa	1,293	1,233	1,144	74.6	2.6	4.8	13.3	25.1	39.6	1,158	5.4	28.8	40.3	25.5	67.0	13.7
Kansas	1,185	1,131	1,044	72.1	3.1	5.0	16.4	30.6	27.6	1,059	4.9	30.9	40.2	24.1	70.6	18.1
Kentucky	1,843	1,751	1,507	66.5	2.3	14.7	27.4	32.6	17.5	1,607	7.7	32.5	40.5	19.4	40.9	43.6
Louisiana	1,920	1,847	1,716	64.0	4.1	12.6	18.2	39.5	15.0	1,673	10.5	37.1	37.8	14.6	42.8	51.7
Maine	677	652	587	67.1	2.2	10.2	16.3	28.4	37.3	535	6.4	31.9	41.7	20.1	3.9	4.8
Maryland	2,250	2,145	1,892	52.5	20.4	1.9	20.4	32.0	20.7	2,048	9.6	32.6	37.2	20.6	47.3	33.3
Massachusetts	2,672	2,622	2,473	53.5	4.6	1.0	9.9	22.7	43.3	2,436	10.6	36.0	38.4	15.0	44.1	13.6
Michigan	4,433	4,235	3,848	70.9	4.6	6.2	17.7	25.5	28.7	3,884	7.0	33.1	40.7	19.3	77.7	7.4
Minnesota	2,213	2,066	1,849	69.7	6.3	3.5	18.4	30.2	28.9	2,012	6.1	30.0	41.7	22.2	68.4	11.6
Mississippi	1,221	1,162	1,010	69.8	1.2	14.5	27.5	38.2	10.8	1,056	7.7	32.9	38.4	21.1	38.7	41.6
Missouri	2,564	2,442	2,199	69.9	3.4	7.1	20.9	29.9	23.7	2,285	6.6	31.4	40.8	21.2	57.4	25.5
Montana	423	413	361	69.0	2.8	13.5	18.4	34.7	24.1	366	4.3	28.9	39.7	27.1	54.9	16.9
Nebraska	758	723	661	72.4	3.4	4.9	16.2	27.9	31.8	675	5.8	30.1	39.4	24.8	68.0	21.2
Nevada	976	827	519	55.6	4.2	7.9	43.9	39.1	3.6	834	7.4	36.9	38.9	16.9	57.8	33.4
New Hampshire	576	547	504	63.6	5.1	6.3	14.6	38.4	27.5	493	4.4	28.6	43.7	23.4	18.1	8.4
New Jersey	3,415	3,310	3,075	54.1	9.3	0.9	13.2	25.0	30.2	3,123	11.1	33.2	38.8	16.9	69.8	10.0
New Mexico	826	781	632	61.8	4.1	18.7	24.3	39.9	12.4	698	6.6	34.3	37.3	21.9	67.4	14.7
New York	7,819	7,679	7,227	41.0	4.9	2.6	8.4	18.7	43.8	7,119	28.2	32.5	27.6	11.7	49.5	8.3
North Carolina	3,860	3,522	2,818	63.6	2.7	17.6	31.8	35.5	12.1	3,271	6.7	31.7	39.2	22.5	23.3	50.6
North Dakota	301	290	276	63.1	4.2	7.3	14.5	36.0	25.5	254	4.6	30.2	37.1	28.1	42.5	29.5
Ohio	4,967	4,783	4,372	68.5	4.3	4.1	16.3	23.9	30.6	4,480	7.3	32.6	39.2	20.9	68.7	18.2
Oklahoma	1,573	1,514	1,406	72.2	2.0	9.4	16.4	39.4	17.8	1,341	5.7	34.6	40.5	19.3	60.7	27.4
Oregon	1,535	1,453	1,194	62.6	4.0	9.1	24.1	34.6	20.1	1,409	7.2	31.7	39.4	21.7	40.5	44.8
Pennsylvania	5,386	5,250	4,938	56.7	18.4	4.7	11.9	21.5	41.7	4,801	11.7	34.6	37.6	16.1	54.0	16.2
Rhode Island	446	440	415	53.9	3.0	1.4	9.5	23.2	44.0	412	7.9	35.7	39.2	17.2	47.7	7.2
South Carolina	1,891	1,754	1,424	60.8	2.3	17.9	32.3	37.1	10.4	1,568	8.0	34.1	37.7	20.2	26.1	61.8
South Dakota	343	323	292	66.5	2.6	11.2	18.8	31.1	29.3	299	4.9	26.3	40.7	28.2	53.8	20.8
Tennessee	2,595	2,439	2,026	68.5	2.5	9.1	26.5	34.1	15.1	2,296	6.6	31.3	39.8	22.3	36.5	53.9
Texas	8,847	8,158	7,009	64.3	2.6	8.0	26.2	40.9	10.2	7,635	6.5	34.8	41.5	17.3	42.3	51.5
Utah	849	769	598	68.3	5.4	4.5	31.5	35.6	12.3	752	3.5	26.9	42.2	27.5	85.8	9.6
Vermont	304	294	271	64.9	3.1	7.0	15.0	34.5	35.0	242	5.8	32.1	42.2	20.0	13.5	4.5
Virginia	3,117	2,904	2,497	61.3	10.2	6.4	24.6	36.5	14.8	2,790	6.4	30.4	39.5	23.8	34.9	45.6
Washington	2,607	2,451	2,032	61.8	2.9	7.7	25.9	34.5	18.5	2,382	6.7	30.8	39.0	23.5	32.4	52.5
West Virginia	867	845	781	67.8	1.8	17.5	19.0	30.4	27.6	732	9.6	34.0	37.8	18.7	43.5	36.2
Wisconsin	2,464	2,321	2,056	65.5	3.3	6.1	19.4	26.5	30.2	2,159	6.7	32.3	40.3	20.6	64.1	12.7
Wyoming	233	224	203	65.6	3.2	15.2	16.5	44.4	19.0	199	3.0	27.9	39.5	29.6	62.7	21.2

[1]The April 1, 2000, Housing Unit Estimates base reflects modifications to the Census 2000 housing units as documented in the Count Question Resolution program and geographic program revisions.

[2]The April 1, 1990, census counts include corrections processed through December 1996, results of post-1990 census corrections of political boundaries, geographic misallocations, or documented undernumerations or overenumerations and geographic boundary updates.

Survey, Census, or Data Collection Method: Housing units—Based on the Census of Population and Housing; for information, see Appendix B, Limitations of the Data and Methodology, and Internet sites <http://www.census.gov/main/www/cen2000.html> and <http://www.census.gov/popest/topics/methodology/>; Characteristics—Based on the American Community Survey; for information, see Appendix B, Limitations of the Data and Methodology, and Internet site <http://www.census.gov/acs/www/AdvMeth/index.htm>.

Sources: Housing units—U.S. Census Bureau, "Table 1: Annual Estimates of Housing Units for the United States and States: April 1, 2000 to July 1, 2004" (HU-EST2004-01), published 21 July 2005, Internet site <http://www.census.gov/popest/housing/HU-EST2004.html>; and "Housing Units, Households, Households by Age of Householder, and Persons per Household: April 1, 1990" (ST-98-47), published 8 December 1999, Internet site <http://www.census.gov/popest/archives/1990s/ST-98-47.txt>; Characteristics—U.S. Census Bureau, American Community Survey, Multi-Year Profiles 2003—Housing Characteristics, accessed 24 June 2005, see Internet site <http://www.census.gov/acs/www/Products/Profiles/Chg/2003/ACS/index.htm>.

Table A-38. States — Specified Owner- and Renter-Occupied Units—Value and Gross Rent

Geographic area	Total units, 2003 (1,000)	Median value in constant (2003) dollars ($1,000)			Value in 2003, percent				Total units, 2003 (1,000)	Median gross rent in constant (2003) dollars			Gross rent in 2003, percent[3]			
		2003	2002	2000	Less than $100,000	$100,000–$199,999	$200,000–$299,999	$300,000 and over		2003	2002	2000	Less than $300	$300–$499	$500–$749	$750 or more
United States . . .	58,809	147	140	129	29.6	36.9	15.0	18.6	35,545	679	668	649	8.4	17.6	33.0	41.0
Alabama	947	96	96	92	52.8	35.0	7.1	5.2	484	498	497	472	15.8	34.6	34.8	14.7
Alaska	112	174	166	155	13.2	50.9	25.3	10.7	85	780	771	734	3.7	11.4	30.5	54.4
Arizona	1,165	146	140	130	20.5	52.2	15.2	12.2	646	662	670	675	5.6	16.7	41.7	36.0
Arkansas	556	84	81	78	63.1	28.5	5.2	3.3	337	513	511	500	11.9	35.0	40.9	12.3
California	5,921	334	282	230	5.1	17.8	20.3	56.8	4,941	890	856	815	4.0	8.5	22.7	64.8
Colorado	1,062	210	204	180	4.3	41.1	31.9	22.6	532	754	742	727	5.8	9.6	34.0	50.6
Connecticut	765	226	201	179	4.7	37.4	24.0	33.9	427	766	741	734	8.4	9.4	30.1	52.1
Delaware	185	166	148	143	14.5	49.6	20.6	15.2	82	718	692	694	8.8	12.4	33.7	45.1
District of Columbia	76	248	217	178	9.1	31.5	15.5	44.0	143	721	705	677	11.4	10.2	31.7	46.7
Florida	3,508	145	131	115	26.4	44.4	15.7	13.5	1,971	724	714	699	7.0	12.3	34.6	46.0
Georgia	1,745	141	134	121	28.0	45.9	14.0	12.1	989	687	675	676	8.0	18.4	31.6	42.0
Hawaii	185	325	298	307	6.2	16.0	21.8	56.1	181	863	849	876	5.4	6.8	24.3	63.5
Idaho	284	118	118	112	35.4	49.0	10.4	5.2	125	565	540	510	10.2	29.5	40.3	20.0
Illinois	2,563	161	151	139	27.8	35.5	18.6	18.2	1,438	699	680	660	7.3	15.6	34.0	43.0
Indiana	1,419	107	103	101	45.5	43.1	7.2	4.2	646	581	558	556	7.8	24.8	45.0	22.4
Iowa	688	91	90	85	56.6	34.5	6.3	2.7	293	531	507	507	13.9	29.2	39.8	17.1
Kansas	611	100	96	90	49.9	37.0	8.5	4.7	322	535	554	534	12.3	31.4	34.3	22.0
Kentucky	812	104	100	94	47.5	39.6	8.5	4.6	459	491	487	478	16.3	35.7	34.5	13.5
Louisiana	892	99	97	90	50.6	37.0	7.2	5.3	546	525	503	516	13.5	31.9	37.0	17.6
Maine	267	135	124	110	31.6	43.0	15.0	10.4	154	562	558	523	16.0	25.0	35.0	24.0
Maryland	1,255	186	170	157	16.6	38.1	20.6	24.7	623	817	752	734	7.2	8.7	25.7	58.5
Massachusetts	1,259	310	255	206	3.5	19.9	24.3	52.3	862	820	813	763	12.2	9.6	21.0	57.1
Michigan	2,417	141	136	125	28.6	45.5	14.8	11.1	977	608	594	584	10.8	20.5	41.0	27.7
Minnesota	1,259	170	159	132	20.0	44.3	21.8	13.9	455	657	663	612	12.8	16.2	33.2	37.9
Mississippi	560	85	81	81	61.3	30.3	6.1	2.3	309	525	524	486	15.8	29.4	38.4	16.4
Missouri	1,256	109	105	97	45.2	39.8	8.9	6.1	656	556	548	523	9.7	28.8	39.7	21.8
Montana	173	119	109	106	38.8	45.7	10.7	4.8	107	506	488	478	15.7	33.1	37.6	13.6
Nebraska	389	101	96	92	49.6	39.8	6.5	4.0	209	540	545	525	12.4	29.9	37.8	19.9
Nevada	433	170	161	150	9.3	54.3	20.4	16.1	317	771	778	744	2.9	9.7	33.9	53.5
New Hampshire	280	208	178	148	9.3	37.4	30.5	22.8	132	780	744	703	7.3	10.0	28.7	53.9
New Jersey	1,795	246	215	185	8.1	28.4	23.4	40.0	1,039	856	824	813	7.0	5.5	22.5	65.0
New Mexico	363	119	119	113	38.1	45.6	9.4	7.0	211	523	538	511	12.1	32.8	36.8	18.3
New York	2,804	199	180	161	26.9	23.3	16.5	33.3	3,243	770	739	728	8.4	12.4	26.8	52.4
North Carolina	1,678	125	124	115	34.9	44.9	11.8	8.4	1,020	601	602	592	9.4	23.4	41.9	25.4
North Dakota	129	82	82	79	64.3	30.6	3.9	1.2	80	456	443	463	19.2	41.6	31.3	7.9
Ohio	2,727	119	116	110	37.8	45.4	11.1	5.8	1,314	575	568	543	9.5	26.1	40.9	23.6
Oklahoma	749	86	82	79	63.3	30.2	4.3	2.2	421	519	515	493	10.6	35.4	37.1	16.8
Oregon	709	171	164	160	9.2	54.7	22.1	14.0	509	657	677	659	6.9	14.0	44.4	34.7
Pennsylvania	3,002	110	105	101	45.0	37.0	10.2	7.8	1,334	602	587	551	10.0	24.7	35.6	29.4
Rhode Island	212	205	169	147	4.6	43.4	27.6	24.5	151	686	636	594	11.5	12.6	36.1	39.8
South Carolina	818	121	119	111	37.4	41.0	11.4	10.3	466	586	577	576	11.1	24.5	41.1	23.2
South Dakota	146	97	92	88	52.7	38.3	6.3	2.7	87	490	494	456	17.3	34.8	35.4	12.4
Tennessee	1,281	110	109	103	43.8	40.4	10.0	5.8	688	548	550	551	12.7	28.4	38.2	20.7
Texas	4,179	99	97	89	50.6	34.8	8.4	6.2	2,695	639	642	616	6.9	20.0	39.6	33.6
Utah	488	157	155	154	11.2	60.8	18.5	9.5	201	632	679	639	5.3	16.3	46.1	32.3
Vermont	111	138	133	123	27.3	49.3	15.6	7.8	67	624	616	578	12.2	16.0	40.6	31.1
Virginia	1,632	162	149	135	25.2	35.2	16.8	22.8	841	751	722	692	6.9	15.4	27.6	50.2
Washington	1,254	200	193	181	9.1	40.8	26.3	23.7	845	734	725	697	6.1	12.4	33.8	47.7
West Virginia	387	86	84	78	62.0	30.5	4.8	2.7	186	432	459	431	21.7	40.1	28.8	9.5
Wisconsin	1,193	132	125	117	29.9	49.7	13.6	6.8	646	595	592	574	8.6	23.6	42.5	25.4
Wyoming	105	116	113	105	38.5	44.7	7.3	9.5	53	494	485	476	12.1	39.3	31.4	17.2

[1]Specified owner-occupied units are owner-occupied, one-family, attached and detached houses on less than 10 acres without a business or medical office on the property.
[2]Specified renter-occupied units include all renter-occupied units except 1-unit attached or detached houses on 10 acres or more.
[3]For units with cash rent.

Survey, Census, or Data Collection Method: Based on the American Community Survey; for information, see Appendix B, Limitations of the Data and Methodology, and Internet site <http://www.census.gov/acs/www/AdvMeth/index.htm>.

Source: U.S. Census Bureau, American Community Survey, Multi-Year Profiles 2003—Housing Characteristics, accessed 24 June 2005. See Internet site <http://www.census.gov/acs/www/Products/Profiles/Chg/2003/ACS/index.htm>.

Geographic area	Homeownership rate[1] (percent)			Vacancy rates, 2004 (percent)		Existing home sales (1,000)					Housing starts (1,000)						
	2004	2000	1990	Rental[2]	Home-owner[3]	2004	2003	2002	2001	2000	2006 esti-mate	2005 esti-mate	2004 esti-mate	2003	2002	2001	2000
United States . . .	**69.0**	**67.4**	**63.9**	**10.2**	**1.7**	**6,784.0**	**6,183.0**	**5,631.0**	**5,332.0**	**5,171.0**	**1,614.0**	**1,658.0**	**1,724.0**	**1,800.0**	**1,711.0**	**1,601.0**	**1,573.0**
Alabama	78.0	73.2	68.4	14.8	2.5	112.0	93.7	82.2	70.5	67.0	21.1	20.9	20.8	21.7	20.2	19.1	21.2
Alaska	67.2	66.4	58.4	7.0	1.8	23.0	18.4	17.2	17.5	14.3	2.3	2.3	2.3	2.5	2.8	2.6	2.0
Arizona	68.7	68.0	64.5	11.3	1.6	186.8	149.6	128.2	116.4	104.8	60.1	61.9	64.4	68.9	64.0	59.5	59.4
Arkansas	69.1	68.9	67.8	13.5	2.3	60.9	53.8	52.2	48.6	45.0	13.6	13.6	13.8	14.2	12.7	10.8	12.5
California	59.7	57.1	53.8	5.4	0.9	610.1	577.6	565.1	533.7	573.5	154.2	165.0	177.7	176.7	153.9	137.4	137.1
Colorado	71.1	68.3	59.0	12.7	2.8	126.0	112.4	109.4	110.3	111.5	37.7	36.8	35.9	37.3	46.3	52.1	52.5
Connecticut	71.7	70.0	67.9	8.4	0.9	72.5	63.5	64.2	65.6	61.5	8.5	8.5	8.6	9.1	8.9	8.5	8.9
Delaware	77.3	72.0	67.7	11.0	1.4	18.9	15.8	14.5	13.1	12.9	5.7	5.9	6.2	6.4	6.2	4.9	4.4
District of Columbia	45.6	41.9	36.4	11.3	2.4	13.4	12.1	11.2	10.0	10.6	0.4	0.4	0.4	0.4	0.6	0.4	0.4
Florida	72.2	68.4	65.1	11.7	1.7	526.5	476.1	429.3	392.5	393.6	165.4	173.6	185.7	197.3	177.0	161.2	147.9
Georgia	70.9	69.8	64.3	16.3	2.2	215.8	174.0	173.9	162.5	143.6	84.1	86.1	89.3	93.6	96.2	93.2	90.4
Hawaii	60.6	55.2	55.5	7.7	1.3	35.5	34.4	28.1	23.3	22.1	6.2	6.5	6.8	6.7	5.6	4.7	4.7
Idaho.	73.7	70.5	69.4	9.8	1.4	32.0	27.6	25.7	28.7	24.1	12.8	13.1	13.5	14.0	13.4	11.7	11.3
Illinois	72.7	67.9	63.0	14.8	1.7	307.5	275.1	269.0	250.5	246.8	56.6	58.5	61.5	63.8	60.8	54.4	51.3
Indiana	75.8	74.9	67.0	12.9	2.5	130.5	120.4	125.2	115.5	111.0	38.8	39.4	40.4	42.1	40.9	40.8	38.2
Iowa	73.2	75.2	70.7	9.4	2.4	71.1	62.4	58.4	55.7	53.3	14.1	14.6	15.3	15.9	15.4	12.9	12.8
Kansas	69.9	69.3	69.0	13.6	2.8	73.4	65.3	60.0	57.3	52.6	13.8	13.8	14.0	14.2	13.7	15.1	13.4
Kentucky	73.3	73.4	65.8	11.3	2.1	89.3	81.1	73.5	71.5	66.0	20.5	20.4	20.4	21.3	20.7	19.2	21.8
Louisiana	70.6	68.1	67.8	7.3	1.3	79.6	76.2	71.7	70.4	66.8	17.7	18.0	18.7	19.0	18.4	16.0	15.5
Maine	74.7	76.5	74.2	6.8	0.8	33.6	30.7	28.8	27.5	27.6	6.5	6.8	7.3	7.3	6.8	5.6	6.3
Maryland	72.1	69.9	64.9	8.2	1.8	140.6	120.8	117.6	108.2	100.5	27.0	27.1	27.4	27.3	28.1	28.6	28.7
Massachusetts	63.8	59.9	58.6	6.5	0.7	141.7	118.3	115.9	110.4	112.3	16.0	16.0	16.2	16.8	16.2	15.9	17.1
Michigan	77.1	77.2	72.3	13.0	2.2	213.4	207.4	203.5	194.0	185.0	50.7	51.7	53.4	55.6	50.9	50.9	50.4
Minnesota	76.4	76.1	68.0	9.1	1.1	137.4	126.7	122.6	99.3	96.3	37.1	39.0	41.7	43.5	40.3	35.3	32.9
Mississippi	74.0	75.2	69.4	12.5	1.4	58.1	51.5	48.0	44.0	38.7	12.9	12.8	12.8	13.2	12.3	11.9	14.1
Missouri	72.4	74.2	64.0	10.3	3.1	141.8	131.1	115.2	113.5	110.2	27.5	27.5	27.7	29.1	29.0	25.1	27.4
Montana	72.4	70.2	69.1	9.7	1.7	24.2	23.2	22.6	20.0	17.4	2.8	2.9	2.9	3.2	3.5	2.5	2.4
Nebraska	71.2	70.2	67.3	9.5	1.5	39.8	38.0	34.3	32.8	32.3	9.7	10.0	10.5	10.7	9.5	8.4	9.2
Nevada	65.7	64.0	55.8	10.6	3.2	99.8	80.9	63.5	55.3	44.6	35.0	36.1	37.8	40.2	33.8	33.4	31.0
New Hampshire.	73.3	69.2	65.0	4.8	0.9	27.2	25.4	23.8	26.1	26.7	6.6	7.0	7.4	7.9	7.9	6.2	6.4
New Jersey	68.8	66.2	65.0	6.2	0.7	188.7	174.3	166.8	157.3	160.8	26.1	26.5	27.2	27.7	27.1	25.9	31.4
New Mexico	71.5	73.7	68.6	8.1	1.6	50.6	43.3	38.9	38.5	29.9	10.1	10.3	10.6	11.4	9.9	8.1	7.3
New York	54.8	53.4	53.3	6.1	1.3	307.5	282.6	290.4	286.6	273.3	37.5	38.8	41.0	44.3	44.8	42.7	41.1
North Carolina.	69.8	71.1	69.0	13.3	2.5	192.6	156.3	142.1	132.7	134.2	70.2	71.1	72.8	76.6	77.8	80.5	76.1
North Dakota	70.0	70.7	67.2	10.4	1.5	14.5	12.9	12.3	11.6	10.8	3.3	3.4	3.6	3.7	3.2	2.6	2.4
Ohio	73.1	71.3	68.7	13.0	2.1	275.7	253.1	237.0	228.7	216.4	48.8	49.7	51.2	53.9	52.0	50.7	47.8
Oklahoma	71.1	72.7	70.3	13.9	2.7	93.6	85.1	79.5	77.0	67.3	14.2	14.3	14.6	15.6	14.5	12.9	14.1
Oregon	69.0	65.3	64.4	11.8	1.7	90.7	78.3	72.1	71.3	62.6	20.0	19.6	19.2	21.6	21.3	19.7	18.8
Pennsylvania	74.9	74.7	73.8	11.7	1.4	244.6	219.6	204.7	198.3	194.0	39.0	39.4	40.4	42.0	41.6	38.7	39.2
Rhode Island	61.5	61.5	58.5	6.1	0.6	19.2	16.9	17.1	18.1	17.0	2.4	2.4	2.4	2.4	2.7	2.2	2.6
South Carolina	76.2	76.5	71.4	14.7	1.9	99.3	83.0	72.7	65.4	64.3	32.3	33.4	35.1	36.9	33.5	30.0	31.6
South Dakota	68.5	71.2	66.2	11.2	1.6	17.3	15.6	14.9	12.8	12.6	4.8	4.9	5.2	5.3	5.3	4.5	4.4
Tennessee	71.6	70.9	68.3	10.0	2.4	156.1	128.8	112.0	105.0	100.4	34.3	34.2	34.3	35.2	34.4	33.6	34.6
Texas	65.5	63.8	59.7	13.9	2.2	485.5	425.4	412.4	387.7	381.8	149.1	154.9	163.3	173.4	161.5	147.4	145.0
Utah	74.9	72.7	70.1	8.9	1.9	43.6	43.9	40.9	39.9	35.5	19.8	19.9	20.2	21.6	19.3	18.2	18.1
Vermont.	72.0	68.7	72.6	4.7	0.8	14.2	14.5	13.0	11.7	12.1	2.6	2.7	2.8	2.9	2.9	2.6	2.6
Virginia	73.4	73.9	69.8	11.4	1.0	186.0	158.3	150.1	135.8	130.0	50.6	51.8	53.4	55.2	57.8	52.7	47.5
Washington	66.0	63.6	61.8	9.6	1.3	147.6	132.3	116.3	115.3	112.4	38.2	38.3	38.8	41.6	38.8	36.5	36.9
West Virginia	80.3	75.9	72.0	10.0	1.5	36.0	28.9	28.1	25.3	22.9	5.4	5.4	5.4	5.6	5.7	4.6	5.3
Wisconsin.	73.3	71.8	68.3	9.1	1.5	116.8	105.9	105.5	97.9	91.6	35.8	36.7	38.1	39.4	37.9	36.8	32.6
Wyoming	72.8	71.0	68.9	5.6	1.2	13.2	11.4	10.6	11.7	9.6	2.3	2.2	2.2	2.2	2.1	1.8	1.9

[1]Proportion of owner households to occupied households.
[2]Proportion of the rental inventory that is vacant for rent.
[3]Proportion of the homeowner inventory that is vacant for sale.

Survey, Census, or Data Collection Method: Homeownership and vacancy rates—Based on the Current Population Survey/Housing Vacancy Survey (CPS/HVS); for information, see Appendix B, Limitations of the Data and Methodology, and Internet site <http://www.census.gov/hhes/www/housing/hvs/annual04/ann04src.html>; Home sales—Based on a monthly survey of local associations/boards and multiple listing services (MLS) nationwide; for information, see Internet site <http://www.realtor.org/Research.nsf/Pages/EHSMeth>; Housing starts—For information, see Internet site <http://www.nahb.org>.

Sources: Homeownership and vacancy rates—U.S. Census Bureau, "Housing Vacancies and Home Ownership Annual Statistics: 2004," Internet site <http://www.census.gov/hhes/www/housing/hvs/annual04/ann04ind.html> (accessed 31 Mar 2005); Home sales—NATIONAL ASSOCIATION OF REALTORS®, Washington, DC, *Real Estate Outlook: Market Trends & Insights*, monthly (copyright), see Internet site <http://www.realtor.org/research>; Housing starts—National Association of Home Builders, Economics Division, Washington, DC, data provided by the Econometric Forecasting Service.

Table A-40. States — Cost of Living Indicators—Housing, Hospital Stays, Public University, Utilities, Gasoline, and Tax Rates

Geographic area	Housing prices of single-family homes[1] ($1,000)						Average costs per full-time–equivalent student in public colleges and universities (dol.)					
	All housing			Previously owned			Public 4-year institutions[6]			Public 2-year institutions[7]		
	2004	2003	2000	2004	2003	2000	2003–2004	2002–2003	1999–2000	2003–2004	2002–2003	1999–2000
United States . . .	211.7	197.9	162.9	196.0	188.0	155.5	10,720	9,787	8,275	1,670	1,483	1,338
Alabama	139.9	127.5	124.5	136.0	125.5	118.1	8,983	7,903	6,743	2,479	2,128	1,486
Alaska	179.5	173.1	174.0	171.7	170.0	172.0	10,118	9,459	8,346	1,943	1,789	2,028
Arizona	169.0	156.5	140.6	165.0	155.0	135.0	10,140	8,728	7,368	1,140	1,029	902
Arkansas	125.0	122.0	93.0	122.5	120.0	89.3	8,349	7,740	6,408	1,641	1,507	1,068
California	399.9	340.0	262.0	406.0	341.0	257.0	12,275	10,812	9,179	485	316	317
Colorado	234.0	225.0	202.0	234.0	227.5	198.0	9,751	9,150	7,992	1,784	1,727	1,553
Connecticut	289.0	250.0	207.0	282.5	247.0	200.0	12,772	11,803	10,087	2,307	2,008	1,895
Delaware	270.0	255.0	164.0	214.5	215.0	158.5	12,496	11,461	9,875	1,992	1,878	1,616
District of Columbia	370.0	309.0	243.5	373.0	309.0	245.0	(X)	(X)	(X)	(X)	(X)	(X)
Florida	185.0	161.0	132.4	182.5	159.0	130.0	9,207	8,714	7,483	1,576	1,493	1,333
Georgia	177.5	168.0	159.9	172.5	164.8	159.0	9,090	8,784	7,308	1,411	1,363	1,366
Hawaii	344.0	306.4	248.0	335.0	303.0	225.1	8,760	8,184	8,048	1,118	1,069	1,051
Idaho	150.0	138.9	134.5	149.9	137.0	132.9	8,091	7,560	6,312	1,658	1,541	1,253
Illinois	227.0	218.0	175.0	220.0	210.0	166.3	11,804	10,984	8,998	1,783	1,660	1,499
Indiana	120.0	115.0	120.0	117.0	115.0	115.7	11,637	10,595	8,851	2,483	2,363	2,125
Iowa	108.0	105.0	110.0	99.0	97.0	105.0	10,878	9,190	7,209	2,686	2,555	2,056
Kansas	147.0	145.0	121.0	140.0	140.0	112.0	8,604	7,751	6,312	1,792	1,639	1,308
Kentucky	144.6	145.0	135.0	138.0	140.0	132.5	8,521	7,673	6,480	2,264	1,867	1,321
Louisiana	145.4	140.0	138.0	140.0	135.0	135.0	7,494	6,905	5,946	1,285	1,062	912
Maine	185.0	191.0	130.5	179.9	190.0	130.0	11,010	10,322	9,089	2,772	2,764	2,592
Maryland	290.0	275.0	211.6	250.0	220.0	190.0	13,419	12,283	10,352	2,601	2,354	2,260
Massachusetts	340.0	295.0	225.5	339.5	292.5	220.0	12,250	10,764	9,248	2,725	2,347	1,927
Michigan	156.0	155.5	147.5	154.9	153.0	145.0	12,208	11,357	9,506	1,868	1,813	1,741
Minnesota	218.0	203.7	154.0	212.5	200.0	150.0	10,845	9,957	7,717	3,414	2,866	2,372
Mississippi	131.9	126.0	122.0	124.5	114.9	114.0	8,547	8,008	6,475	1,392	1,453	971
Missouri	139.9	134.9	116.0	136.0	133.0	111.5	10,320	9,407	8,180	1,940	1,789	1,441
Montana	164.0	158.0	126.9	160.0	159.0	123.8	9,348	8,941	7,460	2,580	2,313	1,955
Nebraska	141.9	143.0	128.0	130.0	133.0	125.0	9,620	8,413	7,275	1,678	1,566	1,369
Nevada	252.0	195.0	156.8	248.9	188.0	151.8	10,333	8,973	7,802	1,507	1,456	1,211
New Hampshire.	255.0	211.0	165.0	250.0	209.0	160.0	13,852	9,416	11,044	4,828	4,481	3,744
New Jersey	310.0	292.0	210.0	315.0	291.5	204.0	15,109	13,903	11,458	2,443	2,315	2,155
New Mexico	126.2	121.5	137.0	125.0	120.0	135.0	8,238	7,951	6,608	997	942	824
New York	243.0	256.0	192.0	239.0	275.0	189.0	12,002	10,916	10,018	2,949	2,728	2,554
North Carolina.	173.5	167.0	153.0	168.0	160.0	144.4	8,805	8,305	6,480	1,166	1,111	778
North Dakota	139.9	124.0	112.6	130.0	120.0	108.5	8,028	7,369	7,008	2,419	2,229	1,891
Ohio	180.0	189.9	144.0	145.0	147.4	135.0	13,319	12,216	9,900	2,793	2,595	2,374
Oklahoma	122.5	117.5	110.0	120.0	115.0	105.4	7,901	6,828	5,747	1,650	1,290	1,239
Oregon	205.0	187.0	163.0	206.5	186.0	163.0	11,626	10,510	9,062	2,421	1,968	1,587
Pennsylvania	190.0	179.9	134.0	147.0	140.0	126.0	13,754	12,899	10,544	2,514	2,384	2,117
Rhode Island	265.0	238.0	175.0	265.0	235.0	169.0	12,763	12,231	10,608	2,120	2,014	1,746
South Carolina	159.2	151.0	132.5	157.0	145.0	129.8	12,710	11,024	7,709	2,635	2,174	1,343
South Dakota	147.0	152.0	138.0	140.0	149.5	136.0	8,379	7,682	6,513	2,812	3,166	2,752
Tennessee	151.2	145.9	127.0	146.0	140.0	122.5	8,936	8,298	6,569	2,076	1,751	1,315
Texas	138.5	140.8	132.0	134.0	139.0	129.0	9,202	8,636	7,512	1,171	1,031	890
Utah	183.4	170.0	164.0	183.6	170.0	164.0	7,865	7,367	6,291	1,946	1,804	1,497
Vermont	130.0	164.9	124.9	130.0	163.9	123.5	14,766	13,969	12,484	3,604	3,652	2,846
Virginia	289.0	260.0	194.2	260.0	225.0	183.0	10,900	9,516	8,618	1,799	1,272	1,139
Washington	232.5	220.0	190.0	232.9	220.0	189.9	11,353	10,723	8,303	2,230	2,097	1,649
West Virginia	164.9	176.8	100.0	128.5	128.0	95.0	8,751	8,175	7,100	1,754	1,743	1,592
Wisconsin.	169.9	165.0	131.9	161.0	164.7	128.0	9,066	8,157	7,273	2,583	2,557	2,107
Wyoming	149.0	147.9	137.9	145.0	154.0	135.8	8,485	7,977	7,091	1,613	1,561	1,320

See footnotes at end of table.

Cost of Living Indicators—Housing, Hospital Stays, Public University, Utilities, Gasoline, and Tax Rates—Con.

Geographic area	Hospital cost per day (dol.)				Energy expenditures, per capita[2,3] (dol.)		Regular gasoline prices[4] (dollars per gallon)			Residential utility prices					
										No. 2 heating oil[4] (dollars per gallon)			Natural gas (dollars per 1,000 cubic feet)		
	2003	2002	2001	2000	2001	2000	2004	2003	2000	2004	2003	2000	2004	2003	2000
United States . . .	**1,379**	**1,290**	**1,217**	**1,149**	**2,433**	**2,499**	**1.40**	**1.11**	**1.07**	**1.55**	**1.36**	**1.31**	**10.74**	**9.52**	**7.76**
Alabama	1,166	1,155	1,009	980	2,592	2,719	1.36	1.04	1.02	(NA)	(NA)	(NA)	13.41	11.81	9.19
Alaska	1,952	1,791	1,756	1,495	4,396	4,341	1.69	1.46	1.31	1.52	1.24	1.34	4.88	4.39	3.58
Arizona	1,570	1,465	1,349	1,311	2,015	2,059	1.55	1.29	1.11	(NA)	(NA)	(NA)	12.11	11.31	9.43
Arkansas	1,130	1,041	938	908	2,726	2,740	1.34	1.05	1.00	(NA)	(NA)	(NA)	11.71	10.33	7.43
California	1,763	1,596	1,527	1,438	2,112	2,098	1.62	1.30	1.16	(NA)	(NA)	(NA)	9.93	9.13	8.21
Colorado	1,551	1,505	1,363	1,280	2,096	2,020	1.41	1.12	1.08	(NA)	(NA)	(NA)	8.40	6.61	6.14
Connecticut	1,684	1,482	1,406	1,373	2,348	2,430	1.45	1.15	1.13	1.52	1.36	1.29	14.04	12.77	11.43
Delaware	1,508	1,396	1,305	1,311	2,495	2,644	1.41	1.10	1.09	1.57	1.43	1.27	12.16	10.53	8.33
District of Columbia	1,824	1,748	1,745	1,512	2,598	2,675	(D)	(D)	1.08	(NA)	(D)	(D)	14.31	13.29	10.81
Florida	1,387	1,264	1,208	1,161	1,933	1,951	1.37	1.07	1.01	(NA)	(NA)	(NA)	18.47	16.17	12.93
Georgia	1,044	1,034	1,059	978	2,307	2,416	1.36	1.05	0.99	(NA)	(NA)	(NA)	13.75	11.86	8.38
Hawaii	1,350	1,204	1,147	1,088	2,301	2,174	1.75	1.50	1.29	(NA)	(NA)	(NA)	27.15	27.27	21.87
Idaho	1,235	1,310	1,109	1,003	2,378	2,441	1.45	1.17	1.13	1.50	1.19	1.17	9.06	7.59	6.28
Illinois	1,497	1,431	1,369	1,278	2,347	2,425	1.41	1.13	1.12	1.41	1.20	1.10	9.43	8.65	7.33
Indiana	1,352	1,278	1,222	1,132	2,785	2,801	1.37	1.09	1.07	1.54	1.20	1.21	10.02	9.40	6.42
Iowa	952	897	822	740	2,784	2,841	1.34	1.07	1.06	(NA)	(NA)	(NA)	(NA)	9.14	7.81
Kansas	952	895	838	837	2,622	2,749	1.35	1.08	1.03	(NA)	(NA)	(NA)	10.76	8.95	7.64
Kentucky	1,106	1,060	1,029	929	2,709	2,809	1.39	1.09	1.06	(NA)	(NA)	(NA)	11.02	9.18	7.41
Louisiana	1,177	1,116	1,072	1,075	4,036	4,638	1.34	1.03	1.01	(NA)	(NA)	(NA)	11.21	10.20	8.34
Maine	1,416	1,280	1,169	1,148	2,817	2,959	1.46	1.15	1.12	1.51	1.31	1.30	14.04	12.77	9.71
Maryland	1,571	1,508	1,422	1,315	2,128	2,227	1.40	1.10	1.04	1.63	1.46	1.35	12.40	11.01	9.78
Massachusetts	1,631	1,538	1,493	1,467	2,495	2,435	1.44	1.16	1.15	1.56	1.39	1.27	(NA)	12.46	9.91
Michigan	1,382	1,293	1,175	1,211	2,190	2,284	1.40	1.12	1.08	1.54	1.32	(NA)	8.47	7.31	5.11
Minnesota	1,109	1,034	971	932	2,496	2,485	1.42	1.15	1.13	1.43	1.22	1.16	9.56	8.58	7.13
Mississippi	882	867	747	719	2,609	2,623	1.37	1.08	1.05	(NA)	(NA)	(NA)	(NA)	9.74	7.49
Missouri	1,403	1,336	1,264	1,185	2,450	2,372	1.35	1.07	1.04	(NA)	(NA)	(NA)	11.04	9.49	7.85
Montana	733	674	595	579	2,740	3,162	1.40	1.12	1.13	(NA)	(NA)	(NA)	9.27	7.08	6.03
Nebraska	1,043	934	795	743	2,567	2,526	1.35	1.07	1.06	(NA)	(NA)	(NA)	9.02	7.83	6.43
Nevada	1,608	1,419	1,410	1,285	2,447	2,419	1.61	1.27	1.22	(NA)	(NA)	(NA)	10.05	8.96	6.63
New Hampshire.	1,389	1,299	1,218	1,201	2,484	2,611	1.45	1.17	1.14	1.50	1.31	1.28	13.20	11.42	10.07
New Jersey	1,411	1,499	1,409	1,299	2,372	2,572	1.45	1.16	1.13	1.66	1.49	1.40	11.59	8.51	7.28
New Mexico	1,563	1,413	1,398	1,388	2,354	2,259	1.43	1.14	1.10	(NA)	(NA)	(NA)	9.50	8.41	6.10
New York	1,402	1,299	1,196	1,118	2,091	2,243	1.43	1.13	1.09	1.63	1.44	1.44	12.42	11.58	9.86
North Carolina	1,200	1,144	1,080	1,061	2,301	2,405	1.34	1.03	1.00	(NA)	(NA)	(NA)	12.65	11.48	9.53
North Dakota	859	824	822	747	3,525	3,233	1.45	1.15	1.14	(NA)	(NA)	(NA)	9.03	7.25	6.37
Ohio	1,504	1,426	1,372	1,198	2,553	2,611	1.37	1.10	1.07	1.48	1.28	1.22	10.45	9.16	7.70
Oklahoma	1,177	1,064	994	1,031	2,937	2,706	1.32	1.04	1.01	(NA)	(NA)	(NA)	10.24	8.89	7.37
Oregon	1,842	1,664	1,548	1,461	2,133	2,234	1.51	1.24	1.18	1.59	1.30	1.37	11.10	9.84	8.12
Pennsylvania	1,326	1,204	1,154	1,080	2,430	2,482	1.36	1.07	1.03	1.49	1.30	1.22	12.26	10.87	8.49
Rhode Island	1,591	1,485	1,371	1,313	2,185	2,271	1.40	1.12	1.09	1.51	1.34	1.26	13.24	11.85	9.83
South Carolina	1,355	1,271	1,142	1,101	2,430	2,537	1.36	1.05	1.00	(NA)	(NA)	(NA)	12.46	11.02	9.15
South Dakota	747	701	638	476	2,481	2,585	1.41	1.14	1.14	(NA)	(NA)	(NA)	9.52	8.49	7.34
Tennessee	1,187	1,105	1,190	1,078	2,402	2,424	1.34	1.04	0.99	(NA)	(NA)	(NA)	10.39	9.64	7.49
Texas	1,482	1,400	1,338	1,274	3,405	3,551	1.33	1.03	0.99	(NA)	(NA)	(NA)	(NA)	9.22	7.41
Utah	1,654	1,689	1,473	1,375	1,987	2,042	1.40	1.13	1.06	(NA)	(NA)	(NA)	8.12	7.33	6.20
Vermont	1,148	986	896	888	2,709	2,675	1.49	1.18	1.13	1.51	1.31	1.26	11.03	10.05	8.13
Virginia	1,277	1,244	1,154	1,057	2,267	2,372	1.36	1.07	1.04	1.46	1.31	1.27	13.38	11.84	9.98
Washington	1,827	1,691	1,595	1,511	2,154	2,236	1.47	1.19	1.15	1.75	1.49	1.45	(NA)	8.43	7.16
West Virginia	993	934	892	844	2,385	2,452	1.41	1.11	1.06	1.49	1.30	1.25	10.87	8.92	7.46
Wisconsin.	1,282	1,170	1,076	1,055	2,471	2,435	1.42	1.13	1.09	1.47	1.27	1.17	10.13	9.27	7.55
Wyoming	943	844	756	677	4,698	4,541	1.43	1.15	1.12	(NA)	(NA)	(NA)	8.56	7.14	6.11

See footnotes at end of table.

Geographic area	Residential utility prices — Electric energy (dollars per 1,000 kilowatthours)			State individual income tax collections per capita[3] (dol.)		State tax rates[5] — General sales tax (cents per dollar)			State tax rates[5] — Gasoline (cents per gallon)		
	2004	2003	2000	2004	2000	2005	2004	2000	2005	2004	2000
United States . . .	89.4	87.0	82.4	674	693	(X)	(X)	(X)	(X)	(X)	(X)
Alabama	75.5	73.9	70.5	495	466	4.000	4.000	4.000	[8]18.00	[8]18.00	[8]18.00
Alaska	123.9	119.8	114.5	(X)	(X)	(X)	(X)	(X)	8.00	8.00	8.00
Arizona	84.7	83.5	84.4	403	447	5.600	5.600	5.000	[9]18.00	[9]18.00	[9]18.00
Arkansas	74.4	72.4	74.5	612	550	[10,11]7.250	5.125	4.625	21.50	21.50	19.70
California	117.8	120.0	108.9	1,014	1,168	[11]7.250	[11]7.250	6.000	18.00	18.00	18.00
Colorado	83.2	81.4	73.1	742	846	2.900	2.900	3.000	22.00	22.00	22.00
Connecticut	116.4	113.1	108.6	1,233	1,167	6.000	6.000	6.000	25.00	25.00	32.00
Delaware	88.0	85.9	85.4	941	935	(X)	(X)	(X)	23.00	[12]23.00	[12]23.00
District of Columbia	81.4	76.6	80.3	(X)	(X)	5.750	5.750	5.750	22.50	20.00	20.00
Florida	89.5	85.5	77.7	(X)	(X)	6.000	6.000	6.000	[13]14.50	[13]13.90	[13]13.10
Georgia	79.4	77.0	76.0	774	777	4.000	4.000	4.000	7.50	7.50	7.50
Hawaii	180.6	167.3	164.1	926	878	4.000	4.000	4.000	[8]16.00	[8]16.00	[8]16.00
Idaho	60.8	62.4	53.9	652	746	6.000	6.000	[14]5.000	25.00	26.00	26.00
Illinois	85.1	83.8	88.3	640	615	[10]6.250	6.250	[15]6.250	[8,9]20.10	[8,9]19.80	[8,9]19.30
Indiana	73.2	70.4	68.7	610	617	6.000	6.000	5.000	[9]18.00	[9]18.00	[9]15.00
Iowa	90.6	85.7	83.7	663	646	5.000	5.000	5.000	20.50	20.10	20.00
Kansas	78.2	77.1	76.5	700	693	5.300	5.300	[14]4.900	24.00	24.00	20.00
Kentucky	60.8	58.1	54.7	680	668	6.000	6.000	6.000	[9,16]17.40	[9,16]16.40	[9,16]16.40
Louisiana	80.9	78.4	76.7	484	354	4.000	4.000	4.000	20.00	20.00	20.00
Maine	126.3	123.7	124.9	881	845	5.000	5.000	5.500	[12]25.20	[12]24.60	22.00
Maryland	80.0	77.3	79.5	950	871	5.000	5.000	5.000	23.50	23.50	23.50
Massachusetts	118.5	116.8	105.3	1,376	1,424	5.000	5.000	5.000	21.00	21.00	[16]21.00
Michigan	85.5	83.5	85.2	650	724	6.000	6.000	6.000	19.00	19.00	19.00
Minnesota	80.6	76.5	75.2	1,119	1,128	6.500	6.500	6.500	20.00	20.00	20.00
Mississippi	81.7	76.0	69.3	366	354	7.000	7.000	7.000	18.40	18.40	18.40
Missouri	70.6	69.6	70.4	647	635	4.225	4.225	4.225	17.03	17.03	17.05
Montana	78.4	75.6	64.9	653	572	(X)	(X)	(X)	27.00	27.00	27.00
Nebraska	69.1	68.7	65.3	711	686	5.500	5.500	5.000	[12]26.30	[12]25.70	[12]24.80
Nevada	97.0	90.2	72.8	(X)	(X)	6.500	6.500	6.500	[8]23.00	[8]24.00	[8]24.00
New Hampshire	125.1	119.8	131.5	42	53	(X)	(X)	(X)	19.50	19.50	18.70
New Jersey	112.4	106.9	102.7	851	856	6.000	6.000	6.000	14.50	14.50	10.50
New Mexico	87.8	86.9	83.6	529	484	5.000	5.000	5.000	18.90	18.90	18.00
New York	145.8	143.1	139.7	1,282	1,222	4.250	4.250	4.000	23.20	22.60	[9,16]18.00
North Carolina	84.4	83.2	79.7	849	896	[17]4.500	4.500	4.000	[16]26.85	[16]24.55	[16]22.25
North Dakota	67.7	64.9	64.4	338	309	5.000	5.000	5.000	21.00	21.00	21.00
Ohio	84.7	82.7	86.1	760	726	6.000	6.000	5.000	26.00	22.00	22.00
Oklahoma	76.7	74.7	70.3	658	619	4.500	4.500	4.500	17.00	17.00	17.00
Oregon	71.2	70.6	58.8	1,188	1,198	(X)	(X)	(X)	[8]24.00	[8]24.00	[8]29.00
Pennsylvania	96.6	95.5	95.3	590	551	6.000	6.000	6.000	30.00	25.90	25.90
Rhode Island	121.9	116.2	112.8	833	791	7.000	7.000	7.000	31.00	31.00	29.00
South Carolina	80.5	80.1	75.8	581	610	5.000	5.000	5.000	16.00	16.00	16.00
South Dakota	76.4	74.7	74.2	(X)	(X)	4.000	4.000	[14]4.000	[8]22.00	[8]22.00	[8]22.00
Tennessee	68.8	65.5	63.3	25	32	7.000	7.000	7.000	[8]21.40	[8]21.40	[8]21.40
Texas	96.0	91.6	79.6	(X)	(X)	6.250	6.250	6.250	20.00	20.00	20.00
Utah	72.4	69.0	62.9	708	740	4.750	4.750	4.750	24.50	24.50	24.75
Vermont	130.7	128.2	123.0	692	709	6.000	6.000	[14]5.000	20.00	20.00	[18]20.00
Virginia	79.9	77.6	75.2	995	965	[11]5.000	[11]4.500	3.500	[8,18]17.50	[8,18]17.50	[8,18]17.50
Washington	63.6	63.1	51.3	(X)	(X)	6.500	6.500	6.500	28.00	28.00	23.00
West Virginia	62.3	62.4	62.7	589	534	6.000	6.000	6.000	27.00	25.35	25.35
Wisconsin	91.0	86.7	75.3	917	1,110	5.000	5.000	5.000	[12]29.10	[12]28.50	[12]25.80
Wyoming	71.0	70.4	65.0	(X)	(X)	[10]4.000	[10]4.000	[10,14]4.000	14.00	14.00	14.00

D Data withheld to avoid disclosure of individual company data.   NA Not available.   X Not applicable.

[1]Median price of single-family nonfarm homes.   [2]Based on total population residing in area.   [3]Population enumerated as of April 1 for 2000; estimated as of July 1 for all other years.
[4]Excludes federal and state taxes. Includes sales of No. 2 fuel oil and high- and low-sulfur diesel fuels.   [5]As of January 1 of the year shown.   [6]Costs include in-state tuition and required fees, room, and board.   [7]Costs include in-state tuition only and do not include room or board   [8]Does not include local option taxes.   [9]Carriers pay an additional surcharge equal to: Arizona, 8 cents; Illinois, 6.3 cents; Indiana, 11 cents; Kentucky, 2 percent; New York, 22.21 cents.   [10]Tax rate may be adjusted annually according to a formula based on balances in the unappropriated general fund and the school foundation fund.   [11]Includes statewide local tax of 1.25 percent in California and 1.0 percent in Virginia.   [12]A portion of the rate is adjustable based on maintenance costs, sales volume, or cost of fuel to state government.   [13]Local taxes for gasoline vary from 9.7 cents to 17.7 cents in 2005 (5.5 cents to 17 cents for all other years), plus a 2.07 cents/gallon pollution tax.   [14]State taxes food, but allows an (income) tax credit to compensate poor households.   [15]1.25 percent of the tax in Illinois is distributed to local governments.   [16]Tax rate is based on the average wholesale price and is adjusted quarterly.   [17]Tax rate scheduled to decrease to 4.0 after June 30, 2005.   [18]Large trucks pay a higher tax: Vermont, total of 25 cents/gallon; Virginia, additional 3.5 cents.

Survey, Census, or Data Collection Method: Housing prices—Based on the Finance Board Monthly Interest Rate Survey (MIRS); for information, see Internet site <http://www.fhfb.gov/>;   Public university—Based on the Integrated Postsecondary Education Data System (IPEDS) "Fall Enrollment" surveys; for information, see Appendix B, Limitations of the Data and Methodology, and Internet site <http://nces.ed.gov/ipeds/>;   Hospital stays—For information, see Internet site <http://www.healthforum.com/healthforum/index.jsp>;   Energy expenditures—Based on the State Energy Data System (SEDS); for information, see Technical Notes at Internet site <http://www.eia.doe.gov/emeu/states/_seds.html>;   Energy and Gas Information Retrieval System; for information, see Internet site <http://www.eia.doe.gov/>;   Electric energy prices—Based on Form EIA-861, "Annual Electric Power Industry Report"; for information, see Internet site <http://www.eia.doe.gov/cneaf/electricity/epa/epa_sum.html>;   State individual income tax—Based on the Annual Survey of State Government Tax Collection; for information, see Internet site <http://www.census.gov/govs/www/statetaxtechdoc2004.html>;   State tax rates—For information, see Internet site <http://www.taxadmin.org/>.

Sources: Housing prices—Federal Housing Finance Board, "Monthly Interest Rate Survey"; see Internet site <http://www.fhfb.gov/>;   Public university—U.S. National Center for Education Statistics, *Digest of Education Statistics 2003*, and prior years; see Internet site <http://nces.ed.gov/programs/digest/>;   Hospital stays—Health Forum, An American Hospital Association Company, Chicago, IL, *Hospital Statistics* 2003 edition, and prior years (copyright);   Energy expenditures—U.S. Energy Information Administration, *State Energy Price and Expenditure Report*, annual; see also Internet site <http://www.eia.doe.gov/>;   Gasoline prices—U.S. Energy Information Administration, *Petroleum Marketing 2004*, and prior years; see also Internet site <http://www.eia.doe.gov/>;   Utility prices—U.S. Energy Information Administration, "Petroleum Product Prices" and "Natural Gas Prices"; see Internet site <http://www.eia.doe.gov/emeu/states/_states.html> (accessed 12 September 2005); and *Electric Power Monthly*, March 2005 and *Electric Power Annual 2003*, and prior years; see also Internet site <http://www.eia.doe.gov/>;   State individual income tax—U.S. Census Bureau, "State Government Tax Collections"; see Internet site <http://www.census.gov/govs/www/statetax.html>;   State tax rates—Federation of Tax Administrators, 2005 and previous years; see Internet site <http://www.taxadmin.org/fta/rate/tax_stru.html>.

Gross State Product in Current and Real (2000) Dollars and by Selected Large Industry

Geographic area	Current dollars (mil. dol.)						Chained (2000) dollars[1] (mil. dol.)					
	2004	2003	2002	2001	2000	1990	2004	2003	2002	2001	2000	1990
United States . . .	11,649,827	10,923,849	10,412,244	10,058,156	9,749,104	5,674,013	10,720,296	10,289,220	10,009,433	9,836,571	9,749,104	6,939,733
Alabama	138,534	130,792	123,763	118,263	114,204	71,085	126,875	122,675	118,205	115,235	114,204	86,582
Alaska	33,876	31,704	29,741	27,358	27,590	24,987	28,983	28,103	28,703	26,432	27,590	31,904
Arizona	199,660	183,272	173,052	164,263	157,639	69,322	187,271	175,536	167,980	162,407	157,639	81,143
Arkansas	80,056	74,540	71,221	68,574	66,176	38,109	72,812	69,734	68,060	66,656	66,176	45,066
California	1,543,835	1,438,134	1,363,577	1,307,880	1,291,113	788,322	1,438,737	1,369,235	1,324,277	1,288,775	1,291,113	955,881
Colorado	199,953	188,397	181,246	177,526	171,363	74,206	185,169	178,327	174,682	174,187	171,363	91,346
Connecticut	187,086	174,085	167,235	165,434	160,685	98,976	172,355	164,137	160,115	161,595	160,685	124,587
Delaware	54,500	50,486	46,991	45,049	42,359	20,118	49,413	46,952	44,545	43,802	42,359	28,059
District of Columbia	75,264	70,668	67,176	63,223	58,425	40,056	66,871	64,137	62,582	61,087	58,425	55,080
Florida	594,525	553,709	522,340	496,861	470,120	257,242	543,845	517,855	497,740	484,433	470,120	320,500
Georgia	340,719	321,199	307,443	299,507	291,014	139,526	314,325	302,966	294,780	292,880	291,014	172,127
Hawaii	50,134	46,671	43,806	41,720	40,176	31,898	45,370	42,964	41,398	40,532	40,176	41,020
Idaho	43,351	40,358	38,276	36,571	35,206	17,769	40,802	38,849	37,413	36,182	35,206	19,550
Illinois	528,904	499,731	486,182	476,851	464,257	277,241	485,231	470,101	465,826	465,299	464,257	336,301
Indiana	227,271	213,342	203,296	195,769	194,683	110,084	208,434	201,263	194,993	190,876	194,683	131,012
Iowa	114,269	102,400	97,810	92,891	90,815	55,876	103,297	95,569	93,227	90,306	90,815	64,503
Kansas	99,090	93,263	89,875	87,206	83,427	51,274	89,896	86,814	85,765	84,696	83,427	62,391
Kentucky	135,412	128,315	121,633	116,545	112,737	67,508	124,079	120,508	116,269	113,530	112,737	81,317
Louisiana	151,993	144,321	134,360	137,567	134,755	93,591	133,289	130,733	130,596	132,355	134,755	121,745
Maine	43,279	40,829	39,027	37,094	35,662	23,343	39,536	38,097	37,110	36,138	35,662	29,255
Maryland	226,513	213,073	202,840	192,425	179,978	113,723	206,375	198,334	192,482	187,245	179,978	145,184
Massachusetts	317,684	297,113	287,191	283,422	276,786	158,903	298,020	284,286	278,213	279,434	276,786	195,734
Michigan	372,756	359,440	347,014	335,793	337,185	189,748	345,980	340,972	333,714	328,228	337,185	234,181
Minnesota	225,625	210,184	199,271	190,567	185,431	100,327	207,793	198,526	191,718	186,611	185,431	121,527
Mississippi	76,205	71,872	68,550	65,725	64,133	38,768	68,857	66,646	65,222	63,736	64,133	46,664
Missouri	203,208	193,828	187,090	182,048	176,443	104,097	185,834	181,638	178,589	177,460	176,443	127,995
Montana	27,701	25,584	23,913	22,636	21,367	13,417	24,654	23,493	22,621	21,838	21,367	16,157
Nebraska	67,891	65,399	60,571	57,771	55,727	33,776	61,216	60,672	57,599	56,158	55,727	40,271
Nevada	99,372	89,711	82,389	78,092	74,797	31,820	90,350	83,603	78,167	75,892	74,797	40,507
New Hampshire	52,097	48,202	46,106	44,394	43,584	23,784	48,550	45,874	44,475	43,691	43,584	27,711
New Jersey	415,891	394,040	377,824	362,336	343,959	214,845	383,725	371,806	363,045	354,390	343,959	266,565
New Mexico	60,940	57,078	53,414	50,908	50,419	26,871	56,415	54,183	52,506	50,465	50,419	28,724
New York	899,660	838,035	802,866	797,145	769,403	503,608	843,084	801,038	777,099	783,183	769,403	624,344
North Carolina	335,398	315,456	301,254	287,281	274,306	140,272	307,601	295,897	286,943	279,893	274,306	173,593
North Dakota	23,581	21,597	20,007	18,800	18,076	11,480	21,088	19,909	19,037	18,198	18,076	13,533
Ohio	418,258	398,918	385,657	374,771	371,228	228,343	384,049	375,740	369,354	365,791	371,228	274,921
Oklahoma	107,236	101,168	95,343	92,609	89,851	57,709	96,688	93,750	91,793	90,267	89,851	69,977
Oregon	128,126	119,973	115,113	111,352	112,964	57,275	121,411	116,113	112,943	110,925	112,964	63,203
Pennsylvania	468,833	443,709	424,820	407,880	391,501	248,307	427,825	415,281	404,630	396,814	391,501	305,168
Rhode Island	41,921	39,363	37,040	35,489	33,835	21,537	38,017	36,547	35,025	34,493	33,835	27,243
South Carolina	135,253	127,963	122,274	117,779	112,831	65,710	124,137	119,973	116,437	114,539	112,831	78,975
South Dakota	29,419	27,337	25,826	24,104	23,230	12,825	26,774	25,609	24,691	23,544	23,230	14,910
Tennessee	216,939	203,071	191,394	180,232	174,349	94,553	199,547	191,186	183,168	175,936	174,349	115,483
Texas	880,936	821,943	775,459	751,405	722,832	384,136	803,734	769,410	755,448	734,864	722,832	462,002
Utah	82,353	76,674	73,646	70,490	67,889	31,444	75,098	71,605	70,086	68,666	67,889	38,799
Vermont	22,114	20,544	19,419	18,656	17,661	11,727	20,608	19,562	18,748	18,350	17,661	13,762
Virginia	326,630	304,116	288,840	277,214	260,257	147,026	299,402	283,922	274,458	270,072	260,257	187,926
Washington	259,768	245,143	233,971	225,656	221,314	115,650	238,286	229,680	223,456	220,096	221,314	145,628
West Virginia	49,774	46,726	45,259	43,512	41,690	28,336	44,310	43,158	42,703	42,065	41,690	33,210
Wisconsin	211,727	198,096	189,508	182,373	176,244	100,313	194,093	186,350	181,153	177,842	176,244	119,126
Wyoming	24,308	22,279	20,326	19,138	17,427	13,150	20,736	19,940	19,533	18,417	17,427	15,181

See footnotes at end of table.

Geographic area	Total[3]	Construction	Manufacturing	Wholesale trade	Retail trade	Transportation and warehousing	Information	Finance and insurance	Real estate, renting, and leasing	Professional and technical services	Management of companies and enterprises	Educational services	Health care and social assistance	Arts, entertainment, and recreation	Accommodation and food services	Government
United States . . .	10,289,220	424,053	1,439,998	630,977	788,387	314,238	502,439	856,322	1,244,084	701,845	186,469	77,819	669,330	95,619	265,216	1,175,255
Alabama	122,675	4,931	21,614	7,201	11,341	3,405	3,988	6,593	12,469	7,178	831	488	8,074	510	2,754	18,961
Alaska	28,103	1,360	610	655	1,758	2,982	859	1,005	2,724	1,045	174	82	1,626	244	786	5,494
Arizona	175,536	9,238	25,954	10,047	16,013	5,134	5,945	14,471	21,742	9,629	2,352	842	10,887	1,675	5,445	20,346
Arkansas	69,734	2,891	13,386	4,697	3,532	3,532	3,105	3,165	6,229	2,388	1,868	248	5,091	347	1,524	8,624
California	1,369,235	53,848	181,488	80,081	106,886	33,201	85,449	96,304	203,549	109,048	22,996	8,428	75,336	16,675	33,804	142,909
Colorado	178,327	9,657	14,781	9,939	13,158	5,465	17,231	12,396	24,067	15,053	2,228	833	9,753	2,214	5,182	20,370
Connecticut	164,137	4,876	21,082	9,198	11,437	2,632	6,770	27,122	21,101	12,729	5,055	2,023	11,622	1,468	2,867	13,840
Delaware	46,952	1,400	4,841	1,756	2,368	537	923	15,232	5,302	2,849	2,192	177	2,207	292	693	3,765
District of Columbia	64,137	655	201	686	998	463	4,675	3,614	5,126	12,733	430	1,475	2,867	375	1,861	22,118
Florida	517,855	26,748	30,976	35,292	47,401	15,891	24,598	37,311	80,302	31,443	6,834	2,958	36,972	8,528	18,460	59,023
Georgia	302,960	13,379	42,996	23,689	22,810	12,547	21,311	18,795	32,616	18,786	5,705	1,987	16,238	2,004	7,384	37,223
Hawaii	42,964	1,970	776	1,604	3,626	1,770	1,336	2,022	7,093	2,012	495	384	2,871	517	3,613	9,192
Idaho	38,849	2,205	7,090	2,098	3,507	1,059	849	1,610	4,232	2,456	576	164	2,407	320	901	5,028
Illinois	470,101	20,298	66,223	33,980	31,442	17,671	20,498	46,760	55,934	38,107	10,237	4,012	28,596	4,189	10,140	43,868
Indiana	201,263	8,478	58,358	10,978	14,969	6,762	4,938	12,026	19,132	7,391	2,273	1,211	13,395	2,608	4,218	18,599
Iowa	95,569	3,523	20,510	5,830	7,293	3,215	3,323	9,932	8,645	2,965	605	684	6,230	967	1,859	10,716
Kansas	86,814	3,381	12,943	5,708	7,251	3,380	7,445	5,496	7,612	3,862	851	382	5,773	423	1,989	11,523
Kentucky	120,508	4,777	26,519	7,236	9,483	5,803	3,293	5,871	10,713	5,274	1,264	538	8,771	679	2,975	16,762
Louisiana	130,733	5,378	14,082	7,300	10,803	5,099	3,763	5,242	13,223	6,060	1,982	889	8,823	2,184	4,015	16,639
Maine	38,097	1,600	4,918	2,113	3,987	906	1,189	2,618	4,971	1,713	409	313	3,704	313	1,148	5,175
Maryland	198,334	10,256	13,528	11,007	15,044	4,350	7,887	14,053	29,389	20,096	1,100	1,983	13,972	1,427	5,345	32,263
Massachusetts	284,286	12,704	37,957	17,492	17,493	5,012	13,630	33,237	36,949	27,652	5,767	5,740	21,918	2,187	6,634	23,261
Michigan	340,972	13,544	76,418	20,308	25,985	8,778	10,005	19,761	37,597	27,130	7,753	1,515	22,159	2,815	6,903	33,496
Minnesota	198,526	9,109	28,807	14,331	14,675	7,025	7,436	20,863	22,134	11,740	6,536	1,275	14,666	1,657	4,255	19,342
Mississippi	66,646	2,574	10,947	3,613	6,576	2,332	1,902	2,945	6,207	2,277	738	318	4,602	717	2,822	11,066
Missouri	181,638	7,933	28,844	11,754	14,697	7,401	9,236	11,617	17,700	10,405	6,255	1,764	12,714	2,329	4,562	20,094
Montana	23,493	1,252	1,228	1,370	2,131	1,026	796	1,220	2,672	1,150	169	77	2,048	324	791	3,790
Nebraska	60,672	2,407	7,843	4,118	4,530	4,251	2,282	4,984	5,067	2,563	926	400	4,067	358	1,210	8,489
Nevada	83,603	7,283	3,069	3,547	7,479	2,987	2,255	6,855	10,329	4,259	1,633	143	4,035	2,281	12,523	8,051
New Hampshire	45,874	2,218	6,609	3,032	4,566	815	1,460	3,942	6,131	2,820	553	661	3,494	417	1,341	3,972
New Jersey	371,806	13,976	43,274	32,041	27,472	11,486	18,003	32,519	54,945	30,273	8,202	2,812	23,658	3,094	8,875	35,389
New Mexico	54,183	2,125	7,090	2,041	4,302	1,456	1,691	2,041	6,029	3,585	291	218	3,373	391	1,599	10,091
New York	801,038	23,494	60,626	43,792	48,633	15,569	56,960	138,273	99,894	65,983	22,069	10,090	58,539	8,448	17,396	78,467
North Carolina	295,897	11,396	68,740	16,834	21,793	7,538	9,927	29,123	27,789	13,931	5,965	1,678	16,476	1,908	6,444	35,427
North Dakota	19,909	779	2,121	1,630	1,708	780	717	1,253	1,570	757	166	72	1,697	110	496	3,014
Ohio	375,740	13,647	80,791	23,423	30,258	11,095	11,567	27,978	38,645	20,087	9,150	2,289	27,581	2,651	7,988	39,416
Oklahoma	93,750	3,590	11,210	5,123	8,367	3,203	4,189	4,854	9,125	4,361	1,265	424	6,250	448	2,177	15,280
Oregon	116,113	4,798	21,433	8,073	7,853	3,355	4,017	6,473	15,632	5,683	2,336	623	8,102	780	2,795	13,841
Pennsylvania	415,281	16,348	72,215	24,219	31,698	13,733	17,188	31,045	48,213	27,904	6,467	6,540	34,674	2,996	8,659	38,360
Rhode Island	36,547	2,010	3,879	1,946	2,750	605	1,488	4,907	4,646	1,949	799	667	3,142	314	1,018	4,194
South Carolina	119,973	6,077	24,816	6,824	10,658	2,809	3,400	5,773	13,045	5,145	730	512	6,450	911	3,818	17,606
South Dakota	25,609	961	3,197	1,440	2,302	652	740	4,385	1,838	627	232	143	2,063	248	682	3,095
Tennessee	191,186	6,744	35,138	13,158	18,125	9,384	6,280	11,776	19,663	9,027	2,263	1,405	14,798	1,768	5,783	22,100
Texas	769,410	32,060	101,342	54,340	61,272	29,302	38,509	50,625	78,123	49,442	10,017	3,443	44,749	4,628	19,109	86,102
Utah	71,605	3,628	7,954	3,854	6,274	2,861	2,938	6,596	8,465	4,383	1,538	612	3,835	591	1,809	9,896
Vermont	19,562	787	3,188	1,064	1,806	408	790	1,158	2,291	1,036	44	316	1,693	157	858	2,420
Virginia	283,922	11,958	36,375	12,825	19,797	7,741	16,566	18,888	33,990	29,333	6,293	1,578	14,138	1,500	6,416	45,912
Washington	229,680	9,671	21,035	14,137	18,467	6,618	21,376	13,842	33,231	15,402	3,634	999	14,308	1,783	5,569	31,185
West Virginia	43,158	1,627	5,080	2,147	3,962	1,401	1,356	1,722	4,053	1,697	291	185	3,961	400	1,204	7,131
Wisconsin	186,350	7,457	43,631	10,622	13,865	5,841	5,952	13,634	20,290	7,739	3,877	1,185	14,063	1,292	3,900	19,488
Wyoming	19,940	1,048	1,259	786	1,410	1,225	370	589	1,726	604	55	35	883	157	635	2,818

[1]For chained (2000) dollar estimates, states will not add to U.S. total.
[2]As of the June 2005 release, Gross State Product estimates by industry were not available for 2004.
[3]Includes industries not shown separately.

Survey, Census, or Data Collection Method: Based on the Regional Economic Information System; for information, see Internet site <http://www.bea.gov/bea/regional/articles.cfm?section=methods>.

Source: Bureau of Economic Analysis, *Survey of Current Business*, June 2005. Internet site <http://www.bea.gov/bea/regional/gsp.htm> (released 23 June 2005).

Table A-42. States — **Personal Income**

Geographic area	Personal income										
	Current dollars (bil. dol.)				Constant (2000) dollars[1]						
					Number (bil. dol.)				Percent change, 2000–2004	Percent distribution	
	2004 prel.	2003	2002	2000	2004 prel.	2003	2002	2000		2004	2000
United States . . .	9,672.2	9,151.7	8,869.8	8,422.1	8,970.4	8,673.7	8,565.9	8,422.1	6.51	100.0	100.0
Alabama	125.9	119.4	114.7	105.8	116.8	113.1	110.8	105.8	10.37	1.3	1.3
Alaska	22.6	21.5	20.9	18.7	20.9	20.4	20.2	18.7	11.75	0.2	0.2
Arizona	163.4	151.9	145.1	132.6	151.5	144.0	140.1	132.6	14.30	1.7	1.6
Arkansas	70.8	66.5	63.5	58.7	65.7	63.0	61.4	58.7	11.83	0.7	0.7
California	1,257.0	1,185.0	1,149.2	1,103.8	1,165.8	1,123.1	1,109.8	1,103.8	5.61	13.0	13.1
Colorado	165.9	157.2	154.0	144.4	153.9	149.0	148.7	144.4	6.58	1.7	1.7
Connecticut	159.1	149.8	147.1	141.6	147.5	142.0	142.0	141.6	4.20	1.6	1.7
Delaware	29.8	28.0	26.7	24.3	27.6	26.5	25.8	24.3	13.76	0.3	0.3
District of Columbia . . .	28.7	27.0	26.2	23.1	26.6	25.6	25.3	23.1	15.11	0.3	0.3
Florida	547.2	511.6	492.9	457.5	507.5	484.9	476.0	457.5	10.92	5.7	5.4
Georgia	265.3	251.6	245.0	230.4	246.1	238.5	236.6	230.4	6.82	2.7	2.7
Hawaii	40.6	38.0	36.5	34.5	37.7	36.0	35.2	34.5	9.33	0.4	0.4
Idaho	37.8	35.4	34.4	31.3	35.0	33.6	33.2	31.3	11.91	0.4	0.4
Illinois	436.7	417.0	409.1	400.4	405.0	395.2	395.1	400.4	1.17	4.5	4.8
Indiana	187.7	178.8	172.2	165.3	174.1	169.4	166.3	165.3	5.33	1.9	2.0
Iowa	90.3	83.4	81.7	77.8	83.7	79.0	78.9	77.8	7.68	0.9	0.9
Kansas	84.3	80.2	78.3	74.6	78.2	76.0	75.6	74.6	4.82	0.9	0.9
Kentucky	114.9	109.4	105.4	98.8	106.5	103.7	101.8	98.8	7.79	1.2	1.2
Louisiana	124.6	118.2	114.5	103.2	115.5	112.1	110.5	103.2	11.98	1.3	1.2
Maine	40.3	38.2	36.6	33.2	37.3	36.2	35.3	33.2	12.57	0.4	0.4
Maryland	218.1	206.4	198.9	182.0	202.3	195.6	192.1	182.0	11.18	2.3	2.2
Massachusetts	268.2	253.6	249.9	240.2	248.8	240.4	241.4	240.2	3.56	2.8	2.9
Michigan	323.1	314.3	301.8	294.2	299.7	297.9	291.4	294.2	1.86	3.3	3.5
Minnesota	182.9	172.3	166.7	158.0	169.7	163.3	161.0	158.0	7.40	1.9	1.9
Mississippi	71.6	67.6	64.6	59.8	66.4	64.1	62.3	59.8	10.91	0.7	0.7
Missouri.	176.1	168.5	163.1	152.7	163.4	159.7	157.5	152.7	6.96	1.8	1.8
Montana	24.9	23.3	22.4	20.7	23.1	22.1	21.6	20.7	11.44	0.3	0.2
Nebraska	54.8	52.4	49.5	47.3	50.8	49.7	47.8	47.3	7.30	0.6	0.6
Nevada	78.0	71.5	66.9	61.4	72.3	67.8	64.6	61.4	17.76	0.8	0.7
New Hampshire.	48.1	45.3	44.1	41.4	44.6	42.9	42.6	41.4	7.75	0.5	0.5
New Jersey	359.5	342.0	334.3	323.6	333.5	324.2	322.9	323.6	3.06	3.7	3.8
New Mexico	49.8	47.0	44.9	40.3	46.2	44.5	43.4	40.3	14.67	0.5	0.5
New York	735.0	693.8	676.6	663.0	681.7	657.6	653.4	663.0	2.82	7.6	7.9
North Carolina.	249.8	236.4	229.7	218.7	231.7	224.0	221.9	218.7	5.95	2.6	2.6
North Dakota	19.9	18.3	16.9	16.1	18.5	17.4	16.4	16.1	14.76	0.2	0.2
Ohio	358.9	344.6	333.5	320.5	332.9	326.6	322.1	320.5	3.85	3.7	3.8
Oklahoma	99.0	93.7	90.5	84.3	91.8	88.8	87.4	84.3	8.87	1.0	1.0
Oregon	107.7	102.4	100.3	96.4	99.9	97.1	96.8	96.4	3.64	1.1	1.1
Pennsylvania	413.7	394.8	382.6	364.8	383.7	374.1	369.5	364.8	5.17	4.3	4.3
Rhode Island	36.5	34.5	33.2	30.7	33.8	32.7	32.0	30.7	10.14	0.4	0.4
South Carolina	114.1	108.5	104.6	98.3	105.8	102.8	101.1	98.3	7.65	1.2	1.2
South Dakota	23.8	22.1	20.4	19.4	22.1	20.9	19.7	19.4	13.49	0.2	0.2
Tennessee	177.1	167.4	160.3	148.8	164.2	158.7	154.8	148.8	10.33	1.8	1.8
Texas	679.7	642.6	623.9	593.1	630.4	609.1	602.5	593.1	6.28	7.0	7.0
Utah	63.6	59.8	58.1	53.6	59.0	56.6	56.1	53.6	10.06	0.7	0.6
Vermont.	20.4	19.1	18.4	16.9	18.9	18.1	17.8	16.9	11.86	0.2	0.2
Virginia	264.7	248.4	239.8	220.8	245.4	235.5	231.6	220.8	11.14	2.7	2.6
Washington	219.0	203.9	198.4	187.9	203.1	193.2	191.6	187.9	8.11	2.3	2.2
West Virginia	47.0	44.5	43.0	39.6	43.6	42.1	41.6	39.6	10.05	0.5	0.5
Wisconsin.	177.2	168.0	162.9	153.5	164.3	159.2	157.3	153.5	7.00	1.8	1.8
Wyoming	17.4	16.3	15.5	14.1	16.1	15.4	15.0	14.1	14.60	0.2	0.2

See footnotes at end of table.

Geographic area	Disposable personal income								
	Current dollars (bil. dol.)				Constant (2000) dollars[1]				
					Number (bil. dol.)				Percent change, 2000–2004
	2004 prel.	2003	2002	2000	2004 prel.	2003	2002	2000	
United States . . .	**8,634.7**	**8,151.2**	**7,819.9**	**7,187.6**	**8,008.2**	**7,725.5**	**7,551.9**	**7,187.6**	**11.42**
Alabama	115.1	108.8	103.7	93.7	106.8	103.2	100.2	93.7	13.96
Alaska	20.6	19.6	18.8	16.6	19.1	18.6	18.2	16.6	15.31
Arizona	148.0	137.4	130.1	115.3	137.3	130.2	125.7	115.3	19.02
Arkansas	64.6	60.5	57.3	51.9	59.9	57.4	55.4	51.9	15.37
California	1,111.4	1,045.0	1,002.9	908.4	1,030.8	990.4	968.5	908.4	13.47
Colorado	148.2	139.8	135.3	122.2	137.4	132.5	130.7	122.2	12.50
Connecticut	135.1	127.1	123.2	113.9	125.3	120.5	119.0	113.9	9.99
Delaware	26.5	24.8	23.4	20.7	24.6	23.5	22.6	20.7	18.87
District of Columbia	25.0	23.5	22.6	19.1	23.2	22.3	21.8	19.1	21.66
Florida	496.1	462.6	441.3	398.2	460.1	438.4	426.2	398.2	15.55
Georgia	237.4	224.6	216.6	198.0	220.2	212.9	209.2	198.0	11.23
Hawaii	36.4	34.1	32.4	30.1	33.7	32.3	31.3	30.1	12.05
Idaho	34.4	32.2	31.1	27.2	31.9	30.5	30.0	27.2	17.13
Illinois	389.2	370.5	359.6	341.0	361.0	351.2	347.3	341.0	5.86
Indiana	169.2	160.7	153.3	144.1	156.9	152.3	148.0	144.1	8.93
Iowa	82.1	75.5	73.5	68.5	76.2	71.6	71.0	68.5	11.18
Kansas	76.0	72.2	69.8	64.8	70.5	68.4	67.4	64.8	8.92
Kentucky	103.4	98.1	93.8	86.4	95.9	93.0	90.6	86.4	10.91
Louisiana	114.1	108.2	103.9	92.0	105.8	102.5	100.3	92.0	15.03
Maine	36.2	34.3	32.6	28.7	33.6	32.5	31.4	28.7	17.00
Maryland	190.5	180.2	171.9	153.0	176.7	170.8	166.0	153.0	15.52
Massachusetts	232.1	219.4	213.7	192.8	215.2	207.9	206.3	192.8	11.61
Michigan	290.4	282.0	267.7	253.2	269.3	267.2	258.5	253.2	6.36
Minnesota	161.7	151.7	145.2	134.1	150.0	143.8	140.2	134.1	11.81
Mississippi	66.3	62.5	59.1	53.9	61.4	59.2	57.1	53.9	13.92
Missouri	158.9	151.6	145.3	132.7	147.4	143.6	140.3	132.7	11.03
Montana	22.6	21.1	20.1	18.3	20.9	20.0	19.4	18.3	14.43
Nebraska	49.5	47.3	44.2	41.3	45.9	44.9	42.7	41.3	11.18
Nevada	70.5	64.5	59.7	53.1	65.3	61.1	57.7	53.1	23.01
New Hampshire	43.5	40.8	39.3	35.4	40.3	38.6	37.9	35.4	13.77
New Jersey	315.1	298.5	288.4	270.0	292.2	282.9	278.5	270.0	8.25
New Mexico	45.5	42.7	40.6	35.7	42.2	40.5	39.2	35.7	18.45
New York	629.5	595.8	574.1	548.7	583.9	564.7	554.4	548.7	6.41
North Carolina	224.1	211.2	203.4	189.0	207.8	200.2	196.4	189.0	9.94
North Dakota	18.4	16.9	15.5	14.5	17.1	16.0	14.9	14.5	17.94
Ohio	320.6	306.8	293.4	275.7	297.4	290.8	283.3	275.7	7.85
Oklahoma	89.8	84.8	81.3	74.3	83.3	80.4	78.5	74.3	12.10
Oregon	95.5	90.7	88.2	82.0	88.6	85.9	85.2	82.0	8.04
Pennsylvania	369.6	352.2	338.1	314.2	342.7	333.8	326.5	314.2	9.09
Rhode Island	32.4	30.6	29.2	26.3	30.1	29.0	28.2	26.3	14.18
South Carolina	103.7	98.4	94.1	86.5	96.2	93.3	90.9	86.5	11.22
South Dakota	22.1	20.5	18.7	17.5	20.5	19.4	18.1	17.5	17.26
Tennessee	164.0	154.7	146.8	133.5	152.1	146.6	141.8	133.5	13.94
Texas	623.5	587.4	564.5	523.0	578.2	556.8	545.2	523.0	10.56
Utah	57.6	54.1	52.1	46.7	53.4	51.2	50.3	46.7	14.54
Vermont	18.4	17.2	16.4	14.6	17.1	16.3	15.8	14.6	16.64
Virginia	233.3	218.5	209.4	186.2	216.4	207.1	202.2	186.2	16.20
Washington	199.9	185.0	178.2	161.4	185.4	175.4	172.1	161.4	14.83
West Virginia	43.0	40.6	38.9	35.3	39.9	38.4	37.6	35.3	12.90
Wisconsin	157.8	149.2	143.5	131.7	146.4	141.4	138.6	131.7	11.16
Wyoming	15.7	14.7	13.8	12.1	14.5	13.9	13.4	12.1	20.20

[1]Constant dollar estimates are computed by the U.S. Census Bureau using the national implicit price deflator for personal consumption expenditures from the Bureau of Economic Analysis. Any regional differences in the rate of inflation are not reflected in these constant dollar estimates.

Survey, Census, or Data Collection Method: Based on the Regional Economic Information System. For more information, see "State Personal Income Methodologies" at <http://www.bea.gov/bea/regional/articles/spi2003/>.

Source: Except as noted, U.S. Bureau of Economic Analysis, *Survey of Current Business*, April 2005. See also <http://www.bea.gov/bea/regional/spi/> (released 28 March 2005).

Table A-43. States — **Personal Income Per Capita**

Geographic area	Personal income per capita												
	Current dollars					Constant (2000) dollars[1]					Income rank	
	2004 prel.	2003	2002	2001	2000	2004 prel.	2003	2002	2001	2000	2004	2000
United States . . .	**32,937**	**31,472**	**30,804**	**30,575**	**29,845**	**30,547**	**29,828**	**29,749**	**29,948**	**29,845**	**(X)**	**(X)**
Alabama	27,795	26,505	25,595	24,714	23,764	25,778	25,121	24,718	24,207	23,764	40	44
Alaska	34,454	33,213	32,582	31,704	29,867	31,954	31,478	31,466	31,054	29,867	13	15
Arizona	28,442	27,232	26,680	26,214	25,660	26,378	25,810	25,766	25,676	25,660	38	37
Arkansas	25,725	24,384	23,470	23,018	21,925	23,858	23,110	22,666	22,546	21,925	49	48
California	35,019	33,415	32,845	32,877	32,464	32,478	31,670	31,720	32,203	32,464	12	8
Colorado	36,063	34,561	34,228	34,491	33,370	33,446	32,756	33,055	33,784	33,370	7	7
Connecticut	45,398	42,972	42,521	42,920	41,489	42,104	40,728	41,064	42,040	41,489	1	1
Delaware	35,861	34,199	33,085	32,097	30,869	33,259	32,413	31,951	31,439	30,869	8	13
District of Columbia	51,803	48,446	46,407	44,827	40,456	48,044	45,916	44,817	43,908	40,456	(X)	(X)
Florida	31,455	30,098	29,549	29,268	28,509	29,173	28,526	28,537	28,668	28,509	23	20
Georgia	30,051	29,000	28,689	28,675	27,989	27,870	27,485	27,706	28,087	27,989	34	26
Hawaii	32,160	30,441	29,552	28,745	28,422	29,826	28,851	28,539	28,155	28,422	20	22
Idaho	27,098	25,902	25,597	25,018	24,075	25,132	24,549	24,720	24,505	24,075	44	42
Illinois	34,351	32,965	32,510	32,532	32,185	31,858	31,243	31,396	31,865	32,185	14	9
Indiana	30,094	28,838	27,960	27,397	27,132	27,910	27,332	27,002	26,835	27,132	33	31
Iowa	30,560	28,340	27,854	27,103	26,554	28,342	26,860	26,900	26,547	26,554	31	33
Kansas	30,811	29,438	28,850	28,714	27,694	28,575	27,900	27,861	28,125	27,694	28	27
Kentucky	27,709	26,575	25,777	24,914	24,412	25,698	25,187	24,894	24,403	24,412	41	40
Louisiana	27,581	26,312	25,565	24,685	23,078	25,580	24,938	24,689	24,179	23,078	42	45
Maine	30,566	29,164	28,177	27,286	25,969	28,348	27,641	27,212	26,726	25,969	30	35
Maryland	39,247	37,446	36,557	35,628	34,257	36,399	35,490	35,304	34,897	34,257	4	5
Massachusetts	41,801	39,504	38,973	38,949	37,756	38,768	37,441	37,638	38,150	37,756	2	3
Michigan	31,954	31,178	30,048	29,940	29,552	29,635	29,550	29,018	29,326	29,552	22	17
Minnesota	35,861	34,031	33,180	32,609	32,017	33,259	32,254	32,043	31,940	32,017	9	10
Mississippi	24,650	23,466	22,511	21,950	21,005	22,861	22,240	21,740	21,500	21,005	50	50
Missouri	30,608	29,464	28,719	27,813	27,241	28,387	27,925	27,735	27,243	27,241	29	30
Montana	26,857	25,406	24,557	24,672	22,929	24,908	24,079	23,716	24,166	22,929	45	46
Nebraska	31,339	30,179	28,672	28,684	27,625	29,065	28,603	27,690	28,096	27,625	25	29
Nevada	33,405	31,910	30,855	30,721	30,437	30,981	30,243	29,798	30,091	30,437	17	14
New Hampshire	37,040	35,140	34,543	33,850	33,396	34,352	33,305	33,359	33,156	33,396	6	6
New Jersey	41,332	39,577	38,979	39,142	38,365	38,333	37,510	37,643	38,339	38,365	3	2
New Mexico	26,191	24,995	24,228	24,088	22,135	24,291	23,689	23,398	23,594	22,135	47	47
New York	38,228	36,112	35,330	35,622	34,897	35,454	34,226	34,119	34,891	34,897	5	4
North Carolina	29,246	28,071	27,640	27,493	27,068	27,124	26,605	26,693	26,929	27,068	37	32
North Dakota	31,398	28,922	26,742	25,876	25,106	29,120	27,411	25,826	25,345	25,106	24	38
Ohio	31,322	30,129	29,230	28,594	28,207	29,049	28,555	28,228	28,008	28,207	26	24
Oklahoma	28,089	26,719	25,958	26,009	24,407	26,051	25,323	25,069	25,476	24,407	39	41
Oregon	29,971	28,734	28,464	28,502	28,097	27,796	27,233	27,489	27,917	28,097	36	25
Pennsylvania	33,348	31,911	31,034	30,275	29,695	30,928	30,244	29,971	29,654	29,695	18	16
Rhode Island	33,733	32,038	31,042	30,680	29,214	31,285	30,365	29,978	30,051	29,214	16	18
South Carolina	27,172	26,144	25,485	24,985	24,424	25,200	24,778	24,612	24,473	24,424	43	39
South Dakota	30,856	28,856	26,865	26,944	25,720	28,617	27,349	25,944	26,391	25,720	27	36
Tennessee	30,005	28,641	27,678	26,864	26,097	27,828	27,145	26,730	26,313	26,097	35	34
Texas	30,222	29,074	28,721	29,044	28,313	28,029	27,555	27,737	28,448	28,313	32	23
Utah	26,606	25,407	25,041	24,809	23,878	24,675	24,080	24,183	24,300	23,878	46	43
Vermont	32,770	30,888	29,855	28,944	27,680	30,392	29,275	28,832	28,350	27,680	19	28
Virginia	35,477	33,730	32,964	32,534	31,087	32,903	31,968	31,835	31,867	31,087	10	12
Washington	35,299	33,254	32,696	32,289	31,779	32,738	31,517	31,576	31,627	31,779	11	11
West Virginia	25,872	24,542	23,841	23,256	21,900	23,995	23,260	23,024	22,779	21,900	48	49
Wisconsin	32,157	30,685	29,937	29,392	28,570	29,824	29,082	28,911	28,789	28,570	21	19
Wyoming	34,306	32,433	31,122	30,301	28,460	31,817	30,739	30,056	29,680	28,460	15	21

See footnotes at end of table.

Geographic area	Disposable personal income per capita											
	Current dollars					Constant (2000) dollars[1]					Percent of U.S. average	
	2004 prel.	2003	2002	2001	2000	2004 prel.	2003	2002	2001	2000	2004	2000
United States ...	**29,404**	**28,031**	**27,158**	**26,240**	**25,471**	**27,270**	**26,567**	**26,227**	**25,702**	**25,471**	**100.0**	**100.0**
Alabama	25,416	24,169	23,147	21,991	21,046	23,572	22,907	22,354	21,540	21,046	86.4	82.6
Alaska	31,454	30,228	29,412	28,148	26,425	29,172	28,649	28,404	27,571	26,425	107.0	103.7
Arizona	25,770	24,625	23,926	22,947	22,326	23,900	23,339	23,106	22,476	22,326	87.6	87.7
Arkansas	23,453	22,193	21,173	20,439	19,375	21,751	21,034	20,448	20,020	19,375	79.8	76.1
California	30,964	29,467	28,664	27,506	26,716	28,717	27,928	27,682	26,942	26,716	105.3	104.9
Colorado	32,207	30,743	30,083	29,584	28,235	29,870	29,137	29,052	28,977	28,235	109.5	110.9
Connecticut	38,559	36,461	35,617	34,610	33,383	35,761	34,557	34,397	33,900	33,383	131.1	131.1
Delaware	31,900	30,301	28,980	27,259	26,278	29,585	28,718	27,987	26,700	26,278	108.5	103.2
District of Columbia	45,213	42,220	40,062	37,665	33,408	41,932	40,015	38,689	36,892	33,408	153.8	131.2
Florida	28,515	27,212	26,456	25,612	24,810	26,446	25,791	25,550	25,087	24,810	97.0	97.4
Georgia	26,891	25,885	25,363	24,767	24,054	24,940	24,533	24,494	24,259	24,054	91.5	94.4
Hawaii	28,808	27,296	26,272	25,124	24,842	26,718	25,870	25,372	24,609	24,842	98.0	97.5
Idaho	24,692	23,559	23,123	21,908	20,959	22,900	22,328	22,331	21,459	20,959	84.0	82.3
Illinois	30,616	29,292	28,572	27,866	27,412	28,394	27,762	27,593	27,294	27,412	104.1	107.6
Indiana	27,125	25,926	24,892	23,920	23,647	25,157	24,572	24,039	23,429	23,647	92.2	92.8
Iowa	27,794	25,666	25,061	23,926	23,390	25,777	24,325	24,202	23,435	23,390	94.5	91.8
Kansas	27,799	26,497	25,712	25,057	24,047	25,782	25,113	24,831	24,543	24,047	94.5	94.4
Kentucky	24,929	23,826	22,944	21,765	21,344	23,120	22,582	22,158	21,319	21,344	84.8	83.8
Louisiana	25,256	24,068	23,206	22,032	20,574	23,423	22,811	22,411	21,580	20,574	85.9	80.8
Maine	27,512	26,200	25,086	23,711	22,489	25,516	24,832	24,226	23,225	22,489	93.6	88.3
Maryland	34,282	32,683	31,585	30,063	28,800	31,794	30,976	30,503	29,446	28,800	116.6	113.1
Massachusetts	36,169	34,174	33,320	31,803	30,310	33,544	32,389	32,178	31,151	30,310	123.0	119.0
Michigan	28,719	27,967	26,654	25,995	25,435	26,635	26,506	25,741	25,462	25,435	97.7	99.9
Minnesota	31,702	29,960	28,894	27,826	27,187	29,402	28,395	27,904	27,255	27,187	107.8	106.7
Mississippi	22,823	21,669	20,615	19,834	18,935	21,167	20,537	19,909	19,427	18,935	77.6	74.3
Missouri	27,614	26,499	25,575	24,181	23,676	25,610	25,115	24,699	23,685	23,676	93.9	93.0
Montana	24,334	22,989	22,074	21,887	20,233	22,568	21,788	21,318	21,438	20,233	82.8	79.4
Nebraska	28,316	27,249	25,591	25,124	24,090	26,261	25,826	24,714	24,609	24,090	96.3	94.6
Nevada	30,177	28,767	27,540	26,783	26,322	27,987	27,264	26,596	26,234	26,322	102.6	103.3
New Hampshire	33,453	31,637	30,782	29,205	28,566	31,026	29,985	29,727	28,606	28,566	113.8	112.2
New Jersey	36,223	34,544	33,620	32,817	32,010	33,595	32,740	32,468	32,144	32,010	123.2	125.7
New Mexico	23,929	22,732	21,859	21,496	19,578	22,193	21,545	21,110	21,055	19,578	81.4	76.9
New York	32,743	31,010	29,978	29,169	28,881	30,367	29,390	28,951	28,571	28,881	111.4	113.4
North Carolina	26,232	25,081	24,468	23,837	23,396	24,329	23,771	23,630	23,348	23,396	89.2	91.9
North Dakota	29,041	26,647	24,396	23,200	22,596	26,934	25,255	23,560	22,724	22,596	98.8	88.7
Ohio	27,981	26,825	25,711	24,674	24,263	25,951	25,424	24,830	24,168	24,263	95.2	95.3
Oklahoma	25,496	24,191	23,313	23,000	21,517	23,646	22,927	22,514	22,528	21,517	86.7	84.5
Oregon	26,580	25,442	25,042	24,506	23,905	24,651	24,113	24,184	24,003	23,905	90.4	93.9
Pennsylvania	29,789	28,472	27,426	26,130	25,573	27,627	26,985	26,486	25,594	25,573	101.3	100.4
Rhode Island	29,996	28,427	27,304	26,402	25,059	27,819	26,942	26,368	25,860	25,059	102.0	98.4
South Carolina	24,712	23,727	22,922	22,063	21,501	22,919	22,488	22,137	21,610	21,501	84.0	84.4
South Dakota	28,711	26,747	24,624	24,325	23,163	26,628	25,350	23,780	23,826	23,163	97.6	90.9
Tennessee	27,794	26,467	25,343	24,150	23,409	25,777	25,085	24,475	23,655	23,409	94.5	91.9
Texas	27,722	26,577	25,987	25,719	24,965	25,710	25,189	25,097	25,191	24,965	94.3	98.0
Utah	24,122	22,980	22,465	21,755	20,801	22,372	21,780	21,695	21,309	20,801	82.0	81.7
Vermont	29,640	27,842	26,592	25,218	24,010	27,489	26,388	25,681	24,701	24,010	100.8	94.3
Virginia	31,277	29,672	28,786	27,574	26,215	29,007	28,122	27,800	27,008	26,215	106.4	102.9
Washington	32,219	30,178	29,368	28,182	27,309	29,881	28,602	28,362	27,604	27,309	109.6	107.2
West Virginia	23,676	22,393	21,572	20,771	19,535	21,958	21,223	20,833	20,345	19,535	80.5	76.7
Wisconsin	28,645	27,258	26,374	25,317	24,498	26,566	25,834	25,470	24,798	24,498	97.4	96.2
Wyoming	30,972	29,194	27,699	26,348	24,497	28,725	27,669	26,750	25,808	24,497	105.3	96.2

X Not applicable.

[1]Constant dollar estimates are computed by the U.S. Census Bureau using the national implicit price deflator for personal consumption expenditures from the Bureau of Economic Analysis. Any regional differences in the rate of inflation are not reflected in these constant dollar estimates.

Survey, Census, or Data Collection Method: Based on the Regional Economic Information System. For more information, see "State Personal Income Methodologies" at <http://www.bea.gov/bea/regional/articles/spi2003/>.

Source: Except as noted, U.S. Bureau of Economic Analysis, *Survey of Current Business*, April 2005. See also <http://www.bea.gov/bea/regional/spi/> (released 28 March 2005).

Geographic area	Farm earnings (mil. dol.)	Forestry, fishing, related activities, and other	Mining	Utilities	Construction	Manufacturing	Wholesale trade	Retail trade	Information	Finance and insurance
						Private earnings (mil. dol.)				
United States . . .	**54,785**	**28,117**	**63,073**	**78,071**	**463,816**	**983,917**	**387,439**	**500,698**	**293,577**	**580,387**
Alabama	1,522	665	708	1,497	5,809	16,146	4,492	6,892	1,882	4,596
Alaska	13	278	1,170	207	1,570	739	357	1,286	458	582
Arizona	913	470	715	1,116	10,912	12,861	6,494	10,239	3,121	8,419
Arkansas	1,917	537	390	572	2,664	9,255	2,511	3,584	1,782	2,123
California	8,927	5,871	2,879	10,131	65,452	121,732	47,032	67,631	57,492	71,953
Colorado	749	238	2,732	1,075	10,982	11,140	6,579	8,437	11,132	9,149
Connecticut	171	73	167	1,580	6,977	17,502	5,850	7,811	3,912	19,906
Delaware	209	22	28	246	1,606	2,783	1,156	1,650	539	3,852
District of Columbia	–	1,350	8	266	799	273	423	623	2,739	2,524
Florida	1,518	1,800	465	2,965	27,232	23,383	20,561	30,024	12,844	26,241
Georgia	2,319	744	537	2,917	12,685	25,561	14,559	14,070	12,798	13,459
Hawaii	219	66	51	282	2,210	870	960	2,226	798	1,287
Idaho	982	428	135	321	2,294	3,576	1,220	2,312	489	1,127
Illinois	2,042	337	1,594	3,084	20,333	47,750	21,863	19,822	11,058	32,602
Indiana	1,013	204	564	1,593	9,150	39,131	6,966	9,314	2,481	6,712
Iowa	3,585	241	142	876	4,181	12,830	3,529	4,946	1,767	5,446
Kansas	753	221	818	716	3,549	11,182	3,569	4,369	3,549	3,684
Kentucky	699	363	1,511	528	4,889	16,526	4,392	6,103	1,536	4,201
Louisiana	645	566	4,189	975	6,078	10,822	4,038	6,347	2,034	3,716
Maine	65	366	9	300	1,947	3,698	1,213	2,600	670	1,748
Maryland	315	139	120	2,542	11,802	10,684	6,700	10,066	4,520	9,734
Massachusetts	81	458	373	1,419	12,295	26,327	11,463	12,507	8,476	25,409
Michigan	764	367	758	2,849	14,153	59,366	12,030	15,941	4,882	12,276
Minnesota	2,185	374	452	1,477	9,187	22,952	9,536	9,328	4,374	12,277
Mississippi	1,351	560	510	618	2,488	8,190	1,891	3,842	880	1,863
Missouri	820	399	413	1,143	9,028	19,242	7,314	9,377	5,259	8,095
Montana	273	205	543	283	1,433	1,075	744	1,659	415	838
Nebraska	1,603	153	143	527	2,683	5,093	2,291	2,933	1,262	3,079
Nevada	88	37	850	603	7,086	2,799	2,286	4,641	1,145	3,856
New Hampshire	36	133	46	421	2,465	5,619	2,171	3,424	955	2,447
New Jersey	228	139	218	2,282	14,462	29,349	19,223	18,352	11,588	23,979
New Mexico	729	138	1,323	328	2,499	2,248	1,174	2,936	781	1,407
New York	913	1,348	1,224	6,075	24,315	43,643	27,890	30,373	35,835	102,424
North Carolina	1,747	688	278	1,425	12,543	33,612	10,381	13,368	5,200	11,678
North Dakota	1,398	97	292	367	966	1,323	910	1,118	421	796
Ohio	1,172	297	1,044	2,144	14,896	55,486	14,661	18,517	6,218	17,189
Oklahoma	1,222	184	3,777	1,174	3,459	10,912	2,873	5,179	2,213	3,238
Oregon	887	1,510	134	789	5,498	13,127	5,279	6,190	2,362	4,284
Pennsylvania	1,172	566	1,738	3,678	17,774	46,472	15,507	20,797	9,205	22,085
Rhode Island	20	61	20	279	1,498	3,264	1,129	1,750	959	2,075
South Carolina	339	389	103	1,096	5,960	15,346	3,739	6,757	1,701	4,022
South Dakota	1,302	93	63	173	1,040	1,862	828	1,361	369	1,237
Tennessee	182	360	284	341	8,241	24,912	8,006	11,081	3,056	8,756
Texas	3,694	1,466	23,857	10,044	35,158	71,302	33,649	37,165	21,264	37,379
Utah	253	54	592	382	4,002	6,399	2,366	4,129	1,670	3,163
Vermont	177	86	55	228	1,095	2,343	591	1,268	348	715
Virginia	382	345	767	1,630	13,927	17,672	8,085	12,533	9,680	12,194
Washington	1,611	1,982	295	617	11,147	19,970	8,411	11,598	11,451	10,113
West Virginia	–83	150	1,919	551	1,903	3,963	1,214	2,405	613	1,108
Wisconsin	1,512	452	248	1,131	8,469	30,973	6,914	8,950	3,214	8,953
Wyoming	149	49	1,823	203	1,026	633	422	868	182	393

See footnotes at end of table.

Geographic area	Private earnings (mil. dol.)								Government and government enterprises (mil. dol.)		
	Real estate and rental and leasing	Professional and technical services	Management of companies and enterprises	Administrative and waste services	Educational services	Health care and social assistance	Arts, entertainment, and recreation	Accommodation and food services	Federal, civilian	Military	State and local
United States . . .	**196,979**	**687,149**	**162,525**	**273,867**	**98,552**	**712,238**	**82,769**	**207,807**	**223,754**	**117,323**	**869,900**
Alabama	1,682	7,139	769	2,616	623	8,537	464	2,126	4,031	1,933	12,220
Alaska	336	1,010	96	466	102	1,786	210	644	1,395	1,575	2,882
Arizona	4,507	9,557	1,869	6,743	1,171	11,835	1,396	4,170	3,981	2,021	14,798
Arkansas	791	2,504	1,763	1,270	312	5,497	303	1,168	1,522	890	6,801
California	33,379	106,712	21,168	37,133	10,599	78,766	16,760	27,110	20,080	13,004	119,015
Colorado	5,244	14,686	2,304	5,082	1,062	10,139	1,746	4,077	4,203	2,703	13,751
Connecticut	2,453	12,042	3,626	3,742	2,544	12,320	987	2,343	1,495	777	12,491
Delaware	422	2,835	985	711	224	2,416	272	609	370	478	2,669
District of Columbia	972	13,523	244	1,648	1,848	3,142	358	1,482	20,117	1,819	2,478
Florida	11,619	32,184	6,150	25,945	3,886	39,790	7,336	14,307	9,936	6,606	43,847
Georgia	5,724	18,088	4,598	9,048	2,543	17,191	1,711	5,864	7,331	5,704	22,751
Hawaii	804	1,985	590	1,333	465	2,932	452	2,825	2,493	3,444	3,985
Idaho	619	2,350	592	976	207	2,563	288	698	968	526	3,763
Illinois	8,840	37,072	9,710	12,774	5,037	30,172	3,217	8,119	7,027	2,622	36,782
Indiana	2,904	6,971	2,250	4,547	1,525	14,239	1,727	3,436	2,716	805	15,765
Iowa	1,021	2,896	624	1,713	854	6,662	609	1,462	1,285	543	9,144
Kansas	1,206	3,960	671	2,011	464	6,104	341	1,544	1,903	1,694	8,266
Kentucky	1,199	4,892	1,343	2,337	690	9,155	583	2,335	2,433	2,750	10,409
Louisiana	2,221	6,134	1,360	2,691	1,132	9,309	1,458	2,829	2,638	2,183	12,971
Maine	502	1,667	391	726	394	4,123	273	929	1,111	487	3,724
Maryland	4,605	19,910	907	5,603	2,601	14,858	1,305	4,152	14,240	3,014	16,269
Massachusetts	4,836	27,642	5,910	6,836	7,238	23,798	2,117	5,504	4,120	983	19,199
Michigan	7,845	24,849	7,597	10,037	1,973	23,653	2,356	5,400	4,179	849	28,639
Minnesota	2,968	11,283	6,547	4,075	1,613	15,547	1,344	3,260	2,554	724	16,643
Mississippi	715	2,325	645	1,089	398	4,847	442	2,053	1,867	1,789	7,940
Missouri	2,628	10,047	5,523	4,089	2,245	13,370	1,813	3,655	4,152	1,805	14,769
Montana	739	1,112	58	432	101	2,208	224	653	980	441	2,670
Nebraska	635	2,552	1,041	1,322	490	4,356	264	926	1,156	912	5,523
Nevada	1,802	4,183	1,680	2,481	195	4,308	1,214	9,722	1,387	871	6,651
New Hampshire	880	2,710	749	1,057	850	3,740	385	1,049	631	169	3,294
New Jersey	6,956	29,202	7,724	10,435	3,140	25,312	2,259	6,900	5,099	1,274	32,016
New Mexico	697	3,260	283	1,412	281	3,556	351	1,251	2,224	1,150	7,174
New York	16,877	64,737	16,407	18,212	12,721	62,054	8,418	13,168	10,262	2,631	72,704
North Carolina	4,253	12,945	5,537	6,440	2,161	17,212	1,727	4,993	4,364	7,470	24,921
North Dakota	195	696	181	285	99	1,851	77	372	626	741	2,003
Ohio	5,521	19,602	8,257	9,340	2,886	29,534	2,295	6,481	6,215	1,863	32,488
Oklahoma	1,442	4,204	865	2,638	551	6,672	364	1,684	3,553	2,278	9,528
Oregon	1,995	5,546	2,136	2,712	809	8,683	716	2,449	2,342	509	11,228
Pennsylvania	6,949	28,235	6,649	9,592	8,225	37,958	2,810	6,965	8,014	1,775	30,054
Rhode Island	466	1,987	903	783	833	3,366	267	808	841	447	3,171
South Carolina	1,888	4,872	701	3,847	639	6,704	734	2,959	2,015	3,018	12,159
South Dakota	358	594	223	389	184	2,265	216	501	751	449	2,095
Tennessee	3,211	9,099	1,707	6,377	1,832	16,114	1,542	4,255	3,949	976	14,460
Texas	18,078	48,466	4,317	21,513	4,454	47,782	3,846	14,837	13,760	10,218	59,956
Utah	1,196	4,253	1,179	1,824	777	4,105	489	1,370	2,430	850	6,494
Vermont	242	1,016	23	325	401	1,818	135	615	461	157	1,984
Virginia	5,620	29,827	6,519	6,921	2,101	14,957	1,338	5,065	14,581	11,501	22,188
Washington	4,156	14,119	3,124	5,825	1,317	14,726	1,672	4,239	5,729	4,414	21,301
West Virginia	382	1,716	190	785	217	4,272	343	892	1,660	371	4,974
Wisconsin	2,025	7,367	3,764	3,458	1,491	15,005	1,055	3,067	2,043	762	16,828
Wyoming	369	587	74	222	46	932	156	483	536	350	2,060

– Represents zero.

Survey, Census, or Data Collection Method: Based on the Regional Economic Information System; for information, see Internet site <http://www.bea.gov/bea/regional/articles/spi2003/>.

Source: U.S. Bureau of Economic Analysis, *Survey of Current Business*, April 2005. See Internet site <http://www.bea.gov/bea/regional/spi/>.

Geographic area	Doctoral scientists[1,2]		Doctoral engineers[1,2]		S&E[3] doctorates awarded[4]		Federal R&D[5] obligations (mil. dol.)		
	2001	1999	2001	1999	2002	2001	2002	2001	1999
United States . . .	**541,630**	**517,550**	**112,540**	**106,900**	**24,499**	**25,412**	**83,629**	**77,915**	**73,645**
Alabama	5,040	5,620	1,340	1,230	307	287	2,705	2,333	1,807
Alaska	1,350	1,240	80	90	19	26	274	212	115
Arizona	6,720	6,320	2,000	1,830	417	403	2,057	1,781	1,117
Arkansas	2,670	2,850	370	270	70	62	141	184	106
California	70,650	66,800	21,040	19,980	3,232	3,334	15,686	12,651	15,600
Colorado	12,150	11,470	2,070	2,070	457	485	1,609	1,341	1,439
Connecticut	9,620	9,470	1,410	1,320	353	370	1,917	1,377	655
Delaware	3,530	3,660	840	730	100	128	79	70	52
District of Columbia	13,410	13,260	1,150	960	282	291	2,850	2,606	2,452
Florida	16,330	14,550	3,080	2,990	762	781	2,301	2,648	2,284
Georgia	11,860	10,920	1,780	1,360	637	608	2,019	3,396	2,023
Hawaii	2,550	2,490	310	170	76	107	375	293	199
Idaho	2,090	1,830	570	520	50	51	231	209	201
Illinois	20,680	20,540	3,940	4,020	1,210	1,323	1,694	1,694	1,316
Indiana	9,080	8,560	1,790	1,480	589	667	526	535	414
Iowa	4,500	4,480	560	560	354	376	405	324	264
Kansas	4,170	3,700	550	520	275	264	291	307	192
Kentucky	4,950	4,520	450	400	185	172	321	272	147
Louisiana	5,270	5,320	870	880	293	334	432	276	219
Maine	2,120	2,310	280	260	30	30	255	451	151
Maryland	22,150	21,510	3,440	3,440	638	664	7,192	9,290	8,094
Massachusetts	26,970	24,880	4,890	4,850	1,461	1,448	4,659	4,318	3,129
Michigan	14,630	13,770	4,570	4,530	967	906	1,244	1,176	840
Minnesota	10,680	10,610	1,950	1,870	403	455	1,151	901	885
Mississippi	2,930	2,880	660	620	136	129	623	402	352
Missouri	8,850	9,050	1,440	1,380	409	439	1,203	909	929
Montana	1,730	1,830	100	110	57	42	113	137	95
Nebraska	2,820	2,670	330	310	150	164	145	125	94
Nevada	1,790	1,760	540	420	61	52	336	295	279
New Hampshire	2,350	2,020	650	590	82	76	297	419	292
New Jersey	20,660	19,740	4,690	4,750	521	621	2,021	1,592	2,661
New Mexico	6,800	6,730	2,340	2,130	176	147	2,746	2,581	2,068
New York	42,610	41,230	6,490	6,230	2,124	2,128	3,747	3,336	2,689
North Carolina	16,780	15,500	2,340	2,200	697	726	1,390	1,401	1,008
North Dakota	1,150	1,290	130	140	46	43	102	78	60
Ohio	18,580	18,140	4,780	4,840	987	1,061	2,103	2,327	3,688
Oklahoma	4,240	4,150	920	880	196	238	272	226	166
Oregon	7,260	6,940	1,460	1,300	233	262	502	523	408
Pennsylvania	24,630	23,820	4,650	4,290	1,207	1,247	3,162	2,602	1,907
Rhode Island	2,370	2,440	500	540	157	162	501	437	392
South Carolina	5,030	4,550	980	810	240	216	371	314	216
South Dakota	1,160	1,070	90	80	36	34	59	55	39
Tennessee	8,680	7,470	1,660	1,750	343	377	961	845	685
Texas	28,610	27,170	8,910	8,340	1,462	1,598	3,374	2,925	3,853
Utah	4,700	4,350	1,220	1,150	265	236	409	395	305
Vermont	1,800	1,720	240	300	49	52	136	113	62
Virginia	16,960	15,770	3,400	3,190	603	628	5,756	4,810	5,750
Washington	14,540	13,250	2,610	2,370	460	457	1,999	1,545	1,307
West Virginia	1,980	2,060	380	380	81	67	254	353	227
Wisconsin	8,520	8,330	1,610	1,410	520	530	595	488	378
Wyoming	940	910	100	50	34	38	40	37	35

See footnotes at end of table.

State and Metropolitan Area Data Book: 2006

U.S. Census Bureau

Table A-45. States — **Science and Engineering Indicators**—Con.

Geographic area	Total R&D[5] performance (mil. dol.)		Industry R&D[1, 5] (mil. dol.)		Academic R&D[5] (mil. dol.)		Number of SBIR[6] awards		Utility patents[7] issued to state residents	
	2002	2000	2002	2000	2002	2001	1999–2002	1995–2000	2002	2001
United States ...	**255,707**	**244,855**	**182,403**	**187,544**	**36,244**	**32,652**	**19,380**	**26,420**	**86,955**	**87,594**
Alabama	2,323	1,730	846	607	503	445	347	486	398	382
Alaska	308	196	51	9	129	116	11	19	43	50
Arizona	4,096	3,107	3,201	2,445	531	501	399	542	1,588	1,540
Arkansas	427	454	225	273	140	141	33	33	184	180
California	51,388	55,093	39,664	45,769	4,882	4,422	3,923	5,510	18,829	18,598
Colorado	4,218	4,230	2,823	3,140	645	573	984	1,196	1,939	1,927
Connecticut	6,774	4,888	6,077	4,371	538	499	349	627	1,805	1,853
Delaware	1,319	1,532	1,219	1,444	88	80	81	112	354	382
District of Columbia	2,706	2,296	194	112	252	228	83	84	61	67
Florida	5,498	4,663	3,707	3,212	1,086	997	442	586	2,397	2,649
Georgia	3,935	2,796	2,107	1,579	1,076	989	205	240	1,295	1,370
Hawaii	456	291	103	44	173	157	82	105	73	95
Idaho	1,370	1,434	992	1,338	93	82	45	39	1,828	1,697
Illinois	10,190	12,767	7,616	10,661	1,441	1,281	300	393	3,470	3,640
Indiana	4,326	3,252	3,572	2,668	651	584	116	142	1,397	1,358
Iowa	1,346	1,017	753	538	486	440	45	35	630	751
Kansas	1,865	1,420	1,427	1,140	300	269	71	73	421	312
Kentucky	1,128	866	656	582	333	297	54	61	450	481
Louisiana	858	627	248	126	483	432	48	58	445	520
Maine	429	319	250	201	69	68	63	66	153	145
Maryland	9,030	8,634	3,800	2,032	1,880	1,644	958	1,255	1,460	1,483
Massachusetts	14,316	13,004	10,279	9,863	1,706	1,577	2,792	3,958	3,608	3,667
Michigan	15,082	18,892	13,565	17,640	1,233	1,107	331	525	3,862	3,854
Minnesota	5,247	4,299	4,460	3,722	504	469	275	409	2,751	2,635
Mississippi	691	513	224	101	285	242	41	41	156	166
Missouri	2,478	2,583	1,592	1,893	706	678	88	113	837	841
Montana	236	170	66	28	122	108	105	73	138	145
Nebraska	663	439	342	199	267	242	35	36	212	215
Nevada	524	377	339	248	127	116	57	52	308	313
New Hampshire	1,435	775	1,153	586	220	197	243	313	609	598
New Jersey	13,020	13,133	11,566	12,062	683	609	573	803	3,762	3,869
New Mexico	4,689	3,085	331	1,158	293	274	351	488	371	376
New York	13,354	13,556	9,234	10,539	2,774	2,476	751	1,112	6,360	6,349
North Carolina	5,135	5,045	3,443	3,672	1,277	1,137	231	310	1,822	1,946
North Dakota	295	146	154	51	106	85	26	31	73	97
Ohio	8,310	7,662	6,230	5,962	1,117	996	733	960	3,329	3,274
Oklahoma	793	660	412	333	282	255	63	72	466	576
Oregon	2,892	2,116	2,320	1,651	387	366	249	369	1,450	1,259
Pennsylvania	9,763	9,842	7,064	7,873	1,913	1,687	663	889	3,343	3,534
Rhode Island	1,639	1,501	1,121	1,090	163	143	71	70	260	287
South Carolina	1,668	1,126	1,054	781	400	361	72	62	599	565
South Dakota	111	85	53	44	38	32	25	37	76	76
Tennessee	2,568	2,057	1,289	1,215	491	423	159	233	831	813
Texas	14,223	11,552	10,744	8,961	2,535	2,244	740	1,004	6,029	6,371
Utah	1,572	1,361	1,116	979	360	338	195	268	675	715
Vermont	398	465	286	396	90	77	54	89	487	453
Virginia	5,895	5,069	2,920	2,718	694	611	1,076	1,466	1,160	1,115
Washington	10,511	10,516	8,579	9,265	748	707	461	661	2,098	1,969
West Virginia	542	457	264	235	97	79	36	26	151	148
Wisconsin	3,585	2,693	2,649	1,981	806	729	205	250	1,864	1,837
Wyoming	80	61	21	7	42	42	40	38	48	51

[1]The reliability varies by state because the sample allocation was not based on geography.
[2]Includes all graduate degree (except M.D.) candidates and recipients in science and engineering fields, including health fields.
[3]Science and engineering.
[4]Does not include health fields.
[5]Research and development.
[6]Small Business Innovation Research.
[7]May be granted to anyone who invents or discovers any new, useful, and nonobvious process, machine, article, or manufacture, or composition of matter, or any new and useful improvement thereof.

Survey, Census, or Data Collection Method: For information, see Internet site <http://www.nsf.gov/statistics/states/>.

Source: National Science Foundation, *Science and Engineering State Profiles: 2001–03*, and previous editions. See also <http://www.nsf.gov/statistics/states/>.

Employer Firm Births and Terminations and Business Bankruptcies

Geographic area	Number of employer firms[1]			Employer firm births[2]					
				Number			Rate[4]		
	2003	2002	2001	2003	2002	2001	2003	2002	2001
United States[5]...	**5,696,600**	**5,678,500**	**5,657,774**	**572,900**	**589,700**	**585,140**	**101**	**104**	**104**
Alabama............	85,768	85,895	86,007	9,014	9,534	10,060	105	111	114
Alaska.............	16,825	16,511	16,398	2,441	2,270	2,438	148	138	151
Arizona............	109,692	107,894	106,680	13,322	14,291	14,541	123	134	140
Arkansas...........	60,416	60,668	59,757	7,253	5,381	3,990	120	90	67
California..........	1,063,230	1,022,192	985,846	113,500	130,840	128,885	111	133	137
Colorado..........	143,821	140,704	138,411	22,400	25,290	24,730	159	183	184
Connecticut........	95,969	96,677	96,916	8,501	8,726	9,074	88	90	94
Delaware..........	25,280	25,097	25,199	3,439	3,223	3,352	137	128	135
District of Columbia	26,633	26,503	26,312	4,052	4,157	4,090	153	158	156
Florida............	426,245	413,476	392,756	69,711	72,720	60,370	169	185	157
Georgia	196,921	194,062	192,736	24,217	28,756	23,211	125	149	123
Hawaii............	29,217	28,800	28,569	3,658	3,555	3,811	127	124	136
Idaho.............	41,539	40,633	40,459	5,998	5,039	5,534	148	125	142
Illinois	281,869	278,839	279,627	28,933	27,342	28,426	104	98	102
Indiana	125,129	124,673	125,119	13,452	13,530	13,903	108	108	112
Iowa..............	68,737	68,466	68,704	5,534	5,660	5,659	81	82	82
Kansas	68,095	67,757	67,197	7,625	6,703	7,026	113	100	104
Kentucky..........	81,407	87,589	88,138	8,155	8,526	8,713	93	97	98
Louisiana..........	94,437	93,989	95,829	9,298	9,810	9,816	99	102	102
Maine	39,691	39,180	38,907	4,033	4,428	4,667	103	114	121
Maryland	134,447	133,536	132,049	20,687	20,576	20,072	155	156	154
Massachusetts	175,827	173,896	170,026	18,984	21,262	18,166	109	125	108
Michigan	210,803	211,567	212,608	22,022	22,799	23,060	104	107	108
Minnesota	133,419	131,646	130,348	14,652	13,683	12,700	111	105	98
Mississippi	53,641	53,409	53,303	6,020	6,256	6,164	113	117	115
Missouri...........	131,464	129,777	129,404	15,947	16,337	14,360	123	126	112
Montana	33,991	33,339	32,891	4,548	3,569	3,608	136	109	111
Nebraska..........	45,595	45,342	45,019	4,311	4,372	4,419	95	97	99
Nevada	48,929	47,340	46,339	9,749	8,826	8,864	206	190	198
New Hampshire.......	39,508	39,211	39,542	4,653	4,562	4,398	119	115	111
New Jersey	268,203	274,966	277,425	29,236	29,916	36,747	106	108	138
New Mexico	41,731	42,066	41,616	5,508	5,281	5,753	131	127	139
New York	478,270	474,425	473,471	60,569	59,571	62,730	128	126	133
North Carolina.......	179,580	178,560	175,461	22,465	22,950	22,436	126	131	130
North Dakota	18,817	18,639	18,544	1,456	1,356	1,419	78	73	76
Ohio..............	229,648	230,705	232,266	22,227	22,379	22,951	96	96	99
Oklahoma	75,486	75,250	75,177	8,802	8,702	9,940	117	116	133
Oregon	102,862	100,726	99,943	13,842	13,160	13,246	137	132	133
Pennsylvania........	271,459	268,723	265,451	31,214	31,939	33,497	116	120	129
Rhode Island	32,594	32,295	33,011	3,465	3,397	3,547	107	103	109
South Carolina	90,998	89,634	89,300	10,759	10,266	11,372	120	115	128
South Dakota	23,161	22,803	22,759	1,338	1,389	1,953	59	61	87
Tennessee	110,427	108,928	109,376	17,700	15,982	16,488	162	146	149
Texas	398,928	394,303	390,390	52,677	54,009	53,271	134	138	137
Utah	58,507	56,346	54,461	10,656	10,431	10,745	189	192	207
Vermont...........	20,922	20,755	21,247	2,122	2,331	2,226	102	110	106
Virginia	167,527	165,185	162,459	22,069	21,438	21,371	134	132	133
Washington	206,699	200,909	199,233	36,136	37,562	39,641	180	189	203
West Virginia	37,144	37,364	37,805	4,126	3,944	3,691	110	104	95
Wisconsin..........	123,800	122,249	122,051	12,400	12,172	12,025	101	100	99
Wyoming	19,616	19,339	19,141	2,419	2,275	2,558	125	119	138

See footnotes at end of table.

Geographic area	Employer firm terminations[2]						Business bankruptcies[3]		
	Number			Rate[4]					
	2003	2002	2001	2003	2002	2001	2003	2002	2001
United States[5] . . .	554,800	569,000	553,291	98	101	98	35,037	38,540	40,099
Alabama	10,927	12,062	14,781	127	140	168	287	381	428
Alaska	2,507	2,541	2,575	152	155	159	121	120	104
Arizona	15,488	17,642	16,371	144	165	158	701	756	753
Arkansas	6,918	4,491	4,746	114	75	80	429	282	290
California	140,435	156,858	149,831	137	159	159	4,501	5,141	5,238
Colorado	13,243	10,332	6,954	94	75	52	552	590	467
Connecticut	11,044	11,383	11,348	114	117	118	187	181	156
Delaware	3,148	3,891	3,122	125	154	126	505	649	1,374
District of Columbia	3,874	3,973	4,013	146	151	153	55	52	49
Florida	56,665	52,241	54,573	137	133	142	1,534	1,803	1,896
Georgia	25,898	31,479	24,352	133	163	129	1,585	1,359	1,162
Hawaii	4,010	3,994	4,080	139	140	145	72	53	68
Idaho.	6,742	7,040	5,851	166	174	150	225	260	303
Illinois	41,112	32,093	31,976	147	115	115	991	1,240	1,547
Indiana	15,137	16,156	15,839	121	129	127	640	661	604
Iowa	7,378	7,480	7,770	108	109	113	323	354	289
Kansas	8,392	6,876	8,055	124	102	119	303	238	220
Kentucky	10,801	11,614	9,883	123	132	112	327	445	474
Louisiana	12,171	14,416	13,319	129	150	138	499	672	716
Maine	4,715	5,042	5,401	120	130	140	105	101	151
Maryland	21,697	20,927	20,667	162	158	158	523	873	758
Massachusetts	21,870	20,532	18,268	126	121	109	396	380	427
Michigan	24,748	26,975	26,535	117	127	124	684	802	688
Minnesota	17,928	12,851	6,770	136	99	53	1,379	1,729	1,887
Mississippi	7,267	7,160	7,557	136	134	141	282	309	289
Missouri.	20,190	21,653	18,188	156	167	142	378	394	505
Montana	4,679	4,445	3,881	140	135	119	98	120	149
Nebraska	5,050	5,234	5,394	111	116	121	238	152	144
Nevada	8,939	8,667	8,252	189	187	184	321	462	419
New Hampshire	4,598	5,418	5,264	117	137	133	178	212	334
New Jersey	36,827	31,571	27,890	134	114	105	734	689	730
New Mexico	5,770	7,949	5,495	137	191	132	774	693	620
New York	61,199	63,631	65,616	129	134	139	1,987	2,585	2,432
North Carolina.	23,234	22,184	23,217	130	126	134	528	576	613
North Dakota	2,049	1,893	2,112	110	102	113	105	116	115
Ohio	23,544	24,269	25,460	102	104	109	1,426	1,538	1,794
Oklahoma	8,434	8,923	9,498	112	119	127	612	607	941
Oregon	14,194	14,793	15,512	141	148	156	1,591	1,606	1,389
Pennsylvania	32,917	35,859	33,426	122	135	129	1,193	1,263	1,541
Rhode Island	4,103	4,981	4,152	127	151	127	48	65	64
South Carolina	10,711	11,491	12,893	119	129	145	142	178	147
South Dakota	1,899	2,098	2,156	83	92	96	110	119	164
Tennessee	16,315	16,514	17,637	150	151	160	597	735	886
Texas	55,461	58,114	59,342	141	149	153	3,153	2,994	3,155
Utah	10,368	11,272	13,565	184	207	261	519	602	475
Vermont	2,584	3,501	2,578	125	165	123	78	91	97
Virginia	20,539	20,305	21,449	124	125	133	956	969	924
Washington	35,345	40,782	41,122	176	205	211	737	698	642
West Virginia	5,550	5,595	5,741	149	148	148	290	357	322
Wisconsin.	12,629	13,651	14,135	103	112	116	722	856	734
Wyoming	2,921	2,895	2,969	151	151	160	44	47	45

[1]Employer firm estimates are the previous year's figure plus the difference between birth and termination estimates. As of end of year.

[2]From prior year's March through current year's March. On occasion, some state terminations result in successor firms, which are not listed as new firms.

[3]A business bankruptcy is the legal recognition that a company is insolvent (i.e., not able to satisfy creditors or discharge liabilities) and must restructure or completely liquidate under Chapter 7, 11, 12, or 13 of the federal bankruptcy laws.

[4]Per 1,000 employer firms. Based on the number of firms at the end of the previous year.

[5]State totals do not add to the U.S. totals as firms enter and exit multiple states and the U.S. data is based upon a different source.

Survey, Census, or Data Collection Method: For information, see Internet site <http://www.sba.gov/advo/research/sbei.html>.

Source: U.S. Small Business Administration, Office of Advocacy, "Small Business Economic Indicators for 2003," published August 2004; see Internet site <http://www.sba.gov/advo/research/sbei.html>.

Geographic area	Firms (1,000)				Employment, 2002 (1,000)			Annual payroll, 2002 (mil. dol.)			Nonemployer establishments			
			By employment-size of enterprise, 2002			By employment-size of enterprise			By employment-size of enterprise		Number (1,000)		Receipts (mil. dol.)	
	2002	2000	Fewer than 20 employees	Fewer than 500 employees	Total	Fewer than 20 employees	Fewer than 500 employees	Total	Fewer than 20 employees	Fewer than 500 employees	2002	2000	2002	2000
United States . . .	**5,697.8**	**5,652.5**	**5,090.3**	**5,680.9**	**112,401**	**20,583**	**56,366**	**3,943,180**	**617,584**	**1,777,050**	**17,646.1**	**16,530.0**	**770,032**	**709,379**
Alabama	78.7	79.9	67.2	76.6	1,581	289	786	45,466	7,068	20,580	239.6	223.1	9,738	8,827
Alaska	16.0	15.9	14.1	15.5	214	53	128	8,439	1,861	4,545	47.1	47.7	1,771	1,721
Arizona	95.9	93.0	81.8	93.2	1,945	329	930	61,108	9,474	26,880	289.3	269.0	13,102	11,931
Arkansas	52.1	52.4	45.1	50.6	975	185	476	25,913	4,271	11,174	162.5	152.9	6,101	5,738
California	674.6	664.6	591.1	669.1	12,856	2,390	6,811	510,841	82,859	243,423	2,252.4	2,103.2	114,113	106,592
Colorado	119.6	116.2	104.8	116.8	1,912	386	981	67,812	11,998	31,676	350.9	333.4	15,426	14,278
Connecticut	77.3	78.5	66.0	75.2	1,556	278	759	68,478	10,261	29,536	228.1	217.3	12,580	11,563
Delaware	20.2	20.2	16.3	18.8	389	64	171	14,716	1,891	5,413	44.5	41.1	2,234	1,854
District of Columbia	16.4	16.3	12.3	15.3	419	54	201	21,358	2,665	9,859	34.2	32.9	1,582	1,503
Florida	370.8	354.0	335.8	366.7	6,367	1,182	2,856	192,932	34,988	85,642	1,189.5	1,074.0	53,987	48,137
Georgia	164.3	160.4	141.9	160.4	3,381	555	1,493	113,752	16,596	45,792	523.8	468.4	23,300	21,143
Hawaii	24.9	24.3	21.2	24.1	440	89	253	13,352	2,533	7,117	76.4	73.8	3,055	2,836
Idaho	33.2	32.2	29.0	32.2	454	112	259	12,562	2,692	6,425	89.3	84.4	3,379	3,103
Illinois	253.7	254.1	218.5	249.4	5,224	885	2,577	197,828	29,295	88,717	720.8	668.2	29,267	26,162
Indiana	116.0	116.3	98.3	113.2	2,517	431	1,254	79,365	11,061	35,019	328.7	319.4	12,106	11,426
Iowa	65.1	65.6	56.0	63.5	1,230	231	642	34,820	5,354	16,385	176.3	171.5	5,734	5,464
Kansas	60.9	61.6	51.9	59.1	1,099	213	588	33,153	5,294	15,674	162.7	156.9	5,880	5,467
Kentucky	71.9	72.3	60.8	69.8	1,463	263	734	42,537	6,358	18,812	236.5	226.2	8,909	8,124
Louisiana	81.7	81.7	69.5	79.7	1,583	303	853	45,628	7,573	21,901	253.7	234.1	9,844	9,267
Maine	34.4	34.1	30.3	33.6	487	116	292	14,375	3,022	7,976	102.6	98.5	3,950	3,602
Maryland	108.0	106.0	92.2	105.4	2,063	381	1,087	75,032	12,218	36,475	343.1	322.8	14,040	12,829
Massachusetts	146.1	148.2	125.8	143.2	3,023	513	1,481	127,902	18,589	57,734	424.2	410.5	21,045	19,811
Michigan	192.3	193.9	166.7	189.3	3,890	709	1,976	142,419	21,454	62,969	555.7	527.0	22,569	20,910
Minnesota	118.7	116.2	102.0	116.2	2,360	408	1,206	84,528	12,049	37,648	333.3	317.9	12,966	12,163
Mississippi	48.0	48.3	41.1	46.5	904	174	452	22,773	3,880	10,430	145.2	134.9	5,763	5,365
Missouri	119.6	118.1	102.6	116.9	2,354	415	1,173	74,124	10,959	33,124	329.9	311.8	12,388	11,201
Montana	28.8	28.0	25.7	28.2	301	96	210	7,429	2,101	4,805	73.0	70.2	2,557	2,352
Nebraska	41.5	41.4	35.7	40.2	749	146	383	21,740	3,423	9,884	106.4	103.3	3,592	3,406
Nevada	42.5	40.3	35.3	40.7	936	137	402	29,308	4,546	12,705	128.1	113.7	7,174	5,900
New Hampshire	32.3	32.1	27.4	31.2	551	113	302	18,652	3,599	9,995	94.2	88.9	4,677	4,153
New Jersey	203.5	202.2	179.5	200.3	3,597	691	1,796	152,370	24,783	67,822	513.5	482.7	27,390	25,100
New Mexico	35.6	35.5	30.2	34.2	554	124	319	15,108	3,042	7,897	103.3	81.4	3,580	2,433
New York	428.4	424.8	383.6	424.3	7,235	1,418	3,756	329,811	50,025	143,307	1,302.7	1,202.9	58,700	53,764
North Carolina	165.0	163.6	143.3	161.8	3,322	597	1,571	101,827	15,670	43,324	492.8	462.2	19,534	18,255
North Dakota	17.2	17.2	14.6	16.6	254	59	161	6,554	1,321	3,791	40.6	39.6	1,386	1,285
Ohio	211.0	212.5	180.1	207.3	4,743	796	2,328	154,820	22,207	68,385	623.6	602.9	24,424	23,132
Oklahoma	70.3	70.2	61.0	68.5	1,200	247	645	33,564	5,896	16,083	228.1	219.0	8,885	8,293
Oregon	85.1	85.1	74.4	83.2	1,329	296	736	43,522	7,731	21,167	218.3	212.2	9,159	8,436
Pennsylvania	237.4	237.5	204.8	233.6	5,046	875	2,498	169,236	24,443	75,489	656.0	632.5	28,328	27,029
Rhode Island	25.5	25.2	21.7	24.6	416	86	238	13,547	2,594	7,291	63.3	59.4	2,726	2,496
South Carolina	78.6	78.4	67.5	76.5	1,539	284	739	43,999	7,120	18,977	221.7	206.8	9,370	8,558
South Dakota	20.9	20.6	18.0	20.2	304	73	189	7,750	1,591	4,424	50.0	48.2	1,687	1,556
Tennessee	100.7	102.4	85.3	97.9	2,292	363	1,033	71,272	9,844	29,765	364.6	339.4	15,432	14,098
Texas	373.1	369.0	324.8	368.1	7,994	1,355	3,759	277,847	40,795	114,686	1,388.3	1,271.4	62,847	58,278
Utah	49.3	46.2	42.3	47.6	900	163	430	26,174	4,352	12,039	144.4	135.8	6,181	5,652
Vermont	19.0	19.1	16.5	18.4	258	66	162	7,436	1,691	4,382	54.3	51.2	1,944	1,828
Virginia	142.6	139.7	122.8	139.5	2,915	513	1,403	101,693	15,216	45,339	398.8	373.4	16,130	14,393
Washington	138.3	138.2	121.6	135.7	2,186	474	1,196	83,127	13,966	38,589	334.9	326.4	14,250	13,979
West Virginia	32.7	33.5	28.0	31.6	561	119	303	14,811	2,531	7,015	84.2	81.8	2,582	2,376
Wisconsin	116.0	115.6	98.8	113.6	2,356	430	1,267	75,313	11,514	35,797	283.4	268.3	11,302	10,417
Wyoming	16.5	15.9	14.3	15.9	178	56	123	5,051	1,320	3,164	37.4	35.7	1,367	1,194

Survey, Census, or Data Collection Method: Employer firms—Based on the Statistics of U.S. Businesses database; for information, see Internet site <http://www.sba.gov/advo/research/data.html#st>;   Nonemployer establishments—Based on business income tax returns filed with the Internal Revenue Service; for information, see Appendix B, Limitations of the Data and Methodology, and Internet site <http://www.census.gov/epcd/nonemployer/view/covmeth.htm>.

Sources: Employer firms—U.S. Small Business Administration, Office of Advocacy, "Statistics of U.S. Businesses and Nonemployer Statistics: Firm Size Data provided by U.S. Census Bureau"; see Internet site <http://www.sba.gov/advo/research/data.html>, accessed 4 May 2005;   Nonemployer establishments—U.S. Census Bureau, "Nonemployer Statistics," annual; see Internet site <http://www.census.gov/epcd/nonemployer/pdf.html>.

Table A-48. States — Private Nonfarm Establishments, Employment, and Payroll

Geographic area	Establishments			By employment-size class of establishment, 2002				Employment (1,000)		By employment-size class of establishment, 2002				Annual payroll (bil. dol.)	
	2002	2000	Net change, 2000-2002	Under 20	20 to 99	100 to 499	500 or more	2002	2000	Under 20	20 to 99	100 to 499	500 or more	2002	2000
United States . . .	7,200,770	7,070,048	130,722	6,198,512	835,205	148,944	18,109	112,401	114,065	28,116	33,335	28,101	22,848	3,943	3,879
Alabama	99,931	99,817	114	85,493	12,101	2,057	280	1,581	1,653	412	476	393	299	45	44
Alaska	18,856	18,501	355	16,905	1,667	253	31	214	205	72	64	51	28	8	8
Arizona	119,740	114,804	4,936	102,054	14,682	2,688	316	1,945	1,919	468	582	498	398	61	58
Arkansas	63,869	63,185	684	55,417	7,128	1,134	190	975	991	255	281	227	212	26	25
California	820,997	799,863	21,134	700,702	101,336	17,086	1,873	12,856	12,885	3,158	4,065	3,166	2,468	511	514
Colorado	142,247	137,528	4,719	124,631	14,878	2,468	270	1,912	1,913	523	591	458	341	68	68
Connecticut	92,375	92,436	-61	79,208	10,826	2,113	228	1,556	1,546	367	434	392	362	68	67
Delaware	24,377	23,771	606	21,192	2,599	501	85	389	377	90	104	93	102	15	14
District of Columbia	19,930	19,655	275	16,396	2,842	619	73	419	415	81	116	117	105	21	20
Florida	450,188	428,438	21,750	397,748	43,424	8,047	969	6,367	6,217	1,609	1,756	1,485	1,517	193	177
Georgia	206,323	200,442	5,881	176,246	24,892	4,600	585	3,381	3,484	790	993	887	712	114	113
Hawaii	30,633	29,853	780	26,440	3,546	577	70	440	432	124	142	108	66	13	12
Idaho	38,842	37,429	1,413	34,746	3,547	488	61	454	451	150	136	89	79	13	12
Illinois	309,980	308,067	1,913	264,125	37,780	7,163	912	5,224	5,501	1,196	1,528	1,352	1,148	198	201
Indiana	147,304	146,321	983	124,440	19,021	3,445	398	2,517	2,651	612	755	659	491	79	79
Iowa	81,042	80,890	152	70,227	9,024	1,578	213	1,230	1,265	326	361	300	242	35	34
Kansas	75,077	74,939	138	64,886	8,582	1,464	145	1,099	1,129	298	340	277	184	33	32
Kentucky	90,493	89,921	572	76,988	11,167	2,107	231	1,463	1,514	375	438	405	244	43	41
Louisiana	101,885	101,016	869	87,014	12,647	1,963	261	1,583	1,592	423	507	361	293	46	43
Maine	40,292	39,466	826	35,873	3,733	623	63	487	492	155	146	117	69	14	13
Maryland	131,815	128,467	3,348	112,426	16,036	3,098	255	2,063	2,058	522	643	574	323	75	71
Massachusetts	175,991	176,222	-231	150,285	21,008	4,192	506	3,023	3,087	683	850	785	705	128	131
Michigan	237,616	236,912	704	203,356	28,521	5,144	595	3,890	4,073	965	1,131	960	834	142	145
Minnesota	143,953	139,080	4,873	123,028	17,259	3,290	376	2,360	2,395	559	694	619	488	85	82
Mississippi	59,902	59,788	114	51,901	6,719	1,114	168	904	957	245	262	211	187	23	23
Missouri	147,977	144,755	3,222	127,098	17,443	3,037	399	2,354	2,399	581	699	576	498	74	72
Montana	32,972	31,849	1,123	29,824	2,831	294	23	301	296	123	107	50	(D)	7	7
Nebraska	50,259	49,623	636	43,708	5,486	919	146	749	751	200	218	170	162	22	20
Nevada	51,383	48,178	3,205	43,984	6,105	1,090	204	936	903	195	244	203	293	29	27
New Hampshire	37,928	37,414	514	32,815	4,330	711	72	551	546	150	170	136	95	19	18
New Jersey	237,505	233,559	3,946	206,823	25,175	4,919	588	3,597	3,548	881	1,006	932	778	152	147
New Mexico	43,213	42,782	431	37,672	4,806	671	64	554	549	174	187	128	64	15	14
New York	498,921	492,073	6,848	439,445	49,118	9,006	1,352	7,235	7,353	1,804	1,947	1,755	1,729	330	331
North Carolina	207,562	203,903	3,659	177,442	25,300	4,263	557	3,322	3,385	827	1,003	822	670	102	100
North Dakota	20,422	20,139	283	17,929	2,137	332	24	254	255	81	85	62	26	7	6
Ohio	271,181	270,509	672	228,078	35,541	6,819	743	4,743	5,002	1,128	1,432	1,274	909	155	155
Oklahoma	86,029	85,094	935	74,795	9,595	1,455	184	1,200	1,202	339	381	276	204	34	32
Oregon	101,933	100,645	1,288	89,388	10,706	1,663	176	1,329	1,355	399	417	312	201	44	44
Pennsylvania	297,257	294,741	2,516	253,405	35,961	7,009	882	5,046	5,087	1,210	1,445	1,327	1,064	169	165
Rhode Island	28,860	28,534	326	25,029	3,199	571	61	416	415	110	128	105	73	14	13
South Carolina	98,357	97,146	1,211	84,477	11,714	1,907	259	1,539	1,602	397	463	372	306	44	43
South Dakota	24,439	23,783	656	21,635	2,381	388	35	304	307	96	93	74	40	8	7
Tennessee	130,556	130,876	-320	109,994	16,941	3,211	410	2,292	2,390	533	676	612	470	71	69
Texas	482,169	471,509	10,660	410,586	59,646	10,603	1,334	7,994	8,026	1,926	2,400	2,019	1,648	278	270
Utah	58,788	55,379	3,409	51,064	6,461	1,118	145	900	917	225	259	212	204	26	25
Vermont	21,624	21,564	60	19,271	2,026	298	29	258	254	84	78	57	39	7	7
Virginia	180,501	175,582	4,919	153,908	22,313	3,771	509	2,915	2,904	732	889	721	572	102	98
Washington	165,933	164,018	1,915	145,857	17,036	2,785	255	2,186	2,267	639	664	510	372	83	88
West Virginia	40,488	41,047	-559	35,223	4,489	686	90	561	558	169	175	130	87	15	14
Wisconsin	142,086	140,415	1,671	120,385	17,889	3,405	407	2,356	2,415	581	715	643	416	75	73
Wyoming	18,769	18,120	649	16,950	1,611	201	7	178	175	73	60	39	(D)	5	5

D Figure withheld to avoid disclosure.

Survey, Census, or Data Collection Method: Based on tabulations of data extracted from the U.S. Census Bureau's Business Register; for information, see Internet site <http://www.census.gov/epcd/cbp/view/cbpview.html>.

Source: U.S. Census Bureau, *County Business Patterns*, annual. See also Internet site <http://www.census.gov/epcd/cbp/view/cbpview.html>.

Geographic area	U.S. affiliates[1]								U.S. exports[2]					U.S. agricultural exports (mil. dol.)		
	Gross book value (mil. dol.)				Employment (1,000)				2004			2003 (mil. dol.)	2000 (mil. dol.)			
	2002	2001	2000	1990	2002	2001	2000	1990	Total exports (mil. dol.)	Rank	Percent change 2000–2004			2004	2003	2000
United States . . .	912,452	1,054,827	1,070,422	552,902	5,394.2	6,237.5	6,498.3	4,704.4	769,304	(X)	8.0	676,409	712,055	[3]62,297	[3]56,209	[3]50,744
Alabama	15,210	17,037	16,646	7,300	72.7	92.0	77.9	55.7	9,037	24	23.5	8,340	7,317	568	388	392
Alaska	30,064	(D)	28,964	19,435	11.2	12.2	12.0	13.2	3,157	37	28.1	2,739	2,464	1	1	1
Arizona	8,442	9,390	10,716	7,234	55.4	65.6	73.2	57.1	13,423	17	-6.4	13,323	14,334	460	453	718
Arkansas	4,724	6,103	4,613	2,344	32.9	40.7	40.9	29.2	3,493	32	34.4	2,962	2,599	1,900	1,445	980
California	91,936	118,426	121,040	75,768	616.4	707.0	749.4	555.9	109,968	2	-8.1	93,995	119,640	9,197	8,156	6,867
Colorado	12,580	12,654	15,319	6,544	76.7	91.2	102.6	56.3	6,651	27	0.9	6,109	6,593	762	871	946
Connecticut	12,789	14,468	13,604	5,357	113.0	126.0	118.0	75.9	8,559	26	6.4	8,136	8,047	59	50	116
Delaware	6,433	6,603	6,114	5,818	23.3	28.0	31.8	43.1	2,053	43	-6.6	1,886	2,197	139	115	114
District of Columbia	4,433	5,187	4,247	3,869	17.0	18.6	17.1	11.4	1,164	(X)	16.1	809	1,003	(NA)	(NA)	(NA)
Florida	28,446	35,481	38,755	18,659	244.9	305.3	312.1	205.7	28,982	8	9.2	24,953	26,543	1,359	1,299	1,277
Georgia	24,973	29,362	29,510	16,729	190.1	220.7	227.9	161.0	19,633	11	31.5	16,286	14,925	1,276	923	909
Hawaii	8,198	9,787	10,369	11,830	38.3	41.0	44.8	53.0	405	50	4.6	368	387	75	71	79
Idaho	2,131	2,598	2,749	776	12.5	14.1	14.2	11.7	2,915	38	-18.1	2,096	3,559	789	836	776
Illinois	41,723	48,910	48,425	23,420	268.4	315.8	325.8	245.8	30,214	7	-3.9	26,473	31,438	3,654	3,203	3,026
Indiana	28,139	29,744	30,179	13,426	137.4	164.3	168.2	126.9	19,109	13	24.2	16,402	15,386	1,858	1,563	1,402
Iowa	6,017	7,169	7,186	2,712	37.4	45.6	40.9	32.8	6,394	28	43.2	5,236	4,466	3,676	3,651	3,177
Kansas	4,837	5,098	9,036	5,134	33.8	39.7	61.0	29.6	4,931	30	-4.2	4,553	5,145	2,928	2,975	3,156
Kentucky	23,731	23,116	22,091	9,229	87.7	100.8	106.0	65.7	12,992	19	35.2	10,734	9,612	984	904	740
Louisiana	27,182	32,551	31,160	17,432	48.9	58.9	61.3	61.4	19,922	10	18.5	18,390	16,814	661	476	427
Maine	5,873	5,266	5,087	2,080	33.0	34.1	33.9	26.6	2,432	40	36.7	2,188	1,779	70	61	60
Maryland	10,191	12,866	13,157	5,713	106.3	114.8	112.9	79.6	5,746	29	25.1	4,941	4,593	248	215	224
Massachusetts	23,265	25,563	23,875	8,890	191.0	221.7	226.8	131.2	21,837	9	6.4	18,663	20,514	158	126	157
Michigan	40,201	52,465	39,238	12,012	204.1	220.1	249.9	139.6	35,625	4	5.3	32,941	33,845	919	892	831
Minnesota	9,763	12,089	13,472	11,972	93.9	102.9	106.2	89.8	12,678	21	23.1	11,266	10,303	2,891	2,699	2,275
Mississippi	4,924	4,800	4,121	2,989	22.2	27.9	24.2	23.6	3,179	35	16.6	2,558	2,726	1,140	793	605
Missouri	15,044	14,918	15,773	5,757	96.7	113.1	107.4	73.7	8,997	25	38.5	7,234	6,497	1,385	1,207	1,074
Montana	1,716	(D)	3,099	2,181	5.8	7.3	6.8	5.1	565	49	4.5	361	541	436	393	350
Nebraska	1,748	2,106	2,737	776	19.3	23.5	21.7	14.9	2,316	41	-7.8	2,724	2,511	3,015	3,123	3,013
Nevada	6,532	8,164	10,128	5,450	26.5	31.7	36.3	22.7	2,907	39	96.1	2,033	1,482	53	35	16
New Hampshire	4,300	5,321	5,124	1,446	38.4	42.5	46.5	25.9	2,286	42	-3.7	1,931	2,373	11	8	6
New Jersey	31,829	36,918	35,115	18,608	228.6	268.5	272.2	227.0	19,192	12	3.0	16,818	18,638	152	147	104
New Mexico	4,454	5,482	5,801	4,312	12.7	15.9	16.7	17.4	2,046	44	-14.4	2,326	2,391	155	137	97
New York	63,047	68,860	68,522	36,424	394.7	469.3	479.1	347.5	44,401	3	3.6	39,181	42,846	502	453	476
North Carolina	20,571	22,875	29,931	15,234	212.7	238.6	264.8	181.0	18,115	15	0.9	16,199	17,946	1,638	1,300	1,318
North Dakota	830	1,753	1,824	1,251	7.6	9.7	7.7	3.1	1,008	46	61.0	854	626	1,892	1,556	1,180
Ohio	32,000	35,158	37,530	20,549	212.8	244.1	260.3	219.1	31,208	6	18.6	29,764	26,322	1,572	1,190	1,174
Oklahoma	7,301	7,743	7,635	6,049	36.5	42.2	41.9	43.6	3,178	36	3.4	2,660	3,072	808	619	531
Oregon	9,286	12,265	13,178	3,427	48.8	56.3	62.1	39.1	11,172	23	-2.4	10,357	11,441	825	722	626
Pennsylvania	30,666	33,528	34,106	16,587	233.4	260.4	283.4	221.6	18,487	14	-1.6	16,299	18,792	1,049	1,008	929
Rhode Island	3,055	3,310	3,394	1,120	21.8	24.1	24.2	13.3	1,286	45	8.5	1,178	1,186	6	3	2
South Carolina	20,272	22,762	23,563	10,067	123.4	137.7	138.4	104.7	13,376	18	56.2	11,773	8,565	386	251	263
South Dakota	684	1,157	1,011	553	7.1	7.7	6.9	4.5	826	47	21.5	672	679	1,238	899	1,067
Tennessee	18,650	20,961	20,842	10,280	131.0	150.8	153.2	116.9	16,123	16	39.1	12,612	11,592	861	662	488
Texas	85,802	103,573	110,032	57,079	351.4	417.5	445.2	299.5	117,245	1	12.9	98,846	103,866	3,363	3,419	3,137
Utah	10,463	13,552	14,340	3,918	31.1	34.6	38.1	21.0	4,718	31	46.5	4,115	3,221	230	253	248
Vermont	1,537	2,614	2,146	631	12.0	11.7	11.5	7.7	3,283	33	-19.9	2,627	4,097	42	31	16
Virginia	15,332	20,668	23,570	10,702	146.4	171.3	181.9	113.3	11,631	22	-0.6	10,853	11,698	511	445	459
Washington	16,098	18,946	22,257	7,985	84.1	99.4	106.8	77.5	33,793	5	4.9	34,173	32,215	1,887	1,912	1,562
West Virginia	7,299	7,115	7,061	7,975	22.4	28.0	28.1	34.9	3,262	34	47.0	2,380	2,219	38	35	31
Wisconsin	17,192	15,842	13,961	5,088	112.5	111.9	110.3	81.4	12,706	20	20.9	11,510	10,508	1,369	1,408	1,378
Wyoming	10,539	10,215	8,072	2,782	8.1	10.4	7.8	5.8	680	48	35.4	582	503	47	36	43

D Withheld to avoid disclosure of individual companies.   NA Not available.   X Not applicable.

[1]U.S. business enterprises in which one foreign owner (individual, branch, partnership, association, trust corporation, or government) has a direct or indirect voting interest of 10 percent or more.
[2]Excludes unreported, not specified, 2nd special category exports, and estimated shipments, and reexports.
[3]The U.S. totals include unallocated exports not included in states.

Survey, Census, or Data Collection Method: U.S. affiliates—Based on the Bureau of Economic Analysis 2002 Benchmark Survey; for information, see the following document at <http://www.bea.gov/bea/ARTICLES/2004/08August/0804FDIUS.pdf>;   U.S. exports—Based on documents collected by the U.S. Customs Service; for information, see the following document at <http://www.census.gov/foreign-trade/Press-Release/explain.pdf>;   U.S. agricultural exports—Based on Custom District-level export data compiled by the U.S. Census Bureau and State-level agricultural production data supplied by the U.S. Department of Agriculture's National Agricultural Statistical Service (NASS); for information, see Internet site <http://www.ers.usda.gov/data/stateexports/>.

Sources: U.S. affiliates—U.S. Bureau of Economic Analysis, *Survey of Current Business*, August 2004 and prior issues; *Foreign Direct Investment in the United States, Operations of U.S. Affiliates of Foreign Companies*, annual;   U.S. exports—U.S. Census Bureau, U.S. International Trade in Goods and Services, series FT-900, December issues. For most recent release, see <http://www.census.gov/foreign-trade/Press-Release/2004pr/12/#ft900> (released 10 February 2005);   U.S. agricultural exports—U.S. Department of Agriculture, Economic Research Service, U.S. Agricultural Trade database, Internet site <http://www.ers.usda.gov/publications/fau/july05/fau10201/fau10201.pdf> (released 8 July 2005).

State and Metropolitan Area Data Book: 2006

U.S. Census Bureau

Table A-50. States — Farms and Farm Earnings

Geographic area	Farms (USDA)[1] (as of June 1)									Farm earnings (BEA)[2] (mil. dol.)		
	Number (1,000)			Land in farms (mil. acres)			Average acreage per farm					
	2004	2003	2000	2004	2003	2000	2004	2003	2000	2003	2002	2000
United States . . .	2,113	2,127	2,167	936.6	938.7	945.1	443	441	436	45,594	32,257	44,482
Alabama	44	45	47	8.7	8.9	9.0	198	198	191	1,146	815	955
Alaska	1	1	1	0.9	0.9	0.9	1,452	1,475	1,569	14	16	15
Arizona	10	10	11	26.4	26.5	26.9	2,588	2,573	2,514	861	1,079	684
Arkansas	48	48	48	14.4	14.4	14.6	303	303	304	1,503	563	1,218
California	77	79	83	26.7	27.1	28.0	347	345	337	8,479	7,907	8,089
Colorado	31	31	30	30.9	31.0	31.6	1,000	987	1,053	724	524	567
Connecticut	4	4	4	0.4	0.4	0.4	86	86	86	185	150	191
Delaware	2	2	3	0.5	0.5	0.6	230	230	215	120	56	122
District of Columbia	(X)	(X)	(X)	(X)	(X)	(X)	(X)	(X)	(X)	–	–	–
Florida	43	44	44	10.1	10.2	10.4	235	232	236	1,597	1,940	1,750
Georgia	49	49	49	10.7	10.8	10.9	218	219	222	2,251	1,384	1,650
Hawaii	6	6	6	1.3	1.3	1.4	236	236	251	221	217	212
Idaho	25	25	25	11.8	11.8	11.9	472	472	486	924	995	867
Illinois	73	73	77	27.5	27.5	27.5	377	377	357	1,066	563	1,338
Indiana	59	60	63	15.0	15.0	15.2	253	253	240	653	41	553
Iowa	90	90	94	31.7	31.7	32.5	353	352	346	1,191	1,572	1,656
Kansas	65	65	65	47.2	47.2	47.5	732	732	736	778	190	705
Kentucky	85	87	90	13.8	13.8	13.7	162	159	152	614	315	1,442
Louisiana	27	27	29	7.9	7.9	8.0	289	289	277	588	207	502
Maine	7	7	7	1.4	1.4	1.4	190	190	190	96	89	146
Maryland	12	12	12	2.1	2.1	2.1	169	170	172	289	138	354
Massachusetts	6	6	6	0.5	0.5	0.5	85	85	89	111	98	116
Michigan	53	53	53	10.1	10.1	10.2	190	189	192	550	412	560
Minnesota	80	80	81	27.6	27.7	27.9	346	346	344	892	539	1,016
Mississippi	42	43	42	11.1	11.1	11.2	262	260	266	914	257	724
Missouri	106	106	109	30.1	30.1	30.2	284	284	277	760	82	657
Montana	28	28	28	60.1	60.1	59.3	2,146	2,146	2,133	179	166	244
Nebraska	48	49	52	45.9	45.9	46.1	950	946	887	1,943	629	963
Nevada	3	3	3	6.3	6.3	6.4	2,100	2,100	2,065	99	81	97
New Hampshire	3	3	3	0.5	0.5	0.4	132	132	133	39	29	42
New Jersey	10	10	10	0.8	0.8	0.8	83	83	86	264	256	304
New Mexico	18	18	18	44.7	44.7	44.9	2,554	2,554	2,494	640	539	504
New York	36	37	38	7.6	7.7	7.7	211	207	205	791	612	770
North Carolina	52	54	56	9.0	9.1	9.2	173	170	166	1,433	1,210	2,579
North Dakota	30	30	31	39.4	39.4	39.4	1,300	1,300	1,279	931	344	962
Ohio	77	78	79	14.6	14.6	14.8	189	188	187	791	102	936
Oklahoma	84	84	85	33.7	33.7	33.8	404	404	400	1,193	749	715
Oregon	40	40	40	17.2	17.2	17.3	430	430	433	963	768	849
Pennsylvania	58	58	59	7.7	7.7	7.7	132	132	130	1,024	485	1,148
Rhode Island	1	1	1	0.1	0.1	0.1	71	71	75	17	14	16
South Carolina	24	24	24	4.9	4.9	4.9	199	199	203	525	152	489
South Dakota	32	32	32	43.8	43.8	44.0	1,386	1,386	1,358	994	29	1,116
Tennessee	85	87	88	11.6	11.6	11.8	136	133	134	141	–88	383
Texas	229	229	228	130.0	130.5	130.9	568	570	573	3,569	3,289	2,765
Utah	15	15	16	11.6	11.6	11.6	758	758	748	262	196	201
Vermont	6	7	7	1.3	1.3	1.3	195	192	192	130	112	163
Virginia	48	48	49	8.6	8.6	8.7	181	181	180	381	106	521
Washington	35	36	37	15.2	15.3	15.6	434	431	420	1,476	1,490	1,607
West Virginia	21	21	21	3.6	3.6	3.6	173	173	173	–35	–69	26
Wisconsin	77	77	78	15.5	15.6	16.0	203	204	206	1,119	805	877
Wyoming	9	9	9	34.4	34.4	34.5	3,743	3,743	3,750	199	106	115

– Represents zero.   X Not applicable.

[1] U.S. Department of Agriculture.
[2] Bureau of Economic Analysis.

Survey, Census, or Data Collection Method: Farms—Based on the National Agricultural Statistics Service (NASS) June Agricultural Survey; for information, see the report listed above at <http://usda.mannlib.cornell.edu/reports/nassr/other/zfl-bb/>;   Income—Based on the Regional Economic Information System; for information, see Internet site <http://www.bea.gov/bea/regional/articles/spi2003/>.

Sources: Farms—U.S. Department of Agriculture, National Agricultural Statistics Service, *Farm Numbers and Land in Farms, Final Estimates, 1998–2002;* and *Farms, Land in Farms, and Livestock Operations 2004 Summary,* January 2005;   Income—U.S. Bureau of Economic Analysis, *Survey of Current Business,* April 2005, see Internet site <http://www.bea.gov/bea/regional/spi/>.

Table A-51. States — **Farm Finances and Income**

Geographic area	Balance sheet of farming sector (USDA)[1]						Farm income (USDA)[1]		
	Assets (mil. dol.)			Debt (mil. dol.)			Value of agricultural sector production (mil. dol.)		
	2003	2002	2000	2003	2002	2000	2003	2002	2000
United States[2]...	1,378,757	1,304,049	1,203,215	197,998	193,312	177,637	240,915	219,744	218,381
Alabama	18,917	17,919	16,521	2,361	2,288	2,054	4,128	3,722	3,927
Alaska	685	655	624	26	25	24	57	56	58
Arizona	44,348	41,734	35,823	1,575	1,550	1,448	3,029	3,501	2,624
Arkansas	25,973	24,664	22,372	4,884	4,746	4,315	5,952	5,111	5,251
California	96,678	92,970	88,124	19,955	19,477	17,837	29,377	28,307	27,086
Colorado	27,150	25,687	25,108	4,143	4,039	3,686	5,562	5,216	5,045
Connecticut	2,824	2,642	2,318	338	328	284	561	528	589
Delaware	1,906	1,813	1,795	433	421	378	859	797	829
District of Columbia	(X)	(X)	(X)	(X)	(X)	(X)	(X)	(X)	(X)
Florida	34,550	32,711	28,959	5,372	5,215	4,771	6,833	7,036	7,082
Georgia	30,027	28,185	24,535	4,115	3,988	3,600	6,195	5,324	5,775
Hawaii	4,463	4,175	3,808	283	277	254	600	583	556
Idaho	18,883	17,925	16,874	3,289	3,244	3,012	4,440	4,554	3,832
Illinois	87,558	81,893	76,078	10,480	10,195	9,383	9,289	8,075	7,894
Indiana	46,035	43,078	40,218	6,391	6,199	5,655	5,957	5,084	5,230
Iowa	83,330	77,600	73,326	14,434	14,097	13,117	13,122	12,784	11,710
Kansas	38,248	36,901	36,983	7,820	7,664	7,141	10,365	8,290	8,655
Kentucky	29,843	28,553	25,704	3,907	3,785	3,433	4,299	3,821	4,604
Louisiana	12,925	12,327	11,798	1,976	1,932	1,777	2,272	1,964	1,953
Maine	2,212	2,106	1,923	423	421	395	563	528	573
Maryland	9,184	8,609	7,887	1,283	1,238	1,087	1,757	1,603	1,725
Massachusetts	4,257	4,012	3,490	445	435	387	469	476	471
Michigan	30,403	28,171	24,548	3,513	3,423	3,074	4,403	4,104	3,795
Minnesota	56,585	51,633	46,958	9,982	9,754	8,969	9,249	8,921	8,352
Mississippi	17,194	16,281	15,197	3,202	3,124	2,887	3,934	3,319	3,309
Missouri.	53,787	50,575	45,005	6,725	6,539	6,015	5,728	5,293	5,442
Montana	27,160	25,786	24,516	2,900	2,850	2,685	2,382	2,213	1,980
Nebraska	47,932	45,461	44,121	10,085	9,910	9,325	11,960	9,727	9,492
Nevada	3,550	3,432	3,311	303	294	259	460	435	454
New Hampshire.	1,148	1,097	988	123	120	104	181	173	174
New Jersey	7,239	6,774	5,972	539	523	465	963	965	954
New Mexico	12,143	11,963	11,441	1,612	1,569	1,419	2,275	2,125	2,193
New York	15,725	14,943	13,967	2,808	2,755	2,509	3,581	3,510	3,386
North Carolina.	30,726	29,022	26,880	4,235	4,119	3,688	8,840	8,151	9,473
North Dakota	25,995	24,810	22,485	4,357	4,292	3,981	4,377	3,668	3,411
Ohio	44,514	41,737	38,537	4,898	4,739	4,239	6,012	4,899	5,392
Oklahoma	30,310	29,073	26,587	4,717	4,656	4,413	5,041	4,531	4,618
Oregon	21,026	20,234	18,659	2,763	2,710	2,519	3,990	3,695	3,691
Pennsylvania	26,636	25,125	23,442	3,230	3,129	2,828	5,034	4,583	4,829
Rhode Island	457	418	377	46	45	39	66	64	62
South Carolina	9,703	9,232	8,338	1,330	1,298	1,143	1,959	1,546	1,757
South Dakota	28,661	26,551	24,696	4,479	4,434	4,198	4,787	3,692	4,331
Tennessee	30,649	29,756	26,990	3,013	2,917	2,605	2,953	2,740	2,665
Texas	112,521	107,480	98,539	13,286	13,000	11,970	17,966	15,624	14,895
Utah	13,249	12,687	11,424	951	933	857	1,385	1,285	1,195
Vermont	3,178	3,034	2,699	435	424	378	562	561	589
Virginia	24,800	23,696	21,619	2,441	2,356	2,069	2,761	2,613	2,884
Washington	22,483	21,774	20,786	3,788	3,727	3,504	5,921	5,865	5,962
West Virginia	5,458	5,121	4,567	456	444	408	503	489	508
Wisconsin.	43,642	40,780	36,065	6,699	6,532	5,983	6,756	6,601	6,069
Wyoming	11,884	11,244	10,217	1,150	1,132	1,067	1,204	990	1,052

See footnotes at end of table.

Geographic area	Value of production, 2003 (dol.)		Farm income (USDA)[1]						Net farm income, 2003 (dol.)	
			Government payments (mil. dol.)		Net farm income (mil. dol.)					
	Per operation	Per acre	2003	2000	2003	2002	2000		Per operation	Per acre
United States[2]...	**113,273**	**257**	**15,949**	**22,896**	**59,229**	**37,277**	**47,897**		**27,848**	**63**
Alabama	91,725	464	220	171	1,604	1,106	1,195		35,654	180
Alaska	92,971	63	2	2	10	11	16		16,491	11
Arizona	294,033	114	135	107	1,078	1,435	720		104,635	41
Arkansas	125,309	413	844	901	1,914	931	1,591		40,301	133
California	374,235	1,084	654	667	8,475	6,168	5,402		107,959	313
Colorado	177,149	179	320	351	1,172	698	711		37,313	38
Connecticut	133,457	1,557	8	18	93	45	183		22,118	258
Delaware	373,533	1,621	19	25	156	64	144		67,686	294
District of Columbia	(X)	(X)	(X)	(X)	(X)	(X)	(X)		(X)	(X)
Florida	155,294	670	135	57	1,831	2,428	2,627		41,614	180
Georgia	125,656	574	552	380	2,971	1,830	2,010		60,265	275
Hawaii	109,027	461	1	12	122	118	112		22,170	94
Idaho	177,598	376	152	261	1,218	1,196	957		48,708	103
Illinois	127,244	338	866	1,944	1,657	839	1,502		22,699	60
Indiana	100,114	396	446	938	1,328	373	852		22,315	88
Iowa	145,796	414	1,051	2,302	2,023	2,044	2,341		22,474	64
Kansas	160,700	220	808	1,232	1,387	252	1,016		21,502	29
Kentucky	49,412	312	147	448	864	411	1,677		9,928	63
Louisiana	83,542	289	442	452	711	212	504		26,138	91
Maine	78,137	411	12	14	84	56	137		11,724	62
Maryland	145,204	853	67	88	327	133	390		27,009	159
Massachusetts	76,815	901	14	11	40	27	69		6,577	77
Michigan	82,612	436	255	381	444	298	259		8,340	44
Minnesota	115,607	334	787	1,502	1,568	738	1,301		19,605	57
Mississippi	91,910	354	476	464	1,148	335	750		26,832	103
Missouri	54,034	190	512	869	1,539	555	955		14,519	51
Montana	85,070	40	356	490	576	250	260		20,571	10
Nebraska	246,606	261	726	1,407	3,228	822	1,374		66,554	70
Nevada	153,485	73	12	4	111	82	100		37,093	18
New Hampshire	53,102	401	6	5	17	2	20		4,855	37
New Jersey	97,223	1,174	12	22	127	125	248		12,861	155
New Mexico	129,986	51	92	79	716	537	501		40,894	16
New York	96,793	468	161	160	597	387	569		16,141	78
North Carolina	165,233	971	362	447	1,629	1,246	3,296		30,444	179
North Dakota	144,469	111	652	1,170	1,315	525	1,027		43,410	33
Ohio	77,468	412	399	678	1,470	528	1,241		18,948	101
Oklahoma	60,369	150	358	440	2,037	1,130	996		24,391	60
Oregon	99,756	232	111	137	493	381	409		12,330	29
Pennsylvania	86,499	654	183	148	1,107	467	1,100		19,017	144
Rhode Island	77,308	1,095	1	1	10	6	12		11,516	163
South Carolina	80,302	404	129	144	681	163	547		27,894	140
South Dakota	151,475	109	549	790	1,321	320	1,358		41,801	30
Tennessee	33,940	255	176	299	480	136	541		5,519	41
Texas	78,454	138	1,666	1,647	5,939	5,246	3,868		25,935	46
Utah	90,519	119	56	36	368	254	232		24,044	32
Vermont	86,394	449	28	26	102	84	144		15,733	82
Virginia	58,121	321	177	152	529	210	690		11,129	61
Washington	166,795	387	265	353	680	971	1,005		19,166	44
West Virginia	24,193	140	13	24	15	−40	45		713	4
Wisconsin	88,310	433	484	603	1,626	1,008	756		21,255	104
Wyoming	130,854	35	51	34	291	134	137		31,679	8

X Not applicable.

[1] U.S. Department of Agriculture.
[2] The U.S. total exceeds the sum of the states in some cases because data for some states are not included in the state's statistics due to disclosure issues.

Survey, Census, or Data Collection Method: Based on the Agricultural Resource Management Survey (ARMS); for information, see Internet site <http://www.ers.usda.gov/Briefing/ARMS/>.

Source: U.S. Department of Agriculture, Economic Research Service, "Farm Income Summary Totals for 50 States"; see Internet site <http://www.ers.usda.gov/Data/FarmIncome/50State/50stmenu.htm>, accessed 12 October 2004; "Farm Business Balance Sheet and Financial Ratios," published 3 December 2004; see Internet site <http://www.ers.usda.gov/data/farmbalancesheet/fbsdmu.htm>.

Table A-52. States — **Farm Marketings and Principal Commodities**

Geographic area	Farm marketings											
	Total marketings (mil. dol.)			Crops (mil. dol.)			Livestock and products (mil. dol.)			Principal commodities, 2003		
	2003	2002	2000	2003	2002	2000	2003	2002	2000	Top	2nd	3rd
United States . . .	**211,647**	**195,072**	**192,078**	**106,176**	**101,257**	**92,494**	**105,471**	**93,816**	**99,585**	**Cattle[1]**	**Dairy products**	**Corn**
Alabama	3,415	2,920	3,271	676	534	625	2,739	2,386	2,646	Broilers	Cattle[1]	Chicken eggs
Alaska	51	50	53	23	22	20	28	28	33	Greenhouse[2]	Hay	Dairy products
Arizona	2,586	3,065	2,234	1,327	1,972	1,181	1,259	1,093	1,054	Cattle[1]	Dairy products	Lettuce
Arkansas	5,298	4,505	4,547	2,083	1,547	1,292	3,215	2,959	3,255	Broilers	Soybeans	Rice
California	27,805	26,606	25,266	20,812	20,345	19,014	6,993	6,261	6,253	Dairy products	Greenhouse[2]	Grapes
Colorado	4,964	4,958	4,616	1,289	1,458	1,285	3,676	3,500	3,330	Cattle[1]	Dairy products	Greenhouse[2]
Connecticut	485	472	505	320	310	329	165	162	175	Greenhouse[2]	Dairy products	Chicken eggs
Delaware	760	718	733	168	171	178	593	547	555	Broilers	Soybeans	Corn
District of Columbia	(X)	(X)	(X)	(X)	(X)	(X)	(X)	(X)	(X)	(X)	(X)	(X)
Florida	6,450	6,663	6,786	5,244	5,448	5,470	1,206	1,214	1,316	Greenhouse[2]	Oranges	Cane for sugar
Georgia	5,246	4,475	5,030	2,024	1,585	1,923	3,222	2,889	3,107	Broilers	Cotton	Chicken eggs
Hawaii	549	540	523	464	454	431	86	86	92	Pineapples	Greenhouse[2]	Cane for sugar
Idaho.	3,953	3,985	3,395	1,776	1,986	1,766	2,177	1,999	1,629	Cattle[1]	Dairy products	Potatoes
Illinois	8,290	7,732	6,996	6,490	6,183	5,324	1,800	1,549	1,672	Corn	Soybeans	Hogs
Indiana	5,162	4,719	4,518	3,363	3,183	2,830	1,799	1,536	1,688	Corn	Soybeans	Hogs
Iowa	12,633	11,394	10,773	6,560	6,248	4,949	6,073	5,146	5,824	Corn	Hogs	Soybeans
Kansas	9,046	8,070	8,040	2,867	2,747	2,535	6,179	5,323	5,505	Cattle[1]	Wheat	Corn
Kentucky	3,469	3,166	3,641	1,243	1,193	1,263	2,226	1,973	2,379	Horses[3]	Cattle[1]	Broilers
Louisiana	1,993	1,723	1,655	1,296	1,073	1,002	697	649	652	Cane for sugar	Cotton	Cattle[1]
Maine	499	465	520	227	214	239	272	251	281	Potatoes	Dairy products	Chicken eggs
Maryland	1,467	1,396	1,443	620	612	608	847	784	835	Broilers	Greenhouse[2]	Dairy products
Massachusetts	385	388	400	298	298	303	87	89	97	Greenhouse[2]	Cranberries	Dairy products
Michigan	3,821	3,465	3,322	2,422	2,175	1,983	1,399	1,290	1,339	Dairy products	Greenhouse[2]	Corn
Minnesota	8,588	7,866	7,374	4,516	4,245	3,491	4,072	3,622	3,883	Corn	Soybeans	Hogs
Mississippi	3,411	2,841	2,729	1,246	890	692	2,165	1,952	2,036	Broilers	Cotton	Soybeans
Missouri.	4,973	4,263	4,561	2,344	1,979	1,879	2,628	2,284	2,681	Cattle[1]	Soybeans	Corn
Montana	1,892	1,768	1,844	787	767	737	1,105	1,001	1,107	Cattle[1]	Wheat	Barley
Nebraska	10,621	9,422	8,956	3,754	3,582	3,040	6,867	5,840	5,916	Cattle[1]	Corn	Soybeans
Nevada	396	362	387	141	149	150	254	213	237	Cattle[1]	Hay	Dairy products
New Hampshire.	150	147	154	88	85	91	62	63	63	Greenhouse[2]	Dairy products	Apples
New Jersey	846	869	844	658	680	652	188	189	192	Greenhouse[2]	Horses[3]	Blueberries
New Mexico	2,140	1,970	2,108	543	573	495	1,597	1,398	1,613	Dairy products	Cattle[1]	Hay
New York	3,139	3,115	3,130	1,225	1,241	1,199	1,915	1,875	1,931	Dairy products	Greenhouse[2]	Hay
North Carolina.	6,916	6,600	7,309	2,759	2,660	3,009	4,158	3,940	4,300	Hogs	Broilers	Greenhouse[2]
North Dakota	3,778	3,344	2,748	2,907	2,546	2,087	870	798	661	Wheat	Cattle[1]	Soybeans
Ohio	4,662	4,372	4,347	2,853	2,742	2,593	1,809	1,629	1,754	Soybeans	Corn	Dairy products
Oklahoma	4,526	3,835	4,251	1,022	912	816	3,504	2,923	3,434	Cattle[1]	Wheat	Hogs
Oregon	3,284	3,098	3,095	2,479	2,288	2,265	805	809	829	Greenhouse[2]	Cattle[1]	Dairy products
Pennsylvania	4,266	4,065	4,121	1,407	1,389	1,356	2,859	2,676	2,765	Dairy products	Cattle[1]	Greenhouse[2]
Rhode Island	57	56	53	49	47	45	9	8	8	Greenhouse[2]	Dairy products	Corn, sweet
South Carolina	1,644	1,449	1,502	754	688	708	890	761	793	Broilers	Greenhouse[2]	Turkeys
South Dakota	4,018	3,775	3,731	1,899	1,730	1,714	2,119	2,046	2,016	Cattle[1]	Soybeans	Corn
Tennessee	2,339	2,054	1,926	1,268	1,120	935	1,071	934	991	Cattle[1]	Broilers	Greenhouse[2]
Texas	15,342	12,594	12,969	5,031	4,505	3,809	10,311	8,089	9,160	Cattle[1]	Cotton	Greenhouse[2]
Utah	1,138	1,067	1,020	258	254	247	880	813	774	Cattle[1]	Dairy products	Hogs
Vermont.	482	475	507	79	76	75	403	399	432	Dairy products	Cattle[1]	Greenhouse[2]
Virginia	2,227	2,155	2,296	695	703	726	1,532	1,451	1,570	Broilers	Cattle[1]	Dairy products
Washington	5,345	5,267	5,126	3,818	3,715	3,413	1,527	1,553	1,713	Apples	Dairy products	Cattle[1]
West Virginia	390	363	397	73	70	58	317	294	339	Broilers	Cattle[1]	Chicken eggs
Wisconsin.	5,876	5,521	5,367	1,782	1,729	1,497	4,094	3,792	3,870	Dairy products	Cattle[1]	Corn
Wyoming	874	887	959	150	136	161	724	751	799	Cattle[1]	Hay	Sugar beets

X Not applicable.

[1]Includes calves.
[2]Includes nursery.
[3]Includes mules.

Survey, Census, or Data Collection Method: Based on the Agricultural Resource Management Survey (ARMS); for information, see Internet site <http://www.ers.usda.gov/Briefing/ARMS/>.

Source: U.S. Department of Agriculture, Economic Research Service, "Farm Income," published 2 September 2004; see Internet site <http://www.ers.usda.gov/Data/farmincome/finfidmu.htm>.

Geographic area	Agriculture								2002	
	Number of farms (1,000)		Land in farms (mil. acres)		Average size of farm (acres)		Value of land and buildings[1] (mil. dol.)		Market value of agricultural products sold and government payments (mil. dol.)	
	2002	1997	2002	1997	2002	1997	2002	1997	Total	Products sold
United States . . .	**2,129.0**	**2,215.9**	**938.3**	**954.8**	**441**	**431**	**1,144.9**	**921.6**	**207,192**	**200,646**
Alabama	45.1	49.9	8.9	9.5	197	191	15.1	14.1	3,343	3,265
Alaska	0.6	0.5	0.9	0.9	1,479	1,608	0.3	0.3	48	46
Arizona	7.3	8.5	26.6	27.2	3,645	3,194	10.6	11.0	2,427	2,395
Arkansas	47.5	49.5	14.5	14.8	305	300	21.2	17.5	5,189	4,950
California	79.6	88.0	27.6	28.8	346	327	96.1	73.8	25,906	25,737
Colorado	31.4	30.2	31.1	32.4	991	1,071	23.8	20.3	4,651	4,525
Connecticut	4.2	4.9	0.4	0.4	85	83	3.5	2.5	474	471
Delaware	2.4	2.7	0.5	0.6	226	221	2.3	1.5	627	619
District of Columbia	(X)	(X)	(X)	(X)	(X)	(X)	(X)	(X)	(X)	(X)
Florida	44.1	45.8	10.4	10.7	236	233	29.3	24.8	6,264	6,242
Georgia	49.3	49.3	10.7	11.3	218	228	22.6	17.9	5,030	4,912
Hawaii	5.4	5.5	1.3	1.4	241	263	4.6	3.5	534	533
Idaho	25.0	25.6	11.8	12.1	470	470	15.3	12.5	4,002	3,908
Illinois	73.0	79.1	27.3	27.7	374	350	66.7	58.2	8,089	7,676
Indiana	60.3	66.7	15.1	15.5	250	233	38.4	32.4	5,008	4,783
Iowa	90.7	96.7	31.7	32.3	350	334	64.2	54.1	12,813	12,274
Kansas	64.4	65.5	47.2	46.7	733	712	32.6	27.3	9,074	8,746
Kentucky	86.5	91.2	13.8	13.9	160	153	25.5	20.3	3,174	3,080
Louisiana	27.4	30.4	7.8	8.4	286	275	12.2	10.3	1,939	1,816
Maine	7.2	7.4	1.4	1.3	190	177	2.3	1.7	472	464
Maryland	12.2	13.3	2.1	2.2	170	165	8.5	7.1	1,326	1,293
Massachusetts	6.1	7.3	0.5	0.6	85	79	4.6	3.1	389	384
Michigan	53.3	53.5	10.1	10.4	190	195	27.1	18.0	3,917	3,772
Minnesota	80.8	78.8	27.5	27.6	340	350	41.8	31.4	8,926	8,576
Mississippi	42.2	42.2	11.1	11.4	263	271	15.6	12.6	3,262	3,116
Missouri	106.8	111.0	29.9	30.2	280	272	45.3	32.7	5,248	4,983
Montana	27.9	27.6	59.6	58.4	2,139	2,115	23.3	18.0	2,093	1,882
Nebraska	49.4	54.5	45.9	45.9	930	841	35.7	30.0	10,051	9,704
Nevada	3.0	3.2	6.3	6.4	2,118	2,000	2.8	2.5	451	447
New Hampshire	3.4	3.9	0.4	0.5	132	118	1.4	1.2	149	145
New Jersey	9.9	10.0	0.8	0.9	81	85	7.4	5.7	754	750
New Mexico	15.2	17.9	44.8	46.2	2,954	2,583	10.6	9.7	1,750	1,700
New York	37.3	38.3	7.7	7.8	206	204	12.9	10.4	3,228	3,118
North Carolina	53.9	59.1	9.1	9.4	168	160	28.0	20.7	7,059	6,962
North Dakota	30.6	32.3	39.3	39.7	1,283	1,227	15.8	16.0	3,526	3,233
Ohio	77.8	78.7	14.6	14.7	187	187	39.6	30.3	4,461	4,264
Oklahoma	83.3	84.0	33.7	34.1	404	405	23.8	21.6	4,606	4,456
Oregon	40.0	40.0	17.1	17.7	427	442	20.4	17.7	3,248	3,195
Pennsylvania	58.1	60.2	7.7	7.8	133	130	26.3	19.9	4,343	4,257
Rhode Island	0.9	1.0	0.1	0.1	71	65	0.6	0.4	56	56
South Carolina	24.5	25.8	4.8	5.0	197	193	10.1	7.6	1,528	1,490
South Dakota	31.7	33.2	43.8	44.1	1,380	1,330	19.6	15.7	4,050	3,835
Tennessee	87.6	91.5	11.7	12.0	133	131	28.5	22.4	2,259	2,200
Texas	228.9	228.2	129.9	134.0	567	587	100.5	82.5	14,664	14,135
Utah	15.3	15.8	11.7	12.0	768	760	9.0	7.2	1,143	1,116
Vermont	6.6	7.1	1.2	1.3	189	186	2.5	2.1	497	473
Virginia	47.6	49.4	8.6	8.8	181	177	23.3	17.6	2,416	2,361
Washington	35.9	40.1	15.3	15.8	426	393	22.4	20.9	5,465	5,331
West Virginia	20.8	21.5	3.6	3.7	172	172	4.8	4.2	488	483
Wisconsin	77.1	79.5	15.7	16.2	204	204	35.8	20.6	5,871	5,623
Wyoming	9.4	9.4	34.4	34.3	3,651	3,633	10.2	7.6	902	864

See footnotes at end of table.

Geographic area	Total number of farm operators (1,000)	2002 Farms by value of sales (1,000)						Cropland (1,000 acres)
		Less than $2,500	$2,500– $9,999	$10,000– $24,999	$25,000– $49,999	$50,000– $99,999	$100,000 or more	
United States . . .	**3,115**	**826.56**	**436.49**	**256.16**	**157.91**	**140.48**	**311.39**	**434,165**
Alabama	63	19.56	12.51	5.21	1.93	1.25	4.67	3,733
Alaska	1	0.21	0.16	0.09	0.05	0.03	0.07	98
Arizona	12	3.45	1.25	0.68	0.43	0.31	1.19	1,262
Arkansas	70	16.41	12.21	6.31	2.18	1.87	8.51	9,576
California	125	23.36	13.30	9.46	7.13	6.80	19.59	10,994
Colorado	50	13.02	5.95	3.78	2.52	2.18	3.93	11,531
Connecticut	7	1.90	0.92	0.50	0.24	0.19	0.44	171
Delaware	4	0.61	0.27	0.16	0.15	0.18	1.02	457
District of Columbia	(X)	(X)	(X)	(X)	(X)	(X)	(X)	(X)
Florida	64	19.11	8.83	5.24	3.31	2.49	5.11	3,715
Georgia	67	23.99	10.18	4.88	2.41	1.59	6.27	4,677
Hawaii	8	1.41	1.63	1.06	0.51	0.31	0.49	211
Idaho	39	11.59	4.12	2.44	1.60	1.37	3.89	6,153
Illinois	102	20.80	9.46	7.98	7.26	8.05	19.47	24,171
Indiana	86	21.62	10.93	7.33	5.11	4.95	10.36	12,909
Iowa	127	23.44	8.64	9.41	10.04	11.72	27.42	27,153
Kansas	90	20.44	10.70	9.26	6.72	6.28	11.02	29,542
Kentucky	123	32.92	25.34	13.15	6.53	3.49	5.12	8,412
Louisiana	39	11.84	6.40	3.04	1.42	1.30	3.43	5,072
Maine	11	3.63	1.46	0.73	0.39	0.31	0.68	537
Maryland	19	5.12	2.27	1.32	0.73	0.67	2.10	1,487
Massachusetts	10	2.59	1.27	0.72	0.42	0.39	0.69	208
Michigan	80	23.29	9.86	6.43	4.02	3.23	6.49	7,984
Minnesota	114	29.02	9.91	8.10	7.24	8.02	18.54	22,729
Mississippi	58	22.45	8.83	3.89	1.59	1.07	4.36	5,823
Missouri	158	36.11	26.91	18.09	9.34	6.93	9.42	18,885
Montana	43	10.12	3.94	3.04	2.72	3.03	5.03	18,316
Nebraska	71	9.82	5.25	5.85	6.03	6.62	15.78	22,521
Nevada	5	1.11	0.55	0.31	0.21	0.23	0.58	940
New Hampshire	6	1.76	0.73	0.30	0.19	0.13	0.25	129
New Jersey	15	5.23	1.81	0.95	0.49	0.38	1.06	548
New Mexico	23	7.51	2.85	1.59	0.89	0.74	1.59	2,575
New York	58	14.24	6.59	4.18	2.73	3.07	6.45	4,841
North Carolina	76	22.10	12.28	5.86	2.70	2.21	8.79	5,472
North Dakota	42	9.31	2.48	3.08	3.07	3.85	8.83	26,506
Ohio	114	28.92	17.74	10.64	6.33	5.30	8.87	11,424
Oklahoma	121	29.93	22.38	12.83	7.37	4.34	6.45	14,843
Oregon	66	18.87	8.78	3.91	2.41	1.88	4.19	5,417
Pennsylvania	87	24.39	11.02	5.98	3.29	3.82	9.60	5,121
Rhode Island	1	0.29	0.21	1.30	0.65	0.56	0.11	24
South Carolina	34	14.50	4.75	2.12	0.92	0.60	1.66	2,270
South Dakota	46	6.95	3.19	3.53	3.84	4.56	9.67	20,318
Tennessee	123	42.74	25.17	10.01	3.69	2.13	3.85	6,993
Texas	335	102.07	61.60	28.59	13.23	8.77	14.66	38,658
Utah	24	7.29	2.85	1.73	1.03	0.79	1.59	2,067
Vermont	11	2.67	1.31	0.63	0.40	0.39	1.17	568
Virginia	70	18.42	13.62	6.74	3.06	1.85	3.92	4,194
Washington	56	15.01	6.35	3.45	2.38	2.16	6.60	8,038
West Virginia	30	12.05	5.11	1.88	0.70	0.38	0.70	1,173
Wisconsin	118	30.49	11.18	8.36	5.93	7.24	13.93	10,729
Wyoming	16	2.90	1.51	1.22	0.99	1.00	1.81	2,990

X Not applicable.

[1]Based on reports for a sample of farms.

Survey, Census, or Data Collection Method: Based on the 2002 Census of Agriculture; for information, see Appendix B, Limitations of the Data and Methodology, and Internet site <http://www.nass.usda.gov/Census_of_Agriculture/index.asp>.

Source: U.S. Department of Agriculture, National Agricultural Statistics Service, *2002 Census of Agriculture,* Vol. 1; see also <http://www.nass.usda.gov/Census_of_Agriculture/index.asp>.

Table A-54. States — **Natural Resource Industries and Minerals**

Geographic area	Establishments 2002	Establishments 2000	Number of employees 2002 — Total	Number of employees 2002 — Percent of all industries	Number of employees 2000	Annual payroll (bil. dol.) 2002	Annual payroll (bil. dol.) 2000	Value of nonfuel mineral production (mil. dol.) 2004 prel.	Value of nonfuel mineral production (mil. dol.) 2003	Value of nonfuel mineral production (mil. dol.) 2000	Crude petroleum Quantity (mil. bbl.)	Crude petroleum Value (mil. dol.)	Natural gas Quantity (mil. cubic feet)	Natural gas Value (mil. dol.)	Coal Quantity (1,000 short tons)	Coal Value (mil. dol.)
United States . . .	73,021	72,932	1,676,938	1.49	1,791,320	66,675	66,576	44,000[3]	38,000[3]	40,100[3]	2,073	57,144	19,911,802[4]	97,250[4]	1,071,753[5]	19,131[5]
Alabama	1,907	1,954	(D)	(D)	57,636	(D)	2,073	982	863	1,070	8	228	346,145	2,051	20,118	679
Alaska	445	497	(D)	(D)	(D)	(D)	(D)	1,320	1,060	1,140	356	8,503	489,757	1,179	1,081	(NA)
Arizona	676	652	22,009	1.13	24,518	708	813	3,000	2,100	2,550	(Z)	(NA)	443	2	12,059	(NA)
Arkansas	1,622	1,649	36,260	3.72	38,457	1,214	1,221	514	445	506	7	192	169,599	877	8	(NA)
California	5,111	4,991	111,061	0.86	118,975	4,170	4,213	3,620	3,170	3,350	250	6,608	337,216	1,698	(X)	(X)
Colorado	1,528	1,507	20,751	1.09	21,655	1,036	970	762	672	566	21	648	1,011,285	4,591	35,831	652
Connecticut	396	401	8,434	0.54	8,729	361	359	132[6]	142[6]	100[6]	(X)	(X)	(X)	(X)	(X)	(X)
Delaware	99	104	(D)	(D)	(D)	(D)	(D)	21[6]	16[6]	12[6]	(X)	(X)	(X)	(X)	(X)	(X)
District of Columbia	9	(NA)	(D)	(D)	(D)	(D)	(D)	(NA)	(NA)	(NA)	(X)	(X)	(X)	(X)	(X)	(X)
Florida	2,168	2,106	46,496	0.73	46,187	1,500	1,361	2,220	2,000	1,920	3	(NA)	3,087	–	(X)	(X)
Georgia	2,178	2,122	(D)	(D)	71,686	(D)	2,426	1,830	1,670	1,660	(X)	(X)	(X)	(X)	(X)	(X)
Hawaii	89	95	(D)	(D)	(D)	(D)	(D)	75	74[6]	91	(X)	(X)	(X)	(X)	(X)	(X)
Idaho	918	947	(D)	(D)	(D)	(D)	(D)	322	294	398	(X)	(X)	(X)	(X)	(X)	(X)
Illinois	1,818	1,760	45,378	0.87	50,435	1,805	1,923	1,030	911	907	12	340	174	–	31,640	763
Indiana	1,373	1,346	39,964	1.59	42,385	1,396	1,378	774	734	729	2	53	1,464	8	35,355	795
Iowa	710	674	18,794	1.53	19,803	661	671	533	477	510	(X)	(X)	(X)	(X)	(X)	(X)
Kansas	1,219	1,208	13,502	1.23	13,287	465	438	741	688	624	34	974	418,893	1,815	154	(NA)
Kentucky	1,483	1,459	45,199	3.09	46,356	1,660	1,600	674	559	497	3	69	87,608	398	112,680	3,172
Louisiana	2,521	2,599	68,155	4.30	66,584	3,122	2,949	364	331	404	90	2,750	1,350,399	7,614	4,028	(NA)
Maine	1,107	1,064	(D)	(D)	(D)	(D)	(D)	122	100	102	(X)	(X)	(X)	(X)	(X)	(X)
Maryland	521	533	13,108	0.64	(D)	464	(D)	478	382[6]	357[6]	(NA)	(NA)	48	(Z)	5,056	115
Massachusetts	961	926	21,143	0.70	23,427	843	904	221[6]	186[6]	210	(X)	(X)	(X)	(X)	(X)	(X)
Michigan	1,864	1,959	36,776	0.95	42,631	1,430	1,607	1,530	1,350	1,670	7	190	236,987	950	(X)	(X)
Minnesota	1,170	1,150	36,461	1.55	41,085	1,621	1,705	1,590[6]	1,230[6]	1,570	(X)	(X)	(X)	(X)	(X)	(X)
Mississippi	1,562	1,619	(D)	(D)	34,592	(D)	1,043	189	174	157	17	456	133,901	688	3,695	(NA)
Missouri	1,291	1,304	26,219	1.11	29,285	824	872	1,540	1,290	1,320	(Z)	(NA)	(X)	(X)	533	(NA)
Montana	838	831	(D)	(D)	(D)	(D)	(D)	582	492	582	19	554	86,027	321	36,994	348
Nebraska	407	399	(D)	(D)	6,257	(D)	191	95[6]	94[6]	170	3	79	1,454	5	(X)	(X)
Nevada	326	331	10,630	1.14	12,045	545	598	3,250	2,940	2,800	(Z)	(NA)	76[7]	–	(X)	(X)
New Hampshire	434	447	6,937	1.26	7,778	253	273	65[6]	64[6]	59[6]	(X)	(X)	(X)	(X)	(X)	(X)
New Jersey	787	740	21,910	0.61	23,394	931	981	330	272	286[6]	(X)	(X)	(X)	(X)	(X)	(X)
New Mexico	780	735	16,205	2.92	15,863	697	648	811	533	812	66	1,952	1,604,015	7,307	26,389	612
New York	2,051	2,025	37,611	0.52	42,372	1,435	1,507	1,060	978	970	(Z)	(NA)	36,137	209	(X)	(X)
North Carolina	2,209	2,233	57,966	1.74	65,173	1,917	2,068	822	676	779	(X)	(X)	(X)	(X)	(X)	(X)
North Dakota	359	347	(D)	(D)	(D)	(D)	(D)	52	38	42	29	861	55,693	197	30,775	270
Ohio	2,201	2,197	56,681	1.20	63,055	2,082	2,223	1,090	968	1,060	6	159	93,641	552	22,009	486
Oklahoma	2,536	2,458	(D)	(D)	33,963	(D)	1,374	498	479	453	65	1,942	1,558,155	7,737	1,565	44
Oregon	2,275	2,319	51,880	3.90	58,428	1,915	1,974	356	311	439	(NA)	(NA)	731	3	(X)	(X)
Pennsylvania	2,879	2,887	74,489	1.48	77,926	2,822	2,786	1,400[6]	1,260[6]	1,250[6]	2	72	159,827	–	63,725	1,705
Rhode Island	146	162	(D)	(D)	(D)	(D)	(D)	37[6]	26[6]	24[6]	(X)	(X)	(X)	(X)	(X)	(X)
South Carolina	1,091	1,107	29,167	1.90	32,073	1,073	1,106	586[6]	484[6]	560	(X)	(X)	(X)	(X)	(X)	(X)
South Dakota	244	230	3,792	1.25		127		210	206	260	1	36	1,103	5	(X)	(X)
Tennessee	1,306	1,361	39,220	1.71	43,671	1,287	1,407	660	606	770	(Z)	(NA)			2,564	74
Texas	8,367	8,412	172,332	2.16	168,687	8,731	7,659	2,400	2,030	2,050	406	11,821	5,243,567	27,171	47,517	701
Utah	551	507	12,500	1.39	12,958	516	516	1,740	1,260	1,420	13	378	268,058	1,103	23,069	394
Vermont	354	360	(D)	(D)	(D)	(D)	(D)	69[6]	73[6]	43[6]	(X)	(X)	(X)	(X)	(X)	(X)
Virginia	1,771	1,801	47,809	1.64	49,717	1,788	1,723	868	727	692	(Z)	(NA)	81,086	–	31,596	957
Washington	2,499	2,601	47,188	2.16	54,268	1,953	2,068	447	430	691	(X)	(X)	(X)	(X)	6,232	(NA)
West Virginia	1,298	1,307	33,375	5.94	29,882	1,335	1,141	179	168	182	1	37	187,723	–	139,711	4,194
Wisconsin	1,697	1,705	71,859	3.05	77,602	2,833	2,931	487[6]	404[6]	349[6]	(X)	(X)	(X)	(X)	(X)	(X)
Wyoming	869	796	(D)	(D)	(D)	(D)	(D)	1,090	1,010	922	52	1,396	1,539,318	6,362	376,270	2,536

– Represents zero. D Withheld to avoid disclosure of individual company data. NA Not available. X Not applicable. Z Less than $500,000 or 500,000 barrels.

[1]Includes Agriculture, forestry, fishing and hunting (NAICS 11), Mining (NAICS 21), Wood product manufacturing (NAICS 321), and Paper manufacturing (NAICS 322).
[2]Covers full- and part-time employees who are on the payroll in the pay period including March 12.
[3]Includes concealed data not distributed by state.
[4]States may not add to U.S. totals due to independent rounding.
[5]U.S. total includes refuse recovery not distributed by state.
[6]Partial data only; excludes values withheld to avoid disclosing individual company data. Concealed data included in U.S. total.
[7]All of Nevada's marketed production was consumed as lease fuel.

Survey, Census, or Data Collection Method: Natural resource industries—Based on tabulations of data extracted from the U.S. Census Bureau's Business Register; for information, see Internet site <http://www.census.gov/epcd/cbp/view/cbpview.html>; Nonfuel minerals—Based on U.S. Geological Survey Mineral Industry Surveys; for information, see Internet site <http://minerals.usgs.gov/minerals/>; Crude petroleum—Based on the Petroleum Supply Reporting System (PSRS); for information, see the above reports at <http://eia.doe.gov/>; Natural gas—Based on Energy Information Administration Survey Form EIA-895, "Monthly and Annual Quantity and Value of Natural Gas Production Report"; for information, see the following report at <http://www.eia.doe.gov/oil_gas/natural_gas/data_publications/natural_gas_annual/nga.html>; Coal—Based on U.S. Department of Labor, Mine Safety and Health Administration, Form 7000-2, "Quarterly Mine Employment and Coal Production Report" and Energy Information Administration Form EIA-7A, "Coal Production Report"; for information, see the following report at <http://www.eia.doe.gov/cneaf/coal/page/acr/acr.pdf>.

Sources: Natural resource industries—U.S. Census Bureau, *County Business Patterns*, annual, see Internet site <http://www.census.gov/epcd/cbp/view/cbpview.html>; Nonfuel minerals—U.S. Geological Survey, *Mineral Commodity Summaries*, annual, see also <http://minerals.usgs.gov/minerals/pubs/mcs/2005/mcs2005.pdf>; Crude petroleum—U.S. Energy Information Administration, *Petroleum Supply Annual,* and *Petroleum Marketing Annual*, see Internet site <http://eia.doe.gov/>; Natural gas—U.S. Energy Information Administration, *Natural Gas Annual, 2003*, see Internet site <http://www.eia.doe.gov/oil_gas/natural_gas/data_publications/natural_gas_annual/nga.html>; Coal—U.S. Energy Information Administration, *Annual Coal Report, 2003*, see Internet site <http://www.eia.doe.gov/cneaf/coal/page/acr/acr_sum.html>.

Table A-55. States — **Utilities**

Geographic area	Private utilities[1] Establishments 2002	2000	Number of employees 2002 Total	Percent of all industries	2000	Annual payroll ($1,000) 2002	2000	Water systems, 2004 Number of systems Total	Community[5]	Non-transient, non-community[6]	Transient, non-community[7]	Population served (1,000) Total	Community[5]	Non-transient, non-community[6]	Transient, non-community[7]
United States . . .	18,432	17,301	648,254	0.58	655,230	41,845	40,651	157,760	51,407	19,025	87,328	289,947	265,832	5,690	18,425
Alabama	507	489	15,022	0.95	14,616	954	893	720	619	31	70	5,203	5,177	19	7
Alaska.	99	97	1,960	0.92	1,810	129	123	1,625	436	220	969	609	465	47	97
Arizona	276	261	10,448	0.54	9,923	662	606	1,591	789	197	605	5,162	4,913	129	120
Arkansas	435	409	8,203	0.84	7,517	417	382	1,109	728	40	341	2,531	2,504	10	17
California	1,166	981	50,733	0.39	51,289	3,485	3,415	7,596	3,123	1,418	3,055	39,396	32,878	423	6,095
Colorado	383	367	7,517	0.39	7,851	453	446	1,937	830	163	944	5,329	4,986	73	271
Connecticut	154	143	10,919	0.70	11,343	763	788	2,981	586	658	1,737	2,897	2,707	129	61
Delaware	42	42	2,548	0.65	2,399	188	148	508	226	105	177	874	792	25	57
District of Columbia	34	44	2,319	0.55	(9)	159	(D)	6	3	3	(NA)	611	606	5	(NA)
Florida.	685	638	30,240	0.47	29,885	1,698	1,754	6,231	1,881	1,009	3,341	17,767	17,206	265	296
Georgia	609	603	23,825	0.70	23,373	1,697	1,402	2,481	1,689	242	550	7,523	7,364	71	88
Hawaii	44	44	2,482	0.56	2,480	167	164	131	115	13	3	1,292	1,280	11	–
Idaho.	184	190	3,455	0.76	3,375	215	184	2,025	752	244	1,029	1,119	953	52	114
Illinois	512	442	34,059	0.65	31,173	2,670	2,318	5,897	1,792	405	3,700	12,103	11,568	144	391
Indiana	524	490	15,322	0.61	18,156	929	1,017	4,423	840	686	2,897	5,273	4,668	197	408
Iowa	294	288	7,344	0.60	7,769	388	391	1,999	1,142	144	713	2,695	2,560	48	88
Kansas	278	274	6,614	0.60	7,688	378	410	1,064	911	52	101	2,586	2,563	19	4
Kentucky	320	346	7,711	0.53	9,940	442	545	532	417	50	65	4,621	4,594	18	9
Louisiana	632	557	12,784	0.81	12,989	762	722	1,602	1,111	179	312	5,029	4,886	70	73
Maine	116	110	2,770	0.57	3,120	134	150	1,989	399	369	1,221	885	616	72	197
Maryland	125	120	10,860	0.53	12,034	711	813	3,696	502	573	2,621	5,186	4,845	169	172
Massachusetts	264	254	13,271	0.44	11,904	1,030	881	1,712	523	250	939	9,219	8,976	69	174
Michigan	458	440	24,421	0.63	25,216	1,519	1,681	11,910	1,438	1,631	8,841	8,672	7,279	355	1,039
Minnesota	310	269	12,492	0.53	13,372	829	818	7,801	965	563	6,273	4,564	3,964	89	511
Mississippi	624	616	8,465	0.94	9,121	447	451	1,383	1,170	95	118	3,139	3,041	74	24
Missouri	425	405	15,637	0.66	17,242	934	1,023	2,720	1,463	241	1,016	5,112	4,910	74	128
Montana	226	213	2,831	0.94	3,098	168	176	2,060	676	227	1,157	916	681	60	174
Nebraska	145	139	2,557	0.34	1,499	100	106	1,377	606	188	583	1,548	1,416	44	88
Nevada	118	109	5,717	0.61	5,293	387	362	610	253	106	251	1,961	1,895	38	28
New Hampshire.	100	102	3,278	0.60	3,276	194	197	2,279	698	444	1,137	1,127	803	91	233
New Jersey	330	314	21,089	0.59	20,958	1,297	1,505	4,121	607	870	2,644	8,490	7,891	217	381
New Mexico	220	205	5,041	0.91	5,508	263	260	1,275	645	147	483	1,760	1,590	39	131
New York	449	411	43,321	0.60	40,260	3,314	2,761	10,005	2,816	757	6,432	21,144	17,901	327	2,916
North Carolina	419	393	18,463	0.56	19,551	1,127	1,079	7,062	2,174	566	4,322	6,947	6,436	156	355
North Dakota	119	120	3,302	1.30	3,175	191	168	523	320	29	174	572	552	4	15
Ohio	652	663	27,213	0.57	27,940	1,638	1,630	5,479	1,318	970	3,191	10,757	10,037	237	483
Oklahoma	455	494	9,225	0.77	9,652	489	517	1,610	1,135	120	355	3,489	3,443	20	27
Oregon	245	226	6,636	0.50	8,225	429	514	2,648	874	337	1,437	3,224	2,925	76	224
Pennsylvania	764	699	34,985	0.69	35,112	2,400	2,493	9,892	2,135	1,213	6,544	11,808	10,453	513	842
Rhode Island	35	34	1,638	0.39	(8)	104	(D)	482	83	78	321	1,060	977	27	55
South Carolina	315	288	10,824	0.70	11,766	584	620	1,406	659	171	576	3,515	3,425	55	36
South Dakota	153	134	2,219	0.73	(8)	111	(D)	689	467	28	194	698	659	12	27
Tennessee	173	171	3,932	0.17	3,367	185	137	1,151	681	46	424	5,435	5,346	29	60
Texas	2,458	2,216	50,173	0.63	49,927	3,145	3,029	6,499	4,489	785	1,225	23,242	22,675	322	245
Utah	167	152	4,717	0.52	5,354	346	304	947	451	63	433	2,586	2,490	28	68
Vermont.	66	64	1,767	0.68	(8)	125	(D)	1,347	435	234	678	722	514	43	165
Virginia	340	295	16,534	0.57	16,163	1,125	971	3,158	1,263	602	1,293	6,606	6,084	306	216
Washington	342	321	5,309	0.24	6,237	330	365	4,130	2,274	315	1,541	6,151	5,597	139	415
West Virginia	233	238	7,502	1.34	7,943	428	412	1,224	536	154	534	1,522	1,442	45	35
Wisconsin.	294	266	16,262	0.69	14,192	1,065	845	11,369	1,086	907	9,376	4,739	3,859	191	689
Wyoming	114	115	2,298	1.29	2,612	139	142	748	276	87	385	534	439	19	76

See footnotes at end of table.

Geographic area	Gas utilities									
	Customers[2] (1,000)				Sales[3] (trillion Btu)				Prices, 2003 (dollars per million Btu)	
	2003				2003					
	All customers	Residential	2002	2000	All customers	Residential	2002	2000	All customers	Residential
United States . . .	**62,610**	**57,802**	**62,034**	**64,115**	**8,927**	**4,722**	**8,864**	**9,052**	**8.13**	**9.25**
Alabama	877	809	869	877	105	48	104	113	9.41	11.46
Alaska	114	100	110	104	113	17	113	24	2.36	4.35
Arizona	1,014	957	981	898	83	36	88	84	8.76	11.11
Arkansas	625	553	626	633	72	39	74	88	8.79	10.08
California	10,224	9,765	10,149	9,801	708	494	757	717	8.67	9.04
Colorado	1,593	1,454	1,550	1,525	198	125	213	195	6.18	6.57
Connecticut	515	467	509	508	85	46	86	96	11.00	12.50
Delaware	142	130	138	122	21	11	19	23	9.14	10.27
District of Columbia	121	113	125	131	16	11	15	19	13.06	12.91
Florida	649	607	647	752	45	16	45	75	11.56	15.75
Georgia	353	319	347	339	56	19	57	66	8.57	10.79
Hawaii	33	30	34	68	3	1	3	6	18.00	15.00
Idaho.	307	274	293	320	31	20	34	39	7.03	7.20
Illinois	3,787	3,548	3,801	3,821	555	430	545	545	8.34	8.53
Indiana	1,737	1,588	1,756	1,803	264	164	248	279	8.37	8.74
Iowa	929	832	922	906	120	74	121	120	8.51	9.15
Kansas	935	850	928	1,708	102	71	109	199	8.44	8.87
Kentucky	800	720	793	1,000	111	60	104	142	8.28	8.88
Louisiana	1,023	959	1,021	838	185	50	197	187	6.97	9.74
Maine	26	18	25	48	5	1	5	11	11.40	15.00
Maryland	886	831	867	868	98	73	86	85	10.76	11.00
Massachusetts	1,438	1,315	1,414	1,572	230	130	169	202	10.50	12.08
Michigan	3,251	3,011	3,244	3,327	522	374	501	523	6.93	7.10
Minnesota	1,433	1,308	1,406	1,373	280	138	280	276	7.75	8.58
Mississippi	491	439	487	473	85	28	75	75	7.55	9.25
Missouri	1,486	1,344	1,481	1,485	176	116	180	176	9.02	9.37
Montana	264	233	259	257	32	21	34	31	6.88	6.90
Nebraska	457	418	450	521	63	36	64	74	7.25	7.83
Nevada	645	611	614	552	80	34	82	47	7.44	7.82
New Hampshire.	103	88	102	121	17	8	15	19	10.47	11.38
New Jersey	2,646	2,437	2,523	2,625	397	241	363	601	7.94	8.18
New Mexico	544	499	533	525	53	33	61	60	7.51	8.06
New York	4,269	3,930	4,307	4,467	550	360	513	650	10.82	11.69
North Carolina	1,064	954	1,011	978	145	68	139	174	9.36	11.04
North Dakota	126	110	125	121	24	12	25	24	7.00	7.17
Ohio	2,225	2,056	2,346	3,078	299	215	286	416	9.11	9.34
Oklahoma	953	872	957	1,000	109	67	115	109	8.09	8.67
Oregon	701	625	634	663	75	38	78	93	8.53	9.66
Pennsylvania	2,558	2,349	2,527	2,501	357	248	319	362	10.24	10.54
Rhode Island	244	221	242	123	30	21	27	16	11.03	11.38
South Carolina	574	516	566	528	122	30	143	95	8.04	10.70
South Dakota	171	151	167	161	25	13	24	23	7.56	8.62
Tennessee	1,158	1,024	1,132	1,065	173	73	165	169	8.24	9.36
Texas	4,186	3,860	4,130	3,987	1,417	213	1,497	895	6.03	8.95
Utah	731	679	712	1,360	90	58	94	181	6.39	6.91
Vermont	35	31	35	59	8	3	8	10	7.88	10.33
Virginia	1,007	924	987	942	134	78	121	129	10.15	11.41
Washington	986	896	951	1,012	132	73	139	172	7.59	8.22
West Virginia	395	360	1,672	407	59	35	250	69	7.85	8.37
Wisconsin.	1,699	1,541	395	1,604	255	143	52	245	8.44	9.21
Wyoming	83	73	137	159	13	7	19	25	6.31	6.86

See footnotes at end of table.

Table A-55. States — **Utilities**—Con.

Geographic area	Net generation (bil. kWh)			Generation by selected major source, 2003—percent					Net summer capacity (mil. kW)			Sales to customers (bil. of kWh)				Prices, 2003[4] (cents per kWh)	
												2003					
	2003	2002	2000	Coal	Petro-leum	Natural gas	Nuclear	Hydro-electric	2003	2002	2000	All cus-tomers	Resi-dential	2002	2000	All cus-tomers	Resi-dential
United States . . .	3,883.2	3,858.5	3,802.1	50.83	3.07	16.74	19.67	7.10	948.4	905.3	809.4	3,488.2	1,273.5	3,462.5	3,309.6	7.42	8.70
Alabama	137.5	132.9	124.4	55.78	0.24	8.91	23.04	9.21	30.2	26.6	23.5	83.8	29.4	83.1	83.5	5.88	7.39
Alaska	6.3	6.8	6.2	8.67	13.35	52.92	–	24.97	1.9	2.0	2.1	5.6	2.0	5.5	5.3	10.50	11.98
Arizona	94.4	94.1	88.9	40.35	0.05	20.06	30.28	7.49	23.5	19.4	15.3	64.1	27.7	62.6	61.0	7.34	8.35
Arkansas	50.4	47.6	43.9	46.63	0.57	14.49	29.15	5.27	13.5	11.3	9.7	43.1	15.6	42.4	41.6	5.57	7.24
California	192.8	184.2	208.1	1.21	1.24	47.43	18.46	18.87	57.9	56.7	51.9	238.7	80.7	235.2	221.3	11.62	12.00
Colorado	46.6	45.6	44.2	77.47	0.07	19.79	–	2.71	10.4	9.4	8.4	46.5	15.7	45.9	43.0	6.77	8.14
Connecticut	29.5	31.3	33.0	14.22	6.98	17.13	54.42	1.91	7.6	7.4	6.4	31.8	13.2	30.9	30.0	10.17	11.31
Delaware	7.4	6.0	6.0	54.47	23.23	19.80	–	–	3.4	3.4	2.1	12.6	4.2	11.6	10.8	6.96	8.59
District of Columbia	0.1	0.3	0.1	–	100.00	–	–	–	0.8	0.8	0.8	10.9	1.9	11.1	10.6	7.43	7.66
Florida	212.6	203.4	191.8	31.83	17.50	32.12	14.57	0.12	49.4	47.1	41.5	217.4	112.6	210.5	195.8	7.72	8.55
Georgia	124.1	126.5	123.9	63.38	0.96	3.45	26.80	3.34	34.8	34.6	27.8	123.7	48.2	123.8	119.2	6.32	7.70
Hawaii	11.0	11.7	10.6	14.98	77.46	–	–	0.82	2.3	2.3	2.4	10.4	3.0	9.9	9.7	14.47	16.73
Idaho	10.4	9.8	11.9	0.87	(Z)	13.19	–	80.15	3.0	3.3	3.0	21.2	7.1	20.7	22.8	5.22	6.24
Illinois	189.1	188.1	178.5	46.54	0.59	2.06	50.11	0.07	45.5	44.7	36.3	136.0	43.2	137.7	125.6	6.88	8.38
Indiana	124.9	125.6	127.8	94.29	0.36	2.44	–	0.34	25.6	25.3	23.3	100.5	30.7	101.4	97.8	5.37	7.04
Iowa	42.1	42.5	41.5	85.05	0.24	0.74	9.47	1.87	10.1	9.3	9.1	41.2	12.8	40.9	39.1	6.11	8.57
Kansas	46.6	47.2	44.8	75.40	2.07	2.63	19.09	0.03	10.9	10.4	10.1	36.7	12.6	36.7	35.9	6.35	7.71
Kentucky	91.7	92.1	93.0	91.65	3.21	0.48	–	4.30	19.1	19.1	16.8	85.2	24.7	87.3	78.3	4.42	5.81
Louisiana	94.9	95.0	92.9	24.12	3.10	47.88	17.00	0.94	25.7	25.6	21.0	77.8	28.6	79.3	80.7	6.93	7.84
Maine	19.0	22.5	14.0	1.98	10.12	49.75	–	16.72	4.3	4.3	4.2	12.0	4.2	9.6	6.4	9.79	12.37
Maryland	52.2	48.3	51.1	57.31	6.84	2.29	26.21	5.07	12.5	11.9	10.4	71.3	26.7	66.9	60.6	6.45	7.73
Massachusetts	48.4	42.0	38.7	22.52	15.42	46.34	10.29	2.22	13.9	12.2	12.4	54.7	19.3	52.4	48.9	10.63	11.68
Michigan	111.3	117.9	104.2	60.87	0.96	10.22	25.10	1.24	30.4	29.3	25.8	108.9	33.7	107.3	104.4	6.85	8.35
Minnesota	55.1	52.8	51.4	64.77	1.59	3.35	24.37	1.48	11.5	11.3	10.3	63.1	20.6	62.2	59.8	6.01	7.65
Mississippi	40.1	42.9	37.6	42.55	4.06	23.61	27.16	–	17.3	13.7	9.0	45.5	17.7	45.5	45.3	6.46	7.60
Missouri	87.2	81.2	76.6	85.08	0.18	3.01	11.12	0.75	20.0	19.8	17.3	74.2	31.4	75.0	72.6	6.02	6.96
Montana	26.3	25.5	26.5	64.90	1.53	0.10	–	33.13	5.2	5.2	5.2	12.7	4.1	12.6	12.5	6.16	7.56
Nebraska	30.5	31.6	29.1	68.80	0.16	1.25	26.26	3.22	6.7	6.1	6.0	25.9	8.9	25.7	24.3	5.64	6.87
Nevada	33.2	32.1	35.5	51.47	0.05	39.92	–	5.29	7.5	6.9	6.7	30.1	10.3	29.2	27.8	8.29	9.02
New Hampshire	21.6	16.0	15.0	18.17	9.47	19.29	42.95	6.16	4.2	3.4	2.9	11.0	4.3	10.5	10.0	10.80	11.98
New Jersey	57.4	61.6	58.1	17.06	2.69	25.74	51.76	0.07	18.6	18.4	16.5	76.6	27.3	74.5	62.8	9.46	10.69
New Mexico	32.7	30.7	34.0	88.02	0.15	10.75	–	0.52	6.3	5.9	5.6	19.3	5.4	19.2	18.8	7.00	8.69
New York	137.6	139.6	138.1	17.13	14.02	20.46	29.55	17.63	36.7	36.0	35.6	144.2	47.1	143.6	124.5	12.44	14.31
North Carolina	127.6	124.5	122.3	58.61	0.61	1.24	32.06	5.64	27.3	26.7	24.5	121.3	49.3	122.7	119.9	6.86	8.32
North Dakota	31.3	31.3	31.3	93.95	0.17	0.03	–	5.50	4.7	4.7	4.7	10.5	3.7	10.2	9.4	5.47	6.49
Ohio	146.6	147.1	149.1	91.91	0.28	1.22	5.78	0.35	34.1	31.5	28.4	151.4	49.5	156.0	161.1	6.75	8.27
Oklahoma	60.6	59.2	55.6	60.50	0.27	36.00	–	2.97	18.2	16.2	14.1	50.4	20.2	49.5	49.6	6.35	7.47
Oregon	49.0	47.1	51.8	8.79	0.09	20.92	–	67.90	12.9	12.5	11.3	45.2	17.7	45.3	50.3	6.18	7.06
Pennsylvania	206.3	204.3	201.7	56.22	2.20	2.67	36.04	1.62	42.4	39.8	36.7	141.0	49.8	140.8	98.1	7.98	9.55
Rhode Island	5.6	7.1	6.0	–	1.04	97.04	–	0.11	1.7	1.7	1.2	7.8	3.0	7.5	7.1	10.47	11.62
South Carolina	93.8	96.6	93.3	39.92	0.49	1.77	53.77	3.91	20.7	20.4	18.7	77.1	26.4	77.8	77.0	6.08	8.01
South Dakota	7.9	7.7	9.7	43.19	0.20	2.22	–	53.83	2.7	2.9	2.8	9.1	3.7	8.9	8.3	6.35	7.47
Tennessee	92.2	96.1	95.8	59.55	0.44	0.68	26.19	13.02	20.9	20.7	19.5	97.5	37.7	98.2	95.7	5.84	6.55
Texas	379.2	385.6	377.7	38.76	0.66	48.76	8.82	0.24	99.6	94.5	81.7	322.7	121.4	320.8	318.3	7.50	9.16
Utah	38.0	36.6	36.6	94.62	0.09	3.64	–	1.11	5.8	5.8	5.2	23.9	7.2	23.3	23.2	5.41	6.90
Vermont	6.0	5.5	6.3	–	0.38	0.03	73.73	19.14	1.0	1.0	1.1	5.4	2.0	5.6	5.6	10.98	12.82
Virginia	75.3	75.0	77.2	49.25	7.68	6.13	32.95	2.37	21.3	20.2	19.4	101.5	40.9	100.5	96.7	6.27	7.76
Washington	100.1	102.8	108.2	11.08	0.07	7.08	7.61	71.69	27.7	27.1	26.1	78.1	31.9	76.5	93.2	5.86	6.31
West Virginia	94.7	94.8	92.9	97.63	0.26	0.29	–	1.43	16.1	16.2	15.0	28.3	10.5	28.5	27.7	5.13	6.24
Wisconsin	60.1	58.4	59.6	69.39	0.79	4.12	20.32	3.07	14.3	14.2	13.6	67.2	21.4	67.0	65.1	6.64	8.67
Wyoming	43.6	43.8	45.5	97.05	0.10	0.64	–	1.36	6.6	6.3	6.2	13.3	2.3	12.9	12.4	4.76	7.04

– Represents zero.　D Data withheld to avoid disclosure.　NA Not available.　Z Less than .005 percent.

[1]Covers Utilities (NAICS 22).
[2]Averages for the year.
[3]Excludes sales for resale.
[4]Includes both bundled and unbundled consumers.
[5]Includes any public water system that supplies water to the same population year-round.
[6]Includes any public water system that regularly supplies water to at least 25 of the same people at least six months per year, but not year-round.
[7]Includes any public water system that provides water in a place such as a gas station or a campground where people do not remain for long periods of time.
[8]1,000–2,499 employees.
[9]2,500–4,999 employees.

Survey, Census, or Data Collection Method:　Private utilities—Based on tabulations of data extracted from the U.S. Census Bureau's Business Register; for information, see Internet site <http://www.census.gov/epcd/cbp/view/cbpview.html>;　Water systems—Based on the Safe Drinking Water Information System/Federal version (SDWIS/Fed); for information, see Internet site <http://www.epa.gov/safewater/sdwisfed/sdwis.htm>;　Gas utilities—Based on the American Gas Storage Survey (AGSS); for information, see Internet site <http://www.aga.org/StatsStudies/>;　Electric industry—Based on the Office of Coal, Nuclear, Electric and Alternate Fuels (CNEAF) Internet Data Collection System (IDC); for information, see the following document at <http://www.eia.doe.gov/cneaf/electricity/epa/epa.pdf>.

Sources:　Private utilities—U.S. Census Bureau, *County Business Patterns*, annual, see Internet site <http://www.census.gov/epcd/cbp/view/cbpview.html>;　Water systems—Environmental Protection Agency, *FACTOIDS: Drinking Water and Ground Water Statistics, 2004*; see Internet site <http://www.epa.gov/safewater/data/pdfs/data_factoids_2004.pdf>;　Gas utilities—American Gas Association, Arlington, VA, *Gas Facts*, annual (copyright);　Electric industry—U.S. Energy Information Administration, *Electric Power Annual, 2003*, and previous editions; see also Internet site <http://www.eia.doe.gov/cneaf/electricity/epa/epa_sum.html> (accessed June 1, 2005); and *Electric Sales and Revenue 2003*, and previous editions; see also Internet site <http://www.eia.doe.gov/cneaf/electricity/esr/esr_sum.html> (issued January 2005).

Table A-56. States — **Energy Consumption**

Geographic area	2001 Total[2] (tril. Btu)	2001 Per capita[3] (mil. Btu)	2001 Percent change, 1990–2001	2000[2] (tril. Btu)	1990[2] (tril. Btu)	Resi-dential	Com-mercial	Indus-trial[2]	Trans-porta-tion	Petro-leum	Natural gas (dry)[4]	Coal	Hydro-electric power[5]	Nuclear electric power
United States . . .	96,275	338	13.8	98,786	84,623	20,241	17,332	32,431	26,272	38,333	22,845	21,905	2,118	8,033
Alabama	1,943	435	14.7	2,129	1,693	380	254	863	446	540	342	846	85	317
Alaska	737	1,164	26.0	638	585	53	65	413	206	292	413	16	14	–
Arizona	1,353	255	42.3	1,335	951	344	312	221	476	524	245	424	80	300
Arkansas	1,106	411	29.0	1,154	857	219	148	462	278	379	232	274	26	154
California	7,853	227	4.1	7,995	7,541	1,446	1,509	1,928	2,971	3,604	2,514	68	256	347
Colorado	1,270	287	35.7	1,251	936	303	287	294	386	462	385	400	13	–
Connecticut	853	249	10.6	855	771	267	215	134	238	439	149	40	3	161
Delaware	293	368	16.0	307	252	62	52	113	66	147	52	38	–	–
District of Columbia	168	294	–4.5	187	176	34	104	4	26	34	31	1	–	–
Florida	4,135	253	26.2	4,138	3,277	1,193	958	598	1,386	1,990	570	726	2	330
Georgia	2,881	343	25.0	2,984	2,305	642	503	876	860	1,034	363	772	21	352
Hawaii	282	230	–13.0	280	324	35	39	77	132	240	3	18	1	–
Idaho.	501	379	24.3	537	403	105	95	180	122	155	82	11	74	–
Illinois	3,870	309	8.3	4,006	3,575	928	829	1,173	939	1,304	971	994	2	965
Indiana	2,802	457	11.5	2,914	2,513	504	397	1,296	604	837	514	1,567	6	–
Iowa	1,151	392	19.6	1,176	962	229	179	472	270	401	225	445	9	40
Kansas	1,044	387	–0.8	1,095	1,052	215	192	385	252	391	274	355	(Z)	108
Kentucky	1,880	462	25.7	1,878	1,495	339	246	846	449	704	217	1,011	39	–
Louisiana	3,500	784	–2.6	3,971	3,592	348	264	2,135	753	1,491	1,340	240	7	181
Maine	491	382	5.0	532	467	111	74	199	107	233	101	8	27	–
Maryland	1,420	264	12.6	1,444	1,262	391	372	252	405	568	191	317	12	143
Massachusetts	1,549	242	9.3	1,547	1,417	461	379	261	447	762	364	109	(Z)	54
Michigan	3,120	312	9.5	3,252	2,851	790	598	928	804	1,042	929	797	4	279
Minnesota	1,745	350	25.8	1,788	1,387	381	336	526	502	674	345	353	9	123
Mississippi	1,173	410	15.3	1,227	1,017	234	163	427	349	486	341	198	–	104
Missouri	1,815	322	19.6	1,785	1,518	496	389	374	556	719	289	716	9	88
Montana	366	404	4.4	408	350	70	60	128	108	168	67	184	67	–
Nebraska	627	365	20.1	631	522	152	130	182	163	218	124	228	11	91
Nevada	629	301	57.6	627	399	147	108	169	205	250	181	189	26	–
New Hampshire.	322	256	22.0	328	264	87	65	68	102	178	25	40	10	91
New Jersey	2,500	294	7.0	2,523	2,336	573	554	491	882	1,246	586	112	–1	318
New Mexico	679	371	13.6	677	598	107	122	220	230	251	262	297	2	–
New York.	4,135	217	10.0	4,246	3,757	1,194	1,303	667	970	1,713	1,206	315	225	422
North Carolina.	2,591	316	24.1	2,669	2,088	641	513	743	694	950	216	757	26	395
North Dakota	407	640	29.4	383	315	61	56	203	88	138	63	420	14	–
Ohio	3,982	350	4.0	4,264	3,828	892	682	1,429	979	1,305	836	1,343	5	162
Oklahoma	1,540	444	10.5	1,469	1,393	298	233	544	466	588	548	377	23	–
Oregon	1,064	307	7.4	1,141	991	252	208	298	307	368	236	43	291	–
Pennsylvania	3,923	319	6.1	3,954	3,696	931	709	1,286	997	1,454	669	1,379	11	770
Rhode Island	227	215	8.7	223	209	73	63	26	66	100	99	(Z)	(Z)	–
South Carolina	1,549	382	20.0	1,610	1,291	322	235	609	383	470	147	414	2	521
South Dakota	248	327	17.5	259	211	60	50	54	83	112	37	44	35	–
Tennessee	2,195	382	19.0	2,201	1,845	500	369	746	581	708	265	688	63	299
Texas	12,029	564	21.1	12,074	9,933	1,570	1,356	6,426	2,677	5,521	4,435	1,493	12	399
Utah	725	318	31.6	750	551	140	140	233	213	261	168	390	5	–
Vermont	164	267	20.7	165	136	48	33	31	52	89	8	(Z)	9	44
Virginia	2,315	322	17.8	2,386	1,965	549	534	547	685	911	247	482	–13	269
Washington	2,034	339	–1.4	2,222	2,064	471	377	586	600	843	323	100	557	86
West Virginia	762	423	–7.6	774	825	157	111	311	183	215	152	872	10	–
Wisconsin.	1,863	345	26.5	1,904	1,473	401	313	729	422	668	363	495	21	120
Wyoming	439	890	9.0	431	403	39	51	238	111	157	104	500	9	–

– Represents zero.   Z Less than .5 trillion Btu.

[1]End-use sector data include electricity sales and associated electrical system energy losses.
[2]U.S. total energy and U.S. industrial sector include net imports of coal coke that is not allocated to the states. State and U.S. totals include net imports of electricity generated from nonrenewable energy sources.
[3]Based on estimated resident population as of July 1.
[4]Includes supplemental gaseous fuels.
[5]Includes net imports of hydroelectricity. A negative number in this column results from pumped storage for which, overall, more electricity is expended than created to provide electricity during peak demand periods.

Survey, Census, or Data Collection Method: Based on the State Energy Data System (SEDS); for information, see "Technical Notes" at Internet site <http://www.eia.doe.gov/emeu/states/_seds.html>.

Source: U.S. Energy Information Administration, *State Energy Data 2001* (formerly *State Energy Data Report*), Internet site <http://www.eia.doe.gov/emeu/states/_seds.html> (released December 2004).

Table A-57. States — Energy Expenditures

Geographic area	Current dollars					Constant (2000) dollars[1]			End-use sector, 2001 (mil. dol.)				Selected source, 2001 (mil. dol.)				
	2001			2000[3] (mil. dol.)	1990[3] (mil. dol.)	2001 (mil. dol.)	2000 (mil. dol.)	1990 (mil. dol.)	Resi-dential	Com-mercial	Indus-trial[3]	Trans-porta-tion	Petroleum product		Natural gas	Coal	Electric pur-chasers
	Total[2, 3] (mil. dol.)	Per capita[4] (dol.)	Percent change, 1990–2001										Total	Motor gas-oline			
United States . . .	693,599	2,433	47.0	703,188	471,786	678,071	703,188	576,713	168,618	125,772	137,820	261,390	336,362	185,892	139,526	28,195	244,814
Alabama	11,580	2,592	38.0	12,094	8,394	11,321	12,094	10,260	2,798	1,628	2,827	4,327	5,142	3,185	2,077	1,219	4,345
Alaska	2,780	4,396	30.5	2,722	2,130	2,718	2,722	2,604	428	453	310	1,589	2,071	435	250	31	567
Arizona	10,672	2,015	63.4	10,562	6,530	10,433	10,562	7,983	2,664	2,046	1,136	4,826	5,351	3,516	1,381	540	4,526
Arkansas	7,340	2,726	56.1	7,326	4,703	7,175	7,326	5,749	1,702	915	1,968	2,755	3,510	1,837	1,419	250	2,464
California	72,924	2,112	49.9	71,058	48,660	71,291	71,058	59,482	15,504	15,832	10,676	30,913	33,751	22,426	20,824	99	27,483
Colorado	9,279	2,096	76.6	8,690	5,255	9,072	8,690	6,423	2,268	1,653	1,155	4,203	4,864	3,148	2,092	374	2,638
Connecticut	8,062	2,348	31.5	8,275	6,130	7,882	8,275	7,493	2,672	1,743	886	2,762	4,273	2,298	1,125	67	2,937
Delaware	1,985	2,495	40.8	2,072	1,410	1,941	2,072	1,723	522	352	425	686	1,020	566	338	80	744
District of Columbia	1,479	2,598	36.5	1,530	1,084	1,446	1,530	1,325	310	826	25	318	381	275	363	1	740
Florida	31,605	1,933	51.1	31,178	20,916	30,898	31,178	25,567	9,257	6,341	2,891	13,116	16,036	9,780	3,195	1,250	15,376
Georgia	19,361	2,307	49.6	19,782	12,938	18,928	19,782	15,816	4,935	3,198	3,441	7,788	9,072	5,699	2,616	1,294	7,484
Hawaii	2,812	2,301	31.3	2,634	2,141	2,749	2,634	2,617	519	515	474	1,304	1,849	754	48	22	1,349
Idaho	3,142	2,378	70.7	3,158	1,841	3,072	3,158	2,250	660	483	712	1,287	1,583	909	517	19	1,037
Illinois	29,387	2,347	36.4	30,122	21,544	28,729	30,122	26,335	7,737	5,578	5,687	10,384	12,676	7,733	7,469	1,220	9,311
Indiana	17,066	2,785	40.5	17,033	12,149	16,684	17,033	14,851	3,710	2,211	5,117	6,028	7,311	4,311	4,122	1,966	5,130
Iowa	8,161	2,784	57.8	8,314	5,170	7,978	8,314	6,320	1,847	1,108	2,387	2,820	4,085	2,130	1,593	403	2,408
Kansas	7,082	2,622	34.0	7,392	5,287	6,923	7,392	6,462	1,667	1,208	1,792	2,416	3,457	1,764	1,500	373	2,223
Kentucky	11,018	2,709	50.3	11,356	7,331	10,771	11,356	8,961	2,005	1,292	3,232	4,489	6,082	3,015	1,475	1,158	3,361
Louisiana	18,026	4,036	32.0	20,726	13,659	17,622	20,726	16,697	2,696	1,891	7,487	5,952	8,991	2,974	4,960	314	5,070
Maine	3,625	2,817	39.8	3,772	2,592	3,544	3,772	3,169	1,112	651	660	1,201	2,131	909	409	15	1,270
Maryland	11,446	2,128	45.5	11,796	7,867	11,189	11,796	9,617	3,179	2,433	1,170	4,663	5,777	3,799	1,891	496	3,983
Massachusetts	15,957	2,495	50.8	15,459	10,582	15,599	15,459	12,936	4,966	3,790	2,130	5,071	7,394	4,134	3,176	183	6,062
Michigan	21,913	2,190	31.4	22,704	16,680	21,422	22,704	20,389	5,551	3,881	3,996	8,484	10,711	6,985	4,440	1,057	7,068
Minnesota	12,447	2,496	65.5	12,224	7,520	12,168	12,224	9,192	2,932	2,050	2,135	5,330	6,495	3,944	2,305	376	3,618
Mississippi	7,459	2,609	48.2	7,462	5,032	7,292	7,462	6,152	1,788	1,088	1,611	2,972	3,886	1,993	1,493	324	2,719
Missouri	13,822	2,450	47.1	13,277	9,397	13,512	13,277	11,487	3,786	2,404	1,914	5,717	7,005	4,154	2,531	700	4,414
Montana	2,484	2,740	46.4	2,852	1,696	2,428	2,852	2,074	469	361	489	1,164	1,408	752	343	177	720
Nebraska	4,412	2,567	41.3	4,323	3,122	4,314	4,323	3,816	1,040	740	904	1,729	2,216	1,215	869	134	1,333
Nevada	5,127	2,447	112.2	4,834	2,416	5,012	4,834	2,953	1,218	808	962	2,139	2,459	1,449	1,447	239	2,172
New Hampshire	3,128	2,484	57.6	3,227	1,985	3,058	3,227	2,427	927	600	446	1,155	1,768	991	239	67	1,129
New Jersey	20,178	2,372	26.7	21,639	15,922	19,727	21,639	19,463	4,951	4,433	2,732	8,063	10,236	5,484	3,659	255	6,785
New Mexico	4,313	2,354	45.1	4,109	2,973	4,216	4,109	3,634	921	825	629	1,938	2,418	1,265	769	437	1,316
New York	39,903	2,091	44.8	42,563	27,557	39,010	42,563	33,685	13,371	12,961	3,297	10,274	15,374	8,032	9,889	463	16,449
North Carolina	18,865	2,301	50.2	19,351	12,557	18,443	19,351	15,350	5,170	3,170	3,414	7,111	9,167	5,554	1,786	1,210	7,804
North Dakota	2,243	3,525	43.1	2,077	1,568	2,193	2,077	1,916	417	307	707	812	1,296	511	241	412	535
Ohio	29,071	2,553	38.3	29,645	21,024	28,420	29,645	25,700	7,375	5,198	6,212	10,286	12,376	7,325	6,404	1,790	10,200
Oklahoma	10,181	2,937	64.4	9,337	6,193	9,953	9,337	7,570	2,193	1,441	2,349	4,197	4,920	2,340	3,011	348	3,016
Oregon	7,411	2,133	48.0	7,644	5,007	7,245	7,644	6,121	1,605	1,129	1,306	3,372	3,855	2,377	1,335	48	2,494
Pennsylvania	29,888	2,430	35.1	30,484	22,122	29,218	30,484	27,041	8,713	5,393	5,632	10,150	13,222	7,149	5,736	1,796	10,757
Rhode Island	2,313	2,185	43.3	2,381	1,614	2,261	2,381	1,972	771	578	209	755	1,067	618	601	(Z)	847
South Carolina	9,867	2,430	43.1	10,176	6,897	9,646	10,176	8,431	2,397	1,447	2,228	3,795	4,412	2,905	1,012	665	4,317
South Dakota	1,881	2,481	37.9	1,952	1,364	1,839	1,952	1,667	449	301	282	849	1,127	619	220	46	548
Tennessee	13,808	2,402	41.7	13,792	9,743	13,499	13,792	11,910	3,217	2,304	2,799	5,489	6,319	3,795	1,971	864	5,325
Texas	72,653	3,405	66.0	74,045	43,777	71,026	74,045	53,513	12,999	9,310	26,995	23,349	38,721	14,245	17,441	1,993	22,979
Utah	4,533	1,987	65.0	4,561	2,748	4,432	4,561	3,359	959	749	659	2,166	2,442	1,394	889	454	1,198
Vermont	1,660	2,709	57.0	1,629	1,058	1,623	1,629	1,293	536	310	200	615	991	503	61	(Z)	607
Virginia	16,290	2,267	44.4	16,791	11,284	15,926	16,791	13,794	4,325	2,963	2,025	6,977	8,523	5,323	1,917	784	5,928
Washington	12,906	2,154	48.8	13,180	8,675	12,617	13,180	10,604	2,920	2,048	1,927	6,012	7,014	4,029	2,316	115	4,141
West Virginia	4,297	2,385	10.8	4,434	3,879	4,201	4,434	4,742	999	603	986	1,710	2,148	1,179	656	1,116	1,392
Wisconsin	13,358	2,471	64.6	13,059	8,113	13,059	13,059	9,918	3,190	1,951	3,361	4,855	6,645	3,690	2,727	552	3,931
Wyoming	2,322	4,698	51.6	2,242	1,531	2,270	2,242	1,872	275	275	746	1,026	1,339	479	384	402	564

Z Less than $500,000.

[1] Constant dollar estimates are computed by the U.S. Census Bureau using the price deflator for Gross Domestic Purchases of energy goods and services from the Bureau of Economic Analysis (Table 1.6.4 of the National Income and Product Accounts Table). See <http://www.bea.gov/bea/dn/nipaweb/SelectTable.asp?Selected=N> (revised 31 August 2005).
[2] Includes sources not shown separately. Total expenditures are the sum of purchases for each source (including electricity sales) less electric utility purchases of fuel.
[3] U.S. total includes coal coke net imports, which are not included in the states.
[4] Based on estimated population as of July 1.

Survey, Census, or Data Collection Method: Based on the State Energy Data System (SEDS); for information, see "Technical Notes" at Internet site <http://www.eia.doe.gov/emeu/states/_seds.html>.

Source: Except as noted, U.S. Energy Information Administration, *State Energy Price and Expenditure Report*, annual. See also <http://www.eia.doe.gov/emeu/states/_seds.html>.

Table A-58. States — **Construction**

Geographic area	Construction[1]						Value of construction contracts[4] (mil. dol.)						New private housing units authorized by building permits[5] (1,000)			
	Nonfarm employment (BLS)[2] (1,000)			Earnings (BEA)[3] (mil. dol.)													
	2004	2003	2000	2004	2003	2001	2004	2003	2002	2001	2000	1990	2004	2003	2002	2000
United States ...	[6]6,964.0	[6]6,735.0	[6]6,787.0	463,816	430,782	408,573	586,986	530,712	504,115	496,602	472,930	246,022	2,070.1	1,889.2	1,747.7	1,592.3
Alabama	103.5	99.7	105.6	5,809	5,374	5,251	8,329	7,510	6,979	8,387	7,225	2,939	27.4	22.3	18.4	17.4
Alaska............	17.6	16.9	14.2	1,570	1,476	1,213	1,919	1,836	1,971	1,600	1,327	1,919	3.1	3.5	3.0	2.1
Arizona	190.1	176.2	168.1	10,912	9,731	8,932	21,188	17,793	14,410	14,706	13,966	4,553	90.6	75.0	66.0	61.5
Arkansas	51.6	50.8	53.0	2,664	2,489	2,451	4,421	3,999	3,592	4,645	3,739	1,438	15.9	14.8	12.4	9.2
California	847.3	795.9	731.0	65,452	58,288	54,516	65,984	60,321	57,912	55,128	52,858	37,318	207.4	191.9	159.6	145.6
Colorado	151.3	149.9	163.6	10,982	10,390	10,565	13,950	11,543	12,227	12,389	12,491	3,235	46.5	39.6	47.9	54.6
Connecticut	[7]65.8	[7]61.9	[7]64.5	6,977	6,151	5,858	5,080	4,820	4,778	4,305	5,181	3,058	11.8	10.4	9.7	9.4
Delaware	[7]26.4	[7]24.4	[7]24.6	1,606	1,423	1,315	1,455	1,555	1,437	1,357	1,350	787	7.9	7.8	6.3	4.6
District of Columbia	[7]12.3	[7]12.9	[7]11.2	799	815	675	1,663	1,806	2,508	1,689	1,763	795	1.9	1.4	1.6	0.8
Florida............	490.6	446.8	406.4	27,232	23,667	20,913	58,162	49,501	42,587	39,377	35,079	16,975	255.9	213.6	185.4	155.3
Georgia	198.0	195.0	204.4	12,685	11,881	11,496	23,628	20,202	19,620	19,316	20,419	7,120	108.4	96.7	97.5	91.8
Hawaii............	[7]29.3	[7]27.9	[7]24.7	2,210	2,038	1,690	2,363	2,308	1,808	1,984	1,409	2,831	9.0	7.3	5.9	4.9
Idaho............	39.6	36.8	36.4	2,294	2,053	2,016	3,867	3,060	2,619	2,520	2,521	986	18.1	15.1	13.5	10.9
Illinois	266.9	274.8	269.7	20,333	19,967	19,016	21,251	19,071	20,823	19,366	17,167	10,796	59.8	62.2	61.0	51.9
Indiana	148.1	144.8	149.9	9,150	8,622	8,142	13,155	12,680	11,270	11,988	11,011	6,350	39.2	39.4	39.6	37.9
Iowa	68.4	65.1	63.9	4,181	3,824	3,510	5,832	6,514	4,774	4,204	3,776	2,034	16.3	16.1	14.8	12.5
Kansas	63.4	62.7	65.6	3,549	3,424	3,329	4,943	4,568	4,962	4,190	4,463	2,193	13.3	15.0	13.0	12.5
Kentucky	83.5	83.1	87.6	4,889	4,734	4,550	7,559	7,147	6,765	6,356	6,625	3,174	22.6	20.4	19.5	18.5
Louisiana	117.1	119.0	129.0	6,078	5,946	5,859	6,193	6,602	5,251	4,675	5,528	3,191	23.0	22.2	18.4	14.7
Maine	31.0	30.5	29.2	1,947	1,814	1,680	2,246	2,096	1,842	1,669	1,710	897	8.8	7.9	7.2	6.2
Maryland	[7]177.6	[7]169.6	[7]161.0	11,802	10,727	9,801	9,416	9,170	8,839	8,925	7,836	6,056	27.4	29.9	29.3	30.4
Massachusetts	138.4	136.8	129.1	12,295	11,817	11,377	9,856	8,806	9,866	10,325	11,983	5,135	22.5	20.3	17.5	18.0
Michigan	190.3	190.6	209.6	14,153	13,592	13,740	14,319	13,975	13,042	14,280	14,735	7,646	54.7	53.9	50.0	52.5
Minnesota	126.5	124.9	118.8	9,187	8,707	8,108	10,974	10,455	9,288	9,463	8,838	4,953	41.8	42.0	39.0	32.8
Mississippi	49.3	50.6	54.4	2,488	2,508	2,388	3,995	3,665	3,445	5,576	2,917	1,569	14.5	12.0	11.3	11.3
Missouri..........	137.5	134.2	138.4	9,028	8,553	8,334	10,061	9,406	8,734	8,256	7,498	3,833	32.8	29.3	28.3	24.3
Montana	[7]24.9	[7]23.1	[7]20.4	1,433	1,310	1,134	1,206	974	951	1,033	1,004	332	5.0	3.8	3.6	2.6
Nebraska	[7]48.2	[7]47.4	[7]45.2	2,683	2,545	2,333	3,400	3,475	3,346	3,036	2,646	1,318	10.9	10.3	9.3	9.1
Nevada	117.6	100.3	89.4	7,086	5,959	5,111	11,206	9,512	8,106	8,284	6,978	3,334	44.6	43.4	35.6	32.3
New Hampshire.......	29.6	28.9	24.9	2,465	2,274	2,051	2,576	2,171	2,419	2,113	2,514	1,021	8.7	8.6	8.7	6.7
New Jersey	166.0	160.5	149.5	14,462	13,294	12,467	11,233	11,813	11,427	11,451	10,940	6,141	35.9	33.0	30.4	34.6
New Mexico	50.1	47.0	44.8	2,499	2,269	2,161	3,949	3,108	2,898	2,667	3,140	1,124	12.6	13.8	12.1	8.9
New York	318.4	319.1	327.3	24,315	23,580	22,736	23,064	21,202	24,223	22,707	20,756	14,137	53.5	49.7	49.1	44.1
North Carolina	216.8	211.4	230.0	12,543	11,512	11,566	21,488	18,934	17,757	17,640	17,258	6,614	93.1	79.2	79.8	78.4
North Dakota	17.2	16.0	15.8	966	838	774	1,194	1,115	1,022	747	854	506	4.0	3.7	3.3	2.1
Ohio	235.1	231.2	246.1	14,896	14,169	13,795	18,394	16,777	17,279	18,305	16,270	9,885	51.7	53.0	51.2	49.7
Oklahoma	62.2	63.6	61.8	3,459	3,420	3,350	5,449	5,129	4,656	6,322	5,330	2,164	17.1	15.0	13.0	11.1
Oregon	82.3	77.0	82.9	5,498	5,008	5,074	7,719	7,334	6,321	6,464	6,020	3,101	27.3	25.0	22.2	19.9
Pennsylvania	248.2	245.7	247.3	17,774	16,943	16,019	15,881	14,820	16,368	15,863	14,861	10,117	49.7	47.4	45.1	41.1
Rhode Island	20.8	20.8	18.1	1,498	1,446	1,215	1,314	1,163	1,331	1,105	1,063	594	2.5	2.3	2.8	2.6
South Carolina	113.3	112.4	114.5	5,960	5,622	5,243	11,731	9,737	8,843	8,140	7,759	3,664	43.2	38.2	34.1	32.8
South Dakota	19.8	19.3	18.0	1,040	985	876	1,541	1,209	1,279	1,038	1,221	468	5.8	5.0	4.8	4.2
Tennessee	117.5	115.4	125.7	8,241	7,797	7,149	12,037	10,138	9,338	9,189	10,148	4,388	44.8	37.5	34.3	32.2
Texas	542.6	552.0	567.1	35,158	33,948	33,033	48,535	44,789	41,935	43,523	41,124	13,197	188.8	177.2	165.0	141.2
Utah	72.5	67.6	72.5	4,002	3,598	3,492	6,528	4,962	5,177	4,309	4,420	1,884	24.3	22.5	19.3	17.6
Vermont..........	16.7	15.4	14.9	1,095	948	873	1,177	891	946	683	602	515	3.6	2.8	3.1	2.5
Virginia	230.8	217.5	210.1	13,927	12,335	11,310	15,840	14,966	14,140	12,509	13,634	7,180	63.2	55.9	59.4	48.4
Washington	163.5	156.2	160.5	11,147	10,319	9,865	14,193	13,285	11,073	11,542	10,332	6,185	50.1	42.8	40.2	39.0
West Virginia	34.5	32.7	34.0	1,903	1,657	1,765	2,053	1,699	1,871	1,354	1,856	1,253	5.7	5.1	4.9	3.8
Wisconsin	126.3	124.1	124.8	8,469	7,984	7,518	12,352	10,070	8,987	8,882	8,044	4,654	40.0	40.9	38.2	34.2
Wyoming	19.2	19.5	18.5	1,026	1,009	939	1,121	1,028	1,071	1,018	778	462	3.3	2.8	2.0	1.6

[1]Covers Construction (NAICS 23).
[2]Bureau of Labor Statistics.
[3]Bureau of Economic Analysis.
[4]Represents value of contruction in states in which work was actually done; includes new structures and additions.
[5]1990 to 2003, based on 19,000 places in the United States having building permits systems; 2004 based on 20,000 places. See source for details.
[6]United States totals differ from the sum of the state figures because of differing benchmarks among states and differing industrial and geographic stratification.
[7]Figure includes natural resources and mining and construction.

Survey, Census, or Data Collection Method: Employment—Based on the Current Employment Statistics (CES) survey; for information, see Appendix B, Limitations of the Data and Methodology, and Internet site <http://www.bls.gov/opub/hom/homch2_a.htm>;   Earnings—Based on the Regional Economic Information System; for information, see "State Personal Income Methodologies" at <http://www.bea.gov/bea/regional/articles/spi2003/>;   Value of construction—For information, see <http://fwdodge.construction.com/>;   New housing units—Based on a survey of local building permit officials using Form C-404; for information, see Internet site <http://www.census.gov/const/www/newresconstdoc.html>.

Sources: Employment—U.S. Bureau of Labor Statistics, Current Employment Statistics Program, see Internet site <http://www.bls.gov/sae/home.htm>;   Earnings—U.S. Bureau of Economic Analysis, *Survey of Current Business*, April 2005, see Internet site <http://www.bea.gov/bea/regional/spi/>;   Value of construction—McGraw-Hill Construction Dodge, a Division of the McGraw-Hill Companies, New York, NY (copyright);   New housing units—U.S. Census Bureau, Construction Reports, Series C40, Building Permits, monthly; publication discontinued in 2001. See Internet site <http://www.census.gov/const/www/newresconstindex.html> and New Residential Construction, monthly.

Table A-59. States — **Manufactures**

Geographic area	Nonfarm employment (BLS)[1] (1,000)					Earnings (BEA)[2] (mil. dol.)			
	2004	2003	2002	2001	2000	2004	2003	2002	2001
United States ...	[4]14,329	[4]14,510	[4]15,259	[4]16,441	[4]17,263	983,917	954,525	925,361	932,482
Alabama	291	294	307	326	351	16,146	15,527	15,023	14,800
Alaska	12	12	11	12	12	739	681	613	632
Arizona	176	175	184	202	210	12,861	12,238	11,955	12,340
Arkansas	204	206	214	227	240	9,255	8,924	8,710	8,658
California	1,533	1,548	1,638	1,786	1,858	121,732	115,869	113,278	118,420
Colorado	155	156	166	182	191	11,140	10,916	10,835	11,096
Connecticut	198	200	211	227	236	17,502	16,712	16,573	16,740
Delaware	35	36	37	39	42	2,783	2,827	2,455	2,420
District of Columbia	3	3	3	3	4	273	251	(D)	290
Florida	388	388	406	432	455	23,383	22,406	22,005	21,608
Georgia	445	452	467	498	531	25,561	24,403	24,273	24,241
Hawaii	15	15	15	16	16	870	795	760	787
Idaho	62	62	65	68	70	3,576	3,426	3,383	3,453
Illinois	697	714	754	815	871	47,750	46,603	46,166	46,711
Indiana	572	573	588	615	664	39,131	38,030	35,347	33,899
Iowa	223	220	227	240	251	12,830	12,059	11,575	11,507
Kansas	176	175	184	195	201	11,182	10,268	10,213	10,410
Kentucky	264	265	275	292	310	16,526	16,128	15,019	14,572
Louisiana	152	156	161	172	177	10,822	10,373	9,790	9,322
Maine	63	64	68	75	80	3,698	3,626	3,578	3,643
Maryland	143	147	157	168	174	10,684	10,343	10,307	10,260
Massachusetts	314	324	349	389	408	26,327	25,623	25,519	26,770
Michigan	696	716	760	820	897	59,366	61,980	55,617	54,979
Minnesota	343	343	356	379	397	22,952	21,821	20,925	20,539
Mississippi	179	179	188	201	223	8,190	7,863	7,531	7,535
Missouri	312	315	325	345	365	19,242	18,733	17,907	17,417
Montana	19	19	20	21	23	1,075	1,018	985	995
Nebraska	101	102	106	111	114	5,093	4,954	4,821	4,686
Nevada	46	44	43	44	43	2,799	2,598	2,371	2,377
New Hampshire	80	80	85	97	103	5,619	5,302	5,229	5,652
New Jersey	339	350	368	401	422	29,349	28,418	27,651	27,517
New Mexico	36	37	38	41	42	2,248	2,159	2,097	2,146
New York	596	613	652	708	751	43,643	42,634	41,949	42,787
North Carolina	580	599	644	704	758	33,612	32,805	32,810	33,340
North Dakota	25	24	24	24	24	1,323	1,202	1,124	1,106
Ohio	825	843	885	953	1,021	55,486	55,625	52,894	52,612
Oklahoma	142	143	152	170	178	10,912	10,354	9,894	11,112
Oregon	200	195	202	216	223	13,127	12,160	11,837	12,324
Pennsylvania	691	712	759	821	862	46,472	45,870	45,646	45,299
Rhode Island	57	59	62	68	71	3,264	3,205	3,253	3,326
South Carolina	269	276	290	314	336	15,346	15,091	14,699	14,522
South Dakota	39	38	38	41	44	1,862	1,722	1,648	1,679
Tennessee	412	413	429	454	488	24,912	24,093	23,016	22,212
Texas	890	900	949	1,027	1,068	71,302	68,010	65,724	68,300
Utah	115	112	114	122	126	6,399	6,108	5,817	5,928
Vermont	37	38	41	46	46	2,343	2,285	2,338	2,445
Virginia	299	305	320	341	364	17,672	17,233	16,892	16,610
Washington	264	267	285	316	332	19,970	19,260	19,943	19,786
West Virginia	63	65	69	72	76	3,963	3,842	3,847	3,802
Wisconsin	502	504	528	560	594	30,973	29,567	28,705	28,312
Wyoming	10	9	10	10	10	633	586	(D)	557

See footnotes at end of table.

Geographic area	Establishments		Average hourly earnings of production workers (dol.)			Value of shipments[3] (mil. dol.)			
	2002	Net change, 2000–2002	2003	2002	2001	2003	2002	2001	2000
United States . . .	344,341	–10,157	15.74	15.29	14.76	3,977,165	3,918,851	3,970,500	4,208,582
Alabama	5,053	–208	13.56	13.10	12.76	70,048	66,686	67,172	70,224
Alaska	495	6	12.16	13.24	11.70	4,371	3,832	3,987	4,034
Arizona	4,796	–105	14.38	14.16	13.80	44,900	41,911	42,168	47,042
Arkansas	3,146	–99	13.55	13.30	12.90	47,560	46,721	46,530	47,798
California	47,558	–1,579	15.05	14.89	14.69	378,468	378,661	414,762	441,363
Colorado	5,250	–142	16.89	15.85	14.72	33,775	34,661	35,627	39,273
Connecticut	5,280	–223	17.74	17.25	16.42	41,587	45,053	47,055	46,465
Delaware	688	1	16.90	16.62	16.56	14,445	16,418	16,664	17,134
District of Columbia	144	–30	15.80	15.39	15.14	293	246	178	210
Florida	14,880	–465	14.09	13.30	12.68	78,900	78,475	76,541	80,721
Georgia	8,636	–84	14.08	13.39	12.50	125,099	126,157	127,624	135,206
Hawaii	915	4	12.90	13.07	13.18	3,880	3,460	3,196	3,732
Idaho	1,763	94	13.72	13.80	13.85	15,788	15,174	15,076	22,328
Illinois	16,556	–756	15.20	14.99	14.66	190,421	188,365	196,449	212,785
Indiana	9,053	–209	17.84	17.16	16.42	167,437	160,924	154,264	162,520
Iowa	3,718	–6	15.70	15.31	14.67	70,323	65,042	65,428	66,393
Kansas	3,181	–48	15.83	15.98	15.48	50,368	50,898	53,031	54,523
Kentucky	4,166	–43	16.02	15.73	15.44	89,652	88,513	84,180	89,809
Louisiana	3,427	–36	16.86	17.03	16.18	94,387	89,541	85,488	94,559
Maine	1,827	–51	16.28	15.55	14.71	13,925	13,852	15,066	16,917
Maryland	3,929	19	15.75	15.21	14.56	35,456	36,363	36,038	36,767
Massachusetts	8,686	–482	16.53	16.25	15.75	78,023	77,997	79,851	85,872
Michigan	14,947	–603	21.28	20.48	19.45	223,853	221,433	209,003	229,292
Minnesota	7,953	–142	15.43	15.06	14.76	82,691	80,624	82,304	86,686
Mississippi	2,766	–77	12.88	12.32	11.93	39,995	38,276	38,560	41,024
Missouri	7,112	–195	18.21	16.79	16.11	95,941	92,909	89,682	90,388
Montana	1,201	1	14.02	14.43	14.03	5,334	4,988	5,423	5,652
Nebraska	1,930	–16	14.86	14.05	13.64	32,962	30,611	31,133	30,860
Nevada	1,728	35	14.63	14.62	13.79	9,103	8,466	7,581	7,131
New Hampshire	2,184	–88	14.85	14.20	13.98	16,205	15,235	16,975	19,565
New Jersey	10,454	–584	15.46	15.20	14.74	96,325	96,600	98,230	101,641
New Mexico	1,545	–18	13.19	13.43	13.27	10,670	10,168	11,464	15,241
New York	20,778	–1,351	16.78	16.74	16.24	142,252	147,317	146,455	155,666
North Carolina	10,548	–449	13.66	13.18	12.81	157,359	156,822	167,124	176,472
North Dakota	689	–11	14.04	13.17	12.77	6,419	6,857	6,517	5,957
Ohio	17,189	–515	18.00	17.49	16.79	240,066	243,904	241,902	258,010
Oklahoma	3,960	18	14.13	14.12	13.66	41,345	39,924	40,063	44,436
Oregon	5,521	–95	15.20	15.06	14.74	44,512	45,865	43,271	49,730
Pennsylvania	16,399	–363	14.98	14.75	14.37	183,721	181,462	178,613	187,354
Rhode Island	2,086	–170	12.88	12.75	12.68	10,653	10,818	10,958	11,622
South Carolina	4,360	–71	14.19	14.00	13.79	84,526	81,133	78,738	78,481
South Dakota	897	–9	13.13	12.60	12.11	10,356	10,710	11,093	12,185
Tennessee	6,833	–260	13.56	13.15	12.88	113,789	109,293	104,109	104,157
Texas	21,051	–358	13.94	13.93	14.04	326,718	310,816	321,361	347,130
Utah	3,018	101	14.90	14.12	13.76	25,624	25,104	25,908	27,766
Vermont	1,140	–68	14.54	14.33	14.18	9,469	9,661	8,926	9,417
Virginia	5,773	–65	15.88	15.25	14.49	82,760	83,953	92,874	95,932
Washington	7,365	–219	18.03	18.15	17.96	79,891	79,314	89,280	90,309
West Virginia	1,454	1	16.05	15.40	14.80	19,463	18,911	16,201	16,906
Wisconsin	9,771	–133	16.12	15.86	15.44	131,134	124,664	126,542	130,078
Wyoming	542	–11	16.74	17.73	17.26	4,924	4,062	3,835	3,818

D Figure withheld to avoid disclosure.

[1]Bureau of Labor Statistics.
[2]Bureau of Economic Analysis.
[3]Includes extensive and unmeasurable duplication from shipments between establishments in the same industry classification.
[4]United States totals differ from the sum of the state figures because of differing benchmarks among states and differing industrial and geographic stratification.

Survey, Census, or Data Collection Method: Employment and average hourly earnings—Based on the Current Employment Statistics (CES) survey; for information, see Appendix B, Limitations of the Data and Methodology, and Internet site <http://www.bls.gov/opub/hom/homch2_a.htm>; Earnings—Based on the Regional Economic Information System; for information, see "State Personal Income Methodologies" at <http://www.bea.gov/bea/regional/articles/spi2003/>; Establishments—Based on tabulations of data extracted from the U.S. Census Bureau's Business Register; for information, see Internet site <http://www.census.gov/epcd/cbp/view/cbpview.html>; Value of shipments—Based on the Annual Survey of Manufactures and the 2002 Economic Census; for information, see Appendix B, Limitations of the Data and Methodology, and Internet sites <http://www.census.gov/mcd/asmhome.html> and <http://www.census.gov/econ/census02/>.

Sources: Employment and average hourly earnings—U.S. Bureau of Labor Statistics, Current Employment Statistics Program, see Internet site <http://www.bls.gov/sae/home.htm>; Earnings—U.S. Bureau of Economic Analysis, *Survey of Current Business*, April 2005, see Internet site <http://www.bea.gov/bea/regional/spi/>; Establishments—U.S. Census Bureau, *County Business Patterns*, annual, see Internet site <http://www.census.gov/epcd/cbp/view/cbpview.html>; Value of shipments—U.S. Census Bureau, *Annual Survey of Manufactures, Geographic Area Statistics*, series M03(AS)-3 and earlier reports, see Internet site <http://www.census.gov/prod/2005pubs/am0331as1.pdf> (released May 2005); and 2002 Economic Census, *Manufacturing, Geographic Area Series*, see also <http://www.census.gov/econ/census02/guide/geosumm.htm> (issued September 2005).

Manufactures Summary and Export-Related Shipments and Employment

Geographic area	Manufactures summary, 2003										Export-related, 2001[1]			
	All employees[2]				Production workers[2]			Value added by manufactures[3]		Value of ship-ments[4] (mil. dol.)	Export-related shipments (mil. dol.)	Export-related manufac-turing employ-ment (1,000)	Export-related as percent of all manufacturers	
	Number	Net change, 2000–2003	Payroll		Total	Hours (mil.)	Wages (mil. dol.)	Total (mil. dol.)	Per production worker (dol.)				Ship-ments	Employ-ment
			Total (mil. dol.)	Per employee (dol.)										
United States . . .	[5]13,865,811	[5]–2,786,093	[5]564,771	40,731	[5]9,794,556	[5]19,883	[5]329,730	[5]1,909,616	137,721	[5]3,977,165	806,189.2	3,251.7	20.3	20.5
Alabama	260,343	–74,879	9,406	36,130	205,276	416	6,434	29,768	114,342	70,048	12,451.6	46.4	18.5	14.7
Alaska	11,357	–1,049	371	32,647	9,668	21	276	1,413	124,424	4,371	599.3	1.5	15.0	11.9
Arizona	161,235	–39,679	7,120	44,159	101,000	206	3,367	29,017	179,964	44,900	11,218.1	47.5	26.6	25.5
Arkansas	192,952	–42,121	6,120	31,717	154,465	315	4,379	22,730	117,800	47,560	7,421.0	29.8	15.9	13.1
California	1,523,323	–316,536	64,840	42,565	978,081	1,949	30,195	197,547	129,682	378,468	110,597.4	471.1	26.7	26.3
Colorado	141,943	–25,291	6,338	44,650	90,368	183	3,161	17,243	121,478	33,775	7,112.6	34.1	20.0	20.9
Connecticut	194,502	–43,160	9,248	47,547	116,954	244	4,478	25,771	132,499	41,587	11,510.5	55.2	24.5	24.0
Delaware	36,490	–4,207	1,630	44,667	25,817	53	965	4,607	126,240	14,445	1,131.3	3.7	6.8	9.7
District of Columbia	1,944	–974	84	43,383	717	1	18	196	100,722	293	0.5	(D)	0.3	(D)
Florida	358,308	–64,118	13,972	38,994	233,396	474	6,919	42,391	118,310	78,900	11,560.5	58.8	15.1	14.7
Georgia	430,768	–82,324	15,422	35,801	330,211	682	10,082	58,683	136,229	125,099	20,387.2	72.6	16.0	15.0
Hawaii	13,564	–1,119	434	32,022	8,988	18	269	1,224	90,275	3,880	197.3	1.3	6.2	9.0
Idaho	58,207	–4,664	2,159	37,087	44,292	90	1,434	7,701	132,311	15,788	4,040.2	15.6	26.8	24.4
Illinois	704,739	–160,931	29,021	41,180	492,542	1,005	16,611	93,534	132,722	190,421	37,335.6	151.2	19.0	18.6
Indiana	536,413	–101,737	22,484	41,916	407,958	840	15,219	80,988	150,981	167,437	31,066.9	120.3	20.1	20.1
Iowa	217,838	–28,954	8,183	37,567	158,392	323	5,148	32,739	150,290	70,323	10,622.7	41.0	16.2	17.4
Kansas	167,731	–27,920	6,702	39,959	116,569	237	3,988	20,429	121,794	50,368	6,986.5	26.1	13.2	13.5
Kentucky	251,650	–40,823	10,108	40,168	192,276	392	6,825	35,562	141,317	89,652	14,967.1	49.5	17.8	17.9
Louisiana	144,766	–17,252	6,392	44,152	105,104	219	4,158	30,605	211,407	94,387	11,691.2	22.1	13.7	14.1
Maine	64,492	–15,296	2,535	39,312	48,125	95	1,682	7,377	114,393	13,925	2,499.8	11.6	16.6	14.9
Maryland	143,771	–23,084	6,515	45,312	91,790	179	3,118	18,490	128,611	35,456	4,948.1	24.3	13.7	15.0
Massachusetts	325,758	–59,794	14,962	45,929	200,989	410	6,864	46,266	142,025	78,023	20,720.6	98.0	25.9	26.0
Michigan	685,392	–122,302	32,549	47,489	505,779	1,052	21,951	97,552	142,330	223,853	47,699.6	190.1	22.8	25.4
Minnesota	333,385	–56,970	14,045	42,127	224,149	452	7,615	41,451	124,335	82,691	12,793.9	68.4	15.5	18.2
Mississippi	167,606	–47,337	5,257	31,363	134,000	260	3,628	17,169	102,437	39,995	4,750.2	19.5	12.3	9.9
Missouri	306,062	–54,827	12,405	40,532	226,072	446	8,111	43,120	140,887	95,941	13,486.3	56.3	15.0	16.2
Montana	16,565	–4,841	587	35,412	12,166	23	379	1,794	108,273	5,334	442.4	1.3	8.2	6.4
Nebraska	100,862	–9,518	3,388	33,592	77,938	162	2,296	11,844	117,426	32,962	4,581.0	15.4	14.7	14.7
Nevada	44,278	4,431	1,821	41,116	28,409	60	947	5,040	113,829	9,103	1,119.8	6.4	14.8	15.8
New Hampshire	83,730	–17,434	3,563	42,549	54,045	112	1,730	8,909	106,398	16,205	3,655.8	20.1	21.5	20.8
New Jersey	345,217	–42,201	15,386	44,569	226,139	460	7,902	51,979	150,570	96,325	15,933.3	64.2	16.2	16.9
New Mexico	29,900	–6,226	1,169	39,087	21,911	44	723	6,150	205,683	10,670	3,367.7	7.6	29.4	23.2
New York	592,077	–144,265	24,434	41,269	397,789	807	13,169	80,199	135,453	142,252	29,325.1	139.5	20.0	19.7
North Carolina	569,379	–174,054	19,792	34,761	433,775	877	12,590	89,017	156,340	157,359	28,667.6	139.6	17.2	20.1
North Dakota	21,206	–2,673	721	34,006	15,984	33	469	2,520	118,813	6,419	666.1	1.9	10.2	8.1
Ohio	811,161	–171,000	34,337	42,330	596,281	1,232	22,446	109,282	134,723	240,066	53,213.6	215.2	22.0	23.3
Oklahoma	138,583	–33,670	5,158	37,223	102,097	205	3,314	17,686	127,619	41,345	6,100.3	27.0	15.2	16.7
Oregon	176,114	–29,165	6,984	39,653	125,092	244	4,205	25,109	142,575	44,512	12,016.1	49.7	27.8	24.9
Pennsylvania	675,602	–118,571	26,880	39,787	478,934	966	16,125	93,777	138,805	183,721	29,667.1	133.2	16.6	17.3
Rhode Island	60,388	–13,298	2,296	38,020	40,652	81	1,211	6,039	100,007	10,653	1,925.1	12.3	17.6	17.6
South Carolina	279,328	–53,016	10,412	37,275	212,349	431	6,756	39,228	140,438	84,526	20,046.0	80.0	25.5	25.6
South Dakota	35,954	–5,883	1,138	31,639	27,433	56	769	3,776	105,013	10,356	2,191.8	6.8	19.8	17.2
Tennessee	384,719	–82,891	14,345	37,286	290,530	587	9,259	51,130	132,902	113,789	17,403.9	77.2	16.7	17.5
Texas	806,797	–187,857	33,636	41,690	558,257	1,150	18,647	123,846	153,503	326,718	69,444.0	215.7	21.6	22.7
Utah	105,841	–18,608	3,980	37,608	71,215	141	2,162	12,720	120,177	25,624	4,800.0	22.9	18.5	18.8
Vermont	41,545	–2,146	1,716	41,309	27,759	57	936	4,972	119,669	9,469	4,048.3	17.6	45.4	38.4
Virginia	295,858	–55,778	11,530	38,973	218,251	450	7,221	46,849	158,349	82,760	14,071.0	57.0	15.2	17.4
Washington	258,610	–65,700	10,930	42,266	164,950	332	5,535	38,896	150,404	79,891	44,120.7	126.8	49.4	41.0
West Virginia	64,617	–4,899	2,613	40,435	48,824	97	1,720	8,205	126,972	19,463	3,026.2	11.5	18.7	10.0
Wisconsin	481,862	–90,326	19,239	39,925	352,222	700	12,021	65,355	135,630	131,134	18,356.1	86.5	14.5	15.9
Wyoming	11,075	841	416	37,552	8,580	19	301	1,722	155,466	4,924	204.4	0.4	5.3	4.4

D Data withheld to avoid disclosure of individual companies.

[1]Exports includes both "direct" exports (exports manufactured in the United States and consumed in foreign markets) and "indirect" exports (intermediate goods and services required to manufacture export goods).

[2]Includes employment and payroll at administrative offices and auxiliary units. All employees represents the average of production workers plus all other employees for the payroll period ended nearest the 12th of March. Production workers represents the average of the employment for the payroll periods ended nearest the 12th of March, May, August, and November.

[3]Adjusted value added; takes into account (a) value added by merchandising operations (that is, difference between the sales value and cost of merchandise sold without further manufacture, processing, or assembly), plus (b) net change in finished goods and work-in-process inventories between beginning and end of year.

[4]Includes extensive and unmeasurable duplication from shipments between establishments in the same industry classification.

[5]Sum of state totals may not add to U.S. total because U.S. and state figures were independently derived.

Survey, Census, or Data Collection Method: Manufactures summary—Based on the Annual Survey of Manufactures; for information, see Appendix B, Limitations of the Data and Methodology, and Internet site <http://www.census.gov/mcd/asmhome.html>; Export-related—Based on tabulations of data from 3 sources: the 2001 Annual Survey of Manufactures, the U.S. Census Bureau's 2001 edition of U.S. International Trade in Goods and Services, and the Bureau of Economic Analysis' Input-Output (I/O) Accounts of the U.S. Economy for 1992; for information, see the following document at <http://www.census.gov/mcd/exports/ar01.pdf>.

Sources: Manufactures summary—U.S. Census Bureau, *Annual Survey of Manufactures, Geographic Area Statistics*, Series M03(AS)-3. See also <http://www.census.gov/prod/2005pubs/am0331as1.pdf> (released May 2005); Export-related—U.S. Census Bureau, *Exports from Manufacturing Establishments: 2001*, Series AR(01)-1, see Internet site <http://www.census.gov/mcd/exports/ar01.pdf> (released July 2004).

Table A-61. States — Major Manufacturing Sectors: 2003

Geographic area	Apparel and textiles[1] (NAICS 313–315) Employment Total	Percent of total manu-facturing	Percent change, 2000–2003	Value of ship-ments (mil. dol.)	Machinery (NAICS 333) Employment Total	Percent of total manu-facturing	Percent change, 2000–2003	Value of ship-ments (mil. dol.)	Computer and electronic products (NAICS 334) Employment Total	Percent of total manu-facturing	Percent change, 2000–2003	Value of ship-ments (mil. dol.)	Motor vehicle and parts[2] (NAICS 3361–3363) Employment Total	Percent of total manu-facturing	Percent change, 2000–2003	Value of ship-ments (mil. dol.)
United States . . .	715,464	5.2	−34.6	114,355	1,098,974	7.9	−21.6	252,984	1,163,493	8.4	−29.2	353,767	1,009,008	7.3	−13.8	486,137
Alabama	30,930	11.9	−43.1	5,683	11,774	4.5	−38.9	2,737	12,096	4.6	−19.5	3,535	19,563	7.5	(NA)	10,162
Alaska.	(NA)	(NA)	(NA)	(NA)	(NA)	(NA)	(NA)	(NA)	(NA)	(NA)	(NA)	(NA)	(NA)	(NA)	(NA)	(NA)
Arizona	(NA)	(NA)	(NA)	(NA)	7,861	4.9	−25.1	1,621	30,926	19.2	−35.0	15,766	(NA)	(NA)	(NA)	(NA)
Arkansas	(NA)	(NA)	(NA)	(NA)	15,057	7.8	−21.1	3,114	5,277	2.7	13.5	1,285	9,706	5.0	(NA)	(NA)
California	117,436	7.7	−28.4	16,209	86,568	5.7	−20.8	17,215	272,573	17.9	−30.0	82,493	43,330	2.8	−6.4	13,782
Colorado	(NA)	(NA)	(NA)	(NA)	9,466	6.7	−19.2	1,824	26,819	18.9	−30.6	6,531	(NA)	(NA)	(NA)	(NA)
Connecticut	(NA)	(NA)	(NA)	(NA)	17,771	9.1	−21.4	3,532	19,426	10.0	−17.2	3,371	(NA)	(NA)	(NA)	(NA)
Delaware	(NA)	(NA)	(NA)	(NA)	(NA)	(NA)	(NA)	(NA)	2,359	6.5	89.9	522	(NA)	(NA)	(NA)	(NA)
District of Columbia	(NA)	(NA)	(NA)	(NA)	(NA)	(NA)	(NA)	(NA)	(NA)	(NA)	(NA)	(NA)	(NA)	(NA)	(NA)	(NA)
Florida	14,773	4.1	−41.6	1,999	19,826	5.5	−24.3	4,287	51,576	14.4	−23.3	12,561	(NA)	(NA)	(NA)	(NA)
Georgia	78,614	18.2	−26.5	18,049	23,537	5.5	−22.4	6,486	10,727	2.5	−17.7	2,585	19,663	4.6	−11.0	10,212
Hawaii	(NA)	(NA)	(NA)	(NA)	(NA)	(NA)	(NA)	(NA)	(NA)	(NA)	(NA)	(NA)	(NA)	(NA)	(NA)	(NA)
Idaho.	(NA)	(NA)	(NA)	(NA)	3,162	5.4	38.7	447	13,512	23.2	−28.9	5,039	(NA)	(NA)	(NA)	(NA)
Illinois	(NA)	(NA)	(NA)	(NA)	82,465	11.7	−21.4	20,964	38,956	5.5	−45.3	10,059	36,928	5.2	−14.6	13,292
Indiana	(NA)	(NA)	(NA)	(NA)	37,676	7.0	−21.1	9,955	17,471	3.3	−31.0	3,896	122,044	22.8	−13.4	51,478
Iowa	(NA)	(NA)	(NA)	(NA)	31,699	14.6	−14.5	10,989	11,310	5.2	−5.5	1,996	(NA)	(NA)	(NA)	(NA)
Kansas	(NA)	(NA)	(NA)	(NA)	17,006	10.1	−18.6	3,721	6,100	3.6	−5.4	1,606	7,412	4.4	(NA)	(NA)
Kentucky	11,467	4.6	−41.9	1,659	17,909	7.1	−30.7	3,677	7,200	2.9	−37.3	3,069	(NA)	(NA)	(NA)	(NA)
Louisiana	(NA)	(NA)	(NA)	(NA)	8,692	6.0	0.9	1,668	1,306	0.9	−45.6	214	(NA)	(NA)	(NA)	(NA)
Maine	(NA)	(NA)	(NA)	(NA)	2,825	4.4	−10.8	487	3,843	6.0	−44.0	729	(NA)	(NA)	(NA)	(NA)
Maryland	5,042	3.5	(NA)	876	8,948	6.2	−22.2	2,110	23,503	16.3	−22.5	6,054	(NA)	(NA)	(NA)	(NA)
Massachusetts	18,059	5.5	−23.6	2,448	25,638	7.9	−18.6	4,856	67,450	20.7	−26.3	22,540	(NA)	(NA)	(NA)	(NA)
Michigan	(NA)	(NA)	(NA)	(NA)	79,120	11.5	−19.3	16,608	19,147	2.8	−16.7	4,754	210,473	30.7	−16.9	118,032
Minnesota	(NA)	(NA)	(NA)	(NA)	31,298	9.4	−22.5	6,780	48,656	14.6	−16.9	12,520	8,751	2.6	(NA)	3,802
Mississippi	9,009	5.4	−45.8	1,274	10,978	6.5	−25.6	2,434	2,583	1.5	−47.8	488	10,440	6.2	(NA)	(NA)
Missouri	(NA)	(NA)	(NA)	(NA)	31,563	10.3	−11.3	5,293	8,231	2.7	−35.2	2,044	31,882	10.4	(NA)	(NA)
Montana	(NA)	(NA)	(NA)	(NA)	1,216	7.3	(NA)	244	(NA)	(NA)	(NA)	(NA)	(NA)	(NA)	(NA)	(NA)
Nebraska	(NA)	(NA)	(NA)	(NA)	9,231	9.2	−25.7	2,018	4,282	4.2	−38.5	839	(NA)	(NA)	(NA)	(NA)
Nevada	(NA)	(NA)	(NA)	(NA)	4,662	10.5	(NA)	638	3,063	6.9	(NA)	560	(NA)	(NA)	(NA)	(NA)
New Hampshire.	(NA)	(NA)	(NA)	(NA)	8,768	10.5	−10.0	1,707	17,243	20.6	−31.9	4,683	(NA)	(NA)	(NA)	(NA)
New Jersey	22,036	6.4	−21.2	2,966	19,125	5.5	−23.1	3,830	28,312	8.2	−24.8	7,465	(NA)	(NA)	(NA)	(NA)
New Mexico	(NA)	(NA)	(NA)	(NA)	1,477	4.9	7.3	220	5,518	18.5	−53.3	4,033	(NA)	(NA)	(NA)	(NA)
New York	53,399	9.0	−41.1	8,061	44,464	7.5	−33.8	10,160	66,258	11.2	−17.8	13,591	(NA)	(NA)	(NA)	(NA)
North Carolina.	110,468	19.4	−35.4	17,184	31,919	5.6	−23.7	9,676	28,555	5.0	−44.6	5,866	25,412	4.5	(NA)	9,793
North Dakota	(NA)	(NA)	(NA)	(NA)	4,040	19.1	−0.3	1,493	1,564	7.4	−34.1	466	(NA)	(NA)	(NA)	(NA)
Ohio	8,545	1.1	−27.5	1,112	76,998	9.5	−25.9	14,913	25,193	3.1	−30.2	6,275	126,952	15.7	−13.2	65,371
Oklahoma	(NA)	(NA)	(NA)	(NA)	22,257	16.1	−12.0	5,104	4,706	3.4	−61.3	1,116	13,090	9.4	(NA)	(NA)
Oregon	(NA)	(NA)	(NA)	(NA)	11,224	6.4	−9.2	1,864	28,795	16.4	−23.1	12,629	8,833	5.0	−8.5	1,897
Pennsylvania	33,750	5.0	−24.9	5,992	53,314	7.9	−20.0	9,961	38,010	5.6	−37.2	7,865	(NA)	(NA)	(NA)	(NA)
Rhode Island	(NA)	(NA)	(NA)	(NA)	3,429	5.7	−19.7	609	6,240	10.3	−15.5	1,194	(NA)	(NA)	(NA)	(NA)
South Carolina	52,311	18.7	−33.4	9,352	21,011	7.5	−14.7	13,937	8,408	3.0	−40.6	2,587	26,170	9.4	15.9	(NA)
South Dakota	(NA)	(NA)	(NA)	(NA)	4,153	11.6	−19.6	841	3,505	9.7	−46.7	3,121	(NA)	(NA)	(NA)	(NA)
Tennessee	17,146	4.5	−52.1	2,980	30,958	8.0	−29.6	9,224	12,165	3.2	−15.9	13,206	52,373	13.6	1.6	(NA)
Texas	24,103	3.0	−44.4	3,229	65,435	8.1	−21.7	14,475	94,195	11.7	−31.7	41,290	25,762	3.2	(NA)	16,568
Utah	(NA)	(NA)	(NA)	(NA)	4,687	4.4	−29.3	855	10,111	9.6	−38.6	2,519	(NA)	(NA)	(NA)	(NA)
Vermont.	(NA)	(NA)	(NA)	(NA)	3,745	9.0	−1.3	533	10,188	24.5	(NA)	3,604	(NA)	(NA)	(NA)	(NA)
Virginia	23,118	7.8	−38.0	4,508	16,117	5.4	−16.2	3,343	18,342	6.2	−25.5	4,980	11,507	3.9	(NA)	(NA)
Washington	(NA)	(NA)	(NA)	(NA)	12,995	5.0	−22.8	2,383	29,272	11.3	−34.3	7,062	(NA)	(NA)	(NA)	(NA)
West Virginia	(NA)	(NA)	(NA)	(NA)	2,914	4.5	−23.1	494	1,564	2.4	33.3	281	(NA)	(NA)	(NA)	(NA)
Wisconsin.	4,822	1.0	−33.8	642	61,301	12.7	−26.1	13,345	16,234	3.4	−28.0	4,753	28,633	5.9	(NA)	(NA)
Wyoming	(NA)	(NA)	(NA)	(NA)	1,905	17.2	(NA)	161	(NA)	(NA)	(NA)	(NA)	(NA)	(NA)	(NA)	(NA)

NA Not available.

[1]Includes Textile mills (NAICS 313), Textile product mills (NAICS 314), and Apparel manufacturing (NAICS 315).
[2]Includes Motor vehicle manufacturing (NAICS 3361), Motor vehicle body and trailer manufacturing (NAICS 3362), and Motor vehicle parts manufacturing (NAICS 3363).

Survey, Census, or Data Collection Method: Based on the Annual Survey of Manufactures; for information, see Appendix B, Limitations of the Data and Methodology, and Internet site <http://www.census.gov/mcd/asmhome.html>.

Source: U.S. Census Bureau, *Annual Survey of Manufactures, Geographic Area Statistics*, Series M03(AS)-3 (released May 2005) and Series M00(AS)-3RV (issued September 2002); see also Internet site <http://www.census.gov/mcd/asm-as3.html>.

Wholesale and Retail Trade and Shopping Centers

| Geographic area | Wholesale and retail nonfarm employment (BLS)[1,2] (1,000) | | | Wholesale trade[3] | | | | Retail trade[4] | | | | Shopping centers | | | |
| | | | | Earnings (BEA)[5] (mil. dol.) | | Establishments | | Earnings (BEA)[5] (mil. dol.) | | Establishments | | Retail sales (bil. dol.) | | Retail sales per square foot (dol.) | |
	2004	2003	2000	2004	2001	2002	Net change, 2000–2002	2004	2001	2002	Net change, 2000–2002	2004	2000	2004	2000
United States . . .	[6]20,690	[6]20,525	[6]21,213	387,439	350,889	436,900	−9,337	500,698	457,313	1,125,693	12,120	1,432.6	1,181.1	241	212
Alabama	310	306	317	4,492	3,983	5,792	−340	6,892	6,129	19,601	−122	20.5	17.4	246	226
Alaska	41	40	40	357	316	748	−4	1,286	1,100	2,683	−50	3.0	2.4	395	312
Arizona	384	369	364	6,494	5,778	6,636	−95	10,239	8,690	17,431	520	34.4	28.2	236	221
Arkansas	177	174	178	2,511	2,107	3,535	30	3,584	3,199	12,151	−60	9.7	8.3	253	225
California	2,270	2,237	2,204	47,032	42,310	58,700	374	67,631	61,363	110,510	2,523	171.4	141.8	231	201
Colorado	334	332	345	6,579	6,447	7,458	6	8,437	7,905	19,200	452	32.8	26.5	275	255
Connecticut	259	257	266	5,850	5,525	4,796	−280	7,811	7,172	14,060	−51	27.6	21.8	272	227
Delaware	67	66	65	1,156	867	953	−56	1,650	1,403	3,800	58	6.4	5.1	269	223
District of Columbia	22	22	22	423	339	338	−34	623	555	1,930	−15	2.4	2.0	222	210
Florida	1,269	1,235	1,252	20,561	17,737	30,760	89	30,024	26,843	70,622	3,226	134.3	108.3	282	246
Georgia	650	650	677	14,559	13,854	13,618	−274	14,070	13,378	34,531	743	42.8	35.7	213	195
Hawaii	84	81	83	960	803	1,828	19	2,226	1,923	4,997	73	6.7	5.1	321	251
Idaho	99	97	103	1,220	1,120	1,978	−34	2,312	2,037	5,920	49	4.4	3.7	216	186
Illinois	924	928	971	21,863	20,517	20,597	−912	19,822	18,654	43,623	−177	59.1	48.2	212	183
Indiana	451	452	484	6,966	6,350	8,440	−202	9,314	8,796	24,358	97	28.9	24.2	221	199
Iowa	247	246	258	3,529	3,171	5,003	−152	4,946	4,616	13,937	−445	10.2	8.5	201	191
Kansas	209	210	220	3,569	3,220	4,719	−157	4,369	4,130	11,980	−281	15.7	13.2	255	226
Kentucky	285	284	298	4,392	3,723	4,713	−226	6,103	5,518	16,985	−3	18.6	15.7	266	231
Louisiana	300	299	311	4,038	3,626	5,965	−227	6,347	5,723	17,746	−9	25.3	21.2	281	249
Maine	109	107	105	1,213	1,010	1,707	−33	2,600	2,283	7,096	81	6.2	4.9	323	280
Maryland	389	386	392	6,700	6,024	6,022	−76	10,066	9,018	19,734	195	34.5	28.5	256	218
Massachusetts	490	489	502	11,463	10,777	9,439	−296	12,507	11,405	25,932	119	33.2	26.9	276	232
Michigan	686	691	746	12,030	11,417	13,055	−521	15,941	15,244	38,829	−33	34.7	28.8	226	202
Minnesota	430	429	436	9,536	8,436	9,166	−128	9,328	8,499	21,095	233	19.3	15.9	258	229
Mississippi	174	174	182	1,891	1,634	2,968	−148	3,842	3,512	12,644	−150	10.5	9.1	230	205
Missouri	431	429	435	7,314	6,607	8,701	−371	9,377	8,548	23,803	−108	31.0	25.8	244	223
Montana	71	69	69	744	630	1,566	29	1,659	1,425	5,193	92	2.8	2.3	274	232
Nebraska	148	148	153	2,291	2,074	2,972	−89	2,933	2,683	8,222	−26	7.8	6.5	198	179
Nevada	161	154	143	2,286	2,001	2,586	30	4,641	3,816	7,310	370	9.5	7.7	152	156
New Hampshire.	125	123	120	2,171	1,954	2,045	−60	3,424	2,968	6,678	133	6.9	5.2	258	209
New Jersey	700	699	705	19,223	18,299	16,548	−609	18,352	16,819	35,410	569	40.8	32.8	218	187
New Mexico	114	113	114	1,174	1,057	2,089	−73	2,936	2,545	7,261	12	8.6	7.2	265	237
New York	1,220	1,211	1,262	27,890	25,344	35,628	−978	30,373	27,204	77,532	2,032	61.1	50.8	231	202
North Carolina.	598	594	616	10,381	8,588	12,071	−293	13,368	12,588	36,082	297	39.5	32.9	198	183
North Dakota	60	59	59	910	782	1,517	−26	1,118	997	3,435	−	2.9	2.4	294	257
Ohio	853	860	919	14,661	13,742	16,203	−443	18,517	17,873	42,608	−100	56.4	47.1	211	187
Oklahoma	223	224	236	2,873	2,662	4,835	−170	5,179	4,728	13,942	−205	16.9	14.6	274	240
Oregon	264	259	267	5,279	4,453	5,815	−21	6,190	5,701	14,328	72	13.3	10.8	214	183
Pennsylvania	893	888	907	15,507	13,273	16,272	−524	20,797	19,174	48,444	−74	56.0	46.1	210	186
Rhode Island	69	70	69	1,129	998	1,481	−49	1,750	1,482	4,203	−139	5.3	4.3	228	217
South Carolina	292	287	300	3,739	3,179	4,940	−151	6,757	6,178	18,487	−132	21.0	17.7	227	210
South Dakota	66	65	65	828	715	1,342	−48	1,361	1,212	4,272	91	1.7	1.5	250	209
Tennessee	447	440	447	8,006	6,747	7,614	−392	11,081	9,877	24,288	−336	31.5	26.1	225	191
Texas	1,546	1,529	1,573	33,649	31,970	31,876	−755	37,165	35,107	76,973	2,215	119.3	99.3	299	264
Utah	174	170	172	2,366	2,132	3,346	52	4,129	3,580	8,275	323	8.6	7.3	211	201
Vermont.	50	50	49	591	514	869	−20	1,268	1,105	3,926	−48	2.6	2.1	294	248
Virginia	528	516	524	8,085	7,231	7,636	−257	12,533	11,004	29,194	400	44.7	36.4	242	210
Washington	429	422	436	8,411	7,312	9,672	−197	11,598	10,416	22,706	6	24.9	20.4	235	200
West Virginia	112	110	117	1,214	1,094	1,708	−161	2,405	2,195	7,510	−278	4.8	4.2	205	182
Wisconsin.	432	431	447	6,914	6,094	7,801	−127	8,950	8,215	21,366	12	20.3	16.7	249	215
Wyoming	37	37	36	422	344	833	43	868	777	2,850	−31	1.8	1.5	291	255

− Represents zero.

[1]Bureau of Labor Statistics.
[2]Includes Wholesale trade (NAICS 42) and Retail trade (NAICS 44).
[3]Covers Wholesale trade (NAICS 42).
[4]Covers Retail trade (NAICS 44).
[5]Bureau of Economic Analysis.
[6]United States totals differ from the sum of the state figures because of differing benchmarks among states and differing industrial and geographic stratification.

Survey, Census, or Data Collection Method: Employment—Based on the Current Employment Statistics (CES) survey; for information, see Appendix B, Limitations of the Data and Methodology, and see Internet site <http://www.bls.gov/opub/hom/homch2_a.htm>;   Earnings—Based on the Regional Economic Information System; for information, see "State Personal Income Methodologies" at <http://www.bea.gov/bea/regional/articles/spi2003/>;   Establishments—Based on tabulations of data extracted from the U.S. Census Bureau's Business Register; for information, see Internet site <http://www.census.gov/epcd/cbp/view/cbpview.html>;   Shopping centers—For information, see Internet site <http://www.icsc.org/>.

Sources: Employment—U.S. Bureau of Labor Statistics, Current Employment Statistics Program, see Internet site <http://www.bls.gov/sae/home.htm>;   Earnings—U.S. Bureau of Economic Analysis, Survey of Current Business, April 2005, see Internet site <http://www.bea.gov/bea/regional/spi/>;   Establishments—U.S. Census Bureau, County Business Patterns, annual, see Internet site <http://www.census.gov/epcd/cbp/view/cbpview.html>;   Shopping centers—National Research Bureau, Chicago, IL. Data for 1995–2004 published by International Council of Shopping Centers in Shopping Centers Today, April issues (copyright, Trade Dimensions International, Inc.).

State and Metropolitan Area Data Book: 2006

U.S. Census Bureau

Geographic area	All retail stores[1] (NAICS 44, 45) (mil. dol.)			Sales per household			Food and beverage stores (NAICS 445) (mil. dol.)		General merchandise stores (mil. dol.)			
									Total (NAICS 452)		Department stores (NAICS 4521)	
	2004	2003	2001	2004 (dol.)	2001 (dol.)	Percent change, 2003–2004	2004	2003	2004	2003	2004	2003
United States . . .	3,522,754	3,367,086	3,324,957	32,040	31,307	4.1	526,194	489,332	504,356	483,234	337,780	323,094
Alabama	45,859	43,234	45,174	25,789	26,161	6.3	6,090	5,761	8,820	8,231	5,998	5,584
Alaska	8,028	7,389	7,549	34,519	33,976	8.1	1,353	1,294	1,826	1,672	858	785
Arizona	67,909	65,581	64,152	32,289	32,192	1.4	9,388	8,560	10,189	9,792	6,701	6,432
Arkansas	28,926	27,531	27,368	26,968	26,237	4.9	3,234	3,065	6,099	5,827	4,352	4,153
California	428,851	413,238	392,114	35,426	33,466	2.7	70,435	64,889	56,316	53,823	36,602	34,891
Colorado	61,285	59,450	58,342	34,727	33,563	2.8	9,272	8,921	8,703	8,354	5,647	5,458
Connecticut	48,829	46,651	46,624	36,316	36,020	4.3	8,685	7,982	3,986	3,783	2,751	2,605
Delaware	11,909	11,149	11,180	37,645	36,935	6.0	1,472	1,324	1,590	1,550	1,122	1,101
District of Columbia	2,783	2,657	2,540	11,298	10,334	6.8	668	625	87	95	73	79
Florida	209,355	200,009	195,869	30,585	30,364	3.0	32,838	31,331	25,911	24,786	18,142	17,315
Georgia	103,516	100,254	99,789	32,106	32,261	2.4	15,870	14,867	14,283	13,901	10,173	9,893
Hawaii	14,260	13,680	12,308	33,484	29,953	3.4	2,854	2,569	2,769	2,806	1,153	1,154
Idaho	18,211	16,137	15,563	36,256	32,235	11.1	2,456	2,183	2,884	2,561	1,606	1,422
Illinois	144,755	137,124	138,373	30,839	30,047	5.5	23,488	21,035	17,734	17,190	13,405	12,984
Indiana	72,222	69,538	73,717	30,048	31,432	3.7	8,808	8,454	12,109	11,845	7,795	7,613
Iowa	37,089	35,870	34,875	31,888	30,302	3.4	5,229	4,935	5,341	5,202	3,667	3,561
Kansas	34,263	33,664	34,662	32,422	33,229	1.6	4,878	4,760	6,777	6,567	4,797	4,649
Kentucky	41,326	39,519	41,201	25,154	26,335	4.4	5,589	5,340	7,683	7,388	5,220	5,017
Louisiana	47,385	44,995	45,044	28,176	27,426	5.5	6,663	6,190	8,906	8,440	6,132	5,788
Maine	19,001	18,127	17,793	35,063	35,451	4.2	3,742	3,520	2,119	2,099	1,374	1,357
Maryland	69,072	64,219	60,240	33,140	30,467	7.2	13,341	11,966	8,518	7,874	6,164	5,693
Massachusetts	83,465	80,287	81,369	33,447	33,462	4.4	14,953	13,896	9,090	8,859	6,401	6,232
Michigan	123,244	119,825	124,085	31,794	33,095	3.1	15,785	14,597	21,820	21,583	13,588	13,377
Minnesota	74,127	71,046	73,837	37,709	39,018	4.1	9,642	8,983	9,493	9,253	7,356	7,185
Mississippi	28,192	26,897	28,351	26,350	27,114	5.2	3,875	3,729	5,150	4,738	3,106	2,857
Missouri	68,687	64,900	67,548	30,456	30,911	5.7	8,553	7,833	11,597	10,836	8,402	7,832
Montana	9,577	8,851	9,133	25,953	25,617	7.4	1,691	1,551	1,704	1,530	1,080	969
Nebraska	21,486	20,459	20,214	31,488	30,366	4.6	2,997	2,887	2,939	2,907	1,741	1,726
Nevada	29,721	27,602	26,257	34,652	32,678	4.4	4,367	3,953	3,667	3,330	2,536	2,303
New Hampshire	25,328	23,743	22,720	50,411	47,923	6.3	3,651	3,330	3,345	3,219	2,248	2,165
New Jersey	116,147	109,105	104,969	36,655	34,153	6.2	19,018	17,201	12,708	12,283	9,050	8,748
New Mexico	20,859	19,795	20,125	29,384	29,837	4.6	2,614	2,515	3,660	3,389	2,524	2,332
New York	205,165	195,874	185,761	28,655	26,376	4.8	33,300	31,131	23,525	22,260	15,837	14,994
North Carolina	94,049	91,712	93,780	28,368	29,587	1.9	13,074	12,447	13,057	12,527	9,159	8,767
North Dakota	8,374	8,085	7,844	32,673	30,859	3.8	841	801	1,279	1,266	926	912
Ohio	139,302	133,937	135,446	30,853	30,872	4.5	18,683	17,310	22,837	22,346	14,037	13,682
Oklahoma	38,292	36,828	35,455	27,862	26,494	3.8	4,470	4,276	7,553	7,314	5,252	5,070
Oregon	44,357	42,625	45,834	31,684	33,771	3.2	6,722	6,202	8,074	7,641	3,624	3,416
Pennsylvania	140,302	135,599	134,331	29,007	28,316	3.8	22,867	21,544	15,694	15,798	11,565	11,632
Rhode Island	10,990	9,932	10,136	25,863	25,264	10.4	1,941	1,712	1,105	1,002	785	710
South Carolina	45,705	43,237	45,266	28,279	29,916	5.2	6,785	6,290	6,893	6,643	4,580	4,414
South Dakota	15,516	14,724	14,448	52,403	50,358	5.4	1,356	1,352	1,396	1,315	938	864
Tennessee	73,920	70,166	70,106	31,866	31,310	5.0	12,338	11,472	12,532	12,049	8,532	8,168
Texas	288,967	274,981	262,791	36,476	34,470	3.9	35,674	33,264	45,371	42,052	31,364	28,976
Utah	27,310	26,134	26,877	36,574	36,859	3.3	4,428	4,201	4,341	4,089	2,679	2,514
Vermont	8,175	7,712	7,466	32,920	31,370	6.0	1,459	1,338	537	543	272	275
Virginia	92,453	86,194	81,954	32,391	30,340	6.5	12,960	11,878	13,634	12,925	8,663	8,204
Washington	74,935	71,587	72,294	31,461	31,242	3.9	11,178	10,474	13,368	12,725	6,945	6,585
West Virginia	18,126	17,288	17,415	24,295	24,175	4.7	2,573	2,422	3,217	3,158	2,070	2,029
Wisconsin	74,044	71,360	68,292	34,377	33,291	3.8	10,892	10,137	10,870	10,702	7,939	7,833
Wyoming	7,109	6,585	6,376	35,752	33,312	8.2	1,151	1,035	1,250	1,165	849	788

See footnotes at end of table.

Geographic area	Motor vehicle and parts dealers (NAICS 441) (mil. dol.)		Food services and drinking places (NAICS 772) (mil. dol.)		Total retail sales + food and drink (mil. dol.)		Furniture and home furnishings (NAICS 442) (mil. dol.)		Electronics and appliances (NAICS 443) (mil. dol.)		Building and material supply (NAICS 444) (mil. dol.)	
	2004	2003	2004	2003	2004	2003	2004	2003	2004	2003	2004	2003
United States . . .	**906,076**	**889,259**	**383,728**	**357,906**	**3,906,482**	**3,724,992**	**104,986**	**98,993**	**98,252**	**98,775**	**355,220**	**330,901**
Alabama	12,200	11,724	4,759	4,480	50,618	47,715	1,185	1,093	744	704	4,581	4,311
Alaska.	1,697	1,592	1,048	959	9,076	8,348	132	112	172	151	1,100	930
Arizona	18,436	18,535	6,946	6,514	74,855	72,096	2,203	2,105	1,867	1,985	5,930	5,604
Arkansas	8,170	7,845	2,538	2,390	31,464	29,921	663	593	482	470	3,041	2,742
California	111,604	109,959	53,044	48,764	481,895	462,002	13,186	12,647	19,075	20,537	41,457	38,764
Colorado	15,999	15,874	7,141	6,514	68,426	65,964	2,429	2,393	1,942	1,905	7,262	6,711
Connecticut	11,560	11,423	4,985	4,613	53,814	51,264	1,508	1,410	1,414	1,353	5,180	4,760
Delaware	3,122	2,914	1,327	1,250	13,236	12,399	585	522	376	369	1,425	1,259
District of Columbia	122	110	1,897	1,774	4,681	4,431	119	125	100	87	277	236
Florida	63,010	61,063	20,601	18,982	229,956	218,991	6,348	5,938	5,704	5,686	17,747	16,280
Georgia	28,583	28,449	11,695	10,995	115,211	111,249	3,446	3,313	2,334	2,401	12,945	12,549
Hawaii	2,306	2,116	2,425	2,272	16,685	15,952	253	233	215	210	954	848
Idaho.	4,881	4,275	1,354	1,279	19,564	17,416	505	447	442	410	2,463	2,128
Illinois	35,026	34,848	17,456	16,550	162,211	153,674	4,167	3,918	4,054	4,052	13,950	13,157
Indiana	18,839	18,699	7,527	7,097	79,750	76,635	1,726	1,688	1,584	1,510	8,049	7,526
Iowa	9,436	9,502	3,013	2,850	40,101	38,721	943	884	920	896	5,254	5,001
Kansas	8,615	8,726	2,952	2,848	37,215	36,512	982	954	994	1,042	3,512	3,296
Kentucky	10,182	9,874	5,174	4,824	46,500	44,343	860	812	661	642	4,835	4,468
Louisiana	12,409	12,140	5,425	5,079	52,810	50,074	1,074	979	744	680	4,835	4,460
Maine	4,138	4,074	1,547	1,432	20,547	19,559	368	351	229	233	1,967	1,833
Maryland	17,301	16,394	7,308	6,724	76,380	70,943	2,165	1,961	2,253	2,204	6,545	5,735
Massachusetts	20,257	19,887	11,428	10,738	94,893	91,025	2,274	2,139	1,812	1,821	7,592	7,108
Michigan	33,550	33,013	12,382	11,676	135,626	131,501	3,501	3,414	2,783	2,881	11,169	10,663
Minnesota	17,209	17,059	6,805	6,392	80,931	77,438	2,607	2,381	2,197	2,183	9,594	9,022
Mississippi	7,499	7,439	2,692	2,458	30,884	29,355	822	748	426	402	3,260	3,057
Missouri.	17,963	17,765	7,359	6,887	76,046	71,787	1,704	1,601	1,494	1,442	6,778	6,358
Montana	2,280	2,174	1,147	1,070	10,723	9,921	235	207	187	176	1,358	1,215
Nebraska	4,802	4,773	2,077	1,961	23,563	22,420	1,090	1,036	437	450	2,819	2,598
Nevada	6,762	6,477	4,125	3,736	33,846	31,338	1,064	890	787	781	2,871	2,702
New Hampshire.	7,184	6,967	1,937	1,793	27,265	25,535	707	628	876	815	2,142	1,919
New Jersey	29,067	27,829	10,793	9,655	126,940	118,760	4,232	3,892	3,696	3,539	9,324	8,365
New Mexico	4,883	4,733	2,182	2,022	23,040	21,818	635	605	393	394	1,802	1,639
New York	44,139	42,587	24,236	22,450	229,401	218,324	6,255	6,055	5,602	5,780	18,477	16,897
North Carolina.	25,471	25,456	10,715	10,066	104,764	101,778	3,516	3,378	2,062	2,154	11,885	11,368
North Dakota	1,855	1,865	723	674	9,097	8,759	219	204	187	187	1,719	1,604
Ohio	35,807	35,401	14,786	13,983	154,089	147,920	4,081	3,868	3,912	3,982	13,955	13,213
Oklahoma	11,229	10,971	4,077	3,830	42,369	40,657	922	873	1,019	995	3,196	2,902
Oregon	11,312	11,073	4,734	4,524	49,091	47,148	1,161	1,130	1,057	1,016	5,150	4,767
Pennsylvania	35,614	35,624	15,121	14,212	155,423	149,811	3,544	3,349	2,780	2,781	12,925	12,338
Rhode Island	2,547	2,397	1,921	1,755	12,911	11,687	311	276	239	219	824	692
South Carolina	11,995	11,431	5,375	4,972	51,079	48,208	1,202	1,161	710	726	6,204	5,834
South Dakota	2,379	2,466	917	856	16,433	15,579	218	208	174	179	1,476	1,434
Tennessee	19,586	19,075	7,653	7,111	81,572	77,277	2,033	1,875	1,283	1,247	7,066	6,545
Texas	82,487	81,868	30,236	28,487	319,203	303,468	8,650	8,141	9,148	9,036	25,172	22,842
Utah	7,122	6,882	2,398	2,234	29,708	28,368	1,015	987	876	834	3,464	3,292
Vermont.	2,104	2,050	730	681	8,905	8,394	190	173	186	177	1,045	964
Virginia	22,821	21,741	9,022	8,480	101,475	94,674	3,436	3,067	3,548	3,060	9,889	9,160
Washington	16,493	16,180	9,226	8,807	84,161	80,394	2,106	1,983	1,906	1,911	8,671	8,167
West Virginia	4,561	4,419	1,750	1,642	19,875	18,930	343	315	204	201	1,828	1,677
Wisconsin.	17,837	17,940	6,400	6,005	80,444	77,365	1,931	1,803	1,864	1,787	9,522	9,327
Wyoming	1,626	1,578	618	556	7,727	7,141	135	126	100	89	736	634

See footnotes at end of table.

Table A-63. States — **Retail Sales**—Con.

Geographic area	Health and personal care (NAICS 446) (mil. dol.)		Gasoline stations (NAICS 447) (mil. dol.)		Clothing and clothing accessories (NAICS 448) (mil. dol.)		Sporting goods, hobby, book and music stores (NAICS 451) (mil. dol.)		Miscellaneous stores (NAICS 453) (mil. dol.)		Nonstore retailers (NAICS 454) (mil. dol.)	
	2004	2003	2004	2003	2004	2003	2004	2003	2004	2003	2004	2003
United States . . .	215,424	198,080	249,258	228,063	184,752	179,674	81,733	93,052	99,566	113,481	196,938	228,063
Alabama	2,745	2,454	4,232	3,859	2,086	1,986	771	836	1,323	1,452	1,082	3,859
Alaska	133	118	503	451	353	348	192	212	192	212	374	451
Arizona	3,887	3,591	5,438	5,048	2,493	2,368	1,561	1,773	2,715	3,019	3,802	5,048
Arkansas	1,305	1,196	2,794	2,659	1,107	1,079	495	566	829	924	708	2,659
California	27,118	24,860	27,174	23,963	25,284	24,650	11,937	13,897	12,122	13,954	13,146	23,963
Colorado	2,021	1,825	4,097	3,801	2,562	2,568	2,183	2,532	2,082	2,375	2,733	3,801
Connecticut	3,299	3,063	2,481	2,277	2,846	2,877	1,204	1,373	1,240	1,403	5,426	2,277
Delaware	812	805	591	531	681	643	361	407	378	404	514	531
District of Columbia	417	372	234	216	390	364	167	210	136	169	66	216
Florida	14,234	13,271	12,323	11,499	11,736	11,415	4,037	4,712	5,734	6,616	9,733	11,499
Georgia	4,688	4,230	9,024	8,310	5,095	4,860	1,815	2,016	2,761	3,139	2,672	8,310
Hawaii	1,245	1,154	1,029	918	1,584	1,629	357	412	561	681	134	918
Idaho	557	461	1,289	1,087	532	477	514	530	560	604	1,127	1,087
Illinois	11,044	9,880	8,719	7,829	8,824	8,792	3,019	3,419	3,574	4,004	11,155	7,829
Indiana	4,489	4,119	5,970	5,608	2,468	2,416	1,231	1,384	1,708	1,982	5,242	5,608
Iowa	1,956	1,794	4,007	3,689	1,238	1,239	661	754	769	876	1,334	3,689
Kansas	1,534	1,411	2,900	2,751	1,563	1,579	775	852	915	1,055	819	2,751
Kentucky	2,765	2,532	4,286	3,953	1,456	1,438	689	769	1,340	1,531	978	3,953
Louisiana	3,106	2,806	4,646	4,298	2,150	2,101	745	837	1,180	1,321	927	4,298
Maine	756	688	1,540	1,380	809	790	370	429	465	528	2,497	1,380
Maryland	4,287	3,988	4,049	3,606	4,398	4,314	2,033	2,218	1,860	2,061	2,321	3,606
Massachusetts	5,702	5,351	4,683	4,295	5,663	5,688	2,351	2,677	2,341	2,759	6,747	4,295
Michigan	10,038	9,254	7,465	6,855	5,245	5,139	3,697	4,272	4,299	5,041	3,891	6,855
Minnesota	3,494	3,157	5,847	5,489	2,792	2,815	2,170	2,508	2,003	2,279	7,080	5,489
Mississippi	1,534	1,376	2,992	2,781	1,012	954	338	385	720	829	564	2,781
Missouri	3,592	3,207	6,875	6,277	2,457	2,314	1,406	1,497	1,930	2,165	4,337	6,277
Montana	312	275	749	686	273	258	292	314	262	281	234	686
Nebraska	1,040	941	1,792	1,630	863	857	391	450	421	472	1,895	1,630
Nevada	1,456	1,320	1,759	1,608	2,260	2,148	639	719	1,366	1,494	2,724	1,608
New Hampshire	1,014	915	1,420	1,270	1,091	1,049	676	731	588	663	2,635	1,270
New Jersey	9,965	9,213	5,462	4,920	7,484	7,180	3,512	3,934	3,143	3,550	8,535	4,920
New Mexico	1,129	1,022	1,944	1,749	855	794	514	575	1,101	1,261	1,329	1,749
New York	18,133	16,921	10,471	9,526	20,293	19,450	5,868	6,788	7,154	8,279	11,948	9,526
North Carolina	5,228	4,885	7,220	6,733	4,310	4,336	1,609	1,839	3,251	3,788	3,366	6,733
North Dakota	498	452	660	626	242	233	248	274	203	238	424	626
Ohio	10,483	9,851	9,720	8,731	6,089	5,964	2,719	3,008	3,299	3,718	7,719	8,731
Oklahoma	2,170	1,929	3,833	3,592	1,060	1,046	763	862	1,089	1,251	987	3,592
Oregon	1,407	1,317	2,465	2,350	1,703	1,661	1,241	1,450	1,514	1,752	2,550	2,350
Pennsylvania	10,891	10,216	8,919	8,449	7,648	7,454	2,817	3,244	3,118	3,554	13,484	8,449
Rhode Island	1,161	1,061	702	614	683	636	271	303	283	297	921	614
South Carolina	2,332	2,011	4,332	3,857	2,280	2,153	628	702	1,562	1,767	782	3,857
South Dakota	409	393	916	874	302	304	210	242	235	298	6,446	874
Tennessee	4,127	3,514	6,251	5,718	3,664	3,564	1,324	1,454	2,034	2,293	1,680	5,718
Texas	12,671	11,452	21,918	20,070	14,367	13,651	5,830	6,658	7,862	8,836	19,816	20,070
Utah	460	426	1,952	1,843	1,151	1,098	775	906	504	538	1,222	1,843
Vermont	404	375	711	633	309	301	203	229	190	222	837	633
Virginia	4,384	4,084	7,894	7,137	4,890	4,679	2,072	2,238	2,051	2,270	4,873	7,137
Washington	3,720	3,591	4,094	3,808	3,043	2,998	2,317	2,660	2,538	2,916	5,500	3,808
West Virginia	1,685	1,563	1,888	1,714	712	676	268	304	456	520	391	1,714
Wisconsin	3,446	3,257	5,913	5,499	2,176	2,175	1,326	1,539	1,386	1,609	6,881	5,499
Wyoming	143	134	1,084	999	179	167	137	152	217	234	351	999

[1]Includes other types of stores, not shown separately.

Survey, Census, or Data Collection Method: For information, see Internet site <http://www.claritas.com/>.

Source: Market Statistics, a division of Claritas Inc., Arlington, VA, *The Survey of Buying Power Data Service*, annual (copyright).

Table A-64. States — **Transportation and Warehousing**

Geographic area	Transportation and warehousing[1] Nonfarm employment (BLS)[2] (1,000)			Earnings (BEA)[3] (mil. dol.)			Establishments		Vehicle miles of travel (bil.)		Commodity shipments (bil. ton-miles)		Railroad shipments[4] (1,000 tons)		Waterborne shipments[5] (1,000 short tons)	
	2004	2003	2000	2004	2003	2001	2002	Net change, 2000–2002	2003	2001	2002	1997	2002	2001	2002	2001
United States . . .	[6]4,250	[6]4,185	[6]4,410	244,582	231,926	235,477	195,143	5,099	2,890	2,796	3,138	2,593	1,876,993	1,898,840	[7]2,340,292	[7]2,386,558
Alabama	52	52	53	2,817	2,645	2,599	2,984	−121	59	57	61	44	43,208	42,311	66,888	68,244
Alaska	19	19	19	1,270	1,187	1,197	1,048	70	5	5	8	7	7,451	7,784	67,479	67,238
Arizona	66	65	64	3,836	3,524	3,311	2,698	115	54	50	16	17	5,167	5,926	(X)	(X)
Arkansas	[8]65	[8]66	[8]64	2,931	2,810	2,699	2,437	−2	31	29	38	31	20,517	20,562	13,166	11,639
California	426	425	461	27,100	25,575	26,013	18,455	957	324	311	167	131	54,718	57,610	190,093	186,480
Colorado	66	65	66	3,719	3,568	3,748	2,969	121	43	43	61	47	37,327	36,163	(X)	(X)
Connecticut	41	40	42	2,203	2,068	1,974	1,603	35	31	31	5	12	1,896	1,703	17,610	18,267
Delaware	11	11	12	559	474	485	679	29	9	9	4	4	1,263	1,588	38,603	37,192
District of Columbia	3	4	5	379	384	(D)	207	3	4	4	(Z)	(Z)	126	145	557	663
Florida	205	203	218	11,448	10,881	10,977	11,131	526	186	171	61	55	65,127	64,414	122,516	121,765
Georgia	158	154	162	9,633	9,175	9,184	5,313	72	109	108	68	61	36,259	34,410	23,258	22,023
Hawaii	25	24	26	1,290	1,206	1,239	752	36	9	9	(S)	1	–	–	22,637	23,113
Idaho	17	17	17	839	787	774	1,451	63	14	14	21	14	10,519	10,416	999	1,335
Illinois	231	230	245	13,472	12,818	13,081	9,646	324	107	103	167	145	116,462	119,525	120,349	122,739
Indiana	111	107	116	5,419	5,158	5,115	4,732	195	73	72	83	57	53,174	55,818	71,522	71,013
Iowa	50	49	49	2,606	2,410	2,280	3,439	181	31	30	108	57	43,270	43,044	16,745	14,347
Kansas	45	45	48	2,453	2,353	2,281	2,461	−13	29	28	45	47	21,960	23,312	1,726	2,339
Kentucky	81	80	90	4,769	4,505	4,301	2,980	−41	47	46	100	101	103,604	109,670	100,082	101,101
Louisiana	[8]81	[8]82	[8]81	4,149	4,011	4,044	3,570	−138	44	43	131	115	38,240	36,990	484,927	496,218
Maine	15	15	15	721	683	664	1,279	−30	15	14	11	8	4,037	4,073	29,140	30,586
Maryland	69	67	69	3,588	3,295	3,253	3,492	220	55	52	15	10	7,741	7,716	47,289	49,903
Massachusetts	73	74	82	3,898	3,822	3,906	3,511	100	54	53	14	13	2,599	2,582	26,117	26,446
Michigan	104	105	[8]135	6,930	6,687	6,733	5,157	−4	101	99	69	70	36,416	32,875	73,778	76,617
Minnesota	81	80	91	5,072	4,864	5,045	4,287	257	55	53	154	121	69,156	74,389	47,834	44,031
Mississippi	39	38	37	1,846	1,757	1,682	2,218	−53	37	36	38	28	13,959	12,851	47,735	46,261
Missouri	90	92	[8]122	5,150	5,179	5,104	4,913	−19	68	68	73	49	18,224	19,632	30,043	34,705
Montana	13	13	14	704	672	658	1,128	11	11	10	62	67	37,179	38,739	(X)	(X)
Nebraska	47	45	43	2,897	2,727	2,853	2,230	110	19	18	33	48	23,068	24,176	219	178
Nevada	38	37	37	1,884	1,719	1,585	1,086	90	19	18	9	5	2,789	2,915	(X)	(X)
New Hampshire.	13	13	14	623	601	584	811	23	13	12	5	5	762	1,364	4,108	4,447
New Jersey	161	163	177	9,211	8,784	8,696	6,961	189	70	69	41	35	10,843	10,939	110,120	93,834
New Mexico	19	19	19	1,010	927	891	1,151	1	23	23	10	16	15,672	16,332	(X)	(X)
New York	224	223	239	12,202	11,704	11,779	11,316	474	135	131	55	40	10,357	10,042	88,059	103,253
North Carolina.	113	111	120	5,714	5,439	5,748	5,372	−36	94	92	47	45	13,399	13,707	9,674	10,667
North Dakota	10	10	8	596	558	533	999	66	7	7	21	28	21,638	21,730	(X)	(X)
Ohio	164	162	172	8,979	8,551	8,355	7,151	274	109	107	127	102	62,925	61,036	119,362	119,539
Oklahoma	42	43	47	2,706	2,545	2,985	2,376	116	46	44	27	24	21,510	20,299	4,440	4,133
Oregon	52	51	52	2,714	2,539	2,511	2,756	25	35	34	49	39	15,346	16,044	31,681	35,830
Pennsylvania	198	197	195	11,098	10,480	10,485	7,239	350	106	103	90	76	61,729	59,816	115,316	125,090
Rhode Island	10	10	10	444	439	(D)	619	17	8	8	3	1	209	157	8,437	9,170
South Carolina	49	49	52	2,365	2,254	2,176	2,355	14	48	47	32	22	15,162	15,251	26,508	24,668
South Dakota	9	10	10	513	486	489	1,031	10	9	9	18	17	7,891	10,326	(X)	(X)
Tennessee	136	135	135	7,954	7,551	7,115	4,304	12	69	68	54	40	19,570	19,200	46,174	46,733
Texas	349	340	356	24,821	23,105	26,844	14,175	96	223	216	230	205	112,756	108,589	442,251	454,765
Utah	41	40	44	2,266	2,128	2,106	1,513	104	24	23	38	38	23,253	26,534	(X)	(X)
Vermont.	7	7	7	329	316	303	528	−8	8	8	3	2	764	1,289	(X)	(X)
Virginia	107	107	115	5,614	5,373	5,393	4,884	112	77	74	44	48	48,137	54,337	47,494	61,840
Washington	85	84	91	5,323	4,987	4,895	4,302	74	55	54	47	50	21,799	21,263	100,894	104,975
West Virginia	19	19	20	1,106	1,053	1,055	1,445	−57	20	20	78	71	119,227	127,283	80,120	79,450
Wisconsin	96	94	92	4,777	4,578	4,382	5,288	68	60	57	71	47	18,612	16,453	42,464	37,438
Wyoming	10	10	10	634	585	(D)	711	81	9	9	421	276	379,977	375,511	(X)	(X)

– Represents zero.   D Figure withheld to avoid disclosure.   S Withheld due to high sampling variability or poor response quality.   X Not applicable.   Z Less than 500 mil. ton-miles.

[1] Covers Transportation and warehousing (NAICS 48, 49).
[2] Bureau of Labor Statistics.
[3] Bureau of Economic Analysis.
[4] Rail shipments of all commodities originating in state.
[5] Includes domestic and foreign shipments terminating and originating in state and intrastate shipments. U.S. and state totals exclude duplication.
[6] United States totals differ from the sum of the state figures because of differing benchmarks among states and differing industrial and geographic stratification.
[7] Includes Guam, the Virgin Islands, the Pacific Islands, Puerto Rico, other territories, and trans-shipments.
[8] Figure includes Transportation and warehousing (NAICS 48, 49) and Utilities (NAICS 22).

Survey, Census, or Data Collection Method: Employment—Based on Current Employment Statistics (CES) survey; for information, see Appendix B, Limitations of the Data and Methodology, and Internet site <http://www.bls.gov/opub/hom/homch2_a.htm>;   Earnings—Based on the Regional Economic Information System; for information, see Internet site <http://www.bea.gov/bea/regional/articles/spi2003/>;   Establishments—Based on tabulations of data extracted from the U.S. Census Bureau's Business Register; for information, see Internet site <http://www.census.gov/epcd/cbp/view/cbpview.html>;   Vehicle miles of travel—Based on the Highway Performance Monitoring System (HPMS); for information, see Internet site <http://www.bts.gov/>;   Commodity shipments—Based on the Commodity Flow Survey; for information, see Appendix B, Limitations of the Data and Methodology, and Internet site <http://www.census.gov/econ/www/cfsnew.html>;   Railroad shipments—Based on the Association of American Railroads (AAR) database; for information, see Internet site <http://www.bts.gov/>;   Waterborne shipments—Based on the U.S. Army Corps of Engineers' (Corps) Navigation Data Center (NDC) database; for information, see Internet site <http://www.bts.gov/>.

Sources: Employment—U.S. Bureau of Labor Statistics, Current Employment Statistics Program, see Internet site <http://www.bls.gov/sae/home.htm>;   Earnings—U.S. Bureau of Economic Analysis, *Survey of Current Business*, April 2005, see Internet site <http://www.bea.gov/bea/regional/spi/>;   Establishments—U.S. Census Bureau, *County Business Patterns*, annual, see Internet site <http://www.census.gov/epcd/cbp/view/cbpview.html>;   Vehicle miles of travel—U.S. Federal Highway Administration, *Highway Statistics*, annual, see Internet site <http://www.fhwa.dot.gov/policy/ohpi/hss/hsspubs.htm>;   Commodity shipments—U.S. Bureau of Transportation Statistics and U.S. Census Bureau, 2002 Economic Census, *Transportation, Commodity Flow Survey*, Individual State Reports, issued December 2004, see Internet site <http://www.census.gov/econ/www/cfsnew.html>. Data for the District of Columbia are on the CD-ROM;   Railroad and waterborne shipments—U.S. Bureau of Transportation Statistics, *State Transportation Statistics 2004* and previous years, see Internet site <http://www.bts.gov/>.

Geographic area	All trucks[1] 2002 (1,000)	1997 (1,000)	Percent change, 1997–2002	Pick-ups 2002 (1,000)	1997 (1,000)	Percent change, 1997–2002	SUVs[2] 2002 (1,000)	1997 (1,000)	Percent change, 1997–2002	Minivans 2002 (1,000)	1997 (1,000)	Percent change, 1997–2002	Commodity transportation, 2002 Shipments Value (mil. dol.)	Weight (1,000 tons)	Percent going out of state Value	Weight
United States . . .	85,174.8	72,800.3	17.0	37,991.1	36,191.8	5.0	24,204.4	15,533.1	55.8	12,207.3	9,837.9	24.1	8,397,210	11,667,919	(X)	(X)
Alabama	1,720.7	1,538.6	11.8	957.1	943.2	1.5	450.2	251.1	79.3	131.0	116.1	12.8	127,727	216,383	68.4	43.3
Alaska	274.2	248.4	10.4	139.9	138.6	1.0	86.4	64.1	34.7	24.1	16.1	49.4	8,032	36,498	10.9	3.9
Arizona	1,500.1	1,390.0	7.9	740.6	784.8	−5.6	374.9	333.2	12.5	171.3	96.1	78.3	111,273	100,872	55.9	20.4
Arkansas	996.9	899.2	10.9	605.4	627.6	−3.5	222.7	127.8	74.2	91.9	77.5	18.5	91,967	120,127	76.0	50.9
California	9,245.6	8,818.8	4.8	4,100.8	4,367.3	−6.1	2,750.3	1,982.5	38.7	1,434.6	1,277.0	12.3	923,669	903,954	39.6	9.0
Colorado	1,677.4	1,422.0	18.0	736.3	697.9	5.5	634.6	422.8	50.1	136.4	135.3	0.9	93,184	150,476	54.1	40.3
Connecticut	797.2	751.5	6.1	250.4	277.8	−9.9	313.6	264.7	18.5	125.5	102.9	22.0	82,477	48,894	75.3	26.5
Delaware	248.6	206.3	20.5	90.8	86.0	5.6	80.7	53.9	49.6	43.9	34.5	27.4	20,348	30,988	76.6	43.5
District of Columbia	42.6	33.0	29.1	6.6	7.5	−12.2	21.6	11.9	81.2	8.4	6.3	31.9	3,707	1,407	84.1	(S)
Florida	4,329.3	3,460.2	25.1	1,723.4	1,498.2	15.0	1,109.4	808.3	37.3	780.2	597.4	30.6	296,989	455,084	34.4	9.7
Georgia	2,733.2	2,258.4	21.0	1,349.3	1,235.4	9.2	892.4	416.5	114.3	205.3	272.8	−24.7	270,703	339,846	63.6	29.3
Hawaii	351.4	294.2	19.4	157.9	144.2	9.5	108.5	64.4	68.7	53.2	51.0	4.3	13,480	23,659	5.1	5.2
Idaho	666.4	550.6	21.0	356.9	336.8	6.0	142.7	112.6	26.7	53.5	36.9	45.0	28,471	34,971	67.0	53.4
Illinois	3,277.2	2,674.6	22.5	1,026.2	1,039.6	−1.3	882.1	521.0	69.3	823.2	524.4	57.0	442,130	718,351	62.7	37.7
Indiana	2,222.2	1,852.5	20.0	1,016.5	943.1	7.8	560.9	275.8	103.4	322.8	301.6	7.0	291,458	397,829	71.6	36.6
Iowa	1,165.6	979.3	19.0	600.1	530.4	13.1	271.2	137.6	97.1	153.6	116.5	31.9	115,396	232,544	74.5	48.5
Kansas	1,079.1	1,082.6	−0.3	562.3	595.5	−5.6	226.4	174.5	29.7	108.0	123.3	−12.4	95,285	192,854	72.8	33.8
Kentucky	1,355.4	1,348.0	0.5	737.7	800.6	−7.9	296.6	205.0	44.7	142.9	136.2	4.9	189,390	336,341	78.0	57.6
Louisiana	1,441.3	1,210.1	19.1	805.0	735.0	9.5	332.0	177.2	87.3	152.4	146.9	3.7	139,843	495,703	45.5	30.4
Maine	390.0	377.6	3.3	199.3	208.9	−4.6	91.8	77.3	18.7	56.9	44.8	26.9	32,355	32,121	67.8	44.8
Maryland	1,375.7	1,192.0	15.4	473.0	471.9	0.2	463.3	290.8	59.3	260.3	215.2	20.9	121,356	165,399	61.9	33.2
Massachusetts	1,530.7	1,240.8	23.4	462.7	430.5	7.5	579.9	401.5	44.4	277.2	226.6	22.3	200,813	75,123	71.0	30.8
Michigan	3,581.3	2,734.5	31.0	1,445.2	1,176.0	22.9	1,106.7	645.5	71.5	624.6	513.1	21.7	388,571	331,190	51.2	29.6
Minnesota	1,698.4	1,461.9	16.2	732.6	688.8	6.4	493.6	276.1	78.8	260.5	260.0	0.2	166,430	336,237	58.5	43.2
Mississippi	741.1	813.0	−8.8	471.3	553.2	−14.8	155.8	107.3	45.2	43.8	65.1	−32.7	94,897	98,720	76.8	53.4
Missouri	1,739.5	1,626.7	6.9	934.5	894.2	4.5	380.8	315.8	20.6	221.5	177.1	25.1	185,392	254,827	69.4	49.6
Montana	473.5	417.2	13.5	286.0	259.4	10.2	95.7	71.5	33.8	32.2	27.3	17.8	12,447	89,547	43.5	58.6
Nebraska	717.0	639.7	12.1	353.8	343.0	3.1	154.2	98.8	56.0	93.5	62.0	50.9	61,797	101,684	66.4	33.5
Nevada	646.5	539.7	19.8	307.6	283.8	8.4	212.0	149.8	41.6	62.8	43.8	43.3	40,756	44,210	70.7	28.7
New Hampshire	403.2	416.6	−3.2	173.0	194.1	−10.9	124.0	105.9	17.1	62.7	57.4	9.2	31,191	33,751	83.1	33.5
New Jersey	2,122.3	1,514.3	40.2	493.3	393.4	25.4	912.6	530.7	72.0	385.1	292.7	31.6	286,580	237,847	72.8	37.6
New Mexico	741.9	715.9	3.6	418.5	432.0	−3.1	200.7	126.2	59.0	63.7	64.5	−1.3	14,907	48,841	51.2	37.0
New York	3,527.6	2,863.9	23.2	937.4	952.3	−1.6	1,296.8	881.1	47.2	776.6	521.6	48.9	318,775	249,551	61.2	33.8
North Carolina	2,528.3	1,996.1	26.7	1,193.4	1,036.7	15.1	688.7	398.1	73.0	278.1	255.9	8.7	293,604	276,004	60.6	25.6
North Dakota	377.0	340.9	10.6	197.4	184.0	7.2	72.6	49.3	47.1	41.0	24.3	68.9	18,921	88,302	55.7	26.8
Ohio	3,499.3	2,985.1	17.2	1,431.7	1,362.5	5.1	881.7	476.9	84.9	610.3	530.1	15.1	494,278	546,095	65.8	38.8
Oklahoma	1,484.6	1,373.5	8.1	751.1	802.9	−6.4	260.8	168.5	54.8	117.7	127.0	−7.3	77,576	136,033	67.2	34.0
Oregon	1,476.5	1,411.7	4.6	775.1	777.7	−0.3	374.9	276.7	35.5	191.9	156.8	22.4	102,600	158,053	59.8	26.4
Pennsylvania	3,088.7	2,605.9	18.5	1,207.8	1,074.7	12.4	957.2	682.0	40.3	563.4	428.7	31.4	354,399	399,764	66.8	41.5
Rhode Island	216.7	190.7	13.6	81.6	73.7	10.7	55.6	56.8	−2.2	41.6	28.9	43.8	21,035	19,389	83.8	51.0
South Carolina	1,173.3	1,140.7	2.9	582.5	643.1	−9.4	303.2	208.3	45.6	156.4	120.1	30.2	143,194	142,708	71.4	37.9
South Dakota	346.6	361.5	−4.1	187.4	202.9	−7.6	73.7	57.7	27.8	36.6	38.7	−5.6	26,430	52,286	72.8	45.3
Tennessee	2,030.5	1,502.4	35.2	1,055.5	851.0	24.0	581.2	231.7	150.8	179.1	148.6	20.5	286,576	270,265	79.6	41.2
Texas	6,412.0	4,410.6	45.4	3,326.7	2,578.9	29.0	1,782.2	906.5	96.6	693.8	383.5	80.9	589,064	1,082,596	37.9	15.4
Utah	723.0	563.7	28.3	336.1	284.6	18.1	240.5	146.6	64.0	81.1	58.4	38.9	61,515	109,672	58.1	43.3
Vermont	244.1	194.5	25.5	114.8	102.6	12.0	67.7	38.9	74.1	36.1	25.2	43.4	16,238	16,218	74.2	36.5
Virginia	1,983.9	1,891.6	4.9	818.0	938.4	−12.8	621.8	429.3	44.9	290.6	229.5	26.6	164,557	268,935	57.1	31.3
Washington	1,923.1	1,903.5	1.0	933.3	1,026.1	−9.0	520.9	438.0	18.9	282.0	207.3	36.0	177,395	259,594	31.1	23.4
West Virginia	665.3	446.0	49.2	362.6	262.6	38.1	158.9	86.9	82.9	60.0	36.5	64.4	38,479	275,583	75.5	66.5
Wisconsin	1,907.6	1,618.5	17.9	817.5	742.3	10.1	477.5	341.0	40.0	346.9	282.7	22.7	217,451	229,502	65.8	44.0
Wyoming	281.2	291.3	−3.5	167.1	175.9	−5.0	60.0	56.7	5.8	17.3	15.6	10.8	12,106	401,092	62.3	87.4

S Estimate does not meet publication standards.   X Not applicable.

[1]Includes other truck types not shown separately.
[2]Sport utility vehicles.

Survey, Census, or Data Collection Method: Trucks, pick-ups, SUVs, and minivans—Based on the 2002 and 1997 Vehicle Inventory and Use Surveys; for information, see Appendix B, Limitations of the Data and Methodology, and Internet site <http://www.census.gov/svsd/www/methods.html>;   Commodity transportation—Based on the 2002 Commodity Flow Survey; for information, see Appendix B, Limitations of the Data and Methodology, and Internet site <http://www.census.gov/econ/www/cfsnew.html>.

Sources: Trucks, pick-ups, SUVs, and minivans—U.S. Census Bureau, 2002 Economic Census, *Vehicle Inventory and Use Survey, Geographic Area Series*, issued December 2004, see Internet site <http://www.census.gov/svsd/www/vius/products.html>;   Commodity transportation—U.S. Bureau of Transportation Statistics and U.S. Census Bureau, 2002 Economic Census, *Transportation, Commodity Flow Survey*, issued December 2004, see Internet site <http://www.census.gov/econ/www/cfsnew.html>. Data for the District of Columbia are on the CD-ROM.

Motor Vehicle Registrations, Motorcycle Registrations, Highway Mileage, Bridges, and Driver's Licenses

Geographic area	Motor vehicle registrations						Motorcycle registrations (1,000)	
	2003				2000		2003	2000
	Number (1,000)			Rate per 1,000 persons[1]	Number (1,000)	Rate per 1,000 persons[1]		
	Total[2]	Automobile	Trucks					
United States . . .	**231,390**	**135,670**	**94,944**	**795.7**	**221,475**	**787.0**	**5,328**	**4,304**
Alabama	4,329	1,771	2,549	961.3	3,960	890.5	70	54
Alaska	637	261	373	982.3	594	948.1	20	16
Arizona	3,574	1,992	1,577	640.6	3,795	739.6	208	164
Arkansas	1,889	955	926	692.3	1,840	688.3	38	25
California	30,248	18,699	11,496	853.0	27,698	817.7	547	434
Colorado	2,027	888	1,134	445.8	3,626	842.9	8	98
Connecticut	2,964	2,041	3912	849.9	2,853	837.9	63	54
Delaware	687	419	266	839.5	630	804.6	15	11
District of Columbia	228	184	41	409.5	242	423.2	1	1
Florida	14,526	8,564	5,915	854.5	11,781	737.1	386	249
Georgia	7,730	4,192	3,519	891.0	7,155	874.0	118	87
Hawaii	903	525	373	723.0	738	608.8	22	20
Idaho	1,301	554	743	951.8	1,178	910.2	44	42
Illinois	9,250	5,769	3,464	731.3	8,973	722.5	261	195
Indiana	5,739	3,252	2,458	925.8	5,571	916.2	144	117
Iowa	3,369	1,883	1,477	1,145.1	3,106	1,061.5	140	126
Kansas	2,314	834	1,477	849.4	2,296	854.0	56	50
Kentucky	3,389	1,959	1,416	822.9	2,826	699.2	51	44
Louisiana	3,714	1,997	1,695	826.4	3,557	795.9	57	48
Maine	1,052	619	430	803.3	1,024	803.3	35	29
Maryland	3,877	2,479	1,386	703.3	3,848	726.4	64	49
Massachusetts	5,479	3,615	1,853	853.4	5,265	829.3	130	107
Michigan	8,540	4,805	3,709	847.1	8,436	848.8	214	182
Minnesota	4,525	2,502	2,007	893.6	4,630	941.1	174	143
Mississippi	1,951	1,139	803	676.8	2,289	804.8	27	32
Missouri	4,460	2,600	1,848	779.8	4,580	818.3	74	61
Montana	1,010	437	571	1,100.6	1,026	1,137.5	66	26
Nebraska	1,677	855	815	965.3	1,619	946.0	27	21
Nevada	1,222	624	596	544.9	1,220	610.4	37	24
New Hampshire	1,145	656	3487	888.5	1,052	851.1	60	49
New Jersey	6,712	4,449	32,240	776.6	6,390	759.4	140	111
New Mexico	1,509	694	812	803.5	1,529	840.3	32	28
New York	10,802	8,313	32,428	562.2	10,235	539.3	150	106
North Carolina	6,119	3,654	2,433	726.6	6,223	773.3	95	82
North Dakota	694	346	346	1,096.1	694	1,080.4	19	17
Ohio	10,536	6,519	3,977	921.2	10,467	922.0	285	254
Oklahoma	3,074	1,623	1,433	876.6	3,014	873.6	72	57
Oregon	3,061	1,545	1,501	858.7	3,022	883.1	75	69
Pennsylvania	9,724	6,121	33,567	786.1	9,260	754.0	268	215
Rhode Island	806	549	3255	748.8	760	724.6	25	19
South Carolina	3,162	1,915	1,230	762.1	3,095	771.4	57	51
South Dakota	827	388	436	1,081.1	793	1,049.9	38	29
Tennessee	4,796	2,782	1,996	820.4	4,820	847.2	94	71
Texas	14,889	7,842	6,963	673.6	14,070	674.8	258	182
Utah	2,006	1,014	991	853.0	1,628	728.8	38	28
Vermont	516	272	242	833.3	515	845.7	26	22
Virginia	6,346	4,044	2,284	861.6	6,046	854.1	73	60
Washington	5,379	2,969	2,400	877.3	5,116	868.0	141	118
West Virginia	1,409	756	649	777.7	1,442	797.3	19	26
Wisconsin	4,647	2,578	2,055	848.9	4,366	813.9	240	179
Wyoming	620	232	385	1,234.5	586	1,186.1	28	19

See footnotes at end of table.

Geographic area	Highway mileage, 2003 (1,000)					Bridges, 2004		Driver's licenses (1,000)	
	Total	Interstate	Other arterial	Collector	Local	Number	Number deficient and obsolete	2003	2000
United States ...	3,974,107	46,508	383,392	788,926	2,745,411	591,750	157,269	196,166	190,625
Alabama	94,434	905	8,795	20,530	64,183	15,648	4,679	3,598	3,521
Alaska	14,230	1,082	1,513	2,753	8,882	1,187	353	481	465
Arizona	57,529	1,167	4,664	8,549	42,999	7,119	717	3,819	3,434
Arkansas	98,541	656	6,839	20,077	70,879	12,456	3,132	1,998	1,948
California	169,549	2,458	27,133	32,074	106,450	23,823	6,668	22,657	21,244
Colorado	86,821	956	8,191	16,586	60,809	8,182	1,387	2,975	3,107
Connecticut	21,089	346	2,785	3,037	14,685	4,167	1,363	2,660	2,653
Delaware	5,894	41	630	939	4,270	850	122	585	557
District of Columbia	1,536	13	264	152	1,085	251	157	313	348
Florida	120,375	1,471	12,162	14,194	92,078	11,469	2,118	12,906	12,853
Georgia	116,534	1,245	13,126	23,342	78,698	14,461	2,948	5,758	5,550
Hawaii	4,309	55	752	831	2,637	1,099	513	834	769
Idaho	46,927	611	3,841	10,075	32,400	4,047	730	921	884
Illinois	138,526	2,170	14,030	21,701	100,537	25,727	4,361	8,054	7,961
Indiana	94,597	1,169	7,963	22,663	62,666	18,171	4,016	4,536	3,976
Iowa	113,516	782	9,680	31,485	71,569	24,902	6,958	1,978	1,953
Kansas	135,012	874	9,197	33,364	91,444	25,525	5,900	1,987	1,908
Kentucky	77,011	763	5,850	16,040	54,293	13,500	4,104	2,800	2,694
Louisiana	60,937	904	5,246	10,132	44,621	13,362	4,324	3,120	2,759
Maine	22,693	367	2,288	5,975	14,045	2,371	843	932	920
Maryland	30,688	481	3,732	4,825	21,363	5,064	1,479	3,552	3,382
Massachusetts	35,590	569	6,188	4,836	23,709	4,954	2,546	4,646	4,490
Michigan	122,222	1,243	12,101	25,814	82,758	10,818	3,121	7,065	6,925
Minnesota	131,893	912	12,702	29,602	88,524	13,026	1,633	3,036	2,941
Mississippi	74,105	685	7,372	15,286	50,716	16,838	4,697	1,886	2,008
Missouri	124,685	1,181	9,414	24,976	88,788	23,791	8,244	3,966	3,856
Montana	69,450	1,192	6,038	16,368	45,852	5,043	1,074	705	679
Nebraska	93,198	482	8,007	20,778	63,910	15,455	3,975	1,311	1,195
Nevada	33,977	560	2,875	5,210	25,280	1,611	198	1,488	1,371
New Hampshire	15,630	235	1,609	2,789	10,960	2,357	788	968	930
New Jersey	38,952	431	5,538	3,839	28,742	6,484	2,370	5,729	5,655
New Mexico	63,953	1,000	5,028	7,234	50,686	3,839	724	1,236	1,239
New York	113,124	1,674	13,502	20,557	76,593	17,301	6,552	11,357	10,871
North Carolina	102,160	1,019	8,937	17,621	74,284	17,340	5,196	6,015	5,690
North Dakota	86,782	572	5,879	11,736	68,595	4,507	1,062	460	459
Ohio	123,522	1,574	10,868	22,518	88,078	27,907	7,102	7,656	8,206
Oklahoma	112,578	930	8,163	25,305	77,994	23,312	8,757	2,348	2,295
Oregon	65,951	728	6,818	17,503	40,849	7,261	1,848	2,590	2,495
Pennsylvania	120,423	1,758	13,194	19,802	85,153	22,253	9,404	8,370	8,229
Rhode Island	6,415	71	832	879	4,548	749	405	731	654
South Carolina	66,230	842	6,876	13,378	45,063	9,201	2,130	2,919	2,843
South Dakota	83,688	679	6,352	19,234	57,423	5,961	1,490	555	544
Tennessee	88,518	1,073	8,935	17,905	60,459	19,688	4,499	4,204	4,251
Texas	301,987	3,233	28,537	63,508	205,539	48,950	10,195	13,498	13,462
Utah	42,716	940	3,360	7,838	30,571	2,805	506	1,548	1,463
Vermont	14,359	320	1,299	3,129	9,592	2,690	954	543	506
Virginia	71,242	1,118	8,250	14,081	47,569	13,160	3,348	5,046	4,837
Washington	82,264	764	7,324	16,807	57,079	7,543	2,056	4,407	4,155
West Virginia	36,993	549	3,170	8,777	24,488	6,881	2,555	1,272	1,347
Wisconsin	113,270	745	11,870	21,408	79,009	13,611	2,339	3,766	3,770
Wyoming	27,482	913	3,673	10,884	12,007	3,033	629	378	371

[1]Based on total population residing in area; population enumerated as of April 1 for 2000; estimated as of July 1 for all other years.
[2]Includes buses not shown separately.
[3]Figure does not include farm trucks registered at a nominal fee and restricted to use in the vicinity of the owner's farm.

Survey, Census, or Data Collection Method: Registrations and driver's licenses—Based on data provided to the U.S. Federal Highway Administration by individual states; for information, see Internet sites <http://www.fhwa.dot.gov/policy/ohim/hs03/mvinfo.htm> and <http://www.fhwa.dot.gov/policy/ohim/hs03/dlinfo.htm>; Highway mileage—Based on the Highway Performance Monitoring System (HPMS); for information, see Internet site <http://www.fhwa.dot.gov/policy/ohim/hs03/misuse.htm>; Bridges—Based on the National Bridge Inventory (NBI); for information, see Internet site <http://www.fhwa.dot.gov/bridge/nbi.htm>.

Sources: Registrations, highway mileage, and driver's licenses—U.S. Federal Highway Administration, *Highway Statistics,* annual, see Internet site <http://www.fhwa.dot.gov/policy/ohpi/hss/hsspubs.htm>; Bridges—U.S. Federal Highway Administration, Office of Bridge Technology, see Internet site <http://www.fhwa.dot.gov/bridge/britab.htm>.

Traffic Fatalities and Shoulder Belt Use

Geographic area	Traffic fatalities						Persons killed in alcohol-related crashes								Percent of drivers and passengers in the front right seat using safety belts		
	Number			Fatality rate[1]					Percent of all persons killed in crashes		By highest BAC in crash[2]						
											0.01 to 0.07		0.08 or more				
	2003	2002	2000	2003	2002	2000	2003	2002	2003	2002	2003	2002	2003	2002	2004	2003	2001
United States ...	42,643	43,005	41,945	1.5	1.5	1.5	17,013	17,524	40	41	2,383	2,432	14,630	15,093	80.0	79.0	73.0
Alabama	1,001	1,038	996	1.7	1.8	1.8	415	410	41	40	40	44	376	366	80.0	77.4	79.4
Alaska	95	89	106	1.9	1.8	2.3	35	37	37	41	3	2	31	35	76.7	78.9	62.6
Arizona	1,120	1,132	1,036	2.1	2.2	2.1	470	489	42	43	63	61	408	428	95.3	86.2	74.4
Arkansas	627	640	652	2.1	2.1	2.2	254	241	41	38	51	35	203	206	64.2	62.8	54.5
California	4,215	4,088	3,753	1.3	1.3	1.2	1,626	1,628	39	40	249	302	1,378	1,326	90.4	91.2	91.1
Colorado	632	743	681	1.5	1.7	1.6	246	314	39	42	26	38	221	276	79.3	77.7	72.1
Connecticut	294	325	341	0.9	1.0	1.1	131	144	45	44	17	19	114	125	82.9	78.0	78.0
Delaware	142	124	123	1.6	1.4	1.5	60	50	42	41	9	8	51	42	82.3	74.9	67.3
District of Columbia	67	47	48	1.6	1.3	1.4	34	24	50	52	4	2	29	22	87.1	84.9	83.6
Florida	3,169	3,136	2,999	1.7	1.8	2.0	1,274	1,279	40	41	185	172	1,089	1,107	76.3	72.6	69.5
Georgia	1,603	1,524	1,541	1.5	1.4	1.5	488	533	30	35	68	88	420	445	86.7	84.5	79.0
Hawaii	135	119	132	1.5	1.3	1.5	72	47	53	39	18	7	54	39	95.1	91.8	82.5
Idaho	293	264	276	2.1	1.9	2.0	107	91	37	34	18	16	90	75	74.0	71.7	60.4
Illinois	1,453	1,420	1,418	1.4	1.4	1.4	639	653	44	46	99	96	539	556	83.0	80.1	71.4
Indiana	834	792	886	1.2	1.1	1.3	262	262	31	33	40	45	223	216	83.4	82.3	67.4
Iowa	441	405	445	1.4	1.3	1.5	145	137	33	34	26	27	119	110	86.4	86.8	80.9
Kansas	471	507	461	1.6	1.8	1.6	206	227	44	45	24	27	182	200	68.3	63.6	60.8
Kentucky	928	915	820	2.0	2.0	1.8	276	302	30	33	36	38	240	263	66.0	65.5	61.9
Louisiana	894	907	938	2.0	2.1	2.3	406	427	45	47	44	62	363	365	75.0	73.8	68.1
Maine	207	216	169	1.4	1.5	1.2	75	50	36	23	6	4	69	47	72.3	(NA)	(NA)
Maryland	649	661	588	1.2	1.2	1.2	281	276	43	42	73	54	208	223	89.0	87.9	82.9
Massachusetts	462	459	433	0.9	0.9	0.8	207	224	45	49	37	33	170	191	63.3	61.7	56.0
Michigan	1,283	1,277	1,382	1.3	1.3	1.4	481	494	37	39	86	68	395	425	90.5	84.8	82.3
Minnesota	657	657	625	1.2	1.2	1.2	267	256	41	39	36	45	231	211	82.1	79.4	73.9
Mississippi	871	885	949	2.3	2.4	2.7	320	335	37	38	32	40	288	295	63.2	62.2	61.6
Missouri	1,232	1,208	1,157	1.8	1.8	1.7	504	518	41	43	80	70	425	448	75.9	72.9	67.9
Montana	262	269	237	2.4	2.6	2.4	128	126	49	47	20	19	108	107	80.9	79.5	76.3
Nebraska	293	307	276	1.5	1.6	1.5	121	117	41	38	22	20	99	96	79.2	76.1	70.2
Nevada	368	381	323	1.9	2.1	1.8	182	165	50	43	24	22	159	143	86.6	78.7	74.5
New Hampshire	127	127	126	1.0	1.0	1.0	52	50	41	39	8	5	43	45	(NA)	49.6	(NA)
New Jersey	747	771	731	1.1	1.1	1.1	275	281	37	36	35	41	240	240	82.0	81.2	77.6
New Mexico	439	449	432	1.9	2.0	1.9	198	219	45	49	28	26	170	192	89.7	87.2	87.8
New York	1,491	1,530	1,460	1.1	1.2	1.1	529	482	35	32	71	78	458	403	85.0	84.6	80.3
North Carolina	1,531	1,576	1,557	1.6	1.7	1.7	554	592	36	38	80	66	474	527	86.1	86.1	82.7
North Dakota	105	97	86	1.4	1.3	1.2	52	49	50	50	6	8	47	40	67.4	63.7	57.9
Ohio	1,277	1,418	1,366	1.2	1.3	1.3	467	558	37	39	66	67	402	491	74.1	74.7	66.9
Oklahoma	668	739	650	1.5	1.6	1.5	255	251	38	34	35	36	220	215	80.3	76.7	67.9
Oregon	512	436	451	1.5	1.3	1.3	207	180	40	41	32	27	175	153	92.6	90.4	87.5
Pennsylvania	1,577	1,614	1,520	1.5	1.5	1.5	618	649	39	40	77	93	542	556	81.8	79.0	70.5
Rhode Island	104	84	80	1.2	1.0	1.0	57	46	55	55	5	9	52	37	76.2	74.2	63.2
South Carolina	968	1,053	1,065	2.0	2.2	2.3	488	549	50	52	64	64	423	485	65.7	72.8	69.6
South Dakota	203	180	173	2.4	2.1	2.1	98	92	48	51	8	13	90	79	69.4	69.9	63.3
Tennessee	1,193	1,177	1,307	1.7	1.7	2.0	447	485	37	41	43	73	404	412	72.0	68.5	68.3
Texas	3,675	3,823	3,779	1.6	1.7	1.7	1,709	1,810	47	47	209	201	1,500	1,610	83.2	84.3	76.1
Utah	309	328	373	1.3	1.3	1.7	46	71	15	22	8	7	39	65	85.7	85.2	77.8
Vermont	69	78	76	0.8	1.0	1.1	29	27	41	35	8	5	21	22	79.9	82.4	67.4
Virginia	943	914	929	1.2	1.2	1.2	364	379	39	41	55	52	309	327	79.9	74.6	72.3
Washington	600	658	631	1.1	1.2	1.2	259	299	43	45	31	33	228	267	94.2	94.8	82.6
West Virginia	394	439	411	2.0	2.2	2.1	148	179	37	41	22	18	126	161	75.8	73.6	52.3
Wisconsin	848	803	799	1.4	1.4	1.4	387	360	46	45	47	38	340	322	72.4	69.8	68.7
Wyoming	165	176	152	1.8	2.0	1.9	62	67	38	38	12	7	50	60	70.1	(NA)	(NA)

NA Not available.

[1] Deaths per 100 million vehicle miles traveled.
[2] BAC means blood alcohol concentration. BAC is measured in grams per deciliter (g/dl).

Survey, Census, or Data Collection Method: Traffic fatalities and persons killed in alcohol-related crashes—Based on the Fatality Analysis Reporting System (FARS); for information, see Appendix B, Limitations of the Data and Methodology, and Internet site <http://www-nrd.nhtsa.dot.gov/departments/nrd-01/summaries/FARS_98.html>; Safety belts—For states, based on surveys conducted in accordance with Section 157, Title 23, U.S. Code; For national figures, based on the National Occupant Protection Use Survey (NOPUS); for information, see Internet site <http://www.nrd.nhtsa.dot.gov/pdf/nrd-30/NCSA/RNotes/2004/809813.pdf>.

Sources: Traffic fatalities and persons killed in alcohol-related crashes—U.S. National Highway Traffic Safety Administration, *Traffic Safety Facts*, annual, see Internet site <http://www.nhtsa.dot.gov/people/Crash/Index.html>; Safety belts—U.S. Department of Transportation, National Highway Traffic Safety Administration, *Safety Belt Use in 2004—Use Rates in the States and Territories*, Washington, DC: November 2004, see Internet site <http://www-nrd.nhtsa.dot.gov/pdf/nrd-30/NCSA/RNotes/2004/809813.pdf>.

Table A-68. States — Communications

Geographic area	Percent of households with telephones		Mobile wireless telephone subscribers[1] (1,000)		Percent of— Households with computers		Households with Internet access		High-speed telecommunication lines (1,000) Total		By type of users, Dec. 2004 Residential and small business	Other[2]	Telecommunications revenue (mil. dol.) 2003 prel.	2000
	2004	1984	2004	2000	2003	1998	2003	1998	2004	2000				
United States . . .	93.8	91.6	[3]181,105	[3]101,043	61.8	42.1	54.6	26.2	[3]37,891	[3]7,070	[3]35,266	[3]2,624	288,322	290,524
Alabama	92.2	88.4	2,581	1,386	53.9	34.3	45.7	21.6	410	63	360	50	4,335	4,008
Alaska	95.6	86.5	321	(D)	72.7	62.4	67.6	44.1	110	1	101	9	816	717
Arizona	91.8	86.9	3,299	1,855	64.3	44.3	55.2	29.3	751	154	699	52	4,891	4,972
Arkansas	88.6	86.6	1,459	744	50.0	29.8	42.4	14.7	220	29	211	9	2,466	2,315
California	96.0	92.5	23,458	12,711	66.3	47.5	59.6	30.7	5,383	1,387	4,972	411	34,048	33,577
Colorado	95.8	93.2	2,808	1,856	70.0	55.3	63.0	34.5	623	105	582	40	5,005	5,290
Connecticut	95.5	95.5	2,181	1,277	69.2	43.8	62.9	31.8	603	112	581	23	3,878	3,924
Delaware	96.0	94.3	646	371	59.5	40.5	53.2	25.1	93	7	90	3	873	875
District of Columbia	91.9	94.9	658	355	64.3	41.4	56.8	24.2	115	28	92	23	1,335	1,648
Florida	93.4	88.7	13,169	6,370	61.0	39.5	55.6	27.8	2,683	461	2,438	245	18,585	18,308
Georgia	91.2	86.2	5,730	2,755	60.6	35.8	53.5	23.9	1,229	204	1,043	186	9,417	8,919
Hawaii	95.4	93.5	881	524	63.3	42.3	55.0	27.9	(D)	(D)	(D)	(D)	1,210	1,177
Idaho	94.8	90.7	706	345	69.2	50.0	56.4	27.4	126	16	123	3	1,235	1,210
Illinois	90.1	94.2	8,076	5,144	60.0	42.7	51.1	26.5	1,535	242	1,409	126	11,911	13,516
Indiana	91.8	91.6	3,158	1,715	59.6	43.5	51.0	26.1	642	60	606	35	5,284	5,552
Iowa	95.4	96.2	1,558	832	64.7	41.4	57.1	21.8	267	58	257	10	2,707	2,340
Kansas	94.8	94.3	1,454	801	63.8	43.7	54.3	25.7	387	69	373	15	2,470	2,571
Kentucky	91.4	88.1	2,189	1,026	58.1	35.9	49.6	21.1	361	33	324	37	3,611	3,573
Louisiana	90.9	89.7	2,835	1,306	52.3	31.1	44.1	17.8	486	75	445	41	4,224	3,964
Maine	96.6	93.4	663	360	67.8	43.4	57.9	26.0	143	26	138	5	1,357	1,328
Maryland	93.4	95.7	3,900	2,299	66.0	46.3	59.2	31.0	796	124	759	37	6,064	5,783
Massachusetts	96.4	95.9	4,043	2,649	64.1	43.4	58.1	28.1	1,144	289	1,096	48	6,973	7,428
Michigan	93.7	92.8	5,767	3,552	59.9	44.0	52.0	25.4	1,097	198	1,041	56	9,340	9,937
Minnesota	97.1	95.8	2,973	1,851	67.9	47.6	61.6	29.0	652	117	620	32	4,675	4,877
Mississippi	89.6	82.4	1,518	787	48.3	25.7	38.9	13.6	169	12	150	19	2,671	2,486
Missouri	93.7	91.5	3,109	1,767	60.7	41.8	53.0	24.3	591	100	543	49	5,667	5,688
Montana	93.5	91.0	(D)	(D)	59.5	40.9	50.4	21.5	73	7	69	4	909	937
Nebraska	95.7	95.7	1,046	659	66.1	42.9	55.4	22.9	217	54	205	12	1,796	1,760
Nevada	92.2	90.4	1,463	685	61.3	41.6	55.2	26.5	344	60	317	27	2,264	1,954
New Hampshire	96.4	94.3	728	387	71.5	54.2	65.2	37.1	216	42	209	7	1,371	1,429
New Jersey	95.1	94.8	7,389	3,575	65.5	48.1	60.5	31.3	1,473	285	1,391	82	10,040	10,670
New Mexico	91.4	82.0	988	443	53.9	42.2	44.5	25.8	146	28	138	8	1,703	1,515
New York	94.5	91.8	10,835	5,918	60.0	37.3	53.3	23.7	2,809	603	2,623	186	20,626	20,903
North Carolina	93.3	88.3	5,364	3,106	57.7	35.0	51.1	19.9	1,121	137	1,025	95	8,308	8,619
North Dakota	95.0	94.6	373	(D)	61.2	40.2	53.2	20.6	48	4	47	1	640	731
Ohio	94.9	92.4	6,628	4,150	58.8	40.7	52.5	24.6	1,347	231	1,249	98	10,402	10,902
Oklahoma	91.0	90.3	1,760	1,124	55.4	37.8	48.4	20.4	392	95	375	17	3,204	2,915
Oregon	95.5	90.6	2,029	1,201	67.0	51.3	61.0	32.7	511	77	490	21	3,326	3,159
Pennsylvania	95.6	94.9	7,037	4,129	60.2	39.3	54.7	24.9	1,405	177	1,329	77	12,069	12,200
Rhode Island	95.3	93.6	607	356	62.3	41.0	55.7	27.1	165	31	161	5	963	1,012
South Carolina	93.4	83.7	2,369	1,393	54.9	35.7	45.6	21.4	416	64	378	38	4,180	4,047
South Dakota	93.6	93.2	429	(D)	62.1	41.6	53.6	23.9	40	3	39	1	667	763
Tennessee	92.8	88.5	3,531	1,986	56.7	37.5	48.9	21.3	630	122	569	61	5,457	5,256
Texas	91.8	88.4	13,092	7,549	59.0	40.9	51.8	24.5	2,598	523	2,442	155	21,472	21,405
Utah	96.3	92.5	1,345	750	74.1	60.1	62.6	35.8	238	36	226	12	1,984	1,998
Vermont	95.9	92.3	(D)	(D)	65.5	48.7	58.1	31.8	72	8	70	2	628	717
Virginia	94.0	93.1	4,240	2,708	66.8	46.4	60.3	27.9	998	140	949	50	8,095	8,013
Washington	95.5	93.0	3,771	2,286	71.4	56.3	62.3	36.6	889	196	848	41	6,081	6,253
West Virginia	93.2	87.7	762	392	55.0	28.3	47.6	17.6	155	6	151	4	1,671	1,625
Wisconsin	95.5	95.2	2,997	1,699	63.8	43.0	57.4	25.1	650	76	616	33	4,852	5,195
Wyoming	94.6	89.9	302	(D)	65.4	46.1	57.7	22.7	46	(D)	29	17	566	563

D Data withheld to avoid disclosure of individual company data.

[1] Carriers with under 10,000 subscribers in a state were not required to report.
[2] Includes medium and large business, institutional, and government customers.
[3] Includes disclosed data for states shown here and island areas not shown here.

Survey, Census, or Data Collection Method: Households with telephones, computers, and Internet access—Based on the Current Population Survey; for information, see Appendix B, Limitations of the Data and Methodology, and the following document at <http://www.census.gov/prod/2002pubs/tp63rv.pdf>; Mobile wireless subscribers—Based on the Federal Communications Commission's Local Competition and Broadband Data Reporting Program (FCC Form 477); for information, see Internet site <http://www.fcc.gov/wcb/iatd/comp.html>; High-speed lines—Based on the Federal Communications Commission's (FCC) Form 477; for information, see Internet site <http://www.fcc.gov/wcb/iatd/comp.html>; Revenue—Based on FCC Form 499-A and FCC Form 499-Q; for information, see Internet site <http://www.fcc.gov/wcb/iatd/trends.html>.

Sources: Households with telephones—Federal Communications Commission, *Telephone Subscribership in the United States* (released March 2005), see Internet site <http://www.fcc.gov/wcb/iatd/lec.html>; Mobile wireless subscribers—Federal Communications Commission, *Local Telephone Competition: Status as of December 31, 2004* (released July 2005), see Internet site <http://www.fcc.gov/wcb/iatd/comp.html>; Households with computers and Internet—U.S. Department of Commerce, National Telecommunications and Information Administration, *Falling through the Net: Defining the Digital Divide*, July 1999, and *A Nation Online, 2004*; High-speed lines—Federal Communications Commission, *High-Speed Services for Internet Access: Status as of December 31, 2004* (released July 2005), see Internet site <http://www.fcc.gov/wcb/iatd/comp.html>; Revenue—Federal Communications Commission, *Trends in Telephone Service 2005* (released June 2005), see Internet site <http://www.fcc.gov/wcb/iatd/trends.html>.

Geographic area	Information industries[1] Nonfarm employment (BLS)[3] (1,000)			Earnings (BEA)[4] (mil. dol.)			Establishments		Daily newspapers[2] Number		Net paid circulation[5] (1,000)		Circulation, per capita[6]	
	2004	2003	2000	2004	2003	2001	2002	Net change, 2000–2002	2004	2000	2004	2000	2004	2000
United States . . .	[7]3,138.0	[7]3,188.0	[7]3,631.0	293,577	276,104	284,582	138,590	5,000	1,456	1,480	54,626	55,773	0.19	0.20
Alabama	31.2	31.8	35.6	1,882	1,771	1,886	1,682	87	24	24	619	658	0.14	0.15
Alaska	6.9	6.9	7.5	458	428	409	405	40	7	7	105	107	0.16	0.17
Arizona	47.9	49.5	54.3	3,121	2,987	3,045	2,165	211	16	16	750	778	0.13	0.15
Arkansas	20.2	20.3	20.5	1,782	1,613	1,373	1,008	86	28	30	467	472	0.17	0.18
California	482.5	476.2	575.4	57,492	51,044	54,132	20,778	422	90	92	5,764	6,175	0.16	0.18
Colorado	81.0	84.6	108.4	11,132	10,905	11,296	3,270	−178	30	29	990	1,267	0.22	0.29
Connecticut	39.1	39.6	46.4	3,912	3,611	3,635	1,832	106	17	17	679	727	0.19	0.21
Delaware	7.1	7.4	8.1	539	521	524	383	29	2	2	132	140	0.16	0.18
District of Columbia	23.8	24.5	25.3	2,739	2,576	(D)	779	16	2	2	808	865	1.46	1.51
Florida	168.2	171.3	187.9	12,844	11,943	11,815	7,832	508	40	42	3,044	3,067	0.17	0.19
Georgia	118.5	123.4	143.5	12,798	12,156	12,084	4,154	263	34	34	1,007	1,047	0.11	0.13
Hawaii	10.7	10.4	12.2	798	701	709	581	48	6	6	267	221	0.21	0.18
Idaho	9.8	9.2	9.7	489	421	408	679	61	12	12	210	211	0.15	0.16
Illinois	120.7	127.5	147.6	11,058	11,148	11,278	5,730	3	67	68	2,284	2,342	0.18	0.19
Indiana	40.9	41.3	45.9	2,481	2,250	2,199	2,230	30	68	68	1,257	1,313	0.20	0.22
Iowa	33.5	33.6	40.3	1,767	1,638	1,676	1,577	10	37	37	594	621	0.20	0.21
Kansas	42.0	44.4	47.3	3,549	3,482	3,152	1,517	−25	43	45	403	442	0.15	0.16
Kentucky	28.8	29.7	33.1	1,536	1,459	1,497	1,534	54	23	23	583	612	0.14	0.15
Louisiana	29.2	29.0	29.8	2,034	1,857	1,725	1,442	41	26	26	692	726	0.15	0.16
Maine	11.6	11.4	12.1	670	611	584	732	32	7	7	227	232	0.17	0.18
Maryland	50.6	51.1	58.5	4,520	4,146	4,332	2,551	97	13	14	558	612	0.10	0.12
Massachusetts	86.6	91.3	111.1	8,476	7,947	9,151	3,950	173	32	32	1,535	1,631	0.24	0.26
Michigan	68.0	70.3	76.7	4,882	4,621	4,605	3,860	178	48	49	1,637	1,723	0.16	0.17
Minnesota	60.2	61.9	69.2	4,374	4,068	4,156	2,774	151	25	25	864	848	0.17	0.17
Mississippi	14.5	15.1	17.3	880	843	868	1,003	−18	23	23	363	385	0.13	0.14
Missouri	64.2	66.4	76.3	5,259	4,942	4,887	2,555	64	42	43	926	937	0.16	0.17
Montana	7.8	7.7	7.9	415	375	344	646	49	11	11	187	184	0.20	0.20
Nebraska	21.5	21.5	26.9	1,262	1,214	1,186	888	40	17	17	407	437	0.23	0.26
Nevada	14.8	15.5	19.2	1,145	1,122	1,175	1,015	105	8	8	304	296	0.13	0.15
New Hampshire	12.5	12.2	13.9	955	861	921	773	29	11	12	217	234	0.17	0.19
New Jersey	98.6	102.0	126.9	11,588	11,119	11,582	4,132	118	17	19	1,273	1,367	0.15	0.16
New Mexico	14.6	15.8	16.7	781	764	757	821	27	18	18	274	285	0.14	0.16
New York	270.6	276.2	319.1	35,835	33,394	33,224	11,157	154	59	59	6,843	6,393	0.36	0.34
North Carolina	71.5	74.7	81.8	5,200	5,160	(D)	3,188	45	47	47	1,308	1,334	0.15	0.17
North Dakota	7.7	7.7	8.4	421	381	349	396	14	10	10	159	167	0.25	0.26
Ohio	92.9	96.5	107.2	6,218	5,904	6,127	4,143	202	84	84	2,286	2,399	0.20	0.21
Oklahoma	31.1	32.4	35.6	2,213	2,057	1,982	1,511	73	42	43	605	639	0.17	0.19
Oregon	33.0	33.6	39.5	2,362	2,189	2,347	1,894	123	19	19	662	681	0.18	0.20
Pennsylvania	112.4	120.4	135.7	9,205	9,134	9,007	5,149	233	81	84	2,596	2,742	0.21	0.22
Rhode Island	10.9	11.0	10.9	959	848	776	395	16	6	6	217	221	0.20	0.21
South Carolina	26.2	27.1	30.5	1,701	1,568	1,515	1,236	4	16	15	611	625	0.15	0.16
South Dakota	6.8	6.8	6.9	369	334	305	464	22	11	11	153	156	0.20	0.21
Tennessee	49.5	51.2	54.7	3,056	2,902	2,822	2,428	−36	26	25	836	856	0.14	0.15
Texas	225.8	233.9	272.2	21,264	20,008	20,805	9,514	720	85	87	2,923	2,926	0.13	0.14
Utah	30.2	30.0	35.4	1,670	1,541	1,671	1,291	186	6	6	331	330	0.14	0.15
Vermont	6.4	6.5	6.8	348	325	308	511	28	8	8	116	122	0.19	0.20
Virginia	100.4	101.4	118.9	9,680	9,069	11,305	3,799	213	25	28	3,209	2,721	0.43	0.38
Washington	92.4	92.3	97.6	11,451	12,480	13,626	3,096	149	23	24	1,059	1,107	0.17	0.19
West Virginia	11.9	12.5	14.1	613	619	582	718	24	20	22	327	363	0.18	0.20
Wisconsin	49.9	50.3	53.6	3,214	2,887	2,779	2,065	−57	35	35	871	944	0.16	0.18
Wyoming	4.3	4.2	3.9	182	159	(D)	357	30	9	9	87	87	0.17	0.18

D Figure withheld to avoid disclosure.

[1]Covers Information (NAICS 51).
[2]For English-language newspapers only.
[3]Bureau of Labor Statistics.
[4]Bureau of Economic Analysis.
[5]Circulation figures based on the principal community served by a newspaper, which is not necessarily the same location as the publisher's office.
[6]Based on estimated resident population as of July 1, except 2000, enumerated as of April 1.
[7]United States totals differ from the sum of the state figures because of differing benchmarks among states and differing industrial and geographic stratification.

Survey, Census, or Data Collection Method: Employment—Based on the Current Employment Statistics (CES) survey; for information, see Appendix B, Limitations of the Data and Methodology, and see Internet site <http://www.bls.gov/opub/hom/homch2_a.htm>; Earnings—Based on the Regional Economic Information System; for information, see "State Personal Income Methodologies" at <http://www.bea.gov/bea/regional/articles/spi2003/>; Establishments—Based on tabulations of data extracted from the U.S. Census Bureau's Business Register; for information, see Internet site <http://www.census.gov/epcd/cbp/view/cbpview.html>; Newspapers—For information, see Internet site <http://www.editorandpublisher.com>.

Sources: Employment—U.S. Bureau of Labor Statistics, Current Employment Statistics Program, see Internet site <http://www.bls.gov/sae/home.htm>; Earnings—U.S. Bureau of Economic Analysis, *Survey of Current Business*, April 2005, see Internet site <http://www.bea.gov/bea/regional/spi/>; Establishments—U.S. Census Bureau, *County Business Patterns*, annual, see Internet site <http://www.census.gov/epcd/cbp/view/cbpview.html>; Newspapers—Editor & Publisher Co., New York, NY, *Editor & Publisher International Year Book*, annual (copyright).

Table A-70. States — **Financial Activities**

Geographic area	Financial activities[1]								FDIC-insured financial institutions						
	Nonfarm employment (BLS)[4] (1,000)			Earnings (BEA)[5] (mil. dol.)			Establishments		Number of institutions		Assets (bil. dol.)				
											Total		By asset-size of bank, 2004		
	2004	2003	2000	2004	2003	2001	2002	Net change, 2000–2002	2004	2000	2004	2000	Less than $1 bil.	$1 bil. to $10 bil.	Greater than $10 bil.
United States . . .	[9]8,052.0	[9]7,977.0	[9]7,687.0	777,366	707,611	662,293	773,446	49,542	8,958	9,888	10,009.8	7,462.9	1,409.6	1,287.6	7,312.7
Alabama	96.5	96.3	98.9	6,278	5,850	5,003	9,970	472	164	170	237.3	183.7	25.5	6.0	205.7
Alaska	14.6	14.4	13.9	918	853	757	1,494	78	7	8	3.9	6.5	1.7	2.1	–
Arizona	163.8	160.0	150.9	12,926	11,776	10,269	14,741	1,213	49	49	59.3	62.7	7.3	7.6	44.4
Arkansas	51.0	50.4	49.3	2,914	2,680	2,390	6,574	553	168	194	40.7	28.9	28.3	12.4	–
California	902.8	885.6	795.1	105,332	94,705	84,443	88,897	7,790	295	351	838.5	673.5	56.1	145.6	636.8
Colorado	155.1	154.1	147.0	14,393	13,438	12,493	17,861	1,797	177	191	39.4	47.4	27.9	11.5	–
Connecticut	140.7	142.7	143.0	22,359	20,110	19,043	9,106	183	57	69	60.7	49.6	15.1	18.1	27.5
Delaware	44.7	45.3	39.0	4,274	3,888	3,811	2,975	183	34	38	436.0	164.4	5.2	35.6	395.2
District of Columbia	30.5	30.8	33.2	3,496	3,085	2,924	1,852	–5	6	7	0.9	1.0	0.9	–	–
Florida	501.0	485.6	463.0	37,860	34,715	30,048	53,764	5,008	295	311	127.3	82.6	58.5	68.8	–
Georgia	218.3	216.4	209.4	19,183	17,598	16,088	23,001	1,764	344	361	224.7	175.3	59.2	34.7	130.8
Hawaii	28.7	28.4	29.4	2,091	1,900	1,704	3,355	173	8	10	33.8	30.9	1.1	22.2	10.6
Idaho	27.9	27.0	25.2	1,746	1,587	1,383	4,003	327	17	20	5.5	3.1	5.5	–	–
Illinois	399.6	401.8	404.1	41,442	38,222	35,551	34,883	1,834	746	828	340.6	394.8	116.3	69.0	155.3
Indiana	140.2	141.3	144.7	9,616	8,965	8,366	15,423	432	197	219	102.8	101.5	38.9	35.4	28.5
Iowa	96.7	95.2	89.6	6,467	5,928	5,077	8,579	597	414	456	51.1	49.0	44.8	6.3	–
Kansas	70.0	69.5	65.6	4,890	4,603	4,015	8,448	506	372	393	57.8	49.3	34.9	22.9	–
Kentucky	87.2	86.6	83.8	5,400	4,950	4,250	9,399	452	237	267	51.5	55.7	33.0	18.5	–
Louisiana	102.8	101.5	99.8	5,937	5,494	5,097	11,592	260	166	182	59.8	56.1	25.0	12.6	22.3
Maine	34.9	35.1	34.0	2,250	2,119	1,909	3,366	268	39	41	43.0	15.1	11.5	2.8	28.7
Maryland	155.6	156.1	146.9	14,339	13,261	11,220	13,264	682	116	137	46.2	55.2	24.0	22.2	–
Massachusetts	219.9	223.7	228.0	30,245	26,454	26,419	15,696	758	200	229	224.2	173.7	52.5	39.0	132.7
Michigan	217.6	218.3	209.4	20,121	18,695	17,960	22,466	1,025	173	190	194.6	170.0	30.7	21.8	142.2
Minnesota	175.8	175.6	164.8	15,245	14,492	12,772	15,377	1,456	478	514	63.5	190.0	47.0	4.0	12.4
Mississippi	45.9	45.9	45.9	2,578	2,408	2,166	6,742	317	102	109	42.1	35.1	15.7	15.5	10.8
Missouri	163.4	162.8	158.3	10,723	10,168	9,257	16,022	972	373	401	91.8	71.6	50.2	28.8	12.8
Montana	21.1	20.3	18.5	1,577	1,413	1,316	3,251	301	80	89	14.6	12.5	10.5	4.2	–
Nebraska	63.0	62.4	60.5	3,714	3,433	3,061	5,702	450	263	291	46.1	45.2	21.3	13.4	11.5
Nevada	61.5	58.5	52.5	5,658	5,058	4,711	7,422	968	38	34	56.1	38.7	5.4	32.3	18.3
New Hampshire	37.6	37.0	34.1	3,327	3,068	2,555	3,267	148	30	35	31.2	31.6	7.8	10.1	13.4
New Jersey	277.8	276.2	266.8	30,935	28,602	26,339	22,462	1,737	139	153	167.7	143.1	32.2	58.3	77.2
New Mexico	34.6	33.9	33.4	2,104	1,972	1,808	4,815	207	58	64	15.8	18.6	9.2	6.6	–
New York	701.5	696.5	746.9	119,301	105,583	116,838	58,476	1,530	200	230	1,166.2	1,436.6	44.5	101.1	1,020.5
North Carolina	192.2	190.4	178.9	15,931	14,499	12,708	21,023	1,536	108	118	1,302.3	988.0	26.7	9.5	1,266.1
North Dakota	18.6	18.4	16.8	991	918	796	2,211	139	103	113	15.4	18.5	9.8	5.6	–
Ohio	312.4	311.8	305.2	22,710	20,856	18,904	28,016	1,248	290	339	1,579.7	435.5	44.5	39.4	1,495.8
Oklahoma	84.4	83.2	81.7	4,680	4,273	3,823	9,404	448	274	294	56.4	49.8	28.2	16.6	11.6
Oregon	96.6	97.1	94.7	6,279	6,004	5,262	11,047	948	40	48	23.6	19.5	7.1	16.5	–
Pennsylvania	336.3	337.9	338.1	29,034	26,621	24,296	27,588	1,590	262	303	331.0	265.3	60.7	73.5	196.9
Rhode Island	34.2	33.7	31.1	2,541	2,342	2,090	2,431	207	15	13	246.1	184.0	2.6	13.2	230.2
South Carolina	93.0	91.5	87.4	5,910	5,491	4,788	10,582	861	96	108	44.5	31.7	16.2	28.2	–
South Dakota	27.9	27.7	26.2	1,595	1,462	1,314	2,713	222	91	101	442.5	38.3	12.8	8.7	421.0
Tennessee	141.9	139.8	139.2	11,967	10,910	9,740	14,225	534	208	221	133.5	92.0	36.0	6.4	91.1
Texas	594.5	585.9	567.9	55,457	50,782	47,017	55,543	3,690	681	759	215.4	233.4	88.9	80.6	45.9
Utah	64.8	64.7	59.0	4,359	4,038	3,553	7,461	602	67	61	193.3	104.5	10.2	13.6	169.5
Vermont	13.3	13.2	13.0	957	896	786	1,680	31	19	23	7.9	8.6	3.7	4.2	–
Virginia	189.0	186.4	178.8	17,814	16,401	14,246	18,324	1,154	140	162	221.2	91.2	31.4	17.9	172.0
Washington	151.8	151.9	142.3	14,269	12,703	11,060	18,022	1,128	98	102	78.5	72.1	21.6	30.1	26.8
West Virginia	30.5	30.8	31.2	1,490	1,418	1,274	3,625	54	72	77	19.8	18.3	9.9	10.0	–
Wisconsin	157.6	156.9	149.1	10,978	10,222	8,974	13,565	576	308	355	118.4	97.9	45.9	24.3	48.2
Wyoming	10.5	10.2	9.1	762	696	619	1,741	138	44	50	5.7	7.9	5.7	–	–

See footnotes at end of table.

Table A-70. States — **Financial Activities**—Con.

Geographic area	FDIC-insured financial institutions				Credit unions				Average insurance premium, 2002[2] (dol.)		Life insurance, 2003 (mil. dol.)			Automobile insurance— average expenditures per insured vehicle[3] (dol.)	
	Number of offices		Deposits (bil. dol.)		Number		Assets (mil. dol.)		Renters[6]	Home-owners[7]	Total pay-ments	Death pay-ments	Annuity pay-ments[8]		
	2004	2000	2004	2000	2004	2000	2004	2000						2002	2000
United States . . .	89,153	84,867	5,416.4	3,970.0	8,989	10,291	646,229	437,649	186	593	311,935	51,757	64,985	774	687
Alabama	1,446	1,429	62.6	52.7	158	186	9,778	6,990	182	533	3,098	848	537	626	594
Alaska	129	134	6.0	4.6	12	13	3,812	2,594	167	668	483	73	89	884	770
Arizona	1,071	938	61.8	43.2	64	68	10,239	6,608	215	543	6,981	765	1,149	877	792
Arkansas	1,341	1,247	38.7	32.7	73	82	1,553	1,188	213	616	1,712	426	308	670	606
California	6,423	6,195	671.1	453.8	555	632	96,828	64,356	260	660	30,640	4,877	6,109	778	667
Colorado	1,418	1,265	64.5	48.8	145	175	11,856	8,393	183	660	4,026	725	1,030	914	755
Connecticut	1,188	1,183	73.8	58.3	160	195	6,371	4,817	193	652	12,137	838	5,515	965	871
Delaware	255	242	105.8	61.6	35	41	1,377	985	150	390	2,885	251	360	907	849
District of Columbia	199	207	18.6	11.9	64	75	4,618	3,341	165	697	1,093	122	319	1,040	996
Florida	4,897	4,661	301.0	207.9	229	250	35,561	22,032	217	786	17,763	3,342	3,720	870	746
Georgia	2,596	2,329	132.0	96.5	199	224	12,226	8,822	210	517	6,122	1,731	1,046	739	674
Hawaii	294	305	23.1	18.2	97	102	6,443	4,104	201	565	1,184	186	283	736	702
Idaho	478	448	13.8	10.6	48	50	2,465	1,540	150	382	1,101	190	209	560	505
Illinois	4,394	3,978	281.9	239.1	450	548	19,279	14,237	182	516	15,453	2,551	3,294	726	652
Indiana	2,275	2,245	81.1	70.5	211	236	13,107	9,659	174	508	5,972	1,187	1,079	646	570
Iowa	1,541	1,486	51.2	43.1	165	193	5,190	3,731	139	450	3,871	611	772	547	479
Kansas	1,485	1,398	46.5	38.5	121	134	3,029	2,245	172	684	2,696	520	578	586	540
Kentucky	1,724	1,617	56.9	48.3	109	128	4,069	3,176	155	480	3,034	653	561	685	616
Louisiana	1,525	1,476	55.2	46.4	260	284	5,822	4,290	244	840	3,480	888	585	926	806
Maine	505	512	16.7	13.6	77	82	3,858	2,756	128	416	995	178	203	585	528
Maryland	1,676	1,711	82.1	64.1	116	128	13,123	8,608	145	477	7,647	1,033	1,164	837	757
Massachusetts	2,115	1,972	172.7	133.9	257	285	21,535	14,643	198	611	12,868	1,291	2,326	984	946
Michigan	3,001	2,967	136.1	117.2	413	465	30,621	22,317	184	577	10,748	1,937	2,162	839	702
Minnesota	1,715	1,577	94.4	70.6	174	189	12,651	8,599	151	590	7,729	804	884	800	696
Mississippi	1,124	1,102	33.5	28.8	114	131	2,570	1,770	240	668	1,588	491	218	679	654
Missouri	2,189	2,096	87.1	75.4	171	188	8,165	6,045	177	550	5,823	1,091	1,184	666	612
Montana	365	344	11.9	9.3	69	76	2,457	1,614	152	547	671	124	144	628	530
Nebraska	997	945	32.9	27.6	79	86	2,540	1,855	145	596	2,052	344	654	589	533
Nevada	474	413	40.5	18.4	20	23	2,307	1,897	220	531	1,797	312	337	887	829
New Hampshire.	415	414	29.4	25.2	27	32	3,213	2,275	150	482	1,720	203	291	731	665
New Jersey	3,157	3,010	211.3	156.3	248	284	9,462	6,384	173	538	14,355	1,986	2,646	1,113	977
New Mexico	490	499	18.2	14.1	54	56	4,322	2,947	200	490	1,567	248	598	699	674
New York	4,837	4,558	637.6	444.0	557	643	35,232	22,780	207	661	26,281	3,557	6,320	1,087	939
North Carolina	2,510	2,448	163.9	112.9	140	171	21,107	12,774	164	527	7,638	1,677	1,197	588	564
North Dakota	421	410	11.4	10.2	60	65	1,424	1,053	121	528	706	95	108	533	477
Ohio	3,950	3,887	200.2	164.1	422	509	14,472	10,865	155	410	12,658	2,276	2,573	639	579
Oklahoma	1,242	1,141	46.3	37.3	86	94	6,300	4,604	269	800	2,647	575	589	650	603
Oregon	1,030	985	39.2	29.7	96	114	11,241	7,246	158	398	3,440	502	859	682	625
Pennsylvania	4,608	4,530	210.7	177.0	669	776	22,521	15,876	141	477	15,895	2,464	3,577	783	699
Rhode Island	233	220	19.9	14.5	31	39	3,446	2,274	176	606	1,182	238	291	937	825
South Carolina	1,269	1,245	48.1	38.2	86	99	6,173	4,482	176	604	5,028	816	436	702	620
South Dakota	448	427	53.3	12.9	56	61	1,473	1,008	119	469	544	126	21	540	482
Tennessee	2,094	1,976	90.2	72.2	212	249	10,767	7,791	193	536	4,654	1,161	821	632	592
Texas	5,480	4,801	310.3	217.4	641	714	47,799	32,585	269	1,238	16,411	3,449	3,111	791	678
Utah	583	576	102.0	38.2	118	137	9,210	5,940	150	416	2,022	347	417	700	620
Vermont	273	267	9.0	7.8	36	44	1,613	1,016	138	493	695	97	148	644	568
Virginia	2,377	2,451	147.8	87.9	226	256	45,530	25,668	142	476	6,075	1,394	1,120	625	576
Washington	1,799	1,691	87.4	60.2	140	167	20,044	14,639	168	501	5,254	839	1,344	788	722
West Virginia	638	621	22.7	20.5	119	132	2,195	1,665	154	447	1,283	309	288	776	680
Wisconsin	2,254	2,116	96.1	75.4	287	343	14,102	9,796	107	340	5,745	930	1,275	609	545
Wyoming	205	176	7.9	8.1	33	37	1,135	769	152	551	485	78	138	580	496

– Represents zero.

[1]Includes Finance and insurance (NAICS 52) and Real estate and rental and leasing (NAICS 53).   [2]Average premium equals premiums divided by exposure per house-years. A house-year is equal to 365 days of insured coverage for a single dwelling and is the standard measurement for homeowners insurance.   [3]Average expenditure equals total premiums written divided by liability car-years. A car-year is equal to 365 days of insured coverage for a single vehicle. The average expenditures for automobile insurance in a state are affected by a number of factors, including the underlying rate structure, the coverages purchased, the deductibles and limits selected, the types of vehicles insured, and the distribution of driver characteristics.   [4]Bureau of Labor Statistics.   [5]Bureau of Economic Analysis.   [6]Based on the HO-4 renters insurance policy for tenants. Includes broad named-peril coverage for the personal property of tenants.   [7]Based on the HO-3 homeowner package policy for owner-occupied dwellings, 1–4 family units. Provides "all risks" coverage (except those specifically excluded in the policy) on buildings, broad named-peril coverage on personal property, and is the most common package written.   [8]Excludes payments from deposit-type contracts.   [9]United States totals differ from the sum of the state figures because of differing benchmarks among states and differing industrial and geographic stratification.

Survey, Census, or Data Collection Method: Employment—Based on the Current Employment Statistics (CES) survey; for information, see Appendix B, Limitations of the Data and Methodology;   Earnings—Based on the Regional Economic Information System;   Establishments—Based on tabulations of data extracted from the U.S. Census Bureau's Business Register;   Credit unions—Natural Credit Union Administration Yearend Call Report;   FDIC-insured financial institutions number and assets—Based on Federal Financial Institution Examination Council (FFIEC) Call Reports and the Office of Thrift Supervision (OTS) Thrift Financial Reports;   FDIC-insured financial institutions offices and deposits—Based on surveys of every FDIC-insured bank and savings association as of June 30 each year conducted by the Federal Deposit Insurance Corporation (FDIC) and the Office of Thrift Supervision (OTS);   Insurance premiums—For information, see Internet site <http://www.naic.org>;   Life insurance—Based on American Council of Life Insurers (ACLI) tabulations of National Association of Insurance Commissioners (NAIC) statutory data;   Automobile insurance—For information, see Internet site <http://www.naic.org>.

Sources: Employment—U.S. Bureau of Labor Statistics, Current Employment Statistics Program, see Internet site <http://www.bls.gov/sae/home.htm>;   Earnings—U.S. Bureau of Economic Analysis, *Survey of Current Business*, April 2005, see Internet site <http://www.bea.gov/bea/regional/spi/>;   Establishments—U.S. Census Bureau, *County Business Patterns*, annual;   Credit unions—National Credit Union Administration, *Yearend Statistics for Federally Insured Credit Unions*, annual, see Internet site <http://www.ncua.gov/>;   FDIC-insured financial institutions number and assets—U.S. Federal Deposit Insurance Corporation, *Statistics on Banking*, annual;   FDIC-insured financial institutions offices and deposits—U.S. Federal Deposit Insurance Corporation, *Bank and Thrift Branch Office Data Book*, annual;   Insurance premiums—National Association of Insurance Commissioners (NAIC), Kansas City, MO, *Dwelling Fire, Homeowners Owner-Occupied, and Home-owners Tenant and Condominium/Cooperative Unit Owners Insurance*, annual (copyright). Reprinted with permission of the NAIC. Further reprint or distribution strictly prohibited without prior written permission of the NAIC;   Life insurance—American Council of Life Insurers, Washington, DC, *Life Insurers Fact Book*, biennial (copyright);   Automobile insurance—National Association of Insurance Commissioners (NAIC), Kansas City, MO, *Auto Insurance Database Report*, annual (copyright). Reprinted with permission of the NAIC. Further reprint or distribution strictly prohibited without prior written permission of the NAIC.

Table A-71. States — **Professional and Business Services and Education and Health Services**

Geographic area	Professional and business services[1]								Education and health services[2]							
	Nonfarm employment (BLS)[3] (1,000)			Earnings (BEA)[4] (mil. dol.)			Establishments		Nonfarm employment (BLS)[3] (1,000)			Earnings (BEA)[4] (mil. dol.)			Establishments	
								Net change, 2000–2002								Net change, 2000–2002
	2004	2003	2000	2004	2003	2001	2002		2004	2003	2000	2004	2003	2001	2002	
United States ...	[5]16,414	[5]15,987	[5]16,666	1,123,541	1,047,000	1,021,011	1,165,292	43,679	[5]16,954	[5]16,588	[5]15,109	810,790	763,681	664,794	777,241	50,668
Alabama	197	187	184	10,524	9,832	8,708	13,121	448	192	187	176	9,160	8,611	7,661	10,072	677
Alaska	23	23	24	1,572	1,476	1,424	2,720	61	35	33	26	1,888	1,727	1,389	1,999	154
Arizona	334	320	326	18,169	16,379	15,519	21,299	1,419	260	247	212	13,006	11,790	9,693	13,596	1,372
Arkansas	108	104	102	5,537	5,102	4,714	7,815	248	143	140	127	5,809	5,423	4,741	6,896	474
California	2,099	2,080	2,246	165,013	156,723	159,019	145,281	5,311	1,562	1,536	1,398	89,365	84,371	71,717	97,870	7,094
Colorado	299	288	315	22,072	20,262	20,688	27,390	1,625	219	213	193	11,201	10,562	9,232	13,256	932
Connecticut	198	197	216	19,410	18,531	18,885	16,493	226	268	264	245	14,864	14,090	12,480	10,686	494
Delaware	62	59	74	4,531	4,269	4,263	5,836	423	52	50	46	2,640	2,462	2,117	2,301	172
District of Columbia ...	143	142	133	15,415	14,213	13,258	5,557	9	92	89	92	4,990	4,744	4,158	2,592	151
Florida	1,290	1,229	1,180	64,279	58,871	53,772	86,529	6,230	919	888	807	43,676	40,580	35,343	48,644	4,084
Georgia	511	490	537	31,734	29,780	29,653	35,231	1,331	407	395	347	19,734	18,542	16,199	19,811	1,581
Hawaii	71	70	61	3,908	3,621	3,107	4,918	248	67	65	60	3,397	3,170	2,814	3,687	248
Idaho	73	70	61	3,918	3,612	3,399	5,239	449	65	62	53	2,770	2,576	2,226	3,888	388
Illinois	796	777	843	59,556	55,498	55,757	53,836	603	728	718	681	35,209	33,514	29,901	31,050	1,672
Indiana	266	254	259	13,768	12,669	12,123	19,518	589	369	360	330	15,764	14,918	13,230	14,810	1,055
Iowa	107	106	108	5,233	4,924	4,586	9,423	278	191	190	182	7,516	7,093	6,361	7,962	210
Kansas	127	124	130	6,642	6,254	6,215	10,548	195	160	157	148	6,568	6,234	5,602	7,718	550
Kentucky	162	155	163	8,572	7,974	7,383	11,656	256	231	228	204	9,845	9,298	8,118	10,408	921
Louisiana	184	181	183	10,185	9,565	9,080	15,466	692	252	245	224	10,441	9,845	8,639	11,658	672
Maine	50	50	52	2,784	2,662	2,571	5,244	242	111	107	97	4,517	4,152	3,618	4,813	426
Maryland	373	363	362	26,420	24,416	22,420	25,955	1,325	348	340	309	17,459	16,475	14,278	15,654	908
Massachusetts	449	441	493	40,388	37,419	39,346	31,974	307	582	576	546	31,036	29,459	25,717	19,643	851
Michigan	584	586	639	42,483	40,585	39,682	35,392	878	553	543	502	25,626	24,280	21,485	26,528	1,131
Minnesota	302	296	319	21,905	20,327	20,273	23,191	652	377	369	325	17,160	16,036	13,605	13,872	1,312
Mississippi	83	79	79	4,059	3,786	3,459	6,862	295	119	116	105	5,245	4,941	4,277	6,048	477
Missouri	303	301	317	19,659	18,540	18,173	20,548	661	359	353	336	15,615	14,841	13,272	15,200	937
Montana	33	33	31	1,602	1,507	1,359	4,298	381	54	53	49	2,309	2,158	1,854	3,288	218
Nebraska	94	92	97	4,915	4,552	4,340	6,500	200	127	123	111	4,846	4,603	3,973	4,872	374
Nevada	133	121	110	8,344	7,279	6,229	10,376	948	80	76	63	4,503	4,108	3,457	5,046	624
New Hampshire	57	55	59	4,516	4,028	4,047	6,073	131	95	93	84	4,590	4,283	3,634	3,772	79
New Jersey	582	578	599	47,361	45,193	44,039	45,546	834	547	538	496	28,452	27,097	23,708	26,310	1,542
New Mexico	90	89	86	4,955	4,741	4,336	6,378	156	103	99	82	3,837	3,583	2,928	4,556	306
New York	1,054	1,043	1,118	99,356	93,441	92,957	80,780	2,027	1,521	1,495	1,380	74,775	70,799	61,788	55,899	3,516
North Carolina	429	418	442	24,922	23,273	21,667	30,348	1,438	446	429	378	19,373	18,081	15,908	19,825	1,855
North Dakota	24	24	25	1,162	1,079	970	2,194	90	49	48	46	1,950	1,840	1,614	1,728	69
Ohio	624	612	645	37,199	34,679	33,324	40,077	782	744	730	680	32,420	30,775	27,384	28,965	1,256
Oklahoma	161	157	165	7,707	7,234	6,937	12,584	441	179	176	163	7,223	6,785	5,996	9,657	626
Oregon	177	171	182	10,394	9,744	9,656	15,342	531	193	189	173	9,492	8,891	7,721	11,080	717
Pennsylvania	633	609	611	44,476	40,425	38,956	43,783	1,433	996	979	917	46,183	43,553	38,304	35,438	1,140
Rhode Island	54	50	51	3,673	3,254	2,822	4,658	189	93	91	83	4,199	3,961	3,396	3,302	204
South Carolina	192	187	195	9,420	8,818	8,280	13,607	555	176	177	156	7,343	6,943	6,133	9,366	756
South Dakota	24	24	27	1,206	1,171	1,197	2,592	130	57	56	52	2,449	2,274	1,903	2,236	126
Tennessee	301	288	301	17,183	15,704	14,893	17,444	220	320	313	279	17,946	16,679	14,192	14,125	660
Texas	1,088	1,054	1,098	74,296	68,126	67,869	78,850	3,645	1,145	1,120	1,003	52,236	49,118	42,191	51,896	3,468
Utah	138	132	138	7,256	6,697	6,657	9,491	1,072	123	119	104	4,882	4,552	3,943	5,839	543
Vermont	21	20	21	1,364	1,261	1,184	2,985	86	53	52	46	2,219	2,073	1,763	2,327	151
Virginia	577	549	568	43,267	39,235	36,343	33,424	1,797	380	370	332	17,058	15,998	13,886	17,505	1,124
Washington	302	291	304	23,068	21,484	19,848	25,576	731	319	313	292	16,043	15,136	13,336	18,376	1,138
West Virginia	58	57	56	2,691	2,487	2,323	4,537	9	111	109	100	4,489	4,219	3,766	4,867	266
Wisconsin	251	244	247	14,589	13,488	12,541	18,390	715	376	365	340	16,496	15,532	13,387	14,642	847
Wyoming	15	16	15	883	811	761	2,417	137	22	21	18	978	900	754	1,662	120

[1]Professional, scientific, and technical services; management of companies and enterprises; administrative and support and waste management and remediation services.
[2]Education services; health care and social assistance.
[3]Bureau of Labor Statistics.
[4]Bureau of Economic Analysis.
[5]United States totals differ from the sum of the state figures because of differing benchmarks among states and differing industrial and geographic stratification.

Survey, Census, or Data Collection Method: Employment—Based on the Current Employment Statistics (CES) survey; for information, see Appendix B, Limitations of the Data and Methodology, and Internet site <http://www.bls.gov/opub/hom/homch2_a.htm>; Earnings—Based on the Regional Economic Information System; for information, see Internet site <http://www.bea.gov/bea/regional/articles/spi2003/>; Establishments—Based on tabulations of data extracted from the U.S. Census Bureau's Business Register; for information, see Internet site <http://www.census.gov/epcd/cbp/view/cbpview.html>.

Sources: Employment—U.S. Bureau of Labor Statistics, Current Employment Statistics Program, see Internet site <http://www.bls.gov/sae/home.htm>; Earnings—U.S. Bureau of Economic Analysis, *Survey of Current Business*, April 2005, see Internet site <http://www.bea.gov/bea/regional/spi>; Establishments—U.S. Census Bureau, *County Business Patterns*, annual, see Internet site <http://www.census.gov/epcd/cbp/view/cbpview.html>.

Table A-72. States — Leisure and Hospitality Services

Geographic area	Arts, entertainment, and recreation services								Accommodation and food services							
	Nonfarm employment (BLS)[1] (1,000)			Earnings (BEA)[2] (mil. dol.)			Establishments		Nonfarm employment (BLS)[1] (1,000)			Earnings (BEA)[2] (mil. dol.)			Establishments	
	2004	2003	2000	2004	2003	2001	2002	Net change, 2000–2002	2004	2003	2000	2004	2003	2001	2002	Net change, 2000–2002
United States . . .	[3]1,833	[3]1,813	[3]1,788	82,769	77,378	69,495	110,375	6,559	[3]10,646	[3]10,360	[3]10,074	207,807	195,271	179,657	565,149	22,738
Alabama	16	15	15	464	431	385	1,020	−6	144	140	134	2,126	2,044	(D)	7,070	185
Alaska	4	4	4	210	198	163	471	16	26	26	24	644	605	525	1,882	116
Arizona	30	29	28	1,396	1,309	1,244	1,542	121	211	204	201	4,170	3,865	3,552	9,913	630
Arkansas	9	9	9	303	286	249	832	50	82	79	77	1,168	1,096	1,004	4,676	255
California	239	232	216	16,760	15,295	12,917	16,295	1,282	1,204	1,168	1,117	27,110	25,077	22,766	66,543	3,337
Colorado	42	41	43	1,746	1,728	1,703	2,137	150	209	205	204	4,077	3,863	3,638	10,810	615
Connecticut	25	24	23	987	902	866	1,588	90	103	101	98	2,343	2,208	1,989	7,032	275
Delaware	9	9	7	272	263	220	347	15	31	30	28	609	562	515	1,568	8
District of Columbia . . .	6	6	5	358	359	359	268	27	45	44	43	1,482	1,357	(D)	1,780	136
Florida	163	158	160	7,336	6,721	6,299	6,259	397	691	655	620	14,307	13,073	11,820	30,203	1,886
Georgia	37	37	37	1,711	1,668	1,565	2,338	131	321	312	295	5,864	5,513	5,104	15,512	1,080
Hawaii	12	11	11	452	420	367	490	8	92	89	89	2,825	2,534	2,288	3,079	58
Idaho	8	8	7	288	259	244	623	29	48	47	46	698	656	604	3,081	209
Illinois	81	81	76	3,217	3,027	2,775	4,144	162	426	416	410	8,119	7,627	7,210	24,118	695
Indiana	45	45	43	1,727	1,645	1,549	1,987	34	230	226	223	3,436	3,262	3,083	11,791	93
Iowa	(NA)	(NA)	(NA)	609	570	534	1,368	77	107	105	106	1,462	1,386	1,307	6,573	46
Kansas	13	13	14	341	314	293	1,054	73	98	96	95	1,544	1,455	1,378	5,610	74
Kentucky	18	18	18	583	546	467	1,239	38	142	138	134	2,335	2,211	2,024	6,689	97
Louisiana	38	37	38	1,458	1,369	1,254	1,307	16	166	162	158	2,829	2,683	2,426	7,566	303
Maine	8	8	7	273	263	228	839	64	52	51	49	929	873	790	3,700	49
Maryland	36	34	32	1,305	1,218	1,133	1,935	69	189	185	175	4,152	3,972	3,610	9,442	593
Massachusetts	46	46	40	2,117	1,982	1,715	2,854	227	245	242	235	5,504	5,218	4,879	14,999	419
Michigan	62	62	64	2,356	2,218	2,024	3,492	146	341	336	336	5,400	5,203	4,858	18,925	315
Minnesota	36	36	33	1,344	1,298	1,114	2,553	254	200	195	189	3,260	3,108	2,874	10,265	361
Mississippi	13	13	21	442	409	596	632	29	112	110	102	2,053	1,984	1,691	4,327	166
Missouri	44	43	42	1,813	1,736	1,544	2,029	88	224	218	212	3,655	3,485	3,207	11,303	404
Montana	10	9	8	224	212	174	896	72	45	43	42	653	619	565	3,230	86
Nebraska	11	11	10	264	254	232	793	67	67	67	67	926	907	838	3,982	18
Nevada	29	28	27	1,214	1,140	1,027	1,084	91	284	275	278	9,722	9,095	8,553	4,262	355
New Hampshire	12	11	10	385	359	306	677	39	52	50	48	1,049	983	895	3,142	115
New Jersey	50	48	43	2,259	2,108	1,850	3,188	224	277	274	261	6,900	6,543	5,972	17,484	1,041
New Mexico	8	8	7	351	332	265	611	38	75	74	70	1,251	1,185	1,058	3,756	79
New York	132	126	122	8,418	7,768	7,012	9,887	708	530	521	516	13,168	12,336	11,439	39,324	1,661
North Carolina	45	45	44	1,727	1,610	1,493	2,988	125	300	291	277	4,993	4,659	4,277	15,731	666
North Dakota	4	3	3	77	73	59	385	12	27	27	26	372	355	325	1,758	28
Ohio	68	68	70	2,295	2,259	2,182	3,862	85	427	420	413	6,481	6,226	5,864	22,763	355
Oklahoma	14	13	14	364	333	302	1,026	62	115	113	113	1,684	1,623	1,531	6,518	189
Oregon	21	20	26	716	682	642	1,444	102	135	132	128	2,449	2,316	2,120	8,785	361
Pennsylvania	78	76	71	2,810	2,654	2,330	4,286	255	397	394	378	6,965	6,644	6,129	24,729	690
Rhode Island	7	7	7	267	258	220	493	41	43	42	40	808	766	679	2,707	110
South Carolina	25	25	26	734	693	630	1,441	−117	176	168	161	2,959	2,770	2,496	8,202	214
South Dakota	6	6	6	216	202	172	573	36	35	34	33	501	475	422	2,200	11
Tennessee	29	28	26	1,542	1,450	1,182	2,111	83	225	219	207	4,255	4,039	3,650	10,053	423
Texas	100	97	91	3,846	3,708	3,232	5,502	394	783	763	728	14,837	14,035	13,079	36,710	1,720
Utah	16	16	16	489	457	453	708	68	86	84	81	1,370	1,295	1,200	4,100	216
Vermont	4	4	3	135	123	105	448	41	29	29	30	615	580	536	1,956	107
Virginia	44	42	(NA)	1,338	1,282	1,127	2,434	127	276	266	256	5,065	4,680	4,248	13,310	779
Washington	44	43	45	1,672	1,493	1,380	2,489	182	210	206	206	4,239	4,000	3,707	13,743	692
West Virginia	10	10	8	343	315	241	560	13	58	57	54	892	857	775	3,285	47
Wisconsin	34	34	33	1,055	1,032	944	2,458	196	216	211	204	3,067	2,916	2,660	13,229	374
Wyoming	3	3	3	156	145	132	388	28	29	28	27	483	445	377	1,733	−4

D Figure withheld to avoid disclosure.   NA Not available.

[1]Bureau of Labor Statistics.
[2]Bureau of Economic Analysis.
[3]United States totals differ from the sum of the state figures because of differing benchmarks among states and differing industrial and geographic stratification.

Survey, Census, or Data Collection Method: Employment—Based on the Current Employment Statistics (CES) survey; for information, see Appendix B, Limitations of the Data and Methodology, and Internet site <http://www.bls.gov/opub/hom/homch2_a.htm>;   Earnings—Based on the Regional Economic Information System; for information, see Internet site <http://www.bea.gov/bea/regional/articles/spi2003/>;   Establishments—Based on tabulations of data extracted from the U.S. Census Bureau's Business Register; for information, see Internet site <http://www.census.gov/epcd/cbp/view/cbpview.html>.

Sources: Employment—U.S. Bureau of Labor Statistics, Current Employment Statistics Program, see Internet site <http://www.bls.gov/sae/home.htm>;   Earnings—U.S. Bureau of Economic Analysis, *Survey of Current Business,* April 2005, see Internet site <http://www.bea.gov/bea/regional/spi/>;   Establishments—U.S. Census Bureau, *County Business Patterns,* annual, see Internet site <http://www.census.gov/epcd/cbp/view/cbpview.html>.

Table A-73. States — Travel and Tourism Indicators

Geographic area	Domestic travel expenditures[1] (mil. dol.)			Impact of international travel on state economy						Overseas visitors to the state[2] (1,000)		Visitors to — (1,000)			
				Travel expenditures (mil. dol.)		Travel-generated employment (1,000)		Travel-generated tax receipts (mil. dol.)				National parks		State parks[3]	
	2003	2002	2001	2003	2001	2003	2001	2003	2001	2003	2000	2003	2000	2003	2000
United States ...	490,870	473,601	479,016	64,509.0	71,893.0	814.5	944.5	10,291.6	11,879.4	18,026	25,975	263,924	283,846	734,990	786,610
Alabama	5,549	5,294	5,348	(NA)	(NA)	(NA)	(NA)	(NA)	(NA)	72	78	752	608	4,871	5,878
Alaska	1,380	1,341	1,343	(NA)	(NA)	(NA)	(NA)	(NA)	(NA)	(4)	52	2,190	2,026	4,301	3,888
Arizona	9,153	8,502	8,686	1,384.0	1,469.7	20.9	23.4	221.1	240.1	487	883	10,556	11,526	2,201	2,371
Arkansas	3,973	3,886	3,921	(NA)	(NA)	(NA)	(NA)	(NA)	(NA)	(4)	(4)	2,402	2,244	9,970	6,643
California	61,075	58,017	60,560	10,485.1	11,957.3	130.2	152.2	1,770.0	2,055.5	3,984	6,364	34,177	34,411	85,779	98,520
Colorado	9,193	8,896	9,121	616.4	707.5	9.8	11.6	135.1	161.8	288	519	5,596	5,807	11,378	10,284
Connecticut	6,709	6,437	6,602	202.4	216.6	1.8	2.0	32.5	35.4	252	260	15	16	7,033	7,567
Delaware	1,135	1,113	1,067	(NA)	(NA)	(NA)	(NA)	(NA)	(NA)	(4)	(4)	(X)	(X)	5,549	3,910
District of Columbia	4,280	4,098	4,129	1,400.9	1,487.8	12.7	14.1	207.2	224.2	(4)	(4)	22,027	28,802	(X)	(X)
Florida	42,893	40,648	40,525	13,372.4	15,642.0	187.8	227.7	2,076.5	2,502.5	4,200	6,026	9,633	8,915	18,241	16,672
Georgia	14,524	14,124	14,349	1,124.5	1,234.7	16.3	18.7	257.3	296.2	451	805	6,231	6,023	12,405	16,124
Hawaii	7,487	6,939	7,073	5,416.0	5,878.8	62.3	70.6	783.8	877.1	1,947	2,727	4,749	5,185	4,499	18,171
Idaho	2,206	2,120	2,164	(NA)	(NA)	(NA)	(NA)	(NA)	(NA)	(4)	(4)	474	437	2,438	2,573
Illinois	21,595	20,706	20,949	1,368.4	1,507.5	18.2	21.4	282.5	321.8	829	1,377	383	368	37,137	44,484
Indiana	6,689	6,504	6,456	209.1	169.2	3.2	2.7	33.1	28.2	144	156	2,205	2,109	14,798	18,475
Iowa	4,629	4,464	4,415	(NA)	(NA)	(NA)	(NA)	(NA)	(NA)	(4)	(4)	263	270	14,534	15,152
Kansas	3,846	3,694	3,637	(NA)	(NA)	(NA)	(NA)	(NA)	(NA)	(4)	(4)	133	116	8,250	7,202
Kentucky	5,433	5,248	5,116	(NA)	(NA)	(NA)	(NA)	(NA)	(NA)	72	78	3,377	3,852	7,668	7,792
Louisiana	9,055	8,820	8,701	363.6	565.7	4.6	7.4	49.5	77.8	216	390	684	895	2,064	1,715
Maine	1,988	1,904	1,920	(NA)	(NA)	(NA)	(NA)	(NA)	(NA)	(4)	104	2,431	2,469	2,542	2,265
Maryland	9,012	8,693	8,683	319.0	386.4	4.4	5.5	64.9	79.2	198	312	3,443	3,180	10,219	10,004
Massachusetts	9,952	9,817	10,074	1,246.6	1,808.9	14.3	20.0	222.3	307.2	829	1,429	9,073	10,251	10,512	12,775
Michigan	11,990	11,612	11,785	582.0	638.2	7.5	8.9	106.9	120.3	361	494	1,554	1,639	22,430	27,534
Minnesota	7,952	7,664	7,702	329.7	489.6	5.7	9.3	101.1	164.8	90	364	521	598	7,782	8,496
Mississippi	5,432	5,291	5,174	(NA)	(NA)	(NA)	(NA)	(NA)	(NA)	90	(4)	6,867	7,006	3,051	4,198
Missouri	9,177	9,341	9,313	121.4	162.5	2.0	2.7	23.3	31.4	90	156	4,292	5,339	17,016	18,174
Montana	2,059	1,961	1,964	(NA)	(NA)	(NA)	(NA)	(NA)	(NA)	(4)	(4)	3,825	3,696	1,575	1,367
Nebraska	2,773	2,699	2,692	(NA)	(NA)	(NA)	(NA)	(NA)	(NA)	(4)	(4)	172	181	9,726	9,619
Nevada	19,319	18,272	18,760	2,021.1	2,022.6	34.8	36.5	291.4	301.2	1,370	2,364	6,024	6,647	3,288	3,451
New Hampshire	2,688	2,585	2,606	120.7	109.3	1.2	1.1	11.6	10.9	90	130	31	37	5,472	5,127
New Jersey	14,728	14,357	14,732	688.5	813.1	9.2	11.3	127.0	152.5	685	909	5,637	5,542	14,943	15,073
New Mexico	4,076	3,991	3,949	(NA)	(NA)	(NA)	(NA)	(NA)	(NA)	90	104	1,825	1,766	3,983	4,639
New York	27,726	26,856	27,072	7,708.0	8,376.1	89.4	102.0	1,582.5	1,780.5	4,200	5,922	14,791	18,533	57,001	59,126
North Carolina	12,632	12,458	12,375	417.8	451.6	6.8	7.6	73.3	81.8	252	416	20,380	21,068	13,213	12,400
North Dakota	1,237	1,166	1,167	(NA)	(NA)	(NA)	(NA)	(NA)	(NA)	(4)	(4)	551	484	1,134	1,111
Ohio	12,419	12,198	12,490	556.0	649.7	7.2	8.6	96.9	114.1	324	390	3,229	3,586	57,238	55,340
Oklahoma	4,208	4,145	4,206	(NA)	(NA)	(NA)	(NA)	(NA)	(NA)	(4)	(4)	1,708	1,808	14,247	16,148
Oregon	5,557	5,380	5,451	303.0	310.1	4.3	4.6	45.9	49.0	162	234	938	831	39,244	38,563
Pennsylvania	15,237	14,695	14,714	1,181.6	1,300.9	16.5	19.5	204.6	244.0	613	649	7,830	8,326	36,031	36,717
Rhode Island	1,427	1,365	1,414	(NA)	(NA)	(NA)	(NA)	(NA)	(NA)	72	(4)	54	56	6,572	6,231
South Carolina	7,215	6,976	6,845	514.2	582.6	7.8	9.0	76.4	89.2	144	156	1,501	938	7,544	9,247
South Dakota	1,521	1,483	1,463	(NA)	(NA)	(NA)	(NA)	(NA)	(NA)	(4)	(4)	4,089	3,772	9,081	7,038
Tennessee	10,580	10,298	10,126	270.0	381.1	3.9	5.8	58.8	84.3	162	286	7,933	8,349	27,020	30,182
Texas	31,471	31,159	31,922	3,118.7	3,184.8	47.8	51.2	573.5	606.9	829	1,169	4,941	5,878	17,620	18,751
Utah	3,725	3,782	3,788	318.3	305.4	7.2	7.1	66.0	62.4	252	416	7,780	8,844	5,806	6,737
Vermont	1,372	1,339	1,351	(NA)	(NA)	(NA)	(NA)	(NA)	(NA)	(4)	(4)	33	46	674	719
Virginia	13,890	13,333	13,138	413.7	480.9	6.2	7.5	66.4	80.2	234	364	21,905	24,029	5,623	5,717
Washington	8,040	7,648	7,891	779.0	841.5	10.2	11.8	138.6	154.0	342	468	7,123	7,276	44,991	46,444
West Virginia	1,798	1,766	1,707	(NA)	(NA)	(NA)	(NA)	(NA)	(NA)	(4)	(4)	1,743	1,942	8,343	7,990
Wisconsin	7,157	6,913	6,841	229.2	257.8	4.0	4.6	39.6	46.8	108	208	311	367	15,739	15,470
Wyoming	1,708	1,604	1,538	(NA)	(NA)	(NA)	(NA)	(NA)	(NA)	(4)	(4)	5,542	5,754	2,214	2,538

NA Not available.   X Not applicable.

[1] Represents U.S. spending on domestic overnight trips and day trips of 50 miles or more, one way, away from home. Excludes spending by foreign visitors and by U.S. residents in U.S. territories and abroad. Includes travelers' expenditures in Indian casino gaming.

[2] Includes travelers for business and pleasure, international travelers in transit from the United States, and students; excludes travel by international personnel and international businessmen employed in the United States. Excludes Canada and Mexico.

[3] For year ending June 30. Data are shown as reported by state park directors. In some states, park agency has under its control forests, fish and wildlife areas, and/or other areas. In other states, agency is responsible for state parks only. Includes overnight visitors.

[4] Data not shown due to low sampling size of overseas visitors. For more information, please contact the Office of Travel and Tourism Industries.

Survey, Census, or Data Collection Method: Domestic travel and impact of international travel—For information, see Internet site <http://www.tia.org/index.html>;   Overseas visitors to the state—Based on the Survey of International Air Travelers (In-Flight Survey) Program and the Visitors Arrival Program (I-94 Form); for information, see Internet site <http://www.tinet.ita.doc.gov/cat/f-2004-45-540.html>;   National parks—Based on the National Park Service Social Science Program; for information, see Internet site <http://www2.nature.nps.gov/stats/>;   State parks—For information, see Internet site <http://naspd.indstate.edu/index.html>.

Sources: Domestic travel and impact of international travel—Travel Industry Association of America, Washington, DC, *Impact of Travel on State Economies*, annual (copyright), see Internet site <http://www.tia.org/index.html>;   Overseas visitors to the state—International Trade Administration, U.S. Department of Commerce, "Overseas Visitors to Select U.S. States and Territories 2003–2004" and previous years, Internet site <http://www.tinet.ita.doc.gov>;   National parks—National Park Service, Public Use Statistics Office, *National Park Service Statistical Abstract*, annual, see also Internet site <http://www2.nature.nps.gov/stats/>;   State parks—National Association of State Park Directors, *Annual Information Exchange*, see Internet site <http://www.naspd.org/>.

Geographic area	Nonfarm employment (BLS)[1] (1,000)			Earnings (BEA)[2] (mil. dol.)			Federal tax collections[3] (mil. dol.)			State tax collections (mil. dol.)		
	2004	2003	2000	2004	2003	2001	2004	2003	2000	2004	2003	2000
United States . . .	[4]21,618.0	[4]21,583.0	[4]20,790.0	1,210,977	1,163,988	1,048,681	2,002,296	1,930,649	2,076,044	593,489	548,991	539,655
Alabama	359.9	358.4	351.7	18,184	17,701	15,838	18,489	17,907	18,869	7,018	6,416	6,438
Alaska	81.2	81.6	74.4	5,852	5,595	4,938	3,267	3,249	2,977	1,288	1,120	1,423
Arizona	400.7	393.5	366.6	20,800	19,475	16,941	25,345	23,231	25,173	9,606	8,692	8,101
Arkansas	200.7	198.5	190.7	9,213	8,630	7,652	20,576	19,849	17,743	5,581	5,146	4,871
California	2,390.3	2,425.5	2,318.1	152,099	147,897	133,820	237,931	227,611	258,601	85,721	79,198	83,808
Colorado	359.2	356.2	337.0	20,657	19,791	17,512	34,661	33,739	37,371	7,051	6,636	7,075
Connecticut	242.4	246.0	241.8	14,763	14,155	13,233	41,909	38,746	40,344	10,291	9,509	10,171
Delaware	58.1	57.2	56.6	3,517	3,345	2,864	11,151	10,481	11,841	2,375	2,116	2,132
District of Columbia	230.6	230.6	223.9	24,414	23,713	21,015	16,931	19,413	(5)	(NA)	(NA)	(NA)
Florida	1,069.0	1,053.0	1,001.7	60,389	56,544	50,183	94,278	91,247	97,339	30,768	26,993	24,817
Georgia	638.4	632.4	597.2	35,786	34,360	30,184	59,084	56,847	61,040	14,571	13,412	13,511
Hawaii	120.1	119.1	114.6	9,922	9,317	8,086	8,395	5,262	6,237	3,849	3,570	3,335
Idaho	114.2	113.0	108.8	5,257	4,948	4,410	6,480	6,757	7,330	2,648	2,344	2,377
Illinois	843.9	853.2	839.6	46,431	45,135	42,112	108,477	105,855	115,149	25,491	22,212	22,789
Indiana	426.1	422.6	410.3	19,286	18,502	17,041	32,192	33,066	33,891	11,957	11,216	10,104
Iowa	244.3	244.8	243.3	10,972	10,532	9,670	14,543	14,559	14,646	5,133	4,922	5,185
Kansas	252.0	250.4	244.9	11,863	11,212	10,136	15,897	15,516	17,815	5,284	5,008	4,848
Kentucky	309.4	312.5	305.1	15,592	15,064	13,658	17,515	16,812	17,899	8,463	8,319	7,695
Louisiana	382.5	379.3	373.4	17,792	16,897	14,798	20,341	19,878	16,200	8,026	7,450	6,512
Maine	104.9	103.7	99.5	5,322	5,094	4,478	5,487	5,194	5,570	2,897	2,697	2,661
Maryland	465.7	467.1	452.5	33,523	32,992	29,615	40,893	38,251	57,985	12,315	10,980	10,354
Massachusetts	407.6	412.6	423.9	24,302	23,682	22,175	59,060	56,054	64,307	16,699	15,608	16,153
Michigan	682.1	685.4	681.6	33,667	33,099	30,723	63,745	64,764	75,674	24,061	22,748	22,756
Minnesota	411.1	412.5	407.6	19,921	19,137	17,359	58,068	57,906	55,241	14,735	13,981	13,339
Mississippi	242.5	240.8	233.8	11,596	10,984	9,664	8,951	9,014	9,759	5,125	4,999	4,712
Missouri	429.3	432.2	426.2	20,726	20,167	18,454	38,326	38,120	40,653	9,120	8,627	8,572
Montana	87.0	85.8	80.3	4,091	3,903	3,420	3,134	3,096	3,675	1,626	1,487	1,411
Nebraska	160.1	159.8	154.4	7,591	7,233	6,390	14,393	13,867	12,662	3,640	3,348	2,981
Nevada	138.5	134.9	121.7	8,909	8,141	7,014	13,294	13,170	11,892	4,739	4,129	3,717
New Hampshire	89.7	90.1	83.5	4,094	3,938	3,389	7,183	7,366	7,942	2,005	1,959	1,696
New Jersey	634.1	621.9	588.8	38,389	36,344	32,595	91,082	86,514	95,860	20,981	19,936	18,148
New Mexico	198.3	195.1	183.0	10,548	10,000	8,735	6,050	6,271	6,197	4,002	3,607	3,743
New York	1,483.3	1,487.8	1,467.7	85,597	82,207	76,268	171,949	168,462	191,362	45,834	42,253	41,736
North Carolina	650.7	641.4	622.2	36,755	34,551	30,617	53,979	48,365	44,947	16,576	15,849	15,315
North Dakota	74.6	75.3	73.0	3,370	3,201	2,747	2,825	2,721	2,873	1,229	1,178	1,172
Ohio	801.8	802.6	785.0	40,566	39,547	35,814	87,854	85,242	88,641	22,476	20,652	19,676
Oklahoma	301.6	295.8	287.7	15,359	14,673	13,429	20,419	19,635	19,113	6,427	5,906	5,840
Oregon	269.5	267.7	267.3	14,079	13,470	12,651	18,880	17,540	20,068	6,103	5,702	5,946
Pennsylvania	745.1	745.6	725.1	39,843	38,990	35,374	87,841	81,812	88,350	25,347	23,187	22,467
Rhode Island	65.8	66.2	64.3	4,459	4,329	3,954	8,545	8,664	8,258	2,409	2,257	2,035
South Carolina	327.5	326.1	322.8	17,192	16,401	14,904	15,357	14,999	16,455	6,804	6,353	6,381
South Dakota	74.3	74.3	70.3	3,295	3,115	2,780	3,294	3,375	4,111	1,063	1,013	927
Tennessee	414.0	411.1	399.0	19,385	18,513	16,587	36,802	35,251	36,710	9,536	8,812	7,740
Texas	1,655.6	1,646.1	1,561.9	83,934	81,112	71,197	152,691	141,935	152,583	30,752	29,099	27,424
Utah	198.7	196.6	185.4	9,774	9,440	8,391	9,594	9,306	10,023	4,189	3,955	3,979
Vermont	52.4	52.0	49.4	2,602	2,410	2,076	3,079	3,035	3,467	1,767	1,559	1,483
Virginia	651.5	637.5	624.7	48,270	46,001	41,514	47,017	47,095	50,091	14,233	12,969	12,648
Washington	523.3	520.6	483.3	31,444	30,060	26,596	42,168	41,906	47,845	13,895	12,960	12,567
West Virginia	143.1	142.5	143.1	7,005	6,779	6,110	5,226	4,830	5,016	3,749	3,594	3,343
Wisconsin	412.1	412.9	405.6	19,633	18,881	17,171	34,711	34,153	35,890	12,531	12,090	12,575
Wyoming	64.6	63.5	60.7	2,946	2,780	2,397	2,934	2,712	2,357	1,505	1,217	964

NA Not available.

[1]Bureau of Labor Statistics.
[2]Bureau of Economic Analysis.
[3]Excludes excise taxes collected by the Customs Service and the Alcohol and Tobacco Tax and Trade Bureau.
[4]United States totals differ from the sum of the state figures because of differing benchmarks among states and differing industrial and geographic stratification.
[5]Data for the District of Columbia included with Maryland.

Survey, Census, or Data Collection Method: Employment—Based on the Current Employment Statistics (CES) survey; for information, see Appendix B, Limitations of the Data and Methodology, and Internet site <http://www.bls.gov/opub/hom/homch2_a.htm>; Earnings—Based on the Regional Economic Information System; for information, see Internet site <http://www.bea.gov/bea/regional/articles/spi2003/>; Federal tax collections—Based on the IRS's Statistics of Income (SOI) program; for information, see Internet site <http://www.irs.gov/taxstats/index.html>; State tax collections—Based on surveys to appropriate state government offices directly involved with state-administered taxes; for information, see Internet site <http://www.census.gov/govs/www/statetaxtechdoc2004.html>.

Sources: Employment—U.S. Bureau of Labor Statistics, Current Employment Statistics Program, see Internet site <http://www.bls.gov/sae/home.htm>; Earnings—U.S. Bureau of Economic Analysis, *Survey of Current Business*, April 2005, see Internet site <http://www.bea.gov/bea/regional/spi>; Federal tax collections—Internal Revenue Service, *Data Book 2004*, Publication 55B, Washington, DC, and previous years, see Internet site <http://www.irs.gov/taxstats/index.html>; State tax collections—U.S. Census Bureau, State Government Tax Collections (STC) report, see Internet site <http://www.census.gov/govs/www/statetax.html>.

Table A-75. States — State Government Employment and Finances

Geographic area	Employment (full-time equivalent)				Finances				
	Number (1,000)		Per 10,000 population[1]		Revenue (mil. dol.)				
					Total		General, 2002		
	2003	2000	2003	2000	2002	2000	Total[2]	Intergovernmental from federal government	Taxes
United States . . .	**4,191**	**4,083**	**144**	**145**	**1,097,829**	**1,260,829**	**1,062,305**	**317,581**	**535,241**
Alabama	86	80	190	179	14,942	16,857	15,986	5,795	6,510
Alaska	25	23	383	365	5,019	8,584	5,423	1,551	1,090
Arizona	65	65	117	126	17,298	16,315	15,860	4,875	8,477
Arkansas	54	49	198	183	10,297	10,789	10,533	3,410	5,226
California	389	355	110	105	151,245	172,481	141,481	40,843	77,755
Colorado	67	66	148	153	11,809	17,060	13,875	3,806	6,923
Connecticut	60	66	172	193	16,993	18,007	15,382	3,686	9,033
Delaware	24	24	299	303	4,842	5,162	4,633	891	2,174
District of Columbia	(X)	(X)	(X)	(X)	(X)	(X)	(X)	(X)	(X)
Florida	187	185	110	116	47,890	51,621	46,995	12,786	25,352
Georgia	121	120	140	147	24,847	29,630	26,114	8,541	13,772
Hawaii	57	55	460	453	5,869	6,941	6,042	1,365	3,421
Idaho	23	23	171	175	4,488	5,576	4,375	1,324	2,271
Illinois	134	128	106	103	41,095	48,524	40,340	10,449	22,475
Indiana	91	83	146	136	20,116	20,456	20,011	5,886	10,201
Iowa	53	55	179	189	11,130	11,340	11,026	3,320	5,006
Kansas	44	43	161	158	9,694	10,394	9,179	2,964	4,808
Kentucky	79	74	191	183	16,073	19,451	15,810	5,102	7,975
Louisiana	90	95	201	212	18,079	18,788	17,659	5,994	7,357
Maine	22	21	167	161	5,451	6,294	5,600	1,817	2,627
Maryland	92	91	166	173	20,788	21,366	19,909	5,260	10,821
Massachusetts	91	96	142	151	26,885	32,011	26,476	5,061	14,823
Michigan	137	142	136	143	43,950	49,511	40,886	11,241	21,864
Minnesota	75	73	149	149	22,439	26,889	21,910	5,282	13,224
Mississippi	56	56	195	195	11,052	12,181	11,044	4,374	4,729
Missouri	91	91	159	163	19,085	20,309	18,654	6,693	8,729
Montana	19	18	204	199	4,033	4,204	3,721	1,419	1,443
Nebraska	34	30	193	174	6,002	6,185	5,987	1,780	2,993
Nevada	25	22	110	112	6,888	7,285	6,167	1,281	3,945
New Hampshire	20	19	158	152	4,636	4,993	4,391	1,189	1,897
New Jersey	147	133	170	158	32,709	42,340	33,897	8,235	18,329
New Mexico	46	48	247	263	8,746	10,570	8,478	2,760	3,628
New York	248	251	129	132	104,534	111,397	92,897	32,197	43,262
North Carolina	131	123	156	153	31,524	34,361	29,972	9,466	15,537
North Dakota	18	16	284	246	3,017	3,295	2,868	1,022	1,117
Ohio	137	136	120	120	45,439	55,274	40,232	12,328	20,130
Oklahoma	66	64	187	187	13,134	13,116	12,761	4,044	6,053
Oregon	57	53	160	156	14,815	21,011	14,305	5,625	5,164
Pennsylvania	159	150	129	122	46,165	54,517	46,544	13,685	22,136
Rhode Island	20	20	187	187	4,891	5,589	4,836	1,637	2,128
South Carolina	77	79	186	196	16,997	15,966	14,477	5,028	6,088
South Dakota	13	13	171	177	2,491	2,901	2,604	1,045	977
Tennessee	83	81	143	143	17,952	18,970	17,620	7,078	7,798
Texas	266	269	120	129	60,588	72,323	62,181	20,672	28,662
Utah	48	49	203	221	8,468	10,227	8,623	2,267	3,925
Vermont	14	14	219	224	3,260	3,292	3,229	1,041	1,518
Virginia	116	119	157	168	23,577	29,409	24,843	5,377	12,781
Washington	113	112	184	191	23,813	30,616	22,775	6,216	12,629
West Virginia	37	32	205	177	9,130	8,591	8,053	2,847	3,552
Wisconsin	71	64	130	119	20,874	32,119	22,874	5,913	11,814
Wyoming	12	11	241	227	2,770	5,740	2,768	1,113	1,094

See footnotes at end of table.

Table A-75. States — **State Government Employment and Finances**—Con.

Geographic area	Finances						
	Expenditures (mil. dol.)						
	Total		General, 2002				
			Total[2]	Inter-governmental	Direct		
	2002	2000			Education	Public welfare	Highways
United States . . .	**1,280,290**	**1,084,548**	**1,109,227**	**364,789**	**162,054**	**239,903**	**71,248**
Alabama	17,996	15,873	16,160	4,096	3,231	4,110	1,064
Alaska	7,402	6,611	6,702	1,056	882	1,029	667
Arizona	18,119	16,574	16,246	6,969	2,212	2,780	1,127
Arkansas	11,521	9,589	10,634	3,071	1,832	2,578	942
California	184,928	149,772	158,235	74,687	17,289	23,014	5,696
Colorado	16,823	13,930	14,662	4,295	3,009	2,283	1,134
Connecticut	20,117	16,723	17,536	3,735	2,218	3,362	817
Delaware	4,646	4,211	4,233	823	733	659	332
District of Columbia	(X)	(X)	(X)	(X)	(X)	(X)	(X)
Florida	51,834	45,208	47,287	14,054	5,105	11,874	4,707
Georgia	30,053	24,813	27,166	8,645	5,011	6,013	1,990
Hawaii	7,446	6,605	6,684	130	2,257	1,112	236
Idaho	5,234	4,493	4,625	1,407	704	1,003	383
Illinois	49,131	41,183	42,678	13,091	6,128	9,429	2,983
Indiana	22,205	20,289	20,585	6,557	4,146	4,805	1,255
Iowa	12,721	11453	11,436	3,326	2,140	2,573	939
Kansas	10,592	9,124	9,617	2,971	1,578	1,963	967
Kentucky	18,407	15,682	16,376	3,560	2,981	4,762	1,614
Louisiana	18,319	16,554	16,162	4,168	2,771	3,311	951
Maine	6,265	5,448	5,670	1,010	699	1,762	439
Maryland	23,317	19,370	20,704	5,236	3,414	4,625	1,196
Massachusetts	32,848	29,478	28,471	6,284	3,188	5,665	2,628
Michigan	49,184	42,749	43,827	19,067	6,590	9,069	1,250
Minnesota	26,693	23,326	23,478	8,271	3,496	6,071	1,080
Mississippi	12,742	10972	11,462	3,457	1,698	3,214	776
Missouri	20,841	17,293	18,708	5,073	2,556	5,377	1,609
Montana	4,265	3,718	3,785	911	637	643	436
Nebraska	6,537	5,772	6,219	1,820	1,116	1,647	526
Nevada	7,348	6,047	6,242	2,433	904	1,004	568
New Hampshire	4,823	4,366	4,177	1,179	630	879	347
New Jersey	41,988	34783	32,936	9,320	4,558	5,663	1,977
New Mexico	10,084	8,701	9,214	2,768	1,468	2,028	925
New York	119,199	96,925	96,529	38,982	7,619	23,328	3,222
North Carolina	33,124	29,615	29,537	9,451	4,602	6,522	2,574
North Dakota	3,020	2,856	2,813	586	563	626	311
Ohio	52,594	44,631	42,362	15,052	6,515	9,723	2,255
Oklahoma	14,727	10,630	12,904	3,377	2,520	3,156	1,010
Oregon	18,029	15,776	14,884	4,213	2,040	3,796	587
Pennsylvania	55,171	47,682	47,147	12,788	7,304	12,160	4,066
Rhode Island	5,767	4,648	4,843	749	672	1,659	260
South Carolina	20,009	16,237	17,048	4,241	2,763	4,360	1,276
South Dakota	2,772	2,403	2,554	506	377	593	390
Tennessee	20,029	16,853	18,489	4,478	3,315	6,319	1,206
Texas	70,274	60,425	61,771	16,681	11,558	14,607	5,111
Utah	10,107	8,592	9,143	2,171	2,351	1,573	728
Vermont	3,512	3,219	3,291	919	524	756	239
Virginia	28,044	24,314	25,546	8,369	4,657	3,622	2,587
Washington	30,378	25,902	25,160	6,806	4,825	6,151	1,254
West Virginia	9,409	7,552	7,560	1,454	1,181	2,136	986
Wisconsin	26,749	23,027	23,119	9,523	3,197	4,136	1,272
Wyoming	2,948	2,553	2,609	975	287	372	354

X Not applicable.

[1]Based on resident population enumerated as of April 1 for 2000 and July 1 for all other years.
[2]Includes categories not shown separately.

Survey, Census, or Data Collection Method: Employment—Based on the Annual Survey of Government Employment; for information, see Internet site <http://www.census.gov/govs/www/apestechdoc.html>; Finances—Annual Survey of Government Finances; for information, see Internet site <http://www.census.gov/govs/www/statetechdoc2002.html>.

Sources: Employment—U.S. Census Bureau, *State Government Employment and Payroll Data*, March 2004 (accessed 10 June 2005), see Internet site <http://www.census.gov/govs/www/apesst.html>; Finances—U.S. Census Bureau, "State Government Finances" (accessed 8 April 2005), see Internet site <http://www.census.gov/govs/www/state.html>.

Table A-76. States — State Resources, Expenditures, and Balances

Geographic area	Expenditures by fund source (mil. dol.) 2004[1] Total[5]	General fund	Federal fund	Total, 2003	Total, 2002	State general fund (mil. dol.) Resources[2,3] 2004[1]	2003	2002	Expenditures[3] 2004[1]	2003	2002	Balance[4] 2004[1]	2003	2002
United States . . .	1,187,444	516,095	358,417	1,136,694	1,088,207	544,912	524,428	527,793	523,539	508,285	513,479	18,625	10,219	14,013
Alabama	19,922	5,523	7,880	16,012	15,313	5,792	5,585	5,347	5,491	5,473	5,362	261	[6]113	[6]25
Alaska	7,578	2,331	2,792	6,496	6,031	2,301	2,496	(NA)	2,301	2,496	(NA)	–	[6]–	[6](NA)
Arizona	20,764	6,474	6,454	19,550	18,414	6,884	6,218	6,330	6,517	6,026	6,329	368	[6]192	[6]2
Arkansas	14,577	3,526	5,070	12,631	12,070	3,526	3,251	3,250	3,526	3,251	3,250	–	–	–
California	165,850	78,028	57,972	161,512	145,843	80,760	79,089	79,865	77,634	77,482	78,380	[6]3,127	[6]1,607	1,486
Colorado	13,372	5,580	3,201	13,213	12,747	6,035	6,138	6,705	5,689	5,913	6,711	346	225	57
Connecticut	21,948	12,530	4,321	20,533	20,328	12,881	12,023	11,686	12,678	12,120	11,899	202	–97	–123
Delaware	6,145	2,545	990	5,825	5,684	3,200	2,918	2,844	2,554	2,454	2,524	[6]646	[6]464	[6]320
District of Columbia	(NA)	(NA)	(NA)	(NA)	(NA)	(NA)	(NA)	(NA)	(NA)	(NA)	(NA)	(NA)	(NA)	(NA)
Florida	53,950	21,615	15,985	48,560	46,952	23,852	21,196	19,736	21,542	20,514	19,267	2,310	[6]682	[6]469
Georgia	28,670	15,446	11,824	27,981	26,416	17,348	17,292	17,300	16,265	16,025	16,074	[6]1,083	[6]1,268	[6]1,226
Hawaii	7,599	3,823	1,467	8,029	7,812	4,025	3,923	3,834	3,840	3,806	3,624	185	[6]117	[6]210
Idaho	4,901	1,994	1,860	4,359	4,242	2,087	1,941	2,002	1,987	1,926	2,002	100	[6]16	–
Illinois	41,290	19,027	10,403	37,653	39,537	26,996	25,161	25,476	22,632	21,893	24,826	182	[6]317	[6]650
Indiana	20,259	11,323	6,239	19,288	18,313	11,535	10,751	9,594	11,244	10,309	9,579	291	[6]442	[6]16
Iowa	13,641	4,489	3,805	13,480	12,154	4,513	4,484	4,603	4,561	4,531	4,600	26	[6]–46	[6]3
Kansas	10,209	4,332	2,719	10,083	9,803	4,644	4,260	4,702	4,317	4,138	4,528	327	123	174
Kentucky	19,534	7,236	6,683	18,376	17,223	7,620	7,444	7,429	7,294	7,179	7,251	250	163	[6]24
Louisiana	19,465	6,536	6,371	16,989	17,414	6,826	6,662	6,476	6,743	6,457	6,426	45	[6]23	[6]50
Maine	6,116	2,556	2,233	6,064	5,717	2,658	2,586	2,507	2,643	2,533	2,593	15	[6]29	–86
Maryland	24,106	10,275	5,852	23,037	22,521	10,493	10,469	11,132	10,262	10,347	10,677	230	[6]123	[6]456
Massachusetts	27,372	20,287	4,876	26,058	26,487	23,949	23,376	24,621	22,470	22,439	22,831	[6]1,479	[6]752	[6]1,790
Michigan	39,424	8,813	11,806	39,844	39,816	8,707	8,909	9,290	8,695	8,735	9,290	12	[6]174	–
Minnesota	23,539	13,387	5,700	23,099	20,620	14,658	14,263	14,142	13,734	13,894	12,755	[6]924	369	1,387
Mississippi	12,052	3,477	4,756	11,708	10,672	3,594	3,498	3,422	3,591	3,458	3,584	3	[6]41	[6]5
Missouri	18,665	6,786	6,462	17,460	17,111	7,150	6,598	7,830	6,662	6,382	7,734	488	[6]216	[6]96
Montana	3,977	1,333	1,559	3,649	3,238	1,419	1,327	1,503	1,287	1,283	1,339	132	43	165
Nebraska	7,649	2,674	2,380	6,809	6,583	2,752	2,622	2,821	2,576	2,619	2,593	177	[6]3	[6]121
Nevada	6,271	2,260	1,663	5,756	5,868	2,461	2,146	1,946	2,320	2,037	1,847	141	[6]108	[6]138
New Hampshire	4,095	1,313	1,240	4,065	3,751	1,321	1,260	1,138	1,305	1,260	1,150	16	–	[6]–12
New Jersey	37,451	23,855	8,702	36,217	34,975	24,761	23,941	21,730	23,939	23,568	21,207	[6]822	373	500
New Mexico	11,779	4,502	3,807	11,464	10,618	5,025	4,339	4,400	4,383	4,051	3,988	[6]480	245	401
New York	97,327	42,065	35,995	89,056	85,044	41,242	40,328	43,532	42,065	37,613	41,455	[6]1,077	[6]815	[6]2,077
North Carolina	29,319	14,700	8,466	28,780	28,136	15,187	14,271	14,713	14,704	13,856	14,530	287	251	[6]1
North Dakota	2,646	884	1,018	2,520	2,440	971	875	887	894	860	847	77	[6]15	[6]40
Ohio	48,775	24,076	8,216	46,905	45,542	24,083	22,558	21,830	23,839	22,653	21,778	157	[6]53	[6]153
Oklahoma	13,986	4,287	4,711	12,922	13,053	4,936	4,687	5,181	4,833	4,653	5,136	102	[6]34	[6]45
Oregon	19,685	5,720	3,564	15,086	16,382	5,001	3,958	5,140	5,479	3,865	5,074	–478	93	66
Pennsylvania	48,752	21,462	16,740	47,292	43,728	22,152	20,679	20,736	21,926	20,400	20,770	77	209	[6]300
Rhode Island	6,146	2,796	1,927	5,509	5,355	2,834	2,741	2,642	2,790	2,691	2,625	44	[6]43	[6]17
South Carolina	15,425	4,954	5,543	16,704	15,479	5,162	5,040	5,409	4,865	4,995	5,348	[6]55	46	62
South Dakota	2,815	904	1,222	2,861	3,242	892	891	864	889	884	853	[6]–	[6]–	[6]–
Tennessee	21,781	8,656	8,706	20,275	18,549	8,767	8,049	7,610	8,357	7,914	7,568	349	[6]64	[6]–
Texas	59,269	29,434	19,814	59,057	56,620	29,787	31,105	32,510	29,434	30,656	30,572	981	[6]88	[6]1,421
Utah	7,930	3,582	2,065	7,542	7,515	3,668	3,552	3,805	3,569	3,536	3,805	53	[6]16	[6]–
Vermont	2,896	901	991	2,674	2,844	973	882	894	915	888	872	–	[6]–	[6]–
Virginia	27,989	11,299	5,756	26,925	26,575	12,660	12,204	12,241	12,387	12,118	12,131	274	[6]86	[6]109
Washington	26,055	11,381	5,800	25,137	24,372	11,958	11,739	11,228	11,452	11,334	11,217	506	[6]405	[6]10
West Virginia	16,208	2,959	3,454	15,678	13,931	3,319	3,139	2,994	3,019	2,933	2,976	291	[6]196	[6]2
Wisconsin	23,841	10,852	6,416	31,770	31,175	10,759	10,772	11,259	10,654	11,054	11,074	[6]105	–282	151
Wyoming	4,429	1,307	941	4,201	3,952	792	792	659	788	788	630	4	[6]4	[6]10

– Represents zero.   NA Not available.

[1] Estimated.
[2] Includes funds budgeted, adjustments, and balances from previous year.
[3] May or may not include budget stabilization fund transfers, depending on state accounting practices.
[4] Resources less expenditures.
[5] Includes bonds and other state funds not shown separately.
[6] Ending balance is held in a budget stabilization fund.

Survey, Census, or Data Collection Method: Based on surveys completed by governors' state budget officers in the 50 states; for information, see Internet site <http://www.nasbo.org/>.

Source: National Association of State Budget Officers, Washington, DC, *2003 State Expenditure Report*, and *State General Fund from NASBO*, Fiscal Survey of the States, semiannual (copyright).

Geographic area	State government tax collections, 2004													
	Total[1] ($1,000)	Per capita (dol.)	Per- cent change, 2003– 2004	Type of tax ($1,000)										
						Sales and gross receipts								
				Total	General sales and gross receipts	Total	Selective sales taxes							
							Alcoholic beverages	Amuse- ments	Insur- ance premiums	Motor fuels	Pari- mutuels	Public utilities	Tobacco products	Other selective sales
United States ...	**593,488,853**	**2,025**	**8.11**	**294,104,344**	**198,431,303**	**95,673,041**	**4,614,804**	**4,990,713**	**13,775,340**	**33,605,402**	**301,879**	**11,482,059**	**12,300,310**	**14,602,534**
Alabama	7,018,242	1,549	9.38	3,675,562	1,892,560	1,783,002	137,222	97	245,577	535,493	3,226	600,558	93,270	167,559
Alaska	1,288,164	1,967	15.00	168,392	(X)	168,392	28,262	2,413	49,873	40,660	(X)	3,962	43,222	(X)
Arizona	5,580,678	1,672	10.52	2,934,030	2,149,527	784,503	41,240	(X)	91,330	453,148	4,574	(X)	146,485	47,726
Arkansas	85,721,483	2,027	8.46	33,984,188	26,506,911	7,477,277	312,826	(X)	2,114,980	3,324,883	42,143	520,589	1,081,588	80,268
California	7,051,457	2,388	8.24	2,894,035	1,909,246	984,789	31,317	99,145	177,782	597,558	4,504	9,339	65,144	(X)
Colorado	9,606,318	1,533	6.26	6,070,737	4,719,642	1,351,095	55,954	625	312,852	671,765	566	34,617	274,716	(X)
Connecticut	10,291,289	2,937	8.23	4,900,376	3,127,221	1,773,155	44,026	435,061	218,202	456,805	10,660	195,646	277,333	135,422
Delaware	2,375,482	2,862	12.24	383,383	(X)	383,383	13,385	(X)	68,009	112,435	188	35,536	75,479	78,351
District of Columbia	(X)	(X)	(X)	(X)	(X)	(X)	(X)	(X)	(X)	(X)	(X)	(X)	(X)	(X)
Florida	30,767,561	1,769	13.98	23,707,430	17,355,404	6,352,026	591,551	(X)	573,100	1,823,349	26,749	2,504,220	446,406	386,651
Georgia	14,570,573	1,650	8.64	6,468,785	4,921,337	1,547,448	149,801	(X)	317,463	755,994	(X)	(X)	227,348	96,842
Hawaii	3,849,135	3,048	7.82	2,470,299	1,900,377	569,922	41,250	(X)	81,916	84,378	(X)	99,504	79,387	183,487
Idaho	2,647,790	1,901	12.94	1,403,155	1,036,924	366,231	6,609	(X)	82,283	218,019	(X)	1,827	52,271	5,222
Illinois	25,490,593	2,005	14.76	12,526,542	6,922,587	5,603,955	147,883	785,922	378,517	1,421,927	12,042	1,704,655	760,226	392,783
Indiana	11,957,470	1,917	6.61	6,906,954	4,759,445	2,147,509	38,509	765,707	178,303	802,168	4,762	10,573	338,716	8,771
Iowa	5,133,126	1,738	4.28	2,437,323	1,617,505	819,818	12,709	213,522	138,229	357,835	3,241	(X)	94,282	(X)
Kansas	5,283,676	1,931	5.50	2,723,152	1,932,927	790,225	87,637	651	121,827	428,985	3,531	740	124,586	22,268
Kentucky	8,463,400	2,041	1.74	4,006,307	2,466,033	1,540,274	79,104	232	331,903	476,605	15,466	(X)	20,627	616,337
Louisiana	8,025,507	1,777	7.73	4,610,512	2,680,716	1,929,796	53,422	524,119	342,353	560,769	20,420	7,467	101,040	320,206
Maine	2,896,759	2,200	7.40	1,360,152	917,248	442,904	39,279	(X)	77,770	220,410	4,509	8,310	92,626	(X)
Maryland	12,314,799	2,216	12.15	5,212,424	2,945,060	2,267,364	26,863	10,432	279,089	746,044	3,028	137,373	272,066	792,469
Massachusetts	16,698,723	2,602	6.99	5,462,094	3,743,204	1,718,890	68,522	5,255	399,764	684,242	5,697	(X)	425,421	129,989
Michigan	24,061,065	2,379	5.77	10,844,250	7,894,458	2,949,792	149,424	99,455	230,272	1,081,259	11,825	28,561	992,793	356,203
Minnesota	14,734,921	2,889	5.39	6,384,318	4,066,790	2,317,528	69,497	55,784	265,970	648,428	1,489	50	190,116	1,086,194
Mississippi	5,124,730	1,765	2.51	3,391,202	2,482,908	908,294	39,793	167,327	161,201	464,748	(X)	12,067	55,587	7,571
Missouri	9,119,664	1,585	5.71	4,468,508	2,950,055	1,518,453	28,026	307,062	304,848	726,705	(X)	(X)	109,653	42,159
Montana	1,625,692	1,754	9.33	437,051	(X)	437,051	20,570	50,496	61,063	197,605	97	28,169	45,209	33,842
Nebraska	3,639,811	2,083	8.73	1,988,078	1,524,591	463,487	23,159	6,136	38,460	302,899	296	3,107	71,220	18,210
Nevada	4,738,877	2,030	14.77	3,824,602	2,264,749	1,559,853	33,867	861,511	194,228	293,595	(X)	9,651	129,055	37,946
New Hampshire	2,005,389	1,543	2.36	674,354	(X)	674,354	12,239	1,777	79,450	129,913	4,115	65,581	100,014	281,265
New Jersey	20,981,428	2,412	5.24	9,740,284	6,261,700	3,478,584	87,357	468,072	417,873	546,952	(X)	942,744	777,512	238,074
New Mexico	4,001,780	2,103	10.94	2,038,440	1,443,300	595,140	37,503	38,543	87,448	210,863	1,188	18,141	52,718	148,736
New York	45,833,652	2,384	8.47	16,478,965	10,050,291	6,428,674	191,128	570	833,073	518,557	36,067	821,911	1,009,595	3,017,773
North Carolina	16,576,316	1,941	4.59	7,269,203	4,351,823	2,917,380	212,224	11,504	432,975	1,272,611	(X)	319,731	43,733	624,602
North Dakota	1,228,890	1,938	4.34	666,738	367,304	299,434	5,910	10,079	30,928	118,744	2,585	34,098	21,167	75,923
Ohio	22,475,528	1,961	8.83	10,783,304	7,881,510	2,901,794	88,267	(X)	423,078	1,541,151	15,918	275,811	557,569	(X)
Oklahoma	6,426,713	1,824	8.82	2,339,028	1,594,246	744,782	68,420	5,356	144,186	415,318	2,822	21,172	63,398	24,110
Oregon	6,103,071	1,698	7.04	748,882	(X)	748,882	13,306	84	52,167	404,547	2,893	10,537	265,348	(X)
Pennsylvania	25,346,869	2,043	9.31	12,529,644	7,773,131	4,756,513	221,408	565	639,578	1,785,200	26,616	1,016,641	981,253	85,252
Rhode Island	2,408,861	2,228	6.74	1,305,374	804,647	500,727	10,607	(X)	43,350	133,415	4,651	88,640	115,503	104,561
South Carolina	6,803,568	1,621	7.09	3,689,986	2,726,657	963,329	146,658	39,627	106,643	489,322	(X)	45,071	29,742	106,266
South Dakota	1,062,722	1,378	4.91	865,262	586,389	278,873	12,435	26	55,339	126,017	880	1,949	27,644	54,583
Tennessee	9,536,031	1,616	8.22	7,344,662	5,845,206	1,499,456	92,062	(X)	351,111	832,168	(X)	4,761	119,482	99,872
Texas	30,751,860	1,367	5.68	24,620,778	15,460,221	9,160,557	601,841	23,086	1,130,499	2,918,842	11,793	793,107	534,577	3,146,812
Utah	4,189,172	1,754	5.93	2,138,897	1,556,332	582,565	28,174	(X)	105,965	344,121	(X)	13,845	61,663	28,797
Vermont	1,766,719	2,845	13.34	687,595	256,958	430,637	16,894	(X)	49,018	85,994	(X)	10,769	51,182	216,780
Virginia	14,233,065	1,908	9.75	5,212,063	2,977,401	2,234,662	146,019	50	351,278	909,468	(X)	128,815	16,199	682,833
Washington	13,895,346	2,240	7.22	10,864,600	8,423,160	2,441,440	192,618	60	345,614	925,723	1,770	353,136	352,527	269,992
West Virginia	3,749,013	2,066	4.31	2,093,253	1,021,365	1,071,888	8,624	(X)	102,181	309,274	9,537	188,412	107,609	346,251
Wisconsin	12,531,098	2,275	3.65	5,795,187	3,899,395	1,895,792	48,071	362	138,388	1,028,516	1,804	367,650	307,425	3,576
Wyoming	1,504,777	2,968	23.63	574,004	462,842	111,162	1,332	(X)	18,034	69,975	227	3,016	18,578	(X)

See footnotes at end of table.

State and Metropolitan Area Data Book: 2006

U.S. Census Bureau

Geographic area	Alcoholic beverages	Amusements	Corporation	Hunting and fishing	Motor vehicle	Occupation and business, NEC	Individual income	Corporation net income	Death and gift	2003	2002	2000	Centers for Medicare and Medicaid Services[2]	Highway trust fund[3]	FEMA[4]	Title 1 programs[5]
	Licenses						*Other taxes*			*Total*			*Selected programs, 2003*			
United States ...	385,659	222,061	6,339,370	1,233,601	17,412,024	10,881,425	197,421,360	30,801,302	5,734,958	379,978	355,690	286,144	164,041	28,521	4,609	8,233
Alabama	2,491	(X)	73,183	14,700	172,815	107,177	2,243,537	292,051	29,467	5,896	5,557	4,570	2,682	530	50	147
Alaska	1,829	1	1,319	23,713	43,782	9,090	(X)	339,564	2,251	2,407	2,250	2,260	535	381	5	–
Arizona	1,652	2,162	8,595	21,246	109,831	20,779	1,685,585	181,830	21,394	7,028	6,314	4,501	3,258	469	11	163
Arkansas	43,841	5,191	70,580	83,013	2,155,042	3,062,827	36,398,983	6,925,916	574,510	3,851	3,559	2,657	1,903	392	36	102
California	5,632	752	7,232	66,073	192,923	50,297	3,413,891	239,591	50,145	46,211	41,627	33,158	17,643	2,727	530	1,413
Colorado	3,732	28	14,048	18,253	161,398	63,308	2,315,865	525,650	42,292	4,232	3,951	3,273	1,417	401	15	95
Connecticut	6,092	66	15,747	4,049	197,418	118,424	4,319,546	379,822	130,464	4,483	4,492	3,771	1,908	387	9	102
Delaware	614	380	568,190	1,036	33,592	220,992	781,212	217,768	11,725	1,025	958	818	401	97	4	28
District of Columbia	(X)	(X)	(X)	(X)	(X)	(X)	(X)	(X)	(X)	3,633	4,025	2,963	833	152	3	35
Florida	34,492	4,583	161,423	14,520	1,124,851	255,501	(X)	1,345,780	383,030	17,256	15,044	11,676	7,475	1,650	164	473
Georgia	2,331	(X)	53,227	24,020	279,991	117,376	6,830,486	494,701	66,018	8,949	9,300	7,192	4,401	778	23	–
Hawaii	(X)	(X)	2,114	275	89,268	19,484	1,169,205	58,119	9,829	1,515	1,460	1,221	495	115	3	27
Idaho	1,309	398	1,754	29,455	107,269	42,094	907,795	103,784	7,418	1,651	1,560	1,229	635	209	2	32
Illinois	10,838	2,163	169,449	30,025	1,370,405	718,979	8,139,558	2,068,574	221,733	14,000	13,296	11,271	5,216	869	(Z)	399
Indiana	9,648	4,049	5,298	17,119	158,542	40,284	3,807,861	644,787	139,995	6,283	5,997	5,142	2,923	615	15	160
Iowa	8,710	7,401	38,999	24,693	377,672	75,977	1,958,697	89,826	67,896	3,383	3,391	2,639	1,473	345	12	54
Kansas	2,460	219	47,170	18,241	161,497	22,510	1,915,530	166,609	48,064	2,759	2,889	2,315	1,184	358	14	–
Kentucky	5,104	3,828	198,245	21,345	205,314	85,419	2,819,393	381,538	67,679	5,968	5,719	4,720	2,857	509	34	142
Louisiana	(X)	(X)	186,912	27,507	114,090	76,956	2,187,050	236,745	45,784	6,486	6,820	5,248	3,344	514	153	–
Maine	3,090	775	3,600	12,144	81,740	49,464	1,160,028	111,616	32,076	2,404	2,049	1,850	1,259	181	5	38
Maryland	960	31	53,264	11,920	282,167	131,948	5,277,844	447,487	152,251	6,330	5,660	5,538	2,560	425	20	173
Massachusetts	2,937	445	25,575	6,836	292,688	140,493	8,830,334	1,301,076	194,706	9,841	9,202	7,500	4,222	497	27	228
Michigan	13,079	(X)	19,344	48,304	1,064,774	171,844	6,576,065	1,841,010	75,543	11,514	11,185	9,486	4,850	776	10	376
Minnesota	1,039	727	6,814	56,535	517,447	283,517	5,709,584	637,183	87,022	5,710	5,776	4,599	2,589	367	35	–
Mississippi	2,346	3,825	89,763	12,833	117,892	59,525	1,061,704	243,846	15,440	4,927	4,605	3,420	2,443	364	24	137
Missouri	3,886	62	90,862	30,349	254,740	135,328	3,720,749	224,366	69,657	7,140	7,137	5,671	3,645	725	35	–
Montana	1,976	4,884	1,112	37,208	144,651	37,855	605,582	67,723	11,431	1,435	1,654	1,439	459	1	3	34
Nebraska	285	(X)	6,731	13,770	88,780	63,980	1,242,603	167,429	26,423	2,079	2,028	1,682	892	222	7	37
Nevada	(X)	95,668	52,760	7,171	139,467	308,850	(X)	(X)	24,548	1,911	1,646	1,244	629	180	2	40
New Hampshire	17,514	354	4,041	9,031	84,431	61,597	54,769	407,603	30,536	1,425	1,326	1,116	542	140	6	26
New Jersey	3,960	66,430	249,969	12,162	398,691	407,712	7,400,733	1,896,998	516,008	10,169	10,239	8,212	4,228	720	37	273
New Mexico	963	258	2,651	17,126	121,246	21,575	1,007,248	138,196	7,392	3,766	3,418	2,774	1,599	261	10	82
New York	46,000	47	57,682	4,293	793,597	146,388	24,647,225	2,044,504	736,004	43,463	38,637	30,038	20,831	1,250	2,443	991
North Carolina	13,796	(X)	337,740	14,891	440,180	131,728	7,250,837	837,085	145,109	10,067	9,510	7,911	4,824	815	116	206
North Dakota	259	452	(X)	12,838	54,707	46,226	213,982	49,807	2,883	1,203	1,189	1,155	343	182	15	25
Ohio	29,843	(X)	297,031	30,826	713,149	666,510	8,705,161	1,060,594	64,242	13,233	13,262	10,560	6,551	918	31	–
Oklahoma	5,204	4,731	41,960	21,571	552,799	199,713	2,319,123	133,309	111,143	4,726	4,510	3,587	1,828	398	34	118
Oregon	2,610	798	4,257	39,882	418,903	131,592	4,270,740	320,065	73,608	4,716	4,457	3,597	1,808	378	30	76
Pennsylvania	14,765	100	787,502	64,809	792,430	763,240	7,323,364	1,677,998	708,587	16,655	15,603	12,765	7,561	1,347	22	436
Rhode Island	99	403	3,982	1,881	56,986	30,031	899,939	69,479	25,313	1,855	1,794	1,526	894	142	4	–
South Carolina	8,076	2,198	72,898	19,275	122,056	113,236	2,438,712	196,510	32,765	4,914	4,883	4,017	2,667	438	9	–
South Dakota	296	134	2,718	22,129	42,167	57,993	(X)	47,108	9,322	1,376	1,350	1,131	391	204	6	–
Tennessee	2,444	785	506,776	24,997	255,137	203,248	146,851	694,798	96,534	8,153	7,374	6,160	4,450	532	13	139
Texas	38,515	6,923	1,896,287	79,988	1,232,494	681,645	1,692,277	145,005	151,131	24,353	21,955	17,350	10,306	2,595	228	831
Utah	1,147	(X)	2,628	20,674	91,372	27,232	1,692,277	145,005	9,674	2,337	2,208	1,910	853	215	7	41
Vermont	520	143	4,604	6,105	62,566	18,873	429,817	62,228	14,712	1,185	1,087	900	495	108	3	25
Virginia	8,209	57	46,342	20,145	340,085	147,815	7,422,071	422,119	149,647	6,200	6,233	4,615	2,020	697	16	153
Washington	10,045	75	18,616	30,399	334,244	190,476	(X)	(X)	139,855	7,474	7,103	5,707	2,953	554	30	123
West Virginia	10,489	12	8,033	15,933	83,663	39,790	1,068,212	181,515	9,301	3,301	3,034	2,542	1,510	328	21	83
Wisconsin	527	523	14,016	60,642	330,291	289,639	5,051,612	681,990	86,357	6,773	6,173	4,504	3,032	579	13	147
Wyoming	5	(X)	6,327	27,801	50,784	14,888	(X)	(X)	6,044	1,420	1,192	1,014	223	233	6	23

– Represents zero. X Not applicable. Z Less than $500,000.

[1]Includes items not shown separately.
[2]Program of the Department of Health and Human Services.
[3]Program of the Department of Transportation.
[4]FEMA = Federal Emergency Management Agency, part of the Department of Homeland Security.
[5]Program of the Department of Education.

Survey, Census, or Data Collection Method: Tax collections—Based on the Annual Survey of State Government Tax Collection; for information, see Internet site <http://www.census.gov/govs/www/statetaxdoc2004.html>;   Federal aid—Based on a survey of federal government departments and agencies; for information, see Internet site <http://www.census.gov/prod/www/abs/fas.html>.

Sources: Tax collections—U.S. Census Bureau, "State Government Tax Collections," see Internet site <http://www.census.gov/govs/www/statetax.html> (accessed 27 April 2005);   Federal aid—U.S. Census Bureau, *Federal Aid to States for Fiscal Year 2003, 2002, 2001, 2000*, see also <http://www.census.gov/prod/www/abs/fas.html>.

Table A-78. States — **Federal Government**

Geographic area	Nonfarm employment (BLS)[1] (1,000)			Federal earnings (BEA)[2] (mil. dol.) Civilian			Federal earnings (BEA)[2] (mil. dol.) Military			Federal funds and grants Total (mil. dol.)		Defense, 2003 Per cent	Defense, 2003 Per capita (dol.)	Selected object categories, 2003 (mil. dol.) Direct payments for individuals	Selected object categories, 2003 (mil. dol.) Grants to state and local government	Selected object categories, 2003 (mil. dol.) Salaries and wages
	2004	2003	2000	2004	2003	2001	2004	2003	2001	2003	2000					
United States ...	[3]2,728.0	[3]2,761.0	[3]2,865.0	223,754	219,213	201,864	117,323	109,607	84,859	2,009,585	1,604,670	14.9	1,030	1,073,228	435,050	207,293
Alabama	51.1	50.3	53.4	4,031	4,009	3,681	1,933	1,831	1,338	36,871	29,250	21.4	1,757	19,930	6,649	3,224
Alaska	17.1	17.1	17.1	1,395	1,338	1,239	1,575	1,405	1,108	7,944	5,963	29.0	3,556	1,625	3,022	1,617
Arizona	50.9	50.5	48.7	3,981	3,681	3,292	2,021	1,891	1,399	37,801	29,282	26.2	1,771	18,675	7,235	3,335
Arkansas	20.8	21.0	22.4	1,522	1,474	1,368	890	823	525	18,340	14,847	7.9	530	11,596	4,541	1,339
California	250.2	255.4	272.9	20,080	19,849	18,596	13,004	12,322	9,995	219,706	175,967	17.9	1,106	110,716	51,329	20,611
Colorado	52.8	53.5	54.8	4,203	4,136	3,853	2,703	2,492	1,915	28,874	22,929	18.0	1,139	13,389	6,014	4,329
Connecticut	20.1	20.8	23.4	1,495	1,519	1,507	777	734	582	28,595	19,527	29.9	2,453	13,218	5,376	1,516
Delaware	5.5	5.3	5.8	370	367	373	478	447	297	5,061	3,962	11.1	690	3,146	1,181	489
District of Columbia	191.9	192.4	183.6	20,117	19,644	17,449	1,819	1,659	1,356	34,750	27,418	9.6	5,894	4,304	4,310	14,760
Florida	126.8	126.3	125.0	9,936	9,507	8,522	6,606	6,272	4,960	113,341	92,882	14.1	938	75,233	17,463	9,746
Georgia	93.5	94.4	97.7	7,331	7,296	6,571	5,704	5,294	4,206	51,910	42,525	17.3	1,037	28,092	10,561	8,015
Hawaii	31.5	31.6	30.9	2,493	2,375	2,091	3,444	3,129	2,729	11,269	9,036	39.8	3,566	4,516	1,911	2,864
Idaho	13.2	13.6	13.6	968	911	841	526	469	330	8,654	7,012	7.5	478	4,431	1,858	834
Illinois	89.9	92.0	100.6	7,027	6,977	6,640	2,622	2,502	2,178	73,020	60,046	6.8	390	45,018	15,720	6,553
Indiana	36.3	37.1	43.2	2,716	2,680	2,582	805	760	429	35,525	28,743	10.3	589	22,572	7,313	2,338
Iowa	18.3	19.0	20.8	1,285	1,283	1,218	543	471	257	17,550	14,761	5.7	342	11,434	3,877	1,129
Kansas	26.0	26.2	27.7	1,903	1,829	1,718	1,694	1,578	1,203	18,208	14,282	13.8	925	10,665	3,415	2,108
Kentucky	37.0	37.4	39.2	2,433	2,457	2,271	2,750	2,542	2,132	31,153	24,472	17.0	1,285	16,288	6,634	3,112
Louisiana	34.4	35.1	37.3	2,638	2,555	2,381	2,183	2,023	1,445	31,646	25,995	11.4	802	17,983	7,820	2,648
Maine	14.4	14.1	14.3	1,111	1,059	958	487	460	340	9,966	7,853	18.2	1,389	5,156	2,610	888
Maryland	127.7	128.2	128.1	14,240	13,990	12,537	3,014	2,855	2,368	57,646	45,365	19.8	2,071	22,467	8,632	10,331
Massachusetts	50.7	52.0	57.0	4,120	4,222	4,024	983	932	591	51,265	40,860	14.5	1,154	26,133	13,328	3,446
Michigan	55.5	56.1	60.4	4,179	4,078	3,804	849	822	466	57,870	46,851	6.0	343	37,598	12,970	3,418
Minnesota	33.7	34.2	36.1	2,554	2,499	2,312	724	697	381	27,580	23,013	7.7	419	16,141	6,914	2,120
Mississippi	25.4	25.8	27.1	1,867	1,808	1,660	1,789	1,686	1,256	21,741	18,389	16.8	1,265	11,827	5,318	1,970
Missouri	54.4	55.3	59.6	4,152	4,135	3,928	1,805	1,674	1,200	43,874	35,730	18.2	1,401	23,396	8,655	3,832
Montana	13.8	13.8	13.4	980	953	851	441	405	278	7,092	5,920	7.8	606	3,812	1,938	845
Nebraska	16.6	16.7	16.6	1,156	1,123	1,012	912	846	620	11,000	9,617	10.0	632	6,688	2,512	1,192
Nevada	16.4	16.5	15.2	1,387	1,236	1,067	871	792	539	11,637	8,633	11.8	611	6,988	1,955	1,222
New Hampshire	7.9	8.0	8.2	631	607	569	169	165	83	7,349	5,805	11.3	642	4,174	1,865	571
New Jersey	62.4	63.3	68.3	5,099	5,052	4,780	1,274	1,198	866	53,679	43,654	9.9	617	32,578	11,481	4,159
New Mexico	29.7	29.9	30.4	2,224	2,205	2,054	1,150	1,046	765	18,736	14,484	11.5	1,151	6,669	4,322	1,926
New York	129.9	135.1	147.0	10,262	10,017	9,522	2,631	2,424	1,719	137,898	110,459	4.6	328	74,030	47,575	8,535
North Carolina	61.2	61.4	67.0	4,364	4,258	3,931	7,470	6,919	5,438	51,766	41,414	14.5	893	29,818	11,613	6,541
North Dakota	10.1	10.1	9.6	626	600	554	741	679	484	5,726	5,246	12.4	1,123	3,074	1,537	717
Ohio	78.2	79.5	87.2	6,215	6,258	6,002	1,863	1,716	1,063	69,902	57,387	9.7	593	42,305	15,687	5,362
Oklahoma	46.1	46.1	47.9	3,553	3,388	3,149	2,278	2,098	1,624	25,254	20,758	15.8	1,135	14,277	5,136	3,353
Oregon	30.2	30.7	31.6	2,342	2,267	2,101	509	486	275	21,253	16,568	5.2	308	13,171	5,103	1,781
Pennsylvania	107.6	108.0	114.3	8,014	8,011	7,633	1,775	1,649	992	90,350	73,745	8.9	651	57,228	18,624	6,363
Rhode Island	10.0	10.2	10.8	841	850	798	447	448	401	8,036	6,879	13.4	1,003	4,326	2,234	817
South Carolina	28.1	28.1	31.3	2,015	1,978	1,841	3,018	2,779	2,210	28,038	22,323	15.2	1,027	15,592	5,969	2,863
South Dakota	11.2	11.3	11.4	751	731	682	449	410	265	6,202	5,141	8.1	656	3,450	1,698	673
Tennessee	50.6	51.3	53.6	3,949	3,899	3,706	976	890	552	42,602	33,588	8.2	598	22,666	9,057	3,357
Texas	180.8	180.4	186.2	13,760	13,444	12,246	10,218	9,480	7,395	140,451	106,671	21.6	1,372	68,266	28,423	13,939
Utah	34.7	35.7	32.8	2,430	2,438	2,194	850	801	495	13,500	10,043	23.0	1,319	5,943	2,845	2,047
Vermont	6.3	6.3	6.1	461	434	378	157	147	79	4,443	3,364	13.7	986	2,186	1,331	360
Virginia	152.4	147.7	153.0	14,581	14,156	12,697	11,501	10,976	9,567	82,454	62,808	39.6	4,425	28,973	7,886	14,756
Washington	69.7	70.2	69.9	5,729	5,494	4,816	4,414	4,162	3,354	43,368	33,923	17.8	1,256	22,100	8,881	5,758
West Virginia	21.8	21.9	22.5	1,660	1,612	1,484	371	343	197	14,226	11,751	3.6	282	8,711	3,562	1,289
Wisconsin	29.5	29.8	32.6	2,043	2,024	1,926	762	654	374	30,237	24,308	6.0	330	18,900	7,544	1,785
Wyoming	7.6	7.6	7.4	536	502	459	350	321	235	4,226	3,221	8.8	747	1,754	1,616	510

[1]Bureau of Labor Statistics.
[2]Bureau of Economic Analysis.
[3]United States totals differ from the sum of the state figures because of differing benchmarks among states and differing industrial and geographic stratification.

Survey, Census, or Data Collection Method: Employment—Based on the Current Employment Statistics (CES) survey; for information, see Appendix B, Limitations of the Data and Methodology, and Internet site <http://www.bls.gov/opub/hom/homch2_a.htm>; Earnings—Based on the Regional Economic Information System; for information, see Internet site <http://www.bea.gov/bea/regional/articles/spi2003/>; Federal funds and grants—Based on information systems in various federal government agencies; for information, see Internet site <http://www.census.gov/govs/www/cffr.html>.

Sources: Employment—U.S. Bureau of Labor Statistics, Current Employment Statistics Program, see Internet site <http://www.bls.gov/sae/home.htm>; Earnings—U.S. Bureau of Economic Analysis, *Survey of Current Business*, April 2005, and see Internet site <http://www.bea.gov/bea/regional/spi/>; Federal funds and grants—U.S. Census Bureau, *Consolidated Federal Funds Report*, annual, see Internet site <http://www.census.gov/govs/www/cffr.html>.

Geographic area	Federal individual income tax returns								Federal civilian employment[4]		Federally owned property, 2003		Federal lands, 2003[5]	
	Number of returns[1] (1,000)		Adjusted gross income[2] (mil. dol.)		Adjusted gross income per return (dol.)		Income tax[3] (mil. dol.)			Percent change, 2000–2002	Number of buildings[6]	Building area (mil. sq. ft.)	Total (1,000 acres)	Percent of total land
	2002	2000	2002	2000	2002	2000	2002	2000	2002 (1,000)					
United States[7]...	131,357	130,122	6,199,925	6,307,009	47,199	48,470	751,617	980,064	2,653	−0.8	432,791	3,032	671,759	29.6
Alabama	1,884	1,904	74,843	72,591	39,730	38,126	7,897	9,476	48	–	8,018	54	1,203	3.7
Alaska	343	329	14,833	13,964	43,240	42,444	1,796	2,064	14	–	8,645	55	243,847	66.7
Arizona	2,285	2,153	102,846	98,821	45,003	45,899	11,482	14,165	46	7.0	5,664	24	36,495	50.2
Arkansas	1,122	1,118	41,364	39,706	36,882	35,515	4,138	5,087	20	–	14,228	54	3,956	11.8
California	15,172	14,867	803,512	864,645	52,961	58,159	101,142	146,454	245	−1.2	60,475	380	46,980	46.9
Colorado	2,079	2,096	105,025	112,909	50,516	53,869	12,715	18,243	52	2.0	9,405	57	23,174	34.9
Connecticut	1,654	1,672	111,029	117,734	67,136	70,415	17,141	22,682	20	−4.8	2,046	16	15	0.5
Delaware	388	378	19,284	18,647	49,665	49,331	2,313	2,794	5	–	1,556	66	29	2.3
District of Columbia	276	279	16,145	16,271	58,573	58,319	2,371	2,839	189	4.4	937	8	10	26.3
Florida...........	7,850	7,499	350,664	348,609	44,673	46,487	44,497	56,618	122	8.0	14,180	111	4,606	13.3
Georgia	3,709	3,637	168,864	168,486	45,524	46,326	19,128	24,693	91	2.2	13,160	113	2,314	6.2
Hawaii	591	572	25,718	23,929	43,510	41,834	2,754	3,124	25	8.7	16,459	86	672	16.4
Idaho...........	578	559	22,254	22,572	38,507	40,379	2,156	2,922	11	–	7,127	77	35,136	66.4
Illinois	5,723	5,787	290,425	302,994	50,749	52,358	37,309	49,472	92	−2.1	4,877	33	652	1.8
Indiana	2,817	2,837	119,765	119,554	42,522	42,141	12,963	16,416	36	−2.7	2,327	13	534	2.3
Iowa	1,325	1,351	54,107	54,016	40,840	39,982	5,442	6,896	18	–	6,246	19	303	0.8
Kansas	1,219	1,223	52,503	53,410	43,066	43,671	5,730	7,491	25	–	6,058	43	642	1.2
Kentucky	1,741	1,747	68,276	66,933	39,220	38,313	6,986	8,617	31	3.3	7,182	56	1,707	6.7
Louisiana	1,880	1,874	70,865	69,184	37,701	36,918	7,506	9,261	33	–	6,430	48	1,502	5.2
Maine	615	606	24,727	24,374	40,201	40,221	2,503	3,151	14	7.7	4,418	35	164	0.8
Maryland	2,602	2,563	145,389	139,963	55,879	54,609	17,870	20,950	133	2.3	10,364	109	193	3.0
Massachusetts	3,052	3,110	178,244	202,426	58,408	65,089	24,505	36,438	53	–	2,135	13	106	2.1
Michigan	4,546	4,620	209,646	217,648	46,113	47,110	24,061	31,781	57	−1.7	6,321	33	3,639	10.0
Minnesota	2,384	2,386	119,930	120,028	50,310	50,305	14,184	17,687	34	–	2,953	19	3,535	6.9
Mississippi	1,170	1,173	40,610	39,170	34,720	33,393	3,827	4,666	24	–	6,605	50	2,101	7.0
Missouri..........	2,564	2,565	107,992	108,519	42,120	42,308	11,834	15,270	54	–	6,720	43	2,238	5.1
Montana	434	424	15,198	14,523	35,057	34,252	1,474	1,766	12	9.1	6,934	15	29,239	31.3
Nebraska	803	809	33,043	33,605	41,165	41,539	3,515	4,561	15	–	540	4	1,459	3.0
Nevada	1,044	954	52,307	48,858	50,101	51,214	6,783	7,845	15	15.4	16,244	91	64,589	91.9
New Hampshire.......	635	629	32,337	34,469	50,952	54,800	3,997	5,673	9	12.5	5,688	53	830	14.4
New Jersey	4,082	4,067	247,077	253,294	60,527	62,280	34,778	44,470	63	1.6	14,790	67	180	3.7
New Mexico	814	728	29,959	23,655	36,817	32,493	3,032	2,721	26	4.0	11,196	105	26,518	34.1
New York	8,590	8,577	465,512	474,337	54,193	55,303	64,517	80,907	133	−0.7	4,705	27	242	0.8
North Carolina.......	3,681	3,636	157,402	156,022	42,763	42,910	16,646	21,231	57	–	3,245	19	3,602	11.5
North Dakota	302	303	11,285	10,735	37,314	35,429	1,140	1,333	8	–	7,744	32	1,333	3.0
Ohio	5,444	5,575	227,754	231,057	41,835	41,445	24,760	31,612	80	−4.8	5,048	71	458	1.7
Oklahoma	1,461	1,465	56,019	54,835	38,344	37,430	5,834	7,150	44	2.3	8,813	56	1,331	3.0
Oregon	1,572	1,562	67,956	70,282	43,233	44,995	7,097	9,723	29	–	7,072	23	30,639	49.7
Pennsylvania	5,772	5,806	261,846	262,961	45,367	45,291	30,944	39,214	106	−0.9	7,509	82	725	2.5
Rhode Island	498	494	23,701	23,015	47,585	46,589	2,817	3,316	11	10.0	1,333	13	5	0.8
South Carolina	1,805	1,802	70,931	69,543	39,301	38,592	7,045	8,804	27	3.8	9,828	63	1,236	6.4
South Dakota	357	355	13,475	13,233	37,698	37,276	1,448	1,824	10	11.1	3,187	18	2,314	4.7
Tennessee	2,565	2,567	105,526	103,066	41,140	40,150	12,129	14,590	49	−2.0	8,402	73	2,016	7.5
Texas	9,299	9,052	415,647	417,263	44,699	46,096	51,853	67,590	166	2.5	24,200	214	3,172	1.9
Utah	970	942	41,015	40,270	42,291	42,749	3,964	4,964	33	10.0	8,359	51	35,025	66.5
Vermont	302	299	12,525	12,632	41,445	42,247	1,330	1,705	6	–	476	2	450	7.6
Virginia	3,432	3,338	180,640	171,060	52,637	51,246	22,232	26,051	143	−1.4	17,812	207	2,617	10.3
Washington	2,809	2,773	141,431	149,598	50,357	53,948	17,928	25,254	65	4.8	13,589	85	13,247	31.0
West Virginia	744	750	26,629	25,645	35,771	34,193	2,598	3,102	19	5.6	1,600	14	1,266	8.2
Wisconsin..........	2,590	2,597	117,029	116,346	45,188	44,800	12,865	15,900	29	−3.3	5,096	22	1,982	5.7
Wyoming	241	235	11,092	11,020	46,027	46,894	1,389	1,820	6	–	4,845	11	31,532	50.6

– Represents zero.

[1] Includes returns constructed by Internal Revenue Service for certain self-employment tax returns.
[2] Less deficit.
[3] Includes additional tax for tax preferences, self-employment tax, tax from investment credit recapture, and other income-related taxes. Total is before earned income credit.
[4] Excludes Central Intelligence Agency, Defense Intelligence Agency, seasonal and on-call employees, and National Security Agency.
[5] Excludes trust properties.
[6] Excludes data for Department of Defense military functions outside of the United States.
[7] For federal individual income tax returns, the states will not sum to U.S. totals. Totals include returns filed from Army Post Office and Fleet Post Office addresses by members of the armed forces stationed overseas; returns by other U.S. citizens abroad; and returns filed by residents of Puerto Rico with income from sources outside of Puerto Rico or with income earned as U.S. government employees.

Survey, Census, or Data Collection Method: Tax returns—Based on the IRS's Statistics of Income (SOI) program; for information, see Internet site <www.irs.gov/taxstats/index.html>; Federal civilian employment—Based on the Central Personnel Data File (CPDF); for information, see Internet site <http://www.opm.gov/feddata/html/acpdf.asp>; Property and land—Based on annual agency reports; for information, see Internet site <www.gsa.gov/>.

Sources: Tax returns—U.S. Internal Revenue Service, *Statistics of Income Bulletin*, quarterly; Federal civilian employment—U.S. Office of Personnel Management, *Biennial Report of Employment by Geographic Area, 2002*; see Internet site <http://www.opm.gov/feddata/geograph/geograph.asp>; Property and land—U.S. General Services Administration, *Federal Real Property Profile*, annual, see Internet site <http://www.gsa.gov/> (released 11 March 2003).

Table A-80. States — Social Security, Food Stamps, and School Lunch Programs

Geographic area	Social security benefits — Beneficiaries (Dec. 31) (1,000) Total		Retired workers and dependents[4]		Payments[1] (mil. dol.) Total		Retired workers and dependents[4]		Federal food stamp program — Participants (Sept. 30) (1,000)		Federal cost[2] (mil. dol.)		National school lunch program — Participants (1,000)		Federal cost[3] (mil. dol.)	
	2004	2000	2004	2000	2004	2000	2004	2000	2004	2000	2004	2000	2004	2000	2004	2000
United States . . .	46,531	44,324	32,278	31,090	485,123	401,044	322,792	271,185	23,819	17,156	24,560	14,927	28,515	26,845	7,489	6,016
Alabama	884	827	536	516	8,697	6,942	5,062	4,186	498	396	513	344	558	541	143	121
Alaska	63	55	41	35	618	465	388	291	49	38	64	46	52	50	21	17
Arizona	888	791	634	575	9,282	7,163	6,377	5,026	530	259	578	240	545	447	160	112
Arkansas	546	517	341	332	5,228	4,250	3,151	2,633	346	247	347	206	322	312	85	71
California	4,412	4,208	3,162	3,046	45,788	38,138	31,216	26,460	1,859	1,830	1,990	1,639	2,795	2,634	997	830
Colorado	571	535	406	376	5,822	4,698	3,926	3,148	242	156	251	127	335	321	75	60
Connecticut	584	579	435	436	6,642	5,711	4,808	4,219	196	165	198	138	292	265	67	50
Delaware	149	135	105	96	1,618	1,268	1,098	872	56	32	57	31	78	72	17	13
District of Columbia	72	74	50	52	653	579	435	384	89	81	98	77	47	47	16	15
Florida.	3,382	3,193	2,497	2,381	34,976	28,700	24,782	20,622	1,202	882	1,269	771	1,464	1,322	428	344
Georgia	1,192	1,106	771	712	11,958	9,503	7,464	5,947	867	559	924	489	1,170	1,065	309	228
Hawaii	199	184	154	143	2,039	1,628	1,516	1,230	99	118	152	166	124	143	31	30
Idaho.	219	194	156	140	2,202	1,697	1,495	1,176	91	58	91	46	153	143	34	27
Illinois	1,884	1,842	1,337	1,320	20,456	17,530	13,869	12,060	1,070	817	1,211	777	1,080	1,058	304	249
Indiana	1,038	994	719	695	11,259	9,380	7,520	6,336	526	300	550	268	679	622	148	100
Iowa	546	540	396	396	5,689	4,891	3,926	3,417	179	123	176	100	385	383	68	55
Kansas	447	440	319	317	4,745	4,057	3,260	2,821	170	117	158	83	323	308	66	53
Kentucky	785	739	459	438	7,656	6,203	4,247	3,505	545	403	543	337	528	499	129	102
Louisiana	739	711	440	429	7,121	5,906	3,960	3,350	706	500	754	448	630	646	178	154
Maine	265	251	175	170	2,548	2,075	1,617	1,360	142	102	140	81	106	107	23	20
Maryland	761	723	541	519	8,076	6,622	5,460	4,541	274	219	287	199	426	392	97	81
Massachusetts	1,067	1,064	748	759	11,195	9,696	7,561	6,691	335	232	304	182	549	528	110	95
Michigan	1,716	1,645	1,172	1,138	19,067	15,892	12,497	10,585	944	603	896	457	858	803	199	160
Minnesota	775	739	567	545	8,080	6,633	5,640	4,673	247	196	249	165	583	563	105	82
Mississippi	546	516	319	303	5,092	4,101	2,889	2,364	377	276	361	226	399	397	125	107
Missouri.	1,046	1,005	703	687	10,686	8,881	6,918	5,876	700	423	663	358	611	587	143	111
Montana	166	158	119	111	1,653	1,376	1,122	926	77	59	79	51	79	79	18	16
Nebraska	291	284	211	209	2,963	2,533	2,049	1,778	114	82	109	61	226	220	45	36
Nevada	341	287	249	212	3,594	2,609	2,504	1,849	120	61	120	57	146	114	43	28
New Hampshire.	219	200	154	145	2,327	1,849	1,584	1,298	48	36	44	28	112	104	18	14
New Jersey	1,370	1,352	1,007	1,000	15,777	13,521	11,191	9,712	369	345	378	304	617	586	153	130
New Mexico	304	281	205	191	2,871	2,303	1,858	1,508	223	169	217	140	208	192	68	53
New York	3,045	3,006	2,162	2,147	33,354	28,691	22,849	19,916	1,598	1,439	1,876	1,361	1,804	1,790	490	455
North Carolina.	1,467	1,350	977	906	14,779	11,651	9,565	7,652	747	488	753	403	886	822	239	179
North Dakota	115	114	82	81	1,125	972	746	645	41	32	40	25	78	80	14	13
Ohio	1,951	1,918	1,346	1,334	20,609	17,724	13,480	11,698	945	610	1,009	520	1,047	996	230	178
Oklahoma	623	594	420	408	6,234	5,141	3,993	3,358	412	253	398	208	389	374	108	86
Oregon	611	568	445	420	6,437	5,200	4,458	3,684	420	234	415	198	284	266	73	55
Pennsylvania	2,405	2,357	1,703	1,708	25,893	22,121	17,477	15,315	961	777	933	656	1,087	1,013	236	190
Rhode Island	192	192	135	139	2,007	1,739	1,371	1,237	78	74	74	59	83	63	22	18
South Carolina	751	689	489	448	7,538	5,908	4,761	3,760	497	295	501	249	473	471	135	111
South Dakota	140	136	101	97	1,340	1,124	913	766	53	43	54	37	104	105	22	19
Tennessee	1,070	996	688	642	10,679	8,537	6,635	5,332	806	496	812	415	648	622	161	124
Texas	2,865	2,638	1,939	1,811	28,664	22,883	18,429	14,963	2,259	1,333	2,307	1,215	2,777	2,451	826	617
Utah	262	242	191	178	2,710	2,152	1,892	1,530	123	82	123	68	289	269	63	46
Vermont.	110	105	77	73	1,117	918	756	624	43	41	40	32	55	52	11	9
Virginia	1,114	1,035	757	704	11,381	9,060	7,408	5,929	486	336	476	263	705	665	146	118
Washington	913	845	658	618	9,833	7,898	6,785	5,564	453	295	455	241	506	466	124	97
West Virginia	407	390	237	233	4,189	3,488	2,268	1,947	256	227	232	185	201	202	48	43
Wisconsin.	937	900	685	665	10,000	8,347	7,018	5,936	324	193	269	129	569	536	108	83
Wyoming	83	77	60	56	856	690	598	485	26	22	25	19	49	52	10	9

[1] Unnegotiated checks not deducted.
[2] Includes benefits only and excludes administrative expenditures.
[3] Includes cash payments and commodity costs.
[4] Includes special benefits for persons age 72 and over not insured under regular or transitional provisions of Social Security Act.

Survey, Census, or Data Collection Method: Social security—Based on a 10 percent sample of administrative records; for information, see Internet site <http://www.ssa.gov/policy/>;   Federal food stamp and national school lunch programs—Based on administrative records; for information, see Internet site <www.fns.usda.gov/pd/>.

Sources: Social security—U.S. Social Security Administration, *Annual Statistical Supplement to the Social Security Bulletin*, see Internet site <http://www.ssa.gov/policy/docs/statcomps/supplement/2004/index.html>;   Federal food stamp and national school lunch programs—U.S. Department of Agriculture, Food and Nutrition Service, "Food and Nutrition Service, Program Data"; see Internet site <http://www.fns.usda.gov/pd/>.

Table A-81. States — Social Welfare Programs and Workers' Compensation

Geographic area	Public aid recipients as percent of population[1]		Supplemental security income (SSI)[2]				Temporary Assistance for Needy Families (TANF)[3]				State unemployment insurance[4]				Workers' compensation payments[5] (mil. dol.)		
			Recipients (Dec.) (1,000)		Annual payments (mil. dol.)		Recipients (Dec.) (1,000)		Annual payments[6] (mil. dol.)		Beneficiaries, first payments (1,000)		Benefits paid (mil. dol.)				
	2003	2000	2003	2000	2003	2000	2003	2000	2003	2000	2004	2000	2004	2000	2002	2000	1990
United States . . .	4.0	4.4	[7]6,902	[7]6,601	[7]34,696	[7]30,669	4,867	5,678	26,340	24,781	8,272	6,915	34,240	20,251	[8]53,443	[8]48,284	[8]38,238
Alabama	4.7	4.6	164	159	738	659	46	45	171	96	119	134	241	203	565	529	444
Alaska	4.0	4.8	11	9	47	37	15	21	88	93	46	44	126	110	188	146	113
Arizona	3.7	3.2	92	81	429	355	116	84	342	261	96	69	295	162	528	515	371
Arkansas	4.1	4.3	87	85	361	333	25	29	54	139	85	80	243	179	222	198	229
California	6.4	6.9	1,163	1,088	7,573	6,386	1,107	1,262	5,851	6,481	1,111	973	5,132	2,407	11,283	8,968	6,065
Colorado	2.0	1.9	54	54	246	228	37	28	236	205	88	52	389	158	807	835	595
Connecticut	2.7	3.3	51	49	244	216	43	64	450	436	128	103	590	349	748	667	694
Delaware	3.2	3.1	13	12	59	50	13	12	56	55	28	27	107	74	169	146	75
District of Columbia	11.3	11.4	20	20	105	93	43	45	166	157	17	15	91	66	102	89	86
Florida	3.1	3.2	409	377	1,908	1,621	120	142	852	781	300	224	1,016	662	2,306	2,545	1,976
Georgia	3.8	3.9	200	197	888	785	134	125	501	386	208	178	585	317	1,083	996	735
Hawaii	3.8	5.5	22	21	113	104	25	46	134	162	24	25	112	102	268	231	216
Idaho	1.7	1.5	20	18	91	76	3	2	43	43	50	45	145	103	233	179	105
Illinois	2.7	3.9	255	249	1,267	1,174	92	234	989	879	392	309	2,059	1,212	2,232	2,049	1,607
Indiana	3.7	3.1	94	88	441	382	138	101	313	342	187	129	686	311	577	546	350
Iowa	3.2	3.2	42	40	176	158	52	53	156	163	89	84	309	210	428	357	231
Kansas	2.9	2.5	38	36	170	151	41	32	150	151	68	54	279	174	405	342	266
Kentucky	6.2	6.5	179	174	819	741	77	87	191	203	121	111	421	271	527	479	383
Louisiana	5.0	5.3	168	166	769	715	57	71	267	118	90	72	284	183	499	494	575
Maine	4.4	4.5	31	30	136	116	26	28	100	108	33	28	116	77	293	267	380
Maryland	2.8	3.0	91	88	441	400	62	71	366	336	109	93	443	271	784	730	505
Massachusetts	4.3	4.2	168	168	855	807	109	100	697	690	239	172	1,460	790	807	828	1,235
Michigan	4.2	4.1	217	210	1,086	988	206	198	1,205	1,264	462	359	1,882	921	1,512	1,474	1,205
Minnesota	3.2	3.6	69	64	316	272	94	114	498	381	147	109	678	398	921	798	582
Mississippi	5.9	5.7	126	129	550	512	45	34	120	62	60	60	158	122	287	269	198
Missouri	3.8	4.2	115	112	528	471	101	125	299	321	166	137	534	333	1,226	909	496
Montana	3.4	3.0	14	14	64	57	17	13	56	44	22	25	69	57	191	170	150
Nebraska	2.8	2.6	22	21	95	85	27	24	79	79	43	28	128	59	293	211	137
Nevada	2.5	2.1	31	25	144	108	24	16	85	69	66	68	258	204	353	361	339
New Hampshire	2.1	2.1	13	12	58	49	14	14	72	73	21	14	84	31	217	182	169
New Jersey	2.9	3.2	150	146	732	672	104	125	842	321	332	246	1,943	1,126	1,471	1,299	844
New Mexico	5.1	6.4	50	47	223	193	45	69	123	149	32	27	127	73	191	146	228
New York	5.0	6.9	625	617	3,400	3,197	336	695	4,463	3,512	513	424	2,584	1,687	3,142	2,909	1,752
North Carolina	3.3	3.6	194	191	825	732	83	98	457	440	273	256	855	487	1,014	853	480
North Dakota	2.7	2.3	8	8	32	30	9	7	42	33	13	12	40	40	74	74	60
Ohio	3.8	4.2	244	240	1,204	1,114	187	235	1,007	995	306	248	1,234	742	2,388	2,099	1,960
Oklahoma	3.2	3.1	75	72	339	302	37	35	203	130	60	41	204	104	490	485	369
Oregon	2.8	2.6	57	52	271	228	43	38	226	169	148	147	653	430	448	412	573
Pennsylvania	4.2	4.3	311	284	1,599	1,367	214	241	1,109	1,327	487	396	2,266	1,462	2,532	2,403	2,019
Rhode Island	5.9	6.9	29	28	150	130	35	44	162	172	41	38	203	136	131	114	219
South Carolina	3.8	3.7	106	107	461	429	51	42	148	245	123	101	352	204	690	597	277
South Dakota	2.5	2.6	13	13	52	48	6	7	26	21	10	8	30	16	79	67	56
Tennessee	5.9	5.5	161	164	719	664	185	147	274	293	168	178	472	364	679	642	463
Texas	3.5	3.6	455	409	1,901	1,575	318	347	911	727	422	322	1,656	989	2,275	2,005	2,896
Utah	1.8	1.8	21	20	99	87	22	21	131	100	45	41	155	95	240	188	187
Vermont	4.2	4.8	13	13	57	51	13	16	67	62	23	18	79	44	148	112	61
Virginia	2.5	2.8	134	132	587	535	47	69	273	418	126	96	385	197	700	681	507
Washington	4.0	4.2	109	101	546	484	135	148	572	535	208	205	1,049	873	1,714	1,528	883
West Virginia	6.4	5.8	75	71	357	318	41	33	157	134	44	49	147	112	829	690	389
Wisconsin	2.5	2.3	89	85	398	357	50	38	489	382	269	230	843	528	894	768	561
Wyoming	1.4	1.4	6	6	25	23	1	1	71	34	14	11	43	26	104	83	49

[1]Total SSI and TANF recipients as of December as a percentage of resident population estimated as of July 1 for 2003 and enumerated as of April 1 for 2000.
[2]Data cover federal SSI payments and/or federally administered state supplementation.
[3]Prior to TANF, the cash assistance program to families was called Aid to Families with Dependent Children (1980–1996). Under the new welfare law (Personal Responsibility and Work Opportunity Reconciliation Act of 1996), the program became TANF.
[4]Includes unemployment compensation for state and local government employees where covered by state law.
[5]Payments represent compensation and medical benefits and include insurance losses paid by private insurance carriers (compiled from state workers' compensation agencies and A.M. Best Co.); disbursements of state funds (compiled from the A.M. Best Co. and state workers' compensation agencies); and self-insurance payments (compiled from state workers' compensation agencies and authors' estimates).
[6]Represents federal and state funds expended in fiscal year.
[7]Includes data not distributed by state.
[8]Includes federal benefits not distributed by state. Federal benefits include: those paid under the Federal Employees Compensation Act for civilian employees; the portion of the Black Lung benefit program that is financed by employers; and a portion of benefits under the Longshore and Harbor Workers Compensation Act that are not reflected in state data, namely, benefits paid by self-insured employers and by special funds under the LHWCA.

Survey, Census, or Data Collection Method: SSI—Based on Social Security Administration administrative records; for information, see Internet site <http://www.ssa.gov/policy/>; TANF—For information, see Internet site <http://www.acf.hhs.gov/>; State unemployment insurance—For information, see Internet site <http://www.doleta.gov/>; Workers' compensation—For information, see Internet site <http://www.nasi.org/>.

Sources: Public aid recipients—Compiled by the U.S. Census Bureau. Data from U.S. Social Security Administration, *Annual Statistical Supplement to the Social Security Bulletin*, and U.S. Administration for Children and Families, *Unemployment Insurance Financial Data Handbook*; SSI—U.S. Social Security Administration, *Annual Statistical Supplement to the Social Security Bulletin*; TANF—U.S. Administration for Children and Families, *Temporary Assistance for Needy Families (TANF) Program, Annual Report to Congress*, and unpublished data; State unemployment insurance—U.S. Employment and Training Administration, *Unemployment Insurance Financial Data Handbook*, annual; Workers' compensation—National Academy of Social Insurance, Washington, DC, *Workers' Compensation: Benefits, Coverage, and Costs*, annual for data beginning in 2000. See Internet site <http://www.nasi.org/>. For 1990 data, U.S. Social Security Administration, *Social Security Bulletin*.

Table A-82. States — Government Transfer Payments to Individuals

Geographic area	Total government transfer payments					Program area, 2003 (mil. dol.)						
	2003			2002 (mil. dol.)	2000 (mil. dol.)	Retirement and disability insurance benefits	Medical payments	Income maintenance benefits	Unemployment insurance benefits	Veterans benefits	Federal education and training assistance payments[2]	Other[3]
	Total (mil. dol.)	Percent change, 2000–2003	Per capita[1] (dol.)									
United States ...	1,275,144	25.2	4,385	1,219,759	1,018,106	493,132	548,986	130,464	53,512	31,916	13,708	3,426
Alabama	20,651	24.1	4,585	19,565	16,643	8,517	8,287	2,412	412	739	270	14
Alaska	3,164	6.7	4,881	3,232	2,966	596	1,244	336	166	117	14	691
Arizona	22,242	39.4	3,987	20,490	15,959	9,157	9,222	2,090	511	743	341	177
Arkansas	12,596	25.9	4,618	12,098	10,006	5,149	4,986	1,354	406	522	169	11
California	145,642	27.1	4,107	138,572	114,559	49,747	63,463	20,621	7,281	2,694	1,648	188
Colorado	14,264	27.7	3,137	13,633	11,169	5,714	5,734	1,327	710	563	181	35
Connecticut	16,662	18.3	4,778	16,245	14,086	6,642	7,420	1,285	927	259	96	32
Delaware	3,650	27.7	4,461	3,410	2,857	1,565	1,526	284	159	83	28	5
District of Columbia	3,290	21.4	5,899	3,202	2,709	666	1,821	505	116	116	47	19
Florida	80,866	25.9	4,757	76,619	64,208	34,274	34,919	6,811	1,622	2,441	742	56
Georgia	30,630	29.3	3,530	30,377	23,696	11,699	12,683	3,708	1,038	1,096	373	34
Hawaii	4,642	20.8	3,718	4,468	3,844	1,972	1,685	604	167	170	40	4
Idaho	4,966	30.5	3,633	4,692	3,804	2,248	1,794	398	251	177	88	10
Illinois	51,277	22.9	4,054	49,067	41,726	20,577	21,102	5,202	3,020	748	577	51
Indiana	24,606	22.5	3,969	23,738	20,081	11,199	9,447	2,176	959	480	329	16
Iowa	12,119	20.6	4,119	12,160	10,046	5,672	4,684	852	468	257	173	13
Kansas	10,746	20.6	3,944	10,532	8,908	4,818	4,133	826	525	292	140	12
Kentucky	19,004	20.4	4,615	18,481	15,778	7,750	7,587	2,243	644	536	235	9
Louisiana	20,701	24.8	4,607	20,525	16,582	6,981	9,583	2,868	400	575	282	12
Maine	6,746	27.1	5,153	6,193	5,307	2,496	3,118	613	165	294	54	6
Maryland	21,579	27.1	3,915	20,157	16,981	8,175	10,061	1,814	752	551	190	36
Massachusetts	32,668	23.4	5,088	31,989	26,471	11,097	15,713	2,515	2,362	693	239	49
Michigan	45,090	22.9	4,472	42,861	36,675	18,657	18,097	4,637	2,563	695	419	23
Minnesota	20,402	29.6	4,029	19,365	15,748	8,146	8,907	1,596	1,030	488	215	20
Mississippi	13,803	27.8	4,789	13,225	10,803	4,956	6,034	1,883	269	415	230	16
Missouri	26,145	25.1	4,571	24,993	20,904	10,655	11,411	2,389	775	631	256	28
Montana	3,697	18.2	4,026	3,570	3,127	1,775	1,260	336	103	154	55	13
Nebraska	6,981	22.6	4,018	6,687	5,694	3,032	2,850	585	170	254	86	4
Nevada	7,716	38.1	3,441	7,230	5,588	3,441	2,893	639	390	275	57	21
New Hampshire	4,803	22.6	3,727	4,711	3,918	2,223	1,914	294	154	173	40	6
New Jersey	41,097	24.2	4,755	40,123	33,092	16,233	18,354	2,641	2,678	592	298	301
New Mexico	7,955	32.3	4,235	7,450	6,014	2,816	3,435	942	180	367	117	98
New York	117,583	22.8	6,120	112,278	95,735	35,083	62,713	12,588	3,945	1,385	1,137	732
North Carolina	35,759	27.2	4,246	34,148	28,108	14,222	14,477	4,024	1,413	1,189	410	24
North Dakota	2,592	11.6	4,092	2,535	2,322	1,192	1,004	191	59	79	42	24
Ohio	53,176	23.2	4,649	50,679	43,149	22,789	22,071	4,973	1,789	1,011	501	43
Oklahoma	15,114	26.0	4,310	14,418	11,999	6,251	5,887	1,566	397	777	211	24
Oregon	15,293	24.9	4,291	14,939	12,243	6,664	5,255	1,369	1,303	507	172	24
Pennsylvania	66,136	20.4	5,346	63,454	54,928	26,446	29,259	5,060	3,608	1,205	514	45
Rhode Island	5,827	22.7	5,415	5,632	4,748	2,146	2,687	532	261	133	60	7
South Carolina	18,212	27.0	4,390	17,417	14,340	7,412	7,246	2,124	570	618	215	27
South Dakota	2,995	20.2	3,915	2,921	2,490	1,311	1,181	240	39	125	48	50
Tennessee	27,345	25.1	4,678	25,734	21,864	10,415	12,052	3,063	773	754	264	24
Texas	77,966	30.1	3,527	73,433	59,911	27,896	33,521	9,553	3,001	2,715	1,064	216
Utah	6,373	28.4	2,709	6,001	4,962	2,866	2,286	549	289	169	172	42
Vermont	2,844	26.7	4,592	2,681	2,245	1,090	1,247	277	120	84	25	2
Virginia	25,059	25.8	3,402	23,951	19,916	11,248	9,359	2,311	790	1,030	274	48
Washington	26,493	27.3	4,321	25,196	20,817	11,057	9,683	2,195	2,285	975	249	47
West Virginia	11,555	29.9	6,379	10,900	8,894	5,620	4,110	1,068	256	387	106	9
Wisconsin	22,414	25.2	4,094	21,902	17,902	9,805	8,856	1,843	1,179	515	193	22
Wyoming	2,011	27.0	4,005	1,879	1,583	976	724	155	61	66	25	4

[1]Based on estimated resident population as of July 1.

[2]Excludes veterans. Consists largely of federal fellowship payments (National Science Foundation, fellowships and traineeships, subsistence payments to state maritime academy cadets, and other federal fellowships), interest subsidy on higher education loans, basic educational opportunity grants, and Job Corps payments.

[3]Consists largely of Bureau of Indian Affairs payments, education exchange payments, Alaska Permanent Fund dividend payments, compensation of survivors of public safety officers, compensation of victims of crime, disaster relief payments, compensation for Japanese internment, and other special payments to individuals.

Survey, Census, or Data Collection Method: Based on the Regional Economic Information System. For more information, see "State Personal Income Methodologies" at <http://www.bea.gov/bea/regional/articles/spi2003/>.

Source: U.S. Bureau of Economic Analysis, "Regional Accounts Data, Annual State Personal Income"; see Internet site <http://www.bea.gov/bea/regional/spi/> (accessed 3 May 2005).

Geographic area	Medicare enrollment (1,000)				Medicaid				State Children's Health Insurance Program (SCHIP)			
					Enrollment[1] (1,000)		Payments[2] (mil. dol.)		Enrollment[3] (1,000)		Expenditures[4] (mil. dol.)	
	2003	2002	2001	2000	2002	2000	2002	2000	2004	2000	2004	2000
United States . . .	[5]40,173	[5]39,594	[5]39,149	[5]38,762	49,755	42,887	213,491	168,443	6,059	3,357	4,600.7	1,928.8
Alabama	719	706	695	685	765	619	3,204	2,393	79	38	19.4	31.9
Alaska	48	46	44	42	110	96	687	473	19	13	72.8	18.1
Arizona	729	708	691	675	878	681	2,882	2,112	88	60	258.9	29.4
Arkansas	453	446	442	439	579	489	2,015	1,543	(NA)	2	28.5	1.5
California	4,078	4,009	3,955	3,901	9,301	7,918	23,636	17,105	1,036	484	661.6	187.3
Colorado	493	484	476	467	426	381	2,166	1,809	57	35	37.6	13.9
Connecticut	522	518	516	515	479	420	3,245	2,839	21	20	17.2	12.8
Delaware	119	116	114	112	167	115	651	529	10	4	5.3	1.5
District of Columbia	74	74	75	75	193	139	1,027	793	6	2	7.2	5.8
Florida	2,921	2,876	2,838	2,804	2,676	2,373	9,827	7,433	420	227	176.5	125.7
Georgia	974	951	933	916	1,637	1,369	4,796	3,624	280	121	215.0	48.7
Hawaii	175	171	168	165	200	194	695	600	19	(Z)	10.5	0.4
Idaho.	178	173	169	165	176	131	792	594	17	12	14.4	7.5
Illinois	1,661	1,646	1,640	1,635	1,731	1,519	9,122	7,807	234	63	309.8	32.7
Indiana	878	865	858	852	849	706	3,725	2,977	81	44	65.4	53.7
Iowa	482	479	478	477	353	314	1,856	1,477	41	20	37.3	15.5
Kansas	394	392	391	390	289	263	1,501	1,227	44	26	39.6	12.8
Kentucky	648	637	630	623	808	764	3,459	2,921	95	56	71.5	60.0
Louisiana	620	612	605	602	899	761	3,234	2,632	106	50	94.4	25.3
Maine	227	223	219	216	276	194	1,717	1,310	29	23	25.2	11.4
Maryland	674	664	655	645	693	626	3,662	3,003	111	93	106.4	92.2
Massachusetts	966	963	961	961	1,066	1,060	6,387	5,413	167	113	119.1	44.2
Michigan	1,445	1,426	1,414	1,403	1,450	1,352	5,919	4,881	(NA)	55	159.5	36.2
Minnesota	676	667	660	654	621	558	4,439	3,280	5	(Z)	72.7	(Z)
Mississippi	437	429	423	419	712	605	2,500	1,808	83	12	101.9	21.1
Missouri	884	874	867	861	1,036	890	4,072	3,274	176	73	80.2	41.2
Montana	142	140	138	137	104	104	533	422	15	8	14.3	4.3
Nebraska	257	256	255	254	256	229	1,255	960	33	11	35.3	6.1
Nevada	274	261	251	240	202	138	724	516	39	16	20.6	9.0
New Hampshire.	180	176	173	170	104	97	746	651	11	4	7.3	1.6
New Jersey	1,220	1,213	1,208	1,203	954	822	5,497	4,714	127	89	221.9	46.9
New Mexico	250	244	238	234	799	376	1,797	1,249	21	8	21.4	3.4
New York	2,763	2,747	2,729	2,715	3,921	3,420	31,489	26,148	827	769	296.9	401.0
North Carolina.	1,205	1,178	1,155	1,133	1,355	1,214	6,041	4,834	174	104	166.2	65.5
North Dakota	103	103	103	103	70	63	423	358	5	3	6.9	1.8
Ohio	1,727	1,713	1,705	1,701	1,656	1,305	9,186	7,115	220	118	167.1	53.1
Oklahoma	521	515	511	508	631	507	2,238	1,604	101	58	46.1	51.3
Oregon	513	504	496	489	621	558	2,136	1,714	47	37	25.3	12.5
Pennsylvania	2,110	2,101	2,095	2,095	1,627	1,492	8,524	6,366	177	120	126.6	70.7
Rhode Island	172	172	172	172	199	179	1,251	1,070	26	12	25.2	10.4
South Carolina	606	592	580	568	809	689	3,383	2,765	76	60	50.8	46.6
South Dakota	122	121	120	119	118	102	504	402	13	6	10.9	3.1
Tennessee	872	855	842	829	1,732	1,568	4,748	3,491	(NA)	15	4.5	41.7
Texas	2,390	2,338	2,300	2,265	2,953	2,633	11,121	9,277	651	131	282.5	41.4
Utah	220	215	210	206	275	225	1,216	960	39	25	28.0	12.8
Vermont.	93	91	90	89	154	139	607	480	7	4	3.2	1.4
Virginia	946	927	910	893	665	627	3,018	2,479	100	38	63.0	18.6
Washington	775	759	746	736	1,039	896	4,373	2,435	17	3	39.7	0.6
West Virginia	347	343	340	338	362	342	1,578	1,394	37	22	30.8	9.7
Wisconsin.	804	794	787	783	716	577	3,606	2,968	68	47	93.7	21.4
Wyoming	69	67	66	65	59	46	280	215	6	3	5.2	1.0

NA Not available.   Z Less than 500 or $50,000.

[1]Persons who had payments made on their behalf at any time during the fiscal year.

[2]Payments are for fiscal year and reflect federal and state hospital share payments. Data exclude disproportionate hospital share payments. Disproportionate share hospitals receive higher Medicaid reimbursement than other hospitals because they treat a disproportionate share of Medicaid patients.

[3]Number of children ever enrolled in SCHIP.

[4]Expenditures for which states are entitled to federal reimbursement under Title XXI and that reconcile any advance of Title XXI federal funds made on the basis of estimates.

[5]Includes enrollees from unknown areas.

Survey, Census, or Data Collection Method: Medicare—For information, see Internet site <http://www.cms.hhs.gov/>;   Medicaid—Based on the Medicaid Statistical Information System (MSIS) and CMS-64 reports; for information, see Internet site <http://www.cms.hhs.gov/MedicaidDataSourcesGenInfo/02_MSISData.asp#TopOfPage>;   SCHIP—Based on the SCHIP Statistical Enrollment Data System (SEDS); for information, see Internet site <http://www.cms.hhs.gov/NationalSCHIPPolicy/SCHIPER/list.asp#TopOfPage>.

Sources: Medicare enrollment—U.S. Centers for Medicare and Medicaid Services, "Medicare Beneficiaries Enrolled by State as of July 1, 1999–2003," published September 2004, see Internet site <http://www.cms.hhs.gov/MedicareEnrpts/>;   Medicaid—U.S. Centers for Medicare and Medicaid Services, Medicaid Statistical Information System, MSIS, see Internet site <http://www.cms.hhs.gov/MedicaidDataSourcesGenInfo/02_MSISData.asp#TopOfPage>;   SCHIP—U.S. Centers for Medicare and Medicaid Services, *The State Children's Health Insurance Program, Annual Enrollment Report* and the Statement of Expenditures for the SCHIP Program (CMS-21), see Internet site <http://www.cms.hhs.gov/NationalSCHIPPolicy/SCHIPER/list.asp#TopOfPage>.

Geographic area	Department of Defense												Number of veterans[1] (1,000)	
	Personnel						Expenditures (mil. dol.)							
	Total		2004				Total		2004					
	2004	2000	Active duty military	Civilian	Reserve and National Guard	Selected major location	2004	2000	Payroll	Contracts	Grants		2004	2000
United States . . .	2,763,823	2,791,331	1,055,314	634,185	1,074,324	Fort Bragg, NC	345,891	229,072	139,490	203,389	3,012		24,523	26,210
Alabama	63,343	63,333	10,276	21,155	31,912	Redstone Arsenal	9,172	5,704	3,284	5,849	39		426	445
Alaska.	27,602	25,986	17,385	4,536	5,681	Elmendorf AFB	2,581	1,750	1,282	1,262	38		67	71
Arizona	49,449	48,126	22,793	9,002	17,654	Davis-Monthan AFB	11,200	6,598	2,678	8,430	91		555	560
Arkansas	24,650	25,015	5,257	3,933	15,460	Little Rock AFB	1,658	1,146	1,128	494	37		268	280
California	275,224	263,173	128,277	58,062	88,885	Camp Pendleton	43,277	29,821	15,017	27,875	384		2,311	2,546
Colorado	59,765	61,230	29,790	10,345	19,630	Fort Carson	6,226	4,638	3,025	3,151	49		428	444
Connecticut	14,953	17,712	3,467	2,452	9,034	Groton	9,719	2,745	717	8,959	43		269	306
Delaware	11,145	10,941	3,949	1,448	5,748	Dover AFB	628	436	417	194	17		81	84
District of Columbia	36,114	35,171	12,266	15,174	8,674	Washington	5,535	3,176	1,983	3,515	36		37	44
Florida	126,646	127,677	52,300	27,076	47,270	Jacksonville	17,803	13,454	9,334	8,386	83		1,788	1,862
Georgia	134,260	133,663	67,642	30,623	35,995	Fort Benning	10,587	8,642	6,633	3,905	48		760	767
Hawaii	62,972	62,111	35,061	16,576	11,335	Schofield Barracks	5,135	3,731	3,374	1,714	47		107	120
Idaho.	12,907	12,489	4,619	1,532	6,756	Mountain Home AFB	751	632	535	187	29		133	136
Illinois	73,975	84,045	26,650	13,111	34,214	Great Lakes	6,099	4,018	3,025	3,004	69		897	994
Indiana	33,217	36,929	988	9,088	23,141	Crane	4,521	2,591	1,299	3,173	49		551	586
Iowa	17,232	18,556	364	1,522	15,346	Des Moines	1,245	905	481	734	31		266	289
Kansas	37,043	37,255	16,294	6,048	14,701	Fort Riley	2,967	2,044	1,529	1,412	26		246	265
Kentucky	59,239	60,709	35,162	8,314	15,763	Fort Campbell	6,568	2,779	2,432	4,119	18		360	378
Louisiana	49,925	50,968	17,380	7,093	25,452	Fort Polk	4,498	3,386	1,871	2,544	82		367	390
Maine	14,963	14,918	2,350	6,290	6,323	Kittery	2,393	1,366	805	1,556	32		144	153
Maryland	84,006	87,002	29,531	31,611	22,864	Fort Meade	14,368	8,786	4,999	9,206	162		486	521
Massachusetts	28,534	33,039	2,468	6,707	19,359	Hanscom AFB	8,208	5,713	1,103	6,961	144		491	552
Michigan	33,558	36,976	1,140	8,110	24,308	Warren	3,973	2,418	1,241	2,612	120		837	906
Minnesota	25,976	25,948	667	2,544	22,765	St. Paul	2,108	1,943	708	1,337	63		427	461
Mississippi	43,017	42,834	14,483	9,088	19,446	Keesler AFB	3,740	2,993	1,828	1,867	45		240	248
Missouri.	51,539	53,743	15,302	9,208	27,029	Fort Leonard Wood	8,662	6,123	2,112	6,502	48		555	588
Montana	10,838	10,654	3,789	1,274	5,775	Malmstrom AFB	645	392	404	207	34		103	108
Nebraska	20,032	20,120	7,332	3,769	8,931	Offutt AFB	1,349	907	925	401	23		159	172
Nevada	17,716	16,118	9,251	2,089	6,376	Nellis AFB	1,621	1,106	1,168	439	14		244	238
New Hampshire.	6,305	6,809	218	1,059	5,028	Hanover	1,123	693	384	716	23		131	138
New Jersey	41,765	44,016	6,392	13,628	21,745	McGuire AFB	6,117	4,514	1,860	4,196	61		583	664
New Mexico	26,187	26,303	11,994	6,805	7,388	Kirtland AFB	2,551	1,777	1,447	1,071	33		180	190
New York	77,597	79,443	22,714	11,409	43,474	Fort Drum	7,825	5,721	2,443	5,244	139		1,172	1,344
North Carolina.	147,045	137,176	101,033	16,942	29,070	Fort Bragg	8,865	5,901	6,569	2,213	82		767	789
North Dakota	14,914	14,474	7,840	1,706	5,368	Minot AFB	841	549	498	310	33		55	61
Ohio	66,744	71,679	7,211	21,704	37,829	Wright Patterson AFB	7,600	5,300	2,894	4,637	69		1,052	1,135
Oklahoma	64,530	66,529	23,476	21,860	19,194	Tinker AFB	4,533	3,810	2,976	1,524	33		355	374
Oregon	17,509	18,447	667	3,276	13,566	Portland	1,346	857	805	530	11		367	386
Pennsylvania	73,173	78,642	2,837	25,079	45,257	Philadelphia	9,269	6,311	2,912	6,203	154		1,146	1,267
Rhode Island	12,593	13,683	2,336	4,370	5,887	Newport	1,052	939	621	418	13		91	101
South Carolina	70,084	73,865	38,213	9,382	22,489	Fort Jackson	4,950	3,538	3,306	1,599	45		414	420
South Dakota	10,621	10,451	3,698	1,161	5,762	Ellsworth AFB	650	360	397	236	17		73	79
Tennessee	31,773	37,243	2,430	5,390	23,953	Millington	3,765	2,273	1,614	2,116	35		541	557
Texas	225,246	228,790	109,760	39,385	76,101	Fort Hood	32,253	20,901	11,082	21,044	127		1,682	1,747
Utah	33,875	31,556	5,756	14,715	13,404	Hill AFB	3,451	2,023	1,548	1,878	25		151	160
Vermont.	5,160	5,509	60	613	4,487	South Burlington	603	348	140	452	11		58	62
Virginia	205,602	198,095	90,088	78,792	36,722	Arlington	39,604	25,106	15,992	23,543	69		751	784
Washington	88,312	84,071	37,906	23,433	26,973	Fort Lewis	8,677	6,271	5,301	3,325	51		633	667
West Virginia	12,898	13,937	503	1,810	10,585	Huntington	728	361	411	280	38		188	200
Wisconsin.	24,137	26,331	502	2,847	20,788	Milwaukee	2,434	1,253	648	1,746	41		475	510
Wyoming	7,913	7,841	3,447	1,039	3,427	F.E. Warren AFB	418	326	302	115	1		55	58

[1]Veterans serving in more than one period of service are counted only once in the total. Includes the Gulf War (no prior wartime service), Vietnam era (no prior wartime service), Korean conflict (no prior wartime service), World War II, and all peacetime periods.

Survey, Census, or Data Collection Method: Department of Defense—For information, see Internet site <http://siadapp.dior.whs.mil/index.html>; Veterans—Based on the U.S. Department of Veterans Affairs administrative data; for information, see Internet site <http://www.va.gov/vetdata/demographics/>.

Sources: Department of Defense—U.S. Department of Defense, *Atlas/Data Abstract for the United States and Selected Areas*, annual, see Internet site <http://siadapp.dior.whs.mil/index.html>; Veterans—U.S. Department of Veterans Affairs, Office of Policy, Planning, and Preparedness; see Internet site <http://www.va.gov/vetdata/demographics>.

Table A-85. States — **Elections**

Geographic area	Voting-age population[1] (1,000) 2004	2000	Percent of voting-age population casting votes for President 2004	2000	Electoral votes cast for President[2] 2004	2000[4]	Popular vote for President 2004 Total[3] (1,000)	Percent of total Demo-cratic	Repub-lican	2000 Total[3] (1,000)	Percent of total Demo-cratic	Repub-lican	Votes cast for U.S. Senators 2004 Total[3] (1,000)	Percent of total Demo-cratic	Repub-lican	2002 Total[3] (1,000)	Percent of total Demo-cratic	Repub-lican
United States . . .	220,377	209,831	55.5	50.2	R-286	R-271	122,349	48.1	50.6	105,397	48.4	47.9	86,969	50.2	45.9	44,265	46.2	50.1
Alabama	3,436	3,330	54.8	50.0	R-9	R-9	1,883	36.8	62.5	1,666	41.6	56.5	1,839	32.4	67.5	1,353	39.8	58.6
Alaska.	467	437	66.9	65.3	R-3	R-3	313	35.5	61.1	286	27.7	58.6	308	45.5	48.6	230	10.5	78.2
Arizona	4,197	3,788	48.0	40.4	R-10	R-8	2,013	44.4	54.9	1,532	44.7	51.0	1,962	20.6	76.7	(X)	(X)	(X)
Arkansas	2,076	1,998	50.8	46.1	R-6	R-6	1,055	44.5	54.3	922	45.9	51.3	1,039	55.9	44.1	804	53.9	46.1
California	26,297	24,728	47.2	44.3	D-55	D-54	12,421	54.3	44.4	10,966	53.4	41.7	12,053	57.7	37.8	(X)	(X)	(X)
Colorado	3,423	3,219	62.2	54.1	R-9	R-8	2,130	47.0	51.7	1,741	42.4	50.8	2,107	51.3	46.5	1,416	45.8	50.7
Connecticut	2,665	2,570	59.2	56.8	D-7	D-8	1,579	54.3	43.9	1,460	55.9	38.4	1,425	66.4	32.1	(X)	(X)	(X)
Delaware	637	592	58.9	55.3	D-3	D-3	375	53.3	45.8	328	55.0	41.9	(X)	(X)	(X)	232	58.2	40.8
District of Columbia	444	456	51.3	44.2	D-3	D-2	228	89.2	9.3	202	85.2	9.0	(X)	(X)	(X)	(X)	(X)	(X)
Florida.	13,394	12,383	56.8	48.2	R-27	R-25	7,610	47.1	52.1	5,963	48.8	48.8	7,430	48.3	49.4	(X)	(X)	(X)
Georgia	6,497	6,050	50.8	42.9	R-15	R-13	3,302	41.4	58.0	2,597	43.0	54.7	3,221	40.0	57.9	2,032	45.9	52.7
Hawaii	964	917	44.5	40.1	D-4	D-4	429	54.0	45.3	368	55.8	37.5	415	75.5	21.0	(X)	(X)	(X)
Idaho.	1,021	930	58.6	53.9	R-4	R-4	598	30.3	68.4	502	27.6	67.2	504	(X)	99.2	409	32.5	65.2
Illinois	9,475	9,192	55.7	51.6	D-21	D-22	5,274	54.8	44.5	4,742	54.6	42.6	5,142	70.0	27.0	3,487	60.3	38.0
Indiana	4,637	4,515	53.2	48.7	R-11	R-12	2,468	39.3	59.9	2,199	41.0	56.6	2,428	61.6	37.2	(X)	(X)	(X)
Iowa	2,274	2,198	66.3	59.8	R-7	D-7	1,507	49.2	49.9	1,316	48.5	48.2	1,479	27.9	70.2	1,023	54.2	43.8
Kansas	2,052	1,981	57.9	54.1	R-6	R-6	1,188	36.6	62.0	1,072	37.2	58.0	1,129	27.5	69.2	767	(NA)	83.6
Kentucky	3,166	3,055	56.7	50.5	R-8	R-8	1,796	39.7	59.5	1,544	41.4	56.5	1,724	49.3	50.7	1,131	35.3	64.7
Louisiana	3,351	3,253	58.0	54.3	R-9	R-9	1,943	42.2	56.7	1,766	44.9	52.6	1,848	47.5	51.0	2,482	49.8	49.5
Maine	1,035	978	71.6	66.7	D-4	D-4	741	53.6	44.6	652	49.1	44.0	(X)	(X)	(X)	505	41.6	58.4
Maryland	4,163	3,953	57.3	51.1	D-10	D-10	2,384	56.0	43.2	2,020	56.5	40.3	2,322	64.8	33.7	(X)	(X)	(X)
Massachusetts	4,952	4,864	59.1	55.6	D-12	D-12	2,927	61.6	36.6	2,703	59.8	32.5	(X)	(X)	(X)	2,007	80.0	(NA)
Michigan	7,579	7,362	63.8	57.5	D-17	D-18	4,839	51.2	47.8	4,233	51.3	46.1	(X)	(X)	(X)	3,129	60.6	37.9
Minnesota	3,861	3,650	73.3	66.8	D-9	D-10	2,828	51.1	47.6	2,439	47.9	45.5	(X)	(X)	(X)	2,255	47.8	49.5
Mississippi	2,153	2,076	52.9	47.9	R-6	R-7	1,140	40.2	59.0	994	40.7	57.6	(X)	(X)	(X)	630	(NA)	84.6
Missouri.	4,370	4,182	62.5	56.4	R-11	R-11	2,731	46.1	53.3	2,360	47.1	50.4	2,706	42.8	56.1	1,878	48.7	49.8
Montana	719	675	62.7	60.9	R-3	R-3	450	38.6	59.1	411	33.4	58.4	(X)	(X)	(X)	327	62.7	31.7
Nebraska	1,313	1,264	59.3	55.1	R-5	R-5	778	32.7	65.9	697	33.3	62.2	(X)	(X)	(X)	480	14.6	82.8
Nevada	1,731	1,500	47.9	40.6	R-5	R-4	830	47.9	50.5	609	46.0	49.5	810	61.1	35.1	(X)	(X)	(X)
New Hampshire.	995	931	68.2	61.1	D-4	R-4	678	50.2	48.8	569	46.8	48.1	657	33.7	66.2	447	46.4	50.8
New Jersey	6,543	6,342	55.2	50.3	D-15	D-15	3,612	52.9	46.2	3,187	56.1	40.3	(X)	(X)	(X)	2,113	53.9	43.9
New Mexico	1,411	1,315	53.6	45.5	R-5	D-5	756	49.0	49.8	599	47.9	47.8	(X)	(X)	(X)	483	35.0	65.0
New York	14,655	14,314	50.8	47.7	D-31	D-33	7,448	56.1	37.7	6,822	60.2	35.2	7,448	58.9	21.8	(X)	(X)	(X)
North Carolina.	6,423	6,104	54.5	47.7	R-15	R-14	3,501	43.6	56.0	2,911	43.2	56.0	3,472	47.0	51.6	2,331	45.0	53.6
North Dakota	495	482	63.1	59.8	R-3	R-3	313	35.5	62.9	288	33.1	60.7	311	68.3	31.7	(X)	(X)	(X)
Ohio	8,680	8,480	64.8	55.4	R-20	R-21	5,628	48.7	50.8	4,702	46.4	50.0	5,426	36.1	63.8	(X)	(X)	(X)
Oklahoma	2,664	2,565	55.0	48.1	R-7	R-8	1,464	34.4	65.6	1,234	38.4	60.3	1,447	41.2	52.8	1,018	36.3	57.3
Oregon	2,742	2,583	67.0	59.4	D-7	D-7	1,837	51.3	47.2	1,534	47.0	46.5	1,781	63.4	31.7	1,267	39.6	56.2
Pennsylvania	9,569	9,371	60.3	52.4	D-21	D-23	5,770	50.9	48.4	4,913	50.6	46.4	5,559	42.0	52.6	(X)	(X)	(X)
Rhode Island	837	803	52.2	50.9	D-4	D-4	437	59.4	38.7	409	61.0	31.9	(X)	(X)	(X)	324	78.4	21.6
South Carolina	3,173	3,014	51.0	45.9	R-8	R-8	1,618	40.9	58.0	1,383	40.9	56.8	1,597	44.1	53.7	1,103	44.2	54.4
South Dakota	580	554	66.9	57.1	R-3	R-3	388	38.4	59.9	316	37.6	60.3	391	49.4	50.6	338	49.6	49.5
Tennessee	4,510	4,305	54.0	48.2	R-11	R-11	2,437	42.5	56.8	2,076	47.3	51.1	(X)	(X)	(X)	1,642	44.3	54.3
Texas	16,223	15,040	45.7	42.6	R-34	R-32	7,411	38.2	61.1	6,408	38.0	59.3	(X)	(X)	(X)	4,514	43.3	55.3
Utah	1,649	1,522	56.3	50.6	R-5	R-5	928	26.0	71.5	771	26.3	66.8	912	28.4	68.7	(X)	(X)	(X)
Vermont.	487	464	64.2	63.5	D-3	D-3	312	58.9	38.8	294	50.6	40.7	307	70.6	24.5	(X)	(X)	(X)
Virginia	5,655	5,361	56.5	51.1	R-13	R-13	3,195	45.5	53.7	2,739	44.4	52.5	(X)	(X)	(X)	1,489	(NA)	82.6
Washington	4,718	4,398	60.6	56.6	D-11	D-11	2,859	52.8	45.6	2,487	50.2	44.6	2,819	55.0	42.7	(X)	(X)	(X)
West Virginia	1,431	1,407	52.8	46.1	R-5	R-5	756	43.2	56.1	648	45.6	51.9	(X)	(X)	(X)	436	63.1	36.9
Wisconsin	4,201	4,010	71.3	64.8	D-10	D-11	2,997	49.7	49.3	2,599	47.8	47.6	2,950	55.4	44.1	(X)	(X)	(X)
Wyoming	390	366	62.6	59.6	R-3	R-3	244	29.0	68.7	218	27.7	67.8	(X)	(X)	(X)	183	27.0	73.0

NA Not available.   X Not applicable.

[1]Estimated population, 18 years and over. Excludes states without registration. Includes armed forces stationed in each state, aliens, and institutionalized population.
[2]By major political party. D=Democratic, R=Republican.
[3]Includes other parties not shown separately.
[4]Excludes one electoral vote left blank by a Democratic elector in the District of Columbia.

Survey, Census, or Data Collection Method: Voting-age population—Based on the Census of Population and Housing; for information, see Appendix B, Limitations of the Data and Methodology, and Internet site <http://www.census.gov/popest/topics/methodology/2004_st_char_meth.html>;   Percent of voting-age population voting for President—For information on 2004 data, see Internet site <http://clerk.house.gov/index.html>. For information on 2000 data, see Internet site <http://www.cq.com/>;   Votes—For information through 2002, see Internet site <http://www.cq.com/>. For electoral votes 2004, see Internet site <http://www.fec.gov/>. For popular vote and votes for U.S. Senators 2004, see Internet site <http://clerk.house.gov/index.html>.

Sources: Voting-age population—U.S. Census Bureau, "Annual Estimates of the Population by Selected Age Groups and Sex for the United States: April 1, 2000 to July 1, 2004" (NC-EST2004-02); also see <http://www.census.gov/popest/states/asrh/>;   Percent of voting-age population voting for President—For 2004 data, U.S. Congress, Clerk of the House, *Statistics of the Presidential and Congressional Election*, biennial; for 2000 data, CQ Press, Washington, DC, *America Votes*, biennial (copyright; printed with permission of CQ Press);   Electoral votes, votes for President, and votes for Senators—Through 2002, CQ Press, Washington, DC, *America Votes*, biennial (copyright; printed with permission of CQ Press). For electoral votes 2004, U.S. Federal Elections Commission, Federal Elections 2004, May 2005. For popular vote and votes for U.S. Senators 2004, Office of the Clerk, *Statistics of the Presidential and Congressional Election*, June 7, 2005.

Table A-86. States — **Composition of Congress**

Geographic area	Votes cast for U.S. Representatives[1] 2004 Total[7] (1,000)	2004 Percent of total Democratic	2004 Republican	2002 Total[7] (1,000)	2002 Percent of total Democratic	2002 Republican	Composition of 109th Congress, 2005[2] Senate[4] Democratic	Senate[4] Republican	House of Representatives[5,6] Democratic	House Republican	Composition of 108th Congress, 2003[3] Senate[4] Democratic	Senate[4] Republican	House of Representatives[5] Democratic	House Republican
United States . . .	113,192	46.6	49.2	73,845	45.9	50.5	44	55	202	231	48	51	205	229
Alabama	1,793	39.5	60.2	1,269	40.0	54.7	–	2	2	5	–	2	2	5
Alaska	791	53.9	45.2	228	17.3	74.5	–	2	–	1	–	2	–	1
Arizona	1,871	31.9	60.3	1,194	39.5	57.1	–	2	2	6	–	2	2	6
Arkansas[8]	791	53.9	45.2	688	57.0	41.2	2	–	3	1	2	–	3	1
California	11,624	53.5	43.3	7,258	51.4	44.4	2	–	33	20	2	–	33	20
Colorado	2,039	48.8	48.6	1,397	42.2	53.9	1	1	3	4	–	2	2	5
Connecticut	1,429	55.0	44.1	989	51.5	47.1	2	–	2	3	2	–	2	3
Delaware	356	29.7	69.1	228	26.7	72.1	2	–	–	1	2	–	–	1
District of Columbia	(X)	(X)	(X)	(X)	(X)	(X)	(X)	(X)	(X)	(X)	(X)	(X)	(X)	(X)
Florida[8]	5,627	39.3	59.0	3,767	40.8	57.4	1	1	7	18	2	–	7	18
Georgia	2,961	38.5	61.5	1,919	42.4	57.6	–	2	6	7	1	1	5	8
Hawaii	417	62.9	35.6	360	64.5	32.4	2	–	2	–	2	–	2	–
Idaho	572	29.9	70.1	405	34.1	63.3	–	2	–	2	–	2	–	2
Illinois	4,989	53.6	45.5	3,429	50.8	48.3	2	–	10	9	1	1	9	10
Indiana	2,416	41.3	57.2	1,521	42.1	55.3	1	1	2	7	1	1	3	6
Iowa	1,458	42.8	56.4	1,013	44.8	54.0	1	1	1	4	1	1	1	4
Kansas	1,156	33.5	62.6	830	31.3	64.6	–	2	1	3	–	2	1	3
Kentucky[8]	1,635	36.8	62.2	1,094	32.1	63.4	–	2	1	5	–	2	1	5
Louisiana[8]	1,259	38.0	62.0	1,325	33.8	59.9	1	1	2	5	2	–	3	4
Maine	710	58.9	39.9	495	58.5	41.5	–	2	2	–	–	2	2	–
Maryland	2,254	58.2	39.8	1,662	54.4	45.3	2	–	6	2	2	–	6	2
Massachusetts	2,927	70.4	14.9	1,841	83.0	15.8	2	–	10	–	2	–	10	–
Michigan	4,631	48.4	49.4	3,056	49.3	48.2	2	–	6	9	2	–	6	9
Minnesota	2,722	51.4	45.4	2,202	49.9	46.8	1	1	4	4	1	1	4	4
Mississippi	1,116	30.0	59.0	678	47.2	50.0	–	2	2	2	–	2	2	2
Missouri	2,667	44.7	53.6	1,854	44.7	53.2	–	2	4	5	–	2	4	5
Montana	444	32.8	64.4	331	32.7	64.6	1	1	–	1	1	1	–	1
Nebraska	765	30.2	67.3	474	9.9	81.6	1	1	–	3	1	1	–	3
Nevada	791	42.2	53.2	500	34.2	60.2	1	1	1	2	1	1	1	2
New Hampshire	652	37.4	60.8	443	39.7	57.5	–	2	–	2	–	2	–	2
New Jersey	3,285	52.4	46.1	2,006	51.4	46.6	2	–	7	6	2	–	7	6
New Mexico	743	51.8	48.2	438	59.9	40.1	1	1	1	2	1	1	1	2
New York	7,448	46.4	29.7	3,822	46.3	40.0	2	–	20	9	2	–	19	10
North Carolina	3,413	48.9	51.1	2,244	43.3	53.9	–	2	6	7	1	1	6	7
North Dakota	311	59.6	40.4	231	52.4	47.6	2	–	1	–	2	–	1	–
Ohio	5,184	48.5	51.1	3,158	42.2	56.2	–	2	6	11	–	2	6	12
Oklahoma	1,375	28.3	63.7	1,002	39.1	54.6	–	2	1	4	–	2	1	4
Oregon	1,772	53.7	43.0	1,240	54.6	42.7	1	1	4	1	1	1	4	1
Pennsylvania	5,151	48.1	49.8	3,310	40.7	56.2	1	1	7	12	–	2	7	12
Rhode Island	402	69.5	28.1	329	68.3	29.5	1	1	2	–	1	1	2	–
South Carolina	1,439	33.8	63.5	985	35.1	57.8	–	2	2	4	1	1	2	4
South Dakota	389	53.4	45.9	337	45.6	53.4	1	1	1	–	2	–	–	1
Tennessee	2,219	46.5	52.3	1,529	46.3	50.4	–	2	5	4	–	2	5	4
Texas	6,959	39.0	57.7	4,295	43.9	53.3	–	2	11	21	–	2	17	15
Utah	909	39.8	57.3	557	39.7	57.8	–	2	1	2	–	2	1	2
Vermont	305	7.1	24.4	225	(X)	32.3	1	–	–	–	1	–	–	–
Virginia	3,004	34.1	60.5	1,516	29.0	66.5	–	2	3	8	–	2	3	8
Washington	2,730	58.9	40.1	1,739	52.2	44.8	2	–	6	3	2	–	6	3
West Virginia	722	57.6	42.0	400	66.0	33.9	2	–	2	1	2	–	2	1
Wisconsin	2,822	48.5	48.9	1,638	41.3	54.3	2	–	4	4	2	–	4	4
Wyoming	239	41.8	55.2	182	36.2	60.5	–	2	–	1	–	2	–	1

– Represents zero.   X Not applicable.

[1]In each state, totals represent the sum of votes cast in each Congressional District or votes cast for Representative at Large in states where only one member is elected. In all years, there are numerous districts within the state where either the Republican or Democratic party had no candidate. In some states, the Republican and Democratic vote includes votes cast for the party candidate by endorsing parties.
[2]As of June 28, 2005.
[3]Vermont had one Independent Senator.
[4]As of January 3.
[5]Vermont had one Independent Representative.
[6]Vacancy due to the resignation of Rob Portman (OH) April 29, 2005.
[7]Includes vote cast for minor parties not shown separately.
[8]State law does not require tabulation of votes for unopposed candidates.

Survey, Census, or Data Collection Method: Votes—For information on 2002 data, see Internet site <http://www.cq.com/>. For information on 2004 data, see Internet site <http://clerk.house.gov/members/index.html>;   Composition of Congress—For information, see Internet site <http://clerk.house.gov/members/index.html>.

Sources: Votes—For 2002 data, CQ Press, Washington, DC, *America Votes*, biennial (copyright; printed with permission of CQ Press). For 2004 data, Office of the Clerk, *Statistics of the Presidential and Congressional Election*, June 7, 2005;   Composition of Congress—Office of the Clerk, *Official List of Members by State*, annual. See also <http://clerk.house.gov/members/index.html>.

Table A-87. States — Composition of Governors and State Legislatures

Geographic area	Votes cast for Governor[1] 2004 — Candidate elected at most recent election	Votes cast for Governor[1] 2004 — Totals[7]	Votes cast for Governor[1] 2004 — Percent for leading party	Votes cast for Governor[1] 2002 — Totals[7]	Votes cast for Governor[1] 2002 — Percent for leading party	Composition of state legislatures,[2] 2005 — Lower House[5] Democratic	Lower House[5] Republican	Upper House[6] Democratic	Upper House[6] Republican
United States . . .	(X)	(X)	(X)	(X)	(X)	**2,704**	**2,683**	**951**	**963**
Alabama[12]	Bob Riley	(X)	(X)	1,367	R-49.2	62	40	25	10
Alaska[13]	Frank H. Murkowski	(X)	(X)	231	R-55.8	14	26	8	12
Arizona[14]	Janet Napolitano	(X)	(X)	1,226	D-46.2	22	38	12	18
Arkansas[13]	Mike Huckabee	(X)	(X)	806	R-53.0	72	28	27	8
California[13]	Arnold Schwarzenegger[16]	8,658	R-48.6	7,476	D-47.3	48	32	25	15
Colorado[13]	Bill Owens	(X)	(X)	1,413	R-62.6	35	30	18	17
Connecticut[14]	John G. Rowland	(X)	(X)	1,023	R-56.1	99	52	24	12
Delaware[13]	Ruth Ann Minner	365	D-50.9	(X)	(X)	15	25	13	8
District of Columbia	(X)	(X)	(X)	(X)	(X)	(X)	(X)	(X)	(X)
Florida[13]	Jeb Bush	(X)	(X)	5,101	R-56.0	36	84	14	26
Georgia[14]	Sonny Perdue	(X)	(X)	2,027	R-51.4	80	99	22	34
Hawaii[13]	Linda Lingle	(X)	(X)	382	R-51.6	41	10	20	5
Idaho[14]	Dirk Kempthorne	(X)	(X)	411	R-56.3	13	57	7	28
Illinois[15]	Rod R. Blagojevich	(X)	(X)	3,539	D-52.2	65	53	31	27
Indiana[13]	Mitch Daniels	2,448	R-53.2	(X)	(X)	48	52	17	33
Iowa[13]	Tom Vilsack	(X)	(X)	1,026	D-52.7	49	51	25	25
Kansas[13]	Kathleen Sebelius	(X)	(X)	836	D-52.9	42	83	10	30
Kentucky[13]	Ernie Fletcher	1,083	R-55.0	[18]1,083	R-55.0	57	43	15	22
Louisiana[12]	Kathleen Babineaux Blanco	1,408	D-51.9	[18]1,407	D-51.9	67	37	24	15
Maine[14]	John Baldacci	(X)	(X)	505	D-47.1	76	73	19	16
Maryland[12]	Robert L. Ehrlich Jr.	(X)	(X)	1,706	R-51.6	98	43	33	14
Massachusetts[14]	Mitt Romney	(X)	(X)	2,194	R-49.8	136	21	34	6
Michigan[13]	Jennifer M. Granholm	(X)	(X)	3,178	D-51.4	52	58	16	22
Minnesota[13]	Tim Pawlenty	(X)	(X)	2,252	R-44.4	66	68	35	31
Mississippi[12]	Haley Barbour	894	R-52.6	[18]894	D-52.6	75	47	28	24
Missouri[13]	Matt Blunt	2,720	R-50.8	(X)	(X)	66	97	10	22
Montana[13]	Brian Schweitzer	446	D-50.4	(X)	(X)	49	50	27	23
Nebraska	Mike Johanns	(X)	(X)	481	R-68.7	([19])	([19])	([19])	([19])
Nevada[13]	Kenny Guinn	(X)	(X)	504	R-68.2	26	16	9	12
New Hampshire[14]	John Lynch	667	D-51.0	443	R-58.6	147	250	8	16
New Jersey[13]	James E. McGreevey	(X)	(X)	2,227	D-56.4	47	33	22	18
New Mexico[13]	Bill Richardson	(X)	(X)	484	D-55.5	42	28	24	18
New York[14]	George E. Pataki	(X)	(X)	4,579	R-49.4	104	46	28	34
North Carolina[14]	Michael F. Easley	3,487	D-55.6	(X)	(X)	63	57	29	21
North Dakota[12]	John Hoeven	310	R-71.3	(X)	(X)	27	67	15	32
Ohio[13]	Bob Taft	(X)	(X)	3,229	R-57.8	40	59	11	22
Oklahoma[13]	Brad Henry	(X)	(X)	1,036	D-43.3	44	57	26	22
Oregon[13]	Theodore R. Kulongoski	(X)	(X)	1,260	D-49.0	27	33	18	12
Pennsylvania[13]	Edward G. Rendell	(X)	(X)	3,583	D-53.4	93	110	18	29
Rhode Island[14]	Donald L. Carcieri	(X)	(X)	333	R-54.7	60	15	33	5
South Carolina[13]	Mark Sanford	(X)	(X)	1,108	R-52.8	50	74	20	26
South Dakota[14]	Mike Rounds	(X)	(X)	335	R-56.8	19	51	10	25
Tennessee[13]	Phil Bredesen	(X)	(X)	1,653	D-50.6	53	46	16	17
Texas[13]	Rick Perry	(X)	(X)	4,554	R-57.8	63	87	12	19
Utah[13]	Jon Huntsman, Jr.	920	R-57.7	(X)	(X)	19	56	8	21
Vermont[14]	Jim Douglas	309	R-58.7	230	R-44.9	83	60	21	9
Virginia[13]	Mark Warner	(X)	(X)	1,887	D-52.2	38	60	16	24
Washington[13]	Christine Gregoire	2,810	D-48.9	(X)	(X)	55	43	26	23
West Virginia[13]	Joe Manchin III	744	D-63.5	(X)	(X)	68	32	21	13
Wisconsin[13]	James E. Doyle	(X)	(X)	1,775	D-45.1	39	60	14	19
Wyoming[13]	Dave Freudenthal	(X)	(X)	185	D-50.0	14	46	7	23

See footnotes at end of table.

Geographic area	Black elected officials, 2001[3]		Hispanic public officials, 2004		Women holding state public offices, 2004[3]		Apportionment of membership in House of Representatives by state[4]		
	Total[8]	U.S. and state legislatures[9]	Total	State executives and legislators[10]	Statewide elective executive office[11]	State legislature	2000	1990	1980
United States . . .	**9,061**	**633**	**4,651**	**231**	**81**	**1,659**	**435**	**435**	**435**
Alabama[12]	756	36	–	–	5	14	7	7	7
Alaska[13]	3	1	–	–	–	12	1	1	1
Arizona[14]	12	1	354	15	3	25	8	6	5
Arkansas[13]	502	15	–	–	–	22	4	4	4
California[13]	224	10	981	28	–	36	53	52	45
Colorado[13]	18	4	134	8	2	34	7	6	6
Connecticut[14]	72	14	28	5	4	55	5	6	6
Delaware[13]	24	4	2	1	3	18	1	1	1
District of Columbia	176	2[17]	–	–	(X)	(X)	(X)	(X)	(X)
Florida[13]	243	25	109	16	1	40	25	23	19
Georgia[14]	611	53	7	3	3	51	13	11	10
Hawaii[13]	–	–	1	1	1	21	2	2	2
Idaho[14]	2	–	1	1	1	27	2	2	2
Illinois[15]	624	28	70	11	2	50	19	20	22
Indiana[13]	86	13	12	1	3	27	9	10	10
Iowa[13]	13	1	–	–	2	32	5	5	6
Kansas[13]	17	7	8	2	3	46	4	4	5
Kentucky[13]	60	5	–	–	1	15	6	6	7
Louisiana[12]	705	32	2	–	1	24	7	7	8
Maine[14]	1	–	–	–	–	50	2	2	2
Maryland[12]	175	40	6	4	–	64	8	8	8
Massachusetts[14]	60	6	18	4	1	50	10	10	11
Michigan[13]	346	25	15	1	2	35	15	16	18
Minnesota[13]	20	2	4	1	3	55	8	8	8
Mississippi[12]	892	46	–	–	1	22	4	5	5
Missouri[13]	201	19	1	–	2	42	9	9	9
Montana[13]	–	–	1	–	2	37	1	1	2
Nebraska	8	1	2	1	2	9	3	3	3
Nevada[13]	14	5	7	3	2	18	3	2	2
New Hampshire[14]	5	5	2	1	–	117	2	2	2
New Jersey[13]	249	16	100	5	–	19	13	13	14
New Mexico[13]	4	1	627	50	3	34	3	3	3
New York[14]	325	34	61	15	1	48	29	31	34
North Carolina[14]	491	28	4	2	4	36	13	12	11
North Dakota[12]	–	–	1	–	2	23	1	1	1
Ohio[13]	313	20	5	–	2	28	18	19	21
Oklahoma[13]	105	6	1	–	4	19	5	6	6
Oregon[13]	6	3	14	3	1	26	5	5	5
Pennsylvania[13]	185	19	17	1	2	36	19	21	23
Rhode Island[14]	8	7	6	3	–	23	2	2	2
South Carolina[13]	534	32	1	1	1	16	6	6	6
South Dakota[14]	–	–	–	–	–	17	1	1	1
Tennessee[13]	180	18	2	1	–	23	9	9	9
Texas[13]	460	19	2,013	38	2	35	32	30	27
Utah[13]	5	1	3	–	1	22	3	3	3
Vermont[14]	1	1	–	–	2	56	1	1	1
Virginia[13]	246	16	1	–	–	20	11	11	10
Washington[13]	26	2	14	3	2	52	9	9	8
West Virginia[13]	19	2	–	–	–	25	3	3	4
Wisconsin[13]	33	8	13	1	3	37	8	9	9
Wyoming[13]	1	–	3	1	1	16	1	1	1

– Represents zero.   X Not applicable.

[1]D=Democratic, R=Republican.   [2]As of February 2005. Figures include immediate results of elections, including holdover members in state houses that do not have all of their members running for reelection.   [3]As of January of the year shown.   [4]Total membership includes representatives assigned to newly admitted states after the apportionment acts. Population figures used for apportionment purposes are those determined for states by each decennial census.   [5]In general, Lower House refers to body consisting of state representatives.   [6]In general, Upper House refers to body consisting of state senators.   [7]Includes minor party and scattered votes.   [8]Includes city and county offices, law enforcement, and education officials not shown separately.   [9]Includes elected state administrators.   [10]Includes U.S. Representatives.   [11]Excludes women elected to the judiciary, women appointed to state cabinet-level positions, women elected to executive posts by the legislature, and elected members of university Board of Trustees or Board of Education.   [12]Members of both houses of state legislatures serve 4-year terms.   [13]Members of the Upper House of state legislatures serve 4-year terms, and Lower House members serve 2-year terms.   [14]Members of both houses of state legislatures serve 2-year terms.   [15]Members serve 4- and 2-year terms, depending on the district.   [16]Recall election in 2003; Arnold Schwarzenegger (Republican) was elected Governor.   [17]Includes one shadow senator.   [18]Voting year 2003.   [19]Members serve 4-year term; Nebraska is the only state to have a nonpartisan legislature.

Survey, Census, or Data Collection Method: Votes for Governor—For information, see Internet site <http://www.cqpress.com/gethome.asp>;   Composition of state legislatures—For information, see Internet site <http://www.ncsl.org/>;   Black officials—For information, see Internet site <http://jointcenter.org/DB/>;   Hispanic officials—For information, see Internet site <http://www.naleo.org/>;   Women holding offices—For information, see Internet site <http://www.cawp.rutgers.edu>;   Apportionment—Based on the decennial census; for information, see Appendix B, Limitations of the Data and Methodology, and Internet site <http://www.census.gov/population/www/censusdata/apportionment.html>.

Sources: Votes for Governor—CQ Press, Washington, DC, *America Votes*, biennial (copyright; printed with permission of CQ Press);   Composition of state legislatures—The Council of State Governments, Lexington, KY, *State Elective Officials and the Legislatures*, annual (copyright);   Black officials—Joint Center for Political and Economic Studies, Washington, DC, *Black Elected Officials: A Statistical Summary*, annual (copyright) and <http://www.jointcenter.org/publications1/BEO.php> (accessed 17 April 2003);   Hispanic officials—National Association of Latino Elected and Appointed Officials (NALEO) Educational Fund, Los Angeles, CA, *National Directory of Latino Elected Officials*, formerly published as *National Roster of Hispanic Elected Officials*, annual;   Women holding offices—Center for American Women and Politics, Eagleton Institute of Politics, Rutgers University, New Brunswick, NJ, information releases (copyright);   Apportionment—U.S. Census Bureau, *Congressional Apportionment, Census 2000 Brief*, C2KBR/01-7, issued July 2001; see also <http://www.census.gov/population/www/censusdata/apportionment.html>.

Metropolitan Areas   Table B

Page

Note:

Table B covers 361
metropolitan statistical
areas and 11 metro-
politan statistical areas
with 29 metropolitan
divisions defined by the
Office of Management
and Budget as of June 6,
2003, and subsequently
updated in December
2003 and November
2004. For more
information, see OMB
Bulletin 05-02 at
*<http://www.whitehouse
.gov/omb/bulletins/fy05
/b05-02_appendix.pdf>*.

For additional
information, see
Appendix C, Geographic
Concepts and Codes.

Metropolitan Areas

You may visit us on the Web at
http://www.census.gov/compendia/smadb

Table B

Metropolitan statistical area **Metropolitan statistical area with metropolitan divisions** *Metropolitan division*	Area, 2000 (square miles)		Population									
					2000[1]	1990[2]	Rank			Persons per square mile of land area[3]		
	Total	Rank	2005 (July 1)	2004 (July 1)	(estimates base)	(April 1)	2005	2000	1990	2005	2000	1990
Abilene, TX.	2,757.6	111	158,291	158,449	160,241	148,004	239	230	222	57.7	58.4	53.9
Akron, OH	927.2	280	702,235	701,837	694,960	657,575	69	67	65	776.0	767.9	726.6
Albany, GA	1,958.0	162	162,842	162,348	157,866	146,583	231	233	226	84.2	81.6	75.8
Albany-Schenectady-Troy, NY	2,878.3	101	848,879	844,961	825,875	809,642	57	56	52	301.3	293.2	287.3
Albuquerque, NM	9,297.0	10	797,940	781,380	729,653	599,416	61	65	70	85.9	78.6	64.5
Alexandria, LA	2,026.5	155	147,965	146,951	145,035	149,082	255	251	221	75.2	73.7	75.8
Allentown-Bethlehem-Easton, PA-NJ	1,475.7	220	790,535	779,730	740,394	686,688	63	64	58	541.8	507.5	470.0
Altoona, PA	527.1	343	126,795	127,202	129,144	130,542	288	275	254	241.1	245.5	248.2
Amarillo, TX	3,682.3	77	238,664	235,696	226,522	196,111	180	179	176	65.2	61.9	53.6
Ames, IA	573.7	338	79,952	80,239	79,981	74,252	353	354	350	139.5	139.6	129.6
Anchorage, AK	27,220.9	2	351,049	346,233	319,605	266,021	138	143	149	13.3	12.1	10.1
Anderson, IN	452.9	350	130,412	130,482	133,358	130,669	280	267	253	288.5	295.0	289.1
Anderson, SC	757.5	310	175,514	173,547	165,740	145,177	224	224	228	244.4	230.8	202.2
Ann Arbor, MI	722.5	315	341,847	338,782	322,770	282,937	141	140	139	481.5	454.6	398.5
Anniston-Oxford, AL	612.3	333	112,141	111,982	112,243	116,032	313	304	274	184.4	184.6	190.5
Appleton, WI	1,041.4	263	215,143	212,864	201,722	174,801	193	191	197	224.1	210.1	182.1
Asheville, NC	2,041.1	153	392,831	387,366	369,172	307,999	125	124	128	193.2	181.6	151.5
Athens-Clarke County, GA	1,035.2	264	175,085	175,415	166,079	136,025	225	223	241	169.8	161.1	131.8
Atlanta-Sandy Springs-Marietta, GA	8,480.3	15	4,917,717	4,796,268	4,248,018	3,068,975	9	11	12	587.1	507.2	366.3
Atlantic City, NJ.	671.5	323	271,015	268,311	252,552	224,327	164	165	165	483.1	450.2	399.9
Auburn-Opelika, AL	615.6	331	123,254	120,537	115,092	87,146	296	296	334	202.4	189.0	143.1
Augusta-Richmond County, GA-SC	3,324.5	87	520,332	516,338	499,649	435,799	95	89	88	158.7	152.4	132.9
Austin-Round Rock, TX.	4,279.9	57	1,452,529	1,411,199	1,249,753	846,227	38	40	48	343.9	295.9	200.2
Bakersfield, CA	8,161.4	17	756,825	734,077	661,653	544,981	66	70	75	93.0	81.3	66.9
Baltimore-Towson, MD	3,104.5	93	2,655,675	2,644,744	2,552,994	2,382,172	19	19	19	1,017.9	978.5	913.1
Bangor, ME	3,556.1	80	147,068	146,698	144,919	146,601	256	252	225	43.3	42.7	43.2
Barnstable Town, MA	1,305.6	237	226,514	227,984	222,230	186,605	188	184	186	572.0	561.2	471.2
Baton Rouge, LA.	4,214.6	59	733,802	727,413	705,967	623,850	67	66	68	182.1	175.2	154.8
Battle Creek, MI	718.4	316	139,191	139,505	137,985	135,982	271	264	242	196.3	194.6	191.8
Bay City, MI	630.9	326	109,029	109,139	110,157	111,723	323	309	279	245.6	248.1	251.6
Beaumont-Port Arthur, TX	2,388.2	132	383,530	383,251	385,090	361,218	126	117	109	178.1	178.8	167.7
Bellingham, WA.	2,503.6	128	183,471	180,205	166,826	127,780	214	222	256	86.5	78.7	60.3
Bend, OR.	3,054.8	94	141,382	134,618	115,367	74,976	267	295	349	46.8	38.2	24.8
Billings, MT.	4,711.2	49	146,593	144,576	138,904	121,499	257	263	264	31.3	29.7	25.9
Binghamton, NY	1,238.4	245	248,422	249,345	252,320	264,497	173	166	150	202.6	205.8	215.7
Birmingham-Hoover, AL	5,369.8	41	1,090,126	1,081,722	1,051,306	956,646	48	48	45	205.8	198.4	180.6
Bismarck, ND	3,613.3	79	99,346	97,885	94,719	83,831	339	341	337	27.9	26.6	23.5
Blacksburg-Christiansburg-Radford, VA	1,089.6	254	151,057	150,597	151,324	140,715	251	241	234	140.4	140.6	130.7
Bloomington, IN.	1,345.1	232	177,709	177,297	175,506	156,669	221	211	210	134.5	132.9	118.5
Bloomington-Normal, IL.	1,186.3	249	159,013	157,847	150,433	129,180	238	243	255	134.3	127.1	109.1
Boise City-Nampa, ID	11,833.1	5	544,201	524,789	464,840	319,596	88	97	125	46.2	39.4	27.1
Boston-Cambridge-Quincy, MA-NH	**4,511.5**	**52**	**4,411,835**	**4,418,758**	**4,392,340**	**4,133,895**	**11**	**10**	**6**	**1,258.0**	**1,252.4**	**1,179.8**
Boston-Quincy, MA.	*1,657.5*	*(X)*	*1,800,432*	*1,807,863*	*1,812,937*	*1,715,269*	*(X)*	*(X)*	*(X)*	*1,609.0*	*1,620.1*	*1,532.9*
Cambridge-Newton-Framingham, MA.	*847.5*	*(X)*	*1,459,011*	*1,462,822*	*1,466,394*	*1,398,468*	*(X)*	*(X)*	*(X)*	*1,772.8*	*1,781.8*	*1,697.2*
Essex County, MA	*828.5*	*(X)*	*738,301*	*737,447*	*723,419*	*670,080*	*(X)*	*(X)*	*(X)*	*1,473.7*	*1,444.0*	*1,345.5*
Rockingham County-Strafford County, NH.	*1,177.9*	*(X)*	*414,091*	*410,626*	*389,590*	*350,078*	*(X)*	*(X)*	*(X)*	*389.2*	*366.2*	*329.0*
Boulder, CO[4]	751.4	311	280,440	279,551	269,787	225,339	161	159	164	378.0	363.6	303.7
Bowling Green, KY.	855.7	295	110,990	109,047	104,166	88,077	317	323	332	130.9	122.8	103.9
Bremerton-Silverdale, WA	566.0	339	240,661	241,436	231,969	189,731	178	177	180	607.7	585.8	479.1
Bridgeport-Stamford-Norwalk, CT	837.0	297	902,775	901,819	882,567	827,645	54	51	51	1,442.1	1,409.9	1,322.1
Brownsville-Harlingen, TX	1,276.3	239	378,311	370,829	335,227	260,120	129	137	151	417.6	370.0	287.1
Brunswick, GA	1,607.1	201	98,433	97,569	93,044	82,207	342	342	338	75.7	71.6	63.2
Buffalo-Niagara Falls, NY	2,366.7	133	1,147,711	1,153,753	1,170,111	1,189,340	47	42	37	732.4	746.7	758.5
Burlington, NC.	434.8	351	140,533	138,452	130,794	108,213	270	271	288	326.8	304.2	251.1
Burlington-South Burlington, VT	1,506.3	215	205,230	204,510	198,889	177,059	198	193	193	163.0	158.0	140.6
Canton-Massillon, OH.	979.9	273	409,996	410,005	406,934	394,106	115	110	98	422.2	419.1	405.9
Cape Coral-Fort Myers, FL	1,211.9	246	544,758	514,923	440,888	335,113	87	103	122	677.6	548.4	416.8
Carson City, NV.	155.7	361	56,062	55,926	52,457	40,443	361	361	361	392.0	366.8	280.9
Casper, WY	5,375.7	40	69,799	68,988	66,533	61,226	358	359	357	13.1	12.5	11.5
Cedar Rapids, IA.	2,019.7	157	246,412	244,306	237,230	210,640	175	174	168	122.7	118.1	104.8
Champaign-Urbana, IL	1,924.3	165	215,742	214,989	210,279	202,848	192	187	174	112.2	109.3	105.5
Charleston, WV.	2,547.0	126	306,435	307,243	309,635	307,689	150	147	129	121.0	122.3	121.5
Charleston-North Charleston, SC	3,162.9	91	594,899	583,472	548,972	506,877	81	85	81	229.6	211.9	195.6
Charlotte-Gastonia-Concord, NC-SC	3,147.2	92	1,521,278	1,474,843	1,330,419	1,024,690	36	37	42	491.1	429.4	330.5
Charlottesville, VA	1,657.9	194	188,424	185,554	174,021	144,151	212	215	229	114.3	105.5	87.4
Chattanooga, TN-GA	2,137.9	146	492,126	488,661	476,501	433,210	98	94	89	235.6	228.1	207.2
Cheyenne, WY	2,687.6	117	85,163	85,033	81,607	73,142	351	352	352	31.7	30.4	27.2
Chicago-Naperville-Joliet, IL-IN-WI	**9,579.2**	**9**	**9,443,356**	**9,393,259**	**9,098,615**	**8,182,076**	**3**	**3**	**3**	**1,309.4**	**1,261.6**	**1,134.0**
Chicago-Naperville-Joliet, IL.	*5,344.3*	*(X)*	*7,882,729*	*7,850,994*	*7,628,447*	*6,894,440*	*(X)*	*(X)*	*(X)*	*1,708.1*	*1,653.0*	*1,493.3*
Gary, IN.	*2,112.7*	*(X)*	*697,401*	*690,891*	*675,971*	*643,037*	*(X)*	*(X)*	*(X)*	*371.6*	*360.1*	*342.6*
Lake County-Kenosha County, IL-WI.	*2,122.3*	*(X)*	*863,226*	*851,374*	*794,197*	*644,599*	*(X)*	*(X)*	*(X)*	*1,198.9*	*1,103.1*	*894.0*

See footnotes at end of table.

State and Metropolitan Area Data Book: 2006

U.S. Census Bureau

Table B-1. Metropolitan Areas — **Area and Population**—Con.

Metropolitan statistical area / Metropolitan statistical area with metropolitan divisions / Metropolitan division	Area, 2000 (square miles) Total	Area, 2000 (square miles) Rank	Population 2005 (July 1)	Population 2004 (July 1)	Population 2000[1] (estimates base)	Population 1990[2] (April 1)	Rank 2005	Rank 2000	Rank 1990	Persons per square mile of land area[3] 2005	Persons per square mile of land area[3] 2000	Persons per square mile of land area[3] 1990
Chico, CA.	1,677.1	187	214,185	212,698	203,171	182,120	194	190	189	130.7	124.0	111.0
Cincinnati-Middletown, OH-KY-IN	4,465.9	54	2,070,441	2,056,843	2,009,657	1,844,915	25	24	23	470.8	456.9	419.4
Clarksville, TN-KY	2,242.2	139	243,665	238,225	232,044	189,279	176	176	182	112.7	107.3	87.5
Cleveland, TN	773.9	305	108,036	106,984	104,015	87,355	325	324	333	141.4	136.1	114.3
Cleveland-Elyria-Mentor, OH	3,978.9	67	2,126,318	2,133,778	2,148,010	2,102,248	23	23	21	1,061.0	1,071.9	1,048.5
Coeur d'Alene, ID	1,315.7	236	127,668	122,447	108,685	69,795	287	314	355	102.5	87.3	56.1
College Station-Bryan, TX	2,133.7	147	189,735	188,745	184,885	150,998	209	204	216	90.1	87.8	71.7
Colorado Springs, CO.	2,688.5	116	587,500	579,416	537,484	409,482	84	86	95	218.9	200.3	152.6
Columbia, MO.	1,161.9	251	153,283	151,144	145,666	122,010	247	250	263	133.2	126.6	106.0
Columbia, SC.	3,833.9	71	689,878	680,039	647,261	548,936	70	73	74	186.4	174.9	148.3
Columbus, GA-AL	1,960.0	161	284,299	284,453	281,768	266,452	158	154	148	146.8	145.5	137.6
Columbus, IN	409.4	354	73,540	72,853	71,435	63,657	357	358	356	180.7	175.5	156.4
Columbus, OH	4,013.6	65	1,708,625	1,690,721	1,612,837	1,405,168	32	31	33	428.9	404.8	352.7
Corpus Christi, TX	2,401.4	130	413,553	409,645	403,280	367,786	111	111	106	232.5	226.7	206.6
Corvallis, OR	679.0	321	78,640	78,383	78,139	70,811	356	356	354	116.3	115.6	104.6
Cumberland, MD-WV	759.0	309	100,667	101,025	102,008	101,643	336	332	301	133.7	135.5	135.0
Dallas-Fort Worth-Arlington, TX.	**9,284.2**	**11**	**5,819,475**	**5,696,045**	**5,161,518**	**3,989,294**	**5**	**5**	**9**	**647.3**	**574.1**	**443.7**
Dallas-Plano-Irving, TX	*5,819.4*	*(X)*	*3,893,123*	*3,810,195*	*3,451,248*	*2,622,562*	*(X)*	*(X)*	*(X)*	*696.6*	*617.5*	*469.2*
Fort Worth-Arlington, TX	*3,464.8*	*(X)*	*1,926,352*	*1,885,850*	*1,710,270*	*1,366,732*	*(X)*	*(X)*	*(X)*	*566.4*	*502.9*	*401.9*
Dalton, GA.	637.5	325	131,701	129,551	120,061	98,609	278	288	311	207.7	189.4	155.5
Danville, IL	902.1	285	82,344	82,647	83,924	88,257	352	349	329	91.6	93.4	98.2
Danville, VA	1,022.1	266	107,997	108,263	110,156	108,728	326	310	287	106.5	108.6	107.2
Davenport-Moline-Rock Island, IA-IL	2,313.8	135	376,309	375,293	376,054	368,145	130	121	105	165.8	165.7	162.2
Dayton, OH	1,716.1	184	843,577	844,850	848,153	843,835	59	54	49	493.9	496.6	494.0
Decatur, AL	1,317.1	235	148,345	147,400	145,867	131,556	253	249	250	116.3	114.3	103.1
Decatur, IL	585.4	336	110,167	110,502	114,706	117,206	322	298	272	189.6	197.4	201.7
Deltona-Daytona Beach-Ormond Beach, FL	1,432.4	224	490,055	478,951	443,343	370,737	100	101	102	444.3	401.9	335.2
Denver-Aurora, CO[4]	8,387.2	16	2,359,994	2,326,310	2,179,320	1,650,489	22	22	24	282.3	260.7	197.4
Des Moines, IA	2,912.2	99	522,454	512,340	481,398	416,346	93	93	94	181.5	167.2	144.6
Detroit-Warren-Livonia, MI.	**4,235.1**	**58**	**4,488,335**	**4,489,523**	**4,452,557**	**4,248,699**	**10**	**9**	**5**	**1,146.7**	**1,137.6**	**1,085.5**
Detroit-Livonia-Dearborn, MI.	*672.0*	*(X)*	*1,998,217*	*2,013,771*	*2,061,162*	*2,111,687*	*(X)*	*(X)*	*(X)*	*3,254.4*	*3,356.9*	*3,439.2*
Warren-Farmington Hills-Troy, MI.	*3,562.9*	*(X)*	*2,490,118*	*2,475,752*	*2,391,395*	*2,137,012*	*(X)*	*(X)*	*(X)*	*754.6*	*724.7*	*647.6*
Dothan, AL	1,728.9	183	136,594	135,011	130,861	120,352	273	270	266	79.5	76.2	70.0
Dover, DE	800.1	301	143,968	139,118	126,700	110,993	260	278	281	244.0	214.7	187.8
Dubuque, IA	616.6	330	91,631	91,079	89,156	86,403	347	347	335	150.7	146.6	142.1
Duluth, MN-WI	9,215.1	12	275,413	275,780	275,486	269,230	162	156	145	32.8	32.8	32.1
Durham, NC	1,812.1	172	456,187	450,260	423,803	344,645	103	105	116	258.5	240.1	195.2
Eau Claire, WI.	1,686.6	186	154,039	152,989	148,337	137,543	245	245	240	93.5	90.0	83.5
El Centro, CA.	4,481.7	53	155,823	152,345	142,361	109,303	244	257	286	37.3	34.1	26.2
Elizabethtown, KY	893.6	288	110,646	109,286	107,543	100,919	319	318	304	124.2	120.7	113.3
Elkhart-Goshen, IN.	467.9	349	195,362	191,629	182,791	156,198	205	205	211	421.0	393.9	336.6
Elmira, NY	410.8	353	89,512	89,952	91,070	95,195	348	344	317	219.4	223.2	233.3
El Paso, TX	1,014.7	269	721,598	712,617	679,622	591,610	68	69	71	712.3	670.9	584.0
Erie, PA	1,558.4	209	280,446	280,844	280,843	275,572	160	155	143	349.7	350.2	343.6
Eugene-Springfield, OR	4,721.8	48	335,180	331,567	322,977	282,912	143	139	140	73.6	70.9	62.1
Evansville, IN-KY.	2,348.0	134	349,543	347,833	342,815	324,858	139	133	124	152.6	149.6	141.8
Fairbanks, AK.	7,444.0	21	87,560	86,904	82,840	77,720	349	351	346	11.9	11.2	10.6
Fargo, ND-MN.	2,820.7	105	184,857	182,649	174,367	153,296	213	214	213	65.8	62.1	54.5
Farmington, NM.	5,538.4	38	126,208	124,196	113,801	91,605	290	299	323	22.9	20.6	16.6
Fayetteville, NC.	1,050.8	260	345,536	346,136	336,613	297,569	140	136	132	331.0	322.4	285.0
Fayetteville-Springdale-Rogers, AR-MO.	3,213.0	90	405,101	390,944	347,045	239,464	117	130	158	127.7	109.4	75.5
Flagstaff, AZ.	18,661.2	3	123,866	122,687	116,320	96,591	295	293	314	6.7	6.2	5.2
Flint, MI.	649.3	324	443,883	443,497	436,148	430,459	107	104	92	693.6	681.5	672.6
Florence, SC.	1,370.5	230	198,443	197,273	193,155	176,195	202	198	194	145.8	141.9	129.5
Florence-Muscle Shoals, AL.	1,342.4	233	142,351	142,194	142,950	131,327	266	256	252	112.6	113.1	103.9
Fond du Lac, WI.	765.8	308	99,337	98,648	97,296	90,083	340	338	326	137.4	134.6	124.6
Fort Collins-Loveland, CO.	2,633.9	120	271,927	268,960	251,494	186,136	163	167	187	104.5	96.7	71.6
Fort Smith, AR-OK.	4,092.8	63	284,994	282,006	273,171	234,078	157	158	159	71.2	68.3	58.5
Fort Walton Beach-Crestview-Destin, FL	1,082.0	257	182,172	180,910	170,498	143,777	217	217	231	194.6	182.2	153.6
Fort Wayne, IN	1,368.4	231	404,414	401,750	390,156	354,435	118	116	113	296.7	286.2	260.0
Fresno, CA.	6,017.4	32	877,584	865,620	799,407	667,490	56	58	62	147.2	134.1	111.9
Gadsden, AL.	548.8	342	103,189	103,096	103,459	99,840	333	327	307	192.9	193.4	186.6
Gainesville, FL	1,324.6	234	240,254	238,489	232,392	191,263	179	175	179	196.4	190.0	156.4
Gainesville, GA.	429.2	352	165,771	160,788	139,315	95,434	229	261	316	420.7	353.6	242.2
Glens Falls, NY	1,777.5	177	128,572	127,774	124,345	118,539	285	280	271	75.4	72.9	69.5
Goldsboro, NC	556.7	340	114,448	114,215	113,329	104,666	308	300	296	207.0	204.9	189.3
Grand Forks, ND-MN	3,437.6	82	97,073	97,024	97,478	103,272	344	337	299	28.5	28.6	30.3
Grand Junction, CO	3,341.1	85	129,872	127,281	116,935	93,145	281	292	322	39.0	35.1	28.0
Grand Rapids-Wyoming, MI.	2,890.7	100	771,185	766,202	740,482	645,918	65	63	67	272.7	261.8	228.4
Great Falls, MT.	2,711.7	113	79,569	79,938	80,357	77,691	354	353	347	29.5	29.8	28.8
Greeley, CO[4]	4,021.6	64	228,943	219,961	180,861	131,821	184	208	249	57.4	45.3	33.0
Green Bay, WI	2,849.0	104	297,493	295,049	282,497	243,698	154	153	157	159.2	151.1	130.4
Greensboro-High Point, NC	2,020.0	156	674,500	666,427	643,447	540,030	73	74	77	336.7	321.2	269.5
Greenville, NC.	920.7	281	162,596	160,360	152,693	123,864	233	237	260	177.3	166.5	135.1

See footnotes at end of table.

Metropolitan statistical area **Metropolitan statistical area with metropolitan divisions** *Metropolitan division*	Area, 2000 (square miles)		Population									
					2000[1] (estimates base)	1990[2] (April 1)	Rank			Persons per square mile of land area[3]		
	Total	Rank	2005 (July 1)	2004 (July 1)			2005	2000	1990	2005	2000	1990
Greenville, SC	2,030.8	154	591,251	583,917	559,922	472,155	83	84	85	295.3	279.7	235.8
Gulfport-Biloxi, MS	1,976.8	159	255,383	252,826	246,190	207,875	170	171	171	169.9	163.8	138.3
Hagerstown-Martinsburg, MD-WV	1,018.8	267	251,311	244,206	222,771	192,774	171	181	178	249.3	221.0	191.2
Hanford-Corcoran, CA	1,391.5	228	143,420	142,291	129,461	101,469	262	273	302	103.1	93.1	73.1
Harrisburg-Carlisle, PA	1,664.4	191	521,812	518,744	509,074	474,242	94	87	84	320.3	312.5	291.1
Harrisonburg, VA	870.9	290	111,689	110,796	108,167	88,189	315	316	330	128.5	124.5	101.5
Hartford-West Hartford-East Hartford, CT	1,606.7	202	1,188,241	1,182,817	1,148,618	1,123,678	44	44	38	784.3	758.2	741.7
Hattiesburg, MS	1,620.9	199	131,871	129,944	123,812	109,603	276	282	285	81.9	76.9	68.0
Hickory-Lenoir-Morganton, NC	1,665.8	190	355,654	353,097	341,820	292,405	136	135	136	217.1	208.7	178.4
Hinesville-Fort Stewart, GA	1,006.0	271	68,627	71,412	71,914	58,947	359	357	358	74.6	78.2	64.1
Holland-Grand Haven, MI	1,632.0	197	255,406	252,945	238,314	187,768	169	173	185	451.2	421.0	331.7
Honolulu, HI	2,126.9	148	905,266	899,562	876,156	836,231	53	52	50	1,508.8	1,460.3	1,393.7
Hot Springs, AR	734.6	312	93,551	92,222	88,068	73,397	346	348	351	138.2	130.1	108.3
Houma-Bayou Cane-Thibodaux, LA	3,552.1	81	199,670	198,409	194,477	182,842	200	195	188	85.3	83.1	78.1
Houston-Sugar Land-Baytown, TX	10,061.9	6	5,280,077	5,176,667	4,715,407	3,767,233	7	8	10	591.4	528.2	421.9
Huntington-Ashland, WV-KY-OH	1,773.8	179	286,012	286,237	288,649	288,189	156	151	137	163.5	165.0	164.8
Huntsville, AL	1,419.9	227	368,661	362,800	342,627	293,047	133	134	135	268.5	249.5	213.4
Idaho Falls, ID	3,006.2	98	113,436	110,560	101,677	88,750	309	333	328	38.3	34.3	29.9
Indianapolis, IN	3,887.9	69	1,640,591	1,617,414	1,525,104	1,294,217	34	34	34	424.7	394.8	334.9
Iowa City, IA	1,194.1	247	138,524	137,558	131,676	115,731	272	269	276	117.1	111.3	97.8
Ithaca, NY	491.6	347	100,018	100,080	96,501	94,097	338	339	320	210.1	202.7	197.7
Jackson, MI	723.8	314	163,629	162,653	158,422	149,756	230	232	219	231.4	224.1	211.8
Jackson, MS	3,795.3	73	522,580	517,060	497,197	446,941	92	90	86	140.3	133.4	119.9
Jackson, TN	847.4	296	110,857	110,042	107,365	90,801	318	319	324	131.0	126.9	107.3
Jacksonville, FL	3,698.1	76	1,248,371	1,223,741	1,122,750	925,213	42	45	47	387.6	348.6	287.2
Jacksonville, NC	908.6	283	152,440	154,587	150,355	149,838	249	244	218	198.7	196.0	195.4
Janesville, WI	726.2	313	157,538	156,207	152,307	139,510	240	239	237	218.8	211.5	193.5
Jefferson City, MO	2,278.4	138	143,867	142,377	140,052	120,704	261	260	265	63.9	62.2	53.6
Johnson City, TN	863.9	292	188,944	187,217	181,607	160,369	211	206	205	221.2	212.7	188.0
Johnstown, PA	693.4	317	148,073	148,646	152,598	163,062	254	238	200	215.2	221.8	237.0
Jonesboro, AR	1,476.4	219	112,084	111,064	107,762	93,620	314	317	321	76.3	73.4	63.7
Joplin, MO	1,268.0	241	166,178	164,031	157,322	134,910	228	234	244	131.3	124.3	106.6
Kalamazoo-Portage, MI	1,670.4	189	319,348	318,272	314,866	293,471	145	146	134	272.2	268.4	250.2
Kankakee-Bradley, IL	681.4	319	107,972	107,038	103,833	96,255	327	325	315	159.5	153.4	142.0
Kansas City, MO-KS	7,949.4	20	1,947,694	1,927,240	1,836,418	1,636,527	27	26	25	247.9	233.7	208.3
Kennewick-Richland-Pasco, WA	3,025.5	96	220,961	215,552	191,822	150,033	191	201	217	75.0	65.1	50.9
Killeen-Temple-Fort Hood, TX	2,858.6	102	351,528	345,949	330,712	268,820	137	138	146	124.5	117.1	95.2
Kingsport-Bristol-Bristol, TN-VA	2,047.1	152	301,294	299,983	298,484	275,678	152	149	142	149.7	148.4	137.0
Kingston, NY	1,160.8	252	182,693	181,824	177,749	165,304	216	210	199	162.2	157.9	146.7
Knoxville, TN	1,931.7	164	655,400	646,979	616,079	534,917	78	76	79	352.9	331.8	288.1
Kokomo, IN	554.3	341	101,362	101,129	101,541	96,946	335	334	313	183.3	183.6	175.3
La Crosse, WI-MN	1,048.8	262	128,899	128,401	126,838	116,401	283	277	273	127.5	125.5	115.1
Lafayette, IN	1,284.5	238	183,340	181,427	178,541	158,848	215	209	208	143.5	139.7	124.3
Lafayette, LA	1,086.8	255	247,824	245,719	238,936	208,859	174	172	170	245.4	236.6	206.8
Lake Charles, LA	3,025.9	95	194,977	194,261	193,568	177,394	207	197	192	81.8	81.2	74.4
Lakeland, FL	2,010.0	158	542,912	524,286	483,924	405,382	89	92	96	289.7	258.2	216.2
Lancaster, PA	983.8	272	490,562	486,361	470,658	422,822	99	96	93	516.9	496.0	445.5
Lansing-East Lansing, MI	1,714.5	185	455,315	455,594	447,822	432,684	104	99	90	266.7	262.3	253.5
Laredo, TX	3,375.5	84	224,695	218,806	193,117	133,239	189	200	247	66.9	57.5	39.7
Las Cruces, NM	3,814.6	72	189,444	185,524	174,682	135,510	210	213	243	49.8	45.9	35.6
Las Vegas-Paradise, NV	8,090.7	19	1,710,551	1,648,524	1,375,738	741,368	31	36	56	216.3	173.9	93.7
Lawrence, KS	474.5	348	102,914	102,738	99,965	81,798	334	335	340	225.2	218.7	179.0
Lawton, OK	1,083.8	256	112,429	113,058	114,996	111,486	312	297	280	105.2	107.6	104.3
Lebanon, PA	362.6	359	125,578	124,087	120,327	113,744	292	287	278	346.9	332.4	314.2
Lewiston, ID-WA	1,497.1	216	59,109	58,640	57,961	51,359	360	360	359	39.8	39.1	34.6
Lewiston-Auburn, ME	497.2	346	108,039	107,125	103,793	105,259	324	326	294	229.9	220.8	224.0
Lexington-Fayette, KY	1,484.1	218	429,889	424,649	408,326	348,428	110	109	115	290.7	276.1	235.6
Lima, OH	406.9	355	106,234	106,333	108,473	109,755	328	315	284	263.0	268.5	271.7
Lincoln, NE	1,422.4	226	281,553	278,509	266,787	229,091	159	160	162	199.1	188.7	162.0
Little Rock-North Little Rock, AR	4,198.2	60	643,272	635,764	610,518	534,943	80	77	78	157.3	149.3	130.8
Logan, UT-ID	1,841.4	171	110,426	109,291	102,720	79,415	321	330	343	60.3	56.1	43.4
Longview, TX	1,807.7	173	201,501	199,966	194,042	180,053	199	196	190	112.9	108.7	100.9
Longview, WA	1,166.3	250	97,325	96,208	92,948	82,119	343	343	339	85.4	81.6	72.1
Los Angeles-Long Beach-Santa Ana, CA	**5,700.3**	**35**	**12,923,547**	**12,899,425**	**12,365,619**	**11,273,720**	**2**	**2**	**2**	**2,664.6**	**2,549.6**	**2,324.5**
Los Angeles-Long Beach-Glendale, CA	*4,752.3*	*(X)*	*9,935,475*	*9,917,331*	*9,519,330*	*8,863,052*	*(X)*	*(X)*	*(X)*	*2,446.6*	*2,344.1*	*2,183.0*
Santa Ana-Anaheim-Irvine, CA	*948.0*	*(X)*	*2,988,072*	*2,982,094*	*2,846,289*	*2,410,668*	*(X)*	*(X)*	*(X)*	*3,787.2*	*3,607.5*	*3,051.5*
Louisville, KY-IN	4,196.3	61	1,208,452	1,199,424	1,162,415	1,056,156	43	43	40	292.2	281.1	255.4
Lubbock, TX	1,802.4	175	258,970	257,835	249,700	229,940	167	169	160	144.0	138.8	127.8
Lynchburg, VA	2,146.7	145	236,910	233,876	228,616	206,226	181	178	173	111.5	107.6	97.0
Macon, GA	1,737.7	182	228,712	227,955	222,385	206,786	186	183	172	132.6	128.9	119.9
Madera, CA	2,153.3	143	142,788	138,895	123,109	88,090	263	284	331	66.8	57.6	41.2
Madison, WI	2,802.1	106	537,039	531,256	501,774	432,323	90	88	91	196.1	183.3	157.8

See footnotes at end of table.

State and Metropolitan Area Data Book: 2006

U.S. Census Bureau

Metropolitan statistical area **Metropolitan statistical area with metropolitan divisions** *Metropolitan division*	Area, 2000 (square miles)		Population									
					2000[1] (estimates base)	1990[2] (April 1)	Rank			Persons per square mile of land area[3]		
	Total	Rank	2005 (July 1)	2004 (July 1)			2005	2000	1990	2005	2000	1990
Manchester-Nashua, NH	892.2	289	401,291	398,355	380,841	335,838	120	119	121	458.1	434.8	383.4
Mansfield, OH	500.3	345	127,949	128,095	128,852	126,137	286	276	258	257.4	259.3	253.8
McAllen-Edinburg-Mission, TX	1,582.7	203	678,275	657,310	569,463	383,545	72	81	100	432.0	362.7	244.5
Medford, OR	2,801.8	107	195,322	193,016	181,275	146,387	206	207	227	70.1	65.1	52.6
Memphis, TN-MS-AR	4,699.6	50	1,260,905	1,248,492	1,205,194	1,067,263	41	41	39	275.8	263.6	233.4
Merced, CA	1,971.9	160	241,706	236,857	210,554	178,403	177	186	191	125.3	109.2	92.5
Miami-Fort Lauderdale-Miami Beach, FL	**6,137.2**	**30**	**5,422,200**	**5,355,903**	**5,007,988**	**4,056,228**	**6**	**6**	**8**	**1,057.8**	**977.0**	**781.8**
Fort Lauderdale-Pompano Beach-Deerfield Beach, FL	*1,319.6*	*(X)*	*1,777,638*	*1,753,000*	*1,623,018*	*1,255,531*	*(X)*	*(X)*	*(X)*	*1,475.2*	*1,346.9*	*1,038.5*
Miami-Miami Beach-Kendall, FL	*2,431.3*	*(X)*	*2,376,014*	*2,358,714*	*2,253,779*	*1,937,194*	*(X)*	*(X)*	*(X)*	*1,221.0*	*1,158.2*	*996.5*
West Palm Beach-Boca Raton-Boynton Beach, FL	*2,386.3*	*(X)*	*1,268,548*	*1,244,189*	*1,131,191*	*863,503*	*(X)*	*(X)*	*(X)*	*642.6*	*573.0*	*424.5*
Michigan City-La Porte, IN	613.0	332	110,512	109,741	110,106	107,066	320	311	290	184.8	184.1	179.0
Midland, TX	902.0	286	121,371	120,014	116,009	106,611	298	294	293	134.9	128.9	118.5
Milwaukee-Waukesha-West Allis, WI	3,322.3	88	1,512,855	1,513,319	1,500,744	1,432,149	37	35	31	1,036.2	1,027.9	980.9
Minneapolis-St. Paul-Bloomington, MN-WI	6,364.1	27	3,142,779	3,112,877	2,968,817	2,538,776	16	16	16	518.4	489.7	418.7
Missoula, MT	2,618.3	121	100,086	99,063	95,802	78,687	337	340	344	38.5	36.9	30.3
Mobile, AL	1,644.0	195	401,427	400,107	399,843	378,643	119	113	101	325.6	324.3	307.1
Modesto, CA	1,514.7	213	505,505	497,599	446,997	370,522	97	100	103	338.4	299.2	247.8
Monroe, LA	1,538.0	211	171,138	171,089	170,053	162,987	226	219	201	115.0	114.3	109.5
Monroe, MI	680.0	320	153,935	152,451	145,945	133,600	246	248	245	279.4	264.9	242.5
Montgomery, AL	2,786.5	108	357,244	354,243	346,528	305,175	135	131	130	131.1	127.2	112.0
Morgantown, WV	1,017.3	268	114,501	113,883	111,200	104,546	307	306	297	113.5	110.2	103.5
Morristown, TN	792.5	302	130,575	128,794	123,081	100,591	279	285	305	182.6	172.1	140.7
Mount Vernon-Anacortes, WA	1,920.5	166	113,171	111,131	102,979	79,545	311	329	342	65.2	59.4	45.8
Muncie, IN	395.9	357	116,362	117,501	118,769	119,659	303	291	268	296.1	302.2	304.5
Muskegon-Norton Shores, MI	1,459.3	222	175,554	174,146	170,200	158,983	223	218	207	344.9	334.4	312.3
Myrtle Beach-Conway-North Myrtle Beach, SC	1,255.0	242	226,992	217,635	196,629	144,053	187	194	230	200.2	173.4	127.0
Napa, CA	788.3	304	132,764	132,394	124,308	110,765	275	281	283	176.1	164.9	146.9
Naples-Marco Island, FL	2,304.9	137	307,242	296,675	251,377	152,099	149	168	214	151.7	124.1	75.1
Nashville-Davidson-Murfreesboro, TN	5,762.7	34	1,422,544	1,394,960	1,311,793	1,048,216	39	39	41	250.1	230.7	184.3
New Haven-Milford, CT	862.0	293	846,766	844,342	824,008	804,219	58	57	53	1,397.3	1,359.7	1,327.1
New Orleans-Metairie-Kenner, LA	7,097.0	23	1,319,367	1,317,990	1,316,512	1,264,383	40	38	35	418.4	417.5	401.0
New York-Northern New Jersey-Long Island, NY-NJ-PA	**9,212.2**	**13**	**18,747,320**	**18,754,585**	**18,323,382**	**16,846,046**	**1**	**1**	**1**	**2,787.3**	**2,724.3**	**2,502.4**
Edison, NJ	*2,208.6*	*(X)*	*2,303,709*	*2,288,043*	*2,173,869*	*1,898,352*	*(X)*	*(X)*	*(X)*	*1,337.0*	*1,261.7*	*1,101.1*
Nassau-Suffolk, NY	*2,826.2*	*(X)*	*2,808,064*	*2,812,212*	*2,753,913*	*2,609,212*	*(X)*	*(X)*	*(X)*	*2,342.0*	*2,296.8*	*2,178.0*
Newark-Union, NJ-PA	*2,256.7*	*(X)*	*2,152,978*	*2,148,774*	*2,097,519*	*1,959,855*	*(X)*	*(X)*	*(X)*	*980.0*	*954.7*	*892.1*
New York-White Plains-Wayne, NY-NJ	*1,920.8*	*(X)*	*11,482,569*	*11,505,556*	*11,298,081*	*10,378,627*	*(X)*	*(X)*	*(X)*	*7,140.9*	*7,026.2*	*6,430.4*
Niles-Benton Harbor, MI	1,581.4	204	162,611	162,825	162,455	161,378	232	229	203	284.8	284.5	282.6
Norwich-New London, CT	771.7	307	266,618	266,107	259,106	254,957	166	161	155	400.3	389.0	382.8
Ocala, FL	1,663.0	193	303,442	291,768	258,916	194,833	151	162	177	192.2	164.0	123.4
Ocean City, NJ	620.3	328	99,286	100,461	102,326	95,089	341	331	318	389.4	401.3	372.9
Odessa, TX	901.7	287	125,339	124,293	121,123	118,934	293	286	269	139.1	134.4	132.0
Ogden-Clearfield, UT	1,904.0	169	486,842	477,343	442,656	351,799	101	102	114	327.0	297.3	236.3
Oklahoma City, OK	5,581.8	36	1,156,812	1,142,390	1,095,421	971,042	46	47	44	209.6	198.5	175.9
Olympia, WA	773.6	306	228,867	224,661	207,355	161,238	185	189	204	314.8	285.2	221.8
Omaha-Council Bluffs, NE-IA	4,406.2	55	813,170	802,247	767,140	685,797	60	60	59	186.4	175.8	157.2
Orlando-Kissimmee, FL	4,011.8	66	1,933,255	1,863,086	1,644,563	1,224,844	28	30	36	553.8	471.1	350.9
Oshkosh-Neenah, WI	578.7	337	159,482	158,664	156,763	140,320	237	235	236	363.3	357.1	319.6
Owensboro, KY	931.4	279	111,599	111,028	109,875	104,681	316	312	295	123.3	121.4	115.5
Oxnard-Thousand Oaks-Ventura, CA	2,208.2	142	796,106	796,165	753,197	669,016	62	61	61	431.5	408.2	362.4
Palm Bay-Melbourne-Titusville, FL	1,557.0	210	531,250	518,812	476,230	398,978	91	95	97	521.9	467.8	391.9
Panama City-Lynn Haven, FL	1,033.3	265	161,558	157,811	148,217	126,994	236	246	257	211.5	194.0	166.2
Parkersburg-Marietta-Vienna, WV-OH	1,386.5	229	162,529	162,931	164,624	161,907	234	225	202	119.0	120.5	118.5
Pascagoula, MS	1,526.9	212	157,199	155,847	150,564	131,916	242	242	248	130.5	124.9	109.5
Pensacola-Ferry Pass-Brent, FL	2,049.1	151	439,877	434,812	412,153	344,406	109	108	117	262.0	245.5	205.1
Peoria, IL	2,518.3	127	369,161	367,451	366,875	358,552	132	127	111	149.5	148.5	145.1
Philadelphia-Camden-Wilmington, PA-NJ-DE-MD	**4,870.6**	**44**	**5,823,233**	**5,798,956**	**5,687,141**	**5,435,550**	**4**	**4**	**4**	**1,257.7**	**1,228.3**	**1,174.0**
Camden, NJ	*1,383.9*	*(X)*	*1,245,902*	*1,237,060*	*1,186,996*	*1,127,972*	*(X)*	*(X)*	*(X)*	*921.5*	*878.0*	*834.3*
Philadelphia, PA	*2,202.8*	*(X)*	*3,890,181*	*3,882,313*	*3,849,644*	*3,728,991*	*(X)*	*(X)*	*(X)*	*1,796.0*	*1,777.3*	*1,721.6*
Wilmington, DE-MD-NJ	*1,284.0*	*(X)*	*687,150*	*679,583*	*650,501*	*578,587*	*(X)*	*(X)*	*(X)*	*617.9*	*585.0*	*520.3*
Phoenix-Mesa-Scottsdale, AZ	14,598.4	4	3,865,077	3,713,291	3,251,876	2,238,498	14	14	20	265.2	223.1	153.6
Pine Bluff, AR	2,084.7	150	104,865	105,223	107,345	106,958	331	320	291	51.3	52.5	52.3
Pittsburgh, PA	5,343.1	42	2,386,074	2,397,767	2,431,087	2,468,289	21	20	18	451.9	460.4	467.7
Pittsfield, MA	946.3	278	131,868	132,397	134,953	139,352	277	266	238	141.6	145.0	149.7
Pocatello, ID	2,590.1	124	85,908	85,658	83,103	73,112	350	350	353	34.1	33.0	29.0
Portland-South Portland-Biddeford, ME	2,858.4	103	514,227	511,036	487,568	441,257	96	91	87	247.2	234.4	212.0
Portland-Vancouver-Beaverton, OR-WA	6,817.8	24	2,095,861	2,062,109	1,927,881	1,523,741	24	25	27	313.6	288.4	228.0
Port St. Lucie-Fort Pierce, FL	1,440.9	223	381,033	364,803	319,426	251,071	128	144	156	337.8	283.2	222.6
Poughkeepsie-Newburgh-Middletown, NY	1,663.9	192	667,742	662,833	621,517	567,109	75	75	73	412.7	384.1	350.5
Prescott, AZ	8,127.8	18	198,701	190,737	167,517	107,714	201	220	289	24.5	20.6	13.3
Providence-New Bedford-Fall River, RI-MA	2,236.2	140	1,622,520	1,627,194	1,582,997	1,509,789	35	32	28	1,013.4	988.8	943.0
Provo-Orem, UT	5,547.3	37	452,851	443,109	376,778	269,407	105	120	144	84.0	69.9	50.0
Pueblo, CO	2,397.7	131	151,322	149,954	141,472	123,051	250	259	261	63.3	59.2	51.5

See footnotes at end of table.

Metropolitan statistical area **Metropolitan statistical area with metropolitan divisions** *Metropolitan division*	Area, 2000 (square miles)		Population				Rank			Persons per square mile of land area[3]		
	Total	Rank	2005 (July 1)	2004 (July 1)	2000[1] (estimates base)	1990[2] (April 1)	2005	2000	1990	2005	2000	1990
Punta Gorda, FL	859.1	294	157,536	157,324	141,627	110,975	241	258	282	227.0	204.1	159.9
Racine, WI	791.9	303	195,708	193,862	188,831	175,034	204	202	196	587.7	567.1	525.6
Raleigh-Cary, NC	2,147.6	144	949,681	914,963	797,026	544,020	51	59	76	448.8	376.7	257.0
Rapid City, SD	6,266.8	29	118,203	117,553	112,818	103,221	301	302	300	18.9	18.1	16.5
Reading, PA	865.7	291	396,314	391,447	373,638	336,523	123	123	120	461.4	435.0	391.8
Redding, CA	3,847.4	70	179,904	177,829	163,256	147,036	220	228	224	47.5	43.1	38.8
Reno-Sparks, NV	6,815.1	25	393,946	384,343	342,885	257,193	124	132	154	59.6	51.9	38.9
Richmond, VA	5,841.7	33	1,175,654	1,156,849	1,096,957	949,244	45	46	46	205.8	192.0	166.2
Riverside-San Bernardino-Ontario, CA	27,408.5	1	3,909,954	3,785,883	3,254,821	2,588,793	13	13	14	143.4	119.4	94.9
Roanoke, VA	1,896.7	170	292,983	291,177	288,254	268,513	155	152	147	156.3	153.8	143.4
Rochester, MN	1,644.0	196	176,984	174,821	163,618	141,945	222	227	233	109.4	101.1	87.7
Rochester, NY	4,870.1	45	1,039,028	1,041,060	1,037,831	1,002,410	49	49	43	354.5	354.1	341.9
Rockford, IL	801.2	300	339,178	334,754	320,204	283,719	142	142	138	426.6	402.8	356.9
Rocky Mount, NC	1,049.3	261	145,507	145,033	142,991	133,369	259	255	246	139.2	136.8	127.6
Rome, GA	518.5	344	94,198	94,053	90,565	81,251	345	345	341	183.6	176.5	158.4
Sacramento-Arden-Arcade-Roseville, CA	5,309.3	43	2,042,283	2,014,594	1,796,857	1,481,220	26	27	29	400.9	352.7	290.8
Saginaw-Saginaw Township North, MI	815.8	299	208,356	209,249	210,042	211,946	195	188	167	257.5	259.6	262.0
St. Cloud, MN	1,802.9	174	181,159	179,176	167,396	149,509	219	221	220	103.3	95.5	85.3
St. George, UT	2,429.9	129	118,885	110,425	90,354	48,560	299	346	360	49.0	37.2	20.0
St. Joseph, MO-KS	1,673.9	188	121,961	122,011	123,822	115,816	297	283	275	73.4	74.5	69.7
St. Louis, MO-IL[5]	8,844.0	8	2,778,518	2,768,641	2,698,672	2,580,720	18	18	13	321.3	312.0	298.3
Salem, OR	1,938.3	163	375,560	369,573	347,218	278,024	131	129	141	195.1	180.4	144.4
Salinas, CA	3,771.1	75	412,104	414,551	401,762	355,660	112	112	112	124.1	120.9	107.1
Salisbury, MD	1,010.6	270	116,247	114,372	109,391	97,779	305	313	312	165.1	155.4	138.9
Salt Lake City, UT	9,977.0	7	1,034,484	1,018,514	968,883	768,075	50	50	54	108.4	101.6	80.4
San Angelo, TX	2,592.1	123	105,367	105,538	105,781	100,087	330	321	306	40.9	41.1	38.9
San Antonio, TX	7,384.7	22	1,889,797	1,852,508	1,711,726	1,407,745	29	29	32	257.5	233.2	191.8
San Diego-Carlsbad-San Marcos, CA	4,525.5	51	2,933,462	2,935,190	2,813,833	2,498,016	17	17	17	698.4	670.0	594.2
Sandusky, OH	626.2	327	78,665	78,976	79,551	76,779	355	355	348	308.5	312.0	301.1
San Francisco-Oakland-Fremont, CA	**3,424.4**	**83**	**4,152,688**	**4,146,980**	**4,123,742**	**3,684,112**	**12**	**12**	**11**	**1,679.2**	**1,667.5**	**1,489.7**
Oakland-Fremont-Hayward, CA	*1,623.3*	*(X)*	*2,466,692*	*2,459,702*	*2,392,557*	*2,080,434*	*(X)*	*(X)*	*(X)*	*1,691.8*	*1,641.0*	*1,426.9*
San Francisco-San Mateo-Redwood City, CA	*1,801.1*	*(X)*	*1,685,996*	*1,687,278*	*1,731,185*	*1,603,678*	*(X)*	*(X)*	*(X)*	*1,659.4*	*1,703.9*	*1,578.4*
San Jose-Sunnyvale-Santa Clara, CA	2,694.7	115	1,754,988	1,737,961	1,735,819	1,534,274	30	28	26	654.8	647.7	572.5
San Luis Obispo-Paso Robles, CA	3,615.5	78	255,478	254,436	246,681	217,162	168	170	166	77.3	74.7	65.7
Santa Barbara-Santa Maria, CA	3,789.1	74	400,762	401,708	399,347	369,608	121	114	104	146.4	145.9	135.0
Santa Cruz-Watsonville, CA	607.2	334	249,666	250,837	255,602	229,734	172	163	161	561.0	574.4	515.1
Santa Fe, NM	1,910.8	167	140,855	139,166	129,288	98,928	268	274	310	73.8	67.7	51.8
Santa Rosa-Petaluma, CA	1,768.2	180	466,477	467,932	458,614	388,222	102	98	99	296.0	291.0	246.3
Sarasota-Bradenton-Venice, FL	1,617.9	200	673,035	651,696	589,963	489,483	74	79	82	512.6	449.3	372.8
Savannah, GA	1,569.6	207	313,883	310,327	293,299	257,899	148	150	153	231.0	215.8	189.4
Scranton-Wilkes-Barre, PA	1,776.4	178	550,546	551,214	560,625	575,322	86	83	72	315.1	320.9	329.3
Seattle-Tacoma-Bellevue, WA	**6,309.4**	**28**	**3,203,314**	**3,167,729**	**3,043,885**	**2,559,136**	**15**	**15**	**15**	**543.5**	**516.4**	**434.3**
Seattle-Bellevue-Everett, WA	*4,502.9*	*(X)*	*2,449,527*	*2,421,951*	*2,343,067*	*1,972,933*	*(X)*	*(X)*	*(X)*	*581.1*	*555.9*	*468.0*
Tacoma, WA	*1,806.5*	*(X)*	*753,787*	*745,778*	*700,818*	*586,203*	*(X)*	*(X)*	*(X)*	*448.9*	*417.4*	*349.8*
Sheboygan, WI	1,271.0	240	114,610	113,899	112,656	103,877	306	303	298	223.0	219.2	202.1
Sherman-Denison, TX	979.2	274	116,834	115,855	110,595	95,019	302	308	319	125.1	118.4	101.7
Shreveport-Bossier City, LA	2,698.3	114	383,233	380,785	375,965	359,687	127	122	110	147.5	144.7	138.4
Sioux City, IA-NE-SD	2,094.6	149	142,571	143,116	143,053	131,350	264	254	251	68.8	69.0	63.4
Sioux Falls, SD	2,586.9	125	207,918	203,186	187,093	153,500	196	203	212	80.6	72.5	59.5
South Bend-Mishawaka, IN-MI	969.4	275	318,156	317,490	316,661	296,529	146	145	133	334.9	333.3	312.1
Spartanburg, SC	819.1	298	266,809	264,106	253,782	226,793	165	164	163	329.0	312.9	279.6
Spokane, WA	1,780.7	176	440,706	435,146	417,939	361,333	108	107	108	249.8	236.9	204.8
Springfield, IL	1,192.4	248	205,527	205,056	201,440	189,550	197	192	181	173.9	170.4	160.2
Springfield, MA	1,904.3	168	687,264	687,296	680,014	672,970	71	68	60	371.7	367.8	363.8
Springfield, MO	3,020.8	97	398,124	390,917	368,374	298,818	122	125	131	132.3	122.4	99.3
Springfield, OH	403.6	356	142,376	142,394	144,741	147,548	265	253	223	355.9	361.9	368.9
State College, PA	1,111.9	253	140,561	139,948	135,758	124,812	269	265	259	126.9	122.5	112.6
Stockton, CA	1,426.3	225	664,116	649,241	563,598	480,628	76	82	83	474.7	402.9	343.6
Sumter, SC	682.0	318	105,517	105,699	104,636	101,276	329	322	303	158.7	157.3	152.3
Syracuse, NY	2,779.4	110	651,763	653,128	650,154	659,924	79	72	64	272.8	272.1	276.1
Tallahassee, FL	2,602.7	122	334,886	331,252	320,304	259,107	144	141	152	140.3	134.2	108.5
Tampa-St. Petersburg-Clearwater, FL	3,330.9	86	2,647,658	2,586,417	2,396,013	2,067,959	20	21	22	1,036.7	938.1	809.7
Terre Haute, IN	1,484.8	217	168,059	168,482	170,954	166,578	227	216	198	114.7	116.7	113.7
Texarkana, TX-Texarkana, AR	1,560.3	208	133,805	132,698	129,749	120,132	274	272	267	88.5	85.8	79.5
Toledo, OH	2,208.9	141	656,696	657,925	659,188	654,157	77	71	66	405.4	406.9	403.8
Topeka, KS	3,290.2	89	229,075	227,609	224,551	210,257	183	180	169	70.7	69.3	64.8
Trenton-Ewing, NJ	228.8	360	366,256	364,381	350,761	325,824	134	128	123	1,620.6	1,552.0	1,441.7
Tucson, AZ	9,188.8	14	924,786	906,540	843,746	666,957	52	55	63	100.7	91.9	72.6
Tulsa, OK	6,460.2	26	887,715	880,713	859,530	761,019	55	53	55	141.3	136.8	121.2
Tuscaloosa, AL	2,667.6	119	196,885	195,103	193,134	176,173	203	199	195	75.3	73.9	67.4
Tyler, TX	949.5	277	190,594	186,822	174,706	151,309	208	212	215	205.4	188.3	162.9

See footnotes at end of table.

Metropolitan statistical area **Metropolitan statistical area with metropolitan divisions** *Metropolitan division*	Area, 2000 (square miles)		Population									
							Rank			Persons per square mile of land area[3]		
	Total	Rank	2005 (July 1)	2004 (July 1)	2000[1] (estimates base)	1990[2] (April 1)	2005	2000	1990	2005	2000	1990
Utica-Rome, NY	2,715.5	112	297,885	298,438	299,896	316,645	153	148	126	113.5	114.3	120.6
Valdosta, GA	1,629.0	198	124,838	123,725	119,566	99,244	294	290	309	78.6	75.2	62.5
Vallejo-Fairfield, CA	906.7	284	411,593	411,896	394,513	339,471	113	115	119	496.5	475.9	410.0
Vero Beach, FL	616.9	329	128,594	124,676	112,947	90,208	284	301	325	255.7	224.5	179.3
Victoria, TX	2,780.2	109	113,356	113,251	111,663	99,394	310	305	308	50.4	49.7	44.2
Vineland-Millville-Bridgeton, NJ	676.6	322	153,252	151,020	146,438	138,053	248	247	239	313.4	299.5	282.3
Virginia Beach-Norfolk-Newport News, VA-NC	3,896.5	68	1,647,346	1,641,671	1,576,917	1,450,855	33	33	30	626.8	600.0	552.1
Visalia-Porterville, CA	4,839.1	47	410,874	400,952	368,021	311,921	114	126	127	85.2	76.3	64.7
Waco, TX	1,060.2	259	224,668	222,765	213,513	189,123	190	185	183	215.6	204.9	181.5
Warner Robins, GA	379.8	358	126,163	123,773	110,765	89,208	291	307	327	334.6	293.8	236.6
Washington-Arlington-Alexandria, DC-VA-MD-WV	**6,028.0**	**31**	**5,214,666**	**5,157,608**	**4,796,182**	**4,122,259**	**8**	**7**	**7**	**926.7**	**852.4**	**732.5**
Bethesda-Gaithersburg-Frederick, MD	*1,174.5*	*(X)*	*1,148,284*	*1,139,087*	*1,069,441*	*907,235*	*(X)*	*(X)*	*(X)*	*991.6*	*923.5*	*783.4*
Washington-Arlington-Alexandria, DC-VA-MD-WV	*4,853.5*	*(X)*	*4,066,382*	*4,018,521*	*3,726,741*	*3,215,024*	*(X)*	*(X)*	*(X)*	*909.9*	*833.9*	*719.1*
Waterloo-Cedar Falls, IA	1,514.1	214	161,897	161,596	163,707	158,640	235	226	209	107.4	108.6	105.2
Wausau, WI	1,576.1	206	128,941	127,823	125,834	115,400	282	279	277	83.5	81.4	74.7
Weirton-Steubenville, WV-OH	591.5	335	126,464	127,495	132,008	142,523	289	268	232	217.7	227.2	244.9
Wenatchee, WA	4,842.3	46	104,768	103,323	99,219	78,455	332	336	345	22.1	20.9	16.5
Wheeling, WV-OH	962.4	276	148,677	149,437	153,178	159,301	252	236	206	156.3	161.1	167.5
Wichita, KS	4,181.1	62	587,055	583,860	571,168	511,111	85	80	80	141.5	137.7	123.2
Wichita Falls, TX	2,675.0	118	146,276	147,751	151,524	140,375	258	240	235	55.5	57.5	53.3
Williamsport, PA	1,243.8	244	118,395	118,505	120,044	118,710	300	289	270	95.9	97.2	96.1
Wilmington, NC	2,310.6	136	315,144	303,258	274,550	200,124	147	157	175	163.8	142.7	104.0
Winchester, VA-WV	1,069.6	258	116,267	113,107	102,997	84,168	304	328	336	109.1	96.6	79.0
Winston-Salem, NC	1,473.2	221	448,629	441,472	421,957	361,448	106	106	107	306.9	288.6	247.2
Worcester, MA	1,579.0	205	783,262	778,608	749,973	709,705	64	62	57	517.7	495.7	469.1
Yakima, WA	4,311.6	56	231,586	229,515	222,581	188,823	182	182	184	53.9	51.8	44.0
York-Hanover, PA	910.3	282	408,801	401,063	381,751	339,574	116	118	118	452.2	422.3	375.2
Youngstown-Warren-Boardman, OH-PA	1,740.7	181	593,168	596,262	602,964	613,622	82	78	69	348.1	353.9	360.3
Yuba City, CA	1,252.3	243	156,029	151,146	139,149	122,643	243	262	262	126.5	112.9	99.5
Yuma, AZ	5,519.0	39	181,277	175,629	160,026	106,895	218	231	292	32.9	29.0	19.4

X Not applicable.

[1]The April 1, 2000, Population Estimates base reflects modifications to the Census 2000 population as documented in the Count Question Resolution program and geographic program revisions.
[2]The April 1, 1990, census counts include corrections processed through August 1997, results of special censuses and test censuses, and do not include adjustments for census coverage errors.
[3]Persons per square mile were calculated on the basis of land area data from the 2000 census.
[4]The Denver-Aurora metropolitan statistical area includes Broomfield County. Broomfield County, CO, was formed from parts of Adams, Boulder, Jefferson, and Weld counties on November 15, 2001, and is coextensive with Broomfield city. For the purposes of defining and presenting data for the Denver-Aurora metropolitan statistical area, Broomfield city is treated as if it were a county when data are available to do so. In many cases, the data will not be available.
[5]The portion of Sullivan city in Crawford County, MO, is legally part of the St. Louis, MO-IL MSA. That portion is not included in these figures for the St. Louis MSA.

Note: Covers metropolitan statistical areas and metropolitan divisions as defined by the Office of Management and Budget as of June 6, 2003, and subsequently updated in December 2003 and November 2004. For more information, see OMB Bulletin 05-02 at <http://www.whitehouse.gov/omb/bulletins/fy05/b05-02_appendix.pdf>.

Survey, Census, or Data Collection Method: Based on the 2000 Census of Population and Housing and, for population estimates, the "component of population change method"; for more information, see Appendix B, Limitations of the Data and Methodology, and also <http://www.census.gov/prod/cen2000/doc/sf1.pdf> and <http://www.census.gov/popest/topics/methodology/>.

Sources: Area—U.S. Census Bureau, 2000 Census of Population and Housing, *Summary Population and Housing Characteristics*, Series PHC-1; and unpublished data on American FactFinder; Population—U.S. Census Bureau, 1990 "Population Estimates: Annual Time Series," archive 1990 (revised data for April 1, 1990, Population Estimates base), <http://www.census.gov/popest/archives/1990s/CO-99-02.html>. 2000 to 2005 compiled from "Population Estimates by County," published 16 March 2006; <http://www.census.gov/popest/counties/CO-EST2005-01.html>.

U.S. Census Bureau

Metropolitan statistical area **Metropolitan statistical area** **with metropolitan divisions** *Metropolitan division*	Components of population change, April 1, 2000, to July 1, 2005						Population change, April 1, 1990, to April 1, 2000	
	Number					Percent change, 2000– 2005	Number	Percent change
	Total population change[1]	Natural increase			Net inter- national migration			
		Total	Births	Deaths				
Abilene, TX.	−1,950	4,371	12,328	7,957	942	−1.2	12,237	8.3
Akron, OH	7,275	9,714	44,354	34,640	3,808	1.0	37,385	5.7
Albany, GA	4,976	5,318	12,452	7,134	707	3.2	11,283	7.7
Albany-Schenectady-Troy, NY	23,004	9,445	49,576	40,131	7,177	2.8	16,233	2.0
Albuquerque, NM.	68,287	30,409	57,366	26,957	11,189	9.4	130,237	21.7
Alexandria, LA.	2,930	3,271	11,571	8,300	422	2.0	−4,047	−2.7
Allentown-Bethlehem-Easton, PA-NJ	50,141	7,691	46,084	38,393	8,366	6.8	53,706	7.8
Altoona, PA	−2,349	−955	7,520	8,475	164	−1.8	−1,398	−1.1
Amarillo, TX	12,142	8,065	18,996	10,931	2,864	5.4	30,411	15.5
Ames, IA	−29	2,330	4,743	2,413	3,008	0.0	5,729	7.7
Anchorage, AK	31,444	18,962	27,038	8,076	3,468	9.8	53,584	20.1
Anderson, IN	−2,946	717	8,482	7,765	463	−2.2	2,689	2.1
Anderson, SC	9,774	2,223	11,648	9,425	668	5.9	20,563	14.2
Ann Arbor, MI	19,077	12,026	21,867	9,841	11,896	5.9	39,833	14.1
Anniston-Oxford, AL	−102	860	7,797	6,937	359	−0.1	−3,789	−3.3
Appleton, WI.	13,421	7,732	14,857	7,125	1,250	6.7	26,921	15.4
Asheville, NC	23,659	1,234	23,157	21,923	4,583	6.4	61,173	19.9
Athens-Clarke County, GA.	9,006	5,492	11,577	6,085	4,125	5.4	30,054	22.1
Atlanta-Sandy Springs-Marietta, GA	669,699	251,881	397,491	145,610	144,564	15.8	1,179,043	38.4
Atlantic City, NJ.	18,463	4,268	18,396	14,128	6,830	7.3	28,225	12.6
Auburn-Opelika, AL	8,162	3,170	7,360	4,190	937	7.1	27,946	32.1
Augusta-Richmond County, GA-SC	20,683	14,977	39,234	24,257	2,675	4.1	63,850	14.7
Austin-Round Rock, TX.	202,776	82,522	117,386	34,864	47,204	16.2	403,526	47.7
Bakersfield, CA	95,172	37,998	64,895	26,897	16,713	14.4	116,672	21.4
Baltimore-Towson, MD	102,681	57,190	180,997	123,807	27,625	4.0	170,822	7.2
Bangor, ME	2,149	1,035	8,052	7,017	714	1.5	−1,682	−1.1
Barnstable Town, MA	4,284	−4,191	10,396	14,587	2,137	1.9	35,625	19.1
Baton Rouge, LA.	27,835	25,475	55,602	30,127	4,993	3.9	82,117	13.2
Battle Creek, MI	1,206	2,393	9,980	7,587	903	0.9	2,003	1.5
Bay City, MI	−1,128	714	6,610	5,896	165	−1.0	−1,566	−1.4
Beaumont-Port Arthur, TX	−1,560	6,349	27,229	20,880	3,189	−0.4	23,872	6.6
Bellingham, WA.	16,645	3,746	10,485	6,739	3,425	10.0	39,046	30.6
Bend, OR.	26,015	2,998	8,122	5,124	486	22.5	40,391	53.9
Billings, MT.	7,689	2,933	9,587	6,654	178	5.5	17,405	14.3
Binghamton, NY	−3,898	707	14,041	13,334	2,112	−1.5	−12,177	−4.6
Birmingham-Hoover, AL	38,820	20,326	78,528	58,202	7,375	3.7	94,660	9.9
Bismarck, ND	4,627	2,232	6,188	3,956	257	4.9	10,888	13.0
Blacksburg-Christiansburg-Radford, VA	−267	1,312	7,864	6,552	2,375	−0.2	10,609	7.5
Bloomington, IN.	2,203	2,933	9,849	6,916	3,078	1.3	18,837	12.0
Bloomington-Normal, IL.	8,580	5,245	10,834	5,589	1,698	5.7	21,253	16.5
Boise City-Nampa, ID	79,361	26,298	43,265	16,967	6,733	17.1	145,244	45.4
Boston-Cambridge-Quincy, MA-NH	**19,495**	**115,563**	**303,982**	**188,419**	**132,759**	**0.4**	**258,445**	**6.3**
Boston-Quincy, MA	*−12,505*	*49,233*	*128,991*	*79,758*	*61,909*	*−0.7*	*97,668*	*5.7*
Cambridge-Newton-Framingham, MA.	*−7,383*	*37,027*	*97,126*	*60,099*	*53,762*	*−0.5*	*67,926*	*4.9*
Essex County, MA	*14,882*	*19,258*	*53,618*	*34,360*	*14,988*	*2.1*	*53,339*	*8.0*
Rockingham County-Strafford County, NH.	*24,501*	*10,045*	*24,247*	*14,202*	*2,100*	*6.3*	*39,512*	*11.3*
Boulder, CO[2]	10,653	11,317	18,398	7,081	8,553	3.9	44,448	19.7
Bowling Green, KY.	6,824	2,587	7,353	4,766	2,000	6.6	16,089	18.3
Bremerton-Silverdale, WA	8,692	6,146	15,549	9,403	1,278	3.7	42,238	22.3
Bridgeport-Stamford-Norwalk, CT	20,208	27,469	63,450	35,981	35,546	2.3	54,922	6.6
Brownsville-Harlingen, TX	43,084	34,793	44,402	9,609	11,797	12.9	75,107	28.9
Brunswick, GA	5,389	1,818	6,908	5,090	713	5.8	10,837	13.2
Buffalo-Niagara Falls, NY	−22,400	3,760	68,911	65,151	7,792	−1.9	−19,229	−1.6
Burlington, NC	9,739	2,783	9,784	7,001	3,577	7.4	22,581	20.9
Burlington-South Burlington, VT	6,341	4,639	11,978	7,339	2,640	3.2	21,830	12.3
Canton-Massillon, OH.	3,062	3,597	25,584	21,987	655	0.8	12,828	3.3
Cape Coral-Fort Myers, FL	103,870	1,166	28,987	27,821	10,075	23.6	105,775	31.6
Carson City, NV.	3,605	398	3,750	3,352	1,094	6.9	12,014	29.7
Casper, WY	3,266	1,740	4,868	3,128	235	4.9	5,307	8.7
Cedar Rapids, IA.	9,182	7,319	17,138	9,819	1,582	3.9	26,590	12.6
Champaign-Urbana, IL	5,463	5,700	13,784	8,084	5,804	2.6	7,431	3.7
Charleston, WV.	−3,200	513	19,711	19,198	488	−1.0	1,946	0.6
Charleston-North Charleston, SC	45,927	19,085	42,723	23,638	4,672	8.4	42,095	8.3
Charlotte-Gastonia-Concord, NC-SC	190,859	63,448	117,627	54,179	33,849	14.3	305,729	29.8
Charlottesville, VA	14,403	4,527	11,717	7,190	3,197	8.3	29,870	20.7
Chattanooga, TN-GA	15,625	6,468	32,209	25,741	3,099	3.3	43,291	10.0
Cheyenne, WY	3,556	2,600	6,178	3,578	353	4.4	8,465	11.6
Chicago-Naperville-Joliet, IL-IN-WI.	**344,741**	**379,103**	**747,424**	**368,321**	**306,954**	**3.8**	**916,539**	**11.2**
Chicago-Naperville-Joliet, IL	*254,282*	*323,572*	*632,040*	*308,468*	*280,459*	*3.3*	*734,007*	*10.6*
Gary, IN	*21,430*	*16,203*	*49,467*	*33,264*	*4,293*	*3.2*	*32,934*	*5.1*
Lake County-Kenosha County, IL-WI	*69,029*	*39,328*	*65,917*	*26,589*	*22,202*	*8.7*	*149,598*	*23.2*

See footnotes at end of table.

Metropolitan statistical area **Metropolitan statistical area with metropolitan divisions** *Metropolitan division*	Components of population change, April 1, 2000, to July 1, 2005						Population change, April 1, 1990, to April 1, 2000	
	Number							
	Total population change[1]	Natural increase			Net inter-national migration	Percent change, 2000–2005	Number	Percent change
		Total	Births	Deaths				
Chico, CA.	11,014	448	12,086	11,638	2,523	5.4	21,051	11.6
Cincinnati-Middletown, OH-KY-IN	60,784	60,330	152,804	92,474	13,977	3.0	164,742	8.9
Clarksville, TN-KY	11,621	12,741	22,021	9,280	1,351	5.0	42,765	22.6
Cleveland, TN.	4,021	1,720	7,140	5,420	677	3.9	16,660	19.1
Cleveland-Elyria-Mentor, OH	−21,692	30,834	143,200	112,366	19,524	−1.0	45,762	2.2
Coeur d'Alene, ID	18,983	3,185	7,877	4,692	278	17.5	38,890	55.7
College Station-Bryan, TX	4,850	8,136	14,187	6,051	6,402	2.6	33,887	22.4
Colorado Springs, CO.	50,016	28,852	46,025	17,173	7,143	9.3	128,002	31.3
Columbia, MO.	7,617	5,060	10,192	5,132	2,385	5.2	23,656	19.4
Columbia, SC	42,617	18,635	47,880	29,245	6,382	6.6	98,325	17.9
Columbus, GA-AL	2,531	8,737	22,917	14,180	2,519	0.9	15,316	5.7
Columbus, IN	2,105	1,843	5,215	3,372	1,219	2.9	7,778	12.2
Columbus, OH	95,788	65,151	131,937	66,786	24,430	5.9	207,669	14.8
Corpus Christi, TX	10,273	17,097	33,478	16,381	3,122	2.5	35,494	9.7
Corvallis, OR	501	1,519	4,009	2,490	1,973	0.6	7,328	10.3
Cumberland, MD-WV	−1,341	−1,143	5,179	6,322	145	−1.3	365	0.4
Dallas-Fort Worth-Arlington, TX.	**657,957**	**333,544**	**503,993**	**170,449**	**232,235**	**12.7**	**1,172,224**	**29.4**
Dallas-Plano-Irving, TX	*441,875*	*235,263*	*343,541*	*108,278*	*179,862*	*12.8*	*828,686*	*31.6*
Fort Worth-Arlington, TX	*216,082*	*98,281*	*160,452*	*62,171*	*52,373*	*12.6*	*343,538*	*25.1*
Dalton, GA.	11,640	7,134	12,233	5,099	5,391	9.7	21,452	21.8
Danville, IL	−1,580	715	5,831	5,116	279	−1.9	−4,333	−4.9
Danville, VA	−2,159	−75	6,875	6,950	473	−2.0	1,428	1.3
Davenport-Moline-Rock Island, IA-IL	255	7,431	25,783	18,352	2,882	0.1	7,909	2.1
Dayton, OH	−4,576	15,460	57,785	42,325	3,862	−0.5	4,318	0.5
Decatur, AL	2,478	2,578	9,944	7,366	1,029	1.7	14,311	10.9
Decatur, IL	−4,539	1,246	7,468	6,222	285	−4.0	−2,500	−2.1
Deltona-Daytona Beach-Ormond Beach, FL	46,712	−6,034	24,853	30,887	4,554	10.5	72,606	19.6
Denver-Aurora, CO[2]	181,600	120,201	190,714	70,513	74,060	8.3	527,905	32.0
Des Moines, IA	41,056	20,395	39,931	19,536	8,182	8.5	65,052	15.6
Detroit-Warren-Livonia, MI.	**35,778**	**113,878**	**319,742**	**205,864**	**72,285**	**0.8**	**203,858**	**4.8**
Detroit-Livonia-Dearborn, MI.	*−62,945*	*54,668*	*158,718*	*104,050*	*32,976*	*−3.1*	*−50,525*	*−2.4*
Warren-Farmington Hills-Troy, MI.	*98,723*	*59,210*	*161,024*	*101,814*	*39,309*	*4.1*	*254,383*	*11.9*
Dothan, AL.	5,733	2,442	9,692	7,250	385	4.4	10,509	8.7
Dover, DE	17,268	4,700	10,484	5,784	840	13.6	15,707	14.2
Dubuque, IA	2,475	2,035	6,217	4,182	651	2.8	2,753	3.2
Duluth, MN-WI	−73	−60	15,263	15,323	737	0.0	6,256	2.3
Durham, NC	32,384	16,465	33,532	17,067	17,449	7.6	79,158	23.0
Eau Claire, WI.	5,702	2,967	9,240	6,273	452	3.8	10,794	7.8
El Centro, CA.	13,462	10,046	14,469	4,423	6,153	9.5	33,058	30.2
Elizabethtown, KY	3,103	4,019	8,409	4,390	707	2.9	6,624	6.6
Elkhart-Goshen, IN.	12,571	9,039	16,559	7,520	4,868	6.9	26,593	17.0
Elmira, NY	−1,558	721	5,653	4,932	281	−1.7	−4,125	−4.3
El Paso, TX	41,976	53,769	74,019	20,250	25,116	6.2	88,012	14.9
Erie, PA.	−397	3,597	17,555	13,958	2,317	−0.1	5,271	1.9
Eugene-Springfield, OR	12,203	3,824	18,974	15,150	4,088	3.8	40,065	14.2
Evansville, IN-KY.	6,728	4,737	23,219	18,482	1,206	2.0	17,957	5.5
Fairbanks, AK	4,720	6,310	8,087	1,777	649	5.7	5,120	6.6
Fargo, ND-MN.	10,490	6,294	12,402	6,108	2,128	6.0	21,071	13.7
Farmington, NM.	12,407	6,355	10,330	3,975	706	10.9	22,196	24.2
Fayetteville, NC.	8,923	20,442	32,569	12,127	3,391	2.7	39,044	13.1
Fayetteville-Springdale-Rogers, AR-MO	58,056	16,115	30,919	14,804	8,109	16.7	107,581	44.9
Flagstaff, AZ.	7,546	6,737	9,935	3,198	1,175	6.5	19,729	20.4
Flint, MI	7,735	12,451	33,244	20,793	1,047	1.8	5,689	1.3
Florence, SC.	5,288	4,261	15,003	10,742	585	2.7	16,960	9.6
Florence-Muscle Shoals, AL.	−599	202	8,341	8,139	362	−0.4	11,623	8.9
Fond du Lac, WI	2,041	1,394	6,025	4,631	594	2.1	7,213	8.0
Fort Collins-Loveland, CO	20,433	9,602	17,539	7,937	3,473	8.1	65,358	35.1
Fort Smith, AR-OK.	11,823	7,043	21,314	14,271	3,097	4.3	39,093	16.7
Fort Walton Beach-Crestview-Destin, FL	11,674	5,612	13,086	7,474	1,045	6.8	26,721	18.6
Fort Wayne, IN	14,258	14,748	31,519	16,771	4,319	3.7	35,721	10.1
Fresno, CA.	78,177	48,004	77,660	29,656	26,772	9.8	131,917	19.8
Gadsden, AL.	−270	−310	6,817	7,127	497	−0.3	3,619	3.6
Gainesville, FL.	7,862	5,103	14,180	9,077	4,577	3.4	41,129	21.5
Gainesville, GA.	26,456	9,632	15,122	5,490	9,147	19.0	43,881	46.0
Glens Falls, NY.	4,227	83	6,547	6,464	311	3.4	5,806	4.9
Goldsboro, NC	1,119	3,676	9,183	5,507	1,454	1.0	8,663	8.3
Grand Forks, ND-MN	−405	2,143	6,313	4,170	917	−0.4	−5,794	−5.6
Grand Junction, CO	12,937	1,986	8,231	6,245	687	11.1	23,790	25.5
Grand Rapids-Wyoming, MI.	30,703	31,517	60,017	28,500	12,467	4.1	94,564	14.6
Great Falls, MT.	−788	1,566	5,636	4,070	192	−1.0	2,666	3.4
Greeley, CO[2]	48,082	12,414	18,503	6,089	5,018	26.6	49,040	37.2
Green Bay, WI	14,996	9,508	20,464	10,956	2,689	5.3	38,799	15.9
Greensboro-High Point, NC	31,053	17,233	46,988	29,755	15,499	4.8	103,417	19.2
Greenville, NC.	9,903	5,448	12,045	6,597	2,163	6.5	28,829	23.3

See footnotes at end of table.

Metropolitan statistical area **Metropolitan statistical area with metropolitan divisions** *Metropolitan division*	Components of population change, April 1, 2000, to July 1, 2005						Population change, April 1, 1990, to April 1, 2000	
	Number					Percent change, 2000– 2005	Number	Percent change
	Total population change[1]	Natural increase			Net inter- national migration			
		Total	Births	Deaths				
Greenville, SC	31,329	13,606	39,743	26,137	8,862	5.6	87,767	18.6
Gulfport-Biloxi, MS	9,193	7,054	19,372	12,318	1,232	3.7	38,315	18.4
Hagerstown-Martinsburg, MD-WV	28,540	3,841	15,346	11,505	565	12.8	29,997	15.6
Hanford-Corcoran, CA	13,959	8,035	12,060	4,025	3,230	10.8	27,992	27.6
Harrisburg-Carlisle, PA	12,738	6,035	31,491	25,456	4,278	2.5	34,832	7.3
Harrisonburg, VA	3,522	2,768	7,140	4,372	2,248	3.3	19,978	22.7
Hartford-West Hartford-East Hartford, CT	39,623	19,006	71,985	52,979	20,208	3.4	24,940	2.2
Hattiesburg, MS	8,059	4,192	10,143	5,951	741	6.5	14,209	13.0
Hickory-Lenoir-Morganton, NC	13,834	6,293	23,176	16,883	5,325	4.0	49,415	16.9
Hinesville-Fort Stewart, GA	−3,287	6,221	8,095	1,874	906	−4.6	12,967	22.0
Holland-Grand Haven, MI	17,092	10,632	18,474	7,842	1,947	7.2	50,546	26.9
Honolulu, HI	29,110	35,977	70,118	34,141	23,631	3.3	39,925	4.8
Hot Springs, AR	5,483	−1,244	5,565	6,809	355	6.2	14,671	20.0
Houma-Bayou Cane-Thibodaux, LA	5,193	7,167	15,449	8,282	624	2.7	11,635	6.4
Houston-Sugar Land-Baytown, TX	564,670	297,973	454,251	156,278	210,440	12.0	948,174	25.2
Huntington-Ashland, WV-KY-OH	−2,637	−332	17,681	18,013	489	−0.9	460	0.2
Huntsville, AL	26,034	8,494	23,324	14,830	3,066	7.6	49,580	16.9
Idaho Falls, ID	11,759	6,387	10,215	3,828	816	11.6	12,927	14.6
Indianapolis, IN	115,487	63,806	129,967	66,161	16,562	7.6	230,887	17.8
Iowa City, IA	6,848	5,277	9,149	3,872	3,012	5.2	15,945	13.8
Ithaca, NY	3,517	1,644	4,701	3,057	4,290	3.6	2,404	2.6
Jackson, MI	5,207	2,764	10,731	7,967	592	3.3	8,666	5.8
Jackson, MS	25,383	18,886	42,091	23,205	1,633	5.1	50,256	11.2
Jackson, TN	3,492	2,672	8,111	5,439	831	3.3	16,564	18.2
Jacksonville, FL	125,621	33,745	89,397	55,652	11,541	11.2	197,537	21.4
Jacksonville, NC	2,085	12,736	16,805	4,069	733	1.4	517	0.3
Janesville, WI	5,231	3,714	10,589	6,875	1,517	3.4	12,797	9.2
Jefferson City, MO	3,815	3,273	9,458	6,185	719	2.7	19,348	16.0
Johnson City, TN	7,337	−66	10,891	10,957	726	4.0	21,238	13.2
Johnstown, PA	−4,525	−2,201	7,819	10,020	302	−3.0	−10,464	−6.4
Jonesboro, AR	4,322	2,315	8,301	5,986	714	4.0	14,142	15.1
Joplin, MO	8,856	4,131	12,646	8,515	1,032	5.6	22,412	16.6
Kalamazoo-Portage, MI	4,482	8,090	21,797	13,707	3,400	1.4	21,395	7.3
Kankakee-Bradley, IL	4,139	2,289	8,049	5,760	780	4.0	7,578	7.9
Kansas City, MO-KS	111,276	69,971	149,366	79,395	23,459	6.1	199,891	12.2
Kennewick-Richland-Pasco, WA	29,139	10,993	17,819	6,826	6,019	15.2	41,789	27.9
Killeen-Temple-Fort Hood, TX	20,816	24,864	35,974	11,110	3,541	6.3	61,892	23.0
Kingsport-Bristol-Bristol, TN-VA	2,810	−1,413	16,821	18,234	765	0.9	22,806	8.3
Kingston, NY	4,944	1,190	9,458	8,268	1,229	2.8	12,445	7.5
Knoxville, TN	39,321	7,279	40,400	33,121	3,642	6.4	81,162	15.2
Kokomo, IN	−179	1,486	7,235	5,749	322	−0.2	4,595	4.7
La Crosse, WI-MN	2,061	1,984	7,539	5,555	445	1.6	10,437	9.0
Lafayette, IN	4,799	5,407	12,031	6,624	5,817	2.7	19,693	12.4
Lafayette, LA	8,888	9,803	19,489	9,686	1,398	3.7	30,077	14.4
Lake Charles, LA	1,409	5,721	15,115	9,394	520	0.7	16,174	9.1
Lakeland, FL	58,988	9,258	36,939	27,681	6,876	12.2	78,542	19.4
Lancaster, PA	19,904	12,526	34,991	22,465	2,919	4.2	47,836	11.3
Lansing-East Lansing, MI	7,493	13,392	30,032	16,640	7,308	1.7	15,138	3.5
Laredo, TX	31,578	26,362	30,901	4,539	9,258	16.4	59,878	44.9
Las Cruces, NM	14,762	10,739	16,226	5,487	4,321	8.5	39,172	28.9
Las Vegas-Paradise, NV	334,813	65,234	125,201	59,967	52,899	24.3	634,370	85.6
Lawrence, KS	2,949	3,441	6,271	2,830	2,154	3.0	18,167	22.2
Lawton, OK	−2,567	5,520	10,072	4,552	495	−2.2	3,510	3.1
Lebanon, PA	5,251	774	7,458	6,684	663	4.4	6,583	5.8
Lewiston, ID-WA	1,148	470	3,717	3,247	169	2.0	6,602	12.9
Lewiston-Auburn, ME	4,246	1,165	6,640	5,475	389	4.1	−1,466	−1.4
Lexington-Fayette, KY	21,563	13,470	30,436	16,966	7,777	5.3	59,898	17.2
Lima, OH	−2,239	2,099	7,927	5,828	176	−2.1	−1,282	−1.2
Lincoln, NE	14,766	11,418	21,142	9,724	5,374	5.5	37,696	16.5
Little Rock-North Little Rock, AR	32,754	19,285	47,977	28,692	3,407	5.4	75,575	14.1
Logan, UT-ID	7,706	10,376	13,118	2,742	2,264	7.5	23,305	29.3
Longview, TX	7,459	3,889	15,339	11,450	2,170	3.8	13,989	7.8
Longview, WA	4,377	1,317	6,248	4,931	765	4.7	10,829	13.2
Los Angeles-Long Beach-Santa Ana, CA	**557,928**	**632,567**	**1,032,433**	**399,866**	**646,907**	**4.5**	**1,091,899**	**9.7**
Los Angeles-Long Beach-Glendale, CA	*416,145*	*486,669*	*797,844*	*311,175*	*506,016*	*4.4*	*656,278*	*7.4*
Santa Ana-Anaheim-Irvine, CA	*141,783*	*145,898*	*234,589*	*88,691*	*140,891*	*5.0*	*435,621*	*18.1*
Louisville, KY-IN	46,037	25,781	83,924	58,143	9,783	4.0	106,259	10.1
Lubbock, TX	9,270	10,574	21,229	10,655	1,602	3.7	19,760	8.6
Lynchburg, VA	8,294	1,931	13,985	12,054	1,171	3.6	22,390	10.9
Macon, GA	6,327	6,204	17,944	11,740	976	2.8	15,599	7.5
Madera, CA	19,679	6,772	11,599	4,827	4,743	16.0	35,019	39.8
Madison, WI	35,265	16,737	34,146	17,409	10,089	7.0	69,451	16.1

See footnotes at end of table.

Metropolitan statistical area **Metropolitan statistical area** **with metropolitan divisions** *Metropolitan division*	Components of population change, April 1, 2000, to July 1, 2005						Population change, April 1, 1990, to April 1, 2000	
	Number					Percent change, 2000– 2005		
	Total population change[1]	Natural increase			Net inter- national migration		Number	Percent change
		Total	Births	Deaths				
Manchester-Nashua, NH	20,450	11,613	25,873	14,260	6,719	5.4	45,003	13.4
Mansfield, OH	−903	1,953	8,333	6,380	300	−0.7	2,715	2.2
McAllen-Edinburg-Mission, TX	108,812	68,118	82,362	14,244	26,572	19.1	185,918	48.5
Medford, OR	14,047	800	10,978	10,178	1,498	7.7	34,888	23.8
Memphis, TN-MS-AR	55,711	47,538	103,781	56,243	10,753	4.6	137,931	12.9
Merced, CA	31,152	13,687	21,415	7,728	7,236	14.8	32,151	18.0
Miami-Fort Lauderdale-Miami Beach, FL	**414,212**	**130,627**	**373,544**	**242,917**	**332,229**	**8.3**	**951,760**	**23.5**
Fort Lauderdale-Pompano Beach-Deerfield Beach, FL	*154,620*	*38,311*	*120,738*	*82,427*	*82,027*	*9.5*	*367,487*	*29.3*
Miami-Miami Beach-Kendall, FL	*122,235*	*85,358*	*176,141*	*90,783*	*208,877*	*5.4*	*316,585*	*16.3*
West Palm Beach-Boca Raton-Boynton Beach, FL	*137,357*	*6,958*	*76,665*	*69,707*	*41,325*	*12.1*	*267,688*	*31.0*
Michigan City-La Porte, IN	406	1,584	7,131	5,547	509	0.4	3,040	2.8
Midland, TX	5,362	4,671	9,605	4,934	967	4.6	9,398	8.8
Milwaukee-Waukesha-West Allis, WI	12,111	44,937	113,112	68,175	18,537	0.8	68,595	4.8
Minneapolis-St. Paul-Bloomington, MN-WI	173,962	135,386	234,117	98,731	58,143	5.9	430,041	16.9
Missoula, MT	4,284	2,377	5,916	3,539	471	4.5	17,115	21.8
Mobile, AL	1,584	10,942	31,758	20,816	2,593	0.4	21,200	5.6
Modesto, CA	58,508	21,743	40,736	18,993	11,723	13.1	76,475	20.6
Monroe, LA	1,085	5,395	13,943	8,548	333	0.6	7,066	4.3
Monroe, MI	7,990	2,838	8,958	6,120	605	5.5	12,345	9.2
Montgomery, AL	10,716	10,929	27,491	16,562	1,048	3.1	41,353	13.6
Morgantown, WV	3,301	1,199	6,282	5,083	1,282	3.0	6,654	6.4
Morristown, TN	7,494	1,535	8,386	6,851	2,096	6.1	22,490	22.4
Mount Vernon-Anacortes, WA	10,192	1,852	7,205	5,353	2,230	9.9	23,434	29.5
Muncie, IN	−2,407	798	7,054	6,256	748	−2.0	−890	−0.7
Muskegon-Norton Shores, MI	5,354	4,047	12,492	8,445	600	3.1	11,217	7.1
Myrtle Beach-Conway-North Myrtle Beach, SC	30,363	3,482	13,827	10,345	2,249	15.4	52,576	36.5
Napa, CA	8,456	1,643	8,353	6,710	4,554	6.8	13,543	12.2
Naples-Marco Island, FL	55,865	6,231	18,889	12,658	13,608	22.2	99,278	65.3
Nashville-Davidson-Murfreesboro, TN	110,751	45,802	103,818	58,016	20,263	8.4	263,577	25.1
New Haven-Milford, CT	22,758	13,482	53,538	40,056	15,916	2.8	19,789	2.5
New Orleans-Metairie-Kenner, LA	2,855	36,919	101,758	64,839	8,574	0.2	52,129	4.1
New York-Northern New Jersey-Long Island, NY-NJ-PA	**423,938**	**634,481**	**1,387,673**	**753,192**	**865,533**	**2.3**	**1,477,336**	**8.8**
Edison, NJ	*129,840*	*52,170*	*156,570*	*104,400*	*70,107*	*6.0*	*275,517*	*14.5*
Nassau-Suffolk, NY	*54,151*	*70,577*	*189,158*	*118,581*	*50,538*	*2.0*	*144,701*	*5.5*
Newark-Union, NJ-PA	*55,459*	*66,694*	*156,180*	*89,486*	*74,505*	*2.6*	*137,664*	*7.0*
New York-White Plains-Wayne, NY-NJ	*184,488*	*445,040*	*885,765*	*440,725*	*670,383*	*1.6*	*919,454*	*8.9*
Niles-Benton Harbor, MI	156	2,955	11,275	8,320	2,299	0.1	1,077	0.7
Norwich-New London, CT	7,512	4,557	16,333	11,776	2,261	2.9	4,149	1.6
Ocala, FL	44,526	−3,332	15,696	19,028	1,887	17.2	64,081	32.9
Ocean City, NJ	−3,040	−1,587	5,232	6,819	305	−3.0	7,237	7.6
Odessa, TX	4,216	6,314	11,698	5,384	1,154	3.5	2,189	1.8
Ogden-Clearfield, UT	44,186	35,185	48,678	13,493	5,228	10.0	90,857	25.8
Oklahoma City, OK	61,391	37,613	88,825	51,212	16,853	5.6	124,379	12.8
Olympia, WA	21,512	4,624	13,381	8,757	1,837	10.4	46,117	28.6
Omaha-Council Bluffs, NE-IA	46,030	33,861	65,266	31,405	10,041	6.0	81,343	11.9
Orlando-Kissimee, FL	288,692	60,566	131,291	70,725	50,685	17.6	419,719	34.3
Oshkosh-Neenah, WI	2,719	2,671	9,361	6,690	985	1.7	16,443	11.7
Owensboro, KY	1,724	2,512	8,201	5,689	253	1.6	5,194	5.0
Oxnard-Thousand Oaks-Ventura, CA	42,909	35,963	61,156	25,193	22,310	5.7	84,181	12.6
Palm Bay-Melbourne-Titusville, FL	55,020	−2,170	26,081	28,251	3,855	11.6	77,252	19.4
Panama City-Lynn Haven, FL	13,341	3,069	10,637	7,568	699	9.0	21,223	16.7
Parkersburg-Marietta-Vienna, WV-OH	−2,095	−45	9,642	9,687	164	−1.3	2,717	1.7
Pascagoula, MS	6,635	4,279	11,552	7,273	870	4.4	18,648	14.1
Pensacola-Ferry Pass-Brent, FL	27,724	9,020	29,080	20,060	2,361	6.7	67,747	19.7
Peoria, IL	2,286	6,075	25,318	19,243	1,746	0.6	8,323	2.3
Philadelphia-Camden-Wilmington, PA-NJ-DE-MD	**136,092**	**119,728**	**401,888**	**282,160**	**75,799**	**2.4**	**251,591**	**4.6**
Camden, NJ	*58,906*	*24,231*	*80,457*	*56,226*	*10,404*	*5.0*	*59,024*	*5.2*
Philadelphia, PA	*40,537*	*76,797*	*273,868*	*197,071*	*56,243*	*1.1*	*120,653*	*3.2*
Wilmington, DE-MD-NJ	*36,649*	*18,700*	*47,563*	*28,863*	*9,152*	*5.6*	*71,914*	*12.4*
Phoenix-Mesa-Scottsdale, AZ	613,201	183,656	314,367	130,711	134,412	18.9	1,013,378	45.3
Pine Bluff, AR	−2,480	1,985	7,815	5,830	363	−2.3	387	0.4
Pittsburgh, PA	−45,013	−16,086	132,931	149,017	12,951	−1.9	−37,202	−1.5
Pittsfield, MA	−3,085	−1,803	6,471	8,274	866	−2.3	−4,399	−3.2
Pocatello, ID	2,805	4,749	8,121	3,372	542	3.4	9,991	13.7
Portland-South Portland-Biddeford, ME	26,659	6,470	28,819	22,349	2,617	5.5	46,311	10.5
Portland-Vancouver-Beaverton, OR-WA	167,980	68,024	145,599	77,575	55,277	8.7	404,140	26.5
Port St. Lucie-Fort Pierce, FL	61,607	−2,163	18,875	21,038	5,065	19.3	68,355	27.2
Poughkeepsie-Newburgh-Middletown, NY	46,225	18,676	43,587	24,911	8,349	7.4	54,408	9.6
Prescott, AZ	31,184	−1,291	9,549	10,840	1,922	18.6	59,803	55.5
Providence-New Bedford-Fall River, RI-MA	39,523	22,798	101,783	78,985	23,285	2.5	73,208	4.8
Provo-Orem, UT	76,073	46,273	55,319	9,046	8,009	20.2	107,371	39.9
Pueblo, CO	9,850	2,910	10,398	7,488	975	7.0	18,421	15.0

See footnotes at end of table.

Metropolitan statistical area **Metropolitan statistical area** **with metropolitan divisions** *Metropolitan division*	Components of population change, April 1, 2000, to July 1, 2005						Population change, April 1, 1990, to April 1, 2000	
	Number					Percent change, 2000– 2005		
	Total population change[1]	Natural increase			Net inter- national migration		Number	Percent change
		Total	Births	Deaths				
Punta Gorda, FL	15,909	−6,012	5,397	11,409	972	11.2	30,652	27.6
Racine, WI	6,877	5,500	13,494	7,994	1,475	3.6	13,797	7.9
Raleigh-Cary, NC	152,655	47,046	72,810	25,764	27,150	19.2	253,006	46.5
Rapid City, SD	5,385	4,884	9,581	4,697	465	4.8	9,597	9.3
Reading, PA	22,676	6,371	25,073	18,702	3,556	6.1	37,115	11.0
Redding, CA	16,648	952	10,373	9,421	665	10.2	16,220	11.0
Reno-Sparks, NV	51,061	12,570	27,357	14,787	9,814	14.9	85,692	33.3
Richmond, VA	78,697	28,399	80,114	51,715	11,022	7.2	147,713	15.6
Riverside-San Bernardino-Ontario, CA	655,133	168,684	297,762	129,078	79,267	20.1	666,028	25.7
Roanoke, VA	4,729	1,038	17,621	16,583	1,739	1.6	19,741	7.4
Rochester, MN	13,366	7,557	13,277	5,720	3,668	8.2	21,673	15.3
Rochester, NY	1,197	17,810	64,979	47,169	10,932	0.1	35,421	3.5
Rockford, IL	18,974	9,640	24,146	14,506	5,208	5.9	36,485	12.9
Rocky Mount, NC	2,516	2,696	10,576	7,880	1,142	1.8	9,622	7.2
Rome, GA	3,633	2,090	7,321	5,231	1,324	4.0	9,314	11.5
Sacramento-Arden-Arcade-Roseville, CA	245,426	67,953	141,614	73,661	50,732	13.7	315,637	21.3
Saginaw-Saginaw Township North, MI	−1,686	3,385	14,209	10,824	806	−0.8	−1,904	−0.9
St. Cloud, MN	13,763	6,626	12,265	5,639	1,212	8.2	17,887	12.0
St. George, UT	28,531	6,548	10,416	3,868	939	31.6	41,794	86.1
St. Joseph, MO-KS	−1,861	1,050	7,694	6,644	223	−1.5	8,006	6.9
St. Louis, MO-IL[3]	79,846	57,722	191,468	133,746	22,309	3.0	117,952	4.6
Salem, OR	28,342	11,293	27,591	16,298	10,483	8.2	69,194	24.9
Salinas, CA	10,342	25,259	37,701	12,442	22,815	2.6	46,102	13.0
Salisbury, MD	6,856	1,920	7,590	5,670	977	6.3	11,612	11.9
Salt Lake City, UT	65,601	73,893	102,847	28,954	31,683	6.8	200,808	26.1
San Angelo, TX	−414	3,166	8,368	5,202	696	−0.4	5,694	5.7
San Antonio, TX	178,071	87,022	151,918	64,896	27,063	10.4	303,981	21.6
San Diego-Carlsbad-San Marcos, CA	119,629	129,527	232,321	102,794	91,725	4.3	315,817	12.6
Sandusky, OH	−886	624	4,891	4,267	132	−1.1	2,772	3.6
San Francisco-Oakland-Fremont, CA	**28,946**	**138,062**	**292,414**	**154,352**	**198,685**	**0.7**	**439,630**	**11.9**
Oakland-Fremont-Hayward, CA	*74,135*	*95,080*	*181,820*	*86,740*	*107,551*	*3.1*	*312,123*	*15.0*
San Francisco-San Mateo-Redwood City, CA	*−45,189*	*42,982*	*110,594*	*67,612*	*91,134*	*−2.6*	*127,507*	*8.0*
San Jose-Sunnyvale-Santa Clara, CA	19,169	96,148	142,829	46,681	129,039	1.1	201,545	13.1
San Luis Obispo-Paso Robles, CA	8,797	2,377	13,099	10,722	3,206	3.6	29,519	13.6
Santa Barbara-Santa Maria, CA	1,415	15,091	29,981	14,890	14,528	0.4	29,739	8.0
Santa Cruz-Watsonville, CA	−5,936	9,148	17,932	8,784	7,935	−2.3	25,868	11.3
Santa Fe, NM	11,567	4,526	8,380	3,854	3,880	8.9	30,360	30.7
Santa Rosa-Petaluma, CA	7,863	9,548	29,872	20,324	13,055	1.7	70,392	18.1
Sarasota-Bradenton-Venice, FL	83,072	−9,236	32,756	41,992	10,701	14.1	100,480	20.5
Savannah, GA	20,584	10,322	24,528	14,206	2,660	7.0	35,400	13.7
Scranton-Wilkes-Barre, PA	−10,079	−11,287	28,410	39,697	1,645	−1.8	−14,697	−2.6
Seattle-Tacoma-Bellevue, WA	**159,429**	**101,696**	**212,753**	**111,057**	**86,035**	**5.2**	**484,749**	**18.9**
Seattle-Bellevue-Everett, WA	*106,460*	*77,473*	*159,933*	*82,460*	*76,029*	*4.5*	*370,134*	*18.8*
Tacoma, WA	*52,969*	*24,223*	*52,820*	*28,597*	*10,006*	*7.6*	*114,615*	*19.6*
Sheboygan, WI	1,954	1,328	6,710	5,382	954	1.7	8,779	8.5
Sherman-Denison, TX	6,239	1,668	8,172	6,504	1,254	5.6	15,576	16.4
Shreveport-Bossier City, LA	7,268	10,203	30,093	19,890	1,082	1.9	16,278	4.5
Sioux City, IA-NE-SD	−482	5,404	11,858	6,454	3,084	−0.3	11,703	8.9
Sioux Falls, SD	20,825	8,199	15,926	7,727	2,390	11.1	33,593	21.9
South Bend-Mishawaka, IN-MI	1,495	7,491	22,679	15,188	3,602	0.5	20,132	6.8
Spartanburg, SC	13,027	4,361	17,885	13,524	2,577	5.1	26,989	11.9
Spokane, WA	22,767	9,268	28,573	19,305	4,640	5.4	56,606	15.7
Springfield, IL	4,087	3,952	14,160	10,208	602	2.0	11,890	6.3
Springfield, MA	7,250	6,515	40,359	33,844	10,123	1.1	7,044	1.0
Springfield, MO	29,750	7,569	26,221	18,652	1,238	8.1	69,556	23.3
Springfield, OH	−2,365	928	9,634	8,706	170	−1.6	−2,807	−1.9
State College, PA	4,803	1,989	6,670	4,681	3,665	3.5	10,946	8.8
Stockton, CA	100,518	29,386	53,041	23,655	17,183	17.8	82,970	17.3
Sumter, SC	881	4,100	9,037	4,937	389	0.8	3,360	3.3
Syracuse, NY	1,609	11,042	41,065	30,023	6,065	0.2	−9,770	−1.5
Tallahassee, FL	14,582	10,079	22,539	12,460	3,225	4.6	61,197	23.6
Tampa-St. Petersburg-Clearwater, FL	251,645	6,866	156,273	149,407	47,022	10.5	328,054	15.9
Terre Haute, IN	−2,895	410	11,016	10,606	778	−1.7	4,376	2.6
Texarkana, TX-Texarkana, AR	4,056	1,898	9,035	7,137	426	3.1	9,617	8.0
Toledo, OH	−2,492	12,979	45,784	32,805	3,616	−0.4	5,031	0.8
Topeka, KS	4,524	4,489	16,346	11,857	1,250	2.0	14,294	6.8
Trenton-Ewing, NJ	15,495	9,012	24,081	15,069	12,030	4.4	24,937	7.7
Tucson, AZ	81,040	26,426	65,914	39,488	18,186	9.6	176,789	26.5
Tulsa, OK	28,185	26,784	68,806	42,022	10,237	3.3	98,511	12.9
Tuscaloosa, AL	3,751	4,294	13,859	9,565	1,308	1.9	16,961	9.6
Tyler, TX	15,888	5,467	14,694	9,227	3,100	9.1	23,397	15.5

See footnotes at end of table.

State and Metropolitan Area Data Book: 2006

U.S. Census Bureau

Table B-2. Metropolitan Areas — **Components of Population Change**—Con.

Metropolitan statistical area **Metropolitan statistical area with metropolitan divisions** *Metropolitan division*	Components of population change, April 1, 2000, to July 1, 2005						Population change, April 1, 1990, to April 1, 2000	
	Number							
	Total population change[1]	Natural increase			Net inter-national migration	Percent change, 2000–2005	Number	Percent change
		Total	Births	Deaths				
Utica-Rome, NY	−2,011	−540	16,867	17,407	4,260	−0.7	−16,749	−5.3
Valdosta, GA	5,272	4,639	9,996	5,357	884	4.4	20,322	20.5
Vallejo-Fairfield, CA	17,080	16,765	30,657	13,892	9,076	4.3	55,042	16.2
Vero Beach, FL	15,647	−2,315	6,103	8,418	1,645	13.9	22,739	25.2
Victoria, TX	1,693	4,147	9,006	4,859	1,094	1.5	12,269	12.3
Vineland-Millville-Bridgeton, NJ	6,814	3,161	11,201	8,040	2,579	4.7	8,385	6.1
Virginia Beach-Norfolk-Newport News, VA-NC.	70,429	61,340	125,625	64,285	10,578	4.5	126,062	8.7
Visalia-Porterville, CA	42,853	25,240	38,978	13,738	13,103	11.6	56,100	18.0
Waco, TX	11,155	6,940	17,477	10,537	3,278	5.2	24,390	12.9
Warner Robins, GA	15,398	4,979	9,434	4,455	807	13.9	21,557	24.2
Washington-Arlington-Alexandria, DC-VA-MD-WV	**418,484**	**244,950**	**404,529**	**159,579**	**200,031**	**8.7**	**673,923**	**16.3**
Bethesda-Gaithersburg-Frederick, MD	*78,843*	*50,013*	*86,232*	*36,219*	*52,780*	*7.4*	*162,206*	*17.9*
Washington-Arlington-Alexandria, DC-VA-MD-WV.	*339,641*	*194,937*	*318,297*	*123,360*	*147,251*	*9.1*	*511,717*	*15.9*
Waterloo-Cedar Falls, IA	−1,810	2,438	10,133	7,695	2,241	−1.1	5,067	3.2
Wausau, WI	3,107	2,895	7,870	4,975	564	2.5	10,434	9.0
Weirton-Steubenville, WV-OH.	−5,544	−2,653	6,764	9,417	131	−4.2	−10,515	−7.4
Wenatchee, WA	5,549	2,848	7,197	4,349	2,463	5.6	20,764	26.5
Wheeling, WV-OH	−4,501	−2,333	7,853	10,186	200	−2.9	−6,123	−3.8
Wichita, KS.	15,887	21,286	47,159	25,873	8,050	2.8	60,057	11.8
Wichita Falls, TX	−5,248	3,181	10,798	7,617	1,317	−3.5	11,149	7.9
Williamsport, PA	−1,649	356	6,873	6,517	129	−1.4	1,334	1.1
Wilmington, NC	40,594	4,464	17,926	13,462	2,562	14.8	74,426	37.2
Winchester, VA-WV	13,270	2,924	7,502	4,578	1,000	12.9	18,829	22.4
Winston-Salem, NC	26,672	11,253	31,732	20,479	8,824	6.3	60,509	16.7
Worcester, MA	33,289	17,180	52,874	35,694	14,029	4.4	40,268	5.7
Yakima, WA	9,005	13,217	22,282	9,065	6,034	4.0	33,758	17.9
York-Hanover, PA	27,050	7,350	24,517	17,167	1,573	7.1	42,177	12.4
Youngstown-Warren-Boardman, OH-PA	−9,796	−1,407	34,638	36,045	1,090	−1.6	−10,658	−1.7
Yuba City, CA	16,880	5,812	12,495	6,683	4,341	12.1	16,506	13.5
Yuma, AZ.	21,251	10,725	16,345	5,620	6,151	13.3	53,131	49.7

[1]Includes net internal migration and residual not shown separately.
[2]The Denver-Aurora metropolitan statistical area includes Broomfield County. Broomfield County, CO, was formed from parts of Adams, Boulder, Jefferson, and Weld counties on November 15, 2001, and is coextensive with Broomfield city. For the purposes of defining and presenting data for the Denver-Aurora metropolitan statistical area, Broomfield city is treated as if it were a county when data are available to do so. In many cases, the data will not be available.
[3]The portion of Sullivan city in Crawford County, MO, is legally part of the St. Louis, MO-IL MSA. That portion is not included in these figures for the St. Louis MSA.

Note: Covers metropolitan statistical areas and metropolitan divisions and component counties defined by the Office of Management and Budget as of June 6, 2003, and subsequently updated in December 2003 and November 2004. For more information, see OMB Bulletin 05-02 at <http://www.whitehouse.gov/omb/bulletins/fy05/b05-02_appendix.pdf>.

Survey, Census, or Data Collection Method: Based on population estimates and the "component of populaton change method"; for more information, see Appendix B, Limitations of the Data and Methodology, and also <http://www.census.gov/popest/topics/methodology/>.

Sources: Population—U.S. Census Bureau, Components of Population Change, "Population Estimates, Cumulative Estimates of the Components of Population Change for Counties: April 1, 2000 to July 1, 2005," <http://www.census.gov/popest/counties/CO-EST2005-05.html>; Population change—Census 2000, Demographic Profiles 1; 1990 census, 100 percent data, STF1 <http://www.census.gov/main/www/cen2000.html>; Net international migration—U.S. Census Bureau, <http://www.census.gov/popest/states/NST-comp-chg.html>; Births—U.S. National Center for Health Statistics, *Vital Statistics of the United States*, Vol. I, Natality, annual, and unpublished data; Deaths—U.S. National Center for Health Statistics, *Vital Statistics of the United States*, Vol. II, Mortality, annual, and unpublished data.

U.S. Census Bureau

Metropolitan statistical area / Metropolitan statistical area with metropolitan divisions / Metropolitan division	Under 5 years	5 to 14 years	15 to 24 years	25 to 34 years	35 to 44 years	45 to 54 years	55 to 64 years	65 to 74 years	75 years and over	White alone	Black or African American alone	Asian alone	American Indian, Alaska Native alone	Native Hawaiian and Other Pacific Islander alone	Hispanic or Latino origin,[1] (percent)	Males per 100 females
Abilene, TX	7.4	14.0	17.4	13.0	13.8	12.6	8.7	7.0	6.2	89.9	6.8	1.1	0.7	0.1	18.7	99.6
Akron, OH	6.2	13.7	13.9	12.7	15.2	15.0	9.9	6.6	6.8	85.8	11.2	1.6	0.2	0.0	0.9	93.8
Albany, GA	7.6	15.3	16.1	13.2	13.9	13.7	9.1	5.9	5.2	49.3	49.2	0.7	0.3	0.0	1.2	90.9
Albany-Schenectady-Troy, NY	5.5	12.7	14.3	12.9	15.5	15.0	10.4	6.5	7.2	88.7	7.3	2.6	0.2	0.0	3.1	94.8
Albuquerque, NM	7.0	14.3	14.5	13.3	15.0	14.6	9.9	6.0	5.4	87.3	2.9	1.9	6.0	0.1	42.9	96.4
Alexandria, LA	7.3	14.4	15.0	12.1	14.3	13.8	10.0	7.0	6.1	69.0	28.4	0.9	0.8	0.0	1.6	93.0
Allentown-Bethlehem-Easton, PA-NJ	5.6	13.2	13.3	11.7	15.8	15.0	10.3	7.1	8.0	93.3	3.4	2.0	0.2	0.1	8.1	94.6
Altoona, PA	5.5	12.2	13.7	11.1	14.1	15.1	11.0	8.2	9.1	97.7	1.2	0.5	0.1	0.0	0.5	92.4
Amarillo, TX	7.6	15.0	15.3	13.9	14.1	13.5	8.7	6.2	5.7	90.3	6.0	1.8	0.8	0.0	21.0	98.4
Ames, IA	5.2	9.4	27.2	18.3	11.3	11.5	7.2	4.7	5.2	90.8	1.9	6.2	0.2	0.0	1.6	105.6
Anchorage, AK	7.4	16.3	15.6	13.2	16.5	16.2	8.7	3.8	2.3	76.4	5.3	4.9	7.5	0.8	5.7	103.6
Anderson, IN	6.4	13.6	13.2	12.4	14.2	14.1	11.0	7.6	7.5	90.4	8.0	0.4	0.2	0.0	1.7	97.2
Anderson, SC	6.5	13.8	12.8	13.0	14.7	14.1	11.4	7.4	6.3	81.5	17.0	0.5	0.2	0.0	1.3	93.7
Ann Arbor, MI	6.0	12.2	18.2	17.7	15.1	13.8	8.6	4.3	4.0	77.6	12.3	7.6	0.4	0.0	2.8	99.3
Anniston-Oxford, AL	6.5	12.9	14.3	12.8	13.9	14.6	10.7	8.0	6.3	78.6	19.4	0.7	0.4	0.1	1.8	92.4
Appleton, WI	6.6	14.9	14.6	12.8	17.1	14.4	8.7	5.4	5.6	94.7	0.6	2.4	1.4	0.0	2.0	99.8
Asheville, NC	5.7	12.1	12.0	12.6	14.2	14.4	11.5	8.7	8.7	93.0	5.0	0.7	0.4	0.0	3.8	93.6
Athens-Clarke County, GA	6.1	11.8	21.6	19.4	12.7	11.5	7.9	4.8	4.3	76.8	19.8	2.2	0.2	0.0	5.6	96.4
Atlanta-Sandy Springs-Marietta, GA	7.8	14.8	13.4	16.7	17.3	13.8	8.5	4.3	3.3	65.6	29.2	3.7	0.3	0.1	7.7	98.2
Atlantic City, NJ	6.5	14.4	12.8	12.5	16.5	14.3	9.6	6.8	6.6	74.4	18.2	5.7	0.3	0.1	13.3	94.3
Auburn-Opelika, AL	5.7	12.8	22.7	18.4	13.0	11.6	7.5	4.7	3.6	73.9	23.2	1.9	0.2	0.0	1.5	97.0
Augusta-Richmond County, GA-SC	7.2	14.9	15.0	13.0	14.8	14.3	9.5	6.2	5.0	61.6	35.3	1.5	0.3	0.1	2.2	94.2
Austin-Round Rock, TX	8.0	13.9	15.4	18.8	16.2	13.2	7.3	4.0	3.2	86.0	7.9	4.0	0.7	0.1	28.3	104.1
Bakersfield, CA	8.1	17.2	16.5	14.4	14.8	12.2	7.7	4.9	4.3	86.1	6.3	3.6	1.7	0.3	41.5	106.1
Baltimore-Towson, MD	6.5	14.0	13.6	13.0	16.3	14.8	10.0	6.1	5.9	68.0	27.3	3.1	0.3	0.1	2.1	93.0
Bangor, ME	5.1	11.9	15.8	12.0	15.5	15.8	10.5	7.1	6.1	96.9	0.5	0.8	0.9	0.0	0.6	95.5
Barnstable Town, MA	4.4	11.0	10.6	10.2	14.4	14.6	11.9	10.8	12.0	95.7	2.1	0.8	0.6	0.0	1.5	90.3
Baton Rouge, LA	7.2	14.2	16.8	14.3	14.7	13.9	9.0	5.3	4.5	63.2	34.4	1.5	0.2	0.0	1.9	96.3
Battle Creek, MI	6.5	14.3	14.3	12.1	14.4	14.5	10.1	6.9	6.7	85.3	11.0	1.3	0.6	0.0	3.3	95.1
Bay City, MI	5.9	13.3	13.4	11.2	14.8	15.6	10.9	7.1	7.8	96.4	1.4	0.5	0.6	0.0	4.0	94.9
Beaumont-Port Arthur, TX	6.8	14.5	14.9	12.5	14.4	14.2	9.5	6.8	6.4	71.2	25.4	2.1	0.4	0.0	8.8	99.6
Bellingham, WA	5.6	12.9	17.4	14.7	13.5	14.5	9.4	5.9	6.1	90.9	0.8	3.1	2.9	0.2	5.5	97.3
Bend, OR	5.8	13.2	13.4	13.5	14.5	15.5	10.8	7.1	6.2	96.2	0.3	0.8	0.8	0.1	4.2	98.9
Billings, MT	6.2	13.4	14.0	12.1	14.6	15.6	10.3	6.8	6.9	94.0	0.5	0.6	3.1	0.1	3.7	95.9
Binghamton, NY	5.3	12.5	15.4	11.2	14.7	14.6	10.5	7.6	8.2	92.5	3.4	2.7	0.2	0.0	2.2	94.5
Birmingham-Hoover, AL	6.7	13.7	13.4	13.8	15.0	14.8	10.0	6.6	6.1	70.0	28.1	0.9	0.3	0.0	2.1	93.0
Bismarck, ND	5.8	13.0	16.2	12.3	14.6	15.4	9.4	6.7	6.6	95.4	0.3	0.5	3.0	0.0	0.7	97.1
Blacksburg-Christiansburg-Radford, VA	4.8	9.7	24.6	16.8	11.8	11.7	9.4	5.9	5.3	92.1	4.4	2.5	0.2	0.0	1.3	103.5
Bloomington, IN	5.3	11.3	22.4	16.2	13.0	12.4	8.5	5.6	5.3	93.6	2.0	2.8	0.3	0.0	1.5	96.8
Bloomington-Normal, IL	6.3	12.8	20.5	16.1	14.1	12.8	7.8	4.8	4.8	89.2	6.6	2.8	0.2	0.0	3.2	93.9
Boise City-Nampa, ID	7.8	15.4	14.7	15.1	15.1	13.5	8.6	4.9	4.9	95.1	0.7	1.6	0.8	0.2	9.9	100.6
Boston-Cambridge-Quincy, MA-NH	**6.4**	**13.0**	**12.8**	**14.3**	**16.7**	**14.5**	**9.8**	**6.1**	**6.4**	**85.6**	**7.5**	**5.4**	**0.3**	**0.1**	**7.0**	**94.1**
Boston-Quincy, MA	*6.4*	*12.7*	*13.3*	*15.5*	*16.4*	*13.9*	*9.5*	*6.0*	*6.3*	*79.9*	*12.9*	*5.6*	*0.3*	*0.1*	*7.7*	*93.4*
Cambridge-Newton-Framingham, MA	*6.2*	*12.5*	*12.2*	*14.7*	*17.1*	*14.6*	*9.9*	*6.3*	*6.5*	*87.1*	*4.0*	*7.6*	*0.2*	*0.0*	*4.8*	*94.8*
Essex County, MA	*6.8*	*14.0*	*12.5*	*12.0*	*16.3*	*15.0*	*9.9*	*6.4*	*7.2*	*90.3*	*4.7*	*2.8*	*0.3*	*0.1*	*13.2*	*92.8*
Rockingham County-Strafford County, NH	*5.8*	*14.1*	*13.5*	*11.6*	*18.0*	*16.1*	*10.2*	*5.7*	*5.0*	*96.8*	*0.7*	*1.4*	*0.2*	*0.0*	*1.2*	*96.9*
Boulder, CO[2]	6.2	12.3	15.7	17.7	16.0	15.4	8.6	4.3	3.7	93.1	1.0	3.7	0.7	0.1	11.8	103.1
Bowling Green, KY	6.3	12.7	17.7	15.2	14.1	13.5	9.6	6.0	5.0	89.2	8.0	1.3	0.3	0.1	2.9	96.8
Bremerton-Silverdale, WA	6.2	14.4	15.1	12.3	15.3	15.6	10.3	5.5	5.3	86.0	2.9	4.5	1.7	0.8	4.6	103.8
Bridgeport-Stamford-Norwalk, CT	6.7	14.6	11.5	11.5	17.0	15.0	10.6	6.4	6.7	84.0	10.7	3.8	0.3	0.1	12.9	94.3
Brownsville-Harlingen, TX	10.7	18.4	16.1	13.6	12.4	10.8	7.2	5.7	5.2	97.8	0.7	0.5	0.6	0.1	85.7	91.9
Brunswick, GA	6.6	14.2	13.8	12.4	14.4	14.1	10.9	7.2	6.4	74.9	23.5	0.5	0.3	0.0	2.7	93.8
Buffalo-Niagara Falls, NY	5.6	13.0	13.6	11.9	15.0	15.0	10.3	7.4	8.2	84.2	12.6	1.6	0.7	0.0	3.4	92.4
Burlington, NC	6.8	13.6	14.1	13.9	14.8	13.2	9.7	7.0	6.8	78.6	18.7	1.2	0.5	0.0	8.8	93.2
Burlington-South Burlington, VT	5.4	13.3	15.6	13.5	16.7	15.5	9.7	5.4	4.8	95.5	0.8	1.8	0.5	0.0	1.0	96.5
Canton-Massillon, OH	6.1	13.7	13.4	11.3	14.4	15.3	10.7	7.4	7.8	91.1	6.7	0.6	0.3	0.0	0.9	93.1
Cape Coral-Fort Myers, FL	5.7	11.4	10.8	10.7	12.9	12.4	12.3	12.1	11.7	90.1	7.6	1.0	0.4	0.1	12.2	96.6
Carson City, NV	6.7	13.0	12.5	12.4	14.6	14.4	11.2	7.9	7.4	92.9	1.7	1.6	2.4	0.1	15.6	105.5
Casper, WY	6.6	13.6	15.5	11.8	13.8	15.9	10.1	6.7	5.9	96.1	0.9	0.5	1.2	0.0	4.9	98.5
Cedar Rapids, IA	6.7	13.7	14.1	13.1	15.4	14.4	9.6	6.4	6.7	94.6	2.5	1.4	0.2	0.1	1.4	97.8
Champaign-Urbana, IL	6.0	11.6	22.2	16.6	12.8	12.3	7.8	5.3	5.4	81.9	9.7	6.5	0.2	0.0	3.2	100.6
Charleston, WV	5.9	12.2	12.2	12.2	14.4	16.4	11.4	8.0	7.2	93.1	4.8	0.8	0.2	0.0	0.5	93.3
Charleston-North Charleston, SC	6.9	14.0	15.4	14.3	15.2	13.8	9.6	5.9	4.8	65.2	31.6	1.6	0.4	0.1	2.4	96.4
Charlotte-Gastonia-Concord, NC-SC	7.5	14.5	13.1	16.1	16.6	13.7	8.9	5.2	4.4	73.0	23.2	2.4	0.5	0.0	6.5	97.0
Charlottesville, VA	5.8	12.3	17.1	14.1	14.0	14.0	9.7	6.7	5.8	82.3	13.5	2.8	0.2	0.0	2.5	91.3
Chattanooga, TN-GA	6.2	13.0	13.4	13.4	14.6	14.8	10.9	7.3	6.3	83.6	14.0	1.1	0.3	0.1	1.6	93.2
Cheyenne, WY	6.8	13.8	14.5	13.7	15.1	14.6	9.9	6.3	5.4	92.7	3.1	1.0	0.9	0.2	11.6	100.8
Chicago-Naperville-Joliet, IL-IN-WI	**7.4**	**14.9**	**13.7**	**14.8**	**15.7**	**13.8**	**9.0**	**5.5**	**5.3**	**75.1**	**18.5**	**4.9**	**0.3**	**0.1**	**17.9**	**96.2**
Chicago-Naperville-Joliet, IL	*7.4*	*14.8*	*13.6*	*15.2*	*15.7*	*13.7*	*9.0*	*5.5*	*5.3*	*73.5*	*19.7*	*5.3*	*0.4*	*0.1*	*18.9*	*95.9*
Gary, IN	*6.8*	*14.9*	*14.3*	*12.2*	*14.4*	*15.0*	*10.0*	*6.4*	*6.1*	*79.2*	*18.5*	*0.9*	*0.3*	*0.1*	*10.3*	*94.1*
Lake County-Kenosha County, IL-WI	*7.5*	*16.0*	*14.6*	*13.0*	*16.6*	*14.4*	*8.8*	*4.9*	*4.3*	*87.0*	*6.9*	*4.3*	*0.4*	*0.1*	*15.0*	*101.0*

See footnotes at end of table.

Metropolitan statistical area **Metropolitan statistical area with metropolitan divisions** *Metropolitan division*	Population characteristics, 2003														
	Age (percent)									One race (percent)					
	Under 5 years	5 to 14 years	15 to 24 years	25 to 34 years	35 to 44 years	45 to 54 years	55 to 64 years	65 to 74 years	75 years and over	White alone	Black or African American alone	Asian alone	American Indian, Alaska Native alone	Native Hawaiian and Other Pacific Islander alone	Hispanic or Latino origin,[1] (percent)	Males per 100 females
Chico, CA	5.4	12.8	17.4	14.0	12.3	13.6	9.6	6.7	8.3	89.7	1.5	3.8	1.8	0.2	11.3	96.6
Cincinnati-Middletown, OH-KY-IN	6.9	14.4	14.3	13.4	15.7	14.5	9.3	6.0	5.6	85.7	11.5	1.5	0.2	0.0	1.2	95.1
Clarksville, TN-KY	8.9	15.6	15.1	16.8	15.0	11.5	7.5	5.4	4.2	74.7	20.2	1.7	0.6	0.3	3.9	101.8
Cleveland, TN	6.3	12.7	14.4	14.0	14.9	13.7	11.2	7.3	5.4	94.5	3.5	0.7	0.3	0.0	2.1	96.5
Cleveland-Elyria-Mentor, OH	6.3	14.1	12.7	12.0	15.3	15.0	10.1	6.9	7.5	77.3	19.6	1.7	0.2	0.0	3.5	92.1
Coeur d'Alene, ID	6.5	14.5	14.4	12.1	14.3	14.8	10.5	6.8	6.1	96.4	0.3	0.5	1.3	0.1	2.6	97.9
College Station-Bryan, TX	6.8	11.9	26.7	18.6	11.1	9.8	6.5	4.5	4.1	83.0	12.2	3.4	0.4	0.1	18.7	100.9
Colorado Springs, CO	7.7	15.2	14.9	14.2	16.2	14.4	8.6	4.9	3.8	85.9	6.9	2.8	1.0	0.3	11.6	100.7
Columbia, MO	6.2	12.5	20.4	17.2	13.8	13.0	7.7	4.7	4.5	86.1	8.6	3.2	0.4	0.0	1.8	94.0
Columbia, SC	6.7	13.8	15.2	14.2	15.3	14.5	9.7	5.7	4.9	63.0	34.2	1.4	0.3	0.1	2.6	94.0
Columbus, GA-AL	7.4	14.7	16.9	13.7	14.2	13.2	8.7	6.0	5.2	56.2	40.3	1.4	0.4	0.2	3.5	99.6
Columbus, IN	7.1	15.2	12.0	12.8	14.8	14.6	10.8	6.9	5.7	95.0	1.7	2.3	0.2	0.0	2.7	97.0
Columbus, OH	7.2	14.0	14.1	15.8	16.0	14.0	8.9	5.3	4.7	81.6	13.6	2.9	0.3	0.0	2.1	96.9
Corpus Christi, TX	8.0	15.6	15.1	12.5	14.1	13.8	9.2	6.3	5.4	93.5	3.5	1.2	0.8	0.2	55.1	96.2
Corvallis, OR	5.0	10.9	21.5	16.1	12.2	14.9	8.9	5.0	5.6	90.9	0.9	5.2	0.7	0.3	5.1	100.1
Cumberland, MD-WV	5.1	11.5	15.2	12.3	13.8	15.2	13.8	11.3	8.2	94.2	4.7	0.5	0.1	0.0	0.7	98.4
Dallas-Fort Worth-Arlington, TX	**8.4**	**15.5**	**14.2**	**16.3**	**16.5**	**13.2**	**8.1**	**4.4**	**3.4**	**79.7**	**14.0**	**4.3**	**0.6**	**0.1**	**24.3**	**100.2**
Dallas-Plano-Irving, TX	*8.6*	*15.5*	*14.1*	*16.8*	*16.6*	*13.0*	*7.9*	*4.2*	*3.3*	*78.1*	*15.2*	*4.8*	*0.6*	*0.1*	*26.1*	*100.7*
Fort Worth-Arlington, TX	*8.1*	*15.6*	*14.5*	*15.2*	*16.1*	*13.5*	*8.5*	*4.8*	*3.7*	*82.8*	*11.6*	*3.5*	*0.6*	*0.1*	*20.8*	*99.4*
Dalton, GA	8.8	15.4	14.1	14.9	15.1	12.6	9.3	5.7	4.1	95.0	2.8	0.8	0.4	0.1	20.0	100.3
Danville, IL	6.6	13.6	13.3	12.1	13.8	14.0	10.5	7.9	8.2	87.2	11.0	0.6	0.2	0.1	3.3	96.9
Danville, VA	6.0	12.5	13.1	10.8	14.2	15.3	11.6	8.3	8.3	66.1	33.0	0.4	0.2	0.0	1.5	90.3
Davenport-Moline-Rock Island, IA-IL	6.5	13.3	14.1	12.5	14.2	14.8	10.5	6.8	7.2	90.9	6.1	1.4	0.3	0.0	6.1	95.7
Dayton, OH	6.4	13.4	14.7	12.4	14.5	14.6	10.4	7.0	6.5	82.2	14.5	1.6	0.2	0.0	1.2	93.9
Decatur, AL	6.4	14.0	13.2	12.6	15.7	14.5	11.0	7.1	5.6	84.3	11.9	0.4	1.8	0.1	3.4	96.3
Decatur, IL	6.4	13.5	14.3	11.0	13.2	15.2	10.7	7.7	8.0	83.2	14.5	0.8	0.2	0.0	1.1	91.0
Deltona-Daytona Beach-Ormond Beach, FL	5.1	11.5	12.7	10.8	13.4	13.7	11.5	10.5	10.8	87.6	10.0	1.2	0.3	0.0	7.9	95.2
Denver-Aurora, CO[2]	7.6	14.1	13.1	16.4	16.4	14.6	8.8	4.8	4.2	87.8	5.8	3.4	1.0	0.1	20.3	100.7
Des Moines, IA	7.2	13.9	13.6	14.5	15.9	14.3	9.4	5.6	5.6	91.8	4.0	2.7	0.3	0.1	4.5	95.5
Detroit-Warren-Livonia, MI	**6.7**	**15.0**	**12.7**	**13.3**	**15.9**	**14.9**	**9.7**	**5.8**	**6.0**	**72.4**	**23.0**	**2.9**	**0.3**	**0.0**	**3.1**	**95.0**
Detroit-Livonia-Dearborn, MI	*7.2*	*16.2*	*13.1*	*13.5*	*15.1*	*14.2*	*9.0*	*5.7*	*6.0*	*53.6*	*42.4*	*2.1*	*0.4*	*0.0*	*4.2*	*92.5*
Warren-Farmington Hills-Troy, MI	*6.2*	*14.0*	*12.4*	*13.1*	*16.6*	*15.5*	*10.3*	*6.0*	*6.0*	*87.8*	*7.0*	*3.5*	*0.3*	*0.0*	*2.3*	*97.1*
Dothan, AL	6.6	13.5	13.4	12.3	14.3	14.3	10.9	7.8	7.0	74.9	23.5	0.5	0.4	0.0	1.5	91.7
Dover, DE	7.2	14.8	15.4	12.8	15.3	13.1	9.3	6.8	5.2	74.9	20.7	1.8	0.6	0.0	3.5	93.3
Dubuque, IA	6.2	13.5	15.3	11.3	14.4	14.5	9.9	7.3	7.6	97.1	1.1	0.7	0.2	0.1	1.2	95.2
Duluth, MN-WI	5.1	11.8	16.4	11.4	13.8	15.8	10.2	7.1	8.3	94.7	0.9	0.7	2.4	0.0	0.8	97.7
Durham, NC	6.8	12.6	15.3	17.5	15.1	13.8	8.6	5.2	5.1	66.1	28.7	3.6	0.4	0.0	8.0	94.1
Eau Claire, WI	5.9	13.0	17.7	13.1	14.1	14.0	9.2	6.2	6.9	96.0	0.4	2.2	0.5	0.0	0.8	96.0
El Centro, CA	8.1	16.7	16.9	13.8	15.0	12.2	7.1	5.5	4.8	90.6	4.3	2.1	2.0	0.3	74.7	108.4
Elizabethtown, KY	7.0	14.5	15.7	12.8	16.0	14.1	9.0	6.1	4.8	83.8	11.4	1.9	0.4	0.1	2.9	100.3
Elkhart-Goshen, IN	8.3	16.2	14.3	13.7	14.6	13.2	8.8	5.5	5.4	92.0	5.1	1.1	0.3	0.1	10.7	99.6
Elmira, NY	5.8	12.8	14.3	11.8	14.7	14.8	10.3	7.3	8.2	91.1	6.5	1.0	0.2	0.0	2.2	97.5
El Paso, TX	9.4	17.5	15.9	13.4	13.9	12.1	7.7	5.6	4.5	94.2	2.8	1.0	1.0	0.2	81.3	92.4
Erie, PA	6.0	13.6	15.9	11.9	14.0	14.8	9.7	6.6	7.6	91.7	6.3	0.7	0.2	0.0	2.2	95.8
Eugene-Springfield, OR	5.5	12.2	15.4	14.3	13.4	15.3	10.5	6.4	7.1	92.6	0.9	2.4	1.1	0.2	5.1	97.0
Evansville, IN-KY	6.4	13.6	14.4	12.2	14.7	14.8	10.0	6.9	7.0	92.5	5.6	0.7	0.2	0.0	1.1	93.6
Fairbanks, AK	8.4	16.1	17.2	15.6	15.3	14.7	7.8	3.1	1.9	78.6	6.7	2.0	7.3	0.3	4.7	108.9
Fargo, ND-MN	6.0	12.7	18.8	16.2	14.0	13.8	7.9	5.0	5.5	95.3	1.1	1.4	1.1	0.1	1.8	98.7
Farmington, NM	8.1	17.0	17.6	12.2	14.0	13.5	8.3	5.4	3.9	57.9	0.6	0.3	39.5	0.1	15.4	98.3
Fayetteville, NC	8.9	16.0	16.7	15.8	15.2	11.9	7.1	5.0	3.2	54.5	37.7	2.1	2.7	0.3	5.6	102.5
Fayetteville-Springdale-Rogers, AR-MO	7.4	14.4	15.4	15.3	14.4	12.4	9.1	6.1	5.4	93.4	1.5	1.5	1.5	0.4	9.8	99.7
Flagstaff, AZ	7.8	15.5	18.4	15.1	13.5	14.1	8.2	4.7	2.7	65.1	1.0	0.9	31.4	0.1	11.1	99.7
Flint, MI	6.9	15.4	13.8	12.9	14.9	14.6	9.8	6.4	5.5	76.3	20.3	0.9	0.5	0.0	2.4	92.7
Florence, SC	6.9	14.2	14.0	12.8	14.2	14.8	10.8	6.6	5.6	57.5	41.1	0.6	0.2	0.0	1.1	89.3
Florence-Muscle Shoals, AL	5.8	12.7	13.7	12.3	14.1	14.5	11.4	8.2	7.4	86.1	12.5	0.4	0.3	0.1	1.1	92.1
Fond du Lac, WI	5.6	13.2	15.3	11.5	15.4	14.9	9.7	6.7	7.6	97.0	1.0	0.9	0.4	0.0	2.5	96.2
Fort Collins-Loveland, CO	6.1	12.8	16.8	16.6	14.5	14.8	8.7	5.0	4.6	95.0	0.8	1.8	0.7	0.1	8.9	100.3
Fort Smith, AR-OK	7.2	14.5	14.1	12.7	14.4	13.6	10.4	7.0	6.1	84.9	3.7	2.0	5.8	0.1	5.3	97.6
Fort Walton Beach-Crestview-Destin, FL	7.0	13.9	14.0	12.9	15.9	14.0	9.4	8.2	4.7	84.3	9.4	2.8	0.6	0.1	4.3	102.1
Fort Wayne, IN	7.6	15.7	13.9	13.2	14.5	14.3	9.1	5.7	5.9	86.8	9.8	1.5	0.4	0.0	4.2	96.7
Fresno, CA	8.1	17.3	16.9	14.4	13.9	12.1	7.6	4.9	4.9	81.8	5.7	8.6	1.9	0.2	46.0	100.8
Gadsden, AL	6.2	13.0	13.2	12.6	13.4	14.5	11.1	8.1	7.8	83.7	14.8	0.4	0.3	0.0	2.0	92.1
Gainesville, FL	5.5	10.9	22.7	17.9	12.1	12.6	8.2	5.3	4.7	74.8	19.9	3.6	0.3	0.0	5.7	96.6
Gainesville, GA	8.7	14.8	14.8	17.0	15.0	11.9	8.5	5.3	4.0	90.3	6.9	1.4	0.4	0.3	22.6	103.9
Glens Falls, NY	4.9	12.7	13.8	12.1	15.6	15.0	11.2	7.5	7.2	96.7	2.0	0.5	0.2	0.0	1.9	100.0
Goldsboro, NC	7.6	14.6	14.1	13.4	15.2	13.7	9.5	6.9	5.2	63.9	33.6	1.0	0.4	0.1	5.5	97.5
Grand Forks, ND-MN	5.6	12.7	20.0	14.4	13.4	13.4	8.3	5.6	6.6	94.3	1.2	1.0	2.0	0.1	2.8	101.8
Grand Junction, CO	6.1	13.2	15.0	12.6	13.5	14.6	9.6	7.6	7.8	96.5	0.5	0.6	0.9	0.1	10.3	95.9
Grand Rapids-Wyoming, MI	7.4	15.2	15.1	13.9	15.4	14.0	8.5	5.3	5.3	88.2	7.9	1.7	0.5	0.1	6.9	99.3
Great Falls, MT	6.4	13.7	14.3	11.5	14.7	14.4	10.4	7.5	7.1	90.4	1.5	0.9	4.7	0.1	2.6	97.8
Greeley, CO[2]	7.8	15.3	17.8	16.0	14.3	12.7	7.8	4.4	3.8	95.8	0.8	1.0	1.1	0.2	29.7	101.3
Green Bay, WI	6.5	14.1	14.7	13.1	16.5	14.6	9.0	5.7	5.8	93.7	1.2	2.0	2.0	0.1	3.7	99.5
Greensboro-High Point, NC	6.8	13.7	13.4	14.4	15.3	14.0	10.1	6.5	5.9	72.6	23.8	2.2	0.5	0.0	5.2	93.8
Greenville, NC	7.0	13.1	18.5	17.0	13.7	12.8	8.0	5.3	4.6	62.8	35.1	1.0	0.3	0.0	4.5	92.2

See footnotes at end of table.

Table B-3. Metropolitan Areas — **Population by Age, Race, and Sex**—Con.

Population characteristics, 2003

Metropolitan statistical area / **Metropolitan statistical area with metropolitan divisions** / *Metropolitan division*	Under 5 years	5 to 14 years	15 to 24 years	25 to 34 years	35 to 44 years	45 to 54 years	55 to 64 years	65 to 74 years	75 years and over	White alone	Black or African American alone	Asian alone	American Indian, Alaska Native alone	Native Hawaiian and Other Pacific Islander alone	Hispanic or Latino origin,[1] (percent)	Males per 100 females
Greenville, SC	6.5	13.5	14.5	14.1	15.1	13.9	10.4	6.4	5.6	80.1	17.5	1.4	0.2	0.1	4.0	96.3
Gulfport-Biloxi, MS	7.2	14.2	14.7	13.6	15.0	13.6	9.7	6.8	5.2	76.0	19.5	2.4	0.5	0.1	2.3	98.8
Hagerstown-Martinsburg, MD-WV	6.1	13.3	13.2	13.9	16.0	14.3	10.1	6.9	6.2	91.5	6.5	0.7	0.2	0.0	1.4	102.1
Hanford-Corcoran, CA	7.7	15.7	16.9	17.8	16.8	11.3	6.6	3.9	3.4	84.1	8.7	3.2	1.9	0.3	45.4	134.0
Harrisburg-Carlisle, PA	5.7	12.8	13.5	12.3	15.2	15.7	10.5	7.1	7.2	86.9	9.7	2.1	0.2	0.0	2.7	94.4
Harrisonburg, VA	5.8	11.5	23.4	13.5	12.8	12.2	8.6	6.1	6.1	93.9	3.4	1.4	0.2	0.0	6.4	94.8
Hartford-West Hartford-East Hartford, CT	5.8	13.4	13.3	12.0	16.3	15.1	10.4	6.4	7.3	84.9	10.7	2.8	0.3	0.1	9.8	94.1
Hattiesburg, MS	7.1	14.1	18.0	15.5	13.7	12.3	8.5	5.8	5.0	71.9	26.5	0.8	0.2	0.0	1.3	91.7
Hickory-Lenoir-Morganton, NC	6.4	13.7	12.7	13.8	15.2	14.0	11.0	7.3	5.9	89.6	6.8	2.5	0.3	0.1	5.0	98.4
Hinesville-Fort Stewart, GA	12.3	18.6	17.9	16.8	14.7	9.5	5.3	2.9	1.9	55.4	38.6	1.9	0.7	0.5	6.4	110.6
Holland-Grand Haven, MI	7.1	15.3	17.3	12.9	15.2	13.4	8.4	5.1	5.3	94.9	1.2	2.4	0.4	0.0	7.4	97.0
Honolulu, HI	6.8	12.6	13.7	13.8	14.9	14.1	10.3	6.7	7.1	22.3	3.1	46.9	0.3	8.7	6.8	100.3
Hot Springs, AR	5.8	11.8	12.1	11.2	13.1	13.6	11.8	10.6	10.1	89.3	8.1	0.6	0.6	0.0	2.7	94.7
Houma-Bayou Cane-Thibodaux, LA	7.1	14.9	16.1	12.6	15.4	13.6	9.5	6.1	4.7	78.4	15.7	0.8	4.0	0.0	1.7	96.2
Houston-Sugar Land-Baytown, TX	8.3	16.0	14.6	15.4	15.8	13.9	8.3	4.5	3.3	76.1	16.8	5.4	0.5	0.1	31.1	99.9
Huntington-Ashland, WV-KY-OH	5.7	12.1	13.9	13.0	13.7	14.7	11.5	8.2	7.2	96.0	2.5	0.5	0.2	0.0	0.7	93.7
Huntsville, AL	6.4	14.1	14.0	13.2	16.6	14.2	10.0	6.8	4.7	74.3	21.5	1.9	0.7	0.1	2.2	97.2
Idaho Falls, ID	8.3	17.1	16.7	11.8	13.6	13.5	8.9	5.3	4.9	96.8	0.6	0.8	0.7	0.1	8.5	99.9
Indianapolis, IN	7.6	15.2	13.3	14.5	16.2	14.0	8.8	5.5	5.0	82.5	14.4	1.6	0.3	0.1	3.3	96.2
Iowa City, IA	5.8	11.1	20.4	19.0	13.9	13.1	7.7	4.4	4.6	91.0	2.8	4.6	0.3	0.1	2.6	98.0
Ithaca, NY	4.1	9.5	27.6	16.7	12.2	12.3	8.2	4.6	4.8	84.7	4.0	9.0	0.3	0.0	3.6	98.9
Jackson, MI	6.1	14.2	13.7	12.8	15.8	14.9	9.8	6.2	6.4	89.5	7.9	0.6	0.4	0.1	2.4	104.4
Jackson, MS	7.4	14.8	15.4	14.0	14.8	14.1	8.9	5.7	5.0	52.4	46.1	0.8	0.1	0.0	1.1	91.8
Jackson, TN	6.8	13.8	16.0	13.4	14.4	13.9	9.4	6.2	6.2	68.4	29.9	0.7	0.2	0.0	1.8	93.1
Jacksonville, FL	7.1	14.6	13.9	13.4	15.8	14.4	9.8	6.1	4.9	72.9	22.7	2.6	0.4	0.1	4.1	95.4
Jacksonville, NC	10.8	13.8	25.6	15.6	12.3	9.3	5.3	4.6	2.6	74.9	18.7	2.2	0.7	0.3	4.8	128.6
Janesville, WI	6.6	14.5	14.1	12.2	15.5	14.5	9.8	6.5	6.3	92.8	4.6	0.9	0.3	0.1	4.5	97.5
Jefferson City, MO	6.2	13.4	15.0	14.0	16.0	14.4	9.4	5.9	5.6	90.7	7.2	0.7	0.4	0.0	1.3	106.4
Johnson City, TN	5.4	11.4	13.5	14.4	14.8	14.4	11.4	7.7	7.1	95.5	2.8	0.6	0.2	0.0	1.5	96.1
Johnstown, PA	4.9	11.3	13.6	10.9	13.6	15.7	10.7	8.6	10.7	95.9	3.0	0.4	0.1	0.0	1.0	94.9
Jonesboro, AR	7.0	13.6	15.7	14.8	13.7	13.0	10.0	6.5	5.8	89.5	8.8	0.5	0.3	0.0	2.2	94.6
Joplin, MO	7.3	14.1	14.8	13.1	13.8	13.4	10.0	6.8	6.7	94.2	1.3	0.7	1.6	0.2	3.7	95.4
Kalamazoo-Portage, MI	6.5	13.7	16.9	13.9	13.9	14.3	9.3	5.8	5.8	87.1	8.7	1.7	0.5	0.0	4.1	95.2
Kankakee-Bradley, IL	7.1	14.7	15.2	12.7	14.1	13.8	9.5	6.5	6.4	82.3	15.6	0.8	0.2	0.0	5.9	95.0
Kansas City, MO-KS	7.2	14.4	13.5	14.0	15.8	14.4	9.5	5.8	5.6	83.2	12.7	2.0	0.5	0.1	5.7	96.1
Kennewick-Richland-Pasco, WA	7.8	16.1	16.0	13.3	14.2	14.0	9.0	5.0	4.6	93.7	1.6	2.2	0.9	0.1	23.1	102.7
Killeen-Temple-Fort Hood, TX	9.8	15.8	16.6	16.5	14.6	11.0	7.0	4.7	4.0	73.9	19.4	2.5	0.9	0.5	17.1	101.5
Kingsport-Bristol-Bristol, TN-VA	5.4	11.9	12.1	12.3	14.6	14.9	12.6	8.6	7.6	96.9	1.9	0.4	0.2	0.0	0.8	93.2
Kingston, NY	5.0	12.6	14.1	12.3	16.2	15.7	11.0	6.7	6.5	90.6	6.4	1.5	0.3	0.0	7.0	98.8
Knoxville, TN	5.9	12.3	13.7	13.9	15.1	14.6	10.8	7.2	6.5	91.1	6.3	1.2	0.3	0.1	1.4	94.1
Kokomo, IN	6.9	14.5	12.9	12.2	14.1	14.4	11.3	7.3	6.5	91.7	5.8	1.0	0.4	0.0	1.7	94.3
La Crosse, WI-MN	5.6	12.9	17.9	13.3	14.0	14.3	8.9	6.3	6.8	94.8	0.9	3.0	0.4	0.0	0.9	94.9
Lafayette, IN	6.0	12.3	23.3	16.8	12.4	11.6	7.8	4.8	5.0	92.0	2.2	4.5	0.3	0.0	5.2	105.4
Lafayette, LA	7.3	14.6	16.1	14.2	15.2	14.2	8.5	5.5	4.4	71.8	26.0	1.3	0.3	0.0	1.7	95.4
Lake Charles, LA	7.2	14.4	15.5	12.7	14.5	14.1	9.4	6.6	5.5	74.4	23.7	0.7	0.3	0.0	1.5	95.6
Lakeland, FL	6.8	13.9	13.3	11.8	13.3	12.5	10.6	9.2	8.5	82.8	14.7	1.1	0.4	0.1	11.4	96.9
Lancaster, PA	6.7	14.7	14.2	11.7	14.7	14.1	9.6	6.8	7.4	93.8	3.3	1.6	0.2	0.1	6.0	95.6
Lansing-East Lansing, MI	6.1	13.4	17.9	14.3	14.1	14.4	9.3	5.3	5.1	85.8	8.6	3.1	0.5	0.1	4.9	95.0
Laredo, TX	12.5	19.6	16.3	14.9	13.0	9.9	6.3	4.1	3.5	98.2	0.5	0.4	0.6	0.1	95.1	93.0
Las Cruces, NM	7.9	15.9	17.9	13.7	13.0	12.1	8.3	6.3	5.0	93.7	2.2	1.0	1.6	0.2	64.9	97.0
Las Vegas-Paradise, NV	7.6	14.8	12.6	16.4	15.5	12.7	9.7	6.4	4.3	81.3	9.1	5.5	0.9	0.5	24.4	103.6
Lawrence, KS	5.7	10.8	24.8	19.6	12.3	11.7	6.9	4.0	4.1	87.3	4.1	3.6	2.6	0.1	3.5	99.1
Lawton, OK	8.1	15.1	18.0	15.0	14.4	11.7	7.6	5.8	4.4	66.5	20.8	2.3	5.4	0.5	7.3	107.0
Lebanon, PA	5.6	13.0	13.1	11.5	14.8	14.7	10.8	7.9	8.6	96.7	1.5	0.9	0.2	0.0	5.2	95.3
Lewiston, ID-WA	6.0	12.9	13.8	11.5	13.4	14.6	10.8	8.0	9.1	93.8	0.3	0.7	3.9	0.0	1.9	94.9
Lewiston-Auburn, ME	5.7	12.8	14.1	11.9	16.3	14.7	10.3	6.9	7.2	96.8	0.9	0.7	0.3	0.1	1.1	95.0
Lexington-Fayette, KY	6.7	12.7	14.8	16.6	15.6	14.2	9.2	5.5	4.8	85.9	10.6	2.1	0.2	0.0	3.4	96.6
Lima, OH	7.0	13.9	15.2	11.7	14.2	14.4	9.8	6.7	7.2	85.4	12.2	0.8	0.2	0.0	1.5	100.1
Lincoln, NE	7.0	12.6	17.7	16.2	14.0	13.7	8.3	5.2	5.4	91.8	2.8	3.2	0.7	0.1	3.5	100.2
Little Rock-North Little Rock, AR	7.0	14.1	14.0	14.3	15.0	14.2	9.8	6.2	5.3	74.9	22.3	1.1	0.4	0.0	2.1	94.4
Logan, UT-ID	10.6	16.3	21.7	18.7	10.2	9.2	5.5	3.8	4.0	96.0	0.5	1.9	0.7	0.2	7.3	97.9
Longview, TX	7.1	14.3	14.9	12.3	14.0	13.8	9.8	7.3	6.5	80.1	17.8	0.6	0.6	0.0	9.2	97.2
Longview, WA	6.2	14.5	14.1	12.0	14.0	14.8	10.9	6.7	6.8	94.2	0.6	1.3	1.6	0.1	5.2	98.2
Los Angeles-Long Beach-Santa Ana, CA	**7.4**	**15.5**	**14.0**	**15.7**	**16.0**	**13.1**	**8.4**	**5.2**	**4.8**	**75.6**	**8.1**	**13.2**	**1.0**	**0.3**	**43.0**	**98.3**
Los Angeles-Long Beach-Glendale, CA	*7.5*	*15.6*	*14.2*	*15.9*	*15.8*	*13.0*	*8.2*	*5.1*	*4.8*	*74.3*	*9.9*	*12.7*	*1.1*	*0.3*	*46.3*	*98.0*
Santa Ana-Anaheim-Irvine, CA	*7.4*	*15.0*	*13.3*	*15.1*	*16.5*	*13.4*	*9.0*	*5.3*	*4.9*	*80.0*	*1.8*	*14.9*	*0.9*	*0.3*	*32.1*	*99.4*
Louisville, KY-IN	6.7	13.9	13.1	13.5	15.6	15.0	10.0	6.4	5.8	84.0	13.3	1.2	0.3	0.1	2.0	94.9
Lubbock, TX	7.6	13.9	18.4	15.7	12.8	12.3	8.1	5.9	5.3	89.4	7.8	1.3	0.7	0.1	29.6	96.0
Lynchburg, VA	5.7	13.0	14.8	11.7	14.2	14.6	11.2	7.8	7.0	79.8	18.3	0.8	0.3	0.0	1.0	92.5
Macon, GA	7.3	14.8	14.5	13.4	14.6	14.0	9.5	6.2	5.7	56.1	42.1	1.0	0.2	0.0	1.3	88.3
Madera, CA	7.6	15.9	16.1	14.4	14.2	12.5	8.4	5.7	5.0	89.3	4.0	1.5	3.0	0.4	47.2	94.0
Madison, WI	6.1	12.4	16.0	16.0	15.9	14.7	8.9	4.9	5.0	90.8	3.7	3.7	0.4	0.0	3.4	98.8

See footnotes at end of table.

Metropolitan statistical area **Metropolitan statistical area with metropolitan divisions** *Metropolitan division*	Population characteristics, 2003														
	Age (percent)									One race (percent)					His-panic or Latino ori-gin,[1] (per-cent)	Males per 100 females
	Under 5 years	5 to 14 years	15 to 24 years	25 to 34 years	35 to 44 years	45 to 54 years	55 to 64 years	65 to 74 years	75 years and over	White alone	Black or Afri-can Ameri-can alone	Asian alone	Ameri-can Indian, Alaska Native alone	Native Hawai-ian and Other Pacific Islander alone		
Manchester-Nashua, NH	6.3	14.6	12.6	12.5	18.0	15.4	9.9	5.4	5.2	94.4	1.7	2.5	0.3	0.0	3.6	98.0
Mansfield, OH	6.2	13.4	13.6	11.9	14.6	14.9	10.7	7.7	7.1	88.5	9.5	0.6	0.2	0.0	0.9	101.4
McAllen-Edinburg-Mission, TX	11.3	19.2	16.7	14.8	12.4	9.9	6.3	4.9	4.5	97.7	0.7	0.7	0.6	0.1	89.2	94.6
Medford, OR	5.6	13.3	13.9	11.9	13.0	15.3	11.2	7.5	8.4	95.0	0.5	1.0	1.1	0.2	7.4	94.4
Memphis, TN-MS-AR	7.6	15.4	14.4	14.3	15.3	14.2	9.0	5.3	4.6	52.4	44.9	1.6	0.2	0.0	2.6	93.1
Merced, CA	8.4	18.6	17.5	14.0	13.9	11.3	7.3	4.9	4.1	85.3	4.1	6.5	1.6	0.2	49.5	101.1
Miami-Fort Lauderdale-Miami Beach, FL	**6.5**	**13.4**	**12.2**	**12.7**	**15.8**	**13.5**	**9.9**	**7.6**	**8.3**	**75.7**	**20.9**	**1.9**	**0.3**	**0.1**	**36.8**	**94.1**
Fort Lauderdale-Pompano Beach-Deerfield Beach, FL	6.6	13.8	11.7	12.9	16.7	14.1	9.6	6.5	8.1	71.3	24.3	2.7	0.3	0.1	20.2	94.2
Miami-Miami Beach-Kendall, FL	6.8	13.7	13.1	13.5	15.9	13.3	10.1	7.3	6.2	76.2	20.9	1.4	0.3	0.1	60.5	93.9
West Palm Beach-Boca Raton-Boynton Beach, FL	5.8	12.3	11.2	11.0	14.4	13.1	10.1	9.6	12.5	80.8	15.9	1.8	0.4	0.1	14.9	94.5
Michigan City-La Porte, IN	6.4	13.9	13.4	12.6	15.1	14.9	10.2	6.6	6.9	87.9	10.1	0.5	0.3	0.0	3.5	106.0
Midland, TX	7.6	16.1	15.7	11.6	13.9	14.9	8.2	6.3	5.6	90.6	6.9	1.0	0.7	0.0	31.8	93.6
Milwaukee-Waukesha-West Allis, WI	6.9	14.5	13.8	12.8	15.5	14.7	9.3	6.1	6.3	79.2	16.4	2.5	0.6	0.1	6.9	94.6
Minneapolis-St. Paul-Bloomington, MN-WI	7.0	14.4	13.8	14.6	17.0	14.5	8.9	4.8	4.8	86.9	5.9	4.7	0.7	0.1	3.8	98.0
Missoula, MT	5.6	11.8	17.4	15.8	14.0	15.5	9.9	5.1	5.0	94.1	0.4	1.2	2.5	0.1	1.7	100.2
Mobile, AL	7.3	15.0	14.6	12.9	14.2	14.0	9.8	6.4	5.7	62.3	34.4	1.7	0.7	0.0	1.2	91.8
Modesto, CA	7.6	16.9	16.2	14.3	14.6	12.5	8.0	5.1	4.9	87.7	3.0	4.7	1.4	0.5	36.0	97.8
Monroe, LA	7.4	14.7	16.2	13.7	13.5	13.2	9.0	6.7	5.7	65.1	33.4	0.7	0.2	0.0	1.5	90.8
Monroe, MI	5.8	14.7	14.6	12.1	15.8	15.5	10.2	6.0	5.3	96.0	2.0	0.6	0.3	0.0	2.2	98.5
Montgomery, AL	7.2	14.3	15.2	13.9	14.9	13.8	9.2	6.2	5.3	56.5	41.4	0.9	0.3	0.0	1.3	94.0
Morgantown, WV	4.9	10.5	20.3	16.5	13.1	13.6	9.3	6.0	5.6	93.8	2.7	2.2	0.2	0.1	0.9	101.6
Morristown, TN	6.1	12.5	13.4	14.0	14.9	13.5	11.9	8.0	5.6	95.6	2.9	0.5	0.3	0.1	4.4	98.2
Mount Vernon-Anacortes, WA	6.1	13.9	15.0	12.2	13.8	14.5	10.2	6.8	7.5	94.0	0.5	1.7	2.0	0.2	12.5	98.1
Muncie, IN	5.9	12.4	19.3	13.6	12.6	12.6	10.1	6.9	6.7	91.2	6.7	0.8	0.2	0.1	1.1	92.3
Muskegon-Norton Shores, MI	6.7	15.0	14.5	12.5	14.9	14.5	9.3	6.2	6.5	82.8	14.2	0.5	0.8	0.1	3.8	98.7
Myrtle Beach-Conway-North Myrtle Beach, SC	6.1	11.8	12.5	14.4	14.6	13.5	11.6	9.2	6.4	81.7	15.9	0.9	0.4	0.1	3.1	96.8
Napa, CA	5.9	13.2	13.8	12.8	14.4	14.6	10.7	6.7	7.8	90.7	1.8	4.2	1.0	0.4	26.6	100.3
Naples-Marco Island, FL	6.1	11.4	11.0	11.1	12.9	11.6	12.0	12.8	11.1	92.2	6.0	0.8	0.4	0.1	23.3	102.1
Nashville-Davidson-Murfreesboro, TN	7.0	13.4	13.9	15.3	16.3	14.5	9.4	5.6	4.7	81.5	15.1	1.9	0.3	0.1	3.8	96.9
New Haven-Milford, CT	6.0	13.6	13.3	12.7	15.9	14.5	10.0	6.2	7.7	83.0	12.4	2.9	0.3	0.1	11.1	93.0
New Orleans-Metairie-Kenner, LA	7.1	14.2	14.6	13.2	15.0	14.7	9.7	5.9	5.5	58.2	37.9	2.5	0.4	0.0	4.7	92.2
New York-Northern New Jersey-Long Island, NY-NJ-PA	**6.7**	**13.6**	**12.5**	**14.3**	**16.3**	**14.0**	**9.9**	**6.4**	**6.3**	**69.2**	**20.2**	**8.6**	**0.5**	**0.1**	**20.9**	**92.8**
Edison, NJ	6.5	13.9	12.0	12.5	16.4	14.5	9.8	6.8	7.4	82.2	7.8	8.7	0.2	0.0	10.0	94.8
Nassau-Suffolk, NY	6.2	13.9	12.4	11.8	16.5	15.0	10.7	6.9	6.5	84.3	9.8	4.5	0.3	0.1	12.1	95.0
Newark-Union, NJ-PA	6.9	14.6	12.3	12.5	16.8	14.7	10.2	6.1	5.9	71.6	22.7	4.4	0.3	0.1	14.4	94.0
New York-White Plains-Wayne, NY-NJ	6.9	13.3	12.7	15.5	16.2	13.7	9.6	6.3	6.0	62.5	24.7	10.3	0.6	0.1	26.4	91.7
Niles-Benton Harbor, MI	6.4	14.1	14.0	11.3	14.4	14.7	10.6	7.2	7.3	80.9	15.0	1.4	0.4	0.1	3.4	94.4
Norwich-New London, CT	5.8	13.5	13.5	12.2	16.7	15.0	10.2	6.4	6.6	88.1	6.1	2.6	0.9	0.1	5.5	97.9
Ocala, FL	5.4	12.1	11.9	10.1	12.8	12.2	11.5	12.4	11.5	85.8	12.0	0.9	0.5	0.0	7.0	93.5
Ocean City, NJ	5.0	12.4	11.9	9.8	14.1	14.6	12.0	9.8	10.4	93.4	5.0	0.6	0.2	0.1	3.6	92.7
Odessa, TX	8.6	16.4	16.2	12.5	13.5	13.4	8.3	6.1	4.9	92.8	4.7	0.6	1.1	0.1	45.7	94.8
Ogden-Clearfield, UT	9.5	17.6	17.9	14.8	12.8	11.5	7.1	4.7	4.0	94.6	1.4	1.6	0.7	0.2	9.3	101.2
Oklahoma City, OK	7.1	13.6	15.4	14.5	14.5	14.0	9.5	6.1	5.3	78.9	10.9	2.9	3.9	0.1	7.4	96.8
Olympia, WA	5.8	13.3	14.8	13.5	14.8	15.9	10.4	5.7	5.8	87.2	2.6	4.7	1.6	0.6	4.8	96.1
Omaha-Council Bluffs, NE-IA	7.5	14.5	14.6	14.3	15.3	14.0	9.0	5.7	5.2	88.4	7.8	1.8	0.5	0.1	5.8	97.2
Orlando-Kissimee, FL	6.8	14.1	13.6	14.5	15.9	14.0	9.2	6.7	5.6	79.1	15.7	3.2	0.4	0.1	19.0	97.5
Oshkosh-Neenah, WI	5.8	12.8	15.7	13.4	15.9	14.6	9.3	6.1	6.4	95.5	1.2	2.1	0.5	0.0	2.1	99.7
Owensboro, KY	7.1	13.9	14.0	12.0	14.5	14.3	10.6	7.2	6.5	94.6	3.9	0.4	0.1	0.0	1.0	94.1
Oxnard-Thousand Oaks-Ventura, CA	7.0	15.6	14.4	13.1	15.8	14.3	9.3	5.4	5.1	88.4	2.2	5.8	1.2	0.3	35.3	100.2
Palm Bay-Melbourne-Titusville, FL	5.1	12.4	12.2	9.7	14.9	14.2	11.4	10.6	9.4	87.4	9.0	1.7	0.4	0.1	5.2	96.4
Panama City-Lynn Haven, FL	6.4	13.5	13.2	12.3	15.5	14.4	10.6	8.3	5.8	84.5	11.1	1.9	0.8	0.1	2.1	97.9
Parkersburg-Marietta-Vienna, WV-OH	5.6	12.7	13.2	11.3	14.6	15.4	11.8	8.1	7.4	97.4	1.0	0.6	0.2	0.1	0.5	94.6
Pascagoula, MS	7.2	15.0	14.7	13.0	15.1	13.8	10.3	6.5	4.4	76.8	20.1	1.7	0.3	0.1	2.1	99.5
Pensacola-Ferry Pass-Brent, FL	6.5	13.7	15.6	12.4	14.7	13.9	9.9	7.6	5.7	77.1	17.6	2.2	0.9	0.1	2.1	99.0
Peoria, IL	6.5	13.6	13.9	12.5	13.8	14.6	10.3	7.2	7.5	88.6	8.8	1.3	0.2	0.0	1.8	94.7
Philadelphia-Camden-Wilmington, PA-NJ-DE-MD	**6.3**	**14.0**	**13.6**	**12.7**	**15.8**	**14.5**	**9.9**	**6.5**	**6.7**	**74.2**	**20.6**	**3.8**	**0.2**	**0.0**	**5.4**	**93.0**
Camden, NJ	6.3	14.4	13.5	12.5	16.5	14.7	9.8	6.2	6.0	78.6	16.5	3.2	0.2	0.1	6.8	95.3
Philadelphia, PA	6.3	13.9	13.6	12.7	15.5	14.5	9.9	6.6	7.0	72.1	22.3	4.3	0.2	0.0	4.9	91.9
Wilmington, DE-MD-NJ	6.5	14.0	14.2	13.5	16.0	14.4	9.8	6.0	5.6	78.0	17.9	2.6	0.3	0.1	5.1	95.3
Phoenix-Mesa-Scottsdale, AZ	8.2	15.4	13.9	15.7	14.7	12.1	8.6	6.0	5.4	89.4	4.0	2.4	2.5	0.2	28.1	101.6
Pine Bluff, AR	6.9	13.8	15.8	12.6	14.5	13.8	9.9	6.5	6.3	52.1	46.4	0.6	0.3	0.0	1.1	102.2
Pittsburgh, PA	5.3	12.3	12.6	11.3	14.9	15.7	10.7	8.0	9.3	89.7	8.0	1.3	0.1	0.0	0.7	91.9
Pittsfield, MA	4.7	12.1	14.0	10.5	14.4	15.2	11.4	8.2	9.6	95.5	2.2	1.2	0.2	0.1	2.0	92.4
Pocatello, ID	8.5	14.9	17.0	14.4	12.4	13.6	8.6	5.4	5.1	93.5	0.6	1.0	3.3	0.2	6.8	97.7
Portland-South Portland-Biddeford, ME	5.4	13.0	12.8	11.8	16.7	16.3	10.7	6.7	6.7	96.5	0.9	1.3	0.3	0.1	1.0	94.9
Portland-Vancouver-Beaverton, OR-WA	6.8	14.0	13.3	15.5	15.7	15.1	9.5	5.0	5.2	88.1	2.9	5.2	0.9	0.3	8.7	99.2
Port St. Lucie-Fort Pierce, FL	5.2	12.1	11.6	9.8	13.2	12.9	11.3	11.6	12.3	85.5	12.2	0.9	0.4	0.1	9.4	96.7
Poughkeepsie-Newburgh-Middletown, NY	6.2	14.7	15.0	12.5	16.6	14.5	9.7	5.7	5.2	85.4	10.2	2.6	0.4	0.1	11.5	100.3
Prescott, AZ	5.1	11.9	12.4	9.8	11.7	14.1	13.3	11.7	10.2	96.0	0.4	0.6	1.7	0.1	10.5	96.7
Providence-New Bedford-Fall River, RI-MA	5.8	13.2	14.2	13.0	15.8	14.3	9.8	6.3	7.6	90.7	5.1	2.3	0.5	0.1	7.8	93.0
Provo-Orem, UT	12.0	17.7	21.0	19.3	10.1	8.2	5.1	3.4	3.1	95.7	0.4	1.2	0.7	0.6	7.5	98.2
Pueblo, CO	6.7	14.1	14.7	13.5	13.7	13.4	9.1	7.3	7.5	93.6	2.3	0.7	1.9	0.2	39.3	96.2

See footnotes at end of table.

Metropolitan statistical area / **Metropolitan statistical area with metropolitan divisions** / *Metropolitan division*	Population characteristics, 2003														
	Age (percent)									One race (percent)					His-panic or Latino ori-gin,[1] (per-cent)	Males per 100 females
	Under 5 years	5 to 14 years	15 to 24 years	25 to 34 years	35 to 44 years	45 to 54 years	55 to 64 years	65 to 74 years	75 years and over	White alone	Black or African American alone	Asian alone	American Indian, Alaska Native alone	Native Hawaiian and Other Pacific Islander alone		
Punta Gorda, FL	3.8	9.1	9.1	7.7	10.6	11.7	14.0	16.9	17.2	93.3	4.9	1.0	0.2	0.0	3.8	91.2
Racine, WI	6.8	14.6	14.1	11.6	16.1	14.9	9.8	6.1	6.1	86.5	10.9	0.8	0.4	0.1	8.6	98.2
Raleigh-Cary, NC	7.6	14.4	13.5	17.2	17.5	13.7	8.3	4.4	3.5	75.0	20.1	3.3	0.4	0.1	7.0	99.3
Rapid City, SD	7.4	14.1	15.7	12.9	14.4	14.5	8.9	6.4	5.6	88.7	1.3	0.9	6.4	0.1	2.5	99.4
Reading, PA	6.0	13.6	14.0	11.9	15.5	14.3	10.1	7.0	7.5	93.0	4.4	1.2	0.2	0.1	10.6	96.5
Redding, CA	5.4	13.6	15.0	11.2	13.6	14.9	11.3	7.6	7.5	91.3	0.9	2.0	2.5	0.1	6.6	95.5
Reno-Sparks, NV	6.9	14.1	13.5	14.6	15.2	14.7	10.3	6.1	4.8	89.4	1.9	4.2	2.0	0.5	18.4	103.3
Richmond, VA	6.4	13.9	13.8	13.4	16.0	15.1	9.9	5.9	5.5	65.6	30.8	2.1	0.4	0.1	2.6	93.8
Riverside-San Bernardino-Ontario, CA	7.5	17.2	16.0	14.4	15.0	12.2	7.6	5.2	4.9	83.1	8.2	4.6	1.4	0.4	40.9	100.0
Roanoke, VA	5.8	12.7	12.5	11.7	14.8	15.5	11.5	7.8	7.8	85.3	12.5	1.2	0.2	0.0	1.4	92.1
Rochester, MN	6.8	14.1	13.9	13.6	16.4	14.3	9.2	5.8	6.0	92.4	2.4	3.9	0.3	0.0	2.4	97.4
Rochester, NY	5.8	13.7	14.5	12.2	15.5	15.0	10.3	6.2	6.7	84.5	11.8	2.2	0.3	0.0	5.2	94.6
Rockford, IL	6.9	14.8	13.7	13.4	15.1	14.0	9.7	6.2	6.2	86.7	9.6	1.8	0.4	0.1	9.5	96.8
Rocky Mount, NC	7.0	14.8	13.3	12.4	14.9	14.9	10.2	6.7	5.8	54.4	44.1	0.5	0.5	0.0	3.5	90.4
Rome, GA	7.1	13.7	15.2	13.7	14.1	13.0	9.6	7.1	6.5	84.5	13.2	1.0	0.3	0.2	6.5	94.4
Sacramento-Arden-Arcade-Roseville, CA	6.6	14.9	14.8	14.5	15.3	14.0	8.9	5.7	5.4	77.1	7.5	10.0	1.1	0.5	16.9	96.8
Saginaw-Saginaw Township North, MI	6.5	14.7	14.3	11.8	14.1	14.7	10.3	6.7	6.8	77.8	19.4	0.9	0.4	0.0	6.9	93.0
St. Cloud, MN	6.3	13.2	19.5	14.6	14.7	12.9	7.8	5.5	5.5	95.9	1.2	1.6	0.3	0.0	1.5	100.6
St. George, UT	8.8	16.0	17.9	14.3	10.0	9.0	7.1	8.3	8.6	95.9	0.3	0.5	1.6	0.5	5.7	97.7
St. Joseph, MO-KS	6.0	13.0	15.1	13.0	15.3	13.9	9.3	6.8	7.7	93.4	4.6	0.5	0.5	0.0	2.0	104.0
St. Louis, MO-IL[3]	6.5	14.2	14.0	12.8	15.5	14.6	9.7	6.4	6.3	78.8	18.1	1.7	0.2	0.0	1.7	93.2
Salem, OR	7.1	14.7	15.3	14.2	13.6	13.4	9.1	5.9	6.7	93.0	1.0	1.8	1.7	0.4	17.8	100.8
Salinas, CA	8.0	15.6	15.8	15.2	14.9	12.6	8.1	5.0	4.9	85.4	4.0	6.3	1.4	0.6	49.7	107.4
Salisbury, MD	6.0	12.6	17.3	12.8	14.6	13.9	9.8	6.6	6.4	70.4	26.9	1.6	0.3	0.0	2.0	95.9
Salt Lake City, UT	9.3	16.3	16.6	16.5	13.7	12.2	7.3	4.2	3.8	92.2	1.3	2.8	1.0	1.3	13.0	102.3
San Angelo, TX	7.3	14.0	17.2	12.5	13.3	13.0	9.0	7.0	6.8	93.3	3.9	0.9	0.8	0.1	32.9	93.9
San Antonio, TX	7.8	15.6	15.3	14.2	14.7	13.1	8.6	5.7	5.0	90.0	6.2	1.5	1.0	0.2	52.1	95.9
San Diego-Carlsbad-San Marcos, CA	7.2	14.4	14.8	15.4	15.7	13.3	8.4	5.4	5.6	80.3	5.9	9.4	1.0	0.5	28.7	101.4
Sandusky, OH	5.8	13.4	12.9	10.3	14.3	15.6	11.8	8.0	7.9	89.3	8.6	0.5	0.2	0.0	2.2	95.0
San Francisco-Oakland-Fremont, CA	**6.4**	**12.5**	**11.5**	**15.3**	**17.0**	**15.2**	**10.2**	**5.9**	**5.9**	**65.2**	**9.5**	**20.9**	**0.6**	**0.7**	**18.9**	**98.1**
Oakland-Fremont-Hayward, CA	*6.9*	*14.2*	*12.8*	*14.3*	*16.5*	*14.9*	*9.8*	*5.4*	*5.3*	*64.2*	*12.5*	*18.6*	*0.7*	*0.6*	*20.2*	*96.6*
San Francisco-San Mateo-Redwood City, CA	*5.7*	*10.1*	*9.5*	*16.7*	*17.8*	*15.7*	*10.8*	*6.7*	*6.9*	*66.7*	*5.2*	*24.3*	*0.5*	*0.8*	*17.1*	*100.3*
San Jose-Sunnyvale-Santa Clara, CA	7.5	13.7	12.1	15.7	17.6	14.2	9.3	5.4	4.6	65.7	2.8	27.8	0.8	0.4	25.4	103.3
San Luis Obispo-Paso Robles, CA	4.7	11.6	17.0	13.3	13.9	15.4	9.9	6.8	7.5	91.8	2.1	2.8	1.0	0.1	17.3	105.6
Santa Barbara-Santa Maria, CA	6.6	13.8	16.8	14.1	14.2	13.1	8.7	6.1	6.7	89.5	2.4	4.2	1.6	0.3	36.1	100.3
Santa Cruz-Watsonville, CA	6.3	12.7	15.6	13.6	15.2	16.7	10.0	4.8	5.1	91.5	1.1	3.7	1.2	0.2	27.7	100.0
Santa Fe, NM	5.7	12.9	13.2	12.1	15.0	17.3	12.3	6.5	5.0	93.2	0.9	1.1	3.4	0.1	49.5	96.2
Santa Rosa-Petaluma, CA	5.9	13.3	14.0	12.2	15.0	16.4	10.7	5.8	6.7	90.6	1.6	3.6	1.3	0.3	19.8	97.6
Sarasota-Bradenton-Venice, FL	5.0	10.7	10.0	9.7	12.5	12.9	12.2	12.4	14.6	91.4	6.5	1.0	0.3	0.1	7.9	92.6
Savannah, GA	7.3	14.4	15.1	14.5	14.6	13.4	9.2	5.9	5.5	62.6	34.4	1.7	0.3	0.1	2.0	94.0
Scranton-Wilkes-Barre, PA	4.9	11.8	13.3	11.2	14.4	14.7	11.1	8.3	10.3	97.0	1.7	0.7	0.1	0.0	1.5	92.3
Seattle-Tacoma-Bellevue, WA	**6.3**	**13.3**	**13.3**	**15.0**	**17.0**	**15.3**	**9.5**	**5.1**	**5.1**	**79.8**	**5.5**	**9.5**	**1.2**	**0.6**	**6.2**	**99.5**
Seattle-Bellevue-Everett, WA	*6.1*	*12.9*	*12.7*	*15.4*	*17.3*	*15.7*	*9.7*	*5.0*	*5.1*	*79.7*	*4.9*	*10.7*	*1.1*	*0.5*	*6.1*	*99.6*
Tacoma, WA	*6.8*	*14.8*	*15.3*	*14.0*	*15.9*	*14.1*	*9.0*	*5.3*	*4.8*	*80.3*	*7.3*	*5.4*	*1.5*	*0.9*	*6.3*	*99.2*
Sheboygan, WI	5.7	13.8	14.1	11.9	15.9	15.2	9.6	6.5	7.3	93.7	1.1	4.0	0.4	0.0	3.9	101.3
Sherman-Denison, TX	6.9	13.9	14.7	12.1	13.9	13.7	10.2	7.5	7.2	90.5	5.6	0.6	1.3	0.0	8.0	94.8
Shreveport-Bossier City, LA	7.3	14.4	15.0	13.2	13.9	13.9	9.4	6.7	6.2	58.8	38.8	1.0	0.4	0.1	2.1	91.9
Sioux City, IA-NE-SD	7.4	14.9	14.7	13.0	14.1	14.0	9.0	6.1	6.7	92.2	1.8	2.8	1.8	0.0	10.9	97.1
Sioux Falls, SD	7.3	14.2	15.0	14.3	15.6	13.9	8.3	5.6	5.9	94.3	1.7	1.1	1.7	0.1	2.0	99.0
South Bend-Mishawaka, IN-MI	6.9	14.5	15.6	12.3	13.9	14.1	9.3	6.2	7.2	85.6	10.6	1.5	0.5	0.0	4.7	94.7
Spartanburg, SC	6.4	14.0	13.5	13.5	15.0	14.3	10.8	6.6	5.9	75.9	21.3	1.7	0.3	0.0	3.4	94.9
Spokane, WA	6.3	13.7	15.6	13.4	14.5	14.4	9.5	5.9	6.4	92.3	1.7	1.9	1.5	0.2	3.1	96.7
Springfield, IL	6.4	13.6	13.0	12.7	15.3	15.5	10.2	6.5	6.9	87.7	9.6	1.3	0.2	0.0	1.3	91.8
Springfield, MA	5.6	13.2	16.3	12.3	14.7	14.6	9.7	6.2	7.4	89.2	7.1	1.9	0.3	0.3	12.1	91.6
Springfield, MO	6.3	13.0	15.8	14.3	14.2	13.4	9.6	6.7	6.6	95.3	1.7	0.9	0.7	0.1	1.7	95.7
Springfield, OH	6.6	13.6	14.2	11.4	13.7	14.6	11.2	7.4	7.4	88.7	8.8	0.6	0.3	0.0	1.3	93.0
State College, PA	4.2	9.6	26.3	17.6	12.5	11.5	7.9	5.4	5.0	92.0	2.7	4.3	0.2	0.1	1.5	105.1
Stockton, CA	7.7	16.8	16.4	14.2	14.6	12.4	8.0	4.9	5.0	74.3	7.6	13.0	1.3	0.5	33.4	100.5
Sumter, SC	8.0	15.3	15.2	12.4	14.9	13.3	8.9	6.5	5.4	48.7	48.9	1.0	0.3	0.1	1.6	93.2
Syracuse, NY	6.0	13.7	15.3	12.1	15.3	14.7	9.9	6.4	6.7	88.3	7.7	2.0	0.7	0.0	2.6	93.6
Tallahassee, FL	6.2	12.0	19.2	16.6	13.6	13.9	9.1	5.2	4.2	64.0	33.1	1.6	0.3	0.0	3.9	93.9
Tampa-St. Petersburg-Clearwater, FL	6.0	12.7	11.8	12.1	14.8	13.9	10.7	8.6	9.3	84.8	11.2	2.2	0.4	0.1	12.0	93.9
Terre Haute, IN	6.1	13.2	16.2	13.0	13.7	13.9	9.7	6.6	7.4	93.4	4.3	1.0	0.3	0.0	0.9	99.3
Texarkana, TX-Texarkana, AR	6.8	14.0	14.3	13.5	14.4	13.7	10.1	6.6	6.7	73.8	24.0	0.5	0.6	0.1	3.6	99.4
Toledo, OH	6.5	14.0	15.3	13.3	14.2	14.6	9.5	6.2	6.5	84.8	12.2	1.3	0.3	0.0	4.6	94.1
Topeka, KS	6.7	13.8	13.9	11.8	14.4	15.1	10.3	7.0	6.9	88.5	7.1	0.9	1.4	0.1	6.5	95.8
Trenton-Ewing, NJ	6.3	13.6	14.6	13.1	15.9	14.6	9.6	6.0	6.2	71.5	20.6	6.3	0.2	0.1	10.9	95.5
Tucson, AZ	6.9	13.9	14.5	13.8	13.6	13.4	9.7	7.3	6.9	89.0	3.2	2.3	3.7	0.2	31.9	95.8
Tulsa, OK	7.2	14.4	14.2	13.2	14.6	14.3	10.0	6.4	5.7	77.8	9.0	1.4	7.3	0.1	5.3	96.1
Tuscaloosa, AL	6.6	13.2	17.8	14.9	13.3	13.8	8.9	6.2	5.3	62.8	35.4	0.9	0.2	0.0	1.3	93.7
Tyler, TX	7.3	14.5	15.2	12.8	13.4	13.2	9.6	7.4	6.6	79.1	18.7	0.8	0.5	0.1	13.0	92.5

See footnotes at end of table.

Table B-3. Metropolitan Areas — Population by Age, Race, and Sex—Con.

Metropolitan statistical area / Metropolitan statistical area with metropolitan divisions / *Metropolitan division*	Population characteristics, 2003														
	Age (percent)									One race (percent)					Hispanic or Latino origin,[1] (percent)	Males per 100 females
	Under 5 years	5 to 14 years	15 to 24 years	25 to 34 years	35 to 44 years	45 to 54 years	55 to 64 years	65 to 74 years	75 years and over	White alone	Black or African American alone	Asian alone	American Indian, Alaska Native alone	Native Hawaiian and Other Pacific Islander alone		
Utica-Rome, NY	5.2	12.7	14.3	11.7	14.9	14.5	10.6	7.3	8.7	92.5	5.1	1.3	0.2	0.0	3.3	98.1
Valdosta, GA	7.2	14.4	17.4	16.1	14.6	12.2	8.1	5.4	4.6	65.0	32.5	1.0	0.4	0.0	3.0	98.9
Vallejo-Fairfield, CA	7.0	15.8[2]	14.7	13.3	15.8	14.5	8.9	5.3	4.7	64.6	15.4	13.5	0.9	0.9	19.9	101.3
Vero Beach, FL	4.9	10.8	11.2	9.3	12.0	12.6	11.4	12.7	15.1	89.7	8.6	0.9	0.3	0.0	7.6	94.4
Victoria, TX	7.8	15.7	14.6	11.7	13.9	13.7	9.7	6.8	6.0	91.9	5.6	1.3	0.6	0.1	40.9	96.2
Vineland-Millville-Bridgeton, NJ	6.8	14.1	13.6	14.4	15.7	13.4	9.3	6.3	6.4	74.6	21.6	1.1	1.0	0.2	21.0	104.9
Virginia Beach-Norfolk-Newport News, VA-NC	7.1	14.6	15.7	13.8	16.0	13.6	8.8	5.6	4.9	62.6	32.0	2.9	0.4	0.1	3.1	97.4
Visalia-Porterville, CA	8.9	18.1	17.3	13.7	13.4	11.6	7.6	4.9	4.6	91.1	1.9	3.4	1.9	0.3	53.8	100.8
Waco, TX	7.5	14.4	18.8	13.3	12.8	12.3	8.4	6.2	6.3	82.0	15.1	1.2	0.6	0.1	19.8	94.6
Warner Robins, GA	7.1	15.5	15.2	13.5	16.5	13.7	8.8	5.9	3.8	71.2	25.0	1.8	0.4	0.1	2.9	96.7
Washington-Arlington-Alexandria, DC-VA-MD-WV	**7.1**	**14.0**	**12.8**	**14.9**	**17.1**	**14.9**	**10.0**	**5.0**	**4.2**	**63.5**	**26.4**	**7.7**	**0.4**	**0.1**	**10.1**	**95.3**
Bethesda-Gaithersburg-Frederick, MD	*7.0*	*14.2*	*11.9*	*12.8*	*17.1*	*15.7*	*10.3*	*5.6*	*5.5*	*73.6*	*13.3*	*10.8*	*0.3*	*0.1*	*10.6*	*93.5*
Washington-Arlington-Alexandria, DC-VA-MD-WV	*7.2*	*13.9*	*13.0*	*15.5*	*17.2*	*14.7*	*9.9*	*4.8*	*3.8*	*60.6*	*30.1*	*6.9*	*0.4*	*0.1*	*10.0*	*95.8*
Waterloo-Cedar Falls, IA	5.7	12.3	17.5	12.6	12.6	14.5	9.9	6.8	7.9	91.2	6.5	1.1	0.2	0.1	1.7	92.8
Wausau, WI	5.9	14.5	14.3	11.5	15.8	15.1	9.7	6.3	6.9	93.6	0.3	5.1	0.4	0.0	0.9	99.6
Weirton-Steubenville, WV-OH	5.1	11.5	12.8	10.7	13.5	16.2	11.6	9.4	9.3	94.7	4.0	0.4	0.2	0.0	0.6	91.9
Wenatchee, WA	6.8	14.9	14.9	11.1	14.1	14.7	9.8	6.8	7.0	96.6	0.4	0.7	1.1	0.2	20.4	98.6
Wheeling, WV-OH	5.1	11.8	13.4	11.0	13.8	16.0	11.1	8.4	9.5	95.6	3.1	0.5	0.1	0.0	0.5	94.0
Wichita, KS	7.5	15.2	14.4	13.2	14.8	14.3	8.7	5.9	6.0	85.8	7.8	3.1	1.1	0.1	8.1	98.3
Wichita Falls, TX	7.0	13.9	17.9	12.2	14.1	13.1	8.8	7.0	6.1	86.7	8.7	1.7	1.0	0.1	12.1	104.0
Williamsport, PA	5.3	12.4	15.0	11.0	14.4	15.0	10.6	7.8	8.3	94.4	4.2	0.5	0.2	0.0	0.6	96.4
Wilmington, NC	5.9	12.0	13.4	14.6	14.2	13.8	11.6	8.3	6.2	81.6	16.4	0.6	0.5	0.1	2.8	95.7
Winchester, VA-WV	6.0	13.9	13.8	13.3	16.0	14.2	10.3	6.9	5.7	93.7	4.3	0.8	0.2	0.0	3.5	99.1
Winston-Salem, NC	6.9	13.8	12.8	13.9	15.4	14.2	10.2	6.9	6.0	77.6	20.3	1.0	0.3	0.1	7.3	93.4
Worcester, MA	6.4	14.1	13.5	13.0	16.7	14.6	9.3	5.8	6.8	91.6	3.6	3.3	0.3	0.1	7.3	95.8
Yakima, WA	8.7	17.1	15.8	12.9	13.3	12.6	8.5	5.4	5.7	91.1	1.2	1.0	4.8	0.2	38.3	99.8
York-Hanover, PA	5.8	13.5	12.9	12.0	16.1	15.4	10.7	6.9	6.7	93.9	4.0	1.0	0.2	0.0	3.2	96.9
Youngstown-Warren-Boardman, OH-PA	5.7	13.1	13.3	11.0	13.8	15.3	10.8	8.0	9.0	87.5	10.8	0.5	0.2	0.0	1.7	93.2
Yuba City, CA	7.4	16.0	15.9	13.3	14.4	12.6	9.0	6.1	5.2	81.9	2.6	10.0	2.0	0.2	22.3	100.0
Yuma, AZ	8.8	16.6	15.1	11.0	12.5	10.4	8.6	9.5	7.5	93.6	2.2	1.1	1.8	0.3	54.4	100.6

[1]Persons of Hispanic origin may be any race.

[2]The Denver-Aurora metropolitan statistical area includes Broomfield County. Broomfield County, CO, was formed from parts of Adams, Boulder, Jefferson, and Weld counties on November 15, 2001, and is coextensive with Broomfield city. For the purposes of defining and presenting data for the Denver-Aurora metropolitan statistical area, Broomfield city is treated as if it were a county when data are available to do so. In many cases, the data will not be available.

[3]The portion of Sullivan city in Crawford County, MO, is legally part of the St. Louis, MO-IL MSA. That portion is not included in these figures for the St. Louis MSA.

Note: Covers metropolitan statistical areas and metropolitan divisions and component counties defined by the Office of Management and Budget as of June 6, 2003, and subsequently updated in December 2003 and November 2004. For more information, see OMB Bulletin 05-02 at <http://www.whitehouse.gov/omb/bulletins/fy05/b05-02_appendix.pdf>.

Survey, Census, or Data Collection Method: Based on population estimates and the "component of population change method"; for more information, see Appendix B, Limitations of the Data and Methodology, and also <http://www.census.gov/popest/topics/methodology/>.

Source: U.S. Census Bureau, Population Estimates, County Population datasets, <http://www.census.gov/popest/datasets.html>.

Metropolitan statistical area / **Metropolitan statistical area with metropolitan divisions** / *Metropolitan division*	Households Total	Households Family with children under 18 (percent of total)	Educational attainment[1] High school graduate or higher (percent)	Educational attainment[1] Bachelor's degree or higher (percent)	Foreign-born population (percent of total)	Speaking language other than English at home[2] (percent)	Living in same house in 1995 and 2000[2] (percent)	Workers who drove alone to work[3] (percent)	Households with income of $75,000 or more in 1999 (percent)	Persons below poverty in 1999 level (percent)
Abilene, TX.	58,475	37.7	78.7	19.6	3.5	13.8	47.6	80.8	12.6	14.6
Akron, OH	274,237	33.6	85.7	24.3	3.0	5.3	57.8	85.4	21.7	9.6
Albany, GA.	57,403	40.7	73.2	15.7	1.6	3.8	55.2	79.4	15.0	20.9
Albany-Schenectady-Troy, NY	330,246	32.5	86.1	29.1	4.8	8.1	59.3	79.6	23.1	9.0
Albuquerque, NM.	281,052	36.6	83.7	28.1	7.8	30.1	50.6	77.5	19.0	13.7
Alexandria, LA.	54,193	39.4	74.4	15.7	1.4	4.6	60.2	78.6	12.1	20.0
Allentown-Bethlehem-Easton, PA-NJ	285,808	33.5	81.3	21.7	5.2	12.0	60.9	81.9	23.2	8.0
Altoona, PA	51,518	31.9	83.8	13.9	1.0	3.1	66.7	82.2	10.8	12.3
Amarillo, TX	85,272	37.8	80.1	20.8	6.0	16.4	48.7	82.0	15.5	13.0
Ames, IA	29,383	28.2	93.5	44.5	6.9	9.4	39.3	71.3	19.9	12.4
Anchorage, AK	115,378	42.2	89.9	27.0	7.1	12.0	43.1	73.5	32.1	7.9
Anderson, IN	53,052	33.1	80.1	14.4	1.2	3.1	59.7	81.8	17.4	9.0
Anderson, SC	65,649	35.3	73.4	15.9	1.5	3.3	58.8	83.3	14.9	11.8
Ann Arbor, MI	125,327	31.1	91.5	48.1	10.3	13.2	43.0	76.0	32.8	10.4
Anniston-Oxford, AL	45,307	33.5	73.9	15.2	1.7	3.5	57.1	85.1	12.2	15.8
Appleton, WI	75,440	37.9	88.0	22.2	2.9	5.7	58.2	84.2	22.9	4.4
Asheville, NC	154,290	29.6	80.9	23.1	3.9	5.9	54.8	80.1	14.7	11.0
Athens-Clarke County, GA.	63,406	31.5	79.4	32.4	6.2	9.0	43.8	77.6	16.6	19.7
Atlanta-Sandy Springs-Marietta, GA	1,554,154	39.5	83.5	31.4	10.0	13.0	45.0	77.0	30.1	9.3
Atlantic City, NJ.	95,024	35.7	78.2	18.7	11.8	20.3	57.6	73.1	22.0	10.3
Auburn-Opelika, AL	45,702	32.8	81.4	27.9	2.7	5.1	44.1	84.1	15.1	21.0
Augusta-Richmond County, GA-SC.	184,801	40.0	78.3	20.4	3.0	5.8	55.3	80.3	17.8	15.0
Austin-Round Rock, TX.	471,855	35.7	84.8	36.7	12.2	25.8	39.4	76.5	28.1	10.8
Bakersfield, CA.	208,652	46.8	68.5	13.5	16.9	33.4	47.2	73.8	17.2	19.8
Baltimore-Towson, MD	974,071	36.1	81.9	29.2	5.7	8.4	57.0	75.5	28.7	9.5
Bangor, ME	58,096	32.2	85.7	20.3	2.5	4.6	58.4	79.2	13.2	13.1
Barnstable Town, MA	94,822	26.1	91.8	33.6	4.9	6.8	57.6	81.3	24.3	6.8
Baton Rouge, LA.	256,637	39.9	79.4	22.8	2.6	6.5	55.9	81.8	18.9	16.5
Battle Creek, MI	54,100	35.0	83.2	16.0	2.4	4.8	57.1	82.3	16.9	10.9
Bay City, MI	43,930	33.0	82.4	14.2	1.4	5.0	65.1	87.3	18.8	9.6
Beaumont-Port Arthur, TX	142,327	38.2	78.7	14.7	4.7	10.4	58.4	83.1	16.8	15.1
Bellingham, WA.	64,446	32.5	87.5	27.2	9.8	9.2	45.4	75.9	18.2	13.8
Bend, OR.	45,595	34.3	88.4	25.0	2.8	5.4	40.6	75.2	19.9	9.2
Billings, MT.	56,149	33.4	88.4	26.2	1.4	4.7	52.6	80.4	14.9	10.9
Binghamton, NY	100,474	31.7	84.0	22.0	4.5	7.9	60.6	79.7	16.2	11.4
Birmingham-Hoover, AL	412,376	35.9	78.8	22.7	2.1	4.2	56.8	83.3	19.3	13.3
Bismarck, ND	37,559	34.4	85.8	25.5	1.3	7.3	56.8	82.2	15.9	8.0
Blacksburg-Christiansburg-Radford, VA	58,443	27.7	79.4	25.7	3.7	5.3	46.6	79.1	13.1	18.2
Bloomington, IN.	68,552	28.8	84.5	29.0	3.9	6.3	45.9	74.8	15.7	14.6
Bloomington-Normal, IL.	56,746	33.1	90.7	36.2	3.3	6.0	46.4	79.7	25.2	9.0
Boise City-Nampa, ID.	170,291	39.4	85.9	25.5	5.7	10.9	44.8	79.4	19.9	9.1
Boston-Cambridge-Quincy, MA-NH	**1,679,659**	**32.9**	**86.7**	**37.0**	**13.7**	**19.1**	**57.6**	**71.1**	**34.3**	**8.3**
Boston-Quincy, MA	*695,910*	*31.9*	*85.5*	*35.2*	*15.6*	*20.7*	*57.6*	*64.4*	*31.9*	*10.2*
Cambridge-Newton-Framingham, MA	*561,220*	*32.1*	*88.5*	*43.6*	*15.2*	*20.4*	*57.9*	*72.1*	*39.4*	*6.3*
Essex County, MA	*275,419*	*35.2*	*84.6*	*31.3*	*11.3*	*19.4*	*58.7*	*78.7*	*32.1*	*8.7*
Rockingham County-Strafford County, NH	*147,110*	*37.1*	*89.4*	*30.2*	*3.6*	*6.3*	*55.2*	*83.5*	*30.7*	*5.7*
Boulder, CO[4]	114,680	32.3	92.8	52.4	9.4	13.6	40.8	70.8	35.3	9.2
Bowling Green, KY.	40,013	34.4	78.0	22.3	3.8	6.0	47.7	79.5	15.3	14.9
Bremerton-Silverdale, WA	86,416	38.5	90.8	25.3	5.7	8.3	48.7	66.3	24.1	8.4
Bridgeport-Stamford-Norwalk, CT	324,232	36.8	84.4	39.9	16.9	23.9	57.3	74.7	43.6	6.8
Brownsville-Harlingen, TX	97,267	52.7	55.2	13.4	25.6	79.0	58.5	73.2	10.1	32.6
Brunswick, GA	36,846	35.8	79.5	19.7	2.7	5.0	55.4	79.3	17.4	15.5
Buffalo-Niagara Falls, NY	468,719	32.2	83.0	23.2	4.4	8.4	63.5	81.7	18.9	11.6
Burlington, NC.	51,584	34.4	76.5	19.2	6.3	9.3	54.5	81.5	16.3	10.8
Burlington-South Burlington, VT	75,978	35.1	88.5	34.8	5.4	7.6	54.2	75.4	23.4	8.4
Canton-Massillon, OH.	159,442	33.8	83.2	17.3	1.7	4.2	62.1	86.0	17.1	9.1
Cape Coral-Fort Myers, FL	188,599	24.8	82.3	21.1	9.2	13.5	47.7	78.7	18.8	9.6
Carson City, NV.	20,171	32.7	82.5	18.5	9.9	14.9	46.1	77.7	19.8	9.4
Casper, WY	26,819	34.8	88.3	20.0	1.8	5.1	51.0	82.7	14.9	11.6
Cedar Rapids, IA.	94,059	33.9	89.8	24.9	2.2	4.5	53.9	81.3	20.8	6.4
Champaign-Urbana, IL	82,711	29.9	90.4	34.5	7.0	10.4	45.7	71.1	18.0	13.4
Charleston, WV.	129,229	31.7	77.6	17.9	1.1	2.7	63.1	80.8	14.7	15.4
Charleston-North Charleston, SC.	207,957	37.2	81.3	25.0	3.3	6.0	50.9	78.1	18.8	13.6
Charlotte-Gastonia-Concord, NC-SC	510,516	36.9	81.3	28.0	6.9	9.8	49.1	80.7	25.3	9.2
Charlottesville, VA	67,575	31.8	82.6	38.3	5.7	7.7	48.8	73.5	23.5	10.9
Chattanooga, TN-GA	189,607	34.0	76.7	19.4	2.4	4.4	56.4	82.7	16.3	11.7
Cheyenne, WY	31,927	35.6	89.1	23.4	2.9	8.0	46.3	80.4	16.4	8.7
Chicago-Naperville-Joliet, IL-IN-WI	**3,280,055**	**37.6**	**81.1**	**29.0**	**16.1**	**25.1**	**56.5**	**70.4**	**30.3**	**10.3**
Chicago-Naperville-Joliet, IL	*2,755,393*	*37.1*	*80.5*	*29.4*	*17.4*	*26.9*	*56.5*	*68.6*	*30.1*	*10.7*
Gary, IN	*252,308*	*37.3*	*82.4*	*17.3*	*4.6*	*11.3*	*60.6*	*81.9*	*21.8*	*10.3*
Lake County-Kenosha County, IL-WI	*272,354*	*43.0*	*86.0*	*34.9*	*12.9*	*19.2*	*52.9*	*77.5*	*39.8*	*5.9*

See footnotes at end of table.

Metropolitan statistical area **Metropolitan statistical area** **with metropolitan divisions** *Metropolitan division*	Households		Educational attainment[1]		Foreign-born population (percent of total)	Speaking language other than English at home[2] (percent)	Living in same house in 1995 and 2000[2] (percent)	Workers who drove alone to work[3] (percent)	Households with income of $75,000 or more in 1999 (percent)	Persons below poverty in 1999 level (percent)
	Total	Family with children under 18 years (percent of total)	High school graduate or higher (percent)	Bachelor's degree or higher (percent)						
Chico, CA	79,566	31.2	82.3	21.8	7.7	12.5	47.9	74.3	13.8	19.3
Cincinnati-Middletown, OH-KY-IN	779,226	36.5	82.4	24.8	2.6	4.6	54.2	81.3	23.8	9.3
Clarksville, TN-KY	83,332	42.6	80.8	16.2	3.5	7.6	43.6	79.2	12.4	11.2
Cleveland, TN	40,729	35.1	71.5	14.5	2.0	4.1	55.5	82.5	13.8	12.0
Cleveland-Elyria-Mentor, OH	853,165	33.3	83.0	23.9	5.3	9.8	60.2	81.3	22.3	10.5
Coeur d'Alene, ID	41,308	37.4	87.3	19.1	2.4	3.7	46.8	80.8	14.7	10.3
College Station-Bryan, TX	67,744	31.4	78.7	31.5	9.0	18.8	37.2	76.3	15.2	23.5
Colorado Springs, CO	200,402	39.2	91.4	31.8	6.3	11.1	40.5	77.9	24.3	7.7
Columbia, MO	56,930	32.3	88.6	39.9	4.3	6.8	41.1	77.2	17.9	13.4
Columbia, SC	245,347	36.8	82.1	26.6	3.3	6.1	53.8	79.2	19.8	11.8
Columbus, GA-AL	103,982	39.5	76.6	18.3	4.0	7.3	48.7	75.6	14.7	14.9
Columbus, IN	27,936	36.5	83.8	22.0	3.8	5.3	54.4	84.4	21.5	7.2
Columbus, OH	636,602	35.0	85.7	28.3	4.5	7.2	49.1	82.1	23.3	9.6
Corpus Christi, TX	141,590	41.9	73.9	17.7	5.9	40.9	53.2	76.3	16.2	17.9
Corvallis, OR	30,145	29.9	93.1	47.4	7.6	10.0	42.3	70.7	23.3	13.6
Cumberland, MD-WV	40,106	30.2	80.0	13.4	1.1	2.5	65.1	80.2	10.0	13.8
Dallas-Fort Worth-Arlington, TX	**1,881,056**	**40.5**	**79.9**	**28.5**	**15.2**	**24.4**	**44.5**	**78.7**	**27.5**	**10.6**
Dallas-Plano-Irving, TX	*1,255,247*	*40.4*	*79.5*	*30.4*	*17.0*	*26.6*	*43.9*	*77.6*	*28.8*	*10.8*
Fort Worth-Arlington, TX	*625,809*	*40.8*	*80.8*	*24.8*	*11.4*	*20.0*	*45.8*	*81.1*	*24.9*	*10.1*
Dalton, GA	42,671	42.0	62.4	11.1	12.7	17.4	53.7	78.0	15.8	11.7
Danville, IL	33,406	33.3	78.7	12.5	1.7	4.3	59.7	81.6	11.5	12.8
Danville, VA	45,291	32.6	67.8	11.3	1.2	3.1	63.5	81.2	10.5	15.1
Davenport-Moline-Rock Island, IA-IL	149,726	33.8	84.5	19.9	3.4	6.3	57.6	83.6	18.4	9.9
Dayton, OH	338,979	33.6	84.0	22.8	2.4	4.5	54.6	84.2	20.7	9.7
Decatur, AL	57,140	37.0	73.8	15.8	2.2	3.9	58.9	85.2	15.9	12.9
Decatur, IL	46,561	32.4	83.2	16.9	1.4	3.3	55.8	84.4	16.7	12.5
Deltona-Daytona Beach-Ormond Beach, FL	184,723	27.0	82.0	17.6	6.4	10.8	51.7	78.7	14.2	11.3
Denver-Aurora, CO[4]	844,017	35.2	86.5	34.2	10.7	17.0	44.6	71.7	29.7	7.8
Des Moines, IA	189,371	35.2	88.5	27.9	5.1	7.8	51.5	81.5	23.0	7.3
Detroit-Warren-Livonia, MI	**1,696,943**	**36.2**	**82.3**	**23.2**	**7.6**	**11.0**	**58.3**	**84.7**	**29.4**	**10.4**
Detroit-Livonia-Dearborn, MI	*768,440*	*37.7*	*77.0*	*17.2*	*6.7*	*10.8*	*60.0*	*80.1*	*22.2*	*16.1*
Warren-Farmington Hills-Troy, MI	*928,503*	*34.9*	*86.7*	*28.1*	*8.3*	*11.1*	*56.9*	*88.0*	*35.3*	*5.5*
Dothan, AL	52,836	35.6	73.1	15.9	1.4	2.8	57.5	84.8	13.2	16.2
Dover, DE	47,224	39.3	79.4	18.6	4.0	7.9	55.6	79.7	18.0	10.3
Dubuque, IA	33,690	34.5	85.2	21.3	1.9	4.0	60.0	81.9	15.4	7.4
Duluth, MN-WI	112,491	30.2	86.7	20.5	1.8	4.8	61.4	79.1	14.4	11.0
Durham, NC	168,704	32.1	82.8	38.8	9.3	12.1	46.7	74.0	23.3	12.4
Eau Claire, WI	57,178	32.9	87.1	22.1	1.8	5.0	55.2	80.6	15.2	9.5
El Centro, CA	39,384	53.4	59.0	10.3	32.2	67.8	52.1	72.7	14.3	20.8
Elizabethtown, KY	39,772	40.4	80.8	14.8	4.0	7.1	50.0	79.5	13.9	10.3
Elkhart-Goshen, IN	66,154	39.6	75.7	15.5	7.1	14.4	51.3	79.4	19.0	7.7
Elmira, NY	35,049	33.9	82.1	18.6	2.2	4.3	60.0	81.1	14.7	12.1
El Paso, TX	210,022	51.3	65.8	16.6	27.4	73.3	55.2	75.9	12.8	23.4
Erie, PA	106,507	34.3	84.6	20.9	2.7	5.9	60.2	79.9	14.6	11.4
Eugene-Springfield, OR	130,453	31.0	87.5	25.5	4.9	7.9	46.8	71.6	15.9	14.1
Evansville, IN-KY	136,768	34.1	82.3	17.4	1.3	3.3	57.1	84.6	16.7	9.7
Fairbanks, AK	29,777	43.6	91.8	27.0	4.0	7.8	39.4	72.8	26.8	7.5
Fargo, ND-MN	69,985	32.0	89.7	29.4	3.0	6.1	47.6	81.8	16.2	10.5
Farmington, NM	37,711	47.1	76.8	13.5	2.4	32.7	57.2	78.7	13.6	21.3
Fayetteville, NC	118,731	43.9	83.8	18.3	5.3	10.8	46.1	77.1	13.9	12.5
Fayetteville-Springdale-Rogers, AR-MO	131,939	36.3	78.8	20.9	6.6	10.0	45.2	78.7	14.3	12.8
Flagstaff, AZ	40,448	39.0	83.8	29.9	4.3	28.2	46.2	68.1	18.3	17.7
Flint, MI	169,825	37.3	83.1	16.2	2.1	4.5	56.8	84.3	22.1	12.9
Florence, SC	72,940	38.5	71.8	16.9	1.5	3.7	61.2	80.4	14.1	17.3
Florence-Muscle Shoals, AL	58,549	33.3	75.2	16.8	1.0	2.4	60.8	86.0	13.8	14.0
Fond du Lac, WI	36,931	34.5	84.2	16.9	2.0	4.8	59.5	80.8	17.4	5.6
Fort Collins-Loveland, CO	97,164	33.4	92.3	39.5	4.3	8.5	41.5	77.4	26.6	9.0
Fort Smith, AR-OK	104,506	37.7	73.2	13.2	4.0	6.7	52.9	80.1	11.0	15.4
Fort Walton Beach-Crestview-Destin, FL	66,269	35.9	88.0	24.2	5.3	7.9	46.4	82.8	18.9	8.5
Fort Wayne, IN	150,858	36.7	85.8	21.3	3.6	6.9	54.0	84.2	20.2	8.4
Fresno, CA	252,940	45.8	67.5	17.5	21.1	40.8	51.0	74.2	16.7	22.4
Gadsden, AL	41,615	33.6	74.1	13.4	1.6	3.0	61.6	84.5	12.0	15.4
Gainesville, FL	92,530	28.3	87.0	36.7	6.9	11.1	41.1	74.8	15.8	21.0
Gainesville, GA	47,381	41.5	70.5	18.7	16.2	20.7	47.8	76.4	22.3	12.2
Glens Falls, NY	48,184	34.4	82.0	18.9	2.2	3.9	62.2	79.9	15.6	9.2
Goldsboro, NC	42,612	38.7	77.2	15.0	4.2	7.2	53.0	80.5	12.8	13.3
Grand Forks, ND-MN	37,505	33.7	86.6	24.2	2.9	6.8	49.0	79.4	13.0	11.2
Grand Junction, CO	45,823	33.9	85.0	22.0	3.0	8.0	45.1	77.1	14.3	10.0
Grand Rapids-Wyoming, MI	272,130	38.4	84.3	22.7	5.4	8.7	54.2	83.0	21.9	8.5
Great Falls, MT	32,547	34.2	87.1	21.5	2.4	5.1	52.8	80.5	11.2	13.2
Greeley, CO[4]	63,247	40.5	79.6	21.6	9.3	20.3	42.5	78.5	20.1	12.2
Green Bay, WI	108,897	35.3	85.4	20.1	3.3	6.3	55.4	83.3	20.3	6.6
Greensboro-High Point, NC	256,315	34.3	78.2	23.4	5.8	8.2	53.3	81.2	19.3	10.4
Greenville, NC	59,235	34.1	78.0	23.9	3.8	6.3	46.7	80.3	14.9	19.4

See footnotes at end of table.

Metropolitan statistical area / **Metropolitan statistical area with metropolitan divisions** / *Metropolitan division*	Households Total	Family with children under 18 years (percent of total)	High school graduate or higher (percent)	Bachelor's degree or higher (percent)	Foreign-born population (percent of total)	Speaking language other than English at home[2] (percent)	Living in same house in 1995 and 2000[2] (percent)	Workers who drove alone to work[3] (percent)	Households with income of $75,000 or more in 1999 (percent)	Persons below poverty in 1999 level (percent)
Greenville, SC	217,152	35.2	76.9	23.1	4.0	6.2	53.0	81.2	18.6	11.2
Gulfport-Biloxi, MS	93,182	37.5	79.5	17.9	3.0	6.1	50.7	79.0	14.3	14.2
Hagerstown-Martinsburg, MD-WV	85,440	34.8	77.6	14.5	1.8	3.3	56.8	80.4	15.9	9.8
Hanford-Corcoran, CA	34,418	51.0	68.8	10.4	16.0	36.7	42.3	73.5	15.8	16.5
Harrisburg-Carlisle, PA	202,380	32.3	84.2	24.3	3.4	6.9	59.0	80.0	21.3	7.9
Harrisonburg, VA	38,488	32.3	73.6	21.4	5.5	8.7	51.5	76.5	15.0	14.3
Hartford-West Hartford-East Hartford, CT	445,870	33.7	84.0	30.5	10.3	18.7	58.3	82.6	31.7	7.9
Hattiesburg, MS	45,999	37.9	79.8	22.6	1.6	3.6	51.0	81.1	12.5	18.5
Hickory-Lenoir-Morganton, NC	133,966	34.9	70.3	13.6	4.6	7.2	58.9	81.3	14.0	9.6
Hinesville-Fort Stewart, GA	22,957	53.4	84.9	13.2	5.6	12.4	34.7	72.4	9.4	14.5
Holland-Grand Haven, MI	81,662	41.2	86.6	26.0	4.9	8.9	55.0	85.9	26.9	5.3
Honolulu, HI	286,450	37.8	84.8	27.9	19.2	28.9	56.3	61.4	31.6	9.6
Hot Springs, AR	37,813	28.0	78.3	18.0	2.6	4.8	52.6	78.9	12.8	14.3
Houma-Bayou Cane-Thibodaux, LA	68,054	43.3	66.7	12.3	1.5	17.0	64.5	79.1	13.8	17.6
Houston-Sugar Land-Baytown, TX	1,656,799	42.7	76.3	26.4	19.0	31.7	48.8	77.0	26.1	13.5
Huntington-Ashland, WV-KY-OH	117,697	31.8	76.6	14.9	0.9	2.3	61.2	83.9	11.4	17.5
Huntsville, AL	134,643	36.2	83.3	30.9	3.5	5.2	52.1	83.9	23.5	10.6
Idaho Falls, ID	34,654	44.1	87.2	24.2	4.3	8.4	54.5	76.7	18.3	10.1
Indianapolis, IN	594,874	36.6	84.3	26.5	3.5	5.7	49.7	82.8	24.5	8.3
Iowa City, IA	52,136	28.4	91.6	42.0	5.6	9.9	43.6	68.8	20.9	12.9
Ithaca, NY	36,420	27.4	91.4	47.5	10.5	13.9	41.9	59.8	18.7	15.4
Jackson, MI	58,168	36.6	84.2	16.3	1.7	4.4	59.0	83.5	20.2	8.5
Jackson, MS	180,556	40.3	79.9	26.2	1.2	3.4	54.5	80.7	18.0	16.4
Jackson, TN	41,212	37.1	77.2	20.1	2.0	3.7	51.7	83.5	16.0	13.4
Jacksonville, FL	432,627	37.4	83.4	22.6	5.3	8.5	49.2	80.3	20.9	10.5
Jacksonville, NC	48,122	45.7	84.3	14.8	4.1	9.4	35.8	66.7	10.1	11.3
Janesville, WI	58,617	36.3	83.9	16.7	3.3	6.1	55.3	83.1	20.8	7.1
Jefferson City, MO	51,637	36.7	81.7	21.2	1.6	4.1	54.5	77.7	16.5	8.0
Johnson City, TN	75,197	30.9	73.7	18.5	1.5	3.1	57.1	84.2	11.4	14.3
Johnstown, PA	60,531	29.2	80.0	13.7	1.3	4.1	71.7	81.7	9.7	11.9
Jonesboro, AR	42,327	35.6	73.5	17.3	1.7	3.5	50.0	82.5	12.0	16.3
Joplin, MO	61,552	35.4	79.6	16.4	2.2	4.7	49.3	81.5	10.5	13.2
Kalamazoo-Portage, MI	121,461	33.8	86.3	26.9	3.9	7.2	52.5	82.9	20.4	11.4
Kankakee-Bradley, IL	38,182	37.8	79.8	15.0	3.5	6.4	57.3	81.1	18.8	11.0
Kansas City, MO-KS	717,761	36.0	86.6	28.0	4.4	7.4	51.5	82.6	23.9	8.4
Kennewick-Richland-Pasco, WA	67,706	42.5	80.1	23.3	12.8	21.9	50.6	77.8	23.6	12.4
Killeen-Temple-Fort Hood, TX	112,011	44.5	83.5	18.0	6.8	17.1	40.2	76.5	14.0	10.7
Kingsport-Bristol-Bristol, TN-VA	124,021	31.4	73.1	15.5	1.0	2.2	61.2	85.4	12.0	13.4
Kingston, NY	67,499	33.3	81.7	25.0	5.9	10.1	61.6	78.1	21.5	10.9
Knoxville, TN	253,005	31.8	80.2	24.6	2.2	4.0	54.4	84.6	17.8	11.9
Kokomo, IN	41,269	34.0	83.4	17.1	1.6	3.7	57.2	84.9	22.8	8.7
La Crosse, WI-MN	49,232	32.0	89.0	24.6	2.3	5.3	53.2	80.2	16.6	9.5
Lafayette, IN	66,502	31.4	87.1	29.2	7.1	10.2	42.4	77.7	18.5	12.6
Lafayette, LA	89,536	40.3	76.4	22.0	2.2	20.8	56.4	82.8	16.6	16.5
Lake Charles, LA	72,205	39.8	76.6	16.4	1.4	9.0	56.1	83.4	16.3	14.9
Lakeland, FL	187,233	33.0	74.8	14.9	6.9	12.1	51.1	79.9	14.5	12.6
Lancaster, PA	172,560	35.9	77.4	20.5	3.2	13.1	60.2	78.2	20.6	7.6
Lansing-East Lansing, MI	172,413	34.1	88.6	28.4	4.6	8.1	51.3	80.4	23.0	10.6
Laredo, TX	50,740	60.8	53.0	13.9	29.0	91.9	58.8	71.5	11.9	30.7
Las Cruces, NM	59,556	43.0	70.0	22.3	18.7	54.4	53.1	77.2	12.1	24.6
Las Vegas-Paradise, NV	512,253	35.4	79.5	17.3	18.0	26.0	34.5	74.6	22.6	10.6
Lawrence, KS	38,486	28.9	92.4	42.7	5.2	8.5	37.0	76.9	18.1	14.5
Lawton, OK	39,808	42.8	85.2	19.1	5.4	11.3	42.6	73.3	12.0	14.2
Lebanon, PA	46,551	32.8	78.6	15.4	2.4	8.0	62.6	81.0	17.1	7.3
Lewiston, ID-WA	23,650	32.4	85.6	18.6	1.9	3.6	53.5	83.1	13.9	13.1
Lewiston-Auburn, ME	42,028	32.9	79.8	14.4	2.6	16.4	56.7	78.0	13.1	10.7
Lexington-Fayette, KY	163,854	32.8	83.2	29.8	4.4	6.6	45.3	80.2	20.9	11.4
Lima, OH	40,646	35.8	82.5	13.4	1.0	3.4	58.8	84.9	15.0	11.4
Lincoln, NE	105,200	31.9	90.3	32.0	5.2	8.5	47.1	80.2	19.1	8.9
Little Rock-North Little Rock, AR	241,094	36.0	83.0	24.2	2.3	4.6	50.8	81.5	17.7	11.8
Logan, UT-ID	31,019	46.1	90.1	29.6	6.3	10.5	45.8	73.2	15.1	12.5
Longview, TX	73,341	37.4	77.3	16.2	4.6	8.2	55.7	82.3	14.3	14.4
Longview, WA	35,850	36.0	83.2	13.3	3.7	6.0	52.6	81.6	16.4	13.7
Los Angeles-Long Beach-Santa Ana, CA	4,069,061	41.1	72.2	26.3	34.8	51.2	51.1	71.9	28.1	15.9
Los Angeles-Long Beach-Glendale, CA	3,133,774	41.3	69.9	24.9	36.2	54.1	52.0	70.4	25.3	17.6
Santa Ana-Anaheim-Irvine, CA	935,287	40.5	79.5	30.8	29.9	41.4	48.0	76.5	37.4	10.2
Louisville, KY-IN	462,241	35.3	80.9	21.2	2.6	4.5	54.6	81.8	20.0	10.7
Lubbock, TX	95,028	35.5	77.9	24.0	3.4	22.9	47.7	80.6	14.1	17.4
Lynchburg, VA	89,736	33.7	75.9	18.7	1.9	3.6	59.0	81.6	15.3	10.9
Macon, GA	84,338	37.9	76.1	18.7	1.6	3.7	56.9	81.0	17.5	16.5
Madera, CA	36,155	45.2	65.4	12.0	20.1	37.0	52.8	73.1	15.6	19.9
Madison, WI	202,687	30.9	91.3	36.9	5.5	8.6	48.3	74.7	24.7	8.6

See footnotes at end of table.

State and Metropolitan Area Data Book: 2006

U.S. Census Bureau

Table B-4. Metropolitan Areas — **Population Characteristics 2000 Census**—Con.

Metropolitan statistical area / **Metropolitan statistical area with metropolitan divisions** / *Metropolitan division*	Households Total	Households Family with children under 18 years (percent of total)	Educational attainment[1] High school graduate or higher (percent)	Educational attainment[1] Bachelor's degree or higher (percent)	Foreign-born population (percent of total)	Speaking language other than English at home[2] (percent)	Living in same house in 1995 and 2000[2] (percent)	Workers who drove alone to work[3] (percent)	Households with income of $75,000 or more in 1999 (percent)	Persons below poverty in 1999 level (percent)
Manchester-Nashua, NH	144,455	37.2	87.0	30.1	6.8	12.7	53.6	83.3	30.5	6.1
Mansfield, OH	49,534	33.9	80.2	12.6	1.8	4.5	59.4	84.7	15.6	10.0
McAllen-Edinburg-Mission, TX	156,824	56.5	50.5	12.9	29.5	83.1	61.1	73.7	9.4	35.4
Medford, OR	71,532	33.0	85.0	22.3	4.9	7.7	46.5	77.4	16.4	12.3
Memphis, TN-MS-AR	448,473	39.8	79.0	22.0	3.2	5.6	52.1	80.7	20.0	15.3
Merced, CA	63,815	50.0	63.8	11.0	24.8	45.2	50.5	72.9	15.0	21.4
Miami-Fort Lauderdale-Miami Beach, FL	**1,905,394**	**33.7**	**76.2**	**24.1**	**35.0**	**44.7**	**49.1**	**77.3**	**22.1**	**13.8**
Fort Lauderdale-Pompano Beach-Deerfield Beach, FL	*654,445*	*32.2*	*82.0*	*24.5*	*25.3*	*28.8*	*47.1*	*80.0*	*22.9*	*11.4*
Miami-Miami Beach-Kendall, FL	*776,774*	*39.0*	*67.9*	*21.7*	*50.9*	*67.9*	*50.2*	*73.8*	*18.9*	*17.6*
West Palm Beach-Boca Raton-Boynton Beach, FL	*474,175*	*27.3*	*83.6*	*27.7*	*17.4*	*21.7*	*49.5*	*79.6*	*26.3*	*9.8*
Michigan City-La Porte, IN	41,050	35.1	80.6	14.0	2.5	5.9	58.3	83.6	17.2	8.2
Midland, TX	42,745	42.4	79.2	24.8	7.6	25.8	54.0	83.3	20.9	12.7
Milwaukee-Waukesha-West Allis, WI	587,657	34.2	84.5	27.0	5.4	10.3	54.8	79.7	24.5	10.4
Minneapolis-St. Paul-Bloomington, MN-WI	1,136,615	35.9	90.6	33.3	7.1	10.2	54.3	78.3	31.4	6.6
Missoula, MT	38,439	31.0	91.0	32.8	2.3	4.8	45.4	73.3	13.7	14.3
Mobile, AL	150,179	39.1	76.7	18.6	2.3	4.6	58.1	82.7	14.4	18.1
Modesto, CA	145,146	45.8	70.4	14.1	18.3	32.4	50.8	76.9	19.0	15.8
Monroe, LA	64,073	38.4	77.6	21.2	1.0	3.0	56.8	81.7	15.0	19.8
Monroe, MI	53,762	39.1	83.1	14.3	1.9	4.0	61.0	88.1	29.0	7.0
Montgomery, AL	129,717	38.2	78.9	24.2	1.6	3.6	53.5	82.9	17.5	15.0
Morgantown, WV	44,990	28.1	80.8	26.0	3.0	5.4	55.1	76.1	12.1	20.4
Morristown, TN	48,636	34.3	68.4	12.2	3.2	4.8	57.4	83.3	10.4	14.4
Mount Vernon-Anacortes, WA	38,852	35.6	84.0	20.8	8.8	11.7	50.2	77.1	20.0	10.9
Muncie, IN	47,131	30.4	81.6	20.4	1.5	3.5	52.0	81.2	15.6	14.2
Muskegon-Norton Shores, MI	63,330	37.8	83.1	13.9	1.9	4.4	58.6	84.0	15.3	11.0
Myrtle Beach-Conway-North Myrtle Beach, SC	81,800	29.5	81.1	18.7	4.0	6.3	49.3	79.0	14.2	11.9
Napa, CA	45,402	34.4	80.4	26.4	18.1	25.2	53.0	72.7	31.8	8.0
Naples-Marco Island, FL	102,973	25.2	81.8	27.9	18.3	25.1	44.2	74.4	29.0	10.1
Nashville-Davidson-Murfreesboro, TN	510,222	35.9	80.3	25.6	4.5	6.7	48.7	80.5	21.9	10.0
New Haven-Milford, CT	319,040	33.8	83.0	27.6	9.0	17.7	58.5	80.7	28.7	9.2
New Orleans-Metairie-Kenner, LA	498,587	37.8	77.7	22.8	4.9	9.3	59.3	72.9	17.7	18.0
New York-Northern New Jersey-Long Island, NY-NJ-PA	**6,676,963**	**35.8**	**78.7**	**30.3**	**26.4**	**35.8**	**61.5**	**52.7**	**32.0**	**13.4**
Edison, NJ	*799,437*	*35.8*	*85.7*	*32.0*	*15.3*	*21.4*	*58.9*	*77.6*	*38.2*	*6.1*
Nassau-Suffolk, NY	*916,686*	*39.6*	*86.4*	*31.3*	*14.4*	*20.0*	*67.2*	*73.9*	*45.0*	*5.5*
Newark-Union, NJ-PA	*751,513*	*38.4*	*82.2*	*32.2*	*18.6*	*25.7*	*60.0*	*72.2*	*37.7*	*9.2*
New York-White Plains-Wayne, NY-NJ	*4,209,327*	*34.6*	*74.8*	*29.4*	*33.0*	*44.3*	*60.8*	*37.5*	*27.0*	*17.5*
Niles-Benton Harbor, MI	63,569	34.5	81.9	19.6	4.9	7.1	57.7	81.6	17.9	12.4
Norwich-New London, CT	99,835	34.7	86.0	26.2	5.4	10.3	55.2	81.1	27.8	6.1
Ocala, FL	106,755	27.8	78.2	13.7	5.2	8.8	50.3	80.6	11.1	12.7
Ocean City, NJ	42,148	28.6	81.9	22.0	3.2	6.6	61.1	80.1	23.1	8.4
Odessa, TX	43,846	43.4	68.0	12.0	10.6	37.1	57.1	81.7	11.1	18.4
Ogden-Clearfield, UT	138,945	48.2	88.9	24.6	4.8	9.8	52.0	78.7	24.7	6.9
Oklahoma City, OK	429,743	35.6	83.5	24.2	5.6	9.4	48.9	81.6	16.5	13.1
Olympia, WA	81,625	35.4	89.5	29.8	6.1	9.2	48.1	77.2	22.6	8.7
Omaha-Council Bluffs, NE-IA	294,502	36.4	87.8	27.1	4.5	7.6	52.9	82.7	22.1	8.2
Orlando-Kissimee, FL	625,248	35.4	82.8	24.8	12.0	21.9	44.0	80.6	20.7	10.5
Oshkosh-Neenah, WI	61,157	32.4	86.3	22.8	2.8	5.7	53.7	84.5	18.9	6.3
Owensboro, KY	43,232	35.9	79.5	15.6	1.0	3.0	56.0	85.1	14.3	12.5
Oxnard-Thousand Oaks-Ventura, CA	243,234	43.6	80.1	26.9	20.7	33.0	51.7	75.9	37.8	9.1
Palm Bay-Melbourne-Titusville, FL	198,195	29.2	86.3	23.6	6.5	8.7	51.6	83.4	18.9	9.3
Panama City-Lynn Haven, FL	59,597	33.8	81.0	17.7	3.6	6.4	49.4	81.0	14.2	12.7
Parkersburg-Marietta-Vienna, WV-OH	66,583	32.8	82.2	14.7	0.8	2.1	61.8	84.1	13.5	12.8
Pascagoula, MS	54,418	41.8	79.6	15.5	2.5	4.8	57.3	80.5	15.6	13.0
Pensacola-Ferry Pass-Brent, FL	154,842	35.5	83.0	21.5	3.5	6.4	47.9	78.6	15.7	12.9
Peoria, IL	143,607	33.6	84.7	20.8	2.1	4.3	58.3	83.6	20.3	9.5
Philadelphia-Camden-Wilmington, PA-NJ-DE-MD	**2,134,404**	**35.6**	**82.4**	**27.7**	**6.9**	**12.0**	**61.4**	**73.1**	**28.3**	**10.5**
Camden, NJ	*430,832*	*38.4*	*83.6*	*25.2*	*5.9*	*11.7*	*62.5*	*79.0*	*31.1*	*7.3*
Philadelphia, PA	*1,459,119*	*34.6*	*81.7*	*28.8*	*7.4*	*12.5*	*62.0*	*69.9*	*27.2*	*11.9*
Wilmington, DE-MD-NJ	*244,453*	*36.6*	*84.3*	*26.3*	*5.5*	*9.4*	*56.5*	*80.0*	*29.9*	*8.1*
Phoenix-Mesa-Scottsdale, AZ	1,194,250	36.1	81.9	25.1	14.1	24.2	41.9	74.6	23.9	11.8
Pine Bluff, AR	38,093	38.7	73.3	14.1	1.1	3.1	56.8	79.9	12.5	18.3
Pittsburgh, PA	995,505	29.9	84.9	23.4	2.6	5.1	66.5	77.5	17.8	10.6
Pittsfield, MA	56,006	29.4	85.1	26.0	3.7	6.4	61.5	79.2	18.7	9.0
Pocatello, ID	29,752	39.5	86.4	24.0	2.9	7.7	50.5	78.1	15.5	13.7
Portland-South Portland-Biddeford, ME	196,669	33.0	88.6	29.2	3.3	7.2	55.9	79.8	21.0	7.9
Portland-Vancouver-Beaverton, OR-WA	745,531	34.9	87.2	28.8	10.8	14.3	45.5	73.1	24.9	9.3
Port St. Lucie-Fort Pierce, FL	132,221	27.0	80.8	19.7	9.5	12.8	51.1	79.7	18.6	11.4
Poughkeepsie-Newburgh-Middletown, NY	214,324	40.0	82.8	24.9	8.4	15.4	59.1	77.4	31.2	8.8
Prescott, AZ	70,171	26.3	84.7	21.1	5.9	9.7	44.1	75.1	14.5	11.7
Providence-New Bedford-Fall River, RI-MA	613,835	33.8	76.3	23.7	11.5	20.3	59.5	80.7	22.4	10.9
Provo-Orem, UT	102,393	51.3	90.7	31.0	6.2	11.3	43.5	72.4	22.2	11.7
Pueblo, CO	54,579	35.2	81.3	18.3	3.0	16.1	51.5	79.4	13.0	14.5

See footnotes at end of table.

Metropolitan statistical area **Metropolitan statistical area** **with metropolitan divisions** *Metropolitan division*	Households		Educational attainment[1]		Foreign-born population (percent of total)	Speaking language other than English at home[2] (percent)	Living in same house in 1995 and 2000[2] (percent)	Workers who drove alone to work[3] (percent)	House-holds with income of $75,000 or more in 1999 (percent)	Persons below poverty in 1999 level (percent)
	Total	Family with children under 18 years (percent of total)	High school graduate or higher (percent)	Bachelor's degree or higher (percent)						
Punta Gorda, FL	63,864	19.5	82.1	17.6	8.0	8.2	52.5	81.7	14.3	8.1
Racine, WI	70,819	37.3	82.9	20.3	4.1	8.4	57.3	83.6	23.8	8.2
Raleigh-Cary, NC	306,478	36.7	86.3	37.6	8.7	11.4	44.3	80.8	30.0	8.6
Rapid City, SD	43,446	37.1	87.8	23.3	2.0	4.9	48.2	82.1	14.4	10.8
Reading, PA	141,570	34.3	78.0	18.5	4.3	12.7	61.1	81.1	21.8	9.2
Redding, CA	63,426	35.0	83.3	16.6	4.0	6.5	50.0	79.7	14.6	15.0
Reno-Sparks, NV	133,546	33.9	84.0	23.7	14.0	19.8	41.3	75.4	24.1	9.8
Richmond, VA	425,100	36.4	81.4	27.6	4.2	6.6	54.0	81.7	24.5	9.1
Riverside-San Bernardino-Ontario, CA	1,034,812	46.1	74.6	16.3	18.8	33.5	47.5	73.5	22.5	14.7
Roanoke, VA	119,366	31.4	79.4	21.0	2.4	4.3	57.6	83.4	17.3	9.2
Rochester, MN	62,504	37.0	89.9	30.5	6.5	8.6	56.8	76.8	26.0	6.2
Rochester, NY	397,303	35.0	84.3	27.7	5.9	10.0	58.4	81.7	23.4	10.1
Rockford, IL	122,577	36.8	81.3	18.8	6.3	10.3	55.7	83.3	21.9	9.1
Rocky Mount, NC	54,036	38.0	71.8	13.9	2.6	5.4	56.8	80.7	14.0	15.5
Rome, GA	34,028	36.3	71.5	15.8	5.2	7.8	53.8	79.8	14.9	13.8
Sacramento-Arden-Arcade-Roseville, CA . . .	665,298	37.3	84.6	26.5	14.5	21.9	47.4	75.3	25.6	12.5
Saginaw-Saginaw Township North, MI	80,430	35.9	81.6	15.9	2.0	6.4	61.5	85.9	19.5	13.6
St. Cloud, MN	60,669	36.4	86.0	21.0	2.3	6.0	56.8	78.0	18.0	8.0
St. George, UT	29,939	39.5	87.6	21.0	4.1	7.6	42.5	75.8	13.9	11.1
St. Joseph, MO-KS	46,531	34.2	81.4	16.4	1.0	3.1	55.9	81.7	12.6	10.8
St. Louis, MO-IL[5]	1,048,279	36.0	83.1	24.8	3.0	5.2	56.9	82.5	22.9	9.8
Salem, OR	124,699	37.0	80.4	20.8	11.5	17.8	45.4	73.1	17.5	12.7
Salinas, CA	121,236	43.5	68.4	22.5	29.0	47.3	48.8	68.7	27.2	12.9
Salisbury, MD	40,579	35.0	78.1	19.5	3.6	5.4	55.8	78.3	16.0	13.2
Salt Lake City, UT	318,150	43.6	87.0	27.6	10.0	15.7	49.4	76.0	25.6	7.7
San Angelo, TX	40,197	36.6	76.3	19.5	5.9	26.5	48.6	79.4	12.5	14.5
San Antonio, TX	601,265	41.3	77.1	22.1	9.8	40.2	51.6	76.2	18.8	14.7
San Diego-Carlsbad-San Marcos, CA	994,677	37.2	82.6	29.5	21.5	33.0	45.1	73.9	27.2	12.0
Sandusky, OH	31,727	33.3	84.0	16.6	1.5	3.8	61.7	88.1	19.9	8.1
San Francisco-Oakland-Fremont, CA	**1,551,948**	**32.5**	**84.2**	**38.8**	**27.4**	**35.8**	**53.2**	**62.8**	**39.9**	**9.0**
Oakland-Fremont-Hayward, CA	*867,495*	*37.4*	*84.2*	*35.0*	*24.0*	*32.5*	*51.7*	*67.9*	*38.1*	*9.5*
San Francisco-San Mateo-Redwood City, CA.	*684,453*	*26.3*	*84.2*	*43.6*	*32.0*	*40.3*	*55.2*	*56.5*	*42.3*	*8.3*
San Jose-Sunnyvale-Santa Clara, CA	581,748	38.9	83.2	39.8	33.6	45.1	51.1	77.2	49.3	7.5
San Luis Obispo-Paso Robles, CA	92,739	30.5	85.6	26.7	8.9	14.7	46.7	73.9	22.5	12.1
Santa Barbara-Santa Maria, CA	136,622	35.6	79.2	29.4	21.2	32.8	48.3	69.4	27.6	13.8
Santa Cruz-Watsonville, CA	91,139	34.7	83.2	34.2	18.2	27.8	50.6	69.5	34.6	11.5
Santa Fe, NM	52,482	33.2	84.5	36.9	10.1	36.9	53.4	71.4	24.0	11.8
Santa Rosa-Petaluma, CA	172,403	34.7	84.9	28.5	14.3	19.8	52.0	74.7	31.6	7.9
Sarasota-Bradenton-Venice, FL	262,397	22.4	84.7	24.6	8.9	11.3	49.6	80.3	20.2	8.6
Savannah, GA	111,105	37.4	79.9	23.2	3.5	6.0	50.6	77.8	20.2	14.1
Scranton-Wilkes-Barre, PA	227,667	29.1	81.5	17.5	2.0	5.2	68.9	81.4	14.2	10.5
Seattle-Tacoma-Bellevue, WA	**1,196,568**	**34.0**	**89.3**	**32.7**	**12.6**	**15.6**	**47.3**	**71.6**	**29.6**	**8.4**
Seattle-Bellevue-Everett, WA	*935,768*	*32.7*	*90.0*	*36.1*	*14.0*	*16.8*	*47.5*	*70.3*	*31.6*	*7.8*
Tacoma, WA	*260,800*	*38.9*	*86.9*	*20.6*	*8.1*	*11.8*	*46.9*	*76.4*	*22.3*	*10.2*
Sheboygan, WI	43,545	33.8	84.4	17.9	4.3	8.7	59.3	81.0	19.0	5.0
Sherman-Denison, TX	42,849	35.7	80.2	17.2	3.9	7.1	51.3	80.8	16.6	10.9
Shreveport-Bossier City, LA	144,293	37.5	79.2	19.2	1.7	4.3	54.6	80.8	15.0	19.0
Sioux City, IA-NE-SD	53,586	37.4	80.9	18.5	7.8	12.7	55.2	78.2	15.6	9.8
Sioux Falls, SD	72,492	36.1	88.1	25.1	3.4	6.0	50.7	82.8	18.1	6.9
South Bend-Mishawaka, IN-MI	120,419	34.8	82.1	21.7	4.1	7.9	56.1	81.4	18.5	9.9
Spartanburg, SC	97,735	36.4	73.1	18.2	3.7	6.3	56.3	82.2	16.1	12.0
Spokane, WA	163,611	34.7	89.1	25.0	4.5	6.6	50.8	76.7	16.4	11.9
Springfield, IL	83,595	33.1	88.1	28.1	1.8	3.5	55.2	81.8	21.3	9.1
Springfield, MA	260,745	33.4	82.4	25.2	6.7	18.2	57.9	79.3	20.1	12.4
Springfield, MO	145,304	33.3	83.0	21.3	1.5	4.0	46.8	81.3	13.1	11.9
Springfield, OH	56,648	34.6	81.2	14.9	1.2	3.0	57.7	82.6	17.8	10.4
State College, PA	49,323	27.0	88.2	36.3	5.8	8.0	46.9	66.7	16.9	16.8
Stockton, CA	181,629	45.3	71.2	14.5	19.5	33.7	51.2	74.6	21.6	17.2
Sumter, SC	37,728	41.7	74.3	15.8	2.1	4.6	55.0	80.4	12.0	15.7
Syracuse, NY	252,043	35.0	84.5	25.2	4.5	7.6	58.7	80.0	19.9	11.8
Tallahassee, FL	125,533	32.2	84.7	34.1	4.3	7.1	46.2	78.6	18.1	16.9
Tampa-St. Petersburg-Clearwater, FL	1,009,316	28.7	81.5	21.7	9.8	15.3	49.1	79.7	17.6	11.0
Terre Haute, IN	65,795	33.4	81.2	17.4	1.4	3.4	56.1	82.3	12.7	11.5
Texarkana, TX-Texarkana, AR	48,695	37.5	76.4	15.0	1.4	4.7	53.4	83.1	13.5	17.1
Toledo, OH	259,973	34.2	84.1	21.2	2.8	6.4	56.9	84.6	19.6	11.8
Topeka, KS	89,600	34.2	88.0	23.6	2.2	5.2	55.5	81.9	17.3	8.9
Trenton-Ewing, NJ	125,807	36.2	81.8	34.0	13.9	20.2	57.4	73.3	36.1	8.1
Tucson, AZ	332,350	32.5	83.4	26.7	11.9	27.5	46.2	73.8	17.4	14.3
Tulsa, OK	337,215	36.4	83.2	22.5	3.9	6.7	50.2	80.9	17.4	11.5
Tuscaloosa, AL	74,863	34.6	76.8	21.9	1.9	4.1	53.6	83.2	15.1	18.0
Tyler, TX	65,692	37.0	80.2	22.5	6.6	12.0	51.0	81.8	17.9	13.5

See footnotes at end of table.

State and Metropolitan Area Data Book: 2006

U.S. Census Bureau

Metropolitan statistical area **Metropolitan statistical area** **with metropolitan divisions** *Metropolitan division*	Households		Educational attainment[1]		Foreign-born population (percent of total)	Speaking language other than English at home[2] (percent)	Living in same house in 1995 and 2000[2] (percent)	Workers who drove alone to work[3] (percent)	House-holds with income of $75,000 or more in 1999 (percent)	Persons below poverty in 1999 level (percent)
	Total	Family with children under 18 years (percent of total)	High school graduate or higher (percent)	Bachelor's degree or higher (percent)						
Utica-Rome, NY	116,230	32.7	79.1	17.7	4.5	8.6	64.1	79.6	14.0	12.2
Valdosta, GA	42,666	39.3	75.0	17.4	2.8	5.1	48.5	78.9	12.6	18.2
Vallejo-Fairfield, CA	130,403	44.6	83.8	21.4	16.9	24.6	49.9	73.3	31.8	7.9
Vero Beach, FL	49,137	24.3	81.6	23.1	8.1	10.4	52.1	80.4	20.1	9.1
Victoria, TX	40,157	41.0	74.6	15.2	5.0	28.2	54.0	77.8	17.3	13.6
Vineland-Millville-Bridgeton, NJ	49,143	39.3	68.5	11.7	6.2	20.4	60.9	78.3	17.9	13.9
Virginia Beach-Norfolk-Newport News, VA-NC	580,278	39.5	84.6	23.7	4.5	7.6	48.0	78.8	20.1	10.2
Visalia-Porterville, CA	110,385	50.0	61.7	11.5	22.6	43.8	53.1	72.2	14.9	23.5
Waco, TX	78,859	37.0	76.6	19.1	6.1	15.6	48.2	79.1	15.0	16.8
Warner Robins, GA	40,911	42.0	84.3	19.8	3.4	6.1	47.3	83.3	19.9	10.0
Washington-Arlington-Alexandria, DC-VA-MD-WV	**1,800,263**	**36.6**	**87.0**	**42.5**	**17.3**	**21.3**	**50.1**	**67.5**	**40.7**	**7.2**
Bethesda-Gaithersburg-Frederick, MD	*394,625*	*37.9*	*89.8*	*50.2*	*22.5*	*26.8*	*53.1*	*70.8*	*45.6*	*5.2*
Washington-Arlington-Alexandria, DC-VA-MD-WV	*1,405,638*	*36.2*	*86.1*	*40.2*	*15.8*	*19.7*	*49.2*	*66.5*	*39.3*	*7.8*
Waterloo-Cedar Falls, IA	63,527	31.9	86.6	22.3	3.2	5.9	56.6	81.9	15.4	10.8
Wausau, WI	47,702	35.5	83.8	18.3	3.5	7.4	61.7	81.1	18.7	6.5
Weirton-Steubenville, WV-OH	54,491	29.3	81.6	12.1	1.4	4.3	68.8	85.3	10.5	13.1
Wenatchee, WA	36,747	38.3	78.9	20.0	13.1	19.6	52.7	74.1	16.8	12.9
Wheeling, WV-OH	62,249	30.2	81.2	14.6	1.0	3.4	66.2	81.8	10.9	14.8
Wichita, KS	220,440	37.2	85.4	24.3	5.7	9.5	50.6	84.4	19.7	9.0
Wichita Falls, TX	56,109	37.0	80.0	19.2	4.7	11.2	47.9	78.2	12.5	11.8
Williamsport, PA	47,003	32.3	80.6	15.1	1.2	3.3	61.0	80.3	12.1	11.0
Wilmington, NC	114,675	29.5	82.6	24.2	3.2	5.2	49.2	81.1	17.7	12.7
Winchester, VA-WV	40,053	35.8	76.4	18.3	3.0	5.3	55.6	78.5	17.0	9.6
Winston-Salem, NC	169,685	34.1	79.8	24.0	5.5	8.1	55.2	80.8	20.0	10.3
Worcester, MA	283,927	35.9	83.5	26.9	7.9	15.0	59.0	82.6	27.3	8.9
Yakima, WA	73,993	43.9	68.7	15.3	16.9	31.8	53.8	77.5	14.3	19.4
York-Hanover, PA	148,219	34.9	80.7	18.4	2.2	5.3	60.2	84.3	19.5	6.6
Youngstown-Warren-Boardman, OH-PA	238,319	32.1	82.6	16.3	2.0	6.1	64.4	86.1	15.2	11.1
Yuba City, CA	47,568	42.3	72.5	13.2	16.6	26.7	49.7	76.1	15.3	17.4
Yuma, AZ	53,848	40.6	65.8	11.8	24.0	45.5	46.1	73.7	12.5	18.5

[1]Persons 25 years and over.
[2]Persons 5 years and over.
[3]Workers 16 years and over.
[4]The Denver-Aurora metropolitan statistical area includes Broomfield County. Broomfield County, CO, was formed from parts of Adams, Boulder, Jefferson, and Weld counties on November 15, 2001, and is coextensive with Broomfield city. For the purposes of defining and presenting data for the Denver-Aurora metropolitan statistical area, Broomfield city is treated as if it were a county when data are available to do so. In many cases, the data will not be available.
[5]The portion of Sullivan city in Crawford County, MO, is legally part of the St. Louis, MO-IL MSA. That portion is not included in these figures for the St. Louis MSA.

Note: Covers metropolitan statistical areas and metropolitan divisions and component counties defined by the Office of Management and Budget as of June 6, 2003, and subsequently updated in December 2003 and November 2004. For more information, see OMB Bulletin 05-02 at <http://www.whitehouse.gov/omb/bulletins/fy05/b05-02_appendix.pdf>.

Survey, Census, or Data Collection Method: Based on the Census of Population and Housing; for more information, see Appendix B, Limitations of the Data and Methodology, and also 2000 Census of Population and Housing, Demographic Profile Technical Documentation (revised August 2002) at <http://www.census.gov/prod/cen2000/doc/ProfileTD.pdf>; Census 2000 Summary File 1, Technical Documentation, SF1/13 (RV) (issued March 2005) at <http://www.census.gov/prod/cen2000/doc/sf1.pdf>; and Census 2000 Summary File 3, Technical Documentation, SF3/15 (RV) (issued March 2005) at <http://www.census.gov/prod/cen2000/doc/sf3.pdf>.

Sources: Households—U.S. Census Bureau, 2000 Census of Population and Housing, "Census 2000 Profiles of General Demographic Characteristics" data files (DP1) (accessed 14 June 2002) and related Internet site at <http://censtats.census.gov/pub/Profiles.shtml>. See also 2000 Census of Population and Housing, *Summary File 1* (SF1) and related Internet site <http://www.census.gov/Press-Release/www/2001/sumfile1.html> and 2000 Census of Population and Housing, *Summary Population and Housing Characteristics*, PHC-1-1 to 52, and related Internet site at <http://www.census.gov/prod/cen2000/index.html>; Educational attainment, foreign born, language, residence, commuting, income, and poverty—U.S. Census Bureau, 2000 Census of Population and Housing, *Summary File 3* (SF3) (accessed 12 January 2004) and related Internet site at <http://www.census.gov/Press-Release/www/2002/sumfile3.html> and 2000 Census of Population and Housing, *Summary Social, Economic, and Housing Characteristics*, PHC-2-1 to 52, and related Internet site at <http://www.census.gov/prod/cen2000/index.html>.

Table B-5. Metropolitan Areas — **Births, Deaths, Infant Deaths**

Metropolitan statistical area **Metropolitan statistical area with metropolitan divisions** *Metropolitan division*	Births				Deaths				Infant deaths[2]					
	Number		Rate per 1,000[1]		Number		Rate per 1,000[1]		Number			Rate per 1,000 live births[3]		
	2002	2000	2002	2000	2002	2000	2002	2000	2002	2000	1990	2002	2000	1990
Abilene, TX...............	2,259	2,371	14.3	14.8	1,520	1,527	9.6	9.5	26	8	26	11.5	3.4	10.5
Akron, OH................	8,443	8,822	12.1	12.7	6,611	6,430	9.5	9.3	44	65	75	5.2	7.4	7.6
Albany, GA................	2,251	2,467	14.1	15.6	1,381	1,321	8.6	8.4	16	26	37	7.1	10.5	13.8
Albany-Schenectady-Troy, NY ..	9,328	9,689	11.2	11.7	7,759	7,688	9.3	9.3	75	66	93	8.0	6.8	7.9
Albuquerque, NM...........	11,192	10,733	14.9	14.7	5,638	5,130	7.5	7.0	85	65	85	7.6	6.1	8.3
Alexandria, LA.............	2,095	2,254	14.4	15.5	1,558	1,555	10.7	10.7	25	23	18	11.9	10.2	7.9
Allentown-Bethlehem-Easton, PA-NJ ..	8,858	8,594	11.7	11.6	7,481	7,413	9.9	10.0	56	52	65	6.3	6.1	6.7
Altoona, PA...............	1,461	1,500	11.4	11.6	1,667	1,590	13.1	12.3	8	6	16	5.5	4.0	10.0
Amarillo, TX..............	3,612	3,538	15.6	15.6	2,150	1,948	9.3	8.6	43	39	21	11.9	11.0	6.1
Ames, IA.................	923	940	11.4	11.8	471	474	5.8	5.9	6	6	10	6.5	6.4	10.8
Anchorage, AK............	4,985	4,986	15.0	15.6	1,523	1,368	4.6	4.3	21	23	55	4.2	4.6	9.8
Anderson, IN..............	1,605	1,648	12.2	12.4	1,476	1,449	11.2	10.9	16	15	19	10.0	9.1	10.5
Anderson, SC.............	2,144	2,218	12.6	13.4	1,770	1,700	10.4	10.3	19	21	25	8.9	9.5	11.7
Ann Arbor, MI.............	4,203	4,137	12.6	12.8	1,806	1,895	5.4	5.9	25	33	33	5.9	8.0	7.9
Anniston-Oxford, AL.........	1,455	1,528	13.1	13.6	1,234	1,365	11.1	12.2	14	19	24	9.6	12.4	14.1
Appleton, WI..............	2,904	2,803	13.9	13.9	1,369	1,360	6.6	6.7	18	11	24	6.2	3.9	8.7
Asheville, NC.............	4,428	4,428	11.7	12.0	4,239	4,187	11.2	11.3	25	35	42	5.6	7.9	10.4
Athens-Clarke County, GA.....	2,215	2,134	13.1	12.8	1,158	1,162	6.8	7.0	13	16	29	5.9	7.5	14.5
Atlanta-Sandy Springs-Marietta, GA ..	73,534	71,734	16.3	16.9	27,736	26,813	6.2	6.3	606	526	612	8.2	7.3	11.3
Atlantic City, NJ...........	3,559	3,403	13.7	13.5	2,793	2,537	10.8	10.0	42	35	53	11.8	10.3	13.0
Auburn-Opelika, AL.........	1,413	1,457	12.0	12.7	735	771	6.3	6.7	5	15	14	3.5	10.3	10.7
Augusta-Richmond County, GA-SC ..	7,191	7,571	14.2	15.2	4,579	4,372	9.0	8.7	68	82	104	9.5	10.8	13.1
Austin-Round Rock, TX.......	22,484	21,780	16.7	17.4	6,742	6,408	5.0	5.1	105	100	98	4.7	4.6	6.6
Bakersfield, CA............	12,217	11,689	17.6	17.7	5,131	4,643	7.4	7.0	76	86	129	6.2	7.4	10.3
Baltimore-Towson, MD	33,691	34,781	13.0	13.6	23,725	23,994	9.1	9.4	249	274	376	7.4	7.9	9.4
Bangor, ME..............	1,502	1,541	10.2	10.6	1,392	1,403	9.5	9.7	6	5	10	4.0	3.2	5.1
Barnstable Town, MA........	1,971	1,996	8.7	9.0	2,717	2,769	11.9	12.5	10	13	25	5.1	6.5	10.1
Baton Rouge, LA...........	10,210	10,812	14.3	15.3	5,854	5,452	8.2	7.7	95	85	118	9.3	7.9	11.2
Battle Creek, MI...........	1,855	1,874	13.4	13.6	1,474	1,427	10.6	10.3	15	15	26	8.1	8.0	11.6
Bay City, MI..............	1,293	1,289	11.8	11.7	1,124	1,135	10.2	10.3	7	6	12	5.4	4.7	7.1
Beaumont-Port Arthur, TX.....	5,104	5,292	13.3	13.7	3,897	3,940	10.2	10.2	41	38	45	8.0	7.2	8.1
Bellingham, WA...........	1,957	2,077	11.2	12.5	1,304	1,228	7.5	7.4	8	7	14	4.1	3.4	7.9
Bend, OR...............	1,489	1,439	11.9	12.5	973	916	7.7	7.9	5	10	5	3.4	6.9	4.7
Billings, MT..............	1,857	1,779	13.1	12.8	1,342	1,230	9.5	8.9	16	7	15	8.6	3.9	8.5
Binghamton, NY...........	2,673	2,825	10.6	11.2	2,555	2,607	10.2	10.3	26	20	26	9.7	7.1	6.8
Birmingham-Hoover, AL.......	14,489	15,194	13.6	14.4	11,043	10,609	10.4	10.1	147	172	163	10.1	11.3	10.9
Bismarck, ND.............	1,167	1,168	12.1	12.3	788	794	8.2	8.4	12	6	3	10.3	5.1	2.5
Blacksburg-Christiansburg-Radford, VA ..	1,446	1,652	9.6	10.9	1,209	1,233	8.0	8.2	4	6	16	2.8	3.6	9.7
Bloomington, IN............	1,900	1,920	10.8	10.9	1,363	1,244	7.8	7.1	11	17	16	5.8	8.9	8.2
Bloomington-Normal, IL.......	2,100	1,991	13.5	13.2	1,036	986	6.7	6.6	16	7	8	7.6	3.5	4.4
Boise City-Nampa, ID........	8,250	7,804	16.5	16.8	3,119	3,116	6.3	6.7	55	53	55	6.7	6.8	10.3
Boston-Cambridge-Quincy, MA-NH	57,315	58,222	12.9	13.3	36,432	36,250	8.2	8.3	255	266	459	4.4	4.6	7.1
Boston-Quincy, MA............	24,296	24,551	13.3	13.5	15,308	15,227	8.4	8.4	116	114	201	4.8	4.6	7.3
Cambridge-Newton-Framingham, MA..	18,795	19,393	12.8	13.2	11,760	11,859	8.0	8.1	74	81	133	3.9	4.2	6.5
Essex County, MA............	9,583	9,563	13.0	13.2	6,661	6,540	9.0	9.0	41	53	90	4.3	5.5	8.2
Rockingham County-Strafford County, NH..........	4,641	4,715	11.5	12.1	2,703	2,624	6.7	6.7	24	18	35	5.2	3.8	6.1
Boulder, CO[4].............	3,700	3,878	13.3	13.3	1,433	1,420	5.1	4.9	18	20	23	4.9	5.2	6.9
Bowling Green, KY..........	1,422	1,345	13.4	12.9	920	833	8.7	8.0	13	10	10	9.1	7.4	8.4
Bremerton-Silverdale, WA.....	2,945	3,109	12.4	13.4	1,766	1,723	7.4	7.4	20	19	24	6.8	6.1	7.0
Bridgeport-Stamford-Norwalk, CT ..	11,943	12,430	13.3	14.1	7,130	7,072	8.0	8.0	83	55	95	6.9	4.4	7.3
Brownsville-Harlingen, TX.....	8,639	8,318	24.5	24.8	2,128	1,808	6.0	5.4	43	30	40	5.0	3.6	6.0
Brunswick, GA............	1,252	1,304	13.1	14.0	961	908	10.1	9.8	17	10	15	13.6	7.7	11.4
Buffalo-Niagara Falls, NY.....	13,080	13,788	11.3	11.8	12,427	12,402	10.7	10.6	108	105	149	8.3	7.6	8.4
Burlington, NC.............	1,815	1,903	13.4	14.5	1,289	1,342	9.5	10.3	19	30	16	10.5	15.8	10.6
Burlington-South Burlington, VT ..	2,269	2,332	11.2	11.7	1,378	1,345	6.8	6.8	10	20	19	4.4	8.6	6.8
Canton-Massillon, OH........	4,806	5,276	11.8	13.0	4,089	4,142	10.0	10.2	37	36	36	7.7	6.8	6.3
Cape Coral-Fort Myers, FL.....	5,389	5,200	11.3	11.8	5,465	5,087	11.5	11.5	40	36	31	7.4	6.9	6.8
Carson City, NV...........	723	719	13.3	13.7	640	549	11.7	10.5	1	4	2	1.4	5.6	3.3
Casper, WY..............	895	906	13.3	13.6	615	567	9.1	8.5	6	4	10	6.7	4.4	10.7
Cedar Rapids, IA..........	3,262	3,269	13.5	13.8	1,933	1,845	8.0	7.8	17	14	30	5.2	4.3	9.3
Champaign-Urbana, IL........	2,539	2,705	11.9	12.9	1,530	1,480	7.2	7.0	25	29	23	9.8	10.7	7.8
Charleston, WV............	3,817	3,763	12.4	12.2	3,638	3,658	11.9	11.8	32	33	37	8.4	8.8	9.3
Charleston-North Charleston, SC ..	7,899	7,931	14.0	14.4	4,593	4,499	8.1	8.2	85	58	117	10.8	7.3	11.7
Charlotte-Gastonia-Concord, NC-SC ..	21,920	21,811	15.6	16.4	10,422	10,094	7.4	7.6	164	194	193	7.5	8.9	11.1
Charlottesville, VA..........	2,158	2,206	12.1	12.7	1,375	1,421	7.7	8.2	16	17	21	7.4	7.7	10.1
Chattanooga, TN-GA	6,058	6,242	12.5	13.1	4,970	4,917	10.3	10.3	53	66	63	8.7	10.6	9.7
Cheyenne, WY............	1,203	1,162	14.5	14.2	667	660	8.0	8.1	11	7	12	9.1	6.0	10.0
Chicago-Naperville-Joliet, IL-IN-WI	140,181	143,767	15.1	15.8	70,757	71,432	7.6	7.9	1054	1218	1701	7.5	8.5	11.3
Chicago-Naperville-Joliet, IL.........	118,535	121,574	15.3	15.9	59,297	60,119	7.6	7.9	897	1084	1524	7.6	8.9	11.8
Gary, IN.................	9,183	9,471	13.5	14.0	6,357	6,414	9.3	9.5	96	74	93	10.5	7.8	9.5
Lake County-Kenosha County, IL-WI	12,463	12,722	15.0	16.0	5,103	4,899	6.2	6.2	61	60	84	4.9	4.7	7.1

See footnotes at end of table.

State and Metropolitan Area Data Book: 2006

U.S. Census Bureau

Table B-5. Metropolitan Areas — **Births, Deaths, Infant Deaths**—Con.

Metropolitan statistical area / **Metropolitan statistical area with metropolitan divisions** / *Metropolitan division*	Births Number		Births Rate per 1,000[1]		Deaths Number		Deaths Rate per 1,000[1]		Infant deaths[2] Number			Infant deaths Rate per 1,000 live births[3]		
	2002	2000	2002	2000	2002	2000	2002	2000	2002	2000	1990	2002	2000	1990
Chico, CA	2,265	2,197	10.9	10.8	2,262	2,141	10.8	10.5	18	14	21	7.9	6.4	7.9
Cincinnati-Middletown, OH-KY-IN	28,852	30,130	14.2	15.0	18,134	17,347	8.9	8.6	216	228	294	7.5	7.6	9.8
Clarksville, TN-KY	4,179	4,472	17.8	19.3	1,769	1,752	7.6	7.6	35	40	27	8.4	8.9	7.4
Cleveland, TN	1,377	1,414	13.0	13.6	970	999	9.2	9.6	13	9	8	9.4	6.4	6.4
Cleveland-Elyria-Mentor, OH	26,762	28,451	12.5	13.2	21,951	21,401	10.2	10.0	246	246	420	9.2	8.6	12.6
Coeur d'Alene, ID	1,470	1,507	12.9	13.9	897	873	7.8	8.0	7	10	7	4.8	6.6	7.0
College Station-Bryan, TX	2,738	2,767	14.7	15.0	1,123	1,117	6.0	6.0	12	12	13	4.4	4.3	5.5
Colorado Springs, CO	8,790	8,502	15.6	15.8	3,281	3,010	5.8	5.6	58	72	70	6.6	8.5	9.3
Columbia, MO	1,905	1,913	12.8	13.1	994	956	6.7	6.6	13	18	23	6.8	9.4	12.8
Columbia, SC	8,789	8,991	13.3	13.9	5,468	5,499	8.3	8.5	77	74	105	8.8	8.2	11.6
Columbus, GA-AL	4,175	4,549	14.6	16.1	2,797	2,699	9.8	9.6	43	68	71	10.3	14.9	14.5
Columbus, IN	982	1,069	13.7	15.0	618	628	8.6	8.8	7	9	5	7.1	8.4	5.0
Columbus, OH	24,932	25,112	15.0	15.6	12,747	12,434	7.7	7.7	206	199	230	8.3	7.9	10.1
Corpus Christi, TX	6,317	6,720	15.6	16.7	3,269	3,358	8.1	8.3	44	49	54	7.0	7.3	8.2
Corvallis, OR	779	760	9.9	9.7	483	440	6.1	5.6	–	1	6	0.0	1.3	6.8
Cumberland, MD-WV	1,024	1,129	10.1	11.1	1,239	1,246	12.3	12.2	10	6	11	9.8	5.3	8.9
Dallas-Fort Worth-Arlington, TX	96,375	92,310	17.6	17.9	33,235	31,737	6.1	6.1	613	494	681	6.4	5.4	9.0
Dallas-Plano-Irving, TX	65,730	63,208	17.9	18.3	21,055	20,177	5.7	5.8	401	314	428	6.1	5.0	8.5
Fort Worth-Arlington, TX	30,645	29,102	16.9	17.0	12,180	11,560	6.7	6.8	212	180	253	6.9	6.2	9.9
Dalton, GA	2,437	2,341	19.4	19.5	960	974	7.7	8.1	15	11	11	6.2	4.7	6.3
Danville, IL	1,100	1,208	13.2	14.4	1,013	939	12.2	11.2	6	11	12	5.5	9.1	9.5
Danville, VA	1,246	1,333	11.4	12.1	1,394	1,330	12.8	12.1	11	12	20	8.8	9.0	13.3
Davenport-Moline-Rock Island, IA-IL	4,963	5,047	13.2	13.4	3,580	3,521	9.5	9.4	24	49	54	4.8	9.7	9.9
Dayton, OH	10,682	11,395	12.6	13.4	8,153	8,141	9.6	9.6	76	82	111	7.1	7.2	8.7
Decatur, AL	1,868	2,019	12.8	13.8	1,397	1,400	9.5	9.6	10	16	15	5.4	7.9	7.5
Decatur, IL	1,466	1,445	13.0	12.6	1,181	1,153	10.5	10.1	9	11	20	6.1	7.6	11.6
Deltona-Daytona Beach-Ormond Beach, FL	4,533	4,456	9.9	10.1	6,108	5,694	13.3	12.8	28	39	39	6.2	8.8	8.2
Denver-Aurora, CO[4]	37,297	35,021	16.4	16.2	14,005	13,078	6.2	6.1	218	209	259	5.8	6.0	9.3
Des Moines, IA	7,590	7,630	15.3	15.8	3,800	3,731	7.7	7.8	39	55	59	5.1	7.2	9.0
Detroit-Warren-Livonia, MI	59,672	63,070	13.3	14.2	39,682	39,407	8.9	8.9	517	541	884	8.7	8.6	12.0
Detroit-Livonia-Dearborn, MI	29,281	31,149	14.4	15.1	20,016	20,299	9.8	9.8	343	338	661	11.7	10.9	16.2
Warren-Farmington Hills-Troy, MI	30,391	31,921	12.5	13.3	19,666	19,108	8.1	8.0	174	203	223	5.7	6.4	6.8
Dothan, AL	1,772	1,903	13.4	14.5	1,321	1,389	10.0	10.6	14	18	16	7.9	9.5	8.7
Dover, DE	1,886	1,942	14.3	15.3	1,120	1,024	8.5	8.1	27	21	29	14.3	10.8	14.2
Dubuque, IA	1,151	1,221	12.9	13.7	785	855	8.8	9.6	5	9	16	4.3	7.4	12.7
Duluth, MN-WI	2,872	2,927	10.4	10.6	3,005	2,949	10.9	10.7	19	19	25	6.6	6.5	7.7
Durham, NC	6,491	6,196	14.7	14.5	3,229	3,308	7.3	7.8	52	45	57	8.0	7.3	10.7
Eau Claire, WI	1,797	1,790	11.9	12.1	1,237	1,177	8.2	7.9	12	4	9	6.7	2.2	4.7
El Centro, CA	2,674	2,640	18.4	18.5	964	862	6.6	6.1	10	12	24	3.7	4.5	8.3
Elizabethtown, KY	1,690	1,652	15.5	15.4	866	845	8.0	7.9	12	14	12	7.1	8.5	6.2
Elkhart-Goshen, IN	3,004	3,305	16.2	18.1	1,472	1,468	7.9	8.0	19	31	27	6.3	9.4	9.9
Elmira, NY	1,072	1,089	11.8	12.0	912	962	10.0	10.6	7	3	15	6.5	2.8	10.8
El Paso, TX	14,061	14,293	20.3	21.0	4,245	3,948	6.1	5.8	51	63	90	3.6	4.4	6.0
Erie, PA	3,374	3,479	11.9	12.4	2,727	2,745	9.7	9.8	38	23	58	11.3	6.6	13.8
Eugene-Springfield, OR	3,495	3,705	10.7	11.5	2,980	2,845	9.1	8.8	30	28	25	8.6	7.6	6.4
Evansville, IN-KY	4,348	4,483	12.6	13.1	3,500	3,544	10.2	10.3	37	34	52	8.5	7.6	10.8
Fairbanks, AK	1,515	1,538	17.9	18.6	281	330	3.3	4.0	7	12	14	4.6	7.8	8.1
Fargo, ND-MN	2,298	2,208	13.0	12.7	1,233	1,132	7.0	6.5	6	26	18	2.6	11.8	8.1
Farmington, NM	1,976	1,953	16.5	17.2	773	709	6.4	6.2	13	13	23	6.6	6.7	11.8
Fayetteville, NC	6,106	6,334	17.9	18.8	2,272	2,262	6.7	6.7	70	64	57	11.5	10.1	9.2
Fayetteville-Springdale-Rogers, AR-MO	5,999	5,378	16.3	15.5	2,848	2,793	7.8	8.0	36	32	33	6.0	6.0	9.0
Flagstaff, AZ	1,883	1,876	15.7	16.1	602	507	5.0	4.4	13	16	22	6.9	8.5	11.2
Flint, MI	6,219	6,360	14.1	14.6	4,117	3,920	9.3	9.0	81	78	93	13.0	12.3	12.1
Florence, SC	2,730	2,820	14.0	14.6	2,048	2,069	10.5	10.7	29	34	50	10.6	12.1	17.0
Florence-Muscle Shoals, AL	1,548	1,662	10.9	11.6	1,562	1,511	11.0	10.6	7	10	11	4.5	6.0	6.1
Fond du Lac, WI	1,132	1,151	11.6	11.8	877	908	9.0	9.3	6	8	9	5.3	7.0	7.1
Fort Collins-Loveland, CO	3,269	3,254	12.4	12.9	1,557	1,498	5.9	6.0	16	16	17	4.9	4.9	6.1
Fort Smith, AR-OK	4,132	4,165	14.9	15.2	2,882	2,757	10.4	10.1	22	31	22	5.3	7.4	5.9
Fort Walton Beach-Crestview-Destin, FL	2,455	2,363	14.0	13.9	1,361	1,327	7.8	7.8	24	15	22	9.8	6.3	8.8
Fort Wayne, IN	5,915	5,998	14.9	15.4	3,233	3,095	8.1	7.9	38	40	53	6.4	6.7	8.6
Fresno, CA	14,770	14,265	17.8	17.8	5,803	5,379	7.0	6.7	102	102	132	6.9	7.2	8.5
Gadsden, AL	1,265	1,384	12.3	13.4	1,319	1,320	12.8	12.8	5	11	19	4.0	7.9	14.1
Gainesville, FL	2,603	2,784	11.0	12.0	1,657	1,706	7.0	7.3	34	31	33	13.1	11.1	11.5
Gainesville, GA	2,923	2,887	19.3	20.7	1,076	1,021	7.1	7.3	25	16	13	8.6	5.5	7.5
Glens Falls, NY	1,291	1,239	10.3	10.0	1,147	1,228	9.1	9.9	8	6	13	6.2	4.8	7.5
Goldsboro, NC	1,659	1,764	14.7	15.6	1,036	1,098	9.2	9.7	16	20	20	9.6	11.3	11.7
Grand Forks, ND-MN	1,232	1,257	12.9	12.9	833	786	8.7	8.1	2	6	14	1.6	4.8	8.3
Grand Junction, CO	1,554	1,473	12.7	12.7	1,222	1,136	10.0	9.8	16	8	12	10.3	5.4	9.4
Grand Rapids-Wyoming, MI	11,273	11,803	14.9	15.7	5,416	5,484	7.2	7.4	85	106	106	7.5	9.0	8.8
Great Falls, MT	1,081	1,008	13.6	12.5	763	792	9.6	9.9	9	10	12	8.3	9.9	8.9
Greeley, CO[4]	3,532	3,171	17.3	17.5	1,220	1,112	6.0	6.1	21	18	17	5.9	5.7	7.7
Green Bay, WI	3,901	3,819	13.5	13.5	2,079	2,139	7.2	7.6	18	24	26	4.6	6.3	6.8
Greensboro-High Point, NC	8,732	9,250	13.3	14.4	5,695	5,770	8.7	9.0	84	71	77	9.6	7.7	9.7
Greenville, NC	2,225	2,290	14.2	15.0	1,238	1,234	7.9	8.1	26	19	30	11.7	8.3	15.8

See footnotes at end of table.

Metropolitan statistical area **Metropolitan statistical area with metropolitan divisions** *Metropolitan division*	Births				Deaths				Infant deaths[2]					
	Number		Rate per 1,000[1]		Number		Rate per 1,000[1]		Number			Rate per 1,000 live births[3]		
	2002	2000	2002	2000	2002	2000	2002	2000	2002	2000	1990	2002	2000	1990
Greenville, SC	7,452	7,543	13.0	13.5	5,021	4,968	8.8	8.9	57	41	76	7.6	5.4	10.5
Gulfport-Biloxi, MS	3,670	3,783	14.7	15.4	2,442	2,428	9.8	9.9	27	40	34	7.4	10.6	9.7
Hagerstown-Martinsburg, MD-WV	2,965	2,820	12.8	12.7	2,137	2,064	9.2	9.3	29	18	20	9.8	6.4	7.3
Hanford-Corcoran, CA	2,311	2,180	17.2	16.8	732	714	5.4	5.5	15	13	28	6.5	6.0	12.3
Harrisburg-Carlisle, PA	5,808	5,878	11.3	11.5	4,859	4,800	9.4	9.4	44	35	57	7.6	6.0	8.4
Harrisonburg, VA	1,406	1,311	12.8	12.1	803	835	7.3	7.7	6	5	3	4.3	3.8	2.6
Hartford-West Hartford-East Hartford, CT	13,191	14,646	11.3	12.8	10,045	10,568	8.6	9.2	91	124	147	6.9	8.5	8.8
Hattiesburg, MS	1,899	1,870	15.0	15.1	1,178	1,175	9.3	9.5	16	18	22	8.4	9.6	12.2
Hickory-Lenoir-Morganton, NC	4,472	4,828	12.8	14.1	3,116	3,187	8.9	9.3	30	41	45	6.7	8.5	10.7
Hinesville-Fort Stewart, GA	1,588	1,620	22.2	22.5	333	346	4.7	4.8	23	22	17	14.5	13.6	10.5
Holland-Grand Haven, MI	3,486	3,667	14.1	15.4	1,537	1,466	6.2	6.2	23	26	21	6.6	7.1	6.6
Honolulu, HI	12,868	12,651	14.5	14.4	6,226	5,835	7.0	6.7	99	105	103	7.7	8.3	6.7
Hot Springs, AR	1,007	1,016	11.2	11.5	1,307	1,229	14.5	14.0	8	7	6	7.9	6.9	6.5
Houma-Bayou Cane-Thibodaux, LA	2,928	3,016	14.9	15.5	1,574	1,477	8.0	7.6	29	38	33	9.9	12.6	10.1
Houston-Sugar Land-Baytown, TX	86,712	83,446	17.5	17.7	30,372	28,319	6.1	6.0	540	431	605	6.2	5.2	8.2
Huntington-Ashland, WV-KY-OH	3,414	3,471	11.9	12.0	3,483	3,395	12.2	11.8	30	25	28	8.8	7.2	7.8
Huntsville, AL	4,354	4,710	12.3	13.8	2,764	2,761	7.8	8.1	40	25	45	9.2	5.3	9.3
Idaho Falls, ID	1,905	1,789	18.1	17.6	712	635	6.8	6.2	6	12	14	3.1	6.7	8.3
Indianapolis, IN	24,471	24,432	15.5	16.0	12,440	12,492	7.9	8.2	194	200	253	7.9	8.2	11.2
Iowa City, IA	1,751	1,672	13.0	12.7	785	709	5.8	5.4	6	8	14	3.4	4.8	8.2
Ithaca, NY	832	839	8.5	8.7	566	573	5.8	5.9	3	11	8	3.6	13.1	7.0
Jackson, MI	2,005	2,122	12.4	13.4	1,486	1,442	9.2	9.1	11	21	25	5.5	9.9	10.4
Jackson, MS	7,496	7,851	14.8	15.8	4,524	4,335	9.0	8.7	76	93	103	10.1	11.8	13.3
Jackson, TN	1,498	1,569	13.7	14.6	1,016	1,074	9.3	10.0	16	16	17	10.7	10.2	12.0
Jacksonville, FL	16,356	16,438	13.9	14.6	9,813	9,579	8.4	8.5	144	147	184	8.8	8.9	11.0
Jacksonville, NC	3,114	3,331	20.8	22.2	757	751	5.1	5.0	26	29	42	8.3	8.7	12.2
Janesville, WI	1,968	2,077	12.8	13.6	1,301	1,335	8.4	8.8	13	20	20	6.6	9.6	9.2
Jefferson City, MO	1,781	1,728	12.5	12.3	1,205	1,239	8.5	8.8	11	19	17	6.2	11.0	9.7
Johnson City, TN	2,056	2,113	11.2	11.6	2,030	1,952	11.0	10.7	15	17	18	7.3	8.0	9.2
Johnstown, PA	1,453	1,570	9.7	10.3	1,919	2,014	12.8	13.2	11	16	15	7.6	10.2	7.9
Jonesboro, AR	1,542	1,646	14.1	15.3	1,135	1,040	10.4	9.7	15	16	14	9.7	9.7	9.8
Joplin, MO	2,441	2,423	15.2	15.4	1,627	1,640	10.2	10.4	23	18	14	9.4	7.4	7.2
Kalamazoo-Portage, MI	4,076	4,260	12.8	13.5	2,651	2,548	8.3	8.1	40	31	46	9.8	7.3	9.8
Kankakee-Bradley, IL	1,578	1,562	15.0	15.0	1,053	1,120	10.0	10.8	18	21	19	11.4	13.4	11.1
Kansas City, MO-KS	28,438	27,811	15.1	15.1	15,552	15,093	8.2	8.2	194	169	241	6.8	6.1	8.9
Kennewick-Richland-Pasco, WA	3,355	3,176	16.5	16.6	1,344	1,255	6.6	6.5	19	23	30	5.7	7.2	10.6
Killeen-Temple-Fort Hood, TX	6,761	6,637	20.0	20.1	2,204	2,093	6.5	6.3	64	48	55	9.5	7.2	9.4
Kingsport-Bristol-Bristol, TN-VA	3,176	3,429	10.6	11.5	3,424	3,309	11.5	11.1	21	27	24	6.6	7.9	7.1
Kingston, NY	1,795	1,781	9.9	10.0	1,632	1,553	9.0	8.7	5	10	11	2.8	5.6	4.3
Knoxville, TN	7,541	7,606	11.9	12.3	6,334	6,037	10.0	9.8	47	37	61	6.2	4.9	8.3
Kokomo, IN	1,339	1,363	13.2	13.4	1,097	1,019	10.8	10.0	9	10	18	6.7	7.3	12.2
La Crosse, WI-MN	1,442	1,452	11.3	11.4	1,067	1,083	8.3	8.5	7	10	7	4.9	6.9	4.1
Lafayette, IN	2,296	2,296	12.8	12.8	1,246	1,314	6.9	7.4	22	22	17	9.6	9.6	7.7
Lafayette, LA	3,660	3,631	15.1	15.2	1,845	1,781	7.6	7.4	32	31	34	8.7	8.5	9.4
Lake Charles, LA	2,823	2,921	14.6	15.1	1,773	1,749	9.2	9.0	31	28	32	11.0	9.6	11.1
Lakeland, FL	6,818	6,877	13.6	14.2	5,291	5,316	10.6	11.0	66	48	67	9.7	7.0	10.3
Lancaster, PA	6,752	6,871	14.1	14.6	4,313	4,265	9.0	9.1	53	45	72	7.8	6.5	9.9
Lansing-East Lansing, MI	5,692	5,867	12.6	13.1	3,175	3,168	7.0	7.1	37	41	72	6.5	7.0	10.8
Laredo, TX	5,941	5,777	28.7	29.9	1,004	904	4.9	4.7	28	35	23	4.7	6.1	5.9
Las Cruces, NM	3,078	3,034	17.2	17.4	1,170	1,057	6.6	6.1	13	14	27	4.2	4.6	9.3
Las Vegas-Paradise, NV	23,815	22,304	15.7	16.2	11,463	10,320	7.6	7.5	150	143	117	6.3	6.4	8.6
Lawrence, KS	1,208	1,182	11.9	11.8	558	540	5.5	5.4	8	7	5	6.6	5.9	4.7
Lawton, OK	1,904	1,934	17.0	16.8	875	808	7.8	7.0	19	7	15	10.0	3.6	7.0
Lebanon, PA	1,534	1,447	12.6	12.0	1,262	1,285	10.4	10.7	11	8	14	7.2	5.5	9.2
Lewiston, ID-WA	698	673	12.1	11.6	668	595	11.6	10.3	2	6	8	2.9	8.9	11.3
Lewiston-Auburn, ME	1,256	1,136	11.9	10.9	1,045	1,023	9.9	9.9	5	9	8	4.0	7.9	5.3
Lexington-Fayette, KY	5,628	5,755	13.5	14.1	3,361	3,244	8.1	7.9	32	50	30	5.7	8.7	5.7
Lima, OH	1,485	1,582	13.7	14.6	1,119	1,116	10.3	10.3	12	14	18	8.1	8.8	9.9
Lincoln, NE	3,981	3,966	14.6	14.9	1,902	1,798	7.0	6.7	28	23	23	7.0	5.8	7.0
Little Rock-North Little Rock, AR	9,001	9,102	14.5	14.9	5,406	5,317	8.7	8.7	85	88	88	9.4	9.7	9.9
Logan, UT-ID	2,526	2,405	23.5	23.4	518	530	4.8	5.2	16	12	11	6.3	5.0	5.9
Longview, TX	3,012	2,831	15.3	14.6	2,106	2,208	10.7	11.4	23	28	28	7.6	9.9	9.9
Longview, WA	1,243	1,290	13.1	13.9	983	953	10.4	10.3	9	11	14	7.2	8.5	10.3
Los Angeles-Long Beach-Santa Ana, CA	196,006	204,530	15.4	16.5	76,758	75,957	6.0	6.1	1,049	1,012	2,031	5.4	4.9	7.9
Los Angeles-Long Beach-Glendale, CA	151,192	157,508	15.5	16.5	59,862	59,352	6.1	6.2	831	780	1634	5.5	5.0	8.0
Santa Ana-Anaheim-Irvine, CA	44,814	47,022	15.3	16.5	16,896	16,605	5.8	5.8	218	232	397	4.9	4.9	7.7
Louisville, KY-IN	15,709	16,341	13.3	14.1	11,247	11,069	9.5	9.5	106	112	139	6.7	6.9	8.7
Lubbock, TX	4,042	3,975	15.9	15.9	2,059	2,011	8.1	8.1	15	31	36	3.7	7.8	8.8
Lynchburg, VA	2,597	2,730	11.3	11.9	2,267	2,291	9.9	10.0	14	19	20	5.4	7.0	6.8
Macon, GA	3,286	3,363	14.6	15.1	2,276	2,256	10.1	10.1	39	36	60	11.9	10.7	17.2
Madera, CA	2,146	2,109	16.7	17.1	880	883	6.8	7.2	13	12	6	6.1	5.7	3.3
Madison, WI	6,488	6,439	12.5	12.8	3,386	3,219	6.5	6.4	39	31	42	6.0	4.8	6.7

See footnotes at end of table.

State and Metropolitan Area Data Book: 2006

U.S. Census Bureau

Metropolitan statistical area **Metropolitan statistical area with metropolitan divisions** *Metropolitan division*	Births				Deaths				Infant deaths[2]					
	Number		Rate per 1,000[1]		Number		Rate per 1,000[1]		Number			Rate per 1,000 live births[3]		
	2002	2000	2002	2000	2002	2000	2002	2000	2002	2000	1990	2002	2000	1990
Manchester-Nashua, NH...............	5,043	5,016	12.9	13.2	2,781	2,788	7.1	7.3	22	27	43	4.4	5.4	7.4
Mansfield, OH........................	1,534	1,598	11.9	12.4	1,226	1,211	9.6	9.4	16	10	25	10.4	6.3	13.3
McAllen-Edinburg-Mission, TX........	15,675	15,361	25.6	27.0	3,038	2,729	5.0	4.8	67	77	58	4.3	5.0	5.4
Medford, OR.........................	2,112	2,051	11.3	11.3	1,946	1,878	10.4	10.4	18	6	18	8.5	2.9	8.6
Memphis, TN-MS-AR..................	19,073	19,784	15.5	16.4	10,827	10,904	8.8	9.0	255	244	284	13.4	12.3	14.1
Merced, CA..........................	4,027	3,875	17.9	18.4	1,451	1,320	6.5	6.3	28	19	33	7.0	4.9	7.6
Miami-Fort Lauderdale-Miami Beach, FL.............	68,146	67,725	13.1	13.5	48,064	47,632	9.2	9.5	444	410	646	6.5	6.1	9.8
Fort Lauderdale-Pompano Beach-Deerfield Beach, F	22,134	22,093	13.0	13.6	16,259	16,023	9.5	9.9	133	129	174	6.0	5.8	9.3
Miami-Miami Beach-Kendall, FL	32,125	32,306	13.9	14.3	18,176	18,540	7.9	8.2	192	186	337	6.0	5.8	9.8
West Palm Beach-Boca Raton-Boynton Beach, FL	13,887	13,326	11.7	11.8	13,629	13,069	11.5	11.6	119	95	135	8.6	7.1	10.4
Michigan City-La Porte, IN.............	1,363	1,442	12.4	13.1	1,015	1,069	9.2	9.7	12	10	12	8.8	6.9	7.7
Midland, TX..........................	1,851	1,844	15.8	15.9	883	894	7.5	7.7	11	12	18	5.9	6.5	8.4
Milwaukee-Waukesha-West Allis, WI	21,060	21,574	13.9	14.4	13,302	13,251	8.8	8.8	178	180	222	8.5	8.3	9.5
Minneapolis-St. Paul-Bloomington, MN-WI	44,542	44,288	14.6	14.9	19,258	18,856	6.3	6.4	214	221	332	4.8	5.0	7.7
Missoula, MT........................	1,117	1,142	11.4	11.9	660	642	6.7	6.7	9	7	14	8.1	6.1	12.8
Mobile, AL...........................	5,830	6,359	14.6	15.9	3,934	3,995	9.8	10.0	60	68	72	10.3	10.7	10.9
Modesto, CA.........................	7,932	7,249	16.5	16.2	3,736	3,412	7.8	7.6	63	51	64	7.9	7.0	8.1
Monroe, LA..........................	2,561	2,700	15.1	15.9	1,566	1,671	9.2	9.8	26	35	33	10.2	13.0	12.1
Monroe, MI..........................	1,777	1,859	11.9	12.7	1,214	1,172	8.1	8.0	16	9	9	9.0	4.8	4.8
Montgomery, AL......................	5,057	5,449	14.4	15.7	3,183	3,003	9.1	8.7	52	36	68	10.3	6.6	12.3
Morgantown, WV.....................	1,233	1,133	11.0	10.2	1,008	1,032	9.0	9.3	8	6	18	6.5	5.3	13.9
Morristown, TN.......................	1,621	1,642	12.9	13.3	1,309	1,248	10.4	10.1	7	9	15	4.3	5.5	11.1
Mount Vernon-Anacortes, WA..........	1,390	1,396	13.0	13.6	951	940	8.9	9.1	6	11	10	4.3	7.9	8.1
Muncie, IN...........................	1,302	1,435	10.9	12.1	1,183	1,188	9.9	10.0	19	21	17	14.6	14.6	10.9
Muskegon-Norton Shores, MI..........	2,313	2,393	13.4	14.1	1,573	1,623	9.1	9.5	14	18	24	6.1	7.5	8.7
Myrtle Beach-Conway-North Myrtle Beach, SC	2,531	2,570	12.3	13.1	1,921	1,941	9.3	9.9	27	23	24	10.7	8.9	10.3
Napa, CA............................	1,565	1,496	12.0	12.0	1,269	1,300	9.8	10.5	6	6	10	3.8	4.0	6.7
Naples-Marco Island, FL..............	3,600	3,067	13.1	12.2	2,396	2,363	8.7	9.4	13	17	19	3.6	5.5	7.6
Nashville-Davidson—Murfreesboro, TN	19,393	19,521	14.3	14.9	11,039	10,544	8.2	8.0	165	136	147	8.5	7.0	8.7
New Haven-Milford, CT................	10,168	10,139	12.2	12.3	7,843	7,973	9.4	9.7	65	65	98	6.4	6.4	7.9
New Orleans-Metairie-Kenner, LA......	18,553	19,411	14.1	14.7	12,515	12,137	9.5	9.2	185	133	250	10.0	6.9	11.4
New York-Northern New Jersey-Long Island, NY-NJ-PA ..	259,620	264,414	14.0	14.4	145,918	147,476	7.8	8.0	1390	1573	2804	5.4	5.9	9.9
Edison, NJ.	30,011	29,558	13.4	13.6	19,954	20,254	8.9	9.3	116	155	219	3.9	5.2	7.5
Nassau-Suffolk, NY.	36,204	37,295	13.0	13.5	22,931	22,431	8.2	8.1	182	190	320	5.0	5.1	8.1
Newark-Union, NJ-PA	29,495	29,966	13.8	14.3	17,269	17,723	8.1	8.4	165	194	306	5.6	6.5	9.7
New York-White Plains-Wayne, NY-NJ	163,910	167,595	14.4	14.8	85,764	87,068	7.5	7.7	927	1034	1959	5.7	6.2	10.7
Niles-Benton Harbor, MI	2,034	2,235	12.5	13.8	1,572	1,604	9.7	9.9	18	19	41	8.8	8.5	15.6
Norwich-New London, CT.............	3,577	2,455	13.6	9.5	2,386	1,957	9.1	7.6	23	18	37	6.4	7.3	9.1
Ocala, FL............................	2,912	2,902	10.7	11.2	3,697	3,389	13.6	13.1	28	19	26	9.6	6.5	9.4
Ocean City, NJ.......................	1,021	1,047	10.0	10.2	1,301	1,361	12.8	13.3	6	8	10	5.9	7.6	7.3
Odessa, TX..........................	2,279	2,147	18.6	17.7	1,053	1,015	8.6	8.4	19	22	17	8.3	10.2	7.5
Ogden-Clearfield, UT.................	9,246	8,877	20.1	20.1	2,619	2,494	5.7	5.6	40	49	60	4.3	5.5	8.5
Oklahoma City, OK...................	16,956	16,266	15.1	14.8	9,834	9,719	8.8	8.9	125	158	169	7.4	9.7	11.3
Olympia, WA.........................	2,440	2,549	11.2	12.3	1,624	1,550	7.5	7.5	16	10	16	6.6	3.9	6.8
Omaha-Council Bluffs, NE-IA..........	12,615	11,964	16.1	15.6	6,061	5,757	7.7	7.5	97	91	85	7.7	7.6	7.2
Orlando-Kissimee, FL.................	24,174	23,643	13.8	14.4	13,629	13,032	7.8	7.9	171	131	155	7.1	5.5	7.6
Oshkosh-Neenah, WI.................	1,846	1,926	11.6	12.3	1,282	1,196	8.1	7.6	12	16	10	6.5	8.3	5.2
Owensboro, KY.......................	1,489	1,607	13.5	14.6	1,090	1,119	9.9	10.2	12	13	12	8.1	8.1	7.9
Oxnard-Thousand Oaks-Ventura, CA....	11,603	11,768	14.9	15.6	4,846	4,802	6.2	6.4	58	48	99	5.0	4.1	7.8
Palm Bay-Melbourne-Titusville, FL.....	4,807	5,015	9.7	10.5	5,507	5,282	11.1	11.1	43	26	32	8.9	5.2	5.6
Panama City-Lynn Haven, FL..........	1,997	2,012	13.1	13.6	1,492	1,433	9.8	9.7	23	10	22	11.5	5.0	10.7
Parkersburg-Marietta-Vienna, WV-OH...	1,856	1,858	11.3	11.3	1,852	1,863	11.3	11.3	15	9	24	8.1	4.8	11.1
Pascagoula, MS......................	2,164	2,257	14.1	15.0	1,392	1,392	9.1	9.2	16	17	11	7.4	7.5	5.3
Pensacola-Ferry Pass-Brent, FL.......	5,418	5,346	12.8	13.0	3,828	3,725	9.0	9.0	46	54	51	8.5	10.1	8.7
Peoria, IL............................	4,837	4,913	13.2	13.4	3,759	3,611	10.3	9.8	41	45	61	8.5	9.2	11.6
Philadelphia-Camden-Wilmington, PA-NJ-DE-MD.......	74,756	76,079	13.0	13.4	54,477	55,252	9.5	9.7	604	573	958	8.1	7.5	10.6
Camden, NJ.	15,297	15,437	12.6	13.0	10,965	10,544	9.0	8.9	121	100	159	7.9	6.5	8.6
Philadelphia, PA.	50,418	51,569	13.0	13.4	38,116	39,209	9.9	10.2	415	390	703	8.2	7.6	11.3
Wilmington, DE-MD-NJ.	9,041	9,073	13.6	13.9	5,396	5,499	8.1	8.5	68	83	96	7.5	9.1	10.2
Phoenix-Mesa-Scottsdale, AZ..........	59,408	57,119	17.0	17.6	25,363	24,272	7.3	7.5	379	383	380	6.4	6.7	8.9
Pine Bluff, AR........................	1,456	1,554	13.7	14.5	1,162	1,134	10.9	10.6	15	13	18	10.3	8.4	10.4
Pittsburgh, PA........................	25,044	26,235	10.4	10.8	28,890	28,229	12.0	11.6	181	215	289	7.2	8.2	9.0
Pittsfield, MA.........................	1,234	1,205	9.3	8.9	1,590	1,560	11.9	11.6	7	3	12	5.7	2.5	6.6
Pocatello, ID.........................	1,539	1,494	18.5	18.0	655	606	7.9	7.3	9	9	11	5.8	6.0	8.7
Portland-South Portland-Biddeford, ME..	5,475	5,478	10.9	11.2	4,476	4,295	8.9	8.8	24	29	41	4.4	5.3	6.2
Portland-Vancouver-Beaverton, OR-WA..	28,024	28,467	13.9	14.8	14,976	14,349	7.4	7.4	137	134	194	4.9	4.7	7.9
Port St. Lucie-Fort Pierce, FL.........	3,488	3,491	10.3	10.9	3,903	3,962	11.6	12.4	30	26	42	8.6	7.4	11.1
Poughkeepsie-Newburgh-Middletown, NY	8,326	8,364	12.9	13.5	4,875	4,689	7.6	7.5	40	44	64	4.8	5.3	6.9
Prescott, AZ.........................	1,920	1,755	10.7	10.5	2,051	1,914	11.4	11.4	9	13	8	4.7	7.4	6.5
Providence-New Bedford-Fall River, RI-MA.	19,576	19,258	12.1	12.2	15,503	15,137	9.6	9.6	126	109	157	6.4	5.7	6.8
Provo-Orem, UT......................	10,773	10,050	26.9	26.7	1,772	1,607	4.4	4.3	64	51	47	5.9	5.1	6.9
Pueblo, CO..........................	2,061	1,945	14.0	13.7	1,505	1,387	10.2	9.8	17	8	17	8.2	4.1	9.6

See footnotes at end of table.

Table B-5. Metropolitan Areas — **Births, Deaths, Infant Deaths**—Con.

Metropolitan statistical area **Metropolitan statistical area with metropolitan divisions** *Metropolitan division*	Births				Deaths				Infant deaths[2]					
	Number		Rate per 1,000[1]		Number		Rate per 1,000[1]		Number			Rate per 1,000 live births[3]		
	2002	2000	2002	2000	2002	2000	2002	2000	2002	2000	1990	2002	2000	1990
Punta Gorda, FL	994	1,034	6.6	7.3	2,287	2,206	15.3	15.6	8	8	9	8.0	7.7	8.5
Racine, WI	2,543	2,651	13.3	14.0	1,489	1,614	7.8	8.5	28	17	26	11.0	6.4	9.6
Raleigh-Cary, NC	13,650	12,995	15.9	16.3	4,768	4,662	5.5	5.8	78	97	86	5.7	7.5	9.7
Rapid City, SD	1,792	1,726	15.5	15.3	881	828	7.6	7.3	13	17	16	7.3	9.8	7.8
Reading, PA	4,725	4,711	12.4	12.6	3,642	3,624	9.5	9.7	43	31	44	9.1	6.6	8.9
Redding, CA	1,963	1,831	11.4	11.2	1,931	1,651	11.2	10.1	15	11	20	7.6	6.0	8.7
Reno-Sparks, NV	5,361	5,014	14.7	14.6	2,767	2,557	7.6	7.5	21	34	39	3.9	6.8	8.6
Richmond, VA	14,821	14,884	13.2	13.6	9,707	9,731	8.6	8.9	139	124	176	9.4	8.3	11.3
Riverside-San Bernardino-Ontario, CA	56,393	53,568	16.1	16.5	24,638	23,333	7.0	7.2	399	368	550	7.1	6.9	9.4
Roanoke, VA	3,219	3,392	11.1	11.8	3,234	3,141	11.2	10.9	33	30	42	10.3	8.8	11.6
Rochester, MN	2,536	2,399	14.9	14.7	1,148	1,065	6.8	6.5	22	15	20	8.7	6.3	8.3
Rochester, NY	12,284	13,037	11.8	12.6	8,988	8,981	8.6	8.7	83	109	156	6.8	8.4	9.5
Rockford, IL	4,603	4,610	14.1	14.4	2,848	2,790	8.7	8.7	44	43	41	9.6	9.3	8.9
Rocky Mount, NC	1,947	2,158	13.5	15.1	1,526	1,535	10.6	10.7	18	27	22	9.2	12.5	9.8
Rome, GA	1,357	1,329	14.7	14.7	1,013	1,019	10.9	11.3	11	11	21	8.1	8.3	15.7
Sacramento—Arden-Arcade—Roseville, CA . .	26,913	25,169	14.0	14.0	14,091	13,145	7.3	7.3	158	146	225	5.9	5.8	8.5
Saginaw-Saginaw Township North, MI	2,657	2,831	12.7	13.5	2,030	2,031	9.7	9.7	24	28	46	9.0	9.9	12.4
St. Cloud, MN	2,341	2,324	13.4	13.9	1,117	1,126	6.4	6.7	12	15	19	5.1	6.5	8.5
St. George, UT	1,979	1,814	19.9	20.1	739	670	7.4	7.4	13	9	6	6.6	5.0	6.4
St. Joseph, MO-KS	1,510	1,567	12.3	12.8	1,292	1,316	10.5	10.8	8	9	13	5.3	5.7	8.0
St. Louis, MO-IL[5]	35,590	36,660	13.0	13.6	26,243	25,357	9.6	9.4	323	287	412	9.1	7.8	9.7
Salem, OR	5,199	5,281	14.5	15.2	3,143	2,917	8.7	8.4	28	33	36	5.4	6.2	7.9
Salinas, CA	6,900	6,717	16.8	16.7	2,403	2,364	5.8	5.9	45	39	61	6.5	5.8	7.7
Salisbury, MD	1,415	1,443	12.7	13.2	1,055	1,100	9.5	10.1	10	19	17	7.1	13.2	11.9
Salt Lake City, UT	20,031	19,766	20.1	20.4	5,568	5,342	5.6	5.5	122	109	119	6.1	5.5	7.6
San Angelo, TX	1,595	1,625	15.2	15.4	1,057	1,036	10.0	9.8	11	18	9	6.9	11.1	5.4
San Antonio, TX	29,414	28,449	16.5	16.6	13,137	12,721	7.4	7.4	207	145	181	7.0	5.1	7.1
San Diego-Carlsbad-San Marcos, CA	43,960	44,337	15.2	15.8	19,481	19,741	6.7	7.0	197	263	367	4.5	5.9	7.2
Sandusky, OH	922	951	11.7	12.0	828	811	10.5	10.2	6	8	10	6.5	8.4	9.3
San Francisco-Oakland-Fremont, CA	56,313	57,297	13.5	13.9	29,520	29,642	7.1	7.2	235	268	449	4.2	4.7	7.4
Oakland-Fremont-Hayward, CA	35,119	35,385	14.3	14.8	16,667	16,565	6.8	6.9	146	168	292	4.2	4.7	7.9
San Francisco-San Mateo-Redwood City, CA .	21,194	21,912	12.4	12.7	12,853	13,077	7.5	7.6	89	100	157	4.2	4.6	6.5
San Jose-Sunnyvale-Santa Clara, CA	28,041	28,562	16.2	16.5	8,941	9,130	5.2	5.3	101	128	159	3.6	4.5	5.5
San Luis Obispo-Paso Robles, CA	2,368	2,436	9.4	9.9	2,042	1,987	8.1	8.1	7	11	26	3.0	4.5	8.6
Santa Barbara-Santa Maria, CA	5,699	5,685	14.2	14.2	2,940	2,932	7.3	7.3	26	33	45	4.6	5.8	6.7
Santa Cruz-Watsonville, CA	3,529	3,675	13.9	14.4	1,626	1,698	6.4	6.6	13	16	20	3.7	4.4	4.6
Santa Fe, NM	1,622	1,640	12.1	12.7	794	764	5.9	5.9	7	13	11	4.3	7.9	7.6
Santa Rosa-Petaluma, CA	5,678	5,652	12.2	12.3	3,875	3,843	8.3	8.4	29	27	29	5.1	4.8	4.7
Sarasota-Bradenton-Venice, FL	6,231	5,957	10.0	10.1	8,079	8,286	13.0	14.0	36	46	65	5.8	7.7	11.4
Savannah, GA	4,563	4,467	15.1	15.2	2,667	2,642	8.8	9.0	47	35	57	10.3	7.8	11.9
Scranton—Wilkes-Barre, PA	5,338	5,475	9.6	9.8	7,442	7,702	13.4	13.7	33	36	41	6.2	6.6	6.0
Seattle-Tacoma-Bellevue, WA	40,254	41,226	12.9	13.5	21,042	20,570	6.7	6.8	222	201	303	5.5	4.9	7.2
Seattle-Bellevue-Everett, WA	30,231	31,049	12.6	13.3	15,600	15,393	6.5	6.6	145	138	205	4.8	4.4	6.6
Tacoma, WA	10,023	10,177	13.7	14.5	5,442	5,177	7.4	7.4	77	63	98	7.7	6.2	9.3
Sheboygan, WI	1,381	1,439	12.2	12.8	1,095	1,084	9.7	9.6	9	14	9	6.5	9.7	6.4
Sherman-Denison, TX	1,530	1,550	13.5	14.0	1,221	1,306	10.7	11.8	8	8	12	5.2	5.2	8.3
Shreveport-Bossier City, LA	5,590	5,788	14.8	15.4	3,700	3,707	9.8	9.9	71	76	68	12.7	13.1	10.9
Sioux City, IA-NE-SD	2,311	2,324	16.2	16.2	1,314	1,300	9.2	9.1	15	10	31	6.5	4.3	14.2
Sioux Falls, SD	3,061	2,835	15.7	15.2	1,404	1,412	7.2	7.5	15	13	26	4.9	4.6	10.5
South Bend-Mishawaka, IN-MI	4,281	4,556	13.5	14.4	2,833	2,873	8.9	9.1	30	33	49	7.0	7.2	10.7
Spartanburg, SC	3,434	3,344	13.2	13.2	2,523	2,602	9.7	10.3	32	22	34	9.3	6.6	9.9
Spokane, WA	5,562	5,667	13.0	13.6	3,705	3,670	8.7	8.8	43	27	37	7.7	4.8	6.6
Springfield, IL	2,587	2,796	12.7	13.9	1,922	1,921	9.4	9.5	22	21	22	8.5	7.5	7.7
Springfield, MA	7,694	7,857	11.2	11.6	6,534	6,722	9.5	9.9	53	31	69	6.9	3.9	7.0
Springfield, MO	4,930	5,075	13.0	13.8	3,627	3,483	9.6	9.5	32	39	31	6.5	7.7	7.5
Springfield, OH	1,826	1,928	12.7	13.3	1,612	1,628	11.2	11.2	10	9	20	5.5	4.7	9.4
State College, PA	1,259	1,278	9.1	9.4	852	864	6.1	6.4	10	3	15	7.9	2.3	9.8
Stockton, CA	10,167	9,606	16.6	17.0	4,604	4,221	7.5	7.5	74	66	86	7.3	6.9	8.7
Sumter, SC	1,575	1,742	15.0	16.6	924	948	8.8	9.1	18	15	23	11.4	8.6	12.1
Syracuse, NY	7,694	8,272	11.8	12.8	5,779	5,762	8.9	8.9	64	67	90	8.3	8.1	8.5
Tallahassee, FL	4,065	4,123	12.5	12.9	2,410	2,375	7.4	7.4	53	42	52	13.0	10.2	13.1
Tampa-St. Petersburg-Clearwater, FL	29,106	29,208	11.7	12.2	28,827	28,577	11.6	11.9	225	209	296	7.7	7.2	10.2
Terre Haute, IN	2,132	2,172	12.6	12.7	2,036	2,074	12.0	12.1	13	16	26	6.1	7.4	11.4
Texarkana, TX-Texarkana, AR	1,711	1,813	13.1	14.0	1,404	1,373	10.7	10.6	10	12	18	5.8	6.6	9.8
Toledo, OH	8,480	9,067	12.9	13.8	6,202	6,366	9.4	9.7	78	63	96	9.2	6.9	9.0
Topeka, KS	3,166	3,089	14.0	13.8	2,238	2,295	9.9	10.2	19	29	28	6.0	9.4	9.0
Trenton-Ewing, NJ	4,599	4,705	12.9	13.4	2,819	3,091	7.9	8.8	33	39	56	7.2	8.3	11.1
Tucson, AZ	12,491	12,516	14.2	14.8	7,745	7,364	8.8	8.7	90	76	93	7.2	6.1	8.1
Tulsa, OK	13,064	13,151	14.9	15.3	8,005	7,832	9.1	9.1	116	110	105	8.9	8.4	8.5
Tuscaloosa, AL	2,521	2,746	13.0	14.3	1,809	1,784	9.3	9.3	35	40	28	13.9	14.6	10.8
Tyler, TX	2,748	2,653	15.2	15.2	1,709	1,703	9.5	9.7	34	25	18	12.4	9.4	7.7

See footnotes at end of table.

State and Metropolitan Area Data Book: 2006

U.S. Census Bureau

Metropolitan statistical area **Metropolitan statistical area with metropolitan divisions** *Metropolitan division*	Births				Deaths				Infant deaths[2]					
	Number		Rate per 1,000[1]		Number		Rate per 1,000[1]		Number			Rate per 1,000 live births[3]		
	2002	2000	2002	2000	2002	2000	2002	2000	2002	2000	1990	2002	2000	1990
Utica-Rome, NY	3,171	3,163	10.6	10.5	3,300	3,303	11.1	11.0	29	32	33	9.1	10.1	7.2
Valdosta, GA	1,799	1,811	14.9	15.1	960	1,022	7.9	8.5	22	20	28	12.2	11.0	16.4
Vallejo-Fairfield, CA	5,864	5,902	14.3	15.0	2,650	2,590	6.5	6.6	47	27	57	8.0	4.6	8.5
Vero Beach, FL	1,056	1,129	9.0	10.0	1,571	1,497	13.3	13.3	6	10	9	5.7	8.9	8.1
Victoria, TX	1,758	1,754	15.6	15.7	985	900	8.7	8.1	14	10	20	8.0	5.7	12.0
Vineland-Millville-Bridgeton, NJ	2,087	2,032	14.1	13.9	1,473	1,531	10.0	10.5	16	27	20	7.7	13.3	8.6
Virginia Beach-Norfolk-Newport News, VA-NC	23,182	23,533	14.4	14.9	12,299	11,895	7.7	7.5	239	210	384	10.3	8.9	14.1
Visalia-Porterville, CA	7,416	7,261	19.5	19.7	2,711	2,646	7.1	7.2	42	49	57	5.7	6.7	7.9
Waco, TX	3,289	3,288	15.1	15.4	1,958	1,990	9.0	9.3	28	25	22	8.5	7.6	7.2
Warner Robins, GA	1,608	1,596	13.8	14.4	843	761	7.2	6.9	13	14	18	8.1	8.8	11.9
Washington-Arlington-Alexandria, DC-VA-MD-WV	75,328	73,578	15.1	15.3	30,421	29,838	6.1	6.2	509	466	764	6.8	6.3	10.6
Bethesda-Gaithersburg-Frederick, MD	16,256	16,070	14.6	15.0	6,541	6,524	5.9	6.1	89	55	111	5.5	3.4	7.2
Washington-Arlington-Alexandria, DC-VA-MD-WV	59,072	57,508	15.2	15.4	23,880	23,314	6.1	6.3	420	411	653	7.1	7.1	11.4
Waterloo-Cedar Falls, IA	1,984	1,936	12.2	11.8	1,448	1,507	8.9	9.2	12	15	18	6.0	7.7	8.6
Wausau, WI	1,504	1,521	11.9	12.1	992	923	7.8	7.3	9	9	16	6.0	5.9	9.5
Weirton-Steubenville, WV-OH	1,288	1,410	10.0	10.7	1,747	1,749	13.5	13.2	6	10	12	4.7	7.1	7.9
Wenatchee, WA	1,354	1,437	13.5	14.5	851	814	8.5	8.2	5	4	13	3.7	2.8	9.0
Wheeling, WV-OH	1,488	1,579	9.9	10.3	1,856	1,912	12.3	12.5	16	13	16	10.8	8.2	8.3
Wichita, KS	9,104	9,384	15.7	16.4	5,009	4,887	8.6	8.6	87	64	103	9.6	6.8	11.3
Wichita Falls, TX	2,086	2,068	14.0	13.6	1,509	1,444	10.1	9.5	20	25	18	9.6	12.1	8.1
Williamsport, PA	1,270	1,342	10.7	11.2	1,208	1,267	10.2	10.6	10	8	14	7.9	6.0	8.2
Wilmington, NC	3,339	3,366	11.6	12.3	2,543	2,436	8.8	8.9	16	19	20	4.8	5.6	6.8
Winchester, VA-WV	1,385	1,404	12.8	13.6	926	835	8.6	8.1	7	8	10	5.1	5.7	7.4
Winston-Salem, NC	5,892	6,122	13.6	14.5	3,928	3,927	9.1	9.3	55	72	61	9.3	11.8	11.4
Worcester, MA	10,066	10,012	13.1	13.3	6,908	6,715	9.0	8.9	56	50	86	5.6	5.0	7.6
Yakima, WA	4,042	4,253	18.0	19.1	1,758	1,694	7.8	7.6	21	31	45	5.2	7.3	11.2
York-Hanover, PA	4,578	4,526	11.7	11.9	3,314	3,353	8.5	8.8	21	26	32	4.6	5.7	6.5
Youngstown-Warren-Boardman, OH-PA	6,161	7,057	10.3	11.7	6,929	7,104	11.6	11.8	62	56	88	10.1	7.9	10.7
Yuba City, CA	2,392	2,225	16.5	16.0	1,240	1,267	8.6	9.1	16	17	25	6.7	7.6	9.5
Yuma, AZ	3,095	3,030	18.6	18.9	1,159	968	7.0	6.0	8	16	20	2.6	5.3	7.4

[1]Per resident population estimated as of July 1 of the year indicated.
[2]Deaths of infants under 1 year.
[3]Infant deaths per 1,000 live registered births.
[4]The Denver-Aurora metropolitan statistical area includes Broomfield County. Broomfield County, CO, was formed from parts of Adams, Boulder, Jefferson, and Weld counties on November 15, 2001, and is coextensive with Broomfield city. For the purposes of defining and presenting data for the Denver-Aurora metropolitan statistical area, Broomfield city is treated as if it were a county when data are available to do so. In many cases, the data will not be available.
[5]The portion of Sullivan city in Crawford County, MO, is legally part of the St. Louis, MO-IL MSA. That portion is not included in these figures for the St. Louis MSA.

Note: Covers metropolitan statistical areas and metropolitan divisions as defined by the Office of Management and Budget as of June 6, 2003, and subsequently updated in December 2003 and November 2004. For more information, see OMB Bulletin 05-02 at <http://www.whitehouse.gov/omb/bulletins/fy05/b05-02_appendix.pdf>.

Survey, Census, or Data Collection Method: For information about these data collections and surveys, see the following organization and Web sites: National Vital Statistics System; <http://www.cdc.gov/nchs> and <http://cdc.gov/nchs/data/statab/techap99/pdf>. Also see Appendix B, Limitations of the Data and Methodology.

Sources: Births—U.S. National Center for Health Statistics, *Vital Statistics of the United States*, Vol. I, Natality, annual, and unpublished data. Deaths and infant deaths—U.S. National Center for Health Statistics, *Vital Statistics of the United States*, Vol. II, Mortality, and unpublished data.

Metropolitan statistical area / **Metropolitan statistical area with metropolitan divisions** / *Metropolitan division*	Physicians, 2003[1] Number	Physicians, 2003[1] Rate per 100,000 persons[2]	Community hospitals, 2003[3] Number	Beds Number	Beds Rate per 100,000 persons[2]	Medicare program enrollment, 2003[4] Total	Medicare Percent change, 2000–2003	Medicare Rate per 100,000 persons[2]	Social security program beneficiaries, December 2004 Number	Rate per 100,000 persons[2]	Percent change, 2000–2004	Retired workers, number	Supplemental security income program recipients, 2004 Number	Rate per 100,000 persons[2]
Abilene, TX	313	198	5	614	388	23,997	2.1	15,168	27,615	17,455	1.9	16,925	3,637	2,294
Akron, OH	1,899	271	7	1,825	260	104,034	1.4	14,841	117,390	16,746	0.2	74,235	12,863	1,832
Albany, GA	340	210	3	635	392	20,735	3.8	12,816	24,920	15,402	1.4	14,015	6,720	4,128
Albany-Schenectady-Troy, NY	2,969	353	11	2,567	305	131,617	1.4	15,657	149,570	17,793	1.6	69,980	17,146	2,028
Albuquerque, NM	2,950	385	11	1,449	189	97,991	7.3	12,782	114,525	14,939	7.8	69,980	16,929	2,166
Alexandria, LA	451	308	5	705	482	23,615	3.2	16,149	26,630	18,211	1.5	13,310	7,020	4,771
Allentown-Bethlehem-Easton, PA-NJ	2,007	261	10	2,206	287	129,191	1.9	16,793	148,525	19,306	3.6	100,460	14,208	1,822
Altoona, PA	340	267	5	469	368	25,027	0.6	19,634	25,500	20,005	3.8	16,115	4,606	3,613
Amarillo, TX	685	293	3	875	375	29,830	3.2	12,772	33,575	14,376	2.9	20,900	3,759	1,592
Ames, IA	173	216	2	292	364	9,020	4.3	11,239	9,865	12,291	3.2	7,080	532	662
Anchorage, AK	991	292	4	734	216	24,346	16.1	7,176	30,395	8,959	13.8	17,780	5,883	1,705
Anderson, IN	200	153	2	231	176	22,828	1.1	17,408	26,740	20,391	1.1	17,040	2,717	2,080
Anderson, SC	354	206	1	420	244	28,369	5.4	16,511	35,690	20,772	5.8	21,805	3,493	2,013
Ann Arbor, MI	3,435	1,023	5	1,515	451	32,544	7.1	9,691	37,955	11,303	11.1	24,415	3,868	1,140
Anniston-Oxford, AL	220	196	3	447	399	21,741	5.0	19,395	25,045	22,342	3.4	13,310	4,579	4,073
Appleton, WI	404	191	4	407	193	25,164	5.7	11,927	29,830	14,138	4.3	19,820	1,902	893
Asheville, NC	1,489	389	5	1,213	317	76,397	5.1	19,970	87,520	22,877	5.1	56,820	8,641	2,231
Athens-Clarke County, GA	406	236	2	617	359	18,697	6.5	10,885	22,305	12,985	7.4	13,365	3,983	2,292
Atlanta-Sandy Springs-Marietta, GA	11,948	259	41	9,061	197	404,586	8.2	8,786	488,925	10,618	8.3	298,555	71,993	1,529
Atlantic City, NJ	644	244	4	806	305	39,508	4.4	14,973	45,140	17,108	5.0	30,435	5,170	1,924
Auburn-Opelika, AL	192	161	1	273	229	11,506	9.2	9,657	15,080	12,657	6.5	8,615	2,747	2,276
Augusta-Richmond County, GA-SC	1,039	204	9	1,830	359	67,240	5.7	13,173	82,715	16,205	5.9	47,615	14,179	2,752
Austin-Round Rock, TX	3,206	233	16	2,448	178	108,630	9.8	7,890	128,630	9,343	11.7	80,265	16,784	1,188
Bakersfield, CA	1,121	157	10	1,498	210	78,689	6.4	11,029	94,080	13,187	6.4	52,445	30,476	4,147
Baltimore-Towson, MD	12,491	475	23	6,889	262	344,409	2.1	13,110	391,010	14,884	1.7	253,210	54,104	2,050
Bangor, ME	489	330	4	466	315	25,114	5.3	16,964	29,005	19,592	5.1	15,970	4,568	3,082
Barnstable Town, MA	844	368	2	306	134	57,608	2.6	25,149	63,295	27,632	2.3	45,965	3,372	1,475
Baton Rouge, LA	1,639	227	13	2,079	288	80,643	5.7	11,178	98,115	13,599	5.8	50,580	19,953	2,738
Battle Creek, MI	256	184	3	517	372	22,972	2.4	16,539	27,245	19,615	3.3	16,645	4,095	2,945
Bay City, MI	172	157	2	335	306	18,613	3.1	16,993	22,420	20,469	3.5	13,500	2,436	2,225
Beaumont-Port Arthur, TX	708	185	10	1,412	369	58,169	1.4	15,193	69,150	18,061	2.4	38,030	10,598	2,764
Bellingham, WA	495	280	1	226	128	23,740	10.3	13,447	27,825	15,761	9.9	18,000	3,202	1,777
Bend, OR	409	316	2	220	170	18,952	12.4	14,630	23,350	18,025	12.3	16,200	1,429	1,063
Billings, MT	536	375	3	670	468	21,715	4.0	15,176	24,460	17,094	4.0	15,945	2,124	1,470
Binghamton, NY	681	272	2	665	265	46,273	1.2	18,465	53,405	21,311	1.1	35,075	6,612	2,653
Birmingham-Hoover, AL	4,187	390	20	4,752	442	163,760	3.4	15,248	195,380	18,192	3.0	104,745	32,866	3,037
Bismarck, ND	340	351	2	475	490	14,558	4.7	15,009	16,180	16,682	2.9	10,280	1,261	1,288
Blacksburg-Christiansburg-Radford, VA	290	192	4	304	202	21,274	4.0	14,105	24,530	16,264	4.8	14,470	2,740	1,816
Bloomington, IN	392	222	2	836	473	22,005	4.3	12,442	26,230	14,831	5.5	16,880	2,248	1,266
Bloomington-Normal, IL	334	213	2	395	252	17,106	4.4	10,905	19,295	12,301	4.3	12,795	1,393	882
Boise City-Nampa, ID	1,195	234	6	1,062	208	56,800	10.1	11,102	67,440	13,182	11.4	43,575	7,377	1,405
Boston-Cambridge-Quincy, MA-NH	**24,178**	**546**	**54**	**11,120**	**251**	**618,468**	**0.7**	**13,960**	**673,925**	**15,211**	**0.0**	**443,955**	**99,614**	**2,251**
Boston-Quincy, MA	*13,213*	*727*	*24*	*6,029*	*332*	*250,643*	*0.2*	*13,789*	*269,875*	*14,847*	*-0.7*	*172,200*	*51,659*	*2,854*
Cambridge-Newton-Framingham, MA	*8,288*	*565*	*14*	*2,925*	*199*	*205,867*	*0.1*	*14,037*	*221,055*	*15,073*	*-0.6*	*151,400*	*24,630*	*1,682*
Essex County, MA	*1,835*	*249*	*10*	*1,566*	*212*	*111,346*	*0.2*	*15,082*	*122,570*	*16,602*	*-0.4*	*80,325*	*20,353*	*2,754*
Rockingham County-Strafford County, NH	*842*	*206*	*6*	*600*	*147*	*50,612*	*7.1*	*12,407*	*60,425*	*14,813*	*7.1*	*40,030*	*2,972*	*724*
Boulder, CO[5]	997	359	3	458	165	30,658	9.4	11,049	27,590	9,944	-1.3	18,360	2,481	890
Bowling Green, KY	274	255	3	777	723	14,869	5.9	13,832	17,595	16,368	5.3	9,920	3,843	3,523
Bremerton-Silverdale, WA	619	258	1	255	106	29,277	7.9	12,211	33,375	13,921	8.2	21,475	3,954	1,653
Bridgeport-Stamford-Norwalk, CT	3,613	402	6	1,707	190	124,839	0.4	13,876	137,055	15,234	-0.4	98,160	10,467	1,159
Brownsville-Harlingen, TX	550	152	5	975	269	38,107	5.6	10,516	44,335	12,235	6.0	24,875	17,613	4,737
Brunswick, GA	255	263	1	278	287	15,187	5.6	15,690	18,850	19,475	5.9	10,895	2,550	2,601
Buffalo-Niagara Falls, NY	4,070	351	14	5,182	447	207,164	-0.7	17,889	234,705	20,268	-0.7	147,130	30,670	2,657
Burlington, NC	247	181	1	319	233	22,534	3.6	16,494	26,055	19,071	4.6	17,635	2,406	1,738
Burlington-South Burlington, VT	1,321	649	2	571	281	23,971	5.5	11,781	28,060	13,790	5.4	17,825	3,398	1,662
Canton-Massillon, OH	934	228	5	1,445	352	71,055	1.9	17,316	77,350	18,850	1.3	49,000	7,233	1,761
Cape Coral-Fort Myers, FL	1,374	279	5	1,735	352	106,110	5.2	21,546	121,810	24,734	5.6	88,610	7,088	1,378
Carson City, NV	161	291	1	131	237	10,596	8.5	19,154	10,440	18,872	5.6	7,350	670	1,197
Casper, WY	180	264	1	205	300	9,929	3.1	14,551	11,425	16,743	0.8	7,450	1,097	1,590
Cedar Rapids, IA	464	191	4	843	347	35,138	3.8	14,480	40,770	16,801	4.0	27,890	2,937	1,201
Champaign-Urbana, IL	631	294	4	676	315	25,466	3.4	11,874	27,955	13,035	3.0	18,090	2,720	1,264
Charleston, WV	996	324	6	1,287	419	58,627	3.0	19,075	68,595	22,318	3.0	35,070	11,931	3,877
Charleston-North Charleston, SC	2,652	463	7	1,586	277	70,506	7.3	12,317	85,015	14,852	7.1	48,895	12,518	2,146
Charlotte-Gastonia-Concord, NC-SC	3,555	247	12	3,300	229	164,334	7.0	11,419	194,700	13,529	7.1	125,155	22,315	1,513
Charlottesville, VA	1,902	1,057	2	687	382	25,054	7.1	13,926	28,210	15,680	5.8	19,155	2,574	1,423
Chattanooga, TN-GA	1,410	290	8	1,971	405	76,843	4.2	15,794	90,790	18,661	4.3	55,275	11,648	2,379
Cheyenne, WY	232	275	1	198	235	11,498	7.4	13,625	12,605	14,937	6.2	8,100	1,110	1,301
Chicago-Naperville-Joliet, IL-IN-WI	**31,150**	**334**	**96**	**24,226**	**260**	**1,089,802**	**2.0**	**11,681**	**1,224,775**	**13,128**	**1.7**	**798,755**	**191,863**	**2,043**
Chicago-Naperville-Joliet, IL	*27,192*	*348*	*79*	*20,569*	*264*	*908,105*	*1.5*	*11,635*	*1,009,620*	*12,936*	*1.2*	*663,660*	*171,166*	*2,181*
Gary, IN	*1,345*	*196*	*9*	*2,595*	*378*	*97,775*	*2.5*	*14,241*	*116,500*	*16,969*	*2.5*	*69,520*	*12,980*	*1,876*
Lake County-Kenosha County, IL-WI	*2,613*	*312*	*8*	*1,062*	*127*	*83,922*	*6.4*	*10,010*	*98,655*	*11,767*	*6.9*	*65,575*	*7,717*	*906*

See footnotes at end of table.

Metropolitan statistical area / Metropolitan statistical area with metropolitan divisions / *Metropolitan division*	Physicians, 2003[1] Number	Physicians Rate per 100,000 persons[2]	Community hospitals, 2003[3] Number	Beds Number	Beds Rate per 100,000 persons[2]	Medicare program enrollment, 2003[4] Total	Medicare Percent change, 2000–2003	Medicare Rate per 100,000 persons[2]	Social security program beneficiaries, December 2004 Number	SS Rate per 100,000 persons[2]	SS Percent change, 2000–2004	Retired workers, number	Supplemental security income program recipients, 2004 Number	SSI Rate per 100,000 persons[2]
Chico, CA	505	239	4	450	213	37,160	2.5	17,599	42,415	20,088	2.1	26,310	10,296	4,835
Cincinnati-Middletown, OH-KY-IN	6,294	307	23	4,886	239	277,165	2.4	13,540	317,280	15,500	2.0	191,010	39,681	1,928
Clarksville, TN-KY	364	154	3	365	155	26,365	6.6	11,160	32,585	13,793	6.6	18,670	5,496	2,301
Cleveland, TN	166	156	3	278	262	16,705	8.9	15,721	20,625	19,410	8.9	11,930	2,800	2,611
Cleveland-Elyria-Mentor, OH	9,240	432	27	7,392	345	337,978	-0.5	15,791	372,305	17,394	-1.0	242,825	48,736	2,281
Coeur d'Alene, ID	257	219	1	246	209	17,754	14.2	15,095	21,605	18,369	14.4	13,615	1,887	1,542
College Station-Bryan, TX	426	227	3	423	225	17,793	6.1	9,462	20,400	10,849	4.4	12,490	3,149	1,662
Colorado Springs, CO	1,338	235	2	868	152	57,709	7.0	10,133	67,230	11,805	6.2	41,710	5,790	1,005
Columbia, MO	1,102	734	4	918	611	16,866	6.8	11,235	19,695	13,119	7.1	12,110	2,192	1,449
Columbia, SC	2,012	300	7	1,852	276	82,855	5.7	12,346	100,165	14,925	6.1	60,975	13,578	1,998
Columbus, GA-AL	657	237	4	1,025	369	38,635	2.6	13,919	45,170	16,273	2.3	26,140	8,863	3,171
Columbus, IN	197	272	1	256	354	10,575	7.7	14,619	12,875	17,799	9.4	8,095	1,125	1,541
Columbus, OH	5,024	300	16	4,612	275	192,187	4.1	11,459	218,605	13,035	4.2	133,065	30,723	1,814
Corpus Christi, TX	1,000	246	6	1,635	402	53,587	3.6	13,191	62,800	15,459	3.9	35,235	12,725	3,106
Corvallis, OR	275	347	1	134	169	8,656	6.4	10,929	10,600	13,384	6.8	7,340	683	861
Cumberland, MD-WV	235	233	3	450	446	20,271	0.9	20,076	21,605	21,397	1.4	13,050	2,562	2,536
Dallas-Fort Worth-Arlington, TX	**12,343**	**221**	**71**	**12,200**	**218**	**486,884**	**7.1**	**8,716**	**568,685**	**10,181**	**8.0**	**353,385**	**75,395**	**1,323**
Dallas-Plano-Irving, TX	*9,361*	*250*	*45*	*8,194*	*219*	*312,979*	*7.2*	*8,375*	*363,445*	*9,725*	*8.2*	*226,760*	*51,385*	*1,348*
Fort Worth-Arlington, TX	*2,982*	*161*	*26*	*4,008*	*217*	*173,905*	*6.9*	*9,407*	*205,240*	*11,102*	*7.5*	*126,625*	*24,010*	*1,272*
Dalton, GA	206	162	2	290	228	15,855	8.1	12,445	19,135	15,019	7.1	11,405	2,648	2,037
Danville, IL	159	192	2	289	349	15,773	0.9	19,030	17,745	21,409	0.4	10,805	2,560	3,092
Danville, VA	195	179	1	350	322	21,660	1.4	19,913	26,070	23,967	2.2	16,150	4,024	3,722
Davenport-Moline-Rock Island, IA-IL	760	203	7	1,097	293	59,014	1.8	15,740	68,015	18,140	2.0	44,675	6,457	1,720
Dayton, OH	2,438	288	9	2,426	287	132,487	2.4	15,668	147,245	17,413	1.7	90,620	16,720	1,977
Decatur, AL	217	147	4	558	379	22,730	6.7	15,422	27,910	18,937	7.4	15,690	4,398	2,979
Decatur, IL	286	257	2	494	444	20,177	0.9	18,124	22,655	20,349	1.5	14,320	3,063	2,760
Deltona-Daytona Beach-Ormond Beach, FL	995	213	6	1,473	315	104,449	3.1	22,335	119,140	25,476	3.4	81,530	9,381	1,960
Denver-Aurora, CO[5]	7,598	330	18	4,538	197	223,773	4.5	9,721	255,640	11,106	4.1	166,880	25,567	1,097
Des Moines, IA	1,111	221	8	1,443	287	63,709	3.5	12,651	73,210	14,537	3.1	49,510	6,594	1,288
Detroit-Warren-Livonia, MI	**13,042**	**291**	**40**	**10,460**	**233**	**613,075**	**0.8**	**13,662**	**712,945**	**15,888**	**1.2**	**431,620**	**104,623**	**2,328**
Detroit-Livonia-Dearborn, MI	*4,935*	*243*	*17*	*5,414*	*267*	*287,693*	*-2.4*	*14,177*	*332,540*	*16,387*	*-2.1*	*185,770*	*75,219*	*3,731*
Warren-Farmington Hills-Troy, MI	*8,107*	*330*	*23*	*5,046*	*205*	*325,382*	*3.8*	*13,237*	*380,405*	*15,475*	*4.2*	*245,850*	*29,404*	*1,187*
Dothan, AL	345	258	3	749	561	20,822	6.6	15,585	28,320	21,197	5.0	16,350	5,506	4,071
Dover, DE	228	169	1	325	241	18,154	11.8	13,488	22,725	16,884	12.9	14,135	2,835	2,043
Dubuque, IA	236	261	2	447	494	15,114	4.3	16,700	17,160	18,961	3.5	11,410	1,407	1,546
Duluth, MN-WI	821	297	11	1,567	567	49,355	0.5	17,860	55,110	19,942	1.8	33,770	6,318	2,291
Durham, NC	4,934	1,108	6	1,811	407	51,580	5.0	11,579	61,645	13,839	5.0	39,800	7,576	1,679
Eau Claire, WI	480	317	5	594	393	22,502	2.2	14,871	25,955	17,153	2.5	16,695	2,661	1,738
El Centro, CA	139	93	2	206	138	18,825	7.3	12,641	21,950	14,739	1.3	12,570	9,647	6,328
Elizabethtown, KY	225	206	2	308	282	14,640	9.0	13,425	16,985	15,575	7.4	9,170	3,297	3,010
Elkhart-Goshen, IN	275	146	2	421	223	23,188	5.0	12,270	27,005	14,290	5.3	18,225	2,288	1,193
Elmira, NY	276	306	2	489	542	16,716	0.8	18,520	19,395	21,488	0.6	12,240	2,905	3,228
El Paso, TX	1,353	193	8	1,649	235	79,128	6.4	11,262	88,945	12,659	6.0	49,210	23,932	3,356
Erie, PA	622	220	6	1,170	413	45,799	1.3	16,182	52,525	18,558	2.0	33,150	9,031	3,198
Eugene-Springfield, OR	896	271	4	604	183	51,244	6.0	15,520	59,135	17,910	6.2	38,455	5,785	1,745
Evansville, IN-KY	920	265	8	1,543	445	56,300	2.0	16,244	65,510	18,901	2.4	40,040	7,247	2,080
Fairbanks, AK	207	243	1	217	255	5,233	8.6	6,140	6,795	7,973	10.8	4,120	676	787
Fargo, ND-MN	616	344	2	532	297	21,247	2.6	11,876	23,670	13,230	2.7	15,070	2,070	1,140
Farmington, NM	181	148	1	151	123	12,891	9.4	10,527	15,865	12,956	7.5	8,530	3,634	2,927
Fayetteville, NC	719	209	1	537	156	34,778	9.5	10,088	43,625	12,654	7.5	22,795	8,957	2,576
Fayetteville-Springdale-Rogers, AR-MO	711	188	8	860	227	50,698	5.2	13,396	61,165	16,162	5.6	37,530	5,787	1,481
Flagstaff, AZ	324	267	2	267	220	14,208	10.7	11,725	13,425	11,079	8.2	7,485	3,052	2,486
Flint, MI	996	225	3	1,207	273	65,570	5.4	14,812	77,725	17,557	3.2	44,545	13,481	3,037
Florence, SC	488	248	5	945	481	29,981	5.9	15,265	35,205	17,925	5.6	19,735	8,303	4,209
Florence-Muscle Shoals, AL	274	193	3	552	389	26,830	5.1	18,923	32,430	22,872	5.4	17,685	4,691	3,296
Fond du Lac, WI	180	183	3	149	152	16,165	2.1	16,466	17,135	17,454	2.4	11,775	1,148	1,164
Fort Collins-Loveland, CO	671	252	3	445	167	28,548	7.2	10,708	32,770	12,291	7.3	21,925	1,868	695
Fort Smith, AR-OK	502	179	8	975	348	45,185	4.6	16,146	55,370	19,785	5.8	29,415	9,313	3,301
Fort Walton Beach-Crestview-Destin, FL	483	272	4	472	265	26,727	9.7	15,029	29,935	16,833	7.4	18,900	2,458	1,355
Fort Wayne, IN	1,028	257	7	1,612	403	52,445	2.8	13,106	61,675	15,413	3.3	40,600	5,457	1,357
Fresno, CA	1,839	216	12	2,273	267	94,572	5.0	11,118	105,300	12,379	4.3	63,910	39,033	4,503
Gadsden, AL	218	211	2	415	402	19,773	2.4	19,175	24,265	23,531	2.5	12,495	4,298	4,163
Gainesville, FL	1,928	812	4	1,139	480	29,482	6.2	12,422	32,865	13,847	6.1	20,100	5,488	2,295
Gainesville, GA	349	223	1	418	267	17,273	9.9	11,047	21,105	13,498	10.4	13,540	2,178	1,353
Glens Falls, NY	288	227	1	342	270	21,873	5.3	17,244	25,525	20,123	5.6	16,085	3,023	2,363
Goldsboro, NC	199	175	1	256	226	17,762	5.4	15,664	20,995	18,516	5.2	11,690	4,364	3,820
Grand Forks, ND-MN	271	283	4	646	675	12,833	-0.1	13,402	14,305	14,940	0.9	9,290	1,166	1,214
Grand Junction, CO	366	293	3	716	574	21,588	7.7	17,304	24,020	19,254	5.9	15,715	2,123	1,668
Grand Rapids-Wyoming, MI	1,822	239	8	2,106	276	92,647	4.1	12,140	110,445	14,481	5.4	69,990	14,223	1,853
Great Falls, MT	245	307	1	490	614	13,233	3.4	16,587	15,055	18,871	2.8	9,685	1,535	1,922
Greeley, CO[5]	333	157	1	276	130	19,380	7.9	9,147	23,325	11,009	4.9	14,130	2,415	1,101
Green Bay, WI	653	224	5	669	229	37,330	4.6	12,790	44,345	15,193	5.4	28,605	3,866	1,308
Greensboro-High Point, NC	1,481	224	5	2,117	320	96,334	5.8	14,551	112,785	17,035	5.6	74,750	12,569	1,883
Greenville, NC	923	582	1	720	454	19,612	6.8	12,371	23,695	14,947	5.2	13,110	5,679	3,532

See footnotes at end of table.

Metropolitan statistical area **Metropolitan statistical area with metropolitan divisions** *Metropolitan division*	Physicians, 2003[1]		Community hospitals, 2003[3]			Medicare program enrollment, 2003[4]			Social security program beneficiaries, December 2004				Supplemental security income program recipients, 2004	
				Beds										
	Number	Rate per 100,000 persons[2]	Number	Number	Rate per 100,000 persons[2]	Total	Percent change, 2000–2003	Rate per 100,000 persons[2]	Number	Rate per 100,000 persons[2]	Percent change, 2000–2004	Retired workers, number	Number	Rate per 100,000 persons[2]
Greenville, SC	1,528	264	8	1,364	236	84,136	6.2	14,553	99,755	17,254	6.8	61,885	11,260	1,929
Gulfport-Biloxi, MS	672	269	6	1,036	415	37,267	7.7	14,927	44,125	17,674	5.8	24,370	7,777	3,077
Hagerstown-Martinsburg, MD-WV	467	196	3	472	198	35,310	6.7	14,839	41,080	17,264	8.4	25,785	4,204	1,717
Hanford-Corcoran, CA	144	104	3	141	102	11,430	7.4	8,240	13,965	10,068	7.0	7,760	4,377	3,070
Harrisburg-Carlisle, PA	1,910	369	6	1,687	326	82,134	3.3	15,879	89,170	17,240	3.8	61,960	7,933	1,528
Harrisonburg, VA	255	231	1	244	221	13,750	3.4	12,439	17,225	15,583	5.2	11,680	1,281	1,151
Hartford-West Hartford-East Hartford, CT	4,464	378	12	2,525	214	180,643	2.0	15,310	202,445	17,157	1.4	141,445	19,304	1,630
Hattiesburg, MS	421	328	2	748	583	17,846	5.7	13,907	21,830	17,012	4.8	11,500	4,439	3,415
Hickory-Lenoir-Morganton, NC	701	200	5	1,136	324	53,658	6.8	15,303	65,490	18,678	7.3	42,845	5,998	1,700
Hinesville-Fort Stewart, GA	60	85	1	94	133	4,121	13.6	5,841	5,605	7,945	11.8	2,770	1,151	1,584
Holland-Grand Haven, MI	349	140	3	316	127	29,533	8.3	11,835	34,135	13,679	8.1	23,165	2,070	820
Honolulu, HI	3,478	389	13	2,160	242	126,752	5.2	14,188	136,730	15,305	4.7	99,140	16,226	1,804
Hot Springs, AR	297	326	3	465	510	23,127	2.6	25,361	24,615	26,992	2.4	16,325	2,692	2,922
Houma-Bayou Cane-Thibodaux, LA	332	168	5	653	331	26,492	4.6	13,409	33,775	17,096	3.7	14,140	7,020	3,533
Houston-Sugar Land-Baytown, TX	14,750	291	59	12,721	251	432,380	7.5	8,522	510,670	10,066	8.5	300,830	90,321	1,743
Huntington-Ashland, WV-KY-OH	947	330	5	1,452	506	55,613	3.1	19,379	61,455	21,415	3.6	30,610	14,391	5,014
Huntsville, AL	849	237	4	973	272	46,661	10.6	13,048	54,080	15,123	9.9	32,920	7,757	2,140
Idaho Falls, ID	226	210	2	299	278	12,830	7.4	11,939	15,760	14,666	8.6	9,775	1,622	1,469
Indianapolis, IN	6,180	386	18	4,997	312	190,606	4.5	11,907	225,295	14,074	4.7	144,260	22,070	1,361
Iowa City, IA	1,761	1,294	3	950	698	14,032	5.6	10,310	16,260	11,947	5.9	10,935	1,323	963
Ithaca, NY	269	271	1	148	149	11,004	3.9	11,070	12,790	12,867	4.0	8,565	1,608	1,606
Jackson, MI	211	130	2	476	293	24,460	2.7	15,050	28,775	17,705	3.7	18,115	3,589	2,202
Jackson, MS	2,126	417	13	2,947	578	66,653	5.0	13,062	81,165	15,906	4.2	45,120	17,676	3,417
Jackson, TN	421	385	2	733	670	15,792	3.3	14,429	18,925	17,292	3.5	11,245	3,202	2,906
Jacksonville, FL	3,749	313	12	3,160	264	151,482	7.3	12,652	177,840	14,853	6.3	108,685	23,600	1,926
Jacksonville, NC	250	165	1	133	88	13,248	11.6	8,741	16,075	10,607	10.4	9,300	2,507	1,625
Janesville, WI	333	215	3	394	254	22,752	4.2	14,683	26,990	17,418	4.8	17,825	2,960	1,891
Jefferson City, MO	199	139	3	332	232	19,503	3.3	13,623	23,750	16,590	4.4	14,655	1,962	1,377
Johnson City, TN	853	458	6	885	475	32,949	6.1	17,692	39,165	21,029	6.6	21,895	5,400	2,883
Johnstown, PA	430	287	3	581	388	32,844	-2.4	21,956	36,215	24,210	-1.6	21,210	4,759	3,205
Jonesboro, AR	288	262	3	476	432	16,753	4.7	15,212	20,370	18,497	8.0	11,200	4,220	3,784
Joplin, MO	293	181	4	780	481	26,397	3.5	16,266	31,265	19,266	4.0	18,260	3,736	2,275
Kalamazoo-Portage, MI	1,058	331	5	928	290	43,818	3.3	13,702	52,270	16,344	4.4	33,480	6,688	2,095
Kankakee-Bradley, IL	185	174	2	445	419	16,616	2.1	15,636	18,995	17,875	2.1	11,075	2,553	2,382
Kansas City, MO-KS	5,430	285	37	5,911	310	245,834	3.3	12,897	282,605	14,826	3.0	182,870	25,779	1,339
Kennewick-Richland-Pasco, WA	389	185	4	431	205	22,589	7.4	10,746	26,855	12,775	6.7	17,070	3,226	1,497
Killeen-Temple-Fort Hood, TX	1,086	316	5	924	269	32,656	9.1	9,494	38,885	11,305	10.4	22,575	5,676	1,640
Kingsport-Bristol-Bristol, TN-VA	833	278	6	1,147	382	60,055	6.4	20,015	72,605	24,198	6.8	39,445	10,144	3,374
Kingston, NY	375	207	3	431	238	27,798	2.8	15,322	33,120	18,255	2.7	20,520	4,257	2,342
Knoxville, TN	2,293	358	9	2,353	367	101,631	5.2	15,864	119,125	18,595	4.7	71,635	15,177	2,345
Kokomo, IN	187	185	4	462	456	16,315	2.7	16,103	19,760	19,503	4.9	12,990	1,884	1,861
La Crosse, WI-MN	576	448	2	484	377	18,833	2.7	14,656	21,235	16,525	2.4	14,520	2,165	1,683
Lafayette, IN	419	231	1	451	249	20,029	3.8	11,064	24,000	13,257	4.9	15,745	1,723	949
Lafayette, LA	707	290	7	1,028	421	28,439	6.1	11,652	34,685	14,211	5.2	17,410	6,808	2,766
Lake Charles, LA	407	210	8	890	459	27,580	4.3	14,223	32,805	16,918	3.2	16,510	5,233	2,689
Lakeland, FL	954	187	4	1,190	233	93,608	5.0	18,324	112,470	22,017	6.1	73,255	14,071	2,683
Lancaster, PA	910	188	4	1,034	214	73,091	4.9	15,130	83,225	17,227	5.3	58,860	7,473	1,533
Lansing-East Lansing, MI	1,073	236	5	1,128	248	55,388	5.1	12,195	65,310	14,379	4.4	40,975	7,997	1,754
Laredo, TX	226	106	2	492	231	18,329	9.2	8,617	21,105	9,922	9.7	11,055	9,054	4,126
Las Cruces, NM	318	174	2	314	172	22,166	9.8	12,142	25,490	13,963	8.0	15,535	5,936	3,190
Las Vegas-Paradise, NV	3,091	196	10	2,751	175	182,306	14.7	11,572	218,970	13,899	14.5	147,410	23,948	1,451
Lawrence, KS	220	216	1	108	106	9,567	5.5	9,377	10,925	10,708	6.0	7,160	930	905
Lawton, OK	235	213	2	445	403	13,205	5.2	11,972	15,795	14,320	5.2	9,070	2,520	2,280
Lebanon, PA	301	245	1	198	161	21,824	4.4	17,735	24,980	20,300	4.3	17,730	1,808	1,452
Lewiston, ID-WA	143	245	2	197	338	11,311	6.1	19,411	13,140	22,549	5.1	8,095	1,495	2,549
Lewiston-Auburn, ME	282	266	2	360	339	18,740	4.4	17,659	21,455	20,218	3.3	12,935	3,374	3,153
Lexington-Fayette, KY	2,189	520	10	1,754	417	51,148	5.7	12,153	60,450	14,363	6.3	36,095	10,014	2,358
Lima, OH	276	258	2	568	530	16,855	-0.5	15,736	19,635	18,331	-0.3	12,225	2,480	2,321
Lincoln, NE	733	265	4	1,113	402	32,950	3.6	11,914	36,970	13,368	3.0	24,940	3,554	1,277
Little Rock-North Little Rock, AR	2,773	441	14	3,008	478	84,220	6.5	13,383	103,955	16,519	6.1	60,350	15,323	2,407
Logan, UT-ID	169	156	2	188	173	9,075	7.7	8,374	10,695	9,869	5.0	7,055	589	537
Longview, TX	377	190	4	664	334	33,182	3.6	16,688	37,110	18,664	0.6	21,710	5,449	2,719
Longview, WA	213	224	1	202	212	15,448	6.0	16,236	18,790	19,748	9.8	11,185	2,549	2,650
Los Angeles-Long Beach-Santa Ana, CA	**39,402**	**307**	**126**	**28,403**	**222**	**1,338,861**	**4.8**	**10,443**	**1,356,400**	**10,580**	**3.6**	**894,715**	**457,300**	**3,538**
Los Angeles-Long Beach-Glendale, CA	*29,860*	*303*	*97*	*23,191*	*235*	*1,029,780*	*4.3*	*10,444*	*1,030,955*	*10,456*	*3.1*	*671,285*	*394,311*	*3,968*
Santa Ana-Anaheim-Irvine, CA	*9,542*	*322*	*29*	*5,212*	*176*	*309,081*	*6.5*	*10,441*	*325,445*	*10,994*	*5.0*	*223,430*	*62,989*	*2,108*
Louisville, KY-IN	4,042	340	18	3,909	328	173,845	3.0	14,606	202,485	17,013	3.0	118,920	29,017	2,416
Lubbock, TX	1,056	411	6	1,442	562	31,878	3.9	12,415	36,760	14,316	3.7	22,215	5,263	2,043
Lynchburg, VA	489	211	2	984	425	42,556	5.6	18,397	47,340	20,465	5.4	29,795	5,240	2,253
Macon, GA	820	362	5	955	421	33,606	3.2	14,827	39,755	17,540	3.4	21,815	8,193	3,591
Madera, CA	150	112	2	352	263	19,091	6.9	14,279	19,155	14,327	4.4	11,970	4,554	3,277
Madison, WI	2,679	510	7	1,467	279	60,530	5.2	11,528	68,705	13,085	4.9	47,085	6,492	1,221

See footnotes at end of table.

State and Metropolitan Area Data Book: 2006

Table B-6. Metropolitan Areas — **Physicians, Community Hospitals, Medicare, Social Security, and SSI**—Con.

Metropolitan statistical area **Metropolitan statistical area with metropolitan divisions** *Metropolitan division*	Physicians, 2003[1]		Community hospitals, 2003[3]			Medicare program enrollment, 2003[4]			Social security program beneficiaries, December 2004				Supplemental security income program recipients, 2004	
				Beds										
	Number	Rate per 100,000 persons[2]	Number	Number	Rate per 100,000 persons[2]	Total	Percent change, 2000–2003	Rate per 100,000 persons[2]	Number	Rate per 100,000 persons[2]	Percent change, 2000–2004	Retired workers, number	Number	Rate per 100,000 persons[2]
Manchester-Nashua, NH.	947	240	5	825	209	48,117	3.9	12,177	56,680	14,345	4.5	37,115	4,189	1,051
Mansfield, OH.	236	184	1	365	285	21,933	3.4	17,105	24,675	19,243	3.9	15,675	2,777	2,168
McAllen-Edinburg-Mission, TX	753	119	7	1,405	221	58,418	8.9	9,194	68,910	10,845	9.3	38,240	30,356	4,612
Medford, OR	601	316	3	539	283	33,915	6.0	17,816	39,415	20,705	5.2	26,530	3,133	1,623
Memphis, TN-MS-AR.	3,677	297	17	4,038	326	146,180	2.9	11,800	176,480	14,245	4.0	99,140	40,882	3,270
Merced, CA	256	111	2	289	125	21,018	5.6	9,083	28,230	12,200	5.1	16,195	10,336	4,361
Miami-Fort Lauderdale-Miami Beach, FL	**18,096**	**343**	**57**	**15,105**	**286**	**812,930**	**1.6**	**15,404**	**878,380**	**16,644**	**1.6**	**612,245**	**170,988**	**3,189**
Fort Lauderdale-Pompano Beach-Deerfield Beach, FL	*4,612*	*267*	*17*	*4,921*	*285*	*244,892*	*−2.1*	*14,164*	*273,865*	*15,840*	*−1.8*	*187,475*	*31,563*	*1,799*
Miami-Miami Beach-Kendall, FL	*9,183*	*393*	*26*	*7,210*	*309*	*321,353*	*4.1*	*13,756*	*332,530*	*14,234*	*4.0*	*224,495*	*123,521*	*5,226*
West Palm Beach-Boca Raton-Boynton Beach, FL.	*4,301*	*355*	*14*	*2,974*	*245*	*246,685*	*2.3*	*20,347*	*271,985*	*22,434*	*2.3*	*200,275*	*15,904*	*1,279*
Michigan City-La Porte, IN	203	185	2	444	405	16,605	1.6	15,129	19,650	17,903	2.9	12,580	1,712	1,560
Midland, TX	223	188	2	373	314	14,662	5.3	12,335	17,410	14,647	3.8	10,785	2,141	1,779
Milwaukee-Waukesha-West Allis, WI.	5,659	374	19	4,241	280	213,907	0.7	14,131	242,680	16,032	0.8	161,945	35,397	2,335
Minneapolis-St. Paul-Bloomington, MN-WI	9,410	305	32	6,177	200	330,821	4.6	10,724	376,260	12,197	4.7	254,260	41,751	1,340
Missoula, MT	394	400	2	346	351	11,664	4.6	11,840	13,345	13,546	4.4	8,280	1,638	1,654
Mobile, AL	1,167	292	6	1,478	370	59,320	3.8	14,832	72,950	18,240	4.5	38,165	13,682	3,416
Modesto, CA	901	183	4	1,198	244	58,154	5.9	11,844	66,870	13,619	4.7	39,225	19,751	3,963
Monroe, LA	444	260	7	1,057	619	23,965	2.2	14,037	27,695	16,221	3.1	15,415	6,083	3,552
Monroe, MI	142	94	1	177	117	19,848	6.1	13,154	24,210	16,044	0.2	14,425	1,986	1,302
Montgomery, AL	765	217	8	1,033	293	49,636	5.4	14,065	59,580	16,883	5.7	33,120	13,747	3,870
Morgantown, WV.	843	743	4	728	641	15,026	2.0	13,239	17,860	15,735	3.2	9,965	2,788	2,450
Morristown, TN.	192	151	3	336	264	22,588	8.8	17,729	26,755	20,999	9.9	14,880	4,151	3,218
Mount Vernon-Anacortes, WA	296	271	1	43	39	17,462	4.8	15,984	20,175	18,468	4.7	13,600	1,811	1,631
Muncie, IN.	361	305	1	393	332	18,631	2.0	15,732	22,030	18,602	1.8	13,650	451	383
Muskegon-Norton Shores, MI	272	157	2	382	220	27,920	3.1	16,112	33,510	19,338	4.2	18,985	5,426	3,111
Myrtle Beach-Conway-North Myrtle Beach, SC	419	199	3	571	271	33,827	12.8	16,031	45,520	21,572	13.5	29,905	4,429	2,035
Napa, CA.	561	426	2	421	320	22,036	0.7	16,725	22,055	16,740	1.3	14,835	2,249	1,699
Naples-Marco Island, FL.	1,106	387	1	539	188	54,158	10.0	18,928	62,080	21,697	9.0	46,035	2,174	733
Nashville-Davidson-Murfreesboro, TN	5,089	371	23	4,499	328	162,946	6.4	11,875	194,260	14,158	5.9	119,985	23,170	1,660
New Haven-Milford, CT	4,406	524	9	2,145	255	131,800	0.4	15,664	146,070	17,359	−0.1	99,645	15,475	1,830
New Orleans-Metairie-Kenner, LA.	6,050	460	23	5,723	435	179,082	2.7	13,610	210,865	16,025	2.4	111,380	49,528	3,753
New York-Northern New Jersey-Long Island, NY-NJ-PA	**83,731**	**448**	**154**	**58,510**	**313**	**2,527,769**	**1.6**	**13,539**	**2,721,495**	**14,577**	**0.6**	**1,837,450**	**562,691**	**3,007**
Edison, NJ	*7,601*	*335*	*17*	*5,037*	*222*	*342,666*	*2.3*	*15,096*	*387,370*	*17,066*	*2.2*	*274,350*	*23,842*	*1,041*
Nassau-Suffolk, NY	*13,589*	*484*	*25*	*8,410*	*299*	*427,077*	*1.9*	*15,205*	*481,890*	*17,157*	*1.5*	*320,090*	*37,373*	*1,328*
Newark-Union, NJ-PA	*8,014*	*374*	*19*	*6,960*	*325*	*278,439*	*1.2*	*12,992*	*310,330*	*14,480*	*0.9*	*210,880*	*40,208*	*1,868*
New York-White Plains-Wayne, NY-NJ	*54,527*	*476*	*93*	*38,103*	*333*	*1,479,587*	*1.4*	*12,924*	*1,541,905*	*13,469*	*−0.2*	*1,032,130*	*461,268*	*4,028*
Niles-Benton Harbor, MI	320	196	2	414	254	29,034	2.9	17,828	32,180	19,760	2.6	20,655	4,897	3,002
Norwich-New London, CT	732	276	2	417	157	39,390	3.1	14,854	44,330	16,717	2.2	29,635	3,179	1,193
Ocala, FL.	535	190	2	610	217	72,671	6.7	25,848	84,365	30,007	7.9	59,625	6,548	2,248
Ocean City, NJ	158	155	1	208	204	22,252	1.4	21,853	25,265	24,812	0.6	17,595	1,497	1,486
Odessa, TX	255	207	2	438	356	15,937	4.2	12,953	18,630	15,142	2.9	10,020	3,501	2,812
Ogden-Clearfield, UT	765	163	4	718	153	44,492	7.5	9,491	48,980	10,449	7.3	32,330	3,982	834
Oklahoma City, OK	3,267	288	21	3,721	328	140,357	4.4	12,385	166,030	14,650	4.9	105,815	20,139	1,760
Olympia, WA	639	289	2	434	196	29,554	9.5	13,375	35,160	15,912	8.3	22,415	3,727	1,659
Omaha-Council Bluffs, NE-IA.	2,944	371	14	2,745	346	98,110	3.6	12,380	111,240	14,036	3.3	71,995	10,708	1,332
Orlando-Kissimee, FL.	4,172	231	13	6,725	373	248,436	9.5	13,784	284,245	15,771	8.1	182,060	39,405	2,117
Oshkosh-Neenah, WI.	459	289	2	338	213	22,481	2.2	14,179	26,385	16,641	3.3	18,000	1,851	1,164
Owensboro, KY	219	198	1	345	311	18,725	4.3	16,894	22,325	20,142	5.7	13,030	3,666	3,302
Oxnard-Thousand Oaks-Ventura, CA	1,889	239	7	1,353	171	91,182	7.3	11,534	101,275	12,811	5.8	66,365	15,092	1,892
Palm Bay-Melbourne-Titusville, FL.	1,231	243	5	1,188	235	103,480	8.0	20,460	120,435	23,813	6.6	81,915	8,519	1,640
Panama City-Lynn Haven, FL.	355	229	2	547	353	25,461	10.3	16,438	29,710	19,182	7.3	17,810	3,867	2,448
Parkersburg-Marietta-Vienna, WV-OH	317	194	2	764	468	30,095	4.0	18,430	34,495	21,125	2.7	19,590	5,374	3,298
Pascagoula, MS	333	216	2	441	286	20,469	9.5	13,268	27,585	17,881	9.4	14,590	3,339	2,137
Pensacola-Ferry Pass-Brent, FL.	1,259	293	6	1,442	336	64,956	10.5	15,131	78,295	18,238	10.0	46,615	10,405	2,380
Peoria, IL.	1,094	299	5	1,332	364	59,809	0.9	16,336	68,235	18,637	1.4	44,465	6,744	1,833
Philadelphia-Camden-Wilmington, PA-NJ-DE-MD	**23,154**	**401**	**67**	**17,698**	**307**	**841,688**	**1.1**	**14,582**	**949,280**	**16,445**	**0.9**	**616,550**	**150,032**	**2,586**
Camden, NJ	*3,357*	*274*	*10*	*2,578*	*210*	*167,371*	*3.4*	*13,651*	*194,090*	*15,830*	*3.1*	*125,830*	*20,669*	*1,670*
Philadelphia, PA.	*17,902*	*462*	*52*	*13,599*	*351*	*585,929*	*0.0*	*15,127*	*650,470*	*16,794*	*−0.3*	*424,960*	*118,735*	*3,058*
Wilmington, DE-MD-NJ	*1,895*	*282*	*5*	*1,521*	*226*	*88,388*	*4.0*	*13,135*	*104,720*	*15,561*	*4.3*	*65,760*	*10,628*	*1,562*
Phoenix-Mesa-Scottsdale, AZ	8,583	239	31	7,004	195	416,913	7.2	11,603	498,170	13,864	8.3	327,320	50,496	1,359
Pine Bluff, AR.	184	173	1	377	355	16,073	0.5	15,128	18,720	17,620	0.8	9,975	4,348	4,107
Pittsburgh, PA.	9,249	384	41	9,089	377	460,650	−1.2	19,117	517,005	21,456	−0.6	320,375	63,226	2,633
Pittsfield, MA	535	402	3	435	327	26,737	0.4	20,093	30,225	22,714	0.7	19,795	3,806	2,873
Pocatello, ID.	180	217	2	369	445	10,306	4.7	12,439	11,245	13,573	4.8	6,775	1,583	1,904
Portland-South Portland-Biddeford, ME	1,891	373	9	1,320	260	78,328	5.5	15,438	89,645	17,668	5.0	57,115	8,166	1,599
Portland-Vancouver-Beaverton, OR-WA.	6,995	343	16	3,386	166	234,359	5.3	11,481	268,330	13,146	6.3	177,540	31,372	1,520
Port St. Lucie-Fort Pierce, FL.	838	240	3	847	243	79,114	6.0	22,667	93,395	26,758	5.7	66,290	6,459	1,771
Poughkeepsie-Newburgh-Middletown, NY	1,647	251	7	1,521	232	85,648	4.4	13,063	100,335	15,303	3.9	61,270	11,109	1,674
Prescott, AZ	421	228	2	227	123	39,042	10.5	21,152	49,885	27,027	11.4	34,680	2,943	1,544
Providence-New Bedford-Fall River, RI-MA	4,990	307	15	3,595	221	261,178	0.7	16,091	294,285	18,131	1.0	193,780	48,355	2,969
Provo-Orem, UT	595	147	6	675	166	29,215	7.6	7,197	34,980	8,617	6.7	21,360	3,275	794
Pueblo, CO	416	279	2	543	364	25,964	3.5	17,424	28,160	18,898	1.7	15,630	4,900	3,263

See footnotes at end of table.

State and Metropolitan Area Data Book: 2006   153

U.S. Census Bureau

Metropolitan statistical area **Metropolitan statistical area with metropolitan divisions** *Metropolitan division*	Physicians, 2003[1]		Community hospitals, 2003[3]			Medicare program enrollment, 2003[4]			Social security program beneficiaries, December 2004				Supplemental security income program recipients, 2004	
				Beds										
	Number	Rate per 100,000 persons[2]	Number	Number	Rate per 100,000 persons[2]	Total	Percent change, 2000–2003	Rate per 100,000 persons[2]	Number	Rate per 100,000 persons[2]	Percent change, 2000–2004	Retired workers, number	Number	Rate per 100,000 persons[2]
Punta Gorda, FL	425	278	3	722	472	41,473	6.2	27,140	52,115	34,104	3.8	38,905	1,632	1,039
Racine, WI	375	195	3	438	227	28,541	3.0	14,822	32,535	16,896	3.3	21,110	3,679	1,895
Raleigh-Cary, NC	2,036	229	6	1,739	196	85,016	11.0	9,579	101,005	11,381	11.3	62,375	13,388	1,464
Rapid City, SD	362	312	2	491	423	16,486	6.9	14,212	19,425	16,746	6.2	12,095	1,873	1,594
Reading, PA	785	203	3	978	253	61,325	1.2	15,860	71,085	18,384	3.3	49,790	7,220	1,844
Redding, CA	517	294	3	492	280	33,800	7.7	19,242	38,770	22,072	7.3	22,630	9,165	5,154
Reno-Sparks, NV	1,176	314	5	1,017	271	45,320	12.7	12,094	53,520	14,282	12.8	36,230	4,822	1,254
Richmond, VA	4,060	357	11	3,369	296	149,328	5.1	13,116	176,625	15,514	5.4	111,585	22,189	1,922
Riverside-San Bernardino-Ontario, CA	6,366	175	32	6,150	169	399,208	7.6	10,952	463,525	12,717	7.5	290,775	109,262	2,881
Roanoke, VA	1,154	398	3	1,265	436	50,139	3.3	17,276	58,215	20,059	4.5	36,470	6,027	2,070
Rochester, MN	2,964	1,720	4	1,374	797	21,630	7.2	12,551	25,380	14,727	6.8	17,855	1,922	1,099
Rochester, NY	4,013	386	11	3,050	293	158,696	2.8	15,245	185,275	17,798	2.7	122,415	24,927	2,393
Rockford, IL	850	257	4	886	267	46,764	4.6	14,115	55,600	16,782	5.5	36,150	5,945	1,773
Rocky Mount, NC	235	162	2	431	298	23,523	4.1	16,265	27,480	19,001	2.7	15,370	6,057	4,165
Rome, GA	341	365	2	500	535	15,212	3.3	16,282	18,285	19,572	2.8	10,910	2,823	3,003
Sacramento-Arden-Arcade-Roseville, CA	5,738	290	15	3,584	181	245,669	8.3	12,436	267,360	13,534	6.6	167,300	68,111	3,377
Saginaw-Saginaw Township North, MI	560	267	3	1,108	529	34,090	2.3	16,278	40,415	19,298	3.4	23,505	7,193	3,441
St. Cloud, MN	447	252	4	850	478	22,627	6.2	12,733	25,110	14,130	6.4	15,640	2,154	1,202
St. George, UT	197	189	1	196	188	16,219	15.6	15,521	19,550	18,708	15.7	13,840	784	713
St. Joseph, MO-KS	185	150	1	460	374	19,916	−0.6	16,180	23,125	18,787	−0.1	14,465	2,384	1,951
St. Louis, MO-IL[6]	9,079	330	43	9,802	356	400,667	1.5	14,550	461,890	16,773	0.8	289,550	51,920	1,878
Salem, OR	727	199	4	520	143	51,191	4.2	14,035	58,965	16,167	4.3	39,590	6,150	1,665
Salinas, CA	960	232	4	637	154	43,750	1.7	10,557	49,470	11,937	0.9	31,505	8,869	2,139
Salisbury, MD	348	308	4	598	529	16,500	4.9	14,587	19,225	16,996	4.9	12,930	2,391	2,086
Salt Lake City, UT	3,544	352	12	2,036	202	88,603	5.1	8,811	103,625	10,305	5.1	67,300	9,802	962
San Angelo, TX	229	217	2	385	364	16,387	2.5	15,513	18,635	17,641	1.9	11,405	2,457	2,329
San Antonio, TX	5,997	330	25	5,037	277	216,513	6.4	11,920	252,195	13,885	6.6	147,130	46,398	2,503
San Diego-Carlsbad-San Marcos, CA	10,126	347	19	5,827	200	350,167	2.6	11,997	375,965	12,881	1.4	246,510	79,911	2,726
Sandusky, OH	141	179	2	373	473	13,908	3.1	17,633	15,095	19,138	1.4	9,875	1,234	1,562
San Francisco-Oakland-Fremont, CA	**18,316**	**441**	**39**	**10,934**	**263**	**526,857**	**1.7**	**12,676**	**532,340**	**12,808**	**0.8**	**356,460**	**134,292**	**3,233**
Oakland-Fremont-Hayward, CA	*7,575*	*308*	*19*	*5,351*	*218*	*280,877*	*2.4*	*11,424*	*296,135*	*12,044*	*1.4*	*190,815*	*72,225*	*2,931*
San Francisco-San Mateo-Redwood City, CA	*10,741*	*633*	*20*	*5,583*	*329*	*245,980*	*0.8*	*14,490*	*236,205*	*13,914*	*0.1*	*165,645*	*62,067*	*3,674*
San Jose-Sunnyvale-Santa Clara, CA	6,611	382	13	3,334	192	177,959	3.6	10,274	180,255	10,407	2.8	122,430	44,382	2,549
San Luis Obispo-Paso Robles, CA	818	323	4	366	145	40,110	2.3	15,849	44,985	17,776	2.1	29,940	5,247	2,061
Santa Barbara-Santa Maria, CA	1,322	328	6	900	223	56,246	2.1	13,964	61,505	15,270	0.7	40,190	9,640	2,399
Santa Cruz-Watsonville, CA	739	294	3	368	146	28,062	−0.8	11,148	31,135	12,369	0.0	20,155	5,615	2,240
Santa Fe, NM	553	405	1	246	180	16,964	11.5	12,410	19,815	14,496	9.8	12,780	2,071	1,493
Santa Rosa-Petaluma, CA	1,479	316	8	824	176	64,105	1.1	13,718	71,245	15,246	0.9	46,965	9,506	2,029
Sarasota-Bradenton-Venice, FL	2,352	371	7	1,899	299	161,625	2.5	25,474	175,580	27,674	2.7	129,855	7,559	1,160
Savannah, GA	983	322	4	1,120	367	40,120	2.5	13,150	46,775	15,331	2.1	27,840	7,214	2,322
Scranton-Wilkes-Barre, PA	1,404	254	14	2,140	387	115,273	−2.2	20,855	131,200	23,737	−0.7	85,525	15,062	2,731
Seattle-Tacoma-Bellevue, WA	**11,729**	**373**	**25**	**5,247**	**167**	**354,128**	**3.7**	**11,270**	**395,905**	**12,600**	**3.5**	**261,375**	**53,450**	**1,688**
Seattle-Bellevue-Everett, WA	*9,836*	*410*	*20*	*4,188*	*174*	*267,541*	*3.0*	*11,140*	*294,645*	*12,268*	*2.5*	*199,625*	*38,220*	*1,578*
Tacoma, WA	*1,893*	*256*	*5*	*1,059*	*143*	*86,587*	*6.1*	*11,693*	*101,260*	*13,675*	*6.5*	*61,750*	*15,230*	*2,043*
Sheboygan, WI	205	181	3	392	345	17,618	1.4	15,515	20,020	17,630	2.3	14,010	1,302	1,143
Sherman-Denison, TX	248	216	3	607	528	19,015	2.4	16,531	21,415	18,618	3.3	13,615	2,182	1,882
Shreveport-Bossier City, LA	1,714	453	9	2,235	590	55,367	2.8	14,622	63,285	16,714	2.4	36,760	13,800	3,614
Sioux City, IA-NE-SD	286	200	2	468	327	21,436	−0.7	14,980	23,640	16,520	−1.2	15,050	2,265	1,582
Sioux Falls, SD	763	384	6	1,218	613	25,453	4.9	12,809	29,455	14,823	4.7	19,470	2,263	1,113
South Bend-Mishawaka, IN-MI	736	232	4	786	248	47,718	0.1	15,033	54,790	17,261	0.8	37,040	5,144	1,617
Spartanburg, SC	612	234	3	626	239	41,603	6.0	15,891	49,690	18,980	6.5	28,770	6,099	2,308
Spokane, WA	1,388	322	6	1,312	304	61,613	4.5	14,288	69,715	16,167	4.6	43,560	10,252	2,353
Springfield, IL	1,033	505	2	1,023	500	31,300	1.8	15,300	36,675	17,927	2.5	23,275	4,734	2,312
Springfield, MA	2,149	313	10	1,810	263	108,877	1.3	15,841	122,525	17,827	0.8	76,025	27,130	3,943
Springfield, MO	978	254	4	1,432	373	60,220	7.1	15,665	69,425	18,060	6.8	41,945	7,771	1,988
Springfield, OH	237	166	2	392	274	24,374	0.6	17,066	27,120	18,988	1.1	16,120	3,549	2,489
State College, PA	320	229	2	253	181	16,231	5.3	11,609	18,695	13,371	6.4	12,630	1,705	1,214
Stockton, CA	1,022	162	7	1,080	171	71,307	5.0	11,285	81,180	12,847	4.5	48,075	26,933	4,144
Sumter, SC	156	148	1	236	223	14,509	6.6	13,720	17,620	16,661	4.8	10,155	3,989	3,765
Syracuse, NY	2,508	384	8	1,958	300	102,118	2.0	15,631	118,345	18,115	1.4	75,175	16,384	2,505
Tallahassee, FL	801	245	4	833	254	35,472	6.6	10,831	42,010	12,828	6.0	26,390	7,860	2,370
Tampa-St. Petersburg-Clearwater, FL	7,455	295	33	8,387	331	469,339	0.9	18,542	537,040	21,217	1.4	357,410	56,485	2,183
Terre Haute, IN	355	209	5	583	344	28,423	−1.1	16,763	32,670	19,268	−1.1	19,760	3,747	2,220
Texarkana, TX-Texarkana, AR	349	265	4	575	437	20,191	2.2	15,332	23,290	17,685	4.0	13,120	4,515	3,402
Toledo, OH	2,212	335	11	2,778	421	96,759	0.5	14,672	107,770	16,342	0.3	66,035	15,891	2,414
Topeka, KS	564	249	5	750	331	36,974	2.4	16,300	40,910	18,036	1.5	26,280	4,306	1,890
Trenton-Ewing, NJ	1,484	411	6	1,296	359	52,272	1.1	14,472	56,975	15,774	0.1	38,370	7,578	2,075
Tucson, AZ	3,375	379	9	2,034	228	134,558	6.6	15,102	152,730	17,142	6.3	98,635	16,422	1,810
Tulsa, OK	1,863	212	21	2,915	331	121,391	3.7	13,796	143,490	16,307	4.9	89,505	15,343	1,740
Tuscaloosa, AL	509	262	4	665	342	28,204	3.7	14,508	35,000	18,003	5.7	18,130	8,174	4,189
Tyler, TX	743	404	5	958	521	28,959	5.5	15,751	32,965	17,930	5.9	20,750	4,172	2,238

See footnotes at end of table.

State and Metropolitan Area Data Book: 2006

U.S. Census Bureau

Metropolitan statistical area **Metropolitan statistical area with metropolitan divisions** *Metropolitan division*	Physicians, 2003[1]		Community hospitals, 2003[3]			Medicare program enrollment, 2003[4]			Social security program beneficiaries, December 2004				Supplemental security income program recipients, 2004	
				Beds										
	Number	Rate per 100,000 persons[2]	Number	Number	Rate per 100,000 persons[2]	Total	Percent change, 2000–2003	Rate per 100,000 persons[2]	Number	Rate per 100,000 persons[2]	Percent change, 2000–2004	Retired workers, number	Number	Rate per 100,000 persons[2]
Utica-Rome, NY	664	223	5	1,138	382	56,305	−0.9	18,888	64,430	21,614	−0.4	40,280	9,187	3,074
Valdosta, GA	220	180	4	486	398	14,623	5.6	11,971	17,915	14,666	5.8	10,025	3,784	3,059
Vallejo-Fairfield, CA	874	212	4	525	128	42,954	8.8	10,435	49,420	12,006	6.5	29,845	10,242	2,480
Vero Beach, FL	430	358	3	766	637	32,651	2.4	27,154	36,335	30,217	5.5	26,305	1,419	1,143
Victoria, TX	245	217	3	656	581	16,135	4.9	14,279	19,075	16,881	4.9	11,045	2,794	2,463
Vineland-Millville-Bridgeton, NJ	217	145	1	457	306	22,649	2.1	15,150	25,955	17,361	1.2	16,035	4,657	3,080
Virginia Beach-Norfolk-Newport News, VA-NC	4,870	300	14	3,018	186	192,331	5.8	11,835	224,235	13,799	4.9	137,870	29,861	1,816
Visalia-Porterville, CA	527	135	3	736	188	42,622	4.1	10,898	51,120	13,071	4.7	29,935	17,503	4,359
Waco, TX	507	231	2	825	376	31,068	2.3	14,150	35,450	16,146	2.7	21,560	5,418	2,436
Warner Robins, GA	187	156	2	231	192	13,146	12.4	10,949	15,195	12,655	10.8	8,795	2,415	1,951
Washington-Arlington-Alexandria, DC-VA-MD-WV	**22,334**	**440**	**39**	**9,342**	**184**	**480,361**	**7.0**	**9,473**	**511,194**	**10,081**	**6.0**	**343,848**	**67,122**	**1,306**
Bethesda-Gaithersburg-Frederick, MD	*8,762*	*776*	*7*	*1,684*	*149*	*123,970*	*6.6*	*10,984*	*127,995*	*11,340*	*5.4*	*90,585*	*12,654*	*1,111*
Washington-Arlington-Alexandria, DC-VA-MD-WV	*13,572*	*344*	*32*	*7,658*	*194*	*356,391*	*7.1*	*9,041*	*383,199*	*9,721*	*6.2*	*253,263*	*54,468*	*1,362*
Waterloo-Cedar Falls, IA	333	206	6	709	438	26,717	1.1	16,521	30,670	18,966	1.2	20,000	3,046	1,881
Wausau, WI	333	262	1	253	199	17,507	3.4	13,756	20,980	16,485	3.6	13,940	1,838	1,439
Weirton-Steubenville, WV-OH	182	142	2	576	448	27,888	−0.5	21,692	31,215	24,280	−0.7	17,515	3,624	2,838
Wenatchee, WA	279	274	2	193	190	15,331	6.5	15,069	17,670	17,368	6.0	12,335	1,599	1,546
Wheeling, WV-OH	406	271	6	1,036	690	30,302	−0.3	20,190	34,875	23,237	−0.6	20,705	4,303	2,878
Wichita, KS	1,515	260	11	1,997	343	78,040	2.3	13,405	89,560	15,384	2.9	58,535	9,095	1,556
Wichita Falls, TX	379	255	5	479	322	22,014	0.7	14,809	25,080	16,871	1.5	15,450	3,208	2,170
Williamsport, PA	268	226	2	438	369	21,787	1.7	18,363	24,690	20,809	3.1	16,210	3,329	2,808
Wilmington, NC	904	308	4	890	303	49,311	11.2	16,785	59,720	20,329	11.1	37,940	6,725	2,218
Winchester, VA-WV	336	304	2	444	402	15,766	9.8	14,279	18,840	17,063	9.2	12,250	1,910	1,691
Winston-Salem, NC	2,018	462	6	1,901	435	66,298	6.0	15,165	76,180	17,426	5.6	50,440	7,878	1,784
Worcester, MA	2,753	355	10	1,634	211	112,188	0.2	14,461	126,480	16,304	−0.5	80,890	18,941	2,430
Yakima, WA	438	193	4	513	226	28,709	3.2	12,655	33,365	14,707	3.4	21,680	5,497	2,399
York-Hanover, PA	758	192	4	727	184	58,951	6.2	14,902	69,645	17,605	7.1	48,010	6,125	1,525
Youngstown-Warren-Boardman, OH-PA	1,296	219	8	1,902	321	113,408	−0.8	19,122	128,170	21,611	−1.1	78,145	15,798	2,677
Yuba City, CA	272	183	2	213	144	20,038	5.2	13,515	22,900	15,445	3.4	13,260	7,185	4,746
Yuma, AZ	219	128	1	277	162	20,451	10.1	11,987	24,295	14,241	10.4	15,735	2,929	1,663

[1]Active, nonfederal physicians as of December 31.
[2]Based on resident population estimated as of July 1 of the year shown.
[3]Nonfederal, short-term general, and other special hospitals except hospital units of institutions.
[4]Unduplicated count of persons enrolled in either hospital and/or supplemental medical insurance as of July 1.
[5]The Denver-Aurora metropolitan statistical area includes Broomfield County. Broomfield County, CO, was formed from parts of Adams, Boulder, Jefferson, and Weld counties on November 15, 2001, and is coextensive with Broomfield city. For the purposes of defining and presenting data for the Denver-Aurora metropolitan statistical area, Broomfield city is treated as if it were a county when data are available to do so. In many cases, the data will not be available.
[6]The portion of Sullivan city in Crawford County, MO, is legally part of the St. Louis, MO-IL MSA. That portion is not included in these figures for the St. Louis MSA.

Note: Covers metropolitan statistical areas and metropolitan divisions as defined by the Office of Management and Budget as of June 6, 2003, and subsequently updated in December 2003 and November 2004. For more information, see OMB Bulletin 05-02 at <http://www.whitehouse.gov/omb/bulletins/fy05/b05-02_appendix.pdf>.

Survey, Census, or Data Collection Method: For information about these data collections and surveys, see the following organizations and their Web sites: American Medical Association, *Physician Characteristics and Distribution in the U.S.* <http://www.ama-assn.org/>; American Hospital Association (AHA) *Hospital Statistics* <http://www.aha.org/aha/index.jsp>; CMS Statistics, Medicare Enrollment, <http://www.cms.hhs.gov/MedicareEnrollment/>; Social Security, OASDI Beneficiaries by State and County, <http://www.ssa.gov/policy/docs/statcomps/oasdi_sc/2003/index.html>; and SSI Monthly Statistics, Supplemental Security Income, <http://www.ssa.gov/policy/docs/statcomps/ssi_sc/2003/index.html>; SSI Recipients by State and County, updated annually, <http://www.ssa.gov/policy/docs/statcomps/ssi_sc/2004/index.html>.

Sources: Physicians—American Medical Association, Chicago, IL, *Physician Characteristics and Distribution in the U.S.*, annual (copyright) (accessed 13 May 2005); Hospitals—Health Forum LLC, an American Hospital Association (AHA) Company, Chicago, IL, *Hospital Statistics*, and unpublished data (copyright) (e-mail accessed 26 May 2005); Medicare program enrollment—Centers for Medicare and Medicaid Services, CMS Statistics: Medicare Enrollment (accessed 17 June 2005); Social security—U.S. Social Security Administration, Office of Research and Statistics, *OASDI Beneficiaries by State and County* (accessed 9 June 2005); Supplemental security income—U.S. Social Security Administration, Office of Research, Evaluation, and Statistics, *SSI Recipients by State and County* (accessed 6 June 2005).

Metropolitan statistical area **Metropolitan statistical area with metropolitan divisions** *Metropolitan division*	Housing units							Housing 2000, percent		New private housing units authorized by building permits		
				Change 2000–2004		Units per square mile of land		Home owner-ship rate	Units in multi-unit struc-tures	Cum-ulative 2000–2003 period	2003	2002
	2004 (July 1)	2000[1] (esti-mates base)	1990 (April 1)	Number	Per-cent	2004	1990					
Abilene, TX	66,821	65,216	63,130	1,605	2.5	24.3	23.0	58.3	25.3	1,380	221	188
Akron, OH	302,154	290,976	263,776	11,178	3.8	333.8	291.4	66.4	26.1	12,396	3,190	2,634
Albany, GA	67,118	63,755	56,075	3,363	5.3	34.7	29.0	55.6	37.2	2,982	907	684
Albany-Schenectady-Troy, NY	372,924	363,740	339,151	9,184	2.5	132.4	120.4	58.5	40.4	11,916	3,222	3,225
Albuquerque, NM	331,838	305,840	246,561	25,998	8.5	35.7	26.5	62.4	33.0	25,656	7,936	7,022
Alexandria, LA	62,782	60,569	58,733	2,213	3.7	31.9	29.8	62.5	29.2	2,004	580	534
Allentown-Bethlehem-Easton, PA-NJ	322,020	307,269	277,649	14,751	4.8	220.7	190.0	66.7	24.2	16,837	4,376	4,563
Altoona, PA	55,753	55,061	54,349	692	1.3	106.0	103.4	68.2	26.3	1,164	362	321
Amarillo, TX	95,263	91,594	84,506	3,669	4.0	26.0	23.1	61.3	27.8	3,543	1,050	920
Ames, IA	33,660	30,630	26,847	3,030	9.9	58.8	46.9	55.9	40.2	2,796	744	878
Anchorage, AK	135,158	127,697	115,106	7,461	5.8	5.1	4.4	57.3	37.4	8,199	2,547	2,196
Anderson, IN	58,427	56,939	53,353	1,488	2.6	129.2	118.0	69.1	20.4	1,751	581	441
Anderson, SC	78,354	73,213	60,745	5,141	7.0	109.1	84.6	68.4	30.3	5,165	1,384	1,554
Ann Arbor, MI	141,941	130,974	111,256	10,967	8.4	199.9	156.7	57.1	39.0	8,945	2,527	2,333
Anniston-Oxford, AL	52,841	51,322	46,753	1,519	3.0	86.8	76.8	64.0	29.1	991	163	233
Appleton, WI	86,252	78,372	64,388	7,880	10.1	89.8	67.1	71.2	24.7	7,944	1,741	2,163
Asheville, NC	189,236	175,331	143,724	13,905	7.9	93.1	70.7	64.9	31.7	13,361	3,269	3,768
Athens-Clarke County, GA	74,978	67,542	54,896	7,436	11.0	72.7	53.2	53.1	43.0	7,003	1,956	2,262
Atlanta-Sandy Springs-Marietta, GA	1,916,351	1,644,587	1,267,685	271,764	16.5	228.8	151.3	63.1	31.1	267,199	66,377	68,359
Atlantic City, NJ	121,192	114,090	106,877	7,102	6.2	216.0	190.5	55.3	36.3	7,615	2,285	2,020
Auburn-Opelika, AL	55,546	50,329	36,636	5,217	10.4	91.3	60.2	56.4	48.8	4,020	1,167	1,316
Augusta-Richmond County, GA-SC	216,791	204,600	173,961	12,191	6.0	66.1	53.0	62.9	32.7	12,292	3,592	3,555
Austin-Round Rock, TX	573,921	496,004	370,310	77,917	15.7	135.9	87.6	55.4	39.1	72,106	15,317	17,201
Bakersfield, CA	247,426	231,567	198,636	15,859	6.8	30.4	24.4	56.0	28.9	16,886	5,813	4,509
Baltimore-Towson, MD	1,082,523	1,048,046	938,979	34,477	3.3	414.9	359.9	62.2	26.6	44,836	11,133	10,991
Bangor, ME	68,727	66,847	61,359	1,880	2.8	20.2	18.1	60.6	36.8	2,086	638	533
Barnstable Town, MA	152,583	147,083	135,192	5,500	3.7	385.8	341.6	50.2	13.4	6,122	1,228	1,393
Baton Rouge, LA	300,066	282,511	246,833	17,555	6.2	74.5	61.2	63.0	32.5	16,907	5,351	4,273
Battle Creek, MI	60,208	58,691	55,619	1,517	2.6	85.0	78.5	67.3	26.5	1,751	394	462
Bay City, MI	47,617	46,423	44,234	1,194	2.6	107.2	99.6	75.1	22.2	1,438	438	361
Beaumont-Port Arthur, TX	161,294	156,697	149,807	4,597	2.9	74.9	69.5	64.1	26.1	4,196	1,384	897
Bellingham, WA	80,637	73,897	55,742	6,740	9.1	38.0	26.3	55.3	36.1	6,926	2,320	1,537
Bend, OR	64,861	54,583	35,928	10,278	18.8	21.5	11.9	60.4	26.9	10,105	3,145	2,533
Billings, MT	62,462	60,057	53,609	2,405	4.0	13.3	11.4	65.0	31.3	2,675	911	712
Binghamton, NY	110,575	110,227	108,223	348	0.3	90.2	88.3	61.6	38.0	1,331	378	390
Birmingham-Hoover, AL	477,954	454,338	397,184	23,616	5.2	90.2	75.0	65.3	30.7	22,392	6,673	5,309
Bismarck, ND	42,480	39,591	33,270	2,889	7.3	11.9	9.3	66.4	38.7	3,088	953	864
Blacksburg-Christiansburg-Radford, VA	65,624	62,755	55,104	2,869	4.6	61.0	51.2	57.4	37.2	2,849	773	912
Bloomington, IN	80,539	75,752	63,296	4,787	6.3	61.0	47.9	56.4	38.7	3,725	1,176	1,043
Bloomington-Normal, IL	65,492	59,972	49,164	5,520	9.2	55.3	41.5	62.9	33.9	5,800	1,643	1,698
Boise City-Nampa, ID	209,234	181,170	124,937	28,064	15.5	17.8	10.6	67.5	25.2	27,655	7,724	6,999
Boston-Cambridge-Quincy, MA-NH	**1,784,647**	**1,751,585**	**1,654,580**	**33,062**	**1.9**	**508.9**	**472.1**	**58.4**	**47.1**	**47,961**	**14,041**	**11,030**
Boston-Quincy, MA	*740,574*	*729,198*	*694,647*	*11,376*	*1.6*	*661.8*	*620.9*	*54.2*	*52.0*	*18,222*	*5,674*	*4,120*
Cambridge-Newton-Framingham, MA	*583,879*	*576,681*	*543,796*	*7,198*	*1.2*	*709.1*	*660.3*	*60.1*	*46.6*	*12,378*	*3,388*	*2,841*
Essex County, MA	*292,125*	*287,144*	*271,977*	*4,981*	*1.7*	*583.5*	*546.1*	*61.0*	*43.1*	*7,570*	*2,058*	*1,597*
Rockingham County-Strafford County, NH	*168,069*	*158,562*	*144,160*	*9,507*	*6.0*	*158.0*	*135.5*	*67.1*	*33.2*	*9,791*	*2,921*	*2,472*
Boulder, CO[2]	119,889	111,440	94,621	8,449	7.6	161.5	127.4	61.9	31.9	9,246	1,428	1,717
Bowling Green, KY	48,023	44,454	36,074	3,569	8.0	56.6	42.5	59.9	35.8	3,224	1,046	739
Bremerton-Silverdale, WA	97,245	92,644	74,038	4,601	5.0	245.6	187.0	62.9	30.0	4,938	1,460	1,229
Bridgeport-Stamford-Norwalk, CT	345,195	339,466	324,355	5,729	1.7	551.6	518.3	66.1	34.9	8,341	1,964	1,879
Brownsville-Harlingen, TX	133,926	119,654	88,759	14,272	11.9	147.9	98.0	55.0	36.7	13,566	3,444	3,917
Brunswick, GA	48,340	44,861	36,404	3,479	7.8	37.2	28.0	58.1	40.6	3,256	838	963
Buffalo-Niagara Falls, NY	518,182	511,583	492,516	6,599	1.3	330.7	314.2	60.6	40.2	11,341	2,925	2,960
Burlington, NC	59,889	55,461	45,312	4,428	8.0	139.3	105.2	65.2	30.7	4,469	1,163	1,411
Burlington-South Burlington, VT	86,407	82,718	73,480	3,689	4.5	68.6	58.4	63.0	34.0	4,030	956	1,122
Canton-Massillon, OH	174,327	170,040	158,446	4,287	2.5	179.6	163.2	68.4	23.4	5,367	1,556	1,400
Cape Coral-Fort Myers, FL	292,830	245,405	189,051	47,425	19.3	364.4	235.3	58.8	45.2	46,900	15,675	11,146
Carson City, NV	22,401	21,283	16,628	1,118	5.3	156.3	115.8	59.8	39.5	1,199	203	336
Casper, WY	30,433	29,882	29,082	551	1.8	5.7	5.4	62.8	29.3	609	174	150
Cedar Rapids, IA	107,105	99,054	84,848	8,051	8.1	53.3	42.2	70.0	26.5	7,074	1,815	1,776
Champaign-Urbana, IL	92,854	88,139	80,761	4,715	5.3	48.3	42.0	55.4	37.2	5,095	1,373	1,579
Charleston, WV	143,971	141,666	133,124	2,305	1.6	56.9	52.6	67.5	29.8	1,762	461	479
Charleston-North Charleston, SC	256,543	232,957	199,879	23,586	10.1	99.0	77.1	59.4	36.2	23,446	7,394	5,981
Charlotte-Gastonia-Concord, NC-SC	634,930	546,423	415,715	88,507	16.2	204.9	134.1	63.1	30.2	81,349	18,833	19,270
Charlottesville, VA	81,325	73,869	58,995	7,456	10.1	49.3	35.8	58.8	27.7	7,607	2,008	2,636
Chattanooga, TN-GA	217,028	205,322	181,276	11,706	5.7	103.9	86.7	64.7	29.0	11,613	3,266	2,934
Cheyenne, WY	35,875	34,213	30,507	1,662	4.9	13.4	11.4	64.4	29.9	1,821	779	478
Chicago-Naperville-Joliet, IL-IN-WI	**3,627,825**	**3,462,286**	**3,147,530**	**165,539**	**4.8**	**503.0**	**436.3**	**61.8**	**42.6**	**187,013**	**49,954**	**49,198**
Chicago-Naperville-Joliet, IL	*3,037,420*	*2,906,717*	*2,668,471*	*130,703*	*4.5*	*658.2*	*577.9*	*60.3*	*46.1*	*150,464*	*39,695*	*40,447*
Gary, IN	*283,408*	*269,570*	*244,514*	*13,838*	*5.1*	*151.0*	*130.3*	*66.7*	*25.2*	*14,960*	*4,407*	*3,418*
Lake County-Kenosha County, IL-WI	*306,997*	*285,999*	*234,545*	*20,998*	*7.3*	*426.2*	*325.5*	*72.4*	*24.0*	*21,589*	*5,852*	*5,333*

See footnotes at end of table.

State and Metropolitan Area Data Book: 2006

U.S. Census Bureau

Table B-7. Metropolitan Areas — **Housing Units and Building Permits**—Con.

Metropolitan statistical area / Metropolitan statistical area with metropolitan divisions / Metropolitan division	2004 (July 1)	2000[1] (estimates base)	1990 (April 1)	Change 2000–2004 Number	Change 2000–2004 Percent	Units per square mile of land 2004	Units per square mile of land 1990	Housing 2000 percent Home ownership rate	Housing 2000 percent Units in multiunit structures	New private housing units authorized by building permits Cumulative 2000–2003 period	2003	2002
Chico, CA	90,310	85,523	76,115	4,787	5.6	55.1	46.4	56.5	36.8	5,182	1,769	1,186
Cincinnati-Middletown, OH-KY-IN	880,073	833,075	732,567	46,998	5.6	200.1	166.5	62.9	33.6	50,733	13,181	12,820
Clarksville, TN-KY	100,234	92,024	70,330	8,210	8.9	46.4	32.5	57.1	28.1	7,276	2,133	1,687
Cleveland, TN	46,828	44,189	35,221	2,639	6.0	61.3	46.1	65.0	31.7	2,264	725	525
Cleveland-Elyria-Mentor, OH	931,197	911,329	858,921	19,868	2.2	464.6	428.4	63.7	30.8	27,554	7,040	6,803
Coeur d'Alene, ID	52,411	46,607	31,964	5,804	12.5	42.1	25.7	66.0	27.8	5,769	1,837	1,414
College Station-Bryan, TX	82,466	75,094	63,181	7,372	9.8	39.2	30.0	46.1	46.2	6,553	1,884	1,839
Colorado Springs, CO	238,861	212,790	172,621	26,071	12.3	89.0	64.3	61.5	29.6	26,466	5,449	7,062
Columbia, MO	67,545	61,024	48,720	6,521	10.7	58.7	42.3	54.8	39.5	6,373	2,101	1,798
Columbia, SC	290,545	269,244	215,346	21,301	7.9	78.5	58.2	63.9	34.5	21,276	6,439	5,198
Columbus, GA-AL	122,518	115,747	103,609	6,771	5.8	63.3	53.5	53.7	32.9	6,823	1,991	1,437
Columbus, IN	30,727	29,853	25,432	874	2.9	75.5	62.5	69.5	23.8	849	283	131
Columbus, OH	743,500	680,457	569,758	63,043	9.3	186.6	143.0	59.0	33.3	64,622	16,423	17,115
Corpus Christi, TX	167,923	160,753	147,341	7,170	4.5	94.4	82.8	55.7	30.8	6,922	1,997	1,981
Corvallis, OR	33,969	31,980	27,024	1,989	6.2	50.2	39.9	54.0	37.0	1,867	439	369
Cumberland, MD-WV	45,768	45,078	43,443	690	1.5	60.8	57.7	64.3	25.0	983	217	208
Dallas-Fort Worth-Arlington, TX	**2,201,825**	**1,997,943**	**1,672,538**	**203,882**	**10.2**	**244.9**	**186.0**	**56.7**	**36.3**	**198,805**	**52,813**	**51,520**
Dallas-Plano-Irving, TX	*1,472,450*	*1,332,518*	*1,104,094*	*139,932*	*10.5*	*263.5*	*197.5*	*55.1*	*38.1*	*137,368*	*35,649*	*34,376*
Fort Worth-Arlington, TX	*729,375*	*665,425*	*568,444*	*63,950*	*9.6*	*214.5*	*167.1*	*59.8*	*32.7*	*61,437*	*17,164*	*17,144*
Dalton, GA	48,854	45,063	39,039	3,791	8.4	77.0	61.5	65.8	37.9	3,559	859	716
Danville, IL	36,710	36,350	37,061	360	1.0	40.8	41.2	66.0	22.9	262	70	62
Danville, VA	52,321	51,119	46,158	1,202	2.4	51.6	45.5	62.1	29.2	1,254	328	262
Davenport-Moline-Rock Island, IA-IL	162,207	158,528	152,831	3,679	2.3	71.5	67.4	67.7	24.6	4,727	1,279	1,301
Dayton, OH	374,764	364,407	342,217	10,357	2.8	219.4	200.3	62.4	26.1	12,823	4,109	3,246
Decatur, AL	64,711	62,397	52,631	2,314	3.7	50.7	41.3	69.1	30.0	1,550	429	409
Decatur, IL	51,380	50,241	50,049	1,139	2.3	88.5	86.2	66.4	21.9	1,505	526	393
Deltona-Daytona Beach-Ormond Beach, FL	230,718	211,938	180,972	18,780	8.9	209.1	163.6	65.6	33.5	19,459	6,416	4,940
Denver-Aurora, CO[2]	988,603	876,377	734,643	112,306	12.8	118.3	87.9	64.0	32.2	94,975	17,359	22,336
Des Moines, IA	219,876	199,394	171,122	20,482	10.3	76.4	59.4	67.3	27.9	17,567	5,502	4,864
Detroit-Warren-Livonia, MI	**1,864,404**	**1,797,185**	**1,666,039**	**67,219**	**3.7**	**476.3**	**425.6**	**68.6**	**25.3**	**75,813**	**19,900**	**19,034**
Detroit-Livonia-Dearborn, MI	*834,620*	*826,145*	*832,710*	*8,475*	*1.0*	*1,359.0*	*1,355.9*	*62.0*	*26.6*	*18,823*	*5,638*	*4,842*
Warren-Farmington Hills-Troy, MI	*1,029,784*	*971,040*	*833,329*	*58,744*	*6.0*	*312.1*	*252.5*	*74.2*	*24.1*	*56,990*	*14,262*	*14,192*
Dothan, AL	62,299	59,723	50,668	2,576	4.3	36.3	29.5	64.7	31.3	1,938	455	403
Dover, DE	56,304	50,481	42,106	5,823	11.5	95.5	71.3	65.5	33.2	5,495	2,167	1,452
Dubuque, IA	37,326	35,508	32,053	1,818	5.1	61.4	52.7	69.7	29.1	1,820	541	497
Duluth, MN-WI	133,828	129,877	128,355	3,951	3.0	15.9	15.3	64.9	24.9	4,584	1,349	1,091
Durham, NC	200,646	180,022	145,583	20,624	11.5	113.7	82.4	55.3	37.0	20,106	5,103	4,696
Eau Claire, WI	65,325	60,295	53,765	5,030	8.3	39.6	32.6	65.4	29.1	5,123	1,162	1,370
El Centro, CA	47,775	43,891	36,559	3,884	8.8	11.4	8.8	52.3	38.4	4,052	1,201	1,021
Elizabethtown, KY	46,810	43,532	37,199	3,278	7.5	52.5	41.7	62.7	32.6	3,075	957	799
Elkhart-Goshen, IN	75,012	69,791	60,182	5,221	7.5	161.7	129.7	68.5	28.4	5,131	1,175	1,606
Elmira, NY	38,033	37,745	37,290	288	0.8	93.2	91.4	64.0	33.0	643	145	141
El Paso, TX	240,600	224,447	187,473	16,153	7.2	237.5	185.1	59.5	31.7	15,622	5,271	3,710
Erie, PA	116,307	114,322	108,585	1,985	1.7	145.0	135.4	64.5	32.8	2,831	769	643
Eugene-Springfield, OR	144,372	138,954	116,676	5,418	3.9	31.7	25.6	58.4	34.0	5,874	1,534	1,625
Evansville, IN-KY	154,784	147,763	137,264	7,021	4.8	67.6	59.9	66.5	26.8	6,817	1,904	1,778
Fairbanks, AK	33,780	33,291	31,823	489	1.5	4.6	4.3	48.3	39.5	734	257	170
Fargo, ND-MN	80,602	73,536	60,953	7,066	9.6	28.7	21.7	56.1	43.4	7,258	2,266	2,159
Farmington, NM	44,359	43,221	34,248	1,138	2.6	8.0	6.2	65.7	42.8	989	367	280
Fayetteville, NC	139,833	130,943	106,359	8,890	6.8	133.9	101.8	55.2	31.9	8,522	2,267	2,836
Fayetteville-Springdale-Rogers, AR-MO	163,309	144,435	101,302	18,874	13.1	51.5	32.0	60.9	28.7	17,116	6,287	3,996
Flagstaff, AZ	57,224	53,443	42,914	3,781	7.1	3.1	2.3	46.5	36.8	3,614	1,189	865
Flint, MI	193,626	183,635	170,808	9,991	5.4	302.7	267.0	67.7	24.7	10,420	2,240	2,403
Florence, SC	82,873	80,778	66,810	2,095	2.6	60.9	49.1	67.2	37.2	1,998	251	701
Florence-Muscle Shoals, AL	67,468	65,404	55,334	2,064	3.2	53.4	43.8	66.4	25.3	1,341	442	326
Fond du Lac, WI	41,102	39,271	34,548	1,831	4.7	56.9	47.8	68.6	27.3	1,993	484	529
Fort Collins-Loveland, CO	119,416	105,392	77,811	14,024	13.3	45.9	29.9	62.4	27.8	13,227	3,003	3,036
Fort Smith, AR-OK	119,973	115,381	98,903	4,592	4.0	30.0	24.7	63.8	27.5	3,331	914	997
Fort Walton Beach-Crestview-Destin, FL	85,065	78,593	62,569	6,472	8.2	90.9	66.9	55.9	32.8	6,613	1,749	1,936
Fort Wayne, IN	172,293	162,420	143,703	9,873	6.1	126.4	105.4	67.5	25.2	10,275	2,631	2,913
Fresno, CA	286,072	270,767	235,563	15,305	5.7	48.0	39.5	52.8	31.5	16,514	5,753	3,837
Gadsden, AL	47,397	45,959	41,787	1,438	3.1	88.6	78.1	67.4	24.2	1,232	335	328
Gainesville, FL	108,888	101,019	83,093	7,869	7.8	89.0	67.9	51.9	48.6	8,091	1,763	1,884
Gainesville, GA	58,848	51,056	38,315	7,792	15.3	149.5	97.3	66.0	28.0	7,569	1,830	1,919
Glens Falls, NY	63,753	61,646	55,953	2,107	3.4	37.4	32.8	56.2	26.3	2,509	778	736
Goldsboro, NC	49,510	47,313	39,483	2,197	4.6	89.6	71.4	58.8	37.6	1,972	690	433
Grand Forks, ND-MN	42,556	41,381	41,360	1,175	2.8	12.5	12.1	54.6	38.5	1,402	674	371
Grand Junction, CO	54,539	48,718	39,208	5,821	11.9	16.4	11.8	68.8	28.8	5,528	1,589	1,370
Grand Rapids-Wyoming, MI	309,632	293,084	253,364	16,548	5.6	109.5	89.6	67.9	29.9	17,080	4,284	4,633
Great Falls, MT	35,568	35,225	33,063	343	1.0	13.2	12.3	59.9	33.6	587	201	120
Greeley, CO[2]	83,132	66,165	51,138	16,967	25.6	20.8	12.8	65.6	29.8	17,044	3,963	4,411
Green Bay, WI	128,697	118,235	101,116	10,462	8.8	68.8	54.1	63.4	29.3	10,779	3,111	2,800
Greensboro-High Point, NC	296,729	275,027	226,103	21,702	7.9	148.1	112.8	62.4	30.8	21,663	4,816	5,668
Greenville, NC	73,448	65,733	49,014	7,715	11.7	80.1	53.4	54.0	47.0	7,285	1,736	1,880

See footnotes at end of table.

Metropolitan statistical area **Metropolitan statistical area** **with metropolitan divisions** *Metropolitan division*	Housing units							Housing 2000, percent		New private housing units authorized by building permits		
	2004 (July 1)	2000[1] (estimates base)	1990 (April 1)	Change 2000–2004 Number	Change 2000–2004 Percent	Units per square mile of land 2004	Units per square mile of land 1990	Home owner-ship rate	Units in multi-unit struc-tures	Cum-ulative 2000–2003 period	2003	2002
Greenville, SC	255,791	239,037	190,711	16,754	7.0	127.8	95.3	63.9	33.8	17,349	4,469	4,305
Gulfport-Biloxi, MS	115,113	106,051	88,522	9,062	8.5	76.6	58.9	58.6	33.2	7,165	1,962	1,577
Hagerstown-Martinsburg, MD-WV	103,326	93,961	79,590	9,365	10.0	102.5	78.9	63.5	28.6	9,605	2,832	2,907
Hanford-Corcoran, CA	39,216	36,563	30,843	2,653	7.3	28.2	22.2	52.6	24.7	2,823	1,017	701
Harrisburg-Carlisle, PA	224,981	217,025	196,855	7,956	3.7	138.1	120.8	65.0	28.1	9,264	2,831	2,386
Harrisonburg, VA	43,739	41,010	33,514	2,729	6.7	50.3	38.6	60.7	30.6	2,751	728	793
Hartford-West Hartford-East Hartford, CT	483,173	471,877	450,082	11,296	2.4	319.0	297.1	62.7	36.1	14,752	4,137	3,846
Hattiesburg, MS	52,333	50,453	43,881	1,880	3.7	32.5	27.2	61.6	34.3	1,168	133	451
Hickory-Lenoir-Morganton, NC	153,626	144,866	121,418	8,760	6.0	93.8	74.1	68.7	32.3	8,116	1,619	1,875
Hinesville-Fort Stewart, GA	27,719	26,209	19,414	1,510	5.8	30.1	21.1	46.5	47.9	1,296	336	406
Holland-Grand Haven, MI	95,536	86,856	66,624	8,680	10.0	168.9	117.8	76.0	24.1	8,715	2,451	1,975
Honolulu, HI	325,775	315,988	281,683	9,787	3.1	543.2	469.3	49.4	45.3	10,090	3,473	2,673
Hot Springs, AR	46,100	44,953	37,966	1,147	2.6	68.1	56.0	59.9	32.3	472	129	125
Houma-Bayou Cane-Thibodaux, LA	78,452	74,973	66,748	3,479	4.6	33.5	28.5	69.6	28.2	3,254	1,053	794
Houston-Sugar Land-Baytown, TX	1,987,809	1,799,627	1,556,545	188,182	10.5	222.6	174.3	56.1	36.7	177,297	56,571	47,088
Huntington-Ashland, WV-KY-OH	131,302	129,864	121,397	1,438	1.1	75.1	69.4	65.5	28.2	960	179	212
Huntsville, AL	156,942	147,185	119,310	9,757	6.6	114.3	86.9	65.2	28.4	6,895	2,397	1,659
Idaho Falls, ID	40,220	36,771	31,402	3,449	9.4	13.6	10.6	72.0	25.4	3,545	1,183	932
Indianapolis, IN	708,938	644,873	535,871	64,065	9.9	183.5	138.7	62.4	28.2	64,409	15,784	16,388
Iowa City, IA	60,006	54,374	45,076	5,632	10.4	50.7	38.1	57.1	40.8	5,337	1,555	1,331
Ithaca, NY	40,016	38,625	35,338	1,391	3.6	84.1	74.2	50.7	47.2	1,590	336	399
Jackson, MI	66,354	62,906	57,979	3,448	5.5	93.9	82.0	70.7	23.5	3,623	831	928
Jackson, MS	208,815	196,546	172,127	12,269	6.2	56.0	46.2	64.2	29.6	12,005	3,569	3,438
Jackson, TN	47,478	44,379	36,753	3,099	7.0	56.2	43.5	63.5	28.6	2,898	761	684
Jacksonville, FL	527,288	475,043	390,335	52,245	11.0	163.7	121.2	61.5	34.7	53,614	15,821	14,361
Jacksonville, NC	60,330	55,726	47,526	4,604	8.3	78.7	62.0	50.2	37.2	4,172	1,048	1,042
Janesville, WI	65,520	62,187	54,840	3,333	5.4	90.9	76.1	67.1	24.2	3,644	988	972
Jefferson City, MO	60,153	56,729	48,399	3,424	6.0	26.7	21.5	66.3	28.7	2,542	496	655
Johnson City, TN	85,356	81,913	67,233	3,443	4.2	100.0	78.8	65.3	33.3	2,595	944	747
Johnstown, PA	66,067	65,796	67,374	271	0.4	96.0	97.9	68.8	22.0	875	237	213
Jonesboro, AR	48,555	46,184	38,705	2,371	5.1	33.1	26.4	59.2	28.8	2,086	690	533
Joplin, MO	70,711	67,468	57,938	3,243	4.8	55.8	45.8	64.0	23.5	2,060	599	476
Kalamazoo-Portage, MI	140,764	133,225	120,485	7,539	5.7	120.0	102.7	62.9	31.3	7,729	2,462	1,710
Kankakee-Bradley, IL	42,350	40,610	37,001	1,740	4.3	62.6	54.6	65.3	27.7	1,981	671	468
Kansas City, MO-KS	822,608	767,761	688,078	54,847	7.1	104.7	87.6	63.8	25.7	57,071	14,935	13,976
Kennewick-Richland-Pasco, WA	78,789	72,047	58,541	6,742	9.4	26.7	19.9	64.0	37.6	7,059	2,249	2,247
Killeen-Temple-Fort Hood, TX	133,110	122,159	101,120	10,951	9.0	47.1	35.8	51.9	33.5	9,865	2,675	2,968
Kingsport-Bristol-Bristol, TN-VA	141,627	136,277	116,762	5,350	3.9	70.4	58.0	69.2	28.7	4,605	1,250	1,306
Kingston, NY	79,846	77,656	71,716	2,190	2.8	70.9	63.7	59.1	29.3	2,773	805	848
Knoxville, TN	293,060	276,142	228,128	16,918	6.1	157.8	122.9	64.3	28.8	15,235	3,899	4,163
Kokomo, IN	46,086	44,452	40,247	1,634	3.7	83.3	72.7	67.8	22.4	1,792	403	500
La Crosse, WI-MN	54,077	51,647	45,496	2,430	4.7	53.5	45.0	64.4	34.1	2,594	680	624
Lafayette, IN	77,243	70,836	60,398	6,407	9.0	60.4	47.2	56.1	34.7	6,381	1,519	1,432
Lafayette, LA	104,169	98,367	85,023	5,802	5.9	103.2	84.2	62.9	34.3	5,258	1,574	1,556
Lake Charles, LA	86,351	81,331	71,457	5,020	6.2	36.2	30.0	64.1	31.9	4,547	1,458	986
Lakeland, FL	246,661	226,376	186,225	20,285	9.0	131.6	99.3	60.7	44.0	21,062	6,823	4,972
Lancaster, PA	188,486	179,990	156,462	8,496	4.7	198.6	164.8	67.9	25.0	9,521	2,690	2,548
Lansing-East Lansing, MI	192,283	181,844	165,018	10,439	5.7	112.6	96.7	63.8	30.5	10,347	3,156	2,406
Laredo, TX	62,825	55,206	37,197	7,619	13.8	18.7	11.1	60.4	30.2	7,098	1,671	1,805
Las Cruces, NM	70,400	65,210	49,148	5,190	8.0	18.5	12.9	61.6	43.8	4,956	1,767	1,213
Las Vegas-Paradise, NV	683,244	559,784	317,188	123,460	22.1	86.4	40.1	54.1	42.5	121,819	36,732	29,156
Lawrence, KS	44,032	40,251	31,782	3,781	9.4	96.4	69.6	49.6	38.9	3,848	1,060	948
Lawton, OK	45,976	45,416	43,589	560	1.2	43.0	40.8	52.9	23.5	604	162	162
Lebanon, PA	51,629	49,320	44,634	2,309	4.7	142.7	123.4	68.7	24.2	2,677	744	810
Lewiston, ID-WA	25,785	25,314	21,982	471	1.9	17.4	14.8	63.7	29.7	609	155	143
Lewiston-Auburn, ME	47,198	45,960	43,815	1,238	2.7	100.4	93.2	58.0	46.3	1,509	508	378
Lexington-Fayette, KY	189,984	175,262	145,229	14,722	8.4	128.5	98.2	56.0	33.6	14,917	3,975	3,934
Lima, OH	44,863	44,245	42,758	618	1.4	110.9	105.7	66.2	23.4	925	284	190
Lincoln, NE	118,208	110,645	92,642	7,563	6.8	83.6	65.5	58.1	33.5	8,061	2,498	1,998
Little Rock-North Little Rock, AR	278,356	261,917	223,788	16,439	6.3	68.1	54.7	61.3	32.1	14,426	4,098	4,536
Logan, UT-ID	36,403	32,907	25,293	3,496	10.6	19.9	13.8	62.6	29.1	3,322	988	731
Longview, TX	83,184	81,146	76,668	2,038	2.5	46.6	42.9	64.2	29.1	1,129	332	321
Longview, WA	40,261	38,624	33,304	1,637	4.2	35.4	29.2	62.8	31.4	1,842	436	481
Los Angeles-Long Beach-Santa Ana, CA	**4,329,148**	**4,240,390**	**4,038,415**	**88,758**	**2.1**	**892.6**	**832.7**	**48.9**	**42.2**	**114,794**	**30,151**	**28,250**
Los Angeles-Long Beach-Glendale, CA	*3,319,806*	*3,270,906*	*3,163,343*	*48,900*	*1.5*	*817.5*	*779.2*	*45.8*	*43.9*	*72,619*	*20,903*	*16,454*
Santa Ana-Anaheim-Irvine, CA	*1,009,342*	*969,484*	*875,072*	*39,858*	*4.1*	*1,278.6*	*1,108.1*	*59.2*	*36.6*	*42,175*	*9,248*	*11,796*
Louisville, KY-IN	524,401	492,296	432,133	32,105	6.5	126.8	104.5	65.3	28.5	-	(X)	(X)
Lubbock, TX	111,395	103,797	95,082	7,598	7.3	61.9	52.8	54.4	31.7	7,485	2,956	1,873
Lynchburg, VA	103,367	98,057	84,018	5,310	5.4	48.7	39.5	68.0	27.6	5,320	1,421	1,458
Macon, GA	99,229	94,063	82,512	5,166	5.5	57.5	47.8	59.1	33.3	5,295	1,871	1,040
Madera, CA	43,897	40,387	30,831	3,510	8.7	20.6	14.4	59.3	20.3	3,645	1,227	981
Madison, WI	232,911	212,662	175,329	20,249	9.5	85.1	64.0	57.3	38.2	21,119	6,117	4,938

See footnotes at end of table.

Metropolitan statistical area **Metropolitan statistical area with metropolitan divisions** *Metropolitan division*	Housing units							Housing 2000, percent		New private housing units authorized by building permits		
	2004 (July 1)	2000[1] (esti-mates base)	1990 (April 1)	Change 2000–2004		Units per square mile of land		Home owner-ship rate	Units in multi-unit struc-tures	Cum-ulative 2000–2003 period	2003	2002
				Number	Per-cent	2004	1990					
Manchester-Nashua, NH	157,453	149,961	135,622	7,492	5.0	179.7	154.7	62.6	38.4	8,198	2,051	2,426
Mansfield, OH	54,698	53,062	50,350	1,636	3.1	110.1	101.3	66.8	24.7	1,964	490	446
McAllen-Edinburg-Mission, TX	222,809	192,658	128,241	30,151	15.7	141.9	81.7	59.5	36.5	28,062	8,060	7,477
Medford, OR	82,297	75,737	60,376	6,560	8.7	29.5	21.7	62.8	33.8	6,639	2,138	1,548
Memphis, TN-MS-AR	518,296	480,841	415,777	37,455	7.8	113.4	90.9	61.5	28.6	37,483	9,605	9,084
Merced, CA	75,110	68,373	58,410	6,737	9.9	38.9	30.3	54.8	26.1	6,967	2,742	1,753
Miami-Fort Lauderdale-Miami Beach, FL	**2,294,911**	**2,149,890**	**1,861,613**	**145,021**	**6.7**	**447.7**	**358.9**	**58.5**	**48.1**	**149,670**	**39,595**	**39,594**
Fort Lauderdale-Pompano Beach-Deerfield Beach, FL	*782,384*	*741,043*	*628,660*	*41,341*	*5.6*	*649.1*	*520.0*	*61.3*	*51.3*	*42,977*	*8,218*	*12,028*
Miami-Miami Beach-Kendall, FL	*906,877*	*852,414*	*771,288*	*54,463*	*6.4*	*466.0*	*396.7*	*52.7*	*47.4*	*56,610*	*15,533*	*14,606*
West Palm Beach-Boca Raton-Boynton Beach, FL	*605,650*	*556,433*	*461,665*	*49,217*	*8.8*	*306.8*	*226.9*	*63.6*	*44.8*	*50,083*	*15,844*	*12,960*
Michigan City-La Porte, IN	47,158	45,621	42,268	1,537	3.4	78.8	70.6	67.7	22.9	1,712	417	413
Midland, TX	49,013	48,060	45,181	953	2.0	54.4	50.2	61.8	31.4	799	260	227
Milwaukee-Waukesha-West Allis, WI	637,701	618,245	562,031	19,456	3.1	436.8	385.0	58.1	40.2	23,913	6,467	5,936
Minneapolis-St. Paul-Bloomington, MN-WI	1,265,792	1,169,776	1,015,235	96,016	8.2	208.8	167.4	70.4	29.9	98,659	27,623	25,751
Missoula, MT	44,351	41,319	33,466	3,032	7.3	17.1	12.9	57.6	36.9	3,168	947	1,127
Mobile, AL	172,738	165,101	151,220	7,637	4.6	140.1	122.6	62.6	27.2	7,929	1,684	1,728
Modesto, CA	163,880	150,807	132,027	13,073	8.7	109.7	88.3	59.6	22.6	13,530	4,119	3,173
Monroe, LA	73,296	71,027	65,604	2,269	3.2	49.3	44.1	60.0	31.7	1,913	543	491
Monroe, MI	62,081	56,471	48,312	5,610	9.9	112.6	87.7	77.1	23.6	4,137	1,160	954
Montgomery, AL	151,297	144,635	121,546	6,662	4.6	55.5	44.6	62.7	29.3	6,172	1,772	1,613
Morgantown, WV	51,265	50,139	43,700	1,126	2.2	50.8	43.3	59.8	38.8	340	90	71
Morristown, TN	56,815	53,744	42,185	3,071	5.7	79.4	59.0	69.1	31.7	2,342	598	524
Mount Vernon-Anacortes, WA	45,724	42,681	33,580	3,043	7.1	26.4	19.4	63.5	28.0	3,187	904	887
Muncie, IN	52,441	51,032	48,793	1,409	2.8	133.3	124.1	62.1	27.2	1,614	563	313
Muskegon-Norton Shores, MI	72,069	68,556	61,962	3,513	5.1	141.6	121.7	71.8	22.5	3,695	969	992
Myrtle Beach-Conway-North Myrtle Beach, SC	140,628	122,085	89,960	18,543	15.2	124.0	79.4	48.9	52.6	17,907	5,130	4,017
Napa, CA	51,326	48,554	44,199	2,772	5.7	68.1	58.6	60.9	26.3	3,063	607	1,003
Naples-Marco Island, FL	174,564	144,536	94,165	30,028	20.8	86.2	46.5	53.8	54.8	29,230	5,820	7,282
Nashville-Davidson-Murfreesboro, TN	594,091	543,271	437,463	50,820	9.4	104.5	76.9	62.7	31.7	48,085	13,549	11,782
New Haven-Milford, CT	345,094	340,732	327,079	4,362	1.3	569.8	539.9	59.1	41.3	7,031	1,826	1,701
New Orleans-Metairie-Kenner, LA	563,028	548,629	533,488	14,399	2.6	178.5	169.2	55.9	34.2	20,117	6,129	5,383
New York-Northern New Jersey-Long Island, NY-NJ-PA	**7,238,782**	**7,091,153**	**6,638,677**	**147,629**	**2.1**	**1,076.3**	**986.1**	**47.8**	**56.7**	**189,222**	**49,812**	**46,390**
Edison, NJ	*914,028*	*875,255*	*781,098*	*38,773*	*4.4*	*530.6*	*453.2*	*68.0*	*25.6*	*42,400*	*10,331*	*9,435*
Nassau-Suffolk, NY	*994,466*	*980,474*	*927,609*	*13,992*	*1.4*	*829.5*	*774.3*	*74.8*	*16.8*	*21,582*	*4,182*	*5,351*
Newark-Union, NJ-PA	*824,179*	*804,577*	*763,901*	*19,602*	*2.4*	*375.2*	*347.7*	*58.0*	*41.1*	*25,915*	*7,277*	*6,187*
New York-White Plains-Wayne, NY-NJ	*4,506,109*	*4,430,847*	*4,166,069*	*75,262*	*1.7*	*2,802.7*	*2,582.0*	*35.9*	*74.6*	*99,325*	*28,022*	*25,417*
Niles-Benton Harbor, MI	75,444	73,445	69,532	1,999	2.7	132.1	121.8	62.5	23.5	2,273	608	614
Norwich-New London, CT	113,666	110,674	104,461	2,992	2.7	170.7	156.8	60.1	31.6	3,774	1,222	956
Ocala, FL	140,344	122,663	94,567	17,681	14.4	88.9	59.9	69.4	38.2	18,161	6,475	6,161
Ocean City, NJ	96,405	91,047	85,537	5,358	5.9	377.8	335.2	34.4	39.3	5,760	1,693	1,422
Odessa, TX	50,577	49,500	48,789	1,077	2.2	56.1	54.1	60.8	35.7	712	173	200
Ogden-Clearfield, UT	162,948	146,726	115,309	16,222	11.1	109.4	77.4	72.4	22.5	15,863	4,422	3,980
Oklahoma City, OK	497,594	472,084	430,605	25,510	5.4	90.2	78.0	59.3	27.2	25,729	8,082	6,289
Olympia, WA	93,039	86,652	66,464	6,387	7.4	128.0	91.4	62.7	33.6	6,627	2,014	1,835
Omaha-Council Bluffs, NE-IA	334,009	311,587	275,262	22,422	7.2	76.6	63.1	63.2	27.0	23,314	6,370	5,919
Orlando-Kissimmee, FL	786,786	683,551	524,197	103,235	15.1	225.4	150.2	60.6	35.7	102,684	28,233	26,208
Oshkosh-Neenah, WI	69,258	64,721	56,123	4,537	7.0	157.9	128.0	64.2	30.4	4,947	1,460	1,375
Owensboro, KY	49,868	46,424	42,163	3,444	7.4	55.1	46.6	67.2	27.8	3,296	603	1,094
Oxnard-Thousand Oaks-Ventura, CA	264,339	251,711	228,478	12,628	5.0	143.2	123.8	65.3	25.4	13,505	3,567	2,525
Palm Bay-Melbourne-Titusville, FL	243,652	222,072	185,150	21,580	9.7	239.3	181.8	66.6	33.9	22,119	6,169	6,622
Panama City-Lynn Haven, FL	86,013	78,435	65,999	7,578	9.7	112.6	86.4	52.1	41.7	7,815	3,676	1,616
Parkersburg-Marietta-Vienna, WV-OH	75,168	74,025	69,301	1,143	1.5	55.0	50.7	67.6	26.4	1,031	229	234
Pascagoula, MS	63,278	59,191	52,205	4,087	6.9	52.5	43.3	69.9	26.4	3,751	897	820
Pensacola-Ferry Pass-Brent, FL	186,802	173,766	145,061	13,036	7.5	111.2	86.4	63.2	29.2	13,707	4,801	3,213
Peoria, IL	158,426	153,285	144,491	5,141	3.4	64.1	58.5	68.1	20.8	5,935	1,757	1,411
Philadelphia-Camden-Wilmington, PA-NJ-DE-MD	**2,342,807**	**2,281,823**	**2,133,715**	**60,984**	**2.7**	**506.0**	**460.8**	**65.5**	**26.0**	**77,455**	**21,095**	**18,994**
Camden, NJ	*473,962*	*456,043*	*415,840*	*17,919*	*3.9*	*350.7*	*307.6*	*70.6*	*22.9*	*20,403*	*5,598*	*5,321*
Philadelphia, PA	*1,596,115*	*1,565,640*	*1,491,310*	*30,475*	*1.9*	*737.0*	*688.5*	*63.7*	*27.0*	*43,608*	*11,692*	*10,280*
Wilmington, DE-MD-NJ	*272,730*	*260,140*	*226,565*	*12,590*	*4.8*	*245.2*	*203.7*	*66.7*	*25.4*	*13,444*	*3,805*	*3,393*
Phoenix-Mesa-Scottsdale, AZ	1,527,894	1,331,385	1,004,773	196,509	14.8	104.8	68.9	61.0	35.4	194,169	54,860	47,899
Pine Bluff, AR	44,197	43,139	40,928	1,058	2.5	21.6	20.0	60.6	28.2	657	214	147
Pittsburgh, PA	1,096,567	1,078,481	1,046,965	18,086	1.7	207.7	198.4	66.0	26.6	27,015	6,513	7,040
Pittsfield, MA	67,146	66,301	64,324	845	1.3	72.1	69.1	56.5	35.7	1,547	417	459
Pocatello, ID	33,105	31,946	28,395	1,159	3.6	13.1	11.3	66.1	31.1	1,307	412	354
Portland-South Portland-Biddeford, ME	245,624	233,323	204,464	12,301	5.3	118.1	98.3	58.5	31.1	13,246	3,505	3,455
Portland-Vancouver-Beaverton, OR-WA	844,347	790,876	624,011	53,471	6.8	126.3	93.4	59.3	34.0	57,253	16,003	14,378
Port St. Lucie-Fort Pierce, FL	179,702	156,733	128,042	22,969	14.7	159.3	113.5	66.5	36.5	23,275	9,690	6,032
Poughkeepsie-Newburgh-Middletown, NY	239,906	228,857	208,446	11,049	4.8	148.3	128.8	63.6	31.0	12,379	2,909	3,259
Prescott, AZ	93,254	81,730	54,805	11,524	14.1	11.5	6.7	63.0	36.7	10,787	2,984	3,264
Providence-New Bedford-Fall River, RI-MA	667,992	656,755	615,807	11,237	1.7	417.3	384.6	56.6	43.4	16,734	4,035	4,551
Provo-Orem, UT	125,226	107,126	75,131	18,100	16.9	23.2	13.9	64.2	28.3	15,869	4,341	3,799
Pueblo, CO	63,972	58,926	50,872	5,046	8.6	26.8	21.3	65.2	24.2	5,073	1,282	1,303

See footnotes at end of table.

Metropolitan statistical area **Metropolitan statistical area with metropolitan divisions** *Metropolitan division*	Housing units			Change 2000–2004		Units per square mile of land		Housing 2000, percent		New private housing units authorized by building permits		
	2004 (July 1)	2000[1] (estimates base)	1990 (April 1)	Number	Percent	2004	1990	Home owner-ship rate	Units in multi-unit struc-tures	Cumulative 2000–2003 period	2003	2002
Punta Gorda, FL	87,954	79,758	64,641	8,196	10.3	126.8	93.2	67.0	30.9	8,310	2,522	1,992
Racine, WI	78,028	74,718	66,965	3,310	4.4	234.2	201.0	66.9	29.1	3,804	1,188	951
Raleigh-Cary, NC	383,121	329,493	226,275	53,628	16.3	181.1	106.9	63.0	32.7	52,322	12,660	11,678
Rapid City, SD	50,524	47,398	41,333	3,126	6.6	8.1	6.6	61.1	36.1	3,061	858	994
Reading, PA	157,157	150,222	134,482	6,935	4.6	183.0	156.5	69.7	22.5	7,952	1,991	2,121
Redding, CA	73,250	68,810	60,552	4,440	6.5	19.4	16.0	61.0	30.8	4,693	1,358	1,341
Reno-Sparks, NV	164,650	145,504	113,278	19,146	13.2	24.9	17.1	54.6	41.3	19,277	5,033	4,716
Richmond, VA	485,593	452,684	389,331	32,909	7.3	85.0	68.2	64.6	24.8	34,333	9,177	9,733
Riverside-San Bernardino-Ontario, CA	1,306,004	1,186,043	1,026,179	119,961	10.1	47.9	37.6	58.1	29.0	123,639	42,252	32,474
Roanoke, VA	135,697	129,589	114,986	6,108	4.7	72.4	61.4	65.1	27.4	6,513	1,627	1,613
Rochester, MN	73,343	65,130	55,579	8,213	12.6	45.3	34.4	74.6	26.6	7,802	2,016	1,952
Rochester, NY	436,636	427,172	399,088	9,464	2.2	149.0	136.1	63.2	31.4	12,702	3,422	2,991
Rockford, IL	137,211	129,818	113,143	7,393	5.7	172.6	142.3	67.1	27.2	8,154	2,625	1,980
Rocky Mount, NC	64,515	61,052	52,851	3,463	5.7	61.7	50.6	58.7	34.2	3,271	762	912
Rome, GA	38,552	36,615	32,821	1,937	5.3	75.1	63.9	62.1	26.6	2,057	502	722
Sacramento-Arden-Arcade-Roseville, CA	794,166	714,981	609,904	79,185	11.1	155.9	119.7	57.0	28.3	80,158	22,832	22,099
Saginaw-Saginaw Township North, MI	87,972	85,507	81,931	2,465	2.9	108.8	101.3	69.5	23.3	2,831	699	630
St. Cloud, MN	70,359	63,754	55,327	6,605	10.4	40.1	31.6	68.8	28.6	6,705	2,015	1,848
St. George, UT	44,909	36,478	19,523	8,431	23.1	18.5	8.0	60.7	25.3	8,185	2,729	2,083
St. Joseph, MO-KS	51,800	50,564	48,188	1,236	2.4	31.2	29.0	64.5	25.0	1,131	304	285
St. Louis, MO-IL[3]	1,183,069	1,133,255	1,064,366	49,814	4.4	136.8	123.0	66.3	28.6	53,225	14,754	14,157
Salem, OR	139,725	132,637	105,847	7,088	5.3	72.6	55.0	60.1	33.0	7,413	1,979	1,960
Salinas, CA	136,549	131,708	121,224	4,841	3.7	41.1	36.5	50.3	30.3	5,347	1,355	1,222
Salisbury, MD	47,927	44,493	39,501	3,434	7.7	68.0	56.1	61.2	25.3	3,636	1,298	915
Salt Lake City, UT	367,935	342,297	278,105	25,648	7.5	38.6	29.1	64.7	29.9	27,273	8,145	6,632
San Angelo, TX	45,915	44,830	40,977	1,085	2.4	17.8	15.9	57.7	27.4	1,012	265	251
San Antonio, TX	701,046	648,587	548,023	52,459	8.1	95.5	74.7	59.8	31.0	50,728	13,375	13,241
San Diego-Carlsbad-San Marcos, CA	1,099,235	1,040,149	946,240	59,086	5.7	261.7	225.1	53.0	39.6	62,712	18,031	13,684
Sandusky, OH	36,820	35,909	32,827	911	2.5	144.5	129.0	63.6	25.5	1,095	334	204
San Francisco-Oakland-Fremont, CA	**1,654,724**	**1,606,855**	**1,500,289**	**47,869**	**3.0**	**669.1**	**606.6**	**53.5**	**41.0**	**53,583**	**14,828**	**12,541**
Oakland-Fremont-Hayward, CA	*928,689*	*894,760*	*820,279*	*33,929*	*3.8*	*637.2*	*562.7*	*58.6*	*33.9*	*38,373*	*11,352*	*9,319*
San Francisco-San Mateo-Redwood City, CA	*726,035*	*712,095*	*680,010*	*13,940*	*2.0*	*714.9*	*669.6*	*47.1*	*49.9*	*15,210*	*3,476*	*3,222*
San Jose-Sunnyvale-Santa Clara, CA	618,317	595,828	552,470	22,489	3.8	230.7	206.1	58.7	34.5	25,202	7,103	4,621
San Luis Obispo-Paso Robles, CA	109,798	102,275	90,200	7,523	7.4	33.2	27.3	55.7	29.5	7,869	2,260	1,993
Santa Barbara-Santa Maria, CA	147,831	142,901	138,149	4,930	3.4	54.0	50.4	53.6	35.3	5,050	1,461	1,696
Santa Cruz-Watsonville, CA	101,040	98,873	91,878	2,167	2.2	226.9	206.1	55.3	27.7	2,819	1,066	608
Santa Fe, NM	60,278	57,701	41,464	2,577	4.5	31.6	21.7	62.4	31.5	2,097	561	604
Santa Rosa-Petaluma, CA	191,689	183,153	161,062	8,536	4.7	121.6	102.2	60.3	23.9	9,268	2,252	1,928
Sarasota-Bradenton-Venice, FL	355,803	320,595	272,300	35,208	11.0	271.1	207.4	62.8	41.3	35,969	9,025	10,186
Savannah, GA	133,020	122,527	106,219	10,493	8.6	97.9	78.0	58.3	33.2	10,447	2,526	2,691
Scranton-Wilkes-Barre, PA	255,885	252,761	242,288	3,124	1.2	146.5	138.7	62.8	30.2	5,447	1,530	1,518
Seattle-Tacoma-Bellevue, WA	**1,338,140**	**1,255,504**	**1,060,127**	**82,636**	**6.6**	**227.0**	**179.9**	**59.2**	**37.2**	**84,921**	**20,601**	**20,887**
Seattle-Bellevue-Everett, WA	*1,040,502*	*978,444*	*831,285*	*62,058*	*6.3*	*246.9*	*197.2*	*59.1*	*38.4*	*63,880*	*15,449*	*15,420*
Tacoma, WA	*297,638*	*277,060*	*228,842*	*20,578*	*7.4*	*177.3*	*136.6*	*59.8*	*32.8*	*21,041*	*5,152*	*5,467*
Sheboygan, WI	48,277	45,951	40,695	2,326	5.1	94.0	79.2	67.7	30.7	2,579	599	680
Sherman-Denison, TX	50,007	48,315	44,223	1,692	3.5	53.6	47.4	62.6	26.8	1,162	337	356
Shreveport-Bossier City, LA	166,178	159,786	153,528	6,392	4.0	64.0	59.1	59.7	31.0	5,661	2,243	1,420
Sioux City, IA-NE-SD	57,997	56,940	52,456	1,057	1.9	28.0	25.3	65.3	26.0	1,635	437	416
Sioux Falls, SD	85,005	75,603	61,774	9,402	12.4	33.0	24.0	64.8	31.9	9,347	2,520	2,057
South Bend-Mishawaka, IN-MI	136,416	130,897	120,600	5,519	4.2	143.7	127.0	67.5	20.5	6,005	1,366	1,413
Spartanburg, SC	114,726	106,986	89,927	7,740	7.2	141.5	110.9	65.8	30.2	7,206	2,081	1,986
Spokane, WA	184,401	175,005	150,105	9,396	5.4	104.6	85.1	61.2	31.1	8,933	2,550	2,066
Springfield, IL	94,137	90,746	81,523	3,391	3.7	79.6	68.9	65.0	27.0	3,853	1,075	930
Springfield, MA	279,968	276,459	263,487	3,509	1.3	151.4	142.4	59.5	38.7	5,978	1,663	1,652
Springfield, MO	170,427	156,493	124,252	13,934	8.9	56.6	41.3	62.9	25.2	12,098	3,455	3,486
Springfield, OH	61,807	61,055	58,377	752	1.2	154.6	145.9	66.3	24.8	1,124	273	292
State College, PA	56,372	53,161	46,195	3,211	6.0	50.9	41.7	55.8	37.9	3,448	1,022	995
Stockton, CA	211,678	189,160	166,274	22,518	11.9	151.3	118.8	58.0	25.7	22,915	7,041	6,143
Sumter, SC	43,455	41,747	35,016	1,708	4.1	65.3	52.6	62.8	36.5	1,709	653	404
Syracuse, NY	282,750	278,110	266,067	4,640	1.7	118.3	111.3	60.7	34.6	6,799	1,703	1,921
Tallahassee, FL	148,572	136,748	107,166	11,824	8.6	62.2	44.9	57.3	41.7	12,150	3,526	3,320
Tampa-St. Petersburg-Clearwater, FL	1,233,984	1,143,995	1,025,064	89,989	7.9	483.2	401.3	62.4	40.8	93,881	29,281	23,542
Terre Haute, IN	74,619	72,509	70,584	2,110	2.9	50.9	48.2	65.3	24.4	1,724	359	399
Texarkana, TX-Texarkana, AR	56,568	54,190	50,406	2,378	4.4	37.4	33.3	62.9	29.5	1,700	651	388
Toledo, OH	294,954	285,491	270,583	9,463	3.3	182.1	167.1	62.0	29.9	11,204	3,205	2,651
Topeka, KS	100,543	96,404	89,046	4,139	4.3	31.0	27.5	65.9	23.9	4,613	1,378	1,371
Trenton-Ewing, NJ	137,573	133,280	123,666	4,293	3.2	608.9	547.3	63.3	29.3	5,254	1,188	1,428
Tucson, AZ	397,150	366,737	298,207	30,413	8.3	43.2	32.5	58.2	38.5	30,308	7,910	7,147
Tulsa, OK	383,373	366,194	335,728	17,179	4.7	61.0	53.4	62.1	28.4	16,859	4,354	4,545
Tuscaloosa, AL	89,839	84,302	69,272	5,537	6.6	34.4	26.5	58.2	39.7	4,416	1,194	1,338
Tyler, TX	75,047	71,701	64,369	3,346	4.7	80.8	69.3	63.8	29.2	2,368	657	631

See footnotes at end of table.

Metropolitan statistical area **Metropolitan statistical area with metropolitan divisions** *Metropolitan division*	Housing units							Housing 2000, percent		New private housing units authorized by building permits		
	2004 (July 1)	2000[1] (esti- mates base)	1990 (April 1)	Change 2000–2004		Units per square mile of land		Home owner- ship rate	Units in multi- unit struc- tures	Cum- ulative 2000– 2003 period	2003	2002
				Number	Per- cent	2004	1990					
Utica-Rome, NY	135,385	134,829	132,050	556	0.4	51.6	50.3	58.7	38.7	1,779	481	474
Valdosta, GA	51,711	48,165	38,022	3,546	7.4	32.5	23.9	57.2	37.0	3,356	1,050	799
Vallejo-Fairfield, CA	144,005	134,513	119,533	9,492	7.1	173.7	144.3	63.2	24.2	9,917	2,642	2,474
Vero Beach, FL	66,177	57,902	47,128	8,275	14.3	131.5	93.6	65.8	37.4	8,227	2,430	1,894
Victoria, TX	48,000	46,609	41,556	1,391	3.0	21.3	18.5	59.6	28.7	1,026	244	323
Vineland-Millville-Bridgeton, NJ	53,736	52,863	50,294	873	1.7	109.8	102.8	63.2	28.4	1,195	374	310
Virginia Beach-Norfolk-Newport News, VA-NC	657,757	622,629	561,928	35,128	5.6	250.3	213.8	58.8	29.1	36,809	10,353	10,211
Visalia-Porterville, CA	126,792	119,639	105,013	7,153	6.0	26.3	21.8	56.8	22.6	7,662	2,270	1,993
Waco, TX	88,372	84,793	78,857	3,579	4.2	84.8	75.7	56.0	29.8	3,321	891	793
Warner Robins, GA	51,207	44,509	34,785	6,698	15.0	135.9	92.3	63.0	29.3	6,614	1,648	1,411
Washington-Arlington-Alexandria, DC-VA-MD-WV	**2,033,679**	**1,890,036**	**1,633,371**	**143,643**	**7.6**	**361.4**	**290.2**	**60.7**	**33.9**	**149,060**	**35,847**	**38,566**
Bethesda-Gaithersburg-Frederick, MD	*434,555*	*407,648*	*350,595*	*26,907*	*6.6*	*375.1*	*302.9*	*67.7*	*28.4*	*27,785*	*6,265*	*6,591*
Washington-Arlington-Alexandria, DC-VA-MD-WV	*1,599,124*	*1,482,388*	*1,282,776*	*116,736*	*7.9*	*357.8*	*286.9*	*58.8*	*35.4*	*121,275*	*29,582*	*31,975*
Waterloo-Cedar Falls, IA	68,964	66,401	63,693	2,563	3.9	45.7	42.2	68.0	23.8	2,560	690	630
Wausau, WI	54,426	50,360	43,774	4,066	8.1	35.2	28.3	71.7	23.9	4,193	1,395	922
Weirton-Steubenville, WV-OH	59,593	59,169	59,446	424	0.7	102.5	102.2	69.5	22.7	673	156	187
Wenatchee, WA	45,202	43,351	35,688	1,851	4.3	9.5	7.5	56.5	32.2	2,037	663	526
Wheeling, WV-OH	69,487	69,219	69,434	268	0.4	73.1	73.0	66.2	26.2	184	55	44
Wichita, KS	249,931	238,566	213,290	11,365	4.8	60.2	51.4	62.9	26.6	12,374	3,648	3,221
Wichita Falls, TX	63,829	62,167	59,801	1,662	2.7	24.2	22.7	58.7	23.9	1,656	534	494
Williamsport, PA	53,416	52,464	49,580	952	1.8	43.3	40.1	62.2	27.7	1,345	289	355
Wilmington, NC	173,153	151,862	109,627	21,291	14.0	90.0	57.0	54.3	37.6	20,502	6,455	5,497
Winchester, VA-WV	49,156	45,091	36,489	4,065	9.0	46.1	34.2	63.8	23.6	4,090	1,137	1,351
Winston-Salem, NC	196,697	183,129	155,292	13,568	7.4	134.5	106.2	64.9	30.2	13,344	3,406	3,549
Worcester, MA	308,387	298,159	279,428	10,228	3.4	203.8	184.7	61.1	40.2	12,592	3,629	3,313
Yakima, WA	80,887	79,174	70,852	1,713	2.2	18.8	16.5	60.2	32.8	2,078	606	534
York-Hanover, PA	166,175	156,720	134,761	9,455	6.0	183.7	149.0	72.0	22.7	10,298	3,148	2,956
Youngstown-Warren-Boardman, OH-PA	260,844	256,738	247,137	4,106	1.6	153.1	145.1	68.7	22.9	5,999	1,431	1,622
Yuba City, CA	54,245	50,955	45,408	3,290	6.5	44.0	36.8	54.4	29.1	3,608	1,597	1,041
Yuma, AZ	80,604	74,140	46,541	6,464	8.7	14.6	8.4	52.4	58.1	6,239	1,915	1,726

X Not applicable.

[1]The April 1, 2000, housing estimates base reflects changes to the 2000 Census of Population and Housing as documented in the Count Question Resolution program, and geographic program revisions.
[2]The Denver-Aurora metropolitan statistical area includes Broomfield County. Broomfield County, CO, was formed from parts of Adams, Boulder, Jefferson, and Weld counties on November 15, 2001, and is coextensive with Broomfield city. For the purposes of defining and presenting data for the Denver-Aurora metropolitan statistical area, Broomfield city is treated as if it were a county when data are available to do so. In many cases, the data will not be available.
[3]The portion of Sullivan city in Crawford County, MO, is legally part of the St. Louis, MO-IL MSA. That portion is not included in these figures for the St. Louis MSA.

Note: Covers metropolitan statistical areas and metropolitan divisions and component counties defined by the Office of Management and Budget as of June 6, 2003, and subsequently updated in December 2003 and November 2004. For more information, see OMB Bulletin 05-02 at <http://www.whitehouse.gov/omb/bulletins/fy05/b05-02_appendix.pdf>.

Survey, Census, or Data Collection Method: Based on the Census of Population and Housing and, for population estimates, the "component of population change method"; for more information, see Appendix B, Limitations of the Data and Methodology, and also <http://www.census.gov/prod/cen2000/doc/sf1.pdf> and <http://www.census.gov/popest/topics/methodology/>; New housing units—Based on a survey of local building permit officials using Form C-404; for information, see Internet site <http://www.census.gov/const/www/newresconstdoc.html>.

Sources: Housing units 2000 and 2004—U.S. Census Bureau, Population Estimates by Housing Units, *Annual Estimates of Housing Units for Counties: April 1, 2000 to July 1, 2004*, <http://www.census.gov/popest/housing/> (accessed 14 November 2005); Housing units 1990—U.S. Census Bureau, 1990 Census of Population and Housing, *Summary Tape File (STF) 1C* on CD-ROM (archive); Housing 2000—U.S. Census Bureau, 2000 Census of Population and Housing, *Census 2000 Profiles of General Demographic Characteristics* data files, <http://factfinder.census.gov/servlet/SAFFHousing?_sse=on> (accessed 7 August 2002); Building permits—U.S. Census Bureau, "New Residential Construction—Building Permits," e-mail from Manufacturing, Mining, and Construction Statistics Branch, subject: building permits by place 2000.

Table B-8. Metropolitan Areas — **Personal Income and Earnings by Industry**

	Personal income							Earnings, 2002					
	Total (mil. dol.)			Per capita[1] (dol.)		Percent change					Percent by selected major industries		
Metropolitan statistical area **Metropolitan statistical area with metropolitan divisions** *Metropolitan division*											Professional and technical services	Health care and social services	Government and government enterprises
	2002	2001	2000	2002	2000	2001–2002	2000–2002	Total[2] (mil. dol.)	Manufacturing	Retail trade			
Abilene, TX.	3,836.7	3,673.6	3,880.2	24,252	24,232	4.4	−1.1	2,699.3	4.5	8.4	(NA)	(NA)	30.1
Akron, OH	21,147.3	20,601.6	20,592.8	30,205	29,591	2.6	2.7	14,808.9	18.8	7.8	5.7	11.0	14.9
Albany, GA	3,661.7	3,517.1	3,371.3	22,862	21,372	4.1	8.6	2,701.9	(NA)	7.5	(NA)	(NA)	22.9
Albany-Schenectady-Troy, NY	26,966.7	26,178.9	25,167.9	32,297	30,445	3.0	7.1	21,560.1	7.8	6.3	10.3	(NA)	26.8
Albuquerque, NM.	21,421.0	20,524.7	18,910.3	28,471	25,848	4.4	13.3	16,481.1	8.7	7.8	13.4	(NA)	22.7
Alexandria, LA.	3,761.6	3,612.2	3,317.9	25,887	22,863	4.1	13.4	2,393.9	10.8	8.0	4.8	16.9	26.7
Allentown-Bethlehem-Easton, PA-NJ	23,541.8	22,762.4	22,219.5	31,073	29,952	3.4	6.0	15,640.6	21.3	8.0	5.3	13.0	11.1
Altoona, PA	3,165.2	3,061.2	3,057.4	24,815	23,692	3.4	3.5	2,365.8	16.1	10.5	5.0	15.3	15.8
Amarillo, TX	5,827.9	5,626.8	5,564.9	25,255	24,508	3.6	4.7	4,431.1	7.5	9.2	(NA)	(NA)	17.1
Ames, IA	2,173.5	2,103.5	2,066.8	26,479	25,775	3.3	5.2	1,782.7	12.3	6.2	4.3	6.8	44.2
Anchorage, AK	11,874.2	11,335.3	10,329.6	35,623	32,235	4.8	15.0	9,402.6	2.1	7.5	8.2	9.2	27.1
Anderson, IN	3,429.7	3,365.6	3,304.6	26,005	24,795	1.9	3.8	2,037.1	36.4	7.3	2.6	11.4	14.6
Anderson, SC	4,251.7	4,199.0	4,037.3	24,983	24,274	1.3	5.3	2,563.6	31.6	10.1	2.8	7.1	17.9
Ann Arbor, MI	11,801.1	11,458.5	11,541.0	35,282	35,575	3.0	2.3	11,197.8	18.7	5.5	14.0	8.5	27.0
Anniston-Oxford, AL	2,618.1	2,493.0	2,382.4	23,504	21,397	5.0	9.9	1,877.6	19.3	8.4	3.9	8.4	29.8
Appleton, WI.	6,232.1	6,062.3	5,872.7	29,891	28,999	2.8	6.1	4,845.1	24.7	8.0	(NA)	8.8	10.1
Asheville, NC	10,103.1	9,857.3	9,683.7	26,757	26,145	2.5	4.3	6,505.7	17.5	9.0	5.2	(NA)	16.0
Athens-Clarke County, GA.	4,109.3	3,960.8	3,784.7	24,171	22,694	3.8	8.6	3,130.2	14.0	7.6	4.0	(NA)	32.3
Atlanta-Sandy Springs-Marietta, GA	149,973.9	147,307.4	141,816.9	33,257	33,120	1.8	5.8	128,414.9	8.2	6.5	(NA)	(NA)	11.5
Atlantic City, NJ.	8,210.4	7,887.0	7,975.4	31,702	31,517	4.1	2.9	7,259.2	3.2	8.3	6.2	9.5	16.7
Auburn-Opelika, AL	2,529.9	2,436.8	2,337.7	21,445	20,248	3.8	8.2	1,606.8	15.7	9.6	(NA)	7.0	34.5
Augusta-Richmond County, GA-SC	13,016.3	12,505.5	11,963.5	25,666	23,911	4.1	8.8	9,504.5	14.0	7.1	(NA)	(NA)	26.8
Austin-Round Rock, TX.	42,671.2	43,152.2	41,157.3	31,677	32,546	−1.1	3.7	37,221.1	14.6	6.3	11.6	(NA)	17.9
Bakersfield, CA	15,674.5	14,727.0	13,891.4	22,635	20,931	6.4	12.8	11,904.9	4.4	7.3	5.0	8.0	27.1
Baltimore-Towson, MD	92,409.6	89,050.4	85,143.9	35,556	33,294	3.8	8.5	68,078.7	8.3	6.6	11.4	10.5	21.9
Bangor, ME	3,816.5	3,666.7	3,422.3	26,123	23,621	4.1	11.5	3,001.4	13.6	9.8	4.6	17.2	20.1
Barnstable Town, MA	9,020.7	8,713.9	7,979.9	39,589	35,745	3.5	13.0	4,613.6	3.2	11.2	8.6	13.2	15.8
Baton Rouge, LA.	18,494.2	17,840.8	17,206.0	25,841	24,325	3.7	7.5	14,407.6	13.9	6.7	(NA)	(NA)	19.8
Battle Creek, MI	3,621.4	3,477.0	3,471.4	26,097	25,138	4.2	4.3	3,034.6	31.8	6.6	5.6	9.9	19.2
Bay City, MI	2,860.8	2,828.6	2,857.8	26,067	25,951	1.1	0.1	1,726.2	20.5	10.9	10.7	12.3	16.9
Beaumont-Port Arthur, TX	9,689.2	9,374.8	9,169.1	25,352	23,832	3.4	5.7	7,162.6	20.5	7.9	(NA)	(NA)	15.4
Bellingham, WA.	4,508.6	4,341.0	4,063.5	25,902	24,245	3.9	11.0	3,051.1	13.8	8.6	5.8	10.3	18.4
Bend, OR.	3,540.0	3,366.9	3,139.7	28,193	26,929	5.1	12.8	2,387.9	9.5	11.0	7.3	13.3	14.3
Billings, MT.	3,985.6	3,845.7	3,651.0	28,156	26,246	3.6	9.2	3,012.9	6.5	9.6	7.5	(NA)	13.7
Binghamton, NY	6,503.2	6,370.9	6,314.7	25,809	25,054	2.1	3.0	4,823.9	26.4	6.8	4.9	11.5	19.6
Birmingham-Hoover, AL	32,650.9	31,493.6	29,898.1	30,661	28,386	3.7	9.2	25,515.7	9.7	7.5	(NA)	(NA)	13.8
Bismarck, ND	2,657.5	2,571.0	2,434.8	27,649	25,675	3.4	9.2	2,047.9	7.8	8.7	5.3	(NA)	21.5
Blacksburg-Christiansburg-Radford, VA	3,261.9	3,144.6	3,040.2	21,399	20,078	3.7	7.3	2,596.7	26.2	7.1	(NA)	(NA)	29.0
Bloomington, IN.	4,182.1	4,048.4	3,955.7	23,633	22,501	3.3	5.7	2,852.7	15.8	7.5	4.4	(NA)	29.3
Bloomington-Normal, IL.	4,798.5	4,619.4	4,409.9	30,892	29,229	3.9	8.8	4,383.6	10.8	5.8	3.6	8.8	12.7
Boise City-Nampa, ID.	14,397.4	13,976.2	13,415.8	28,878	28,622	3.0	7.3	11,440.2	18.0	7.6	(NA)	(NA)	14.3
Boston-Cambridge-Quincy, MA-NH	**188,418.0**	**188,379.6**	**182,380.4**	**42,436**	**41,435**	**0.0**	**3.3**	**160,711.3**	**11.4**	**5.3**	**14.6**	**9.6**	**10.1**
Boston-Quincy, MA	*77,390.6*	*76,863.4*	*73,221.3*	*42,353*	*40,326*	*0.7*	*5.7*	*76,590.6*	*5.6*	*4.4*	*12.8*	*11.3*	*10.9*
Cambridge-Newton-Framingham, MA	*68,484.6*	*69,183.7*	*68,073.8*	*46,499*	*46,339*	*−1.0*	*0.6*	*58,174.9*	*15.5*	*4.9*	*19.3*	*7.1*	*8.4*
Essex County, MA	*28,203.5*	*28,150.0*	*27,301.5*	*38,309*	*37,635*	*0.2*	*3.3*	*16,516.9*	*22.1*	*7.6*	*9.8*	*11.8*	*12.0*
Rockingham County-Strafford County, NH.	*14,339.3*	*14,182.5*	*13,783.8*	*35,518*	*35,218*	*1.1*	*4.0*	*9,428.9*	*14.0*	*10.3*	*8.7*	*8.5*	*11.1*
Boulder, CO[3]	11,280.5	12,083.5	11,825.5	40,474	40,364	−6.6	−4.6	9,598.5	17.9	5.6	18.1	6.7	14.1
Bowling Green, KY.	2,574.3	2,463.4	2,454.8	24,242	23,502	4.5	4.9	2,025.7	21.5	8.6	4.0	(NA)	16.9
Bremerton-Silverdale, WA	7,570.4	7,159.3	6,852.9	31,740	29,472	5.7	10.5	4,689.0	1.5	7.1	5.3	8.1	54.5
Bridgeport-Stamford-Norwalk, CT	53,432.7	54,393.1	52,189.9	59,727	58,998	−1.8	2.4	39,532.7	12.0	5.8	12.8	7.4	6.7
Brownsville-Harlingen, TX	5,697.0	5,340.4	5,023.1	16,126	14,915	6.7	13.4	3,854.2	9.8	9.0	3.6	17.3	27.0
Brunswick, GA	2,615.6	2,496.8	2,410.9	27,409	25,851	4.8	8.5	1,564.3	11.5	8.6	(NA)	(NA)	26.2
Buffalo-Niagara Falls, NY	33,076.3	32,168.7	31,806.5	28,489	27,209	2.8	4.0	24,352.3	20.0	6.5	7.0	10.8	17.8
Burlington, NC.	3,587.1	3,523.7	3,431.0	26,459	26,102	1.8	4.5	2,483.7	24.0	7.9	4.6	10.4	9.8
Burlington-South Burlington, VT	6,474.2	6,328.1	6,026.0	31,981	30,206	2.3	7.4	5,440.5	21.3	8.2	8.5	(NA)	15.8
Canton-Massillon, OH.	11,061.3	10,791.2	10,748.7	27,185	26,412	2.5	2.9	7,519.5	26.5	8.9	(NA)	(NA)	12.0
Cape Coral-Fort Myers, FL	15,009.4	14,294.6	12,874.8	31,562	29,011	5.0	16.6	8,168.7	4.8	12.4	6.7	9.4	15.4
Carson City, NV.	1,773.7	1,720.8	1,683.8	32,522	32,049	3.1	5.3	1,445.6	10.8	9.3	5.5	7.6	36.4
Casper, WY	2,294.5	2,219.7	2,256.8	34,018	33,911	3.4	1.7	1,670.7	5.8	7.6	5.5	11.4	13.5
Cedar Rapids, IA.	7,328.9	7,253.7	7,111.9	30,341	29,910	1.0	3.1	5,929.9	21.6	7.5	(NA)	(NA)	11.0
Champaign-Urbana, IL	5,862.4	5,684.3	5,447.2	27,294	25,870	3.1	7.6	4,469.2	10.8	6.3	5.8	(NA)	34.2
Charleston, WV.	8,653.7	8,408.8	8,023.7	28,230	25,934	2.9	7.9	6,843.8	10.1	6.8	(NA)	(NA)	18.2
Charleston-North Charleston, SC	15,176.0	14,433.2	13,933.2	26,965	25,316	5.1	8.9	11,585.2	10.4	8.3	7.7	8.6	26.4
Charlotte-Gastonia-Concord, NC-SC	46,511.8	44,965.3	43,120.0	33,083	32,187	3.4	7.9	41,457.8	14.0	6.4	(NA)	6.0	10.2
Charlottesville, VA	5,755.2	5,575.7	5,333.4	32,053	30,513	3.2	7.9	4,267.5	0.1	6.9	(NA)	(NA)	32.5
Chattanooga, TN-GA	13,333.5	12,991.4	12,862.7	27,603	26,958	2.6	3.7	10,314.1	16.8	9.5	(NA)	(NA)	16.2
Cheyenne, WY	2,569.8	2,425.1	2,292.5	30,949	28,057	6.0	12.1	1,898.1	4.4	8.1	5.4	6.7	40.2
Chicago-Naperville-Joliet, IL-IN-WI.	**329,814.5**	**325,965.3**	**318,438.8**	**35,583**	**34,921**	**1.2**	**3.6**	**264,160.1**	**13.1**	**5.6**	**(NA)**	**(NA)**	**11.7**
Chicago-Naperville-Joliet, IL.	*275,388.8*	*272,406.8*	*265,915.8*	*35,493*	*34,790*	*1.1*	*3.6*	*227,895.3*	*11.8*	*5.3*	*(NA)*	*7.7*	*11.4*
Gary, IN.	*18,740.1*	*18,617.8*	*18,385.6*	*27,501*	*27,175*	*0.7*	*1.9*	*11,762.0*	*22.6*	*7.8*	*(NA)*	*(NA)*	*13.7*
Lake County-Kenosha County, IL-WI	*35,685.5*	*34,940.6*	*34,137.4*	*43,076*	*42,743*	*2.1*	*4.5*	*24,502.8*	*21.3*	*8.1*	*8.4*	*6.6*	*14.2*

See footnotes at end of table.

State and Metropolitan Area Data Book: 2006

Metropolitan statistical area **Metropolitan statistical area with metropolitan divisions** *Metropolitan division*	Personal income							Earnings, 2002					
	Total (mil. dol.)			Per capita[1] (dol.)		Percent change				Percent by selected major industries			
											Profes- sional and tech- nical ser- vices	Health care and social ser- vices	Govern- ment and govern- ment enter- prises
	2002	2001	2000	2002	2000	2001– 2002	2000– 2002	Total[2] (mil. dol.)	Manu- factur- ing	Retail trade			
Chico, CA.	4,999.0	4,782.9	4,570.6	23,944	22,430	4.5	9.4	3,035.6	5.1	11.0	6.3	15.6	21.9
Cincinnati-Middletown, OH-KY-IN	64,768.9	62,995.7	61,393.0	31,804	30,477	2.8	5.5	49,815.5	16.2	6.6	(NA)	(NA)	12.3
Clarksville, TN-KY	5,801.7	5,520.1	5,305.4	24,716	22,799	5.1	9.4	4,449.7	16.0	6.5	(NA)	(NA)	48.5
Cleveland, TN.	2,654.7	2,586.5	2,332.7	25,149	22,372	2.6	13.8	1,891.2	30.5	7.2	3.2	(NA)	11.7
Cleveland-Elyria-Mentor, OH	69,059.6	68,363.9	67,934.8	32,244	31,626	1.0	1.7	54,533.6	18.5	6.2	9.6	10.7	13.7
Coeur d'Alene, ID	2,761.2	2,638.5	2,520.7	24,164	23,014	4.6	9.5	1,735.9	8.9	11.4	6.2	10.4	19.4
College Station-Bryan, TX.	3,976.3	3,841.9	3,673.1	21,028	19,814	3.5	8.3	3,064.9	7.4	7.8	(NA)	(NA)	37.7
Colorado Springs, CO.	16,894.9	16,533.6	15,990.3	29,892	29,603	2.2	5.7	13,333.1	(NA)	7.1	11.0	7.1	27.6
Columbia, MO.	4,131.4	3,989.3	3,845.8	27,658	26,339	3.6	7.4	3,308.0	7.4	7.8	(NA)	(NA)	36.8
Columbia, SC	18,385.5	17,844.2	17,429.2	27,730	26,855	3.0	5.5	14,615.8	11.3	7.6	(NA)	(NA)	25.5
Columbus, GA-AL	7,410.1	7,158.8	6,740.1	25,899	23,887	3.5	9.9	5,805.2	(NA)	6.2	(NA)	7.9	32.7
Columbus, IN	2,172.3	2,125.9	2,183.4	30,261	30,450	2.2	–0.5	1,972.9	43.1	5.2	4.1	7.2	11.3
Columbus, OH	53,061.2	51,420.2	49,769.8	32,043	30,740	3.2	6.6	45,202.4	12.2	8.3	(NA)	(NA)	16.2
Corpus Christi, TX	10,163.5	9,771.5	9,348.0	25,119	23,183	4.0	8.7	7,625.3	10.3	7.8	(NA)	11.9	23.0
Corvallis, OR	2,399.4	2,333.9	2,259.4	30,421	28,907	2.8	6.2	1,827.6	26.3	4.7	6.4	10.7	27.0
Cumberland, MD-WV	2,263.8	2,167.3	2,099.9	22,377	20,619	4.5	7.8	1,427.2	16.4	8.7	2.2	(NA)	24.5
Dallas-Fort Worth-Arlington, TX.	**185,167.0**	**182,207.4**	**176,530.1**	**33,816**	**33,973**	**1.6**	**4.9**	**164,953.3**	**(NA)**	**7.2**	**(NA)**	**(NA)**	**9.6**
Dallas-Plano-Irving, TX.	*130,174.0*	*128,431.6*	*125,748.5*	*35,506*	*36,187*	*1.4*	*3.5*	*122,645.7*	*(NA)*	*6.9*	*(NA)*	*7.2*	*9.0*
Fort Worth-Arlington, TX.	*54,993.0*	*53,775.8*	*50,781.6*	*30,391*	*29,504*	*2.3*	*8.3*	*42,307.6*	*16.1*	*8.3*	*(NA)*	*(NA)*	*11.6*
Dalton, GA.	3,083.0	2,971.7	2,869.5	24,609	23,735	3.7	7.4	2,943.8	42.1	6.3	(NA)	7.0	9.4
Danville, IL	1,870.1	1,842.2	1,807.4	22,484	21,563	1.5	3.5	1,243.3	21.9	6.9	3.2	10.0	23.4
Danville, VA.	2,470.0	2,391.2	2,364.1	22,660	21,488	3.3	4.5	1,573.9	33.6	8.8	2.2	12.1	15.5
Davenport-Moline-Rock Island, IA-IL	10,644.1	10,411.2	10,172.9	28,384	27,066	2.2	4.6	7,993.6	16.7	7.6	(NA)	(NA)	16.7
Dayton, OH	25,189.6	24,689.0	24,210.5	29,796	28,549	2.0	4.0	20,048.0	20.5	6.2	(NA)	11.0	20.4
Decatur, AL	3,642.1	3,635.0	3,461.9	24,884	23,702	0.2	5.2	2,400.5	36.0	7.4	2.8	(NA)	14.5
Decatur, IL.	3,157.5	3,168.9	3,129.5	28,094	27,336	–0.4	0.9	2,465.8	29.2	7.5	3.5	10.8	10.1
Deltona-Daytona Beach-Ormond Beach, FL	11,380.4	10,865.0	10,380.7	24,747	23,329	4.7	9.6	5,638.6	7.4	10.9	5.9	15.3	16.5
Denver-Aurora, CO[3].	86,526.4	85,893.5	82,196.3	38,008	37,852	0.7	5.3	73,210.3	(NA)	5.9	(NA)	(NA)	12.3
Des Moines, IA	16,434.2	15,781.7	15,218.9	33,129	31,508	4.1	8.0	14,069.9	7.2	7.7	6.3	(NA)	13.3
Detroit-Warren-Livonia, MI.	**152,799.6**	**151,682.4**	**151,792.6**	**34,129**	**34,048**	**0.7**	**0.7**	**124,888.5**	**21.6**	**5.8**	**13.3**	**8.6**	**10.1**
Detroit-Livonia-Dearborn, MI.	*56,477.0*	*56,507.5*	*56,659.6*	*27,684*	*27,515*	*–0.1*	*–0.3*	*50,218.6*	*20.7*	*5.2*	*10.1*	*9.4*	*13.2*
Warren-Farmington Hills-Troy, MI.	*96,322.5*	*95,174.9*	*95,133.0*	*39,524*	*39,656*	*1.2*	*1.3*	*74,669.9*	*22.1*	*6.2*	*15.5*	*8.1*	*8.0*
Dothan, AL.	3,357.5	3,239.8	3,018.5	25,462	23,029	3.6	11.2	2,274.7	13.7	10.0	(NA)	(NA)	16.6
Dover, DE.	3,285.9	3,088.5	3,020.9	24,987	23,769	6.4	8.8	2,528.4	(NA)	7.8	(NA)	9.2	39.8
Dubuque, IA	2,442.1	2,361.6	2,293.1	27,294	25,691	3.4	6.5	1,987.4	23.7	9.0	4.7	14.5	8.1
Duluth, MN-WI	7,437.1	7,153.6	7,000.5	26,927	25,404	4.0	6.2	5,361.0	8.1	7.6	3.8	(NA)	21.8
Durham, NC	13,903.3	13,547.6	12,996.6	31,435	30,507	2.6	7.0	14,327.2	27.2	4.7	(NA)	11.1	17.9
Eau Claire, WI.	4,009.8	3,873.0	3,803.7	26,685	25,595	3.5	5.4	3,001.9	17.4	8.5	4.8	14.3	16.2
El Centro, CA.	2,972.5	2,734.2	2,530.3	20,382	17,753	8.7	17.5	2,189.1	4.4	8.4	2.3	4.0	35.7
Elizabethtown, KY.	2,765.9	2,702.5	2,620.7	25,324	24,315	2.3	5.5	2,256.6	16.7	7.0	2.5	(NA)	45.7
Elkhart-Goshen, IN.	5,144.9	4,920.9	4,871.0	27,665	26,544	4.6	5.6	5,215.2	53.7	4.9	2.5	6.6	6.3
Elmira, NY.	2,230.1	2,203.4	2,217.0	24,558	24,351	1.2	0.6	1,591.4	20.5	9.1	3.5	14.5	21.6
El Paso, TX	13,992.3	13,313.6	12,649.9	20,129	18,556	5.1	10.6	11,178.4	12.2	8.2	3.7	10.2	27.6
Erie, PA	7,095.2	6,949.0	6,888.2	25,301	24,541	2.1	3.0	5,303.1	26.4	8.3	4.0	14.4	13.9
Eugene-Springfield, OR	8,646.6	8,434.7	8,247.5	26,416	25,502	2.5	4.8	5,936.3	14.8	8.9	6.0	12.6	19.3
Evansville, IN-KY.	10,021.4	9,716.6	9,294.0	29,116	27,098	3.1	7.8	7,813.0	26.6	6.5	4.5	(NA)	9.2
Fairbanks, AK.	2,560.7	2,425.9	2,303.3	30,081	27,832	5.6	11.2	2,178.2	1.4	6.3	3.2	7.5	46.9
Fargo, ND-MN.	5,113.6	4,895.6	4,820.7	28,869	27,596	4.5	6.1	4,229.1	8.7	8.8	5.8	(NA)	15.0
Farmington, NM.	2,457.5	2,365.0	2,166.7	20,511	18,974	3.9	13.4	1,949.1	3.3	8.0	(NA)	8.3	22.0
Fayetteville, NC.	8,626.3	8,088.1	7,823.1	25,409	23,232	6.7	10.3	7,389.2	8.4	6.1	2.3	(NA)	58.3
Fayetteville-Springdale-Rogers, AR-MO	9,097.0	8,635.5	7,979.1	24,788	22,834	5.3	14.0	7,480.5	17.4	6.0	(NA)	(NA)	12.0
Flagstaff, AZ.	2,942.5	2,792.0	2,661.7	24,543	22,820	5.4	10.6	2,057.4	6.8	9.4	3.8	13.4	33.8
Flint, MI.	11,446.2	11,270.0	11,550.2	25,977	26,434	1.6	–0.9	8,119.7	28.2	7.3	7.8	11.6	14.6
Florence, SC.	4,862.9	4,740.7	4,486.2	24,943	23,212	2.6	8.4	3,691.6	25.4	8.2	4.2	(NA)	17.4
Florence-Muscle Shoals, AL.	3,225.9	3,212.7	3,113.5	22,769	21,773	0.4	3.6	1,965.7	17.0	10.5	(NA)	9.1	27.3
Fond du Lac, WI.	2,880.7	2,798.5	2,699.5	29,487	27,721	2.9	6.7	2,092.6	35.2	6.2	2.9	9.8	11.5
Fort Collins-Loveland, CO.	8,296.1	8,098.6	7,657.1	31,420	30,272	2.4	8.3	6,058.9	20.2	7.6	(NA)	8.6	19.2
Fort Smith, AR-OK.	6,398.9	6,253.1	5,889.2	23,021	21,506	2.3	8.7	4,669.0	23.3	7.2	7.8	(NA)	13.3
Fort Walton Beach-Crestview-Destin, FL	5,254.0	4,871.3	4,610.5	29,938	26,969	7.9	14.0	4,174.2	3.5	7.3	(NA)	6.1	44.4
Fort Wayne, IN	11,485.8	11,277.1	11,211.1	28,965	28,670	1.9	2.4	9,482.0	23.2	6.3	4.8	(NA)	9.7
Fresno, CA.	19,544.1	18,401.4	17,627.7	23,492	21,979	6.2	10.9	14,465.5	8.6	7.9	4.9	11.9	21.8
Gadsden, AL.	2,365.2	2,291.6	2,212.0	22,999	21,413	3.2	6.9	1,393.3	19.1	8.8	3.4	18.5	14.7
Gainesville, FL.	5,933.6	5,719.8	5,521.1	25,033	23,712	3.7	7.5	4,693.5	4.3	7.2	6.4	(NA)	37.6
Gainesville, GA.	3,794.9	3,669.9	3,485.4	25,040	24,741	3.4	8.9	2,863.4	27.0	7.3	(NA)	12.3	12.3
Glens Falls, NY.	3,149.3	3,040.1	3,008.8	25,092	24,197	3.6	4.7	2,034.0	16.8	9.5	3.4	13.3	21.0
Goldsboro, NC.	2,641.0	2,566.6	2,503.8	23,376	22,093	2.9	5.5	1,836.5	14.7	7.8	2.2	10.7	35.1
Grand Forks, ND-MN	2,475.3	2,363.4	2,308.7	25,831	23,740	4.7	7.2	1,945.5	6.9	8.7	3.5	(NA)	32.7
Grand Junction, CO.	3,166.7	3,009.5	2,928.1	25,940	24,926	5.2	8.1	2,130.0	6.7	10.5	5.2	14.9	17.6
Grand Rapids-Wyoming, MI.	21,688.5	21,256.9	20,818.4	28,659	28,026	2.0	4.2	18,715.1	26.4	7.1	(NA)	9.8	9.6
Great Falls, MT.	2,113.0	2,033.4	1,968.1	26,546	24,545	3.9	7.4	1,494.4	2.9	9.3	5.6	16.6	30.8
Greeley, CO[3].	5,000.2	4,885.8	4,586.4	24,495	25,040	2.3	9.0	3,533.7	15.5	7.4	3.6	8.2	13.4
Green Bay, WI.	8,641.3	8,327.4	8,137.2	29,905	28,729	3.8	6.2	7,162.7	21.6	6.9	4.7	(NA)	11.8
Greensboro-High Point, NC.	18,708.5	18,382.9	18,138.0	28,508	28,109	1.8	3.1	15,572.0	21.7	7.5	6.2	(NA)	11.2
Greenville, NC.	3,789.5	3,701.9	3,666.8	24,212	23,944	2.4	3.3	2,704.4	15.7	7.9	3.9	10.7	32.5

See footnotes at end of table.

U.S. Census Bureau

Metropolitan statistical area **Metropolitan statistical area with metropolitan divisions** *Metropolitan division*	Personal income Total (mil. dol.) 2002	2001	2000	Per capita[1] (dol.) 2002	2000	Percent change 2001–2002	2000–2002	Earnings, 2002 Total[2] (mil. dol.)	Manufacturing	Retail trade	Professional and technical services	Health care and social services	Government and government enterprises
Greenville, SC	15,572.6	15,342.0	15,073.3	27,179	26,834	1.5	3.3	12,564.8	21.1	8.4	(NA)	(NA)	13.6
Gulfport-Biloxi, MS	6,212.8	5,965.2	5,826.7	24,971	23,627	4.2	6.6	5,010.5	6.1	6.8	5.1	(NA)	35.3
Hagerstown-Martinsburg, MD-WV	6,027.9	5,777.7	5,453.7	26,051	24,395	4.3	10.5	3,929.9	15.1	9.3	4.8	(NA)	20.2
Hanford-Corcoran, CA	2,504.7	2,338.6	2,117.6	18,581	16,306	7.1	18.3	1,867.4	9.0	6.0	1.8	7.3	47.1
Harrisburg-Carlisle, PA	16,366.2	15,717.9	15,143.4	31,821	29,729	4.1	8.1	15,189.7	9.3	6.7	7.1	10.5	22.1
Harrisonburg, VA	2,562.5	2,533.9	2,385.2	23,270	22,051	1.1	7.4	2,188.7	28.1	9.1	4.2	9.4	15.2
Hartford-West Hartford-East Hartford, CT	44,402.6	43,659.2	42,567.6	37,995	36,987	1.7	4.3	37,920.8	15.1	6.1	8.6	10.5	14.3
Hattiesburg, MS	2,893.0	2,754.3	2,555.0	22,781	20,557	5.0	13.2	2,072.2	11.1	9.9	(NA)	15.2	25.7
Hickory-Lenoir-Morganton, NC	8,887.0	8,816.5	8,635.9	25,507	25,178	0.8	2.9	6,638.4	37.2	7.3	(NA)	(NA)	12.8
Hinesville-Fort Stewart, GA	1,290.4	1,230.1	1,191.8	17,919	16,617	4.9	8.3	1,419.3	(NA)	2.7	(NA)	(NA)	79.7
Holland-Grand Haven, MI	6,769.3	6,672.5	6,677.7	27,485	27,885	1.5	1.4	5,267.7	42.0	6.2	3.9	5.1	11.9
Honolulu, HI	28,300.7	26,914.8	26,604.8	31,707	30,383	5.1	6.4	22,415.0	2.1	6.7	7.3	9.0	34.2
Hot Springs, AR	2,292.4	2,215.6	2,118.0	25,482	23,964	3.5	8.2	1,266.7	11.3	10.7	3.6	21.0	15.0
Houma-Bayou Cane-Thibodaux, LA	4,773.2	4,597.2	4,198.5	24,330	21,588	3.8	13.7	3,445.5	11.2	7.1	3.5	8.0	13.4
Houston-Sugar Land-Baytown, TX	173,756.8	170,557.7	161,397.6	34,969	34,041	1.9	7.7	152,994.5	13.2	5.6	11.5	(NA)	9.8
Huntington-Ashland, WV-KY-OH	6,630.2	6,411.7	6,203.6	23,139	21,514	3.4	6.9	4,486.0	12.9	8.5	(NA)	(NA)	18.5
Huntsville, AL	10,222.8	9,850.4	9,476.7	28,959	27,589	3.8	7.9	9,646.3	22.2	6.1	17.6	(NA)	27.0
Idaho Falls, ID	2,604.9	2,494.4	2,321.1	24,837	22,730	4.4	12.2	1,909.9	5.4	9.2	19.6	11.3	14.4
Indianapolis, IN	51,841.5	50,762.5	48,861.5	32,916	31,920	2.1	6.1	43,281.3	17.1	6.7	(NA)	(NA)	12.4
Iowa City, IA	4,087.3	3,949.7	3,815.3	30,163	28,886	3.5	7.1	3,423.2	8.8	6.6	4.8	(NA)	41.8
Ithaca, NY	2,520.6	2,422.2	2,320.9	25,242	24,002	4.1	8.6	2,191.2	10.1	5.4	6.6	(NA)	12.5
Jackson, MI	4,030.0	3,929.3	3,966.2	25,011	24,987	2.6	1.6	2,705.2	21.4	9.4	3.2	11.6	17.8
Jackson, MS	13,549.9	13,144.2	12,667.9	26,848	25,424	3.1	7.0	10,474.1	7.8	7.7	8.0	(NA)	21.1
Jackson, TN	2,765.8	2,682.4	2,663.6	25,310	24,766	3.1	3.8	2,469.6	23.7	9.6	3.3	(NA)	18.6
Jacksonville, FL	35,337.6	33,973.8	33,150.7	30,037	29,439	4.0	6.6	27,280.3	6.7	7.7	(NA)	9.7	18.4
Jacksonville, NC	3,808.4	3,596.2	3,437.2	25,317	22,881	5.9	10.8	3,180.5	1.2	4.7	1.5	3.1	75.2
Janesville, WI	4,138.0	4,009.6	3,992.8	26,865	26,176	3.2	3.6	2,977.1	33.7	8.2	2.5	11.4	12.8
Jefferson City, MO	3,708.0	3,637.0	3,445.3	26,112	24,554	2.0	7.6	3,002.1	9.5	8.0	(NA)	(NA)	36.0
Johnson City, TN	4,204.5	4,065.9	3,892.9	22,897	21,395	3.4	8.0	2,869.6	19.0	8.9	(NA)	(NA)	20.2
Johnstown, PA	3,590.5	3,498.2	3,413.4	23,885	22,422	2.6	5.2	2,196.7	9.0	9.7	7.0	18.0	19.5
Jonesboro, AR	2,398.8	2,336.2	2,247.9	21,968	20,793	2.7	6.7	1,720.8	19.8	8.7	3.6	17.0	16.9
Joplin, MO	3,747.1	3,653.6	3,533.3	23,418	22,405	2.6	6.1	2,848.5	25.0	9.1	2.5	14.8	11.0
Kalamazoo-Portage, MI	8,672.7	8,446.3	8,325.2	27,265	26,410	2.7	4.2	6,581.4	27.0	7.7	4.7	10.6	15.5
Kankakee-Bradley, IL	2,716.1	2,650.8	2,570.7	25,901	24,747	2.5	5.7	1,716.6	21.2	9.2	(NA)	15.6	15.7
Kansas City, MO-KS	61,254.9	59,737.0	58,247.1	32,467	31,612	2.5	5.2	50,141.1	9.9	6.6	(NA)	(NA)	14.6
Kennewick-Richland-Pasco, WA	5,468.9	5,138.5	4,755.9	26,905	24,687	6.4	15.0	4,335.0	6.7	6.7	19.2	7.7	17.9
Killeen-Temple-Fort Hood, TX	8,230.8	7,823.0	7,458.6	24,287	22,458	5.2	10.4	6,564.0	5.9	6.5	(NA)	8.3	54.8
Kingsport-Bristol-Bristol, TN-VA	7,317.2	7,121.7	6,834.1	24,481	22,898	2.7	7.1	5,149.3	30.5	8.7	(NA)	12.2	11.5
Kingston, NY	4,864.2	4,709.6	4,545.7	27,013	25,553	3.3	7.0	2,488.9	10.4	11.3	4.6	13.7	26.0
Knoxville, TN	17,921.7	17,156.2	16,569.0	28,466	26,836	4.5	8.2	14,499.2	14.5	10.1	9.3	11.4	15.1
Kokomo, IN	2,892.4	2,825.1	2,929.1	28,543	28,851	2.4	-1.3	2,770.7	58.9	5.8	2.9	(NA)	10.3
La Crosse, WI-MN	3,611.6	3,480.0	3,302.7	28,222	26,004	3.8	9.4	2,870.0	17.8	7.0	3.5	(NA)	14.4
Lafayette, IN	4,548.7	4,490.6	4,392.6	25,006	24,554	1.3	3.6	3,771.5	27.0	6.7	3.2	(NA)	24.6
Lafayette, LA	6,636.4	6,478.5	6,048.3	27,385	25,281	2.4	9.7	5,668.3	6.1	8.1	7.8	(NA)	10.8
Lake Charles, LA	4,701.2	4,582.0	4,312.9	24,370	22,292	2.6	9.0	3,643.9	20.7	(NA)	5.8	(NA)	14.2
Lakeland, FL	12,890.7	12,315.8	11,517.0	25,777	23,727	4.7	11.9	8,098.7	12.7	9.6	5.8	10.9	15.1
Lancaster, PA	14,000.6	13,603.2	13,569.5	29,266	28,770	2.9	3.2	10,256.6	25.6	8.9	5.8	10.0	8.8
Lansing-East Lansing, MI	12,614.5	12,268.0	12,066.7	27,806	26,909	2.8	4.5	10,676.2	16.3	6.8	(NA)	9.1	27.6
Laredo, TX	3,436.6	3,216.0	2,933.7	16,593	15,071	6.9	17.1	2,711.2	1.4	10.3	4.3	10.2	26.4
Las Cruces, NM	3,674.2	3,424.3	3,120.0	20,573	17,831	7.3	17.8	2,332.3	4.9	7.5	6.5	12.2	35.6
Las Vegas-Paradise, NV	44,572.4	42,457.2	41,239.3	29,396	29,601	5.0	8.1	35,133.6	3.1	7.8	6.6	6.7	13.4
Lawrence, KS	2,658.2	2,587.0	2,423.4	26,010	24,190	2.8	9.7	1,812.4	9.0	6.8	8.1	7.4	30.7
Lawton, OK	2,685.5	2,583.7	2,452.6	23,725	21,408	3.9	9.5	2,139.7	9.6	6.1	3.4	5.8	56.5
Lebanon, PA	3,379.7	3,294.6	3,175.3	27,836	26,369	2.6	6.4	1,848.2	24.5	9.2	3.4	14.2	17.9
Lewiston, ID-WA	1,515.1	1,470.8	1,418.6	26,246	24,484	3.0	6.8	1,052.7	15.2	9.6	3.9	15.1	18.4
Lewiston-Auburn, ME	2,809.2	2,661.9	2,532.0	26,721	24,378	5.5	10.9	1,933.2	15.1	10.4	8.2	16.2	12.1
Lexington-Fayette, KY	12,967.5	12,575.8	12,387.6	31,136	30,251	3.1	4.7	11,351.8	20.8	7.0	(NA)	(NA)	16.4
Lima, OH	2,728.5	2,673.7	2,633.0	25,237	24,258	2.0	3.6	2,375.3	29.5	8.0	2.3	16.2	14.2
Lincoln, NE	8,221.7	7,905.3	7,774.8	30,022	29,041	4.0	5.7	6,758.8	13.4	6.2	7.8	(NA)	21.2
Little Rock-North Little Rock, AR	17,831.1	17,292.8	16,498.2	28,659	26,960	3.1	8.1	14,396.8	8.7	6.9	(NA)	(NA)	22.2
Logan, UT-ID	2,098.5	2,028.3	1,932.0	19,772	18,744	3.5	8.6	1,495.1	20.5	7.5	5.4	6.7	25.0
Longview, TX	5,061.6	4,932.3	4,775.2	25,727	24,611	2.6	6.0	3,489.1	12.8	10.3	(NA)	(NA)	11.7
Longview, WA	2,373.4	2,338.6	2,201.9	25,104	23,668	1.5	7.8	1,706.0	25.5	8.0	2.6	11.5	14.5
Los Angeles-Long Beach-Santa Ana, CA	**413,164.9**	**402,423.7**	**385,053.4**	**32,547**	**31,049**	**2.7**	**7.3**	**343,260.8**	**12.3**	**6.6**	**11.3**	**7.7**	**12.4**
Los Angeles-Long Beach-Glendale, CA	*300,898.1*	*293,228.7*	*279,049.5*	*30,804*	*29,235*	*2.6*	*7.8*	*254,950.3*	*11.8*	*6.3*	*11.4*	*8.0*	*13.4*
Santa Ana-Anaheim-Irvine, CA	*112,266.8*	*109,195.0*	*106,003.9*	*38,367*	*37,110*	*2.8*	*5.9*	*88,310.5*	*13.5*	*7.2*	*11.2*	*6.8*	*9.4*
Louisville, KY-IN	36,194.6	35,463.4	34,249.6	30,666	29,398	2.1	5.7	27,655.8	18.6	6.7	(NA)	(NA)	12.2
Lubbock, TX	6,365.1	6,109.4	6,055.4	25,027	24,227	4.2	5.1	4,785.7	5.8	10.2	4.6	15.3	22.2
Lynchburg, VA	5,849.6	5,773.3	5,626.4	25,422	24,579	1.3	4.0	3,982.8	28.3	8.7	(NA)	(NA)	13.1
Macon, GA	6,213.5	5,948.8	5,662.1	27,635	25,458	4.4	9.7	4,349.3	(NA)	7.3	(NA)	(NA)	14.3
Madera, CA	2,527.1	2,379.1	2,265.1	19,617	18,321	6.2	11.6	1,573.3	9.2	8.2	(NA)	14.1	22.0
Madison, WI	18,000.9	17,199.2	16,468.9	34,650	32,688	4.7	9.3	15,192.9	11.6	8.4	8.3	(NA)	24.1

See footnotes at end of table.

Table B-8. Metropolitan Areas — **Personal Income and Earnings by Industry**—Con.

Metropolitan statistical area **Metropolitan statistical area with metropolitan divisions** *Metropolitan division*	Personal income							Earnings, 2002					
	Total (mil. dol.)			Per capita[1] (dol.)		Percent change			Percent by selected major industries				
	2002	2001	2000	2002	2000	2001–2002	2000–2002	Total[2] (mil. dol.)	Manufacturing	Retail trade	Professional and technical services	Health care and social services	Government and government enterprises
Manchester-Nashua, NH	13,913.6	13,837.2	13,770.0	35,496	36,016	0.6	1.0	10,750.9	20.3	9.1	9.3	9.9	9.6
Mansfield, OH	3,222.1	3,120.4	3,024.2	25,098	23,482	3.3	6.5	2,514.4	34.5	8.0	2.5	11.3	16.6
McAllen-Edinburg-Mission, TX	9,055.6	8,442.8	7,792.9	14,769	13,578	7.3	16.2	6,180.3	4.9	11.1	4.1	18.3	26.7
Medford, OR	4,942.0	4,738.3	4,530.9	26,477	24,917	4.3	9.1	3,245.9	9.2	13.0	4.5	14.0	16.2
Memphis, TN-MS-AR	37,495.9	36,298.8	34,458.8	30,557	28,520	3.3	8.8	31,854.0	10.3	7.5	(NA)	(NA)	14.1
Merced, CA	4,639.7	4,428.9	4,133.9	20,623	19,533	4.8	12.2	2,869.6	13.6	8.6	2.4	8.8	20.8
Miami-Fort Lauderdale-Miami Beach, FL	**168,638.8**	**163,369.5**	**157,014.7**	**32,373**	**31,226**	**3.2**	**7.4**	**112,053.7**	**5.2**	**8.1**	**10.0**	**9.7**	**14.1**
Fort Lauderdale-Pompano Beach-Deerfield Beach, FL	*54,172.8*	*52,525.8*	*50,137.6*	*31,785*	*30,713*	*3.1*	*8.0*	*33,309.3*	*5.6*	*9.7*	*9.0*	*9.3*	*14.3*
Miami-Miami Beach-Kendall, FL	*62,037.2*	*59,875.9*	*57,922.3*	*26,780*	*25,627*	*3.6*	*7.1*	*50,944.3*	*4.9*	*7.3*	*10.1*	*9.3*	*16.1*
West Palm Beach-Boca Raton-Boynton Beach, FL	*52,428.8*	*50,967.8*	*48,954.8*	*44,120*	*43,107*	*2.9*	*7.1*	*27,800.1*	*5.4*	*7.7*	*11.1*	*11.1*	*10.4*
Michigan City-La Porte, IN	2,729.4	2,697.7	2,683.0	24,773	24,350	1.2	1.7	1,853.2	24.6	7.5	2.7	12.5	16.4
Midland, TX	3,956.2	3,925.1	4,092.3	33,728	35,422	0.8	-3.3	2,943.9	3.4	6.2	6.4	6.3	11.7
Milwaukee-Waukesha-West Allis, WI	51,798.5	50,691.3	49,151.3	34,308	32,722	2.2	5.4	41,648.4	20.4	5.7	7.6	11.6	11.2
Minneapolis-St. Paul-Bloomington, MN-WI	115,502.5	113,143.2	109,817.8	37,787	36,840	2.1	5.2	97,006.7	14.2	6.0	(NA)	8.2	12.0
Missoula, MT	2,625.5	2,496.5	2,342.8	26,823	24,383	5.2	12.1	2,149.7	6.2	10.0	6.9	15.6	18.7
Mobile, AL	9,033.4	8,862.8	8,638.2	22,620	21,592	1.9	4.6	7,189.1	12.7	8.2	7.9	11.0	17.3
Modesto, CA	11,372.1	10,908.2	10,572.6	23,642	23,506	4.3	7.6	7,552.9	13.4	10.5	4.2	11.6	17.1
Monroe, LA	4,223.5	4,027.0	3,838.8	24,857	22,581	4.9	10.0	3,104.3	13.2	8.4	7.7	(NA)	16.3
Monroe, MI	4,327.9	4,235.2	4,281.3	29,015	29,228	2.2	1.1	2,297.9	32.3	7.6	(NA)	6.5	12.9
Montgomery, AL	9,665.0	9,261.0	8,864.9	27,533	25,549	4.4	9.0	7,550.3	9.9	6.5	8.7	(NA)	29.3
Morgantown, WV	2,777.6	2,662.6	2,449.0	24,576	22,018	4.3	13.4	2,177.3	9.5	6.2	5.2	(NA)	35.2
Morristown, TN	2,873.3	2,768.9	2,621.0	22,909	21,218	3.8	9.6	2,001.5	38.3	8.4	(NA)	(NA)	11.3
Mount Vernon-Anacortes, WA	3,135.4	3,019.7	2,823.4	29,377	27,288	3.8	11.1	2,061.3	13.5	10.4	7.0	8.8	19.2
Muncie, IN	2,991.6	2,945.2	2,898.1	25,313	24,421	1.6	3.2	2,139.1	22.1	7.7	4.3	17.9	19.4
Muskegon-Norton Shores, MI	4,081.8	4,013.0	3,943.4	23,707	23,126	1.7	3.5	2,765.4	27.2	10.9	4.0	12.8	16.0
Myrtle Beach-Conway-North Myrtle Beach, SC	5,059.5	4,890.1	4,740.0	24,584	23,936	3.5	6.7	3,552.6	5.4	13.0	5.9	8.1	13.9
Napa, CA	4,982.9	4,846.4	4,713.5	38,361	37,834	2.8	5.7	3,449.5	19.1	6.8	6.7	9.8	13.6
Naples-Marco Island, FL	11,601.4	11,142.5	10,012.0	42,050	39,406	4.1	15.9	5,578.8	2.3	9.9	7.9	10.8	9.6
Nashville-Davidson-Murfreesboro, TN	43,317.3	42,029.7	40,309.3	32,026	30,605	3.1	7.5	36,629.1	13.1	7.5	(NA)	(NA)	10.8
New Haven-Milford, CT	29,532.1	28,950.3	28,379.2	35,339	34,400	2.0	4.1	20,928.7	14.9	7.6	9.4	13.4	13.2
New Orleans-Metairie-Kenner, LA	38,084.9	36,767.1	34,605.7	28,995	26,304	3.6	10.1	29,088.4	7.8	6.5	(NA)	(NA)	17.0
New York-Northern New Jersey-Long Island, NY-NJ-PA	**755,390.0**	**751,487.5**	**732,799.3**	**40,680**	**39,920**	**0.5**	**3.1**	**599,666.9**	**6.4**	**5.2**	**12.5**	**9.3**	**12.3**
Edison, NJ	*90,194.1*	*88,846.9*	*86,490.0*	*40,183*	*39,625*	*1.5*	*4.3*	*61,962.4*	*11.2*	*7.5*	*14.0*	*8.7*	*12.8*
Nassau-Suffolk, NY	*121,159.1*	*119,997.0*	*116,297.9*	*43,349*	*42,131*	*1.0*	*4.2*	*69,335.7*	*7.9*	*8.0*	*9.7*	*12.7*	*16.0*
Newark-Union, NJ-PA	*92,243.4*	*91,115.8*	*89,531.3*	*43,326*	*42,616*	*1.2*	*3.0*	*69,121.8*	*11.6*	*6.3*	*13.0*	*8.5*	*13.3*
New York-White Plains-Wayne, NY-NJ	*451,793.5*	*451,527.8*	*440,480.0*	*39,629*	*38,937*	*0.1*	*2.6*	*399,247.0*	*4.5*	*4.2*	*12.7*	*8.9*	*11.4*
Niles-Benton Harbor, MI	4,305.2	4,225.8	4,239.4	26,482	26,071	1.9	1.6	3,021.4	33.2	7.0	3.9	9.2	11.8
Norwich-New London, CT	9,202.7	8,873.6	8,513.5	35,106	32,813	3.7	8.1	7,294.7	18.6	6.5	8.3	9.2	31.9
Ocala, FL	6,437.0	6,168.0	5,893.9	23,637	22,643	4.4	9.2	3,255.3	11.7	12.5	4.9	12.4	18.0
Ocean City, NJ	3,548.9	3,363.4	3,239.4	34,879	31,666	5.5	9.6	1,720.5	1.9	11.7	4.6	9.5	26.1
Odessa, TX	2,731.9	2,658.1	2,546.5	22,342	21,097	2.8	7.3	2,088.7	10.3	10.8	(NA)	8.5	17.3
Ogden-Clearfield, UT	11,587.1	11,143.7	10,772.1	25,168	24,212	4.0	7.6	7,696.1	14.6	7.8	(NA)	7.7	33.0
Oklahoma City, OK	31,219.1	30,441.2	29,092.1	27,877	26,503	2.6	7.3	24,858.7	13.4	7.3	(NA)	(NA)	24.3
Olympia, WA	6,719.3	6,461.3	6,093.0	30,828	29,242	4.0	10.3	4,175.5	4.0	9.0	4.2	10.8	42.2
Omaha-Council Bluffs, NE-IA	26,011.7	25,248.8	24,230.4	33,200	31,509	3.0	7.4	20,867.0	7.5	7.2	(NA)	(NA)	15.1
Orlando-Kissimee, FL	48,431.4	46,354.1	44,750.8	27,587	27,018	4.5	8.2	39,861.7	6.5	7.8	9.8	9.3	11.3
Oshkosh-Neenah, WI	4,680.6	4,541.8	4,430.8	29,537	28,217	3.1	5.6	4,221.4	42.3	4.6	3.5	9.5	11.9
Owensboro, KY	2,758.6	2,735.7	2,698.4	25,014	24,530	0.8	2.2	2,000.3	24.9	7.8	(NA)	(NA)	16.8
Oxnard-Thousand Oaks-Ventura, CA	27,006.3	26,173.3	25,364.4	34,572	33,523	3.2	6.5	17,215.4	16.6	7.4	7.7	7.2	16.5
Palm Bay-Melbourne-Titusville, FL	13,770.3	13,281.4	12,865.5	27,762	26,925	3.7	7.0	8,962.0	16.7	8.0	9.6	11.4	17.1
Panama City-Lynn Haven, FL	3,889.4	3,656.7	3,521.8	25,536	23,757	6.4	10.4	2,734.2	5.5	9.2	5.9	13.1	29.3
Parkersburg-Marietta-Vienna, WV-OH	4,053.5	3,896.9	3,784.6	24,774	23,013	4.0	7.1	3,003.7	(NA)	8.9	(NA)	(NA)	16.1
Pascagoula, MS	3,496.6	3,447.1	3,302.6	22,833	21,860	1.4	5.9	2,281.2	33.7	6.5	(NA)	6.6	23.9
Pensacola-Ferry Pass-Brent, FL	10,544.0	10,229.2	9,702.7	24,884	23,507	3.1	8.7	6,889.0	5.3	7.8	6.3	12.5	33.4
Peoria, IL	10,684.9	10,497.9	10,256.6	29,170	27,974	1.8	4.2	7,960.4	25.0	6.0	(NA)	(NA)	11.5
Philadelphia-Camden-Wilmington, PA-NJ-DE-MD	**205,346.1**	**199,176.5**	**193,919.1**	**35,753**	**34,062**	**3.1**	**5.9**	**156,460.5**	**12.1**	**6.5**	**(NA)**	**11.3**	**12.5**
Camden, NJ	*40,353.4*	*38,792.0*	*37,034.7*	*33,300*	*31,157*	*4.0*	*9.0*	*26,398.5*	*12.4*	*8.5*	*8.7*	*11.3*	*17.5*
Philadelphia, PA	*142,093.2*	*138,099.2*	*135,225.3*	*36,752*	*35,106*	*2.9*	*5.1*	*110,653.5*	*12.2*	*6.1*	*13.2*	*11.7*	*11.4*
Wilmington, DE-MD-NJ	*22,899.4*	*22,285.4*	*21,659.1*	*34,413*	*33,192*	*2.8*	*5.7*	*19,408.6*	*11.0*	*5.8*	*(NA)*	*9.1*	*11.7*
Phoenix-Mesa-Scottsdale, AZ	99,387.0	96,477.3	92,974.8	28,481	28,365	3.0	6.9	79,135.8	11.2	8.3	(NA)	8.4	12.6
Pine Bluff, AR	2,180.1	2,137.7	2,045.5	20,501	19,073	2.0	6.6	1,555.0	21.2	6.6	(NA)	(NA)	27.7
Pittsburgh, PA	78,241.3	76,386.0	74,360.8	32,381	30,610	2.4	5.2	58,326.4	13.9	7.0	10.4	12.3	11.2
Pittsfield, MA	4,437.1	4,260.2	4,081.8	33,263	30,278	4.2	8.7	2,938.2	16.8	8.8	6.0	16.7	11.4
Pocatello, ID	1,885.6	1,829.9	1,731.7	22,643	20,840	3.0	8.9	1,347.4	12.9	8.3	(NA)	(NA)	26.8
Portland-South Portland-Biddeford, ME	15,849.1	15,296.1	14,576.1	31,678	29,791	3.6	8.7	11,742.5	9.4	8.6	7.5	13.0	17.3
Portland-Vancouver-Beaverton, OR-WA	64,754.8	63,892.2	62,190.0	32,167	32,127	1.4	4.1	51,231.7	15.5	6.6	8.6	9.0	13.3
Port St. Lucie-Fort Pierce, FL	10,663.2	10,180.8	9,649.8	31,638	30,103	4.7	10.5	4,540.6	5.4	10.7	7.1	14.3	15.4
Poughkeepsie-Newburgh-Middletown, NY	19,702.1	19,256.5	18,378.4	30,618	29,459	2.3	7.2	11,879.7	16.7	8.4	6.0	12.1	22.7
Prescott, AZ	3,927.1	3,713.4	3,574.1	21,936	21,153	5.8	9.9	1,919.1	6.1	10.8	5.3	11.7	21.6
Providence-New Bedford-Fall River, RI-MA	49,645.1	48,076.4	45,975.9	30,796	28,976	3.3	8.0	32,998.6	16.0	7.9	(NA)	13.0	16.7
Provo-Orem, UT	7,849.6	7,703.8	7,433.3	19,594	19,606	1.9	5.6	6,008.9	12.5	8.4	8.5	8.8	14.6
Pueblo, CO	3,489.2	3,371.5	3,261.5	23,689	22,995	3.5	7.0	2,145.2	10.6	9.7	2.7	17.3	22.7

See footnotes at end of table.

Table B-8. Metropolitan Areas — **Personal Income and Earnings by Industry**—Con.

| Metropolitan statistical area / **Metropolitan statistical area with metropolitan divisions** / *Metropolitan division* | Personal income | | | | | | | Earnings, 2002 | | | | | |
| | Total (mil. dol.) | | | Per capita[1] (dol.) | | Percent change | | | Percent by selected major industries | | | | |
	2002	2001	2000	2002	2000	2001–2002	2000–2002	Total[2] (mil. dol.)	Manufacturing	Retail trade	Professional and technical services	Health care and social services	Government and government enterprises
Punta Gorda, FL	4,036.1	3,797.4	3,649.6	26,932	25,653	6.3	10.6	1,651.3	2.5	12.1	6.9	19.4	13.7
Racine, WI	5,784.9	5,657.8	5,438.8	30,331	28,779	2.2	6.4	3,623.2	36.2	6.4	4.8	11.4	12.8
Raleigh-Cary, NC	28,613.4	28,270.9	27,062.3	33,293	33,658	1.2	5.7	21,797.8	9.9	7.5	(NA)	6.6	17.1
Rapid City, SD	3,170.7	3,045.2	2,917.6	27,429	25,819	4.1	8.7	2,317.7	7.1	9.0	4.3	(NA)	26.3
Reading, PA	11,261.6	10,959.6	10,778.2	29,531	28,783	2.8	4.5	7,792.6	24.4	7.7	7.2	10.0	11.3
Redding, CA	4,557.8	4,311.7	4,004.8	26,532	24,445	5.7	13.8	2,969.6	5.1	10.8	5.9	16.1	20.2
Reno-Sparks, NV	13,424.7	13,136.0	12,418.4	36,763	36,026	2.2	8.1	9,640.9	8.1	7.7	7.0	(NA)	14.7
Richmond, VA	36,060.6	35,207.5	33,603.1	32,067	30,548	2.4	7.3	29,156.0	10.4	6.2	(NA)	(NA)	19.4
Riverside-San Bernardino-Ontario, CA	84,300.7	80,077.1	74,787.1	24,073	22,810	5.3	12.7	51,718.8	10.6	9.4	4.6	9.5	21.5
Roanoke, VA	8,467.4	8,182.9	7,807.6	29,283	27,073	3.5	8.5	6,725.9	(NA)	8.1	(NA)	(NA)	13.7
Rochester, MN	5,740.8	5,501.3	5,102.7	33,829	31,044	4.4	12.5	4,973.1	20.2	5.8	4.2	(NA)	9.3
Rochester, NY	31,716.1	31,203.1	30,455.4	30,499	29,329	1.6	4.1	24,169.6	24.1	6.4	(NA)	(NA)	14.2
Rockford, IL	8,861.0	8,668.6	8,721.7	27,138	27,169	2.2	1.6	6,826.5	30.8	6.8	3.6	(NA)	10.6
Rocky Mount, NC	3,548.4	3,532.2	3,421.7	24,650	23,919	0.5	3.7	2,585.3	24.3	7.8	2.6	(NA)	16.7
Rome, GA	2,346.2	2,245.5	2,110.1	25,337	23,240	4.5	11.2	1,698.7	26.7	7.1	3.3	16.5	14.2
Sacramento-Arden-Arcade-Roseville, CA	59,829.2	57,496.5	54,235.5	31,069	29,993	4.1	10.3	46,801.1	7.2	7.5	8.3	8.1	28.7
Saginaw-Saginaw Township North, MI	5,305.5	5,254.6	5,373.9	25,297	25,596	1.0	-1.3	4,494.4	31.6	7.5	3.8	13.3	12.6
St. Cloud, MN	4,593.0	4,379.4	4,219.4	26,626	25,104	4.9	8.9	3,745.6	19.3	9.9	(NA)	(NA)	15.4
St. George, UT	1,994.4	1,877.4	1,751.9	20,059	19,206	6.2	13.8	1,273.4	6.0	13.1	4.5	12.6	14.8
St. Joseph, MO-KS	2,939.5	2,860.7	2,815.6	23,885	22,718	2.8	4.4	2,059.6	18.1	8.2	(NA)	(NA)	17.5
St. Louis, MO-IL[4]	88,409.5	86,138.5	84,221.8	32,462	31,174	2.6	5.0	67,284.2	(NA)	6.2	(NA)	(NA)	12.8
Salem, OR	9,031.8	8,733.1	8,515.3	25,214	24,453	3.4	6.1	6,184.6	9.2	7.3	4.1	12.8	30.4
Salinas, CA	13,091.5	12,699.2	12,097.1	31,842	30,015	3.1	8.2	9,355.8	5.1	7.5	5.3	6.6	21.8
Salisbury, MD	2,712.2	2,639.5	2,502.6	24,312	22,832	2.8	8.4	1,945.1	10.8	8.3	(NA)	(NA)	21.2
Salt Lake City, UT	28,540.0	27,936.7	27,080.5	28,674	27,852	2.2	5.4	26,381.4	10.1	7.5	(NA)	(NA)	15.6
San Angelo, TX	2,683.6	2,624.0	2,522.8	25,556	23,864	2.3	6.4	1,857.7	10.1	7.5	(NA)	14.8	27.5
San Antonio, TX	48,883.8	47,317.4	45,996.8	27,368	26,752	3.3	6.3	38,016.2	6.5	7.9	(NA)	(NA)	22.9
San Diego-Carlsbad-San Marcos, CA	101,292.6	97,140.8	92,654.0	34,872	32,797	4.3	9.3	79,407.3	9.9	6.7	12.6	7.0	22.8
Sandusky, OH	2,378.3	2,340.4	2,280.3	30,155	28,652	1.6	4.3	1,766.2	32.1	6.4	2.4	9.5	13.9
San Francisco-Oakland-Fremont, CA	**195,395.7**	**200,184.6**	**199,988.7**	**46,920**	**48,347**	**-2.4**	**-2.3**	**154,842.3**	**8.2**	**6.5**	**15.9**	**7.3**	**12.6**
Oakland-Fremont-Hayward, CA	*99,477.9*	*100,157.3*	*98,208.6*	*40,516*	*40,853*	*-0.7*	*1.3*	*69,615.7*	*12.4*	*7.1*	*11.6*	*9.4*	*14.7*
San Francisco-San Mateo-Redwood City, CA	*95,917.7*	*100,027.3*	*101,780.0*	*56,120*	*58,746*	*-4.1*	*-5.8*	*85,226.7*	*4.7*	*6.0*	*19.5*	*5.6*	*11.0*
San Jose-Sunnyvale-Santa Clara, CA	79,595.9	85,585.6	92,947.2	45,925	53,408	-7.0	-14.4	79,958.9	29.3	4.9	17.9	5.3	7.6
San Luis Obispo-Paso Robles, CA	7,598.5	7,300.0	6,801.0	30,145	27,459	4.1	11.7	4,765.5	6.6	9.9	7.3	10.0	21.1
Santa Barbara-Santa Maria, CA	13,701.2	13,271.7	12,911.0	34,103	32,298	3.2	6.1	9,510.6	9.4	8.0	10.1	8.7	19.8
Santa Cruz-Watsonville, CA	9,707.0	9,841.4	10,014.5	38,323	39,153	-1.4	-3.1	5,552.5	9.6	9.7	10.0	9.5	16.1
Santa Fe, NM	4,417.5	4,147.3	3,846.0	32,932	29,627	6.5	14.9	2,850.0	2.6	10.7	10.0	9.6	26.0
Santa Rosa-Petaluma, CA	17,390.9	17,208.7	16,778.0	37,331	36,447	1.1	3.7	10,772.7	15.8	8.5	8.0	10.3	13.5
Sarasota-Bradenton-Venice, FL	23,264.5	22,345.3	21,027.0	37,509	35,476	4.1	10.6	11,932.5	8.4	9.6	10.0	13.1	9.6
Savannah, GA	8,449.1	8,126.7	7,879.3	28,054	26,863	4.0	7.2	6,014.2	14.7	7.7	5.3	(NA)	19.7
Scranton-Wilkes-Barre, PA	15,279.3	14,901.3	14,643.0	27,602	26,171	2.5	4.3	10,501.7	17.8	8.5	5.1	14.4	14.2
Seattle-Tacoma-Bellevue, WA	**118,739.4**	**117,090.2**	**115,202.9**	**38,037**	**37,746**	**1.4**	**3.1**	**101,196.1**	**14.1**	**6.4**	**9.3**	**7.6**	**14.4**
Seattle-Bellevue-Everett, WA	*97,371.9*	*96,461.0*	*95,786.2*	*40,753*	*40,793*	*0.9*	*1.7*	*88,193.4*	*15.0*	*6.3*	*10.1*	*6.9*	*12.0*
Tacoma, WA	*21,367.6*	*20,629.1*	*19,416.7*	*29,221*	*27,582*	*3.6*	*10.0*	*13,002.7*	*8.4*	*7.8*	*4.4*	*12.6*	*30.6*
Sheboygan, WI	3,465.0	3,360.9	3,249.5	30,612	28,819	3.1	6.6	2,745.0	46.3	5.4	3.8	9.1	9.8
Sherman-Denison, TX	2,644.2	2,609.3	2,559.0	23,274	23,052	1.3	3.3	1,765.6	24.3	9.9	3.5	16.0	12.5
Shreveport-Bossier City, LA	9,789.4	9,490.3	9,064.5	25,984	24,103	3.2	8.0	7,235.0	10.8	7.1	(NA)	(NA)	23.8
Sioux City, IA-NE-SD	3,869.2	3,816.4	3,712.3	27,112	25,953	1.4	4.2	3,073.2	(NA)	6.7	(NA)	(NA)	12.2
Sioux Falls, SD	6,223.3	5,977.4	5,648.3	31,947	30,005	4.1	10.2	5,212.0	10.2	8.2	4.1	(NA)	9.4
South Bend-Mishawaka, IN-MI	8,946.7	8,704.1	8,314.8	28,153	26,228	2.8	7.6	6,409.0	23.5	7.2	6.5	(NA)	10.7
Spartanburg, SC	6,522.8	6,327.3	6,189.6	25,182	24,331	3.1	5.4	5,388.9	32.9	7.7	4.1	7.2	13.9
Spokane, WA	11,381.7	11,071.9	10,890.5	26,637	26,012	2.8	4.5	8,664.1	10.1	9.6	6.5	14.6	20.3
Springfield, IL	6,416.5	6,266.3	5,995.6	31,430	29,745	2.4	7.0	5,247.6	3.4	6.0	6.3	(NA)	32.8
Springfield, MA	20,066.2	19,420.4	18,765.8	29,302	27,578	3.3	6.9	13,173.6	14.3	7.7	5.2	14.2	19.6
Springfield, MO	9,705.3	9,332.9	8,792.1	25,622	23,789	4.0	10.4	7,306.0	15.1	10.7	(NA)	(NA)	13.2
Springfield, OH	3,761.6	3,762.7	3,734.9	26,159	25,825	(Z)	0.7	2,174.4	25.3	10.2	3.2	14.0	16.0
State College, PA	3,560.3	3,393.9	3,266.2	25,394	24,020	4.9	9.0	3,023.3	10.5	6.5	6.3	7.8	42.4
Stockton, CA	14,788.5	14,273.6	13,757.1	24,119	24,213	3.6	7.5	9,658.8	10.0	9.4	4.2	9.8	19.9
Sumter, SC	2,269.9	2,176.3	2,150.1	21,577	20,528	4.3	5.6	1,715.3	21.3	6.5	2.0	8.5	36.4
Syracuse, NY	18,422.8	17,726.0	17,565.9	28,257	27,007	3.9	4.9	14,464.1	16.3	6.6	7.1	(NA)	17.0
Tallahassee, FL	8,547.0	8,287.8	7,957.5	26,302	24,791	3.1	7.4	6,956.0	2.5	6.3	(NA)	(NA)	40.0
Tampa-St. Petersburg-Clearwater, FL	73,985.8	71,521.8	68,891.0	29,728	28,655	3.4	7.4	52,941.9	7.4	8.2	9.1	11.0	13.0
Terre Haute, IN	3,934.4	3,838.1	3,771.5	23,196	22,081	2.5	4.3	2,726.6	21.7	11.1	2.9	(NA)	19.4
Texarkana, TX-Texarkana, AR	3,128.5	3,008.6	2,884.8	23,931	22,237	4.0	8.4	2,140.4	13.0	10.1	0.0	16.1	23.1
Toledo, OH	18,891.5	18,451.8	18,305.4	28,612	27,767	2.4	3.2	14,985.4	23.5	7.3	(NA)	(NA)	15.5
Topeka, KS	6,401.5	6,233.3	6,022.6	28,398	26,787	2.7	6.3	4,832.4	9.3	8.1	(NA)	(NA)	23.4
Trenton-Ewing, NJ	14,581.7	14,262.8	13,871.7	40,711	39,455	2.2	5.1	12,976.7	4.4	4.9	13.9	8.3	24.0
Tucson, AZ	22,213.3	21,245.6	20,513.6	25,278	24,172	4.6	8.3	14,887.1	13.3	8.0	7.1	11.6	24.6
Tulsa, OK	26,827.2	26,335.8	24,984.0	30,627	29,008	1.9	7.4	21,220.8	21.0	7.4	(NA)	(NA)	9.6
Tuscaloosa, AL	4,871.5	4,704.6	4,516.7	25,152	23,362	3.5	7.9	3,635.8	21.2	7.2	3.8	(NA)	24.6
Tyler, TX	5,144.5	4,945.6	4,922.0	28,466	28,061	4.0	4.5	3,983.9	13.2	12.1	5.7	17.9	12.5

See footnotes at end of table.

Table B-8. Metropolitan Areas — **Personal Income and Earnings by Industry**—Con.

Metropolitan statistical area **Metropolitan statistical area with metropolitan divisions** *Metropolitan division*	Personal income Total (mil. dol.) 2002	2001	2000	Per capita[1] (dol.) 2002	2000	Percent change 2001–2002	2000–2002	Earnings, 2002 Total[2] (mil. dol.)	Manufacturing	Retail trade	Professional and technical services	Health care and social services	Government and government enterprises
Utica-Rome, NY	7,348.1	7,148.2	7,046.6	24,668	23,520	2.8	4.3	5,029.9	13.2	7.8	4.2	13.8	25.4
Valdosta, GA	2,789.7	2,595.3	2,484.7	23,059	20,765	7.5	12.3	2,002.8	(NA)	9.7	(NA)	(NA)	34.3
Vallejo-Fairfield, CA	11,912.2	11,600.9	10,953.3	29,089	27,579	2.7	8.8	6,428.8	9.3	9.6	3.5	11.4	29.2
Vero Beach, FL	4,698.7	4,547.6	4,207.7	39,830	37,114	3.3	11.7	1,797.6	6.2	11.4	7.2	16.5	13.1
Victoria, TX	2,908.0	2,873.0	2,809.3	25,844	25,162	1.2	3.5	2,147.8	(NA)	9.5	1.0	(NA)	14.4
Vineland-Millville-Bridgeton, NJ	3,823.1	3,609.3	3,421.0	25,856	23,371	5.9	11.8	2,782.8	19.4	9.2	3.4	11.7	25.8
Virginia Beach-Norfolk-Newport News, VA-NC	45,773.2	43,856.4	39,634.8	28,365	26,355	4.4	9.9	37,209.0	(NA)	5.8	(NA)	(NA)	38.3
Visalia-Porterville, CA	8,075.5	7,739.3	7,218.7	21,193	19,571	4.3	11.9	5,492.3	8.9	8.1	3.0	7.0	22.9
Waco, TX	5,211.8	5,007.0	4,862.0	24,003	22,719	4.1	7.2	4,010.4	18.0	7.7	3.9	10.5	17.3
Warner Robins, GA	3,027.2	2,828.4	2,713.5	25,876	24,378	7.0	11.6	2,638.3	6.6	5.8	6.0	4.8	61.1
Washington-Arlington-Alexandria, DC-VA-MD-WV	**214,440.7**	**208,097.5**	**196,093.1**	**42,773**	**40,665**	**3.0**	**9.4**	**193,515.6**	**(NA)**	**4.5**	**20.3**	**(NA)**	**27.6**
Bethesda-Gaithersburg-Frederick, MD	*54,247.0*	*52,263.5*	*50,002.5*	*48,517*	*46,541*	*3.8*	*8.5*	*36,321.8*	*5.3*	*5.8*	*18.8*	*8.0*	*21.0*
Washington-Arlington-Alexandria, DC-VA-MD-WV	*160,193.7*	*155,834.1*	*146,090.6*	*41,124*	*38,980*	*2.8*	*9.7*	*157,193.8*	*(NA)*	*4.2*	*20.6*	*(NA)*	*29.1*
Waterloo-Cedar Falls, IA	4,354.1	4,204.5	4,055.9	26,846	24,795	3.6	7.4	3,389.5	26.6	7.6	4.3	(NA)	15.6
Wausau, WI	3,691.6	3,555.4	3,430.6	29,103	27,248	3.8	7.6	2,955.5	28.1	8.5	(NA)	8.7	10.6
Weirton-Steubenville, WV-OH	3,072.2	2,981.9	2,937.2	23,750	22,307	3.0	4.6	1,992.1	32.6	6.5	2.1	(NA)	12.5
Wenatchee, WA	2,644.2	2,523.1	2,377.9	26,321	23,923	4.8	11.2	1,809.9	5.9	9.8	3.4	14.8	21.2
Wheeling, WV-OH	3,776.1	3,679.6	3,539.9	24,993	23,159	2.6	6.7	2,399.5	13.1	8.8	(NA)	(NA)	17.0
Wichita, KS	17,158.2	16,829.5	15,918.1	29,587	27,828	2.0	7.8	13,708.3	32.5	6.4	(NA)	10.9	12.7
Wichita Falls, TX	3,981.8	3,822.3	3,712.3	26,583	24,513	4.2	7.3	2,921.3	14.0	7.5	(NA)	11.2	34.5
Williamsport, PA	2,980.1	2,932.1	2,761.9	25,096	23,029	1.6	7.9	2,155.1	29.1	8.6	3.7	12.8	16.8
Wilmington, NC	7,688.7	7,476.7	7,118.2	26,753	25,820	2.8	8.0	5,045.8	11.1	9.5	(NA)	(NA)	19.4
Winchester, VA-WV	2,955.0	2,837.4	2,648.9	27,308	25,577	4.1	11.6	2,230.6	26.4	9.1	3.7	(NA)	11.6
Winston-Salem, NC	12,775.1	12,500.1	12,412.4	29,485	29,323	2.2	2.9	9,630.0	19.8	7.3	(NA)	(NA)	9.5
Worcester, MA	25,579.7	25,377.0	24,539.3	33,229	32,604	0.8	4.2	16,585.1	17.5	7.2	8.3	12.6	14.4
Yakima, WA	5,323.7	5,120.1	4,916.1	23,714	22,074	4.0	8.3	3,654.2	11.4	7.9	3.2	13.2	19.3
York-Hanover, PA	11,221.5	10,890.7	11,018.5	28,810	28,790	3.0	1.8	7,481.4	29.5	8.0	4.4	10.6	11.4
Youngstown-Warren-Boardman, OH-PA	15,107.5	14,748.6	14,805.9	25,358	24,588	2.4	2.0	10,129.2	27.2	9.3	3.5	14.1	13.8
Yuba City, CA	3,416.5	3,251.6	3,093.9	23,617	22,177	5.1	10.4	2,149.5	6.4	9.0	4.1	11.3	32.9
Yuma, AZ	3,430.7	2,967.9	2,653.8	20,561	16,513	15.6	29.3	2,591.1	3.2	7.1	1.8	8.0	28.2

NA Not available.   Z Less than .05%.

[1]Based on resident population estimated as of July 1, 2000 and 2002.

[2]Includes construction; wholesale; transportation and warehousing; information; finance and insurance; management of companies and enterprises; administrative and waste services; educational services; arts, entertainment, and recreation; accommodation and food services; and other services (except public administration); not shown separately.

[3]The Denver-Aurora metropolitan statistical area includes Broomfield County. Broomfield County, CO, was formed from parts of Adams, Boulder, Jefferson, and Weld counties on November 15, 2001, and is coextensive with Broomfield city. For the purposes of defining and presenting data for the Denver-Aurora metropolitan statistical area, Broomfield city is treated as if it were a county when data are available to do so. In many cases, the data will not be available.

[4]The portion of Sullivan city in Crawford County, MO, is legally part of the St. Louis, MO-IL MSA. That portion is not included in these figures for the St. Louis MSA.

Note: Covers metropolitan statistical areas and metropolitan divisions and component counties defined by the Office of Management and Budget as of June 6, 2003, and subsequently updated in December 2003 and November 2004. For more information, see OMB Bulletin 05-02 at <http://www.whitehouse.gov/omb/bulletins/fy05/b05-02_appendix.pdf>.

Survey, Census, or Data Collection Method: Based on the Regional Economic Information System; for more information, see Appendix B, Limitations of the Data and Methodology, and also <http://www.bea.gov/bea/regional/articles.cfm?section=methods> and <http://www.bea.gov/bea/regional/articles/lapi2003/lapi2003.pdf>.

Source: Personal income and earnings—U.S. Bureau of Economic Analysis, *Regional Economic Information System (REIS) 1969–2002* on CD-ROM, and related Internet site at <http://www.bea.gov/bea/regional/reis/>.

Labor Force and Private Business Establishments and Employment

Metropolitan statistical area **Metropolitan statistical area with metropolitan divisions** *Metropolitan division*	Civilian labor force							Private nonfarm businesses					
	Total			Number of unemployed		Unemployment rate[1]		Establishments		Employment[2]		Annual payroll per employee, 2002	
	2004	Change, 2000–2004	2000	2004	2000	2004	2000	2002	Change, 2000–2002	2002	Change, 2000–2002	Amount (dollars)	Percent of national average
Abilene, TX.	80,240	5,012	75,228	3,909	3,117	4.9	4.1	3,915	–102	54,004	700	23,141	66.0
Akron, OH.	373,273	9,785	363,488	22,354	14,896	6.0	4.1	17,758	209	289,151	–13,008	33,118	94.4
Albany, GA.	72,439	946	71,493	3,768	3,372	5.2	4.7	3,357	65	50,369	–2,499	27,068	77.2
Albany-Schenectady-Troy, NY	452,566	16,396	436,170	19,037	14,991	4.2	3.4	19,743	465	317,209	–2,335	33,012	94.1
Albuquerque, NM.	391,796	21,567	370,229	20,513	15,304	5.2	4.1	18,087	122	274,426	–6,400	29,893	85.2
Alexandria, LA.	64,660	1,258	63,402	3,714	3,297	5.7	5.2	3,337	50	48,222	–1,518	25,561	72.9
Allentown-Bethlehem-Easton, PA-NJ	404,991	19,721	385,270	21,551	14,259	5.3	3.7	18,073	360	288,496	1,090	33,849	96.5
Altoona, PA	65,809	3,446	62,363	3,633	2,905	5.5	4.7	3,259	–30	49,193	–2,658	25,870	73.7
Amarillo, TX.	128,349	10,675	117,674	5,578	4,492	4.3	3.8	5,767	–15	83,504	–1,132	28,006	79.8
Ames, IA.	46,560	–116	46,676	1,472	876	3.2	1.9	1,902	–31	27,080	–1,422	24,796	70.7
Anchorage, AK.	178,647	9,454	169,193	11,388	8,995	6.4	5.3	9,613	304	127,135	4,728	42,496	121.1
Anderson, IN.	63,421	–329	63,750	3,746	1,908	5.9	3.0	2,686	–87	38,421	–3,925	27,403	78.1
Anderson, SC.	83,733	330	83,403	5,977	2,492	7.1	3.0	3,796	71	55,028	–3,970	27,213	77.6
Ann Arbor, MI.	188,183	2,203	185,980	8,160	4,422	4.3	2.4	8,296	44	150,487	–6,977	41,491	118.3
Anniston-Oxford, AL.	54,324	755	53,569	2,931	2,428	5.4	4.5	2,570	4	38,373	–2,241	25,003	71.3
Appleton, WI.	121,974	4,352	117,622	5,565	3,352	4.6	2.8	5,623	141	105,127	–4,285	32,127	91.6
Asheville, NC.	195,625	11,225	184,400	8,373	6,027	4.3	3.3	10,696	393	143,332	–3,900	26,716	76.2
Athens-Clarke County, GA.	95,181	5,957	89,224	3,238	2,891	3.4	3.2	4,035	206	54,513	93	25,608	73.0
Atlanta-Sandy Springs-Marietta, GA.	2,454,115	81,620	2,372,495	112,927	73,906	4.6	3.1	119,863	4,148	2,066,678	–71,597	38,356	109.3
Atlantic City, NJ.	134,390	5,422	128,968	7,483	6,007	5.6	4.7	6,533	156	125,928	5,370	29,592	84.4
Auburn-Opelika, AL.	62,818	3,984	58,834	2,622	2,101	4.2	3.6	2,077	85	33,307	1,036	24,053	68.6
Augusta-Richmond County, GA-SC.	246,659	13,528	233,131	13,355	9,009	5.4	3.9	10,094	87	180,422	3,198	30,887	88.0
Austin-Round Rock, TX.	778,097	39,898	738,199	39,391	22,662	5.1	3.1	33,362	1,540	549,172	–1,246	38,111	108.6
Bakersfield, CA.	318,655	24,212	294,443	31,210	24,344	9.8	8.3	11,268	375	154,185	3,875	30,746	87.6
Baltimore-Towson, MD.	1,346,001	20,017	1,325,984	61,195	50,333	4.5	3.8	63,694	1,445	1,049,283	4,762	36,431	103.8
Bangor, ME.	78,822	3,623	75,199	4,271	2,844	5.4	3.8	4,166	–7	57,427	585	27,924	79.6
Barnstable Town, MA.	123,131	9,761	113,370	5,956	3,751	4.8	3.3	8,596	257	74,340	2,153	31,479	89.7
Baton Rouge, LA.	351,569	12,673	338,896	21,321	16,122	6.1	4.8	16,308	227	278,604	–2,560	30,399	86.7
Battle Creek, MI.	73,138	3,360	69,778	5,096	2,921	7.0	4.2	2,999	–30	56,235	–4,484	33,473	95.4
Bay City, MI.	56,851	107	56,744	4,300	2,300	7.6	4.1	2,571	15	33,815	–1,521	30,078	85.7
Beaumont-Port Arthur, TX.	179,733	3,138	176,595	15,069	11,432	8.4	6.5	8,009	–98	125,925	–3,222	30,638	87.3
Bellingham, WA.	100,935	12,623	88,312	5,803	4,567	5.7	5.2	5,583	197	58,451	–1,186	29,662	84.6
Bend, OR.	71,064	9,492	61,572	4,771	3,322	6.7	5.4	4,947	457	45,386	2,500	27,299	77.8
Billings, MT.	82,549	6,159	76,390	2,920	3,153	3.5	4.1	5,336	140	60,549	–273	27,071	77.2
Binghamton, NY	122,618	–2,475	125,093	6,556	4,468	5.3	3.6	5,126	27	91,069	–279	27,827	79.3
Birmingham-Hoover, AL.	533,028	–1,665	534,693	25,810	18,563	4.8	3.5	25,867	233	450,925	–14,705	33,683	96.0
Bismarck, ND.	58,320	3,642	54,678	1,733	1,344	3.0	2.5	3,053	81	42,337	224	26,888	76.6
Blacksburg-Christiansburg-Radford, VA.	76,157	3,392	72,765	3,155	2,361	4.1	3.2	3,220	79	46,201	–2,990	26,983	76.9
Bloomington, IN.	93,852	2,877	90,975	4,279	2,723	4.6	3.0	3,880	–4	55,529	–1,309	25,449	72.5
Bloomington-Normal, IL.	84,940	–412	85,352	3,834	2,893	4.5	3.4	3,536	–6	78,612	–4,113	37,082	105.7
Boise City-Nampa, ID.	267,602	16,176	251,426	11,626	9,376	4.3	3.7	14,431	746	198,012	356	30,840	87.9
Boston-Cambridge-Quincy, MA-NH	**2,373,906**	**–5,419**	**2,379,325**	**115,721**	**59,626**	**4.9**	**2.5**	**125,649**	**273**	**2,303,251**	**–49,269**	**45,709**	**130.3**
Boston-Quincy, MA.	*950,724*	*–9,025*	*959,749*	*48,263*	*25,315*	*5.1*	*2.6*	*52,065*	*159*	*1,063,635*	*7,193*	*47,418*	*135.2*
Cambridge-Newton-Framingham, MA.	*811,419*	*–10,782*	*822,201*	*35,826*	*17,761*	*4.4*	*2.2*	*42,890*	*–184*	*797,012*	*–55,942*	*48,173*	*137.3*
Essex County, MA.	*375,684*	*3,117*	*372,567*	*21,524*	*10,130*	*5.7*	*2.7*	*18,610*	*22*	*276,507*	*–5,859*	*38,024*	*108.4*
Rockingham County-Strafford County, NH.	*236,079*	*11,271*	*224,808*	*10,108*	*6,420*	*4.3*	*2.9*	*12,084*	*276*	*166,097*	*5,339*	*35,730*	*101.8*
Boulder, CO[3]	166,160	6,040	160,120	8,181	3,758	4.9	2.3	10,586	–542	143,549	–14,352	40,589	115.7
Bowling Green, KY.	57,773	2,605	55,168	2,569	2,138	4.4	3.9	2,670	68	44,221	–185	26,830	76.5
Bremerton-Silverdale, WA.	121,067	14,736	106,331	7,086	5,394	5.9	5.1	5,566	326	51,818	1,929	27,229	77.6
Bridgeport-Stamford-Norwalk, CT.	454,667	8,869	445,798	19,943	9,440	4.4	2.1	28,385	–202	462,542	17,612	56,000	159.6
Brownsville-Harlingen, TX.	143,006	15,832	127,174	12,549	8,890	8.8	7.0	6,046	250	88,506	2,009	20,372	58.1
Brunswick, GA.	50,236	3,694	46,542	2,027	1,693	4.0	3.6	2,830	56	34,394	360	24,090	68.7
Buffalo-Niagara Falls, NY.	586,572	7,365	579,207	34,122	24,773	5.8	4.3	27,248	412	469,860	–7,791	30,621	87.3
Burlington, NC.	69,671	583	69,088	4,299	2,194	6.2	3.2	3,308	–40	54,710	–5,268	26,162	74.6
Burlington-South Burlington, VT.	118,840	5,325	113,515	4,137	2,661	3.5	2.3	7,190	576	97,612	2,176	33,430	95.3
Canton-Massillon, OH.	204,989	–1,176	206,165	13,547	8,543	6.6	4.1	9,813	–151	163,383	–6,243	28,198	80.4
Cape Coral-Fort Myers, FL.	247,719	40,332	207,387	9,556	6,699	3.9	3.2	13,768	1,375	155,807	12,753	28,412	81.0
Carson City, NV.	27,240	738	26,502	1,355	994	5.0	3.8	2,281	–69	22,743	–2,042	30,207	86.1
Casper, WY.	39,872	3,335	36,537	1,485	1,438	3.7	3.9	2,683	58	28,121	564	28,243	80.5
Cedar Rapids, IA.	137,073	817	136,256	6,936	3,290	5.1	2.4	6,539	95	118,162	–5,614	31,298	89.2
Champaign-Urbana, IL.	114,737	–556	115,293	5,249	4,125	4.6	3.6	4,924	62	76,004	–1,619	27,601	78.7
Charleston, WV.	138,639	–6,570	145,209	6,874	7,643	5.0	5.3	7,683	–162	123,444	5,265	29,301	83.5
Charleston-North Charleston, SC.	290,125	25,386	264,739	15,514	8,216	5.3	3.1	14,660	590	208,693	–10,806	27,869	79.4
Charlotte-Gastonia-Concord, NC-SC.	778,270	46,975	731,295	43,513	24,582	5.6	3.4	39,926	1,129	734,833	11,439	36,636	104.4
Charlottesville, VA.	93,585	5,961	87,624	2,917	1,822	3.1	2.1	5,242	232	70,948	151	30,515	87.0
Chattanooga, TN-GA.	249,313	2,641	246,672	11,074	8,280	4.4	3.4	11,266	–69	208,768	–3,746	28,839	82.2
Cheyenne, WY.	42,699	2,464	40,235	1,935	1,514	4.5	3.8	2,387	99	27,580	679	26,133	74.5
Chicago-Naperville-Joliet, IL-IN-WI.	**4,733,077**	**–34,733**	**4,767,810**	**288,055**	**207,287**	**6.1**	**4.3**	**230,115**	**2,515**	**4,028,005**	**–214,298**	**40,878**	**116.5**
Chicago-Naperville-Joliet, IL.	*3,982,271*	*–40,199*	*4,022,470*	*245,565*	*180,538*	*6.2*	*4.5*	*193,284*	*1,537*	*3,431,123*	*–209,928*	*41,171*	*117.4*
Gary, IN.	*323,188*	*–3,192*	*326,380*	*18,836*	*11,029*	*5.8*	*3.4*	*14,621*	*221*	*230,582*	*–12,061*	*31,179*	*88.9*
Lake County-Kenosha County, IL-WI.	*427,618*	*8,658*	*418,960*	*23,654*	*15,720*	*5.5*	*3.8*	*22,210*	*757*	*366,300*	*7,691*	*44,236*	*126.1*

See footnotes at end of table.

	Civilian labor force							Private nonfarm businesses					
Metropolitan statistical area **Metropolitan statistical area with metropolitan divisions** *Metropolitan division*	Total			Number of unemployed		Unemployment rate[1]		Establishments		Employment[2]		Annual payroll per employee, 2002	
	2004	Change, 2000–2004	2000	2004	2000	2004	2000	2002	Change, 2000–2002	2002	Change, 2000–2002	Amount (dollars)	Percent of national average
Chico, CA	98,004	4,853	93,151	7,055	5,725	7.2	6.1	4,758	161	56,283	2,507	24,066	68.6
Cincinnati-Middletown, OH-KY-IN	1,083,362	40,454	1,042,908	57,394	37,266	5.3	3.6	47,748	217	916,575	−42,072	34,824	99.3
Clarksville, TN-KY	102,692	5,153	97,539	5,451	4,094	5.3	4.2	4,011	49	62,102	2,094	23,839	68.0
Cleveland, TN	53,322	249	53,073	2,751	1,990	5.2	3.7	2,127	−4	38,016	−4,146	27,620	78.7
Cleveland-Elyria-Mentor, OH	1,100,716	−23,015	1,123,731	64,815	42,886	5.9	3.8	56,335	−616	970,650	−86,684	35,139	100.2
Coeur d'Alene, ID	63,799	7,433	56,366	3,510	3,520	5.5	6.2	3,692	29	35,947	−1,065	26,233	74.8
College Station-Bryan, TX	101,571	8,222	93,349	4,534	3,602	4.5	3.9	3,903	183	54,942	3,173	24,719	70.5
Colorado Springs, CO	296,726	20,077	276,649	16,817	7,802	5.7	2.8	14,992	687	209,821	−5,466	31,919	91.0
Columbia, MO	90,576	5,829	84,747	3,374	1,872	3.7	2.2	4,063	51	64,221	−107	26,601	75.8
Columbia, SC	349,852	16,245	333,607	20,019	10,224	5.7	3.1	16,195	80	267,755	−4,301	29,400	83.8
Columbus, GA-AL	123,146	−1,897	125,043	6,336	5,621	5.2	4.5	5,721	62	96,507	−8,961	26,593	75.8
Columbus, IN	36,213	−1,278	37,491	1,578	943	4.4	2.5	1,854	−118	35,589	−2,976	36,219	103.2
Columbus, OH	916,311	37,862	878,449	49,559	28,299	5.4	3.2	39,642	1,002	785,150	−14,365	34,907	99.5
Corpus Christi, TX	197,774	12,616	185,158	13,201	9,993	6.7	5.4	9,447	85	129,676	−3,029	27,916	79.6
Corvallis, OR	42,371	1,080	41,291	2,296	1,627	5.4	3.9	1,991	64	27,638	380	34,268	97.7
Cumberland, MD-WV	45,001	−678	45,679	2,843	2,646	6.3	5.8	2,312	−15	30,462	326	24,836	70.8
Dallas-Fort Worth-Arlington, TX	2,965,577	115,774	2,849,803	174,761	102,753	5.9	3.6	130,270	3,453	2,501,040	−45,791	39,359	112.2
Dallas-Plano-Irving, TX	1,987,225	69,619	1,917,606	119,670	69,063	6.0	3.6	90,844	2,020	1,821,159	−31,597	41,438	118.1
Fort Worth-Arlington, TX	978,352	46,155	932,197	55,091	33,690	5.6	3.6	39,426	1,433	679,881	−14,194	33,792	96.3
Dalton, GA	63,925	524	63,401	2,631	2,191	4.1	3.5	3,041	-	64,548	−2,468	30,650	87.4
Danville, IL	37,470	−1,351	38,821	3,128	2,306	8.3	5.9	1,735	−19	27,504	−1,479	27,506	78.4
Danville, VA	52,600	−241	52,841	3,884	1,976	7.4	3.7	2,440	7	37,675	−1,301	25,201	71.8
Davenport-Moline-Rock Island, IA-IL	196,151	−3,743	199,894	10,843	8,257	5.5	4.1	9,488	−101	159,127	−9,336	31,101	88.7
Dayton, OH	428,304	−1,669	429,973	26,693	16,701	6.2	3.9	18,969	−130	358,042	−24,594	32,342	92.2
Decatur, AL	72,206	−1,593	73,799	4,420	2,892	6.1	3.9	3,191	41	49,518	−2,527	27,906	79.5
Decatur, IL	51,956	−4,170	56,126	3,780	2,910	7.3	5.2	2,674	−48	51,065	−6,070	31,668	90.3
Deltona-Daytona Beach-Ormond Beach, FL	231,766	22,446	209,320	10,580	7,065	4.6	3.4	11,246	444	133,177	1,917	24,012	68.4
Denver-Aurora, CO[3]	1,296,362	78,429	1,217,933	74,633	30,477	5.8	2.5	69,993	2,614	1,055,380	−6,271	39,322	112.1
Des Moines, IA	290,000	12,435	277,565	13,531	6,731	4.7	2.4	14,075	311	267,473	1,334	34,027	97.0
Detroit-Warren-Livonia, MI	2,206,277	−84,522	2,290,799	157,141	83,515	7.1	3.6	105,651	−250	1,892,160	−106,394	41,443	118.1
Detroit-Livonia-Dearborn, MI	918,630	−36,307	954,937	78,785	40,776	8.6	4.3	35,955	−56	714,125	−43,362	40,582	115.7
Warren-Farmington Hills-Troy, MI	1,287,647	−48,215	1,335,862	78,356	42,739	6.1	3.2	69,696	−194	1,178,035	−63,032	41,965	119.6
Dothan, AL	65,607	−240	65,847	3,093	2,704	4.7	4.1	3,615	54	54,812	−26	26,187	74.6
Dover, DE	69,332	5,345	63,987	2,479	2,290	3.6	3.6	2,991	30	46,157	1,757	26,545	75.7
Dubuque, IA	49,054	220	48,834	2,310	1,629	4.7	3.3	2,631	−28	47,196	−2,792	27,073	77.2
Duluth, MN-WI	145,511	2,866	142,645	8,497	6,349	5.8	4.5	7,392	61	100,026	−2,225	27,494	78.4
Durham, NC	241,836	10,808	231,028	10,586	6,790	4.4	2.9	10,675	154	223,105	−13	39,256	111.9
Eau Claire, WI	86,973	3,613	83,360	4,115	2,938	4.7	3.5	4,007	85	63,745	213	27,195	77.5
El Centro, CA	59,885	3,766	56,119	10,212	9,811	17.1	17.5	2,324	51	25,535	182	25,370	72.3
Elizabethtown, KY	52,486	3,258	49,228	2,763	2,168	5.3	4.4	2,282	104	33,086	−1,542	26,183	74.6
Elkhart-Goshen, IN	100,003	2,728	97,275	4,169	2,458	4.2	2.5	5,102	90	108,296	−10,058	31,994	91.2
Elmira, NY	40,584	−2,244	42,828	2,463	1,843	6.1	4.3	1,932	15	34,242	−913	26,569	75.7
El Paso, TX	290,119	14,845	275,274	22,700	18,721	7.8	6.8	12,403	93	194,012	−5,869	23,411	66.7
Erie, PA	140,830	542	140,288	8,886	6,363	6.3	4.5	6,807	−156	118,018	−4,382	28,066	80.0
Eugene-Springfield, OR	173,146	2,269	170,877	12,783	9,236	7.4	5.4	9,585	−105	117,253	−2,272	29,030	82.7
Evansville, IN-KY	180,580	1,616	178,964	8,322	5,725	4.6	3.2	8,824	−86	157,880	−7,360	30,542	87.1
Fairbanks, AK	43,514	2,580	40,934	2,855	2,453	6.6	6.0	2,263	88	24,597	2,989	35,531	101.3
Fargo, ND-MN	112,620	8,073	104,547	3,267	2,531	2.9	2.4	5,497	177	88,369	329	27,817	79.3
Farmington, NM	53,564	3,959	49,605	3,250	2,865	6.1	5.8	2,588	101	34,726	386	28,657	81.7
Fayetteville, NC	139,622	6,326	133,296	7,852	6,169	5.6	4.6	5,600	12	87,496	−6,358	25,048	71.4
Fayetteville-Springdale-Rogers, AR-MO	207,116	30,685	176,431	7,522	5,106	3.6	2.9	8,936	513	157,773	12,220	28,697	81.8
Flagstaff, AZ	67,044	4,449	62,595	3,667	2,829	5.5	4.5	3,608	150	39,167	250	24,631	70.2
Flint, MI	213,704	−749	214,453	17,807	9,607	8.3	4.5	8,997	−120	139,377	−12,362	33,644	95.9
Florence, SC	95,670	4,191	91,479	7,813	3,858	8.2	4.2	4,562	25	76,853	−1,064	27,199	77.5
Florence-Muscle Shoals, AL	66,618	−3,649	70,267	4,341	3,268	6.5	4.7	3,325	−39	43,258	−7,404	23,553	67.1
Fond du Lac, WI	57,401	1,511	55,890	2,635	1,666	4.6	3.0	2,491	−25	43,382	−1,724	28,632	81.6
Fort Collins-Loveland, CO	162,927	16,577	146,350	7,511	3,550	4.6	2.4	8,500	483	96,336	2,758	31,617	90.1
Fort Smith, AR-OK	132,182	5,194	126,988	6,807	4,674	5.1	3.7	5,940	113	103,052	−4,344	25,642	73.1
Fort Walton Beach-Crestview-Destin, FL	92,689	12,425	80,264	3,220	2,955	3.5	3.7	4,906	108	57,709	−587	25,798	73.5
Fort Wayne, IN	209,628	861	208,767	10,868	5,374	5.2	2.6	10,440	187	189,584	−12,454	32,397	92.3
Fresno, CA	409,472	20,243	389,229	42,464	40,517	10.4	10.4	15,553	273	220,182	7,232	29,157	83.1
Gadsden, AL	47,268	−1,493	48,761	2,977	2,551	6.3	5.2	2,173	18	32,472	−1,873	23,601	67.3
Gainesville, FL	127,621	5,217	122,404	4,421	3,722	3.5	3.0	5,471	130	83,414	932	26,290	74.9
Gainesville, GA	78,439	5,226	73,213	2,983	2,170	3.8	3.0	3,531	169	56,685	−1,170	30,753	87.7
Glens Falls, NY	66,679	3,182	63,497	3,194	2,508	4.8	3.9	3,419	26	43,823	−1,425	27,640	78.8
Goldsboro, NC	51,526	814	50,712	2,806	2,041	5.4	4.0	2,338	−2	37,854	137	24,535	69.9
Grand Forks, ND-MN	54,875	2,558	52,317	2,046	1,787	3.7	3.4	2,573	3	35,756	−641	24,883	70.9
Grand Junction, CO	68,915	10,085	58,830	3,533	1,824	5.1	3.1	3,940	46	42,915	−435	27,293	77.8
Grand Rapids-Wyoming, MI	400,969	−1,891	402,860	27,876	13,139	7.0	3.3	18,668	577	359,094	−9,506	33,819	96.4
Great Falls, MT	39,209	922	38,287	1,643	1,901	4.2	5.0	2,510	−54	27,710	−48	22,877	65.2
Greeley, CO[3]	108,615	15,077	93,538	5,829	2,430	5.4	2.6	4,418	352	58,663	1,822	31,914	91.0
Green Bay, WI	172,444	9,840	162,604	8,098	4,714	4.7	2.9	7,750	112	141,024	−5,111	32,517	92.7
Greensboro-High Point, NC	357,938	7,777	350,161	19,985	12,367	5.6	3.5	18,139	−85	322,040	−20,046	30,834	87.9
Greenville, NC	81,156	2,976	78,180	4,639	3,337	5.7	4.3	3,483	57	53,205	−1,864	25,662	73.1

See footnotes at end of table.

Table B-9. Metropolitan Areas — **Labor Force and Private Business Establishments and Employment**—Con.

Metropolitan statistical area **Metropolitan statistical area with metropolitan divisions** *Metropolitan division*	Civilian labor force							Private nonfarm businesses					
	Total			Number of unemployed		Unemployment rate[1]		Establishments		Employment[2]		Annual payroll per employee, 2002	
	2004	Change, 2000–2004	2000	2004	2000	2004	2000	2002	Change, 2000–2002	2002	Change, 2000–2002	Amount (dollars)	Percent of national average
Greenville, SC	295,086	1,006	294,080	18,327	7,925	6.2	2.7	14,509	-215	270,129	-20,668	32,068	91.4
Gulfport-Biloxi, MS	119,933	2,469	117,464	6,157	5,703	5.1	4.9	5,525	21	87,535	-4,695	25,531	72.8
Hagerstown-Martinsburg, MD-WV	114,984	1,874	113,110	4,932	4,125	4.3	3.6	5,167	148	82,575	1,762	27,905	79.5
Hanford-Corcoran, CA	54,424	5,065	49,359	5,889	4,964	10.8	10.1	1,591	52	20,459	1,919	26,959	76.8
Harrisburg-Carlisle, PA	279,913	11,500	268,413	12,588	9,117	4.5	3.4	12,965	66	264,726	7,289	31,745	90.5
Harrisonburg, VA	63,020	7,321	55,699	1,862	1,048	3.0	1.9	2,836	141	48,277	48	26,395	75.2
Hartford-West Hartford-East Hartford, CT	607,091	17,054	590,037	30,827	14,416	5.1	2.4	29,891	-74	561,896	-12,686	41,444	118.1
Hattiesburg, MS	62,337	1,739	60,598	3,214	2,936	5.2	4.8	3,045	41	44,537	1,208	24,440	69.7
Hickory-Lenoir-Morganton, NC	179,873	-7,693	187,566	12,078	5,636	6.7	3.0	8,128	1	153,231	-14,897	26,640	75.9
Hinesville-Fort Stewart, GA	26,850	2,924	23,926	1,470	1,223	5.5	5.1	802	20	9,671	-39	22,582	64.4
Holland-Grand Haven, MI	133,594	-1,997	135,591	7,519	3,639	5.6	2.7	5,911	21	103,121	-4,684	33,002	94.1
Honolulu, HI	431,677	-528	432,205	13,692	16,961	3.2	3.9	20,952	315	317,533	1,671	31,756	90.5
Hot Springs, AR	40,904	2,560	38,344	2,425	1,624	5.9	4.2	2,681	110	31,423	492	23,446	66.8
Houma-Bayou Cane-Thibodaux, LA	92,539	5,886	86,653	4,699	3,723	5.1	4.3	4,653	119	65,845	2,318	29,887	85.2
Houston-Sugar Land-Baytown, TX	2,573,882	182,523	2,391,359	162,229	103,796	6.3	4.3	110,685	2,816	1,992,206	24,705	40,435	115.3
Huntington-Ashland, WV-KY-OH	130,228	4,446	125,782	7,218	7,159	5.5	5.7	6,244	-84	92,464	-1,176	26,954	76.8
Huntsville, AL	192,749	8,642	184,107	8,829	5,908	4.6	3.2	8,505	197	144,850	770	34,183	97.4
Idaho Falls, ID	56,420	5,888	50,532	1,953	1,744	3.5	3.5	3,116	166	41,070	-28	29,485	84.0
Indianapolis, IN	867,103	46,862	820,241	40,419	19,771	4.7	2.4	40,999	649	765,159	-15,003	35,727	101.8
Iowa City, IA	98,319	19,155	79,164	3,146	1,600	3.2	2.0	3,392	17	56,848	-131	27,790	79.2
Ithaca, NY	54,015	2,926	51,089	1,967	1,697	3.6	3.3	2,168	43	43,706	1,906	26,472	75.5
Jackson, MI	79,260	-43	79,303	5,987	2,706	7.6	3.4	3,452	41	51,053	-3,643	31,279	89.2
Jackson, MS	260,934	11,922	249,012	13,418	11,880	5.1	4.8	12,342	295	202,604	-11,042	28,056	80.0
Jackson, TN	53,971	-589	54,560	3,008	2,074	5.6	3.8	2,827	-38	53,398	-3,253	29,186	83.2
Jacksonville, FL	608,406	20,115	588,291	29,404	19,030	4.8	3.2	30,379	1,761	491,231	11,376	31,220	89.0
Jacksonville, NC	55,315	2,329	52,986	3,047	2,324	5.5	4.4	2,552	-50	29,166	-11	19,223	54.8
Janesville, WI	84,074	1,261	82,813	4,691	3,433	5.6	4.1	3,425	65	57,417	-3,336	33,167	94.5
Jefferson City, MO	79,696	2,974	76,722	3,393	2,078	4.3	2.7	3,546	82	52,110	-1,701	26,492	75.5
Johnson City, TN	95,180	3,865	91,315	5,098	4,168	5.4	4.6	3,762	12	61,465	-3,908	25,159	71.7
Johnstown, PA	67,642	1,022	66,620	4,731	4,055	7.0	6.1	3,546	-2	49,317	-2,097	23,891	68.1
Jonesboro, AR	55,735	1,674	54,061	3,135	2,212	5.6	4.1	2,723	58	39,486	459	24,355	69.4
Joplin, MO	84,184	2,136	82,048	4,339	2,694	5.2	3.3	4,248	167	66,671	-4,675	25,755	73.4
Kalamazoo-Portage, MI	172,239	-642	172,881	10,643	5,584	6.2	3.2	7,347	-104	128,449	566	33,084	94.3
Kankakee-Bradley, IL	51,954	-359	52,313	3,946	2,408	7.6	4.6	2,320	31	37,500	-22,239	28,196	80.4
Kansas City, MO-KS	1,034,715	35,423	999,292	62,048	33,086	6.0	3.3	50,471	447	889,834	-15,737	35,091	100.0
Kennewick-Richland-Pasco, WA	115,089	15,736	99,353	7,248	5,459	6.3	5.5	4,626	202	65,686	1,203	34,480	98.3
Killeen-Temple-Fort Hood, TX	145,987	11,990	133,997	8,353	5,965	5.7	4.5	5,314	145	85,436	-968	26,077	74.3
Kingsport-Bristol-Bristol, TN-VA	141,222	1,425	139,797	7,808	5,301	5.5	3.8	6,352	-105	105,396	-4,372	29,244	83.4
Kingston, NY	92,002	3,052	88,950	4,417	3,170	4.8	3.6	4,597	239	47,759	2,030	25,980	74.1
Knoxville, TN	337,030	19,308	317,722	13,850	10,754	4.1	3.4	15,988	-12	280,453	2,848	30,745	87.6
Kokomo, IN	47,452	-2,954	50,406	3,045	1,493	6.4	3.0	2,349	59	41,858	-6,744	37,747	107.6
La Crosse, WI-MN	74,632	2,113	72,519	3,130	2,400	4.2	3.3	3,395	70	60,842	-205	27,509	78.4
Lafayette, IN	92,621	-1,134	93,755	4,312	2,412	4.7	2.6	3,820	-33	67,737	-4,856	30,101	85.8
Lafayette, LA	121,685	3,297	118,388	5,669	4,849	4.7	4.1	7,571	254	111,033	71	28,620	81.6
Lake Charles, LA	91,669	943	90,726	5,134	4,330	5.6	4.8	4,458	42	71,833	739	27,996	79.8
Lakeland, FL	248,359	17,521	230,838	12,426	9,528	5.0	4.1	9,807	198	156,908	-4,557	28,372	80.9
Lancaster, PA	266,749	16,177	250,572	10,560	7,084	4.0	2.8	11,605	165	214,288	-292	30,538	87.0
Lansing-East Lansing, MI	251,020	2,123	248,897	14,973	7,184	6.0	2.9	10,419	134	171,044	-1,765	32,410	92.4
Laredo, TX	83,598	12,636	70,962	5,700	4,367	6.8	6.2	4,332	252	55,987	2,771	21,194	60.4
Las Cruces, NM	82,835	6,537	76,298	5,297	4,700	6.4	6.2	3,245	34	40,233	3,183	21,954	62.6
Las Vegas-Paradise, NV	827,958	99,671	728,287	36,184	33,822	4.4	4.6	32,567	2,936	665,118	25,963	31,171	88.9
Lawrence, KS	63,455	5,527	57,928	2,622	1,691	4.1	2.9	2,662	38	36,948	-537	23,125	65.9
Lawton, OK	46,478	3,207	43,271	2,083	1,589	4.5	3.7	2,144	-55	28,554	961	23,831	67.9
Lebanon, PA	69,658	5,521	64,137	2,826	2,026	4.1	3.2	2,566	-2	37,629	-1	27,573	78.6
Lewiston, ID-WA	28,692	434	28,258	1,558	1,451	5.4	5.1	1,610	-51	19,716	-964	28,181	80.3
Lewiston-Auburn, ME	57,087	1,686	55,401	2,560	1,938	4.5	3.5	2,765	-21	45,076	-790	27,916	79.6
Lexington-Fayette, KY	226,237	-2,261	228,498	9,187	7,012	4.1	3.1	11,235	132	200,602	-8,705	31,459	89.7
Lima, OH	52,437	1,067	51,370	3,453	2,247	6.6	4.4	2,834	-5	48,423	-3,416	29,094	82.9
Lincoln, NE	167,097	8,358	158,739	5,624	3,724	3.4	2.3	7,683	134	131,201	-998	28,616	81.6
Little Rock-North Little Rock, AR	324,531	13,533	310,998	16,444	11,250	5.1	3.6	16,600	80	274,540	-6,848	29,794	84.9
Logan, UT-ID	60,743	7,648	53,095	2,370	1,507	3.9	2.8	2,682	81	34,337	1,451	23,261	66.3
Longview, TX	99,846	7,110	92,736	5,978	4,813	6.0	5.2	5,173	94	72,970	2,029	26,986	76.9
Longview, WA	43,705	406	43,299	3,729	2,766	8.5	6.4	2,306	-29	30,848	-1,666	32,544	92.8
Los Angeles-Long Beach-Santa Ana, CA	**6,396,271**	**233,068**	**6,163,203**	**383,333**	**305,863**	**6.0**	**5.0**	**313,622**	**8,784**	**5,174,665**	**-67,923**	**38,732**	**110.4**
Los Angeles-Long Beach-Glendale, CA	*4,809,764*	*128,464*	*4,681,300*	*315,724*	*253,484*	*6.6*	*5.4*	*231,948*	*5,666*	*3,791,362*	*-72,509*	*38,439*	*109.6*
Santa Ana-Anaheim-Irvine, CA	*1,586,507*	*104,604*	*1,481,903*	*67,609*	*52,379*	*4.3*	*3.5*	*81,674*	*3,118*	*1,383,303*	*4,586*	*39,533*	*112.7*
Louisville, KY-IN	602,059	-9,034	611,093	30,601	21,866	5.1	3.6	29,817	374	525,004	-25,833	32,014	91.3
Lubbock, TX	140,654	9,643	131,011	6,451	4,709	4.6	3.6	6,690	64	95,979	1,538	24,295	69.3
Lynchburg, VA	113,280	205	113,075	4,861	2,512	4.3	2.2	5,845	35	91,244	-5,286	29,358	83.7
Macon, GA	106,855	2,693	104,162	5,185	4,307	4.9	4.1	5,341	-54	84,726	-6,530	28,126	80.2
Madera, CA	63,159	8,079	55,080	5,559	4,782	8.8	8.7	1,935	70	23,607	447	27,485	78.3
Madison, WI	332,612	22,830	309,782	11,008	7,658	3.3	2.5	14,854	437	254,924	4,860	33,185	94.6

See footnotes at end of table.

Table B-9. Metropolitan Areas — **Labor Force and Private Business Establishments and Employment**—Con.

Metropolitan statistical area / Metropolitan statistical area with metropolitan divisions / *Metropolitan division*	Civilian labor force							Private nonfarm businesses					
	Total			Number of unemployed		Unemployment rate[1]		Establishments		Employment[2]		Annual payroll per employee, 2002	
	2004	Change, 2000–2004	2000	2004	2000	2004	2000	2002	Change, 2000–2002	2002	Change, 2000–2002	Amount (dollars)	Percent of national average
Manchester-Nashua, NH	225,241	10,326	214,915	8,841	5,410	3.9	2.5	10,869	−35	176,136	−812	37,944	108.2
Mansfield, OH	63,344	353	62,991	4,564	3,186	7.2	5.1	3,022	4	49,073	−2,714	29,134	83.0
McAllen-Edinburg-Mission, TX	254,431	43,139	211,292	23,207	19,418	9.1	9.2	8,782	462	122,326	7,471	21,523	61.4
Medford, OR	98,817	7,004	91,813	7,002	5,098	7.1	5.6	5,625	261	63,461	1,207	27,149	77.4
Memphis, TN-MS-AR	597,092	4,370	592,722	35,499	22,606	5.9	3.8	26,253	−109	528,944	−40,419	33,498	95.5
Merced, CA	98,860	8,359	90,501	10,670	8,699	10.8	9.6	2,989	30	39,777	231	26,008	74.1
Miami-Fort Lauderdale-Miami Beach, FL	**2,621,674**	**125,014**	**2,496,660**	**135,984**	**110,319**	**5.2**	**4.4**	**160,867**	**7,520**	**1,900,015**	**−22,426**	**33,228**	**94.7**
Fort Lauderdale-Pompano Beach-Deerfield Beach, FL	*917,342*	*63,428*	*853,914*	*43,339*	*31,084*	*4.7*	*3.6*	*52,744*	*2,416*	*621,950*	*2,549*	*32,370*	*92.3*
Miami-Miami Beach-Kendall, FL	*1,107,950*	*7,671*	*1,100,279*	*62,202*	*56,427*	*5.6*	*5.1*	*69,345*	*2,836*	*820,215*	*−34,174*	*33,251*	*94.8*
West Palm Beach-Boca Raton-Boynton Beach, FL	*596,382*	*53,915*	*542,467*	*30,443*	*22,808*	*5.1*	*4.2*	*38,778*	*2,268*	*457,850*	*9,199*	*34,354*	*97.9*
Michigan City-La Porte, IN	52,965	−1,210	54,175	3,199	1,795	6.0	3.3	2,573	−62	36,693	−3,584	27,497	78.4
Midland, TX	64,312	6,096	58,216	2,907	2,446	4.5	4.2	3,982	−56	46,328	328	30,377	86.6
Milwaukee-Waukesha-West Allis, WI	801,566	−4,976	806,542	43,290	29,081	5.4	3.6	39,731	−139	759,715	−30,847	35,998	102.6
Minneapolis-St. Paul-Bloomington, MN-WI	1,849,010	86,535	1,762,475	82,331	48,831	4.5	2.8	87,843	3,311	1,591,041	−38,498	40,197	114.6
Missoula, MT	57,504	3,322	54,182	2,275	2,219	4.0	4.1	3,760	137	41,975	658	25,908	73.9
Mobile, AL	180,685	−6,657	187,342	11,756	8,273	6.5	4.4	9,153	−78	153,632	−2,809	28,025	79.9
Modesto, CA	226,124	18,076	208,048	20,606	16,196	9.1	7.8	8,668	411	131,702	11,069	29,587	84.3
Monroe, LA	83,395	3,599	79,796	4,746	3,648	5.7	4.6	4,482	42	64,863	−6,093	26,845	76.5
Monroe, MI	77,483	262	77,221	4,879	2,460	6.3	3.2	2,574	88	38,679	−876	34,800	99.2
Montgomery, AL	167,029	1,293	165,736	9,142	6,238	5.5	3.8	7,965	−76	128,173	−7,781	27,816	79.3
Morgantown, WV	57,330	2,621	54,709	2,205	2,562	3.8	4.7	2,567	−53	36,985	1,401	27,011	77.0
Morristown, TN	62,464	519	61,945	3,652	2,633	5.8	4.3	2,282	−17	42,119	−3,814	27,717	79.0
Mount Vernon-Anacortes, WA	56,305	4,213	52,092	3,855	3,044	6.8	5.8	3,350	93	34,944	−713	29,036	82.8
Muncie, IN	57,036	−1,891	58,927	3,397	1,954	6.0	3.3	2,653	−45	45,502	−4,961	26,628	75.9
Muskegon-Norton Shores, MI	89,530	3,807	85,723	7,062	3,511	7.9	4.1	3,663	76	54,471	−2,993	30,766	87.7
Myrtle Beach-Conway-North Myrtle Beach, SC	118,119	12,880	105,239	6,694	3,665	5.7	3.5	7,409	222	87,396	1,106	22,828	65.1
Napa, CA	72,272	5,612	66,660	3,311	2,356	4.6	3.5	3,963	216	52,547	3,021	35,647	101.6
Naples-Marco Island, FL	136,834	20,876	115,958	5,511	4,312	4.0	3.7	9,201	726	97,794	5,570	30,380	86.6
Nashville-Davidson-Murfreesboro, TN	732,403	17,091	715,312	31,375	22,843	4.3	3.2	34,926	343	637,295	−12,451	34,015	97.0
New Haven-Milford, CT	429,670	15,370	414,300	22,384	10,694	5.2	2.6	20,705	−70	333,360	−5,568	37,425	106.7
New Orleans-Metairie-Kenner, LA	613,148	−12,170	625,318	27,983	29,204	4.6	4.7	31,599	71	525,160	−6,385	30,339	86.5
New York-Northern New Jersey-Long Island, NY-NJ-PA	**9,092,696**	**165,555**	**8,927,141**	**514,588**	**397,153**	**5.7**	**4.4**	**521,372**	**6,313**	**7,470,229**	**−97,818**	**50,172**	**143.0**
Edison, NJ	*1,158,703*	*42,143*	*1,116,560*	*51,198*	*36,370*	*4.4*	*3.3*	*61,549*	*1,512*	*893,901*	*916*	*42,415*	*120.9*
Nassau-Suffolk, NY	*1,460,015*	*42,324*	*1,417,691*	*67,062*	*47,918*	*4.6*	*3.4*	*92,319*	*1,653*	*1,073,035*	*−12,115*	*38,415*	*109.5*
Newark-Union, NJ-PA	*1,075,964*	*15,468*	*1,060,496*	*51,503*	*38,398*	*4.8*	*3.6*	*60,580*	*339*	*945,448*	*4,321*	*47,148*	*134.4*
New York-White Plains-Wayne, NY-NJ	*5,398,014*	*65,620*	*5,332,394*	*344,825*	*274,467*	*6.4*	*5.1*	*306,924*	*2,809*	*4,557,845*	*−90,940*	*55,089*	*157.0*
Niles-Benton Harbor, MI	78,577	−6,018	84,595	6,130	3,105	7.8	3.7	4,065	74	61,007	508	31,626	90.1
Norwich-New London, CT	143,277	11,520	131,757	6,360	3,070	4.4	2.3	5,891	162	110,111	4,341	36,453	103.9
Ocala, FL	116,911	7,839	109,072	5,357	4,408	4.6	4.0	5,794	311	74,105	970	24,745	70.5
Ocean City, NJ	57,942	2,445	55,497	4,003	3,532	6.9	6.4	4,158	138	25,665	−280	30,234	86.2
Odessa, TX	61,646	5,066	56,580	3,702	3,059	6.0	5.4	3,140	129	41,306	2,681	27,849	79.4
Ogden-Clearfield, UT	237,670	15,113	222,557	12,592	8,119	5.3	3.6	9,722	689	126,871	−6,499	26,512	75.6
Oklahoma City, OK	576,297	24,293	552,004	25,560	15,120	4.4	2.7	30,202	467	437,342	155	28,080	80.0
Olympia, WA	121,240	12,632	108,608	6,930	4,994	5.7	4.6	5,250	200	55,393	2,424	28,824	82.2
Omaha-Council Bluffs, NE-IA	442,019	14,626	427,393	19,056	11,840	4.3	2.8	20,848	424	382,328	835	32,629	93.0
Orlando-Kissimee, FL	960,639	67,015	893,624	43,685	27,973	4.5	3.1	47,229	2,300	793,083	−21,508	30,735	87.6
Oshkosh-Neenah, WI	92,788	2,913	89,875	4,203	2,448	4.5	2.7	3,685	−33	78,151	−3,645	35,111	100.1
Owensboro, KY	54,729	−1,053	55,782	2,826	2,494	5.2	4.5	2,696	−21	43,823	−1,961	26,920	76.7
Oxnard-Thousand Oaks-Ventura, CA	416,060	23,103	392,957	22,259	17,803	5.3	4.5	17,949	743	251,825	13,823	36,690	104.6
Palm Bay-Melbourne-Titusville, FL	249,982	18,309	231,673	11,092	8,414	4.4	3.6	11,878	518	167,108	9,410	31,764	90.5
Panama City-Lynn Haven, FL	78,426	6,558	71,868	3,599	3,335	4.6	4.6	4,252	44	55,142	1,210	24,092	68.7
Parkersburg-Marietta-Vienna, WV-OH	80,350	1,068	79,282	4,716	3,994	5.9	5.0	4,045	−60	61,672	−896	26,857	76.6
Pascagoula, MS	69,778	−2,485	72,263	4,326	4,464	6.2	6.2	2,615	−66	44,471	−1,115	28,795	82.1
Pensacola-Ferry Pass-Brent, FL	196,364	9,226	187,138	9,266	7,437	4.7	4.0	8,818	289	126,005	1,607	25,357	72.3
Peoria, IL	183,606	−3,244	186,850	10,529	7,953	5.7	4.3	8,835	4	156,960	−6,536	32,226	91.9
Philadelphia-Camden-Wilmington, PA-NJ-DE-MD	**2,916,970**	**70,451**	**2,846,519**	**151,909**	**110,568**	**5.2**	**3.9**	**144,549**	**2,011**	**2,497,789**	**−18,266**	**39,379**	**112.3**
Camden, NJ	*644,950*	*34,507*	*610,443*	*31,003*	*21,609*	*4.8*	*3.5*	*28,882*	*339*	*429,769*	*−5,780*	*34,525*	*98.4*
Philadelphia, PA	*1,925,827*	*39,871*	*1,885,956*	*105,562*	*77,356*	*5.5*	*4.1*	*96,179*	*1,316*	*1,738,700*	*−19,825*	*40,295*	*114.9*
Wilmington, DE-MD-NJ	*346,193*	*−3,927*	*350,120*	*15,344*	*11,603*	*4.4*	*3.3*	*19,488*	*356*	*329,320*	*7,339*	*40,876*	*116.5*
Phoenix-Mesa-Scottsdale, AZ	1,851,316	185,661	1,665,655	82,196	55,961	4.4	3.4	77,539	3,484	1,390,433	11,053	33,323	95.0
Pine Bluff, AR	46,132	1,388	44,744	3,612	2,550	7.8	5.7	1,891	17	28,224	−2,803	25,231	71.9
Pittsburgh, PA	1,217,830	26,554	1,191,276	70,287	51,615	5.8	4.3	60,828	46	1,055,581	−1,972	32,917	93.8
Pittsfield, MA	72,596	2,534	70,062	3,322	1,990	4.6	2.8	4,310	−73	55,974	−2,961	30,281	86.3
Pocatello, ID	43,485	1,565	41,920	2,084	1,981	4.8	4.7	2,067	24	25,329	−745	24,718	70.5
Portland-South Portland-Biddeford, ME	286,977	16,533	270,444	10,289	7,116	3.6	2.6	16,826	598	212,531	−3,019	32,777	93.4
Portland-Vancouver-Beaverton, OR-WA	1,094,183	16,729	1,077,454	78,376	48,302	7.2	4.5	57,429	699	844,882	−22,376	36,473	104.0
Port St. Lucie-Fort Pierce, FL	165,346	21,639	143,707	9,361	7,398	5.7	5.1	8,613	538	91,520	1,279	27,243	77.7
Poughkeepsie-Newburgh-Middletown, NY	321,040	18,351	302,689	14,205	10,031	4.4	3.3	15,543	706	196,208	11,199	32,502	92.6
Prescott, AZ	86,965	11,384	75,581	3,704	2,959	4.3	3.9	5,382	397	49,244	3,181	23,669	67.5
Providence-New Bedford-Fall River, RI-MA	849,649	28,480	821,169	46,500	32,187	5.5	3.9	58,680	16,927	599,074	−3,813	32,027	91.3
Provo-Orem, UT	195,722	12,168	183,554	9,483	5,446	4.8	3.0	8,225	950	134,191	−9,914	26,324	75.0
Pueblo, CO	68,767	4,917	63,850	4,976	2,329	7.2	3.6	3,233	46	44,835	−3,518	25,934	73.9

See footnotes at end of table.

Metropolitan statistical area / **Metropolitan statistical area with metropolitan divisions** / *Metropolitan division*	Civilian labor force							Private nonfarm businesses					
	Total			Number of unemployed		Unemployment rate[1]		Establishments		Employment[2]		Annual payroll per employee, 2002	
	2004	Change, 2000–2004	2000	2004	2000	2004	2000	2002	Change, 2000–2002	2002	Change, 2000–2002	Amount (dollars)	Percent of national average
Punta Gorda, FL	60,501	5,356	55,145	3,022	2,042	5.0	3.7	3,393	320	31,486	−199	24,818	70.7
Racine, WI	100,667	921	99,746	6,049	3,892	6.0	3.9	4,258	110	71,400	−2,027	33,256	94.8
Raleigh-Cary, NC	484,107	31,195	452,912	21,059	11,529	4.4	2.5	24,698	921	378,506	7,976	33,646	95.9
Rapid City, SD	65,340	4,155	61,185	2,183	1,546	3.3	2.5	3,886	154	47,027	204	25,953	74.0
Reading, PA	197,732	3,117	194,615	10,523	7,659	5.3	3.9	8,405	250	145,505	−3,358	31,689	90.3
Redding, CA	83,543	8,721	74,822	6,172	4,493	7.4	6.0	4,552	84	48,851	2,735	28,131	80.2
Reno-Sparks, NV	208,568	11,642	196,926	8,386	7,337	4.0	3.7	11,484	269	172,303	2,496	32,174	91.7
Richmond, VA	600,345	36,023	564,322	23,183	11,635	3.9	2.1	29,360	709	502,829	5,809	34,003	96.9
Riverside-San Bernardino-Ontario, CA	1,647,915	227,378	1,420,537	93,946	71,834	5.7	5.1	57,650	4,006	914,837	56,404	29,093	82.9
Roanoke, VA	147,311	−315	147,626	5,458	3,239	3.7	2.2	8,287	127	135,599	−3,700	28,547	81.4
Rochester, MN	103,853	8,187	95,666	4,227	2,667	4.1	2.8	4,318	269	90,080	3,427	35,137	100.2
Rochester, NY	530,253	−4,793	535,046	28,236	19,479	5.3	3.6	23,307	316	432,379	−10,910	33,722	96.1
Rockford, IL	162,832	−5,400	168,232	12,605	7,803	7.7	4.6	7,755	7	137,321	−10,055	32,543	92.8
Rocky Mount, NC	68,698	392	68,306	5,023	3,474	7.3	5.1	3,234	−26	56,508	−1,448	26,944	76.8
Rome, GA	48,664	3,884	44,780	2,227	1,679	4.6	3.7	2,057	41	36,121	−1,823	26,061	74.3
Sacramento-Arden-Arcade-Roseville, CA	1,003,214	98,069	905,145	53,792	38,898	5.4	4.3	42,752	2,353	653,250	39,831	34,575	98.6
Saginaw-Saginaw Township North, MI	101,030	−343	101,373	8,784	4,093	8.7	4.0	5,006	−17	85,294	−7,319	32,837	93.6
St. Cloud, MN	104,379	5,028	99,351	4,876	3,227	4.7	3.2	5,016	324	86,052	2,728	27,642	78.8
St. George, UT	50,392	11,318	39,074	2,225	1,379	4.4	3.5	2,794	283	29,996	3,357	23,696	67.5
St. Joseph, MO-KS	65,711	5,145	60,566	3,902	2,046	5.9	3.4	3,022	72	42,919	16	25,972	74.0
St. Louis, MO-IL[4]	1,453,133	25,391	1,427,742	86,535	50,029	6.0	3.5	69,287	1,015	1,214,875	−9,242	34,607	98.6
Salem, OR	184,729	7,203	177,526	13,691	9,623	7.4	5.4	8,686	93	103,340	−4,068	27,674	78.9
Salinas, CA	212,218	8,353	203,865	17,450	15,023	8.2	7.4	8,898	323	109,812	4,744	32,123	91.6
Salisbury, MD	60,849	4,054	56,795	2,837	2,568	4.7	4.5	2,937	−2	41,015	539	27,020	77.0
Salt Lake City, UT	534,889	13,744	521,145	28,830	16,735	5.4	3.2	28,833	942	492,324	−10,474	31,910	91.0
San Angelo, TX	53,200	1,577	51,623	2,595	2,000	4.9	3.9	2,619	−15	35,691	665	26,103	74.4
San Antonio, TX	883,166	64,002	819,164	49,835	32,586	5.6	4.0	36,897	1,132	640,934	3,136	29,188	83.2
San Diego-Carlsbad-San Marcos, CA	1,490,333	113,684	1,376,649	70,292	53,973	4.7	3.9	71,330	3,408	1,083,047	30,833	37,412	106.6
Sandusky, OH	43,516	1,548	41,968	2,763	1,771	6.3	4.2	2,045	4	29,458	−3,606	28,872	82.3
San Francisco-Oakland-Fremont, CA	**2,178,653**	**−104,663**	**2,283,316**	**121,318**	**77,184**	**5.6**	**3.4**	**118,782**	**−1,744**	**1,912,175**	**−94,152**	**49,720**	**141.7**
Oakland-Fremont-Hayward, CA	*1,259,397*	*−10,990*	*1,270,387*	*72,481*	*45,640*	*5.8*	*3.6*	*59,211*	*755*	*972,754*	*1,257*	*44,380*	*126.5*
San Francisco-San Mateo-Redwood City, CA	*919,256*	*−93,673*	*1,012,929*	*48,837*	*31,544*	*5.3*	*3.1*	*59,571*	*−2,499*	*939,421*	*−95,409*	*55,249*	*157.5*
San Jose-Sunnyvale-Santa Clara, CA	854,249	−113,545	967,794	57,002	31,136	6.7	3.2	45,333	−1,287	906,018	−104,282	62,395	177.9
San Luis Obispo-Paso Robles, CA	130,739	8,236	122,503	5,718	4,888	4.4	4.0	7,492	548	81,056	7,431	28,004	79.8
Santa Barbara-Santa Maria, CA	214,137	11,566	202,571	9,990	8,796	4.7	4.3	11,062	178	139,876	−320	34,230	97.6
Santa Cruz-Watsonville, CA	145,419	−3,119	148,538	10,231	7,613	7.0	5.1	7,028	56	78,674	−586	34,118	97.3
Santa Fe, NM	75,811	5,169	70,642	3,273	2,571	4.3	3.6	4,866	197	46,006	1,311	27,814	79.3
Santa Rosa-Petaluma, CA	256,820	3,469	253,351	12,680	8,459	4.9	3.3	13,666	247	166,357	3,357	35,607	101.5
Sarasota-Bradenton-Venice, FL	298,354	26,347	272,007	12,087	8,665	4.1	3.2	17,999	1,127	207,513	−34,987	28,499	81.2
Savannah, GA	155,061	12,549	142,512	6,274	4,916	4.0	3.4	7,648	129	121,773	6,159	28,909	82.4
Scranton-Wilkes-Barre, PA	278,004	5,144	272,860	17,978	13,261	6.5	4.9	13,600	−114	223,592	−5,313	26,712	76.1
Seattle-Tacoma-Bellevue, WA	**1,698,510**	**54,877**	**1,643,633**	**95,815**	**71,090**	**5.6**	**4.3**	**90,730**	**54**	**1,373,253**	**−72,565**	**43,193**	**123.1**
Seattle-Bellevue-Everett, WA	*1,331,242*	*28,653*	*1,302,589*	*69,788*	*53,960*	*5.2*	*4.1*	*74,797*	*−329*	*1,173,703*	*−63,896*	*45,134*	*128.7*
Tacoma, WA	*367,268*	*26,224*	*341,044*	*26,027*	*17,130*	*7.1*	*5.0*	*15,933*	*383*	*199,550*	*−8,669*	*31,774*	*90.6*
Sheboygan, WI	64,662	139	64,523	2,863	1,592	4.4	2.5	2,699	95	56,288	−940	30,492	86.9
Sherman-Denison, TX	57,169	868	56,301	3,518	2,238	6.2	4.0	2,577	−3	36,693	−2,826	28,209	80.4
Shreveport-Bossier City, LA	175,564	3,310	172,254	10,622	8,292	6.1	4.8	8,627	55	144,732	1,528	26,570	75.7
Sioux City, IA-NE-SD	74,597	−2,850	77,447	3,855	2,130	5.2	2.8	3,893	−7	68,493	−3,608	26,670	76.0
Sioux Falls, SD	119,418	8,033	111,385	3,792	2,357	3.2	2.1	6,466	272	108,128	1,273	28,944	82.5
South Bend-Mishawaka, IN-MI	160,589	−1,515	162,104	7,973	4,996	5.0	3.1	7,279	−98	127,395	−6,809	29,993	85.5
Spartanburg, SC	131,026	1,735	129,291	10,023	4,447	7.6	3.4	6,425	142	117,817	−4,135	31,607	90.1
Spokane, WA	224,981	13,084	211,897	14,693	11,051	6.5	5.2	11,787	98	164,194	−4,079	30,294	86.4
Springfield, IL	109,117	−3,068	112,185	6,015	4,134	5.5	3.7	5,558	−52	82,985	−2,457	29,481	84.0
Springfield, MA	352,473	7,355	345,118	18,657	9,902	5.3	2.9	15,890	−1,097	247,409	−4,561	30,681	87.5
Springfield, MO	211,403	12,204	199,199	9,598	5,587	4.5	2.8	10,637	291	160,713	−3,382	25,318	72.2
Springfield, OH	70,600	−1,459	72,059	4,776	3,107	6.8	4.3	2,699	−11	47,153	−3,918	26,565	75.7
State College, PA	72,253	3,785	68,468	3,165	2,418	4.4	3.5	3,156	29	43,165	−3,589	25,894	73.8
Stockton, CA	285,200	26,032	259,168	24,244	18,014	8.5	7.0	10,831	644	161,040	6,635	30,952	88.2
Sumter, SC	45,664	1,041	44,623	3,693	1,834	8.1	4.1	1,949	85	33,356	−3,664	25,686	73.2
Syracuse, NY	328,548	2,913	325,635	17,913	12,337	5.5	3.8	15,350	348	267,078	−6,342	32,316	92.1
Tallahassee, FL	173,345	1,108	172,237	6,870	5,500	4.0	3.2	7,927	331	107,501	3,880	27,395	78.1
Tampa-St. Petersburg-Clearwater, FL	1,268,218	68,868	1,199,350	57,816	40,370	4.6	3.4	63,864	2,378	1,009,648	−23,097	32,704	93.2
Terre Haute, IN	81,425	109	81,316	5,748	3,324	7.1	4.1	3,811	−35	58,065	−4,618	27,121	77.3
Texarkana, TX-Texarkana, AR	61,286	2,686	58,600	3,543	2,794	5.8	4.8	2,849	−21	40,772	−2,695	25,284	72.1
Toledo, OH	336,451	162	336,289	23,598	14,573	7.0	4.3	16,079	75	291,866	−9,610	32,000	91.2
Topeka, KS	125,105	5,272	119,833	7,585	4,850	6.1	4.0	5,719	−18	87,049	−7,222	28,364	80.9
Trenton-Ewing, NJ	190,469	10,326	180,143	7,993	5,881	4.2	3.3	10,344	695	186,454	12,337	43,228	123.2
Tucson, AZ	439,127	29,961	409,166	20,219	15,310	4.6	3.7	19,147	515	293,113	−269	29,586	84.3
Tulsa, OK	443,241	3,424	439,817	22,014	12,970	5.0	2.9	23,446	306	370,917	−6,420	31,950	91.1
Tuscaloosa, AL	94,918	1,517	93,401	4,661	3,507	4.9	3.8	4,298	−21	71,198	−2,935	27,634	78.8
Tyler, TX	94,195	7,856	86,339	5,009	3,767	5.3	4.4	5,040	179	76,492	2,594	29,849	85.1

See footnotes at end of table.

State and Metropolitan Area Data Book: 2006

U.S. Census Bureau

Metropolitan statistical area **Metropolitan statistical area with metropolitan divisions** *Metropolitan division*	Civilian labor force							Private nonfarm businesses					
	Total			Number of unemployed		Unemployment rate[1]		Establishments		Employment[2]		Annual payroll per employee, 2002	
	2004	Change, 2000–2004	2000	2004	2000	2004	2000	2002	Change, 2000–2002	2002	Change, 2000–2002	Amount (dollars)	Percent of national average
Utica-Rome, NY	142,009	−671	142,680	7,512	5,626	5.3	3.9	6,218	69	100,070	−1,605	26,574	75.8
Valdosta, GA	61,609	5,261	56,348	2,139	2,521	3.5	4.5	2,844	98	41,362	1,830	23,056	65.7
Vallejo-Fairfield, CA	208,356	9,547	198,809	12,258	9,033	5.9	4.5	6,820	315	105,894	11,375	32,808	93.5
Vero Beach, FL	56,240	5,208	51,032	3,696	2,617	6.6	5.1	3,580	128	38,619	16	26,624	75.9
Victoria, TX	56,108	337	55,771	3,261	2,161	5.8	3.9	2,742	12	36,748	−1,514	29,446	83.9
Vineland-Millville-Bridgeton, NJ	68,698	3,162	65,536	4,552	3,800	6.6	5.8	3,113	87	47,471	1,647	31,262	89.1
Virginia Beach-Norfolk-Newport News, VA-NC	777,793	58,254	719,539	32,260	18,164	4.1	2.5	35,284	810	583,509	2,901	28,234	80.5
Visalia-Porterville, CA	182,888	10,579	172,309	20,984	17,904	11.5	10.4	6,009	83	80,663	3,501	26,668	76.0
Waco, TX	110,305	6,530	103,775	5,861	4,279	5.3	4.1	4,821	−19	88,422	−2,241	25,935	73.9
Warner Robins, GA	59,586	5,838	53,748	2,265	1,825	3.8	3.4	2,093	127	31,223	4,504	22,801	65.0
Washington-Arlington-Alexandria, DC-VA-MD-WV	**2,801,375**	**140,347**	**2,661,028**	**103,874**	**72,759**	**3.7**	**2.7**	**129,718**	**4,445**	**2,216,101**	**22,314**	**44,152**	**125.9**
Bethesda-Gaithersburg-Frederick, MD	*613,211*	*16,457*	*596,754*	*19,394*	*15,728*	*3.2*	*2.6*	*31,258*	*689*	*470,137*	*−6,357*	*42,464*	*121.0*
Washington-Arlington-Alexandria, DC-VA-MD-WV	*2,188,164*	*123,890*	*2,064,274*	*84,480*	*57,031*	*3.9*	*2.8*	*98,460*	*3,756*	*1,745,964*	*28,671*	*44,607*	*127.2*
Waterloo-Cedar Falls, IA	90,972	2,431	88,541	4,327	2,487	4.8	2.8	4,075	−43	69,582	−1,643	27,476	78.3
Wausau, WI	74,730	2,474	72,256	3,218	2,349	4.3	3.3	3,321	−116	63,252	−385	29,109	83.0
Weirton-Steubenville, WV-OH	58,099	−992	59,091	4,521	3,042	7.8	5.1	2,654	−30	41,634	−2,390	27,867	79.4
Wenatchee, WA	59,577	4,856	54,721	4,006	3,495	6.7	6.4	2,870	45	28,185	−229	28,055	80.0
Wheeling, WV-OH	67,662	−1,585	69,247	4,087	3,766	6.0	5.4	3,699	−67	53,917	718	24,468	69.7
Wichita, KS	304,798	7,049	297,749	18,780	12,430	6.2	4.2	14,715	183	254,068	−5,499	31,602	90.1
Wichita Falls, TX	74,452	2,712	71,740	3,844	3,182	5.2	4.4	3,584	−27	48,200	−471	24,739	70.5
Williamsport, PA	60,753	1,502	59,251	3,782	2,567	6.2	4.3	2,849	−30	46,941	−2,506	25,711	73.3
Wilmington, NC	154,626	12,608	142,018	7,153	5,634	4.6	4.0	8,847	457	99,823	−865	27,009	77.0
Winchester, VA-WV	59,987	5,257	54,730	1,903	1,249	3.2	2.3	2,857	94	48,613	3,416	28,788	82.1
Winston-Salem, NC	230,040	7,720	222,320	11,564	7,514	5.0	3.4	10,537	77	192,949	−4,633	32,836	93.6
Worcester, MA	400,729	12,785	387,944	21,936	10,463	5.5	2.7	18,294	380	291,262	−2,116	35,155	100.2
Yakima, WA	119,787	6,389	113,398	10,339	8,713	8.6	7.7	4,693	−66	59,160	−1,104	27,766	79.1
York-Hanover, PA	216,502	7,571	208,931	9,960	6,980	4.6	3.3	8,402	204	157,700	4,609	30,415	86.7
Youngstown-Warren-Boardman, OH-PA	280,415	−2,960	283,375	20,303	14,186	7.2	5.0	14,056	−67	210,102	−24,014	27,985	79.8
Yuba City, CA	65,824	3,554	62,270	6,719	5,492	10.2	8.8	2,538	50	28,026	1,790	27,829	79.3
Yuma, AZ	73,938	9,568	64,370	11,415	10,662	15.4	16.6	2,560	23	36,268	5,035	21,320	60.8

[1]Civilian unemployed as percent of total civilian labor force.

[2]For pay period including March 12 of the year shown.

[3]The Denver-Aurora metropolitan statistical area includes Broomfield County. Broomfield County, CO, was formed from parts of Adams, Boulder, Jefferson, and Weld counties on November 15, 2001, and is coextensive with Broomfield city. For the purposes of defining and presenting data for the Denver-Aurora metropolitan statistical area, Broomfield city is treated as if it were a county when data are available to do so. In many cases, the data will not be available.

[4]The portion of Sullivan city in Crawford County, MO, is legally part of the St. Louis, MO-IL MSA. That portion is not included in these figures for the St. Louis MSA.

Note: Covers metropolitan statistical areas and metropolitan divisions and component counties defined by the Office of Management and Budget as of June 6, 2003, and subsequently updated in December 2003 and November 2004. For more information, see OMB Bulletin 05-02 at <http://www.whitehouse.gov/omb/bulletins/fy05/b05-02_appendix.pdf>.

Survey, Census, or Data Collection Method: Civilian labor force—Based on the Current Population Survey (CPS); for information, see Appendix B, Limitations of the Data and Methodology, and the following document at <http://www.census.gov/prod/2002pubs/tp63rv.pdf>. For data extracted from the U.S. Census Bureau's County Business Patterns, see Internet site <http://www.census.gov/epcd/cbp/view/cbpview.html>.

Sources: Civilian labor force—U.S. Bureau of Labor Statistics, *Local Area Unemployment Statistics, Annual Averages*; see Internet site <http://www.bls.gov/lau> (accessed 18 August 2005). Private nonfarm businesses—U.S. Bureau, *County Business Patterns* on CD-ROM; issued April 2003 and December 2004.

Metropolitan statistical area / Metropolitan statistical area with metropolitan divisions / *Metropolitan division*	Banking,[1] 2004		Retail trade[2] (NAICS 44–45), 2002						Accommodation and food services[2] (NAICS 72), 2002					
			Estab-lish-ments	Sales					Estab-lish-ments	Sales				
				Total (mil. dol.)	Per cap-ita[3] (dol.)	Percent				Total (mil. dol.)	Per cap-ita[3] (dol.)	Percent		
	Num-ber of offices	Depos-its (mil. dol.)				Change, 1997–2002	Gen-eral mer-chan-dise stores[4]	Paid employ-ees[5]				Change, 1997–2002	Food ser-vices[6]	Paid employ-ees[5]
Abilene, TX.	52	1,669	690	1,796	11,361	17.7	(NA)	8,461	297	195	1,232	23.1	(NA)	5,769
Akron, OH	230	9,395	2,491	7,473	10,683	12.7	12.1	38,273	1,424	890	1,272	20.8	87.6	25,923
Albany, GA	49	1,661	700	1,458	9,104	6.4	(NA)	8,153	254	(NA)	(NA)	(NA)	(NA)	4,056
Albany-Schenectady-Troy, NY	304	16,116	3,177	9,363	11,225	28.3	(NA)	47,963	1,825	1,093	1,311	27.2	80.2	26,205
Albuquerque, NM	169	7,742	2,579	8,842	11,732	23.1	(NA)	38,605	1,425	1,217	1,615	26.4	(NA)	30,318
Alexandria, LA	55	1,547	616	1,513	10,398	22.2	(NA)	7,542	197	(NA)	(NA)	(NA)	(NA)	3,781
Allentown-Bethlehem-Easton, PA-NJ	290	11,502	2,835	8,098	10,680	24.2	(NA)	40,230	1,478	838	1,105	14.8	85.9	20,742
Altoona, PA	62	1,748	611	1,695	13,277	27.3	20.5	8,544	270	155	1,213	42.3	87.7	4,711
Amarillo, TX	62	2,883	975	2,844	12,324	18.6	(NA)	12,691	483	337	1,462	(NA)	(NA)	8,756
Ames, IA	39	1,183	339	800	9,909	26.7	18.7	4,643	210	111	1,374	24.5	80.1	3,812
Anchorage, AK	47	3,038	1,137	4,397	13,210	22.4	27.6	18,018	822	815	2,448	31.9	72.9	14,557
Anderson, IN	56	1,294	464	1,277	9,678	13.7	16.4	6,264	240	142	1,076	1.5	94.7	4,195
Anderson, SC	60	1,932	734	1,658	9,736	22.9	17.0	8,818	312	175	1,029	21.2	92.9	5,018
Ann Arbor, MI	98	4,445	1,160	4,072	12,247	20.7	14.7	18,790	614	512	1,540	19.0	83.5	13,876
Anniston-Oxford, AL	31	1,340	570	1,160	10,413	18.2	20.9	6,223	188	131	1,177	14.7	87.3	3,877
Appleton, WI	79	2,874	859	2,860	13,712	31.9	(NA)	14,557	456	271	1,300	25.0	83.2	8,282
Asheville, NC	122	4,929	1,946	4,570	12,092	23.1	(NA)	22,018	913	701	1,854	39.1	64.7	16,027
Athens-Clarke County, GA	59	2,188	713	1,763	10,414	26.9	(NA)	10,024	326	233	1,373	(NA)	(NA)	6,381
Atlanta-Sandy Springs-Marietta, GA	1,311	80,583	16,348	52,509	11,658	27.8	(NA)	250,438	8,568	8,005	1,777	(NA)	(NA)	170,471
Atlantic City, NJ	81	3,656	1,182	3,311	12,768	31.7	14.1	15,016	749	4,866	18,767	-3.0	8.0	56,112
Auburn-Opelika, AL	34	1,332	416	1,013	8,617	30.8	(NA)	5,589	205	139	1,186	26.5	84.6	4,491
Augusta-Richmond County, GA-SC	134	5,100	1,923	4,900	9,666	23.5	(NA)	25,066	778	548	1,081	22.0	(NA)	15,459
Austin-Round Rock, TX.	329	13,842	4,657	21,024	15,612	11.4	(NA)	69,746	2,579	2,474	1,837	54.1	78.8	56,551
Bakersfield, CA	95	4,272	1,909	5,601	8,082	32.6	15.0	25,134	1,048	643	927	30.3	87.4	15,434
Baltimore-Towson, MD	793	40,460	9,306	28,317	10,906	30.6	10.9	134,961	4,582	3,905	1,504	33.6	79.9	87,863
Bangor, ME	54	1,613	798	2,088	14,212	26.2	13.9	10,386	302	186	1,266	22.9	78.5	5,229
Barnstable Town, MA	122	5,652	1,663	3,394	14,911	34.7	4.7	15,625	1,141	757	3,327	21.3	68.4	11,966
Baton Rouge, LA	228	8,946	2,726	6,831	9,552	14.7	(NA)	37,894	1,103	786	1,100	(NA)	(NA)	22,269
Battle Creek, MI	42	973	534	1,398	10,080	12.9	25.5	7,910	291	161	1,161	9.2	93.0	4,721
Bay City, MI	36	1,225	509	1,281	11,670	16.2	21.3	6,384	241	127	1,158	19.3	92.8	3,844
Beaumont-Port Arthur, TX	81	3,721	1,507	4,160	10,873	20.0	(NA)	19,811	565	401	1,047	18.9	89.5	11,079
Bellingham, WA	68	2,342	819	1,777	10,205	6.2	16.8	9,332	451	246	1,412	25.5	81.1	6,251
Bend, OR	52	1,692	763	1,863	14,836	43.7	22.3	8,557	373	267	2,125	37.2	62.6	6,145
Billings, MT	48	1,919	796	1,995	14,079	24.0	(NA)	9,842	432	289	2,040	31.7	78.5	7,840
Binghamton, NY	72	2,682	949	2,457	9,763	24.0	15.9	13,850	564	292	1,161	27.9	85.2	8,422
Birmingham-Hoover, AL	326	20,141	4,445	12,375	11,611	23.7	(NA)	57,915	1,719	1,281	1,201	(NA)	(NA)	32,765
Bismarck, ND	41	1,547	467	1,270	13,205	25.7	16.1	6,698	192	141	1,470	25.7	75.3	4,377
Blacksburg-Christiansburg-Radford, VA	62	1,797	627	1,388	9,190	18.5	(NA)	7,883	298	180	1,190	30.3	(NA)	5,491
Bloomington, IN	66	1,829	657	1,619	9,221	22.3	(NA)	9,261	365	245	1,397	(NA)	(NA)	7,572
Bloomington-Normal, IL	60	7,994	585	1,742	11,220	18.2	17.0	8,999	324	243	1,563	21.0	80.2	8,247
Boise City-Nampa, ID	165	5,637	1,871	5,217	10,455	22.3	(NA)	26,296	1,011	608	1,219	34.4	84.3	17,154
Boston-Cambridge-Quincy, MA-NH	**1,422**	**141,814**	**17,263**	**53,092**	**11,977**	**23.7**	**7.5**	**255,184**	**10,130**	**8,694**	**1,961**	**27.6**	**78.5**	**172,305**
Boston-Quincy, MA	*589*	*86,247*	*7,023*	*21,084*	*11,562*	*23.5*	*8.2*	*101,068*	*4,411*	*4,406*	*2,416*	*28.9*	*75.5*	*83,973*
Cambridge-Newton-Framingham, MA	*478*	*35,720*	*5,393*	*16,876*	*11,491*	*16.7*	*9.3*	*82,873*	*3,126*	*2,562*	*1,744*	*24.5*	*78.2*	*50,752*
Essex County, MA	*248*	*13,910*	*2,722*	*8,169*	*11,091*	*32.7*	*8.4*	*39,321*	*1,624*	*1,109*	*1,506*	*27.1*	*87.5*	*23,436*
Rockingham County-Strafford County, NH.	*107*	*5,937*	*2,125*	*6,963*	*17,237*	*32.9*	*(NA)*	*31,922*	*969*	*618*	*1,529*	*31.8*	*85.2*	*14,144*
Boulder, CO[7]	99	4,894	1,279	3,464	12,448	(NA)	13.7	18,243	720	539	1,938	(NA)	82.0	13,773
Bowling Green, KY	43	1,332	568	1,269	11,972	12.6	(NA)	7,604	208	(NA)	(NA)	(NA)	(NA)	5,651
Bremerton-Silverdale, WA	67	1,928	809	2,267	9,507	31.6	22.2	10,783	434	235	986	30.4	89.0	6,234
Bridgeport-Stamford-Norwalk, CT	328	23,106	3,876	13,931	15,569	20.5	7.4	54,834	1,874	1,369	1,529	22.9	82.7	24,678
Brownsville-Harlingen, TX	64	3,396	1,120	2,757	7,808	44.8	20.6	15,005	570	371	1,052	33.5	77.8	10,012
Brunswick, GA	40	1,288	613	1,124	11,755	32.6	(NA)	5,879	262	354	3,707	35.0	46.0	7,449
Buffalo-Niagara Falls, NY	307	24,048	4,255	11,658	10,050	20.9	12.3	64,046	2,588	1,425	1,229	24.7	85.6	41,692
Burlington, NC	47	2,030	607	1,630	12,018	30.9	12.0	7,884	258	195	1,436	34.3	91.2	4,770
Burlington-South Burlington, VT	72	3,129	1,167	2,869	14,172	31.1	(NA)	14,759	532	335	1,656	(NA)	71.7	8,596
Canton-Massillon, OH.	125	4,791	1,591	4,271	10,446	12.4	15.7	23,641	821	464	1,135	16.0	94.6	14,151
Cape Coral-Fort Myers, FL	178	8,396	2,181	6,366	13,386	45.8	14.1	29,122	929	840	1,766	20.1	65.4	18,322
Carson City, NV.	21	990	273	861	15,786	26.9	(NA)	3,387	124	110	2,019	18.3	61.4	2,328
Casper, WY	18	934	370	876	12,979	35.7	21.8	4,503	177	98	1,449	23.9	80.0	2,854
Cedar Rapids, IA	108	3,750	993	2,928	12,115	26.8	16.3	15,223	490	287	1,187	12.9	84.3	8,662
Champaign-Urbana, IL	96	3,825	803	2,151	10,109	21.1	(NA)	12,120	498	303	1,424	(NA)	(NA)	9,250
Charleston, WV	103	4,229	1,271	3,355	10,936	10.7	(NA)	17,373	541	389	1,268	(NA)	82.1	9,753
Charleston-North Charleston, SC	155	6,142	2,558	6,217	11,029	37.0	(NA)	31,937	1,211	1,198	2,126	43.3	65.9	27,347
Charlotte-Gastonia-Concord, NC-SC	400	78,456	5,698	17,091	12,160	28.1	12.8	81,100	2,843	2,256	1,604	31.6	65.9	54,522
Charlottesville, VA	63	2,408	807	2,072	11,627	35.1	(NA)	10,899	394	361	2,024	33.9	(NA)	8,295
Chattanooga, TN-GA	168	6,310	2,031	5,169	10,696	21.6	(NA)	25,500	894	635	1,314	(NA)	(NA)	17,465
Cheyenne, WY	24	916	366	1,191	14,313	39.2	14.8	5,156	177	139	1,668	30.6	77.6	3,683
Chicago-Naperville-Joliet, IL-IN-WI.	**2,745**	**220,456**	**29,620**	**100,306**	**10,824**	**24.6**	**(NA)**	**434,544**	**17,053**	**15,581**	**1,681**	**39.8**	**73.1**	**314,064**
Chicago-Naperville-Joliet, IL.	*2,252*	*193,093*	*24,112*	*78,415*	*10,109*	*20.4*	*(NA)*	*351,599*	*14,132*	*13,271*	*1,711*	*29.7*	*73.3*	*261,629*
Gary, IN.	*237*	*8,864*	*2,505*	*7,320*	*10,735*	*26.9*	*(NA)*	*35,292*	*1,273*	*1,117*	*1,638*	*(NA)*	*58.5*	*24,673*
Lake County-Kenosha County, IL-WI.	*256*	*18,499*	*3,003*	*14,572*	*17,580*	*51.2*	*7.4*	*47,653*	*1,648*	*1,193*	*1,439*	*31.2*	*84.0*	*27,762*

See footnotes at end of table.

State and Metropolitan Area Data Book: 2006

U.S. Census Bureau

Metropolitan statistical area **Metropolitan statistical area with metropolitan divisions** *Metropolitan division*	Banking,[1] 2004		Retail trade[2] (NAICS 44–45), 2002						Accommodation and food services[2] (NAICS 72), 2002					
				Sales						Sales				
						Percent						Percent		
	Number of offices	Deposits (mil. dol.)	Establishments	Total (mil. dol.)	Per capita[3] (dol.)	Change, 1997–2002	General merchandise stores[4]	Paid employees[5]	Establishments	Total (mil. dol.)	Per capita[3] (dol.)	Change, 1997–2002	Food services[6]	Paid employees[5]
Chico, CA	48	2,547	770	2,027	9,714	34.9	17.6	10,644	381	223	1,067	42.5	89.5	6,353
Cincinnati-Middletown, OH-KY-IN	768	43,045	7,108	21,528	10,574	18.1	(NA)	111,562	3,904	3,546	(NA)	(NA)	(NA)	84,519
Clarksville, TN-KY	77	2,207	865	2,092	8,933	20.5	(NA)	11,022	378	246	1,050	24.7	(NA)	7,859
Cleveland, TN	42	1,313	426	900	8,517	13.5	18.6	4,667	154	107	1,016	23.8	(NA)	3,104
Cleveland-Elyria-Mentor, OH	737	62,259	7,835	23,715	11,070	19.9	(NA)	111,220	4,412	2,905	1,356	16.4	85.3	76,420
Coeur d'Alene, ID	39	1,271	540	1,288	11,265	25.9	15.7	6,262	307	222	1,944	61.4	55.0	5,031
College Station-Bryan, TX	51	2,091	707	1,745	9,368	18.7	(NA)	9,133	359	264	1,420	44.6	(NA)	7,650
Colorado Springs, CO	137	4,735	2,033	6,193	10,991	21.6	(NA)	30,004	1,147	1,066	1,891	22.9	63.4	24,039
Columbia, MO	59	2,022	656	1,785	12,004	19.4	(NA)	9,389	351	235	1,580	28.3	(NA)	6,865
Columbia, SC	179	8,689	2,680	6,725	10,149	16.6	(NA)	36,150	1,187	860	1,297	(NA)	(NA)	24,546
Columbus, GA-AL	74	4,280	1,040	2,732	9,548	21.6	(NA)	13,922	477	389	1,359	(NA)	(NA)	9,447
Columbus, IN	26	2,404	323	732	10,186	7.5	18.0	4,180	121	95	1,319	-7.4	82.4	2,734
Columbus, OH	469	26,103	5,812	20,283	12,238	17.1	(NA)	100,175	3,323	2,752	1,661	32.0	84.5	71,670
Corpus Christi, TX	104	3,819	1,457	3,866	9,560	18.7	(NA)	18,766	921	590	1,459	24.2	82.6	16,158
Corvallis, OR	15	648	269	538	6,811	13.6	14.6	3,319	182	97	1,228	12.9	86.8	2,703
Cumberland, MD-WV	34	800	440	917	9,065	13.7	(NA)	5,524	220	121	1,193	36.1	(NA)	3,746
Dallas-Fort Worth-Arlington, TX	1,340	93,059	18,259	62,298	11,383	24.7	(NA)	276,521	9,639	9,157	(NA)	(NA)	(NA)	205,313
Dallas-Plano-Irving, TX	*908*	*73,989*	*12,156*	*41,951*	*11,449*	*23.9*	*(NA)*	*184,036*	*6,351*	*6,315*	*1,723*	*27.0*	*(NA)*	*137,044*
Fort Worth-Arlington, TX	*432*	*19,070*	*6,103*	*20,347*	*11,250*	*26.4*	*(NA)*	*92,485*	*2,946*	*2,622*	*1,450*	*34.7*	*86.0*	*63,657*
Dalton, GA	37	1,673	625	1,458	11,619	18.0	13.5	6,864	209	143	1,140	27.7	85.3	3,586
Danville, IL	35	987	321	717	8,618	12.3	22.2	4,012	168	73	873	6.1	89.7	2,441
Danville, VA	44	1,392	496	980	8,984	10.6	19.7	5,794	167	102	934	19.2	(NA)	3,026
Davenport-Moline-Rock Island, IA-IL	148	5,440	1,571	4,112	10,964	10.6	(NA)	22,436	842	711	1,897	63.9	(NA)	16,740
Dayton, OH	264	9,364	2,958	9,249	10,943	15.8	(NA)	47,597	1,589	1,180	1,396	19.4	89.3	33,483
Decatur, AL	48	1,563	661	1,356	9,257	8.2	17.3	7,129	222	137	938	19.9	(NA)	3,895
Decatur, IL	46	1,618	477	1,277	11,344	13.1	22.9	6,689	218	133	1,177	7.3	84.4	3,948
Deltona-Daytona Beach-Ormond Beach, FL	150	6,891	1,888	4,714	10,260	21.3	16.6	24,312	972	735	1,599	15.6	72.3	18,167
Denver-Aurora, CO[7]	635	35,892	8,256	27,989	12,296	(NA)	13.8	123,541	4,692	4,374	1,922	41.3	75.7	95,251
Des Moines, IA	190	11,155	2,002	6,185	12,459	22.2	(NA)	33,333	1,107	735	1,481	27.6	(NA)	19,765
Detroit-Warren-Livonia, MI	1,123	76,202	16,393	51,765	11,558	15.6	15.3	226,616	7,888	5,671	1,266	18.3	87.7	144,761
Detroit-Livonia-Dearborn, MI	*391*	*28,080*	*6,593*	*17,444*	*8,550*	*10.0*	*15.1*	*78,991*	*3,254*	*2,306*	*1,130*	*14.0*	*85.3*	*58,299*
Warren-Farmington Hills-Troy, MI	*732*	*48,122*	*9,800*	*34,321*	*14,074*	*18.7*	*15.4*	*147,625*	*4,634*	*3,365*	*1,380*	*21.4*	*89.4*	*86,462*
Dothan, AL	48	1,917	795	1,703	12,904	15.0	(NA)	8,525	229	142	1,077	(NA)	82.1	3,889
Dover, DE	32	1,377	568	1,719	13,061	29.7	21.7	8,416	211	153	1,163	29.3	82.1	3,817
Dubuque, IA	40	1,588	502	1,094	12,232	17.0	19.1	6,358	240	115	1,289	21.8	82.6	3,912
Duluth, MN-WI	99	2,969	1,340	3,037	10,997	23.8	(NA)	16,417	832	442	1,601	21.5	66.7	12,508
Durham, NC	119	5,205	1,692	4,124	9,355	23.3	(NA)	23,351	909	730	1,657	(NA)	76.2	17,210
Eau Claire, WI	64	1,834	687	1,924	12,796	26.8	18.9	10,463	377	184	1,220	22.1	83.4	6,095
El Centro, CA	14	1,208	481	1,345	9,234	36.0	23.6	6,423	214	127	870	42.0	83.0	2,909
Elizabethtown, KY	49	1,338	491	1,154	10,612	22.9	19.2	5,836	166	139	1,273	(NA)	88.4	3,824
Elkhart-Goshen, IN	57	1,848	727	1,932	10,394	-2.1	21.1	9,594	352	225	1,210	18.7	88.7	6,218
Elmira, NY	25	1,144	401	1,043	11,489	19.1	20.3	5,766	208	105	1,152	21.3	89.5	3,262
El Paso, TX	73	4,390	2,138	5,807	8,373	23.6	25.3	29,951	1,090	772	1,113	9.8	86.9	20,736
Erie, PA	87	3,028	1,159	3,076	10,895	20.1	15.5	16,418	612	320	1,135	20.8	85.9	10,033
Eugene-Springfield, OR	94	3,068	1,421	3,720	11,376	12.0	19.2	19,048	781	465	1,421	19.7	83.1	11,579
Evansville, IN-KY	120	4,853	1,493	4,098	11,895	20.5	(NA)	21,681	665	552	1,602	(NA)	(NA)	14,891
Fairbanks, AK	18	761	332	1,113	13,126	19.9	(NA)	4,758	195	155	1,829	38.3	68.2	2,914
Fargo, ND-MN	83	3,059	790	2,508	14,169	17.9	(NA)	13,379	396	267	1,510	13.4	(NA)	8,566
Farmington, NM	23	888	470	1,239	10,325	25.0	21.8	6,157	177	137	1,146	37.4	83.6	3,832
Fayetteville, NC	69	2,213	1,110	3,090	9,069	17.4	18.7	15,627	514	374	1,096	15.3	(NA)	10,602
Fayetteville-Springdale-Rogers, AR-MO	165	5,504	1,502	3,788	10,324	46.2	(NA)	19,589	664	435	1,186	49.3	(NA)	12,023
Flagstaff, AZ	27	783	671	1,340	11,174	24.0	17.7	7,896	455	424	3,538	4.1	51.8	8,923
Flint, MI	93	3,782	1,703	5,027	11,401	11.2	18.4	24,353	717	443	1,004	9.7	94.4	12,693
Florence, SC	70	2,108	1,051	2,187	11,207	15.7	17.8	11,599	343	206	1,056	15.5	81.8	6,207
Florence-Muscle Shoals, AL	58	1,937	698	1,525	10,748	16.5	21.8	7,832	234	137	966	20.8	92.5	4,228
Fond du Lac, WI	37	1,332	411	1,029	10,519	15.5	16.1	6,279	222	112	1,144	20.4	89.8	3,695
Fort Collins-Loveland, CO	78	3,447	1,251	3,165	11,996	29.7	18.5	15,809	702	477	1,806	38.4	79.4	12,248
Fort Smith, AR-OK	116	3,399	1,113	2,500	8,987	15.4	(NA)	13,115	439	255	917	16.3	87.7	7,471
Fort Walton Beach-Crestview-Destin, FL	78	2,843	968	2,476	14,131	41.1	19.1	12,181	422	357	2,040	36.6	84.3	8,857
Fort Wayne, IN	129	4,520	1,565	4,448	11,207	13.5	(NA)	24,411	749	514	1,295	13.5	(NA)	15,874
Fresno, CA	143	7,416	2,475	7,259	8,724	30.2	16.5	32,591	1,290	824	990	30.3	88.5	21,110
Gadsden, AL	28	1,069	454	912	8,858	23.6	17.7	4,581	171	103	996	20.6	91.9	3,231
Gainesville, FL	66	2,416	953	2,406	10,199	22.5	(NA)	13,923	453	331	1,405	(NA)	(NA)	9,241
Gainesville, GA	51	2,322	551	1,493	9,834	20.3	17.8	6,729	232	199	1,308	33.8	(NA)	4,263
Glens Falls, NY	48	1,701	682	1,500	11,937	34.4	10.2	7,402	494	235	1,872	18.0	(NA)	4,107
Goldsboro, NC	32	959	519	1,024	9,049	-0.9	23.2	5,818	170	103	914	22.6	90.1	3,152
Grand Forks, ND-MN	43	1,288	484	1,321	13,791	15.2	(NA)	7,137	243	134	1,403	13.1	83.7	4,726
Grand Junction, CO	42	1,495	600	1,662	13,603	44.2	20.1	7,682	250	180	1,477	44.7	76.2	4,740
Grand Rapids-Wyoming, MI	240	10,941	2,669	9,162	12,104	25.0	(NA)	43,533	1,252	861	1,137	24.5	84.7	24,400
Great Falls, MT	24	885	431	1,012	12,683	26.0	21.9	5,552	257	130	1,625	18.2	81.6	3,908
Greeley, CO[7]	59	2,236	582	1,673	8,187	(NA)	(NA)	7,331	320	158	775	(NA)	94.9	4,841
Green Bay, WI	116	4,998	1,165	3,382	11,696	18.2	(NA)	17,618	707	368	1,273	14.6	83.8	11,489
Greensboro-High Point, NC	208	9,129	2,798	7,725	11,765	16.3	12.4	37,926	1,276	958	1,459	23.8	81.1	24,290
Greenville, NC	44	1,400	694	1,734	11,079	21.1	(NA)	8,314	276	195	1,246	24.7	88.9	6,325

See footnotes at end of table.

Metropolitan statistical area **Metropolitan statistical area with metropolitan divisions** *Metropolitan division*	Banking,[1] 2004		Retail trade[2] (NAICS 44–45), 2002						Accommodation and food services[2] (NAICS 72), 2002					
			Estab-lish-ments	Sales					Estab-lish-ments	Sales				
						Percent						Percent		
	Num-ber of offices	Depos-its (mil. dol.)		Total (mil. dol.)	Per cap-ita[3] (dol.)	Change, 1997–2002	Gen-eral mer-chan-dise stores[4]	Paid employ-ees[5]		Total (mil. dol.)	Per cap-ita[3] (dol.)	Change, 1997–2002	Food ser-vices[6]	Paid employ-ees[5]
Greenville, SC	203	8,961	2,302	5,859	10,227	7.5	15.8	29,920	1,084	731	1,276	15.0	83.9	20,641
Gulfport-Biloxi, MS	85	2,803	1,119	2,533	10,168	33.9	(NA)	13,539	530	1,587	6,371	(NA)	(NA)	24,258
Hagerstown-Martinsburg, MD-WV	90	2,641	993	2,500	10,798	36.9	18.6	13,352	435	269	1,162	30.0	78.7	7,366
Hanford-Corcoran, CA	19	818	307	724	5,378	15.0	19.1	3,530	156	87	644	33.0	89.8	2,087
Harrisburg-Carlisle, PA	220	8,284	2,104	6,484	12,611	17.9	(NA)	31,744	1,143	827	1,609	28.4	68.7	19,383
Harrisonburg, VA	48	1,363	563	1,367	12,432	30.6	(NA)	6,934	210	148	1,346	18.9	(NA)	4,348
Hartford-West Hartford-East Hartford, CT	386	26,148	4,477	12,723	10,883	16.3	10.0	63,740	2,316	1,632	1,396	28.6	83.3	36,558
Hattiesburg, MS	56	1,568	671	1,414	11,148	21.3	(NA)	7,985	219	143	1,126	(NA)	87.5	4,706
Hickory-Lenoir-Morganton, NC	102	4,057	1,456	3,555	10,190	21.1	(NA)	17,466	621	373	1,069	24.7	92.2	10,865
Hinesville-Fort Stewart, GA	13	293	189	328	4,590	25.3	(NA)	2,025	84	44	622	20.4	94.0	1,380
Holland-Grand Haven, MI	86	3,275	819	2,142	8,693	11.5	23.2	11,687	348	217	881	25.4	93.5	6,235
Honolulu, HI	195	18,402	3,065	8,817	9,948	6.7	20.0	41,968	2,119	2,957	3,337	-2.6	55.0	49,864
Hot Springs, AR	51	1,260	533	1,107	12,301	26.4	(NA)	5,841	249	158	1,757	31.5	71.0	4,426
Houma-Bayou Cane-Thibodaux, LA	79	2,383	817	1,833	9,335	12.1	(NA)	11,737	333	199	1,013	28.7	90.8	5,646
Houston-Sugar Land-Baytown, TX	1,190	83,930	16,000	52,301	10,529	30.4	(NA)	230,260	7,761	7,136	1,437	33.4	82.3	161,029
Huntington-Ashland, WV-KY-OH	110	3,452	1,236	2,922	10,199	21.2	(NA)	15,905	501	316	1,102	15.1	(NA)	8,785
Huntsville, AL	90	4,480	1,488	3,828	10,847	27.0	(NA)	19,386	615	486	1,376	24.0	85.3	12,910
Idaho Falls, ID	32	941	507	1,293	12,311	30.2	(NA)	6,649	219	120	1,142	(NA)	82.1	3,464
Indianapolis, IN	533	23,608	5,803	19,132	12,126	19.2	(NA)	95,598	3,123	2,654	1,682	27.3	80.9	66,403
Iowa City, IA	48	2,038	628	1,420	10,525	23.9	(NA)	9,333	326	203	1,506	31.1	80.9	6,549
Ithaca, NY	33	1,203	366	804	8,181	30.5	7.8	4,631	317	157	1,597	38.8	78.0	3,815
Jackson, MI	52	1,552	600	1,549	9,606	20.1	26.1	8,183	282	159	986	16.0	90.6	4,617
Jackson, MS	198	7,071	2,108	5,625	11,136	25.1	(NA)	27,806	841	651	1,289	(NA)	84.3	17,421
Jackson, TN	47	1,418	596	1,469	13,430	13.3	20.0	7,737	204	159	1,452	10.1	84.7	4,780
Jacksonville, FL	269	19,693	4,735	13,615	11,598	30.6	(NA)	65,063	2,166	1,849	1,575	27.6	71.7	43,422
Jacksonville, NC	24	698	572	1,441	9,622	32.2	18.4	6,807	250	170	1,138	33.3	87.3	5,364
Janesville, WI	46	1,599	558	1,754	11,384	9.6	18.0	8,366	353	184	1,193	21.6	90.7	5,356
Jefferson City, MO	58	2,693	593	1,723	12,114	46.9	(NA)	9,705	237	152	1,067	(NA)	(NA)	3,900
Johnson City, TN	62	2,266	724	1,886	10,265	30.3	(NA)	9,379	298	203	1,102	19.5	(NA)	6,158
Johnstown, PA	81	2,248	613	1,404	9,332	12.7	19.1	7,639	295	129	860	16.2	90.3	4,040
Jonesboro, AR	62	1,846	555	1,186	10,869	22.0	(NA)	6,589	174	120	1,098	33.6	93.1	3,508
Joplin, MO	76	1,932	788	1,871	11,684	29.5	(NA)	9,760	312	188	1,177	18.1	87.0	5,939
Kalamazoo-Portage, MI	93	3,043	1,155	3,217	10,121	11.3	(NA)	17,631	604	401	1,261	28.4	86.7	12,506
Kankakee-Bradley, IL	39	1,514	396	1,105	10,495	21.9	20.0	5,786	207	112	1,063	11.5	91.9	3,347
Kansas City, MO-KS	706	31,123	6,880	21,864	11,585	18.7	(NA)	105,736	3,466	3,202	1,697	(NA)	68.2	74,199
Kennewick-Richland-Pasco, WA	55	1,773	771	2,245	11,039	32.4	(NA)	10,262	381	234	1,149	36.9	81.9	5,835
Killeen-Temple-Fort Hood, TX	77	2,776	1,045	2,945	8,710	40.5	(NA)	13,619	509	316	936	(NA)	(NA)	8,803
Kingsport-Bristol-Bristol, TN-VA	118	3,674	1,317	2,954	9,878	13.9	(NA)	15,150	502	224	748	(NA)	(NA)	9,431
Kingston, NY	55	2,228	827	1,838	10,188	43.8	14.5	8,995	473	273	1,512	26.5	56.9	6,549
Knoxville, TN	230	8,692	2,730	8,512	13,463	17.9	(NA)	40,617	1,158	997	1,577	33.1	85.1	26,681
Kokomo, IN	38	1,065	459	1,259	12,431	16.8	22.3	6,361	207	144	1,423	16.0	(NA)	3,857
La Crosse, WI-MN	49	1,875	553	1,602	12,522	4.8	(NA)	9,125	330	173	1,350	16.1	(NA)	6,344
Lafayette, IN	67	2,107	680	1,989	11,081	21.3	(NA)	11,129	373	252	1,401	(NA)	(NA)	7,328
Lafayette, LA	99	3,224	1,136	2,908	11,997	9.4	18.8	15,851	486	419	1,727	(NA)	(NA)	11,148
Lake Charles, LA	77	1,959	830	2,063	10,688	26.2	(NA)	11,429	322	401	2,080	30.2	(NA)	9,812
Lakeland, FL	125	4,562	1,713	4,522	9,041	17.6	18.8	22,457	649	452	905	7.9	85.5	11,901
Lancaster, PA	196	7,380	2,002	5,379	11,240	15.1	10.6	29,751	857	588	1,229	16.1	77.6	15,425
Lansing-East Lansing, MI	129	4,926	1,687	5,085	11,241	17.8	(NA)	27,246	854	582	1,287	18.8	(NA)	17,658
Laredo, TX	38	4,259	728	2,035	9,845	33.5	22.2	10,429	288	241	1,164	66.2	84.7	5,645
Las Cruces, NM	42	1,236	513	1,252	7,012	18.2	21.1	6,499	245	155	870	27.6	87.7	4,513
Las Vegas-Paradise, NV	313	28,526	4,750	19,302	12,734	56.7	(NA)	79,005	2,787	16,441	10,846	32.5	15.3	212,136
Lawrence, KS	54	1,363	422	878	8,647	15.7	17.6	5,988	265	157	1,547	30.1	83.4	5,487
Lawton, OK	38	855	422	901	8,059	30.2	28.0	4,999	190	122	1,087	25.4	91.0	3,768
Lebanon, PA	49	1,519	446	1,283	10,544	6.1	15.2	6,272	206	94	772	23.5	89.4	2,773
Lewiston, ID-WA	22	620	271	691	11,959	10.6	(NA)	3,413	138	73	1,256	22.6	79.9	2,092
Lewiston-Auburn, ME	32	1,129	481	1,468	13,951	17.7	13.9	6,704	195	113	1,072	45.7	87.3	2,882
Lexington-Fayette, KY	177	6,503	1,750	5,512	13,265	26.5	(NA)	28,329	861	768	1,848	21.7	(NA)	19,858
Lima, OH	38	1,700	512	1,341	12,402	3.8	27.1	7,367	228	147	1,359	15.3	92.1	4,435
Lincoln, NE	125	4,435	1,108	2,969	10,872	26.3	(NA)	17,528	595	394	1,443	19.0	(NA)	11,816
Little Rock-North Little Rock, AR	299	9,165	2,650	7,493	12,037	19.0	(NA)	35,003	1,074	806	1,294	(NA)	(NA)	22,021
Logan, UT-ID	25	932	391	805	7,482	9.2	(NA)	5,413	149	82	760	51.9	89.7	2,665
Longview, TX	67	2,698	990	2,304	11,687	22.4	(NA)	11,261	335	204	1,036	18.1	84.3	5,869
Longview, WA	20	569	392	938	9,914	15.6	18.6	4,510	219	112	1,188	15.9	91.4	2,984
Los Angeles-Long Beach-Santa Ana, CA	**2,160**	**246,643**	**38,195**	**127,837**	**10,072**	**33.6**	**11.8**	**522,275**	**22,985**	**19,804**	**1,560**	**29.2**	**78.9**	**405,651**
Los Angeles-Long Beach-Glendale, CA	*1,572*	*188,911*	*28,636*	*92,100*	*9,433*	*32.5*	*11.6*	*378,933*	*17,074*	*14,212*	*1,456*	*28.2*	*80.5*	*290,380*
Santa Ana-Anaheim-Irvine, CA	*588*	*57,732*	*9,559*	*35,737*	*12,205*	*36.5*	*12.2*	*143,342*	*5,911*	*5,592*	*1,910*	*31.6*	*74.8*	*115,271*
Louisville, KY-IN	463	19,336	4,509	12,573	10,651	21.4	(NA)	66,025	2,109	1,992	(NA)	(NA)	(NA)	48,268
Lubbock, TX	81	4,015	1,083	3,315	13,043	22.1	(NA)	15,820	528	416	1,635	24.7	(NA)	11,806
Lynchburg, VA	82	3,168	1,032	2,498	10,855	21.7	(NA)	13,647	355	210	913	(NA)	(NA)	6,724
Macon, GA	65	3,074	1,008	2,402	10,676	13.7	(NA)	13,820	414	291	(NA)	(NA)	(NA)	7,424
Madera, CA	23	878	334	705	5,474	33.7	(NA)	3,500	170	93	725	27.9	68.1	2,070
Madison, WI	210	10,340	2,119	7,923	15,289	22.3	(NA)	38,450	1,299	824	1,590	(NA)	82.0	23,044

See footnotes at end of table.

State and Metropolitan Area Data Book: 2006

U.S. Census Bureau

Metropolitan statistical area / **Metropolitan statistical area with metropolitan divisions** / *Metropolitan division*	Banking,[1] 2004 Number of offices	Banking,[1] 2004 Deposits (mil. dol.)	Retail trade[2] (NAICS 44–45), 2002 Establishments	Sales Total (mil. dol.)	Sales Per capita[3] (dol.)	Percent Change, 1997–2002	Percent General merchandise stores[4]	Paid employees[5]	Accommodation and food services[2] (NAICS 72), 2002 Establishments	Sales Total (mil. dol.)	Sales Per capita[3] (dol.)	Percent Change, 1997–2002	Food services[6]	Paid employees[5]
Manchester-Nashua, NH	99	6,489	1,703	6,183	15,761	25.5	14.5	27,247	753	554	1,413	34.0	85.6	13,018
Mansfield, OH	46	1,493	527	1,484	11,557	14.3	23.6	7,734	270	153	1,188	8.9	91.7	4,685
McAllen-Edinburg-Mission, TX	114	6,350	1,713	5,023	8,196	50.5	19.0	24,012	692	525	856	49.0	84.4	13,341
Medford, OR	69	2,219	898	2,580	13,803	24.3	17.5	11,018	552	299	1,599	45.6	80.4	7,149
Memphis, TN-MS-AR	373	25,947	4,379	12,734	10,381	17.3	(NA)	63,237	1,982	2,939	2,396	24.8	45.5	57,244
Merced, CA	30	1,603	544	1,602	7,124	45.4	19.3	6,975	278	141	626	29.5	89.0	3,763
Miami-Fort Lauderdale-Miami Beach, FL	**1,446**	**123,861**	**22,632**	**63,061**	**12,114**	**25.0**	**11.3**	**278,569**	**9,603**	**9,228**	**1,773**	**25.8**	**69.6**	**188,687**
Fort Lauderdale-Pompano Beach-Deerfield Beach, FL	*426*	*30,504*	*7,193*	*22,012*	*12,917*	*22.4*	*11.3*	*96,645*	*3,363*	*2,800*	*1,643*	*13.2*	*76.1*	*60,130*
Miami-Miami Beach-Kendall, FL	*572*	*62,369*	*10,113*	*24,568*	*10,616*	*18.6*	*11.5*	*110,975*	*3,935*	*4,162*	*1,799*	*30.1*	*65.2*	*81,610*
West Palm Beach-Boca Raton-Boynton Beach, FL	*448*	*30,988*	*5,326*	*16,481*	*13,879*	*40.5*	*11.1*	*70,949*	*2,305*	*2,266*	*1,908*	*36.5*	*69.9*	*46,947*
Michigan City-La Porte, IN	33	1,261	496	1,128	10,234	8.3	18.4	6,041	233	341	3,093	221.3	(NA)	5,029
Midland, TX	39	2,090	529	1,294	11,014	5.5	18.4	6,443	240	170	1,447	37.2	87.9	4,641
Milwaukee-Waukesha-West Allis, WI	560	38,461	5,062	16,222	10,745	13.4	13.7	83,547	2,870	1,952	1,293	25.4	85.3	52,862
Minneapolis-St. Paul-Bloomington, MN-WI	750	52,380	10,896	38,700	12,667	24.0	(NA)	189,192	5,475	4,944	1,618	31.6	82.0	125,153
Missoula, MT	33	1,242	557	1,525	15,590	42.7	19.8	7,888	329	206	2,105	41.4	78.1	5,202
Mobile, AL	105	4,803	1,647	4,074	10,194	19.7	18.9	21,045	637	439	1,098	18.6	85.9	12,289
Modesto, CA	93	5,205	1,433	4,919	10,242	49.9	16.2	21,925	751	499	1,038	58.9	90.7	13,117
Monroe, LA	72	1,976	798	1,873	11,023	18.9	23.0	9,789	282	206	1,211	(NA)	(NA)	5,689
Monroe, MI	44	1,639	441	1,398	9,365	35.1	15.8	7,043	247	132	883	34.4	91.5	4,124
Montgomery, AL	109	5,024	1,461	3,538	10,073	11.2	(NA)	18,318	551	412	1,174	(NA)	84.8	11,024
Morgantown, WV	41	1,541	470	1,006	8,950	22.0	16.9	5,913	236	133	1,183	30.1	78.2	3,915
Morristown, TN	42	1,288	488	1,180	9,405	23.9	(NA)	5,577	167	112	894	(NA)	(NA)	3,241
Mount Vernon-Anacortes, WA	45	1,530	618	1,604	15,029	49.8	18.5	7,263	295	187	1,750	58.0	68.2	3,973
Muncie, IN	40	1,426	525	1,323	11,121	18.2	21.5	7,418	225	147	1,233	15.8	92.0	4,542
Muskegon-Norton Shores, MI	41	1,292	623	1,536	8,920	12.5	28.0	8,558	317	177	1,028	15.1	87.5	5,370
Myrtle Beach-Conway-North Myrtle Beach, SC	106	3,806	1,585	3,224	15,647	28.7	17.3	15,962	1,052	1,065	5,170	20.8	56.4	20,870
Napa, CA	40	2,338	551	1,390	10,696	46.0	7.6	6,618	343	351	2,700	22.2	61.8	6,678
Naples-Marco Island, FL	126	8,132	1,465	4,197	15,222	59.8	11.3	18,943	586	698	2,531	30.0	57.0	13,104
Nashville-Davidson-Murfreesboro, TN	452	23,141	5,579	15,845	11,712	21.2	(NA)	79,778	2,521	2,508	1,853	(NA)	(NA)	54,794
New Haven-Milford, CT	262	15,601	3,218	9,268	11,102	20.0	11.9	44,627	1,674	1,012	1,212	25.7	88.5	22,068
New Orleans-Metairie-Kenner, LA	355	19,794	5,005	12,916	9,833	17.8	(NA)	69,141	2,917	3,151	2,399	33.4	63.1	69,171
New York-Northern New Jersey-Long Island, NY-NJ-PA	**5,074**	**708,689**	**75,123**	**183,728**	**9,883**	**28.2**	**8.5**	**790,694**	**36,146**	**28,045**	**1,509**	**30.0**	**76.4**	**477,314**
Edison, NJ	*805*	*58,488*	*8,742*	*27,877*	*12,424*	*27.9*	*11.6*	*121,795*	*4,477*	*2,995*	*1,335*	*33.9*	*83.0*	*59,981*
Nassau-Suffolk, NY	*840*	*75,300*	*13,369*	*38,117*	*13,638*	*27.1*	*10.9*	*157,498*	*5,813*	*3,699*	*1,323*	*31.6*	*88.9*	*72,219*
Newark-Union, NJ-PA	*819*	*47,249*	*8,390*	*23,322*	*10,947*	*26.6*	*(NA)*	*96,857*	*4,177*	*2,744*	*1,288*	*19.8*	*79.9*	*52,940*
New York-White Plains-Wayne, NY-NJ	*2,610*	*527,652*	*44,622*	*94,412*	*8,267*	*29.2*	*8.8*	*414,544*	*21,679*	*18,607*	*1,629*	*30.7*	*72.3*	*292,174*
Niles-Benton Harbor, MI	60	1,919	624	1,318	8,113	1.2	18.3	7,777	413	191	1,176	16.8	82.8	5,548
Norwich-New London, CT	87	3,935	1,119	3,012	11,464	25.2	15.9	14,752	589	2,380	9,060	614.9	12.0	28,640
Ocala, FL	77	3,548	1,063	2,860	10,496	28.8	20.7	14,139	378	241	884	19.9	88.5	5,988
Ocean City, NJ	58	2,361	772	1,383	13,587	43.9	(NA)	5,816	933	498	4,888	35.2	49.7	6,192
Odessa, TX	28	1,166	497	1,358	11,091	19.1	22.0	6,591	219	154	1,257	28.4	90.0	4,073
Ogden-Clearfield, UT	93	3,061	1,352	4,194	9,118	16.9	(NA)	21,722	637	381	829	23.2	88.0	11,613
Oklahoma City, OK	350	14,854	4,335	11,678	10,429	15.4	(NA)	58,681	2,177	1,570	1,402	(NA)	(NA)	43,709
Olympia, WA	63	2,060	757	2,236	10,299	38.3	20.1	10,154	399	245	1,128	27.0	88.7	6,418
Omaha-Council Bluffs, NE-IA	298	13,804	2,931	9,840	12,567	23.5	(NA)	50,067	1,614	1,337	1,707	(NA)	(NA)	32,638
Orlando-Kissimee, FL	471	25,711	7,392	21,266	12,118	26.1	(NA)	102,604	3,303	6,060	3,453	12.2	44.4	103,829
Oshkosh-Neenah, WI	46	1,581	553	1,511	9,535	1.4	12.6	8,072	352	167	1,056	8.8	88.5	5,162
Owensboro, KY	60	1,966	510	1,125	10,196	21.8	(NA)	6,376	173	136	1,230	(NA)	(NA)	4,033
Oxnard-Thousand Oaks-Ventura, CA	153	10,976	2,429	9,025	11,557	39.3	12.6	36,622	1,287	987	1,264	27.3	82.9	22,571
Palm Bay-Melbourne-Titusville, FL	125	5,791	1,913	5,233	10,555	34.2	17.3	26,449	839	604	1,219	22.0	78.0	15,741
Panama City-Lynn Haven, FL	47	2,113	813	1,865	12,249	24.6	23.0	9,819	449	373	2,451	11.0	65.9	8,874
Parkersburg-Marietta-Vienna, WV-OH	70	2,177	735	2,021	12,350	30.9	(NA)	10,265	327	195	(NA)	(NA)	(NA)	5,521
Pascagoula, MS	46	1,288	549	1,069	6,986	2.7	22.6	6,426	234	133	866	(NA)	(NA)	3,858
Pensacola-Ferry Pass-Brent, FL	113	4,068	1,587	4,146	9,776	20.7	(NA)	19,542	636	477	1,125	18.0	88.8	12,494
Peoria, IL	157	5,173	1,427	3,895	10,633	13.0	(NA)	19,681	861	606	1,655	(NA)	(NA)	15,534
Philadelphia-Camden-Wilmington, PA-NJ-DE-MD	**1,847**	**181,749**	**21,082**	**67,476**	**11,752**	**25.7**	**10.4**	**306,842**	**10,787**	**7,558**	**1,316**	**28.9**	**81.3**	**162,363**
Camden, NJ	*359*	*17,386*	*4,479*	*15,681*	*12,933*	*36.8*	*11.0*	*64,437*	*2,092*	*1,346*	*1,110*	*30.2*	*87.3*	*31,139*
Philadelphia, PA	*1,269*	*71,350*	*14,030*	*43,500*	*11,258*	*21.4*	*9.7*	*203,363*	*7,534*	*5,287*	*1,368*	*30.3*	*79.1*	*110,146*
Wilmington, DE-MD-NJ	*219*	*93,013*	*2,573*	*8,295*	*12,467*	*30.0*	*12.8*	*39,042*	*1,161*	*926*	*1,391*	*19.2*	*84.8*	*21,078*
Phoenix-Mesa-Scottsdale, AZ	701	43,718	10,399	38,501	11,036	28.3	(NA)	174,829	5,851	5,638	1,616	30.0	72.2	132,226
Pine Bluff, AR	36	954	399	810	7,610	9.7	(NA)	4,490	153	77	(NA)	(NA)	(NA)	2,200
Pittsburgh, PA	879	53,279	9,377	25,138	10,411	14.5	14.7	132,572	5,039	3,296	1,365	25.8	81.6	88,798
Pittsfield, MA	57	2,609	794	1,571	11,785	22.7	9.9	8,740	511	327	2,455	32.3	54.3	7,554
Pocatello, ID	27	549	381	841	10,099	13.3	(NA)	4,696	184	94	1,123	20.5	79.8	2,988
Portland-South Portland-Biddeford, ME	181	7,095	2,669	6,445	12,849	22.2	11.0	32,624	1,629	1,001	1,995	33.3	66.7	20,080
Portland-Vancouver-Beaverton, OR-WA	510	22,963	6,806	21,750	10,804	12.7	(NA)	100,696	4,465	3,015	1,498	20.5	82.4	71,328
Port St. Lucie-Fort Pierce, FL	116	6,012	1,339	3,808	11,294	34.0	(NA)	18,649	535	390	1,157	23.7	81.4	10,263
Poughkeepsie-Newburgh-Middletown, NY	211	8,467	2,607	7,129	11,064	34.3	14.7	33,132	1,285	676	1,048	32.8	80.7	15,007
Prescott, AZ	47	2,472	789	1,608	8,978	33.7	17.4	9,028	490	313	1,747	73.5	55.1	7,279
Providence-New Bedford-Fall River, RI-MA	387	27,544	6,550	17,695	10,972	39.7	11.4	85,666	3,846	2,460	1,525	38.3	86.3	57,233
Provo-Orem, UT	83	2,492	1,172	3,349	8,367	32.5	(NA)	18,658	493	334	835	41.5	79.6	10,316
Pueblo, CO	38	1,213	542	1,431	9,708	21.2	24.3	7,344	338	176	1,193	23.5	86.0	5,495

See footnotes at end of table.

Metropolitan statistical area / **Metropolitan statistical area with metropolitan divisions** / *Metropolitan division*	Banking,[1] 2004		Retail trade[2] (NAICS 44–45), 2002						Accommodation and food services[2] (NAICS 72), 2002					
			Estab-lish-ments	Sales				Paid employ-ees[5]	Estab-lish-ments	Sales				Paid employ-ees[5]
				Total (mil. dol.)	Per cap-ita[3] (dol.)	Percent				Total (mil. dol.)	Per cap-ita[3] (dol.)	Percent		
	Num-ber of offices	Depos-its (mil. dol.)				Change, 1997–2002	Gen-eral mer-chan-dise stores[4]					Change, 1997–2002	Food ser-vices[6]	
Punta Gorda, FL	55	2,869	558	1,435	9,570	34.9	26.7	7,862	238	138	922	11.9	89.5	3,654
Racine, WI	67	2,462	689	1,895	9,924	21.2	16.8	9,815	349	186	975	20.3	87.7	5,473
Raleigh-Cary, NC	252	11,730	3,513	11,145	12,943	32.3	12.2	49,561	1,590	1,239	1,439	(NA)	83.0	29,949
Rapid City, SD	34	1,456	690	1,688	14,632	35.3	(NA)	8,037	373	235	2,034	30.9	64.2	5,493
Reading, PA	137	6,260	1,374	3,846	10,072	15.5	13.1	19,099	688	369	966	11.6	89.0	10,028
Redding, CA	42	1,927	705	1,972	11,471	45.6	18.1	8,904	376	231	1,346	43.1	75.6	5,355
Reno-Sparks, NV	80	9,099	1,428	4,996	13,681	32.9	(NA)	21,369	828	2,005	5,490	10.2	20.7	35,569
Richmond, VA	366	33,149	4,422	12,657	11,255	31.3	(NA)	66,208	1,925	1,454	(NA)	(NA)	(NA)	37,371
Riverside-San Bernardino-Ontario, CA	478	31,399	8,876	32,270	9,211	47.0	15.9	133,530	5,019	4,202	1,199	44.9	76.3	94,812
Roanoke, VA	128	4,585	1,336	3,714	12,841	17.9	(NA)	19,818	597	397	(NA)	(NA)	(NA)	10,855
Rochester, MN	59	2,199	756	2,243	13,221	37.8	(NA)	11,904	331	275	1,621	(NA)	(NA)	7,323
Rochester, NY	280	12,597	3,621	10,310	9,919	17.0	12.8	56,321	2,019	1,126	1,083	15.8	86.9	29,785
Rockford, IL	92	5,176	1,124	3,490	10,678	18.2	16.7	17,602	588	367	1,124	13.1	88.9	10,034
Rocky Mount, NC	45	1,401	665	1,356	9,417	8.5	16.3	7,361	247	146	1,011	8.8	86.8	4,568
Rome, GA	28	1,147	424	960	10,366	18.8	23.6	4,663	185	121	1,310	38.3	94.1	3,066
Sacramento-Arden-Arcade-Roseville, CA	355	24,983	5,899	21,122	10,968	49.6	(NA)	89,589	3,560	2,811	1,460	49.5	75.4	62,034
Saginaw-Saginaw Township North, MI	66	1,717	1,052	2,703	12,880	9.1	18.3	13,900	415	339	1,617	25.4	82.3	9,495
St. Cloud, MN	66	2,816	850	2,496	14,269	34.8	(NA)	12,902	365	228	1,304	28.7	86.3	7,113
St. George, UT	33	1,096	459	1,157	11,615	31.6	21.8	6,012	200	156	1,561	37.4	60.7	3,681
St. Joseph, MO-KS	61	1,777	504	1,168	9,481	20.1	(NA)	6,361	225	120	976	8.1	(NA)	3,802
St. Louis, MO-IL[8]	802	44,028	10,042	30,088	10,998	22.0	11.5	147,393	5,267	4,517	1,651	(NA)	(NA)	110,070
Salem, OR	95	3,269	1,227	3,264	9,075	12.4	(NA)	16,195	679	569	(NA)	(NA)	(NA)	11,662
Salinas, CA	76	5,585	1,542	4,063	9,873	33.8	14.3	17,811	958	1,034	2,512	23.5	47.7	18,462
Salisbury, MD	53	1,420	524	1,296	11,610	22.0	(NA)	7,181	192	127	1,138	30.6	88.9	3,743
Salt Lake City, UT	268	92,458	3,669	12,151	12,209	14.3	(NA)	58,643	1,897	1,697	1,705	28.3	70.9	42,797
San Angelo, TX	28	1,118	472	1,137	10,803	27.4	(NA)	5,855	195	128,329	(NA)	(NA)	(NA)	3,811
San Antonio, TX	333	27,961	5,600	18,780	10,543	37.6	(NA)	83,190	3,279	3,060	1,718	(NA)	(NA)	69,390
San Diego-Carlsbad-San Marcos, CA	539	43,813	9,486	31,586	10,906	42.2	14.1	138,363	5,761	6,331	2,186	49.1	61.2	120,065
Sandusky, OH	25	850	350	834	10,569	14.0	21.0	4,595	267	181	2,294	7.9	58.5	4,411
San Francisco-Oakland-Fremont, CA	**958**	**154,040**	**14,202**	**48,253**	**11,591**	**31.5**	**11.6**	**206,977**	**10,100**	**8,778**	**2,109**	**16.1**	**72.0**	**161,596**
Oakland-Fremont-Hayward, CA	*488*	*47,062*	*7,121*	*26,621*	*10,854*	*34.6*	*12.7*	*110,894*	*4,545*	*3,235*	*1,319*	*30.6*	*84.9*	*66,503*
San Francisco-San Mateo-Redwood City, CA	*470*	*106,978*	*7,081*	*21,632*	*12,647*	*28.0*	*10.3*	*96,083*	*5,555*	*5,542*	*3,240*	*9.1*	*64.5*	*95,093*
San Jose-Sunnyvale-Santa Clara, CA	328	47,230	5,277	20,421	11,802	20.5	(NA)	85,350	3,775	3,083	1,782	17.6	79.6	59,605
San Luis Obispo-Paso Robles, CA	70	3,999	1,205	2,668	10,587	49.9	8.9	13,634	760	600	2,382	56.7	57.4	12,467
Santa Barbara-Santa Maria, CA	98	8,076	1,633	4,311	10,788	35.4	14.3	20,685	975	841	2,094	32.5	67.0	17,805
Santa Cruz-Watsonville, CA	51	3,970	979	2,618	10,335	32.9	12.2	12,714	606	426	1,683	39.0	78.1	10,060
Santa Fe, NM	39	1,751	910	1,809	13,484	27.2	(NA)	9,196	353	376	2,803	23.4	59.8	7,846
Santa Rosa-Petaluma, CA	119	8,392	1,870	5,732	12,303	38.2	12.8	26,106	1,068	724	1,554	46.9	74.3	15,536
Sarasota-Bradenton-Venice, FL	268	14,233	2,691	7,138	11,508	24.2	13.6	35,068	1,123	877	1,413	21.2	76.3	20,308
Savannah, GA	91	4,028	1,338	3,239	10,748	19.2	(NA)	17,401	733	602	1,997	(NA)	85.0	14,813
Scranton-Wilkes-Barre, PA	236	9,699	2,449	6,174	11,148	22.6	(NA)	33,223	1,293	679	1,226	27.9	85.0	18,742
Seattle-Tacoma-Bellevue, WA	**870**	**56,990**	**11,202**	**37,994**	**12,170**	**25.9**	**14.0**	**160,703**	**7,148**	**5,260**	**1,685**	**21.6**	**79.0**	**114,391**
Seattle-Bellevue-Everett, WA	*673*	*50,272*	*8,953*	*30,905*	*12,928*	*25.1*	*13.2*	*129,881*	*5,904*	*4,478*	*1,873*	*20.3*	*77.3*	*94,616*
Tacoma, WA	*197*	*6,718*	*2,249*	*7,090*	*9,694*	*29.7*	*17.3*	*30,822*	*1,244*	*782*	*1,070*	*29.4*	*88.9*	*19,775*
Sheboygan, WI	42	1,682	423	1,149	10,144	26.2	18.0	6,266	250	139	1,224	30.9	61.9	4,401
Sherman-Denison, TX	41	1,422	468	1,369	12,039	25.3	24.0	5,889	190	116	1,021	10.8	89.1	2,941
Shreveport-Bossier City, LA	104	3,698	1,492	4,078	10,815	24.0	16.9	19,475	592	1,339	3,552	(NA)	27.7	21,407
Sioux City, IA-NE-SD	68	2,042	639	1,309	9,161	29.2	(NA)	12,312	331	190	1,333	29.1	(NA)	5,701
Sioux Falls, SD	120	43,737	961	2,732	14,016	27.1	(NA)	14,360	473	355	1,824	50.6	(NA)	9,370
South Bend-Mishawaka, IN-MI	83	3,215	1,144	3,472	10,938	18.0	19.7	17,580	591	369	1,161	13.3	86.9	10,061
Spartanburg, SC	77	2,716	1,102	2,724	10,503	17.8	13.7	13,809	511	300	1,155	22.7	93.1	8,567
Spokane, WA	124	4,805	1,699	4,868	11,394	18.1	17.7	24,543	908	579	1,354	27.4	80.8	15,060
Springfield, IL	86	4,015	858	2,427	11,888	18.4	(NA)	12,617	524	332	1,628	(NA)	(NA)	8,614
Springfield, MA	217	9,973	2,661	6,810	9,954	28.6	(NA)	36,081	1,430	788	1,151	24.6	88.6	21,024
Springfield, MO	173	6,136	1,775	4,677	12,349	19.5	(NA)	24,197	801	529	1,397	32.0	(NA)	14,980
Springfield, OH	39	1,407	508	1,328	9,233	20.4	16.2	7,228	251	153	1,066	15.4	90.4	4,861
State College, PA	64	1,741	576	1,403	10,123	21.6	15.9	8,520	295	209	1,509	35.1	74.4	6,039
Stockton, CA	107	36,847	1,661	5,474	8,936	48.8	15.9	23,716	938	572	933	51.7	88.2	13,839
Sumter, SC	18	684	455	854	8,114	9.2	13.4	4,930	132	79	749	12.6	89.8	2,372
Syracuse, NY	197	8,107	2,469	6,765	10,387	21.2	12.8	36,216	1,490	823	1,264	25.4	84.8	22,647
Tallahassee, FL	90	4,298	1,272	3,086	9,518	21.8	(NA)	17,961	588	422	1,302	31.7	(NA)	11,366
Tampa-St. Petersburg-Clearwater, FL	694	40,169	9,507	30,090	12,096	24.4	13.1	135,646	4,250	3,587	1,442	21.5	73.9	83,051
Terre Haute, IN	57	2,140	716	2,817	16,610	3.2	(NA)	11,359	374	208	1,227	(NA)	(NA)	6,274
Texarkana, TX-Texarkana, AR	40	1,488	586	1,462	11,168	22.4	(NA)	7,375	207	190	1,450	47.5	92.4	4,103
Toledo, OH	215	8,216	2,528	7,245	10,989	12.6	(NA)	37,700	1,492	982	1,490	18.8	88.0	27,844
Topeka, KS	123	4,054	973	2,199	9,741	20.1	(NA)	12,414	432	333	(NA)	(NA)	(NA)	8,153
Trenton-Ewing, NJ	135	8,847	1,409	4,191	11,719	31.7	10.8	19,525	741	554	1,548	40.6	77.9	10,895
Tucson, AZ	151	8,941	2,818	8,693	9,906	26.8	16.9	43,549	1,599	1,388	1,581	33.2	67.0	35,894
Tulsa, OK	268	13,022	3,242	8,886	10,141	17.4	(NA)	45,071	1,700	1,117	1,275	24.2	(NA)	29,394
Tuscaloosa, AL	53	2,316	851	1,976	10,201	21.4	(NA)	10,662	347	240	1,240	(NA)	(NA)	6,950
Tyler, TX	63	2,650	831	2,332	12,902	24.8	18.4	10,656	297	237	1,309	35.1	88.1	6,465

See footnotes at end of table.

Table B-10. Metropolitan Areas — **Banking, Retail Trade, and Accommodation and Food Services**—Con.

Metropolitan statistical area **Metropolitan statistical area with metropolitan divisions** *Metropolitan division*	Banking,[1] 2004		Retail trade[2] (NAICS 44–45), 2002						Accommodation and food services[2] (NAICS 72), 2002					
				Sales						Sales				
						Percent						Percent		
	Number of offices	Deposits (mil. dol.)	Establishments	Total (mil. dol.)	Per capita[3] (dol.)	Change, 1997–2002	General merchandise stores[4]	Paid employees[5]	Establishments	Total (mil. dol.)	Per capita[3] (dol.)	Change, 1997–2002	Food services[6]	Paid employees[5]
Utica-Rome, NY	87	3,757	1,136	2,744	9,212	27.1	(NA)	14,637	652	278	932	25.8	80.5	7,779
Valdosta, GA	37	1,624	655	1,405	11,610	28.2	(NA)	7,329	225	188	1,554	(NA)	(NA)	5,372
Vallejo-Fairfield, CA	62	3,110	1,124	4,156	10,148	49.0	17.4	17,882	669	434	1,059	48.6	89.6	10,248
Vero Beach, FL	58	3,077	667	1,525	12,922	33.3	17.4	8,504	211	140	1,185	24.5	91.3	3,589
Victoria, TX	28	1,663	462	1,172	10,411	17.6	(NA)	5,638	218	113	1,001	15.6	(NA)	3,310
Vineland-Millville-Bridgeton, NJ	47	1,746	553	1,519	10,259	23.8	11.6	7,008	212	104	705	32.5	89.5	2,644
Virginia Beach-Norfolk-Newport News, VA-NC	355	14,965	6,089	15,642	9,745	23.0	(NA)	84,281	3,078	2,548	(NA)	(NA)	(NA)	63,472
Visalia-Porterville, CA	64	2,831	1,059	2,931	7,687	37.2	18.7	13,275	474	259	678	11.3	89.1	6,620
Waco, TX	46	2,571	818	2,199	10,123	22.3	19.1	10,919	400	293	1,348	32.7	86.5	7,658
Warner Robins, GA	26	974	428	1,218	10,460	29.4	18.9	6,100	201	150	1,291	46.8	83.4	4,085
Washington-Arlington-Alexandria, DC-VA-MD-WV	**1,455**	**119,795**	**16,539**	**55,882**	**11,177**	**30.4**	**(NA)**	**255,349**	**9,249**	**10,052**	**2,011**	**(NA)**	**(NA)**	**189,351**
Bethesda-Gaithersburg-Frederick, MD	*361*	*23,832*	*3,732*	*13,737*	*12,319*	*27.7*	*(NA)*	*59,672*	*1,866*	*1,603*	*1,437*	*27.7*	*80.7*	*33,425*
Washington-Arlington-Alexandria, DC-VA-MD-WV	*1,094*	*95,963*	*12,807*	*42,145*	*10,850*	*31.3*	*10.5*	*195,677*	*7,383*	*8,449*	*2,175*	*(NA)*	*(NA)*	*155,926*
Waterloo-Cedar Falls, IA	64	1,993	715	1,829	11,280	17.9	(NA)	10,602	343	177	1,093	(NA)	(NA)	5,959
Wausau, WI	50	2,041	528	1,844	14,530	29.7	17.9	10,582	273	128	1,009	21.7	85.9	4,328
Weirton-Steubenville, WV-OH	55	1,723	487	949	7,338	14.5	(NA)	5,593	282	101	784	(NA)	(NA)	3,047
Wenatchee, WA	34	1,344	495	1,028	10,229	16.4	22.4	5,329	294	153	1,523	27.1	63.8	3,524
Wheeling, WV-OH	77	2,476	677	1,540	10,195	15.8	15.8	8,931	332	177	1,171	19.9	88.7	5,214
Wichita, KS	230	8,062	2,237	5,792	9,990	17.8	(NA)	29,928	1,187	738	1,273	11.9	85.8	20,773
Wichita Falls, TX	44	1,681	609	1,547	10,382	21.3	(NA)	8,036	277	185	1,241	14.0	(NA)	5,154
Williamsport, PA	49	1,438	553	1,277	10,744	11.1	15.7	7,396	254	118	993	11.2	87.2	3,392
Wilmington, NC	110	4,087	1,535	3,815	13,266	24.8	(NA)	18,211	758	462	1,606	26.9	82.6	12,830
Winchester, VA-WV	53	1,746	516	1,650	15,237	49.5	(NA)	7,396	211	151	1,395	31.7	75.9	3,710
Winston-Salem, NC	127	10,901	1,809	5,166	11,921	23.0	(NA)	23,862	786	576	1,328	(NA)	86.0	15,412
Worcester, MA	226	9,919	2,710	8,093	10,517	29.9	11.2	38,350	1,536	940	1,221	31.2	87.6	22,414
Yakima, WA	58	2,016	800	1,900	8,463	9.1	20.3	9,397	404	203	902	13.4	85.2	4,878
York-Hanover, PA	143	5,282	1,413	3,848	9,873	18.4	18.2	21,490	662	410	1,051	28.5	88.4	11,437
Youngstown-Warren-Boardman, OH-PA	204	7,856	2,537	5,861	9,838	1.5	16.4	32,863	1,191	665	1,116	16.1	91.4	20,016
Yuba City, CA	23	1,306	424	1,115	7,714	31.0	(NA)	5,288	199	111	766	46.0	87.9	3,027
Yuma, AZ	22	1,111	457	1,337	8,021	29.1	22.3	6,516	271	174	1,044	33.4	72.1	4,618

NA Not available.

[1] As of June 30. Covers all FDIC-insured commercial banks and savings institutions.
[2] Includes only establishments with payroll.
[3] Based on resident population estimated as of July 1, 2002.
[4] Represents NAICS code 452.
[5] For pay period including March 12.
[6] Includes full-service restaurants, limited-service eating places, and special food services, and drinking places (alcoholic beverages).
[7] The Denver-Aurora metropolitan statistical area includes Broomfield County. Broomfield County, CO, was formed from parts of Adams, Boulder, Jefferson, and Weld counties on November 15, 2001, and is coextensive with Broomfield city. For the purposes of defining and presenting data for the Denver-Aurora metropolitan statistical area, Broomfield city is treated as if it were a county when data are available to do so. In many cases, the data will not be available.
[8] The portion of Sullivan city in Crawford County, MO, is legally part of the St. Louis, MO-IL MSA. That portion is not included in these figures for the St. Louis MSA.

Note: Covers metropolitan statistical areas and metropolitan divisions and component counties defined by the Office of Management and Budget as of June 6, 2003, and subsequently updated in December 2003 and November 2004. For more information, see OMB Bulletin 05-02 at <http://www.whitehouse.gov/omb/bulletins/fy05/b05-02_appendix.pdf>.

Survey, Census, or Data Collection Method: Banking—Based on surveys of every FDIC-insured bank and savings association as of June 30 each year conducted by the Federal Deposit Insurance Corporation (FDIC) and the Office of Thrift Supervision (OTS); for information, see Internet site <http://www2.fdic.gov/sod/sodPublications.asp?barItem=5>; Retail trade and accommodation and food services—Based on the economic census; for more information, see Appendix B, Limitations of the Data and Methodology, and also <http://www.census.gov/econ/census02>.

Sources: Banking—U.S. Federal Deposit Insurance Corporation (FDIC) and Office of Thrift Supervision (OTS), 2004 Bank and Thrift Branch Office Data Book: Summary of Deposits, <http://www2.fdic.gov/sod/index.asp> (accessed 5 April 2005); Retail trade—U.S. Census Bureau, 1997 and 2002 economic censuses, Geographic Area Series reports, <http://www.census.gov/econ/census02/> (accessed 6 June 2005); Accommodation and food services—U.S. Census Bureau, 1997 and 2002 Geographic Area Series reports, <http://www.census.gov/econ/census02/> (accessed 13 July 2005).

Metropolitan statistical area **Metropolitan statistical area with metropolitan divisions** *Metropolitan division*	Federal funds and grants					Government							
						Earnings				Employment			
	2003					2002				2002			
	Expenditures total (mil. dol.)	Percent change, 2002–2003	Per capita[1] (dol.)	Percent for direct payments to individuals	2000 (mil. dol.)	Total (mil. dol.)	Percent of total earnings	Percent change, 2000–2002	2000 (mil. dol.)	Total	Percent of total employment	Percent change, 2000–2002	2000
Abilene, TX	1,098.1	3.1	6,941	52.5	942.4	812.0	19.5	12.9	719.4	18,472	2.3	−0.2	18,504
Akron, OH	3,705.6	8.2	5,286	62.4	2,970.1	2,208.2	31.7	14.3	1,932.1	50,706	2.3	3.5	49,013
Albany, GA	1,141.8	8.9	7,057	47.6	926.0	617.8	26.2	4.9	589.1	14,594	2.4	−5.8	15,485
Albany-Schenectady-Troy, NY	13,953.9	10.3	16,600	25.5	8,589.9	5,785.6	14.5	9.3	5,292.0	110,085	1.9	0.9	109,153
Albuquerque, NM	7,472.5	8.3	9,747	33.1	5,729.3	3,734.9	20.5	16.4	3,207.8	78,896	2.1	3.7	76,077
Alexandria, LA	1,091.6	10.2	7,465	54.4	818.6	640.0	22.8	18.1	542.1	15,939	2.5	2.4	15,573
Allentown-Bethlehem-Easton, PA-NJ	3,722.0	−1.8	4,838	74.6	3,147.7	1,732.4	44.4	9.9	1,576.7	40,775	2.4	2.6	39,745
Altoona, PA	824.8	5.3	6,471	69.4	718.6	372.7	34.2	5.6	353.0	9,461	2.5	1.9	9,284
Amarillo, TX	1,468.1	−4.6	6,286	46.4	1,866.4	759.2	30.8	8.7	698.4	18,530	2.4	0.6	18,428
Ames, IA	488.6	4.6	6,087	40.4	362.6	788.2	10.2	5.6	746.5	19,266	2.4	−3.0	19,871
Anchorage, AK	3,379.0	5.6	9,959	21.1	2,443.6	2,543.9	13.3	11.6	2,279.8	43,589	1.7	3.7	42,052
Anderson, IN	710.0	2.2	5,414	75.5	608.8	296.6	44.2	6.0	279.9	7,274	2.5	−0.3	7,296
Anderson, SC	770.0	4.4	4,481	74.3	631.7	459.1	37.4	8.2	424.2	12,086	2.6	−1.3	12,248
Ann Arbor, MI	1,943.9	8.4	5,789	39.6	1,558.7	3,019.1	11.1	14.4	2,639.5	69,189	2.3	3.3	66,956
Anniston-Oxford, AL	1,071.0	9.2	9,554	54.4	919.5	560.4	20.0	14.3	490.3	12,158	2.2	0.2	12,130
Appleton, WI	746.2	11.6	3,537	63.6	552.1	488.9	43.2	8.3	451.2	11,926	2.4	1.5	11,753
Asheville, NC	2,242.9	4.4	5,863	68.4	1,864.0	1,041.8	36.7	5.3	989.6	25,901	2.5	−0.4	26,005
Athens-Clarke County, GA	870.5	4.6	5,067	48.9	681.8	1,011.2	17.0	12.2	901.3	22,272	2.2	2.3	21,762
Atlanta-Sandy Springs-Marietta, GA	21,495.8	−7.4	4,668	47.5	18,732.6	14,820.8	31.1	14.5	12,949.0	307,015	2.1	4.8	292,993
Atlantic City, NJ	1,601.4	−7.0	6,069	57.7	1,361.5	1,208.8	21.8	15.4	1,047.8	21,714	1.8	6.1	20,473
Auburn-Opelika, AL	461.3	7.3	3,872	61.8	365.6	554.5	21.5	4.4	530.9	13,717	2.5	−7.4	14,808
Augusta-Richmond County, GA-SC	4,863.6	3.8	9,529	35.5	4,140.7	2,547.3	20.0	9.4	2,329.1	54,590	2.1	−0.8	55,022
Austin-Round Rock, TX	9,516.7	2.3	6,913	31.3	6,731.6	6,666.9	20.6	18.5	5,626.5	147,014	2.2	5.1	139,840
Bakersfield, CA	3,856.0	2.8	5,405	50.2	3,562.6	3,227.4	22.1	13.8	2,835.7	59,797	1.9	4.3	57,331
Baltimore-Towson, MD	22,638.7	15.0	8,617	42.0	18,779.0	14,899.1	17.6	13.9	13,076.0	265,668	1.8	1.4	261,896
Bangor, ME	963.2	6.1	6,506	56.0	795.9	603.1	24.5	11.4	541.2	14,935	2.5	−0.8	15,053
Barnstable Town, MA	1,767.5	9.0	7,716	69.3	1,503.2	729.5	31.4	8.8	670.8	14,959	2.1	−1.1	15,130
Baton Rouge, LA	4,459.7	−0.6	6,181	50.3	3,438.3	2,846.7	25.3	12.0	2,541.7	76,670	2.7	−0.5	77,057
Battle Creek, MI	971.2	5.7	6,992	55.9	800.1	581.4	23.9	4.3	557.3	11,547	2.0	−2.4	11,837
Bay City, MI	582.9	7.7	5,322	71.9	476.9	291.0	37.6	1.5	286.6	6,941	2.4	−3.2	7,173
Beaumont-Port Arthur, TX	2,342.2	7.9	6,117	63.1	2,035.9	1,100.3	34.8	7.8	1,020.7	27,319	2.5	−1.6	27,753
Bellingham, WA	878.8	7.0	4,978	56.3	811.9	562.7	31.4	26.4	445.0	14,203	2.5	8.9	13,048
Bend, OR	532.1	7.4	4,108	74.8	412.1	340.8	38.0	7.3	317.6	7,358	2.2	−5.0	7,747
Billings, MT	781.2	0.8	5,460	58.0	671.0	412.4	34.7	6.1	388.8	9,770	2.4	1.5	9,622
Binghamton, NY	1,889.8	11.7	7,541	48.4	1,669.3	943.7	26.6	5.9	891.2	23,121	2.5	3.1	22,421
Birmingham-Hoover, AL	6,440.5	8.0	5,997	63.3	5,277.7	3,526.2	30.5	7.4	3,282.0	80,275	2.3	−1.0	81,109
Bismarck, ND	789.4	1.5	8,138	40.0	689.4	440.6	22.0	12.4	391.9	11,384	2.6	2.2	11,141
Blacksburg-Christiansburg-Radford, VA	789.5	−0.4	5,235	58.6	626.7	754.1	20.0	8.6	694.5	19,195	2.5	−1.0	19,395
Bloomington, IN	871.6	5.6	4,928	55.2	766.6	835.9	21.2	3.0	811.5	22,557	2.7	−2.9	23,227
Bloomington-Normal, IL	529.3	−12.3	3,374	65.9	435.5	555.9	28.2	9.1	509.4	14,469	2.6	1.0	14,323
Boise City-Nampa, ID	2,542.5	1.9	4,970	49.5	2,037.6	1,638.4	31.2	15.3	1,420.9	39,414	2.4	4.3	37,793
Boston-Cambridge-Quincy, MA-NH	**35,269.1**	**9.3**	**7,961**	**42.7**	**28,586.7**	**16,283.5**	**27.2**	**5.8**	**15,386.4**	**313,789**	**1.9**	**−1.0**	**316,954**
Boston-Quincy, MA	*15,563.4*	*7.5*	*8,562*	*42.6*	*12,861.9*	*8,384.4*	*21.7*	*1.4*	*8,272.2*	*154,572*	*1.8*	*−4.4*	*161,674*
Cambridge-Newton-Framingham, MA	*12,515.4*	*7.7*	*8,534*	*38.0*	*10,117.6*	*4,872.1*	*30.1*	*11.8*	*4,356.6*	*90,061*	*1.8*	*2.5*	*87,886*
Essex County, MA	*5,356.7*	*20.3*	*7,256*	*47.2*	*4,135.3*	*1,979.1*	*37.3*	*7.8*	*1,835.7*	*42,391*	*2.1*	*2.3*	*41,431*
Rockingham County-Strafford County, NH	*1,833.6*	*6.0*	*4,495*	*61.8*	*1,471.9*	*1,047.9*	*38.9*	*13.7*	*921.9*	*26,765*	*2.6*	*3.1*	*25,963*
Boulder, CO[2]	1,864.1	7.6	6,718	34.0	1,499.2	1,353.4	20.5	13.4	1,193.0	28,085	2.1	0.8	27,873
Bowling Green, KY	539.2	−13.8	5,016	61.9	446.0	343.1	31.3	8.7	315.5	9,721	2.8	3.9	9,360
Bremerton-Silverdale, WA	2,809.5	15.6	11,718	32.0	2,366.8	2,557.3	9.4	16.7	2,190.6	41,053	1.6	4.7	39,194
Bridgeport-Stamford-Norwalk, CT	5,777.6	11.5	6,422	48.5	4,483.6	2,642.0	34.1	9.6	2,409.8	48,456	1.8	3.2	46,974
Brownsville-Harlingen, TX	1,665.3	5.1	4,596	50.5	1,354.5	1,041.0	34.8	13.2	919.3	26,768	2.6	2.4	26,150
Brunswick, GA	681.7	−1.9	7,043	57.3	593.5	409.3	23.6	11.3	367.8	8,894	2.2	0.1	8,886
Buffalo-Niagara Falls, NY	7,531.8	7.5	6,504	59.2	6,472.4	4,335.3	26.7	4.6	4,146.6	91,304	2.1	0.8	90,567
Burlington, NC	584.6	6.1	4,279	74.8	481.3	243.5	56.1	9.1	223.1	6,595	2.7	−2.4	6,754
Burlington-South Burlington, VT	1,538.3	15.5	7,560	33.8	1,134.7	857.9	23.7	14.2	751.0	18,815	2.2	2.8	18,309
Canton-Massillon, OH	1,994.1	7.1	4,860	73.0	1,676.7	902.3	45.5	13.1	797.8	22,118	2.5	2.3	21,619
Cape Coral-Fort Myers, FL	2,615.3	5.9	5,310	86.1	2,167.5	1,257.1	39.2	10.4	1,138.4	27,764	2.2	1.1	27,474
Carson City, NV	648.5	6.1	11,722	35.7	489.6	526.5	10.5	12.6	467.4	10,420	2.0	4.4	9,982
Casper, WY	351.1	10.4	5,145	59.5	317.2	226.2	30.2	10.5	204.8	5,611	2.5	−3.0	5,782
Cedar Rapids, IA	1,458.0	3.7	6,008	48.0	1,474.9	650.6	37.3	9.1	596.5	16,240	2.5	−0.1	16,249
Champaign-Urbana, IL	1,081.0	−4.0	5,041	48.9	955.2	1,529.1	14.0	13.1	1,352.1	35,004	2.3	0.7	34,760
Charleston, WV	2,644.6	2.1	8,604	54.2	2,113.3	1,244.0	24.7	9.0	1,141.1	28,725	2.3	−0.5	28,863
Charleston-North Charleston, SC	4,368.1	8.9	7,631	45.7	3,622.7	3,062.7	18.7	10.6	2,770.2	65,694	2.1	0.3	65,520
Charlotte-Gastonia-Concord, NC-SC	5,579.9	7.6	3,877	62.8	4,616.3	4,237.5	34.0	11.7	3,792.4	98,203	2.3	3.4	94,993
Charlottesville, VA	1,106.4	6.2	6,150	50.6	875.3	1,386.5	13.0	13.2	1,224.7	29,867	2.2	4.3	28,636
Chattanooga, TN-GA	3,473.7	1.3	7,140	53.5	3,049.3	1,675.8	29.0	11.3	1,506.0	37,598	2.2	6.0	35,477
Cheyenne, WY	994.4	12.2	11,784	32.2	774.2	762.8	11.1	18.0	646.7	15,867	2.1	0.9	15,730
Chicago-Naperville-Joliet, IL-IN-WI	**46,091.1**	**7.1**	**4,940**	**57.0**	**39,192.9**	**31,018.2**	**30.1**	**7.9**	**28,759.7**	**607,761**	**2.0**	**0.9**	**602,434**
Chicago-Naperville-Joliet, IL	*38,760.4*	*7.0*	*4,966*	*56.6*	*32,949.3*	*25,917.5*	*30.1*	*8.5*	*23,889.3*	*495,451*	*1.9*	*1.4*	*488,714*
Gary, IN	*3,448.3*	*5.8*	*5,023*	*69.3*	*2,866.6*	*1,609.7*	*42.7*	*3.0*	*1,562.1*	*41,658*	*2.6*	*−0.9*	*42,048*
Lake County-Kenosha County, IL-WI	*3,882.3*	*9.1*	*4,631*	*49.6*	*3,377.1*	*3,491.0*	*24.0*	*5.5*	*3,308.2*	*70,652*	*2.0*	*−1.4*	*71,672*

See footnotes at end of table.

Table B-11. Metropolitan Areas — **Government**—Con.

Metropolitan statistical area / **Metropolitan statistical area with metropolitan divisions** / *Metropolitan division*	Federal funds and grants 2003					Government Earnings 2002				Government Employment 2002			
	Expenditures total (mil. dol.)	Percent change, 2002–2003	Per capita[1] (dol.)	Percent for direct payments to individuals	2000 (mil. dol.)	Total (mil. dol.)	Percent of total earnings	Percent change, 2000–2002	2000 (mil. dol.)	Total	Percent of total employment	Percent change, 2000–2002	2000
Chico, CA	1,190.7	3.7	5,639	70.8	997.1	663.4	31.8	10.9	598.0	15,883	2.4	-2.8	16,341
Cincinnati-Middletown, OH-KY-IN	11,587.1	9.4	5,661	52.4	9,717.8	6,124.9	33.4	12.5	5,445.5	136,489	2.2	3.4	132,033
Clarksville, TN-KY	2,494.5	12.6	10,559	31.3	1,950.7	2,158.2	10.9	13.1	1,908.4	43,519	2.0	1.6	42,815
Cleveland, TN	493.8	6.4	4,647	74.2	397.3	220.6	48.2	6.5	207.1	6,209	2.8	-1.0	6,273
Cleveland-Elyria-Mentor, OH	12,708.0	6.2	5,937	62.0	10,697.9	7,490.4	28.6	11.1	6,740.9	150,166	2.0	1.5	147,984
Coeur d'Alene, ID	607.8	-3.7	5,168	61.7	428.8	337.1	34.9	14.5	294.4	8,885	2.6	2.8	8,645
College Station-Bryan, TX	2,029.2	133.0	10,791	21.0	753.4	1,156.0	16.3	12.1	1,030.9	31,731	2.7	3.5	30,652
Colorado Springs, CO	5,294.3	9.5	9,296	34.1	4,023.3	3,680.9	15.5	16.1	3,169.6	70,653	1.9	3.5	68,251
Columbia, MO	769.9	5.2	5,128	53.1	662.5	1,216.1	12.3	6.9	1,137.3	31,282	2.6	-2.1	31,940
Columbia, SC	4,843.8	3.3	7,218	45.6	3,950.0	3,732.8	18.0	1.5	3,678.5	89,610	2.4	-6.8	96,103
Columbus, GA-AL	2,562.4	9.2	9,231	43.5	2,141.1	1,896.3	14.6	12.1	1,691.8	42,827	2.3	2.3	41,877
Columbus, IN	369.7	8.0	5,111	59.1	282.4	223.8	32.3	9.3	204.7	5,600	2.5	-0.1	5,603
Columbus, OH	10,399.2	3.1	6,201	42.9	8,153.0	7,304.6	23.0	22.0	6,495.9	160,513	2.2	2.7	156,251
Corpus Christi, TX	2,722.5	8.8	6,702	50.1	2,312.9	1,755.3	23.1	8.1	1,623.9	38,180	2.2	-1.4	38,734
Corvallis, OR	393.4	9.3	4,967	50.5	319.9	493.6	16.0	19.4	413.3	12,399	2.5	11.5	11,122
Cumberland, MD-WV	713.2	10.3	7,063	69.1	665.2	349.4	28.9	11.9	312.2	8,114	2.3	-1.1	8,204
Dallas-Fort Worth-Arlington, TX	**32,528.1**	**30.5**	**5,823**	**36.0**	**22,214.4**	**15,902.8**	**35.1**	**15.2**	**13,809.5**	**345,513**	**2.2**	**4.4**	**331,051**
Dallas-Plano-Irving, TX	*16,046.8*	*5.5*	*4,294*	*46.3*	*12,827.4*	*10,979.3*	*34.0*	*16.1*	*9,458.7*	*236,357*	*2.2*	*5.3*	*224,358*
Fort Worth-Arlington, TX	*16,481.3*	*69.5*	*8,915*	*25.9*	*9,387.0*	*4,923.5*	*37.5*	*13.2*	*4,350.8*	*109,156*	*2.2*	*2.3*	*106,693*
Dalton, GA	436.0	2.2	3,422	73.2	370.2	275.7	46.2	13.8	242.2	7,322	2.7	4.5	7,009
Danville, IL	529.3	-2.6	6,386	65.7	460.1	290.9	28.5	5.8	275.0	6,423	2.2	-1.0	6,491
Danville, VA	611.4	2.0	5,621	66.6	501.8	243.8	44.6	9.6	222.5	6,795	2.8	3.1	6,591
Davenport-Moline-Rock Island, IA-IL	2,115.3	0.3	5,642	63.4	1,864.0	1,333.1	28.1	7.5	1,239.9	28,609	2.1	-0.6	28,787
Dayton, OH	6,883.7	6.3	8,141	44.7	6,038.0	4,089.1	20.7	9.6	3,729.4	73,124	1.8	0.7	72,643
Decatur, AL	742.6	-0.9	5,039	67.7	661.3	348.2	42.3	8.2	321.8	9,635	2.8	0.6	9,578
Decatur, IL	599.4	-2.7	5,384	72.0	526.5	249.3	44.7	2.7	242.7	6,869	2.8	-4.0	7,157
Deltona-Daytona Beach-Ormond Beach, FL	2,878.3	8.2	6,155	78.0	2,332.3	930.3	50.3	7.4	866.1	22,226	2.4	0.1	22,200
Denver-Aurora, CO[2]	12,713.9	5.9	5,523	42.2	11,190.0	8,975.2	25.6	14.3	7,852.1	176,309	2.0	4.5	168,656
Des Moines, IA	2,986.2	-4.7	5,930	49.1	2,414.4	1,873.2	26.9	9.2	1,715.4	40,834	2.2	0.4	40,685
Detroit-Warren-Livonia, MI	**24,589.7**	**4.6**	**5,480**	**62.3**	**20,612.1**	**12,634.5**	**35.5**	**6.8**	**11,832.8**	**251,742**	**2.0**	**-0.2**	**252,278**
Detroit-Livonia-Dearborn, MI	*13,268.4*	*4.1*	*6,539*	*59.5*	*11,467.2*	*6,639.0*	*30.6*	*4.3*	*6,362.2*	*129,961*	*2.0*	*-2.6*	*133,433*
Warren-Farmington Hills-Troy, MI	*11,321.3*	*5.2*	*4,606*	*65.5*	*9,144.9*	*5,995.6*	*41.0*	*9.6*	*5,470.6*	*121,781*	*2.0*	*2.5*	*118,845*
Dothan, AL	879.3	16.5	6,581	61.0	670.2	376.7	35.5	12.3	335.3	10,552	2.8	2.5	10,297
Dover, DE	1,158.7	10.6	8,609	41.2	904.3	1,005.7	13.4	15.9	867.8	20,575	2.0	1.4	20,295
Dubuque, IA	438.3	2.0	4,843	67.6	355.3	160.4	56.4	8.3	148.1	4,342	2.7	0.1	4,336
Duluth, MN-WI	1,785.9	6.8	6,463	60.0	1,449.1	1,167.1	23.7	8.5	1,075.9	27,753	2.4	-3.2	28,682
Durham, NC	3,391.3	8.7	7,613	34.2	2,555.9	2,558.1	17.4	11.7	2,289.4	52,486	2.1	2.4	51,246
Eau Claire, WI	701.9	7.1	4,639	63.5	556.2	486.6	31.1	6.2	458.4	12,088	2.5	-0.6	12,166
El Centro, CA	765.9	3.5	5,143	50.6	648.1	782.0	19.0	20.3	650.1	16,230	2.1	9.4	14,841
Elizabethtown, KY	1,013.4	6.0	9,293	42.9	968.5	1,030.7	10.6	2.1	1,009.8	21,240	2.1	-7.2	22,893
Elkhart-Goshen, IN	594.4	4.9	3,145	75.7	497.0	326.1	58.0	7.3	304.0	8,279	2.5	3.6	7,989
Elmira, NY	539.2	3.5	5,973	63.7	462.3	344.0	26.2	9.5	314.1	7,390	2.1	-5.1	7,784
El Paso, TX	4,317.6	12.0	6,145	46.3	3,368.2	3,082.5	22.8	12.0	2,751.1	69,152	2.2	1.9	67,870
Erie, PA	1,512.9	8.0	5,345	66.8	1,268.2	738.1	38.3	6.7	692.0	17,630	2.4	0.8	17,494
Eugene-Springfield, OR	1,741.0	7.9	5,273	64.0	1,404.0	1,143.4	28.9	10.3	1,036.4	26,634	2.3	-2.0	27,174
Evansville, IN-KY	1,888.2	4.1	5,448	64.2	1,584.6	717.1	48.3	3.6	692.0	18,554	2.6	-1.0	18,746
Fairbanks, AK	1,142.2	-1.2	13,403	14.8	915.8	1,021.5	8.3	15.2	886.9	19,035	1.9	6.0	17,951
Fargo, ND-MN	901.8	-3.2	5,040	49.2	773.6	634.4	28.2	9.7	578.2	16,201	2.6	-0.9	16,352
Farmington, NM	575.5	-0.9	4,699	49.8	466.8	428.5	28.6	11.9	382.8	11,604	2.7	4.4	11,114
Fayetteville, NC	4,296.1	10.8	12,461	27.4	3,449.8	4,305.4	8.0	14.7	3,753.4	80,905	1.9	3.4	78,211
Fayetteville-Springdale-Rogers, AR-MO	1,396.1	5.1	3,689	72.6	1,168.3	898.0	42.1	12.5	798.4	23,870	2.7	3.7	23,017
Flagstaff, AZ	799.3	5.0	6,596	42.0	635.7	696.0	17.4	11.9	622.3	16,168	2.3	2.8	15,727
Flint, MI	2,292.2	4.1	5,178	71.3	1,941.7	1,187.0	37.3	2.3	1,160.1	26,547	2.2	-2.2	27,149
Florence, SC	1,120.2	6.5	5,703	61.1	890.6	641.9	30.6	7.9	594.9	16,936	2.6	-0.7	17,048
Florence-Muscle Shoals, AL	940.5	4.3	6,633	67.0	792.3	536.3	26.4	5.1	510.4	12,832	2.4	-3.0	13,231
Fond du Lac, WI	423.8	7.1	4,317	71.0	356.6	240.1	40.9	8.5	221.3	6,154	2.6	0.1	6,145
Fort Collins-Loveland, CO	1,088.2	10.6	4,082	54.3	844.6	1,165.0	22.9	17.3	992.9	25,872	2.2	2.9	25,154
Fort Smith, AR-OK	1,482.5	3.9	5,297	68.2	1,203.0	619.1	45.2	8.6	570.2	16,799	2.7	1.3	16,576
Fort Walton Beach-Crestview-Destin, FL	2,939.9	13.4	16,532	31.7	2,143.5	1,851.3	9.6	18.8	1,558.9	30,599	1.7	5.1	29,101
Fort Wayne, IN	1,978.8	-1.6	4,945	55.3	1,657.0	921.2	43.4	6.0	869.6	22,372	2.4	-0.1	22,385
Fresno, CA	4,074.2	7.9	4,789	50.5	3,411.7	3,160.6	26.9	16.7	2,708.1	66,651	2.1	5.3	63,286
Gadsden, AL	627.0	6.0	6,081	76.8	520.1	205.2	50.3	3.4	198.4	5,771	2.8	-4.5	6,043
Gainesville, FL	1,419.8	1.4	5,982	50.6	1,169.8	1,763.3	13.5	8.8	1,620.8	44,524	2.5	3.1	43,177
Gainesville, GA	565.8	4.2	3,619	64.4	430.4	351.6	44.5	17.2	299.9	9,112	2.6	7.0	8,514
Glens Falls, NY	636.3	8.4	5,016	67.4	522.6	427.8	29.7	7.2	399.1	10,350	2.4	1.1	10,241
Goldsboro, NC	903.9	3.5	7,971	66.9	763.3	644.1	17.6	9.4	588.6	14,419	2.2	-0.1	14,434
Grand Forks, ND-MN	796.2	-2.3	8,315	33.3	704.9	635.8	15.1	12.9	563.0	15,540	2.4	1.1	15,377
Grand Junction, CO	641.2	6.0	5,140	67.5	543.6	374.1	33.4	11.1	336.8	8,447	2.3	-0.3	8,476
Grand Rapids-Wyoming, MI	2,935.8	0.4	3,849	65.4	2,547.5	1,787.6	42.7	5.6	1,692.3	38,624	2.2	0.2	38,532
Great Falls, MT	768.2	6.9	9,629	63.2	661.3	461.0	11.8	9.5	411.8	9,367	2.0	0.7	9,305
Greeley, CO[2]	651.9	2.8	3,077	61.3	528.4	474.2	44.7	16.5	406.8	13,125	2.8	4.4	12,569
Green Bay, WI	1,141.8	-2.4	3,912	63.4	995.3	848.3	34.4	8.8	779.5	20,442	2.4	1.0	20,235
Greensboro-High Point, NC	3,184.2	7.4	4,809	62.1	2,635.0	1,749.0	37.9	6.5	1,643.0	42,257	2.4	-1.7	42,987
Greenville, NC	723.9	1.8	4,566	60.6	605.8	878.2	18.1	8.0	813.2	20,297	2.3	2.3	19,842

See footnotes at end of table.

Table B-11. Metropolitan Areas — **Government**—Con.

Metropolitan statistical area / **Metropolitan statistical area with metropolitan divisions** / *Metropolitan division*	Federal funds and grants 2003 Expenditures total (mil. dol.)	Per cent change, 2002–2003	Per capita[1] (dol.)	Per cent for direct payments to individuals	2000 (mil. dol.)	Government Earnings 2002 Total (mil. dol.)	Per cent of total earnings	Per cent change, 2000–2002	2000 (mil. dol.)	Government Employment 2002 Total	Per cent of total employment	Per cent change, 2000–2002	2000
Greenville, SC	2,791.5	16.5	4,828	61.4	2,131.8	1,712.8	33.8	11.5	1,536.4	41,615	2.4	2.3	40,687
Gulfport-Biloxi, MS	2,462.4	6.5	9,863	42.8	2,100.8	1,771.0	14.1	12.2	1,578.5	36,027	2.0	1.3	35,559
Hagerstown-Martinsburg, MD-WV	1,326.1	12.7	5,573	60.2	1,150.2	793.7	30.0	9.8	722.7	16,033	2.0	-0.8	16,164
Hanford-Corcoran, CA	776.8	8.1	5,600	37.1	677.0	880.4	15.8	23.2	714.3	18,065	2.1	11.6	16,185
Harrisburg-Carlisle, PA	5,971.9	0.3	11,546	39.1	4,659.7	3,362.7	15.4	10.1	3,053.9	67,027	2.0	2.4	65,484
Harrisonburg, VA	398.7	15.6	3,607	77.3	308.4	333.7	33.1	6.9	312.1	9,386	2.8	2.3	9,175
Hartford-West Hartford-East Hartford, CT	10,751.0	17.0	9,112	37.5	6,343.7	5,404.1	21.8	10.0	4,910.6	98,316	1.8	1.8	96,602
Hattiesburg, MS	663.5	(Z)	5,171	65.9	557.3	532.3	24.1	6.5	499.8	15,808	3.0	2.3	15,458
Hickory-Lenoir-Morganton, NC	1,505.3	14.4	4,293	68.8	1,115.2	851.8	41.2	3.6	822.2	23,596	2.8	-1.8	24,019
Hinesville-Fort Stewart, GA	339.7	12.6	4,815	49.5	247.9	1,131.8	6.2	11.6	1,014.5	22,302	2.0	0.7	22,148
Holland-Grand Haven, MI	801.3	5.2	3,211	68.3	684.7	625.1	39.9	11.6	560.2	14,719	2.4	4.4	14,095
Honolulu, HI	9,056.3	8.7	10,137	34.1	7,249.7	7,676.5	11.6	15.1	6,669.1	143,976	1.9	2.8	140,028
Hot Springs, AR	628.3	6.1	6,890	80.6	537.7	190.5	47.9	14.8	165.9	4,913	2.6	5.3	4,664
Houma-Bayou Cane-Thibodaux, LA	978.7	13.2	4,954	64.0	763.9	463.1	42.7	7.2	432.1	14,967	3.2	-1.1	15,134
Houston-Sugar Land-Baytown, TX	24,184.0	14.1	4,767	43.8	19,689.3	14,936.3	34.0	12.7	13,257.6	335,546	2.2	2.9	326,211
Huntington-Ashland, WV-KY-OH	1,981.8	7.0	6,906	64.6	1,666.1	831.1	34.5	4.5	795.4	19,835	2.4	-5.0	20,882
Huntsville, AL	7,123.9	11.5	19,921	18.0	5,019.9	2,606.3	13.7	12.0	2,327.2	43,377	1.7	0.9	42,984
Idaho Falls, ID	1,421.0	12.5	13,223	19.1	1,276.3	275.3	39.0	9.2	252.2	6,888	2.5	-0.2	6,900
Indianapolis, IN	9,500.1	6.7	5,935	50.9	7,520.6	5,363.5	29.8	8.5	4,942.5	117,320	2.2	2.1	114,941
Iowa City, IA	746.2	-2.7	5,482	38.0	645.7	1,432.1	9.5	9.6	1,306.8	30,790	2.1	1.8	30,241
Ithaca, NY	607.2	2.2	6,108	38.9	513.3	273.2	36.4	7.5	254.2	6,532	2.4	-0.7	6,577
Jackson, MI	722.6	2.6	4,446	73.0	617.4	481.9	33.7	9.0	442.0	10,744	2.2	2.3	10,503
Jackson, MS	3,792.0	2.4	7,431	45.0	3,091.9	2,211.8	23.1	5.2	2,102.2	58,767	2.7	-0.3	58,938
Jackson, TN	577.7	5.1	5,278	63.6	481.5	460.1	23.8	9.2	421.2	12,263	2.7	2.7	11,945
Jacksonville, FL	8,596.7	17.8	7,180	48.4	6,603.9	5,031.0	23.8	11.9	4,496.5	94,797	1.9	3.5	91,549
Jacksonville, NC	2,079.2	19.0	13,720	21.8	1,592.6	2,391.9	6.3	14.8	2,084.1	52,243	2.2	7.2	48,744
Janesville, WI	745.5	4.6	4,811	61.1	582.1	380.0	40.8	5.9	358.9	9,349	2.5	0.2	9,330
Jefferson City, MO	1,792.9	-0.9	12,524	33.3	1,308.6	1,081.6	13.2	6.7	1,014.0	28,125	2.6	2.8	27,353
Johnson City, TN	1,720.2	53.1	9,236	42.7	1,002.0	579.4	32.1	8.2	535.6	15,387	2.7	1.4	15,173
Johnstown, PA	1,203.8	5.6	8,047	63.6	1,061.8	427.7	35.0	5.2	406.7	10,416	2.4	-1.9	10,620
Jonesboro, AR	623.1	-8.6	5,658	58.8	532.5	290.3	37.9	8.5	267.6	8,368	2.9	0.9	8,291
Joplin, MO	951.7	1.5	5,865	58.4	963.8	312.2	52.0	9.1	286.2	9,613	3.1	2.0	9,422
Kalamazoo-Portage, MI	1,435.2	2.8	4,488	65.0	1,225.3	1,020.6	31.3	9.3	933.5	23,549	2.3	-5.0	24,784
Kankakee-Bradley, IL	522.8	-0.2	4,920	71.8	469.3	270.0	39.4	7.2	251.9	6,619	2.5	-0.5	6,654
Kansas City, MO-KS	11,732.3	6.8	6,155	50.9	9,272.1	7,322.2	26.0	10.7	6,611.8	156,844	2.1	1.6	154,436
Kennewick-Richland-Pasco, WA	3,225.0	4.7	15,342	15.6	2,250.4	774.7	27.1	14.9	674.1	15,676	2.0	5.3	14,892
Killeen-Temple-Fort Hood, TX	3,881.6	13.5	11,285	27.7	3,093.5	3,599.8	9.6	13.3	3,178.4	73,851	2.1	3.1	71,633
Kingsport-Bristol-Bristol, TN-VA	1,775.8	-1.3	5,918	69.7	1,404.7	593.0	50.6	6.3	557.7	16,502	2.8	-0.6	16,594
Kingston, NY	863.2	7.1	4,758	65.5	705.3	647.0	28.0	5.0	616.0	14,704	2.3	1.9	14,427
Knoxville, TN	6,523.6	8.4	10,183	36.2	5,239.8	2,195.0	29.2	10.5	1,985.7	54,175	2.5	4.4	51,901
Kokomo, IN	485.1	-1.3	4,788	75.5	415.6	285.3	35.5	7.7	264.9	7,792	2.7	-0.5	7,832
La Crosse, WI-MN	629.7	13.5	4,900	58.7	479.8	412.5	31.2	6.5	387.5	10,889	2.6	-0.2	10,912
Lafayette, IN	743.1	-4.5	4,105	57.5	652.9	926.9	19.5	9.1	849.4	22,972	2.5	0.7	22,802
Lafayette, LA	1,030.2	4.4	4,221	62.6	843.6	611.9	39.9	11.2	550.3	15,420	2.5	-3.2	15,933
Lake Charles, LA	1,075.7	13.1	5,548	60.6	748.7	517.1	37.5	11.5	463.7	15,135	2.9	-0.9	15,277
Lakeland, FL	2,549.2	9.7	4,990	77.8	2,037.4	1,225.7	41.7	19.3	1,027.8	28,355	2.3	-0.6	28,515
Lancaster, PA	1,972.5	4.2	4,083	72.0	1,677.2	905.7	53.3	9.7	826.0	21,534	2.4	4.2	20,660
Lansing-East Lansing, MI	4,230.9	-4.7	9,315	40.0	3,316.7	2,950.8	15.4	6.8	2,762.3	60,840	2.1	0.0	60,822
Laredo, TX	896.2	7.2	4,213	44.5	721.9	715.9	29.7	16.7	613.5	17,448	2.4	7.7	16,194
Las Cruces, NM	1,241.1	4.3	6,799	42.5	1,001.6	829.2	22.0	13.0	734.0	20,255	2.4	6.1	19,087
Las Vegas-Paradise, NV	7,170.4	10.8	4,552	59.4	5,311.4	4,713.6	33.4	15.7	4,075.1	85,978	1.8	8.7	79,105
Lawrence, KS	398.2	6.7	3,903	52.8	312.8	555.9	18.4	12.2	495.5	16,402	3.0	0.5	16,315
Lawton, OK	1,286.5	3.0	11,664	51.5	1,166.4	1,208.3	9.1	9.4	1,104.8	25,623	2.1	-0.1	25,641
Lebanon, PA	746.9	9.7	6,070	59.3	575.8	330.6	37.2	8.6	304.4	7,416	2.2	1.6	7,299
Lewiston, ID-WA	373.5	-2.1	6,409	63.8	314.5	193.6	30.1	5.7	183.1	5,332	2.8	-3.4	5,521
Lewiston-Auburn, ME	597.3	9.0	5,628	64.7	507.0	234.2	45.3	14.1	205.3	6,083	2.6	2.6	5,931
Lexington-Fayette, KY	2,271.1	11.2	5,396	53.1	2,222.0	1,865.6	22.9	9.5	1,703.0	42,567	2.3	-2.0	43,442
Lima, OH	711.3	5.6	6,641	72.2	596.9	336.2	31.9	9.3	307.7	7,947	2.4	-0.6	7,998
Lincoln, NE	1,705.6	0.8	6,167	43.8	1,362.8	1,435.7	19.3	15.2	1,246.5	33,139	2.3	2.3	32,395
Little Rock-North Little Rock, AR	4,694.0	10.2	7,459	47.2	3,512.1	3,200.9	19.7	12.2	2,854.0	70,602	2.2	2.8	68,696
Logan, UT-ID	407.1	7.9	3,756	50.9	302.6	374.3	29.0	13.9	328.6	10,710	2.9	4.6	10,236
Longview, TX	992.1	6.2	4,990	74.7	854.0	407.5	48.8	7.8	378.0	11,905	2.9	1.9	11,684
Longview, WA	487.3	1.8	5,121	69.4	420.9	248.0	38.4	12.2	221.0	5,983	2.4	2.8	5,820
Los Angeles-Long Beach-Santa Ana, CA	68,977.7	8.1	5,380	46.1	56,535.0	42,396.7	30.2	13.9	37,220.9	793,551	1.9	3.5	766,709
Los Angeles-Long Beach-Glendale, CA	56,540.1	6.9	5,734	43.7	46,940.7	34,084.3	28.9	13.4	30,049.4	630,333	1.8	3.6	608,253
Santa Ana-Anaheim-Irvine, CA	12,437.5	14.4	4,202	56.7	9,594.3	8,312.4	35.6	15.9	7,171.5	163,218	2.0	3.0	158,456
Louisville, KY-IN	8,223.1	12.0	6,909	47.1	5,445.9	3,370.4	35.3	8.3	3,110.9	76,856	2.3	-4.8	80,769
Lubbock, TX	1,283.8	7.8	5,000	63.6	1,315.9	1,062.5	24.2	9.2	972.9	24,604	2.3	1.2	24,323
Lynchburg, VA	1,766.2	33.7	7,635	48.6	1,291.9	520.1	44.5	5.6	492.5	14,870	2.9	0.2	14,835
Macon, GA	1,420.3	7.5	6,266	62.3	1,143.1	621.0	36.5	10.7	560.9	15,752	2.5	2.6	15,357
Madera, CA	522.3	4.4	3,907	66.4	436.8	345.5	38.7	9.9	314.5	8,310	2.4	5.0	7,918
Madison, WI	3,794.9	0.1	7,227	36.3	2,952.1	3,662.8	14.3	10.8	3,305.2	78,701	2.1	1.4	77,629

See footnotes at end of table.

State and Metropolitan Area Data Book: 2006

U.S. Census Bureau

Table B-11. Metropolitan Areas — **Government**—Con.

Metropolitan statistical area **Metropolitan statistical area with metropolitan divisions** *Metropolitan division*	Federal funds and grants 2003					Government — Earnings 2002				Government — Employment 2002			
	Expenditures total (mil. dol.)	Percent change, 2002-2003	Per capita[1] (dol.)	Percent for direct payments to individuals	2000 (mil. dol.)	Total (mil. dol.)	Percent of total earnings	Percent change, 2000-2002	2000 (mil. dol.)	Total	Percent of total employment	Percent change, 2000-2002	2000
Manchester-Nashua, NH	2,137.2	2.3	5,409	49.6	1,769.1	1,028.1	38.4	14.1	901.0	21,808	2.1	5.8	20,614
Mansfield, OH	635.3	3.4	4,954	68.6	533.7	418.5	30.6	16.1	360.5	10,006	2.4	4.8	9,552
McAllen-Edinburg-Mission, TX	2,608.3	10.8	4,105	48.7	1,940.3	1,652.6	38.4	14.9	1,438.2	44,689	2.7	5.2	42,480
Medford, OR	1,013.2	5.7	5,322	68.5	851.8	525.8	36.2	9.7	479.4	11,544	2.2	-4.2	12,051
Memphis, TN-MS-AR	8,480.1	14.8	6,845	44.4	6,731.6	4,489.9	27.6	13.0	3,973.5	98,314	2.2	3.0	95,408
Merced, CA	964.5	8.2	4,168	58.7	815.8	596.7	38.8	19.0	501.4	14,223	2.4	4.0	13,681
Miami-Fort Lauderdale-Miami Beach, FL	29,054.8	8.9	5,505	68.9	25,359.5	15,844.9	33.3	9.1	14,527.3	315,357	2.0	3.7	304,020
Fort Lauderdale-Pompano Beach-Deerfield Beach, FL	8,104.9	5.9	4,688	79.2	6,803.2	4,755.7	36.4	9.2	4,355.8	96,862	2.0	4.4	92,742
Miami-Miami Beach-Kendall, FL	14,036.7	18.1	6,008	56.8	11,639.0	8,193.3	28.5	10.7	7,403.3	156,697	1.9	3.7	151,074
West Palm Beach-Boca Raton-Boynton Beach, FL	6,913.2	-3.2	5,702	81.5	6,917.2	2,895.9	41.9	4.6	2,768.1	61,798	2.1	2.6	60,204
Michigan City-La Porte, IN	494.0	1.1	4,501	74.8	419.3	304.0	36.1	4.0	292.2	8,144	2.7	0.5	8,107
Midland, TX	427.6	4.6	3,597	75.2	353.5	343.5	34.6	11.1	309.3	8,657	2.5	0.2	8,641
Milwaukee-Waukesha-West Allis, WI	7,963.1	6.5	5,261	59.8	6,783.3	4,647.9	32.6	6.1	4,380.5	97,051	2.1	-0.1	97,151
Minneapolis-St. Paul-Bloomington, MN-WI	14,802.0	4.6	4,798	48.9	12,495.1	11,592.9	26.6	10.2	10,518.4	236,385	2.0	0.5	235,287
Missoula, MT	540.5	8.5	5,486	50.7	451.1	401.0	24.6	15.1	348.5	10,099	2.5	10.2	9,165
Mobile, AL	2,320.3	3.8	5,801	67.2	2,016.9	1,240.6	32.2	7.8	1,150.7	30,741	2.5	-0.4	30,870
Modesto, CA	2,046.9	8.3	4,169	62.7	1,650.5	1,294.1	37.9	16.5	1,110.9	27,435	2.1	5.7	25,948
Monroe, LA	897.7	6.0	5,258	65.6	748.4	505.4	33.8	9.3	462.2	14,992	3.0	-0.3	15,034
Monroe, MI	574.9	4.3	3,810	76.8	471.3	296.2	50.9	10.6	267.7	6,822	2.3	1.7	6,705
Montgomery, AL	3,741.8	1.8	10,603	49.9	3,084.4	2,215.2	15.9	12.2	1,975.1	44,495	2.0	0.8	44,126
Morgantown, WV	783.9	8.1	6,906	46.8	762.9	766.3	14.8	6.6	718.6	18,067	2.4	-0.4	18,131
Morristown, TN	666.5	5.5	5,232	71.5	534.8	225.4	56.5	7.8	209.1	6,767	3.0	-1.1	6,843
Mount Vernon-Anacortes, WA	539.0	-1.7	4,934	72.2	451.9	395.0	27.7	8.9	362.8	10,091	2.6	2.4	9,857
Muncie, IN	596.1	6.2	5,033	68.2	489.8	414.3	28.6	6.1	390.3	11,088	2.7	2.2	10,850
Muskegon-Norton Shores, MI	877.4	-12.6	5,063	66.4	742.1	441.6	39.2	6.9	413.0	9,944	2.3	0.3	9,917
Myrtle Beach-Conway-North Myrtle Beach, SC	1,023.4	9.4	4,850	70.8	848.7	494.5	42.7	12.9	438.0	12,208	2.5	2.0	11,969
Napa, CA	702.1	11.3	5,329	72.2	563.3	467.5	28.2	16.5	401.3	9,806	2.1	3.0	9,524
Naples-Marco Island, FL	1,224.6	4.3	4,280	86.2	996.0	537.7	53.2	17.8	456.4	12,079	2.2	10.1	10,974
Nashville-Davidson-Murfreesboro, TN	7,838.1	3.7	5,712	51.4	6,257.1	3,958.5	34.7	9.9	3,600.4	91,789	2.3	0.7	91,185
New Haven-Milford, CT	5,199.6	5.6	6,179	58.4	4,365.2	2,762.2	30.5	9.3	2,527.4	51,571	1.9	-3.2	53,273
New Orleans-Metairie-Kenner, LA	9,928.6	9.2	7,546	49.0	8,867.1	4,941.4	26.6	12.5	4,392.5	113,947	2.3	-1.1	115,190
New York-Northern New Jersey-Long Island, NY-NJ-PA	112,902.7	6.5	6,047	54.3	95,044.1	73,701.0	25.3	8.1	68,209.5	1,278,525	1.7	0.6	1,271,253
Edison, NJ	12,349.9	10.0	5,441	62.1	10,080.0	7,909.6	28.7	9.0	7,255.7	143,110	1.8	0.3	142,653
Nassau-Suffolk, NY	16,001.4	7.3	5,697	62.1	13,398.1	11,100.6	25.3	7.6	10,316.2	189,942	1.7	1.1	187,879
Newark-Union, NJ-PA	11,184.6	4.6	5,219	58.7	9,653.3	9,223.1	23.2	11.3	8,285.7	158,867	1.7	2.2	155,411
New York-White Plains-Wayne, NY-NJ	73,366.8	6.0	6,409	50.6	61,912.8	45,467.8	25.2	7.4	42,351.9	786,606	1.7	0.2	785,310
Niles-Benton Harbor, MI	876.4	1.4	5,381	69.5	752.7	355.3	45.8	4.0	341.5	8,952	2.5	-4.6	9,388
Norwich-New London, CT	3,993.7	12.3	15,060	23.5	2,422.2	2,325.9	11.4	16.4	1,997.9	49,138	2.1	7.6	45,680
Ocala, FL	1,647.3	5.4	5,859	85.4	1,393.8	586.3	48.0	4.3	562.0	15,809	2.7	0.7	15,697
Ocean City, NJ	688.1	8.2	6,757	74.6	589.4	449.1	22.7	11.9	401.3	10,133	2.3	-0.1	10,148
Odessa, TX	500.9	10.6	4,071	73.2	405.7	361.9	34.0	8.8	332.7	9,484	2.6	-2.3	9,707
Ogden-Clearfield, UT	3,912.2	16.0	8,346	32.1	2,743.0	2,537.6	18.5	17.7	2,155.1	50,695	2.0	7.3	47,246
Oklahoma City, OK	8,762.5	-0.5	7,732	43.8	7,283.5	6,030.1	18.8	11.5	5,406.3	121,726	2.0	1.2	120,243
Olympia, WA	2,283.3	-2.6	10,333	38.3	1,645.1	1,763.8	12.5	10.7	1,593.8	36,053	2.0	1.4	35,556
Omaha-Council Bluffs, NE-IA	4,535.7	3.3	5,723	51.8	3,824.5	3,145.9	25.2	11.6	2,818.7	66,285	2.1	1.8	65,130
Orlando-Kissimee, FL	9,792.0	7.8	5,433	59.3	8,118.7	4,515.5	39.9	8.6	4,158.3	103,628	2.3	6.7	97,161
Oshkosh-Neenah, WI	1,239.0	4.0	7,815	35.8	966.1	502.4	31.6	8.1	464.8	12,384	2.5	0.8	12,281
Owensboro, KY	555.0	3.0	5,007	70.4	453.0	336.2	33.0	9.2	307.9	9,352	2.8	1.3	9,236
Oxnard-Thousand Oaks-Ventura, CA	4,065.6	5.8	5,143	50.9	3,328.3	2,845.1	27.8	13.6	2,505.3	51,544	1.8	4.0	49,544
Palm Bay-Melbourne-Titusville, FL	5,545.5	8.9	10,965	45.9	4,311.9	1,536.0	32.9	12.1	1,370.7	30,317	2.0	3.0	29,443
Panama City-Lynn Haven, FL	1,324.0	4.6	8,548	54.3	1,257.0	802.1	19.3	14.0	703.5	15,128	1.9	3.7	14,592
Parkersburg-Marietta-Vienna, WV-OH	1,058.9	1.3	6,484	62.2	892.7	484.9	33.7	8.4	447.3	10,980	2.3	-1.3	11,126
Pascagoula, MS	2,146.5	-1.9	13,914	25.1	1,487.3	545.9	28.3	7.7	506.8	13,875	2.5	0.6	13,786
Pensacola-Ferry Pass-Brent, FL	3,501.6	11.1	8,157	54.8	2,793.7	2,302.6	18.6	10.0	2,093.3	45,156	2.0	0.4	44,997
Peoria, IL	1,916.7	0.1	5,235	65.1	1,697.1	917.7	39.9	8.7	844.6	22,474	2.4	1.0	22,250
Philadelphia-Camden-Wilmington, PA-NJ-DE-MD	38,985.6	6.6	6,754	55.2	32,417.5	19,494.9	29.6	9.6	17,790.8	371,416	1.9	0.8	368,304
Camden, NJ	7,746.7	10.1	6,318	53.1	6,334.4	4,615.4	26.6	11.8	4,127.2	89,248	1.9	2.6	86,979
Philadelphia, PA	27,814.7	5.8	7,181	54.9	23,314.9	12,600.5	30.7	8.3	11,639.0	234,460	1.9	0.3	233,812
Wilmington, DE-MD-NJ	3,424.1	6.3	5,088	62.5	2,768.2	2,279.1	29.5	12.6	2,024.6	47,708	2.1	0.4	47,513
Phoenix-Mesa-Scottsdale, AZ	20,089.6	9.6	5,591	49.3	14,468.1	9,964.7	36.1	16.4	8,561.9	218,635	2.2	6.2	205,894
Pine Bluff, AR	951.4	12.6	8,955	42.4	767.0	430.3	24.7	11.7	385.2	10,576	2.5	1.3	10,444
Pittsburgh, PA	18,584.8	5.7	7,713	62.0	16,121.0	6,536.9	36.9	8.1	6,046.3	137,743	2.1	-0.4	138,275
Pittsfield, MA	1,087.9	5.5	8,175	53.5	862.8	334.2	39.8	3.2	323.9	8,433	2.5	0.4	8,403
Pocatello, ID	403.2	-7.7	4,867	61.2	343.4	360.4	23.0	10.5	326.1	9,822	2.7	0.1	9,816
Portland-South Portland-Biddeford, ME	3,818.9	6.9	7,527	43.8	3,015.1	2,029.2	25.0	14.9	1,766.6	41,871	2.1	3.5	40,436
Portland-Vancouver-Beaverton, OR-WA	9,441.4	7.9	4,625	56.2	7,751.4	6,818.4	29.9	12.9	6,039.2	133,814	2.0	1.6	131,756
Port St. Lucie-Fort Pierce, FL	2,078.3	6.2	5,955	86.5	1,700.5	701.0	49.8	7.2	653.7	16,095	2.3	0.3	16,051
Poughkeepsie-Newburgh-Middletown, NY	3,387.8	1.5	5,167	55.5	2,719.1	2,700.7	24.3	11.5	2,422.0	56,267	2.1	2.7	54,796
Prescott, AZ	980.9	5.5	5,314	79.8	760.5	414.3	44.6	15.7	358.0	10,744	2.6	7.2	10,024
Providence-New Bedford-Fall River, RI-MA	10,817.7	7.2	6,665	53.3	9,377.4	5,517.5	29.4	9.6	5,035.5	105,689	1.9	0.4	105,245
Provo-Orem, UT	1,063.9	10.9	2,621	62.9	832.2	877.4	46.3	14.6	765.5	24,809	2.8	6.1	23,381
Pueblo, CO	930.9	6.9	6,247	65.4	773.2	486.3	30.6	10.1	441.5	11,845	2.4	0.4	11,794

See footnotes at end of table.

Metropolitan statistical area **Metropolitan statistical area with metropolitan divisions** *Metropolitan division*	Federal funds and grants					Government							
						Earnings				Employment			
	2003					2002				2002			
	Expenditures total (mil. dol.)	Percent change, 2002–2003	Per capita[1] (dol.)	Percent for direct payments to individuals	2000 (mil. dol.)	Total (mil. dol.)	Percent of total earnings	Percent change, 2000–2002	2000 (mil. dol.)	Total	Percent of total employment	Percent change, 2000–2002	2000
Punta Gorda, FL	970.8	4.4	6,353	94.4	816.2	225.9	67.6	5.9	213.4	5,425	2.4	–3.5	5,624
Racine, WI	822.9	2.9	4,273	70.6	682.6	463.6	41.5	9.0	425.2	10,256	2.2	0.4	10,219
Raleigh-Cary, NC	4,895.3	5.2	5,516	42.0	4,492.4	3,738.1	23.7	9.6	3,409.3	83,378	2.2	2.9	81,011
Rapid City, SD	897.4	6.7	7,736	44.6	758.7	610.4	19.0	11.9	545.5	13,312	2.2	1.6	13,108
Reading, PA	1,670.8	3.3	4,321	76.0	1,405.6	881.8	43.8	8.7	811.2	21,864	2.5	3.5	21,116
Redding, CA	1,061.2	4.8	6,041	70.0	883.5	599.7	29.3	14.0	526.0	14,444	2.4	6.1	13,618
Reno-Sparks, NV	1,743.0	1.6	4,651	58.0	1,345.4	1,413.7	26.5	14.4	1,235.8	25,540	1.8	9.9	23,235
Richmond, VA	7,547.5	3.1	6,629	49.9	6,077.0	5,662.8	20.1	7.9	5,245.9	122,960	2.2	0.8	121,950
Riverside-San Bernardino-Ontario, CA	14,663.2	8.5	4,023	64.2	12,001.9	11,145.2	32.7	17.1	9,516.6	233,044	2.1	8.2	215,382
Roanoke, VA	1,781.6	13.1	6,139	60.9	1,422.8	919.4	31.6	6.3	865.2	20,721	2.3	–1.5	21,037
Rochester, MN	827.7	5.5	4,803	49.9	684.4	462.6	37.3	10.0	420.6	10,777	2.3	2.2	10,546
Rochester, NY	5,836.5	7.3	5,607	60.6	4,680.2	3,426.0	30.4	13.5	3,017.4	78,405	2.3	2.9	76,211
Rockford, IL	1,355.7	3.0	4,092	68.5	1,139.6	723.9	45.8	7.2	675.6	17,147	2.4	3.1	16,639
Rocky Mount, NC	831.3	7.7	5,748	60.0	721.8	430.5	33.6	6.4	404.5	11,348	2.6	1.1	11,228
Rome, GA	440.4	3.9	4,714	74.3	357.8	241.6	38.7	8.9	221.9	6,521	2.7	2.3	6,373
Sacramento-Arden-Arcade-Roseville, CA	17,706.0	–6.4	8,963	37.9	14,225.7	13,447.2	14.7	14.0	11,799.6	239,568	1.8	3.9	230,554
Saginaw-Saginaw Township North, MI	1,153.2	2.5	5,506	66.9	999.1	566.1	37.0	4.4	542.2	12,811	2.3	0.9	12,702
St. Cloud, MN	716.8	0.2	4,034	60.3	576.0	576.3	30.8	10.9	519.8	13,052	2.3	0.7	12,965
St. George, UT	406.5	4.0	3,890	77.4	314.4	188.4	55.5	8.7	173.4	5,430	2.9	6.9	5,080
St. Joseph, MO-KS	664.9	2.6	5,402	67.5	558.1	360.9	34.1	3.8	347.8	10,313	2.9	–2.8	10,605
St. Louis, MO-IL[3]	21,989.5	5.8	7,985	44.2	17,728.9	8,585.1	32.1	9.3	7,853.3	186,372	2.2	–0.5	187,306
Salem, OR	2,331.3	3.2	6,392	49.7	1,801.3	1,881.4	19.4	11.3	1,691.0	38,990	2.1	0.2	38,911
Salinas, CA	2,106.6	3.5	5,083	52.5	1,778.4	2,036.5	20.3	17.7	1,729.6	36,170	1.8	3.3	35,003
Salisbury, MD	570.1	19.1	5,040	63.2	516.3	411.7	27.5	13.7	361.9	9,695	2.4	2.5	9,458
Salt Lake City, UT	5,112.4	5.4	5,084	40.7	4,044.8	4,111.9	24.5	12.0	3,671.0	95,619	2.3	2.9	92,959
San Angelo, TX	678.4	5.3	6,422	54.5	569.0	510.8	20.7	11.4	458.6	12,434	2.4	0.4	12,380
San Antonio, TX	14,255.2	12.4	7,848	45.2	10,868.9	8,714.9	20.8	10.9	7,856.5	181,475	2.1	3.4	175,455
San Diego-Carlsbad-San Marcos, CA	24,045.1	3.8	8,238	37.6	18,991.0	18,091.0	16.1	16.4	15,544.1	340,913	1.9	7.5	317,049
Sandusky, OH	420.5	0.1	5,331	69.8	351.3	245.3	32.2	15.7	212.0	6,036	2.5	6.0	5,695
San Francisco-Oakland-Fremont, CA	**25,998.6**	**4.5**	**6,255**	**46.5**	**22,158.7**	**19,587.4**	**21.2**	**12.9**	**17,355.9**	**315,126**	**1.6**	**(Z)**	**315,178**
Oakland-Fremont-Hayward, CA	*14,289.7*	*2.7*	*5,812*	*46.8*	*12,248.4*	*10,207.2*	*24.1*	*12.1*	*9,105.2*	*171,426*	*1.7*	*–0.2*	*171,814*
San Francisco-San Mateo-Redwood City, CA	*11,708.9*	*6.9*	*6,897*	*46.0*	*9,910.3*	*9,380.1*	*18.1*	*13.7*	*8,250.6*	*143,700*	*1.5*	*0.2*	*143,364*
San Jose-Sunnyvale-Santa Clara, CA	11,408.1	13.3	6,586	33.5	9,037.2	6,067.4	28.5	13.4	5,351.2	102,441	1.7	0.1	102,298
San Luis Obispo-Paso Robles, CA	1,113.7	7.4	4,401	74.3	966.8	1,005.0	25.2	15.5	870.1	21,735	2.2	5.5	20,599
Santa Barbara-Santa Maria, CA	2,724.0	11.3	6,763	45.4	2,282.7	1,880.3	21.4	15.0	1,634.4	38,171	2.0	4.6	36,492
Santa Cruz-Watsonville, CA	992.7	3.8	3,944	64.1	862.0	893.4	28.2	18.9	751.4	19,350	2.2	4.9	18,454
Santa Fe, NM	1,173.4	–0.4	8,584	34.5	879.9	741.4	18.4	14.7	646.7	17,513	2.4	–0.6	17,624
Santa Rosa-Petaluma, CA	2,039.1	4.1	4,363	70.6	1,731.0	1,451.3	32.2	14.4	1,268.7	30,410	2.1	2.0	29,819
Sarasota-Bradenton-Venice, FL	3,999.2	7.0	6,303	87.1	3,307.2	1,146.4	55.3	8.8	1,054.1	25,942	2.3	0.9	25,710
Savannah, GA	2,861.0	15.8	9,378	37.8	2,268.9	1,183.4	25.8	11.3	1,063.6	26,006	2.2	0.7	25,825
Scranton-Wilkes-Barre, PA	4,013.3	2.2	7,261	70.5	3,399.8	1,495.6	37.0	8.7	1,376.4	33,264	2.2	0.5	33,113
Seattle-Tacoma-Bellevue, WA	**18,729.8**	**10.2**	**5,961**	**45.6**	**15,188.4**	**14,553.5**	**21.6**	**12.2**	**12,968.9**	**287,775**	**2.0**	**3.3**	**278,607**
Seattle-Bellevue-Everett, WA	*13,677.2*	*10.3*	*5,695*	*45.1*	*11,131.3*	*10,579.4*	*22.7*	*11.1*	*9,521.1*	*209,742*	*2.0*	*2.8*	*203,996*
Tacoma, WA	*5,052.6*	*9.9*	*6,823*	*47.0*	*4,057.1*	*3,974.1*	*18.6*	*15.3*	*3,447.9*	*78,033*	*2.0*	*4.6*	*74,611*
Sheboygan, WI	452.7	1.3	3,987	71.9	393.6	269.1	42.2	7.2	251.0	6,499	2.4	(Z)	6,497
Sherman-Denison, TX	561.4	0.6	4,880	78.9	500.1	220.5	52.2	8.0	204.2	6,108	2.8	(Z)	6,109
Shreveport-Bossier City, LA	2,506.1	6.5	6,618	55.8	2,025.2	1,719.8	22.0	11.2	1,546.6	38,358	2.2	0.4	38,192
Sioux City, IA-NE-SD	852.0	–9.2	5,954	52.2	744.2	374.3	38.2	8.0	346.7	9,602	2.6	–1.6	9,754
Sioux Falls, SD	994.2	–2.4	5,004	57.1	853.2	492.1	40.4	10.1	446.9	12,042	2.4	1.1	11,906
South Bend-Mishawaka, IN-MI	2,163.8	16.3	6,817	46.4	1,598.6	683.7	46.4	6.3	643.3	17,327	2.5	–1.4	17,578
Spartanburg, SC	1,115.6	5.2	4,261	74.7	912.5	748.4	35.0	9.8	681.4	18,223	2.4	2.4	17,795
Spokane, WA	2,554.2	6.5	5,923	59.1	2,133.2	1,762.0	24.5	12.9	1,561.3	37,741	2.1	4.7	36,058
Springfield, IL	3,216.4	–6.9	15,722	31.0	2,396.3	1,718.8	11.9	8.7	1,580.7	31,784	1.8	–1.2	32,172
Springfield, MA	4,076.4	3.4	5,931	59.0	3,516.9	2,584.0	26.6	8.6	2,380.3	59,225	2.3	2.4	57,822
Springfield, MO	1,822.7	5.5	4,741	68.8	1,475.7	961.5	40.0	9.6	877.6	25,013	2.6	0.7	24,835
Springfield, OH	837.3	0.7	5,862	68.7	708.9	347.1	41.2	9.6	316.7	8,426	2.4	–0.1	8,437
State College, PA	961.1	10.8	6,874	39.8	767.6	1,280.8	10.9	14.0	1,123.6	38,460	3.0	5.8	36,357
Stockton, CA	2,675.1	4.6	4,234	61.2	2,226.8	1,921.3	32.9	18.8	1,617.5	39,318	2.0	9.0	36,085
Sumter, SC	877.5	14.2	8,298	44.3	708.1	624.2	16.9	16.0	538.1	13,127	2.1	2.2	12,843
Syracuse, NY	3,749.7	6.3	5,740	57.4	3,232.7	2,464.0	26.5	10.2	2,236.5	55,882	2.3	1.4	55,129
Tallahassee, FL	4,111.4	–7.7	12,554	27.6	3,307.6	2,782.3	11.8	4.3	2,667.9	64,056	2.3	–0.4	64,296
Tampa-St. Petersburg-Clearwater, FL	16,181.1	6.6	6,393	70.1	13,469.6	6,899.4	36.7	9.0	6,331.0	146,960	2.1	1.9	144,255
Terre Haute, IN	1,052.2	–9.7	6,205	62.0	867.6	528.4	32.1	4.7	504.8	13,638	2.6	–3.1	14,071
Texarkana, TX-Texarkana, AR	971.0	–5.4	7,373	56.7	795.5	493.5	26.7	6.2	464.7	11,248	2.3	–2.0	11,473
Toledo, OH	3,328.6	4.1	5,047	66.8	2,881.1	2,328.2	28.3	15.9	2,009.0	53,203	2.3	3.6	51,332
Topeka, KS	1,974.4	–3.2	8,704	47.3	1,616.6	1,130.0	20.1	9.3	1,033.6	27,936	2.5	1.4	27,542
Trenton-Ewing, NJ	3,730.2	–5.8	10,327	40.0	3,153.6	3,116.7	11.6	10.5	2,820.2	51,895	1.7	2.0	50,894
Tucson, AZ	8,108.7	4.3	9,101	39.8	6,382.0	3,669.5	24.3	15.8	3,168.2	82,071	2.2	2.4	80,130
Tulsa, OK	4,102.6	5.0	4,663	67.4	3,463.7	2,042.7	43.1	8.5	1,882.5	52,091	2.6	–0.5	52,350
Tuscaloosa, AL	1,189.1	8.1	6,117	58.0	978.4	893.9	21.7	8.1	826.6	23,127	2.6	0.5	23,017
Tyler, TX	921.7	7.7	5,013	69.4	759.0	498.8	36.9	6.8	467.0	12,574	2.5	–0.4	12,622

See footnotes at end of table.

Table B-11. Metropolitan Areas — **Government**—Con.

Metropolitan statistical area / **Metropolitan statistical area with metropolitan divisions** / *Metropolitan division*	Federal funds and grants 2003 Expenditures total (mil. dol.)	Per cent change, 2002–2003	Per capita[1] (dol.)	Per cent for direct payments to indivi-duals	2000 (mil. dol.)	Government Earnings 2002 Total (mil. dol.)	Per cent of total earn-ings	Per cent change, 2000–2002	2000 (mil. dol.)	Government Employment 2002 Total	Per cent of total employ-ment	Per cent change, 2000–2002	2000
Utica-Rome, NY	1,982.4	7.0	6,650	60.7	1,694.5	1,277.5	23.3	8.8	1,174.5	27,740	2.2	-2.3	28,383
Valdosta, GA	838.6	1.0	6,865	46.3	663.9	686.9	17.8	16.4	590.1	15,547	2.3	4.3	14,899
Vallejo-Fairfield, CA	2,442.4	14.8	5,933	49.2	1,948.8	1,875.6	21.9	18.5	1,583.4	35,710	1.9	7.2	33,312
Vero Beach, FL	832.3	8.6	6,921	86.1	677.5	235.1	51.1	8.1	217.6	5,249	2.2	1.5	5,173
Victoria, TX	532.1	6.1	4,709	66.5	437.9	309.3	36.5	6.5	290.4	8,893	2.9	0.4	8,861
Vineland-Millville-Bridgeton, NJ	874.8	5.5	5,851	60.5	737.9	717.6	20.8	11.1	646.1	14,391	2.0	1.7	14,152
Virginia Beach-Norfolk-Newport News, VA-NC	18,213.7	-0.9	11,208	33.0	15,281.5	14,243.9	11.4	12.9	12,613.7	264,088	1.9	2.2	258,441
Visalia-Porterville, CA	1,634.1	4.8	4,178	56.1	1,342.3	1,259.4	31.1	13.4	1,110.5	30,325	2.4	3.7	29,239
Waco, TX	1,236.2	7.1	5,630	61.8	1,080.4	693.7	31.6	11.6	621.4	16,893	2.4	5.0	16,093
Warner Robins, GA	1,769.9	9.9	14,741	26.5	1,304.2	1,612.9	7.4	18.1	1,366.1	25,650	1.6	7.5	23,855
Washington-Arlington-Alexandria, DC-VA-MD-WV	98,384.7	10.9	19,403	17.0	75,122.6	53,358.7	9.5	14.8	46,459.9	696,389	1.3	3.2	675,034
Bethesda-Gaithersburg-Frederick, MD	15,215.4	16.1	13,481	22.2	11,541.9	7,627.0	14.8	14.4	6,667.3	105,861	1.4	4.2	101,641
Washington-Arlington-Alexandria, DC-VA-MD-WV	83,169.3	10.0	21,098	16.1	63,580.7	45,731.8	8.6	14.9	39,792.6	590,528	1.3	3.0	573,393
Waterloo-Cedar Falls, IA	805.1	-7.3	4,978	69.3	723.9	528.7	30.6	5.4	501.5	14,451	2.7	-1.6	14,682
Wausau, WI	537.6	2.1	4,224	62.0	426.5	313.4	40.6	8.6	288.5	7,859	2.5	1.5	7,744
Weirton-Steubenville, WV-OH	870.1	7.2	6,768	74.6	727.1	249.1	51.6	5.3	236.7	6,896	2.8	-2.6	7,079
Wenatchee, WA	513.7	9.9	5,049	61.0	415.1	383.7	26.5	10.7	346.7	8,467	2.2	-0.9	8,547
Wheeling, WV-OH	974.1	4.4	6,490	69.7	807.3	407.8	36.8	6.7	382.2	10,839	2.7	-2.5	11,122
Wichita, KS	3,488.4	2.6	5,992	51.5	2,881.7	1,746.3	33.3	11.0	1,572.9	43,519	2.5	1.4	42,921
Wichita Falls, TX	1,295.7	3.2	8,716	45.0	1,101.6	1,008.4	14.7	17.1	860.9	23,864	2.4	5.4	22,641
Williamsport, PA	652.4	3.8	5,498	68.9	567.1	362.7	32.7	27.3	284.9	9,114	2.5	34.3	6,788
Wilmington, NC	1,648.6	9.9	5,612	65.8	1,312.6	981.0	29.9	13.9	861.4	23,709	2.4	4.9	22,606
Winchester, VA-WV	441.6	2.7	4,000	76.3	403.3	259.3	42.6	11.6	232.3	6,787	2.6	3.8	6,536
Winston-Salem, NC	2,038.7	6.7	4,663	66.6	1,603.8	913.7	47.8	5.5	866.1	23,752	2.6	0.4	23,666
Worcester, MA	3,926.5	4.1	5,061	64.8	3,361.4	2,387.0	32.5	9.5	2,179.0	51,557	2.2	0.3	51,407
Yakima, WA	1,171.5	9.5	5,164	54.4	994.1	704.3	32.2	9.1	645.8	16,870	2.4	2.0	16,545
York-Hanover, PA	2,074.9	2.7	5,245	57.6	1,716.2	850.2	46.5	10.3	770.4	18,838	2.2	1.9	18,478
Youngstown-Warren-Boardman, OH-PA	3,532.9	6.8	5,957	73.3	2,992.4	1,397.0	42.5	8.7	1,285.6	35,256	2.5	-0.9	35,571
Yuba City, CA	966.2	1.5	6,517	52.2	839.2	706.7	21.0	17.0	603.9	14,639	2.1	5.6	13,859
Yuma, AZ	1,021.7	13.4	5,989	48.2	791.4	729.7	23.4	15.7	630.7	16,380	2.2	4.3	15,703

Z Less than .05%.

[1] Based on resident population estimated as of July 1, 2003.

[2] The Denver-Aurora metropolitan statistical area includes Broomfield County. Broomfield County, CO, was formed from parts of Adams, Boulder, Jefferson, and Weld counties on November 15, 2001, and is coextensive with Broomfield city. For the purposes of defining and presenting data for the Denver-Aurora metropolitan statistical area, Broomfield city is treated as if it were a county when data are available to do so. In many cases, the data will not be available.

[3] The portion of Sullivan city in Crawford County, MO, is legally part of the St. Louis, MO-IL MSA. That portion is not included in these figures for the St. Louis MSA.

Note: Covers metropolitan statistical areas and metropolitan divisions and component counties defined by the Office of Management and Budget as of June 6, 2003, and subsequently updated in December 2003 and November 2004. For more information, see OMB Bulletin 05-02 at <http://www.whitehouse.gov/omb/bulletins/fy05/b05-02_appendix.pdf>.

Survey, Census, or Data Collection Method: Federal funds and grants—Based on information systems in various federal government agencies; for information, see Internet site <http://www.census.gov/govs/www/cffr.html>; Government earnings and employment—Based on the Regional Economic Information System; for more information, see Appendix B, Limitations of the Data and Methodology, and also <http://www.bea.gov/bea/regional/articles.cfm?section=methods> and <http://www.bea.gov/bea/regional/articles/lapi2003/lapi2003.pdf>.

Sources: Federal funds and grants—U.S. Census Bureau, Consolidated Federal Funds Report, annual, see Internet site <http://www.census.gov/govs/www/cffr.html>. Government earnings and employment—U.S. Bureau of Economic Analysis, *Regional Economic Information System (REIS) 1969–2002* on CD-ROM (related Internet site: <http://www.bea.gov/bea/regional/data.htm>).

Metro Counties

Table C

You may visit us on the Web at
http://www.census.gov/compendia/smadb

Metro Counties

Table C

Metropolitan statistical area **Metropolitan statistical area with metropolitan divisions** *Metropolitan division* Component county	Population				Net change		Percent change		Percent—			
	2005 (July 1)	2004 (July 1)	2000[1] (estimates base)	1990[2] (April 1)	2000–2005[3]	1990–2000	2000–2005[3]	1990–2000	65 years and over, 2003	Black or African american alone, 2003	Asian alone, 2003	Hispanic or Latino origin, 2003[4]
Abilene, TX.................	158,291	158,449	160,241	148,004	−1,950	12,237	−1.2	8.3	13.2	6.8	1.1	18.7
Callahan County, TX.................	13,516	13,332	12,905	11,859	611	1,046	4.7	8.8	17.7	0.4	0.5	7.5
Jones County, TX.................	19,736	20,026	20,785	16,490	−1,049	4,295	−5.0	26.0	13.5	12.1	0.5	21.4
Taylor County, TX.................	125,039	125,091	126,551	119,655	−1,512	6,896	−1.2	5.8	12.7	6.6	1.3	19.5
Akron, OH.................	702,235	701,837	694,960	657,575	7,275	37,385	1.0	5.7	13.4	11.2	1.6	0.9
Portage County, OH.................	155,631	155,229	152,061	142,585	3,570	9,476	2.3	6.6	11.2	3.4	1.1	0.7
Summit County, OH.................	546,604	546,608	542,899	514,990	3,705	27,909	0.7	5.4	14.0	13.4	1.7	0.9
Albany, GA.................	162,842	162,348	157,866	146,583	4,976	11,283	3.2	7.7	11.1	49.2	0.7	1.2
Baker County, GA.................	4,154	4,216	4,074	3,615	80	459	2.0	12.7	12.4	52.0	–	2.9
Dougherty County, GA.................	94,882	95,222	96,065	96,321	−1,183	−256	−1.2	−0.3	11.8	62.3	0.8	1.2
Lee County, GA.................	31,099	29,987	24,757	16,250	6,342	8,507	25.6	52.4	6.8	15.2	1.1	1.1
Terrell County, GA.................	10,711	10,932	10,970	10,653	−259	317	−2.4	3.0	12.7	61.3	0.5	1.3
Worth County, GA.................	21,996	21,991	22,000	19,744	−4	2,256	(Z)	11.4	12.5	29.5	0.3	1.2
Albany-Schenectady-Troy, NY.................	848,879	844,961	825,875	809,642	23,004	16,233	2.8	2.0	13.7	7.3	2.6	3.1
Albany County, NY.................	297,414	297,910	294,565	292,793	2,849	1,772	1.0	0.6	14.0	12.4	3.7	3.8
Rensselaer County, NY.................	155,251	154,460	152,538	154,429	2,713	−1,891	1.8	−1.2	13.2	5.7	2.2	2.7
Saratoga County, NY.................	214,859	212,586	200,635	181,276	14,224	19,359	7.1	10.7	11.7	1.7	1.5	2.2
Schenectady County, NY.................	149,078	148,065	146,555	149,285	2,523	−2,730	1.7	−1.8	16.1	8.0	2.8	4.0
Schoharie County, NY.................	32,277	31,940	31,582	31,859	695	−277	2.2	−0.9	15.1	1.4	0.4	2.2
Albuquerque, NM.................	797,940	781,380	729,653	599,416	68,287	130,237	9.4	21.7	11.4	2.9	1.9	42.9
Bernalillo County, NM.................	603,562	592,538	556,002	480,577	47,560	75,425	8.6	15.7	11.6	3.2	2.2	43.5
Sandoval County, NM.................	107,460	102,725	90,584	63,319	16,876	27,265	18.6	43.1	10.9	2.1	1.1	31.2
Torrance County, NM.................	17,501	17,544	16,915	10,285	586	6,630	3.5	64.5	10.5	2.0	0.4	38.4
Valencia County, NM.................	69,417	68,573	66,152	45,235	3,265	20,917	4.9	46.2	10.6	1.5	0.5	55.7
Alexandria, LA.................	147,965	146,951	145,035	149,082	2,930	−4,047	2.0	−2.7	13.1	28.4	0.9	1.6
Grant Parish, LA.................	19,503	19,144	18,698	17,526	805	1,172	4.3	6.7	12.6	11.6	0.2	1.4
Rapides Parish, LA.................	128,462	127,807	126,337	131,556	2,125	−5,219	1.7	−4.0	13.1	30.9	1.0	1.6
Allentown-Bethlehem-Easton, PA-NJ.................	790,535	779,730	740,394	686,688	50,141	53,706	6.8	7.8	15.1	3.4	2.0	8.1
Warren County, NJ.................	110,376	109,795	102,433	91,607	7,943	10,826	7.8	11.8	12.5	2.6	1.7	4.9
Carbon County, PA.................	61,959	61,032	58,802	56,846	3,157	1,956	5.4	3.4	17.7	0.9	0.4	1.6
Lehigh County, PA.................	330,433	325,570	312,090	291,130	18,343	20,960	5.9	7.2	15.5	4.4	2.6	11.4
Northampton County, PA.................	287,767	283,333	267,069	247,105	20,698	19,964	7.8	8.1	15.1	3.2	1.7	6.9
Altoona, PA.................	126,795	127,202	129,144	130,542	−2,349	−1,398	−1.8	−1.1	17.3	1.2	0.5	0.5
Blair County, PA.................	126,795	127,202	129,144	130,542	−2,349	−1,398	−1.8	−1.1	17.3	1.2	0.5	0.5
Amarillo, TX.................	238,664	235,696	226,522	196,111	12,142	30,411	5.4	15.5	11.9	6.0	1.8	21.0
Armstrong County, TX.................	2,173	2,134	2,148	2,021	25	127	1.2	6.3	19.7	0.4	–	5.8
Carson County, TX.................	6,586	6,494	6,516	6,576	70	−60	1.1	−0.9	15.7	0.8	0.1	8.3
Potter County, TX.................	119,852	118,324	113,546	97,841	6,306	15,705	5.6	16.1	11.7	10.4	2.3	30.8
Randall County, TX.................	110,053	108,744	104,312	89,673	5,741	14,639	5.5	16.3	11.8	1.6	1.3	11.3
Ames, IA.................	79,952	80,239	79,981	74,252	−29	5,729	(Z)	7.7	9.9	1.9	6.2	1.6
Story County, IA.................	79,952	80,239	79,981	74,252	−29	5,729	(Z)	7.7	9.9	1.9	6.2	1.6
Anchorage, AK.................	351,049	346,233	319,605	266,021	31,444	53,584	9.8	20.1	6.1	5.3	4.9	5.7
Anchorage Borough, AK.................	275,043	274,067	260,283	226,338	14,760	33,945	5.7	15.0	6.0	6.4	6.0	6.4
Matanuska-Susitna Borough, AK.................	76,006	72,166	59,322	39,683	16,684	19,639	28.1	49.5	6.3	0.9	0.7	2.9
Anderson, IN.................	130,412	130,482	133,358	130,669	−2,946	2,689	−2.2	2.1	15.0	8.0	0.4	1.7
Madison County, IN.................	130,412	130,482	133,358	130,669	−2,946	2,689	−2.2	2.1	15.0	8.0	0.4	1.7
Anderson, SC.................	175,514	173,547	165,740	145,177	9,774	20,563	5.9	14.2	13.7	17.0	0.5	1.3
Anderson County, SC.................	175,514	173,547	165,740	145,177	9,774	20,563	5.9	14.2	13.7	17.0	0.5	1.3
Ann Arbor, MI.................	341,847	338,782	322,770	282,937	19,077	39,833	5.9	14.1	8.3	12.3	7.6	2.8
Washtenaw County, MI.................	341,847	338,782	322,770	282,937	19,077	39,833	5.9	14.1	8.3	12.3	7.6	2.8
Anniston-Oxford, AL.................	112,141	111,982	112,243	116,032	−102	−3,789	−0.1	−3.3	14.3	19.4	0.7	1.8
Calhoun County, AL.................	112,141	111,982	112,243	116,032	−102	−3,789	−0.1	−3.3	14.3	19.4	0.7	1.8
Appleton, WI.................	215,143	212,864	201,722	174,801	13,421	26,921	6.7	15.4	11.0	0.6	2.4	2.0
Calumet County, WI.................	44,137	43,768	40,631	34,291	3,506	6,340	8.6	18.5	10.6	0.5	2.0	1.5
Outagamie County, WI.................	171,006	169,096	161,091	140,510	9,915	20,581	6.2	14.6	11.1	0.7	2.6	2.1
Asheville, NC.................	392,831	387,366	369,172	307,999	23,659	61,173	6.4	19.9	17.5	5.0	0.7	3.8
Buncombe County, NC.................	218,876	215,705	206,289	174,819	12,587	31,470	6.1	18.0	15.3	7.3	0.8	3.2
Haywood County, NC.................	56,482	56,140	54,034	46,942	2,448	7,092	4.5	15.1	19.6	1.3	0.3	1.5
Henderson County, NC.................	97,217	95,474	89,214	69,285	8,003	19,929	9.0	28.8	21.5	3.0	0.7	6.9
Madison County, NC.................	20,256	20,047	19,635	16,953	621	2,682	3.2	15.8	16.1	0.9	0.3	1.5
Athens-Clarke County, GA.................	175,085	175,415	166,079	136,025	9,006	30,054	5.4	22.1	9.1	19.8	2.2	5.6
Clarke County, GA.................	104,439	105,750	101,489	87,594	2,950	13,895	2.9	15.9	8.2	26.6	3.0	7.5
Madison County, GA.................	27,289	27,196	25,730	21,050	1,559	4,680	6.1	22.2	11.1	8.4	0.4	2.1
Oconee County, GA.................	29,748	28,908	26,225	17,618	3,523	8,607	13.4	48.9	9.0	6.4	1.7	3.1
Oglethorpe County, GA.................	13,609	13,561	12,635	9,763	974	2,872	7.7	29.4	11.8	19.1	0.3	2.5
Atlanta-Sandy Springs-Marietta, GA.................	4,917,717	4,796,268	4,248,018	3,068,975	669,699	1,179,043	15.8	38.4	7.7	29.2	3.7	7.7
Barrow County, GA.................	59,954	56,656	46,144	29,721	13,810	16,423	29.9	55.3	8.4	9.9	2.7	4.4
Bartow County, GA.................	89,229	86,914	76,019	55,915	13,210	20,104	17.4	36.0	9.3	8.4	0.5	4.6
Butts County, GA.................	21,045	20,587	19,523	15,326	1,522	4,197	7.8	27.4	9.8	27.0	0.4	1.7
Carroll County, GA.................	105,453	102,143	87,268	71,422	18,185	15,846	20.8	22.2	9.6	16.1	0.7	3.4
Cherokee County, GA.................	184,211	174,851	141,907	90,204	42,304	51,703	29.8	57.3	6.8	3.4	1.2	6.9
Clayton County, GA.................	267,966	264,227	236,517	181,436	31,449	55,081	13.3	30.4	6.6	58.8	5.1	9.5
Cobb County, GA.................	663,818	654,649	607,751	447,745	56,067	160,006	9.2	35.7	7.4	20.0	3.6	9.3
Coweta County, GA.................	109,903	105,395	89,215	53,853	20,688	35,362	23.2	65.7	8.4	16.9	0.9	4.1
Dawson County, GA.................	19,731	19,041	15,999	9,429	3,732	6,570	23.3	69.7	10.2	0.6	0.4	2.3
DeKalb County, GA.................	677,959	674,335	666,072	546,174	11,887	119,898	1.8	22.0	8.1	55.5	3.8	8.8
Douglas County, GA.................	112,760	107,084	92,284	71,120	20,476	21,164	22.2	29.8	7.5	25.0	1.2	3.6

See footnotes at end of table.

Table C-1. Metropolitan Areas With Component Counties — Population and Population Characteristics—Con.

Metropolitan statistical area / **Metropolitan statistical area with metropolitan divisions** / *Metropolitan division* / Component county	Population 2005 (July 1)	Population 2004 (July 1)	Population 2000[1] (estimates base)	Population 1990[2] (April 1)	Net change 2000–2005[3]	Net change 1990–2000	Percent change 2000–2005[3]	Percent change 1990–2000	Percent— 65 years and over, 2003	Percent— Black or African American alone, 2003	Percent— Asian alone, 2003	Percent— Hispanic or Latino origin, 2003[4]
Atlanta-Sandy Springs-Marietta, GA—Con.												
Fayette County, GA	104,248	101,200	91,263	62,415	12,985	28,848	14.2	46.2	9.6	13.6	2.8	2.6
Forsyth County, GA	140,393	131,950	98,407	44,083	41,986	54,324	42.7	123.2	6.8	1.3	2.0	6.5
Fulton County, GA	915,623	905,802	815,806	648,776	99,817	167,030	12.2	25.7	7.7	43.1	3.5	6.7
Gwinnett County, GA	726,273	700,577	588,448	352,910	137,825	235,538	23.4	66.7	5.6	15.7	8.6	13.8
Haralson County, GA	28,338	27,965	25,690	21,966	2,648	3,724	10.3	17.0	13.0	5.4	0.2	0.7
Heard County, GA	11,346	11,266	11,012	8,628	334	2,384	3.0	27.6	10.8	10.5	0.1	1.0
Henry County, GA	167,848	158,939	119,370	58,741	48,478	60,629	40.6	103.2	7.3	20.9	2.3	3.2
Jasper County, GA	13,147	12,778	11,426	8,453	1,721	2,973	15.1	35.2	11.1	24.7	0.1	2.7
Lamar County, GA	16,378	16,326	15,912	13,038	466	2,874	2.9	22.0	12.3	28.9	0.4	1.3
Meriwether County, GA	22,919	22,790	22,534	22,411	385	123	1.7	0.5	13.8	40.9	0.2	1.4
Newton County, GA	86,713	81,624	62,001	41,808	24,712	20,193	39.9	48.3	9.1	27.3	1.0	2.7
Paulding County, GA	112,411	106,035	81,568	41,611	30,843	39,957	37.8	96.0	5.6	10.4	0.5	2.6
Pickens County, GA	28,442	27,798	22,979	14,432	5,463	8,547	23.8	59.2	13.4	1.3	0.3	2.5
Pike County, GA	16,128	15,689	13,688	10,224	2,440	3,464	17.8	33.9	10.8	12.4	0.4	1.6
Rockdale County, GA	78,545	76,858	70,111	54,091	8,434	16,020	12.0	29.6	9.2	27.3	2.0	7.3
Spalding County, GA	61,289	60,745	58,417	54,457	2,872	3,960	4.9	7.3	11.6	32.2	0.7	1.9
Walton County, GA	75,647	72,044	60,687	38,586	14,960	22,101	24.7	57.3	10.2	14.0	0.8	2.1
Atlantic City, NJ	271,015	268,311	252,552	224,327	18,463	28,225	7.3	12.6	13.4	18.2	5.7	13.3
Atlantic County, NJ	271,015	268,311	252,552	224,327	18,463	28,225	7.3	12.6	13.4	18.2	5.7	13.3
Auburn-Opelika, AL	123,254	120,537	115,092	87,146	8,162	27,946	7.1	32.1	8.3	23.2	1.9	1.5
Lee County, AL	123,254	120,537	115,092	87,146	8,162	27,946	7.1	32.1	8.3	23.2	1.9	1.5
Augusta-Richmond County, GA-SC	520,332	516,338	499,649	435,799	20,683	63,850	4.1	14.7	11.2	35.3	1.5	2.2
Burke County, GA	23,299	23,122	22,243	20,579	1,056	1,664	4.7	8.1	10.2	50.4	0.4	1.3
Columbia County, GA	103,812	100,554	89,288	66,031	14,524	23,257	16.3	35.2	8.8	11.5	3.3	2.5
McDuffie County, GA	21,743	21,559	21,231	20,119	512	1,112	2.4	5.5	11.8	38.1	0.4	1.5
Richmond County, GA	195,769	196,922	199,775	189,719	−4,006	10,056	−2.0	5.3	10.9	51.0	1.5	2.2
Aiken County, SC	150,181	148,879	142,552	120,991	7,629	21,561	5.4	17.8	13.3	26.1	0.8	2.4
Edgefield County, SC	25,528	25,302	24,560	18,360	968	6,200	3.9	33.8	10.7	41.2	0.3	2.1
Austin-Round Rock, TX	1,452,529	1,411,199	1,249,753	846,227	202,776	403,526	16.2	47.7	7.2	7.9	4.0	28.3
Bastrop County, TX	69,932	68,519	57,716	38,263	12,216	19,453	21.2	50.8	9.9	8.8	0.6	26.5
Caldwell County, TX	36,523	36,384	32,192	26,392	4,331	5,800	13.5	22.0	11.3	8.5	0.5	43.1
Hays County, TX	124,432	119,274	97,566	65,614	26,866	31,952	27.5	48.7	7.6	4.0	0.9	31.1
Travis County, TX	888,185	868,873	812,312	576,407	75,873	235,905	9.3	40.9	6.8	9.0	5.0	30.9
Williamson County, TX	333,457	318,149	249,967	139,551	83,490	110,416	33.4	79.1	7.3	5.8	3.5	18.9
Bakersfield, CA	756,825	734,077	661,653	544,981	95,172	116,672	14.4	21.4	9.2	6.3	3.6	41.5
Kern County, CA	756,825	734,077	661,653	544,981	95,172	116,672	14.4	21.4	9.2	6.3	3.6	41.5
Baltimore-Towson, MD	2,655,675	2,644,744	2,552,994	2,382,172	102,681	170,822	4.0	7.2	11.9	27.3	3.1	2.1
Anne Arundel County, MD	510,878	508,356	489,656	427,239	21,222	62,417	4.3	14.6	10.2	13.3	2.5	2.7
Baltimore County, MD	786,113	781,171	754,292	692,134	31,821	62,158	4.2	9.0	14.5	22.1	3.6	2.0
Carroll County, MD	168,541	166,489	150,897	123,372	17,644	27,525	11.7	22.3	10.9	2.4	1.1	1.1
Harford County, MD	239,259	235,290	218,590	182,132	20,669	36,458	9.5	20.0	10.6	9.6	1.6	1.8
Howard County, MD	269,457	266,532	247,842	187,328	21,615	60,514	8.7	32.3	8.0	14.3	9.7	3.3
Queen Anne's County, MD	45,612	44,963	40,563	33,953	5,049	6,610	12.4	19.5	12.6	7.8	0.8	1.0
Baltimore city, MD	635,815	641,943	651,154	736,014	−15,339	−84,860	−2.4	−11.5	12.5	64.9	1.6	1.8
Bangor, ME	147,068	146,698	144,919	146,601	2,149	−1,682	1.5	−1.1	13.3	0.5	0.8	0.6
Penobscot County, ME	147,068	146,698	144,919	146,601	2,149	−1,682	1.5	−1.1	13.3	0.5	0.8	0.6
Barnstable Town, MA	226,514	227,984	222,230	186,605	4,284	35,625	1.9	19.1	22.9	2.1	0.8	1.5
Barnstable County, MA	226,514	227,984	222,230	186,605	4,284	35,625	1.9	19.1	22.9	2.1	0.8	1.5
Baton Rouge, LA	733,802	727,413	705,967	623,850	27,835	82,117	3.9	13.2	9.8	34.4	1.5	1.9
Ascension Parish, LA	90,501	87,019	76,627	58,214	13,874	18,413	18.1	31.6	7.5	19.5	0.7	3.0
East Baton Rouge Parish, LA	411,417	411,564	412,852	380,105	−1,435	32,747	−0.3	8.6	10.2	41.9	2.4	2.0
East Feliciana Parish, LA	20,823	20,870	21,360	19,211	−537	2,149	−2.5	11.2	11.1	45.9	0.3	0.8
Iberville Parish, LA	32,386	32,483	33,320	31,049	−934	2,271	−2.8	7.3	11.0	50.1	0.3	1.1
Livingston Parish, LA	109,206	105,758	91,808	70,523	17,398	21,285	19.0	30.2	8.5	3.9	0.3	1.3
Pointe Coupee Parish, LA	22,377	22,444	22,763	22,540	−386	223	−1.7	1.0	14.4	37.4	0.3	1.1
St. Helena Parish, LA	10,259	10,309	10,525	9,874	−266	651	−2.5	6.6	11.6	53.8	0.1	1.3
West Baton Rouge Parish, LA	21,634	21,855	21,601	19,419	33	2,182	0.2	11.2	10.2	34.6	0.4	2.0
West Feliciana Parish, LA	15,199	15,111	15,111	12,915	88	2,196	0.6	17.0	7.4	50.0	0.2	1.1
Battle Creek, MI	139,191	139,505	137,985	135,982	1,206	2,003	0.9	1.5	13.7	11.0	1.3	3.3
Calhoun County, MI	139,191	139,505	137,985	135,982	1,206	2,003	0.9	1.5	13.7	11.0	1.3	3.3
Bay City, MI	109,029	109,139	110,157	111,723	−1,128	−1,566	−1.0	−1.4	14.9	1.4	0.5	4.0
Bay County, MI	109,029	109,139	110,157	111,723	−1,128	−1,566	−1.0	−1.4	14.9	1.4	0.5	4.0
Beaumont-Port Arthur, TX	383,530	383,251	385,090	361,218	−1,560	23,872	−0.4	6.6	13.2	25.4	2.1	8.8
Hardin County, TX	50,976	50,218	48,073	41,320	2,903	6,753	6.0	16.3	12.5	6.6	0.3	2.9
Jefferson County, TX	247,571	248,308	252,051	239,389	−4,480	12,662	−1.8	5.3	13.5	34.9	3.0	11.7
Orange County, TX	84,983	84,725	84,966	80,509	17	4,457	(Z)	5.3	13.1	8.3	0.8	4.0
Bellingham, WA	183,471	180,205	166,826	127,780	16,645	39,046	10.0	30.6	12.0	0.8	3.1	5.5
Whatcom County, WA	183,471	180,205	166,826	127,780	16,645	39,046	10.0	30.6	12.0	0.8	3.1	5.5
Bend, OR	141,382	134,618	115,367	74,976	26,015	40,391	22.5	53.9	13.3	0.3	0.8	4.2
Deschutes County, OR	141,382	134,618	115,367	74,976	26,015	40,391	22.5	53.9	13.3	0.3	0.8	4.2
Billings, MT	146,593	144,576	138,904	121,499	7,689	17,405	5.5	14.3	13.7	0.5	0.6	3.7
Carbon County, MT	9,902	9,770	9,552	8,080	350	1,472	3.7	18.2	16.1	0.4	0.5	1.8
Yellowstone County, MT	136,691	134,806	129,352	113,419	7,339	15,933	5.7	14.0	13.5	0.5	0.6	3.8
Binghamton, NY	248,422	249,345	252,320	264,497	−3,898	−12,177	−1.5	−4.6	15.8	3.4	2.7	2.2
Broome County, NY	196,947	197,926	200,536	212,160	−3,589	−11,624	−1.8	−5.5	16.4	4.1	3.3	2.4
Tioga County, NY	51,475	51,419	51,784	52,337	−309	−553	−0.6	−1.1	13.7	0.7	0.8	1.4

See footnotes at end of table.

Metropolitan statistical area **Metropolitan statistical area with metropolitan divisions** *Metropolitan division* Component county	Population				Net change		Percent change		Percent—			
	2005 (July 1)	2004 (July 1)	2000[1] (estimates base)	1990[2] (April 1)	2000–2005[3]	1990–2000	2000–2005[3]	1990–2000	65 years and over, 2003	Black or African American alone, 2003	Asian alone, 2003	Hispanic or Latino origin, 2003[4]
Birmingham-Hoover, AL	1,090,126	1,081,722	1,051,306	956,646	38,820	94,660	3.7	9.9	12.7	28.1	0.9	2.1
Bibb County, AL	21,516	21,290	19,889	16,576	1,627	3,313	8.2	20.0	11.8	22.8	0.1	1.3
Blount County, AL	55,725	54,973	51,036	39,248	4,689	11,788	9.2	30.0	13.0	1.2	0.2	5.9
Chilton County, AL	41,744	41,377	39,593	32,458	2,151	7,135	5.4	22.0	12.7	10.8	0.3	3.3
Jefferson County, AL	657,229	658,468	662,040	651,520	–4,811	10,520	–0.7	1.6	13.4	40.7	1.1	1.9
St. Clair County, AL	72,330	70,275	64,742	49,811	7,588	14,931	11.7	30.0	12.1	7.9	0.2	1.2
Shelby County, AL	171,465	165,463	143,293	99,363	28,172	43,930	19.7	44.2	8.7	8.2	1.4	2.6
Walker County, AL	70,117	69,876	70,713	67,670	–596	3,043	–0.8	4.5	15.3	6.4	0.2	1.1
Bismarck, ND	99,346	97,885	94,719	83,831	4,627	10,888	4.9	13.0	13.3	0.3	0.5	0.7
Burleigh County, ND	73,818	72,563	69,416	60,131	4,402	9,285	6.3	15.4	12.8	0.3	0.5	0.7
Morton County, ND	25,528	25,322	25,303	23,700	225	1,603	0.9	6.8	14.8	0.2	0.4	0.8
Blacksburg-Christiansburg-Radford, VA	151,057	150,597	151,324	140,715	–267	10,609	–0.2	7.5	11.2	4.4	2.5	1.3
Giles County, VA	17,098	16,925	16,657	16,366	441	291	2.6	1.8	16.0	1.6	0.2	0.6
Montgomery County, VA	84,303	83,901	83,681	73,913	622	9,768	0.7	13.2	8.6	3.7	3.9	1.6
Pulaski County, VA	35,081	35,104	35,127	34,496	–46	631	–0.1	1.8	15.6	6.0	0.4	1.1
Radford city, VA	14,575	14,667	15,859	15,940	–1,284	–81	–8.1	–0.5	10.0	7.9	1.5	1.3
Bloomington, IN	177,709	177,297	175,506	156,669	2,203	18,837	1.3	12.0	10.9	2.0	2.8	1.5
Greene County, IN	33,479	33,465	33,157	30,410	322	2,747	1.0	9.0	15.0	0.2	0.3	0.8
Monroe County, IN	121,407	120,910	120,563	108,978	844	11,585	0.7	10.6	9.5	2.8	4.0	1.8
Owen County, IN	22,823	22,922	21,786	17,281	1,037	4,505	4.8	26.1	12.5	0.3	0.2	0.7
Bloomington-Normal, IL	159,013	157,847	150,433	129,180	8,580	21,253	5.7	16.5	9.5	6.6	2.8	3.2
McLean County, IL	159,013	157,847	150,433	129,180	8,580	21,253	5.7	16.5	9.5	6.6	2.8	3.2
Boise City-Nampa, ID	544,201	524,789	464,840	319,596	79,361	145,244	17.1	45.4	9.9	0.7	1.6	9.9
Ada County, ID	344,727	332,545	300,904	205,775	43,823	95,129	14.6	46.2	9.3	0.8	2.0	5.1
Boise County, ID	7,535	7,379	6,670	3,509	865	3,161	13.0	90.1	10.8	0.1	0.3	3.4
Canyon County, ID	164,593	157,883	131,441	90,076	33,152	41,365	25.2	45.9	10.3	0.6	0.9	19.9
Gem County, ID	16,273	15,962	15,181	11,844	1,092	3,337	7.2	28.2	15.8	0.1	0.5	7.5
Owyhee County, ID	11,073	11,020	10,644	8,392	429	2,252	4.0	26.8	12.7	0.3	0.6	23.5
Boston-Cambridge-Quincy, MA-NH	**4,411,835**	**4,418,758**	**4,392,340**	**4,133,895**	**19,495**	**258,445**	**0.4**	**6.3**	**12.5**	**7.5**	**5.4**	**7.0**
Boston-Quincy, MA	*1,800,432*	*1,807,863*	*1,812,937*	*1,715,269*	*–12,505*	*97,668*	*–0.7*	*5.7*	*12.3*	*12.9*	*5.6*	*7.7*
Norfolk County, MA	653,595	653,621	650,308	616,087	3,287	34,221	0.5	5.6	14.2	4.0	6.8	2.1
Plymouth County, MA	492,409	489,979	472,822	435,276	19,587	37,546	4.1	8.6	11.7	7.4	1.1	2.7
Suffolk County, MA	654,428	664,263	689,807	663,906	–35,379	25,901	–5.1	3.9	11.0	25.5	7.6	16.5
Cambridge-Newton-Framingham, MA	*1,459,011*	*1,462,822*	*1,466,394*	*1,398,468*	*–7,383*	*67,926*	*–0.5*	*4.9*	*12.7*	*4.0*	*7.6*	*4.8*
Middlesex County, MA	1,459,011	1,462,822	1,466,394	1,398,468	–7,383	67,926	–0.5	4.9	12.7	4.0	7.6	4.8
Essex County, MA	*738,301*	*737,447*	*723,419*	*670,080*	*14,882*	*53,339*	*2.1*	*8.0*	*13.5*	*4.7*	*2.8*	*13.2*
Essex County, MA	738,301	737,447	723,419	670,080	14,882	53,339	2.1	8.0	13.5	4.7	2.8	13.2
Rockingham County-Strafford County, NH	*414,091*	*410,626*	*389,590*	*350,078*	*24,501*	*39,512*	*6.3*	*11.3*	*10.6*	*0.7*	*1.4*	*1.2*
Rockingham County, NH	295,076	292,346	277,357	245,845	17,719	31,512	6.4	12.8	10.4	0.7	1.3	1.3
Strafford County, NH	119,015	118,280	112,233	104,233	6,782	8,000	6.0	7.7	11.1	0.7	1.6	1.1
Boulder, CO[5]	280,440	279,551	269,787	225,339	10,653	44,448	3.9	19.7	8.0	1.0	3.7	11.8
Boulder County, CO[5]	280,440	279,551	269,787	225,339	10,653	44,448	3.9	19.7	8.0	1.0	3.7	11.8
Bowling Green, KY	110,990	109,047	104,166	88,077	6,824	16,089	6.6	18.3	10.9	8.0	1.3	2.9
Edmonson County, KY	12,030	11,884	11,644	10,357	386	1,287	3.3	12.4	14.2	0.6	0.1	0.6
Warren County, KY	98,960	97,163	92,522	77,720	6,438	14,802	7.0	19.0	10.5	8.9	1.5	3.2
Bremerton-Silverdale, WA	240,661	241,436	231,969	189,731	8,692	42,238	3.7	22.3	10.8	2.9	4.5	4.6
Kitsap County, WA	240,661	241,436	231,969	189,731	8,692	42,238	3.7	22.3	10.8	2.9	4.5	4.6
Bridgeport-Stamford-Norwalk, CT	902,775	901,819	882,567	827,645	20,208	54,922	2.3	6.6	13.0	10.7	3.8	12.9
Fairfield County, CT	902,775	901,819	882,567	827,645	20,208	54,922	2.3	6.6	13.0	10.7	3.8	12.9
Brownsville-Harlingen, TX	378,311	370,829	335,227	260,120	43,084	75,107	12.9	28.9	10.9	0.7	0.5	85.7
Cameron County, TX	378,311	370,829	335,227	260,120	43,084	75,107	12.9	28.9	10.9	0.7	0.5	85.7
Brunswick, GA	98,433	97,569	93,044	82,207	5,389	10,837	5.8	13.2	13.6	23.5	0.5	2.7
Brantley County, GA	15,491	15,427	14,629	11,077	862	3,552	5.9	32.1	10.5	4.8	0.1	1.1
Glynn County, GA	71,874	71,047	67,568	62,496	4,306	5,072	6.4	8.1	14.4	25.9	0.6	3.3
McIntosh County, GA	11,068	11,095	10,847	8,634	221	2,213	2.0	25.6	12.8	34.2	0.4	0.8
Buffalo-Niagara Falls, NY	1,147,711	1,153,753	1,170,111	1,189,340	–22,400	–19,229	–1.9	–1.6	15.6	12.6	1.6	3.4
Erie County, NY	930,703	935,946	950,265	968,584	–19,562	–18,319	–2.1	–1.9	15.7	13.9	1.8	3.7
Niagara County, NY	217,008	217,807	219,846	220,756	–2,838	–910	–1.3	–0.4	15.2	6.8	0.8	1.7
Burlington, NC	140,533	138,452	130,794	108,213	9,739	22,581	7.4	20.9	13.9	18.7	1.2	8.8
Alamance County, NC	140,533	138,452	130,794	108,213	9,739	22,581	7.4	20.9	13.9	18.7	1.2	8.8
Burlington-South Burlington, VT	205,230	204,510	198,889	177,059	6,341	21,830	3.2	12.3	10.2	0.8	1.8	1.0
Chittenden County, VT	149,613	149,379	146,571	131,761	3,042	14,810	2.1	11.2	9.9	1.0	2.3	1.1
Franklin County, VT	47,914	47,498	45,417	39,980	2,497	5,437	5.5	13.6	11.0	0.3	0.3	0.6
Grand Isle County, VT	7,703	7,633	6,901	5,318	802	1,583	11.6	29.8	12.1	0.2	0.2	0.4
Canton-Massillon, OH	409,996	410,005	406,934	394,106	3,062	12,828	0.8	3.3	15.2	6.7	0.6	0.9
Carroll County, OH	29,388	29,460	28,836	26,521	552	2,315	1.9	8.7	14.6	0.5	0.2	0.6
Stark County, OH	380,608	380,545	378,098	367,585	2,510	10,513	0.7	2.9	15.2	7.2	0.6	0.9
Cape Coral-Fort Myers, FL	544,758	514,923	440,888	335,113	103,870	105,775	23.6	31.6	23.8	7.6	1.0	12.2
Lee County, FL	544,758	514,923	440,888	335,113	103,870	105,775	23.6	31.6	23.8	7.6	1.0	12.2
Carson City, NV	56,062	55,926	52,457	40,443	3,605	12,014	6.9	29.7	15.3	1.7	1.6	15.6
Carson City, NV	56,062	55,926	52,457	40,443	3,605	12,014	6.9	29.7	15.3	1.7	1.6	15.6
Casper, WY	69,799	68,988	66,533	61,226	3,266	5,307	4.9	8.7	12.7	0.9	0.5	4.9
Natrona County, WY	69,799	68,988	66,533	61,226	3,266	5,307	4.9	8.7	12.7	0.9	0.5	4.9

See footnotes at end of table.

Table C-1. Metropolitan Areas With Component Counties — **Population and Population Characteristics**—Con.

Metropolitan statistical area / **Metropolitan statistical area with metropolitan divisions** / *Metropolitan division* / Component county	Population				Net change		Percent change		Percent—			
	2005 (July 1)	2004 (July 1)	2000[1] (estimates base)	1990[2] (April 1)	2000–2005[3]	1990–2000	2000–2005[3]	1990–2000	65 years and over, 2003	Black or African-american alone, 2003	Asian alone, 2003	Hispanic or Latino origin, 2003[4]
Cedar Rapids, IA	246,412	244,306	237,230	210,640	9,182	26,590	3.9	12.6	13.0	2.5	1.4	1.4
Benton County, IA	27,000	26,747	25,308	22,429	1,692	2,879	6.7	12.8	14.6	0.3	0.3	0.7
Jones County, IA	20,509	20,554	20,221	19,444	288	777	1.4	4.0	15.9	2.0	0.3	1.1
Linn County, IA	198,903	197,005	191,701	168,767	7,202	22,934	3.8	13.6	12.5	2.8	1.6	1.5
Champaign-Urbana, IL	215,742	214,989	210,279	202,848	5,463	7,431	2.6	3.7	10.7	9.7	6.5	3.2
Champaign County, IL	184,905	184,265	179,669	173,025	5,236	6,644	2.9	3.8	9.7	11.2	7.5	3.5
Ford County, IL	14,157	14,226	14,241	14,275	-84	-34	-0.6	-0.2	18.1	0.4	0.4	1.6
Piatt County, IL	16,680	16,498	16,369	15,548	311	821	1.9	5.3	16.0	0.4	0.3	0.8
Charleston, WV	306,435	307,243	309,635	307,689	-3,200	1,946	-1.0	0.6	15.2	4.8	0.8	0.5
Boone County, WV	25,703	25,674	25,535	25,870	168	-335	0.7	-1.3	13.3	0.7	0.1	0.5
Clay County, WV	10,356	10,438	10,330	9,983	26	347	0.3	3.5	14.0	0.1	–	0.4
Kanawha County, WV	193,559	194,941	200,073	207,619	-6,514	-7,546	-3.3	-3.6	16.6	7.2	1.0	0.5
Lincoln County, WV	22,374	22,414	22,108	21,382	266	726	1.2	3.4	13.3	(Z)	0.1	0.6
Putnam County, WV	54,443	53,776	51,589	42,835	2,854	8,754	5.5	20.4	12.1	0.9	0.7	0.5
Charleston-North Charleston, SC	594,899	583,472	548,972	506,877	45,927	42,095	8.4	8.3	10.7	31.6	1.6	2.4
Berkeley County, SC	151,673	148,865	142,651	128,776	9,022	13,875	6.3	10.8	8.9	28.5	2.2	2.5
Charleston County, SC	330,368	327,403	309,980	295,041	20,388	14,939	6.6	5.1	11.9	34.8	1.4	2.5
Dorchester County, SC	112,858	107,204	96,341	83,060	16,517	13,281	17.1	16.0	9.5	25.8	1.3	2.1
Charlotte-Gastonia-Concord, NC-SC	1,521,278	1,474,843	1,330,419	1,024,690	190,859	305,729	14.3	29.8	9.6	23.2	2.4	6.5
Anson County, NC	25,499	25,742	25,275	23,474	224	1,801	0.9	7.7	14.1	48.7	0.7	1.1
Cabarrus County, NC	150,244	146,018	131,063	98,935	19,181	32,128	14.6	32.5	11.0	13.9	1.2	6.6
Gaston County, NC	196,137	194,154	190,316	175,093	5,821	15,223	3.1	8.7	12.7	14.3	1.0	4.1
Mecklenburg County, NC	796,372	771,573	695,370	511,481	101,002	183,889	14.5	36.0	8.5	29.4	3.7	8.0
Union County, NC	162,929	153,720	123,772	84,210	39,157	39,562	31.6	47.0	8.7	11.9	0.8	7.8
York County, SC	190,097	183,636	164,623	131,497	25,474	33,126	15.5	25.2	10.4	19.8	1.2	2.4
Charlottesville, VA	188,424	185,554	174,021	144,151	14,403	29,870	8.3	20.7	12.4	13.5	2.8	2.5
Albemarle County, VA	90,717	89,017	84,197	68,172	6,520	16,025	7.7	23.5	11.9	9.5	4.0	3.0
Fluvanna County, VA	24,751	23,835	20,047	12,429	4,704	7,618	23.5	61.3	13.6	17.6	0.4	1.5
Greene County, VA	17,418	17,007	15,244	10,297	2,174	4,947	14.3	48.0	10.1	6.5	0.5	1.6
Nelson County, VA	15,101	14,950	14,445	12,778	656	1,667	4.5	13.0	17.0	14.2	0.2	2.2
Charlottesville city, VA	40,437	40,745	40,088	40,475	349	-387	0.9	-1.0	12.1	23.1	3.5	2.6
Chattanooga, TN-GA	492,126	488,661	476,501	433,210	15,625	43,291	3.3	10.0	13.6	14.0	1.1	1.6
Catoosa County, GA	60,813	59,745	53,252	42,464	7,561	10,788	14.2	25.4	12.1	1.2	0.9	1.2
Dade County, GA	16,040	15,949	15,154	13,147	886	2,007	5.8	15.3	12.0	1.1	0.4	1.0
Walker County, GA	63,890	63,214	61,053	58,340	2,837	2,713	4.6	4.7	13.7	3.5	0.4	0.9
Hamilton County, TN	310,935	309,729	307,896	285,536	3,039	22,360	1.0	7.8	13.9	20.6	1.5	2.0
Marion County, TN	27,757	27,696	27,776	24,860	-19	2,916	-0.1	11.7	13.4	4.2	0.2	0.8
Sequatchie County, TN	12,691	12,328	11,370	8,863	1,321	2,507	11.6	28.3	12.2	0.8	0.3	0.8
Cheyenne, WY	85,163	85,033	81,607	73,142	3,556	8,465	4.4	11.6	11.7	3.1	1.0	11.6
Laramie County, WY	85,163	85,033	81,607	73,142	3,556	8,465	4.4	11.6	11.7	3.1	1.0	11.6
Chicago-Naperville-Joliet, IL-IN-WI	**9,443,356**	**9,393,259**	**9,098,615**	**8,182,076**	**344,741**	**916,539**	**3.8**	**11.2**	**10.7**	**18.5**	**4.9**	**17.9**
Chicago-Naperville-Joliet, IL	*7,882,729*	*7,850,994*	*7,628,447*	*6,894,440*	*254,282*	*734,007*	*3.3*	*10.6*	*10.8*	*19.7*	*5.3*	*18.9*
Cook County, IL	5,303,683	5,327,165	5,376,822	5,105,044	-73,139	271,778	-1.4	5.3	11.6	26.4	5.4	21.5
DeKalb County, IL	97,665	95,306	88,969	77,932	8,696	11,037	9.8	14.2	9.5	4.8	2.5	7.4
DuPage County, IL	929,113	928,126	904,152	781,689	24,961	122,463	2.8	15.7	10.0	3.6	9.5	10.7
Grundy County, IL	43,838	41,178	37,535	32,337	6,303	5,198	16.8	16.1	12.0	0.4	0.4	5.0
Kane County, IL	482,113	472,761	404,120	317,471	77,993	86,649	19.3	27.3	8.0	5.7	2.5	26.2
Kendall County, IL	79,514	72,704	54,520	39,413	24,994	15,107	45.8	38.3	8.7	2.4	1.4	9.9
McHenry County, IL	303,990	296,260	260,062	183,241	43,928	76,821	16.9	41.9	8.3	0.8	2.1	9.2
Will County, IL	642,813	617,494	502,267	357,313	140,546	144,954	28.0	40.6	8.0	10.4	2.9	10.7
Gary, IN	*697,401*	*690,891*	*675,971*	*643,037*	*21,430*	*32,934*	*3.2*	*5.1*	*12.5*	*18.5*	*0.9*	*10.3*
Jasper County, IN	31,876	31,605	30,043	24,960	1,833	5,083	6.1	20.4	12.7	0.4	0.3	3.1
Lake County, IN	493,297	490,089	484,564	475,594	8,733	8,970	1.8	1.9	13.0	25.5	0.9	12.6
Newton County, IN	14,456	14,371	14,566	13,551	-110	1,015	-0.8	7.5	12.8	0.2	0.3	3.4
Porter County, IN	157,772	154,826	146,798	128,932	10,974	17,866	7.5	13.9	11.1	1.4	1.1	5.1
Lake County-Kenosha County, IL-WI	*863,226*	*851,374*	*794,197*	*644,599*	*69,029*	*149,598*	*8.7*	*23.2*	*9.1*	*6.9*	*4.3*	*15.0*
Lake County, IL	702,682	692,869	644,620	516,418	58,062	128,202	9.0	24.8	8.7	7.2	5.0	16.6
Kenosha County, WI	160,544	158,505	149,577	128,181	10,967	21,396	7.3	16.7	11.1	5.5	1.2	7.7
Chico, CA	214,185	212,698	203,171	182,120	11,014	21,051	5.4	11.6	15.0	1.5	3.8	11.3
Butte County, CA	214,185	212,698	203,171	182,120	11,014	21,051	5.4	11.6	15.0	1.5	3.8	11.3
Cincinnati-Middletown, OH-KY-IN	2,070,441	2,056,843	2,009,657	1,844,915	60,784	164,742	3.0	8.9	11.6	11.5	1.5	1.2
Dearborn County, IN	49,082	48,609	46,130	38,835	2,952	7,295	6.4	18.8	11.3	0.6	0.4	0.6
Franklin County, IN	23,085	22,876	22,151	19,580	934	2,571	4.2	13.1	13.0	(Z)	0.3	0.5
Ohio County, IN	5,874	5,797	5,623	5,315	251	308	4.5	5.8	14.3	0.5	0.2	0.4
Boone County, KY	106,272	101,431	85,992	57,589	20,280	28,403	23.6	49.3	8.1	2.0	1.7	2.2
Bracken County, KY	8,670	8,694	8,279	7,766	391	513	4.7	6.6	13.3	0.6	0.1	0.6
Campbell County, KY	87,251	87,285	88,616	83,866	-1,365	4,750	-1.5	5.7	12.6	1.9	0.6	1.0
Gallatin County, KY	8,134	7,982	7,870	5,393	264	2,477	3.4	45.9	10.3	1.7	0.3	1.4
Grant County, KY	24,610	24,339	22,384	15,737	2,226	6,647	9.9	42.2	9.1	0.3	0.4	1.1
Kenton County, KY	153,665	153,019	151,463	142,031	2,202	9,432	1.5	6.6	10.8	4.3	0.8	1.3
Pendleton County, KY	15,125	15,082	14,390	12,036	735	2,354	5.1	19.6	10.3	0.5	0.1	0.7
Brown County, OH	44,398	44,162	42,285	34,966	2,113	7,319	5.0	20.9	12.0	1.0	0.2	0.3
Butler County, OH	350,412	346,123	332,705	291,479	17,707	41,226	5.3	14.1	10.7	5.8	1.9	1.7
Clermont County, OH	190,589	188,062	177,451	150,167	13,138	27,284	7.4	18.2	9.9	0.9	0.9	0.9
Hamilton County, OH	806,652	813,639	845,276	866,228	-38,624	-20,952	-4.6	-2.4	13.4	24.0	1.9	1.2
Warren County, OH	196,622	189,743	159,042	113,927	37,580	45,115	23.6	39.6	9.2	2.9	2.2	1.2
Clarksville, TN-KY	243,665	238,225	232,044	189,279	11,621	42,765	5.0	22.6	9.6	20.2	1.7	3.9
Christian County, KY	70,145	70,364	72,309	68,941	-2,164	3,368	-3.0	4.9	10.1	26.1	1.1	4.5
Trigg County, KY	13,349	13,262	12,597	10,361	752	2,236	6.0	21.6	16.9	9.7	0.3	0.9
Montgomery County, TN	147,202	141,806	134,768	100,498	12,434	34,270	9.2	34.1	8.2	19.9	2.1	4.1
Stewart County, TN	12,969	12,793	12,370	9,479	599	2,891	4.8	30.5	14.6	2.0	1.5	1.1

See footnotes at end of table.

Metropolitan statistical area **Metropolitan statistical area with metropolitan divisions** *Metropolitan division* Component county	Population				Net change		Percent change		Percent—			
	2005 (July 1)	2004 (July 1)	2000[1] (estimates base)	1990[2] (April 1)	2000–2005[3]	1990–2000	2000–2005[3]	1990–2000	65 years and over, 2003	Black or African American alone, 2003	Asian alone, 2003	Hispanic or Latino origin, 2003[4]
Cleveland, TN	108,036	106,984	104,015	87,355	4,021	16,660	3.9	19.1	12.7	3.5	0.7	2.1
Bradley County, TN	92,092	91,044	87,965	73,712	4,127	14,253	4.7	19.3	12.3	4.1	0.8	2.3
Polk County, TN	15,944	15,940	16,050	13,643	–106	2,407	–0.7	17.6	14.9	0.5	0.1	0.9
Cleveland-Elyria-Mentor, OH	2,126,318	2,133,778	2,148,010	2,102,248	–21,692	45,762	–1.0	2.2	14.4	19.6	1.7	3.5
Cuyahoga County, OH	1,335,317	1,349,047	1,393,845	1,412,140	–58,528	–18,295	–4.2	–1.3	15.3	28.4	2.2	3.5
Geauga County, OH	95,218	94,473	90,895	81,129	4,323	9,766	4.8	12.0	12.9	1.3	0.5	0.5
Lake County, OH	232,466	232,034	227,511	215,499	4,955	12,012	2.2	5.6	14.4	2.2	1.1	2.1
Lorain County, OH	296,307	293,532	284,664	271,126	11,643	13,538	4.1	5.0	12.6	8.6	0.7	7.0
Medina County, OH	167,010	164,692	151,095	122,354	15,915	28,741	10.5	23.5	10.8	0.9	0.8	1.0
Coeur d'Alene, ID	127,668	122,447	108,685	69,795	18,983	38,890	17.5	55.7	12.9	0.3	0.5	2.6
Kootenai County, ID	127,668	122,447	108,685	69,795	18,983	38,890	17.5	55.7	12.9	0.3	0.5	2.6
College Station-Bryan, TX	189,735	188,745	184,885	150,998	4,850	33,887	2.6	22.4	8.5	12.2	3.4	18.7
Brazos County, TX	156,305	155,662	152,415	121,862	3,890	30,553	2.6	25.1	7.0	10.8	4.0	19.4
Burleson County, TX	17,238	17,073	16,470	13,625	768	2,845	4.7	20.9	16.0	14.5	0.2	15.8
Robertson County, TX	16,192	16,010	16,000	15,511	192	489	1.2	3.2	16.2	24.1	0.3	15.0
Colorado Springs, CO	587,500	579,416	537,484	409,482	50,016	128,002	9.3	31.3	8.8	6.9	2.8	11.6
El Paso County, CO	565,582	557,752	516,929	397,014	48,653	119,915	9.4	30.2	8.8	7.1	2.9	11.9
Teller County, CO	21,918	21,664	20,555	12,468	1,363	8,087	6.6	64.9	8.4	0.7	0.7	4.3
Columbia, MO	153,283	151,144	145,666	122,010	7,617	23,656	5.2	19.4	9.2	8.6	3.2	1.8
Boone County, MO	143,326	141,216	135,454	112,379	7,872	23,075	5.8	20.5	8.7	8.7	3.4	1.9
Howard County, MO	9,957	9,928	10,212	9,631	–255	581	–2.5	6.0	16.0	6.7	0.1	0.7
Columbia, SC	689,878	680,039	647,261	548,936	42,617	98,325	6.6	17.9	10.6	34.2	1.4	2.6
Calhoun County, SC	15,100	15,248	15,184	12,753	–84	2,431	–0.6	19.1	13.7	47.6	0.1	1.6
Fairfield County, SC	24,047	24,144	23,454	22,295	593	1,159	2.5	5.2	13.2	59.5	0.4	1.2
Kershaw County, SC	56,486	55,374	52,647	43,599	3,839	9,048	7.3	20.8	12.7	26.3	0.4	1.9
Lexington County, SC	235,272	230,861	216,014	167,611	19,258	48,403	8.9	28.9	10.7	13.7	1.1	2.3
Richland County, SC	340,078	335,597	320,781	286,321	19,297	34,460	6.0	12.0	9.7	47.4	2.0	2.7
Saluda County, SC	18,895	18,815	19,181	16,357	–286	2,824	–1.5	17.3	14.2	29.5	(Z)	10.2
Columbus, GA-AL	284,299	284,453	281,768	266,452	2,531	15,316	0.9	5.7	11.2	40.3	1.4	3.5
Russell County, AL	49,326	49,164	49,756	46,860	–430	2,896	–0.9	6.2	13.5	42.6	0.5	2.0
Chattahoochee County, GA	14,679	15,646	14,882	16,934	–203	–2,052	–1.4	–12.1	1.5	29.6	2.0	11.0
Harris County, GA	27,779	26,847	23,695	17,788	4,084	5,907	17.2	33.2	11.5	18.3	0.5	1.3
Marion County, GA	7,244	7,134	7,144	5,590	100	1,554	1.4	27.8	10.4	33.6	0.3	6.9
Muscogee County, GA	185,271	185,662	186,291	179,280	–1,020	7,011	–0.5	3.9	11.6	44.1	1.7	3.3
Columbus, IN	73,540	72,853	71,435	63,657	2,105	7,778	2.9	12.2	12.7	1.7	2.3	2.7
Bartholomew County, IN	73,540	72,853	71,435	63,657	2,105	7,778	2.9	12.2	12.7	1.7	2.3	2.7
Columbus, OH	1,708,625	1,690,721	1,612,837	1,405,168	95,788	207,669	5.9	14.8	10.0	13.6	2.9	2.1
Delaware County, OH	150,268	142,747	109,989	66,929	40,279	43,060	36.6	64.3	8.0	3.0	3.1	1.1
Fairfield County, OH	138,423	135,913	122,881	103,472	15,542	19,409	12.6	18.8	11.1	4.5	0.9	1.0
Franklin County, OH	1,090,771	1,087,462	1,068,869	961,437	21,902	107,432	2.0	11.2	9.7	19.1	3.8	2.7
Licking County, OH	154,806	152,792	145,621	128,300	9,185	17,321	6.3	13.5	12.0	2.2	0.7	0.7
Madison County, OH	41,295	41,003	40,213	37,068	1,082	3,145	2.7	8.5	11.4	6.4	0.6	0.7
Morrow County, OH	34,322	34,076	31,628	27,749	2,694	3,879	8.5	14.0	11.5	0.4	0.3	0.6
Pickaway County, OH	52,989	51,999	52,727	48,244	262	4,483	0.5	9.3	11.6	5.1	0.2	0.7
Union County, OH	45,751	44,729	40,909	31,969	4,842	8,940	11.8	28.0	9.4	2.9	0.7	0.9
Corpus Christi, TX	413,553	409,645	403,280	367,786	10,273	35,494	2.5	9.7	11.7	3.5	1.2	55.1
Aransas County, TX	24,640	23,999	22,497	17,892	2,143	4,605	9.5	25.7	20.2	1.6	2.5	21.7
Nueces County, TX	319,704	317,317	313,645	291,145	6,059	22,500	1.9	7.7	11.3	4.1	1.3	58.4
San Patricio County, TX	69,209	68,329	67,138	58,749	2,071	8,389	3.1	14.3	10.8	1.9	0.6	51.6
Corvallis, OR	78,640	78,383	78,139	70,811	501	7,328	0.6	10.3	10.6	0.9	5.2	5.1
Benton County, OR	78,640	78,383	78,139	70,811	501	7,328	0.6	10.3	10.6	0.9	5.2	5.1
Cumberland, MD-WV	100,667	101,025	102,008	101,643	–1,341	365	–1.3	0.4	17.1	4.7	0.5	0.7
Allegany County, MD	73,639	73,999	74,930	74,946	–1,291	–16	–1.7	(Z)	17.8	5.3	0.5	0.8
Mineral County, WV	27,028	27,026	27,078	26,697	–50	381	–0.2	1.4	15.0	2.9	0.4	0.6
Dallas-Fort Worth-Arlington, TX	**5,819,475**	**5,696,045**	**5,161,518**	**3,989,294**	**657,957**	**1,172,224**	**12.7**	**29.4**	**7.8**	**14.0**	**4.3**	**24.3**
Dallas-Plano-Irving, TX	*3,893,123*	*3,810,195*	*3,451,248*	*2,622,562*	*441,875*	*828,686*	*12.8*	*31.6*	*7.4*	*15.2*	*4.8*	*26.1*
Collin County, TX	659,457	628,426	491,777	264,036	167,680	227,741	34.1	86.3	5.6	5.9	8.7	11.6
Dallas County, TX	2,305,454	2,291,071	2,218,842	1,852,810	86,612	366,032	3.9	19.8	8.1	20.7	4.2	34.3
Delta County, TX	5,480	5,528	5,327	4,857	153	470	2.9	9.7	17.4	8.2	0.2	3.4
Denton County, TX	554,642	530,982	432,962	273,525	121,680	159,437	28.1	58.3	5.0	6.4	5.2	14.3
Ellis County, TX	133,474	128,631	111,360	85,167	22,114	26,193	19.9	30.8	8.9	8.3	0.4	20.2
Hunt County, TX	82,543	81,688	76,596	64,343	5,947	12,253	7.8	19.0	12.2	9.1	0.6	9.5
Kaufman County, TX	89,129	85,447	71,310	52,220	17,819	19,090	25.0	36.6	9.9	10.1	0.6	12.7
Rockwall County, TX	62,944	58,422	43,074	25,604	19,870	17,470	46.1	68.2	8.1	4.1	1.6	12.5
Fort Worth-Arlington, TX	*1,926,352*	*1,885,850*	*1,710,270*	*1,366,732*	*216,082*	*343,538*	*12.6*	*25.1*	*8.5*	*11.6*	*3.5*	*20.8*
Johnson County, TX	146,376	143,231	126,811	97,165	19,565	29,646	15.4	30.5	9.4	2.6	0.6	13.6
Parker County, TX	102,801	100,170	88,494	64,785	14,307	23,709	16.2	36.6	10.3	1.9	0.4	7.6
Tarrant County, TX	1,620,479	1,587,019	1,446,172	1,170,103	174,307	276,069	12.1	23.6	8.3	13.3	4.0	22.5
Wise County, TX	56,696	55,430	48,793	34,679	7,903	14,114	16.2	40.7	10.3	1.1	0.3	12.0
Dalton, GA	131,701	129,551	120,061	98,609	11,640	21,452	9.7	21.8	9.8	2.8	0.8	20.0
Murray County, GA	40,812	40,326	36,503	26,147	4,309	10,356	11.8	39.6	8.5	0.9	0.2	9.7
Whitfield County, GA	90,889	89,225	83,558	72,462	7,331	11,096	8.8	15.3	10.4	3.6	1.1	24.7
Danville, IL	82,344	82,647	83,924	88,257	–1,580	–4,333	–1.9	–4.9	16.1	11.0	0.6	3.3
Vermilion County, IL	82,344	82,647	83,924	88,257	–1,580	–4,333	–1.9	–4.9	16.1	11.0	0.6	3.3
Danville, VA	107,997	108,263	110,156	108,728	–2,159	1,428	–2.0	1.3	16.6	33.0	0.4	1.5
Pittsylvania County, VA	61,854	61,790	61,745	55,672	109	6,073	0.2	10.9	14.1	23.7	0.2	1.4
Danville city, VA	46,143	46,473	48,411	53,056	–2,268	–4,645	–4.7	–8.8	19.9	45.1	0.7	1.6
Davenport-Moline-Rock Island, IA-IL	376,309	375,293	376,054	368,145	255	7,909	0.1	2.1	14.0	6.1	1.4	6.1
Henry County, IL	50,591	50,568	51,020	51,159	–429	–139	–0.8	–0.3	16.1	1.3	0.3	3.2
Mercer County, IL	16,912	16,991	16,957	17,290	–45	–333	–0.3	–1.9	16.0	0.5	0.2	1.3
Rock Island County, IL	147,808	147,609	149,388	148,723	–1,580	665	–1.1	0.4	15.2	8.1	1.2	9.8
Scott County, IA	160,998	160,125	158,689	150,973	2,309	7,716	1.5	5.1	11.9	6.3	2.0	4.1

See footnotes at end of table.

Table C-1. Metropolitan Areas With Component Counties — **Population and Population Characteristics**—Con.

Metropolitan statistical area **Metropolitan statistical area with metropolitan divisions** *Metropolitan division* Component county	Population				Net change		Percent change		Percent—			
	2005 (July 1)	2004 (July 1)	2000[1] (estimates base)	1990[2] (April 1)	2000–2005[3]	1990–2000	2000–2005[3]	1990–2000	65 years and over, 2003	Black or African American alone, 2003	Asian alone, 2003	Hispanic or Latino origin, 2003[4]
Dayton, OH	843,577	844,850	848,153	843,835	–4,576	4,318	–0.5	0.5	13.5	14.5	1.6	1.2
Greene County, OH	151,996	151,991	147,886	136,731	4,110	11,155	2.8	8.2	12.0	6.2	2.4	1.3
Miami County, OH	101,619	100,786	98,868	93,182	2,751	5,686	2.8	6.1	13.5	1.9	1.1	0.8
Montgomery County, OH	547,435	549,553	559,062	573,809	–11,627	–14,747	–2.1	–2.6	14.0	20.2	1.6	1.3
Preble County, OH	42,527	42,520	42,337	40,113	190	2,224	0.4	5.5	13.7	0.4	0.3	0.5
Decatur, AL	148,345	147,400	145,867	131,556	2,478	14,311	1.7	10.9	12.6	11.9	0.4	3.4
Lawrence County, AL	34,605	34,470	34,803	31,513	–198	3,290	–0.6	10.4	12.4	12.7	0.1	1.2
Morgan County, AL	113,740	112,930	111,064	100,043	2,676	11,021	2.4	11.0	12.7	11.6	0.5	4.1
Decatur, IL	110,167	110,502	114,706	117,206	–4,539	–2,500	–4.0	–2.1	15.7	14.5	0.8	1.1
Macon County, IL	110,167	110,502	114,706	117,206	–4,539	–2,500	–4.0	–2.1	15.7	14.5	0.8	1.1
Deltona-Daytona Beach-Ormond Beach, FL	490,055	478,951	443,343	370,737	46,712	72,606	10.5	19.6	21.3	10.0	1.2	7.9
Volusia County, FL	490,055	478,951	443,343	370,737	46,712	72,606	10.5	19.6	21.3	10.0	1.2	7.9
Denver-Aurora, CO[5]	2,359,994	2,326,310	2,179,320	1,650,489	180,674	528,831	8.3	32.0	9.0	5.8	3.4	20.3
Adams County, CO[5]	399,426	388,064	347,963	265,038	51,463	82,925	14.8	31.3	7.9	3.2	3.4	31.7
Arapahoe County, CO	529,090	522,346	488,896	391,511	40,194	97,385	8.2	24.9	9.0	9.3	4.7	14.5
Broomfield County, CO[5]	43,478	42,456	39,198	24,638	4,280	14,560	10.9	59.1	6.6	1.0	4.5	10.5
Clear Creek County, CO	9,197	9,173	9,322	7,619	–125	1,703	–1.3	22.4	7.6	0.5	0.8	4.0
Denver County, CO	557,917	555,991	553,693	467,610	4,224	86,083	0.8	18.4	10.9	11.3	3.2	34.8
Douglas County, CO	249,416	237,551	175,766	60,391	73,650	115,375	41.9	191.0	4.2	1.3	3.3	6.0
Elbert County, CO	22,788	22,455	19,872	9,646	2,916	10,226	14.7	106.0	6.4	0.9	0.5	4.7
Gilpin County, CO	4,932	4,866	4,757	3,070	175	1,687	3.7	55.0	6.1	0.6	0.9	3.8
Jefferson County, CO[5]	526,801	526,648	525,330	438,430	1,471	86,900	0.3	19.8	10.3	1.0	2.6	11.1
Park County, CO	16,949	16,760	14,523	7,174	2,426	7,349	16.7	102.4	7.7	0.5	0.5	4.7
Des Moines, IA	522,454	512,340	481,398	416,346	41,056	65,052	8.5	15.6	11.3	4.0	2.7	4.5
Dallas County, IA	51,762	49,455	40,750	29,755	11,012	10,995	27.0	37.0	9.9	0.9	1.4	5.5
Guthrie County, IA	11,547	11,550	11,353	10,935	194	418	1.7	3.8	19.9	0.1	0.2	1.4
Madison County, IA.	15,158	14,905	14,019	12,483	1,139	1,536	8.1	12.3	13.8	0.1	0.2	0.8
Polk County, IA	401,006	394,031	374,605	327,140	26,401	47,465	7.0	14.5	11.0	5.0	3.2	5.0
Warren County, IA	42,981	42,399	40,671	36,033	2,310	4,638	5.7	12.9	12.0	0.3	0.4	1.1
Detroit-Warren-Livonia, MI.	**4,488,335**	**4,489,523**	**4,452,557**	**4,248,699**	**35,778**	**203,858**	**0.8**	**4.8**	**11.8**	**23.0**	**2.9**	**3.1**
Detroit-Livonia-Dearborn, MI.	*1,998,217*	*2,013,771*	*2,061,162*	*2,111,687*	*–62,945*	*–50,525*	*–3.1*	*–2.4*	*11.7*	*42.4*	*2.1*	*4.2*
Wayne County, MI	1,998,217	2,013,771	2,061,162	2,111,687	–62,945	–50,525	–3.1	–2.4	11.7	42.4	2.1	4.2
Warren-Farmington Hills-Troy, MI.	*2,490,118*	*2,475,752*	*2,391,395*	*2,137,012*	*98,723*	*254,383*	*4.1*	*11.9*	*11.9*	*7.0*	*3.5*	*2.3*
Lapeer County, MI.	93,361	92,368	87,904	74,768	5,457	13,136	6.2	17.6	9.9	0.9	0.5	3.4
Livingston County, MI.	181,517	177,271	156,951	115,645	24,566	41,306	15.7	35.7	8.8	0.6	0.7	1.4
Macomb County, MI.	829,453	822,965	788,149	717,400	41,304	70,749	5.2	9.9	13.5	4.1	2.8	1.8
Oakland County, MI.	1,214,361	1,212,181	1,194,156	1,083,592	20,205	110,564	1.7	10.2	11.4	11.1	5.1	2.6
St. Clair County, MI.	171,426	170,967	164,235	145,607	7,191	18,628	4.4	12.8	12.1	2.1	0.4	2.3
Dothan, AL	136,594	135,011	130,861	120,352	5,733	10,509	4.4	8.7	14.8	23.5	0.5	1.5
Geneva County, AL.	25,735	25,562	25,767	23,647	–32	2,120	–0.1	9.0	16.9	10.6	0.2	1.9
Henry County, AL.	16,610	16,535	16,310	15,374	300	936	1.8	6.1	16.5	31.5	(Z)	1.8
Houston County, AL	94,249	92,914	88,784	81,331	5,465	7,453	6.2	9.2	13.9	25.6	0.7	1.4
Dover, DE	143,968	139,118	126,700	110,993	17,268	15,707	13.6	14.2	12.1	20.7	1.8	3.5
Kent County, DE	143,968	139,118	126,700	110,993	17,268	15,707	13.6	14.2	12.1	20.7	1.8	3.5
Dubuque, IA	91,631	91,079	89,156	86,403	2,475	2,753	2.8	3.2	14.8	1.1	0.7	1.2
Dubuque County, IA	91,631	91,079	89,156	86,403	2,475	2,753	2.8	3.2	14.8	1.1	0.7	1.2
Duluth, MN-WI	275,413	275,780	275,486	269,230	–73	6,256	(Z)	2.3	15.4	0.9	0.7	0.8
Carlton County, MN	34,026	33,610	31,671	29,259	2,355	2,412	7.4	8.2	14.9	1.1	0.5	0.9
St. Louis County, MN	197,179	198,135	200,528	198,213	–3,349	2,315	–1.7	1.2	15.8	0.9	0.7	0.8
Douglas County, WI	44,208	44,035	43,287	41,758	921	1,529	2.1	3.7	14.2	0.6	0.8	0.8
Durham, NC	456,187	450,260	423,803	344,645	32,384	79,158	7.6	23.0	10.2	28.7	3.6	8.0
Chatham County, NC	58,002	56,861	49,329	38,759	8,673	10,570	17.6	27.3	14.2	15.4	1.5	10.9
Durham County, NC	242,582	239,468	223,314	181,855	19,268	41,459	8.6	22.8	9.4	39.4	3.7	9.8
Orange County, NC	118,386	117,141	115,537	93,851	2,849	21,686	2.5	23.1	9.0	13.5	5.2	5.0
Person County, NC	37,217	36,790	35,623	30,180	1,594	5,443	4.5	18.0	13.7	28.6	0.2	2.2
Eau Claire, WI.	154,039	152,989	148,337	137,543	5,702	10,794	3.8	7.8	13.1	0.4	2.2	0.8
Chippewa County, WI	59,950	58,867	55,205	52,360	4,745	2,845	8.6	5.4	14.4	0.3	1.1	0.7
Eau Claire County, WI	94,089	94,122	93,132	85,183	957	7,949	1.0	9.3	12.3	0.6	2.8	0.9
El Centro, CA	155,823	152,345	142,361	109,303	13,462	33,058	9.5	30.2	10.3	4.3	2.1	74.7
Imperial County, CA	155,823	152,345	142,361	109,303	13,462	33,058	9.5	30.2	10.3	4.3	2.1	74.7
Elizabethtown, KY	110,646	109,286	107,543	100,919	3,103	6,624	2.9	6.6	10.9	11.4	1.9	2.9
Hardin County, KY	96,947	95,788	94,170	89,240	2,777	4,930	2.9	5.5	10.2	12.6	2.1	3.2
Larue County, KY	13,699	13,498	13,373	11,679	326	1,694	2.4	14.5	15.3	3.1	0.2	1.1
Elkhart-Goshen, IN.	195,362	191,629	182,791	156,198	12,571	26,593	6.9	17.0	10.8	5.1	1.1	10.7
Elkhart County, IN	195,362	191,629	182,791	156,198	12,571	26,593	6.9	17.0	10.8	5.1	1.1	10.7
Elmira, NY	89,512	89,952	91,070	95,195	–1,558	–4,125	–1.7	–4.3	15.5	6.5	1.0	2.2
Chemung County, NY	89,512	89,952	91,070	95,195	–1,558	–4,125	–1.7	–4.3	15.5	6.5	1.0	2.2
El Paso, TX	721,598	712,617	679,622	591,610	41,976	88,012	6.2	14.9	10.1	2.8	1.0	81.3
El Paso County, TX	721,598	712,617	679,622	591,610	41,976	88,012	6.2	14.9	10.1	2.8	1.0	81.3
Erie, PA	280,446	280,844	280,843	275,572	–397	5,271	–0.1	1.9	14.2	6.3	0.7	2.2
Erie County, PA	280,446	280,844	280,843	275,572	–397	5,271	–0.1	1.9	14.2	6.3	0.7	2.2
Eugene-Springfield, OR	335,180	331,567	322,977	282,912	12,203	40,065	3.8	14.2	13.5	0.9	2.4	5.1
Lane County, OR	335,180	331,567	322,977	282,912	12,203	40,065	3.8	14.2	13.5	0.9	2.4	5.1

See footnotes at end of table.

State and Metropolitan Area Data Book: 2006

193

U.S. Census Bureau

Table C-1. Metropolitan Areas With Component Counties — **Population and Population Characteristics**—Con.

Metropolitan statistical area **Metropolitan statistical area with metropolitan divisions** *Metropolitan division* Component county	Population				Net change		Percent change		Percent—			
	2005 (July 1)	2004 (July 1)	2000[1] (estimates base)	1990[2] (April 1)	2000– 2005[3]	1990– 2000	2000– 2005[3]	1990– 2000	65 years and over, 2003	Black or African American alone, 2003	Asian alone, 2003	Hispanic or Latino origin, 2003[4]
Evansville, IN-KY	349,543	347,833	342,815	324,858	6,728	17,957	2.0	5.5	13.8	5.6	0.7	1.1
Gibson County, IN	33,408	33,241	32,500	31,913	908	587	2.8	1.8	15.2	2.0	0.6	0.7
Posey County, IN	26,852	26,891	27,061	25,968	−209	1,093	−0.8	4.2	12.6	0.9	0.2	0.4
Vanderburgh County, IN	173,187	172,898	171,922	165,058	1,265	6,864	0.7	4.2	14.7	8.2	1.0	1.0
Warrick County, IN	56,362	55,350	52,383	44,920	3,979	7,463	7.6	16.6	11.1	1.2	0.8	0.9
Henderson County, KY	45,573	45,363	44,829	43,044	744	1,785	1.7	4.1	13.1	7.3	0.4	1.3
Webster County, KY	14,161	14,090	14,120	13,955	41	165	0.3	1.2	14.8	4.4	(Z)	3.6
Fairbanks, AK	87,560	86,904	82,840	77,720	4,720	5,120	5.7	6.6	5.0	6.7	2.0	4.7
Fairbanks North Star Borough, AK	87,560	86,904	82,840	77,720	4,720	5,120	5.7	6.6	5.0	6.7	2.0	4.7
Fargo, ND-MN	184,857	182,649	174,367	153,296	10,490	21,071	6.0	13.7	10.6	1.1	1.4	1.8
Clay County, MN	53,838	53,066	51,229	50,422	2,609	807	5.1	1.6	12.6	0.6	1.0	2.9
Cass County, ND	131,019	129,583	123,138	102,874	7,881	20,264	6.4	19.7	9.8	1.3	1.5	1.4
Farmington, NM	126,208	124,196	113,801	91,605	12,407	22,196	10.9	24.2	9.3	0.6	0.3	15.4
San Juan County, NM	126,208	124,196	113,801	91,605	12,407	22,196	10.9	24.2	9.3	0.6	0.3	15.4
Fayetteville, NC	345,536	346,136	336,613	297,569	8,923	39,044	2.7	13.1	8.3	37.7	2.1	5.6
Cumberland County, NC	304,520	306,943	302,967	274,713	1,553	28,254	0.5	10.3	8.4	37.6	2.2	5.2
Hoke County, NC	41,016	39,193	33,646	22,856	7,370	10,790	21.9	47.2	7.3	38.3	1.1	8.5
Fayetteville-Springdale-Rogers, AR-MO	405,101	390,944	347,045	239,464	58,056	107,581	16.7	44.9	11.5	1.5	1.5	9.8
Benton County, AR	186,938	179,609	153,404	97,499	33,534	55,905	21.9	57.3	13.3	0.8	1.4	10.2
Madison County, AR	14,962	14,670	14,243	11,618	719	2,625	5.0	22.6	13.7	0.2	(Z)	2.9
Washington County, AR	180,357	174,265	157,717	113,409	22,640	44,308	14.4	39.1	9.6	2.5	1.9	9.9
McDonald County, MO	22,844	22,400	21,681	16,938	1,163	4,743	5.4	28.0	11.2	0.3	0.3	10.1
Flagstaff, AZ	123,866	122,687	116,320	96,591	7,546	19,729	6.5	20.4	7.4	1.0	0.9	11.1
Coconino County, AZ	123,866	122,687	116,320	96,591	7,546	19,729	6.5	20.4	7.4	1.0	0.9	11.1
Flint, MI	443,883	443,497	436,148	430,459	7,735	5,689	1.8	1.3	11.8	20.3	0.9	2.4
Genesee County, MI	443,883	443,497	436,148	430,459	7,735	5,689	1.8	1.3	11.8	20.3	0.9	2.4
Florence, SC	198,443	197,273	193,155	176,195	5,288	16,960	2.7	9.6	12.2	41.1	0.6	1.1
Darlington County, SC	67,346	67,588	67,394	61,851	−48	5,543	−0.1	9.0	12.4	42.6	0.2	0.9
Florence County, SC	131,097	129,685	125,761	114,344	5,336	11,417	4.2	10.0	12.1	40.4	0.9	1.1
Florence-Muscle Shoals, AL	142,351	142,194	142,950	131,327	−599	11,623	−0.4	8.9	15.5	12.5	0.4	1.1
Colbert County, AL	54,660	54,728	54,984	51,666	−324	3,318	−0.6	6.4	15.7	17.0	0.4	1.2
Lauderdale County, AL	87,691	87,466	87,966	79,661	−275	8,305	−0.3	10.4	15.4	9.7	0.4	1.1
Fond du Lac, WI	99,337	98,648	97,296	90,083	2,041	7,213	2.1	8.0	14.3	1.0	0.9	2.5
Fond du Lac County, WI	99,337	98,648	97,296	90,083	2,041	7,213	2.1	8.0	14.3	1.0	0.9	2.5
Fort Collins-Loveland, CO	271,927	268,960	251,494	186,136	20,433	65,358	8.1	35.1	9.6	0.8	1.8	8.9
Larimer County, CO	271,927	268,960	251,494	186,136	20,433	65,358	8.1	35.1	9.6	0.8	1.8	8.9
Fort Smith, AR-OK	284,994	282,006	273,171	234,078	11,823	39,093	4.3	16.7	13.0	3.7	2.0	5.3
Crawford County, AR	57,630	56,641	53,247	42,493	4,383	10,754	8.2	25.3	11.4	0.9	1.4	3.7
Franklin County, AR	18,218	18,025	17,771	14,897	447	2,874	2.5	19.3	16.1	0.8	0.4	1.9
Sebastian County, AR	118,750	117,632	115,070	99,590	3,680	15,480	3.2	15.5	12.7	6.6	3.8	7.9
Le Flore County, OK	49,528	49,155	48,111	43,270	1,417	4,841	2.9	11.2	13.8	2.3	0.3	4.7
Sequoyah County, OK	40,868	40,553	38,972	33,828	1,896	5,144	4.9	15.2	13.7	1.9	0.3	2.2
Fort Walton Beach-Crestview-Destin, FL	182,172	180,910	170,498	143,777	11,674	26,721	6.8	18.6	12.8	9.4	2.8	4.3
Okaloosa County, FL	182,172	180,910	170,498	143,777	11,674	26,721	6.8	18.6	12.8	9.4	2.8	4.3
Fort Wayne, IN	404,414	401,750	390,156	354,435	14,258	35,721	3.7	10.1	11.6	9.8	1.5	4.2
Allen County, IN	344,006	341,816	331,849	300,836	12,157	31,013	3.7	10.3	11.2	11.5	1.7	4.7
Wells County, IN	28,085	28,025	27,600	25,948	485	1,652	1.8	6.4	14.5	0.2	0.3	1.6
Whitley County, IN	32,323	31,909	30,707	27,651	1,616	3,056	5.3	11.1	12.8	0.2	0.3	0.9
Fresno, CA	877,584	865,620	799,407	667,490	78,177	131,917	9.8	19.8	9.7	5.7	8.6	46.0
Fresno County, CA	877,584	865,620	799,407	667,490	78,177	131,917	9.8	19.8	9.7	5.7	8.6	46.0
Gadsden, AL	103,189	103,096	103,459	99,840	−270	3,619	−0.3	3.6	15.9	14.8	0.4	2.0
Etowah County, AL	103,189	103,096	103,459	99,840	−270	3,619	−0.3	3.6	15.9	14.8	0.4	2.0
Gainesville, FL	240,254	238,489	232,392	191,263	7,862	41,129	3.4	21.5	10.1	19.9	3.6	5.7
Alachua County, FL	223,852	222,568	217,955	181,596	5,897	36,359	2.7	20.0	9.7	20.8	3.9	5.9
Gilchrist County, FL	16,402	15,921	14,437	9,667	1,965	4,770	13.6	49.3	14.7	6.6	0.2	3.1
Gainesville, GA	165,771	160,788	139,315	95,434	26,456	43,881	19.0	46.0	9.2	6.9	1.4	22.6
Hall County, GA	165,771	160,788	139,315	95,434	26,456	43,881	19.0	46.0	9.2	6.9	1.4	22.6
Glens Falls, NY	128,572	127,774	124,345	118,539	4,227	5,806	3.4	4.9	14.7	2.0	0.5	1.9
Warren County, NY	65,548	65,029	63,303	59,209	2,245	4,094	3.5	6.9	15.4	0.8	0.6	1.5
Washington County, NY	63,024	62,745	61,042	59,330	1,982	1,712	3.2	2.9	13.9	3.2	0.3	2.3
Goldsboro, NC	114,448	114,215	113,329	104,666	1,119	8,663	1.0	8.3	12.0	33.6	1.0	5.5
Wayne County, NC	114,448	114,215	113,329	104,666	1,119	8,663	1.0	8.3	12.0	33.6	1.0	5.5
Grand Forks, ND-MN	97,073	97,024	97,478	103,272	−405	−5,794	−0.4	−5.6	12.2	1.2	1.0	2.8
Polk County, MN	31,133	31,010	31,369	32,589	−236	−1,220	−0.8	−3.7	17.2	0.4	0.4	4.2
Grand Forks County, ND	65,940	66,014	66,109	70,683	−169	−4,574	−0.3	−6.5	9.8	1.6	1.3	2.1
Grand Junction, CO	129,872	127,281	116,935	93,145	12,937	23,790	11.1	25.5	15.3	0.5	0.6	10.3
Mesa County, CO	129,872	127,281	116,935	93,145	12,937	23,790	11.1	25.5	15.3	0.5	0.6	10.3
Grand Rapids-Wyoming, MI	771,185	766,202	740,482	645,918	30,703	94,564	4.1	14.6	10.5	7.9	1.7	6.9
Barry County, MI	59,892	59,240	56,755	50,057	3,137	6,698	5.5	13.4	12.0	0.3	0.3	1.7
Ionia County, MI	64,608	64,276	61,518	57,024	3,090	4,494	5.0	7.9	9.9	5.1	0.4	2.7
Kent County, MI	596,666	592,999	574,335	500,631	22,331	73,704	3.9	14.7	10.2	9.5	2.1	8.1
Newaygo County, MI	50,019	49,687	47,874	38,206	2,145	9,668	4.5	25.3	12.9	1.3	0.3	4.4

See footnotes at end of table.

State and Metropolitan Area Data Book: 2006

U.S. Census Bureau

Metropolitan statistical area **Metropolitan statistical area with metropolitan divisions** *Metropolitan division* Component county	Population				Net change		Percent change		Percent—			
	2005 (July 1)	2004 (July 1)	2000[1] (estimates base)	1990[2] (April 1)	2000–2005[3]	1990–2000	2000–2005[3]	1990–2000	65 years and over, 2003	Black or African can alone, 2003	Asian alone, 2003	Hispanic or Latino origin, 2003[4]
Great Falls, MT	79,569	79,938	80,357	77,691	−788	2,666	−1.0	3.4	14.6	1.5	0.9	2.6
Cascade County, MT	79,569	79,938	80,357	77,691	−788	2,666	−1.0	3.4	14.6	1.5	0.9	2.6
Greeley, CO[5]	228,943	219,961	180,861	131,821	48,082	49,040	26.6	37.2	8.2	0.8	1.0	29.7
Weld County, CO[5]	228,943	219,961	180,861	131,821	48,082	49,040	26.6	37.2	8.2	0.8	1.0	29.7
Green Bay, WI	297,493	295,049	282,497	243,698	14,996	38,799	5.3	15.9	11.5	1.2	2.0	3.7
Brown County, WI	238,987	236,870	226,658	194,594	12,329	32,064	5.4	16.5	10.7	1.4	2.4	4.5
Kewaunee County, WI	20,840	20,689	20,187	18,878	653	1,309	3.2	6.9	14.8	0.2	0.1	0.7
Oconto County, WI	37,666	37,490	35,652	30,226	2,014	5,426	5.6	18.0	14.5	0.3	0.2	0.8
Greensboro-High Point, NC	674,500	666,427	643,447	540,030	31,053	103,417	4.8	19.2	12.4	23.8	2.2	5.2
Guilford County, NC	443,519	437,879	421,048	347,420	22,471	73,628	5.3	21.2	11.9	30.5	3.0	4.5
Randolph County, NC	138,367	136,295	130,471	106,546	7,896	23,925	6.1	22.5	12.3	5.5	0.8	8.3
Rockingham County, NC	92,614	92,253	91,928	86,064	686	5,864	0.7	6.8	15.0	19.6	0.3	3.8
Greenville, NC	162,596	160,360	152,693	123,864	9,903	28,829	6.5	23.3	9.9	35.1	1.0	4.5
Greene County, NC	20,026	20,113	18,974	15,384	1,052	3,590	5.5	23.3	11.7	40.5	(Z)	9.7
Pitt County, NC	142,570	140,247	133,719	108,480	8,851	25,239	6.6	23.3	9.6	34.3	1.1	3.7
Greenville, SC	591,251	583,917	559,922	472,155	31,329	87,767	5.6	18.6	12.0	17.5	1.4	4.0
Greenville County, SC	407,383	401,019	379,632	320,167	27,751	59,465	7.3	18.6	11.8	18.9	1.6	4.8
Laurens County, SC	70,293	70,094	69,533	58,092	760	11,441	1.1	19.7	13.0	26.3	0.2	2.7
Pickens County, SC	113,575	112,804	110,757	93,896	2,818	16,861	2.5	18.0	11.9	6.8	1.2	2.0
Gulfport-Biloxi, MS	255,383	252,826	246,190	207,875	9,193	38,315	3.7	18.4	12.0	19.5	2.4	2.3
Hancock County, MS	46,711	45,899	42,967	31,760	3,744	11,207	8.7	35.3	14.3	6.6	1.0	1.9
Harrison County, MS	193,810	192,458	189,601	165,365	4,209	24,236	2.2	14.7	11.6	22.6	2.9	2.4
Stone County, MS	14,862	14,469	13,622	10,750	1,240	2,872	9.1	26.7	10.9	20.0	0.2	1.4
Hagerstown-Martinsburg, MD-WV	251,311	244,206	222,771	192,774	28,540	29,997	12.8	15.6	13.1	6.5	0.7	1.4
Washington County, MD	141,895	139,193	131,923	121,393	9,972	10,530	7.6	8.7	14.1	8.0	0.8	1.3
Berkeley County, WV	93,394	89,267	75,905	59,253	17,489	16,652	23.0	28.1	10.8	5.2	0.6	1.7
Morgan County, WV	16,022	15,746	14,943	12,128	1,079	2,815	7.2	23.2	16.7	0.6	0.3	0.9
Hanford-Corcoran, CA	143,420	142,291	129,461	101,469	13,959	27,992	10.8	27.6	7.3	8.7	3.2	45.4
Kings County, CA	143,420	142,291	129,461	101,469	13,959	27,992	10.8	27.6	7.3	8.7	3.2	45.4
Harrisburg-Carlisle, PA	521,812	518,744	509,074	474,242	12,738	34,832	2.5	7.3	14.4	9.7	2.1	2.7
Cumberland County, PA	223,089	221,135	213,674	195,257	9,415	18,417	4.4	9.4	15.0	2.5	2.1	1.4
Dauphin County, PA	253,995	253,060	251,798	237,813	2,197	13,985	0.9	5.9	14.2	17.5	2.4	4.2
Perry County, PA	44,728	44,549	43,602	41,172	1,126	2,430	2.6	5.9	12.3	0.7	0.2	0.7
Harrisonburg, VA	111,689	110,796	108,167	88,189	3,522	19,978	3.3	22.7	12.1	3.4	1.4	6.4
Rockingham County, VA	71,251	70,151	67,714	57,482	3,537	10,232	5.2	17.8	13.9	1.6	0.3	3.6
Harrisonburg city, VA	40,438	40,645	40,453	30,707	−15	9,746	(Z)	31.7	9.2	6.4	3.3	10.9
Hartford-West Hartford-East Hartford, CT	1,188,241	1,182,817	1,148,618	1,123,678	39,623	24,940	3.4	2.2	13.7	10.7	2.8	9.8
Hartford County, CT	877,393	873,879	857,183	851,783	20,210	5,400	2.4	0.6	14.3	13.2	3.0	12.2
Middlesex County, CT	163,214	162,169	155,071	143,196	8,143	11,875	5.3	8.3	13.6	4.6	1.8	3.3
Tolland County, CT	147,634	146,769	136,364	128,699	11,270	7,665	8.3	6.0	10.4	3.0	2.6	3.0
Hattiesburg, MS	131,871	129,944	123,812	109,603	8,059	14,209	6.5	13.0	10.8	26.5	0.8	1.3
Forrest County, MS	75,095	74,464	72,604	68,314	2,491	4,290	3.4	6.3	11.3	34.5	1.0	1.4
Lamar County, MS	44,616	43,245	39,070	30,424	5,546	8,646	14.2	28.4	9.6	13.3	0.7	1.1
Perry County, MS	12,160	12,235	12,138	10,865	22	1,273	0.2	11.7	12.0	22.5	0.2	1.0
Hickory-Lenoir-Morganton, NC	355,654	353,097	341,820	292,405	13,834	49,415	4.0	16.9	13.1	6.8	2.5	5.0
Alexander County, NC.	35,492	35,333	33,612	27,544	1,880	6,068	5.6	22.0	12.5	4.6	1.3	2.7
Burke County, NC.	89,399	89,435	89,145	75,740	254	13,405	0.3	17.7	14.0	6.5	3.7	4.2
Caldwell County, NC.	79,122	78,855	77,386	70,709	1,736	6,677	2.2	9.4	13.7	5.3	0.5	3.4
Catawba County, NC.	151,641	149,474	141,677	118,412	9,964	23,265	7.0	19.6	12.5	8.3	3.3	7.0
Hinesville-Fort Stewart, GA	68,627	71,412	71,914	58,947	−3,287	12,967	−4.6	22.0	4.8	38.6	1.9	6.4
Liberty County, GA	57,544	60,493	61,610	52,745	−4,066	8,865	−6.6	16.8	4.6	41.4	2.1	6.0
Long County, GA	11,083	10,919	10,304	6,202	779	4,102	7.6	66.1	6.2	23.1	0.8	8.6
Holland-Grand Haven, MI	255,406	252,945	238,314	187,768	17,092	50,546	7.2	26.9	10.4	1.2	2.4	7.4
Ottawa County, MI	255,406	252,945	238,314	187,768	17,092	50,546	7.2	26.9	10.4	1.2	2.4	7.4
Honolulu, HI	905,266	899,562	876,156	836,231	29,110	39,925	3.3	4.8	13.7	3.1	46.9	6.8
Honolulu County, HI	905,266	899,562	876,156	836,231	29,110	39,925	3.3	4.8	13.7	3.1	46.9	6.8
Hot Springs, AR	93,551	92,222	88,068	73,397	5,483	14,671	6.2	20.0	20.7	8.1	0.6	2.7
Garland County, AR	93,551	92,222	88,068	73,397	5,483	14,671	6.2	20.0	20.7	8.1	0.6	2.7
Houma-Bayou Cane-Thibodaux, LA	199,670	198,409	194,477	182,842	5,193	11,635	2.7	6.4	10.8	15.7	0.8	1.7
Lafourche Parish, LA	92,179	91,955	89,974	85,860	2,205	4,114	2.5	4.8	11.5	13.1	0.8	1.5
Terrebonne Parish, LA	107,491	106,454	104,503	96,982	2,988	7,521	2.9	7.8	10.2	18.0	0.9	1.8
Houston-Sugar Land, Baytown, TX	5,280,077	5,176,667	4,715,407	3,767,233	564,670	948,174	12.0	25.2	7.8	16.8	5.4	31.1
Austin County, TX.	26,123	25,690	23,590	19,832	2,533	3,758	10.7	18.9	14.4	10.2	0.4	17.6
Brazoria County, TX	278,484	270,870	241,767	191,707	36,717	50,060	15.2	26.1	8.6	9.1	3.1	24.1
Chambers County, TX	28,411	28,129	26,031	20,088	2,380	5,943	9.1	29.6	8.8	9.9	1.0	12.6
Fort Bend County, TX	463,650	442,389	354,445	225,421	109,205	129,024	30.8	57.2	5.9	20.4	14.0	21.7
Galveston County, TX	277,563	272,024	250,158	217,396	27,405	32,762	11.0	15.1	10.8	15.1	2.5	19.1
Harris County, TX.	3,693,050	3,641,114	3,400,580	2,818,101	292,470	582,479	8.6	20.7	7.5	18.5	5.5	36.0
Liberty County, TX	75,141	74,962	70,159	52,726	4,982	17,433	7.1	33.1	10.0	12.2	0.4	12.1
Montgomery County, TX	378,033	362,192	293,768	182,201	84,265	111,567	28.7	61.2	8.7	3.6	1.3	14.6
San Jacinto County, TX.	24,801	24,562	22,246	16,372	2,555	5,874	11.5	35.9	14.8	12.3	0.4	6.1
Waller County, TX.	34,821	34,735	32,663	23,389	2,158	9,274	6.6	39.7	9.3	27.3	0.5	21.1
Huntington-Ashland, WV-KY-OH	286,012	286,237	288,649	288,189	−2,637	460	−0.9	0.2	15.4	2.5	0.5	0.7
Boyd County, KY	49,594	49,578	49,752	51,150	−158	−1,398	−0.3	−2.7	15.4	2.7	0.3	1.3
Greenup County, KY	37,184	37,109	36,891	36,742	293	149	0.8	0.4	15.2	0.6	0.4	0.6
Lawrence County, OH	63,112	62,657	62,319	61,834	793	485	1.3	0.8	14.5	2.0	0.3	0.5
Cabell County, WV	94,031	94,517	96,784	96,827	−2,753	−43	−2.8	(Z)	16.2	4.4	1.0	0.6
Wayne County, WV.	42,091	42,376	42,903	41,636	−812	1,267	−1.9	3.0	15.1	0.2	0.2	0.5

See footnotes at end of table.

Table C-1. Metropolitan Areas With Component Counties — **Population and Population Characteristics**—Con.

Metropolitan statistical area **Metropolitan statistical area with metropolitan divisions** *Metropolitan division* Component county	Population				Net change		Percent change		Percent—			
	2005 (July 1)	2004 (July 1)	2000[1] (estimates base)	1990[2] (April 1)	2000– 2005[3]	1990– 2000	2000– 2005[3]	1990– 2000	65 years and over, 2003	Black or African american alone, 2003	Asian alone, 2003	Hispanic or Latino origin, 2003[4]
Huntsville, AL	368,661	362,800	342,627	293,047	26,034	49,580	7.6	16.9	11.5	21.5	1.9	2.2
Limestone County, AL	70,469	69,202	65,676	54,135	4,793	11,541	7.3	21.3	11.5	13.2	0.4	3.0
Madison County, AL	298,192	293,598	276,951	238,912	21,241	38,039	7.7	15.9	11.6	23.4	2.2	2.0
Idaho Falls, ID	113,436	110,560	101,677	88,750	11,759	12,927	11.6	14.6	10.2	0.6	0.8	8.5
Bonneville County, ID	91,856	89,733	82,522	72,207	9,334	10,315	11.3	14.3	10.4	0.6	0.9	8.2
Jefferson County, ID	21,580	20,827	20,827	16,543	2,425	2,612	12.7	15.8	9.4	0.4	0.3	9.6
Indianapolis, IN	1,640,591	1,617,414	1,525,104	1,294,217	115,487	230,887	7.6	17.8	10.5	14.4	1.6	3.3
Boone County, IN	52,061	50,820	46,107	38,147	5,954	7,960	12.9	20.9	11.2	0.5	0.8	1.2
Brown County, IN	15,154	15,214	14,957	14,080	197	877	1.3	6.2	13.2	0.3	0.4	0.9
Hamilton County, IN	240,685	229,840	182,740	108,936	57,945	73,804	31.7	67.7	7.4	2.4	3.5	2.0
Hancock County, IN	63,138	60,965	55,391	45,527	7,747	9,864	14.0	21.7	11.5	0.8	0.6	1.1
Hendricks County, IN	127,483	123,467	104,093	75,717	23,390	28,376	22.5	37.5	9.9	2.4	1.2	1.6
Johnson County, IN	128,436	125,682	115,209	88,109	13,227	27,100	11.5	30.8	11.0	0.9	1.0	1.6
Marion County, IN	863,133	861,847	860,454	797,159	2,679	63,295	0.3	7.9	10.9	25.3	1.6	4.8
Morgan County, IN	69,778	69,188	66,689	55,920	3,089	10,769	4.6	19.3	10.9	0.1	0.3	0.8
Putnam County, IN	36,957	36,680	36,019	30,315	938	5,704	2.6	18.8	12.6	2.8	0.6	1.2
Shelby County, IN.	43,766	43,711	43,445	40,307	321	3,138	0.7	7.8	12.5	0.8	0.9	1.9
Iowa City, IA	138,524	137,558	131,676	115,731	6,848	15,945	5.2	13.8	9.1	2.8	4.6	2.6
Johnson County, IA.	117,067	116,226	111,006	96,119	6,061	14,887	5.5	15.5	7.6	3.3	5.4	2.6
Washington County, IA	21,457	21,332	20,670	19,612	787	1,058	3.8	5.4	17.1	0.3	0.3	3.0
Ithaca, NY	100,018	100,080	96,501	94,097	3,517	2,404	3.6	2.6	9.4	4.0	9.0	3.6
Tompkins County, NY	100,018	100,080	96,501	94,097	3,517	2,404	3.6	2.6	9.4	4.0	9.0	3.6
Jackson, MI	163,629	162,653	158,422	149,756	5,207	8,666	3.3	5.8	12.6	7.9	0.6	2.4
Jackson County, MI	163,629	162,653	158,422	149,756	5,207	8,666	3.3	5.8	12.6	7.9	0.6	2.4
Jackson, MS	522,580	517,060	497,197	446,941	25,383	50,256	5.1	11.2	10.7	46.1	0.8	1.1
Copiah County, MS	29,164	29,117	28,757	27,592	407	1,165	1.4	4.2	12.5	51.0	0.2	1.3
Hinds County, MS.	249,345	249,828	250,800	254,441	-1,455	-3,641	-0.6	-1.4	10.8	63.6	0.6	0.8
Madison County, MS	84,286	81,935	74,674	53,794	9,612	20,880	12.9	38.8	10.0	37.3	1.7	1.1
Rankin County, MS	131,841	128,593	115,327	87,161	16,514	28,166	14.3	32.3	10.1	18.0	0.9	1.4
Simpson County, MS	27,944	27,587	27,639	23,953	305	3,686	1.1	15.4	13.3	34.8	0.2	1.5
Jackson, TN	110,857	110,042	107,365	90,801	3,492	16,564	3.3	18.2	12.3	29.9	0.7	1.8
Chester County, TN	15,941	15,813	15,528	12,819	413	2,709	2.7	21.1	13.5	9.0	0.3	1.2
Madison County, TN	94,916	94,229	91,837	77,982	3,079	13,855	3.4	17.8	12.1	33.5	0.8	1.9
Jacksonville, FL	1,248,371	1,223,741	1,122,750	925,213	125,621	197,537	11.2	21.4	11.0	22.7	2.6	4.1
Baker County, FL	24,569	23,946	22,259	18,486	2,310	3,773	10.4	20.4	9.7	14.0	0.5	1.9
Clay County, FL	171,095	164,387	140,814	105,986	30,281	34,828	21.5	32.9	10.0	7.4	2.3	4.8
Duval County, FL	826,436	819,623	778,866	672,971	47,570	105,895	6.1	15.7	10.2	30.0	3.1	4.5
Nassau County, FL	64,746	63,061	57,663	43,941	7,083	13,722	12.3	31.2	13.6	7.3	0.6	1.7
St. Johns County, FL.	161,525	152,724	123,148	83,829	38,377	39,319	31.2	46.9	15.1	6.2	1.1	2.8
Jacksonville, NC	152,440	154,587	150,355	149,838	2,085	517	1.4	0.3	7.2	18.7	2.2	4.8
Onslow County, NC	152,440	154,587	150,355	149,838	2,085	517	1.4	0.3	7.2	18.7	2.2	4.8
Janesville, WI	157,538	156,207	152,307	139,510	5,231	12,797	3.4	9.2	12.8	4.6	0.9	4.5
Rock County, WI	157,538	156,207	152,307	139,510	5,231	12,797	3.4	9.2	12.8	4.6	0.9	4.5
Jefferson City, MO	143,867	142,377	140,052	120,704	3,815	19,348	2.7	16.0	11.5	7.2	0.7	1.3
Callaway County, MO	42,541	42,060	40,766	32,809	1,775	7,957	4.4	24.3	10.5	5.4	0.6	0.9
Cole County, MO	72,757	72,030	71,397	63,579	1,360	7,818	1.9	12.3	11.3	10.3	1.0	1.5
Moniteau County, MO	15,084	14,967	14,827	12,298	257	2,529	1.7	20.6	13.5	3.6	0.3	2.4
Osage County, MO	13,485	13,320	13,062	12,018	423	1,044	3.2	8.7	13.8	0.2	(Z)	0.6
Johnson City, TN	188,944	187,217	181,607	160,369	7,337	21,238	4.0	13.2	14.7	2.8	0.9	1.5
Carter County, TN	58,865	58,627	56,742	51,505	2,123	5,237	3.7	10.2	14.6	1.5	0.3	1.0
Unicoi County, TN	17,572	17,663	17,667	16,549	-95	1,118	-0.5	6.8	18.3	0.6	0.1	2.5
Washington County, TN	112,507	110,927	107,198	92,315	5,309	14,883	5.0	16.1	14.2	3.9	0.9	1.6
Johnstown, PA	148,073	148,646	152,598	163,062	-4,525	-10,464	-3.0	-6.4	19.3	3.0	0.4	1.0
Cambria County, PA	148,073	148,646	152,598	163,062	-4,525	-10,464	-3.0	-6.4	19.3	3.0	0.4	1.0
Jonesboro, AR	112,084	111,064	107,762	93,620	4,322	14,142	4.0	15.1	12.3	8.8	0.5	2.2
Craighead County, AR	86,735	85,791	82,148	68,956	4,587	13,192	5.6	19.1	11.6	9.3	0.6	2.3
Poinsett County, AR	25,349	25,273	25,614	24,664	-265	950	-1.0	3.9	14.3	7.3	0.2	1.6
Joplin, MO	166,178	164,031	157,322	134,910	8,856	22,412	5.6	16.6	13.5	1.3	0.7	3.7
Jasper County, MO	110,624	109,338	104,686	90,465	5,938	14,221	5.7	15.7	13.3	1.6	0.8	4.2
Newton County, MO	55,554	54,693	52,636	44,445	2,918	8,191	5.5	18.4	13.8	0.8	0.4	2.6
Kalamazoo-Portage, MI	319,348	318,272	314,866	293,471	4,482	21,395	1.4	7.3	11.6	8.7	1.7	4.1
Kalamazoo County, MI	240,536	239,748	238,603	223,411	1,933	15,192	0.8	6.8	11.3	10.0	2.2	2.8
Van Buren County, MI	78,812	78,524	76,263	70,060	2,549	6,203	3.3	8.9	12.4	5.0	0.4	8.2
Kankakee-Bradley, IL	107,972	107,038	103,833	96,255	4,139	7,578	4.0	7.9	12.9	15.6	0.8	5.9
Kankakee County, IL	107,972	107,038	103,833	96,255	4,139	7,578	4.0	7.9	12.9	15.6	0.8	5.9
Kansas City, MO-KS.	1,947,694	1,927,240	1,813,064	1,636,527	134,630	176,537	7.4	10.8	11.3	12.7	2.0	5.7
Franklin County, KS	26,247	26,130	24,784	21,994	1,463	2,790	5.9	12.7	13.9	1.3	0.4	2.8
Johnson County, KS	506,562	496,892	451,476	355,021	55,086	96,455	12.2	27.2	9.9	3.4	3.7	4.6
Leavenworth County, KS	73,113	72,443	68,691	64,371	4,422	4,320	6.4	6.7	9.6	10.6	1.3	3.9
Linn County, KS.	9,914	9,748	9,570	8,254	344	1,316	3.6	15.9	17.4	0.6	0.2	1.0
Miami County, KS.	30,496	29,811	28,351	23,466	2,145	4,885	7.6	20.8	11.7	1.6	0.2	1.6
Wyandotte County, KS	155,750	155,981	157,882	162,026	-2,132	-4,144	-1.4	-2.6	11.1	28.4	1.9	19.2
Bates County, MO	17,027	16,967	16,653	15,025	374	1,628	2.2	10.8	16.3	0.7	0.2	1.2

See footnotes at end of table.

State and Metropolitan Area Data Book: 2006

U.S. Census Bureau

Table C-1. Metropolitan Areas With Component Counties — **Population and Population Characteristics**—Con.

Metropolitan statistical area **Metropolitan statistical area with metropolitan divisions** *Metropolitan division* Component county	Population				Net change		Percent change		Percent—			
	2005 (July 1)	2004 (July 1)	2000¹ (estimates base)	1990² (April 1)	2000–2005³	1990–2000	2000–2005³	1990–2000	65 years and over, 2003	Black or African American alone, 2003	Asian alone, 2003	Hispanic or Latino origin, 2003⁴
Kansas City, MO-KS—Con.												
Caldwell County, MO	9,307	9,244	8,969	8,380	338	589	3.8	7.0	16.3	0.2	0.1	0.7
Cass County, MO	94,232	91,809	82,092	63,808	12,140	18,284	14.8	28.7	11.7	2.0	0.6	2.6
Clay County, MO	202,078	197,725	184,006	153,411	18,072	30,595	9.8	19.9	10.7	3.4	1.7	3.9
Clinton County, MO	20,715	20,625	18,975	16,595	1,740	2,380	9.2	14.3	13.8	1.5	0.2	1.1
Jackson County, MO	662,959	662,185	654,880	633,234	8,079	21,646	1.2	3.4	12.3	24.1	1.5	5.9
Lafayette County, MO	33,108	32,998	32,960	31,107	148	1,853	0.4	6.0	15.2	2.3	0.3	1.2
Platte County, MO	82,085	80,724	73,775	57,867	8,310	15,908	11.3	27.5	9.1	4.1	1.9	3.2
Ray County, MO.	24,101	23,958	23,354	21,968	747	1,386	3.2	6.3	12.5	1.4	0.2	1.1
Kennewick-Richland-Pasco, WA	220,961	215,552	191,822	150,033	29,139	41,789	15.2	27.9	9.6	1.6	2.2	23.1
Benton County, WA	157,950	155,901	142,475	112,560	15,475	29,915	10.9	26.6	10.3	1.2	2.4	13.7
Franklin County, WA	63,011	59,651	49,347	37,473	13,664	11,874	27.7	31.7	7.7	2.7	1.8	48.9
Killeen-Temple-Fort Hood, TX	351,528	345,949	330,712	268,820	20,816	61,892	6.3	23.0	8.7	19.4	2.5	17.1
Bell County, TX	256,057	250,466	237,974	191,073	18,083	46,901	7.6	24.5	9.1	20.2	2.8	18.3
Coryell County, TX	75,802	74,851	74,976	64,226	826	10,750	1.1	16.7	6.3	20.8	1.8	13.6
Lampasas County, TX	19,669	20,632	17,762	13,521	1,907	4,241	10.7	31.4	14.0	3.3	0.8	15.4
Kingsport-Bristol-Bristol, TN-VA	301,294	299,983	298,484	275,678	2,810	22,806	0.9	8.3	16.2	1.9	0.4	0.8
Hawkins County, TN	56,196	55,589	53,563	44,565	2,633	8,998	4.9	20.2	13.6	1.6	0.3	0.8
Sullivan County, TN	152,716	152,263	153,048	143,596	-332	9,452	-0.2	6.6	16.4	2.0	0.5	0.7
Scott County, VA	22,962	23,000	23,403	23,204	-441	199	-1.9	0.9	18.3	0.8	0.1	0.5
Washington County, VA	52,085	51,786	51,103	45,887	982	5,216	1.9	11.4	15.7	1.3	0.3	0.7
Bristol city, VA	17,335	17,345	17,367	18,426	-32	-1,059	-0.2	-5.7	21.3	5.6	0.6	1.2
Kingston, NY	182,693	181,824	177,749	165,304	4,944	12,445	2.8	7.5	13.2	6.4	1.5	7.0
Ulster County, NY	182,693	181,824	177,749	165,304	4,944	12,445	2.8	7.5	13.2	6.4	1.5	7.0
Knoxville, TN	655,400	646,979	616,079	534,917	39,321	81,162	6.4	15.2	13.6	6.3	1.2	1.4
Anderson County, TN	72,430	72,045	71,330	68,250	1,100	3,080	1.5	4.5	16.5	3.7	1.0	1.2
Blount County, TN	115,535	113,444	105,823	85,969	9,712	19,854	9.2	23.1	14.1	2.7	1.0	1.1
Knox County, TN	404,972	400,340	382,032	335,749	22,940	46,283	6.0	13.8	12.7	8.7	1.5	1.4
Loudon County, TN	43,387	42,267	39,086	31,255	4,301	7,831	11.0	25.1	17.3	1.2	0.3	2.6
Union County, TN.	19,076	18,883	17,808	13,694	1,268	4,114	7.1	30.0	11.4	0.5	0.2	0.8
Kokomo, IN	101,362	101,129	101,541	96,946	-179	4,595	-0.2	4.7	13.7	5.8	1.0	1.7
Howard County, IN	84,977	84,586	84,964	80,827	13	4,137	(Z)	5.1	13.6	6.9	1.1	1.8
Tipton County, IN	16,385	16,543	16,577	16,119	-192	458	-1.2	2.8	14.3	0.2	0.3	1.3
La Crosse, WI-MN	128,899	128,401	126,838	116,401	2,061	10,437	1.6	9.0	13.1	0.9	3.0	0.9
Houston County, MN	19,941	19,866	19,718	18,497	223	1,221	1.1	6.6	16.5	0.5	0.5	0.6
La Crosse County, WI	108,958	108,535	107,120	97,904	1,838	9,216	1.7	9.4	12.5	1.0	3.4	0.9
Lafayette, IN	183,340	181,427	178,541	158,848	4,799	19,693	2.7	12.4	9.8	2.2	4.5	5.2
Benton County, IN	9,039	9,109	9,421	9,441	-382	-20	-4.1	-0.2	15.1	0.3	0.1	2.6
Carroll County, IN	20,426	20,296	20,165	18,809	261	1,356	1.3	7.2	13.8	0.3	(Z)	3.4
Tippecanoe County, IN	153,875	152,022	148,955	130,598	4,920	18,357	3.3	14.1	9.0	2.6	5.3	5.6
Lafayette, LA	247,824	245,719	238,936	208,859	8,888	30,077	3.7	14.4	9.9	26.0	1.3	1.7
Lafayette Parish, LA	197,390	195,401	190,353	164,762	7,037	25,591	3.7	15.5	9.8	24.5	1.3	1.9
St. Martin Parish, LA	50,434	50,318	48,583	44,097	1,851	4,486	3.8	10.2	10.1	32.1	1.0	0.9
Lake Charles, LA	194,977	194,261	193,568	177,394	1,409	16,174	0.7	9.1	12.1	23.7	0.7	1.5
Calcasieu Parish, LA	185,419	184,635	183,577	168,134	1,842	15,443	1.0	9.2	12.1	24.7	0.8	1.5
Cameron Parish, LA	9,558	9,626	9,991	9,260	-433	731	-4.3	7.9	11.5	4.3	0.5	2.4
Lakeland, FL	542,912	524,286	483,924	405,382	58,988	78,542	12.2	19.4	17.8	14.7	1.1	11.4
Polk County, FL	542,912	524,286	483,924	405,382	58,988	78,542	12.2	19.4	17.8	14.7	1.1	11.4
Lancaster, PA	490,562	486,361	470,658	422,822	19,904	47,836	4.2	11.3	14.2	3.3	1.6	6.0
Lancaster County, PA	490,562	486,361	470,658	422,822	19,904	47,836	4.2	11.3	14.2	3.3	1.6	6.0
Lansing-East Lansing, MI	455,315	455,594	447,822	432,684	7,493	15,138	1.7	3.5	10.3	8.6	3.1	4.9
Clinton County, MI	69,329	68,675	64,753	57,893	4,576	6,860	7.1	11.8	11.2	1.1	0.6	2.6
Eaton County, MI	107,394	106,826	103,655	92,879	3,739	10,776	3.6	11.6	11.7	5.9	1.4	3.5
Ingham County, MI	278,592	280,093	279,414	281,912	-822	-2,498	-0.3	-0.9	9.6	11.4	4.3	6.0
Laredo, TX	224,695	218,806	193,117	133,239	31,578	59,878	16.4	44.9	7.6	0.5	0.4	95.1
Webb County, TX	224,695	218,806	193,117	133,239	31,578	59,878	16.4	44.9	7.6	0.5	0.4	95.1
Las Cruces, NM	189,444	185,524	174,682	135,510	14,762	39,172	8.5	28.9	11.3	2.2	1.0	64.9
Dona Ana County, NM.	189,444	185,524	174,682	135,510	14,762	39,172	8.5	28.9	11.3	2.2	1.0	64.9
Las Vegas-Paradise, NV	1,710,551	1,648,524	1,375,738	741,368	334,813	634,370	24.3	85.6	10.8	9.1	5.5	24.4
Clark County, NV	1,710,551	1,648,524	1,375,738	741,368	334,813	634,370	24.3	85.6	10.8	9.1	5.5	24.4
Lawrence, KS	102,914	102,738	99,965	81,798	2,949	18,167	3.0	22.2	8.1	4.1	3.6	3.5
Douglas County, KS	102,914	102,738	99,965	81,798	2,949	18,167	3.0	22.2	8.1	4.1	3.6	3.5
Lawton, OK	112,429	113,058	114,996	111,486	-2,567	3,510	-2.2	3.1	10.2	20.8	2.3	7.3
Comanche County, OK	112,429	113,058	114,996	111,486	-2,567	3,510	-2.2	3.1	10.2	20.8	2.3	7.3
Lebanon, PA	125,578	124,087	120,327	113,744	5,251	6,583	4.4	5.8	16.5	1.5	0.9	5.2
Lebanon County, PA	125,578	124,087	120,327	113,744	5,251	6,583	4.4	5.8	16.5	1.5	0.9	5.2
Lewiston, ID-WA	59,109	58,640	57,961	51,359	1,148	6,602	2.0	12.9	17.1	0.3	0.7	1.9
Nez Perce County, ID	37,931	37,730	37,410	33,754	521	3,656	1.4	10.8	17.0	0.4	0.8	1.8
Asotin County, WA	21,178	20,910	20,551	17,605	627	2,946	3.1	16.7	17.2	0.2	0.5	2.1
Lewiston-Auburn, ME	108,039	107,125	103,793	105,259	4,246	-1,466	4.1	-1.4	14.2	0.9	0.7	1.1
Androscoggin County, ME	108,039	107,125	103,793	105,259	4,246	-1,466	4.1	-1.4	14.2	0.9	0.7	1.1

See footnotes at end of table.

Metropolitan statistical area **Metropolitan statistical area with metropolitan divisions** *Metropolitan division* Component county	Population				Net change		Percent change		Percent—			
	2005 (July 1)	2004 (July 1)	2000[1] (estimates base)	1990[2] (April 1)	2000–2005[3]	1990–2000	2000–2005[3]	1990–2000	65 years and over, 2003	Black or African American alone, 2003	Asian alone, 2003	Hispanic or Latino origin, 2003[4]
Lexington-Fayette, KY	429,889	424,649	408,326	348,428	21,563	59,898	5.3	17.2	10.3	10.6	2.1	3.4
Bourbon County, KY	19,833	19,694	19,360	19,236	473	124	2.4	0.6	13.6	6.9	0.2	3.3
Clark County, KY	34,887	34,408	33,144	29,496	1,743	3,648	5.3	12.4	12.3	4.8	0.3	1.4
Fayette County, KY	268,080	266,451	260,512	225,366	7,568	35,146	2.9	15.6	10.1	14.0	3.0	4.2
Jessamine County, KY	43,463	42,256	39,041	30,508	4,422	8,533	11.3	28.0	9.8	3.1	0.7	1.4
Scott County, KY	39,380	37,901	33,061	23,867	6,319	9,194	19.1	38.5	8.6	5.3	1.0	1.8
Woodford County, KY	24,246	23,939	23,208	19,955	1,038	3,253	4.5	16.3	10.9	5.4	0.4	3.7
Lima, OH	106,234	106,333	108,473	109,755	−2,239	−1,282	−2.1	−1.2	13.9	12.2	0.8	1.5
Allen County, OH	106,234	106,333	108,473	109,755	−2,239	−1,282	−2.1	−1.2	13.9	12.2	0.8	1.5
Lincoln, NE	281,553	278,509	266,787	229,091	14,766	37,696	5.5	16.5	10.5	2.8	3.2	3.5
Lancaster County, NE	264,814	261,742	250,291	213,641	14,523	36,650	5.8	17.2	10.2	3.0	3.4	3.7
Seward County, NE	16,739	16,767	16,496	15,450	243	1,046	1.5	6.8	15.4	0.3	0.5	1.4
Little Rock-North Little Rock, AR	643,272	635,764	610,518	534,943	32,754	75,575	5.4	14.1	11.5	22.3	1.1	2.1
Faulkner County, AR	97,147	95,074	86,014	60,006	11,133	26,008	12.9	43.3	9.6	9.2	0.8	2.1
Grant County, AR	17,348	17,190	16,464	13,948	884	2,516	5.4	18.0	12.3	2.7	0.2	1.3
Lonoke County, AR	60,658	58,623	52,828	39,268	7,830	13,560	14.8	34.5	10.5	6.4	0.5	1.8
Perry County, AR	10,468	10,435	10,209	7,969	259	2,240	2.5	28.1	15.3	1.9	0.1	1.2
Pulaski County, AR	366,463	365,228	361,474	349,569	4,989	11,905	1.4	3.4	11.6	34.4	1.4	2.4
Saline County, AR	91,188	89,214	83,529	64,183	7,659	19,346	9.2	30.1	13.3	2.3	0.7	1.5
Logan, UT-ID	110,426	109,291	102,720	79,415	7,706	23,305	7.5	29.3	7.8	0.5	1.9	7.3
Franklin County, ID	12,371	12,154	11,329	9,232	1,042	2,097	9.2	22.7	11.7	0.1	0.2	5.9
Cache County, UT	98,055	97,137	91,391	70,183	6,664	21,208	7.3	30.2	7.3	0.5	2.1	7.5
Longview, TX	201,501	199,966	194,042	180,053	7,459	13,989	3.8	7.8	13.8	17.8	0.6	9.2
Gregg County, TX	115,649	114,827	111,379	104,948	4,270	6,431	3.8	6.1	13.1	20.1	0.8	10.8
Rusk County, TX	47,971	47,855	47,372	43,735	599	3,637	1.3	8.3	14.7	18.8	0.3	9.5
Upshur County, TX	37,881	37,284	35,291	31,370	2,590	3,921	7.3	12.5	14.5	9.6	0.3	4.3
Longview, WA	97,325	96,208	92,948	82,119	4,377	10,829	4.7	13.2	13.5	0.6	1.3	5.2
Cowlitz County, WA	97,325	96,208	92,948	82,119	4,377	10,829	4.7	13.2	13.5	0.6	1.3	5.2
Los Angeles-Long Beach-Santa Ana, CA	**12,923,547**	**12,899,425**	**12,365,619**	**11,273,720**	**557,928**	**1,091,899**	**4.5**	**9.7**	**10.0**	**8.1**	**13.2**	**43.0**
Los Angeles-Long Beach-Glendale, CA	*9,935,475*	*9,917,331*	*9,519,330*	*8,863,052*	*416,145*	*656,278*	*4.4*	*7.4*	*9.9*	*9.9*	*12.7*	*46.3*
Los Angeles County, CA	9,935,475	9,917,331	9,519,330	8,863,052	416,145	656,278	4.4	7.4	9.9	9.9	12.7	46.3
Santa Ana-Anaheim-Irvine, CA	*2,988,072*	*2,982,094*	*2,846,289*	*2,410,668*	*141,783*	*435,621*	*5.0*	*18.1*	*10.2*	*1.8*	*14.9*	*32.1*
Orange County, CA	2,988,072	2,982,094	2,846,289	2,410,668	141,783	435,621	5.0	18.1	10.2	1.8	14.9	32.1
Louisville, KY-IN	1,208,452	1,199,424	1,162,415	1,056,156	46,037	106,259	4.0	10.1	12.2	13.3	1.2	2.0
Clark County, IN	101,592	100,463	96,472	87,774	5,120	8,698	5.3	9.9	12.4	6.6	0.6	2.1
Floyd County, IN	71,997	71,513	70,823	64,404	1,174	6,419	1.7	10.0	12.2	4.4	0.7	1.2
Harrison County, IN	36,827	36,343	34,325	29,890	2,502	4,435	7.3	14.8	11.4	0.4	0.2	1.1
Washington County, IN	27,885	27,835	27,223	23,717	662	3,506	2.4	14.8	11.9	0.2	0.2	0.7
Bullitt County, KY	68,474	66,816	61,236	47,567	7,238	13,669	11.8	28.7	8.2	0.6	0.3	0.7
Henry County, KY	15,903	15,802	15,060	12,823	843	2,237	5.6	17.4	12.0	3.6	0.4	2.6
Jefferson County, KY	699,827	698,903	693,604	665,123	6,223	28,481	0.9	4.3	13.3	19.8	1.7	2.1
Meade County, KY	28,447	28,281	26,349	24,170	2,098	2,179	8.0	9.0	8.6	4.0	0.6	2.2
Nelson County, KY	41,088	40,415	37,477	29,710	3,611	7,767	9.6	26.1	10.8	5.3	0.8	1.1
Oldham County, KY	53,533	52,081	46,618	33,263	6,915	13,355	14.8	40.1	7.1	4.3	0.7	1.7
Shelby County, KY	38,205	37,131	33,337	24,824	4,868	8,513	14.6	34.3	10.2	8.7	0.6	6.7
Spencer County, KY	15,651	14,840	11,766	6,801	3,885	4,965	33.0	73.0	8.2	1.5	0.2	1.1
Trimble County, KY	9,023	9,001	8,125	6,090	898	2,035	11.1	33.4	10.9	0.3	0.1	1.3
Lubbock, TX	258,970	257,835	249,700	229,940	9,270	19,760	3.7	8.6	11.2	7.8	1.3	29.6
Crosby County, TX	6,686	6,653	7,072	7,304	−386	−232	−5.5	−3.2	15.7	4.4	–	48.9
Lubbock County, TX	252,284	251,182	242,628	222,636	9,656	19,992	4.0	9.0	11.1	7.9	1.3	29.1
Lynchburg, VA	236,910	233,876	228,616	206,226	8,294	22,390	3.6	10.9	14.8	18.3	0.8	1.0
Amherst County, VA	32,134	31,912	31,894	28,578	240	3,316	0.8	11.6	14.2	20.2	0.4	1.0
Appomattox County, VA	13,967	13,936	13,705	12,298	262	1,407	1.9	11.4	15.2	22.6	0.2	0.5
Bedford County, VA	65,286	63,919	60,385	45,552	4,901	14,833	8.1	32.6	12.9	6.1	0.5	0.7
Campbell County, VA	52,339	51,619	51,105	47,572	1,234	3,533	2.4	7.4	14.0	15.2	0.7	0.9
Bedford city, VA	6,211	6,222	6,299	6,177	−88	122	−1.4	2.0	22.4	23.3	0.7	0.7
Lynchburg city, VA	66,973	66,268	65,228	66,049	1,745	−821	2.7	−1.2	16.9	30.2	1.5	1.5
Macon, GA	228,712	227,955	222,385	206,786	6,327	15,599	2.8	7.5	11.9	42.1	1.0	1.3
Bibb County, GA	154,918	154,861	153,887	150,137	1,031	3,750	0.7	2.5	12.6	49.3	1.3	1.4
Crawford County, GA	12,874	12,876	12,495	8,991	379	3,504	3.0	39.0	8.7	22.1	0.2	2.4
Jones County, GA	26,836	26,335	23,639	20,739	3,197	2,900	13.5	14.0	10.8	22.6	0.7	0.5
Monroe County, GA	23,785	23,411	21,774	17,113	2,011	4,661	9.2	27.2	10.5	26.2	0.4	1.4
Twiggs County, GA	10,299	10,472	10,590	9,806	−291	784	−2.7	8.0	10.9	42.3	0.2	1.2
Madera, CA	142,788	138,895	123,109	88,090	19,679	35,019	16.0	39.8	10.8	4.0	1.5	47.2
Madera County, CA	142,788	138,895	123,109	88,090	19,679	35,019	16.0	39.8	10.8	4.0	1.5	47.2
Madison, WI	537,039	531,256	501,774	432,323	35,265	69,451	7.0	16.1	10.0	3.7	3.7	3.4
Columbia County, WI	55,364	54,831	52,468	45,088	2,896	7,380	5.5	16.4	14.1	1.0	0.3	1.5
Dane County, WI	458,106	453,051	426,526	367,085	31,580	59,441	7.4	16.2	9.3	4.3	4.3	3.7
Iowa County, WI	23,569	23,374	22,780	20,150	789	2,630	3.5	13.1	13.2	0.2	0.3	0.4
Manchester-Nashua, NH	401,291	398,355	380,841	335,838	20,450	45,003	5.4	13.4	10.6	1.7	2.5	3.6
Hillsborough County, NH	401,291	398,355	380,841	335,838	20,450	45,003	5.4	13.4	10.6	1.7	2.5	3.6
Mansfield, OH	127,949	128,095	128,852	126,137	−903	2,715	−0.7	2.2	14.8	9.5	0.6	0.9
Richland County, OH	127,949	128,095	128,852	126,137	−903	2,715	−0.7	2.2	14.8	9.5	0.6	0.9
McAllen-Edinburg-Mission, TX	678,275	657,310	569,463	383,545	108,812	185,918	19.1	48.5	9.4	0.7	0.7	89.2
Hidalgo County, TX	678,275	657,310	569,463	383,545	108,812	185,918	19.1	48.5	9.4	0.7	0.7	89.2
Medford, OR	195,322	193,016	181,275	146,387	14,047	34,888	7.7	23.8	15.9	0.5	1.0	7.4
Jackson County, OR	195,322	193,016	181,275	146,387	14,047	34,888	7.7	23.8	15.9	0.5	1.0	7.4

See footnotes at end of table.

Table C-1. Metropolitan Areas With Component Counties — **Population and Population Characteristics**—Con.

Metropolitan statistical area **Metropolitan statistical area with metropolitan divisions** *Metropolitan division* Component county	Population				Net change		Percent change		Percent—			
	2005 (July 1)	2004 (July 1)	2000[1] (estimates base)	1990[2] (April 1)	2000–2005[3]	1990–2000	2000–2005[3]	1990–2000	65 years and over, 2003	Black or African can alone, 2003	Asian alone, 2003	Hispanic or Latino origin, 2003[4]
Memphis, TN-MS-AR	1,260,905	1,248,492	1,205,194	1,067,263	55,711	137,931	4.6	12.9	9.9	44.9	1.6	2.6
Crittenden County, AR	51,882	51,541	50,866	49,939	1,016	927	2.0	1.9	9.8	50.3	0.6	1.4
DeSoto County, MS	137,004	130,704	107,199	67,910	29,805	39,289	27.8	57.9	9.1	15.0	0.9	2.7
Marshall County, MS	35,659	35,419	34,993	30,361	666	4,632	1.9	15.3	11.2	50.5	0.1	1.3
Tate County, MS	26,548	26,267	25,370	21,432	1,178	3,938	4.6	18.4	11.4	30.5	0.1	1.1
Tunica County, MS	10,321	10,078	9,227	8,164	1,094	1,063	11.9	13.0	9.4	72.8	0.4	2.6
Fayette County, TN	34,458	33,562	28,796	25,559	5,662	3,237	19.7	12.7	12.3	30.8	0.9	1.2
Shelby County, TN	909,035	906,287	897,472	826,330	11,563	71,142	1.3	8.6	9.8	50.7	1.9	2.9
Tipton County, TN	55,998	54,634	51,271	37,568	4,727	13,703	9.2	36.5	10.0	19.1	0.4	1.3
Merced, CA	241,706	236,857	210,554	178,403	31,152	32,151	14.8	18.0	9.0	4.1	6.5	49.5
Merced County, CA	241,706	236,857	210,554	178,403	31,152	32,151	14.8	18.0	9.0	4.1	6.5	49.5
Miami-Fort Lauderdale-Miami Beach, FL	**5,422,200**	**5,355,903**	**5,007,988**	**4,056,228**	**414,212**	**951,760**	**8.3**	**23.5**	**15.9**	**20.9**	**1.9**	**36.8**
Fort Lauderdale-Pompano Beach-Deerfield Beach, FL	*1,777,638*	*1,753,000*	*1,623,018*	*1,255,531*	*154,620*	*367,487*	*9.5*	*29.3*	*14.7*	*24.3*	*2.7*	*20.2*
Broward County, FL	1,777,638	1,753,000	1,623,018	1,255,531	154,620	367,487	9.5	29.3	14.7	24.3	2.7	20.2
Miami-Miami Beach-Kendall, FL	*2,376,014*	*2,358,714*	*2,253,779*	*1,937,194*	*122,235*	*316,585*	*5.4*	*16.3*	*13.6*	*20.9*	*1.4*	*60.5*
Miami-Dade County, FL	2,376,014	2,358,714	2,253,779	1,937,194	122,235	316,585	5.4	16.3	13.6	20.9	1.4	60.5
West Palm Beach-Boca Raton-Boynton Beach, FL	*1,268,548*	*1,244,189*	*1,131,191*	*863,503*	*137,357*	*267,688*	*12.1*	*31.0*	*22.1*	*15.9*	*1.8*	*14.9*
Palm Beach County, FL	1,268,548	1,244,189	1,131,191	863,503	137,357	267,688	12.1	31.0	22.1	15.9	1.8	14.9
Michigan City-La Porte, IN	110,512	109,741	110,106	107,066	406	3,040	0.4	2.8	13.5	10.1	0.5	3.5
LaPorte County, IN	110,512	109,741	110,106	107,066	406	3,040	0.4	2.8	13.5	10.1	0.5	3.5
Midland, TX	121,371	120,014	116,009	106,611	5,362	9,398	4.6	8.8	11.9	6.9	1.0	31.8
Midland County, TX	121,371	120,014	116,009	106,611	5,362	9,398	4.6	8.8	11.9	6.9	1.0	31.8
Milwaukee-Waukesha-West Allis, WI	1,512,855	1,513,319	1,500,744	1,432,149	12,111	68,595	0.8	4.8	12.4	16.4	2.5	6.9
Milwaukee County, WI	921,654	926,764	940,164	959,275	-18,510	-19,111	-2.0	-2.0	12.3	26.2	3.0	9.8
Ozaukee County, WI	86,072	85,697	82,317	72,831	3,755	9,486	4.6	13.0	13.3	1.1	1.3	1.4
Washington County, WI	126,158	124,382	117,496	95,328	8,662	22,168	7.4	23.3	11.5	0.5	0.8	1.4
Waukesha County, WI	378,971	376,476	360,767	304,715	18,204	56,052	5.0	18.4	12.6	0.9	2.0	2.7
Minneapolis-St. Paul-Bloomington, MN-WI	3,142,779	3,112,877	2,968,817	2,538,776	173,962	430,041	5.9	16.9	9.6	5.9	4.7	3.8
Anoka County, MN	323,996	319,548	298,084	243,641	25,912	54,443	8.7	22.3	7.7	2.3	2.6	2.0
Carver County, MN	84,864	81,851	70,205	47,915	14,659	22,290	20.9	46.5	7.3	0.9	2.1	2.8
Chisago County, MN	49,400	48,253	41,101	30,521	8,299	10,580	20.2	34.7	9.5	0.8	1.0	1.5
Dakota County, MN	383,592	378,343	355,904	275,189	27,688	80,715	7.8	29.3	7.8	3.0	3.6	3.4
Hennepin County, MN	1,119,364	1,119,866	1,116,039	1,032,431	3,325	83,608	0.3	8.1	10.9	9.8	5.4	4.9
Isanti County, MN	37,664	36,526	31,287	25,921	6,377	5,366	20.4	20.7	10.2	0.4	0.5	1.1
Ramsey County, MN	494,920	499,206	511,202	485,783	-16,282	25,419	-3.2	5.2	12.0	8.7	9.4	5.7
Scott County, MN	119,825	114,765	89,498	57,846	30,327	31,652	33.9	54.7	5.9	1.4	3.8	3.2
Sherburne County, MN	81,752	78,621	64,415	41,945	17,337	22,470	26.9	53.6	7.0	0.9	0.8	1.5
Washington County, MN	220,426	216,153	201,130	145,858	19,296	55,272	9.6	37.9	8.1	2.3	3.3	2.2
Wright County, MN	110,730	107,062	89,993	68,710	20,737	21,283	23.0	31.0	8.5	0.4	0.8	1.3
Pierce County, WI	39,102	38,449	36,804	32,765	2,298	4,039	6.2	12.3	9.5	0.3	0.7	0.8
St. Croix County, WI	77,144	74,234	63,155	50,251	13,989	12,904	22.2	25.7	9.4	0.4	0.9	0.8
Missoula, MT	100,086	99,063	95,802	78,687	4,284	17,115	4.5	21.8	10.1	0.4	1.2	1.7
Missoula County, MT	100,086	99,063	95,802	78,687	4,284	17,115	4.5	21.8	10.1	0.4	1.2	1.7
Mobile, AL	401,427	400,107	399,843	378,643	1,584	21,200	0.4	5.6	12.1	34.4	1.7	1.2
Mobile County, AL	401,427	400,107	399,843	378,643	1,584	21,200	0.4	5.6	12.1	34.4	1.7	1.2
Modesto, CA	505,505	497,599	446,997	370,522	58,508	76,475	13.1	20.6	10.0	3.0	4.7	36.0
Stanislaus County, CA	505,505	497,599	446,997	370,522	58,508	76,475	13.1	20.6	10.0	3.0	4.7	36.0
Monroe, LA	171,138	171,089	170,053	162,987	1,085	7,066	0.6	4.3	12.3	33.4	0.7	1.5
Ouachita Parish, LA	148,237	148,238	147,250	142,191	987	5,059	0.7	3.6	11.9	34.2	0.8	1.3
Union Parish, LA	22,901	22,851	22,803	20,796	98	2,007	0.4	9.7	14.9	27.8	0.3	2.6
Monroe, MI	153,935	152,451	145,945	133,600	7,990	12,345	5.5	9.2	11.4	2.0	0.6	2.2
Monroe County, MI	153,935	152,451	145,945	133,600	7,990	12,345	5.5	9.2	11.4	2.0	0.6	2.2
Montgomery, AL	357,244	354,243	346,528	305,175	10,716	41,353	3.1	13.6	11.5	41.4	0.9	1.3
Autauga County, AL	48,612	47,458	43,671	34,222	4,941	9,449	11.3	27.6	10.4	17.2	0.6	1.3
Elmore County, AL	73,937	71,829	65,876	49,210	8,061	16,666	12.2	33.9	10.9	21.1	0.5	1.4
Lowndes County, AL	13,076	13,154	13,471	12,658	-395	813	-2.9	6.4	12.8	72.5	0.1	0.6
Montgomery County, AL	221,619	221,802	223,510	209,085	-1,891	14,425	-0.8	6.9	11.9	51.0	1.2	1.3
Morgantown, WV	114,501	113,883	111,200	104,546	3,301	6,654	3.0	6.4	11.7	2.7	2.2	0.9
Monongalia County, WV	84,386	84,061	81,866	75,509	2,520	6,357	3.1	8.4	10.5	3.5	2.9	1.0
Preston County, WV	30,115	29,822	29,334	29,037	781	297	2.7	1.0	15.1	0.4	0.2	0.6
Morristown, TN	130,575	128,794	123,081	100,591	7,494	22,490	6.1	22.4	13.6	2.9	0.5	4.4
Grainger County, TN	22,283	21,885	20,659	17,095	1,624	3,564	7.9	20.8	13.0	0.4	0.1	1.2
Hamblen County, TN	59,898	59,368	58,128	50,480	1,770	7,648	3.0	15.2	13.8	4.2	0.7	7.8
Jefferson County, TN	48,394	47,541	44,294	33,016	4,100	11,278	9.3	34.2	13.5	2.3	0.4	1.7
Mount Vernon-Anacortes, WA	113,171	111,131	102,979	79,545	10,192	23,434	9.9	29.5	14.3	0.5	1.7	12.5
Skagit County, WA	113,171	111,131	102,979	79,545	10,192	23,434	9.9	29.5	14.3	0.5	1.7	12.5
Muncie, IN	116,362	117,501	118,769	119,659	-2,407	-890	-2.0	-0.7	13.6	6.7	0.8	1.1
Delaware County, IN	116,362	117,501	118,769	119,659	-2,407	-890	-2.0	-0.7	13.6	6.7	0.8	1.1
Muskegon-Norton Shores, MI	175,554	174,146	170,200	158,983	5,354	11,217	3.1	7.1	12.7	14.2	0.5	3.8
Muskegon County, MI	175,554	174,146	170,200	158,983	5,354	11,217	3.1	7.1	12.7	14.2	0.5	3.8
Myrtle Beach-Conway-North Myrtle Beach, SC	226,992	217,635	196,629	144,053	30,363	52,576	15.4	36.5	15.6	15.9	0.9	3.1
Horry County, SC	226,992	217,635	196,629	144,053	30,363	52,576	15.4	36.5	15.6	15.9	0.9	3.1

See footnotes at end of table.

Metropolitan statistical area **Metropolitan statistical area with metropolitan divisions** *Metropolitan division* Component county	Population 2005 (July 1)	Population 2004 (July 1)	Population 2000[1] (estimates base)	Population 1990[2] (April 1)	Net change 2000–2005[3]	Net change 1990–2000	Percent change 2000–2005[3]	Percent change 1990–2000	65 years and over, 2003	Black or African American alone, 2003	Asian alone, 2003	Hispanic or Latino origin, 2003[4]
Napa, CA	132,764	132,394	124,308	110,765	8,456	13,543	6.8	12.2	14.4	1.8	4.2	26.6
Napa County, CA	132,764	132,394	124,308	110,765	8,456	13,543	6.8	12.2	14.4	1.8	4.2	26.6
Naples-Marco Island, FL	307,242	296,675	251,377	152,099	55,865	99,278	22.2	65.3	23.8	6.0	0.8	23.3
Collier County, FL	307,242	296,675	251,377	152,099	55,865	99,278	22.2	65.3	23.8	6.0	0.8	23.3
Nashville-Davidson-Murfreesboro, TN	1,422,544	1,394,960	1,311,793	1,048,216	110,751	263,577	8.4	25.1	10.3	15.1	1.9	3.8
Cannon County, TN	13,337	13,285	12,826	10,467	511	2,359	4.0	22.5	13.7	1.4	0.1	1.8
Cheatham County, TN	38,603	37,982	35,912	27,140	2,691	8,772	7.5	32.3	9.2	1.4	0.3	1.4
Davidson County, TN	575,261	571,948	569,892	510,786	5,369	59,106	0.9	11.6	11.1	27.3	2.8	5.6
Dickson County, TN	45,894	45,366	43,160	35,061	2,734	8,099	6.3	23.1	11.9	4.5	0.3	1.2
Hickman County, TN	23,793	23,670	22,295	16,754	1,498	5,541	6.7	33.1	12.1	4.2	0.1	1.0
Macon County, TN	21,549	21,355	20,386	15,906	1,163	4,480	5.7	28.2	12.5	0.3	0.2	2.5
Robertson County, TN	60,379	59,197	54,433	41,492	5,946	12,941	10.9	31.2	10.9	8.4	0.4	3.9
Rutherford County, TN	218,292	209,739	182,023	118,570	36,269	63,453	19.9	53.5	7.6	10.2	2.4	3.5
Smith County, TN	18,647	18,397	17,712	14,143	935	3,569	5.3	25.2	12.9	2.7	0.2	1.3
Sumner County, TN	145,009	141,732	130,449	103,281	14,560	27,168	11.2	26.3	11.0	6.1	0.8	2.1
Trousdale County, TN	7,677	7,504	7,259	5,920	418	1,339	5.8	22.6	13.6	11.7	0.2	2.0
Williamson County, TN	153,595	146,992	126,638	81,021	26,957	45,617	21.3	56.3	8.1	4.8	1.8	2.9
Wilson County, TN	100,508	97,793	88,808	67,675	11,700	21,133	13.2	31.2	9.9	6.3	0.6	1.5
New Haven-Milford, CT	846,766	844,342	824,008	804,219	22,758	19,789	2.8	2.5	13.9	12.4	2.9	11.1
New Haven County, CT	846,766	844,342	824,008	804,219	22,758	19,789	2.8	2.5	13.9	12.4	2.9	11.1
New Orleans-Metairie-Kenner, LA	1,319,367	1,317,990	1,316,512	1,264,383	2,855	52,129	0.2	4.1	11.5	37.9	2.5	4.7
Jefferson Parish, LA	452,824	453,089	455,466	448,306	−2,642	7,160	−0.6	1.6	12.2	25.3	3.6	7.6
Orleans Parish, LA	454,863	461,115	484,674	496,938	−29,811	−12,264	−6.2	−2.5	11.5	67.5	2.5	3.1
Plaquemines Parish, LA.	28,995	28,971	26,757	25,575	2,238	1,182	8.4	4.6	10.0	22.7	3.6	2.2
St. Bernard Parish, LA	65,364	65,636	67,229	66,631	−1,865	598	−2.8	0.9	13.8	9.0	1.5	5.2
St. Charles Parish, LA.	50,633	49,955	48,067	42,437	2,566	5,630	5.3	13.3	9.2	25.9	0.8	3.5
St. John the Baptist Parish, LA	46,393	45,530	43,049	39,996	3,344	3,053	7.8	7.6	7.8	47.0	0.7	3.3
St. Tammany Parish, LA	220,295	213,694	191,270	144,500	29,025	46,770	15.2	32.4	10.4	10.8	1.0	2.8
New York-Northern New Jersey-Long Island, NY-NJ-PA	**18,747,320**	**18,754,585**	**18,323,382**	**16,846,046**	**423,938**	**1,477,336**	**2.3**	**8.8**	**12.7**	**20.2**	**8.6**	**20.9**
Edison, NJ	*2,303,709*	*2,288,043*	*2,173,869*	*1,898,352*	*129,840*	*275,517*	*6.0*	*14.5*	*14.2*	*7.8*	*8.7*	*10.0*
Middlesex County, NJ	789,516	783,665	750,162	671,811	39,354	78,351	5.2	11.7	12.0	10.3	16.5	15.3
Monmouth County, NJ	635,952	635,062	615,301	553,093	20,651	62,208	3.4	11.2	12.5	8.2	4.5	7.0
Ocean County, NJ	558,341	553,093	510,916	433,203	47,425	77,713	9.3	17.9	21.3	3.3	1.4	5.8
Somerset County, NJ	319,900	316,223	297,490	240,245	22,410	57,245	7.5	23.8	10.9	8.5	10.5	10.2
Nassau-Suffolk, NY.	*2,808,064*	*2,812,212*	*2,753,913*	*2,609,212*	*54,151*	*144,701*	*2.0*	*5.5*	*13.4*	*9.8*	*4.5*	*12.1*
Nassau County, NY	1,333,137	1,337,693	1,334,544	1,287,444	−1,407	47,100	−0.1	3.7	14.9	11.7	6.1	11.7
Suffolk County, NY	1,474,927	1,474,519	1,419,369	1,321,768	55,558	97,601	3.9	7.4	12.0	8.2	3.1	12.5
Newark-Union, NJ-PA	*2,152,978*	*2,148,774*	*2,097,519*	*1,959,855*	*55,459*	*137,664*	*2.6*	*7.0*	*11.9*	*22.7*	*4.4*	*14.4*
Essex County, NJ	791,057	795,015	792,305	777,964	−1,248	14,341	−0.2	1.8	11.6	43.2	4.0	16.8
Hunterdon County, NJ	130,404	129,318	121,989	107,802	8,415	14,187	6.9	13.2	11.0	2.6	2.3	3.4
Morris County, NJ	490,593	487,437	470,212	421,361	20,381	48,851	4.3	11.6	12.0	3.0	7.1	8.9
Sussex County, NJ	153,130	152,117	144,170	130,943	8,960	13,227	6.2	10.1	9.4	1.4	1.5	4.3
Union County, NJ	531,457	530,846	522,541	493,819	8,916	28,722	1.7	5.8	13.1	22.5	4.1	22.4
Pike County, PA	56,337	54,041	46,302	27,966	10,035	18,336	21.7	65.6	14.7	4.4	0.7	4.8
New York-White Plains-Wayne, NY-NJ	*11,482,569*	*11,505,556*	*11,298,081*	*10,378,627*	*184,488*	*919,454*	*1.6*	*8.9*	*12.3*	*24.7*	*10.3*	*26.4*
Bergen County, NJ	902,561	901,745	884,118	825,380	18,443	58,738	2.1	7.1	15.0	5.8	12.3	12.1
Hudson County, NJ	603,521	605,359	608,975	553,099	−5,454	55,876	−0.9	10.1	11.2	15.3	10.2	41.1
Passaic County, NJ	499,060	498,939	490,377	453,302	8,683	37,075	1.8	8.2	11.8	15.4	4.1	32.5
Bronx County, NY	1,357,589	1,362,523	1,332,650	1,203,789	24,939	128,861	1.9	10.7	10.1	42.5	3.4	51.3
Kings County, NY	2,486,235	2,497,859	2,465,525	2,300,664	20,710	164,861	0.8	7.2	11.9	39.4	8.7	20.3
New York County, NY	1,593,200	1,590,911	1,537,372	1,487,536	55,828	49,836	3.6	3.4	12.4	20.4	10.5	27.4
Putnam County, NY	100,507	100,378	95,843	83,941	4,664	11,902	4.9	14.2	9.9	2.4	1.6	8.5
Queens County, NY	2,241,600	2,250,718	2,229,379	1,951,598	12,221	277,781	0.5	14.2	13.0	21.9	20.6	26.2
Richmond County, NY	464,573	462,695	443,728	378,977	20,845	64,751	4.7	17.1	11.7	11.2	6.8	14.3
Rockland County, NY	292,916	293,049	286,753	265,475	6,163	21,278	2.1	8.0	12.4	12.5	6.5	12.0
Westchester County, NY	940,807	941,380	923,361	874,866	17,446	48,495	1.9	5.5	13.8	15.6	5.3	17.9
Niles-Benton Harbor, MI	162,611	162,825	162,455	161,378	156	1,077	0.1	0.7	14.5	15.9	1.4	3.4
Berrien County, MI	162,611	162,825	162,455	161,378	156	1,077	0.1	0.7	14.5	15.9	1.4	3.4
Norwich-New London, CT	266,618	266,107	259,106	254,957	7,512	4,149	2.9	1.6	13.0	6.1	2.6	5.5
New London County, CT	266,618	266,107	259,106	254,957	7,512	4,149	2.9	1.6	13.0	6.1	2.6	5.5
Ocala, FL	303,442	291,768	258,916	194,835	44,526	64,081	17.2	32.9	23.9	12.0	0.9	7.0
Marion County, FL	303,442	291,768	258,916	194,835	44,526	64,081	17.2	32.9	23.9	12.0	0.9	7.0
Ocean City, NJ	99,286	100,461	102,326	95,089	−3,040	7,237	−3.0	7.6	20.3	5.0	0.6	3.6
Cape May County, NJ	99,286	100,461	102,326	95,089	−3,040	7,237	−3.0	7.6	20.3	5.0	0.6	3.6
Odessa, TX	125,339	124,293	121,123	118,934	4,216	2,189	3.5	1.8	11.1	4.7	0.6	45.7
Ector County, TX	125,339	124,293	121,123	118,934	4,216	2,189	3.5	1.8	11.1	4.7	0.6	45.7
Ogden-Clearfield, UT	486,842	477,343	442,656	351,799	44,186	90,857	10.0	25.8	8.8	1.4	1.6	9.3
Davis County, UT	268,187	261,395	238,994	187,941	29,193	51,053	12.2	27.2	7.7	1.3	1.8	5.9
Morgan County, UT	7,906	7,633	7,129	5,528	777	1,601	10.9	29.0	9.4	0.1	0.1	1.3
Weber County, UT	210,749	208,315	196,533	158,330	14,216	38,203	7.2	24.1	10.1	1.5	1.4	13.9
Oklahoma City, OK	1,156,812	1,142,390	1,095,421	971,042	61,391	124,379	5.6	12.8	11.4	10.9	2.9	7.4
Canadian County, OK	98,701	95,581	87,697	74,409	11,004	13,288	12.5	17.9	10.0	2.2	2.6	4.2
Cleveland County, OK	224,898	221,124	208,016	174,253	16,882	33,763	8.1	19.4	8.9	3.9	3.6	4.2
Grady County, OK	49,369	48,265	45,516	41,747	3,853	3,769	8.5	9.0	12.7	3.0	0.4	3.0
Lincoln County, OK	32,311	32,294	32,080	29,216	231	2,864	0.7	9.8	13.9	2.6	0.3	1.6
Logan County, OK	36,894	36,514	33,924	29,011	2,970	4,913	8.8	16.9	11.8	11.5	0.5	2.8
McClain County, OK	30,096	29,114	27,740	22,795	2,356	4,945	8.5	21.7	12.6	0.7	0.2	5.3
Oklahoma County, OK	684,543	679,498	660,448	599,611	24,095	60,837	3.6	10.1	12.1	15.7	3.3	9.8

See footnotes at end of table.

Table C-1. Metropolitan Areas With Component Counties — Population and Population Characteristics—Con.

Metropolitan statistical area / Metropolitan statistical area with metropolitan divisions / Metropolitan division / Component county	Population 2005 (July 1)	Population 2004 (July 1)	Population 2000[1] (estimates base)	Population 1990[2] (April 1)	Net change 2000–2005[3]	Net change 1990–2000	Percent change 2000–2005[3]	Percent change 1990–2000	Percent 65 years and over, 2003	Percent Black or African American alone, 2003	Percent Asian alone, 2003	Percent Hispanic or Latino origin, 2003[4]
Olympia, WA	228,867	224,661	207,355	161,238	21,512	46,117	10.4	28.6	11.5	2.6	4.7	4.8
Thurston County, WA	228,867	224,661	207,355	161,238	21,512	46,117	10.4	28.6	11.5	2.6	4.7	4.8
Omaha-Council Bluffs, NE-IA	813,170	802,247	767,140	685,797	46,030	81,343	6.0	11.9	10.9	7.8	1.8	5.8
Harrison County, IA	15,884	15,811	15,666	14,730	218	936	1.4	6.4	17.2	0.1	0.2	0.8
Mills County, IA	15,284	14,995	14,547	13,202	737	1,345	5.1	10.2	12.3	0.3	0.3	1.4
Pottawattamie County, IA	89,738	89,208	87,803	82,628	1,935	5,175	2.2	6.3	13.7	0.9	0.7	3.5
Cass County, NE	25,734	25,553	24,334	21,318	1,400	3,016	5.8	14.1	12.2	0.2	0.5	1.5
Douglas County, NE	486,929	481,203	463,585	416,444	23,344	47,141	5.0	11.3	10.7	11.6	2.3	7.6
Sarpy County, NE	139,371	135,707	122,595	102,583	16,776	20,012	13.7	19.5	7.3	4.2	2.1	4.3
Saunders County, NE	20,458	20,235	19,830	18,285	628	1,545	3.2	8.4	15.1	0.1	0.2	1.2
Washington County, NE	19,772	19,535	18,780	16,607	992	2,173	5.3	13.1	12.9	0.5	0.4	1.1
Orlando - Kissimee, FL	1,933,255	1,863,086	1,644,563	1,224,844	288,692	419,719	17.6	34.3	12.3	15.7	3.2	19.0
Lake County, FL	277,035	261,845	210,527	152,104	66,508	58,423	31.6	38.4	26.0	8.7	1.1	7.6
Orange County, FL	1,023,023	989,873	896,344	677,491	126,679	218,853	14.1	32.3	9.7	20.8	4.0	21.2
Osceola County, FL	231,578	220,127	172,493	107,728	59,085	64,765	34.3	60.1	11.1	9.2	2.5	34.3
Seminole County, FL	401,619	391,241	365,199	287,521	36,420	77,678	10.0	27.0	10.7	10.5	3.0	12.6
Oshkosh-Neenah, WI	159,482	158,664	156,763	140,320	2,719	16,443	1.7	11.7	12.5	1.2	2.1	2.1
Winnebago County, WI	159,482	158,664	156,763	140,320	2,719	16,443	1.7	11.7	12.5	1.2	2.1	2.1
Owensboro, KY	111,599	111,028	109,875	104,681	1,724	5,194	1.6	5.0	13.7	3.9	0.4	1.0
Daviess County, KY	93,060	92,646	91,545	87,189	1,515	4,356	1.7	5.0	13.9	4.5	0.5	1.0
Hancock County, KY	8,613	8,445	8,392	7,864	221	528	2.6	6.7	11.0	0.9	0.2	1.0
McLean County, KY	9,926	9,937	9,938	9,628	−12	310	−0.1	3.2	14.2	0.4	0.1	1.1
Oxnard-Thousand Oaks-Ventura, CA	796,106	796,165	753,197	669,016	42,909	84,181	5.7	12.6	10.5	2.2	5.8	35.3
Ventura County, CA	796,106	796,165	753,197	669,016	42,909	84,181	5.7	12.6	10.5	2.2	5.8	35.3
Palm Bay-Melbourne-Titusville, FL	531,250	518,812	476,230	398,978	55,020	77,252	11.6	19.4	20.0	9.0	1.7	5.2
Brevard County, FL	531,250	518,812	476,230	398,978	55,020	77,252	11.6	19.4	20.0	9.0	1.7	5.2
Panama City-Lynn Haven, FL	161,558	157,811	148,217	126,994	13,341	21,223	9.0	16.7	14.0	11.1	1.9	2.1
Bay County, FL	161,558	157,811	148,217	126,994	13,341	21,223	9.0	16.7	14.0	11.1	1.9	2.1
Parkersburg-Marietta-Vienna, WV-OH	162,529	162,931	164,624	161,907	−2,095	2,717	−1.3	1.7	15.5	1.0	0.6	0.5
Washington County, OH	62,210	62,630	63,251	62,254	−1,041	997	−1.6	1.6	15.5	1.0	0.5	0.5
Pleasants County, WV	7,376	7,437	7,514	7,546	−138	−32	−1.8	−0.4	14.8	0.6	0.3	0.4
Wirt County, WV	5,896	5,850	5,873	5,192	23	681	0.4	13.1	14.1	0.4	0.3	0.3
Wood County, WV	87,047	87,014	87,986	86,915	−939	1,071	−1.1	1.2	15.8	1.1	0.6	0.5
Pascagoula, MS	157,199	155,847	150,564	131,916	6,635	18,648	4.4	14.1	10.9	20.1	1.7	2.1
George County, MS	21,259	20,750	19,144	16,673	2,115	2,471	11.0	14.8	10.7	9.0	0.2	2.1
Jackson County, MS	135,940	135,097	131,420	115,243	4,520	16,177	3.4	14.0	10.9	21.8	1.9	2.1
Pensacola-Ferry Pass-Brent, FL	439,877	434,812	412,153	344,406	27,724	67,747	6.7	19.7	13.2	17.6	2.2	2.1
Escambia County, FL	296,772	296,739	294,410	262,798	2,362	31,612	0.8	12.0	13.9	23.7	2.6	2.0
Santa Rosa County, FL	143,105	138,073	117,743	81,608	25,362	36,135	21.5	44.3	11.7	4.2	1.5	2.5
Peoria, IL	369,161	367,451	366,875	358,552	2,286	8,323	0.6	2.3	14.7	8.8	1.3	1.8
Marshall County, IL	13,217	13,190	13,156	12,846	61	310	0.5	2.4	18.7	0.4	0.3	1.5
Peoria County, IL	182,328	182,129	183,433	182,827	−1,105	606	−0.6	0.3	14.0	16.8	2.1	2.5
Stark County, IL	6,169	6,186	6,332	6,534	−163	−202	−2.6	−3.1	18.8	0.1	0.2	0.9
Tazewell County, IL	129,999	129,007	128,485	123,692	1,514	4,793	1.2	3.9	15.2	0.9	0.6	1.2
Woodford County, IL	37,448	36,939	35,469	32,653	1,979	2,816	5.6	8.6	14.3	0.5	0.4	0.8
Philadelphia-Camden-Wilmington, PA-NJ-DE-MD	**5,823,233**	**5,798,956**	**5,687,141**	**5,435,550**	**136,092**	**251,591**	**2.4**	**4.6**	**13.1**	**20.6**	**3.8**	**5.4**
Camden, NJ	*1,245,902*	*1,237,060*	*1,186,996*	*1,127,972*	*58,906*	*59,024*	*5.0*	*5.2*	*12.2*	*16.5*	*3.2*	*6.8*
Burlington County, NJ	450,743	448,656	423,391	395,066	27,352	28,325	6.5	7.2	12.6	16.4	3.2	4.7
Camden County, NJ	518,249	515,620	508,932	502,824	9,317	6,108	1.8	1.2	12.3	20.2	4.0	10.7
Gloucester County, NJ	276,910	272,784	254,673	230,082	22,237	24,591	8.7	10.7	11.5	9.6	1.7	2.9
Philadelphia, PA	*3,890,181*	*3,882,313*	*3,849,644*	*3,728,991*	*40,537*	*120,653*	*1.1*	*3.2*	*13.7*	*22.3*	*4.3*	*4.9*
Bucks County, PA	621,342	617,214	597,632	541,174	23,710	56,458	4.0	10.4	12.8	3.2	2.9	2.4
Chester County, PA	474,027	466,043	433,501	376,396	40,526	57,105	9.3	15.2	11.9	6.0	2.6	3.6
Delaware County, PA	555,648	554,426	551,974	547,651	3,674	4,323	0.7	0.8	14.9	16.3	3.9	1.6
Montgomery County, PA	775,883	773,375	748,987	678,193	26,896	70,794	3.6	10.4	14.8	7.8	4.9	2.2
Philadelphia County, PA	1,463,281	1,471,255	1,517,550	1,585,577	−54,269	−68,027	−3.6	−4.3	13.5	45.1	5.1	9.1
Wilmington, DE-MD-NJ	*687,150*	*679,583*	*650,501*	*578,587*	*36,649*	*71,914*	*5.6*	*12.4*	*11.6*	*17.9*	*2.6*	*5.1*
New Castle County, DE	523,008	518,728	500,265	441,946	22,743	58,319	4.5	13.2	11.4	20.9	3.2	5.9
Cecil County, MD	97,796	95,536	85,951	71,347	11,845	14,604	13.8	20.5	10.5	3.7	0.7	1.5
Salem County, NJ	66,346	65,319	64,285	65,294	2,061	−1,009	3.2	−1.5	14.3	15.2	0.7	4.4
Phoenix-Mesa-Scottsdale, AZ	3,865,077	3,713,291	3,251,876	2,238,498	613,201	1,013,378	18.9	45.3	11.4	4.0	2.4	28.1
Maricopa County, AZ	3,635,528	3,498,587	3,072,335	2,122,101	563,193	950,234	18.3	44.8	11.2	4.0	2.5	28.0
Pinal County, AZ	229,549	214,704	179,541	116,397	50,008	63,144	27.9	54.2	15.0	3.2	0.8	30.5
Pine Bluff, AR	104,865	105,223	107,345	106,958	−2,480	387	−2.3	0.4	12.8	46.4	0.6	1.1
Cleveland County, AR	8,903	8,770	8,571	7,781	332	790	3.9	10.2	14.2	13.8	0.1	1.9
Jefferson County, AR	81,700	82,162	84,282	85,487	−2,582	−1,205	−3.1	−1.4	12.8	52.1	0.8	1.0
Lincoln County, AR	14,262	14,291	14,492	13,690	−230	802	−1.6	5.9	12.0	33.3	0.1	1.6
Pittsburgh, PA	2,386,074	2,397,767	2,431,087	2,468,289	−45,013	−37,202	−1.9	−1.5	17.3	8.0	1.3	0.7
Allegheny County, PA	1,235,841	1,247,512	1,281,666	1,336,449	−45,825	−54,783	−3.6	−4.1	17.3	12.7	2.1	0.9
Armstrong County, PA	70,586	71,373	72,392	73,478	−1,806	−1,086	−2.5	−1.5	17.9	0.9	0.1	0.5
Beaver County, PA	177,377	178,120	181,412	186,093	−4,035	−4,681	−2.2	−2.6	18.3	6.0	0.3	0.8
Butler County, PA	182,087	180,664	174,083	152,013	8,004	22,070	4.6	14.5	14.3	0.9	0.7	0.5
Fayette County, PA	146,142	146,842	148,644	145,351	−2,502	3,293	−1.7	2.3	17.9	3.6	0.3	0.4
Washington County, PA	206,406	205,319	202,897	204,584	3,509	−1,687	1.7	−0.8	17.3	3.3	0.5	0.6
Westmoreland County, PA	367,635	367,937	369,993	370,321	−2,358	−328	−0.6	−0.1	18.2	2.1	0.6	0.5
Pittsfield, MA	131,868	132,397	134,953	139,352	−3,085	−4,399	−2.3	−3.2	17.8	2.2	1.2	2.0
Berkshire County, MA	131,868	132,397	134,953	139,352	−3,085	−4,399	−2.3	−3.2	17.8	2.2	1.2	2.0

See footnotes at end of table.

Table C-1. Metropolitan Areas With Component Counties — **Population and Population Characteristics**—Con.

Metropolitan statistical area **Metropolitan statistical area with metropolitan divisions** *Metropolitan division* Component county	Population				Net change		Percent change		Percent—			
	2005 (July 1)	2004 (July 1)	2000[1] (estimates base)	1990[2] (April 1)	2000–2005[3]	1990–2000	2000–2005[3]	1990–2000	65 years and over, 2003	Black or African American alone, 2003	Asian alone, 2003	Hispanic or Latino origin, 2003[4]
Pocatello, ID	85,908	85,658	83,103	73,112	2,805	9,991	3.4	13.7	10.5	0.6	1.0	6.8
Bannock County, ID	78,155	77,941	75,565	66,026	2,590	9,539	3.4	14.4	10.4	0.7	1.1	5.1
Power County, ID	7,753	7,717	7,538	7,086	215	452	2.9	6.4	11.4	0.2	0.4	23.6
Portland-South Portland-Biddeford, ME	514,227	511,036	487,568	441,257	26,659	46,311	5.5	10.5	13.4	0.9	1.3	1.0
Cumberland County, ME	274,950	273,622	265,612	243,135	9,338	22,477	3.5	9.2	13.3	1.3	1.7	1.1
Sagadahoc County, ME	36,962	36,901	35,214	33,535	1,748	1,679	5.0	5.0	12.7	1.0	0.7	1.1
York County, ME	202,315	200,513	186,742	164,587	15,573	22,155	8.3	13.5	13.6	0.5	0.8	0.8
Portland-Vancouver-Beaverton, OR-WA	2,095,861	2,062,109	1,927,881	1,523,741	167,980	404,140	8.7	26.5	10.2	2.9	5.2	8.7
Clackamas County, OR	368,470	362,681	338,408	278,850	30,062	59,558	8.9	21.4	11.5	0.8	3.0	5.7
Columbia County, OR	48,065	46,998	43,560	37,557	4,505	6,003	10.3	16.0	11.4	0.4	0.7	3.0
Multnomah County, OR	672,906	671,363	660,469	583,887	12,437	76,582	1.9	13.1	10.6	6.0	6.3	8.9
Washington County, OR	499,794	487,548	445,342	311,554	54,452	133,788	12.2	42.9	8.7	1.4	8.0	13.0
Yamhill County, OR	92,196	90,599	84,992	65,551	7,204	19,441	8.5	29.7	11.5	0.9	1.1	12.4
Clark County, WA	403,766	392,364	345,238	238,053	58,528	107,185	17.0	45.0	9.5	2.0	3.3	5.5
Skamania County, WA	10,664	10,556	9,872	8,289	792	1,583	8.0	19.1	11.0	0.4	0.6	4.8
Port St. Lucie-Fort Pierce, FL	381,033	364,803	319,426	251,071	61,607	68,355	19.3	27.2	23.9	12.2	0.9	9.4
Martin County, FL	139,728	137,693	126,731	100,900	12,997	25,831	10.3	25.6	27.1	5.4	0.7	8.5
St. Lucie County, FL	241,305	227,110	192,695	150,171	48,610	42,524	25.2	28.3	21.8	16.5	1.1	10.0
Poughkeepsie-Newburgh-Middletown, NY	667,742	662,833	621,517	567,109	46,225	54,408	7.4	9.6	10.9	10.2	2.6	11.5
Dutchess County, NY	294,849	293,322	280,150	259,462	14,699	20,688	5.2	8.0	12.0	10.4	3.2	7.9
Orange County, NY	372,893	369,511	341,367	307,647	31,526	33,720	9.2	11.0	10.0	10.1	2.0	14.5
Prescott, AZ	198,701	190,737	167,517	107,714	31,184	59,803	18.6	55.5	21.9	0.4	0.6	10.5
Yavapai County, AZ	198,701	190,737	167,517	107,714	31,184	59,803	18.6	55.5	21.9	0.4	0.6	10.5
Providence-New Bedford-Fall River, RI-MA	1,622,520	1,627,194	1,582,997	1,509,789	39,523	73,208	2.5	4.8	13.9	5.1	2.3	7.8
Bristol County, MA	546,331	547,278	534,678	506,325	11,653	28,353	2.2	5.6	13.7	3.3	1.6	4.3
Bristol County, RI	52,743	52,899	50,648	48,859	2,095	1,789	4.1	3.7	16.4	0.8	1.2	1.2
Kent County, RI	171,590	171,703	167,090	161,135	4,500	5,955	2.7	3.7	14.6	1.3	1.8	1.9
Newport County, RI	83,740	84,846	85,433	87,194	−1,693	−1,761	−2.0	−2.0	14.8	3.6	1.5	2.2
Providence County, RI	639,653	641,874	621,602	596,270	18,051	25,332	2.9	4.2	13.8	8.9	3.4	14.9
Washington County, RI	128,463	128,594	123,546	110,006	4,917	13,540	4.0	12.3	13.1	1.0	1.8	1.4
Provo-Orem, UT	452,851	443,109	376,778	269,407	76,073	107,371	20.2	39.9	6.5	0.4	1.2	7.5
Juab County, UT	9,113	8,995	8,238	5,817	875	2,421	10.6	41.6	10.3	0.2	0.4	2.5
Utah County, UT	443,738	434,114	368,540	263,590	75,198	104,950	20.4	39.8	6.4	0.4	1.2	7.7
Pueblo, CO	151,322	149,954	141,472	123,051	9,850	18,421	7.0	15.0	14.8	2.3	0.7	39.3
Pueblo County, CO	151,322	149,954	141,472	123,051	9,850	18,421	7.0	15.0	14.8	2.3	0.7	39.3
Punta Gorda, FL	157,536	157,324	141,627	110,975	15,909	30,652	11.2	27.6	34.1	4.9	1.0	3.8
Charlotte County, FL	157,536	157,324	141,627	110,975	15,909	30,652	11.2	27.6	34.1	4.9	1.0	3.8
Racine, WI	195,708	193,862	188,831	175,034	6,877	13,797	3.6	7.9	12.2	10.9	0.8	8.6
Racine County, WI	195,708	193,862	188,831	175,034	6,877	13,797	3.6	7.9	12.2	10.9	0.8	8.6
Raleigh-Cary, NC	949,681	914,963	797,026	544,020	152,655	253,006	19.2	46.5	7.9	20.1	3.3	7.0
Franklin County, NC	54,429	53,469	47,260	36,414	7,169	10,846	15.2	29.8	10.6	28.5	0.3	5.9
Johnston County, NC	146,437	141,761	121,900	81,306	24,537	40,594	20.1	49.9	9.4	16.0	0.4	9.4
Wake County, NC	748,815	719,733	627,866	426,300	120,949	201,566	19.3	47.3	7.4	20.3	4.1	6.6
Rapid City, SD	118,203	117,553	112,818	103,221	5,385	9,597	4.8	9.3	12.0	1.3	0.9	2.5
Meade County, SD	24,623	24,657	24,245	21,878	378	2,367	1.6	10.8	10.7	2.2	0.9	2.1
Pennington County, SD	93,580	92,896	88,573	81,343	5,007	7,230	5.7	8.9	12.4	1.0	1.0	2.6
Reading, PA	396,314	391,447	373,638	336,523	22,676	37,115	6.1	11.0	14.5	4.4	1.2	10.6
Berks County, PA	396,314	391,447	373,638	336,523	22,676	37,115	6.1	11.0	14.5	4.4	1.2	10.6
Redding, CA	179,904	177,829	163,256	147,036	16,648	16,220	10.2	11.0	15.0	0.9	2.0	6.6
Shasta County, CA	179,904	177,829	163,256	147,036	16,648	16,220	10.2	11.0	15.0	0.9	2.0	6.6
Reno-Sparks, NV	393,946	384,343	342,885	257,193	51,061	85,692	14.9	33.3	10.8	1.9	4.2	18.4
Storey County, NV	4,074	3,731	3,399	2,526	675	873	19.9	34.6	12.1	0.3	1.2	5.1
Washoe County, NV	389,872	380,612	339,486	254,667	50,386	84,819	14.8	33.3	10.8	1.9	4.2	18.6
Richmond, VA	1,175,654	1,156,849	1,096,957	949,244	78,697	147,713	7.2	15.6	11.4	30.8	2.1	2.6
Amelia County, VA	12,273	11,941	11,400	8,787	873	2,613	7.7	29.7	13.9	25.5	0.2	0.8
Caroline County, VA	25,563	24,000	22,121	19,217	3,442	2,904	15.6	15.1	13.1	32.3	0.4	1.6
Charles City County, VA	7,119	7,117	6,926	6,282	193	644	2.8	10.3	13.2	51.5	0.1	0.6
Chesterfield County, VA	288,876	282,470	259,848	209,564	29,028	50,284	11.2	24.0	7.7	19.9	2.5	3.8
Cumberland County, VA	9,378	9,171	9,017	7,825	361	1,192	4.0	15.2	15.8	36.1	0.5	2.0
Dinwiddie County, VA	25,391	25,111	24,533	22,319	858	2,214	3.5	9.9	11.9	33.1	0.4	1.2
Goochland County, VA	19,360	18,676	16,863	14,163	2,497	2,700	14.8	19.1	12.1	24.1	0.7	1.1
Hanover County, VA	97,426	96,019	86,320	63,306	11,106	23,014	12.9	36.4	11.2	9.5	1.0	1.1
Henrico County, VA	280,581	275,962	262,193	217,849	18,388	44,344	7.0	20.4	12.3	26.4	4.2	2.6
King and Queen County, VA	6,796	6,757	6,630	6,289	166	341	2.5	5.4	16.7	33.3	0.3	1.1
King William County, VA	14,732	14,331	13,146	10,913	1,586	2,233	12.1	20.5	11.4	21.2	0.4	1.2
Louisa County, VA	30,020	28,797	25,627	20,325	4,393	5,302	17.1	26.1	13.3	20.5	0.3	0.8
New Kent County, VA	16,107	15,500	13,462	10,445	2,645	3,017	19.6	28.9	9.3	15.3	0.6	1.5
Powhatan County, VA	26,598	25,823	22,377	15,328	4,221	7,049	18.9	46.0	8.9	15.2	0.2	1.0
Prince George County, VA	36,725	36,462	33,108	27,394	3,617	5,714	10.9	20.9	6.9	33.4	1.9	5.2
Sussex County, VA	12,071	12,167	12,504	10,248	−433	2,256	−3.5	22.0	13.9	62.3	0.2	1.1
Colonial Heights city, VA	17,567	17,465	16,897	16,064	670	833	4.0	5.2	19.0	8.2	2.9	1.7
Hopewell city, VA	22,690	22,401	22,277	23,101	413	−824	1.9	−3.6	14.5	36.5	1.0	3.1
Petersburg city, VA	32,604	32,764	33,756	37,027	−1,152	−3,271	−3.4	−8.8	15.8	80.7	0.7	1.6
Richmond city, VA	193,777	193,915	197,952	202,798	−4,175	−4,846	−2.1	−2.4	13.6	57.8	1.3	3.1

See footnotes at end of table.

Metropolitan statistical area / **Metropolitan statistical area with metropolitan divisions** / *Metropolitan division* / Component county	Population				Net change		Percent change		Percent—			
	2005 (July 1)	2004 (July 1)	2000[1] (estimates base)	1990[2] (April 1)	2000–2005[3]	1990–2000	2000–2005[3]	1990–2000	65 years and over, 2003	Black or African American alone, 2003	Asian alone, 2003	Hispanic or Latino origin, 2003[4]
Riverside-San Bernardino-Ontario, CA	3,909,954	3,785,883	3,254,821	2,588,793	655,133	666,028	20.1	25.7	10.0	8.2	4.6	40.9
Riverside County, CA	1,946,419	1,869,465	1,545,387	1,170,413	401,032	374,974	26.0	32.0	11.9	6.6	4.2	39.1
San Bernardino County, CA	1,963,535	1,916,418	1,709,434	1,418,380	254,101	291,054	14.9	20.5	8.3	9.7	5.1	42.6
Roanoke, VA	292,983	291,177	288,254	268,513	4,729	19,741	1.6	7.4	15.6	12.5	1.2	1.4
Botetourt County, VA	32,027	31,747	30,496	24,992	1,531	5,504	5.0	22.0	13.7	3.9	0.7	0.7
Craig County, VA	5,154	5,173	5,091	4,372	63	719	1.2	16.4	13.4	0.5	0.2	0.3
Franklin County, VA	50,345	49,669	47,283	39,549	3,062	7,734	6.5	19.6	14.9	8.9	0.3	1.3
Roanoke County, VA	88,172	87,511	85,726	79,294	2,446	6,432	2.9	8.1	15.5	4.1	1.7	1.3
Roanoke city, VA	92,631	92,570	94,911	96,509	−2,280	−1,598	−2.4	−1.7	16.6	27.5	1.3	1.9
Salem city, VA	24,654	24,507	24,747	23,797	−93	950	−0.4	4.0	16.7	6.4	1.0	1.1
Rochester, MN	176,984	174,821	163,618	141,945	13,366	21,673	8.2	15.3	11.7	2.4	3.9	2.4
Dodge County, MN	19,595	19,357	17,731	15,731	1,864	2,000	10.5	12.7	11.5	0.2	0.5	3.0
Olmsted County, MN	135,189	133,268	124,277	106,470	10,912	17,807	8.8	16.7	11.2	3.1	5.0	2.4
Wabasha County, MN	22,200	22,196	21,610	19,744	590	1,866	2.7	9.5	15.0	0.3	0.5	2.0
Rochester, NY	1,039,028	1,041,060	1,037,831	1,002,410	1,197	35,421	0.1	3.5	13.0	11.8	2.2	5.2
Livingston County, NY	64,205	64,511	64,328	62,372	−123	1,956	−0.2	3.1	11.7	3.2	0.9	2.6
Monroe County, NY	733,366	735,816	735,343	713,968	−1,977	21,375	−0.3	3.0	13.1	15.2	2.8	6.1
Ontario County, NY	104,461	103,415	100,224	95,101	4,237	5,123	4.2	5.4	13.5	2.5	0.8	2.8
Orleans County, NY	43,387	43,583	44,171	41,846	−784	2,325	−1.8	5.6	12.7	7.3	0.4	3.9
Wayne County, NY	93,609	93,735	93,765	89,123	−156	4,642	−0.2	5.2	12.5	3.4	0.6	3.0
Rockford, IL	339,178	334,754	320,204	283,719	18,974	36,485	5.9	12.9	12.4	9.6	1.8	9.5
Boone County, IL	50,483	48,471	41,786	30,806	8,697	10,980	20.8	35.6	10.4	1.4	0.8	15.4
Winnebago County, IL	288,695	286,283	278,418	252,913	10,277	25,505	3.7	10.1	12.7	11.0	2.0	8.5
Rocky Mount, NC	145,507	145,033	142,991	133,369	2,516	9,622	1.8	7.2	12.5	44.1	0.5	3.5
Edgecombe County, NC	54,129	54,350	55,606	56,692	−1,477	−1,086	−2.7	−1.9	12.1	58.5	0.2	3.2
Nash County, NC	91,378	90,683	87,385	76,677	3,993	10,708	4.6	14.0	12.8	35.2	0.6	3.7
Rome, GA	94,198	94,053	90,565	81,251	3,633	9,314	4.0	11.5	13.6	13.2	1.0	6.5
Floyd County, GA	94,198	94,053	90,565	81,251	3,633	9,314	4.0	11.5	13.6	13.2	1.0	6.5
Sacramento-Arden-Arcade-Roseville, CA	2,042,283	2,014,594	1,796,857	1,481,220	245,426	315,637	13.7	21.3	11.2	7.5	10.0	16.9
El Dorado County, CA	176,841	172,723	156,299	125,995	20,542	30,304	13.1	24.1	11.9	0.8	2.3	10.4
Placer County, CA	317,028	306,305	248,399	172,796	68,629	75,603	27.6	43.8	13.5	1.2	3.8	10.4
Sacramento County, CA	1,363,482	1,351,428	1,223,499	1,041,219	139,983	182,280	11.4	17.5	10.8	10.4	12.3	17.7
Yolo County, CA	184,932	184,138	168,660	141,210	16,272	27,450	9.6	19.4	9.3	2.4	10.7	27.1
Saginaw-Saginaw Township North, MI	208,356	209,249	210,042	211,946	−1,686	−1,904	−0.8	−0.9	13.5	19.4	0.9	6.9
Saginaw County, MI	208,356	209,249	210,042	211,946	−1,686	−1,904	−0.8	−0.9	13.5	19.4	0.9	6.9
St. Cloud, MN	181,159	179,176	167,396	149,509	13,763	17,887	8.2	12.0	11.1	1.2	1.6	1.5
Benton County, MN	38,505	38,105	34,227	30,185	4,278	4,042	12.5	13.4	10.3	1.3	1.2	1.0
Stearns County, MN	142,654	141,071	133,169	119,324	9,485	13,845	7.1	11.6	11.3	1.2	1.7	1.6
St. George, UT	118,885	110,425	90,354	48,560	28,531	41,794	31.6	86.1	16.9	0.3	0.5	5.7
Washington County, UT	118,885	110,425	90,354	48,560	28,531	41,794	31.6	86.1	16.9	0.3	0.5	5.7
St. Joseph, MO-KS	121,961	122,011	123,822	115,816	−1,861	8,006	−1.5	6.9	14.5	4.6	0.5	2.0
Doniphan County, KS	7,816	7,990	8,249	8,134	−433	115	−5.2	1.4	15.5	2.5	0.3	1.6
Andrew County, MO	16,899	16,882	16,492	14,632	407	1,860	2.5	12.7	13.4	0.7	0.3	0.9
Buchanan County, MO	84,904	84,801	86,004	83,083	−1,100	2,921	−1.3	3.5	14.8	4.4	0.6	2.4
DeKalb County, MO	12,342	12,338	13,077	9,967	−735	3,110	−5.6	31.2	13.4	11.7	0.3	1.2
St. Louis, MO-IL[6]	2,778,518	2,768,641	2,698,672	2,580,720	79,846	117,952	3.0	4.6	12.8	18.1	1.7	1.7
Bond County, IL	18,027	18,041	17,631	14,991	396	2,640	2.2	17.6	14.4	7.0	0.3	2.0
Calhoun County, IL	5,163	5,156	5,084	5,322	79	−238	1.6	−4.5	18.8	0.1	0.2	0.7
Clinton County, IL	36,095	36,107	35,531	33,944	564	1,587	1.6	4.7	14.6	4.0	0.3	1.9
Jersey County, IL	22,456	22,344	21,668	20,539	788	1,129	3.6	5.5	14.5	0.7	0.3	0.7
Macoupin County, IL	49,111	49,073	49,019	47,679	92	1,340	0.2	2.8	16.9	1.0	0.2	0.7
Madison County, IL	264,309	263,443	258,952	249,238	5,357	9,714	2.1	3.9	13.9	7.6	0.7	1.8
Monroe County, IL	31,040	30,491	27,619	22,422	3,421	5,197	12.4	23.2	13.3	0.1	0.3	1.2
St. Clair County, IL	260,067	259,123	256,067	262,852	4,000	−6,785	1.6	−2.6	12.8	29.3	1.1	2.8
Franklin County, MO	99,090	98,029	93,807	80,603	5,283	13,204	5.6	16.4	12.3	0.9	0.3	0.7
Jefferson County, MO	213,669	210,466	198,099	171,380	15,570	26,719	7.9	15.6	9.5	0.7	0.5	1.1
Lincoln County, MO	47,727	45,733	38,944	28,892	8,783	10,052	22.6	34.8	10.0	1.8	0.2	1.2
St. Charles County, MO	329,940	320,459	283,893	212,751	46,047	71,142	16.2	33.4	9.3	3.2	1.2	1.6
St. Louis County, MO	1,004,666	1,007,723	1,016,300	993,508	−11,634	22,792	−1.1	2.3	14.0	20.8	2.8	1.5
Warren County, MO	28,764	27,822	24,525	19,534	4,239	4,991	17.3	25.6	12.7	2.2	0.2	1.6
Washington County, MO	24,032	23,926	23,344	20,380	688	2,964	2.9	14.5	11.9	2.8	0.2	0.8
St. Louis city, MO	344,362	350,705	348,189	396,685	−3,827	−48,496	−1.1	−12.2	12.7	52.0	2.2	2.1
Salem, OR	375,560	369,573	347,218	278,024	28,342	69,194	8.2	24.9	12.5	1.0	1.8	17.8
Marion County, OR	305,265	301,702	284,838	228,483	20,427	56,355	7.2	24.7	12.0	1.0	1.9	19.7
Polk County, OR	70,295	67,871	62,380	49,541	7,915	12,839	12.7	25.9	15.0	0.6	1.3	9.3
Salinas, CA	412,104	414,551	401,762	355,660	10,342	46,102	2.6	13.0	9.9	4.0	6.3	49.7
Monterey County, CA	412,104	414,551	401,762	355,660	10,342	46,102	2.6	13.0	9.9	4.0	6.3	49.7
Salisbury, MD	116,247	114,372	109,391	97,779	6,856	11,612	6.3	11.9	13.0	26.9	1.6	2.0
Somerset County, MD	25,845	25,764	24,747	23,440	1,098	1,307	4.4	5.6	13.5	40.6	0.7	1.5
Wicomico County, MD	90,402	88,608	84,644	74,339	5,758	10,305	6.8	13.9	12.8	22.8	1.9	2.2
Salt Lake City, UT	1,034,484	1,018,514	968,883	768,075	65,601	200,808	6.8	26.1	8.0	1.3	2.8	13.0
Salt Lake County, UT	948,172	934,838	898,412	725,956	49,760	172,456	5.5	23.8	8.2	1.3	3.0	13.4
Summit County, UT	35,001	33,937	29,736	15,518	5,265	14,218	17.7	91.6	5.2	0.3	1.1	9.0
Tooele County, UT	51,311	49,739	40,735	26,601	10,576	14,134	26.0	53.1	6.7	1.5	0.7	9.1

See footnotes at end of table.

Metropolitan statistical area **Metropolitan statistical area with metropolitan divisions** *Metropolitan division* Component county	Population				Net change		Percent change		Percent—			
	2005 (July 1)	2004 (July 1)	2000[1] (estimates base)	1990[2] (April 1)	2000–2005[3]	1990–2000	2000–2005[3]	1990–2000	65 years and over, 2003	Black or African American alone, 2003	Asian alone, 2003	Hispanic or Latino origin, 2003[4]
San Angelo, TX	105,367	105,538	105,781	100,087	–414	5,694	–0.4	5.7	13.8	3.9	0.9	32.9
Irion County, TX	1,756	1,729	1,771	1,629	–15	142	–0.8	8.7	14.8	1.8	–	25.5
Tom Green County, TX	103,611	103,809	104,010	98,458	–399	5,552	–0.4	5.6	13.8	3.9	0.9	33.0
San Antonio, TX	1,889,797	1,852,508	1,711,726	1,407,745	178,071	303,981	10.4	21.6	10.7	6.2	1.5	52.1
Atascosa County, TX	43,226	42,688	38,628	30,533	4,598	8,095	11.9	26.5	10.7	0.9	0.4	59.8
Bandera County, TX	19,988	19,686	17,645	10,562	2,343	7,083	13.3	67.1	15.6	0.4	0.3	14.5
Bexar County, TX	1,518,370	1,492,361	1,392,931	1,185,394	125,439	207,537	9.0	17.5	10.3	7.2	1.8	56.5
Comal County, TX	96,018	91,839	78,021	51,832	17,997	26,189	23.1	50.5	14.3	1.1	0.5	23.1
Guadalupe County, TX	103,032	99,541	89,046	64,873	13,986	24,173	15.7	37.3	11.7	5.1	0.9	33.8
Kendall County, TX	28,607	27,342	23,743	14,589	4,864	9,154	20.5	62.7	13.0	0.4	0.3	18.5
Medina County, TX	43,027	42,312	39,304	27,312	3,723	11,992	9.5	43.9	12.2	2.3	0.4	46.2
Wilson County, TX	37,529	36,739	32,408	22,650	5,121	9,758	15.8	43.1	10.8	1.5	0.4	37.3
San Diego-Carlsbad-San Marcos, CA . .	2,933,462	2,935,190	2,813,833	2,498,016	119,629	315,817	4.3	12.6	11.0	5.9	9.4	28.7
San Diego County, CA	2,933,462	2,935,190	2,813,833	2,498,016	119,629	315,817	4.3	12.6	11.0	5.9	9.4	28.7
Sandusky, OH	78,665	78,976	79,551	76,779	–886	2,772	–1.1	3.6	15.9	8.6	0.5	2.2
Erie County, OH	78,665	78,976	79,551	76,779	–886	2,772	–1.1	3.6	15.9	8.6	0.5	2.2
San Francisco-Oakland-Fremont, CA . .	**4,152,688**	**4,146,980**	**4,123,742**	**3,684,112**	**28,946**	**439,630**	**0.7**	**11.9**	**11.9**	**9.5**	**20.9**	**18.9**
Oakland-Fremont-Hayward, CA . . .	*2,466,692*	*2,459,702*	*2,392,557*	*2,080,434*	*74,135*	*312,123*	*3.1*	*15.0*	*10.7*	*12.5*	*18.6*	*20.2*
Alameda County, CA	1,448,905	1,452,096	1,443,741	1,276,702	5,164	167,039	0.4	13.1	10.3	14.5	23.0	20.2
Contra Costa County, CA	1,017,787	1,007,606	948,816	803,732	68,971	145,084	7.3	18.1	11.2	9.6	12.1	20.1
San Francisco-San Mateo-Redwood City, CA . . .	*1,685,996*	*1,687,278*	*1,731,185*	*1,603,678*	*–45,189*	*127,507*	*–2.6*	*8.0*	*13.6*	*5.2*	*24.3*	*17.1*
Marin County, CA	246,960	245,929	247,289	230,096	–329	17,193	–0.1	7.5	14.0	3.0	4.9	12.0
San Francisco County, CA . . .	739,426	743,193	776,733	723,959	–37,307	52,774	–4.8	7.3	14.3	7.7	32.5	14.0
San Mateo County, CA	699,610	698,156	707,163	649,623	–7,553	57,540	–1.1	8.9	12.7	3.4	22.3	22.3
San Jose-Sunnyvale-Santa Clara, CA . .	1,754,988	1,737,961	1,735,819	1,534,274	19,169	201,545	1.1	13.1	10.0	2.8	27.8	25.4
San Benito County, CA	55,936	55,981	53,234	36,697	2,702	16,537	5.1	45.1	8.0	1.2	2.8	50.2
Santa Clara County, CA	1,699,052	1,681,980	1,682,585	1,497,577	16,467	185,008	1.0	12.4	10.1	2.8	28.6	24.5
San Luis Obispo-Paso Robles, CA	255,478	254,436	246,681	217,162	8,797	29,519	3.6	13.6	14.3	2.1	2.8	17.3
San Luis Obispo County, CA . .	255,478	254,436	246,681	217,162	8,797	29,519	3.6	13.6	14.3	2.1	2.8	17.3
Santa Barbara-Santa Maria, CA	400,762	401,708	399,347	369,608	1,415	29,739	0.4	8.0	12.8	2.4	4.2	36.1
Santa Barbara County, CA . . .	400,762	401,708	399,347	369,608	1,415	29,739	0.4	8.0	12.8	2.4	4.2	36.1
Santa Cruz-Watsonville, CA	249,666	250,837	255,602	229,734	–5,936	25,868	–2.3	11.3	9.9	1.1	3.7	27.7
Santa Cruz County, CA	249,666	250,837	255,602	229,734	–5,936	25,868	–2.3	11.3	9.9	1.1	3.7	27.7
Santa Fe, NM	140,855	139,166	129,288	98,928	11,567	30,360	8.9	30.7	11.4	0.9	1.1	49.5
Santa Fe County, NM	140,855	139,166	129,288	98,928	11,567	30,360	8.9	30.7	11.4	0.9	1.1	49.5
Santa Rosa-Petaluma, CA	466,477	467,932	458,614	388,222	7,863	70,392	1.7	18.1	12.4	1.6	3.6	19.8
Sonoma County, CA	466,477	467,932	458,614	388,222	7,863	70,392	1.7	18.1	12.4	1.6	3.6	19.8
Sarasota-Bradenton-Venice, FL	673,035	651,696	589,963	489,483	83,072	100,480	14.1	20.5	26.9	6.5	1.0	7.9
Manatee County, FL	306,779	295,974	264,002	211,707	42,777	52,295	16.2	24.7	23.2	9.0	1.1	10.8
Sarasota County, FL	366,256	355,722	325,961	277,776	40,295	48,185	12.4	17.3	30.0	4.5	0.9	5.5
Savannah, GA	313,883	310,327	293,299	257,899	20,584	35,400	7.0	13.7	11.4	34.4	1.7	2.0
Bryan County, GA	28,549	27,473	23,417	15,438	5,132	7,979	21.9	51.7	6.9	13.8	0.8	2.2
Chatham County, GA	238,410	238,339	232,347	216,774	6,063	15,573	2.6	7.2	12.6	40.6	2.0	2.0
Effingham County, GA	46,924	44,515	37,535	25,687	9,389	11,848	25.0	46.1	7.9	12.7	0.5	1.7
Scranton—Wilkes-Barre, PA	550,546	551,214	560,625	575,322	–10,079	–14,697	–1.8	–2.6	18.7	1.7	0.7	1.5
Lackawanna County, PA	209,525	209,950	213,295	219,097	–3,770	–5,802	–1.8	–2.6	18.8	1.5	0.8	1.6
Luzerne County, PA	312,861	313,088	319,250	328,149	–6,389	–8,899	–2.0	–2.7	19.0	1.9	0.7	1.5
Wyoming County, PA	28,160	28,176	28,080	28,076	80	4	0.3	(Z)	13.9	0.5	0.3	0.7
Seattle-Tacoma-Bellevue, WA	**3,203,314**	**3,167,729**	**3,043,885**	**2,559,136**	**159,429**	**484,749**	**5.2**	**18.9**	**10.1**	**5.5**	**9.5**	**6.2**
Seattle-Bellevue-Everett, WA . . .	*2,449,527*	*2,421,951*	*2,343,067*	*1,972,933*	*106,460*	*370,134*	*4.5*	*18.8*	*10.1*	*4.9*	*10.7*	*6.1*
King County, WA	1,793,583	1,777,746	1,737,043	1,507,305	56,540	229,738	3.3	15.2	10.5	6.0	12.2	6.3
Snohomish County, WA	655,944	644,205	606,024	465,628	49,920	140,396	8.2	30.2	9.3	2.0	6.8	5.6
Tacoma, WA	*753,787*	*745,778*	*700,818*	*586,203*	*52,969*	*114,615*	*7.6*	*19.6*	*10.2*	*7.3*	*5.4*	*6.3*
Pierce County, WA	753,787	745,778	700,818	586,203	52,969	114,615	7.6	19.6	10.2	7.3	5.4	6.3
Sheboygan, WI	114,610	113,899	112,656	103,877	1,954	8,779	1.7	8.5	13.8	1.1	4.0	3.9
Sheboygan County, WI	114,610	113,899	112,656	103,877	1,954	8,779	1.7	8.5	13.8	1.1	4.0	3.9
Sherman-Denison, TX	116,834	115,855	110,595	95,019	6,239	15,576	5.6	16.4	14.7	5.6	0.6	8.0
Grayson County, TX	116,834	115,855	110,595	95,019	6,239	15,576	5.6	16.4	14.7	5.6	0.6	8.0
Shreveport-Bossier City, LA	383,233	380,785	375,965	359,687	7,268	16,278	1.9	4.5	13.0	38.8	1.0	2.1
Bossier Parish, LA	105,541	103,722	98,357	86,088	7,184	12,269	7.3	14.3	11.0	21.1	1.4	3.4
Caddo Parish, LA	251,309	250,893	252,116	248,253	–807	3,863	–0.3	1.6	13.7	45.8	0.9	1.6
De Soto Parish, LA	26,383	26,170	25,492	25,346	891	146	3.5	0.6	13.6	40.5	0.1	1.7
Sioux City, IA-NE-SD	142,571	143,116	143,053	131,350	–482	11,703	–0.3	8.9	12.8	1.8	2.8	10.9
Woodbury County, IA	102,605	103,206	103,877	98,276	–1,272	5,601	–1.2	5.7	13.0	2.2	2.8	9.6
Dakota County, NE	20,349	20,518	20,253	16,742	96	3,511	0.5	21.0	10.4	1.0	3.7	24.4
Dixon County, NE	6,155	6,122	6,339	6,143	–184	196	–2.9	3.2	17.0	(Z)	0.4	6.6
Union County, SD	13,462	13,270	12,584	10,189	878	2,395	7.0	23.5	13.1	0.7	2.2	1.5
Sioux Falls, SD	207,918	203,186	187,093	153,500	20,825	33,593	11.1	21.9	11.4	1.7	1.1	2.0
Lincoln County, SD	33,381	31,524	24,147	15,427	9,234	8,720	38.2	56.5	8.8	0.6	1.0	0.7
McCook County, SD	5,930	5,893	5,832	5,688	98	144	1.7	2.5	18.4	0.1	0.2	0.8
Minnehaha County, SD	160,087	157,158	148,265	123,809	11,822	24,456	8.0	19.8	11.2	2.1	1.2	2.4
Turner County, SD	8,520	8,611	8,849	8,576	–329	273	–3.7	3.2	19.3	0.2	0.2	0.4
South Bend-Mishawaka, IN-MI	318,156	317,490	316,661	296,529	1,495	20,132	0.5	6.8	13.4	10.6	1.5	4.7
St. Joseph County, IN	266,160	265,718	265,559	247,052	601	18,507	0.2	7.5	13.3	11.5	1.6	5.1
Cass County, MI	51,996	51,772	51,102	49,477	894	1,625	1.7	3.3	14.0	6.0	0.6	2.4

See footnotes at end of table.

Metropolitan statistical area **Metropolitan statistical area with metropolitan divisions** *Metropolitan division* Component county	Population				Net change		Percent change		Percent—			
	2005 (July 1)	2004 (July 1)	2000[1] (estimates base)	1990[2] (April 1)	2000–2005[3]	1990–2000	2000–2005[3]	1990–2000	65 years and over, 2003	Black or African American alone, 2003	Asian alone, 2003	Hispanic or Latino origin, 2003[4]
Spartanburg, SC	266,809	264,106	253,782	226,793	13,027	26,989	5.1	11.9	12.6	21.3	1.7	3.4
Spartanburg County, SC	266,809	264,106	253,782	226,793	13,027	26,989	5.1	11.9	12.6	21.3	1.7	3.4
Spokane, WA	440,706	435,146	417,939	361,333	22,767	56,606	5.4	15.7	12.3	1.7	1.9	3.1
Spokane County, WA	440,706	435,146	417,939	361,333	22,767	56,606	5.4	15.7	12.3	1.7	1.9	3.1
Springfield, IL	205,527	205,056	201,440	189,550	4,087	11,890	2.0	6.3	13.3	9.6	1.3	1.3
Menard County, IL	12,738	12,741	12,486	11,164	252	1,322	2.0	11.8	13.6	0.5	0.2	0.9
Sangamon County, IL	192,789	192,315	188,954	178,386	3,835	10,568	2.0	5.9	13.3	10.2	1.4	1.3
Springfield, MA	687,264	687,296	680,014	672,970	7,250	7,044	1.1	1.0	13.6	7.1	1.9	12.1
Franklin County, MA	72,334	72,214	71,535	70,092	799	1,443	1.1	2.1	13.9	1.1	1.0	2.1
Hampden County, MA	461,591	461,491	456,226	456,310	5,365	−84	1.2	(Z)	14.1	9.6	1.5	16.6
Hampshire County, MA	153,339	153,591	152,253	146,568	1,086	5,685	0.7	3.9	11.9	2.3	3.6	3.6
Springfield, MO	398,124	390,917	368,374	298,818	29,750	69,556	8.1	23.3	13.2	1.7	0.9	1.7
Christian County, MO	67,266	64,222	54,285	32,644	12,981	21,641	23.9	66.3	10.7	0.3	0.4	1.6
Dallas County, MO	16,437	16,347	15,661	12,646	776	3,015	5.0	23.8	14.9	0.1	0.1	1.2
Greene County, MO	250,784	247,992	240,391	207,949	10,393	32,442	4.3	15.6	13.7	2.4	1.2	1.8
Polk County, MO	28,892	28,316	26,992	21,826	1,900	5,166	7.0	23.7	15.5	0.4	0.3	1.5
Webster County, MO	34,745	34,040	31,045	23,753	3,700	7,292	11.9	30.7	11.8	1.3	0.4	1.3
Springfield, OH	142,376	142,394	144,741	147,548	−2,365	−2,807	−1.6	−1.9	14.8	8.8	0.6	1.3
Clark County, OH	142,376	142,394	144,741	147,548	−2,365	−2,807	−1.6	−1.9	14.8	8.8	0.6	1.3
State College, PA	140,561	139,948	135,758	124,812	4,803	10,946	3.5	8.8	10.4	2.7	4.3	1.5
Centre County, PA	140,561	139,948	135,758	124,812	4,803	10,946	3.5	8.8	10.4	2.7	4.3	1.5
Stockton, CA	664,116	649,241	563,598	480,628	100,518	82,970	17.8	17.3	9.9	7.6	13.0	33.4
San Joaquin County, CA	664,116	649,241	563,598	480,628	100,518	82,970	17.8	17.3	9.9	7.6	13.0	33.4
Sumter, SC	105,517	105,699	104,636	101,276	881	3,360	0.8	3.3	11.9	48.9	1.0	1.6
Sumter County, SC	105,517	105,699	104,636	101,276	881	3,360	0.8	3.3	11.9	48.9	1.0	1.6
Syracuse, NY	651,763	653,128	650,154	659,924	1,609	−9,770	0.2	−1.5	13.1	7.7	2.0	2.6
Madison County, NY	70,337	70,392	69,441	69,166	896	275	1.3	0.4	12.6	1.5	0.7	1.4
Onondaga County, NY	458,053	458,870	458,336	468,973	−283	−10,637	−0.1	−2.3	13.6	10.5	2.5	3.0
Oswego County, NY	123,373	123,866	122,377	121,785	996	592	0.8	0.5	11.4	0.7	0.5	1.6
Tallahassee, FL	334,886	331,252	320,304	259,107	14,582	61,197	4.6	23.6	9.4	33.1	1.6	3.9
Gadsden County, FL	46,428	46,083	45,087	41,116	1,341	3,971	3.0	9.7	12.1	58.4	0.3	6.7
Jefferson County, FL	14,490	14,392	12,902	11,296	1,588	1,606	12.3	14.2	13.9	38.1	0.3	3.4
Leon County, FL	245,756	243,703	239,452	192,493	6,304	46,959	2.6	24.4	8.4	30.3	2.1	3.6
Wakulla County, FL	28,212	27,074	22,863	14,202	5,349	8,661	23.4	61.0	11.5	12.7	0.3	2.4
Tampa-St. Petersburg-Clearwater, FL	2,647,658	2,586,417	2,396,013	2,067,959	251,645	328,054	10.5	15.9	17.9	11.2	2.2	12.0
Hernando County, FL	158,409	150,540	130,802	101,115	27,607	29,687	21.1	29.4	28.4	4.5	0.8	6.3
Hillsborough County, FL	1,132,152	1,100,333	998,948	834,054	133,204	164,894	13.3	19.8	11.6	16.3	2.6	20.2
Pasco County, FL	429,065	408,046	344,768	281,131	84,297	63,637	24.5	22.6	23.9	2.8	1.2	7.0
Pinellas County, FL	928,032	927,498	921,495	851,659	6,537	69,836	0.7	8.2	21.2	10.0	2.5	5.6
Terre Haute, IN	168,059	168,482	170,954	166,578	−2,895	4,376	−1.7	2.6	14.1	4.3	1.0	0.9
Clay County, IN	27,142	27,068	26,567	24,705	575	1,862	2.2	7.5	14.9	0.5	0.2	0.7
Sullivan County, IN	21,763	21,862	21,751	18,993	12	2,758	0.1	14.5	13.5	4.3	0.2	0.9
Vermillion County, IN	16,562	16,544	16,788	16,773	−226	15	−1.3	0.1	15.8	0.3	0.1	0.7
Vigo County, IN	102,592	103,008	105,848	106,107	−3,256	−259	−3.1	−0.2	13.7	5.9	1.5	1.0
Texarkana, TX-Texarkana, AR	133,805	132,698	129,749	120,132	4,056	9,617	3.1	8.0	13.3	24.0	0.5	3.6
Miller County, AR	43,162	42,518	40,443	38,467	2,719	1,976	6.7	5.1	13.2	25.2	0.5	1.1
Bowie County, TX	90,643	90,180	89,306	81,665	1,337	7,641	1.5	9.4	13.4	23.3	0.5	4.8
Toledo, OH	656,696	657,925	659,188	654,157	−2,492	5,031	−0.4	0.8	12.7	12.2	1.3	4.6
Fulton County, OH	42,955	42,817	42,084	38,498	871	3,586	2.1	9.3	12.6	0.3	0.5	6.0
Lucas County, OH	448,229	450,304	455,054	462,361	−6,825	−7,307	−1.5	−1.6	12.8	17.3	1.4	4.8
Ottawa County, OH	41,583	41,412	40,985	40,029	598	956	1.5	2.4	16.5	0.6	0.3	3.8
Wood County, OH	123,929	123,392	121,065	113,269	2,864	7,796	2.4	6.9	11.1	1.3	1.2	3.5
Topeka, KS	229,075	227,609	224,551	210,257	4,524	14,294	2.0	6.8	13.9	7.1	0.9	6.5
Jackson County, KS	13,535	13,193	12,657	11,525	878	1,132	6.9	9.8	14.6	0.5	0.2	2.0
Jefferson County, KS	19,106	18,951	18,426	15,905	680	2,521	3.7	15.9	13.2	0.5	0.2	1.5
Osage County, KS	17,150	17,050	16,715	15,248	435	1,467	2.6	9.6	15.6	0.4	0.2	1.7
Shawnee County, KS	172,365	171,553	169,868	160,976	2,497	8,892	1.5	5.5	13.7	9.3	1.2	8.0
Wabaunsee County, KS	6,919	6,862	6,885	6,603	34	282	0.5	4.3	15.5	0.5	0.1	2.0
Trenton-Ewing, NJ	366,256	364,381	350,761	325,824	15,495	24,937	4.4	7.7	12.3	20.6	6.3	10.9
Mercer County, NJ	366,256	364,381	350,761	325,824	15,495	24,937	4.4	7.7	12.3	20.6	6.3	10.9
Tucson, AZ	924,786	906,540	843,746	666,957	81,040	176,789	9.6	26.5	14.2	3.2	2.3	31.9
Pima County, AZ	924,786	906,540	843,746	666,957	81,040	176,789	9.6	26.5	14.2	3.2	2.3	31.9
Tulsa, OK	887,715	880,713	859,530	761,019	28,185	98,511	3.3	12.9	12.1	9.0	1.4	5.3
Creek County, OK	68,708	68,647	67,369	60,915	1,339	6,454	2.0	10.6	13.5	2.5	0.4	2.2
Okmulgee County, OK	39,732	39,764	39,685	36,490	47	3,195	0.1	8.8	14.7	10.1	0.2	2.1
Osage County, OK	45,416	45,073	44,434	41,645	982	2,789	2.2	6.7	13.7	10.9	0.3	2.2
Pawnee County, OK	16,860	16,793	16,612	15,575	248	1,037	1.5	6.7	14.2	0.7	0.3	1.1
Rogers County, OK	80,757	79,032	70,638	55,170	10,119	15,468	14.3	28.0	11.7	0.9	0.4	2.3
Tulsa County, OK	572,059	568,611	563,301	503,341	8,758	59,960	1.6	11.9	11.7	11.4	1.9	7.0
Wagoner County, OK	64,183	62,793	57,491	47,883	6,692	9,608	11.6	20.1	10.8	4.1	0.7	2.6
Tuscaloosa, AL	196,885	195,103	193,134	176,173	3,751	16,961	1.9	9.6	11.5	35.4	0.9	1.3
Greene County, AL	9,661	9,697	9,974	10,153	−313	−179	−3.1	−1.8	14.3	80.4	0.1	0.6
Hale County, AL	18,316	18,228	18,285	15,498	31	2,787	0.2	18.0	12.4	59.6	0.1	0.9
Tuscaloosa County, AL	168,908	167,178	164,875	150,522	4,033	14,353	2.4	9.5	11.3	30.0	1.0	1.4

See footnotes at end of table.

Metropolitan statistical area **Metropolitan statistical area with metropolitan divisions** *Metropolitan division* Component county	Population				Net change		Percent change		Percent—			
	2005 (July 1)	2004 (July 1)	2000[1] (estimates base)	1990[2] (April 1)	2000– 2005[3]	1990– 2000	2000– 2005[3]	1990– 2000	65 years and over, 2003	Black or African American alone, 2003	Asian alone, 2003	Hispanic or Latino origin, 2003[4]
Tyler, TX	190,594	186,822	174,706	151,309	15,888	23,397	9.1	15.5	14.0	18.7	0.8	13.0
Smith County, TX	190,594	186,822	174,706	151,309	15,888	23,397	9.1	15.5	14.0	18.7	0.8	13.0
Utica-Rome, NY	297,885	298,438	299,896	316,645	−2,011	−16,749	−0.7	−5.3	16.1	5.1	1.3	3.3
Herkimer County, NY	63,780	63,824	64,437	65,809	−657	−1,372	−1.0	−2.1	16.4	0.7	0.6	1.1
Oneida County, NY	234,105	234,614	235,459	250,836	−1,354	−15,377	−0.6	−6.1	16.0	6.3	1.5	3.8
Valdosta, GA	124,838	123,725	119,566	99,244	5,272	20,322	4.4	20.5	10.0	32.5	1.0	3.0
Brooks County, GA	16,327	16,327	16,450	15,398	−123	1,052	−0.7	6.8	14.5	38.7	0.2	3.5
Echols County, GA	4,253	4,111	3,750	2,334	503	1,416	13.4	60.7	7.7	8.2	0.1	24.0
Lanier County, GA	7,553	7,422	7,241	5,531	312	1,710	4.3	30.9	10.8	26.3	0.4	2.0
Lowndes County, GA	96,705	95,865	92,125	75,981	4,580	16,144	5.0	21.2	9.2	33.0	1.2	2.2
Vallejo-Fairfield, CA	411,593	411,896	394,513	339,471	17,080	55,042	4.3	16.2	10.0	15.4	13.5	19.9
Solano County, CA	411,593	411,896	394,513	339,471	17,080	55,042	4.3	16.2	10.0	15.4	13.5	19.9
Vero Beach, FL	128,594	124,676	112,947	90,208	15,647	22,739	13.9	25.2	27.8	8.6	0.9	7.6
Indian River County, FL	128,594	124,676	112,947	90,208	15,647	22,739	13.9	25.2	27.8	8.6	0.9	7.6
Victoria, TX	113,356	113,251	111,663	99,394	1,693	12,269	1.5	12.3	12.8	5.6	1.3	40.9
Calhoun County, TX	20,606	20,537	20,647	19,053	−41	1,594	−0.2	8.4	14.1	2.6	3.5	43.9
Goliad County, TX	7,102	7,079	6,928	5,980	174	948	2.5	15.9	16.5	5.7	0.2	35.3
Victoria County, TX	85,648	85,635	84,088	74,361	1,560	9,727	1.9	13.1	12.2	6.3	0.9	40.7
Vineland-Millville-Bridgeton, NJ	153,252	151,020	146,438	138,053	6,814	8,385	4.7	6.1	12.7	21.6	1.1	21.0
Cumberland County, NJ	153,252	151,020	146,438	138,053	6,814	8,385	4.7	6.1	12.7	21.6	1.1	21.0
Virginia Beach-Norfolk-Newport News, VA-NC	1,647,346	1,641,671	1,576,917	1,450,855	70,429	126,062	4.5	8.7	10.5	32.0	2.9	3.1
Currituck County, NC	23,112	22,055	18,190	13,736	4,922	4,454	27.1	32.4	11.6	6.5	0.5	1.3
Gloucester County, VA	37,787	37,118	34,780	30,131	3,007	4,649	8.6	15.4	12.3	9.9	0.7	1.6
Isle of Wight County, VA	33,417	32,635	29,728	25,053	3,689	4,675	12.4	18.7	12.4	25.4	0.4	1.1
James City County, VA	57,525	55,500	48,102	34,970	9,423	13,132	19.6	37.6	17.6	13.4	1.5	2.0
Mathews County, VA	9,194	9,158	9,207	8,348	−13	859	−0.1	10.3	22.2	10.7	0.2	0.9
Surry County, VA	7,013	6,990	6,829	6,145	184	684	2.7	11.1	13.6	51.3	0.2	0.9
York County, VA	61,758	60,804	56,297	42,434	5,461	13,863	9.7	32.7	9.8	13.2	3.7	3.0
Chesapeake city, VA	218,968	214,830	199,184	151,982	19,784	47,202	9.9	31.1	9.3	29.6	1.8	2.2
Hampton city, VA	145,579	145,001	146,437	133,811	−858	12,626	−0.6	9.4	10.8	47.6	1.8	2.8
Newport News city, VA	179,899	181,917	180,697	171,439	−798	9,258	−0.4	5.4	10.2	41.9	2.5	4.1
Norfolk city, VA	231,954	237,347	234,403	261,250	−2,449	−26,847	−1.0	−10.3	10.0	45.3	2.8	3.8
Poquoson city, VA	11,811	11,673	11,566	11,005	245	561	2.1	5.1	12.9	1.0	1.9	1.2
Portsmouth city, VA	100,169	99,404	100,565	103,910	−396	−3,345	−0.4	−3.2	13.4	52.7	0.7	1.6
Suffolk city, VA	78,994	76,529	63,677	52,143	15,317	11,534	24.1	22.1	10.5	42.8	1.0	1.5
Virginia Beach city, VA	438,415	439,224	425,257	393,089	13,158	32,168	3.1	8.2	9.1	19.9	5.3	4.3
Williamsburg city, VA	11,751	11,486	11,998	11,409	−247	589	−2.1	5.2	13.8	12.5	4.6	2.5
Visalia-Porterville, CA	410,874	400,952	368,021	311,921	42,853	56,100	11.6	18.0	9.4	1.9	3.4	53.8
Tulare County, CA	410,874	400,952	368,021	311,921	42,853	56,100	11.6	18.0	9.4	1.9	3.4	53.8
Waco, TX	224,668	222,765	213,513	189,123	11,155	24,390	5.2	12.9	12.5	15.1	1.2	19.8
McLennan County, TX	224,668	222,765	213,513	189,123	11,155	24,390	5.2	12.9	12.5	15.1	1.2	19.8
Warner Robins, GA	126,163	123,773	110,765	89,208	15,398	21,557	13.9	24.2	9.7	25.0	1.8	2.9
Houston County, GA	126,163	123,773	110,765	89,208	15,398	21,557	13.9	24.2	9.7	25.0	1.8	2.9
Washington-Arlington-Alexandria, DC-VA-MD-WV	**5,214,666**	**5,157,608**	**4,796,182**	**4,122,259**	**418,484**	**673,923**	**8.7**	**16.3**	**9.1**	**26.4**	**7.7**	**10.1**
Bethesda-Gaithersburg-Frederick, MD	*1,148,284*	*1,139,087*	*1,069,441*	*907,235*	*78,843*	*162,206*	*7.4*	*17.9*	*11.1*	*13.3*	*10.8*	*10.6*
Frederick County, MD	220,701	217,456	195,276	150,208	25,425	45,068	13.0	30.0	9.7	6.4	2.1	2.9
Montgomery County, MD	927,583	921,631	874,165	757,027	53,418	117,138	6.1	15.5	11.4	14.9	12.8	12.3
Washington-Arlington-Alexandria, DC-VA-MD-WV	*4,066,382*	*4,018,521*	*3,726,741*	*3,215,024*	*339,641*	*511,717*	*9.1*	*15.9*	*8.6*	*30.1*	*6.9*	*10.0*
District of Columbia, DC	550,521	554,239	572,059	606,900	−21,538	−34,841	−3.8	−5.7	12.0	58.8	3.1	9.4
Calvert County, MD	87,925	86,293	74,563	51,372	13,362	23,191	17.9	45.1	8.9	12.0	1.0	1.7
Charles County, MD	138,822	135,702	120,546	101,154	18,276	19,392	15.2	19.2	7.8	29.9	1.9	2.2
Prince George's County, MD	846,123	841,642	800,691	728,553	45,432	72,138	5.7	9.9	8.1	64.8	3.9	8.5
Arlington County, VA	195,965	197,955	189,453	170,897	6,512	18,556	3.4	10.9	9.3	9.0	8.5	18.1
Clarke County, VA	14,205	13,840	12,652	12,101	1,553	551	12.3	4.6	14.2	6.6	0.5	1.7
Fairfax County, VA	1,006,529	1,002,488	969,749	818,358	36,780	151,391	3.8	18.5	8.5	8.7	14.9	12.3
Fauquier County, VA	64,997	63,049	55,145	48,860	9,852	6,285	17.9	12.9	10.6	8.5	0.8	2.7
Loudoun County, VA	255,518	239,325	169,599	86,129	85,919	83,470	50.7	96.9	5.3	7.2	8.5	7.6
Prince William County, VA	348,588	336,525	280,813	215,677	67,775	65,136	24.1	30.2	5.2	19.6	5.1	14.5
Spotsylvania County, VA	116,549	111,805	90,395	57,403	26,154	32,992	28.9	57.5	7.9	13.6	1.5	3.9
Stafford County, VA	117,874	114,513	92,446	61,236	25,428	31,210	27.5	51.0	5.6	15.1	1.8	4.9
Warren County, VA	35,556	34,494	31,578	26,142	3,978	5,436	12.6	20.8	12.1	4.9	0.5	1.8
Alexandria city, VA	135,337	136,635	128,283	111,182	7,054	17,101	5.5	15.4	9.9	21.7	5.3	14.5
Fairfax city, VA	21,963	21,989	21,498	19,894	465	1,604	2.2	8.1	13.6	5.8	13.3	13.2
Falls Church city, VA	10,781	10,574	10,377	9,522	404	855	3.9	9.0	13.1	4.5	7.0	8.1
Fredericksburg city, VA	20,732	20,776	19,279	19,027	1,453	252	7.5	1.3	13.8	21.2	1.4	5.8
Manassas city, VA	37,569	37,626	35,135	27,957	2,434	7,178	6.9	25.7	6.3	13.5	3.8	20.4
Manassas Park city, VA	11,622	11,469	10,290	6,734	1,332	3,556	12.9	52.8	5.1	11.4	4.7	24.1
Jefferson County, WV	49,206	47,582	42,190	35,926	7,016	6,264	16.6	17.4	10.8	6.2	0.7	2.0
Waterloo-Cedar Falls, IA	161,897	161,596	163,707	158,640	−1,810	5,067	−1.1	3.2	14.7	6.5	1.1	1.7
Black Hawk County, IA	125,891	125,707	128,013	123,798	−2,122	4,215	−1.7	3.4	14.1	8.2	1.2	2.0
Bremer County, IA	23,677	23,525	23,325	22,813	352	512	1.5	2.2	16.0	0.4	0.7	0.6
Grundy County, IA	12,329	12,364	12,369	12,029	−40	340	−0.3	2.8	18.7	0.1	0.3	0.6
Wausau, WI	128,941	127,823	125,834	115,400	3,107	10,434	2.5	9.0	13.2	0.3	5.1	0.9
Marathon County, WI	128,941	127,823	125,834	115,400	3,107	10,434	2.5	9.0	13.2	0.3	5.1	0.9

See footnotes at end of table.

Table C-1. Metropolitan Areas With Component Counties — **Population and Population Characteristics**—Con.

Metropolitan statistical area **Metropolitan statistical area with metropolitan divisions** *Metropolitan division* Component county	Population				Net change		Percent change		Percent—			
	2005 (July 1)	2004 (July 1)	2000[1] (estimates base)	1990[2] (April 1)	2000–2005[3]	1990–2000	2000–2005[3]	1990–2000	65 years and over, 2003	Black or African American alone, 2003	Asian alone, 2003	Hispanic or Latino origin, 2003[4]
Weirton-Steubenville, WV-OH	126,464	127,495	132,008	142,523	−5,544	−10,515	−4.2	−7.4	18.6	4.0	0.4	0.6
Jefferson County, OH	70,599	71,358	73,894	80,298	−3,295	−6,404	−4.5	−8.0	18.6	5.7	0.4	0.7
Brooke County, WV	24,515	24,724	25,447	26,992	−932	−1,545	−3.7	−5.7	18.3	1.0	0.5	0.4
Hancock County, WV	31,350	31,413	32,667	35,233	−1,317	−2,566	−4.0	−7.3	18.9	2.5	0.4	0.8
Wenatchee, WA	104,768	103,323	99,219	78,455	5,549	20,764	5.6	26.5	13.8	0.4	0.7	20.4
Chelan County, WA	69,791	68,897	66,616	52,250	3,175	14,366	4.8	27.5	14.1	0.3	0.7	20.1
Douglas County, WA	34,977	34,426	32,603	26,205	2,374	6,398	7.3	24.4	13.1	0.4	0.6	21.0
Wheeling, WV-OH	148,677	149,437	153,178	159,301	−4,501	−6,123	−2.9	−3.8	17.9	3.1	0.5	0.5
Belmont County, OH	69,228	69,460	70,226	71,074	−998	−848	−1.4	−1.2	18.0	3.9	0.3	0.4
Marshall County, WV	34,337	34,617	35,519	37,356	−1,182	−1,837	−3.3	−4.9	16.4	0.5	0.3	0.7
Ohio County, WV	45,112	45,360	47,433	50,871	−2,321	−3,438	−4.9	−6.8	18.8	3.8	0.9	0.4
Wichita, KS	587,055	583,860	571,168	511,111	15,887	60,057	2.8	11.8	11.9	7.8	3.1	8.1
Butler County, KS	62,354	61,694	59,484	50,580	2,870	8,904	4.8	17.6	12.6	1.5	0.5	2.5
Harvey County, KS	33,843	33,697	32,869	31,028	974	1,841	3.0	5.9	16.6	1.7	0.7	8.3
Sedgwick County, KS	466,061	463,383	452,869	403,662	13,192	49,207	2.9	12.2	11.3	9.4	3.8	9.1
Sumner County, KS	24,797	25,086	25,946	25,841	−1,149	105	−4.4	0.4	16.0	1.0	0.3	3.6
Wichita Falls, TX	146,276	147,751	151,524	140,375	−5,248	11,149	−3.5	7.9	13.0	8.7	1.7	12.1
Archer County, TX	9,095	9,239	8,854	7,973	241	881	2.7	11.0	13.2	0.1	0.2	5.4
Clay County, TX	11,287	11,205	11,006	10,024	281	982	2.6	9.8	14.6	0.4	(Z)	4.1
Wichita County, TX	125,894	127,307	131,664	122,378	−5,770	9,286	−4.4	7.6	12.9	10.1	1.9	13.2
Williamsport, PA	118,395	118,505	120,044	118,710	−1,649	1,334	−1.4	1.1	16.2	4.2	0.5	0.6
Lycoming County, PA	118,395	118,505	120,044	118,710	−1,649	1,334	−1.4	1.1	16.2	4.2	0.5	0.6
Wilmington, NC	315,144	303,258	274,550	200,124	40,594	74,426	14.8	37.2	14.5	16.4	0.6	2.8
Brunswick County, NC	89,162	84,590	73,141	50,985	16,021	22,156	21.9	43.5	17.6	13.4	0.3	3.1
New Hanover County, NC	179,553	173,627	160,327	120,284	19,226	40,043	12.0	33.3	13.1	16.4	0.9	2.2
Pender County, NC	46,429	45,041	41,082	28,855	5,347	12,227	13.0	42.4	14.2	22.3	0.2	4.4
Winchester, VA-WV	116,267	113,107	102,997	84,168	13,270	18,829	12.9	22.4	12.6	4.3	0.8	3.5
Frederick County, VA	69,123	66,696	59,209	45,723	9,914	13,486	16.7	29.5	10.8	3.0	0.7	2.7
Winchester city, VA	25,119	24,862	23,585	21,947	1,534	1,638	6.5	7.5	15.5	10.8	1.6	8.1
Hampshire County, WV	22,025	21,549	20,203	16,498	1,822	3,705	9.0	22.5	14.5	0.9	0.2	0.6
Winston-Salem, NC	448,629	441,472	421,957	361,448	26,672	60,509	6.3	16.7	12.9	20.3	1.0	7.3
Davie County, NC	39,136	37,940	34,835	27,859	4,301	6,976	12.3	25.0	13.8	6.8	0.4	4.6
Forsyth County, NC	325,967	320,780	306,063	265,878	19,904	40,185	6.5	15.1	12.6	26.1	1.2	8.3
Stokes County, NC	45,858	45,449	44,711	37,223	1,147	7,488	2.6	20.1	12.9	4.6	0.3	1.8
Yadkin County, NC	37,668	37,303	36,348	30,488	1,320	5,860	3.6	19.2	14.7	3.3	0.2	7.8
Worcester, MA	783,262	778,608	749,973	709,705	33,289	40,268	4.4	5.7	12.5	3.6	3.3	7.3
Worcester County, MA	783,262	778,608	749,973	709,705	33,289	40,268	4.4	5.7	12.5	3.6	3.3	7.3
Yakima, WA	231,586	229,515	222,581	188,823	9,005	33,758	4.0	17.9	11.1	1.2	1.0	38.3
Yakima County, WA	231,586	229,515	222,581	188,823	9,005	33,758	4.0	17.9	11.1	1.2	1.0	38.3
York-Hanover, PA	408,801	401,063	381,751	339,574	27,050	42,177	7.1	12.4	13.6	4.0	1.0	3.2
York County, PA	408,801	401,063	381,751	339,574	27,050	42,177	7.1	12.4	13.6	4.0	1.0	3.2
Youngstown-Warren-Boardman, OH-PA	593,168	596,262	602,964	613,622	−9,796	−10,658	−1.6	−1.7	17.0	10.8	0.5	1.7
Mahoning County, OH	254,274	255,995	257,555	264,806	−3,281	−7,251	−1.3	−2.7	17.4	15.9	0.6	3.0
Trumbull County, OH	219,296	220,552	225,116	227,813	−5,820	−2,697	−2.6	−1.2	16.0	8.0	0.5	0.8
Mercer County, PA	119,598	119,715	120,293	121,003	−695	−710	−0.6	−0.6	17.8	5.2	0.5	0.7
Yuba City, CA	156,029	151,146	139,149	122,643	16,880	16,506	12.1	13.5	11.3	2.6	10.0	22.3
Sutter County, CA	88,876	86,676	78,930	64,415	9,946	14,515	12.6	22.5	12.3	2.1	12.3	24.1
Yuba County, CA	67,153	64,470	60,219	58,228	6,934	1,991	11.5	3.4	10.1	3.3	7.0	20.0
Yuma, AZ	181,277	175,629	160,026	106,895	21,251	53,131	13.3	49.7	17.0	2.2	1.1	54.4
Yuma County, AZ	181,277	175,629	160,026	106,895	21,251	53,131	13.3	49.7	17.0	2.2	1.1	54.4

– Represents zero.   Z Less than .05%.

[1]The 2000 Population Estimates base reflects modifications to the Census 2000 population as documented in the Count Question Resolution program and geographic program revisions.

[2]The April 1, 1990, census counts include corrections processed through August 1997 and results of special censuses and test censuses, and do not include adjustments for census coverage errors.

[3]Period refers to April 1, 2000, to July 1, 2005.

[4]Persons of Hispanic or Latino origin may be any race.

[5]The Denver-Aurora metropolitan statistical area includes Broomfield County. Broomfield County, CO, was formed from parts of Adams, Boulder, Jefferson, and Weld counties on November 15, 2001, and is coextensive with Broomfield city. For the purposes of defining and presenting data for the Denver-Aurora metropolitan statistical area, Broomfield city is treated as if it were a county when data are available to do so. In many cases, the data will not be available.

[6]The portion of Sullivan city in Crawford County, MO, is legally part of the St. Louis, MO-IL MSA. That portion is not included in these figures for the St. Louis MSA.

Note: Covers metropolitan statistical areas and metropolitan divisions and component counties defined by the Office of Management and Budget as of June 6, 2003, and subsequently updated in December 2003 and November 2004. For more information, see OMB Bulletin 05-02 at <http://www.whitehouse.gov/omb/bulletins/fy05/b05-02_appendix.pdf>.

Survey, Census, or Data Collection Method: Based on the 2000 Census of Population and Housing and, for population estimates, the "component of population change method" and "County Characteristic Population Estimates Data"; see Appendix B, Limitations of the Data and Methodology, and also <http://www.census.gov/prod/cen2000/doc/sf1.pdf> and <http://www.census.gov/popest/topics/methodology/>.

Source: U.S. Census Bureau, 2000 to 2005 compiled from "Population Estimates by County" <http://www.census.gov/popest/counties/CO-EST2005-01.html> and "Population Estimates, Cumulative Estimates of the Components of Population Change for Counties: April 1, 2000 to July 1, 2005" <http://www.census.gov/popest/counties/CO-EST2005-05.html>; 1990, "Population Estimates: Annual Time Series," archive 1990 (revised data for April 1, 1990, Population Estimates base) <http://www.census.gov/popest/archives/1990s/CO-99-02.html>;   Age, race, and Hispanic population—U.S. Census Bureau, "County Characteristic Population Estimates Data," <http://www.census.gov/popest/estimates.php>.

Table C-2. Metropolitan Areas With Component Counties —

Population Characteristics and Housing Units

Metropolitan statistical area / **Metropolitan statistical area with metropolitan divisions** / *Metropolitan division* / Component county	2000				Persons below poverty level in 1999		Housing units			
	Educational attainment, percent with bachelor's degree or higher[1]	Percent foreign born	Workers 16 years and over		Total persons	Percent of persons below poverty level in 1999	2004 (July 1)	2000[2] (estimates base)	Change 2000–2004[3]	
			Total workers	Percent of workers who drove alone to work					Number	Percent
Abilene, TX	19.6	3.5	77,848	73.8	21,846	13.6	66,821	65,216	1,605	2.5
Callahan County, TX	12.3	1.4	5,919	73.3	1,563	12.1	6,086	5,925	161	2.7
Jones County, TX	8.2	1.6	7,331	74.9	2,653	12.8	7,411	7,236	175	2.4
Taylor County, TX	22.5	4.0	64,598	73.7	17,630	13.9	53,324	52,055	1,269	2.4
Akron, OH	24.3	3.0	360,811	79.7	66,386	9.6	302,154	290,976	11,178	3.8
Portage County, OH	21.0	2.0	83,571	78.4	13,395	8.8	63,436	60,096	3,340	5.6
Summit County, OH	25.1	3.3	277,240	80.0	52,991	9.8	238,718	230,880	7,838	3.4
Albany, GA	15.7	1.6	72,016	71.4	33,002	20.9	67,118	63,755	3,363	5.3
Baker County, GA	10.7	1.9	1,742	69.3	951	23.3	1,782	1,740	42	2.4
Dougherty County, GA	17.8	1.7	43,126	68.9	22,974	23.9	40,944	39,656	1,288	3.2
Lee County, GA	17.0	1.7	12,480	81.3	1,958	7.9	10,446	8,813	1,633	18.5
Terrell County, GA	10.7	1.7	4,573	64.2	3,069	28.0	4,617	4,460	157	3.5
Worth County, GA	8.6	1.0	10,095	73.2	4,050	18.4	9,329	9,086	243	2.7
Albany-Schenectady-Troy, NY	29.1	4.8	430,282	73.6	73,946	9.0	372,924	363,740	9,184	2.5
Albany County, NY	33.3	6.5	155,220	70.2	29,745	10.1	132,113	129,972	2,141	1.6
Rensselaer County, NY	23.7	3.7	80,147	72.7	14,011	9.2	67,546	66,120	1,426	2.2
Saratoga County, NY	30.9	3.1	108,283	78.5	11,238	5.6	91,453	86,701	4,752	5.5
Schenectady County, NY	26.3	5.3	71,491	75.0	15,560	10.6	65,607	65,032	575	0.9
Schoharie County, NY	17.3	2.4	15,141	70.5	3,392	10.7	16,205	15,915	290	1.8
Albuquerque, NM	28.1	7.8	360,542	71.7	99,746	13.7	331,838	305,840	25,998	8.5
Bernalillo County, NM	30.5	8.6	282,693	71.7	74,987	13.5	259,500	239,074	20,426	8.5
Sandoval County, NM	24.8	4.3	41,599	73.7	10,847	12.1	38,631	34,866	3,765	10.8
Torrance County, NM	14.4	4.2	7,229	64.3	3,106	18.4	7,548	7,257	291	4.0
Valencia County, NM	14.8	6.4	29,021	71.1	10,806	16.3	26,159	24,643	1,516	6.2
Alexandria, LA	15.7	1.4	62,382	71.8	29,045	20.0	62,782	60,569	2,213	3.7
Grant Parish, LA	9.8	0.5	7,685	71.8	3,948	21.1	8,793	8,531	262	3.1
Rapides Parish, LA	16.5	1.6	54,697	71.8	25,097	19.9	53,989	52,038	1,951	3.7
Allentown-Bethlehem-Easton, PA-NJ	21.7	5.2	372,922	76.8	59,500	8.0	322,020	307,269	14,751	4.8
Warren County, NJ	24.4	5.8	53,293	76.9	5,492	5.4	44,088	41,156	2,932	7.1
Carbon County, PA	11.0	1.8	28,020	75.5	5,509	9.4	31,491	30,492	999	3.3
Lehigh County, PA	23.3	6.2	157,506	76.7	28,095	9.0	133,848	128,910	4,938	3.8
Northampton County, PA	21.2	4.6	134,103	77.1	20,404	7.6	112,593	106,711	5,882	5.5
Altoona, PA	13.9	1.0	61,655	75.6	15,840	12.3	55,753	55,061	692	1.3
Blair County, PA	13.9	1.0	61,655	75.6	15,840	12.3	55,753	55,061	692	1.3
Amarillo, TX	20.8	6.0	111,613	76.1	29,426	13.0	95,263	91,594	3,669	4.0
Armstrong County, TX	20.5	0.9	1,009	76.1	219	10.2	937	920	17	1.8
Carson County, TX	15.5	2.7	3,124	79.6	468	7.2	2,879	2,815	64	2.3
Potter County, TX	13.5	9.4	50,317	71.8	20,478	18.0	46,674	44,598	2,076	4.7
Randall County, TX	28.9	2.6	57,163	79.7	8,261	7.9	44,773	43,261	1,512	3.5
Ames, IA	44.5	6.9	46,694	67.0	9,921	12.4	33,660	30,630	3,030	9.9
Story County, IA	44.5	6.9	46,694	67.0	9,921	12.4	33,660	30,630	3,030	9.9
Anchorage, AK	27.0	7.1	171,573	66.8	25,101	7.9	135,158	127,697	7,461	5.8
Anchorage Borough, AK	28.9	8.2	143,350	68.1	18,682	7.2	107,248	100,368	6,880	6.9
Matanuska-Susitna Borough, AK	18.3	2.6	28,223	60.2	6,419	10.8	27,910	27,329	581	2.1
Anderson, IN	14.4	1.2	63,897	75.4	11,941	9.0	58,427	56,939	1,488	2.6
Madison County, IN	14.4	1.2	63,897	75.4	11,941	9.0	58,427	56,939	1,488	2.6
Anderson, SC	15.9	1.5	81,305	78.0	19,639	11.8	78,354	73,213	5,141	7.0
Anderson County, SC	15.9	1.5	81,305	78.0	19,639	11.8	78,354	73,213	5,141	7.0
Ann Arbor, MI	48.1	10.3	179,279	71.7	33,450	10.4	141,941	130,974	10,967	8.4
Washtenaw County, MI	48.1	10.3	179,279	71.7	33,450	10.4	141,941	130,974	10,967	8.4
Anniston-Oxford, AL	15.2	1.7	51,402	78.2	17,695	15.8	52,841	51,322	1,519	3.0
Calhoun County, AL	15.2	1.7	51,402	78.2	17,695	15.8	52,841	51,322	1,519	3.0
Appleton, WI	22.2	2.9	111,228	80.6	8,826	4.4	86,252	78,372	7,880	10.1
Calumet County, WI	20.8	2.1	22,747	79.7	1,409	3.5	17,926	15,758	2,168	13.8
Outagamie County, WI	22.5	3.1	88,481	80.9	7,417	4.6	68,326	62,614	5,712	9.1
Asheville, NC	23.1	3.9	182,007	74.8	40,438	11.0	189,236	175,331	13,905	7.9
Buncombe County, NC	25.3	3.9	106,066	74.4	22,920	11.1	101,518	93,966	7,552	8.0
Haywood County, NC	16.0	1.6	25,258	76.3	6,112	11.3	30,527	28,640	1,887	6.6
Henderson County, NC	24.1	5.9	41,450	75.5	8,526	9.6	46,861	43,003	3,858	9.0
Madison County, NC	16.1	1.7	9,233	73.3	2,880	14.7	10,330	9,722	608	6.3
Athens-Clarke County, GA	32.4	6.2	87,853	70.0	32,650	19.7	74,978	67,542	7,436	11.0
Clarke County, GA	39.8	8.4	55,218	65.6	26,337	26.0	47,029	42,126	4,903	11.6
Madison County, GA	10.9	2.0	12,849	76.2	2,964	11.5	11,200	10,520	680	6.5
Oconee County, GA	39.8	4.4	13,596	78.3	1,688	6.4	11,010	9,528	1,482	15.6
Oglethorpe County, GA	15.6	0.8	6,190	78.7	1,661	13.1	5,739	5,368	371	6.9
Atlanta-Sandy Springs-Marietta, GA	31.6	10.1	2,241,668	71.8	391,208	9.3	1,888,550	1,622,087	266,463	16.4
Barrow County, GA	10.9	3.6	23,898	73.6	3,787	8.2	21,841	17,304	4,537	26.2
Bartow County, GA	14.1	2.5	38,215	75.6	6,445	8.5	34,075	28,751	5,324	18.5
Butts County, GA	8.6	0.9	8,457	75.4	2,017	10.3	8,544	7,393	1,151	15.6
Carroll County, GA	16.5	2.9	42,630	73.6	11,495	13.2	41,407	34,067	7,340	21.5
Cherokee County, GA	27.0	5.8	77,534	77.5	7,474	5.3	67,442	51,937	15,505	29.9
Clayton County, GA	16.6	10.9	122,396	70.2	23,493	9.9	99,087	86,461	12,626	14.6
Cobb County, GA	39.8	11.6	343,473	76.5	38,910	6.4	261,659	237,522	24,137	10.2
Coweta County, GA	20.6	3.7	46,015	76.7	6,888	7.7	40,373	33,182	7,191	21.7
Dawson County, GA	18.1	1.4	8,454	75.4	1,210	7.6	8,712	7,163	1,549	21.6
DeKalb County, GA	36.3	15.2	368,086	65.3	70,484	10.6	288,457	261,231	27,226	10.4
Douglas County, GA	19.2	3.9	48,921	77.1	7,080	7.7	42,821	34,858	7,963	22.8

See footnotes at end of table.

Metropolitan statistical area **Metropolitan statistical area with metropolitan divisions** *Metropolitan division* Component county	2000				Persons below poverty level in 1999		Housing units			
	Educational attainment, percent with bachelor's degree or higher[1]	Percent foreign born	Workers 16 years and over		Total persons	Percent of persons below poverty level in 1999	2004 (July 1)	2000[2] (estimates base)	Change 2000–2004[3]	
			Total workers	Percent of workers who drove alone to work					Number	Percent
Atlanta-Sandy Springs-Marietta, GA—Con.										
Fayette County, GA	36.2	5.0	47,090	81.2	2,386	2.6	36,583	32,726	3,857	11.8
Forsyth County, GA	34.6	6.0	52,904	79.0	5,382	5.5	48,580	36,505	12,075	33.1
Fulton County, GA	41.4	9.6	431,553	63.8	124,241	15.2	389,799	348,634	41,165	11.8
Gwinnett County, GA	34.1	16.9	325,379	75.9	33,067	5.6	255,265	209,682	45,583	21.7
Haralson County, GA	9.0	0.9	11,751	71.2	3,914	15.2	11,484	10,719	765	7.1
Heard County, GA	7.3	0.7	4,902	66.6	1,480	13.4	4,789	4,512	277	6.1
Henry County, GA	19.5	3.4	63,081	79.4	5,821	4.9	60,841	43,166	17,675	40.9
Jasper County, GA	11.5	2.1	5,517	69.2	1,604	14.0	5,516	4,806	710	14.8
Lamar County, GA	11.3	1.0	7,667	71.9	1,682	10.6	6,752	6,145	607	9.9
Meriwether County, GA	10.8	0.7	9,845	69.1	3,931	17.4	10,016	9,211	805	8.7
Newton County, GA	14.5	2.5	30,745	75.6	6,079	9.8	31,526	23,033	8,493	36.9
Paulding County, GA	15.2	2.1	42,755	79.8	4,454	5.5	40,815	29,241	11,574	39.6
Pickens County, GA	15.6	2.0	11,542	75.8	2,080	9.1	12,638	10,687	1,951	18.3
Pike County, GA	14.0	1.0	6,544	75.0	1,275	9.3	5,978	5,068	910	18.0
Rockdale County, GA	23.4	7.6	35,166	74.7	5,673	8.1	28,634	25,082	3,552	14.2
Spalding County, GA	12.5	2.2	27,148	69.9	8,856	15.2	24,916	23,001	1,915	8.3
Walton County, GA	13.0	2.0	30,409	75.5	5,829	9.6	27,801	22,500	5,301	23.6
Atlantic City, NJ	18.7	11.8	125,696	65.5	25,906	10.3	121,192	114,090	7,102	6.2
Atlantic County, NJ	18.7	11.8	125,696	65.5	25,906	10.3	121,192	114,090	7,102	6.2
Auburn-Opelika, AL	27.9	2.7	56,547	77.6	24,119	21.0	55,546	50,329	5,217	10.4
Lee County, AL	27.9	2.7	56,547	77.6	24,119	21.0	55,546	50,329	5,217	10.4
Augusta-Richmond County, GA-SC	20.4	3.0	237,567	73.5	74,945	15.0	216,791	204,600	12,191	6.0
Burke County, GA	9.5	0.8	9,108	70.3	6,348	28.5	9,106	8,842	264	3.0
Columbia County, GA	32.0	4.8	45,831	81.8	4,540	5.1	38,363	33,321	5,042	15.1
McDuffie County, GA	11.7	0.6	9,712	72.1	3,882	18.3	9,200	8,916	284	3.2
Richmond County, GA	18.7	3.4	94,690	68.5	37,313	18.7	85,111	82,312	2,799	3.4
Aiken County, SC	19.9	2.3	67,969	75.4	19,455	13.6	65,372	61,987	3,385	5.5
Edgefield County, SC	12.5	1.3	10,257	74.1	3,407	13.9	9,639	9,222	417	4.5
Austin-Round Rock, TX	36.7	12.2	689,602	72.0	134,589	10.8	573,921	496,004	77,917	15.7
Bastrop County, TX	17.0	8.1	27,642	70.5	6,456	11.2	23,929	22,254	1,675	7.5
Caldwell County, TX	13.3	5.1	14,206	69.7	3,971	12.3	12,838	11,901	937	7.9
Hays County, TX	31.3	5.6	53,942	70.3	13,039	13.4	42,338	35,643	6,695	18.8
Travis County, TX	40.6	15.1	460,525	70.5	99,388	12.2	381,542	335,881	45,661	13.6
Williamson County, TX	33.6	7.4	133,287	78.7	11,735	4.7	113,274	90,325	22,949	25.4
Bakersfield, CA	13.5	16.9	267,603	63.4	130,949	19.8	247,426	231,567	15,859	6.8
Kern County, CA	13.5	16.9	267,603	63.4	130,949	19.8	247,426	231,567	15,859	6.8
Baltimore-Towson, MD	29.2	5.7	1,313,310	70.4	243,792	9.5	1,082,523	1,048,046	34,477	3.3
Anne Arundel County, MD	30.6	4.7	269,772	76.1	24,335	5.0	197,331	186,937	10,394	5.6
Baltimore County, MD	30.6	7.1	396,897	75.0	47,603	6.3	323,070	313,734	9,336	3.0
Carroll County, MD	24.8	2.0	80,767	79.8	5,617	3.7	59,496	54,260	5,236	9.6
Harford County, MD	27.3	3.4	116,981	79.6	10,695	4.9	90,415	83,146	7,269	8.7
Howard County, MD	52.9	11.3	139,885	79.0	9,491	3.8	99,415	92,818	6,597	7.1
Queen Anne's County, MD	25.4	2.4	21,849	75.6	2,537	6.3	18,454	16,674	1,780	10.7
Baltimore city, MD	19.1	4.6	287,159	47.5	143,514	22.0	294,342	300,477	−6,135	−2.0
Bangor, ME	20.3	2.5	74,297	73.2	18,956	13.1	68,727	66,847	1,880	2.8
Penobscot County, ME	20.3	2.5	74,297	73.2	18,956	13.1	68,727	66,847	1,880	2.8
Barnstable Town, MA	33.6	4.9	107,184	75.3	15,021	6.8	152,583	147,083	5,500	3.7
Barnstable County, MA	33.6	4.9	107,184	75.3	15,021	6.8	152,583	147,083	5,500	3.7
Baton Rouge, LA	22.8	2.6	335,375	75.3	116,199	16.5	300,066	282,511	17,555	6.2
Ascension Parish, LA	14.5	1.8	37,203	79.1	9,808	12.8	33,424	29,172	4,252	14.6
East Baton Rouge Parish, LA	30.8	3.7	205,905	74.6	71,276	17.3	176,463	169,073	7,390	4.4
East Feliciana Parish, LA	11.3	0.6	8,557	70.4	4,352	20.4	8,139	7,915	224	2.8
Iberville Parish, LA	9.6	0.7	12,364	73.1	6,909	20.7	12,328	11,953	375	3.1
Livingston Parish, LA	11.4	0.8	42,978	77.8	10,339	11.3	40,312	36,212	4,100	11.3
Pointe Coupee Parish, LA	12.8	0.9	9,626	72.4	5,172	22.7	10,724	10,297	427	4.1
St. Helena Parish, LA	11.2	0.3	4,135	69.2	2,804	26.6	5,145	5,034	111	2.2
West Baton Rouge Parish, LA	11.1	0.9	9,976	76.0	3,564	16.5	8,776	8,370	406	4.9
West Feliciana Parish, LA	10.6	0.5	4,631	77.2	1,975	13.1	4,755	4,485	270	6.0
Battle Creek, MI	16.0	2.4	66,943	75.7	15,094	10.9	60,208	58,691	1,517	2.6
Calhoun County, MI	16.0	2.4	66,943	75.7	15,094	10.9	60,208	58,691	1,517	2.6
Bay City, MI	14.2	1.4	54,312	80.5	10,605	9.6	47,617	46,423	1,194	2.6
Bay County, MI	14.2	1.4	54,312	80.5	10,605	9.6	47,617	46,423	1,194	2.6
Beaumont-Port Arthur, TX	14.7	4.7	169,288	74.9	57,974	15.1	161,294	156,697	4,597	2.9
Hardin County, TX	13.0	1.3	21,877	78.5	5,314	11.1	20,646	19,836	810	4.1
Jefferson County, TX	16.3	6.2	108,633	73.8	41,142	16.3	104,826	102,080	2,746	2.7
Orange County, TX	11.0	2.1	38,778	75.7	11,518	13.6	35,822	34,781	1,041	3.0
Bellingham, WA	27.2	9.8	87,365	68.8	23,003	13.8	80,637	73,897	6,740	9.1
Whatcom County, WA	27.2	9.8	87,365	68.8	23,003	13.8	80,637	73,897	6,740	9.1
Bend, OR	25.0	2.8	58,836	69.9	10,613	9.2	64,861	54,583	10,278	18.8
Deschutes County, OR	25.0	2.8	58,836	69.9	10,613	9.2	64,861	54,583	10,278	18.8
Billings, MT	26.2	1.4	73,490	75.6	15,121	10.9	62,462	60,057	2,405	4.0
Carbon County, MT	23.3	1.6	4,792	61.6	1,089	11.4	5,571	5,494	77	1.4
Yellowstone County, MT	26.4	1.4	68,698	76.6	14,032	10.8	56,891	54,563	2,328	4.3
Binghamton, NY	22.0	4.5	122,581	74.0	28,854	11.4	110,575	110,227	348	0.3
Broome County, NY	22.7	5.3	96,563	73.8	24,559	12.2	88,931	88,817	114	0.1
Tioga County, NY	19.7	1.7	26,018	75.0	4,295	8.3	21,644	21,410	234	1.1

See footnotes at end of table.

Metropolitan statistical area **Metropolitan statistical area with metropolitan divisions** *Metropolitan division* Component county	2000				Persons below poverty level in 1999		Housing units			
			Workers 16 years and over						Change	
									2000–2004[3]	
	Educational attainment, percent with bachelor's degree or higher[1]	Percent foreign born	Total workers	Percent of workers who drove alone to work	Total persons	Percent of persons below poverty level in 1999	2004 (July 1)	2000[2] (estimates base)	Number	Percent
Birmingham-Hoover, AL	22.7	2.1	504,786	77.3	139,841	13.3	477,954	454,338	23,616	5.2
Bibb County, AL	7.1	0.4	8,521	73.5	4,091	19.6	8,578	8,345	233	2.8
Blount County, AL	9.6	3.1	23,896	73.4	5,930	11.6	21,634	21,158	476	2.2
Chilton County, AL	9.9	1.9	18,240	74.2	6,152	15.5	18,281	17,651	630	3.6
Jefferson County, AL	24.6	2.3	317,658	76.7	95,674	14.5	298,362	288,162	10,200	3.5
St. Clair County, AL	11.1	0.6	29,492	76.9	7,584	11.7	29,228	27,303	1,925	7.1
Shelby County, AL	36.8	2.4	77,111	82.5	8,932	6.2	68,606	59,302	9,304	15.7
Walker County, AL	9.1	0.7	29,868	76.9	11,478	16.2	33,265	32,417	848	2.6
Bismarck, ND	25.5	1.3	52,375	78.5	7,623	8.0	42,480	39,591	2,889	7.3
Burleigh County, ND	28.7	1.5	38,986	79.6	5,237	7.5	31,366	29,004	2,362	8.1
Morton County, ND	17.0	0.9	13,389	75.2	2,386	9.4	11,114	10,587	527	5.0
Blacksburg-Christiansburg-Radford, VA	25.7	3.7	74,606	72.9	27,467	18.2	65,624	62,755	2,869	4.6
Giles County, VA	12.4	0.8	7,794	74.0	1,582	9.5	8,015	7,732	283	3.7
Montgomery County, VA	35.9	5.8	41,747	71.1	17,341	20.7	34,520	32,561	1,959	6.0
Pulaski County, VA	12.5	0.6	17,389	79.1	4,444	12.7	16,799	16,325	474	2.9
Radford city, VA	34.1	2.5	7,676	68.1	4,100	25.9	6,290	6,137	153	2.5
Bloomington, IN	29.0	3.9	91,744	69.7	25,667	14.6	80,539	75,752	4,787	6.3
Greene County, IN	10.5	0.5	16,115	72.8	3,566	10.8	15,750	15,053	697	4.6
Monroe County, IN	39.6	5.4	64,772	68.6	20,095	16.7	54,575	50,846	3,729	7.3
Owen County, IN	9.2	0.4	10,857	71.3	2,006	9.2	10,214	9,853	361	3.7
Bloomington-Normal, IL	36.2	3.3	86,065	73.5	13,488	9.0	65,492	59,972	5,520	9.2
McLean County, IL	36.2	3.3	86,065	73.5	13,488	9.0	65,492	59,972	5,520	9.2
Boise City-Nampa, ID	25.5	5.7	242,306	74.8	42,501	9.1	209,234	181,170	28,064	15.5
Ada County, ID	31.2	4.3	163,955	76.8	22,471	7.5	135,717	118,516	17,201	14.5
Boise County, ID	19.9	2.4	3,357	60.2	852	12.8	4,699	4,349	350	8.0
Canyon County, ID	14.9	8.6	63,525	71.5	15,438	11.7	57,874	47,965	9,909	20.7
Gem County, ID	11.4	4.9	6,753	70.7	1,959	12.9	6,311	5,888	423	7.2
Owyhee County, ID	10.2	11.9	4,716	63.4	1,781	16.7	4,633	4,452	181	4.1
Boston-Cambridge-Quincy, MA-NH	**37.0**	**13.7**	**2,340,913**	**66.8**	**362,866**	**8.3**	**1,784,647**	**1,751,585**	**33,062**	**1.9**
Boston-Quincy, MA	*35.2*	*15.6*	*950,335*	*59.9*	*184,944*	*10.2*	*740,574*	*729,198*	*11,376*	*1.6*
Norfolk County, MA	42.9	11.8	348,897	69.3	29,377	4.5	259,617	255,154	4,463	1.7
Plymouth County, MA	27.8	6.3	246,330	76.1	30,649	6.5	187,574	181,524	6,050	3.3
Suffolk County, MA	32.5	25.5	355,108	39.5	124,918	18.1	293,383	292,520	863	0.3
Cambridge-Newton-Framingham, MA	*43.6*	*15.2*	*805,662*	*68.3*	*92,705*	*6.3*	*583,879*	*576,681*	*7,198*	*1.2*
Middlesex County, MA	43.6	15.2	805,662	68.3	92,705	6.3	583,879	576,681	7,198	1.2
Essex County, MA	*31.3*	*11.3*	*366,950*	*73.7*	*63,137*	*8.7*	*292,125*	*287,144*	*4,981*	*1.7*
Essex County, MA	31.3	11.3	366,950	73.7	63,137	8.7	292,125	287,144	4,981	1.7
Rockingham County-Strafford County, NH	*30.2*	*3.6*	*217,966*	*79.4*	*22,080*	*5.7*	*168,069*	*158,562*	*9,507*	*6.0*
Rockingham County, NH	31.7	3.7	155,700	81.0	12,347	4.5	119,679	113,023	6,656	5.9
Strafford County, NH	26.4	3.4	62,266	75.3	9,733	8.7	48,390	45,539	2,851	6.3
Boulder, CO[4]	52.4	9.4	169,972	66.5	26,818	9.2	119,889	111,440	8,449	7.6
Boulder County, CO[4]	52.4	9.4	169,972	66.5	26,818	9.2	119,889	111,440	8,449	7.6
Bowling Green, KY	22.3	3.8	54,736	73.6	15,550	14.9	48,023	44,454	3,569	8.0
Edmonson County, KY	4.9	0.4	4,977	71.1	2,117	18.2	6,334	6,104	230	3.8
Warren County, KY	24.7	4.3	49,759	73.9	13,433	14.5	41,689	38,350	3,339	8.7
Bremerton-Silverdale, WA	25.3	5.7	115,055	61.6	19,601	8.4	97,245	92,644	4,601	5.0
Kitsap County, WA	25.3	5.7	115,055	61.6	19,601	8.4	97,245	92,644	4,601	5.0
Bridgeport-Stamford-Norwalk, CT	39.9	16.9	448,096	69.9	59,689	6.8	345,195	339,466	5,729	1.7
Fairfield County, CT	39.9	16.9	448,096	69.9	59,689	6.8	345,195	339,466	5,729	1.7
Brownsville-Harlingen, TX	13.4	25.6	123,112	63.5	109,288	32.6	133,926	119,654	14,272	11.9
Cameron County, TX	13.4	25.6	123,112	63.5	109,288	32.6	133,926	119,654	14,272	11.9
Brunswick, GA	19.7	2.7	45,082	73.6	14,376	15.5	48,340	44,861	3,479	7.8
Brantley County, GA	6.2	0.9	6,521	71.0	2,266	15.5	6,683	6,490	193	3.0
Glynn County, GA	23.8	3.3	33,858	74.3	10,120	15.0	35,472	32,636	2,836	8.7
McIntosh County, GA	11.1	1.0	4,703	72.7	1,990	18.3	6,185	5,735	450	7.8
Buffalo-Niagara Falls, NY	23.2	4.4	572,973	74.2	135,192	11.6	518,182	511,583	6,599	1.3
Erie County, NY	24.5	4.5	465,413	73.3	112,358	11.8	421,092	415,868	5,224	1.3
Niagara County, NY	17.4	3.9	107,560	78.1	22,834	10.4	97,090	95,715	1,375	1.4
Burlington, NC	19.2	6.3	68,394	75.9	14,183	10.8	59,889	55,461	4,428	8.0
Alamance County, NC	19.2	6.3	68,394	75.9	14,183	10.8	59,889	55,461	4,428	8.0
Burlington-South Burlington, VT	34.8	5.4	112,207	71.0	16,803	8.4	86,407	82,718	3,689	4.5
Chittenden County, VT	41.2	5.9	84,556	71.7	12,267	8.4	61,379	58,864	2,515	4.3
Franklin County, VT	16.6	3.7	24,000	68.9	4,011	8.8	20,179	19,191	988	5.1
Grand Isle County, VT	25.0	4.2	3,651	70.1	525	7.6	4,849	4,663	186	4.0
Canton-Massillon, OH	17.3	1.7	203,026	80.5	37,110	9.1	174,327	170,040	4,287	2.5
Carroll County, OH	9.1	0.6	13,807	78.1	3,245	11.3	13,096	13,016	80	0.6
Stark County, OH	17.9	1.8	189,219	80.7	33,865	9.0	161,231	157,024	4,207	2.7
Cape Coral-Fort Myers, FL	21.1	9.2	193,814	74.1	42,316	9.6	292,830	245,405	47,425	19.3
Lee County, FL	21.1	9.2	193,814	74.1	42,316	9.6	292,830	245,405	47,425	19.3
Carson City, NV	18.5	9.9	24,834	72.8	4,923	9.4	22,401	21,283	1,118	5.3
Carson City, NV	18.5	9.9	24,834	72.8	4,923	9.4	22,401	21,283	1,118	5.3
Casper, WY	20.0	1.8	35,081	76.9	7,695	11.6	30,433	29,882	551	1.8
Natrona County, WY	20.0	1.8	35,081	76.9	7,695	11.6	30,433	29,882	551	1.8

See footnotes at end of table.

State and Metropolitan Area Data Book: 2006

U.S. Census Bureau

Metropolitan statistical area / Metropolitan statistical area with metropolitan divisions / Metropolitan division / Component county	2000		Workers 16 years and over		Persons below poverty level in 1999		Housing units		Change 2000–2004[3]	
	Educational attainment, percent with bachelor's degree or higher[1]	Percent foreign born	Total workers	Percent of workers who drove alone to work	Total persons	Percent of persons below poverty level in 1999	2004 (July 1)	2000[2] (estimates base)	Number	Percent
Cedar Rapids, IA	24.9	2.2	130,927	77.3	15,268	6.4	107,105	99,054	8,051	8.1
Benton County, IA	13.9	0.6	13,185	73.7	1,522	6.0	10,872	10,377	495	4.8
Jones County, IA	12.7	0.8	10,128	73.1	1,596	7.9	8,314	8,126	188	2.3
Linn County, IA	27.7	2.6	107,614	78.1	12,150	6.3	87,919	80,551	7,368	9.1
Champaign-Urbana, IL	34.5	7.0	114,720	66.0	28,215	13.4	92,854	88,139	4,715	5.3
Champaign County, IL	38.0	8.0	98,835	64.2	26,460	14.7	79,634	75,280	4,354	5.8
Ford County, IL	13.9	1.1	7,117	74.4	956	6.7	6,173	6,060	113	1.9
Piatt County, IL	21.0	0.6	8,768	79.7	799	4.9	7,047	6,799	248	3.6
Charleston, WV	17.9	1.1	141,028	74.4	47,693	15.4	143,971	141,666	2,305	1.6
Boone County, WV	7.2	0.4	9,615	73.9	5,584	21.9	11,683	11,575	108	0.9
Clay County, WV	7.3	0.1	3,614	66.8	2,816	27.3	4,940	4,836	104	2.2
Kanawha County, WV	20.6	1.4	94,658	73.7	28,374	14.2	94,591	93,788	803	0.9
Lincoln County, WV	5.9	0.0	8,041	69.1	6,134	27.7	10,051	9,846	205	2.1
Putnam County, WV	19.7	1.0	25,100	79.9	4,785	9.3	22,706	21,621	1,085	5.0
Charleston-North Charleston, SC	25.0	3.3	273,253	72.6	74,504	13.6	256,543	232,957	23,586	10.1
Berkeley County, SC	14.4	3.1	70,410	73.7	16,066	11.3	59,517	54,717	4,800	8.8
Charleston County, SC	30.7	3.6	155,555	70.9	49,330	15.9	155,602	141,025	14,577	10.3
Dorchester County, SC	21.4	2.8	47,288	76.8	9,108	9.4	41,424	37,215	4,209	11.3
Charlotte-Gastonia-Concord, NC-SC	28.0	6.9	719,296	75.1	122,312	9.2	634,930	546,423	88,507	16.2
Anson County, NC	9.2	0.7	10,756	69.9	4,235	16.8	10,441	10,221	220	2.2
Cabarrus County, NC	19.1	4.7	70,000	78.5	9,108	6.9	60,654	52,848	7,806	14.8
Gaston County, NC	14.2	3.3	96,898	77.2	20,309	10.7	83,650	78,815	4,835	6.1
Mecklenburg County, NC	37.1	9.8	389,714	73.8	62,652	9.0	345,761	292,755	53,006	18.1
Union County, NC	21.3	5.7	65,074	76.6	9,926	8.0	57,009	45,723	11,286	24.7
York County, SC	20.9	2.4	86,854	75.6	16,082	9.8	77,415	66,061	11,354	17.2
Charlottesville, VA	38.3	5.7	88,552	69.6	19,033	10.9	81,325	73,869	7,456	10.1
Albemarle County, VA	47.7	7.3	41,043	75.1	5,232	6.6	37,839	33,740	4,099	12.1
Fluvanna County, VA	24.5	2.3	10,134	74.6	1,121	5.6	9,568	8,018	1,550	19.3
Greene County, VA	19.8	1.6	8,313	75.1	987	6.5	6,811	5,986	825	13.8
Nelson County, VA	20.8	1.9	7,143	65.7	1,743	12.1	9,068	8,554	514	6.0
Charlottesville city, VA	40.8	6.9	21,919	56.0	9,950	22.1	18,039	17,571	468	2.7
Chattanooga, TN-GA	19.4	2.4	240,455	77.1	55,863	11.7	217,028	205,322	11,706	5.7
Catoosa County, GA	13.8	1.7	28,092	81.4	4,966	9.3	24,053	21,773	2,280	10.5
Dade County, GA	10.9	1.4	7,471	71.6	1,404	9.3	6,397	6,224	173	2.8
Walker County, GA	10.2	1.0	29,025	78.0	7,466	12.2	27,193	25,577	1,616	6.3
Hamilton County, TN	23.9	3.0	157,919	76.6	36,308	11.8	141,211	134,692	6,519	4.8
Marion County, TN	9.5	0.5	12,742	75.7	3,867	13.9	13,057	12,140	917	7.6
Sequatchie County, TN	10.2	1.2	5,206	77.0	1,852	16.3	5,117	4,916	201	4.1
Cheyenne, WY	23.4	2.9	41,881	75.7	7,104	8.7	35,875	34,213	1,662	4.9
Laramie County, WY	23.4	2.9	41,881	75.7	7,104	8.7	35,875	34,213	1,662	4.9
Chicago-Naperville-Joliet, IL-IN-WI	**29.0**	**16.1**	**4,559,787**	**64.7**	**934,512**	**10.3**	**3,627,825**	**3,462,286**	**165,539**	**4.8**
Chicago-Naperville-Joliet, IL	*29.4*	*17.4*	*3,814,721*	*63.0*	*818,086*	*10.7*	*3,037,420*	*2,906,717*	*130,703*	*4.5*
Cook County, IL	28.0	19.8	2,620,175	56.9	713,040	13.3	2,134,456	2,096,122	38,334	1.8
DeKalb County, IL	26.8	5.8	48,904	71.1	9,203	10.3	35,659	32,988	2,671	8.1
DuPage County, IL	41.7	15.3	492,352	75.9	32,163	3.6	350,387	335,621	14,766	4.4
Grundy County, IL	15.2	2.7	19,468	80.0	1,786	4.8	16,605	15,040	1,565	10.4
Kane County, IL	27.7	15.7	206,024	74.7	26,587	6.6	159,302	138,998	20,304	14.6
Kendall County, IL	25.3	5.3	29,697	79.1	1,636	3.0	25,938	19,519	6,419	32.9
McHenry County, IL	27.7	7.2	140,203	78.4	9,446	3.6	106,501	92,905	13,596	14.6
Will County, IL	25.5	7.1	257,898	77.7	24,225	4.8	208,572	175,524	33,048	18.8
Gary, IN	*17.3*	*4.6*	*329,905*	*74.9*	*69,797*	*10.3*	*283,408*	*269,570*	*13,838*	*5.1*
Jasper County, IN	13.0	1.5	14,785	75.2	1,923	6.4	12,324	11,236	1,088	9.7
Lake County, IN	16.2	5.3	230,901	73.0	58,380	12.0	202,916	194,992	7,924	4.1
Newton County, IN	9.6	2.3	7,259	76.2	993	6.8	5,986	5,726	260	4.5
Porter County, IN	22.6	3.0	76,960	80.5	8,501	5.8	62,182	57,616	4,566	7.9
Lake County-Kenosha County, IL-WI	*34.9*	*12.9*	*415,161*	*72.8*	*46,629*	*5.9*	*306,997*	*285,999*	*20,998*	*7.3*
Lake County, IL	38.6	14.8	337,181	71.9	35,714	5.5	242,583	226,010	16,573	7.3
Kenosha County, WI	19.2	4.8	77,980	76.5	10,915	7.3	64,414	59,989	4,425	7.4
Chico, CA	21.8	7.7	91,098	65.9	39,148	19.3	90,310	85,523	4,787	5.6
Butte County, CA	21.8	7.7	91,098	65.9	39,148	19.3	90,310	85,523	4,787	5.6
Cincinnati-Middletown, OH-KY-IN	24.8	2.6	1,027,076	76.5	186,697	9.1	880,073	833,075	46,998	5.6
Dearborn County, IN	15.4	0.8	23,905	78.9	3,011	6.5	19,258	17,797	1,461	8.2
Franklin County, IN	12.5	0.6	11,126	76.3	1,556	7.0	9,082	8,596	486	5.7
Ohio County, IN	11.6	0.1	2,964	78.6	398	7.1	2,596	2,424	172	7.1
Boone County, KY	22.8	3.0	46,791	80.5	4,785	5.6	40,145	33,351	6,794	20.4
Bracken County, KY	9.5	0.3	4,085	66.9	888	10.7	3,831	3,715	116	3.1
Campbell County, KY	20.5	1.4	45,176	75.0	8,093	9.1	38,094	36,898	1,196	3.2
Gallatin County, KY	6.9	0.4	3,758	72.6	1,035	13.2	3,475	3,362	113	3.4
Grant County, KY	9.4	1.0	11,249	71.8	2,436	10.9	10,082	9,306	776	8.3
Kenton County, KY	22.9	1.6	80,078	76.8	13,487	8.9	67,064	63,571	3,493	5.5
Pendleton County, KY	9.7	0.5	6,954	70.9	1,627	11.3	5,916	5,756	160	2.8
Brown County, OH	8.8	0.4	20,128	73.3	4,856	11.5	17,825	17,193	632	3.7
Butler County, OH	23.5	2.7	170,576	79.1	27,946	8.4	137,220	129,749	7,471	5.8
Clermont County, OH	20.8	1.6	93,287	80.0	12,462	7.0	75,465	69,226	6,239	9.0
Hamilton County, OH	29.2	3.4	426,778	73.6	97,692	11.6	380,585	373,393	7,192	1.9
Warren County, OH	28.4	2.3	80,221	82.0	6,425	4.1	69,435	58,738	10,697	18.2
Clarksville, TN-KY	16.2	3.5	117,796	73.4	25,980	11.2	100,234	92,024	8,210	8.9
Christian County, KY	12.5	2.5	35,688	68.4	9,935	13.7	28,337	27,182	1,155	4.2
Trigg County, KY	12.0	0.8	5,853	76.5	1,537	12.2	6,944	6,698	246	3.7
Montgomery County, TN	19.3	4.4	70,666	75.9	12,982	9.6	58,759	52,167	6,592	12.6
Stewart County, TN	10.2	1.7	5,589	71.2	1,526	12.3	6,194	5,977	217	3.6

See footnotes at end of table.

Metropolitan statistical area **Metropolitan statistical area with metropolitan divisions** *Metropolitan division* Component county	2000				Persons below poverty level in 1999		Housing units			
			Workers 16 years and over						Change	
	Educational attainment, percent with bachelor's degree or higher[1]	Percent foreign born	Total workers	Percent of workers who drove alone to work	Total persons	Percent of persons below poverty level in 1999	2004 (July 1)	2000[2] (estimates base)	2000–2004[3]	
									Number	Percent
Cleveland, TN	14.5	2.0	52,030	76.3	12,529	12.0	46,828	44,189	2,639	6.0
Bradley County, TN	15.9	2.2	44,724	77.3	10,463	11.9	39,117	36,820	2,297	6.2
Polk County, TN	7.5	0.8	7,306	70.1	2,066	12.9	7,711	7,369	342	4.6
Cleveland-Elyria-Mentor, OH	23.9	5.3	1,068,907	75.6	226,498	10.5	931,197	911,329	19,868	2.2
Cuyahoga County, OH	25.1	6.4	676,874	72.5	179,372	12.9	619,448	616,876	2,572	0.4
Geauga County, OH	31.7	2.8	46,454	78.9	4,096	4.5	34,499	32,805	1,694	5.2
Lake County, OH	21.5	4.3	123,182	82.9	11,372	5.0	96,211	93,487	2,724	2.9
Lorain County, OH	16.6	2.6	141,833	79.1	24,809	8.7	118,432	111,368	7,064	6.3
Medina County, OH	24.8	3.0	80,564	82.6	6,849	4.5	62,607	56,793	5,814	10.2
Coeur d'Alene, ID	19.1	2.4	54,471	73.2	11,229	10.3	52,411	46,607	5,804	12.5
Kootenai County, ID	19.1	2.4	54,471	73.2	11,229	10.3	52,411	46,607	5,804	12.5
College Station-Bryan, TX	31.5	9.0	93,231	68.5	43,473	23.5	82,466	75,094	7,372	9.8
Brazos County, TX	37.0	10.3	79,136	68.2	37,417	24.5	65,867	59,023	6,844	11.6
Burleson County, TX	13.2	3.0	7,360	71.4	2,813	17.1	8,510	8,197	313	3.8
Robertson County, TX	12.7	3.3	6,735	68.0	3,243	20.3	8,089	7,874	215	2.7
Colorado Springs, CO	31.8	6.3	292,067	73.2	41,414	7.7	238,861	212,790	26,071	12.3
El Paso County, CO	31.8	6.4	280,574	73.4	40,318	7.8	227,386	202,428	24,958	12.3
Teller County, CO	31.7	1.8	11,493	70.1	1,096	5.3	11,475	10,362	1,113	10.7
Columbia, MO	39.9	4.3	82,411	72.0	19,468	13.4	67,545	61,024	6,521	10.7
Boone County, MO	41.7	4.5	77,188	72.2	18,366	13.6	63,082	56,678	6,404	11.3
Howard County, MO	17.9	1.0	5,223	68.3	1,102	10.8	4,463	4,346	117	2.7
Columbia, SC	26.6	3.3	339,343	73.4	76,293	11.8	290,545	269,244	21,301	7.9
Calhoun County, SC	14.2	1.0	6,978	71.8	2,439	16.1	7,229	6,864	365	5.3
Fairfield County, SC	11.7	0.5	10,838	70.3	4,518	19.3	10,695	10,383	312	3.0
Kershaw County, SC	16.3	1.7	26,519	73.8	6,668	12.7	24,146	22,683	1,463	6.4
Lexington County, SC	24.6	2.9	115,110	78.9	19,331	8.9	97,791	90,978	6,813	7.5
Richland County, SC	32.5	3.9	170,704	70.1	40,386	12.6	141,931	129,793	12,138	9.4
Saluda County, SC	11.9	5.9	9,194	71.3	2,951	15.4	8,753	8,543	210	2.5
Columbus, GA-AL	18.3	4.0	136,838	69.7	42,042	14.9	122,518	115,747	6,771	5.8
Russell County, AL	9.7	2.0	21,672	75.1	9,743	19.6	24,158	22,831	1,327	5.8
Chattahoochee County, GA	25.0	6.0	9,032	48.8	1,051	7.1	3,329	3,316	13	0.4
Harris County, GA	21.1	1.9	12,368	81.1	1,929	8.1	11,733	10,288	1,445	14.0
Marion County, GA	8.9	5.0	3,147	65.0	1,578	22.1	3,217	3,130	87	2.8
Muscogee County, GA	20.3	4.7	90,619	69.1	27,741	14.9	80,081	76,182	3,899	5.1
Columbus, IN	22.0	3.8	37,181	79.7	5,164	7.2	30,727	29,853	874	2.9
Bartholomew County, IN	22.0	3.8	37,181	79.7	5,164	7.2	30,727	29,853	874	2.9
Columbus, OH	28.3	4.5	863,882	77.3	155,402	9.6	743,500	680,457	63,043	9.3
Delaware County, OH	41.0	2.6	60,918	81.7	4,118	3.7	54,906	42,374	12,532	29.6
Fairfield County, OH	20.8	1.3	63,714	81.1	7,064	5.8	53,591	47,934	5,657	11.8
Franklin County, OH	31.8	6.0	584,391	75.9	121,843	11.4	507,039	471,007	36,032	7.6
Licking County, OH	18.4	1.1	75,423	78.8	10,602	7.3	63,541	58,798	4,743	8.1
Madison County, OH	13.0	1.1	18,802	79.2	2,790	6.9	15,172	14,399	773	5.4
Morrow County, OH	9.5	0.5	16,024	77.4	2,820	8.9	12,458	12,132	326	2.7
Pickaway County, OH	11.4	0.7	23,277	79.3	4,402	8.3	19,401	18,596	805	4.3
Union County, OH	15.9	1.0	21,333	80.0	1,763	4.3	17,392	15,217	2,175	14.3
Corpus Christi, TX	17.7	5.9	183,553	69.3	72,330	17.9	167,923	160,753	7,170	4.5
Aransas County, TX	16.7	5.7	9,344	68.1	4,429	19.7	13,763	12,848	915	7.1
Nueces County, TX	18.8	6.5	145,403	69.3	56,097	17.9	127,722	123,041	4,681	3.8
San Patricio County, TX	13.0	3.3	28,806	69.6	11,804	17.6	26,438	24,864	1,574	6.3
Corvallis, OR	47.4	7.6	40,427	66.0	10,665	13.6	33,969	31,980	1,989	6.2
Benton County, OR	47.4	7.6	40,427	66.0	10,665	13.6	33,969	31,980	1,989	6.2
Cumberland, MD-WV	13.4	1.1	45,523	72.5	14,041	13.8	45,768	45,078	690	1.5
Allegany County, MD	14.1	1.2	32,996	72.3	10,149	13.5	33,037	32,984	53	0.2
Mineral County, WV	11.7	0.6	12,527	73.2	3,892	14.4	12,731	12,094	637	5.3
Dallas-Fort Worth-Arlington, TX	**28.5**	**15.2**	**2,681,811**	**73.6**	**547,385**	**10.6**	**2,201,825**	**1,997,943**	**203,882**	**10.2**
Dallas-Plano-Irving, TX	*30.4*	*17.0*	*1,800,113*	*72.4*	*374,218*	*10.8*	*1,472,450*	*1,332,518*	*139,932*	*10.5*
Collin County, TX	47.3	13.3	275,351	79.9	23,784	4.8	239,181	194,946	44,235	22.7
Dallas County, TX	27.0	20.9	1,123,518	69.2	293,267	13.2	903,877	854,048	49,829	5.8
Delta County, TX	13.9	0.5	2,403	72.0	911	17.1	2,461	2,410	51	2.1
Denton County, TX	36.6	9.4	248,793	77.7	28,039	6.5	199,418	168,069	31,349	18.7
Ellis County, TX	17.1	7.1	56,473	74.9	9,401	8.4	44,617	39,071	5,546	14.2
Hunt County, TX	16.8	4.7	36,737	71.2	9,518	12.4	33,426	32,490	936	2.9
Kaufman County, TX	12.3	5.7	34,843	73.1	7,313	10.3	28,938	26,133	2,805	10.7
Rockwall County, TX	32.7	7.8	21,995	80.1	1,985	4.6	20,532	15,351	5,181	33.8
Fort Worth-Arlington, TX	*24.8*	*11.4*	*881,698*	*75.8*	*173,167*	*10.1*	*729,375*	*665,425*	*63,950*	*9.6*
Johnson County, TX	13.8	5.2	62,376	75.3	10,921	8.6	49,684	46,269	3,415	7.4
Parker County, TX	18.6	2.6	43,493	75.4	7,069	8.0	36,478	34,084	2,394	7.0
Tarrant County, TX	26.6	12.7	752,129	76.0	150,488	10.4	622,966	565,830	57,136	10.1
Wise County, TX	13.0	5.1	23,700	72.3	4,689	9.6	20,247	19,242	1,005	5.2
Dalton, GA	11.1	12.7	59,644	73.7	14,077	11.7	48,854	45,063	3,791	8.4
Murray County, GA	7.2	3.6	18,556	75.4	4,583	12.6	15,333	14,320	1,013	7.1
Whitfield County, GA	12.8	16.6	41,088	72.9	9,494	11.4	33,521	30,743	2,778	9.0
Danville, IL	12.5	1.7	38,705	73.7	10,704	12.8	36,710	36,350	360	1.0
Vermilion County, IL	12.5	1.7	38,705	73.7	10,704	12.8	36,710	36,350	360	1.0
Danville, VA	11.3	1.2	52,844	74.0	16,586	15.1	52,321	51,119	1,202	2.4
Pittsylvania County, VA	9.3	1.0	30,949	76.7	7,217	11.7	29,118	28,011	1,107	4.0
Danville city, VA	13.9	1.4	21,895	70.3	9,369	19.4	23,203	23,108	95	0.4
Davenport-Moline-Rock Island, IA-IL	19.9	3.4	194,944	77.7	37,194	9.9	162,207	158,528	3,679	2.3
Henry County, IL	15.7	1.7	26,184	77.5	4,038	7.9	21,543	21,270	273	1.3
Mercer County, IL	12.6	0.6	8,534	76.6	1,304	7.7	7,214	7,109	105	1.5
Rock Island County, IL	17.1	4.6	76,299	76.2	15,523	10.4	64,883	64,493	390	0.6
Scott County, IA	24.9	3.1	83,927	79.3	16,329	10.3	68,567	65,656	2,911	4.4

See footnotes at end of table.

State and Metropolitan Area Data Book: 2006

U.S. Census Bureau

Metropolitan statistical area **Metropolitan statistical area with metropolitan divisions** *Metropolitan division* Component county	2000 Educational attainment, percent with bachelor's degree or higher[1]	2000 Percent foreign born	2000 Workers 16 years and over Total workers	2000 Workers 16 years and over Percent of workers who drove alone to work	Persons below poverty level 1999 Total persons	Persons below poverty level 1999 Percent of persons below poverty level in 1999	Housing units 2004 (July 1)	Housing units 2000[2] (estimates base)	Housing units Change 2000–2004[3] Number	Housing units Change 2000–2004[3] Percent
Dayton, OH	22.8	2.4	431,604	78.5	82,370	9.7	374,764	364,407	10,357	2.8
Greene County, OH	31.1	3.4	78,098	78.9	11,847	8.0	62,642	58,224	4,418	7.6
Miami County, OH	16.3	1.5	52,381	82.2	6,531	6.6	41,580	40,554	1,026	2.5
Montgomery County, OH	22.8	2.5	279,635	77.7	61,440	11.0	252,728	248,443	4,285	1.7
Preble County, OH	10.1	0.6	21,490	78.6	2,552	6.0	17,814	17,186	628	3.7
Decatur, AL	15.8	2.2	69,343	79.0	18,747	12.9	64,711	62,397	2,314	3.7
Lawrence County, AL	7.5	0.5	15,774	77.5	5,271	15.1	15,466	15,009	457	3.0
Morgan County, AL	18.4	2.7	53,569	79.4	13,476	12.1	49,245	47,388	1,857	3.9
Decatur, IL	16.9	1.4	56,708	77.0	14,316	12.5	51,380	50,241	1,139	2.3
Macon County, IL	16.9	1.4	56,708	77.0	14,316	12.5	51,380	50,241	1,139	2.3
Deltona-Daytona Beach-Ormond Beach, FL	17.6	6.4	201,913	72.5	49,907	11.3	230,718	211,938	18,780	8.9
Volusia County, FL	17.6	6.4	201,913	72.5	49,907	11.3	230,718	211,938	18,780	8.9
Denver-Aurora, CO[4]	34.2	10.9	1,193,561	71.7	170,649	7.9	988,683	876,377	112,306	12.8
Adams County, CO[4]	17.4	12.5	190,881	71.1	32,036	8.8	149,389	127,088	22,301	17.5
Arapahoe County, CO	37.0	11.0	273,207	75.1	27,987	5.7	220,306	197,192	23,114	11.7
Broomfield County, CO[4]	(X)	(X)	(X)	(X)	1,588	(X)	17,790	(X)	(X)	(X)
Clear Creek County, CO	38.8	1.9	5,776	70.0	501	5.4	5,378	5,128	250	4.9
Denver County, CO	34.5	17.4	301,714	63.1	77,813	14.0	265,101	251,069	14,032	5.6
Douglas County, CO	51.9	5.2	98,970	78.7	3,706	2.1	85,040	63,333	21,707	34.3
Elbert County, CO	26.6	1.9	11,056	72.9	791	4.0	8,154	7,113	1,041	14.6
Gilpin County, CO	31.2	3.4	3,150	69.5	191	4.0	3,200	2,929	271	9.3
Jefferson County, CO[4]	36.5	5.4	300,673	75.8	26,821	5.1	222,078	211,828	10,250	4.8
Park County, CO	30.3	2.2	8,134	62.8	803	5.5	12,247	10,697	1,550	14.5
Des Moines, IA	27.9	5.1	269,708	76.8	35,082	7.3	219,876	199,394	20,482	10.3
Dallas County, IA	26.8	4.0	22,636	78.3	2,250	5.5	18,806	16,529	2,277	13.8
Guthrie County, IA	14.9	1.2	5,884	69.9	888	7.8	5,655	5,467	188	3.4
Madison County, IA	14.4	0.6	7,394	74.0	920	6.6	6,101	5,661	440	7.8
Polk County, IA	29.7	5.9	210,961	77.0	29,051	7.8	172,904	156,448	16,456	10.5
Warren County, IA	21.2	1.1	22,833	75.8	1,973	4.9	16,410	15,289	1,121	7.3
Detroit-Warren-Livonia, MI	**23.2**	**7.6**	**2,186,795**	**77.9**	**464,642**	**10.4**	**1,864,404**	**1,797,185**	**67,219**	**3.7**
Detroit-Livonia-Dearborn, MI	*17.2*	*6.7*	*930,640*	*71.2*	*332,598*	*16.1*	*834,620*	*826,145*	*8,475*	*1.0*
Wayne County, MI	17.2	6.7	930,640	71.2	332,598	16.1	834,620	826,145	8,475	1.0
Warren-Farmington Hills-Troy, MI	*28.1*	*8.3*	*1,256,155*	*82.9*	*132,044*	*5.5*	*1,029,784*	*971,040*	*58,744*	*6.0*
Lapeer County, MI	12.7	2.2	43,411	77.3	4,654	5.3	34,771	32,732	2,039	6.2
Livingston County, MI	28.2	3.0	83,868	82.8	5,228	3.3	68,377	58,919	9,458	16.1
Macomb County, MI	17.6	8.8	408,563	83.5	44,010	5.6	341,420	320,276	21,144	6.6
Oakland County, MI	38.2	10.0	637,937	83.5	65,478	5.5	513,148	492,006	21,142	4.3
St. Clair County, MI	12.6	2.7	82,376	77.7	12,674	7.7	72,068	67,107	4,961	7.4
Dothan, AL	15.9	1.4	61,756	78.5	21,226	16.2	62,299	59,723	2,576	4.3
Geneva County, AL	8.7	0.8	11,799	74.4	5,010	19.4	12,372	12,115	257	2.1
Henry County, AL	14.1	1.1	7,237	75.3	3,070	18.8	8,280	8,037	243	3.0
Houston County, AL	18.4	1.6	42,720	80.2	13,146	14.8	41,647	39,571	2,076	5.2
Dover, DE	18.6	4.0	64,387	74.0	13,083	10.3	56,304	50,481	5,823	11.5
Kent County, DE	18.6	4.0	64,387	74.0	13,083	10.3	56,304	50,481	5,823	11.5
Dubuque, IA	21.3	1.9	47,961	77.1	6,639	7.4	37,326	35,508	1,818	5.1
Dubuque County, IA	21.3	1.9	47,961	77.1	6,639	7.4	37,326	35,508	1,818	5.1
Duluth, MN-WI	20.5	1.8	138,792	72.5	30,205	11.0	133,828	129,877	3,951	3.0
Carlton County, MN	14.9	1.6	15,270	75.9	2,389	7.5	14,794	13,721	1,073	7.8
St. Louis County, MN	21.9	1.9	101,258	71.8	23,211	11.6	97,818	95,800	2,018	2.1
Douglas County, WI	18.3	1.6	22,264	73.3	4,605	10.6	21,216	20,356	860	4.2
Durham, NC	38.8	9.3	229,178	69.3	52,821	12.4	200,646	180,022	20,624	11.5
Chatham County, NC	27.6	8.7	25,874	73.3	4,723	9.6	23,742	21,358	2,384	11.2
Durham County, NC	40.1	10.9	120,651	69.7	28,557	12.8	107,996	95,452	12,544	13.1
Orange County, NC	51.5	9.1	65,009	65.6	15,318	13.0	52,509	47,708	4,801	10.1
Person County, NC	10.3	1.3	17,644	74.2	4,223	11.9	16,399	15,504	895	5.8
Eau Claire, WI	22.1	1.8	80,957	75.6	14,023	9.5	65,325	60,295	5,030	8.3
Chippewa County, WI	14.7	0.9	28,970	76.5	4,442	8.0	25,083	22,821	2,262	9.9
Eau Claire County, WI	27.0	2.2	51,987	75.1	9,581	10.3	40,242	37,474	2,768	7.4
El Centro, CA	10.3	32.2	50,788	61.8	29,681	20.8	47,775	43,891	3,884	8.8
Imperial County, CA	10.3	32.2	50,788	61.8	29,681	20.8	47,775	43,891	3,884	8.8
Elizabethtown, KY	14.8	4.0	54,416	74.0	11,081	10.3	46,810	43,532	3,278	7.5
Hardin County, KY	15.4	4.5	48,182	73.8	9,051	9.6	40,545	37,672	2,873	7.6
Larue County, KY	10.9	0.4	6,234	75.5	2,030	15.2	6,265	5,860	405	6.9
Elkhart-Goshen, IN	15.5	7.1	96,532	75.5	14,058	7.7	75,012	69,791	5,221	7.5
Elkhart County, IN	15.5	7.1	96,532	75.5	14,058	7.7	75,012	69,791	5,221	7.5
Elmira, NY	18.6	2.2	42,550	73.3	11,063	12.1	38,033	37,745	288	0.8
Chemung County, NY	18.6	2.2	42,550	73.3	11,063	12.1	38,033	37,745	288	0.8
El Paso, TX	16.6	27.4	274,811	67.5	158,722	23.4	240,600	224,447	16,153	7.2
El Paso County, TX	16.6	27.4	274,811	67.5	158,722	23.4	240,600	224,447	16,153	7.2
Erie, PA	20.9	2.7	137,485	73.7	32,108	11.4	116,307	114,322	1,985	1.7
Erie County, PA	20.9	2.7	137,485	73.7	32,108	11.4	116,307	114,322	1,985	1.7
Eugene-Springfield, OR	25.5	4.9	166,126	65.8	45,423	14.1	144,372	138,954	5,418	3.9
Lane County, OR	25.5	4.9	166,126	65.8	45,423	14.1	144,372	138,954	5,418	3.9

See footnotes at end of table.

Metropolitan statistical area **Metropolitan statistical area with metropolitan divisions** *Metropolitan division* Component county	2000				Persons below poverty level in 1999		Housing units			
			Workers 16 years and over						Change	
	Educational attainment, percent with bachelor's degree or higher[1]	Percent foreign born	Total workers	Percent of workers who drove alone to work	Total persons	Percent of persons below poverty level in 1999	2004 (July 1)	2000[2] (estimates base)	2000–2004[3]	
									Number	Percent
Evansville, IN-KY	17.4	1.3	177,387	78.9	33,267	9.7	154,784	147,763	7,021	4.8
Gibson County, IN	12.4	0.9	16,657	78.4	2,607	8.0	14,757	14,125	632	4.5
Posey County, IN	14.8	0.5	13,719	80.9	1,972	7.3	11,485	11,076	409	3.7
Vanderburgh County, IN	19.3	1.6	90,182	77.8	18,414	10.7	79,591	76,300	3,291	4.3
Warrick County, IN	21.8	1.3	27,892	84.8	2,751	5.3	22,429	20,546	1,883	9.2
Henderson County, KY	13.8	1.1	22,422	76.9	5,393	12.0	20,125	19,466	659	3.4
Webster County, KY	7.1	1.9	6,515	71.9	2,130	15.1	6,397	6,250	147	2.4
Fairbanks, AK	27.0	4.0	45,008	65.5	6,206	7.5	33,780	33,291	489	1.5
Fairbanks North Star Borough, AK	27.0	4.0	45,008	65.5	6,206	7.5	33,780	33,291	489	1.5
Fargo, ND-MN	29.4	3.0	100,863	77.2	18,259	10.5	80,602	73,536	7,066	9.6
Clay County, MN	24.7	2.6	27,318	72.0	6,272	12.2	21,195	19,746	1,449	7.3
Cass County, ND	31.3	3.2	73,545	79.1	11,987	9.7	59,407	53,790	5,617	10.4
Farmington, NM	13.5	2.4	49,000	70.1	24,196	21.3	44,359	43,221	1,138	2.6
San Juan County, NM	13.5	2.4	49,000	70.1	24,196	21.3	44,359	43,221	1,138	2.6
Fayetteville, NC	18.3	5.3	172,833	70.2	42,122	12.5	139,833	130,943	8,890	6.8
Cumberland County, NC	19.1	5.3	157,249	70.3	36,391	12.0	125,622	118,425	7,197	6.1
Hoke County, NC	10.9	5.8	15,584	69.1	5,731	17.0	14,211	12,518	1,693	13.5
Fayetteville-Springdale-Rogers, AR-MO	20.9	6.6	175,138	73.3	44,368	12.8	163,309	144,435	18,874	13.1
Benton County, AR	20.3	6.4	74,545	76.8	15,201	9.9	72,810	64,281	8,529	13.3
Madison County, AR	10.1	1.8	6,675	66.5	2,616	18.4	6,770	6,537	233	3.6
Washington County, AR	24.5	7.4	83,716	71.8	22,104	14.0	74,074	64,330	9,744	15.1
McDonald County, MO	7.0	5.6	10,202	63.5	4,447	20.5	9,655	9,287	368	4.0
Flagstaff, AZ	29.9	4.3	59,688	61.9	20,609	17.7	57,224	53,443	3,781	7.1
Coconino County, AZ	29.9	4.3	59,688	61.9	20,609	17.7	57,224	53,443	3,781	7.1
Flint, MI	16.2	2.1	207,808	76.1	56,480	12.9	193,626	183,635	9,991	5.4
Genesee County, MI	16.2	2.1	207,808	76.1	56,480	12.9	193,626	183,635	9,991	5.4
Florence, SC	16.9	1.5	91,795	72.4	33,489	17.3	82,873	80,778	2,095	2.6
Darlington County, SC	13.5	0.9	31,299	72.1	13,426	19.9	29,715	28,942	773	2.7
Florence County, SC	18.7	1.8	60,496	72.6	20,063	16.0	53,158	51,836	1,322	2.6
Florence-Muscle Shoals, AL	16.8	1.0	65,685	79.9	20,034	14.0	67,468	65,404	2,064	3.2
Colbert County, AL	14.1	0.9	24,388	80.7	7,592	13.8	25,815	24,980	835	3.3
Lauderdale County, AL	18.5	1.0	41,297	79.4	12,442	14.1	41,653	40,424	1,229	3.0
Fond du Lac, WI	16.9	2.0	53,717	76.3	5,471	5.6	41,102	39,271	1,831	4.7
Fond du Lac County, WI	16.9	2.0	53,717	76.3	5,471	5.6	41,102	39,271	1,831	4.7
Fort Collins-Loveland, CO	39.5	4.3	143,110	72.8	22,600	9.0	119,416	105,392	14,024	13.3
Larimer County, CO	39.5	4.3	143,110	72.8	22,600	9.0	119,416	105,392	14,024	13.3
Fort Smith, AR-OK	13.2	4.0	126,312	74.3	42,043	15.4	119,973	115,381	4,592	4.0
Crawford County, AR	9.7	2.4	24,762	76.0	7,500	14.1	22,406	21,315	1,091	5.1
Franklin County, AR	11.0	1.3	8,103	71.7	2,663	15.0	7,856	7,673	183	2.4
Sebastian County, AR	16.6	6.9	55,925	75.9	15,410	13.4	51,288	49,310	1,978	4.0
Le Flore County, OK	11.3	2.5	20,537	70.8	8,857	18.4	20,731	20,143	588	2.9
Sequoyah County, OK	10.9	0.7	16,985	72.1	7,613	19.5	17,692	16,940	752	4.4
Fort Walton Beach-Crestview-Destin, FL	24.2	5.3	87,000	78.2	14,562	8.5	85,065	78,593	6,472	8.2
Okaloosa County, FL	24.2	5.3	87,000	78.2	14,562	8.5	85,065	78,593	6,472	8.2
Fort Wayne, IN	21.3	3.6	207,002	79.2	32,880	8.4	172,293	162,420	9,873	6.1
Allen County, IN	22.7	4.0	175,606	78.8	29,807	9.0	147,408	138,905	8,503	6.1
Wells County, IN	14.3	0.8	14,674	80.8	1,589	5.8	11,473	10,970	503	4.6
Whitley County, IN	13.3	0.8	16,722	82.0	1,484	4.8	13,412	12,545	867	6.9
Fresno, CA	17.5	21.1	341,944	64.0	179,085	22.4	286,072	270,767	15,305	5.7
Fresno County, CA	17.5	21.1	341,944	64.0	179,085	22.4	286,072	270,767	15,305	5.7
Gadsden, AL	13.4	1.6	46,225	77.9	15,938	15.4	47,397	45,959	1,438	3.1
Etowah County, AL	13.4	1.6	46,225	77.9	15,938	15.4	47,397	45,959	1,438	3.1
Gainesville, FL	36.7	6.9	119,369	67.9	48,783	21.0	108,888	101,019	7,869	7.8
Alachua County, FL	38.7	7.3	113,346	67.7	46,939	21.5	102,700	95,113	7,587	8.0
Gilchrist County, FL	9.4	1.7	6,023	71.5	1,844	12.8	6,188	5,906	282	4.8
Gainesville, GA	18.7	16.2	69,294	72.1	16,980	12.2	58,848	51,056	7,792	15.3
Hall County, GA	18.7	16.2	69,294	72.1	16,980	12.2	58,848	51,056	7,792	15.3
Glens Falls, NY	18.9	2.2	60,613	74.1	11,429	9.2	63,753	61,646	2,107	3.4
Warren County, NY	23.2	2.4	31,788	74.7	6,025	9.5	36,269	34,852	1,417	4.1
Washington County, NY	14.3	1.9	28,825	73.5	5,404	8.9	27,484	26,794	690	2.6
Goldsboro, NC	15.0	4.2	53,790	74.2	15,097	13.3	49,510	47,313	2,197	4.6
Wayne County, NC	15.0	4.2	53,790	74.2	15,097	13.3	49,510	47,313	2,197	4.6
Grand Forks, ND-MN	24.2	2.9	52,481	74.5	10,906	11.2	42,556	41,381	1,175	2.8
Polk County, MN	17.6	2.2	15,270	71.7	3,284	10.5	14,427	14,008	419	3.0
Grand Forks County, ND	27.8	3.2	37,211	75.6	7,622	11.5	28,129	27,373	756	2.8
Grand Junction, CO	22.0	3.0	58,382	71.4	11,651	10.0	54,539	48,718	5,821	11.9
Mesa County, CO	22.0	3.0	58,382	71.4	11,651	10.0	54,539	48,718	5,821	11.9
Grand Rapids-Wyoming, MI	22.7	5.4	381,804	77.8	63,250	8.5	309,632	293,084	16,548	5.6
Barry County, MI	14.7	0.8	28,907	77.5	3,089	5.4	25,295	23,876	1,419	5.9
Ionia County, MI	10.8	1.2	28,371	76.7	4,858	7.9	23,427	22,006	1,421	6.5
Kent County, MI	25.8	6.6	302,688	78.3	49,832	8.7	236,522	224,000	12,522	5.6
Newaygo County, MI	11.4	1.8	21,838	72.6	5,471	11.4	24,388	23,202	1,186	5.1

See footnotes at end of table.

Table C-2. Metropolitan Areas With Component Counties — **Population Characteristics and Housing Units**—Con.

Metropolitan statistical area / **Metropolitan statistical area with metropolitan divisions** / *Metropolitan division* / Component county	2000 Educational attainment, percent with bachelor's degree or higher[1]	2000 Percent foreign born	2000 Workers 16 years and over Total workers	2000 Workers 16 years and over Percent of workers who drove alone to work	Persons below poverty level in 1999 Total persons	Persons below poverty level in 1999 Percent of persons below poverty level in 1999	Housing units 2004 (July 1)	Housing units 2000[2] (estimates base)	Housing units Change 2000–2004[3] Number	Housing units Change 2000–2004[3] Percent
Great Falls, MT	21.5	2.4	40,135	74.8	10,605	13.2	35,568	35,225	343	1.0
Cascade County, MT	21.5	2.4	40,135	74.8	10,605	13.2	35,568	35,225	343	1.0
Greeley, CO[4]	21.6	9.3	92,841	72.9	22,019	12.2	83,132	66,165	16,967	25.6
Weld County, CO[4]	21.6	9.3	92,841	72.9	22,019	12.2	83,132	66,165	16,967	25.6
Green Bay, WI	20.1	3.3	154,827	79.0	18,785	6.6	128,697	118,235	10,462	8.8
Brown County, WI	22.5	3.9	125,437	80.3	15,123	6.7	98,258	90,199	8,059	8.9
Kewaunee County, WI	11.4	0.9	10,984	73.8	1,165	5.8	8,760	8,221	539	6.6
Oconto County, WI	10.6	0.7	18,406	73.8	2,497	7.0	21,679	19,815	1,864	9.4
Greensboro-High Point, NC	23.4	5.8	344,254	75.6	66,648	10.4	296,729	275,027	21,702	7.9
Guilford County, NC	30.3	6.5	229,864	75.3	43,227	10.3	197,036	180,391	16,645	9.2
Randolph County, NC	11.1	5.7	69,346	77.2	11,802	9.0	57,904	54,428	3,476	6.4
Rockingham County, NC	10.8	2.7	45,044	74.5	11,619	12.6	41,789	40,208	1,581	3.9
Greenville, NC	23.9	3.8	77,947	73.0	29,592	19.4	73,448	65,733	7,715	11.7
Greene County, NC	8.2	4.9	8,528	69.6	3,591	18.9	7,566	7,368	198	2.7
Pitt County, NC	26.4	3.6	69,419	73.4	26,001	19.4	65,882	58,365	7,517	12.9
Greenville, SC	23.1	4.0	287,919	75.7	62,678	11.2	255,791	239,037	16,754	7.0
Greenville County, SC	26.2	4.9	197,900	76.5	38,825	10.2	175,585	162,804	12,781	7.9
Laurens County, SC	11.7	1.6	33,689	72.7	9,648	13.9	31,177	30,233	944	3.1
Pickens County, SC	19.1	2.9	56,330	74.7	14,205	12.8	49,029	46,000	3,029	6.6
Gulfport-Biloxi, MS	17.9	3.0	120,065	72.9	35,005	14.2	115,113	106,051	9,062	8.5
Hancock County, MS	17.3	1.4	18,904	71.1	6,137	14.3	22,996	21,072	1,924	9.1
Harrison County, MS	18.4	3.6	94,847	73.3	26,597	14.0	86,556	79,636	6,920	8.7
Stone County, MS	12.4	1.0	6,314	72.0	2,271	16.7	5,561	5,343	218	4.1
Hagerstown-Martinsburg, MD-WV	14.5	1.8	108,707	76.0	21,784	9.8	103,326	93,961	9,365	10.0
Washington County, MD	14.6	1.9	63,714	76.6	11,697	8.9	56,691	52,972	3,719	7.0
Berkeley County, WV	15.1	1.7	38,040	75.8	8,556	11.3	37,802	32,913	4,889	14.9
Morgan County, WV	11.2	1.4	6,953	71.6	1,531	10.2	8,833	8,076	757	9.4
Hanford-Corcoran, CA	10.4	16.0	49,044	62.8	21,307	16.5	39,216	36,563	2,653	7.3
Kings County, CA	10.4	16.0	49,044	62.8	21,307	16.5	39,216	36,563	2,653	7.3
Harrisburg-Carlisle, PA	24.3	3.4	262,657	75.7	40,094	7.9	224,981	217,025	7,956	3.7
Cumberland County, PA	27.9	3.2	111,105	78.2	13,102	6.1	91,256	86,951	4,305	5.0
Dauphin County, PA	23.5	4.1	128,945	73.8	23,706	9.4	114,145	111,133	3,012	2.7
Perry County, PA	11.3	0.9	22,607	73.6	3,286	7.5	19,580	18,941	639	3.4
Harrisonburg, VA	21.4	5.5	56,692	70.6	15,434	14.3	43,739	41,010	2,729	6.7
Rockingham County, VA	17.6	3.3	35,873	75.6	5,415	8.0	29,123	27,325	1,798	6.6
Harrisonburg city, VA	31.2	9.2	20,819	62.1	10,019	24.8	14,616	13,685	931	6.8
Hartford-West Hartford-East Hartford, CT	30.5	10.3	600,167	76.5	91,303	7.9	483,173	471,877	11,296	2.4
Hartford County, CT	29.6	11.7	438,197	75.8	77,440	9.0	358,811	353,022	5,789	1.6
Middlesex County, CT	33.8	6.0	86,327	79.1	6,911	4.5	70,209	67,285	2,924	4.3
Tolland County, CT	32.8	5.9	75,643	77.9	6,952	5.1	54,153	51,570	2,583	5.0
Hattiesburg, MS	22.6	1.6	59,258	74.0	22,885	18.5	52,333	50,453	1,880	3.7
Forrest County, MS	22.8	2.0	35,018	72.2	15,089	20.8	31,171	29,913	1,258	4.2
Lamar County, MS	26.8	1.1	19,240	78.5	5,150	13.2	15,896	15,433	463	3.0
Perry County, MS	7.7	0.5	5,000	70.0	2,646	21.8	5,266	5,107	159	3.1
Hickory-Lenoir-Morganton, NC	13.6	4.6	182,914	77.0	32,802	9.6	153,626	144,866	8,760	6.0
Alexander County, NC	9.3	2.4	18,707	78.9	2,821	8.4	14,874	14,098	776	5.5
Burke County, NC	12.8	4.8	45,094	76.6	9,132	10.2	38,802	37,427	1,375	3.7
Caldwell County, NC	10.4	1.9	41,256	75.5	8,161	10.5	35,172	33,420	1,752	5.2
Catawba County, NC	17.0	6.5	77,857	77.5	12,688	9.0	64,778	59,921	4,857	8.1
Hinesville-Fort Stewart, GA	13.2	5.6	36,025	66.6	10,450	14.5	27,719	26,209	1,510	5.8
Liberty County, GA	14.5	5.7	31,136	66.5	8,464	13.7	23,355	21,977	1,378	6.3
Long County, GA	5.8	5.4	4,889	67.0	1,986	19.3	4,364	4,232	132	3.1
Holland-Grand Haven, MI	26.0	4.9	128,356	81.0	12,655	5.3	95,536	86,856	8,680	10.0
Ottawa County, MI	26.0	4.9	128,356	81.0	12,655	5.3	95,536	86,856	8,680	10.0
Honolulu, HI	27.9	19.2	447,320	56.6	83,937	9.6	325,775	315,988	9,787	3.1
Honolulu County, HI	27.9	19.2	447,320	56.6	83,937	9.6	325,775	315,988	9,787	3.1
Hot Springs, AR	18.0	2.6	38,577	74.0	12,565	14.3	46,100	44,953	1,147	2.6
Garland County, AR	18.0	2.6	38,577	74.0	12,565	14.3	46,100	44,953	1,147	2.6
Houma-Bayou Cane-Thibodaux, LA	12.3	1.5	83,659	72.6	34,167	17.6	78,452	74,973	3,479	4.6
Lafourche Parish, LA	12.4	1.5	39,587	72.0	14,560	16.2	36,360	35,045	1,315	3.8
Terrebonne Parish, LA	12.3	1.5	44,072	73.2	19,607	18.8	42,092	39,928	2,164	5.4
Houston-Sugar Land, Baytown, TX	26.4	19.0	2,284,849	70.8	635,349	13.5	1,987,809	1,799,627	188,182	10.5
Austin County, TX	17.3	7.3	11,268	74.9	2,814	11.9	10,665	10,205	460	4.5
Brazoria County, TX	19.6	8.5	112,904	76.9	23,465	9.7	101,475	90,628	10,847	12.0
Chambers County, TX	12.1	5.1	12,353	78.3	2,833	10.9	11,877	10,336	1,541	14.9
Fort Bend County, TX	36.9	18.3	174,803	76.4	24,953	7.0	131,840	115,991	15,849	13.7
Galveston County, TX	22.7	8.3	122,894	71.7	32,510	13.0	122,742	111,733	11,009	9.9
Harris County, TX	26.9	22.2	1,653,892	69.4	503,234	14.8	1,422,519	1,298,130	124,389	9.6
Liberty County, TX	8.1	5.1	28,548	71.4	9,296	13.3	27,613	26,359	1,254	4.8
Montgomery County, TX	25.3	8.6	143,259	74.9	27,376	9.3	133,916	112,770	21,146	18.8
San Jacinto County, TX	9.6	2.5	9,032	68.3	4,150	18.7	11,901	11,520	381	3.3
Waller County, TX	16.8	9.4	15,896	62.4	4,718	14.4	13,261	11,955	1,306	10.9
Huntington-Ashland, WV-KY-OH	14.9	0.9	125,050	75.4	50,496	17.5	131,302	129,864	1,438	1.1
Boyd County, KY	14.1	1.1	21,365	76.0	7,393	14.9	22,267	21,976	291	1.3
Greenup County, KY	11.5	0.6	15,517	76.1	5,130	13.9	16,261	15,977	284	1.8
Lawrence County, OH	10.3	0.5	25,978	77.2	11,645	18.7	27,475	27,189	286	1.1
Cabell County, WV	20.9	1.3	44,851	72.8	17,983	18.6	45,942	45,615	327	0.7
Wayne County, WV	11.9	0.6	17,339	77.9	8,345	19.5	19,357	19,107	250	1.3

See footnotes at end of table.

Metropolitan statistical area **Metropolitan statistical area with metropolitan divisions** *Metropolitan division* Component county	2000				Persons below poverty level in 1999		Housing units			
	Educational attainment, percent with bachelor's degree or higher[1]	Percent foreign born	Workers 16 years and over		Total persons	Percent of persons below poverty level in 1999	2004 (July 1)	2000[2] (estimates base)	Change 2000–2004[3]	
			Total workers	Percent of workers who drove alone to work					Number	Percent
Huntsville, AL	30.9	3.5	175,445	78.1	36,179	10.6	156,942	147,185	9,757	6.6
Limestone County, AL	16.9	1.7	31,103	79.0	7,771	11.8	28,290	26,897	1,393	5.2
Madison County, AL	34.3	4.0	144,342	78.0	28,408	10.3	128,652	120,288	8,364	7.0
Idaho Falls, ID	24.2	4.3	49,052	71.9	10,244	10.1	40,220	36,771	3,449	9.4
Bonneville County, ID	26.1	3.9	40,370	72.6	8,260	10.0	33,360	30,484	2,876	9.4
Jefferson County, ID	15.2	5.9	8,682	69.0	1,984	10.4	6,860	6,287	573	9.1
Indianapolis, IN	26.5	3.5	809,790	77.7	126,503	8.3	708,938	644,873	64,065	9.9
Boone County, IN	27.6	1.5	23,820	79.9	2,337	5.1	20,056	17,929	2,127	11.9
Brown County, IN	18.5	1.0	7,743	77.3	1,310	8.8	7,750	7,163	587	8.2
Hamilton County, IN	48.9	4.0	98,100	84.0	5,300	2.9	87,504	69,478	18,026	25.9
Hancock County, IN	22.2	0.9	29,807	81.5	1,623	2.9	25,420	21,750	3,670	16.9
Hendricks County, IN	23.1	1.6	55,521	85.1	3,665	3.5	49,279	39,229	10,050	25.6
Johnson County, IN	23.1	1.7	62,226	81.5	6,337	5.5	50,779	45,095	5,684	12.6
Marion County, IN	25.4	4.6	457,567	74.6	95,827	11.1	407,994	387,183	20,811	5.4
Morgan County, IN	12.6	0.9	34,825	78.9	4,367	6.5	27,923	25,908	2,015	7.8
Putnam County, IN	13.1	1.1	17,004	73.1	2,516	7.0	14,018	13,505	513	3.8
Shelby County, IN	12.7	1.6	23,177	79.0	3,221	7.4	18,215	17,633	582	3.3
Iowa City, IA	42.0	5.6	78,045	65.0	16,930	12.9	60,006	54,374	5,632	10.4
Johnson County, IA	47.6	6.4	66,978	64.2	15,406	13.9	51,193	45,831	5,362	11.7
Washington County, IA	16.4	1.5	11,067	69.5	1,524	7.4	8,813	8,543	270	3.2
Ithaca, NY	47.5	10.5	51,187	55.4	14,905	15.4	40,016	38,625	1,391	3.6
Tompkins County, NY	47.5	10.5	51,187	55.4	14,905	15.4	40,016	38,625	1,391	3.6
Jackson, MI	16.3	1.7	75,917	77.3	13,417	8.5	66,354	62,906	3,448	5.5
Jackson County, MI	16.3	1.7	75,917	77.3	13,417	8.5	66,354	62,906	3,448	5.5
Jackson, MS	26.2	1.2	239,707	73.9	81,608	16.4	208,815	196,546	12,269	6.2
Copiah County, MS	11.6	0.8	12,357	65.8	6,979	24.3	11,360	11,101	259	2.3
Hinds County, MS	27.2	1.1	119,165	71.2	48,193	19.2	103,578	100,287	3,291	3.3
Madison County, MS	37.9	1.7	37,241	77.4	10,155	13.6	32,388	28,781	3,607	12.5
Rankin County, MS	23.8	1.6	59,555	80.0	10,462	9.1	49,979	45,070	4,909	10.9
Simpson County, MS	10.9	0.9	11,389	68.2	5,819	21.1	11,510	11,307	203	1.8
Jackson, TN	20.1	2.0	54,433	76.4	14,414	13.4	47,478	44,379	3,099	7.0
Chester County, TN	11.2	0.5	7,615	72.4	2,065	13.3	6,517	6,174	343	5.6
Madison County, TN	21.5	2.3	46,818	77.1	12,349	13.4	40,961	38,205	2,756	7.2
Jacksonville, FL	22.6	5.3	574,062	75.1	118,116	10.5	527,288	475,043	52,245	11.0
Baker County, FL	8.2	1.1	9,819	74.3	2,961	13.3	8,074	7,592	482	6.3
Clay County, FL	20.1	4.5	71,993	79.1	9,437	6.7	62,501	53,748	8,753	16.3
Duval County, FL	21.9	5.9	401,657	74.0	90,828	11.7	357,721	329,778	27,943	8.5
Nassau County, FL	18.9	2.7	28,726	74.7	5,192	9.0	29,028	25,917	3,111	12.0
St. Johns County, FL	33.1	4.9	61,867	77.3	9,698	7.9	69,964	58,008	11,956	20.6
Jacksonville, NC	14.8	4.1	85,054	62.3	16,917	11.3	60,330	55,726	4,604	8.3
Onslow County, NC	14.8	4.1	85,054	62.3	16,917	11.3	60,330	55,726	4,604	8.3
Janesville, WI	16.7	3.3	80,895	77.1	10,880	7.1	65,520	62,187	3,333	5.4
Rock County, WI	16.7	3.3	80,895	77.1	10,880	7.1	65,520	62,187	3,333	5.4
Jefferson City, MO	21.2	1.6	72,050	73.9	11,254	8.0	60,153	56,729	3,424	6.0
Callaway County, MO	16.5	1.1	20,578	74.5	3,142	7.7	17,032	16,167	865	5.4
Cole County, MO	27.4	2.2	37,697	75.9	5,709	8.0	31,072	28,915	2,157	7.5
Moniteau County, MO	13.0	1.6	6,964	70.6	1,335	9.0	5,936	5,742	194	3.4
Osage County, MO	10.4	0.5	6,811	64.4	1,068	8.2	6,113	5,905	208	3.5
Johnson City, TN	18.5	1.5	89,777	78.0	25,966	14.3	85,356	81,913	3,443	4.2
Carter County, TN	12.8	0.8	27,249	75.7	9,309	16.4	26,599	25,920	679	2.6
Unicoi County, TN	10.6	1.4	8,101	79.0	2,269	12.8	8,494	8,214	280	3.4
Washington County, TN	22.9	1.9	54,427	79.1	14,388	13.4	50,263	47,779	2,484	5.2
Johnstown, PA	13.7	1.3	67,088	73.4	18,111	11.9	66,067	65,796	271	0.4
Cambria County, PA	13.7	1.3	67,088	73.4	18,111	11.9	66,067	65,796	271	0.4
Jonesboro, AR	17.3	1.7	53,906	76.1	17,586	16.3	48,555	46,184	2,371	5.1
Craighead County, AR	20.9	2.0	42,505	76.8	12,246	14.9	37,218	35,133	2,085	5.9
Poinsett County, AR	6.3	0.9	11,401	73.6	5,340	20.8	11,337	11,051	286	2.6
Joplin, MO	16.4	2.2	78,729	75.3	20,819	13.2	70,711	67,468	3,243	4.8
Jasper County, MO	16.5	2.6	52,597	75.6	14,808	14.1	47,838	45,571	2,267	5.0
Newton County, MO	16.1	1.4	26,132	74.5	6,011	11.4	22,873	21,897	976	4.5
Kalamazoo-Portage, MI	26.9	3.9	167,273	75.8	35,817	11.4	140,764	133,225	7,539	5.7
Kalamazoo County, MI	31.2	4.0	129,426	75.8	27,483	11.5	104,945	99,250	5,695	5.7
Van Buren County, MI	14.3	3.5	37,847	75.9	8,334	10.9	35,819	33,975	1,844	5.4
Kankakee-Bradley, IL	15.0	3.5	51,561	74.4	11,445	11.0	42,350	40,610	1,740	4.3
Kankakee County, IL	15.0	3.5	51,561	74.4	11,445	11.0	42,350	40,610	1,740	4.3
Kansas City, MO-KS	28.2	4.5	952,535	77.9	152,464	8.4	812,757	758,390	54,367	7.2
Franklin County, KS	16.5	1.3	12,803	72.3	1,857	7.5	10,843	10,229	614	6.0
Johnson County, KS	47.7	5.7	253,160	83.5	15,323	3.4	203,222	181,800	21,422	11.8
Leavenworth County, KS	23.1	2.7	32,624	77.5	4,128	6.0	26,451	24,401	2,050	8.4
Linn County, KS	12.7	0.3	4,640	67.0	1,041	10.9	4,901	4,720	181	3.8
Miami County, KS	19.4	0.6	14,787	78.7	1,531	5.4	11,739	10,984	755	6.9
Wyandotte County, KS	12.0	9.5	74,269	70.1	25,773	16.3	66,333	65,892	441	0.7
Bates County, MO	10.1	0.9	7,775	70.0	2,372	14.2	7,476	7,247	229	3.2

See footnotes at end of table.

State and Metropolitan Area Data Book: 2006

U.S. Census Bureau

Table C-2. Metropolitan Areas With Component Counties — **Population Characteristics and Housing Units**—Con.

Metropolitan statistical area **Metropolitan statistical area with metropolitan divisions** *Metropolitan division* Component county	2000				Persons below poverty level in 1999		Housing units			
			Workers 16 years and over						Change	
									2000–2004[3]	
	Educational attainment, percent with bachelor's degree or higher[1]	Percent foreign born	Total workers	Percent of workers who drove alone to work	Total persons	Percent of persons below poverty level in 1999	2004 (July 1)	2000[2] (estimates base)	Number	Percent
Kansas City, MO-KS—Con.										
Caldwell County, MO	11.7	0.4	4,188	71.2	1,048	11.7	4,607	4,493	114	2.5
Cass County, MO	17.7	1.6	42,590	78.9	4,664	5.7	35,736	31,677	4,059	12.8
Clay County, MO	24.9	2.9	101,627	80.9	9,898	5.4	81,063	76,230	4,833	6.3
Clinton County, MO	14.5	0.5	9,530	75.5	1,728	9.1	8,550	7,877	673	8.5
Jackson County, MO	23.4	4.3	335,322	74.6	76,808	11.7	303,527	288,231	15,296	5.3
Lafayette County, MO	13.8	0.7	16,644	74.4	2,816	8.5	14,171	13,707	464	3.4
Platte County, MO	33.3	3.7	42,576	82.6	3,477	4.7	34,138	30,902	3,236	10.5
Ray County, MO	10.8	0.4	11,632	74.0	1,557	6.7	9,851	9,371	480	5.1
Kennewick-Richland-Pasco, WA	23.3	12.8	92,458	71.1	23,797	12.4	78,789	72,047	6,742	9.4
Benton County, WA	26.3	8.5	70,583	74.2	14,517	10.2	60,108	55,963	4,145	7.4
Franklin County, WA	13.6	25.2	21,875	60.8	9,280	18.8	18,681	16,084	2,597	16.1
Killeen-Temple-Fort Hood, TX	18.0	6.8	165,863	71.2	35,531	10.7	133,110	122,159	10,951	9.0
Bell County, TX	19.8	7.3	121,181	73.3	27,607	11.6	102,700	92,782	9,918	10.7
Coryell County, TX	12.4	5.3	36,234	63.7	5,481	7.3	22,529	21,776	753	3.5
Lampasas County, TX	16.2	6.0	8,448	74.2	2,443	13.8	7,881	7,601	280	3.7
Kingsport-Bristol-Bristol, TN-VA	15.5	1.0	137,841	79.8	39,856	13.4	141,627	136,277	5,350	3.9
Hawkins County, TN	10.0	0.7	24,007	79.4	8,338	15.6	25,486	24,416	1,070	4.4
Sullivan County, TN	18.1	1.3	71,474	80.9	19,453	12.7	71,668	69,052	2,616	3.8
Scott County, VA	8.3	0.3	9,827	74.5	3,882	16.6	11,671	11,355	316	2.8
Washington County, VA	16.1	0.9	24,849	80.3	5,468	10.7	24,135	22,985	1,150	5.0
Bristol city, VA	17.0	1.4	7,684	76.8	2,715	15.6	8,667	8,469	198	2.3
Kingston, NY	25.0	5.9	89,555	71.2	19,338	10.9	79,846	77,656	2,190	2.8
Ulster County, NY	25.0	5.9	89,555	71.2	19,338	10.9	79,846	77,656	2,190	2.8
Knoxville, TN	24.6	2.2	309,756	79.2	73,225	11.9	293,060	276,142	16,918	6.1
Anderson County, TN	20.8	1.9	33,076	80.2	9,255	13.0	33,468	32,451	1,017	3.1
Blount County, TN	17.9	1.5	52,693	79.3	10,084	9.5	49,705	47,059	2,646	5.6
Knox County, TN	29.0	2.5	197,352	79.1	46,572	12.2	183,033	171,439	11,594	6.8
Loudon County, TN	17.0	1.8	18,752	78.9	3,858	9.9	18,289	17,277	1,012	5.9
Union County, TN	5.8	0.3	7,883	75.0	3,456	19.4	8,565	7,916	649	8.2
Kokomo, IN	17.1	1.6	49,985	79.6	8,786	8.7	46,086	44,452	1,634	3.7
Howard County, IN	18.1	1.8	41,471	79.0	7,944	9.3	39,044	37,604	1,440	3.8
Tipton County, IN	12.4	1.0	8,514	82.3	842	5.1	7,042	6,848	194	2.8
La Crosse, WI-MN	24.6	2.3	70,075	75.5	12,105	9.5	54,077	51,647	2,430	4.7
Houston County, MN	20.5	1.1	10,519	71.9	1,264	6.4	8,452	8,168	284	3.5
La Crosse County, WI	25.4	2.5	59,556	76.2	10,841	10.1	45,625	43,479	2,146	4.9
Lafayette, IN	29.2	7.1	95,947	71.1	22,420	12.6	77,243	70,836	6,407	9.0
Benton County, IN	13.0	0.8	4,829	75.0	505	5.4	3,876	3,818	58	1.5
Carroll County, IN	12.9	2.2	10,499	75.4	1,348	6.7	9,104	8,675	429	4.9
Tippecanoe County, IN	33.2	8.2	80,619	70.3	20,567	13.8	64,263	58,343	5,920	10.1
Lafayette, LA	22.0	2.2	116,220	75.3	39,477	16.5	104,169	98,367	5,802	5.9
Lafayette Parish, LA	25.5	2.5	95,292	76.4	29,216	15.3	83,052	78,122	4,930	6.3
St. Martin Parish, LA	8.5	0.9	20,928	70.4	10,261	21.1	21,117	20,245	872	4.3
Lake Charles, LA	16.4	1.4	89,799	76.1	28,802	14.9	86,351	81,331	5,020	6.2
Calcasieu Parish, LA	16.9	1.4	85,415	76.1	27,582	15.0	80,779	75,995	4,784	6.3
Cameron Parish, LA	7.9	1.6	4,384	74.2	1,220	12.2	5,572	5,336	236	4.4
Lakeland, FL	14.9	6.9	219,246	73.7	60,953	12.6	246,661	226,376	20,285	9.0
Polk County, FL	14.9	6.9	219,246	73.7	60,953	12.6	246,661	226,376	20,285	9.0
Lancaster, PA	20.5	3.2	243,203	74.5	35,553	7.6	188,486	179,990	8,496	4.7
Lancaster County, PA	20.5	3.2	243,203	74.5	35,553	7.6	188,486	179,990	8,496	4.7
Lansing-East Lansing, MI	28.4	4.6	241,342	74.7	47,332	10.6	192,283	181,844	10,439	5.7
Clinton County, MI	21.2	1.2	33,996	79.2	2,963	4.6	28,309	24,630	3,679	14.9
Eaton County, MI	21.7	2.2	55,940	78.1	5,948	5.7	44,667	42,118	2,549	6.1
Ingham County, MI	33.0	6.3	151,406	72.4	38,421	13.8	119,307	115,096	4,211	3.7
Laredo, TX	13.9	29.0	69,019	63.4	59,339	30.7	62,825	55,206	7,619	13.8
Webb County, TX	13.9	29.0	69,019	63.4	59,339	30.7	62,825	55,206	7,619	13.8
Las Cruces, NM	22.3	18.7	74,974	68.7	43,054	24.6	70,400	65,210	5,190	8.0
Dona Ana County, NM	22.3	18.7	74,974	68.7	43,054	24.6	70,400	65,210	5,190	8.0
Las Vegas-Paradise, NV	17.3	18.0	688,917	68.4	145,855	10.6	683,244	559,784	123,460	22.1
Clark County, NV	17.3	18.0	688,917	68.4	145,855	10.6	683,244	559,784	123,460	22.1
Lawrence, KS	42.7	5.2	58,044	72.2	14,486	14.5	44,032	40,251	3,781	9.4
Douglas County, KS	42.7	5.2	58,044	72.2	14,486	14.5	44,032	40,251	3,781	9.4
Lawton, OK	19.1	5.4	56,461	67.1	16,276	14.2	45,976	45,416	560	1.2
Comanche County, OK	19.1	5.4	56,461	67.1	16,276	14.2	45,976	45,416	560	1.2
Lebanon, PA	15.4	2.4	62,467	76.3	8,728	7.3	51,629	49,320	2,309	4.7
Lebanon County, PA	15.4	2.4	62,467	76.3	8,728	7.3	51,629	49,320	2,309	4.7
Lewiston, ID-WA	18.6	1.9	28,619	77.3	7,600	13.1	25,785	25,314	471	1.9
Nez Perce County, ID	18.9	1.9	18,752	78.1	4,468	11.9	16,538	16,203	335	2.1
Asotin County, WA	18.0	1.8	9,867	75.6	3,132	15.2	9,247	9,111	136	1.5
Lewiston-Auburn, ME	14.4	2.6	54,529	72.8	11,115	10.7	47,198	45,960	1,238	2.7
Androscoggin County, ME	14.4	2.6	54,529	72.8	11,115	10.7	47,198	45,960	1,238	2.7

See footnotes at end of table.

Metropolitan statistical area **Metropolitan statistical area with metropolitan divisions** *Metropolitan division* Component county	2000 Educational attainment, percent with bachelor's degree or higher[1]	2000 Percent foreign born	2000 Workers 16 years and over Total workers	2000 Workers 16 years and over Percent of workers who drove alone to work	Persons below poverty level in 1999 Total persons	Persons below poverty level in 1999 Percent of persons below poverty level in 1999	Housing units 2004 (July 1)	Housing units 2000[2] (estimates base)	Housing units Change 2000–2004[3] Number	Housing units Change 2000–2004[3] Percent
Lexington-Fayette, KY	29.8	4.4	223,816	75.0	46,438	11.4	189,984	175,262	14,722	8.4
Bourbon County, KY	13.5	2.0	9,638	73.9	2,670	13.8	8,753	8,349	404	4.8
Clark County, KY	15.6	1.0	16,477	78.9	3,476	10.5	15,096	13,749	1,347	9.8
Fayette County, KY	35.6	5.9	147,226	74.2	31,963	12.3	124,907	116,167	8,740	7.5
Jessamine County, KY	21.5	1.8	20,068	73.9	3,904	10.0	16,734	14,646	2,088	14.3
Scott County, KY	20.3	1.9	17,563	75.6	2,764	8.4	14,515	12,977	1,538	11.9
Woodford County, KY	25.9	2.7	12,844	80.1	1,661	7.2	9,979	9,374	605	6.5
Lima, OH	13.4	1.0	50,866	78.6	12,374	11.4	44,863	44,245	618	1.4
Allen County, OH	13.4	1.0	50,866	78.6	12,374	11.4	44,863	44,245	618	1.4
Lincoln, NE	32.0	5.2	154,323	76.3	23,787	8.9	118,208	110,645	7,563	6.8
Lancaster County, NE	32.6	5.4	145,342	76.7	22,722	9.1	111,523	104,217	7,306	7.0
Seward County, NE	22.6	1.7	8,981	70.3	1,065	6.5	6,685	6,428	257	4.0
Little Rock-North Little Rock, AR	24.2	2.3	312,865	76.1	71,904	11.8	278,356	261,917	16,439	6.3
Faulkner County, AR	25.2	1.7	45,646	72.2	10,333	12.0	38,232	34,546	3,686	10.7
Grant County, AR	11.0	0.6	7,900	77.6	1,654	10.0	7,227	6,960	267	3.8
Lonoke County, AR	14.6	1.4	26,411	77.6	5,490	10.4	23,092	20,749	2,343	11.3
Perry County, AR	11.1	0.8	4,661	72.0	1,408	13.8	4,836	4,702	134	2.8
Pulaski County, AR	28.1	3.0	186,483	76.1	47,129	13.0	167,538	161,135	6,403	4.0
Saline County, AR	16.4	1.3	41,764	79.7	5,890	7.1	37,431	33,825	3,606	10.7
Logan, UT-ID	29.6	6.3	52,091	68.2	12,849	12.5	36,403	32,907	3,496	10.6
Franklin County, ID	13.6	3.4	5,190	67.8	832	7.3	4,148	3,872	276	7.1
Cache County, UT	31.9	6.7	46,901	68.3	12,017	13.1	32,255	29,035	3,220	11.1
Longview, TX	16.2	4.6	88,156	75.8	28,022	14.4	83,184	81,146	2,038	2.5
Gregg County, TX	19.5	5.4	52,708	76.2	16,329	14.7	47,444	46,349	1,095	2.4
Rusk County, TX	12.8	4.4	19,914	76.8	6,526	13.8	20,341	19,867	474	2.4
Upshur County, TX	11.1	2.0	15,534	73.2	5,167	14.6	15,399	14,930	469	3.1
Longview, WA	13.3	3.7	43,307	74.1	12,765	13.7	40,261	38,624	1,637	4.2
Cowlitz County, WA	13.3	3.7	43,307	74.1	12,765	13.7	40,261	38,624	1,637	4.2
Los Angeles-Long Beach-Santa Ana, CA	**26.3**	**34.8**	**5,724,165**	**65.0**	**1,964,074**	**15.9**	**4,329,148**	**4,240,390**	**88,758**	**2.1**
Los Angeles-Long Beach-Glendale, CA	*24.9*	*36.2*	*4,312,264*	*63.0*	*1,674,599*	*17.6*	*3,319,806*	*3,270,906*	*48,900*	*1.5*
Los Angeles County, CA	24.9	36.2	4,312,264	63.0	1,674,599	17.6	3,319,806	3,270,906	48,900	1.5
Santa Ana-Anaheim-Irvine, CA	*30.8*	*29.9*	*1,411,901*	*71.2*	*289,475*	*10.2*	*1,009,342*	*969,484*	*39,858*	*4.1*
Orange County, CA	30.8	29.9	1,411,901	71.2	289,475	10.2	1,009,342	969,484	39,858	4.1
Louisville, KY-IN	21.2	2.6	595,942	76.6	124,257	10.7	524,401	492,296	32,105	6.5
Clark County, IN	14.3	1.7	51,728	78.7	7,683	8.0	45,067	41,176	3,891	9.4
Floyd County, IN	20.4	1.2	37,408	80.7	6,096	8.6	30,618	29,087	1,531	5.3
Harrison County, IN	13.1	0.9	18,355	77.1	2,159	6.3	14,565	13,699	866	6.3
Washington County, IN	10.2	0.5	13,813	74.6	2,845	10.5	11,779	11,191	588	5.3
Bullitt County, KY	9.2	0.6	32,120	81.0	4,806	7.8	26,338	23,160	3,178	13.7
Henry County, KY	9.8	1.4	7,495	71.5	2,041	13.6	6,789	6,381	408	6.4
Jefferson County, KY	24.8	3.4	353,318	75.3	84,143	12.1	319,112	305,835	13,277	4.3
Meade County, KY	11.3	2.0	12,535	75.9	2,965	11.3	10,753	10,293	460	4.5
Nelson County, KY	13.4	1.2	18,682	77.0	4,497	12.0	16,900	14,934	1,966	13.2
Oldham County, KY	30.6	1.6	22,618	82.1	1,717	3.7	18,590	15,691	2,899	18.5
Shelby County, KY	18.7	3.9	17,693	74.7	3,198	9.6	14,596	12,857	1,739	13.5
Spencer County, KY	11.1	1.2	6,218	79.4	1,015	8.6	5,735	4,555	1,180	25.9
Trimble County, KY	7.6	1.1	3,959	71.4	1,092	13.4	3,559	3,437	122	3.5
Lubbock, TX	24.0	3.4	124,800	74.5	43,496	17.4	111,395	103,797	7,598	7.3
Crosby County, TX	10.5	3.9	2,886	70.2	1,954	27.6	3,218	3,202	16	0.5
Lubbock County, TX	24.4	3.3	121,914	74.6	41,542	17.1	108,177	100,595	7,582	7.5
Lynchburg, VA	18.7	1.9	113,428	76.7	24,900	10.9	103,367	98,057	5,310	5.4
Amherst County, VA	13.1	1.2	15,431	74.4	3,238	10.2	13,421	12,958	463	3.6
Appomattox County, VA	10.5	1.4	6,593	78.2	1,547	11.3	6,107	5,828	279	4.8
Bedford County, VA	20.9	1.8	31,345	81.3	4,263	7.1	29,019	26,841	2,178	8.1
Campbell County, VA	14.6	1.1	25,914	81.3	5,329	10.4	23,225	22,088	1,137	5.1
Bedford city, VA	15.2	1.6	2,865	62.5	1,160	18.4	2,752	2,702	50	1.9
Lynchburg city, VA	25.2	3.2	31,280	70.2	9,363	14.3	28,843	27,640	1,203	4.4
Macon, GA	18.7	1.6	102,366	74.0	36,771	16.5	99,229	94,063	5,166	5.5
Bibb County, GA	21.3	1.9	69,936	72.3	28,370	18.4	70,017	67,194	2,823	4.2
Crawford County, GA	6.8	0.5	5,667	78.2	1,904	15.2	5,456	4,872	584	12.0
Jones County, GA	15.0	1.0	11,347	79.6	2,375	10.0	10,345	9,272	1,073	11.6
Monroe County, GA	17.1	1.0	10,801	79.3	2,069	9.5	8,997	8,434	563	6.7
Twiggs County, GA	5.4	0.8	4,615	69.0	2,053	19.4	4,414	4,291	123	2.9
Madera, CA	12.0	20.1	48,667	61.5	24,514	19.9	43,897	40,387	3,510	8.7
Madera County, CA	12.0	20.1	48,667	61.5	24,514	19.9	43,897	40,387	3,510	8.7
Madison, WI	36.9	5.5	297,688	70.7	43,111	8.6	232,911	212,662	20,249	9.5
Columbia County, WI	16.7	1.3	28,369	75.8	2,656	5.1	24,253	22,685	1,568	6.9
Dane County, WI	40.6	6.3	256,180	70.2	38,815	9.1	198,191	180,398	17,793	9.9
Iowa County, WI	18.5	0.6	13,139	70.8	1,640	7.2	10,467	9,579	888	9.3
Manchester-Nashua, NH	30.1	6.8	209,738	79.0	23,358	6.1	157,453	149,961	7,492	5.0
Hillsborough County, NH	30.1	6.8	209,738	79.0	23,358	6.1	157,453	149,961	7,492	5.0
Mansfield, OH	12.6	1.8	61,318	78.9	12,941	10.0	54,698	53,062	1,636	3.1
Richland County, OH	12.6	1.8	61,318	78.9	12,941	10.0	54,698	53,062	1,636	3.1
McAllen-Edinburg-Mission, TX	12.9	29.5	204,906	63.4	201,865	35.4	222,809	192,658	30,151	15.7
Hidalgo County, TX	12.9	29.5	204,906	63.4	201,865	35.4	222,809	192,658	30,151	15.7
Medford, OR	22.3	4.9	87,189	70.3	22,269	12.3	82,297	75,737	6,560	8.7
Jackson County, OR	22.3	4.9	87,189	70.3	22,269	12.3	82,297	75,737	6,560	8.7

See footnotes at end of table.

State and Metropolitan Area Data Book: 2006

Metropolitan statistical area / Metropolitan statistical area with metropolitan divisions / *Metropolitan division* / Component county	2000 Educational attainment, percent with bachelor's degree or higher[1]	2000 Percent foreign born	2000 Workers 16 years and over Total workers	2000 Workers 16 years and over Percent of workers who drove alone to work	Persons below poverty level in 1999 Total persons	Persons below poverty level in 1999 Percent of persons below poverty level in 1999	Housing units 2004 (July 1)	Housing units 2000[2] (estimates base)	Housing units Change 2000–2004[3] Number	Housing units Change 2000–2004[3] Percent
Memphis, TN-MS-AR	22.0	3.2	587,466	74.0	184,381	15.3	518,296	480,841	37,455	7.8
Crittenden County, AR	12.8	1.2	22,102	72.6	12,688	24.9	21,665	20,507	1,158	5.6
DeSoto County, MS	14.3	1.9	55,827	80.7	7,571	7.1	50,464	40,795	9,669	23.7
Marshall County, MS	9.0	1.0	15,168	68.8	7,282	20.8	13,805	13,252	553	4.2
Tate County, MS	12.3	0.2	11,914	68.0	3,287	13.0	10,144	9,354	790	8.4
Tunica County, MS	9.1	0.9	4,004	65.8	2,999	32.5	4,344	3,705	639	17.2
Fayette County, TN	12.8	0.7	13,526	74.6	4,053	14.1	12,117	11,210	907	8.1
Shelby County, TN	25.3	3.8	440,141	73.4	140,398	15.6	384,367	362,954	21,413	5.9
Tipton County, TN	10.8	0.8	24,784	77.5	6,103	11.9	21,390	19,064	2,326	12.2
Merced, CA	11.0	24.8	86,678	61.7	45,059	21.4	75,110	68,373	6,737	9.9
Merced County, CA	11.0	24.8	86,678	61.7	45,059	21.4	75,110	68,373	6,737	9.9
Miami-Fort Lauderdale-Miami Beach, FL	**24.1**	**35.0**	**2,324,501**	**70.5**	**692,014**	**13.8**	**2,294,911**	**2,149,890**	**145,021**	**6.7**
Fort Lauderdale-Pompano Beach-Deerfield Beach, FL	*24.5*	*25.3*	*803,157*	*74.1*	*184,589*	*11.4*	*782,384*	*741,043*	*41,341*	*5.6*
Broward County, FL	24.5	25.3	803,157	74.1	184,589	11.4	782,384	741,043	41,341	5.6
Miami-Miami Beach-Kendall, FL	*21.7*	*50.9*	*1,010,965*	*65.7*	*396,995*	*17.6*	*906,877*	*852,414*	*54,463*	*6.4*
Miami-Dade County, FL	21.7	50.9	1,010,965	65.7	396,995	17.6	906,877	852,414	54,463	6.4
West Palm Beach-Boca Raton-Boynton Beach, FL	*27.7*	*17.4*	*510,379*	*74.2*	*110,430*	*9.8*	*605,650*	*556,433*	*49,217*	*8.8*
Palm Beach County, FL	27.7	17.4	510,379	74.2	110,430	9.8	605,650	556,433	49,217	8.8
Michigan City-La Porte, IN	14.0	2.5	53,431	78.4	8,994	8.2	47,158	45,621	1,537	3.4
LaPorte County, IN	14.0	2.5	53,431	78.4	8,994	8.2	47,158	45,621	1,537	3.4
Midland, TX	24.8	7.6	54,645	77.5	14,758	12.7	49,013	48,060	953	2.0
Midland County, TX	24.8	7.6	54,645	77.5	14,758	12.7	49,013	48,060	953	2.0
Milwaukee-Waukesha-West Allis, WI	27.0	5.4	782,552	74.0	155,664	10.4	637,701	618,245	19,456	3.1
Milwaukee County, WI	23.6	6.8	469,688	68.3	139,747	14.9	403,863	400,093	3,770	0.9
Ozaukee County, WI	38.6	3.3	45,255	81.5	2,078	2.5	34,236	32,034	2,202	6.9
Washington County, WI	21.9	1.9	66,549	81.8	4,204	3.6	49,718	45,809	3,909	8.5
Waukesha County, WI	34.1	3.6	201,060	83.3	9,635	2.7	149,884	140,309	9,575	6.8
Minneapolis-St. Paul-Bloomington, MN-WI	33.3	7.1	1,679,836	74.4	195,253	6.6	1,265,792	1,169,776	96,016	8.2
Anoka County, MN	21.3	3.6	170,915	78.4	12,367	4.1	118,013	108,091	9,922	9.2
Carver County, MN	34.3	3.4	39,072	78.9	2,391	3.4	30,506	24,883	5,623	22.6
Chisago County, MN	15.3	1.2	21,840	77.1	2,052	5.0	18,232	15,533	2,699	17.4
Dakota County, MN	34.9	5.1	206,500	79.9	12,757	3.6	147,976	133,750	14,226	10.6
Hennepin County, MN	39.1	9.9	641,557	70.9	90,384	8.1	487,947	468,824	19,123	4.1
Isanti County, MN	14.5	1.3	17,120	75.2	1,753	5.6	14,194	12,061	2,133	17.7
Ramsey County, MN	34.3	10.6	277,129	70.5	52,673	10.3	210,830	206,448	4,382	2.1
Scott County, MN	29.4	4.0	50,862	80.2	2,979	3.3	40,624	31,609	9,015	28.5
Sherburne County, MN	19.4	1.5	35,429	78.1	2,776	4.3	28,230	22,827	5,403	23.7
Washington County, MN	33.9	3.4	111,853	80.5	5,765	2.9	81,988	73,635	8,353	11.3
Wright County, MN	17.9	1.1	49,527	76.6	4,211	4.7	42,597	34,357	8,240	24.0
Pierce County, WI	24.6	1.0	22,165	70.6	2,652	7.2	14,832	13,493	1,339	9.9
St. Croix County, WI	26.3	1.1	35,867	77.4	2,493	3.9	29,823	24,265	5,558	22.9
Missoula, MT	32.8	2.3	53,808	67.3	13,691	14.3	44,351	41,319	3,032	7.3
Missoula County, MT	32.8	2.3	53,808	67.3	13,691	14.3	44,351	41,319	3,032	7.3
Mobile, AL	18.6	2.3	179,280	74.9	72,549	18.1	172,738	165,101	7,637	4.6
Mobile County, AL	18.6	2.3	179,280	74.9	72,549	18.1	172,738	165,101	7,637	4.6
Modesto, CA	14.1	18.3	197,448	66.2	70,406	15.8	163,880	150,807	13,073	8.7
Stanislaus County, CA	14.1	18.3	197,448	66.2	70,406	15.8	163,880	150,807	13,073	8.7
Monroe, LA	21.2	1.0	79,910	73.7	33,663	19.8	73,296	71,027	2,269	3.2
Ouachita Parish, LA	22.7	1.0	69,940	74.0	29,515	20.0	61,958	60,154	1,804	3.0
Union Parish, LA	11.8	1.2	9,970	71.3	4,148	18.2	11,338	10,873	465	4.3
Monroe, MI	14.3	1.9	72,941	83.2	10,161	7.0	62,081	56,471	5,610	9.9
Monroe County, MI	14.3	1.9	72,941	83.2	10,161	7.0	62,081	56,471	5,610	9.9
Montgomery, AL	24.2	1.6	161,764	76.5	51,943	15.0	151,297	144,635	6,662	4.6
Autauga County, AL	18.0	1.2	21,167	77.9	4,738	10.8	18,975	17,662	1,313	7.4
Elmore County, AL	16.6	1.1	30,056	79.0	6,187	9.4	27,612	25,735	1,877	7.3
Lowndes County, AL	11.0	0.3	5,061	66.3	4,209	31.2	5,859	5,801	58	1.0
Montgomery County, AL	28.5	2.0	105,480	76.0	36,809	16.5	98,851	95,437	3,414	3.6
Morgantown, WV	26.0	3.0	53,488	69.5	22,696	20.4	51,265	50,139	1,126	2.2
Monongalia County, WV	32.4	3.8	40,551	69.2	17,394	21.2	37,533	36,695	838	2.3
Preston County, WV	10.8	0.6	12,937	70.4	5,302	18.1	13,732	13,444	288	2.1
Morristown, TN	12.2	3.2	59,927	77.9	17,740	14.4	56,815	53,744	3,071	5.7
Grainger County, TN	7.8	1.1	9,397	76.1	3,809	18.4	10,121	9,732	389	4.0
Hamblen County, TN	13.3	5.3	28,662	79.8	8,236	14.2	25,750	24,693	1,057	4.3
Jefferson County, TN	12.8	1.5	21,868	76.1	5,695	12.9	20,944	19,319	1,625	8.4
Mount Vernon-Anacortes, WA	20.8	8.8	49,692	70.6	11,244	10.9	45,724	42,681	3,043	7.1
Skagit County, WA	20.8	8.8	49,692	70.6	11,244	10.9	45,724	42,681	3,043	7.1
Muncie, IN	20.4	1.5	60,139	73.5	16,862	14.2	52,441	51,032	1,409	2.8
Delaware County, IN	20.4	1.5	60,139	73.5	16,862	14.2	52,441	51,032	1,409	2.8
Muskegon-Norton Shores, MI	13.9	1.9	81,221	77.9	18,752	11.0	72,069	68,556	3,513	5.1
Muskegon County, MI	13.9	1.9	81,221	77.9	18,752	11.0	72,069	68,556	3,513	5.1
Myrtle Beach-Conway-North Myrtle Beach, SC	18.7	4.0	102,356	73.9	23,356	11.9	140,628	122,085	18,543	15.2
Horry County, SC	18.7	4.0	102,356	73.9	23,356	11.9	140,628	122,085	18,543	15.2

See footnotes at end of table.

Metropolitan statistical area **Metropolitan statistical area with metropolitan divisions** *Metropolitan division* Component county	2000				Persons below poverty level in 1999		Housing units			
			Workers 16 years and over						Change	
	Educational attainment, percent with bachelor's degree or higher[1]	Percent foreign born	Total workers	Percent of workers who drove alone to work	Total persons	Percent of persons below poverty level in 1999	2004 (July 1)	2000[2] (estimates base)	2000–2004[3]	
									Number	Percent
Napa, CA	26.4	18.1	61,208	68.1	9,913	8.0	51,326	48,554	2,772	5.7
Napa County, CA	26.4	18.1	61,208	68.1	9,913	8.0	51,326	48,554	2,772	5.7
Naples-Marco Island, FL	27.9	18.3	109,476	70.1	25,449	10.1	174,564	144,536	30,028	20.8
Collier County, FL	27.9	18.3	109,476	70.1	25,449	10.1	174,564	144,536	30,028	20.8
Nashville-Davidson—Murfreesboro, TN	25.6	4.5	700,392	75.4	131,548	10.0	594,091	543,271	50,820	9.4
Cannon County, TN	8.4	0.8	6,217	71.4	1,609	12.5	5,617	5,420	197	3.6
Cheatham County, TN	15.1	1.1	18,933	75.1	2,635	7.3	14,824	13,508	1,316	9.7
Davidson County, TN	30.5	6.9	307,653	73.1	70,960	12.5	266,234	252,978	13,256	5.2
Dickson County, TN	11.3	0.7	21,657	74.2	4,334	10.0	19,083	17,614	1,469	8.3
Hickman County, TN	6.7	0.8	9,529	71.5	2,986	13.4	9,228	8,904	324	3.6
Macon County, TN	5.6	1.8	10,014	68.1	3,038	14.9	9,267	8,894	373	4.2
Robertson County, TN	11.9	2.5	28,585	76.2	4,840	8.9	23,527	20,995	2,532	12.1
Rutherford County, TN	22.9	3.6	101,245	77.5	15,808	8.7	84,753	70,616	14,137	20.0
Smith County, TN	9.3	0.9	8,625	76.6	2,141	12.1	7,987	7,665	322	4.2
Sumner County, TN	18.6	2.4	68,565	78.3	10,463	8.0	56,907	51,657	5,250	10.2
Trousdale County, TN	8.9	1.7	3,423	72.2	954	13.1	3,241	3,095	146	4.7
Williamson County, TN	44.4	3.9	67,362	80.2	5,933	4.7	54,314	47,005	7,309	15.5
Wilson County, TN	19.6	1.4	48,584	78.6	5,847	6.6	39,109	34,920	4,189	12.0
New Haven-Milford, CT	27.6	9.0	421,514	74.3	75,733	9.2	345,094	340,732	4,362	1.3
New Haven County, CT	27.6	9.0	421,514	74.3	75,733	9.2	345,094	340,732	4,362	1.3
New Orleans-Metairie-Kenner, LA	22.8	4.9	616,770	66.5	236,747	18.0	563,028	548,629	14,399	2.6
Jefferson Parish, LA	21.5	7.5	226,332	72.7	61,608	13.5	191,451	187,907	3,544	1.9
Orleans Parish, LA	25.8	4.2	213,819	53.2	130,896	27.0	212,781	215,091	–2,310	–1.1
Plaquemines Parish, LA	10.8	2.8	10,973	70.5	4,682	17.5	11,142	10,481	661	6.3
St. Bernard Parish, LA	8.9	3.0	31,267	72.4	8,687	12.9	27,229	26,790	439	1.6
St. Charles Parish, LA	17.5	2.5	22,818	77.9	5,424	11.3	18,362	17,430	932	5.3
St. John the Baptist Parish, LA	12.9	2.3	19,218	72.5	7,114	16.5	16,632	15,532	1,100	7.1
St. Tammany Parish, LA	28.3	2.4	92,343	75.7	18,336	9.6	85,431	75,398	10,033	13.3
New York-Northern New Jersey-Long Island, NY-NJ-PA	**30.3**	**26.4**	**8,754,250**	**48.0**	**2,451,775**	**13.4**	**7,238,782**	**7,091,153**	**147,629**	**2.1**
Edison, NJ	*32.0*	*15.3*	*1,087,185*	*72.5*	*132,453*	*6.1*	*914,028*	*875,255*	*38,773*	*4.4*
Middlesex County, NJ	33.0	24.2	391,203	69.1	48,205	6.4	280,757	273,637	7,120	2.6
Monmouth County, NJ	34.6	10.4	311,406	71.0	38,242	6.2	249,852	240,884	8,968	3.7
Ocean County, NJ	19.5	6.5	225,604	76.8	34,945	6.8	265,447	248,711	16,736	6.7
Somerset County, NJ	46.5	18.1	158,972	77.7	11,061	3.7	117,972	112,023	5,949	5.3
Nassau-Suffolk, NY	*31.3*	*14.4*	*1,367,434*	*69.7*	*151,802*	*5.5*	*994,466*	*980,474*	*13,992*	*1.4*
Nassau County, NY	35.4	17.9	655,809	65.5	68,631	5.1	458,004	458,151	–147	0.0
Suffolk County, NY	27.5	11.2	711,625	73.6	83,171	5.9	536,462	522,323	14,139	2.7
Newark-Union, NJ-PA	*32.2*	*18.6*	*1,045,063*	*66.4*	*193,095*	*9.2*	*824,179*	*804,577*	*19,602*	*2.4*
Essex County, NJ	27.5	21.2	370,939	54.4	120,006	15.1	304,878	301,011	3,867	1.3
Hunterdon County, NJ	41.8	6.3	65,107	79.1	3,027	2.5	47,527	45,032	2,495	5.5
Morris County, NJ	44.1	15.4	252,892	77.0	17,872	3.8	181,257	174,379	6,878	3.9
Sussex County, NJ	27.2	5.7	76,705	79.6	5,693	3.9	59,045	56,529	2,516	4.5
Union County, NJ	28.5	25.1	258,641	65.5	43,319	8.3	194,227	192,945	1,282	0.7
Pike County, PA	19.0	5.0	20,779	73.1	3,178	6.9	37,245	34,681	2,564	7.4
New York-White Plains-Wayne, NY-NJ	*29.4*	*33.0*	*5,254,568*	*33.6*	*1,974,425*	*17.5*	*4,506,109*	*4,430,847*	*75,262*	*1.7*
Bergen County, NJ	38.2	25.1	453,774	68.6	43,417	4.9	344,721	339,820	4,901	1.4
Hudson County, NJ	25.3	38.5	297,702	37.3	93,149	15.3	244,332	240,618	3,714	1.5
Passaic County, NJ	21.2	26.6	232,485	64.5	59,072	12.1	170,978	170,048	930	0.5
Bronx County, NY	14.6	29.0	500,716	22.4	395,263	29.7	498,593	490,659	7,934	1.6
Kings County, NY	21.8	37.8	1,039,512	19.4	610,476	24.8	943,531	930,867	12,664	1.4
New York County, NY	49.4	29.4	841,633	6.8	298,231	19.4	817,462	798,144	19,318	2.4
Putnam County, NY	33.9	8.8	50,709	75.1	4,110	4.3	36,216	35,030	1,186	3.4
Queens County, NY	24.3	46.1	1,037,238	30.8	321,102	14.4	827,259	817,250	10,009	1.2
Richmond County, NY	23.2	16.4	207,766	50.0	43,866	9.9	172,247	163,993	8,254	5.0
Rockland County, NY	37.5	19.1	140,516	69.4	26,772	9.3	96,411	94,973	1,438	1.5
Westchester County, NY	40.9	22.2	452,517	57.8	78,967	8.6	354,359	349,445	4,914	1.4
Niles-Benton Harbor, MI	19.6	4.9	81,078	75.6	20,202	12.4	75,444	73,445	1,999	2.7
Berrien County, MI	19.6	4.9	81,078	75.6	20,202	12.4	75,444	73,445	1,999	2.7
Norwich-New London, CT	26.2	5.4	137,406	76.5	15,780	6.1	113,666	110,674	2,992	2.7
New London County, CT	26.2	5.4	137,406	76.5	15,780	6.1	113,666	110,674	2,992	2.7
Ocala, FL	13.7	5.2	104,422	74.4	32,918	12.7	140,344	122,663	17,681	14.4
Marion County, FL	13.7	5.2	104,422	74.4	32,918	12.7	140,344	122,663	17,681	14.4
Ocean City, NJ	22.0	3.2	49,201	71.6	8,549	8.4	96,405	91,047	5,358	5.9
Cape May County, NJ	22.0	3.2	49,201	71.6	8,549	8.4	96,405	91,047	5,358	5.9
Odessa, TX	12.0	10.6	54,197	74.0	22,310	18.4	50,577	49,500	1,077	2.2
Ector County, TX	12.0	10.6	54,197	74.0	22,310	18.4	50,577	49,500	1,077	2.2
Ogden-Clearfield, UT	24.6	4.8	221,334	73.7	30,375	6.9	162,948	146,726	16,222	11.1
Davis County, UT	28.8	3.6	119,468	74.5	11,984	5.0	83,611	74,114	9,497	12.8
Morgan County, UT	23.3	2.7	3,307	71.7	369	5.2	2,415	2,158	257	11.9
Weber County, UT	19.9	6.4	98,559	72.9	18,022	9.2	76,922	70,454	6,468	9.2
Oklahoma City, OK	24.2	5.6	551,170	76.3	143,729	13.1	497,594	472,084	25,510	5.4
Canadian County, OK	20.9	3.2	45,422	81.4	6,751	7.7	37,279	33,969	3,310	9.7
Cleveland County, OK	28.0	4.4	111,190	79.0	20,977	10.1	91,633	84,844	6,789	8.0
Grady County, OK	14.4	1.1	21,681	75.6	6,209	13.6	20,086	19,444	642	3.3
Lincoln County, OK	11.1	0.8	14,706	71.8	4,591	14.3	14,070	13,712	358	2.6
Logan County, OK	19.1	1.5	16,979	72.3	4,170	12.3	14,214	13,906	308	2.2
McClain County, OK	15.7	2.6	13,525	76.7	2,886	10.4	11,944	11,189	755	6.7
Oklahoma County, OK	25.4	7.2	327,667	75.2	98,145	14.9	308,368	295,020	13,348	4.5

See footnotes at end of table.

State and Metropolitan Area Data Book: 2006

U.S. Census Bureau

Table C-2. Metropolitan Areas With Component Counties — **Population Characteristics and Housing Units**—Con.

Metropolitan statistical area / **Metropolitan statistical area with metropolitan divisions** / *Metropolitan division* / Component county	2000 Educational attainment, percent with bachelor's degree or higher[1]	2000 Percent foreign born	2000 Workers 16 years and over — Total workers	2000 Workers — Percent of workers who drove alone to work	Persons below poverty level in 1999 — Total persons	Persons below poverty — Percent of persons below poverty level in 1999	Housing units 2004 (July 1)	Housing units 2000[2] (estimates base)	Housing units Change 2000–2004[3] Number	Housing units Change Percent
Olympia, WA	29.8	6.1	108,808	71.6	17,992	8.7	93,039	86,652	6,387	7.4
Thurston County, WA	29.8	6.1	108,808	71.6	17,992	8.7	93,039	86,652	6,387	7.4
Omaha-Council Bluffs, NE-IA	27.1	4.5	415,588	78.5	62,703	8.2	334,009	311,587	22,422	7.2
Harrison County, IA	12.7	0.8	7,839	71.1	1,093	7.0	6,858	6,602	256	3.9
Mills County, IA	16.3	1.0	7,780	74.3	1,151	7.9	5,900	5,671	229	4.0
Pottawattamie County, IA	15.0	2.0	46,671	77.0	7,200	8.2	37,913	35,808	2,105	5.9
Cass County, NE	18.7	1.2	13,086	78.3	1,239	5.1	10,802	10,179	623	6.1
Douglas County, NE	30.6	5.9	250,082	78.0	44,553	9.6	203,611	192,672	10,939	5.7
Sarpy County, NE	30.2	3.7	69,079	82.9	5,092	4.2	52,370	44,981	7,389	16.4
Saunders County, NE	16.9	1.2	10,554	77.2	1,291	6.5	8,740	8,266	474	5.7
Washington County, NE	22.7	1.6	10,497	79.7	1,084	5.8	7,815	7,408	407	5.5
Orlando - Kissimee, FL	24.8	12.0	840,887	75.3	172,476	10.5	786,786	683,551	103,235	15.1
Lake County, FL	16.6	5.1	86,307	76.1	19,907	9.5	121,564	102,829	18,735	18.2
Orange County, FL	26.1	14.4	471,974	74.4	106,233	11.9	409,685	361,349	48,336	13.4
Osceola County, FL	15.7	14.0	84,142	72.4	19,532	11.3	93,352	72,293	21,059	29.1
Seminole County, FL	31.0	9.1	198,464	78.5	26,804	7.3	162,185	147,080	15,105	10.3
Oshkosh-Neenah, WI	22.8	2.8	85,874	79.8	9,940	6.3	69,258	64,721	4,537	7.0
Winnebago County, WI	22.8	2.8	85,874	79.8	9,940	6.3	69,258	64,721	4,537	7.0
Owensboro, KY	15.6	1.0	54,287	78.7	13,713	12.5	49,868	46,424	3,444	7.4
Daviess County, KY	17.0	1.0	45,681	78.8	11,024	12.0	41,662	38,432	3,230	8.4
Hancock County, KY	8.1	0.8	4,007	80.9	1,127	13.4	3,672	3,600	72	2.0
McLean County, KY	8.7	0.7	4,599	76.3	1,562	15.7	4,534	4,392	142	3.2
Oxnard-Thousand Oaks-Ventura, CA	26.9	20.7	372,020	70.5	68,540	9.1	264,339	251,711	12,628	5.0
Ventura County, CA	26.9	20.7	372,020	70.5	68,540	9.1	264,339	251,711	12,628	5.0
Palm Bay-Melbourne-Titusville, FL	23.6	6.5	220,413	77.6	44,218	9.3	243,652	222,072	21,580	9.7
Brevard County, FL	23.6	6.5	220,413	77.6	44,218	9.3	243,652	222,072	21,580	9.7
Panama City-Lynn Haven, FL	17.7	3.6	72,124	75.8	18,882	12.7	86,013	78,435	7,578	9.7
Bay County, FL	17.7	3.6	72,124	75.8	18,882	12.7	86,013	78,435	7,578	9.7
Parkersburg-Marietta-Vienna, WV-OH	14.7	0.8	77,570	77.0	21,111	12.8	75,168	74,025	1,143	1.5
Washington County, OH	15.0	0.6	30,918	76.8	7,002	11.1	28,081	27,760	321	1.2
Pleasants County, WV	9.7	0.5	3,194	78.2	992	13.2	3,242	3,214	28	0.9
Wirt County, WV	9.9	0.3	2,412	71.1	1,138	19.4	3,361	3,266	95	2.9
Wood County, WV	15.2	1.1	41,046	77.4	11,979	13.6	40,484	39,785	699	1.8
Pascagoula, MS	15.5	2.5	71,293	73.7	19,644	13.0	63,278	59,191	4,087	6.9
George County, MS	9.1	1.3	8,116	61.6	3,140	16.4	7,730	7,513	217	2.9
Jackson County, MS	16.5	2.7	63,177	75.3	16,504	12.6	55,548	51,678	3,870	7.5
Pensacola-Ferry Pass-Brent, FL	21.5	3.5	195,138	72.6	53,260	12.9	186,802	173,766	13,036	7.5
Escambia County, FL	21.0	3.7	139,584	70.7	41,978	14.3	132,017	124,647	7,370	5.9
Santa Rosa County, FL	22.9	3.0	55,554	77.4	11,282	9.6	54,785	49,119	5,666	11.5
Peoria, IL	20.8	2.1	184,290	78.3	34,760	9.5	158,426	153,285	5,141	3.4
Marshall County, IL	14.5	1.0	6,837	75.8	715	5.4	6,087	5,896	191	3.2
Peoria County, IL	23.3	3.2	90,729	76.7	24,228	13.2	80,526	78,204	2,322	3.0
Stark County, IL	13.4	0.4	2,865	71.6	534	8.4	2,803	2,725	78	2.9
Tazewell County, IL	18.1	1.1	65,680	80.5	7,806	6.1	54,754	52,973	1,781	3.4
Woodford County, IL	21.1	1.0	18,179	79.6	1,477	4.2	14,256	13,487	769	5.7
Philadelphia-Camden-Wilmington, PA-NJ-DE-MD	**27.7**	**6.9**	**2,825,656**	**67.3**	**598,949**	**10.5**	**2,342,807**	**2,281,823**	**60,984**	**2.7**
Camden, NJ	*25.2*	*5.9*	*603,361*	*73.3*	*86,796*	*7.3*	*473,962*	*456,043*	*17,919*	*3.9*
Burlington County, NJ	28.4	6.3	219,871	78.0	19,280	4.6	169,905	161,310	8,595	5.3
Camden County, NJ	24.0	6.9	250,704	68.0	52,121	10.2	202,772	199,679	3,093	1.5
Gloucester County, NJ	22.0	3.4	132,786	75.5	15,395	6.0	101,285	95,054	6,231	6.6
Philadelphia, PA	*28.8*	*7.4*	*1,882,518*	*64.1*	*459,397*	*11.9*	*1,596,115*	*1,565,640*	*30,475*	*1.9*
Bucks County, PA	31.2	5.9	320,110	78.7	26,562	4.4	235,423	225,497	9,926	4.4
Chester County, PA	42.5	5.5	229,631	76.7	22,032	5.1	175,474	163,773	11,701	7.1
Delaware County, PA	30.0	6.7	272,268	70.3	42,411	7.7	219,732	216,978	2,754	1.3
Montgomery County, PA	38.7	7.0	403,574	75.8	32,215	4.3	306,687	297,434	9,253	3.1
Philadelphia County, PA	17.9	9.0	656,935	42.7	336,177	22.2	658,799	661,958	-3,159	-0.5
Wilmington, DE-MD-NJ	*26.3*	*5.5*	*339,777*	*74.4*	*52,756*	*8.1*	*272,730*	*260,140*	*12,590*	*4.8*
New Castle County, DE	29.5	6.6	263,440	73.5	40,710	8.1	207,669	199,521	8,148	4.1
Cecil County, MD	16.4	1.8	44,866	78.0	6,066	7.1	38,271	34,461	3,810	11.1
Salem County, NJ	15.2	2.5	31,471	76.5	5,980	9.3	26,790	26,158	632	2.4
Phoenix-Mesa-Scottsdale, AZ	25.1	14.1	1,571,024	69.7	383,484	11.8	1,527,894	1,331,385	196,509	14.8
Maricopa County, AZ	25.9	14.4	1,504,252	69.8	355,668	11.6	1,429,101	1,250,231	178,870	14.3
Pinal County, AZ	11.9	9.0	66,772	66.3	27,816	15.5	98,793	81,154	17,639	21.7
Pine Bluff, AR	14.1	1.1	45,176	72.2	19,689	18.3	44,197	43,139	1,058	2.5
Cleveland County, AR	10.0	1.4	3,867	71.7	1,297	15.1	3,941	3,834	107	2.8
Jefferson County, AR	15.7	1.1	36,322	72.6	16,203	19.2	35,176	34,350	826	2.4
Lincoln County, AR	7.6	0.7	4,987	69.6	2,189	15.1	5,080	4,955	125	2.5
Pittsburgh, PA	23.4	2.6	1,174,504	71.8	256,990	10.6	1,096,567	1,078,481	18,086	1.7
Allegheny County, PA	28.3	3.8	630,964	66.5	139,505	10.9	589,348	583,646	5,702	1.0
Armstrong County, PA	10.4	0.7	32,338	75.5	8,350	11.5	32,805	32,387	418	1.3
Beaver County, PA	15.8	1.7	87,264	77.8	16,635	9.2	78,825	77,765	1,060	1.4
Butler County, PA	23.5	1.4	86,400	79.7	15,269	8.8	74,032	69,868	4,164	6.0
Fayette County, PA	11.5	0.6	64,371	74.8	26,434	17.8	67,145	66,490	655	1.0
Washington County, PA	18.8	1.2	96,043	76.9	19,513	9.6	90,252	87,267	2,985	3.4
Westmoreland County, PA	20.2	1.4	177,124	79.0	31,284	8.5	164,160	161,058	3,102	1.9
Pittsfield, MA	26.0	3.7	68,806	73.7	12,204	9.0	67,146	66,301	845	1.3
Berkshire County, MA	26.0	3.7	68,806	73.7	12,204	9.0	67,146	66,301	845	1.3

See footnotes at end of table.

Metropolitan statistical area **Metropolitan statistical area with metropolitan divisions** *Metropolitan division* Component county	2000 Educational attainment, percent with bachelor's degree or higher[1]	2000 Percent foreign born	Workers 16 years and over Total workers	Workers 16 years and over Percent of workers who drove alone to work	Persons below poverty level in 1999 Total persons	Persons below poverty level in 1999 Percent of persons below poverty level in 1999	Housing units 2004 (July 1)	Housing units 2000[2] (estimates base)	Change 2000–2004[3] Number	Change 2000–2004[3] Percent
Pocatello, ID	24.0	2.9	41,857	71.6	11,381	13.7	33,105	31,946	1,159	3.6
Bannock County, ID	24.9	2.2	38,369	71.9	10,181	13.5	30,169	29,102	1,067	3.7
Power County, ID	14.3	10.5	3,488	67.8	1,200	15.9	2,936	2,844	92	3.2
Portland-South Portland-Biddeford, ME	29.2	3.3	263,255	75.4	38,369	7.9	245,624	233,323	12,301	5.3
Cumberland County, ME	34.2	3.8	145,269	74.6	20,352	7.7	128,734	122,600	6,134	5.0
Sagadahoc County, ME	25.0	2.4	18,952	73.6	3,014	8.6	17,149	16,489	660	4.0
York County, ME	22.9	2.8	99,034	77.0	15,003	8.0	99,741	94,234	5,507	5.8
Portland-Vancouver-Beaverton, OR-WA	28.8	10.8	1,031,059	67.8	179,809	9.3	844,347	790,876	53,471	6.8
Clackamas County, OR	28.4	7.1	178,724	73.1	21,969	6.5	144,766	136,954	7,812	5.7
Columbia County, OR	14.0	1.8	21,419	72.4	3,910	9.0	18,813	17,572	1,241	7.1
Multnomah County, OR	30.7	12.7	365,188	60.2	81,711	12.4	299,975	288,561	11,414	4.0
Washington County, OR	34.5	14.2	244,449	70.6	32,575	7.3	193,836	178,913	14,923	8.3
Yamhill County, OR	20.6	7.6	41,891	69.3	7,336	8.6	33,221	30,270	2,951	9.7
Clark County, WA	22.1	8.5	174,500	73.4	31,027	9.0	148,993	134,030	14,963	11.2
Skamania County, WA	16.8	3.5	4,888	66.2	1,281	13.0	4,743	4,576	167	3.6
Port St. Lucie-Fort Pierce, FL	19.7	9.5	135,540	74.4	36,308	11.4	179,702	156,733	22,969	14.7
Martin County, FL	26.3	8.1	53,332	74.6	10,844	8.6	71,572	65,471	6,101	9.3
St. Lucie County, FL	15.1	10.5	82,208	74.2	25,464	13.2	108,130	91,262	16,868	18.5
Poughkeepsie-Newburgh-Middletown, NY	24.9	8.4	303,673	71.6	54,530	8.8	239,906	228,857	11,049	4.8
Dutchess County, NY	27.6	8.4	138,815	72.6	19,858	7.1	109,896	106,103	3,793	3.6
Orange County, NY	22.5	8.4	164,858	70.8	34,672	10.2	130,010	122,754	7,256	5.9
Prescott, AZ	21.1	5.9	71,822	70.2	19,552	11.7	93,254	81,730	11,524	14.1
Yavapai County, AZ	21.1	5.9	71,822	70.2	19,552	11.7	93,254	81,730	11,524	14.1
Providence-New Bedford-Fall River, RI-MA	23.7	11.5	809,475	74.2	172,784	10.9	667,992	656,755	11,237	1.7
Bristol County, MA	19.9	11.7	275,122	75.5	52,236	9.8	221,687	216,918	4,769	2.2
Bristol County, RI	34.3	10.0	26,200	76.2	3,009	5.9	20,120	19,881	239	1.2
Kent County, RI	24.8	4.9	89,909	80.7	10,862	6.5	71,511	70,365	1,146	1.6
Newport County, RI	38.3	4.9	46,750	74.8	5,906	6.9	40,373	39,561	812	2.1
Providence County, RI	21.3	15.6	303,889	70.4	92,164	14.8	254,832	253,214	1,618	0.6
Washington County, RI	35.5	4.2	67,605	76.9	8,607	7.0	59,469	56,816	2,653	4.7
Provo-Orem, UT	31.0	6.2	178,172	67.8	44,117	11.7	125,226	107,126	18,100	16.9
Juab County, UT	12.2	1.4	3,547	64.2	847	10.3	3,132	2,810	322	11.5
Utah County, UT	31.5	6.3	174,625	67.9	43,270	11.7	122,094	104,316	17,778	17.0
Pueblo, CO	18.3	3.0	63,895	73.0	20,449	14.5	63,972	58,926	5,046	8.6
Pueblo County, CO	18.3	3.0	63,895	73.0	20,449	14.5	63,972	58,926	5,046	8.6
Punta Gorda, FL	17.6	8.0	52,542	77.2	11,419	8.1	87,954	79,758	8,196	10.3
Charlotte County, FL	17.6	8.0	52,542	77.2	11,419	8.1	87,954	79,758	8,196	10.3
Racine, WI	20.3	4.1	96,933	77.2	15,491	8.2	78,028	74,718	3,310	4.4
Racine County, WI	20.3	4.1	96,933	77.2	15,491	8.2	78,028	74,718	3,310	4.4
Raleigh-Cary, NC	37.6	8.7	444,143	76.3	68,874	8.6	383,121	329,493	53,628	16.3
Franklin County, NC	13.2	3.6	23,863	73.1	5,790	12.3	22,335	20,364	1,971	9.7
Johnston County, NC	15.9	5.9	62,248	75.3	15,399	12.6	57,313	50,175	7,138	14.2
Wake County, NC	43.9	9.7	358,032	76.7	47,685	7.6	303,473	258,954	44,519	17.2
Rapid City, SD	23.3	2.0	60,889	77.5	12,162	10.8	50,524	47,398	3,126	6.6
Meade County, SD	16.8	1.4	13,150	74.9	2,195	9.1	10,835	10,149	686	6.8
Pennington County, SD	25.0	2.1	47,739	78.2	9,967	11.3	39,689	37,249	2,440	6.6
Reading, PA	18.5	4.3	190,703	75.6	34,201	9.2	157,157	150,222	6,935	4.6
Berks County, PA	18.5	4.3	190,703	75.6	34,201	9.2	157,157	150,222	6,935	4.6
Redding, CA	16.6	4.0	72,193	71.2	24,556	15.0	73,250	68,810	4,440	6.5
Shasta County, CA	16.6	4.0	72,193	71.2	24,556	15.0	73,250	68,810	4,440	6.5
Reno-Sparks, NV	23.7	14.0	182,843	70.4	33,513	9.8	164,650	145,504	19,146	13.2
Storey County, NV	18.0	2.2	1,880	72.2	195	5.7	1,707	1,596	111	7.0
Washoe County, NV	23.7	14.1	180,963	70.3	33,318	9.8	162,943	143,908	19,035	13.2
Richmond, VA	27.6	4.2	570,130	76.9	99,314	9.1	485,593	452,684	32,909	7.3
Amelia County, VA	9.8	0.7	5,731	74.8	948	8.3	4,962	4,609	353	7.7
Caroline County, VA	12.1	1.7	11,025	72.8	2,008	9.1	9,815	8,889	926	10.4
Charles City County, VA	10.5	1.3	3,575	75.0	735	10.6	3,055	2,895	160	5.5
Chesterfield County, VA	32.6	5.2	140,775	81.9	11,586	4.5	108,794	97,707	11,087	11.3
Cumberland County, VA	11.8	1.3	4,189	72.9	1,360	15.1	4,307	4,085	222	5.4
Dinwiddie County, VA	11.0	1.4	11,977	80.4	2,185	8.9	10,444	9,707	737	7.6
Goochland County, VA	29.4	2.0	8,650	79.7	1,068	6.3	7,591	6,555	1,036	15.8
Hanover County, VA	28.7	1.8	46,256	82.8	3,065	3.6	35,944	32,196	3,748	11.6
Henrico County, VA	34.9	6.7	143,197	81.1	15,917	6.1	121,038	112,570	8,468	7.5
King and Queen County, VA	10.3	0.9	3,149	71.2	713	10.8	3,156	3,010	146	4.9
King William County, VA	14.8	1.2	6,925	78.7	713	5.4	5,656	5,189	467	9.0
Louisa County, VA	14.0	1.3	12,643	72.2	2,586	10.1	13,426	11,855	1,571	13.3
New Kent County, VA	16.3	0.9	7,282	79.7	644	4.8	6,029	5,203	826	15.9
Powhatan County, VA	19.1	1.2	10,839	82.0	1,133	5.1	8,725	7,509	1,216	16.2
Prince George County, VA	19.4	4.5	16,951	71.7	2,234	6.8	11,590	10,726	864	8.1
Sussex County, VA	10.0	1.0	4,505	74.8	1,597	12.8	4,709	4,653	56	1.2
Colonial Heights city, VA	19.0	4.9	8,496	84.2	913	5.4	7,588	7,340	248	3.4
Hopewell city, VA	10.2	1.9	10,142	75.2	3,263	14.6	9,909	9,749	160	1.6
Petersburg city, VA	14.8	2.3	14,814	65.3	6,461	19.1	15,879	15,955	−76	−0.5
Richmond city, VA	29.5	3.9	99,009	63.4	40,185	20.3	92,976	92,282	694	0.8

See footnotes at end of table.

Metropolitan statistical area **Metropolitan statistical area with metropolitan divisions** *Metropolitan division* Component county	2000				Persons below poverty level in 1999		Housing units			
	Educational attainment, percent with bachelor's degree or higher[1]	Percent foreign born	Workers 16 years and over			Percent of persons below poverty level in 1999	2004 (July 1)	2000[2] (estimates base)	Change 2000–2004[3]	
			Total workers	Percent of workers who drove alone to work	Total persons				Number	Percent
Riverside-San Bernardino-Ontario, CA	16.3	18.8	1,389,976	66.1	477,496	14.7	1,306,004	1,186,043	119,961	10.1
Riverside County, CA	16.6	19.0	654,387	66.3	214,084	13.9	670,202	584,674	85,528	14.6
San Bernardino County, CA	15.9	18.6	735,589	65.9	263,412	15.4	635,802	601,369	34,433	5.7
Roanoke, VA	21.0	2.4	147,721	78.9	26,630	9.2	135,697	129,589	6,108	4.7
Botetourt County, VA	19.6	0.9	16,171	83.3	1,559	5.1	13,405	12,571	834	6.6
Craig County, VA	10.8	0.3	2,443	75.6	520	10.2	2,712	2,554	158	6.2
Franklin County, VA	14.8	1.4	23,900	75.5	4,481	9.5	24,668	22,717	1,951	8.6
Roanoke County, VA	28.2	3.1	45,040	84.5	3,732	4.4	38,200	36,087	2,113	5.9
Roanoke city, VA	18.7	3.1	47,258	73.7	14,793	15.6	46,108	45,257	851	1.9
Salem city, VA	19.8	2.1	12,909	79.5	1,545	6.2	10,604	10,403	201	1.9
Rochester, MN	30.5	6.5	90,916	72.8	10,105	6.2	73,343	65,130	8,213	12.6
Dodge County, MN	17.1	2.5	9,707	73.8	1,020	5.8	7,444	6,642	802	12.1
Olmsted County, MN	34.7	7.9	69,525	73.2	7,806	6.3	56,123	49,422	6,701	13.6
Wabasha County, MN	16.9	2.0	11,684	69.9	1,279	5.9	9,776	9,066	710	7.8
Rochester, NY	27.7	5.9	528,343	75.5	104,742	10.1	436,636	427,172	9,464	2.2
Livingston County, NY	19.2	2.6	32,547	71.1	6,018	9.4	24,709	24,023	686	2.9
Monroe County, NY	31.2	7.3	374,449	75.6	79,311	10.8	310,613	304,388	6,225	2.0
Ontario County, NY	24.7	2.7	53,238	76.7	7,106	7.1	44,277	42,647	1,630	3.8
Orleans County, NY	13.0	2.7	20,116	72.7	4,378	9.9	17,463	17,347	116	0.7
Wayne County, NY	17.0	2.3	47,993	77.0	7,929	8.5	39,574	38,767	807	2.1
Rockford, IL	18.8	6.3	164,477	77.2	29,152	9.1	137,211	129,818	7,393	5.7
Boone County, IL	14.5	7.5	21,079	75.8	2,892	6.9	17,207	15,414	1,793	11.6
Winnebago County, IL	19.4	6.1	143,398	77.3	26,260	9.4	120,004	114,404	5,600	4.9
Rocky Mount, NC	13.9	2.6	67,169	73.3	22,161	15.5	64,515	61,052	3,463	5.7
Edgecombe County, NC	8.5	2.1	25,155	68.3	10,683	19.2	24,947	24,002	945	3.9
Nash County, NC	17.2	3.0	42,014	76.3	11,478	13.1	39,568	37,050	2,518	6.8
Rome, GA	15.8	5.2	43,331	72.9	12,538	13.8	38,552	36,615	1,937	5.3
Floyd County, GA	15.8	5.2	43,331	72.9	12,538	13.8	38,552	36,615	1,937	5.3
Sacramento—Arden-Arcade—Roseville, CA	26.5	14.5	871,760	69.1	224,922	12.5	794,166	714,981	79,185	11.1
El Dorado County, CA	26.5	7.2	78,086	70.0	11,079	7.1	78,351	71,278	7,073	9.9
Placer County, CA	30.3	7.1	123,875	75.3	14,272	5.7	132,672	107,302	25,370	23.6
Sacramento County, CA	24.8	16.1	587,086	68.8	169,784	13.9	516,104	474,814	41,290	8.7
Yolo County, CA	34.1	20.3	82,713	61.1	29,787	17.7	67,039	61,587	5,452	8.9
Saginaw-Saginaw Township North, MI	15.9	2.0	98,640	77.6	28,603	13.6	87,972	85,507	2,465	2.9
Saginaw County, MI	15.9	2.0	98,640	77.6	28,603	13.6	87,972	85,507	2,465	2.9
St. Cloud, MN	21.0	2.3	94,922	74.1	13,434	8.0	70,359	63,754	6,605	10.4
Benton County, MN	17.2	2.1	19,602	77.4	2,397	7.0	15,324	13,461	1,863	13.8
Stearns County, MN	22.0	2.4	75,320	73.2	11,037	8.3	55,035	50,293	4,742	9.4
St. George, UT	21.0	4.1	37,740	70.4	9,988	11.1	44,909	36,478	8,431	23.1
Washington County, UT	21.0	4.1	37,740	70.4	9,988	11.1	44,909	36,478	8,431	23.1
St. Joseph, MO-KS	16.4	1.0	58,449	76.3	13,194	10.8	51,800	50,564	1,236	2.4
Doniphan County, KS	14.8	0.8	4,178	73.0	930	11.3	3,540	3,489	51	1.5
Andrew County, MO	18.8	0.6	8,449	77.6	1,339	8.1	6,925	6,662	263	3.9
Buchanan County, MO	16.9	1.1	41,638	76.8	9,978	11.6	37,292	36,574	718	2.0
DeKalb County, MO	10.7	1.0	4,184	72.3	947	8.2	4,043	3,839	204	5.3
St. Louis, MO-IL[5]	24.8	3.0	1,376,248	76.7	264,721	9.8	1,183,069	1,133,255	49,814	4.4
Bond County, IL	15.0	0.8	8,154	71.3	1,413	8.0	6,973	6,689	284	4.2
Calhoun County, IL	9.4	1.0	2,451	68.0	450	8.9	2,770	2,681	89	3.3
Clinton County, IL	13.0	1.2	17,906	76.5	2,138	6.0	14,441	13,802	639	4.6
Jersey County, IL	12.6	1.0	10,999	76.1	1,473	6.8	9,327	8,918	409	4.6
Macoupin County, IL	11.8	0.5	23,931	76.1	4,487	9.2	21,823	21,097	726	3.4
Madison County, IL	19.2	1.3	130,809	78.1	24,774	9.6	113,914	108,949	4,965	4.6
Monroe County, IL	20.4	0.8	14,898	83.3	915	3.3	11,927	10,749	1,178	11.0
St. Clair County, IL	19.3	2.1	123,339	75.1	36,358	14.2	109,668	104,437	5,231	5.0
Franklin County, MO	12.8	0.8	47,717	77.6	6,494	6.9	40,848	38,295	2,553	6.7
Jefferson County, MO	12.1	1.0	104,725	78.9	13,253	6.7	81,937	75,586	6,351	8.4
Lincoln County, MO	9.7	0.6	19,583	77.0	3,168	8.1	16,704	15,511	1,193	7.7
St. Charles County, MO	26.3	2.1	156,972	82.8	11,177	3.9	122,829	105,517	17,312	16.4
St. Louis County, MO	35.4	4.2	530,355	79.8	68,552	6.7	430,624	423,730	6,894	1.6
Warren County, MO	11.1	1.5	12,721	76.1	2,095	8.5	12,633	11,046	1,587	14.4
Washington County, MO	7.5	0.7	9,459	67.9	4,586	19.6	10,319	9,894	425	4.3
St. Louis city, MO	19.1	5.6	162,229	59.8	83,388	23.9	176,332	176,354	−22	0.0
Salem, OR	20.8	11.5	168,623	66.6	44,047	12.7	139,725	132,637	7,088	5.3
Marion County, OR	19.8	12.6	137,444	66.1	37,104	13.0	113,796	108,176	5,620	5.2
Polk County, OR	25.3	6.5	31,179	68.8	6,943	11.1	25,929	24,461	1,468	6.0
Salinas, CA	22.5	29.0	184,789	61.2	51,692	12.9	136,549	131,708	4,841	3.7
Monterey County, CA	22.5	29.0	184,789	61.2	51,692	12.9	136,549	131,708	4,841	3.7
Salisbury, MD	19.5	3.6	55,204	71.9	14,456	13.2	47,927	44,493	3,434	7.7
Somerset County, MD	11.6	2.5	10,389	66.4	3,993	16.1	10,414	10,092	322	3.2
Wicomico County, MD	21.9	3.9	44,815	73.2	10,463	12.4	37,513	34,401	3,112	9.0
Salt Lake City, UT	27.6	10.0	503,514	71.4	74,938	7.7	367,935	342,297	25,638	7.5
Salt Lake County, UT	27.4	10.4	467,256	71.7	70,714	7.9	331,749	310,996	20,753	6.7
Summit County, UT	45.5	7.7	17,037	71.1	1,609	5.4	19,802	17,489	2,313	13.2
Tooele County, UT	15.9	3.7	19,221	62.8	2,615	6.4	16,384	13,812	2,572	18.6

See footnotes at end of table.

Metropolitan statistical area **Metropolitan statistical area with metropolitan divisions** *Metropolitan division* Component county	2000		Workers 16 years and over		Persons below poverty level in 1999		Housing units		Change 2000–2004[3]	
	Educational attainment, percent with bachelor's degree or higher[1]	Percent foreign born	Total workers	Percent of workers who drove alone to work	Total persons	Percent of persons below poverty level in 1999	2004 (July 1)	2000[2] (estimates base)	Number	Percent
San Angelo, TX	19.5	5.9	52,630	72.6	15,341	14.5	45,915	44,830	1,085	2.4
Irion County, TX	21.5	3.5	872	78.4	148	8.4	939	914	25	2.7
Tom Green County, TX	19.5	5.9	51,758	72.5	15,193	14.6	44,976	43,916	1,060	2.4
San Antonio, TX	22.1	9.8	808,627	70.5	252,311	14.7	701,046	648,587	52,459	8.1
Atascosa County, TX	10.5	5.1	16,441	68.0	7,701	19.9	15,511	14,877	634	4.3
Bandera County, TX	19.4	3.9	8,254	70.2	1,895	10.7	9,861	9,503	358	3.8
Bexar County, TX	22.7	10.9	658,509	69.9	215,736	15.5	560,820	521,359	39,461	7.6
Comal County, TX	26.2	4.8	37,958	76.3	6,585	8.4	38,512	32,718	5,794	17.7
Guadalupe County, TX	19.1	6.5	44,206	74.2	8,568	9.6	37,002	33,585	3,417	10.2
Kendall County, TX	31.4	5.6	11,321	74.5	2,443	10.3	11,272	9,609	1,663	17.3
Medina County, TX	13.3	4.1	17,160	69.4	5,794	14.7	15,410	14,826	584	3.9
Wilson County, TX	12.8	3.3	14,778	71.0	3,589	11.1	12,658	12,110	548	4.5
San Diego-Carlsbad-San Marcos, CA	29.5	21.5	1,407,152	68.2	338,399	12.0	1,099,235	1,040,149	59,086	5.7
San Diego County, CA	29.5	21.5	1,407,152	68.2	338,399	12.0	1,099,235	1,040,149	59,086	5.7
Sandusky, OH	16.6	1.5	39,502	82.5	6,439	8.1	36,820	35,909	911	2.5
Erie County, OH	16.6	1.5	39,502	82.5	6,439	8.1	36,820	35,909	911	2.5
San Francisco-Oakland-Fremont, CA	**38.8**	**27.4**	**2,164,856**	**58.6**	**371,257**	**9.0**	**1,654,724**	**1,606,855**	**47,869**	**3.0**
Oakland-Fremont-Hayward, CA	*35.0*	*24.0*	*1,209,224*	*62.9*	*228,379*	*9.5*	*928,689*	*894,760*	*33,929*	*3.8*
Alameda County, CA	34.9	27.2	734,555	61.3	156,804	10.9	552,258	540,183	12,075	2.2
Contra Costa County, CA	35.0	19.0	474,669	65.4	71,575	7.5	376,431	354,577	21,854	6.2
San Francisco-San Mateo-Redwood City, CA	*43.6*	*32.0*	*955,632*	*53.2*	*142,878*	*8.3*	*726,035*	*712,095*	*13,940*	*2.0*
Marin County, CA	51.3	16.6	133,052	62.3	15,601	6.3	106,598	104,990	1,608	1.5
San Francisco County, CA	45.0	36.8	448,669	37.8	86,585	11.1	353,930	346,527	7,403	2.1
San Mateo County, CA	39.0	32.3	373,911	68.5	40,692	5.8	265,507	260,578	4,929	1.9
San Jose-Sunnyvale-Santa Clara, CA	39.8	33.6	904,279	72.8	129,711	7.5	618,317	595,828	22,489	3.8
San Benito County, CA	17.1	18.8	25,347	66.6	5,241	9.8	17,632	16,499	1,133	6.9
Santa Clara County, CA	40.5	34.1	878,932	72.9	124,470	7.4	600,685	579,329	21,356	3.7
San Luis Obispo-Paso Robles, CA	26.7	8.9	116,868	68.1	29,775	12.1	109,798	102,275	7,523	7.4
San Luis Obispo County, CA	26.7	8.9	116,868	68.1	29,775	12.1	109,798	102,275	7,523	7.4
Santa Barbara-Santa Maria, CA	29.4	21.2	196,304	63.4	55,086	13.8	147,831	142,901	4,930	3.4
Santa Barbara County, CA	29.4	21.2	196,304	63.4	55,086	13.8	147,831	142,901	4,930	3.4
Santa Cruz-Watsonville, CA	34.2	18.2	137,734	63.7	29,383	11.5	101,040	98,873	2,167	2.2
Santa Cruz County, CA	34.2	18.2	137,734	63.7	29,383	11.5	101,040	98,873	2,167	2.2
Santa Fe, NM	36.9	10.1	68,236	66.6	15,241	11.8	60,278	57,701	2,577	4.5
Santa Fe County, NM	36.9	10.1	68,236	66.6	15,241	11.8	60,278	57,701	2,577	4.5
Santa Rosa-Petaluma, CA	28.5	14.3	240,198	70.0	36,349	7.9	191,689	183,153	8,536	4.7
Sonoma County, CA	28.5	14.3	240,198	70.0	36,349	7.9	191,689	183,153	8,536	4.7
Sarasota-Bradenton-Venice, FL	24.6	8.9	257,741	75.9	50,921	8.6	355,803	320,595	35,208	11.0
Manatee County, FL	20.8	8.4	117,077	75.5	26,104	9.9	154,424	138,128	16,296	11.8
Sarasota County, FL	27.4	9.3	140,664	76.2	24,817	7.6	201,379	182,467	18,912	10.4
Savannah, GA	23.2	3.5	142,821	72.5	41,216	14.1	133,020	122,527	10,493	8.6
Bryan County, GA	19.3	2.5	11,505	79.0	2,715	11.6	10,278	8,675	1,603	18.5
Chatham County, GA	25.0	4.0	113,087	70.8	35,043	15.1	106,405	99,683	6,722	6.7
Effingham County, GA	13.6	1.3	18,229	78.8	3,458	9.2	16,337	14,169	2,168	15.3
Scranton—Wilkes-Barre, PA	17.5	2.0	267,166	75.6	58,727	10.5	255,885	252,761	3,124	1.2
Lackawanna County, PA	19.6	2.3	101,831	74.8	21,802	10.2	96,405	95,362	1,043	1.1
Luzerne County, PA	16.4	1.9	151,869	76.1	34,136	10.7	146,411	144,686	1,725	1.2
Wyoming County, PA	15.4	1.2	13,466	75.3	2,789	9.9	13,069	12,713	356	2.8
Seattle-Tacoma-Bellevue, WA	**32.7**	**12.6**	**1,649,977**	**66.6**	**254,886**	**8.4**	**1,338,140**	**1,255,504**	**82,636**	**6.6**
Seattle-Bellevue-Everett, WA	*36.1*	*14.0*	*1,297,300*	*65.7*	*183,570*	*7.8*	*1,040,502*	*978,444*	*62,058*	*6.3*
King County, WA	40.0	15.4	974,767	64.3	142,546	8.2	781,976	742,239	39,737	5.4
Snohomish County, WA	24.4	9.7	322,533	69.9	41,024	6.8	258,526	236,205	22,321	9.4
Tacoma, WA	*20.6*	*8.1*	*352,677*	*70.2*	*71,316*	*10.2*	*297,638*	*277,060*	*20,578*	*7.4*
Pierce County, WA	20.6	8.1	352,677	70.2	71,316	10.2	297,638	277,060	20,578	7.4
Sheboygan, WI	17.9	4.3	61,080	77.6	5,658	5.0	48,277	45,951	2,326	5.1
Sheboygan County, WI	17.9	4.3	61,080	77.6	5,658	5.0	48,277	45,951	2,326	5.1
Sherman-Denison, TX	17.2	3.9	53,380	75.7	12,109	10.9	50,007	48,315	1,692	3.5
Grayson County, TX	17.2	3.9	53,380	75.7	12,109	10.9	50,007	48,315	1,692	3.5
Shreveport-Bossier City, LA	19.2	1.7	176,280	72.9	71,383	19.0	166,178	159,786	6,392	4.0
Bossier Parish, LA	18.1	2.5	48,990	77.5	13,184	13.4	43,936	40,306	3,630	9.0
Caddo Parish, LA	20.6	1.5	116,718	71.2	51,903	20.6	110,712	108,276	2,436	2.2
De Soto Parish, LA	10.2	1.0	10,572	69.8	6,296	24.7	11,530	11,204	326	2.9
Sioux City, IA-NE-SD	18.5	7.8	74,893	74.0	14,000	9.8	57,997	56,940	1,057	1.9
Woodbury County, IA	18.9	7.2	54,240	74.3	10,434	10.0	41,741	41,394	347	0.8
Dakota County, NE	12.4	15.6	10,511	72.0	2,264	11.2	7,722	7,528	194	2.6
Dixon County, NE	14.1	3.4	3,247	69.3	621	9.8	2,730	2,673	57	2.1
Union County, SD	26.3	2.4	6,895	77.3	681	5.4	5,804	5,345	459	8.6
Sioux Falls, SD	25.1	3.4	106,637	79.4	12,918	6.9	85,005	75,603	9,402	12.4
Lincoln County, SD	25.5	1.1	13,651	80.9	1,053	4.4	12,495	9,131	3,364	36.8
McCook County, SD	16.3	0.7	2,840	67.6	458	7.9	2,507	2,383	124	5.2
Minnehaha County, SD	26.0	4.1	85,601	80.1	10,790	7.3	66,064	60,237	5,827	9.7
Turner County, SD	17.0	0.5	4,545	68.9	617	7.0	3,939	3,852	87	2.3
South Bend-Mishawaka, IN-MI	21.7	4.1	161,299	75.6	31,213	9.9	136,416	130,897	5,519	4.2
St. Joseph County, IN	23.6	4.6	135,196	75.3	26,226	9.9	111,341	107,013	4,328	4.0
Cass County, MI	12.1	1.9	26,103	76.9	4,987	9.8	25,075	23,884	1,191	5.0

See footnotes at end of table.

State and Metropolitan Area Data Book: 2006

Metropolitan statistical area **Metropolitan statistical area with metropolitan divisions** *Metropolitan division* Component county	2000				Persons below poverty level in 1999		Housing units			
	Educational attainment, percent with bachelor's degree or higher[1]	Percent foreign born	Workers 16 years and over		Total persons	Percent of persons below poverty level in 1999	2004 (July 1)	2000[2] (estimates base)	Change	
			Total workers	Percent of workers who drove alone to work					2000–2004[3]	
									Number	Percent
Spartanburg, SC	18.2	3.7	126,914	75.9	30,394	12.0	114,726	106,986	7,740	7.2
Spartanburg County, SC	18.2	3.7	126,914	75.9	30,394	12.0	114,726	106,986	7,740	7.2
Spokane, WA	25.0	4.5	210,968	69.5	49,859	11.9	184,401	175,005	9,396	5.4
Spokane County, WA	25.0	4.5	210,968	69.5	49,859	11.9	184,401	175,005	9,396	5.4
Springfield, IL	28.1	1.8	108,765	77.4	18,351	9.1	94,137	90,746	3,391	3.7
Menard County, IL	20.5	0.7	6,771	76.9	1,011	8.1	5,569	5,285	284	5.4
Sangamon County, IL	28.6	1.9	101,994	77.4	17,340	9.2	88,568	85,461	3,107	3.6
Springfield, MA	25.2	6.7	345,718	73.6	84,243	12.4	279,968	276,459	3,509	1.3
Franklin County, MA	29.1	3.6	39,413	74.5	6,634	9.3	32,534	31,939	595	1.9
Hampden County, MA	20.5	7.2	218,853	75.2	65,024	14.3	187,432	185,876	1,556	0.8
Hampshire County, MA	37.9	6.6	87,452	69.0	12,585	8.3	60,002	58,644	1,358	2.3
Springfield, MO	21.3	1.5	190,721	76.0	43,847	11.9	170,427	156,493	13,934	8.9
Christian County, MO	20.9	0.9	28,763	79.1	4,869	9.0	25,339	21,827	3,512	16.1
Dallas County, MO	9.5	0.5	6,823	71.8	2,768	17.7	7,212	6,914	298	4.3
Greene County, MO	24.2	1.9	128,323	76.2	27,630	11.5	113,156	104,517	8,639	8.3
Polk County, MO	14.6	1.5	12,549	71.8	4,142	15.3	11,818	11,183	635	5.7
Webster County, MO	11.0	0.8	14,263	73.2	4,438	14.3	12,902	12,052	850	7.1
Springfield, OH	14.9	1.2	71,629	76.0	15,054	10.4	61,807	61,055	752	1.2
Clark County, OH	14.9	1.2	71,629	76.0	15,054	10.4	61,807	61,055	752	1.2
State College, PA	36.3	5.8	68,550	61.4	22,742	16.8	56,372	53,161	3,211	6.0
Centre County, PA	36.3	5.8	68,550	61.4	22,742	16.8	56,372	53,161	3,211	6.0
Stockton, CA	14.5	19.5	244,516	65.2	97,105	17.2	211,678	189,160	22,518	11.9
San Joaquin County, CA	14.5	19.5	244,516	65.2	97,105	17.2	211,678	189,160	22,518	11.9
Sumter, SC	15.8	2.1	48,696	73.2	16,451	15.7	43,455	41,747	1,708	4.1
Sumter County, SC	15.8	2.1	48,696	73.2	16,451	15.7	43,455	41,747	1,708	4.1
Syracuse, NY	25.2	4.5	323,383	73.3	76,991	11.8	282,750	278,110	4,640	1.7
Madison County, NY	21.6	2.2	35,174	71.3	6,313	9.1	29,099	28,646	453	1.6
Onondaga County, NY	28.5	5.7	228,431	74.2	54,208	11.8	200,040	196,633	3,407	1.7
Oswego County, NY	14.4	1.6	59,778	71.3	16,470	13.5	53,611	52,831	780	1.5
Tallahassee, FL	34.1	4.3	170,540	70.8	54,064	16.9	148,572	136,748	11,824	8.6
Gadsden County, FL	12.9	4.1	19,547	67.3	8,509	18.9	18,033	17,703	330	1.9
Jefferson County, FL	16.9	1.2	5,781	70.9	2,040	15.8	5,501	5,251	250	4.8
Leon County, FL	41.7	4.7	134,177	71.0	41,078	17.2	113,554	103,974	9,580	9.2
Wakulla County, FL	15.7	1.5	11,035	74.7	2,437	10.7	11,484	9,820	1,664	16.9
Tampa-St. Petersburg-Clearwater, FL	21.7	9.8	1,142,022	74.3	262,439	11.0	1,233,984	1,143,995	89,989	7.9
Hernando County, FL	12.7	5.3	46,581	75.6	13,307	10.2	69,984	62,727	7,257	11.6
Hillsborough County, FL	25.1	11.5	509,059	73.5	122,872	12.3	477,626	425,962	51,664	12.1
Pasco County, FL	13.1	7.0	140,895	74.6	36,201	10.5	194,333	173,719	20,614	11.9
Pinellas County, FL	22.9	9.5	445,487	74.9	90,059	9.8	492,041	481,587	10,454	2.2
Terre Haute, IN	17.4	1.4	81,859	75.4	19,701	11.5	74,619	72,509	2,110	2.9
Clay County, IN	12.8	0.6	12,819	76.3	2,265	8.5	11,572	11,097	475	4.3
Sullivan County, IN	9.4	0.3	9,245	76.5	2,123	9.8	9,136	8,804	332	3.8
Vermillion County, IN	11.2	0.8	8,076	78.9	1,558	9.3	7,578	7,405	173	2.3
Vigo County, IN	21.4	2.0	51,719	74.5	13,755	13.0	46,333	45,203	1,130	2.5
Texarkana, TX-Texarkana, AR	15.0	1.4	56,815	76.3	22,230	17.1	56,568	54,190	2,378	4.4
Miller County, AR	12.5	1.1	18,119	77.8	7,602	18.8	18,700	17,727	973	5.5
Bowie County, TX	16.1	1.5	38,696	75.6	14,628	16.4	37,868	36,463	1,405	3.9
Toledo, OH	21.2	2.8	335,831	77.8	77,558	11.8	294,954	285,491	9,463	3.3
Fulton County, OH	13.2	1.3	21,987	80.4	2,255	5.4	16,886	16,232	654	4.0
Lucas County, OH	21.3	3.2	226,450	77.4	62,026	13.6	201,158	196,259	4,899	2.5
Ottawa County, OH	16.0	1.1	20,711	80.1	2,374	5.8	26,461	25,532	929	3.6
Wood County, OH	26.2	2.4	66,683	77.6	10,903	9.0	50,449	47,468	2,981	6.3
Topeka, KS	23.6	2.2	116,408	77.6	19,996	8.9	100,543	96,404	4,139	4.3
Jackson County, KS	15.4	0.5	6,378	71.7	1,091	8.6	5,317	5,094	223	4.4
Jefferson County, KS	17.9	0.6	9,380	73.5	1,219	6.6	7,931	7,491	440	5.9
Osage County, KS	14.3	0.6	8,459	75.0	1,370	8.2	7,310	7,019	291	4.1
Shawnee County, KS	26.0	2.7	88,593	78.8	15,824	9.3	76,831	73,767	3,064	4.2
Wabaunsee County, KS	17.3	0.7	3,598	74.0	492	7.1	3,154	3,033	121	4.0
Trenton-Ewing, NJ	34.0	13.9	180,299	66.4	28,570	8.1	137,573	133,280	4,293	3.2
Mercer County, NJ	34.0	13.9	180,299	66.4	28,570	8.1	137,573	133,280	4,293	3.2
Tucson, AZ	26.7	11.9	397,215	68.7	120,778	14.3	397,150	366,737	30,413	8.3
Pima County, AZ	26.7	11.9	397,215	68.7	120,778	14.3	397,150	366,737	30,413	8.3
Tulsa, OK	22.5	3.9	429,226	75.6	99,150	11.5	383,373	366,194	17,179	4.7
Creek County, OK	11.7	0.7	31,034	75.1	8,924	13.2	28,894	27,986	908	3.2
Okmulgee County, OK	11.4	0.7	17,015	69.2	7,292	18.4	17,594	17,316	278	1.6
Osage County, OK	14.6	1.0	20,409	74.1	5,651	12.7	19,496	18,826	670	3.6
Pawnee County, OK	12.1	0.6	7,659	72.1	2,136	12.9	7,609	7,464	145	1.9
Rogers County, OK	16.9	1.3	34,604	78.7	5,999	8.5	29,448	27,475	1,973	7.2
Tulsa County, OK	26.9	5.4	290,038	75.5	64,062	11.4	254,128	243,953	10,175	4.2
Wagoner County, OK	15.4	1.8	28,467	78.7	5,086	8.8	26,204	23,174	3,030	13.1
Tuscaloosa, AL	21.9	1.9	89,352	76.4	34,555	18.0	89,839	84,302	5,537	6.6
Greene County, AL	10.5	0.7	3,578	65.0	3,391	34.0	5,264	5,117	147	2.9
Hale County, AL	8.1	0.3	6,349	69.6	4,531	26.4	8,069	7,756	313	4.0
Tuscaloosa County, AL	24.0	2.1	79,425	77.5	26,633	16.2	76,506	71,429	5,077	7.1

See footnotes at end of table.

Table C-2. Metropolitan Areas With Component Counties — Population Characteristics and Housing Units—Con.

Metropolitan statistical area / Metropolitan statistical area with metropolitan divisions / Metropolitan division / Component county	2000 Educational attainment, percent with bachelor's degree or higher[1]	2000 Percent foreign born	Workers 16 years and over Total workers	Workers 16 years and over Percent of workers who drove alone to work	Persons below poverty level in 1999 Total persons	Persons below poverty level in 1999 Percent of persons below poverty level in 1999	Housing units 2004 (July 1)	Housing units 2000[2] (estimates base)	Housing units Change 2000–2004[3] Number	Housing units Change 2000–2004[3] Percent
Tyler, TX	22.5	6.6	82,955	75.2	23,543	13.5	75,047	71,701	3,346	4.7
Smith County, TX	22.5	6.6	82,955	75.2	23,543	13.5	75,047	71,701	3,346	4.7
Utica-Rome, NY	17.7	4.5	140,870	73.1	36,685	12.2	135,385	134,829	556	0.4
Herkimer County, NY	15.7	2.0	31,374	70.5	7,921	12.3	32,292	32,026	266	0.8
Oneida County, NY	18.3	5.2	109,496	73.8	28,764	12.2	103,093	102,803	290	0.3
Valdosta, GA	17.4	2.8	56,874	73.1	21,751	18.2	51,711	48,165	3,546	7.4
Brooks County, GA	11.3	1.7	7,250	70.6	3,785	23.0	7,265	7,118	147	2.1
Echols County, GA	8.4	12.6	1,755	66.5	1,060	28.2	1,526	1,482	44	3.0
Lanier County, GA	8.8	1.1	3,296	70.4	1,284	17.7	3,131	3,011	120	4.0
Lowndes County, GA	19.7	2.7	44,573	74.0	15,622	17.0	39,789	36,554	3,235	8.8
Vallejo-Fairfield, CA	21.4	16.9	190,243	67.2	31,344	7.9	144,005	134,513	9,492	7.1
Solano County, CA	21.4	16.9	190,243	67.2	31,344	7.9	144,005	134,513	9,492	7.1
Vero Beach, FL	23.1	8.1	47,737	75.6	10,325	9.1	66,177	57,902	8,275	14.3
Indian River County, FL	23.1	8.1	47,737	75.6	10,325	9.1	66,177	57,902	8,275	14.3
Victoria, TX	15.2	5.0	52,320	72.6	15,140	13.6	48,000	46,609	1,391	3.0
Calhoun County, TX	12.1	8.5	8,922	71.4	3,340	16.2	10,651	10,238	413	4.0
Goliad County, TX	12.3	2.8	3,047	70.8	1,119	16.2	3,534	3,426	108	3.2
Victoria County, TX	16.2	4.3	40,351	73.0	10,681	12.7	33,815	32,945	870	2.6
Vineland-Millville-Bridgeton, NJ	11.7	6.2	65,642	68.5	20,367	13.9	53,736	52,863	873	1.7
Cumberland County, NJ	11.7	6.2	65,642	68.5	20,367	13.9	53,736	52,863	873	1.7
Virginia Beach-Norfolk-Newport News, VA-NC	23.7	4.5	818,481	73.6	160,249	10.2	657,757	622,629	35,128	5.6
Currituck County, NC	13.3	1.4	9,065	75.7	1,922	10.6	12,588	10,687	1,901	17.8
Gloucester County, VA	17.6	1.9	17,879	75.2	2,644	7.6	15,426	14,494	932	6.4
Isle of Wight County, VA	17.5	1.1	14,851	79.4	2,449	8.2	13,316	12,066	1,250	10.4
James City County, VA	41.5	4.1	23,128	77.7	3,001	6.2	24,752	20,772	3,980	19.2
Mathews County, VA	19.2	2.2	4,242	71.6	550	6.0	5,552	5,333	219	4.1
Surry County, VA	12.8	0.5	3,376	70.0	734	10.7	3,533	3,294	239	7.3
York County, VA	37.4	5.2	29,669	82.5	1,947	3.5	23,454	20,701	2,753	13.3
Chesapeake city, VA	24.7	3.0	102,470	79.4	14,259	7.2	77,938	72,672	5,266	7.2
Hampton city, VA	21.8	3.9	71,790	73.4	15,088	10.3	58,585	57,311	1,274	2.2
Newport News city, VA	19.9	4.8	92,586	73.4	24,027	13.3	76,801	74,117	2,684	3.6
Norfolk city, VA	19.6	5.0	123,360	60.7	40,857	17.4	95,722	94,416	1,306	1.4
Poquoson city, VA	31.6	2.9	5,908	84.1	512	4.4	4,460	4,300	160	3.7
Portsmouth city, VA	13.8	1.6	48,163	66.4	15,471	15.4	42,252	41,605	647	1.6
Suffolk city, VA	17.3	1.9	30,345	75.2	8,264	13.0	29,483	24,704	4,779	19.3
Virginia Beach city, VA	28.1	6.6	234,257	78.0	27,163	6.4	169,420	162,277	7,143	4.4
Williamsburg city, VA	45.0	5.2	7,392	38.2	1,361	11.3	4,475	3,880	595	15.3
Visalia-Porterville, CA	11.5	22.6	153,805	61.4	86,572	23.5	126,792	119,639	7,153	6.0
Tulare County, CA	11.5	22.6	153,805	61.4	86,572	23.5	126,792	119,639	7,153	6.0
Waco, TX	19.1	6.1	102,001	71.7	35,977	16.8	88,372	84,793	3,579	4.2
McLennan County, TX	19.1	6.1	102,001	71.7	35,977	16.8	88,372	84,793	3,579	4.2
Warner Robins, GA	19.8	3.4	56,550	78.2	11,058	10.0	51,207	44,509	6,698	15.0
Houston County, GA	19.8	3.4	56,550	78.2	11,058	10.0	51,207	44,509	6,698	15.0
Washington-Arlington-Alexandria, DC-VA-MD-WV	**42.5**	**17.3**	**2,648,831**	**63.6**	**345,860**	**7.2**	**2,033,679**	**1,890,036**	**143,643**	**7.6**
Bethesda-Gaithersburg-Frederick, MD	*50.2*	*22.5*	*584,274*	*67.6*	*55,574*	*5.2*	*434,555*	*407,648*	*26,907*	*6.6*
Frederick County, MD	30.0	4.0	107,151	75.7	8,550	4.4	81,504	73,016	8,488	11.6
Montgomery County, MD	54.6	26.7	477,123	65.8	47,024	5.4	353,051	334,632	18,419	5.5
Washington-Arlington-Alexandria, DC-VA-MD-WV	*40.2*	*15.8*	*2,064,557*	*62.4*	*290,286*	*7.8*	*1,599,124*	*1,482,388*	*116,736*	*7.9*
District of Columbia, DC	39.1	12.9	298,225	33.6	109,500	19.1	276,600	274,845	1,755	0.6
Calvert County, MD	22.5	2.2	39,341	74.1	3,235	4.3	31,166	27,576	3,590	13.0
Charles County, MD	20.0	2.9	64,983	73.5	6,518	5.4	49,221	43,903	5,318	12.1
Prince George's County, MD	27.2	13.8	431,120	61.5	60,196	7.5	313,068	302,378	10,690	3.5
Arlington County, VA	60.2	27.8	120,803	52.8	14,371	7.6	91,559	90,426	1,133	1.3
Clarke County, VA	23.9	2.5	6,712	75.0	811	6.4	5,862	5,388	474	8.8
Fairfax County, VA	54.8	24.5	548,812	70.6	43,396	4.5	380,637	359,411	21,226	5.9
Fauquier County, VA	27.1	3.6	29,446	74.4	2,964	5.4	23,881	21,045	2,836	13.5
Loudoun County, VA	47.2	11.3	95,686	78.7	4,637	2.7	86,915	62,160	24,755	39.8
Prince William County, VA	31.5	11.5	157,254	69.6	12,182	4.3	120,072	98,052	22,020	22.5
Spotsylvania County, VA	22.8	3.2	47,747	75.3	4,247	4.7	40,583	33,329	7,254	21.8
Stafford County, VA	29.6	4.0	50,424	71.1	3,138	3.4	38,427	31,405	7,022	22.4
Warren County, VA	15.0	2.1	16,257	68.4	2,631	8.3	14,388	13,300	1,088	8.2
Alexandria city, VA	54.3	25.4	80,949	59.9	11,279	8.8	67,699	64,251	3,448	5.4
Fairfax city, VA	45.7	25.4	12,361	70.4	1,205	5.6	8,576	8,204	372	4.5
Falls Church city, VA	63.7	16.1	6,072	60.8	432	4.2	4,691	4,725	−34	−0.7
Fredericksburg city, VA	30.5	5.2	10,906	62.6	2,632	13.7	9,084	8,888	196	2.2
Manassas city, VA	28.1	14.2	19,118	71.3	2,151	6.1	12,556	12,114	442	3.6
Manassas Park city, VA	20.3	15.0	5,672	70.6	530	5.2	3,995	3,365	630	18.7
Jefferson County, WV	21.6	2.1	22,669	67.0	4,231	10.0	20,144	17,623	2,521	14.3
Waterloo-Cedar Falls, IA	22.3	3.2	86,561	76.4	17,725	10.8	68,964	66,401	2,563	3.9
Black Hawk County, IA	23.0	3.7	67,444	77.2	16,050	12.5	53,596	51,760	1,836	3.5
Bremer County, IA	21.5	1.2	12,757	72.8	1,111	4.8	9,818	9,337	481	5.2
Grundy County, IA	17.2	0.8	6,360	75.2	564	4.6	5,550	5,304	246	4.6
Wausau, WI	18.3	3.5	69,216	76.9	8,163	6.5	54,426	50,360	4,066	8.1
Marathon County, WI	18.3	3.5	69,216	76.9	8,163	6.5	54,426	50,360	4,066	8.1

See footnotes at end of table.

Table C-2. Metropolitan Areas With Component Counties — **Population Characteristics and Housing Units**—Con.

Metropolitan statistical area **Metropolitan statistical area with metropolitan divisions** *Metropolitan division* Component county	2000				Persons below poverty level in 1999		Housing units			
	Educational attainment, percent with bachelor's degree or higher[1]	Percent foreign born	Workers 16 years and over		Total persons	Percent of persons below poverty level in 1999	2004 (July 1)	2000[2] (estimates base)	Change 2000–2004[3]	
			Total workers	Percent of workers who drove alone to work					Number	Percent
Weirton-Steubenville, WV-OH	12.1	1.4	58,712	77.9	17,304	13.1	59,593	59,169	424	0.7
Jefferson County, OH	11.8	1.3	31,829	76.7	10,862	14.7	33,584	33,291	293	0.9
Brooke County, WV	13.4	1.1	11,526	79.2	2,862	11.2	11,190	11,150	40	0.4
Hancock County, WV	11.5	1.8	15,357	79.5	3,580	11.0	14,819	14,728	91	0.6
Wenatchee, WA	20.0	13.1	47,410	65.6	12,787	12.9	45,202	43,351	1,851	4.3
Chelan County, WA	21.9	12.9	31,844	64.6	8,147	12.2	31,512	30,407	1,105	3.6
Douglas County, WA	16.2	13.5	15,566	67.7	4,640	14.2	13,690	12,944	746	5.8
Wheeling, WV-OH	14.6	1.0	68,887	73.9	22,630	14.8	69,487	69,219	268	0.4
Belmont County, OH	11.1	1.0	30,626	76.6	9,768	13.9	31,371	31,236	135	0.4
Marshall County, WV	10.7	0.7	15,628	73.8	5,769	16.2	15,957	15,814	143	0.9
Ohio County, WV	23.1	1.3	22,633	70.2	7,093	15.0	22,159	22,169	−10	0.0
Wichita, KS	24.3	5.7	291,566	79.3	51,228	9.0	249,931	238,566	11,365	4.8
Butler County, KS	20.4	1.3	29,271	80.0	4,187	7.0	24,844	23,178	1,666	7.2
Harvey County, KS	23.0	3.7	16,922	77.3	2,010	6.1	13,914	13,378	536	4.0
Sedgwick County, KS	25.4	6.6	232,983	79.6	42,605	9.4	200,085	191,133	8,952	4.7
Sumner County, KS	15.7	0.8	12,390	74.9	2,426	9.4	11,088	10,877	211	1.9
Wichita Falls, TX	19.2	4.7	75,860	72.8	17,805	11.8	63,829	62,167	1,662	2.7
Archer County, TX	15.9	2.3	4,502	76.3	788	8.9	3,950	3,871	79	2.0
Clay County, TX	13.9	1.4	5,542	75.3	1,121	10.2	5,125	4,992	133	2.7
Wichita County, TX	20.0	5.1	65,816	72.4	15,896	12.1	54,754	53,304	1,450	2.7
Williamsport, PA	15.1	1.2	58,610	74.0	13,205	11.0	53,416	52,464	952	1.8
Lycoming County, PA	15.1	1.2	58,610	74.0	13,205	11.0	53,416	52,464	952	1.8
Wilmington, NC	24.2	3.2	139,955	75.2	34,969	12.7	173,153	151,862	21,291	14.0
Brunswick County, NC	16.1	2.9	34,240	73.3	9,095	12.4	61,117	51,430	9,687	18.8
New Hanover County, NC	31.0	3.2	86,628	76.2	20,445	12.8	89,309	79,634	9,675	12.1
Pender County, NC	13.6	3.6	19,087	74.5	5,429	13.2	22,727	20,798	1,929	9.3
Winchester, VA-WV	18.3	3.0	53,620	74.2	9,939	9.6	49,156	45,091	4,065	9.0
Frederick County, VA	18.6	2.4	31,787	79.7	3,727	6.3	26,182	23,319	2,863	12.3
Winchester city, VA	23.7	6.8	12,777	67.3	2,991	12.7	11,185	10,587	598	5.6
Hampshire County, WV	11.3	0.6	9,056	64.3	3,221	15.9	11,789	11,185	604	5.4
Winston-Salem, NC	24.0	5.5	217,720	75.5	43,256	10.3	196,697	183,129	13,568	7.4
Davie County, NC	17.6	3.4	17,601	78.6	2,952	8.5	16,327	14,953	1,374	9.2
Forsyth County, NC	28.7	6.5	158,215	75.2	32,699	10.7	143,840	133,093	10,747	8.1
Stokes County, NC	9.3	1.5	23,629	75.0	4,022	9.0	20,056	19,262	794	4.1
Yadkin County, NC	10.3	4.4	18,275	75.6	3,583	9.9	16,474	15,821	653	4.1
Worcester, MA	26.9	7.9	383,764	77.5	67,136	8.9	308,387	298,159	10,228	3.4
Worcester County, MA	26.9	7.9	383,764	77.5	67,136	8.9	308,387	298,159	10,228	3.4
Yakima, WA	15.3	16.9	99,238	67.7	43,070	19.4	80,887	79,174	1,713	2.2
Yakima County, WA	15.3	16.9	99,238	67.7	43,070	19.4	80,887	79,174	1,713	2.2
York-Hanover, PA	18.4	2.2	203,496	80.0	25,269	6.6	166,175	156,720	9,455	6.0
York County, PA	18.4	2.2	203,496	80.0	25,269	6.6	166,175	156,720	9,455	6.0
Youngstown-Warren-Boardman, OH-PA	16.3	2.0	280,207	79.2	67,208	11.1	260,844	256,738	4,106	1.6
Mahoning County, OH	17.5	2.4	118,973	79.4	31,328	12.2	113,378	111,762	1,616	1.4
Trumbull County, OH	14.5	1.8	105,683	80.4	22,788	10.1	96,395	95,117	1,278	1.3
Mercer County, PA	17.3	1.6	55,551	76.6	13,092	10.9	51,071	49,859	1,212	2.4
Yuba City, CA	13.2	16.6	60,642	65.7	24,236	17.4	54,245	50,955	3,290	6.5
Sutter County, CA	15.3	19.3	35,470	67.0	12,031	15.2	30,496	28,319	2,177	7.7
Yuba County, CA	10.3	13.2	25,172	64.0	12,205	20.3	23,749	22,636	1,113	4.9
Yuma, AZ	11.8	24.0	59,601	63.9	29,670	18.5	80,604	74,140	6,464	8.7
Yuma County, AZ	11.8	24.0	59,601	63.9	29,670	18.5	80,604	74,140	6,464	8.7

X Not applicable.

[1]Persons 25 years and over.

[2]The April 1, 2000, housing unit estimates base reflects modifications to the Census 2000 housing units as documented in the Count Question Resolution program and geographic program revisions.

[3]Period refers to April 1, 2000, to July 1, 2004.

[4]The Denver-Aurora metropolitan statistical area includes Broomfield County. Broomfield County, CO, was formed from parts of Adams, Boulder, Jefferson, and Weld counties on November 15, 2001, and is coextensive with Broomfield city. For the purposes of defining and presenting data for the Denver-Aurora metropolitan statistical area, Broomfield city is treated as if it were a county when data are available to do so. In many cases, the data will not be available.

[5]The portion of Sullivan city in Crawford County, MO, is legally part of the St. Louis, MO-IL MSA. That portion is not included in these figures for the St. Louis MSA.

Note: Covers metropolitan statistical areas and metropolitan divisions and component counties defined by the Office of Management and Budget as of June 6, 2003, and subsequently updated in December 2003 and November 2004. For more information, see OMB Bulletin 05-02 at <http://www.whitehouse.gov/omb/bulletins/fy05/b05-02_appendix.pdf>.

Survey, Census, or Data Collection Method: Educational attainment, foreign born, commuting, and poverty are based on the Census of Population and Housing; for more information, see Appendix B, Limitations of the Data and Methodology, and also 2000 Census of Population and Housing, Demographic Profile Technical Documentation (revised August 2002) at <http://www.census.gov/prod/cen2000/doc/ProfileTD.pdf> and Census 2000 Summary File 3, Technical Documentation, SF3/15 (RV) (issued March 2005) at <http://www.census.gov/prod/cen2000/doc/sf3.pdf>. Housing units are based on the "Estimates and Projections Area Documentation, State and County Housing Units Estimates" at <http://www.census.gov/popest/topics/methodology/2004_hu_meth.html> (issued 20 July 2005).

Sources: Educational attainment, foreign born, commuting, and poverty—U.S. Census Bureau, 2000 Census of Population and Housing, *Summary File 3* (SF3) (accessed 12 January 2004) and related Internet site at <http://www.census.gov/Press-Release/www/2002/sumfile3.html> and 2000 Census of Population and Housing, Summary Social, Economic, and Housing Characteristics, PHC-2-1 to 52 and related Internet site at <http://www.census.gov/prod/cen2000/index.html>; Housing units—U.S. Census Bureau, *Annual Estimates of Housing Units for Counties: April 1, 2000 to July 1, 2004* at <http://www.census.gov/popest/housing/> (accessed 14 November 2005).

Table C-3. Metropolitan Areas With Component Counties — **Personal Income and Earnings by Industry**

	Personal income										
Metropolitan statistical area **Metropolitan statistical area with metropolitan divisions** *Metropolitan division* Component county	Total (million dollars)			Per capita[1] (dollars)			Earnings—percent by selected industries				
	2002	2001	2000	2002	2000	Percent change,[2] 2000–2002	Manu-fac-turing	Retail trade	Profes-sional and technical services	Health care and social assis-tance	Govern-ment and govern-ment enter-prises
Abilene, TX	3,837	3,674	3,880	24,252	24,232	-1.1	4.5	8.4	(NA)	(NA)	30.1
Callahan County, TX	288	275	265	22,337	20,539	8.7	5.8	10.2	(D)	(D)	27.9
Jones County, TX	360	355	336	17,746	16,213	6.9	2.8	6.5	1.9	5.6	50.5
Taylor County, TX	3,189	3,044	3,278	25,505	25,924	-2.7	4.6	8.5	4.7	14.5	28.6
Akron, OH	21,147	20,602	20,593	30,205	29,591	2.7	18.8	7.8	5.7	11.0	14.9
Portage County, OH	4,131	4,016	3,999	26,834	26,245	3.3	27.6	7.3	3.1	4.7	27.3
Summit County, OH	17,016	16,586	16,594	31,155	30,529	2.5	17.1	7.9	6.2	12.2	12.6
Albany, GA	3,662	3,517	3,371	22,862	21,372	8.6	(NA)	7.5	(NA)	(NA)	22.9
Baker County, GA	86	80	82	21,273	20,155	4.7	(D)	2.6	(D)	(D)	20.8
Dougherty County, GA	2,251	2,165	2,073	23,500	21,614	8.6	19.0	7.5	5.4	13.7	22.4
Lee County, GA	614	593	566	22,158	22,725	8.6	1.5	6.1	(D)	7.1	26.6
Terrell County, GA	227	216	205	20,973	18,675	10.8	14.0	7.2	3.0	(D)	25.9
Worth County, GA	484	463	446	22,186	20,355	8.3	5.2	10.4	1.4	8.9	24.1
Albany-Schenectady-Troy, NY	26,967	26,179	25,168	32,297	30,445	7.1	7.8	6.3	10.3	(NA)	26.8
Albany County, NY	10,598	10,265	9,810	35,763	33,301	8.0	4.1	5.4	9.1	10.0	32.7
Rensselaer County, NY	4,441	4,327	4,171	28,978	27,331	6.5	6.6	7.6	7.4	13.0	23.2
Saratoga County, NY	6,500	6,344	6,176	31,420	30,655	5.2	11.8	9.4	9.0	8.2	19.3
Schenectady County, NY	4,678	4,504	4,274	31,845	29,187	9.4	18.8	6.0	18.3	12.3	14.4
Schoharie County, NY	751	739	738	23,733	23,345	1.8	2.9	9.7	2.8	(D)	36.8
Albuquerque, NM	21,421	20,525	18,910	28,471	25,848	13.3	8.7	7.8	13.4	(NA)	22.7
Bernalillo County, NM	17,295	16,559	15,079	30,204	27,046	14.7	6.2	7.8	14.7	9.7	22.6
Sandoval County, NM	2,412	2,347	2,169	25,211	23,932	11.2	41.0	5.7	3.4	3.1	18.4
Torrance County, NM	325	309	299	19,521	17,630	8.4	2.5	11.3	1.3	(D)	37.3
Valencia County, NM	1,390	1,310	1,363	20,598	20,513	2.0	7.1	10.7	2.4	7.7	32.5
Alexandria, LA	3,762	3,612	3,318	25,887	22,863	13.4	10.8	8.0	4.8	16.9	26.7
Grant Parish, LA	366	351	331	19,538	17,666	10.8	13.8	4.2	0.8	3.4	46.7
Rapides Parish, LA	3,395	3,262	2,987	26,827	23,632	13.7	10.6	8.2	5.0	17.7	25.5
Allentown-Bethlehem-Easton, PA-NJ	23,542	22,762	22,220	31,073	29,952	6.0	21.3	8.0	5.3	13.0	11.1
Warren County, NJ	3,529	3,425	3,366	32,824	32,687	4.8	26.1	13.1	4.5	10.2	14.7
Carbon County, PA	1,511	1,460	1,424	25,320	24,199	6.2	15.4	10.2	2.9	14.9	17.8
Lehigh County, PA	10,257	9,940	9,708	32,374	31,059	5.7	21.3	6.6	5.7	15.5	8.4
Northampton County, PA	8,245	7,937	7,722	30,133	28,869	6.8	20.0	8.2	5.1	8.8	14.0
Altoona, PA	3,165	3,061	3,057	24,815	23,692	3.5	16.1	10.5	5.0	15.3	15.8
Blair County, PA	3,165	3,061	3,057	24,815	23,692	3.5	16.1	10.5	5.0	15.3	15.8
Amarillo, TX	5,828	5,627	5,565	25,255	24,508	4.7	7.5	9.2	(NA)	(NA)	17.1
Armstrong County, TX	52	52	49	24,596	22,446	6.1	(D)	3.4	(D)	(D)	21.6
Carson County, TX	171	172	175	25,879	26,921	-2.4	(D)	1.4	(D)	(D)	8.4
Potter County, TX	2,790	2,666	2,711	24,125	23,841	2.9	8.0	9.7	6.6	16.3	17.1
Randall County, TX	2,815	2,737	2,630	26,456	25,127	7.0	8.8	10.6	4.8	6.3	20.4
Ames, IA	2,173	2,103	2,067	26,479	25,775	5.2	12.3	6.2	4.3	6.8	44.2
Story County, IA	2,173	2,103	2,067	26,479	25,775	5.2	12.3	6.2	4.3	6.8	44.2
Anchorage, AK	11,874	11,335	10,330	35,623	32,235	15.0	2.1	7.5	8.2	9.2	27.1
Anchorage Borough, AK	10,043	9,610	8,778	37,442	33,691	14.4	2.1	7.0	8.5	9.0	27.4
Matanuska-Susitna Borough, AK	1,831	1,725	1,552	28,128	25,905	18.0	2.9	13.5	4.4	12.1	23.1
Anderson, IN	3,430	3,366	3,305	26,005	24,795	3.8	36.4	7.3	2.6	11.4	14.6
Madison County, IN	3,430	3,366	3,305	26,005	24,795	3.8	36.4	7.3	2.6	11.4	14.6
Anderson, SC	4,252	4,199	4,037	24,983	24,274	5.3	31.6	10.1	2.8	7.1	17.9
Anderson County, SC	4,252	4,199	4,037	24,983	24,274	5.3	31.6	10.1	2.8	7.1	17.9
Ann Arbor, MI	11,801	11,458	11,541	35,282	35,575	2.3	18.7	5.5	14.0	8.5	27.0
Washtenaw County, MI	11,801	11,458	11,541	35,282	35,575	2.3	18.7	5.5	14.0	8.5	27.0
Anniston-Oxford, AL	2,618	2,493	2,382	23,504	21,397	9.9	19.3	8.4	3.9	8.4	29.8
Calhoun County, AL	2,618	2,493	2,382	23,504	21,397	9.9	19.3	8.4	3.9	8.4	29.8
Appleton, WI	6,232	6,062	5,873	29,891	28,999	6.1	24.7	8.0	(NA)	8.8	10.1
Calumet County, WI	1,277	1,247	1,167	30,050	28,664	9.4	39.0	5.7	(D)	5.8	10.1
Outagamie County, WI	4,955	4,816	4,705	29,850	29,083	5.3	22.9	8.3	4.5	9.2	10.1
Asheville, NC	10,103	9,857	9,684	26,757	26,145	4.3	17.5	9.0	5.2	(NA)	16.0
Buncombe County, NC	5,739	5,609	5,525	27,288	26,693	3.9	14.7	8.6	6.2	17.8	15.9
Haywood County, NC	1,334	1,288	1,262	24,261	23,322	5.8	17.0	12.4	4.3	(D)	21.2
Henderson County, NC	2,610	2,543	2,488	28,252	27,763	4.9	25.8	9.3	3.0	9.9	13.7
Madison County, NC	419	417	410	21,097	20,786	2.4	17.3	5.1	2.1	(D)	20.8
Athens-Clarke County, GA	4,109	3,961	3,785	24,171	22,694	8.6	14.0	7.6	4.0	(NA)	32.3
Clarke County, GA	2,353	2,242	2,162	22,860	21,237	8.9	15.0	7.6	3.6	14.2	34.9
Madison County, GA	634	624	583	23,762	22,549	8.7	10.4	6.0	4.0	(D)	21.6
Oconee County, GA	825	799	766	30,263	29,015	7.7	9.7	8.2	8.4	6.4	16.4
Oglethorpe County, GA	297	295	274	22,624	21,529	8.5	4.9	6.1	2.3	(D)	23.8
Atlanta-Sandy Springs-Marietta, GA	149,974	147,307	141,817	33,257	33,120	5.8	8.2	6.5	(NA)	(NA)	11.5
Barrow County, GA	1,204	1,178	1,082	23,501	23,250	11.3	18.6	12.3	3.9	5.3	18.9
Bartow County, GA	2,133	2,051	1,981	25,860	25,825	7.7	27.9	8.4	3.6	5.7	13.8
Butts County, GA	477	459	429	22,270	21,745	11.1	16.7	7.1	2.4	(D)	24.8
Carroll County, GA	2,120	2,042	1,902	22,339	21,608	11.4	27.6	9.1	3.0	11.6	17.3
Cherokee County, GA	4,855	4,764	4,480	30,450	31,156	8.4	8.3	11.0	6.2	7.6	15.3
Clayton County, GA	5,471	5,329	5,154	21,585	21,611	6.2	5.7	6.9	4.8	7.0	11.2
Cobb County, GA	23,332	23,143	22,321	36,357	36,427	4.5	4.9	7.5	14.4	7.0	8.3
Coweta County, GA	2,633	2,565	2,440	26,932	27,070	7.9	19.2	11.4	4.3	9.8	16.4
Dawson County, GA	478	466	433	27,106	26,579	10.4	10.7	16.0	(D)	2.9	16.7
DeKalb County, GA	22,983	22,519	21,434	34,118	32,072	7.2	6.9	6.3	8.4	9.5	13.8
Douglas County, GA	2,570	2,513	2,437	26,085	26,282	5.5	10.5	15.0	4.1	8.7	15.5

See footnotes at end of table.

State and Metropolitan Area Data Book: 2006

U.S. Census Bureau

Table C-3. Metropolitan Areas With Component Counties — **Personal Income and Earnings by Industry**—Con.

Metropolitan statistical area / Metropolitan statistical area with metropolitan divisions / Metropolitan division / Component county	Total (million dollars)			Per capita[1] (dollars)		Percent change,[2] 2000–2002	Manu-fac-turing	Retail trade	Profes-sional and technical services	Health care and social assis-tance	Govern-ment and govern-ment enter-prises
	2002	2001	2000	2002	2000						
Atlanta-Sandy Springs-Marietta, GA—Con.											
Fayette County, GA	3,626	3,538	3,383	37,553	36,725	7.2	13.7	9.5	6.4	9.1	12.9
Forsyth County, GA	3,861	3,827	3,637	33,108	36,179	6.2	17.7	6.8	10.3	4.3	10.0
Fulton County, GA	38,921	38,302	37,497	47,478	45,894	3.8	5.9	4.0	15.3	5.8	11.3
Gwinnett County, GA	19,553	19,379	19,008	30,138	31,868	2.9	11.0	9.6	9.3	4.6	8.1
Haralson County, GA	600	575	544	22,320	21,087	10.3	31.0	8.2	(D)	5.8	21.2
Heard County, GA	215	211	208	19,117	18,773	3.3	(D)	1.4	0.7	(D)	14.3
Henry County, GA	3,732	3,612	3,285	26,658	27,006	13.6	10.5	11.2	3.8	8.3	22.4
Jasper County, GA	283	274	255	23,226	22,180	11.1	35.9	3.6	2.8	(D)	19.2
Lamar County, GA	379	365	337	23,347	21,090	12.3	24.6	7.5	1.5	(D)	25.5
Meriwether County, GA	474	457	459	20,764	20,386	3.3	22.3	10.0	2.2	(D)	28.6
Newton County, GA	1,632	1,574	1,485	22,749	23,598	9.9	30.1	7.4	(D)	10.2	17.3
Paulding County, GA	2,189	2,131	1,959	23,207	23,597	11.7	7.5	13.1	5.4	5.2	23.1
Pickens County, GA	712	688	619	27,743	26,502	14.9	12.6	9.1	5.1	(D)	16.9
Pike County, GA	345	334	310	23,615	22,455	11.2	16.1	3.0	3.9	(D)	24.6
Rockdale County, GA	2,114	2,042	1,964	28,903	27,836	7.7	20.7	9.1	4.9	8.8	10.4
Spalding County, GA	1,439	1,381	1,324	24,126	22,640	8.7	24.9	9.5	(D)	10.3	18.6
Walton County, GA	1,643	1,589	1,450	24,502	23,526	13.4	17.1	11.2	3.0	(D)	19.6
Atlantic City, NJ	8,210	7,887	7,975	31,702	31,517	2.9	3.2	8.3	6.2	9.5	16.7
Atlantic County, NJ	8,210	7,887	7,975	31,702	31,517	2.9	3.2	8.3	6.2	9.5	16.7
Auburn-Opelika, AL	2,530	2,437	2,338	21,445	20,248	8.2	15.7	9.6	(NA)	7.0	34.5
Lee County, AL	2,530	2,437	2,338	21,445	20,248	8.2	15.7	9.6	(D)	7.0	34.5
Augusta-Richmond County, GA-SC	13,016	12,506	11,963	25,666	23,911	8.8	14.0	7.1	(NA)	(NA)	26.8
Burke County, GA	417	405	388	18,300	17,410	7.5	17.3	5.4	(D)	(D)	16.6
Columbia County, GA	2,881	2,770	2,672	30,345	29,750	7.8	16.1	10.9	(D)	7.9	15.5
McDuffie County, GA	523	507	481	24,529	22,590	8.9	21.1	10.0	2.4	(D)	21.0
Richmond County, GA	4,755	4,527	4,411	23,994	22,105	7.8	12.6	6.8	4.0	12.7	38.4
Aiken County, SC	3,922	3,798	3,546	27,019	24,838	10.6	14.1	6.7	4.2	5.6	12.2
Edgefield County, SC	517	499	465	20,930	18,899	11.3	20.6	4.9	1.0	(D)	32.1
Austin-Round Rock, TX	42,671	43,152	41,157	31,677	32,546	3.7	14.6	6.3	11.6	(NA)	17.9
Bastrop County, TX	1,417	1,395	1,307	22,057	22,419	8.4	7.2	13.5	6.0	6.0	32.8
Caldwell County, TX	706	693	642	20,223	19,774	10.0	4.0	9.2	2.9	(D)	24.4
Hays County, TX	2,623	2,566	2,323	23,910	23,464	12.9	11.6	12.7	5.6	8.5	24.4
Travis County, TX	30,091	30,275	28,865	35,492	35,208	4.2	15.7	5.7	13.0	7.4	18.0
Williamson County, TX	7,833	8,224	8,019	26,979	31,453	-2.3	8.4	7.7	4.6	8.1	12.9
Bakersfield, CA	15,674	14,727	13,891	22,635	20,931	12.8	4.4	7.3	5.0	8.0	27.1
Kern County, CA	15,674	14,727	13,891	22,635	20,931	12.8	4.4	7.3	5.0	8.0	27.1
Baltimore-Towson, MD	92,410	89,050	85,144	35,556	33,294	8.5	8.3	6.6	11.4	10.5	21.9
Anne Arundel County, MD	19,756	18,910	17,917	39,273	36,463	10.3	9.6	6.6	10.6	5.9	33.6
Baltimore County, MD	29,376	28,465	27,083	38,159	35,828	8.5	10.4	8.8	9.9	11.9	17.9
Carroll County, MD	5,434	5,194	4,909	34,117	32,379	10.7	11.7	9.2	5.6	10.8	14.9
Harford County, MD	7,558	7,263	6,874	33,249	31,320	9.9	6.2	10.0	8.6	8.0	34.0
Howard County, MD	11,830	11,353	10,893	45,464	43,648	8.6	5.6	8.0	20.2	6.3	9.8
Queen Anne's County, MD	1,506	1,452	1,390	35,172	34,093	8.3	11.0	12.3	6.8	4.1	19.2
Baltimore city, MD	16,949	16,414	16,077	26,629	24,789	5.4	6.7	3.1	11.1	14.6	21.2
Bangor, ME	3,817	3,667	3,422	26,123	23,621	11.5	13.6	9.8	4.6	17.2	20.1
Penobscot County, ME	3,817	3,667	3,422	26,123	23,621	11.5	13.6	9.8	4.6	17.2	20.1
Barnstable Town, MA	9,021	8,714	7,980	39,589	35,745	13.0	3.2	11.2	8.6	13.2	15.8
Barnstable County, MA	9,021	8,714	7,980	39,589	35,745	13.0	3.2	11.2	8.6	13.2	15.8
Baton Rouge, LA	18,494	17,841	17,206	25,841	24,325	7.5	13.9	6.7	(NA)	(NA)	19.8
Ascension Parish, LA	2,078	2,000	1,840	25,432	23,790	12.9	29.0	6.3	4.5	6.6	9.0
East Baton Rouge Parish, LA	11,704	11,321	10,993	28,474	26,633	6.5	8.7	6.9	9.0	9.8	20.7
East Feliciana Parish, LA	455	432	417	21,571	19,528	9.0	7.5	4.7	2.3	(D)	54.7
Iberville Parish, LA	689	658	614	20,796	18,450	12.1	47.1	3.5	1.8	(D)	15.0
Livingston Parish, LA	2,110	2,022	1,960	21,336	21,172	7.7	10.7	11.3	(D)	6.1	22.8
Pointe Coupee Parish, LA	489	475	466	21,701	20,488	4.9	8.6	9.8	3.2	(D)	20.6
St. Helena Parish, LA	188	184	172	18,034	16,391	9.2	9.6	4.0	(D)	(D)	29.7
West Baton Rouge Parish, LA	517	497	499	23,859	23,132	3.7	28.2	4.4	1.3	(D)	11.0
West Feliciana Parish, LA	264	253	243	17,377	16,065	8.4	19.6	1.8	(D)	2.3	35.3
Battle Creek, MI	3,621	3,477	3,471	26,097	25,138	4.3	31.8	6.6	5.6	9.9	19.2
Calhoun County, MI	3,621	3,477	3,471	26,097	25,138	4.3	31.8	6.6	5.6	9.9	19.2
Bay City, MI	2,861	2,829	2,858	26,067	25,951	0.1	20.5	10.9	10.7	12.3	16.9
Bay County, MI	2,861	2,829	2,858	26,067	25,951	0.1	20.5	10.9	10.7	12.3	16.9
Beaumont-Port Arthur, TX	9,689	9,375	9,169	25,352	23,832	5.7	20.5	7.9	(NA)	(NA)	15.4
Hardin County, TX	1,159	1,125	1,092	23,596	22,687	6.2	11.3	12.0	4.5	(D)	20.3
Jefferson County, TX	6,491	6,274	6,124	26,096	24,336	6.0	18.6	7.7	12.2	11.8	15.1
Orange County, TX	2,038	1,976	1,953	24,182	22,990	4.4	33.6	7.6	(D)	7.1	14.9
Bellingham, WA	4,509	4,341	4,063	25,902	24,245	11.0	13.8	8.6	5.8	10.3	18.4
Whatcom County, WA	4,509	4,341	4,063	25,902	24,245	11.0	13.8	8.6	5.8	10.3	18.4
Bend, OR	3,540	3,367	3,140	28,193	26,929	12.8	9.5	11.0	7.3	13.3	14.3
Deschutes County, OR	3,540	3,367	3,140	28,193	26,929	12.8	9.5	11.0	7.3	13.3	14.3
Billings, MT	3,986	3,846	3,651	28,156	26,246	9.2	6.5	9.6	7.5	(NA)	13.7
Carbon County, MT	251	244	230	25,792	24,050	9.1	4.4	11.5	4.3	(D)	22.9
Yellowstone County, MT	3,735	3,602	3,421	28,330	26,408	9.2	6.6	9.6	7.5	15.8	13.4
Binghamton, NY	6,503	6,371	6,315	25,809	25,054	3.0	26.4	6.8	4.9	11.5	19.6
Broome County, NY	5,223	5,110	5,075	26,088	25,339	2.9	22.1	7.0	5.3	12.6	20.3
Tioga County, NY	1,281	1,261	1,239	24,732	23,948	3.3	53.4	5.4	2.4	4.5	15.2

See footnotes at end of table.

Metropolitan statistical area / Metropolitan statistical area with metropolitan divisions / *Metropolitan division* / Component county	Personal income						Earnings—percent by selected industries				
	Total (million dollars)			Per capita[1] (dollars)		Percent change,[2] 2000–2002	Manu-fac-turing	Retail trade	Profes-sional and technical services	Health care and social assis-tance	Govern-ment and govern-ment enter-prises
	2002	2001	2000	2002	2000						
Birmingham-Hoover, AL	32,651	31,494	29,898	30,661	28,386	9.2	9.7	7.5	(NA)	(NA)	13.8
Bibb County, AL	395	378	353	18,800	17,727	11.9	9.7	7.9	3.1	(D)	30.5
Blount County, AL	1,123	1,108	1,023	21,169	19,974	9.8	14.5	11.1	2.9	(D)	18.3
Chilton County, AL	857	829	782	21,185	19,656	9.5	15.4	13.3	(D)	(D)	18.8
Jefferson County, AL	21,777	21,006	20,130	33,057	30,408	8.2	8.5	7.0	10.4	13.0	13.8
St. Clair County, AL	1,540	1,486	1,387	22,873	21,308	11.0	19.8	10.2	(D)	6.5	18.3
Shelby County, AL	5,353	5,138	4,758	34,819	32,919	12.5	17.3	8.1	9.1	6.6	9.4
Walker County, AL	1,606	1,548	1,464	22,766	20,715	9.7	6.5	13.8	5.6	(D)	17.6
Bismarck, ND	2,658	2,571	2,435	27,649	25,675	9.2	7.8	8.7	5.3	(NA)	21.5
Burleigh County, ND	2,079	1,999	1,876	29,305	26,984	10.8	6.0	8.5	5.7	17.8	22.5
Morton County, ND	579	572	559	22,983	22,080	3.5	17.3	9.7	2.7	(D)	16.4
Blacksburg-Christiansburg-Radford, VA	3,262	3,145	3,040	21,399	20,078	7.3	26.2	7.1	(NA)	(NA)	29.0
Giles County, VA	363	353	348	21,463	20,814	4.4	38.6	8.5	(D)	(D)	13.3
Montgomery County, VA	[5]2,050	[5]1,971	[5]1,887	[5]20,392	[5]18,950	[5]8.6	[5]19.6	[5]7.4	(D)	[5]7.8	[5]35.7
Pulaski County, VA	849	821	805	24,258	22,926	5.5	42.7	5.5	2.2	(D)	13.9
Radford city, VA	(5)	(5)	(5)	(5)	(5)	(5)	(5)	(5)	(5)	(5)	(5)
Bloomington, IN	4,182	4,048	3,956	23,633	22,501	5.7	15.8	7.5	4.4	(NA)	29.3
Greene County, IN	752	731	700	22,714	21,082	7.4	5.9	9.9	7.3	(D)	26.9
Monroe County, IN	2,939	2,841	2,796	24,212	23,162	5.1	15.5	7.3	4.2	12.1	30.4
Owen County, IN	491	477	460	21,862	21,006	6.8	36.0	7.1	2.7	5.4	18.0
Bloomington-Normal, IL	4,798	4,619	4,410	30,892	29,229	8.8	10.8	5.8	3.6	8.8	12.7
McLean County, IL	4,798	4,619	4,410	30,892	29,229	8.8	10.8	5.8	3.6	8.8	12.7
Boise City-Nampa, ID	14,397	13,976	13,416	28,878	28,622	7.3	18.0	7.6	(NA)	(NA)	14.3
Ada County, ID	10,892	10,561	10,156	34,072	33,518	7.3	17.9	7.3	8.0	9.9	14.0
Boise County, ID	157	150	145	22,309	21,538	8.3	4.3	4.6	(D)	(D)	41.2
Canyon County, ID	2,824	2,747	2,624	19,432	19,715	7.6	20.6	9.3	3.8	10.4	14.2
Gem County, ID	308	307	295	19,753	19,377	4.3	3.0	8.4	(D)	(D)	27.8
Owyhee County, ID	217	211	196	19,799	18,371	10.3	4.7	4.1	1.1	3.2	20.5
Boston-Cambridge-Quincy, MA-NH	**188,418**	**188,380**	**182,380**	**42,436**	**41,435**	**3.3**	**11.4**	**5.3**	**14.6**	**9.6**	**10.1**
Boston-Quincy, MA	77,391	76,863	73,221	42,353	40,326	5.7	5.6	4.4	12.8	11.3	10.9
Norfolk County, MA	31,469	31,510	30,494	48,081	46,824	3.2	10.3	7.7	10.0	9.0	8.1
Plymouth County, MA	17,548	17,193	16,413	36,214	34,595	6.9	7.8	9.1	8.1	12.7	17.1
Suffolk County, MA	28,374	28,160	26,314	41,227	38,134	7.8	3.2	2.1	15.0	12.0	11.0
Cambridge-Newton-Framingham, MA	68,485	69,184	68,074	46,499	46,339	0.6	15.5	4.9	19.3	7.1	8.4
Middlesex County, MA	68,485	69,184	68,074	46,499	46,339	0.6	15.5	4.9	19.3	7.1	8.4
Essex County, MA	28,204	28,150	27,302	38,309	37,635	3.3	22.1	7.6	9.8	11.8	12.0
Essex County, MA	28,204	28,150	27,302	38,309	37,635	3.3	22.1	7.6	9.8	11.8	12.0
Rockingham County-Strafford County, NH	14,339	14,183	13,784	35,518	35,218	4.0	14.0	10.3	8.7	8.5	11.1
Rockingham County, NH	11,098	10,982	10,726	38,592	38,483	3.5	13.0	10.6	9.7	7.6	8.3
Strafford County, NH	3,241	3,200	3,058	27,906	27,140	6.0	17.9	9.2	5.1	11.5	21.2
Boulder, CO[3]	11,281	12,084	11,825	40,474	40,364	(X)	17.9	5.6	18.1	6.7	14.1
Boulder County, CO[3]	11,281	12,084	11,825	40,474	40,364	(X)	17.9	5.6	18.1	6.7	14.1
Bowling Green, KY	2,574	2,463	2,455	24,242	23,502	4.9	21.5	8.6	4.0	(NA)	16.9
Edmonson County, KY	198	191	185	16,728	15,830	7.1	(D)	6.8	2.5	(D)	51.2
Warren County, KY	2,377	2,272	2,270	25,183	24,467	4.7	22.1	8.6	4.0	12.4	16.0
Bremerton-Silverdale, WA	7,570	7,159	6,853	31,740	29,472	10.5	1.5	7.1	5.3	8.1	54.5
Kitsap County, WA	7,570	7,159	6,853	31,740	29,472	10.5	1.5	7.1	5.3	8.1	54.5
Bridgeport-Stamford-Norwalk, CT	53,433	54,393	52,190	59,727	58,998	2.4	12.0	5.8	12.8	7.4	6.7
Fairfield County, CT	53,433	54,393	52,190	59,727	58,998	2.4	12.0	5.8	12.8	7.4	6.7
Brownsville-Harlingen, TX	5,697	5,340	5,023	16,126	14,915	13.4	9.8	9.0	3.6	17.3	27.0
Cameron County, TX	5,697	5,340	5,023	16,126	14,915	13.4	9.8	9.0	3.6	17.3	27.0
Brunswick, GA	2,616	2,497	2,411	27,409	25,851	8.5	11.5	8.6	(NA)	(NA)	26.2
Brantley County, GA	290	275	260	19,114	17,682	11.5	7.1	5.9	(D)	(D)	29.3
Glynn County, GA	2,111	2,019	1,959	30,459	28,949	7.8	12.4	8.6	4.2	8.9	25.8
McIntosh County, GA	215	203	192	19,599	17,639	11.7	1.6	12.0	(D)	4.3	29.0
Buffalo-Niagara Falls, NY	33,076	32,169	31,806	28,489	27,209	4.0	20.0	6.5	7.0	10.8	17.8
Erie County, NY	27,537	26,767	26,426	29,208	27,836	4.2	18.2	6.4	7.6	10.9	17.6
Niagara County, NY	5,539	5,402	5,380	25,381	24,501	2.9	31.7	7.5	3.3	10.4	18.8
Burlington, NC	3,587	3,524	3,431	26,459	26,102	4.5	24.0	7.9	4.6	10.4	9.8
Alamance County, NC	3,587	3,524	3,431	26,459	26,102	4.5	24.0	7.9	4.6	10.4	9.8
Burlington-South Burlington, VT	6,474	6,328	6,026	31,981	30,206	7.4	21.3	8.2	8.5	(NA)	15.8
Chittenden County, VT	5,066	4,958	4,739	34,103	32,243	6.9	21.8	7.9	9.3	12.2	14.6
Franklin County, VT	1,195	1,162	1,091	25,663	23,931	9.5	19.3	10.2	2.9	11.2	23.2
Grand Isle County, VT	213	208	196	29,105	28,299	8.4	2.8	8.4	8.1	(D)	26.6
Canton-Massillon, OH	11,061	10,791	10,749	27,185	26,412	2.9	26.5	8.9	(NA)	(NA)	12.0
Carroll County, OH	669	652	635	22,878	21,990	5.4	27.8	7.5	(D)	(D)	12.5
Stark County, OH	10,392	10,139	10,114	27,519	26,750	2.8	26.5	8.9	4.6	13.3	12.0
Cape Coral-Fort Myers, FL	15,009	14,295	12,875	31,562	29,011	16.6	4.8	12.4	6.7	9.4	15.4
Lee County, FL	15,009	14,295	12,875	31,562	29,011	16.6	4.8	12.4	6.7	9.4	15.4
Carson City, NV	1,774	1,721	1,684	32,522	32,049	5.3	10.8	9.3	5.5	7.6	36.4
Carson City, NV	1,774	1,721	1,684	32,522	32,049	5.3	10.8	9.3	5.5	7.6	36.4
Casper, WY	2,294	2,220	2,257	34,018	33,911	1.7	5.8	7.6	5.5	11.4	13.5
Natrona County, WY	2,294	2,220	2,257	34,018	33,911	1.7	5.8	7.6	5.5	11.4	13.5

See footnotes at end of table.

Metropolitan statistical area / **Metropolitan statistical area with metropolitan divisions** / *Metropolitan division* / Component county	Personal income										
	Total (million dollars)			Per capita[1] (dollars)			Earnings—percent by selected industries				
	2002	2001	2000	2002	2000	Percent change,[2] 2000–2002	Manu-fac-turing	Retail trade	Profes-sional and technical services	Health care and social assis-tance	Govern-ment and govern-ment enter-prises
Cedar Rapids, IA	7,329	7,254	7,112	30,341	29,910	3.1	21.6	7.5	(NA)	(NA)	11.0
Benton County, IA	692	682	648	26,509	25,580	6.7	15.0	10.8	(D)	(D)	21.7
Jones County, IA	455	451	437	22,415	21,610	4.1	17.6	10.8	3.9	(D)	23.5
Linn County, IA	6,183	6,120	6,027	31,677	31,354	2.6	22.0	7.2	5.5	9.4	10.0
Champaign-Urbana, IL	5,862	5,684	5,447	27,294	25,870	7.6	10.8	6.3	5.8	(NA)	34.2
Champaign County, IL	4,967	4,791	4,579	26,947	25,446	8.5	10.4	6.2	5.9	11.6	35.5
Ford County, IL	403	399	381	28,485	26,772	5.9	17.6	7.3	3.0	11.8	15.7
Piatt County, IL	492	495	487	30,192	29,746	1.0	14.3	6.9	5.0	(D)	20.5
Charleston, WV	8,654	8,409	8,024	28,230	25,934	7.9	10.1	6.8	(NA)	(NA)	18.2
Boone County, WV	506	483	493	19,705	19,329	2.7	0.8	5.3	2.9	(D)	14.9
Clay County, WV	158	153	142	15,202	13,716	11.4	(D)	5.4	(D)	6.6	24.7
Kanawha County, WV	6,233	6,064	5,746	31,821	28,777	8.5	9.8	7.0	9.7	14.9	18.9
Lincoln County, WV	370	354	343	16,611	15,522	7.6	1.0	8.2	3.6	10.0	38.3
Putnam County, WV	1,387	1,355	1,299	26,501	25,110	6.7	19.0	6.2	7.0	(D)	12.1
Charleston-North Charleston, SC	15,176	14,433	13,933	26,965	25,316	8.9	10.4	8.3	7.7	8.6	26.4
Berkeley County, SC	3,223	3,046	2,884	22,225	20,171	11.8	28.0	6.6	2.6	3.7	20.4
Charleston County, SC	9,613	9,167	8,924	30,361	28,725	7.7	5.5	8.4	8.8	9.6	28.5
Dorchester County, SC	2,340	2,220	2,125	23,134	21,973	10.1	26.3	9.6	5.5	7.4	18.0
Charlotte-Gastonia-Concord, NC-SC	46,512	44,965	43,120	33,083	32,187	7.9	14.0	6.4	(NA)	6.0	10.2
Anson County, NC	558	569	531	22,066	21,035	5.1	23.5	5.0	(D)	5.0	25.0
Cabarrus County, NC	4,155	3,986	3,871	29,733	29,280	7.3	23.5	9.1	3.2	6.3	16.7
Gaston County, NC	5,242	5,115	5,026	27,173	26,364	4.3	34.5	7.8	3.1	12.1	12.4
Mecklenburg County, NC	28,332	27,267	26,104	38,556	37,279	8.5	9.7	5.8	8.7	5.2	8.7
Union County, NC	3,654	3,605	3,289	26,227	26,175	11.1	26.3	6.9	4.0	4.6	13.3
York County, SC	4,570	4,424	4,299	26,300	25,945	6.3	20.2	8.2	(D)	9.2	14.4
Charlottesville, VA	6 5,755	6 5,576	6 5,333	6 32,053	30,513	7.9	0.1	6.9	(NA)	(NA)	32.5
Albemarle County, VA	6 4,452	6 4,318	6 4,162	6 35,254	6 33,370	6 7.0	(D)	6 7.0	6 8.2	6 8.5	6 33.5
Fluvanna County, VA	530	512	470	23,845	23,236	12.7	(D)	4.6	(D)	(D)	29.8
Greene County, VA	385	370	340	23,603	22,154	13.0	(D)	8.1	(D)	(D)	19.2
Nelson County, VA	388	376	361	26,344	24,938	7.6	4.6	6.4	6.4	4.4	19.0
Charlottesville city, VA	(6)	(6)	(6)	(6)	(6)	(6)	(6)	(6)	(6)	(6)	(6)
Chattanooga, TN-GA	13,333	12,991	12,863	27,603	26,958	3.7	16.8	9.5	(NA)	(NA)	16.2
Catoosa County, GA	1,303	1,261	1,201	23,086	22,376	8.5	15.8	11.6	2.5	16.6	12.9
Dade County, GA	338	326	316	21,463	20,810	6.8	26.5	11.3	3.2	2.0	17.8
Walker County, GA	1,378	1,325	1,335	22,201	21,835	3.3	37.9	8.2	2.9	(D)	20.3
Hamilton County, TN	9,454	9,237	9,186	30,572	29,825	2.9	15.1	9.2	6.7	8.7	16.2
Marion County, TN	625	612	607	22,496	21,852	3.0	24.6	15.1	(D)	(D)	15.9
Sequatchie County, TN	236	231	219	20,026	19,180	7.7	27.1	8.0	2.4	7.2	19.4
Cheyenne, WY	2,570	2,425	2,293	30,949	28,057	12.1	4.4	8.1	5.4	6.7	40.2
Laramie County, WY	2,570	2,425	2,293	30,949	28,057	12.1	4.4	8.1	5.4	6.7	40.2
Chicago-Naperville-Joliet, IL-IN-WI	**329,814**	**325,965**	**318,439**	**35,583**	**34,921**	**3.6**	**13.1**	**5.6**	**12.8**	**7.8**	**11.7**
Chicago-Naperville-Joliet, IL	*275,389*	*272,407*	*265,916*	*35,493*	*34,790*	*3.6*	*11.8*	*5.3*	*(NA)*	*7.7*	*11.4*
Cook County, IL	189,054	187,092	182,394	35,224	33,920	3.7	10.7	4.6	15.1	7.9	11.7
DeKalb County, IL	2,419	2,384	2,327	26,208	26,053	4.0	17.0	8.7	2.8	10.3	29.8
DuPage County, IL	41,663	41,472	41,923	45,214	46,238	-0.6	11.6	6.7	12.8	6.4	7.1
Grundy County, IL	1,191	1,138	1,090	30,767	28,936	9.3	12.1	5.8	2.5	6.8	9.6
Kane County, IL	13,434	13,210	12,507	30,394	30,681	7.4	21.3	7.1	6.6	8.6	14.3
Kendall County, IL	1,884	1,848	1,720	30,530	31,156	9.5	32.1	7.9	(D)	2.6	13.9
McHenry County, IL	9,299	9,097	8,731	33,507	33,371	6.5	24.1	8.4	5.5	8.5	12.2
Will County, IL	16,445	16,166	15,224	29,461	29,955	8.0	14.5	8.2	4.6	8.3	15.7
Gary, IN	*18,740*	*18,618*	*18,386*	*27,501*	*27,175*	*1.9*	*22.6*	*7.8*	*(NA)*	*(NA)*	*13.7*
Jasper County, IN	777	773	759	25,331	25,141	2.4	15.1	9.8	9.6	(D)	15.0
Lake County, IN	12,987	12,895	12,756	26,730	26,323	1.8	21.0	7.9	3.8	13.1	13.4
Newton County, IN	326	321	315	22,701	21,672	3.3	31.6	4.3	(D)	2.2	20.0
Porter County, IN	4,650	4,629	4,555	30,892	30,939	2.1	29.1	7.2	4.5	8.0	14.2
Lake County-Kenosha County, IL-WI	*35,686*	*34,941*	*34,137*	*43,076*	*42,743*	*4.5*	*21.3*	*8.1*	*8.4*	*6.6*	*14.2*
Lake County, IL	31,253	30,649	29,976	46,343	46,217	4.3	20.4	8.2	9.0	6.2	14.0
Kenosha County, WI	4,432	4,291	4,161	28,775	27,728	6.5	29.8	7.0	3.1	10.5	16.1
Chico, CA	4,999	4,783	4,571	23,944	22,430	9.4	5.1	11.0	6.3	15.6	21.9
Butte County, CA	4,999	4,783	4,571	23,944	22,430	9.4	5.1	11.0	6.3	15.6	21.9
Cincinnati-Middletown, OH-KY-IN	64,769	62,996	61,393	31,804	30,477	5.5	16.2	6.6	(NA)	(NA)	12.3
Dearborn County, IN	1,343	1,305	1,273	28,438	27,476	5.5	18.1	9.1	2.2	6.5	15.8
Franklin County, IN	617	599	565	27,418	25,427	9.2	11.3	8.7	3.2	(D)	23.6
Ohio County, IN	142	139	134	24,661	23,789	6.0	(D)	3.0	(D)	3.6	15.0
Boone County, KY	2,781	2,691	2,588	29,703	29,740	7.5	16.2	7.5	2.9	3.4	7.0
Bracken County, KY	176	174	177	20,887	21,302	(Z)	(D)	7.9	(D)	5.4	28.1
Campbell County, KY	2,479	2,416	2,355	28,049	26,562	5.3	14.2	8.5	6.1	11.8	19.9
Gallatin County, KY	163	159	161	20,828	20,487	1.1	41.2	5.2	1.4	(D)	15.7
Grant County, KY	498	481	477	21,195	21,158	4.5	21.9	16.8	2.2	8.7	20.1
Kenton County, KY	4,600	4,463	4,428	30,332	29,199	3.9	9.4	5.4	7.5	14.2	12.0
Pendleton County, KY	303	296	302	20,445	20,797	0.5	17.7	5.3	2.0	6.2	23.9
Brown County, OH	990	971	934	22,815	21,945	6.0	12.0	10.2	3.6	(D)	30.0
Butler County, OH	9,996	9,754	9,547	29,415	28,612	4.7	20.2	7.4	4.3	9.8	15.1
Clermont County, OH	5,431	5,272	5,177	29,638	28,980	4.9	20.8	9.8	6.3	8.0	12.5
Hamilton County, OH	29,845	29,014	28,330	35,883	33,564	5.4	15.0	5.7	10.0	10.8	10.9
Warren County, OH	5,402	5,262	4,946	30,955	30,770	9.2	22.8	10.4	7.1	5.5	13.4
Clarksville, TN-KY	5,802	5,520	5,305	24,716	22,799	9.4	16.0	6.5	(NA)	(NA)	48.5
Christian County, KY	1,666	1,581	1,526	23,444	21,137	9.2	12.1	3.2	2.0	4.0	68.1
Trigg County, KY	324	310	295	25,419	23,302	10.1	37.2	8.3	(D)	(D)	20.6
Montgomery County, TN	3,548	3,375	3,245	25,689	23,959	9.4	20.5	11.6	(D)	10.4	19.4
Stewart County, TN	263	253	240	20,560	19,300	9.4	15.7	8.2	0.5	3.2	52.5

See footnotes at end of table.

Metropolitan statistical area / Metropolitan statistical area with metropolitan divisions / *Metropolitan division* / Component county	Personal income						Earnings—percent by selected industries				
	Total (million dollars)			Per capita[1] (dollars)		Percent change,[2] 2000–2002	Manu-fac-turing	Retail trade	Profes-sional and technical services	Health care and social assis-tance	Govern-ment and govern-ment enter-prises
	2002	2001	2000	2002	2000						
Cleveland, TN	2,655	2,587	2,333	25,149	22,372	13.8	30.5	7.2	3.2	(NA)	11.7
Bradley County, TN	2,302	2,240	2,004	25,733	22,732	14.9	31.5	6.6	3.3	(D)	10.9
Polk County, TN	353	347	328	21,902	20,401	7.4	13.8	17.0	1.2	8.5	25.4
Cleveland-Elyria-Mentor, OH	69,060	68,364	67,935	32,244	31,626	1.7	18.5	6.2	9.6	10.7	13.7
Cuyahoga County, OH	45,866	45,378	45,277	33,382	32,524	1.3	15.3	5.6	11.0	11.1	13.6
Geauga County, OH	3,507	3,475	3,397	37,868	37,236	3.2	30.3	6.3	4.9	7.4	11.1
Lake County, OH	7,059	6,987	6,943	30,860	30,500	1.7	30.3	8.7	6.2	9.0	12.9
Lorain County, OH	7,768	7,750	7,646	26,964	26,809	1.6	31.8	7.7	3.0	10.3	17.2
Medina County, OH	4,859	4,772	4,672	30,685	30,766	4.0	20.7	9.3	6.8	8.6	13.0
Coeur d'Alene, ID	2,761	2,639	2,521	24,164	23,014	9.5	8.9	11.4	6.2	10.4	19.4
Kootenai County, ID	2,761	2,639	2,521	24,164	23,014	9.5	8.9	11.4	6.2	10.4	19.4
College Station-Bryan, TX	3,976	3,842	3,673	21,028	19,814	8.3	7.4	7.8	(NA)	(NA)	37.7
Brazos County, TX	3,255	3,143	3,006	20,806	19,675	8.3	7.0	7.8	6.9	10.9	39.2
Burleson County, TX	368	356	350	21,957	21,126	5.2	8.1	9.8	(D)	(D)	22.2
Robertson County, TX	353	343	317	22,236	19,790	11.4	14.6	5.2	1.4	6.5	23.8
Colorado Springs, CO	16,895	16,534	15,990	29,892	29,603	5.7	(NA)	7.1	11.0	7.1	27.6
El Paso County, CO	16,256	15,910	15,373	29,903	29,593	5.7	10.8	7.1	11.1	7.1	27.8
Teller County, CO	639	624	617	29,604	29,841	3.6	(D)	7.0	5.3	3.0	16.5
Columbia, MO	4,131	3,989	3,846	27,658	26,339	7.4	7.4	7.8	(NA)	(NA)	36.8
Boone County, MO	3,894	3,758	3,623	27,947	26,671	7.5	7.2	7.8	3.8	10.9	37.1
Howard County, MO	237	231	223	23,644	21,916	6.3	16.7	7.5	(D)	(D)	21.5
Columbia, SC	18,385	17,844	17,429	27,730	26,855	5.5	11.3	7.6	(NA)	(NA)	25.5
Calhoun County, SC	360	355	339	23,632	22,220	6.2	41.9	5.1	2.2	(D)	16.4
Fairfield County, SC	503	488	472	21,078	20,049	6.6	30.2	8.6	(D)	(D)	18.6
Kershaw County, SC	1,353	1,295	1,234	25,171	23,358	9.6	35.6	6.9	(D)	4.9	16.0
Lexington County, SC	6,452	6,270	6,268	28,981	28,906	2.9	16.3	10.5	(D)	6.5	16.5
Richland County, SC	9,301	9,021	8,713	28,318	27,114	6.8	6.1	6.7	8.3	10.2	30.0
Saluda County, SC	416	416	403	21,816	20,992	3.4	31.5	6.1	0.7	(D)	22.3
Columbus, GA-AL	7,410	7,159	6,740	25,899	23,887	9.9	(NA)	6.2	(NA)	7.9	32.7
Russell County, AL	1,034	1,016	965	20,978	19,411	7.1	32.7	9.6	2.7	(NA)	18.7
Chattahoochee County, GA	261	249	236	13,525	15,741	10.5	(D)	0.6	0.2	(D)	94.9
Harris County, GA	792	766	727	31,554	30,543	8.9	16.2	5.4	(D)	(D)	20.1
Marion County, GA	156	154	138	21,678	19,226	12.6	37.0	5.1	1.1	4.8	19.7
Muscogee County, GA	5,168	4,974	4,674	27,892	25,065	10.6	12.3	6.9	7.5	10.1	23.1
Columbus, IN	2,172	2,126	2,183	30,261	30,450	−0.5	43.1	5.2	4.1	7.2	11.3
Bartholomew County, IN	2,172	2,126	2,183	30,261	30,450	−0.5	43.1	5.2	4.1	7.2	11.3
Columbus, OH	53,061	51,420	49,770	32,043	30,740	6.6	12.2	8.3	(NA)	(NA)	16.2
Delaware County, OH	5,336	5,103	4,686	42,419	41,940	13.9	10.3	8.9	13.3	5.5	10.5
Fairfield County, OH	3,716	3,611	3,467	28,786	28,092	7.2	18.3	9.4	5.0	9.9	23.7
Franklin County, OH	35,729	34,589	33,798	32,947	31,535	5.7	8.7	8.3	10.2	9.3	16.2
Licking County, OH	4,108	4,030	3,918	27,631	26,824	4.9	19.1	11.6	(D)	9.9	15.5
Madison County, OH	1,062	1,041	957	26,313	23,790	11.0	32.2	6.5	4.6	12.1	22.5
Morrow County, OH	741	730	691	22,484	21,729	7.2	24.3	7.6	(D)	(D)	25.8
Pickaway County, OH	1,194	1,190	1,152	23,110	21,805	3.6	35.4	6.4	(D)	(D)	28.1
Union County, OH	1,175	1,128	1,101	27,349	26,725	6.7	58.6	2.8	(D)	1.9	8.4
Corpus Christi, TX	10,163	9,771	9,348	25,119	23,183	8.7	10.3	7.8	(NA)	11.9	23.0
Aransas County, TX	579	557	544	25,094	24,122	6.4	3.8	13.5	(D)	5.4	17.0
Nueces County, TX	8,152	7,851	7,499	25,961	23,926	8.7	9.5	8.0	6.8	13.0	21.4
San Patricio County, TX	1,433	1,364	1,306	21,215	19,409	9.7	18.3	5.1	(D)	4.7	37.2
Corvallis, OR	2,399	2,334	2,259	30,421	28,907	6.2	26.3	4.7	6.4	10.7	27.0
Benton County, OR	2,399	2,334	2,259	30,421	28,907	6.2	26.3	4.7	6.4	10.7	27.0
Cumberland, MD-WV	2,264	2,167	2,100	22,377	20,619	7.8	16.4	8.7	2.2	(NA)	24.5
Allegany County, MD	1,681	1,604	1,557	22,703	20,813	8.0	14.0	8.6	2.7	18.6	25.0
Mineral County, WV	583	563	543	21,487	20,083	7.3	26.4	9.4	(D)	(D)	22.3
Dallas-Fort Worth-Arlington, TX	**185,167**	**182,207**	**176,530**	**33,816**	**33,973**	**4.9**	**(NA)**	**7.2**	**9.7**	**7.4**	**9.6**
Dallas-Plano-Irving, TX	*130,174*	*128,432*	*125,748*	*35,506*	*36,187*	*3.5*	*12.4*	*6.9*	*(NA)*	*7.2*	*9.0*
Collin County, TX	23,231	23,078	22,708	40,831	45,410	2.3	14.6	8.8	7.5	6.9	9.8
Dallas County, TX	82,527	81,281	80,217	36,289	36,047	2.9	11.6	6.3	12.2	7.1	7.9
Delta County, TX	106	103	102	19,553	18,997	4.2	(D)	6.0	(D)	10.1	27.3
Denton County, TX	15,444	15,294	14,507	31,603	33,060	6.5	12.4	11.0	5.9	8.7	19.0
Ellis County, TX	3,276	3,177	3,009	27,294	26,757	8.9	36.8	8.5	(D)	6.3	14.8
Hunt County, TX	1,875	1,836	1,766	23,424	22,942	6.2	29.8	9.0	3.4	5.9	23.2
Kaufman County, TX	1,941	1,907	1,819	24,892	25,219	6.7	20.0	11.6	(D)	8.0	21.1
Rockwall County, TX	1,775	1,754	1,620	34,825	36,948	9.5	8.8	11.5	(D)	13.7	12.7
Fort Worth-Arlington, TX	*54,993*	*53,776*	*50,782*	*30,391*	*29,504*	*8.3*	*16.1*	*8.3*	*(NA)*	*(NA)*	*11.6*
Johnson County, TX	3,348	3,262	3,088	24,677	24,121	8.4	21.3	12.0	(D)	8.8	15.8
Parker County, TX	2,666	2,582	2,549	28,180	28,552	4.6	8.5	12.9	6.2	5.6	20.1
Tarrant County, TX	47,785	46,785	44,068	31,307	30,299	8.4	16.2	8.0	6.0	8.4	11.2
Wise County, TX	1,193	1,147	1,076	22,563	21,769	10.9	11.9	10.9	(D)	(D)	16.0
Dalton, GA	3,083	2,972	2,869	24,609	23,735	7.4	42.1	6.3	(NA)	7.0	9.4
Murray County, GA	788	756	734	20,400	19,933	7.4	48.9	5.4	(D)	3.3	12.8
Whitfield County, GA	2,295	2,216	2,136	26,485	25,398	7.5	40.8	6.5	11.8	7.7	8.8
Danville, IL	1,870	1,842	1,807	22,484	21,563	3.5	21.9	6.9	3.2	10.0	23.4
Vermilion County, IL	1,870	1,842	1,807	22,484	21,563	3.5	21.9	6.9	3.2	10.0	23.4
Danville, VA	2,470	2,391	2,364	22,660	21,488	4.5	33.6	8.8	2.2	12.1	15.5
Pittsylvania County, VA	[7]2,470	[7]2,391	[7]2,364	[7]22,660	[7]21,488	[7]4.5	[7]33.6	[7]8.8	[7]2.2	[7]12.1	[7]15.5
Danville city, VA	(7)	(7)	(7)	(7)	(7)	(7)	(7)	(7)	(7)	(7)	(7)
Davenport-Moline-Rock Island, IA-IL	10,644	10,411	10,173	28,384	27,066	4.6	16.7	7.6	(NA)	(NA)	16.7
Henry County, IL	1,357	1,340	1,303	26,912	25,529	4.1	10.7	10.0	3.2	9.1	21.4
Mercer County, IL	436	430	416	25,613	24,540	4.7	10.6	7.6	2.4	(D)	32.0
Rock Island County, IL	4,079	3,994	3,984	27,469	26,717	2.4	15.6	5.7	(D)	8.3	21.6
Scott County, IA	4,772	4,647	4,469	30,000	28,158	6.8	18.9	9.3	5.9	12.7	10.1

See footnotes at end of table.

Table C-3. Metropolitan Areas With Component Counties — **Personal Income and Earnings by Industry**—Con.

Metropolitan statistical area / Metropolitan statistical area with metropolitan divisions / Metropolitan division / Component county	Total (million dollars)			Per capita[1] (dollars)		Percent change,[2] 2000–2002	Manu-fac-turing	Retail trade	Profes-sional and technical services	Health care and social assis-tance	Govern-ment and govern-ment enter-prises
	2002	2001	2000	2002	2000						
Dayton, OH	25,190	24,689	24,210	29,796	28,549	4.0	20.5	6.2	(NA)	11.0	20.4
Greene County, OH	4,500	4,362	4,272	29,951	28,825	5.3	6.6	6.8	11.0	5.5	48.5
Miami County, OH	2,797	2,775	2,760	28,076	27,878	1.3	34.8	8.7	2.8	9.4	12.5
Montgomery County, OH	16,884	16,551	16,168	30,528	28,950	4.4	21.5	5.7	8.2	12.7	14.7
Preble County, OH	1,009	1,001	1,011	23,751	23,869	−0.2	42.5	7.3	(D)	4.5	17.8
Decatur, AL	3,642	3,635	3,462	24,884	23,702	5.2	36.0	7.4	2.8	(NA)	14.5
Lawrence County, AL	715	739	696	20,570	19,951	2.8	35.8	7.2	1.9	(D)	18.4
Morgan County, AL	2,927	2,896	2,766	26,227	24,878	5.8	36.0	7.4	2.9	7.4	13.9
Decatur, IL	3,157	3,169	3,130	28,094	27,336	0.9	29.2	7.5	3.5	10.8	10.1
Macon County, IL	3,157	3,169	3,130	28,094	27,336	0.9	29.2	7.5	3.5	10.8	10.1
Deltona-Daytona Beach-Ormond Beach, FL	11,380	10,865	10,381	24,747	23,329	9.6	7.4	10.9	5.9	15.3	16.5
Volusia County, FL	11,380	10,865	10,381	24,747	23,329	9.6	7.4	10.9	5.9	15.3	16.5
Denver-Aurora, CO[3]	86,526	85,894	82,196	38,008	37,852	(X)	(NA)	5.9	(NA)	(NA)	12.3
Adams County, CO[3]	10,205	10,294	9,811	27,389	26,729	(X)	11.5	8.5	3.8	5.7	12.6
Arapahoe County, CO	21,993	22,036	21,053	43,109	42,832	4.5	3.4	6.1	13.3	7.0	7.6
Broomfield County, CO[3]	1,321	(X)	(X)	32,366	(X)	(X)	15.1	7.6	24.2	1.9	2.4
Clear Creek County, CO	356	351	321	37,276	34,445	10.9	(D)	5.0	4.3	(D)	17.5
Denver County, CO	22,585	22,655	21,746	40,448	39,153	3.9	4.7	3.7	12.4	7.3	14.5
Douglas County, CO	8,289	8,446	7,844	39,176	43,478	5.7	3.7	11.7	9.7	3.8	11.3
Elbert County, CO	673	668	626	30,543	31,125	7.4	2.5	6.6	(D)	(D)	20.7
Gilpin County, CO	175	174	164	36,124	34,229	6.5	(D)	0.3	0.7	(D)	6.6
Jefferson County, CO[3]	20,477	20,816	20,198	38,600	38,239	(X)	12.9	7.8	12.8	7.9	15.8
Park County, CO	453	454	432	28,140	29,434	4.7	3.1	5.6	10.6	(D)	28.0
Des Moines, IA	16,434	15,782	15,219	33,129	31,508	8.0	7.2	7.7	6.3	(NA)	13.3
Dallas County, IA	1,413	1,358	1,238	31,912	30,166	14.1	13.5	6.4	4.4	10.1	14.8
Guthrie County, IA	298	288	273	26,380	24,052	9.3	6.5	5.3	2.6	(D)	23.4
Madison County, IA	395	378	350	27,437	24,913	12.7	23.9	7.3	3.7	(D)	21.1
Polk County, IA	13,188	12,666	12,299	34,287	32,731	7.2	6.8	7.6	6.5	9.7	12.8
Warren County, IA	1,140	1,092	1,058	27,507	25,941	7.8	7.3	12.9	4.0	9.8	22.0
Detroit-Warren-Livonia, MI	**152,800**	**151,682**	**151,793**	**34,129**	**34,048**	**0.7**	**21.6**	**5.8**	**13.3**	**8.6**	**10.1**
Detroit-Livonia-Dearborn, MI	*56,477*	*56,507*	*56,660*	*27,684*	*27,515*	*−0.3*	*20.7*	*5.2*	*10.1*	*9.4*	*13.2*
Wayne County, MI	56,477	56,507	56,660	27,684	27,515	−0.3	20.7	5.2	10.1	9.4	13.2
Warren-Farmington Hills-Troy, MI	*96,323*	*95,175*	*95,133*	*39,524*	*39,656*	*1.3*	*22.1*	*6.2*	*15.5*	*8.1*	*8.0*
Lapeer County, MI	2,496	2,463	2,481	27,547	28,092	0.6	24.5	9.9	4.0	4.4	21.2
Livingston County, MI	5,851	5,764	5,675	34,639	35,809	3.1	24.0	8.1	4.6	5.4	11.6
Macomb County, MI	26,282	25,934	26,057	32,571	32,948	0.9	37.6	7.0	6.7	7.2	11.5
Oakland County, MI	57,033	56,443	56,335	47,394	47,079	1.2	16.2	5.6	20.0	8.4	6.0
St. Clair County, MI	4,660	4,571	4,585	27,864	27,836	1.7	20.9	8.7	3.6	13.4	15.7
Dothan, AL	3,358	3,240	3,018	25,462	23,029	11.2	13.7	10.0	(NA)	(NA)	16.6
Geneva County, AL	579	571	520	22,711	20,150	11.3	10.2	8.8	(D)	4.1	20.5
Henry County, AL	372	354	324	22,778	19,795	15.0	24.7	5.3	2.2	(D)	14.2
Houston County, AL	2,407	2,315	2,175	26,728	24,459	10.7	13.0	10.6	3.4	15.5	16.3
Dover, DE	3,286	3,088	3,021	24,987	23,769	8.8	(NA)	7.8	(NA)	9.2	39.8
Kent County, DE	3,286	3,088	3,021	24,987	23,769	8.8	(D)	7.8	(D)	9.2	39.8
Dubuque, IA	2,442	2,362	2,293	27,294	25,691	6.5	23.7	9.0	4.7	14.5	8.1
Dubuque County, IA	2,442	2,362	2,293	27,294	25,691	6.5	23.7	9.0	4.7	14.5	8.1
Duluth, MN-WI	7,437	7,154	7,000	26,927	25,404	6.2	8.1	7.6	3.8	(NA)	21.8
Carlton County, MN	830	788	759	25,503	23,913	9.3	22.9	5.8	2.0	(D)	28.9
St. Louis County, MN	5,573	5,365	5,260	27,879	26,246	5.9	6.1	7.6	4.3	18.5	21.2
Douglas County, WI	1,035	1,000	981	23,639	22,611	5.5	8.3	8.8	2.6	(D)	19.3
Durham, NC	13,903	13,548	12,997	31,435	30,507	7.0	27.2	4.7	(NA)	11.1	17.9
Chatham County, NC	1,890	1,861	1,702	35,151	34,242	11.0	28.1	7.7	(D)	8.5	11.4
Durham County, NC	7,211	7,030	6,888	30,813	30,675	4.7	33.0	3.8	11.1	13.1	9.1
Orange County, NC	3,937	3,814	3,583	33,375	30,885	9.9	4.2	6.7	7.3	4.9	51.9
Person County, NC	866	843	824	23,690	23,037	5.1	35.7	8.9	1.6	8.0	17.0
Eau Claire, WI	4,010	3,873	3,804	26,685	25,595	5.4	17.4	8.5	4.8	14.3	16.2
Chippewa County, WI	1,441	1,410	1,385	25,655	25,026	4.1	33.5	8.9	2.3	9.9	16.1
Eau Claire County, WI	2,568	2,463	2,419	27,301	25,933	6.2	10.7	8.3	5.8	16.2	16.3
El Centro, CA	2,973	2,734	2,530	20,382	17,753	17.5	4.4	8.4	2.3	4.0	35.7
Imperial County, CA	2,973	2,734	2,530	20,382	17,753	17.5	4.4	8.4	2.3	4.0	35.7
Elizabethtown, KY	2,766	2,702	2,621	25,324	24,315	5.5	16.7	7.0	2.5	(NA)	45.7
Hardin County, KY	2,439	2,384	2,304	25,468	24,411	5.9	16.5	6.9	2.5	6.7	46.7
Larue County, KY	327	319	317	24,295	23,638	3.2	22.0	9.8	2.4	(D)	22.8
Elkhart-Goshen, IN	5,145	4,921	4,871	27,665	26,544	5.6	53.7	4.9	2.5	6.6	6.3
Elkhart County, IN	5,145	4,921	4,871	27,665	26,544	5.6	53.7	4.9	2.5	6.6	6.3
Elmira, NY	2,230	2,203	2,217	24,558	24,351	0.6	20.5	9.1	3.5	14.5	21.6
Chemung County, NY	2,230	2,203	2,217	24,558	24,351	0.6	20.5	9.1	3.5	14.5	21.6
El Paso, TX	13,992	13,314	12,650	20,129	18,556	10.6	12.2	8.2	3.7	10.2	27.6
El Paso County, TX	13,992	13,314	12,650	20,129	18,556	10.6	12.2	8.2	3.7	10.2	27.6
Erie, PA	7,095	6,949	6,888	25,301	24,541	3.0	26.4	8.3	4.0	14.4	13.9
Erie County, PA	7,095	6,949	6,888	25,301	24,541	3.0	26.4	8.3	4.0	14.4	13.9
Eugene-Springfield, OR	8,647	8,435	8,248	26,416	25,502	4.8	14.8	8.9	6.0	12.6	19.3
Lane County, OR	8,647	8,435	8,248	26,416	25,502	4.8	14.8	8.9	6.0	12.6	19.3

See footnotes at end of table.

Table C-3. Metropolitan Areas With Component Counties — **Personal Income and Earnings by Industry**—Con.

Metropolitan statistical area / Metropolitan statistical area with metropolitan divisions / *Metropolitan division* / Component county	Personal income						Earnings—percent by selected industries				
	Total (million dollars)			Per capita[1] (dollars)		Percent change,[2] 2000–2002	Manu-fac-turing	Retail trade	Profes-sional and technical services	Health care and social assis-tance	Govern-ment and govern-ment enter-prises
	2002	2001	2000	2002	2000						
Evansville, IN-KY.	10,021	9,717	9,294	29,116	27,098	7.8	26.6	6.5	4.5	(NA)	9.2
Gibson County, IN.	835	801	768	25,555	23,596	8.8	50.9	5.1	2.7	4.8	7.1
Posey County, IN.	767	762	746	28,401	27,569	2.7	48.6	4.3	3.9	(D)	10.1
Vanderburgh County, IN.	5,298	5,115	4,860	30,842	28,283	9.0	18.7	7.4	5.5	13.9	8.7
Warrick County, IN.	1,623	1,567	1,497	30,240	28,486	8.4	37.0	4.7	3.3	10.3	11.5
Henderson County, KY.	1,141	1,106	1,075	25,356	23,980	6.2	36.3	5.8	2.1	10.5	10.9
Webster County, KY.	358	366	347	25,417	24,586	3.1	11.1	4.3	0.7	(D)	10.6
Fairbanks, AK.	2,561	2,426	2,303	30,081	27,832	11.2	1.4	6.3	3.2	7.5	46.9
Fairbanks North Star Borough, AK.	2,561	2,426	2,303	30,081	27,832	11.2	1.4	6.3	3.2	7.5	46.9
Fargo, ND-MN.	5,114	4,896	4,821	28,869	27,596	6.1	8.7	8.8	5.8	(NA)	15.0
Clay County, MN.	1,268	1,215	1,174	24,470	22,872	8.0	7.4	10.6	3.1	(D)	27.8
Cass County, ND.	3,846	3,680	3,647	30,687	29,561	5.5	8.9	8.5	6.3	13.7	12.8
Farmington, NM.	2,458	2,365	2,167	20,511	18,974	13.4	3.3	8.0	(NA)	8.3	22.0
San Juan County, NM.	2,458	2,365	2,167	20,511	18,974	13.4	3.3	8.0	2.6	8.3	22.0
Fayetteville, NC.	8,626	8,088	7,823	25,409	23,232	10.3	8.4	6.1	2.3	(NA)	58.3
Cumberland County, NC.	7,985	7,471	7,238	26,323	23,899	10.3	7.6	6.1	2.4	4.8	59.2
Hoke County, NC.	641	617	586	17,739	17,269	9.5	31.9	3.5	(D)	(D)	30.8
Fayetteville-Springdale-Rogers, AR-MO.	9,097	8,636	7,979	24,788	22,834	14.0	17.4	6.0	(NA)	(NA)	12.0
Benton County, AR.	4,427	4,177	3,873	26,789	25,017	14.3	15.7	4.7	(D)	5.0	7.0
Madison County, AR.	288	283	267	20,112	18,651	8.0	26.7	6.5	(D)	(D)	15.9
Washington County, AR.	3,946	3,755	3,463	23,810	21,823	13.9	17.6	7.5	4.4	10.9	17.3
McDonald County, MO.	436	420	377	20,107	17,394	15.7	38.3	7.8	1.1	3.4	14.5
Flagstaff, AZ.	2,943	2,792	2,662	24,543	22,820	10.6	6.8	9.4	3.8	13.4	33.8
Coconino County, AZ.	2,943	2,792	2,662	24,543	22,820	10.6	6.8	9.4	3.8	13.4	33.8
Flint, MI.	11,446	11,270	11,550	25,977	26,434	-0.9	28.2	7.3	7.8	11.6	14.6
Genesee County, MI.	11,446	11,270	11,550	25,977	26,434	-0.9	28.2	7.3	7.8	11.6	14.6
Florence, SC.	4,863	4,741	4,486	24,943	23,212	8.4	25.4	8.2	4.2	(NA)	17.4
Darlington County, SC.	1,591	1,558	1,493	23,455	22,118	6.6	39.0	6.7	2.4	(D)	12.8
Florence County, SC.	3,272	3,183	2,994	25,738	23,798	9.3	20.6	8.7	4.8	11.9	19.0
Florence-Muscle Shoals, AL.	3,226	3,213	3,113	22,769	21,773	3.6	17.0	10.5	(NA)	9.1	27.3
Colbert County, AL.	1,191	1,179	1,168	21,808	21,219	2.0	19.9	9.4	(D)	6.7	31.3
Lauderdale County, AL.	2,035	2,033	1,946	23,372	22,119	4.6	14.4	11.5	4.1	11.3	23.9
Fond du Lac, WI.	2,881	2,799	2,700	29,487	27,721	6.7	35.2	6.2	2.9	9.8	11.5
Fond du Lac County, WI.	2,881	2,799	2,700	29,487	27,721	6.7	35.2	6.2	2.9	9.8	11.5
Fort Collins-Loveland, CO.	8,296	8,099	7,657	31,420	30,272	8.3	20.2	7.6	(NA)	8.6	19.2
Larimer County, CO.	8,296	8,099	7,657	31,420	30,272	8.3	20.2	7.6	7.7	8.6	19.2
Fort Smith, AR-OK.	6,399	6,253	5,889	23,021	21,506	8.7	23.3	7.2	7.8	(NA)	13.3
Crawford County, AR.	1,088	1,061	1,003	19,798	18,795	8.5	18.9	6.5	2.4	6.1	12.4
Franklin County, AR.	372	370	345	20,790	19,457	7.9	17.6	7.4	(D)	(D)	27.1
Sebastian County, AR.	3,219	3,157	2,923	27,543	25,308	10.1	27.2	6.4	10.6	14.3	9.0
Le Flore County, OK.	961	939	886	19,776	18,408	8.4	13.8	11.2	(D)	(D)	28.0
Sequoyah County, OK.	759	726	731	19,144	18,715	3.8	10.7	12.0	6.3	15.8	29.4
Fort Walton Beach-Crestview-Destin, FL.	5,254	4,871	4,611	29,938	26,969	14.0	3.5	7.3	(NA)	6.1	44.4
Okaloosa County, FL.	5,254	4,871	4,611	29,938	26,969	14.0	3.5	7.3	7.4	6.1	44.4
Fort Wayne, IN.	11,486	11,277	11,211	28,965	28,670	2.4	23.2	6.3	4.8	(NA)	9.7
Allen County, IN.	9,948	9,755	9,677	29,493	29,090	2.8	21.7	6.3	5.2	14.2	9.4
Wells County, IN.	704	701	716	25,300	25,916	-1.6	35.2	6.0	1.9	(D)	12.1
Whitley County, IN.	833	820	818	26,539	26,604	1.9	41.7	7.6	(D)	6.0	13.2
Fresno, CA.	19,544	18,401	17,628	23,492	21,979	10.9	8.6	7.9	4.9	11.9	21.8
Fresno County, CA.	19,544	18,401	17,628	23,492	21,979	10.9	8.6	7.9	4.9	11.9	21.8
Gadsden, AL.	2,365	2,292	2,212	22,999	21,413	6.9	19.1	8.8	3.4	18.5	14.7
Etowah County, AL.	2,365	2,292	2,212	22,999	21,413	6.9	19.1	8.8	3.4	18.5	14.7
Gainesville, FL.	5,934	5,720	5,521	25,033	23,712	7.5	4.3	7.2	6.4	(NA)	37.6
Alachua County, FL.	5,612	5,408	5,238	25,280	23,996	7.1	4.3	7.2	6.5	16.6	37.5
Gilchrist County, FL.	322	312	283	21,383	19,446	13.9	4.6	7.6	1.6	(D)	38.7
Gainesville, GA.	3,795	3,670	3,485	25,040	24,741	8.9	27.0	7.3	(NA)	12.3	12.3
Hall County, GA.	3,795	3,670	3,485	25,040	24,741	8.9	27.0	7.3	3.6	12.3	12.3
Glens Falls, NY.	3,149	3,040	3,009	25,092	24,197	4.7	16.8	9.5	3.4	13.3	21.0
Warren County, NY.	1,795	1,722	1,705	28,020	26,923	5.2	13.1	10.8	5.1	16.2	13.6
Washington County, NY.	1,354	1,318	1,303	22,039	21,366	3.9	24.3	6.9	(D)	7.2	36.2
Goldsboro, NC.	2,641	2,567	2,504	23,376	22,093	5.5	14.7	7.8	2.2	10.7	35.1
Wayne County, NC.	2,641	2,567	2,504	23,376	22,093	5.5	14.7	7.8	2.2	10.7	35.1
Grand Forks, ND-MN.	2,475	2,363	2,309	25,831	23,740	7.2	6.9	8.7	3.5	(NA)	32.7
Polk County, MN.	751	735	722	24,292	23,006	4.0	14.7	6.6	3.4	(D)	25.1
Grand Forks County, ND.	1,725	1,629	1,587	26,563	24,090	8.7	4.7	9.3	3.5	14.0	34.8
Grand Junction, CO.	3,167	3,010	2,928	25,940	24,926	8.1	6.7	10.5	5.2	14.9	17.6
Mesa County, CO.	3,167	3,010	2,928	25,940	24,926	8.1	6.7	10.5	5.2	14.9	17.6
Grand Rapids-Wyoming, MI.	21,688	21,257	20,818	28,659	28,026	4.2	26.4	7.1	(NA)	9.8	9.6
Barry County, MI.	1,658	1,628	1,575	28,530	27,670	5.3	25.7	7.8	(D)	10.6	16.7
Ionia County, MI.	1,347	1,323	1,291	21,329	20,942	4.3	27.0	8.1	4.3	6.2	27.5
Kent County, MI.	17,638	17,271	16,938	30,068	29,395	4.1	26.5	7.0	7.5	10.0	8.2
Newaygo County, MI.	1,046	1,035	1,014	21,375	21,122	3.1	25.0	8.7	4.4	8.9	23.0

See footnotes at end of table.

Table C-3. Metropolitan Areas With Component Counties — **Personal Income and Earnings by Industry**—Con.

Metropolitan statistical area / **Metropolitan statistical area with metropolitan divisions** / *Metropolitan division* / Component county	Total (million dollars)			Per capita[1] (dollars)		Percent change,[2] 2000–2002	Manu-fac-turing	Retail trade	Profes-sional and technical services	Health care and social assis-tance	Govern-ment and govern-ment enter-prises
	2002	2001	2000	2002	2000						
Great Falls, MT	2,113	2,033	1,968	26,546	24,545	7.4	2.9	9.3	5.6	16.6	30.8
Cascade County, MT	2,113	2,033	1,968	26,546	24,545	7.4	2.9	9.3	5.6	16.6	30.8
Greeley, CO[3]	5,000	4,886	4,586	24,495	25,040	(X)	15.5	7.4	3.6	8.2	13.4
Weld County, CO[3]	5,000	4,886	4,586	24,495	25,040	(X)	15.5	7.4	3.6	8.2	13.4
Green Bay, WI	8,641	8,327	8,137	29,905	28,729	6.2	21.6	6.9	4.7	(NA)	11.8
Brown County, WI	7,210	6,927	6,776	31,095	29,815	6.4	21.0	6.9	4.8	11.9	11.2
Kewaunee County, WI	523	517	506	25,499	25,045	3.3	28.4	6.2	2.5	3.8	17.4
Oconto County, WI	908	884	856	24,836	23,911	6.2	28.3	8.2	3.1	(D)	19.5
Greensboro-High Point, NC	18,708	18,383	18,138	28,508	28,109	3.1	21.7	7.5	6.2	(NA)	11.2
Guilford County, NC	13,429	13,162	13,001	31,225	30,789	3.3	18.2	7.7	7.1	10.1	10.8
Randolph County, NC	3,158	3,141	3,093	23,629	23,594	2.1	34.5	6.6	2.4	6.4	12.2
Rockingham County, NC	2,122	2,081	2,044	22,930	22,233	3.8	38.5	7.6	2.2	(D)	14.2
Greenville, NC	3,790	3,702	3,667	24,212	23,944	3.3	15.7	7.9	3.9	10.7	32.5
Greene County, NC	401	416	404	20,567	21,190	-0.6	11.5	5.7	2.4	8.8	32.5
Pitt County, NC	3,388	3,286	3,263	24,731	24,335	3.8	15.9	8.0	3.9	10.8	32.5
Greenville, SC	15,573	15,342	15,073	27,179	26,834	3.3	21.1	8.4	(NA)	(NA)	13.6
Greenville County, SC	11,547	11,393	11,314	29,544	29,695	2.1	20.1	8.6	8.7	6.9	10.9
Laurens County, SC	1,506	1,487	1,421	21,490	20,394	6.0	30.2	5.8	(D)	(D)	21.5
Pickens County, SC	2,520	2,462	2,338	22,486	21,056	7.8	23.4	8.1	(D)	8.0	29.9
Gulfport-Biloxi, MS	6,213	5,965	5,827	24,971	23,627	6.6	6.1	6.8	5.1	(NA)	35.3
Hancock County, MS	1,043	998	928	23,370	21,452	12.4	11.2	5.1	12.7	(D)	33.8
Harrison County, MS	4,883	4,695	4,632	25,693	24,423	5.4	4.9	7.0	3.9	7.6	35.7
Stone County, MS	286	273	266	20,302	19,468	7.6	20.4	8.5	2.8	6.4	30.9
Hagerstown-Martinsburg, MD-WV	6,028	5,778	5,454	26,051	24,395	10.5	15.1	9.3	4.8	(NA)	20.2
Washington County, MD	3,643	3,501	3,323	27,052	25,149	9.7	17.3	10.2	4.2	13.4	14.5
Berkeley County, WV	1,979	1,889	1,777	24,310	23,253	11.3	9.8	7.3	6.5	10.0	31.9
Morgan County, WV	406	388	354	26,508	23,575	14.7	21.6	10.0	2.7	(D)	22.8
Hanford-Corcoran, CA	2,505	2,339	2,118	18,581	16,306	18.3	9.0	6.0	1.8	7.3	47.1
Kings County, CA	2,505	2,339	2,118	18,581	16,306	18.3	9.0	6.0	1.8	7.3	47.1
Harrisburg-Carlisle, PA	16,366	15,718	15,143	31,821	29,729	8.1	9.3	6.7	7.1	10.5	22.1
Cumberland County, PA	7,152	6,892	6,652	32,854	31,090	7.5	8.5	8.5	7.9	10.4	17.3
Dauphin County, PA	8,075	7,725	7,422	31,955	29,477	8.8	9.9	5.3	6.6	10.7	25.5
Perry County, PA	1,139	1,100	1,069	25,932	24,511	6.6	11.5	12.1	3.6	4.7	24.7
Harrisonburg, VA	2,562	2,534	2,385	23,270	22,051	7.4	28.1	9.1	4.2	9.4	15.2
Rockingham County, VA	[8]2,563	[8]2,534	[8]2,385	[8]23,270	[8]22,051	[8]7.4	[8]28.1	[8]9.1	[8]4.2	[8]9.4	[8]15.2
Harrisonburg city, VA	(8)	(8)	(8)	(8)	(8)	(8)	(8)	(8)	(8)	(8)	(8)
Hartford-West Hartford-East Hartford, CT	44,403	43,659	42,568	37,995	36,987	4.3	15.1	6.1	8.6	10.5	14.3
Hartford County, CT	33,422	32,878	32,152	38,579	37,460	3.9	14.7	5.9	9.1	10.4	12.9
Middlesex County, CT	6,198	6,077	5,898	38,854	37,894	5.1	20.7	6.9	6.4	11.8	13.9
Tolland County, CT	4,782	4,704	4,517	33,496	32,991	5.9	9.3	8.1	5.8	10.6	36.1
Hattiesburg, MS	2,893	2,754	2,555	22,781	20,557	13.2	11.1	9.9	(NA)	15.2	25.7
Forrest County, MS	1,751	1,669	1,553	23,804	21,339	12.7	9.0	9.1	4.4	13.8	30.9
Lamar County, MS	933	883	823	22,683	20,913	13.5	8.5	13.5	(D)	21.8	11.3
Perry County, MS	209	202	180	16,994	14,740	16.4	50.6	5.1	(D)	5.0	16.3
Hickory-Lenoir-Morganton, NC	8,887	8,816	8,636	25,507	25,178	2.9	37.2	7.3	(NA)	(NA)	12.8
Alexander County, NC	835	837	816	24,299	24,248	2.3	46.4	6.7	3.4	(D)	12.8
Burke County, NC	2,131	2,104	2,049	23,890	22,961	4.0	32.3	6.1	4.2	12.3	20.6
Caldwell County, NC	1,984	1,925	1,855	25,235	23,900	7.0	37.8	7.0	(D)	7.4	11.2
Catawba County, NC	3,936	3,950	3,915	26,925	27,483	0.5	37.9	8.0	2.4	9.3	10.4
Hinesville-Fort Stewart, GA	1,290	1,230	1,192	17,919	16,617	8.3	(NA)	2.7	(NA)	(NA)	79.7
Liberty County, GA	1,115	1,065	1,037	18,210	16,890	7.6	3.4	2.8	(D)	1.4	80.4
Long County, GA	175	165	155	16,265	14,997	13.1	(D)	(D)	(D)	(D)	47.4
Holland-Grand Haven, MI	6,769	6,673	6,678	27,485	27,885	1.4	42.0	6.2	3.9	5.1	11.9
Ottawa County, MI	6,769	6,673	6,678	27,485	27,885	1.4	42.0	6.2	3.9	5.1	11.9
Honolulu, HI	28,301	26,915	26,605	31,707	30,383	6.4	2.1	6.7	7.3	9.0	34.2
Honolulu County, HI	28,301	26,915	26,605	31,707	30,383	6.4	2.1	6.7	7.3	9.0	34.2
Hot Springs, AR	2,292	2,216	2,118	25,482	23,964	8.2	11.3	10.7	3.6	21.0	15.0
Garland County, AR	2,292	2,216	2,118	25,482	23,964	8.2	11.3	10.7	3.6	21.0	15.0
Houma-Bayou Cane-Thibodaux, LA	4,773	4,597	4,198	24,330	21,588	13.7	11.2	7.1	3.5	8.0	13.4
Lafourche Parish, LA	2,344	2,250	2,028	25,835	22,543	15.6	10.1	6.3	3.2	5.7	17.5
Terrebonne Parish, LA	2,429	2,348	2,171	23,036	20,767	11.9	12.0	7.7	3.7	9.6	10.4
Houston-Sugar Land, Baytown, TX	173,757	170,558	161,398	34,969	34,041	7.7	13.2	5.6	11.5	(NA)	9.8
Austin County, TX	686	662	630	27,918	26,503	9.0	23.6	6.4	7.8	3.4	12.9
Brazoria County, TX	7,099	6,915	6,574	27,639	27,028	8.0	28.7	7.3	5.4	5.0	14.7
Chambers County, TX	760	745	723	28,026	27,628	5.1	35.8	4.8	1.7	2.5	16.0
Fort Bend County, TX	13,160	12,875	12,088	33,000	33,676	8.9	14.1	7.0	7.4	6.3	14.4
Galveston County, TX	7,971	7,722	7,385	30,541	29,453	7.9	14.8	7.2	5.4	6.6	31.7
Harris County, TX	130,404	128,261	121,593	36,825	35,606	7.2	12.6	5.3	12.2	6.1	8.5
Liberty County, TX	1,694	1,649	1,490	23,015	21,088	13.7	20.6	11.1	2.8	(D)	19.0
Montgomery County, TX	10,736	10,523	9,815	32,688	32,990	9.4	8.6	9.8	9.8	9.2	12.2
San Jacinto County, TX	490	476	448	21,044	19,968	9.3	5.8	7.0	7.8	(D)	30.4
Waller County, TX	757	730	652	22,258	19,844	16.1	22.3	14.5	3.8	(D)	31.2
Huntington-Ashland, WV-KY-OH	6,630	6,412	6,204	23,139	21,514	6.9	12.9	8.5	(NA)	(NA)	18.5
Boyd County, KY	1,281	1,228	1,201	25,795	24,196	6.6	18.4	8.8	7.9	16.7	12.1
Greenup County, KY	839	808	780	22,795	21,183	7.6	10.3	7.1	(D)	(D)	13.4
Lawrence County, OH	1,272	1,236	1,195	20,472	19,192	6.4	5.8	12.8	(D)	10.9	29.0
Cabell County, WV	2,444	2,369	2,285	25,588	23,638	7.0	12.1	8.2	5.2	21.8	17.3
Wayne County, WV	794	771	741	18,718	17,279	7.1	9.7	6.2	(D)	(D)	38.7

See footnotes at end of table.

Metropolitan statistical area / Metropolitan statistical area with metropolitan divisions / Metropolitan division / Component county	Total (million dollars) 2002	2001	2000	Per capita[1] (dollars) 2002	2000	Percent change,[2] 2000–2002	Manu-fac-turing	Retail trade	Profes-sional and technical services	Health care and social assis-tance	Govern-ment and govern-ment enter-prises
Huntsville, AL	10,223	9,850	9,477	28,959	27,589	7.9	22.2	6.1	17.6	(NA)	27.0
Limestone County, AL	1,590	1,558	1,468	23,546	22,262	8.3	35.3	6.6	8.8	(D)	25.3
Madison County, AL	8,633	8,293	8,009	30,239	28,855	7.8	20.5	6.1	18.7	5.9	27.2
Idaho Falls, ID	2,605	2,494	2,321	24,837	22,730	12.2	5.4	9.2	19.6	11.3	14.4
Bonneville County, ID	2,198	2,120	1,961	25,815	23,656	12.1	4.5	9.6	21.7	12.7	13.9
Jefferson County, ID	407	374	360	20,619	18,741	12.9	12.4	6.0	2.3	(D)	18.5
Indianapolis, IN	51,841	50,763	48,862	32,916	31,920	6.1	17.1	6.7	(NA)	(NA)	12.4
Boone County, IN	1,868	1,828	1,704	38,585	36,734	9.6	12.1	7.4	5.8	6.9	13.6
Brown County, IN	450	437	434	29,476	28,946	3.7	6.5	10.3	8.7	5.3	21.0
Hamilton County, IN	8,847	8,698	8,020	42,891	43,260	10.3	6.8	8.1	8.1	6.3	8.2
Hancock County, IN	1,965	1,930	1,865	33,741	33,518	5.4	18.0	7.5	12.9	5.6	15.6
Hendricks County, IN	3,441	3,355	3,242	29,999	30,764	6.1	6.5	12.6	4.6	6.2	18.6
Johnson County, IN	3,635	3,549	3,453	29,936	29,774	5.3	18.6	11.8	5.4	8.2	14.7
Marion County, IN	27,711	27,117	26,403	32,129	30,688	5.0	18.3	5.8	8.1	10.0	12.2
Morgan County, IN	1,853	1,815	1,774	27,294	26,526	4.5	18.3	12.2	(D)	8.7	19.5
Putnam County, IN	883	865	803	24,250	22,248	9.9	32.7	6.5	(D)	(D)	20.5
Shelby County, IN	1,187	1,170	1,162	27,093	26,657	2.1	42.3	5.7	2.2	(D)	14.2
Iowa City, IA	4,087	3,950	3,815	30,163	28,886	7.1	8.8	6.6	4.8	(NA)	41.8
Johnson County, IA	3,503	3,381	3,251	30,636	29,191	7.8	8.0	6.5	4.9	7.2	43.7
Washington County, IA	584	569	565	27,607	27,244	3.4	18.2	8.4	3.7	(D)	18.2
Ithaca, NY	2,521	2,422	2,321	25,242	24,002	8.6	10.1	5.4	6.6	(NA)	12.5
Tompkins County, NY	2,521	2,422	2,321	25,242	24,002	8.6	10.1	5.4	6.6	(D)	12.5
Jackson, MI	4,030	3,929	3,966	25,011	24,987	1.6	21.4	9.4	3.2	11.6	17.8
Jackson County, MI	4,030	3,929	3,966	25,011	24,987	1.6	21.4	9.4	3.2	11.6	17.8
Jackson, MS	13,550	13,144	12,668	26,848	25,424	7.0	7.8	7.7	8.0	(NA)	21.1
Copiah County, MS	544	528	491	18,922	17,063	10.8	29.5	7.5	2.9	6.3	24.0
Hinds County, MS	6,594	6,386	6,210	26,494	24,782	6.2	5.8	6.8	9.0	12.7	24.8
Madison County, MS	2,561	2,467	2,380	32,896	31,712	7.6	9.9	9.9	10.1	7.9	10.6
Rankin County, MS	3,287	3,198	3,081	27,034	26,515	6.7	10.8	8.6	4.8	9.1	15.5
Simpson County, MS	564	565	506	20,425	18,289	11.5	2.9	10.8	1.8	(D)	22.0
Jackson, TN	2,766	2,682	2,664	25,310	24,766	3.8	23.7	9.6	3.3	(NA)	18.6
Chester County, TN	340	333	309	21,366	19,982	10.0	15.2	13.8	2.2	(D)	18.1
Madison County, TN	2,425	2,350	2,354	25,983	25,590	3.0	24.2	9.4	3.4	11.9	18.7
Jacksonville, FL	35,338	33,974	33,151	30,037	29,439	6.6	6.7	7.7	(NA)	9.7	18.4
Baker County, FL	478	448	431	20,618	19,257	10.9	3.9	6.8	(D)	6.6	46.7
Clay County, FL	4,065	3,878	3,730	26,739	26,330	9.0	4.6	12.8	5.7	13.4	17.4
Duval County, FL	23,829	22,932	22,549	29,624	28,923	5.7	6.4	7.2	7.5	9.6	18.3
Nassau County, FL	1,896	1,836	1,747	31,298	30,149	8.5	12.6	7.9	5.6	4.4	25.6
St. Johns County, FL	5,070	4,880	4,693	37,191	37,709	8.0	9.5	9.9	5.6	10.2	15.3
Jacksonville, NC	3,808	3,596	3,437	25,317	22,881	10.8	1.2	4.7	1.5	3.1	75.2
Onslow County, NC	3,808	3,596	3,437	25,317	22,881	10.8	1.2	4.7	1.5	3.1	75.2
Janesville, WI	4,138	4,010	3,993	26,865	26,176	3.6	33.7	8.2	2.5	11.4	12.8
Rock County, WI	4,138	4,010	3,993	26,865	26,176	3.6	33.7	8.2	2.5	11.4	12.8
Jefferson City, MO	3,708	3,637	3,445	26,112	24,554	7.6	9.5	8.0	(NA)	(NA)	36.0
Callaway County, MO	901	881	847	21,340	20,690	6.4	14.8	5.8	1.8	4.1	26.6
Cole County, MO	2,164	2,113	1,987	30,149	27,807	8.9	6.3	8.4	4.2	10.3	40.1
Moniteau County, MO	320	322	307	21,428	20,705	4.1	23.4	8.9	2.2	(D)	24.1
Osage County, MO	323	320	304	24,703	23,241	6.2	26.9	10.7	(D)	4.6	19.1
Johnson City, TN	4,205	4,066	3,893	22,897	21,395	8.0	19.0	8.9	(NA)	(NA)	20.2
Carter County, TN	1,151	1,109	1,062	20,233	18,692	8.3	14.7	11.4	3.4	(D)	19.0
Unicoi County, TN	400	381	382	22,671	21,628	4.8	38.2	3.7	(D)	4.8	15.8
Washington County, TN	2,654	2,577	2,449	24,323	22,787	8.4	17.9	8.9	5.1	15.0	20.8
Johnstown, PA	3,590	3,498	3,413	23,885	22,422	5.2	9.0	9.7	7.0	18.0	19.5
Cambria County, PA	3,590	3,498	3,413	23,885	22,422	5.2	9.0	9.7	7.0	18.0	19.5
Jonesboro, AR	2,399	2,336	2,248	21,968	20,793	6.7	19.8	8.7	3.6	17.0	16.9
Craighead County, AR	1,927	1,859	1,793	23,002	21,733	7.5	19.2	9.1	3.9	18.5	16.3
Poinsett County, AR	472	477	455	18,563	17,765	3.6	23.7	6.1	1.8	6.6	20.9
Joplin, MO	3,747	3,654	3,533	23,418	22,405	6.1	25.0	9.1	2.5	14.8	11.0
Jasper County, MO	2,501	2,440	2,393	23,407	22,800	4.5	24.0	9.3	3.0	11.9	11.3
Newton County, MO	1,246	1,214	1,140	23,439	21,619	9.3	27.7	8.5	1.1	22.6	10.1
Kalamazoo-Portage, MI	8,673	8,446	8,325	27,265	26,410	4.2	27.0	7.7	4.7	10.6	15.5
Kalamazoo County, MI	6,918	6,732	6,643	28,742	27,809	4.1	28.0	7.6	4.8	11.6	14.2
Van Buren County, MI	1,755	1,714	1,682	22,673	22,034	4.3	21.0	8.4	4.2	4.5	23.6
Kankakee-Bradley, IL	2,716	2,651	2,571	25,901	24,747	5.7	21.2	9.2	(NA)	15.6	15.7
Kankakee County, IL	2,716	2,651	2,571	25,901	24,747	5.7	21.2	9.2	(D)	15.6	15.7
Kansas City, MO-KS	61,255	59,737	58,247	32,467	31,612	5.2	9.9	6.6	(NA)	(NA)	14.6
Franklin County, KS	620	603	573	24,499	23,054	8.1	12.0	8.5	2.2	(D)	18.2
Johnson County, KS	20,581	20,121	20,079	43,237	44,176	2.5	7.1	7.6	11.9	7.8	8.0
Leavenworth County, KS	1,831	1,768	1,695	25,806	24,591	8.1	2.7	4.2	7.5	(D)	56.1
Linn County, KS	219	220	202	22,550	21,066	8.2	3.7	6.8	1.7	3.0	28.0
Miami County, KS	807	783	745	27,884	26,155	8.3	8.6	12.6	3.7	(D)	24.1
Wyandotte County, KS	3,364	3,270	3,121	21,332	19,776	7.8	21.7	(D)	2.6	7.2	22.8
Bates County, MO	389	393	354	22,945	21,187	9.7	10.1	9.4	4.1	(D)	26.0

See footnotes at end of table.

Table C-3. Metropolitan Areas With Component Counties — **Personal Income and Earnings by Industry**—Con.

Metropolitan statistical area / Metropolitan statistical area with metropolitan divisions / Metropolitan division / Component county	Personal income						Earnings—percent by selected industries				
	Total (million dollars)			Per capita[1] (dollars)		Percent change,[2] 2000–2002	Manu-fac-turing	Retail trade	Profes-sional and technical services	Health care and social assis-tance	Govern-ment and govern-ment enter-prises
	2002	2001	2000	2002	2000						
Kansas City, MO-KS—Con.											
Caldwell County, MO	215	210	202	23,722	22,454	6.2	1.1	9.8	1.8	(D)	26.5
Cass County, MO	2,385	2,322	2,199	27,380	26,610	8.5	5.7	13.0	3.4	6.5	21.4
Clay County, MO	5,960	5,775	5,558	31,171	30,079	7.2	23.1	10.5	9.4	6.7	12.0
Clinton County, MO	495	486	464	25,206	24,363	6.7	4.0	12.1	2.1	(D)	26.4
Jackson County, MO	20,257	19,743	19,223	30,714	29,323	5.4	7.8	5.9	11.7	9.1	15.7
Lafayette County, MO	890	875	814	26,959	24,651	9.4	9.9	11.5	(D)	(D)	22.3
Platte County, MO	2,652	2,593	2,460	34,083	33,155	7.8	9.7	5.2	5.0	4.9	8.8
Ray County, MO	590	575	557	24,855	23,819	5.9	13.3	9.5	(D)	5.3	24.2
Kennewick-Richland-Pasco, WA	5,469	5,139	4,756	26,905	24,687	15.0	6.7	6.7	19.2	7.7	17.9
Benton County, WA	4,372	4,103	3,801	29,086	26,566	15.0	6.2	6.3	23.5	7.2	16.8
Franklin County, WA	1,097	1,035	955	20,715	19,263	14.9	8.8	8.3	1.9	9.7	22.0
Killeen-Temple-Fort Hood, TX	8,231	7,823	7,459	24,287	22,458	10.4	5.9	6.5	(NA)	8.3	54.8
Bell County, TX	6,274	5,960	5,676	25,581	23,751	10.5	5.8	6.1	3.0	8.6	56.1
Coryell County, TX	1,513	1,438	1,373	20,235	18,260	10.1	3.2	9.8	(D)	4.4	50.1
Lampasas County, TX	444	425	409	23,524	22,837	8.5	14.4	12.1	2.9	7.5	21.8
Kingsport-Bristol-Bristol, TN-VA	7,317	7,122	6,834	24,481	22,898	7.1	30.5	8.7	(NA)	12.2	11.5
Hawkins County, TN	1,180	1,133	1,087	21,564	20,253	8.5	44.5	9.9	(D)	4.2	16.3
Sullivan County, TN	4,018	3,908	3,751	26,306	24,530	7.1	31.0	7.8	4.5	15.2	8.6
Scott County, VA	455	444	417	19,715	17,860	9.0	13.6	13.7	2.8	9.7	25.2
Washington County, VA	9 1,664	9 1,638	9 1,578	9 24,343	9 23,048	9 5.5	9 25.3	9 9.9	(D)	9 8.1	9 15.5
Bristol city, VA	(9)	(9)	(9)	(9)	(9)	(9)	(9)	(9)	(9)	(9)	(9)
Kingston, NY	4,864	4,710	4,546	27,013	25,553	7.0	10.4	11.3	4.6	13.7	26.0
Ulster County, NY	4,864	4,710	4,546	27,013	25,553	7.0	10.4	11.3	4.6	13.7	26.0
Knoxville, TN	17,922	17,156	16,569	28,466	26,836	8.2	14.5	10.1	9.3	11.4	15.1
Anderson County, TN	1,942	1,852	1,785	27,100	25,038	8.8	29.8	5.2	19.2	8.2	13.3
Blount County, TN	2,784	2,643	2,544	25,353	23,948	9.4	25.9	12.1	2.9	5.7	12.6
Knox County, TN	11,792	11,312	10,931	30,327	28,554	7.9	8.6	10.8	8.9	13.4	15.8
Loudon County, TN	1,069	1,025	996	26,212	25,403	7.2	28.2	9.8	3.1	6.2	16.9
Union County, TN	335	324	313	18,096	17,496	7.3	31.8	7.9	1.2	6.2	24.4
Kokomo, IN	2,892	2,825	2,929	28,543	28,851	−1.3	58.9	5.8	2.9	(NA)	10.3
Howard County, IN	2,408	2,350	2,435	28,402	28,659	−1.1	61.1	5.3	2.9	5.5	9.4
Tipton County, IN	484	475	494	29,269	29,836	−2.0	28.9	12.8	3.1	(D)	23.2
La Crosse, WI-MN	3,612	3,480	3,303	28,222	26,004	9.4	17.8	7.0	3.5	(NA)	14.4
Houston County, MN	559	542	512	28,071	25,945	9.1	13.0	8.3	3.5	(D)	19.7
La Crosse County, WI	3,052	2,938	2,790	28,250	26,015	9.4	18.1	6.9	3.5	17.7	14.0
Lafayette, IN	4,549	4,491	4,393	25,006	24,554	3.6	27.0	6.7	3.2	(NA)	24.6
Benton County, IN	230	230	230	24,731	24,523	−0.2	17.3	7.3	1.4	4.9	23.8
Carroll County, IN	552	556	548	27,146	27,191	0.6	36.3	7.1	3.0	(D)	13.1
Tippecanoe County, IN	3,767	3,705	3,614	24,737	24,200	4.2	26.7	6.7	3.2	11.6	25.3
Lafayette, LA	6,636	6,478	6,048	27,385	25,281	9.7	6.1	8.1	7.8	(NA)	10.8
Lafayette Parish, LA	5,717	5,568	5,216	29,646	27,370	9.6	5.9	7.9	8.2	11.6	10.0
St. Martin Parish, LA	919	910	832	18,572	17,103	10.4	9.3	12.2	2.2	(D)	24.8
Lake Charles, LA	4,701	4,582	4,313	24,370	22,292	9.0	20.7	(NA)	5.8	(NA)	14.2
Calcasieu Parish, LA	4,526	4,403	4,134	24,708	22,529	9.5	21.1	6.9	5.9	10.0	14.0
Cameron Parish, LA	176	179	178	18,031	17,932	−1.6	10.1	(D)	3.9	(D)	19.8
Lakeland, FL	12,891	12,316	11,517	25,777	23,727	11.9	12.7	9.6	5.8	10.9	15.1
Polk County, FL	12,891	12,316	11,517	25,777	23,727	11.9	12.7	9.6	5.8	10.9	15.1
Lancaster, PA	14,001	13,603	13,570	29,266	28,770	3.2	25.6	8.9	5.8	10.0	8.8
Lancaster County, PA	14,001	13,603	13,570	29,266	28,770	3.2	25.6	8.9	5.8	10.0	8.8
Lansing-East Lansing, MI	12,614	12,268	12,067	27,806	26,909	4.5	16.3	6.8	(NA)	9.1	27.6
Clinton County, MI	1,999	1,941	1,862	29,978	28,661	7.3	21.5	8.3	(D)	7.0	19.8
Eaton County, MI	2,927	2,845	2,804	27,748	26,984	4.4	9.5	9.5	5.7	5.4	20.2
Ingham County, MI	7,689	7,482	7,401	27,313	26,474	3.9	17.0	6.2	7.3	9.8	29.5
Laredo, TX	3,437	3,216	2,934	16,593	15,071	17.1	1.4	10.3	4.3	10.2	26.4
Webb County, TX	3,437	3,216	2,934	16,593	15,071	17.1	1.4	10.3	4.3	10.2	26.4
Las Cruces, NM	3,674	3,424	3,120	20,573	17,831	17.8	4.9	7.5	6.5	12.2	35.6
Dona Ana County, NM	3,674	3,424	3,120	20,573	17,831	17.8	4.9	7.5	6.5	12.2	35.6
Las Vegas-Paradise, NV	44,572	42,457	41,239	29,396	29,601	8.1	3.1	7.8	6.6	6.7	13.4
Clark County, NV	44,572	42,457	41,239	29,396	29,601	8.1	3.1	7.8	6.6	6.7	13.4
Lawrence, KS	2,658	2,587	2,423	26,010	24,190	9.7	9.0	6.8	8.1	7.4	30.7
Douglas County, KS	2,658	2,587	2,423	26,010	24,190	9.7	9.0	6.8	8.1	7.4	30.7
Lawton, OK	2,686	2,584	2,453	23,725	21,408	9.5	9.6	6.1	3.4	5.8	56.5
Comanche County, OK	2,686	2,584	2,453	23,725	21,408	9.5	9.6	6.1	3.4	5.8	56.5
Lebanon, PA	3,380	3,295	3,175	27,836	26,369	6.4	24.5	9.2	3.4	14.2	17.9
Lebanon County, PA	3,380	3,295	3,175	27,836	26,369	6.4	24.5	9.2	3.4	14.2	17.9
Lewiston, ID-WA	1,515	1,471	1,419	26,246	24,484	6.8	15.2	9.6	3.9	15.1	18.4
Nez Perce County, ID	988	959	931	26,578	24,903	6.1	16.8	9.3	3.8	15.0	18.1
Asotin County, WA	527	512	488	25,647	23,721	8.1	9.0	10.8	4.6	15.9	19.4
Lewiston-Auburn, ME	2,809	2,662	2,532	26,721	24,378	10.9	15.1	10.4	8.2	16.2	12.1
Androscoggin County, ME	2,809	2,662	2,532	26,721	24,378	10.9	15.1	10.4	8.2	16.2	12.1

See footnotes at end of table.

Table C-3. Metropolitan Areas With Component Counties —

Personal Income and Earnings by Industry—Con.

Metropolitan statistical area / **Metropolitan statistical area with metropolitan divisions** / *Metropolitan division* / Component county	Personal income										
	Total (million dollars)			Per capita[1] (dollars)			Earnings—percent by selected industries				
	2002	2001	2000	2002	2000	Percent change,[2] 2000–2002	Manufacturing	Retail trade	Professional and technical services	Health care and social assistance	Government and government enterprises
Lexington-Fayette, KY	12,967	12,576	12,388	31,136	30,251	4.7	20.8	7.0	(NA)	(NA)	16.4
Bourbon County, KY	547	538	562	28,045	28,988	-2.6	25.6	6.3	(D)	(D)	11.6
Clark County, KY	906	875	862	26,944	25,920	5.1	30.0	8.4	4.6	8.6	10.4
Fayette County, KY	8,681	8,401	8,135	32,932	31,175	6.7	11.8	7.5	11.3	11.1	19.8
Jessamine County, KY	1,036	1,008	1,013	25,429	25,827	2.3	19.7	12.2	(D)	(D)	13.4
Scott County, KY	993	967	980	28,022	29,324	1.3	65.8	2.6	1.3	(D)	5.0
Woodford County, KY	804	786	836	34,135	35,922	-3.8	29.7	4.1	5.3	(D)	7.4
Lima, OH	2,728	2,674	2,633	25,237	24,258	3.6	29.5	8.0	2.3	16.2	14.2
Allen County, OH	2,728	2,674	2,633	25,237	24,258	3.6	29.5	8.0	2.3	16.2	14.2
Lincoln, NE	8,222	7,905	7,775	30,022	29,041	5.7	13.4	6.2	7.8	(NA)	21.2
Lancaster County, NE	7,766	7,450	7,341	30,192	29,226	5.8	13.1	6.2	7.8	12.9	21.4
Seward County, NE	456	455	434	27,402	26,227	5.1	20.9	5.0	6.6	(D)	16.8
Little Rock-North Little Rock, AR	17,831	17,293	16,498	28,659	26,960	8.1	8.7	6.9	(NA)	(NA)	22.2
Faulkner County, AR	2,121	2,070	1,941	23,578	22,472	9.3	19.4	7.7	15.7	9.9	16.7
Grant County, AR	405	395	365	24,167	22,133	10.7	23.8	7.6	4.4	(D)	21.6
Lonoke County, AR	1,288	1,256	1,171	23,296	22,027	10.0	14.7	9.8	3.5	9.1	19.7
Perry County, AR	230	225	207	22,060	20,220	11.2	3.3	6.4	(D)	6.0	25.1
Pulaski County, AR	11,661	11,289	10,859	32,072	30,021	7.4	6.8	6.1	6.9	11.3	23.0
Saline County, AR	2,126	2,058	1,955	24,674	23,288	8.7	12.9	17.8	3.7	10.0	20.7
Logan, UT-ID	2,099	2,028	1,932	19,772	18,744	8.6	20.5	7.5	5.4	6.7	25.0
Franklin County, ID	231	227	212	19,610	18,641	8.9	9.8	8.2	2.6	3.3	22.5
Cache County, UT	1,868	1,801	1,720	19,792	18,757	8.6	21.3	7.4	5.6	7.0	25.2
Longview, TX	5,062	4,932	4,775	25,727	24,611	6.0	12.8	10.3	(NA)	(NA)	11.7
Gregg County, TX	3,213	3,131	3,028	28,418	27,208	6.1	13.8	11.0	5.2	14.5	10.2
Rusk County, TX	1,057	1,029	997	22,399	21,044	6.1	10.9	7.3	(D)	6.2	13.8
Upshur County, TX	791	772	751	21,693	21,217	5.4	7.6	9.9	4.6	(D)	22.1
Longview, WA	2,373	2,339	2,202	25,104	23,668	7.8	25.5	8.0	2.6	11.5	14.5
Cowlitz County, WA	2,373	2,339	2,202	25,104	23,668	7.8	25.5	8.0	2.6	11.5	14.5
Los Angeles-Long Beach-Santa Ana, CA	**413,165**	**402,424**	**385,053**	**32,547**	**31,049**	**7.3**	**12.3**	**6.6**	**11.3**	**7.7**	**12.4**
Los Angeles-Long Beach-Glendale, CA	*300,898*	*293,229*	*279,050*	*30,804*	*29,235*	*7.8*	*11.8*	*6.3*	*11.4*	*8.0*	*13.4*
Los Angeles County, CA	300,898	293,229	279,050	30,804	29,235	7.8	11.8	6.3	11.4	8.0	13.4
Santa Ana-Anaheim-Irvine, CA	*112,267*	*109,195*	*106,004*	*38,367*	*37,110*	*5.9*	*13.5*	*7.2*	*11.2*	*6.8*	*9.4*
Orange County, CA	112,267	109,195	106,004	38,367	37,110	5.9	13.5	7.2	11.2	6.8	9.4
Louisville, KY-IN	36,195	35,463	34,250	30,666	29,398	5.7	18.6	6.7	(NA)	(NA)	12.2
Clark County, IN	2,699	2,653	2,551	27,541	26,354	5.8	19.2	9.5	2.5	7.4	16.8
Floyd County, IN	2,202	2,164	2,139	30,865	30,179	2.9	26.0	7.4	5.3	10.2	18.7
Harrison County, IN	901	888	878	25,564	25,447	2.6	26.9	8.4	(D)	(D)	15.6
Washington County, IN	619	624	616	22,382	22,595	0.5	33.9	8.2	2.3	4.9	21.6
Bullitt County, KY	1,524	1,502	1,474	23,927	23,907	3.4	24.7	8.9	(D)	3.4	17.6
Henry County, KY	356	353	352	23,222	23,316	1.1	28.8	10.7	2.3	5.5	22.9
Jefferson County, KY	23,300	22,774	21,859	33,466	31,506	6.6	16.9	6.2	7.6	12.1	10.7
Meade County, KY	595	595	567	21,687	21,359	4.8	14.7	12.4	1.8	(D)	22.7
Nelson County, KY	1,001	968	938	25,732	24,878	6.7	33.3	7.7	4.1	9.5	11.5
Oldham County, KY	1,580	1,557	1,521	32,120	32,345	3.9	9.1	7.8	(D)	9.0	24.6
Shelby County, KY	982	955	960	28,034	28,601	2.3	44.4	7.0	(D)	7.9	10.2
Spencer County, KY	287	286	265	21,150	22,042	8.6	(D)	10.0	2.6	(D)	35.3
Trimble County, KY	148	144	129	17,109	15,844	14.2	(D)	4.5	(D)	7.5	33.8
Lubbock, TX	6,365	6,109	6,055	25,027	24,227	5.1	5.8	10.2	(NA)	15.3	22.2
Crosby County, TX	162	152	152	23,594	21,594	6.3	2.6	5.8	(D)	7.9	24.7
Lubbock County, TX	6,203	5,957	5,903	25,067	24,303	5.1	5.9	10.3	4.5	15.4	22.2
Lynchburg, VA	5,850	5,773	5,626	25,422	24,579	4.0	28.3	8.7	(NA)	(NA)	13.1
Amherst County, VA	695	684	669	21,841	20,960	4.0	23.2	6.8	2.8	(D)	27.5
Appomattox County, VA	329	325	322	24,997	23,505	2.3	18.4	9.6	(D)	3.6	20.8
Bedford County, VA	[10]1,992	[10]1,954	[10]1,868	[10]29,228	[10]27,909	[10]6.6	[10]21.2	[10]7.1	(D)	[10]8.0	[10]14.3
Campbell County, VA	[11]2,833	[11]2,811	[11]2,768	[11]24,340	[11]23,782	[11]2.4	[11]31.3	[11]9.3	[11]3.7	[11]12.2	[11]10.4
Bedford city, VA	[10]	[10]	[10]	[10]	[10]	[10]	[10]	[10]	[10]	[10]	[10]
Lynchburg city, VA	[11]	[11]	[11]	[11]	[11]	[11]	[11]	[11]	[11]	[11]	[11]
Macon, GA	6,214	5,949	5,662	27,635	25,458	9.7	(NA)	7.3	(NA)	(NA)	14.3
Bibb County, GA	4,568	4,365	4,161	29,587	27,055	9.8	17.2	7.5	6.9	16.9	12.7
Crawford County, GA	272	261	245	21,658	19,633	11.2	3.7	7.0	2.2	6.5	26.0
Jones County, GA	595	571	552	23,998	23,313	7.7	1.7	6.9	2.8	7.4	27.3
Monroe County, GA	572	554	520	25,275	23,795	10.0	3.9	4.8	3.0	(D)	31.5
Twiggs County, GA	207	197	184	19,742	17,345	12.7	(D)	2.5	(D)	2.5	18.2
Madera, CA	2,527	2,379	2,265	19,617	18,321	11.6	9.2	8.2	(NA)	14.1	22.0
Madera County, CA	2,527	2,379	2,265	19,617	18,321	11.6	9.2	8.2	(D)	14.1	22.0
Madison, WI	18,001	17,199	16,469	34,650	32,688	9.3	11.6	8.4	8.3	(NA)	24.1
Columbia County, WI	1,631	1,574	1,522	30,528	28,936	7.1	29.2	8.6	2.7	9.6	17.0
Dane County, WI	15,687	15,000	14,366	35,414	33,534	9.2	10.8	6.5	8.9	8.6	25.1
Iowa County, WI	683	626	581	29,532	25,452	17.6	7.0	55.0	1.4	(D)	10.1
Manchester-Nashua, NH	13,914	13,837	13,770	35,496	36,016	1.0	20.3	9.1	9.3	9.9	9.6
Hillsborough County, NH	13,914	13,837	13,770	35,496	36,016	1.0	20.3	9.1	9.3	9.9	9.6
Mansfield, OH	3,222	3,120	3,024	25,098	23,482	6.5	34.5	8.0	2.5	11.3	16.6
Richland County, OH	3,222	3,120	3,024	25,098	23,482	6.5	34.5	8.0	2.5	11.3	16.6
McAllen-Edinburg-Mission, TX	9,056	8,443	7,793	14,769	13,578	16.2	4.9	11.1	4.1	18.3	26.7
Hidalgo County, TX	9,056	8,443	7,793	14,769	13,578	16.2	4.9	11.1	4.1	18.3	26.7
Medford, OR	4,942	4,738	4,531	26,477	24,917	9.1	9.2	13.0	4.5	14.0	16.2
Jackson County, OR	4,942	4,738	4,531	26,477	24,917	9.1	9.2	13.0	4.5	14.0	16.2

See footnotes at end of table.

State and Metropolitan Area Data Book: 2006

Metropolitan statistical area / **Metropolitan statistical area with metropolitan divisions** / *Metropolitan division* / Component county	Personal income						Earnings—percent by selected industries				
	Total (million dollars)			Per capita[1] (dollars)		Percent change,[2] 2000–2002	Manu-fac-turing	Retail trade	Profes-sional and technical services	Health care and social assis-tance	Govern-ment and govern-ment enter-prises
	2002	2001	2000	2002	2000						
Memphis, TN-MS-AR	37,496	36,299	34,459	30,557	28,520	8.8	10.3	7.5	(NA)	(NA)	14.1
Crittenden County, AR	1,087	1,064	1,008	21,278	19,766	7.8	12.5	9.2	2.6	9.4	17.3
DeSoto County, MS	3,231	3,100	2,832	27,261	26,074	14.1	17.8	10.7	3.9	8.4	9.9
Marshall County, MS	669	645	610	19,019	17,399	9.6	17.9	11.3	1.9	(D)	18.8
Tate County, MS	567	550	536	22,175	21,050	5.9	13.1	14.4	(D)	(D)	23.9
Tunica County, MS	172	178	160	17,763	17,328	7.6	3.0	1.8	0.6	(D)	5.4
Fayette County, TN	813	793	737	26,073	25,293	10.4	26.7	5.6	3.7	(D)	16.3
Shelby County, TN	29,704	28,747	27,394	32,914	30,499	8.4	9.5	7.3	5.7	9.5	14.2
Tipton County, TN	1,252	1,223	1,183	23,468	22,943	5.8	26.4	8.8	1.8	(D)	19.0
Merced, CA	4,640	4,429	4,134	20,623	19,533	12.2	13.6	8.6	2.4	8.8	20.8
Merced County, CA	4,640	4,429	4,134	20,623	19,533	12.2	13.6	8.6	2.4	8.8	20.8
Miami-Fort Lauderdale-Miami Beach, FL	**168,639**	**163,369**	**157,015**	**32,373**	**31,226**	**7.4**	**5.2**	**8.1**	**10.0**	**9.7**	**14.1**
Fort Lauderdale-Pompano Beach-Deerfield Beach, FL .	*54,173*	*52,526*	*50,138*	*31,785*	*30,713*	*8.0*	*5.6*	*9.7*	*9.0*	*9.3*	*14.3*
Broward County, FL	54,173	52,526	50,138	31,785	30,713	8.0	5.6	9.7	9.0	9.3	14.3
Miami-Miami Beach-Kendall, FL	*62,037*	*59,876*	*57,922*	*26,780*	*25,627*	*7.1*	*4.9*	*7.3*	*10.1*	*9.3*	*16.1*
Miami-Dade County, FL	62,037	59,876	57,922	26,780	25,627	7.1	4.9	7.3	10.1	9.3	16.1
West Palm Beach-Boca Raton-Boynton Beach, FL ..	*52,429*	*50,968*	*48,955*	*44,120*	*43,107*	*7.1*	*5.4*	*7.7*	*11.1*	*11.1*	*10.4*
Palm Beach County, FL	52,429	50,968	48,955	44,120	43,107	7.1	5.4	7.7	11.1	11.1	10.4
Michigan City-La Porte, IN	2,729	2,698	2,683	24,773	24,350	1.7	24.6	7.5	2.7	12.5	16.4
LaPorte County, IN	2,729	2,698	2,683	24,773	24,350	1.7	24.6	7.5	2.7	12.5	16.4
Midland, TX	3,956	3,925	4,092	33,728	35,422	–3.3	3.4	6.2	6.4	6.3	11.7
Midland County, TX	3,956	3,925	4,092	33,728	35,422	–3.3	3.4	6.2	6.4	6.3	11.7
Milwaukee-Waukesha-West Allis, WI ..	51,798	50,691	49,151	34,308	32,722	5.4	20.4	5.7	7.6	11.6	11.2
Milwaukee County, WI	28,470	27,811	26,521	30,456	28,229	7.3	16.9	5.3	7.9	13.6	13.1
Ozaukee County, WI	3,980	3,903	3,806	47,418	46,091	4.6	30.6	6.1	6.4	8.9	9.2
Washington County, WI	4,128	4,051	3,965	34,149	33,612	4.1	33.9	8.2	3.3	7.2	11.1
Waukesha County, WI	15,221	14,927	14,860	41,114	41,041	2.4	24.4	5.8	7.8	8.1	7.0
Minneapolis-St. Paul-Bloomington, MN-WI ...	115,502	113,143	109,818	37,787	36,840	5.2	14.2	6.0	(NA)	8.2	12.0
Anoka County, MN	9,733	9,482	9,226	31,385	30,776	5.5	28.5	7.9	3.8	9.3	12.1
Carver County, MN	3,012	2,968	2,758	39,611	38,917	9.2	33.6	5.3	6.9	8.4	10.5
Chisago County, MN	1,274	1,225	1,157	28,424	27,833	10.2	18.0	8.4	(D)	19.5	18.0
Dakota County, MN	13,755	13,383	13,090	37,289	36,583	5.1	13.5	8.3	7.8	6.3	11.3
Hennepin County, MN	49,702	49,077	48,143	44,302	43,074	3.2	11.7	5.3	12.8	7.8	9.6
Isanti County, MN	933	889	830	27,546	26,314	12.5	18.0	9.9	(D)	(D)	17.9
Ramsey County, MN	18,033	17,576	17,076	35,304	33,394	5.6	13.3	5.4	6.7	9.9	16.8
Scott County, MN	3,362	3,265	3,072	32,391	33,718	9.4	16.6	5.1	8.2	5.8	20.0
Sherburne County, MN	1,869	1,791	1,671	25,998	25,597	11.8	15.8	10.6	2.9	5.8	18.3
Washington County, MN	7,928	7,762	7,383	37,679	36,437	7.4	22.5	9.4	4.9	9.0	13.7
Wright County, MN	2,761	2,670	2,509	28,083	27,638	10.1	17.0	10.5	(D)	7.6	16.1
Pierce County, WI	1,035	1,008	951	27,676	25,773	8.8	9.9	5.8	5.2	7.9	32.7
St. Croix County, WI	2,104	2,049	1,953	30,756	30,672	7.7	25.8	9.3	5.7	8.8	12.9
Missoula, MT	2,626	2,497	2,343	26,823	24,383	12.1	6.2	10.0	6.9	15.6	18.7
Missoula County, MT	2,626	2,497	2,343	26,823	24,383	12.1	6.2	10.0	6.9	15.6	18.7
Mobile, AL	9,033	8,863	8,638	22,620	21,592	4.6	12.7	8.2	7.9	11.0	17.3
Mobile County, AL	9,033	8,863	8,638	22,620	21,592	4.6	12.7	8.2	7.9	11.0	17.3
Modesto, CA	11,372	10,908	10,573	23,642	23,506	7.6	13.4	10.5	4.2	11.6	17.1
Stanislaus County, CA	11,372	10,908	10,573	23,642	23,506	7.6	13.4	10.5	4.2	11.6	17.1
Monroe, LA	4,224	4,027	3,839	24,857	22,581	10.0	13.2	8.4	7.7	(NA)	16.3
Ouachita Parish, LA	3,730	3,551	3,402	25,354	23,109	9.6	14.1	8.5	8.1	13.8	16.2
Union Parish, LA	494	476	437	21,655	19,172	13.1	(D)	6.5	2.1	(D)	16.9
Monroe, MI	4,328	4,235	4,281	29,015	29,228	1.1	32.3	7.6	(NA)	6.5	12.9
Monroe County, MI	4,328	4,235	4,281	29,015	29,228	1.1	32.3	7.6	(D)	6.5	12.9
Montgomery, AL	9,665	9,261	8,865	27,533	25,549	9.0	9.9	6.5	8.7	(NA)	29.3
Autauga County, AL	1,128	1,095	1,011	24,736	23,024	11.6	23.8	11.4	3.2	4.4	15.9
Elmore County, AL	1,648	1,580	1,530	23,846	23,091	7.7	18.3	9.2	4.8	(D)	23.2
Lowndes County, AL	245	244	236	18,219	17,479	4.2	37.6	6.1	1.8	2.9	17.5
Montgomery County, AL	6,643	6,342	6,089	29,813	27,262	9.1	7.5	6.0	9.6	9.8	31.1
Morgantown, WV	2,778	2,663	2,449	24,576	22,018	13.4	9.5	6.2	5.2	(NA)	35.2
Monongalia County, WV	2,171	2,082	1,911	26,022	23,321	13.7	8.6	5.8	5.6	16.4	37.0
Preston County, WV	606	580	538	20,496	18,375	12.6	15.2	8.7	2.9	(D)	23.2
Morristown, TN	2,873	2,769	2,621	22,909	21,218	9.6	38.3	8.4	(NA)	(NA)	11.3
Grainger County, TN	432	408	393	20,363	18,948	9.9	38.0	7.7	2.4	4.3	18.0
Hamblen County, TN	1,446	1,393	1,318	24,747	22,632	9.7	43.5	8.1	(D)	8.1	9.3
Jefferson County, TN	996	968	911	21,742	20,426	9.3	23.6	9.4	2.1	(D)	14.9
Mount Vernon-Anacortes, WA	3,135	3,020	2,823	29,377	27,288	11.1	13.5	10.4	7.0	8.8	19.2
Skagit County, WA	3,135	3,020	2,823	29,377	27,288	11.1	13.5	10.4	7.0	8.8	19.2
Muncie, IN	2,992	2,945	2,898	25,313	24,421	3.2	22.1	7.7	4.3	17.9	19.4
Delaware County, IN	2,992	2,945	2,898	25,313	24,421	3.2	22.1	7.7	4.3	17.9	19.4
Muskegon-Norton Shores, MI	4,082	4,013	3,943	23,707	23,126	3.5	27.2	10.9	4.0	12.8	16.0
Muskegon County, MI	4,082	4,013	3,943	23,707	23,126	3.5	27.2	10.9	4.0	12.8	16.0
Myrtle Beach-Conway-North Myrtle Beach, SC	5,059	4,890	4,740	24,584	23,936	6.7	5.4	13.0	5.9	8.1	13.9
Horry County, SC	5,059	4,890	4,740	24,584	23,936	6.7	5.4	13.0	5.9	8.1	13.9

See footnotes at end of table.

Metropolitan statistical area **Metropolitan statistical area with metropolitan divisions** *Metropolitan division* Component county	Personal income						Earnings—percent by selected industries				
	Total (million dollars)			Per capita[1] (dollars)		Percent change,[2] 2000–2002	Manu-fac-turing	Retail trade	Profes-sional and technical services	Health care and social assis-tance	Govern-ment and govern-ment enter-prises
	2002	2001	2000	2002	2000						
Napa, CA	4,983	4,846	4,714	38,361	37,834	5.7	19.1	6.8	6.7	9.8	13.6
Napa County, CA	4,983	4,846	4,714	38,361	37,834	5.7	19.1	6.8	6.7	9.8	13.6
Naples-Marco Island, FL	11,601	11,143	10,012	42,050	39,406	15.9	2.3	9.9	7.9	10.8	9.6
Collier County, FL	11,601	11,143	10,012	42,050	39,406	15.9	2.3	9.9	7.9	10.8	9.6
Nashville-Davidson—Murfreesboro, TN	43,317	42,030	40,309	32,026	30,605	7.5	13.1	7.5	(NA)	(NA)	10.8
Cannon County, TN	313	300	284	23,924	22,026	10.2	13.7	13.5	2.5	(D)	18.5
Cheatham County, TN	962	935	898	25,956	24,874	7.1	39.4	7.3	(D)	2.8	14.1
Davidson County, TN	20,476	19,919	19,029	35,959	33,390	7.6	8.0	7.0	9.5	17.3	10.6
Dickson County, TN	1,057	1,034	1,020	23,893	23,533	3.7	28.9	12.5	3.9	9.8	14.7
Hickman County, TN	420	407	394	18,083	17,541	6.7	19.6	10.2	(D)	6.9	26.1
Macon County, TN	443	437	428	21,262	20,925	3.6	15.0	13.5	2.7	(D)	18.0
Robertson County, TN	1,453	1,406	1,390	25,413	25,335	4.5	37.4	9.7	2.6	(D)	16.0
Rutherford County, TN	5,270	5,025	4,885	26,946	26,630	7.9	30.1	7.7	3.0	10.9	11.2
Smith County, TN	427	415	400	23,533	22,477	6.7	32.0	11.0	2.1	11.1	11.6
Sumner County, TN	3,738	3,650	3,549	27,410	27,067	5.3	23.6	8.3	5.1	8.8	13.6
Trousdale County, TN	156	152	150	21,129	20,432	4.3	22.4	7.2	3.5	5.6	24.5
Williamson County, TN	5,790	5,616	5,209	42,370	40,668	11.1	4.4	7.8	13.9	14.1	7.7
Wilson County, TN	2,811	2,735	2,673	30,120	29,939	5.2	27.2	8.7	(D)	8.5	9.1
New Haven-Milford, CT	29,532	28,950	28,379	35,339	34,400	4.1	14.9	7.6	9.4	13.4	13.2
New Haven County, CT	29,532	28,950	28,379	35,339	34,400	4.1	14.9	7.6	9.4	13.4	13.2
New Orleans-Metairie-Kenner, LA	38,085	36,767	34,606	28,995	26,304	10.1	7.8	6.5	(NA)	(NA)	17.0
Jefferson Parish, LA	13,678	13,259	12,616	30,280	27,747	8.4	8.1	9.2	8.8	11.0	10.7
Orleans Parish, LA	13,767	13,271	12,342	29,100	25,522	11.5	3.7	4.2	11.0	8.9	21.5
Plaquemines Parish, LA	631	615	561	23,091	20,984	12.4	18.2	(D)	(D)	(D)	18.0
St. Bernard Parish, LA	1,589	1,533	1,450	23,944	21,639	9.6	17.9	8.6	3.2	(D)	15.8
St. Charles Parish, LA	1,237	1,188	1,167	25,202	24,212	6.0	40.3	4.0	2.3	2.0	11.5
St. John the Baptist Parish, LA	948	903	851	21,477	19,726	11.4	28.1	6.3	2.5	7.1	12.8
St. Tammany Parish, LA	6,235	5,998	5,618	30,899	29,221	11.0	3.5	11.0	7.8	15.1	19.7
New York-Northern New Jersey-Long Island, NY-NJ-PA	**755,390**	**751,488**	**732,799**	**40,680**	**39,920**	**3.1**	**6.4**	**5.2**	**12.5**	**9.3**	**12.3**
Edison, NJ	*90,194*	*88,847*	*86,490*	*40,183*	*39,625*	*4.3*	*11.2*	*7.5*	*14.0*	*8.7*	*12.8*
Middlesex County, NJ	28,926	28,644	27,477	37,449	36,483	5.3	15.4	6.2	15.5	6.4	12.0
Monmouth County, NJ	27,419	27,054	26,318	43,684	42,646	4.2	4.7	8.2	15.4	11.9	16.7
Ocean County, NJ	16,907	16,301	15,582	31,497	30,339	8.5	4.7	13.7	6.4	17.4	20.5
Somerset County, NJ	16,942	16,849	17,113	55,057	57,262	-1.0	13.5	6.1	13.2	5.5	6.3
Nassau-Suffolk, NY	*121,159*	*119,997*	*116,298*	*43,349*	*42,131*	*4.2*	*7.9*	*8.0*	*9.7*	*12.7*	*16.0*
Nassau County, NY	66,351	66,079	63,409	49,543	47,449	4.6	5.6	8.2	10.6	14.5	13.7
Suffolk County, NY	54,808	53,918	52,889	37,650	37,140	3.6	10.5	7.8	8.5	10.6	18.7
Newark-Union, NJ-PA	*92,243*	*91,116*	*89,531*	*43,326*	*42,616*	*3.0*	*11.6*	*6.3*	*13.0*	*8.5*	*13.3*
Essex County, NJ	30,493	30,136	29,355	38,312	37,045	3.9	8.8	4.5	11.8	10.3	18.7
Hunterdon County, NJ	6,974	6,859	6,479	55,050	52,846	7.6	6.9	15.6	17.7	7.6	12.3
Morris County, NJ	26,804	26,498	26,479	56,002	56,175	1.2	10.3	6.1	14.5	6.3	8.0
Sussex County, NJ	5,609	5,499	5,349	37,676	36,975	4.9	5.4	9.8	11.1	12.8	19.4
Union County, NJ	21,098	20,911	20,749	39,889	39,661	1.7	19.9	6.8	12.1	8.5	11.7
Pike County, PA	1,266	1,213	1,120	25,292	24,008	13.0	6.2	9.5	5.1	6.2	24.0
New York-White Plains-Wayne, NY-NJ	*451,793*	*451,528*	*440,480*	*39,629*	*38,937*	*2.6*	*4.5*	*4.2*	*12.7*	*8.9*	*11.4*
Bergen County, NJ	47,287	46,873	45,380	52,867	51,234	4.2	11.8	7.7	11.8	10.4	7.6
Hudson County, NJ	18,456	18,319	17,633	30,259	28,936	4.7	5.3	5.6	6.8	6.0	15.5
Passaic County, NJ	15,552	15,224	14,954	31,323	30,463	4.0	15.1	8.9	7.0	10.7	16.4
Bronx County, NY	28,457	27,455	25,817	20,950	19,350	10.2	3.7	6.1	3.0	30.3	15.6
Kings County, NY	62,232	61,077	60,470	25,138	24,519	2.9	6.7	7.4	6.2	26.9	10.7
New York County, NY	131,576	135,365	132,138	84,591	85,789	-0.4	2.0	2.5	15.8	4.7	11.2
Putnam County, NY	3,885	3,846	3,737	39,434	38,884	4.0	7.1	6.9	7.5	15.2	20.5
Queens County, NY	64,314	63,377	62,299	28,877	27,926	3.2	7.3	6.3	3.3	16.0	9.0
Richmond County, NY	15,929	15,848	15,230	34,980	34,194	4.6	(D)	8.5	6.3	25.6	10.4
Rockland County, NY	12,031	11,813	11,828	41,311	41,150	1.7	14.4	7.2	10.9	14.0	17.0
Westchester County, NY	52,074	52,331	50,992	55,522	55,072	2.1	7.5	5.9	12.2	11.2	13.1
Niles-Benton Harbor, MI	4,305	4,226	4,239	26,482	26,071	1.6	33.2	7.0	3.9	9.2	11.8
Berrien County, MI	4,305	4,226	4,239	26,482	26,071	1.6	33.2	7.0	3.9	9.2	11.8
Norwich-New London, CT	9,203	8,874	8,514	35,106	32,813	8.1	18.6	6.5	8.3	9.2	31.9
New London County, CT	9,203	8,874	8,514	35,106	32,813	8.1	18.6	6.5	8.3	9.2	31.9
Ocala, FL	6,437	6,168	5,894	23,637	22,643	9.2	11.7	12.5	4.9	12.4	18.0
Marion County, FL	6,437	6,168	5,894	23,637	22,643	9.2	11.7	12.5	4.9	12.4	18.0
Ocean City, NJ	3,549	3,363	3,239	34,879	31,666	9.6	1.9	11.7	4.6	9.5	26.1
Cape May County, NJ	3,549	3,363	3,239	34,879	31,666	9.6	1.9	11.7	4.6	9.5	26.1
Odessa, TX	2,732	2,658	2,546	22,342	21,097	7.3	10.3	10.8	(NA)	8.5	17.3
Ector County, TX	2,732	2,658	2,546	22,342	21,097	7.3	10.3	10.8	(D)	8.5	17.3
Ogden-Clearfield, UT	11,587	11,144	10,772	25,168	24,212	7.6	14.6	7.8	(NA)	7.7	33.0
Davis County, UT	6,471	6,217	6,024	25,947	25,064	7.4	11.0	7.3	6.4	5.9	38.6
Morgan County, UT	167	167	156	22,397	21,749	7.2	16.0	7.9	(D)	1.3	19.0
Weber County, UT	4,949	4,760	4,593	24,315	23,263	7.8	19.2	8.4	4.0	10.1	26.1
Oklahoma City, OK	31,219	30,441	29,092	27,877	26,503	7.3	13.4	7.3	(NA)	(NA)	24.3
Canadian County, OK	2,326	2,249	2,210	25,527	25,058	5.2	21.2	8.4	4.2	4.6	24.3
Cleveland County, OK	5,660	5,399	5,236	26,240	25,129	8.1	5.4	10.2	6.8	8.5	32.4
Grady County, OK	1,047	995	928	22,407	20,361	12.8	26.2	8.2	(D)	6.5	19.1
Lincoln County, OK	671	648	611	20,813	18,999	9.9	7.6	8.2	2.7	4.5	24.8
Logan County, OK	837	802	761	24,004	22,428	9.9	3.5	9.3	8.9	(D)	26.6
McClain County, OK	664	632	614	23,677	22,059	8.0	5.1	14.4	2.9	3.9	21.7
Oklahoma County, OK	20,015	19,716	18,731	29,818	28,313	6.9	14.0	6.7	6.4	9.8	23.4

See footnotes at end of table.

Metropolitan statistical area **Metropolitan statistical area with metropolitan divisions** *Metropolitan division* Component county	Personal income										
	Total (million dollars)			Per capita[1] (dollars)		Percent change,[2] 2000–2002	Earnings—percent by selected industries				
	2002	2001	2000	2002	2000		Manu-fac-turing	Retail trade	Profes-sional and technical services	Health care and social assis-tance	Govern-ment and govern-ment enter-prises
Olympia, WA.	6,719	6,461	6,093	30,828	29,242	10.3	4.0	9.0	4.2	10.8	42.2
Thurston County, WA.	6,719	6,461	6,093	30,828	29,242	10.3	4.0	9.0	4.2	10.8	42.2
Omaha-Council Bluffs, NE-IA.	26,012	25,249	24,230	33,200	31,509	7.4	7.5	7.2	(NA)	(NA)	15.1
Harrison County, IA.	400	389	384	25,650	24,481	3.9	6.5	11.0	(D)	(D)	21.7
Mills County, IA.	465	433	420	31,575	28,832	10.8	4.9	8.8	3.9	(D)	41.7
Pottawattamie County, IA.	2,402	2,322	2,249	27,256	25,566	6.8	15.0	11.2	3.8	12.6	15.9
Cass County, NE	714	699	670	28,802	27,466	6.5	15.0	9.1	3.1	6.3	23.1
Douglas County, NE	17,342	16,906	16,126	36,765	34,717	7.5	7.0	6.9	7.8	9.9	11.0
Sarpy County, NE.	3,574	3,413	3,324	27,638	26,986	7.5	4.6	5.9	6.0	2.8	38.3
Saunders County, NE	543	537	511	27,263	25,761	6.1	8.7	8.5	3.7	(D)	22.6
Washington County, NE.	572	550	544	29,616	28,959	5.1	14.8	9.2	(D)	(D)	24.6
Orlando - Kissimee, FL.	48,431	46,354	44,751	27,587	27,018	8.2	6.5	7.8	9.8	9.3	11.3
Lake County, FL.	6,128	5,820	5,460	26,085	25,653	12.2	5.5	10.6	5.4	16.8	15.5
Orange County, FL.	26,164	25,047	24,437	27,695	27,083	7.1	6.7	6.5	10.6	8.8	10.7
Osceola County, FL.	3,883	3,647	3,503	19,992	20,113	10.9	3.6	10.6	2.7	11.5	18.6
Seminole County, FL.	12,256	11,839	11,351	32,110	30,927	8.0	6.6	11.5	10.6	8.2	10.1
Oshkosh-Neenah, WI	4,681	4,542	4,431	29,537	28,217	5.6	42.3	4.6	3.5	9.5	11.9
Winnebago County, WI	4,681	4,542	4,431	29,537	28,217	5.6	42.3	4.6	3.5	9.5	11.9
Owensboro, KY.	2,759	2,736	2,698	25,014	24,530	2.2	24.9	7.8	(NA)	(NA)	16.8
Daviess County, KY.	2,326	2,274	2,257	25,310	24,639	3.0	17.8	8.7	(D)	10.9	18.7
Hancock County, KY	171	171	173	20,219	20,531	−1.4	79.6	2.1	(D)	1.4	5.9
McLean County, KY.	262	291	268	26,351	26,903	−2.3	5.2	7.1	1.0	(D)	13.9
Oxnard-Thousand Oaks-Ventura, CA.	27,006	26,173	25,364	34,572	33,523	6.5	16.6	7.4	7.7	7.2	16.5
Ventura County, CA.	27,006	26,173	25,364	34,572	33,523	6.5	16.6	7.4	7.7	7.2	16.5
Palm Bay-Melbourne-Titusville, FL.	13,770	13,281	12,865	27,762	26,925	7.0	16.7	8.0	9.6	11.4	17.1
Brevard County, FL.	13,770	13,281	12,865	27,762	26,925	7.0	16.7	8.0	9.6	11.4	17.1
Panama City-Lynn Haven, FL.	3,889	3,657	3,522	25,536	23,757	10.4	5.5	9.2	5.9	13.1	29.3
Bay County, FL.	3,889	3,657	3,522	25,536	23,757	10.4	5.5	9.2	5.9	13.1	29.3
Parkersburg-Marietta-Vienna, WV-OH	4,054	3,897	3,785	24,774	23,013	7.1	(NA)	8.9	(NA)	(NA)	16.1
Washington County, OH.	1,577	1,492	1,437	25,230	22,737	9.8	22.8	7.8	3.6	11.6	12.4
Pleasants County, WV.	174	167	160	22,892	21,255	9.3	31.8	3.6	(D)	(D)	17.9
Wirt County, WV.	101	99	95	17,379	16,087	7.2	(D)	8.8	(D)	10.8	41.0
Wood County, WV.	2,200	2,139	2,094	25,105	23,824	5.1	21.3	10.1	3.0	14.7	18.0
Pascagoula, MS.	3,497	3,447	3,303	22,833	21,860	5.9	33.7	6.5	(NA)	6.6	23.9
George County, MS.	388	375	360	19,385	18,749	7.7	9.6	13.2	(D)	4.7	30.4
Jackson County, MS.	3,109	3,073	2,943	23,350	22,313	5.7	35.3	6.1	4.7	6.7	23.5
Pensacola-Ferry Pass-Brent, FL.	10,544	10,229	9,703	24,884	23,507	8.7	5.3	7.8	6.4	12.5	33.4
Escambia County, FL.	7,404	7,225	6,852	25,017	23,284	8.1	5.6	7.6	6.6	13.2	33.8
Santa Rosa County, FL.	3,140	3,004	2,851	24,576	24,061	10.1	4.1	8.8	4.6	9.1	31.4
Peoria, IL.	10,685	10,498	10,257	29,170	27,974	4.2	25.0	6.0	(NA)	(NA)	11.5
Marshall County, IL.	355	352	340	27,206	25,866	4.3	36.3	5.6	1.6	(D)	13.6
Peoria County, IL.	5,389	5,288	5,157	29,496	28,150	4.5	15.8	5.7	12.2	19.7	12.0
Stark County, IL.	159	167	159	25,439	25,147	0.2	10.3	12.5	(D)	6.6	22.4
Tazewell County, IL.	3,772	3,696	3,629	29,403	28,249	3.9	40.6	6.2	2.3	5.1	9.7
Woodford County, IL.	1,010	995	971	28,039	27,351	4.0	26.0	8.4	2.9	7.1	16.5
Philadelphia-Camden-Wilmington, PA-NJ-DE-MD.	**205,346**	**199,176**	**193,919**	**35,753**	**34,062**	**5.9**	**12.1**	**6.5**	**12.4**	**11.3**	**12.5**
Camden, NJ	*40,353*	*38,792*	*37,035*	*33,300*	*31,157*	*9.0*	*12.4*	*8.5*	*8.7*	*11.3*	*17.5*
Burlington County, NJ.	15,985	15,376	14,882	36,513	35,047	7.4	12.0	8.2	8.2	9.6	16.9
Camden County, NJ.	16,430	15,804	14,968	32,108	29,424	9.8	11.5	7.8	10.3	13.8	17.9
Gloucester County, NJ.	7,939	7,611	7,184	30,265	28,139	10.5	15.9	11.1	5.9	9.1	18.0
Philadelphia, PA	*142,093*	*138,099*	*135,225*	*36,752*	*35,106*	*5.1*	*12.2*	*6.1*	*13.2*	*11.7*	*11.4*
Bucks County, PA.	24,199	23,668	22,922	39,717	38,242	5.6	15.9	9.8	10.5	10.5	9.3
Chester County, PA.	21,012	20,482	20,245	46,737	46,461	3.8	15.2	7.8	12.0	8.6	7.2
Delaware County, PA.	21,327	20,669	20,328	38,508	36,817	4.9	13.9	7.4	12.4	13.1	9.5
Montgomery County, PA.	36,298	35,386	34,536	47,461	45,990	5.1	16.5	6.1	13.9	10.7	6.2
Philadelphia County, PA.	39,257	37,893	37,194	26,369	24,572	5.5	5.7	3.7	14.4	13.7	18.5
Wilmington, DE-MD-NJ	*22,900*	*22,285*	*21,659*	*34,413*	*33,192*	*5.7*	*11.0*	*5.8*	*(NA)*	*9.1*	*11.7*
New Castle County, DE.	18,398	17,940	17,440	36,047	34,751	5.5	9.7	5.6	14.5	9.1	10.8
Cecil County, MD.	2,626	2,534	2,442	29,078	28,244	7.5	19.8	9.1	(D)	8.6	21.4
Salem County, NJ.	1,875	1,812	1,777	28,977	27,669	5.5	19.4	5.7	3.0	9.3	15.6
Phoenix-Mesa-Scottsdale, AZ	99,387	96,477	92,975	28,481	28,365	6.9	11.2	8.3	(NA)	8.4	12.6
Maricopa County, AZ.	95,619	92,913	89,772	29,020	28,993	6.5	11.4	8.3	8.6	8.4	12.1
Pinal County, AZ.	3,768	3,564	3,203	19,356	17,655	17.6	6.0	7.2	(D)	7.5	34.6
Pine Bluff, AR.	2,180	2,138	2,046	20,501	19,073	6.6	21.2	6.6	(NA)	(NA)	27.7
Cleveland County, AR.	190	193	178	22,062	20,768	6.8	5.2	(D)	0.4	(D)	25.2
Jefferson County, AR.	1,771	1,721	1,654	21,277	19,635	7.1	22.4	7.0	(D)	12.1	26.7
Lincoln County, AR.	219	224	214	15,128	14,800	2.5	14.4	4.7	0.8	5.2	40.5
Pittsburgh, PA.	78,241	76,386	74,361	32,381	30,610	5.2	13.9	7.0	10.4	12.3	11.2
Allegheny County, PA.	46,303	45,269	44,298	36,500	34,608	4.5	11.7	5.8	12.4	12.6	10.2
Armstrong County, PA.	1,789	1,759	1,668	24,929	23,074	7.2	13.1	11.2	4.1	12.3	15.6
Beaver County, PA.	4,720	4,632	4,495	26,357	24,814	5.0	18.5	7.9	6.8	13.6	14.2
Butler County, PA.	5,308	5,180	5,028	29,780	28,801	5.6	23.9	10.4	4.8	8.8	13.9
Fayette County, PA.	3,519	3,380	3,265	23,988	21,987	7.8	12.0	12.6	4.4	13.9	16.4
Washington County, PA.	6,057	5,889	5,656	29,740	27,863	7.1	16.8	7.4	6.0	12.3	12.1
Westmoreland County, PA.	10,545	10,278	9,950	28,635	26,909	6.0	21.2	10.8	5.6	11.5	13.1
Pittsfield, MA.	4,437	4,260	4,082	33,263	30,278	8.7	16.8	8.8	6.0	16.7	11.4
Berkshire County, MA.	4,437	4,260	4,082	33,263	30,278	8.7	16.8	8.8	6.0	16.7	11.4

See footnotes at end of table.

Table C-3. Metropolitan Areas With Component Counties — **Personal Income and Earnings by Industry**—Con.

Metropolitan statistical area / Metropolitan statistical area with metropolitan divisions / *Metropolitan division* / Component county	Total (million dollars)			Per capita[1] (dollars)		Percent change,[2] 2000–2002	Earnings—percent by selected industries				
	2002	2001	2000	2002	2000		Manu-facturing	Retail trade	Profes-sional and technical services	Health care and social assis-tance	Govern-ment and govern-ment enter-prises
Pocatello, ID	1,886	1,830	1,732	22,643	20,840	8.9	12.9	8.3	(NA)	(NA)	26.8
Bannock County, ID	1,726	1,684	1,577	22,754	20,860	9.5	10.5	9.1	4.7	10.5	28.3
Power County, ID	160	146	155	21,512	20,640	2.9	31.5	2.8	(D)	(D)	14.9
Portland-South Portland-Biddeford, ME	15,849	15,296	14,576	31,678	29,791	8.7	9.4	8.6	7.5	13.0	17.3
Cumberland County, ME	9,278	8,946	8,475	34,498	31,864	9.5	8.0	8.4	8.9	14.2	14.3
Sagadahoc County, ME	1,005	971	918	27,955	26,039	9.5	(D)	5.1	4.2	4.9	16.4
York County, ME	5,566	5,380	5,184	28,482	27,561	7.4	16.0	9.9	4.4	11.9	25.9
Portland-Vancouver-Beaverton, OR-WA	64,755	63,892	62,190	32,167	32,127	4.1	15.5	6.6	8.6	9.0	13.3
Clackamas County, OR	12,526	12,318	12,416	35,543	36,564	0.9	15.3	7.9	8.0	9.9	11.8
Columbia County, OR	1,238	1,216	1,168	27,234	26,749	6.0	24.2	8.2	3.3	5.2	20.1
Multnomah County, OR	22,857	22,505	21,384	33,840	32,332	6.9	9.3	5.7	10.1	9.5	15.6
Washington County, OR	14,904	14,902	14,881	31,578	33,183	0.2	28.1	7.2	6.1	6.6	7.1
Yamhill County, OR	2,206	2,160	2,078	25,088	24,363	6.1	22.5	7.3	3.3	10.1	16.6
Clark County, WA	10,797	10,566	10,040	29,191	28,894	7.5	12.4	7.3	9.8	11.3	17.2
Skamania County, WA	229	225	222	22,728	22,450	2.8	10.8	3.7	5.4	1.4	45.7
Port St. Lucie-Fort Pierce, FL	10,663	10,181	9,650	31,638	30,103	10.5	5.4	10.7	7.1	14.3	15.4
Martin County, FL	5,850	5,658	5,347	44,330	42,071	9.4	6.0	11.2	9.6	14.1	10.2
St. Lucie County, FL	4,813	4,523	4,302	23,458	22,240	11.9	4.7	10.1	4.5	14.4	21.0
Poughkeepsie-Newburgh-Middletown, NY	19,702	19,256	18,378	30,618	29,459	7.2	16.7	8.4	6.0	12.1	22.7
Dutchess County, NY	9,379	9,273	8,858	32,604	31,540	5.9	26.1	6.9	5.3	12.6	17.8
Orange County, NY	10,323	9,983	9,521	29,013	27,755	8.4	7.2	10.0	6.7	11.6	27.7
Prescott, AZ	3,927	3,713	3,574	21,936	21,153	9.9	6.1	10.8	5.3	11.7	21.6
Yavapai County, AZ	3,927	3,713	3,574	21,936	21,153	9.9	6.1	10.8	5.3	11.7	21.6
Providence-New Bedford-Fall River, RI-MA	49,645	48,076	45,976	30,796	28,976	8.0	16.0	7.9	(NA)	13.0	16.7
Bristol County, MA	16,678	16,198	15,279	30,674	28,505	9.2	21.2	10.1	5.4	12.8	13.9
Bristol County, RI	1,953	1,895	1,841	38,252	36,286	6.1	17.9	7.4	(D)	10.6	17.1
Kent County, RI	5,533	5,324	5,170	32,555	30,865	7.0	16.9	10.2	8.2	11.2	13.3
Newport County, RI	3,172	3,044	3,012	36,908	35,151	5.3	9.9	6.4	9.6	6.9	38.5
Providence County, RI	17,949	17,425	16,611	28,301	26,673	8.1	12.9	5.7	6.9	14.9	15.2
Washington County, RI	4,360	4,191	4,064	34,289	32,768	7.3	17.5	10.4	(D)	10.9	22.3
Provo-Orem, UT	7,850	7,704	7,433	19,594	19,606	5.6	12.5	8.4	8.5	8.8	14.6
Juab County, UT	166	155	149	19,224	18,031	10.9	15.4	7.5	7.0	3.9	19.8
Utah County, UT	7,684	7,549	7,284	19,603	19,641	5.5	12.5	8.4	8.5	8.8	14.5
Pueblo, CO	3,489	3,372	3,262	23,689	22,995	7.0	10.6	9.7	2.7	17.3	22.7
Pueblo County, CO	3,489	3,372	3,262	23,689	22,995	7.0	10.6	9.7	2.7	17.3	22.7
Punta Gorda, FL	4,036	3,797	3,650	26,932	25,653	10.6	2.5	12.1	6.9	19.4	13.7
Charlotte County, FL	4,036	3,797	3,650	26,932	25,653	10.6	2.5	12.1	6.9	19.4	13.7
Racine, WI	5,785	5,658	5,439	30,331	28,779	6.4	36.2	6.4	4.8	11.4	12.8
Racine County, WI	5,785	5,658	5,439	30,331	28,779	6.4	36.2	6.4	4.8	11.4	12.8
Raleigh-Cary, NC	28,613	28,271	27,062	33,293	33,658	5.7	9.9	7.5	(NA)	6.6	17.1
Franklin County, NC	1,214	1,202	1,158	24,043	24,329	4.8	25.0	8.8	3.4	8.0	19.2
Johnston County, NC	3,387	3,340	3,137	25,502	25,442	8.0	25.2	9.6	(D)	5.7	16.8
Wake County, NC	24,012	23,729	22,767	35,515	35,959	5.5	8.4	7.3	12.6	6.6	17.1
Rapid City, SD	3,171	3,045	2,918	27,429	25,819	8.7	7.1	9.0	4.3	(NA)	26.3
Meade County, SD	644	626	570	26,210	23,515	13.1	5.1	6.0	3.3	(D)	37.6
Pennington County, SD	2,526	2,420	2,348	27,759	26,448	7.6	7.5	9.5	4.4	16.1	24.6
Reading, PA	11,262	10,960	10,778	29,531	28,783	4.5	24.4	7.7	7.2	10.0	11.3
Berks County, PA	11,262	10,960	10,778	29,531	28,783	4.5	24.4	7.7	7.2	10.0	11.3
Redding, CA	4,558	4,312	4,005	26,532	24,445	13.8	5.1	10.8	5.9	16.1	20.2
Shasta County, CA	4,558	4,312	4,005	26,532	24,445	13.8	5.1	10.8	5.9	16.1	20.2
Reno-Sparks, NV	13,425	13,136	12,418	36,763	36,026	8.1	8.1	7.7	7.0	(NA)	14.7
Storey County, NV	101	100	96	29,609	28,266	5.5	24.7	4.2	2.4	(D)	20.9
Washoe County, NV	13,324	13,036	12,323	36,831	36,103	8.1	8.1	7.7	7.1	9.8	14.6
Richmond, VA	36,061	35,208	33,603	32,067	30,548	7.3	10.4	6.2	(NA)	(NA)	19.4
Amelia County, VA	288	288	265	24,635	23,056	9.0	9.6	6.1	2.6	(D)	19.1
Caroline County, VA	603	568	527	26,689	23,824	14.4	6.8	8.6	(NA)	2.5	24.1
Charles City County, VA	185	182	162	26,273	23,366	14.5	17.2	(D)	(D)	(D)	19.4
Chesterfield County, VA	[12]9,096	[12]8,860	[12]8,410	[12]33,586	[12]32,225	[12]8.2	[12]14.4	[12]9.2	[12]6.6	[12]6.7	[12]16.0
Cumberland County, VA	185	181	177	20,480	19,629	4.6	(D)	11.3	2.1	3.7	26.0
Dinwiddie County, VA	[13]1,945	[13]1,895	[13]1,841	[13]25,957	[13]24,505	[13]5.7	[13]14.2	[13]11.0	(D)	(D)	[13]32.0
Goochland County, VA	779	764	687	44,028	40,587	13.3	4.0	4.6	7.1	(D)	16.2
Hanover County, VA	3,063	2,991	2,737	33,366	31,457	11.9	10.0	8.6	5.2	(D)	11.3
Henrico County, VA	9,623	9,426	9,254	35,928	35,148	4.0	7.2	7.6	9.1	9.7	7.1
King and Queen County, VA	163	159	155	24,747	23,366	5.4	12.5	4.3	3.9	(D)	36.1
King William County, VA	394	385	360	28,594	27,293	9.4	35.9	7.7	(D)	(D)	15.6
Louisa County, VA	732	705	661	27,039	25,658	10.7	17.9	4.7	(D)	(D)	12.5
New Kent County, VA	410	400	370	28,757	27,339	10.8	5.0	10.2	(D)	(D)	21.5
Powhatan County, VA	676	657	614	27,867	27,174	10.0	1.8	5.7	5.0	(D)	38.4
Prince George County, VA	[14]1,325	[14]1,285	[14]1,252	[14]23,474	[14]22,552	[14]5.8	[14]5.9	(D)	(D)	(D)	[14]53.7
Sussex County, VA	257	251	238	21,199	19,025	8.0	7.9	6.9	(D)	(D)	41.3
Colonial Heights city, VA	(12)	(12)	(12)	(12)	(12)	(12)	(12)	(12)	(12)	(12)	(12)
Hopewell city, VA	(14)	(14)	(14)	(14)	(14)	(14)	(14)	(14)	(14)	(14)	(14)
Petersburg city, VA	(13)	(13)	(13)	(13)	(13)	(13)	(13)	(13)	(13)	(13)	(13)
Richmond city, VA	6,337	6,209	5,894	32,237	29,852	7.5	9.6	3.1	13.0	6.2	27.3

See footnotes at end of table.

State and Metropolitan Area Data Book: 2006

Table C-3. Metropolitan Areas With Component Counties — Personal Income and Earnings by Industry—Con.

Metropolitan statistical area / Metropolitan statistical area with metropolitan divisions / Metropolitan division / Component county	Total (million dollars) 2002	2001	2000	Per capita[1] (dollars) 2002	2000	Percent change,[2] 2000–2002	Manufacturing	Retail trade	Professional and technical services	Health care and social assistance	Government and government enterprises
Riverside-San Bernardino-Ontario, CA	84,301	80,077	74,787	24,073	22,810	12.7	10.6	9.4	4.6	9.5	21.5
Riverside County, CA	42,068	39,794	37,015	24,814	23,730	13.7	10.1	9.9	4.8	9.0	20.6
San Bernardino County, CA	42,232	40,284	37,772	23,379	21,974	11.8	11.1	9.0	4.3	10.0	22.4
Roanoke, VA	8,467	8,183	7,808	29,283	27,073	8.5	(NA)	8.1	(NA)	(NA)	13.7
Botetourt County, VA	980	946	882	31,482	28,844	11.1	28.3	4.7	4.7	(D)	12.6
Craig County, VA	116	113	111	22,763	21,741	4.6	(D)	7.0	(D)	(D)	34.0
Franklin County, VA	1,192	1,152	1,112	24,582	23,441	7.1	24.9	9.1	2.8	(D)	15.5
Roanoke County, VA	[15]3,654	[15]3,542	[15]3,363	[15]32,911	[15]30,425	[15]8.7	[15]21.0	[15]7.8	[15]6.2		[15]15.3
Roanoke city, VA	2,526	2,431	2,340	27,033	24,697	8.0	6.8	8.7	9.1	16.7	12.1
Salem city, VA	([15])	([15])	([15])	([15])	([15])	([15])	([15])	([15])	([15])	([15])	([15])
Rochester, MN	5,741	5,501	5,103	33,829	31,044	12.5	20.2	5.8	4.2	(NA)	9.3
Dodge County, MN	536	511	472	28,883	26,414	13.7	25.2	5.1	2.9	(D)	17.9
Olmsted County, MN	4,572	4,381	4,064	35,389	32,556	12.5	19.2	5.8	4.4	39.4	8.5
Wabasha County, MN	633	609	567	28,835	26,149	11.7	32.3	7.5	2.0	11.6	15.2
Rochester, NY	31,716	31,203	30,455	30,499	29,329	4.1	24.1	6.4	(NA)	(NA)	14.2
Livingston County, NY	1,522	1,495	1,475	23,512	22,914	3.2	12.2	9.6	3.0	8.3	40.8
Monroe County, NY	23,927	23,536	22,905	32,506	31,134	4.5	25.2	5.8	7.9	10.4	11.1
Ontario County, NY	2,930	2,896	2,827	28,788	28,155	3.7	19.6	11.2	4.0	12.4	19.1
Orleans County, NY	942	912	901	21,623	20,391	4.6	14.5	6.4	(D)	(D)	41.8
Wayne County, NY	2,395	2,364	2,348	25,551	25,039	2.0	25.4	8.0	5.4	7.0	29.4
Rockford, IL	8,861	8,669	8,722	27,138	27,169	1.6	30.8	6.8	(NA)	(NA)	10.6
Boone County, IL	1,225	1,201	1,178	27,357	28,002	4.0	44.3	6.5	(D)	(D)	9.2
Winnebago County, IL	7,636	7,468	7,544	27,103	27,044	1.2	29.2	6.8	4.0	13.8	10.8
Rocky Mount, NC	3,548	3,532	3,422	24,650	23,919	3.7	24.3	7.8	2.6	(NA)	16.7
Edgecombe County, NC	1,236	1,230	1,206	22,469	21,808	2.5	19.8	6.7	1.6	(D)	21.3
Nash County, NC	2,313	2,302	2,216	25,998	25,249	4.4	26.8	8.4	3.2	8.1	14.1
Rome, GA	2,346	2,245	2,110	25,337	23,240	11.2	26.7	7.1	3.3	16.5	14.2
Floyd County, GA	2,346	2,245	2,110	25,337	23,240	11.2	26.7	7.1	3.3	16.5	14.2
Sacramento—Arden-Arcade—Roseville, CA	59,829	57,497	54,236	31,069	29,993	10.3	7.2	7.5	8.3	8.1	28.7
El Dorado County, CA	6,051	5,805	5,596	36,561	35,602	8.1	3.9	9.2	15.6	9.7	16.2
Placer County, CA	10,328	9,869	9,153	37,083	36,425	12.8	12.6	11.2	6.3	8.9	11.2
Sacramento County, CA	38,569	37,102	35,017	29,631	28,468	10.1	6.2	6.8	8.5	8.2	32.7
Yolo County, CA	4,881	4,720	4,470	27,114	26,330	9.2	8.3	6.8	5.7	5.4	31.6
Saginaw-Saginaw Township North, MI	5,306	5,255	5,374	25,297	25,596	-1.3	31.6	7.5	3.8	13.3	12.6
Saginaw County, MI	5,306	5,255	5,374	25,297	25,596	-1.3	31.6	7.5	3.8	13.3	12.6
St. Cloud, MN	4,593	4,379	4,219	26,626	25,104	8.9	19.3	9.9	(NA)	(NA)	15.4
Benton County, MN	975	937	862	26,877	24,996	13.2	29.7	7.3	(D)	(D)	10.0
Stearns County, MN	3,618	3,443	3,357	26,559	25,132	7.7	17.4	10.4	3.8	13.8	16.4
St. George, UT	1,994	1,877	1,752	20,059	19,206	13.8	6.0	13.1	4.5	12.6	14.8
Washington County, UT	1,994	1,877	1,752	20,059	19,206	13.8	6.0	13.1	4.5	12.6	14.8
St. Joseph, MO-KS	2,940	2,861	2,816	23,885	22,718	4.4	18.1	8.2	(NA)	(NA)	17.5
Doniphan County, KS	173	169	163	21,186	19,706	6.6	20.2	3.8	(D)	(D)	23.9
Andrew County, MO	443	435	415	26,528	25,099	6.6	2.9	14.1	4.3	7.7	22.4
Buchanan County, MO	2,139	2,072	2,056	25,103	23,889	4.0	19.9	8.1	3.0	14.1	15.2
DeKalb County, MO	185	185	182	14,218	13,919	1.4	(D)	8.2	1.2	(D)	50.0
St. Louis, MO-IL[4]	88,410	86,138	84,222	32,462	31,174	5.0	(NA)	6.2	(NA)	(NA)	12.8
Bond County, IL	438	427	413	24,541	23,382	6.2	15.4	6.0	(D)	(D)	26.0
Calhoun County, IL	119	116	114	23,718	22,386	4.2	(D)	12.1	(D)	(D)	24.6
Clinton County, IL	1,008	989	946	28,131	26,605	6.5	9.5	11.0	3.7	10.3	21.6
Jersey County, IL	582	571	543	26,449	25,043	7.2	2.7	13.7	5.5	(D)	26.7
Macoupin County, IL	1,209	1,188	1,176	24,671	24,001	2.8	9.8	8.0	3.8	(D)	20.4
Madison County, IL	7,290	7,067	6,840	27,947	26,401	6.6	24.8	8.7	4.9	10.8	15.9
Monroe County, IL	915	902	855	31,488	30,779	7.0	4.3	12.7	6.2	7.5	15.8
St. Clair County, IL	6,928	6,649	6,445	26,909	25,151	7.5	7.6	7.2	7.8	12.2	32.2
Franklin County, MO	2,571	2,504	2,421	26,783	25,776	6.2	31.3	9.8	3.5	8.3	12.1
Jefferson County, MO	5,190	5,065	4,879	25,465	24,542	6.4	12.5	10.2	3.2	10.1	18.1
Lincoln County, MO	977	938	884	23,050	22,506	10.5	18.0	11.0	2.2	(D)	19.5
St. Charles County, MO	9,151	8,803	8,528	30,181	29,800	7.3	17.3	9.3	6.1	9.8	11.7
St. Louis County, MO	41,755	40,929	40,644	41,126	39,989	2.7	14.2	6.4	9.4	9.2	7.6
Warren County, MO	662	638	595	25,398	24,063	11.3	30.2	10.3	(D)	(D)	14.9
Washington County, MO	423	405	380	17,893	16,208	11.3	17.3	9.5	0.9	(D)	37.8
St. Louis city, MO	9,194	8,948	8,561	27,352	24,687	7.4	12.4	2.2	10.2	10.2	17.0
Salem, OR	9,032	8,733	8,515	25,214	24,453	6.1	9.2	7.3	4.1	12.8	30.4
Marion County, OR	7,398	7,166	6,981	25,208	24,443	6.0	8.6	7.6	4.2	13.3	30.1
Polk County, OR	1,634	1,567	1,535	25,241	24,499	6.5	14.0	5.6	2.9	8.4	33.3
Salinas, CA	13,091	12,699	12,097	31,842	30,015	8.2	5.1	7.5	5.3	6.6	21.8
Monterey County, CA	13,091	12,699	12,097	31,842	30,015	8.2	5.1	7.5	5.3	6.6	21.8
Salisbury, MD	2,712	2,640	2,503	24,312	22,832	8.4	10.8	8.3	(NA)	(NA)	21.2
Somerset County, MD	499	494	455	19,594	18,400	9.7	2.1	5.8	1.8	(D)	46.5
Wicomico County, MD	2,213	2,146	2,048	25,708	24,123	8.1	12.2	8.7	(D)	17.1	17.0
Salt Lake City, UT	28,540	27,937	27,081	28,674	27,852	5.4	10.1	7.5	(NA)	(NA)	15.6
Salt Lake County, UT	26,184	25,658	24,924	28,539	27,674	5.1	10.2	7.5	10.0	7.4	15.3
Summit County, UT	1,439	1,402	1,336	45,121	44,546	7.7	4.0	8.3	7.4	3.9	11.4
Tooele County, UT	917	877	820	19,947	19,683	11.8	12.2	5.8	(D)	(D)	36.1

See footnotes at end of table.

	Personal income										
Metropolitan statistical area **Metropolitan statistical area with metropolitan divisions** *Metropolitan division* Component county	Total (million dollars)			Per capita[1] (dollars)			Earnings—percent by selected industries				
						Percent change,[2] 2000– 2002	Manu- fac- turing	Retail trade	Profes- sional and technical services	Health care and social assis- tance	Govern- ment and govern- ment enter- prises
	2002	2001	2000	2002	2000						
San Angelo, TX	2,684	2,624	2,523	25,556	23,864	6.4	10.1	7.5	(NA)	14.8	27.5
Irion County, TX	44	42	41	25,241	22,997	7.7	1.9	(D)	(D)	1.5	24.2
Tom Green County, TX	2,640	2,582	2,482	25,562	23,879	6.4	10.1	7.6	3.3	14.9	27.5
San Antonio, TX	48,884	47,317	45,997	27,368	26,752	6.3	6.5	7.9	(NA)	(NA)	22.9
Atascosa County, TX	809	779	743	19,654	19,087	8.9	3.3	10.5	3.5	(D)	20.9
Bandera County, TX	486	465	460	25,625	25,765	5.8	1.3	10.6	4.7	6.2	24.8
Bexar County, TX	40,373	39,175	38,190	27,910	27,321	5.7	5.5	7.4	7.0	9.8	23.3
Comal County, TX	2,471	2,364	2,296	29,171	29,137	7.7	16.3	15.2	4.4	9.4	12.8
Guadalupe County, TX	2,257	2,170	2,077	23,919	23,103	8.7	29.4	8.8	(D)	(D)	19.6
Kendall County, TX	841	799	736	33,206	30,715	14.2	8.9	19.0	7.0	5.9	15.1
Medina County, TX	842	810	777	20,672	19,692	8.3	4.9	9.9	3.6	(D)	32.9
Wilson County, TX	805	755	719	23,421	21,969	11.9	5.4	10.3	2.8	(D)	32.5
San Diego-Carlsbad-San Marcos, CA	101,293	97,141	92,654	34,872	32,797	9.3	9.9	6.7	12.6	7.0	22.8
San Diego County, CA	101,293	97,141	92,654	34,872	32,797	9.3	9.9	6.7	12.6	7.0	22.8
Sandusky, OH	2,378	2,340	2,280	30,155	28,652	4.3	32.1	6.4	2.4	9.5	13.9
Erie County, OH	2,378	2,340	2,280	30,155	28,652	4.3	32.1	6.4	2.4	9.5	13.9
San Francisco-Oakland-Fremont, CA	**195,396**	**200,185**	**199,989**	**46,920**	**48,347**	**-2.3**	**8.2**	**6.5**	**15.9**	**7.3**	**12.6**
Oakland-Fremont-Hayward, CA	*99,478*	*100,157*	*98,209*	*40,516*	*40,853*	*1.3*	*12.4*	*7.1*	*11.6*	*9.4*	*14.7*
Alameda County, CA	55,624	56,378	55,791	37,945	38,466	-0.3	14.1	6.8	11.8	9.3	16.5
Contra Costa County, CA	43,854	43,780	42,418	44,326	44,484	3.4	9.1	7.5	11.1	9.6	11.2
San Francisco-San Mateo-Redwood City, CA	*95,918*	*100,027*	*101,780*	*56,120*	*58,746*	*-5.8*	*4.7*	*6.0*	*19.5*	*5.6*	*11.0*
Marin County, CA	16,945	17,215	16,766	68,650	67,710	1.1	2.8	8.7	17.6	10.0	9.1
San Francisco County, CA	41,634	43,188	43,284	54,639	55,735	-3.8	2.0	4.8	21.2	4.8	14.0
San Mateo County, CA	37,339	39,624	41,730	53,315	58,913	-10.5	9.8	7.1	17.3	5.7	6.7
San Jose-Sunnyvale-Santa Clara, CA	79,596	85,586	92,947	45,925	53,408	-14.4	29.3	4.9	17.9	5.3	7.6
San Benito County, CA	1,598	1,607	1,561	28,660	28,990	2.4	14.8	9.7	3.3	3.6	18.4
Santa Clara County, CA	77,998	83,979	91,386	46,499	54,188	-14.7	29.4	4.8	18.0	5.3	7.5
San Luis Obispo-Paso Robles, CA	7,599	7,300	6,801	30,145	27,459	11.7	6.6	9.9	7.3	10.0	21.1
San Luis Obispo County, CA	7,599	7,300	6,801	30,145	27,459	11.7	6.6	9.9	7.3	10.0	21.1
Santa Barbara-Santa Maria, CA	13,701	13,272	12,911	34,103	32,298	6.1	9.4	8.0	10.1	8.7	19.8
Santa Barbara County, CA	13,701	13,272	12,911	34,103	32,298	6.1	9.4	8.0	10.1	8.7	19.8
Santa Cruz-Watsonville, CA	9,707	9,841	10,015	38,323	39,153	-3.1	9.6	9.7	10.0	9.5	16.1
Santa Cruz County, CA	9,707	9,841	10,015	38,323	39,153	-3.1	9.6	9.7	10.0	9.5	16.1
Santa Fe, NM	4,417	4,147	3,846	32,932	29,627	14.9	2.6	10.7	10.0	9.6	26.0
Santa Fe County, NM	4,417	4,147	3,846	32,932	29,627	14.9	2.6	10.7	10.0	9.6	26.0
Santa Rosa-Petaluma, CA	17,391	17,209	16,778	37,331	36,447	3.7	15.8	8.5	8.0	10.3	13.5
Sonoma County, CA	17,391	17,209	16,778	37,331	36,447	3.7	15.8	8.5	8.0	10.3	13.5
Sarasota-Bradenton-Venice, FL	23,264	22,345	21,027	37,509	35,476	10.6	8.4	9.6	10.0	13.1	9.6
Manatee County, FL	9,093	8,772	8,088	32,469	30,440	12.4	11.7	9.0	12.4	9.1	10.4
Sarasota County, FL	14,171	13,573	12,939	41,658	39,567	9.5	5.9	10.1	8.2	16.1	9.0
Savannah, GA	8,449	8,127	7,879	28,054	26,863	7.2	14.7	7.7	5.3	(NA)	19.7
Bryan County, GA	637	613	567	25,235	24,075	12.3	5.5	9.1	5.5	(D)	23.7
Chatham County, GA	6,877	6,612	6,459	29,274	27,842	6.5	13.8	7.7	5.4	13.1	19.4
Effingham County, GA	936	902	854	22,802	22,588	9.6	35.9	7.4	3.5	(D)	23.0
Scranton—Wilkes-Barre, PA	15,279	14,901	14,643	27,602	26,171	4.3	17.8	8.5	5.1	14.4	14.2
Lackawanna County, PA	6,090	5,954	5,755	28,846	27,031	5.8	18.4	9.8	5.6	16.0	13.2
Luzerne County, PA	8,529	8,314	8,249	27,120	25,893	3.4	15.8	7.9	5.0	13.8	15.3
Wyoming County, PA	660	634	639	23,618	22,803	3.3	38.7	5.8	1.9	7.6	10.3
Seattle-Tacoma-Bellevue, WA	**118,739**	**117,090**	**115,203**	**38,037**	**37,746**	**3.1**	**14.1**	**6.4**	**9.3**	**7.6**	**14.4**
Seattle-Bellevue-Everett, WA	*97,372*	*96,461*	*95,786*	*40,735*	*40,793*	*1.7*	*15.0*	*6.3*	*10.1*	*6.9*	*12.0*
King County, WA	77,524	76,977	77,272	44,135	44,437	0.3	12.7	6.0	10.9	6.7	11.2
Snohomish County, WA	19,848	19,484	18,515	31,312	30,393	7.2	30.0	7.9	4.6	7.9	17.6
Tacoma, WA	*21,368*	*20,629*	*19,417*	*29,221*	*27,582*	*10.0*	*8.4*	*7.8*	*4.4*	*12.6*	*30.6*
Pierce County, WA	21,368	20,629	19,417	29,221	27,582	10.0	8.4	7.8	4.4	12.6	30.6
Sheboygan, WI	3,465	3,361	3,249	30,612	28,819	6.6	46.3	5.4	3.8	9.1	9.8
Sheboygan County, WI	3,465	3,361	3,249	30,612	28,819	6.6	46.3	5.4	3.8	9.1	9.8
Sherman-Denison, TX	2,644	2,609	2,559	23,274	23,052	3.3	24.3	9.9	3.5	16.0	12.5
Grayson County, TX	2,644	2,609	2,559	23,274	23,052	3.3	24.3	9.9	3.5	16.0	12.5
Shreveport-Bossier City, LA	9,789	9,490	9,064	25,984	24,103	8.0	10.8	7.1	(NA)	(NA)	23.8
Bossier Parish, LA	2,399	2,304	2,235	23,811	22,667	7.3	5.8	7.6	(D)	7.3	40.3
Caddo Parish, LA	6,856	6,667	6,332	27,397	25,136	8.3	11.8	7.1	5.5	15.7	19.0
De Soto Parish, LA	535	518	497	20,757	19,464	7.7	21.2	5.4	1.8	(D)	16.9
Sioux City, IA-NE-SD	3,869	3,816	3,712	27,112	25,953	4.2	(NA)	6.7	(NA)	(NA)	12.2
Woodbury County, IA	2,778	2,723	2,653	26,877	25,548	4.7	14.3	8.7	4.3	16.2	14.7
Dakota County, NE	452	441	431	22,194	21,266	4.7	49.7	4.6	1.3	(D)	8.5
Dixon County, NE	160	160	158	25,849	25,027	1.1	(D)	2.1	(D)	(D)	14.9
Union County, SD	480	492	470	37,416	37,296	2.1	18.3	1.4	3.5	7.1	4.7
Sioux Falls, SD	6,223	5,977	5,648	31,947	30,005	10.2	10.2	8.2	4.1	(NA)	9.4
Lincoln County, SD	817	779	697	29,428	28,375	17.4	13.6	7.8	3.7	(D)	9.2
McCook County, SD	163	162	166	27,916	28,323	-1.7	5.2	9.3	3.3	(D)	14.1
Minnehaha County, SD	5,001	4,792	4,545	32,776	30,506	10.0	10.2	8.2	4.1	16.8	9.3
Turner County, SD	242	244	241	28,109	27,206	0.4	4.1	6.8	3.3	9.9	16.6
South Bend-Mishawaka, IN-MI	8,947	8,704	8,315	28,153	26,228	7.6	23.5	7.2	6.5	(NA)	10.7
St. Joseph County, IN	7,656	7,442	7,049	28,742	26,515	8.6	23.0	7.2	6.8	12.7	9.9
Cass County, MI	1,290	1,262	1,265	25,100	24,735	2.0	30.0	7.6	2.8	(D)	21.3

See footnotes at end of table.

State and Metropolitan Area Data Book: 2006

U.S. Census Bureau

Table C-3. Metropolitan Areas With Component Counties — **Personal Income and Earnings by Industry**—Con.

Metropolitan statistical area / **Metropolitan statistical area with metropolitan divisions** / *Metropolitan division* / Component county	Personal income — Total (million dollars)			Per capita[1] (dollars)		Percent change,[2] 2000–2002	Earnings—percent by selected industries — Manufacturing	Retail trade	Professional and technical services	Health care and social assistance	Government and government enterprises
	2002	2001	2000	2002	2000						
Spartanburg, SC	6,523	6,327	6,190	25,182	24,331	5.4	32.9	7.7	4.1	7.2	13.9
Spartanburg County, SC	6,523	6,327	6,190	25,182	24,331	5.4	32.9	7.7	4.1	7.2	13.9
Spokane, WA	11,382	11,072	10,890	26,637	26,012	4.5	10.1	9.6	6.5	14.6	20.3
Spokane County, WA	11,382	11,072	10,890	26,637	26,012	4.5	10.1	9.6	6.5	14.6	20.3
Springfield, IL	6,416	6,266	5,996	31,430	29,745	7.0	3.4	6.0	6.3	(NA)	32.8
Menard County, IL	355	354	340	28,223	27,168	4.5	0.7	7.9	4.7	(D)	26.5
Sangamon County, IL	6,061	5,913	5,656	31,640	29,916	7.2	3.4	6.0	6.3	15.8	32.9
Springfield, MA	20,066	19,420	18,766	29,302	27,578	6.9	14.3	7.7	5.2	14.2	19.6
Franklin County, MA	2,183	2,101	2,022	30,291	28,272	8.0	22.8	7.4	4.3	10.9	16.0
Hampden County, MA	13,422	13,017	12,569	29,239	27,535	6.8	14.9	7.7	5.2	15.5	17.6
Hampshire County, MA	4,461	4,302	4,174	29,026	27,380	6.9	8.2	7.8	5.6	10.8	28.7
Springfield, MO	9,705	9,333	8,792	25,622	23,789	10.4	15.1	10.7	(NA)	(NA)	13.2
Christian County, MO	1,389	1,330	1,253	23,449	22,809	10.8	13.4	12.8	(D)	5.6	14.9
Dallas County, MO	338	322	302	21,244	19,242	12.0	8.5	13.6	(D)	6.3	20.7
Greene County, MO	6,842	6,581	6,192	28,122	25,732	10.5	15.6	10.4	5.8	16.2	12.1
Polk County, MO	528	509	480	19,085	17,745	9.9	7.4	10.9	2.6	(D)	25.7
Webster County, MO	608	591	565	18,606	18,068	7.7	16.7	13.0	(D)	(D)	20.8
Springfield, OH	3,762	3,763	3,735	26,159	25,825	0.7	25.3	10.2	3.2	14.0	16.0
Clark County, OH	3,762	3,763	3,735	26,159	25,825	0.7	25.3	10.2	3.2	14.0	16.0
State College, PA	3,560	3,394	3,266	25,394	24,020	9.0	10.5	6.5	6.3	7.8	42.4
Centre County, PA	3,560	3,394	3,266	25,394	24,020	9.0	10.5	6.5	6.3	7.8	42.4
Stockton, CA	14,788	14,274	13,757	24,119	24,213	7.5	10.0	9.4	4.2	9.8	19.9
San Joaquin County, CA	14,788	14,274	13,757	24,119	24,213	7.5	10.0	9.4	4.2	9.8	19.9
Sumter, SC	2,270	2,176	2,150	21,577	20,528	5.6	21.3	6.5	2.0	8.5	36.4
Sumter County, SC	2,270	2,176	2,150	21,577	20,528	5.6	21.3	6.5	2.0	8.5	36.4
Syracuse, NY	18,423	17,726	17,566	28,257	27,007	4.9	16.3	6.6	7.1	(NA)	17.0
Madison County, NY	1,839	1,786	1,748	26,357	25,167	5.2	14.1	8.6	7.7	(D)	20.9
Onondaga County, NY	13,839	13,312	13,174	30,119	28,736	5.0	16.4	6.3	7.6	10.8	15.7
Oswego County, NY	2,745	2,628	2,644	22,365	21,580	3.8	17.0	7.2	2.5	9.5	25.8
Tallahassee, FL	8,547	8,288	7,958	26,302	24,791	7.4	2.5	6.3	(NA)	(NA)	40.0
Gadsden County, FL	935	899	883	20,563	19,589	5.9	9.7	5.6	(D)	3.6	38.8
Jefferson County, FL	321	310	308	23,362	23,821	4.4	2.4	6.0	4.7	(D)	38.8
Leon County, FL	6,749	6,547	6,255	28,056	26,061	7.9	1.6	6.4	12.2	10.6	30.9
Wakulla County, FL	542	532	512	21,514	22,269	5.8	14.7	5.8	6.4	(D)	40.5
Tampa-St. Petersburg-Clearwater, FL	73,986	71,522	68,891	29,728	28,655	7.4	7.4	8.2	9.1	11.0	13.0
Hernando County, FL	3,374	3,225	3,087	24,401	23,479	9.3	4.4	11.8	4.4	17.9	18.9
Hillsborough County, FL	31,151	29,829	28,646	29,602	28,558	8.7	5.8	7.4	10.0	8.5	13.5
Pasco County, FL	8,774	8,367	7,844	23,529	22,583	11.8	4.6	13.7	4.6	19.7	19.3
Pinellas County, FL	30,688	30,101	29,314	33,167	31,787	4.7	10.3	8.5	8.8	12.9	11.2
Terre Haute, IN	3,934	3,838	3,771	23,196	22,081	4.3	21.7	11.1	2.9	(NA)	19.4
Clay County, IN	593	580	597	22,359	22,473	-0.7	29.8	12.0	2.4	6.5	16.1
Sullivan County, IN	434	434	423	19,849	19,466	2.4	8.6	7.7	1.9	(D)	38.2
Vermillion County, IN	403	398	387	24,308	23,081	4.1	32.8	9.4	(D)	(D)	13.4
Vigo County, IN	2,505	2,427	2,364	23,930	22,362	6.0	20.7	11.5	3.4	11.9	18.6
Texarkana, TX-Texarkana, AR	3,128	3,009	2,885	23,931	22,237	8.4	13.0	10.1	0.0	16.1	23.1
Miller County, AR	960	931	849	23,275	20,994	13.0	27.0	8.2	(D)	5.0	12.7
Bowie County, TX	2,168	2,077	2,036	24,233	22,799	6.5	7.7	10.8	(D)	20.3	27.0
Toledo, OH	18,891	18,452	18,305	28,612	27,767	3.2	23.5	7.3	(NA)	(NA)	15.5
Fulton County, OH	1,147	1,135	1,128	27,097	26,775	1.7	47.9	5.4	(D)	(D)	10.8
Lucas County, OH	13,093	12,767	12,669	28,799	27,851	3.3	19.8	7.7	6.4	14.4	15.1
Ottawa County, OH	1,220	1,201	1,193	29,768	29,107	2.2	20.5	9.1	(D)	(D)	16.8
Wood County, OH	3,432	3,349	3,314	28,055	27,344	3.6	31.4	5.8	4.2	6.0	18.7
Topeka, KS	6,401	6,233	6,023	28,398	26,787	6.3	9.3	8.1	(NA)	(NA)	23.4
Jackson County, KS	333	326	310	25,947	24,430	7.6	7.4	10.3	2.6	(D)	25.7
Jefferson County, KS	449	438	418	24,009	22,661	7.3	6.7	5.5	2.7	(D)	29.6
Osage County, KS	382	380	362	22,760	21,617	5.5	9.4	11.6	(D)	(D)	42.1
Shawnee County, KS	5,068	4,921	4,770	29,757	28,052	6.2	9.4	8.0	5.7	12.9	22.7
Wabaunsee County, KS	169	169	162	24,960	23,541	4.3	18.3	5.8	(D)	4.7	26.4
Trenton-Ewing, NJ	14,582	14,263	13,872	40,711	39,455	5.1	4.4	4.9	13.9	8.3	24.0
Mercer County, NJ	14,582	14,263	13,872	40,711	39,455	5.1	4.4	4.9	13.9	8.3	24.0
Tucson, AZ	22,213	21,246	20,514	25,278	24,172	8.3	13.3	8.0	7.1	11.6	24.6
Pima County, AZ	22,213	21,246	20,514	25,278	24,172	8.3	13.3	8.0	7.1	11.6	24.6
Tulsa, OK	26,827	26,336	24,984	30,627	29,008	7.4	21.0	7.4	(NA)	(NA)	9.6
Creek County, OK	1,510	1,491	1,421	22,003	21,040	6.3	23.0	8.3	3.2	11.4	15.9
Okmulgee County, OK	761	732	690	19,178	17,399	10.3	19.8	10.4	2.5	(D)	32.7
Osage County, OK	1,012	972	922	22,420	20,687	9.8	10.9	5.7	(D)	4.9	30.3
Pawnee County, OK	361	349	332	21,482	19,882	8.9	4.8	11.6	(D)	12.4	28.4
Rogers County, OK	1,880	1,828	1,730	24,998	24,249	8.6	29.1	7.3	(D)	6.1	18.1
Tulsa County, OK	19,965	19,659	18,669	35,030	33,115	6.9	20.8	7.3	7.8	9.2	7.9
Wagoner County, OK	1,337	1,305	1,220	22,106	21,139	9.6	20.0	9.6	3.6	(D)	23.2
Tuscaloosa, AL	4,871	4,705	4,517	25,152	23,362	7.9	21.2	7.2	3.8	(NA)	24.6
Greene County, AL	187	181	175	18,862	17,551	6.9	14.9	5.1	0.8	(D)	27.5
Hale County, AL	325	311	298	17,806	16,293	8.9	25.8	5.5	2.1	(D)	24.6
Tuscaloosa County, AL	4,360	4,213	4,044	26,339	24,497	7.8	21.2	7.3	3.9	7.5	24.5

See footnotes at end of table.

Metropolitan statistical area / Metropolitan statistical area with metropolitan divisions / Metropolitan division / Component county	Personal income										
	Total (million dollars)			Per capita[1] (dollars)		Percent change,[2] 2000–2002	Earnings—percent by selected industries				
	2002	2001	2000	2002	2000		Manu-facturing	Retail trade	Profes-sional and technical services	Health care and social assis-tance	Govern-ment and govern-ment enter-prises
Tyler, TX	5,144	4,946	4,922	28,466	28,061	4.5	13.2	12.1	5.7	17.9	12.5
Smith County, TX	5,144	4,946	4,922	28,466	28,061	4.5	13.2	12.1	5.7	17.9	12.5
Utica-Rome, NY	7,348	7,148	7,047	24,668	23,520	4.3	13.2	7.8	4.2	13.8	25.4
Herkimer County, NY	1,453	1,421	1,377	22,807	21,391	5.5	20.7	9.2	2.4	9.3	25.1
Oneida County, NY	5,895	5,728	5,669	25,174	24,103	4.0	12.1	7.6	4.4	14.5	25.5
Valdosta, GA	2,790	2,595	2,485	23,059	20,765	12.3	(NA)	9.7	(NA)	(NA)	34.3
Brooks County, GA	348	335	333	21,308	20,239	4.2	13.5	6.8	1.7	(D)	20.1
Echols County, GA	64	60	57	16,661	15,019	12.3	(D)	1.2	(D)	1.4	22.9
Lanier County, GA	148	137	134	20,693	18,468	10.6	(D)	8.5	(D)	(D)	31.1
Lowndes County, GA	2,230	2,064	1,960	23,808	21,277	13.8	11.3	10.1	3.5	9.4	35.5
Vallejo-Fairfield, CA	11,912	11,601	10,953	29,089	27,579	8.8	9.3	9.6	3.5	11.4	29.2
Solano County, CA	11,912	11,601	10,953	29,089	27,579	8.8	9.3	9.6	3.5	11.4	29.2
Vero Beach, FL	4,699	4,548	4,208	39,830	37,114	11.7	6.2	11.4	7.2	16.5	13.1
Indian River County, FL	4,699	4,548	4,208	39,830	37,114	11.7	6.2	11.4	7.2	16.5	13.1
Victoria, TX	2,908	2,873	2,809	25,844	25,162	3.5	(NA)	9.5	1.0	(NA)	14.4
Calhoun County, TX	434	438	435	21,251	21,045	-0.2	56.2	3.8	(NA)	(D)	9.9
Goliad County, TX	151	148	143	21,449	20,555	5.6	(D)	8.6	(D)	4.4	31.9
Victoria County, TX	2,323	2,287	2,231	27,310	26,557	4.1	11.0	11.5	(D)	13.1	15.4
Vineland-Millville-Bridgeton, NJ	3,823	3,609	3,421	25,856	23,371	11.8	19.4	9.2	3.4	11.7	25.8
Cumberland County, NJ	3,823	3,609	3,421	25,856	23,371	11.8	19.4	9.2	3.4	11.7	25.8
Virginia Beach-Norfolk-Newport News, VA-NC	45,773	43,856	41,659	28,365	26,355	9.9	(NA)	5.8	(NA)	(NA)	38.3
Currituck County, NC	520	490	468	26,481	25,522	11.1	2.6	15.0	4.1	(D)	23.7
Gloucester County, VA	941	909	853	26,260	24,463	10.3	3.8	12.9	4.5	11.2	29.0
Isle of Wight County, VA	871	849	811	28,150	27,128	7.4	50.1	3.8	(D)	(D)	9.5
James City County, VA	[16]2,357	[16]2,262	[16]2,107	[16]37,322	[16]34,825	[16]11.8	(D)	[16]7.5	[16]6.2	[16]7.9	[16]22.3
Mathews County, VA	319	311	281	34,588	30,508	13.7	7.4	9.6	6.1	4.4	22.7
Surry County, VA	156	153	145	22,448	21,252	7.5	(D)	1.0	2.2	(D)	13.0
York County, VA	[17]2,262	[17]2,154	[17]2,025	[17]31,673	[17]29,678	[17]11.7	(D)	[17]7.1	[17]5.0	[17]5.2	[17]38.1
Chesapeake city, VA	5,956	5,669	5,380	28,910	26,838	10.7	7.4	9.6	8.3	5.8	19.6
Hampton city, VA	3,831	3,692	3,505	26,280	23,927	9.3	6.4	6.0	11.8	5.8	50.9
Newport News city, VA	4,315	4,183	3,956	23,986	21,968	9.1	28.5	5.6	8.1	8.0	26.2
Norfolk city, VA	6,015	5,754	5,511	24,873	23,509	9.1	5.3	3.3	4.9	7.2	52.8
Poquoson city, VA	(17)	(17)	(17)	(17)	(17)	(17)	(17)	(17)	(17)	(17)	(17)
Portsmouth city, VA	2,376	2,257	2,149	23,835	21,401	10.5	4.5	3.1	2.1	8.5	58.4
Suffolk city, VA	1,822	1,753	1,626	26,059	25,308	12.1	12.4	8.9	4.8	(D)	24.5
Virginia Beach city, VA	14,032	13,419	12,842	32,374	30,098	9.3	2.8	7.1	10.4	6.8	30.1
Williamsburg city, VA	(16)	(16)	(16)	(16)	(16)	(16)	(16)	(16)	(16)	(16)	(16)
Visalia-Porterville, CA	8,076	7,739	7,219	21,193	19,571	11.9	8.9	8.1	3.0	7.0	22.9
Tulare County, CA	8,076	7,739	7,219	21,193	19,571	11.9	8.9	8.1	3.0	7.0	22.9
Waco, TX	5,212	5,007	4,862	24,003	22,719	7.2	18.0	7.7	3.9	10.5	17.3
McLennan County, TX	5,212	5,007	4,862	24,003	22,719	7.2	18.0	7.7	3.9	10.5	17.3
Warner Robins, GA	3,027	2,828	2,714	25,876	24,378	11.6	6.6	5.8	6.0	4.8	61.1
Houston County, GA	3,027	2,828	2,714	25,876	24,378	11.6	6.6	5.8	6.0	4.8	61.1
Washington-Arlington-Alexandria, DC-VA-MD-WV	**214,441**	**208,098**	**196,093**	**42,773**	**40,665**	**9.4**	**(NA)**	**4.5**	**20.3**	**5.8**	**27.6**
Bethesda-Gaithersburg-Frederick, MD	54,247	52,263	50,002	48,517	46,541	8.5	5.3	5.8	18.8	8.0	21.0
Frederick County, MD	7,215	6,947	6,427	34,478	32,693	12.3	8.9	8.0	12.2	9.0	19.3
Montgomery County, MD	47,032	45,316	43,575	51,750	49,642	7.9	4.9	5.5	19.6	7.8	21.2
Washington-Arlington-Alexandria, DC-VA-MD-WV	160,194	155,834	146,091	41,124	38,980	9.7	(NA)	4.2	20.6	(NA)	29.1
District of Columbia, DC	26,636	25,935	23,102	46,800	40,428	15.3	(D)	1.0	21.9	5.1	41.0
Calvert County, MD	2,650	2,526	2,352	32,932	31,283	12.6	4.9	8.0	8.8	12.6	19.4
Charles County, MD	4,156	3,953	3,730	32,254	30,753	11.4	3.6	13.0	5.5	8.5	29.0
Prince George's County, MD	25,287	24,138	23,195	30,489	28,863	9.0	4.1	7.7	9.7	7.4	32.0
Arlington County, VA	10,428	10,209	9,378	55,148	49,536	11.2	(D)	2.4	21.3	3.1	37.8
Clarke County, VA	419	408	394	31,723	30,983	6.3	26.7	4.9	4.3	(D)	14.4
Fairfax County, VA	[18]53,589	[18]52,463	[18]50,393	[18]52,199	[18]50,027	[18]6.3	[18]2.0	[18]5.0	[18]5.7	[18]5.7	[18]14.3
Fauquier County, VA	2,369	2,312	2,165	39,881	38,953	9.4	5.2	8.7	10.1	10.1	15.0
Loudoun County, VA	7,438	7,651	7,154	36,455	41,129	4.0	4.1	5.5	10.9	3.8	15.0
Prince William County, VA	[19]11,294	[19]10,894	[19]10,228	[19]31,436	[19]31,036	[19]10.4	(D)	[19]10.5	[19]11.8	(D)	[19]25.6
Spotsylvania County, VA	[20]3,566	[20]3,388	[20]3,145	[20]29,072	[20]28,360	[20]13.4	(D)	[20]12.6	[20]6.4	[20]13.8	[20]16.3
Stafford County, VA	3,068	2,926	2,690	29,278	28,732	14.1	2.7	5.0	6.2	3.4	26.1
Warren County, VA	883	852	822	26,701	25,927	7.4	(D)	8.8	4.4	10.0	17.1
Alexandria city, VA	7,156	6,968	6,212	55,071	48,100	15.2	(D)	5.1	23.0	4.9	26.7
Fairfax city, VA	(18)	(18)	(18)	(18)	(18)	(18)	(18)	(18)	(18)	(18)	(18)
Falls Church city, VA	(18)	(18)	(18)	(18)	(18)	(18)	(18)	(18)	(18)	(18)	(18)
Fredericksburg city, VA	(20)	(20)	(20)	(20)	(20)	(20)	(20)	(20)	(20)	(20)	(20)
Manassas city, VA	(19)	(19)	(19)	(19)	(19)	(19)	(19)	(19)	(19)	(19)	(19)
Manassas Park city, VA	(19)	(19)	(19)	(19)	(19)	(19)	(19)	(19)	(19)	(19)	(19)
Jefferson County, WV	1,255	1,210	1,130	27,957	26,624	11.0	11.4	10.4	5.5	7.8	27.0
Waterloo-Cedar Falls, IA	4,354	4,204	4,056	26,846	24,795	7.4	26.6	7.6	4.3	(NA)	15.6
Black Hawk County, IA	3,349	3,220	3,118	26,470	24,377	7.4	28.3	7.7	4.7	12.4	16.0
Bremer County, IA	653	636	612	28,022	26,261	6.7	19.1	6.8	2.6	(D)	13.6
Grundy County, IA	352	348	326	28,488	26,359	7.8	14.1	7.9	2.2	(D)	13.5
Wausau, WI	3,692	3,555	3,431	29,103	27,248	7.6	28.1	8.5	(NA)	8.7	10.6
Marathon County, WI	3,692	3,555	3,431	29,103	27,248	7.6	28.1	8.5	4.5	8.7	10.6

See footnotes at end of table.

State and Metropolitan Area Data Book: 2006

U.S. Census Bureau

Metropolitan statistical area **Metropolitan statistical area with metropolitan divisions** *Metropolitan division* Component county	Personal income										
	Total (million dollars)			Per capita[1] (dollars)			Earnings—percent by selected industries				
	2002	2001	2000	2002	2000	Percent change,[2] 2000–2002	Manu-fac-turing	Retail trade	Profes-sional and technical services	Health care and social assis-tance	Govern-ment and govern-ment enter-prises
Weirton-Steubenville, WV-OH.	3,072	2,982	2,937	23,750	22,307	4.6	32.6	6.5	2.1	(NA)	12.5
Jefferson County, OH	1,707	1,656	1,632	23,622	22,147	4.6	18.6	8.1	2.5	15.3	15.1
Brooke County, WV	592	579	568	23,614	22,387	4.2	39.7	6.7	(D)	(D)	11.4
Hancock County, WV.	773	747	737	24,147	22,607	4.9	50.4	4.0	2.5	(D)	9.1
Wenatchee, WA	2,644	2,523	2,378	26,321	23,923	11.2	5.9	9.8	3.4	14.8	21.2
Chelan County, WA.	1,869	1,786	1,675	27,812	25,106	11.6	6.5	9.7	3.6	16.6	19.6
Douglas County, WA	775	737	703	23,309	21,506	10.3	3.4	10.4	2.4	6.5	29.1
Wheeling, WV-OH	3,776	3,680	3,540	24,993	23,159	6.7	13.1	8.8	(NA)	(NA)	17.0
Belmont County, OH	1,632	1,582	1,514	23,390	21,595	7.8	8.0	14.3	3.0	15.3	19.9
Marshall County, WV.	789	775	741	22,541	20,942	6.5	34.6	4.6	(D)	(D)	15.1
Ohio County, WV	1,354	1,323	1,284	29,265	27,133	5.4	5.8	6.7	7.6	23.4	15.7
Wichita, KS.	17,158	16,830	15,918	29,587	27,828	7.8	32.5	6.4	(NA)	10.9	12.7
Butler County, KS	1,674	1,639	1,579	27,710	26,445	6.1	15.0	8.3	(D)	11.1	23.9
Harvey County, KS	904	881	830	27,106	25,238	9.0	26.0	7.4	(D)	16.0	10.8
Sedgwick County, KS	13,959	13,700	12,900	30,302	28,449	8.2	34.1	6.2	4.4	10.7	11.9
Sumner County, KS.	621	609	609	24,358	23,454	1.9	18.3	8.4	2.4	8.2	27.5
Wichita Falls, TX.	3,982	3,822	3,712	26,583	24,513	7.3	14.0	7.5	(NA)	11.2	34.5
Archer County, TX	245	240	227	27,107	25,300	8.0	1.4	5.4	(D)	3.8	21.0
Clay County, TX.	271	265	235	24,113	21,179	15.2	8.0	8.5	4.8	7.5	17.6
Wichita County, TX.	3,466	3,317	3,250	26,761	24,742	6.6	14.6	7.5	3.5	11.6	35.6
Williamsport, PA	2,980	2,932	2,762	25,096	23,029	7.9	29.1	8.6	3.7	12.8	16.8
Lycoming County, PA.	2,980	2,932	2,762	25,096	23,029	7.9	29.1	8.6	3.7	12.8	16.8
Wilmington, NC.	7,689	7,477	7,118	26,753	25,820	8.0	11.1	9.5	(NA)	(NA)	19.4
Brunswick County, NC.	1,885	1,825	1,653	23,908	22,416	14.0	7.5	9.0	5.1	6.9	16.9
New Hanover County, NC	4,873	4,736	4,588	29,408	28,559	6.2	12.1	9.7	8.6	10.3	19.4
Pender County, NC.	930	916	877	21,720	21,244	6.1	10.1	8.2	(D)	(D)	27.1
Winchester, VA-WV.	2,955	2,837	2,649	27,308	25,577	11.6	26.4	9.1	3.7	(NA)	11.6
Frederick County, VA.	[21]2,536	[21]2,437	[21]2,268	[21]29,063	[21]27,242	[21]11.8	[21]28.0	[21]9.2	[21]3.6	[21]14.1	[21]10.2
Winchester city, VA.	[21]	[21]	[21]	[21]	[21]	[21]	[21]	[21]	[21]	[21]	[21]
Hampshire County, WV	419	400	381	20,000	18,759	10.0	5.2	8.2	4.9	(D)	30.9
Winston-Salem, NC.	12,775	12,500	12,412	29,485	29,323	2.9	19.8	7.3	(NA)	(NA)	9.5
Davie County, NC	1,056	1,033	1,026	28,827	29,272	2.9	33.0	8.5	(D)	5.9	13.6
Forsyth County, NC.	9,821	9,582	9,519	31,236	31,019	3.2	19.0	7.2	8.1	13.9	8.6
Stokes County, NC	1,035	1,028	1,023	23,040	22,813	1.2	13.9	8.3	3.4	(D)	23.5
Yadkin County, NC	863	857	844	23,134	23,113	2.2	28.5	8.9	(D)	6.5	16.2
Worcester, MA	25,580	25,377	24,539	33,229	32,604	4.2	17.5	7.2	8.3	12.6	14.4
Worcester County, MA.	25,580	25,377	24,539	33,229	32,604	4.2	17.5	7.2	8.3	12.6	14.4
Yakima, WA	5,324	5,120	4,916	23,714	22,074	8.3	11.4	7.9	3.2	13.2	19.3
Yakima County, WA.	5,324	5,120	4,916	23,714	22,074	8.3	11.4	7.9	3.2	13.2	19.3
York-Hanover, PA	11,222	10,891	11,019	28,810	28,790	1.8	29.5	8.0	4.4	10.6	11.4
York County, PA.	11,222	10,891	11,019	28,810	28,790	1.8	29.5	8.0	4.4	10.6	11.4
Youngstown-Warren-Boardman, OH-PA	15,107	14,749	14,806	25,358	24,588	2.0	27.2	9.3	3.5	14.1	13.8
Mahoning County, OH	6,553	6,410	6,370	25,924	24,783	2.9	11.0	11.3	4.6	17.1	16.4
Trumbull County, OH.	5,614	5,506	5,619	25,156	24,980	-0.1	44.4	7.4	2.6	9.6	11.7
Mercer County, PA	2,940	2,833	2,816	24,541	23,433	4.4	26.4	9.1	3.1	17.1	12.5
Yuba City, CA.	3,416	3,252	3,094	23,617	22,177	10.4	6.4	9.0	4.1	11.3	32.9
Sutter County, CA.	2,114	2,015	1,939	25,698	24,495	9.0	7.9	12.5	4.0	13.1	15.4
Yuba County, CA.	1,302	1,236	1,155	20,873	19,136	12.8	4.6	4.9	4.1	9.2	53.4
Yuma, AZ.	3,431	2,968	2,654	20,561	16,513	29.3	3.2	7.1	1.8	8.0	28.2
Yuma County, AZ.	3,431	2,968	2,654	20,561	16,513	29.3	3.2	7.1	1.8	8.0	28.2

D Data withheld to avoid disclosure.   NA Not available.   X Not applicable.   Z Less than .05%.

[1]Based on resident population estimated as of July 1, 2000 and 2002.

[2]Includes construction; wholesale; transportation and warehousing; information; finance and insurance; management of companies and enterprises; administrative and waste services; educational services; arts, entertainment, and recreation; accommodation and food services; and other services (except public administration); not shown separately.

[3]The Denver-Aurora metropolitan statistical area includes Broomfield County. Broomfield County, CO, was formed from parts of Adams, Boulder, Jefferson, and Weld counties on November 15, 2001, and is coextensive with Broomfield city. For the purposes of defining and presenting data for the Denver-Aurora metropolitan statistical area, Broomfield city is treated as if it were a county when data are available to do so. In many cases, the data will not be available.

[4]The portion of Sullivan city in Crawford County, MO, is legally part of the St. Louis, MO-IL MSA. That portion is not included in these figures for the St. Louis MSA.

[5]Radford city included with Montgomery County, VA, in the Blacksburg-Christiansburg-Radford, VA MSA.

[6]Charlottesville city included with Albemarle County, VA, in the Charlottesville, VA MSA.

[7]Danville city included with Pittsylvania County, VA, in the Danville, VA MSA.

[8]Harrisonburg city included with Rockingham County, VA, in the Harrisonburg, VA MSA.

[9]Bristol city included with Washington County, VA, in the Kingsport-Bristol-Bristol, TN-VA MSA.

[10]Bedford city included with Bedford County, VA, in the Lynchburg, VA MSA.

[11]Lynchburg city included with Campbell County, VA, in the Lynchburg, VA MSA.

[12]Colonial Heights city included with Chesterfield County, VA, in the Richmond, VA MSA.

[13]Petersburg city included with Dinwiddie County, VA, in the Richmond, VA MSA.

[14]Hopewell city included with Prince George County, VA, in the Richmond, VA MSA.

[15]Salem city included with Roanoke County, VA, in the Roanoke, VA MSA.

[16]Williamsburg city included with James City County, VA, in the Virginia Beach-Norfold-Newport News, VA-NC MSA.

[17]Poquoson city included with York County, VA, in the Virginia Beach-Norfolk-Newport News, VA-NC MSA.

[18]Fairfax and Falls Church cities included with Fairfax County, VA, in the Washington-Arlington-Alexandria, DC-VA-MD MSA.

[19]Manassas and Manassas Park cities included with Prince William County, VA, in the Washington-Arlington-Alexandria, DC-VA-MD MSA.

[20]Fredericksburg city included with Spotsylvania County, VA, in the Washington-Arlington-Alexandria, DC-VA-MD MSA.

[21]Winchester city included with Frederick County, VA, in the Winchester, VA-WV MSA.

Note: Covers metropolitan statistical areas and metropolitan divisions and component counties defined by the Office of Management and Budget as of June 6, 2003, and subsequently updated in December 2003 and November 2004. For more information, see OMB Bulletin 05-02 at <http://www.whitehouse.gov/omb/bulletins/fy05/b05-02_appendix.pdf>.

Survey, Census, or Data Collection Method: Based on the Regional Economic Information System; for more information, see Appendix B, Limitations of the Data and Methodology, and also <http://www.bea.gov/bea/regional/articles.cfm?section=methods> and <http://www.bea.gov/bea/regional/articles/lapi2003/lapi2003.pdf>.

Source: Personal income and earnings—U.S. Bureau of Economic Analysis, *Regional Economic Information System (REIS) 1969–2002* on CD-ROM (related Internet site <http://www.bea.gov/bea/regional/data.htm>).

Table C-4. Metropolitan Areas With Component Counties — Civilian Labor Force and Private Nonfarm Businesses

Metropolitan statistical area / Metropolitan statistical area with metropolitan divisions / Metropolitan division / Component county	Civilian labor force							Private nonfarm businesses					
	Total			Number of unemployed		Unemployment rate[1]		Establishments		Employment[2]		Annual payroll per employee, 2002	
	2004	Net change, 2000–2004	2000	2004	2000	2004	2000	2002	Net change, 2000–2002	2002	Net change, 2000–2002	Amount (dollars)	Percent of national average
Abilene, TX	80,240	5,012	75,228	3,909	3,117	4.9	4.1	3,915	−102	54,004	700	23,141	66.0
Callahan County, TX	6,786	582	6,204	317	238	4.7	3.8	205	7	1,154	156	19,668	56.1
Jones County, TX	8,008	334	7,674	490	392	6.1	5.1	316	−2	2,881	−268	19,961	56.9
Taylor County, TX	65,446	4,096	61,350	3,102	2,487	4.7	4.1	3,394	−107	49,969	812	23,405	66.7
Akron, OH	373,273	9,785	363,488	22,354	14,896	6.0	4.1	17,758	209	289,151	−13,008	33,118	94.4
Portage County, OH	87,329	2,936	84,393	5,031	3,288	5.8	3.9	3,181	73	41,085	−5,687	28,456	81.1
Summit County, OH	285,944	6,849	279,095	17,323	11,608	6.1	4.2	14,577	136	248,066	−7,321	33,890	96.6
Albany, GA	72,439	946	71,493	3,768	3,372	5.2	4.7	3,357	65	50,369	−2,499	27,068	77.2
Baker County, GA	1,824	78	1,746	76	74	4.2	4.2	25	4	388	174	17,830	50.8
Dougherty County, GA	41,128	−470	41,598	2,445	2,160	5.9	5.2	2,573	−11	42,681	−2,958	28,297	80.7
Lee County, GA	14,763	1,583	13,180	474	445	3.2	3.4	275	67	3,153	679	21,066	60.0
Terrell County, GA	4,565	−102	4,667	266	245	5.8	5.2	193	2	1,865	−243	18,680	53.2
Worth County, GA	10,159	−143	10,302	507	448	5.0	4.3	291	3	2,282	−151	20,794	59.3
Albany-Schenectady-Troy, NY	452,566	16,396	436,170	19,037	14,991	4.2	3.4	19,743	465	317,209	−2,335	33,012	94.1
Albany County, NY	160,394	4,857	155,537	6,587	5,189	4.1	3.3	9,017	141	164,977	−3,532	34,173	97.4
Rensselaer County, NY	83,768	2,529	81,239	3,818	2,938	4.6	3.6	2,776	46	41,812	−142	30,513	87.0
Saratoga County, NY	117,745	6,555	111,190	4,452	3,682	3.8	3.3	4,430	293	55,992	2,199	29,666	84.6
Schenectady County, NY	74,976	2,039	72,937	3,329	2,532	4.4	3.5	2,924	−38	48,961	−637	35,972	102.5
Schoharie County, NY	15,683	416	15,267	851	650	5.4	4.3	596	23	5,467	−223	24,835	70.8
Albuquerque, NM	391,796	21,567	370,229	20,513	15,304	5.2	4.1	18,087	122	274,426	−6,400	29,893	85.2
Bernalillo County, NM	305,411	16,074	289,337	15,682	11,669	5.1	4.0	15,669	−1	241,224	−9,050	30,034	85.6
Sandoval County, NM	47,747	4,540	43,207	2,632	1,845	5.5	4.3	1,315	94	21,294	1,546	33,700	96.1
Torrance County, NM	7,562	−10	7,572	440	380	5.8	5.0	229	6	2,072	226	18,252	52.0
Valencia County, NM	31,076	963	30,113	1,759	1,410	5.7	4.7	874	23	9,836	878	20,657	58.9
Alexandria, LA	64,660	1,258	63,402	3,714	3,297	5.7	5.2	3,337	50	48,222	−1,518	25,561	72.9
Grant Parish, LA	8,075	197	7,878	550	467	6.8	5.9	226	24	1,581	127	22,486	64.1
Rapides Parish, LA	56,585	1,061	55,524	3,164	2,830	5.6	5.1	3,111	26	46,641	−1,645	25,665	73.2
Allentown-Bethlehem-Easton, PA-NJ	404,991	19,721	385,270	21,551	14,259	5.3	3.7	18,073	360	288,496	1,090	33,849	96.5
Warren County, NJ	58,676	3,015	55,661	2,465	1,619	4.2	2.9	2,821	99	31,972	780	36,667	104.5
Carbon County, PA	30,098	1,106	28,992	1,962	1,494	6.5	5.2	1,129	−9	13,532	−894	21,921	62.5
Lehigh County, PA	169,830	7,388	162,442	9,176	5,939	5.4	3.7	8,219	40	158,452	−2,977	35,799	102.0
Northampton County, PA	146,387	8,212	138,175	7,948	5,207	5.4	3.8	5,904	230	84,540	4,181	31,039	88.5
Altoona, PA	65,809	3,446	62,363	3,633	2,905	5.5	4.7	3,259	−30	49,193	−2,658	25,870	73.7
Blair County, PA	65,809	3,446	62,363	3,633	2,905	5.5	4.7	3,259	−30	49,193	−2,658	25,870	73.7
Amarillo, TX	128,349	10,675	117,674	5,578	4,492	4.3	3.8	5,767	−15	83,504	−1,132	28,006	79.8
Armstrong County, TX	1,102	14	1,088	46	34	4.2	3.1	40	8	312	−63	25,093	71.5
Carson County, TX	3,574	223	3,351	149	109	4.2	3.3	116	−11	3,738	2,900	55,927	159.4
Potter County, TX	57,889	4,929	52,960	3,261	2,842	5.6	5.4	3,571	−61	55,969	−6,020	27,655	78.8
Randall County, TX	65,784	5,509	60,275	2,122	1,507	3.2	2.5	2,040	49	23,485	2,051	24,436	69.7
Ames, IA	46,560	−116	46,676	1,472	876	3.2	1.9	1,902	−31	27,080	−1,422	24,796	70.7
Story County, IA	46,560	−116	46,676	1,472	876	3.2	1.9	1,902	−31	27,080	−1,422	24,796	70.7
Anchorage, AK	178,647	9,454	169,193	11,388	8,995	6.4	5.3	9,613	304	127,135	4,728	42,496	121.1
Anchorage Borough, AK	145,787	5,396	140,391	8,673	6,937	5.9	4.9	8,036	148	116,914	4,150	43,495	124.0
Matanuska-Susitna Borough, AK	32,860	4,058	28,802	2,715	2,058	8.3	7.1	1,577	156	10,221	578	31,071	88.6
Anderson, IN	63,421	−329	63,750	3,746	1,908	5.9	3.0	2,686	−87	38,421	−3,925	27,403	78.1
Madison County, IN	63,421	−329	63,750	3,746	1,908	5.9	3.0	2,686	−87	38,421	−3,925	27,403	78.1
Anderson, SC	83,733	330	83,403	5,977	2,492	7.1	3.0	3,796	71	55,028	−3,970	27,213	77.6
Anderson County, SC	83,733	330	83,403	5,977	2,492	7.1	3.0	3,796	71	55,028	−3,970	27,213	77.6
Ann Arbor, MI	188,183	2,203	185,980	8,160	4,422	4.3	2.4	8,296	44	150,487	−6,977	41,491	118.3
Washtenaw County, MI	188,183	2,203	185,980	8,160	4,422	4.3	2.4	8,296	44	150,487	−6,977	41,491	118.3
Anniston-Oxford, AL	54,324	755	53,569	2,931	2,428	5.4	4.5	2,570	4	38,373	−2,241	25,003	71.3
Calhoun County, AL	54,324	755	53,569	2,931	2,428	5.4	4.5	2,570	4	38,373	−2,241	25,003	71.3
Appleton, WI	121,974	4,352	117,622	5,565	3,352	4.6	2.8	5,623	141	105,127	−4,285	32,127	91.6
Calumet County, WI	25,524	1,357	24,167	1,009	649	4.0	2.7	798	29	13,744	1,322	28,533	81.3
Outagamie County, WI	96,450	2,995	93,455	4,556	2,703	4.7	2.9	4,825	112	91,383	−5,607	32,668	93.1
Asheville, NC	195,625	11,225	184,400	8,373	6,027	4.3	3.3	10,696	393	143,332	−3,900	26,716	76.2
Buncombe County, NC	113,520	6,263	107,257	4,805	3,388	4.2	3.2	6,529	148	93,830	−5,195	26,988	76.9
Haywood County, NC	27,056	1,284	25,772	1,212	1,011	4.5	3.9	1,443	41	15,153	108	22,910	65.3
Henderson County, NC	45,315	3,284	42,031	1,850	1,276	4.1	3.0	2,406	201	30,906	911	28,582	81.5
Madison County, NC	9,734	394	9,340	506	352	5.2	3.8	318	3	3,443	276	19,304	55.0
Athens-Clarke County, GA	95,181	5,957	89,224	3,238	2,891	3.4	3.2	4,035	206	54,513	93	25,608	73.0
Clarke County, GA	57,199	2,815	54,384	2,036	1,870	3.6	3.4	2,799	202	44,869	3,589	26,093	74.4
Madison County, GA	14,980	1,150	13,830	536	451	3.6	3.3	393	−118	2,887	−4,054	22,188	63.2
Oconee County, GA	15,766	1,397	14,369	411	368	2.6	2.6	682	103	5,936	578	24,355	69.4
Oglethorpe County, GA	7,236	595	6,641	255	202	3.5	3.0	161	19	821	−20	20,181	57.5
Atlanta-Sandy Springs-Marietta, GA	2,454,115	81,620	2,372,495	112,927	73,906	4.6	3.1	119,863	4,148	2,066,678	−71,597	38,356	109.3
Barrow County, GA	27,718	2,521	25,197	1,179	759	4.3	3.0	900	89	10,707	1,157	26,841	76.5
Bartow County, GA	43,031	2,386	40,645	2,152	1,498	5.0	3.7	1,709	110	27,375	825	28,035	79.9
Butts County, GA	9,682	575	9,107	487	418	5.0	4.6	350	10	4,389	89	22,909	65.3
Carroll County, GA	48,059	3,092	44,967	2,255	1,678	4.7	3.7	1,894	48	25,420	−2,329	28,912	82.4
Cherokee County, GA	91,823	8,862	82,961	3,283	2,147	3.6	2.6	3,739	492	31,018	1,735	26,894	76.7
Clayton County, GA	133,263	6,761	126,502	7,423	4,268	5.6	3.4	4,190	−184	74,897	−13,625	27,752	79.1
Cobb County, GA	368,324	6,763	361,561	15,373	10,140	4.2	2.8	18,344	393	302,068	−10,807	39,843	113.6
Coweta County, GA	52,169	3,375	48,794	1,997	1,611	3.8	3.3	1,801	136	24,013	314	27,187	77.5
Dawson County, GA	9,852	809	9,043	359	244	3.6	2.7	514	19	4,723	502	22,270	63.5
DeKalb County, GA	371,973	−9,925	381,898	19,767	12,652	5.3	3.3	15,694	−1,273	283,358	−45,030	36,203	103.2
Douglas County, GA	54,548	3,013	51,535	2,536	1,535	4.6	3.0	2,275	170	30,778	1,557	24,080	68.6

See footnotes at end of table.

Metropolitan statistical area **Metropolitan statistical area with metropolitan divisions** *Metropolitan division* Component county	Civilian labor force							Private nonfarm businesses					
	Total			Number of unemployed		Unemployment rate[1]		Establishments		Employment[2]		Annual payroll per employee, 2002	
	2004	Net change, 2000–2004	2000	2004	2000	2004	2000	2002	Net change, 2000–2002	2002	Net change, 2000–2002	Amount (dollars)	Percent of national average
Atlanta-Sandy Springs-Marietta, GA—Con.													
Fayette County, GA.	51,044	1,164	49,880	1,760	1,331	3.4	2.7	2,683	272	34,270	4,678	29,923	85.3
Forsyth County, GA.	67,310	9,930	57,380	2,094	1,373	3.1	2.4	3,315	947	43,166	13,479	33,146	94.5
Fulton County, GA.	416,408	−14,874	431,282	22,245	14,977	5.3	3.5	31,600	654	731,167	−37,349	45,849	130.7
Gwinnett County, GA.	375,143	28,084	347,059	14,917	9,514	4.0	2.7	18,851	1,066	291,476	4,010	36,851	105.0
Haralson County, GA.	12,672	249	12,423	625	444	4.9	3.6	472	28	5,389	−209	25,559	72.9
Heard County, GA.	4,942	−195	5,137	259	205	5.2	4.0	126	7	1,271	−172	21,122	60.2
Henry County, GA.	79,947	12,311	67,636	3,194	1,803	4.0	2.7	2,742	471	32,705	4,267	25,146	71.7
Jasper County, GA	6,066	275	5,791	286	187	4.7	3.2	174	14	2,092	251	24,699	70.4
Lamar County, GA	7,829	−241	8,070	431	363	5.5	4.5	241	4	2,490	−637	22,102	63.0
Meriwether County, GA	9,898	−262	10,160	629	463	6.4	4.6	341	−1	4,232	−787	24,785	70.7
Newton County, GA.	37,655	5,294	32,361	1,835	1,054	4.9	3.3	1,313	132	17,349	1,760	29,871	85.1
Paulding County, GA.	52,958	7,089	45,869	2,093	1,222	4.0	2.7	1,219	235	10,404	1,223	24,391	69.5
Pickens County, GA	13,711	1,197	12,514	498	375	3.6	3.0	550	66	5,349	341	24,841	70.8
Pike County, GA.	7,251	254	6,997	336	258	4.6	3.7	206	11	1,019	−202	21,396	61.0
Rockdale County, GA.	37,770	805	36,965	1,805	1,153	4.8	3.1	2,001	19	32,942	1,414	30,876	88.0
Spalding County, GA	28,014	−171	28,185	1,648	1,221	5.9	4.3	1,222	39	19,164	−126	23,774	67.8
Walton County, GA.	35,055	2,479	32,576	1,461	1,013	4.2	3.1	1,397	174	13,447	2,074	26,411	75.3
Atlantic City, NJ.	134,390	5,422	128,968	7,483	6,007	5.6	4.7	6,533	156	125,928	5,370	29,592	84.4
Atlantic County, NJ.	134,390	5,422	128,968	7,483	6,007	5.6	4.7	6,533	156	125,928	5,370	29,592	84.4
Auburn-Opelika, AL.	62,818	3,984	58,834	2,622	2,101	4.2	3.6	2,077	85	33,307	1,036	24,053	68.6
Lee County, AL.	62,818	3,984	58,834	2,622	2,101	4.2	3.6	2,077	85	33,307	1,036	24,053	68.6
Augusta-Richmond County, GA-SC.	246,659	13,528	233,131	13,355	9,009	5.4	3.9	10,094	87	180,422	3,198	30,887	88.0
Burke County, GA.	9,813	615	9,198	666	463	6.8	5.0	339	20	5,210	−171	29,423	83.9
Columbia County, GA	52,686	5,358	47,328	1,936	1,369	3.7	2.9	1,784	−20	22,050	−1,204	25,853	73.7
McDuffie County, GA.	10,320	395	9,925	591	437	5.7	4.4	478	8	6,762	−663	22,814	65.0
Richmond County, GA.	89,700	2,295	87,405	5,291	3,850	5.9	4.4	4,531	77	89,352	5,610	30,079	85.7
Aiken County, SC	73,342	4,410	68,932	4,224	2,528	5.8	3.7	2,625	5	52,021	−411	36,444	103.9
Edgefield County, SC	10,798	455	10,343	647	362	6.0	3.5	337	−3	5,027	37	22,191	63.3
Austin-Round Rock, TX.	778,097	39,898	738,199	39,391	22,662	5.1	3.1	33,362	1,540	549,172	−1,246	38,111	108.6
Bastrop County, TX.	33,157	3,448	29,709	1,845	1,032	5.6	3.5	850	60	7,739	495	21,898	62.4
Caldwell County, TX.	16,060	958	15,102	1,016	629	6.3	4.2	514	20	3,965	−261	19,270	54.9
Hays County, TX.	63,076	6,412	56,664	3,066	1,853	4.9	3.3	2,435	249	28,461	4,421	24,163	68.9
Travis County, TX.	499,134	7,477	491,657	26,188	15,114	5.2	3.1	24,249	701	422,941	−23,148	38,648	110.2
Williamson County, TX.	166,670	21,603	145,067	7,276	4,034	4.4	2.8	5,314	510	86,066	17,247	42,410	120.9
Bakersfield, CA.	318,655	24,212	294,443	31,210	24,344	9.8	8.3	11,268	375	154,185	3,875	30,746	87.6
Kern County, CA.	318,655	24,212	294,443	31,210	24,344	9.8	8.3	11,268	375	154,185	3,875	30,746	87.6
Baltimore-Towson, MD.	1,346,001	20,017	1,325,984	61,195	50,333	4.5	3.8	63,694	1,445	1,049,283	4,762	36,431	103.8
Anne Arundel County, MD.	272,165	4,801	267,364	9,903	8,063	3.6	3.0	13,017	842	194,857	10,040	36,572	104.2
Baltimore County, MD.	414,355	6,368	407,987	18,082	15,093	4.4	3.7	19,803	813	318,130	3,731	34,231	97.6
Carroll County, MD.	88,867	5,002	83,865	2,930	2,487	3.3	3.0	4,195	123	45,679	2,154	26,560	75.7
Harford County, MD.	125,136	5,351	119,785	4,865	3,883	3.9	3.2	5,006	173	58,957	120	28,082	80.0
Howard County, MD.	151,028	6,521	144,507	4,682	3,624	3.1	2.5	7,560	218	135,024	34	43,078	122.8
Queen Anne's County, MD.	24,159	1,479	22,680	824	693	3.4	3.1	1,283	86	9,671	96	25,357	72.3
Baltimore city, MD.	270,291	−9,505	279,796	19,909	16,490	7.4	5.9	12,830	−810	286,965	−11,413	39,307	112.0
Bangor, ME.	78,822	3,623	75,199	4,271	2,844	5.4	3.8	4,166	−7	57,427	585	27,924	79.6
Penobscot County, ME.	78,822	3,623	75,199	4,271	2,844	5.4	3.8	4,166	−7	57,427	585	27,924	79.6
Barnstable Town, MA.	123,131	9,761	113,370	5,956	3,751	4.8	3.3	8,596	257	74,340	2,153	31,479	89.7
Barnstable County, MA.	123,131	9,761	113,370	5,956	3,751	4.8	3.3	8,596	257	74,340	2,153	31,479	89.7
Baton Rouge, LA.	351,569	12,673	338,896	21,321	16,122	6.1	4.8	16,308	227	278,604	−2,560	30,399	86.7
Ascension Parish, LA.	42,406	4,123	38,283	2,665	1,903	6.3	5.0	1,639	121	24,761	−574	33,809	96.4
East Baton Rouge Parish, LA.	209,336	2,839	206,497	11,775	8,967	5.6	4.3	11,412	−87	209,893	−3,533	30,047	85.6
East Feliciana Parish, LA.	8,292	49	8,243	589	445	7.1	5.4	249	−3	4,670	1,209	25,338	72.2
Iberville Parish, LA.	12,699	139	12,560	1,136	834	8.9	6.6	546	4	10,384	−253	41,187	117.4
Livingston Parish, LA.	49,762	5,127	44,635	3,126	2,369	6.3	5.3	1,353	125	12,418	184	21,955	62.6
Pointe Coupee Parish, LA.	9,794	81	9,713	730	577	7.5	5.9	366	16	3,932	156	22,374	63.8
St. Helena Parish, LA.	4,021	−23	4,044	267	220	6.6	5.4	96	6	1,041	295	20,905	59.6
West Baton Rouge Parish, LA.	10,404	271	10,133	698	504	6.7	5.0	459	29	8,657	−198	30,683	87.5
West Feliciana Parish, LA.	4,855	67	4,788	335	303	6.9	6.3	188	16	2,848	154	46,168	131.6
Battle Creek, MI.	73,138	3,360	69,778	5,096	2,921	7.0	4.2	2,999	−30	56,235	−4,484	33,473	95.4
Calhoun County, MI.	73,138	3,360	69,778	5,096	2,921	7.0	4.2	2,999	−30	56,235	−4,484	33,473	95.4
Bay City, MI.	56,851	107	56,744	4,300	2,300	7.6	4.1	2,571	15	33,815	−1,521	30,078	85.7
Bay County, MI.	56,851	107	56,744	4,300	2,300	7.6	4.1	2,571	15	33,815	−1,521	30,078	85.7
Beaumont-Port Arthur, TX.	179,733	3,138	176,595	15,069	11,432	8.4	6.5	8,009	−98	125,925	−3,222	30,638	87.3
Hardin County, TX.	24,457	1,271	23,186	1,832	1,290	7.5	5.6	726	−11	8,012	−801	22,440	64.0
Jefferson County, TX.	113,919	1,152	112,767	9,534	7,330	8.4	6.5	5,863	−46	98,448	−1,954	31,085	88.6
Orange County, TX.	41,357	715	40,642	3,703	2,812	9.0	6.9	1,420	−41	19,465	−467	31,754	90.5
Bellingham, WA.	100,935	12,623	88,312	5,803	4,567	5.7	5.2	5,583	197	58,451	−1,186	29,662	84.6
Whatcom County, WA.	100,935	12,623	88,312	5,803	4,567	5.7	5.2	5,583	197	58,451	−1,186	29,662	84.6
Bend, OR.	71,064	9,492	61,572	4,771	3,322	6.7	5.4	4,947	457	45,386	2,500	27,299	77.8
Deschutes County, OR	71,064	9,492	61,572	4,771	3,322	6.7	5.4	4,947	457	45,386	2,500	27,299	77.8
Billings, MT.	82,549	6,159	76,390	2,920	3,153	3.5	4.1	5,336	140	60,549	−273	27,071	77.2
Carbon County, MT.	5,366	378	4,988	210	221	3.9	4.4	350	44	1,911	−45	18,049	51.4
Yellowstone County, MT.	77,183	5,781	71,402	2,710	2,932	3.5	4.1	4,986	96	58,638	−228	27,365	78.0
Binghamton, NY.	122,618	−2,475	125,093	6,556	4,468	5.3	3.6	5,126	27	91,069	−279	27,827	79.3
Broome County, NY.	96,456	−2,039	98,495	5,200	3,559	5.4	3.6	4,343	44	82,750	−253	28,208	80.4
Tioga County, NY.	26,162	−436	26,598	1,356	909	5.2	3.4	783	−17	8,319	−26	24,029	68.5

See footnotes at end of table.

Table C-4. Metropolitan Areas With Component Counties — **Civilian Labor Force and Private Nonfarm Businesses**—Con.

Metropolitan statistical area / Metropolitan statistical area with metropolitan divisions / Metropolitan division / Component county	Civilian labor force							Private nonfarm businesses					
	Total			Number of unemployed		Unemployment rate[1]		Establishments		Employment[2]		Annual payroll per employee, 2002	
	2004	Net change, 2000–2004	2000	2004	2000	2004	2000	2002	Net change, 2000–2002	2002	Net change, 2000–2002	Amount (dollars)	Percent of national average
Birmingham-Hoover, AL	533,028	−1,665	534,693	25,810	18,563	4.8	3.5	25,867	233	450,925	−14,705	33,683	96.0
Bibb County, AL	8,945	274	8,671	482	412	5.4	4.8	315	−16	2,586	−817	22,460	64.0
Blount County, AL	26,179	710	25,469	1,052	795	4.0	3.1	696	−46	6,973	−895	22,370	63.8
Chilton County, AL	19,690	−52	19,742	909	758	4.6	3.8	779	4	6,495	−325	22,142	63.1
Jefferson County, AL	325,242	−8,371	333,613	17,107	11,836	5.3	3.5	17,516	50	346,939	−15,181	34,882	99.4
St. Clair County, AL	32,787	990	31,797	1,574	1,067	4.8	3.4	1,139	17	11,197	−1,313	24,032	68.5
Shelby County, AL	89,425	5,896	83,529	2,824	2,037	3.2	2.4	4,055	300	61,665	4,584	33,872	96.6
Walker County, AL	30,760	−1,112	31,872	1,862	1,658	6.1	5.2	1,367	−76	15,070	−758	24,609	70.1
Bismarck, ND	58,320	3,642	54,678	1,733	1,344	3.0	2.5	3,053	81	42,337	224	26,688	76.6
Burleigh County, ND	43,754	3,110	40,644	1,210	932	2.8	2.3	2,366	42	35,340	253	26,688	76.1
Morton County, ND	14,566	532	14,034	523	412	3.6	2.9	687	39	6,997	−29	27,899	79.5
Blacksburg-Christiansburg-Radford, VA	76,157	3,392	72,765	3,155	2,361	4.1	3.2	3,220	79	46,201	−2,990	26,983	76.9
Giles County, VA	8,113	398	7,715	398	326	4.9	4.2	324	−3	3,887	−732	29,793	84.9
Montgomery County, VA	42,832	2,378	40,454	1,368	1,019	3.2	2.5	1,845	52	25,588	1,431	24,785	70.6
Pulaski County, VA	17,896	690	17,206	1,049	778	5.9	4.5	692	27	12,164	−1,138	28,509	81.3
Radford city, VA	7,316	−74	7,390	340	238	4.6	3.2	359	3	4,562	−2,551	32,849	93.6
Bloomington, IN	93,852	2,877	90,975	4,279	2,723	4.6	3.0	3,880	−4	55,529	−1,309	25,449	72.5
Greene County, IN	16,267	188	16,079	961	740	5.9	4.6	631	−12	5,687	−277	19,957	56.9
Monroe County, IN	66,115	2,010	64,105	2,730	1,664	4.1	2.6	2,924	−2	45,942	−1,405	26,355	75.1
Owen County, IN	11,470	679	10,791	588	319	5.1	3.0	325	10	3,900	373	22,774	64.9
Bloomington-Normal, IL	84,940	−412	85,352	3,834	2,893	4.5	3.4	3,536	−6	78,612	−4,113	37,082	105.7
McLean County, IL	84,940	−412	85,352	3,834	2,893	4.5	3.4	3,536	−6	78,612	−4,113	37,082	105.7
Boise City-Nampa, ID	267,602	16,176	251,426	11,626	9,376	4.3	3.7	14,431	746	198,012	356	30,840	87.9
Ada County, ID	178,469	8,192	170,277	6,944	5,739	3.9	3.4	10,622	483	156,764	3,585	32,294	92.1
Boise County, ID	3,566	140	3,426	171	167	4.8	4.9	136	12	563	49	20,108	57.3
Canyon County, ID	73,656	7,746	65,910	3,997	2,925	5.4	4.4	3,189	240	37,596	−2,600	25,777	73.5
Gem County, ID	7,109	83	7,026	386	359	5.4	5.1	331	18	1,956	−349	19,044	54.3
Owyhee County, ID	4,802	15	4,787	128	186	2.7	3.9	153	−7	1,133	−329	23,365	66.6
Boston-Cambridge-Quincy, MA-NH	2,373,906	−5,419	2,379,325	115,721	59,626	4.9	2.5	125,649	273	2,303,251	−49,269	45,709	130.3
Boston-Quincy, MA	950,724	−9,025	959,749	48,263	25,315	5.1	2.6	52,065	159	1,063,635	7,193	47,418	135.2
Norfolk County, MA	353,195	−4,036	357,231	15,813	8,155	4.5	2.3	19,663	−15	351,072	13,506	42,912	122.3
Plymouth County, MA	255,382	4,031	251,351	13,101	6,680	5.1	2.7	12,074	435	149,160	1,401	34,022	97.0
Suffolk County, MA	342,147	−9,020	351,167	19,349	10,480	5.7	3.0	20,328	−261	563,403	−7,714	53,773	153.3
Cambridge-Newton-Framingham, MA	811,419	−10,782	822,201	35,826	17,761	4.4	2.2	42,890	−184	797,012	−55,942	48,173	137.3
Middlesex County, MA	811,419	−10,782	822,201	35,826	17,761	4.4	2.2	42,890	−184	797,012	−55,942	48,173	137.3
Essex County, MA	375,684	3,117	372,567	21,524	10,130	5.7	2.7	18,610	22	276,507	−5,859	38,024	108.4
Essex County, MA	375,684	3,117	372,567	21,524	10,130	5.7	2.7	18,610	22	276,507	−5,859	38,024	108.4
Rockingham County-Strafford County, NH	236,079	11,271	224,808	10,108	6,420	4.3	2.9	12,084	276	166,097	5,339	35,730	101.8
Rockingham County, NH	169,213	6,901	162,312	7,859	4,767	4.6	2.9	9,552	207	129,047	3,705	36,484	104.0
Strafford County, NH	66,866	4,370	62,496	2,249	1,653	3.4	2.6	2,532	69	37,050	1,634	33,105	94.4
Boulder, CO[3]	166,160	(X)	160,120	8,181	3,758	4.9	2.3	10,586	(X)	143,549	(X)	40,589	115.7
Boulder County, CO[3]	166,160	(X)	160,120	8,181	3,758	4.9	2.3	10,586	(X)	143,549	(X)	40,589	115.7
Bowling Green, KY	57,773	2,605	55,168	2,569	2,138	4.4	3.9	2,670	68	44,221	−185	26,830	76.5
Edmonson County, KY	5,200	173	5,027	296	253	5.7	5.0	112	10	814	55	17,656	50.3
Warren County, KY	52,573	2,432	50,141	2,273	1,885	4.3	3.8	2,558	58	43,407	−240	27,002	77.0
Bremerton-Silverdale, WA	121,067	14,736	106,331	7,086	5,394	5.9	5.1	5,566	326	51,818	1,929	27,229	77.6
Kitsap County, WA	121,067	14,736	106,331	7,086	5,394	5.9	5.1	5,566	326	51,818	1,929	27,229	77.6
Bridgeport-Stamford-Norwalk, CT	454,667	8,869	445,798	19,943	9,440	4.4	2.1	28,385	−202	462,542	17,612	56,000	159.6
Fairfield County, CT	454,667	8,869	445,798	19,943	9,440	4.4	2.1	28,385	−202	462,542	17,612	56,000	159.6
Brownsville-Harlingen, TX	143,006	15,832	127,174	12,549	8,890	8.8	7.0	6,046	250	88,506	2,009	20,372	58.1
Cameron County, TX	143,006	15,832	127,174	12,549	8,890	8.8	7.0	6,046	250	88,506	2,009	20,372	58.1
Brunswick, GA	50,236	3,694	46,542	2,027	1,693	4.0	3.6	2,830	56	34,394	360	24,090	68.7
Brantley County, GA	7,400	601	6,799	347	281	4.7	4.1	191	12	1,523	61	19,903	56.7
Glynn County, GA	37,737	2,890	34,847	1,452	1,207	3.8	3.5	2,416	49	31,026	480	24,704	70.4
McIntosh County, GA	5,099	203	4,896	228	205	4.5	4.2	223	−5	1,845	−181	17,223	49.1
Buffalo-Niagara Falls, NY	586,572	7,365	579,207	34,122	24,773	5.8	4.3	27,248	412	469,860	−7,791	30,621	87.3
Erie County, NY	474,789	5,779	469,010	27,175	19,619	5.7	4.2	22,707	365	408,186	−4,312	30,695	87.5
Niagara County, NY	111,783	1,586	110,197	6,947	5,154	6.2	4.7	4,541	47	61,674	−3,479	30,131	85.9
Burlington, NC	69,671	583	69,088	4,299	2,194	6.2	3.2	3,308	−40	54,710	−5,268	26,162	74.6
Alamance County, NC	69,671	583	69,088	4,299	2,194	6.2	3.2	3,308	−40	54,710	−5,268	26,162	74.6
Burlington-South Burlington, VT	118,840	5,325	113,515	4,137	2,661	3.5	2.3	7,190	576	97,612	2,176	33,430	95.3
Chittenden County, VT	88,638	3,423	85,215	2,873	1,833	3.2	2.2	5,363	55	86,110	2,317	34,304	97.8
Franklin County, VT	26,008	1,487	24,521	1,064	688	4.1	2.8	1,077	−45	11,502	−141	26,888	76.6
Grand Isle County, VT	4,194	415	3,779	200	140	4.8	3.7	750	566	(D)	(D)	(D)	(D)
Canton-Massillon, OH	204,989	−1,176	206,165	13,547	8,543	6.6	4.1	9,813	−151	163,383	−6,243	28,198	80.4
Carroll County, OH	14,431	323	14,108	1,036	612	7.2	4.3	481	−3	5,260	120	21,611	61.6
Stark County, OH	190,558	−1,499	192,057	12,511	7,931	6.6	4.1	9,332	−148	158,123	−6,363	28,417	81.0
Cape Coral-Fort Myers, FL	247,719	40,332	207,387	9,556	6,699	3.9	3.2	13,768	1,375	155,807	12,753	28,422	81.0
Lee County, FL	247,719	40,332	207,387	9,556	6,699	3.9	3.2	13,768	1,375	155,807	12,753	28,422	81.0
Carson City, NV	27,240	738	26,502	1,355	994	5.0	3.8	2,281	−69	22,743	−2,042	30,207	86.1
Carson City, NV	27,240	738	26,502	1,355	994	5.0	3.8	2,281	−69	22,743	−2,042	30,207	86.1
Casper, WY	39,872	3,335	36,537	1,485	1,438	3.7	3.9	2,683	58	28,121	564	28,243	80.5
Natrona County, WY	39,872	3,335	36,537	1,485	1,438	3.7	3.9	2,683	58	28,121	564	28,243	80.5

See footnotes at end of table.

Metropolitan statistical area / Metropolitan statistical area with metropolitan divisions / Metropolitan division / Component county	Civilian labor force							Private nonfarm businesses					
	Total			Number of unemployed		Unemployment rate[1]		Establishments		Employment[2]		Annual payroll per employee, 2002	
	2004	Net change, 2000–2004	2000	2004	2000	2004	2000	2002	Net change, 2000–2002	2002	Net change, 2000–2002	Amount (dollars)	Percent of national average
Cedar Rapids, IA	137,073	817	136,256	6,936	3,290	5.1	2.4	6,539	95	118,162	−5,614	31,298	89.2
Benton County, IA	14,050	257	13,793	686	332	4.9	2.4	626	−9	4,645	8	24,183	68.9
Jones County, IA	10,390	−108	10,498	563	289	5.4	2.8	509	8	4,442	−104	21,833	62.2
Linn County, IA	112,633	668	111,965	5,687	2,669	5.0	2.4	5,404	96	109,075	−5,518	31,986	91.2
Champaign-Urbana, IL	114,737	−556	115,293	5,249	4,125	4.6	3.6	4,924	62	76,004	−1,619	27,601	78.7
Champaign County, IL	98,952	−14	98,966	4,428	3,517	4.5	3.6	4,155	103	69,101	−1,574	28,087	80.1
Ford County, IL	7,024	−280	7,304	382	278	5.4	3.8	403	−20	3,810	−276	22,890	65.2
Piatt County, IL	8,761	−262	9,023	439	330	5.0	3.7	366	−21	3,093	231	22,546	64.3
Charleston, WV	138,639	−6,570	145,209	6,874	7,643	5.0	5.3	7,683	−162	123,444	5,265	29,301	83.5
Boone County, WV	9,408	−409	9,817	470	666	5.0	6.8	369	−25	6,743	1,220	40,686	116.0
Clay County, WV	3,492	−154	3,646	263	308	7.5	8.4	138	2	1,257	36	28,849	82.2
Kanawha County, WV	91,990	−5,387	97,377	4,454	4,815	4.8	4.9	5,804	−187	100,513	3,791	28,580	81.5
Lincoln County, WV	7,828	−312	8,140	497	596	6.3	7.3	249	17	1,781	-	21,594	61.6
Putnam County, WV	25,921	−308	26,229	1,190	1,258	4.6	4.8	1,123	31	13,150	218	30,055	85.7
Charleston-North Charleston, SC	290,125	25,386	264,739	15,514	8,216	5.3	3.1	14,660	590	208,693	−10,806	27,869	79.4
Berkeley County, SC	70,823	5,391	65,432	3,930	2,052	5.5	3.1	2,065	260	30,156	3,567	30,282	86.3
Charleston County, SC	166,024	13,739	152,285	8,973	4,789	5.4	3.1	10,719	233	158,745	−11,048	28,059	80.0
Dorchester County, SC	53,278	6,256	47,022	2,611	1,375	4.9	2.9	1,876	97	19,792	−3,325	22,664	64.6
Charlotte-Gastonia-Concord, NC-SC	778,270	46,975	731,295	43,513	24,582	5.6	3.4	39,926	1,129	734,833	11,439	36,636	104.4
Anson County, NC	10,999	28	10,971	960	582	8.7	5.3	453	−6	5,478	−741	24,848	70.8
Cabarrus County, NC	77,466	5,788	71,678	4,728	2,187	6.1	3.1	3,409	234	52,010	−811	30,626	87.3
Gaston County, NC	98,706	−916	99,622	6,293	5,512	6.4	5.5	4,019	−182	60,973	−9,795	26,520	75.6
Mecklenburg County, NC	419,632	25,496	394,136	21,225	11,691	5.1	3.0	24,713	468	519,735	21,041	39,908	113.8
Union County, NC	76,847	9,902	66,945	3,555	1,883	4.6	2.8	3,377	471	41,272	2,067	28,785	82.1
York County, SC	94,620	6,677	87,943	6,752	2,727	7.1	3.1	3,955	144	55,365	−322	29,725	84.7
Charlottesville, VA	93,585	5,961	87,624	2,917	1,822	3.1	2.1	5,242	232	70,948	151	30,515	87.0
Albemarle County, VA	45,692	2,630	43,062	1,163	741	2.5	1.7	1,919	173	24,261	1,388	30,792	87.8
Fluvanna County, VA	11,871	1,762	10,109	332	200	2.8	2.0	351	26	2,470	359	25,784	73.5
Greene County, VA	9,297	995	8,302	260	153	2.8	1.8	277	17	2,661	900	28,159	80.3
Nelson County, VA	7,362	410	6,952	249	162	3.4	2.3	401	15	3,233	654	17,500	49.9
Charlottesville city, VA	19,363	164	19,199	913	566	4.7	2.9	2,294	1	38,323	−3,150	31,907	90.9
Chattanooga, TN-GA	249,313	2,641	246,672	11,074	8,280	4.4	3.4	11,266	−69	208,768	−3,746	28,839	82.2
Catoosa County, GA	32,681	2,929	29,752	1,093	794	3.3	2.7	796	39	10,831	15	25,669	73.2
Dade County, GA	8,232	509	7,723	324	231	3.9	3.0	237	15	3,242	721	19,905	56.7
Walker County, GA	31,674	1,175	30,499	1,317	1,078	4.2	3.5	892	−16	15,492	−1,120	24,599	70.1
Hamilton County, TN	158,196	−2,038	160,234	7,223	5,369	4.6	3.4	8,729	−117	171,703	−3,067	29,898	85.2
Marion County, TN	13,003	−106	13,109	819	598	6.3	4.6	440	6	5,482	87	21,935	62.5
Sequatchie County, TN	5,527	172	5,355	298	210	5.4	3.9	172	4	2,018	−382	21,405	61.0
Cheyenne, WY	42,699	2,464	40,235	1,935	1,514	4.5	3.8	2,387	99	27,580	679	26,133	74.5
Laramie County, WY	42,699	2,464	40,235	1,935	1,514	4.5	3.8	2,387	99	27,580	679	26,133	74.5
Chicago-Naperville-Joliet, IL-IN-WI	**4,733,077**	**−34,733**	**4,767,810**	**288,055**	**207,287**	**6.1**	**4.3**	**230,115**	**2,515**	**4,028,005**	**−214,298**	**40,878**	**116.5**
Chicago-Naperville-Joliet, IL	*3,982,271*	*−40,199*	*4,022,470*	*245,565*	*180,538*	*6.2*	*4.5*	*193,284*	*1,537*	*3,431,123*	*−209,928*	*41,171*	*117.4*
Cook County, IL	2,633,630	−100,221	2,733,851	172,535	132,459	6.6	4.8	127,337	−828	2,353,456	−200,550	42,604	121.4
DeKalb County, IL	52,311	953	51,358	2,755	1,852	5.3	3.6	1,978	31	25,561	−507	26,512	75.6
DuPage County, IL	523,093	−7,614	530,707	25,505	17,728	4.9	3.3	32,261	−115	605,044	−15,636	41,581	118.5
Grundy County, IL	21,657	523	21,134	1,689	1,109	7.8	5.2	978	62	12,238	1,310	41,269	117.6
Kane County, IL	240,960	18,828	222,132	14,335	9,534	5.9	4.3	11,031	738	179,889	−1,685	32,812	93.5
Kendall County, IL	37,838	5,422	32,416	1,892	1,061	5.0	3.3	1,276	126	13,528	691	28,288	80.6
McHenry County, IL	160,295	8,669	151,626	8,338	5,433	5.2	3.6	7,240	395	89,314	−2,849	34,015	97.0
Will County, IL	312,487	33,241	279,246	18,516	11,362	5.9	4.1	11,183	1,128	152,093	9,298	35,068	100.0
Gary, IN	*323,188*	*−3,192*	*326,380*	*18,836*	*11,029*	*5.8*	*3.4*	*14,621*	*221*	*230,582*	*−12,061*	*31,179*	*88.9*
Jasper County, IN	14,839	68	14,771	840	482	5.7	3.3	798	16	10,295	260	26,718	76.2
Lake County, IN	222,936	−3,527	226,463	13,935	8,207	6.3	3.6	10,076	34	168,194	−11,029	31,302	89.2
Newton County, IN	7,026	−268	7,294	350	207	5.0	2.8	300	11	3,121	−87	24,570	70.0
Porter County, IN	78,387	535	77,852	3,711	2,133	4.7	2.7	3,447	160	48,972	−1,205	32,115	91.5
Lake County-Kenosha County, IL-WI	*427,618*	*8,658*	*418,960*	*23,654*	*15,720*	*5.5*	*3.8*	*22,210*	*757*	*366,300*	*7,691*	*44,236*	*126.1*
Lake County, IL	344,507	6,650	337,857	18,840	12,458	5.5	3.7	19,122	806	318,976	9,663	46,433	132.4
Kenosha County, WI	83,111	2,008	81,103	4,814	3,262	5.8	4.0	3,088	−49	47,324	−1,972	29,426	83.9
Chico, CA	98,004	4,853	93,151	7,055	5,725	7.2	6.1	4,758	161	56,283	2,507	24,066	68.6
Butte County, CA	98,004	4,853	93,151	7,055	5,725	7.2	6.1	4,758	161	56,283	2,507	24,066	68.6
Cincinnati-Middletown, OH-KY-IN	1,083,362	40,454	1,042,908	57,394	37,266	5.3	3.6	47,748	217	916,575	−42,072	34,824	99.3
Dearborn County, IN	25,666	1,084	24,582	1,344	778	5.2	3.2	997	24	13,520	198	27,634	78.8
Franklin County, IN	11,793	425	11,368	652	382	5.5	3.4	372	12	3,914	−74	23,149	66.0
Ohio County, IN	3,083	85	2,998	167	98	5.4	3.3	83	6	1,488	−307	26,259	74.9
Boone County, KY	54,440	5,422	49,018	2,270	1,462	4.2	3.0	2,563	161	54,810	−3,682	32,229	91.9
Bracken County, KY	4,304	123	4,181	245	149	5.7	3.6	118	2	950	−164	21,541	61.4
Campbell County, KY	46,040	−500	46,540	2,168	1,549	4.7	3.3	1,635	20	24,819	1,448	28,526	81.3
Gallatin County, KY	3,973	64	3,909	220	156	5.5	4.0	98	3	1,106	−323	20,460	58.3
Grant County, KY	12,250	693	11,557	640	448	5.2	3.9	415	−32	4,258	−567	23,043	65.7
Kenton County, KY	82,921	15	82,909	3,784	2,710	4.6	3.3	3,178	−51	62,834	−997	32,283	92.0
Pendleton County, KY	7,406	252	7,154	348	250	4.7	3.5	200	−4	1,823	113	23,905	68.1
Brown County, OH	21,749	1,191	20,558	1,499	1,055	6.9	5.1	604	7	5,757	−877	24,389	69.5
Butler County, OH	182,743	9,938	172,805	9,830	6,202	5.4	3.6	6,754	449	122,910	8,488	32,607	92.9
Clermont County, OH	101,941	6,604	95,337	5,536	3,480	5.4	3.7	3,537	260	47,846	−260	28,880	82.3
Hamilton County, OH	429,081	2,013	427,068	24,198	15,800	5.6	3.7	23,945	−951	510,618	−45,945	37,603	107.2
Warren County, OH	95,969	13,045	82,924	4,493	2,747	4.7	3.3	3,249	311	59,922	877	33,325	95.0
Clarksville, TN-KY	102,692	5,153	97,539	5,451	4,094	5.3	4.2	4,011	49	62,102	2,094	23,839	68.0
Christian County, KY	26,532	166	26,366	1,642	1,273	6.2	4.8	1,338	16	22,966	374	25,705	73.3
Trigg County, KY	6,227	289	5,938	312	266	5.0	4.5	237	−14	2,721	−19	22,103	63.0
Montgomery County, TN	64,016	4,308	59,708	3,102	2,283	4.8	3.8	2,278	35	34,751	1,240	22,919	65.3
Stewart County, TN	5,917	390	5,527	395	272	6.7	4.9	158	12	1,664	499	20,142	57.4

See footnotes at end of table.

Metropolitan statistical area **Metropolitan statistical area with metropolitan divisions** *Metropolitan division* Component county	Civilian labor force							Private nonfarm businesses					
	Total			Number of unemployed		Unemployment rate[1]		Establishments		Employment[2]		Annual payroll per employee, 2002	
	2004	Net change, 2000–2004	2000	2004	2000	2004	2000	2002	Net change, 2000–2002	2002	Net change, 2000–2002	Amount (dollars)	Percent of national average
Cleveland, TN	53,322	249	53,073	2,751	1,990	5.2	3.7	2,127	−4	38,016	−4,146	27,620	78.7
Bradley County, TN	45,910	358	45,552	2,329	1,647	5.1	3.6	1,883	12	36,074	−4,054	27,926	79.6
Polk County, TN	7,412	−109	7,521	422	343	5.7	4.6	244	−16	1,942	−92	21,941	62.5
Cleveland-Elyria-Mentor, OH	1,100,716	−23,015	1,123,731	64,815	42,886	5.9	3.8	56,335	−616	970,650	−86,684	35,139	100.2
Cuyahoga County, OH	679,639	−25,283	704,922	42,214	28,076	6.2	4.0	37,337	−869	711,881	−67,028	36,748	104.7
Geauga County, OH	50,256	342	49,914	2,365	1,527	4.7	3.1	2,664	49	28,417	−754	30,469	86.9
Lake County, OH	129,693	−1,621	131,314	7,016	4,387	5.4	3.3	6,439	59	89,556	−7,647	31,756	90.5
Lorain County, OH	151,221	−51	151,272	8,812	6,148	5.8	4.1	5,980	157	91,812	−6,986	30,411	86.7
Medina County, OH	89,907	3,598	86,309	4,408	2,748	4.9	3.2	3,915	−12	48,984	−4,269	29,517	84.1
Coeur d'Alene, ID	63,799	7,433	56,366	3,510	3,520	5.5	6.2	3,692	29	35,947	−1,065	26,233	74.8
Kootenai County, ID	63,799	7,433	56,366	3,510	3,520	5.5	6.2	3,692	29	35,947	−1,065	26,233	74.8
College Station-Bryan, TX	101,571	8,222	93,349	4,534	3,602	4.5	3.9	3,903	183	54,942	3,173	24,719	70.5
Brazos County, TX	86,019	7,336	78,683	3,662	2,960	4.3	3.8	3,366	150	50,111	2,736	24,819	70.7
Burleson County, TX	8,326	617	7,709	456	314	5.5	4.1	292	13	2,668	377	22,212	63.3
Robertson County, TX	7,226	269	6,957	416	328	5.8	4.7	245	20	2,163	60	25,484	72.6
Colorado Springs, CO	296,726	20,077	276,649	16,817	7,802	5.7	2.8	14,992	687	209,821	−5,466	31,919	91.0
El Paso County, CO	284,080	19,308	264,772	16,128	7,467	5.7	2.8	14,346	680	204,667	−5,322	32,079	91.4
Teller County, CO	12,646	769	11,877	689	335	5.4	2.8	646	7	5,154	−144	25,554	72.8
Columbia, MO	90,576	5,829	84,747	3,374	1,872	3.7	2.2	4,063	51	64,221	−107	26,601	75.8
Boone County, MO	85,093	5,739	79,354	3,120	1,715	3.7	2.2	3,857	54	62,578	71	26,752	76.3
Howard County, MO	5,483	90	5,393	254	157	4.6	2.9	206	−3	1,643	−178	20,845	59.4
Columbia, SC	349,852	16,245	333,607	20,019	10,224	5.7	3.1	16,195	80	267,755	−4,301	29,400	83.8
Calhoun County, SC	7,252	183	7,069	482	257	6.6	3.6	209	7	2,161	73	25,778	73.5
Fairfield County, SC	11,382	366	11,016	914	527	8.0	4.8	335	12	5,514	−1,353	33,564	95.7
Kershaw County, SC	28,200	1,192	27,008	1,747	972	6.2	3.6	1,162	−24	14,656	−566	24,071	68.6
Lexington County, SC	124,321	6,365	117,956	6,042	3,064	4.9	2.6	5,225	257	75,164	7,094	27,018	77.0
Richland County, SC	169,131	7,928	161,203	10,117	5,074	6.0	3.1	9,038	−153	167,948	−7,666	30,971	88.3
Saluda County, SC	9,566	211	9,355	717	330	7.5	3.5	226	−19	2,312	−1,883	19,986	57.0
Columbus, GA-AL	123,146	−1,897	125,043	6,366	5,621	5.2	4.5	5,721	62	96,507	−8,961	26,593	75.8
Russell County, AL	21,003	−1,285	22,288	1,278	922	6.1	4.1	841	−64	9,437	−1,728	21,721	61.9
Chattahoochee County, GA	3,270	632	2,638	223	215	6.8	8.2	65	8	636	−711	21,858	62.3
Harris County, GA	13,794	862	12,932	506	404	3.7	3.1	418	2	4,362	66	19,224	54.8
Marion County, GA	3,277	−53	3,330	164	131	5.0	3.9	88	11	1,943	−228	19,118	54.5
Muscogee County, GA	81,802	−2,053	83,855	4,195	3,949	5.1	4.7	4,309	105	80,129	−6,360	27,786	79.2
Columbus, IN	36,213	−1,278	37,491	1,578	943	4.4	2.5	1,854	−118	35,589	−2,976	36,219	103.2
Bartholomew County, IN	36,213	−1,278	37,491	1,578	943	4.4	2.5	1,854	−118	35,589	−2,976	36,219	103.2
Columbus, OH	916,311	37,862	878,449	49,559	28,299	5.4	3.2	39,642	1,002	785,150	−14,365	34,907	99.5
Delaware County, OH	74,221	11,703	62,518	2,975	1,684	4.0	2.7	3,067	548	53,048	10,174	36,021	102.7
Fairfield County, OH	70,695	5,333	65,362	3,830	2,167	5.4	3.3	2,604	63	30,874	−238	24,407	69.6
Franklin County, OH	606,603	14,814	591,789	32,863	18,654	5.4	3.2	28,176	209	603,696	−23,145	35,838	102.2
Licking County, OH	80,310	3,120	77,190	4,779	2,859	6.0	3.7	2,920	56	46,961	−1,676	27,262	77.7
Madison County, OH	19,688	406	19,282	1,162	665	5.9	3.4	750	25	11,066	−200	28,219	80.4
Morrow County, OH	17,439	1,051	16,388	1,047	624	6.0	3.8	436	27	4,384	−725	23,245	66.3
Pickaway County, OH	23,766	−32	23,798	1,749	969	7.4	4.1	828	14	12,133	7	28,185	80.3
Union County, OH	23,589	1,467	22,122	1,154	677	4.9	3.1	861	60	22,988	1,438	46,579	132.8
Corpus Christi, TX	197,774	12,616	185,158	13,201	9,993	6.7	5.4	9,447	85	129,676	−3,029	27,916	79.6
Aransas County, TX	10,919	1,192	9,727	919	578	8.4	5.9	503	26	3,523	−69	19,438	55.4
Nueces County, TX	157,208	9,235	147,973	9,938	7,794	6.3	5.3	7,931	58	115,367	−1,424	28,349	80.8
San Patricio County, TX	29,647	2,189	27,458	2,344	1,621	7.9	5.9	1,013	1	10,786	−1,536	26,047	74.2
Corvallis, OR	42,371	1,080	41,291	2,296	1,627	5.4	3.9	1,991	64	27,638	380	34,268	97.7
Benton County, OR	42,371	1,080	41,291	2,296	1,627	5.4	3.9	1,991	64	27,638	380	34,268	97.7
Cumberland, MD-WV	45,001	−678	45,679	2,843	2,646	6.3	5.8	2,312	−15	30,462	326	24,836	70.8
Allegany County, MD	32,520	−240	32,760	2,082	1,942	6.4	5.9	1,831	−16	25,212	76	25,006	71.3
Mineral County, WV	12,481	−438	12,919	761	704	6.1	5.4	481	1	5,250	250	24,020	68.5
Dallas-Fort Worth-Arlington, TX	2,965,577	115,774	2,849,803	174,761	102,753	5.9	3.6	130,270	3,453	2,501,040	−45,791	39,359	112.2
Dallas-Plano-Irving, TX	1,987,225	69,619	1,917,606	119,670	69,063	6.0	3.6	90,844	2,020	1,821,159	−31,597	41,438	118.1
Collin County, TX	341,633	41,921	299,712	16,437	8,564	4.8	2.9	12,961	1,880	217,088	33,764	44,501	126.8
Dallas County, TX	1,174,623	−12,308	1,186,931	79,901	46,638	6.8	3.9	62,844	−963	1,402,914	−75,202	42,648	121.6
Delta County, TX	2,508	−60	2,568	183	132	7.3	5.1	66	−6	619	148	16,220	46.2
Denton County, TX	296,034	28,549	267,485	13,095	7,615	4.4	2.8	8,774	752	123,008	12,393	30,899	88.1
Ellis County, TX	63,539	3,403	60,136	3,568	2,172	5.6	3.6	2,122	74	28,192	−290	27,157	77.4
Hunt County, TX	39,007	123	38,884	2,367	1,665	6.1	4.3	1,323	33	17,561	−2,939	32,050	91.4
Kaufman County, TX	41,018	3,421	37,597	2,706	1,540	6.6	4.1	1,556	93	19,008	−1,306	25,166	71.7
Rockwall County, TX	28,863	4,570	24,293	1,413	737	4.9	3.0	1,198	157	12,769	1,835	27,797	79.2
Fort Worth-Arlington, TX	978,352	46,155	932,197	55,091	33,690	5.6	3.6	39,426	1,433	679,881	−14,194	33,792	96.3
Johnson County, TX	70,499	4,082	66,417	4,159	2,534	5.9	3.8	2,249	73	26,160	−407	24,503	69.8
Parker County, TX	49,101	2,793	46,308	2,500	1,668	5.1	3.6	1,740	187	16,260	602	23,201	66.1
Tarrant County, TX	831,646	37,488	794,158	47,063	28,608	5.7	3.6	34,461	1,093	626,555	−14,372	34,562	98.5
Wise County, TX	27,106	1,792	25,314	1,369	880	5.1	3.5	976	80	10,906	−17	27,628	78.8
Dalton, GA	63,925	524	63,401	2,631	2,191	4.1	3.5	3,041	-	64,548	−2,468	30,650	87.4
Murray County, GA	20,155	497	19,658	785	658	3.9	3.3	463	−3	9,732	−1,090	25,059	71.4
Whitfield County, GA	43,770	27	43,743	1,846	1,533	4.2	3.5	2,578	3	54,816	−1,378	31,642	90.2
Danville, IL	37,470	−1,351	38,821	3,128	2,306	8.3	5.9	1,735	−19	27,504	−1,479	27,506	78.4
Vermilion County, IL	37,470	−1,351	38,821	3,128	2,306	8.3	5.9	1,735	−19	27,504	−1,479	27,506	78.4
Danville, VA	52,600	−241	52,841	3,884	1,976	7.4	3.7	2,440	7	37,675	−1,301	25,201	71.8
Pittsylvania County, VA	31,545	−108	31,653	1,943	1,048	6.2	3.3	908	−30	10,172	−1,590	21,446	61.1
Danville city, VA	21,055	−133	21,188	1,941	928	9.2	4.4	1,532	37	27,503	289	26,589	75.8
Davenport-Moline-Rock Island, IA-IL	196,151	−3,743	199,894	10,843	8,257	5.5	4.1	9,488	−101	159,127	−9,336	31,101	88.7
Henry County, IL	26,484	−783	27,267	1,501	1,334	5.7	4.9	1,133	−30	12,126	−2,703	22,883	65.2
Mercer County, IL	8,713	−110	8,823	605	496	6.9	5.6	319	−31	2,205	−198	20,450	58.3
Rock Island County, IL	75,447	−2,044	77,491	4,221	3,550	5.6	4.6	3,573	−72	65,337	−4,122	34,357	97.9
Scott County, IA	85,507	−806	86,313	4,516	2,877	5.3	3.3	4,463	32	79,459	−2,313	29,974	85.4

See footnotes at end of table.

State and Metropolitan Area Data Book: 2006

U.S. Census Bureau

Table C-4. Metropolitan Areas With Component Counties — **Civilian Labor Force and Private Nonfarm Businesses**—Con.

Metropolitan statistical area / Metropolitan statistical area with metropolitan divisions / *Metropolitan division* / Component county	Civilian labor force — Total 2004	Net change, 2000–2004	Total 2000	Number of unemployed 2004	2000	Unemployment rate 2004	2000	Establishments 2002	Net change, 2000–2002	Employment 2002	Net change, 2000–2002	Annual payroll per employee, 2002 Amount (dollars)	Percent of national average
Dayton, OH	428,304	−1,669	429,973	26,693	16,701	6.2	3.9	18,969	−130	358,042	−24,594	32,342	92.2
Greene County, OH	77,007	980	76,027	4,263	2,822	5.5	3.7	2,924	37	46,340	1,178	27,636	78.8
Miami County, OH	54,180	467	53,713	3,087	1,891	5.7	3.5	2,269	41	38,416	−92	28,631	81.6
Montgomery County, OH	275,327	−3,084	278,411	18,014	11,150	6.5	4.0	13,041	−222	263,770	−25,828	33,913	96.7
Preble County, OH	21,790	−32	21,822	1,329	838	6.1	3.8	735	14	9,516	148	26,682	76.1
Decatur, AL	72,206	−1,593	73,799	4,420	2,892	6.1	3.9	3,191	41	49,518	−2,527	27,906	79.5
Lawrence County, AL	16,121	−665	16,786	1,029	748	6.4	4.5	421	6	4,334	−1,055	34,151	97.3
Morgan County, AL	56,085	−928	57,013	3,391	2,144	6.0	3.8	2,770	35	45,184	−1,472	27,307	77.8
Decatur, IL	51,956	−4,170	56,126	3,780	2,910	7.3	5.2	2,674	−48	51,065	−6,070	31,668	90.3
Macon County, IL	51,956	−4,170	56,126	3,780	2,910	7.3	5.2	2,674	−48	51,065	−6,070	31,668	90.3
Deltona-Daytona Beach-Ormond Beach, FL	231,766	22,446	209,320	10,580	7,065	4.6	3.4	11,246	444	133,177	1,917	24,012	68.4
Volusia County, FL	231,766	22,446	209,320	10,580	7,065	4.6	3.4	11,246	444	133,177	1,917	24,012	68.4
Denver-Aurora, CO[3]	1,296,362	78,429	1,217,933	74,633	30,477	5.8	2.5	69,993	2,614	1,055,380	−6,271	39,322	112.1
Adams County, CO[3]	202,362	(X)	186,664	12,945	4,972	6.4	2.7	7,690	(X)	130,778	(X)	33,322	95.0
Arapahoe County, CO	294,372	12,553	281,819	16,317	6,674	5.5	2.4	17,024	612	280,035	−12,372	40,274	114.8
Broomfield County, CO[3]	24,060	(NA)	(X)	1,324	(X)	5.5	(X)	1,303	(NA)	26,601	(NA)	53,654	152.9
Clear Creek County, CO	6,137	96	6,041	339	157	5.5	2.6	351	17	2,380	−383	23,803	67.8
Denver County, CO	306,567	1,547	305,020	20,455	8,872	6.7	2.9	21,792	−629	382,217	−29,086	41,817	119.2
Douglas County, CO	128,816	23,230	105,586	5,443	2,112	4.2	2.0	5,199	1,121	50,758	12,856	38,638	110.1
Elbert County, CO	12,659	1,054	11,605	577	255	4.6	2.2	515	62	2,504	185	25,494	72.7
Gilpin County, CO	3,318	11	3,307	180	79	5.4	2.4	86	3	4,185	468	30,820	87.9
Jefferson County, CO[3]	308,615	(X)	309,368	16,566	7,146	5.4	2.3	15,599	(X)	174,739	(X)	35,560	101.4
Park County, CO	9,456	933	8,523	487	210	5.2	2.5	434	36	1,183	−153	24,117	68.7
Des Moines, IA	290,000	12,435	277,565	13,531	6,731	4.7	2.4	14,075	311	267,473	1,334	34,027	97.0
Dallas County, IA	26,553	2,854	23,699	955	477	3.6	2.0	1,038	221	13,679	3,883	29,370	83.7
Guthrie County, IA	6,174	76	6,098	283	169	4.6	2.8	322	22	2,093	225	22,123	63.1
Madison County, IA	7,913	243	7,670	404	250	5.1	3.3	370	25	2,923	149	22,096	63.0
Polk County, IA	224,962	8,547	216,415	10,866	5,304	4.8	2.5	11,573	50	240,997	−3,125	35,005	99.8
Warren County, IA	24,398	715	23,683	1,023	531	4.2	2.2	772	−7	7,781	202	19,628	56.0
Detroit-Warren-Livonia, MI	**2,206,277**	**−84,522**	**2,290,799**	**157,141**	**83,515**	**7.1**	**3.6**	**105,651**	**−250**	**1,892,160**	**−106,394**	**41,443**	**118.1**
Detroit-Livonia-Dearborn, MI	*918,630*	*−36,307*	*954,937*	*78,785*	*40,776*	*8.6*	*4.3*	*35,955*	*−56*	*714,125*	*−43,362*	*40,582*	*115.7*
Wayne County, MI	918,630	−36,307	954,937	78,785	40,776	8.6	4.3	35,955	−56	714,125	−43,362	40,582	115.7
Warren-Farmington Hills-Troy, MI	*1,287,647*	*−48,215*	*1,335,862*	*78,356*	*42,739*	*6.1*	*3.2*	*69,696*	*−194*	*1,178,035*	*−63,032*	*41,965*	*119.6*
Lapeer County, MI	45,093	−943	46,036	3,451	1,968	7.7	4.3	1,839	18	18,896	−2,821	27,718	79.0
Livingston County, MI	91,678	1,776	89,902	4,375	2,336	4.8	2.6	4,014	215	43,397	−1,130	32,472	92.6
Macomb County, MI	422,696	−12,272	434,968	28,215	15,562	6.7	3.6	18,972	132	305,885	−29,365	38,131	108.7
Oakland County, MI	643,206	−34,477	677,683	35,789	19,227	5.6	2.8	41,291	−608	765,163	−25,927	45,081	128.5
St. Clair County, MI	84,974	−2,299	87,273	6,526	3,646	7.7	4.2	3,580	49	44,694	−3,789	30,112	85.8
Dothan, AL	65,607	−240	65,847	3,093	2,704	4.7	4.1	3,615	54	54,812	−26	26,187	74.6
Geneva County, AL	11,892	−444	12,336	575	561	4.8	4.5	492	36	3,943	−467	20,629	58.8
Henry County, AL	7,653	−80	7,733	422	341	5.5	4.4	331	6	3,853	−332	23,393	66.7
Houston County, AL	46,062	284	45,778	2,096	1,802	4.6	3.9	2,792	12	47,016	773	26,882	76.6
Dover, DE	69,332	5,345	63,987	2,479	2,290	3.6	3.6	2,991	30	46,157	1,757	26,545	75.7
Kent County, DE	69,332	5,345	63,987	2,479	2,290	3.6	3.6	2,991	30	46,157	1,757	26,545	75.7
Dubuque, IA	49,054	220	48,834	2,310	1,629	4.7	3.3	2,631	−28	47,196	−2,792	27,073	77.2
Dubuque County, IA	49,054	220	48,834	2,310	1,629	4.7	3.3	2,631	−28	47,196	−2,792	27,073	77.2
Duluth, MN-WI	145,511	2,866	142,645	8,497	6,349	5.8	4.5	7,392	61	100,026	−2,225	27,494	78.4
Carlton County, MN	16,983	1,025	15,958	1,068	788	6.3	4.9	750	67	7,908	−1,153	32,934	93.9
St. Louis County, MN	105,293	1,409	103,884	6,101	4,594	5.8	4.4	5,539	-	78,399	−777	27,730	79.0
Douglas County, WI	23,235	432	22,803	1,328	967	5.7	4.2	1,103	−6	13,719	−295	23,013	65.6
Durham, NC	241,836	10,808	231,028	10,586	6,790	4.4	2.9	10,675	154	223,105	−13	39,256	111.9
Chatham County, NC	29,480	2,782	26,698	1,130	742	3.8	2.8	993	58	12,926	−210	23,898	68.1
Durham County, NC	128,061	6,403	121,658	5,716	3,617	4.5	3.0	5,942	−9	164,125	955	43,002	122.6
Orange County, NC	65,547	952	64,595	2,508	1,637	3.8	2.5	2,953	65	35,807	−218	30,628	87.3
Person County, NC	18,748	671	18,077	1,232	794	6.6	4.4	787	40	10,247	−540	28,778	82.0
Eau Claire, WI	86,973	3,613	83,360	4,115	2,938	4.7	3.5	4,007	85	63,745	213	27,195	77.5
Chippewa County, WI	31,738	1,700	30,038	1,773	1,250	5.6	4.2	1,441	205	18,066	462	27,329	77.9
Eau Claire County, WI	55,235	1,913	53,322	2,342	1,688	4.2	3.2	2,566	−120	45,679	−249	27,142	77.4
El Centro, CA	59,885	3,766	56,119	10,212	9,811	17.1	17.5	2,324	51	25,535	182	25,370	72.3
Imperial County, CA	59,885	3,766	56,119	10,212	9,811	17.1	17.5	2,324	51	25,535	182	25,370	72.3
Elizabethtown, KY	52,486	3,258	49,228	2,763	2,168	5.3	4.4	2,282	104	33,086	−1,542	26,183	74.6
Hardin County, KY	45,790	2,947	42,843	2,429	1,882	5.3	4.4	2,066	109	31,069	−1,630	26,532	75.6
Larue County, KY	6,696	311	6,385	334	286	5.0	4.5	216	−5	2,017	88	20,807	59.3
Elkhart-Goshen, IN	100,003	2,728	97,275	4,169	2,458	4.2	2.5	5,102	90	108,296	−10,058	31,994	91.2
Elkhart County, IN	100,003	2,728	97,275	4,169	2,458	4.2	2.5	5,102	90	108,296	−10,058	31,994	91.2
Elmira, NY	40,584	−2,244	42,828	2,463	1,843	6.1	4.3	1,932	15	34,242	−913	26,569	75.7
Chemung County, NY	40,584	−2,244	42,828	2,463	1,843	6.1	4.3	1,932	15	34,242	−913	26,569	75.7
El Paso, TX	290,119	14,845	275,274	22,700	18,721	7.8	6.8	12,403	93	194,012	−5,869	23,411	66.7
El Paso County, TX	290,119	14,845	275,274	22,700	18,721	7.8	6.8	12,403	93	194,012	−5,869	23,411	66.7
Erie, PA	140,830	542	140,288	8,886	6,363	6.3	4.5	6,807	−156	118,018	−4,382	28,066	80.0
Erie County, PA	140,830	542	140,288	8,886	6,363	6.3	4.5	6,807	−156	118,018	−4,382	28,066	80.0
Eugene-Springfield, OR	173,146	2,269	170,877	12,783	9,236	7.4	5.4	9,585	−105	117,253	−2,272	29,030	82.7
Lane County, OR	173,146	2,269	170,877	12,783	9,236	7.4	5.4	9,585	−105	117,253	−2,272	29,030	82.7

See footnotes at end of table.

Table C-4. Metropolitan Areas With Component Counties — Civilian Labor Force and Private Nonfarm Businesses—Con.

Metropolitan statistical area / **Metropolitan statistical area with metropolitan divisions** / *Metropolitan division* / Component county	Civilian labor force							Private nonfarm businesses					
	Total			Number of unemployed		Unemployment rate[1]		Establishments		Employment[2]		Annual payroll per employee, 2002	
	2004	Net change, 2000–2004	2000	2004	2000	2004	2000	2002	Net change, 2000–2002	2002	Net change, 2000–2002	Amount (dollars)	Percent of national average
Evansville, IN-KY	180,580	1,616	178,964	8,322	5,725	4.6	3.2	8,824	−86	157,880	−7,360	30,542	87.1
Gibson County, IN	17,079	268	16,811	787	532	4.6	3.2	724	−25	12,136	71	37,239	106.2
Posey County, IN	13,841	−76	13,917	598	405	4.3	2.9	524	−7	7,327	−228	41,845	119.3
Vanderburgh County, IN	90,655	532	90,123	4,390	2,771	4.8	3.1	5,190	−62	104,671	−6,471	29,186	83.2
Warrick County, IN	29,660	1,118	28,542	1,240	900	4.2	3.2	1,051	14	12,474	813	31,574	90.0
Henderson County, KY	22,767	−39	22,806	1,027	805	4.5	3.5	1,078	−7	18,576	−1,424	28,660	81.7
Webster County, KY	6,578	−187	6,765	280	312	4.3	4.6	257	1	2,696	−121	30,519	87.0
Fairbanks, AK	43,514	2,580	40,934	2,855	2,453	6.6	6.0	2,263	88	24,597	2,989	35,531	101.3
Fairbanks North Star Borough, AK	43,514	2,580	40,934	2,855	2,453	6.6	6.0	2,263	88	24,597	2,989	35,531	101.3
Fargo, ND-MN	112,620	8,073	104,547	3,267	2,531	2.9	2.4	5,497	177	88,369	329	27,817	79.3
Clay County, MN	30,864	2,665	28,199	1,116	931	3.6	3.3	1,161	14	14,238	−472	20,229	57.7
Cass County, ND	81,756	5,408	76,348	2,151	1,600	2.6	2.1	4,336	163	74,131	801	29,274	83.4
Farmington, NM	53,564	3,959	49,605	3,250	2,865	6.1	5.8	2,588	101	34,726	386	28,657	81.7
San Juan County, NM	53,564	3,959	49,605	3,250	2,865	6.1	5.8	2,588	101	34,726	386	28,657	81.7
Fayetteville, NC	139,622	6,326	133,296	7,852	6,169	5.6	4.6	5,600	12	87,496	−6,358	25,048	71.4
Cumberland County, NC	123,223	4,364	118,859	6,875	5,336	5.6	4.5	5,294	−11	83,030	−6,098	25,170	71.7
Hoke County, NC	16,399	1,962	14,437	977	833	6.0	5.8	306	23	4,466	−260	22,790	65.0
Fayetteville-Springdale-Rogers, AR-MO	207,116	30,685	176,431	7,522	5,106	3.6	2.9	8,936	513	157,773	12,220	28,697	81.8
Benton County, AR	92,300	15,663	76,637	3,121	2,120	3.4	2.8	3,965	308	77,065	9,587	30,495	86.9
Madison County, AR	7,537	635	6,902	302	214	4.0	3.1	195	−3	2,345	401	22,289	63.5
Washington County, AR	95,200	13,181	82,019	3,513	2,410	3.7	2.9	4,438	209	73,563	2,277	27,489	78.4
McDonald County, MO	12,079	1,206	10,873	586	362	4.9	3.3	338	−1	4,800	−45	21,474	61.2
Flagstaff, AZ	67,044	4,449	62,595	3,667	2,829	5.5	4.5	3,608	150	39,167	250	24,631	70.2
Coconino County, AZ	67,044	4,449	62,595	3,667	2,829	5.5	4.5	3,608	150	39,167	250	24,631	70.2
Flint, MI	213,704	−749	214,453	17,807	9,607	8.3	4.5	8,997	−120	139,377	−12,362	33,644	95.9
Genesee County, MI	213,704	−749	214,453	17,807	9,607	8.3	4.5	8,997	−120	139,377	−12,362	33,644	95.9
Florence, SC	95,670	4,191	91,479	7,813	3,858	8.2	4.2	4,562	25	76,853	−1,064	27,199	77.5
Darlington County, SC	32,322	949	31,373	2,599	1,475	8.0	4.7	1,264	−12	20,294	−1,273	29,021	82.7
Florence County, SC	63,348	3,242	60,106	5,214	2,383	8.2	4.0	3,298	37	56,559	209	26,545	75.7
Florence-Muscle Shoals, AL	66,618	−3,649	70,267	4,341	3,268	6.5	4.7	3,325	−39	43,258	−7,404	23,553	67.1
Colbert County, AL	24,967	−1,297	26,264	1,731	1,306	6.9	5.0	1,326	−34	17,941	−1,446	24,516	69.9
Lauderdale County, AL	41,651	−2,352	44,003	2,610	1,962	6.3	4.5	1,999	−5	25,317	−5,958	22,870	65.2
Fond du Lac, WI	57,401	1,511	55,890	2,635	1,666	4.6	3.0	2,491	−25	43,382	−1,724	28,632	81.6
Fond du Lac County, WI	57,401	1,511	55,890	2,635	1,666	4.6	3.0	2,491	−25	43,382	−1,724	28,632	81.6
Fort Collins-Loveland, CO	162,927	16,577	146,350	7,511	3,550	4.6	2.4	8,500	483	96,336	2,758	31,617	90.1
Larimer County, CO	162,927	16,577	146,350	7,511	3,550	4.6	2.4	8,500	483	96,336	2,758	31,617	90.1
Fort Smith, AR-OK	132,182	5,194	126,988	6,807	4,674	5.1	3.7	5,940	113	103,052	−4,344	25,642	73.1
Crawford County, AR	26,130	1,427	24,703	1,326	877	5.1	3.6	965	50	15,637	−1,135	24,714	70.4
Franklin County, AR	8,287	238	8,049	399	270	4.8	3.4	280	−1	3,355	211	20,931	59.7
Sebastian County, AR	57,995	1,660	56,335	2,791	1,881	4.8	3.3	3,333	28	69,658	−3,271	27,537	78.5
Le Flore County, OK	21,615	900	20,715	1,199	894	5.5	4.3	746	23	7,645	−218	19,717	56.2
Sequoyah County, OK	18,155	969	17,186	1,092	752	6.0	4.4	616	13	6,757	69	17,299	49.3
Fort Walton Beach-Crestview-Destin, FL	92,689	12,425	80,264	3,220	2,955	3.5	3.7	4,906	108	57,709	−587	25,798	73.5
Okaloosa County, FL	92,689	12,425	80,264	3,220	2,955	3.5	3.7	4,906	108	57,709	−587	25,798	73.5
Fort Wayne, IN	209,628	861	208,767	10,868	5,374	5.2	2.6	10,440	187	189,584	−12,454	32,397	92.3
Allen County, IN	177,333	692	176,641	9,170	4,602	5.2	2.6	9,125	176	168,433	−10,550	33,093	94.3
Wells County, IN	14,836	−117	14,953	726	351	4.9	2.3	612	4	10,244	−1,175	25,898	73.8
Whitley County, IN	17,459	286	17,173	972	421	5.6	2.5	703	7	10,907	−729	27,756	79.1
Fresno, CA	409,472	20,243	389,229	42,464	40,517	10.4	10.4	15,553	273	220,182	7,232	29,157	83.1
Fresno County, CA	409,472	20,243	389,229	42,464	40,517	10.4	10.4	15,553	273	220,182	7,232	29,157	83.1
Gadsden, AL	47,268	−1,493	48,761	2,977	2,551	6.3	5.2	2,173	18	32,472	−1,873	23,601	67.3
Etowah County, AL	47,268	−1,493	48,761	2,977	2,551	6.3	5.2	2,173	18	32,472	−1,873	23,601	67.3
Gainesville, FL	127,621	5,217	122,404	4,421	3,722	3.5	3.0	5,471	130	83,414	932	26,290	74.9
Alachua County, FL	120,629	4,641	115,988	4,151	3,492	3.4	3.0	5,283	112	82,235	826	26,371	75.2
Gilchrist County, FL	6,992	576	6,416	270	230	3.9	3.6	188	18	1,179	106	20,602	58.7
Gainesville, GA	78,439	5,226	73,213	2,983	2,170	3.8	3.0	3,531	169	56,685	−1,170	30,753	87.7
Hall County, GA	78,439	5,226	73,213	2,983	2,170	3.8	3.0	3,531	169	56,685	−1,170	30,753	87.7
Glens Falls, NY	66,679	3,182	63,497	3,194	2,508	4.8	3.9	3,419	26	43,823	−1,425	27,640	78.8
Warren County, NY	35,087	1,744	33,343	1,709	1,388	4.9	4.2	2,322	3	33,440	−1,692	28,176	80.3
Washington County, NY	31,592	1,438	30,154	1,485	1,120	4.7	3.7	1,097	23	10,383	267	25,916	73.9
Goldsboro, NC	51,526	814	50,712	2,806	2,041	5.4	4.0	2,338	−2	37,854	137	24,535	69.9
Wayne County, NC	51,526	814	50,712	2,806	2,041	5.4	4.0	2,338	−2	37,854	137	24,535	69.9
Grand Forks, ND-MN	54,875	2,558	52,317	2,046	1,787	3.7	3.4	2,573	3	35,756	−641	24,883	70.9
Polk County, MN	17,207	1,297	15,910	901	779	5.2	4.9	815	−16	9,062	320	22,347	63.7
Grand Forks County, ND	37,668	1,261	36,407	1,145	1,008	3.0	2.8	1,758	19	26,694	−961	25,744	73.4
Grand Junction, CO	68,915	10,085	58,830	3,533	1,824	5.1	3.1	3,940	46	42,915	−435	27,293	77.8
Mesa County, CO	68,915	10,085	58,830	3,533	1,824	5.1	3.1	3,940	46	42,915	−435	27,293	77.8
Grand Rapids-Wyoming, MI	400,969	−1,891	402,860	27,876	13,139	7.0	3.3	18,668	577	359,094	−9,506	33,819	96.4
Barry County, MI	30,164	−296	30,460	1,784	1,017	5.9	3.3	1,018	10	10,837	−892	27,226	77.6
Ionia County, MI	30,288	252	30,036	2,455	1,106	8.1	3.7	993	−43	11,199	−757	28,569	81.4
Kent County, MI	317,604	−1,695	319,299	21,790	9,952	6.9	3.1	15,821	548	328,391	−7,598	34,349	97.9
Newaygo County, MI	22,913	−152	23,065	1,847	1,064	8.1	4.6	836	62	8,667	−259	28,764	82.0

See footnotes at end of table.

Metropolitan statistical area / Metropolitan statistical area with metropolitan divisions / Metropolitan division / Component county	Civilian labor force							Private nonfarm businesses					
	Total			Number of unemployed		Unemployment rate[1]		Establishments		Employment[2]		Annual payroll per employee, 2002	
	2004	Net change, 2000–2004	2000	2004	2000	2004	2000	2002	Net change, 2000–2002	2002	Net change, 2000–2002	Amount (dollars)	Percent of national average
Great Falls, MT	39,209	922	38,287	1,643	1,901	4.2	5.0	2,510	-54	27,710	-48	22,877	65.2
Cascade County, MT	39,209	922	38,287	1,643	1,901	4.2	5.0	2,510	-54	27,710	-48	22,877	65.2
Greeley, CO[3]	108,615	(X)	93,538	5,829	2,430	5.4	2.6	4,418	(X)	58,663	(X)	31,914	91.0
Weld County, CO[3]	108,615	(X)	93,538	5,829	2,430	5.4	2.6	4,418	(X)	58,663	(X)	31,914	91.0
Green Bay, WI	172,444	9,840	162,604	8,098	4,714	4.7	2.9	7,750	112	141,024	-5,111	32,517	92.7
Brown County, WI	139,419	7,921	131,498	6,295	3,721	4.5	2.8	6,434	139	127,466	-4,410	33,007	94.1
Kewaunee County, WI	12,143	502	11,641	529	309	4.4	2.7	505	13	5,118	-434	27,249	77.7
Oconto County, WI	20,882	1,417	19,465	1,274	684	6.1	3.5	811	-40	8,440	-267	28,317	80.7
Greensboro-High Point, NC	357,938	7,777	350,161	19,985	12,367	5.6	3.5	18,139	-85	322,040	-20,046	30,834	87.9
Guilford County, NC	237,818	5,673	232,145	12,817	7,654	5.4	3.3	13,585	-76	251,444	-14,645	32,511	92.7
Randolph County, NC	73,726	1,678	72,048	3,745	2,483	5.1	3.4	2,723	-55	43,424	-3,699	24,178	68.9
Rockingham County, NC	46,394	426	45,968	3,423	2,230	7.4	4.9	1,831	46	27,172	-1,702	25,951	74.0
Greenville, NC	81,156	2,976	78,180	4,639	3,337	5.7	4.3	3,483	57	53,205	-1,864	25,662	73.1
Greene County, NC	9,013	445	8,568	556	401	6.2	4.7	226	19	1,743	-279	18,689	53.3
Pitt County, NC	72,143	2,531	69,612	4,083	2,936	5.7	4.2	3,257	38	51,462	-1,585	25,898	73.8
Greenville, SC	295,086	1,006	294,080	18,327	7,925	6.2	2.7	14,509	-215	270,129	-20,668	32,068	91.4
Greenville County, SC	204,636	1,793	202,843	12,074	5,172	5.9	2.5	11,431	-194	227,127	-14,736	33,574	95.7
Laurens County, SC	33,374	-416	33,790	2,382	1,068	7.1	3.2	904	-11	14,589	-2,562	25,207	71.9
Pickens County, SC	57,076	-371	57,447	3,871	1,685	6.8	2.9	2,174	-10	28,413	-3,370	23,550	67.1
Gulfport-Biloxi, MS	119,933	2,469	117,464	6,157	5,703	5.1	4.9	5,525	21	87,535	-4,695	25,531	72.8
Hancock County, MS	20,641	1,038	19,603	1,012	949	4.9	4.8	796	43	9,784	-194	27,072	77.2
Harrison County, MS	92,389	1,135	91,254	4,770	4,374	5.2	4.8	4,465	6	75,338	-4,547	25,440	72.5
Stone County, MS	6,903	296	6,607	375	380	5.4	5.8	264	-28	2,413	46	22,134	63.1
Hagerstown-Martinsburg, MD-WV	114,984	1,874	113,110	4,932	4,125	4.3	3.6	5,167	148	82,575	1,762	27,905	79.5
Washington County, MD	66,981	777	66,204	2,939	2,409	4.4	3.6	3,376	48	58,626	22	28,480	81.2
Berkeley County, WV	41,034	1,416	39,618	1,704	1,431	4.2	3.6	1,526	83	21,637	1,833	26,782	76.3
Morgan County, WV	6,969	-319	7,288	289	285	4.1	3.9	265	17	2,312	-9	23,856	68.0
Hanford-Corcoran, CA	54,424	5,065	49,359	5,889	4,964	10.8	10.1	1,591	52	20,459	1,919	26,959	76.8
Kings County, CA	54,424	5,065	49,359	5,889	4,964	10.8	10.1	1,591	52	20,459	1,919	26,959	76.8
Harrisburg-Carlisle, PA	279,913	11,500	268,413	12,588	9,117	4.5	3.4	12,965	66	264,726	7,289	31,745	90.5
Cumberland County, PA	119,654	5,839	113,815	4,723	3,603	3.9	3.2	5,514	-56	117,293	1,873	31,154	88.8
Dauphin County, PA	135,984	4,683	131,301	6,648	4,643	4.9	3.5	6,663	83	141,214	5,097	32,740	93.3
Perry County, PA	24,275	978	23,297	1,217	871	5.0	3.7	788	39	6,219	319	20,295	57.9
Harrisonburg, VA	63,020	7,321	55,699	1,862	1,048	3.0	1.9	2,836	141	48,277	48	26,395	75.2
Rockingham County, VA	40,832	4,765	36,067	1,121	604	2.7	1.7	1,198	48	20,668	-2,500	27,888	79.5
Harrisonburg city, VA	22,188	2,556	19,632	741	444	3.3	2.3	1,638	93	27,609	2,548	25,278	72.1
Hartford-West Hartford-East Hartford, CT	607,091	17,054	590,037	30,827	14,416	5.1	2.4	29,891	-74	561,896	-12,686	41,444	118.1
Hartford County, CT	438,416	9,448	428,968	23,927	11,173	5.5	2.6	23,083	-115	470,077	-6,563	42,835	122.1
Middlesex County, CT	88,819	3,402	85,417	3,684	1,802	4.1	2.1	4,315	79	63,587	3,145	36,516	104.1
Tolland County, CT	79,856	4,204	75,652	3,216	1,441	4.0	1.9	2,493	-38	28,232	-9,268	29,371	83.7
Hattiesburg, MS	62,337	1,739	60,598	3,214	2,936	5.2	4.8	3,045	41	44,537	1,208	24,440	69.7
Forrest County, MS	35,853	583	35,270	1,957	1,772	5.5	5.0	2,123	-10	33,919	249	24,696	70.4
Lamar County, MS	21,227	1,114	20,113	874	832	4.1	4.1	767	47	8,652	945	22,403	63.9
Perry County, MS	5,257	42	5,215	383	332	7.3	6.4	155	4	1,966	14	28,972	82.6
Hickory-Lenoir-Morganton, NC	179,873	-7,693	187,566	12,078	5,636	6.7	3.0	8,128	1	153,231	-14,897	26,640	75.9
Alexander County, NC	18,624	-677	19,301	1,116	535	6.0	2.8	573	-4	8,054	-691	22,561	64.3
Burke County, NC	43,197	-2,892	46,089	2,877	1,642	6.7	3.6	1,604	37	27,109	-6,534	26,636	75.9
Caldwell County, NC	40,581	-1,668	42,249	3,008	1,239	7.4	2.9	1,551	-17	27,608	-3,470	24,860	70.9
Catawba County, NC	77,471	-2,456	79,927	5,077	2,220	6.6	2.8	4,400	-15	90,460	-4,202	27,547	78.5
Hinesville-Fort Stewart, GA	26,850	2,924	23,926	1,470	1,223	5.5	5.1	802	20	9,671	-39	22,582	64.4
Liberty County, GA	21,677	2,065	19,612	1,260	1,062	5.8	5.4	744	9	9,273	-217	22,909	65.3
Long County, GA	5,173	859	4,314	210	161	4.1	3.7	58	11	398	178	14,955	42.6
Holland-Grand Haven, MI	133,594	-1,997	135,591	7,519	3,639	5.6	2.7	5,911	21	103,121	-4,684	33,002	94.1
Ottawa County, MI	133,594	-1,997	135,591	7,519	3,639	5.6	2.7	5,911	21	103,121	-4,684	33,002	94.1
Honolulu, HI	431,677	-528	432,205	13,692	16,961	3.2	3.9	20,952	315	317,533	1,671	31,756	90.5
Honolulu County, HI	431,677	-528	432,205	13,692	16,961	3.2	3.9	20,952	315	317,533	1,671	31,756	90.5
Hot Springs, AR	40,904	2,560	38,344	2,425	1,624	5.9	4.2	2,681	110	31,423	492	23,446	66.8
Garland County, AR	40,904	2,560	38,344	2,425	1,624	5.9	4.2	2,681	110	31,423	492	23,446	66.8
Houma-Bayou Cane-Thibodaux, LA	92,539	5,886	86,653	4,699	3,723	5.1	4.3	4,653	119	65,845	2,318	29,887	85.2
Lafourche Parish, LA	43,735	2,765	40,970	2,179	1,728	5.0	4.2	1,853	17	26,139	1,874	29,140	83.1
Terrebonne Parish, LA	48,804	3,121	45,683	2,520	1,995	5.2	4.4	2,800	102	39,706	444	30,379	86.6
Houston-Sugar Land, Baytown, TX	2,573,882	182,523	2,391,359	162,229	103,796	6.3	4.3	110,685	2,816	1,992,206	24,705	40,435	115.3
Austin County, TX	12,653	646	12,007	687	478	5.4	4.0	588	40	6,501	702	27,067	77.2
Brazoria County, TX	130,607	10,572	120,035	9,153	6,000	7.0	5.0	4,018	181	61,786	910	34,765	99.1
Chambers County, TX	13,822	718	13,104	813	564	5.9	4.3	387	11	4,413	-1,963	31,209	89.0
Fort Bend County, TX	217,361	31,847	185,514	11,482	6,672	5.3	3.6	6,615	607	82,953	4,305	34,940	99.6
Galveston County, TX	136,955	8,974	127,981	9,524	6,319	7.0	4.9	4,861	60	68,266	-892	28,103	80.1
Harris County, TX	1,827,239	102,156	1,725,083	116,959	75,205	6.4	4.4	85,314	522	1,654,636	13,598	42,107	120.0
Liberty County, TX	32,260	2,022	30,238	2,889	1,801	9.0	6.0	1,043	3	11,426	-242	23,103	65.9
Montgomery County, TX	176,724	24,048	152,676	9,020	5,627	5.1	3.7	6,787	986	90,063	4,523	33,488	95.5
San Jacinto County, TX	10,049	656	9,393	663	445	6.6	4.7	170	25	1,076	33	17,654	50.3
Waller County, TX	16,212	884	15,328	1,039	685	6.4	4.5	902	381	11,086	3,731	27,525	78.5
Huntington-Ashland, WV-KY-OH	130,228	4,446	125,782	7,218	7,159	5.5	5.7	6,244	-84	92,464	-1,176	26,954	76.8
Boyd County, KY	22,844	1,416	21,428	1,368	1,247	6.0	5.8	1,494	17	24,594	-892	30,125	85.9
Greenup County, KY	16,924	1,130	15,794	1,021	925	6.0	5.9	528	16	6,229	1,335	26,286	74.9
Lawrence County, OH	28,280	2,244	26,036	1,766	1,919	6.2	7.4	883	-36	9,835	-441	19,794	56.4
Cabell County, WV	44,505	-325	44,830	2,125	2,142	4.8	4.8	2,748	-44	44,759	-306	26,323	75.0
Wayne County, WV	17,675	-19	17,694	938	926	5.3	5.2	591	-37	7,047	-872	30,484	86.9

See footnotes at end of table.

Metropolitan statistical area / Metropolitan statistical area with metropolitan divisions / Metropolitan division / Component county	Civilian labor force							Private nonfarm businesses					
	Total			Number of unemployed		Unemployment rate[1]		Establishments		Employment[2]		Annual payroll per employee, 2002	
	2004	Net change, 2000–2004	2000	2004	2000	2004	2000	2002	Net change, 2000–2002	2002	Net change, 2000–2002	Amount (dollars)	Percent of national average
Huntsville, AL	192,749	8,642	184,107	8,829	5,908	4.6	3.2	8,505	197	144,850	770	34,183	97.4
Limestone County, AL	34,733	1,420	33,313	1,743	1,131	5.0	3.4	1,130	39	15,496	−1,813	31,317	89.3
Madison County, AL	158,016	7,222	150,794	7,086	4,777	4.5	3.2	7,375	158	129,354	2,583	34,527	98.4
Idaho Falls, ID	56,420	5,888	50,532	1,953	1,744	3.5	3.5	3,116	166	41,070	−28	29,485	84.0
Bonneville County, ID	46,357	4,837	41,520	1,578	1,408	3.4	3.4	2,747	144	38,230	282	30,261	86.3
Jefferson County, ID	10,063	1,051	9,012	375	336	3.7	3.7	369	22	2,840	−310	19,035	54.3
Indianapolis, IN	867,103	46,862	820,241	40,419	19,771	4.7	2.4	40,999	649	765,159	−15,003	35,727	101.8
Boone County, IN	26,166	1,773	24,393	983	493	3.8	2.0	1,300	36	13,172	431	26,427	75.3
Brown County, IN	8,201	288	7,913	427	220	5.2	2.8	384	1	2,225	−46	19,218	54.8
Hamilton County, IN	119,532	17,699	101,833	3,727	1,821	3.1	1.8	5,829	509	83,399	3,534	36,963	105.4
Hancock County, IN	32,870	2,310	30,560	1,258	664	3.8	2.2	1,316	51	14,880	745	33,111	94.4
Hendricks County, IN	65,667	7,885	57,782	2,378	1,093	3.6	1.9	2,319	172	31,091	4,580	27,410	78.1
Johnson County, IN	68,333	4,755	63,578	2,813	1,304	4.1	2.1	2,815	182	42,544	2,805	25,822	73.6
Marion County, IN	467,380	9,789	457,591	25,038	12,252	5.4	2.7	24,042	−346	538,036	−26,629	37,814	107.8
Morgan County, IN	37,135	1,402	35,733	1,683	844	4.5	2.4	1,341	34	13,630	−173	25,155	71.7
Putnam County, IN	17,777	585	17,192	964	478	5.4	2.8	707	24	10,938	−47	25,511	72.7
Shelby County, IN	24,042	376	23,666	1,148	602	4.8	2.5	946	−14	15,244	−203	29,704	84.7
Iowa City, IA	98,319	19,155	79,164	3,146	1,600	3.2	2.0	3,392	17	56,848	−131	27,790	79.2
Johnson County, IA	84,183	16,411	67,772	2,558	1,332	3.0	2.0	2,725	59	51,016	−71	28,404	81.0
Washington County, IA	14,136	2,744	11,392	588	268	4.2	2.4	667	−42	5,832	−60	22,426	63.9
Ithaca, NY	54,015	2,926	51,089	1,967	1,697	3.6	3.3	2,168	43	43,706	1,906	26,472	75.5
Tompkins County, NY	54,015	2,926	51,089	1,967	1,697	3.6	3.3	2,168	43	43,706	1,906	26,472	75.5
Jackson, MI	79,260	−43	79,303	5,987	2,706	7.6	3.4	3,452	41	51,053	−3,643	31,279	89.2
Jackson County, MI	79,260	−43	79,303	5,987	2,706	7.6	3.4	3,452	41	51,053	−3,643	31,279	89.2
Jackson, MS	260,934	11,922	249,012	13,418	11,880	5.1	4.8	12,342	295	202,604	−11,042	28,056	80.0
Copiah County, MS	12,592	348	12,244	878	795	7.0	6.5	435	−23	5,765	−242	21,706	61.9
Hinds County, MS	124,364	2,013	122,351	7,134	6,429	5.7	5.3	6,506	−195	117,742	−17,773	29,392	83.8
Madison County, MS	42,660	3,373	39,287	2,025	1,700	4.7	4.3	2,119	162	30,766	3,235	26,892	76.7
Rankin County, MS	69,264	5,980	63,284	2,738	2,360	4.0	3.7	2,832	322	42,947	3,121	27,323	77.9
Simpson County, MS	12,054	208	11,846	643	596	5.3	5.0	450	29	5,384	617	18,149	51.7
Jackson, TN	53,971	−589	54,560	3,008	2,074	5.6	3.8	2,827	−38	53,398	−3,253	29,186	83.2
Chester County, TN	7,549	−109	7,658	428	317	5.7	4.1	250	6	3,028	−370	20,237	57.7
Madison County, TN	46,422	−480	46,902	2,580	1,757	5.6	3.7	2,577	−44	50,370	−2,883	29,724	84.7
Jacksonville, FL	608,406	20,115	588,291	29,404	19,030	4.8	3.2	30,379	1,761	491,231	11,376	31,220	89.0
Baker County, FL	10,479	102	10,377	456	313	4.4	3.0	319	41	5,008	1,184	23,190	66.1
Clay County, FL	79,088	5,347	73,741	3,409	2,232	4.3	3.0	3,035	219	32,846	1,568	22,303	63.6
Duval County, FL	414,882	7,284	407,598	21,528	13,524	5.2	3.3	21,863	949	397,861	3,755	32,870	93.7
Nassau County, FL	30,889	664	30,225	1,304	999	4.2	3.3	1,285	83	12,699	−48	28,527	81.3
St. Johns County, FL	73,068	6,718	66,350	2,707	1,962	3.7	3.0	3,877	469	42,817	4,917	24,464	69.7
Jacksonville, NC	55,315	2,329	52,986	3,047	2,324	5.5	4.4	2,552	−50	29,166	−11	19,223	54.8
Onslow County, NC	55,315	2,329	52,986	3,047	2,324	5.5	4.4	2,552	−50	29,166	−11	19,223	54.8
Janesville, WI	84,074	1,261	82,813	4,691	3,433	5.6	4.1	3,425	65	57,417	−3,336	33,167	94.5
Rock County, WI	84,074	1,261	82,813	4,691	3,433	5.6	4.1	3,425	65	57,417	−3,336	33,167	94.5
Jefferson City, MO	79,696	2,974	76,722	3,393	2,078	4.3	2.7	3,546	82	52,110	−1,701	26,492	75.5
Callaway County, MO	23,151	1,243	21,908	1,059	596	4.6	2.7	673	−6	9,643	−1,114	28,277	80.6
Cole County, MO	41,273	1,357	39,916	1,627	992	3.9	2.5	2,246	58	36,955	−294	26,690	76.1
Moniteau County, MO	7,729	238	7,491	363	221	4.7	3.0	347	10	2,866	−256	20,535	58.5
Osage County, MO	7,543	136	7,407	344	269	4.6	3.6	280	20	2,646	−37	23,676	67.5
Johnson City, TN	95,180	3,865	91,315	5,098	4,168	5.4	4.6	3,762	12	61,465	−3,908	25,159	71.7
Carter County, TN	29,111	1,343	27,768	1,698	1,352	5.8	4.9	760	17	9,489	−502	22,590	64.4
Unicoi County, TN	8,382	52	8,330	528	580	6.3	7.0	275	16	4,070	337	28,090	80.1
Washington County, TN	57,687	2,470	55,217	2,872	2,236	5.0	4.0	2,727	−21	47,906	−3,743	25,418	72.5
Johnstown, PA	67,642	1,022	66,620	4,731	4,055	7.0	6.1	3,546	−2	49,317	−2,097	23,891	68.1
Cambria County, PA	67,642	1,022	66,620	4,731	4,055	7.0	6.1	3,546	−2	49,317	−2,097	23,891	68.1
Jonesboro, AR	55,735	1,674	54,061	3,135	2,212	5.6	4.1	2,723	58	39,486	459	24,355	69.4
Craighead County, AR	44,262	1,612	42,650	2,403	1,676	5.4	3.9	2,295	50	35,203	1,011	24,738	70.5
Poinsett County, AR	11,473	62	11,411	732	536	6.4	4.7	428	8	4,283	−552	21,207	60.4
Joplin, MO	84,184	2,136	82,048	4,339	2,694	5.2	3.3	4,248	167	66,671	−4,675	25,755	73.4
Jasper County, MO	55,909	1,579	54,330	2,854	1,695	5.1	3.1	3,214	135	51,228	−4,045	26,119	74.5
Newton County, MO	28,275	557	27,718	1,485	999	5.3	3.6	1,034	32	15,443	−630	24,548	70.0
Kalamazoo-Portage, MI	172,239	−642	172,881	10,643	5,584	6.2	3.2	7,347	−104	128,449	566	33,084	94.3
Kalamazoo County, MI	132,171	−996	133,167	7,695	3,985	5.8	3.0	5,883	−21	111,971	1,125	34,227	97.6
Van Buren County, MI	40,068	354	39,714	2,948	1,599	7.4	4.0	1,464	−83	16,478	−559	25,318	72.2
Kankakee-Bradley, IL	51,954	−359	52,313	3,946	2,408	7.6	4.6	2,320	31	37,500	−22,239	28,196	80.4
Kankakee County, IL	51,954	−359	52,313	3,946	2,408	7.6	4.6	2,320	31	37,500	−22,239	28,196	80.4
Kansas City, MO-KS	1,034,715	35,423	999,292	62,048	33,086	6.0	3.3	50,471	447	889,834	−15,737	35,091	100.0
Franklin County, KS	13,698	577	13,121	848	500	6.2	3.8	600	17	7,612	−100	24,888	70.9
Johnson County, KS	283,203	21,687	261,516	13,963	7,825	4.9	3.0	16,117	223	286,164	3,512	37,718	107.5
Leavenworth County, KS	32,792	1,681	31,111	2,098	1,294	6.4	4.2	1,113	−10	14,425	−619	29,067	82.9
Linn County, KS	4,866	152	4,714	370	235	7.6	5.0	167	−26	1,216	−165	29,660	84.5
Miami County, KS	15,818	554	15,264	842	517	5.3	3.4	705	87	6,655	−213	23,785	67.8
Wyandotte County, KS	75,427	1,461	73,966	7,008	4,635	9.3	6.3	3,036	−45	59,201	−2,387	35,662	101.7
Bates County, MO	8,254	57	8,197	569	286	6.9	3.5	405	15	3,032	−21	18,761	53.5

See footnotes at end of table.

State and Metropolitan Area Data Book: 2006

U.S. Census Bureau

Table C-4. Metropolitan Areas With Component Counties — Civilian Labor Force and Private Nonfarm Businesses—Con.

Metropolitan statistical area / **Metropolitan statistical area with metropolitan divisions** / *Metropolitan division* / Component county	Civilian labor force							Private nonfarm businesses					
	Total			Number of unemployed		Unemployment rate[1]		Establishments		Employment[2]		Annual payroll per employee, 2002	
	2004	Net change, 2000–2004	2000	2004	2000	2004	2000	2002	Net change, 2000–2002	2002	Net change, 2000–2002	Amount (dollars)	Percent of national average
Kansas City, MO-KS—Con.													
Caldwell County, MO	4,498	16	4,482	260	142	5.8	3.2	182	−2	959	−45	20,475	58.4
Cass County, MO	47,891	2,766	45,125	2,587	1,186	5.4	2.6	1,835	54	16,343	860	22,886	65.2
Clay County, MO	111,283	3,659	107,624	5,296	2,499	4.8	2.3	4,821	132	81,648	−2,945	34,117	97.3
Clinton County, MO	10,456	438	10,018	586	283	5.6	2.8	462	40	4,105	672	19,492	55.6
Jackson County, MO	349,443	295	349,148	23,814	11,758	6.8	3.4	17,844	−158	360,416	−15,770	35,846	102.2
Lafayette County, MO	17,314	−300	17,614	973	537	5.6	3.0	805	7	7,012	−75	18,993	54.1
Platte County, MO	47,528	2,271	45,257	2,092	974	4.4	2.2	1,956	96	37,436	1,670	28,704	81.8
Ray County, MO	12,244	109	12,135	742	415	6.1	3.4	423	17	3,610	−111	20,392	58.1
Kennewick-Richland-Pasco, WA	115,089	15,736	99,353	7,248	5,459	6.3	5.5	4,626	202	65,686	1,203	34,480	98.3
Benton County, WA	87,439	11,114	76,325	5,161	3,796	5.9	5.0	3,451	152	52,763	2,226	36,489	104.0
Franklin County, WA	27,650	4,622	23,028	2,087	1,663	7.5	7.2	1,175	50	12,923	−1,023	26,274	74.9
Killeen-Temple-Fort Hood, TX	145,987	11,990	133,997	8,353	5,965	5.7	4.5	5,314	145	85,436	−968	26,077	74.3
Bell County, TX	111,013	9,603	101,410	6,198	4,326	5.6	4.3	4,244	171	74,137	−1,140	27,187	77.5
Coryell County, TX	25,206	1,251	23,955	1,712	1,304	6.8	5.4	694	−31	7,569	14	18,746	53.4
Lampasas County, TX	9,768	1,136	8,632	443	335	4.5	3.9	376	5	3,730	158	18,895	53.9
Kingsport-Bristol-Bristol, TN-VA	141,222	1,425	139,797	7,808	5,301	5.5	3.8	6,352	−105	105,396	−4,372	29,244	83.4
Hawkins County, TN	25,163	542	24,621	1,529	1,052	6.1	4.3	573	−57	9,987	−2,108	26,727	76.2
Sullivan County, TN.	72,974	−170	73,144	4,054	2,754	5.6	3.8	3,583	−60	62,851	−1,535	31,799	90.6
Scott County, VA	9,791	112	9,679	542	370	5.5	3.8	334	6	3,409	159	21,624	61.6
Washington County, VA	25,587	678	24,909	1,214	889	4.7	3.6	1,195	31	14,735	252	24,929	71.1
Bristol city, VA	7,707	263	7,444	469	236	6.1	3.2	667	−25	14,414	−1,140	26,064	74.3
Kingston, NY	92,002	3,052	88,950	4,417	3,170	4.8	3.6	4,597	239	47,759	2,030	25,980	74.1
Ulster County, NY	92,002	3,052	88,950	4,417	3,170	4.8	3.6	4,597	239	47,759	2,030	25,980	74.1
Knoxville, TN	337,030	19,308	317,722	13,850	10,754	4.1	3.4	15,988	−12	280,453	2,848	30,745	87.6
Anderson County, TN	35,201	1,238	33,963	1,711	1,435	4.9	4.2	1,668	−52	40,515	951	38,829	110.7
Blount County, TN.	58,412	4,205	54,207	2,431	1,953	4.2	3.6	2,233	59	36,847	−1,573	32,950	93.9
Knox County, TN	213,244	11,357	201,887	8,336	6,343	3.9	3.1	11,075	−99	190,404	3,206	28,951	82.5
Loudon County, TN	21,358	1,799	19,559	936	706	4.4	3.6	814	71	10,641	279	26,707	76.1
Union County, TN	8,815	709	8,106	436	317	4.9	3.9	198	9	2,046	−15	18,926	53.9
Kokomo, IN	47,452	−2,954	50,406	3,045	1,493	6.4	3.0	2,349	59	41,858	−6,744	37,747	107.6
Howard County, IN	39,365	−2,324	41,689	2,625	1,270	6.7	3.0	2,003	33	38,178	−6,631	38,557	109.9
Tipton County, IN	8,087	−630	8,717	420	223	5.2	2.6	346	26	3,680	−113	29,346	83.7
La Crosse, WI-MN	74,632	2,113	72,519	3,130	2,400	4.2	3.3	3,395	70	60,842	−205	27,509	78.4
Houston County, MN	11,511	512	10,999	588	452	5.1	4.1	453	63	4,120	90	21,294	60.7
La Crosse County, WI	63,121	1,601	61,520	2,542	1,948	4.0	3.2	2,942	7	56,722	−295	27,960	79.7
Lafayette, IN	92,621	−1,134	93,755	4,312	2,412	4.7	2.6	3,820	−33	67,737	−4,856	30,101	85.8
Benton County, IN.	4,568	−280	4,848	243	135	5.3	2.8	238	−14	1,861	−245	22,731	64.8
Carroll County, IN	10,351	−190	10,541	583	286	5.6	2.7	418	9	4,561	−517	24,167	68.9
Tippecanoe County, IN	77,702	−664	78,366	3,486	1,991	4.5	2.5	3,164	−28	61,315	−4,094	30,766	87.7
Lafayette, LA	121,685	3,297	118,388	5,669	4,849	4.7	4.1	7,571	254	111,033	71	28,620	81.6
Lafayette Parish, LA	99,750	2,639	97,111	4,446	3,737	4.5	3.8	6,855	194	103,844	1,328	29,136	83.1
St. Martin Parish, LA	21,935	658	21,277	1,223	1,112	5.6	5.2	716	60	7,189	−1,257	21,168	60.3
Lake Charles, LA.	91,669	943	90,726	5,134	4,330	5.6	4.8	4,458	42	71,833	739	27,996	79.8
Calcasieu Parish, LA	87,231	1,028	86,203	4,903	4,117	5.6	4.8	4,276	36	70,144	926	27,859	79.4
Cameron Parish, LA	4,438	−85	4,523	231	213	5.2	4.7	182	6	1,689	−187	33,659	95.9
Lakeland, FL.	248,359	17,521	230,838	12,426	9,528	5.0	4.1	9,807	198	156,908	−4,557	28,372	80.9
Polk County, FL	248,359	17,521	230,838	12,426	9,528	5.0	4.1	9,807	198	156,908	−4,557	28,372	80.9
Lancaster, PA	266,749	16,177	250,572	10,560	7,084	4.0	2.8	11,605	165	214,288	−292	30,538	87.0
Lancaster County, PA	266,749	16,177	250,572	10,560	7,084	4.0	2.8	11,605	165	214,288	−292	30,538	87.0
Lansing-East Lansing, MI	251,020	2,123	248,897	14,973	7,184	6.0	2.9	10,419	134	171,044	−1,765	32,410	92.4
Clinton County, MI	36,753	1,014	35,739	1,959	936	5.3	2.6	1,209	40	12,427	−1,258	29,312	83.6
Eaton County, MI	58,596	506	58,090	3,171	1,641	5.4	2.8	1,899	−88	27,098	−4,175	27,378	78.0
Ingham County, MI	155,671	603	155,068	9,843	4,607	6.3	3.0	7,311	182	131,519	3,668	33,739	96.2
Laredo, TX	83,598	12,636	70,962	5,700	4,367	6.8	6.2	4,332	252	55,987	2,771	21,194	60.4
Webb County, TX	83,598	12,636	70,962	5,700	4,367	6.8	6.2	4,332	252	55,987	2,771	21,194	60.4
Las Cruces, NM	82,835	6,537	76,298	5,297	4,700	6.4	6.2	3,245	34	40,233	3,183	21,954	62.6
Dona Ana County, NM	82,835	6,537	76,298	5,297	4,700	6.4	6.2	3,245	34	40,233	3,183	21,954	62.6
Las Vegas-Paradise, NV	827,958	99,671	728,287	36,184	33,822	4.4	4.6	32,567	2,936	665,118	25,963	31,171	88.9
Clark County, NV	827,958	99,671	728,287	36,184	33,822	4.4	4.6	32,567	2,936	665,118	25,963	31,171	88.9
Lawrence, KS	63,455	5,527	57,928	2,622	1,691	4.1	2.9	2,662	38	36,948	−537	23,125	65.9
Douglas County, KS	63,455	5,527	57,928	2,622	1,691	4.1	2.9	2,662	38	36,948	−537	23,125	65.9
Lawton, OK	46,478	3,207	43,271	2,083	1,589	4.5	3.7	2,144	−55	28,554	961	23,831	67.9
Comanche County, OK	46,478	3,207	43,271	2,083	1,589	4.5	3.7	2,144	−55	28,554	961	23,831	67.9
Lebanon, PA	69,658	5,521	64,137	2,826	2,026	4.1	3.2	2,566	−2	37,629	−1	27,573	78.6
Lebanon County, PA	69,658	5,521	64,137	2,826	2,026	4.1	3.2	2,566	−2	37,629	−1	27,573	78.6
Lewiston, ID-WA	28,692	434	28,258	1,558	1,451	5.4	5.1	1,610	−51	19,716	−964	28,181	80.3
Nez Perce County, ID	18,572	2	18,570	886	959	4.8	5.2	1,195	−23	15,750	−798	29,007	82.7
Asotin County, WA	10,120	432	9,688	672	492	6.6	5.1	415	−28	3,966	−166	24,902	71.0
Lewiston-Auburn, ME	57,087	1,686	55,401	2,560	1,938	4.5	3.5	2,765	−21	45,076	−790	27,916	79.6
Androscoggin County, ME	57,087	1,686	55,401	2,560	1,938	4.5	3.5	2,765	−21	45,076	−790	27,916	79.6

See footnotes at end of table.

Metropolitan statistical area / Metropolitan statistical area with metropolitan divisions / *Metropolitan division* / Component county	Civilian labor force							Private nonfarm businesses					
	Total			Number of unemployed		Unemployment rate[1]		Establishments		Employment[2]		Annual payroll per employee, 2002	
	2004	Net change, 2000–2004	2000	2004	2000	2004	2000	2002	Net change, 2000–2002	2002	Net change, 2000–2002	Amount (dollars)	Percent of national average
Lexington-Fayette, KY	226,237	−2,261	228,498	9,187	7,012	4.1	3.1	11,235	132	200,602	−8,705	31,459	89.7
Bourbon County, KY	9,716	−255	9,971	450	336	4.6	3.4	405	9	5,517	85	29,070	82.9
Clark County, KY	16,693	−291	16,984	821	640	4.9	3.8	787	23	13,123	654	25,957	74.0
Fayette County, KY	146,473	−2,746	149,219	5,785	4,461	3.9	3.0	7,808	−82	139,587	−11,596	31,344	89.3
Jessamine County, KY	20,998	358	20,640	856	620	4.1	3.0	935	46	13,538	1,076	24,352	69.4
Scott County, KY	19,319	1,018	18,301	811	580	4.2	3.2	768	114	21,339	1,878	40,404	115.2
Woodford County, KY	13,038	−345	13,383	464	375	3.6	2.8	532	22	7,498	−802	32,357	92.2
Lima, OH	52,437	1,067	51,370	3,453	2,247	6.6	4.4	2,834	−5	48,423	−3,416	29,094	82.9
Allen County, OH	52,437	1,067	51,370	3,453	2,247	6.6	4.4	2,834	−5	48,423	−3,416	29,094	82.9
Lincoln, NE	167,097	8,358	158,739	5,624	3,724	3.4	2.3	7,683	134	131,201	−998	28,616	81.6
Lancaster County, NE	157,658	8,182	149,476	5,347	3,507	3.4	2.3	7,252	125	125,814	−572	28,907	82.4
Seward County, NE	9,439	176	9,263	277	217	2.9	2.3	431	9	5,387	−426	21,830	62.2
Little Rock-North Little Rock, AR	324,531	13,533	310,998	16,444	11,250	5.1	3.6	16,600	80	274,540	−6,848	29,794	84.9
Faulkner County, AR	49,014	3,679	45,335	2,399	1,631	4.9	3.6	1,925	142	30,245	977	24,444	69.7
Grant County, AR	8,421	350	8,071	460	318	5.5	3.9	277	5	2,630	−387	26,687	76.1
Lonoke County, AR	28,529	2,176	26,353	1,310	866	4.6	3.3	981	38	9,367	512	21,599	61.6
Perry County, AR	4,938	144	4,794	279	236	5.7	4.9	113	−8	648	31	19,103	54.5
Pulaski County, AR	188,527	4,685	183,842	9,931	6,815	5.3	3.7	11,750	−293	214,944	−9,028	31,406	89.5
Saline County, AR	45,102	2,499	42,603	2,065	1,384	4.6	3.2	1,554	196	16,706	1,047	24,246	69.1
Logan, UT-ID	60,743	7,648	53,095	2,370	1,507	3.9	2.8	2,682	81	34,337	1,451	23,261	66.3
Franklin County, ID	5,925	712	5,213	231	167	3.9	3.2	249	5	1,692	9	20,825	59.4
Cache County, UT	54,818	6,936	47,882	2,139	1,340	3.9	2.8	2,433	76	32,645	1,442	23,388	66.7
Longview, TX	99,846	7,110	92,736	5,978	4,813	6.0	5.2	5,173	94	72,970	2,029	26,986	76.9
Gregg County, TX	59,453	4,274	55,179	3,603	2,979	6.1	5.4	3,968	100	60,122	2,648	27,239	77.6
Rusk County, TX	22,208	1,145	21,063	1,323	1,034	6.0	4.9	738	−44	8,846	−671	27,941	79.6
Upshur County, TX	18,185	1,691	16,494	1,052	800	5.8	4.9	467	38	4,002	52	21,075	60.1
Longview, WA	43,705	406	43,299	3,729	2,766	8.5	6.4	2,306	−29	30,848	−1,666	32,544	92.8
Cowlitz County, WA	43,705	406	43,299	3,729	2,766	8.5	6.4	2,306	−29	30,848	−1,666	32,544	92.8
Los Angeles-Long Beach-Santa Ana, CA	**6,396,271**	**233,068**	**6,163,203**	**383,333**	**305,863**	**6.0**	**5.0**	**313,622**	**8,784**	**5,174,665**	**−67,923**	**38,732**	**110.4**
Los Angeles-Long Beach-Glendale, CA	*4,809,764*	*128,464*	*4,681,300*	*315,724*	*253,484*	*6.6*	*5.4*	*231,948*	*5,666*	*3,791,362*	*−72,509*	*38,439*	*109.6*
Los Angeles County, CA	4,809,764	128,464	4,681,300	315,724	253,484	6.6	5.4	231,948	5,666	3,791,362	−72,509	38,439	109.6
Santa Ana-Anaheim-Irvine, CA	*1,586,507*	*104,604*	*1,481,903*	*67,609*	*52,379*	*4.3*	*3.5*	*81,674*	*3,118*	*1,383,303*	*4,586*	*39,533*	*112.7*
Orange County, CA	1,586,507	104,604	1,481,903	67,609	52,379	4.3	3.5	81,674	3,118	1,383,303	4,586	39,533	112.7
Louisville, KY-IN	602,059	−9,034	611,093	30,601	21,866	5.1	3.6	29,817	374	525,004	−25,833	32,014	91.3
Clark County, IN	52,564	−158	52,722	2,638	1,807	5.0	3.4	2,547	94	40,281	−1,709	28,481	81.2
Floyd County, IN	37,204	−1,013	38,217	1,807	1,252	4.9	3.3	1,780	59	24,123	−2,636	27,736	79.1
Harrison County, IN	18,977	177	18,800	1,007	601	5.3	3.2	691	40	11,309	2,843	22,340	63.7
Washington County, IN	14,006	−87	14,093	881	512	6.3	3.6	486	18	5,546	−308	23,242	66.3
Bullitt County, KY	33,923	487	33,436	1,633	1,091	4.8	3.3	958	34	11,322	625	23,631	67.4
Henry County, KY	7,692	−72	7,764	358	249	4.7	3.2	210	−39	1,928	−756	24,351	69.4
Jefferson County, KY	351,160	−10,677	361,837	18,387	13,432	5.2	3.7	19,782	−50	393,330	−23,060	33,868	96.5
Meade County, KY	11,741	35	11,706	671	476	5.7	4.1	308	3	2,570	−452	24,153	68.8
Nelson County, KY	19,706	99	19,607	980	825	5.0	4.2	911	33	11,970	−458	25,356	72.3
Oldham County, KY	24,642	626	24,016	913	717	3.7	3.0	1,096	101	9,666	373	24,773	70.6
Shelby County, KY	18,794	493	18,301	796	553	4.2	3.0	781	58	11,482	−295	29,287	83.5
Spencer County, KY	7,447	933	6,514	315	196	4.2	3.0	188	17	888	−60	19,257	54.9
Trimble County, KY	4,203	123	4,080	215	155	5.1	3.8	79	6	589	60	25,730	73.3
Lubbock, TX	140,654	9,643	131,011	6,451	4,709	4.6	3.6	6,690	64	95,979	1,538	24,295	69.3
Crosby County, TX	2,989	10	2,979	187	137	6.3	4.6	119	−8	961	37	23,035	65.7
Lubbock County, TX	137,665	9,633	128,032	6,264	4,572	4.6	3.6	6,571	72	95,018	1,501	24,308	69.3
Lynchburg, VA	113,280	205	113,075	4,861	2,512	4.3	2.2	5,845	35	91,244	−5,286	29,358	83.7
Amherst County, VA	15,174	−85	15,259	673	324	4.4	2.1	612	14	7,123	−96	24,620	70.2
Appomattox County, VA	6,642	−60	6,702	294	166	4.4	2.5	249	−29	2,499	−640	22,183	63.2
Bedford County, VA	32,461	663	31,798	1,163	612	3.6	1.9	1,280	338	9,494	874	27,734	79.1
Campbell County, VA	26,092	−154	26,246	1,104	607	4.2	2.3	1,054	86	13,061	−987	26,614	75.9
Bedford city, VA	2,579	−2	2,581	119	64	4.6	2.5	332	−153	4,380	−1,585	22,281	63.5
Lynchburg city, VA	30,332	−157	30,489	1,508	739	5.0	2.4	2,318	−221	54,687	−2,852	31,807	90.7
Macon, GA	106,855	2,693	104,162	5,185	4,307	4.9	4.1	5,341	−54	84,726	−6,530	28,126	80.2
Bibb County, GA	71,353	867	70,486	3,624	3,009	5.1	4.3	4,487	−102	77,497	−6,114	28,523	81.3
Crawford County, GA	5,985	103	5,882	287	232	4.8	3.9	94	18	689	42	18,556	52.9
Jones County, GA	12,755	941	11,814	530	450	4.2	3.8	287	48	1,964	−146	22,958	65.4
Monroe County, GA	12,159	786	11,373	497	415	4.1	3.6	382	−16	3,696	123	25,106	71.6
Twiggs County, GA	4,603	−4	4,607	247	201	5.4	4.4	91	−2	880	−435	24,853	70.8
Madera, CA	63,159	8,079	55,080	5,559	4,782	8.8	8.7	1,935	70	23,607	447	27,485	78.3
Madera County, CA	63,159	8,079	55,080	5,559	4,782	8.8	8.7	1,935	70	23,607	447	27,485	78.3
Madison, WI	332,612	22,830	309,782	11,008	7,658	3.3	2.5	14,854	437	254,924	4,860	33,185	94.6
Columbia County, WI	31,609	1,709	29,900	1,451	1,073	4.6	3.6	1,532	90	18,952	725	26,180	74.6
Dane County, WI	286,627	20,426	266,201	8,995	6,197	3.1	2.3	12,725	345	226,805	5,351	33,895	96.6
Iowa County, WI	14,376	695	13,681	562	388	3.9	2.8	597	2	9,167	−1,216	30,099	85.8
Manchester-Nashua, NH	225,241	10,326	214,915	8,841	5,410	3.9	2.5	10,869	−35	176,136	−812	37,944	108.2
Hillsborough County, NH	225,241	10,326	214,915	8,841	5,410	3.9	2.5	10,869	−35	176,136	−812	37,944	108.2
Mansfield, OH	63,344	353	62,991	4,564	3,186	7.2	5.1	3,022	4	49,073	−2,714	29,134	83.0
Richland County, OH	63,344	353	62,991	4,564	3,186	7.2	5.1	3,022	4	49,073	−2,714	29,134	83.0
McAllen-Edinburg-Mission, TX	254,431	43,139	211,292	23,207	19,418	9.1	9.2	8,782	462	122,326	7,471	21,523	61.4
Hidalgo County, TX	254,431	43,139	211,292	23,207	19,418	9.1	9.2	8,782	462	122,326	7,471	21,523	61.4
Medford, OR	98,817	7,004	91,813	7,002	5,098	7.1	5.6	5,625	261	63,461	1,207	27,149	77.4
Jackson County, OR	98,817	7,004	91,813	7,002	5,098	7.1	5.6	5,625	261	63,461	1,207	27,149	77.4

See footnotes at end of table.

State and Metropolitan Area Data Book: 2006

U.S. Census Bureau

Table C-4. Metropolitan Areas With Component Counties — Civilian Labor Force and Private Nonfarm Businesses—Con.

Metropolitan statistical area / **Metropolitan statistical area with metropolitan divisions** / *Metropolitan division* / Component county	Civilian labor force — Total			Number of unemployed		Unemployment rate[1]		Private nonfarm businesses — Establishments		Employment[2]		Annual payroll per employee, 2002	
	2004	Net change, 2000–2004	2000	2004	2000	2004	2000	2002	Net change, 2000–2002	2002	Net change, 2000–2002	Amount (dollars)	Percent of national average
Memphis, TN-MS-AR	597,092	4,370	592,722	35,499	22,606	5.9	3.8	26,253	−109	528,944	−40,419	33,498	95.5
Crittenden County, AR	21,960	69	21,891	1,539	897	7.0	4.1	974	26	14,649	−1,137	23,831	67.9
DeSoto County, MS	67,317	8,166	59,151	2,347	1,477	3.5	2.5	1,966	125	31,802	760	26,029	74.2
Marshall County, MS	15,768	448	15,320	1,197	662	7.6	4.3	438	3	6,881	−291	19,935	56.8
Tate County, MS	12,000	243	11,757	720	442	6.0	3.8	408	−6	4,756	−820	21,027	59.9
Tunica County, MS	4,440	387	4,053	381	211	8.6	5.2	218	19	17,423	−1,144	22,837	65.1
Fayette County, TN	15,121	1,068	14,053	945	643	6.2	4.6	431	−15	4,333	121	26,900	76.7
Shelby County, TN	434,521	−6,730	441,251	26,745	17,324	6.2	3.9	21,096	−247	440,078	−37,221	35,376	100.8
Tipton County, TN	25,965	719	25,246	1,625	950	6.3	3.8	722	−14	9,022	−687	24,583	70.1
Merced, CA	98,860	8,359	90,501	10,670	8,699	10.8	9.6	2,989	30	39,777	231	26,008	74.1
Merced County, CA	98,860	8,359	90,501	10,670	8,699	10.8	9.6	2,989	30	39,777	231	26,008	74.1
Miami-Fort Lauderdale-Miami Beach, FL	**2,621,674**	**125,014**	**2,496,660**	**135,984**	**110,319**	**5.2**	**4.4**	**160,867**	**7,520**	**1,900,015**	**−22,426**	**33,228**	**94.7**
Fort Lauderdale-Pompano Beach-Deerfield Beach, FL	917,342	63,428	853,914	43,339	31,084	4.7	3.6	52,744	2,416	621,950	2,549	32,370	92.3
Broward County, FL	917,342	63,428	853,914	43,339	31,084	4.7	3.6	52,744	2,416	621,950	2,549	32,370	92.3
Miami-Miami Beach-Kendall, FL	1,107,950	7,671	1,100,279	62,202	56,427	5.6	5.1	69,345	2,836	820,215	−34,174	33,251	94.8
Miami-Dade County, FL	1,107,950	7,671	1,100,279	62,202	56,427	5.6	5.1	69,345	2,836	820,215	−34,174	33,251	94.8
West Palm Beach-Boca Raton-Boynton Beach, FL	596,382	53,915	542,467	30,443	22,808	5.1	4.2	38,778	2,268	457,850	9,199	34,354	97.9
Palm Beach County, FL	596,382	53,915	542,467	30,443	22,808	5.1	4.2	38,778	2,268	457,850	9,199	34,354	97.9
Michigan City-La Porte, IN	52,965	−1,210	54,175	3,199	1,795	6.0	3.3	2,573	−62	36,693	−3,584	27,497	78.4
LaPorte County, IN	52,965	−1,210	54,175	3,199	1,795	6.0	3.3	2,573	−62	36,693	−3,584	27,497	78.4
Midland, TX	64,312	6,096	58,216	2,907	2,446	4.5	4.2	3,982	−56	46,328	328	30,377	86.6
Midland County, TX	64,312	6,096	58,216	2,907	2,446	4.5	4.2	3,982	−56	46,328	328	30,377	86.6
Milwaukee-Waukesha-West Allis, WI	801,566	−4,976	806,542	43,290	29,081	5.4	3.6	39,731	−139	759,715	−30,847	35,998	102.6
Milwaukee County, WI	468,503	−9,327	477,830	29,463	20,307	6.3	4.2	21,153	−162	458,394	−22,178	36,268	103.4
Ozaukee County, WI	47,815	171	47,644	1,728	1,179	3.6	2.5	2,751	−131	36,177	−1,181	35,297	100.6
Washington County, WI	71,313	1,313	70,000	3,176	1,936	4.5	2.8	3,248	144	48,292	951	30,437	86.8
Waukesha County, WI	213,935	2,867	211,068	8,923	5,659	4.2	2.7	12,579	10	216,852	−8,439	36,784	104.9
Minneapolis-St. Paul-Bloomington, MN-WI	1,849,010	86,535	1,762,475	82,331	48,831	4.5	2.8	87,843	3,311	1,591,041	−38,498	40,197	114.6
Anoka County, MN	191,465	11,488	179,977	8,668	5,007	4.5	2.8	7,088	467	102,652	1,412	38,179	108.8
Carver County, MN	46,458	5,232	41,226	1,789	1,019	3.9	2.5	1,971	221	29,663	2,116	35,774	102.0
Chisago County, MN	26,284	2,949	23,335	1,398	870	5.3	3.7	1,153	54	11,062	393	26,838	76.5
Dakota County, MN	230,487	12,504	217,983	9,370	5,443	4.1	2.5	9,299	696	146,344	−7,773	35,939	102.4
Hennepin County, MN	681,440	12,116	669,324	30,565	18,545	4.5	2.8	39,020	−117	823,307	−42,061	43,773	124.8
Isanti County, MN	20,509	2,496	18,013	1,062	626	5.2	3.5	774	24	8,005	680	25,786	73.5
Ramsey County, MN	289,548	1,723	287,825	13,722	8,481	4.7	2.9	13,940	239	299,412	−5,732	39,113	111.5
Scott County, MN	65,619	11,077	54,542	2,526	1,455	3.8	2.7	2,632	420	32,709	1,654	33,084	94.3
Sherburne County, MN	44,208	6,174	38,034	2,175	1,173	4.9	3.1	1,585	273	15,410	1,037	29,151	83.1
Washington County, MN	126,494	7,963	118,531	5,073	3,001	4.0	2.5	4,959	457	63,330	5,321	34,223	97.6
Wright County, MN	60,469	7,676	52,793	2,945	1,718	4.9	3.3	2,688	322	27,477	1,810	27,703	79.0
Pierce County, WI	23,387	504	22,883	984	583	4.2	2.5	839	43	6,840	5	24,918	71.0
St. Croix County, WI	42,642	4,633	38,009	2,054	910	4.8	2.4	1,895	212	24,830	2,640	33,531	95.6
Missoula, MT	57,504	3,322	54,182	2,275	2,219	4.0	4.1	3,760	137	41,975	658	25,908	73.9
Missoula County, MT	57,504	3,322	54,182	2,275	2,219	4.0	4.1	3,760	137	41,975	658	25,908	73.9
Mobile, AL	180,685	−6,657	187,342	11,756	8,273	6.5	4.4	9,153	−78	153,632	−2,809	28,025	79.9
Mobile County, AL	180,685	−6,657	187,342	11,756	8,273	6.5	4.4	9,153	−78	153,632	−2,809	28,025	79.9
Modesto, CA	226,124	18,076	208,048	20,606	16,196	9.1	7.8	8,668	411	131,702	11,069	29,587	84.3
Stanislaus County, CA	226,124	18,076	208,048	20,606	16,196	9.1	7.8	8,668	411	131,702	11,069	29,587	84.3
Monroe, LA	83,395	3,599	79,796	4,746	3,648	5.7	4.6	4,482	42	64,863	−6,093	26,845	76.5
Ouachita Parish, LA	72,752	3,110	69,642	4,060	3,104	5.6	4.5	4,150	46	60,453	−5,356	27,414	78.1
Union Parish, LA	10,643	489	10,154	686	544	6.4	5.4	332	−4	4,410	−737	19,056	54.3
Monroe, MI	77,483	262	77,221	4,879	2,460	6.3	3.2	2,574	88	38,679	−876	34,800	99.2
Monroe County, MI	77,483	262	77,221	4,879	2,460	6.3	3.2	2,574	88	38,679	−876	34,800	99.2
Montgomery, AL	167,029	1,293	165,736	9,142	6,238	5.5	3.8	7,965	−76	128,173	−7,781	27,816	79.3
Autauga County, AL	22,950	928	22,022	1,057	796	4.6	3.6	833	64	9,962	847	22,673	64.6
Elmore County, AL	33,043	1,613	31,430	1,542	1,115	4.7	3.5	1,052	−39	11,445	2,073	23,318	66.5
Lowndes County, AL	5,086	−21	5,107	458	316	9.0	6.2	148	−2	2,233	842	39,688	113.1
Montgomery County, AL	105,950	−1,227	107,177	6,085	4,011	5.7	3.7	5,932	−99	104,533	−10,783	28,545	81.4
Morgantown, WV	57,330	2,621	54,709	2,205	2,562	3.8	4.7	2,567	−53	36,985	1,401	27,011	77.0
Monongalia County, WV	43,397	2,088	41,309	1,484	1,811	3.4	4.4	1,970	−25	31,984	1,861	27,707	79.0
Preston County, WV	13,933	533	13,400	721	751	5.2	5.6	597	−28	5,001	−460	22,560	64.3
Morristown, TN	62,464	519	61,945	3,652	2,633	5.8	4.3	2,282	−17	42,119	−3,814	27,717	79.0
Grainger County, TN	9,854	119	9,735	597	447	6.1	4.6	234	−12	2,333	−577	21,852	62.3
Hamblen County, TN	29,345	−331	29,676	1,633	1,203	5.6	4.1	1,385	−19	29,635	−2,752	29,725	84.7
Jefferson County, TN	23,265	731	22,534	1,422	983	6.1	4.4	663	14	10,151	−485	23,205	66.1
Mount Vernon-Anacortes, WA	56,305	4,213	52,092	3,855	3,044	6.8	5.8	3,350	93	34,944	−713	29,036	82.8
Skagit County, WA	56,305	4,213	52,092	3,855	3,044	6.8	5.8	3,350	93	34,944	−713	29,036	82.8
Muncie, IN	57,036	−1,891	58,927	3,397	1,954	6.0	3.3	2,653	−45	45,502	−4,961	26,628	75.9
Delaware County, IN	57,036	−1,891	58,927	3,397	1,954	6.0	3.3	2,653	−45	45,502	−4,961	26,628	75.9
Muskegon-Norton Shores, MI	89,530	3,807	85,723	7,062	3,511	7.9	4.1	3,663	76	54,471	−2,993	30,766	87.7
Muskegon County, MI	89,530	3,807	85,723	7,062	3,511	7.9	4.1	3,663	76	54,471	−2,993	30,766	87.7
Myrtle Beach-Conway-North Myrtle Beach, SC	118,119	12,880	105,239	6,694	3,665	5.7	3.5	7,409	222	87,396	1,106	22,828	65.1
Horry County, SC	118,119	12,880	105,239	6,694	3,665	5.7	3.5	7,409	222	87,396	1,106	22,828	65.1

See footnotes at end of table.

Metropolitan statistical area / Metropolitan statistical area with metropolitan divisions / Metropolitan division / Component county	Civilian labor force							Private nonfarm businesses					
	Total			Number of unemployed		Unemployment rate[1]		Establishments		Employment[2]		Annual payroll per employee, 2002	
	2004	Net change, 2000–2004	2000	2004	2000	2004	2000	2002	Net change, 2000–2002	2002	Net change, 2000–2002	Amount (dollars)	Percent of national average
Napa, CA	72,272	5,612	66,660	3,311	2,356	4.6	3.5	3,963	216	52,547	3,021	35,647	101.6
Napa County, CA	72,272	5,612	66,660	3,311	2,356	4.6	3.5	3,963	216	52,547	3,021	35,647	101.6
Naples-Marco Island, FL	136,834	20,876	115,958	5,511	4,312	4.0	3.7	9,201	726	97,794	5,570	30,380	86.6
Collier County, FL	136,834	20,876	115,958	5,511	4,312	4.0	3.7	9,201	726	97,794	5,570	30,380	86.6
Nashville-Davidson—Murfreesboro, TN	732,403	17,091	715,312	31,375	22,843	4.3	3.2	34,926	343	637,295	-12,451	34,015	97.0
Cannon County, TN	6,410	18	6,392	286	230	4.5	3.6	147	-21	1,383	31	21,631	61.7
Cheatham County, TN	20,024	417	19,607	859	551	4.3	2.8	532	8	4,209	-2,501	24,314	69.3
Davidson County, TN	305,870	-4,842	310,712	13,594	9,950	4.4	3.2	18,156	-444	379,303	-19,244	35,059	99.9
Dickson County, TN	22,710	475	22,235	1,119	811	4.9	3.6	893	7	13,144	-260	26,235	74.8
Hickman County, TN	10,128	288	9,840	590	410	5.8	4.2	326	19	2,624	286	20,263	57.8
Macon County, TN	10,390	150	10,240	549	389	5.3	3.8	323	15	3,421	-654	21,047	60.0
Robertson County, TN	30,941	1,222	29,719	1,408	1,070	4.6	3.6	887	-77	12,363	-1,535	24,513	69.9
Rutherford County, TN	111,353	8,300	103,053	4,316	3,202	3.9	3.1	3,658	208	70,658	-1,036	33,979	96.9
Smith County, TN	9,090	144	8,946	585	393	6.4	4.4	308	2	4,765	-160	26,549	75.7
Sumner County, TN	73,459	2,712	70,747	3,092	2,322	4.2	3.3	2,727	182	36,831	1,754	27,430	78.2
Trousdale County, TN	3,603	36	3,567	199	124	5.5	3.5	118	-2	1,029	-204	18,317	52.2
Williamson County, TN	75,936	5,680	70,256	2,527	1,784	3.3	2.5	4,670	308	75,659	5,747	37,408	106.6
Wilson County, TN	52,489	2,491	49,998	2,251	1,607	4.3	3.2	2,181	138	31,906	5,325	34,085	97.2
New Haven-Milford, CT	429,670	15,370	414,300	22,384	10,694	5.2	2.6	20,705	-70	333,360	-5,568	37,425	106.7
New Haven County, CT	429,670	15,370	414,300	22,384	10,694	5.2	2.6	20,705	-70	333,360	-5,568	37,425	106.7
New Orleans-Metairie-Kenner, LA	613,148	-12,170	625,318	27,983	29,204	4.6	4.7	31,599	71	525,160	-6,385	30,339	86.5
Jefferson Parish, LA	225,432	-6,053	231,485	9,608	9,904	4.3	4.3	12,655	-187	209,974	-6,808	29,446	83.9
Orleans Parish, LA	200,185	-10,338	210,523	10,459	10,688	5.2	5.1	10,516	-103	207,852	-673	31,217	89.0
Plaquemines Parish, LA	11,196	200	10,996	529	596	4.7	5.4	742	9	10,558	-1,027	38,693	110.3
St. Bernard Parish, LA	30,936	-1,210	32,146	1,471	1,633	4.8	5.1	1,190	-1	13,873	-56	27,264	77.7
St. Charles Parish, LA	23,748	-124	23,872	1,063	1,239	4.5	5.2	903	21	18,080	371	42,810	122.0
St. John the Baptist Parish, LA	20,220	254	19,966	1,202	1,264	5.9	6.3	643	17	10,767	-466	32,589	92.9
St. Tammany Parish, LA	101,431	5,101	96,330	3,651	3,880	3.6	4.0	4,950	315	54,056	2,274	24,977	71.2
New York-Northern New Jersey-Long Island, NY-NJ-PA	9,092,696	165,555	8,927,141	514,588	397,153	5.7	4.4	521,372	6,313	7,470,229	-97,818	50,172	143.0
Edison, NJ	1,158,703	42,143	1,116,560	51,198	36,370	4.4	3.3	61,549	1,512	893,901	916	42,415	120.9
Middlesex County, NJ	415,094	13,955	401,139	18,530	13,341	4.5	3.3	21,217	619	384,967	-5,100	43,389	123.7
Monmouth County, NJ	325,295	7,300	317,995	14,307	10,186	4.4	3.2	18,977	301	219,153	3,857	37,529	107.0
Ocean County, NJ	246,341	14,364	231,977	12,117	8,583	4.9	3.7	11,691	709	118,189	6,317	29,389	83.8
Somerset County, NJ	171,973	6,524	165,449	6,244	4,260	3.6	2.6	9,664	-117	171,592	-4,158	55,443	158.0
Nassau-Suffolk, NY	1,460,015	42,324	1,417,691	67,062	47,918	4.6	3.4	92,319	1,653	1,073,035	-12,115	38,415	109.5
Nassau County, NY	689,777	9,978	679,799	31,227	22,607	4.5	3.3	46,787	-414	536,245	-26,105	38,973	111.1
Suffolk County, NY	770,238	32,346	737,892	35,835	25,311	4.7	3.4	45,532	2,067	536,790	13,990	37,858	107.9
Newark-Union, NJ-PA	1,075,964	15,468	1,060,496	51,503	38,398	4.8	3.6	60,580	339	945,448	4,321	47,148	134.4
Essex County, NJ	366,807	845	365,962	21,710	16,465	5.9	4.5	20,183	426	334,345	7,399	42,213	120.3
Hunterdon County, NJ	70,485	2,551	67,934	2,276	1,586	3.2	2.3	4,028	126	46,503	3,944	43,985	125.4
Morris County, NJ	265,365	4,147	261,218	9,255	6,926	3.5	2.7	17,395	-166	294,195	-8,112	58,065	165.5
Sussex County, NJ	82,619	3,091	79,528	3,389	2,347	4.1	3.0	3,621	78	31,204	680	29,468	84.0
Union County, NJ	266,408	1,739	264,669	13,475	10,268	5.1	3.9	14,584	-175	233,029	-317	44,103	125.7
Pike County, PA	24,280	3,095	21,185	1,398	806	5.8	3.8	769	50	6,172	727	22,267	63.5
New York-White Plains-Wayne, NY-NJ	5,398,014	65,620	5,332,394	344,825	274,467	6.4	5.1	306,924	2,809	4,557,845	-90,940	55,089	157.0
Bergen County, NJ	464,740	-4,375	469,115	19,289	14,775	4.2	3.1	33,200	25	465,483	-3,692	45,957	131.0
Hudson County, NJ	290,976	-6,715	297,691	17,721	14,349	6.1	4.8	13,559	295	232,153	14,294	46,364	132.2
Passaic County, NJ	235,749	-446	236,195	14,374	10,807	6.1	4.6	12,160	273	169,077	-936	35,921	102.4
Bronx County, NY	503,926	17,644	486,282	45,908	34,825	9.1	7.2	15,061	966	209,469	3,097	33,419	95.3
Kings County, NY	1,051,732	9,647	1,042,085	80,569	66,541	7.7	6.4	40,302	2,147	435,948	4,156	31,961	91.1
New York County, NY	873,482	18,122	855,360	54,429	43,453	6.2	5.1	103,698	-4,083	1,991,801	-89,074	75,350	214.8
Putnam County, NY	55,185	2,604	52,581	2,165	1,524	3.9	2.9	2,812	188	20,538	1,441	33,824	96.4
Queens County, NY	1,065,668	1,904	1,063,764	67,997	56,605	6.4	5.3	38,612	2,303	468,585	-7,085	35,815	102.1
Richmond County, NY	225,327	8,276	217,051	14,209	11,069	6.3	5.1	7,677	214	85,676	1,003	31,086	88.6
Rockland County, NY	150,724	5,026	145,698	6,700	4,777	4.4	3.3	8,692	100	100,815	295	35,867	102.2
Westchester County, NY	480,505	13,933	466,572	21,464	15,742	4.5	3.4	31,151	381	378,300	-14,439	47,804	136.3
Niles-Benton Harbor, MI	78,577	-6,018	84,595	6,130	3,105	7.8	3.7	4,065	74	61,007	508	31,626	90.1
Berrien County, MI	78,577	-6,018	84,595	6,130	3,105	7.8	3.7	4,065	74	61,007	508	31,626	90.1
Norwich-New London, CT	143,277	11,520	131,757	6,360	3,070	4.4	2.3	5,891	162	110,111	4,341	36,453	103.9
New London County, CT	143,277	11,520	131,757	6,360	3,070	4.4	2.3	5,891	162	110,111	4,341	36,453	103.9
Ocala, FL	116,911	7,839	109,072	5,357	4,408	4.6	4.0	5,794	311	74,105	970	24,745	70.5
Marion County, FL	116,911	7,839	109,072	5,357	4,408	4.6	4.0	5,794	311	74,105	970	24,745	70.5
Ocean City, NJ	57,942	2,445	55,497	4,003	3,532	6.9	6.4	4,158	138	25,665	-280	30,234	86.2
Cape May County, NJ	57,942	2,445	55,497	4,003	3,532	6.9	6.4	4,158	138	25,665	-280	30,234	86.2
Odessa, TX	61,646	5,066	56,580	3,702	3,059	6.0	5.4	3,140	129	41,306	2,681	27,849	79.4
Ector County, TX	61,646	5,066	56,580	3,702	3,059	6.0	5.4	3,140	129	41,306	2,681	27,849	79.4
Ogden-Clearfield, UT	237,670	15,113	222,557	12,592	8,119	5.3	3.6	9,722	689	126,871	-6,499	26,512	75.6
Davis County, UT	128,663	9,351	119,312	6,257	3,742	4.9	3.1	5,053	447	62,262	271	26,149	74.5
Morgan County, UT	3,599	207	3,392	175	117	4.9	3.4	171	22	1,169	108	27,848	79.4
Weber County, UT	105,408	5,555	99,853	6,160	4,260	5.8	4.3	4,498	220	63,440	-6,878	26,844	76.5
Oklahoma City, OK	576,297	24,293	552,004	25,560	15,120	4.4	2.7	30,202	467	437,342	155	28,080	80.0
Canadian County, OK	49,489	2,920	46,569	1,919	1,115	3.9	2.4	1,734	32	17,325	-1,713	22,716	64.8
Cleveland County, OK	118,393	7,033	111,360	4,310	2,597	3.6	2.3	4,486	216	54,756	7,091	23,527	67.1
Grady County, OK	23,074	1,099	21,975	1,026	650	4.4	3.0	909	-19	10,209	-468	23,560	67.2
Lincoln County, OK	15,136	260	14,876	742	443	4.9	3.0	522	16	4,707	-317	20,381	58.1
Logan County, OK	17,850	861	16,989	689	432	3.9	2.5	599	72	5,028	156	19,381	55.2
McClain County, OK	14,370	535	13,835	619	358	4.3	2.6	624	51	5,041	-11	21,085	60.1
Oklahoma County, OK	337,985	11,585	326,400	16,255	9,525	4.8	2.9	21,328	99	340,276	-4,583	29,560	84.3

See footnotes at end of table.

Table C-4. Metropolitan Areas With Component Counties — **Civilian Labor Force and Private Nonfarm Businesses**—Con.

Metropolitan statistical area **Metropolitan statistical area with metropolitan divisions** *Metropolitan division* Component county	Civilian labor force							Private nonfarm businesses					
	Total			Number of unemployed		Unemployment rate[1]		Establishments		Employment[2]		Annual payroll per employee, 2002	
	2004	Net change, 2000–2004	2000	2004	2000	2004	2000	2002	Net change, 2000–2002	2002	Net change, 2000–2002	Amount (dollars)	Percent of national average
Olympia, WA	121,240	12,632	108,608	6,930	4,994	5.7	4.6	5,250	200	55,393	2,424	28,824	82.2
Thurston County, WA	121,240	12,632	108,608	6,930	4,994	5.7	4.6	5,250	200	55,393	2,424	28,824	82.2
Omaha-Council Bluffs, NE-IA	442,019	14,626	427,393	19,056	11,840	4.3	2.8	20,848	424	382,328	835	32,629	93.0
Harrison County, IA	8,017	−126	8,143	439	226	5.5	2.8	351	−15	2,456	−786	21,065	60.0
Mills County, IA	8,007	55	7,952	361	165	4.5	2.1	270	30	2,886	185	24,765	70.6
Pottawattamie County, IA	48,228	−198	48,426	2,642	1,184	5.5	2.4	1,932	23	31,537	2,468	24,331	69.4
Cass County, NE	14,203	540	13,663	573	378	4.0	2.8	520	1	3,644	−355	23,668	67.5
Douglas County, NE	269,238	8,623	260,615	11,947	7,802	4.4	3.0	14,252	94	298,931	−6,829	34,493	98.3
Sarpy County, NE	71,606	5,133	66,473	2,327	1,508	3.2	2.3	2,558	262	33,852	6,319	27,974	79.7
Saunders County, NE	11,242	87	11,155	407	313	3.6	2.8	467	11	3,306	−5	22,456	64.0
Washington County, NE	11,478	512	10,966	360	264	3.1	2.4	498	18	5,716	−162	29,016	82.7
Orlando - Kissimee, FL	960,639	67,015	893,624	43,685	27,973	4.5	3.1	47,229	2,300	793,083	−21,508	30,735	87.6
Lake County, FL	105,989	12,853	93,136	4,763	3,341	4.5	3.6	4,910	294	55,055	571	24,457	69.7
Orange County, FL	528,933	30,123	498,810	24,402	15,274	4.6	3.1	27,335	944	548,294	−26,639	31,300	89.2
Osceola County, FL	104,733	15,309	89,424	4,986	2,942	4.8	3.3	3,787	439	48,679	610	23,161	66.0
Seminole County, FL	220,984	8,730	212,254	9,534	6,416	4.3	3.0	11,197	623	141,055	3,950	33,601	95.8
Oshkosh-Neenah, WI	92,788	2,913	89,875	4,203	2,448	4.5	2.7	3,685	−33	78,151	−3,645	35,111	100.1
Winnebago County, WI	92,788	2,913	89,875	4,203	2,448	4.5	2.7	3,685	−33	78,151	−3,645	35,111	100.1
Owensboro, KY	54,729	−1,053	55,782	2,826	2,494	5.2	4.5	2,696	−21	43,823	−1,961	26,920	76.7
Daviess County, KY	46,055	−776	46,831	2,314	2,032	5.0	4.3	2,387	−22	38,812	−2,443	25,646	73.1
Hancock County, KY	4,068	−118	4,186	224	214	5.5	5.1	137	8	3,781	714	41,315	117.8
McLean County, KY	4,606	−159	4,765	288	248	6.3	5.2	172	−7	1,230	−232	22,859	65.2
Oxnard-Thousand Oaks-Ventura, CA	416,060	23,103	392,957	22,259	17,803	5.3	4.5	17,949	743	251,825	13,823	36,690	104.6
Ventura County, CA	416,060	23,103	392,957	22,259	17,803	5.3	4.5	17,949	743	251,825	13,823	36,690	104.6
Palm Bay-Melbourne-Titusville, FL	249,982	18,309	231,673	11,092	8,414	4.4	3.6	11,878	518	167,108	9,410	31,764	90.5
Brevard County, FL	249,982	18,309	231,673	11,092	8,414	4.4	3.6	11,878	518	167,108	9,410	31,764	90.5
Panama City-Lynn Haven, FL	78,426	6,558	71,868	3,599	3,335	4.6	4.6	4,252	44	55,142	1,210	24,092	68.7
Bay County, FL	78,426	6,558	71,868	3,599	3,335	4.6	4.6	4,252	44	55,142	1,210	24,092	68.7
Parkersburg-Marietta-Vienna, WV-OH	80,350	1,068	79,282	4,716	3,994	5.9	5.0	4,045	−60	61,672	−896	26,857	76.6
Washington County, OH	33,086	1,901	31,185	2,081	1,702	6.3	5.5	1,569	−5	22,704	−551	27,284	77.8
Pleasants County, WV	3,279	−47	3,326	199	192	6.1	5.8	123	−13	1,738	−73	35,842	102.2
Wirt County, WV	2,477	−87	2,564	175	179	7.1	7.0	67	−7	359	53	15,476	44.1
Wood County, WV	41,508	−699	42,207	2,261	1,921	5.4	4.6	2,286	−35	36,871	−325	26,281	74.9
Pascagoula, MS	69,778	−2,485	72,263	4,326	4,464	6.2	6.2	2,615	−66	44,471	−1,115	28,795	82.1
George County, MS	8,581	137	8,444	763	665	8.9	7.9	306	2	2,934	−13	21,626	61.6
Jackson County, MS	61,197	−2,622	63,819	3,563	3,799	5.8	6.0	2,309	−68	41,537	−1,102	29,301	83.5
Pensacola-Ferry Pass-Brent, FL	196,364	9,226	187,138	9,266	7,437	4.7	4.0	8,818	289	126,005	1,607	25,357	72.3
Escambia County, FL	134,347	2,112	132,235	6,624	5,334	4.9	4.0	6,740	157	106,609	15	25,947	74.0
Santa Rosa County, FL	62,017	7,114	54,903	2,642	2,103	4.3	3.8	2,078	132	19,396	1,592	22,117	63.0
Peoria, IL	183,606	−3,244	186,850	10,529	7,953	5.7	4.3	8,835	4	156,960	−6,536	32,226	91.9
Marshall County, IL	6,783	−204	6,987	347	290	5.1	4.2	278	−19	2,932	34	24,509	69.9
Peoria County, IL	89,336	−1,804	91,140	5,400	4,108	6.0	4.5	4,802	−40	102,436	−5,866	34,070	97.1
Stark County, IL	2,775	−109	2,884	198	173	7.1	6.0	137	5	862	−144	21,753	62.0
Tazewell County, IL	65,899	−1,214	67,113	3,726	2,744	5.7	4.1	2,877	43	42,279	−304	29,936	85.3
Woodford County, IL	18,813	87	18,726	858	638	4.6	3.4	741	15	8,451	−256	25,080	71.5
Philadelphia-Camden-Wilmington, PA-NJ-DE-MD	**2,916,970**	**70,451**	**2,846,519**	**151,909**	**110,568**	**5.2**	**3.9**	**144,549**	**2,011**	**2,497,789**	**−18,266**	**39,379**	**112.3**
Camden, NJ	*644,950*	*34,507*	*610,443*	*31,003*	*21,609*	*4.8*	*3.5*	*28,882*	*339*	*429,769*	*−5,780*	*34,525*	*98.4*
Burlington County, NJ	236,864	15,486	221,378	9,908	6,872	4.2	3.1	10,518	200	170,813	−3,077	36,631	104.4
Camden County, NJ	263,725	9,488	254,237	14,118	9,860	5.4	3.9	12,598	17	177,348	−6,535	33,951	96.8
Gloucester County, NJ	144,361	9,533	134,828	6,977	4,877	4.8	3.6	5,766	122	81,608	3,832	31,366	89.4
Philadelphia, PA	*1,925,827*	*39,871*	*1,885,956*	*105,562*	*77,356*	*5.5*	*4.1*	*96,179*	*1,316*	*1,738,700*	*−19,825*	*40,295*	*114.9*
Bucks County, PA	340,117	11,036	329,081	15,912	11,281	4.7	3.4	18,231	433	243,624	−3,948	33,567	95.7
Chester County, PA	248,735	12,930	235,805	9,424	7,206	3.8	3.1	13,058	881	205,120	14,968	45,590	130.0
Delaware County, PA	281,514	4,449	277,065	14,516	10,449	5.2	3.8	13,222	−84	210,264	−6,814	39,423	112.4
Montgomery County, PA	423,280	14,450	408,830	18,076	12,970	4.3	3.2	25,663	−137	497,803	589	43,314	123.5
Philadelphia County, PA	632,181	−2,994	635,175	47,634	35,450	7.5	5.6	26,005	223	581,889	−24,620	38,978	111.1
Wilmington, DE-MD-NJ	*346,193*	*−3,927*	*350,120*	*15,344*	*11,603*	*4.4*	*3.3*	*19,488*	*356*	*329,320*	*7,339*	*40,876*	*116.5*
New Castle County, DE	267,682	−5,070	272,752	11,680	8,777	4.4	3.2	16,468	277	288,744	6,613	41,817	119.2
Cecil County, MD	47,447	1,621	45,826	2,038	1,609	4.3	3.5	1,691	47	21,410	581	30,324	86.4
Salem County, NJ	31,064	−478	31,542	1,626	1,217	5.2	3.9	1,329	32	19,166	145	38,474	109.7
Phoenix-Mesa-Scottsdale, AZ	1,851,316	185,661	1,665,655	82,196	55,961	4.4	3.4	77,539	3,484	1,390,433	11,053	33,323	95.0
Maricopa County, AZ	1,771,778	175,727	1,596,051	77,565	52,736	4.4	3.3	75,292	3,278	1,361,929	7,680	33,531	95.6
Pinal County, AZ	79,538	9,934	69,604	4,631	3,225	5.8	4.6	2,247	206	28,504	3,373	23,419	66.8
Pine Bluff, AR	46,132	1,388	44,744	3,612	2,550	7.8	5.7	1,891	17	28,224	−2,803	25,231	71.9
Cleveland County, AR	4,119	228	3,891	277	191	6.7	4.9	101	−11	753	−37	19,003	54.2
Jefferson County, AR	36,820	988	35,832	2,927	2,054	7.9	5.7	1,630	28	25,813	−2,747	25,577	72.9
Lincoln County, AR	5,193	172	5,021	408	305	7.9	6.1	160	-	1,658	−19	22,679	64.6
Pittsburgh, PA	1,217,830	26,554	1,191,276	70,287	51,615	5.8	4.3	60,828	46	1,055,581	−1,972	32,917	93.8
Allegheny County, PA	644,892	9,042	635,850	34,811	25,715	5.4	4.0	34,733	−118	687,285	−3,942	35,451	101.1
Armstrong County, PA	33,850	722	33,128	2,428	1,882	7.2	5.7	1,458	−32	15,732	−934	23,668	67.5
Beaver County, PA	90,433	1,613	88,820	5,328	3,801	5.9	4.3	3,465	−12	48,079	−1,505	27,697	79.0
Butler County, PA	94,712	5,653	89,059	5,312	3,633	5.6	4.1	4,344	90	62,886	−471	29,616	84.4
Fayette County, PA	65,927	1,414	64,513	5,165	3,658	7.8	5.7	2,881	92	34,761	731	22,198	63.3
Washington County, PA	101,783	3,436	98,347	5,969	4,512	5.9	4.6	5,025	120	79,981	5,711	30,351	86.5
Westmoreland County, PA	186,233	4,674	181,559	11,274	8,414	6.1	4.6	8,922	−94	126,857	−1,562	28,508	81.3
Pittsfield, MA	72,596	2,534	70,062	3,322	1,990	4.6	2.8	4,310	−73	55,974	−2,961	30,281	86.3
Berkshire County, MA	72,596	2,534	70,062	3,322	1,990	4.6	2.8	4,310	−73	55,974	−2,961	30,281	86.3

See footnotes at end of table.

Metropolitan statistical area / Metropolitan statistical area with metropolitan divisions / Metropolitan division / Component county	Civilian labor force							Private nonfarm businesses					
	Total			Number of unemployed		Unemployment rate[1]		Establishments		Employment[2]		Annual payroll per employee, 2002	
	2004	Net change, 2000–2004	2000	2004	2000	2004	2000	2002	Net change, 2000–2002	2002	Net change, 2000–2002	Amount (dollars)	Percent of national average
Pocatello, ID	43,485	1,565	41,920	2,084	1,981	4.8	4.7	2,067	24	25,329	−745	24,718	70.5
Bannock County, ID	39,800	1,484	38,316	1,858	1,774	4.7	4.6	1,911	17	23,621	−486	24,877	70.9
Power County, ID	3,685	81	3,604	226	207	6.1	5.7	156	7	1,708	−259	22,512	64.2
Portland-South Portland-Biddeford, ME	286,977	16,533	270,444	10,289	7,116	3.6	2.6	16,826	598	212,531	−3,019	32,777	93.4
Cumberland County, ME	157,029	8,067	148,962	5,258	3,793	3.3	2.5	10,574	266	148,683	−1,414	34,018	97.0
Sagadahoc County, ME	18,789	325	18,464	685	514	3.6	2.8	847	63	13,499	−416	36,128	103.0
York County, ME	111,159	8,141	103,018	4,346	2,809	3.9	2.7	5,405	269	50,349	−1,189	28,215	80.4
Portland-Vancouver-Beaverton, OR-WA	1,094,183	16,729	1,077,454	78,376	48,302	7.2	4.5	57,429	699	844,882	−22,376	36,473	104.0
Clackamas County, OR	189,545	1,659	187,886	12,838	7,736	6.8	4.1	10,017	392	122,746	7,037	34,221	97.5
Columbia County, OR	23,108	599	22,509	2,127	1,255	9.2	5.6	888	42	8,756	−280	33,046	94.2
Multnomah County, OR	374,146	−5,778	379,924	28,532	18,032	7.6	4.7	23,215	−357	381,845	−22,997	36,055	102.8
Washington County, OR	264,193	5,658	258,535	16,711	10,162	6.3	3.9	12,725	277	212,600	−1,832	41,631	118.7
Yamhill County, OR	43,899	81	43,818	3,250	2,198	7.4	5.0	2,080	41	23,649	−445	27,417	78.2
Clark County, WA	194,341	14,384	179,957	14,491	8,622	7.5	4.8	8,337	301	94,221	−3,698	32,163	91.7
Skamania County, WA	4,951	126	4,825	427	297	8.6	6.2	167	3	1,065	−161	26,331	75.1
Port St. Lucie-Fort Pierce, FL	165,346	21,639	143,707	9,361	7,398	5.7	5.1	8,613	538	91,520	1,279	27,243	77.7
Martin County, FL	63,400	7,091	56,309	3,035	2,353	4.8	4.2	4,525	257	47,568	−1,093	28,125	80.2
St. Lucie County, FL	101,946	14,548	87,398	6,326	5,045	6.2	5.8	4,088	281	43,952	2,372	26,288	74.9
Poughkeepsie-Newburgh-Middletown, NY	321,040	18,351	302,689	14,205	10,031	4.4	3.3	15,543	706	196,208	11,199	32,502	92.6
Dutchess County, NY	146,342	6,530	139,812	6,150	4,509	4.2	3.2	7,077	316	99,029	7,981	35,779	102.0
Orange County, NY	174,698	11,821	162,877	8,055	5,522	4.6	3.4	8,466	390	97,179	3,218	29,163	83.1
Prescott, AZ	86,965	11,384	75,581	3,704	2,959	4.3	3.9	5,382	397	49,244	3,181	23,669	67.5
Yavapai County, AZ	86,965	11,384	75,581	3,704	2,959	4.3	3.9	5,382	397	49,244	3,181	23,669	67.5
Providence-New Bedford-Fall River, RI-MA	849,649	28,480	821,169	46,500	32,187	5.5	3.9	58,680	16,927	599,074	−3,813	32,027	91.3
Bristol County, MA	287,360	9,143	278,217	17,524	10,157	6.1	3.7	13,517	297	198,582	−4,565	30,572	87.1
Bristol County, RI	27,143	318	26,825	1,201	960	4.4	3.6	17,500	16,369	(D)	(D)	(D)	(D)
Kent County, RI	95,732	2,979	92,753	4,688	3,555	4.9	3.8	4,949	26	69,143	−2,554	31,550	89.9
Newport County, RI	45,453	492	44,961	2,082	1,645	4.6	3.7	2,735	33	29,420	875	31,132	88.7
Providence County, RI	321,356	11,993	309,363	17,985	13,598	5.6	4.4	16,262	−19	264,097	476	33,663	96.0
Washington County, RI	72,605	3,555	69,050	3,020	2,272	4.2	3.3	3,717	221	37,832	1,955	29,804	85.0
Provo-Orem, UT	195,722	12,168	183,554	9,483	5,446	4.8	3.0	8,225	950	134,191	−9,914	26,324	75.0
Juab County, UT	3,961	237	3,724	247	133	6.2	3.6	162	14	1,778	30	23,266	66.3
Utah County, UT	191,761	11,931	179,830	9,236	5,313	4.8	3.0	8,063	936	132,413	−9,944	26,365	75.2
Pueblo, CO	68,767	4,917	63,850	4,976	2,329	7.2	3.6	3,233	46	44,835	−3,518	25,934	73.9
Pueblo County, CO	68,767	4,917	63,850	4,976	2,329	7.2	3.6	3,233	46	44,835	−3,518	25,934	73.9
Punta Gorda, FL	60,501	5,356	55,145	3,022	2,042	5.0	3.7	3,393	320	31,486	−199	24,818	70.7
Charlotte County, FL	60,501	5,356	55,145	3,022	2,042	5.0	3.7	3,393	320	31,486	−199	24,818	70.7
Racine, WI	100,667	921	99,746	6,049	3,892	6.0	3.9	4,258	110	71,400	−2,027	33,256	94.8
Racine County, WI	100,667	921	99,746	6,049	3,892	6.0	3.9	4,258	110	71,400	−2,027	33,256	94.8
Raleigh-Cary, NC	484,107	31,195	452,912	21,059	11,529	4.4	2.5	24,698	921	378,506	7,976	33,646	95.9
Franklin County, NC	25,828	1,510	24,318	1,317	795	5.1	3.3	836	80	8,224	74	26,450	75.4
Johnston County, NC	68,596	4,776	63,820	3,029	1,864	4.4	2.9	2,753	192	30,218	582	25,320	72.2
Wake County, NC	389,683	24,909	364,774	16,713	8,870	4.3	2.4	21,109	649	340,064	7,320	34,560	98.5
Rapid City, SD	65,340	4,155	61,185	2,183	1,546	3.3	2.5	3,886	154	47,027	204	25,953	74.0
Meade County, SD	12,967	686	12,281	447	319	3.4	2.6	576	57	5,293	641	25,138	71.7
Pennington County, SD	52,373	3,469	48,904	1,736	1,227	3.3	2.5	3,310	97	41,734	−437	26,056	74.3
Reading, PA	197,732	3,117	194,615	10,523	7,659	5.3	3.9	8,405	250	145,505	−3,358	31,689	90.3
Berks County, PA	197,732	3,117	194,615	10,523	7,659	5.3	3.9	8,405	250	145,505	−3,358	31,689	90.3
Redding, CA	83,543	8,721	74,822	6,172	4,493	7.4	6.0	4,552	84	48,851	2,735	28,131	80.2
Shasta County, CA	83,543	8,721	74,822	6,172	4,493	7.4	6.0	4,552	84	48,851	2,735	28,131	80.2
Reno-Sparks, NV	208,568	11,642	196,926	8,386	7,337	4.0	3.7	11,484	269	172,303	2,496	32,174	91.7
Storey County, NV	2,014	16	1,998	68	65	3.4	3.3	78	-	298	−166	17,768	50.6
Washoe County, NV	206,554	11,626	194,928	8,318	7,272	4.0	3.7	11,406	269	172,005	2,662	32,199	91.8
Richmond, VA	600,345	36,023	564,322	23,183	11,635	3.9	2.1	29,360	709	502,829	5,809	34,000	96.9
Amelia County, VA	6,093	269	5,824	212	116	3.5	2.0	281	27	1,921	179	21,523	61.4
Caroline County, VA	11,745	823	10,922	460	237	3.9	2.2	386	22	3,284	309	24,807	70.7
Charles City County, VA	3,808	219	3,589	187	88	4.9	2.5	187	58	1,940	493	25,293	72.1
Chesterfield County, VA	153,150	11,830	141,320	4,831	2,521	3.2	1.8	5,893	396	89,339	7,417	31,376	89.4
Cumberland County, VA	4,396	188	4,208	170	94	3.9	2.2	148	16	899	103	18,535	52.8
Dinwiddie County, VA	12,374	419	11,955	471	249	3.8	2.1	348	98	4,835	−22	25,786	73.5
Goochland County, VA	9,750	895	8,855	319	154	3.3	1.7	492	62	4,680	1,368	33,975	96.8
Hanover County, VA	52,014	4,859	47,155	1,484	777	2.9	1.6	2,805	128	35,440	1,247	28,378	80.9
Henrico County, VA	152,386	7,838	144,548	5,207	2,613	3.4	1.8	7,079	−133	141,809	−6,597	35,682	101.7
King and Queen County, VA	3,183	45	3,138	119	80	3.7	2.5	129	26	736	167	22,774	64.9
King William County, VA	7,627	648	6,979	246	131	3.2	1.9	327	17	3,095	−88	33,395	95.2
Louisa County, VA	14,200	1,402	12,798	506	303	3.6	2.4	493	1	4,049	−139	34,373	98.0
New Kent County, VA	8,147	897	7,250	265	132	3.3	1.8	259	−5	1,890	−315	26,944	76.8
Powhatan County, VA	12,523	1,351	11,172	363	202	2.9	1.8	511	46	3,119	−2,051	25,503	72.7
Prince George County, VA	13,995	848	13,147	588	335	4.2	2.5	387	31	7,058	2,658	32,191	91.8
Sussex County, VA	4,421	−79	4,500	290	165	6.6	3.7	201	5	2,334	−596	24,980	71.2
Colonial Heights city, VA	8,967	404	8,563	354	192	3.9	2.2	661	6	9,523	−662	20,465	58.3
Hopewell city, VA	10,194	387	9,807	562	278	5.5	2.8	472	−5	7,734	−374	30,922	88.1
Petersburg city, VA	14,331	513	13,818	1,094	470	7.6	3.4	745	−134	13,215	−831	29,696	84.6
Richmond city, VA	97,041	2,267	94,774	5,455	2,498	5.6	2.6	7,556	47	165,929	3,543	37,696	107.5

See footnotes at end of table.

Metropolitan statistical area **Metropolitan statistical area with metropolitan divisions** *Metropolitan division* Component county	Civilian labor force							Private nonfarm businesses					
	Total			Number of unemployed		Unemployment rate[1]		Establishments		Employment[2]		Annual payroll per employee, 2002	
	2004	Net change, 2000–2004	2000	2004	2000	2004	2000	2002	Net change, 2000–2002	2002	Net change, 2000–2002	Amount (dollars)	Percent of national average
Riverside-San Bernardino-Ontario, CA	1,647,915	227,378	1,420,537	93,946	71,834	5.7	5.1	57,650	4,006	914,837	56,404	29,093	82.9
Riverside County, CA	810,655	129,768	680,887	46,840	36,432	5.8	5.4	28,954	2,389	427,580	34,774	28,679	81.7
San Bernardino County, CA	837,260	97,610	739,650	47,106	35,402	5.6	4.8	28,696	1,617	487,257	21,630	29,457	84.0
Roanoke, VA	147,311	–315	147,626	5,458	3,239	3.7	2.2	8,287	127	135,599	–3,700	28,547	81.4
Botetourt County, VA	16,598	282	16,316	521	290	3.1	1.8	679	95	6,608	260	28,735	81.9
Craig County, VA	2,479	1	2,478	93	59	3.8	2.4	62	3	318	–25	20,525	58.5
Franklin County, VA	24,544	404	24,140	920	719	3.7	3.0	1,035	81	11,103	–109	23,466	66.9
Roanoke County, VA	45,909	337	45,572	1,444	791	3.1	1.7	2,110	680	34,664	11,223	25,899	73.8
Roanoke city, VA	45,159	–1,107	46,266	2,055	1,133	4.6	2.4	3,437	–736	59,918	–15,417	30,004	85.5
Salem city, VA	12,622	–232	12,854	425	247	3.4	1.9	964	4	22,988	368	31,252	89.1
Rochester, MN	103,853	8,187	95,666	4,227	2,667	4.1	2.8	4,318	269	90,080	3,427	35,137	100.2
Dodge County, MN	11,266	990	10,276	484	313	4.3	3.0	454	41	3,806	–238	28,606	81.5
Olmsted County, MN	79,495	6,471	73,024	3,172	1,987	4.0	2.7	3,261	269	78,872	3,574	36,388	103.7
Wabasha County, MN	13,092	726	12,366	571	367	4.4	3.0	603	–41	7,402	91	25,161	71.7
Rochester, NY	530,253	–4,793	535,046	28,236	19,479	5.3	3.6	23,307	316	432,379	–10,910	33,722	96.1
Livingston County, NY	32,819	–208	33,027	1,923	1,342	5.9	4.1	1,257	18	12,437	–103	23,536	67.1
Monroe County, NY	374,017	–3,889	377,906	19,574	13,379	5.2	3.5	16,877	38	351,760	–11,013	35,148	100.2
Ontario County, NY	55,021	325	54,696	2,753	1,939	5.0	3.5	2,713	157	40,429	896	29,546	84.2
Orleans County, NY	19,888	–461	20,349	1,286	949	6.5	4.7	692	8	7,607	239	22,596	64.4
Wayne County, NY	48,508	–560	49,068	2,700	1,870	5.6	3.8	1,768	95	20,146	–929	27,692	78.9
Rockford, IL	162,832	–5,400	168,232	12,605	7,803	7.7	4.6	7,755	7	137,321	–10,055	32,543	92.8
Boone County, IL	22,749	743	22,006	1,736	1,077	7.6	4.9	761	59	10,967	–673	38,471	109.7
Winnebago County, IL	140,083	–6,143	146,226	10,869	6,726	7.8	4.6	6,994	–52	126,354	–9,382	32,028	91.3
Rocky Mount, NC	68,698	392	68,306	5,023	3,474	7.3	5.1	3,234	–26	56,508	–1,448	26,944	76.8
Edgecombe County, NC	24,809	–152	24,961	2,171	1,469	8.8	5.9	1,007	53	24,209	7,028	27,780	79.2
Nash County, NC	43,889	544	43,345	2,852	2,005	6.5	4.6	2,227	–79	32,299	–8,476	26,318	75.0
Rome, GA	48,664	3,884	44,780	2,227	1,679	4.6	3.7	2,057	41	36,121	–1,823	26,061	74.3
Floyd County, GA	48,664	3,884	44,780	2,227	1,679	4.6	3.7	2,057	41	36,121	–1,823	26,061	74.3
Sacramento—Arden-Arcade—Roseville, CA	1,003,214	98,069	905,145	53,792	38,898	5.4	4.3	42,752	2,353	653,250	39,831	34,575	98.6
El Dorado County, CA	89,023	7,225	81,798	4,558	3,400	5.1	4.2	4,262	306	40,114	1,899	29,420	83.9
Placer County, CA	154,923	23,435	131,488	7,060	4,733	4.6	3.6	8,276	979	109,719	15,788	35,494	101.2
Sacramento County, CA	665,612	59,569	606,043	36,635	26,426	5.5	4.4	26,670	948	445,167	21,284	35,195	100.3
Yolo County, CA	93,656	7,840	85,816	5,539	4,339	5.9	5.1	3,544	120	58,250	860	31,662	90.3
Saginaw-Saginaw Township North, MI	101,030	–343	101,373	8,784	4,093	8.7	4.0	5,006	–17	85,294	–7,319	32,837	93.6
Saginaw County, MI	101,030	–343	101,373	8,784	4,093	8.7	4.0	5,006	–17	85,294	–7,319	32,837	93.6
St. Cloud, MN	104,379	5,028	99,351	4,876	3,227	4.7	3.2	5,016	324	86,052	2,728	27,642	78.8
Benton County, MN	22,508	1,833	20,675	1,162	730	5.2	3.5	895	144	13,267	1,870	28,161	80.3
Stearns County, MN	81,871	3,195	78,676	3,714	2,497	4.5	3.2	4,121	180	72,785	858	27,547	78.5
St. George, UT	50,392	11,318	39,074	2,225	1,379	4.4	3.5	2,794	283	29,996	3,357	23,696	67.5
Washington County, UT	50,392	11,318	39,074	2,225	1,379	4.4	3.5	2,794	283	29,996	3,357	23,696	67.5
St. Joseph, MO-KS	65,711	5,145	60,566	3,902	2,046	5.9	3.4	3,022	72	42,919	16	25,972	74.0
Doniphan County, KS	4,579	488	4,091	351	202	7.7	4.9	171	–10	1,479	–568	22,439	64.0
Andrew County, MO	9,805	923	8,882	490	256	5.0	2.9	239	–3	1,541	–742	20,201	57.6
Buchanan County, MO	45,951	3,321	42,630	2,764	1,421	6.0	3.3	2,415	80	38,675	1,594	26,523	75.6
DeKalb County, MO	5,376	413	4,963	297	167	5.5	3.4	197	5	1,224	–268	20,103	57.3
St. Louis, MO-IL[4]	1,453,133	25,391	1,427,742	86,535	50,029	6.0	3.5	69,287	1,015	1,214,875	–9,242	34,607	98.6
Bond County, IL	8,391	77	8,314	562	388	6.7	4.7	338	–14	3,709	–474	24,948	71.1
Calhoun County, IL	2,498	–38	2,536	180	140	7.2	5.5	101	–8	609	–88	18,609	53.0
Clinton County, IL	18,408	72	18,336	1,018	722	5.5	3.9	874	52	8,890	779	21,602	61.6
Jersey County, IL	11,226	96	11,130	662	510	5.9	4.6	416	–1	4,590	–48	19,404	55.3
Macoupin County, IL	24,203	–161	24,364	1,583	1,104	6.5	4.5	1,046	–25	9,885	–518	24,116	68.7
Madison County, IL	132,745	140	132,605	8,347	5,814	6.3	4.4	5,915	108	83,041	–2,238	29,062	82.8
Monroe County, IL	16,337	838	15,499	751	511	4.6	3.3	714	55	7,041	801	27,161	77.4
St. Clair County, IL	119,753	196	119,557	8,499	6,068	7.1	5.1	5,472	37	77,768	2,477	27,063	77.1
Franklin County, MO	53,104	1,753	51,351	3,038	1,740	5.7	3.4	2,551	132	31,362	–459	26,349	75.1
Jefferson County, MO	116,164	5,120	111,044	6,427	3,352	5.5	3.0	3,632	139	36,378	699	24,394	69.5
Lincoln County, MO	23,530	2,727	20,803	1,297	650	5.5	3.1	823	63	7,855	933	27,073	77.2
St. Charles County, MO	182,040	14,646	167,394	7,744	3,955	4.3	2.4	6,687	433	100,342	4,808	30,395	86.6
St. Louis County, MO	560,629	1,772	558,857	30,280	15,722	5.4	2.8	29,974	–187	570,586	–16,262	36,803	104.9
Warren County, MO	14,817	1,199	13,618	781	423	5.3	3.1	571	15	5,740	–227	23,271	66.3
Washington County, MO	10,262	300	9,962	866	553	8.4	5.6	448	129	2,837	–89	17,676	50.4
St. Louis city, MO	159,026	–3,346	162,372	14,500	8,377	9.1	5.2	9,725	87	264,242	664	39,930	113.8
Salem, OR	184,729	7,203	177,526	13,691	9,623	7.4	5.4	8,686	93	103,340	–4,068	27,674	78.9
Marion County, OR	149,988	5,594	144,394	11,411	8,027	7.6	5.6	7,497	47	91,716	–2,899	27,968	79.7
Polk County, OR	34,741	1,609	33,132	2,280	1,596	6.6	4.8	1,189	46	11,624	–1,169	25,361	72.3
Salinas, CA	212,218	8,353	203,865	17,450	15,023	8.2	7.4	8,898	323	109,812	4,744	32,123	91.6
Monterey County, CA	212,218	8,353	203,865	17,450	15,023	8.2	7.4	8,898	323	109,812	4,744	32,123	91.6
Salisbury, MD	60,849	4,054	56,795	2,837	2,568	4.7	4.5	2,937	–2	41,015	539	27,020	77.0
Somerset County, MD	11,209	738	10,471	706	650	6.3	6.2	392	–13	3,712	542	26,540	75.7
Wicomico County, MD	49,640	3,316	46,324	2,131	1,918	4.3	4.1	2,545	11	37,303	–3	27,068	77.2
Salt Lake City, UT	534,889	13,744	521,145	28,830	16,735	5.4	3.2	28,833	942	492,324	–10,474	31,910	91.0
Salt Lake County, UT	492,264	9,367	482,897	26,546	15,357	5.4	3.2	26,691	756	467,970	–12,905	32,284	92.0
Summit County, UT	19,742	1,611	18,131	1,044	634	5.3	3.5	1,619	129	17,233	1,791	22,542	64.3
Tooele County, UT	22,883	2,766	20,117	1,240	744	5.4	3.7	523	57	7,121	640	30,019	85.6

See footnotes at end of table.

Metropolitan statistical area / **Metropolitan statistical area with metropolitan divisions** / *Metropolitan division* / Component county	Civilian labor force							Private nonfarm businesses					
	Total			Number of unemployed		Unemployment rate[1]		Establishments		Employment[2]		Annual payroll per employee, 2002	
	2004	Net change, 2000–2004	2000	2004	2000	2004	2000	2002	Net change, 2000–2002	2002	Net change, 2000–2002	Amount (dollars)	Percent of national average
San Angelo, TX	53,200	1,577	51,623	2,595	2,000	4.9	3.9	2,619	−15	35,691	665	26,103	74.4
Irion County, TX	959	16	943	41	30	4.3	3.2	47	5	262	8	30,695	87.5
Tom Green County, TX	52,241	1,561	50,680	2,554	1,970	4.9	3.9	2,572	−20	35,429	657	26,069	74.3
San Antonio, TX	883,166	64,002	819,164	49,835	32,586	5.6	4.0	36,897	1,132	640,934	3,136	29,188	83.2
Atascosa County, TX	18,837	1,619	17,218	1,073	710	5.7	4.1	574	29	5,959	43	20,845	59.4
Bandera County, TX	9,565	863	8,702	470	317	4.9	3.6	376	55	1,982	321	20,533	58.5
Bexar County, TX	709,784	47,810	661,974	41,061	26,909	5.8	4.1	30,225	426	566,881	−5,019	29,753	84.8
Comal County, TX	45,746	5,376	40,370	2,342	1,421	5.1	3.5	2,220	170	27,876	2,897	25,808	73.6
Guadalupe County, TX	49,705	4,363	45,342	2,384	1,546	4.8	3.4	1,588	229	22,988	3,870	26,122	74.5
Kendall County, TX	13,370	1,279	12,091	603	405	4.5	3.3	852	126	6,678	479	27,911	79.6
Medina County, TX	19,214	1,254	17,960	1,058	713	5.5	4.0	616	42	4,895	−12	20,465	58.3
Wilson County, TX	16,945	1,438	15,507	844	565	5.0	3.6	446	55	3,675	557	19,035	54.3
San Diego-Carlsbad-San Marcos, CA	1,490,333	113,684	1,376,649	70,292	53,973	4.7	3.9	71,330	3,408	1,083,047	30,833	37,412	106.6
San Diego County, CA	1,490,333	113,684	1,376,649	70,292	53,973	4.7	3.9	71,330	3,408	1,083,047	30,833	37,412	106.6
Sandusky, OH	43,516	1,548	41,968	2,763	1,771	6.3	4.2	2,045	4	29,458	−3,606	28,872	82.3
Erie County, OH	43,516	1,548	41,968	2,763	1,771	6.3	4.2	2,045	4	29,458	−3,606	28,872	82.3
San Francisco-Oakland-Fremont, CA	2,178,653	−104,663	2,283,316	121,318	77,184	5.6	3.4	118,782	−1,744	1,912,175	−94,152	49,720	141.7
Oakland-Fremont-Hayward, CA	1,259,397	−10,990	1,270,387	72,481	45,640	5.8	3.6	59,211	755	972,754	1,257	44,380	126.5
Alameda County, CA	751,698	−17,634	769,332	44,887	27,832	6.0	3.6	36,772	381	653,437	−2,293	44,697	127.4
Contra Costa County, CA	507,699	6,644	501,055	27,594	17,808	5.4	3.6	22,439	374	319,317	3,550	43,731	124.7
San Francisco-San Mateo-Redwood City, CA	919,256	−93,673	1,012,929	48,837	31,544	5.3	3.1	59,571	−2,499	939,421	−95,409	55,249	157.5
Marin County, CA	129,928	−11,889	141,817	5,773	4,038	4.4	2.8	10,183	−74	102,449	−3,826	42,619	121.5
San Francisco County, CA	425,970	−46,908	472,878	25,073	16,098	5.9	3.4	29,599	−1,807	501,768	−53,879	56,717	161.7
San Mateo County, CA	363,358	−34,876	398,234	17,991	11,408	5.0	2.9	19,789	−618	335,204	−37,704	56,911	162.2
San Jose-Sunnyvale-Santa Clara, CA	854,249	−113,545	967,794	57,002	31,136	6.7	3.2	45,333	−1,287	906,018	−104,282	62,395	177.9
San Benito County, CA	25,429	−2,001	27,430	2,412	1,654	9.5	6.0	1,029	64	10,813	32	30,167	86.0
Santa Clara County, CA	828,820	−111,544	940,364	54,590	29,482	6.6	3.1	44,304	−1,351	895,205	−104,314	62,784	179.0
San Luis Obispo-Paso Robles, CA	130,739	8,236	122,503	5,718	4,888	4.4	4.0	7,492	548	81,056	7,431	28,004	79.8
San Luis Obispo County, CA	130,739	8,236	122,503	5,718	4,888	4.4	4.0	7,492	548	81,056	7,431	28,004	79.8
Santa Barbara-Santa Maria, CA	214,137	11,566	202,571	9,990	8,796	4.7	4.3	11,062	178	139,876	−320	34,230	97.6
Santa Barbara County, CA	214,137	11,566	202,571	9,990	8,796	4.7	4.3	11,062	178	139,876	−320	34,230	97.6
Santa Cruz-Watsonville, CA	145,419	−3,119	148,538	10,231	7,613	7.0	5.1	7,028	56	78,674	−586	34,118	97.3
Santa Cruz County, CA	145,419	−3,119	148,538	10,231	7,613	7.0	5.1	7,028	56	78,674	−586	34,118	97.3
Santa Fe, NM	75,811	5,169	70,642	3,273	2,571	4.3	3.6	4,866	197	46,006	1,311	27,814	79.3
Santa Fe County, NM	75,811	5,169	70,642	3,273	2,571	4.3	3.6	4,866	197	46,006	1,311	27,814	79.3
Santa Rosa-Petaluma, CA	256,820	3,469	253,351	12,680	8,459	4.9	3.3	13,666	247	166,357	3,357	35,607	101.5
Sonoma County, CA	256,820	3,469	253,351	12,680	8,459	4.9	3.3	13,666	247	166,357	3,357	35,607	101.5
Sarasota-Bradenton-Venice, FL	298,354	26,347	272,007	12,087	8,665	4.1	3.2	17,999	1,127	207,513	−34,987	28,499	81.2
Manatee County, FL	136,556	13,348	123,208	5,619	3,912	4.1	3.2	6,207	605	73,016	−8,448	27,636	78.8
Sarasota County, FL	161,798	12,999	148,799	6,468	4,753	4.0	3.2	11,792	522	134,497	−26,539	28,967	82.6
Savannah, GA	155,061	12,549	142,512	6,274	4,916	4.0	3.4	7,648	129	121,773	6,159	28,909	82.4
Bryan County, GA	13,601	1,960	11,641	454	359	3.3	3.1	437	39	3,270	118	22,200	63.3
Chatham County, GA	118,919	7,116	111,803	5,021	3,965	4.2	3.5	6,667	45	112,680	5,571	29,032	82.8
Effingham County, GA	22,541	3,473	19,068	799	592	3.5	3.1	544	45	5,823	470	30,301	86.4
Scranton—Wilkes-Barre, PA	278,004	5,144	272,860	17,978	13,261	6.5	4.9	13,600	−114	223,592	−5,313	26,712	76.1
Lackawanna County, PA	105,710	2,085	103,625	6,394	4,639	6.0	4.5	5,336	−86	90,351	−3,032	26,104	74.4
Luzerne County, PA	158,007	2,575	155,432	10,699	7,962	6.8	5.1	7,634	−27	124,838	−2,490	26,823	76.5
Wyoming County, PA	14,287	484	13,803	885	660	6.2	4.8	630	−1	8,403	209	31,605	90.1
Seattle-Tacoma-Bellevue, WA	1,698,510	54,877	1,643,633	95,815	71,090	5.6	4.3	90,730	54	1,373,253	−72,565	43,193	123.1
Seattle-Bellevue-Everett, WA	1,331,242	28,653	1,302,589	69,788	53,960	5.2	4.1	74,797	−329	1,173,703	−63,896	45,134	128.7
King County, WA	993,458	12,560	980,898	50,826	39,529	5.1	4.0	59,191	−620	971,829	−61,057	46,962	133.9
Snohomish County, WA	337,784	16,093	321,691	18,962	14,431	5.6	4.5	15,606	291	201,874	−2,839	36,338	103.6
Tacoma, WA	367,268	26,224	341,044	26,027	17,130	7.1	5.0	15,933	383	199,550	−8,669	31,774	90.6
Pierce County, WA	367,268	26,224	341,044	26,027	17,130	7.1	5.0	15,933	383	199,550	−8,669	31,774	90.6
Sheboygan, WI	64,662	139	64,523	2,863	1,592	4.4	2.5	2,699	95	56,288	−940	30,492	86.9
Sheboygan County, WI	64,662	139	64,523	2,863	1,592	4.4	2.5	2,699	95	56,288	−940	30,492	86.9
Sherman-Denison, TX	57,169	868	56,301	3,518	2,238	6.2	4.0	2,577	−3	36,693	−2,826	28,209	80.4
Grayson County, TX	57,169	868	56,301	3,518	2,238	6.2	4.0	2,577	−3	36,693	−2,826	28,209	80.4
Shreveport-Bossier City, LA	175,564	3,310	172,254	10,622	8,292	6.1	4.8	8,627	55	144,732	1,528	26,570	75.7
Bossier Parish, LA	48,981	2,036	46,945	2,625	2,111	5.4	4.5	2,059	91	30,609	−136	22,751	64.9
Caddo Parish, LA	115,450	897	114,553	7,177	5,555	6.2	4.8	6,208	−50	109,937	1,796	27,601	78.7
De Soto Parish, LA	11,133	377	10,756	820	626	7.4	5.8	360	14	4,186	−132	27,410	78.1
Sioux City, IA-NE-SD	74,597	−2,850	77,447	3,855	2,130	5.2	2.8	3,893	−7	68,493	−3,608	26,670	76.0
Woodbury County, IA	53,252	−2,579	55,831	2,934	1,503	5.5	2.7	2,881	−51	46,561	−988	25,123	71.6
Dakota County, NE	10,783	−157	10,940	478	348	4.4	3.2	460	18	10,190	−696	25,877	73.8
Dixon County, NE	3,176	−194	3,370	112	85	3.5	2.5	128	2	1,296	592	27,994	79.8
Union County, SD	7,386	80	7,306	331	194	4.5	2.7	424	24	10,446	−2,516	34,173	97.4
Sioux Falls, SD	119,418	8,033	111,385	3,792	2,357	3.2	2.1	6,466	272	108,128	1,273	28,944	82.5
Lincoln County, SD	17,531	3,010	14,521	418	267	2.4	1.8	711	105	6,078	871	28,590	81.5
McCook County, SD	3,041	52	2,989	98	71	3.2	2.4	183	5	1,233	−40	18,509	52.8
Minnehaha County, SD	94,111	5,029	89,082	3,103	1,902	3.3	2.1	5,299	163	99,169	434	29,276	83.5
Turner County, SD	4,735	−58	4,793	173	117	3.7	2.4	273	−1	1,648	8	18,104	51.6
South Bend-Mishawaka, IN-MI	160,589	−1,515	162,104	7,973	4,996	5.0	3.1	7,279	−98	127,395	−6,809	29,993	85.5
St. Joseph County, IN	133,572	−1,342	134,914	6,705	4,139	5.0	3.1	6,417	−140	118,863	−6,229	30,224	86.2
Cass County, MI	27,017	−173	27,190	1,268	857	4.7	3.2	862	42	8,532	−580	26,774	76.3

See footnotes at end of table.

State and Metropolitan Area Data Book: 2006

U.S. Census Bureau

Table C-4. Metropolitan Areas With Component Counties — Civilian Labor Force and Private Nonfarm Businesses—Con.

Metropolitan statistical area **Metropolitan statistical area with metropolitan divisions** *Metropolitan division* Component county	Civilian labor force							Private nonfarm businesses					
	Total			Number of unemployed		Unemployment rate[1]		Establishments		Employment[2]		Annual payroll per employee, 2002	
	2004	Net change, 2000–2004	2000	2004	2000	2004	2000	2002	Net change, 2000–2002	2002	Net change, 2000–2002	Amount (dollars)	Percent of national average
Spartanburg, SC	131,026	1,735	129,291	10,023	4,447	7.6	3.4	6,425	142	117,817	−4,135	31,607	90.1
Spartanburg County, SC	131,026	1,735	129,291	10,023	4,447	7.6	3.4	6,425	142	117,817	−4,135	31,607	90.1
Spokane, WA	224,981	13,084	211,897	14,693	11,051	6.5	5.2	11,787	98	164,194	−4,079	30,294	86.4
Spokane County, WA	224,981	13,084	211,897	14,693	11,051	6.5	5.2	11,787	98	164,194	−4,079	30,294	86.4
Springfield, IL	109,117	−3,068	112,185	6,015	4,134	5.5	3.7	5,558	−52	82,985	−2,457	29,481	84.0
Menard County, IL	6,756	−244	7,000	367	251	5.4	3.6	245	−2	1,517	116	23,295	66.4
Sangamon County, IL	102,361	−2,824	105,185	5,648	3,883	5.5	3.7	5,313	−50	81,468	−2,573	29,596	84.4
Springfield, MA	352,473	7,355	345,118	18,657	9,902	5.3	2.9	15,890	−1,097	247,409	−4,561	30,681	87.5
Franklin County, MA	39,771	545	39,226	1,676	941	4.2	2.4	1,702	−97	25,868	1,110	25,629	73.1
Hampden County, MA	224,098	4,898	219,200	13,597	7,112	6.1	3.2	10,657	−943	174,766	−6,441	32,506	92.7
Hampshire County, MA	88,604	1,912	86,692	3,384	1,849	3.8	2.1	3,531	−57	46,775	770	26,656	76.0
Springfield, MO	211,403	12,204	199,199	9,598	5,587	4.5	2.8	10,637	291	160,713	−3,382	25,318	72.2
Christian County, MO	35,131	4,339	30,792	1,508	824	4.3	2.7	1,330	125	11,162	−4	20,904	59.6
Dallas County, MO	7,522	318	7,204	426	304	5.7	4.2	251	−22	2,516	−270	14,619	41.7
Greene County, MO	138,403	5,552	132,851	6,185	3,577	4.5	2.7	7,786	133	135,133	−1,996	26,313	75.0
Polk County, MO	13,971	812	13,159	702	385	5.0	2.9	638	45	7,201	−471	19,380	55.2
Webster County, MO	16,376	1,183	15,193	777	497	4.7	3.3	632	10	4,701	−641	22,040	62.8
Springfield, OH	70,600	−1,459	72,059	4,776	3,107	6.8	4.3	2,699	−11	47,153	−3,918	26,565	75.7
Clark County, OH	70,600	−1,459	72,059	4,776	3,107	6.8	4.3	2,699	−11	47,153	−3,918	26,565	75.7
State College, PA	72,253	3,785	68,468	3,165	2,418	4.4	3.5	3,156	29	43,165	−3,589	25,894	73.8
Centre County, PA	72,253	3,785	68,468	3,165	2,418	4.4	3.5	3,156	29	43,165	−3,589	25,894	73.8
Stockton, CA	285,200	26,032	259,168	24,244	18,014	8.5	7.0	10,831	644	161,040	6,635	30,952	88.2
San Joaquin County, CA	285,200	26,032	259,168	24,244	18,014	8.5	7.0	10,831	644	161,040	6,635	30,952	88.2
Sumter, SC	45,664	1,041	44,623	3,693	1,834	8.1	4.1	1,949	85	33,356	−3,664	25,686	73.2
Sumter County, SC	45,664	1,041	44,623	3,693	1,834	8.1	4.1	1,949	85	33,356	−3,664	25,686	73.2
Syracuse, NY	328,548	2,913	325,635	17,913	12,337	5.5	3.8	15,350	348	267,078	−6,342	32,316	92.1
Madison County, NY	35,676	508	35,168	1,986	1,354	5.6	3.9	1,405	28	19,904	−144	25,486	72.6
Onondaga County, NY	233,001	1,474	231,527	11,812	8,162	5.1	3.5	11,886	284	223,065	−5,650	33,024	94.1
Oswego County, NY	59,871	931	58,940	4,115	2,821	6.9	4.8	2,059	36	24,109	−548	31,406	89.5
Tallahassee, FL	173,345	1,108	172,237	6,870	5,500	4.0	3.2	7,927	331	107,501	3,880	27,395	78.1
Gadsden County, FL	19,735	−178	19,913	1,005	798	5.1	4.0	580	5	9,804	421	25,253	72.0
Jefferson County, FL	6,449	395	6,054	253	223	3.9	3.7	254	15	1,888	267	20,954	59.7
Leon County, FL	134,146	−451	134,597	5,157	4,104	3.8	3.0	6,726	290	93,204	3,079	27,877	79.5
Wakulla County, FL	13,015	1,342	11,673	455	375	3.5	3.2	367	21	2,605	113	22,861	65.2
Tampa-St. Petersburg-Clearwater, FL	1,268,218	68,868	1,199,350	57,816	40,370	4.6	3.4	63,864	2,378	1,009,648	−23,097	32,704	93.2
Hernando County, FL	54,434	4,873	49,561	3,059	2,157	5.6	4.4	2,560	191	24,494	886	23,600	67.3
Hillsborough County, FL	568,523	39,840	528,683	24,811	17,237	4.4	3.3	28,315	1,481	515,199	12,365	35,493	101.2
Pasco County, FL	169,319	19,129	150,190	8,424	5,536	5.0	3.7	6,737	544	65,515	274	23,675	67.5
Pinellas County, FL	475,942	5,026	470,916	21,522	15,440	4.5	3.3	26,252	162	404,440	−36,622	31,165	88.8
Terre Haute, IN	81,425	109	81,316	5,748	3,324	7.1	4.1	3,811	−35	58,065	−4,618	27,121	77.3
Clay County, IN	13,037	137	12,900	840	510	6.4	4.0	516	−13	5,011	−988	24,459	69.7
Sullivan County, IN	9,303	47	9,256	676	467	7.3	5.0	374	−13	3,505	−366	24,485	69.8
Vermillion County, IN	8,168	4	8,164	645	365	7.9	4.5	286	−2	4,376	−495	37,730	107.6
Vigo County, IN	50,917	−79	50,996	3,587	1,982	7.0	3.9	2,635	−7	45,173	−2,769	26,593	75.8
Texarkana, TX-Texarkana, AR	61,286	2,686	58,600	3,543	2,794	5.8	4.8	2,849	−21	40,772	−2,695	25,284	72.1
Miller County, AR	18,843	685	18,158	912	805	4.8	4.4	742	3	11,221	−99	25,815	73.6
Bowie County, TX	42,443	2,001	40,442	2,631	1,989	6.2	4.9	2,107	−24	29,551	−2,596	25,082	71.5
Toledo, OH	336,451	162	336,289	23,598	14,573	7.0	4.3	16,079	75	291,866	−9,610	32,000	91.2
Fulton County, OH	22,607	13	22,594	1,425	908	6.3	4.0	1,102	4	18,262	−2,156	30,335	86.5
Lucas County, OH	225,842	−490	226,332	16,612	10,264	7.4	4.5	11,084	−31	214,756	−5,963	32,200	91.8
Ottawa County, OH	21,446	140	21,306	1,742	1,083	8.1	5.1	1,122	−35	11,225	−1,006	32,269	92.0
Wood County, OH	66,556	499	66,057	3,819	2,318	5.7	3.5	2,771	137	47,623	−485	31,675	90.3
Topeka, KS	125,105	5,272	119,833	7,585	4,850	6.1	4.0	5,719	−18	87,049	−7,222	28,364	80.9
Jackson County, KS	7,033	414	6,619	425	282	6.0	4.3	276	−9	3,347	49	18,830	53.7
Jefferson County, KS	10,229	517	9,712	583	383	5.7	3.9	366	−9	2,309	104	25,144	71.7
Osage County, KS	9,136	341	8,795	603	401	6.6	4.6	309	−40	3,264	−214	14,553	41.5
Shawnee County, KS	94,932	3,943	90,989	5,790	3,659	6.1	4.0	4,636	36	77,392	−7,197	29,526	84.2
Wabaunsee County, KS	3,775	57	3,718	184	125	4.9	3.4	132	4	737	36	20,912	59.6
Trenton-Ewing, NJ	190,469	10,326	180,143	7,993	5,881	4.2	3.3	10,344	695	186,454	12,337	43,228	123.2
Mercer County, NJ	190,469	10,326	180,143	7,993	5,881	4.2	3.3	10,344	695	186,454	12,337	43,228	123.2
Tucson, AZ	439,127	29,961	409,166	20,219	15,310	4.6	3.7	19,147	515	293,113	−269	29,586	84.3
Pima County, AZ	439,127	29,961	409,166	20,219	15,310	4.6	3.7	19,147	515	293,113	−269	29,586	84.3
Tulsa, OK	443,241	3,424	439,817	22,014	12,970	5.0	2.9	23,446	306	370,917	−6,420	31,950	91.1
Creek County, OK	32,220	283	31,937	1,830	1,044	5.7	3.3	1,279	4	15,710	−123	24,839	70.8
Okmulgee County, OK	16,996	−102	17,098	1,212	773	7.1	4.5	710	43	7,004	466	23,590	67.2
Osage County, OK	20,861	43	20,818	1,091	669	5.2	3.2	516	−16	3,413	−820	18,059	51.5
Pawnee County, OK	7,858	−61	7,919	454	297	5.8	3.8	292	−18	2,371	−340	22,280	63.5
Rogers County, OK	38,372	2,275	36,097	1,678	981	4.4	2.7	1,382	75	17,014	1,440	28,021	79.9
Tulsa County, OK	295,838	−665	296,503	14,321	8,439	4.8	2.8	18,470	187	318,772	−6,093	33,126	94.4
Wagoner County, OK	31,096	1,651	29,445	1,428	767	4.6	2.6	797	31	6,633	−950	21,791	62.1
Tuscaloosa, AL	94,918	1,517	93,401	4,661	3,507	4.9	3.8	4,298	−21	71,198	−2,935	27,634	78.8
Greene County, AL	3,603	56	3,547	303	217	8.4	6.1	131	−3	1,393	76	20,182	57.5
Hale County, AL	7,156	99	7,057	504	380	7.0	5.4	214	−16	2,651	−555	22,203	63.3
Tuscaloosa County, AL	84,159	1,362	82,797	3,854	2,910	4.6	3.5	3,953	−2	67,154	−2,456	28,003	79.8

See footnotes at end of table.

Table C-4. Metropolitan Areas With Component Counties — Civilian Labor Force and Private Nonfarm Businesses—Con.

Metropolitan statistical area **Metropolitan statistical area with metropolitan divisions** *Metropolitan division* Component county	Civilian labor force							Private nonfarm businesses					
	Total			Number of unemployed		Unemployment rate[1]		Establishments		Employment[2]		Annual payroll per employee, 2002	
	2004	Net change, 2000–2004	2000	2004	2000	2004	2000	2002	Net change, 2000–2002	2002	Net change, 2000–2002	Amount (dollars)	Percent of national average
Tyler, TX	94,195	7,856	86,339	5,009	3,767	5.3	4.4	5,040	179	76,492	2,594	29,849	85.1
Smith County, TX	94,195	7,856	86,339	5,009	3,767	5.3	4.4	5,040	179	76,492	2,594	29,849	85.1
Utica-Rome, NY	142,009	−671	142,680	7,512	5,626	5.3	3.9	6,218	69	100,070	−1,605	26,574	75.8
Herkimer County, NY	31,413	−296	31,709	1,782	1,345	5.7	4.2	1,177	−6	13,240	−643	24,277	69.2
Oneida County, NY	110,596	−375	110,971	5,730	4,281	5.2	3.9	5,041	75	86,830	−962	26,925	76.7
Valdosta, GA	61,609	5,261	56,348	2,139	2,521	3.5	4.5	2,844	98	41,362	1,830	23,056	65.7
Brooks County, GA	7,992	414	7,578	284	350	3.6	4.6	200	−8	1,914	−475	23,059	65.7
Echols County, GA	2,117	253	1,864	63	64	3.0	3.4	15	3	56	33	24,089	68.7
Lanier County, GA	3,612	272	3,340	130	164	3.6	4.9	113	−5	745	−237	18,882	53.8
Lowndes County, GA	47,888	4,322	43,566	1,662	1,943	3.5	4.5	2,516	108	38,647	2,509	23,135	65.9
Vallejo-Fairfield, CA	208,356	9,547	198,809	12,258	9,033	5.9	4.5	6,820	315	105,894	11,375	32,808	93.5
Solano County, CA	208,356	9,547	198,809	12,258	9,033	5.9	4.5	6,820	315	105,894	11,375	32,808	93.5
Vero Beach, FL	56,240	5,208	51,032	3,696	2,617	6.6	5.1	3,580	128	38,619	16	26,624	75.9
Indian River County, FL	56,240	5,208	51,032	3,696	2,617	6.6	5.1	3,580	128	38,619	16	26,624	75.9
Victoria, TX	56,108	337	55,771	3,261	2,161	5.8	3.9	2,742	12	36,748	−1,514	29,446	83.9
Calhoun County, TX	9,289	−55	9,344	700	436	7.5	4.7	421	10	7,084	−971	40,536	115.5
Goliad County, TX	3,379	47	3,332	194	126	5.7	3.8	112	-	811	99	23,803	67.8
Victoria County, TX	43,440	345	43,095	2,367	1,599	5.4	3.7	2,209	2	28,853	−642	26,882	76.6
Vineland-Millville-Bridgeton, NJ	68,698	3,162	65,536	4,552	3,800	6.6	5.8	3,113	87	47,471	1,647	31,262	89.1
Cumberland County, NJ	68,698	3,162	65,536	4,552	3,800	6.6	5.8	3,113	87	47,471	1,647	31,262	89.1
Virginia Beach-Norfolk-Newport News, VA-NC	777,793	58,254	719,539	32,260	18,164	4.1	2.5	35,284	810	583,509	2,901	28,234	80.5
Currituck County, NC	10,824	1,649	9,175	318	255	2.9	2.8	537	86	3,912	775	21,752	62.0
Gloucester County, VA	18,969	1,547	17,422	562	336	3.0	1.9	862	54	6,486	201	19,752	56.3
Isle of Wight County, VA	16,328	1,567	14,761	538	320	3.3	2.2	551	22	10,615	1,040	32,594	92.9
James City County, VA	26,419	3,343	23,076	839	453	3.2	2.0	1,179	143	15,183	2,834	27,530	78.5
Mathews County, VA	4,358	141	4,217	133	92	3.1	2.2	223	8	1,210	−2	18,525	52.8
Surry County, VA	3,565	203	3,362	144	97	4.0	2.9	76	−8	1,344	−66	56,945	162.3
York County, VA	29,738	3,107	26,631	863	518	2.9	1.9	1,275	93	13,301	−644	23,316	66.5
Chesapeake city, VA	106,164	9,113	97,051	3,883	2,213	3.7	2.3	4,732	233	78,465	2,015	26,704	76.1
Hampton city, VA	66,955	3,197	63,758	3,304	1,720	4.9	2.7	2,449	−2	47,343	−1,392	25,548	72.8
Newport News city, VA	86,350	4,492	81,858	4,053	2,136	4.7	2.6	3,714	20	82,201	−2,676	31,410	89.5
Norfolk city, VA	99,974	7,726	92,248	5,431	3,016	5.4	3.3	5,604	145	118,129	1,206	32,745	93.3
Poquoson city, VA	6,107	329	5,778	175	106	2.9	1.8	188	11	1,370	−43	18,161	51.8
Portsmouth city, VA	44,161	1,622	42,539	2,489	1,446	5.6	3.4	1,784	105	27,196	1,558	26,813	76.4
Suffolk city, VA	34,679	5,625	29,054	1,371	728	4.0	2.5	1,174	19	17,052	743	26,783	76.3
Virginia Beach city, VA	218,520	14,479	204,041	7,796	4,530	3.6	2.2	10,267	10	143,404	−1,807	26,129	74.5
Williamsburg city, VA	4,682	114	4,568	361	198	7.7	4.3	669	−129	16,298	−841	23,051	65.7
Visalia-Porterville, CA	182,888	10,579	172,309	20,984	17,904	11.5	10.4	6,009	83	80,663	3,501	26,668	76.0
Tulare County, CA	182,888	10,579	172,309	20,984	17,904	11.5	10.4	6,009	83	80,663	3,501	26,668	76.0
Waco, TX	110,305	6,530	103,775	5,861	4,279	5.3	4.1	4,821	−19	88,422	−2,241	25,935	73.9
McLennan County, TX	110,305	6,530	103,775	5,861	4,279	5.3	4.1	4,821	−19	88,422	−2,241	25,935	73.9
Warner Robins, GA	59,586	5,838	53,748	2,265	1,825	3.8	3.4	2,093	127	31,223	4,504	22,801	65.0
Houston County, GA	59,586	5,838	53,748	2,265	1,825	3.8	3.4	2,093	127	31,223	4,504	22,801	65.0
Washington-Arlington-Alexandria, DC-VA-MD-WV	**2,801,375**	**140,347**	**2,661,028**	**103,874**	**72,759**	**3.7**	**2.7**	**129,718**	**4,445**	**2,216,101**	**22,314**	**44,152**	**125.9**
Bethesda-Gaithersburg-Frederick, MD	*613,211*	*16,457*	*596,754*	*19,394*	*15,728*	*3.2*	*2.6*	*31,258*	*689*	*470,137*	*−6,357*	*42,464*	*121.0*
Frederick County, MD	115,994	6,491	109,503	3,732	2,961	3.2	2.6	5,434	496	78,558	6,214	32,991	94.0
Montgomery County, MD	497,217	9,966	487,251	15,662	12,767	3.1	2.6	25,824	193	391,579	−12,571	44,364	126.5
Washington-Arlington-Alexandria, DC-VA-MD-WV	*2,188,164*	*123,890*	*2,064,274*	*84,480*	*57,031*	*3.9*	*2.8*	*98,460*	*3,756*	*1,745,964*	*28,671*	*44,607*	*127.2*
District of Columbia, DC	298,958	−10,538	309,496	24,493	17,663	8.2	5.7	19,930	275	418,755	3,772	51,005	145.4
Calvert County, MD	44,236	3,918	40,318	1,455	1,211	3.3	3.0	1,631	141	15,893	971	30,047	85.6
Charles County, MD	70,078	5,039	65,039	2,358	1,917	3.4	2.9	2,665	257	32,626	3,193	26,075	74.3
Prince George's County, MD	441,741	13,027	428,714	20,281	15,770	4.6	3.7	14,211	383	253,508	2,814	34,775	99.1
Arlington County, VA	119,393	1,218	118,175	3,071	1,850	2.6	1.6	5,298	71	111,895	−2,845	50,031	142.6
Clarke County, VA	7,342	504	6,838	201	108	2.7	1.6	351	50	3,579	302	29,907	85.3
Fairfax County, VA	570,177	24,945	545,232	15,396	8,880	2.7	1.6	25,987	407	494,893	−14,248	50,735	144.6
Fauquier County, VA	33,550	3,642	29,908	872	462	2.6	1.5	1,686	171	15,199	1,666	30,137	85.9
Loudoun County, VA	128,602	29,551	99,051	2,945	1,404	2.3	1.4	5,449	940	93,004	24,969	47,459	135.3
Prince William County, VA	178,193	26,112	152,081	4,912	2,687	2.8	1.8	5,324	941	69,901	7,942	28,982	82.6
Spotsylvania County, VA	57,600	9,570	48,030	1,467	819	2.5	1.7	1,722	381	23,693	5,535	25,851	73.7
Stafford County, VA	58,223	10,264	47,959	1,475	809	2.5	1.7	1,644	199	20,966	3,088	26,604	75.8
Warren County, VA	17,894	1,480	16,414	576	332	3.2	2.0	775	15	7,897	−158	22,938	65.4
Alexandria city, VA	81,527	1,392	80,135	2,332	1,422	2.9	1.8	4,609	−32	81,256	−257	43,338	123.5
Fairfax city, VA	12,929	543	12,386	350	167	2.7	1.3	2,289	121	31,552	−2,672	41,798	119.1
Falls Church city, VA	6,294	182	6,112	204	98	3.2	1.6	865	−2	15,736	355	43,278	123.4
Fredericksburg city, VA	11,067	846	10,221	540	235	4.9	2.3	1,474	−195	21,256	−2,534	28,613	81.6
Manassas city, VA	20,508	1,432	19,076	630	320	3.1	1.7	1,456	−493	20,083	−4,240	40,603	115.7
Manassas Park city, VA	6,229	498	5,731	170	80	2.7	1.4	259	97	3,496	975	36,313	103.5
Jefferson County, WV	23,623	265	23,358	752	797	3.2	3.4	835	29	10,776	43	22,681	64.7
Waterloo-Cedar Falls, IA	90,972	2,431	88,541	4,327	2,487	4.8	2.8	4,075	−43	69,582	−1,643	27,476	78.3
Black Hawk County, IA	70,871	1,793	69,078	3,521	1,999	5.0	2.9	3,144	−25	59,300	−1,026	27,426	78.2
Bremer County, IA	13,348	453	12,895	547	331	4.1	2.6	626	−15	7,468	−562	27,694	78.9
Grundy County, IA	6,753	185	6,568	259	157	3.8	2.4	305	−3	2,814	−55	27,972	79.7
Wausau, WI	74,730	2,474	72,256	3,218	2,349	4.3	3.3	3,321	−116	63,252	−385	29,109	83.0
Marathon County, WI	74,730	2,474	72,256	3,218	2,349	4.3	3.3	3,321	−116	63,252	−385	29,109	83.0

See footnotes at end of table.

Table C-4. Metropolitan Areas With Component Counties — **Civilian Labor Force and Private Nonfarm Businesses**—Con.

Metropolitan statistical area **Metropolitan statistical area with metropolitan divisions** *Metropolitan division* Component county	Civilian labor force							Private nonfarm businesses					
	Total			Number of unemployed		Unemployment rate[1]		Establishments		Employment[2]		Annual payroll per employee, 2002	
	2004	Net change, 2000–2004	2000	2004	2000	2004	2000	2002	Net change, 2000–2002	2002	Net change, 2000–2002	Amount (dollars)	Percent of national average
Weirton-Steubenville, WV-OH..............	58,099	−992	59,091	4,521	3,042	7.8	5.1	2,654	−30	41,634	−2,390	27,867	79.4
Jefferson County, OH.................	32,094	509	31,585	2,570	1,800	8.0	5.7	1,555	−8	21,116	−1,210	26,577	75.8
Brooke County, WV...................	11,206	−603	11,809	822	536	7.3	4.5	437	−10	10,851	3,324	35,716	101.8
Hancock County, WV..................	14,799	−898	15,697	1,129	706	7.6	4.5	662	−12	9,667	−4,504	21,874	62.4
Wenatchee, WA........................	59,577	4,856	54,721	4,006	3,495	6.7	6.4	2,870	45	28,185	−229	28,055	80.0
Chelan County, WA...................	39,701	3,095	36,606	2,749	2,384	6.9	6.5	2,278	−7	23,460	−760	28,572	81.4
Douglas County, WA..................	19,876	1,761	18,115	1,257	1,111	6.3	6.1	592	52	4,725	531	25,484	72.6
Wheeling, WV-OH......................	67,662	−1,585	69,247	4,087	3,766	6.0	5.4	3,699	−67	53,917	718	24,468	69.7
Belmont County, OH..................	31,848	962	30,886	2,126	1,871	6.7	6.1	1,608	−19	19,921	450	21,981	62.7
Marshall County, WV.................	14,970	−925	15,895	903	902	6.0	5.7	539	−15	7,001	276	27,192	77.5
Ohio County, WV.....................	20,844	−1,622	22,466	1,058	993	5.1	4.4	1,552	−33	26,995	−8	25,596	73.0
Wichita, KS..........................	304,798	7,049	297,749	18,780	12,430	6.2	4.2	14,715	183	254,068	−5,499	31,602	90.1
Butler County, KS...................	31,329	875	30,454	1,904	1,248	6.1	4.1	1,282	1	11,766	−228	23,819	67.9
Harvey County, KS...................	17,784	289	17,495	883	635	5.0	3.6	820	2	12,031	315	25,755	73.4
Sedgwick County, KS.................	243,225	6,222	237,003	15,196	9,945	6.2	4.2	12,070	182	225,716	−5,280	32,525	92.7
Sumner County, KS...................	12,460	−337	12,797	797	602	6.4	4.7	543	−2	4,555	−306	21,432	61.1
Wichita Falls, TX....................	74,452	2,712	71,740	3,844	3,182	5.2	4.4	3,584	−27	48,200	−471	24,739	70.5
Archer County, TX...................	5,219	353	4,866	195	154	3.7	3.2	144	−7	757	42	23,715	67.6
Clay County, TX.....................	6,278	332	5,946	251	210	4.0	3.5	129	1	927	−78	24,000	68.4
Wichita County, TX..................	62,955	2,027	60,928	3,398	2,818	5.4	4.6	3,311	−21	46,516	−435	24,771	70.6
Williamsport, PA.....................	60,753	1,502	59,251	3,782	2,567	6.2	4.3	2,849	−30	46,941	−2,506	25,711	73.3
Lycoming County, PA.................	60,753	1,502	59,251	3,782	2,567	6.2	4.3	2,849	−30	46,941	−2,506	25,711	73.3
Wilmington, NC.......................	154,626	12,608	142,018	7,153	5,634	4.6	4.0	8,847	457	99,823	−865	27,009	77.0
Brunswick County, NC................	40,029	4,714	35,315	2,074	1,612	5.2	4.6	1,903	220	17,488	−188	25,743	73.4
New Hanover County, NC..............	93,655	6,326	87,329	4,077	3,219	4.4	3.7	6,163	153	76,529	−910	27,731	79.0
Pender County, NC...................	20,942	1,568	19,374	1,002	803	4.8	4.1	781	84	5,806	233	21,308	60.7
Winchester, VA-WV....................	59,987	5,257	54,730	1,903	1,249	3.2	2.3	2,857	94	48,613	3,416	28,788	82.1
Frederick County, VA................	36,776	4,182	32,594	1,039	661	2.8	2.0	1,201	16	20,661	1,844	26,932	76.8
Winchester city, VA.................	13,767	982	12,785	443	283	3.2	2.2	1,303	58	25,193	1,585	31,354	89.4
Hampshire County, WV................	9,444	93	9,351	421	305	4.5	3.3	353	20	2,759	−13	19,256	54.9
Winston-Salem, NC....................	230,040	7,720	222,320	11,564	7,514	5.0	3.4	10,537	77	192,949	−4,633	32,836	93.6
Davie County, NC....................	19,280	916	18,364	945	778	4.9	4.2	725	33	9,303	460	24,041	68.5
Forsyth County, NC..................	167,214	6,098	161,116	8,335	5,211	5.0	3.2	8,532	39	169,843	−4,656	34,135	97.3
Stokes County, NC...................	24,064	223	23,841	1,274	841	5.3	3.5	638	30	5,503	−71	22,426	63.9
Yadkin County, NC...................	19,482	483	18,999	1,010	684	5.2	3.6	642	−25	8,300	−366	22,997	65.6
Worcester, MA........................	400,729	12,785	387,944	21,936	10,463	5.5	2.7	18,294	380	291,262	−2,116	35,155	100.2
Worcester County, MA................	400,729	12,785	387,944	21,936	10,463	5.5	2.7	18,294	380	291,262	−2,116	35,155	100.2
Yakima, WA...........................	119,787	6,389	113,398	10,339	8,713	8.6	7.7	4,693	−66	59,160	−1,104	27,766	79.1
Yakima County, WA...................	119,787	6,389	113,398	10,339	8,713	8.6	7.7	4,693	−66	59,160	−1,104	27,766	79.1
York-Hanover, PA.....................	216,502	7,571	208,931	9,960	6,980	4.6	3.3	8,402	204	157,700	4,609	30,415	86.7
York County, PA.....................	216,502	7,571	208,931	9,960	6,980	4.6	3.3	8,402	204	157,700	4,609	30,415	86.7
Youngstown-Warren-Boardman, OH-PA	280,415	−2,960	283,375	20,303	14,186	7.2	5.0	14,056	−67	210,102	−24,014	27,985	79.8
Mahoning County, OH.................	118,023	−1,702	119,725	8,727	6,063	7.4	5.1	6,311	−130	90,070	−9,705	26,974	76.9
Trumbull County, OH.................	106,456	−578	107,034	7,959	5,320	7.5	5.0	4,724	−6	75,541	−12,394	30,619	87.3
Mercer County, PA...................	55,936	−680	56,616	3,617	2,803	6.5	5.0	3,021	69	44,491	−1,915	25,558	72.9
Yuba City, CA........................	65,824	3,554	62,270	6,719	5,492	10.2	8.8	2,538	50	28,026	1,790	27,829	79.3
Sutter County, CA...................	40,270	2,345	37,925	4,247	3,559	10.5	9.4	1,712	62	19,112	1,849	28,178	80.3
Yuba County, CA.....................	25,554	1,209	24,345	2,472	1,933	9.7	7.9	826	−12	8,914	−59	27,080	77.2
Yuma, AZ.............................	73,938	9,568	64,370	11,415	10,662	15.4	16.6	2,560	23	36,268	5,035	21,320	60.8
Yuma County, AZ.....................	73,938	9,568	64,370	11,415	10,662	15.4	16.6	2,560	23	36,268	5,035	21,320	60.8

- Represents zero.   D Data withheld to avoid disclosure.   X Not applicable.

[1]Civilian unemployed as percent of total civilian labor force.
[2]For pay period including March 12 of the year shown.
[3]The Denver-Aurora metropolitan statistical area includes Broomfield County. Broomfield County, CO, was formed from parts of Adams, Boulder, Jefferson, and Weld counties on November 15, 2001, and is coextensive with Broomfield city. For the purposes of defining and presenting data for the Denver-Aurora metropolitan statistical area, Broomfield city is treated as if it were a county when data are available to do so. In many cases, the data will not be available.
[4]The portion of Sullivan city in Crawford County, MO, is legally part of the St. Louis, MO-IL MSA. That portion is not included in these figures for the St. Louis MSA.

Note: Covers metropolitan statistical areas and metropolitan divisions and component counties defined by the Office of Management and Budget as of June 6, 2003, and subsequently updated in December 2003 and November 2004. For more information, see OMB Bulletin 05-02 at <http://www.whitehouse.gov/omb/bulletins/fy05/b05-02_appendix.pdf>.

Survey, Census, or Data Collection Method: Civilian labor force data are based on Local Area Unemployment Statistics methodology at <http://www.bls.gov/lau/laumthd.htm> (released 10 March 2005).   For data extracted from the U.S. Census Bureau's County Business Patterns, see Internet site <http://www.census.gov/epcd/cbp/view/cbpview.html> and Appendix B, Limitations of the Data and Methodology.

Sources: Civilian labor force—U.S. Bureau of Labor Statistics, *Local Area Unemployment Statistics, Annual Averages*; see Internet site <http://www.bls.gov/lau> (accessed 18 August 2005);   Private nonfarm businesses—U.S. Census Bureau, *County Business Patterns* on CD-ROM; annual.

Micropolitan Areas Table D

Page

Note:

Table D presents data for the 575 micropolitan areas defined by the Office of Management and Budget as of June 6, 2003, and subsequently updated in December 2003 and November 2004. For more information, see OMB Bulletin 05-02 at *<http://www.whitehouse .gov/omb/bulletins/fy05 /b05-02_appendix.pdf>*.

For additional information, see Appendix C, Geographic Concepts and Codes.

270   Population and Personal Income

You may visit us on the Web at
http://www.census.gov/compendia/smadb

Table D

Micropolitan statistical area Component counties	Population				Net change		Percent change		Personal income Total (mil. dol.)		Per capita[3] (dollars)		Percent change
	2005 (July 1)	2004 (July 1)	2000[1] (esti-mates base)	1990[2] (April 1)	2000–2005	1990–2000	2000–2005	1990–2000	2002	2000	2002	2000	2000–2002
Abbeville, LA.	55,195	54,624	53,953	50,055	1,242	3,898	2.3	7.8	1,073.1	1,007.5	19,842	18,730	6.5
Vermilion Parish, LA	55,195	54,624	53,953	50,055	1,242	3,898	2.3	7.8	1,073.1	1,007.5	19,842	18,730	6.5
Aberdeen, SD.	38,818	38,829	39,730	39,936	–912	–206	–2.3	–0.5	1,198.2	1,109.4	30,610	27,928	8.0
Brown County, SD	34,706	34,733	35,377	35,580	–671	–203	–1.9	–0.6	1,078.5	988.0	30,925	27,932	9.2
Edmunds County, SD	4,112	4,096	4,353	4,356	–241	–3	–5.5	–0.1	119.7	121.4	28,035	27,895	–1.4
Aberdeen, WA.	70,900	70,335	67,200	64,175	3,700	3,025	5.5	4.7	1,578.1	1,475.2	22,986	21,957	7.0
Grays Harbor County, WA	70,900	70,335	67,200	64,175	3,700	3,025	5.5	4.7	1,578.1	1,475.2	22,986	21,957	7.0
Ada, OK.	35,346	35,059	35,143	34,119	203	1,024	0.6	3.0	754.9	728.1	21,638	20,718	3.7
Pontotoc County, OK.	35,346	35,059	35,143	34,119	203	1,024	0.6	3.0	754.9	728.1	21,638	20,718	3.7
Adrian, MI.	102,033	101,762	99,127	91,476	2,906	7,651	2.9	8.4	2,638.2	2,577.1	26,276	26,003	2.4
Lenawee County, MI.	102,033	101,762	99,127	91,476	2,906	7,651	2.9	8.4	2,638.2	2,577.1	26,276	26,003	2.4
Alamogordo, NM	63,538	63,571	62,245	51,928	1,293	10,317	2.1	19.9	1,204.7	1,053.7	19,459	16,916	14.3
Otero County, NM.	63,538	63,571	62,245	51,928	1,293	10,317	2.1	19.9	1,204.7	1,053.7	19,459	16,916	14.3
Albany-Lebanon, OR.	108,914	107,219	103,054	91,227	5,860	11,827	5.7	13.0	2,524.6	2,328.0	24,067	22,598	8.4
Linn County, OR.	108,914	107,219	103,054	91,227	5,860	11,827	5.7	13.0	2,524.6	2,328.0	24,067	22,598	8.4
Albemarle, NC.	58,964	58,721	58,187	51,765	777	6,422	1.3	12.4	1,362.7	1,346.0	23,193	23,135	1.2
Stanly County, NC	58,964	58,721	58,187	51,765	777	6,422	1.3	12.4	1,362.7	1,346.0	23,193	23,135	1.2
Albert Lea, MN	31,946	31,986	32,555	33,060	–609	–505	–1.9	–1.5	823.1	780.3	25,659	23,968	5.5
Freeborn County, MN	31,946	31,986	32,555	33,060	–609	–505	–1.9	–1.5	823.1	780.3	25,659	23,968	5.5
Albertville, AL	85,634	84,767	82,313	70,832	3,321	11,481	4.0	16.2	2,010.7	1,773.6	24,172	21,549	13.4
Marshall County, AL	85,634	84,767	82,313	70,832	3,321	11,481	4.0	16.2	2,010.7	1,773.6	24,172	21,549	13.4
Alexander City, AL	51,879	52,080	53,593	49,889	–1,714	3,704	–3.2	7.4	1,157.5	1,102.8	21,996	20,581	5.0
Coosa County, AL.	11,162	11,306	11,883	11,063	–721	820	–6.1	7.4	227.9	216.9	19,661	18,258	5.1
Tallapoosa County, AL.	40,717	40,774	41,710	38,826	–993	2,884	–2.4	7.4	929.6	885.8	22,656	21,243	4.9
Alexandria, MN	35,138	34,588	32,910	28,674	2,228	4,236	6.8	14.8	895.2	829.9	26,594	25,221	7.9
Douglas County, MN.	35,138	34,588	32,910	28,674	2,228	4,236	6.8	14.8	895.2	829.9	26,594	25,221	7.9
Alice, TX	40,951	40,811	39,389	37,679	1,562	1,710	4.0	4.5	810.5	734.7	20,242	18,656	10.3
Jim Wells County, TX	40,951	40,811	39,389	37,679	1,562	1,710	4.0	4.5	810.5	734.7	20,242	18,656	10.3
Allegan, MI.	113,174	112,205	106,128	90,509	7,046	15,619	6.6	17.3	2,924.5	2,801.3	26,769	26,401	4.4
Allegan County, MI	113,174	112,205	106,128	90,509	7,046	15,619	6.6	17.3	2,924.5	2,801.3	26,769	26,401	4.4
Alma, MI	42,345	42,321	42,314	38,982	31	3,332	0.1	8.5	916.7	848.3	21,661	20,049	8.1
Gratiot County, MI	42,345	42,321	42,314	38,982	31	3,332	0.1	8.5	916.7	848.3	21,661	20,049	8.1
Alpena, MI	30,428	30,682	31,293	30,605	–865	688	–2.8	2.2	748.1	730.2	24,151	23,335	2.5
Alpena County, MI	30,428	30,682	31,293	30,605	–865	688	–2.8	2.2	748.1	730.2	24,151	23,335	2.5
Altus, OK.	26,518	27,100	28,256	28,764	–1,738	–508	–6.2	–1.8	645.3	592.4	23,566	20,958	8.9
Jackson County, OK.	26,518	27,100	28,256	28,764	–1,738	–508	–6.2	–1.8	645.3	592.4	23,566	20,958	8.9
Americus, GA	37,034	37,138	37,031	33,816	3	3,215	0.0	9.5	828.0	774.4	22,289	20,913	6.9
Schley County, GA	4,122	4,032	3,784	3,588	338	196	8.9	5.5	75.7	74.9	19,262	19,794	1.1
Sumter County, GA.	32,912	33,106	33,247	30,228	–335	3,019	–1.0	10.0	752.3	699.5	22,647	21,040	7.5
Amsterdam, NY.	48,968	49,121	49,680	51,981	–712	–2,301	–1.4	–4.4	1,259.3	1,193.3	25,546	24,021	5.5
Montgomery County, NY	48,968	49,121	49,680	51,981	–712	–2,301	–1.4	–4.4	1,259.3	1,193.3	25,546	24,021	5.5
Andrews, TX.	12,748	12,858	12,938	14,338	–190	–1,400	–1.5	–9.8	278.7	264.7	21,564	20,465	5.3
Andrews County, TX	12,748	12,858	12,938	14,338	–190	–1,400	–1.5	–9.8	278.7	264.7	21,564	20,465	5.3
Angola, IN	33,773	33,657	33,310	27,446	463	5,864	1.4	21.4	834.5	849.2	24,913	25,493	–1.7
Steuben County, IN.	33,773	33,657	33,310	27,446	463	5,864	1.4	21.4	834.5	849.2	24,913	25,493	–1.7
Arcadia, FL.	35,406	34,842	32,303	23,865	3,103	8,438	9.6	35.4	579.9	531.5	17,613	16,459	9.1
DeSoto County, FL.	35,406	34,842	32,303	23,865	3,103	8,438	9.6	35.4	579.9	531.5	17,613	16,459	9.1
Ardmore, OK.	56,251	55,986	54,423	51,076	1,828	3,347	3.4	6.6	1,247.0	1,229.6	22,702	22,596	1.4
Carter County, OK	47,125	46,906	45,597	42,919	1,528	2,678	3.4	6.2	1,066.3	1,066.3	23,145	23,389	(Z)
Love County, OK.	9,126	9,080	8,826	8,157	300	669	3.4	8.2	180.7	163.3	20,394	18,502	10.6
Arkadelphia, AR.	22,916	23,055	23,500	21,437	–584	2,063	–2.5	9.6	489.1	442.1	20,795	18,809	10.6
Clark County, AR.	22,916	23,055	23,500	21,437	–584	2,063	–2.5	9.6	489.1	442.1	20,795	18,809	10.6
Ashland, OH.	54,123	53,897	52,570	47,507	1,553	5,063	3.0	10.7	1,209.4	1,175.3	22,744	22,359	2.9
Ashland County, OH.	54,123	53,897	52,570	47,507	1,553	5,063	3.0	10.7	1,209.4	1,175.3	22,744	22,359	2.9
Ashtabula, OH.	103,221	102,992	102,788	99,821	433	2,967	0.4	3.0	2,403.1	2,304.9	23,335	22,428	4.3
Ashtabula County, OH.	103,221	102,992	102,788	99,821	433	2,967	0.4	3.0	2,403.1	2,304.9	23,335	22,428	4.3
Astoria, OR.	36,798	36,300	35,590	33,301	1,208	2,289	3.4	6.9	898.1	861.8	25,196	24,213	4.2
Clatsop County, OR.	36,798	36,300	35,590	33,301	1,208	2,289	3.4	6.9	898.1	861.8	25,196	24,213	4.2
Atchison, KS.	16,804	16,860	16,760	16,932	44	–172	0.3	–1.0	361.7	343.0	21,596	20,469	5.4
Atchison County, KS.	16,804	16,860	16,760	16,932	44	–172	0.3	–1.0	361.7	343.0	21,596	20,469	5.4
Athens, OH.	62,062	62,200	62,306	59,549	–244	2,757	–0.4	4.6	1,266.8	1,113.8	19,885	17,854	13.7
Athens County, OH.	62,062	62,200	62,306	59,549	–244	2,757	–0.4	4.6	1,266.8	1,113.8	19,885	17,854	13.7
Athens, TN.	51,327	50,832	49,176	42,383	2,151	6,793	4.4	16.0	1,073.9	1,009.2	21,407	20,521	6.4
McMinn County, TN	51,327	50,832	49,176	42,383	2,151	6,793	4.4	16.0	1,073.9	1,009.2	21,407	20,521	6.4
Athens, TX	80,017	79,287	73,593	58,543	6,424	15,050	8.7	25.7	1,796.0	1,677.2	23,796	22,793	7.1
Henderson County, TX	80,017	79,287	73,593	58,543	6,424	15,050	8.7	25.7	1,796.0	1,677.2	23,796	22,793	7.1
Auburn, IN.	41,659	41,420	40,404	35,324	1,255	5,080	3.1	14.4	1,080.4	1,027.9	26,551	25,445	5.1
De Kalb County, IN.	41,659	41,420	40,404	35,324	1,255	5,080	3.1	14.4	1,080.4	1,027.9	26,551	25,445	5.1
Auburn, NY.	81,454	81,445	81,942	82,313	–488	–371	–0.6	–0.5	1,999.1	1,859.8	24,526	22,698	7.5
Cayuga County, NY	81,454	81,445	81,942	82,313	–488	–371	–0.6	–0.5	1,999.1	1,859.8	24,526	22,698	7.5
Augusta-Waterville, ME.	120,986	120,150	117,224	115,904	3,762	1,320	3.2	1.1	3,238.8	2,981.1	27,324	25,434	8.6
Kennebec County, ME.	120,986	120,150	117,224	115,904	3,762	1,320	3.2	1.1	3,238.8	2,981.1	27,324	25,434	8.6
Austin, MN	38,799	38,951	38,702	37,385	97	1,317	0.3	3.5	1,052.9	979.1	27,149	25,299	7.5
Mower County, MN	38,799	38,951	38,702	37,385	97	1,317	0.3	3.5	1,052.9	979.1	27,149	25,299	7.5
Bainbridge, GA	28,618	28,562	28,243	25,511	375	2,732	1.3	10.7	594.3	562.9	21,162	19,928	5.6
Decatur County, GA	28,618	28,562	28,243	25,511	375	2,732	1.3	10.7	594.3	562.9	21,162	19,928	5.6
Baraboo, WI.	57,746	57,089	55,349	46,975	2,397	8,374	4.3	17.8	1,581.0	1,458.3	28,298	26,348	8.4
Sauk County, WI.	57,746	57,089	55,349	46,975	2,397	8,374	4.3	17.8	1,581.0	1,458.3	28,298	26,348	8.4
Barre, VT	59,478	59,118	58,073	54,928	1,405	3,145	2.4	5.7	1,815.0	1,649.0	30,831	28,393	10.1
Washington County, VT	59,478	59,118	58,073	54,928	1,405	3,145	2.4	5.7	1,815.0	1,649.0	30,831	28,393	10.1
Bartlesville, OK.	49,149	49,066	48,996	48,066	153	930	0.3	1.9	1,475.6	1,371.1	30,028	27,988	7.6
Washington County, OK.	49,149	49,066	48,996	48,066	153	930	0.3	1.9	1,475.6	1,371.1	30,028	27,988	7.6
Bastrop, LA.	29,989	30,383	30,983	31,938	–994	–955	–3.2	–3.0	596.9	564.3	19,560	18,215	5.8
Morehouse Parish, LA.	29,989	30,383	30,983	31,938	–994	–955	–3.2	–3.0	596.9	564.3	19,560	18,215	5.8

See footnotes at end of table.

Table D-1. Micropolitan Areas — **Population and Personal Income**—Con.

Micropolitan statistical area Component counties	Population								Personal income				
	2005 (July 1)	2004 (July 1)	2000[1] (esti-mates base)	1990[2] (April 1)	Net change		Percent change		Total (mil. dol.)		Per capita[3] (dollars)		Percent change
					2000– 2005	1990– 2000	2000– 2005	1990– 2000	2002	2000	2002	2000	2000– 2002
Batavia, NY	59,257	59,608	60,336	60,060	−1,079	276	−1.8	0.5	1,499.7	1,435.5	25,024	23,796	4.5
Genesee County, NY	59,257	59,608	60,336	60,060	−1,079	276	−1.8	0.5	1,499.7	1,435.5	25,024	23,796	4.5
Batesville, AR	34,737	34,622	34,293	31,192	444	3,101	1.3	9.9	757.1	699.9	22,080	20,409	8.2
Independence County, AR	34,737	34,622	34,293	31,192	444	3,101	1.3	9.9	757.1	699.9	22,080	20,409	8.2
Bay City, TX	37,849	38,027	37,957	36,928	−108	1,029	−0.3	2.8	808.5	779.9	21,277	20,555	3.7
Matagorda County, TX	37,849	38,027	37,957	36,928	−108	1,029	−0.3	2.8	808.5	779.9	21,277	20,555	3.7
Beatrice, NE	23,306	23,404	22,986	22,794	320	192	1.4	0.8	622.0	584.9	26,744	25,448	6.3
Gage County, NE	23,306	23,404	22,986	22,794	320	192	1.4	0.8	622.0	584.9	26,744	25,448	6.3
Beaver Dam, WI	88,103	87,913	86,020	76,559	2,083	9,461	2.4	12.4	2,231.3	2,194.7	25,684	25,515	1.7
Dodge County, WI	88,103	87,913	86,020	76,559	2,083	9,461	2.4	12.4	2,231.3	2,194.7	25,684	25,515	1.7
Beckley, WV	79,167	79,195	79,092	76,819	75	2,273	0.1	3.0	1,903.5	1,714.1	24,050	21,675	11.1
Raleigh County, WV	79,167	79,195	79,092	76,819	75	2,273	0.1	3.0	1,903.5	1,714.1	24,050	21,675	11.1
Bedford, IN	46,403	46,233	45,949	42,836	454	3,113	1.0	7.3	1,130.5	1,087.6	24,540	23,671	3.9
Lawrence County, IN	46,403	46,233	45,949	42,836	454	3,113	1.0	7.3	1,130.5	1,087.6	24,540	23,671	3.9
Beeville, TX	32,873	33,018	32,270	25,135	603	7,135	1.9	28.4	508.0	483.2	15,701	14,976	5.1
Bee County, TX	32,873	33,018	32,270	25,135	603	7,135	1.9	28.4	508.0	483.2	15,701	14,976	5.1
Bellefontaine, OH	46,580	46,544	46,017	42,310	563	3,707	1.2	8.8	1,215.8	1,186.0	26,293	25,776	2.5
Logan County, OH	46,580	46,544	46,017	42,310	563	3,707	1.2	8.8	1,215.8	1,186.0	26,293	25,776	2.5
Bemidji, MN	42,871	42,286	39,786	34,384	3,085	5,402	7.8	15.7	982.0	856.3	23,864	21,519	14.7
Beltrami County, MN	42,871	42,286	39,786	34,384	3,085	5,402	7.8	15.7	982.0	856.3	23,864	21,519	14.7
Bennettsville, SC	28,021	28,328	28,816	29,361	−795	−545	−2.8	−1.9	513.8	485.3	17,956	16,845	5.9
Marlboro County, SC	28,021	28,328	28,816	29,361	−795	−545	−2.8	−1.9	513.8	485.3	17,956	16,845	5.9
Bennington, VT	36,999	37,022	36,992	35,845	7	1,147	0.0	3.2	1,189.5	1,079.8	32,024	29,187	10.2
Bennington County, VT	36,999	37,022	36,992	35,845	7	1,147	0.0	3.2	1,189.5	1,079.8	32,024	29,187	10.2
Berlin, NH-VT	40,257	40,144	39,620	41,233	637	−1,613	1.6	−3.9	995.3	958.4	25,158	24,190	3.9
Coos County, NH	33,655	33,504	33,157	34,828	498	−1,671	1.5	−4.8	869.5	837.0	26,337	25,242	3.9
Essex County, VT	6,602	6,640	6,463	6,405	139	58	2.2	0.9	125.8	121.4	19,214	18,792	3.6
Big Rapids, MI	42,391	42,159	40,651	37,308	1,740	3,343	4.3	9.0	813.6	754.0	19,601	18,544	7.9
Mecosta County, MI	42,391	42,159	40,651	37,308	1,740	3,343	4.3	9.0	813.6	754.0	19,601	18,544	7.9
Big Spring, TX	32,522	32,804	33,465	32,343	−943	1,122	−2.8	3.5	711.9	669.7	21,501	20,011	6.3
Howard County, TX	32,522	32,804	33,465	32,343	−943	1,122	−2.8	3.5	711.9	669.7	21,501	20,011	6.3
Bishop, CA	18,156	18,247	17,925	18,281	231	−356	1.3	−1.9	479.6	435.0	26,246	24,269	10.2
Inyo County, CA	18,156	18,247	17,925	18,281	231	−356	1.3	−1.9	479.6	435.0	26,246	24,269	10.2
Blackfoot, ID	43,739	43,187	41,812	37,583	1,927	4,229	4.6	11.3	883.1	805.6	20,839	19,269	9.6
Bingham County, ID	43,739	43,187	41,812	37,583	1,927	4,229	4.6	11.3	883.1	805.6	20,839	19,269	9.6
Bloomsburg-Berwick, PA	82,971	82,934	82,361	80,937	610	1,424	0.7	1.8	2,121.1	1,927.3	25,685	23,402	10.1
Columbia County, PA	64,939	64,939	64,108	63,202	831	906	1.3	1.4	1,616.9	1,452.0	25,101	22,650	11.4
Montour County, PA	18,032	17,995	18,253	17,735	−221	518	−1.2	2.9	504.2	475.3	27,757	26,046	6.1
Bluefield, WV-VA	106,384	106,561	107,398	110,940	−1,014	−3,542	−0.9	−3.2	2,458.0	2,263.4	23,115	21,076	8.6
Tazewell County, VA	44,795	44,634	44,455	45,960	340	−1,505	0.8	−3.3	985.4	903.6	22,269	20,328	9.1
Mercer County, WV	61,589	61,927	62,943	64,980	−1,354	−2,037	−2.2	−3.1	1,472.7	1,359.8	23,718	21,604	8.3
Blytheville, AR	47,911	48,377	51,852	57,525	−3,941	−5,673	−7.6	−9.9	1,010.7	952.8	20,137	18,380	6.1
Mississippi County, AR	47,911	48,377	51,852	57,525	−3,941	−5,673	−7.6	−9.9	1,010.7	952.8	20,137	18,380	6.1
Bogalusa, LA	44,623	44,096	43,907	43,185	716	722	1.6	1.7	845.4	761.2	19,297	17,338	11.1
Washington Parish, LA	44,623	44,096	43,907	43,185	716	722	1.6	1.7	845.4	761.2	19,297	17,338	11.1
Bonham, TX	33,142	32,588	31,379	24,804	1,763	6,575	5.6	26.5	663.9	625.1	20,847	19,921	6.2
Fannin County, TX	33,142	32,588	31,379	24,804	1,763	6,575	5.6	26.5	663.9	625.1	20,847	19,921	6.2
Boone, IA	26,602	26,436	26,254	25,186	348	1,068	1.3	4.2	761.5	713.2	29,162	27,168	6.8
Boone County, IA	26,602	26,436	26,254	25,186	348	1,068	1.3	4.2	761.5	713.2	29,162	27,168	6.8
Boone, NC	42,472	42,442	42,747	36,952	−275	5,795	−0.6	15.7	1,041.9	960.4	24,265	22,467	8.5
Watauga County, NC	42,472	42,442	42,747	36,952	−275	5,795	−0.6	15.7	1,041.9	960.4	24,265	22,467	8.5
Borger, TX	22,484	22,616	23,779	25,689	−1,295	−1,910	−5.4	−7.4	556.3	556.5	24,026	23,403	(Z)
Hutchinson County, TX	22,484	22,616	23,779	25,689	−1,295	−1,910	−5.4	−7.4	556.3	556.5	24,026	23,403	(Z)
Bozeman, MT	78,210	75,632	68,276	50,463	9,934	17,813	14.5	35.3	1,913.8	1,699.1	26,890	24,880	12.6
Gallatin County, MT	78,210	75,632	68,276	50,463	9,934	17,813	14.5	35.3	1,913.8	1,699.1	26,890	24,880	12.6
Bradford, PA	44,370	44,740	45,802	47,131	−1,432	−1,329	−3.1	−2.8	1,121.8	1,128.1	24,705	24,632	−0.6
McKean County, PA	44,370	44,740	45,802	47,131	−1,432	−1,329	−3.1	−2.8	1,121.8	1,128.1	24,705	24,632	−0.6
Brainerd, MN	88,827	87,653	82,635	66,040	6,192	16,595	7.5	25.1	2,162.0	1,969.5	25,366	23,887	9.8
Cass County, MN	28,910	28,457	27,301	21,791	1,609	5,510	5.9	25.3	729.7	667.6	26,164	24,461	9.3
Crow Wing County, MN	59,917	59,196	55,334	44,249	4,583	11,085	8.3	25.1	1,432.3	1,301.8	24,978	23,530	10.0
Branson, MO	73,916	72,665	68,656	44,639	5,260	24,017	7.7	53.8	1,643.6	1,528.5	23,464	22,265	7.5
Stone County, MO	30,931	30,638	28,739	19,078	2,192	9,661	7.6	50.6	695.8	635.3	23,680	22,104	9.5
Taney County, MO	42,985	41,967	39,917	25,561	3,068	14,356	7.7	56.2	947.8	893.2	23,309	22,380	6.1
Brenham, TX	31,521	31,161	30,433	26,154	1,088	4,279	3.6	16.4	904.1	846.8	29,443	27,828	6.8
Washington County, TX	31,521	31,161	30,433	26,154	1,088	4,279	3.6	16.4	904.1	846.8	29,443	27,828	6.8
Brevard, NC	29,626	29,450	29,379	25,520	247	3,859	0.8	15.1	776.3	770.7	26,342	26,238	0.7
Transylvania County, NC	29,626	29,450	29,379	25,520	247	3,859	0.8	15.1	776.3	770.7	26,342	26,238	0.7
Brigham City, UT	46,440	45,966	42,885	36,485	3,555	6,400	8.3	17.5	948.1	872.7	21,563	20,352	8.6
Box Elder County, UT	46,440	45,966	42,885	36,485	3,555	6,400	8.3	17.5	948.1	872.7	21,563	20,352	8.6
Brookhaven, MS	33,906	33,708	33,176	30,278	730	2,898	2.2	9.6	728.1	653.1	21,699	19,689	11.5
Lincoln County, MS	33,906	33,708	33,176	30,278	730	2,898	2.2	9.6	728.1	653.1	21,699	19,689	11.5
Brookings, OR	22,427	22,147	21,123	19,327	1,304	1,796	6.2	9.3	530.1	499.5	24,679	23,655	6.1
Curry County, OR	22,427	22,147	21,123	19,327	1,304	1,796	6.2	9.3	530.1	499.5	24,679	23,655	6.1
Brookings, SD	28,121	28,045	28,264	25,207	−143	3,057	−0.5	12.1	684.0	673.4	24,094	23,813	1.6
Brookings County, SD	28,121	28,045	28,264	25,207	−143	3,057	−0.5	12.1	684.0	673.4	24,094	23,813	1.6
Brownsville, TN	19,656	19,689	19,825	19,437	−169	388	−0.9	2.0	397.4	399.4	20,292	20,151	−0.5
Haywood County, TN	19,656	19,689	19,825	19,437	−169	388	−0.9	2.0	397.4	399.4	20,292	20,151	−0.5
Brownwood, TX	38,664	38,257	37,716	34,371	948	3,345	2.5	9.7	805.5	765.8	21,221	20,305	5.2
Brown County, TX	38,664	38,257	37,716	34,371	948	3,345	2.5	9.7	805.5	765.8	21,221	20,305	5.2

See footnotes at end of table.

Table D-1. Micropolitan Areas — **Population and Personal Income**—Con.

Micropolitan statistical area / Component counties	Population								Personal income				
					Net change		Percent change		Total (mil. dol.)		Per capita[3] (dollars)		Percent change
	2005 (July 1)	2004 (July 1)	2000[1] (estimates base)	1990[2] (April 1)	2000–2005	1990–2000	2000–2005	1990–2000	2002	2000	2002	2000	2000–2002
Bucyrus, OH	45,774	45,881	46,902	47,870	–1,128	–968	–2.4	–2.0	1,099.6	1,083.0	23,721	23,095	1.5
Crawford County, OH	45,774	45,881	46,902	47,870	–1,128	–968	–2.4	–2.0	1,099.6	1,083.0	23,721	23,095	1.5
Burley, ID	40,338	40,570	41,511	38,893	–1,173	2,618	–2.8	6.7	907.2	812.6	22,115	19,577	11.6
Cassia County, ID	21,324	21,381	21,413	19,532	–89	1,881	–0.4	9.6	524.9	462.0	24,324	21,578	13.6
Minidoka County, ID	19,014	19,189	20,098	19,361	–1,084	737	–5.4	3.8	382.3	350.6	19,664	17,445	9.0
Burlington, IA-IL	48,782	48,908	50,510	50,710	–1,728	–200	–3.4	–0.4	1,327.1	1,288.2	26,754	25,507	3.0
Henderson County, IL	7,972	8,068	8,219	8,096	–247	123	–3.0	1.5	189.9	187.7	23,263	22,848	1.2
Des Moines County, IA	40,810	40,840	42,291	42,614	–1,481	–323	–3.5	–0.8	1,137.2	1,100.4	27,442	26,023	3.3
Butte-Silver Bow, MT	32,982	33,067	34,526	33,941	–1,544	585	–4.5	1.7	857.0	783.4	25,624	22,690	9.4
Silver Bow County, MT	32,982	33,067	34,526	33,941	–1,544	585	–4.5	1.7	857.0	783.4	25,624	22,690	9.4
Cadillac, MI	47,175	46,760	45,101	38,507	2,074	6,594	4.6	17.1	982.7	958.0	21,470	21,244	2.6
Missaukee County, MI	15,299	15,255	14,556	12,147	743	2,409	5.1	19.8	294.2	280.9	19,638	19,303	4.7
Wexford County, MI	31,876	31,505	30,545	26,360	1,331	4,185	4.4	15.9	688.5	677.1	22,362	22,168	1.7
Calhoun, GA	50,279	48,997	44,370	35,072	5,909	9,298	13.3	26.5	1,063.7	975.0	22,806	21,978	9.1
Gordon County, GA	50,279	48,997	44,370	35,072	5,909	9,298	13.3	26.5	1,063.7	975.0	22,806	21,978	9.1
Cambridge, MD	31,401	31,002	30,594	30,236	807	358	2.6	1.2	756.5	719.7	24,725	23,523	5.1
Dorchester County, MD	31,401	31,002	30,594	30,236	807	358	2.6	1.2	756.5	719.7	24,725	23,523	5.1
Cambridge, OH	41,123	41,220	40,796	39,024	327	1,772	0.8	4.5	892.8	809.0	21,705	19,832	10.4
Guernsey County, OH	41,123	41,220	40,796	39,024	327	1,772	0.8	4.5	892.8	809.0	21,705	19,832	10.4
Camden, AR	32,691	32,848	34,434	36,400	–1,743	–1,966	–5.1	–5.4	704.1	658.2	21,060	19,117	7.0
Calhoun County, AR	5,589	5,541	5,731	5,826	–142	–95	–2.5	–1.6	118.9	105.3	21,030	18,366	13.0
Ouachita County, AR	27,102	27,307	28,703	30,574	–1,601	–1,871	–5.6	–6.1	585.2	553.0	21,067	19,267	5.8
Campbellsville, KY	23,754	23,437	22,911	21,146	843	1,765	3.7	8.3	473.5	440.6	20,391	19,229	7.5
Taylor County, KY	23,754	23,437	22,911	21,146	843	1,765	3.7	8.3	473.5	440.6	20,391	19,229	7.5
Canon City, CO	47,766	47,439	46,323	32,273	1,443	14,050	3.1	43.5	912.4	867.5	19,229	18,733	5.2
Fremont County, CO	47,766	47,439	46,323	32,273	1,443	14,050	3.1	43.5	912.4	867.5	19,229	18,733	5.2
Canton, IL	37,708	37,687	38,237	38,080	–529	157	–1.4	0.4	895.7	844.3	23,833	22,082	6.1
Fulton County, IL	37,708	37,687	38,237	38,080	–529	157	–1.4	0.4	895.7	844.3	23,833	22,082	6.1
Cape Girardeau-Jackson, MO-IL	92,413	92,108	90,416	82,878	1,997	7,538	2.2	9.1	2,261.8	2,111.9	24,755	23,356	7.1
Alexander County, IL	8,927	9,228	9,588	10,626	–661	–1,038	–6.9	–9.8	167.0	161.9	17,607	16,891	3.2
Bollinger County, MO	12,325	12,309	12,065	10,619	260	1,446	2.2	13.6	229.6	211.8	18,682	17,548	8.4
Cape Girardeau County, MO	71,161	70,571	68,763	61,633	2,398	7,130	3.5	11.6	1,865.1	1,738.2	26,802	25,277	7.3
Carbondale, IL	57,954	58,186	59,530	61,067	–1,576	–1,537	–2.6	–2.5	1,387.3	1,267.6	23,628	21,276	9.4
Jackson County, IL	57,954	58,186	59,530	61,067	–1,576	–1,537	–2.6	–2.5	1,387.3	1,267.6	23,628	21,276	9.4
Carlsbad-Artesia, NM	51,437	51,661	51,454	48,605	–17	2,849	0.0	5.9	1,218.2	1,059.6	23,763	20,596	15.0
Eddy County, NM	51,437	51,661	51,454	48,605	–17	2,849	0.0	5.9	1,218.2	1,059.6	23,763	20,596	15.0
Cedar City, UT	38,311	36,422	33,966	20,789	4,345	13,177	12.8	63.4	634.6	556.7	17,939	16,389	14.0
Iron County, UT	38,311	36,422	33,966	20,789	4,345	13,177	12.8	63.4	634.6	556.7	17,939	16,389	14.0
Cedartown, GA	40,479	40,128	38,268	33,815	2,211	4,453	5.8	13.2	792.8	716.6	20,107	18,732	10.6
Polk County, GA	40,479	40,128	38,268	33,815	2,211	4,453	5.8	13.2	792.8	716.6	20,107	18,732	10.6
Celina, OH	41,202	41,059	40,921	39,443	281	1,478	0.7	3.7	1,052.5	1,040.8	25,760	25,439	1.1
Mercer County, OH	41,202	41,059	40,921	39,443	281	1,478	0.7	3.7	1,052.5	1,040.8	25,760	25,439	1.1
Central City, KY	31,548	31,635	31,798	31,318	–250	480	–0.8	1.5	654.2	642.4	20,632	20,205	1.8
Muhlenberg County, KY	31,548	31,635	31,798	31,318	–250	480	–0.8	1.5	654.2	642.4	20,632	20,205	1.8
Centralia, IL	40,144	40,428	41,707	41,561	–1,563	146	–3.7	0.4	966.2	946.7	23,515	22,703	2.1
Marion County, IL	40,144	40,428	41,707	41,561	–1,563	146	–3.7	0.4	966.2	946.7	23,515	22,703	2.1
Centralia, WA	72,449	71,299	68,659	59,358	3,790	9,301	5.5	15.7	1,660.2	1,527.4	23,836	22,254	8.7
Lewis County, WA	72,449	71,299	68,659	59,358	3,790	9,301	5.5	15.7	1,660.2	1,527.4	23,836	22,254	8.7
Chambersburg, PA	137,409	134,743	129,546	121,082	7,863	8,464	6.1	7.0	3,370.6	3,223.8	25,622	24,886	4.6
Franklin County, PA	137,409	134,743	129,546	121,082	7,863	8,464	6.1	7.0	3,370.6	3,223.8	25,622	24,886	4.6
Charleston-Mattoon, IL	62,038	62,509	64,306	62,314	–2,268	1,992	–3.5	3.2	1,516.3	1,463.1	24,096	22,753	3.6
Coles County, IL	51,065	51,460	53,042	51,644	–1,977	1,398	–3.7	2.7	1,246.5	1,204.3	24,046	22,706	3.5
Cumberland County, IL	10,973	11,049	11,264	10,670	–291	594	–2.6	5.6	269.7	258.8	24,331	22,976	4.2
Chester, SC	33,228	33,567	34,131	32,170	–903	1,961	–2.6	6.1	716.3	680.6	21,019	19,943	5.2
Chester County, SC	33,228	33,567	34,131	32,170	–903	1,961	–2.6	6.1	716.3	680.6	21,019	19,943	5.2
Chillicothe, OH	75,197	74,832	73,445	69,330	1,752	4,115	2.4	5.9	1,717.5	1,631.8	23,123	22,222	5.2
Ross County, OH	75,197	74,832	73,445	69,330	1,752	4,115	2.4	5.9	1,717.5	1,631.8	23,123	22,222	5.2
City of The Dalles, OR	23,593	23,553	23,815	21,683	–222	2,132	–0.9	9.8	566.1	563.5	24,008	23,656	0.5
Wasco County, OR	23,593	23,553	23,815	21,683	–222	2,132	–0.9	9.8	566.1	563.5	24,008	23,656	0.5
Claremont, NH	43,041	42,475	40,561	38,592	2,480	1,969	6.1	5.1	1,238.1	1,122.0	29,880	27,671	10.3
Sullivan County, NH	43,041	42,475	40,561	38,592	2,480	1,969	6.1	5.1	1,238.1	1,122.0	29,880	27,671	10.3
Clarksburg, WV	92,136	91,931	92,116	91,509	20	607	0.0	0.7	2,192.5	2,048.7	23,963	22,244	7.0
Doddridge County, WV	7,476	7,404	7,416	6,994	60	422	0.8	6.0	137.4	124.0	18,437	16,727	10.8
Harrison County, WV	68,369	68,343	68,598	69,371	–229	–773	–0.3	–1.1	1,753.7	1,648.7	25,817	24,039	6.4
Taylor County, WV	16,291	16,184	16,102	15,144	189	958	1.2	6.3	301.4	276.0	18,704	17,140	9.2
Clarksdale, MS	29,002	29,232	30,569	31,665	–1,567	–1,096	–5.1	–3.5	640.8	602.3	21,404	19,706	6.4
Coahoma County, MS	29,002	29,232	30,569	31,665	–1,567	–1,096	–5.1	–3.5	640.8	602.3	21,404	19,706	6.4
Clearlake, CA	65,147	64,287	58,600	50,631	6,547	7,969	11.2	15.7	1,573.5	1,388.0	25,288	23,689	13.4
Lake County, CA	65,147	64,287	58,600	50,631	6,547	7,969	11.2	15.7	1,573.5	1,388.0	25,288	23,689	13.4
Cleveland, MS	38,641	39,028	40,487	41,875	–1,846	–1,388	–4.6	–3.3	715.3	690.2	18,111	17,051	3.6
Bolivar County, MS	38,641	39,028	40,487	41,875	–1,846	–1,388	–4.6	–3.3	715.3	690.2	18,111	17,051	3.6
Clewiston, FL	39,561	38,113	36,367	25,773	3,194	10,594	8.8	41.1	756.6	657.8	20,604	18,098	15.0
Hendry County, FL	39,561	38,113	36,367	25,773	3,194	10,594	8.8	41.1	756.6	657.8	20,604	18,098	15.0
Clinton, IA	49,717	49,789	50,078	51,040	–361	–962	–0.7	–1.9	1,274.7	1,197.5	25,586	23,916	6.4
Clinton County, IA	49,717	49,789	50,078	51,040	–361	–962	–0.7	–1.9	1,274.7	1,197.5	25,586	23,916	6.4
Clovis, NM	45,846	45,730	44,900	42,207	946	2,693	2.1	6.4	1,077.4	925.8	23,984	20,596	16.4
Curry County, NM	45,846	45,730	44,900	42,207	946	2,693	2.1	6.4	1,077.4	925.8	23,984	20,596	16.4
Coffeyville, KS	34,570	34,850	36,200	38,816	–1,630	–2,616	–4.5	–6.7	794.8	765.8	22,562	21,156	3.8
Montgomery County, KS	34,570	34,850	36,200	38,816	–1,630	–2,616	–4.5	–6.7	794.8	765.8	22,562	21,156	3.8
Coldwater, MI	46,460	46,557	45,871	41,502	589	4,369	1.3	10.5	996.2	962.6	21,419	20,985	3.5
Branch County, MI	46,460	46,557	45,871	41,502	589	4,369	1.3	10.5	996.2	962.6	21,419	20,985	3.5
Columbia, TN	76,292	74,738	69,734	54,812	6,558	14,922	9.4	27.2	1,899.4	1,846.7	26,562	26,486	2.9
Maury County, TN	76,292	74,738	69,734	54,812	6,558	14,922	9.4	27.2	1,899.4	1,846.7	26,562	26,486	2.9

See footnotes at end of table.

Micropolitan statistical area Component counties	Population								Personal income				
			2000[1] (esti-mates base)	1990[2] (April 1)	Net change		Percent change		Total (mil. dol.)		Per capita[3] (dollars)		Percent change
	2005 (July 1)	2004 (July 1)			2000–2005	1990–2000	2000–2005	1990–2000	2002	2000	2002	2000	2000–2002
Columbus, MS	59,895	60,298	61,524	59,308	−1,629	2,216	−2.6	3.7	1,361.4	1,304.0	22,382	21,197	4.4
Lowndes County, MS	59,895	60,298	61,524	59,308	−1,629	2,216	−2.6	3.7	1,361.4	1,304.0	22,382	21,197	4.4
Columbus, NE	31,262	31,282	31,532	29,820	−270	1,712	−0.9	5.7	811.9	775.3	25,937	24,589	4.7
Platte County, NE	31,262	31,282	31,532	29,820	−270	1,712	−0.9	5.7	811.9	775.3	25,937	24,589	4.7
Concord, NH	146,881	145,358	136,716	120,005	10,165	16,711	7.4	13.9	4,548.0	4,225.5	32,121	30,907	7.6
Merrimack County, NH	146,881	145,358	136,716	120,005	10,165	16,711	7.4	13.9	4,548.0	4,225.5	32,121	30,907	7.6
Connersville, IN	24,885	24,967	25,550	26,015	−665	−465	−2.6	−1.8	652.7	621.8	26,004	24,337	5.0
Fayette County, IN	24,885	24,967	25,550	26,015	−665	−465	−2.6	−1.8	652.7	621.8	26,004	24,337	5.0
Cookeville, TN	98,175	97,302	93,685	78,306	4,490	15,379	4.8	19.6	2,159.2	2,003.6	22,592	21,383	7.8
Jackson County, TN	11,072	11,128	11,028	9,297	44	1,731	0.4	18.6	230.0	203.8	20,578	18,481	12.9
Overton County, TN	20,523	20,435	20,194	17,636	329	2,558	1.6	14.5	408.1	371.0	20,172	18,373	10.0
Putnam County, TN	66,580	65,739	62,463	51,373	4,117	11,090	6.6	21.6	1,521.0	1,428.8	23,705	22,868	6.5
Coos Bay, OR	64,711	63,825	62,694	60,273	2,017	2,421	3.2	4.0	1,498.9	1,376.7	23,937	21,961	8.9
Coos County, OR	64,711	63,825	62,694	60,273	2,017	2,421	3.2	4.0	1,498.9	1,376.7	23,937	21,961	8.9
Corbin, KY	38,029	37,586	35,961	33,326	2,068	2,635	5.8	7.9	713.6	656.2	19,388	18,250	8.8
Whitley County, KY	38,029	37,586	35,961	33,326	2,068	2,635	5.8	7.9	713.6	656.2	19,388	18,250	8.8
Cordele, GA	22,017	21,982	21,991	20,011	26	1,980	0.1	9.9	465.5	432.2	21,036	19,661	7.7
Crisp County, GA	22,017	21,982	21,991	20,011	26	1,980	0.1	9.9	465.5	432.2	21,036	19,661	7.7
Corinth, MS	35,306	35,166	34,608	31,722	698	2,886	2.0	9.1	735.1	681.4	21,158	19,690	7.9
Alcorn County, MS	35,306	35,166	34,608	31,722	698	2,886	2.0	9.1	735.1	681.4	21,158	19,690	7.9
Cornelia, GA	39,603	38,948	36,133	27,621	3,470	8,512	9.6	30.8	867.9	791.9	22,981	21,914	9.6
Habersham County, GA	39,603	38,948	36,133	27,621	3,470	8,512	9.6	30.8	867.9	791.9	22,981	21,914	9.6
Corning, NY	98,632	98,790	98,810	99,088	−178	−278	−0.2	−0.3	2,590.5	2,842.3	26,034	28,769	−8.9
Steuben County, NY	98,632	98,790	98,810	99,088	−178	−278	−0.2	−0.3	2,590.5	2,842.3	26,034	28,769	−8.9
Corsicana, TX	48,687	48,215	45,333	39,926	3,354	5,407	7.4	13.5	1,002.0	944.5	21,397	20,841	6.1
Navarro County, TX	48,687	48,215	45,333	39,926	3,354	5,407	7.4	13.5	1,002.0	944.5	21,397	20,841	6.1
Cortland, NY	48,622	48,921	48,578	48,963	44	−385	0.1	−0.8	1,100.2	1,070.8	22,693	22,043	2.7
Cortland County, NY	48,622	48,921	48,578	48,963	44	−385	0.1	−0.8	1,100.2	1,070.8	22,693	22,043	2.7
Coshocton, OH	36,945	37,073	36,704	35,427	241	1,277	0.7	3.6	857.8	851.6	23,206	23,202	0.7
Coshocton County, OH	36,945	37,073	36,704	35,427	241	1,277	0.7	3.6	857.8	851.6	23,206	23,202	0.7
Crawfordsville, IN	38,239	37,900	37,613	34,436	626	3,177	1.7	9.2	938.2	911.5	24,725	24,230	2.9
Montgomery County, IN	38,239	37,900	37,613	34,436	626	3,177	1.7	9.2	938.2	911.5	24,725	24,230	2.9
Crescent City, CA	28,705	28,327	27,479	23,460	1,226	4,019	4.5	17.1	513.3	495.3	18,677	18,031	3.6
Del Norte County, CA	28,705	28,327	27,479	23,460	1,226	4,019	4.5	17.1	513.3	495.3	18,677	18,031	3.6
Crossville, TN	51,346	50,187	47,027	34,736	4,319	12,291	9.2	35.4	1,087.8	1,022.6	22,339	21,750	6.4
Cumberland County, TN	51,346	50,187	47,027	34,736	4,319	12,291	9.2	35.4	1,087.8	1,022.6	22,339	21,750	6.4
Crowley, LA	59,552	59,164	58,838	55,882	714	2,956	1.2	5.3	1,225.5	1,089.3	20,750	18,518	12.5
Acadia Parish, LA	59,552	59,164	58,838	55,882	714	2,956	1.2	5.3	1,225.5	1,089.3	20,750	18,518	12.5
Cullman, AL	79,886	79,092	77,586	67,613	2,300	9,973	3.0	14.8	1,812.0	1,647.9	23,262	21,244	10.0
Cullman County, AL	79,886	79,092	77,586	67,613	2,300	9,973	3.0	14.8	1,812.0	1,647.9	23,262	21,244	10.0
Culpeper, VA	42,530	40,151	34,494	27,791	8,036	6,703	23.3	24.1	1,014.8	909.3	27,545	26,362	11.6
Culpeper County, VA	42,530	40,151	34,494	27,791	8,036	6,703	23.3	24.1	1,014.8	909.3	27,545	26,362	11.6
Danville, KY	53,485	52,969	51,170	45,686	2,315	5,484	4.5	12.0	1,147.2	1,084.6	22,128	21,196	5.8
Boyle County, KY	28,363	28,218	27,698	25,641	665	2,057	2.4	8.0	701.4	664.8	25,327	23,995	5.5
Lincoln County, KY	25,122	24,751	23,472	20,045	1,650	3,427	7.0	17.1	445.8	419.9	18,458	17,892	6.2
Daphne-Fairhope, AL	162,586	156,688	141,416	98,280	21,170	43,136	15.0	43.9	4,037.0	3,693.7	27,224	26,122	9.3
Baldwin County, AL	162,586	156,688	141,416	98,280	21,170	43,136	15.0	43.9	4,037.0	3,693.7	27,224	26,122	9.3
Decatur, IN	33,849	33,778	33,622	31,095	227	2,527	0.7	8.1	786.9	773.4	23,512	23,006	1.7
Adams County, IN	33,849	33,778	33,622	31,095	227	2,527	0.7	8.1	786.9	773.4	23,512	23,006	1.7
Defiance, OH	39,112	39,076	39,455	39,350	−343	105	−0.9	0.3	1,029.5	1,025.7	26,259	26,001	0.4
Defiance County, OH	39,112	39,076	39,455	39,350	−343	105	−0.9	0.3	1,029.5	1,025.7	26,259	26,001	0.4
Del Rio, TX	47,596	47,446	45,017	38,721	2,579	6,296	5.7	16.3	847.2	756.2	18,503	16,802	12.0
Val Verde County, TX	47,596	47,446	45,017	38,721	2,579	6,296	5.7	16.3	847.2	756.2	18,503	16,802	12.0
Deming, NM	26,498	26,090	24,993	18,110	1,505	6,883	6.0	38.0	433.8	364.8	17,195	14,595	18.9
Luna County, NM	26,498	26,090	24,993	18,110	1,505	6,883	6.0	38.0	433.8	364.8	17,195	14,595	18.9
De Ridder, LA	34,562	34,012	33,053	30,083	1,509	2,970	4.6	9.9	666.3	622.5	20,089	18,821	7.0
Beauregard Parish, LA	34,562	34,012	33,053	30,083	1,509	2,970	4.6	9.9	666.3	622.5	20,089	18,821	7.0
Dickinson, ND	22,886	22,967	23,420	23,940	−534	−520	−2.3	−2.2	558.1	514.9	24,198	21,983	8.4
Billings County, ND	813	826	874	1,108	−61	−234	−7.0	−21.1	16.7	16.0	19,151	18,289	4.2
Stark County, ND	22,073	22,141	22,546	22,832	−473	−286	−2.1	−1.3	541.5	498.9	24,396	22,126	8.5
Dillon, SC	30,974	31,142	30,715	29,114	259	1,601	0.8	5.5	569.2	551.8	18,333	17,968	3.2
Dillon County, SC	30,974	31,142	30,715	29,114	259	1,601	0.8	5.5	569.2	551.8	18,333	17,968	3.2
Dixon, IL	35,669	35,677	36,059	34,392	−390	1,667	−1.1	4.8	857.2	834.2	24,084	23,135	2.8
Lee County, IL	35,669	35,677	36,059	34,392	−390	1,667	−1.1	4.8	857.2	834.2	24,084	23,135	2.8
Dodge City, KS	33,751	33,456	32,589	27,463	1,162	5,126	3.6	18.7	742.8	698.8	22,905	21,453	6.3
Ford County, KS	33,751	33,456	32,589	27,463	1,162	5,126	3.6	18.7	742.8	698.8	22,905	21,453	6.3
Douglas, GA	47,704	47,126	45,184	35,805	2,520	9,379	5.6	26.2	972.4	906.5	20,983	20,066	7.3
Atkinson County, GA	8,030	7,949	7,606	6,213	424	1,393	5.6	22.4	143.8	135.8	18,710	17,847	5.9
Coffee County, GA	39,674	39,177	37,578	29,592	2,096	7,986	5.6	27.0	828.6	770.7	21,435	20,515	7.5
Dublin, GA	56,434	56,117	53,535	48,317	2,899	5,218	5.4	10.8	1,220.1	1,125.6	22,231	21,027	8.4
Johnson County, GA	9,538	9,623	8,561	8,329	977	232	11.4	2.8	163.5	155.6	17,368	18,174	5.1
Laurens County, GA	46,896	46,494	44,974	39,988	1,922	4,986	4.3	12.5	1,056.6	970.0	23,238	21,570	8.9
DuBois, PA	82,783	82,883	83,389	78,097	−606	5,292	−0.7	6.8	1,926.5	1,799.8	23,131	21,586	7.0
Clearfield County, PA	82,783	82,883	83,389	78,097	−606	5,292	−0.7	6.8	1,926.5	1,799.8	23,131	21,586	7.0
Dumas, TX	20,348	20,455	20,112	17,865	236	2,247	1.2	12.6	451.5	431.6	22,403	21,462	4.6
Moore County, TX	20,348	20,455	20,112	17,865	236	2,247	1.2	12.6	451.5	431.6	22,403	21,462	4.6
Duncan, OK	42,946	42,773	43,079	42,299	−133	780	−0.3	1.8	987.8	942.6	23,207	21,884	4.8
Stephens County, OK	42,946	42,773	43,079	42,299	−133	780	−0.3	1.8	987.8	942.6	23,207	21,884	4.8
Dunn, NC	103,692	101,370	91,591	67,822	12,101	23,769	13.2	35.0	2,180.7	1,979.8	22,484	21,616	10.1
Harnett County, NC	103,692	101,370	91,591	67,822	12,101	23,769	13.2	35.0	2,180.7	1,979.8	22,484	21,616	10.1
Durango, CO	47,452	46,621	44,177	32,284	3,275	11,893	7.4	36.8	1,334.3	1,210.8	29,127	27,409	10.2
La Plata County, CO	47,452	46,621	44,177	32,284	3,275	11,893	7.4	36.8	1,334.3	1,210.8	29,127	27,409	10.2

See footnotes at end of table.

Micropolitan statistical area Component counties	Population								Personal income				
					Net change		Percent change		Total (mil. dol.)		Per capita[3] (dollars)		Percent change
	2005 (July 1)	2004 (July 1)	2000[1] (estimates base)	1990[2] (April 1)	2000–2005	1990–2000	2000–2005	1990–2000	2002	2000	2002	2000	2000–2002
Durant, OK	37,815	37,623	36,626	32,089	1,189	4,537	3.2	14.1	765.7	694.6	20,733	18,967	10.2
Bryan County, OK	37,815	37,623	36,626	32,089	1,189	4,537	3.2	14.1	765.7	694.6	20,733	18,967	10.2
Dyersburg, TN	37,829	37,508	37,332	34,854	497	2,478	1.3	7.1	895.5	835.2	24,124	22,380	7.2
Dyer County, TN	37,829	37,508	37,332	34,854	497	2,478	1.3	7.1	895.5	835.2	24,124	22,380	7.2
Eagle Pass, TX	51,181	50,485	47,387	36,378	3,794	11,009	8.0	30.3	606.1	545.4	12,432	11,512	11.1
Maverick County, TX	51,181	50,485	47,387	36,378	3,794	11,009	8.0	30.3	606.1	545.4	12,432	11,512	11.1
East Liverpool-Salem, OH	110,928	111,337	112,124	108,276	–1,196	3,848	–1.1	3.6	2,540.6	2,458.9	22,771	21,935	3.3
Columbiana County, OH	110,928	111,337	112,124	108,276	–1,196	3,848	–1.1	3.6	2,540.6	2,458.9	22,771	21,935	3.3
Easton, MD	35,683	35,130	33,906	30,549	1,777	3,357	5.2	11.0	1,459.0	1,287.1	42,497	37,966	13.4
Talbot County, MD	35,683	35,130	33,906	30,549	1,777	3,357	5.2	11.0	1,459.0	1,287.1	42,497	37,966	13.4
East Stroudsburg, PA	163,234	158,816	139,845	95,709	23,389	44,136	16.7	46.1	3,761.3	3,417.7	25,223	24,442	10.1
Monroe County, PA	163,234	158,816	139,845	95,709	23,389	44,136	16.7	46.1	3,761.3	3,417.7	25,223	24,442	10.1
Edwards, CO	55,268	53,895	49,753	27,935	5,515	21,818	11.1	78.1	1,867.1	1,745.1	35,379	35,045	7.0
Eagle County, CO	47,530	46,162	41,943	21,928	5,587	20,015	13.3	91.3	1,705.4	1,584.2	37,923	37,736	7.6
Lake County, CO	7,738	7,733	7,810	6,007	–72	1,803	–0.9	30.0	161.7	160.9	20,718	20,586	0.5
Effingham, IL	34,581	34,640	34,268	31,704	313	2,564	0.9	8.1	911.1	858.6	26,477	25,059	6.1
Effingham County, IL	34,581	34,640	34,268	31,704	313	2,564	0.9	8.1	911.1	858.6	26,477	25,059	6.1
El Campo, TX	41,554	41,411	41,222	39,955	332	1,267	0.8	3.2	999.4	915.8	24,304	22,217	9.1
Wharton County, TX	41,554	41,411	41,222	39,955	332	1,267	0.8	3.2	999.4	915.8	24,304	22,217	9.1
El Dorado, AR	44,186	44,536	45,578	46,719	–1,392	–1,141	–3.1	–2.4	1,308.2	1,157.4	28,974	25,399	13.0
Union County, AR	44,186	44,536	45,578	46,719	–1,392	–1,141	–3.1	–2.4	1,308.2	1,157.4	28,974	25,399	13.0
Elizabeth City, NC	59,317	57,267	53,221	47,649	6,096	5,572	11.5	11.7	1,211.3	1,134.1	22,169	21,310	6.8
Camden County, NC	8,967	8,468	6,929	5,904	2,038	1,025	29.4	17.4	192.2	176.0	25,896	25,394	9.2
Pasquotank County, NC	38,270	37,057	34,879	31,298	3,391	3,581	9.7	11.4	768.7	726.0	21,576	20,814	5.9
Perquimans County, NC	12,080	11,742	11,413	10,447	667	966	5.8	9.2	250.3	232.2	21,603	20,349	7.8
Elk City, OK	18,880	18,388	19,755	18,812	–875	943	–4.4	5.0	391.5	354.4	19,599	17,945	10.5
Beckham County, OK	18,880	18,388	19,755	18,812	–875	943	–4.4	5.0	391.5	354.4	19,599	17,945	10.5
Elko, NV	46,998	45,901	46,924	35,077	74	11,847	0.2	33.8	1,165.1	1,152.7	25,219	24,570	1.1
Elko County, NV	45,570	44,482	45,290	33,530	280	11,760	0.6	35.1	1,126.5	1,114.6	25,266	24,618	1.1
Eureka County, NV	1,428	1,419	1,634	1,547	–206	87	–12.6	5.6	38.6	38.1	23,927	23,242	1.4
Ellensburg, WA	36,841	36,158	33,490	26,725	3,351	6,765	10.0	25.3	837.1	771.2	24,188	23,030	8.5
Kittitas County, WA	36,841	36,158	33,490	26,725	3,351	6,765	10.0	25.3	837.1	771.2	24,188	23,030	8.5
Emporia, KS	38,690	38,922	38,996	37,753	–306	1,243	–0.8	3.3	871.6	825.3	22,440	21,164	5.6
Chase County, KS	3,081	3,082	3,033	3,021	48	12	1.6	0.4	91.4	82.1	29,813	27,088	11.3
Lyon County, KS	35,609	35,840	35,963	34,732	–354	1,231	–1.0	3.5	780.2	743.1	21,808	20,664	5.0
Enid, OK	56,958	57,325	57,683	56,735	–725	948	–1.3	1.7	1,454.2	1,378.9	25,444	23,909	5.5
Garfield County, OK	56,958	57,325	57,683	56,735	–725	948	–1.3	1.7	1,454.2	1,378.9	25,444	23,909	5.5
Enterprise-Ozark, AL	94,315	94,098	92,650	89,873	1,665	2,777	1.8	3.1	2,225.9	2,016.4	23,852	21,761	10.4
Coffee County, AL	45,567	45,077	43,553	40,240	2,014	3,313	4.6	8.2	1,156.3	1,021.5	26,265	23,457	13.2
Dale County, AL	48,748	49,021	49,097	49,633	–349	–536	–0.7	–1.1	1,069.6	995.0	21,696	20,257	7.5
Escanaba, MI	38,347	38,315	38,570	37,780	–223	790	–0.6	2.1	923.9	891.8	24,050	23,125	3.6
Delta County, MI	38,347	38,315	38,570	37,780	–223	790	–0.6	2.1	923.9	891.8	24,050	23,125	3.6
Espanola, NM	40,828	40,768	41,256	34,365	–428	6,891	–1.0	20.1	800.0	702.8	19,537	17,037	13.8
Rio Arriba County, NM	40,828	40,768	41,256	34,365	–428	6,891	–1.0	20.1	800.0	702.8	19,537	17,037	13.8
Eufaula, AL-GA	30,881	31,012	31,651	27,626	–770	4,025	–2.4	14.6	649.8	595.2	20,608	18,806	9.2
Barbour County, AL	28,414	28,545	29,044	25,417	–630	3,627	–2.2	14.3	594.6	546.6	20,524	18,821	8.8
Quitman County, GA	2,467	2,467	2,607	2,209	–140	398	–5.4	18.0	55.2	48.6	21,568	18,644	13.5
Eureka-Arcata-Fortuna, CA	128,376	128,287	126,336	119,118	2,040	7,218	1.6	6.1	3,188.7	2,935.6	25,039	23,240	8.6
Humboldt County, CA	128,376	128,287	126,336	119,118	2,040	7,218	1.6	6.1	3,188.7	2,935.6	25,039	23,240	8.6
Evanston, WY	19,939	19,786	19,709	18,705	230	1,004	1.2	5.4	547.7	455.0	27,725	23,089	20.4
Uinta County, WY	19,939	19,786	19,709	18,705	230	1,004	1.2	5.4	547.7	455.0	27,725	23,089	20.4
Fairmont, MN	21,002	21,067	21,778	22,914	–776	–1,136	–3.6	–5.0	620.5	568.8	29,065	26,118	9.1
Martin County, MN	21,002	21,067	21,778	22,914	–776	–1,136	–3.6	–5.0	620.5	568.8	29,065	26,118	9.1
Fairmont, WV	56,509	56,473	56,512	57,249	–3	–737	0.0	–1.3	1,366.5	1,268.2	24,258	22,439	7.8
Marion County, WV	56,509	56,473	56,512	57,249	–3	–737	0.0	–1.3	1,366.5	1,268.2	24,258	22,439	7.8
Fallon, NV	24,556	24,289	24,025	17,938	531	6,087	2.2	33.9	664.6	601.9	27,234	25,068	10.4
Churchill County, NV	24,556	24,289	24,025	17,938	531	6,087	2.2	33.9	664.6	601.9	27,234	25,068	10.4
Faribault-Northfield, MN	60,949	60,317	56,830	49,183	4,119	7,647	7.2	15.5	1,467.8	1,363.1	24,981	23,987	7.7
Rice County, MN	60,949	60,317	56,830	49,183	4,119	7,647	7.2	15.5	1,467.8	1,363.1	24,981	23,987	7.7
Farmington, MO	61,661	60,730	55,770	48,904	5,891	6,866	10.6	14.0	1,178.6	1,105.3	20,762	19,820	6.6
St. Francois County, MO	61,661	60,730	55,770	48,904	5,891	6,866	10.6	14.0	1,178.6	1,105.3	20,762	19,820	6.6
Fergus Falls, MN	57,658	57,757	57,157	50,714	501	6,443	0.9	12.7	1,423.0	1,310.5	24,461	22,895	8.6
Otter Tail County, MN	57,658	57,757	57,157	50,714	501	6,443	0.9	12.7	1,423.0	1,310.5	24,461	22,895	8.6
Findlay, OH	73,503	73,447	71,315	65,536	2,188	5,779	3.1	8.8	2,140.4	2,026.8	29,425	28,419	5.6
Hancock County, OH	73,503	73,447	71,315	65,536	2,188	5,779	3.1	8.8	2,140.4	2,026.8	29,425	28,419	5.6
Fitzgerald, GA	27,409	27,100	27,468	24,894	–59	2,574	–0.2	10.3	608.5	552.0	22,293	20,094	10.2
Ben Hill County, GA	17,316	17,261	17,497	16,245	–181	1,252	–1.0	7.7	397.6	360.5	22,991	20,603	10.3
Irwin County, GA	10,093	9,839	9,971	8,649	122	1,322	1.2	15.3	210.8	191.5	21,087	19,203	10.1
Forest City, NC	63,771	63,543	62,992	56,918	779	6,074	1.2	10.7	1,415.1	1,341.7	22,355	21,304	5.5
Rutherford County, NC	63,771	63,543	62,992	56,918	779	6,074	1.2	10.7	1,415.1	1,341.7	22,355	21,304	5.5
Forrest City, AR	27,902	28,160	29,289	28,497	–1,387	792	–4.7	2.8	505.2	471.6	17,645	16,103	7.1
St. Francis County, AR	27,902	28,160	29,289	28,497	–1,387	792	–4.7	2.8	505.2	471.6	17,645	16,103	7.1
Fort Dodge, IA	39,003	39,186	40,194	40,342	–1,191	–148	–3.0	–0.4	1,026.1	963.0	25,748	23,959	6.5
Webster County, IA	39,003	39,186	40,194	40,342	–1,191	–148	–3.0	–0.4	1,026.1	963.0	25,748	23,959	6.5
Fort Leonard Wood, MO	44,187	44,377	41,762	41,307	2,425	455	5.8	1.1	1,052.4	950.3	23,884	22,717	10.7
Pulaski County, MO	44,187	44,377	41,762	41,307	2,425	455	5.8	1.1	1,052.4	950.3	23,884	22,717	10.7
Fort Morgan, CO	27,995	28,063	27,261	21,939	734	5,322	2.7	24.3	644.5	593.9	23,327	21,794	8.5
Morgan County, CO	27,995	28,063	27,261	21,939	734	5,322	2.7	24.3	644.5	593.9	23,327	21,794	8.5
Fort Payne, AL	67,271	66,928	64,666	54,651	2,605	10,015	4.0	18.3	1,449.9	1,354.2	22,068	20,945	7.1
DeKalb County, AL	67,271	66,928	64,666	54,651	2,605	10,015	4.0	18.3	1,449.9	1,354.2	22,068	20,945	7.1
Fort Polk South, LA	48,745	49,522	52,497	61,961	–3,752	–9,464	–7.1	–15.3	1,187.4	1,055.2	23,168	20,085	12.5
Vernon Parish, LA	48,745	49,522	52,497	61,961	–3,752	–9,464	–7.1	–15.3	1,187.4	1,055.2	23,168	20,085	12.5
Fort Valley, GA	24,794	24,533	23,810	21,189	984	2,621	4.1	12.4	563.1	514.1	23,370	21,596	9.5
Peach County, GA	24,794	24,533	23,810	21,189	984	2,621	4.1	12.4	563.1	514.1	23,370	21,596	9.5

See footnotes at end of table.

274 State and Metropolitan Area Data Book: 2006

U.S. Census Bureau

Table D-1. Microplitan Areas — **Population and Personal Income**—Con.

Micropolitan statistical area Component counties	Population								Personal income				
					Net change		Percent change		Total (mil. dol.)		Per capita[3] (dollars)		Percent change
	2005 (July 1)	2004 (July 1)	2000[1] (estimates base)	1990[2] (April 1)	2000–2005	1990–2000	2000–2005	1990–2000	2002	2000	2002	2000	2000–2002
Frankfort, IN	34,091	34,038	33,977	30,974	114	3,003	0.3	9.7	774.5	745.1	22,803	21,935	3.9
Clinton County, IN	34,091	34,038	33,977	30,974	114	3,003	0.3	9.7	774.5	745.1	22,803	21,935	3.9
Frankfort, KY	68,601	68,259	67,031	58,352	1,570	8,679	2.3	14.9	1,855.1	1,779.0	27,408	26,540	4.3
Anderson County, KY	20,394	20,080	19,189	14,571	1,205	4,618	6.3	31.7	484.3	463.8	24,766	24,175	4.4
Franklin County, KY	48,207	48,179	47,842	43,781	365	4,061	0.8	9.3	1,370.8	1,315.2	28,481	27,489	4.2
Freeport, IL	47,965	48,125	48,909	48,052	–944	857	–1.9	1.8	1,323.4	1,310.8	27,480	26,804	1.0
Stephenson County, IL	47,965	48,125	48,909	48,052	–944	857	–1.9	1.8	1,323.4	1,310.8	27,480	26,804	1.0
Fremont, NE	36,078	36,000	36,229	34,500	–151	1,729	–0.4	5.0	943.3	904.3	26,234	24,960	4.3
Dodge County, NE	36,078	36,000	36,229	34,500	–151	1,729	–0.4	5.0	943.3	904.3	26,234	24,960	4.3
Fremont, OH	61,676	61,803	61,815	61,963	–139	–148	–0.2	–0.2	1,536.4	1,478.8	24,831	23,926	3.9
Sandusky County, OH	61,676	61,803	61,815	61,963	–139	–148	–0.2	–0.2	1,536.4	1,478.8	24,831	23,926	3.9
Gaffney, SC	53,844	53,655	52,679	44,506	1,165	8,173	2.2	18.4	1,107.2	1,070.1	20,669	20,317	3.5
Cherokee County, SC	53,844	53,655	52,679	44,506	1,165	8,173	2.2	18.4	1,107.2	1,070.1	20,669	20,317	3.5
Gainesville, TX	38,847	38,438	36,469	30,777	2,378	5,692	6.5	18.5	935.2	881.1	24,778	24,166	6.1
Cooke County, TX	38,847	38,438	36,469	30,777	2,378	5,692	6.5	18.5	935.2	881.1	24,778	24,166	6.1
Galesburg, IL	70,867	71,513	74,445	75,574	–3,578	–1,129	–4.8	–1.5	1,720.4	1,668.6	23,462	22,414	3.1
Knox County, IL	53,309	53,799	55,756	56,393	–2,447	–637	–4.4	–1.1	1,329.3	1,288.4	24,189	23,108	3.2
Warren County, IL	17,558	17,714	18,689	19,181	–1,131	–492	–6.1	–2.6	391.2	380.2	21,288	20,344	2.9
Gallup, NM	71,918	72,531	74,938	60,686	–3,020	14,252	–4.0	23.5	1,126.6	1,015.2	15,299	13,551	11.0
McKinley County, NM	71,918	72,531	74,938	60,686	–3,020	14,252	–4.0	23.5	1,126.6	1,015.2	15,299	13,551	11.0
Garden City, KS	38,988	39,170	40,619	33,070	–1,631	7,549	–4.0	22.8	829.0	836.2	21,025	20,587	–0.9
Finney County, KS	38,988	39,170	40,619	33,070	–1,631	7,549	–4.0	22.8	829.0	836.2	21,025	20,587	–0.9
Gardnerville Ranchos, NV	47,017	45,933	41,465	27,637	5,552	13,828	13.4	50.0	1,770.4	1,639.5	40,997	39,547	8.0
Douglas County, NV	47,017	45,933	41,465	27,637	5,552	13,828	13.4	50.0	1,770.4	1,639.5	40,997	39,547	8.0
Georgetown, SC	60,983	59,851	56,107	46,302	4,876	9,805	8.7	21.2	1,536.5	1,360.8	26,460	24,257	12.9
Georgetown County, SC	60,983	59,851	56,107	46,302	4,876	9,805	8.7	21.2	1,536.5	1,360.8	26,460	24,257	12.9
Gettysburg, PA	99,749	98,265	91,615	78,274	8,134	13,341	8.9	17.0	2,548.2	2,308.0	26,957	25,196	10.4
Adams County, PA	99,749	98,265	91,615	78,274	8,134	13,341	8.9	17.0	2,548.2	2,308.0	26,957	25,196	10.4
Gillette, WY	37,405	36,654	33,988	29,370	3,417	4,618	10.1	15.7	1,092.7	929.6	30,253	27,357	17.5
Campbell County, WY	37,405	36,654	33,988	29,370	3,417	4,618	10.1	15.7	1,092.7	929.6	30,253	27,357	17.5
Glasgow, KY	50,270	49,724	48,146	42,964	2,124	5,182	4.4	12.1	1,049.3	1,022.7	21,521	21,247	2.6
Barren County, KY	40,073	39,585	38,129	34,001	1,944	4,128	5.1	12.1	871.8	849.7	22,491	22,288	2.6
Metcalfe County, KY	10,197	10,139	10,017	8,963	180	1,054	1.8	11.8	177.5	173.0	17,761	17,282	2.6
Gloversville, NY	55,625	55,328	55,014	54,191	611	823	1.1	1.5	1,394.7	1,325.2	25,311	24,090	5.2
Fulton County, NY	55,625	55,328	55,014	54,191	611	823	1.1	1.5	1,394.7	1,325.2	25,311	24,090	5.2
Granbury, TX	55,508	53,886	48,354	34,341	7,154	14,013	14.8	40.8	1,466.9	1,317.2	28,727	27,242	11.4
Hood County, TX	47,930	46,426	41,514	28,981	6,416	12,533	15.5	43.2	1,275.2	1,149.9	29,039	27,703	10.9
Somervell County, TX	7,578	7,460	6,840	5,360	738	1,480	10.8	27.6	191.7	167.3	26,808	24,449	14.6
Grand Island, NE	69,878	69,671	68,227	63,022	1,651	5,205	2.4	8.3	1,782.4	1,655.8	26,036	24,272	7.6
Hall County, NE	55,104	54,816	53,502	48,925	1,602	4,577	3.0	9.4	1,430.8	1,329.1	26,582	24,845	7.7
Howard County, NE	6,708	6,727	6,556	6,055	152	501	2.3	8.3	150.8	140.9	23,100	21,499	7.0
Merrick County, NE	8,066	8,128	8,169	8,042	–103	127	–1.3	1.6	200.8	185.8	24,774	22,745	8.1
Grants, NM	27,620	27,556	25,670	23,794	1,950	1,876	7.6	7.9	424.3	383.4	16,221	14,940	10.7
Cibola County, NM	27,620	27,556	25,670	23,794	1,950	1,876	7.6	7.9	424.3	383.4	16,221	14,940	10.7
Grants Pass, OR	80,761	79,810	75,869	62,649	4,892	13,220	6.4	21.1	1,773.6	1,626.5	22,791	21,436	9.0
Josephine County, OR	80,761	79,810	75,869	62,649	4,892	13,220	6.4	21.1	1,773.6	1,626.5	22,791	21,436	9.0
Great Bend, KS	28,105	28,004	28,124	29,382	–19	–1,258	–0.1	–4.3	730.9	681.1	26,465	24,219	7.3
Barton County, KS	28,105	28,004	28,124	29,382	–19	–1,258	–0.1	–4.3	730.9	681.1	26,465	24,219	7.3
Greeneville, TN	65,318	64,581	63,049	55,853	2,269	7,196	3.6	12.9	1,545.3	1,434.3	24,275	22,753	7.7
Greene County, TN	65,318	64,581	63,049	55,853	2,269	7,196	3.6	12.9	1,545.3	1,434.3	24,275	22,753	7.7
Greensburg, IN	25,184	24,944	24,572	23,645	612	927	2.5	3.9	648.0	620.8	26,295	25,266	4.4
Decatur County, IN	25,184	24,944	24,572	23,645	612	927	2.5	3.9	648.0	620.8	26,295	25,266	4.4
Greenville, MS	59,220	59,527	62,767	67,935	–3,547	–5,168	–5.7	–7.6	1,192.4	1,165.5	19,504	18,572	2.3
Washington County, MS	59,220	59,527	62,767	67,935	–3,547	–5,168	–5.7	–7.6	1,192.4	1,165.5	19,504	18,572	2.3
Greenville, OH	52,983	53,092	53,315	53,619	–332	–304	–0.6	–0.6	1,378.6	1,363.1	26,042	25,569	1.1
Darke County, OH	52,983	53,092	53,315	53,619	–332	–304	–0.6	–0.6	1,378.6	1,363.1	26,042	25,569	1.1
Greenwood, MS	46,828	46,966	48,645	46,578	–1,817	2,067	–3.7	4.4	930.5	866.8	19,686	17,822	7.4
Carroll County, MS	10,397	10,512	10,777	9,237	–380	1,540	–3.5	16.7	210.7	194.1	19,972	18,009	8.6
Leflore County, MS	36,431	36,454	37,868	37,341	–1,437	527	–3.8	1.4	719.8	672.7	19,604	17,768	7.0
Greenwood, SC	67,979	67,592	66,334	59,567	1,645	6,767	2.5	11.4	1,582.4	1,531.7	23,552	23,092	3.3
Greenwood County, SC	67,979	67,592	66,334	59,567	1,645	6,767	2.5	11.4	1,582.4	1,531.7	23,552	23,092	3.3
Grenada, MS	22,861	22,748	23,198	21,555	–337	1,643	–1.5	7.6	491.2	460.9	21,372	19,871	6.6
Grenada County, MS	22,861	22,748	23,198	21,555	–337	1,643	–1.5	7.6	491.2	460.9	21,372	19,871	6.6
Guymon, OK	20,112	20,236	20,181	16,419	–69	3,762	–0.3	22.9	488.7	569.9	24,344	28,238	–14.3
Texas County, OK	20,112	20,236	20,181	16,419	–69	3,762	–0.3	22.9	488.7	569.9	24,344	28,238	–14.3
Hammond, LA	106,502	105,002	100,831	85,709	5,671	15,122	5.6	17.6	2,157.5	1,923.0	21,067	19,074	12.2
Tangipahoa Parish, LA	106,502	105,002	100,831	85,709	5,671	15,122	5.6	17.6	2,157.5	1,923.0	21,067	19,074	12.2
Hannibal, MO	38,136	37,930	37,948	36,158	188	1,790	0.5	5.0	868.0	842.7	23,017	22,209	3.0
Marion County, MO	28,375	28,278	28,283	27,682	92	601	0.3	2.2	655.5	630.3	23,384	22,286	4.0
Ralls County, MO	9,761	9,652	9,665	8,476	96	1,189	1.0	14.0	212.5	212.4	21,955	21,985	0.1
Harriman, TN	52,889	52,781	51,954	47,227	935	4,727	1.8	10.0	1,247.3	1,160.6	23,878	22,343	7.5
Roane County, TN	52,889	52,781	51,954	47,227	935	4,727	1.8	10.0	1,247.3	1,160.6	23,878	22,343	7.5
Harrisburg, IL	26,072	26,207	26,647	26,551	–575	96	–2.2	0.4	588.3	546.8	22,451	20,526	7.6
Saline County, IL	26,072	26,207	26,647	26,551	–575	96	–2.2	0.4	588.3	546.8	22,451	20,526	7.6
Harrison, AR	44,245	43,650	42,701	35,963	1,544	6,738	3.6	18.7	894.2	830.9	20,727	19,462	7.6
Boone County, AR	35,793	35,165	34,062	28,297	1,731	5,765	5.1	20.4	749.5	703.4	21,636	20,653	6.6
Newton County, AR	8,452	8,485	8,639	7,666	–187	973	–2.2	12.7	144.7	127.6	17,023	14,768	13.4
Hastings, NE	39,803	39,583	38,200	36,748	1,603	1,452	4.2	4.0	967.1	920.1	25,573	24,087	5.1
Adams County, NE	33,070	32,769	31,168	29,625	1,902	1,543	6.1	5.2	784.4	745.8	25,370	23,931	5.2
Clay County, NE	6,733	6,814	7,032	7,123	–299	–91	–4.3	–1.3	182.7	174.2	26,483	24,777	4.8
Havre, MT	16,304	16,343	16,636	17,654	–332	–1,018	–2.0	–5.8	399.4	372.7	24,437	22,412	7.2
Hill County, MT	16,304	16,343	16,636	17,654	–332	–1,018	–2.0	–5.8	399.4	372.7	24,437	22,412	7.2
Hays, KS	26,767	27,040	27,425	26,004	–658	1,421	–2.4	5.5	733.3	679.4	26,851	24,776	7.9
Ellis County, KS	26,767	27,040	27,425	26,004	–658	1,421	–2.4	5.5	733.3	679.4	26,851	24,776	7.9

See footnotes at end of table.

Micropolitan statistical area Component counties	Population 2005 (July 1)	2004 (July 1)	2000¹ (estimates base)	1990² (April 1)	Net change 2000–2005	1990–2000	Percent change 2000–2005	1990–2000	Personal income Total (mil. dol.) 2002	2000	Per capita³ (dollars) 2002	2000	Percent change 2000–2002
Heber, UT	18,974	18,134	15,436	10,089	3,538	5,347	22.9	53.0	366.0	321.3	21,627	20,819	13.9
Wasatch County, UT	18,974	18,134	15,436	10,089	3,538	5,347	22.9	53.0	366.0	321.3	21,627	20,819	13.9
Helena, MT	69,619	68,795	65,967	55,434	3,652	10,533	5.5	19.0	1,817.4	1,676.4	27,180	25,416	8.4
Jefferson County, MT	11,170	10,863	10,085	7,939	1,085	2,146	10.8	27.0	267.0	252.0	25,696	24,994	5.9
Lewis and Clark County, MT	58,449	57,932	55,882	47,495	2,567	8,387	4.6	17.7	1,550.4	1,424.4	27,453	25,493	8.8
Henderson, NC	43,771	43,721	43,156	38,892	615	4,264	1.4	11.0	960.4	905.1	21,880	20,976	6.1
Vance County, NC	43,771	43,721	43,156	38,892	615	4,264	1.4	11.0	960.4	905.1	21,880	20,976	6.1
Hereford, TX	18,538	18,509	18,519	19,153	19	−634	0.1	−3.3	413.2	451.6	22,498	24,392	−8.5
Deaf Smith County, TX	18,538	18,509	18,519	19,153	19	−634	0.1	−3.3	413.2	451.6	22,498	24,392	−8.5
Hilo, HI	167,293	162,601	149,285	120,317	18,008	28,968	12.1	24.1	3,645.6	3,195.3	23,547	21,409	14.1
Hawaii County, HI	167,293	162,601	149,285	120,317	18,008	28,968	12.1	24.1	3,645.6	3,195.3	23,547	21,409	14.1
Hilton Head Island-Beaufort, SC	159,247	155,155	142,741	101,912	16,506	40,829	11.6	40.1	4,938.1	4,326.4	32,745	30,317	14.1
Beaufort County, SC	137,849	133,883	122,022	86,425	15,827	35,597	13.0	41.2	4,536.5	3,959.9	34,935	32,464	14.6
Jasper County, SC	21,398	21,272	20,719	15,487	679	5,232	3.3	33.8	401.6	366.6	19,171	17,683	9.6
Hobbs, NM	56,719	56,110	55,192	55,765	1,527	−573	2.8	−1.0	1,251.5	1,103.5	22,503	19,998	13.4
Lea County, NM	56,719	56,110	55,192	55,765	1,527	−573	2.8	−1.0	1,251.5	1,103.5	22,503	19,998	13.4
Homosassa Springs, FL	134,370	130,273	118,656	93,515	15,714	25,141	13.2	26.9	2,887.3	2,635.4	23,341	22,215	9.6
Citrus County, FL	134,370	130,273	118,656	93,515	15,714	25,141	13.2	26.9	2,887.3	2,635.4	23,341	22,215	9.6
Hood River, OR	21,284	21,084	20,480	16,903	804	3,577	3.9	21.2	498.6	467.3	24,151	22,821	6.7
Hood River County, OR	21,284	21,084	20,480	16,903	804	3,577	3.9	21.2	498.6	467.3	24,151	22,821	6.7
Hope, AR	23,383	33,003	33,505	31,722	−10,122	1,783	−30.2	5.6	677.8	627.8	20,447	18,742	8.0
Hempstead County, AR	23,383	23,436	23,577	21,621	−194	1,956	−0.8	9.0	475.1	440.4	20,264	18,686	7.9
Nevada County, AR	9,550	9,567	9,928	10,101	−378	−173	−3.8	−1.7	202.7	187.4	20,888	18,874	8.2
Houghton, MI	37,900	37,907	38,274	37,147	−374	1,127	−1.0	3.0	782.9	747.3	20,434	19,507	4.8
Houghton County, MI	35,705	35,692	35,965	35,446	−260	519	−0.7	1.5	733.0	699.0	20,319	19,417	4.9
Keweenaw County, MI	2,195	2,215	2,309	1,701	−114	608	−4.9	35.7	49.9	48.3	22,288	20,900	3.4
Hudson, NY	63,622	63,586	63,076	62,982	546	94	0.9	0.1	1,832.4	1,802.6	28,980	28,580	1.7
Columbia County, NY	63,622	63,586	63,076	62,982	546	94	0.9	0.1	1,832.4	1,802.6	28,980	28,580	1.7
Humboldt, TN	48,148	47,992	48,172	46,315	−24	1,857	0.0	4.0	1,109.1	1,075.8	23,063	22,335	3.1
Gibson County, TN	48,148	47,992	48,172	46,315	−24	1,857	0.0	4.0	1,109.1	1,075.8	23,063	22,335	3.1
Huntingdon, PA	45,947	45,920	45,598	44,164	349	1,434	0.8	3.2	940.8	884.7	20,519	19,403	6.3
Huntingdon County, PA	45,947	45,920	45,598	44,164	349	1,434	0.8	3.2	940.8	884.7	20,519	19,403	6.3
Huntington, IN	38,236	38,110	38,100	35,427	136	2,673	0.4	7.5	982.4	964.0	25,715	25,304	1.9
Huntington County, IN	38,236	38,110	38,100	35,427	136	2,673	0.4	7.5	982.4	964.0	25,715	25,304	1.9
Huntsville, TX	62,735	62,761	61,695	50,917	1,040	10,778	1.7	21.2	1,104.8	1,047.7	17,899	16,985	5.4
Walker County, TX	62,735	62,761	61,695	50,917	1,040	10,778	1.7	21.2	1,104.8	1,047.7	17,899	16,985	5.4
Huron, SD	15,896	16,008	16,978	18,253	−1,082	−1,275	−6.4	−7.0	455.3	456.6	27,501	26,892	−0.3
Beadle County, SD	15,896	16,008	16,978	18,253	−1,082	−1,275	−6.4	−7.0	455.3	456.6	27,501	26,892	−0.3
Hutchinson, KS	63,558	63,556	64,687	62,389	−1,129	2,298	−1.7	3.7	1,586.3	1,549.5	24,789	23,955	2.4
Reno County, KS	63,558	63,556	64,687	62,389	−1,129	2,298	−1.7	3.7	1,586.3	1,549.5	24,789	23,955	2.4
Hutchinson, MN	36,636	36,199	34,874	32,030	1,762	2,844	5.1	8.9	970.5	930.3	27,224	26,678	4.3
McLeod County, MN	36,636	36,199	34,874	32,030	1,762	2,844	5.1	8.9	970.5	930.3	27,224	26,678	4.3
Indiana, PA	88,703	88,929	89,531	89,994	−828	−463	−0.9	−0.5	2,116.5	2,005.3	23,802	22,396	5.5
Indiana County, PA	88,703	88,929	89,531	89,994	−828	−463	−0.9	−0.5	2,116.5	2,005.3	23,802	22,396	5.5
Indianola, MS	32,311	32,558	34,281	32,867	−1,970	1,414	−5.7	4.3	525.9	537.2	15,537	15,672	−2.1
Sunflower County, MS	32,311	32,558	34,281	32,867	−1,970	1,414	−5.7	4.3	525.9	537.2	15,537	15,672	−2.1
Iron Mountain, MI-WI	33,006	32,688	32,582	31,421	424	1,161	1.3	3.7	865.0	805.0	26,720	24,710	7.4
Dickinson County, MI	28,032	27,671	27,481	26,831	551	650	2.0	2.4	743.8	694.1	27,298	25,258	7.2
Florence County, WI	4,974	5,017	5,101	4,590	−127	511	−2.5	11.1	121.2	110.9	23,648	21,759	9.2
Jackson, WY-ID	26,499	26,209	24,466	14,611	2,033	9,855	8.3	67.4	1,462.8	1,267.2	57,632	51,798	15.4
Teton County, ID	7,467	7,208	6,108	3,439	1,359	2,669	22.2	77.6	137.1	113.8	20,072	18,612	20.5
Teton County, WY	19,032	19,001	18,358	11,172	674	7,186	3.7	64.3	1,325.7	1,153.5	71,457	62,852	14.9
Jacksonville, IL	41,134	41,383	42,158	42,041	−1,024	117	−2.4	0.3	981.5	948.7	23,606	22,504	3.5
Morgan County, IL	35,722	35,960	36,609	36,397	−887	212	−2.4	0.6	868.5	835.2	24,079	22,813	4.0
Scott County, IL	5,412	5,423	5,549	5,644	−137	−95	−2.5	−1.7	113.0	113.5	20,509	20,462	−0.4
Jacksonville, TX	48,464	48,096	46,683	41,049	1,781	5,634	3.8	13.7	1,135.7	1,034.7	24,165	22,167	9.8
Cherokee County, TX	48,464	48,096	46,683	41,049	1,781	5,634	3.8	13.7	1,135.7	1,034.7	24,165	22,167	9.8
Jamestown, ND	20,835	20,930	21,853	22,241	−1,018	−388	−4.7	−1.7	550.0	517.5	25,716	23,686	6.3
Stutsman County, ND	20,835	20,930	21,853	22,241	−1,018	−388	−4.7	−1.7	550.0	517.5	25,716	23,686	6.3
Jamestown-Dunkirk-Fredonia, NY	136,409	137,143	139,599	141,895	−3,190	−2,296	−2.3	−1.6	3,078.9	2,985.2	22,263	21,385	3.1
Chautauqua County, NY	136,409	137,143	139,599	141,895	−3,190	−2,296	−2.3	−1.6	3,078.9	2,985.2	22,263	21,385	3.1
Jasper, IN	53,624	53,527	52,524	49,125	1,100	3,399	2.1	6.9	1,537.0	1,461.1	29,045	27,820	5.2
Dubois County, IN	40,858	40,600	39,704	36,616	1,154	3,088	2.9	8.4	1,257.8	1,188.8	31,466	29,941	5.8
Pike County, IN	12,766	12,927	12,820	12,509	−54	311	−0.4	2.5	279.2	272.4	21,571	21,251	2.5
Jennings, LA	31,272	31,179	31,409	30,722	−137	687	−0.4	2.2	573.9	528.0	18,449	16,812	8.7
Jefferson Davis Parish, LA	31,272	31,179	31,409	30,722	−137	687	−0.4	2.2	573.9	528.0	18,449	16,812	8.7
Jesup, GA	28,390	28,092	26,617	22,356	1,773	4,261	6.7	19.1	569.3	536.4	21,037	20,155	6.1
Wayne County, GA	28,390	28,092	26,617	22,356	1,773	4,261	6.7	19.1	569.3	536.4	21,037	20,155	6.1
Juneau, AK	30,987	31,111	30,680	26,751	307	3,929	1.0	14.7	1,110.2	1,066.5	36,086	34,772	4.1
Juneau City and Borough, AK	30,987	31,111	30,680	26,751	307	3,929	1.0	14.7	1,110.2	1,066.5	36,086	34,772	4.1
Kahului-Wailuku, HI	139,884	138,004	128,781	100,374	11,103	28,407	8.6	28.3	3,611.2	3,240.7	27,087	25,141	11.4
Maui County, HI	139,884	138,004	128,781	100,374	11,103	28,407	8.6	28.3	3,611.2	3,240.7	27,087	25,141	11.4
Kalispell, MT	83,172	81,114	74,743	59,218	8,429	15,525	11.3	26.2	1,981.2	1,793.9	25,583	24,004	10.4
Flathead County, MT	83,172	81,114	74,743	59,218	8,429	15,525	11.3	26.2	1,981.2	1,793.9	25,583	24,004	10.4
Kapaa, HI	62,640	61,836	58,536	51,177	4,104	7,359	7.0	14.4	1,506.9	1,410.1	25,132	24,089	6.9
Kauai County, HI	62,640	61,836	58,536	51,177	4,104	7,359	7.0	14.4	1,506.9	1,410.1	25,132	24,089	6.9
Kearney, NE	50,346	50,265	49,201	44,076	1,145	5,125	2.3	11.6	1,261.3	1,157.3	25,392	23,520	9.0
Buffalo County, NE	43,572	43,411	42,316	37,447	1,256	4,869	3.0	13.0	1,071.2	977.1	24,995	23,088	9.6
Kearney County, NE	6,774	6,854	6,885	6,629	−111	256	−1.6	3.9	190.2	180.2	27,892	26,179	5.5
Keene, NH	77,287	76,784	73,994	70,121	3,293	3,873	4.5	5.5	2,236.3	2,087.6	29,842	28,217	7.1
Cheshire County, NH	77,287	76,784	73,994	70,121	3,293	3,873	4.5	5.5	2,236.3	2,087.6	29,842	28,217	7.1
Kendallville, IN	47,448	47,154	46,438	37,877	1,010	8,561	2.2	22.6	1,115.0	1,081.6	23,728	23,292	3.1
Noble County, IN	47,448	47,154	46,438	37,877	1,010	8,561	2.2	22.6	1,115.0	1,081.6	23,728	23,292	3.1
Kennett, MO	32,545	32,420	33,105	33,112	−560	−7	−1.7	0.0	679.5	643.7	20,704	19,445	5.6
Dunklin County, MO	32,545	32,420	33,105	33,112	−560	−7	−1.7	0.0	679.5	643.7	20,704	19,445	5.6

See footnotes at end of table.

Table D-1. Micropolitan Areas — **Population and Personal Income**—Con.

Micropolitan statistical area Component counties	Population				Net change		Percent change		Personal income Total (mil. dol.)		Per capita[3] (dollars)		Percent change
	2005 (July 1)	2004 (July 1)	2000[1] (esti-mates base)	1990[2] (April 1)	2000–2005	1990–2000	2000–2005	1990–2000	2002	2000	2002	2000	2000–2002
Keokuk-Fort Madison, IA-MO	36,705	44,093	45,331	46,234	−8,626	−903	−19.0	−2.0	1,055.0	1,038.2	23,717	22,905	1.6
Lee County, IA	36,705	36,745	37,939	38,687	−1,234	−748	−3.3	−1.9	904.8	888.0	24,455	23,406	1.9
Clark County, MO	7,323	7,348	7,392	7,547	−69	−155	−0.9	−2.1	150.2	150.2	20,067	20,329	0.0
Kerrville, TX	46,496	45,943	43,838	36,304	2,658	7,534	6.1	20.8	1,318.5	1,157.9	29,416	26,420	13.9
Kerr County, TX	46,496	45,943	43,838	36,304	2,658	7,534	6.1	20.8	1,318.5	1,157.9	29,416	26,420	13.9
Ketchikan, AK	13,262	13,229	13,982	13,828	−720	154	−5.1	1.1	501.7	480.9	37,012	34,391	4.3
Ketchikan Gateway Borough, AK	13,262	13,229	13,982	13,828	−720	154	−5.1	1.1	501.7	480.9	37,012	34,391	4.3
Key West-Marathon, FL	76,329	78,016	79,480	78,024	−3,151	1,456	−4.0	1.9	3,075.9	2,941.5	38,905	37,019	4.6
Monroe County, FL	76,329	78,016	79,480	78,024	−3,151	1,456	−4.0	1.9	3,075.9	2,941.5	38,905	37,019	4.6
Kill Devil Hills, NC	33,903	33,584	30,195	22,746	3,708	7,449	12.3	32.7	928.2	810.8	28,908	26,853	14.5
Dare County, NC	33,903	33,584	30,195	22,746	3,708	7,449	12.3	32.7	928.2	810.8	28,908	26,853	14.5
Kingsville, TX	31,174	31,306	31,932	30,734	−758	1,198	−2.4	3.9	632.2	577.9	19,976	18,098	9.4
Kenedy County, TX	417	407	415	460	2	−45	0.5	−9.8	10.5	10.6	25,650	25,504	−0.4
Kleberg County, TX	30,757	30,899	31,517	30,274	−760	1,243	−2.4	4.1	621.6	567.4	19,901	18,000	9.6
Kinston, NC	57,961	58,155	59,499	57,274	−1,538	2,225	−2.6	3.9	1,407.6	1,403.2	23,936	23,589	0.3
Lenoir County, NC	57,961	58,155	59,499	57,274	−1,538	2,225	−2.6	3.9	1,407.6	1,403.2	23,936	23,589	0.3
Kirksville, MO	28,817	28,935	29,098	28,813	−281	285	−1.0	1.0	606.8	567.2	20,791	19,475	7.0
Adair County, MO	24,509	24,626	24,925	24,577	−416	348	−1.7	1.4	524.9	492.2	21,021	19,729	6.6
Schuyler County, MO	4,308	4,309	4,173	4,236	135	−63	3.2	−1.5	82.0	75.0	19,433	17,960	9.3
Klamath Falls, OR	66,192	65,268	63,932	57,702	2,260	6,230	3.5	10.8	1,479.2	1,362.1	23,002	21,307	8.6
Klamath County, OR	66,192	65,268	63,932	57,702	2,260	6,230	3.5	10.8	1,479.2	1,362.1	23,002	21,307	8.6
Kodiak, AK	13,051	13,231	13,980	13,309	−929	671	−6.6	5.0	399.8	373.2	29,255	26,681	7.1
Kodiak Island Borough, AK	13,051	13,231	13,980	13,309	−929	671	−6.6	5.0	399.8	373.2	29,255	26,681	7.1
Laconia, NH	61,547	60,984	56,578	49,216	4,969	7,362	8.8	15.0	1,912.4	1,701.9	32,318	30,082	12.4
Belknap County, NH	61,547	60,984	56,578	49,216	4,969	7,362	8.8	15.0	1,912.4	1,701.9	32,318	30,082	12.4
La Follette, TN	40,686	40,570	39,940	35,079	746	4,861	1.9	13.9	815.2	710.7	20,409	17,795	14.7
Campbell County, TN	40,686	40,570	39,940	35,079	746	4,861	1.9	13.9	815.2	710.7	20,409	17,795	14.7
La Grande, OR	24,540	24,445	24,548	23,598	−8	950	0.0	4.0	586.6	559.0	24,007	22,767	4.9
Union County, OR	24,540	24,445	24,548	23,598	−8	950	0.0	4.0	586.6	559.0	24,007	22,767	4.9
LaGrange, GA	62,015	61,132	58,937	55,536	3,078	3,401	5.2	6.1	1,503.1	1,418.6	25,121	24,073	6.0
Troup County, GA	62,015	61,132	58,937	55,536	3,078	3,401	5.2	6.1	1,503.1	1,418.6	25,121	24,073	6.0
Lake City, FL	64,040	61,710	56,760	42,613	7,280	14,147	12.8	33.2	1,141.7	1,063.4	19,547	18,736	7.4
Columbia County, FL	64,040	61,710	56,760	42,613	7,280	14,147	12.8	33.2	1,141.7	1,063.4	19,547	18,736	7.4
Lake Havasu City-Kingman, AZ	187,200	179,563	156,272	93,497	30,928	62,775	19.8	67.1	3,295.3	2,908.2	19,914	18,613	13.3
Mohave County, AZ	187,200	179,563	156,272	93,497	30,928	62,775	19.8	67.1	3,295.3	2,908.2	19,914	18,613	13.3
Lamesa, TX	14,256	14,257	14,959	14,349	−703	610	−4.7	4.3	279.0	270.1	19,208	18,051	3.3
Dawson County, TX	14,256	14,257	14,959	14,349	−703	610	−4.7	4.3	279.0	270.1	19,208	18,051	3.3
Lancaster, SC	63,113	62,950	61,404	54,516	1,709	6,888	2.8	12.6	1,338.4	1,264.3	21,513	20,594	5.9
Lancaster County, SC	63,113	62,950	61,404	54,516	1,709	6,888	2.8	12.6	1,338.4	1,264.3	21,513	20,594	5.9
Laramie, WY	30,890	31,397	31,833	30,797	−943	1,036	−3.0	3.4	839.1	742.8	26,379	23,322	13.0
Albany County, WY	30,890	31,397	31,833	30,797	−943	1,036	−3.0	3.4	839.1	742.8	26,379	23,322	13.0
Las Vegas, NM	29,530	29,488	30,096	25,743	−566	4,353	−1.9	16.9	590.8	496.2	19,851	16,489	19.0
San Miguel County, NM	29,530	29,488	30,096	25,743	−566	4,353	−1.9	16.9	590.8	496.2	19,851	16,489	19.0
Laurel, MS	84,322	83,787	83,106	79,145	1,216	3,961	1.5	5.0	1,821.2	1,671.6	21,856	20,117	9.0
Jasper County, MS	18,162	18,144	18,124	17,114	38	1,010	0.2	5.9	339.5	301.9	18,571	16,659	12.5
Jones County, MS	66,160	65,643	64,982	62,031	1,178	2,951	1.8	4.8	1,481.8	1,369.7	22,780	21,081	8.2
Laurinburg, NC	37,180	37,077	36,022	33,754	1,158	2,268	3.2	6.7	759.3	739.9	21,284	20,544	2.6
Scotland County, NC	37,180	37,077	36,022	33,754	1,158	2,268	3.2	6.7	759.3	739.9	21,284	20,544	2.6
Lawrenceburg, TN	41,101	40,743	39,962	35,303	1,139	4,659	2.9	13.2	861.1	808.5	21,200	20,235	6.5
Lawrence County, TN	41,101	40,743	39,962	35,303	1,139	4,659	2.9	13.2	861.1	808.5	21,200	20,235	6.5
Lebanon, MO	34,492	33,649	32,594	27,158	1,898	5,436	5.8	20.0	689.0	632.7	20,932	19,410	8.9
Laclede County, MO	34,492	33,649	32,594	27,158	1,898	5,436	5.8	20.0	689.0	632.7	20,932	19,410	8.9
Lebanon, NH-VT	172,023	171,441	167,637	155,133	4,386	12,504	2.6	8.1	5,330.1	4,892.9	31,366	29,183	8.9
Grafton County, NH	84,708	84,187	81,826	74,929	2,882	6,897	3.5	9.2	2,795.7	2,565.1	33,574	31,338	9.0
Orange County, VT	29,287	29,190	28,310	26,149	977	2,161	3.5	8.3	746.6	663.5	25,913	23,438	12.5
Windsor County, VT	58,028	58,064	57,501	54,055	527	3,446	0.9	6.4	1,787.7	1,664.3	30,905	28,944	7.4
Levelland, TX	22,787	22,779	22,664	24,199	123	−1,535	0.5	−6.3	501.1	463.8	22,100	20,463	8.0
Hockley County, TX	22,787	22,779	22,664	24,199	123	−1,535	0.5	−6.3	501.1	463.8	22,100	20,463	8.0
Lewisburg, PA	43,131	42,881	41,659	36,176	1,472	5,483	3.5	15.2	974.6	913.1	23,091	21,917	6.7
Union County, PA	43,131	42,881	41,659	36,176	1,472	5,483	3.5	15.2	974.6	913.1	23,091	21,917	6.7
Lewisburg, TN	28,372	27,950	26,878	21,539	1,494	5,339	5.6	24.8	699.2	659.3	25,524	24,532	6.1
Marshall County, TN	28,372	27,950	26,878	21,539	1,494	5,339	5.6	24.8	699.2	659.3	25,524	24,532	6.1
Lewistown, PA	46,235	46,191	46,498	46,197	−263	301	−0.6	0.7	1,011.9	951.4	21,772	20,464	6.4
Mifflin County, PA	46,235	46,191	46,498	46,197	−263	301	−0.6	0.7	1,011.9	951.4	21,772	20,464	6.4
Lexington, NE	26,637	26,598	26,551	21,868	86	4,683	0.3	21.4	603.7	583.9	22,780	21,988	3.4
Dawson County, NE	24,617	24,551	24,408	19,940	209	4,468	0.9	22.4	550.1	534.1	22,522	21,880	3.0
Gosper County, NE	2,020	2,047	2,143	1,928	−123	215	−5.7	11.2	53.6	49.7	25,818	23,222	7.8
Lexington Park, MD	96,518	94,950	86,529	75,974	9,989	10,555	11.5	13.9	2,763.7	2,511.1	30,658	29,026	10.1
St. Mary's County, MD	96,518	94,950	86,529	75,974	9,989	10,555	11.5	13.9	2,763.7	2,511.1	30,658	29,026	10.1
Liberal, KS	23,274	23,256	22,552	18,743	722	3,809	3.2	20.3	511.0	498.0	22,222	22,093	2.6
Seward County, KS	23,274	23,256	22,552	18,743	722	3,809	3.2	20.3	511.0	498.0	22,222	22,093	2.6
Lincoln, IL	30,603	30,715	31,156	30,798	−553	358	−1.8	1.2	708.5	689.2	22,984	22,123	2.8
Logan County, IL	30,603	30,715	31,156	30,798	−553	358	−1.8	1.2	708.5	689.2	22,984	22,123	2.8
Lincolnton, NC	69,851	68,089	64,049	50,319	5,802	13,730	9.1	27.3	1,565.1	1,493.2	23,638	23,316	4.8
Lincoln County, NC	69,851	68,089	64,049	50,319	5,802	13,730	9.1	27.3	1,565.1	1,493.2	23,638	23,316	4.8
Lock Haven, PA	37,439	37,311	37,929	37,182	−490	747	−1.3	2.0	859.7	791.3	22,888	20,866	8.6
Clinton County, PA	37,439	37,311	37,929	37,182	−490	747	−1.3	2.0	859.7	791.3	22,888	20,866	8.6
Logansport, IN	40,130	40,324	40,979	38,413	−849	2,566	−2.1	6.7	1,014.0	1,005.9	25,000	24,546	0.8
Cass County, IN	40,130	40,324	40,979	38,413	−849	2,566	−2.1	6.7	1,014.0	1,005.9	25,000	24,546	0.8
London, KY	56,338	55,796	52,928	43,438	3,410	9,490	6.4	21.8	1,114.9	1,054.6	20,468	19,928	5.7
Laurel County, KY	56,338	55,796	52,928	43,438	3,410	9,490	6.4	21.8	1,114.9	1,054.6	20,468	19,928	5.7

See footnotes at end of table.

Table D-1. Micropolitan Areas — **Population and Personal Income**—Con.

Micropolitan statistical area Component counties	Population 2005 (July 1)	2004 (July 1)	2000[1] (esti-mates base)	1990[2] (April 1)	Net change 2000–2005	1990–2000	Percent change 2000–2005	1990–2000	Personal income Total (mil. dol.) 2002	2000	Per capita[3] (dollars) 2002	2000	Percent change 2000–2002
Los Alamos, NM	18,822	18,753	18,287	18,115	535	172	2.9	0.9	887.5	762.3	48,485	41,669	16.4
Los Alamos County, NM	18,822	18,753	18,287	18,115	535	172	2.9	0.9	887.5	762.3	48,485	41,669	16.4
Lufkin, TX	81,557	81,272	80,264	69,884	1,293	10,380	1.6	14.9	1,991.2	1,797.8	24,775	22,403	10.8
Angelina County, TX	81,557	81,272	80,264	69,884	1,293	10,380	1.6	14.9	1,991.2	1,797.8	24,775	22,403	10.8
Lumberton, NC	127,586	126,263	123,399	105,179	4,187	18,220	3.4	17.3	2,286.4	2,212.7	18,328	17,935	3.3
Robeson County, NC	127,586	126,263	123,399	105,179	4,187	18,220	3.4	17.3	2,286.4	2,212.7	18,328	17,935	3.3
Macomb, IL	31,966	32,301	32,860	35,244	−894	−2,384	−2.7	−6.8	710.2	682.8	21,516	20,773	4.0
McDonough County, IL	31,966	32,301	32,860	35,244	−894	−2,384	−2.7	−6.8	710.2	682.8	21,516	20,773	4.0
Madison, IN	32,430	32,204	31,726	29,797	704	1,929	2.2	6.5	727.1	681.4	22,546	21,478	6.7
Jefferson County, IN	32,430	32,204	31,726	29,797	704	1,929	2.2	6.5	727.1	681.4	22,546	21,478	6.7
Madisonville, KY	46,705	46,736	46,479	46,126	226	353	0.5	0.8	1,070.2	1,014.2	23,039	21,825	5.5
Hopkins County, KY	46,705	46,736	46,479	46,126	226	353	0.5	0.8	1,070.2	1,014.2	23,039	21,825	5.5
Magnolia, AR	24,695	24,885	25,572	25,691	−877	−119	−3.4	−0.5	597.7	556.9	23,642	21,776	7.3
Columbia County, AR	24,695	24,885	25,572	25,691	−877	−119	−3.4	−0.5	597.7	556.9	23,642	21,776	7.3
Malone, NY	51,033	50,931	51,124	46,540	−91	4,584	−0.2	9.8	1,027.0	962.0	20,232	18,819	6.8
Franklin County, NY	51,033	50,931	51,124	46,540	−91	4,584	−0.2	9.8	1,027.0	962.0	20,232	18,819	6.8
Manhattan, KS	106,540	107,104	108,794	113,720	−2,254	−4,926	−2.1	−4.3	2,700.2	2,487.7	25,386	22,835	8.5
Geary County, KS	24,585	25,145	27,733	30,453	−3,148	−2,720	−11.4	−8.9	715.3	660.2	27,077	23,784	8.3
Pottawatomie County, KS	19,129	18,890	18,286	16,128	843	2,158	4.6	13.4	485.2	437.5	26,330	23,929	10.9
Riley County, KS	62,826	63,069	62,775	67,139	51	−4,364	0.1	−6.5	1,499.7	1,390.0	24,377	22,099	7.9
Manitowoc, WI	81,949	81,822	82,940	80,421	−991	2,519	−1.2	3.1	2,233.2	2,169.1	27,097	26,152	3.0
Manitowoc County, WI	81,949	81,822	82,940	80,421	−991	2,519	−1.2	3.1	2,233.2	2,169.1	27,097	26,152	3.0
Mankato-North Mankato, MN	88,878	88,234	85,819	82,120	3,059	3,699	3.6	4.5	2,418.5	2,242.5	27,702	26,126	7.8
Blue Earth County, MN	58,030	57,385	55,915	54,044	2,115	1,871	3.8	3.5	1,577.2	1,448.8	27,763	25,907	8.9
Nicollet County, MN	30,848	30,849	29,904	28,076	944	1,828	3.2	6.5	841.3	793.8	27,590	26,535	6.0
Marinette, WI-MI	68,402	68,366	68,753	65,468	−351	3,285	−0.5	5.0	1,620.5	1,541.8	23,651	22,430	5.1
Menominee County, MI	24,996	25,119	25,296	24,920	−300	376	−1.2	1.5	559.2	555.1	22,245	21,948	0.7
Marinette County, WI	43,406	43,247	43,457	40,548	−51	2,909	−0.1	7.2	1,061.3	986.7	24,466	22,710	7.6
Marion, IN	70,557	71,256	73,277	74,169	−2,720	−892	−3.7	−1.2	1,763.8	1,641.5	24,474	22,403	7.5
Grant County, IN	70,557	71,256	73,277	74,169	−2,720	−892	−3.7	−1.2	1,763.8	1,641.5	24,474	22,403	7.5
Marion, OH	65,932	66,073	66,147	64,274	−215	1,873	−0.3	2.9	1,574.0	1,490.2	23,759	22,533	5.6
Marion County, OH	65,932	66,073	66,147	64,274	−215	1,873	−0.3	2.9	1,574.0	1,490.2	23,759	22,533	5.6
Marion-Herrin, IL	63,617	63,124	61,244	57,733	2,373	3,511	3.9	6.1	1,496.8	1,367.9	24,101	22,341	9.4
Williamson County, IL	63,617	63,124	61,244	57,733	2,373	3,511	3.9	6.1	1,496.8	1,367.9	24,101	22,341	9.4
Marquette, MI	64,760	64,903	64,614	70,887	146	−6,273	0.2	−8.8	1,504.2	1,441.9	23,262	22,315	4.3
Marquette County, MI	64,760	64,903	64,614	70,887	146	−6,273	0.2	−8.8	1,504.2	1,441.9	23,262	22,315	4.3
Marshall, MN	24,472	24,595	25,434	24,789	−962	645	−3.8	2.6	705.7	660.2	28,259	25,954	6.9
Lyon County, MN	24,472	24,595	25,434	24,789	−962	645	−3.8	2.6	705.7	660.2	28,259	25,954	6.9
Marshall, MO	23,075	23,017	23,742	23,523	−667	219	−2.8	0.9	557.5	534.8	24,231	22,529	4.2
Saline County, MO	23,075	23,017	23,742	23,523	−667	219	−2.8	0.9	557.5	534.8	24,231	22,529	4.2
Marshall, TX	63,459	62,924	62,095	57,483	1,364	4,612	2.2	8.0	1,424.5	1,338.8	22,806	21,565	6.4
Harrison County, TX	63,459	62,924	62,095	57,483	1,364	4,612	2.2	8.0	1,424.5	1,338.8	22,806	21,565	6.4
Marshalltown, IA	39,418	39,441	39,324	38,276	94	1,048	0.2	2.7	1,078.5	1,002.2	27,486	25,485	7.6
Marshall County, IA	39,418	39,441	39,324	38,276	94	1,048	0.2	2.7	1,078.5	1,002.2	27,486	25,485	7.6
Martin, TN	33,732	33,658	34,895	31,972	−1,163	2,923	−3.3	9.1	742.0	716.4	21,625	20,526	3.6
Weakley County, TN	33,732	33,658	34,895	31,972	−1,163	2,923	−3.3	9.1	742.0	716.4	21,625	20,526	3.6
Martinsville, VA	71,426	71,786	73,306	73,104	−1,880	202	−2.6	0.3	1,676.8	1,581.4	23,144	21,578	6.0
Henry County, VA	56,501	56,875	57,972	56,942	−1,471	1,030	−2.5	1.8	[4]1,676.8	[4]1,581.4	[4]23,143.9	[4]21,577.8	[4]6.0
Martinsville city, VA	14,925	14,911	15,334	16,162	−409	−828	−2.7	−5.1	([4])	([4])	([4])	([4])	([4])
Maryville, MO	21,710	21,708	21,864	21,709	−154	155	−0.7	0.7	430.6	415.9	19,717	19,021	3.6
Nodaway County, MO	21,710	21,708	21,864	21,709	−154	155	−0.7	0.7	430.6	415.9	19,717	19,021	3.6
Mason City, IA	52,413	52,581	54,247	54,724	−1,834	−477	−3.4	−0.9	1,461.8	1,389.6	27,526	25,621	5.2
Cerro Gordo County, IA	44,645	44,836	46,336	46,733	−1,691	−397	−3.6	−0.8	1,289.4	1,216.8	28,460	26,265	6.0
Worth County, IA	7,768	7,745	7,911	7,991	−143	−80	−1.8	−1.0	172.4	172.8	22,103	21,848	−0.3
Mayfield, KY	37,625	37,352	37,077	33,550	548	3,527	1.5	10.5	818.5	789.1	22,070	21,288	3.7
Graves County, KY	37,625	37,352	37,077	33,550	548	3,527	1.5	10.5	818.5	789.1	22,070	21,288	3.7
Maysville, KY	31,012	30,769	30,931	29,695	81	1,236	0.3	4.2	598.7	569.9	19,490	18,425	5.1
Lewis County, KY	13,872	13,853	14,133	13,029	−261	1,104	−1.8	8.5	208.4	201.7	15,057	14,272	3.3
Mason County, KY	17,140	16,916	16,798	16,666	342	132	2.0	0.8	390.2	368.2	23,126	21,918	6.0
McAlester, OK	44,641	44,239	43,969	40,581	672	3,388	1.5	8.3	910.7	836.1	20,636	19,017	8.9
Pittsburg County, OK	44,641	44,239	43,969	40,581	672	3,388	1.5	8.3	910.7	836.1	20,636	19,017	8.9
McComb, MS	52,861	52,517	52,576	50,210	285	2,366	0.5	4.7	1,037.1	950.1	19,790	18,074	9.2
Amite County, MS	13,435	13,420	13,584	13,328	−149	256	−1.1	1.9	262.4	236.6	19,429	17,422	10.9
Pike County, MS	39,426	39,097	38,992	36,882	434	2,110	1.1	5.7	774.7	713.5	19,916	18,302	8.6
McMinnville, TN	39,753	39,502	38,405	32,992	1,348	5,413	3.5	16.4	870.8	821.0	22,510	21,377	6.1
Warren County, TN	39,753	39,502	38,405	32,992	1,348	5,413	3.5	16.4	870.8	821.0	22,510	21,377	6.1
McPherson, KS	29,523	29,413	29,584	27,268	−61	2,316	−0.2	8.5	805.6	759.9	27,438	25,684	6.0
McPherson County, KS	29,523	29,413	29,584	27,268	−61	2,316	−0.2	8.5	805.6	759.9	27,438	25,684	6.0
Meadville, PA	89,442	89,725	90,390	86,169	−948	4,221	−1.0	4.9	2,020.0	2,062.7	22,433	22,823	−2.1
Crawford County, PA	89,442	89,725	90,390	86,169	−948	4,221	−1.0	4.9	2,020.0	2,062.7	22,433	22,823	−2.1
Menomonie, WI	41,708	41,460	39,956	35,909	1,752	4,047	4.4	11.3	932.2	877.6	22,859	21,963	6.2
Dunn County, WI	41,708	41,460	39,956	35,909	1,752	4,047	4.4	11.3	932.2	877.6	22,859	21,963	6.2
Meridian, MS	105,134	105,572	106,485	103,224	−1,351	3,261	−1.3	3.2	2,423.3	2,241.5	22,863	21,056	8.1
Clarke County, MS	17,670	17,703	17,969	17,313	−299	656	−1.7	3.8	349.2	313.5	19,578	17,452	11.4
Kemper County, MS	10,246	10,373	10,428	10,356	−182	72	−1.7	0.7	190.7	174.0	18,104	16,693	9.6
Lauderdale County, MS	77,218	77,496	78,088	75,555	−870	2,533	−1.1	3.4	1,883.5	1,754.1	24,264	22,468	7.4
Merrill, WI	30,319	30,205	29,715	26,993	604	2,722	2.0	10.1	737.3	682.9	24,588	22,981	8.0
Lincoln County, WI	30,319	30,205	29,715	26,993	604	2,722	2.0	10.1	737.3	682.9	24,588	22,981	8.0
Mexico, MO	25,759	25,670	25,802	23,599	−43	2,203	−0.2	9.3	572.0	576.1	22,158	22,331	−0.7
Audrain County, MO	25,759	25,670	25,802	23,599	−43	2,203	−0.2	9.3	572.0	576.1	22,158	22,331	−0.7
Miami, OK	32,866	32,818	33,253	30,561	−387	2,692	−1.2	8.8	653.6	621.2	19,880	18,681	5.2
Ottawa County, OK	32,866	32,818	33,253	30,561	−387	2,692	−1.2	8.8	653.6	621.2	19,880	18,681	5.2
Middlesborough, KY	29,665	29,724	30,043	31,506	−378	−1,463	−1.3	−4.6	525.5	497.9	17,521	16,578	5.5
Bell County, KY	29,665	29,724	30,043	31,506	−378	−1,463	−1.3	−4.6	525.5	497.9	17,521	16,578	5.5

See footnotes at end of table.

State and Metropolitan Area Data Book: 2006

Micropolitan statistical area Component counties	Population								Personal income				
			2000[1] (esti- mates base)	1990[2] (April 1)	Net change		Percent change		Total (mil. dol.)		Per capita[3] (dollars)		Percent change
	2005 (July 1)	2004 (July 1)			2000–2005	1990–2000	2000–2005	1990–2000	2002	2000	2002	2000	2000–2002
Midland, MI.	84,064	84,236	83,007	75,651	1,057	7,356	1.3	9.7	2,600.6	2,621.8	30,964	31,579	-0.8
Midland County, MI. . . .	84,064	84,236	83,007	75,651	1,057	7,356	1.3	9.7	2,600.6	2,621.8	30,964	31,579	-0.8
Milledgeville, GA	54,873	55,066	54,796	48,438	77	6,358	0.1	13.1	1,216.9	1,090.5	22,085	19,900	11.6
Baldwin County, GA	45,230	45,234	44,745	39,530	485	5,215	1.1	13.2	1,063.1	952.4	23,596	21,282	11.6
Hancock County, GA	9,643	9,832	10,051	8,908	-408	1,143	-4.1	12.8	153.8	138.2	15,310	13,747	11.3
Minden, LA	41,356	41,273	41,736	41,989	-380	-253	-0.9	-0.6	907.4	833.2	21,856	19,965	8.9
Webster Parish, LA.	41,356	41,273	41,736	41,989	-380	-253	-0.9	-0.6	907.4	833.2	21,856	19,965	8.9
Mineral Wells, TX	27,478	27,250	27,088	25,055	390	2,033	1.4	8.1	632.9	585.5	23,316	21,616	8.1
Palo Pinto County, TX . . .	27,478	27,250	27,088	25,055	390	2,033	1.4	8.1	632.9	585.5	23,316	21,616	8.1
Minot, ND.	63,700	64,489	67,210	67,609	-3,510	-399	-5.2	-0.6	1,779.9	1,656.6	27,283	24,657	7.4
McHenry County, ND	5,511	5,604	5,952	6,528	-441	-576	-7.4	-8.8	124.3	118.4	21,652	19,895	5.0
Renville County, ND	2,422	2,456	2,594	3,160	-172	-566	-6.6	-17.9	63.1	69.3	25,125	26,733	-8.9
Ward County, ND	55,767	56,429	58,664	57,921	-2,897	743	-4.9	1.3	1,592.5	1,468.9	27,946	25,048	8.4
Mitchell, SD	3,747	22,595	21,878	20,497	-18,131	1,381	-82.9	6.7	613.3	575.4	27,716	26,306	6.6
Davison County, SD	18,777	18,892	18,723	17,503	54	1,220	0.3	7.0	545.3	507.6	29,101	27,119	7.4
Hanson County, SD	3,747	3,703	3,155	2,994	592	161	18.8	5.4	68.1	67.8	20,070	21,486	0.5
Moberly, MO	25,336	25,165	24,667	24,370	669	297	2.7	1.2	526.8	493.6	21,327	20,014	6.7
Randolph County, MO . . .	25,336	25,165	24,667	24,370	669	297	2.7	1.2	526.8	493.6	21,327	20,014	6.7
Monroe, WI.	35,165	34,696	33,728	30,339	1,437	3,389	4.3	11.2	956.1	907.6	28,065	26,915	5.3
Green County, WI.	35,165	34,696	33,728	30,339	1,437	3,389	4.3	11.2	956.1	907.6	28,065	26,915	5.3
Montrose, CO	37,482	36,653	33,598	24,423	3,884	9,175	11.6	37.6	843.1	744.0	23,849	22,147	13.3
Montrose County, CO . . .	37,482	36,653	33,598	24,423	3,884	9,175	11.6	37.6	843.1	744.0	23,849	22,147	13.3
Morehead City, NC.	62,525	61,812	59,403	52,556	3,122	6,847	5.3	13.0	1,667.8	1,530.0	27,713	25,755	9.0
Carteret County, NC	62,525	61,812	59,403	52,556	3,122	6,847	5.3	13.0	1,667.8	1,530.0	27,713	25,755	9.0
Morgan City, LA.	51,416	52,008	53,305	58,086	-1,889	-4,781	-3.5	-8.2	1,261.9	1,123.0	24,059	21,069	12.4
St. Mary Parish, LA.	51,416	52,008	53,305	58,086	-1,889	-4,781	-3.5	-8.2	1,261.9	1,123.0	24,059	21,069	12.4
Moscow, ID.	34,714	35,036	34,858	30,617	-144	4,241	-0.4	13.9	846.0	740.7	24,141	21,227	14.2
Latah County, ID	34,714	35,036	34,858	30,617	-144	4,241	-0.4	13.9	846.0	740.7	24,141	21,227	14.2
Moses Lake, WA	81,229	79,983	75,039	54,758	6,190	20,281	8.2	37.0	1,684.6	1,513.6	21,721	20,177	11.3
Grant County, WA	81,229	79,983	75,039	54,758	6,190	20,281	8.2	37.0	1,684.6	1,513.6	21,721	20,177	11.3
Moultrie, GA.	43,915	43,685	42,125	36,645	1,790	5,480	4.2	15.0	863.1	809.9	20,107	19,224	6.6
Colquitt County, GA	43,915	43,685	42,125	36,645	1,790	5,480	4.2	15.0	863.1	809.9	20,107	19,224	6.6
Mountain Home, AR	40,330	39,803	38,466	31,186	1,864	7,280	4.8	23.3	929.3	847.2	23,975	22,029	9.7
Baxter County, AR	40,330	39,803	38,466	31,186	1,864	7,280	4.8	23.3	929.3	847.2	23,975	22,029	9.7
Mountain Home, ID	28,634	28,840	29,088	21,205	-454	7,883	-1.6	37.2	651.6	585.9	22,138	20,132	11.2
Elmore County, ID	28,634	28,840	29,088	21,205	-454	7,883	-1.6	37.2	651.6	585.9	22,138	20,132	11.2
Mount Airy, NC	72,601	72,188	71,235	61,704	1,366	9,531	1.9	15.4	1,729.2	1,674.3	23,999	23,508	3.3
Surry County, NC	72,601	72,188	71,235	61,704	1,366	9,531	1.9	15.4	1,729.2	1,674.3	23,999	23,508	3.3
Mount Pleasant, MI	65,618	65,378	63,360	54,624	2,258	8,736	3.6	16.0	1,396.9	1,301.3	21,770	20,536	7.3
Isabella County, MI	65,618	65,378	63,360	54,624	2,258	8,736	3.6	16.0	1,396.9	1,301.3	21,770	20,536	7.3
Mount Pleasant, TX	29,445	29,160	28,126	24,009	1,319	4,117	4.7	17.1	647.5	583.1	22,957	20,739	11.0
Titus County, TX.	29,445	29,160	28,126	24,009	1,319	4,117	4.7	17.1	647.5	583.1	22,957	20,739	11.0
Mount Sterling, KY	42,691	41,979	40,400	34,345	2,291	6,055	5.7	17.6	817.8	780.5	19,793	19,323	4.8
Bath County, KY	11,626	11,513	11,134	9,692	492	1,442	4.4	14.9	218.0	212.1	19,131	19,050	2.8
Menifee County, KY	6,809	6,784	6,604	5,092	205	1,512	3.1	29.7	102.8	96.4	15,356	14,594	6.7
Montgomery County, KY . .	24,256	23,682	22,662	19,561	1,594	3,101	7.0	15.9	497.0	472.1	21,398	20,835	5.3
Mount Vernon, IL	48,735	48,717	48,673	45,519	62	3,154	0.1	6.9	1,121.1	1,035.1	23,037	21,270	8.3
Hamilton County, IL	8,301	8,394	8,600	8,499	-299	101	-3.5	1.2	182.3	168.8	21,690	19,636	8.0
Jefferson County, IL	40,434	40,323	40,073	37,020	361	3,053	0.9	8.2	938.8	866.3	23,319	21,621	8.4
Mount Vernon, OH	58,398	57,757	54,655	47,473	3,743	7,182	6.8	15.1	1,345.3	1,267.8	23,925	23,202	6.1
Knox County, OH	58,398	57,757	54,655	47,473	3,743	7,182	6.8	15.1	1,345.3	1,267.8	23,925	23,202	6.1
Murray, KY	35,122	34,793	34,149	30,735	973	3,414	2.8	11.1	822.5	816.9	23,927	23,917	0.7
Calloway County, KY	35,122	34,793	34,149	30,735	973	3,414	2.8	11.1	822.5	816.9	23,927	23,917	0.7
Muscatine, IA	54,598	54,399	53,971	51,499	627	2,472	1.2	4.8	1,478.2	1,371.2	27,217	25,408	7.8
Louisa County, IA	11,842	12,041	12,172	11,592	-330	580	-2.7	5.0	301.4	283.4	24,682	23,277	6.4
Muscatine County, IA . . .	42,756	42,358	41,799	39,907	957	1,892	2.3	4.7	1,176.8	1,087.7	27,953	26,029	8.2
Muskogee, OK	70,607	70,478	69,461	68,078	1,146	1,383	1.6	2.0	1,531.3	1,383.0	21,926	19,913	10.7
Muskogee County, OK. . . .	70,607	70,478	69,461	68,078	1,146	1,383	1.6	2.0	1,531.3	1,383.0	21,926	19,913	10.7
Nacogdoches, TX	60,468	60,024	59,231	54,753	1,237	4,478	2.1	8.2	1,277.7	1,154.1	21,577	19,487	10.7
Nacogdoches County, TX. .	60,468	60,024	59,231	54,753	1,237	4,478	2.1	8.2	1,277.7	1,154.1	21,577	19,487	10.7
Natchez, MS-LA	128,454	51,956	54,474	56,184	73,980	-1,710	135.8	-3.0	1,119.4	1,052.4	20,973	19,324	6.4
Concordia Parish, LA . . .	19,273	19,509	20,225	20,828	-952	-603	-4.7	-2.9	355.8	324.6	17,869	16,053	9.6
Adams County, MS.	32,099	32,447	34,249	35,356	-2,150	-1,107	-6.3	-3.1	763.6	727.8	22,821	21,255	4.9
Natchitoches, LA	38,541	38,418	39,090	36,689	-549	2,401	-1.4	6.5	797.9	703.8	20,497	18,007	13.4
Natchitoches Parish, LA . .	38,541	38,418	39,090	36,689	-549	2,401	-1.4	6.5	797.9	703.8	20,497	18,007	13.4
New Bern, NC.	113,841	113,940	114,999	102,399	-1,158	12,600	-1.0	12.3	2,998.3	2,879.7	26,187	25,051	4.1
Craven County, NC.	90,795	90,824	91,660	81,613	-865	10,047	-0.9	12.3	2,458.9	2,370.0	26,917	25,871	3.8
Jones County, NC	10,311	10,394	10,394	9,414	-83	980	-0.8	10.4	223.0	210.1	21,728	20,201	6.2
Pamlico County, NC	12,735	12,722	12,945	11,372	-210	1,573	-1.6	13.8	316.3	299.6	24,565	23,146	5.6
Newberry, SC	37,250	37,096	36,039	33,172	1,211	2,867	3.4	8.6	786.8	742.6	21,397	20,552	6.0
Newberry County, SC . . .	37,250	37,096	36,039	33,172	1,211	2,867	3.4	8.6	786.8	742.6	21,397	20,552	6.0
New Castle, IN	47,244	47,662	48,469	48,139	-1,225	330	-2.5	0.7	1,236.3	1,211.3	25,704	24,995	2.1
Henry County, IN	47,244	47,662	48,469	48,139	-1,225	330	-2.5	0.7	1,236.3	1,211.3	25,704	24,995	2.1
New Castle, PA	92,809	93,148	94,625	96,246	-1,816	-1,621	-1.9	-1.7	2,195.2	2,146.7	23,413	22,690	2.3
Lawrence County, PA . . .	92,809	93,148	94,625	96,246	-1,816	-1,621	-1.9	-1.7	2,195.2	2,146.7	23,413	22,690	2.3
New Iberia, LA	74,388	74,166	73,270	68,297	1,118	4,973	1.5	7.3	1,629.5	1,466.7	22,107	20,020	11.1
Iberia Parish, LA	74,388	74,166	73,270	68,297	1,118	4,973	1.5	7.3	1,629.5	1,466.7	22,107	20,020	11.1
New Philadelphia-Dover, OH .	91,944	92,073	91,044	84,090	900	6,954	1.0	8.3	2,109.4	2,042.6	23,029	22,439	3.3
Tuscarawas County, OH . .	91,944	92,073	91,044	84,090	900	6,954	1.0	8.3	2,109.4	2,042.6	23,029	22,439	3.3
Newport, TN	34,929	34,647	33,622	29,141	1,307	4,481	3.9	15.4	639.5	603.7	18,777	17,957	5.9
Cocke County, TN	34,929	34,647	33,622	29,141	1,307	4,481	3.9	15.4	639.5	603.7	18,777	17,957	5.9
Newton, IA	37,674	37,696	37,251	34,795	423	2,456	1.1	7.1	1,025.7	967.5	27,300	25,975	6.0
Jasper County, IA.	37,674	37,696	37,251	34,795	423	2,456	1.1	7.1	1,025.7	967.5	27,300	25,975	6.0

See footnotes at end of table.

Table D-1. Micropolitan Areas — **Population and Personal Income**—Con.

Micropolitan statistical area Component counties	Population								Personal income				
					Net change		Percent change		Total (mil. dol.)		Per capita[3] (dollars)		Percent change
	2005 (July 1)	2004 (July 1)	2000[1] (estimates base)	1990[2] (April 1)	2000–2005	1990–2000	2000–2005	1990–2000	2002	2000	2002	2000	2000–2002
New Ulm, MN	26,534	26,650	26,870	26,984	–336	–114	–1.3	–0.4	722.2	687.8	27,027	25,599	5.0
Brown County, MN	26,534	26,650	26,870	26,984	–336	–114	–1.3	–0.4	722.2	687.8	27,027	25,599	5.0
Nogales, AZ	42,009	40,777	38,567	29,676	3,442	8,891	8.9	30.0	710.0	650.7	17,902	16,871	9.1
Santa Cruz County, AZ	42,009	40,777	38,567	29,676	3,442	8,891	8.9	30.0	710.0	650.7	17,902	16,871	9.1
Norfolk, NE	49,622	49,826	49,441	46,726	181	2,715	0.4	5.8	1,196.3	1,135.2	23,824	22,961	5.4
Madison County, NE	35,488	35,667	35,165	32,655	323	2,510	0.9	7.7	885.5	831.9	24,614	23,656	6.4
Pierce County, NE	7,600	7,614	7,851	7,827	–251	24	–3.2	0.3	174.0	166.3	22,511	21,188	4.7
Stanton County, NE	6,534	6,545	6,425	6,244	109	181	1.7	2.9	136.8	137.0	21,018	21,322	–0.2
North Platte, NE	36,883	36,350	35,960	33,932	923	2,028	2.6	6.0	908.0	846.5	25,343	23,544	7.3
Lincoln County, NE	35,636	35,104	34,658	32,508	978	2,150	2.8	6.6	884.7	825.7	25,621	23,827	7.1
Logan County, NE	740	719	771	878	–31	–107	–4.0	–12.2	16.4	14.7	21,825	19,018	11.6
McPherson County, NE	507	527	531	546	–24	–15	–4.5	–2.7	6.9	6.2	12,647	11,657	11.8
North Vernon, IN	28,427	28,310	27,697	23,661	730	4,036	2.6	17.1	616.5	604.5	21,876	21,827	2.0
Jennings County, IN	28,427	28,310	27,697	23,661	730	4,036	2.6	17.1	616.5	604.5	21,876	21,827	2.0
North Wilkesboro, NC	67,390	67,000	65,812	59,393	1,578	6,419	2.4	10.8	1,620.3	1,554.8	24,266	23,627	4.2
Wilkes County, NC	67,390	67,000	65,812	59,393	1,578	6,419	2.4	10.8	1,620.3	1,554.8	24,266	23,627	4.2
Norwalk, OH	60,385	60,150	59,611	56,240	774	3,371	1.3	6.0	1,452.2	1,440.7	24,234	24,171	0.8
Huron County, OH	60,385	60,150	59,611	56,240	774	3,371	1.3	6.0	1,452.2	1,440.7	24,234	24,171	0.8
Oak Harbor, WA	79,252	79,742	71,876	60,195	7,376	11,681	10.3	19.4	2,181.1	1,909.5	29,031	26,579	14.2
Island County, WA	79,252	79,742	71,876	60,195	7,376	11,681	10.3	19.4	2,181.1	1,909.5	29,031	26,579	14.2
Oak Hill, WV	46,823	47,008	47,518	47,952	–695	–434	–1.5	–0.9	953.5	866.6	20,218	18,237	10.0
Fayette County, WV	46,823	47,008	47,518	47,952	–695	–434	–1.5	–0.9	953.5	866.6	20,218	18,237	10.0
Ocean Pines, MD	48,750	48,790	46,759	35,028	1,991	11,731	4.3	33.5	1,445.4	1,299.0	29,637	27,780	11.3
Worcester County, MD	48,750	48,790	46,759	35,028	1,991	11,731	4.3	33.5	1,445.4	1,299.0	29,637	27,780	11.3
Ogdensburg-Massena, NY	111,380	111,292	111,850	111,974	–470	–124	–0.4	(Z)	2,299.6	2,225.0	20,629	19,891	3.4
St. Lawrence County, NY	111,380	111,292	111,850	111,974	–470	–124	–0.4	(Z)	2,299.6	2,225.0	20,629	19,891	3.4
Oil City, PA	55,928	56,149	57,476	59,381	–1,548	–1,905	–2.7	–3.2	1,351.5	1,340.2	23,767	23,319	0.8
Venango County, PA	55,928	56,149	57,476	59,381	–1,548	–1,905	–2.7	–3.2	1,351.5	1,340.2	23,767	23,319	0.8
Okeechobee, FL	39,836	39,006	35,908	29,627	3,928	6,281	10.9	21.2	695.4	610.5	18,818	17,004	13.9
Okeechobee County, FL	39,836	39,006	35,908	29,627	3,928	6,281	10.9	21.2	695.4	610.5	18,818	17,004	13.9
Olean, NY	207,994	83,035	83,919	84,234	124,075	–315	147.9	–0.4	1,927.9	1,756.9	23,119	20,937	9.7
Cattaraugus County, NY	82,502	83,035	83,919	84,234	–1,417	–315	–1.7	–0.4	1,927.9	1,756.9	23,119	20,937	9.7
Oneonta, NY	62,746	62,706	61,660	60,517	1,086	1,143	1.8	1.9	1,439.3	1,347.7	23,240	21,859	6.8
Otsego County, NY	62,746	62,706	61,660	60,517	1,086	1,143	1.8	1.9	1,439.3	1,347.7	23,240	21,859	6.8
Ontario, OR-ID	53,527	52,903	52,176	42,472	1,351	9,704	2.6	22.8	1,005.8	986.7	19,176	18,912	1.9
Payette County, ID	22,197	21,577	20,635	16,434	1,562	4,201	7.6	25.6	424.0	386.6	20,016	18,739	9.7
Malheur County, OR	31,330	31,326	31,541	26,038	–211	5,503	–0.7	21.1	581.9	600.1	18,608	19,026	–3.0
Opelousas-Eunice, LA	89,937	89,322	87,770	80,331	2,167	7,439	2.5	9.3	1,693.1	1,532.8	19,171	17,467	10.5
St. Landry Parish, LA	89,937	89,322	87,770	80,331	2,167	7,439	2.5	9.3	1,693.1	1,532.8	19,171	17,467	10.5
Orangeburg, SC	92,167	92,115	91,511	84,803	656	6,708	0.7	7.9	1,955.8	1,803.7	21,418	19,713	8.4
Orangeburg County, SC	92,167	92,115	91,511	84,803	656	6,708	0.7	7.9	1,955.8	1,803.7	21,418	19,713	8.4
Oskaloosa, IA	22,364	22,111	22,308	21,522	56	786	0.3	3.7	561.9	549.9	25,121	24,655	2.2
Mahaska County, IA	22,364	22,111	22,308	21,522	56	786	0.3	3.7	561.9	549.9	25,121	24,655	2.2
Ottawa-Streator, IL	154,028	153,506	153,117	148,331	911	4,786	0.6	3.2	3,985.0	3,910.3	26,024	25,543	1.9
Bureau County, IL	35,330	35,183	35,498	35,688	–168	–190	–0.5	–0.5	929.5	900.9	26,358	25,380	3.2
La Salle County, IL	112,604	112,225	111,529	106,913	1,075	4,616	1.0	4.3	2,903.4	2,857.2	25,980	25,624	1.6
Putnam County, IL	6,094	6,098	6,090	5,730	4	360	0.1	6.3	152.2	152.3	24,902	25,011	–0.1
Ottumwa, IA	35,965	35,793	36,009	35,687	–44	322	–0.1	0.9	853.4	779.1	23,769	21,636	9.5
Wapello County, IA	35,965	35,793	36,009	35,687	–44	322	–0.1	0.9	853.4	779.1	23,769	21,636	9.5
Owatonna, MN	35,755	35,208	33,799	30,729	1,956	3,070	5.8	10.0	977.3	918.9	28,406	27,191	6.4
Steele County, MN	35,755	35,208	33,799	30,729	1,956	3,070	5.8	10.0	977.3	918.9	28,406	27,191	6.4
Owosso, MI	72,945	73,028	71,710	69,770	1,235	1,940	1.7	2.8	1,659.1	1,659.7	22,999	23,148	0.0
Shiawassee County, MI	72,945	73,028	71,710	69,770	1,235	1,940	1.7	2.8	1,659.1	1,659.7	22,999	23,148	0.0
Oxford, MS	40,842	40,237	38,743	31,826	2,099	6,917	5.4	21.7	914.8	801.7	23,147	20,676	14.1
Lafayette County, MS	40,842	40,237	38,743	31,826	2,099	6,917	5.4	21.7	914.8	801.7	23,147	20,676	14.1
Paducah, KY-IL	98,083	97,801	98,686	94,595	–603	4,091	–0.6	4.3	2,682.0	2,564.7	27,413	25,992	4.6
Massac County, IL	15,348	15,294	15,125	14,752	223	373	1.5	2.5	346.7	319.5	22,920	21,130	8.5
Ballard County, KY	8,277	8,229	8,307	7,902	–30	405	–0.4	5.1	214.9	217.0	26,426	26,121	–1.0
Livingston County, KY	9,760	9,714	9,816	9,062	–56	754	–0.6	8.3	222.3	211.6	22,623	21,560	5.1
McCracken County, KY	64,698	64,564	65,438	62,879	–740	2,559	–1.1	4.1	1,898.1	1,816.6	29,313	27,764	4.5
Pahrump, NV	40,477	37,686	32,923	17,781	7,554	15,142	22.9	85.2	893.6	796.8	25,833	24,206	12.2
Nye County, NV	40,477	37,686	32,923	17,781	7,554	15,142	22.9	85.2	893.6	796.8	25,833	24,206	12.2
Palatka, FL	73,568	72,574	70,435	65,070	3,133	5,365	4.4	8.2	1,362.4	1,281.6	19,155	18,198	6.3
Putnam County, FL	73,568	72,574	70,435	65,070	3,133	5,365	4.4	8.2	1,362.4	1,281.6	19,155	18,198	6.3
Palestine, TX	56,408	55,988	55,092	48,024	1,316	7,068	2.4	14.7	1,033.0	973.3	18,950	17,670	6.1
Anderson County, TX	56,408	55,988	55,092	48,024	1,316	7,068	2.4	14.7	1,033.0	973.3	18,950	17,670	6.1
Palm Coast, FL	76,410	69,016	50,581	28,701	25,829	21,880	51.1	76.2	1,382.5	1,194.2	24,041	23,613	15.8
Flagler County, FL	76,410	69,016	50,581	28,701	25,829	21,880	51.1	76.2	1,382.5	1,194.2	24,041	23,613	15.8
Pampa, TX	22,299	22,220	23,469	24,992	–1,170	–1,523	–5.0	–6.1	586.1	576.0	25,802	24,546	1.8
Gray County, TX	21,479	21,393	22,586	23,967	–1,107	–1,381	–4.9	–5.8	565.2	555.4	25,860	24,593	1.8
Roberts County, TX	820	827	883	1,025	–63	–142	–7.1	–13.9	20.9	20.6	24,324	23,331	1.4
Paragould, AR	39,401	38,863	37,513	31,804	1,888	5,709	5.0	18.0	758.1	719.0	19,956	19,168	5.4
Greene County, AR	39,401	38,863	37,513	31,804	1,888	5,709	5.0	18.0	758.1	719.0	19,956	19,168	5.4
Paris, TN	31,511	31,326	31,143	27,888	368	3,255	1.2	11.7	728.2	686.6	23,279	22,043	6.1
Henry County, TN	31,511	31,326	31,143	27,888	368	3,255	1.2	11.7	728.2	686.6	23,279	22,043	6.1
Paris, TX	49,644	49,598	48,634	43,949	1,010	4,685	2.1	10.7	1,107.5	1,079.7	22,598	22,203	2.6
Lamar County, TX	49,644	49,598	48,634	43,949	1,010	4,685	2.1	10.7	1,107.5	1,079.7	22,598	22,203	2.6
Parsons, KS	22,169	22,154	22,749	23,693	–580	–944	–2.5	–4.0	532.4	479.0	23,833	21,053	11.2
Labette County, KS	22,169	22,154	22,749	23,693	–580	–944	–2.5	–4.0	532.4	479.0	23,833	21,053	11.2
Payson, AZ	51,663	51,311	51,377	40,216	286	11,161	0.6	27.8	1,064.0	973.4	20,646	18,950	9.3
Gila County, AZ	51,663	51,311	51,377	40,216	286	11,161	0.6	27.8	1,064.0	973.4	20,646	18,950	9.3
Pecos, TX	11,638	11,828	13,061	15,852	–1,423	–2,791	–10.9	–17.6	214.5	206.8	17,139	15,832	3.7
Reeves County, TX	11,638	11,828	13,061	15,852	–1,423	–2,791	–10.9	–17.6	214.5	206.8	17,139	15,832	3.7
Pella, IA	32,984	32,691	32,120	30,001	864	2,119	2.7	7.1	851.3	849.2	26,143	26,443	0.2
Marion County, IA	32,984	32,691	32,120	30,001	864	2,119	2.7	7.1	851.3	849.2	26,143	26,443	0.2

See footnotes at end of table.

280 State and Metropolitan Area Data Book: 2006

U.S. Census Bureau

Table D-1. Microplitan Areas — **Population and Personal Income**—Con.

Micropolitan statistical area Component counties	Population 2005 (July 1)	2004 (July 1)	2000[1] (estimates base)	1990[2] (April 1)	Net change 2000–2005	1990–2000	Percent change 2000–2005	1990–2000	Personal income Total (mil. dol.) 2002	2000	Per capita[3] (dollars) 2002	2000	Percent change 2000–2002
Pendleton-Hermiston, OR	85,544	85,248	81,744	66,874	3,800	14,870	4.6	22.2	1,869.1	1,740.3	22,514	21,290	7.4
Morrow County, OR	11,666	11,692	11,057	7,625	609	3,432	5.5	45.0	241.7	226.2	20,826	20,445	6.9
Umatilla County, OR	73,878	73,556	70,687	59,249	3,191	11,438	4.5	19.3	1,627.4	1,514.2	22,789	21,422	7.5
Peru, IN	35,620	35,922	36,184	36,897	−564	−713	−1.6	−1.9	795.3	785.1	21,881	21,704	1.3
Miami County, IN	35,620	35,922	36,184	36,897	−564	−713	−1.6	−1.9	795.3	785.1	21,881	21,704	1.3
Phoenix Lake-Cedar Ridge, CA	59,380	56,843	54,679	48,456	4,701	6,223	8.6	12.8	1,402.7	1,268.8	25,044	23,207	10.6
Tuolumne County, CA	59,380	56,843	54,679	48,456	4,701	6,223	8.6	12.8	1,402.7	1,268.8	25,044	23,207	10.6
Picayune, MS	52,659	51,785	48,785	38,714	3,874	10,071	7.9	26.0	957.0	871.1	19,002	17,856	9.9
Pearl River County, MS	52,659	51,785	48,785	38,714	3,874	10,071	7.9	26.0	957.0	871.1	19,002	17,856	9.9
Pierre, SD	19,704	19,635	19,283	17,270	421	2,013	2.2	11.7	547.6	516.5	28,337	26,790	6.0
Hughes County, SD	16,875	16,791	16,501	14,817	374	1,684	2.3	11.4	475.4	441.2	28,646	26,741	7.8
Stanley County, SD.	2,829	2,844	2,782	2,453	47	329	1.7	13.4	72.2	75.3	26,459	27,086	−4.1
Pierre Part, LA	23,196	23,206	23,384	22,753	−188	631	−0.8	2.8	571.8	448.3	24,657	19,167	27.6
Assumption Parish, LA	23,196	23,206	23,384	22,753	−188	631	−0.8	2.8	571.8	448.3	24,657	19,167	27.6
Pittsburg, KS.	38,222	38,167	38,225	35,568	−3	2,657	0.0	7.5	856.8	807.1	22,482	21,117	6.2
Crawford County, KS.	38,222	38,167	38,225	35,568	−3	2,657	0.0	7.5	856.8	807.1	22,482	21,117	6.2
Plainview, TX	36,233	36,329	36,578	34,671	−345	1,907	−0.9	5.5	785.5	756.8	21,965	20,692	3.8
Hale County, TX.	36,233	36,329	36,578	34,671	−345	1,907	−0.9	5.5	785.5	756.8	21,965	20,692	3.8
Platteville, WI	49,671	49,616	49,535	49,264	136	271	0.3	0.6	1,189.3	1,104.1	24,060	22,291	7.7
Grant County, WI	49,671	49,616	49,535	49,264	136	271	0.3	0.6	1,189.3	1,104.1	24,060	22,291	7.7
Plattsburgh, NY.	82,047	81,684	79,940	85,969	2,107	−6,029	2.6	−7.0	1,952.2	1,801.3	24,142	22,534	8.4
Clinton County, NY	82,047	81,684	79,940	85,969	2,107	−6,029	2.6	−7.0	1,952.2	1,801.3	24,142	22,534	8.4
Plymouth, IN	46,945	46,564	45,258	42,182	1,687	3,076	3.7	7.3	1,114.3	1,085.1	24,319	23,984	2.7
Marshall County, IN	46,945	46,564	45,258	42,182	1,687	3,076	3.7	7.3	1,114.3	1,085.1	24,319	23,984	2.7
Point Pleasant, WV-OH.	57,123	57,109	57,057	56,132	66	925	0.1	1.6	1,266.8	1,174.2	22,085	20,580	7.9
Gallia County, OH.	31,362	31,285	31,090	30,954	272	136	0.9	0.4	750.9	687.2	23,973	22,103	9.3
Mason County, WV.	25,761	25,824	25,967	25,178	−206	789	−0.8	3.1	515.9	487.0	19,814	18,755	5.9
Ponca City, OK	46,480	46,802	47,943	48,056	−1,463	−113	−3.1	−0.2	1,186.1	1,095.2	24,890	22,842	8.3
Kay County, OK	46,480	46,802	47,943	48,056	−1,463	−113	−3.1	−0.2	1,186.1	1,095.2	24,890	22,842	8.3
Pontiac, IL	39,186	39,045	39,653	39,301	−467	352	−1.2	0.9	1,071.1	1,007.3	27,230	25,405	6.3
Livingston County, IL.	39,186	39,045	39,653	39,301	−467	352	−1.2	0.9	1,071.1	1,007.3	27,230	25,405	6.3
Poplar Bluff, MO	41,338	41,003	40,826	38,765	512	2,061	1.3	5.3	969.3	891.4	23,752	21,839	8.7
Butler County, MO	41,338	41,003	40,826	38,765	512	2,061	1.3	5.3	969.3	891.4	23,752	21,839	8.7
Portales, NM.	18,238	18,199	17,983	16,702	255	1,281	1.4	7.7	428.8	344.1	23,792	19,115	24.6
Roosevelt County, NM.	18,238	18,199	17,983	16,702	255	1,281	1.4	7.7	428.8	344.1	23,792	19,115	24.6
Port Angeles, WA	69,689	67,991	64,318	56,464	5,371	7,854	8.4	13.9	1,781.8	1,583.3	26,959	24,616	12.5
Clallam County, WA	69,689	67,991	64,318	56,464	5,371	7,854	8.4	13.9	1,781.8	1,583.3	26,959	24,616	12.5
Portsmouth, OH.	76,561	76,634	79,081	80,327	−2,520	−1,246	−3.2	−1.6	1,632.6	1,559.0	20,914	19,716	4.7
Scioto County, OH	76,561	76,634	79,081	80,327	−2,520	−1,246	−3.2	−1.6	1,632.6	1,559.0	20,914	19,716	4.7
Pottsville, PA.	147,447	147,410	150,147	152,585	−2,700	−2,438	−1.8	−1.6	3,562.9	3,435.1	23,947	22,882	3.7
Schuylkill County, PA	147,447	147,410	150,147	152,585	−2,700	−2,438	−1.8	−1.6	3,562.9	3,435.1	23,947	22,882	3.7
Price, UT	19,437	19,612	20,376	20,228	−939	148	−4.6	0.7	462.9	435.1	23,365	21,356	6.4
Carbon County, UT.	19,437	19,612	20,376	20,228	−939	148	−4.6	0.7	462.9	435.1	23,365	21,356	6.4
Prineville, OR	22,067	21,429	19,344	14,111	2,723	5,233	14.1	37.1	440.9	393.8	21,859	20,365	12.0
Crook County, OR	22,067	21,429	19,344	14,111	2,723	5,233	14.1	37.1	440.9	393.8	21,859	20,365	12.0
Pullman, WA.	40,170	40,182	40,664	38,775	−494	1,889	−1.2	4.9	830.7	805.9	20,302	19,802	3.1
Whitman County, WA	40,170	40,182	40,664	38,775	−494	1,889	−1.2	4.9	830.7	805.9	20,302	19,802	3.1
Quincy, IL-MO.	77,226	77,142	78,723	76,323	−1,497	2,400	−1.9	3.1	1,993.1	1,880.3	25,501	23,888	6.0
Adams County, IL.	67,040	66,924	68,204	66,090	−1,164	2,114	−1.7	3.2	1,797.3	1,691.3	26,515	24,801	6.3
Lewis County, MO	10,186	10,218	10,519	10,233	−333	286	−3.2	2.8	195.8	189.0	18,872	17,971	3.6
Raymondville, TX.	20,382	20,203	20,071	17,705	311	2,366	1.5	13.4	300.4	272.0	14,982	13,552	10.4
Willacy County, TX.	20,382	20,203	20,071	17,705	311	2,366	1.5	13.4	300.4	272.0	14,982	13,552	10.4
Red Bluff, CA	61,197	59,976	56,159	49,625	5,038	6,534	9.0	13.2	1,179.9	1,068.6	20,536	19,032	10.4
Tehama County, CA	61,197	59,976	56,159	49,625	5,038	6,534	9.0	13.2	1,179.9	1,068.6	20,536	19,032	10.4
Red Wing, MN	45,585	45,497	44,163	40,690	1,422	3,473	3.2	8.5	1,316.2	1,221.1	29,287	27,650	7.8
Goodhue County, MN	45,585	45,497	44,163	40,690	1,422	3,473	3.2	8.5	1,316.2	1,221.1	29,287	27,650	7.8
Rexburg, ID	43,217	42,546	39,213	34,611	4,004	4,602	10.2	13.3	675.8	593.6	16,548	15,132	13.8
Fremont County, ID.	12,242	12,320	11,792	10,937	450	855	3.8	7.8	241.4	213.1	20,322	18,064	13.3
Madison County, ID	30,975	30,226	27,421	23,674	3,554	3,747	13.0	15.8	434.4	380.6	15,000	13,871	14.1
Richmond, IN	69,192	69,655	71,045	71,951	−1,853	−906	−2.6	−1.3	1,742.0	1,705.4	24,696	24,006	2.1
Wayne County, IN	69,192	69,655	71,045	71,951	−1,853	−906	−2.6	−1.3	1,742.0	1,705.4	24,696	24,006	2.1
Richmond-Berea, KY	94,461	92,820	87,895	72,311	6,566	15,584	7.5	21.6	1,804.3	1,698.9	20,031	19,327	6.2
Madison County, KY	77,749	76,136	71,261	57,508	6,488	13,753	9.1	23.9	1,527.1	1,437.3	20,808	20,167	6.2
Rockcastle County, KY	16,712	16,684	16,634	14,803	78	1,831	0.5	12.4	277.1	261.6	16,615	15,727	6.0
Rio Grande City-Roma, TX	60,941	59,661	53,846	40,518	7,095	13,328	13.2	32.9	588.6	514.7	10,480	9,560	14.4
Starr County, TX	60,941	59,661	53,846	40,518	7,095	13,328	13.2	32.9	588.6	514.7	10,480	9,560	14.4
Riverton, WY	36,491	36,218	35,842	33,662	649	2,180	1.8	6.5	898.8	828.8	24,962	23,124	8.4
Fremont County, WY.	36,491	36,218	35,842	33,662	649	2,180	1.8	6.5	898.8	828.8	24,962	23,124	8.4
Roanoke Rapids, NC	77,506	77,600	79,387	76,314	−1,881	3,073	−2.4	4.0	1,625.6	1,591.4	20,724	20,049	2.1
Halifax County, NC	56,023	56,096	57,297	55,516	−1,274	1,781	−2.2	3.2	1,142.5	1,133.1	20,197	19,777	0.8
Northampton County, NC	21,483	21,504	22,090	20,798	−607	1,292	−2.7	6.2	483.0	458.3	22,084	20,753	5.4
Rochelle, IL	54,290	53,525	51,172	45,957	3,118	5,215	6.1	11.3	1,352.7	1,329.5	25,916	25,984	1.8
Ogle County, IL	54,290	53,525	51,172	45,957	3,118	5,215	6.1	11.3	1,352.7	1,329.5	25,916	25,984	1.8
Rockingham, NC	46,781	46,658	46,583	44,518	198	2,065	0.4	4.6	990.9	942.0	21,163	20,225	5.2
Richmond County, NC.	46,781	46,658	46,583	44,518	198	2,065	0.4	4.6	990.9	942.0	21,163	20,225	5.2
Rockland, ME	41,219	41,050	39,668	36,310	1,521	3,388	3.8	9.3	1,185.8	1,042.6	29,390	26,268	13.7
Knox County, ME	41,219	41,050	39,668	36,310	1,521	3,388	3.8	9.3	1,185.8	1,042.6	29,390	26,268	13.7
Rock Springs, WY	37,975	37,570	37,501	38,823	474	−1,322	1.3	−3.4	1,131.4	1,106.3	30,400	29,511	2.3
Sweetwater County, WY	37,975	37,570	37,501	38,823	474	−1,322	1.3	−3.4	1,131.4	1,106.3	30,400	29,511	2.3
Rolla, MO.	42,125	41,679	39,880	35,248	2,245	4,632	5.6	13.1	953.9	851.4	23,221	21,328	12.0
Phelps County, MO.	42,125	41,679	39,880	35,248	2,245	4,632	5.6	13.1	953.9	851.4	23,221	21,328	12.0
Roseburg, OR.	104,202	103,089	100,484	94,649	3,718	5,835	3.7	6.2	2,492.6	2,275.9	24,644	22,654	9.5
Douglas County, OR.	104,202	103,089	100,484	94,649	3,718	5,835	3.7	6.2	2,492.6	2,275.9	24,644	22,654	9.5
Roswell, NM.	61,860	61,497	61,320	57,849	540	3,471	0.9	6.0	1,367.0	1,165.5	22,727	19,007	17.3
Chaves County, NM.	61,860	61,497	61,320	57,849	540	3,471	0.9	6.0	1,367.0	1,165.5	22,727	19,007	17.3

See footnotes at end of table.

Micropolitan statistical area Component counties	Population								Personal income				
					Net change		Percent change		Total (mil. dol.)		Per capita[3] (dollars)		Percent change
	2005 (July 1)	2004 (July 1)	2000[1] (esti- mates base)	1990[2] (April 1)	2000– 2005	1990– 2000	2000– 2005	1990– 2000	2002	2000	2002	2000	2000– 2002
Russellville, AR	77,971	77,321	75,669	63,642	2,302	12,027	3.0	18.9	1,639.3	1,536.5	21,398	20,310	6.7
Pope County, AR	56,580	56,007	54,490	45,883	2,090	8,607	3.8	18.8	1,206.7	1,138.7	21,836	20,902	6.0
Yell County, AR	21,391	21,314	21,179	17,759	212	3,420	1.0	19.3	432.6	397.8	20,263	18,786	8.7
Ruston, LA	57,243	57,547	57,871	57,450	−628	421	−1.1	0.7	1,289.7	1,179.3	22,451	20,373	9.4
Jackson Parish, LA	15,135	15,262	15,389	15,705	−254	−316	−1.7	−2.0	363.3	344.8	23,794	22,406	5.4
Lincoln Parish, LA	42,108	42,285	42,482	41,745	−374	737	−0.9	1.8	926.4	834.5	21,965	19,637	11.0
Rutland, VT	63,743	63,550	63,419	62,142	324	1,277	0.5	2.1	1,801.3	1,648.1	28,423	25,989	9.3
Rutland County, VT	63,743	63,550	63,419	62,142	324	1,277	0.5	2.1	1,801.3	1,648.1	28,423	25,989	9.3
Safford, AZ	40,594	40,368	42,043	34,562	−1,449	7,481	−3.4	21.6	693.4	646.8	16,883	15,387	7.2
Graham County, AZ	33,073	32,858	33,494	26,554	−421	6,940	−1.3	26.1	532.9	474.2	16,046	14,158	12.4
Greenlee County, AZ	7,521	7,510	8,549	8,008	−1,028	541	−12.0	6.8	160.5	172.7	20,418	20,200	−7.0
St. Marys, GA	45,759	45,082	43,736	30,167	2,023	13,569	4.6	45.0	1,017.3	915.7	22,516	20,936	11.1
Camden County, GA	45,759	45,082	43,736	30,167	2,023	13,569	4.6	45.0	1,017.3	915.7	22,516	20,936	11.1
St. Marys, PA	33,577	33,963	35,045	34,878	−1,468	167	−4.2	0.5	927.0	900.7	26,873	25,709	2.9
Elk County, PA	33,577	33,963	35,045	34,878	−1,468	167	−4.2	0.5	927.0	900.7	26,873	25,709	2.9
Salina, KS	60,042	60,052	59,811	54,935	231	4,876	0.4	8.9	1,636.2	1,626.7	27,225	27,203	0.6
Ottawa County, KS	6,123	6,149	6,195	5,634	−72	561	−1.2	10.0	141.7	137.2	22,863	22,150	3.3
Saline County, KS	53,919	53,903	53,616	49,301	303	4,315	0.6	8.8	1,494.5	1,489.5	27,726	27,787	0.3
Salisbury, NC	135,099	134,030	130,667	110,605	4,432	20,062	3.4	18.1	3,325.4	3,156.1	24,910	24,157	5.4
Rowan County, NC	135,099	134,030	130,667	110,605	4,432	20,062	3.4	18.1	3,325.4	3,156.1	24,910	24,157	5.4
Sanford, NC	55,704	54,417	49,424	41,374	6,280	8,050	12.7	19.5	1,308.7	1,243.2	26,598	25,154	5.3
Lee County, NC	55,704	54,417	49,424	41,374	6,280	8,050	12.7	19.5	1,308.7	1,243.2	26,598	25,154	5.3
Sault Ste. Marie, MI	38,780	38,722	38,568	34,604	212	3,964	0.5	11.5	747.7	718.2	19,298	18,622	4.1
Chippewa County, MI	38,780	38,722	38,568	34,604	212	3,964	0.5	11.5	747.7	718.2	19,298	18,622	4.1
Sayre, PA	62,537	62,496	62,793	60,967	−256	1,826	−0.4	3.0	1,460.7	1,365.9	23,290	21,754	6.9
Bradford County, PA	62,537	62,496	62,793	60,967	−256	1,826	−0.4	3.0	1,460.7	1,365.9	23,290	21,754	6.9
Scottsbluff, NE	37,485	37,445	37,814	36,877	−329	937	−0.9	2.5	916.3	894.2	24,422	23,649	2.5
Banner County, NE	733	759	824	852	−91	−28	−11.0	−3.3	16.2	14.3	21,223	17,362	13.3
Scotts Bluff County, NE	36,752	36,686	36,990	36,025	−238	965	−0.6	2.7	900.0	879.9	24,489	23,789	2.3
Scottsboro, AL	53,650	53,747	54,026	47,796	−376	6,230	−0.7	13.0	1,173.9	1,154.7	21,802	21,374	1.7
Jackson County, AL	53,650	53,747	54,026	47,796	−376	6,230	−0.7	13.0	1,173.9	1,154.7	21,802	21,374	1.7
Scottsburg, IN	23,820	23,590	23,049	20,991	771	2,058	3.3	9.8	506.9	495.9	21,682	21,515	2.2
Scott County, IN	23,820	23,590	23,049	20,991	771	2,058	3.3	9.8	506.9	495.9	21,682	21,515	2.2
Seaford, DE	176,548	172,223	157,468	113,229	19,080	44,239	12.1	39.1	4,178.2	3,816.1	25,471	24,237	9.5
Sussex County, DE	176,548	172,223	157,468	113,229	19,080	44,239	12.1	39.1	4,178.2	3,816.1	25,471	24,237	9.5
Searcy, AR	71,332	70,577	67,410	54,676	3,922	12,734	5.8	23.3	1,400.2	1,267.9	20,210	18,807	10.4
White County, AR	71,332	70,577	67,410	54,676	3,922	12,734	5.8	23.3	1,400.2	1,267.9	20,210	18,807	10.4
Sebring, FL	95,496	93,133	87,453	68,432	8,043	19,021	9.2	27.8	1,980.5	1,770.5	22,004	20,248	11.9
Highlands County, FL	95,496	93,133	87,453	68,432	8,043	19,021	9.2	27.8	1,980.5	1,770.5	22,004	20,248	11.9
Sedalia, MO	40,121	39,690	39,449	35,437	672	4,012	1.7	11.3	941.8	901.3	23,915	22,850	4.5
Pettis County, MO	40,121	39,690	39,449	35,437	672	4,012	1.7	11.3	941.8	901.3	23,915	22,850	4.5
Selinsgrove, PA	38,207	38,113	37,551	36,680	656	871	1.7	2.4	977.2	940.3	25,758	25,045	3.9
Snyder County, PA	38,207	38,113	37,551	36,680	656	871	1.7	2.4	977.2	940.3	25,758	25,045	3.9
Selma, AL	44,366	44,715	46,225	48,130	−1,859	−1,905	−4.0	−4.0	933.4	889.7	20,589	19,248	4.9
Dallas County, AL	44,366	44,715	46,225	48,130	−1,859	−1,905	−4.0	−4.0	933.4	889.7	20,589	19,248	4.9
Seneca, SC	69,577	68,972	66,428	57,494	3,149	8,934	4.7	15.5	1,711.5	1,601.4	25,209	24,109	6.9
Oconee County, SC	69,577	68,972	66,428	57,494	3,149	8,934	4.7	15.5	1,711.5	1,601.4	25,209	24,109	6.9
Seneca Falls, NY	34,855	35,011	33,377	33,683	1,478	−306	4.4	−0.9	815.8	774.6	23,306	23,210	5.3
Seneca County, NY	34,855	35,011	33,377	33,683	1,478	−306	4.4	−0.9	815.8	774.6	23,306	23,210	5.3
Sevierville, TN	79,282	77,153	71,709	51,043	7,573	20,666	10.6	40.5	1,828.4	1,604.4	24,603	22,374	14.0
Sevier County, TN	79,282	77,153	71,709	51,043	7,573	20,666	10.6	40.5	1,828.4	1,604.4	24,603	22,374	14.0
Seymour, IN	42,237	41,848	41,413	37,730	824	3,683	2.0	9.8	1,006.9	959.7	24,227	23,175	4.9
Jackson County, IN	42,237	41,848	41,413	37,730	824	3,683	2.0	9.8	1,006.9	959.7	24,227	23,175	4.9
Shawnee, OK	68,272	67,719	65,705	58,760	2,567	6,945	3.9	11.8	1,436.2	1,328.2	21,522	20,216	8.1
Pottawatomie County, OK	68,272	67,719	65,705	58,760	2,567	6,945	3.9	11.8	1,436.2	1,328.2	21,522	20,216	8.1
Shelby, NC	98,288	98,269	96,577	84,714	1,711	11,863	1.8	14.0	2,248.2	2,210.7	23,020	22,892	1.7
Cleveland County, NC	98,288	98,269	96,577	84,714	1,711	11,863	1.8	14.0	2,248.2	2,210.7	23,020	22,892	1.7
Shelbyville, TN	42,204	41,153	37,830	30,411	4,374	7,419	11.6	24.4	927.5	877.8	23,635	23,212	5.7
Bedford County, TN	42,204	41,153	37,830	30,411	4,374	7,419	11.6	24.4	927.5	877.8	23,635	23,212	5.7
Shelton, WA	54,359	53,110	49,587	38,341	4,772	11,246	9.6	29.3	1,251.0	1,130.2	24,471	22,798	10.7
Mason County, WA	54,359	53,110	49,587	38,341	4,772	11,246	9.6	29.3	1,251.0	1,130.2	24,471	22,798	10.7
Sheridan, WY	27,389	27,236	26,606	23,562	783	3,044	2.9	12.9	878.0	793.6	32,563	29,829	10.6
Sheridan County, WY	27,389	27,236	26,606	23,562	783	3,044	2.9	12.9	878.0	793.6	32,563	29,829	10.6
Sidney, OH	48,736	48,479	47,996	44,915	740	3,081	1.5	6.9	1,297.4	1,270.9	26,801	26,487	2.1
Shelby County, OH	48,736	48,479	47,996	44,915	740	3,081	1.5	6.9	1,297.4	1,270.9	26,801	26,487	2.1
Sierra Vista-Douglas, AZ	126,106	123,864	118,033	97,624	8,073	20,409	6.8	20.9	2,662.8	2,329.3	22,129	19,727	14.3
Cochise County, AZ	126,106	123,864	118,033	97,624	8,073	20,409	6.8	20.9	2,662.8	2,329.3	22,129	19,727	14.3
Sikeston, MO	41,143	40,825	40,392	39,376	751	1,016	1.9	2.6	951.9	884.8	23,493	21,907	7.6
Scott County, MO	41,143	40,825	40,392	39,376	751	1,016	1.9	2.6	951.9	884.8	23,493	21,907	7.6
Silver City, NM	29,747	29,363	30,920	27,676	−1,173	3,244	−3.8	11.7	598.5	578.3	19,762	18,703	3.5
Grant County, NM	29,747	29,363	30,920	27,676	−1,173	3,244	−3.8	11.7	598.5	578.3	19,762	18,703	3.5
Silverthorne, CO	24,892	24,851	23,665	12,881	1,227	10,784	5.2	83.7	830.5	819.4	33,443	34,617	1.4
Summit County, CO	24,892	24,851	23,665	12,881	1,227	10,784	5.2	83.7	830.5	819.4	33,443	34,617	1.4
Snyder, TX	16,217	16,174	16,250	18,634	−33	−2,384	−0.2	−12.8	372.8	333.7	23,305	20,532	11.7
Scurry County, TX	16,217	16,174	16,250	18,634	−33	−2,384	−0.2	−12.8	372.8	333.7	23,305	20,532	11.7
Somerset, KY	59,200	58,693	56,322	49,489	2,878	6,833	5.1	13.8	1,259.2	1,163.1	21,986	20,654	8.3
Pulaski County, KY	59,200	58,693	56,322	49,489	2,878	6,833	5.1	13.8	1,259.2	1,163.1	21,986	20,654	8.3
Somerset, PA	78,907	79,322	80,040	78,218	−1,133	1,822	−1.4	2.3	1,763.0	1,672.2	22,148	20,896	5.4
Somerset County, PA	78,907	79,322	80,040	78,218	−1,133	1,822	−1.4	2.3	1,763.0	1,672.2	22,148	20,896	5.4
Southern Pines-Pinehurst, NC	81,685	80,066	75,155	59,013	6,530	16,142	8.7	27.4	2,503.4	2,370.0	32,107	31,534	5.6
Moore County, NC	81,685	80,066	75,155	59,013	6,530	16,142	8.7	27.4	2,503.4	2,370.0	32,107	31,534	5.6

See footnotes at end of table.

Table D-1. Micropolitan Areas — **Population and Personal Income**—Con.

Micropolitan statistical area Component counties	2005 (July 1)	2004 (July 1)	2000[1] (esti-mates base)	1990[2] (April 1)	Net change 2000–2005	Net change 1990–2000	Percent change 2000–2005	Percent change 1990–2000	Total (mil. dol.) 2002	Total (mil. dol.) 2000	Per capita[3] (dollars) 2002	Per capita[3] (dollars) 2000	Percent change 2000–2002
Spearfish, SD	22,395	22,312	21,764	20,655	631	1,109	2.9	5.4	567.4	481.8	26,252	22,139	17.8
Lawrence County, SD	22,395	22,312	21,764	20,655	631	1,109	2.9	5.4	567.4	481.8	26,252	22,139	17.8
Spencer, IA	16,897	16,955	17,384	17,585	−487	−201	−2.8	−1.1	462.7	444.2	27,061	25,549	4.2
Clay County, IA	16,897	16,955	17,384	17,585	−487	−201	−2.8	−1.1	462.7	444.2	27,061	25,549	4.2
Spirit Lake, IA	16,687	16,580	16,469	14,909	218	1,560	1.3	10.5	515.2	484.7	31,359	29,435	6.3
Dickinson County, IA	16,687	16,580	16,469	14,909	218	1,560	1.3	10.5	515.2	484.7	31,359	29,435	6.3
Starkville, MS	41,247	41,136	42,949	38,375	−1,702	4,574	−4.0	11.9	910.7	809.9	21,426	18,837	12.4
Oktibbeha County, MS	41,247	41,136	42,949	38,375	−1,702	4,574	−4.0	11.9	910.7	809.9	21,426	18,837	12.4
Statesboro, GA	61,454	60,206	56,159	43,125	5,295	13,034	9.4	30.2	1,151.1	1,100.4	20,158	19,594	4.6
Bulloch County, GA	61,454	60,206	56,159	43,125	5,295	13,034	9.4	30.2	1,151.1	1,100.4	20,158	19,594	4.6
Statesville-Mooresville, NC	140,924	136,828	123,610	92,931	17,314	30,679	14.0	33.0	3,503.6	3,326.4	26,863	26,914	5.3
Iredell County, NC	140,924	136,828	123,610	92,931	17,314	30,679	14.0	33.0	3,503.6	3,326.4	26,863	26,914	5.3
Staunton-Waynesboro, VA	114,331	112,604	109,241	97,687	5,090	11,554	4.7	11.8	2,843.5	2,627.6	25,680	24,057	8.2
Augusta County, VA	69,725	68,713	65,792	54,677	3,933	11,115	6.0	20.3	(5)2,843.5	(5)2,627.6	(5)25,680	(5)24,057	(5)8.2
Staunton city, VA	23,337	23,065	23,844	24,461	−507	−617	−2.1	−2.5	(5)	(5)	(5)	(5)	(5)
Waynesboro city, VA	21,269	20,826	19,605	18,549	1,664	1,056	8.5	5.7	(5)	(5)	(5)	(5)	(5)
Stephenville, TX	34,076	33,883	33,036	27,991	1,040	5,045	3.1	18.0	808.9	734.3	24,431	22,229	10.2
Erath County, TX	34,076	33,883	33,036	27,991	1,040	5,045	3.1	18.0	808.9	734.3	24,431	22,229	10.2
Sterling, CO	20,719	20,932	20,660	17,567	59	3,093	0.3	17.6	534.4	501.8	25,436	24,291	6.5
Logan County, CO	20,719	20,932	20,660	17,567	59	3,093	0.3	17.6	534.4	501.8	25,436	24,291	6.5
Sterling, IL	59,863	59,955	60,656	60,186	−793	470	−1.3	0.8	1,475.5	1,493.2	24,473	24,621	−1.2
Whiteside County, IL	59,863	59,955	60,656	60,186	−793	470	−1.3	0.8	1,475.5	1,493.2	24,473	24,621	−1.2
Stevens Point, WI	67,585	67,486	67,244	61,405	341	5,839	0.5	9.5	1,794.8	1,670.1	26,674	24,840	7.5
Portage County, WI	67,585	67,486	67,244	61,405	341	5,839	0.5	9.5	1,794.8	1,670.1	26,674	24,840	7.5
Stillwater, OK	69,151	69,389	68,159	61,507	992	6,652	1.5	10.8	1,516.7	1,434.2	21,627	21,012	5.8
Payne County, OK	69,151	69,389	68,159	61,507	992	6,652	1.5	10.8	1,516.7	1,434.2	21,627	21,012	5.8
Storm Lake, IA	20,151	20,160	20,364	19,965	−213	399	−1.0	2.0	499.3	482.1	24,627	23,680	3.6
Buena Vista County, IA	20,151	20,160	20,364	19,965	−213	399	−1.0	2.0	499.3	482.1	24,627	23,680	3.6
Sturgis, MI	62,984	62,831	62,540	58,913	444	3,627	0.7	6.2	1,458.4	1,444.5	23,352	23,099	1.0
St. Joseph County, MI	62,984	62,831	62,540	58,913	444	3,627	0.7	6.2	1,458.4	1,444.5	23,352	23,099	1.0
Sulphur Springs, TX	33,381	33,121	32,021	28,833	1,360	3,188	4.2	11.1	746.0	721.5	23,071	22,530	3.4
Hopkins County, TX	33,381	33,121	32,021	28,833	1,360	3,188	4.2	11.1	746.0	721.5	23,071	22,530	3.4
Summerville, GA	26,570	26,472	25,499	22,242	1,071	3,257	4.2	14.6	490.6	458.9	18,783	17,996	6.9
Chattooga County, GA	26,570	26,472	25,499	22,242	1,071	3,257	4.2	14.6	490.6	458.9	18,783	17,996	6.9
Sunbury, PA	92,610	92,821	94,478	96,771	−1,868	−2,293	−2.0	−2.4	2,235.9	2,115.2	23,919	22,389	5.7
Northumberland County, PA	92,610	92,821	94,478	96,771	−1,868	−2,293	−2.0	−2.4	2,235.9	2,115.2	23,919	22,389	5.7
Susanville, CA	34,751	34,606	33,767	27,598	984	6,169	2.9	22.4	643.8	589.4	19,174	17,456	9.2
Lassen County, CA	34,751	34,606	33,767	27,598	984	6,169	2.9	22.4	643.8	589.4	19,174	17,456	9.2
Sweetwater, TX	14,878	15,057	15,761	16,594	−883	−833	−5.6	−5.0	331.7	315.8	21,895	20,034	5.0
Nolan County, TX	14,878	15,057	15,761	16,594	−883	−833	−5.6	−5.0	331.7	315.8	21,895	20,034	5.0
Tahlequah, OK	44,671	44,159	42,675	34,049	1,996	8,626	4.7	25.3	821.7	714.9	18,945	16,758	14.9
Cherokee County, OK	44,671	44,159	42,675	34,049	1,996	8,626	4.7	25.3	821.7	714.9	18,945	16,758	14.9
Talladega-Sylacauga, AL	80,457	80,157	80,375	74,107	82	6,268	0.1	8.5	1,775.8	1,528.3	22,134	19,019	16.2
Talladega County, AL	80,457	80,157	80,375	74,107	82	6,268	0.1	8.5	1,775.8	1,528.3	22,134	19,019	16.2
Tallulah, LA	12,457	12,658	13,720	12,463	−1,263	1,257	−9.2	10.1	217.2	191.9	16,461	13,994	13.2
Madison Parish, LA	12,457	12,658	13,720	12,463	−1,263	1,257	−9.2	10.1	217.2	191.9	16,461	13,994	13.2
Taos, NM	31,722	31,501	30,079	23,118	1,643	6,961	5.5	30.1	644.6	541.6	20,912	18,009	19.0
Taos County, NM	31,722	31,501	30,079	23,118	1,643	6,961	5.5	30.1	644.6	541.6	20,912	18,009	19.0
Taylorville, IL	35,176	35,228	35,362	34,418	−186	944	−0.5	2.7	876.4	839.9	24,902	23,756	4.3
Christian County, IL	35,176	35,228	35,362	34,418	−186	944	−0.5	2.7	876.4	839.9	24,902	23,756	4.3
The Villages, FL	64,182	60,569	53,589	31,577	10,593	22,012	19.8	69.7	995.5	826.4	17,249	15,422	20.5
Sumter County, FL	64,182	60,569	53,589	31,577	10,593	22,012	19.8	69.7	995.5	826.4	17,249	15,422	20.5
Thomaston, GA	27,679	27,868	27,637	26,300	42	1,337	0.2	5.1	565.1	555.9	20,339	20,118	1.7
Upson County, GA	27,679	27,868	27,637	26,300	42	1,337	0.2	5.1	565.1	555.9	20,339	20,118	1.7
Thomasville, GA	44,692	43,866	42,845	38,986	1,847	3,859	4.3	9.9	1,115.0	992.6	25,896	23,166	12.3
Thomas County, GA	44,692	43,866	42,845	38,986	1,847	3,859	4.3	9.9	1,115.0	992.6	25,896	23,166	12.3
Thomasville-Lexington, NC	154,623	153,511	147,665	126,677	6,958	20,988	4.7	16.6	3,907.2	3,945.2	25,914	26,723	−1.0
Davidson County, NC	154,623	153,511	147,665	126,677	6,958	20,988	4.7	16.6	3,907.2	3,945.2	25,914	26,723	−1.0
Tiffin, OH	57,483	57,758	58,625	59,733	−1,142	−1,108	−1.9	−1.9	1,380.1	1,353.9	23,822	23,095	1.9
Seneca County, OH	57,483	57,758	58,625	59,733	−1,142	−1,108	−1.9	−1.9	1,380.1	1,353.9	23,822	23,095	1.9
Tifton, GA	40,793	40,204	38,434	34,998	2,359	3,436	6.1	9.8	911.4	841.2	23,342	21,883	8.3
Tift County, GA	40,793	40,204	38,434	34,998	2,359	3,436	6.1	9.8	911.4	841.2	23,342	21,883	8.3
Toccoa, GA	25,060	25,087	25,490	23,257	−430	2,233	−1.7	9.6	611.7	563.4	23,935	22,106	8.6
Stephens County, GA	25,060	25,087	25,490	23,257	−430	2,233	−1.7	9.6	611.7	563.4	23,935	22,106	8.6
Torrington, CT	190,071	189,258	182,667	174,092	7,404	8,575	4.1	4.9	7,140.1	6,948.9	38,309	38,047	2.8
Litchfield County, CT	190,071	189,258	182,667	174,092	7,404	8,575	4.1	4.9	7,140.1	6,948.9	38,309	38,047	2.8
Traverse City, MI	141,011	139,573	131,990	106,497	9,021	25,493	6.8	23.9	3,730.7	3,535.9	27,353	26,791	5.5
Benzie County, MI	17,644	17,376	16,111	12,200	1,533	3,911	9.5	32.1	418.0	381.0	24,949	23,647	9.7
Grand Traverse County, MI	83,971	82,859	77,990	64,273	5,981	13,717	7.7	21.3	2,370.5	2,254.8	29,250	28,917	5.1
Kalkaska County, MI	17,239	17,217	16,627	13,497	612	3,130	3.7	23.2	312.1	305.1	18,340	18,350	2.3
Leelanau County, MI	22,157	22,121	21,262	16,527	895	4,735	4.2	28.7	630.1	594.9	29,201	27,978	5.9
Troy, AL	29,639	29,423	29,726	27,595	−87	2,131	−0.3	7.7	691.1	624.6	23,662	21,009	10.7
Pike County, AL	29,639	29,423	29,726	27,595	−87	2,131	−0.3	7.7	691.1	624.6	23,662	21,009	10.7
Truckee-Grass Valley, CA	98,394	97,447	92,537	78,510	5,857	14,027	6.3	17.9	3,122.9	2,826.4	32,841	30,551	10.5
Nevada County, CA	98,394	97,447	92,537	78,510	5,857	14,027	6.3	17.9	3,122.9	2,826.4	32,841	30,551	10.5
Tullahoma, TN	97,896	96,819	93,291	79,785	4,605	13,506	4.9	16.9	2,234.5	2,058.2	23,453	22,064	8.6
Coffee County, TN	50,869	50,122	48,176	40,339	2,693	7,837	5.6	19.4	1,218.7	1,112.6	24,780	23,099	9.5
Franklin County, TN	41,003	40,716	39,347	34,725	1,656	4,622	4.2	13.3	885.0	826.9	22,048	21,017	7.0
Moore County, TN	6,024	5,981	5,768	4,721	256	1,047	4.4	22.2	130.7	118.6	21,959	20,565	10.2
Tupelo, MS	130,360	129,240	125,606	107,835	4,754	17,771	3.8	16.5	3,139.2	2,859.4	24,701	22,768	9.8
Itawamba County, MS	23,359	23,172	22,857	20,017	502	2,840	2.2	14.2	495.1	443.8	21,562	19,417	11.6
Lee County, MS	78,793	78,105	75,978	65,581	2,815	10,397	3.7	15.9	2,095.3	1,916.7	27,206	25,230	9.3
Pontotoc County, MS	28,208	27,963	26,771	22,237	1,437	4,534	5.4	20.4	548.8	499.0	20,245	18,640	10.0
Tuskegee, AL	22,810	23,164	24,083	24,928	−1,273	−845	−5.3	−3.4	395.9	376.2	16,728	15,624	5.2
Macon County, AL	22,810	23,164	24,083	24,928	−1,273	−845	−5.3	−3.4	395.9	376.2	16,728	15,624	5.2

See footnotes at end of table.

Table D-1. Micropolitan Areas — **Population and Personal Income**—Con.

Micropolitan statistical area Component counties	Population								Personal income				
			2000[1] (esti-mates base)	1990[2] (April 1)	Net change		Percent change		Total (mil. dol.)		Per capita[3] (dollars)		Percent change
	2005 (July 1)	2004 (July 1)			2000–2005	1990–2000	2000–2005	1990–2000	2002	2000	2002	2000	2000–2002
Twin Falls, ID	89,057	87,387	82,789	68,718	6,268	14,071	7.6	20.5	2,087.2	1,803.1	24,808	21,780	15.8
Jerome County, ID	19,638	19,304	18,440	15,138	1,198	3,302	6.5	21.8	463.0	401.8	24,787	21,785	15.2
Twin Falls County, ID	69,419	68,083	64,349	53,580	5,070	10,769	7.9	20.1	1,624.2	1,401.4	24,814	21,778	15.9
Ukiah, CA	88,161	88,407	86,426	80,345	1,735	6,081	2.0	7.6	2,358.3	2,151.2	26,947	24,898	9.6
Mendocino County, CA	88,161	88,407	86,426	80,345	1,735	6,081	2.0	7.6	2,358.3	2,151.2	26,947	24,898	9.6
Union, SC	28,539	28,641	29,879	30,337	–1,340	–458	–4.5	–1.5	644.6	602.9	22,002	20,182	6.9
Union County, SC	28,539	28,641	29,879	30,337	–1,340	–458	–4.5	–1.5	644.6	602.9	22,002	20,182	6.9
Union City, TN-KY	39,430	39,724	40,203	39,988	–773	215	–1.9	0.5	974.4	957.3	24,376	23,816	1.8
Fulton County, KY	7,217	7,337	7,705	8,271	–488	–566	–6.3	–6.8	169.2	166.3	22,398	21,591	1.7
Obion County, TN	32,213	32,387	32,498	31,717	–285	781	–0.9	2.5	805.2	791.0	24,837	24,343	1.8
Urbana, OH	39,698	39,581	38,944	36,019	754	2,925	1.9	8.1	1,010.7	993.5	25,743	25,514	1.7
Champaign County, OH	39,698	39,581	38,944	36,019	754	2,925	1.9	8.1	1,010.7	993.5	25,743	25,514	1.7
Uvalde, TX	26,955	26,663	25,935	23,340	1,020	2,595	3.9	11.1	527.7	484.2	19,839	18,667	9.0
Uvalde County, TX	26,955	26,663	25,935	23,340	1,020	2,595	3.9	11.1	527.7	484.2	19,839	18,667	9.0
Valley, AL	35,460	35,557	36,577	36,876	–1,117	–299	–3.1	–0.8	799.6	730.0	22,141	19,957	9.5
Chambers County, AL	35,460	35,557	36,577	36,876	–1,117	–299	–3.1	–0.8	799.6	730.0	22,141	19,957	9.5
Van Wert, OH	29,154	29,259	29,639	30,464	–485	–825	–1.6	–2.7	711.0	730.9	24,277	24,666	–2.7
Van Wert County, OH	29,154	29,259	29,639	30,464	–485	–825	–1.6	–2.7	711.0	730.9	24,277	24,666	–2.7
Vermillion, SD	12,995	13,019	13,481	13,186	–486	295	–3.6	2.2	322.3	311.3	24,338	23,076	3.6
Clay County, SD	12,995	13,019	13,481	13,186	–486	295	–3.6	2.2	322.3	311.3	24,338	23,076	3.6
Vernal, UT	26,995	26,567	25,272	22,211	1,723	3,061	6.8	13.8	480.6	427.7	18,341	16,928	12.4
Uintah County, UT	26,995	26,567	25,272	22,211	1,723	3,061	6.8	13.8	480.6	427.7	18,341	16,928	12.4
Vernon, TX	13,896	13,934	14,628	15,121	–732	–493	–5.0	–3.3	342.0	324.4	24,455	22,171	5.4
Wilbarger County, TX	13,896	13,934	14,628	15,121	–732	–493	–5.0	–3.3	342.0	324.4	24,455	22,171	5.4
Vicksburg, MS	49,131	49,221	49,585	47,880	–454	1,705	–0.9	3.6	1,336.5	1,241.0	27,189	25,034	7.7
Warren County, MS	49,131	49,221	49,585	47,880	–454	1,705	–0.9	3.6	1,336.5	1,241.0	27,189	25,034	7.7
Vidalia, GA	36,183	35,745	34,400	31,235	1,783	3,165	5.2	10.1	727.7	672.3	20,945	19,548	8.2
Montgomery County, GA	8,909	8,929	8,274	7,163	635	1,111	7.7	15.5	159.0	146.2	18,767	17,669	8.7
Toombs County, GA	27,274	26,816	26,126	24,072	1,148	2,054	4.4	8.5	568.7	526.1	21,647	20,144	8.1
Vincennes, IN	38,366	38,513	39,188	39,884	–822	–696	–2.1	–1.7	966.2	894.6	24,936	22,831	8.0
Knox County, IN	38,366	38,513	39,188	39,884	–822	–696	–2.1	–1.7	966.2	894.6	24,936	22,831	8.0
Wabash, IN	33,843	34,115	34,981	35,069	–1,138	–88	–3.3	–0.3	872.5	868.9	25,282	24,843	0.4
Wabash County, IN	33,843	34,115	34,981	35,069	–1,138	–88	–3.3	–0.3	872.5	868.9	25,282	24,843	0.4
Wahpeton, ND-MN	24,142	24,251	25,079	25,664	–937	–585	–3.7	–2.3	640.8	590.8	26,290	23,557	8.5
Wilkin County, MN	6,802	6,813	7,127	7,516	–325	–389	–4.6	–5.2	165.4	160.9	23,788	22,580	2.8
Richland County, ND	17,340	17,438	17,952	18,148	–612	–196	–3.4	–1.1	475.4	429.9	27,288	23,945	10.6
Walla Walla, WA	57,558	57,238	55,294	48,439	2,264	6,855	4.1	14.2	1,354.1	1,252.0	24,159	22,646	8.2
Walla Walla County, WA	57,558	57,238	55,294	48,439	2,264	6,855	4.1	14.2	1,354.1	1,252.0	24,159	22,646	8.2
Walterboro, SC	39,605	39,502	38,352	34,377	1,253	3,975	3.3	11.6	789.7	732.7	20,298	19,106	7.8
Colleton County, SC	39,605	39,502	38,352	34,377	1,253	3,975	3.3	11.6	789.7	732.7	20,298	19,106	7.8
Wapakoneta, OH	47,242	46,892	46,625	44,585	617	2,040	1.3	4.6	1,291.2	1,305.6	27,652	28,007	–1.1
Auglaize County, OH	47,242	46,892	46,625	44,585	617	2,040	1.3	4.6	1,291.2	1,305.6	27,652	28,007	–1.1
Warren, PA	42,033	42,470	43,796	45,050	–1,763	–1,254	–4.0	–2.8	1,040.4	1,028.0	24,099	23,477	1.2
Warren County, PA	42,033	42,470	43,796	45,050	–1,763	–1,254	–4.0	–2.8	1,040.4	1,028.0	24,099	23,477	1.2
Warrensburg, MO	50,784	50,620	48,437	42,514	2,347	5,923	4.8	13.9	1,095.6	970.3	22,007	20,019	12.9
Johnson County, MO	50,784	50,620	48,437	42,514	2,347	5,923	4.8	13.9	1,095.6	970.3	22,007	20,019	12.9
Warsaw, IN	76,072	75,531	74,235	65,294	1,837	8,941	2.5	13.7	2,045.2	1,948.3	27,287	26,247	5.0
Kosciusko County, IN	76,072	75,531	74,235	65,294	1,837	8,941	2.5	13.7	2,045.2	1,948.3	27,287	26,247	5.0
Washington, IN	30,466	30,287	29,830	27,533	636	2,297	2.1	8.3	686.8	670.8	23,029	22,492	2.4
Daviess County, IN	30,466	30,287	29,830	27,533	636	2,297	2.1	8.3	686.8	670.8	23,029	22,492	2.4
Washington, NC	46,018	45,635	44,989	42,283	1,029	2,706	2.3	6.4	1,009.3	1,009.5	22,311	22,441	(Z)
Beaufort County, NC	46,018	45,635	44,989	42,283	1,029	2,706	2.3	6.4	1,009.3	1,009.5	22,311	22,441	(Z)
Washington, OH	28,199	28,067	28,439	27,466	–240	973	–0.8	3.5	702.2	637.4	24,964	22,416	10.2
Fayette County, OH	28,199	28,067	28,439	27,466	–240	973	–0.8	3.5	702.2	637.4	24,964	22,416	10.2
Watertown, SD	31,717	31,573	31,461	27,672	256	3,789	0.8	13.7	827.1	799.1	26,327	25,405	3.5
Codington County, SD	26,010	25,956	25,910	22,698	100	3,212	0.4	14.2	699.4	676.8	27,091	26,127	3.3
Hamlin County, SD	5,707	5,617	5,551	4,974	156	577	2.8	11.6	127.7	122.3	22,801	22,032	4.4
Watertown-Fort Atkinson, WI	79,328	78,307	75,944	67,783	3,384	8,161	4.5	12.0	2,214.2	2,120.9	28,805	27,929	4.4
Jefferson County, WI	79,328	78,307	75,944	67,783	3,384	8,161	4.5	12.0	2,214.2	2,120.9	28,805	27,929	4.4
Watertown-Fort Drum, NY	116,384	114,424	111,469	110,943	4,915	526	4.4	0.5	2,734.3	2,551.3	23,999	22,884	7.2
Jefferson County, NY	116,384	114,424	111,469	110,943	4,915	526	4.4	0.5	2,734.3	2,551.3	23,999	22,884	7.2
Wauchula, FL	28,286	28,022	26,914	19,499	1,372	7,415	5.1	38.0	496.4	447.3	18,001	16,619	11.0
Hardee County, FL	28,286	28,022	26,914	19,499	1,372	7,415	5.1	38.0	496.4	447.3	18,001	16,619	11.0
Waycross, GA	51,611	51,100	51,173	48,799	438	2,374	0.9	4.9	1,082.4	1,004.7	21,035	19,637	7.7
Pierce County, GA	17,119	16,702	15,714	13,328	1,405	2,386	8.9	17.9	337.3	312.8	21,071	19,907	7.8
Ware County, GA	34,492	34,398	35,459	35,471	–967	–12	–2.7	0.0	745.1	692.0	21,019	19,517	7.7
West Helena, AR	24,107	24,350	26,282	28,838	–2,175	–2,556	–8.3	–8.9	450.2	440.3	17,970	16,756	2.3
Phillips County, AR	24,107	24,350	26,282	28,838	–2,175	–2,556	–8.3	–8.9	450.2	440.3	17,970	16,756	2.3
West Plains, MO	38,400	37,861	37,235	31,447	1,165	5,788	3.1	18.4	761.9	681.4	20,442	18,303	11.8
Howell County, MO	38,400	37,861	37,235	31,447	1,165	5,788	3.1	18.4	761.9	681.4	20,442	18,303	11.8
West Point, MS	21,223	21,540	21,973	21,120	–750	853	–3.4	4.0	457.5	425.7	20,914	19,375	7.5
Clay County, MS	21,223	21,540	21,973	21,120	–750	853	–3.4	4.0	457.5	425.7	20,914	19,375	7.5
Whitewater, WI	99,844	98,089	92,420	75,000	7,424	17,420	8.0	23.2	2,603.1	2,522.4	27,364	27,295	3.2
Walworth County, WI	99,844	98,089	92,420	75,000	7,424	17,420	8.0	23.2	2,603.1	2,522.4	27,364	27,295	3.2
Willimantic, CT	115,826	114,623	109,199	102,525	6,627	6,674	6.1	6.5	3,170.5	2,971.1	28,526	27,211	6.7
Windham County, CT	115,826	114,623	109,199	102,525	6,627	6,674	6.1	6.5	3,170.5	2,971.1	28,526	27,211	6.7
Williston, ND	19,282	19,244	19,660	21,129	–378	–1,469	–1.9	–7.0	486.1	444.9	24,917	22,627	9.3
Williams County, ND	19,282	19,244	19,660	21,129	–378	–1,469	–1.9	–7.0	486.1	444.9	24,917	22,627	9.3
Willmar, MN	41,199	41,169	41,162	38,761	37	2,401	0.1	6.2	1,188.3	1,102.2	29,095	26,776	7.8
Kandiyohi County, MN	41,199	41,169	41,162	38,761	37	2,401	0.1	6.2	1,188.3	1,102.2	29,095	26,776	7.8
Wilmington, OH	42,570	42,202	40,686	35,415	1,884	5,271	4.6	14.9	1,050.6	1,055.6	25,441	25,948	–0.5
Clinton County, OH	42,570	42,202	40,686	35,415	1,884	5,271	4.6	14.9	1,050.6	1,055.6	25,441	25,948	–0.5
Wilson, NC	76,281	75,844	73,932	66,061	2,349	7,871	3.2	11.9	1,813.6	1,730.6	24,205	23,412	4.8
Wilson County, NC	76,281	75,844	73,932	66,061	2,349	7,871	3.2	11.9	1,813.6	1,730.6	24,205	23,412	4.8

See footnotes at end of table.

Table D-1. Micropolitan Areas — **Population and Personal Income**—Con.

Micropolitan statistical area Component counties	Population								Personal income				
					Net change		Percent change		Total (mil. dol.)		Per capita[3] (dollars)		Percent change
	2005 (July 1)	2004 (July 1)	2000[1] (esti- mates base)	1990[2] (April 1)	2000– 2005	1990– 2000	2000– 2005	1990– 2000	2002	2000	2002	2000	2000– 2002
Winfield, KS	35,298	35,697	36,280	36,915	−982	−635	−2.7	−1.7	881.4	818.7	24,239	22,567	7.7
Cowley County, KS.	35,298	35,697	36,280	36,915	−982	−635	−2.7	−1.7	881.4	818.7	24,239	22,567	7.7
Winona, MN	49,276	49,148	50,015	47,828	−739	2,187	−1.5	4.6	1,267.3	1,214.2	25,583	24,270	4.4
Winona County, MN	49,276	49,148	50,015	47,828	−739	2,187	−1.5	4.6	1,267.3	1,214.2	25,583	24,270	4.4
Wisconsin Rapids-Marshfield, WI	75,234	75,228	75,576	73,605	−342	1,971	−0.5	2.7	2,225.9	2,087.6	29,533	27,627	6.6
Wood County, WI	75,234	75,228	75,576	73,605	−342	1,971	−0.5	2.7	2,225.9	2,087.6	29,533	27,627	6.6
Woodward, OK	19,088	18,902	18,439	18,976	649	−537	3.5	−2.8	392.2	366.5	21,257	19,880	7.0
Woodward County, OK	19,088	18,902	18,439	18,976	649	−537	3.5	−2.8	392.2	366.5	21,257	19,880	7.0
Wooster, OH.	113,697	113,169	111,701	101,461	1,996	10,240	1.8	10.1	2,820.4	2,675.7	25,002	23,954	5.4
Wayne County, OH.	113,697	113,169	111,701	101,461	1,996	10,240	1.8	10.1	2,820.4	2,675.7	25,002	23,954	5.4
Worthington, MN	20,508	20,479	20,807	20,098	−299	709	−1.4	3.5	520.4	482.4	25,241	23,182	7.9
Nobles County, MN.	20,508	20,479	20,807	20,098	−299	709	−1.4	3.5	520.4	482.4	25,241	23,182	7.9
Yankton, SD	21,718	21,776	21,610	19,252	108	2,358	0.5	12.2	540.4	532.0	25,147	24,618	1.6
Yankton County, SD	21,718	21,776	21,610	19,252	108	2,358	0.5	12.2	540.4	532.0	25,147	24,618	1.6
Yazoo City, MS	28,195	28,329	28,163	25,506	32	2,657	0.1	10.4	522.1	504.0	18,633	17,901	3.6
Yazoo County, MS	28,195	28,329	28,163	25,506	32	2,657	0.1	10.4	522.1	504.0	18,633	17,901	3.6
Zanesville, OH	85,579	85,487	84,734	82,068	845	2,666	1.0	3.2	2,090.4	1,978.5	24,540	23,350	5.7
Muskingum County, OH.	85,579	85,487	84,734	82,068	845	2,666	1.0	3.2	2,090.4	1,978.5	24,540	23,350	5.7

Z Less than .05%.

[1]The April 1, 2000, Population Estimates base reflects modifications to the Census 2000 population as documented in the Count Question Resolution program and geographic program revisions.
[2]The April 1, 1990, census counts include corrections processed through August 1997 and results of special censuses and test censuses, and do not include adjustments for census coverage errors.
[3]Based on resident population estimated as of July 1, 2000 and 2002.
[4]Independent city of Martinsville is included with Henry County; data not available separately.
[5]Independent cities of Staunton and Waynesboro included with Augusta County; data not available separately.

Note: Covers micropolitan statistical areas and component counties defined by the Office of Management and Budget as of June 6, 2003, and subsequently updated in December 2003 and November 2004. For more information, see OMB Bulletin 05-02 at <http://www.whitehouse.gov/omb/bulletins/fy05/b05-02_appendix.pdf>.

Survey, Census, or Data Collection Method: Population—Based on the 2000 Census of Population and Housing and, for population estimates, the "component of population change method" and "County Characteristic Population Estimates Data"; see Appendix B, Limitations of the Data and Methodology, and also <http://www.census.gov/prod/cen2000/doc/sf1.pdf> and <http://www.census.gov/popest/topics/methodology/>; Personal income—Based on the Regional Economic Information System; for more information, see Appendix B, Limitations of the Data and Methodology, and also <http://www.bea.gov/bea/regional/articles.cfm?section=methods> and <http://www.bea.gov/bea/regional/articles/lapi2003/lapi2003.pdf>.

Sources: Population—U.S. Census Bureau, 2000 to 2005 compiled from "Population Estimates by County," published 16 March 2006; <http://www.census.gov/popest/counties/CO-EST2005-01.html>; and "Population Estimates, Cumulative Estimates of the Components of Population Change for Counties," published 16 March 2006; April 1, 2000, to July 1, 2005, <http://www.census.gov/popest/counties/CO-EST2005-05.html>; 1990, "Population Estimates: Annual Time Series," archive 1990 (revised data for April 1, 1990, Population Estimates base) <http://www.census.gov/popest/archives/1990s/CO-99-02.html>; Personal income—U.S. Bureau of Economic Analysis, *Regional Economic Information System (REIS) 1969-2002* on CD-ROM, and related Internet site at <http://www.bea.gov/bea/regional/reis/> (released 25 May 2004).

Appendixes

You may visit us on the Web at
http://www.census.gov/compendia/smadb

Appendixes

Appendix A.
Source Notes and Explanations

This appendix presents general notes on population and economic and government censuses followed by source notes and explanations of the data items presented in table sets A through D of this publication. These table sets vary in both geographic and data coverage.

Each table set begins with information on the number of data items and tables, as well as specific geographic coverage. For each table, the table number and title are given, followed by a brief listing of the data items on that table, the source citation for these items, and related definitions and other explanatory text on the source.

GENERAL NOTES

Population

Decennial censuses. The population statistics for 2000 and earlier are based on results from the censuses of population and housing, conducted by the U.S. Census Bureau as of April 1 in each of those years. As provided by Article 1, Section 2, of the U.S. Constitution, adopted in 1787, a census has been taken every 10 years commencing with 1790. The original purposes of the census were to apportion the seats in the U.S. House of Representatives based on the population of each state and to derive an equitable tax on each state for the payment of the Revolutionary War debt. Through the years, the nation's needs and interests have become more complex, and the content of the decennial census has changed accordingly. Presently, census data not only are used to apportion seats in the House and to aid legislators in the realignment of legislative district boundaries but are also used in the distribution of billions of federal dollars each year and are vital to state and local governments and to private firms for such functions as market analysis, site selection, and environmental impact studies.

The decennial census uses both short- and long-form questionnaires to gather information. The short form asks a limited number of basic questions. These questions are asked of all people and housing units and are often referred to as 100-percent questions because they are asked of the entire population. The population items include sex, age, race, Hispanic or Latino, household relationship, and group quarters. Housing items include occupancy status, vacancy status, and tenure (owner occupied or renter occupied). The long form asks more detailed information on a sample basis and includes the 100-percent questions as well as questions on education,

employment, income, ancestry, homeowner costs, units in a structure, number of rooms, plumbing facilities, etc. For a more detailed discussion of the information available from the 2000 census, see *Introduction to Census 2000 Data Products* available at <http://www.census.gov/mso /www/prodprof/census2000.pdf>.

Persons enumerated in the census were counted as inhabitants of their usual place of residence, which generally means the place where a person lives and sleeps most of the time. This place is not necessarily the same as the legal residence, voting residence, or domicile. In the vast majority of cases, however, the use of these different bases of classification would produce substantially the same statistics, although appreciable differences may exist for a few areas.

The implementation of this usual-residence practice has resulted in the establishment of residence rules for certain categories of persons whose usual place of residence is not immediately apparent (e.g., college students were counted at their college residence). As in the above example, persons were not always counted as residents of the place where they happened to be staying on census day. However, persons without a usual place of residence were counted where they were enumerated.

For information on procedures and concepts used for the 2000 Census of Population and Housing, as well as a facsimile of the questionnaires and descriptions of the data products resulting from the census, see U.S. Census Bureau, *2000 Census of Population and Housing: Summary File 1, Technical Documentation*, Series SF1/01(RV) released June 2001 and available on the Census Bureau Web site at <http://www.census.gov/prod/cen2000/doc /sf1.pdf> and *2000 Census of Population and Housing, Demographic Profiles of General Demographic Characteristics, Technical Documentation*, released May 2001 and available at <http://www.census.gov/prod/cen2000/doc /ProfilesTD.pdf>.

Population estimates. The Census Bureau annually produces estimates of total resident population for each state and county. County population estimates are produced with a component of population change method, while the state population estimates are solely the sum of the county populations.

The Census Bureau develops county population estimates with a demographic procedure called an "administrative records component of population change" method. A major assumption underlying this approach is that the components of population change are closely approximated by administrative data in a demographic change model. In order to apply the model, Census Bureau demographers estimate each component of population change separately. For the population residing in households, the components of population change are births, deaths, and net migration, including net international migration. For the nonhousehold population, change is represented by the net change in the population living in group quarters facilities.

Each component in this model is represented with data that are symptomatic of some aspect of population change. For example, birth certificates are symptomatic of additions to the population resulting from births, so the Census Bureau uses these data to estimate the birth component for a county. Some other components are derived from death certificates, Internal Revenue Service (IRS) data, medicare enrollment records, armed forces data, group quarters population data, and data from the American Community Survey (ACS).

In cases where the Census Bureau does not have data for all counties for the current estimate year, components of population change are estimated based on one or more simplifying assumptions. When initial population estimates are prepared, the same variant of the component model with these simplifying assumptions is used. In the creation of current vintage population estimates, the initial population estimates from the previous vintage are replaced with "revised" population estimates calculated with the actual data for all components of population change. Calculations of "revised" population estimates also incorporate updates to components of change from previous years.

The estimates of the county populations are produced by starting with the base populations from either Census 2000 or the revised population estimate for the most recent year and then adding or subtracting the demographic components of population change calculated for the time period. Basically, the Census Bureau adds the estimated number of births and subtracts the estimated number of deaths for the time period. The Census Bureau then accounts for net migration, which is calculated using several components including net internal migration, net foreign-born international migration, net movement to/from Puerto Rico, net armed forces movement to/from overseas, the change in group quarters population, and native emigration from the United States

The Census Bureau produces separate population estimates for the populations under age 65 and age 65 and older, mainly because different data are used to measure the internal migration of these two populations. For the population under age 65, data from individual IRS tax returns is used to calculate measures of migration.

Medicare enrollment is used to calculate measures of migration for the population age 65 and older because this population is not always well-represented on tax returns.

The first step in estimating the population under age 65 is to establish the base populations under age 65. The total base population for the estimate of the population under age 65 is either the April 1, 2000, population estimates base or the revised county population estimate for the prior estimate year. For official population estimates, the April 1, 2000, population estimates base is not adjusted for census undercount. In general, the April 1, 2000, population estimates base uses Census 2000 data as its base, but includes certain modifications (geographic updates, Count Question Resolution (CQR) changes to the Census Bureau's program TIGER database). The group quarters population component is primarily a combination of military personnel living in barracks, college students living in dormitories, and persons residing in institutions. The Census Bureau subtracts the base group quarters population under age 65 from the base total population under age 65 to calculate the base household population under age 65.

The components of population change are calculated using resident births, resident deaths to the population under age 65, net internal migration for the population under age 65, and net international migration for the population under age 65. Resident births are recorded by residence of mother, regardless of where the birth occurred; hence, a county need not have a hospital in order to have resident births. Resident deaths to the population under age 65 use death data tabulated by the most recent residence of the decedent, not by the place where the death occurred. Net internal migration for population under age 65 is estimated using household migration derived from federal income tax returns and the change in the group quarters population.

Net international migration for the population under age 65 is estimated from several sources, including the net foreign-born international migration, net movement to/from Puerto Rico, net armed forces movement to/from overseas, and native emigration. National-level data on the net foreign-born international migration of the population under 65 for the current estimate period are distributed to counties based on the county distribution of the noncitizen foreign-born population who entered the U.S. during the 5 years prior to April 1, 2000, from Census 2000. National-level data on the total net movement of the population under age 65 to or from Puerto Rico for the current estimate period are distributed to counties based on the county distribution of the Puerto Rican population who entered the U.S. during the 5 years prior to April 1, 2000. The national-level total armed forces station strength data are distributed to states using armed forces data originally supplied by each branch of the service, and these state-level data are distributed to counties using the military employment data from Census 2000. National-level data on the total number of emigrants from the United States under age 65 for the current estimate period are distributed to counties based on the county distribution of the native-born population from Census 2000.

The first step in estimating the population age 65 and older is to establish the base populations. The total base population for the estimate of the population age 65 and older is either the Census 2000 base (for July 1 population estimate in the decennial year) or the revised county population estimate for the prior estimate year. The base group quarters population age 65 and older is primarily a combination of persons age 65 and older residing in nursing homes and other facilities and persons residing in institutions. This population is subtracted from the total base population to calculate the base household population age 65 and older.

The components of population change for the population 65 and older are resident deaths to populations age 65 and older, net internal migration for population age 65 and older, and net international migration for population age 65 and over. Resident deaths to the population age 65 and older use death data tabulated by the most recent residence of the decedent, not by the place where the death occurred. Net internal migration for population age 65 and older includes household migration derived from medicare enrollment records and the change in the group quarters population. The process used to derive the net international migration for the population age 65 and older is similar to that used for the population under age 65.

A detailed explanation of how population estimates are produced can be found at <http://www.census.gov /popest/topics/methodology/2004_st_co_meth.html>.

American Community Survey

The American Community Survey (ACS) is a new nationwide survey designed to provide communities a fresh look at how they are changing. It is intended to eliminate the need for the long form in the 2010 census. The ACS collects information from U.S. households similar to what was collected on the Census 2000 long form, such as income, commute time to work, home value, veteran status, and other important data. As with the official U.S. census, information about individuals will remain confidential.

The ACS collects and produces population and housing information every year instead of every 10 years. About three million households are surveyed each year. Collecting data every year will reduce the cost of the official

decennial census, and will provide more up-to-date information throughout the decade about trends in the U.S. population at the local community level. A similar program is planned for Puerto Rico.

The ACS began in 1996 and has expanded each subsequent year. Data from the 2003 ACS are available for approximately 862 geographies including the nation, all states, the District of Columbia, most areas with a population of 250,000 or more, and selected areas of 65,000 or more.

The Census Bureau plans to conduct the ACS in every county of the United States, contacting the residents of three million housing units. Within 3 years, data should be available for all areas of 20,000 or more. For small areas less than 20,000, it will take 5 years to accumulate a large enough sample to provide estimates with accuracy similar to the decennial census.

Economic Censuses

The economic census is the major source of facts about the structure and functioning of the nation's economy. It provides essential information for government, business, industry, and the general public. It furnishes an important part of the framework for such composite measures as the gross domestic product estimates, input/output measures, production and price indexes, and other statistical series that measure short-term changes in economic conditions. Title 13 of the United States Code (Sections 131, 191, and 224) directs the Census Bureau to take the economic census every 5 years, covering years ending in "2" and "7." The economic censuses form an integrated program at 5-year intervals since 1967 and before that for 1963, 1958, and 1954. Prior to that time, the individual censuses were taken separately at varying intervals. Prior to 1997, the Census Bureau took the census of agriculture, but beginning in 1997, the census has been done under the direction of the U.S. Department of Agriculture. Beginning with the 1997 Economic Census data found in this publication, the census presents data based on the North American Industry Classification System (NAICS). Previous census data were presented based on the Standard Industrial Classification (SIC) system developed some 60 years ago. Due to this change, comparability between census years and data found in previous books will be limited. This new system of industrial classification was developed by experts on classification in government and private industry under the guidance of the Office of Information and Regulatory Affairs, Office of Management and Budget.

There are 20 NAICS sectors, which are subdivided into 100 subsectors (three-digit codes), 317 industry groups (four-digit codes), and, as implemented in the United States, 1,904 industries (five- and six-digit codes). While many of the individual NAICS industries correspond directly to industries as defined under the SIC system, most of the higher-level groupings do not.

The economic censuses are collected on an establishment basis. A company operating at more than one location is required to file a separate report for each store, factory, shop, or other location. Each establishment is assigned a separate industry classification based on its primary activity and not that of its parent company. Establishments responding to the establishment survey are classified into industries on the basis of their principal product or activity (determined by annual sales volume) in accordance with the "North American Industry Classification System—United States, 2002" manual available from the National Technical Information Service.

More detailed information about the scope, coverage, classification system, data items, and publications for each of the economic censuses and related surveys is published in the Guide to the Economic Censuses and Related Statistics. More information on the methodology, procedures, and history of the censuses is available in the "Guide to the 2002 Economic Census" found on the Census Bureau Web site at <http://www.census.gov/econ/census02 /guide/index.html>.

Data from the 2002 Economic Census were released through the Census Bureau's American FactFinder service, on CD-ROM, and in Adobe Acrobat PDF reports available on the Census Bureau Web site. For more information on these various media of release, see the following page on the Census Bureau Web site <http://www.census.gov /econ/census02/>.

North American Industry Classification System (NAICS) Sectors

The **Agriculture, Forestry, Fishing and Hunting** sector (NAICS 11) comprises establishments primarily engaged in growing crops, raising animals, harvesting timber, and harvesting fish and other animals from a farm, ranch, or their natural habitats.

The establishments in this sector are often described as farms, ranches, dairies, greenhouses, nurseries, orchards, or hatcheries. A farm may consist of a single tract of land or a number of separate tracts, which may be held under different tenures. For example, one tract may be owned by the farm operator and another rented. It may be operated by the operator alone or with the assistance of members of the household or hired employees, or it may be operated by a partnership, corporation, or other type of organization. When a landowner has one or more tenants, renters, croppers, or managers, the land operated by each is considered a farm.

The sector distinguishes two basic activities: agricultural production and agricultural support activities. Agricultural production includes establishments performing the complete farm or ranch operation, such as farm owner-operators, tenant farm operators, and sharecroppers. Agricultural support activities include establishments that

perform one or more activities associated with farm operation, such as soil preparation, planting, harvesting, and management, on a contract or fee basis.

Excluded from the Agriculture, Forestry, Hunting and Fishing sector are establishments primarily engaged in agricultural research and establishments primarily engaged in administering programs for regulating and conserving land, mineral, wildlife, and forest use. These establishments are classified in Industry 54171, Research and Development in the Physical, Engineering, and Life Sciences; and Industry 92412, Administration of Conservation Programs, respectively.

The **Mining** sector (NAICS 21) comprises establishments that extract naturally occurring mineral solids, such as coal and ores; liquid minerals, such as crude petroleum; and gases, such as natural gas. The term mining is used in the broad sense to include quarrying, well operations, beneficiating (e.g., crushing, screening, washing, and flotation), and other preparation customarily performed at the mine site, or as a part of mining activity.

The Mining sector distinguishes two basic activities: mine operation and mining support activities. Mine operation includes establishments operating mines, quarries, or oil and gas wells on their own account or for others on a contract or fee basis. Mining support activities include establishments that perform exploration (except geophysical surveying) and/or other mining services on a contract or fee basis (except mine site preparation and construction of oil/gas pipelines).

Establishments in the Mining sector are grouped and classified according to the natural resource mined or to be mined. Industries include establishments that develop the mine site, extract the natural resources, and/or those that beneficiate (i.e., prepare) the mineral mined. Beneficiation is the process whereby the extracted material is reduced to particles that can be separated into mineral and waste, the former suitable for further processing or direct use. The operations that take place in beneficiation are primarily mechanical, such as grinding, washing, magnetic separation, and centrifugal separation. In contrast, manufacturing operations primarily use chemical and electrochemical processes, such as electrolysis and distillation. However, some treatments, such as heat treatments, take place in both the beneficiation and the manufacturing (i.e., smelting/refining) stages. The range of preparation activities varies by mineral and the purity of any given ore deposit. While some minerals, such as petroleum and natural gas, require little or no preparation, others are washed and screened, while yet others, such as gold and silver, can be transformed into bullion before leaving the mine site.

Mining, beneficiating, and manufacturing activities often occur in a single location. Separate receipts will be collected for these activities whenever possible. When receipts cannot be broken out between mining and manufacturing, establishments that mine or quarry nonmetallic minerals and beneficiate the nonmetallic minerals into more finished manufactured products are classified based on the primary activity of the establishment. A mine that manufactures a small amount of finished products will be classified in Sector 21, Mining. An establishment that mines whose primary output is a more finished manufactured product will be classified in Sector 31–33, Manufacturing.

The **Utilities** sector (NAICS 22) comprises establishments engaged in the provision of the following utility services: electric power, natural gas, steam supply, water supply, and sewage removal. Within this sector, the specific activities associated with the utility services provided vary by utility: electric power includes generation, transmission, and distribution; natural gas includes distribution; steam supply includes provision and/or distribution; water supply includes treatment and distribution; and sewage removal includes collection, treatment, and disposal of waste through sewer systems and sewage treatment facilities. Excluded from this sector are establishments primarily engaged in waste management services classified in Subsector 562, Waste Management and Remediation Services, which also collect, treat, and dispose of waste materials; however, they do not use sewer systems or sewage treatment facilities.

The **Construction** sector (NAICS 23) comprises establishments primarily engaged in the construction of buildings or engineering projects (e.g., highways and utility systems). Establishments primarily engaged in the preparation of sites for new construction and establishments primarily engaged in subdividing land for sale as building sites also are included in this sector.

Construction work done may include new work, additions, alterations, or maintenance and repairs. Activities of these establishments generally are managed at a fixed place of business, but they usually perform construction activities at multiple project sites. Production responsibilities for establishments in this sector are usually specified in (1) contracts with the owners of construction projects (prime contracts) or (2) contracts with other construction establishments (subcontracts).

Establishments primarily engaged in contracts that include responsibility for all aspects of individual construction projects are commonly known as general contractors, but also may be known as design-builders, construction managers, turnkey contractors, or (in cases where two or more establishments jointly secure a general contract) joint-venture contractors. Construction managers that provide oversight and scheduling only (i.e., agency) as well as construction managers that are responsible for the entire

project (i.e., at risk) are included as general contractor-type establishments. Establishments of the "general contractor type" frequently arrange construction of separate parts of their projects through subcontracts with other construction establishments.

Establishments primarily engaged in activities to produce a specific component (e.g., masonry, painting, and electrical work) of a construction project are commonly known as specialty trade contractors. Activities of specialty trade contractors are usually subcontracted from other construction establishments, but especially in remodeling and repair construction, the work may be done directly for the owner of the property.

Establishments primarily engaged in activities to construct buildings to be sold on sites that they own are known as operative builders, but also may be known as speculative builders or merchant builders. Operative builders produce buildings in a manner similar to general contractors, but their production processes also include site acquisition and securing of financial backing. Operative builders are most often associated with the construction of residential buildings. Like general contractors, they may subcontract all or part of the actual construction work on their buildings.

There are substantial differences in the types of equipment, workforce skills, and other inputs required by establishments in this sector. To highlight these differences and variations in the underlying production functions, this sector is divided into three subsectors.

Subsector 236, Construction of Buildings, comprises establishments of the general contractor type and operative builders involved in the construction of buildings. Subsector 237, Heavy and Civil Engineering Construction, comprises establishments involved in the construction of engineering projects. Subsector 238, Specialty Trade Contractors, comprises establishments engaged in specialty trade activities generally needed in the construction of all types of buildings.

Force account construction is construction work performed by an enterprise primarily engaged in some business other than construction for its own account and use, using employees of the enterprise. This activity is not included in the construction sector unless the construction work performed is the primary activity of a separate establishment of the enterprise. The installation and the ongoing repair and maintenance of telecommunications and utility networks is excluded from construction when the establishments performing the work are not independent contractors. Although a growing proportion of this work is subcontracted to independent contractors in the Construction Sector, the operating units of telecommunications and utility companies performing this work are included with the telecommunications or utility activities.

The **Manufacturing** sector (NAICS 31–33) comprises establishments engaged in the mechanical, physical, or chemical transformation of materials, substances, or components into new products. The assembling of component parts of manufactured products is considered manufacturing, except in cases where the activity is appropriately classified in Sector 23, Construction.

Establishments in the Manufacturing sector are often described as plants, factories, or mills and characteristically use power-driven machines and materials-handling equipment. However, establishments that transform materials or substances into new products by hand or in the worker's home and those engaged in selling to the general public products made on the same premises from which they are sold, such as bakeries, candy stores, and custom tailors, may also be included in this sector. Manufacturing establishments may process materials or may contract with other establishments to process their materials for them. Both types of establishments are included in manufacturing.

The materials, substances, or components transformed by manufacturing establishments are raw materials that are products of agriculture, forestry, fishing, mining, or quarrying as well as products of other manufacturing establishments. The materials used may be purchased directly from producers, obtained through customary trade channels, or secured without recourse to the market by transferring the product from one establishment to another, under the same ownership. The new product of a manufacturing establishment may be finished in the sense that it is ready for utilization or consumption, or it may be semifinished to become an input for an establishment engaged in further manufacturing. For example, the product of the alumina refinery is the input used in the primary production of aluminum; primary aluminum is the input to an aluminum wire drawing plant; and aluminum wire is the input for a fabricated wire product manufacturing establishment.

The subsectors in the Manufacturing sector generally reflect distinct production processes related to material inputs, production equipment, and employee skills. In the machinery area, where assembling is a key activity, parts and accessories for manufactured products are classified in the industry of the finished manufactured item when they are made for separate sale. For example, a replacement refrigerator door would be classified with refrigerators, and an attachment for a piece of metalworking machinery would be classified with metalworking machinery. However, components, input from other manufacturing establishments, are classified based on the production function of the component manufacturer. For example, electronic components are classified in Subsector 334, Computer and Electronic Product Manufacturing, and stampings are classified in Subsector 332, Fabricated Metal Product Manufacturing.

Manufacturing establishments often perform one or more activities that are classified outside the Manufacturing sector of NAICS. For instance, almost all manufacturing has some captive research and development or administrative operations, such as accounting, payroll, or management. These captive services are treated the same as captive manufacturing activities. When the services are provided by separate establishments, they are classified to the NAICS sector where such services are primary, not in manufacturing.

The boundaries of manufacturing and the other sectors of the classification system can be somewhat blurry. The establishments in the manufacturing sector are engaged in the transformation of materials into new products. Their output is a new product. However, the definition of what constitutes a new product can be somewhat subjective. As clarification, the following activities are considered manufacturing in NAICS: Milk bottling and pasteurizing; Water bottling and processing; Fresh fish packaging (oyster shucking, fish filleting); Apparel jobbing (assigning of materials to contract factories or shops for fabrication or other contract operations) as well as contracting on materials owned by others; Printing and related activities; Ready-mixed concrete production; Leather converting; Grinding of lenses to prescription; Wood preserving; Electroplating, plating, metal heat treating, and polishing for the trade; Lapidary work for the trade; Fabricating signs and advertising displays; Rebuilding or remanufacturing machinery (i.e., automotive parts); Ship repair and renovation; Machine shops; and Tire retreading. Conversely, there are activities that are sometimes considered manufacturing, but that for NAICS are classified in another sector (i.e., not classified as manufacturing).

They include: (1) Logging, classified in Sector 11, Agriculture, Forestry, Fishing and Hunting, is considered a harvesting operation; (2) The beneficiating of ores and other minerals, classified in Sector 21, Mining, is considered part of the activity of mining; (3) The construction of structures and fabricating operations performed at the site of construction by contractors is classified in Sector 23, Construction; (4) Establishments engaged in breaking of bulk and redistribution in smaller lots, including packaging, repackaging, or bottling products, such as liquors or chemicals; the customized assembly of computers; sorting of scrap; mixing paints to customer order; and cutting metals to customer order, classified in Sector 42, Wholesale Trade or Sector 44–45, Retail Trade, produce a modified version of the same product, not a new product; and (5) Publishing and the combined activity of publishing and printing, classified in Sector 51, Information, perform the transformation of information into a product where the value of the product to the consumer lies in the information content, not in the format in which it is distributed (i.e., the book or software diskette).

Industries in the Wood Product Manufacturing subsector (NAICS 321) manufacture wood products, such as lumber, plywood, veneers, wood containers, wood flooring, wood trusses, manufactured homes (i.e., mobile homes), and prefabricated wood buildings. The production processes of the Wood Product Manufacturing subsector include sawing, planing, shaping, laminating, and assembling of wood products starting from logs that are cut into bolts, or lumber that then may be further cut, or shaped by lathes or other shaping tools. The lumber or other transformed wood shapes may also be subsequently planed or smoothed and assembled into finished products, such as wood containers. The Wood Product Manufacturing subsector includes establishments that make wood products from logs and bolts that are sawed and shaped, and establishments that purchase sawed lumber and make wood products. With the exception of sawmills and wood preservation establishments, the establishments are grouped into industries mainly based on the specific products manufactured.

Industries in the Paper Manufacturing subsector (NAICS 322) make pulp, paper, or converted paper products. The manufacturing of these products is grouped together because they constitute a series of vertically connected processes. More than one is often carried out in a single establishment. There are essentially three activities. The manufacturing of pulp involves separating the cellulose fibers from other impurities in wood or used paper. The manufacturing of paper involves matting these fibers into a sheet. Converted paper products are made from paper and other materials by various cutting and shaping techniques, and include coating and laminating activities.

The Paper Manufacturing subsector is subdivided into two industry groups, the first for the manufacturing of pulp and paper and the second for the manufacturing of converted paper products. Paper making is treated as the core activity of the subsector. Therefore, any establishment that makes paper (including paperboard), either alone or in combination with pulp manufacturing or paper converting, is classified as a paper or paperboard mill. Establishments that make pulp without making paper are classified as pulp mills. Pulp mills, paper mills, and paperboard mills comprise the first industry group.

Establishments that make products from purchased paper and other materials make up the second industry group, Converted Paper Product Manufacturing. This general activity is then subdivided based, for the most part, on process distinctions. Paperboard container manufacturing uses corrugating, cutting, and shaping machinery to form paperboard into containers. Paper bag and coated and treated paper manufacturing establishments cut and coat paper and foil. Stationery product manufacturing establishments make a variety of paper products used for writing, filing, and similar applications. Other converted paper product manufacturing includes, in particular, the conversion of sanitary paper stock into such things as tissue paper and disposable diapers.

An important process used in the Paper Bag and Coated and Treated Paper Manufacturing industry is lamination, often combined with coating. Lamination and coating makes a composite material with improved properties of strength, impermeability, and so on. The laminated materials may be paper, metal foil, or plastics film. While paper is often one of the components, it is not always. Lamination of plastics film to plastics film is classified in the NAICS Subsector 326, Plastics and Rubber Products Manufacturing, because establishments that do this often first make the film. The same situation holds with respect to bags. The manufacturing of bags from plastics only, whether or not laminated, is classified in Subsector 326, Plastics and Rubber Products Manufacturing, but all other bag manufacturing is classified in this subsector. Excluded from this subsector are photosensitive papers. These papers are chemically treated and are classified in Industry 32599, All Other Chemical Product and Preparation Manufacturing.

Industries in the Textile Mills subsector (NAICS 313) group establishments that transform a basic fiber (natural or synthetic) into a product, such as yarn or fabric, that is further manufactured into usable items, such as apparel, sheets towels, and textile bags for individual or industrial consumption. The further manufacturing may be performed in the same establishment and classified in this subsector, or it may be performed at a separate establishment and be classified elsewhere in manufacturing.

Industries in the Textile Product Mills subsector (NAICS 314) group establishments that make textile products (except apparel). With a few exceptions, processes used in these industries are generally cut and sew (i.e., purchasing fabric and cutting and sewing to make nonapparel textile products, such as sheets and towels).

Industries in the Apparel Manufacturing subsector (NAICS 315) group establishments with two distinct manufacturing processes: (1) cut and sew (i.e., purchasing fabric and cutting and sewing to make a garment) and (2) the manufacture of garments in establishments that first knit fabric and then cut and sew the fabric into a garment. The Apparel Manufacturing subsector includes a diverse range of establishments manufacturing full lines of ready-to-wear apparel and custom apparel: apparel contractors, performing cutting or sewing operations on materials owned by others; jobbers performing entrepreneurial functions involved in apparel manufacture; and tailors, manufacturing custom garments for individual clients, are all included. Knitting, when done alone, is classified in the Textile Mills subsector, but when knitting is combined with the production of complete garments, the activity is classified in Apparel Manufacturing.

Industries in the Machinery Manufacturing subsector (NAICS 333) create end products that apply mechanical force; for example, the application of gears and levers, to perform work. Some important processes for the manufacture of machinery are forging, stamping, bending, forming, and machining that are used to shape individual pieces of metal. Processes such as welding and assembling are used to join separate parts together. Although these processes are similar to those used in metal-fabricating establishments, machinery manufacturing is different because it typically employs multiple metal-forming processes in manufacturing the various parts of the machine. Moreover, complex assembly operations are an inherent part of the production process.

Industries in the Computer and Electronic Product Manufacturing subsector (NAICS 334) group establishments that manufacture computers, computer peripherals, communications equipment, and similar electronic products, and establishments that manufacture components for such products. The Computer and Electronic Product Manufacturing industries have been combined in the hierarchy of NAICS because of the economic significance they have attained. Their rapid growth suggests that they will become even more important to the economies of all three North American countries in the future, and in addition, their manufacturing processes are fundamentally different from the manufacturing processes of other machinery and equipment. The design and use of integrated circuits and the application of highly specialized miniaturization technologies are common elements in the production technologies of the computer and electronic subsector. Convergence of technology motivates this NAICS subsector. Digitalization of sound recording, for example, causes both the medium (the compact disc) and the equipment to resemble the technologies for recording, storing, transmitting, and manipulating data. Communications technology and equipment have been converging with computer technology. When technologically related components are in the same sector, it makes it easier to adjust the classification for future changes without needing to redefine its basic structure. The creation of the Computer and Electronic Product Manufacturing subsector will assist in delineating new and emerging industries because the activities that will serve as the probable sources of new industries, such as computer manufacturing and communications equipment manufacturing, or computers and audio equipment, are brought together. As new activities emerge, they are less likely, therefore, to cross the subsector boundaries of the classification.

Industries in the Motor Vehicle Manufacturing industry group (NAICS 3361) combine establishments primarily engaged in manufacturing complete motor vehicles or manufacturing chassis only. Motor vehicles includes automobiles, light duty motor vehicles, light trucks, utility vehicles, and heavy duty trucks.

Industries in the Motor Vehicle Body and Trailer Manufacturing industry group (NAICS 3362) combine establishments primarily engaged in manufacturing motor vehicle bodies, trailers, motor homes, travel trailers, and campers.

Industries in the Motor Vehicle Parts Manufacturing industry group (NAICS 3363) combine establishments primarily engaged in manufacturing and/or rebuilding motor vehicle parts, including gasoline engine and engine parts, carburetors, pistons, piston rings, valves, motor vehicle electrical and electronic equipment, vehicular lighting, steering and suspension components (except spring), brake systems, transmission and power train parts, vehicle seating and interior trim, motor vehicle metal stamping, and other motor vehicle parts.

The **Wholesale Trade** sector (NAICS 42) comprises establishments engaged in wholesaling merchandise, generally without transformation, and rendering services incidental to the sale of merchandise.

The wholesaling process is an intermediate step in the distribution of merchandise. Wholesalers are organized to sell or arrange the purchase or sale of —

1. goods for resale (i.e., goods sold to other wholesalers or retailers),

2. capital or durable nonconsumer goods, or

3. raw and intermediate materials and supplies used in production.

Wholesalers sell merchandise to other businesses and normally operate from a warehouse or office. These warehouses and offices are characterized by having little or no display of merchandise. In addition, neither the design nor the location of the premises is intended to solicit walk-in traffic. Wholesalers do not normally use advertising directed to the general public. Customers are generally reached initially via telephone, in-person marketing, or by specialized advertising that may include Internet and other electronic means. Follow-up orders are either vendor-initiated or client-initiated, generally based on previous sales, and typically exhibit strong ties between sellers and buyers. In fact, transactions are often conducted between wholesalers and clients that have long-standing business relationships.

This sector comprises two main types of wholesalers: those that sell goods on their own account, and those that arrange sales and purchases for others, generally for a commission or fee.

1. Establishments that sell goods on their own account are known as wholesale merchants, distributors, jobbers, drop shippers, and import/export merchants. Also included as wholesale merchants are sales offices and sales branches (but not retail stores) maintained by manufacturing, refining, or mining enterprises apart from their plants or mines for the purpose of

marketing their products. Merchant wholesale establishments typically maintain their own warehouse, where they receive and handle goods for their customers. Goods are generally sold without transformation, but may include integral functions, such as sorting, packaging, labeling, and other marketing services.

2. Establishments arranging for the purchase or sale of goods owned by others or purchasing goods, generally on a commission basis, are known as business-to-business electronic markets, agents and brokers, commission merchants, import/export agents and brokers, auction companies, and manufacturers' representatives. These establishments operate from offices and generally do not own or handle the goods they sell.

Some wholesale establishments may be connected with a single manufacturer and promote and sell the particular manufacturers' products to a wide range of other wholesalers or retailers. Other wholesalers may be connected to a retail chain or a limited number of retail chains and only provide a variety of products needed by the retail operation(s). These wholesalers may obtain the products from a wide range of manufacturers. Still other wholesalers may not take title to the goods, but act as agents and brokers for a commission.

Although wholesaling normally denotes sales in large volumes, durable nonconsumer goods may be sold in single units. Sales of capital or durable nonconsumer goods used in the production of goods and services, such as farm machinery, medium and heavy duty trucks, and industrial machinery, are always included in wholesale trade.

The **Retail Trade** sector (NAICS 44–45) comprises establishments engaged in retailing merchandise, generally without transformation, and rendering services incidental to the sale of merchandise.

The retailing process is the final step in the distribution of merchandise; retailers are, therefore, organized to sell merchandise in small quantities to the general public. This sector comprises two main types of retailers: store and nonstore retailers.

Store retailers operate fixed point-of-sale locations, located and designed to attract a high volume of walk-in customers. In general, retail stores have extensive displays of merchandise and use mass-media advertising to attract customers. They typically sell merchandise to the general public for personal or household consumption, but some also serve business and institutional clients. These include establishments, such as office supply stores, computer and software stores, building materials dealers, plumbing supply stores, and electrical supply stores. Catalog showrooms, gasoline service stations, automotive dealers, and mobile home dealers are treated as store retailers.

In addition to retailing merchandise, some types of store retailers are also engaged in the provision of after-sales services, such as repair and installation. For example, new automobile dealers, electronics and appliance stores, and musical instrument and supplies stores often provide repair services. As a general rule, establishments engaged in retailing merchandise and providing after-sales services are classified in this sector.

The first 11 subsectors of retail trade are store retailers. The establishments are grouped into industries and industry groups typically based on one or more of the following criteria:

1. The merchandise line or lines carried by the store; for example, specialty stores are distinguished from general-line stores.

2. The usual trade designation of the establishments. This criterion applies in cases where a store type is well-recognized by the industry and the public, but difficult to define strictly in terms of merchandise lines carried; for example, pharmacies, hardware stores, and department stores.

3. Capital requirements in terms of display equipment; for example, food stores have equipment requirements not found in other retail industries.

4. Human resource requirements in terms of expertise; for example, the staff of an automobile dealer requires knowledge in financing, registering, and licensing issues that are not necessary in other retail industries.

Nonstore retailers, like store retailers, are organized to serve the general public, but their retailing methods differ. The establishments of this subsector reach customers and market merchandise with methods such as the broadcasting of "infomercials," the broadcasting and publishing of direct-response advertising, the publishing of paper and electronic catalogs, door-to-door solicitation, in-home demonstration, selling from portable stalls (street vendors, except food), and distribution through vending machines. Establishments engaged in the direct sale (nonstore) of products, such as home heating oil dealers and home delivery newspaper routes, are included here.

The buying of goods for resale is a characteristic of retail trade establishments that particularly distinguishes them from establishments in the agriculture, manufacturing, and construction industries. For example, farms that sell their products at or from the point of production are not classified in retail, but rather in agriculture. Similarly, establishments that both manufacture and sell their products to the general public are not classified in retail, but rather in manufacturing. However, establishments that engage in processing activities incidental to retailing are classified in retail. This includes establishments, such as optical goods stores that do in-store grinding of lenses, and meat and seafood markets.

Wholesalers also engage in the buying of goods for resale, but they are not usually organized to serve the general public. They typically operate from a warehouse or office, and neither the design nor the location of these premises is intended to solicit a high volume of walk-in traffic. Wholesalers supply institutional, industrial, wholesale, and retail clients; their operations are, therefore, generally organized to purchase, sell, and deliver merchandise in larger quantities. However, dealers of durable nonconsumer goods, such as farm machinery and heavy duty trucks, are included in wholesale trade even if they often sell these products in single units.

The **Transportation and Warehousing** sector (NAICS 48–49) includes industries providing transportation of passengers and cargo, warehousing and storage for goods, scenic and sightseeing transportation, and support activities related to modes of transportation. Establishments in these industries use transportation equipment or transportation-related facilities as a productive asset. The type of equipment depends on the mode of transportation. The modes of transportation are air, rail, water, road, and pipeline.

The Transportation and Warehousing sector distinguishes three basic types of activities: subsectors for each mode of transportation, a subsector for warehousing and storage, and a subsector for establishments providing support activities for transportation. In addition, there are subsectors for establishments that provide passenger transportation for scenic and sightseeing purposes, postal services, and courier services.

A separate subsector for support activities is established in the sector because, first, support activities for transportation are inherently multimodal, such as freight transportation arrangement, or have multimodal aspects. Secondly, there are production process similarities among the support activity industries.

One of the support activities identified in the support activity subsector is the routine repair and maintenance of transportation equipment (e.g., aircraft at an airport, railroad rolling stock at a railroad terminal, or ships at a harbor or port facility). Such establishments do not perform complete overhauling or rebuilding of transportation equipment (i.e., periodic restoration of transportation equipment to original design specifications) or transportation equipment conversion (i.e., major modification to systems). An establishment that primarily performs factory (or shipyard) overhauls, rebuilding, or conversions of aircraft, railroad rolling stock, or a ship is classified in Subsector 336, Transportation Equipment Manufacturing, according to the type of equipment.

Many of the establishments in this sector often operate on networks, with physical facilities, labor forces, and equipment spread over an extensive geographic area. Warehousing establishments in this sector are distinguished

from merchant wholesaling in that the warehouse establishments do not sell the goods.

Excluded from this sector are establishments primarily engaged in providing travel agent services that support transportation and other establishments, such as hotels, businesses, and government agencies. These establishments are classified in Sector 56, Administrative and Support, Waste Management, and Remediation Services. Also, establishments primarily engaged in providing rental and leasing of transportation equipment without operator are classified in Subsector 532, Rental and Leasing Services.

The **Information** sector (NAICS 51) comprises establishments engaged in the following processes: (1) producing and distributing information and cultural products, (2) providing the means to transmit or distribute these products as well as data or communications, and (3) processing data.

The main components of this sector are the publishing industries, including software publishing, and both traditional publishing and publishing exclusively on the Internet; the motion picture and sound recording industries; the broadcasting industries, including traditional broadcasting and those broadcasting exclusively over the Internet; the telecommunications industries; the industries known as Internet service providers and Web search portals; data processing industries; and the information services industries.

The expressions "information age" and "global information economy" are used with considerable frequency today. The general idea of an "information economy" includes both the notion of industries primarily producing, processing, and distributing information, as well as the idea that every industry is using available information and information technology to reorganize and make themselves more productive.

For the purpose of developing NAICS, it is the transformation of information into a commodity that is produced and distributed by a number of growing industries that is at issue. The Information sector groups three types of establishments: (1) those engaged in producing and distributing information and cultural products; (2) those that provide the means to transmit or distribute these products as well as data or communications; and (3) those that process data. Cultural products are those that directly express attitudes, opinions, ideas, values, and artistic creativity; provide entertainment; or offer information and analysis concerning the past and present. Included in this definition are popular, mass-produced products as well as cultural products that normally have a more limited audience, such as poetry books, literary magazines, or classical records.

The unique characteristics of information and cultural products, and of the processes involved in their production and distribution, distinguish the Information sector from the goods-producing and service-producing sectors. Some of these characteristics are:

1. Unlike traditional goods, an "information or cultural product," such as a newspaper online or television program, does not necessarily have tangible qualities, nor is it necessarily associated with a particular form. A movie can be shown at a movie theater, on a television broadcast, through video-on-demand, or rented at a local video store. A sound recording can be aired on radio, embedded in multimedia products, or sold at a record store.

2. Unlike traditional services, the delivery of these products does not require direct contact between the supplier and the consumer.

3. The value of these products to the consumer lies in their informational, educational, cultural, or entertainment content, not in the format in which they are distributed. Most of these products are protected from unlawful reproduction by copyright laws.

4. The intangible property aspect of information and cultural products makes the processes involved in their production and distribution very different from goods and services. Only those possessing the rights to these works are authorized to reproduce, alter, improve, and distribute them. Acquiring and using these rights often involves significant costs. In addition, technology is revolutionizing the distribution of these products. It is possible to distribute them in a physical form, via broadcast, or online.

5. Distributors of information and cultural products can easily add value to the products they distribute. For instance, broadcasters add advertising not contained in the original product. This capacity means that unlike traditional distributors, they derive revenue not from sale of the distributed product to the final consumer, but from those who pay for the privilege of adding information to the original product. Similarly, a directory and mailing list publisher can acquire the rights to thousands of previously published newspaper and periodical articles and add new value by providing search and software and organizing the information in a way that facilitates research and retrieval. These products often command a much higher price than the original information.

The distribution modes for information commodities may either eliminate the necessity for traditional manufacture, or reverse the conventional order of manufacture-distribute: A newspaper distributed online, for example, can be printed locally or by the final consumer. Similarly, it is anticipated that packaged software, which today is mainly bought through the traditional retail channels, will soon be available mainly online. The NAICS Information sector is designed to make such economic changes transparent as they occur, or to facilitate designing surveys that will monitor the new phenomena and provide data to analyze the changes.

Many of the industries in the NAICS Information sector are engaged in producing products protected by copyright law, or in distributing them (other than distribution by traditional wholesale and retail methods). Examples are traditional publishing industries, software and directory and mailing list publishing industries, and film and sound industries. Broadcasting and telecommunications industries and information providers and processors are also included in the Information sector, because their technologies are so closely linked to other industries in the Information sector.

The **Finance and Insurance** sector (NAICS 52) comprises establishments primarily engaged in financial transactions (transactions involving the creation, liquidation, or change in ownership of financial assets) and/or in facilitating financial transactions. Three principal types of activities are identified:

1. Raising funds by taking deposits and/or issuing securities and, in the process, incurring liabilities. Establishments engaged in this activity use raised funds to acquire financial assets by making loans and/or purchasing securities. Putting themselves at risk, they channel funds from lenders to borrowers and transform or repackage the funds with respect to maturity, scale and risk. This activity is known as financial intermediation.

2. Pooling of risk by underwriting insurance and annuities. Establishments engaged in this activity collect fees, insurance premiums, or annuity considerations; build up reserves; invest those reserves; and make contractual payments. Fees are based on the expected incidence of the insured risk and the expected return on investment.

3. Providing specialized services facilitating or supporting financial intermediation, insurance, and employee benefit programs.

In addition, monetary authorities charged with monetary control are included in this sector.

The subsectors, industry groups, and industries within the NAICS Finance and Insurance sector are defined on the basis of their unique production processes. As with all industries, the production processes are distinguished by their use of specialized human resources and specialized physical capital. In addition, the way in which these establishments acquire and allocate financial capital, their source of funds, and the use of those funds provides a third basis for distinguishing characteristics of the production process. For instance, the production process in raising funds through deposit-taking is different from the process of raising funds in bond or money markets. The process of making loans to individuals also requires different production processes than does the creation of investment pools or the underwriting of securities.

Most of the Finance and Insurance subsectors contain one or more industry groups of (1) intermediaries with similar patterns of raising and using funds and (2) establishments engaged in activities that facilitate, or are otherwise related to, that type of financial or insurance intermediation. Industries within this sector are defined in terms of activities for which a production process can be specified, and many of these activities are not exclusive to a particular type of financial institution. To deal with the varied activities taking place within existing financial institutions, the approach is to split these institutions into components performing specialized services. This requires defining the units engaged in providing those services and developing procedures that allow for their delineation. These units are the equivalents for finance and insurance of the establishments defined for other industries.

The output of many financial services, as well as the inputs and the processes by which they are combined, cannot be observed at a single location and can only be defined at a higher level of the organizational structure of the enterprise. Additionally, a number of independent activities that represent separate and distinct production processes may take place at a single location belonging to a multilocation financial firm. Activities are more likely to be homogeneous with respect to production characteristics than are locations, at least in financial services. The classification defines activities broadly enough that it can be used both by those classifying by location and by those employing a more top-down approach to the delineation of the establishment.

Establishments engaged in activities that facilitate, or are otherwise related to, the various types of intermediation have been included in individual subsectors, rather than in a separate subsector dedicated to services alone because these services are performed by intermediaries, as well as by specialist establishments, and the extent to which the activity of the intermediaries can be separately identified is not clear.

The Finance and Insurance sector has been defined to encompass establishments primarily engaged in financial transactions; that is, transactions involving the creation, liquidation, or change in ownership of financial assets or in facilitating financial transactions. Financial industries are extensive users of electronic means for facilitating the verification of financial balances, authorizing transactions, transferring funds to and from transactors' accounts, notifying banks (or credit card issuers) of the individual transactions, and providing daily summaries. Since these transaction processing activities are integral to the production of finance and insurance services, establishments that principally provide a financial transaction processing service are classified to this sector, rather than to the data processing industry in the Information sector.

Legal entities that hold portfolios of assets on behalf of others are significant, and data on them are required for a variety of purposes. Thus for NAICS, these funds, trusts, and other financial vehicles are the fifth subsector of the Finance and Insurance sector. These entities earn interest, dividends, and other property income, but have little or no employment and no revenue from the sale of services. Separate establishments and employees devoted to the management of funds are classified in Industry Group 5239, Other Financial Investment Activities.

The **Real Estate and Rental and Leasing** sector (NAICS 53) comprises establishments primarily engaged in renting, leasing, or otherwise allowing the use of tangible or intangible assets, and establishments providing related services. The major portion of this sector comprises establishments that rent, lease, or otherwise allow the use of their own assets by others. The assets may be tangible, as is the case of real estate and equipment, or intangible, as is the case with patents and trademarks.

This sector also includes establishments primarily engaged in managing real estate for others, selling, renting and/or buying real estate for others, and appraising real estate. These activities are closely related to this sector's main activity, and it was felt that, from a production basis, they would best be included here. In addition, a substantial proportion of property management is self-performed by lessors.

The main components of this sector are the real estate lessors industries; equipment lessors industries (including motor vehicles, computers, and consumer goods); and lessors of nonfinancial intangible assets (except copyrighted works).

Excluded from this sector are real estate investment trusts (REITS) and establishments primarily engaged in renting or leasing equipment with operators. REITS are classified in Subsector 525, Funds, Trusts, and Other Financial Vehicles, because they are considered investment vehicles. Establishments renting or leasing equipment with operators are classified in various subsectors of NAICS depending on the nature of the services provided (e.g., transportation, construction, agriculture). These activities are excluded from this sector because the client is paying for the expertise and knowledge of the equipment operator in addition to the rental of the equipment. In many cases, such as the rental of heavy construction equipment, the operator is essential to operate the equipment.

The **Professional, Scientific, and Technical Services** sector (NAICS 54) comprises establishments that specialize in performing professional, scientific, and technical activities for others. These activities require a high degree of expertise and training. The establishments in this sector specialize according to expertise and provide these services to clients in a variety of industries and, in some cases, to households. Activities performed include: legal advice and representation; accounting, bookkeeping, and payroll services; architectural, engineering, and specialized design services; computer services; consulting services; research services; advertising services; photographic services; translation and interpretation services; veterinary services; and other professional, scientific, and technical services.

This sector excludes establishments primarily engaged in providing a range of day-to-day office administrative services, such as financial planning, billing and record keeping, personnel, and physical distribution and logistics. These establishments are classified in Sector 56, Administrative and Support and Waste Management and Remediation Services.

The **Management of Companies and Enterprises** sector (NAICS 55) comprises (1) establishments that hold the securities of (or other equity interests in) companies and enterprises for the purpose of owning a controlling interest or influencing management decisions or (2) establishments (except government establishments) that administer, oversee, and manage establishments of the company or enterprise and that normally undertake the strategic or organizational planning and decision-making role of the company or enterprise. Establishments that administer, oversee, and manage may hold the securities of the company or enterprise.

Establishments in this sector perform essential activities that are often undertaken, in-house, by establishments in many sectors of the economy. By consolidating the performance of these activities of the enterprise at one establishment, economies of scale are achieved.

Government establishments primarily engaged in administering, overseeing, and managing governmental programs are classified in Sector 92, Public Administration. Establishments primarily engaged in providing a range of day-to-day office administrative services, such as financial planning, billing and record keeping, personnel, and physical distribution and logistics, are classified in Industry 56111, Office Administrative Services.

The **Administrative and Support and Waste Management and Remediation Services** sector (NAICS 56) comprises establishments performing routine support activities for the day-to-day operations of other organizations. These essential activities are often undertaken in-house by establishments in many sectors of the economy. The establishments in this sector specialize in one or more of these support activities and provide these services to clients in a variety of industries and, in some cases, to households. Activities performed include: office administration, hiring and placing of personnel, document preparation and similar clerical services, solicitation, collection, security and surveillance services, cleaning, and waste disposal services.

The administrative and management activities performed by establishments in this sector are typically on a contract or fee basis. These activities may also be performed by establishments that are part of the company or enterprise. However, establishments involved in administering, overseeing, and managing other establishments of the company or enterprise are classified in Sector 55, Management of Companies and Enterprises. These establishments normally undertake the strategic and organizational planning and decision-making role of the company or enterprise. Government establishments engaged in administering, overseeing, and managing governmental programs are classified in Sector 92, Public Administration.

The **Educational Services** sector (NAICS 61) comprises establishments that provide instruction and training in a wide variety of subjects. This instruction and training is provided by specialized establishments, such as schools, colleges, universities, and training centers. These establishments may be privately owned and operated for profit or not for profit, or they may be publicly owned and operated. They may also offer food and accommodation services to their students.

Educational services are usually delivered by teachers or instructors who explain, tell, demonstrate, supervise, and direct learning. Instruction is imparted in diverse settings, such as educational institutions, the workplace, or the home through correspondence, television, or other means. It can be adapted to the particular needs of the students; for example, sign language can replace verbal language for teaching students with hearing impairments. All industries in the sector share this commonality of process, namely, labor inputs of instructors with the requisite subject matter expertise and teaching ability.

The **Health Care and Social Assistance** sector (NAICS 62) comprises establishments providing health care and social assistance for individuals. The sector includes both health care and social assistance because it is sometimes difficult to distinguish between the boundaries of these two activities. The industries in this sector are arranged on a continuum starting with those establishments providing medical care exclusively, continuing with those providing health care and social assistance, and finally finishing with those providing only social assistance. The services provided by establishments in this sector are delivered by trained professionals. All industries in the sector share this commonality of process, namely, labor inputs of health practitioners or social workers with the requisite expertise. Many of the industries in the sector are defined based on the educational degree held by the practitioners included in the industry.

Excluded from this sector are aerobic classes in Subsector 713, Amusement, Gambling and Recreation Industries, and nonmedical diet and weight-reducing centers in Subsector 812, Personal and Laundry Services. Although these can be viewed as health services, these services are not typically delivered by health practitioners.

Industries in the Ambulatory Health Care Services subsector (NAICS 621) provide health care services directly or indirectly to ambulatory patients and do not usually provide inpatient services. Health practitioners in this subsector provide outpatient services, with the facilities and equipment not usually being the most significant part of the production process.

Industries in the Hospitals subsector (NAICS 622) provide medical, diagnostic, and treatment services that include physician, nursing, and other health services to inpatients and the specialized accommodation services required by inpatients. Hospitals may also provide outpatient services as a secondary activity. Establishments in the Hospitals subsector provide inpatient health services, many of which can only be provided using the specialized facilities and equipment that form a significant and integral part of the production process.

Industries in the Nursing and Residential Care Facilities subsector (NAICS 623) provide residential care combined with either nursing, supervisory, or other types of care as required by the residents. In this subsector, the facilities are a significant part of the production process, and the care provided is a mix of health and social services with the health services being largely some level of nursing services.

The **Arts, Entertainment, and Recreation** sector (NAICS 71) includes a wide range of establishments that operate facilities or provide services to meet varied cultural, entertainment, and recreational interests of their patrons. This sector comprises: (1) establishments that are involved in producing, promoting, or participating in live performances, events, or exhibits intended for public viewing; (2) establishments that preserve and exhibit objects and sites of historical, cultural, or educational interest; and (3) establishments that operate facilities or provide services that enable patrons to participate in recreational activities or pursue amusement, hobby, and leisure-time interests.

Some establishments that provide cultural, entertainment, or recreational facilities and services are classified in other sectors. Excluded from this sector are: (1) establishments that provide both accommodations and recreational facilities, such as hunting and fishing camps and resort and casino hotels, which are classified in Subsector 721, Accommodation; (2) restaurants and night clubs that provide live entertainment in addition to the sale of food and beverages, which are classified in Subsector 722, Food Services and Drinking Places; (3) motion picture theaters, libraries and archives, and publishers of newspapers, magazines, books, periodicals, and computer software, which are classified in Sector 51, Information; and (4) establishments using transportation equipment to provide recreational and entertainment services, such as those operating sightseeing buses, dinner cruises, or helicopter rides, which are classified in Subsector 487, Scenic and Sightseeing Transportation.

The **Accommodation and Food Services** sector (NAICS 72) comprises establishments providing customers with lodging and/or preparing meals, snacks, and beverages for immediate consumption. The sector includes both accommodation and food services establishments because the two activities are often combined at the same establishment. Excluded from this sector are civic and social organizations; amusement and recreation parks; theaters; and other recreation or entertainment facilities providing food and beverage services.

The **Other Services** (except Public Administration) sector (NAICS 81) comprises establishments engaged in providing services not specifically provided for elsewhere in the classification system. Establishments in this sector are primarily engaged in activities such as equipment and machinery repairing, promoting or administering religious activities, grantmaking, advocacy, and providing drycleaning and laundry services, personal care services, death care services, pet care services, photofinishing services, temporary parking services, and dating services.

Private households that engage in employing workers on or about the premises in activities primarily concerned with the operation of the household are included in this sector.

Excluded from this sector are establishments primarily engaged in retailing new equipment and also performing repairs and general maintenance on equipment. These establishments are classified in Sector 44–45, Retail Trade.

The **Public Administration** sector (NAICS 92) consists of establishments of federal, state, and local government agencies that administer, oversee, and manage public programs and have executive, legislative, or judicial authority over other institutions within a given area. These agencies also set policy, create laws, adjudicate civil and criminal legal cases, and provide for public safety and for national defense. In general, government establishments in the Public Administration sector oversee governmental programs and activities that are not performed by private establishments. Establishments in this sector typically are engaged in the organization and financing of the production of public goods and services, most of which are provided for free or at prices that are not economically significant.

Government establishments also engage in a wide range of productive activities covering not only public goods and services but also individual goods and services similar to those produced in sectors typically identified with private-sector establishments. In general, ownership is not a criterion for classification in NAICS. Therefore, government establishments engaged in the production of private sector-like goods and services should be classified in the same industry as private sector establishments engaged in similar activities.

As a practical matter, it is difficult to identify separate establishment detail for many government agencies. To the extent that separate establishment records are available, the administration of governmental programs is classified in Sector 92, Public Administration, while the operation of that same governmental program is classified elsewhere in NAICS based on the activities performed. For example, the governmental administrative authority for an airport is classified in Industry 92612, Regulation and Administration of Transportation Programs, while operating the airport is classified in Industry 48811, Airport Operations. When separate records are not available to distinguish between the administration of a governmental program and the operation of it, the establishment is classified in Sector 92, Public Administration.

Examples of government-provided goods and services that are classified in sectors other than Public Administration include: schools, classified in Sector 61, Educational Services; hospitals, classified in Subsector 622, Hospitals; establishments operating transportation facilities, classified in Sector 48–49, Transportation and Warehousing; the operation of utilities, classified in Sector 22, Utilities; and the Government Printing Office, classified in Subsector 323, Printing and Related Support Activities.

Census of Governments

A census of governments is taken at 5-year intervals as required by law under Title 13, United States Code, Section 161. The 2002 census, similar to those taken since 1957, covers three major subject fields—government organization, public employment, and government finances.

The concept of local governments as defined by the Census Bureau covers three general-purpose governments (county, municipal, and township) and two limited-purpose governments (school district and special district). For information on the history, methodology, and concepts for the census of governments, see the Governments Finance and Employment Classification Manual found at <http://www.census.gov/govs/www/class.html>.

The term "full-time equivalent employment" refers to a computed statistic representing the number of full-time employees that could have been employed if the reported number of hours worked by part-time employees had been worked by full-time employees. This statistic is calculated separately for each function of a government by dividing the "part-time hours paid" by the standard number of hours for full-time employees in the particular government and then adding the resulting quotient to the number of full-time employees.

For a brief discussion of the census of governments, see descriptive text under Local government employment. General revenue covers all government revenue except liquor stores revenue, insurance trust revenue, and utility revenue. Taxes are compulsory contributions exacted by a government for public purposes except employee and

employer assessments for retirement and social insurance purposes, which are classified as insurance trust revenue. All tax revenue is classified as general revenue and comprises amounts received (including interest and penalties but excluding protested amounts and refunds) from all taxes imposed by a government. Local government tax revenue excludes any amounts from shares of state imposed and collected taxes, which are classified as intergovernmental revenue. Property taxes are taxes conditioned on ownership of property and measured by its value. This category includes general property taxes related to property as a whole, real and personal, tangible or intangible, whether taxed at a single rate or at classified rates, and taxes on selected types of property, such as motor vehicles or on certain or all intangibles. Direct expenditure includes payments to employees, suppliers, contractors, beneficiaries, and other final recipients of government payment; i.e., all expenditure other than intergovernmental expenditure, while general expenditure covers all government expenditure other than the specifically enumerated kinds of expenditure classified as utility expenditure, liquor stores expenditure, and employee retirement or other insurance trust expenditure.

TABLE A — STATES

Table A presents 87 tables with 1,539 items of data for each state, the United States as a whole, and the District of Columbia. These tables are numbered A-1 through A-87.

A number of the statistics in tables A-1 through A-87 are also presented for metropolitan areas in tables B-1 through B-11, for metropolitan area component counties in tables C-1 through C-4, and for micropolitan areas in table D-1.

Table A-1. Area and Population

Area, total and rank, 2000;
Population, 2005, 2004, 2000, and 1990;
  Rank and per square mile of land area, 2005, 2000, and 1990;
Population change, net change, net international migration, net internal migration, 2000–2005;
  Percent change, 2000–2005 and 1990–2000.

Sources: Area—U.S. Census Bureau, 2000 Census of Population and Housing, *Summary Population and Housing Characteristics*, Series PHC-1; and unpublished data on American FactFinder; Population—U.S. Census Bureau, 1990 Census of Population and Housing, Population and Housing Unit Counts (CPH-2); "Time Series of Intercensal State Population Estimates: April 1, 1990 to April 1, 2000" (CO-EST2001-12-00), published 11 April 2002; Internet site <http://www.census.gov/popest/archives/2000s /vintage_2001/CO-EST2001-12/CO-EST2001-12-00.html>; and "Annual Estimates of the Population for the United

States and States, and for Puerto Rico: April 1, 2000 to July 1, 2005" (NST-EST2005-01), published 22 December 2005; Internet site <http://www.census.gov/popest/states/NST-ann-est.html>; Rank—"Table 2: Cumulative Estimates of Population Change for the United States and States, and for Puerto Rico and State Rankings: April 1, 2000 to July 1, 2005" (NST-EST2005-02), published 22 December 2005; Internet site <http://www.census.gov/popest/states/NST-pop-chg.html>; Population change—U.S. Census Bureau, "Table 4: Cumulative Estimates of the Components of Population Change for the United States and States: April 1, 2000 to July 1, 2005" (NST-EST2005-04), published 22 December 2005; Internet site <http://www.census.gov/popest/states/NST-comp-chg.html>.

Land area. The Census Bureau provides land area for the decennial censuses. Area was calculated from the specific set of boundaries recorded for the entity (in this case, states and counties) in the Census Bureau's geographic database.

Land area measurements may disagree with the information displayed on census maps and in the TIGER file because, for area measurement purposes, features identified as "intermittent water" and "glacier" are reported as land area. TIGER is an acronym for the new digital (computer-readable) geographic database that automates the mapping and related geographic activities required to support the Census Bureau's census and survey programs; TIGER stands for Topologically Integrated Geographic Encoding and Referencing system.

The accuracy of any area measurement figure is limited by the inaccuracy inherent in (1) the location and shape of the various boundary features in the database, and (2) rounding affecting the last digit in all operations that compute and/or sum the area measurement. Identification of land and inland, coastal, and territorial is for statistical purposes and does not necessarily reflect legal definitions thereof.

Population data for 2005 and revised population data for 2000 through 2004 were released in late December 2005 for states. The population figures from the previous release were used to calculate rates or describe various population characteristics in Tables A-2 through A-87.

The 2000 and 1990 decennial population counts are from the short form questionnaires that were asked of all people and housing units and are often referred to as 100-percent questions because they are asked of the entire population. For more information on the decennial census, see General Notes.

Persons enumerated in the census were counted as inhabitants of their usual place of residence, which generally means the place where a person lives and sleeps most of the time. This place is not necessarily the same as the legal residence, voting residence, or domicile. In the vast

majority of cases, however, the use of these different bases of classification would produce substantially the same statistics, although appreciable differences may exist for a few areas.

The implementation of this usual-residence practice has resulted in the establishment of residence rules for certain categories of persons whose usual place of residence is not immediately apparent (e.g., college students were counted at their college residence). As in the above example, persons were not always counted as residents of the place where they happened to be staying on census day. However, persons without a usual place of residence were counted where they were enumerated.

Rank numbers are assigned on the basis of area size for the rank of area and by population size for rank of population, with each state placed in descending order, largest to smallest. Where ties—two or more states with identical areas or populations—occur, the same rank is assigned to each of the tied states. In such cases, the following rank number(s) is omitted so that the lowest rank is usually equal to the number of states ranked.

Persons per square mile, also known as population density, is the average number of inhabitants per square mile of land area. These figures are derived by dividing the total number of residents by the number of square miles of land area in the specified geographic area. To determine population per square kilometer, multiply the population per square mile by .3861.

Net change represents the increase or decrease between the two years shown.

Refer to the General Notes on population estimates for explanations of **international migration** and **internal migration**.

Percent change represents the increase or decrease between the two years shown as a percentage of the beginning population.

Table A-2. Population by Residence

Metropolitan and micropolitan area population, 2004, 2000, and 1990;
 Percent of total, 2004;
 Percent change, 2000–2004;
Nonmetropolitan area population, 2004, 2000, and 1990;
 Percent change, 2000–2004;
Urban, 2000 and 1990;
 Percent of total population, 2000 and 1990.

Sources: Metropolitan, micropolitan, and nonmetropolitan area population—U.S. Census Bureau, "Annual Estimates of the Population for Counties: April 1, 2000 to July 1, 2004" (CO-EST2004-01), published 14 April 2005; Internet site <http://www.census.gov/popest/counties/CO-EST2004-01.html>; and 2000 Census of Population and

Housing, Population and Housing Unit Counts PHC-1; Urban population—U.S. Census Bureau, 2000 Census of Population and Housing, Population and Housing Unit Counts PHC-3, see Internet site <http://www.census.gov/prod/cen2000/index.html>.

Data for **metropolitan** and **micropolitan** areas refer to 361 metropolitan statistical areas and 575 micropolitan statistical areas defined by the U.S. Office of Management and Budget as of November 2004; **nonmetropolitan** is the area outside metropolitan and micropolitan areas. For more information on metropolitan and micropolitan statistical areas, see Geographic Concepts and Codes.

The Census Bureau classifies as **urban** all territory, population, and housing units located within urbanized areas (UAs) and urban clusters (UCs). It delineates UA and UC boundaries to encompass densely settled territory, which generally consists of (1) a cluster of one or more block groups or census blocks, each of which has a population density of at least 1,000 people per square mile at the time, (2) surrounding block groups and census blocks, each of which has a population density of at least 500 people per square mile at the time, or (3) less densely settled blocks that form enclaves or indentations, or are used to connect discontiguous areas with qualifying densities. All territory located outside of UAs and UCs are classified as rural. Geographic entities such as metropolitan areas and counties often contain both urban and rural territory.

Table A-3. Population Projections

Population projections, 2005, 2006, 2007, 2008, 2009, 2010, 2015, 2020, 2025, and 2030;
Rank, 2010 and 2020;
Percent change, 2000–2010, 2010–2020, and 2020–2030;
Males per 100 females, 2010;
Population by age,
  Under 18 years, 2005 and 2010;
  18 to 44 years, 2005 and 2010;
  45 to 64 years, 2005 and 2010;
  65 to 74 years, 2005 and 2010;
  75 years and over, 2005 and 2010;
Percent of population in 2010, under 18 years and 65 years and over.

Source: U.S. Census Bureau, "State Interim Population Projections by Age and Sex: 2004–2030," published 21 April 2005. See Internet site <http://www.census.gov/population/www/projections/projectionsagesex.html>.

The **population projections** are the results of using the cohort-component method. This method requires separate assumptions for each of the components of population change: births, deaths, internal migration, and international migration. Each of these components was projected separately from 2000 to 2030 based on recent fertility, mortality, and migration trends. Projected fertility and

mortality rates were based on birth and death statistics by state from the National Center for Health Statistics (NCHS). Projected internal migration was based on data on state migration patterns derived from the Internal Revenue Service (IRS) and Census 2000 data. Projected international migration was based on the estimates of net international migration by state derived from the Population Estimates Program and data on the foreign-born population enumerated in Census 2000.

Table A-4. Population by Age Group and Sex

Population by age, 2004, total, under 5, 5 to 17, 18 to 24, 25 to 34, 35 to 44, 45 to 54, 55 to 64, 65 to 74, 75 to 84, and 85 years and over;
Population under 18 years, 2004, 2000, and 1990;
Population 65 years and over, 2004, 2000, and 1990;
Percent of population by age,
  Under 18 years, 2004, 2000, and 1990;
  65 years and over, 2004, 2000, and 1990;
Males per 100 females, 2004.

Source: U.S. Census Bureau, "State Single Year of Age and Sex Population Estimates: April 1, 2000 to July 1, 2004—RESIDENT"; see Internet site <http://www.census.gov/popest/states/files/SC-EST2004-AGESEX_RES.csv>; and "Age and Sex for States and for Puerto Rico: April 1, 2000 to July 1, 2004"; see Internet site <http://www.census.gov/popest/states/asrh/SC-est2004-02.html>; and "Table ST-99-9 Population Estimates for the U.S., Regions, and States by Selected Age Groups and Sex: Annual Time Series, July 1, 1990," published 9 March 2000; see Internet site <http://www.census.gov/popest/archives/1990s/ST-99-09.txt>.

Refer to the General Notes on population estimates for explanations of **population by age and sex**.

Table A-5. Population by Race and Hispanic Origin

All races, 2004 and 2000;
White alone, 2004 and 2000;
Black or African American alone, 2004 and 2000;
American Indian, Alaska Native alone, 2004 and 2000;
Asian alone, 2004 and 2000;
Native Hawaiian and Other Pacific Islander alone, 2004 and 2000;
Two or more races, 2004 and 2000;
Hispanic or Latino origin, 2004 and 2000;
Non-Hispanic White alone, 2004 and 2000;
Percent of total, 2004, White alone; Black or African American alone; American Indian, Alaska Native alone; Asian alone; Native Hawaiian, Other Pacific Islander alone; two or more races; Hispanic or Latino origin; and Non-Hispanic White alone;
Percent change, 2000–2004, White alone; Black or African American alone; American Indian, Alaska Native alone; Asian alone; Native Hawaiian, Other Pacific Islander alone; Two or more races; Hispanic or Latino origin; and Non-Hispanic White alone.

Source: U.S. Census Bureau, "State Population Estimates with Sex, 6 Race Groups (5 Race Alone Groups and One Group with Two or More Race Groups) and Hispanic Origin: April 1, 2000 to July 1, 2004" (SC-EST2004-6RACE), published 11 August 2005; <http://www.census.gov/popest/datasets.html>; "Table 4: Annual Estimates of the Population by Race Alone and Hispanic or Latino Origin for the United States and States: July 1, 2004" (SC-EST2004-04), published 11 August 2005; <http://www.census.gov/popest/states/asrh/SC-EST2004-04.html>.

Race. The racial classifications used by the Census Bureau adhere to the October 30, 1997, *Federal Register Notice* entitled "Revisions to the Standards for the Classification of Federal Data on Race and Ethnicity" issued by the Office of Management and Budget (OMB). These standards govern the categories used to collect and present federal data on race and ethnicity. The OMB requires federal agencies to use a minimum of five race categories: White, Black or African American, American Indian and Alaska Native, Asian, and Native Hawaiian and Other Pacific Islander. For respondents unable to identify with any of these five race categories, the OMB approved including a sixth category, "Some other race," on the Census 2000 questionnaire.

The question on race for Census 2000 was different from the one for the 1990 census in several ways. Most significantly, respondents were given the option of selecting one or more race categories to indicate their racial identities. Because of these changes, the Census 2000 data on race are not directly comparable with data from the 1990 census or earlier censuses. Caution must be used when interpreting changes in the racial composition of the U.S. population over time.

Population estimates by race and Hispanic origin are calculated using a distributive cohort component method. Previously developed resident state population estimates by age and sex and residential national population estimates by age, sex, race, and Hispanic origin are used as a base. Estimated post-censal changes in the corresponding populations are applied with a cohort component model. These distributions are applied to the original state age-sex and national characteristics estimates.

White refers to people having origins in any of the original peoples of Europe, the Middle East, or North Africa. It includes people who indicated their race or races as White or wrote in entries such as Irish, German, Italian, Lebanese, Near Easterner, Arab, or Polish.

Black or African American refers to people having origins in any of the Black racial groups of Africa. It includes people who indicated their race or races as Black, African American, or Negro or wrote in entries such as African American, Afro American, Nigerian, or Haitian.

American Indian and Alaska Native refers to people having origins in any of the original peoples of North and South America (including Central America) and who maintain tribal affiliation or community attachment. It includes people who indicated their race or races by marking this category or writing in their principal or enrolled tribe, such as Rosebud Sioux, Chippewa, or Navajo.

Asian refers to people having origins in any of the original peoples of the Far East, Southeast Asia, or the Indian subcontinent. It includes people who indicated their race or races as Asian Indian, Chinese, Filipino, Korean, Japanese, Vietnamese, or Other Asian or wrote in entries such as Burmese, Hmong, Pakistani, or Thai.

Native Hawaiian and Other Pacific Islander refers to people having origins in any of the original peoples of Hawaii, Guam, Samoa, or other Pacific Islands. It includes people who indicated their race or races as Native Hawaiian, Guamanian or Chamorro, Samoan, or Other Pacific Islander or wrote in entries such as Tahitian, Mariana Islander, or Chuukese.

Two or more races. People may have chosen to provide two or more races either by checking two or more race response check boxes, by providing multiple write-in responses, or by some combination of check boxes and write-in responses. The race response categories shown on the questionnaire were collapsed into the five minimum race groups by the OMB.

Hispanic or Latino. People who identify with the terms "Hispanic" or "Latino" are those who classify themselves in one of the specific Hispanic or Latino categories listed on the questionnaire, such as Mexican, Puerto Rican, or Cuban, as well as those who indicate that they are other Spanish, Hispanic, or Latino. Origin can be viewed as the heritage, nationality group, lineage, or country of birth of the person or the person's parents or ancestors before their arrival in the United States. People who identify their origin as Spanish, Hispanic, or Latino may be any race.

The concept of race, as used by the Census Bureau, reflects self-identification by people according to the race or races with which they most closely identify. These categories are sociopolitical constructs and should not be interpreted as being scientific or anthropological in nature. Furthermore, the race categories include both racial and national-origin groups.

Traditional and current data collection and classification treat race and Hispanic origin as two separate and distinct concepts in accordance with guidelines from the OMB. Race and Hispanic origin are two separate concepts in the federal statistical system. People who are Hispanic may be any race, and people in each race group may be either Hispanic or Non-Hispanic. Also, each person has two attributes, their race (or races) and whether or not they are Hispanic. The overlap of race and Hispanic origin is the main comparability issue. For example, Black Hispanics (Hispanic Blacks) are included in both the number of Blacks and in the number of Hispanics. For further information, see Census Bureau Web page <http://www.census.gov/population/www/socdemo/compraceho.html>.

Table A-6. Households

Total, 2003 and 2000;
Percent of households, 2003,
  Family households,
    Total,
      Households total;
      With own children under 18 years;
    Married-couple families,
      Married-couple families, total;
      With own children under 18 years;
    Female householder, no husband present,
      Female householder, no husband present, total;
      With own children under 18 years;
  Nonfamily households,
    Nonfamily households, total;
    Householder living alone,
      Householder living alone, total;
      65 years and over;
  Households with one or more persons,
    Under 18 years;
    65 years and over;
Persons per household, 2003 and 2000.

Source: U.S. Census Bureau, American Community Survey, Multi-Year Profiles 2003—General Demographics, accessed 24 June 2005. See Internet site <http://www.census.gov/acs/www/Products/Profiles/Chg/2003/ACS/index.htm>.

Household. A household includes all of the people who occupy a housing unit. A housing unit may be a house, an apartment, a mobile home or trailer, a group of rooms, or a single room that is occupied as separate living quarters. Separate living quarters are those in which the occupants live separately from any other individuals in the building and that have direct access from outside the building or through a common hall. People not living in households are classified as living in group quarters. **Persons per household** (or average household size) is a measure obtained by dividing the number of people in households by the total number of households (or householders).

Family household (family). A family includes a householder and one or more people living in the same household who are related to the householder by birth, marriage, or adoption. All people in a household who are related to the householder are regarded as members of his or her family. A family household may contain people not related to the householder, but those people are not included as part of the householder's family in census tabulations. Thus, the number of family households is equal to the number of families, but family households may include more members than do families. A household can contain only one family for purposes of census tabulations. Not all households contain families since a household may comprise a group of unrelated people or one person living alone. **Married-couple family** is a family in which the householder and his or her spouse are enumerated as members of the same household. **Female householder, no husband present** includes a family with a female who maintains a household with no husband of the householder present. **Nonfamily household** is a household in which the householder lives alone or with nonrelatives only.

Own child category is a never-married child under 18 years old who is a son or daughter of the householder by birth, marriage (a stepchild), or adoption.

Table A-7. Marital Status: 2003

Males 15 years and over,
  Total;
  Percent, never married; now married, except separated;
    separated; widowed; and divorced;
Females 15 years and over,
  Total;
  Percent, never married; now married, except separated;
    separated; widowed; and divorced.

Source: U.S. Census Bureau, American Community Survey, Multi-Year Profiles 2003—Social Characteristics, accessed 24 June 2005. See Internet site <http://www.census.gov/acs/www/Products/Profiles/Chg/2003/ACS/index.htm>.

Marital status refers to how people responded when asked if they were now married, widowed, divorced, separated, or never married. Couples who live together (unmarried people, people in common-law marriages) were allowed to report the marital status they considered the most appropriate. **Never married** includes all people who have never been married, including people whose only marriage(s) was annulled. **Now married, except separated** includes people whose current marriage has not ended through widowhood, divorce, or separation (regardless of previous marital history). The category also include couples who live together or people in common-law marriages if they consider this category the most appropriate. **Separated** includes people legally separated or otherwise absent from their spouse because of marital discord. This category also includes people who have been deserted or who have parted because they no longer want to live together but who have not obtained a divorce. **Widowed** includes widows and widowers who have not remarried.

Table A-8. Residence One Year Ago, Immigrants, and Language Spoken at Home

Residence one year ago, population 1 year and over, 2003,
  and percent who lived in same house one year ago;
Immigrants, 2003, 2002, 2001, and 2000;
  Leading countries of origin, 2003, Mexico, India, China,
    Philippines, Vietnam, El Salvador, Cuba, and Bosnia and

Herzegovina; Language spoken at home, 2003, Population 5 years and over; Language other than English, percent, total and Spanish.

Sources: Residence and language spoken—U.S. Census Bureau, American Community Survey, Multi-Year Profiles 2003—Social Characteristics, accessed 24 June 2005. See Internet site <http://www.census.gov/acs/www/Products /Profiles/Chg/2003/ACS/index.htm>; Immigrants—U.S. Department of Homeland Security, Office of Immigration Statistics, *2003 Yearbook of Immigration Statistics*, see Internet site <http://uscis.gov/graphics/shared/aboutus /statistics/ybpage.htm>.

Residence one year ago. People were asked for the city or town, U.S. county, state or foreign country of residence one year ago if reporting that one year ago they lived in a different house from their current residence. This was asked of the population one year and older. Residence one year ago is used in conjunction with location of current residence to determine the extent of residential mobility of the population and the resulting redistribution of the population across the various states, metropolitan areas, and regions of the country. When no information on previous residence was reported for a person, information for other family members, if available, was used to assign a location of residence one year ago. All cases of nonresponse or incomplete response that were not assigned a previous residence based on information from other family members were allocated to the previous residence of another person with similar characteristics who provided complete information.

Immigrant refers to an alien admitted to the United States as a lawful permanent resident. The Immigration and Nationality Act (INA) broadly defines an immigrant as any alien in the United States, except one legally admitted under specific nonimmigrant categories. An illegal alien who entered the United States without inspection, for example, would be strictly defined as an immigrant under the INA but is not a permanent resident alien. Lawful permanent residents are legally accorded the privilege of residing permanently in the United States. They may be issued immigrant visas by the Department of State overseas or adjusted to permanent resident status by the Department of Homeland Security in the United States. Immigration statistics are prepared from entry visas and change of immigration status forms. Data are shown by state of intended residence.

Language spoken at home. People were asked if they sometimes or always spoke a language other than English at home. **Language other than English** includes anyone responding yes to this question but does not include the speaking of a language only at school or if speaking is limited to a few expressions or slang. People reporting they did speak another language at home were asked to identify the language spoken, such as Korean, Italian, Spanish, and Vietnamese.

Table A-9. Place of Birth: 2003

Total population;
Percent, born in state of residence, born in different state, and foreign born;
Foreign born,
  Total;
  Percent,
    Not a citizen;
    Entered 1990 or later;
    Born in—
      Europe,
      Asia, total, China, India, Korea, Philippines, and Vietnam;
      Latin America, total and Mexico.

Source: U.S. Census Bureau, American Community Survey, Multi-Year Profiles 2003—Social Characteristics, accessed 24 June 2005, see Internet site <http://www .census.gov/acs/www/Products/Profiles/Chg/2003/ACS /index.htm>; and "PCT027. Place of Birth for the Foreign-Born Population," see Internet site <http://factfinder .census.gov/servlet/DatasetMainPageServlet?_program =ACS&_lang=en&_ts=>.

Place of birth. People were asked where they were born and were asked to select from two categories: (1) in the United States, (2) outside the United States. Respondents selecting category 1 were then asked to report the name of the state while respondents selecting category 2 were then asked to report the name of the foreign country, or Puerto Rico, Guam, etc. People not reporting a place of birth were assigned the state or country of birth of another family member, or were allocated the response of another individual with similar characteristics. People born outside the United States were asked to report their place of birth according to current international boundaries. Since numerous changes in boundaries of foreign countries have occurred in the last century, some people may have reported their place of birth in terms of boundaries that existed at the time of their birth or emigration, or in accordance with their own national preference. The **foreign-born** population includes anyone who was not a U.S. citizen at birth. This includes respondents who indicated they were a U.S. citizen by naturalization or not a U.S. citizen. This excludes people born in either the United States, Puerto Rico or a U.S. Island Area such as Guam or the U.S. Virgin Islands, or people born in a foreign country to a U.S. citizen parent(s).

Table A-10. Live Births and Birth Rates

Total births, 2003, 2000, and 1990;
Rate, 2003, 2000, and 1990;
Percent with low birth weight, 2003, 2000, and 1990;
Percent to teenage mothers, 2003, 2000, and 1990;
Percent to unmarried women, 2003, 2000, and 1990.

Source: U.S. National Center for Health Statistics, *Vital Statistics of the United States*, annual; *National Vital Statistics Report* (NVSR), formerly *Monthly Vital Statistics Report*; see also <http://www.cdc.gov/nchs/nvss.htm>.

Births. Through the National Vital Statistics System, the National Center for Health Statistics (NCHS) collects and publishes data on births in the United States. The Division of Vital Statistics obtains information on births from the registration offices of all states, New York City, and the District of Columbia. In most areas, practically all births are registered. The most recent test of the completeness of birth registration, conducted on a sample of births from 1964 to 1968, showed that 99.3 percent of all births in the United States during that period were registered.

Birth statistics are limited to events occurring during the year. The data are by place of residence and exclude events occurring to nonresidents of the United States. Births that occur outside the United States are excluded. **Birth rates** represent the number of births per 1,000 resident population estimated as of July 1 for 2003 and enumerated as of April 1 for 1990 and 2000 (decennial census years).

Table A-11. Births and Birth Rates by Race and Hispanic Origin and Fertility Rate: 2002

Births,
   All races;
   White, Non-Hispanic;
   Black, Non-Hispanic;
   American Indian;
   Asian or Pacific Islander;
   Hispanic;
Birth rates,
   All races;
   White, total and Non-Hispanic;
   Black, total and Non-Hispanic;
   American Indian;
   Asian or Pacific Islander;
   Hispanic;
   Fertility rate.

Source: U.S. National Center for Health Statistics, *Vital Statistics of the United States*, annual; and *National Vital Statistics Report* (NVSR), formerly *Monthly Vital Statistics Report*, and unpublished data. See also Internet site <http://www.cdc.gov/nchs/nvss.htm>.

Births by race. Through the National Vital Statistics System, the National Center for Health Statistics (NCHS) collects and publishes data on births in the United States. The Division of Vital Statistics obtains information on births from the registration offices of all states, New York City, and the District of Columbia. Race and Hispanic origin are reported separately on the birth certificate. Beginning with the 1989 data year, NCHS started tabulating its

birth data primarily by race of the mother. In 1988 and prior years, births were tabulated by the race of the child, which was determined from the race of the parents as entered on the birth certificate.

Fertility rate represents the number of births per 1,000 women age 15–44 years estimated.

Table A-12. Deaths and Death Rates

Deaths for all races,
   Number, 2002, 2001, 2000, and 1990;
   Rate, 2002, 2001, 2000, and 1990;
Number of deaths by race, 2002; White; Black, Asian or Pacific Islander; American Indian, Eskimo, or Aleut;
Infant deaths, 2002, 2001, 2000, and 1990;
   Rate,
      All races, 2002, 2001, 2000, and 1990;
      White, 2002, 2001, and 2000;
      Black, 2002, 2001, and 2000.

Source: U.S. National Center for Health Statistics, *Vital Statistics of the United States*, annual; *National Vital Statistics Report* (NVSR), formerly *Monthly Vital Statistics Report*; see also <http://www.cdc.gov/nchs/nvss.htm>.

Deaths. Through the National Vital Statistics System, the National Center for Health Statistics (NCHS) collects and publishes data on deaths in the United States. The Division of Vital Statistics obtains information on deaths from the registration offices of all states, New York City, and the District of Columbia. In most areas, practically all deaths are registered. The most recent test of the completeness of birth registration, conducted on a sample of births from 1964 to 1968, showed that 99.3 percent of all births in the United States during that period were registered. No comparable information is available for deaths, but it is generally believed that death registration in the United States is at least as complete as birth registration.

Death statistics are limited to events occurring during the year. The data are by place of residence and exclude events occurring to nonresidents of the United States. Deaths that occur outside the United States are excluded. **Death rates** represent the number of deaths per 1,000 resident population estimated as of July 1 for 2002 and enumerated as of April 1 for 1990 and 2000 (decennial census years).

Infant death rates are the most commonly used index for measuring the risk of dying during the first year of life. The rates are calculated by dividing the number of infant deaths in a calendar year by the number of live births registered for the same period and are presented as rates per 1,000 live births.

Table A-13. Death Rates by Cause: 2002

Death rates,
   HIV;
   Malignant neoplasms;

Diabetes mellitus;
Alzheimer's disease;
Diseases of the heart;
Cerebrovascular diseases;
Pneumonia and influenza;
Chronic lower respiratory diseases;
Chronic liver diseases and cirrhosis;
Accidents and adverse effects, total and motor vehicle;
Intentional self-harm (suicide);
Assault (homicide);
Injury by firearms.

Source: U.S. National Center for Health Statistics, *National Vital Statistics Report* (NVSR), formerly *Monthly Vital Statistics Report*; see also <http://www.cdc.gov/nchs /nvss.htm>.

Death rates by cause. Mortality statistics by cause of death are compiled in accordance with World Health Organization (WHO) regulations, which specify that member nations classify causes of death according to the current revision of the *International Statistical Classification of Diseases and Related Health Problems* (ICD). Effective with deaths occurring in 1999, the United States began using the Tenth Revision of this classification.

Table A-14. Marriages and Divorces—Number and Rate

Marriages, 2004, 2000, and 1990;
   Rates per 1,000 population, 2004, 2000, and 1990;
Divorces, 2004, 2000, and 1990;
   Rates per 1,000 population, 2004, 2000, and 1990.

Source: U.S. National Center for Health Statistics, *Vital Statistics of the United States*, annual; *National Vital Statistics Report* (NVSR), formerly *Monthly Vital Statistics Report*; see also <http://www.cdc.gov/nchs/products /pubs/pubd/nvsr/nvsr.htm>.

Marriage and divorce. The compilation of nationwide statistics on marriages and divorces in the United States began in 1887–88, when the National Office of Vital Statistics prepared estimates for the years 1867–86. Although periodic updates took place after 1888, marriage and divorce statistics were not collected and published annually until 1944 by that office. In 1957 and 1958, respectively, the same office established marriage- and divorce-registration areas. Beginning in 1957, the marriage-registration area comprised 30 states, plus Alaska, Hawaii, Puerto Rico, and the Virgin Islands; it currently includes 42 states and the District of Columbia. The divorce-registration area, started in 1958 with 14 states, Alaska, Hawaii, and the Virgin Islands, currently includes a total of 31 states and the Virgin Islands. Total counts of events for registration and nonregistration states are gathered by collecting already summarized data on marriages and divorced reported by state offices of vital statistics and by county offices of registration.

Table A-15. Community Hospitals

Number of hospitals, 2003, 2000, and 1990;
Beds, 2003, 2000, and 1990;
Patients admitted, 2003, 2000, and 1990;
Outpatient visits, 2003, 2000, and 1990;
Personnel, 2002, 2000, and 1990.

Source: Health Forum, An American Hospital Association Company, Chicago, IL, *Hospital Statistics*, 2005 edition, and prior years (copyright).

Community hospitals statistics are compiled by the American Hospital Association (AHA) from surveys of all hospitals in the United States and its outlying areas. AHA surveys include unregistered hospitals, as well as those registered by the AHA. Hospitals were asked to report data for a full year ending September 30.

Community hospitals are defined as nonfederal, short-term (average length of stay less than 30 days) general, or special hospitals, excluding psychiatric and tuberculosis hospitals and hospital units of institutions, whose services and facilities are available to the public. Institutions and services commonly referred to as convalescent and resting homes, nursing homes, infirmaries, old-age homes, and sanatoriums are excluded almost entirely.

Data for **beds** represent the number of beds regularly maintained (set up and staffed for use) for inpatients as of the close of the reporting period. This number excludes newborn bassinets. **Personnel** figures represent the number of persons on the hospital payroll at the end of the reporting period. Personnel are recorded as full-time equivalents (FTEs), which are calculated by adding the number of full-time personnel to one-half the number of part-time personnel, excluding medical and dental residents, interns, and other trainees. **Outpatient visits** include visits by patients who are not lodged in the hospital while receiving medical, dental, or other services.

Table A-16. Health Care Services, Physicians, and Nurses

Health care services, 2002,
   Establishments, total, ambulatory health care services, hospitals, and nursing and residential care facilities;
   Employees, total, ambulatory health care services, hospitals, and nursing and residential care facilities;
   Annual payroll;
Physicians, 2003 and 2000;
   Rate per 100,000 population, 2003 and 2000;
Nurses, 2001 and 1992;
   Rate per 100,000 population, 2001 and 1992.

Sources: Health care services—U.S. Census Bureau, *County Business Patterns*, annual, see Internet site <http://www.census.gov/epcd/cbp/view/cbpview.html>; Physicians—American Medical Association, Chicago, IL, *Physician Characteristics and Distribution in the U.S.*, annual (copyright); Nurses—U.S. Department of Health and Human Services, Health Resources and Services Administration, unpublished data.

An **establishment** is a single physical location at which business is conducted or services or industrial operations are performed. It is not necessarily identical with a company or enterprise, which may consist of one or more establishments. When two or more activities are carried on at a single location under a single ownership, all activities generally are grouped together as a single establishment. The entire establishment is classified on the basis of its major activity, and all data are included in that classification. Establishment counts represent the number of locations with paid employees any time during the year.

Paid **employment** consists of full- and part-time employees, including salaried officers and executives of corporations, who are on the payroll in the pay period including March 12. Included are employees on paid sick leave, holidays, and vacations; not included are proprietors and partners of unincorporated businesses.

Total **payroll** includes all forms of compensation, such as salaries, wages, reported tips, commissions, bonuses, vacation allowances, sick-leave pay, employee contributions to qualified pension plans, and the value of taxable fringe benefits. For corporations, it includes amounts paid to officers and executives; for unincorporated businesses, it does not include profit or other compensation of proprietors or partners. Payroll is reported before deductions for social security, income tax, insurance, union dues, etc. First-quarter payroll consists of payroll during the January-to-March quarter.

Health Care Services combines Ambulatory Health Care Services (NAICS 621), Hospitals (NAICS 622), and Nursing and Residential Care Facilities (NAICS 623). Refer to General Notes to see information on these subsectors of the Health Care and Social Assistance industry defined using the North American Industry Classification System (NAICS).

Table A-17. Persons With and Without Health Insurance Coverage

Persons,
   Total persons covered, 2003, 2000, and 1990;
   Number not covered, 2003, 2000, and 1990;
   Percent of persons not covered, 2003, 2000, and 1990;
Children,
   Number not covered, 2003, 2000, and 1990;
   Percent of children not covered, 2003, 2000, and 1990.

Source: U.S. Census Bureau, Current Population Reports, annual, and unpublished data.

Health insurance coverage. The Current Population Survey (CPS) asks about health insurance coverage in the previous calendar year. The questionnaire asks separate questions about the major types of health insurance, and

people who answer "no" to each of these questions are then asked to verify that they were, in fact, not covered by any type of health insurance. Health insurance coverage is broadly defined as private or government coverage. Private health insurance is coverage by a plan provided through an employer or union or purchased by an individual from a private company. Government health insurance includes the federal programs Medicare, Medicaid, and military health care; the State Children's Health Insurance Program (SCHIP); and individual state health plans. People are considered insured if they were covered by any type of health insurance for part or all of the previous year, and everyone else is considered uninsured.

Table A-18. Health Conditions and Chronic Disease-Related Characteristics and Diabetes

High blood pressure, 2001 and 1991;
High blood cholesterol, 2001 and 1991;
Cigarette smoking, 2003 and 1991;
Heavy drinking, 2001 and 1991;
Above healthy weight, 2001 and 1991;
Obesity, 2001 and 1991;
Diagnosed diabetes, 2001 and 1991;
No leisure time physical activity in the past month, 2001 and 1991.

Source: U.S. Centers for Disease Control and Prevention, Atlanta, GA, *Morbidity and Mortality Weekly Report*, Vol. 53, No. 44, November 12, 2004; Vol. 52, No. 53, January 9, 2004; and *Supplemental Summaries* Vol. 52, No. SS-8, August 22, 2003; see Internet site <http://www.cdc.gov/mmwr/>.

Health conditions. The Centers for Disease Control and Prevention's Behavioral Risk Factor Surveillance System (BRFSS) collects prevalence data on risk behaviors and preventive health practices that affect health status. Data are collected monthly by state health departments through telephone surveys and provide health departments, public health officials, and policy makers with necessary behavioral information. When combined with mortality and morbidity statistics, these data enable public health officials to establish policies and priorities and to initiate and assess health promotion strategies. Topics of the surveys include factors such as blood pressure, cholesterol, cigarette smoking, drinking, weight, diabetes, and physical activity.

Table A-19. State Public Health, Children Immunized, and STDs and AIDS

State direct public health expenditures, 2003 and 2000;
   Per capita, 2003 and 2000;
   Percent of total state health, 2003 and 2000;
Percent of children age 19–35 months who were immunized, 2003–2004, 2001–2002, and 2000–2001;
Percent of adults age 65 years and over who received influenza vaccine, 2003, 2002, and 2001;

AIDS cases reported, 2003, 2002, and 2000;
  Rate, 2003, 2002, and 2000;
STD cases, 2003, total, chlamydia, gonorrhea, and
  syphilis.

Sources: State public health expenditures—Milbank
Memorial Fund, the National Association of State Budget
Officers, and the Reforming States Group, *2002–2003
State Health Care Expenditure Report* (copyright) and
2000–2001 State Health Care Expenditure Report (copy-
right); Children immunized—U.S. Centers for Disease
Control and Prevention, Atlanta, GA, *National Immuniza-
tion Survey*, accessed 4 March 2005, see <http://www.cdc
.gov/nip/coverage/>; Adults who received vaccine—U.S.
Centers for Disease Control and Prevention, Atlanta, GA,
Morbidity and Mortality Weekly Report, Vol. 53, No. 43,
November 5, 2004; Vol. 52, No. 41, October 17, 2003;
Vol. 51, No. 45, November 15, 2002, see <http://www.cdc
.gov/mmwr/>; AIDS—U.S. Centers for Disease Control
and Prevention, Atlanta, GA, *HIV/AIDS Surveillance Report*,
annual, see <http://www.cdc.gov/hiv/stats/hasrlink.htm>;
STDs—U.S. Centers for Disease Control and Prevention,
Sexually Transmitted Disease Surveillance, annual, see
<http://www.cdc.gov/nchstp/od/nchstp.html>.

Direct public health care includes local health clinics,
Ryan White AIDS Grant expenditures, and Indian health.
Expenditures may include funds spent on pharmaceutical
assistance for the elderly; childhood immunization;
chronic disease hospitals and programs; hearing aid assistance; adult day care for persons with Alzheimer's disease;
health grants; services for medically handicapped children; the Women, Infant, and Children (WIC) program;
pregnancy outreach and counseling; chronic renal disease
treatment programs; AIDS testing; breast and cervical can-
cer screening; tuberculosis programs; emergency health
services; adult genetics programs; and phenylketonuria
(PKU) testing.

Children immunized. The National Immunization Survey
(NIS) collects data through telephone surveys followed by
mail surveys. The survey covers immunization of U.S. pre-
school children ages 19 to 35 months old. The data shown
in this publication refer to the 4:3:1:3:3 vaccine series and
refers to four or more doses of diphtheria and tetanus tox-
oids and pertussis (DTP) vaccines, three or more doses of
poliovirus vaccine, one or more doses of any measles-
containing vaccine (MCV), three or more doses of Haemo-
philus influenzae type b (Hib) vaccine, and three or more
doses of hepatitis B vaccine.

Influenza vaccine for adults age 65 and over. The
Centers for Disease Control and Prevention's (CDC) Behavioral Risk Factor Surveillance System (BRFSS) collects
prevalence data on risk behaviors and preventive health
practices that affect health status. Vaccination of persons
at risk for complications from influenza and pneumococcal
disease is a key public health strategy for preventing associated morbidity and mortality in the United States.

AIDS cases reported. All 50 states, the District of
Columbia, and U.S. dependencies, possessions, and associated nations report AIDS cases to CDC by using a uniform surveillance case definition and case report form.
Although completeness of reporting AIDS cases to state
and local health departments differs by geographic region
and patient population, studies conducted by state and
local health departments indicate that the reporting of
AIDS cases in most areas of the United States is more than
85 percent complete.

Sexually transmitted disease (STD) cases. Cases of
nationally notifiable STDs are reported to the CDC by the
STD control programs and health departments in the 50
states, the District of Columbia, selected cities, 3,140 U.S.
counties, U.S. dependencies and possessions, and independent nations in free association with the United States.
Although most areas generally adhere to the same case
definitions for STDs, there may be differences in the policies and systems for collecting surveillance data. Comparisons of case numbers and rates among areas should be
interpreted with caution. However, since case definitions
and surveillance activities within a given area remain relatively stable, trends should be minimally affected by these
differences.

Table A-20. Public School Fall Enrollment

Total enrollment, 2002, 2000, 1995, and 1990;
Prekindergarten through grade 8, 2002, 2000, 1995, and
  1990;
Grades 9 through 12, 2002, 2000, 1995, and 1990;
Enrollment rate, 2002, 2000, 1995, and 1990.

Source: U.S. National Center for Education Statistics,
Digest of Education Statistics, annual, see Internet site
<http://www.nces.ed.gov/>.

Public school enrollment data represent fall enrollment
at all levels taught in a public school system, from prekindergarten through grade 12.

These data are from the Common Core of Data (CCD),
which is the National Center for Education Statistics'
(NCES) primary database on elementary and secondary
public education in the United States. The CCD, collected
annually, is a comprehensive, national statistical database
of all public elementary and secondary schools and school
districts and contains data that are comparable across all
states.

Table A-21. Public Elementary and Secondary
Schools—Finances and Teachers

Receipts, 2003–2004,
  Total,
  Revenue receipts,
    Total;
    Source, federal, state, and local;
  Nonrevenue receipts;

Expenditures, 2003–2004,
  Total;
  Per capita;
  Current expenditures,
    Elementary and secondary day schools;
    Average per pupil in average daily attendance,
      amount, and rank;
    Capital outlay;
    Teachers, 2003–2004,
  Number, elementary and secondary;
  Average salary, elementary and secondary.

Source: National Education Association, Washington, DC, Estimates of School Statistics Database (copyright).

Revenue receipts are available for current expenses, other non-day-school programs operated by the public schools, capital outlay, and debt service for public schools. Included among revenue receipts are all appropriations from general funds of federal, state, county, and local governments; receipts from taxes levied for school purposes; income from permanent school funds and endowments; and income from leases of school lands and miscellaneous sources (interest on bank deposits, tuition, gifts, school lunch charges, and so on).

Nonrevenue receipts refer to the amount received by local education agencies from the sale of bonds and real property and equipment, loans, and proceeds from insurance adjustments.

Total **expenditures** for public schools include current expenditures for elementary and secondary day schools, capital outlays, and interest payments.

Current expenditures include those expenditures for operating local public day schools, excluding interest on school debt and capital outlay. These expenditures include such items as salaries for school personnel, fixed charges, student transportation, school books and materials, and energy costs. **Capital outlay** refers to an expenditure that results in the acquisition of fixed assets or additions to fixed assets, which are presumed to have benefits for more than one year. It is an expenditure for land or existing buildings, improvements of grounds, construction of buildings, additions to buildings, remodeling of buildings, or initial, additional, and replacement equipment.

Data on classroom **teachers' salaries** are revised periodically by the National Education Association. Teachers at the elementary and secondary school levels include grades kindergarten through 6 and 7 through 12, respectively. **Average salary** is the arithmetic mean of the salaries of elementary and secondary school teachers. This figure is the average gross salary before deductions for social security, retirement, health insurance, etc.

Table A-22. Public High School Graduates and Educational Attainment

Public high school graduates, 2004, 2000, 1995, and
  1990;

Educational attainment, 2003,
  Population 25 years and over,
    Percent of persons 25 years and over, by highest level completed, not a high school graduate; high school graduate; some college, but no degree; associate's degree; bachelor's degree; and advanced degree.

Sources: Public high school graduates—U.S. National Center for Education Statistics, *Digest of Education Statistics*, annual; Attainment—U.S. Census Bureau, American Community Survey, Multi-Year Profiles 2003—Social Characteristics, accessed 24 June 2005. See Internet site <http://www.census.gov/acs/www/Products/Profiles/Chg/2003/ACS/index.htm>.

Data for **public high school graduates** include graduates of regular day school programs but exclude other programs and persons receiving high school equivalency certificates.

Data on **educational attainment** are derived from questions asked of all respondents to the American Community Survey, and data presented here are tabulated for people 25 years old and over. Respondents are classified according to the highest degree or the highest level of school completed. Persons currently enrolled in school are asked to report the level of the previous grade attended or the highest degree received. **High school graduate** refers to respondents who received a high school diploma or the equivalent, such as passing the test of General Educational Development (G.E.D.), and did not attend college. **Some college, but no degree** refers to respondents who have attended college for some amount of time but have no degree. The category **Associate's degree** includes people whose highest degree is an associate's degree, which generally requires 2 years of college-level work and is either in an occupational program that prepares them for a specific occupation, or an academic program primarily in the arts and sciences. The course work may or may not be transferable to a **bachelor's degree**. **Advanced degree** refers to a graduate or professional degree.

Table A-23. Institutions of Higher Education

Fall enrollment, 2002, 2000, and 1990;
  Public, 2002, 2000, and 1990;
  Private, 2002, 2000, and 1990;
State appropriations for higher education, 2003–2004,
  full-time equivalent enrollment, educational appropriations, educational appropriations per full-time equivalent enrollment, net tuition, and net tuition as a percent of total educational revenue.

Sources: Fall enrollment—U.S. National Center for Education Statistics, *Digest of Education Statistics*, annual; Appropriations—State Higher Education Executive Officers, Denver, CO (copyright).

Higher education is identified by the National Center for Education Statistics (NCES) as the study beyond secondary school at an institution that offers programs terminating in an associate, baccalaureate, or higher degrees. The data shown are based upon the Integrated Postsecondary Education Data System (IPEDS), established as the core postsecondary education data collection program for NCES. IPEDS is a system of surveys designed to collect data from all primary providers of postsecondary education in such areas as enrollment, program completions, faculty, staff, and finances. See the sources for methodological details.

Appropriations refers to money set aside by formal legislative action for a specific use. SHEEO defines **educational appropriations** by the equation: Net State Support plus Local Tax Appropriations minus Research, Agricultural, and Medical (RAM) appropriations. See the source for further information. **Full-time equivalent enrollment** (FTE) is a measure of enrollment equal to one student enrolled full-time for one academic year, based on all credit hours, including summer sessions. The data capture FTE enrollment in public institutions of higher education in those credit or contact hours associated with courses that apply to degree or certificate, excluding noncredit continuing education, adult education, or extension courses. Data for **net tuition** exclude discounts, waivers, and state-appropriated aid to students attending in-state public institutions and excludes medical student tuition.

Table A-24. Degree-Granting Institutions and Educational Services

Degree-granting institutions,
  Degrees conferred, 2001–2002, total, public, private, and bachelor's;
  Full-time faculty on 9/10-month contracts, 2002–2003,
    Total,
    Average salary, total and professors;
Educational services,
  Establishments, 2002, 2001, and 2000;
  Number of employees, 2002, 2001, and 2000;
  Annual payroll, 2002, 2001, and 2000.

Sources: Degrees conferred—U.S. National Center for Education Statistics, *Digest of Education Statistics 2003*, NCES 2005-025, December 2004; Faculty—U.S. National Center for Education Statistics, *Staff in Postsecondary Institutions, Fall 2002, and Salaries of Full-Time Instructional Faculty, 2002–03*, 2005-167, November 2004; Educational services—U.S. Census Bureau, *County Business Patterns*, annual; see Internet site <http://www.census.gov/epcd/cbp/view/cbpview.html>.

Degrees conferred refers to awards conferred by a college, university, or other postsecondary education institution as official recognition for the successful completion of a program of studies. **Full-time faculty** are those members of the instruction/research staff who are employed full-time and whose major regular assignment is instruction, including those with released time for research.

Educational services. Refer to General Notes to see information on the Educational Services industry defined using the North American Industry Classification System (NAICS). See the notes and explanations for Table A-16 for information on establishments, employees, and payroll.

Table A-25. Crimes and Crime Rates

Violent, 2003, 2002, 2000, and 1990;
Property, 2003, 2002, 2000, and 1990;
Offenses by type per 100,000 population, 2003,
  Violent crimes, total, murder, forcible rape, robbery, and aggravated assault;
  Property crimes, total, burglary, larceny/theft, and motor vehicle theft.

Source: U.S. Federal Bureau of Investigation, *Crime in the United States*, annual. See also <http://www.fbi.gov/ucr/02cius.htm/> (released 27 October 2003).

Data presented on crime are through the voluntary contribution of crime statistics by law enforcement agencies across the United States. The Uniform Crime Reporting (UCR) program provides periodic assessments of crime in the nation as measured by offenses coming to the attention of the law enforcement community. The Committee of Uniform Crime Records of the International Association of Chiefs of Police initiated this voluntary national data collection effort in 1930. UCR program contributors compile and submit their crime data in one of two means: either directly to the FBI or through the state UCR programs.

Users of these data are cautioned about comparing data between areas based on these respective Crime Index figures. Assessing criminality and law enforcement's responses from area to area should encompass many elements (i.e., population density and urbanization, population composition, stability of population, modes of transportation, commuting patterns and highway systems, economic conditions, cultural conditions, family conditions, climate, effective strength and emphasis of law enforcement agencies, attitudes of citizenry toward crime, and crime reporting practices). These elements may have a significant impact on crime reporting. Also, not all law enforcement agencies provide data for all 12 months of the year, and some agencies fail to report at all. Data are as reported to the FBI.

Seven offenses, because of their seriousness, frequency of occurrence, and likelihood of being reported to police, were initially selected to serve as an index for evaluating fluctuations in the volume of crime. These crimes, known as the Crime Index offenses, were murder and nonnegligent manslaughter, forcible rape, robbery, aggravated assault, burglary, larceny-theft, and motor vehicle theft. By congressional mandate, arson was added as the eighth Index offense in 1979. Only the Modified Index (not shown in this publication) includes arson.

Violent crimes include four crime categories: (1) Murder and nonnegligent manslaughter, as defined in the UCR program, is the willful (nonnegligent) killing of one human being by another. This offense excludes deaths caused by negligence, suicide, or accident; justifiable homicides; and attempts to murder or assaults to murder. (2) Forcible rape is the carnal knowledge of a female forcibly and against her will. Assaults or attempts to commit rape by force or threat of force are also included; however, statutory rape (without force) and other sex offenses are excluded. (3) Robbery is the taking or attempting to take anything of value from the care, custody, or control of a person or persons by force or threat of force or violence and/or by putting the victim in fear. (4) Aggravated assault is an unlawfulattack by one person upon another for the purpose of inflicting severe or aggravated bodily injury. This type of assault is usually accompanied by the use of a weapon or by means likely to produce death or great bodily harm. Attempts are included since an injury does not necessarily have to result when a gun, knife, or other weapon is used, which could and probably would result in a serious personal injury if the crime were successfully completed.

In general, property crimes include four crime categories: (1) Burglary is the unlawful entry of a structure to commit a felony or theft. (2) Larceny-theft is the unlawful taking, carrying, leading, or riding away of property from the possession or constructive possession of another. It includes crimes such as shoplifting, pocket picking, purse snatching, thefts from motor vehicles, thefts of motor vehicle parts and accessories, bicycle thefts, etc., in which no use of force, violence, or fraud occurs. This crime category does not include embezzlement, "con" games, forgery, worthless checks, and motor vehicle theft. (3) Motor vehicle theft is the theft or attempted theft of a motor vehicle. This definition excludes the taking of a motor vehicle for temporary use by those persons having lawful access. (4) Arson is any willful or malicious burning or attempt to burn, with or without intent to defraud, a dwelling house, public building, motor vehicle or aircraft, personal property of another, etc. Only fires determined through investigation to have been willfully or maliciously set are classified as arson. Fires of suspicious or unknown origins are excluded.

Rates are based on U.S. Census Bureau resident population enumerated as of April 1 for decennial census years and estimated as of July 1 for other years.

Table A-26. Juvenile Arrests, Child Abuse Cases, and Prisoners

Juvenile arrest rate, 2003, violent crime, property crime, drug abuse, and weapons;
Child abuse and neglect cases reported and investigated, 2003, number of reports, number of children subject of investigation, and number of victims;
Prisoners under jurisdiction of federal and state authorities,
  2003, number and rate;
    2000;

Prisoners executed, 2004 and 1977 to 2004;
Prisoners under death sentence, 2003, 2002, 2001, and 2000.

Sources: Juvenile arrests—Office of Justice Programs, *Juvenile Arrests 2003*, see Internet site <http://www.ncjrs.org/pdffiles1/ojjdp/209735.pdf>; Child abuse and neglect—U.S. Department of Health and Human Services, Administration of Children, Youth and Families, *Child Maltreatment 2003* (Washington, DC: U.S. Government Printing Office, 2003); Prisoners under jurisdiction—U.S. Bureau of Justice Statistics, *Prisoners in 2003*, and earlier issues, see Internet site <http://www.ojp.usdoj.gov/bjs/abstract/p03.htm>; Capital punishment—U.S. Bureau of Justice Statistics, *Capital Punishment*, annual, see Internet site <http://www.ojp.usdoj.gov/bjs/correct.htm>.

Data on **juvenile arrest rates** are based on analysis of arrest data from FBI reports and population from the Census Bureau. Rates are calculated by dividing the number of arrests of persons under age 18 for every 100,000 persons ages 10–17. Arrest rates are calculated by dividing the number of youth arrests made in the year by the number of youth living in reporting jurisdictions. While juvenile arrest rates in part reflect juvenile behavior, many other factors can affect the size of these rates. Consequently, comparisons of juvenile arrest rates across states, while informative, should be made with caution.

Data on **child abuse and neglect cases** are collected and analyzed through the National Child Abuse and Neglect Data System (NCANDS) by the Children's Bureau, Administration on Children, Youth and Families in the Administration for Children and Families, U.S. Department of Health and Human Services. The number of investigations includes assessments and is based on the total number of investigations that received a disposition. The number of children subject of an investigation of assessment is based on the total number of children for whom an alleged maltreatment was substantiated, indicated, or assessed to have occurred or the child was at risk of occurrence. Victims are defined as children subject of a substantiated, indicated, or alternative response-victim maltreatment.

Data for **prisoners under federal and state jurisdiction** were collected by the Bureau of Justice Statistics. Adults convicted of criminal activity may be given a prison or jail sentence. The data represent all persons under the jurisdiction of federal and state authorities rather than those in custody of those authorities.

Data on **number of executions** are for persons executed under crime authority. Fifty-nine persons were executed in 2004, bringing to 944 the total executed since 1977.

Data on **persons under sentence of death** are collected annually for the Bureau of Justice Statistics as part of the National Prisoner Statistics Program. Data are obtained from the departments of corrections in each of the 50 states and the District of Columbia. The following states and the District of Columbia did not have the death penalty as of December 31, 2003: Alaska, Hawaii, Iowa, Maine, Massachusetts, Michigan, Minnesota, North Dakota, Rhode Island, Vermont, West Virginia, and Wisconsin. The data exclude prisoners under sentence of death who remained within local correctional systems pending exhaustion of the appellate process or who had not been committed to prison.

Table A-27. State and Local Justice System and State Prisons

Full-time equivalent employment,
  2002, number and percent of total state and local;
  2000;
  Per 10,000 population, 2002, total justice system, police protection, judicial and legal, and corrections;
Expenditures,
  2002, total and percent of state and local;
  2000;
  Per capita, 2002, total justice system, police protection, judicial and legal, and corrections;
State prison expenditures, fiscal year 2001,
  Expenditures, total, operating, and capital;
  Annual operating costs, per inmate and per resident.

Source: U.S. Bureau of Justice Statistics, *Justice Expenditure and Employment Extracts, 2002*, and prior years; and *State Prison Expenditures, 2001*; see also <http://www.ojp.usdoj.gov/bjs/>.

State and local justice system. Full-time employees include those persons whose hours of work represent full-time employment in their employer government. **Expenditure** refers to all amounts of money paid out other than for retirement of debt, investment in securities, extensions of loans, or agency transactions. It includes only external cash payments and excludes any intragovernmental transfers and noncash transactions. It also includes any payments financed from borrowing, fund balances, intergovernmental revenue, and other current revenue.

Data for **police protection** cover all activities concerned with the enforcement of law and order, including coroners' offices, police-training academies, investigation bureaus, and local jails, "lockup," or other detention facilities not intended to serve as correctional facilities. **Judicial and legal** services covers all civil and criminal activities associated with courts, including prosecution and public defense. Data for **corrections** cover all activities pertaining to the confinement and correction of adults and minors accused or convicted of criminal offenses. Any pardon, probation, and parole activities also are included here.

Data on **state prison expenditures** were obtained by extracting corrections data from each state's responses to the Census Bureau's annual Survey of Government Finances. Expenditures are the total amounts paid for prison operations, including interest on indebtedness.

Table A-28. Civilian Labor Force and Employment

Civilian noninstitutionalized population 16 years and over,
  2004, total, male, and female; 2003; 2000; and 1990;
Civilian labor force,
  Total 2004, number, male, and female; 2003; 2000; and 1990;
  Employed, 2004, number, male, and female; 2003; 2000; and 1990.

Source: U.S. Bureau of Labor Statistics, *Geographic Profile of Employment and Unemployment, 2004 Annual Averages*; see Internet site <http://www.bls.gov/gps/> (accessed 2 August 2005); data for prior years, Local Unemployment Statistics Program, see Internet site <http://www.bls.gov/lau/> (accessed 7 September 2005).

Civilian labor force data are based on the Current Population Survey (CPS) and are annual averages of monthly data. An explanation of the technical procedures used to develop labor force estimates appears monthly in the Explanatory Note in the BLS periodical, Employment and Earnings. Information may also be found in the Handbook of Labor Statistics, which may be found at the BLS Web site at <http://www.bls.gov/opub/hom/>.

The **civilian noninstitutionalized population** includes persons 16 years of age and older residing in the 50 states and the District of Columbia who are not inmates of institutions (for example, penal and mental facilities, homes for the aged), and who are not on active duty in the armed forces. The **civilian labor force** comprises all civilians 16 years old and over classified as employed or unemployed. Employed persons are all civilians who, during the survey week, did any work at all as paid employees, in their own business, profession, or on their own farm or who worked 15 hours or more as unpaid workers in an enterprise operated by a member of the family. It also includes all those who were not working but who had jobs or businesses from which they were temporarily absent because of illness, bad weather, vacation, labor-management disputes, job training, or personal reasons, whether they were paid for the time off or were seeking other jobs. Each employed person is counted only once regardless of how many jobs they may have.

Table A-29. Civilian Labor Force and Unemployment

Employment/population ratio, 2004, male and female;
Unemployment,
  Total, 2004, total, male, and female; 2003; 2000; and 1990;
  Rate, 2004, total, male, and female; 2003; 2000; and 1990;
Participation rate, 2004, male and female.

Source: U.S. Bureau of Labor Statistics, *Geographic Profile of Employment and Unemployment, 2004 Annual Averages*; see Internet site <http://www.bls.gov/gps/> (accessed 2 August 2005); data for prior years, Local Unemployment Statistics Program, see Internet site <http://www.bls.gov/lau/> (accessed 7 September 2005).

Unemployed persons are all civilians 16 years old and over who had no employment during the survey week, were available for work, except for temporary illness, and had made specific efforts to find employment some time during the prior 4 weeks. Persons who were laid off or were waiting to report to a new job within 30 days did not need to be looking for work to be classified as unemployed. The unemployment rate for all civilian workers represents the number of unemployed as a percent of the civilian labor force.

Table A-30. Employed Civilians by Occupation: 2003

Total,
Management, professional and related occupations,
   Management, business, and financial operations occupations,
   Professional and related occupations;
Service occupations;
Sales and office occupations,
   Sales and related occupations,
   Office and administrative support occupations;
Natural resources, construction, and maintenance occupations,
   Farming, fishing, and forestry occupations,
   Construction and extraction occupations,
   Installation, maintenance, and repair occupations;
Production, transportation, and material-moving occupations,
   Production occupations,
   Transportation and material-moving occupations.

Source: U.S. Bureau of Labor Statistics, Local Area Unemployment Statistics, *Geographic Profile of Employment and Unemployment, 2003* (published August 2005). See Internet site <http://www.bls.gov/gps/>.

Employed persons are persons 16 years and over in the civilian noninstitutionalized population who, during the reference week, (a) did any work at all (at least 1 hour) as paid employees; worked in their own business, profession, or on their own farm, or worked 15 hours or more as unpaid workers in an enterprise operated by a member of the family; and (b) all those who were not working but who had jobs or businesses from which they were temporarily absent because of vacation, illness, bad weather, child care problems, maternity or paternity leave, labor-management dispute, job training, or other family or personal reasons, whether or not they were paid for the time off or were seeking other jobs. Each employed person is

counted only once, even if he or she holds more than one job. Excluded are persons whose only activity consisted of work around their own house (painting, repairing, or own-home housework) or volunteer work for religious, charitable, and other organizations.

An **occupation** is a set of activities or tasks that employees are paid to perform. Employees who perform essentially the same tasks are in the same occupation, whether or not they work in the same industry. Some occupations are concentrated in a few particular industries; other occupations are found in many industries. These data are based on the occupational classifications derived from the 2000 census. For information concerning the occupations, see the following Bureau of Labor Statistics (BLS) Web site at <http://www.bls.gov/cps/cpsoccind.htm>.

Table A-31. Private Industry Employment and Pay

Employment, 2003, 2002, 2001, and 2000;
   Percent change, 2002–2003 and 2000–2003;
Average annual pay, 2003, 2002, 2001, and 2000;
   Rank, 2003 and 2000;
   Percent change, 2002–2003 and 2000–2003.

Source: U.S. Bureau of Labor Statistics, *Employment and Wages, Annual Averages*, annual, 2003 edition. See Internet sites <http://www.bls.gov/cew/cewbultn03.htm> and <http://www.bls.gov/cew/home.htm> for prior years.

These data for employment and average annual pay are the product of a federal-state cooperative program, the Quarterly Census of Employment and Wages (QCEW) program, also knows as the ES-202 program. The data are derived from summaries of employment and total pay of workers covered by state and federal unemployment insurance (UI) legislation and provided by State Workforce Agencies (SWAs). The summaries are a result of the administration of state unemployment insurance programs that require most employers to pay quarterly taxes based on the employment and wages of workers covered.

Average annual pay was computed by dividing total annual payrolls of employers covered by unemployment insurance programs by average monthly employment for these employers. Included in the annual payroll data are bonuses, the cash value of meals and lodging when supplied, and tips and other gratuities. Average annual pay only approximates annual earnings because an individual may not be employed by the same employer all year or may work for more than one employer.

Table A-32. Industry Employment and Pay

Private industry employment, 2003,
   Total; construction; manufacturing; wholesale trade;
      retail trade; transportation and warehousing; information; finance and insurance; real estate and rental and

leasing; professional and technical services; management of companies and enterprises; educational services; health care and social assistance; arts, entertainment, and recreation; and accommodation and food services;

Government employment, 2003;

Private industry annual pay,

Total; construction; manufacturing; wholesale trade; retail trade; transportation and warehousing; information; finance and insurance; real estate and rental and leasing; professional and technical services; management of companies and enterprises; educational services; health care and social assistance; arts, entertainment, and recreation; and accommodation and food services;

Government average annual pay, 2003.

Source: U.S. Bureau of Labor Statistics, *Employment and Wages, Annual Averages, 2003*, annual. See Internet site <http://www.bls.gov/cew/cewbultn03.htm>.

See the text for Table A-31 for explanations of employment and annual pay data. Refer to General Notes to see information on different industries defined using the North American Industry Classification System (NAICS).

Table A-33. Union Membership

Union members, 2004, 2000, and 1990;
Workers covered by union, 2004, 2000, and 1990;
Percent of workers,
   Union members, 2004, 2000, and 1990;
   Covered by union, 2004, 2000, and 1990;
   Private sector union members, 2004, 2000, and 1990.

Source: The Bureau of National Affairs, Inc., Washington, DC, Union Membership and Earnings Data Book: Compilations from the Current Population Survey, 2004 and prior annual editions (copyright by BNA PLUS); authored by Barry Hirsch of Trinity University, San Antonio, TX, and David Macpherson of Florida State University. See Internet sites <http://www.bna.com/bnaplus/labor/laborrpts .html> and <http://www.unionstats.com>.

Union membership data refer to wage and salary workers who report that they are members of a labor union or an employee association similar to a union. These data are based on the Current Population Survey (CPS) and represent union members by place of residence. Refer to the source for information on the methodology used.

Table A-34. Median Income of Households in Constant (2003) Dollars and Distribution by Income Level

Median household income in (2003) dollars, 2003, 2002, 2001, and 2000;
Total number of households, 2003;
Percent of households by income level, 2003, under $10,000, $10,000–$14,999, $15,000–$24,999,

$25,000–$34,999, $35,000–$49,999, $50,000–$74,999, $75,000–$99,999, $100,000–$149,999, $150,000–$199,999, and $200,000 and over.

Source: U.S. Census Bureau, American Community Survey, Multi-Year Profiles 2003—Economic Characteristics, accessed 24 June 2005. See Internet site <http://www .census.gov/acs/www/Products/Profiles/Chg/2003/ACS /index.htm>.

Income of households includes the income of the householder and all other individuals 15 years old and over in the household, whether they are related to the householder or not. Because many households consist of only one person, average household income is usually less than average family income. Although the household income statistics cover the past 12 months, the characteristics of individuals and the composition of households refer to the time of enumeration. Thus, the income of the household does not include amounts received by individuals who were members of the household during all or part of the past 12 months if these individuals no longer resided in the household at the time of enumeration. Similarly, income amounts reported by individuals who did not reside in the household during the past 12 months but who were members of the household at the time of enumeration are included. However, the composition of most households was the same during the past 12 months as at the time of enumeration. **Median income** divides the income distribution into two equal parts: one-half of the cases falling below the median income and one-half above the median. The median household income is based on the distribution of the total number of households including those with no income.

Table A-35. Median Income of Families in Constant (2003) Dollars and Distribution by Income Level

Median family income in (2003) dollars, 2003, 2002, 2001, and 2000;
Total number of families, 2003;
Percent of families by income level, 2003, under $10,000, $10,000–$14,999, $15,000–$24,999, $25,000–$34,999, $35,000–$49,999, $50,000–$74,999, $75,000–$99,999, $100,000–$149,999, $150,000–$199,999, and $200,000 and over.

Source: U.S. Census Bureau, American Community Survey, Multi-Year Profiles 2003—Economic Characteristics, accessed 24 June 2005. See Internet site <http://www .census.gov/acs/www/Products/Profiles/Chg/2003/ACS /index.htm>.

In compiling statistics on family income, the incomes of all members 15 years old and over related to the householder are summed and treated as a single amount. Although the family income statistics cover the past 12 months, the characteristics of individuals and the composition of families refer to the time of enumeration. Thus, the income of the family does not include amounts received by individuals who were members of the family during all or part of the past 12 months if these individuals no longer resided with the family at the time of enumeration. Similarly, income amounts reported by individuals who did not reside with the family during the past 12 months but who were members of the family at the time of enumeration are included. However, the composition of most families was the same during the past 12 months as at the time of enumeration. **Median income** divides the income distribution into two equal parts: one-half of the cases falling below the median income and one-half above the median. The median family income is based on the distribution of the total number of families including those with no income.

Table A-36. Poverty Status of Families and Individuals in the Past 12 Months

Number below poverty in the past 12 months,
  Families, 2003, 2002, 2001, and 2000;
  Individuals, 2003, 2002, 2001, and 2000;
Percent below poverty in the past 12 months,
  Families, 2003, 2002, 2001, and 2000;
  Individuals, 2003, 2002, 2001, and 2000.

Source: U.S. Census Bureau, American Community Survey, Multi-Year Profiles 2003—Economic Characteristics, accessed 24 June 2005. See Internet site <http://www.census.gov/acs/www/Products/Profiles/Chg/2003/ACS/index.htm>.

Poverty status is determined using thresholds arranged in a two-dimensional matrix. The matrix consists of family size cross-classified by presence and number of family members under age 18 years old. Unrelated individuals and two-person families are further differentiated by age of reference person. To determine a person's poverty status, one compares the person's total family income in the last 12 months with the poverty threshold appropriate for that person's family size and composition. If the total income of that person's family is less than the threshold appropriate for that family, then the person is considered poor or "below the poverty level," together with every member of his or her family. If a person is not living with anyone related by birth, marriage, or adoption, then the person's own income is compared with his or her poverty threshold. The total number of people below the poverty level was the sum of people in families and the number of unrelated individuals with incomes in the last 12 months below the poverty level.

Table A-37. Housing—Units and Characteristics

Total housing units, 2004, 2000, and 1990;
Characteristics, 2003,
  Total units,

Units in structure, percent, 1-unit detached, 1-unit attached, and mobile home;
Year built, percent, 1990 or later, 1970 to 1989, and prior to 1950;
Occupied units,
  Total units;
  Vehicles available, percent, none, 1, 2, and 3 or more;
  House heating fuel, percent, utility gas and electricity.

Sources: Housing units—U.S. Census Bureau, "Table 1: Annual Estimates of Housing Units for the United States and States: April 1, 2000 to July 1, 2004" (HU-EST2004-01), published 21 July 2005, Internet site <http://www.census.gov/popest/housing/HU-EST2004.html>; and "Housing Units, Households, Households by Age of Householder, and Persons per Household: April 1, 1990" (ST-98-47), published 8 December 1999, Internet site <http://www.census.gov/popest/archives/1990s/ST-98-47.txt>; Characteristics—U.S. Census Bureau, American Community Survey, Multi-Year Profiles 2003—Housing Characteristics, accessed 24 June 2005, see Internet site <http://www.census.gov/acs/www/Products/Profiles/Chg/2003/ACS/index.htm>.

Refer to the General Notes to see information on the American Community Survey (ACS).

A **housing unit** is a house, apartment, mobile home or trailer, group of rooms, or single room occupied or, if vacant, intended for occupancy as separate living quarters. Separate living quarters are those in which the occupants do not live and eat with any other persons in the structure and that have direct access from the outside of the building through a common hall. For vacant units, the criteria of separateness and direct access are applied to the intended occupants whenever possible.

Units in structure. A structure is a separate building that either has open spaces on all sides or is separated from other structures by dividing walls that extend from ground to roof. In determining the number of units in a structure, all housing units, both occupied and vacant, are counted. Stores and office space are excluded. The statistics are presented for the number of housing units in structures of specified type and size, not for the number of residential buildings.

Year structure built refers to when the building was first constructed, not when it was remodeled, added to, or converted. Housing units under construction are included as vacant housing if they meet the housing unit definition—that is, all exterior windows, doors, and final usable floors are in place. For mobile homes, houseboats, RVs, etc., the manufacturer's model year was assumed to be the year built. The data relate to the number of units built during the specified periods that were still in existence at the time of enumeration.

A housing unit is classified as **occupied** if it is the current place of residence of the person or group of people living in it at the time of enumeration, or if the occupants are only temporarily absent from the residence for 2 months or less; that is, away on vacation or a business trip. If all the people staying in the unit at the time of the interview are staying there for 2 months or less, the unit is considered to be temporarily occupied, and classified as "vacant." The occupants may be a single family, one person living alone, two or more families living together, or any other group of related or unrelated people who share living quarters. Occupied rooms or suites of rooms in hotel, motels, and similar places are classified as housing units only when occupied by permanent residents, that is, people who consider the hotel as their current place of residence or have no current place of residence elsewhere. If any of the occupants in rooming or boarding houses, congregate housing, or continuing care facilities live separately from others in the building and have direct access, their quarters are classified as separate housing units.

Data on **vehicles available** show the number of passenger cars, vans, and pickup or panel trucks of one-ton capacity or less kept at home and available for the use of household members. Vehicles rented or leased for 1 month or more, company vehicles, and police and government vehicles are included if kept at home and used for nonbusiness purposes. Dismantled or immobile vehicles are excluded. Vehicles kept at home but used only for business purposes also are excluded.

House heating fuel data refer to occupied housing units. The data show the type of fuel used most to heat the house, apartment, or mobile home. Utility gas includes gas piped through underground pipes from a central system to serve the neighborhood. Electricity is generally supplied by means of above or underground electric power lines.

Table A-38. Specified Owner- and Renter-Occupied Units—Value and Gross Rent

Specified owner-occupied units,
   Total units, 2003;
   Median value in constant (2003) dollars, 2003, 2002, and 2000;
   Value in 2003, percent, less than $100,000, $100,000–$199,999, $200,000–$299,999, and $300,000 and over;
Specified renter-occupied units,
   Total units, 2003;
   Median gross rent in constant (2003) dollars, 2003, 2002, and 2000;
   Gross rent for units with case rent in 2003, percent, less than $300, $300–$499, $500–$749, and $750 or more.

Source: U.S. Census Bureau, American Community Survey, Multi-Year Profiles 2003—Housing Characteristics, accessed 24 June 2005. See Internet site <http://www.census.gov/acs/www/Products/Profiles/Chg/2003/ACS/index.htm>.

Refer to the General Notes to see information on the American Community Survey (ACS).

Specified owner-occupied units include only 1-family houses on less than 10 acres without a business or medical office on the property. The data for "specified units" exclude mobile homes, houses with a business or medical office, houses on 10 or more acres, and housing units in multiunit buildings. Value is the respondent's estimate of how much the property (house and lot, mobile home and lot, or condominium unit) would sell for if it were for sale. If the house or mobile home was owned or being bought, but the land on which it sits was not, the respondent was asked to estimate the combined value of the house or mobile home and the land. Median value divides the value distribution into two equal parts: one-half of the cases falling below the **median value** of the property and one-half above the median.

Specified renter-occupied units are renter-occupied (or vacant-for-rent) units that exclude one-family houses on 10 or more acres. Gross rent is the contract rent plus the estimated average monthly cost of utilities (electricity, gas, and water and sewer) and fuels (oil, coal, kerosene, wood, etc.) if these are being paid for by the renter (or paid for the renter by someone else). The **median rent** divides the rent distribution into two equal parts: one-half of the cases falling below the median contract rent and one-half above the median.

Table A-39. Housing Starts, Sales, Vacancy Rates, and Ownership

Homeownership rate, 2004, 2000, and 1990;
Vacancy rates, 2004, rental and homeowner;
Existing home sales, 2004, 2003, 2002, 2001, and 2000;
Housing starts, 2006 estimate, 2005 estimate, 2004 estimate, 2003, 2002, 2001, and 2000.

Sources: Homeownership and vacancy rates—U.S. Census Bureau, "Housing Vacancies and Home Ownership Annual Statistics: 2004," Internet site <http://www.census.gov/hhes/www/housing/hvs/annual04/ann04ind.html> (accessed 31 Mar 2005); Home sales—NATIONAL ASSOCIATION OF REALTORS®, Washington, DC, *Real Estate Outlook: Market Trends & Insights*, monthly (copyright), see Internet site <http://www.realtor.org/research>; Housing starts—National Association of Home Builders, Economics Division, Washington, DC, data provided by the Econometric Forecasting Service.

Vacancy rates and **homeownership rates** are based on data obtained from the Current Population Survey/Housing Vacancy Survey (CPS/HVS). Beginning in 2003, new weighting procedures based on the 2000 decennial census were implemented. Caution should be used when comparing current data with 1990 data shown here.

A housing unit is vacant if no one is living in it at the time of the interview, unless its occupants are only temporarily absent. In addition, a vacant unit may be one that is owned entirely by persons who have a usual residence elsewhere. Rental vacancy rate is the proportion of the rental inventory that is vacant for rent. The homeowner vacancy rate is the proportion of the homeowner inventory that is vacant for sale. The proportion of owner households to occupied households is termed the homeownership rate. It is computed by dividing the number of owner households by the number of occupied households.

Existing home sales data are from the National Association of Realtors. See source for detail of statistics presented (copyright).

Data for housing starts were supplied to the National Association of Home Builders by the Econometric Forecasting Service. For details about the data, please contact the source.

Table A-40. Cost of Living Indicators—Housing, Hospital Stays, Public University, Utilities, Gasoline, and Tax Rates

Housing prices of single-family homes,
  All housing, 2004, 2003, and 2000;
  Previously owned, 2004, 2003, and 2000;
Average costs per full-time-equivalent student in public colleges and universities,
  Public 4-year institutions, 2003–2004, 2002–2003, and 1999–2000;
  Public 2-year institutions, 2003–2004, 2002–2003, and 1999–2000;
Hospital cost per day, 2003, 2002, 2001, and 2000;
Energy expenditures, per capita, 2001 and 2000;
Regular gasoline prices, 2004, 2003, and 2000;
Residential utility prices,
  No. 2 heating oil, 2004, 2003, and 2000;
  Natural gas, 2004, 2003, and 2000;
  Electric energy, 2004, 2003, and 2000;
State individual income tax collections per capita, 2004 and 2000;
State tax rates,
  General sales tax, 2005, 2004, and 2000;
  Gasoline, 2005, 2004, and 2000.

Sources: Housing prices—Federal Housing Finance Board, "Monthly Interest Rate Survey"; see Internet site <http://www.fhfb.gov/>; Public university—U.S. National Center for Education Statistics, *Digest of Education Statistics 2003*, and prior years; see Internet site <http://nces.ed.gov/programs/digest/>; Hospital stays—Health Forum, An American Hospital Association Company, Chicago, IL, *Hospital Statistics* 2003 edition, and prior years (copyright); Energy expenditures—U.S. Energy Information Administration, *State Energy Price and Expenditure Report*, annual; see also Internet site <http://www.eia.doe.gov/>; Gasoline prices—U.S. Energy Information Administration, *Petroleum Marketing Annual 2004*, and prior years; see also Internet site <http://www.eia.doe.gov/>;

Utility prices—U.S. Energy Information Administration, "Petroleum Product Prices" and "Natural Gas Prices"; see Internet site <http://www.eia.doe.gov/emeu/states/_states.html> (accessed 12 September 2005); and *Electric Power Monthly*, March 2005, and *Electric Power Annual 2003*, and prior years; see also Internet site <http://www.eia.doe.gov/>; State individual income tax—U.S. Census Bureau, "State Government Tax Collections"; see Internet site <http://www.census.gov/govs/www/statetax.html>; State tax rates—Federation of Tax Administrators, 2005 and previous years; see Internet site <http://www.taxadmin.org/fta/rate/tax_stru.html>.

Data on **housing prices** are collected through the Federal Housing Finance Board's Monthly Interest Rate Survey (MIRS). This survey provides monthly information on interest rates, loan terms, and house prices by property type, by loan type, and by lender type, as well as information on 15- and 30-year fixed-rate loans.

The **average costs per full-time-equivalent student in public colleges and universities** data shown are based upon the Integrated Postsecondary Education Data System (IPEDS), established as the core postsecondary education data collection program for NCES. IPEDS is a system of surveys designed to collect data from all primary providers of postsecondary education in such areas as enrollment, program completions, faculty, staff, and finances. See the sources for methodological details.

Hospital cost per day. The American Hospital Association (AHA) compiles community hospitals statistics from surveys of all hospitals in the United States and its outlying areas. AHA surveys include unregistered hospitals as well as those registered by the AHA. Hospitals were asked to report data for a full year ending September 30. Data for hospital cost per day are total expenses adjusted per inpatient day. Expenses include payroll, nonpayroll, bad debt, and all nonoperating expenses for the reporting period.

Energy expenditure data refers to money directly spent by consumers to purchase energy. Expenditures equal the amount of energy used by the consumer times the price per unit paid by the consumer. In the calculation of the amount of energy used, process fuel and intermediate products are not included. Population used to calculate per capita data is based on total population residing in the area.

The data on **regular gasoline prices** refer to prices of gasoline having an antiknock, i.e., octane rating, greater than or equal to 88 and less than or equal to 90. Gasoline sales are reported by grade in accordance with their classification at the time of sales. In general, automotive octane requirements are lower at high altitudes. Therefore, in some areas of the United States, such as the Rocky Mountain States, the octane ratings for the gasoline grade may be 2 or more octane points lower. Prices exclude federal and state taxes.

Residential utility prices refer to the price of fuel used in private dwellings, including apartments, for heating, cooking, water heating, and other household uses. Prices for **No. 2 heating oil** include sales of No. 2 fuel oil and high- and low-sulfur diesel fuels. Prices are classified in accordance to what the product was sold as, regardless of the actual specifications of that product. If a No. 2 distillate were sold as a heating oil or fuel oil, the volume and price would be published in the category No. 2 fuel oil even if the product conformed to the higher specifications of a diesel fuel. Prices exclude federal and state taxes. **Natural gas** is a mixture of hydrocarbon compounds and small quantities of various nonhydrocarbons existing in the gaseous phase or solution with oil in natural underground reservoirs at reservoir conditions. The price of **electric energy** is calculated by dividing the total monthly revenue by the corresponding total monthly sales for each sector and geographic area.

Data for **state individual income tax collections** were based on the Annual Survey of State Government Tax Collection. Taxes are defined as all compulsory contributions exacted by a government for public purposes, except employer and employee assessments for retirement and social insurance purposes. For more detailed information on income tax collections, see the source.

The Federation of Tax Administrators collects data on **state tax rates** from various sources. The data shown are as of January 1 of the year shown. States may change these tax rates any time during the year. Data for taxes on fuel are collected by distributor/supplier/retailers in each state. Additional taxes may apply to motor carriers. See the source for more detailed methodological information.

Table A-41. Gross State Product in Current and Real (2000) Dollars and by Selected Large Industry

Current dollars, 2004, 2003, 2002, 2001, 2000, and 1990;
Chained (2000) dollars, 2004, 2003, 2002, 2001, 2000, and 1990;
Chained (2000) dollars by industry, 2003, total; construction; manufacturing; wholesale trade; retail trade; transportation and warehousing; information, finance and insurance; real estate, renting and leasing; professional and technical services; management of companies and enterprises; educational services; health care and social assistance; arts, entertainment, and recreation; accommodation and food services; and government.

Source: Bureau of Economic Analysis, *Survey of Current Business*, June 2005; and Internet site <http://www.bea.gov/bea/regional/gsp.htm > (released 23 June 2005).

Gross state product (GSP) is the value added in production by the labor and property located in a state. GSP for a state is derived as the sum of the gross state product

originating in a state. In concept, an industry's GSP, referred to as its "value added," is equivalent to its gross output minus its intermediate inputs. GSP is often considered the state counterpart of the nation's gross domestic product (GDP), the Bureau of Economic Analysis' (BEA's) featured measure of U.S. output. In practice, GSP estimates are measured as the sum of the costs incurred and incomes earned in the production of GDP.

The BEA prepares estimates of GSP in millions of current dollars and of real GSP in millions of chained (2000) dollars. The estimates of real GSP are derived by applying national implicit price deflators to the current-dollar GSP estimates for the detailed industries. These estimates of real GSP reflect the uniqueness of each state's industry mix, but they do not reflect differences by state in the prices of goods and services produced for local markets.

Table A-42. Personal Income

Personal income,
    Current dollars, 2004, 2003, 2002, and 2000;
    Constant (2000) dollars, 2004, 2003, 2002, and 2000;
        Percent change, 2000–2004;
        Percent distribution, 2004 and 2000.
Disposable personal income,
    Current dollars, 2004, 2003, 2002, and 2000;
    Constant (2000) dollars, 2004, 2003, 2002, and 2000;
        Percent change, 2000–2004.

Source: Except as noted, U.S. Bureau of Economic Analysis, *Survey of Current Business*, April 2005. See also <http://www.bea.gov/bea/regional/spi/> (released 28 March 2005).

Personal income data are based on the Regional Economic Information System; see Appendix B for additional information on that system.

Personal income is defined as the income received by, or on behalf of, all residents of the state. It consists of the income received by persons from all sources; that is, from participation in production, from both government and business transfer payments, and from government interest (which is treated like a transfer payment). Personal income is the sum of wage and salary disbursements, other labor income, proprietors' income with inventory valuation and capital consumption adjustments, personal dividend income, personal interest income, and transfer payment to persons, less personal contributions for social insurance.

Disposable income is the income that ultimately flows back to households and consumers, after subtracting any taxes that are paid and after adding any transfer payments received by households (such as social security, unemployment insurance, and welfare). It is personal income that is available for spending and saving.

Table A-43. Personal Income Per Capita

Personal income per capita,
    Current dollars, 2004, 2003, 2002, 2001, and 2000;
    Constant (2000) dollars, 2004, 2003, 2002, 2001, and

2000;
 Income rank, 2004 and 2000;
Disposable personal income per capita,
 Current dollars, 2004, 2003, 2002, 2001, and 2000;
 Constant (2000) dollars, 2004, 2003, 2002, 2001, and
 2000; Percent of U.S. average, 2004 and 2000.

Source: Except as noted, U.S. Bureau of Economic Analysis, *Survey of Current Business*, April 2005. See also <http://www.bea.gov/bea/regional/spi/> (released 28 March 2005).

Personal income is defined as the income received by, or on behalf of, all residents of the state. It consists of the income received by persons from all sources; that is, from participation in production, from both government and business transfer payments, and from government interest (which is treated like a transfer payment). Refer to the source explanations for A-42 for more detailed information on personal income and disposable personal income.

Per capita personal income is calculated as the total personal income of the residents of an area divided by the population of the area. Per capita personal income is often used as an indicator of the quality of consumer markets and of the economic well-being of the residents of the area.

Table A-44. Earnings by Industry: 2004

Farm earnings,
Private earnings, forestry, fishing-related activities, and
 other; mining; utilities; construction; manufacturing;
 wholesale trade; retail trade; information; finance and
 insurance; real estate and rental and leasing; professional
 and technical services; management of companies and
 enterprises; administrative and waste services; educational services; health care and social assistance; arts,
 entertainment and recreation; and accommodation and
 food services;
Government and government enterprises, federal, civilian;
 military; and state and local.

Source: U.S. Bureau of Economic Analysis, *Survey of Current Business*, April 2005. See Internet site <http://www.bea.gov/bea/regional/spi/>.

Earnings by industry are a by-product and actual component of the personal income series in Tables A-42 and A-43.

Earnings cover wage and salary disbursements, other labor income, and proprietors' income. Wage and salary disbursements are defined as monetary remuneration of employees, including corporate officers; commissions, tips, and bonuses; and pay-in-kind that represents income to the recipient. They are measured before such deductions as social security contributions and union dues. All disbursements in the current period are covered. Pay-in-kind represents allowances for food, clothing, and lodging

paid in kind to employees, which represent income to them, valued at the cost to the employer. Other labor income consists of employer contributions to privately administered pension and welfare funds and a few small items such as directors' fees, compensation of prison inmates, and miscellaneous judicial fees. Proprietors' income is the monetary income and income in-kind of proprietorships and partnerships, including the independent professions, and of tax-exempt cooperatives. Refer to General Notes for information on industries.

Table A-45. Science and Engineering Indicators

Doctoral scientists, 2001 and 1999;
Doctoral engineers, 2001 and 1999;
S&E doctorates awarded, 2002 and 2001;
Federal R&D obligations, 2002, 2001, and 1999;
Total R&D performance, 2002 and 2000;
Industry R&D, 2002 and 2000;
Academic R&D, 2002 and 2001;
Number of SBIR awards, 1999–2002 and 1995–2000;
Utility patents issued to state residents, 2002 and 2001.

Source: National Science Foundation, *Science and Engineering State Profiles: 2001–03*, and previous editions. See also <http://www.nsf.gov/statistics/states/>.

The Division of Science Resources Statistics (SRS) of the National Science Foundation (NSF) compiles science and engineering (S&E) data that summarize state-specific data on personnel and finances. The SRS survey databases include doctoral scientists and engineers, S&E doctorates awarded, S&E graduate students and postdoctorates, federal research and development (R&D) obligations by agency and performer, total and industrial R&D expenditures, and academic R&D expenditures. See the source for detailed information on these topics.

Table A-46. Employer Firm Births and Terminations and Business Bankruptcies

Number of employer firms, 2003, 2002, and 2001;
Employer firm births, 2003, 2002, and 2001;
 Rate, 2003, 2002, and 2001;
Employer firm terminations, 2003, 2002, and 2001;
 Rate, 2003, 2002, and 2001;
Business bankruptcies, 2003, 2002, and 2001.

Source: U.S. Small Business Administration, Office of Advocacy, "Small Business Economic Indicators for 2003," published August 2004; see Internet site <http://www.sba.gov/advo/research/sbei.html>.

Firms are an aggregation of all establishments owned by a parent company with some annual payroll. Employer **firm births** refers to the formation of new establishments or enterprises. Employer **firm deaths** refers to the voluntary or involuntary closure of a firm or establishment. **Bankruptcy** is a condition in which a business cannot meet its debt obligations and petitions a federal district court for either reorganization of its debts or liquidations of its assets. In the action the property of a debtor is taken over by a receiver or trustee in bankruptcy for the benefit of the creditors. This action is conducted as prescribed by the National Bankruptcy Act, and may be voluntary or involuntary. See the above source for more methodological information.

Table A-47. Employer Firms and Nonemployer Establishments

Firms, 2002 and 2000,
  By employment-size of enterprise, 2002, fewer than 20 employees and fewer than 500 employees;
Employment, 2002,
  Total,
    By employment-size of enterprise, fewer than 20 employees and fewer than 500 employees;
Annual payroll, 2002,
  Total,
    By employment-size of enterprise, fewer than 20 employees and fewer than 500 employees;
Nonemployer establishments, 2002 and 2000,
  Receipts, 2002 and 2000.

Sources: Employer firms—U.S. Small Business Administration, Office of Advocacy, "Statistics of U.S. Businesses and Nonemployer Statistics: Firm Size Data provided by U.S. Census Bureau"; see Internet site <http://www.sba .gov/advo/research/data.html>, accessed 4 May 2005; Nonemployer establishments—U.S. Census Bureau, "Nonemployer Statistics," annual; see Internet site <http:// www.census.gov/epcd/nonemployer/pdf.html>.

See explanations for A-46 in addition to the source for information on firms, employment, and payroll.

The universe of **nonemployer** establishments is created annually in conjunction with identifying the Census Bureau's employer business universe. If the Census Bureau receives information through administrative records that a business has no paid employees, then the business becomes part of the potential nonemployer universe. Name, address, industry classification, and receipts are available for each potential nonemployer establishment. These data are obtained chiefly from the annual business income tax returns filed with the Internal Revenue Service (IRS) and maintained in the Census Bureau's Business Register (see notes for A-48 for explanations of Business Register).

Table A-48. Private Nonfarm Establishments, Employment, and Payroll

Establishments, 2002 and 2000,
  Net change, 2000–2002;
  By employment-size class of establishment, 2002, under 20, 20 to 99, 100 to 499, and 500 or more;

Employment, 2002 and 2000,
  By employment-size class of establishment, 2002, under 20, 20 to 99, 100 to 499, and 500 or more;
Annual payroll, 2002 and 2000.

Source: U.S. Census Bureau, *County Business Patterns*, annual. See also Internet site <http://www.census.gov /epcd/cbp/view/cbpview.html>.

County Business Patterns (CBP) is an annual series that provides subnational economic data by industry. The series is useful for studying the economic activity of small areas; analyzing economic changes over time; and as a benchmark for statistical series, surveys, and databases between economic censuses. CBP covers most of the country's economic activity. The series excludes data on self-employed individuals, employees of private households, railroad employees, agricultural production employees, and most government employees.

CBP data are extracted from the Business Register, the Census Bureau's file of all known single- and multiestablishment companies. The Annual Company Organization Survey and quinquennial economic censuses provide individual establishment data for multilocation firms. Data for single-location firms are obtained from various programs conducted by the Census Bureau, such as the economic censuses, the Annual Survey of Manufactures, and Current Business Surveys, as well as from administrative records of the Internal Revenue Service (IRS), the Social Security Administration (SSA), and the Bureau of Labor Statistics (BLS).

An **establishment** is a single physical location at which business is conducted or where services or industrial operations are performed. It is not necessarily identical with a company or enterprise, which may consist of one establishment or more. When two or more activities are carried on at a single location under a single ownership, all activities generally are grouped together as a single establishment. The entire establishment is classified on the basis of its major activity and all data are included in that classification. Establishment counts represent the number of locations with paid employees at any time during the year. This series excludes governmental establishments except for wholesale liquor establishments, retail liquor stores, federally chartered savings institutions, federally chartered credit unions, and hospitals. Establishments without a fixed location or having an unknown county location within a state are included under a "statewide" geography classification.

Paid **employment** consists of full- and part-time employees, including salaried officers and executives of corporations, who are on the payroll in the pay period including March 12. Included are employees on paid sick leave, holidays, and vacations; not included are proprietors and partners of unincorporated businesses.

Total **payroll** includes all forms of compensation, such as salaries, wages, reported tips, commissions, bonuses, vacation allowances, sick-leave pay, employee contributions to qualified pension plans, and the value of taxable fringe benefits. For corporations, it includes amounts paid to officers and executives; for unincorporated businesses, it does not include profit or other compensation of proprietors or partners. Payroll is reported before deductions for social security, income tax, insurance, union dues, etc.

Table A-49. Foreign Direct Investment in the United States, and U.S. Exports

U.S. affiliates,
   Gross book value, 2002, 2001, 2000, and 1990;
   Employment, 2002, 2001, 2000, and 1990;
U.S. exports, 2004, total exports, rank, and percent
  change, 2000–2004; 2003; and 2000;
U.S. agricultural exports, 2004, 2003, and 2000.

Sources: U.S. affiliates—U.S. Bureau of Economic Analysis, *Survey of Current Business*, August 2004 and prior issues; *Foreign Direct Investment in the United States, Operations of U.S. Affiliates of Foreign Companies*, annual; U.S. exports—U.S. Census Bureau, U.S. International Trade in Goods and Services, series FT-900, December issues. For most recent release, see <http://www.census.gov/foreign-trade/Press-Release/2004pr/12/#ft900> (released 10 February 2005); U.S. agricultural exports— U.S. Department of Agriculture, Economic Research Service, U.S. Agricultural Trade database, Internet site <http://www.ers.usda.gov/publications/fau/july05/fau10201/fau10201.pdf> (released 8 July 2005).

Foreign direct investment data in the United States are based on a survey of operations of nonbank U.S. affiliates that are majority-owned by foreign direct investors.

A **U.S. affiliate** is a U.S. business enterprise in which there is foreign direct investment; that is, in which a single foreign person owns or controls, directly or indirectly, 10 percent or more of the voting securities of an incorporated U.S. business enterprise. "Person" is broadly defined to include any individual, corporation, branch, partnership, associated group, association, estate trust, or other organization and any government. A "foreign person" is any person that resides outside the United States; that is, outside the 50 states, the District of Columbia, the Commonwealth of Puerto Rico, and all U.S. territories and possessions.

The Census Bureau basic goods data are compiled from the documents collected by the U.S. Customs Service and reflect the movement of goods between foreign countries and the 50 states, the District of Columbia, Puerto Rico, the U.S. Virgin Islands, and U.S. Foreign Trade Zones. They include government and nongovernment shipments of goods, and exclude shipments between the United States and its territories and possessions, transactions with U.S.

military, diplomatic and consular installations abroad, U.S. goods returned to the United States by its armed forces, personal and household effects of travelers, and in-transit shipments. **Exports** are valued at the F.A.S. (free alongside ship) value of merchandise at the U.S. port of export, based on the transaction price including inland freight, insurance, and other charges incurred in placing the merchandise alongside the carrier at the U.S. port of exportation. For information on how these data were collected, see Appendix B.

Data on the value of **U.S. agricultural exports** by state of production are not collected by U.S. Customs and Border Protection. Consequently, the Economic Research Service (ERS) estimates state shares of agricultural exports using custom district-level export data compiled by the Census Bureau and state-level agricultural production data supplied by the U.S. Department of Agriculture's (USDA's) National Agricultural Statistics Service (NASS). As noted below, these approximations are adjusted for exports of agricultural products for which NASS does not collect state-level production data. Using these approximations, a state that is the largest producer of an agricultural commodity will also account for the largest share of U.S. exports of that commodity. Countries of destination for each state's exports cannot be determined.

Table A-50. Farms and Farm Earnings

Farms (USDA), 2004, 2003, and 2000;
   Land in farms, 2004, 2003, and 2000;
   Average acreage per farm, 2004, 2003, and 2000;
Farm earnings (BEA), 2003, 2002, and 2000.

Sources: Farms—U.S. Department of Agriculture, National Agricultural Statistics Service, *Farm Numbers and Land in Farms, Final Estimates, 1998–2002*; and *Farms, Land in Farms*, and *Livestock Operations 2004 Summary*, January 2005; Income—U.S. Bureau of Economic Analysis, *Survey of Current Business*, April 2005, see Internet site <http://www.bea.gov/bea/regional/spi/>.

A **farm** is any place from which $1,000 or more of agricultural products were produced and sold, or normally would have been sold, during the year. Government payments are included in sales. Ranches, institutional farms, experimental and research farms, and Indian Reservations are included as farms. Places with the entire acreage enrolled in the Conservation Reserve Program (CRP), Wetlands Reserve Program (WRP), or other government programs are counted as farms.

Land in farms consists of agricultural land used for crops, pasture, or grazing. Also included is woodland and wasteland not actually under cultivation or used for pasture or grazing, provided it was part of the farm operator's total operation. Land in farms includes acres in the Conservation Reserve, Wetlands Reserve Programs, or other government programs. Land in farms includes land owned and operated as well as land rented from others. Land used rent-free is included as land rented from others. All grazing land, except land used under government permits on a per-head basis, is included as land in farms provided it was part of a farm or ranch. Land under the exclusive use of a grazing association is reported by the grazing association and included as land in farms. All land in American Indian reservations used for growing crops or grazing livestock is included as land in farms. Land in reservations not reported by individual American Indians or non-Native Americans is reported in the name of the cooperative group that used the land. In many instances, the entire American Indian reservation is reported as one farm.

Average acreage per farm was calculated by dividing the total land in farms for an area by the number of farms in that area.

Farm earnings is comprised of the net income of sole proprietors, partners and hired laborers arising directly from the current production of agricultural commodities, either livestock or crops. It includes net farm proprietors' income and the wages and salaries, pay-in-kind, and supplements to wages and salaries of hired farm laborers; but specifically excludes the income of nonfamily farm corporations.

Table A-51. Farm Finances and Income

Balance sheet of farming sector (USDA),
   Assets, 2003, 2002, and 2000;
   Debt, 2003, 2002, and 2000;
Farm income (USDA),
   Value of agricultural sector production, 2003, 2002, and 2000;
   Value of production, 2003, per operation and per acre;
   Government payments, 2003 and 2000;
   Net farm income, 2003, 2002, and 2000;
   Net farm income, 2003, per operation and per acre.

Source: U.S. Department of Agriculture, Economic Research Service, "Farm Income Summary Totals for 50 States"; see Internet site <http://www.ers.usda.gov/Data /FarmIncome/50State/50stmenu.htm>, accessed 12 October 2004; "Farm Business Balance Sheet and Financial Ratios," published 3 December 2004; see Internet site <http://www.ers.usda.gov/data/farmbalancesheet /fbsdmu.htm>.

The farm business **balance sheet** accounts assess the wealth of the farm sector. It contains only farm debt and assets, including farmland normally used to produce agricultural products. Farm business **assets** are those items of value that make up the farm firm. Assets include farm real estate assets, machinery and equipment, value of crops stored, livestock and poultry inventories, purchased inputs on hand, investments in cooperatives, and other financial assets such as cash and checkable deposits.

Debt represents claims on the firm's assets by lenders, lessors, and other creditors. Liabilities are obligations owed to those who provide debt capital to the farm firm. Only liabilities incurred by those involved in on-farm agricultural production are included in the balance sheet. Debt held by firms and individuals performing the input supply, processing, distributing, or marketing functions for farms are excluded from the balance sheet.

Net farm income is that portion of the net value added by agriculture to the national economy earned by farm operators. Farm operators typically benefit most from the increases and assimilate most of the declines arising from short-term, unanticipated weather and market conditions. Net farm income is a value of production measure indicating the farm operators' share of the net value added to the national economy within a calendar year, independent of whether it is received in cash or a noncash form such as increases/decreases in inventories and imputed rental for the farm operator's dwelling.

Table A-52. Farm Marketings and Principal Commodities

Farm marketings,
   Total marketings, 2003, 2002, and 2000;
   Crops, 2003, 2002, and 2000;
   Livestock and products, 2003, 2002, and 2000;
   Principal commodities, 2003, top, 2nd, and 3rd.

Source: U.S. Department of Agriculture, Economic Research Service, "Farm Income," published 2 September 2004; see Internet site <http://www.ers.usda.gov/Data /farmincome/finfidmu.htm>.

Farm marketings represent quantities of agricultural products sold by farmers multiplied by prices received per unit of production at the local market. Information on prices received for farm products is generally obtained from surveys of firms (such as grain elevators, packers, and processors) purchasing agricultural commodities directly from producers. In some cases, the price information is obtained directly from the producers. Refer to the source for detailed information on farm income, including farm marketings and commodities.

Table A-53. Agricultural Census

Agriculture,
   Number of farms, 2002 and 1997;
   Land in farms, 2002 and 1997;
   Average size of farm, 2002 and 1997;
   Value of land and buildings, 2002 and 1997;
2002,
   Market value of agricultural products sold and government payments, total and products sold;
   Total number of farm operators;
   Farms by value of sales, less than $2,500, $2,500-$9,999, $10,000-$24,999, $25,000-$49,999, $50,000-$99,999, and $100,000 or more;
Cropland.

Source: U.S. Department of Agriculture, National Agricultural Statistics Service, *2002 Census of Agriculture*, Vol. 1; see also <http://www.nass.usda.gov/Census_of_Agriculture/index.asp>.

Refer to the notes for A-50 for explanations of farms, land in farms, and the average size of farms.

Market value of agricultural products sold. This USDA National Agricultural Statistics Service category represents the gross market value before taxes and production expenses of all agricultural products sold or removed from the place in 2002 regardless of who received the payment. It is equivalent to total sales. It includes sales by the operators as well as the value of any shares received by partners, landlords, contractors, or others associated with the operation. The value of commodities placed in the Commodity Credit Corporation (CCC) loan program is included in this figure. Market value of agricultural products sold does not include payments received for participation in other federal farm programs. Also, it does not include income from farm-related sources such as custom-work and other agricultural services, or income from non-farm sources.

The value of crops sold in 2002 does not necessarily represent the sales from crops harvested in 2002. Data may include sales from crops produced in earlier years and may exclude some crops produced in 2002 but held in storage and not sold. For commodities such as sugarbeets and wool sold through a co-op that made payments in several installments, respondents were requested to report the total value received in 2002.

The value of agricultural products sold was requested of all operators. If the operators failed to report this information, estimates were made based on the amount of crops harvested, livestock or poultry inventory, or number sold. Caution should be used when comparing sales in the 2002 census with sales reported in earlier censuses. Sales figures are expressed in current dollars and have not been adjusted for inflation or deflation. The value of sales of some crops and of some livestock and animal specialties were asked separately in the 1997 census and were combined into categories in the 2002 census.

Government payments consist of direct cash payments received by the farm operators in 2002. It includes disaster payments, loan deficiency payments from prior participation, payments from Conservation Reserve Programs (CRP), the Wetlands Reserve Programs (WRP), other conservation programs, and all other federal farm programs under which payments were made directly to farm operators. Commodity Credit Corporation (CCC) proceeds and federal crop insurance payments were not tabulated in this category.

Operators represent the total reported number of operators on farms and ranches. The 2002 census was the first to ask for the total number of operators associated with an operation. An operator is a person who operates a farm, either doing the work or making day-to-day decisions. A family operation may have more than one operator.

Table A-54. Natural Resource Industries and Minerals

Natural resource industries,
Establishments, 2002 and 2000;
Number of employees, 2002 and 2000,
Percent of all industries, 2002;
Annual payroll, 2002 and 2000;
Value of nonfuel mineral production, 2004, 2003, and 2000;
Mineral fuels, 2003,
Crude petroleum, quantity and value;
Natural gas, quantity and value;
Coal, quantity and value.

Sources: Natural resource industries—U.S. Census Bureau, *County Business Patterns*, annual, see Internet site <http://www.census.gov/epcd/cbp/view/cbpview.html>; Nonfuel minerals—U.S. Geological Survey, *Mineral Commodity Summaries*, annual, see also <http://minerals.usgs.gov/minerals/pubs/mcs/2005/mcs2005.pdf>; Crude petroleum—U.S. Energy Information Administration, *Petroleum Supply Annual*, and *Petroleum Marketing Annual*, see Internet site <http://eia.doe.gov/>; Natural gas—U.S. Energy Information Administration, *Natural Gas Annual, 2003*, see Internet site <http://www.eia.doe.gov/oil_gas/natural_gas/data_publications/natural_gas_annual/nga.html>; Coal—U.S. Energy Information Administration, *Annual Coal Report, 2003*, see Internet site <http://www.eia.doe.gov/cneaf/coal/page/acr/acr_sum.html>.

Natural Resource Industries includes Agriculture, Forestry, Fishing and Hunting (NAICS 11), Mining (NAICS 21), Wood Product Manufacturing (NAICS 321), and Paper Manufacturing (NAICS 322). For general information on establishments, employment, and payroll, see the explanations for Table A-48. For detailed information on industry sectors and subsectors, see the General Notes for the North American Industry Classification System (NAICS). Both Wood Product Manufacturing and Paper Manufacturing are subsectors of Manufacturing.

Nonfuel mineral production. The U.S. Geological Survey (USGS) collects information about the quantity and quality of all mineral resources. Long-term public and commercial planning must be based on the probability of discovering new deposits, on developing economic extraction processes for currently unworkable deposits, and on knowing which resources are immediately available. See the source listed for more detailed information on nonfuel mineral production.

The U.S. Energy Information Administration (EIA) obtains data on **crude petroleum** through the Petroleum Supply Reporting System (PSRS). This system represents a family of data collection survey forms, data processing systems, and publication systems that have been consolidated to achieve comparability and consistency throughout.

Natural gas is a gaseous mixture of hydrocarbon compounds, the primary one being methane. The EIA obtains data on natural gas using Survey Form EIA-895, "Monthly and Annual Quantity and Value of Natural Gas Production Report."

Coal is a readily combustible black or brownish-black rock whose composition, including inherent moisture, consists of more than 50 percent by weight and more than 70 percent by volume of carbonaceous material. The EIA obtains data on coal using the U.S. Department of Labor, Mine Safety and Health Administration, Form 7000-2, "Quarterly Mine Employment and Coal Production Report" and Energy Information Administration Form EIA-7A, "Coal Production Report."

Table A-55. Utilities

Private utilities,
   Establishments, 2002 and 2000;
   Number of employees, 2002 and 2000,
      Percent of all industries, 2002;
   Annual payroll, 2002 and 2000;
Water systems, 2004,
   Number of systems, total, community, nontransient non-
      community, and transient noncommunity;
   Population served, total, community, nontransient non-
      community, and transient noncommunity;
Gas utilities,
   Customers, 2003, all customers and residential; 2002;
      and 2000;
   Sales, 2003, all customers and residential; 2002; and
      2000;
   Prices, 2003, all customers and residential;
Electric industry,
   Net generation, 2003, 2002, and 2000;
   Generation by selected major source, 2003, percent,
      coal, petroleum, natural gas, nuclear, and hydroelectric;
   Net summer capacity, 2003, 2002, and 2000;
   Sales to customers, 2003, all customers and residential;
      2002; and 2000;
   Prices, 2003, all customers and residential.

Sources: Private utilities—U.S. Census Bureau, *County Business Patterns*, annual, see Internet site <http://www.census.gov/epcd/cbp/view/cbpview.html>; Water systems—Environmental Protection Agency, *FACTOIDS: Drinking Water and Ground Water Statistics, 2004*; see Internet site <http://www.epa.gov/safewater/data/pdfs/data_factoids_2004.pdf>; Gas utilities—American Gas Association, Arlington, VA, *Gas Facts*, annual (copyright); Electric industry—U.S. Energy Information Administration, *Electric Power Annual, 2003*, and previous editions; see also Internet site

<http://www.eia.doe.gov/cneaf/electricity/epa/epa_sum.html> (accessed 1 June 2005); and *Electric Sales and Revenue 2003*, and previous editions; see also Internet site <http://www.eia.doe.gov/cneaf/electricity/esr/esr_sum.html> (issued January 2005).

Private utilities. Refer to General Notes to see information on the Private utilities industry defined using the North American Industry Classification System (NAICS). See the notes and explanations for Table A-16 for information on establishments, employees, and payroll.

Data on **water systems** are obtained by the Environmental Protection Agency through the Safe Drinking Water Information System/Federal Version (SDWIS/FED), a database designed and implemented to meet the EPA's needs in the oversight and management of the Safe Drinking Water Act (SDWA). The database contains data submitted by states and EPA regions in conformance with reporting requirements established by statute, regulation, and guidance. Community systems include any public water system that supplies water to the same population year-round. Nontransient noncommunity systems include any public water system that regularly supplies water to at least 25 of the same people at least 6 months per year, but not year-round. Transient noncommunity systems include any public water system that provides water in a place such as a gas station or a campground where people do not remain for long periods of time.

Gas utilities are companies that are primarily distributors of natural gas to ultimate customers in a given geographic area. Utility gases include natural gas, manufactured gas, synthetic gas, liquefied petroleum gas-air mixture, or mixtures of any of these gases. The term customer refers to an individual, firm, or organization that purchases service at one location under one rate classification, contract, or rate schedule. If service is supplied at more than one location or under more than one rate schedule, each location and rate schedule is counted as a separate customer unless the consumption at the several locations is combined before billing and billed on one rate schedule.

Electric industry. Net generation is the gross generation minus plant use from all electric utility-owned plants. The energy required for pumping at a pumped-storage plant is regarded as plant use and must be deducted from the gross generation. Net summer capacity refers to the steady hourly output, which generating equipment is expected to supply to system load exclusive of auxiliary power, as demonstrated by tests at the time of summer peak demand. Sales include the amount of kilowatt-hours sold in a given period of time; they are usually grouped by classes of service, such as residential, commercial, industrial, and other. Other sales include public street and highway lighting, other sales to public authorities and railways, and interdepartmental sales.

Table A-56. Energy Consumption

Energy consumption, 2001, 2000, and 1990,
  Per capita, 2001;
  Percent change, 1990–2001;
End-use sector, 2001, residential, commercial, industrial,
  and transportation;
Selected source, 2001, petroleum, natural gas, coal,
  hydroelectric power, and nuclear electric power.

Source: U.S. Energy Information Administration, *State Energy Data 2001* (formerly *State Energy Data Report*), Internet site <http://www.eia.doe.gov/emeu/states/_seds.html> (released December 2004).

Energy consumption is the use of energy as a source of heat or power or as an input in the manufacturing process. Data on energy consumption are from the State Energy Data System (SEDS), which is maintained and operated by the Energy Information Administration (EIA). This goal in maintaining SEDS is to create historical time series of energy consumption, prices, and expenditures by state that are defined as consistently as possible over time and across sectors. SEDS exists for two principal reasons: (1) to provide state energy consumption, price, and expenditure estimates to members of Congress, federal and state agencies, and the general public and (2) to provide the historical series necessary for EIA's energy models.

Table A-57. Energy Expenditures

Current dollars, 2001, 2000, and 1990,
  Per capita, 2001;
  Percent change, 1990–2001;
Constant (2000) dollars, 2001, 2000, and 1990;
End-use sector, 2001, residential, commercial, industrial,
  and transportation;
Selected source, 2001,
  Petroleum product, total and motor gasoline;
  Natural gas;
  Coal;
  Electric purchasers.

Source: Except as noted, U.S. Energy Information Administration, *State Energy Price and Expenditure Report*, annual. See also <http://www.eia.doe.gov/emeu/states/_seds.html>.

Energy expenditures refer to the money directly spent by consumers to purchase energy. Expenditures equal the amount of energy used by the consumer times the price per unit paid by the consumer. In the calculation of the amount of energy used, process fuel and intermediate products are not included. Data on energy expenditures are from the State Energy Data System (SEDS), which is maintained and operated by the Energy Information Administration (EIA). For more information about the SEDS, see the explanation for Table A-56.

Table A-58. Construction

Construction,
  Nonfarm employment, 2004, 2003, and 2000;
  Earnings, 2004, 2003, and 2001;
Value of construction contracts, 2004, 2003, 2002, 2001,
  2000, and 1990;
New private housing units authorized by building permits,
  2004, 2003, 2002, and 2000.

Sources: Employment—U.S. Bureau of Labor Statistics, Current Employment Statistics Program, see Internet site <http://www.bls.gov/sae/home.htm>; Earnings—U.S. Bureau of Economic Analysis, *Survey of Current Business*, April 2005, see Internet site <http://www.bea.gov/bea/regional/spi/>; Value of construction—McGraw-Hill Construction Dodge, a Division of the McGraw-Hill Companies, New York, NY (copyright); New housing units—U.S. Census Bureau, Construction Reports, Series C40, Building Permits, monthly; publication discontinued in 2001. See Internet site <http://www.census.gov/const/www/newresconstindex.html> and New Residential Construction, monthly.

Construction. Refer to General Notes to see information on the Construction industry defined using the North American Industry Classification System (NAICS).

Data for **employment** are based on the Current Employment Statistics (CES) survey of payroll records covering over 390,000 businesses on a monthly basis. Employment is defined as the total number of persons on establishment payrolls employed full- or part-time who received pay for any part of the pay period, which includes the 12th day of the month. Temporary and intermittent employees are included, as are any workers who are on paid sick leave, on paid holiday, or who work during only part of the specified pay period. A striking worker who only works a small portion of the survey period, and is paid, would be included as employed under the CES definitions. Persons on the payroll of more than one establishment are counted in each establishment. Data exclude proprietors, self-employed, unpaid family or volunteer workers, farm workers, and domestic workers. Persons on layoff the entire pay period, on leave without pay, on strike for the entire period, or who have not yet reported for work are not counted as employed.

Earnings data are based on the Regional Economic Information System. Earnings are defined as the sum of wage and salary disbursements, supplements to wages and salaries, and proprietors' income.

Value of construction contracts includes new structures and additions. The data represent values of construction in states in which the work was actually done. Refer to the source for information about the data and methodology used to obtain the data.

Statistics on **housing units authorized by building permits** include housing units issued in local permit-issuing jurisdictions by a building or zoning permit. Not all areas of the country require a building or zoning permit. The statistics only represent those areas that do require a permit. Current surveys indicate that construction is undertaken for all but a very small percentage of housing units authorized by building permits. A major portion typically gets under way during the month of permit issuance and most of the remainder begin within the three following months. Because of this lag, the housing unit authorization statistics do not represent the number of units actually put into construction for the period shown, and should therefore not be directly interpreted as "housing starts."

Table A-59. Manufactures

Nonfarm employment (BLS), 2004, 2003, 2002, 2001, and 2000;

Earnings (BEA), 2004, 2003, 2002, and 2001;

Establishments, 2002 and net change 2000–2002;

Average hourly earnings of production workers, 2003, 2002, and 2001;

Value of shipments, 2003, 2002, 2001, and 2000.

Sources: Employment and average hourly earnings—U.S. Bureau of Labor Statistics, Current Employment Statistics Program, see Internet site <http://www.bls.gov/sae/home .htm>; Earnings—U.S. Bureau of Economic Analysis, *Survey of Current Business*, April 2005, see Internet site <http://www.bea.gov/bea/regional/spi/>; Establishments—U.S. Census Bureau, *County Business Patterns*, annual, see Internet site <http://www.census.gov /epcd/cbp/view/cbpview.html>; Value of shipments—U.S. Census Bureau, *Annual Survey of Manufactures, Geographic Area Statistics*, series M03(AS)-3 and earlier reports, see Internet site <http://www.census.gov/prod /2005pubs/am0331as1.pdf> (released May 2005); and 2002 Economic Census, *Manufacturing, Geographic Area Series*, see also <http://www.census.gov/econ/census02 /guide/geosumm.htm> (issued September 2005).

Manufactures. Refer to General Notes to see information on the Manufacturing industry defined using the North American Industry Classification System (NAICS). See the notes and explanations for Table A-58 for information on employment and earnings and Table A-16 for information on establishments.

Average hourly earnings are on a "gross" basis. They reflect not only changes in basic hourly and incentive wage rates, but also such variable factors as premium pay for overtime and late-shift work and changes in output of workers paid on an incentive plan. Included is pay for overtime, vacations, holidays, and sick leave. Bonuses, commissions, and other types of noncash payments are excluded unless they are earned and paid regularly (at least once a month). Employee benefits paid by the employers, as well as payments-in-kind, are excluded.

Value of shipments includes the received or receivable net selling values, free on board plant (exclusive of freight and taxes), of all products shipped, both primary and secondary, as well as all miscellaneous receipts, such as receipts for contract work performed for others, installation and repair, sales of scrap, and sales of products bought and sold without further processing. Included are all items made by or for the establishments from material owned by it, whether sold, transferred to other plants of the same company, or shipped on consignment. The net selling value of products made in one plant on a contract basis from materials owned by another was reported by the plant providing the materials. In the case of multiunit companies, the manufacturer was requested to report the value of products transferred to other establishments of the same company at full economic or commercial value, including not only the direct cost of production but also a reasonable proportion of "all other costs" (including company overhead) and profit.

Table A-60. Manufactures Summary and Export-Related Shipments and Employment

Manufactures summary, 2003,

  All employees,

    Number;

    Net change, 2000–2003;

    Payroll, total and per employee;

  Production workers, total, hours, and wages;

  Value added by manufactures, total and per production worker;

  Value of shipments;

Export-related, 2001,

  Export-related shipments;

  Export-related manufacturing employment;

  Export-related as percent of all manufacturers, shipments and employment.

Sources: Manufactures summary—U.S. Census Bureau, *Annual Survey of Manufactures, Geographic Area Statistics*, Series M03(AS)-3. See also <http://www.census.gov /prod/2005pubs/am0331as1.pdf> (released May 2005); Export-related—U.S. Census Bureau, *Exports from Manufacturing Establishments: 2001*, Series AR(01)-1, see Internet site <http://www.census.gov/mcd/exports/ar01.pdf> (released July 2004).

The **all employees** number is the average number of production workers plus the number of other employees in mid-March. Included are all persons on paid sick leave, paid holidays, and paid vacations during the pay period. Officers of corporations are included as employees; proprietors and partners of unincorporated firms are excluded.

Payroll includes all forms of compensation such as salaries, wages, commissions, bonuses, vacation allowances, sick-leave pay, and the value of payments in kind (e.g., free meals and lodgings paid during the year to all employees). Tips and gratuities received by employees from patrons and reported to employers are included. For corporations, it includes amounts paid to officers and executives; for unincorporated businesses, it does not include profit or other compensation of proprietors or partners. Payroll is reported before deductions for social security, income tax, insurance, union dues, etc.

Production workers include workers (up through the line-supervisor level) engaged in fabricating, processing, assembling, inspecting, receiving, storing, handling, packing, warehousing, shipping (but not delivering), maintenance, repair, janitorial and guard services, product development, auxiliary production for plant's own use (e.g., power plant), recordkeeping, and other services closely associated with these production operations. Not included in this classification are all other employees, defined as nonproduction employees, including those engaged in factory supervision above the line-supervisor level.

Value added by manufacture is a measure of manufacturing activity derived by subtracting the cost of materials, supplies, containers, fuel, purchased electricity, and contract work from the value of shipments (products manufactured plus receipts for services rendered). The result of this calculation is adjusted by the addition of value added by merchandising operations (i.e., the difference between the sales value and cost of merchandise sold without further manufacture, processing, or assembly) plus the net change in finished goods and work-in-process between the beginning- and end-of-year inventories. Value added avoids the duplication in the figure for value of shipments that results from the use of products of some establishments as materials by others. Value added is considered to be the best value measure available for comparing the relative economic importance of manufacturing among industries and geographic areas.

Export-related data are based on tabulations of data from 3 sources: the 2001 Annual Survey of Manufactures, the Census Bureau's 2001 edition of U.S. International Trade in Goods and Services, and the Bureau of Economic Analysis' Input-Output (I/O) Accounts of the U.S. Economy for 1992. To provide a means for using these different sources on a comparable basis required substantial manipulations and conversions. For example, each of these sources uses a different classification scheme (NAICS for the economic census, manufacturing sector, the harmonized system for the exports of merchandise, and the SIC for I/O accounts). The I/O accounts originate from 1992 data. Thus, a host of conversions and adjustments were used. The user should bear in mind that each of these conversions and adjustments is imperfect, and a potential source of error in the figures presented. Refer to the source for further discussion of methodology.

Table A-61. Major Manufacturing Sectors: 2003

Apparel and textiles,
  Employment, total, percent of total manufacturing, and
    percent change, 2000–2003;
  Value of shipments;
Machinery,
  Employment, total, percent of total manufacturing, and
    percent change, 2000–2003;
  Value of shipments;
Computer and electronic products,
  Employment, total, percent of total manufacturing, and
    percent change, 2000–2003;
  Value of shipments;
Motor vehicle and parts,
  Employment, total, percent of total manufacturing, and
    percent change, 2000–2003;
  Value of shipments.

Source: U.S. Census Bureau, *Annual Survey of Manufactures, Geographic Area Statistics*, Series M03(AS)-3 (released May 2005) and Series M00(AS)-3RV (issued September 2002); see also Internet site <http://www.census.gov/mcd/asm-as3.html>.

Refer to General Notes to see information on the Manufacturing industry and major sectors defined using the North American Industry Classification System (NAICS). See the notes and explanations for Table A-60 for information on employment and value of shipments.

Table A-62. Wholesale and Retail Trade and Shopping Centers

Wholesale and retail nonfarm employment (BLS), 2004, 2003, and 2000;
Wholesale trade,
  Earnings (BEA), 2004 and 2001;
  Establishments, 2002 and net change, 2000–2002;
Retail trade,
  Earnings (BEA), 2004 and 2001;
  Establishments, 2002 and net change, 2000–2002;
Shopping centers,
  Retail sales, 2004 and 2000;
  Retail sales per square foot, 2004 and 2000.

Sources: Employment—U.S. Bureau of Labor Statistics, Current Employment Statistics Program, see Internet site <http://www.bls.gov/sae/home.htm>; Earnings—U.S. Bureau of Economic Analysis, *Survey of Current Business*, April 2005, see Internet site <http://www.bea.gov/bea/regional/spi/>; Establishments—U.S. Census Bureau, *County Business Patterns*, annual, see Internet site <http://www.census.gov/epcd/cbp/view/cbpview.html>; Shopping centers—National Research Bureau, Chicago, IL. Data for 1995–2004 published by International Council of Shopping Centers in *Shopping Centers Today*, April issues (copyright, Trade Dimensions International, Inc.).

Wholesale and retail trade. Refer to General Notes to see information on the Wholesale Trade and Retail Trade industries defined using the North American Industry Classification System (NAICS). See the notes and explanations for Table A-58 for information on employment and earnings and Table A-16 for information on establishments.

Shopping centers. Data on shopping centers are provided by the International Council of Shopping Centers (ICSC), the global trade association of the shopping center industry. Refer to the source for explanations of the data.

Table A-63. Retail Sales

All retail stores, 2004, 2003, and 2001;
Sales per household, 2004, 2001, and percent change, 2003–2004;
Food and beverage stores, 2004 and 2003;
General merchandise stores,
   Total, 2004 and 2003;
   Department stores, 2004 and 2003;
Motor vehicle and parts dealers, 2004 and 2003;
Food services and drinking places, 2004 and 2003;
Total retail sales plus food and drink, 2004 and 2003;
Furniture and home furnishings, 2004 and 2003;
Electronics and appliances, 2004 and 2003;
Building and material supply, 2004 and 2003;
Health and personal care, 2004 and 2003;
Gasoline stations, 2004 and 2003;
Clothing and clothing accessories, 2004 and 2003;
Sporting goods, hobby, book and music stores, 2004 and 2003;
Miscellaneous stores, 2004 and 2003;
Nonstore retailers, 2004 and 2003.

Source: Market Statistics, a division of Claritas Inc., Arlington, VA, *The Survey of Buying Power Data Service*, annual (copyright).

Refer to General Notes to see information on the Retail Trade industry defined using the North American Industry Classification System (NAICS). For more detailed information on subsectors of the Retail Trade industry, see the list of codes with definitions at Internet site <http://www.census.gov/epcd/www/naics.html>.

Table A-64. Transportation and Warehousing

Transportation and warehousing,
   Nonfarm employment (BLS), 2004, 2003, and 2000;
   Earnings (BEA), 2004, 2003, and 2001;
   Establishments, 2002 and net change, 2000–2002;
Vehicle miles of travel, 2003 and 2001;
Commodity shipments, 2002 and 1997;
Railroad shipments, 2002 and 2001;
Waterborne shipments, 2002 and 2001.

Sources: Employment—U.S. Bureau of Labor Statistics, Current Employment Statistics Program, see Internet site <http://www.bls.gov/sae/home.htm>; Earnings—U.S.

Bureau of Economic Analysis, *Survey of Current Business*, April 2005, see Internet site <http://www.bea.gov/bea /regional/spi/>; Establishments—U.S. Census Bureau, *County Business Patterns*, annual, see Internet site <http://www.census.gov/epcd/cbp/view/cbpview.html>; Vehicle miles of travel—U.S. Federal Highway Administration, *Highway Statistics*, annual, see Internet site <http://www.fhwa.dot.gov/policy/ohpi/hss/hsspubs.htm>; Commodity shipments—U.S. Bureau of Transportation Statistics and U.S. Census Bureau, 2002 Economic Census, *Transportation, Commodity Flow Survey*, Individual State Reports, issued December 2004, see Internet site <http://www.census.gov/econ/www/cfsnew.html>. Data for the District of Columbia are on the CD-ROM; Railroad and waterborne shipments—U.S. Bureau of Transportation Statistics, *State Transportation Statistics 2004* and previous years, see Internet site <http://www.bts.gov/>.

Transportation and warehousing. Refer to General Notes to see information on the Transportation and Warehousing industry defined using the North American Industry Classification System (NAICS). See the notes and explanations for Table A-58 for information on employment and earnings and Table A-16 for information on establishments.

Vehicle miles of travel data are collected by the Federal Highway Administration (FHWA). Vehicle miles of travel are miles of travel by all types of motor vehicles as determined by the states on the basis of actual traffic counts and established estimating procedures.

Commodity shipment data are provided from the Department of Transportation/Department of Commerce, Commodity Flow Survey (CFS) Program. This survey is designed to provide data on the flow of goods and materials by mode of transport. A sample of 50,000 establishments engaging in mining, manufacturing, wholesale trade, and selected auxiliary establishments (warehouses) of in-scope multiunit and retail companies was used to collect data for the 2002 commodity survey. The 1997 survey used a sample of 100,000 establishments.

Railroad shipment data are developed by the Association of American Railroads (AAR) from the Surface Transportation Board's Carload Waybill Sample. The sample contains detailed information on the origination and termination of carloads by commodity and carrier for virtually all U.S. freight railroads. Normal statistical variations and limited sampling of very small railroads may cause limited distortions.

Waterborne shipment data are compiled by the U.S. Army Corps of Engineers and include detailed data on the movements of vessels and commodities at the ports and harbors on the waterways and canals of the United States and its territories. Data on foreign commerce are supplied to the Corps of Engineers by the Census Bureau, U.S. Customs, and purchased from the Journal of Commerce, Port

Import Export Reporting Service. The tonnage figures of shipments represent short tons (2,000 pounds).

Table A-65. Trucks Registered and Commodity Transportation

All trucks, 2002, 1997, and percent change, 1997–2002;
Pick-ups, 2002, 1997, and percent change, 1997–2002;
SUVs, 2002, 1997, and percent change, 1997–2002;
Minivans, 2002, 1997, and percent change, 1997–2002;
Commodity transportation, 2002,
   Shipments, value and weight;
   Percent going out of state, value and weight.

Source: Trucks, pick-ups, SUVs, and minivans—U.S. Census Bureau, 2002 Economic Census, *Vehicle Inventory and Use Survey, Geographic Area Series*, issued December 2004, see Internet site <http://www.census.gov/svsd /www/vius/products.html>; Commodity transportation—U.S. Bureau of Transportation Statistics and U.S. Census Bureau, 2002 Economic Census, *Transportation, Commodity Flow Survey*, issued December 2004, see Internet site <http://www.census.gov/econ/www /cfsnew.html>. Data for the District of Columbia are on the CD-ROM.

Data for **trucks** are based on data from the Vehicle Inventory and Use Survey and administrative records. The survey covers private and commercial trucks registered (or licensed) in the United States as of July 1 of the survey year. The survey excludes vehicles owned by federal, state, or local governments; ambulances; buses; motor homes; farm tractors; unpowered trailer units; and trucks reported to have been sold, junked, or wrecked prior to January 1 of the survey year.

Commodity transportation data are provided from the Department of Transportation/Department of Commerce, Commodity Flow Survey (CFS) Program. This survey is designed to provide data on the flow of goods and materials by mode of transport. A sample of 50,000 establishments engaging in mining, manufacturing, wholesale trade, and selected auxiliary establishments (warehouses) of in-scope multiunit and retail companies was used to collect data. The percent of shipments going out of state was calculated by subtracting the shipments within the state from the total number of shipments and then dividing this number by total shipments.

Table A-66. Motor Vehicle Registrations, Motorcycle Registrations, Highway Mileage, Bridges, and Driver's Licenses

Motor vehicle registrations,
  2003,
    Number, total, automobile, and trucks;
    Rate per 1,000 persons;
  2000, number and rate per 1,000 persons;
Motorcycle registrations, 2003 and 2000;

Highway mileage, 2003, total, interstate, other arterial,
  collector, and local;
Bridges, 2004, number and number deficient and obsolete;
Driver's licenses, 2003 and 2000.

Sources: Registrations, highway mileage, and driver's licenses—U.S. Federal Highway Administration, *Highway Statistics*, annual, see Internet site <http://www.fhwa.dot .gov/policy/ohpi/hss/hsspubs.htm>; Bridges—U.S. Federal Highway Administration, Office of Bridge Technology, see Internet site <http://www.fhwa.dot.gov/bridge /britab.htm>.

Vehicle registration data are collected by the Federal Highway Administration (FHWA) from state motor vehicle registration agencies. Accordingly, registration practices and dates do vary; data presented here are as near to a calendar-year basis as possible.

Total **highway mileage** includes roads and streets in the functional systems, which are assigned to groups according to the character service they are intended to provide. The functional systems are (1) arterial highways that generally handle the long trips, (2) collector facilities that collect and disperse traffic between the arterials and the lower systems, and (3) local roads and streets that primarily serve direct access to residential areas.

The Interstate System connects, as directly as practicable, the nation's principal metropolitan areas, cities, and industrial centers; serves the national defense; and connects at suitable border points with routes of continental importance. Arterial highways include those roads that generally handle the long trips. Collectors collect and disperse traffic between the arterials and the bottom system. Local roads and streets serve the residential areas, individual farms, and other local areas.

Driver's licenses. Each state and the District of Columbia administers its own driver licensing system. Since 1954, all states have required drivers to be licensed, and since 1959, all states have required examination prior to licensing. Tests of knowledge of state driving laws and practices, vision, and driving proficiency are now required for new licensees.

Data on **bridges** are based on the National Bridge Inventory (NBI). The NBI is a compilation of data supplied by states as required by the National Bridge Inspection Standards for bridges located on public roads. The database is maintained in a format prescribed by the Recording and Coding Guide for the Structure Inventory and Appraisal of the Nation's Bridges.

Bridges are structurally deficient if they have been restricted to light vehicles, require immediate rehabilitation to remain open, or are closed. Bridges are functionally obsolete if they have deck geometry, load-carrying capacity, clearance or approach roadway alignment that no longer meet the criteria for the system of which the bridge is carrying a part.

Table A-67. Traffic Fatalities and Shoulder Belt Use

Traffic fatalities, 2003, 2002, and 2000;
  Fatality rate, 2003, 2002, and 2000;
Persons killed in alcohol-related crashes, 2003 and 2002;
  Percent of all persons killed in crashes, 2003 and 2002;
  By highest BAC in crash,
    0.01 to 0.07, 2003 and 2002;
    0.08 or more, 2003 and 2002;
Percent of drivers and passengers in the front right seat using safety belts, 2004, 2003, and 2001.

Source: Traffic fatalities and persons killed in alcohol-related crashes—U.S. National Highway Traffic Safety Administration, *Traffic Safety Facts*, annual, see Internet site <http://www.nhtsa.dot.gov/people/Crash/Index .html>; Safety belts—U.S. Department of Transportation, National Highway Traffic Safety Administration, *Safety Belt Use in 2004—Use Rates in the States and Territories*, Washington, DC: November 2004, see Internet site <http://www-nrd.nhtsa.dot.gov/pdf/nrd-30/NCSA/RNotes /2004/809813.pdf>.

Traffic fatalities. The National Highway Traffic Safety Administration (NHTSA) has a cooperative agreement with an agency in each state's government to provide information on all qualifying fatal crashes in the state. These agreements are managed by regional contracting Officer's Technical Representatives located in the 10 NHTSA regional offices.

A fatal crash involves a motor vehicle in transport on a trafficway in which at least one person dies within 30 days of the crash. Traffic fatality rate is per 100 million vehicle miles traveled.

NHTSA defines a fatal crash as alcohol related if either a driver or a nonmotorist (usually a pedestrian) had a measurable or estimated Blood Alcohol Concentration (BAC) of 0.01 grams per deciliter or above. BAC is measured as a percentage by weight of alcohol in the blood (grams/deciliter). A positive BAC level (0.01 g/dl and higher) indicates that alcohol was consumed by the person tested; a BAC level of 0.01 to 0.07 g/dl indicates that the person was impaired; a BAC level of 0.08 g/dl or more indicates that the person was intoxicated.

Safety belt use. Data for states are based on observational surveys conducted in accordance with Section 157, Title 23, U.S. Code. For national figures, data are based on the National Occupant Protection Use Survey (NOPUS). Motorists observed in the survey were counted as "belted" if they appeared to have a shoulder belt across the front of their body.

Table A-68. Communications

Percent of households with telephones, 2004 and 1984;
Mobile wireless telephone subscribers, 2004 and 2000;
Percent of—
  Households with computers, 2003 and 1998;
  Households with Internet access, 2003 and 1998;
High-speed telecommunication lines, 2004 and 2000;
  By type of users, 2004, residential and small business and other;
Telecommunications revenue, 2003 and 2000.

Sources: Households with telephones—Federal Communications Commission, *Telephone Subscribership in the United States* (released March 2005), see Internet site <http://www.fcc.gov/wcb/iatd/lec.html>; Mobile wireless subscribers—Federal Communications Commission, *Local Telephone Competition: Status as of December 31, 2004* (released July 2005), see Internet site <http://www .fcc.gov/wcb/iatd/comp.html>; Households with computers and Internet—U.S. Department of Commerce, National Telecommunications and Information Administration, *Falling through the Net: Defining the Digital Divide*, July 1999, and *A Nation Online, 2004*; High-speed lines— Federal Communications Commission, *High-Speed Services for Internet Access: Status as of December 31, 2004* (released July 2005), see Internet site <http://www.fcc.gov /wcb/iatd/comp.html>; Revenue—Federal Communications Commission, *Trends in Telephone Service 2005* (released June 2005), see Internet site <http://www.fcc .gov/wcb/iatd/trends.html>.

The Federal Communications Commission (FCC) provides data for **households with telephones, computers, and Internet access** based on the Current Population Survey (CPS) conducted by the Census Bureau. The CPS is a nationwide monthly survey of civilian noninstitutional population 15 years old and over that uses a sample of 60,000.

The FCC's local competition and broadband data gathering program collects data on **mobile wireless** telephone subscribership and high-speed connections from telecommunications carriers twice a year using FCC Form 477. **High-speed lines** are connections that deliver services at speeds exceeding 200 kilobits per second (kbps) in at least one direction.

Revenue. Beginning in 1993, the FCC required all carriers with interstate revenues to begin filing an annual Telecommunications Relay Service (TRS) Fund Worksheet. Because revenues derived from providing access to the interstate network are considered to be interstate, virtually all carriers were required to file information. The FCC Form 499-A Telecommunications Reporting Worksheet was introduced on April 1, 2000. Beginning in 2001, many telecommunications providers also had to file the quarterly FCC Form 499-Q.

Table A-69. Information Industries and Newspapers

Information industries,
 Nonfarm employment (BLS), 2004, 2003, and 2000;
 Earnings (BEA), 2004, 2003, and 2001;
 Establishments, 2002 and net change, 2000–2002;
Daily newspapers, 2004 and 2000;
 Net paid circulation, 2004 and 2000;
 Circulation, per capita, 2004 and 2000.

Sources: Employment—U.S. Bureau of Labor Statistics, Current Employment Statistics Program, see Internet site <http://www.bls.gov/sae/home.htm>; Earnings—U.S. Bureau of Economic Analysis, *Survey of Current Business*, April 2005, see Internet site <http://www.bea.gov/bea /regional/spi/>; Establishments—U.S. Census Bureau, *County Business Patterns*, annual, see Internet site <http://www.census.gov/epcd/cbp/view/cbpview.html>; Newspaper—Editor & Publisher Co., New York, NY, *Editor & Publisher International Year Book*, annual (copyright).

Information industries. Refer to General Notes to see an explanation of the Information industry defined using the North American Industry Classification System (NAICS). See the notes and explanations for Table A-58 for information on employment and earnings and Table A-16 for information on establishments.

Data on **daily newspapers** are provided by Editor & Publisher Co. These data are for English-language newspapers only. Circulation figures are based on the principal community served by a newspaper, which is not necessarily the same location as the publisher's office. Refer to the source for more information.

Table A-70. Financial Activities

Financial activities,
 Nonfarm employment (BLS), 2004, 2003, and 2000;
 Earnings (BEA), 2004, 2003, and 2001;
 Establishments, 2002 and net change, 2000–2002;
FDIC-insured financial institutions,
 Number of institutions, 2004 and 2000;
 Assets,
  Total, 2004 and 2000;
  By asset-size of bank, 2004, less than $1 bil., $1 bil.
   to $10 bil., and greater than $10 bil.;
 Number of offices, 2004 and 2000;
 Deposits, 2004 and 2000;
Credit unions,
 Number, 2004 and 2000;
 Assets, 2004 and 2000;
Average insurance premium, 2002, renters and home-
 owners;
Life insurance, 2003, total payments, death payments, and
 annuity payments;
Automobile insurance—average expenditures per insured
 vehicle, 2002 and 2000.

Sources: Employment—U.S. Bureau of Labor Statistics, Current Employment Statistics Program, see Internet site <http://www.bls.gov/sae/home.htm>; Earnings—U.S. Bureau of Economic Analysis, *Survey of Current Business*, April 2005, see Internet site <http://www.bea.gov/bea /regional/spi/>; Establishments—U.S. Census Bureau, *County Business Patterns*, annual; Credit unions— National Credit Union Administration, *Yearend Statistics for Federally Insured Credit Unions*, annual, see Internet site <http://www.ncua.gov/>; FDIC-insured financial institutions number and assets—U.S. Federal Deposit Insurance Corporation, *Statistics on Banking*, annual; FDIC-insured financial institutions offices and deposits— U.S. Federal Deposit Insurance Corporation, *Bank and Thrift Branch Office Data Book*, annual; Insurance premiums—National Association of Insurance Commis- sioners (NAIC), Kansas City, MO, *Dwelling Fire, Homeown- ers Owner-Occupied, and Homeowners Tenant and Condominium/Cooperative Unit Owners Insurance*, annual (copyright). Reprinted with permission of the NAIC. Fur- ther reprint or distribution strictly prohibited without prior written permission of the NAIC; Life insurance—American Council of Life Insurers, Washington, DC, *Life Insurers Fact Book*, biennial (copyright); Automobile insurance—National Association of Insurance Commissioners (NAIC), Kansas City, MO, *Auto Insurance Database Report*, annual (copy- right). Reprinted with permission of the NAIC. Further reprint or distribution strictly prohibited without prior written permission of the NAIC.

Financial activities. Refer to General Notes to see infor- mation on the Finance and Insurance industry and Real Estate and Rental and Leasing industry defined using the North American Industry Classification System (NAICS). See the notes and explanations for Table A-58 for informa- tion on employment and earnings and Table A-16 for infor- mation on establishments.

FDIC-insured financial institutions includes both FDIC- insured commercial banks and FDIC-insured savings insti- tutions. The category of FDIC-insured commercial banks includes all commercial banks insured by the Federal Deposit Insurance Corporation (FDIC) either through the Bank Insurance Fund (BIF) or through the Savings Associa- tion Insurance Fund (SAIF). These institutions are regulated by and submit financial data to one of the three federal commercial bank regulators. The category of FDIC-insured savings institutions includes all institutions insured by either the FDIC Savings Association Insurance Fund (SAIF) operating under state or federal banking codes applicable to thrift institutions. These institutions are regulated by and submit financial data to the Office of Thrift Supervi- sion or the FDIC.

A **credit union** is a not-for-profit financial institution owned and operated by its members. Each credit union serves the specific field of membership it decides upon. Members share a common bond such as being employed by the same employer, belonging to an organization or church, or living in the same community. Credit unions offer a variety of financial services and products, including savings, loans, check cashing, wire transfers, and financial counseling. Credit union data are collected by the National Credit Union Administration (NCUA) using the Yearend Call Report.

The National Association of Insurance Commissioners (NAIC) publishes data on insurance premiums for renters and homeowners. **Average premium** equals premiums divided by exposure per house-years. A house-year is equal to 365 days of insured coverage for a single dwelling and is the standard measurement for homeowners insurance. Renters insurance premiums are based on HO-4 renters insurance policy for tenants. It includes broad named-peril coverage for the personal property of tenants. Homeowners insurance premiums are based on the HO-3 homeowner package policy for owner-occupied homes. This policy provides "all risks" coverage (except those specifically excluded in the policy) on buildings and broad named-peril coverage on personal property. The HO-3 homeowner package policy is the most common package written.

The NAIC also publishes data on **automobile insurance**. The average expenditure per insured vehicle equals total premiums written divided by liability car-years. A car-year is equal to 365 days of insured coverage for a single vehicle. The average expenditures for automobile insurance in a state are affected by a number of factors, including the underlying rate structure, the coverages purchased, the deductibles and limits selected, the types of vehicles insured, and the distribution of driver characteristics.

Life insurance. The American Council of Life Insurers (ACLI) publishes life insurance data by tabulating NAIC statutory data. Annuity refers to a financial contract that offers tax-deferred savings and a choice of payout options to meet the owner's income needs in retirement: income for life, income for a certain period of time, or a lump sum.

Table A-71. Professional and Business Services and Education and Health Services

Professional and business services,
  Nonfarm employment (BLS), 2004, 2003, and 2000;
  Earnings (BEA), 2004, 2003, and 2001;
  Establishments, 2002 and net change, 2000–2002;
Education and health services,
  Nonfarm employment (BLS), 2004, 2003, and 2000;
  Earnings (BEA), 2004, 2003, and 2001;
  Establishments, 2002 and net change, 2000–2002.

Sources: Employment—U.S. Bureau of Labor Statistics, Current Employment Statistics Program, see Internet site <http://www.bls.gov/sae/home.htm>; Earnings—U.S.

Bureau of Economic Analysis, *Survey of Current Business*, April 2005, see Internet site <http://www.bea.gov/bea /regional/spi>; Establishments—U.S. Census Bureau, *County Business Patterns*, annual, see Internet site <http://www.census.gov/epcd/cbp/view/cbpview.html>.

Professional and Business Services includes Professional, Scientific and Technical Services; Management of Companies and Enterprises; and Administrative and Support and Waste Management and Remediation Services. **Education and Health Services** includes Educational Services and Health Care and Social Assistance. Refer to General Notes to see information on the above industries defined using the North American Industry Classification System (NAICS). See the notes and explanations for Table A-58 for information on employment and earnings and Table A-16 for information on establishments.

Table A-72. Leisure and Hospitality Services

Arts, entertainment, and recreation services,
  Nonfarm employment (BLS), 2004, 2003, and 2000;
  Earnings, 2004, 2003, and 2001;
  Establishments, 2002, and net change, 2000–2002;
Accommodation and food services,
  Nonfarm employment (BLS), 2004, 2003, and 2000;
  Earnings (BEA), 2004, 2003, and 2001;
  Establishments, 2002, and net change, 2000–2002.

Sources: Employment—U.S. Bureau of Labor Statistics, Current Employment Statistics Program, see Internet site <http://www.bls.gov/sae/home.htm>; Earnings—U.S. Bureau of Economic Analysis, *Survey of Current Business*, April 2005, see Internet site <http://www.bea.gov/bea /regional/spi/>; Establishments—U.S. Census Bureau, *County Business Patterns*, annual, see Internet site <http://www.census.gov/epcd/cbp/view/cbpview.html>.

Refer to General Notes to see information on **Arts, Entertainment, and Recreation Services** and **Accommodation and Food Services** industries defined using the North American Industry Classification System (NAICS). See the notes and explanations for Table A-58 for information on employment and earnings and Table A-16 for information on establishments.

Table A-73. Travel and Tourism Indicators

Domestic travel expenditures, 2003, 2002, and 2001;
Impact of international travel on state economy,
  Travel expenditures, 2003 and 2001;
  Travel-generated employment, 2003 and 2001;
  Travel-generated tax receipts, 2003 and 2001;
Overseas visitors to the state, 2003 and 2000;
Visitors to—
  National parks, 2003 and 2000;
  State parks, 2003 and 2000.

Sources: Domestic travel and impact of international travel—Travel Industry Association of America, Washington, DC, *Impact of Travel on State Economies*, annual (copyright), see Internet site <http://www.tia.org/index .html>; Overseas visitors to the state—International Trade Administration, U.S. Department of Commerce, "Overseas Visitors to Select U.S. States and Territories 2003–2004" and previous years, Internet site <http:// www.tinet.ita.doc.gov>; National parks—National Park Service, Public Use Statistics Office, *National Park Service Statistical Abstract*, annual, see also Internet site <http:// www2.nature.nps.gov/stats/>; State parks—National Association of State Park Directors, *Annual Information Exchange*, see Internet site <http://www.naspd.org/>.

Data on **domestic travel expenditures** represent U.S. spending on domestic overnight trips and day trips of 50 miles or more, one way, away from home. This excludes spending by foreign visitors and by U.S. residents in U.S. territories and abroad. Data include travelers' expenditures in Indian casino gaming.

The International Trade Administration collects data on **overseas visitors** to the state using the Survey of International Air Travelers (In-Flight Survey) Program and the Visitors Arrival Program (I-94 Form). The In-Flight Survey is a monthly survey of international air travelers to and from the United States. The program is a public/private partnership between the government and airlines to collect information on the international travel market. The I-94 Form must be completed by all U.S. noncitizens to enter the United States. Canadian and some Mexican citizens are exempt. Data include travelers for business and pleasure, international travelers in transit from the United States, and students. Data exclude travel by international personnel and international businessmen employed in the United States.

Visitors to national parks. A visit is defined as the entry of any person, except National Park Service (NPS) personnel, onto lands or waters administered by the NPS. A visit may occur as a recreation visit or a nonrecreation visit. A same-day reentry, negligible transit, and an entry to a detached portion of the same park on the same day are considered to be a single visit. Visits are reported separately for two contiguous parks.

Data on **visitors to state parks** are collected by the National Association of State Park Directors (NASPD), composed of 50 state park directors. In some states, park agency has under its control forests, fish and wildlife areas, and/or other areas. In other states, park agency is responsible for state parks only. These data include overnight visitors.

Table A-74. Government

Nonfarm employment (BLS), 2004, 2003, and 2000;
Earnings (BEA), 2004, 2003, and 2001;
Federal tax collections, 2004, 2003, and 2000;
State tax collections, 2004, 2003, and 2000.

Sources: Employment—U.S. Bureau of Labor Statistics, Current Employment Statistics Program, see Internet site <http://www.bls.gov/sae/home.htm>; Earnings—U.S. Bureau of Economics Analysis, *Survey of Current Business*, April 2005, see Internet site <http://www.bea.gov/bea /regional/spi/>; Federal tax collections—Internal Revenue Service, *Data Book 2004*, Publication 55B, Washington, DC, and previous years, see Internet site <http:// www.irs.gov/taxstats/index.html>; State tax collections—U.S. Census Bureau, State Government Tax Collections (STC) report, see Internet site <http://www .census.gov/govs/www/statetax.html>.

Government employment and earnings. Refer to the notes and explanations for Table A-58 for information on employment and earnings data. Government employment covers only civilian workers.

Data on **federal tax collections** are provided by the Internal Revenue Service (IRS) through the Statistics of Income (SOI) program. This program pulls data electronically from the master file and augments the data with items captured from the hard copies of taxpayers' returns. The IRS processes about 200 million tax returns each year, and SOI uses about half a million of these for statistics.

State tax collections data are collected by the Census Bureau through an Annual Survey of State Government Tax Collection. These statistics are of all 50 state governments in the United States and are for state governments only. They should not be interpreted as state area data (state plus local government tax collections combined).

Table A-75. State Government Employment and Finances

Employment, 2003 and 2000;
  Per 10,000 population, 2003 and 2000;
Finances,
  Revenue, 2002 and 2000;
    General, 2002, total, intergovernmental from federal
    government, and taxes;
  Expenditures, 2002 and 2000;
    General, 2002,
      Total;
      Intergovernmental;
      Direct, education, public welfare, and highways.

Sources: Employment—U.S. Census Bureau, *State Government Employment and Payroll Data*, March 2004 (accessed 10 June 2005), see Internet site <http://www .census.gov/govs/www/apesst.html>; Finances—U.S. Census Bureau, "State Government Finances" (accessed 8 April 2005), see Internet site <http://www.census.gov /govs/www/state.html>.

The Census Bureau collects data on **state government employment** by conducting an Annual Survey of Government Employment. Alternatively, every 5 years, in years ending in a "2" or "7," a Census of Governments, including an employment portion, is conducted. For both the census and the annual surveys, the employment detail is equivalent.

Employment refers to all persons gainfully employed by and performing services for a government. Employees include all persons paid for personal services performed, including persons paid from federally funded programs, paid elected or appointed officials, persons in a paid leave status, and persons paid on a per-meeting, annual, semiannual, or quarterly basis. Unpaid officials, pensioners, persons whose work is performed on a fee basis, and contractors and their employees are excluded from the count of employees. **Full-time equivalent employment** refers to a computed statistic representing the number of full-time employees who could have been employed if the reported number of hours worked by part-time employees had been worked by full-time employees. This statistic is calculated separately for each function of a government by dividing the "part-time hours paid" by the standard number of hours for full-time employees in the particular government and then adding the resulting quotient to the number of full-time employees.

Finance data are collected by the Census Bureau through the Annual Survey of Government Finances, which covers all state and local governments in the United States. The survey content includes the entire range of government finance activities: revenue, expenditure, debt, and assets.

Revenue includes all amounts of money received by a government from external sources during its fiscal year net of refunds and other correcting transactions, other than issuance of debt, sale of investments, and agency or private trust transactions. Revenue excludes amounts transferred from other funds or agencies of the same government. Revenue comprises amounts received by all agencies, boards, commissions, or other organizations categorized as dependent on the government concerned. Stated in terms of the accounting procedures from which these data originate, revenue covers receipts from all accounting funds of a government, other than intragovernmental service (revolving), agency, and private trust funds.

General revenue comprises all revenue except that classified as liquor store, utility, or insurance trust revenue. Generally, the basis for this distinction is not the fund or administrative unit established to account for and control a particular activity, but rather the nature of the revenue source involved. Within general revenue are four main categories: taxes, intergovernmental revenue, current charges, and miscellaneous general revenue. Each is described in detail below.

Intergovernmental revenue comprises monies from other governments, including grants, shared taxes, and contingent loans and advances for support of particular functions or for general financial support; any significant and identifiable amounts received as reimbursement for performance of governmental services for other governments; and any other form of revenue representing the sharing by other governments in the financing of activities administered by the receiving government. All intergovernmental revenue is reported in the general government sector, even if it is used to support activities in other sectors (such as utilities). Intergovernmental revenue excludes amounts received from the sale of property, commodities, and utility services to other governments (which are reported in different revenue categories). It also excludes amounts received from other governments as the employer share or for support of public employee retirement or other insurance trust funds of the recipient government, which are treated as insurance trust revenue.

Taxes are compulsory contributions exacted by a government for public purposes, other than for employee and employer assessments and contributions to finance retirement and social insurance trust systems and for special assessments to pay capital improvements. Tax revenue comprises gross amounts collected (including interest and penalties) minus amounts paid under protest and amounts refunded during the same period. It consists of all taxes imposed by a government whether the government collects the taxes itself or relies on another government to act as its collection agent.

Expenditure includes all amounts of money paid out by a government during its fiscal year—net of recoveries and other correcting transactions—other than for retirement of debt, purchase of investment securities, extension of loans, and agency or private trust transactions. Under this definition, expenditure relates to external payments of a government and excludes amounts transferred to funds or agencies of the same government (other than payments to intragovernmental service funds).

Expenditure includes payments from all sources of funds, including not only current revenues but also proceeds from borrowing and prior year fund balances. Note, however, that the Census Bureau's finance statistics do not relate expenditure to their source of funding. Expenditure includes amounts spent by all agencies, boards, commissions, or other organizations categorized as dependent on the government concerned.

General expenditure comprises all expenditure except that classified as liquor store, utility, or insurance trust expenditure. As noted above, it includes all such payments regardless of the source of revenue from which they were financed. General government expenditures are classified by function and character and object.

For more information and detailed definitions, see the Governments Finance and Employment Classification Manual at <http://ftp2.census.gov/govs/class/classfull.pdf> (released December 2000).

Table A-76. State Resources, Expenditures, and Balances

Expenditures by fund source, 2004, 2003, and 2002,
   General fund, 2004;
   Federal fund, 2004;
State general fund,
   Resources, 2004, 2003, and 2002;
   Expenditures, 2004, 2003, and 2002;
   Balance, 2004, 2003, and 2002.

Source: National Association of State Budget Officers, Washington, DC, *2003 State Expenditure Report*, and *State General Fund from NASBO*, Fiscal Survey of the States, semiannual (copyright).

State general funds support most ongoing broad-based state services, as opposed to long-term state capital projects, and are available for appropriation to support any governmental activity. These funds exclude special funds earmarked for particular purposes, such as highway trust funds, which are supported by fuel taxes and motor license fees.

Resources include funds budgeted, adjustments, and balances from the previous year. Expenditures may or may not include budget stabilization fund transfers, depending on state accounting practices. Refer to the source for detail.

Table A-77. State Government Tax Collections: 2004, and Federal Aid to State and Local Governments

State government tax collections, 2004,
   Total;
   Per capita;
   Percent change, 2003–2004;
   Type of tax,
      Sales and gross receipts,
         Total;
         General sales and gross receipts;
         Selective sales taxes, total, alcoholic beverages, amusements, insurance premiums, motor fuels, parimutuels, public utilities, tobacco products, and other selective sales;
      Licenses, alcoholic beverages, amusements, corporation, hunting and fishing, motor vehicle, and occupation and business, NEC;
      Other taxes, individual income, corporation net income, and death and gift;
Federal aid to state and local governments, 2003, 2002, and 2000,
   Selected programs, 2003, Centers for Medicare and Medicaid Services, Highway trust fund, FEMA, and Title 1 programs.

Sources: Tax collections—U.S. Census Bureau, "State Government Tax Collections," see Internet site <http://www.census.gov/govs/www/statetax.html> (accessed 27 April 2005);   Federal aid—U.S. Census Bureau, *Federal Aid to States for Fiscal Year 2003, 2002, 2001, 2000*, see also <http://www.census.gov/prod/www/abs/fas.html>.

Data on **state government tax collections** are collected by the Census Bureau by conducting an Annual Survey of State Government Tax Collection. The data are on the fiscal year tax collections of all 50 state governments in the United States and are for state governments only. They should not be interpreted as state area data (state plus local government tax collections combined).

Taxes are compulsory contributions exacted by government for public purposes including interest, penalties, and local shares of state-imposed taxes. Excluded are amounts paid under protest and amounts refunded during the same period. It consists of all taxes imposed by a government whether the government collects the taxes itself or relies on another government to act as its collection agent.

Sales and gross receipts taxes are taxes on goods and services, measured on the basis of the volume or value of their transfer, upon gross receipts or gross income therefrom, or as an amount per unit sold; and related taxes based upon use, storage, production, importation, or consumption of goods and service.

General sales and gross receipts taxes are applicable with only specified exceptions to sales of all types of goods and services or to all gross receipts, whether at a single rate or at classified rates, and sales use taxes.

Individual income tax includes tax on individuals measured by net income and tax on special types of income (e.g. interest, dividends, income from intangible property, etc.).

Corporation net income tax includes taxes on corporations and unincorporated businesses, measured by net income, whether on corporations in general or on specific kinds of corporations, such as financial institutions.

Federal aid to state and local governments. All amounts of federal government grants and other payments to state and local governments represent actual cash outlays made during the fiscal year. Each federal government executive department and agency provides annual data on grants and other payments to governmental units. The data are collected from federal agencies by the Census Bureau.

Data on federal aid include the following: direct cash grants to state and local government units, payments for grants-in-kind, such as purchases of commodities distributed to state or local government institutions (e.g., school programs); payments to nongovernment entities when such payments result in cash or in-kind services passed on to state and local governments; payments to regional commissions and organizations that are redistributed to the state or local level; federal government payments to state or local governments for research and development that is an integral part of the provision of public services; and shared revenues.

Table A-78. Federal Government

Nonfarm employment (BLS), 2004, 2003, and 2000;
Federal earnings (BEA),
   Civilian, 2004, 2003, and 2001;
   Military, 2004, 2003, and 2001;
Federal funds and grants,
   Total, 2003 and 2000;
   Defense, 2003, percent, and per capita;
   Selected object categories, 2003, direct payments for individuals, grants to state and local government, and salaries and wages.

Sources: Employment—U.S. Bureau of Labor Statistics, Current Employment Statistics Program, see Internet site <http://www.bls.gov/sae/home.htm>; Earnings—U.S. Bureau of Economic Analysis, *Survey of Current Business*, April 2005, and see Internet site <http://www.bea.gov /bea/regional/spi/>; Federal funds and grants—U.S. Census Bureau, *Consolidated Federal Funds Report*, annual, see Internet site <http://www.census.gov/govs/www/cffr .html>.

Refer to the notes and explanations for Table A-58 for information on **employment** and **earnings**. See the source for further detail.

Total **federal funds and grants** includes federal government expenditures for grants to state and local governments, salaries and wages, procurement, direct payment for individuals, and other programs for which data are available by state. Data for these items come from a variety of sources within the federal government and represent actual expenditures of the federal government during the fiscal year.

The Defense Department data are computed from Defense Department grants to state and local governments, salaries and wages, retired military pay, procurement, and research grants. Per capita for defense is based on resident population estimated as of July 1.

Direct payment for individuals data are compiled from amounts reported by the Federal Agencies for the Federal Assistance Award Data System (FAADS). The FAADS is a quarterly report of financial assistance awards made by each federal agency. Coverage includes grants, direct payments to individuals and others, insurance, and loans.

All amounts of federal government grants to state and local governments represent actual cash outlays made during the fiscal year. This includes direct cash grants to state and local government units; payments for grants-in-kind, such as purchases of commodities distributed to state and

local government institutions; payments to nongovernment entities when such payments result in cash or in-kind services passed on to state or local governments; payments to regional commissions and organizations that are redistributed to the state or local level; federal government payments to state and local governments for research and development that is an integral part of the provision of public service; and federal revenues shared with state and local governments.

Table A-79. Federal Individual Income Tax Returns

Federal individual income tax returns,
   Number of return, 2002 and 2000;
   Adjusted gross income, 2002 and 2000;
   Adjusted gross income per return, 2002 and 2000;
   Income tax, 2002 and 2000;
Federal civilian employment, 2002, and percent change, 2000–2002;
Federally owned property, 2003, number of buildings and building area;
Federal lands, 2003, total and percent of total land.

Sources: Tax returns—U.S. Internal Revenue Service, *Statistics of Income Bulletin*, quarterly; Federal civilian employment—U.S. Office of Personnel Management, *Biennial Report of Employment by Geographic Area, 2002*; see Internet site <http://www.opm.gov/feddata/geograph /geograph.asp>; Property and land—U.S. General Services Administration, *Federal Real Property Profile*, annual, see Internet site <http://www.gsa.gov/> (released 11 March 2003).

Data for **federal individual income tax returns** are provided by the Internal Revenue Service through the Statistics of Income (SOI) Program. This program pulls data electronically from the master file and augments the data with items captured from the hard copies of taxpayers' returns. The IRS processes about 200 million tax returns each year, and SOI uses about half a million of these for statistics. See the source for more detailed information.

Federal civilian employment data are provided by the Office of Personnel Management (OPM). OPM has government-wide responsibility for the collection and maintenance of accurate information on the federal workforce. The Central Personnel Data File (CPDF) is an automated personnel information system containing information on most of the federal civilian workforce. Data exclude Central Intelligence Agency, Defense Intelligence Agency, seasonal and on-call employees, and National Security Agency. Refer to the source for more information.

Data on **federally owned property** and **federal lands** are collected through the General Services Administration's (GSA's) Federal Real Property Profile (FRPP) reporting system. Contributing agencies provide data annually based on their real property holdings as of September 30. Land acreage is divided into urban and rural categories. Leased land is usually not reported if it is included with a building lease. Buildings are roofed and walled structures built for permanent use. Buildings owned by the government, whether or not located on government-owned land, are included in the data. Buildings under construction are included only if they were available for use as of September 30 of the year shown.

Table A-80. Social Security, Food Stamps, and School Lunch Programs

Social security benefits,
   Beneficiaries, 2004 and 2000,
      Retired workers and dependents, 2004 and 2000;
   Payments, 2004 and 2000,
      Retired workers and dependents, 2004 and 2000;
Federal food stamp program,
   Participants, 2004 and 2000;
   Federal cost, 2004 and 2000;
National school lunch program,
   Participants, 2004 and 2000;
   Federal cost, 2004 and 2000.

Sources: Social security—U.S. Social Security Administration, *Annual Statistical Supplement to the Social Security Bulletin*, see Internet site <http://www.ssa.gov/policy /docs/statcomps/supplement/2004/index.html>; Federal food stamp and national school lunch programs—U.S. Department of Agriculture, Food and Nutrition Service, "Food and Nutrition Service, Program Data"; see Internet site <http://www.fns.usda.gov/pd/>.

Social security. The Old-Age, Survivors, and Disability Insurance Program (OASDI) provides monthly benefits for retired and disabled insured workers and their dependents and to survivors of insured workers. To be eligible for benefits, a worker must have had a specified period of employment in which OASDI taxes were paid. A worker becomes eligible for full retirement benefits at age 65, although reduced benefits may be obtained up to 3 years earlier; the worker's spouse is under the same limitations. Survivor benefits are payable to dependents of deceased insured workers. Disability benefits are payable to an insured worker under age 65 with a prolonged disability and to that person's dependents on the same basis as dependents of a retired worker. Also, disability benefits are payable at age 50 to the disabled widow or widower of a deceased worker who was fully insured at the time of death. A lump-sum benefit is generally payable on the death of an insured worker to a spouse or minor children.

The data were derived from the Master Beneficiary Record (MBR), the principal administrative file of social security beneficiaries. Data for total recipients and retired workers include persons with special age-72 benefits. Special age-72 benefit represents the monthly benefit payable to men who attained age 72 before 1972 and for women who attained age 72 before 1970 and who do not have

sufficient quarters to qualify for a retired-worker benefit under either the fully or the transitionally insured status provision.

The **Food Stamp Program** is designed to help low-income households buy a more nutritious diet. Under the program, single persons and those living in households meeting the nationwide standard for income and assets may receive coupons redeemable for food at most retail food stores. The monthly amount of coupons a unit receives is determined by household size and income. Households without income receive the determined monthly cost of a nutritionally adequate diet for their household size. This amount is updated to account for food price increases. Households with income receive the difference between the amount of a nutritionally adequate diet and 30 percent of their income, after certain allowable deductions. Federal costs include benefits only and exclude administrative expenditures.

The **National School Lunch Program** covers public and private elementary and secondary schools and residential child care institutions. Costs include federal cash reimbursements at rates set by law for each meal served and commodity costs.

Table A-81. Social Welfare Programs and Workers' Compensation

Public aid recipients as percent of population, 2003 and 2000;
Supplemental security income (SSI),
   Recipients, 2003 and 2000;
   Annual payments, 2003 and 2000;
Temporary Assistance for Needy Families (TANF),
   Recipients, 2003 and 2000;
   Annual payments, 2003 and 2000;
State unemployment insurance,
   Beneficiaries, first payments, 2004 and 2000;
   Benefits paid, 2004 and 2000;
Workers' compensation payments, 2002, 2000, and 1990.

Sources: Public aid recipients—Compiled by the U.S. Census Bureau. Data from U.S. Social Security Administration, *Annual Statistical Supplement to the Social Security Bulletin*, and U.S. Administration for Children and Families, *Unemployment Insurance Financial Data Handbook*; SSI—U.S. Social Security Administration, *Annual Statistical Supplement to the Social Security Bulletin*; TANF—U.S. Administration for Children and Families, *Temporary Assistance for Needy Families (TANF) Program, Annual Report to Congress*, and unpublished data; State unemployment insurance—U.S. Employment and Training Administration, *Unemployment Insurance Financial Data Handbook*, annual; Workers' compensation—National Academy of Social Insurance, Washington, DC, *Workers' Compensation: Benefits, Coverage, and Costs*, annual for data beginning in 2000. See Internet site <http://www.nasi.org/>. For 1990 data, U.S. Social Security Administration, *Social Security Bulletin*.

Public aid recipients is defined as total federal Supplemental Security Income (SSI) and Temporary Assistance for Needy Families (TANF) recipients as of June as a percentage of resident population estimated as of July 1 for 2003 and enumerated as of April 1 for 2000.

The **Supplemental Security Income** (SSI) program provides cash payments in accordance with nationwide eligibility requirements to persons with limited income and resources who are aged, blind, or disabled. Under the SSI program, each person living in his or her own household is provided a cash payment from the federal government that is sufficient, when added to the person's countable income (the total gross money income of an individual less certain exclusions), to bring the total monthly income up to a specified level (the federal benefit rate). If the individual or couple is living in another household, the guaranteed level is reduced by one-third.

An aged person is defined as an individual who is 65 years old or over. A blind person is anyone with vision of 20/200 or less with the use of correcting lens in the better eye or with tunnel vision of 20 degrees or less. The disabled classification refers to any person unable to engage in any substantial gainful activity by reason of any medically determinable physical or mental impairment expected to result in death or that has lasted or can be expected to last for a continuous period of at least 12 months. For a child under 18 years, eligibility is based on disability or severity comparable with that of an adult, since the criterion of "substantial gainful activity" is inapplicable for children.

The **Temporary Assistance for Needy Families** (TANF) program is a time-limited program that assists families with children when the parents or other responsible relatives cannot provide for the family's basic needs. The federal government provides grants to states to run the TANF program so that the states decide on the design of the program, the type and amount of assistance payments, the range of other services to be provided, and the rules for determining who is eligible for benefits. Prior to TANF, the cash assistance program to families was called Aid to Families with Dependent Children (1980–1996). Under the new welfare law (Personal Responsibility Reconciliation Act of 1996), the program became TANF.

Unemployment insurance is presently administered by the U.S. Employment and Training Administration and each state's employment security agency. The program provides unemployment benefits to eligible workers who are unemployed through no fault of their own (as determined under state law), and meet other eligibility requirements of state law. Unemployment insurance payments (benefits) are intended to provide temporary assistance to unemployed workers who meet the requirements of state law. Each state administers a separate unemployment insurance program within guidelines established by federal law. Eligibility for unemployment insurance, benefit amounts, and the

length of time benefits are available are determined by the state law under which unemployment insurance claims are established. In the majority of states, benefit funding is based solely on a tax imposed on employers.

Workers' compensation provides protection to workers disabled from work-related injury or illness. The program includes protection under the laws of 50 states, the District of Columbia, and two federal programs (the Federal Employees Compensation Act and the Longshoremen's and Harbor Workers' Compensation Act). Payments represent compensation and medical benefits and include insurance losses paid by private insurance carriers, disbursements of state funds, and self-insurance payments.

Table A-82. Government Transfer Payments to Individuals

Total government transfer payments, 2003, 2002, and 2000,
  Percent change, 2000–2003;
  Per capita, 2003;
Program area, 2003, retirement and disability insurance benefits, medical payments, income maintenance benefits, unemployment insurance benefits, veterans benefits, federal education and training assistance payments, and other.

Source: U.S. Bureau of Economic Analysis, "Regional Accounts Data, Annual State Personal Income"; see Internet site <http://www.bea.gov/bea/regional/spi/> (accessed 3 May 2005).

Government transfer payments to individuals consist of: retirement and disability insurance benefits, medical benefits, income maintenance benefits, unemployment insurance compensation, veterans benefits, federal education and training assistance, and other transfer receipts of individuals from governments.

Retirement and disability insurance benefits consist of Old-Age, Survivors, and Disability (OASDI) benefits; railroad retirement and disability benefits; federal and state workers' compensation; temporary disability benefits; black lung benefits; and Pension Benefit Guaranty benefits.

Medical payments include medical benefits, public assistance medical care, and military medical insurance benefits. Medicare benefits are federal government payments made through intermediaries to beneficiaries for the care provided to individuals under the Medicare program. Public assistance medical care benefits are received by low-income individuals. These payments consist mainly of the payments made through intermediaries to the vendors for care provided to individuals under the federally assisted, state-administered Medicaid program and State Children's Health Insurance Program (SCHIP) and under the general

State and Metropolitan Area Data Book: 2006

assistance medical programs of state and local governments. Military medical insurance benefits are vendor payments made under the TriCare Management Program, formerly called the Civilian Health and Medical Plan of the Uniformed Services program, for the medical care of dependents of active duty military personnel and of retired military personnel and their dependents at nonmilitary medical facilities.

Income maintenance benefits consist largely of supplemental security income payments, family assistance, food stamp payments, and other assistance payments, including general assistance.

Unemployment insurance benefits are made up of state unemployment compensation; unemployment compensation of federal civilian employees, railroad employees, and veterans; and trade adjustment allowances. State unemployment compensation are benefits consisting mainly of the payments received by individuals under state-administered unemployment insurance (UI) programs, but they include the special benefits authorized by federal legislation for periods of high unemployment. The provisions that govern the eligibility, timing, and amount of benefit payments vary among the states, but the provisions that govern the coverage and financing are uniform nationally. Unemployment compensation of federal civilian employees are benefits received by former federal employees under a federal program administered by the state employment security agencies. Unemployment compensation of railroad employees are benefits received by railroad workers who are unemployed because of sickness or because work is unavailable in the railroad industry and in related industries, such as carrier affiliates. This UI program is administered by the Railroad Retirement Board (RRB) under a federal program that is applicable throughout the nation. Unemployment compensation of veterans are benefits that are received by unemployed veterans who have recently separated from military service and who are not eligible for military retirement benefits. The compensation is paid under a federal program that is administered by the state employment security agencies. Trade adjustment allowances are the payments received by workers who are unemployed because of the adverse economic effects of international trade arrangements.

Veterans benefits include veterans pension and disability benefits, veterans readjustment benefits, veterans life insurance benefits, and other assistance to veterans (federal government payments received by paraplegics and by certain other disabled veterans to purchase automobiles and other conveyances, state and local government payments of assistance to indigent veterans, and the state and local government payments of bonuses to veterans).

Federal education and training assistance consists of federal fellowships, higher education student assistance, Job Corps payments, and interest payments on guaranteed student loans. Federal fellowships consist of the payments to outstanding science students who receive National Science Foundation (NSF) grants, the subsistence payments to the cadets at the six state maritime academies, and the payments for all other federal fellowships. Higher education student assistance consists of the federal payments, called Pell Grants, for an undergraduate education for students with low incomes. Job Corps payments are primarily the allowances for living expenses received by economically disadvantaged individuals who are between the ages of 16 and 21 and who are enrolled in the designated vocational and educational training programs. These benefits also include the adjustment allowances received by trainees upon the successful completion of their training. Interest payments on guaranteed student loans are made by the Department of Education to commercial lending institutions on behalf of the individuals who receive low-interest, deferred-payment loans from these institutions in order to pay the expenses of higher education.

Other transfer receipts of individuals from governments consist largely of Bureau of Indian Affairs payments, education exchange payments, Alaska Permanent Fund dividend payments, compensation of survivors of public safety officers, compensation of victims of crime, disaster relief payments, compensation for Japanese internment, and other special payments to individuals.

Table A-83. Medicare, Medicaid, and State Children's Health Insurance Program

Medicare enrollment, 2003, 2002, 2001, and 2000;
Medicaid,
    Enrollment, 2002 and 2000;
    Payments, 2002 and 2000;
State Children's Health Insurance Program (SCHIP),
    Enrollment, 2004 and 2000;
    Expenditures, 2004 and 2000.

Sources: Medicare enrollment—U.S. Centers for Medicare and Medicaid Services, "Medicare Beneficiaries Enrolled by State as of July 1, 1999–2003," published September 2004, see Internet site <http://www.cms.hhs.gov/MedicareEnrpts/>; Medicaid—U.S. Centers for Medicare and Medicaid Services, Medicaid Statistical Information System, MSIS, see Internet site <http://www.cms.hhs.gov/MedicaidDataSourcesGenInfo/02_MSISData.asp#TopOfPage>; SCHIP—U.S. Centers for Medicare and Medicaid Services, *The State Children's Health Insurance Program, Annual Enrollment Report* and the Statement of Expenditures for the SCHIP Program (CMS-21), see Internet site <http://www.cms.hhs.gov/NationalSCHIPPolicy/SCHIPER/list.asp#TopOfPage>.

Medicare. Since July 1966, the federal Medicare program has provided two coordinated plans for nearly all people age 65 and over: (1) a hospital insurance plan, which covers hospital and related services and (2) a voluntary supplementary medical insurance plan, financed partially by monthly premiums paid by participants, which partly covers physicians' and related medical services. Such insurance also applies, since July 1973, to disabled beneficiaries of any age after 24 months of entitlement to cash benefits under the social security or railroad retirement programs and to persons with end-state renal disease.

Medicaid is a health insurance program for certain low-income people. These include: certain low-income families with children; aged, blind, or disabled people on supplemental security income; certain low-income pregnant women and children; and people who have very high medical bills. Medicaid is funded and administered through a state-federal partnership. Although there are broad federal requirements for medicaid, states have a wide degree of flexibility to design their program. States have authority to establish eligibility standards, determine what benefits and services to cover, and set payment rates. All states, however, must cover these basic services: inpatient and outpatient hospital services; doctors' services, family planning, and periodic health checkups; and diagnosis and treatment for children.

The Balanced Budget Act of 1997 created the **State Children's Health Insurance Program** (SCHIP) and provided new funds for states to cover uninsured children. This program represents the largest single expansion of health insurance coverage for children in more than 30 years and aims to improve the quality of life for millions of vulnerable children under 19 years of age. Under title XXI of the Social Security Act, states were given the option to set up a separate child health program, expand medicaid coverage, or have a combination of both a separate child health program and a medicaid expansion.

As of September 1999, all states, territories, and the District of Columbia had approved SCHIP plans in place. States continue to shape their programs through SCHIP state plan amendments. As of September 4, 2003, 169 amendments to SCHIP plans and 10 Section 1115 demonstration projects had been approved to enroll even more children or families. Coverage is now available for children whose income is 200 percent of the Federal Poverty Level (FPL) or higher in 39 states and the District of Columbia. Prior to this legislation, only six states had income eligibility levels at or above 200 percent for infants only.

Table 84. Department of Defense and Veterans

Department of Defense,
  Personnel, 2004 and 2000;
    2004, active duty military, civilian, Reserve and
    National Guard, and selected major location;
  Expenditures, 2004 and 2000;
    2004, payroll, contracts, and grants;
  Number of veterans, 2004 and 2000.

Sources: Department of Defense—U.S. Department of Defense, *Atlas/Data Abstract for the United States and*

Selected Areas, annual, see Internet site <http://siadapp.dior.whs.mil/index.html>; Veterans—U.S. Department of Veterans Affairs, Office of Policy, Planning, and Preparedness; see Internet site <http://www.va.gov/vetdata/demographics/>.

The **Department of Defense** (DOD) is responsible for providing the military forces of the United States. It includes the Office of the Security of Defense, the Joint Chiefs of Staff, the Army, the Navy, the Air Force, and the defense agencies. The President serves as Commander in Chief of the armed forces; from him, the authority flows to the Secretary of Defense and through the Joint Chiefs of Staff to the commanders of unified and specified commands (e.g., U.S. Strategic Command).

DOD personnel data include active duty military, civilian, and Reserve and National Guard. Expenditures include payroll outlays, contracts, and grants. Payroll outlays consist of active duty military pay, civilian pay, Reserve and National Guard pay, and retired military pay. Contracts include supply and equipment contracts, RDT&E contracts, service contracts, construction contracts, and civil function contracts.

Veterans. The Office of Policy in the Department of Veterans Affairs (VA) is responsible for administering a range of programs and analyses concerning veteran surveys, demographics, and population estimates. Within the Office of Policy, the Office of the actuary (OACT) develops estimates and projections of the veteran population and their characteristics. Veterans serving in more than one period of service are counted only once in the total. The data include the Gulf War (no prior wartime service), Vietnam era (no prior wartime service), Korean conflict (no prior wartime service), World War II, and all peacetime periods.

Table A-85. Elections

Voting-age population, 2004 and 2000;
Percent of voting-age population casting votes for President, 2004 and 2000;
Electoral votes cast for President, 2004 and 2000;
Popular vote for President,
  2004,
    Total,
    Percent of total, Democratic and Republican;
  2000,
    Total,
    Percent of total, Democratic and Republican;
Votes cast for U.S. Senators,
  2004,
    Total,
    Percent of total, Democratic and Republican;
  2002,
    Total,
    Percent of total, Democratic and Republican.

Sources: Voting-age population—U.S. Census Bureau, "Annual Estimates of the Population by Selected Age

State and Metropolitan Area Data Book: 2006

Groups and Sex for the United States: April 1, 2000 to July 1, 2004" (NC-EST2004-02); also see <http://www.census .gov/popest/states/asrh/>; Percent of voting-age population voting for President—For 2004 data, U.S. Congress, Clerk of the House, *Statistics of the Presidential and Congressional Election*, biennial; for 2000 data, CQ Press, Washington, DC, *America Votes*, biennial (copyright; printed with permission of CQ Press); Electoral votes, votes for President, and votes for Senators—Through 2002, CQ Press, Washington, DC, *America Votes*, biennial (copyright; printed with permission of CQ Press). For electoral votes 2004, U.S. Federal Elections Commission, Federal Elections 2004, May 2005. For popular vote and votes for U.S. Senators 2004, Office of the Clerk, *Statistics of the Presidential and Congressional Election*, June 7, 2005.

The **voting-age population** relates to persons 18 years old and over in all states and the District of Columbia. Data include armed forces stationed in each state, aliens, and the institutionalized population.

Votes cast for President. The Constitution specifies how the President and Vice President are selected. Each state elects, by popular vote, a group of electors equal in number to its total of members of Congress. The 23rd Amendment, adopted in 1961, grants the District of Columbia three presidential electors, a number equal to that of the least populous state. A majority vote of all electors is necessary to elect the President and Vice President. If no candidate receives a majority, the House of Representatives, with each state having one vote, is empowered to elect the President and Vice President, again, with a majority of votes required.

Votes cast for U.S. Senators. The U.S. Senate is composed of 100 members, two from each state, who are elected to serve for a term of 6 years. One-third of the Senate is elected every 2 years. Senators were originally chosen by the state legislatures. The 17th Amendment to the Constitution, adopted in 1913, prescribed that Senators be elected by popular vote.

Table A-86. Composition of Congress

Votes cast for U.S. Representatives,
  2004,
    Total,
    Percent of total, Democratic and Republican;
  2002,
    Total,
    Percent of total, Democratic and Republican;
Composition of 109th Congress, 2005,
  Senate, Democratic and Republican;
  House of Representatives, Democratic and Republican;
Composition of 108th Congress, 2003,
  Senate, Democratic and Republican;
  House of Representatives, Democratic and Republican.

Sources: Votes—For 2002 data, CQ Press, Washington, DC, *America Votes*, biennial (copyright; printed with permission of CQ Press). For 2004 data, Office of the Clerk, *Statistics of the Presidential and Congressional Election*, June 7, 2005; Composition of Congress—Office of the Clerk, *Official List of Members by State*, annual. See also <http://clerk.house.gov/members/index.html>.

In each state, totals for votes cast for Representatives represent the sum of votes cast in each Congressional District or votes cast for Representatives at Large in states where only one member is elected. In all years, there are numerous districts within the state where either the Republican or Democratic party had no candidate. In some states, the Republican and Democratic vote includes votes cast for the party candidate by endorsing parties. Refer to the notes and explanations for A-85 for information on Senators.

Table A-87. Composition of Governors and State Legislatures

Votes cast for Governor,
  2004, candidate elected at most recent election, totals,
    and percent for leading party;
  2002, totals and percent for leading party;
Composition of state legislatures, 2005,
  Lower House, Democratic and Republican;
  Upper House, Democratic and Republican;
Black elected officials, 2001, total and U.S. and state legislatures;
Hispanic public officials, 2004, total and state executives and legislators;
Women holding state public offices, 2004, statewide elective executive office and state legislature;
Apportionment of membership in House of Representatives by state, 2000, 1990, and 1980.

Sources: Votes for Governor—CQ Press, Washington, DC, *America Votes*, biennial (copyright; printed with permission of CQ Press); Composition of state legislatures—The Council of State Governments, Lexington, KY, *State Elective Officials and the Legislatures*, annual (copyright); Black officials—Joint Center for Political and Economic Studies, Washington, DC, *Black Elected Officials: A Statistical Summary*, annual (copyright) and <http://www.jointcenter.org/publications1/BEO.php> (accessed 17 April 2003); Hispanic officials—National Association of Latino Elected and Appointed Officials (NALEO) Educational Fund, Los Angeles, CA, *National Directory of Latino Elected Officials*, formerly published as *National Roster of Hispanic Elected Officials*, annual; Women holding offices—Center for American Women and Politics, Eagleton Institute of Politics, Rutgers University, New Brunswick, NJ, information releases (copyright); Apportionment—U.S. Census Bureau, *Congressional Apportionment, Census 2000 Brief*, C2KBR/01-7, issued July 2001; see also <http://www.census.gov/population/www /censusdata/apportionment.html>.

Data for **votes cast for Governor** represent total votes cast, including scattered votes. The percentage of votes cast for the leading party represents the percentage of the total votes cast for the party with a majority or plurality.

Data shown for **composition of state legislatures** reflect election results in year shown for most states and to odd-year elections the previous years in a few states. The figures reflect the immediate results of elections, including holdover members in state houses that do not have all of their members running for reelection. Lower House refers to the body consisting of State Representatives. Upper House refers to the body consisting of U.S. Senators.

Black elected officials. As of January 2001, no Black elected officials had been identified in Hawaii, Montana, North Dakota, or South Dakota. The total includes U.S. and state legislatures and elected state administrators, city and county offices, law enforcement, and education officials not shown separately.

Hispanic public officials data include U.S. Representatives, state executives and legislators, county and municipal officials, judicial and law enforcement officials, and education and school boards. In 2004, no Hispanic public officials had been identified in Alabama, Alaska, Arkansas, the District of Columbia, Iowa, Kentucky, Maine, Mississippi, South Dakota, Vermont, or West Virginia.

Data for **women holding state public offices** cover women in statewide elective executive offices and state legislatures, county commissions, mayoralties, townships, and local councils.

Apportionment. Total membership in the House of Representatives includes Representatives assigned to newly admitted states after the apportionment acts. Population figures used for apportionment purposes are those determined for states by each decennial census.

TABLE B — METRO AREAS

Table B consists of 11 tables (B-1 through B-11) with 139 data items for 361 metropolitan statistical areas (MSAs), 11 metropolitan statistical areas with metropolitan divisions, and 29 metropolitan divisions. They are presented alphabetically in each of the 11 tables.

All summaries, including historical data, are presented for the areas as currently defined. Where possible, the original figures have been retabulated to reflect the status of metropolitan area boundaries as of 1 November 2004. For more information on these areas, see Appendix C, Geographic Concepts and Codes.

Table B-1. Area and Population

Total area, 2000;
Population, total, 1990, 2000, 2004, 2005; rank, 1990, 2000, and 2005;
Persons per square mile of land area, 1990, 2000, and 2005.

Sources: Area—U.S. Census Bureau, 2000 Census of Population and Housing, *Summary Population and Housing Characteristics*, Series PHC-1; and unpublished data on American FactFinder; Population—U.S. Census Bureau, 1990 "Population Estimates: Annual Time Series," archive 1990 (revised data for April 1, 1990, Population Estimates base), <http://www.census.gov/popest/archives/1990s/CO-99-02.html>; 2000 to 2005 compiled from "Population Estimates by County," published 16 March 2006; <http://www.census.gov/popest/counties/CO-EST2005-01.html>.

Total area. Area measurement data provide the size, in square units, of geographic entities for which the U.S. Census Bureau tabulates and disseminates data. Area is calculated from the specific boundary recorded for each entity (in this case, states and counties) in the Census Bureau's geographic database.

Area measurements may disagree with the information displayed on the Census Bureau maps and in the TIGER® database because, for area measurement purposes, features identified as "intermittent water" and "glacier" are reported as land area. TIGER® is an acronym for the new digital (computer-readable) geographic database that automates the mapping and related geographic activities required to support the Census Bureau's census and survey programs; TIGER® stands for Topologically Integrated Geographic Encoding and Referencing system. The accuracy of any area measurement data is limited by the accuracy inherent in (1) the location and shape of the various boundary information in the database, (2) the location and shapes of the shorelines of water bodies in that database, and (3) rounding affecting the last digit in all operations that compute and/or sum the area measurements. Identification of land and inland, coastal, and territorial is for statistical purposes and does not necessarily reflect legal definitions thereof.

Population estimates is the estimated population from the calculated number of people living in an area as of July 1. The estimated population is calculated from a component of change model that incorporates information on natural changes (births, deaths) and net migration (net internal migration, net international migration) that has occurred in an area since a Census 2000 reference date.

The Census Bureau develops county population estimates with a demographic procedure called an "administrative records component of change" method. A major assumption underlying this approach is that the components of population change are closely approximated by administrative data in a demographic change model. In order to apply the model, Census Bureau demographers estimate each component of population change separately. In cases where we do not have data for all counties for the current estimate year, we estimate the components of population changes based on one or more simplifying assumptions.

When we prepare our initial population estimates, we use the same variant of the component model with these simplifying assumptions. In the creation of current vintage population estimates, we replace the initial population estimates from the previous vintage with "revised" population estimates calculated with the actual data for all components of population change. Calculations of "revised" population estimates also incorporate updates to components of change from previous years. For more information on the method used for these estimates, see Appendix B, Limitations of the Methodology, and the Web site at <http://www.census.gov/popest/topics/methodology/>.

Rank numbers are assigned on the basis of population size, with each county area placed in descending order, largest to smallest. Where ties—two or more areas with identical populations—occur, the same rank is assigned to each of the tied county areas. In such cases, the following rank number(s) is omitted so that the lowest rank is usually equal to the number of county areas ranked.

Persons per square mile of land area, also known as population density, is the average number of inhabitants per square mile of land area. These figures are derived by dividing the total number of residents by the number of square miles of land area in the specified geographic area.

Table B-2. Components of Population Change

Components of population change—total, natural increase, natural increase of births, natural increase of deaths, net international migration, percent change, April 1, 2000, to July 1, 2005;
Population change—April 1, 1990, to April 1, 2000;
Percent change—April 1, 1990, to April 1, 2000.

Sources: Population—U.S. Census Bureau, Components of Population Change, "Population Estimates, Cumulative Estimates of the Components of Population Change for Counties: April 1, 2000 to July 1, 2005," <http://www.census.gov/popest/counties/CO-EST2005-05.html>; Population change—Census 2000, Demographic Profiles 1; 1990 census, 100 percent data, STF1 <http://www.census.gov/main/www/cen2000.html>; Net international migration—U.S. Census Bureau, <http://www.census.gov/popest/states/NST-comp-chg.html>; Births—U.S. National Center for Health Statistics, *Vital Statistics of the United States*, Vol. 1, Natality, annual, and unpublished data; Deaths—U.S. National Center for Health Statistics, *Vital Statistics of the United States*, Vol. 11, Mortality, annual, and unpublished data.

The U.S. Census Bureau annually produces estimates of total resident population for each state and county. County population estimates are produced with a component of population change method, while the state population estimates are solely the sum of the county populations. The following documentation describes the work that was carried out to produce the July 1, 2004, total resident population estimates at the county level.

The Census Bureau develops county population estimates with a demographic procedure called an "administrative records component of population change" method. A major assumption underlying this approach is that the components of population change are closely approximated by administrative data in a demographic change model. In order to apply the model, Census Bureau demographers estimate each component of population change separately. For the population residing in households, the components of population change are births, deaths, and net migration, including net international migration. For the nonhousehold population, change is represented by the net change in the population living in group quarters facilities.

Each component in our model is represented with data that are symptomatic of some aspect of population change. For example, birth certificates are symptomatic of additions to the population resulting from births, so we used these data to estimate the birth component for a county. Some other components are derived from death certificates, Internal Revenue Service (IRS) data, Medicare enrollment records, Armed Forces data, group quarters population data, and data from the American Community Survey (ACS).

The Census Bureau produces the estimates of the county populations by starting with the base populations from either Census 2000 or the revised population estimate for the most recent year and then adding or subtracting the demographic components of population change calculated for the time period. Basically, the operation is to add the estimated number of births and subtract the estimated number of deaths for the time period. The Census Bureau accounts for net migration, which is calculated using several components including net internal migration, net foreign-born international migration, net movement to/from Puerto Rico, net Armed Forces movement to/from overseas, the change in the group quarters population, and native emigration from the United States. The definitions of these concepts follow.

Natural increase—births minus deaths. The rate of natural increase expresses natural increase during a time period as a percentage of an area's population at the midpoint of the time period.

Net international migration—international migration, in its simplest form, is defined as any movement across U.S. (50 states and District of Columbia) borders. The Census Bureau makes estimates of net international migration for the nation, states, and counties. We estimate net international migration as: (1) net migration of the foreign born, (2) net movement from Puerto Rico, (3) net movement of the U.S. Armed Forces, and (4) emigration of the native born. The largest component, net migration of the foreign born, includes lawful permanent residents (immigrants), temporary migrants (such as students), humanitarian migrants (such as refugees), and people illegally present in the United States. Currently, we do not estimate these components individually.

Percent population change is the difference between the population of an area at the beginning and end of a time period, expressed as a percentage of the beginning population.

Table B-3. Population by Age, Race, and Sex

Population characteristics, 2003,
  Age (percent),
    Under 5 years;
    5 to 14 years;
    15 to 24 years;
    25 to 34 years;
    35 to 44 years;
    45 to 54 years;
    55 to 64 years;
    65 to 74 years;
    75 years and over;
  One race (percent),
    White alone;
    Black or African American alone;
    American Indian and Alaska Native alone;
    Asian alone;
    Native Hawaiian and Other Pacific Islander alone;
  Percent Hispanic or Latino origin;
  Males per 100 females.

Source: U.S. Census Bureau, Population Estimates, County Population datasets, <http://www.census.gov/popest/datasets.html>.

Age, sex, and race estimates are based on the distributed cohort component method. For an overview, see <http://www.census.gov/popest/topics/methodology/2004_co_char_meth.html>.

Age. The age classification is based on the age of the person in complete years as of July 1, 2004. The age of the person usually was derived from their date of birth information. **Median age** represents the age that divides the age distribution into two equal parts, one-half of the cases falling below the median age and one-half above the median. This measure is rounded to the nearest tenth.

Race. The concept of race, as used by the Census Bureau, reflects self-identification by people according to the race or races with which they most closely identify. These categories are sociopolitical constructs and should not be interpreted as being scientific or anthropological in nature. Furthermore, the race categories include both racial and national-origin groups. Caution must be used when interpreting changes in the racial composition of the U.S. population over time. The racial classifications used by the Census Bureau adhere to the December 15, 2000 (revised from October 30, 1997), Federal Register Notice entitled

"Revisions to the Standards for the Classification of Federal Data on Race and Ethnicity" issued by the Office of Management and Budget (OMB), <http://www.whitehouse.gov/omb/inforeg/r_and_e_guidance2000update.pdf>. These standards govern the categories used to collect and present federal data on race and ethnicity. The OMB required federal agencies to use a minimum of five race categories: White, Black or African American, American Indian and Alaska Native, Asian, and Native Hawaiian and Other Pacific Islander. For respondents unable to identify with any of these five race categories, the OMB approved including a sixth category, "Some other race."

The Census 2000 question on race included three areas where respondents could write in a more specific race group. The response categories and write-in answers can be combined to create the five minimum OMB race categories plus "Some other race." People who responded to the question on race by indicating only one race are referred to as the race alone population, or the group that reported only one race category.

White. A person having origins in any of the original peoples of Europe, the Middle East, or North Africa. It includes people who indicated their race as "White" or reported entries such as Irish, German, Italian, Lebanese, Near Easterner, Arab, or Polish.

Black or African American. A person having origins in any of the Black racial groups of Africa. It includes people who indicated their race as "Black, African Am., or Negro," or who provided written entries such as African American, Afro American, Kenyan, Nigerian, or Haitian.

American Indian and Alaska Native. A person having origins in any of the original peoples of North and South America (including Central America) and who maintains tribal affiliation or community attachment. It includes people who classify themselves as described below.

American Indian. Includes people who indicated their race as "American Indian," entered the name of an Indian tribe, or reported such entries as Canadian Indian, French-American Indian, or Spanish-American Indian.

Alaska Native. Includes written responses of Eskimos, Aleuts, and Alaska Indians as well as entries such as Arctic Slope, Inupait, Yupik, Alutiiq, Egeik, and Pribilovian. The Alaska tribes are the Alaskan Athabascan, Tlingit, and Haida.

Asian. A person having origins in any of the original peoples of the Far East, Southeast Asia, or the Indian subcontinent including, for example, Cambodia, China, India, Japan, Korea, Malaysia, Pakistan, the Philippine Islands, Thailand, and Vietnam. It includes "Asian Indian," "Chinese," "Filipino," "Korean," "Japanese," "Vietnamese," and "Other Asian."

Asian Indian includes people who indicated their race as "Asian Indian" or identified themselves as Bengalese, Bharat, Dravidian, East Indian, or Goanese. *Chinese*

includes people who indicated their race as "Chinese" or who identified themselves as Cantonese or Chinese American. In some census tabulations, written entries of Taiwanese are included with Chinese while in others they are shown separately. *Filipino* includes people who indicated their race as "Filipino" or who reported entries such as Philipano, Philipine, or Filipino American. *Japanese* includes people who indicated their race as "Japanese" or who reported entries such as Nipponese or Japanese American. *Korean* includes people who indicated their race as "Korean" or who provided a response of Korean American. *Vietnamese* includes people who indicated their race as "Vietnamese" or who provided a response of Vietnamese American.

Native Hawaiian and Other Pacific Islander. A person having origins in any of the original peoples of Hawaii, Guam, Samoa, or other Pacific Islands. It includes people who indicated their race as "Native Hawaiian," "Guamanian or Chamorro," "Samoan," and "Other Pacific Islander."

Native Hawaiian includes people who indicated their race as "Native Hawaiian" or who identified themselves as "Part Hawaiian" or "Hawaiian." *Guamanian or Chamorro* includes people who indicated their race as such, including written entries of Chamorro or Guam. *Samoan* includes people who indicated their race as "Samoan" or who identified themselves as "American Samoan" or "Western Samoan." *Other Pacific Islander* includes people who provided a write-in response of a Pacific Islander group such as "Tahitian," "Northern Mariana Islander," "Palauan," "Fijian," or a cultural group, such as "Melanesian," "Micronesian," or "Polynesian."

Hispanic or Latino origin. People who identify with the terms "Hispanic" or "Latino" are those who classified themselves in one of the specific Hispanic or Latino categories listed on the questionnaire—"Mexican," "Puerto Rican," or "Cuban"—as well as those who indicated that they are "other Spanish, Hispanic, or Latino." Origin can be viewed as the heritage, nationality group, lineage, or country of birth of the person or the person's parents or ancestors before their arrival in the United States. People who identify their origin as Spanish, Hispanic, or Latino may be any race.

Table B-4. Population Characteristics 2000 Census

Households—total, and percent of family households with children under 18 years;
Persons 25 years and over, percent high school graduate or higher, and percent bachelor's degree or higher;
Foreign-born population, percent of total population;
Persons 5 years and over, percent speaking language other than English at home, percent living in same house in 1995 and 2000;
Persons 16 years and over, percent of workers who drove alone to work;
Percent of households with income of $75,000 or more;
Percent of persons below poverty, percent.

Sources: Households—U.S. Census Bureau, 2000 Census of Population and Housing, "Census 2000 Profiles of General Demographic Characteristics" data files (DP1) (accessed 14 June 2002) and related Internet site at <http://censtats.census.gov/pub/Profiles.shtml>. See also 2000 Census of Population and Housing, *Summary File 1* (SF1) and related Internet site <http://www.census.gov /Press-Release/www/2001/sumfile1.html> and 2000 Census of Population and Housing, *Summary Population and Housing Characteristics*, PHC-1-1 to 52, and related Internet site at <http://www.census.gov/prod/cen2000 /index.html>; Educational attainment, foreign born, language, residence, commuting, income, and poverty—U.S. Census Bureau, 2000 Census of Population and Housing, *Summary File 3* (SF3) (accessed 12 January 2004) and related Internet site at <http://www.census.gov/Press -Release/www/2002/sumfile3.html> and 2000 Census of Population and Housing, *Summary Social, Economic, and Housing Characteristics*, PHC-2-1 to 52, and related Internet site at <http://www.census.gov/prod/cen2000 /index.html>.

Population characteristics in this table are for the 2000 Census of Population and Housing. For information, see General Notes for Population and Decennial censuses, on page A-1.

Household. A household includes all of the people who occupy a housing unit. People not living in households are classified as living in group quarters. Persons per household (or average household size) is a measure obtained by dividing the number of people in households by the total number of households (or householders).

Family household. A family includes a householder and one or more people living in the same household who are related to the householder by birth, marriage, or adoption. All people in a household who are related to the householder are regarded as members of his or her family. A family household may contain people not related to the householder, but those people are not included as part of the householder's family in census tabulations. Thus, the number of family households is equal to the number of families, but family households may include more members than do families. A household can contain only one family for purposes of census tabulations. Not all households contain families since a household may comprise a group of unrelated people or one person living alone.

Educational Attainment

Data on **educational attainment** in 2000 were derived from answers to the questionnaire, which was asked of a sample of persons. Data are tabulated as attainment for persons 25 years old and over. Persons are classified according to the highest level of school completed or the highest degree received. Respondents were asked to report the level of the previous grade attended or the highest degree received for the persons currently enrolled in school. The question included response categories that allowed persons to report completing the 12th grade without receiving a high school diploma and that instructed respondents to report as "high school graduate(s)"— persons who received either a high school diploma or the equivalent; for example, passed the Test of General Educational Development (G.E.D.) and did not attend college. The category "High school graduate or higher" covers persons whose highest degree was a high school diploma or its equivalent, persons who attended college or professional school, and persons who received a college, university, or professional degree. Persons who reported completing the 12th grade but not receiving a diploma are not included.

Foreign-Born Population

The Census Bureau separates the U.S. resident population into two groups based on whether or not a person was a U.S. citizen at the time of birth. Anyone born in the United States or U.S. Island Area (such as Puerto Rico), or born abroad to a U.S. citizen parent, is a U.S. citizen at the time of birth and consequently included in the *native population*. The term *foreign-born population* refers to anyone who is not a U.S. citizen at birth. This includes naturalized U.S. citizens, legal permanent resident aliens (immigrants), temporary migrants (such as students), humanitarian migrants (such as refugees), and people illegally present in the United States.

Household Income and Poverty

Data for household income and persons below poverty level are based on sample data from the 2000 census.

Household income is total money income received in a calendar year by all household members 15 years old and over. Total money income is the sum of amounts reported separately for income from wages or salaries; nonfarm self-employment; farm self-employment; social security; public assistance; and all other regularly received income such as veterans payments, pensions, unemployment compensation, and alimony. Receipts not counted as income include various "lump sum" payments such as capital gains or inheritances. The total represents the amount of income received before deductions for personal income taxes, social security, bond purchases, union dues, Medicare deductions, etc. Household income differs from family income by including income received by all household members, not just those related to the householder, and by persons living alone or in other nonfamily households. Income is derived on a sample basis.

Poverty is defined in relation to family income. Families and unrelated individuals are classified as above or below the poverty level by comparing their total income to an income cutoff or "poverty threshold." The income cutoffs vary by family size, number of children, and age of the family householder or unrelated individual. Poverty status is determined for all families (and, by implication, all family members). Poverty status is also determined for persons not in families, except for inmates of institutions, members of the Armed Forces living in barracks, college students living in dormitories, and unrelated individuals under 15 years old. Poverty status is derived on a sample basis.

Table B-5. Births, Deaths, Infant Deaths

Births, 2002, 2000,
    Number and rate per 1,000;
Deaths, 2002, 2000,
    Number and rate per 1,000;
Infant deaths, 2002, 2000, 1990,
    Number and rate per 1,000.

Sources: Births—U.S. National Center for Health Statistics, *Vital Statistics of the United States*, Vol. 1, Natality, annual, and unpublished data.   Deaths and infant deaths—U.S. National Center for Health Statistics, *Vital Statistics of the United States*, Volume II, Mortality, and unpublished data.

Births and deaths. Through the National Vital Statistics System, the NCHS collects and publishes data on births and deaths in the United States. The Division of Vital Statistics obtains information on births and deaths from the registration offices of all states, New York City, and the District of Columbia. In most areas, practically all births and deaths are registered. The most recent test of the completeness of birth registration, conducted on a sample of births from 1964 to 1968, showed that 99.3 percent of all births in the United States during that period were registered. No comparable information is available for deaths, but it is generally believed that death registration in the United States is at least as complete as birth registration.

Birth and **death** statistics are limited to events occurring during the year. The data are by place of residence and exclude events occurring to nonresidents of the United States. Births or deaths that occur outside the United States are excluded. **Birth** and **death rates** represent the number of births and deaths per 1,000 resident population estimated as of July 1 for 2000 and 2002. **Infant death rates** represent the number of deaths of infants under 1 year of age per 1,000 live births. They exclude fetal deaths.

Table B-6. Physicians, Community Hospitals, Medicare, Social Security, and SSI

Physicians, 2003,
    Number and rate per 100,000 persons;
Community hospitals, 2003,
    Number;
    Beds,
    Number, rate per 100,000 persons, and change

2000–2003;
Medicare program enrollment, 2003,
  Total, percent change 2000–2003, and rate per 100,000
    persons;
Social security program, 2004,
  Beneficiaries, number, rate per 100,000 persons, change
    2000–2003, and number of retired workers;
Supplementary security income program, 2004,
  Number and rate per 100,000 persons.

Sources: Physicians—American Medical Association, Chicago, IL, *Physician Characteristics and Distribution in the U.S.*, annual (copyright) (accessed 13 May 2005); Hospitals—Health Forum LLC, an American Hospital Association (AHA) Company, Chicago, IL, *Hospital Statistics*, and unpublished data (copyright) (e-mail accessed 26 May 2005); Medicare program enrollment—Centers for Medicare and Medicaid Services, CMS Statistics: Medicare Enrollment (accessed 17 June 2005); Social security—U.S. Social Security Administration, Office of Research and Statistics, *OASDI Beneficiaries by State and County* (accessed 9 June 2005); Supplemental security income—U.S. Social Security Administration, Office of Research, Evaluation, and Statistics, *SSI Recipients by State and County* (accessed 6 June 2005).

Physicians

The number of physicians covers active, nonfederal physicians as of December 31 of the year shown. The figures are based on information contained in the AMA Physician master file. The file has been maintained by the AMA since 1906 and includes information on every physician in the country and on those graduates of American medical schools who are temporarily practicing overseas. The file also includes members and nonmembers of the AMA and graduates of foreign medical schools who are in the United States and meet U.S. education standards for primary recognition as physicians. Thus, all physicians comprising the total manpower pool are included on the file. However, this publication excludes data for all federal physicians and nonfederal physicians who are temporarily in foreign locations.

Master file data are obtained from both AMA surveys and inputs from physicians, other organizations, and institutions. Primary sources are as follows: medical schools, hospitals, medical societies, national boards, state licensing agencies, the Educational Commission for Foreign Medical Graduates, the Surgeon General of the U.S. Government, the American Board of Medical Specialties, and physicians.

Physician rate is per 100,000 resident population estimated as of July 1, 2003.

Community Hospitals

Community hospitals are defined as nonfederal, short-term (average length of stay less than 30 days), general, or other special hospitals whose facilities and services are available to the public; psychiatric and tuberculosis hospitals and hospital units of institutions are excluded. Data for beds are based on the average number of beds in the facilities over the reporting period. Rate is per 100,000 resident population estimated as of July 1, 2003.

Medicare Enrollment

When first implemented in 1966, Medicare covered only most persons age 65 and over. By the end of 1966, 3.7 million persons had received at least some health care services covered by Medicare. In 1973, other groups became eligible for Medicare benefits: persons who are entitled to social security or Railroad Retirement disability benefits for at least 24 months; persons with end stage renal disease (ESRD) requiring continuing dialysis or kidney transplant; and certain otherwise noncovered aged persons who elect to buy into Medicare.

Medicare consists of two primary parts: Hospital Insurance (HI), also known as Part A, and Supplementary Medical Insurance (SMI), also known as Part B. Health care services covered under Medicare's Hospital Insurance include inpatient hospital care, skilled nursing facility care, home health agency care, and hospice care. SMI coverage is optional and requires payment of a monthly premium.

Social Security

The Old-Age, Survivors, and Disability Insurance Program (OASDI) provides monthly benefits for retired and disabled insured workers and their dependents and to survivors of insured workers. To be eligible for benefits, a worker must have had a specified period of employment in which OASDI taxes were paid. A worker becomes eligible for full retirement benefits at age 65, although reduced benefits may be obtained up to 3 years earlier; the worker's spouse is under the same limitations. Survivor benefits are payable to dependents of deceased insured workers. Disability benefits are payable to an insured worker under age 65 with a prolonged disability and to that person's dependents on the same basis as dependents of a retired worker. Also, disability benefits are payable at age 50 to the disabled widow or widower of a deceased worker who was fully insured at the time of death. A lump-sum benefit is generally payable on the death of an insured worker to a spouse or minor children.

The data were derived from the Master Beneficiary Record (MBR), the principal administrative file of social security beneficiaries. Data for total recipients and retired workers include persons with special age-72 benefits. Special age-72 benefit represents the monthly benefit payable to men who attained age 72 before 1972 and for women who attained age 72 before 1970 and who do not have sufficient quarters to qualify for a retired-worker benefit under either the fully or the transitionally insured status provision.

Supplemental Security Income

The Supplemental Security Income (SSI) program provides cash payments in accordance with nationwide eligibility requirements to persons with limited income and resources who are aged, blind, or disabled. Under the SSI program, each person living in his or her own household is provided a cash payment from the federal government that is sufficient, when added to the person's countable income (the total gross money income of an individual less certain exclusions), to bring the total monthly income up to a specified level (the federal benefit rate). If the individual or couple is living in another household, the guaranteed level is reduced by one-third.

An aged person is defined as an individual who is 65 years old or over. A blind person is anyone with vision of 20/200 or less with the use of correcting lens in the better eye or with tunnel vision of 20 degrees or less. The disabled classification refers to any person unable to engage in any substantial gainful activity by reason of any medically determinable physical or mental impairment expected to result in death or that has lasted or can be expected to last for a continuous period of at least 12 months. For a child under 18 years, eligibility is based on disability or severity comparable with that of an adult, since the criterion of "substantial gainful activity" is inapplicable for children.

Table B-7. Housing Units and Building Permits

Housing units,
  2004 (July 1), 2000 (estimates base), 1990 (April 1);
  Change 2000–2004, Units per square mile, 2004,
   1990;
Housing 2000,
  Home ownership rate and Units in multiunit structures;
New private housing units authorized by building permits
 2000–2003, 2003, and 2002.

Sources: Housing units 2000 and 2004—U.S. Census Bureau, Population Estimates by Housing Units, *Annual Estimates of Housing Units for Counties: April 1, 2000 to July 1, 2004*, <http://www.census.gov/popest/housing/> (accessed 14 November 2005); Housing units 1990—U.S. Census Bureau, 1990 Census of Population and Housing, *Summary Tape File (STF) 1C* on CD-ROM (archive); Housing 2000—U.S. Census Bureau, 2000 Census of Population and Housing, *Census 2000 Profiles of General Demographic Characteristics* data files, <http://factfinder.census.gov/servlet/SAFFHousing?sse=on> (accessed 7 August 2002); Building permits—U.S. Census Bureau, "New Residential Construction—Building Permits," e-mail from Manufacturing, Mining, and Construction Statistics Branch, subject: building permits by place 2000 (accessed 12 April 2005).

Housing unit estimates are developed by using building permits, mobile home shipments, and estimates of housing unit loss to measure housing unit change since the last census. For more information, see <http://www.census.gov/popest/topics/methodology/2004_hu_meth.html>.

A **housing unit** is a house, apartment, mobile home or trailer, group of rooms, or single room occupied or, if vacant, intended for occupancy as separate living quarters. Separate living quarters are those in which the occupants do not live and eat with any other persons in the structure and that have direct access from the outside of the building through a common hall. A housing unit is classified as occupied if it is the usual place of residence of the person or group of people living in it at the time of census enumeration or if the occupants are only temporarily absent; that is, away on vacation or business. All occupied housing units are classified as either owner-occupied or renter-occupied. A housing unit is owner-occupied if the owner or co-owner lives in the unit even if it is mortgaged or not fully paid for. All occupied housing units that are not owner-occupied, whether they are rented for cash rent or occupied without payment of cash rent, are classified as renter-occupied.

Housing 2000

Homeownership rates are computed by dividing the number of households that are owned by the total number of households. **Multiunit structures** are structures containing 2 or more housing units. For information on home ownership rates and units in multiunit structures, see Census 2000 summary files.

Building permits data are based on reports submitted by local building permit officials in response to a Census Bureau mail survey. They are obtained using Form C-404, "Report of New Privately Owned Residential Building or Zoning Permits Issued." Data are collected from individual permit offices, most of which are municipalities; the remainder are counties, townships, or New England- and Middle Atlantic-type towns. Currently, there are 19,000 permit-issuing places. When a report is not received, missing data are either (1) obtained from the Survey of Use of Permits, which is used to collect information on housing starts, or (2) imputed.

The data relate to new private housing units intended for occupancy on a housekeeping basis. They exclude mobile homes (trailers), hotels, motels, and group residential structures, such as nursing homes and college dormitories. They also exclude conversions of and alterations to existing buildings. A **housing unit** consists of a room or group of rooms intended for occupancy as separate living quarters by a family, by a group of unrelated persons living together, or by a person living alone.

Table B-8. Personal Income and Earnings by Industry

Personal income,
  Total, 2000–2002;
  Personal income per capita, 2002, 2000;

Percent change, 2001–2002 and 2000–2002;
Earnings,
    Total, 2002;
    Percent by selected industries.

Source: Personal income and earnings—U.S. Bureau of Economic Analysis, *Regional Economic Information System (REIS) 1969–2002* on CD-ROM, and related Internet site at <http://www.bea.gov/bea/regional/reis/>.

The **personal income** of an area is defined as the income received by, or on behalf of, all the residents of that area. It consists of the income received by persons from all sources; that is, from participation in production, from both government and business transfer payments, and from government interest. Personal income is the sum of wage and salary disbursements, other labor income, proprietors' income, rental income of persons, personal dividend income, personal interest income, and transfer payments, less personal contributions for social insurance.

Personal income differs by definition from money income, which is prepared by the Census Bureau, in that money income is measured before deduction of personal contributions for social insurance and does not include imputed income, lump sum payments, and income received by quasi-individuals. Money income does include income from private pensions and annuities and from interpersonal transfer, such as child support; therefore, it is not comparable to personal income. Total personal income is adjusted to place of residence.

About 90 percent of the state and county estimates of personal income are based on census data and on administrative records data that are collected by other federal agencies. The data from censuses are mainly collected from the recipient of the income. The most important sources of census data for the state and county estimates are the census of agriculture and the census of population and housing that are conducted by the Census Bureau. The data from administrative records may originate either from the recipients of the income or from the source of the income. These data are a byproduct of the administration of various federal and state government programs. The most important sources of these data are as follows: the state unemployment insurance programs of the Employment and Training Administration, Department of Labor; the social insurance programs of the Social Security Administration and the Health Care Financing Administration, Department of Health and Human Services; the federal income tax program of the Internal Revenue Service, Department of the Treasury; the veterans benefit programs of the Department of Veterans Affairs; and the military payroll systems of the Department of Defense. The remaining 10 percent of the estimates are based on data from other sources. For example, the estimates of the components of farm proprietors' income, a component of personal income, are partly based on the state estimates of farm income and the county estimates of case receipts, crop production, and livestock inventory that are prepared by the Department of Agriculture, which uses sample surveys, along with census data and administrative records data, to derive its estimates.

Total **earnings** cover wage and salary disbursements, other labor income, and proprietors' income. Wage and salary disbursements are defined as monetary remuneration of employees, including corporate officers; commissions, tips, and bonuses; and pay-in-kind that represents income to the recipient. They are measured before such deductions as social security contributions and union dues. All disbursements in the current period are covered. Pay-in-kind represents allowances for food, clothing, and lodging paid in kind to employees, which represent income to them, valued at the cost to the employer. Other labor income consists of employer contributions to privately administered pension and welfare funds and a few small items such as directors' fees, compensation of prison inmates, and miscellaneous judicial fees. Proprietors' income is the monetary income and income in-kind of proprietorships and partnerships, including the independent professions, and of tax-exempt cooperatives.

Table B-9. Labor Force and Private Business Establishments and Employment

Civilian labor force,
    Total, 2003–2004;
    Percent change, 2000–2003;
    Unemployment, total and rate.
Private nonfarm businesses,
    Establishments, 2002;
    Employment, 2002;
    Percent change, 2000–2002;
    Annual payroll per employee, 2002.

Sources: Civilian labor force—U.S. Bureau of Labor Statistics, *Local Area Unemployment Statistics, Annual Averages*; see Internet site <http://www.bls.gov/lau> (accessed 18 August 2005); Private nonfarm businesses—U.S. Census Bureau, *County Business Patterns* on CD-ROM; issued April 2003 and December 2004.

Civilian Labor Force

Civilian labor force data are the product of a federal-state cooperative program in which state employment security agencies prepare labor force and unemployment estimates under concepts, definitions, and technical procedures established by the BLS. These data for substate areas are produced by the BLS primarily for use in allocating funds under various federal legislative programs. Users of these data are cautioned that, because of the small size of many of the areas, as well as limitations of the data inputs, the estimates are subject to considerable, but nonquantifiable, error. An explanation of the technical procedures used to develop monthly and annual local area labor force estimates appears monthly in the Explanatory Note for state and area unemployment data in the BLS periodical *Employment and Earnings*. Additional information may also be found at the BLS Web site at <http://www.bls.gov/opub/hom/>.

The **civilian labor force** comprises all civilians 16 years old and over classified as employed or unemployed. Employed persons are all civilians who, during the survey week, did any work at all as paid employees in their own business, profession, or on their own farm or who worked 15 hours or more as unpaid workers in an enterprise operated by a member of the family. It also includes all those who were not working but who had jobs or businesses from which they were temporarily absent because of illness, bad weather, vacation, labor-management disputes, job training, or personal reasons, whether they were paid for the time off or were seeking other jobs. Each employed person is counted only once. Those who held more than one job are counted in the job at which they worked the greatest number of hours during the survey week, the calendar week including the 12th of the month.

Unemployed persons are all civilians 16 years old and over who had no employment during the survey week, were available for work, except for temporary illness, and had made specific efforts to find employment some time during the prior 4 weeks. Persons who were laid off or were waiting to report to a new job within 30 days did not need to be looking for work to be classified as unemployed. The unemployment rate for all civilian workers represents the number of unemployed as a percent of the civilian labor force.

County Business Patterns (CBP) is an annual series that provides subnational economic data by industry. The series is useful for studying the economic activity of small areas; analyzing economic changes over time; and as a benchmark for statistical series, surveys, and databases between economic censuses. CBP covers most of the country's economic activity. The series excludes data on self-employed individuals, employees of private households, railroad employees, agricultural production employees, and most government employees. The County Business Patterns program has tabulated on a North American Industry Classification System (NAICS) basis since 1998. Data for 1997 and earlier years are based on the Standard Industrial Classification (SIC) System. For more information on the relationship between the two systems, see the Bridge Between NAICS and SIC.

CBP data are extracted from the Business Register, the Census Bureau's file of all known single- and multiestablishment companies. The Annual Company Organization Survey and quinquennial economic censuses provide individual establishment data for multilocation firms. Data for single-location firms are obtained from various programs'

censuses, the Annual Survey of Manufactures, and Current Business Surveys, as well as from administrative records of the Internal Revenue Service (IRS), the Social Security Administration (SSA), and the Bureau of Labor Statistics (BLS).

An **establishment** is a single physical location at which business is conducted or services or industrial operations are performed. It is not necessarily identical with a company or enterprise, which may consist of one or more establishments. When two or more activities are carried on at a single location under a single ownership, all activities generally are grouped together as a single establishment. The entire establishment is classified on the basis of its major activity, and all data are included in that classification.

Establishment-size designations are determined by paid employment in the mid-March pay period. The size group "1 to 4" includes establishments that did not report any paid employees in the mid-March pay period but paid wages to at least one employee at some time during the year.

Establishment counts represent the number of locations with paid employees any time during the year. This series excludes governmental establishments except for wholesale liquor establishments (NAICS 4248), retail liquor stores (NAICS 44531), federally chartered savings institutions (NAICS 522120), federally chartered credit unions (NAICS 522130), and hospitals (NAICS 622).

Total **payroll** includes all forms of compensation, such as salaries, wages, reported tips, commissions, bonuses, vacation allowances, sick-leave pay, employee contributions to qualified pension plans, and the value of taxable fringe benefits. For corporations, it includes amounts paid to officers and executives; for unincorporated businesses, it does not include profit or other compensation of proprietors or partners. Payroll is reported before deductions for social security, income tax, insurance, union dues, etc. First-quarter payroll consists of payroll during the January-to-March quarter.

Paid employment consists of full- and part-time employees, including salaried officers and executives of corporations, who are on the payroll in the pay period including March 12. Included are employees on paid sick leave, holidays, and vacations; not included are proprietors and partners of unincorporated businesses.

Table B-10. Banking, Retail Trade, and Accommodation and Food Services

Banking, 2004,
  Number of offices;
  Deposits (millions of dollars);
Retail trade, 2002,
  Total (NAICS 44–45)—establishments with payroll;

Sales of establishments with payroll;
Annual payroll;
Paid employees;
Accommodation and food services, 2002,
  Total (NAICS 72);
  Accommodation (NAICS 721) and food services and
    drinking places (NAICS 722),
      Establishments with payroll;
      Sales of establishments with payroll;
      Annual payroll;
      Paid employees.

Sources: Banking—U.S. Federal Deposit Insurance Corporation (FDIC) and Office of Thrift Supervision (OTS), 2004 Bank and Thrift Branch Office Data Book: Summary of Deposits, <http://www2.fdic.gov/sod/index.asp> (accessed 5 April 2005); Retail trade—U.S. Census Bureau, 1997 and 2002 economic censuses, Geographic Area Series reports, <http://www.census.gov/econ/census02/> (accessed 6 June 2005); Accommodation and food services—U.S. Census Bureau, 1997 and 2002 Geographic Area Series reports, <http://www.census.gov/econ/census02/> (accessed 13 July 2005).

Banking

The FDIC and OTS collect deposit data on each office of every FDIC-insured bank and saving association as of June 30 of each year in the Summary of Deposits (SOD) survey. The FDIC surveys all FDIC-insured commercial banks, savings banks, and U.S. branches of foreign banks, and the OTS surveys all savings associations. Data presented here exclude U.S. branch offices of foreign banks. For all counties, individual banking offices—not the combined totals of the bank—are the source of the data.

Insured **savings institutions** include all FDIC-insured (OTS-regulated and FDIC-regulated) financial institutions that operate under federal or state banking charters.

The number of **banking offices** in any given area includes every location at which deposit business is transacted. Banking office is defined to include all offices and facilities that actually hold deposits, but to exclude loan production offices, computer centers, and other nondeposit installations, such as automated teller machines (ATMs). The term "offices" includes both main offices and branches. An institution with four branches operates a total of five offices.

Retail trade data presented are based on the North American Industry Classification System (NAICS) for 2002 and are not entirely comparable with previous data for earlier economic censuses (see General Note for Economic Censuses). The data cover only establishments with payroll. The retail sector (NAICS codes 4445) comprises establishments engaged in retailing merchandise, generally without transformation, and rendering services incidental to the sale of merchandise. The retailing process is the final step

in the distribution of merchandise; retailers are, therefore, organized to sell merchandise in small quantities to the general public. This sector comprises two main types of retailers: store (operate fixed point-of-sale locations, located and designed to attract a high volume of walk-in customers) and nonstore retailers (establishments of this subsector reach customers and market merchandise with methods such as the broadcasting of "infomercials," the broadcasting and publishing of direct-response advertising, the publishing of paper and electronic catalogs, door-to-door solicitation, in-home demonstration, selling from portable stalls (street vendors, except food), and distribution through vending machines).

An **establishment** is a single physical location at which business is conducted or where services or industrial operations are performed. It is not necessarily identical with the company or enterprise, which may consist of one or more establishments. The count of establishments represents the number in business at any time during the year.

Sales include merchandise sold for cash or credit at retail and wholesale by establishments primarily engaged in retail trade; amounts received from customers for layaway purchases; receipts from rental of vehicles, equipment, instruments, tools, etc.; receipts for delivery, installation, maintenance, repair, alteration, storage, and other services; the total value of service contracts; gasoline, liquor, tobacco, and other excise taxes that are paid by the manufacturer or wholesaler and passed on to the retailer; and shipping and handling receipts.

Sales are net after deductions for refunds and allowances for merchandise returned by customers. Trade-in allowances are not deducted from sales. Sales do not include carrying or other credit charges; sales and other taxes (including Hawaii's General Excise Tax) collected from customers and forwarded to taxing authorities; gross sales and receipts of departments or concessions operated by other companies; and commissions or receipts from the sale of government lottery tickets.

Sales do not include retail sales made by manufacturers, wholesalers, service establishments, or other businesses whose primary activity is other than retail trade. They do include receipts other than from the sale of merchandise at retail, e.g., service receipts, sales to industrial users, and sales to other retailers, by establishments primarily engaged in retail trade. Sales figures represent the sales of all establishments in business at any time during the year.

Payroll includes all forms of compensation such as salaries, wages, commissions, dismissal pay, bonuses, vacation allowances, sick-leave pay, and employee contributions to qualified pension plans paid during the year to all employees and reported on Internal Revenue Service (IRS) Form 941 as taxable Medicare wages and tips (even if not subject to income or FICA tax). Includes tips and gratuities received by employees from patrons and reported to employers. Excludes payrolls of departments or concessions operated by other companies at the establishment. For corporations, payroll includes amounts paid to officers and executives; for unincorporated businesses, it does not include profit or other compensation of proprietors or partners. Payroll is reported before deductions for social security, income tax, insurance, union dues, etc. This definition of payroll is the same as that used by the IRS on Form 941.

Paid employees consist of full-time and part-time employees, including salaried officers and executives of corporations, who were on the payroll during the pay period including March 12. Included are employees on paid sick leave, paid holidays, and paid vacations; not included are proprietors and partners of unincorporated businesses; employees of departments or concessions operated by other companies at the establishment; full- and part-time leased employees whose payroll was filed under an employee leasing company's Employer Identification Number (EIN); and temporary staffing obtained from a staffing service. The definition of paid employees is the same as that used by the Internal Revenue Service (IRS) on Form 941.

Accommodation and food services data presented are based on the North American Industry Classification System (NAICS) for 2002. The data cover only establishments with payroll. The accommodation and food service sector (NAICS codes 72) comprises establishments providing customers with lodging and/or prepared meals, snacks, and beverages for immediate consumption. This sector is comprised of hotels and other lodging places that were formerly classified in the Standard Industrial Classification (SIC) system in Division I, Services, and eating and drinking places and mobile food services that were classified in SIC Division G, Retail Trade. This new sector includes both accommodation and food services establishments because the two activities are often combined at the same establishment. Excluded from this sector are civic and social organizations, amusement and recreation parks, theaters, and other recreation or entertainment facilities providing food and beverage services.

For definitions of establishments, paid employees, and annual payroll, see Retail Trade above.

Sales in the food services sector cover the industries in the Food Services and Drinking Places subsector that prepares meals, snacks, and beverages to customer order for immediate on-premises and off-premises consumption. There is a wide range of establishments in these industries. Some provide food and drink only, while others provide various combinations of seating space, waiter/waitress services, and incidental amenities, such as limited entertainment. The industries in the subsector are grouped based on the type and level of services provided.

The industry groups are full-service restaurants; limited-service eating places; special food services, such as food service contractors, caterers, and mobile food services, and drinking places.

Table B-11. Government

Federal funds and grants—total, 2000, 2003,
    Total expenditures;
    Percent change, 2002–2003;
    Per capita;
    Percent—direct payments to individuals;

Government,
    Earnings—total, 2000, 2002,
        Percent of total earnings;
        Percent change, 2000–2002;

    Employment—total, 2000, 2002,
        Percent of total employment;
        Percent change, 2000–2002.

Sources: Federal funds and grants—U.S. Census Bureau, Consolidated Federal Funds Report, annual, see Internet site <http://www.census.gov/govs/www/cffr.html>; Government earnings and employment—U.S. Bureau of Economic Analysis, *Regional Economic Information System (REIS) 1969–2002* on CD-ROM (related Internet site: <http://www.bea.gov/bea/regional/data.htm>).

Direct payments for individuals is taken from information reported to the Federal Assistance Awards Data System. The two object areas of direct payments for individuals are (1) direct payments for retirement and disability benefits and (2) all other direct payments for individuals.

Table C-1. Population and Population Characteristics

Population—total, 2005, 2004, 2000, 1990,
    Net change;
    Percent change;
Percent,
    65 years and over, 2003;
    Black or African American alone;
    Asian alone;
    Hispanic or Latino origin.

Sources: U.S. Census Bureau, 2000 to 2005 compiled from "Population Estimates by County" <http://www.census.gov/popest/counties/CO-EST2005-01.html> and "Population Estimates, Cumulative Estimates of the Components of Population Change for Counties: April 1, 2000 to July 1, 2005" <http://www.census.gov/popest/counties/CO-EST2005-05.html>; 1990, "Population Estimates: Annual Time Series," archive 1990 (revised data for April 1, 1990, Population Estimates base) <http://www.census.gov/popest/archives/1990s/CO-99-02.html>; Age, race, and Hispanic population—U.S. Census Bureau, "County Characteristic Population Estimates Data," <http://www.census.gov/popest/estimates.php>.

See Tables B-1, B-2, and B-3, State and Metropolitan Area Data Book: 2006.

For more information, see <http://www.census.gov/hhes /www/income.html>, <http://www.census.gov/popest /estimates.php>, and <http://www.census.gov/popest /counties/CO-EST2004-04.html>.

Table C-2. Population Characteristics and Housing Units

Educational attainment, 2000,
  Percent;
Foreign born, 2000,
  Percent;
Workers 16 years and over,
  Total;
  Percent of workers who drove alone to work;
Persons below poverty level in 1999,
  Total;
  Percent;
Housing units, 2000, 2004,
  Change—number, percent.

Source: Educational attainment, foreign born, commuting, and poverty—U.S. Census Bureau, 2000 Census of Population and Housing, *Summary File 3* (SF3) (accessed 12 January 2004) and related Internet site at <http://www .census.gov/Press-Release/www/2002/sumfile3.html> and 2000 Census of Population and Housing, Summary Social, Economic, and Housing Characteristics, PHC-2-1 to 52 and related Internet site at <http://www.census.gov /prod/cen2000/index.html>; Housing units—U.S. Census Bureau, *Annual Estimates of Housing Units for Counties: April 1, 2000 to July 1, 2004* at <http://www.census.gov /popest/housing/> (accessed 14 November 2005).

See Tables B-4 and B-7, State and Metropolitan Area Data Book: 2006.

For more information, see <http://www.census.gov /popest/housing>.

Table C-3. Personal Income and Earnings by Industry

Personal income, 2000, 2001, 2002,
  Total;
  Per capita;
  Percent change;
  Earnings, percent by selected industries.

Source: Personal income and earnings—U.S. Bureau of Economic Analysis, *Regional Economic Information System (REIS) 1969–2002* on CD-ROM (related Internet site <http://www.bea.gov/bea/regional/data.htm>).

See Table B-8, State and Metropolitan Area Data Book: 2006.

For more information, see Internet site <http://www.bea.gov/bea/regional/reis/>.

Table C-4. Civilian Labor Force and Private Nonfarm Businesses

Civilian labor force, 2000, 2004,
  Total;
  Net change;
  Number of unemployed;
  Unemployment rate;
Private labor force, 2002,
  Establishments—total, change;
  Employment—total, change;
  Annual payroll per employee—total, percent of national average.

Sources: Civilian labor force—U.S. Bureau of Labor Statistics, *Local Area Unemployment Statistics, Annual Averages*; see Internet site <http://www.bls.gov/lau> (accessed 18 August 2005); Private nonfarm businesses—U.S. Census Bureau, *County Business Patterns* on CD-ROM; annual.

See Table B-9, State and Metropolitan Area Data Book: 2006.

For more information, see Internet site <http://www.bls .gov/lau/home.htm>.

Table D-1. Population and Personal Income

Population, 1990, 2000, 2004, 2005,
  Net change, 2000–2005, 1990–2000;
  Percent change, 2000–2005, 1990–2000;
Personal income, total, 2002, 2000,
  Per capita, 2002, 2000;
  Percent change, 2000–2002.

Sources: Population—U.S. Census Bureau, 2000 to 2005 compiled from "Population Estimates by County," published 16 March 2006; <http://www.census.gov/popest /counties/CO-EST2005-01.html>; and "Population Estimates, Cumulative Estimates of the Components of Population Change for Counties," published 16 March 2006; April 1, 2000, to July 1, 2005, <http://www.census.gov /popest/counties/CO-EST2005-05.html>; 1990, "Population Estimates: Annual Time Series," archive 1990 (revised data for April 1, 1990, Population Estimates base) <http://www.census.gov/popest/archives/1990s /CO-99-02.html>; Personal income—U.S. Bureau of Economic Analysis, *Regional Economic Information System (REIS) 1969–2002* on CD-ROM, and related Internet site at <http://www.bea.gov/bea/regional/reis/> (released 25 May 2004).

See Tables B-1 and B-8, State and Metropolitan Area Data Book: 2006.

For more information, see <http://www.census.gov /popest/counties/CO-EST2004-01.html>.

Appendix B.
Limitations of the Data and Methodology

INTRODUCTION

The data presented in this *State and Metropolitan Area Data Book* came from many sources. The sources include not only federal statistical bureaus and other organizations that collect and issue statistics as their principal activity, but also governmental administrative and regulatory agencies, private research bodies, trade associations, insurance companies, health associations, and private organizations such as the National Education Association and philanthropic foundations. Consequently, the data vary considerably as to reference periods, definitions of terms and, for ongoing series, the number and frequency of time periods for which data are available.

The statistics presented were obtained and tabulated by various means. Some statistics are based on complete enumerations or censuses while others are based on samples. Some information is extracted from records kept for administrative or regulatory purposes (school enrollment, hospital records, securities registration, financial accounts, social security records, income tax returns, etc.), while other information is obtained explicitly for statistical purposes through interviews or by mail. The estimation procedures used vary, from highly sophisticated scientific techniques to crude "informed guesses."

Each set of data relates to a group of individuals or units of interest referred to as the *target universe* or *target population*, or simply as the *universe* or *population*. Prior to data collection, the target universe should be clearly defined. For example, if data are to be collected for the universe of households in the United States, it is necessary to define a "household." The target universe may not be completely controllable or ideal. Cost and other considerations may restrict data collection to a survey universe based on some available list; such list may be inaccurate or out of date. This list is called a *survey frame* or *sampling frame*.

The data in many tables are based on data obtained for all population units, a census, or on data obtained for only a portion, or sample, of the population units. When the data presented are based on a sample, the sample is usually a scientifically selected probability sample. This is a sample selected from a list or sampling frame in such a way that every possible sample has a known chance of selection, and usually each unit selected can be assigned a number, greater than 0 and less than or equal to 1, representing its likelihood or probability of selection.

For large-scale sample surveys, the probability sample of units is often selected as a multistage sample. The first stage of a multistage sample is the selection of a probability sample of large groups of population members, referred to as primary sampling units (PSUs). For example, in a national multistage household sample, PSUs are often counties or groups of counties. The second stage of a multistage sample is the selection, within each PSU selected at the first stage, of smaller groups of population units, referred to as secondary sampling units. In subsequent stages of selection, smaller and smaller nested groups are chosen until the ultimate sample of population units is obtained. To qualify a multistage sample as a probability sample, all stages of sampling must be carried out using probability sampling methods.

Prior to selection at each stage of a multistage (or a single-stage) sample, a list of the sampling units or sampling frame for that stage must be obtained. For example, for the first stage of selection of a national household sample, a list of the counties and county groups that form the PSUs must be obtained. For the final stage of selection, lists of households, and sometimes persons within the households, have to be compiled in the field. For surveys of economic entities and for the economic censuses, the Census Bureau generally uses a frame constructed from the Census Bureau's Business Register. The Business Register contains all establishments with payroll in the United States, including small single-establishment firms as well as large multiestablishment firms.

Wherever the quantities in a table refer to an entire universe, but are constructed from data collected in a sample survey, the table quantities are referred to as *sample estimates*. In constructing a sample estimate, an attempt is made to come as close as is feasible to the corresponding universe quantity that would be obtained from a complete census of the universe. Estimates based on a sample will, however, generally differ from the hypothetical census figures. Two classifications of errors are associated with estimates based on sample surveys: (1) *sampling error*—the error arising from the use of a sample, rather than a census, to estimate population quantities—and (2) *nonsampling error*—those errors arising from nonsampling sources. As discussed below, the magnitude of the sampling error for an estimate can usually be estimated from the sample data. However, the magnitude of the nonsampling error for an estimate can rarely be estimated. Consequently, actual error in an estimate exceeds the error that can be estimated.

The particular sample used in a survey is only one of a large number of possible samples of the same size, which could have been selected using the same sampling procedure. Estimates derived from the different samples would, in general, differ from each other. The *standard error* (SE) is a measure of the variation among the estimates derived from all possible samples. The standard error is the most commonly used measure of the sampling error of an estimate. Valid estimates of the standard errors of survey estimates can usually be calculated from the data collected in a probability sample. For convenience, the standard error is sometimes expressed as a percent of the estimate and is called the relative standard error or *coefficient of variation* (CV). For example, an estimate of 200 units with an estimated standard error of 10 units has an estimated CV of 5 percent.

A sample estimate and an estimate of its standard error or CV can be used to construct interval estimates that have a prescribed confidence that the interval includes the average of the estimates derived from all possible samples with a known probability. To illustrate, if all possible samples were selected under essentially the same general conditions, and using the same sample design, and if an estimate and its estimated standard error were calculated from each sample, then: 1) approximately 68 percent of the intervals from one standard error below the estimate to one standard error above the estimate would include the average estimate derived from all possible samples; 2) approximately 90 percent of the intervals from 1.6 standard errors below the estimate to 1.6 standard errors above the estimate would include the average estimate derived from all possible samples; and 3) approximately 95 percent of the intervals from two standard errors below the estimate to two standard errors above the estimate would include the average estimate derived from all possible samples.

Thus, for a particular sample, one can say with the appropriate level of confidence (e.g., 90 percent or 95 percent) that the average of all possible samples is included in the constructed interval. Example of a confidence interval: An estimate is 200 units with a standard error of 10 units. An approximately 90-percent confidence interval (plus or minus 1.6 standard errors) is from 184 to 216.

All surveys and censuses are subject to nonsampling errors. Nonsampling errors are of two kinds: *random* and *nonrandom*. Random nonsampling errors arise because of the varying interpretation of questions (by respondents or interviewers) and varying actions of coders, keyers, and other processors. Some randomness is also introduced when respondents must estimate. Nonrandom nonsampling errors result from total nonresponse (no usable data obtained for a sampled unit), partial or item nonresponse (only a portion of a response may be usable), inability or unwillingness on the part of respondents to provide correct information, difficulty interpreting questions, mistakes in recording or keying data, errors of collection or processing, and coverage problems (overcoverage and undercoverage of the target universe). Random nonresponse errors usually, but not always, result in an understatement of sampling errors and thus an overstatement of the precision of survey estimates. Estimating the magnitude of nonsampling errors would require special experiments or access to independent data and, consequently, the magnitudes are seldom available.

Nearly all types of nonsampling errors that affect surveys also occur in complete censuses. Since surveys can be conducted on a smaller scale than censuses, nonsampling errors can presumably be controlled more tightly. Relatively more funds and effort can perhaps be expended toward eliciting responses, detecting and correcting response error, and reducing processing errors. As a result, survey results can sometimes be more accurate than census results.

To compensate for suspected nonrandom errors, adjustments of the sample estimates are often made. For example, adjustments are frequently made for nonresponse, both total and partial. Adjustments made for either type of nonresponse are often referred to as *imputations*. Imputation for total nonresponse is usually made by substituting the "average" questionnaire response(s) of the respondents for the questionnaire responses of the nonrespondents. These imputations usually are made separately within various groups of sample members, formed by attempting to place respondents and nonrespondents together that have "similar" design or ancillary characteristics. Imputation for item nonresponse is usually made by substituting for a missing item the response to that item of a respondent having characteristics that are "similar" to those of the nonrespondent.

For an estimate calculated from a sample survey, the *total error* in the estimate is composed of the sampling error, which can usually be estimated from the sample, and the nonsampling error, which usually cannot be estimated from the sample. The total error present in a population quantity obtained from a complete census is composed of only nonsampling errors. Ideally, estimates of the total error associated with data given in these tables should be given. However, due to the unavailability of estimates of nonsampling errors, only estimates of the levels of sampling errors, in terms of estimated standard errors or coefficients of variation, are available. To obtain estimates of the estimated standard errors from the sample of interest, obtain a copy of the referenced report that appears at the end of each table.

Source of Additional Material: The Federal Committee on Statistical Methodology (FCSM) is an interagency committee dedicated to improving the quality of federal statistics <http://fcsm.ssd.census.gov>.

Principal databases: Beginning below are brief descriptions of 19 of the sample surveys, censuses, and administrative collections that provide a substantial portion of the data contained in this publication.

U.S. DEPARTMENT OF AGRICULTURE

National Agricultural Statistics Service (NASS)

Census of Agriculture

Universe, Frequency, and Types of Data: Complete count of U.S. farms and ranches conducted once every 5 years with data at the national, state, and county level. Data published on farm numbers and related items/characteristics.

Type of Data Collection Operation: Complete census for number of farms; land in farms; agricultural products sold; total cropland; irrigated land; farm operator characteristics; livestock and poultry inventory and sales; and selected crops harvested. Market value of land and buildings, total farm production expenses, machinery and equipment, fertilizer and chemicals, and farm labor are estimated from a sample of farms.

Data Collection and Imputation Procedures: Data collection takes place by mailing questionnaires to all farmers and ranchers. Nonrespondents are contacted by telephone and correspondence follow-ups. Imputations were made for all nonresponse items/characteristics. Coverage adjustments were made to account for missed farms and ranches.

Estimates of Sampling Error: Variability in the estimates is due to the sample selection and estimation for items collected by sample and census nonresponse and coverage estimation procedures. The CVs for national and state estimates are generally very small. The response rate is approximately 81 percent.

Other (nonsampling) Errors: Nonsampling errors are due to incompleteness of the census mailing list, duplications on the list, respondent reporting errors, errors in editing reported data, and in imputation for missing data. Evaluation studies are conducted to measure certain nonsampling errors such as list coverage and classification error. Results from the evaluation program for the 2002 census indicate the net undercoverage amounted to about 18 percent of the nation's total farms.

Sources of Additional Material: U.S. Department of Agriculture, NASS, *2002 Census of Agriculture*, Volume 1, Subject Series C, Part 1, *Agricultural Atlas of the U.S.*; Part 2, *Coverage Evaluation*; Part 3, *Rankings of States and Counties*.

Multiple Frame Surveys

Universe, Frequency, and Types of Data: Surveys of U.S. farm operators are taken to obtain data on major livestock inventories, selected crop acreage and production, grain stocks, and farm labor characteristics; farm economic data and chemical use data.

Type of Data Collection Operation: Primary frame is obtained from general or special purpose lists, supplemented by a probability sample of land areas used to estimate for list incompleteness.

Data Collection and Imputation Procedures: Mail, telephone, or personal interviews used for initial data collection. Mail nonrespondent follow-up by phone and personal interviews. Imputation based on average of respondents.

Estimates of Sampling Error: Estimated CV for number of hired farm workers is about 3 percent. Estimated CVs range from 1 percent to 2 percent for regional estimates to 3 percent to 6 percent for state estimates of livestock inventories and crop acreage.

Other (nonsampling) Errors: In addition to above, replicated sampling procedures used to monitor effects of changes in survey procedures.

Sources of Additional Material: U.S. Department of Agriculture, National Agricultural Statistics Service, *National Agricultural Statistics Service: The Fact Finders of Agriculture*, September 1994.

U.S. BUREAU OF LABOR STATISTICS

Current Employment Statistics (CES) Program

Universe, Frequency, and Types of Data: Monthly survey drawn from a sampling frame of over 8 million unemployment insurance tax accounts in order to obtain data by industry on employment, hours, and earnings.

Type of Data Collection Operation: In 2004, the CES sample included about 160,000 businesses and government agencies, which represent approximately 400,000 individual work sites.

Data Collection and Imputation Procedures: Each month, the state agencies cooperating with BLS, as well as BLS Data Collection Centers, collect data through various automated collection modes and mail. BLS-Washington staff prepares national estimates of employment, hours, and earnings while states use the data to develop state and area estimates.

Estimates of Sampling Errors: The relative standard error for total nonfarm employment is 0.1 percent.

Other (nonsampling) Errors: Estimates of employment adjusted annually to reflect complete universe. The average adjustment is 0.3 percent over the last decade, with an absolute range from less than 0.05 percent to 0.5 percent.

Sources of Additional Material: U.S. Bureau of Labor Statistics, *Employment and Earnings*, monthly, Explanatory Notes and Estimates of Errors, Tables 2-A through 2-F. See also the BLS Handbook of Methods, Chapter 1, Labor Force

Data Derived from the Current Population Survey, and Chapter 2, Employment, Hours, and Earnings from the Establishment Survey. The BLS Handbook may be found at <http://www.bls.gov/opub/hom/>.

U.S. DEPARTMENT OF COMMERCE

U.S. Bureau of Economic Analysis (BEA)

Regional Economic Information System (REIS)

Universe, Frequency, and Types of Data: The Regional Economic Information System contains estimates of personal income and its components and employment for local areas, such as states, counties, metropolitan areas, and micropolitan areas.

Type of Data Collection Operation: The estimates of personal income are primarily based on administrative records data, census data, and survey data.

Data Collection and Imputation Procedures: The data are collected from administrative records, which may come from the recipients of the income or from the sources of the income. These data are a byproduct of the administration of various federal and state government programs. The most important sources of these data are the state unemployment insurance programs of the Bureau of Labor Statistics, social insurance programs of the Centers for Medicare and Medicaid Services, the federal income tax program of the Internal Revenue Service, veterans benefit programs of the U.S. Department of Veterans Affairs, and military payroll systems of the U.S. Department of Defense.

The data from censuses are mainly collected from the recipients of income. The most important sources for these data are the Census of Agriculture at the U.S. Department of Agriculture (USDA) and the Census of Population and Housing conducted by the U.S. Census Bureau. Other sources may include estimates of farm proprietors' income by the USDA, wages and salaries from County Business Patterns from the Census Bureau, and the Quarterly Census of Employment and Wages by the Department of Labor.

Estimates of Sampling Error: Not applicable, except component variables may be subject to error.

Other (nonsampling) Errors: Nonsampling errors in the administrative datasets may affect personal income estimates.

Sources of Additional Material: U.S. Bureau of Economic Analysis, *Local Area Personal Income and Employment Methodology, 1997–2003*. See also <http://www.bea.gov/bea/regional/articles/lapi2003/lapi2003.pdf>. Methodological information on other BEA datasets such as "State Personal Income" and "Gross State Product" may be found at <http://www.bea.gov/bea/regional/articles.cfm?section=methods>.

U.S. Census Bureau

American Community Survey (ACS)

Universe, Frequency, and Types of Data: Nationwide survey to obtain data about demographic, social, economic, and housing characteristics of people, households, and housing units. Covers household population and excludes the population living in institutions, college dormitories, and other group quarters.

Type of Data Collection Operation: Two-stage stratified annual sample of approximately 829,000 housing units. The ACS samples housing units from the Master Address File (MAF). The first stage of sampling involves dividing the United States into primary sampling units (PSUs), most of which comprise a metropolitan area, a large county, or a group of smaller counties. Every PSU falls within the boundary of a state. The PSUs are then grouped into strata on the basis of independent information; that is, information obtained from the decennial census or other sources. The strata are constructed so that they are as homogeneous as possible with respect to social and economic characteristics that are considered important by ACS data users. A pair of PSUs were selected from each stratum. The probability of selection for each PSU in the stratum is proportional to its estimated 1996 population. In the second stage of sampling, a sample of housing units within the sample PSUs is drawn. Ultimate sampling units (USUs) are housing units. The USUs sampled in the second stage consist of housing units that are systematically drawn from sorted lists of addresses of housing units from the MAF.

Data Collection and Imputation Procedures: The American Community Survey (ACS) is conducted every month on independent samples. Each housing unit in the independent monthly samples is mailed a prenotice letter announcing the selection of the address to participate, a survey questionnaire package, and a reminder postcard. These sample units receive a second (replacement) questionnaire package if the initial questionnaire is not returned by a scheduled date. In the mailout/mailback sites, sample units for which a questionnaire is not returned in the mail and for which a telephone number is available are defined as the telephone nonresponse follow-up universe. Interviewers attempt to contact and interview these mail nonresponse cases. Sample units from all sites that are still unresponsive 2 months after the mailing of the survey questionnaires and directly after the completion of the telephone follow-up operation are subsampled at a rate of 1 in 3. The selected nonresponse units are assigned to field representatives, who visit the units, verify their existence or declare them nonexistent, determine their occupancy status, and conduct interviews. After data collection is completed, any remaining incomplete or inconsistent information was imputed during the final automated edit of the collected data.

Estimates of Sampling Error: The data in the ACS products are estimates of the actual figures that would have been obtained by interviewing the entire population using the same methodology. The estimates from the chosen sample also differ from other samples of housing units and persons within those housing units.

Other (nonsampling) Errors: In addition to sampling error, data users should realize that other types of errors may be introduced during any of the various complex operations used to collect and process survey data. An important goal of the ACS is to minimize the amount of nonsampling error introduced through nonresponse for sample housing units. One way of this is by following up on mail nonrespondents.

Sources of Additional Material: U.S. Census Bureau, American Community Survey Web site available on the Internet, <http://www.census.gov/acs/www/index.html>. U.S. Census Bureau, American Community Survey, Accuracy of the Data documents available on the Internet, <http://www.census.gov/acs/www/UseData/Accuracy /Accuracy1.htm>.

Annual Survey of Manufactures (ASM)

Universe, Frequency, and Types of Data: The Annual Survey of Manufactures (ASM) is conducted annually, except for years ending in 2 and 7, for all manufacturing establishments having one or more paid employees. The purpose of the ASM is to provide key intercensal measures of manufacturing activity, products, and location for the public and private sectors. The ASM provides statistics on employment, payroll, worker hours, payroll supplements, cost of materials, value added by manufacturing, capital expenditures, inventories, and energy consumption. It also provides estimates of value of shipments for 1,800 classes of manufactured products.

Type of Data Collection Operation: The ASM includes approximately 57,000 establishments selected from the census universe of 366,000 manufacturing establishments. Some 27,000 large establishments are selected with certainty, and some 30,000 other establishments are selected with probability proportional to a composite measure of establishment size. The survey is updated from two sources: Internal Revenue Service administrative records are used to include new single-unit manufacturers, and the Company Organization Survey identifies new establishments of multiunit forms.

Data Collection and Imputation Procedures: The survey is conducted by mail with phone and mail follow-ups of nonrespondents. Imputation (for all nonresponse items) is based on previous year reports, or for new establishments in survey, on industry averages.

Estimates of Sampling Error: Estimated standard errors for number of employees, new expenditures, and for value-added totals are given in annual publications. For U.S.-level industry statistics, most estimated standard errors are 2 percent or less, but vary considerably for detailed characteristics.

Other (nonsampling) Errors: Response rate is about 85 percent. Nonsampling errors include those due to collection, reporting, and transcription errors, many of which are corrected through computer and clerical checks.

Sources of Additional Material: U.S. Census Bureau, Annual Survey of Manufactures, and Technical Paper 24; <http://www.census.gov/econ/www/mancen.html>.

Annual Surveys of State and Local Government

Universe, Frequency, and Types of Data: Sample survey conducted annually to obtain data on revenue, expenditure, debt, and employment of state and local governments. Universe is all governmental units in the United States (about 87,500).

Type of Data Collection Operation: Sample survey includes all state governments, county governments with 100,000 and over population, municipalities with 75,000 and over population, townships with 50,000 and over population, all independent school districts with 10,000 and over enrollment in March 2002, all school districts providing college-level (postsecondary) education, and other governments meeting certain criteria; probability sample for remaining units.

Data Collection and Imputation Procedures: Field and office compilation of data from official records and reports for states and large local governments; central collection of local governmental financial data through cooperative agreements with a number of state governments; mail canvass of other units with mail and telephone follow-ups of nonrespondents. Data for nonresponses are imputed from previous year data or obtained from secondary sources, if available.

Estimates of Sampling Error: State and local government totals are generally subject to sampling variability of less than 3 percent.

Other (nonsampling) Errors: Nonresponse rate is less than 10 percent for local governments. Other possible errors may result from undetected inaccuracies in classification, response, and processing.

Sources of Additional Material: U.S. Census Bureau, <http://www.census.gov/prod/www/abs/govern.html>; U.S. Census Bureau, Public Employment in 1992, GE 92, No. 1, Governmental Finances in GF 92, No. 5, and Census of Governments, 1997 and 2002, various reports. Web site references: Census of Governments at <http://www .census.gov/govs/www/cog2002.html> and <http://www .census.gov/govs/www/cog.html>. Employment state and local site: <http://www.census.gov/govs/www/apes.html> and finance state and local site: <http://www.census.gov/govs/www/estimate.html>.

2002 Economic Census
(Industry Series, Geographic Area Series Reports) (for NAICS sectors 22, 31–33, 42, 44–45, 48–49, and 51–81)

Universe, Frequency, and Types of Data: Conducted every 5 years to obtain data on number of establishments, number of employees, total payroll size, total sales/receipts/revenue, and other industry-specific statistics. In 2002, the universe was all employer and nonemployer establishments primarily engaged in wholesale, retail, utilities, finance and insurance, real estate, transportation and warehousing, information, education, health care, and other service industries.

Type of Data Collection Operation: All large employer firms were surveyed (i.e., all employer firms above payroll size cutoffs established to separate large from small employers) plus a 5 percent to 25 percent sample of the small employer firms. Firms with no employees were not required to file a census return.

Data Collection and Imputation Procedures: Mail questionnaires were used with both mail and telephone follow-ups for nonrespondents. Data for nonrespondents and for small employer firms not mailed a questionnaire were obtained from administrative records of other federal agencies or imputed. Nonemployer data were obtained exclusively from IRS 2002 income tax returns.

Estimates of Sampling Error: Not applicable for basic data such as sales, revenue, receipts, payroll, etc.

Other (nonsampling) Errors: Establishment response rates by NAICS sector in 2002 ranged from 80 percent to 89 percent. Item response rates generally ranged from 50 percent to 90 percent, with lower rates for the more detailed questions. Nonsampling errors may occur during the collection, reporting, and keying of data, and due to industry misclassification.

Sources of Additional Material: U.S. Census Bureau, 2002 Economic Census: Geographic Area Series Reports (by NAICS sector), Appendix C, and <http://www.census.gov/econ/census02/guide/index.html>.

Census of Population

Universe, Frequency, and Types of Data: Complete count of U.S. population conducted every 10 years since 1790. Data obtained on number and characteristics of people in the United States.

Type of Data Collection Operation: In 1980, 1990, and 2000, complete census for some items: age, date of birth, sex, race, and relationship to householder. In 1980, approximately 19 percent of the housing units were included in the sample; in 1990 and 2000, approximately 17 percent.

Data Collection and Imputation Procedures: In 1980, 1990, and 2000, mail questionnaires were used extensively, with personal interviews in the remainder. Extensive telephone and personal follow-up for nonrespondents was done in the censuses. Imputations were made for missing characteristics.

Estimates of Sampling Error: Sampling errors for data are estimated for all items collected by sample and vary by characteristic and geographic area. The coefficients of variation (CVs) for national and state estimates are generally very small.

Other (nonsampling) Errors: Since 1950, evaluation programs have been conducted to provide information on the magnitude of some sources of nonsampling errors such as response bias and undercoverage in each census. Results from the evaluation program for the 1990 census indicated that the estimated net undercoverage amounted to about 1.5 percent of the total resident population. For Census 2000, the evaluation program indicates a net overcount of 0.5 percent of the resident population.

Sources of Additional Material: U.S. Census Bureau, 1990 Census of Population and Housing, Content Reinterview Survey: Accuracy of Data for Selected Population and Housing Characteristics as measured by Reinterview, CPH-E-1; 1990 Census of Population and Housing, Effectiveness of Quality Assurance, CPH-E-2; Programs to Improve Coverage in the 1990 Census, CPH-E-3. For Census 2000, see <http://www.census.gov/pred/www>.

County Business Patterns

Universe, Frequency, and Types of Data: County Business Patterns is an annual tabulation of basic data items extracted from the Business Register, a file of all known single- and multilocation companies, maintained and updated by the Census Bureau. Data include number of establishments, number of employees, first quarter and annual payrolls, and number of establishments by employment size class. Data are excluded for self-employed persons, domestic service workers, railroad employees, agricultural production workers, and most government employees.

Type of Data Collection Operation: The annual Company Organization Survey provides individual establishment data for multilocation companies. Data for single establishment companies are obtained from various Census Bureau programs, such as the Annual Survey of Manufactures and Current Business Surveys, as well as from administrative records of the Internal Revenue Service and the Social Security Administration.

Estimates of Sampling Error: Not applicable.

Other (nonsampling) Error: The data are subject to nonsampling errors, such as industry classification errors, as well as errors of response, keying, and nonreporting.

Sources of Additional Material: U.S. Census Bureau, *General Explanation of County Business Patterns*. See also "Frequently Asked County Business Patterns (CBP) Questions" at <http://www.census.gov/epcd/cbp/view/cbpfaq.html>.

Current Population Survey (CPS)

Universe, Frequency, and Types of Data: Nationwide monthly sample survey of civilian noninstitutionalized population, 15 years old or over, to obtain data on employment, unemployment, and a number of other characteristics.

Type of Data Collection Operation: Multistage probability sample of about 50,000 households in 754 PSUs in 1996 expanded to about 60,000 households in July 2001. Oversampling in some states and the largest MSAs to improve reliability for those areas of employment data on annual average basis. A continual sample rotation system is used. Households are in sample 4 months, out for 8 months, and in for 4 more. Month-to-month overlap is 75 percent; year-to-year overlap is 50 percent.

Data Collection and Imputation Procedures: For first and fifth months that a household is in sample, personal interviews; other months, approximately 85 percent of the data is collected by phone. Imputation is done for both item and total nonresponse. Adjustment for total nonresponse is done by a predefined cluster of units, by MSA size and residence; for item nonresponse, imputation varies by subject matter.

Estimates of Sampling Error: Estimated CVs on national annual averages for labor force, total employment, and nonagricultural employment, 0.2 percent; for total unemployment and agricultural employment, 1.0 percent to 2.5 percent. The estimated CVs for family income and poverty rate for all persons are 0.5 percent and 1.5 percent, respectively. CVs for subnational areas, such as states, would be larger and would vary by area.

Other (nonsampling) Errors: Estimates of response bias on unemployment are not available, but estimates of unemployment are usually 5 percent to 9 percent lower than estimates from reinterviews. Six to 7 percent of sample households are unavailable for interviews.

Sources of Additional Material: U.S. Census Bureau and Bureau of Labor Statistics, *Current Population Survey, Design and Methodology*, Technical Paper 63RV, issued March 2002, available at <http://www.census.gov/prod/2002pubs/tp63rv.pdf>; and Bureau of Labor Statistics, *Employment and Earnings*, monthly, Explanatory Notes and Estimates of Error, Household Data and *BLS Handbook of Methods*, Chapter 1, available at <http://www.bls.gov/opub/hom/homch1a.htm>.

Monthly Survey of Construction

Universe, Frequency, and Types of Data: Survey conducted monthly of newly constructed housing units (excluding mobile homes). Data are collected on the start, completion, and sale of housing. (Annual figures are aggregates of monthly estimates.)

Type of Data Collection Operation: For permit-issuing places, probability sample of 850 housing units obtained from 19,000 permit-issuing places. For nonpermit places, multistage probability sample of new housing units selected in 169 PSUs. In those areas, all roads are canvassed in selected enumeration districts.

Data Collection and Imputation Procedures: Data are obtained by telephone inquiry and field visit.

Estimates of Sampling Error: Estimated CV of 3 percent to 4 percent for estimates of national totals, but may be for estimated totals of more detailed characteristics, such as housing units in multiunit structures.

Other (nonsampling) Errors: Response rate is over 90 percent for most items. Nonsampling errors are attributed to definitional problems, differences in interpretation of questions, incorrect reporting, inability to obtain information about all cases in the sample, and processing errors.

Sources of Additional Material: U.S. Census Bureau, "New Residential Construction" at <http://www.census.gov/const/www/newsresconstindex.html>.

Nonemployer Statistics

Universe, Frequency, and Types of Data: Nonemployer statistics are an annual tabulation of economic data by industry for active businesses without paid employees that are subject to federal income tax. Data showing the number of establishments and receipts by industry are available for the United States, states, counties, and metropolitan areas. Most types of businesses covered by the Census Bureau's economic statistics programs are included in the nonemployer statistics. Tax-exempt and agricultural production businesses are excluded from nonemployer statistics.

Type of Data Collection Operation: The universe of nonemployer establishments is created annually as a by-product of the Census Bureau's Business Register processing for employer establishments. If a business is active but without paid employees, then it becomes part of the potential nonemployer universe. Industry classification and receipts are available for each potential nonemployer business. These data are obtained primarily from the annual business income tax returns of the Internal Revenue Service (IRS). The potential nonemployer universe undergoes a series of complex processing, editing, and analytical review procedures at the Census Bureau to distinguish nonemployers from employers, and to correct and complete data items used in creating the data tables.

Estimates of Sampling Error: Not applicable.

Other (nonsampling) Errors: The data are subject to nonsampling errors, such as errors of self-classification by industry on tax forms, as well as errors of response, keying, nonreporting, and coverage.

Sources of Additional Material: U.S. Census Bureau, *Nonemployer Statistics: 2002*, Introduction; Coverage and Methodology. See also <http://www.census.gov/epcd /nonemployer/view/cov&meth.htm>.

Population Estimates

Universe, Frequency, and Types of Data: The U.S. Census Bureau annually produces estimates of total resident population for each state and county. County population estimates are produced with a component of population change method, while the state population estimates are solely the sum of the county populations.

Type of Data Collection Operation: The Census Bureau develops county population estimates with a demographic procedure called an "administrative records component of population change" method. A major assumption underlying this approach is that the components of population change are closely approximated by administrative data in a demographic change model. In order to apply the model, Census Bureau demographers estimate each component of population change separately. For the population residing in households, the components of population change are births, deaths, and net migration, including net international migration. For the nonhousehold population, change is represented by the net change in the population living in group quarters facilities.

Estimates of Sampling Error: Not applicable.

Other (nonsampling) Errors: Not available.

Sources of Additional Material: U.S. Census Bureau, "Estimates and Projections Area Documentation, State and County Total Population Estimates," at <http://www .census.gov/popest/topics/methodology/2004_st_co _meth.pdf>. For methodological information on other population estimates datasets, such as "Housing Unit Estimates" and "State Population Estimates by Age, Sex, Race, and Hispanic Origin," see <http://www.census.gov/popest /topics/methodology/>.

U.S. DEPARTMENT OF EDUCATION

National Center for Education Statistics

Higher Education General Information Survey (HEGIS), Degrees and Other Formal Awards Conferred. Beginning 1986, Integrated Postsecondary Education Data Survey (IPEDS), Completions

Universe, Frequency, and Types of Data: Annual survey of all institutions and branches listed in the Education Directory, Colleges and Universities to obtain data on earned degrees and other formal awards, conferred by field of study, level of degree, sex, and by racial/ethnic characteristics (every other year prior to 1989, then annually).

Type of Data Collection Operation: Complete census.

Data Collection and Imputation Procedures: Data are collected through a Web-based survey in the fall of every year. Missing data are imputed by using data of similar institutions.

Estimates of Sampling Error: Not applicable.

Other (nonsampling) Errors: For 2002–2003, approximately 100.0 percent response rate for degree-granting institutions.

Sources of Additional Material: U.S. Department of Education, National Center for Education Statistics, *Postsecondary Institutions in the United States: Fall 2003 and Degrees and Other Awards Conferred: 2002–03*. For additional information, see Web site at <http://www.nces.ed .gov/ipeds/>.

U.S. FEDERAL BUREAU OF INVESTIGATION

Uniform Crime Reporting (UCR) Program

Universe, Frequency, and Types of Data: Monthly reports on the number of criminal offenses that become known to law enforcement agencies. Data are collected on crimes cleared by arrest; by age, sex, and race of arrestees and for victims and offenders for homicides; on fatal and nonfatal assaults against law enforcement officers; and on hate crimes reported.

Type of Data Collection Operation: Crime statistics are based on reports of crime data submitted either directly to the FBI by contributing law enforcement agencies or through cooperating state UCR programs.

Data Collection and Imputation Procedures: States with UCR programs collect data directly from individual law enforcement agencies and forward reports, prepared in accordance with UCR standards, to the FBI. Accuracy and consistency edits are performed by the FBI.

Estimates of Sampling Error: Not applicable.

Other (nonsampling) Errors: Coverage of 93 percent of the population (95 percent in MSAs, 85 percent in cities outside of metropolitan areas, and 83 percent in nonmetropolitan counties) by UCR Program, through varying number of agencies reporting.

Sources of Additional Material: U.S. Federal Bureau of Investigation, *Crime in the United States*, annual. For additional information, see Web site at <http://www.fbi.gov /ucr.htm>.

U.S. INTERNAL REVENUE SERVICE

Individual Income Tax Returns

Universe, Frequency, and Types of Data: Annual study of unaudited individual income tax returns, forms 1040, 1040A, and 1040EZ, filed by U.S. citizens and residents. Data provided on various financial characteristics by size of adjusted gross income, marital status, and by taxable and nontaxable returns. Data by state, based on 100 percent file, also include returns from 1040NR, filed by non-resident aliens, plus certain self-employment tax returns.

Type of Data Collection Operation: Annual 2002 strati-fied probability sample of approximately 176,000 returns broken into sample strata based on the larger of total income or total loss amounts as well as the size of busi-ness plus farm receipts. Sampling rates for sample strata varied from 0.05 percent to 100 percent.

Data Collection and Imputation Procedures: Com-puter selection of sample of tax return records. Data adjusted during editing for incorrect, missing, or inconsis-tent entries to ensure consistency with other entries on return.

Estimates of Sampling Error: Estimated CVs for tax year 2002: Adjusted gross income less deficit 0.12 per-cent; salaries and wages 0.21 percent; and tax-exempt interest received 1.78 percent. (State data not subject to sampling error.)

Other (nonsampling) Errors: Processing errors and errors arising from the use of tolerance checks for the data.

Sources of Additional Material: U.S. Internal Revenue Service, *Statistics of Income, Individual Income Tax Returns*, annual.

NATIONAL CENTER FOR HEALTH STATISTICS

National Vital Statistics System

Universe, Frequency, and Types of Data: Annual data on births and deaths in the United States.

Type of Data Collection Operation: Mortality data based on complete file of death records, except 1972, based on 50 percent sample. Natality statistics 1951–1971, based on 50 percent sample of birth certifi-cates, except a 20 percent to 50 percent sample in 1967, received by NCHS. Beginning 1972, data from some states received through Vital Statistics Cooperative Program (VSCP) and complete file used; data from other states based on 50 percent sample. Beginning 1986, all reporting areas participated in the VSCP.

Data Collection and Imputation Procedures: Reports based on records from registration offices of all states, District of Columbia, New York City, Puerto Rico, Virgin Islands, Guam, American Samoa, and Northern Mariana Islands.

Estimates of Sampling Error: For recent years, there is no sampling for these files; the files are based on 100 per-cent of events registered.

Other (nonsampling) Errors: Data on births and deaths believed to be at least 99 percent complete.

Sources of Additional Material: U.S. National Center for Health Statistics, *Vital Statistics of the United States*, Vol. I and Vol. II, annual, and National Vital Statistics Reports. NCHS Web site at <http://www.cdc.gov/nchs/nvss.htm>.

National Highway Traffic Safety Administration (NHTSA)

Fatality Analysis Reporting System (FARS)

Universe, Frequency, and Types of Data: FARS is a census of all fatal motor vehicle traffic crashes that occur throughout the United States, including the District of Columbia and Puerto Rico, on roadways customarily open to the public. The crash must be reported to the state/jurisdiction, and at least one directly related fatality must occur within 30 days of the crash.

Type of Data Collection Operation: One or more ana-lysts in each state extract data from the official documents and enter the data into a standardized electronic database.

Data Collection and Imputation Procedures: Detailed data describing the characteristics of the fatal crash and the vehicles and persons involved are obtained from police crash reports, driver and vehicle registration records, autopsy reports, highway department, etc. Com-puterized edit checks monitor the accuracy and complete-ness of the data. The FARS incorporates a sophisticated mathematical multiple imputation procedure to develop a probability distribution of missing blood alcohol concen-tration (BAC) levels in the database for drivers, pedestri-ans, and cyclists.

Estimates of Sampling Error: Since this is census data, there are no sampling errors.

Other (nonsampling) Errors: Fatal motor vehicle traffic crash data are more than 97 percent complete. However, these data are highly dependent on the accuracy of the police accident reports. Errors or omissions within police accident reports may not be detected.

Sources of Additional Material: The FARS Coding and Validation Manual, ANSI D16.1 Manual on Classification of Motor Vehicle Traffic Accidents (sixth edition).

Appendix C.
Geographic Concepts and Codes

Geographic Concepts

STATES

States are the major political units of the United States. The District of Columbia is treated as a state equivalent in this publication. Tables A-1 through A-87 present data for the United States, the 50 states, and the District of Columbia.

For census purposes, states are often grouped into geographic regions and divisions. For reference, these areas are delineated on the state map on the inside of the front cover. However, Table A only uses an alphabetical state presentation.

METROPOLITAN AND MICROPOLITAN STATISTICAL AREAS

The U.S. Office of Management and Budget (OMB) defines metropolitan and micropolitan statistical areas according to published standards that are applied to Census Bureau data. The general concept of a metropolitan or micropolitan statistical area is that of a core area containing a substantial population nucleus, together with adjacent communities having a high degree of economic and social integration with that core. The term "core based statistical area" (CBSA) refers collectively to metropolitan and micropolitan statistical areas.

The major purpose of CBSAs is to enable all federal agencies to use the same geographic definitions in tabulating and publishing data for metropolitan and micropolitan areas. The definitions are designed to serve a wide variety of statistical and analytical purposes; adoption of the area for any specific purpose should be judged in terms of appropriateness for that purpose. While the definitions have been developed for statistical use by federal agencies, state and local governments as well as private business firms have often found the definitions helpful in presenting data for metropolitan and micropolitan areas.

The official 2000 Standards for Defining Metropolitan and Micropolitan Statistical Areas may be found on the OMB Web site at <http://www.whitehouse.gov/omb/fedreg /metroareas122700.pdf>. OMB Bulletin 05-02, which was issued on February 22, 2005, provides the listing of metropolitan and micropolitan statistical areas found in this publication; this document and related documents may be found at

<http://www.whitehouse.gov/omb/bulletins/fy05/b05-02 .html>. OMB recently issued Bulletin 06-01, which contains some minor changes and updates; it may be found at <http://www.whitehouse.gov/omb/bulletins/fy2006 /b06-01.pdf>.

Metropolitan areas presented in tables B-1 through B-11 and C-1 through C-4 and micropolitan areas presented in table D-1 of this publication are those county-based areas defined originally as of June 6, 2003, and subsequently updated in December 2003 and November 2004. A series of maps showing these areas appears on pages C–4 to C–15.

Users who want to become more familiar with the metropolitan and micropolitan statistical area standards and how they are applied may contact the Population Division, U.S. Census Bureau, by e-mail at <pop@census.gov> or by telephone at 301-763-2422. Current metropolitan and micropolitan statistical area definitions and related updates are available through the Subjects A to Z area of the Census Bureau's Internet site <http://www.census .gov>. Copies of metropolitan and micropolitan statistical areas wall maps may be ordered through the Products and Services Staff, Geography Division, U.S. Census Bureau, at 301-763-1128.

Historical development. In 1910, the Bureau of the Census introduced "metropolitan districts" as an area classification. This marked the first use by the Bureau of the Census of a unit for reporting population data for large cities, together with their suburbs. Originally, only cities of at least 200,000 population were designated as the core of a metropolitan district. By 1940, the concept had been expanded to apply to a city of 50,000 or more inhabitants. The metropolitan district was generally defined to include contiguous minor civil divisions (MCDs) and incorporated places having a population density of at least 150 persons per square mile; therefore, the boundaries did not necessarily follow county lines.

A major limitation of the metropolitan district concept, from the standpoint of statistical presentation, was that not many data items beyond those available from the census of population and housing were available for MCDs and smaller places. The applicability of the metropolitan district concept also was limited because other generally similar area classifications were in use (e.g., the industrial areas of the census of manufactures and the labor market areas of the Labor Department's Employment and Training Administration), which were defined in different ways.

The standard metropolitan area (SMA) concept was developed in 1949 by the Bureau of the Budget (now OMB), with the advice of the newly established Federal Committee on Standard Metropolitan Areas, to overcome the above difficulties. It was designed so that a wide variety of statistical data on metropolitan areas might be presented for a uniform set of geographic areas. The SMAs consisted of one or more contiguous counties containing at least one city of 50,000 or more inhabitants. Additional counties had to meet certain criteria of metropolitan character and of social and economic integration with the central county in order to be included in an SMA.

Changes in the official criteria have been made at the time of each census since 1950. None of these changes have involved significant deviations from the basic metropolitan concept. Several modifications have been made in the rules for determining how large a city must be to have a metropolitan division defined. Criteria changes also have been made to reflect changing national conditions. For example, the 1949 rule specified that a county must have less than 25 percent of its workers engaged in agriculture. However, with a rapidly decreasing proportion of the population engaged in farming, this requirement has been eliminated because practically no counties are still affected by it. In 1959, the designation "standard metropolitan area" was changed to "standard metropolitan statistical area" (SMSA) to emphasize the nature and purpose of the areas. The SMSA designation was changed to the MSA/CMSA/PMSA designations in June 1983. The term "core based statistical area" (CBSA) was adopted in 2000 and refers collectively to metropolitan and micropolitan statistical areas.

Currently defined metropolitan and micropolitan statistical areas are based on application of 2000 standards that appeared in the Federal Register on December 27, 2000, to 2000 decennial census data. Current metropolitan and micropolitan statistical area definitions were announced by OMB effective June 6, 2003, and subsequently updated in December 2003 and November 2004.

Defining metropolitan and micropolitan statistical areas. The 2000 standards provide that each CBSA must contain at least one urban area of 10,000 or more population. Each metropolitan statistical area must have at least one urbanized area of 50,000 or more inhabitants. Each micropolitan statistical area must have at least one urban cluster of at least 10,000 but less than 50,000 population.

Under the standards, the county (or counties) in which at least 50 percent of the population resides within urban areas of 10,000 or more population, or that contain at least 5,000 people residing within a single urban area of 10,000 or more population, is identified as a "central county" (counties). Additional "outlying counties" are included in the CBSA if they meet specified requirements of commuting to or from the central counties. Counties or equivalent entities form the geographic "building blocks" for metropolitan and micropolitan statistical areas throughout the United States and Puerto Rico.

If specified criteria are met, a metropolitan statistical area containing a single core with a population of 2.5 million or more may be subdivided to form smaller groupings of counties referred to as "metropolitan divisions."

Principal cities and metropolitan and micropolitan statistical area titles. The largest city in each metropolitan or micropolitan statistical area is designated a "principal city." Additional cities qualify if specified requirements are met concerning population size and employment. The title of each metropolitan or micropolitan statistical area consists of the names of up to three of its principal cities and the name of each state into which the metropolitan or micropolitan statistical area extends. Titles of metropolitan divisions also typically are based on principal city names but in certain cases consist of county names.

Defining New England city and town areas. In view of the importance of cities and towns in New England, the 2000 standards also provide for a set of geographic areas that are defined using cities and towns in the six New England states. The New England city and town areas (NECTAs) are defined using the same criteria as metropolitan and micropolitan statistical areas and are identified as either metropolitan or micropolitan, based, respectively, on the presence of either an urbanized area of 50,000 or more population or an urban cluster of at least 10,000 but less than 50,000 population. If the specified criteria are met, a NECTA containing a single core with a population of at least 2.5 million may be subdivided to form smaller groupings of cities and towns referred to as New England city and town area divisions.

Changes in definitions over time. Changes in the definitions of these statistical areas since the 1950 census have consisted chiefly of—

- The recognition of new areas as they reached the minimum required city or urbanized area population.

- The addition of counties (or cities and towns in New England) to existing areas as new decennial census data showed them to qualify.

In some instances, formerly separate areas have been merged, components of an area have been transferred from one area to another, or components have been dropped from an area. The large majority of changes have taken place on the basis of decennial census data. However, Census Bureau data serve as the basis for intercensal updates in specified circumstances.

Because of these historical changes in geographic definitions, users must be cautious in comparing data for these statistical areas from different dates. For some purposes, comparisons of data for areas as defined at given dates may be appropriate; for other purposes, it may be preferable to maintain consistent area definitions. Historical metropolitan area definitions are available for 1999, 1993, 1990, 1983, 1981, 1973, 1970, 1963, 1960, and 1950.

Special metropolitan area notes found in this publication. This report includes metropolitan statistical areas and consolidated metropolitan statistical areas defined by the Office of Management and Budget as of June 6, 2003, and subsequently updated in December 2003 and November 2004. There are 361 metropolitan statistical areas and 575 micropolitan statistical areas in the United States. In addition, there are 8 metropolitan statistical areas and 5 micropolitan statistical areas in Puerto Rico not covered in this publication. Every state now has at least one metropolitan area; New Jersey and the District of Columbia are wholly included in metropolitan areas.

There are two metropolitan areas that we want to specially note for users. First, the Denver, CO, metropolitan had the special case involving the newly created county of Broomfield. Broomfield County, CO, was formed from parts of Adams, Boulder, Jefferson, and Weld Counties, CO, on November 15, 2001, and is coextensive with Broomfield city. For purposes of defining and presenting data for metropolitan statistical areas, Broomfield city is treated as if it were a county at the time of the 1990 and 2000 censuses. The other area is the St. Louis, MO-IL area. A portion of Sullivan city in Crawford County, MO, is legally part of the St. Louis, MO-IL MSA. Census 2000 tabulations and intercensal estimates for the St. Louis, MO-IL metropolitan statistical area do not include this small area.

COUNTIES

The primary political divisions of most states are termed "counties," which are the basic building blocks for metropolitan areas. In Louisiana, these divisions are known as "parishes." In Alaska, which has no counties, the county equivalents are the organized "boroughs" and the "census areas" that are delineated for statistical purposes by the State of Alaska and the Census Bureau. In four states (Maryland, Missouri, Nevada, and Virginia), there are one or more cities that are independent of any county organization and thus constitute primary divisions of their states. These cities are known as "independent cities" and are treated as equivalent to counties for statistical purposes. The District of Columbia has no primary divisions, and the entire area is considered equivalent to a county for statistical purposes.

Tables C-1 through C-4 present data for the 361 metropolitan statistical areas and their 1,090 component counties defined as of November 2004. Table D-1 presents data for the 575 micropolitan statistical areas and their 692 counties likewise as defined as of November 2004.

Geographic Codes

STATES

Each state and equivalent is assigned a two-digit Federal Information Processing Standards (FIPS) code in alphabetic order by state name; codes range from 01 for Alabama to 56 for Wyoming. These codes are published by the National Institute of Standards and Technology (NIST), U.S. Department of Commerce, in FIPS Publication 5-2 (issued May 28, 1987) and related updates, which can be viewed at Internet site <http://www.itl.nist.gov/fipspubs/>. Each state and equivalent area is also assigned a two-letter FIPS/United States Postal Service (USPS) code. These two codes are included in the Excel spreadsheet version of tables A-1 through A-87 of this publication.

METROPOLITAN AND MICROPOLITAN STATISTICAL AREAS

Each metropolitan and micropolitan statistical area is assigned a five-digit CBSA code, in alphabetical order nationwide. This five-digit code applies to the CBSA and its component counties and metropolitan divisions where appropriate. These codes and updates can be viewed at Internet site <http://www.census.gov/population/www /estimates/metrodef.html>. These codes are included in the CD-ROM version of tables B-1 through B-11, C-1 through C-4, and D-1 of this publication.

COUNTIES

Each county and county equivalent is assigned a three-digit FIPS code that is unique within a state. These codes are designed in alphabetic order of county or county equivalent within a state, except for independent cities, which follow the listing of counties. In most states, the codes begin with 001 and generally continue in increments of two; the county codes for independent cities are assigned in alphabetic sequence beginning with 510 and generally continuing in increments of 10. These codes are published by NIST in FIPS Publication 6-4 (issued August 31, 1990) and related updates, which can be viewed at Internet site <http://www.itl.nist.gov/fipspubs/>. For a county code to be unique for the nation, it is combined with its two-digit FIPS state code. These five-digit codes appear next to the county name on the CD-ROM version of tables C-1 through C-4 and D-1 of this publication.

METROPOLITAN DIVISIONS

Each metropolitan division is assigned a five-digit CBSA division code that it shares with only those counties within the metropolitan division. These codes and updates can be viewed at Internet site <http://www.census.gov /population/www/estimates/metrodef.html>. These codes appear in the Excel spreadsheet versions of all Tables B and C of this publication.

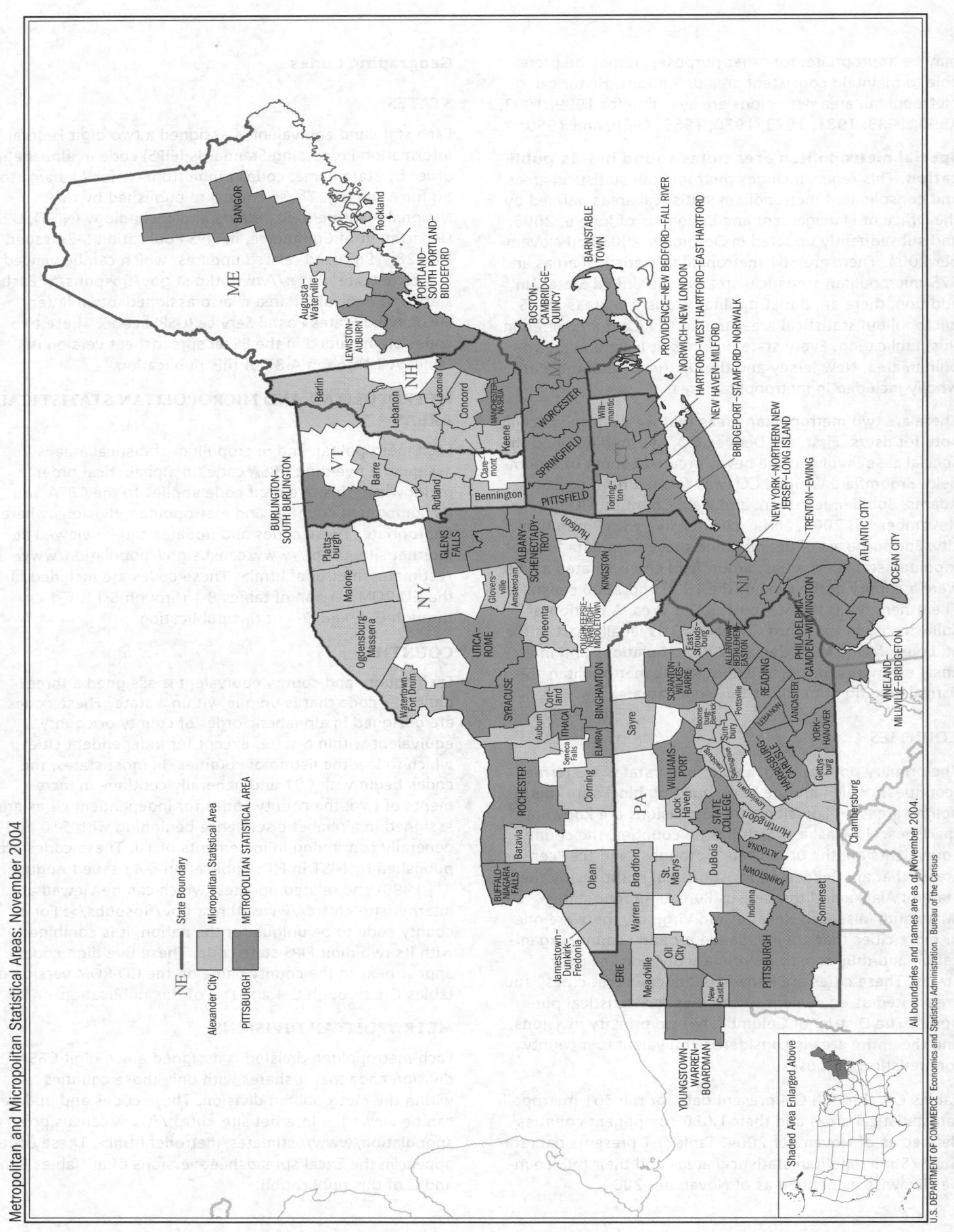

Metropolitan and Micropolitan Statistical Areas: November 2004

NE

State Boundary

Alexander City — Micropolitan Statistical Area

PITTSBURGH — METROPOLITAN STATISTICAL AREA

All boundaries and names are as of November 2004.

U.S. DEPARTMENT OF COMMERCE Economics and Statistics Administration Bureau of the Census

Shaded Area Enlarged Above

Metropolitan and Micropolitan Statistical Areas: November 2004

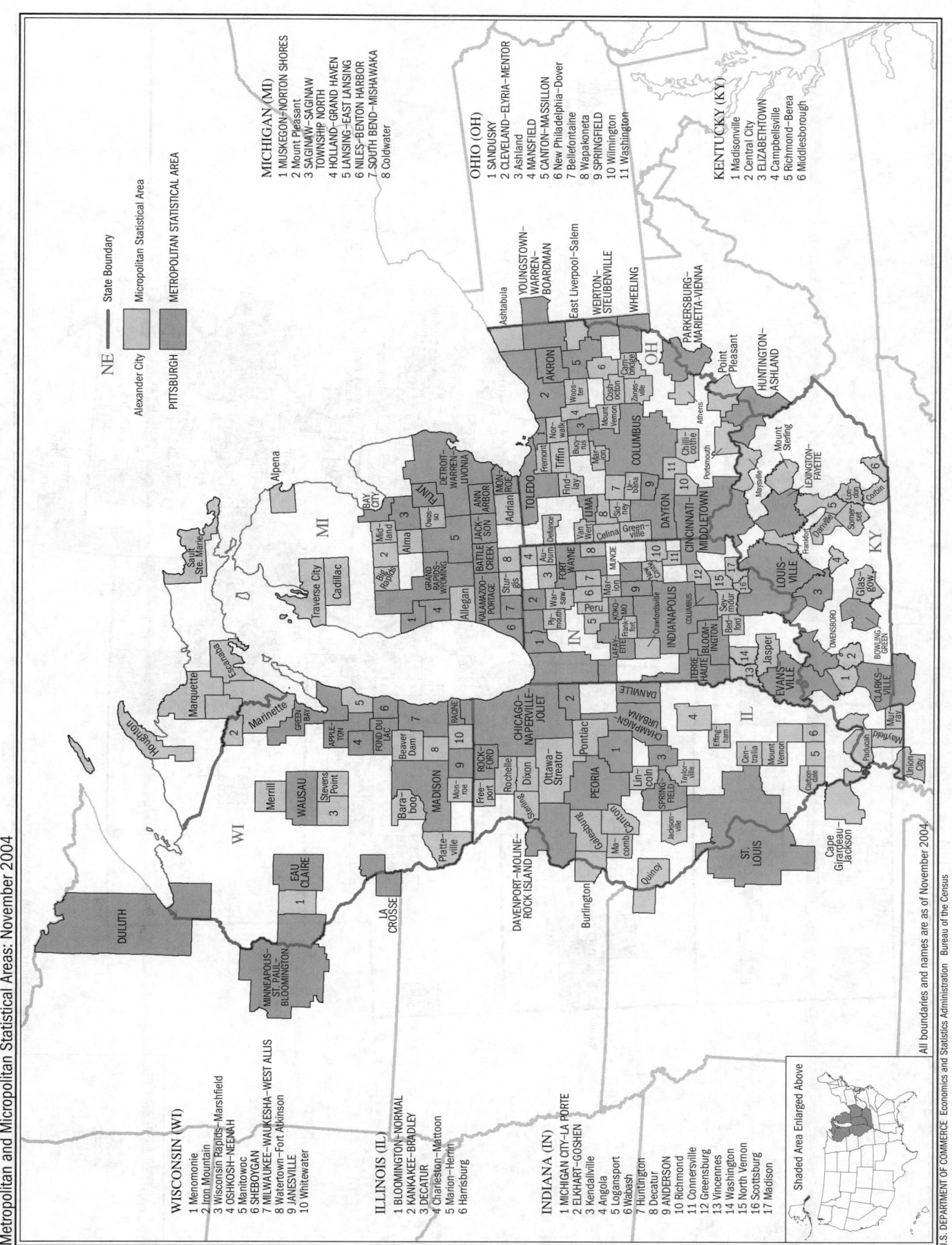

State and Metropolitan Area Data Book: 2006

U.S. Census Bureau

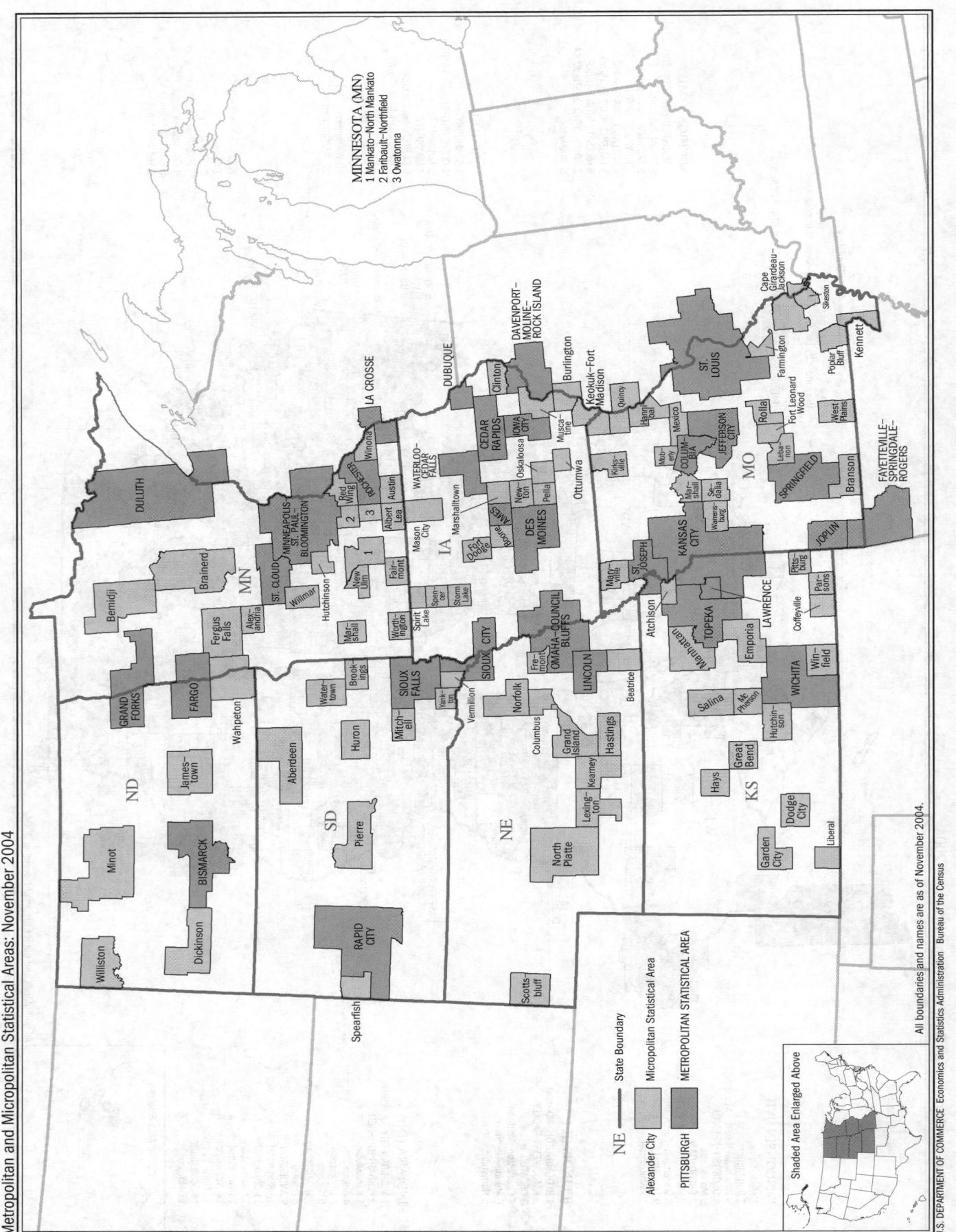

MINNESOTA (MN)
1 Mankato–North Mankato
2 Faribault–Northfield
3 Owatonna

Cape Girardeau–Jackson
Sikeston
Kennett
St. Louis
Poplar Bluff
West Plains
Farmington
Fort Leonard Wood
Rolla
Lebanon
MO
Springfield
Branson
FAYETTEVILLE–SPRINGDALE–ROGERS
JOPLIN

DAVENPORT–MOLINE–ROCK ISLAND
LA CROSSE
DUBUQUE
Burlington
Clinton
Keokuk–Fort Madison
Quincy
Hannibal
Mexico
Moberly
Columbia
Jefferson City
Marshall
Sedalia
Warrensburg
KANSAS CITY
ST. JOSEPH
Atchison
Maryville
Mary-ville
Pittsburg
Coffeyville
Parsons
LAWRENCE
TOPEKA
Manhattan
Emporia
Winfield
WICHITA
Salina
McPherson
Hutchinson
Great Bend
Hays
KS
Dodge City
Liberal
Garden City

Winona
ROCHESTER
Red Wing
Austin
Albert Lea
WATERLOO–CEDAR FALLS
CEDAR RAPIDS
IOWA CITY
Muscatine
New Oskaloosa
ton
Pella
Ottumwa
Kirks-ville
Marshalltown
Mason City
Fort Dodge
Boone
AMES
DES MOINES
IA
New Ulm
Fair-mont
Spirit Lake
Storm Lake
Steen-ber
Wor-thington
Spencer

DULUTH
Bemidji
Brainerd
MN
ST. CLOUD
MINNEAPOLIS ST. PAUL–BLOOMINGTON
Willmar
Hutchinson
Alex-andria
Fergus Falls
Marshall
2
3
1

Minot
Williston
Dickinson
BISMARCK
ND
James-town
GRAND FORKS
FARGO
Wahpeton
Aberdeen
SD
Pierre
Watertown
Brookings
Huron
Mitch-ell
SIOUX FALLS
Yank-ton
Vermillion
SIOUX CITY
Norfolk
Columbus
Fremont
OMAHA–COUNCIL BLUFFS
LINCOLN
Beatrice
NE
Grand Island
Kearney
Hastings
Lexing-ton
North Platte
Scotts-bluff
Spearfish
RAPID CITY

Shaded Area Enlarged Above

NE — State Boundary
Alexander City — Micropolitan Statistical Area
PITTSBURGH — METROPOLITAN STATISTICAL AREA

All boundaries and names are as of November 2004.

U.S. DEPARTMENT OF COMMERCE Economics and Statistics Administration Bureau of the Census

Metropolitan and Micropolitan Statistical Areas: November 2004

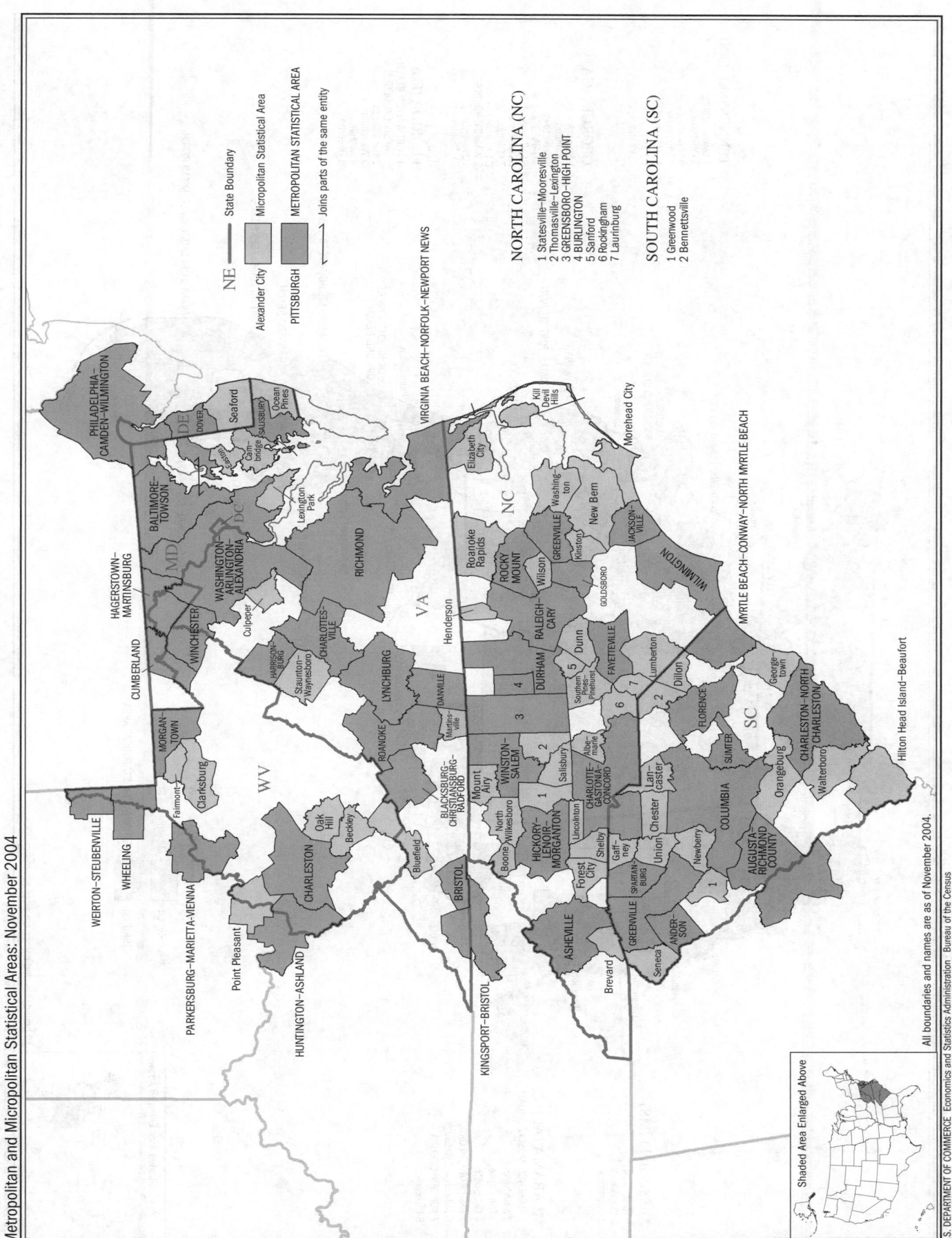

NE ——— State Boundary

Alexander City — Micropolitan Statistical Area

PITTSBURGH — METROPOLITAN STATISTICAL AREA

↑ Joins parts of the same entity

NORTH CAROLINA (NC)
1 Statesville–Mooresville
2 Thomasville–Lexington
3 GREENSBORO–HIGH POINT
4 BURLINGTON
5 Sanford
6 Rockingham
7 Laurinburg

SOUTH CAROLINA (SC)
1 Greenwood
2 Bennettsville

All boundaries and names are as of November 2004.

U.S. DEPARTMENT OF COMMERCE Economics and Statistics Administration Bureau of the Census

Shaded Area Enlarged Above

State and Metropolitan Area Data Book: 2006

U.S. Census Bureau

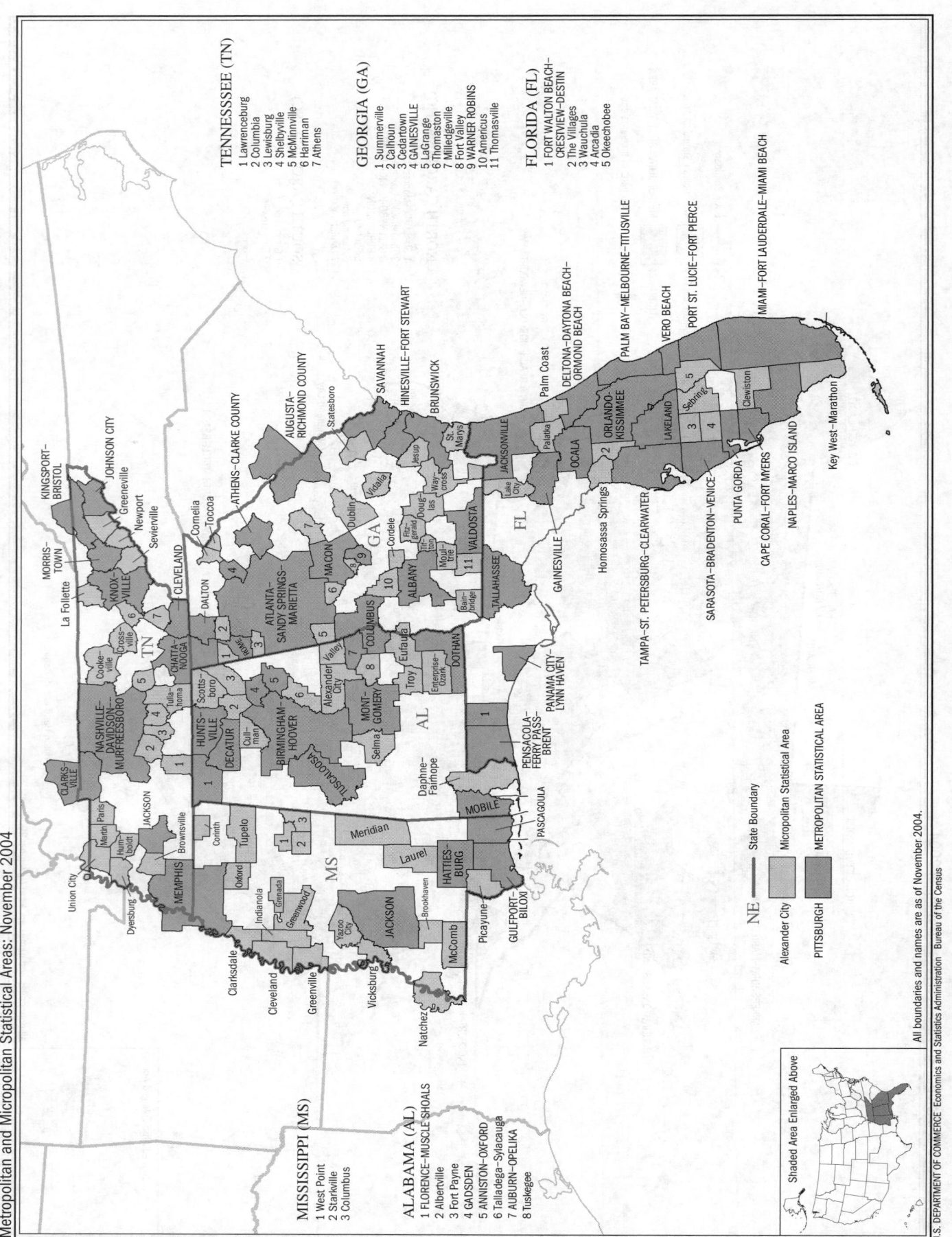

Metropolitan and Micropolitan Statistical Areas: November 2004

TENNESSEE (TN)
1 Lawrenceburg
2 Columbia
3 Lewisburg
4 Shelbyville
5 McMinnville
6 Harriman
7 Athens

GEORGIA (GA)
1 Summerville
2 Calhoun
3 Cedartown
4 GAINESVILLE
5 LaGrange
6 Thomaston
7 Milledgeville
8 Fort Valley
9 WARNER ROBINS
10 Americus
11 Thomasville

FLORIDA (FL)
1 FORT WALTON BEACH–
   CRESTVIEW–DESTIN
2 The Villages
3 Wauchula
4 Arcadia
5 Okeechobee

MISSISSIPPI (MS)
1 West Point
2 Starkville
3 Columbus

ALABAMA (AL)
1 FLORENCE–MUSCLE SHOALS
2 Albertville
3 Fort Payne
4 GADSDEN
5 ANNISTON–OXFORD
6 Talladega–Sylacauga
7 AUBURN–OPELIKA
8 Tuskegee

NE Alexander City
PITTSBURGH

— State Boundary
   Micropolitan Statistical Area
   METROPOLITAN STATISTICAL AREA

All boundaries and names are as of November 2004.

Shaded Area Enlarged Above

U.S. DEPARTMENT OF COMMERCE Economics and Statistics Administration Bureau of the Census

State and Metropolitan Area Data Book: 2006

U.S. Census Bureau

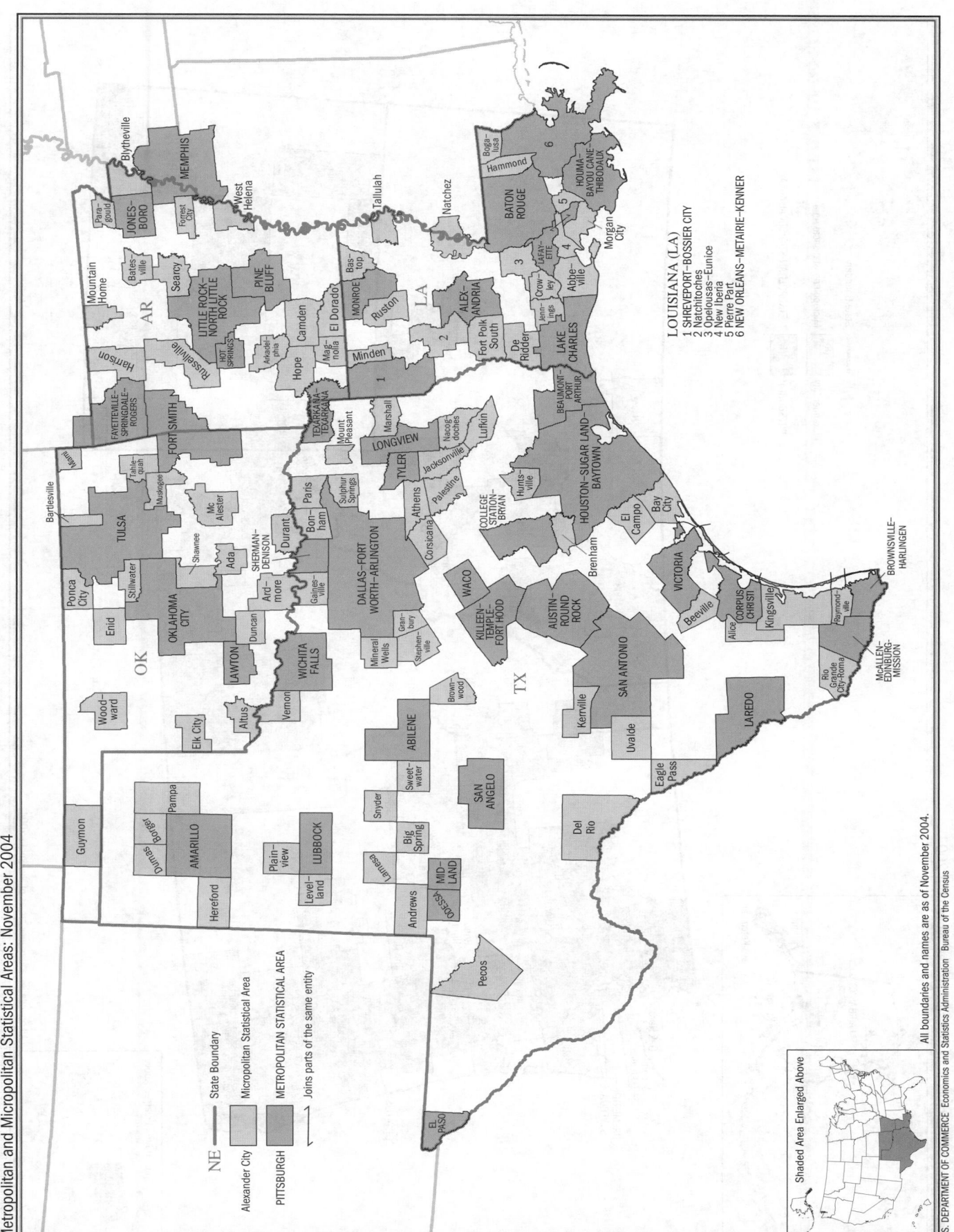

Metropolitan and Micropolitan Statistical Areas: November 2004

NE — State Boundary

Alexander City — Micropolitan Statistical Area

PITTSBURGH — METROPOLITAN STATISTICAL AREA

⌐ Joins parts of the same entity

LOUISIANA (LA)
1 SHREVEPORT–BOSSIER CITY
2 NATCHITOCHES
3 OPELOUSAS–EUNICE
4 NEW IBERIA
5 PIERRE PART
6 NEW ORLEANS–METAIRIE–KENNER

All boundaries and names are as of November 2004.

U.S. DEPARTMENT OF COMMERCE Economics and Statistics Administration Bureau of the Census

Shaded Area Enlarged Above

Metropolitan and Micropolitan Statistical Areas: November 2004

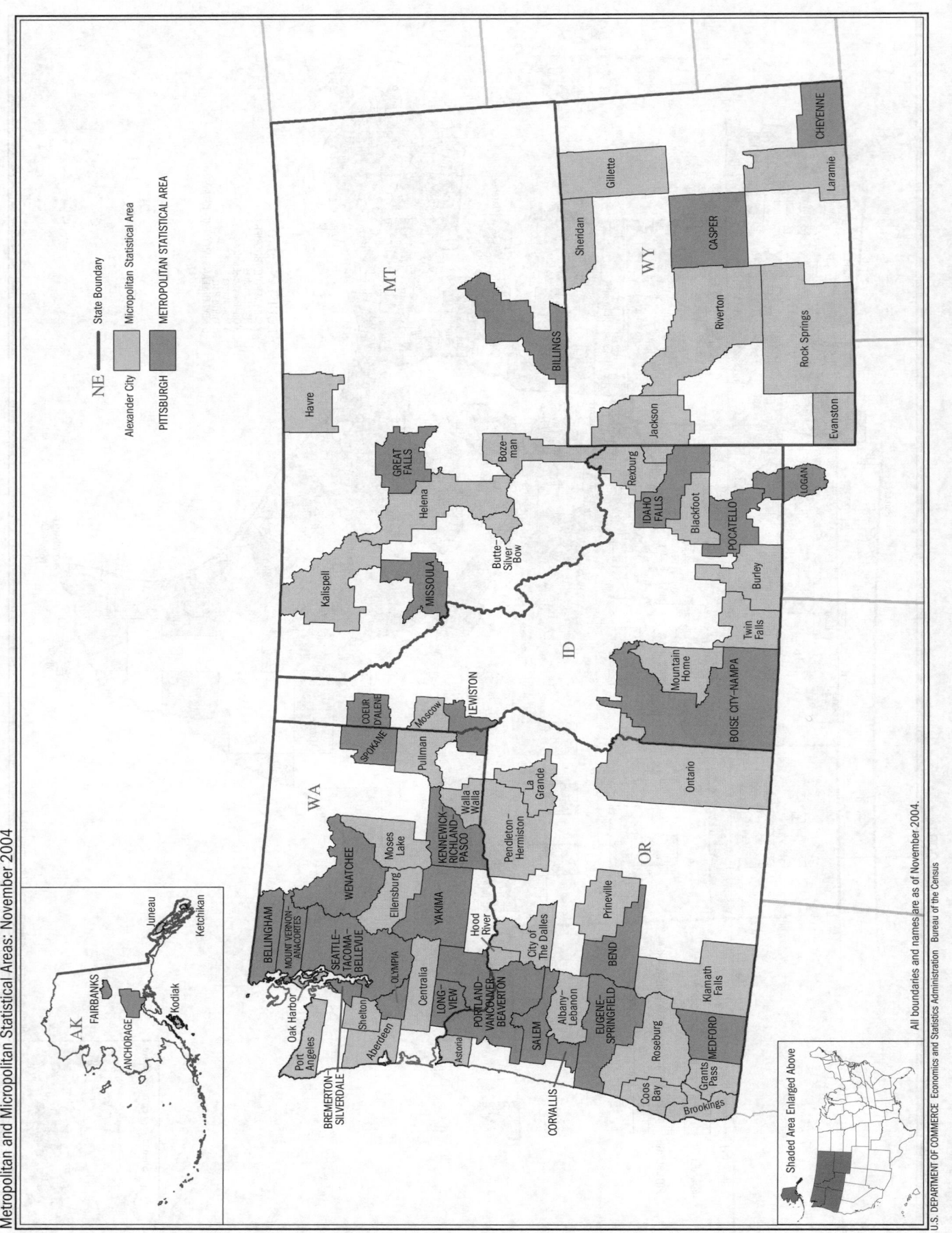

NE

State Boundary

Alexander City — Micropolitan Statistical Area

PITTSBURGH — METROPOLITAN STATISTICAL AREA

Shaded Area Enlarged Above

All boundaries and names are as of November 2004.

U.S. DEPARTMENT OF COMMERCE Economics and Statistics Administration Bureau of the Census

Metropolitan and Micropolitan Statistical Areas: November 2004

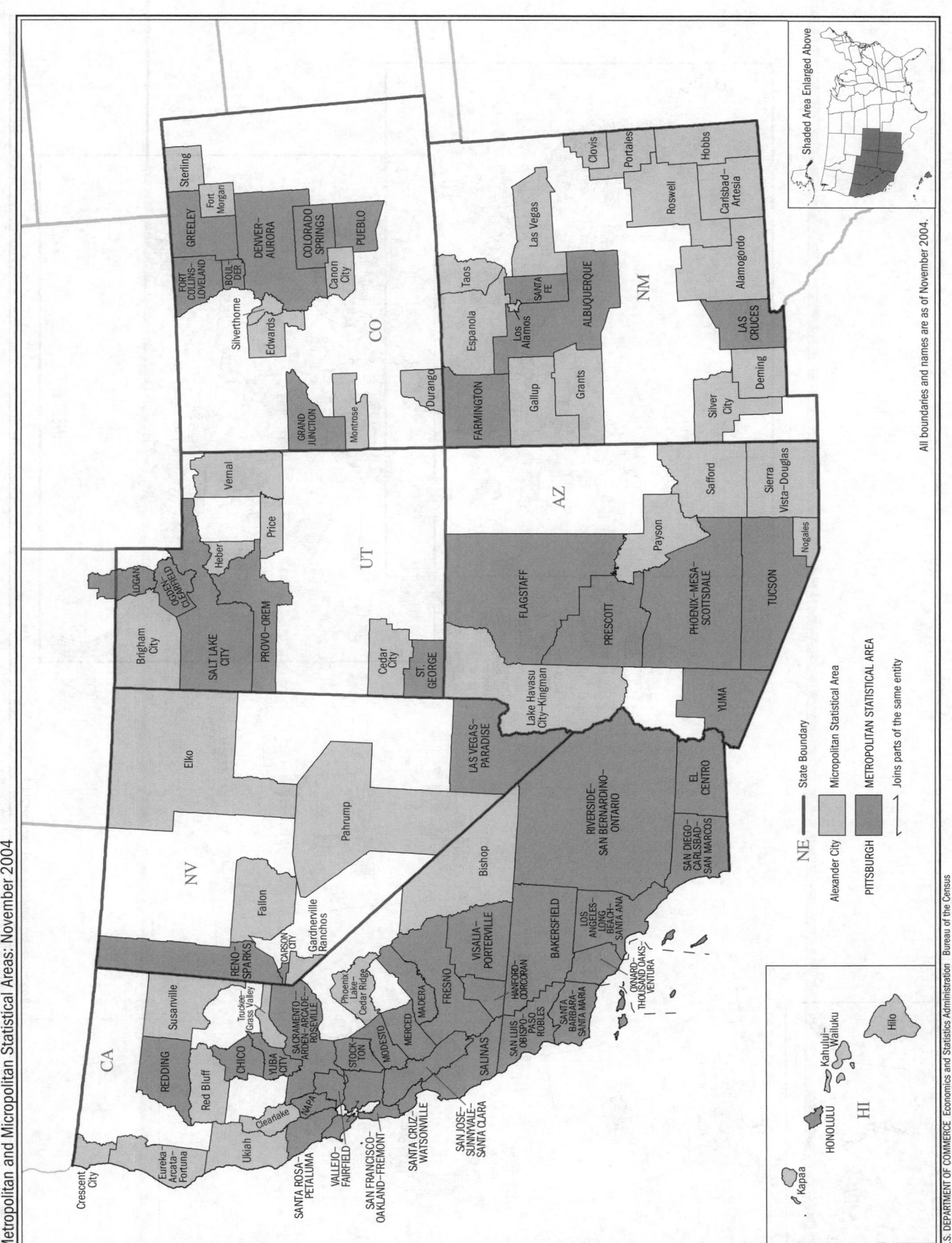

All boundaries and names are as of November 2004.

Shaded Area Enlarged Above

CO

NM

AZ

UT

NV

CA

HI

Sterling
Fort Morgan
GREELEY
FORT COLLINS-LOVELAND
BOULDER
DENVER-AURORA
COLORADO SPRINGS
PUEBLO
Canon City
Silverthorne
Edwards
GRAND JUNCTION
Montrose
Durango

Clovis
Portales
Hobbs
Roswell
Carlsbad-Artesia
Las Vegas
Santa Fe
ALBUQUERQUE
Alamogordo
LAS CRUCES
Taos
Espanola
Los Alamos
Gallup
Grants
FARMINGTON
Silver City
Deming

Safford
Sierra Vista-Douglas
Nogales
Payson
FLAGSTAFF
PRESCOTT
PHOENIX-MESA-SCOTTSDALE
TUCSON
YUMA
Lake Havasu City-Kingman

Vernal
Price
Heber
LOGAN
OGDEN-CLEARFIELD
Brigham City
SALT LAKE CITY
PROVO-OREM
Cedar City
ST GEORGE

Elko
Pahrump
Fallon
Gardnerville Ranchos
CARSON CITY
RENO-SPARKS

LAS VEGAS-PARADISE
Bishop

RIVERSIDE-SAN BERNARDINO-ONTARIO
EL CENTRO
SAN DIEGO-CARLSBAD-SAN MARCOS

Susanville
REDDING
Red Bluff
CHICO
YUBA CITY
Truckee-Grass Valley
SACRAMENTO-ARDEN-ARCADE-ROSEVILLE
Phoenix Lake-Cedar Ridge
STOCKTON
MODESTO
MERCED
MADERA
FRESNO
VISALIA-PORTERVILLE
HANFORD-CORCORAN
BAKERSFIELD
LOS ANGELES-LONG BEACH-SANTA ANA
OXNARD-THOUSAND OAKS-VENTURA
SANTA BARBARA-SANTA MARIA
SAN LUIS OBISPO-PASO ROBLES
SALINAS
SAN JOSE-SUNNYVALE-SANTA CLARA
SANTA CRUZ-WATSONVILLE
SAN FRANCISCO-OAKLAND-FREMONT
VALLEJO-FAIRFIELD
NAPA
Clearlake
Ukiah
SANTA ROSA-PETALUMA
Eureka-Arcata-Fortuna
Crescent City

Kapaa
HONOLULU
Kahului-Wailuku
Hilo

NE — State Boundary
Alexander City — Micropolitan Statistical Area
PITTSBURGH — METROPOLITAN STATISTICAL AREA
Joins parts of the same entity

U.S. DEPARTMENT OF COMMERCE Economics and Statistics Administration Bureau of the Census

State and Metropolitan Area Data Book: 2006

C-11

U.S. Census Bureau

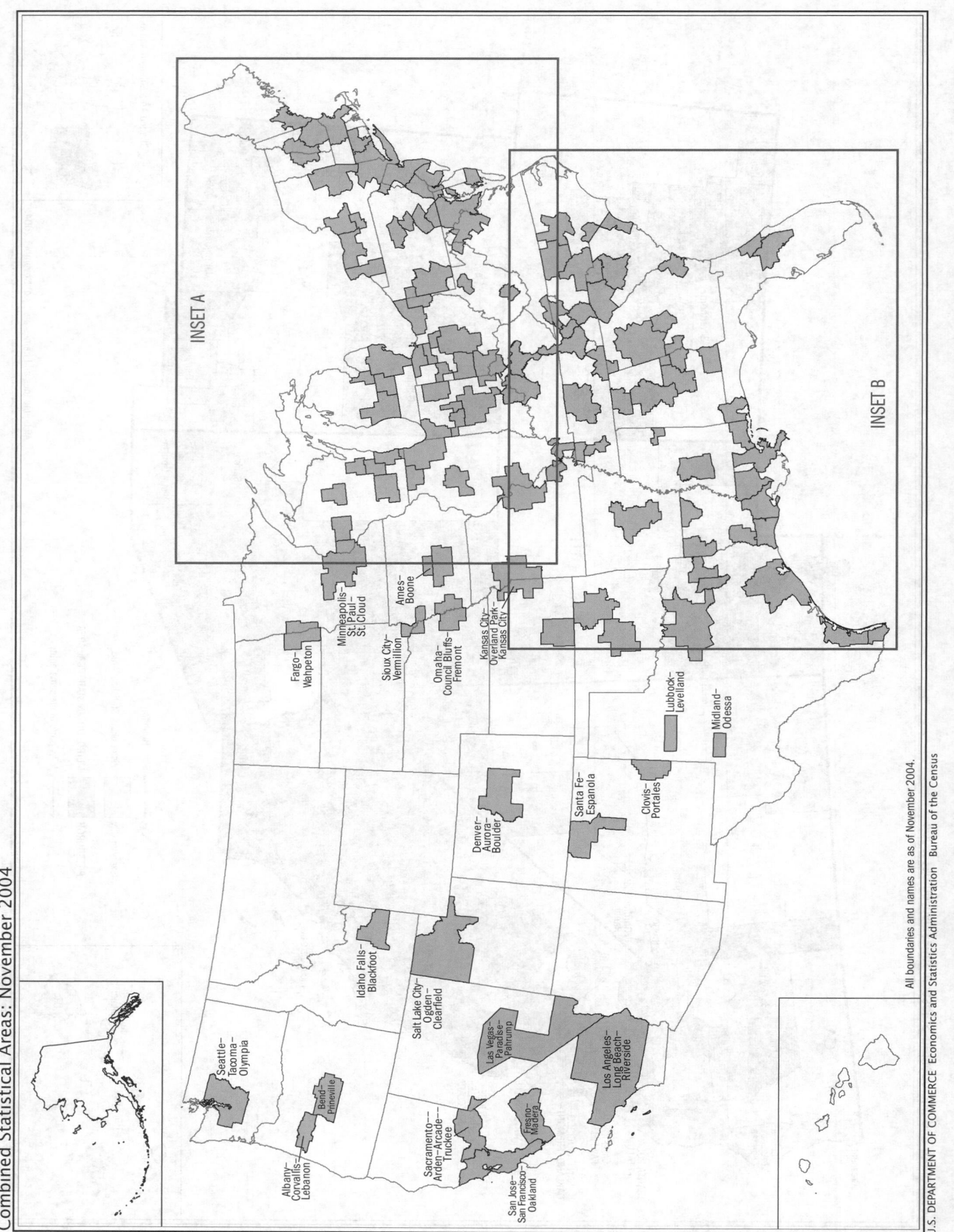

INSET A

INSET B

Fargo–
Wahpeton

Minneapolis–
St. Paul–
St. Cloud

Ames–
Boone

Sioux City–
Vermillion

Omaha–
Council Bluffs–
Fremont

Kansas City–
Overland Park–
Kansas City

Lubbock–
Leveland

Midland–
Odessa

Denver–
Aurora–
Boulder

Santa Fe–
Espanola

Clovis–
Portales

Idaho Falls–
Blackfoot

Salt Lake City–
Ogden–
Clearfield

Seattle–
Tacoma–
Olympia

Bend–
Prineville

Las Vegas–
Paradise–
Pahrump

Los Angeles–
Long Beach–
Riverside

Albany–
Corvallis–
Lebanon

Sacramento–
Arden-Arcade–
Truckee

Fresno–
Madera

San Jose–
San Francisco–
Oakland

All boundaries and names are as of November 2004.

U.S. DEPARTMENT OF COMMERCE Economics and Statistics Administration Bureau of the Census

Combined Statistical Areas: November 2004 - INSET A

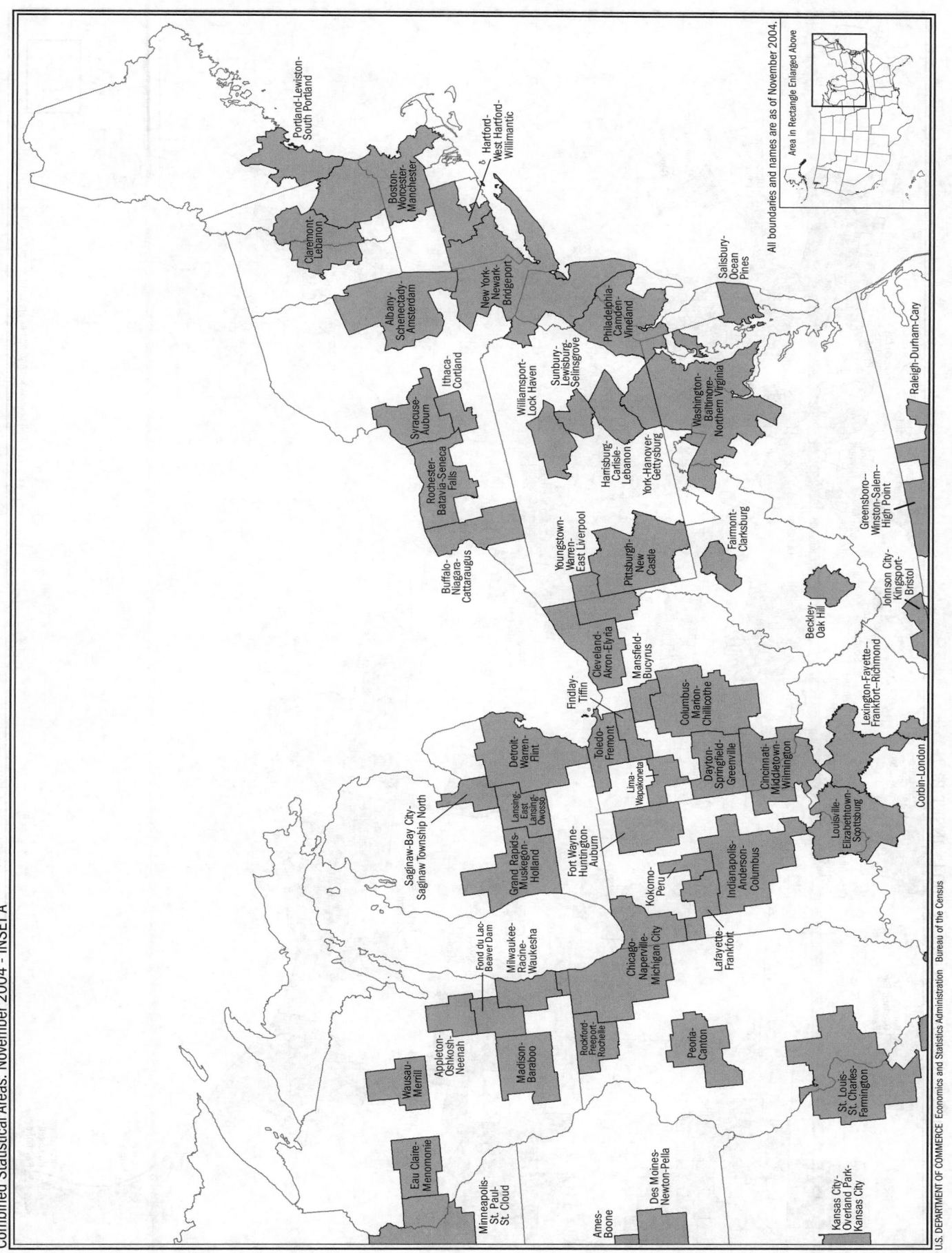

Portland-Lewiston-South Portland

Hartford-West Hartford-Willimantic

Boston-Worcester-Manchester

Claremont-Lebanon

Albany-Schenectady-Amsterdam

New York-Newark-Bridgeport

Philadelphia-Camden-Vineland

Salisbury-Ocean Pines

Ithaca-Cortland

Williamsport-Lock Haven

Sunbury-Lewisburg-Selinsgrove

Washington-Baltimore-Northern Virginia

Raleigh-Durham-Cary

Syracuse-Auburn

Harrisburg-Carlisle-Lebanon

York-Hanover-Gettysburg

Greensboro-Winston-Salem-High Point

Rochester-Batavia-Seneca Falls

Fairmont-Clarksburg

Buffalo-Niagara-Cattaraugus

Youngstown-Warren-East Liverpool

Pittsburgh-New Castle

Johnson City-Kingsport-Bristol

Beckley-Oak Hill

Cleveland-Akron-Elyria

Mansfield-Bucyrus

Lexington-Fayette--Frankfort-Richmond

Findlay-Tiffin

Columbus-Marion-Chillicothe

Corbin-London

Detroit-Warren-Flint

Toledo-Fremont

Dayton-Springfield-Greenville

Cincinnati-Middletown-Wilmington

Louisville-Elizabethtown-Scottsburg

Saginaw-Bay City-Saginaw Township North

Lansing-East Lansing-Owosso

Lima-Wapakoneta

Grand Rapids-Muskegon-Holland

Fort Wayne-Huntington-Auburn

Kokomo-Peru

Indianapolis-Anderson-Columbus

Fond du Lac-Beaver Dam

Milwaukee-Racine-Waukesha

Chicago-Naperville-Michigan City

Lafayette-Frankfort

Appleton-Oshkosh-Neenah

Madison-Baraboo

Rockford-Freeport-Rochelle

Peoria-Canton

Wausau-Merrill

Eau Claire-Menomonie

St. Louis-St. Charles-Farmington

Minneapolis-St. Paul-St. Cloud

Ames-Boone

Des Moines-Newton-Pella

Kansas City-Overland Park-Kansas City

All boundaries and names are as of November 2004.

Area in Rectangle Enlarged Above

U.S. DEPARTMENT OF COMMERCE Economics and Statistics Administration Bureau of the Census

State and Metropolitan Area Data Book: 2006

C-13

U.S. Census Bureau

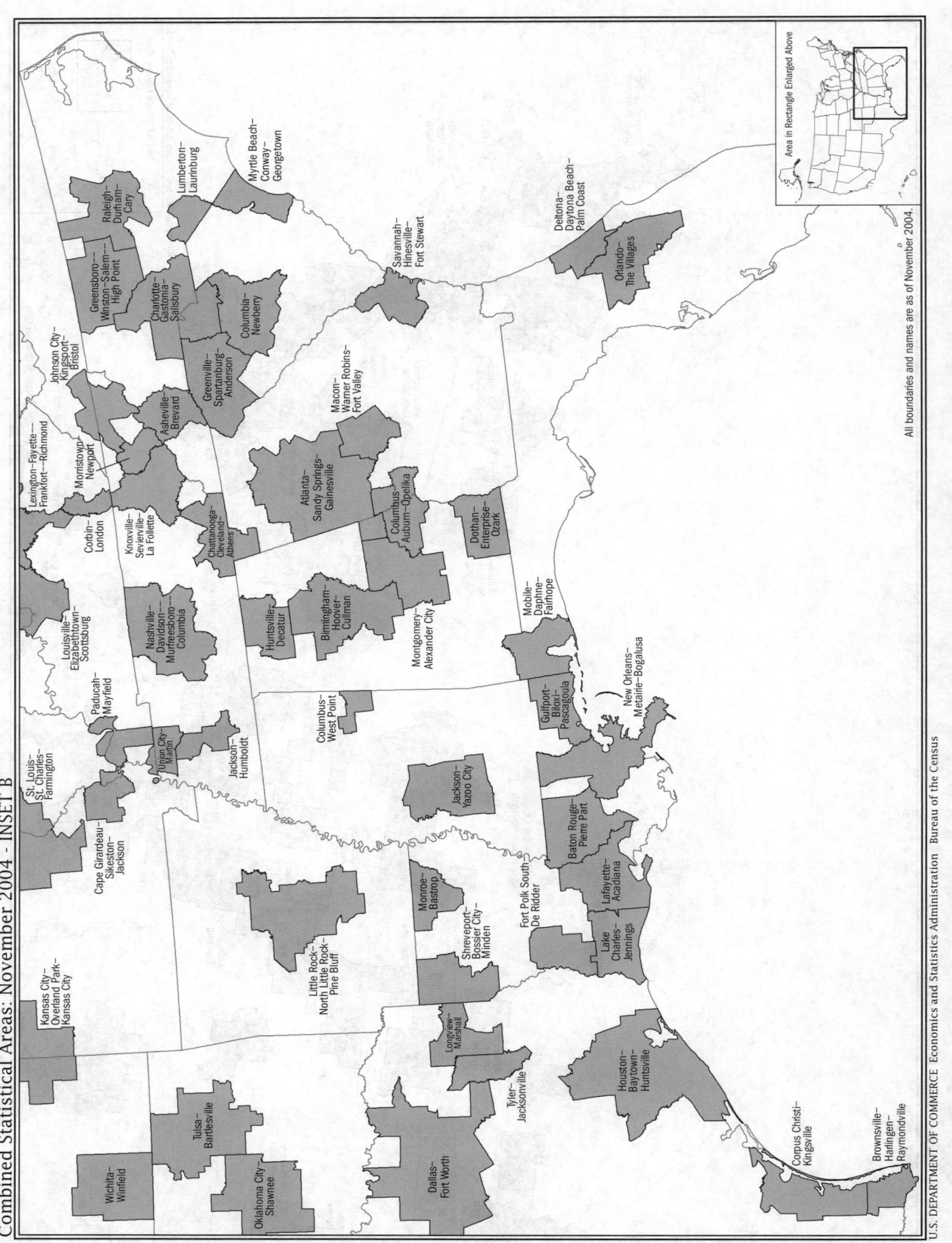

Area in Rectangle Enlarged Above

All boundaries and names are as of November 2004.

Raleigh–Durham–Cary

Lumberton–Laurinburg

Myrtle Beach–Conway–Georgetown

Greensboro–Winston-Salem–High Point

Charlotte–Gastonia–Salisbury

Columbia–Newberry

Deltona–Daytona Beach–Palm Coast

Orlando–The Villages

Savannah–Hinesville–Fort Stewart

Johnson City–Kingsport–Bristol

Greenville–Spartanburg–Anderson

Lexington–Fayette Frankfort–Richmond

Morristown–Newport

Asheville–Brevard

Macon–Warner Robins–Fort Valley

Corbin–London

Knoxville–Sevierville–La Follette

Chattanooga–Cleveland–Athens

Atlanta–Sandy Springs–Gainesville

Columbus–Auburn–Opelika

Dothan–Enterprise–Ozark

Louisville–Elizabethtown–Scottsburg

Nashville–Davidson–Murfreesboro–Columbia

Huntsville–Decatur

Birmingham–Hoover–Cullman

Montgomery–Alexander City

Mobile–Daphne–Fairhope

New Orleans–Metairie–Bogalusa

Paducah–Mayfield

Columbus–West Point

Gulfport–Biloxi–Pascagoula

St. Louis–St. Charles–Farmington

Union City–Martin

Jackson–Humboldt

Jackson–Yazoo City

Baton Rouge–Pierre Part

Cape Girardeau–Sikeston–Jackson

Lafayette–Acadiana

Monroe–Bastrop

Fort Polk South–De Ridder

Lake Charles–Jennings

Kansas City–Overland Park–Kansas City

Little Rock–North Little Rock–Pine Bluff

Shreveport–Bossier City–Minden

Longview–Marshall

Houston–Baytown–Huntsville

Tyler–Jacksonville

Tulsa–Bartlesville

Corpus Christi–Kingsville

Wichita–Winfield

Oklahoma City–Shawnee

Dallas–Fort Worth

Brownsville–Harlingen–Raymondville

U.S. DEPARTMENT OF COMMERCE Economics and Statistics Administration Bureau of the Census

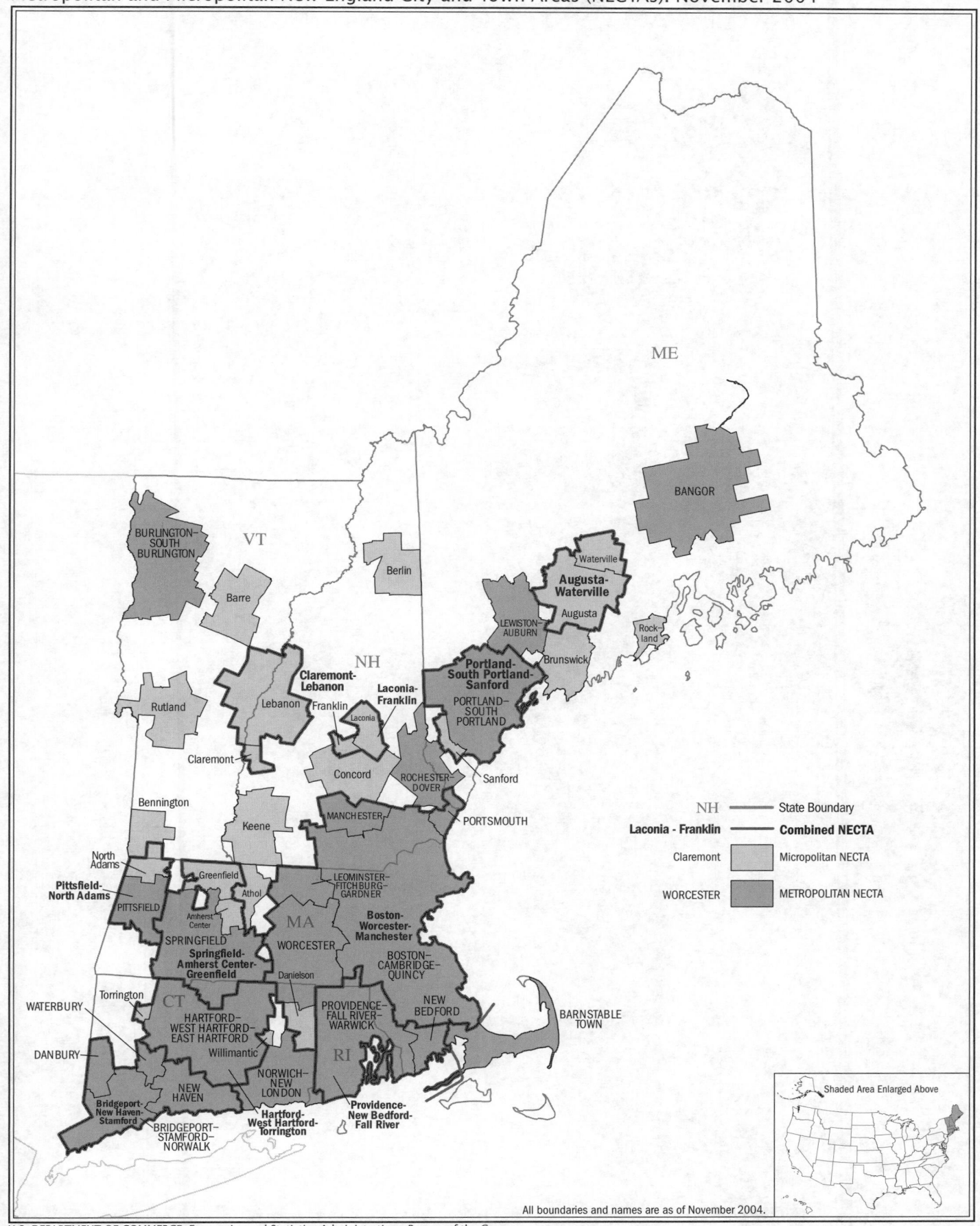

ME

VT

BURLINGTON-
SOUTH
BURLINGTON

Barre

Berlin

BANGOR

Waterville

**Augusta-
Waterville**

Augusta

NH

Rutland

Claremont-
Lebanon

Lebanon

Franklin

Laconia-
Franklin

Laconia

LEWISTON-
AUBURN

Brunswick

Rock-
land

**Portland-
South Portland-
Sanford**

PORTLAND-
SOUTH
PORTLAND

Claremont

Concord

ROCHESTER-
DOVER

Sanford

Bennington

Keene

MANCHESTER

PORTSMOUTH

North
Adams

Greenfield

**Pittsfield-
North Adams**

PITTSFIELD

Athol

LEOMINSTER-
FITCHBURG-
GARDNER

Amherst
Center

MA

**Boston-
Worcester-
Manchester**

SPRINGFIELD

WORCESTER

**Springfield-
Amherst Center-
Greenfield**

Danielson

BOSTON-
CAMBRIDGE-
QUINCY

Torrington

CT

WATERBURY

HARTFORD-
WEST HARTFORD-
EAST HARTFORD

PROVIDENCE-
FALL RIVER-
WARWICK

NEW
BEDFORD

BARNSTABLE
TOWN

DANBURY

Willimantic

RI

**Bridgeport-
New Haven-
Stamford**

NEW
HAVEN

NORWICH-
NEW
LONDON

**Hartford-
West Hartford-
Torrington**

**Providence-
New Bedford-
Fall River**

BRIDGEPORT-
STAMFORD-
NORWALK

Legend:
- NH ——— State Boundary
- **Laconia - Franklin** ——— **Combined NECTA**
- Claremont ☐ Micropolitan NECTA
- WORCESTER ☐ METROPOLITAN NECTA

Shaded Area Enlarged Above

All boundaries and names are as of November 2004.

U.S. DEPARTMENT OF COMMERCE Economics and Statistics Administration Bureau of the Census

Appendix D.
Guide to State Statistical Abstracts and State Information

The bibliography below includes the most recent statistical abstracts for states published since 1999, plus those that will be issued in late 2005. For some states, a near equivalent has been listed in substitution for, or in addition to, a statistical abstract. All sources contain statistical tables on a variety of subjects for the state as a whole, its component parts, or both. Internet sites also contain statistical data.

Alabama

University of Alabama, Center for Business and Economic Research, Box 870221, Tuscaloosa, AL 35487-0221.

205-348-6191. Fax: 205-348-2951. Internet site <http://cber.cba.ua.edu/>.

Economic Abstract of Alabama, 2000. Alabama Economic Outlook, 2005. Revised annually.

Alaska

Department of Community and Economic Development, Division of Community Advocacy, 550 W. 7th Avenue, Suite 1770, Anchorage, AK 99501-2341.

907-269-4580. Fax: 907-269-4539. Internet site <http://www.dced.state.ak.us/dca/home.htm/>.

The Alaska Economic Performance Report, 2004. Online.

Arizona

Economic and Business Research Center, University of Arizona, McClelland Hall, Rm. 103, P.O. Box 210108, Tucson, AZ 85721-0108.

520-621-2155. Fax: 520-621-2150. Internet site <http://www.ebr.eller.arizona.edu/>.

Arizona Statistical Abstract, 2003. Arizona's Economy. Quarterly newsletter. *Arizona Economic Indicators.* Semi-annual. Online.

Arkansas

University of Arkansas at Little Rock, Institute for Economic Advancement, Economic Research, 2801 South University Avenue, Little Rock, AR 72204.

501-569-8519. Fax: 501-569-8538. Internet site <http://www.aiea.ualr.edu/>.

Arkansas State and County Economic Data, 2003. Revised annually. *Arkansas Personal Income Handbook, 2003. Arkansas Statistical Abstract, 2004.* Revised biennially.

California

Department of Finance, 915 L Street, Sacramento, CA 95814.

916-445-3878. Internet site <http://www.dof.ca.gov /HTML/FS_DATA/STAT-ABS/SA_HOME.htm>.

California Statistical Abstract, 2004. Annual. Online only.

Colorado

University of Colorado, University Libraries, 184 UCB, 1720 Pleasant St., Boulder, CO 80309-0184.

303-492-8834. Internet site <http://www.colorado.edu/libraries/govpubs/online.htm>.

Colorado by the Numbers. Online only.

Connecticut

Connecticut Department of Economic and Community Development, 505 Hudson St., Hartford, CT 06106.

1-860-270-8000. Internet site <http://www.ct.gov/ecd/site/default.asp>.

Connecticut Town Profiles, 2003–2004.

Delaware

Delaware Economic Development Office, 99 Kings Highway, Dover, DE 19901.

302-739-4271. Fax: 302-739-2028. Internet site <http://www.state.de.us/dedo/default.shtml>.

Delaware Statistical Overview, 2002–2003.

District of Columbia

Business Resource Center, John A. Wilson Building, 1350 Pennsylvania Avenue, NW, Washington, DC 20004.

202-727-1000. Internet site <http://brc.dc.gov/resources/facts.asp>.

Market Facts and Statistics. Online only.

Florida

University of Florida, Bureau of Economic and Business Research, P.O. Box 117145, 221 Matherly Hall, Gainesville, FL 32611-7145.

352-392-0171, ext. 219. Internet site <http://www.bebr.ufl.edu>.

Florida Statistical Abstract, 2004. 38th edition. Annual. Also available on CD-ROM. *Florida County Perspective, 2004.* One profile for each county. Annual. Also available on CD-ROM. *Florida County Rankings, 2004.* 11th edition. Annual. Also available on CD-ROM.

Georgia

University of Georgia, Selig Center for Economic Growth, Terry College of Business, Athens, GA 30602-6269.

706-542-4085. Internet site <http://www.selig.uga.edu/>.

Georgia Statistical Abstract, 2004–05.

University of Georgia, Center for Agribusiness and Economic Development, 301 Lumpkin House, Athens, GA 30602-7509.

706-542-8938 or 706-542-0760. Fax: 706-542-8934. Internet site <http://www.georgiastats.uga.edu/>.

The Georgia County Guide, 2004. Annual.

Hawaii

Hawaii State Department of Business, and Economic Development and Tourism, Research and Economic Analysis Division, Statistics and Data Support Branch, P.O. Box 2359, Honolulu, HI 96804.

808-586-2423. Internet site <http://www.hawaii.gov/DBEDT/>.

The State of Hawaii Data Book 2003: A Statistical Abstract. Annual.

Idaho

Idaho Commerce and Labor, 700 West State St., P.O. Box 83720, Boise, ID 83720-0093.

208-334-2650. Internet site <http://www.idoc.state.id.us/data/community/>.

County Profiles of Idaho, 2003. Online. *Idaho Community Profiles, 2003.* Online. *Profile of Rural Idaho, 1999.*

Illinois

Institute of Government and Public Affairs, 1007 W. Nevada Street, Urbana, IL 61801.

217-333-3340. Internet site <http://www.igpa.uiuc.edu/default.htm>.

Illinois Statistical Abstract, 2004. Online only.

Indiana

Indiana University, Indiana Business Research Center, Kelley School of Business, Ste 3110, 1275 E. 10th Street, Bloomington, IN 47405.

812-855-4848. Internet site <http://www.stats.indiana.edu/>.

STATS Indiana. Online only.

Iowa

Office of Social and Economic Trend Analysis, 303 East Hall, Ames, IA 50010-1070.

515-294-9903. Fax: 515-294-0592. Internet site <http://www.seta.iastate.edu/>.

Iowa by the Numbers, 2004. CD-ROM.

State Library of Iowa, State Data Center, Ola Babcock Miller Building, East 12th and Grand, Des Moines, IA 50319.

1-800-248-4483. Fax: 515-242-6543. Internet site <http://www.silo.lib.ia.us/specializedservices /datacenter/>.

Kansas

University of Kansas, Policy Research Institute, 1541 Lilac Lane, 607 Blake Hall, Lawrence, KS 66044-3177.

785-864-3701. Fax: 785-864-3683. Internet site <http://www.ku.edu/pri/>.

Kansas Statistical Abstract, 2003. 38th edition. Online only.

Kentucky

Kentucky Cabinet for Economic Development, Division of Research, 300 West Broadway, Frankfort, KY 40601.

1-800-626-2930. Internet site <http://www.thinkkentucky.com/kyedc/resandstat.asp>.

Kentucky Deskbook of Economic Statistics. Online only.

Louisiana

The University of Louisiana at Monroe, 700 University Avenue, Monroe, Louisiana 71209.

318-342-1000. Internet site <http://ulm.edu/>.

Louisiana Electronic Assistance Program. Online only.

Louisiana State Census Data Center, Office of Electronic Services, P.O. Box 94095, Baton Rouge, LA 70804-9095.

225-219-4025. Fax: 225-219-4027. Internet site <http://www.louisiana.gov/wps/portal/>.

Maine

Maine State Planning Office, #38 State House Station, 184 State Street, Augusta, ME 04333.

1-800-662-4545. Fax: 207-287-6489. Internet site <http://www.state.me.us/spo/economics/economics/>.

Maryland

RESI, Towson University, 8000 York Road, Towson, MD 21252-7097.

410-704-7374. Fax 410-704-4115. Internet site <http://wwwnew.towson.edu/outreach/resi/default.asp>.

Maryland Statistical Abstract, 2003.

Massachusetts

MassCHIP, Massachusetts Department of Public Health, 250 Washington Street, 6th Floor, Boston, MA 02108.

617-624-5629. Internet site <http://masschip.state.ma.us>.

Instant Topics. Online only.

Michigan

Michigan Economic Development Coporation, 300 North Washington Square, Lansing, MI 48913.

517-373-9808. Internet site <http://medc.michigan.org/miinfo/>.

Economic Profiler. Online only.

Minnesota

Minnesota Department of Employment and Economic Development, 1st National Bank Building, 332 Minnesota Street, Suite E200, Saint Paul, MN 55101-1351.

1-800-657-3858. Internet site <http://www.deed.state.mn.us/facts/index.htm>.

Compare Minnesota: Profiles of Minnesota's Economy and Population, 2002-2003.

State Demographic Center, 650 Cedar Street, Saint Paul, MN 55155.

651-296-2557. Internet site <http://www.demography.state.mn.us/>.

Mississippi

Mississippi State University, College of Business and Industry, Division of Research, P.O. Box 5288, Mississippi State, MS 39762.

662-325-3817. Fax: 662-325-8686.

Mississippi Statistical Abstract, 2003.

Missouri

University of Missouri, Economic and Policy Analysis Research Center, 10 Professional Building, Columbia, MO 65211.

573-882-4805. Fax: 573-882-5563. Internet site <http://econ.missouri.edu/eparc/>.

Statistical Abstract for Missouri, 2003. Biennial. Online only.

Montana

Census and Economic Information Center, Montana Department of Commerce, 301 S. Park, P.O. Box 200505, Helena, MT 59620-0505.

406-841-2740. Internet site <http://ceic.commerce.state.mt.us/>.

Nebraska

Nebraska Department of Economic Development, P.O. Box 94666, 301 Centennial Mall South, Lincoln, NE 68509-4666.

1-800-426-6505. Fax 402-471-3778. Internet site <http://info.neded.org/>.

Nebraska Data Book. Online only.

Nevada

Department of Administration, Budget and Planning Division, 209 East Musser Street, Suite 200, Carson City, NV 89701.

775-684-0222. Fax: 775-684-0260. Internet site <http://www.budget.state.nv.us/>.

Nevada Statistical Abstract, 2004. Online only.

New Hampshire

New Hampshire Office of Energy and Planning, 57 Regional Drive, Suite 3, Concord, NH 03301-8519.

603-271-2155. Fax 603-271-2615. Internet site <http://www.nh.gov/oep/>.

New Jersey

New Jersey State Data Center, NJ Department of Labor and Workforce Development, P.O. Box 388, Trenton, NJ 08625-0388.

609-984-2595. Fax: 609-984-6833. Internet site <http://www.state.nj.us/labor/lra/>.

Labor Market Information. Online only.

New Mexico

University of New Mexico, Bureau of Business and Economic Research, MSC02 1720, Albuquerque, NM 87131-0001.

505-277-2216. Fax 505-277-7066. Internet site <http://www.unm.edu/~bber/>.

New Mexico Business, Current Economic Report. Monthly. *FOR-UNM Bulletin.* Quarterly.

New York

Nelson A. Rockefeller Institute of Government, 411 State Street, Albany, NY 12203-1003.

518-443-5522. Fax: 518-443-5788. Internet site <http://www.rockinst.org/>.

New York State Statistical Yearbook, 2004. 29th edition.

North Carolina

Office of Governor, Office of State Budget and Management, 116 West Jones Street, Raleigh, NC 27603-8005.

919-733-7061. Fax 919-733-0640. Internet site <http://www.osbm.state.nc.us/osbm/>.

How North Carolina Ranks, 2004. Online only.

North Dakota

University of North Dakota, Bureau of Business and Economic Research, P.O. Box 8369, Grand Forks, ND 58202.

1-800-225-5863. Fax 701-777-3365. Internet site <http://business.und.edu/bber/>.

North Dakota Statistical Abstract. Online only.

Ohio

Office of Strategic Research, Ohio Department of Development, P.O. Box 1001, Columbus, OH 43216-1001.

1-800-848-1300. Internet site <http://www.odod.state.oh.us/research>.

Research products and services. Updated continually. *Ohio County Profiles.* Updated periodically. *Ohio County Indicators.* Updated periodically.

Oklahoma

University of Oklahoma, Center for Economic and Management Research, Michael F. Price College of Business, 307 West Brooks, Room 3, Norman, OK 73019.

405-325-2933. Fax: 405-325-7688. Internet site <http://origins.ou.edu/>.

Statistical Abstract of Oklahoma, 1999.

Oregon

Secretary of State, Archives Division, Archives Bldg., 800 Summer Street, NE, Salem, OR 97310.

503-373-0701. Fax: 503-378-4118. Internet site <http://www.sos.state.or.us/bbook>.

Oregon Blue Book, 2005–2006. Biennial.

Pennsylvania

Pennsylvania State Data Center, Institute of State and Regional Affairs, Penn State Harrisburg, 777 West Harrisburg Pike, Middletown, PA 17057-4898.

717-948-6336. Fax: 717-948-6754. Internet site <http://pasdc.hbg.psu.edu>.

Pennsylvania Statistical Abstract, 2004.

Rhode Island

Rhode Island Economic Development Corporation, One West Exchange Street, Providence, RI 02903.

401-222-2601. Internet site <http://www.riedc.com/>.

RI Data Bank. Online only.

South Carolina

Budget and Control Board, Office of Research and Statistics, 1919 Blanding Street, Columbia, SC 29201.

803-898-9940. Internet site <http://www.ors2.state.sc.us/abstract/index.asp>.

South Carolina Statistical Abstract, 2005.

South Dakota

South Dakota State Data Center, Business Research Bureau, The University of South Dakota, 414 E. Clark Street, Vermillion, SD 57069.

605-677-5287. Fax: 605-677-5427. Internet site <http://www.usd.edu/sdsdc/publications.cfm>.

2003 South Dakota Community Abstracts.

Tennessee

College of Business Administration, The University of Tennessee, Temple Court, Suite 100, 804 Volunteer Blvd., Knoxville, TN 37996-4334.

865-974-5441. Fax: 865-974-3100. Internet site <http://cber.bus.utk.edu/Default.htm>.

Tennessee Statistical Abstract, 2003. Biennial.

Texas

Dallas Morning News, Communications Center, P.O. Box 655237, Dallas, TX 75265-5237.

214-977-8261. Internet site
<http://www.texasalmanac.com/>.

Texas Almanac, 2004–2005.

Texas State Data Center and Office of the State Demographer, Institute for Demographic and Socioeconomic Research, University of Texas at San Antonio, 6900 North Loop, 1604 West, San Antonio, TX 78249-0704.

210-458-6543. Fax: 210-458-6541. Internet site
<http://txsdc.utsa.edu/>.

Utah

Governor's Office of Planning and Budget, Demographic and Economic Analysis, State Capitol Complex, Suite 210, East Office Building, Salt Lake City, UT 84114-2210.

801-538-1027. Fax: 801-538-1547. Internet site
<http://www.governor.utah.gov/dea/>.

2005 Economic Report to the Governor. Annual. *Utah Data Guide Newsletter.* Quarterly.

Vermont

Department of Employment and Training, Labor Market Information, P.O. Box 488, Montpelier, VT 05601-0488.

802-828-4202. Fax: 802-828-4050. Internet site
<http://www.vtlmi.info/>.

Vermont Economic-Demographic Profile, 2005. Annual.

Virginia

Weldon Cooper Center, P.O. Box 400206, Charlottesville, VA 22904-4206.

434-982-5582. Fax: 434-982-4596. Internet site
<http://www.ccps.virginia.edu/demographics/>.

Virginia Statistical Abstract. Online only.

Washington

Washington State Office of Financial Management, Forecasting Division, P.O. Box 43113, Olympia, WA 98504-3113.

360-902-0555. Internet site <http://www.ofm.wa.gov/>.

Washington State Data Book, 2003. Biennial.

West Virginia

West Virginia University, College of Business and Economics, Bureau of Business and Economic Research, P.O. Box 6025, Morgantown, WV 26506-6025.

304-293-7831. Fax: 304-293-5652. Internet site
<http://www.bber.wvu.edu/>.

2004 West Virginia County Data Profiles. West Virginia Economic Outlook, 2005. Annual.

Wisconsin

Wisconsin Legislative Reference Bureau, P.O. Box 2037, Madison, WI 53701-2037.

608-266-0341. Internet site
<http://www.legis.state.wi.us/lrb/bb/>.

2003–2004 Wisconsin Blue Book. Biennial.

Wyoming

Department of Administration and Information, Economic Analysis Division, 1807 Capitol Avenue, Suite 206, Cheyenne, WY 82002-0060.

307-777-7504. Fax: 307-632-1819. Internet site
<http://eadiv.state.wy.us/>.

The Equality State Almanac, 2002.

KEY FEDERAL WEB SITES WITH STATE-LEVEL INFORMATION

Many federal government agencies publish state-level information. The ones selected below have large concentrations of such information in easy-to-locate Web sites.

U.S. BUREAU OF ECONOMIC ANALYSIS

Gross State Product at
<http://www.bea.gov/bea/regional/gsp.htm>.

Personal income at
<http://www.bea.gov/bea/regional/statelocal.htm>.

U.S. BUREAU OF LABOR STATISTICS

Current Employment Statistics at
<http://www.bls.gov/sae/home.htm>.

Geographic Profile of Employment and Unemployment at
<http://www.bls.gov/gps/home.htm>.

State occupational injuries, illnesses, and fatalities at
<http://www.bls.gov/iif/oshstate.htm>.

U.S. CENSUS BUREAU

American Community Survey data at
<http://www.census.gov/acs/www/>.

Annual Survey of Manufactures at
<http://www.census.gov/mcd/asm-as3.html>.

Building permits at
<http://www.census.gov/const/www/C40/table2.html>.

County Business Patterns at
<http://censtats.census.gov/cbpnaic/cbpnaic.shtml>.

2002 Economic Census data at
<http://www.census.gov/econ/census02/guide /geosumm.htm>.

Foreign trade at
<http://www.census.gov/foreign-trade/statistics
/state/>.

Housing unit estimates at
<http://www.census.gov/popest/housing/>.

Population estimates at
<http://www.census.gov/popest/states/>.

State and County QuickFacts profiles at
<http://quickfacts.census.gov/qfd/index.html>.

State government finances at
<http://www.census.gov/govs/www/state.html>.

State government employment at
<http://www.census.gov/govs/www/apesst.html>.

U.S. DEPARTMENT OF AGRICULTURE

Economic Research Service

Agricultural exports at
<http://www.ers.usda.gov/Data/StateExports/>.

Farm income at
<http://www.ers.usda.gov/Data/farmincome
/finfidmu.htm>.

State Fact Sheets at
<http://www.ers.usda.gov/StateFacts/>.

National Agricultural Statistics Service

Census of Agriculture 2002 at
<http://www.nass.usda.gov/census/census02
/volume1/>.

Other reports at
<http://www.usda.gov/nass/pubs/reportname.htm>.

U.S. DEPARTMENT OF HEALTH AND HUMAN SERVICES

Centers for Disease Control and Prevention

Behavioral Risk Factor Surveillance System at
<http://www2.cdc.gov/nccdphp/brfss2/publications
/index.asp>.

Fast Stats A to Z at
<http://www.cdc.gov/nchs/fastats/map_page.htm>.

Substance Abuse and Mental Health Services Administration

State-level data at
<http://oas.samhsa.gov/states.htm>.

ENERGY INFORMATION ADMINISTRATION

Energy consumption at
<http://www.eia.doe.gov/emeu/states/_seds.html>.

General state information at
<http://www.eia.doe.gov/emeu/states/_states.html>.

State Electricity Profiles at
<http://www.eia.doe.gov/cneaf/electricity/st_profiles
/e_profiles_sum.html>.

NATIONAL CENTER OF EDUCATION STATISTICS

State Education Data Profiles at
<http://nces.ed.gov/programs/stateprofiles/>.

NATIONAL SCIENCE FOUNDATION

Science and Engineering State Profiles at
<http://www.nsf.gov/statistics/showpub
.cfm?TopID=11>.

U.S. DEPARTMENT OF TRANSPORTATION

Federal Highway Administration

Highway statistics at
<http://www.fhwa.dot.gov/policy/ohpi/hss
/hsspubs.htm>.

National Highway Traffic Safety Administration

State traffic safety information at
<http://www.nhtsa.dot.gov/stsi/>.

Appendix E.
Ranking Tables

Table E-1. State Rankings — **Area and Population**

Geographic area	Area, 2000 Total (sq. mi.)	Area, 2000 Rank	Population 2005 (1,000)	Population 2000[2] (1,000)	Population 1990[3] (1,000)	Rank 2005	Rank 2000	Rank 1990	Population per square mile of land area[1] 2005	Pop/sq mi 2000	Pop/sq mi 1990	Rank 2005	Rank 2000	Rank 1990	Net change Number (1,000)	Net change Rank	Percent change Number	Percent change Rank
United States ...	3,794,083	(X)	296,410	281,425	248,791	(X)	(X)	(X)	83.8	79.6	70.3	(X)	(X)	(X)	14,985.8	(X)	5.3	(X)
Alabama	52,419	30	4,558	4,447	4,040	23	23	22	89.8	87.6	79.6	26	26	25	110.5	28	2.5	39
Alaska	663,267	1	664	627	550	47	48	49	1.2	1.1	1.0	50	50	50	36.7	43	5.9	18
Arizona	113,998	6	5,939	5,131	3,665	17	20	24	52.3	45.2	32.3	35	36	37	808.7	5	15.8	2
Arkansas	53,179	29	2,779	2,673	2,351	32	33	33	53.4	51.3	45.1	33	34	35	105.8	30	4.0	23
California	163,696	3	36,132	33,872	29,811	1	1	1	231.7	217.2	191.1	11	12	12	2,260.5	1	6.7	13
Colorado	104,094	8	4,665	4,302	3,294	22	24	26	45.0	41.5	31.8	37	37	38	363.2	10	8.4	8
Connecticut	5,543	48	3,510	3,406	3,287	29	29	27	724.5	702.9	678.5	4	4	4	104.7	31	3.1	32
Delaware	2,489	49	844	784	666	45	45	46	431.8	401.1	341.0	6	7	7	59.9	36	7.6	10
District of Columbia	68	(X)	551	572	607	(X)	(X)	(X)	8,966.1	9,316.4	9,884.4	(X)	(X)	(X)	−21.5	(X)	−3.8	(X)
Florida	65,755	22	17,790	15,983	12,938	4	4	4	329.9	296.4	239.9	8	8	10	1,807.0	3	11.3	3
Georgia	59,425	24	9,073	8,187	6,478	9	10	11	156.7	141.4	111.9	18	18	21	885.8	4	10.8	4
Hawaii	10,931	43	1,275	1,212	1,108	42	42	41	198.5	188.6	172.6	13	13	13	63.7	35	5.3	20
Idaho	83,570	14	1,429	1,294	1,007	39	39	42	17.3	15.6	12.2	44	44	44	135.1	25	10.4	6
Illinois	57,914	25	12,763	12,420	11,431	5	5	6	229.6	223.4	205.6	12	11	11	343.7	11	2.8	36
Indiana	36,418	38	6,272	6,081	5,544	15	14	14	174.9	169.5	154.6	17	16	16	191.5	21	3.1	30
Iowa	56,272	26	2,966	2,926	2,777	30	30	30	53.1	52.4	49.7	34	33	33	40.0	42	1.4	44
Kansas	82,277	15	2,745	2,689	2,478	33	32	32	33.5	32.9	30.3	40	40	39	55.9	37	2.1	41
Kentucky	40,409	37	4,173	4,042	3,687	26	25	23	105.0	101.7	92.8	22	23	23	131.1	26	3.2	28
Louisiana	51,840	31	4,524	4,469	4,222	24	22	21	103.8	102.6	96.9	23	22	22	54.7	38	1.2	45
Maine	35,385	39	1,322	1,275	1,228	40	40	38	42.8	41.3	39.8	38	38	36	46.6	41	3.7	25
Maryland	12,407	42	5,600	5,297	4,781	19	19	19	573.0	541.9	489.1	5	5	5	303.9	12	5.7	19
Massachusetts	10,555	44	6,399	6,349	6,016	13	13	13	816.2	809.8	767.4	3	3	3	49.6	39	0.8	48
Michigan	96,716	11	10,121	9,938	9,295	8	8	8	178.2	175.0	163.6	16	15	14	182.4	22	1.8	42
Minnesota	86,939	12	5,133	4,919	4,376	21	21	20	64.5	61.8	55.0	31	31	31	213.3	19	4.3	22
Mississippi	48,430	32	2,921	2,845	2,575	31	31	31	62.3	60.6	54.9	32	32	32	76.4	33	2.7	37
Missouri	69,704	21	5,800	5,597	5,117	18	17	15	84.2	81.2	74.3	28	27	27	203.6	20	3.6	26
Montana	147,042	4	936	902	799	44	44	44	6.4	6.2	5.5	48	48	48	33.5	44	3.7	24
Nebraska	77,354	16	1,759	1,711	1,578	38	38	36	22.9	22.3	20.5	42	42	42	47.5	40	2.8	35
Nevada	110,561	7	2,415	1,998	1,202	35	35	39	22.0	18.2	10.9	43	43	45	416.6	8	20.8	1
New Hampshire	9,350	46	1,310	1,236	1,109	41	41	40	146.1	137.8	123.7	19	20	18	74.2	34	6.0	17
New Jersey	8,721	47	8,718	8,414	7,748	10	9	9	1,175.3	1,134.4	1,044.5	1	1	1	303.6	13	3.6	27
New Mexico	121,590	5	1,928	1,819	1,515	36	36	37	15.9	15.0	12.5	45	45	43	109.3	29	6.0	16
New York	54,556	27	19,255	18,977	17,991	3	3	2	407.8	401.9	381.0	7	6	6	277.8	14	1.5	43
North Carolina	53,819	28	8,683	8,046	6,632	11	11	10	178.3	165.2	136.2	15	17	17	636.8	6	7.9	9
North Dakota	70,700	19	637	642	639	48	47	47	9.2	9.3	9.3	47	47	46	−5.5	50	−0.9	50
Ohio	44,825	34	11,464	11,353	10,847	7	7	7	280.0	277.3	264.9	9	9	9	110.9	27	1.0	47
Oklahoma	69,898	20	3,548	3,451	3,146	28	27	28	51.7	50.3	45.8	36	35	34	97.2	32	2.8	33
Oregon	98,381	9	3,641	3,421	2,842	27	28	29	37.9	35.6	29.6	39	39	40	219.6	18	6.4	14
Pennsylvania	46,055	33	12,430	12,281	11,883	6	6	5	277.3	274.0	265.1	10	10	8	148.6	24	1.2	46
Rhode Island	1,545	50	1,076	1,048	1,003	43	43	43	1,029.9	1,003.2	960.3	2	2	2	27.9	45	2.7	38
South Carolina	32,020	40	4,255	4,012	3,486	25	26	25	141.3	133.2	115.8	21	21	20	243.3	16	6.1	15
South Dakota	77,117	17	776	755	696	46	46	45	10.2	9.9	9.2	46	46	47	21.1	46	2.8	34
Tennessee	42,143	36	5,963	5,689	4,877	16	16	17	144.7	138.0	118.3	20	19	19	273.7	15	4.8	21
Texas	268,581	2	22,860	20,852	16,986	2	2	3	87.3	79.6	64.9	27	28	29	2,008.2	2	9.6	7
Utah	84,899	13	2,470	2,233	1,723	34	34	35	30.1	27.2	21.0	41	41	41	236.4	17	10.6	5
Vermont	9,614	45	623	609	563	49	49	48	67.4	65.8	60.8	30	30	30	14.2	48	2.3	40
Virginia	42,774	35	7,567	7,079	6,189	12	12	12	191.1	178.8	156.3	14	14	15	488.4	7	6.9	11
Washington	71,300	18	6,288	5,894	4,867	14	15	18	94.5	88.6	73.1	25	25	28	393.6	9	6.7	12
West Virginia	24,230	41	1,817	1,808	1,793	37	37	34	75.5	75.1	74.5	29	29	26	8.5	49	0.5	49
Wisconsin	65,498	23	5,536	5,364	4,892	20	18	16	101.9	98.8	90.1	24	24	24	172.5	23	3.2	29
Wyoming	97,814	10	509	494	454	50	50	50	5.2	5.1	4.7	49	49	49	15.5	47	3.1	31

X Not applicable.

[1]Persons per square mile were calculated on the basis of land area data from the 2000 census.
[2]The April 1, 2000, Population Estimates base reflects modifications to the Census 2000 population as documented in the Count Question Resolution program and geographic program revisions.
[3]The April 1, 1990, census counts include corrections processed through August 1997 and results of special censuses and test censuses, and do not include adjustments for census coverage errors.

Note: When states share the same rank, the next lower rank is omitted. States may share the same value but have different ranks due to rounding.

Survey, Census, or Data Collection Method: Based on the Census of Population and Housing; for information, see Appendix B, Limitations of the Data and Methodology, and Internet sites <http://www.census.gov/main/www/cen2000.html> and <http://www.census.gov/popest/topics/methodology/>.

Sources: Area—U.S. Census Bureau, 2000 Census of Population and Housing, *Summary Population and Housing Characteristics*, Series PHC-1; and unpublished data on American FactFinder; Population—U.S. Census Bureau, 1990 Census of Population and Housing, Population and Housing Unit Counts (CPH-2); "Time Series of Intercensal State Population Estimates: April 1, 1990 to April 1, 2000" (CO-EST2001-12-00), published 11 April 2002; Internet site <http://www.census.gov/popest/archives/2000s/vintage_2001/CO-EST2001-12/CO-EST2001-12-00.html>; and "Annual Estimates of the Population for the United States and States, and for Puerto Rico: April 1, 2000 to July 1, 2005" (NST-EST2005-01), published 22 December 2005; Internet site <http://www.census.gov/popest/states/NST-ann-est.html>; Population change—U.S. Census Bureau, "Table 4: Cumulative Estimates of the Components of Population Change for the United States and States: April 1, 2000 to July 1, 2005" (NST-EST2005-04), published 22 December 2005; Internet site <http://www.census.gov/popest/states/NST-comp-chg.html>.

Table E-2. State Rankings — **Population Projections**

Geographic area	Number (1,000)						Rank						Percent change			Rank		
	2005	2010	2015	2020	2025	2030	2005	2010	2015	2020	2025	2030	2000–2010	2010–2020	2020–2030	2000–2010	2010–2020	2020–2030
United States . . .	**295,507**	**308,936**	**322,366**	**335,805**	**349,439**	**363,584**	(X)	(X)	(X)	(X)	(X)	(X)	**9.8**	**8.7**	**8.3**	(X)	(X)	(X)
Alabama	4,527	4,596	4,663	4,729	4,800	4,874	24	24	24	24	24	24	3.4	2.9	3.1	43	36	26
Alaska.	661	694	733	774	821	868	47	47	47	47	46	46	10.7	11.6	12.0	18	11	10
Arizona	5,868	6,637	7,495	8,456	9,532	10,712	17	14	13	13	12	10	29.4	27.4	26.7	2	2	1
Arkansas	2,777	2,875	2,969	3,060	3,151	3,240	32	32	33	31	32	32	7.5	6.4	5.9	23	21	20
California	36,039	38,067	40,123	42,207	44,305	46,445	1	1	1	1	1	1	12.4	10.9	10.0	11	13	13
Colorado	4,618	4,832	5,049	5,279	5,523	5,792	22	22	22	22	22	22	12.3	9.3	9.7	12	16	14
Connecticut	3,503	3,577	3,635	3,676	3,691	3,689	29	29	29	29	30	30	5.0	2.7	0.4	34	37	39
Delaware	837	884	927	963	991	1,013	45	45	45	45	45	45	12.9	8.9	5.1	10	17	21
District of Columbia	551	530	506	481	455	433	(X)	(X)	(X)	(X)	(X)	(X)	−7.4	−9.3	−9.8	(X)	(X)	(X)
Florida.	17,510	19,252	21,204	23,407	25,912	28,686	4	4	3	3	3	3	20.5	21.6	22.6	3	3	3
Georgia	8,926	9,589	10,231	10,844	11,439	12,018	9	9	9	8	9	8	17.1	13.1	10.8	6	9	11
Hawaii	1,277	1,341	1,386	1,412	1,439	1,466	42	42	42	41	41	41	10.7	5.3	3.8	19	24	23
Idaho.	1,407	1,517	1,630	1,741	1,853	1,970	39	39	39	39	37	37	17.3	14.8	13.1	5	6	9
Illinois	12,699	12,917	13,097	13,237	13,341	13,433	5	5	5	5	5	5	4.0	2.5	1.5	41	39	36
Indiana	6,250	6,392	6,518	6,627	6,721	6,810	14	16	16	17	18	18	5.1	3.7	2.8	33	32	29
Iowa	2,974	3,010	3,026	3,020	2,993	2,955	30	30	31	33	34	34	2.9	0.4	−2.2	45	48	48
Kansas	2,752	2,805	2,853	2,891	2,919	2,940	33	33	34	35	35	35	4.4	3.0	1.7	38	35	34
Kentucky	4,163	4,265	4,351	4,424	4,490	4,555	26	26	26	26	27	27	5.5	3.7	3.0	31	31	28
Louisiana	4,534	4,613	4,674	4,719	4,762	4,803	23	23	23	25	25	26	3.2	2.3	1.8	44	41	33
Maine	1,319	1,357	1,389	1,409	1,414	1,411	40	41	41	42	42	42	6.4	3.8	0.2	29	30	40
Maryland	5,601	5,905	6,208	6,498	6,763	7,022	19	19	18	18	17	16	11.5	10.0	8.1	14	15	16
Massachusetts	6,519	6,649	6,759	6,856	6,939	7,012	13	13	15	15	16	17	4.7	3.1	2.3	36	34	31
Michigan	10,207	10,429	10,599	10,696	10,714	10,694	8	8	8	10	10	11	4.9	2.6	0.0	35	38	41
Minnesota	5,175	5,421	5,668	5,901	6,109	6,306	21	21	21	21	20	20	10.2	8.9	6.9	20	18	18
Mississippi	2,916	2,971	3,014	3,045	3,069	3,092	31	31	32	32	33	33	4.5	2.5	1.6	37	40	35
Missouri.	5,765	5,922	6,070	6,200	6,315	6,430	18	18	19	19	19	19	5.8	4.7	3.7	30	28	24
Montana	933	969	999	1,023	1,037	1,045	44	44	44	44	44	44	7.4	5.6	2.2	24	23	32
Nebraska	1,744	1,769	1,789	1,803	1,813	1,820	38	38	38	37	38	38	3.4	1.9	1.0	42	44	37
Nevada	2,352	2,691	3,058	3,452	3,863	4,282	35	34	30	30	28	28	34.6	28.3	24.0	1	1	2
New Hampshire.	1,315	1,386	1,457	1,525	1,586	1,646	41	40	40	40	40	40	12.1	10.0	8.0	13	14	17
New Jersey	8,745	9,018	9,256	9,462	9,637	9,802	10	11	11	11	11	13	7.2	4.9	3.6	25	26	25
New Mexico	1,902	1,980	2,042	2,084	2,107	2,100	36	36	36	36	36	36	8.9	5.3	0.7	22	25	38
New York	19,258	19,444	19,547	19,577	19,540	19,477	3	3	4	4	4	4	2.5	0.7	−0.5	47	46	45
North Carolina.	8,702	9,346	10,011	10,709	11,449	12,228	11	10	10	9	8	7	16.1	14.6	14.2	8	7	7
North Dakota	635	637	635	630	621	607	48	49	49	49	49	49	−0.9	−1.0	−3.7	50	49	49
Ohio	11,478	11,576	11,635	11,644	11,606	11,551	7	7	7	7	7	9	2.0	0.6	−0.8	48	47	46
Oklahoma	3,521	3,592	3,662	3,736	3,821	3,913	28	28	28	28	29	29	4.1	4.0	4.8	40	29	22
Oregon	3,596	3,791	4,013	4,260	4,536	4,834	27	27	27	27	26	25	10.8	12.4	13.5	17	10	8
Pennsylvania	12,427	12,584	12,711	12,787	12,802	12,768	6	6	6	6	6	6	2.5	1.6	−0.1	46	45	43
Rhode Island	1,087	1,117	1,140	1,154	1,158	1,153	43	43	43	43	43	43	6.5	3.4	−0.1	28	33	42
South Carolina	4,239	4,447	4,642	4,823	4,990	5,149	25	25	25	23	23	23	10.8	8.5	6.8	16	20	19
South Dakota	772	786	797	802	802	800	46	46	46	46	47	47	4.2	2.0	−0.2	39	43	44
Tennessee	5,965	6,231	6,502	6,781	7,073	7,381	16	17	17	16	15	15	9.5	8.8	8.8	21	19	15
Texas	22,775	24,649	26,586	28,635	30,865	33,318	2	2	2	2	2	2	18.2	16.2	16.4	4	4	5
Utah	2,418	2,595	2,783	2,990	3,226	3,485	34	35	35	34	31	31	16.2	15.2	16.6	7	5	4
Vermont	631	653	673	691	703	712	49	48	48	48	48	48	7.2	5.9	3.1	26	22	27
Virginia	7,553	8,010	8,467	8,917	9,364	9,825	12	12	12	12	13	12	13.2	11.3	10.2	9	12	12
Washington	6,205	6,542	6,951	7,432	7,996	8,625	15	15	14	14	14	14	11.0	13.6	16.0	15	8	6
West Virginia	1,819	1,829	1,823	1,801	1,766	1,720	37	37	37	38	39	39	1.2	−1.5	−4.5	49	50	50
Wisconsin.	5,554	5,727	5,883	6,005	6,088	6,151	20	20	20	20	21	21	6.8	4.8	2.4	27	27	30
Wyoming	507	520	528	531	529	523	50	50	50	50	50	50	5.3	2.1	−1.5	32	42	47

X Not applicable.

Note: When states share the same rank, the next lower rank is omitted. States may share the same value but have different ranks due to rounding.

Survey, Census, or Data Collection Method: Based on calculations using National Center for Health Statistics (NCHS) fertility and mortality rates, state migration patterns derived from the Internal Revenue Service (IRS) and Census 2000, and international migration derived from the Population Estimates Program and data on the foreign-born population in Census 2000; for information, see Internet site <http://www.census.gov/population/www/methodep.html>.

Source: U.S. Census Bureau, "State Interim Population Projections by Age and Sex: 2004–2030," published 21 April 2005. See Internet site <http://www.census.gov/population/www/projections/projectionsagesex.html>.

Table E-3. State Rankings — **Population by Age Group**

Geographic area	Population under 18 years						Population 65 years and over						Percent of population by age, 2004			
	2004 (1,000)	2000 (1,000)	1990[1] (1,000)	Rank 2004	Rank 2000	Rank 1990	2004 (1,000)	2000 (1,000)	1990[1] (1,000)	Rank 2004	Rank 2000	Rank 1990	Under 18 years Percent	Under 18 years Rank	65 years and over Percent	65 years and over Rank
United States . . .	73,278	72,295	63,941	(X)	(X)	(X)	36,294	34,992	31,082	(X)	(X)	(X)	25.0	(X)	12.4	(X)
Alabama	1,095	1,124	1,064	24	23	22	598	580	520	22	22	20	24.2	28	13.2	17
Alaska	188	191	173	47	47	47	42	36	22	50	50	50	28.7	2	6.4	50
Arizona	1,547	1,367	986	14	19	23	732	668	476	17	18	22	26.9	4	12.7	26
Arkansas	677	680	624	34	34	34	381	374	349	31	31	30	24.6	22	13.8	9
California	9,596	9,250	7,822	1	1	1	3,823	3,596	3,113	1	1	1	26.7	5	10.7	45
Colorado	1,179	1,101	864	22	24	26	451	416	328	29	30	32	25.6	13	9.8	47
Connecticut	839	842	754	29	29	28	474	470	444	26	26	25	23.9	31	13.5	12
Delaware	194	195	164	45	46	48	109	102	80	46	46	47	23.3	39	13.1	19
District of Columbia	110	115	119	(X)	(X)	(X)	67	70	77	(X)	(X)	(X)	19.8	(X)	12.1	(X)
Florida	4,003	3,646	2,884	4	4	5	2,928	2,808	2,356	2	2	2	23.0	42	16.8	1
Georgia	2,333	2,169	1,736	9	9	10	847	785	651	12	13	15	26.4	7	9.6	48
Hawaii	299	296	282	41	42	41	172	161	124	40	40	42	23.7	35	13.6	11
Idaho	372	369	309	39	39	39	159	146	121	41	43	43	26.7	6	11.4	41
Illinois	3,238	3,246	2,961	5	5	4	1,521	1,500	1,429	7	7	6	25.5	14	12.0	38
Indiana	1,600	1,574	1,461	13	13	13	772	753	694	14	15	13	25.7	12	12.4	30
Iowa	680	734	721	33	31	31	433	436	426	30	29	26	23.0	41	14.7	5
Kansas	683	713	663	32	33	32	355	356	342	32	32	31	25.0	17	13.0	23
Kentucky	980	995	957	26	26	24	519	505	465	25	24	24	23.6	36	12.5	27
Louisiana	1,165	1,220	1,233	23	22	18	528	517	467	23	23	23	25.8	11	11.7	39
Maine	282	301	310	42	41	38	190	183	163	39	39	36	21.4	49	14.4	6
Maryland	1,395	1,356	1,168	17	20	21	635	599	514	20	20	21	25.1	15	11.4	40
Massachusetts	1,464	1,500	1,361	16	15	14	854	860	815	11	11	10	22.8	44	13.3	13
Michigan	2,533	2,596	2,468	8	8	8	1,247	1,219	1,104	8	8	8	25.1	16	12.3	31
Minnesota	1,240	1,287	1,170	21	21	20	615	594	546	21	21	19	24.3	25	12.1	35
Mississippi	750	775	750	30	30	29	353	344	319	33	33	33	25.8	10	12.2	32
Missouri	1,385	1,428	1,319	19	16	15	766	755	715	15	14	12	24.1	29	13.3	15
Montana	208	230	223	44	44	44	127	121	106	44	44	44	22.5	46	13.7	10
Nebraska	435	450	430	37	37	37	232	232	223	36	35	35	24.9	18	13.3	16
Nevada	604	512	299	35	35	40	262	219	127	35	36	40	25.9	9	11.2	44
New Hampshire	305	310	280	40	40	42	157	148	125	42	42	41	23.5	38	12.1	37
New Jersey	2,156	2,088	1,817	10	10	9	1,126	1,113	1,026	9	9	9	24.8	20	12.9	24
New Mexico	492	509	449	36	36	35	229	212	162	37	37	37	25.9	8	12.1	36
New York	4,572	4,690	4,292	3	3	3	2,493	2,449	2,340	3	3	3	23.8	32	13.0	22
North Carolina	2,118	1,964	1,616	11	11	11	1,032	969	800	10	10	11	24.8	19	12.1	33
North Dakota	139	161	176	48	48	46	93	94	91	47	47	46	21.9	47	14.7	4
Ohio	2,779	2,888	2,808	7	7	6	1,525	1,508	1,403	6	6	7	24.3	26	13.3	14
Oklahoma	860	892	840	27	27	27	464	456	423	27	27	27	24.4	24	13.2	18
Oregon	852	847	727	28	28	30	460	438	390	28	28	29	23.7	34	12.8	25
Pennsylvania	2,837	2,922	2,807	6	6	7	1,897	1,919	1,821	5	5	4	22.9	43	15.3	3
Rhode Island	244	248	227	43	43	43	151	152	150	43	41	38	22.6	45	13.9	8
South Carolina	1,025	1,010	925	25	25	25	520	485	394	24	25	28	24.4	23	12.4	29
South Dakota	191	203	199	46	45	45	109	108	102	45	45	45	24.8	21	14.2	7
Tennessee	1,391	1,399	1,222	18	17	19	738	703	616	16	16	17	23.6	37	12.5	28
Texas	6,267	5,887	4,858	2	2	2	2,217	2,073	1,708	4	4	5	27.9	3	9.9	46
Utah	740	719	629	31	32	33	208	190	149	38	38	39	31.0	1	8.7	49
Vermont	135	148	144	49	49	49	81	78	66	48	48	48	21.7	48	13.0	20
Virginia	1,805	1,738	1,511	12	12	12	847	792	661	13	12	14	24.2	27	11.4	42
Washington	1,486	1,514	1,267	15	14	17	703	662	573	19	19	18	24.0	30	11.3	43
West Virginia	385	402	445	38	38	36	278	277	268	34	34	34	21.2	50	15.3	2
Wisconsin	1,308	1,369	1,292	20	18	16	716	703	650	18	17	16	23.7	33	13.0	21
Wyoming	117	129	136	50	50	50	61	58	47	49	49	49	23.1	40	12.1	34

X Not applicable.

[1] The April 1, 1990, data shown here do not reflect the corrections referred to in footnote 2 of Table A-1.

Note: When states share the same rank, the next lower rank is omitted. States may share the same value but have different ranks due to rounding.

Survey, Census, or Data Collection Method: Based on the Census of Population and Housing; for information, see Appendix B, Limitations of the Data and Methodology, and sites <http://www.census.gov/main/www/cen2000.html> and <http://www.census.gov/popest/topics/methodology/>.

Source: U.S. Census Bureau, "State Single Year of Age and Sex Population Estimates: April 1, 2000 to July 1, 2004—RESIDENT"; see Internet site <http://www.census.gov/popest/states/files/SC-EST2004-AGESEXRES.csv>; and "Age and Sex for States and for Puerto Rico: April 1, 2000 to July 1, 2004"; see Internet site <http://www.census.gov/popest/states/asrh/SC-est2004-02.html>; and "Table ST-99-9 Population Estimates for the U.S., Regions, and States by Selected Age Groups and Sex: Annual Time Series, July 1, 1990 to July 1, 1999," published 9 March 2000; see Internet site <http://www.census.gov/popest/archives/1990s/ST-99-09.txt>.

Table E-4. State Rankings — # Median Income of Households and Families in Constant (2003) Dollars

Geographic area	Median household income in (2003) dollars				Rank				Median family income in (2003) dollars				Rank			
	2003	2002	2001	2000	2003	2002	2001	2000	2003	2002	2001	2000	2003	2002	2001	2000
United States . . .	43,564	44,049	43,937	44,270	(X)	(X)	(X)	(X)	52,273	52,764	52,754	52,904	(X)	(X)	(X)	(X)
Alabama	35,158	35,937	34,919	35,576	43	45	44	44	43,307	43,249	43,075	43,507	43	46	43	44
Alaska	52,499	57,567	58,292	56,586	6	2	3	3	61,117	67,256	64,509	63,190	8	4	6	6
Arizona	40,762	41,907	42,190	41,171	29	26	26	30	47,219	48,524	48,792	48,876	36	33	33	32
Arkansas	34,246	35,218	34,094	35,312	47	47	47	46	41,072	42,843	41,534	42,168	48	47	48	48
California	50,220	50,574	50,009	49,699	11	9	11	11	56,530	57,486	56,350	56,681	14	14	15	15
Colorado	50,538	49,017	49,237	49,445	10	12	12	12	59,252	58,481	58,263	59,373	12	11	12	9
Connecticut	56,803	57,539	58,427	57,693	3	3	2	2	69,917	70,421	70,807	69,729	2	2	1	2
Delaware	50,583	50,883	50,979	50,983	9	8	9	9	61,270	58,936	59,278	58,919	7	10	10	11
District of Columbia	42,118	44,668	42,264	43,534	(X)	(X)	(X)	(X)	50,243	50,073	49,030	48,890	(X)	(X)	(X)	(X)
Florida	39,871	40,050	39,561	40,626	34	34	36	32	47,442	47,617	46,899	48,340	35	36	38	34
Georgia	42,742	42,725	43,932	44,048	23	22	21	21	50,647	50,503	50,983	49,968	29	30	25	28
Hawaii	50,787	51,400	51,897	54,904	8	7	7	5	60,647	59,977	60,691	63,139	9	8	8	7
Idaho.	39,492	38,034	38,462	40,093	36	39	38	34	46,783	45,683	44,029	46,983	39	41	41	39
Illinois	47,977	47,458	47,853	48,737	14	14	14	13	57,385	57,916	58,326	58,993	13	12	11	10
Indiana	42,067	42,573	43,349	43,496	24	23	23	22	51,338	51,872	52,547	52,411	25	22	20	22
Iowa.	40,526	40,020	40,989	40,767	32	35	30	31	51,336	50,634	50,662	50,463	26	28	27	26
Kansas	41,075	40,789	40,333	42,970	28	31	33	24	51,157	51,353	49,588	52,737	27	25	31	20
Kentucky	34,368	35,650	34,831	35,029	46	46	45	47	41,898	43,838	42,556	43,018	45	44	44	45
Louisiana	34,141	34,092	34,763	32,981	48	48	46	49	41,831	41,696	42,296	41,095	46	48	45	49
Maine	39,838	40,676	39,011	38,980	35	33	37	38	48,541	48,086	45,610	48,911	32	34	39	31
Maryland	57,218	56,858	55,761	55,796	2	4	4	4	69,087	66,985	67,027	66,966	3	5	4	3
Massachusetts	53,610	56,367	54,718	53,204	5	5	5	7	67,527	68,411	67,933	65,908	4	3	3	4
Michigan	44,407	44,723	46,036	46,305	19	20	16	18	55,018	55,118	55,977	56,264	17	17	16	16
Minnesota	50,100	50,320	51,560	50,986	12	10	8	8	61,417	61,534	61,679	61,308	6	7	7	8
Mississippi	32,466	32,566	33,456	34,947	49	49	49	48	39,182	39,372	40,983	42,857	49	50	49	46
Missouri.	40,725	40,967	40,593	39,661	30	30	31	36	49,441	50,779	50,059	47,951	31	27	30	35
Montana	35,399	35,980	34,052	35,438	42	44	48	45	44,503	44,939	41,898	43,997	42	42	46	42
Nebraska	41,406	40,725	41,178	39,899	26	32	29	35	50,756	50,606	50,866	49,791	28	29	26	29
Nevada	45,395	44,846	45,418	45,481	18	18	18	19	52,502	51,183	52,407	52,454	20	26	23	21
New Hampshire.	53,910	55,456	54,693	54,199	4	6	6	6	63,439	65,816	64,767	64,493	5	6	5	5
New Jersey	58,588	60,031	58,429	57,727	1	1	1	1	70,263	72,082	69,856	69,904	1	1	2	1
New Mexico	34,805	36,721	35,561	35,602	45	42	42	43	41,661	43,586	41,645	42,816	47	45	47	47
New York	46,195	45,703	45,567	46,691	17	17	17	17	55,309	55,615	54,650	55,887	16	16	17	18
North Carolina.	38,234	38,972	40,296	40,302	40	36	34	33	45,540	46,926	48,003	47,555	41	39	35	37
North Dakota	37,554	36,895	36,483	36,768	41	41	41	41	48,386	48,072	47,976	45,833	33	35	36	41
Ohio	41,350	41,353	42,212	42,453	27	28	25	25	51,522	50,356	52,507	52,297	23	31	21	23
Oklahoma	35,129	36,228	35,154	36,309	44	43	43	42	43,259	44,234	43,266	43,523	44	43	42	43
Oregon	40,319	41,207	42,012	41,769	33	29	27	28	49,800	51,534	50,345	49,324	30	24	28	30
Pennsylvania	41,478	41,899	42,333	42,319	25	27	24	26	51,339	52,152	52,461	51,689	24	21	22	24
Rhode Island	48,854	46,653	44,373	46,750	13	16	20	16	60,165	56,977	56,598	57,732	11	15	14	14
South Carolina	38,467	38,739	40,143	38,894	37	37	35	39	47,081	47,411	48,935	46,857	37	37	32	40
South Dakota	38,415	38,068	38,140	37,174	38	38	39	40	46,824	47,245	47,529	47,582	38	38	37	36
Tennessee	38,247	37,913	37,541	39,035	39	40	40	37	46,654	46,735	45,155	47,448	40	40	40	38
Texas	40,674	42,184	41,915	42,069	31	24	28	27	47,479	48,967	48,772	48,595	34	32	34	33
Utah	46,873	47,505	47,873	48,461	15	13	13	14	52,481	52,405	54,017	54,916	21	20	19	19
Vermont.	43,697	44,745	43,636	43,207	21	19	22	23	52,895	54,203	51,771	51,328	19	18	24	25
Virginia	50,805	49,879	50,396	50,276	7	11	10	10	60,174	58,980	59,585	58,824	10	9	9	12
Washington	46,868	46,983	47,579	48,120	16	15	15	15	56,461	57,508	58,218	58,146	15	13	13	13
West Virginia	31,008	31,626	30,548	31,102	50	50	50	50	38,568	39,545	38,876	37,375	50	49	50	50
Wisconsin.	44,084	44,667	44,649	45,140	20	21	19	20	54,500	54,140	54,044	55,892	18	19	18	17
Wyoming	43,332	41,925	40,479	41,191	22	25	32	29	51,627	51,716	50,105	49,977	22	23	29	27

X Not applicable.

Note: When states share the same rank, the next lower rank is omitted. States may share the same value but have different ranks due to rounding.

Survey, Census, or Data Collection Method: Based on the American Community Survey; for information, see Appendix B, Limitations of the Data and Methodology, and Internet site <http://www.census.gov/acs/www/AdvMeth/index.htm>.

Source: U.S. Census Bureau, American Community Survey, Multi-Year Profiles 2003—Economic Characteristics, accessed 24 June 2005. See Internet site <http://www.census.gov/acs/www/Products/Profiles/Chg/2003/ACS/index.htm>.

Poverty Status of Families and Individuals in the Past 12 Months

	Number below poverty in past 12 months								Percent below poverty in the past 12 months							
	Families				Individuals				Families				Individuals			
			Rank				Rank				Rank				Rank	
Geographic area	2003 (1,000)	2000 (1,000)	2003	2000	2003 (1,000)	2000 (1,000)	2003	2000	2003	2000	2003	2000	2003	2000	2003	2000
United States ...	7,143	6,615	(X)	(X)	35,846	33,311	(X)	(X)	9.8	9.3	(X)	(X)	12.7	12.2	(X)	(X)
Alabama	164	146	14	15	748	672	14	14	13.7	12.4	6	7	17.1	15.6	6	7
Alaska	13	11	47	49	61	55	48	49	8.0	6.8	30	38	9.7	9.1	40	42
Arizona	166	150	12	13	839	780	12	12	11.9	11.6	10	10	15.4	15.6	10	7
Arkansas	89	96	26	25	421	439	29	27	12.1	13.0	9	6	16.0	17.0	9	5
California	849	832	1	1	4,610	4,520	1	1	10.5	10.7	16	12	13.4	13.7	18	12
Colorado	88	64	27	32	433	363	28	29	7.3	5.7	37	47	9.8	8.7	39	46
Connecticut	58	51	33	34	273	254	35	34	6.4	5.8	45	46	8.1	7.7	48	48
Delaware	12	14	48	46	69	70	47	46	5.8	6.7	48	40	8.7	9.3	45	39
District of Columbia	21	17	(X)	(X)	105	94	(X)	(X)	18.5	15.4	(X)	(X)	19.9	17.5	(X)	(X)
Florida	422	387	4	4	2,174	1,987	4	4	9.7	9.3	19	19	13.1	12.8	20	18
Georgia	234	206	9	8	1,125	999	9	9	10.8	10.0	12	15	13.4	12.6	18	19
Hawaii	21	19	43	43	132	103	41	43	7.4	6.8	36	37	10.9	8.8	30	44
Idaho	35	26	39	39	183	144	38	39	9.8	7.7	18	29	13.8	11.4	15	23
Illinois	265	262	6	5	1,389	1,335	5	5	8.5	8.6	25	20	11.3	11.1	26	26
Indiana	119	113	22	21	633	592	20	20	7.5	7.1	34	34	10.6	10.1	34	31
Iowa	53	53	34	33	286	281	33	33	6.9	7.0	42	35	10.1	10.0	38	34
Kansas	51	43	35	35	284	247	34	35	7.1	6.2	41	44	10.8	9.5	32	38
Kentucky	159	148	15	14	696	640	16	17	14.2	13.5	5	5	17.4	16.4	5	6
Louisiana	191	182	11	11	882	862	11	11	16.6	16.0	1	1	20.3	20.0	1	1
Maine	26	22	40	42	133	124	40	40	7.6	6.6	33	42	10.5	10.1	36	31
Maryland	86	89	29	26	439	477	27	24	6.1	6.6	47	41	8.2	9.3	47	39
Massachusetts	118	110	23	22	582	586	21	21	7.5	7.1	35	33	9.4	9.6	43	36
Michigan	224	196	10	10	1,118	975	10	10	8.6	7.7	24	30	11.4	10.1	25	31
Minnesota	75	66	31	30	383	328	30	30	5.6	5.1	49	49	7.8	6.9	49	49
Mississippi	121	104	20	23	553	498	24	23	16.4	14.2	2	4	19.9	18.2	2	3
Missouri	133	118	17	20	646	606	18	19	8.6	7.7	23	28	11.7	11.2	22	25
Montana	24	23	41	40	126	117	42	41	9.9	9.5	17	17	14.2	13.4	11	14
Nebraska	36	28	38	38	182	158	39	38	8.2	6.5	28	43	10.8	9.6	32	36
Nevada	47	34	36	37	252	194	36	36	8.7	6.9	22	36	11.5	9.9	24	35
New Hampshire	17	11	44	48	96	63	44	47	5.1	3.5	50	50	7.7	5.3	50	50
New Jersey	145	126	16	17	704	651	15	16	6.6	6.0	44	45	8.4	7.9	46	47
New Mexico	70	64	32	31	340	320	31	32	14.8	14.2	4	3	18.6	18.0	3	4
New York	499	491	3	3	2,501	2,391	3	3	10.7	10.7	13	13	13.5	13.1	17	16
North Carolina	239	203	8	9	1,136	1,018	8	8	10.7	9.6	14	16	14.0	13.1	13	16
North Dakota	13	14	46	45	71	71	46	45	8.4	8.1	26	25	11.7	11.6	22	20
Ohio	280	246	5	7	1,343	1,216	6	7	9.4	8.4	21	24	12.1	11.1	21	26
Oklahoma	112	100	24	24	546	459	25	26	12.4	11.0	8	11	16.1	13.8	8	11
Oregon	88	84	28	27	481	439	26	28	9.7	9.5	20	18	13.9	13.2	14	15
Pennsylvania	260	247	7	6	1,296	1,240	7	6	8.2	7.8	27	27	10.9	10.5	30	30
Rhode Island	22	23	42	41	117	108	43	42	8.2	8.5	29	22	11.3	10.7	26	28
South Carolina	121	123	19	19	563	557	22	22	11.3	11.7	11	9	14.1	14.4	12	10
South Dakota	14	16	45	44	81	83	45	44	7.2	8.4	40	23	11.1	11.5	28	22
Tennessee	164	158	13	12	780	745	13	13	10.6	10.5	15	14	13.8	13.5	15	13
Texas	712	639	2	2	3,508	3,056	2	2	13.1	12.3	7	8	16.3	15.1	7	9
Utah	43	40	37	36	244	192	37	37	7.6	7.2	32	32	10.6	8.8	34	44
Vermont	10	12	49	47	57	63	49	48	6.4	7.5	46	31	9.7	10.7	40	28
Virginia	126	124	18	18	642	630	19	18	6.6	6.8	43	39	9.0	9.2	44	41
Washington	121	127	21	16	654	667	17	15	7.9	8.6	31	21	11.0	11.6	29	20
West Virginia	76	72	30	29	326	327	32	31	15.5	14.7	3	2	18.5	18.6	4	2
Wisconsin	101	75	25	28	554	461	23	25	7.2	5.6	39	48	10.5	8.9	36	43
Wyoming	10	10	50	50	47	55	50	50	7.3	7.9	38	26	9.7	11.4	40	23

X Not applicable.

Note: When states share the same rank, the next lower rank is omitted. States may share the same value but have different ranks due to rounding.

Survey, Census, or Data Collection Method: Based on the American Community Survey; for information, see Appendix B, Limitations of the Data and Methodology, and Internet site <http://www.census.gov/acs/www/AdvMeth/index.htm>.

Source: U.S. Census Bureau, American Community Survey, Multi-Year Profiles 2003—Economic Characteristics, accessed 24 June 2005. See Internet site <http://www.census.gov/acs/www/Products/Profiles/Chg/2003/ACS/index.htm>.

Table E-6. State Rankings — **Value and Gross Rent of Specified Owner- and Renter-Occupied Units, Homeownership Rates, Vacancy Rates, and Housing Prices**

Geographic area	Median value of specified owner-occupied units in constant (2003) dollars[1]		Rank		Median gross rent of specified renter-occupied units in constant (2003) dollars[2]		Rank		Homeownership rate, 2004[3]		Vacancy rates, 2004				Housing prices of single-family homes, 2004[4]	
											Rental[5]		Homeowner[6]			
	2003 ($1,000)	2000 ($1,000)	2003	2000	2003	2000	2003	2000	Rate (percent)	Rank	Rate (percent)	Rank	Rate (percent)	Rank	Number ($1,000)	Rank
United States ...	147	129	(X)	(X)	679	649	(X)	(X)	69.0	(X)	10.2	(X)	1.7	(X)	211.7	(X)
Alabama	96	92	44	40	498	472	45	47	78.0	2	14.8	2	2.5	6	139.9	40
Alaska	174	155	12	11	780	734	6	6	67.2	42	7.0	41	1.8	19	179.5	23
Arizona	146	130	20	20	662	675	19	17	68.7	40	11.3	19	1.6	25	169.0	27
Arkansas	84	78	49	49	513	500	43	41	69.1	37	13.5	8	2.3	11	125.0	47
California	334	230	1	2	890	815	1	2	59.7	49	5.4	48	0.9	43	399.9	1
Colorado	210	180	6	6	754	727	11	10	71.1	30	12.7	13	2.8	3	234.0	13
Connecticut	226	179	5	7	766	734	10	6	71.7	26	8.4	36	0.9	43	289.0	6
Delaware	166	143	16	16	718	694	15	14	77.3	3	11.0	22	1.4	32	270.0	8
District of Columbia	248	178	(X)	(X)	721	677	(X)	(X)	45.6	(X)	11.3	(X)	2.4	(X)	370.0	(X)
Florida	145	115	21	26	724	699	14	12	72.2	23	11.7	16	1.7	21	185.0	19
Georgia	141	121	23	23	687	676	17	16	70.9	32	16.3	1	2.2	12	177.5	24
Hawaii	325	307	2	1	863	876	2	1	60.6	48	7.7	39	1.3	36	344.0	2
Idaho	118	112	32	28	565	510	32	39	73.7	12	9.8	28	1.4	32	150.0	33
Illinois	161	139	18	17	699	660	16	18	72.7	20	14.8	2	1.7	21	227.0	15
Indiana	107	101	37	35	581	556	30	29	75.8	7	12.9	12	2.5	6	120.0	49
Iowa	91	85	45	45	531	507	38	40	73.2	17	9.4	32	2.4	9	108.0	50
Kansas	100	90	40	42	535	534	37	33	69.9	35	13.6	7	2.8	3	147.0	36
Kentucky	104	94	38	38	491	478	47	44	73.3	14	11.3	19	2.1	15	144.6	38
Louisiana	99	90	41	41	525	516	39	37	70.6	33	7.3	40	1.3	36	145.4	37
Maine	135	110	25	31	562	523	33	35	74.7	10	6.8	42	0.8	46	185.0	19
Maryland	186	157	11	10	817	734	5	6	72.1	24	8.2	37	1.8	19	290.0	5
Massachusetts	310	206	3	3	820	763	4	4	63.8	46	6.5	43	0.7	48	340.0	3
Michigan	141	125	22	21	608	584	25	25	77.1	4	13.0	10	2.2	12	156.0	31
Minnesota	170	132	15	19	657	612	20	22	76.4	5	9.1	33	1.1	41	218.0	16
Mississippi	85	81	48	46	525	486	39	43	74.0	11	12.5	14	1.4	32	131.9	44
Missouri	109	97	36	37	556	523	34	35	72.4	21	10.3	25	3.1	2	139.9	40
Montana	119	106	30	32	506	478	44	44	72.4	21	9.7	29	1.7	21	164.0	29
Nebraska	101	92	39	39	540	525	36	34	71.2	29	9.5	31	1.5	28	141.9	39
Nevada	170	150	14	13	771	744	8	5	65.7	44	10.6	23	3.2	1	252.0	11
New Hampshire	208	148	7	14	780	703	6	11	73.3	14	4.8	49	0.9	43	255.0	10
New Jersey	246	185	4	4	856	813	3	3	68.8	39	6.2	44	0.7	48	310.0	4
New Mexico	119	113	31	27	523	511	41	38	71.5	28	8.1	38	1.6	25	126.2	46
New York	199	161	10	8	770	728	9	9	54.8	50	6.1	45	1.3	36	243.0	12
North Carolina	125	115	27	25	601	592	27	24	69.8	36	13.3	9	2.5	6	173.5	25
North Dakota	82	79	50	47	456	463	49	48	70.0	34	10.4	24	1.5	28	139.9	40
Ohio	119	110	29	30	575	543	31	32	73.1	18	13.0	10	2.1	15	180.0	22
Oklahoma	86	79	47	48	519	493	42	42	71.1	30	13.9	5	2.7	5	122.5	48
Oregon	171	160	13	9	657	659	20	19	69.0	38	11.8	15	1.7	21	205.0	17
Pennsylvania	110	101	34	36	602	551	26	30	74.9	8	11.7	16	1.4	32	190.0	18
Rhode Island	205	147	8	15	686	594	18	23	61.5	47	6.1	45	0.6	50	265.0	9
South Carolina	121	111	28	29	586	576	29	27	76.2	6	14.7	4	1.9	17	159.2	30
South Dakota	97	88	43	44	490	456	48	49	68.5	41	11.2	21	1.6	25	147.0	35
Tennessee	110	103	35	34	548	551	35	30	71.6	27	10.0	26	2.4	9	151.2	32
Texas	99	89	42	43	639	616	22	21	65.5	45	13.9	5	2.2	12	138.5	43
Utah	157	154	19	12	632	639	23	20	74.9	8	8.9	35	1.9	17	183.4	21
Vermont	138	123	24	22	624	578	24	26	72.0	25	4.7	50	0.8	46	130.0	45
Virginia	162	135	17	18	751	692	12	15	73.4	13	11.4	18	1.0	42	289.0	6
Washington	200	181	9	5	734	697	13	13	66.0	43	9.6	30	1.3	36	232.5	14
West Virginia	86	78	46	50	432	431	50	50	80.3	1	10.0	26	1.5	28	164.9	28
Wisconsin	132	117	26	24	595	574	28	28	73.3	14	9.1	33	1.5	28	169.9	26
Wyoming	116	105	33	33	494	476	46	46	72.8	19	5.6	47	1.2	40	149.0	34

X Not applicable.

[1]Specified owner-occupied units are owner-occupied, one-family, attached and detached houses on less than 10 acres without a business or medical office on the property.
[2]Specified renter-occupied units include all renter-occupied units except 1-unit attached or detached houses on 10 acres or more.
[3]Proportion of owner households to occupied households.
[4]Median price of single-family nonfarm homes.
[5]Proportion of the rental inventory that is vacant for rent.
[6]Proportion of the homeowner inventory that is vacant for sale.

Note: When states share the same rank, the next lower rank is omitted. States may share the same value but have different ranks due to rounding.

Survey, Census, or Data Collection Method: Specified owner- and renter-occupied units—Based on the American Community Survey; for information, see Appendix B, Limitations of the Data and Methodology, and Internet site <http://www.census.gov/acs/www/AdvMeth/index.htm>; Homeownership and vacancy rates—Based on the Current Population Survey/Housing Vacancy Survey (CPS/HVS); for information, see Appendix B, Limitations of the Data and Methodology, and Internet site <http://www.census.gov/hhes/www/housing/hvs/annual04/ann04src.html>; Housing prices—Based on the Finance Board Monthly Interest Rate Survey (MIRS); for information, see Internet site <http://www.fhfb.gov/>.

Source: Specified owner- and renter-occupied units—U.S. Census Bureau, American Community Survey, Multi-Year Profiles 2003—Housing Characteristics, accessed 24 June 2005. See Internet site <http://www.census.gov/acs/www/Products/Profiles/Chg/2003/ACS/index.htm>; Homeownership and vacancy rates—U.S. Census Bureau, "Housing Vacancies and Home Ownership Annual Statistics: 2004," Internet site <http://www.census.gov/hhes/www/housing/hvs/annual04/ann04ind.html> (accessed 31 Mar 2005); Housing prices—Federal Housing Finance Board, "Monthly Interest Rate Survey"; see Internet site <http://www.fhfb.gov/>.

Table E-7. State Rankings — Cost of Living Indicators—Utilities, Gasoline, and Tax Rates

Geographic area	Regular gasoline prices[1] 2004 (dollars per gallon)	Rank	Residential utility prices — No. 2 heating oil[1] 2004 (dollars per gallon)	Rank	Residential utility prices — Natural gas 2004 (dollars per 1,000 cubic feet)	Rank	Residential utility prices — Electric energy 2004 (dollars per 1,000 kilowatt-hours)	Rank	State individual income tax collections per capita[2] 2004 (dollars)	Rank	State tax rates[3] — General sales tax 2005 (cents per dollar)	Rank	State tax rates[3] — Gasoline 2005 (cents per gallon)	Rank
United States . . .	1.40	(X)	1.55	(X)	10.74	(X)	89.4	(X)	674	(X)	(X)	(X)	(X)	(X)
Alabama	1.36	40	(NA)	(X)	13.41	6	75.5	37	495	37	4.000	39	[4]18.00	36
Alaska	1.69	2	1.52	10	4.88	45	123.9	6	(X)	(X)	(X)	(X)	8.00	49
Arizona	1.55	5	(NA)	(X)	12.11	16	84.7	22	403	39	5.600	22	[5]18.00	36
Arkansas	1.34	47	(NA)	(X)	11.71	17	74.4	38	612	31	6.000	10	21.50	22
California	1.62	3	(NA)	(X)	9.93	32	117.8	9	1,014	6	[6, 7]7.250	1	18.00	36
Colorado	1.41	24	(NA)	(X)	8.40	43	83.2	25	742	18	2.900	45	22.00	20
Connecticut	1.45	11	1.52	11	14.04	3	116.4	10	1,233	3	6.000	10	25.00	11
Delaware	1.41	22	1.57	6	12.16	15	88.0	18	941	9	(X)	(X)	23.00	18
District of Columbia	(D)	(X)	(NA)	(X)	14.31	(X)	81.4	(X)	(X)	(X)	5.750	(X)	22.50	(X)
Florida	1.37	33	(NA)	(X)	18.47	2	89.5	17	(X)	(X)	6.000	10	[8]14.50	46
Georgia	1.36	36	(NA)	(X)	13.75	5	79.4	32	774	16	4.000	39	7.50	50
Hawaii	1.75	1	(NA)	(X)	27.15	1	180.6	1	926	10	4.000	39	[4]16.00	44
Idaho	1.45	12	1.50	16	9.06	38	60.8	49	652	27	6.000	10	25.00	11
Illinois	1.41	23	1.41	23	9.43	36	85.1	21	640	30	[6]6.250	8	[4, 5]20.10	27
Indiana	1.37	35	1.54	9	10.02	31	73.2	39	610	32	6.000	10	[5]18.00	36
Iowa	1.34	47	(NA)	(X)	(NA)	(X)	90.6	16	663	24	5.000	25	20.50	26
Kansas	1.35	43	(NA)	(X)	10.76	25	78.2	34	700	21	5.300	24	24.00	14
Kentucky	1.39	31	(NA)	(X)	11.02	23	60.8	49	680	23	6.000	10	[5, 9]17.40	41
Louisiana	1.34	46	(NA)	(X)	11.21	19	80.9	27	484	38	4.000	39	20.00	28
Maine	1.46	9	1.51	12	14.04	3	126.3	4	881	12	5.000	25	[10]25.20	10
Maryland	1.40	28	1.63	3	12.40	13	80.0	30	950	8	5.000	25	23.50	16
Massachusetts	1.44	15	1.56	7	(NA)	(X)	118.5	8	1,376	1	5.000	25	21.00	24
Michigan	1.40	27	1.54	8	8.47	42	85.5	20	650	28	6.000	10	19.00	33
Minnesota	1.42	19	1.43	22	9.56	33	80.6	28	1,119	5	6.500	5	20.00	28
Mississippi	1.37	32	(NA)	(X)	(NA)	(X)	81.7	26	366	40	7.000	2	18.40	35
Missouri	1.35	42	(NA)	(X)	11.04	21	70.6	43	647	29	4.225	38	17.03	42
Montana	1.40	28	(NA)	(X)	9.27	37	78.4	33	653	26	(X)	(X)	27.00	5
Nebraska	1.35	41	(NA)	(X)	9.02	40	69.1	44	711	19	5.500	23	[10]26.30	8
Nevada	1.61	4	(NA)	(X)	10.05	30	97.0	12	(X)	(X)	6.500	5	[4]23.00	18
New Hampshire.	1.45	14	1.50	15	13.20	9	125.1	5	42	42	(X)	(X)	19.50	32
New Jersey	1.45	12	1.66	2	11.59	18	112.4	11	851	13	6.000	10	14.50	46
New Mexico	1.43	18	(NA)	(X)	9.50	35	87.8	19	529	36	5.000	25	18.90	34
New York	1.43	16	1.63	4	12.42	12	145.8	2	1,282	2	4.250	37	23.20	17
North Carolina.	1.34	45	(NA)	(X)	12.65	10	84.4	24	849	14	[11]4.500	35	[9]26.85	7
North Dakota	1.45	10	(NA)	(X)	9.03	39	67.7	46	338	41	5.000	25	21.00	24
Ohio	1.37	34	1.48	19	10.45	26	84.7	22	760	17	6.000	10	26.00	9
Oklahoma	1.32	50	(NA)	(X)	10.24	28	76.7	35	658	25	4.500	35	17.00	43
Oregon	1.51	6	1.59	5	11.10	20	71.2	41	1,188	4	(X)	(X)	[4]24.00	14
Pennsylvania	1.36	37	1.49	18	12.26	14	96.6	13	590	33	6.000	10	30.00	2
Rhode Island	1.40	26	1.51	12	13.24	8	121.9	7	833	15	7.000	2	31.00	1
South Carolina	1.36	39	(NA)	(X)	12.46	11	80.5	29	581	35	5.000	25	16.00	44
South Dakota	1.41	21	(NA)	(X)	9.52	34	76.4	36	(X)	(X)	4.000	39	[4]22.00	20
Tennessee	1.34	44	(NA)	(X)	10.39	27	68.8	45	25	43	7.000	2	[4]21.40	23
Texas	1.33	49	(NA)	(X)	(NA)	(X)	96.0	14	(X)	(X)	6.250	8	20.00	28
Utah	1.40	30	(NA)	(X)	8.12	44	72.4	40	708	20	4.750	34	24.50	13
Vermont	1.49	7	1.51	14	11.03	22	130.7	3	692	22	6.000	10	20.00	28
Virginia	1.36	38	1.46	21	13.38	7	79.9	31	995	7	[7]5.000	25	[4, 12]17.50	40
Washington	1.47	8	1.75	1	(NA)	(X)	63.6	47	(X)	(X)	6.500	5	28.00	4
West Virginia	1.41	24	1.49	17	10.87	24	62.3	48	589	34	6.000	10	27.00	5
Wisconsin	1.42	20	1.47	20	10.13	29	91.0	15	917	11	5.000	25	[10]29.10	3
Wyoming	1.43	16	(NA)	(X)	8.56	41	71.0	42	(X)	(X)	[6]4.000	39	14.00	48

D Data withheld to avoid disclosure of individual company data.   NA Not available.   X Not applicable.

[1]Excludes federal and state taxes. Prices for No. 2 heating oil include sales of No. 2 fuel oil and high- and low-sulfur diesel fuels.
[2]Population estimated as of July 1.
[3]As of January 1 of the year shown.
[4]Does not include local option taxes.
[5]Carriers pay an additional surcharge equal to: Arizona, 8 cents; Illinois, 6.3 cents; Indiana, 11 cents; Kentucky, 2 percent; New York, 22.21 cents.
[6]Tax rate may be adjusted annually according to a formula based on balances in the unappropriated general fund and the school foundation fund.
[7]Includes statewide local tax of 1.25 percent in California and 1.0 percent in Virginia.
[8]Local taxes for gasoline vary from 9.7 cents to 17.7 cents in 2005, plus a 2.07 cents per gallon pollution tax.
[9]Tax rate is based on the average wholesale price and is adjusted quarterly.
[10]A portion of the rate is adjustable based on maintenance costs, sales volume, or cost of fuel to state government.
[11]Tax rate scheduled to decrease to 4.0 after June 30, 2005.
[12]Large trucks pay a higher tax: Vermont, total of 25 cents/gallon; Virginia, additional 3.5 cents.

Note: When states share the same rank, the next lower rank is omitted. States may share the same value but have different ranks due to rounding.

Survey, Census, or Data Collection Method: Gasoline, heating oil, and natural gas prices—Based on the Oil and Gas Information Retrieval System; for information, see Internet site <http://www.eia.doe.gov/>;   Electric energy prices—Based on Form EIA-861, "Annual Electric Power Industry Report"; for information, see Internet site <http://www.eia.doe.gov/cneaf/electricity/epa/epa_sum.html>;   State individual income tax—Based on the Annual Survey of State Government Tax Collection; for information, see Internet site <http://www.census.gov/govs/www/statetaxtechdoc2004.html>;   State tax rates—For information, see Internet site <http://www.taxadmin.org/>.

Sources: Gasoline prices—U.S. Energy Information Administration, *Petroleum Marketing Annual 2004*; see also Internet site <http://www.eia.doe.gov/>;   Utility prices—U.S. Energy Information Administration, "Petroleum Product Prices" and "Natural Gas Prices"; see Internet site <http://www.eia.doe.gov/emeu/states/_states.html> (accessed 12 September 2005); and *Electric Power Monthly*, March 2005; see also Internet site <http://www.eia.doe.gov/>;   State individual income tax—U.S. Census Bureau, "State Government Tax Collections"; see Internet site <http://www.census.gov/govs/www/statetax.html>;   State tax rates—Federation of Tax Administrators, 2005; see Internet site <http://www.taxadmin.org/fta/rate/tax_stru.html>.

Table E-8. State Rankings — Population by Residence

Item	Unit	United States	State	Value	State	Value	State	Value	State	Value	State	Value
Top 5												
Total population, 2004	1,000 . . .	293,655	California	35,894	Texas	22,490	New York	19,227	Florida	17,397	Illinois	12,714
Metropolitan and micropolitan area population, 2004	1,000 . . .	274,114	California	35,637	Texas	21,079	New York	18,794	Florida	17,013	Illinois	12,096
Percent of total	Percent . .	93.3	Connecticut	100.0	Delaware	100.0	New Jersey	100.0	Rhode Island	100.0	Hawaii	100.0
Nonmetropolitan area population, 2004[1]	1,000 . . .	19,542	Texas	1,411	Kentucky	1,016	Iowa	822	Virginia	821	Georgia	812
Percent of total	Percent . .	6.7	Montana	35.4	North Dakota	31.2	Maine	29.6	South Dakota	28.9	Wyoming	28.4
Urban population, 2000	1,000 . . .	222,361	California	31,990	Texas	17,204	New York	16,603	Florida	14,270	Illinois	10,910
Percent of total	Percent . .	79.0	California	94.4	New Jersey	94.4	Nevada	91.5	Hawaii	91.5	Massachusetts	91.4
Bottom 5												
Total population, 2004	1,000 . . .	293,655	Wyoming	507	Vermont	621	North Dakota	634	Alaska	655	South Dakota	771
Metropolitan and micropolitan area population, 2004	1,000 . . .	274,114	Wyoming	362	North Dakota	437	Vermont	458	Alaska	489	South Dakota	548
Percent of total	Percent . .	93.3	Montana	64.6	North Dakota	68.8	Maine	70.4	South Dakota	71.1	Wyoming	71.6
Nonmetropolitan area population, 2004[1]	1,000 . . .	19,542	Connecticut	–	Delaware	–	New Jersey	–	Rhode Island	–	Hawaii	(Z)
Percent of total	Percent . .	6.7	Connecticut	–	Delaware	–	New Jersey	–	Rhode Island	–	Hawaii	(Z)
Urban population, 2000	1,000 . . .	222,361	Vermont	232	Wyoming	321	North Dakota	359	South Dakota	391	Alaska	411
Percent of total	Percent . .	79.0	Vermont	38.2	Maine	40.2	West Virginia	46.1	Mississippi	48.8	South Dakota	51.9

– Represents zero. Z Less than 500 or .05%.

[1] Represents the area outside of metropolitan and micropolitan areas.

Note: If two or more states share the same rank, they are listed alphabetically. When six or more states make up the top 5 or bottom 5 listing due to shared ranks, only five states are listed alphabetically within the table and the remaining states are listed in the corresponding footnote.

Survey, Census, or Data Collection Method: Based on the Census of Population and Housing; for information, see Appendix B, Limitations of the Data and Methodology, and Internet sites <http://www.census.gov/main/www/cen2000.html> and <http://www.census.gov/popest/topics/methodology/>.

Sources: Total, metropolitan, micropolitan, and nonmetropolitan area population—U.S. Census Bureau, "Annual Estimates of the Population for Counties: April 1, 2000 to July 1, 2004" (CO-EST2004-01), published 14 April 2005; Internet site <http://www.census.gov/popest/counties/CO-EST2004-01.html>;   Urban population—U.S. Census Bureau, 2000 Census of Population and Housing, Population and Housing Unit Counts PHC-3, see Internet site <http://www.census.gov/prod/cen2000/index.html>.

Table E-9. State Rankings — Population by Race and Hispanic Origin—Percent of Total: 2004

Race or Hispanic origin	Unit	United States	State	Value	State	Value	State	Value	State	Value	State	Value
Top 5												
White alone	Percent . .	80.4	Maine	96.9	Vermont	96.9	New Hampshire	96.2	Idaho	95.5	West Virginia	95.2
Black or African American alone	Percent . .	12.8	Mississippi	36.8	Louisiana	33.0	Georgia	29.6	South Carolina	29.4	Maryland	29.1
American Indian, Alaska Native alone	Percent . .	1.0	Alaska	15.8	New Mexico	10.1	South Dakota	8.6	Oklahoma	8.1	Montana	6.4
Asian alone	Percent . .	4.2	Hawaii	41.8	California	12.1	New Jersey	7.0	New York	6.5	Washington	6.3
Native Hawaiian, Other Pacific Islander alone . .	Percent . .	0.2	Hawaii	9.1	Utah	0.7	Alaska	0.6	Nevada	0.5	Washington	0.5
Two or more races	Percent . .	1.5	Hawaii	20.1	Alaska	4.7	Oklahoma	4.0	Washington	2.9	Nevada	2.5
Hispanic or Latino origin	Percent . .	14.1	New Mexico	43.3	California	34.7	Texas	34.6	Arizona	28.0	Nevada	22.8
Non-Hispanic White alone	Percent . .	67.4	Maine	96.1	Vermont	96.0	West Virginia	94.4	New Hampshire	94.3	Iowa	91.7
Bottom 5												
White alone	Percent . .	80.4	Hawaii	26.5	Mississippi	61.3	Louisiana	64.1	Maryland	64.5	Georgia	66.4
Black or African American alone	Percent . .	12.8	Montana	0.4	Idaho	0.6	Vermont	0.6	North Dakota	0.7	Maine	0.7
American Indian, Alaska Native alone	Percent . .	1.0	Pennsylvania	0.2	West Virginia	0.2	Kentucky	0.2	Ohio	0.2	New Hampshire	0.2
Asian alone	Percent . .	4.2	Montana	0.5	West Virginia	0.6	Wyoming	0.6	North Dakota	0.7	South Dakota	0.7
Native Hawaiian, Other Pacific Islander alone . .	Percent . .	0.2	West Virginia	(Z)	Vermont	(Z)	Mississippi	(Z)	Ohio	(Z)	Maine	(Z)
Two or more races	Percent . .	1.5	Mississippi	0.6	Louisiana	0.8	West Virginia	0.8	South Carolina	0.8	Alabama	0.9
Hispanic or Latino origin	Percent . .	14.1	West Virginia	0.8	Maine	0.9	Vermont	1.0	North Dakota	1.5	Mississippi	1.7
Non-Hispanic White alone	Percent . .	67.4	Hawaii	23.3	New Mexico	43.5	California	44.5	Texas	49.8	Maryland	59.8

Z Less than .05%.

Note: If two or more states share the same rank, they are listed alphabetically. When six or more states make up the top 5 or bottom 5 listing due to shared ranks, only five states are listed alphabetically within the table and the remaining states are listed in the corresponding footnote.

Survey, Census, or Data Collection Method: Based on the Census of Population and Housing; for information, see Appendix B, Limitations of the Data and Methodology, and Internet sites <http://www.census.gov/main/www/cen2000.html> and <http://www.census.gov/popest/topics/methodology/>.

Sources: U.S. Census Bureau, "State Population Estimates with Sex, 6 Race Groups (5 Race Alone Groups and One Group with Two or More Race Groups) and Hispanic Origin: April 1, 2000 to July 1, 2004" (SC-EST2004-6RACE), published 11 August 2005; <http://www.census.gov/popest/datasets.html>; "Table 4: Annual Estimates of the Population by Race Alone and Hispanic or Latino Origin for the United States and States: July 1, 2004" (SC-EST2004-04), published 11 August 2005; <http://www.census.gov/popest/states/asrh/SC-EST2004-04.html>.

Table E-10. State Rankings — Persons With and Without Health Insurance Coverage: 2003

Insurance item	Unit	United States	State	Value	State	Value	State	Value	State	Value	State	Value
Top 5												
Persons												
Persons covered	1,000	243,320	California	28,895	Texas	16,484	New York	16,104	Florida	13,849	Illinois	10,810
Persons not covered	1,000	44,961	California	6,499	Texas	5,374	Florida	3,071	New York	2,866	Illinois	1,818
Percent not covered	Percent . .	15.6	Texas	24.6	New Mexico	22.1	Louisiana	20.6	Oklahoma	20.4	Montana	19.4
Children												
Children not covered	1,000	8,373	Texas	1,264	California	1,196	Florida	616	New York	432	Illinois	320
Percent not covered	Percent . .	11.4	Texas	20.0	Oklahoma	17.9	Montana	17.7	Nevada	17.4	Florida	15.5
Bottom 5												
Persons												
Persons covered	1,000	243,320	Wyoming	411	Alaska	523	Vermont	553	North Dakota	563	South Dakota	659
Persons not covered	1,000	44,961	Vermont	58	North Dakota	69	Wyoming	78	South Dakota	91	Delaware	91
Percent not covered	Percent . .	15.6	Minnesota	8.7	Vermont	9.5	Hawaii	10.1	Rhode Island	10.2	New Hampshire	10.3
Children												
Children not covered	1,000	8,373	Vermont	5	North Dakota	11	Rhode Island	13	Wyoming	15	South Dakota	16
Percent not covered	Percent . .	11.4	Vermont	3.9	Rhode Island	5.2	New Hampshire	5.5	Michigan	5.8	Maine	6.0

Note: If two or more states share the same rank, they are listed alphabetically. When six or more states make up the top 5 or bottom 5 listing due to shared ranks, only five states are listed alphabetically within the table and the remaining states are listed in the corresponding footnote.

Survey, Census, or Data Collection Method: Based on the Annual Social and Economic Supplement to the Current Population Survey; for information, see Internet site <http://www.census.gov/hhes/income/p60_226sa.pdf>.

Source: U.S. Census Bureau, Current Population Reports, annual, and unpublished data.

Table E-11. State Rankings — Health Conditions and Chronic Disease-Related Characteristics and Diabetes: 2001

Item	Unit	United States[1]	State	Value	State	Value	State	Value	State	Value	State	Value
Top 5												
High blood pressure	Percent . .	25.6	West Virginia	32.5	Alabama	31.6	Mississippi	31.3	Kentucky	30.1	Arkansas	29.7
High blood cholesterol	Percent . .	30.2	West Virginia	37.7	Nevada	36.5	Michigan	33.6	Tennessee	33.2	Rhode Island	33.1
Cigarette smoking[2]	Percent . .	23.2	Kentucky	30.9	Oklahoma	28.7	West Virginia	28.2	Ohio	27.6	Indiana	27.4
Heavy drinking[3]	Percent . .	5.1	Wisconsin	8.7	Nevada	7.8	Rhode Island	7.5	Delaware	7.1	Massachusetts	7.0
Above healthy weight[4]	Percent . .	58.9	Mississippi	63.8	Alaska	63.3	West Virginia	63.0	Kentucky	62.1	Alabama[6]	61.6
Obesity[5]	Percent . .	21.4	Mississippi	27.1	Michigan	25.8	West Virginia	25.3	Texas	25.2	Indiana	25.1
Diagnosed diabetes	Percent . .	6.5	Alabama	9.6	Mississippi	9.3	West Virginia	8.8	Florida	8.2	South Carolina	8.1
No leisure time physical activity in the past month . .	Percent . .	25.4	Louisiana	35.6	Tennessee	35.1	Kentucky[7]	33.4	Mississippi[7]	33.4	Oklahoma	32.8
Bottom 5												
High blood pressure	Percent . .	25.6	New Mexico	20.0	Vermont	21.4	Colorado	21.6	Alaska	21.8	Minnesota	22.3
High blood cholesterol	Percent . .	30.2	New Mexico	24.8	Hawaii	25.1	Louisiana	27.6	Nebraska[9]	27.8	South Carolina	27.8
Cigarette smoking[2]	Percent . .	23.2	Utah	13.2	California	17.2	Massachusetts	19.5	Idaho	19.6	Nebraska	20.2
Heavy drinking[3]	Percent . .	5.1	Tennessee	2.5	Kentucky	2.7	West Virginia	3.0	Utah	3.1	Oklahoma	3.5
Above healthy weight[4]	Percent . .	58.9	Hawaii	51.4	Colorado	51.7	Vermont	52.1	Massachusetts	54.4	Utah	54.8
Obesity[5]	Percent . .	21.4	Colorado	15.5	Massachusetts	17.1	Rhode Island[10]	18.1	Vermont[10]	18.1	Connecticut	18.2
Diagnosed diabetes	Percent . .	6.5	Alaska	4.0	Utah	4.3	Minnesota	4.4	Wyoming	4.5	Colorado	4.6
No leisure time physical activity in the past month . .	Percent . .	25.4	Utah	16.5	Minnesota[11]	17.1	Washington[11]	17.1	Hawaii	18.9	Colorado	19.2

[1]Represents median value among the states and DC.
[2]Has smoked 100 cigarettes or more and currently smokes.
[3]Having consumed an average of more than 2 drinks for males and more than 1 drink for females per day in the past month.
[4]Overweight is defined as having a body mass index greater than or equal to 25.0 and less than or equal to 99.8 kg/m^2.
[5]In adults age 20 years and over. Obesity is defined as having a body mass index greater than or equal to 30.0 and less than or equal to 99.8 kg/m^2.
[6]Alabama and Oklahoma share the same rank.
[7]Kentucky and Mississippi share the same rank.
[8]Minnesota and Utah share the same rank.
[9]Nebraska and South Carolina share the same rank.
[10]Rhode Island and Vermont share the same rank.
[11]Minnesota and Washington share the same rank.

Note: If two or more states share the same rank, they are listed alphabetically. When six or more states make up the top 5 or bottom 5 listing due to shared ranks, only five states are listed alphabetically within the table and the remaining states are listed in the corresponding footnote.

Survey, Census, or Data Collection Method: Based on the Behavioral Risk Factor Surveillance System (BRFSS); for information, see Internet site <http://www.cdc.gov/brfss/>.

Source: U.S. Centers for Disease Control and Prevention, Atlanta, GA, *Morbidity and Mortality Weekly Report, Supplemental Summaries* Vol. 52, No. SS-8, August 22, 2003; see Internet site <http://www.cdc.gov/mmwr/>.

Table E-12. State Rankings — Social Insurance, Human Services, Medicare, Medicaid, and State Children's Health Insurance Program: 2003

Item	Unit	United States	State	Value	State	Value	State	Value	State	Value	State	Value
Top 5												
Social security benefits												
Beneficiaries (Dec. 31)												
Total	1,000..	45,312	California	4,304	Florida	3,278	New York	3,024	Texas	2,731	Pennsylvania	2,377
Retired workers and dependents[1]	1,000..	31,652	California	3,110	Florida	2,433	New York	2,156	Texas	1,865	Pennsylvania	1,703
Payments[2]												
Total	mil. dol..	463,006	California	43,857	Florida	33,305	New York	32,187	Texas	27,068	Pennsylvania	24,919
Retired workers and dependents[1]	mil. dol..	309,918	California	30,115	Florida	23,685	New York	22,188	Texas	17,506	Pennsylvania	16,941
Federal food stamp program												
Participants (Sept. 30)	1,000..	21,222	Texas	1,872	California	1,709	New York	1,436	Florida	1,041	Illinois	954
Federal cost[3]	mil. dol..	21,332	Texas	1,881	California	1,806	New York	1,677	Illinois	1,053	Florida	988
National school lunch program												
Participants	1,000..	27,928	California	2,732	Texas	2,672	New York	1,788	Florida	1,398	Georgia	1,130
Federal cost[4]	mil. dol..	7,051	California	949	Texas	774	New York	489	Florida	411	Illinois	288
Supplemental security income (SSI)[5]												
Recipients (Dec.)	1,000..	6,902	California	1,163	New York	625	Texas	455	Florida	409	Pennsylvania	311
Annual payments	mil. dol..	34,696	California	7,573	New York	3,400	Florida	1,908	Texas	1,901	Pennsylvania	1,599
Temporary Assistance for Needy Families (TANF)[6]												
Recipients (Dec.)	1,000..	4,867	California	1,107	New York	336	Texas	318	Pennsylvania	214	Michigan	206
Annual payments[7]	mil. dol..	26,340	California	5,851	New York	4,463	Michigan	1,205	Pennsylvania	1,109	Ohio	1,007
State unemployment insurance[8]												
Beneficiaries, first payments	1,000..	9,827	California	1,380	New York	599	Pennsylvania	566	Texas	533	Michigan	502
Benefits paid	mil. dol..	41,117	California	6,115	New York	3,124	Pennsylvania	2,678	Illinois	2,455	Texas	2,204
Medicare enrollment[9]	1,000..	40,173	California	4,078	Florida	2,921	New York	2,763	Texas	2,390	Pennsylvania	2,110
Medicaid[9]												
Enrollment[10]	1,000..	49,755	California	9,301	New York	3,921	Texas	2,953	Florida	2,676	Tennessee	1,732
Payments[11]	mil. dol..	213,491	New York	31,489	California	23,636	Texas	11,121	Florida	9,827	Ohio	9,186
State Children's Health Insurance Program (SCHIP)												
Enrollment[12]	1,000..	5,985	California	955	New York	897	Texas	726	Florida	443	Georgia	252
Expenditures[13]	mil. dol..	4,276.4	California	565.0	Texas	405.6	Florida	357.7	New York	352.2	New Jersey	262.6
Bottom 5												
Social security benefits												
Beneficiaries (Dec. 31)												
Total	1,000..	45,312	Alaska	59	Wyoming	79	Vermont	107	North Dakota	114	South Dakota	138
Retired workers and dependents[1]	1,000..	31,652	Alaska	38	Wyoming	58	Vermont	74	North Dakota	82	South Dakota	98
Payments[2]												
Total	mil. dol..	463,006	Alaska	574	Wyoming	809	Vermont	1,066	North Dakota	1,082	South Dakota	1,282
Retired workers and dependents[1]	mil. dol..	309,918	Alaska	364	Wyoming	566	North Dakota	719	Vermont	723	South Dakota	873
Federal food stamp program												
Participants (Sept. 30)	1,000..	21,222	Wyoming	25	North Dakota	40	Vermont	41	New Hampshire	45	Delaware	46
Federal cost[3]	mil. dol..	21,332	Wyoming	24	North Dakota	37	Vermont	38	New Hampshire	40	Delaware	48
National school lunch program												
Participants	1,000..	27,928	Wyoming	49	Alaska	53	Vermont	54	Delaware	75	North Dakota	77
Federal cost[4]	mil. dol..	7,051	Wyoming	10	Vermont	10	North Dakota	13	Delaware	15	New Hampshire	16
Supplemental security income (SSI)[5]												
Recipients (Dec.)	1,000..	6,902	Wyoming	6	North Dakota	8	Alaska	11	Delaware[14]	13	New Hampshire[14]	13
Annual payments	mil. dol..	34,696	Wyoming	25	North Dakota	32	Alaska	47	South Dakota	52	Vermont	57
Temporary Assistance for Needy Families (TANF)[6]												
Recipients (Dec.)	1,000..	4,867	Wyoming	1	Idaho	3	South Dakota	6	North Dakota	9	Delaware[15]	13
Annual payments[7]	mil. dol..	26,340	South Dakota	26	North Dakota	42	Idaho	43	Arkansas	54	Montana	56
State unemployment insurance[8]												
Beneficiaries, first payments	1,000..	9,827	South Dakota	12	North Dakota[16]	16	Wyoming[16]	16	New Hampshire	23	Montana	27
Benefits paid	mil. dol..	41,117	South Dakota	33	North Dakota	47	Wyoming	49	Montana	81	Vermont	101
Medicare enrollment[9]	1,000..	40,173	Alaska	48	Wyoming	69	Vermont	93	North Dakota	103	Delaware	119
Medicaid[9]												
Enrollment[10]	1,000..	49,755	Wyoming	59	North Dakota	70	Montana	104	New Hampshire	104	Alaska	110
Payments[11]	mil. dol..	213,491	Wyoming	280	North Dakota	423	South Dakota	504	Montana	533	Vermont	607
State Children's Health Insurance Program (SCHIP)												
Enrollment[12]	1,000..	5,985	Minnesota	4	North Dakota	5	Wyoming	5	Vermont	7	Washington	10
Expenditures[13]	mil. dol..	4,276.4	Minnesota	(Z)	Vermont	3.1	Wyoming	3.9	New Hampshire	4.4	Delaware	4.6

Z Less than $50,000.

[1] Includes special benefits for persons age 72 and over not insured under regular or transitional provisions of the Social Security Act.
[2] Unnegotiated checks not deducted.
[3] Includes benefits only and excludes administrative expenditures.
[4] Includes cash payments and commodity costs.
[5] Data cover federal SSI payments and/or federally administered state supplementation.
[6] Prior to TANF, the cash assistance program to families was called Aid to Families with Dependent Children (1980–1996). Under the new welfare law (Personal Responsibility and Work Opportunity Reconciliation Act of 1996), the program became TANF.
[7] Represents federal and state funds expended in fiscal year.
[8] Includes unemployment compensation for state and local government employees where covered by state law.
[9] The data presented here are for 2002 because later data were unavailable at the time of this table's preparation.
[10] Persons who had payments made on their behalf at any time during the fiscal year.
[11] Payments are for fiscal year and reflect federal and state hospital share payments. Data exclude disproportionate hospital share payments. Disproportionate share hospitals receive higher Medicaid reimbursement than other hospitals because they treat a disproportionate share of Medicaid patients.
[12] Number of children ever enrolled in SCHIP.
[13] Expenditures for which states are entitled to federal reimbursement under Title XXI and that reconcile any advance of Title XXI federal funds made on the basis of estimates.
[14] Delaware, New Hampshire, South Dakota, and Vermont share the same rank.
[15] Delaware and New Hampshire share the same rank.
[16] North Dakota and Wyoming share the same rank.

Note: If two or more states share the same rank, they are listed alphabetically. When six or more states make up the top 5 or bottom 5 listing due to shared ranks, only five states are listed alphabetically within the table and the remaining states are listed in the corresponding footnote.

Survey, Census, or Data Collection Method: Social security, federal food stamp program, and national school lunch program—For information, please refer to Table A-80. SSI, TANF, and state unemployment insurance—For information, please refer to Table A-81. Medicare, Medicaid, and SCHIP—For information, please refer to Table A-83.

Sources: Social security, federal food stamp program, and national school lunch program—For source information, please refer to Table A-80. SSI, TANF, and state unemployment insurance—For source information, please refer to Table A-81. Medicare, Medicaid, and SCHIP—For source information, please refer to Table A-83.

Metropolitan statistical area	Area, 2000 (square miles) Total	Rank	Population 2005 (July 1)	Rank	Population per square mile of land area[1] 2005 (July 1)	Rank	Population change, April 1, 2000, to July 1, 2005 Total population change[2]	Rank	Percent change, 2000–2005	Rank	Population change, April 1, 1990, to April 1, 2000 Total population change[2]	Rank	Percent change, 1990–2000	Rank
Abilene, TX.	2,757.6	111	158,291	239	57.7	328	−1,950	331	−1.2	332	12,241	256	8.3	242
Akron, OH	927.2	280	702,235	69	776.0	20	7,275	211	1.0	284	37,385	142	5.7	281
Albany, GA	1,958.0	162	162,842	231	84.2	294	4,976	239	3.2	226	11,259	264	7.7	253
Albany-Schenectady-Troy, NY	2,878.3	101	848,879	57	301.3	103	23,004	107	2.8	238	16,432	230	2.0	318
Albuquerque, NM.	9,297.0	9	797,940	61	85.9	295	68,287	43	9.4	68	130,233	43	21.7	79
Alexandria, LA.	2,026.5	155	147,965	255	75.2	309	2,930	274	2.0	260	−4,047	347	−2.7	351
Allentown-Bethlehem-Easton, PA-NJ	1,475.7	220	790,535	63	541.8	36	50,141	55	6.8	106	53,707	103	7.8	250
Altoona, PA	527.1	343	126,795	288	241.1	136	−2,349	336	−1.8	343	−1,398	339	−1.1	339
Amarillo, TX	3,682.3	77	238,664	180	65.2	322	12,142	163	5.4	150	30,378	159	15.5	138
Ames, IA	573.7	338	79,952	353	139.5	225	−29	308	0.0	309	5,729	303	7.7	252
Anchorage, AK	27,220.9	2	351,049	138	13.3	358	31,444	82	9.8	63	53,584	104	20.1	91
Anderson, IN	452.9	350	130,412	280	288.5	109	−2,946	344	−2.2	350	2,689	323	2.1	317
Anderson, SC	757.5	310	175,514	224	244.4	137	9,774	181	5.9	130	20,544	205	14.1	153
Ann Arbor, MI	722.5	315	341,847	141	481.5	46	19,077	125	5.9	129	39,958	132	14.1	156
Anniston-Oxford, AL	612.3	333	112,141	313	184.4	179	−102	310	−0.1	310	−3,785	346	−3.3	353
Appleton, WI.	1,041.4	263	215,143	193	224.1	147	13,421	153	6.7	109	26,801	172	15.3	140
Asheville, NC	2,041.1	153	392,831	125	193.2	178	23,659	106	6.4	115	61,170	92	19.9	93
Athens-Clarke County, GA.	1,035.2	264	175,085	225	169.8	194	9,006	186	5.4	146	30,054	163	22.1	74
Atlanta-Sandy Springs-Marietta, GA	8,480.3	15	4,917,717	9	587.1	34	669,699	1	15.8	24	1,178,556	2	38.4	18
Atlantic City, NJ.	671.5	323	271,015	164	483.1	45	18,463	128	7.3	94	28,225	168	12.6	184
Auburn-Opelika, AL	615.6	331	123,254	296	202.4	168	8,162	196	7.1	97	27,946	170	32.1	26
Augusta-Richmond County, GA-SC	3,324.5	87	520,332	95	158.7	206	20,683	116	4.1	184	63,921	89	14.7	147
Austin-Round Rock, TX.	4,279.9	57	1,452,529	38	343.9	85	202,776	15	16.2	22	403,536	18	47.7	9
Bakersfield, CA	8,161.4	17	756,825	66	93.0	288	95,172	34	14.4	30	118,168	47	21.7	78
Baltimore-Towson, MD	3,104.5	93	2,655,675	19	1,017.9	17	102,681	31	4.0	189	170,822	37	7.2	263
Bangor, ME	3,556.1	80	147,068	256	43.3	339	2,149	285	1.5	278	−1,682	342	−1.1	340
Barnstable Town, MA	1,305.6	237	226,514	188	572.0	32	4,284	251	1.9	266	35,625	146	19.1	102
Baton Rouge, LA.	4,214.6	59	733,802	67	182.1	186	27,835	97	3.9	195	82,120	66	13.2	170
Battle Creek, MI	718.4	316	139,191	271	196.3	170	1,206	298	0.9	288	2,003	328	1.5	324
Bay City, MI	630.9	326	109,029	323	245.6	130	−1,128	322	−1.0	328	−1,566	341	−1.4	343
Beaumont-Port Arthur, TX	2,388.2	132	383,530	126	178.1	189	−1,560	325	−0.4	318	23,864	180	6.6	268
Bellingham, WA.	2,503.6	128	183,471	214	86.5	291	16,645	134	10.0	61	39,034	137	30.5	31
Bend, OR.	3,054.8	94	141,382	267	46.8	337	26,015	104	22.5	5	40,409	130	53.9	6
Billings, MT.	4,711.2	49	146,593	257	31.3	350	7,689	203	5.5	141	17,405	222	14.3	151
Binghamton, NY	1,238.4	245	248,422	173	202.6	164	−3,898	349	−1.5	337	−12,177	357	−4.6	356
Birmingham-Hoover, AL	5,369.8	41	1,090,126	48	205.8	163	38,820	75	3.7	206	95,394	58	10.0	216
Bismarck, ND	3,613.3	79	99,346	339	27.9	353	4,627	246	4.9	161	10,888	267	13.0	172
Blacksburg-Christiansburg-Radford, VA	1,089.6	254	151,057	251	140.4	226	−267	312	−0.2	313	10,557	271	7.5	258
Bloomington, IN.	1,345.1	232	177,709	221	134.5	234	2,203	284	1.3	281	18,837	215	12.0	193
Bloomington-Normal, IL.	1,186.3	249	159,013	238	134.3	237	8,580	193	5.7	133	21,253	198	16.5	126
Boise City-Nampa, ID.	11,833.1	5	544,201	88	46.2	338	79,361	38	17.1	19	145,244	40	45.4	12
Boston-Cambridge-Quincy, MA-NH	**4,511.5**	**52**	**4,411,835**	**11**	**1,258.0**	**9**	**19,495**	**123**	**0.4**	**299**	**257,449**	**25**	**6.2**	**274**
Boulder, CO[3]	751.4	311	280,440	161	378.0	74	10,653	174	3.9	194	65,949	85	29.3	38
Bowling Green, KY.	855.7	295	110,990	317	130.9	246	6,824	217	6.6	111	17,136	223	19.7	95
Bremerton-Silverdale, WA	566.0	339	240,661	178	607.7	29	8,692	192	3.7	202	42,238	122	22.3	72
Bridgeport-Stamford-Norwalk, CT	837.0	297	902,775	54	1,442.1	6	20,208	120	2.3	257	54,922	100	6.6	267
Brownsville-Harlingen, TX.	1,276.3	239	378,311	129	417.6	65	43,084	65	12.9	40	75,107	74	28.9	40
Brunswick, GA	1,607.1	201	98,433	342	75.7	307	5,389	229	5.8	132	10,837	268	13.2	168
Buffalo-Niagara Falls, NY	2,366.7	133	1,147,711	47	732.4	21	−22,400	360	−1.9	346	−19,177	360	−1.6	346
Burlington, NC	434.8	351	140,533	270	326.8	93	9,739	182	7.4	92	22,587	188	20.9	86
Burlington-South Burlington, VT	1,506.3	215	205,230	198	163.0	199	6,341	221	3.2	225	21,830	193	12.3	189
Canton-Massillon, OH.	979.9	273	409,996	115	422.2	59	3,062	272	0.8	292	12,828	251	3.3	303
Cape Coral-Fort Myers, FL	1,211.9	246	544,758	87	677.6	26	103,870	30	23.6	4	105,775	52	31.6	27
Carson City, NV.	155.7	361	56,062	361	392.0	72	3,605	263	6.9	103	12,014	257	29.7	34
Casper, WY	5,375.7	40	69,799	358	13.1	359	3,266	269	4.9	160	5,307	306	8.7	236
Cedar Rapids, IA.	2,019.7	157	246,412	175	122.7	258	9,182	185	3.9	196	26,590	175	12.6	182
Champaign-Urbana, IL	1,924.3	165	215,742	192	112.2	270	5,463	228	2.6	249	7,427	290	3.7	297
Charleston, WV.	2,547.0	126	306,435	150	121.0	259	−3,200	347	−1.0	329	1,946	329	0.6	331
Charleston-North Charleston, SC	3,162.9	91	594,899	81	229.6	145	45,927	62	8.4	78	43,538	124	8.3	239
Charlotte-Gastonia-Concord, NC-SC	3,147.2	92	1,521,278	36	491.1	47	190,859	16	14.3	31	305,805	22	29.8	33
Charlottesville, VA.	1,657.9	194	188,424	212	114.3	272	14,403	146	8.3	80	30,136	162	20.9	85
Chattanooga, TN-GA	2,137.9	146	492,126	98	235.6	139	15,625	139	3.3	222	44,321	120	10.0	215
Cheyenne, WY	2,687.6	117	85,163	351	31.7	349	3,556	264	4.4	178	8,465	284	11.6	200
Chicago-Naperville-Joliet, IL-IN-WI.	**9,579.2**	**8**	**9,443,356**	**3**	**1,309.4**	**8**	**344,741**	**10**	**3.8**	**200**	**916,240**	**8**	**11.2**	**206**
Chico, CA.	1,677.1	187	214,185	194	130.7	242	11,014	172	5.4	147	21,051	203	11.6	201
Cincinnati-Middletown, OH-KY-IN.	4,465.9	54	2,070,441	25	470.8	48	60,784	47	3.0	230	164,715	38	8.9	229
Clarksville, TN-KY	2,242.2	139	243,665	176	112.7	271	11,621	169	5.0	159	42,721	121	22.6	68
Cleveland, TN.	773.9	305	108,036	325	141.4	223	4,021	259	3.9	197	16,660	226	19.1	103
Cleveland-Elyria-Mentor, OH	3,978.9	67	2,126,318	23	1,061.0	12	−21,692	359	−1.0	327	45,895	117	2.2	314
Coeur d'Alene, ID	1,315.7	236	127,668	287	102.5	284	18,983	126	17.5	17	38,890	139	55.7	4
College Station-Bryan, TX	2,133.7	147	189,735	209	90.1	289	4,850	241	2.6	248	33,887	153	22.4	69
Colorado Springs, CO.	2,688.5	116	587,500	84	218.9	155	50,016	56	9.3	69	128,002	44	31.3	28
Columbia, MO.	1,161.9	251	153,283	247	133.2	239	7,617	204	5.2	154	23,656	181	19.4	98
Columbia, SC	3,833.2	71	689,878	70	186.4	182	42,617	68	6.6	110	98,823	56	18.0	110
Columbus, GA-AL	1,960.0	161	284,299	158	146.8	218	2,531	279	0.9	287	15,318	239	5.7	279
Columbus, IN	409.4	354	73,540	357	180.7	188	2,105	286	2.9	234	7,778	288	12.2	190
Columbus, OH	4,013.6	65	1,708,625	32	428.9	58	95,788	33	5.9	127	207,526	29	14.8	146
Corpus Christi, TX.	2,401.4	130	413,553	111	232.5	141	10,273	177	2.5	251	35,494	147	9.7	219

See footnotes at end of table.

Metropolitan statistical area	Area, 2000 (square miles)		Population		Population per square mile of land area[1]		Population change, April 1, 2000, to July 1, 2005				Population change, April 1, 1990, to April 1, 2000			
	Total	Rank	2005 (July 1)	Rank	2005 (July 1)	Rank	Total population change[2]	Rank	Percent change, 2000–2005	Rank	Total population change[2]	Rank	Percent change, 1990–2000	Rank
Corvallis, OR	679.0	321	78,640	356	116.3	261	501	304	0.6	295	7,342	291	10.4	212
Cumberland, MD-WV	759.0	309	100,667	336	133.7	235	−1,341	323	−1.3	334	365	336	0.4	333
Dallas-Fort Worth-Arlington, TX	**9,284.2**	**10**	**5,819,475**	**5**	**647.3**	**27**	**657,957**	**2**	**12.7**	**42**	**1,172,250**	**3**	**29.4**	**36**
Dalton, GA	637.5	325	131,701	278	207.7	162	11,640	168	9.7	65	21,422	196	21.7	80
Danville, IL	902.1	285	82,344	352	91.6	287	−1,580	326	−1.9	345	−4,338	349	−4.9	357
Danville, VA	1,022.1	266	107,997	326	106.5	277	−2,159	334	−2.0	347	1,445	330	1.3	325
Davenport-Moline-Rock Island, IA-IL	2,313.8	135	376,309	130	165.8	196	255	306	0.1	307	7,868	287	2.1	316
Dayton, OH	1,716.1	184	843,577	59	493.9	44	−4,576	353	−0.5	321	4,318	314	0.5	332
Decatur, AL	1,317.1	235	148,345	253	116.3	263	2,478	281	1.7	262	14,311	242	10.9	209
Decatur, IL	585.4	336	110,167	322	189.6	177	−4,539	352	−4.0	359	−2,500	344	−2.1	349
Deltona-Daytona Beach-Ormond Beach, FL	1,432.4	224	490,055	100	444.3	55	46,712	58	10.5	55	72,631	77	19.6	97
Denver-Aurora, CO[3]	8,387.2	16	2,359,994	22	282.3	113	181,600	17	8.3	79	507,267	12	30.7	29
Des Moines, IA	2,912.2	99	522,454	93	181.5	190	41,056	70	8.5	75	65,048	87	15.6	135
Detroit-Warren-Livonia, MI	**4,235.1**	**58**	**4,488,335**	**10**	**1,146.7**	**11**	**35,778**	**76**	**0.8**	**291**	**203,858**	**30**	**4.8**	**288**
Dothan, AL	1,728.9	183	136,594	273	79.5	302	5,733	224	4.4	176	10,509	272	8.7	235
Dover, DE	800.1	301	143,968	260	244.0	138	17,268	129	13.6	36	15,704	237	14.1	153
Dubuque, IA	616.6	330	91,631	347	150.7	210	2,475	282	2.8	241	2,740	320	3.2	305
Duluth, MN-WI	9,215.1	11	275,413	162	32.8	347	−73	309	0.0	308	6,256	301	2.3	312
Durham, NC	1,812.1	172	456,187	103	258.5	125	32,384	80	7.6	88	81,868	67	23.8	62
Eau Claire, WI	1,686.6	186	154,039	245	93.5	286	5,702	225	3.8	199	10,794	270	7.8	249
El Centro, CA	4,481.7	53	155,823	244	37.3	345	13,462	152	9.5	67	33,058	156	30.2	32
Elizabethtown, KY	893.6	288	110,646	319	124.2	253	3,103	271	2.9	236	6,628	297	6.6	270
Elkhart-Goshen, IN	467.9	349	195,362	205	421.0	64	12,571	160	6.9	102	26,593	174	17.0	117
Elmira, NY	410.8	353	89,512	348	219.4	149	−1,558	324	−1.7	341	−4,125	348	−4.3	355
El Paso, TX	1,014.7	269	721,598	68	712.3	22	41,976	69	6.2	121	88,012	61	14.9	145
Erie, PA	1,558.4	209	280,446	160	349.7	79	−397	314	−0.1	311	5,271	307	1.9	320
Eugene-Springfield, OR	4,721.8	48	335,180	143	73.6	313	12,203	162	3.8	201	40,047	131	14.2	152
Evansville, IN-KY	2,348.0	134	349,543	139	152.6	209	6,728	219	2.0	263	17,957	221	5.5	284
Fairbanks, AK	7,444.0	21	87,560	349	11.9	360	4,720	245	5.7	134	5,120	309	6.6	269
Fargo, ND-MN	2,820.7	105	184,857	213	65.8	321	10,490	175	6.0	125	21,071	202	13.7	159
Farmington, NM	5,538.4	38	126,208	290	22.9	355	12,407	161	10.9	53	22,196	192	24.2	58
Fayetteville, NC	1,050.8	260	345,536	140	331.0	88	8,923	188	2.7	247	39,187	134	13.2	169
Fayetteville-Springdale-Rogers, AR-MO	3,213.0	90	405,101	117	127.7	252	58,056	50	16.7	20	107,581	49	44.9	15
Flagstaff, AZ	18,661.2	3	123,866	295	6.7	361	7,546	205	6.5	113	19,729	212	20.4	90
Flint, MI	649.3	324	443,883	107	693.6	24	7,735	201	1.8	267	5,682	305	1.3	326
Florence, SC	1,370.5	230	198,443	202	145.8	217	5,288	233	2.7	243	16,960	225	9.6	220
Florence-Muscle Shoals, AL	1,342.4	233	142,351	266	112.6	268	−599	318	−0.4	320	11,623	262	8.9	231
Fond du Lac, WI	765.8	308	99,337	340	137.4	232	2,041	289	2.1	258	7,213	293	8.0	244
Fort Collins-Loveland, CO	2,633.9	120	271,927	163	104.5	279	20,433	119	8.1	85	65,358	86	35.1	22
Fort Smith, AR-OK	4,092.8	63	284,994	157	71.2	315	11,823	165	4.3	180	39,092	136	16.7	123
Fort Walton Beach-Crestview-Destin, FL	1,082.0	257	182,172	217	194.6	173	11,674	167	6.8	104	26,722	173	18.6	106
Fort Wayne, IN	1,368.4	231	404,414	118	296.7	106	14,258	147	3.7	207	35,721	145	10.1	213
Fresno, CA	6,017.4	32	877,584	56	147.2	216	78,177	40	9.8	64	131,917	42	19.8	94
Gadsden, AL	548.8	342	103,189	333	192.9	174	−270	313	−0.3	314	3,619	316	3.6	298
Gainesville, FL	1,324.6	234	240,254	179	196.4	171	7,862	200	3.4	217	41,129	129	21.5	82
Gainesville, GA	429.2	352	165,771	229	420.7	67	26,456	102	19.0	12	43,849	119	45.9	11
Glens Falls, NY	1,777.5	177	128,572	285	75.4	308	4,227	254	3.4	216	5,806	302	4.9	286
Goldsboro, NC	556.7	340	114,448	308	207.0	161	1,119	301	1.0	285	8,663	283	8.3	240
Grand Forks, ND-MN	3,437.6	82	97,073	344	28.5	352	−405	315	−0.4	319	−5,703	351	−5.5	359
Grand Junction, CO	3,341.1	85	129,872	281	39.0	342	12,937	158	11.1	52	23,110	185	24.8	57
Grand Rapids-Wyoming, MI	2,890.7	100	771,185	65	272.7	118	30,703	87	4.1	183	94,568	59	14.6	148
Great Falls, MT	2,711.7	113	79,569	354	29.5	351	−788	319	−1.0	326	2,666	324	3.4	302
Greeley, CO[3]	4,021.6	64	228,943	184	57.4	330	48,082	57	26.6	2	49,115	112	37.3	19
Green Bay, WI	2,849.0	104	297,493	154	159.2	203	14,996	142	5.3	151	38,901	138	16.0	131
Greensboro-High Point, NC	2,020.0	156	674,500	73	336.7	87	31,053	86	4.8	162	103,400	53	19.1	101
Greenville, NC	920.7	281	162,596	233	177.3	192	9,903	179	6.5	114	29,464	167	23.9	60
Greenville, SC	2,030.8	154	591,251	83	295.3	107	31,329	83	5.6	139	87,787	62	18.6	105
Gulfport-Biloxi, MS	1,976.8	159	255,383	170	169.9	195	9,193	184	3.7	203	38,315	140	18.4	107
Hagerstown-Martinsburg, MD-WV	1,018.8	267	251,311	171	249.3	135	28,540	93	12.8	41	29,997	164	15.6	137
Hanford-Corcoran, CA	1,391.5	228	143,420	262	103.1	281	13,959	149	10.8	54	27,992	169	27.6	44
Harrisburg-Carlisle, PA	1,664.4	191	521,812	94	320.3	96	12,738	159	2.5	252	34,832	152	7.3	261
Harrisonburg, VA	870.9	290	111,689	315	128.5	247	3,522	265	3.3	223	20,004	208	22.7	67
Hartford-West Hartford-East Hartford, CT	1,606.7	202	1,188,241	44	784.3	19	39,623	72	3.4	214	24,940	177	2.2	313
Hattiesburg, MS	1,620.9	199	131,871	276	81.9	299	8,059	197	6.5	112	14,209	244	13.0	173
Hickory-Lenoir-Morganton, NC	1,665.8	190	355,654	136	217.1	154	13,834	150	4.0	186	49,442	110	16.9	119
Hinesville-Fort Stewart, GA	1,006.0	271	68,627	359	74.6	300	−3,287	348	−4.6	361	12,967	249	22.0	75
Holland-Grand Haven, MI	1,632.0	197	255,406	169	451.2	53	17,092	130	7.2	96	50,546	108	26.9	46
Honolulu, HI	2,126.9	148	905,266	53	1,508.8	5	29,110	91	3.3	219	39,925	133	4.8	290
Hot Springs, AR	734.6	312	93,551	346	138.2	233	5,483	227	6.2	120	14,671	241	20.0	92
Houma-Bayou Cane-Thibodaux, LA	3,552.1	81	199,670	200	85.3	292	5,193	238	2.7	246	11,635	261	6.4	272
Houston-Sugar Land-Baytown, TX	10,061.9	6	5,280,077	7	591.4	31	564,670	5	12.0	45	948,072	7	25.2	54
Huntington-Ashland, WV-KY-OH	1,773.8	179	286,012	156	163.5	197	−2,637	342	−0.9	325	460	334	0.2	336
Huntsville, AL	1,419.9	227	368,661	133	268.5	121	26,034	103	7.6	89	49,329	111	16.8	120
Idaho Falls, ID	3,006.2	98	113,436	309	38.3	344	11,759	166	11.6	47	12,927	250	14.6	149
Indianapolis, IN	3,887.9	69	1,640,591	34	424.7	61	115,487	26	7.6	90	230,887	28	17.8	114
Iowa City, IA	1,194.1	247	138,524	272	117.1	262	6,848	216	5.2	156	15,945	234	13.8	158
Ithaca, NY	491.6	347	100,018	338	210.1	157	3,517	266	3.6	208	2,404	325	2.6	309
Jackson, MI	723.8	314	163,629	230	231.4	140	5,207	237	3.3	220	8,666	282	5.8	278

See footnotes at end of table.

Metropolitan statistical area	Area, 2000 (square miles) Total	Rank	Population 2005 (July 1)	Rank	Population per square mile of land area[1] 2005 (July 1)	Rank	Population change, April 1, 2000, to July 1, 2005 Total population change[2]	Rank	Percent change, 2000–2005	Rank	Population change, April 1, 1990, to April 1, 2000 Total population change[2]	Rank	Percent change, 1990–2000	Rank
Jackson, MS	3,795.3	73	522,580	92	140.3	230	25,383	105	5.1	158	50,256	109	11.2	205
Jackson, TN	847.4	296	110,857	318	131.0	241	3,492	267	3.3	224	16,576	227	18.3	108
Jacksonville, FL	3,698.1	76	1,248,371	42	387.6	73	125,621	24	11.2	50	197,537	34	21.4	83
Jacksonville, NC	908.6	283	152,440	249	198.7	166	2,085	287	1.4	280	517	333	0.3	335
Janesville, WI	726.2	313	157,538	240	218.8	152	5,231	236	3.4	215	12,797	252	9.2	224
Jefferson City, MO	2,278.4	138	143,867	261	63.9	324	3,815	260	2.7	244	19,348	214	16.0	130
Johnson City, TN	863.9	292	188,944	211	221.2	151	7,337	210	4.0	188	21,238	199	13.2	166
Johnstown, PA	693.4	317	148,073	254	215.2	153	−4,525	351	−3.0	356	−10,431	354	−6.4	360
Jonesboro, AR	1,476.4	219	112,084	314	76.3	306	4,322	250	4.0	191	14,142	245	15.1	143
Joplin, MO	1,268.0	241	166,178	228	131.3	244	8,856	190	5.6	137	22,412	190	16.6	124
Kalamazoo-Portage, MI	1,670.4	189	319,348	145	272.2	117	4,482	248	1.4	279	21,395	197	7.3	262
Kankakee-Bradley, IL	681.4	319	107,972	327	159.5	202	4,139	256	4.0	192	7,578	289	7.9	248
Kansas City, MO-KS	7,949.4	20	1,947,694	27	247.9	133	111,276	27	6.1	124	199,510	33	12.2	192
Kennewick-Richland-Pasco, WA	3,025.5	96	220,961	191	75.0	312	29,139	90	15.2	26	41,789	126	27.9	42
Killeen-Temple-Fort Hood, TX	2,858.6	102	351,528	137	124.5	257	20,816	115	6.3	118	61,892	90	23.0	66
Kingsport-Bristol-Bristol, TN-VA	2,047.1	152	301,294	152	149.7	211	2,810	276	0.9	286	22,806	186	8.3	241
Kingston, NY	1,160.8	252	182,693	216	162.2	200	4,944	240	2.8	240	12,445	253	7.5	257
Knoxville, TN	1,931.7	164	655,400	78	352.9	80	39,321	74	6.4	116	81,162	69	15.2	142
Kokomo, IN	554.3	341	101,362	335	183.3	185	−179	311	−0.2	312	4,595	312	4.7	291
La Crosse, WI-MN	1,048.8	262	128,899	283	127.5	248	2,061	288	1.6	275	10,437	273	9.0	228
Lafayette, IN	1,284.5	238	183,340	215	143.5	221	4,799	243	2.7	245	19,693	213	12.4	186
Lafayette, LA	1,086.8	255	247,824	174	245.4	134	8,888	189	3.7	204	30,346	161	14.5	150
Lake Charles, LA	3,025.9	95	194,977	207	81.8	298	1,409	297	0.7	293	16,174	233	9.1	225
Lakeland, FL	2,010.0	158	542,912	89	289.7	112	58,988	48	12.2	43	78,542	70	19.4	99
Lancaster, PA	983.8	272	490,562	99	516.9	40	19,904	121	4.2	182	47,836	113	11.3	203
Lansing-East Lansing, MI	1,714.5	185	455,315	104	266.7	119	7,493	208	1.7	273	15,054	240	3.5	301
Laredo, TX	3,375.5	84	224,695	189	66.9	319	31,578	81	16.4	21	59,878	96	44.9	14
Las Cruces, NM	3,814.6	72	189,444	210	49.8	334	14,762	144	8.5	76	39,172	135	28.9	39
Las Vegas-Paradise, NV	8,090.7	19	1,710,551	31	216.3	158	334,813	11	24.3	3	634,306	11	85.5	2
Lawrence, KS	474.5	348	102,914	334	225.2	146	2,949	273	3.0	233	18,164	220	22.2	73
Lawton, OK	1,083.8	256	112,429	312	105.2	280	−2,567	341	−2.2	351	3,510	317	3.1	306
Lebanon, PA	362.6	359	125,578	292	346.9	82	5,251	235	4.4	177	6,583	299	5.8	277
Lewiston, ID-WA	1,497.1	216	59,109	360	39.8	341	1,148	300	2.0	262	6,602	298	12.9	179
Lewiston-Auburn, ME	497.2	346	108,039	324	229.9	143	4,246	253	4.1	185	−1,466	340	−1.4	342
Lexington-Fayette, KY	1,484.1	218	429,889	110	290.7	110	21,563	111	5.3	152	59,898	95	17.2	116
Lima, OH	406.9	355	106,234	328	263.0	120	−2,239	335	−2.1	349	−1,282	338	−1.2	341
Lincoln, NE	1,422.4	226	281,553	159	199.1	169	14,766	143	5.5	142	37,696	141	16.5	125
Little Rock-North Little Rock, AR	4,198.2	60	643,272	80	157.3	207	32,754	79	5.4	149	75,484	73	14.1	157
Logan, UT-ID	1,841.4	171	110,426	321	60.3	326	7,706	202	7.5	91	23,305	184	29.3	37
Longview, TX	1,807.7	173	201,501	199	112.9	269	7,459	209	3.8	198	13,989	246	7.8	251
Longview, WA	1,166.3	250	97,325	343	85.4	293	4,377	249	4.7	164	10,829	269	13.2	167
Los Angeles-Long Beach-Santa Ana, CA	5,700.3	35	12,923,547	2	2,664.6	2	557,928	6	4.5	169	1,091,907	4	9.7	217
Louisville, KY-IN	4,196.3	61	1,208,452	43	292.2	108	46,037	60	4.0	193	106,002	51	10.0	214
Lubbock, TX	1,802.4	175	258,970	167	144.0	219	9,270	183	3.7	205	19,760	211	8.6	237
Lynchburg, VA	2,146.7	145	236,910	181	111.5	273	8,294	195	3.6	210	22,390	191	10.9	210
Macon, GA	1,737.7	182	228,712	186	132.6	238	6,327	222	2.8	237	15,752	236	7.6	255
Madera, CA	2,153.3	143	142,788	263	66.8	320	19,679	122	16.0	23	35,019	149	39.8	17
Madison, WI	2,802.1	106	537,039	90	196.1	172	35,265	77	7.0	99	69,451	80	16.1	129
Manchester-Nashua, NH	892.2	289	401,291	120	458.1	52	20,450	118	5.4	148	44,768	118	13.3	165
Mansfield, OH	500.3	345	127,949	286	257.4	124	−903	321	−0.7	323	2,715	322	2.2	315
McAllen-Edinburg-Mission, TX	1,582.7	203	678,275	72	432.0	62	108,812	29	19.1	11	185,918	35	48.5	8
Medford, OR	2,801.8	107	195,322	206	70.1	317	14,047	148	7.7	87	34,880	151	23.8	61
Memphis, TN-MS-AR	4,699.6	50	1,260,905	41	275.8	116	55,711	52	4.6	166	137,941	41	12.9	176
Merced, CA	1,971.9	160	241,706	177	125.3	254	31,152	85	14.8	28	32,151	157	18.0	110
Miami-Fort Lauderdale-Miami Beach, FL	6,137.2	30	5,422,200	6	1,057.8	13	414,212	9	8.3	81	951,464	6	23.5	64
Michigan City-La Porte, IN	613.0	332	110,512	320	184.8	183	406	305	0.4	301	3,040	318	2.8	307
Midland, TX	902.0	286	121,371	298	134.9	236	5,362	231	4.6	167	9,398	279	8.8	232
Milwaukee-Waukesha-West Allis, WI	3,322.3	88	1,512,855	37	1,036.2	14	12,111	164	0.8	290	68,592	82	4.8	289
Minneapolis-St. Paul-Bloomington, MN-WI	6,364.1	27	3,142,779	16	518.4	39	173,962	19	5.9	131	429,972	15	16.9	118
Missoula, MT	2,618.3	121	100,086	337	38.5	343	4,284	252	4.5	170	17,115	224	21.8	77
Mobile, AL	1,644.0	195	401,427	119	325.6	91	1,584	294	0.4	300	21,200	201	5.6	283
Modesto, CA	1,514.7	213	505,505	97	338.4	86	58,508	49	13.1	38	76,475	72	20.6	87
Monroe, LA	1,538.0	211	171,138	226	115.0	265	1,085	302	0.6	296	7,172	294	4.4	295
Monroe, MI	680.0	320	153,935	246	279.4	114	7,990	198	5.5	143	12,345	254	9.2	223
Montgomery, AL	2,786.5	108	357,244	135	131.1	240	10,716	173	3.1	229	41,353	127	13.6	162
Morgantown, WV	1,017.3	268	114,501	307	113.5	267	3,301	268	3.0	231	6,654	296	6.4	271
Morristown, TN	792.5	302	130,575	279	182.6	187	7,494	207	6.1	122	22,490	189	22.4	71
Mount Vernon-Anacortes, WA	1,920.5	166	113,171	311	65.2	323	10,192	178	9.9	62	23,424	182	29.4	35
Muncie, IN	395.9	357	116,362	303	296.1	104	−2,407	338	−2.0	348	−890	337	−0.7	337
Muskegon-Norton Shores, MI	1,459.3	222	175,554	223	344.9	83	5,354	232	3.1	227	11,217	265	7.1	264
Myrtle Beach-Conway-North Myrtle Beach, SC	1,255.0	242	226,992	187	200.2	175	30,363	88	15.4	25	52,576	106	36.5	21
Napa, CA	788.3	304	132,764	275	176.1	191	8,456	194	6.8	105	13,514	248	12.2	191
Naples-Marco Island, FL	2,304.9	137	307,242	149	151.7	215	55,865	51	22.2	6	99,278	55	65.3	3
Nashville-Davidson-Murfreesboro, TN	5,762.7	34	1,422,544	39	250.1	132	110,751	28	8.4	77	263,573	24	25.1	55
New Haven-Milford, CT	862.0	293	846,766	58	1,397.3	7	22,758	109	2.8	242	19,789	210	2.5	310
New Orleans-Metairie-Kenner, LA	7,097.0	23	1,319,367	40	418.4	63	2,855	275	0.2	304	52,119	107	4.1	296
New York-Northern New Jersey-Long Island, NY-NJ-PA	9,212.2	12	18,747,320	1	2,787.3	1	423,938	7	2.3	256	1,476,956	1	8.8	233
Niles-Benton Harbor, MI	1,581.4	204	162,611	232	284.8	111	156	307	0.1	306	1,075	332	0.7	330

See footnotes at end of table.

Table E-13. Metropolitan Area Rankings — **Population Indicators**—Con.

Metropolitan statistical area	Area, 2000 (square miles) Total	Rank	Population 2005 (July 1)	Rank	Population per square mile of land area[1] 2005 (July 1)	Rank	Population change, April 1, 2000, to July 1, 2005 Total population change[2]	Rank	Percent change, 2000–2005	Rank	Population change, April 1, 1990, to April 1, 2000 Total population change[2]	Rank	Percent change, 1990–2000	Rank
Norwich-New London, CT	771.7	307	266,618	166	400.3	69	7,512	206	2.9	235	4,131	315	1.6	323
Ocala, FL	1,663.0	193	303,442	151	192.2	180	44,526	63	17.2	18	64,083	88	32.9	25
Ocean City, NJ	620.3	328	99,286	341	389.4	71	-3,040	345	-3.0	357	7,237	292	7.6	256
Odessa, TX	901.7	287	125,339	293	139.1	231	4,216	255	3.5	213	2,189	326	1.8	321
Ogden-Clearfield, UT	1,904.0	169	486,842	101	327.0	94	44,186	64	10.0	60	90,857	60	25.8	51
Oklahoma City, OK	5,581.8	36	1,156,812	46	209.6	159	61,391	46	5.6	138	124,379	46	12.8	180
Olympia, WA	773.6	306	228,867	185	314.8	99	21,512	112	10.4	58	46,117	115	28.6	41
Omaha-Council Bluffs, NE-IA	4,406.2	55	813,170	60	186.4	181	46,030	61	6.0	126	81,244	68	11.8	197
Orlando-Kissimee, FL	4,011.8	66	1,933,255	28	553.8	37	288,692	12	17.6	16	419,709	16	34.3	23
Oshkosh-Neenah, WI	578.7	337	159,482	237	363.3	76	2,719	278	1.7	270	16,443	229	11.7	199
Owensboro, KY	931.4	279	111,599	316	123.3	256	1,724	291	1.6	276	5,194	308	5.0	285
Oxnard-Thousand Oaks-Ventura, CA	2,208.2	142	796,106	62	431.5	57	42,909	66	5.7	135	84,181	64	12.6	183
Palm Bay-Melbourne-Titusville, FL	1,557.0	210	531,250	91	521.9	41	55,020	53	11.6	48	77,252	71	19.4	100
Panama City-Lynn Haven, FL	1,033.3	265	161,558	236	211.5	160	13,341	155	9.0	71	21,223	200	16.7	122
Parkersburg-Marietta-Vienna, WV-OH	1,386.5	229	162,529	234	119.0	260	-2,095	333	-1.3	333	2,717	321	1.7	322
Pascagoula, MS	1,526.9	212	157,199	242	130.5	245	6,635	220	4.4	175	18,648	217	14.1	155
Pensacola-Ferry Pass-Brent, FL	2,049.1	151	439,877	109	262.0	122	27,724	98	6.7	108	67,747	84	19.7	96
Peoria, IL	2,518.3	127	369,161	132	149.5	212	2,286	283	0.6	297	8,347	286	2.3	311
Philadelphia-Camden-Wilmington, PA-NJ-DE-MD	**4,870.6**	**44**	**5,823,233**	**4**	**1,257.7**	**10**	**136,092**	**23**	**2.4**	**255**	**251,679**	**27**	**4.6**	**292**
Phoenix-Mesa-Scottsdale, AZ	14,598.4	4	3,865,077	14	265.2	126	613,201	4	18.9	13	1,013,396	5	45.3	13
Pine Bluff, AR	2,084.7	150	104,865	331	51.3	332	-2,480	339	-2.3	353	383	335	0.4	334
Pittsburgh, PA	5,343.1	42	2,386,074	21	451.9	51	-45,013	361	-1.9	344	-37,202	361	-1.5	345
Pittsfield, MA	946.3	278	131,868	277	141.6	220	-3,085	346	-2.3	352	-4,399	350	-3.2	352
Pocatello, ID	2,590.1	124	85,908	350	34.1	346	2,805	277	3.4	218	9,991	275	13.7	160
Portland-South Portland-Biddeford, ME	2,858.4	103	514,227	96	247.2	131	26,659	101	5.5	144	46,311	114	10.5	211
Portland-Vancouver-Beaverton, OR-WA	6,817.8	24	2,095,861	24	313.6	101	167,980	20	8.7	74	404,140	17	26.5	47
Port St. Lucie-Fort Pierce, FL	1,440.9	223	381,033	128	337.8	92	61,607	45	19.3	9	68,355	83	27.2	45
Poughkeepsie-Newburgh-Middletown, NY	1,663.9	192	667,742	75	412.7	66	46,225	59	7.4	93	54,408	101	9.6	221
Prescott, AZ	8,127.8	18	198,701	201	24.5	354	31,184	84	18.6	14	59,803	97	55.5	5
Providence-New Bedford-Fall River, RI-MA	2,236.2	140	1,622,520	35	1,013.4	15	39,523	73	2.5	253	73,208	76	4.8	287
Provo-Orem, UT	5,547.3	37	452,851	105	84.0	305	76,073	41	20.2	7	107,367	50	39.9	16
Pueblo, CO	2,397.7	131	151,322	250	63.3	325	9,850	180	7.0	101	18,421	218	15.0	144
Punta Gorda, FL	859.1	294	157,536	241	227.0	144	15,909	135	11.2	49	30,652	158	27.6	43
Racine, WI	791.9	303	195,708	204	587.7	30	6,877	214	3.6	209	13,797	247	7.9	247
Raleigh-Cary, NC	2,147.6	144	949,681	51	448.8	56	152,655	22	19.2	10	255,971	26	47.3	10
Rapid City, SD	6,266.8	29	118,203	301	18.9	357	5,385	230	4.8	163	9,597	278	9.3	222
Reading, PA	865.7	291	396,314	123	461.4	50	22,676	110	6.1	123	37,115	143	11.0	208
Redding, CA	3,847.4	70	179,904	220	47.5	335	16,648	133	10.2	59	16,220	232	11.0	207
Reno-Sparks, NV	6,815.1	25	393,946	124	59.6	327	51,061	54	14.9	27	85,692	63	33.3	24
Richmond, VA	5,841.7	33	1,175,654	45	205.8	165	78,697	39	7.2	95	147,713	39	15.6	136
Riverside-San Bernardino-Ontario, CA	27,408.5	1	3,909,954	13	143.4	227	655,133	3	20.1	8	666,028	10	25.7	52
Roanoke, VA	1,896.7	170	292,983	155	156.3	208	4,729	244	1.6	274	19,911	209	7.4	259
Rochester, MN	1,644.0	196	176,984	222	109.4	274	13,366	154	8.2	83	21,673	194	15.3	141
Rochester, NY	4,870.1	45	1,039,028	49	354.5	78	1,197	299	0.1	305	35,421	148	3.5	300
Rockford, IL	801.2	300	339,178	142	426.6	60	18,974	127	5.9	128	36,485	144	12.9	178
Rocky Mount, NC	1,049.3	261	145,507	259	139.2	228	2,516	280	1.8	268	9,791	276	7.3	260
Rome, GA	518.5	344	94,198	345	183.6	184	3,633	262	4.0	190	9,314	280	11.5	202
Sacramento-Arden-Arcade-Roseville, CA	5,309.3	43	2,042,283	26	400.9	70	245,426	14	13.7	35	315,755	21	21.3	84
Saginaw-Saginaw Township North, MI	815.8	299	208,356	195	257.5	123	-1,686	328	-0.8	324	-1,907	343	-0.9	338
St. Cloud, MN	1,802.9	174	181,159	219	103.3	282	13,763	151	8.2	82	18,416	219	12.4	187
St. George, UT	2,429.9	129	118,885	299	49.0	336	28,531	94	31.6	1	41,794	125	86.1	1
St. Joseph, MO-KS	1,673.9	188	121,961	297	73.4	311	-1,861	330	-1.5	336	6,520	300	5.6	282
St. Louis, MO-IL[4]	8,844.0	14	2,778,518	18	321.3	95	79,864	37	3.0	232	117,790	48	4.6	293
Salem, OR	1,938.4	163	375,560	131	195.1	176	28,342	95	8.2	84	69,190	81	24.9	56
Salinas, CA	3,771.1	75	412,104	112	124.1	250	10,342	176	2.6	250	46,102	116	13.0	174
Salisbury, MD	1,010.6	270	116,247	305	165.1	198	6,856	215	6.3	119	11,612	263	11.9	195
Salt Lake City, UT	9,977.0	7	1,034,484	50	108.4	276	65,601	44	6.8	107	200,783	32	26.1	50
San Angelo, TX	2,592.1	123	105,367	330	40.9	340	-414	316	-0.4	317	5,694	304	5.7	280
San Antonio, TX	7,384.7	22	1,889,797	29	257.5	127	178,071	18	10.4	57	303,958	23	21.6	81
San Diego-Carlsbad-San Marcos, CA	4,525.5	51	2,933,462	17	698.4	23	119,629	25	4.3	181	315,817	20	12.6	181
Sandusky, OH	626.2	327	78,665	355	308.5	98	-886	320	-1.1	331	2,772	319	3.6	299
San Francisco-Oakland-Fremont, CA	**3,424.4**	**83**	**4,152,688**	**12**	**1,679.2**	**3**	**28,946**	**92**	**0.7**	**294**	**437,148**	**14**	**11.9**	**196**
San Jose-Sunnyvale-Santa Clara, CA	2,694.7	115	1,754,988	30	654.8	25	19,169	124	1.1	282	201,545	31	13.1	171
San Luis Obispo-Paso Robles, CA	3,615.5	78	255,478	168	77.3	304	8,797	191	3.6	211	29,519	166	13.6	161
Santa Barbara-Santa Maria, CA	3,789.1	74	400,762	121	146.4	214	1,415	296	0.4	302	29,739	165	8.0	243
Santa Cruz-Watsonville, CA	607.2	334	249,666	172	561.0	33	-5,936	356	-2.3	354	25,868	176	11.3	204
Santa Fe, NM	1,910.8	167	140,855	268	73.8	314	11,567	170	8.9	72	30,364	160	30.7	30
Santa Rosa-Petaluma, CA	1,768.2	180	466,477	102	296.0	105	7,863	199	1.7	271	70,392	78	18.1	109
Sarasota-Bradenton-Venice, FL	1,617.9	200	673,035	74	512.6	43	83,072	35	14.1	32	100,476	54	20.5	88
Savannah, GA	1,569.6	207	313,883	148	231.0	142	20,584	117	7.0	100	34,940	150	13.5	163
Scranton-Wilkes-Barre, PA	1,776.4	178	550,546	86	315.1	97	-10,079	358	-1.8	342	-14,639	358	-2.5	350
Seattle-Tacoma-Bellevue, WA	**6,309.4**	**28**	**3,203,314**	**15**	**543.5**	**35**	**159,429**	**21**	**5.2**	**153**	**484,714**	**13**	**18.9**	**104**
Sheboygan, WI	1,271.0	240	114,610	306	223.0	148	1,954	290	1.7	269	8,769	281	8.4	238
Sherman-Denison, TX	979.2	274	116,834	302	125.1	251	6,239	223	5.6	136	15,574	238	16.4	127
Shreveport-Bossier City, LA	2,698.5	114	383,233	127	147.5	213	7,268	212	1.9	265	16,278	231	4.5	294
Sioux City, IA-NE-SD	2,094.6	149	142,571	264	68.8	318	-482	317	-0.3	315	11,703	260	8.9	230
Sioux Falls, SD	2,586.9	125	207,918	196	80.6	301	20,825	114	11.1	51	33,593	155	21.9	76
South Bend-Mishawaka, IN-MI	969.4	275	318,156	146	334.9	84	1,495	295	0.5	298	20,134	207	6.8	266

See footnotes at end of table.

Metropolitan statistical area	Area, 2000 (square miles)		Population		Population per square mile of land area[1]		Population change, April 1, 2000, to July 1, 2005				Population change, April 1, 1990, to April 1, 2000			
	Total	Rank	2005 (July 1)	Rank	2005 (July 1)	Rank	Total population change[2]	Rank	Percent change, 2000–2005	Rank	Total population change[2]	Rank	Percent change, 1990–2000	Rank
Spartanburg, SC	819.1	298	266,809	165	329.0	90	13,027	157	5.1	157	26,991	171	11.9	194
Spokane, WA	1,780.7	176	440,706	108	249.8	128	22,767	108	5.4	145	56,575	98	15.7	134
Springfield, IL	1,192.4	248	205,527	197	173.9	193	4,087	257	2.0	259	11,887	259	6.3	273
Springfield, MA	1,904.3	168	687,264	71	371.7	75	7,250	213	1.1	283	7,044	295	1.0	328
Springfield, MO	3,020.8	97	398,124	122	132.3	243	29,750	89	8.1	86	69,556	79	23.3	65
Springfield, OH	403.6	356	142,376	265	355.9	77	-2,365	337	-1.6	339	-2,806	345	-1.9	348
State College, PA	1,111.9	253	140,561	269	126.9	249	4,803	242	3.5	212	11,972	258	9.7	218
Stockton, CA	1,426.3	225	664,116	76	474.7	49	100,518	32	17.8	15	82,970	65	17.3	115
Sumter, SC	682.0	318	105,517	329	158.7	201	881	303	0.8	289	2,009	327	2.0	319
Syracuse, NY	2,779.4	110	651,763	79	272.8	115	1,609	293	0.2	303	-9,710	353	-1.5	344
Tallahassee, FL	2,602.7	122	334,886	144	140.3	229	14,582	145	4.6	168	61,208	91	23.6	63
Tampa-St. Petersburg-Clearwater, FL	3,330.9	86	2,647,658	20	1,036.7	16	251,645	13	10.5	56	328,038	19	15.9	133
Terre Haute, IN	1,484.8	217	168,059	227	114.7	264	-2,895	343	-1.7	340	4,365	313	2.6	308
Texarkana, TX-Texarkana, AR	1,560.3	208	133,805	274	88.5	290	4,056	258	3.1	228	9,617	277	8.0	245
Toledo, OH	2,208.9	141	656,696	77	405.4	68	-2,492	340	-0.4	316	5,031	311	0.8	329
Topeka, KS	3,290.2	89	229,075	183	70.7	316	4,524	247	2.0	261	14,294	243	6.8	265
Trenton-Ewing, NJ	228.8	360	366,256	134	1,620.6	4	15,495	140	4.4	173	24,937	178	7.7	254
Tucson, AZ	9,188.8	13	924,786	52	100.7	283	81,040	36	9.6	66	176,866	36	26.5	48
Tulsa, OK	6,460.2	26	887,715	55	141.3	224	28,185	96	3.3	221	98,513	57	12.9	175
Tuscaloosa, AL	2,667.6	119	196,885	203	75.3	310	3,751	261	1.9	264	15,861	235	9.0	227
Tyler, TX	949.5	277	190,594	208	205.4	167	15,888	136	9.1	70	23,397	183	15.5	139
Utica-Rome, NY	2,715.5	112	297,885	153	113.5	266	-2,011	332	-0.7	322	-16,737	359	-5.3	358
Valdosta, GA	1,629.0	198	124,838	294	78.6	303	5,272	234	4.4	174	20,316	206	20.5	89
Vallejo-Fairfield, CA	906.7	284	411,593	113	496.5	42	17,080	131	4.3	179	54,121	102	15.9	132
Vero Beach, FL	616.9	329	128,594	284	255.7	129	15,647	138	13.9	34	22,739	187	25.2	53
Victoria, TX	2,780.2	109	113,356	310	50.4	333	1,693	292	1.5	277	12,269	255	12.3	188
Vineland-Millville-Bridgeton, NJ	676.6	322	153,252	248	313.4	100	6,814	218	4.7	165	8,385	285	6.1	275
Virginia Beach-Norfolk-Newport News, VA-NC	3,896.5	48	1,647,346	33	626.8	28	70,429	42	4.5	171	126,981	45	8.8	234
Visalia-Porterville, CA	4,839.1	47	410,874	114	85.2	296	42,853	67	11.6	46	56,100	99	18.0	112
Waco, TX	1,060.2	259	224,668	190	215.6	156	11,155	171	5.2	155	24,394	179	12.9	177
Warner Robins, GA	379.8	358	126,163	291	334.6	89	15,398	141	13.9	33	21,557	195	24.2	59
Washington-Arlington-Alexandria, DC-VA-MD-WV	**6,028.0**	**31**	**5,214,666**	**8**	**926.7**	**18**	**418,484**	**8**	**8.7**	**73**	**673,269**	**9**	**16.3**	**128**
Waterloo-Cedar Falls, IA	1,514.1	214	161,897	235	107.4	275	-1,810	329	-1.1	330	5,066	310	3.2	304
Wausau, WI	1,576.1	206	128,941	282	83.5	297	3,107	270	2.5	254	10,434	274	9.0	226
Weirton-Steubenville, WV-OH	591.5	335	126,464	289	217.7	150	-5,544	355	-4.2	360	-10,515	355	-7.4	361
Wenatchee, WA	4,842.3	46	104,768	332	22.1	356	5,549	226	5.6	140	20,764	204	26.5	49
Wheeling, WV-OH	962.4	276	148,677	252	156.3	205	-4,501	350	-2.9	355	-6,129	352	-3.8	354
Wichita, KS	4,181.1	62	587,055	85	141.5	222	15,887	137	2.8	239	60,055	94	11.7	198
Wichita Falls, TX	2,675.0	118	146,276	258	55.5	329	-5,248	354	-3.5	358	11,149	266	7.9	246
Williamsport, PA	1,243.8	244	118,395	300	95.9	285	-1,649	327	-1.4	335	1,334	331	1.1	327
Wilmington, NC	2,310.6	136	315,144	147	163.8	204	40,594	71	14.8	29	74,408	75	37.2	20
Winchester, VA-WV	1,069.6	258	116,267	304	109.1	278	13,270	156	12.9	39	18,829	216	22.4	70
Winston-Salem, NC	1,473.2	221	448,629	106	306.9	102	26,672	100	6.3	117	60,513	93	16.7	121
Worcester, MA	1,579.0	205	783,262	64	517.7	38	33,289	78	4.4	172	41,258	128	5.8	276
Yakima, WA	4,311.6	56	231,586	182	53.9	331	9,005	187	4.0	187	33,758	154	17.9	113
York-Hanover, PA	910.3	282	408,801	116	452.2	54	27,050	99	7.1	98	42,177	123	12.4	185
Youngstown-Warren-Boardman, OH-PA	1,740.7	181	593,168	82	348.1	81	-9,796	357	-1.6	338	-10,658	356	-1.7	347
Yuba City, CA	1,252.3	243	156,029	243	126.5	255	16,880	132	12.1	44	16,506	228	13.5	164
Yuma, AZ	5,519.0	39	181,277	218	32.9	348	21,251	113	13.3	37	53,131	105	49.7	7

[1]Persons per square mile were calculated on the basis of land area data from the 2000 census.
[2]Includes net internal migration and residual not shown separately.
[3]The Denver-Aurora metropolitan statistical area includes Broomfield County. Broomfield County, CO, was formed from parts of Adams, Boulder, Jefferson, and Weld Counties on November 15, 2001, and is coextensive with Broomfield city. For the purposes of defining and presenting data for the Denver-Aurora metropolitan statistical area, Broomfield is treated as if it were a county when data are available to do so. In many cases, the data will not be available.
[4]The portion of Sullivan city in Crawford County, MO, is legally part of the St. Louis, MO-IL MSA. That portion is not included in these figures for the St. Louis MSA.

Source: U.S. Census Bureau. See Tables B-1 and B-2 of the State and Metropolitan Area Data Book: 2006. For more information, see <http://www.census.gov/population>.

Metropolitan statistical area	Black or African American alone, 2003 (percent)	Rank	Asian alone, 2003 (percent)	Rank	Hispanic or Latino origin,[1] 2003 (percent)	Rank	Age, 2003 (percent)				Educational attainment, 2000	
							Under 25 years	Rank	65 years and over	Rank	Bachelor's degree or higher (percent)	Rank
Abilene, TX.	6.8	182	1.1	217	18.7	60	38.7	68	13.2	134	19.6	221
Akron, OH	11.2	122	1.6	172	0.9	343	33.8	259	13.4	123	24.3	124
Albany, GA.	49.2	1	0.7	292	1.2	324	39.0	62	11.1	247	15.7	298
Albany-Schenectady-Troy, NY	7.3	174	2.6	90	3.1	222	32.5	308	13.7	103	29.1	55
Albuquerque, NM.	2.9	254	1.9	136	42.9	19	35.8	160	11.4	234	28.1	63
Alexandria, LA.	28.4	33	0.9	266	1.6	296	36.7	121	13.1	140	15.7	297
Allentown-Bethlehem-Easton, PA-NJ	3.4	244	2.0	129	8.1	108	32.1	321	15.1	53	21.7	181
Altoona, PA	1.2	310	0.5	350	0.5	360	31.4	330	17.3	23	13.9	332
Amarillo, TX	6.0	199	1.8	150	21.0	50	37.9	82	11.9	207	20.8	202
Ames, IA	1.9	284	6.2	21	1.6	297	41.8	19	9.9	305	44.5	5
Anchorage, AK	5.3	210	4.9	30	5.7	146	39.3	54	6.1	359	27.0	79
Anderson, IN	8.0	162	0.4	359	1.7	293	33.3	278	15.0	55	14.4	322
Anderson, SC	17.0	82	0.5	328	1.3	318	33.0	289	13.7	104	15.9	291
Ann Arbor, MI	12.3	111	7.6	16	2.8	230	36.4	132	8.3	342	48.1	2
Anniston-Oxford, AL	19.4	71	0.7	305	1.8	283	33.7	265	14.3	80	15.2	305
Appleton, WI.	0.6	341	2.4	99	2.0	275	36.0	147	11.0	250	22.2	169
Asheville, NC	5.0	214	0.7	304	3.8	191	29.9	345	17.5	21	23.1	151
Athens-Clarke County, GA.	19.8	67	2.2	115	5.6	149	39.5	50	9.1	333	32.4	34
Atlanta-Sandy Springs-Marietta, GA	29.2	31	3.7	53	7.7	114	36.0	148	7.7	352	31.4	38
Atlantic City, NJ.	18.2	78	5.7	23	13.3	70	33.7	262	13.4	121	18.7	236
Auburn-Opelika, AL	23.2	47	1.9	142	1.5	299	41.1	32	8.3	341	27.9	69
Augusta-Richmond County, GA-SC	35.3	16	1.5	180	2.2	252	37.1	109	11.2	242	20.4	208
Austin-Round Rock, TX.	7.9	165	4.0	45	28.3	37	37.3	99	7.2	356	36.7	21
Bakersfield, CA	6.3	193	3.6	54	41.5	20	41.8	20	9.2	331	13.5	337
Baltimore-Towson, MD	27.3	35	3.1	68	2.1	262	34.0	247	11.9	203	29.2	53
Bangor, ME	0.5	345	0.8	283	0.6	355	32.8	300	13.3	127	20.3	210
Barnstable Town, MA	2.1	279	0.8	279	1.5	306	26.1	359	22.9	8	33.6	30
Baton Rouge, LA.	34.4	19	1.5	178	1.9	280	38.2	76	9.8	315	22.8	156
Battle Creek, MI	11.0	125	1.3	203	3.3	215	35.1	191	13.7	106	16.0	290
Bay City, MI	1.4	303	0.5	332	4.0	183	32.6	306	14.9	57	14.2	325
Beaumont-Port Arthur, TX	25.4	40	2.1	118	8.8	102	36.2	141	13.2	131	14.7	317
Bellingham, WA.	0.8	334	3.1	70	5.5	150	35.9	152	12.0	202	27.2	76
Bend, OR.	0.3	357	0.8	272	4.2	179	32.4	310	13.3	129	25.0	111
Billings, MT.	0.5	348	0.6	316	3.7	194	33.6	268	13.7	101	26.2	94
Binghamton, NY	3.4	246	2.7	87	2.2	256	33.2	281	15.8	39	22.0	172
Birmingham-Hoover, AL	28.1	34	0.9	258	2.1	260	33.8	260	12.7	163	22.7	158
Bismarck, ND	0.3	360	0.5	349	0.7	353	35.0	201	13.3	128	25.5	100
Blacksburg-Christiansburg-Radford, VA	4.4	223	2.5	97	1.3	314	39.1	57	11.2	244	25.7	98
Bloomington, IN.	2.0	280	2.8	78	1.5	304	39.0	60	10.9	255	29.0	57
Bloomington-Normal, IL.	6.6	186	2.8	84	3.2	220	39.7	48	9.5	323	36.2	23
Boise City-Nampa, ID.	0.7	338	1.6	171	9.9	94	37.8	85	9.9	309	25.5	102
Boston-Cambridge-Quincy, MA-NH	**7.5**	**173**	**5.4**	**26**	**7.0**	**124**	**32.1**	**315**	**12.5**	**176**	**37.0**	**17**
Boulder, CO[4]	1.0	321	3.7	52	11.8	79	34.3	238	8.0	347	52.4	1
Bowling Green, KY.	8.0	161	1.3	194	2.9	229	36.7	124	10.9	253	22.3	168
Bremerton-Silverdale, WA	2.9	256	4.5	37	4.6	172	35.8	161	10.8	263	25.3	103
Bridgeport-Stamford-Norwalk, CT	10.7	130	3.8	48	12.9	73	32.8	297	13.0	143	39.9	10
Brownsville-Harlingen, TX	0.7	337	0.5	334	85.7	3	45.1	8	10.9	254	13.4	341
Brunswick, GA	23.5	45	0.5	331	2.7	236	34.6	216	13.6	109	19.7	219
Buffalo-Niagara Falls, NY	12.6	107	1.6	166	3.4	213	32.2	311	15.6	43	23.2	149
Burlington, NC	18.7	73	1.2	210	8.8	103	34.5	219	13.9	93	19.2	227
Burlington-South Burlington, VT	0.8	332	1.8	147	1.0	339	34.4	231	10.2	289	34.8	24
Canton-Massillon, OH.	6.7	183	0.6	317	0.9	346	33.1	284	15.2	52	17.3	270
Cape Coral-Fort Myers, FL	7.6	170	1.0	249	12.2	75	27.9	357	23.8	7	21.1	196
Carson City, NV.	1.7	291	1.6	173	15.6	68	32.2	313	15.3	50	18.5	244
Casper, WY	0.9	325	0.5	347	4.9	165	35.7	164	12.7	167	20.0	215
Cedar Rapids, IA	2.5	268	1.4	190	1.4	312	34.4	229	13.0	145	24.9	112
Champaign-Urbana, IL	9.7	137	6.5	18	3.2	218	39.8	45	10.7	269	34.5	25
Charleston, WV.	4.8	217	0.8	278	0.5	358	30.4	340	15.2	51	17.9	255
Charleston-North Charleston, SC	31.6	28	1.6	174	2.4	247	36.3	135	10.7	271	25.0	108
Charlotte-Gastonia-Concord, NC-SC	23.2	48	2.4	100	6.5	134	35.0	199	9.6	319	28.0	65
Charlottesville, VA	13.5	103	2.8	85	2.5	244	35.2	184	12.4	179	38.3	15
Chattanooga, TN-GA	14.0	101	1.1	218	1.6	295	32.8	301	13.6	114	19.4	224
Cheyenne, WY	3.1	250	1.0	230	11.6	81	35.1	195	11.7	215	23.4	143
Chicago-Naperville-Joliet, IL-IN-WI.	**18.5**	**76**	**4.9**	**31**	**17.9**	**63**	**36.0**	**151**	**10.7**	**267**	**29.0**	**56**
Chico, CA.	1.5	299	3.8	49	11.3	84	35.6	168	15.0	56	21.8	179
Cincinnati-Middletown, OH-KY-IN	11.5	119	1.5	175	1.2	323	35.5	170	11.6	217	24.8	116
Clarksville, TN-KY	20.2	62	1.7	157	3.9	186	39.6	49	9.6	321	16.2	287
Cleveland, TN.	3.5	243	0.7	303	2.1	265	33.4	275	12.7	160	14.5	319
Cleveland-Elyria-Mentor, OH	19.6	68	1.7	153	3.5	201	33.1	285	14.4	75	23.9	137
Coeur d'Alene, ID	0.3	361	0.5	327	2.6	241	35.5	176	12.9	153	19.1	230
College Station-Bryan, TX	12.2	113	3.4	61	18.7	61	45.4	7	8.5	340	31.5	37
Colorado Springs, CO.	6.9	180	2.8	81	11.6	80	37.9	83	8.8	338	31.8	36
Columbia, MO.	8.6	155	3.2	66	1.8	282	39.1	58	9.2	330	39.9	9
Columbia, SC.	34.2	21	1.4	185	2.6	237	35.6	165	10.6	273	26.6	86
Columbus, GA-AL	40.3	10	1.4	187	3.5	204	39.0	63	11.2	243	18.3	248
Columbus, IN.	1.7	289	2.3	108	2.7	233	34.3	235	12.7	164	22.0	173
Columbus, OH	13.6	102	2.9	74	2.1	269	35.4	181	10.0	298	28.3	62
Corpus Christi, TX	3.5	242	1.2	207	55.1	7	38.7	67	11.7	214	17.7	259

See footnotes at end of table.

Table E-14. Metropolitan Area Rankings — **Population Characteristics**—Con.

Metropolitan statistical area	Black or African American alone, 2003 (percent)	Rank	Asian alone, 2003 (percent)	Rank	Hispanic or Latino origin,[1] 2003 (percent)	Rank	Age, 2003 (percent) Under 25 years	Rank	65 years and over	Rank	Educational attainment, 2000 Bachelor's degree or higher (percent)	Rank
Corvallis, OR	0.9	328	5.2	27	5.1	162	37.3	98	10.6	274	47.4	4
Cumberland, MD-WV	4.7	219	0.5	347	0.7	351	31.8	325	17.1	24	13.4	338
Dallas-Fort Worth-Arlington, TX.	**14.0**	**100**	**4.3**	**39**	**24.3**	**44**	**38.2**	**78**	**7.8**	**350**	**28.5**	**60**
Dalton, GA	2.8	262	0.8	271	20.0	54	38.2	77	9.8	313	11.1	358
Danville, IL	11.0	124	0.6	320	3.3	214	33.5	270	16.1	33	12.5	348
Danville, VA	33.0	25	0.4	358	1.5	303	31.5	329	16.6	29	11.3	357
Davenport-Moline-Rock Island, IA-IL	6.1	197	1.4	193	6.1	140	33.9	255	14.0	88	19.9	216
Dayton, OH	14.5	96	1.6	168	1.2	327	34.5	221	13.5	115	22.8	154
Decatur, AL	11.9	117	0.4	351	3.4	210	33.5	271	12.6	169	15.8	295
Decatur, IL	14.5	97	0.8	282	1.1	331	34.1	242	15.7	40	16.9	273
Deltona-Daytona Beach-Ormond Beach, FL	10.0	135	1.2	216	7.9	111	29.3	353	21.3	10	17.6	261
Denver-Aurora, CO[4]	5.8	204	3.4	59	20.3	53	34.8	207	9.0	335	34.2	27
Des Moines, IA	4.0	234	2.7	88	4.5	174	34.7	212	11.3	240	27.9	67
Detroit-Warren-Livonia, MI.	**23.0**	**49**	**2.9**	**75**	**3.1**	**223**	**34.3**	**234**	**11.8**	**211**	**23.2**	**148**
Dothan, AL	23.5	46	0.5	338	1.5	300	33.5	274	14.8	60	15.9	292
Dover, DE	20.7	57	1.8	143	3.5	207	37.4	96	12.1	197	18.6	239
Dubuque, IA	1.1	317	0.7	289	1.2	325	35.0	198	14.8	58	21.3	188
Duluth, MN-WI	0.9	327	0.7	300	0.8	349	33.3	277	15.4	47	20.5	207
Durham, NC	28.7	32	3.6	58	8.0	110	34.7	211	10.2	288	38.8	14
Eau Claire, WI	0.4	351	2.2	116	0.8	348	36.5	129	13.1	142	22.1	170
El Centro, CA	4.3	225	2.1	120	74.7	5	41.7	23	10.3	284	10.3	361
Elizabethtown, KY	11.4	120	1.9	138	2.9	228	37.2	104	10.9	258	14.8	315
Elkhart-Goshen, IN	5.1	212	1.1	225	10.7	89	38.8	66	10.8	260	15.5	301
Elmira, NY	6.5	187	1.0	232	2.2	255	32.8	296	15.5	46	18.6	240
El Paso, TX	2.8	261	1.0	243	81.3	4	42.9	12	10.1	295	16.6	279
Erie, PA	6.3	194	0.7	294	2.2	257	35.5	177	14.2	81	20.9	201
Eugene-Springfield, OR	0.9	330	2.4	103	5.1	163	33.1	288	13.5	117	25.5	101
Evansville, IN-KY	5.6	207	0.7	288	1.1	335	34.4	226	13.8	94	17.4	265
Fairbanks, AK	6.7	185	2.0	125	4.7	169	41.7	25	5.0	360	27.0	78
Fargo, ND-MN.	1.1	314	1.4	189	1.8	281	37.5	92	10.6	275	29.4	51
Farmington, NM.	0.6	343	0.3	361	15.4	69	42.7	14	9.3	328	13.5	336
Fayetteville, NC.	37.7	14	2.1	124	5.6	148	41.7	22	8.3	343	18.3	250
Fayetteville-Springdale-Rogers, AR-MO	1.5	298	1.5	179	9.8	96	37.3	101	11.5	222	20.9	200
Flagstaff, AZ	1.0	319	0.9	257	11.1	85	41.7	21	7.4	354	29.9	45
Flint, MI	20.3	60	0.9	263	2.4	250	36.0	146	11.8	210	16.2	289
Florence, SC.	41.1	9	0.6	309	1.1	333	35.2	186	12.2	189	16.9	274
Florence-Muscle Shoals, AL.	12.5	109	0.4	360	1.1	330	32.1	316	15.5	44	16.8	276
Fond du Lac, WI	1.0	318	0.9	264	2.5	246	34.2	241	14.3	79	16.9	275
Fort Collins-Loveland, CO	0.8	333	1.8	146	8.9	101	35.7	162	9.6	320	39.5	12
Fort Smith, AR-OK	3.7	239	2.0	127	5.3	155	35.8	155	13.0	147	13.2	345
Fort Walton Beach-Crestview-Destin, FL	9.4	143	2.8	79	4.3	178	34.8	206	12.8	155	24.2	125
Fort Wayne, IN	9.8	136	1.5	181	4.2	180	37.2	103	11.6	219	21.3	189
Fresno, CA.	5.7	205	8.6	14	46.0	15	42.3	15	9.7	316	17.5	263
Gadsden, AL.	14.8	94	0.4	351	2.0	273	32.5	309	15.9	38	13.4	340
Gainesville, FL.	19.9	66	3.6	55	5.7	147	39.2	55	10.1	296	36.7	20
Gainesville, GA.	6.9	178	1.4	188	22.6	47	38.3	74	9.2	329	18.7	233
Glens Falls, NY	2.0	282	0.5	342	1.9	279	31.4	332	14.7	67	18.9	231
Goldsboro, NC	33.6	22	1.0	227	5.5	151	36.3	137	12.0	198	15.0	309
Grand Forks, ND-MN	1.2	307	1.0	237	2.8	232	38.3	73	12.2	192	24.2	126
Grand Junction, CO	0.5	346	0.6	324	10.3	92	34.4	230	15.3	49	22.0	177
Grand Rapids-Wyoming, MI.	7.9	164	1.7	156	6.9	128	37.7	86	10.5	279	22.7	159
Great Falls, MT	1.5	301	0.9	262	2.6	242	34.4	228	14.6	69	21.5	185
Greeley, CO[4]	0.8	335	1.0	247	29.7	34	40.9	33	8.2	344	21.6	183
Green Bay, WI	1.2	313	2.0	129	3.7	193	35.3	183	11.5	227	20.1	212
Greensboro-High Point, NC	23.8	43	2.2	117	5.2	159	33.8	258	12.4	180	23.4	144
Greenville, NC.	35.1	17	1.0	246	4.5	175	38.6	70	9.9	308	23.9	136
Greenville, SC.	17.5	81	1.4	192	4.0	184	34.5	217	12.0	201	23.1	153
Gulfport-Biloxi, MS	19.5	69	2.4	102	2.3	251	36.1	144	12.0	199	17.9	257
Hagerstown-Martinsburg, MD-WV	6.5	189	0.7	293	1.4	310	32.6	304	13.1	141	14.5	319
Hanford-Corcoran, CA	8.7	151	3.2	66	45.4	17	40.3	41	7.3	355	10.4	360
Harrisburg-Carlisle, PA	9.7	138	2.1	122	2.7	233	32.0	322	14.4	76	24.3	122
Harrisonburg, VA	3.4	245	1.4	184	6.4	138	40.7	35	12.1	193	21.4	186
Hartford-West Hartford-East Hartford, CT	10.7	129	2.8	83	9.8	95	32.5	307	13.7	99	30.5	41
Hattiesburg, MS.	26.5	37	0.8	276	1.3	321	39.2	56	10.8	261	22.6	160
Hickory-Lenoir-Morganton, NC	6.8	181	2.5	93	5.0	164	32.9	294	13.1	136	13.6	335
Hinesville-Fort Stewart, GA	38.6	12	1.9	135	6.4	137	48.8	3	4.8	361	13.2	344
Holland-Grand Haven, MI	1.2	309	2.4	104	7.4	117	39.7	47	10.4	282	26.0	96
Honolulu, HI	3.1	249	46.9	1	6.8	131	33.1	286	13.7	100	27.9	70
Hot Springs, AR.	8.1	158	0.6	322	2.7	235	29.7	348	20.7	11	18.0	253
Houma-Bayou Cane-Thibodaux, LA	15.7	88	0.8	270	1.7	290	38.0	81	10.8	264	12.3	349
Houston-Sugar Land-Baytown, TX	16.8	83	5.4	25	31.1	33	38.8	65	7.8	351	26.4	90
Huntington-Ashland, WV-KY-OH	2.5	269	0.5	332	0.7	354	31.7	326	15.4	48	14.9	313
Huntsville, AL.	21.5	53	1.9	137	2.2	259	34.5	222	11.5	220	30.9	40
Idaho Falls, ID.	0.6	342	0.8	277	8.5	106	42.1	18	10.2	291	24.2	127
Indianapolis, IN.	14.4	98	1.6	167	3.3	216	36.0	150	10.5	278	26.5	88
Iowa City, IA	2.8	258	4.6	36	2.6	238	37.3	100	9.1	334	42.0	8
Ithaca, NY	4.0	230	9.0	12	3.6	196	41.3	29	9.4	325	47.5	3
Jackson, MI	7.9	163	0.6	321	2.4	249	34.0	246	12.6	168	16.3	286

See footnotes at end of table.

Metropolitan statistical area	Black or African American alone, 2003 (percent)	Rank	Asian alone, 2003 (percent)	Rank	Hispanic or Latino origin,[1] 2003 (percent)	Rank	Age, 2003 (percent)				Educational attainment, 2000	
							Under 25 years	Rank	65 years and over	Rank	Bachelor's degree or higher (percent)	Rank
Jackson, MS	46.1	4	0.8	275	1.1	334	37.6	89	10.7	269	26.2	93
Jackson, TN	29.9	30	0.7	299	1.8	284	36.6	125	12.3	185	20.1	213
Jacksonville, FL	22.7	50	2.6	89	4.1	181	35.6	167	11.0	252	22.6	161
Jacksonville, NC	18.7	74	2.2	112	4.8	167	50.2	2	7.2	357	14.8	314
Janesville, WI	4.6	220	0.9	251	4.5	176	35.2	187	12.8	156	16.7	277
Jefferson City, MO	7.2	175	0.7	297	1.3	315	34.6	213	11.5	224	21.2	192
Johnson City, TN	2.8	259	0.6	318	1.5	308	30.3	342	14.7	66	18.5	245
Johnstown, PA	3.0	253	0.4	356	1.0	338	29.9	346	19.3	14	13.7	333
Jonesboro, AR	8.8	148	0.5	329	2.2	258	36.2	138	12.3	187	17.3	269
Joplin, MO	1.3	304	0.7	305	3.7	195	36.2	143	13.5	119	16.4	282
Kalamazoo-Portage, MI	8.7	150	1.7	151	4.1	182	37.1	111	11.6	218	26.9	83
Kankakee-Bradley, IL	15.6	90	0.8	279	5.9	142	37.0	116	12.9	151	15.0	310
Kansas City, MO-KS	12.7	106	2.0	128	5.7	144	35.1	194	11.3	238	28.0	66
Kennewick-Richland-Pasco, WA	1.6	296	2.2	114	23.1	46	39.9	44	9.6	322	23.3	146
Killeen-Temple-Fort Hood, TX	19.4	72	2.5	98	17.1	66	42.2	17	8.7	339	18.0	254
Kingsport-Bristol-Bristol, TN-VA	1.9	283	0.4	357	0.8	350	29.4	352	16.2	31	15.5	302
Kingston, NY	6.4	191	1.5	183	7.0	126	31.7	328	13.2	133	25.0	110
Knoxville, TN	6.3	192	1.2	206	1.4	313	31.9	323	13.6	108	24.6	118
Kokomo, IN	5.8	203	1.0	240	1.7	286	34.3	237	13.7	102	17.1	272
La Crosse, WI-MN	0.9	324	3.0	72	0.9	347	36.5	131	13.1	138	24.6	121
Lafayette, IN	2.2	275	4.5	38	5.2	160	41.6	26	9.8	314	29.2	53
Lafayette, LA	26.0	39	1.3	205	1.7	291	38.1	80	9.9	309	22.0	174
Lake Charles, LA	23.7	44	0.7	290	1.5	301	37.2	106	12.1	195	16.4	281
Lakeland, FL	14.7	95	1.1	219	11.4	83	34.0	250	17.8	20	14.9	311
Lancaster, PA	3.3	247	1.6	163	6.0	141	35.6	166	14.2	83	20.5	206
Lansing-East Lansing, MI	8.6	153	3.1	71	4.9	166	37.5	93	10.3	285	28.4	61
Laredo, TX	0.5	350	0.4	353	95.1	1	48.4	5	7.6	353	13.9	329
Las Cruces, NM	2.2	274	1.0	244	64.9	6	41.7	24	11.3	239	22.3	165
Las Vegas-Paradise, NV	9.1	144	5.5	24	24.4	43	34.9	203	10.8	266	17.3	268
Lawrence, KS	4.1	228	3.6	56	3.5	200	41.4	28	8.1	345	42.7	6
Lawton, OK	20.8	56	2.3	107	7.3	120	41.2	31	10.2	292	19.1	228
Lebanon, PA	1.5	300	0.9	254	5.2	157	31.7	327	16.5	30	15.4	303
Lewiston, ID-WA	0.3	359	0.7	302	1.9	278	32.6	303	17.1	25	18.6	241
Lewiston-Auburn, ME	0.9	326	0.7	307	1.1	332	32.6	305	14.2	84	14.4	323
Lexington-Fayette, KY	10.6	132	2.1	121	3.4	209	34.1	243	10.3	286	29.8	47
Lima, OH	12.2	114	0.8	284	1.5	309	36.1	145	13.9	89	13.4	339
Lincoln, NE	2.8	260	3.2	64	3.5	202	37.3	102	10.5	276	32.0	35
Little Rock-North Little Rock, AR	22.3	51	1.1	223	2.1	263	35.1	190	11.5	222	24.2	131
Logan, UT-ID	0.5	349	1.9	139	7.3	122	48.6	4	7.8	349	29.6	48
Longview, TX	17.8	79	0.6	323	9.2	100	36.3	134	13.8	97	16.2	288
Longview, WA	0.6	339	1.3	201	5.2	156	34.9	205	13.5	118	13.3	342
Los Angeles-Long Beach-Santa Ana, CA	**8.1**	**159**	**13.2**	**5**	**43.0**	**18**	**36.9**	**118**	**10.0**	**302**	**26.3**	**91**
Louisville, KY-IN	13.3	104	1.2	208	2.0	272	33.7	263	12.2	191	21.2	193
Lubbock, TX	7.8	168	1.3	204	29.6	35	39.9	43	11.2	241	24.0	135
Lynchburg, VA	18.3	77	0.8	285	1.0	337	33.5	273	14.8	59	18.7	234
Macon, GA	42.1	7	1.0	239	1.3	316	36.6	125	11.9	206	18.7	237
Madera, CA	4.0	231	1.5	176	47.2	14	39.7	46	10.8	265	12.0	352
Madison, WI	3.7	240	3.7	51	3.4	212	34.5	225	10.0	304	36.9	18
Manchester-Nashua, NH	1.7	295	2.5	94	3.6	198	33.6	269	10.6	272	30.1	44
Mansfield, OH	9.5	142	0.6	318	0.9	342	33.1	283	14.8	63	12.6	347
McAllen-Edinburg-Mission, TX	0.7	336	0.7	298	89.2	2	47.2	6	9.4	326	12.9	346
Medford, OR	0.5	347	1.0	234	7.4	119	32.8	302	15.9	35	22.3	167
Memphis, TN-MS-AR	44.9	5	1.6	170	2.6	239	37.4	97	9.9	312	22.0	176
Merced, CA	4.1	229	6.5	17	49.5	13	44.5	10	9.0	336	11.0	359
Miami-Fort Lauderdale-Miami Beach, FL	**20.9**	**55**	**1.9**	**133**	**36.8**	**25**	**32.1**	**318**	**15.9**	**37**	**24.1**	**132**
Michigan City-La Porte, IN	10.1	134	0.5	346	3.5	203	33.7	261	13.5	120	14.0	328
Midland, TX	6.9	179	1.0	242	31.8	32	39.5	51	11.9	205	24.8	115
Milwaukee-Waukesha-West Allis, WI	16.4	84	2.5	95	6.9	129	35.2	188	12.4	181	27.0	80
Minneapolis-St. Paul-Bloomington, MN-WI	5.9	201	4.7	33	3.8	189	35.1	192	9.6	318	33.3	31
Missoula, MT	0.4	355	1.2	211	1.7	292	34.8	208	10.1	294	32.8	32
Mobile, AL	34.4	18	1.7	160	1.2	326	37.0	117	12.1	194	18.6	238
Modesto, CA	3.0	252	4.7	34	36.0	27	40.7	38	10.0	303	14.1	327
Monroe, LA	33.4	23	0.7	295	1.5	305	38.3	75	12.3	183	21.2	194
Monroe, MI	2.0	281	0.6	312	2.2	253	35.1	196	11.4	235	14.3	324
Montgomery, AL	41.4	8	0.9	254	1.3	320	36.7	122	11.5	221	24.2	128
Morgantown, WV	2.7	265	2.2	113	0.9	345	35.7	163	11.7	216	26.0	95
Morristown, TN	2.9	257	0.5	339	4.4	177	32.1	319	13.6	112	12.2	350
Mount Vernon-Anacortes, WA	0.5	344	1.7	155	12.5	74	35.0	200	14.3	78	20.8	204
Muncie, IN	6.7	184	0.8	286	1.1	329	37.6	87	13.6	113	20.4	209
Muskegon-Norton Shores, MI	14.2	99	0.5	345	3.8	192	36.2	139	12.7	165	13.9	330
Myrtle Beach-Conway-North Myrtle Beach, SC	15.9	86	0.9	261	3.1	224	30.4	339	15.6	41	18.7	235
Napa, CA	1.8	287	4.2	42	26.6	40	32.9	293	14.4	74	26.4	89
Naples-Marco Island, FL	6.0	198	0.8	287	23.3	45	28.5	356	23.8	6	27.9	68
Nashville-Davidson-Murfreesboro, TN	15.1	93	1.9	140	3.8	190	34.3	239	10.3	287	25.6	99
New Haven-Milford, CT	12.4	110	2.9	75	11.1	86	33.0	290	13.9	91	27.6	73
New Orleans-Metairie-Kenner, LA	37.9	13	2.5	95	4.7	170	35.9	153	11.5	228	22.8	157
New York-Northern New Jersey-Long Island, NY-NJ-PA	**20.2**	**63**	**8.6**	**13**	**20.9**	**51**	**32.8**	**295**	**12.7**	**166**	**30.3**	**43**
Niles-Benton Harbor, MI	15.9	87	1.4	191	3.4	211	34.5	218	14.5	73	19.6	220

See footnotes at end of table.

Metropolitan statistical area	Black or African American alone, 2003 (percent)	Rank	Asian alone, 2003 (percent)	Rank	Hispanic or Latino origin,[1] 2003 (percent)	Rank	Age, 2003 (percent)				Educational attainment, 2000	
							Under 25 years	Rank	65 years and over	Rank	Bachelor's degree or higher (percent)	Rank
Norwich-New London, CT	6.1	196	2.6	91	5.5	152	32.8	299	13.0	144	26.2	92
Ocala, FL	12.0	116	0.9	267	7.0	127	29.4	349	23.9	4	13.7	334
Ocean City, NJ	5.0	215	0.6	311	3.6	199	29.3	354	20.3	12	22.0	175
Odessa, TX	4.7	218	0.6	310	45.7	16	41.2	30	11.1	248	12.0	353
Ogden-Clearfield, UT	1.4	302	1.6	165	9.3	99	45.0	9	8.8	337	24.6	119
Oklahoma City, OK	10.9	126	2.9	73	7.4	118	36.2	142	11.4	236	24.2	130
Olympia, WA	2.6	267	4.7	32	4.8	168	33.9	254	11.5	226	29.8	46
Omaha-Council Bluffs, NE-IA	7.8	166	1.8	144	5.8	143	36.6	127	10.9	259	27.1	77
Orlando-Kissimee, FL	15.7	89	3.2	65	19.0	58	34.5	220	12.3	186	24.8	117
Oshkosh-Neenah, WI	1.2	312	2.1	123	2.1	268	34.3	236	12.5	172	22.8	155
Owensboro, KY	3.9	237	0.4	355	1.0	336	34.9	204	13.7	105	15.6	299
Oxnard-Thousand Oaks-Ventura, CA	2.2	276	5.8	22	35.3	28	37.0	113	10.5	280	26.9	81
Palm Bay-Melbourne-Titusville, FL	9.0	145	1.7	152	5.2	158	29.8	347	20.0	13	23.6	142
Panama City-Lynn Haven, FL	11.1	123	1.9	141	2.1	261	33.1	287	14.0	86	17.7	260
Parkersburg-Marietta-Vienna, WV-OH	1.0	320	0.6	326	0.5	359	31.4	331	15.5	45	14.7	316
Pascagoula, MS	20.1	64	1.7	159	2.1	264	36.9	119	10.9	256	15.5	300
Pensacola-Ferry Pass-Brent, FL	17.6	80	2.2	111	2.1	266	35.8	156	13.2	132	21.5	184
Peoria, IL	8.8	149	1.3	197	1.8	284	34.0	247	14.7	65	20.8	205
Philadelphia-Camden-Wilmington, PA-NJ-DE-MD	**20.6**	**59**	**3.8**	**47**	**5.4**	**153**	**34.0**	**251**	**13.1**	**137**	**27.7**	**72**
Phoenix-Mesa-Scottsdale, AZ	4.0	232	2.4	101	28.1	38	37.5	91	11.4	229	25.1	107
Pine Bluff, AR	46.4	3	0.6	314	1.1	328	36.4	133	12.8	157	14.1	326
Pittsburgh, PA	8.0	160	1.3	195	0.7	352	30.1	343	17.3	22	23.4	145
Pittsfield, MA	2.2	273	1.2	214	2.0	270	30.7	336	17.8	19	26.0	97
Pocatello, ID	0.6	340	1.0	234	6.8	132	40.5	40	10.5	277	24.0	134
Portland-South Portland-Biddeford, ME	0.9	323	1.3	199	1.0	340	31.2	334	13.4	124	29.2	52
Portland-Vancouver-Beaverton, OR-WA	2.9	255	5.2	28	8.7	104	34.0	245	10.2	290	28.8	58
Port St. Lucie-Fort Pierce, FL	12.2	112	0.9	251	9.4	98	28.9	355	23.9	5	19.7	218
Poughkeepsie-Newburgh-Middletown, NY	10.2	133	2.6	92	11.5	82	35.8	159	10.9	256	24.9	113
Prescott, AZ	0.4	352	0.6	325	10.5	91	29.4	351	21.9	9	21.1	195
Providence-New Bedford-Fall River, RI-MA	5.1	213	2.3	106	7.8	113	33.2	282	13.9	92	23.7	139
Provo-Orem, UT	0.4	353	1.2	209	7.5	116	50.8	1	6.5	358	31.0	39
Pueblo, CO	2.3	272	0.7	291	39.3	23	35.6	169	14.8	61	18.3	247
Punta Gorda, FL	4.9	216	1.0	230	3.8	188	21.9	361	34.1	1	17.6	262
Racine, WI	10.9	127	0.8	274	8.6	105	35.5	175	12.2	190	20.3	211
Raleigh-Cary, NC	20.1	65	3.3	63	7.0	125	35.5	179	7.9	348	37.6	16
Rapid City, SD	1.3	306	0.9	253	2.5	245	37.1	108	12.0	199	23.3	147
Reading, PA	4.4	222	1.2	212	10.6	90	33.6	267	14.5	72	18.5	242
Redding, CA	0.9	329	2.0	126	6.6	133	34.0	252	15.0	54	16.6	280
Reno-Sparks, NV	1.9	286	4.2	43	18.4	62	34.5	224	10.8	262	23.7	139
Richmond, VA	30.8	29	2.1	119	2.6	240	34.2	240	11.4	233	27.6	74
Riverside-San Bernardino-Ontario, CA	8.2	157	4.6	35	40.9	22	40.7	36	10.0	297	16.3	285
Roanoke, VA	12.5	108	1.2	215	1.4	311	30.9	335	15.6	42	21.0	197
Rochester, MN	2.4	270	3.9	46	2.4	248	34.8	209	11.7	213	30.5	42
Rochester, NY	11.8	118	2.2	110	5.2	161	34.1	244	13.0	149	27.7	71
Rockford, IL	9.6	140	1.8	145	9.5	97	35.4	180	12.4	182	18.8	232
Rocky Mount, NC	44.1	6	0.5	340	3.5	206	35.1	189	12.5	175	13.9	331
Rome, GA	13.2	105	1.0	232	6.5	136	36.0	149	13.6	107	15.8	296
Sacramento-Arden-Arcade-Roseville, CA	7.5	172	10.0	8	16.9	67	36.2	140	11.2	245	26.5	87
Saginaw-Saginaw Township North, MI	19.4	70	0.9	256	6.9	130	35.5	174	13.5	116	15.9	293
St. Cloud, MN	1.2	308	1.6	162	1.5	307	39.0	59	11.1	249	21.0	198
St. George, UT	0.3	358	0.5	335	5.7	145	42.7	13	16.9	28	21.0	198
St. Joseph, MO-KS	4.6	221	0.5	344	2.0	271	34.0	249	14.5	71	16.4	283
St. Louis, MO-IL[5]	18.1	202	1.7	7	1.7	41	34.4	227	11.8	212	24.8	114
Salem, OR	1.0	322	1.8	148	17.8	64	37.1	110	12.5	174	20.8	203
Salinas, CA	4.0	235	6.3	20	49.7	11	39.4	52	9.9	311	22.5	163
Salisbury, MD	26.9	36	1.6	169	2.0	274	35.9	154	13.0	148	19.5	223
Salt Lake City, UT	1.3	305	2.8	82	13.0	71	42.3	16	8.0	346	27.6	75
San Angelo, TX	3.9	238	0.9	265	32.9	30	38.4	72	13.8	96	19.5	222
San Antonio, TX	6.2	195	1.5	177	52.1	10	38.7	69	10.7	268	22.1	171
San Diego-Carlsbad-San Marcos, CA	5.9	200	9.4	11	28.7	36	36.3	136	11.0	251	29.5	49
Sandusky, OH	8.6	156	0.5	341	2.2	254	32.1	320	15.9	36	16.6	278
San Francisco-Oakland-Fremont, CA	**9.5**	**141**	**20.9**	**3**	**18.9**	**59**	**30.4**	**338**	**11.9**	**209**	**38.8**	**13**
San Jose-Sunnyvale-Santa Clara, CA	2.8	263	27.8	2	25.4	42	33.2	280	10.0	300	39.8	11
San Luis Obispo-Paso Robles, CA	2.1	278	2.8	80	17.3	65	33.2	279	14.3	77	26.7	85
Santa Barbara-Santa Maria, CA	2.4	271	4.2	41	36.1	26	37.2	107	12.8	159	29.4	50
Santa Cruz-Watsonville, CA	1.1	316	3.7	50	27.7	39	34.6	214	9.9	307	34.2	26
Santa Fe, NM	0.9	331	1.1	222	49.5	12	31.8	324	11.4	230	36.9	19
Santa Rosa-Petaluma, CA	1.6	297	3.6	57	19.8	57	33.3	276	12.4	178	28.5	59
Sarasota-Bradenton-Venice, FL	6.5	188	1.0	229	7.9	112	25.7	360	26.9	3	24.6	120
Savannah, GA	34.4	20	1.7	161	2.0	277	36.8	120	11.4	231	23.2	150
Scranton-Wilkes-Barre, PA	1.7	294	0.7	296	1.5	302	30.0	344	18.7	15	17.5	264
Seattle-Tacoma-Bellevue, WA	**5.5**	**209**	**9.5**	**10**	**6.2**	**139**	**33.0**	**292**	**10.1**	**293**	**32.7**	**33**
Sheboygan, WI	1.1	315	4.0	44	3.9	185	33.6	266	13.8	95	17.9	256
Sherman-Denison, TX	5.6	206	0.6	315	8.0	109	35.5	178	14.7	68	17.2	271
Shreveport-Bossier City, LA	38.8	11	1.0	245	2.1	267	36.7	123	13.0	150	19.2	226
Sioux City, IA-NE-SD	1.8	288	2.8	86	10.9	88	37.0	112	12.8	158	18.5	243
Sioux Falls, SD	1.7	292	1.1	224	2.0	276	36.5	130	11.4	232	25.1	106
South Bend-Mishawaka, IN-MI	10.6	131	1.5	182	4.7	171	37.0	115	13.4	122	21.7	182

See footnotes at end of table.

| Metropolitan statistical area | Black or African American alone, 2003 (percent) | Rank | Asian alone, 2003 (percent) | Rank | Hispanic or Latino origin,[1] 2003 (percent) | Rank | Age, 2003 (percent) | | | | Educational attainment, 2000 | |
							Under 25 years	Rank	65 years and over	Rank	Bachelor's degree or higher (percent)	Rank
Spartanburg, SC	21.3	54	1.7	154	3.4	208	33.9	257	12.6	171	18.2	252
Spokane, WA	1.7	293	1.9	132	3.1	225	35.5	173	12.3	184	25.0	109
Springfield, IL	9.6	139	1.3	196	1.3	322	33.0	291	13.3	125	28.1	64
Springfield, MA	7.1	177	1.9	134	12.1	76	35.1	193	13.6	111	25.2	105
Springfield, MO	1.7	290	0.9	260	1.7	288	35.2	185	13.2	130	21.3	190
Springfield, OH	8.8	147	0.6	313	1.3	317	34.3	233	14.8	62	14.9	312
State College, PA	2.7	264	4.3	40	1.5	298	40.1	42	10.4	283	36.3	22
Stockton, CA	7.6	171	13.0	6	33.4	29	40.8	34	9.9	306	14.5	321
Sumter, SC	48.9	2	1.0	227	1.6	294	38.6	71	11.9	208	15.8	294
Syracuse, NY	7.7	169	2.0	131	2.6	243	34.9	202	13.1	139	25.2	104
Tallahassee, FL	33.1	24	1.6	164	3.9	186	37.4	95	9.4	327	34.1	28
Tampa-St. Petersburg-Clearwater, FL	11.2	121	2.2	109	12.0	78	30.5	337	17.9	17	21.7	180
Terre Haute, IN	4.3	226	1.0	238	0.9	341	35.5	172	14.1	85	17.4	267
Texarkana, TX-Texarkana, AR	24.0	42	0.5	336	3.6	197	35.1	197	13.3	125	15.0	308
Toledo, OH	12.2	115	1.3	202	4.6	173	35.8	158	12.7	162	21.2	191
Topeka, KS	7.1	176	0.9	259	6.5	135	34.4	232	13.9	90	23.6	141
Trenton-Ewing, NJ	20.6	58	6.3	19	10.9	87	34.6	215	12.3	188	34.0	29
Tucson, AZ	3.2	248	2.3	105	31.9	31	35.3	182	14.2	82	26.7	84
Tulsa, OK	9.0	146	1.4	186	5.3	154	35.8	157	12.1	196	22.5	164
Tuscaloosa, AL	35.4	15	0.9	268	1.3	319	37.6	88	11.5	225	21.9	178
Tyler, TX	18.7	75	0.8	279	13.0	72	37.0	114	14.0	87	22.5	162
Utica-Rome, NY	5.1	211	1.3	200	3.3	217	32.2	312	16.1	34	17.7	258
Valdosta, GA	32.5	26	1.0	236	3.0	226	39.0	61	10.0	299	17.4	266
Vallejo-Fairfield, CA	15.4	91	13.5	4	19.9	55	37.5	90	10.0	301	21.4	187
Vero Beach, FL	8.6	154	0.9	269	7.6	115	26.8	358	27.8	2	23.1	152
Victoria, TX	5.6	208	1.3	198	40.9	21	38.2	79	12.8	154	15.2	306
Vineland-Millville-Bridgeton, NJ	21.6	52	1.1	226	21.0	49	34.5	223	12.7	161	11.7	355
Virginia Beach-Norfolk-Newport News, VA-NC	32.0	27	2.9	77	3.1	221	37.5	94	10.5	281	23.7	138
Visalia-Porterville, CA	1.9	285	3.4	60	53.8	9	44.2	11	9.4	324	11.5	356
Waco, TX	15.1	92	1.2	213	19.8	56	40.7	37	12.5	173	19.1	229
Warner Robins, GA	25.0	41	1.8	149	2.9	227	37.9	84	9.7	317	19.8	217
Washington-Arlington-Alexandria, DC-VA-MD-WV	**26.4**	**38**	**7.7**	**15**	**10.1**	**93**	**33.9**	**256**	**9.1**	**332**	**42.5**	**7**
Waterloo-Cedar Falls, IA	6.5	190	1.1	220	1.7	289	35.5	171	14.7	64	22.3	166
Wausau, WI	0.3	356	5.1	29	0.9	344	34.7	210	13.2	135	18.3	249
Weirton-Steubenville, WV-OH	4.0	233	0.4	354	0.6	357	29.4	350	18.6	16	12.1	351
Wenatchee, WA	0.4	354	0.7	301	20.4	52	36.6	128	13.8	97	20.0	214
Wheeling, WV-OH	3.1	251	0.5	337	0.5	361	30.3	341	17.9	18	14.6	318
Wichita, KS	7.8	167	3.1	69	8.1	107	37.2	105	11.9	204	24.3	123
Wichita Falls, TX	8.7	152	1.7	157	12.1	77	38.8	64	13.0	146	19.2	225
Williamsport, PA	4.2	227	0.5	342	0.6	356	32.8	298	16.2	32	15.1	307
Wilmington, NC	16.4	85	0.6	308	2.8	231	31.3	333	14.5	70	24.2	129
Winchester, VA-WV	4.3	224	0.8	273	3.5	205	33.7	264	12.6	170	18.3	251
Winston-Salem, NC	20.3	61	1.0	250	7.3	123	33.5	272	12.9	152	24.0	133
Worcester, MA	3.6	241	3.3	62	7.3	121	33.9	253	12.5	176	26.9	82
Yakima, WA	1.2	311	1.0	241	38.3	24	41.6	27	11.1	246	15.3	304
York-Hanover, PA	4.0	236	1.0	248	3.2	219	32.2	314	13.6	110	18.4	246
Youngstown-Warren-Boardman, OH-PA	10.8	128	0.5	330	1.7	287	32.1	317	17.0	27	16.3	284
Yuba City, CA	2.6	266	10.0	9	22.3	48	39.3	53	11.3	237	13.2	343
Yuma, AZ	2.2	277	1.1	221	54.4	8	40.5	39	17.0	26	11.8	354

[1]Persons of Hispanic origin may be any race.

[2]The Denver-Aurora metropolitan statistical area includes Broomfield County. Broomfield County, CO, was formed from parts of Adams, Boulder, Jefferson, and Weld Counties on November 15, 2001, and is coextensive with Broomfield city. For the purposes of defining and presenting data for the Denver-Aurora metropolitan statistical area, Broomfield is treated as if it were a county when data are available to do so. In many cases, the data will not be available.

[3]The portion of Sullivan City in Crawford County, MO, is legally part of the St. Louis, MO-IL MSA. That portion is not included in these figures for the St. Louis MSA.

Source: U.S. Census Bureau. See Tables B-3 and B-4 of the State and Metropolitan Area Data Book: 2006. For more information, see <http://www.census.gov/popest/datasets.html>.

Metropolitan statistical area	Birth rate, 2002 Rate per 1,000 persons[4]	Rank	Physicians, 2003[1] Rate per 100,000 persons[5]	Rank	Medicare program enrollment, 2003[2] Rate per 100,000 persons[5]	Rank	Social security program beneficiaries, December 2004 Rate per 100,000 persons[5]	Rank	Housing units, percent change 2000–2004[3] Percent	Rank	Housing units per square mile of land area, 2004 Number	Rank	Home-ownership rate, 2000 (percent) Percent	Rank
Abilene, TX	14.3	122	198	276	15,168	136	17,455	141	2.5	311	24.3	324	58.3	273
Akron, OH	12.1	275	271	153	14,841	156	16,746	177	3.8	254	333.8	22	66.4	70
Albany, GA	14.1	137	210	259	12,816	239	15,402	224	5.3	200	34.7	297	55.6	315
Albany-Schenectady-Troy, NY	11.2	321	353	69	15,657	114	17,793	129	2.5	308	132.4	99	58.5	269
Albuquerque, NM	14.9	97	385	45	12,782	242	14,939	239	8.5	92	35.7	294	62.4	189
Alexandria, LA	14.4	117	308	103	16,149	89	18,211	109	3.7	264	31.9	305	62.5	186
Allentown-Bethlehem-Easton, PA-NJ	11.7	297	261	172	16,793	65	19,306	70	4.8	214	220.7	40	66.7	63
Altoona, PA	11.4	302	267	159	19,634	22	20,005	58	1.3	349	106.0	133	68.2	37
Amarillo, TX	15.6	60	293	124	12,772	243	14,376	260	4.0	247	26.0	322	61.3	210
Ames, IA	11.4	303	216	246	11,239	306	12,291	326	9.9	61	58.8	229	55.9	310
Anchorage, AK	15.0	86	292	127	7,176	359	8,959	358	5.8	175	5.1	359	57.3	287
Anderson, IN	12.2	269	153	338	17,408	55	20,391	48	2.6	302	129.2	103	69.1	24
Anderson, SC	12.6	246	206	266	16,511	75	20,772	44	7.0	138	109.1	130	68.4	36
Ann Arbor, MI	12.6	242	1,023	5	9,691	338	11,303	337	8.4	95	199.9	49	57.1	292
Anniston-Oxford, AL	13.1	204	196	278	19,395	24	22,342	24	3.0	285	86.8	170	64.0	129
Appleton, WI	13.9	149	191	290	11,927	278	14,138	272	10.1	56	89.8	163	71.2	10
Asheville, NC	11.7	295	389	40	19,970	20	22,877	20	7.9	107	93.1	155	64.9	109
Athens-Clarke County, GA	13.1	200	236	208	10,885	323	12,985	308	11.0	41	72.7	197	53.1	338
Atlanta-Sandy Springs-Marietta, GA	16.3	47	259	176	8,786	350	10,618	344	16.5	8	228.8	35	63.1	155
Atlantic City, NJ	13.7	154	244	197	14,973	151	17,108	159	6.2	159	216.0	42	55.3	321
Auburn-Opelika, AL	12.0	277	161	328	9,657	339	12,657	319	10.4	47	91.3	156	56.4	301
Augusta-Richmond County, GA-SC	14.2	127	204	269	13,173	228	16,205	201	6.0	171	66.1	211	62.9	161
Austin-Round Rock, TX	16.7	36	233	213	7,890	357	9,343	357	15.7	11	135.9	95	55.4	316
Bakersfield, CA	17.6	27	157	329	11,029	317	13,187	299	6.8	143	30.4	310	56.0	306
Baltimore-Towson, MD	13.0	215	475	16	13,110	232	14,884	242	3.3	274	414.9	17	62.2	195
Bangor, ME	10.2	342	330	82	16,964	63	19,592	64	2.8	293	20.2	332	60.6	226
Barnstable Town, MA	8.7	359	368	61	25,149	6	27,632	5	3.7	257	385.8	18	50.2	351
Baton Rouge, LA	14.3	123	227	226	11,178	308	13,599	288	6.2	161	74.5	195	63.0	159
Battle Creek, MI	13.4	178	184	303	16,539	72	19,615	63	2.6	304	85.0	175	67.3	54
Bay City, MI	11.8	292	157	329	16,993	62	20,469	46	2.6	305	107.2	132	75.1	3
Beaumont-Port Arthur, TX	13.3	180	185	299	15,193	134	18,061	114	2.9	286	74.9	194	64.1	127
Bellingham, WA	11.2	316	280	142	13,447	217	15,761	214	9.1	74	38.0	288	55.3	318
Bend, OR	11.9	287	316	95	14,630	166	18,025	117	18.8	6	21.5	328	60.4	230
Billings, MT	13.1	197	375	53	15,176	135	17,094	161	4.0	248	13.3	348	65.0	104
Binghamton, NY	10.6	333	272	150	18,465	38	21,311	37	0.3	361	90.2	159	61.6	205
Birmingham-Hoover, AL	13.6	161	390	39	15,248	131	18,192	110	5.2	203	90.2	160	65.3	93
Bismarck, ND	12.1	271	351	71	15,009	149	16,682	183	7.3	128	11.9	352	66.4	68
Blacksburg-Christiansburg-Radford, VA	9.6	354	192	287	14,105	192	16,264	199	4.6	231	61.0	223	57.4	285
Bloomington, IN	10.8	329	222	236	12,442	252	14,831	245	6.3	156	61.0	224	56.4	300
Bloomington-Normal, IL	13.5	166	213	252	10,905	321	12,301	325	9.2	73	55.3	241	62.9	167
Boise City-Nampa, ID	16.5	40	234	211	11,102	312	13,182	300	15.5	13	17.8	340	67.5	49
Boston-Cambridge-Quincy, MA-NH	12.9	217	546	11	13,960	197	15,211	232	1.9	328	508.9	8	58.4	272
Boulder, CO[6]	13.3	185	359	64	11,049	315	9,944	354	7.6	116	161.5	66	61.9	201
Bowling Green, KY	13.4	175	255	183	13,832	202	16,368	193	8.0	104	56.6	234	59.9	238
Bremerton-Silverdale, WA	12.4	260	258	177	12,211	266	13,921	277	5.0	210	245.6	29	62.9	165
Bridgeport-Stamford-Norwalk, CT	13.3	179	402	34	13,876	201	15,234	231	1.7	335	551.6	6	66.1	76
Brownsville-Harlingen, TX	24.5	4	152	339	10,516	330	12,235	328	11.9	34	147.9	80	55.0	323
Brunswick, GA	13.1	198	263	168	15,690	109	19,475	67	7.8	113	37.2	291	58.1	280
Buffalo-Niagara Falls, NY	11.3	313	351	71	17,889	44	20,268	52	1.3	345	330.7	23	60.6	228
Burlington, NC	13.4	177	181	308	16,494	76	19,071	78	8.0	105	139.3	91	65.2	100
Burlington-South Burlington, VT	11.2	318	649	9	11,781	290	13,790	285	4.5	233	68.6	205	63.0	157
Canton-Massillon, OH	11.8	293	228	224	17,316	56	18,850	89	2.5	309	179.6	58	68.4	35
Cape Coral-Fort Myers, FL	11.3	308	279	143	21,546	12	24,734	11	19.3	5	364.4	20	58.8	261
Carson City, NV	13.3	188	291	129	19,154	28	18,872	87	5.3	202	156.3	70	59.8	241
Casper, WY	13.3	187	264	166	14,551	173	16,743	179	1.8	331	5.7	358	62.8	174
Cedar Rapids, IA	13.5	167	191	290	14,480	177	16,801	174	8.1	101	53.3	250	70.0	13
Champaign-Urbana, IL	11.9	282	294	121	11,874	284	13,035	306	5.3	197	48.3	266	55.4	317
Charleston, WV	12.4	255	324	90	19,075	31	22,318	25	1.6	339	56.9	232	67.5	51
Charleston-North Charleston, SC	14.0	139	463	17	12,317	264	14,852	244	10.1	53	99.0	144	59.4	249
Charlotte-Gastonia-Concord, NC-SC	15.6	64	247	192	11,419	302	13,529	292	16.2	10	204.9	46	63.1	154
Charlottesville, VA	12.1	272	1,057	4	13,926	198	15,680	216	10.1	55	49.3	263	58.8	259
Chattanooga, TN-GA	12.5	250	290	133	15,794	102	18,661	94	5.7	180	103.9	138	64.7	113
Cheyenne, WY	14.5	113	275	148	13,625	210	14,937	240	4.9	211	13.4	347	64.4	118
Chicago-Naperville-Joliet, IL-IN-WI	15.1	79	334	80	11,681	292	13,128	302	4.8	215	503.0	10	61.8	203
Chico, CA	10.9	328	239	202	17,599	53	20,088	56	5.6	189	55.1	242	56.5	298
Cincinnati-Middletown, OH-KY-IN	14.2	128	307	106	13,540	213	15,500	220	5.6	187	200.1	48	62.9	163
Clarksville, TN-KY	17.8	25	154	337	11,160	309	13,793	284	8.9	79	46.4	271	57.1	290
Cleveland, TN	13.0	205	156	333	15,721	108	19,410	68	6.0	170	61.3	221	65.0	106
Cleveland-Elyria-Mentor, OH	12.5	254	432	27	15,791	103	17,394	146	2.2	322	464.6	13	63.7	140
Coeur d'Alene, ID	12.9	225	219	240	15,095	144	18,369	104	12.5	30	42.1	280	66.0	78
College Station-Bryan, TX	14.7	102	227	226	9,462	344	10,849	341	9.8	63	39.2	285	46.1	360
Colorado Springs, CO	15.6	63	235	210	10,133	335	11,805	334	12.3	32	89.0	166	61.5	208
Columbia, MO	12.8	229	734	8	11,235	307	13,119	303	10.7	44	58.7	230	54.8	325
Columbia, SC	13.3	186	300	114	12,346	262	14,925	241	7.9	108	78.5	186	63.9	133
Columbus, GA-AL	14.6	108	237	206	13,919	199	16,273	198	5.8	174	63.3	215	53.7	335
Columbus, IN	13.7	157	272	150	14,619	168	17,799	127	2.9	287	75.5	191	69.5	18
Columbus, OH	15.0	84	300	114	11,459	301	13,035	306	9.3	72	186.6	51	59.0	258
Corpus Christi, TX	15.6	61	246	193	13,191	227	15,459	221	4.5	233	94.4	150	55.7	313

See footnotes at end of table.

Table E-15. Metropolitan Area Rankings — **Social and Housing Indicators**—Con.

Metropolitan statistical area	Birth rate, 2002 Rate per 1,000 persons[4]	Rank	Physicians, 2003[1] Rate per 100,000 persons[5]	Rank	Medicare program enrollment, 2003[2] Rate per 100,000 persons[5]	Rank	Social security program beneficiaries, December 2004 Rate per 100,000 persons[5]	Rank	Housing units, percent change 2000–2004[3] Percent	Rank	Housing units per square mile of land area, 2004 Number	Rank	Home-ownership rate, 2000 (percent) Percent	Rank
Corvallis, OR	9.9	349	347	73	10,929	320	13,384	294	6.2	160	50.2	262	54.0	333
Cumberland, MD-WV	10.1	343	233	213	20,076	18	21,397	36	1.5	342	60.8	226	64.3	121
Dallas-Fort Worth-Arlington, TX.	**17.6**	**28**	**221**	**237**	**8,716**	**352**	**10,181**	**350**	**10.2**	**52**	**244.9**	**30**	**56.7**	**295**
Dalton, GA	19.4	14	162	325	12,445	251	15,019	236	8.4	93	77.0	187	65.8	83
Danville, IL	13.2	190	192	287	19,030	32	21,409	35	1.0	354	40.8	282	66.0	80
Danville, VA	11.4	304	179	312	19,913	21	23,967	15	2.4	316	51.6	253	62.1	198
Davenport-Moline-Rock Island, IA-IL	13.2	190	203	270	15,740	105	18,140	111	2.3	317	71.5	201	67.7	45
Dayton, OH	12.6	243	288	137	15,668	110	17,413	145	2.8	290	219.4	41	62.4	193
Decatur, AL	12.8	236	147	344	15,422	123	18,937	84	3.7	260	50.7	259	69.1	23
Decatur, IL	13.0	207	257	180	18,124	43	20,349	49	2.3	318	88.5	169	66.4	67
Deltona-Daytona Beach-Ormond Beach, FL	9.9	348	213	252	22,335	8	25,476	9	8.9	81	209.1	43	65.6	88
Denver-Aurora, CO[6]	16.4	45	330	82	9,721	337	11,106	338	12.8	28	118.3	115	64.0	130
Des Moines, IA	15.3	70	221	237	12,651	248	14,537	256	10.3	51	76.4	190	67.3	55
Detroit-Warren-Livonia, MI.	**13.3**	**181**	**291**	**129**	**13,662**	**209**	**15,888**	**211**	**3.7**	**256**	**476.3**	**12**	**68.6**	**33**
Dothan, AL	13.4	174	258	177	15,585	117	21,197	39	4.3	238	36.3	292	64.7	114
Dover, DE	14.3	120	169	320	13,488	216	16,884	169	11.5	37	95.5	149	65.5	90
Dubuque, IA	12.9	221	261	172	16,700	69	18,961	83	5.1	206	61.4	220	69.7	15
Duluth, MN-WI	10.4	337	297	118	17,860	45	19,942	59	3.0	282	15.9	344	64.9	108
Durham, NC	14.7	101	1,108	3	11,579	296	13,839	282	11.5	38	113.7	118	55.3	319
Eau Claire, WI.	11.9	278	317	94	14,871	154	17,153	157	8.3	96	39.6	284	65.4	92
El Centro, CA	18.4	19	93	360	12,641	249	14,739	248	8.8	82	11.4	354	52.3	344
Elizabethtown, KY	15.5	66	206	266	13,425	218	15,575	218	7.5	117	52.5	251	62.7	177
Elkhart-Goshen, IN.	16.2	50	146	346	12,270	265	14,290	266	7.5	120	161.7	65	68.5	34
Elmira, NY	11.8	291	306	110	18,520	37	21,488	32	0.8	356	93.2	154	64.0	128
El Paso, TX	20.3	8	193	284	11,262	305	12,659	318	7.2	132	237.5	32	59.5	247
Erie, PA	11.9	280	220	239	16,182	87	18,558	99	1.7	333	145.0	82	64.5	117
Eugene-Springfield, OR	10.7	332	271	153	15,520	119	17,910	122	3.9	252	31.7	306	58.4	271
Evansville, IN-KY	12.6	244	265	163	16,244	85	18,901	85	4.8	217	67.6	210	66.5	65
Fairbanks, AK	17.9	24	243	198	6,140	360	7,973	360	1.5	343	4.6	360	48.3	356
Fargo, ND-MN.	13.0	214	344	75	11,876	282	13,230	298	9.6	66	28.7	314	56.1	303
Farmington, NM.	16.5	44	148	342	10,527	329	12,956	309	2.6	300	8.0	357	65.7	86
Fayetteville, NC.	17.9	22	209	262	10,088	336	12,654	321	6.8	145	133.9	97	55.2	322
Fayetteville-Springdale-Rogers, AR-MO	16.3	46	188	295	13,396	222	16,162	204	13.1	27	51.5	255	60.9	219
Flagstaff, AZ	15.7	59	267	159	11,725	291	11,079	339	7.1	136	3.1	361	46.5	359
Flint, MI	14.1	134	225	230	14,812	161	17,557	139	5.4	192	302.7	25	67.7	44
Florence, SC.	14.0	142	248	191	15,265	130	17,925	121	2.6	303	60.9	225	67.2	57
Florence-Muscle Shoals, AL.	10.9	327	193	284	18,923	34	22,872	21	3.2	277	53.4	249	66.4	69
Fond du Lac, WI	11.6	301	183	305	16,466	77	17,454	142	4.7	224	56.9	233	68.6	32
Fort Collins-Loveland, CO	12.4	257	252	187	10,708	327	12,291	326	13.3	25	45.9	273	62.4	191
Fort Smith, AR-OK.	14.9	96	179	312	16,146	90	19,785	60	4.0	250	30.0	312	63.8	137
Fort Walton Beach-Crestview-Destin, FL	14.0	140	272	150	15,029	148	16,833	173	8.2	99	90.9	158	55.9	309
Fort Wayne, IN	14.9	92	257	180	13,106	233	15,413	223	6.1	164	126.4	109	67.5	52
Fresno, CA.	17.8	26	216	246	11,118	311	12,379	323	5.7	185	48.0	267	52.8	341
Gadsden, AL.	12.3	262	211	257	19,175	27	23,531	18	3.1	279	88.6	168	67.4	53
Gainesville, FL	11.0	323	812	6	12,422	256	13,847	281	7.8	111	89.0	165	51.9	347
Gainesville, GA.	19.3	15	223	234	11,047	316	13,498	293	15.3	14	149.5	76	66.0	79
Glens Falls, NY	10.3	341	227	226	17,244	59	20,123	55	3.4	270	37.4	290	56.2	302
Goldsboro, NC	14.7	104	175	315	15,664	112	18,516	100	4.6	226	89.6	164	58.8	260
Grand Forks, ND-MN	12.9	223	283	141	13,402	221	14,940	238	2.8	291	12.5	351	54.6	327
Grand Junction, CO	12.7	237	293	124	17,304	57	19,254	74	11.9	33	16.4	343	68.8	27
Grand Rapids-Wyoming, MI.	14.9	93	239	202	12,147	270	14,481	258	5.6	186	109.5	128	67.9	41
Great Falls, MT	13.6	162	307	106	16,587	71	18,871	88	1.0	355	13.2	349	59.9	237
Greeley, CO[6]	17.3	30	157	329	9,147	347	11,009	340	25.6	1	20.8	330	65.6	87
Green Bay, WI	13.5	169	224	231	12,790	241	15,193	233	8.8	83	68.8	204	63.4	147
Greensboro-High Point, NC	13.3	184	224	231	14,551	173	17,035	163	7.9	109	148.1	79	62.4	187
Greenville, NC.	14.2	125	582	10	12,371	261	14,947	237	11.7	36	80.1	181	54.0	332
Greenville, SC.	13.0	212	264	166	14,553	172	17,254	153	7.0	140	127.8	106	63.9	134
Gulfport-Biloxi, MS	14.7	100	269	158	14,927	152	17,674	133	8.5	91	76.6	188	58.6	267
Hagerstown-Martinsburg, MD-WV	12.8	230	196	278	14,839	157	17,264	151	10.0	58	102.5	141	63.5	145
Hanford-Corcoran, CA	17.2	32	104	358	8,240	356	10,068	352	7.3	130	28.2	315	52.6	342
Harrisburg-Carlisle, PA	11.3	310	369	60	15,879	97	17,240	154	3.7	263	138.1	92	65.0	105
Harrisonburg, VA	12.8	233	231	217	12,439	253	15,583	217	6.7	148	50.3	261	60.7	222
Hartford-West Hartford-East Hartford, CT	11.3	312	378	52	15,310	127	17,157	156	2.4	315	319.0	24	62.7	180
Hattiesburg, MS.	15.0	87	328	87	13,907	200	17,012	165	3.7	259	32.5	304	61.6	206
Hickory-Lenoir-Morganton, NC	12.8	228	200	272	15,303	128	18,678	92	6.0	165	93.8	153	68.7	30
Hinesville-Fort Stewart, GA	22.2	6	85	361	5,841	361	7,945	361	5.8	176	30.1	311	46.5	358
Holland-Grand Haven, MI	14.1	129	140	349	11,835	287	13,679	286	10.0	57	168.9	63	76.0	2
Honolulu, HI	14.5	112	389	40	14,188	187	15,305	227	3.1	280	543.2	7	49.4	353
Hot Springs, AR.	11.2	320	326	89	25,361	5	26,992	7	2.6	306	68.1	207	59.9	239
Houma-Bayou Cane-Thibodaux, LA	14.9	90	168	321	13,409	219	17,096	160	4.6	227	33.5	299	69.6	17
Houston-Sugar Land-Baytown, TX	17.5	29	291	129	8,522	354	10,066	353	10.5	46	222.6	39	56.1	305
Huntington-Ashland, WV-KY-OH	11.9	284	330	82	19,379	25	21,415	34	1.1	353	75.1	193	65.5	89
Huntsville, AL	12.3	261	237	206	13,048	236	15,123	235	6.6	149	114.3	117	65.2	102
Idaho Falls, ID.	18.1	20	210	259	11,939	277	14,666	251	9.4	69	13.6	346	72.0	6
Indianapolis, IN	15.5	68	386	43	11,907	281	14,074	274	9.9	59	183.5	53	62.4	190
Iowa City, IA	13.0	216	1,294	2	10,310	333	11,947	332	10.4	49	50.7	260	57.1	291
Ithaca, NY	8.5	360	271	153	11,070	313	12,867	311	3.6	266	84.1	177	50.7	348
Jackson, MI	12.4	256	130	352	15,050	146	17,705	131	5.5	191	93.9	152	70.7	11

See footnotes at end of table.

Table E-15. Metropolitan Area Rankings — **Social and Housing Indicators**—Con.

Metropolitan statistical area	Birth rate, 2002 Rate per 1,000 persons[4]	Rank	Physicians, 2003[1] Rate per 100,000 persons[5]	Rank	Medicare program enrollment, 2003[2] Rate per 100,000 persons[5]	Rank	Social security program beneficiaries, December 2004 Rate per 100,000 persons[5]	Rank	Housing units, percent change 2000–2004[3] Percent	Rank	Housing units per square mile of land area, 2004 Number	Rank	Home-ownership rate, 2000 (percent) Percent	Rank
Jackson, MS.	14.8	98	417	29	13,062	235	15,906	210	6.2	158	56.0	238	64.2	124
Jackson, TN	13.7	155	385	45	14,429	180	17,292	150	7.0	141	56.2	236	63.5	144
Jacksonville, FL.	13.9	147	313	100	12,652	247	14,853	243	11.0	42	163.7	64	61.5	209
Jacksonville, NC	20.8	7	165	323	8,741	351	10,607	345	8.3	98	78.7	185	50.2	350
Janesville, WI	12.8	235	215	251	14,683	163	17,418	144	5.4	196	90.9	157	67.1	59
Jefferson City, MO	12.5	251	139	350	13,623	211	16,590	187	6.0	167	26.7	319	66.3	73
Johnson City, TN.	11.2	319	458	20	17,692	50	21,029	41	4.2	245	100.0	143	65.3	96
Johnstown, PA	9.7	352	287	139	21,956	9	24,210	13	0.4	358	96.0	147	68.8	28
Jonesboro, AR	14.1	131	262	169	15,212	133	18,497	101	5.1	204	33.1	301	59.2	253
Joplin, MO	15.2	72	181	308	16,266	83	19,266	73	4.8	213	55.8	239	64.0	132
Kalamazoo-Portage, MI	12.8	227	331	81	13,702	208	16,344	194	5.7	184	120.0	113	62.9	168
Kankakee-Bradley, IL	15.0	85	174	317	15,636	115	17,875	125	4.3	240	62.6	216	65.3	97
Kansas City, MO-KS.	15.1	82	285	140	12,897	238	14,826	246	7.1	134	104.7	135	63.8	138
Kennewick-Richland-Pasco, WA	16.5	43	185	299	10,746	325	12,775	316	9.4	70	26.7	318	64.0	131
Killeen-Temple-Fort Hood, TX	20.0	11	316	95	9,494	341	11,305	336	9.0	77	47.1	269	51.9	346
Kingsport-Bristol-Bristol, TN-VA	10.6	336	278	145	20,015	19	24,198	14	3.9	251	70.4	203	69.2	22
Kingston, NY.	9.9	347	207	264	15,322	126	18,255	106	2.8	292	70.9	202	59.1	255
Knoxville, TN	11.9	283	358	65	15,864	98	18,595	98	6.1	163	157.8	69	64.3	120
Kokomo, IN	13.2	191	185	299	16,103	92	19,503	66	3.7	261	83.3	179	67.8	43
La Crosse, WI-MN.	11.3	314	448	22	14,656	165	16,525	188	4.7	220	53.5	248	64.4	119
Lafayette, IN.	12.8	232	231	217	11,064	314	13,257	297	9.0	75	60.4	227	56.1	304
Lafayette, LA	15.1	80	290	133	11,652	293	14,211	270	5.9	172	103.2	139	62.9	169
Lake Charles, LA.	14.6	106	210	259	14,223	185	16,918	167	6.2	162	36.2	293	64.1	126
Lakeland, FL.	13.6	158	187	298	18,324	42	22,017	27	9.0	78	131.6	101	60.7	225
Lancaster, PA	14.1	133	188	295	15,130	140	17,227	155	4.7	218	198.6	50	67.9	42
Lansing-East Lansing, MI	12.6	247	236	208	12,195	267	14,379	259	5.7	177	112.6	121	63.8	139
Laredo, TX.	28.7	1	106	357	8,617	353	9,922	355	13.8	24	18.7	336	60.4	231
Las Cruces, NM	17.2	31	174	317	12,142	271	13,963	276	8.0	106	18.5	338	61.6	204
Las Vegas-Paradise, NV	15.7	56	196	278	11,572	297	13,899	278	22.1	3	86.4	171	54.1	331
Lawrence, KS	11.9	286	216	246	9,377	345	10,708	343	9.4	68	96.4	146	49.6	352
Lawton, OK	17.0	33	213	252	11,972	275	14,320	264	1.2	351	43.0	279	52.9	340
Lebanon, PA.	12.6	245	245	194	17,735	48	20,300	51	4.7	222	142.7	86	68.7	31
Lewiston, ID-WA	12.1	273	245	194	19,411	23	22,549	23	1.9	329	17.4	341	63.7	141
Lewiston-Auburn, ME	11.9	281	266	162	17,659	51	20,218	53	2.7	297	100.4	142	58.0	281
Lexington-Fayette, KY	13.5	163	520	13	12,153	269	14,363	261	8.4	94	128.5	104	56.0	308
Lima, OH	13.7	153	258	177	15,736	106	18,331	105	1.4	344	110.9	124	66.2	74
Lincoln, NE.	14.6	111	265	163	11,914	280	13,368	296	6.8	144	83.6	178	58.1	278
Little Rock-North Little Rock, AR.	14.5	114	441	24	13,383	223	16,519	190	6.3	157	68.1	208	61.3	211
Logan, UT-ID	23.5	5	156	333	8,374	355	9,869	356	10.6	45	19.9	333	62.6	181
Longview, TX	15.3	71	190	292	16,688	70	18,664	93	2.5	310	46.6	270	64.2	123
Longview, WA	13.1	195	224	231	16,236	86	19,748	62	4.2	242	35.4	295	62.8	172
Los Angeles-Long Beach-Santa Ana, CA	**15.4**	**69**	**307**	**106**	**10,443**	**331**	**10,580**	**346**	**2.1**	**325**	**892.6**	**2**	**48.9**	**354**
Louisville, KY-IN[7].	13.3	183	340	78	14,606	169	17,013	164	6.5	153	126.8	108	65.3	95
Lubbock, TX.	15.9	53	411	30	12,445	257	14,316	265	7.3	127	61.9	218	54.4	328
Lynchburg, VA.	11.3	311	211	257	18,397	40	20,465	47	5.4	193	48.7	265	68.0	39
Macon, GA.	14.6	107	362	63	14,827	159	17,540	140	5.5	190	57.5	231	59.1	256
Madera, CA.	16.7	37	112	355	14,279	182	14,327	263	8.7	85	20.6	331	59.3	252
Madison, WI	12.5	252	510	14	11,528	299	13,085	304	9.5	67	85.1	173	57.3	286
Manchester-Nashua, NH	12.9	226	240	200	12,177	268	14,345	262	5.0	209	179.7	57	62.6	184
Mansfield, OH	11.9	278	184	303	17,105	60	19,243	75	3.1	281	110.1	125	66.8	62
McAllen-Edinburg-Mission, TX	25.6	3	119	354	9,194	346	10,845	342	15.7	12	141.9	87	59.5	248
Medford, OR.	11.3	309	316	95	17,816	47	20,705	45	8.7	87	29.5	313	62.8	171
Memphis, TN-MS-AR	15.5	65	297	118	11,800	289	14,245	268	7.8	112	113.4	119	61.5	207
Merced, CA.	17.9	23	111	356	9,083	348	12,200	329	9.9	62	38.9	286	54.8	324
Miami-Fort Lauderdale-Miami Beach, FL.	**13.1**	**199**	**343**	**76**	**15,404**	**124**	**16,644**	**185**	**6.7**	**147**	**447.7**	**14**	**58.5**	**268**
Michigan City-La Porte, IN.	12.4	259	185	299	15,129	141	17,903	123	3.4	271	78.8	184	67.7	47
Midland, TX.	15.8	55	188	295	12,335	263	14,647	254	2.0	327	54.4	245	61.8	202
Milwaukee-Waukesha-West Allis, WI	13.9	146	374	54	14,131	190	16,032	207	3.1	278	436.8	15	58.1	279
Minneapolis-St. Paul-Bloomington, MN-WI	14.6	110	305	111	10,724	326	12,197	330	8.2	100	208.8	44	70.4	12
Missoula, MT	11.4	305	400	37	11,840	286	13,546	290	7.3	126	17.1	342	57.6	284
Mobile, AL	14.6	109	292	127	14,832	158	18,240	107	4.6	228	140.1	90	62.6	182
Modesto, CA.	16.5	41	183	305	11,844	285	13,619	287	8.7	86	109.7	127	59.6	245
Monroe, LA.	15.1	81	260	174	14,037	194	16,221	200	3.2	276	49.3	264	60.0	236
Monroe, MI.	11.9	285	94	359	13,154	229	16,044	206	9.9	60	112.6	120	77.1	1
Montgomery, AL	14.4	118	217	242	14,065	193	16,883	170	4.6	230	55.5	240	62.7	179
Morgantown, WV	11.0	324	743	7	13,239	226	15,735	215	2.2	319	50.8	258	59.8	240
Morristown, TN	12.9	219	151	340	17,729	49	20,999	42	5.7	178	79.4	183	69.1	25
Mount Vernon-Anacortes, WA	13.0	206	271	153	15,984	95	18,468	102	7.1	135	26.4	320	63.5	146
Muncie, IN	10.9	325	305	111	15,732	107	18,602	97	2.8	294	133.3	98	62.1	197
Muskegon-Norton Shores, MI.	13.4	173	157	329	16,112	91	19,338	69	5.1	205	141.6	88	71.8	8
Myrtle Beach-Conway-North Myrtle Beach, SC	12.3	263	199	274	16,031	94	21,572	31	15.2	15	124.0	111	48.9	355
Napa, CA.	12.0	276	426	28	16,725	68	16,740	180	5.7	179	68.1	206	60.9	218
Naples-Marco Island, FL.	13.1	203	387	42	18,928	33	21,697	28	20.8	4	86.2	172	53.8	334
Nashville-Davidson-Murfreesboro, TN	14.3	119	371	57	11,875	283	14,158	271	9.4	71	104.5	137	62.7	178
New Haven-Milford, CT.	12.2	268	524	12	15,664	112	17,359	149	1.3	346	569.8	5	59.1	257
New Orleans-Metairie-Kenner, LA.	14.1	132	460	19	13,610	212	16,025	208	2.6	301	178.5	59	55.9	311
New York-Northern New Jersey-Long Island, NY-NJ-PA . .	**14.0**	**145**	**448**	**22**	**13,539**	**214**	**14,577**	**255**	**2.1**	**326**	**1,076.3**	**1**	**47.8**	**357**
Niles-Benton Harbor, MI	12.5	253	196	278	17,828	46	19,760	61	2.7	295	132.1	100	62.5	185

See footnotes at end of table.

State and Metropolitan Area Data Book: 2006

Metropolitan statistical area	Birth rate, 2002		Physicians, 2003[1]		Medicare program enrollment, 2003[2]		Social security program beneficiaries, December 2004		Housing units, percent change 2000–2004[3]		Housing units per square mile of land area, 2004		Home-ownership rate, 2000 (percent)	
	Rate per 1,000 persons[4]	Rank	Rate per 100,000 persons[5]	Rank	Rate per 100,000 persons[5]	Rank	Rate per 100,000 persons[5]	Rank	Percent	Rank	Number	Rank	Percent	Rank
Norwich-New London, CT...............	13.6	159	276	147	14,854	155	16,717	181	2.7	296	170.7	62	60.1	234
Ocala, FL............................	10.7	333	190	292	25,848	3	30,007	3	14.4	20	88.9	167	69.4	21
Ocean City, NJ......................	10.0	345	155	336	21,853	10	24,812	10	5.9	173	377.8	19	34.4	361
Odessa, TX.........................	18.6	16	207	264	12,953	237	15,142	234	2.2	323	56.1	237	60.8	220
Ogden-Clearfield, UT................	20.1	10	163	324	9,491	342	10,449	347	11.1	40	109.4	129	72.4	5
Oklahoma City, OK..................	15.1	76	288	137	12,385	259	14,650	253	5.4	194	90.2	161	59.3	250
Olympia, WA........................	11.2	317	289	135	13,375	224	15,912	209	7.4	123	128.0	105	62.7	176
Omaha-Council Bluffs, NE-IA........	16.1	51	371	57	12,380	260	14,036	275	7.2	133	76.6	189	63.2	151
Orlando-Kissimee, FL...............	13.8	152	231	217	13,784	204	15,771	213	15.1	16	225.4	38	60.6	227
Oshkosh-Neenah, WI................	11.6	299	289	135	14,179	188	16,641	186	7.0	139	157.9	68	64.2	122
Owensboro, KY.....................	13.5	168	198	276	16,894	64	20,142	54	7.4	121	55.1	243	67.2	56
Oxnard-Thousand Oaks-Ventura, CA..	14.9	95	239	202	11,534	298	12,811	314	5.0	208	143.2	85	65.3	94
Palm Bay-Melbourne-Titusville, FL	9.7	351	243	198	20,460	15	23,813	16	9.7	64	239.3	31	66.6	64
Panama City-Lynn Haven, FL........	13.1	196	229	221	16,438	78	19,182	76	9.7	65	112.6	122	52.1	345
Parkersburg-Marietta-Vienna, WV-OH.	11.3	307	194	283	18,430	39	21,125	40	1.5	341	55.0	244	67.6	48
Pascagoula, MS.....................	14.1	130	216	246	13,268	225	17,881	124	6.9	142	52.5	252	69.9	14
Pensacola-Ferry Pass-Brent, FL.....	12.8	234	293	124	15,131	139	18,238	108	7.5	118	111.2	123	63.2	149
Peoria, IL...........................	13.2	193	299	117	16,336	79	18,637	95	3.4	272	64.1	213	68.1	38
Philadelphia-Camden-Wilmington, PA-NJ-DE-MD......	**13.0**	**207**	**401**	**36**	**14,582**	**171**	**16,445**	**192**	**2.7**	**298**	**506.0**	**9**	**65.5**	**91**
Phoenix-Mesa-Scottsdale, AZ.......	17.0	34	239	202	11,603	295	13,864	280	14.8	18	104.8	134	61.0	216
Pine Bluff, AR......................	13.7	156	173	319	15,128	142	17,620	137	2.5	312	21.6	327	60.6	229
Pittsburgh, PA......................	10.4	338	384	47	19,117	30	21,456	33	1.7	336	207.7	45	66.0	81
Pittsfield, MA.......................	9.3	356	402	34	20,093	17	22,714	22	1.3	347	72.1	200	56.5	297
Pocatello, ID.......................	18.5	18	217	242	12,439	253	13,573	289	3.6	265	13.1	350	66.1	77
Portland-South Portland-Biddeford, ME	10.9	326	373	55	15,438	122	17,668	134	5.3	201	118.1	116	58.5	270
Portland-Vancouver-Beaverton, OR-WA..	13.9	150	343	76	11,481	300	13,146	301	6.8	146	126.3	110	59.3	251
Port St. Lucie-Fort Pierce, FL........	10.3	339	240	200	22,667	7	26,758	8	14.7	19	159.3	67	66.5	66
Poughkeepsie-Newburgh-Middletown, NY	12.9	218	251	189	13,063	234	15,303	228	4.8	212	148.3	78	63.6	143
Prescott, AZ........................	10.7	330	228	224	21,152	13	27,027	6	14.1	22	11.5	353	63.0	156
Providence-New Bedford-Fall River, RI-MA.	12.1	270	307	106	16,091	93	18,131	112	1.7	334	417.3	16	56.6	296
Provo-Orem, UT.....................	26.9	2	147	344	7,197	358	8,617	359	16.9	7	23.2	326	64.2	125
Pueblo, CO.........................	14.0	143	279	143	17,424	54	18,898	86	8.6	90	26.8	317	65.2	101
Punta Gorda, FL....................	6.6	361	278	145	27,140	2	34,104	1	10.3	50	126.8	107	67.0	60
Racine, WI.........................	13.3	182	195	282	14,822	160	16,896	168	4.4	235	234.2	33	66.9	61
Raleigh-Cary, NC...................	15.9	54	229	221	9,579	340	11,381	335	16.3	9	181.1	56	63.0	158
Rapid City, SD.....................	15.5	67	312	102	14,212	186	16,746	177	6.6	150	8.1	356	61.1	215
Reading, PA........................	12.4	258	203	270	15,860	99	18,384	103	4.6	229	183.0	54	69.7	16
Redding, CA........................	11.4	305	294	121	19,242	26	22,072	26	6.5	155	19.4	334	61.0	217
Reno-Sparks, NV....................	14.7	103	314	99	12,094	272	14,282	267	13.2	26	24.9	323	54.6	326
Richmond, VA.......................	13.2	194	357	67	13,116	231	15,514	219	7.3	129	85.0	174	64.6	115
Riverside-San Bernardino-Ontario, CA..	16.1	52	175	315	10,952	318	12,717	317	10.1	54	47.9	268	58.1	277
Roanoke, VA........................	11.1	322	398	38	17,276	58	20,059	57	4.7	219	72.4	199	65.1	103
Rochester, MN.....................	14.9	89	1,720	1	12,551	250	14,727	249	12.6	29	45.3	275	74.6	4
Rochester, NY......................	11.8	289	386	43	15,245	132	17,798	128	2.2	320	149.0	77	63.2	152
Rockford, IL........................	14.1	136	257	180	14,115	191	16,782	175	5.7	181	172.6	61	67.1	58
Rocky Mount, NC...................	13.5	165	162	325	16,265	84	19,001	79	5.7	183	61.7	219	58.7	264
Rome, GA..........................	14.7	105	365	62	16,282	81	19,572	65	5.3	199	75.1	192	62.1	196
Sacramento-Arden-Arcade-Roseville, CA.	14.0	144	290	132	12,436	255	13,534	291	11.1	39	155.9	71	57.0	293
Saginaw-Saginaw Township North, MI.	12.7	241	267	159	16,278	82	19,298	71	2.9	284	108.8	131	69.5	20
St. Cloud, MN......................	13.4	176	252	187	12,733	244	14,130	273	10.4	48	40.1	283	68.8	26
St. George, UT.....................	19.9	12	189	294	15,521	118	18,708	91	23.1	2	18.5	337	60.7	223
St. Joseph, MO-KS.................	12.3	264	150	341	16,180	88	18,787	90	2.4	313	31.2	308	64.5	116
St. Louis, MO-IL[8].................	13.0	212	330	82	14,550	175	16,773	176	4.4	236	136.8	93	66.3	72
Salem, OR..........................	14.5	115	199	274	14,035	195	16,167	202	5.3	198	72.6	198	60.1	235
Salinas, CA........................	16.8	35	232	215	10,557	328	11,937	333	3.7	261	41.1	281	50.3	349
Salisbury, MD......................	12.7	239	308	103	14,587	170	16,996	166	7.7	114	68.0	209	61.2	213
Salt Lake City, UT..................	20.1	9	352	70	8,811	349	10,305	349	7.5	119	38.6	287	64.7	112
San Angelo, TX....................	15.2	75	217	242	15,513	121	17,641	135	2.4	314	17.8	339	57.7	283
San Antonio, TX....................	16.5	42	330	82	11,920	279	13,885	279	8.1	102	95.5	148	59.8	242
San Diego-Carlsbad-San Marcos, CA..	15.2	74	347	73	11,997	273	12,881	310	5.7	182	261.7	27	53.0	339
Sandusky, OH......................	11.7	298	179	312	17,633	52	19,138	77	2.5	307	144.5	83	63.6	142
San Francisco-Oakland-Fremont, CA.......	**13.5**	**164**	**441**	**24**	**12,676**	**245**	**12,808**	**315**	**3.0**	**284**	**669.1**	**3**	**53.5**	**337**
San Jose-Sunnyvale-Santa Clara, CA...	16.2	48	382	50	10,274	334	10,407	348	3.8	255	230.7	34	58.7	266
San Luis Obispo-Paso Robles, CA....	9.4	355	323	91	15,849	100	17,776	130	7.4	125	33.2	300	55.7	314
Santa Barbara-Santa Maria, CA......	14.2	126	328	87	13,964	196	15,270	229	3.4	268	54.0	246	53.6	336
Santa Cruz-Watsonville, CA.........	13.9	148	294	121	11,148	310	12,369	324	2.2	321	226.9	37	55.3	320
Santa Fe, NM.......................	12.1	274	405	32	12,410	258	14,496	257	4.5	232	31.6	307	62.4	192
Santa Rosa-Petaluma, CA...........	12.2	267	316	95	13,718	207	15,246	230	4.7	225	121.6	112	60.3	232
Sarasota-Bradenton-Venice, FL......	10.0	344	371	57	25,474	4	27,674	4	11.0	43	271.1	26	62.8	170
Savannah, GA......................	15.1	77	322	92	13,150	230	15,331	226	8.6	89	97.9	145	58.3	273
Scranton-Wilkes-Barre, PA..........	9.6	353	254	185	20,855	14	23,737	17	1.2	350	146.5	81	62.8	173
Seattle-Tacoma-Bellevue, WA	**12.9**	**220**	**373**	**55**	**11,270**	**304**	**12,600**	**322**	**6.6**	**151**	**227.0**	**36**	**59.2**	**254**
Sheboygan, WI.....................	12.2	266	181	308	15,515	120	17,630	136	5.1	207	94.0	151	67.7	46
Sherman-Denison, TX...............	13.5	172	216	246	16,531	73	18,618	96	3.5	267	53.6	247	62.6	183
Shreveport-Bossier City, LA.........	14.8	99	453	21	14,622	167	16,714	182	4.0	249	64.0	214	59.7	243
Sioux City, IA-NE-SD...............	16.2	49	200	272	14,980	150	16,520	189	1.9	330	28.0	316	65.3	98
Sioux Falls, SD.....................	15.7	57	384	47	12,809	240	14,823	247	12.4	31	33.0	302	64.8	111
South Bend-Mishawaka, IN-MI.......	13.5	170	232	215	15,033	147	17,261	152	4.2	244	143.7	84	67.5	50

See footnotes at end of table.

Metropolitan statistical area	Birth rate, 2002 Rate per 1,000 persons[4]	Rank	Physicians, 2003[1] Rate per 100,000 persons[5]	Rank	Medicare program enrollment, 2003[2] Rate per 100,000 persons[5]	Rank	Social security program beneficiaries, December 2004 Rate per 100,000 persons[5]	Rank	Housing units, percent change 2000–2004[3] Percent	Rank	Housing units per square mile of land area, 2004 Number	Rank	Home-ownership rate, 2000 (percent) Percent	Rank
Spartanburg, SC	13.2	189	234	211	15,891	96	18,980	81	7.2	131	141.5	89	65.8	85
Spokane, WA	13.0	209	322	92	14,288	181	16,167	202	5.4	195	104.6	136	61.2	212
Springfield, IL	12.7	240	505	15	15,300	129	17,927	120	3.7	258	79.6	182	65.0	107
Springfield, MA	11.2	315	313	100	15,841	101	17,827	126	1.3	348	151.4	74	59.5	246
Springfield, MO	13.0	210	254	185	15,665	111	18,060	115	8.9	80	56.6	235	62.9	164
Springfield, OH	12.7	238	166	322	17,066	61	18,988	80	1.2	352	154.6	72	66.3	71
State College, PA	9.1	357	229	221	11,609	294	13,371	295	6.0	166	50.9	257	55.8	312
Stockton, CA	16.6	38	162	325	11,285	303	12,847	312	11.9	35	151.3	75	58.0	282
Sumter, SC	15.0	88	148	342	13,720	206	16,661	184	4.1	246	65.3	212	62.8	174
Syracuse, NY	11.8	290	384	47	15,631	116	18,115	113	1.7	337	118.3	114	60.7	221
Tallahassee, FL	12.5	249	245	194	10,831	324	12,828	313	8.6	88	62.2	217	57.3	288
Tampa-St. Petersburg-Clearwater, FL	11.7	296	295	120	18,542	36	21,217	38	7.9	110	483.2	11	62.4	188
Terre Haute, IN	12.6	248	209	262	16,763	67	19,268	72	2.9	288	50.9	256	65.3	99
Texarkana, TX-Texarkana, AR	13.1	202	265	163	15,332	125	17,685	132	4.4	237	37.4	289	62.9	165
Toledo, OH	12.9	222	335	79	14,672	164	16,342	195	3.3	273	182.1	55	62.0	200
Topeka, KS	14.0	138	249	190	16,300	80	18,036	116	4.3	239	31.0	309	65.9	82
Trenton-Ewing, NJ	12.9	223	411	30	14,472	178	15,774	212	3.2	275	608.9	4	63.3	148
Tucson, AZ	14.2	124	379	51	15,102	143	17,142	158	8.3	97	43.2	278	58.2	275
Tulsa, OK	14.9	91	212	255	13,796	203	16,307	196	4.7	221	61.0	222	62.1	199
Tuscaloosa, AL	13.0	211	262	169	14,508	176	18,003	118	6.6	152	34.4	298	58.2	276
Tyler, TX	15.2	73	404	33	15,751	104	17,930	119	4.7	223	80.8	180	63.8	135
Utica-Rome, NY	10.6	334	223	234	18,888	35	21,614	29	0.4	358	51.6	254	58.7	265
Valdosta, GA	14.9	94	180	311	11,971	276	14,666	251	7.4	124	32.5	303	57.2	289
Vallejo-Fairfield, CA	14.3	121	212	255	10,435	332	12,006	331	7.1	137	173.7	60	63.2	150
Vero Beach, FL	9.0	358	358	65	27,154	1	30,217	2	14.3	21	131.5	102	65.8	84
Victoria, TX	15.6	62	217	242	14,279	182	16,881	171	3.0	283	21.3	329	59.6	244
Vineland-Millville-Bridgeton, NJ	14.1	135	145	347	15,150	138	17,361	148	1.7	338	109.8	126	63.2	153
Virginia Beach-Norfolk-Newport News, VA-NC	14.4	116	300	114	11,835	287	13,799	283	5.6	187	250.3	28	58.8	262
Visalia-Porterville, CA	19.5	13	135	351	10,898	322	13,071	305	6.0	169	26.3	321	56.8	294
Waco, TX	15.1	78	231	217	14,150	189	16,146	205	4.2	243	84.8	176	56.0	307
Warner Robins, GA	13.8	151	156	333	10,949	319	12,655	320	15.0	17	135.9	94	63.0	160
Washington-Arlington-Alexandria, DC-VA-MD-WV	**15.1**	**83**	**440**	**26**	**9,473**	**343**	**10,081**	**351**	**7.6**	**115**	**361.4**	**21**	**60.7**	**224**
Waterloo-Cedar Falls, IA	12.2	265	206	266	16,521	74	18,966	82	3.9	253	45.7	274	68.0	40
Wausau, WI	11.9	288	262	169	13,756	205	16,485	191	8.1	103	35.2	296	71.7	9
Weirton-Steubenville, WV-OH	10.0	346	142	348	21,692	11	24,280	12	0.7	357	102.5	140	69.5	19
Wenatchee, WA	13.5	171	274	149	15,069	145	17,368	147	4.3	241	9.5	355	56.5	299
Wheeling, WV-OH	9.9	350	271	153	20,190	16	23,237	19	0.4	360	73.1	196	66.2	75
Wichita, KS	15.7	58	260	174	13,405	220	15,384	225	4.8	216	60.2	228	62.9	162
Wichita Falls, TX	14.0	141	255	183	14,809	162	16,871	172	2.7	298	24.2	325	58.7	263
Williamsport, PA	10.7	331	226	229	18,363	41	20,809	43	1.8	332	43.3	277	62.2	194
Wilmington, NC	11.6	300	308	103	16,785	66	20,329	50	14.0	23	90.0	162	54.3	330
Winchester, VA-WV	12.8	231	304	113	14,279	182	17,063	162	9.0	76	46.1	272	63.8	136
Winston-Salem, NC	13.6	160	462	18	15,165	137	17,426	143	7.4	122	134.5	96	64.9	110
Worcester, MA	13.1	201	355	68	14,461	179	16,304	197	3.4	269	203.8	47	61.1	214
Yakima, WA	18.0	21	193	284	12,655	246	14,707	250	2.2	324	18.8	335	60.2	233
York-Hanover, PA	11.7	294	192	287	14,902	153	17,605	138	6.0	168	183.7	52	72.0	7
Youngstown-Warren-Boardman, OH-PA	10.3	340	219	240	19,122	29	21,611	30	1.6	340	153.1	73	68.7	29
Yuba City, CA	16.5	39	183	305	13,515	215	15,445	222	6.5	154	44.0	276	54.4	329
Yuma, AZ	18.6	17	128	353	11,987	274	14,241	269	8.7	84	14.6	345	52.4	343

[1]Active, nonfederal physicians as of December 31.
[2]Unduplicated count of persons enrolled in either hospital and/or supplemental medical insurance as of July 1.
[3]The April 1, 2000, housing estimates base reflects changes to the 2000 Census of Population and Housing as documented in the Count Question Resolution program and geographic program revisions.
[4]Per 1,000 resident population estimated as of July 1, 2002.
[5]Based on resident population estimated as of July 1 of the year shown.
[6]The Denver-Aurora metropolitan statistical area includes Broomfield County. Broomfield County, CO, was formed from parts of Adams, Boulder, Jefferson, and Weld Counties on November 15, 2001, and is coextensive with Broomfield city. For the purposes of defining and presenting data for the Denver-Aurora metropolitan statistical area, Broomfield is treated as if it were a county when data are available to do so. In many cases, the data will not be available.

Sources: U.S. Census Bureau. U.S. National Center for Health Statistics, American Medical Association. For more information, see <http://www.census.gov/popest.housing>, <http://cdc.gov/nchs/nvss.htm>, and <http://www.aha.org/aha/index/jsp;>. See Tables B-5, B-6 and B-7 of the State and Metropolitan Area Data Book: 2006.

Table E-16. Metropolitan Area Rankings — **Economic Indicators**

Metropolitan statistical area	Earnings, 2002—percent by selected major industries				Civilian labor force, 2000–2004		Unemployment rate,[2] 2004		New private housing units authorized by building permits, 2000–2003	
	Manufacturing		Government[1]							
	Percent	Rank	Percent	Rank	Net change	Rank	Rate	Rank	Number	Rank
Abilene, TX..................	4.5	318	30.1	51	5,012	177	4.9	222	1,380	320
Akron, OH..................	18.8	114	14.9	227	9,785	108	6.0	102	12,396	99
Albany, GA..................	(NA)	(NA)	22.9	105	946	272	5.2	190	2,982	260
Albany-Schenectady-Troy, NY	7.8	272	26.8	73	16,396	63	4.2	305	11,916	106
Albuquerque, NM	8.7	260	22.7	109	21,567	45	5.2	187	25,656	50
Alexandria, LA..............	10.8	216	26.7	77	1,258	264	5.7	124	2,004	289
Allentown-Bethlehem-Easton, PA-NJ	21.3	87	11.1	328	19,721	51	5.3	178	16,837	78
Altoona, PA.................	16.1	143	15.8	210	3,446	203	5.5	151	1,164	331
Amarillo, TX................	7.5	275	17.1	178	10,675	102	4.3	293	3,543	243
Ames, IA...................	12.3	196	44.2	13	–116	301	3.2	357	2,796	267
Anchorage, AK..............	2.1	338	27.1	68	9,454	114	6.4	73	8,199	134
Anderson, IN...............	36.4	10	14.6	234	–329	305	5.9	110	1,751	304
Anderson, SC...............	31.6	25	17.9	163	330	291	7.1	44	5,165	203
Ann Arbor, MI..............	18.7	115	27.0	72	2,203	244	4.3	295	8,945	127
Anniston-Oxford, AL..........	19.3	110	29.8	52	755	280	5.4	168	991	340
Appleton, WI...............	24.7	62	10.1	341	4,352	184	4.6	262	7,944	142
Asheville, NC...............	17.5	125	16.0	205	11,225	100	4.3	302	13,361	92
Athens-Clarke County, GA......	14.0	167	32.3	46	5,957	151	3.4	349	7,003	163
Atlanta-Sandy Springs-Marietta, GA....	8.2	267	11.5	315	81,620	13	4.6	249	267,199	1
Atlantic City, NJ.............	3.2	331	16.7	191	5,422	159	5.6	146	7,615	149
Auburn-Opelika, AL...........	15.7	149	34.5	33	3,984	189	4.2	309	4,020	227
Augusta-Richmond County, GA-SC ..	14.0	168	26.8	74	13,528	77	5.4	165	12,292	102
Austin-Round Rock, TX........	14.6	162	17.9	162	39,898	26	5.1	208	72,106	21
Bakersfield, CA.............	4.4	321	27.1	67	24,212	40	9.8	8	16,886	76
Baltimore-Towson, MD	8.3	266	21.9	115	20,017	50	4.5	266	44,836	36
Bangor, ME................	13.6	176	20.1	136	3,623	198	5.4	163	2,086	283
Barnstable Town, MA..........	3.2	330	15.8	208	9,761	109	4.8	226	6,122	182
Baton Rouge, LA............	13.9	171	19.8	139	12,673	81	6.1	93	16,907	75
Battle Creek, MI.............	31.8	24	19.2	153	3,360	206	7.0	51	1,751	304
Bay City, MI...............	20.5	97	16.9	185	107	299	7.6	31	1,438	318
Beaumont-Port Arthur, TX.......	20.5	100	15.4	220	3,138	215	8.4	17	4,196	220
Bellingham, WA.............	13.8	173	18.4	157	12,623	84	5.7	123	6,926	165
Bend, OR..................	9.5	243	14.3	244	9,492	113	6.7	59	10,105	117
Billings, MT................	6.5	291	13.7	261	6,159	147	3.5	343	2,675	271
Binghamton, NY.............	26.4	49	19.6	142	–2,475	336	5.3	174	1,331	323
Birmingham-Hoover, AL.........	9.7	240	13.8	258	–1,665	328	4.8	225	22,392	57
Bismarck, ND	7.8	274	21.5	123	3,642	197	3.0	359	3,088	256
Blacksburg-Christiansburg-Radford, VA ..	26.2	54	29.0	57	3,392	205	4.1	312	2,849	262
Bloomington, IN.............	15.8	147	29.3	55	2,877	224	4.6	263	3,725	233
Bloomington-Normal, IL.........	10.8	215	12.7	285	–412	308	4.5	271	5,800	188
Boise City-Nampa, ID..........	18.0	121	14.3	242	16,176	66	4.3	294	27,655	44
Boston-Cambridge-Quincy, MA-NH.............	**11.4**	**206**	**10.1**	**338**	**–5,419**	**350**	**4.9**	**221**	**47,961**	**34**
Boulder, CO[3].............	17.9	122	14.1	252	6,040	149	4.9	218	9,246	126
Bowling Green, KY............	21.5	84	16.9	183	2,605	232	4.4	277	3,224	253
Bremerton-Silverdale, WA	1.5	341	54.5	7	14,736	73	5.9	115	4,938	211
Bridgeport-Stamford-Norwalk, CT	12.0	201	6.7	360	8,869	116	4.4	286	8,341	131
Brownsville-Harlingen, TX.......	9.8	239	27.0	70	15,832	67	8.8	12	13,566	89
Brunswick, GA..............	11.5	204	26.2	81	3,694	196	4.0	321	3,256	251
Buffalo-Niagara Falls, NY........	20.0	105	17.8	168	7,365	135	5.8	118	11,341	108
Burlington, NC..............	24.0	69	9.8	342	583	282	6.2	86	4,469	218
Burlington-South Burlington, VT	21.3	88	15.8	209	5,325	162	3.5	344	4,030	226
Canton-Massillon, OH..........	26.5	48	12.0	304	–1,176	319	6.6	63	5,367	195
Cape Coral-Fort Myers, FL.......	4.8	317	15.4	218	40,332	25	3.9	330	46,900	35
Carson City, NV.............	10.8	217	36.4	24	738	281	5.0	213	1,199	328
Casper, WY................	5.8	304	13.5	266	3,335	207	3.7	336	609	353
Cedar Rapids, IA............	21.6	82	11.0	329	817	278	5.1	209	7,074	160
Champaign-Urbana, IL.........	10.8	214	34.2	36	–556	310	4.6	259	5,095	206
Charleston, WV.............	10.1	229	18.2	160	–6,570	352	5.0	216	1,762	303
Charleston-North Charleston, SC	10.4	222	26.4	78	25,386	38	5.3	174	23,446	53
Charlotte-Gastonia-Concord, NC-SC	14.0	169	10.2	337	46,975	21	5.6	142	81,349	17
Charlottesville, VA............	0.1	345	32.5	44	5,961	150	3.1	358	7,607	150
Chattanooga, TN-GA..........	16.8	131	16.2	199	2,641	230	4.4	278	11,613	107
Cheyenne, WY..............	4.4	319	40.2	17	2,464	239	4.5	268	1,821	299
Chicago-Naperville-Joliet, IL-IN-WI	**13.1**	**186**	**11.7**	**310**	**–34,733**	**358**	**6.1**	**90**	**187,013**	**5**
Chico, CA.................	5.1	312	21.9	116	4,853	180	7.2	42	5,182	202
Cincinnati-Middletown, OH-KY-IN	16.2	142	12.3	296	40,454	24	5.3	182	50,733	31
Clarksville, TN-KY............	16.0	145	48.5	8	5,153	171	5.3	181	7,276	155
Cleveland, TN..............	30.5	29	11.7	313	249	293	5.2	197	2,264	281
Cleveland-Elyria-Mentor, OH	18.5	118	13.7	260	–23,015	357	5.9	112	27,554	45
Coeur d'Alene, ID............	8.9	257	19.4	146	7,433	134	5.5	154	5,769	189
College Station-Bryan, TX.......	7.4	278	37.7	21	8,222	123	4.5	275	6,553	176
Colorado Springs, CO..........	(NA)	(NA)	27.6	62	20,077	49	5.7	132	26,466	48
Columbia, MO..............	7.4	280	36.8	23	5,829	155	3.7	335	6,373	179
Columbia, SC	11.3	207	25.5	87	16,245	64	5.7	126	21,276	60
Columbus, GA-AL............	(NA)	(NA)	32.7	43	–1,897	332	5.2	193	6,823	168
Columbus, IN..............	43.1	4	11.3	321	–1,278	321	4.4	291	849	346
Columbus, OH..............	12.2	198	16.2	202	37,862	27	5.4	166	64,622	22
Corpus Christi, TX...........	10.3	225	23.0	102	12,616	85	6.7	60	6,922	166

See footnotes at end of table.

| Metropolitan statistical area | Earnings, 2002—percent by selected major industries | | | | Civilian labor force, 2000–2004 | | Unemployment rate,[2] 2004 | | New private housing units authorized by building permits, 2000–2003 | |
| | Manufacturing | | Government[1] | | | | | | | |
	Percent	Rank	Percent	Rank	Net change	Rank	Rate	Rank	Number	Rank
Corvallis, OR.	26.3	53	27.0	71	1,080	266	5.4	163	1,867	297
Cumberland, MD-WV	16.4	139	24.5	93	−678	314	6.3	75	983	342
Dallas-Fort Worth-Arlington, TX	**(NA)**	**(NA)**	**9.6**	**346**	**115,774**	**8**	**5.9**	**111**	**198,805**	**2**
Dalton, GA	42.1	6	9.4	354	524	284	4.1	314	3,559	241
Danville, IL	21.9	78	23.4	99	−1,351	322	8.3	18	262	359
Danville, VA	33.6	17	15.5	216	−241	303	7.4	35	1,254	326
Davenport-Moline-Rock Island, IA-IL	16.7	136	16.7	189	−3,743	345	5.5	150	4,727	212
Dayton, OH	20.5	96	20.4	131	−1,669	329	6.2	81	12,823	96
Decatur, AL	36.0	12	14.5	236	−1,593	327	6.1	89	1,550	314
Decatur, IL	29.2	33	10.1	340	−4,170	346	7.3	38	1,505	317
Deltona-Daytona Beach-Ormond Beach, FL	7.4	277	16.5	195	22,446	43	4.6	260	19,459	66
Denver-Aurora, CO[3]	(NA)	(NA)	12.3	299	78,429	14	5.8	122	94,975	14
Des Moines, IA	7.2	281	13.3	271	12,435	88	4.7	239	17,567	70
Detroit-Warren-Livonia, MI	**21.6**	**83**	**10.1**	**339**	**−84,522**	**359**	**7.1**	**45**	**75,813**	**20**
Dothan, AL	13.7	174	16.6	193	−240	302	4.7	235	1,938	295
Dover, DE	(NA)	(NA)	39.8	19	5,345	161	3.6	342	5,495	193
Dubuque, IA	23.7	71	8.1	358	220	294	4.7	236	1,820	300
Duluth, MN-WI	8.1	270	21.8	118	2,866	225	5.8	117	4,584	216
Durham, NC	27.2	41	17.9	166	10,808	101	4.4	288	20,106	65
Eau Claire, WI	17.4	127	16.2	200	3,613	199	4.7	232	5,123	205
El Centro, CA	4.4	320	35.7	27	3,766	195	17.1	1	4,052	225
Elizabethtown, KY	16.7	135	45.7	11	3,258	211	5.3	186	3,075	257
Elkhart-Goshen, IN	53.7	2	6.3	361	2,728	226	4.2	310	5,131	204
Elmira, NY	20.5	99	21.6	120	−2,244	334	6.1	91	643	352
El Paso, TX.	12.2	199	27.6	63	14,845	72	7.8	25	15,622	83
Erie, PA	26.4	49	13.9	255	542	283	6.3	76	2,831	263
Eugene-Springfield, OR.	14.8	158	19.3	150	2,269	243	7.4	36	5,874	187
Evansville, IN-KY	26.6	46	9.2	356	1,616	253	4.6	247	6,817	169
Fairbanks, AK	1.4	343	46.9	10	2,580	233	6.6	66	734	348
Fargo, ND-MN	8.7	261	15.0	226	8,073	126	2.9	361	7,258	156
Farmington, NM	3.3	328	22.0	113	3,959	190	6.1	92	989	341
Fayetteville, NC.	8.4	264	58.3	4	6,326	146	5.6	140	8,522	130
Fayetteville-Springdale-Rogers, AR-MO	17.4	128	12.0	303	30,685	31	3.6	340	17,116	72
Flagstaff, AZ	6.8	285	33.8	37	4,449	181	5.5	159	3,614	239
Flint, MI	28.2	36	14.6	231	−749	315	8.3	19	10,420	113
Florence, SC	25.4	57	17.4	171	4,191	186	8.2	21	1,998	290
Florence-Muscle Shoals, AL	17.0	130	27.3	66	−3,649	344	6.5	68	1,341	322
Fond du Lac, WI	35.2	13	11.5	318	1,511	258	4.6	251	1,993	291
Fort Collins-Loveland, CO	20.2	104	19.2	151	16,577	61	4.6	246	13,227	95
Fort Smith, AR-OK	23.3	74	13.3	273	5,194	169	5.1	200	3,331	246
Fort Walton Beach-Crestview-Destin, FL.	3.5	325	44.4	12	12,425	89	3.5	345	6,613	175
Fort Wayne, IN	23.2	75	9.7	345	861	277	5.2	192	10,275	116
Fresno, CA.	8.6	263	21.8	117	20,243	47	10.4	6	16,514	80
Gadsden, AL	19.1	112	14.7	229	−1,493	324	6.3	78	1,232	327
Gainesville, FL.	4.3	323	37.6	22	5,217	167	3.5	347	8,091	139
Gainesville, GA	27.0	44	12.3	298	5,226	166	3.8	332	7,569	151
Glens Falls, NY	16.8	132	21.0	129	3,182	213	4.8	230	2,509	277
Goldsboro, NC.	14.7	159	35.1	31	814	279	5.4	161	1,972	293
Grand Forks, ND-MN	6.9	284	32.7	42	2,558	235	3.7	334	1,402	319
Grand Junction, CO	6.7	288	17.6	169	10,085	106	5.1	203	5,528	192
Grand Rapids-Wyoming, MI	26.4	51	9.6	351	−1,891	330	7.0	52	17,080	73
Great Falls, MT	2.9	333	30.8	48	922	274	4.2	308	587	356
Greeley, CO[3]	15.5	150	13.4	269	15,077	71	5.4	170	17,044	74
Green Bay, WI.	21.6	81	11.8	308	9,840	107	4.7	237	10,779	111
Greensboro-High Point, NC	21.7	79	11.2	325	7,777	130	5.6	143	21,663	59
Greenville, NC.	15.7	148	32.5	45	2,976	218	5.7	128	7,285	154
Greenville, SC	21.1	92	13.6	264	1,006	271	6.2	83	17,349	71
Gulfport-Biloxi, MS	6.1	298	35.3	29	2,469	238	5.1	202	7,165	158
Hagerstown-Martinsburg, MD-WV	15.1	153	20.2	133	1,874	248	4.3	300	9,605	121
Hanford-Corcoran, CA.	9.0	255	47.1	9	5,065	175	10.8	4	2,823	265
Harrisburg-Carlisle, PA	9.3	248	22.1	112	11,500	97	4.5	272	9,264	125
Harrisonburg, VA	28.1	38	15.2	221	7,321	137	3.0	360	2,751	269
Hartford-West Hartford-East Hartford, CT	15.1	156	14.3	245	17,054	59	5.1	205	14,752	86
Hattiesburg, MS	11.1	211	25.7	86	1,739	249	5.2	198	1,168	330
Hickory-Lenoir-Morganton, NC	37.2	9	12.8	280	−7,693	354	6.7	58	8,116	138
Hinesville-Fort Stewart, GA	(NA)	(NA)	79.7	1	2,924	221	5.5	155	1,296	325
Holland-Grand Haven, MI	42.0	7	11.9	307	−1,997	333	5.6	138	8,715	129
Honolulu, HI	2.1	339	34.2	35	−528	309	3.2	355	10,090	118
Hot Springs, AR.	11.3	208	15.0	225	2,560	234	5.9	109	472	357
Houma-Bayou Cane-Thibodaux, LA.	11.2	210	13.4	268	5,886	153	5.1	205	3,254	252
Houston-Sugar Land-Baytown, TX.	13.2	184	9.8	344	182,523	4	6.3	77	177,297	6
Huntington-Ashland, WV-KY-OH	12.9	191	18.5	156	4,446	182	5.5	148	960	343
Huntsville, AL	22.2	76	27.0	69	8,642	118	4.6	255	6,895	167
Idaho Falls, ID.	5.4	309	14.4	237	5,888	152	3.5	348	3,545	242
Indianapolis, IN	17.1	129	12.4	294	46,862	22	4.7	242	64,409	23
Iowa City, IA	8.8	259	41.8	16	19,155	53	3.2	353	5,337	197
Ithaca, NY	10.1	232	12.5	292	2,926	220	3.6	339	1,590	313
Jackson, MI	21.4	85	17.8	167	−43	300	7.6	32	3,623	238

See footnotes at end of table.

Table E-16. Metropolitan Area Rankings — **Economic Indicators**—Con.

Metropolitan statistical area	Earnings, 2002—percent by selected major industries				Civilian labor force, 2000–2004		Unemployment rate,[2] 2004		New private housing units authorized by building permits, 2000–2003	
	Manufacturing		Government[1]							
	Percent	Rank	Percent	Rank	Net change	Rank	Rate	Rank	Number	Rank
Jackson, MS	7.8	273	21.1	127	11,922	93	5.1	201	12,005	105
Jackson, TN	23.7	70	18.6	155	−589	311	5.6	145	2,898	261
Jacksonville, FL	6.7	287	18.4	157	20,115	48	4.8	227	53,614	27
Jacksonville, NC	1.2	344	75.2	2	2,329	242	5.5	153	4,172	222
Janesville, WI	33.7	16	12.8	282	1,261	263	5.6	144	3,644	236
Jefferson City, MO	9.5	244	36.0	26	2,974	219	4.3	304	2,542	276
Johnson City, TN	19.0	113	20.2	135	3,865	192	5.4	172	2,595	272
Johnstown, PA	9.0	256	19.5	143	1,022	270	7.0	50	875	345
Jonesboro, AR	19.8	107	16.9	184	1,674	252	5.6	139	2,086	283
Joplin, MO	25.0	60	11.0	330	2,136	245	5.2	199	2,060	286
Kalamazoo-Portage, MI	27.0	43	15.5	215	−642	312	6.2	85	7,729	147
Kankakee-Bradley, IL	21.2	90	15.7	211	−359	307	7.6	30	1,981	292
Kansas City, MO-KS	9.9	237	14.6	232	35,423	29	6.0	100	57,071	26
Kennewick-Richland-Pasco, WA	6.7	286	17.9	165	15,736	68	6.3	78	7,059	161
Killeen-Temple-Fort Hood, TX	5.9	303	54.8	6	11,990	92	5.7	126	9,865	120
Kingsport-Bristol-Bristol, TN-VA	30.5	28	11.5	317	1,425	260	5.5	149	4,605	215
Kingston, NY	10.4	223	26.0	84	3,052	217	4.8	228	2,773	268
Knoxville, TN	14.5	163	15.1	222	19,308	52	4.1	315	15,235	84
Kokomo, IN	58.9	1	10.3	336	−2,954	339	6.4	71	1,792	301
La Crosse, WI-MN	17.8	124	14.4	241	2,113	247	4.2	307	2,594	273
Lafayette, IN	27.0	42	24.6	92	−1,134	318	4.7	244	6,381	178
Lafayette, LA	6.1	299	10.8	332	3,297	210	4.7	243	5,258	200
Lake Charles, LA	20.7	95	14.2	248	943	273	5.6	141	4,547	217
Lakeland, FL	12.7	194	15.1	223	17,521	57	5.0	211	21,062	62
Lancaster, PA	25.6	55	8.8	357	16,177	65	4.0	325	9,521	122
Lansing-East Lansing, MI	16.3	141	27.6	61	2,123	246	6.0	104	10,347	114
Laredo, TX	1.4	342	26.4	79	12,636	82	6.8	55	7,098	159
Las Cruces, NM	4.9	315	35.6	28	6,537	143	6.4	72	4,956	209
Las Vegas-Paradise, NV	3.1	332	13.4	270	99,671	10	4.4	290	121,819	10
Lawrence, KS	9.0	254	30.7	49	5,527	157	4.1	313	3,848	229
Lawton, OK	9.6	242	56.5	5	3,207	212	4.5	274	604	355
Lebanon, PA	24.5	64	17.9	164	5,521	158	4.1	318	2,677	270
Lewiston, ID-WA	15.2	152	18.4	159	434	286	5.4	162	609	353
Lewiston-Auburn, ME	15.1	155	12.1	302	1,686	251	4.5	273	1,509	316
Lexington-Fayette, KY	20.8	94	16.4	196	−2,261	335	4.1	317	14,917	85
Lima, OH	29.5	30	14.2	250	1,067	268	6.6	64	925	344
Lincoln, NE	13.4	178	21.2	124	8,358	120	3.4	350	8,061	140
Little Rock-North Little Rock, AR	8.7	262	22.2	110	13,533	76	5.1	207	14,426	87
Logan, UT-ID	20.5	98	25.0	89	7,648	132	3.9	328	3,322	247
Longview, TX	12.8	192	11.7	311	7,110	139	6.0	103	1,129	334
Longview, WA	25.5	56	14.5	235	406	287	8.5	15	1,842	298
Los Angeles-Long Beach-Santa Ana, CA	**12.3**	**197**	**12.4**	**295**	**233,068**	**1**	**6.0**	**101**	**114,794**	**11**
Louisville, KY-IN [4]	18.6	117	12.2	300	−9,034	355	5.1	204	–	361
Lubbock, TX	5.8	305	22.2	111	9,643	110	4.6	253	7,485	152
Lynchburg, VA	28.3	35	13.1	277	205	295	4.3	299	5,320	198
Macon, GA	(NA)	(NA)	14.3	243	2,693	228	4.9	223	5,295	199
Madera, CA	9.2	253	22.0	114	8,079	125	8.8	11	3,645	235
Madison, WI	11.6	203	24.1	95	22,830	42	3.3	352	21,119	61
Manchester-Nashua, NH	20.3	102	9.6	350	10,326	104	3.9	327	8,198	135
Mansfield, OH	34.5	14	16.6	192	353	289	7.2	41	1,964	294
McAllen-Edinburg-Mission, TX	4.9	316	26.7	76	43,139	23	9.1	9	28,062	43
Medford, OR	9.2	251	16.2	201	7,004	141	7.1	46	6,639	172
Memphis, TN-MS-AR	10.3	226	14.1	253	4,370	183	5.9	107	37,483	37
Merced, CA	13.6	175	20.8	130	8,359	119	10.8	5	6,967	164
Miami-Fort Lauderdale-Miami Beach, FL	**5.2**	**311**	**14.1**	**251**	**125,014**	**7**	**5.2**	**191**	**149,670**	**7**
Michigan City-La Porte, IN	24.6	63	16.4	197	−1,210	320	6.0	96	1,712	307
Midland, TX	3.4	326	11.7	312	6,096	148	4.5	270	799	347
Milwaukee-Waukesha-West Allis, WI	20.4	101	11.2	327	−4,976	348	5.4	167	23,913	52
Minneapolis-St. Paul-Bloomington, MN-WI	14.2	165	12.0	305	86,535	12	4.5	276	98,659	13
Missoula, MT	6.2	297	18.7	154	3,322	208	4.0	326	3,168	255
Mobile, AL	12.7	193	17.3	175	−6,657	353	6.5	69	7,929	143
Modesto, CA	13.4	179	17.1	178	18,076	56	9.1	10	13,530	90
Monroe, LA	13.2	185	16.3	198	3,599	200	5.7	131	1,913	296
Monroe, MI	32.3	22	12.9	279	262	292	6.3	80	4,137	223
Montgomery, AL	9.9	238	29.3	53	1,293	262	5.5	157	6,172	181
Morgantown, WV	9.5	245	35.2	30	2,621	231	3.8	331	340	358
Morristown, TN	38.3	8	11.3	324	519	285	5.8	116	2,342	279
Mount Vernon-Anacortes, WA	13.5	177	19.2	152	4,213	185	6.8	54	3,187	254
Muncie, IN	22.1	77	19.4	148	−1,891	330	6.0	105	1,614	312
Muskegon-Norton Shores, MI	27.2	39	16.0	206	3,807	193	7.9	23	3,695	234
Myrtle Beach-Conway-North Myrtle Beach, SC	5.4	307	13.9	254	12,880	79	5.7	133	17,907	69
Napa, CA	19.1	111	13.6	265	5,612	156	4.6	255	3,063	258
Naples-Marco Island, FL	2.3	337	9.6	347	20,876	46	4.0	322	29,230	42
Nashville-Davidson-Murfreesboro, TN	13.1	187	10.8	331	17,091	58	4.3	301	48,085	33
New Haven-Milford, CT	14.9	157	13.2	274	15,370	69	5.2	188	7,031	162
New Orleans-Metairie-Kenner, LA	7.8	271	17.0	182	−12,170	356	4.6	261	20,117	64
New York-Northern New Jersey-Long Island, NY-NJ-PA	**6.4**	**295**	**12.3**	**297**	**165,555**	**5**	**5.7**	**135**	**189,222**	**4**
Niles-Benton Harbor, MI	33.2	18	11.8	309	−6,018	351	7.8	26	2,273	280

See footnotes at end of table.

Metropolitan statistical area	Earnings, 2002—percent by selected major industries				Civilian labor force, 2000–2004		Unemployment rate,[2] 2004		New private housing units authorized by building permits, 2000–2003	
	Manufacturing		Government[1]							
	Percent	Rank	Percent	Rank	Net change	Rank	Rate	Rank	Number	Rank
Norwich-New London, CT	18.6	116	31.9	47	11,520	96	4.4	280	3,774	231
Ocala, FL	11.7	202	18.0	161	7,839	129	4.6	254	18,161	68
Ocean City, NJ	1.9	340	26.1	82	2,445	240	6.9	53	5,760	190
Odessa, TX.	10.3	227	17.3	172	5,066	174	6.0	99	712	349
Ogden-Clearfield, UT	14.6	161	33.0	39	15,113	70	5.3	182	15,863	82
Oklahoma City, OK.	13.4	180	24.3	94	24,293	39	4.4	282	25,729	49
Olympia, WA.	4.0	324	42.2	15	12,632	83	5.7	128	6,627	173
Omaha-Council Bluffs, NE-IA	7.5	276	15.1	224	14,626	74	4.3	297	23,314	54
Orlando-Kissimmee, FL	6.5	292	11.3	322	67,005	17	4.5	265	102,684	12
Oshkosh-Neenah, WI	42.3	5	11.9	306	2,913	222	4.5	269	4,947	210
Owensboro, KY	24.9	61	16.8	187	–1,053	317	5.2	195	3,296	249
Oxnard-Thousand Oaks-Ventura, CA	16.6	138	16.5	194	23,103	41	5.3	173	13,505	91
Palm Bay-Melbourne-Titusville, FL.	16.7	137	17.1	177	18,309	55	4.4	281	22,119	58
Panama City-Lynn Haven, FL.	5.5	306	29.3	54	6,558	142	4.6	252	7,815	145
Parkersburg-Marietta-Vienna, WV-OH	(NA)	(NA)	16.1	203	1,068	267	5.9	114	1,031	337
Pascagoula, MS.	33.7	15	23.9	97	–2,485	337	6.2	84	3,751	232
Pensacola-Ferry Pass-Brent, FL	5.3	310	33.4	38	9,226	115	4.7	233	13,707	88
Peoria, IL	25.0	59	11.5	316	–3,244	343	5.7	125	5,935	186
Philadelphia-Camden-Wilmington, PA-NJ-DE-MD	**12.1**	**200**	**12.5**	**293**	**70,451**	**15**	**5.2**	**189**	**77,455**	**19**
Phoenix-Mesa-Scottsdale, AZ.	11.2	209	12.6	288	185,661	3	4.4	279	194,169	3
Pine Bluff, AR	21.2	89	27.7	60	1,388	261	7.8	24	657	351
Pittsburgh, PA	13.9	172	11.2	326	26,554	34	5.8	121	27,015	47
Pittsfield, MA	16.8	133	11.4	319	2,534	236	5.7	257	1,547	315
Pocatello, ID	12.9	190	26.8	75	1,565	255	4.8	229	1,307	324
Portland-South Portland-Biddeford, ME	9.4	246	17.3	174	16,533	62	3.6	341	13,246	94
Portland-Vancouver-Beaverton, OR-WA	15.5	151	13.3	272	16,729	60	7.2	43	57,253	25
Port St. Lucie-Fort Pierce, FL	5.4	308	15.4	217	21,639	44	5.7	134	23,275	55
Poughkeepsie-Newburgh-Middletown, NY	16.7	134	22.7	107	18,351	54	4.4	284	12,379	100
Prescott, AZ	6.1	300	21.6	121	11,384	98	4.3	303	10,787	110
Providence-New Bedford-Fall River, RI-MA	16.0	144	16.7	188	28,480	33	5.5	157	16,734	79
Provo-Orem, UT.	12.5	195	14.6	233	12,168	91	4.8	224	15,869	81
Pueblo, CO	10.6	220	22.7	108	4,917	178	7.2	40	5,073	207
Punta Gorda, FL	2.5	336	13.7	262	5,356	160	5.0	212	8,310	132
Racine, WI	36.2	11	12.8	281	921	275	6.0	98	3,804	230
Raleigh-Cary, NC	9.9	236	17.1	176	31,195	30	4.4	292	52,322	30
Rapid City, SD	7.1	283	26.3	80	4,155	187	3.3	351	3,061	259
Reading, PA	24.4	65	11.3	323	3,117	216	5.3	177	7,952	141
Redding, CA	5.1	313	20.2	134	8,721	117	7.4	34	4,693	213
Reno-Sparks, NV	8.1	269	14.7	230	11,642	94	4.0	323	19,277	67
Richmond, VA	10.4	224	19.4	145	36,023	28	3.9	329	34,333	40
Riverside-San Bernardino-Ontario, CA	10.6	219	21.5	122	227,378	2	5.7	130	123,639	9
Roanoke, VA.	(NA)	(NA)	13.7	263	–315	304	3.7	338	6,513	177
Rochester, MN.	20.2	103	9.3	355	8,187	124	4.1	316	7,802	146
Rochester, NY.	24.1	68	14.2	249	–4,793	347	5.3	176	12,702	97
Rockford, IL	30.8	27	10.6	334	–5,400	349	7.7	28	8,154	137
Rocky Mount, NC	24.3	66	16.7	190	392	288	7.3	37	3,271	250
Rome, GA.	26.7	45	14.2	247	3,884	191	4.6	257	2,057	287
Sacramento-Arden-Arcade-Roseville, CA	7.2	282	28.7	58	98,069	11	5.4	171	80,158	18
Saginaw-Saginaw Township North, MI	31.6	26	12.6	287	–343	306	8.7	13	2,831	264
St. Cloud, MN	19.3	109	15.4	219	5,028	176	4.7	238	6,705	171
St. George, UT	6.0	301	14.8	228	11,318	99	4.4	285	8,185	136
St. Joseph, MO-KS.	18.1	119	17.5	170	5,145	172	5.9	108	1,131	333
St. Louis, MO-IL[5]	(NA)	(NA)	12.8	283	25,391	37	6.0	106	53,225	29
Salem, OR	9.2	252	30.4	50	7,203	138	7.4	33	7,413	153
Salinas, CA.	5.1	314	21.8	119	8,353	121	8.2	20	5,347	196
Salisbury, MD	10.8	218	21.2	126	4,054	188	4.7	241	3,636	237
Salt Lake City, UT	10.1	230	15.6	213	13,744	75	5.4	169	27,273	46
San Angelo, TX	10.1	233	27.5	65	1,577	254	4.9	220	1,012	339
San Antonio, TX.	6.5	293	22.9	104	64,002	18	5.6	136	50,728	32
San Diego-Carlsbad-San Marcos, CA	9.9	235	22.8	106	113,684	9	4.7	234	62,712	24
Sandusky, OH.	32.1	23	13.9	257	1,548	256	6.3	74	1,095	336
San Francisco-Oakland-Fremont, CA.	**8.2**	**268**	**12.6**	**286**	**–104,663**	**360**	**5.6**	**146**	**53,583**	**28**
San Jose-Sunnyvale-Santa Clara, CA	29.3	32	7.6	359	–113,545	361	6.7	61	25,202	51
San Luis Obispo-Paso Robles, CA	6.6	290	21.1	128	8,236	122	4.4	289	7,869	144
Santa Barbara-Santa Maria, CA	9.4	247	19.8	138	11,566	95	4.7	240	5,050	208
Santa Cruz-Watsonville, CA	9.6	241	16.1	204	–3,119	342	7.0	48	2,819	266
Santa Fe, NM	2.6	334	26.0	83	5,169	170	4.3	296	2,097	282
Santa Rosa-Petaluma, CA	15.8	146	13.5	267	3,469	202	4.9	217	9,268	124
Sarasota-Bradenton-Venice, FL	8.4	265	9.6	349	26,347	35	4.1	319	35,969	39
Savannah, GA.	14.7	160	19.7	140	12,549	87	4.0	320	10,447	112
Scranton-Wilkes-Barre, PA.	17.8	123	14.2	246	5,144	173	6.5	70	5,447	194
Seattle-Tacoma-Bellevue, WA.	**14.1**	**166**	**14.4**	**240**	**54,877**	**20**	**5.6**	**137**	**84,921**	**16**
Sheboygan, WI	46.3	3	9.8	342	139	297	4.4	283	2,579	274
Sherman-Denison, TX.	24.3	67	12.5	291	868	276	6.2	88	1,162	332
Shreveport-Bossier City, LA	10.8	213	23.8	98	3,310	209	6.1	95	5,661	191
Sioux City, IA-NE-SD	(NA)	(NA)	12.2	301	–2,850	338	5.2	194	1,635	311
Sioux Falls, SD	10.2	228	9.4	353	8,033	127	3.2	354	9,347	123
South Bend-Mishawaka, IN-MI	23.5	73	10.7	333	–1,515	325	5.0	215	6,005	183

See footnotes at end of table.

| Metropolitan statistical area | Earnings, 2002—percent by selected major industries | | | | Civilian labor force, 2000–2004 | | Unemployment rate,[2] 2004 | | New private housing units authorized by building permits, 2000–2003 | |
| | Manufacturing | | Government[1] | | | | | | | |
	Percent	Rank	Percent	Rank	Net change	Rank	Rate	Rank	Number	Rank
Spartanburg, SC	32.9	19	13.9	256	1,735	250	7.6	29	7,206	157
Spokane, WA	10.1	231	20.3	132	13,084	78	6.5	67	8,933	128
Springfield, IL	3.4	327	32.8	41	−3,068	341	5.5	152	3,853	228
Springfield, MA	14.3	164	19.6	141	7,355	136	5.3	184	5,978	185
Springfield, MO	15.1	154	13.2	275	12,204	90	4.5	267	12,098	104
Springfield, OH	25.3	58	16.0	207	−1,459	323	6.8	56	1,124	335
State College, PA	10.5	221	42.4	14	3,785	194	4.4	287	3,448	244
Stockton, CA	10.0	234	19.9	137	26,032	36	8.5	16	22,915	56
Sumter, SC	21.3	86	36.4	25	1,041	269	8.1	22	1,709	308
Syracuse, NY	16.3	140	17.0	180	2,913	222	5.5	160	6,799	170
Tallahassee, FL	2.5	335	40.0	18	1,108	265	4.0	324	12,150	103
Tampa-St. Petersburg-Clearwater, FL	7.4	279	13.0	278	68,868	16	4.6	263	93,881	15
Terre Haute, IN	21.7	80	19.4	147	109	298	7.1	47	1,724	306
Texarkana, TX-Texarkana, AR	13.0	189	23.1	101	2,686	229	5.8	120	1,700	309
Toledo, OH	23.5	72	15.5	214	162	296	7.0	49	11,204	109
Topeka, KS	9.3	249	23.4	100	5,272	163	6.1	94	4,613	214
Trenton-Ewing, NJ	4.4	322	24.0	96	10,326	104	4.2	306	5,254	201
Tucson, AZ	13.3	181	24.6	90	29,961	32	4.6	248	30,308	41
Tulsa, OK	21.0	93	9.6	348	3,424	204	5.0	214	16,859	77
Tuscaloosa, AL	21.2	91	24.6	91	1,517	257	4.9	219	4,416	219
Tyler, TX	13.2	182	12.5	289	7,856	128	5.3	179	2,368	278
Utica-Rome, NY	13.2	183	25.4	88	−671	313	5.3	185	1,779	302
Valdosta, GA	(NA)	(NA)	34.3	34	5,261	164	3.5	346	3,356	245
Vallejo-Fairfield, CA	9.3	250	29.2	56	9,547	112	5.9	113	9,917	119
Vero Beach, FL	6.2	296	13.1	276	5,208	168	6.6	65	8,227	133
Victoria, TX	(NA)	(NA)	14.4	238	337	290	5.8	119	1,026	338
Vineland-Millville-Bridgeton, NJ	19.4	108	25.8	85	3,162	214	6.6	62	1,195	329
Virginia Beach-Norfolk-Newport News, VA-NC	(NA)	(NA)	38.3	20	58,254	19	4.1	311	36,809	38
Visalia-Porterville, CA	8.9	258	22.9	103	10,579	103	11.5	3	7,662	148
Waco, TX	18.0	120	17.3	173	6,530	144	5.3	180	3,321	248
Warner Robins, GA	6.6	289	61.1	3	5,838	154	3.8	333	6,614	174
Washington-Arlington-Alexandria, DC-VA-MD-WV	**(NA)**	**(NA)**	**27.6**	**64**	**140,347**	**6**	**3.7**	**337**	**149,060**	**8**
Waterloo-Cedar Falls, IA	26.6	47	15.6	212	2,431	241	4.8	231	2,560	275
Wausau, WI	28.1	37	10.6	335	2,474	237	4.3	298	4,193	221
Weirton-Steubenville, WV-OH	32.6	20	12.5	290	−992	316	7.8	27	673	350
Wenatchee, WA	5.9	302	21.2	125	4,856	179	6.7	57	2,037	288
Wheeling, WV-OH	13.1	188	17.0	181	−1,585	326	6.0	96	184	360
Wichita, KS	32.5	21	12.7	284	7,049	140	6.2	87	12,374	101
Wichita Falls, TX	14.0	170	34.5	32	2,712	227	5.2	196	1,656	310
Williamsport, PA	29.1	34	16.8	186	1,502	259	6.2	82	1,345	321
Wilmington, NC	11.1	211	19.4	144	12,608	86	4.6	245	20,502	63
Winchester, VA-WV	26.4	52	11.6	314	5,257	165	3.2	355	4,090	224
Winston-Salem, NC	19.8	106	9.5	352	7,720	131	5.0	210	13,344	93
Worcester, MA	17.5	126	14.4	239	12,785	80	5.5	156	12,592	98
Yakima, WA	11.4	205	19.3	149	6,389	145	8.6	14	2,078	285
York-Hanover, PA	29.5	31	11.4	320	7,571	133	4.6	250	10,298	115
Youngstown-Warren-Boardman, OH-PA	27.2	40	13.8	259	−2,960	340	7.2	39	5,999	184
Yuba City, CA	6.4	294	32.9	40	3,554	201	10.2	7	3,608	240
Yuma, AZ	3.2	329	28.2	59	9,568	111	15.4	2	6,239	180

− Represents zero.   NA Not available.

[1]Includes government enterprises.

[2]Civilian unemployed as percent of total civilian labor force.

[3]The Denver-Aurora metropolitan statistical area includes Broomfield County. Broomfield County, CO, was formed from parts of Adams, Boulder, Jefferson, and Weld Counties on November 15, 2001, and is coextensive with Broomfield city. For the purposes of defining and presenting data for the Denver-Aurora metropolitan statistical area, Broomfield is treated as if it were a county when data are available to do so. In many cases, the data will not be available.

[4]Excludes Trimble County, KY.

[5]The portion of Sullivan city in Crawford County, MO, is legally part of the St. Louis, MO-IL MSA. That portion is not included in these figures for the St. Louis, MO-IL MSA.

Sources: U.S. Bureau of Economic Analysis, U.S. Bureau of Labor Statistics, and U.S. Census Bureau. For more information, see <http://www.bea.gov/bea/regional/reis/>, <http://www.bls.gov/lau>, and <http://www.census.gov/popest/housing/>. See Tables B-7, B-8, and B-9 of the State and Metropolitan Area Data Book: 2006.

Metropolitan statistical area	Private nonfarm business establishments				Retail trade[1] (NAICS 44–55), sales 2002				Accommodation and food services[1] (NAICS 72), sales 2002		Federal funds and grants, 2003			
	Establishment change, 2000–2003	Rank	Annual payroll per employee, 2002 (dollars)	Rank	Per capita[2] (dollars)	Rank	Percent change, 1997–2002	Rank	Per capita[2] (dollars)	Rank	Total expenditures (million dollars)	Rank	Per capita[3] (dollars)	Rank
Abilene, TX	−102	340	23,141	349	11,361	134	17.7	261	1,232	199	1,098	208	6,941	92
Akron, OH	209	109	33,118	72	10,683	196	12.7	313	1,272	186	3,706	92	5,286	227
Albany, GA	65	199	27,068	250	9,104	317	6.4	344	(NA)	(NA)	1,142	201	7,057	89
Albany-Schenectady-Troy, NY	465	55	33,012	74	11,225	142	28.3	98	1,311	166	13,954	25	16,600	3
Albuquerque, NM	122	151	29,893	150	11,732	105	23.1	161	1,615	84	7,472	49	9,747	33
Alexandria, LA	50	218	25,561	308	10,398	224	22.2	177	(NA)	(NA)	1,092	209	7,465	79
Allentown-Bethlehem-Easton, PA-NJ	360	70	33,849	58	10,680	197	24.2	143	1,105	262	3,722	91	4,838	285
Altoona, PA	−30	297	25,870	300	13,277	35	27.3	105	1,213	211	825	264	6,471	124
Amarillo, TX	−15	280	28,006	204	12,324	67	18.6	237	1,462	120	1,468	177	6,286	134
Ames, IA	−31	301	24,796	323	9,909	272	26.7	115	1,374	150	489	340	6,087	151
Anchorage, AK	304	85	42,496	9	13,210	39	22.4	170	2,448	21	3,379	99	9,959	31
Anderson, IN	−87	336	27,403	237	9,678	289	13.7	299	1,076	274	710	290	5,414	211
Anderson, SC	71	192	27,213	243	9,736	286	22.9	165	1,029	292	770	275	4,481	312
Ann Arbor, MI	44	225	41,491	10	12,247	73	20.7	208	1,540	105	1,944	150	5,789	181
Anniston-Oxford, AL	4	260	25,003	319	10,413	221	18.2	245	1,177	228	1,071	214	9,554	35
Appleton, WI	141	137	32,127	93	13,712	27	31.9	66	1,300	172	746	280	3,537	355
Asheville, NC	393	66	26,716	264	12,092	86	23.1	162	1,854	48	2,243	131	5,863	175
Athens-Clarke County, GA	206	110	25,608	307	10,414	220	26.9	111	1,373	151	870	255	5,067	250
Atlanta-Sandy Springs-Marietta, GA	4,148	6	38,356	22	11,658	112	27.8	103	1,777	56	21,496	15	4,668	300
Atlantic City, NJ	156	130	29,592	155	12,768	53	31.7	67	18,767	1	1,601	172	6,069	154
Auburn-Opelika, AL	85	175	24,053	337	8,617	336	30.8	77	1,186	224	461	343	3,872	347
Augusta-Richmond County, GA-SC	87	173	30,887	122	9,666	290	23.5	159	1,081	272	4,864	64	9,529	36
Austin-Round Rock, TX	1,540	21	38,111	23	15,612	5	11.4	323	1,837	51	9,517	36	6,913	94
Bakersfield, CA	375	68	30,746	127	8,082	346	32.6	61	927	315	3,856	84	5,405	213
Baltimore-Towson, MD	1,445	22	36,431	33	10,906	174	30.6	80	1,504	114	22,639	13	8,617	49
Bangor, ME	−7	276	27,924	208	14,212	18	26.2	119	1,266	188	963	236	6,506	120
Barnstable Town, MA	257	96	31,479	113	14,911	12	34.7	46	3,327	13	1,768	161	7,716	70
Baton Rouge, LA	227	105	30,399	139	9,552	295	14.7	292	1,100	265	4,460	68	6,181	140
Battle Creek, MI	−30	297	33,473	65	10,080	261	12.9	310	1,161	237	971	231	6,992	91
Bay City, MI	15	253	30,078	148	11,670	111	16.2	277	1,158	240	583	317	5,322	222
Beaumont-Port Arthur, TX	−98	337	30,638	132	10,873	178	20.0	220	1,047	288	2,342	125	6,117	148
Bellingham, WA	197	115	29,662	154	10,205	241	6.2	345	1,412	139	879	248	4,978	268
Bend, OR	457	57	27,299	239	14,836	13	43.7	22	2,125	28	532	330	4,108	330
Billings, MT	140	139	27,071	249	14,079	22	24.0	145	2,040	33	781	273	5,460	208
Binghamton, NY	27	242	27,827	217	9,763	283	24.0	147	1,161	237	1,890	152	7,541	77
Birmingham-Hoover, AL	233	103	33,683	61	11,611	116	23.7	154	1,201	215	6,441	54	5,997	158
Bismarck, ND	81	182	26,888	260	13,205	40	25.7	127	1,470	119	789	271	8,138	61
Blacksburg-Christiansburg-Radford, VA	79	186	26,983	255	9,190	314	18.5	238	1,190	220	790	270	5,235	233
Bloomington, IN	−4	272	25,449	310	9,221	311	22.3	173	1,397	144	872	254	4,928	277
Bloomington-Normal, IL	−6	275	37,082	28	11,220	143	18.2	246	1,563	98	529	332	3,374	357
Boise City-Nampa, ID	746	33	30,840	123	10,455	217	22.3	175	1,219	209	2,543	120	4,870	270
Boston-Cambridge-Quincy, MA-NH	273	90	45,709	5	11,977	93	23.7	155	1,961	41	35,269	6	7,961	65
Boulder, CO[4]	−542	357	40,589	14	12,448	61	(NA)	(NA)	1,938	43	1,864	154	6,718	108
Bowling Green, KY	68	197	26,830	263	11,972	94	12.6	314	(NA)	(NA)	539	326	5,016	260
Bremerton-Silverdale, WA	326	75	27,229	242	9,507	299	31.6	69	986	304	2,809	109	11,718	18
Bridgeport-Stamford-Norwalk, CT	−202	354	56,000	2	15,569	7	20.5	213	1,529	106	5,778	57	6,422	126
Brownsville-Harlingen, TX	250	99	20,372	360	7,808	349	44.8	18	1,052	284	1,665	168	4,596	307
Brunswick, GA	56	210	24,090	335	11,755	103	32.6	60	3,707	8	682	294	7,043	90
Buffalo-Niagara Falls, NY	412	63	30,621	133	10,050	265	20.9	207	1,229	201	7,532	48	6,504	121
Burlington, NC	−40	308	26,162	287	12,018	89	30.9	76	1,436	132	585	316	4,279	320
Burlington-South Burlington, VT	576	47	33,430	66	14,172	19	31.1	73	1,656	74	1,538	173	7,560	75
Canton-Massillon, OH	−151	351	28,198	194	10,446	218	12.4	318	1,135	253	1,994	144	4,860	282
Cape Coral-Fort Myers, FL	1,375	23	28,422	188	13,386	34	45.8	15	1,766	58	2,615	115	5,310	225
Carson City, NV	−69	326	30,207	146	15,786	2	26.9	110	2,019	37	648	301	11,722	17
Casper, WY	58	207	28,243	191	12,979	44	35.7	38	1,449	126	351	360	5,145	241
Cedar Rapids, IA	95	163	31,298	115	12,115	81	26.8	114	1,187	223	1,458	178	6,008	157
Champaign-Urbana, IL	62	203	27,601	229	10,109	259	21.1	205	1,424	133	1,081	212	5,041	255
Charleston, WV	−162	353	29,301	163	10,936	173	10.7	328	1,268	187	2,645	114	8,604	51
Charleston-North Charleston, SC	590	45	27,869	213	11,029	161	37.0	35	2,126	27	4,368	69	7,631	73
Charlotte-Gastonia-Concord, NC-SC	1,129	25	36,636	30	12,150	78	28.1	102	1,604	87	5,580	58	3,877	346
Charlottesville, VA	232	104	30,515	136	11,627	113	35.1	42	2,024	36	1,106	207	6,150	145
Chattanooga, TN-GA	−69	326	28,839	177	10,696	193	21.6	190	1,314	165	3,474	96	7,140	87
Cheyenne, WY	99	160	26,133	288	14,313	16	39.2	29	1,668	71	994	224	11,784	16
Chicago-Naperville-Joliet, IL-IN-WI	2,515	15	40,878	13	10,824	183	24.6	139	1,681	70	46,091	4	4,940	275
Chico, CA	161	129	24,066	336	9,714	287	34.9	43	1,067	277	1,191	195	5,639	190
Cincinnati-Middletown, OH-KY-IN	217	107	34,824	46	10,574	204	18.1	247	(NA)	(NA)	11,587	29	5,661	187
Clarksville, TN-KY	49	220	23,839	340	8,933	328	20.5	210	1,050	286	2,494	122	10,559	26
Cleveland, TN	−4	272	27,620	228	8,517	337	13.5	303	1,016	295	494	338	4,647	304
Cleveland-Elyria-Mentor, OH	−616	358	35,139	41	11,070	157	19.9	223	1,356	155	12,708	27	5,937	167
Coeur d'Alene, ID	29	240	26,233	284	11,265	138	25.9	125	1,944	42	608	310	5,168	238
College Station-Bryan, TX	183	119	24,719	326	9,368	303	18.7	235	1,420	136	2,029	143	10,791	24
Colorado Springs, CO	687	41	31,919	101	10,991	166	21.6	191	1,891	46	5,294	60	9,296	39
Columbia, MO	51	216	26,601	271	12,004	90	19.4	226	1,580	95	770	275	5,128	245
Columbia, SC	80	184	29,400	161	10,149	252	16.6	272	1,297	173	4,844	65	7,218	85
Columbus, GA-AL	62	203	26,593	272	9,548	296	21.6	189	1,359	153	2,562	117	9,231	42
Columbus, IN	−118	347	36,219	34	10,186	250	7.5	342	1,319	163	370	359	5,111	247
Columbus, OH	1,002	28	34,907	45	12,238	74	17.1	267	1,661	72	10,399	33	6,201	139
Corpus Christi, TX	85	175	27,916	210	9,560	294	18.7	236	1,459	122	2,723	112	6,702	109

See footnotes at end of table.

Metropolitan statistical area	Private nonfarm business establishments				Retail trade[1] (NAICS 44–55), sales 2002				Accommodation and food services[1] (NAICS 72), sales 2002		Federal funds and grants, 2003			
	Establishment change, 2000–2003	Rank	Annual payroll per employee, 2002 (dollars)	Rank	Per capita[2] (dollars)	Rank	Percent change, 1997–2002	Rank	Per capita[2] (dollars)	Rank	Total expenditures (million dollars)	Rank	Per capita[3] (dollars)	Rank
Corvallis, OR.	64	201	34,268	51	6,811	358	13.6	302	1,228	203	393	357	4,967	271
Cumberland, MD-WV	−15	280	24,836	321	9,065	320	13.7	300	1,193	217	713	288	7,063	88
Dallas-Fort Worth-Arlington, TX	**3,453**	**9**	**39,359**	**18**	**11,383**	**132**	**24.7**	**138**	**(NA)**	**(NA)**	**32,528**	**7**	**5,823**	**179**
Dalton, GA	–	266	30,650	131	11,619	114	18.0	249	1,140	249	436	348	3,422	356
Danville, IL	−19	286	27,506	232	8,618	335	12.3	319	873	326	529	332	6,386	131
Danville, VA	7	258	25,201	316	8,984	324	10.6	329	934	312	611	309	5,621	193
Davenport-Moline-Rock Island, IA-IL	−101	339	31,101	120	10,964	170	10.6	331	1,897	45	2,115	135	5,642	189
Dayton, OH	−130	349	32,342	89	10,943	171	15.8	279	1,396	146	6,884	52	8,141	60
Decatur, AL	41	230	27,906	211	9,257	308	8.2	340	938	310	743	283	5,039	258
Decatur, IL	−48	311	31,668	108	11,344	135	13.1	308	1,177	228	599	312	5,384	216
Deltona-Daytona Beach-Ormond Beach, FL	444	60	24,012	338	10,260	235	21.3	196	1,599	90	2,878	107	6,155	143
Denver-Aurora, CO[4]	2,614	14	39,322	19	12,296	71	(NA)	(NA)	1,922	44	12,714	26	5,523	200
Des Moines, IA	311	82	34,027	55	12,459	60	22.2	178	1,481	117	2,986	104	5,930	171
Detroit-Warren-Livonia, MI	**−250**	**356**	**41,443**	**12**	**11,558**	**122**	**15.6**	**283**	**1,266**	**188**	**24,590**	**10**	**5,480**	**207**
Dothan, AL	54	213	26,187	285	12,904	47	15.0	291	1,077	273	879	248	6,581	118
Dover, DE	30	238	26,545	277	13,061	42	29.7	90	1,163	235	1,159	199	8,609	50
Dubuque, IA	−28	295	27,073	248	12,232	75	17.0	269	1,289	178	438	347	4,843	284
Duluth, MN-WI	61	205	27,494	234	10,997	165	23.8	153	1,601	89	1,786	157	6,463	125
Durham, NC	154	131	39,256	20	9,355	305	23.3	160	1,657	73	3,391	97	7,613	74
Eau Claire, WI	85	175	27,195	245	12,796	52	26.8	113	1,220	208	702	291	4,639	305
El Centro, CA	51	216	25,370	311	9,234	309	36.0	37	870	327	766	278	5,143	242
Elizabethtown, KY	104	158	26,183	286	10,612	202	22.9	166	1,273	183	1,013	222	9,293	40
Elkhart-Goshen, IN	90	170	31,994	99	10,394	225	−2.1	358	1,210	214	594	315	3,145	359
Elmira, NY	15	253	26,569	275	11,489	126	19.1	222	1,152	243	539	326	5,973	162
El Paso, TX.	93	167	23,411	347	8,373	339	23.6	157	1,113	261	4,318	70	6,145	146
Erie, PA	−156	352	28,066	200	10,895	176	20.1	219	1,135	253	1,513	174	5,345	219
Eugene-Springfield, OR.	−105	342	29,030	173	11,376	133	12.0	321	1,421	135	1,741	164	5,273	229
Evansville, IN-KY	−86	335	30,542	134	11,895	98	20.5	211	1,602	88	1,888	153	5,448	209
Fairbanks, AK	88	171	35,531	39	13,126	41	19.9	222	1,829	52	1,142	201	13,403	11
Fargo, ND-MN	177	123	27,817	218	14,169	20	17.9	253	1,510	110	902	244	5,040	256
Farmington, NM	101	159	28,657	182	10,325	231	25.0	134	1,146	246	575	319	4,699	299
Fayetteville, NC	12	255	25,048	318	9,069	319	17.4	264	1,096	268	4,296	71	12,461	15
Fayetteville-Springdale-Rogers, AR-MO	513	52	28,687	181	10,324	232	46.2	13	1,186	224	1,396	183	3,689	351
Flagstaff, AZ	150	133	24,631	328	11,174	147	24.0	149	3,538	10	799	268	6,596	116
Flint, MI	−120	348	33,644	63	11,401	129	11.2	326	1,004	299	2,292	128	5,178	236
Florence, SC	25	244	27,199	244	11,207	144	15.7	281	1,056	282	1,120	204	5,703	186
Florence-Muscle Shoals, AL	−39	307	23,553	345	10,748	188	16.5	273	966	308	940	240	6,633	113
Fond du Lac, WI	−25	292	28,632	183	10,519	211	15.5	285	1,144	247	424	350	4,317	317
Fort Collins-Loveland, CO	483	53	31,617	110	11,996	92	29.7	91	1,806	54	1,088	210	4,082	335
Fort Smith, AR-OK	113	153	25,642	306	8,987	323	15.4	286	917	317	1,482	176	5,297	226
Fort Walton Beach-Crestview-Destin, FL.	108	157	25,798	301	14,131	21	41.1	25	2,040	33	2,940	105	16,532	4
Fort Wayne, IN	187	118	32,397	88	11,207	144	13.5	304	1,295	174	1,979	147	4,945	274
Fresno, CA.	273	90	29,157	167	8,724	331	30.2	85	990	303	4,074	76	4,789	292
Gadsden, AL	18	250	23,601	344	8,558	330	23.6	156	996	301	627	307	6,081	152
Gainesville, FL	130	145	26,290	283	10,199	243	22.5	169	1,405	140	1,420	181	5,982	161
Gainesville, GA	169	124	30,753	126	9,834	280	20.3	215	1,308	169	566	322	3,619	352
Glens Falls, NY	26	243	27,640	226	11,937	96	34.4	47	1,872	47	636	303	5,016	260
Goldsboro, NC	−2	267	24,535	329	9,049	321	−0.9	357	914	318	904	243	7,971	64
Grand Forks, ND-MN	3	264	24,883	320	13,791	26	15.2	288	1,403	141	796	269	8,315	55
Grand Junction, CO	46	221	27,293	240	13,603	29	44.2	19	1,477	118	641	302	5,140	244
Grand Rapids-Wyoming, MI	577	46	33,819	59	12,104	84	25.0	135	1,137	252	2,936	106	3,849	348
Great Falls, MT	−54	316	22,877	352	12,683	55	26.0	123	1,625	79	768	277	9,629	34
Greeley, CO[4]	352	71	31,914	102	8,187	342	(NA)	(NA)	775	335	652	299	3,077	360
Green Bay, WI	112	154	32,517	85	11,696	108	18.2	243	1,273	183	1,142	201	3,912	342
Greensboro-High Point, NC	−85	334	30,834	124	11,765	102	16.3	276	1,459	122	3,184	103	4,809	289
Greenville, NC	57	209	25,662	305	11,079	156	21.1	206	1,246	195	724	285	4,566	308
Greenville, SC	−215	355	32,068	95	10,227	240	7.5	341	1,276	181	2,791	110	4,828	286
Gulfport-Biloxi, MS	21	247	25,531	309	10,168	251	33.9	51	6,371	4	2,462	123	9,863	32
Hagerstown-Martinsburg, MD-WV	148	134	27,905	212	10,798	187	36.9	36	1,162	236	1,326	185	5,573	198
Hanford-Corcoran, CA.	52	215	26,959	256	5,378	360	15.0	290	644	344	777	274	5,600	196
Harrisburg-Carlisle, PA	66	198	31,745	106	12,611	57	17.9	251	1,609	85	5,972	55	11,546	20
Harrisonburg, VA	141	137	26,395	281	12,432	62	30.6	79	1,346	159	399	355	3,607	353
Hartford-West Hartford-East Hartford, CT	−74	330	41,444	11	10,883	177	16.3	275	1,396	146	10,751	32	9,112	43
Hattiesburg, MS	41	230	24,440	331	11,148	149	21.3	195	1,126	256	664	298	5,171	237
Hinesville-Fort Stewart, GA	20	249	22,582	355	4,590	361	25.3	130	622	346	340	361	4,815	287
Holland-Grand Haven, MI	21	247	33,002	75	8,693	333	11.5	322	881	325	801	267	3,211	358
Honolulu, HI	315	80	31,756	105	9,948	268	6.7	343	3,337	12	9,056	39	10,137	30
Hot Springs, AR	110	155	23,446	346	12,301	70	26.4	117	1,757	59	628	306	6,890	98
Houma-Bayou Cane-Thibodaux, LA.	119	152	29,887	151	9,335	306	12.1	320	1,013	296	979	229	4,954	272
Houston-Sugar Land-Baytown, TX.	2,816	13	40,435	15	10,529	209	30.4	83	1,437	131	24,184	11	4,767	294
Huntington-Ashland, WV-KY-OH	−84	333	26,954	257	10,199	243	21.2	199	1,102	263	1,982	145	6,906	96
Huntsville, AL	197	115	34,183	53	10,847	182	27.0	109	1,376	149	7,124	51	19,921	1
Idaho Falls, ID	166	126	29,485	158	12,311	68	30.2	85	1,142	248	1,421	180	13,223	12
Indianapolis, IN	649	42	35,727	36	12,126	79	19.2	227	1,682	69	9,500	37	5,935	168
Iowa City, IA	17	251	27,790	221	10,525	210	23.9	151	1,506	113	746	280	5,482	206
Ithaca, NY	43	227	26,472	280	8,181	343	30.5	81	1,597	92	607	311	6,108	150
Jackson, MI	41	230	31,279	116	9,606	292	20.1	216	986	304	723	286	4,446	313

See footnotes at end of table.

Metropolitan statistical area	Private nonfarm business establishments				Retail trade[1] (NAICS 44–55), sales 2002				Accommodation and food services[1] (NAICS 72), sales 2002		Federal funds and grants, 2003			
	Establishment change, 2000–2003	Rank	Annual payroll per employee, 2002 (dollars)	Rank	Per capita[2] (dollars)	Rank	Percent change, 1997–2002	Rank	Per capita[2] (dollars)	Rank	Total expenditures (million dollars)	Rank	Per capita[3] (dollars)	Rank
Jackson, MS	295	86	28,056	201	11,136	151	25.1	132	1,289	178	3,792	87	7,431	81
Jackson, TN	−38	306	29,186	166	13,430	33	13.3	307	1,452	124	578	318	5,278	228
Jacksonville, FL	1,761	20	31,220	118	11,598	119	30.6	78	1,575	97	8,597	41	7,180	86
Jacksonville, NC	−50	312	19,223	361	9,622	291	32.2	65	1,138	250	2,079	137	13,720	10
Janesville, WI	65	199	33,167	71	11,384	131	9.6	332	1,193	217	745	282	4,811	288
Jefferson City, MO	82	181	26,492	279	12,114	82	46.9	12	1,067	277	1,793	156	12,524	14
Johnson City, TN	12	255	25,159	317	10,265	234	30.3	84	1,102	263	1,720	165	9,236	41
Johnstown, PA	−2	267	23,891	339	9,332	307	12.7	311	860	330	1,204	194	8,047	62
Jonesboro, AR	58	207	24,355	332	10,869	180	22.0	184	1,098	266	623	308	5,658	188
Joplin, MO	167	125	25,755	302	11,684	110	29.5	92	1,177	228	952	238	5,865	174
Kalamazoo-Portage, MI	−104	341	33,084	73	10,121	258	11.3	324	1,261	192	1,435	179	4,488	311
Kankakee-Bradley, IL	31	237	28,196	195	10,495	215	21.9	185	1,063	280	523	334	4,920	278
Kansas City, MO-KS	447	59	35,091	44	11,585	121	18.7	234	1,697	66	11,732	28	6,155	143
Kennewick-Richland-Pasco, WA	202	112	34,480	50	11,039	159	32.4	63	1,149	245	3,225	101	15,342	6
Killeen-Temple-Fort Hood, TX	145	135	26,077	290	8,710	332	40.5	26	936	311	3,882	83	11,285	21
Kingsport-Bristol-Bristol, TN-VA	−105	342	29,244	164	9,878	275	13.9	298	748	340	1,776	159	5,918	173
Kingston, NY	239	102	25,980	293	10,188	249	43.8	21	1,512	109	863	257	4,758	295
Knoxville, TN	−12	279	30,745	128	13,463	32	17.9	255	1,577	96	6,524	53	10,183	29
Kokomo, IN	59	206	37,747	25	12,431	63	16.8	271	1,423	134	485	342	4,788	293
La Crosse, WI-MN	70	194	27,509	231	12,522	59	4.8	349	1,350	157	630	305	4,900	279
Lafayette, IN	−33	302	30,101	147	11,081	155	21.3	198	1,401	143	743	283	4,105	331
Lafayette, LA	254	97	28,620	184	11,997	91	9.4	333	1,727	62	1,030	219	4,221	325
Lake Charles, LA	42	228	27,996	206	10,688	195	26.2	120	2,080	32	1,076	213	5,548	199
Lakeland, FL	198	114	28,372	189	9,041	322	17.6	262	905	320	2,549	119	4,990	266
Lancaster, PA	165	127	30,538	135	11,240	141	15.1	289	1,229	201	1,972	149	4,083	334
Lansing-East Lansing, MI	134	142	32,410	87	11,241	140	17.8	259	1,287	180	4,231	72	9,315	38
Laredo, TX	252	98	21,194	359	9,845	278	33.5	56	1,164	234	896	247	4,213	326
Las Cruces, NM	34	236	21,954	356	7,012	356	18.2	241	870	327	1,241	190	6,799	103
Las Vegas-Paradise, NV	2,936	12	31,171	119	12,734	54	56.7	2	10,846	2	7,170	50	4,552	309
Lawrence, KS	38	234	23,125	350	8,647	334	15.7	280	1,547	104	398	356	3,903	344
Lawton, OK	−55	318	23,831	341	8,059	347	30.2	87	1,087	270	1,287	188	11,664	19
Lebanon, PA	−2	267	27,573	230	10,544	207	6.1	346	772	336	747	279	6,070	153
Lewiston, ID-WA	−51	313	28,181	196	11,959	95	10.6	330	1,256	194	373	358	6,409	128
Lewiston-Auburn, ME	−21	288	27,916	209	13,951	24	17.7	260	1,072	275	597	313	5,628	192
Lexington-Fayette, KY	132	144	31,459	114	13,265	37	26.5	116	1,848	50	2,271	130	5,396	215
Lima, OH	−5	274	29,094	170	12,402	64	3.8	350	1,359	153	711	289	6,641	112
Lincoln, NE	134	142	28,616	185	10,872	179	26.3	118	1,443	128	1,706	166	6,167	142
Little Rock-North Little Rock, AR	80	184	29,794	153	12,037	88	19.0	231	1,294	175	4,694	66	7,459	80
Logan, UT-ID	81	182	23,261	348	7,482	353	9.2	335	760	338	407	352	3,756	350
Longview, TX	94	165	26,986	254	11,687	109	22.4	171	1,036	291	992	227	4,990	266
Longview, WA	−29	296	32,544	83	9,914	271	15.6	282	1,188	221	487	341	5,121	246
Los Angeles-Long Beach-Santa Ana, CA	**8,784**	**2**	**38,732**	**21**	**10,072**	**263**	**33.6**	**55**	**1,560**	**100**	**68,978**	**3**	**5,380**	**218**
Louisville, KY-IN	374	69	32,014	97	10,651	200	21.4	194	(NA)	(NA)	8,223	43	6,909	95
Lubbock, TX	64	201	24,295	333	13,043	43	22.1	180	1,635	77	1,284	189	5,000	265
Lynchburg, VA	35	235	29,358	162	10,855	181	21.7	188	913	319	1,766	162	7,635	72
Macon, GA	−54	316	28,126	198	10,676	199	13.7	301	(NA)	(NA)	1,420	181	6,266	135
Madera, CA	70	194	27,485	235	5,474	359	33.7	53	725	341	522	335	3,907	343
Madison, WI	437	61	33,185	70	15,289	8	22.3	176	1,590	93	3,795	86	7,227	84
Manchester-Nashua, NH	−35	304	37,944	24	15,761	3	25.5	128	1,413	137	2,137	134	5,409	212
Mansfield, OH	4	260	29,134	168	11,557	123	14.3	295	1,188	221	635	304	4,954	272
McAllen-Edinburg-Mission, TX	462	56	21,523	357	8,196	341	50.5	3	856	331	2,608	116	4,105	331
Medford, OR	261	95	27,149	246	13,803	25	24.3	142	1,599	90	1,013	222	5,322	222
Memphis, TN-MS-AR	−109	344	33,498	64	10,381	228	17.3	266	2,396	23	8,480	42	6,845	101
Merced, CA	30	238	26,008	292	7,124	355	45.4	17	626	345	965	235	4,168	329
Miami-Fort Lauderdale-Miami Beach, FL	**7,520**	**3**	**33,228**	**69**	**12,114**	**82**	**25.0**	**133**	**1,773**	**57**	**29,055**	**8**	**5,505**	**203**
Michigan City-La Porte, IN	−62	321	27,497	233	10,234	238	8.3	339	3,093	14	494	338	4,501	310
Midland, TX	−56	319	30,377	141	11,014	163	5.5	348	1,447	127	428	349	3,597	354
Milwaukee-Waukesha-West Allis, WI	−139	350	35,998	35	10,745	190	13.4	305	1,293	176	7,963	45	5,261	230
Minneapolis-St. Paul-Bloomington, MN-WI	3,311	11	40,197	16	12,667	56	24.0	148	1,618	81	14,802	22	4,798	291
Missoula, MT	137	141	25,908	298	15,590	6	42.7	23	2,105	30	540	325	5,486	205
Mobile, AL	−78	332	28,025	203	10,194	247	19.7	224	1,098	266	2,320	127	5,801	180
Modesto, CA	411	64	29,587	156	10,242	237	49.9	4	1,038	290	2,047	140	4,169	328
Monroe, LA	42	228	26,845	262	11,023	162	18.9	232	1,211	213	898	245	5,258	231
Monroe, MI	88	171	34,800	47	9,365	304	35.1	41	883	324	575	319	3,810	349
Montgomery, AL	−76	331	27,816	219	10,073	262	11.2	325	1,174	232	3,742	89	10,603	25
Morgantown, WV	−53	315	27,011	252	8,950	326	22.0	182	1,183	227	784	272	6,906	96
Morristown, TN	−17	283	27,717	223	9,405	302	23.9	150	894	322	667	296	5,232	235
Mount Vernon-Anacortes, WA	93	167	29,036	172	15,029	11	49.8	6	1,750	60	539	326	4,934	276
Muncie, IN	−45	310	26,628	269	11,121	152	18.2	242	1,233	198	596	314	5,033	259
Muskegon-Norton Shores, MI	76	188	30,766	125	8,920	329	12.5	316	1,028	293	877	251	5,063	251
Myrtle Beach-Conway-North Myrtle Beach, SC	222	106	22,828	353	15,647	4	28.7	96	5,170	6	1,023	220	4,850	283
Napa, CA	216	108	35,647	37	10,696	193	46.0	16	2,700	16	702	291	5,329	221
Naples-Marco Island, FL	726	35	30,380	140	15,222	10	59.8	1	2,531	17	1,225	193	4,280	319
Nashville-Davidson-Murfreesboro, TN	343	73	34,015	56	11,712	107	21.2	200	1,853	49	7,838	46	5,712	185
New Haven-Milford, CT	−70	328	37,425	26	11,102	153	20.0	221	1,212	212	5,200	61	6,179	141
New Orleans-Metairie-Kenner, LA	71	192	30,339	142	9,833	281	17.8	257	2,399	22	9,929	34	7,546	76
New York-Northern New Jersey-Long Island, NY-NJ-PA	**6,313**	**4**	**50,172**	**3**	**9,883**	**274**	**28.2**	**100**	**1,509**	**111**	**112,903**	**1**	**6,047**	**155**
Niles-Benton Harbor, MI	74	190	31,626	109	8,113	345	1.2	356	1,176	231	876	252	5,381	217

See footnotes at end of table.

State and Metropolitan Area Data Book: 2006

U.S. Census Bureau

Metropolitan statistical area	Establishment change, 2000–2003	Rank	Annual payroll per employee, 2002 (dollars)	Rank	Per capita[2] (dollars)	Rank	Percent change, 1997–2002	Rank	Per capita[2] (dollars)	Rank	Total expenditures (million dollars)	Rank	Per capita[3] (dollars)	Rank
	Private nonfarm business establishments				Retail trade[1] (NAICS 44–55), sales 2002				Accommodation and food services[1] (NAICS 72), sales 2002		Federal funds and grants, 2003			
Norwich-New London, CT	162	128	36,453	32	11,464	128	25.2	131	9,060	3	3,994	80	15,060	7
Ocala, FL	311	82	24,745	324	10,496	214	28.8	95	884	323	1,647	170	5,859	177
Ocean City, NJ	138	140	30,234	145	13,587	30	43.9	20	4,888	7	688	293	6,757	106
Odessa, TX	129	146	27,849	215	11,091	154	19.1	230	1,257	193	501	337	4,071	336
Ogden-Clearfield, UT	689	40	26,512	278	9,118	316	16.9	270	829	333	3,912	82	8,346	54
Oklahoma City, OK	467	54	28,080	199	10,429	219	15.4	287	1,402	142	8,762	40	7,732	69
Olympia, WA	200	113	28,824	178	10,299	233	38.3	30	1,128	255	2,283	129	10,333	27
Omaha-Council Bluffs, NE-IA	424	62	32,629	82	12,567	58	23.5	158	1,707	64	4,536	67	5,723	184
Orlando-Kissimmee, FL	2,300	18	30,735	129	12,118	80	26.1	122	3,453	11	9,792	35	5,433	210
Oshkosh-Neenah, WI	−33	302	35,111	43	9,535	297	1.4	355	1,056	282	1,239	191	7,815	67
Owensboro, KY	−21	288	26,920	259	10,196	245	21.8	187	1,230	200	555	324	5,007	263
Oxnard-Thousand Oaks-Ventura, CA	743	34	36,690	29	11,557	123	39.3	28	1,264	190	4,066	77	5,143	242
Palm Bay-Melbourne-Titusville, FL	518	50	31,764	104	10,555	206	34.2	49	1,219	209	5,545	59	10,965	23
Panama City-Lynn Haven, FL	44	225	24,092	334	12,249	72	24.6	140	2,451	20	1,324	186	8,548	53
Parkersburg-Marietta-Vienna, WV-OH	−60	320	26,857	261	12,350	65	30.9	75	(NA)	(NA)	1,059	217	6,484	123
Pascagoula, MS	−66	322	28,795	179	6,986	357	2.7	353	866	329	2,146	133	13,914	9
Pensacola-Ferry Pass-Brent, FL	289	88	25,357	312	9,776	282	20.7	209	1,125	257	3,502	94	8,157	59
Peoria, IL	4	260	32,226	91	10,633	201	13.0	309	1,655	75	1,917	151	5,235	233
Philadelphia-Camden-Wilmington, PA-NJ-DE-MD	**2,011**	**19**	**39,379**	**17**	**11,752**	**104**	**25.7**	**126**	**1,316**	**164**	**38,986**	**5**	**6,754**	**107**
Phoenix-Mesa-Scottsdale, AZ	3,484	8	33,323	67	11,036	160	28.3	99	1,616	83	20,090	16	5,591	197
Pine Bluff, AR	17	251	25,231	315	7,610	352	5.7	347	(NA)	(NA)	951	239	8,955	46
Pittsburgh, PA	46	221	32,917	76	10,411	222	14.5	293	1,365	152	18,585	18	7,713	71
Pittsfield, MA	−73	329	30,281	144	11,785	101	22.7	167	2,455	19	1,088	210	8,175	58
Pocatello, ID	24	245	24,718	327	10,099	260	13.3	306	1,123	259	403	354	4,867	281
Portland-South Portland-Biddeford, ME	598	44	32,777	80	12,849	50	22.2	179	1,995	40	3,819	85	7,527	78
Portland-Vancouver-Beaverton, OR-WA	699	38	36,473	31	10,804	185	12.7	312	1,498	115	9,441	38	4,625	306
Port St. Lucie-Fort Pierce, FL	538	49	27,243	241	11,294	136	34.0	50	1,157	241	2,078	138	5,955	165
Poughkeepsie-Newburgh-Middletown, NY	706	37	32,502	86	11,064	158	34.3	48	1,048	287	3,388	98	5,167	239
Prescott, AZ	397	65	23,669	343	8,978	325	33.7	54	1,747	61	981	228	5,314	224
Providence-New Bedford-Fall River, RI-MA	16,927	1	32,027	96	10,972	168	39.7	27	1,525	107	10,818	31	6,665	110
Provo-Orem, UT	950	29	26,324	282	8,367	340	32.5	62	835	332	1,064	215	2,621	361
Pueblo, CO	46	221	25,934	297	9,708	288	21.2	202	1,193	217	931	241	6,247	137
Punta Gorda, FL	320	78	24,818	322	9,570	293	34.9	44	922	316	971	231	6,353	132
Racine, WI	110	155	33,256	68	9,924	269	21.2	203	975	307	823	265	4,273	321
Raleigh-Cary, NC	921	31	33,646	62	12,943	45	32.3	64	1,439	130	4,895	63	5,516	201
Rapid City, SD	154	131	25,953	295	14,632	14	35.3	40	2,034	35	897	246	7,736	68
Reading, PA	250	99	31,689	107	10,072	263	15.5	284	966	309	1,671	167	4,321	316
Redding, CA	84	179	28,131	197	11,471	127	45.6	16	1,346	159	1,061	216	6,041	156
Reno-Sparks, NV	269	93	32,174	92	13,681	28	32.9	58	5,490	5	1,743	163	4,651	303
Richmond, VA	709	36	34,003	57	11,255	139	31.3	72	(NA)	(NA)	7,547	47	6,629	114
Riverside-San Bernardino-Ontario, CA	4,006	7	29,093	171	9,211	313	47.0	11	1,199	216	14,663	23	4,023	338
Roanoke, VA	127	149	28,547	186	12,841	51	17.9	252	(NA)	(NA)	1,782	158	6,139	147
Rochester, MN	269	93	35,137	42	13,221	38	37.8	32	1,621	80	828	263	4,803	290
Rochester, NY	316	79	33,722	60	9,919	270	17.0	268	1,083	271	5,837	56	5,607	195
Rockford, IL	7	258	32,543	84	10,678	198	18.2	244	1,124	258	1,356	184	4,092	333
Rocky Mount, NC	−26	293	26,944	258	9,417	301	8.5	338	1,011	297	831	262	5,748	182
Rome, GA	41	230	26,061	291	10,366	229	18.8	233	1,310	167	440	346	4,714	297
Sacramento-Arden-Arcade-Roseville, CA	2,353	17	34,575	49	10,968	169	49.6	7	1,460	121	17,706	20	8,963	45
Saginaw-Saginaw Township North, MI	−17	283	32,837	77	12,880	49	9.1	336	1,617	82	1,153	200	5,506	202
St. Cloud, MN	324	76	27,642	225	14,269	17	34.8	45	1,304	170	717	287	4,034	337
St. George, UT	283	89	23,696	342	11,615	115	31.6	70	1,561	99	406	353	3,890	345
St. Joseph, MO-KS	72	191	25,972	294	9,481	300	20.1	218	976	306	665	297	5,402	214
St. Louis, MO-IL[5]	1,015	27	34,607	48	10,998	164	22.0	182	1,651	76	21,990	14	7,985	63
Salem, OR	93	167	27,674	224	9,075	318	12.4	317	(NA)	(NA)	2,331	126	6,392	130
Salinas, CA	323	77	32,123	94	9,873	276	33.8	52	2,512	18	2,107	136	5,083	249
Salisbury, MD	−2	267	27,020	251	11,610	117	22.0	181	1,138	250	570	321	5,040	256
Salt Lake City, UT	942	30	31,910	103	12,209	76	14.3	296	1,705	65	5,112	62	5,084	248
San Angelo, TX	−15	280	26,103	289	10,803	186	27.4	104	(NA)	(NA)	678	295	6,422	126
San Antonio, TX	1,132	24	29,188	165	10,543	208	37.6	33	1,718	63	14,255	24	7,848	66
San Diego-Carlsbad-San Marcos, CA	3,408	10	37,412	27	10,906	174	42.2	24	2,186	26	24,045	12	8,238	57
Sandusky, OH	4	260	28,872	176	10,569	205	14.0	297	2,294	25	420	351	5,331	220
San Francisco-Oakland-Fremont, CA	**−1,744**	**361**	**49,720**	**4**	**11,591**	**120**	**31.5**	**71**	**2,109**	**29**	**25,999**	**9**	**6,255**	**136**
San Jose-Sunnyvale-Santa Clara, CA	−1,287	360	62,395	1	11,802	100	20.5	212	1,782	55	11,408	30	6,586	117
San Luis Obispo-Paso Robles, CA	548	48	28,004	205	10,587	203	49.9	5	2,382	24	1,114	206	4,401	314
Santa Barbara-Santa Maria, CA	178	122	34,230	52	10,738	192	35.4	39	2,094	31	2,724	111	6,763	105
Santa Cruz-Watsonville, CA	56	210	34,118	54	10,335	230	32.9	59	1,683	68	993	226	3,944	341
Santa Fe, NM	197	115	27,814	220	13,484	31	27.2	106	2,803	15	1,173	197	8,584	52
Santa Rosa-Petaluma, CA	247	101	35,607	38	12,303	69	38.2	31	1,554	101	2,039	141	4,363	315
Sarasota-Bradenton-Venice, FL	1,127	26	28,499	187	11,508	125	24.2	144	1,413	137	3,999	79	6,303	133
Savannah, GA	129	146	28,909	175	10,748	188	19.2	228	1,997	39	2,861	108	9,378	37
Scranton-Wilkes-Barre, PA	−114	345	26,712	265	11,148	149	22.6	168	1,226	205	4,013	78	7,261	83
Seattle-Tacoma-Bellevue, WA	**54**	**213**	**43,193**	**8**	**12,170**	**77**	**25.9**	**124**	**1,685**	**67**	**18,730**	**17**	**5,961**	**163**
Sheboygan, WI	95	163	30,492	137	10,144	254	26.2	121	1,224	206	453	344	3,987	340
Sherman-Denison, TX	−3	271	28,209	193	12,039	87	25.3	129	1,021	294	561	323	4,880	280
Shreveport-Bossier City, LA	55	212	26,570	274	10,815	184	24.0	146	3,552	9	2,506	121	6,618	115
Sioux City, IA-NE-SD	−7	276	26,670	266	9,161	315	2.9	352	1,333	161	852	258	5,954	166
Sioux Falls, SD	272	92	28,944	174	14,016	23	27.1	108	1,824	53	994	224	5,004	264
South Bend-Mishawaka, IN-MI	−98	337	29,993	149	10,938	172	18.0	250	1,161	237	2,164	132	6,817	102

See footnotes at end of table.

Metropolitan statistical area	Private nonfarm business establishments				Retail trade[1] (NAICS 44–55), sales 2002				Accommodation and food services[1] (NAICS 72), sales 2002		Federal funds and grants, 2003			
	Establishment change, 2000–2003	Rank	Annual payroll per employee, 2002 (dollars)	Rank	Per capita[2] (dollars)	Rank	Percent change, 1997–2002	Rank	Per capita[2] (dollars)	Rank	Total expenditures (million dollars)	Rank	Per capita[3] (dollars)	Rank
Spartanburg, SC	142	136	31,607	111	10,503	213	17.8	256	1,155	242	1,116	205	4,261	322
Spokane, WA	98	161	30,294	143	11,394	130	18.1	248	1,354	156	2,554	118	5,923	172
Springfield, IL	-52	314	29,481	159	11,888	99	18.4	240	1,628	78	3,216	102	15,722	5
Springfield, MA	-1,097	359	30,681	130	9,954	267	28.6	97	1,151	244	4,076	75	5,931	170
Springfield, MO	291	87	25,318	313	12,349	66	19.5	225	1,397	144	1,823	155	4,741	296
Springfield, OH	-11	278	26,565	276	9,233	310	20.4	214	1,066	279	837	260	5,862	176
State College, PA	29	240	25,894	299	10,123	256	21.6	192	1,509	111	961	237	6,874	99
Stockton, CA	644	43	30,952	121	8,936	327	48.8	10	933	313	2,675	113	4,234	323
Sumter, SC	85	175	25,686	304	8,114	344	9.2	334	749	339	878	250	8,298	56
Syracuse, NY	348	72	32,316	90	10,387	226	21.2	201	1,264	190	3,750	88	5,740	183
Tallahassee, FL	331	74	27,395	238	9,518	298	21.8	186	1,302	171	4,111	73	12,554	13
Tampa-St. Petersburg-Clearwater, FL	2,378	16	32,704	81	12,096	85	24.4	141	1,442	129	16,181	21	6,393	129
Terre Haute, IN	-35	304	27,121	247	16,610	1	3.2	351	1,227	204	1,052	218	6,205	138
Texarkana, TX-Texarkana, AR	-21	288	25,284	314	11,168	148	22.4	172	1,450	125	971	231	7,373	82
Toledo, OH	75	189	32,000	98	10,989	167	12.6	315	1,490	116	3,329	100	5,047	254
Topeka, KS	-18	285	28,364	190	9,741	285	20.1	217	(NA)	(NA)	1,974	148	8,704	48
Trenton-Ewing, NJ	695	39	43,228	7	11,719	106	31.7	68	1,548	103	3,730	90	10,327	28
Tucson, AZ	515	51	29,586	157	9,906	273	26.8	112	1,581	94	8,109	44	9,101	44
Tulsa, OK	306	84	31,950	100	10,141	255	17.4	265	1,275	182	4,103	74	4,663	301
Tuscaloosa, AL	-21	288	27,634	227	10,201	242	21.4	193	1,240	197	1,189	196	6,117	148
Tyler, TX	179	121	29,849	152	12,902	48	24.8	136	1,309	168	922	242	5,013	262
Utica-Rome, NY	69	196	26,574	273	9,212	312	27.1	107	932	314	1,982	145	6,650	111
Valdosta, GA	98	161	23,056	351	11,610	117	28.2	101	1,554	101	839	259	6,865	100
Vallejo-Fairfield, CA	315	80	32,808	79	10,148	253	49.0	9	1,059	281	2,442	124	5,933	169
Vero Beach, FL	128	148	26,624	270	12,922	46	33.3	57	1,185	226	832	261	6,921	93
Victoria, TX	12	255	29,446	160	10,411	222	17.6	263	1,001	300	532	330	4,709	298
Vineland-Millville-Bridgeton, NJ	87	173	31,262	117	10,259	236	23.8	152	705	342	875	253	5,851	178
Virginia Beach-Norfolk-Newport News, VA-NC	810	32	28,234	192	9,745	284	23.0	163	(NA)	(NA)	18,214	19	11,208	22
Visalia-Porterville, CA	83	180	26,668	267	7,687	351	37.2	34	678	343	1,634	171	4,178	327
Waco, TX	-19	286	25,935	296	10,123	256	22.3	174	1,348	158	1,236	192	5,630	191
Warner Robins, GA	127	149	22,801	354	10,460	216	29.4	93	1,291	177	1,770	160	14,741	8
Washington-Arlington-Alexandria, DC-VA-MD-WV	**4,445**	**5**	**44,152**	**6**	**11,177**	**146**	**30.4**	**82**	**2,011**	**38**	**98,385**	**2**	**19,403**	**2**
Waterloo-Cedar Falls, IA	-43	309	27,476	236	11,280	137	17.9	254	1,093	269	805	266	4,978	268
Wausau, WI	-116	346	29,109	169	14,530	15	29.7	89	1,009	298	538	329	4,224	324
Weirton-Steubenville, WV-OH	-30	297	27,867	214	7,338	354	14.5	294	784	334	870	255	6,768	104
Wenatchee, WA	45	224	28,055	202	10,229	239	16.4	274	1,523	108	514	336	5,049	253
Wheeling, WV-OH	-67	324	24,468	330	10,195	246	15.8	278	1,171	233	974	230	6,490	122
Wichita, KS	183	119	31,602	112	9,990	266	17.8	258	1,273	183	3,488	95	5,992	159
Wichita Falls, TX	-27	294	24,739	325	10,382	227	21.3	197	1,241	196	1,296	187	8,716	47
Williamsport, PA	-30	297	25,711	303	10,744	191	11.1	327	993	302	652	299	5,498	204
Wilmington, NC	457	57	27,009	253	13,266	36	24.8	137	1,606	86	1,649	169	5,612	194
Winchester, VA-WV	94	165	28,788	180	15,237	9	49.5	8	1,395	148	442	345	4,000	339
Winston-Salem, NC	77	187	32,836	78	11,921	97	23.0	164	1,328	162	2,039	141	4,663	301
Worcester, MA	380	67	35,155	40	10,517	212	29.9	88	1,221	207	3,927	81	5,061	252
Yakima, WA	-66	322	27,766	222	8,463	338	9.1	337	902	321	1,172	198	5,164	240
York-Hanover, PA	204	111	30,415	138	9,873	276	18.4	239	1,051	285	2,075	139	5,245	232
Youngstown-Warren-Boardman, OH-PA	-67	324	27,985	207	9,838	279	1.5	354	1,116	260	3,533	93	5,957	164
Yuba City, CA	50	218	27,829	216	7,714	350	31.0	74	766	337	966	234	6,517	119
Yuma, AZ	23	246	21,320	358	8,021	348	29.1	94	1,044	289	1,022	221	5,989	160

– Represents zero.   NA Not available.

[1]Includes only establishments with payroll.
[2]Based on resident population estimated as of July 1, 2002.
[3]Based on resident population estimated as of July 1, 2003.
[4]The Denver-Aurora metropolitan statistical area includes Broomfield County. Broomfield County, CO, was formed from parts of Adams, Boulder, Jefferson, and Weld Counties on November 15, 2001, and is coextensive with Broomfield city. For the purposes of defining and presenting data for the Denver-Aurora metropolitan statistical area, Broomfield is treated as if it were a county when data are available to do so.
[5]The portion of Sullivan city in Crawford County, MO, is legally part of the St. Louis, MO-IL MSA. That portion is not included in these figures for the St. Louis, MO-IL MSA.

Sources: U.S. Bureau of Labor Statistics, U.S. Census Bureau, U.S. Federal Deposit Insurance Corporation (FDIC), and Office of Thrift Supervision (OTS). For more information, see <http://www.bls.gov/lau>, <http://www.census.gov/govs/www/cffr.html>, and <http://www2.fdic.gov/sod/index.asp>. See Tables B-9, B-10, and B-11 of the State and Metropolitan Area Data Book: 2006.

Subject Index

Note:

This index lists table and page locations for the subjects covered in the four data tables of this publication. It is an alphabetic presentation of subjects. If a subject is not covered for a specific table (geography), the corresponding references are blank.

You may visit us on the Web at
http://www.census.gov/compendia/smadb

Subject Index

Subject Index

State and Metropolitan Area Data Book: 2006

U.S. Census Bureau

	Table A. States		Table B. Metro Areas		Table C. Metro Areas With Counties		Table D. Micropolitan Areas	
	Page	Table	Page	Table	Page	Table	Page	Table
Transportation—Con.								
Commodity shipments	91	A-65						
Cost of living	51–53, E-8	A-40, E-7						
Gross state product	54, 55	A-41						
Transportation and warehousing	90	A-64						
Travel.	101	A-73						
Trucks	91	A-65						
U								
Unemployment.	39	A-29	168–173, E-27–E-31	B-9, E-16				
Unemployment insurance	111, E-11	A-81, E-12						
Union membership	44	A-33						
Universities and colleges.	29, 51-53	A-22, 40	138–143	B-4				
Unmarried women.	15	A-10						
Utilities.	60, 61, 76–78	A-44, 55						
Cost of living	51–53, E-8	A-40, E-7						
V								
Vacancy rates	50	A-39						
Vehicle miles of travel	90	A-64						
Vehicle registrations	91–93	A-65, 66						
Veterans	114	A-84						
Violent crime	32, 33	A-25						
Vital statistics.	15–19	A-10–13						
Voter participation	115	A-85						
Votes:								
Congressional	115, 116	A-85, 86						
Governor.	117, 118	A-87						
Presidential.	115	A-85						
Representatives, U.S.	116	A-86						
Senators, U.S.	115	A-85						
Voting-age population.	115	A-85						
W								
Wages (see also Pay and Salaries)	28, 41–43, 82, 83, 108	A-21, 31, 32, 59, 78						
Water systems.	76–78	A-55						
Waterborne shipments	90	A-64						
Welfare programs	110, 111, E-11	A-80, 81, E-12						
White:								
Births	16	A-11						
Infant mortality rates.	17, 18	A-12						
Population.	9, 10, E-9	A-5, E-9						
Wholesale trade:								
Average annual pay	42, 43	A-32						
Earnings	60, 61, 86	A-44, 62						
Employment.	42, 43	A-32						
Establishments	86	A-62						
Gross state product	54, 55	A-41						
Widows	12	A-7						
Women:								
Births	15, 16	A-10, 11						
Labor force.	37–39	A-28, 29						
Public officials	117, 118	A-87						
Workers' compensation	111	A-81						